FINLAND
Helsinki ✴

•St. Petersburg

tockholm

✴ Tallinn
ESTONIA

Nizhniy Novgorod•

✴ Riga
LATVIA

•Moscow

RUSSIA

LITHUANIA

Vilnius ✴

(RUSSIA)

✴ Minsk

BELARUS

✴ Warsaw

OLAND

•Kiev

•Kharkov

UKRAINE

Dnieper

CARPATHIAN

LOVAKIA

MTS.

MOLDOVA

✴ Kishinev

KAZAKHSTAN

•Budapest

UNGARY

ROMANIA

Bucharest ✴

Caspian

Sea

grade

NA

SERBIA

Black   Sea

CAUCASUS MTS.

GEORGIA ✴ T'bilisi

AZERBAIJAN

MTS.

UGOSLAVIA)

BULGARIA

✴ Sofia

ARMENIA

✴ Baku

9.

Skopje ✴

✴ Yerevan

MACEDONIA

AZERBAIJAN

✴ Tiranë

LBANIA

Ankara ✴

GREECE

Aegean

Sea

TURKEY

IRAN

ian

a

Athens ✴

SYRIA

•Baghdad

Mediterranean

CYPRUS

Crete

LEBANON

IRAQ

Beirut ✴

Damascus

Sea

✴

KUWAIT

Jerusalem ✴

Kuwa

Amman

ISRAEL

Cairo

JORDAN

EGYPT

SAUDI   ARABIA

W9-BNJ-343

WESTERN
CIVIL

The Continuing

D EDITION

Thomas F. X. Noble
University of Virginia

Barry S. Strauss
Cornell University

Duane J. Osheim
University of Virginia

Kristen B. Neuschel
Duke University

William B. Cohen
Indiana University

David D. Roberts
University of Georgia

Houghton Mifflin Company   Boston   New York

Executive Editor: Patricia A. Coryell
Senior Basic Book Editor: Elizabeth M. Welch
Senior Project Editor: Christina M. Horn
Editorial Assistant: Stewart S. Jester
Senior Production/Design Coordinator: Sarah Ambrose
Senior Manufacturing Coordinator: Marie Barnes
Marketing Manager: Sandra McGuire

Chapter opener credits begin on page A-1. Text credits begin on page A-1.

Cover image: Léon Cogniet, *The National Guard of Paris Leaves to Join the Army,* September 1792. Versailles, France. Giraudon/Art Resource, NY.

Cover designer: Tony Saizon

Printed in the U.S.A.

Library of Congress Catalog Card Number: 97-72525

ISBN: 0-395-82900-3

1 2 3 4 5 6 7 8 9-VH-01 00 99 98 97

Brief Contents

1 The Ancestors of the West   3

2 The Book and the Myths: Western Asia and Early Greece   43

3 The Age of the Polis: Greece, ca. 750–350 B.C.   79

4 The Hellenistic World, 323–30 B.C.   119

5 Rome: From Republic to Empire, ca. 509–44 B.C.   153

6 Imperial Rome, 27 B.C.–A.D. 284   193

7 The World of Late Antiquity, ca. 300–600   227

8 Early Medieval Civilizations, ca. 600–900   267

9 The Expansion of Europe, ca. 900–1150   307

10 Medieval Civilization at Its Height, ca. 1150–1300   353

11 The Transformation of Medieval Civilization, 1300–1500   395

12 The Renaissance   437

13 Europe, the Old World and the New   475

14 The Age of the Reformation   509

15 Europe in the Age of Religious War, 1555–1648   547

16 Europe in the Age of Louis XIV, ca. 1610–1715   589

17 A Revolution in World-View   625

18 Europe on the Threshold of Modernity, ca. 1715–1789   659

19 Revolutionary Europe, 1789–1815   699

20 Restoration, Reform, and Revolution, 1814–1848   739

21 The Industrial Transformation of Europe   775

22 New Powers and New Tensions, 1850–1880   811

23 The Age of Optimism, 1850–1880   845

24 Escalating Tensions, 1880–1914   879

25 War and Revolution, 1914–1919   917

26 The Illusion of Stability, 1919–1930   957

27 The Tortured Decade, 1930–1939   995

28 The Era of the Second World War, 1939–1949   1031

29 An Anxious Stability: The Age of the Cold War, 1949–1985   1073

30 The West and the World in the Late Twentieth Century   1113

Contents

Maps   *xix*
Documents   *xx*
Chronologies, Genealogies, and Charts   *xxiii*
Weighing the Evidence   *xxiv*
Preface   *xxv*
About the Authors   *xxxii*

1 The Ancestors of the West   3

Origins, to ca. 3000 B.C.   4
The First Human Beings   4
From the Cave to the Town, ca. 40,000–5000 B.C.   5
Neolithic and Copper Age Europe, 7000–2500 B.C.   9
The Emergence of Civilization   10

Mesopotamia, to ca. 1600 B.C.   12
The City-States of Sumer   12
Conquest and Assimilation, ca. 2350–1900 B.C.   14
The Majesty of the Law   16
Divine Masters   17
Arts and Sciences   19

Egypt, to ca. 1100 B.C.   21
Geography as Destiny   21
Storm over Origins   22
Divine Kingship   23
Life and Afterlife   25

Expansion and Reform, 1540–1293 B.C.   28
Arts and Sciences   31
Encounters with the West: Egyptian Attitudes Toward Foreigners   32

Widening Horizons: Anatolia and the Levant   33
The City-States of Syria-Palestine, ca. 2500–1200 B.C.   33
The Hittites   34
The First International System and Its Collapse, ca. 1500–1150 B.C.   36

Summary   37
Suggested Reading   38

Weighing the Evidence: The Iceman and His World   40

2 The Book and the Myths: Western Asia and Early Greece   43

Assyrians, Neo-Babylonians, Phoenicians, ca. 1200–ca. 500 B.C.   44
The Roar of the Lions   44
Traders the World Honored   48

Israel, ca. 1500–400 B.C.   50
The Hebrew Bible   50
The Emergence of Monotheism, ca. 1500–600 B.C.   51
Exile and Return, 598–ca. 400 B.C.   54
The People of the Covenant   56

Persia, ca. 1000–330 B.C.   57
Building an Empire   59
The King of Kings   60
Zoroastrianism   63

Early Greece, to ca. 750 B.C.   64
The Minoans and Early Greece, 3000–1375 B.C.   64
The Mycenaeans, to ca. 1200 B.C.   67
Between Mycenae and the City-States, ca. 1100–800 B.C.   69
Homer and History   69
World of the Heroes   71

Encounters with the West: Greeks and Trojans   72

Summary   73
Suggested Reading   74

Weighing the Evidence: The Trojan War   76

3 **The Age of the Polis: Greece, ca. 750–350 B.C.**   79

Society and Politics in Archaic Greece, ca. 750–500 B.C.   81
Eighth-Century B.C. Revival and Expansion   81
Emergence of the Polis   82
The Hoplite Phalanx and the Community   83
Tyranny in the Polis   85
Sparta   85
Early Athens   89

The Culture of Archaic Greece   91
Revealing the Self: Lyric Poetry and Sculpture   91
Religious Faith and Practice   92
The Origins of Western Philosophy   94

Classical Athens   95
The Development of Demokratia, 508–321 B.C.   95
How Demokratia Worked   97
Metics, Women, Slaves   99

Struggles for Hegemony   100
The Persian Wars, 499–479 B.C.   100
The Rise of the Athenian Empire   101
Encounters with the West: The Enemy as Barbarian   102
The Peloponnesian War, 431–404 B.C.   103
The Fruitless Wars of the Fourth Century B.C.   103

The Public Culture of Classical Greece   104
Religion and Art   105
The Sophists and Socrates   106
Plato and Aristotle   107
Athenian Drama   111
Historical Thought and Writing   113

Summary   113
Suggested Reading   114

Weighing the Evidence: The Parthenon   116

4 **The Hellenistic World, 323–30 B.C.**   119

Philip and Alexander   120
The Rise of Macedon   120
Alexander the Conqueror   121

The Variety of the Hellenistic Kingdoms   125
Hellenism Redefined   126
Colonialism, Greek Style   126
Macedon and Greece   128
Ptolemaic Egypt   129
Encounters with the West: The Oracle of the Potter   131

Seleucids and Attalids   132
The Greco-Indian Interaction   133

The Alexandrian Moment   134

The Anti-Epic Temperament   135
Advances in Science and Medicine   138
Men and Women in Art and Society   139

**The Turn Inward: New Philosophies,
New Faiths   142**

Stoics, Skeptics, Cynics, and Epicureans   142
The Mystery Religions   144
Hellenistic Judaism   145

**Summary   147
Suggested Reading   148**

*Weighing the Evidence: Images of
Cleopatra   150*

**5   Rome: From Republic to Empire,
ca. 509–44 B.C.   153**

Before the Republic   154

Archaic Rome and Its Neighbors   155
The Roman Monarchy   157

Founding the Roman Republic   158

A Foundation Myth of the Roman Republic   158
The Roman Household   159
Patrons and Clients   160
Religion and World-View   162

**Government and Society in the Early and Middle
Republic, ca. 509–133 B.C.   163**

Political Institutions   163
Conflict of the Orders   165

From Italian City-State to World Empire   166

Republican Expansion: The Conquest of Italy, ca.
  509–265 B.C.   168
Rome Versus Carthage: The Punic Wars,
  264–146 B.C.   172
Victories in the Hellenistic East, ca. 200–133 B.C.   175
The Socioeconomic Consequences of Expansion   175
The Impact of Greece on Rome and Its Empire   176
*Encounters with the West: Roman Attitudes Toward the
Conquered   179*

**The Revolution from the Gracchi to Caesar,
133–44 B.C.   180**

The Gracchi   180

Marius and Sulla   182
Pompey and Caesar   183
The World of Cicero   185

**Summary   187
Suggested Reading   188**

*Weighing the Evidence: Luxury Goods and Gender
Wars in Rome   190*

**6   Imperial Rome,
27 B.C.–A.D. 284   193**

Augustus and the Principate, 27 B.C.–A.D. 68   195

The Political Settlement   195
The Economic and Social Settlement   197
The Culture of the Augustan Age   200
The Julio-Claudians   201

The Roman Peace, A.D. 69–180   203

The Flavians and the "Good Emperors"   203
Prosperity and Romanization in the Provinces   204
The Culture of the Roman Peace   209

**The Crisis of the Third Century, A.D.
180–284   210**

Severan Ambitions   210
Shock and Recovery   211

Encounters with the West: Syria Between Rome and Persia   212

Early Christianity   213

Jesus of Nazareth   213
Paul of Tarsus   216
Expansion, Divergence, Persecution   219
Mystery Religions   220

Summary   221
Suggested Reading   221

Weighing the Evidence: Pompeii   224

7   The World of Late Antiquity, ca. 300–600   227

Rebuilding the Roman Empire   229

The Reforms of Diocletian (r. 284–305)   229
The Reforms of Constantine (r. 306–337)   231
The Legalization of Christianity   233

The Fourth-Century Empire: An Illusory Stability   235

Imperial Politics: Families and Armies   236
Administrative Successes and Failures   236
The Development of the Catholic Church   237
Shifting Social Hierarchies   240

From Empire to Kingdoms: The Ascendancy of the Germanic Peoples   243

Invasions and Migrations   243
Incorporating the Barbarians   244
Encounters with the West: Two Views of the Huns   246
More Kingdoms: The End of Direct Roman Rule in the West   247
The New Old West   249

The Roman Empire in the East   250

Constantinople and Its Rulers   250
The Emperor Justinian (r. 527–565)   251

Christian Culture and Life   254

The True Church: Competing Visions   255
The Rise of Christian Monasticism   255
The Quest for a Catholic Tradition   257

Summary   261
Suggested Reading   262

Weighing the Evidence: The Ravenna Mosaics   264

8   Early Medieval Civilizations, ca. 600–900   267

The Islamic East   268

Arabia Before Muhammad   268
The Prophet and His Faith   269
The Expansion of Islam   271
The Abbassid Revolution   274
The Emergence of Islamic Culture   275

The Byzantine Empire   275

From the Eastern Roman Empire to the Byzantine Empire   276
The Eighth-Century Recovery   276
Ninth-Century Problems   280

Christian Kingdoms in the West   280

Encounters with the West: Muslim and Byzantine "Diplomacy"?   281
The Struggles of Christian Spain   281
Italy and the Papal State   282
The Fate of the British Isles   284

The World of Charlemagne   287

The Rise of the Carolingian Family   287
The Empire of Charlemagne   288
Carolingian Government   292
The Carolingian Renaissance   293

The Fragmentation of the Carolingian Empire   296

Internal Factors in the Carolingian Decline   296
New Waves of Invasions   297

Early Medieval Economies and Societies   298

Trade and Commerce   298
Town and Countryside   299
Social Patterns   299

Summary   302
Suggested Reading   302

Weighing the Evidence: The Manuscript Book   304

9   The Expansion of Europe, ca. 900–1150   307

Signs of Expansion   308

The Growing Population   308
Technological Gains   308
Forms of Enterprise   310

The Traditional Order of Society   311

Those Who Fight: The Nobility   312
Those Who Pray: The Clergy   314
Those Who Work: The Peasants   317
Those Left Out: Townspeople and Jews   318

Germany and the Empire   320

Unifying the Realm: The Saxon and Salian
  Rulers   320
The Investiture Controversy   323

Shaping the Kingdom   326

The Rise of Capetian France   326
Anglo-Saxon England and the Norman
  Conquest   329
The Progress of the Reconquista in Spain   332
Kingdoms and Cities in Italy   332

The Growth of New States   335

The Celtic Realms   335
Scandinavia   337
The Slavic World   337

Cultural Life in an Age of Expansion   339

Schools and Latin Letters   339
The Rise of Vernacular Culture   342
The Romanesque Achievement   343

A Clash of Cultures: The First Crusade   344

The Eastern Mediterranean Background   344
The Western Background   345
The "Pilgrimage" to Jerusalem   346
Encounters with the West: An Arab Perspective on the First Crusade   347

Summary   346
Suggested Reading   348

Weighing the Evidence: The Medieval Castle   350

10   Medieval Civilization at Its Height, ca. 1150–1300   353

The Empire and the Papacy   355

Revival of the Empire, 1152–1190   355
Imperial Authority and the Papal Challenge,
  1190–1272   356
The Papal Monarchy   359

The Evolution of Central Governments   360

France   361
England   364
Spain   366
Italy   367
Russia   368
Encounters with the West: William of Rubruck Reports on the Mongols   369

Economic Life   370

The Roles of Cities and Towns   370
Commercial Growth and Innovation   371
Changing Economic Attitudes   371

Social and Religious Movements   372

Heretics and Dissidents   372
Reform from Within: The Mendicant Orders   373
Communities of Women   375
The Later Crusades   377

The Height of Medieval Culture   379

The University   379
Scholasticism   380
The Gothic Image   381
Latin and Vernacular Culture   384

Boniface VIII and Philip IV: Crisis of Church and State, 1294–1302   386

The Issues   386
The Outcome   388

Summary   388
Suggested Reading   389

*Weighing the Evidence: The Arts of Chartres
Cathedral*   390

11 The Transformation of Medieval Civilization, 1300–1500   395

The Crisis of the Western Christian Church   396

The Babylonian Captivity, 1309–1377   397
Heresy, Reunion, and Reform   400
The Reformed Papacy   401

The Challenge to Medieval Governments   402

England, France, and the Hundred Years' War   402
The Results of the War   407
Italy   410
Germany and Switzerland   412
Scandinavia and Eastern Europe   413

Economy and Society   414

The Black Death and Demographic Crisis   414
Patterns of Economic Change   417
The Popular Revolts   422

**Formation of the Ottoman and Spanish
Empires**   423

The Ottoman Turks   423
The Union of Crowns in Spain   427

*Encounters with the West: A European View of
Constantinople*   428

Summary   431
Suggested Reading   432

*Weighing the Evidence: A Painting of the
Plague*   434

12 The Renaissance   437

Humanism and Culture in Italy, 1300–1500   438

The Emergence of Humanism   438
Vernacular Literatures   439
Early Humanism   441
Humanistic Studies   442
The Transformation of Humanism   444
*Encounters with the West: Rabbi Mordecai Dato Criticizes
the Humanists*   447
Humanism and Political Thought   448

The Arts in Italy, 1250–1550   450

The Artistic Renaissance   450
Art and Patronage   453

The Spread of the Renaissance, 1350–1536   456

The Impact of Printing   456
Humanism Outside Italy   457
Thomas More and Desiderius Erasmus   459
Renaissance Art in the North   461

The Renaissance and Court Society   462

The Elaboration of the Court   462
The Court of Mantua   463
Castiglione and the European Gentleman   464
The Renaissance Papacy   466

Summary   468

Suggested Reading   469

Weighing the Evidence: The Art of Renaissance Florence   470

13 Europe, the Old World and the New   475

The European Background, 1250–1492   476
Navigational Innovations   476
Lands Beyond Christendom   477
The Revolution in Geography   479

Portuguese Voyages of Discovery, 1350–1515   480
The Early Voyages   480
The Search for a Sea Route to Asia   482
The Portuguese in Asia   483

Spanish Voyages of Discovery, 1492–1522   486
The Role of Columbus   486
Columbus's Successors   490

Spain's Colonial Empire, 1492–1600   491
The Americas Before the European Invasion   491
The Spanish Conquests   494
Encounters with the West: An Inca Nobleman Defends His Civilization   495
Colonial Organization   498
The Debate over Indian Rights   499

The Columbian Exchange   500
Disease   501
Plants and Animals   501
Culture   502

Summary   504
Suggested Reading   504

Weighing the Evidence: A Mexican Shrine   506

14 The Age of the Reformation   509

The Reformation Movements, ca.1517–1545   510
The Late Medieval Context   511
Martin Luther and the New Theology   512
The Reformation of the Communities   516
John Calvin and the Reformed Tradition   519
The Radical Reform of the Anabaptists   520

The Empire of Charles V (r. 1519–1556)   521
Imperial Challenges   522
German Politics   523
Encounters with the West: Duels Among Europeans and Turks   524
The Religious Settlement   525

The English Reformation, 1520–1603   527
Henry VIII and the Monarchical Reformation   527
Reform and Counter-Reform Under Edward and Mary   529
The Elizabethan Settlement   530

Reform in Other States, 1523–1560   531
France   531
Eastern Europe   532
Scandinavia   534

The Late Reformation, ca. 1545–1600   534
Catholic Reform   535
Confessionalization   538
The Regulation of Religious Life   538

Summary   540
Suggested Reading   541

Weighing the Evidence: A Reformation Woodcut   542

15 Europe in the Age of Religious War, 1555–1648   547

Society and the State   548
Economic Transformation and the New Elites   548
Economic Change and the Common People   549
Coping with Poverty and Violence   550
The Hunt for Witches and the Illusion of Order   552

Imperial Spain and the Limits of Power   **553**

The Revolt of the Netherlands   553
The Failure of the Invincible Armada   559
Successes at Home and Around the
  Mediterranean   560
Spain in Decline   561

**Religious and Political Crisis in France and
England**   **561**

The French Religious Wars   562
The Consolidation of Royal Authority in France,
  1610–1643   564
England: Precarious Stability, 1558–1603   565
Rising Tensions in England, 1603–1642   569

**The Holy Roman Empire and the Thirty Years'
War**   **571**

Peace Through Diversity, 1555–ca. 1618   571
The Thirty Years' War, 1618–1648   573
The Effects of the War   576

Society and Culture   **578**

Literacy and Literature   578
*Encounters with the West: Montaigne Discusses Barbarity
in the New World and the Old*   579
The Great Age of Theater   580
Sovereignty in Ceremony, Image, and Word   581
Baroque Art and Architecture   582

Summary   **584**
Suggested Reading   **584**

Weighing the Evidence: Signatures   586

16 Europe in the Age of Louis XIV, ca. 1610–1715   589

France in the Age of Absolutism   **590**

The Last Challenge to Absolutism   590
France Under Louis XIV, 1661–1715   591
The Life of the Court   592
Louis XIV and a Half-Century of War   594

The English Revolution   **597**

Civil War and Revolution, 1642–1649   598
The Interregnum, 1649–1660   600
The Restoration, 1660–1685   601
The Glorious Revolution, 1688   602

New Powers in Central and Eastern Europe   **603**

The Consolidation of Austria   603
The Rise of Brandenburg-Prussia   604
Competition Around the Baltic: The Demise of the
  Polish State and the Zenith of Swedish Power   605
The Expansion of Russia: From Ivan "the Terrible"
  Through Peter "the Great"   608

The Rise of Overseas Trade   **611**

The Growth of Trading Empires: The Success of
  the Dutch   611
The "Golden Age" of the Netherlands   613
*Encounters with the West: Agents of the Dutch East India
Company Confront Asian Powers*   614
The Growth of Atlantic Colonies and
  Commerce   616
The Beginning of the End of Traditional Society   619

Summary   **620**
Suggested Reading   **620**

Weighing the Evidence: Table Manners   622

17 A Revolution in World-View   625

The Revolution in Astronomy   **626**

The Inherited World-View and the Sixteenth-Century
  Context   626
The Copernican Challenge   628
The First Copernican Astronomers   630
Galileo and the Triumph of Copernicanism   632

The Scientific Revolution Generalized   **633**

The Promise of the New Science   634

Scientific Thought in France: Descartes and a New
  Cosmology   635
Science and Revolution in England   638
The Newtonian Synthesis: The Copernican Revolution
  Completed   639
Other Branches of Science   640

Science and Society   641

The Rise of Scientific Professionalism   642
The New Science and the Needs of the State   645
Religion and the New Science   646
*Encounters with the West: Jesuits and Astronomy in
China*   648
The Mechanistic World Order and Human Affairs at
  the End of the Seventeenth Century   649

Summary   652
Suggested Reading   653

Weighing the Evidence: Modern Maps   654

**18   Europe on the Threshold of
        Modernity, ca. 1715–1789   659**

The Enlightenment   660

Voltaire and the Enlightenment   660
The Variety of Enlightenment Thought   663
The Growth of Public Opinion   666
Art in the Age of Reason   669

European Rulers and European Society   671

France During the Enlightenment   671
Monarchy and Constitutional Government in Great
  Britain   672
"Enlightened" Monarchy   675
Catherine the Great and the Empire of Russia   677

States in Conflict   680

A Century of Warfare: Circumstances and
  Rationales   680
The Power of Austria and Prussia   682
The Atlantic World: Trade, Colonization,
  Competition   682
*Encounters with the West: An African Recalls the Horrors of
the Slave Ship*   685
Great Britain and France: Wars Overseas   686

Economic Expansion and Social Change   687

More Food and More People   687
The Growth of Industry   689
Control and Resistance   690

Summary   693

Weighing the Evidence: Gardens   694

Suggested Reading   696

**19   Revolutionary Europe,
        1789–1815   699**

Background to Revolution   700

Revolutionary Movements Around Europe   700
The American Revolution and the Kingdom of
  France   701
The Crisis of the Old Regime   702
1789: The Revolution Begins   704

The French Revolutions   710

The First Phase Completed, 1789–1791   710
The Second Revolution and Foreign War,
  1791–1793   713
The Faltering Republic and the Terror,
  1793–1794   715
Thermidorian Reaction and the Directory,
  1794–1799   719

The Napoleonic Era   720

Napoleon: From Soldier to Emperor, 1799–1804   720
Conquering Europe, 1805–1810   723
Defeat and Abdication, 1812–1815   725

**The Impact of Revolution on France and
the World   728**

The Significance of Revolution in France   728
The Impact of the Revolution Overseas   729
The View from Britain   730

Contents   **xiii**

*Encounters with the West: A Planter's Wife on the Haitian
Slave Revolt*   731

Summary   733
Suggested Reading   733

Weighing the Evidence: Political Symbols   734

**20 Restoration, Reform, and
Revolution, 1814–1848**   **739**

**The Search for Stability: The Congress of
Vienna**   **741**
Ideological Confrontations   **742**

Conservatism   742
Romanticism   743
Nationalism   746
Liberalism   747
Socialism   749

Restoration and Reform   **751**

France   751
Great Britain   753
*Encounters with the West: A Moroccan Description of the
French Freedom of the Press*   754
Spain   757
Austria and the German States   758
Italy   759
Russia   760
The Ottoman Empire   761

The Revolutions of 1848   **762**

Roots of Rebellion   762
France   763
Austria   766
Italy   767
The German States   768

Summary   770
Suggested Reading   770

Weighing the Evidence: Raft of the "Medusa"   772

*Encounters with the West: A Persian Discovers the British
Rail System*   777

Industrialization and European Production   **778**

Advances in the Cotton Industry   779
Iron, Steam, and Factories   780
Inventions and Entrepreneurs   782
Britain's Lead in Industrial Innovation   783
The Spread of Industry to the Continent   784

**The Transformation of Europe and Its
Environment**   **787**

Urbanization and Its Discontents   788
The Working Classes and Their Lot   791
Industrialization and the Family   793
The Land, the Water, and the Air   795

Responses to Industrialization   **796**

Economic Liberalism   796
The Growth of Working-Class Solidarity   797
Collective Action   799
Marx and Marxism   802

Summary   805
Suggested Reading   806

Weighing the Evidence: Workers' Wages   808

**21 The Industrial Transformation
of Europe**   **775**

**22 New Powers and New Tensions,
1850–1880**   **811**

Setting the Stage for Industrialization   **776**

Why Europe?   776
Transformations Accompanying
  Industrialization   776

**The Changing Scope of International
Relations**   **812**

The Crimean War as a Turning Point, 1854–1856   812
The Congress of Paris and Its Aftermath   813

Italian Unification   814

Cavour Plots Unification   815
Unification Achieved, 1860   816
The Problems of Unified Italy   818

German Unification   819

The Rise of Bismarck   819
Prussian Wars and German Unity   820
The Franco-Prussian War and Unification,
1870–1871   822
The Character of the New Germany   824

Precarious Supranational Empires   824

The Dual Monarchy in Austria-Hungary   824
The Ailing Ottoman Empire   827

The Emergence of a Powerful United States, 1840–1880   829

Territorial Expansion and Slavery   829
Civil War and National Unity   831
The Frontiers of Democracy   831

Stability in Victorian Britain   833

Parliamentary Government   833
Encounters with the West: A Japanese View of the British Parliament   833
Gladstone, Disraeli, and the Two-Party System   834

France: From Empire to Republic   834

The People's Emperor, Napoleon III   835
The Paris Commune, 1871   836
Creation of the Third Republic, 1871–1875   836

Russia and the Great Reforms   837

The Abolition of Serfdom, 1861   838
Reforms in Russian Institutions   838

Summary   840
Suggested Reading   840

Weighing the Evidence: An Engraving of the British Royal Family   842

23 The Age of Optimism, 1850–1880   845

Industrial Growth and Acceleration   846

The "Second Industrial Revolution," 1850–1914   846
Transportation and Communications   847

Changing Conditions Among Social Groups   849

The Declining Aristocracy   850
The Expanding Middle Classes   850
Middle-Class Lifestyles   851
The Workers' Lot   854
The Transformation of the Countryside   856

Urban Problems and Solutions   857

City Planning and Urban Renovation   857
The Introduction of Public Services   859

Social and Political Initiatives   862

State Intervention in Welfare   862
Educational and Cultural Opportunities   863

Culture in an Age of Optimism   864

Darwin and the Doctrine of Evolution   864
Physics, Chemistry, and Medicine   865
Birth of the Social Sciences   867
The Challenge to Religion   868
Art in the Age of Material Change   870
*Encounters with the West: A Chinese Official's Views of
European Material Progress*   873

Summary   874
Suggested Reading   874

Weighing the Evidence: The Crystal Palace   876

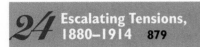

**24 Escalating Tensions,
1880–1914   879**

**From Optimism to Anxiety: Politics and
Culture   880**

The Erosion of the Liberal Consensus   880
The Growth of Socialism and Anarchism   880
The New Right, Racism, and Anti-Semitism   882
Irrationality and Uncertainty   884

The New Imperialism   886

Economic and Social Motives   887
Nationalistic Motives   887
Other Ideological Motives   889
Conquest, Administration, and Westernization   891
*Encounters with the West: Chief Montshiwa Petitions
Queen Victoria*   894
Overseas Migrations and the Spread of
   European Values   897

The Democratic Powers   898

Great Britain   899
France   900
Italy   903

The Autocracies   904

Germany   904
Austria-Hungary   905
The Ottoman Empire   905
Russia   906

The Coming War   909

Power Alignments   909
The Momentum for War   909

Summary   912
Suggested Reading   912

*Weighing the Evidence: The Layout of the British
Museum   914*

**25 War and Revolution,
1914–1919   917**

The Unforeseen Stalemate, 1914–1917   918

August 1914: The Domestic and Military
   Setting   918
Into the Nightmare, 1914   921
Seeking a Breakthrough, 1915–1917   923
1917 as a Turning Point   925

The Experience of Total War   926

Hardship on the Home Front   926
Domestic Mobilization   927
Accelerating Socioeconomic Change   929
Propaganda and the "Mobilization of
   Enthusiasm"   929

**Two Revolutions in Russia: March and November,
1917   931**

The Wartime Crisis of the Russian Autocracy   931
The March Revolution and the Fate of the Provisional
   Government   931
The Bolsheviks Come to Power   933
The Russian Revolution and the War   935

**The New War and the Entente Victory,
1917–1918   935**

The Debate over War Aims   935
The Renewal of the French War Effort   939

The German Gamble, 1918   939
Military Defeat and Political Change in
   Germany   940

The Outcome and the Impact   941

The Costs of War   941
The Search for Peace in a Revolutionary Era   942
The Peace Settlement   943
*Encounters with the West: Prince Faisal at the Peace
Conference   944*

Summary   950
Suggested Reading   952

*Weighing the Evidence: The Poetry of World
War I   954*

26 The Illusion of Stability, 1919–1930 957

**The West and the World after the
Great War   959**

The Erosion of European Power   959
Enforcing the Versailles Settlement   960
*Encounters with the West: Sun Yixien on Chinese
Nationalism   961*

Toward Mass Society   963

Economic Readjustment and the New
   Prosperity   964
Work, Leisure, and the New Popular Culture   965
Society and Politics in the Victorious
   Democracies   968
Democracy Aborted   969

**The Weimar Republic in Germany: A Candle
Burning at Both Ends   969**

Germany's Cautious Revolution, 1919–1920   969
Gustav Stresemann and the Scope for Gradual
   Consolidation, 1920–1929   971
The End of the Weimar Republic, 1929–1933   973

**Communism, Fascism, and the New Political
Spectrum   974**

Consolidating Communist Power in Russia,
   1917–1921   975
From Lenin to Stalin, 1921–1929   978
The Crisis of Liberal Italy and the Creation of Fascism,
   1919–1925   980
Innovation and Compromise in Fascist Italy,
   1925–1930   984

**The Search for Meaning in a Disordered
World   985**

Anxiety, Alienation, and Disillusionment   985
Recasting the Tradition   986
The Search for a New Tradition   987

Summary   989
Suggested Reading   990

Weighing the Evidence: Modern Design   992

27 The Tortured Decade, 1930–1939 995

The Great Depression   996

Sources of the Economic Contraction   996
Consequences and Responses   998
Encounters with the West: Gandhi on Nonviolence   1000

**The Stalinist Revolution in the Soviet
Union   1001**

Crash Industrialization and Forced Collectivization,
   1929–1933   1001
From Opposition to Terror, 1932–1938   1003
Communism and Stalinism   1005

Hitler and Nazism in Germany   1005

The Rise of Nazism, 1919–1933   1005

The Consolidation of Hitler's Power,
  1933–1934   1007
Hitler's World-View   1007
Nazi Aims and German Society   1009

**Fascist Challenge and Antifascist
Response   1013**

The Reorientation of Fascist Italy   1013
Fascism and the Popular Front Response   1014
From Democracy to Civil War in Spain,
  1931–1939   1015
France in the Era of the Popular Front   1018

The Coming of World War II, 1935–1939   1020

Restoring German Sovereignty, 1935–1936   1020
Austria, Czechoslovakia, and Appeasement   1020
Poland, the Nazi-Soviet Pact, and the Coming
  of War   1023

Summary   1025
Suggested Reading   1026

Weighing the Evidence: Film as Propaganda   1028

**28 The Era of the Second World War,
      1939–1949 1031**

The Victory of Nazi Germany, 1939–1941   1032

Initial Conquests and "Phony War"   1032
The Fall of France, 1940   1033
Winston Churchill and the Battle of Britain   1034
Italian Intervention and the Spread of War   1035

**The Assault on the Soviet Union and the Nazi New
Order   1037**

An Ambiguous Outcome, 1941–1942   1039
Hitler's New Order   1039
The Holocaust   1040
Collaboration and Resistance   1043
Toward the Soviet Triumph   1044

A Global War, 1941–1944   1046

Japan and the Origins of the Pacific War   1046
The United States in Europe and the Pacific   1048
*Encounters with the West: Japan's "Pan-Asian"
Mission*   1049
The Search for a Second Front in Europe   1050

**The Shape of the Allied Victory,
1944–1945   1051**

Yalta: Shaping the Postwar World   1052
Victory in Europe   1055

The Potsdam Conference and the Question of
  Germany   1056
The Atomic Bomb and the Capitulation of
  Japan   1057
Death, Disruption, and the Question of Guilt   1058

Toward the Postwar World   1060

Conflicting Visions and the Coming of the Cold
  War   1061
The Division of Germany   1061
The "Iron Curtain" and the Emergence of a Bipolar
  World   1062
The West and the New World Agenda   1063

Summary   1067
Suggested Reading   1068

Weighing the Evidence: Holocaust Testimony   1070

**29 An Anxious Stability: The Age of
      the Cold War, 1949–1985 1073**

The Search for Cultural Bearings   1074

Absurdity and Commitment in Existentialism   1075
Marxists and Traditionalists   1076
The Intellectual Migration and Americanism   1077

**Prosperity, Democracy, and the New Social
Compact in Western Europe   1079**

From Economic Reconstruction to Economic
  Miracle   1079
Social Welfare and the Issue of Gender   1080

Restoration of Democracy in Germany, France, and
    Italy   1082

Western Europe and the World   1086

NATO and the Atlantic Orientation   1086
The Varieties of Decolonization   1087
*Encounters with the West: The Legacy of European
Colonialism   1093*
Economic Integration and the Coming of the European
    Union   1094

**The Soviet Union and the Communist
Bloc   1097**

Dilemmas of the Soviet System in Postwar
    Europe   1097
De-Stalinization Under Khrushchev,
    1955–1964   1098
From Liberalization to Stagnation   1101

**Democracy and Its Discontents, 1968 and
After   1104**

Democratic Consolidation and Political
    Alienation   1104
The Oil Crisis and the Changing Economic
    Framework   1105
Strains in the Welfare State   1106
The Democratic Consensus and Its Limitations   1106

Summary   1107
Suggested Reading   1108

Weighing the Evidence: Pop Art   1110

**30 The West and the World in the
    Late Twentieth Century   1113**

Challenges of Affluence in the West   1114

The Changing Economies: Prosperity, Imbalance,
    Limitation   1115
Affluence and Secularization   1117
The Significance of Gender   1118
Re-evaluating the Role of Government   1119

On the Ruins of the Communist System   1121

Crisis and Innovation in the Soviet Bloc   1121
The Crisis of Communism in the Satellite
    States   1122
The Anticommunist Revolution, 1989–1991   1127
Life After Communism   1130

**Europe and the West After the Bipolar
Peace   1132**

The Changing International Framework   1133
The European Union   1136
Supranational Initiatives and Global Issues   1139
Immigration and Citizenship   1140

**In the Shadow of History: The Experiment
Continues   1141**

Europe and America, Old and New   1141
Technology and the Fragile European
    Environment   1144
The Uncertain Triumph of Democratic
    Capitalism   1144

**Conclusion: Western Civilization in a Global
Age   1147**

*Encounters with the West: The Case of
"Orientalism"   1148*

Suggested Reading   1149

*Weighing the Evidence: The Debate over Western
Civilization   1150*

Chapter Opener Credits   A-1

Text Credits   A-1

Index   A-5

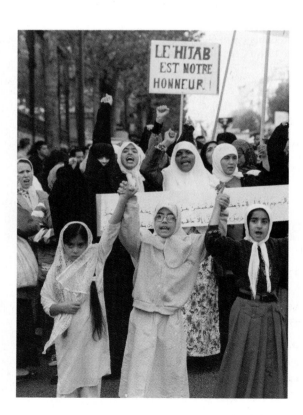

Maps

1.1 Western Asia   8

1.2 Ancient Egypt and the Levant   22

1.3 The International System, ca. 1500– ca. 1200 B.C.   35

2.1 The Assyrian and Persian Empires   45

2.2 Ancient Israel   54

2.3 Aegean Greece   65

3.1 Archaic and Classical Greece   80

3.2 Phoenician and Greek Colonization   83

3.3 Attica   89

3.4 Greece in the Peloponnesian War   104

4.1 Conquests of Philip and Alexander   124

4.2 Hellenistic Kingdoms, Leagues, and City-States, ca. 240 B.C.   125

4.3 The Eastern Mediterranean, ca. 200 B.C.   130

5.1 Early Italy and Region of City of Rome   156

5.2 Roman Italy, ca. 265 B.C.   167

5.3 Roman Expansion, 264–44 B.C.   174

6.1 The Roman World in the Early Empire   194

6.2 The Expansion of Christianity to A.D. 200   214

7.1 Diocletian's Division of the Roman Empire   228

7.2 The Spread of Christianity to A.D. 600   238

7.3 The Germanic Kingdoms in the Sixth Century   249

8.1 The Expansion of Islam to 732   270

8.2 The Byzantine Empire in the Eighth and Ninth Centuries   278

8.3 The Carolingian World   290

9.1 Germany and Its Duchies   321

9.2 French Territorial Principalities   327

9.3 The Christian Reconquista of Muslim Spain   333

9.4 The Communal Movement in Italy   334

9.5 The States of an Expanding Europe   336

10.1 Europe, ca. 1220   354

10.2 The Crusades, 1095–1270   378

11.1 England and France in the Hundred Years' War   406

11.2 The Progress of the Black Death   415

11.3 Turkey and Eastern Europe   426

12.1 The Spread of Printing   457

13.1 Winds and Currents   481

13.2 World Exploration   484

13.3 Mexico and Central America   493

13.4 Peru and Central America   494

14.1 Reform in Germany   518

14.2 Protestants and Catholics in 1555   526

15.1 The Spanish Habsburgs and Europe   554

15.2 The Netherlands, 1559–1609   556

15.3 Territories of the Austrian Habsburgs   573

15.4 Europe in the Thirty Years' War   574

16.1 Territorial Gains of Louis XIV, 1667–1715   596

16.2 New Powers in Central and Eastern Europe   606

16.3 Dutch Commerce in the Seventeenth Century   612

16.4 British and French in North America, ca. 1700   618

18.1 The Partition of Poland and the Expansion of Russia   679

18.2 The Atlantic Economy, ca. 1750   684

18.3 British Gains in North America   688

18.4 Population and Production in Eighteenth-Century Europe   691

19.1 Napoleonic Europe, ca. 1810   724

20.1 Europe in 1815   740

20.2 Major Revolutions and Reforms, 1848–1849   763

21.1 The Industrial Transformation in England, ca. 1850   783

21.2 Continental Industrialization, ca. 1850   785

21.3 Cities Reaching Population Level of 100,000 by 1750, 1800, and 1850   789

22.1 The Unification of Italy, 1859–1870   817

22.2 The Unification of Germany   821

22.3 Austria-Hungary in 1878   826

22.4 U.S. Expansion Through 1853   830

23.1 European Rails, 1850 and 1880   848

23.2 Haussmann's Paris, 1850–1870   859

24.1 Africa in 1914   893

24.2 Asia in 1914   896

24.3 European Migrations, 1820–1910   898

24.4 The Balkans in 1914   911

25.1 Major Fronts of World War I   920

25.2 Stalemate and Decision on the Western Front   922

25.3 The Impact of the War: The Territorial Settlement in Europe and the Middle East   946

25.4 Ethnicity in East-Central Europe, 1919   948

26.1 Foreign Intervention and Civil War in Revolutionary Russia, 1918–1920   976

27.1 The Spanish Civil War, 1936–1939   1016

27.2 The Expansion of Nazi Germany, 1936–1939   1024

28.1 World War II: European Theaters   1036

28.2 The Nazi New Order in Europe, 1942   1038

28.3 The War in East Asia and the Pacific   1050

28.4 The Impact of World War II in Europe   1054

28.5 The Partition of Palestine and the Birth of the State of Israel   1067

29.1 From Colonialism to Independence   1088

29.2 Military Alliances and Multinational Economic Groupings in the Era of the Cold War   1096

30.1 Europe After the Cold War   1126

30.2 Ethnic Conflict in East-Central Europe   1134

30.3 World Population Density, mid-1990s   1138

Documents

King Hammurabi Dispenses Justice   17

Heroism and Death in Mesopotamia   20

Pharaoh the Divine and Invincible   26

Humane Values   29

Encounters with the West: Egyptian Attitudes Toward Foreigners   32

An Assyrian King Attacks Phoenicia and Jerusalem   46

The Covenant   55

Ruth   58

Cyrus and His Subjects' Gods   61

Encounters with the West: Greeks and Trojans   72

Spartan Women   88

The Debate on Democracy   98

Encounters with the West: The Enemy as Barbarian   102

Socrates' Defense   108

"Man Is a Political Animal"   110

Virtues and Vices of Alexander the Great   123

Encounters with the West: The Oracle of the Potter   131

A Seleucid Queen Helps the City of Iasos   141

Early Stoic Ethics and Politics   143

The Jews Struggle over Hellenism   146

The Rape of Lucretia   159

A Roman Triumph   170

Encounters with the West: Roman Attitudes Toward the Conquered   179

Tiberius Gracchus on Rome's Plight   181

Cicero in Defense of Milo   186

Augustus: The Official Story   196

Augustus: A Skeptical View   198

Ordinary People   206

Encounters with the West: Syria Between Rome and Persia   212

Christian Community and Christian Relationships   218

A Contemporary View of Diocletian's Reforms   232

The Valor of a Woman   242

Encounters with the West: Two Views of the Huns   246

Basic Principles of Roman Law   253

Melania the Younger: The Appeal of Monasticism to Women   257

The Moment of Augustine's Spiritual Awakening   260

The Message of the Quran   272

Encounters with the West: Muslim and Byzantine "Diplomacy"?   281

Two English Holy Women: Hilda and Leoba   286

A Contemporary Portrait of Charlemagne   289

Carolingian Women and the Great Estate   293

Feudal Bonds and Obligations   313

Furnishings of a Welsh Household   319

The Issues in the Investiture Controversy   325

Saint Anselm on the Existence of God   341

The Making of a Saint and Scholar: Hildegard of Bingen   342

Encounters with the West: An Arab Perspective on the First Crusade   347

Innocent III on His Rights and Powers   358

A Contemporary View of Saint Louis   364

Encounters with the West: William of Rubruck Reports on the Mongols   369

New Orders for Women: Clares and Beguines   376

Thomas Aquinas's Proof for the Existence of God   382

Saint Catherine and the Avignon Papacy   399

The Inquisition of Joan of Arc   408

The Black Death   417

The Rising of 1381   424

Encounters with the West: A European View of Constantinople   428

Petrarch Responds to His Critics   443

Cassandra Fedele Defends Liberal Arts for Women   445

Encounters with the West: Rabbi Mordecai Dato Criticizes the Humanists   447

Isabella d'Este Orders Art   465

Giovanni della Casa on the Perfect Gentleman   467

Pegalotti on Travel to the East   479

Albuquerque Defends the Portuguese Empire   485

Christopher Columbus Describes His Discoveries   489

Encounters with the West: An Inca Nobleman Defends His Civilization   495

The New World and the Old   503

Martin Luther's Address to the Christian Nobility of the German Nation   515

Encounters with the West: Duels Among Europeans and Turks   524

The Act of Supremacy   529

The Conversion of Jeanne d'Albret   533

Ignatius Loyola's Spiritual Exercises   537

A Woman Defends Her Right to Practice Healing   550

Elite Fears of Popular Religious Unrest in the Netherlands   557

Richelieu Supports the Authority of the State   566

Encounters with the West: Montaigne Discusses Barbarity in the New World and the Old   579

Elizabeth I Addresses Her Troops   582

Politics and Ritual at the Court of Louis XIV   593

The Putney Debates   599

Peter the Great Changes Russia   610

Encounters with the West: Agents of the Dutch East India Company Confront Asian Powers   614

The Disappointments of the Virginia Colony   617

Copernicus's Preface to *On the Revolution of Heavenly Bodies*   629

Galileo Confronts the Church   633

Margaret Cavendish Challenges Male Scientists   645

Encounters with the West: Jesuits and Astronomy in China   648

Locke's View of the Purpose of Government   650

Voltaire on Britain's Commercial Success   662

An English Feminist Criticizes Unenlightened Views of Women   666

Rousseau Discusses the Benefits of Submitting to the General Will   667

Encounters with the West: An African Recalls the Horrors of the Slave Ship   685

The Condition of Serfs in Russia   693

Declaration of the Rights of Man and the Citizen   707

A Young Woman Recounts the March to Versailles   709

Declaration of the Rights of Woman   712

Robespierre Justifies the Terror   716

A Citizen of Paris Suffers Under the Terror   717

Encounters with the West: A Planter's Wife on the Haitian Slave Revolt   731

Metternich's Cure for Europe   744

Adam Smith Describes the Workings of the Market Economy   748

Encounters with the West: A Moroccan Description of the French Freedom of the Press   754

A Plea to Abolish Slavery in the British Colonies   756

A Revolutionary of 1848 Calls for Women's Political Rights   766

Encounters with the West: A Persian Discovers the British Rail System   777

Friedrich Engels Describes an Urban Slum   790

The Young Girl in the Factory   794

The New Discipline of the Factory System   801

The *Communist Manifesto*   804

Florence Nightingale in the Crimean War   813

Cavour and Napoleon III Plot War   816

Bismarck Considers the Dynastic Role in German Unification   825

Encounters with the West: A Japanese View of the British Parliament   833

The Tsar Demands the Freeing of the Serfs   839

Advice on Running the Middle-Class Household   853

Haussmann Justifies the Rebuilding of Paris   860

Darwin's Basic Laws of Evolution   866

Emile Zola on the Novelist as Scientist   872

Encounters with the West: A Chinese Official's Views of European Material Progress   873

The Limits of Intellect   885

Mary Kingsley on Africans and British Imperialism   892

Encounters with the West: Chief Montshiwa Petitions Queen Victoria   894

Pankhurst on Women's Rights   902

A Conspiratorial Revolutionary Party   907

Into the Trenches   924

Domestic Mobilization and the Role of Women   928

The Bolsheviks in Power, November 1917   936

A Meaning to the War: Wilson's Fourteen Points   938

Encounters with the West: Prince Faisal at the Peace Conference   944

Encounters with the West: Sun Yixien on Chinese Nationalism   961

Doubts About Mass Society   966

A Marxist Critique of Communism   978

Toward Fascism: Alfredo Rocco on the Weakness of the Liberal Democratic State   982

Tradition and Women: The Conditions of Independence   988

Retreating from "the New Woman"   999

Encounters with the West: Gandhi on Nonviolence   1000

Carrying out the Stalinist Revolution   1003

Hitler's World-View: Nature, Race, and Struggle   1008

Toward Appeasement: The Longing
  for Peace   1022
Toward the Nazi New Order   1041
Stalingrad: The Diary of a German
  Soldier   1045
*Encounters with the West: Japan's "Pan-Asian"
  Mission   1049*
Discerning the Iron Curtain   1064
The Soviet View of the Cold War   1065
Existentialism and the Loss of Bearings   1076
Human Freedom and the Origins of a
  New Feminism   1083

*Encounters with the West: The Legacy of
  European Colonialism   1093*
Practical Thinking and European
  Integration   1095
Denouncing the Crimes of Stalinism   1100
Toward a Postindustrial Society   1116
Power from Below: Living the Truth   1123
Europe and the American Challenge   1143
The Varieties of Liberal Capitalism   1146
*Encounters with the West: The Case of
  "Orientalism"   1148*

Chronologies, Genealogies, and Charts

Human Origins to ca. 3000 B.C.   5
Early Writing   12
Mesopotamia   13
Egypt   21
Anatolia and the Levant   33
Western Asia   44
Greece and the Aegean   64
Society and Politics in Archaic Greece   81
War and Diplomacy in Classical Greece   101
Foundations of the Hellenistic World   121
Rebellion and Reform   133
Roman Government and Society   163
Roman Expansion   172
Roman Peace and Third-Century Crisis   208
The Evolution of the Roman Empire   233
The Development of Catholic Christianity   239
The Barbarians   245
The Islamic World   269
The Byzantine Empire   275
The Germanic West   287
A Quire   304
Kings and Warriors   326
Monks and Writers   340
The Structure of Romanesque
  Architecture   343

The Development of States, 1150–1300   361
Population Increases in Italian Cities,
  1200–1300   370
Spiritual and Intellectual Leaders of High
  Medieval Europe   379
The Structure of Gothic Architecture   383
The Crisis of the Western Church   398
England and France in the Late Middle
  Ages   403
French and English Succession in the
  Fourteenth Century   404
The Union of Crowns in Spain   429
Overseas Exploration and Conquest   487
The Reformation and Counter-Reformation
  516
The Habsburg Succession, 1493–1556   521
Revolt of the Netherlands   558
The French Succession, 1515–1715   563
The Thirty Years' War, 1618–1648   572
Signatures from English Court
  Depositions   586
Milestones of the Scientific Revolution   630
Major Works of the Enlightenment   663
The French Revolution, 1789–1791   711
The French Revolution, 1792–1793   713

The French Revolution, 1793–1794   715

The French Revolution, 1794–1799   720

European Revolutions, 1820–1831   758

Major Inventions of the Industrial
    Transformation   780

The Increase in Gross National Product per
    Capita in Principal European Countries,
    1830–1913   787

Coal Production in Industrializing
    Nations   795

Wage Differentials in Verviers, Belgium,
    1836–1869   809

German Unification   822

Improvements in Communications and
    Transportation   847

Major Diplomatic Alliances and
    Agreements   910

Plan of the Upper Floor of the British Museum,
    ca. 1880   915

World War I and Its Aftermath   937

Events of the 1920s   985

The Diplomatic Revolution of the 1930s   1015

The Era of World War II   1047

Decolonization   1091

The Era of the Cold War   1099

Beyond the Cold War   1121

Weighing the Evidence

1   The Iceman and His World   40–41

2   The Trojan War   76–77

3   The Parthenon   116–117

4   Images of Cleopatra   150–151

5   Luxury Goods and Gender Wars in
    Rome   190–191

6   Pompeii   224–225

7   The Ravenna Mosaics   264–265

8   The Manuscript Book   304–305

9   The Medieval Castle   350–351

10   The Arts of Chartres Cathedral   390–391

11   A Painting of the Plague   434–435

12   The Art of Renaissance Florence   470–471

13   A Mexican Shrine   506–507

14   A Reformation Woodcut   542–543

15   Signatures   586–587

16   Table Manners   622–623

17   Modern Maps   654–655

18   Gardens   694–695

19   Political Symbols   734–735

20   *Raft of the "Medusa"*   772–773

21   Workers' Wages   808–809

22   An Engraving of the British Royal
    Family   842–843

23   The Crystal Palace   876–877

24   The Layout of the British Museum   914–915

25   The Poetry of World War I   954–955

26   Modern Design   992–993

27   Film as Propaganda   1028–1029

28   Holocaust Testimony   1070–1071

29   Pop Art   1110–1111

30   The Debate over Western
    Civilization   1150–1151

Preface

Miles Davis was once asked what he thought jazz musicians would be playing in ten years, and he said that if he knew that, he would already be playing it. The authors of this book are committed teachers who never lost the thrill of being history students. We do not claim that we have seen into the future, but we can say with real conviction that we have tried to do better, for both instructors and students, than has been done in the past. And as we look back over nearly a decade, to the time when we were planning the first edition of *Western Civilization: The Continuing Experiment*, we can say with a mixture of pride and humility that we anticipated quite well what kind of history would be "playing" in ten years.

The purpose of a Western civilization textbook is to anchor a course that aims to inform students about essential developments within a tradition that has powerfully, although not always positively, affected everyone who is alive today. Although each of us finds something to admire in all of the existing textbooks, none of us was fully happy with any of them. We were disappointed with books that claimed "balance" but actually stressed a single kind of history. We regretted that so many texts were uneven in their command of recent scholarship. Although convinced of both the inherent interest of Western civilization and the importance of teaching the subject, we were disconcerted by the celebratory tone of some books, which portray the West as resting on its laurels instead of creatively facing its future.

As we were planning this book, momentous changes shook the Western world. Most obviously, the Soviet Union collapsed and the communist regimes of Eastern Europe tumbled one after another. Those who reflect on the West today must take account of Islamic minorities in the Slavic Balkans, Turkish workers in Germany, and African workers in France. Unprecedented economic prosperity—to be sure, unevenly distributed—marks all the lands from Ireland to Russia. Thus, the study of Western civilization at the dawn of a new millennium cannot focus narrowly on the peoples of Europe's western fringe, and it cannot take its bearings from a historical landscape whose most prominent features are the Depression of the 1930s, the world wars, and a global population divided by the iron curtain.

We decided to try very hard to produce a book that is balanced and coherent; that addresses the full range of subjects that a Western civilization text needs to address; that provides the student reader with interesting, timely material; that is up-to-date in terms of scholarship and approach; and that is handsome to look at—in short, a book that helps the instructor to teach and the student to learn. We have kept our common vision fresh through frequent meetings, correspondence, E-mail, critical mutual readings, and expert editorial guidance. Six authors have come together as one, and because each of us focused on his or her own area of specialization, we believe we have attained a rare blend of competence, confidence, and enthusiasm.

CENTRAL THEMES AND APPROACH

Western civilization is a story. We therefore aimed at a strong chronological narrative line. Our experience as teachers tells us that students appreciate this clear but gentle orientation. Our experience tells us, too, that an approach that is more chronological than thematic will leave instructors plenty of room to adapt our narrative to their preferred organization.

Although we maintain the familiar, large-scale divisions of a Western civilization book, we also present some innovative adjustments in arrangement. For instance, Chapter 2 treats early Greece together with the whole eastern Mediterranean region in the period from about 1500 to 750 B.C. This approach both links kindred cultures and respects chronological flow better than customary treatments, which take western Asia to a certain point and backtrack to deal with early Greece. We focus an entire chapter on Late Antiquity, the tumultuous and fascinating period from about A.D. 300 to 600 that witnessed the transformation of the Roman Empire into three successors: Byzantine, Islamic, and European. We introduce and analyze the industrial transformation in the middle of the nineteenth century, when it was at its high point, instead of scattering its account through several chapters. Our twentieth-century chapters reflect an understanding of the century formed in its closing years rather than in its middle decades. What is new in our organization represents adjustments grounded in the best scholarship, and what is old represents time-tested approaches.

A chronological narrative that respects the traditional divisions of ancient, medieval, early modern, and modern will inevitably reflect great people and great events. We make no apology for this, and we urge no particular ideology in doing it. Marx was surely right when he said that women and men make history without knowing they are doing so, but it is nonetheless true that Alexander, Charlemagne, Elizabeth I, Napoleon, and Hitler have had a more decisive impact on the development of the West than most ordinary individuals. That is true, but not interesting to teachers or to students until we say why it is true.

This book takes as its point of departure *power* in all its senses: public and private; economic, social, political, and cultural; symbolic and real. We continually ask who had power, and who did not. Through what public and private means was power gained, lost, and exercised in a given time and place? How did people talk about power? What kinds of rituals, ceremonies, or celebrations displayed power? What relationships existed among economic, social, political, and cultural power?

By using power, not old-fashioned high politics, as our organizing principle we believe we have achieved the kind of balance and integration that are frequently promised but seldom attained. We have deliberately avoided putting the occasional paragraph or section on women, children, families, religious minorities, eating habits, or marriage patterns in the middle of a discussion of something else entirely. We maintain a sustained interest in the history of women, often using gender as a tool of analysis and explanation, and we discuss such subjects as diet, clothing, or dwellings when Europeans themselves talked about them, or when there were important changes in these areas. Women are not relegated to a separate section in our account of the Middle Ages, for example, but instead are situated in accounts of politics, society, religion, and culture. Nineteenth-century women appear as workers, writers, or political activists and not under a single heading that would deprive them of contextual participation in their contemporary world.

Our focus on power permits a continuous, nuanced treatment of intellectual history. Major thinkers and key intellectual traditions are consistently integrated into the story rather than treated in-dependently as if they were *the* story of Western civilization, or else a sideshow to the main event. Any understanding of Plato and Aristotle, for instance, must begin in the Greek *polis*. Renaissance humanism cannot be understood apart from its late medieval Italian, urban context. We anchor the Scientific Revolution to Renaissance and Reformation intellectual life, court societies, patronage networks, and the expanding world created by Europe's first overseas empires. We root romanticism in its urban, industrial, nationalistic, and politically restless nineteenth-century world, and we treat existentialism as one response to modern war and totalitarianism.

We thought hard about another issue that textbooks usually take for granted: What is the West? This book was conceived and written after the end of the cold war and the fall of communist regimes in Eastern Europe. Both the West's understanding of itself at any point in time and the historical understanding of the West through succeeding generations have changed in interesting and important ways, never more so than today. Thus, we continually invite our readers to think about the precise object of their study.

In fashioning our picture of the West, we took two unusual steps. First, our West is bigger than the one found in most textbooks. We treat the Celtic world, Scandinavia, and the Slavic world as integral parts of the story. We look often at the lands that border the West—Anatolia/Turkey, western Asia, North Africa, the Eurasian steppes—in order to show the to-and-fro of peoples, ideas, technologies, and products. Second, we continually situate the West in its global context. We must be clear: This is not a world history book. But just as we recognize that the West has influenced the rest of the world, so too we carefully acknowledge that the rest of the world has influenced the West. We begin this story of mutual interaction with the Greeks and Romans, carry it through the European Middle Ages, focus on it in the age of European exploration and conquest, and analyze it closely in the modern world of industry, empire, diplomacy, and questions of citizenship and identity.

We ask, finally, that you note the subtitle of the book: "The Continuing Experiment." It was carefully chosen to convey our resolve to avoid a deterministic approach. For students and teachers, an appreciation of continuity and change, of unity and diversity, can foster sympathetic participation in our often bewildering world. We try to give individual actors, moments, and movements the sense of drama, possibility, and contingency that they actually possessed.

We, with faultless hindsight, always know how things came out. Contemporaries often hadn't a clue. We respect them. Much of the fascination, and the reward, of studying Western civilization lies precisely in its richness, diversity, changeability, unpredictability.

DISTINCTIVE FEATURES

To make this text as accessible as possible to students, we have constantly been aware of its place in a program of teaching. Each chapter begins with a thematic introduction that engages the reader's interest while pointing clearly and in some detail to what will follow. Chronologies help to organize and review major developments. Careful chapter summaries draw together major topics and themes and link the present chapter to the one that follows. To help students strike out on their own to new historical discoveries, we provide for each chapter an annotated reading list of scholarly classics and exciting new works.

In addition to a sound pedagogical framework, and to an engaging full-color design that clarifies and animates the illustrations and text, we have thoroughly integrated all the elements of the book. Our maps, for example, support the text in both traditional and novel ways. Teachers will find "old friends" among them but will make many new acquaintances too. Our diverse array of boxed primary sources—five per chapter—are referred to and tightly anchored in the text and support their surrounding discussion. Here again, classic documents are blended with fresh newcomers. Our photographs, many of which have not previously appeared in textbooks, are never merely decorative, and their captions seek to extend the discussions that they complement.

An example may help to illustrate this integration. The central theme of Chapter 9, which treats Europe from 900 to 1150, is "expansion." Thus the chapter explores population growth, economic development, and foreign military adventures—chiefly the Crusades. But this theme of expansion is developed to reinforce the book's central, unifying themes—power and the West within the wider world. For example, the text discusses the kinds of social and institutional structures that were created or refined to accommodate the expansion of territorial power and responsibility. The maps provide clear evidence of the territorial expansion of both old

states (England, France, Germany) and new ones (in Celtic, Scandinavian, and Slavic areas). The pictures illustrate power in several ways. Kings are depicted on thrones, wearing crowns, holding orbs and scepters, and receiving gifts and obeisance. In other words, their symbolic and ceremonial manifestations of power are displayed. Castles, one of the great military and political technologies of the time, appear in Welsh, French, and Polish forms. A woman of immense power in central Italy is shown receiving the earnest entreaties for help of a German emperor. Boxed documents illustrate personal bonds of homage and fealty, key issues in the period's clashes between secular and ecclesiastical officials, and, on a lesser scale, the division of goods in Welsh law between men and women after a divorce. The various components of this chapter, as of all the chapters, continually reinforce one another, for a careful integration that promotes discussion and enhances learning.

Another important component of this book is the two-page feature "Weighing the Evidence," presented at the end of each chapter. These features introduce students to the fascinating variety of sources that historians use and invite them to think critically about the nature of historical information and inquiry. Each opens with a description of the evidence reproduced in the feature—sources ranging from images of Cleopatra, the Ravenna mosaics, Reformation woodcuts, eighteenth-century political symbols, the layout of the British Museum, and the poetry of World War I—and then discusses how the professional historian examines this evidence to reconstruct the past. When Samuel Butler said that God cannot change history but that historians can and often do, he meant that history itself arises from new or different acts of interpretation. With "Weighing the Evidence," students look over the shoulder of the historian to become active participants in this interpretive process. The sources examined are interesting and instructive in their own right, but the "Weighing the Evidence" features also contribute to the teaching program of the book. As always, they are carefully integrated into the text: There are references to them at appropriate points in the narrative; they themselves contain cross-references where appropriate to other sections or illustrations; and they support ongoing discussions.

This book is also flexible in format as well as substantive organization. Because schools use different academic calendars, organize Western civilization courses according to different chronologies, and require or recommend different parts of the course, we issue this book in four formats, three of which embrace the complete work:

- One-volume hardcover edition (Chapters 1–30)
- Two-volume paperback, Volume I: To 1715 (Chapters 1–17), Volume II: Since 1560 (Chapters 15–30)
- Three-volume paperback, Volume A: To 1500 (Chapters 1–12), Volume B: 1300–1715 (Chapters 11–19), Volume C: Since 1789 (Chapters 19–30)
- And new to this edition, Since 1300 (Chapters 11–30)

Volume II opens with a comprehensive introduction that situates the student reader in the late sixteenth century and surveys the course of Western civilization from ancient times to the early centuries of the modern era. This introduction is designed particularly for students who did not take the first semester of the course, or who are new to this book.

CHANGES IN THE NEW EDITION

In preparing our second edition we thought hard about our own experiences in using the book, and we paid strict attention to the advice given us by many instructors, including those who used the book and those who did not. Five main lines of revision guided our changes:

Organizational Changes

The most obvious change here is that we shrank our book from thirty-two to thirty chapters. The first-edition chapter on "The Frontiers of Latin Europe" was deleted, and its most important conceptual perspectives and substantive material were redistributed among Chapters 8, 9, and 10. Two chapters on later medieval Europe were tightened in focus and organization and turned into one new chapter (11). By cutting out two first-edition chapters in Volume I, it became possible to include Chapter 17 on the Scientific Revolution in both Volumes I and II, a change that accommodates many syllabuses.

Many other organizational changes are less visible but still significant. The revolution from the Gracchi to Caesar in Republican Rome has been moved to Chapter 5, which permits Chapter 6 to have a sharper focus on the crisis of the late Republic and the emergence of the Roman Empire. Some material on medieval church-state controversies that was earlier distributed over several chapters is now consolidated in Chapter 10. Discussions of the late medieval economy are now sharply focused in Chapter 11, and former sections on late medieval and Renaissance art are now found together in Chapter 12. Sections treating the English Revolution, the French Revolution, and the revolutions of 1848 have undergone significant reorganization and revision. The book's final chapters have been rearranged and revised in light of shifting perspectives on postcommunist Eastern Europe.

Thematic Integration

Users and reviewers praised our book's two major themes—power and the shape of the West within the wider world—but in preparing this edition we felt we could do even better. Specifically, we saw opportunities to treat the second theme in more detail and to sharpen our use of gender as a means of explanation. Accordingly, we began at the beginning, so to speak, and incorporated material on Neolithic and Copper Age Europe to complement our treatment of the Mesopotamian and Mediterranean worlds. We paid more attention to the shifting frontiers of medieval Europe. In revising our account of the immensely important political and diplomatic history of the period from about 1500 to 1800, we included more extensive coverage of both Europe's immediate frontiers and the wider world. Our nineteenth-century chapters contain an expanded account of the growing power of the United States and the global significance of European emigration. Our nineteenth- and twentieth-century chapters now contain additional coverage of the mutual relations between Europe and its colonies. The Depression of the 1930s is anchored more firmly in a global context, and the multicultural implications of vast population movements in the late twentieth century are carefully considered.

From the start, our book paid serious attention to the experiences of women and to the exciting possibilities of using gender as a tool of analysis. We were very pleased that users and reviewers affirmed our intentions and achievements. Still, in revising we believed that we could improve our coverage. Readers of the first edition will detect many changes, as in the sections on the Roman Empire, Late Antiquity, the High Middle Ages, exploration and discovery, the Scientific Revolution, nineteenth-century ideologies and social movements, the welfare state, and the problems of identity politics in the very recent past.

New Primary-Source Chapter Feature

To help us achieve our goal of thematic integration, in this edition we have added the primary-source feature "Encounters with the West." Every chapter contains one readily identifiable document that portrays other people commenting on westerners or westerners commenting on the world around them. In these documents, students meet Egyptians and Romans reacting to foreigners, a Franciscan missionary telling about the Mongols, an Inca nobleman describing his civilization, the wife of a wealthy plantation owner stating her views on Haiti's slave revolt, a Moroccan commenting on French press freedoms, Gandhi talking about nonviolence, and the controversial, influential Edward Said discussing "Orientalism."

Improved Chapter Features

We have also revised our existing pedagogical framework to take every opportunity to tighten the book's integration and to enhance its teachability. Every chapter now opens with an arresting full-color illustration that is specifically referenced in the introduction on the facing page. This visual and textual device expresses the main themes and issues raised in that chapter and captures the interest and provokes the imagination of the student reader. To continue our book's close integration of text and artwork, we have replaced about one-third of the in-text illustrations. Each new picture and drawing was chosen specifically to enhance the book's pedagogical force. All maps were scrutinized for accuracy and pedagogical value, and many were revised in subtle ways. We incorporated a number of new boxed documents that work to illustrate or extend our themes. Most chapters, moreover, now contain at least one document that lends itself to a "gendered" reading to help students familiarize themselves with gender as a tool of analysis. About one-third of the "Weighing the Evidence" features are new in this edition. Some of the newcomers are attributable to exciting discoveries, such as "The Ice Man's World." Others, on topics ranging from the invention of modern cartography to the Crystal Palace and pop art, serve to bolster our themes and to provoke discussion.

Incorporation of Recent Scholarship

One important advantage of a six-person author team is that we can keep track of the latest publications across the whole course of Western civilization. Naturally, few periods or problems have been the subject of massive reinterpretation since our first edition, but many small changes in perspective have turned up all over. In line with the most recent, sound work, we have especially revised sections on the Greek phalanx and polis, the Etruscans and early Rome, Jesus and early Christianity, Late Antiquity, the Slavic world, vernacular culture in the Renaissance, the origins of the Reformation, the English Revolution, Napoleon, many aspects of the nineteenth century, the cold war, and the fall of Soviet communism. To incorporate recent findings and perspectives, we have updated all the lists of suggested readings.

SUPPLEMENTS

We have thoroughly revised our array of text supplements provided to aid students in learning and instructors in teaching. These supplements, including a *Study Guide*, a *Computerized Study Guide*, an *Instructor's Resource Manual*, *Test Items*, *Computerized Test Items*, *Map Transparencies*, a *Videodisc* and *Videodisc Guide*, and two new multimedia supplements: a *Power Presentation Manager* and a CD-ROM of interactive maps, are tied closely to the text and to one another, to provide a tightly integrated program of teaching and learning.

The *Study Guide*, written by Miriam Shadis of Ohio University, includes an introductory essay on how to make the best use of your Western Civilization course. For each chapter it gives learning objectives, an annotated outline of the chapter, multiple-choice questions keyed to the text, essay questions with guidelines, analytical questions, and map exercises. The *Study Guide* is published in two volumes, to correspond with Volumes I and II of the text: Volume I contains Chapters 1–17 and Volume II contains Chapters 15–30. The *Study Guide* is also available in a computerized version for use with IBM® PC or compatible computers. This *Computerized Study Guide* contains text page references for all questions and rejoinders to each multiple-choice question that explain why the student's response is or is not correct.

The *Instructor's Resource Manual*, prepared by Janice Liedl of Laurentian University, contains useful teaching strategies and tips for getting the most out of the text. Each chapter includes a summary and outline, learning objectives, lecture suggestions, discussion questions, recommended outside reading, and writing assignment and paper topics. For the new edition we have expanded the *Instructor's Resource Manual* to include recommended film, video, and multimedia resources, as well as collaborative learning activities for students.

Each chapter of the *Test Items,* written by Diane Moczar of Northern Virginia Community College, offers a list of 20 to 30 key terms, 10 to 15 short-answer and essay questions, 2 to 3 map questions, and 40 to 50 multiple-choice questions. Answers to the multiple-choice questions are located at the end of the *Test Items.* We also offer a computerized version of the *Test Items* for use with IBM® PC or compatible computers, to enable teachers to alter, replace, or add questions. Each item in the computerized test item file is numbered according to the printed test item file to ease the creation of customized tests.

An exciting addition to our map program is a CD-ROM of thirty interactive maps, available to both instructors and students. We also offer *The Western Civilization Videodisc/Videotape/Slide* program, a multimedia collection of visual images, as well as a set of full-color *Transparencies* of all the maps in the text.

In addition, we are pleased to provide the *Power Presentation Manager,* a software tool that enables teachers to prepare visual aids for lectures electronically, using both textual and visual materials. Instructors can customize their lectures by incorporating their own material onto the PPM and combining it with the electronic resources provided, including adaptable chapter outlines, tables, illustrations, and maps from the text.

Finally, we are proud to announce the creation of our on-line primary-source collection, *BiblioBase™: Custom Coursepacks in Western Civilization.* This resource will allow instructors to select from over 600 primary-source documents to create their own customized reader.

ACKNOWLEDGMENTS

From the first draft to the last, the authors have benefited from repeated critical readings by many colleagues. We have tried very hard to profit from the vast fund of experience and knowledge that has been placed generously at our disposal. Our thanks to the following instructors: **Lawrence Backlund,** Montgomery County Community College; **John Battick,** University of Maine—Orono; **F. E. Beemon,** Middle Tennessee State University; **Christopher M. Bellitto,** St. Joseph's Seminary, Dunwoodie; **Wayne Bledsoe,** University of Missouri—Rolla; **Donna Bohanan,** Auburn University; **RaGena De Aragon,** Gonzaga University; **Peter Diehl,** Western Wash-

ington University; **Katherine J. Haldane,** The Citadel; **Boyd Hill,** University of Colorado—Boulder; **James Lehning,** University of Utah; **Daniel Lewis,** California State Polytechnic University at Pomona; **Janice Liedl,** Laurentian University; **Raymond Mentzner,** Montana State University; **John Nicols,** University of Oregon; **Byron Nordstrom,** Gustavus Adolphus College; **Beth Plummer,** Wingate University; **Janet Polasky,** University of New Hampshire; **Donald Pryce,** University of South Dakota; **John Rosser,** Boston College; **Arnold Sherman,** Champlain College; **Tom Taylor,** Seattle University; and **James Walter,** Sinclair Community College.

Each of us has also benefited from the close readings and valuable criticisms of our coauthors, although we all assume responsibility for our own chapters. Barry Strauss has written Chapters 1–6; Thomas Noble, Chapters 7–10; Duane Osheim, Chapters 11–14; Kristen Neuschel, Chapters 15–19; William Cohen, Chapters 20–24; and David Roberts, Chapters 25–30.

Many colleagues, friends, and family members have helped us develop this work as well. Thomas Noble wishes to thank Linda L. Noble for her patience and kindness over the years devoted to this project. He is also grateful to John Contreni, Wendy Davies, Thomas Head, Elizabeth Meyer, Richard Sullivan, John Van Engen, Robert Wilken, and Ian Wood.

Barry Strauss is grateful to colleagues at Cornell and at other universities who offered advice and encouragement and responded to scholarly questions. He would also like to thank Sandra Kisner and Elaine Scott for their invaluable assistance. Most important has been the support and forbearance of his family. His daughter, Sylvie, his son, Michael, and, above all, his wife, Marcia, have truly been sources of inspiration.

Duane Osheim wishes to thank his family for support during the writing and revising of this book. He is also grateful to colleagues at the University of Virginia, who helped to clarify the many connections between Western civilization and the wider world. He would specifically like to thank Erik Midelfort, Arthur Field, Janis Gibbs, and Beth Plummer for comments and advice.

Kristen Neuschel thanks her colleagues at Duke University for sharing their expertise. She is especially grateful to Sy Mauskopf, Bill Reddy, John Richards, Tom Robisheaux, Alex Roland, John J. TePaske, Julius Scott, and Peter Wood. She also thanks her husband and fellow historian, Alan Williams, for his wisdom about Western civilization and his support throughout the project, and her children, Jesse and Rachel, for their patience, joy, and curiosity.

William Cohen thanks his wife, Christine Matheu, and his daughters, Natalie, Leslie, and Laurel, for their support and encouragement over the many years that this project has matured.

David Roberts wishes to thank Bonnie Cary, Linda Green, and Nancy Heaton for their able assistance and Joshua Cole, Karl Friday, Thomas Ganschow, John Haag, John Morrow, Miranda Pollard, Ronald Rader, William Stueck, Eve Troutt Powell, and Kirk Willis, colleagues at the University of Georgia, for sharing their expertise in response to questions. He also thanks Beth Roberts for her constant support and interest and her exceedingly critical eye, and Ellen, Trina, and Anthony, for their college-age perspective and advice.

All the authors wish to thank the thousands of students who helped us to learn and to teach Western civilization. Their questions and concerns have shaped much of this work.

We also wish to acknowledge and thank the editors who did so much to bring this book into being. Elizabeth Welch, our Senior Basic Book Editor, sifted our thoughts, sharpened our focus, and smoothed our prose. Christina Horn, our Senior Project Editor, displayed boundless patience and professionalism as she assembled this book from all its constituent parts. Carole Frohlich, our tireless and enterprising picture researcher, often knew better than we did just what we wanted. To Jean Woy, Editor-in-Chief for Social Sciences (and our original Sponsoring Editor), we are grateful for confidence in this project, and in us. Sean Wakely was the Sponsoring Editor who steered this ship safely into port on its first voyage. Patricia Coryell is on the bridge now. We are grateful to them both for smooth passages.

Thomas F. X. Noble

The authors (left to right): Kristen Neuschel, Bill Cohen, David Roberts, Tom Noble (in back), Duane Osheim, Barry Strauss.

About the Authors

Thomas F. X. Noble

After receiving his Ph.D. from Michigan State University, Thomas Noble has taught at Albion College, Michigan State University, Texas Tech University, and since 1980 at the University of Virginia. He is the author of *The Republic of St. Peter: The Birth of the Papal State, 680–825, Religion, Culture and Society in the Early Middle Ages,* and *Soldiers of Christ: Saints and Saints' Lives from Late Antiquity and the Early Middle Ages.* Noble's articles and reviews have appeared in many leading journals, including the *American Historical Review, Byzantinische Zeitschrift, Catholic Historical Review, Revue d'histoire ecclésiastique, Speculum,* and *Studi medievali.* He has also contributed chapters to several books and articles to three encyclopedias. Noble, who was a member of the Institute for Advanced Study in 1994, has been awarded fellowships by the National Endowment for the Humanities (twice) and by the American Philosophical Society.

Barry S. Strauss

Professor of history and Classics at Cornell University, where he is also Director of the Peace Studies Program, Barry S. Strauss holds a Ph.D. from Yale in history. He has been awarded fellowships by the National Endowment for the Humanities, the American School of Classical Studies at Athens, and the Killam Foundation of Canada. He is the recipient of the Clark Award for excellence in teaching from Cornell. His many publications include *Athens After the Peloponnesian War: Class, Faction, and Policy, 403–386 B.C.; Fathers and Sons in Athens: Ideology and Society in the Era of the Peloponnesian War; The Anatomy of Error: Ancient Military Disasters and Their Lessons for Modern Strategists* (with Josiah Ober); and *Hegemonic Rivalry from Thucydides to the Nuclear Age* (co-edited with R. Ned Lebow).

Duane J. Osheim

A Fellow of the American Academy in Rome with a Ph.D. in History from the University of California, Davis, Duane Osheim is a professor of history at the University of Virginia. A specialist in late Medieval and Renaissance social and institutional history, he is author of *A Tuscan Monastery and Its Social World* and *An Italian Lordship: The Bishopric of Lucca in the Late Middle Ages,* as well as numerous studies of religious values and rural life in late Medieval Italy.

Kristen B. Neuschel

Associate professor of history at Duke University, Kristen B. Neuschel received the Ph.D. from Brown University. She is the author of *Word of Honor: Interpreting Noble Culture in Sixteenth-Century France* and articles on French social history and European women's history. In 1988 she received the Alumni Distinguished Undergraduate Teaching Award, which is awarded annually on the basis of student nominations for excellence in teaching at Duke.

William B. Cohen

After receiving his Ph.D. at Stanford University, William Cohen has taught at Northwestern University and Indiana University, where he is now professor of history. At Indiana, he served as chairman of the West European Studies and History departments. A previous president of the Society for French Historical Studies, Cohen has received several academic fellowships, among them a National Endowment for the Humanities and a Fulbright fellowship. Among his many publications are *Rulers of Empire, The French Encounter with Africans, European Empire Building, Robert Delavignette and the French Empire, The Transformation of Modern France,* and *Urban Government and the Rise of the City.*

David D. Roberts

After taking his Ph.D. in modern European history at the University of California, Berkeley, David Roberts taught at the Universities of Virginia and Rochester before becoming professor of history at the University of Georgia in 1988. At Rochester he chaired the Humanities Department of the Eastman School of Music, and he has chaired the History Department at Georgia since 1993. A recipient of Woodrow Wilson and Rockefeller Foundation fellowships, he is the author of *The Syndicalist Tradition and Italian Fascism, Benedetto Croce and the Uses of Historicism,* and *Nothing but History: Reconstruction and Extremity after Metaphysics,* as well as numerous articles and reviews.

WESTERN
CIVILIZATION

CHAPTER I

The Ancestors of the West

More than four thousand years ago in Sumer, in what is today southern Iraq, people had already begun to wonder about the origins of civilization. How did people learn to cultivate "the jewel and ornament of the plain," as a Sumerian poem asks, "the holy furrows . . . [where] grain grows?" How did they learn to live in a "well-supplied" city, "awesome in its appearance," its temples "rich with abundance," its laws "perfected"?[1] Surely, they answered, only the gods could have created civilization.

Today, explanations of the origins of civilization are more diverse and complex. Nevertheless, we can admire people's early investigations of their past, for it is still a difficult subject—and a tantalizing one. There remains much that we do not know, but what we do know is often dramatic and exciting. We know, for instance, that the first modern humans evolved from humanlike ancestors, though scholars debate whether the date was closer to 45,000 or to 70,000 years ago. This chapter begins with those first humans and ends with the collapse of the great civilizations of Egypt and western Asia around 1200 B.C. In between came the most momentous inventions in human history: representational art and religion, technological innovation and specialization, the shift from a food-collecting to a food-producing economy, and the first villages, from which grew the first cities and kingdoms. Consider, for example, the illustration on the opposite page. A west Asian mosaic from about 2650 B.C., it depicts a complex society with ranks of people ranging from servant to king. In the mosaic, power is expressed through the control of agricultural produce (for example, wine) and domesticated animals. The life and death of the first civilizations set

The Standard of Ur,
Peace Panel.

the path followed during the first millennium B.C. by the Greeks, Romans, and ancient Israelites, who in turn laid the foundations of the West.

The period studied in this chapter includes both *prehistory*—the term often used for time before the invention of writing—and recorded history. Writing appeared last among the complex of characteristics that marks the emergence of civilization: that is, a complex and hierarchical society with sufficient agricultural advances to support cities, centers of social and cultural sophistication.

So characterized, civilization emerged around 3500 to 3000 B.C.* in two great river valleys: the valley of the Tigris and Euphrates in what is today Iraq, and the valley of the Nile in Egypt. Two other civilizations emerged before 2000 B.C.: one in what is today Pakistan and northwest India, the other in northern China. In Europe, the main focus of this book, civilization did not gain a firm foothold until around 2000 B.C., first on the Aegean island of Crete and then on the Greek mainland.

Impressive in their own right, Mesopotamia and Egypt around 3100–1200 B.C. influenced a wide range of early civilizations in the eastern Mediterranean region. Among them are the Hittites and the inhabitants of the Syro-Palestinian city-states, who are studied in this chapter, and the Hebrews and the Greeks, who are studied in Chapter 2.

ORIGINS, TO CA. 3000 B.C.

The earth is old; modern human beings are young; and civilization is a very recent innovation. Physical anthropologists, archaeologists, geneticists, and biochemists have made great strides in explaining human origins. Great disagreement still reigns nonetheless. Each decade seems to bring an exciting new discovery that calls for the reassessment of previous theories.

We can be more certain about the series of processes, beginning around 10,000 B.C., that led to

the emergence of civilization by 3500–3000 B.C. Over a period of several thousand years, humans abandoned a mobile existence for a sedentary one. They learned to domesticate animals and to cultivate plants. They replaced a food-collecting economy with a food-producing economy. They developed the first towns, from which, over several millennia, slowly evolved the first urban societies.

The First Human Beings

The human family, the hominids, includes not only anatomically modern people but many ancient and extinct species. Some are our evolutionary ancestors; others are branches from a common genealogical tree. Modern human beings, *Homo sapiens sapiens*—genus *Homo*, species *sapiens*, subspecies *sapiens* (Latin for "wise, wise human being")—first appeared either more than 70,000 or more than 45,000 years ago (depending on which scholarly estimate we follow). Humanlike beings are, however, much older.

The earliest such beings, ancestors of modern people, appeared in the tropics and subtropics of Africa at least 5 million years ago. A little more than 2.5 million years ago they had evolved into humanlike creatures who invented the first technology, simple stone tools. Prehistory is traditionally referred to as the Stone Age, because stone was the primary medium from which hominids made tools. From about 2.0 to 1.6 million years ago, hominids migrated out of Africa to Asia and to the eastern edge of Europe. (Those three continents are sometimes collectively called the "Old World" to distinguish them from the "New World" of the Americas and Australia.) By about 1.6 million years ago they had evolved into *Homo erectus* ("upright person"), hominids with a large brain, who used more complex stone tools and may have acquired language. The next important stage in human evolution is the gradual emergence, from separate *Homo erectus* populations in different places, of various archaic forms of *Homo sapiens*.

For many millennia Europe represented a challenging environment for human habitation because of the ebb and flow of glaciers: the Ice Age, as scholars refer to the period of fluctuating cycles of warm and cold, beginning about 730,000 years ago and ending only about 10,000 years ago. The earliest humans in Europe found great contrasts in

---

*We follow the traditional practice in the West of expressing historical dates in relation to the birth of Jesus Christ (actually, to one calculation of his birthdate, because in fact Jesus was not born in 1 A.D.; see page 214). Dates before his birth are labeled B.C. (which stands for *before Christ*) and dates after his birth are labeled A.D. (*anno Domini*, Latin for "in the year of the Lord"). A widely used alternate refers to these dates as B.C.E. (before the common era) and C.E. (of the common era).

temperature, seasons, and landscapes, requiring considerable adaptation—but adapt they did.

Humans came late to Europe, though not as late as scholars once thought. Indeed, recent finds in Spain show the presence of archaic humans in Europe about 800,000 years ago. Beginning about 400,000 years ago, Europe was home to the ancestors of the best-known archaic people, the Neandertals. Fully evolved by 130,000 years ago, Neandertal people lived in Europe and western Asia for the following 100,000 years, to about 30,000 years ago. They were strong and stocky, an adaptation perhaps to the rugged climate of the Ice Age. The Neandertals were far from being the brutes they are usually imagined to be. They were, for example, among the first people to bury their dead, often with grave offerings suggesting tenderness and sensitivity—for example, flint, animal bones, or flowers.

Neandertals, however, were not modern humans. Modern humans entered Europe from western Asia about 40,000 years ago. Within 10,000 years, Neandertals had disappeared; whether through war or through disease or through intermarriage with modern humans, we do not know. The first modern humans tended to be taller and less muscular than Neandertals and other archaic people. They also had more precise use of the hand and walked more efficiently, and they lived longer. With its high forehead and tucked-in face, the modern human skull is distinctive, but differences between the modern and archaic human brain are a matter of scholarly debate. What no one debates, however, is that around 40,000 years ago modern humans put a revolution into effect. It would not be too much to say that they invented culture.[2]

From the Cave to the Town, ca. 40,000–5000 B.C.

Before the emergence of modern humans, people had relatively little ability to change the natural environment. Modern humans changed all that. They were the first animals to exploit natural resources largely by means of technology and organization. Thus they began the process of human manipulation of the environment that—sometimes brilliantly, sometimes disastrously—has remained a leading theme of the human experience ever since. The key to this change was a dramatic increase in the amount and complexity of infor-

HUMAN ORIGINS TO CA. 3000 B.C.

5 million years ago	Earliest hominids
1.6 million years ago	*Homo erectus*
800,000 years ago	First humans in Europe
130,000–30,000 years ago	Neandertals
70,000–45,000 years ago	*Homo sapiens sapiens*
40,000–10,000 B.C.	Upper Paleolithic era
10,000 B.C.	Last Ice Age ends
9000–2500 B.C.	Neolithic era
3500–3000 B.C.	First civilizations

(All dates in this chapter are approximate.)

mation being communicated: what might be called the first information revolution. The twin symbols of the revolution are cave paintings and notations made on bone, signs that humans were thinking about their environment, representing it, and recording information about it.

These dramatic changes, the foundation of modern human culture, began in the Upper Paleolithic (Greek for "Old Stone") era, about 40,000 to about 10,000 B.C. The beginning of the period witnessed the first human hunter-gatherer societies, complex organizations that survived by a food-collecting economy of hunting, fishing, and gathering fruits and nuts. By the end of the period a second revolution was under way: the invention of a food-producing economy, consisting of the domestication of animals and the cultivation of crops. This revolution went hand in hand with the creation first of villages and then of walled towns.

Archaeology tells us something about early people's way of life, as do analogies from contemporary anthropology, for even today a tiny number of people still exist in hunter-gatherer societies in isolated corners of the globe: for example, in the Kalahari Desert of Africa and in the Arctic. It is reasonable to speculate that early humans lived in small groups, of perhaps twenty-five to fifty persons, related by kinship or marriage. They moved from place to place, following the seasonal migration of game. Hunting was largely a male preserve,

Chauvet Cave Art This black-painted panel shows horses, rhinoceros, and wild oxen. This painting and others in the cave, discovered in 1994 in southern France, are over 30,000 years old, making them perhaps the oldest known paintings in the world. *(Jean Cottes/Ministère de la Culture/Sygma)*

but females played a major role in gathering nuts and berries. Women brought their children to work or used kin or friends for baby-sitting.

It was probably common for men and women to pair off, have children, and establish a family, much as marriage is a near-universal practice among humans today. Compared to other animals, humans produce extremely dependent infants requiring years of attention. In order to ensure the survival of the young to adulthood, males as well as females need to play a role in child rearing. Humans, however, are not naturally monogamous. They tend to seek sexual variety, and hence, in addition to marriage and the family, marital infidelity, divorce, remarriage, and polygamy have all also been found in history, as has homosexuality.[3]

Early people found shelter by building huts or, frequently, by living in caves or rock shelters—hence our notion of the "caveman." Caves offered

shelter, could be heated, and made a naturally good vantage point for observing prey. In the Upper Paleolithic era, about 30,000 years ago, caves were the site of the earliest representational art. The most spectacular Paleolithic paintings discovered so far have been found in caves in southern France (for example, at Lascaux and at Chauvet Cave) and in Spain (at Altamira). European cave paintings of such animals as the bison, horse, reindeer, and woolly mammoth (a huge, extinct member of the elephant family with hairy skin and long, upward-curving tusks) attest to early human artistic skill; the presence of abstract shapes attests to an interest in symbols. The cave paintings are perhaps illustrations of myths or attempts to control the environment through magic—that is, to manipulate it supernaturally.

Other early representational art includes engravings on stone of animals, birds, and stylized human females, as well as female figurines carved from ivory or bone. Usually represented with exaggerated breasts or buttocks, the carvings are called Venus figurines, after Venus, the Greco-Roman goddess of love. They might represent an attempt to control fertility through magic.

Upper Paleolithic craftsmanship is as impressive as the art. The early human tool kit included the first utensils in such malleable materials as antler and ivory. Stone tools became longer and the first polished bone tools appeared, as did the first stone and bone spear points and the first bows and arrows. The presence of bone needles and awls (pointed tools for punching holes) implies sewing, probably of animal skins.

The existence of Paleolithic artists and skilled craftspeople demonstrates at least a limited specialization of skills and division of labor: Upper Paleolithic society required organization, albeit on a limited scale. Hunting was a communal enterprise. Related families are likely to have joined together in clans, which in turn may have formed tribes. It is often thought that each of these groups was patriarchal (literally, "ruled by the father"); that is, the family was governed by the father, the tribe by a male headman or chief. Yet later myths (for example, among the ancient Greeks) argue that women were the rulers of prehistoric society; today some historians see evidence of matriarchy (literally, "rule by the mother") in the Venus figurines. Moreover, some tribes may have had no chief at all but, rather, followed the decision of the community.

About fifteen thousand years ago, humans began to specialize in the wild plants they collected and the animals they hunted. The logical next step was to learn how to control the environment in order to domesticate plants and animals. What triggered these changes is unclear: perhaps environmental pressure, perhaps human curiosity and experimentation. The results are more certain: There was more food.

People seem to have begun by domesticating dogs, which were useful in hunting. Then they learned to keep sheep, goats, and cattle. Next came farming. Humans learned first how to grow wheat and barley, then legumes (beans). With males occupied in hunting, it may well have been females who first unraveled the secrets of agriculture.

Scholars often speak of the domestication of animals and plants as the "Neolithic (literally, "New Stone") Revolution." In truth, the process was evolutionary. It began sometime after 10,000 B.C. in western Asia, in the period of warmer climate following the last Ice Age, when wild cereals spread to that region. By 5000 B.C., farmers and herders were found throughout the Old World.

The earliest area of domestication is a zone of land stretching in a crescent shape west to east from what is today southern Jordan to southern Iran. Scholars call this region of dependable annual rainfall the "Fertile Crescent" (Map 1.1). The Neolithic Revolution may have begun after 10,000 B.C. in the hills and valleys of the northern and eastern parts of the crescent, in the Taurus Mountains of Anatolia (modern Turkey) and in the Zagros Mountains of Iran. With domestication came small agricultural settlements, or villages, which were increasingly common after 7000 B.C. Thus was born the farming village. It is probably the place that most people have called home since the spread of agriculture around the world.

Scholars once thought of Neolithic villages as simple places devoted to subsistence agriculture, with no craft specialization, and as egalitarian societies lacking social hierarchies. In recent years, new evidence and a rethinking of older information have shifted the picture considerably. The Neolithic village site of Çayönü Tepesi in eastern Anatolia, for example, provides evidence of metalworking (of copper) and of specialization of labor (in bead making) from approximately 7000 to 6000 B.C. At Çayönü was found the world's earliest known example of cloth, probably linen, woven around 7000 B.C. Other contemporaneous village sites provide evidence of experiments in ironworking and craft specialization. There was long-distance trade between villages in pottery and in obsidian (a sharp volcanic glass used in tools). Artwork shows men wearing loincloths and headdresses, women wearing pants and halter tops, and both sexes wearing jewelry.

Consider the case of Jericho, in Palestine near the Dead Sea (see Map 1.1), perhaps the oldest town on earth. A small village around 9000 B.C., by about 7000 Jericho had become a town surrounded by massive walls 10 feet thick and 13 or more feet high, probably used for defense. The walls, about 765 yards long, probably enclosed an area of about 10 acres. The most prominent feature of the walls was a great tower 33 feet in diameter and 28 feet high with an interior stairway. Inside

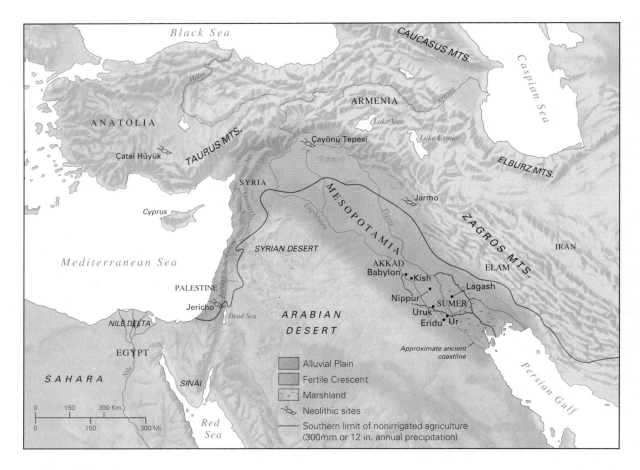

Map 1.1 Western Asia In the Fertile Crescent, an arc-shaped region of dependable annual rainfall, the Neolithic Revolution began after 10,000 B.C. In southern Mesopotamia, between the Tigris and Euphrates Rivers, the world's first urban civilization took root about 3500–3000 B.C.

the walls was a densely packed population of about two thousand people.

An even larger Neolithic town is Çatal Hüyük in south central Anatolia (see Map 1.1). Its population of six thousand people in 6000 B.C. made it the largest settlement of the era by far. It was probably a trading center and perhaps a religious shrine. Carbonization from fire has preserved a wealth of artifacts attesting to Çatal Hüyük's sophistication, including fabrics, obsidian mirrors, wooden vessels, and sticks that were used to apply eye makeup.

Agriculture made human populations richer and more numerous, but the ensuing concentration of population bred disease and war. Survival now depended more on a given piece of farmland

than on shifting hunting grounds. The result was a rise in territoriality, that is, in emotional investment in the land, so much that people were willing to die for it. In addition, more men than ever before were available to fight, because agriculture proved to be so efficient a source of food that it freed people for specialized labor. Some became craftsmen, some artists, some priests—and some warriors.

This is not to say that war in Neolithic times was sophisticated. Indeed, the phenomenon perhaps consisted of group fighting and sporadic raids rather than systematic warfare. People added new weapons to the spear and the bow: the sling, the dagger, and the mace (a heavy war club). Spanish rock art shows a confrontation between two groups of archers, one following what seems to be a leader wearing a plumed hat. The scene may be a ritual rather than a violent conflict, but other evidence is a stronger indication of bloodshed. A cemetery along the Nile River in the Sudan dating from 12,000 to 4500 B.C. contains numerous human skeletons killed by arrowheads, some with multiple wounds. The victims include women and children.

Neolithic and Copper Age Europe, 7000–2500 B.C.

Europe was one day to become the center of Western civilization, but the Continent lagged behind its neighbors at first. Innovations from the east reached Europe after 7000 B.C. and slowly transformed it. Europe was no empty vessel to be filled by eastern technologies, however: Europeans developed their own unique culture.

The term *Europe* refers to one continent with several very distinct regions. Southern Europe is made up of a rugged and hilly Mediterranean coastal strip, connected to northern Africa and western Asia by the sea and by similarities in climate and landscape. Northern Europe, by contrast, consists in large part of forested plain, indented here and there by great rivers. In the southeast the plain becomes open and largely treeless; it stretches from Russia across central Asia to China. High mountains are found in the Alps of south central Europe, from which chains of lower mountains radiate toward the southwest and southeast.

Before 7000 B.C., Europeans lived a traditional hunter-gatherer existence. Farming began in southeastern Europe around 7000 B.C., when migrants from western Asia brought the settled way of life of the Neolithic village. That food-producing economy spread across Europe between about 6000 and 4500 B.C., borne alternately by colonization and by native adaptation of new technologies.

The farmers of Early Neolithic Europe (ca. 7000–ca. 4500 B.C.) were pioneers. They tended to live in hamlets or villages surrounded by larger populations that remained hunters and gatherers. Between about 4500 and 2500 B.C., however, the majority of Europeans slowly adopted a food-producing way of life. The consequent give-and-take

between pioneers and natives led to the development of regional cultures. This era of European prehistory is known as the Late Neolithic, or the Copper Age, because copper came into use on the Continent during this time, as did gold. Both metals were used primarily as status symbols: The most dramatic example is a Bulgarian burial site dating from about 4000 B.C. in which a 45-year-old man is buried with 990 separate gold objects as well as copper and flint weapons.

Between about 4500 and about 3500 B.C., Copper Age Europeans developed their own cultures in relative isolation from the more advanced east. For example, European metallurgy probably developed independently. On Europe's northern and western edges people began to set up stone tombs and monuments, often of huge blocks. Such monuments, known as megaliths, may illustrate an awareness of time created by the spread of agriculture, with its seasonal rhythms.

Between about 3500 and 2500 B.C., Copper Age Europe grew in sophistication. The urbanization of Mesopotamia (in modern-day Iraq; see Map 1.1) had an impact on southeastern Europe, which supplied raw materials for western Asia. Greece underwent the greatest transformation, to the extent that it developed its own urban civilization by about 2000 B.C. (see Chapter 2). Elsewhere, especially in the Balkans, technological innovations came into use, from the wheel, to complex metal-casting, to wine cups (evidence of a new taste). The recent discovery of a Copper Age corpse preserved in the ice of the Italian Alps opens a window into northern Italian society of about 3200 B.C. (See the feature "Weighing the Evidence: The Iceman and His World," on pages 40–41.)

In western Europe stone monuments are the most dramatic symbol of cultural achievement. On the Mediterranean island of Malta, for example, people built grand, elaborate, temple complexes, constructed of large limestone blocks. In Britain, megalithic architecture reached its peak with Stonehenge, built in stages from about 2800 to 1500 B.C. This famous monument consists of a circle of stones oriented precisely on the rising sun of midsummer: a sign both of early Europeans' interest in the calendar and of their skill in technology.

Neolithic and Copper Age sculpture consists of many representations of females and few of males. Consider, for example, the large sculpted female figures found in Malta's temples. The enlarged buttocks and thighs of these statues might be symbols of fertility. Some scholars speculate that early Europeans worshiped goddesses until warlike invaders after 2000 B.C. brought male deities with them. The theory is, however, controversial.

The Emergence of Civilization

Civilization is derived from the Latin *civitas*, meaning "commonwealth," or "city." The first civilizations, beginning in Mesopotamia and Egypt between 3500 and 3000 B.C., did indeed contain the first cities. What differentiated them from their Neolithic predecessors, however, was not so much size (a city versus a town) as complexity. Civilization allowed human beings to think big. With a sufficiently large and specialized labor force, and with a sufficiently strong government, it became possible to expand control over nature, to pursue advances in technology, to trade and compete

over ever widening areas, to free an elite for ever more ambitious projects in art and thought, and to invent writing. In short, the advent of civilization in the fourth millennium B.C. marked a major turning point, when the human horizon expanded forever.

Civilization arose in southern Iraq, in the valley between the Tigris and Euphrates Rivers (see Map 1.1), a region that the Greeks called "Mesopotamia" (literally, "between the rivers"). At around the same time or shortly afterward, civilization also began in the valley of the Nile River in Egypt. A perennial topic of debate among scholars is whether different civilizations develop independently or whether one culture spreads to other locations from an original source. As we shall see, early civilizations are characterized by a combination of contacts and independent developments.

Both Mesopotamia and Egypt are home to valleys containing alluvial land—that is, a relatively flat tract where fertile soil is deposited by a

The Maltese Female This "Sleeping Lady," a terra-cotta statuette of the late fourth millennium B.C. from Malta, shows a reclining woman, perhaps a goddess or priestess. Her double-egg shaped buttocks are thought to symbolize fertility or regeneration. *(Erich Lessing/Art Resource, NY)*

river. Otherwise, the two regions are quite different. Although the Nile Valley is easy to farm, the Tigris-Euphrates plain had to be tamed by would-be farmers. Every summer the Nile flooded in a relatively regular and predictable manner, bringing north to Egypt the waters of the monsoon rains of the Ethiopian highlands, where one branch of the river rises. The spring deluges of the Tigris and Euphrates were more sudden and less predictable. Moreover, the Nile's waters spread so broadly that it took little human effort to irrigate most of the available farmland in the Nile Valley. In southern Mesopotamia, by contrast, most of the soil was alternately so dry or so marshy that agriculture would not have been possible without irrigation and drainage—that is, the use of channels, dikes, or dams to control floodwaters and improve the fertility of the land. One Mesopotamian text describes a farmer as "the man of dike, ditch, and plow." Some scholars argue that the very hostility of Mesopotamia's environment generated the cooperation and control that civilization represents.

The first cities emerged in Mesopotamia through a slow, incremental process of action and reaction. Labor became more specialized and agricultural production was maximized. When part of the population moves to a city, those who remain on the land must work harder or use better farming techniques or increase the amount of land under cultivation. In fourth- and third-millennium B.C. Mesopotamia, farmers did all three. Meanwhile, both the number and variety of settlements increased. Urban populations required the support of people in smaller units—towns, villages, and hamlets—clustered around a city.

In short, river-valley society became more complex, which in turn created a need for cooperation and central direction. By the end of the fourth millennium B.C., Mesopotamia consisted of numerous city-states—that is, independent political units that each contained a rural countryside with villages controlled by a capital city. The urban landscape's most visible sign of centralized authority was the temple.

In early times the Mesopotamian temple was probably the most important authority not only in religion but in politics and economics as well. (In early Egypt, by contrast, the king emerged as the most important authority; see page 23.) A simple structure around 5000 B.C., the temple had become by 4000 B.C. an elaborate, monumental work of architecture built on a raised platform. Each city had at least one temple, the house of its patron god and the common symbol of the community. Temples were wealthy and powerful and commanded loyalty. They had to be, because only a strong institution could control the large amount of manpower that temple-building required.

Along with the growth of cities came the development of writing. Mesopotamia was the first civilization to leave a written record, having invented writing about 3500–3100 B.C. Writing was the child of recordkeeping, so a plausible theory argues, since complex economy requires records and inventories. Before they invented writing, Mesopotamian people used tiny clay or stone tokens to represent objects being counted or traded. By 3500 B.C., with 250 different types of tokens, the system had grown unwieldy enough for people to start using signs to indicate tokens. It was a short step to dispensing with the tokens and placing the signs on a clay tablet, using a reed stylus with a triangular point: the first writing. New words were soon added through pictographs (pictures that stand for particular objects). In time the pictographs evolved into ideograms—that is, abstract symbols that are no longer recognizable as specific objects and thus can be used to denote ideas as well as things.

In the centuries following its introduction, writing became standardized. Scholars call the signs *cuneiform* from the Latin for "wedge-shaped," a good description of what early writing looks like (Figure 1.1). In its first centuries, cuneiform was used almost entirely for economic records or commercial transactions; then it was adapted to make brief records of offerings to the gods. By 2350 B.C., cuneiform had evolved into a mixed system of about six hundred signs, most of them phonetic (syllabic), with relatively few ideograms. Writing became flexible enough to record the spoken language. Cuneiform then became an instrument of infinite potential, one that could be used for poetry as easily as for bookkeeping.

An adaptable system, cuneiform became the standard script of various languages of western Asia for several thousand years. Compared to a modern alphabet, in which a small number of letters stand for the sounds of speech, cuneiform is clumsy, but alphabets were not invented before about 1400 B.C., and they took nearly a thousand

Uruk IV ca. 3100 B.C.	Sumerian ca. 2500 B.C.	Old Babylonian ca. 1800 B.C.	Neo-Babylonian ca. 600 B.C.	SUMERIAN Babylonian
				APIN epinnu plough
				ŠE še'u grain
				ŠAR kirû mountain
				KUR šadû orchard
				GUD alpu ox
				KU(A) nunu fish
				DUG karpatu jar

Figure 1.1 Early Writing The pictographs of early writing evolved into a system of phonetic syllables and abstract symbols. Simplified and standardized, this writing was cuneiform, or "wedge-shaped." It was adapted from Sumerian to Babylonian and other languages throughout western Asia. (*Source:* From *Babylon*, by Joan Oates. Published by Thames and Hudson Ltd., 1978. Used by permission.)

years to displace cuneiform. Clumsy it may have been, but cuneiform was writing, and writing is both a catalyst for change and the historian's best friend. Mesopotamia after 3000 B.C. was dynamic, sophisticated, and, best of all, intelligible to us.

MESOPOTAMIA, TO CA. 1600 B.C.

The people of Mesopotamia after 3000 B.C. flourished and experimented: in government, in cooperation and conflict among different ethnic groups, in law, and in the working out of class and gender relations. Their quest for divine justice laid the foundations on which the Hebrews later built. Their engineering skill, mathematics, and astronomy set ancient science on a grand trajectory. A

keen and often bitter awareness of human limitations and vanity, moreover, gives Mesopotamian civilization a sympathetic quality.

Archaeologists sometimes refer to the third and second millennia in the eastern Mediterranean and western Asia as the "Bronze Age." In this period people mastered the technology of making bronze, an alloy of copper and tin. As a result, bronze frequently replaced stone as a primary material for everyday use.

The City-States of Sumer

The Sumerians live. Their independence ended four thousand years ago; their culture and identity were absorbed by foreigners. Yet whenever someone today counts the minutes, whenever a group of people engage in a political debate, whenever someone quotes the law, the Sumerians live, for these are all legacies of that first literate society.

It is ironic that the first cities emerged in southern Mesopotamia, because farming villages came late to this region, about 5300 B.C. Earlier farmers preferred higher elevations, with dependable rainfall, to the hot and dry southern Mesopotamian lowlands. Why they eventually moved south is unknown; perhaps a problem at home, such as population pressure, or the lure of adventure abroad moved them. In time, with the development of a good irrigation system, the immigrants and their descendants turned southern Mesopotamia into rich farmland. Nature, nonetheless, was never to be taken for granted in this region of extreme heat, scorching winds, and flash floods. Nor could the people of Mesopotamia afford to ignore the outside world. They depended on foreign trade for minerals and timber while, at the same time, they became uneasily aware that the neighboring peoples of the mountains and deserts welcomed the opportunity to conquer their cities.

The formative era of Mesopotamian civilization is called the Uruk Period (ca. 3800–3200 B.C.) after one of its major archaeological sites. The Uruk Period encompassed a series of major technological breakthroughs, including the wheel and the plow, the first orchards—of dates, figs, or olives—and the first sophisticated metal-casting processes. It witnessed the emergence of the first cities, for example, Uruk. Moreover, it marked a dramatic increase in the extent of territory and population, in warfare and political centralization, in social complexity, and in institutional formality. Finally, as if to cap a period of remarkable change, the end of the Uruk Period witnessed the invention of writing.

Mesopotamian cities flourished in this era. By the period that scholars have named the "Early Dynastic Period" (2800–2350 B.C.), named for the first royal dynasties (ruling families), a large Mesopotamian city had grown to the point where it might cover a thousand acres surrounded by more than five miles of walls, within which lived about fifty thousand people. Such a city with its monumental temples and palaces, was not only larger and more impressive than a Çatal Hüyük or Jericho, it was also part of a network of thirty such city-states with a common culture, commerce, and propensity to make war on each other. Hence the

MESOPOTAMIA

3800–3200 B.C.	Uruk Period
3500–3100 B.C.	Writing invented
2800–2350 B.C.	Early Dynastic Period
2371–2316 B.C.	Reign of Sargon
2112–2004 B.C.	Third Dynasty of Ur
1900–1600 B.C.	Old Babylonian Period
1792–1750 B.C.	Reign of Hammurabi

city-states of Mesopotamia may be called the first civilization.

The dominant inhabitants of that civilization are called Sumerians. Present in southern Mesopotamia by 3200 B.C. and probably earlier, the Sumerians entered their great age in the third millennium B.C., when their city-states enjoyed a proud independence. Conscious of the unique achievement represented by their way of living, their economy, politics, art and architecture, language, thought, and literature—in short, by Sumerian culture—the Sumerians called southern Mesopotamia simply "the land" (see Map 1.1).

It was a land where geography was an obstacle to unification and where the scarcity of fresh water led to quarrels among cities over water rights. Separated from each other by desert and swampland, the Sumerian cities were jealous and selfish, even though they had much in common: language, literature, arts and sciences, and even religion.

Each city had its own small urbanized area and a larger agricultural hinterland irrigated by canals. Cities traded with each other and with the outside world. They exported grain, dates, and textiles and other worked products in exchange for raw materials, including copper from Oman or Sinai, gold from Armenia or perhaps Nubia (modern Sudan), timber from the mountains east of the Persian Gulf, and carnelian (a reddish mineral used in jewelry) from India. The primary political units of southern Mesopotamia for most of the third millennium B.C., Sumerian city-states were a laboratory of civilization.

How were the Sumerian city-states governed? A Sumerian might respond that they were governed by the gods, for the Sumerians believed that the gods had created everything and owned everything on earth. As historians, we can trace the evolution of human government among the Sumerians: In each city, power flowed first from the temples to the wealthy land-owning families and then finally to monarchs.

As we have already seen, the temple was the focus of loyalty in the early Sumerian city. The temple controlled large landed estates, so the priests, scribes, and other temple officials were a major economic authority. Yet they were not absolute rulers. By the Early Dynastic Period, political power in a Sumerian city rested largely in the hands of the Council of Elders, whose members were probably wealthy landowners. Some scholars argue that the council shared power with a popular assembly, creating, in effect, a bicameral legislature and perhaps even a primitive democracy. The evidence is ambiguous, however, leaving it highly debatable whether ordinary people took part in Sumerian government.

Ordinary people certainly had a subordinate position in society. Although usually free, they frequently had to rent land from temple or noble. Some peasants were organized in work bands under foremen. There were also slaves in Sumer, originally captives from the mountains. Slaves formed a small group, much outnumbered by free peasants. Sumerian women worked alongside men in most professions. Priestesses were usually noblewomen from wealthy families.

By about 2700 B.C., political power shifted again from the council to the palace. It was a time of chronic intercity warfare, and the times demanded a strong hand. The new ruler was a "big man" (*lugal*) or "governor" (*ensi*)—that is, a king or, occasionally, a queen. The monarch was first and foremost a warrior. He claimed to be the representative on earth of the gods, a position that gave him general responsibility for his subjects' welfare. Accordingly, kings sponsored irrigation works, raised fortification walls, restored temples, and built splendid palaces.

According to a plausible tradition, the earliest Sumerian kings, dating from the period 2700 to 2600 B.C., are Enmebaragesi of the city of Kish, his son and successor, Agga, and Gilgamesh of Uruk, a hero of epic poetry whom many scholars consider a genuine historical personage. In the cities

of Ur and Lagash the king's wife was often a power in her own right. Kish was ruled by Kubaba (r. ca. 2450 B.C.), the first reigning queen of recorded history.

Sumerian monarchs also recognized a responsibility for promoting justice. History's earliest known reformer of law and society is Uru-inim-gina, king of Lagash around 2400 B.C. Surviving documents describe Lagash as a society in which wealthy landowners encroached on the temples and oppressed the poor, and royal administrators mistreated ordinary people. The king's aims seem to have been both to correct abuses and to weaken independent sources of power threatening royal authority. Uru-inim-gina attempted to control the bureaucracy, protect the property of humble people, and guard the temples. He also put into effect the first known attempt to control wages and prices. Uru-inim-gina's proclaimed intention was to promote impartial justice, a goal that he expressed in the formula "[the king] will protect the mother that is in distress, the mighty man shall not oppress the naked and the widow." If at the same time he also managed to increase his own power, then so much the better. As it turned out, Lagash was conquered only a few years later. Uru-inim-gina's reforms nonetheless survived as the precedent for a long Mesopotamian tradition of royal lawgiving.

Several warrior-kings attempted to conquer and unite all the Sumerian cities. The most successful was Sargon (r. 2371–2316 B.C.), an unusual figure who rose from obscurity to a high position under the king of Kish before founding his own capital city, Agade. Even more important, Sargon was a native speaker not of Sumerian but of Akkadian.

Conquest and Assimilation, ca. 2350–1900 B.C.

Cities were rarities in the third millennium B.C. Rude and tough, the surrounding peoples of the desert and the mountains coveted Mesopotamia's wealth. Some conquerors came directly from the hinterland to the walls of the city they were attacking; others, like Sargon, rose to power within the context of the warring Sumerian city-states. Both groups were sufficiently impressed by Sumerian culture to adopt a great many Sumerian customs and ideas as their own. The conquering Akkadians, for example, adopted Sumerian religion and wrote Akkadian in cuneiform.

The Akkadians were originally a seminomadic people who lived on the edge of the desert. Shepherds, they moved their flocks with the seasons. Their language, Akkadian, belongs to the Semitic group of languages, which includes such languages as Arabic and Hebrew. Scholars formerly believed that the Akkadians came directly from the desert to conquer Sumer, but it is now clear that they had begun settling in the northern cities of southern Mesopotamia by the end of the Uruk Period.

The commander of one of history's first professional armies, Sargon conquered all Mesopotamia, and his power extended westward along the Euphrates and eastward into the Iranian Plateau. Recent research suggests that Sargon's armies might have made use of the horse to draw war chariots, thus allowing them to cover much greater distances than earlier forces. Sargon's armies tore down the walls of conquered cities, leaving them defenseless and thereby discouraging rebellion. The old rulers were generally allowed to remain in office because the installation of new men by Sargon might spark local hostility. The Akkadians were satisfied with loose control, as long as they could monopolize trade.

Sargon's dynasty boasted that it reigned over "the peoples of all lands" or "the four quarters of the earth." The Akkadian empire reached its greatest height in the reign of Sargon's grandson, Naram-sin (r. ca. 2250–2220 B.C.), but it did not survive the next reign. Sargon nonetheless proved to be one of western Asia's most influential figures. His ideal of universal empire was one to which future conquerors would lay claim.

Sargon proved adept at using religion to legitimize his rule. A self-made monarch, he was sensitive to the charge of usurpation; indeed, he chose the throne name Sargon (Sharrum-ken in Akkadian) because it means "the king is legitimate." By claiming the status of the gods' representative on earth, Sargon strengthened his authority. He once paraded a defeated enemy in a halter before the temple and priests of Enlil, the chief Sumerian god, confidently proclaiming that Enlil was on his side. Sargon and most of his successors presented themselves as mediators between human beings

Akkadian Bronze This stern-faced, life-size cast-bronze head, with its stylized and elaborately ringleted beard and its carefully arranged hair, shows Mesopotamian craftsmanship at its finest. Sometimes said to be Sargon (r. 2371–2316 B.C.) or Naram-sin (r. ca. 2250–2220 B.C.), it was deliberately mutilated in ancient times. (*Claus Hansmann, München*)

and the gods, but they usually stopped short of claiming to be gods themselves.

Assimilation was another lasting Akkadian legacy. Although Sargon made Akkadian the official language of administration, he made politic concessions to Sumerian sensibilities. For instance, his daughter Enkheduanna, whom he appointed high priestess at Ur and Uruk, wrote poetry in Sumerian, poetry powerful enough to be quoted often in later Sumerian texts. The first known woman poet, Enkheduanna described the union of Sumerians and Akkadians.

Around 2200 B.C. the Akkadian empire broke up into a series of smaller successor states. The Gutians, raiders from the Zagros Mountains on the eastern border of Mesopotamia, played a major role in ending Akkadian power. Ascendant in eastern Mesopotamia for about a century, the Gutians absorbed Sumerian and Akkadian culture. When Gutian power waned, the Sumerians returned to power under the Third Dynasty of Ur (2112–2004 B.C.). Far from excising all Akkadian influence, the revived Sumerian rulers spoke of themselves as "kings of Sumer and Akkad." It was a title that would have a long and potent history; for the next fifteen hundred years many of the great kings of western Asia would label themselves, among other honorifics, "king of Sumer and Akkad." By using this title, the Sumerian kings of Ur showed that they recognized the existence of a composite, common Mesopotamian society.

This society survived renewed political turmoil around 2000 B.C. Various raiders attacked from the mountains and deserts, and individual cities within Mesopotamia rebelled against Ur. A new kingdom, under the rule of the Amorites, one of the raiding peoples, emerged around 1900 B.C. in southern Mesopotamia. The kingdom of the Amorites, Semitic-speakers, shared Mesopotamian culture and traditions. Babylon, northwest of Ur, in the central part of Mesopotamia, became the Amorite capital. From Babylon, Amorite kings issued cuneiform decrees that, except for being in a Semitic language, might have been drafted by a Sumerian monarch.

The Majesty of the Law

Hammurabi (r. 1792–1750 B.C.) ruled in Babylon about six hundred years after Sargon. Much of his forty-two-year reign was devoted to creating a Mesopotamian empire. A careful administrator who ushered in an era of prosperity and cultural flowering, Hammurabi is most famous for the text known as Hammurabi's Code. Although the work was less a "code" than a collection of verdicts—a

kind of treatise on justice glorifying Hammurabi's qualities as a judge—we shall use the familiar name. Hammurabi's Code became both a legal and a literary classic, often copied in later times.

Hammurabi's Code offers a remarkable portrait of Mesopotamian society. The document contains nearly three hundred rulings on topics ranging from family to commercial law, from wage rates to murder. It is a collection of cases rather than of general principles. As such it is very revealing of the pragmatism of Mesopotamian scholarship and science. There was no notion of abstract or universal principles in Mesopotamia; indeed, there was no word for "law."

Hammurabi's Code is often thought of as harsh and early. Harsh it was, but not so early. The earliest known law code was promulgated by King Ur-Nammu of Ur around 2100 B.C., and other codes survive from the three centuries between Ur-Nammu's and Hammurabi's day. There are many similarities among the codes. As a great reformer, however, Hammurabi prided himself on making changes in the law. In some ways his code was more lenient than earlier documents. For example, family members sold or handed over into servitude because of debt were automatically freed after three years. But Hammurabi's was the first code to include such harsh penalties as bodily mutilation, drowning, and impaling; earlier codes are satisfied with payment in silver as recompense for crime. Hammurabi's Code also introduces the law of retaliation for wounds: "If a man has destroyed the eye of a member of the aristocracy: they shall destroy his eye. If he has broken his limb: they shall break the (same) limb." Children could be punished for the crimes of their fathers. (See the box, "King Hammurabi Dispenses Justice.")

Inscribed in stone and put in a prominent public place, Hammurabi's Code and other Mesopotamian legal texts symbolized the notion that the law belonged to everyone. Although ordinary people could not read, it was possible for them to find a patron who could. Yet Hammurabi's society was anything but egalitarian. There were three classes: slaves, free people who owned land, and *mushkenum* (a subordinate class whose members were legally free but landless and often in a dependent position). Punishments were class-biased: Crimes against a free person received harsher pun-

King Hammurabi Dispenses Justice

The Code of Hammurabi, king of Babylon (r. 1792–1750 B.C.), is one of the best-known documents of antiquity. Less a code than a treatise on justice, the text illustrates both the image of himself that the king wished to promote and the class and gender hierarchies of Mesopotamia in the second millennium B.C. The following excerpts are from the preface and body of the text.

[The gods] named me to promote the welfare of the people, me, Hammurabi, the devout, god-fearing prince, to cause justice to prevail in the land, to destroy the wicked and the evil, that the strong might not oppress the weak, to rise like the sun over the black-headed (people), and to light up the land. . . . I established law and justice in the language of the land, thereby promoting the welfare of the people. At that time (I decreed):

128: If a seignior acquired a wife but did not draw up the contracts for her, that woman is no wife.

129: If the wife of a seignior has been caught while lying with another man, they shall bind them and throw them into the water [that is, submit to the water ordeal, with the river as divine judge]. If the husband of the woman wishes to spare his wife, then the king in turn may spare his subject.

170: When a seignior's first wife bore him children and his female slave also bore him children, if the father during this lifetime has ever said "My children!" to the children whom the slave bore him, thus having counted them with the children of his first wife, after the father has gone to (his) fate, the children of the first wife and the children of the slave shall share equally in the goods of the paternal estate, with the first-born, the son of the first wife, receiving a preferential share.

196: If a seignior has destroyed the eye of a member of the aristocracy, they shall destroy his eye.

198: If he has destroyed the eye of a commoner or broken the bone of a commoner, he shall pay one mina of silver.

202: If a seignior has struck the cheek of a seignior who is superior to him, he shall be beaten sixty (times) with an oxtail whip in the assembly.

237: When a seignior hired a boatman and a boat and loaded it with grain, wool, oil, dates, or any kind of freight, if that boatman was so careless that he has sunk the boat and lost what was in it as well, the boatman shall make good the boat which he sank and whatever he lost that was in it.

Source: James B. Pritchard, ed., *Ancient Near Eastern Texts Relating to the Old Testament*, 3d ed., with Supplement (Princeton: Princeton University Press, 1969), pp. 164, 171, 173, 175–176.

ishment than crimes against a slave or a mushkenum. Debt seems to have been a serious and widespread problem, frequently leading debtors to sell their children, especially daughters, into slavery. Women could own and inherit property and testify in court. The overall direction of the code, however, is patriarchal. It enshrines the power of the male head of family.

Divine Masters

The Sumerians left their stamp on Mesopotamian religion; the Old Babylonian period (1900–1600 B.C.) was a second era of great religious creativity. Many Sumerian gods arose out of the forces of nature: An, the sky-god; Enki, the earth-god and freshwater-god; Enlil, the air-god; Nanna, the moon-god; and

Utu (Semitic, Shamash), the sun-god. Other Sumerian gods embodied human passions or notions about the afterlife: Inanna (Semitic, Ishtar), goddess of love and war; Ereshkigal, goddess of the underworld. The Sumerians were polytheists—that is, they had many gods—and their gods (like the later gods of Greece) were anthropomorphic, or human in form. Indeed, Sumerian (and Greek) gods were thought to be much like human beings, by turns wise and foolish, except that they were immortal and superpowerful.

We can speak of the Sumerian pantheon—that is, the association of all the Sumerian gods. The Sumerians sometimes envisioned their gods holding an assembly, based perhaps on a boisterous Sumerian prototype. The Sumerians and Akkadians considered Enlil, city-god of Nippur, to be the chief god. The Babylonians replaced him with Marduk, city-god of Babylon.

Every Mesopotamian city had its main temple complex, the most striking feature of which was a *ziggurat*, a stepped tower. Constructed originally as simple raised terraces, ziggurats eventually became seven-stage structures. Unlike the pyramids of Egypt, ziggurats were not tombs but "stairways" providing a way for the god to descend from heaven to earth. A typical ziggurat had two temples: a "high temple" at the top, to serve the god in the sky, and a "low temple" for the god to reach the earth. The "low temple" was the chief sanctuary of the city.

The keynote of Mesopotamian religion is a certain pessimism about the human condition. It is not surprising that the Mesopotamians, living in a difficult natural environment, regarded the gods with fear and awe. Indeed, they saw their deities as masters or parents who were to be obeyed. Although the gods communicated with humans, their language was mysterious. To understand the divine will, the Mesopotamians engaged in various kinds of divination: the interpretation of dreams, the examination of the entrails of slaughtered animals,

The Uruk Vase This panel, from an alabaster vase of late-third-millennium-B.C. Uruk, is thought to depict either the goddess Inanna or one of her priestesses. She accepts a basket of gifts. Behind her are two bundles of reeds with streamers, symbols of the goddess. *(Frank Scherschel/Life Magazine © Time, Inc.)*

the study of the stars (which stimulated great advances in astronomy, as we will see). By building temples, offering prayers and animal sacrifices, and participating in public rituals and processions, Mesopotamians hoped to propitiate their gods.

Most people expected nothing glorious in the afterlife, merely a shadowy existence. It was thought that with a person's last breath his or her spirit went on a long journey to the Netherworld, a place under the earth. More than one Mesopotamian text describes the Netherworld as the "Land-of-no-return" and "the house wherein the dwellers are bereft of light,/Where dust is their fare and clay their food,/Where they see no light, residing in darkness."[4] The dead resided there permanently, though in some texts their spirits return to earth, often with hostile intent toward the living.

Archaeological evidence might indicate a shift in such attitudes toward death, at least on the part of the Mesopotamian upper classes, by the late third millennium B.C. The kings and nobles of the Third Dynasty of Ur were buried with rich grave goods and with their servants, apparently the victims of human sacrifice upon the master's death. Perhaps the rulers now expected to have the opportunity to use their wealth again in a comfortable immortality, possibly influenced by Egyptian ideas (see pages 26–28).

Arts and Sciences

From Sumer to Babylon, the people of Mesopotamia were deeply inquisitive. They focused on the beginning and the end of things. "How did the world come into being?" and "What happens to us when we die?" are perhaps the two fundamental questions of their rich literature. The Babylonian creation epic known from its first line as *Enuma Elish* ("When on high") is a poem about the triumph of the gods of order over the forces of chaos. It also commemorates the political ascendancy of Babylon. This poem was recited annually during the New Year's festival by Babylonian priests. Another important Babylonian literary genre, known as wisdom literature, responds to life's vicissitudes with precepts that are sometimes simple, sometimes sophisticated. It proved eventually to influence the wisdom literature of the Hebrew Bible.

The best-known example of Mesopotamian literature is the *Epic of Gilgamesh*. Frequently translated and adapted by various west Asian peoples, *Gilgamesh* may be a Sumerian work perhaps dating back to about 2500 B.C. An epic poem is the story of heroic deeds, in this case those of Gilgamesh, king of Uruk. Gilgamesh was probably a real historical personage, but the poem primarily concerns his fictionalized personal life, in particular the painful wisdom he gains as he grows from arrogant youth to maturity. The main themes are friendship, loss, and the inevitability of death. Much of the poem discusses Gilgamesh's close relationship with Enkidu, who is first his rival, then his friend, and finally his educator. Enkidu's untimely death makes Gilgamesh aware of his own mortality. Alone, Gilgamesh is incapable of introspection or self-awareness; only through his intense and ultimately tragic friendship with Enkidu does Gilgamesh become aware of himself. Distraught by his friend's death, Gilgamesh goes on a quest for immortality, but in vain. The *Epic of Gilgamesh* contains stories that presage the later biblical Eden and Flood narratives; there is little doubt that those narratives found their way from Mesopotamia to the Hebrew Bible. (See the box, "Heroism and Death in Mesopotamia.")

As we have seen in connection with Hammurabi's Code, Mesopotamian thinkers had no concept of abstract or universal principles. They did, however, demonstrate the ability to observe critically, to separate the typical from the particular, and to arrange their thoughts in a logical order. We know, for example, of an Akkadian medical treatise consisting of cases rather than principles, but they are typical rather than particular cases: "a man who is feverish and has a burning abdomen" rather than the specific case of so-and-so. Symptoms are arranged according to the part of the body affected, and the ability to observe carefully and to make comparisons and analogies is clear. The description of the course of a particular disease shows a clear awareness of cause and effect. In short, however limited Mesopotamian science seems when judged by later standards, it was a great contribution in its day.

The Mesopotamians made advances in mathematics, astronomy, medicine, and engineering, as well as in divination, which they considered to be every inch a science. The Sumerians had two

Heroism and Death in Mesopotamia

The **Epic of Gilgamesh** *sheds light on categories of gender and power in Mesopotamia. Men like King Gilgamesh and his friend Enkidu have heroic adventures and risk death. Women lead quieter lives but are wiser and more realistic, as the following excerpts show.*

[Gilgamesh mourns the death of Enkidu.]

"Hear me, O elders and give ear unto me! It is for Enkidu, my friend, that I weep, Moaning bitterly like a wailing woman. The axe at my side, my hand's trust, The dirk in my belt, the shield in front of me, My festal robe, my richest trimming—An evil demon rose up and robbed me! O my younger friend, thou chasedst The wild ass of the hills, the panther of the steppe! Enkidu, my younger friend, thou who chasedst The wild ass of the hills, the panther of the steppe! We who have conquered all things, scaled the mountains, Who seized the Bull and slew him, Brought affliction on Hubaba, who dwelled in the Cedar Forest! What, now, is this sleep that has laid hold on thee? Thou art benighted and canst not hear me!" But he lifts not up his head; he touched his heart but it does not beat.

[Beginning lost. Gilgamesh is addressing Siduri, the ale-wife:]
"He who with me underwent all hardships—Enkidu, whom I loved dearly, who with me underwent all hardships—has now gone to the fate of mankind! Day and night I have wept over him. I would not give him up for burial—in case my friend should rise at my plaint—seven days and seven nights, until a worm fell out of his nose. Since his passing I have not found life, I have roamed like a hunter in the midst of the steppe. O ale-wife, now that I have seen thy face, let me not see the death which I ever dread."

The ale-wife said to him, to Gilgamesh: "Gilgamesh, whither rovest thou? The life thou pursuest thou shalt not find. When the gods created mankind, death for mankind they set aside, Life in their own hands retaining. Thou, Gilgamesh, let full be thy belly, make thou merry by day and by night. Of each day make thou a feast of rejoicing, day and night dance thou and play! Let thy garments be sparkling fresh, thy head be washed; bathe thou in water. Pay heed to the little one that holds on to thy hand, let thy spouse delight in thy bosom! For this is the task of mankind!"

Source: James B. Pritchard, ed., *Ancient Near Eastern Texts Relating to the Old Testament*, 3d ed., with Supplement (Princeton: Princeton University Press, 1969), pp. 89–90.

systems of numeration: a decimal system (powers of ten) for administration and business and a sexagesimal system (powers of sixty) for weights and mathematical or astronomical calculations. Like the Babylonians, we still divide hours by sixty today. Furthermore, our modern system of numerical place-value notation—for example, the difference between 42 and 24—is derived, through Hindu-Arabic intermediaries, from the Babylonian place-value numerical system. The Babylonians were adept at arithmetic and could solve problems for which we would use algebra. A millennium before the Greek mathematician Pythagoras (who claimed to have studied the Mesopotamian tradition) proved the validity of the theorem that bears his name, they were familiar with the proposition that in a right triangle the square of the longest side is equal to the sum of the squares of the two shortest sides. In the first millennium B.C. the Babylonians developed a sophisticated mathematical astronomy (see page 48). As early as the seventeenth century B.C., however, they made systematic, if not always accurate, recordings of the movements of the planet Venus.

In medical matters they demonstrated considerable critical ability, as we have seen. Physicians made advances in the use of plant products for medicines and in very rudimentary surgery. The Babylonians had a simple pregnancy test of moderate accuracy, and they may have been able to perform delivery by cesarean section. They were able to extract an aching tooth. When they became ill, however, most people in Mesopotamia set more store by magic and incantations than by surgery or herbal medicine.

Mesopotamian sculptors, particularly the Sumerians, were adept and sophisticated. They did not produce realistic representations of reality—that was not their purpose. Rather, they aimed at creating symbols of religious piety or political or military power. Sumerian statues tend to be stiff and solemn. The head and face are carved in detail, and the body is neglected and sometimes merely represented by a geometrical form.

The most common type of Mesopotamian sculpture is relief sculpture, in which figures or forms are projected from a flat surface. Steles (upright stone slabs or pillars), plaques, and cylinder seals (small, carved stone or metal cylinders rolled over wet clay to render an impression, often indicating ownership) are all found.

EGYPT, TO CA. 1100 B.C.

From Babylon to the valley of the Nile River, the distance was about 750 miles by way of the caravan routes through Syria and Palestine: close enough to exchange customs, goods, and, if necessary, blows, but far enough for a distinct Egyptian civilization to emerge. As in Sumer, so too in Egypt a great civilization arose in a river valley. Egypt developed writing around 3100 B.C., slightly after Mesopotamia (and possibly under Mesopotamian influence), but was much earlier than Mesopotamia in becoming a unified kingdom under one ruler.

With its unique contributions in religion, politics, the arts, and science, and with its wealth of huge, surviving stone monuments, Egypt has impressed both scholars and lay people as few other

EGYPT	
3100 B.C.	Unification of Nile Valley
3100–2695 B.C.	Archaic Period
2695–2160 B.C.	Old Kingdom
2160–1963 B.C.	First Intermediate Period
1963–1786 B.C.	Middle Kingdom
1786–1550 B.C.	Second Intermediate Period; Hyksos
1550–1070 B.C.	New Kingdom

ancient civilizations have. In the ancient world, Egyptian culture was distinct but influential, from the spread of such Egyptian notions as a Last Judgment in the afterlife to Egyptian techniques in architecture and sculpture.

Geography as Destiny

Ancient Egypt is a product of the unique characteristics of the Nile River (Map 1.2). Egypt was "the gift of the Nile," to use the well-known phrase of Herodotus, a Greek historian who visited Egypt in the fifth century B.C.

Yet most of Egypt is desert; only about 5 percent is habitable by humans, including a few oases, the Nile Delta, and the Nile Valley itself, which extends about 760 miles from Cairo to Egypt's modern southern border: so-called Upper Egypt, a long and narrow valley never more than about 14 miles wide. North of Cairo, in so-called Lower Egypt, the Nile branches out into the wide, low-lying delta before flowing into the Mediterranean Sea.

The alluvial plain of the Nile was much friendlier to would-be farmers than was the valley of the Tigris and Euphrates. Unlike those rivers, the Nile was rarely given to damaging floods; its course was remarkably regular and predictable. Its annual floods, which took place between late summer and autumn (in contrast to Mesopotamia's spring floods), were generally benign. As a result, Egyptian agriculture was one of the wealthiest in the ancient world. Bread and beer were the national staples.

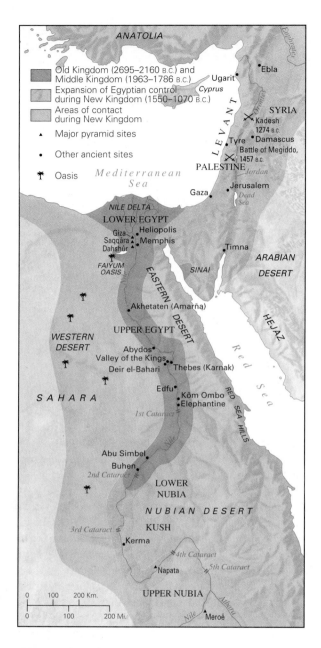

Map 1.2 Ancient Egypt and the Levant The unique geography of the Nile Valley left a stamp on ancient Egypt. Fertile soil made Egypt wealthy, and the surrounding desert led to periods of isolation from nearby African and Asian cultures.

Another result of the Nile's fertility was the relative optimism of ancient Egypt's world-view. "Hail to Thee, O Nile, that gushest forth from the earth and comest to nourish Egypt!" So proclaims an ancient hymn that indicates the Egyptians' grat-

itude toward and confidence in the benevolence of the environment. With its plentiful water and fertile land, Egypt did not suffer the chronic warfare that relative scarcity encouraged in Mesopotamia. Nor was Egypt easily reached by invaders. The Nile was cut off by deserts to the east and west, by rapids to the south, and by the Mediterranean to the north.

Egyptian art and literature betray little of the despair over the unpredictability of the universe that developed in the harsher climatic conditions of Mesopotamia. The behavior of the Nile, furthermore, encouraged a static quality in Egyptian ideology. Change seemed virtually impossible. Even death appeared to be a minor event compared with the regularity of the Nile, which may help explain the prominence in Egyptian religion of belief in the afterlife. In addition, the static outlook helped promote the idea of an absolute, all-powerful, and all-providing king—that is, pharaoh.

Storm over Origins

Early Egypt developed a distinctive civilization, with no major invasion for over a thousand years after the beginning of the historical period around 3100 B.C. Just how isolated was early Egypt, however, and just how distinctive was its civilization? Debate has arisen in recent years about the relationship of Egypt with western Asia, Europe, and the rest of Africa. Before World War II, most Egyptologists tended to see Egypt more as part of the Near East (that is, of the culture of western Asia) than as part of Africa. Many imagined that ancient Egyptians looked much like modern Europeans: part of "the Great White Race."[5] More recently, with the liberation after World War II of Europe's former African colonies and with the awakening of a growing interest in Africa by African Americans, some people have argued that Egypt was primarily African in character and that the ancient Egyptians were black.

The truth lies in between these two positions. Much of Egypt's earliest culture, for example, from Neolithic artwork and pottery to the notion that the ruler represents the ancestors and guarantees the fertility of the soil, is African. Yet in its late Neolithic era (ca. 3400–3050 B.C.), Egypt witnessed new styles and techniques in art, architecture, ceramics, and metallurgy that were imported from western Asia. As for the population, it seems, from the fourth millennium B.C. if not earlier, to have consisted of Africans mixed with immigrants from western Asia. The Egyptians considered themselves a distinct ethnic and racial group, unlike their neighbors in Africa or elsewhere. Egyptians were generally darker skinned than the ancient peoples of Europe or western Asia but often lighter skinned than the peoples of Africa south of the Sahara: They included a considerable variety of skin colors and body types. The farther south in Egypt one traveled, the more likely one was to see the dark skin and facial features characteristic of sub-Saharan Africans.

Much discussion has focused on the influence of Egypt on ancient Greek civilization, the first civilization of Europe. Egypt had a limited but significant impact on early Greece, as did the cultures of western Asia. The Greeks borrowed, among other things, Egyptian techniques in architecture and sculpture, Egyptian religious notions, and western Asian artisanship and shipbuilding, poetry and mythology. Much of what the Greeks borrowed, however, they transformed into something different.

Within Africa itself, Egypt was in continual contact with other regions, particularly the neighboring areas of ancient Libya and Nubia (roughly, the modern Sudan). The people of Nubia, who were black Africans, borrowed from Egypt and were perhaps borrowed from in turn. Some scholars believe, for example, that the early Egyptian notion of monarchy originated in Nubia. In West Africa certain important institutions—including sacred royalty, the cult of the ram, and belief in the afterlife existence of a double of one's physical person—may possibly be of Egyptian origin.

The debate over Egyptian origins highlights both Egypt's wide influence and its idiosyncrasy. Egypt was one of several influences on Greece; Greece was one of several countries influenced by Egypt; yet Greece and Egypt remained fundamentally distinct.

Divine Kingship

Agriculture and settled village life emerged in Egypt around 5000 B.C. By 4000, villages had grown into towns, each controlling a strip of territory. About one thousand years later, around 3100 B.C., the Nile Valley had become one unified kingdom of Egypt, with a capital city perhaps at Mem-

phis. We do not know precisely how this process was carried out. Egyptians writing after 3000 B.C. assumed that the Nile Valley was originally home to two kingdoms roughly corresponding to Upper and Lower Egypt, which, they said, had come into existence by the fourth millennium B.C. Then, around 3100, a certain Menes, king of Upper Egypt, is said to have conquered Lower Egypt and united the two into one combined kingdom controlling the entire Nile Valley.

We do not know how much (if any) of this tradition is true. But it is clear that between about 5000 and 3100 B.C., Egyptian communities up and down the Nile Valley succeeded in clearing marshes and expanding the amount of land under cultivation, which in turn could support a larger population. By 3100 B.C., monumental architecture, writing, and kingship appeared, a combination of indigenous invention and borrowing from Mesopotamia and perhaps Nubia, as already discussed. For several centuries Egyptians consolidated their institutions. Although few specifics are known about this so-called Archaic Period (3100–2695 B.C.), it is clear that it laid the groundwork for the next era. Around 2700 B.C., a remarkable, distinctive, and relatively well-documented period of creativity began, the so-called Third (2695–2600) and Fourth (2600–2500) Dynasties (that is, ruling families) of the Old Kingdom.

The history of third- and second-millennium B.C. Egypt is usually divided into three distinct eras of great prosperity: the Old Kingdom (2695–2160 B.C.), the Middle Kingdom (1963–1786 B.C.), and the New Kingdom (1550–1070 B.C.). Central authority broke down in the so-called Intermediate Periods between the kingdoms. Broadly speaking, one might characterize the Old Kingdom as a spectacular era of creativity and originality, symbolized by the building of the Great Pyramids; the Middle Kingdom as an era of introspection and literary production; and the New Kingdom as an era in which Egypt's traditional isolation gave way to international diplomacy and expansion.

The early Egyptian government was the first to govern a large territory. Indeed, a chart of Egypt's power structure would be strictly hierarchical, resembling a pyramid, with a broad base of laborers and artisans supporting a commanding elite. The occupant of this high point of power was considered so important that for centuries Egyptians referred to the office rather than to the person, calling it "the Great House": in Egyptian, *per-aa*, or "pharaoh," as the ruler himself (or occasionally herself) was eventually called.

The pyramids of pharaonic Egypt symbolized the king's power. The ancients built thirty-five major and many smaller pyramids, of which the best known are the Great Pyramids of Giza—three gigantic, perfectly symmetrical limestone tombs constructed during the Fourth Dynasty. Nearly five thousand years since it was built, the pyramid of King Khufu (r. 2589–2566 B.C., better known by his Greek name, Cheops) is still the largest all-stone building in human history. Nearby the Great Pyramids stands the Great Sphinx, a human-headed lion carved out of a huge rock outcropping, perhaps representing Khufu's son, King Khepren (r. 2558–2532 B.C.), for whom the second pyramid at Giza was built.

When the Great Pyramids were constructed, the kingdom of Egypt was still young. The power of the king to control the vast area of Lower and Upper Egypt was still open both to question and to armed revolt. By ordering the construction of an astonishingly large project focused on his person, the king made a statement of his power: an eloquent, simple, and irrefutable statement. The sheer size of the Great Pyramids demonstrated the king's ability to organize a vast labor force. Indeed, it has plausibly been suggested that the encampment of workers at Giza represents the largest gathering of human beings to that date. Moreover, the pyramids and the rows of tombs surrounding them reinforced the hierarchical structure of Egyptian society, of which the king was the capstone. Only princes and some officials were given the privilege of erecting a tomb beside the royal pyramids, a privilege that Fourth Dynasty Egyptians viewed as a prerequisite to gaining access to eternal life. The principal royal wives were permitted to be buried in small pyramids of their own.

The "Lord of the Two Lands" (Lower and Upper Egypt), to use just one of his several titles, the king in theory owned all the land. In practice Egypt's economy was a mixture of private enterprise and centralized control. The king was thought to watch over Egypt carefully. In the Middle Kingdom, for example, he was represented as a good shepherd, appointed by the sun-god, Re, as one text says, "to keep alive the people and

the folk, not sleeping by night as well as by day in seeking out every beneficial act, in looking for possibilities of usefulness." Even sleepless pharaohs needed help, however, and they delegated authority to a large group of officials. Indeed, Old Kingdom Egypt was one of the earliest great bureaucracies. The country was supervised by provincial governors, military commanders, judges, treasurers, engineers, agricultural overseers, scribes, and others. The highest official was the vizier, a sort of prime minister who had more day-to-day power than pharaoh himself.

The essence of good government was what the Egyptians called *ma'at*, whose basic meaning is "order"—in government, society, or the universe. *Ma'at* can also mean "truth" or "justice." The god-king embodied what we would call law, but the administration of justice rested mainly on others' shoulders. Egypt had a well-functioning system of judges who heard lawsuits, and it probably also had a detailed law code, although few written laws survive.

Bureaucratic and with claims to absolute power, Egyptian kingship was sacred monarchy. In Mesopotamia, the king generally claimed to have been appointed by the gods. In Egypt, pharaoh was deemed actually *to be* a god. He was called the "good god" in his lifetime and the "great god" after death. Considered the physical child of the sun-god Re, he was also deemed to be the sky-god Horus, and after dying he became Osiris, god of the underworld. Just as Egyptian myth recounted how the world was created when a god, sitting on a hill, made the waters recede, so pharaoh was thought to make the Nile rise and fall each year. (See the box, "Pharaoh the Divine and Invincible.")

A wall of language and ceremony separated kings from ordinary human beings. Egyptians did not speak "to" the king but rather "in his presence." He was outfitted with a variety of crowns, headdresses, and scepters. Pharaoh's exalted status was apparent on the occasion of a ceremonial "glorious appearance" before his subjects, especially at the Sed festival or jubilee, a celebration of the anniversary of his reign. The most traditional part of the ceremony was the appearance of the king and queen at the palace door on jubilee day wearing special jubilee clothes, but there were other elements of pageantry. The well-documented Sed festivals of Amenhotep III

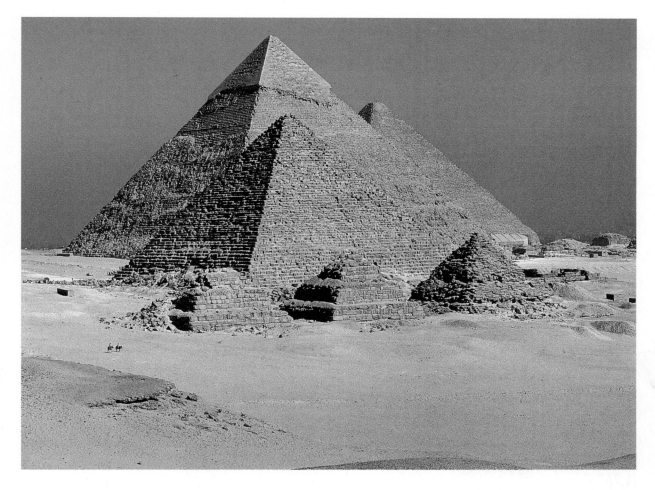

Great Pyramids of Giza Royal funerary monuments of three Egyptian kings of the twenty-sixth century B.C., the pyramids symbolize the power and ambition of the Old Kingdom. The pyramid of King Khufu (or Cheops, rearmost in the photo) is still the largest all-stone building in human history. *(Michael Holford)*

(r. 1390–1352 B.C.), who celebrated three of them, included such grand features as an elaborate procession of boats on the Nile, the assembling of officials and foreign dignitaries standing according to rank, distribution of gifts and a special breakfast (bread, beef, fowl, and beer), and the erection of festival buildings.

Life and Afterlife

Later peoples, beginning with the Greeks, have assumed that the ordinary Egyptian chafed under royal power. It is true that Egyptians were burdened with a variety of taxes (paid in agricultural produce) and that free people, both men and women, had an obligation of forced labor service on public works, from irrigation projects to the pyramids. Sometimes this service caused resentment. We hear of worker discipline maintained by beatings, of fugitives, of the pious hope that there be no forced labor in the afterlife, and even, in one unusual case, of a workers' strike.

Both piety and practicality, however, dictated that most people make peace with their public burdens. Far from resenting the king's claim to divinity, ordinary people might have been reassured to be ruled by a god. Nor were the pyramid-builders slaves laboring under a tyrant, as Greek

Pharaoh the Divine and Invincible

Egypt's rulers presented themselves as god-kings. Excerpt (a), a selection from the grave stele of a high official of the Twelfth Dynasty of the Middle Kingdom (ca. 1850 B.C.), states pharaoh's divinity unhesitatingly. Excerpt (b), from an inscription about Amenhotep II (r. 1427–1400 B.C.), shows the emphasis that the warrior-pharaohs of the New Kingdom placed on their invincibility in combat—in sport as well as in battle.

(a)

Now, further, his majesty appeared as king as a goodly youth. When he had matured and completed eighteen years on his thighs in valor, he was one who knew every task of Montu [the war-god]; there was no one like him on the field of battle. He was one who knew horses: there was not his like in this numerous army. There was not one therein who could draw his bow. He could not be approached in running.

Worship King Nimaatre, living forever, within your bodies and associate with his majesty in your hearts. He is Perception which is in men's hearts, and his eyes search out every body. He is Re, by whose beams one sees, He is one who illumines the Two Lands more than the sun disc.

He is one who makes the land greener than does a high Nile, for he has filled the Two Lands with strength and life. The nostrils are chilled when he inclines toward rage, but when he is merciful, they will breathe the air. He gives food to them who are in his service, and he supplies them who tread his path.

(b)

Strong of arms, one who did not weary when he took the oar, he [Amenhotep II] rowed at the stern of his falcon-boat as the stroke for two hundred men. When there was a pause, after they had attained half an iter's course [about two-thirds of a mile], they were weak, their bodies were limp, they could not draw a breath, while his majesty was (still) strong under his oar of twenty cubits [about 34 feet] in its length. He left off and moored his falcon-boat only after he had attained three iters [about four miles] in rowing, without letting down in pulling. Faces were bright at the sight of him, when he did this.

Source: James B. Pritchard, ed., *Ancient Near Eastern Texts Relating to the Old Testament*, 3d ed., with Supplement (Princeton: Princeton University Press), pp. 244, 431.

writers assumed. In fact, they might have given their labor gladly to raising the man-god's tomb, as an act of faith, just as people centuries later donated time and money to build medieval cathedrals. There were material compensations, too: ration supplements for ordinary laborers, steady employment for specialized craftsmen.

Herodotus, that Greek visitor to Egypt, remarked that the Egyptians were the most religious people in the world. Egypt indeed offered a great variety of religious experience, from ritual and festival to ethical teaching to magic. This experience is difficult to summarize, not only because of variations over time and place but because of the tendency of Egyptian religion toward syncretism—that is, the combining of mutually opposed beliefs, principles, or practices. For example, Egyptian mythology taught that the sky was a cow or was held up by a god or by a post or that it was a goddess stretched over the earth. No one was troubled by the inconsistency, as a modern worshiper might be, because it was thought that a fundamental unity underlay the manifold varieties of nature.

In addition to syncretism, Egyptian religion also tended toward henotheism. Monotheism, which is familiar today to Christians, Jews, and Muslims, is the belief in one god and only one god. Henotheists like the ancient Egyptians emphasize the worship of one god without denying the existence of others. For example, the most important Egyptian god was Re, the sun, often called "universal lord." From time to time, Re was syncretized with other gods to create a powerful new god: for example, Re-Atum, a combination of Re and a creator-god; Re-Harakhty, Re-Horus-of-the-Horizon; and Amon-Re, a combination of Re and the invisible, omnipresent Amon. One text even refers to Amon-Re-Atum-Harakhty!

Egypt's religion had an abundance of greater and lesser deities, including human, animal, and composite gods. Various animals, from cats and dogs to crocodiles and serpents, were thought to represent the divine. There were innumerable local deities, spirits, and demons as well as gods and goddesses of all Egypt. In addition to Re and his various syncretized forms, important deities included Thoth, the moon-god and god of wisdom; Nut, goddess of the sky; Ptah, who replaced Atum in a separate myth as creator-god; Osiris, who invented agriculture and became lord of the dead; Horus, son of Osiris, a sky-god imagined as a giant falcon; and Isis, wife of Osiris and mother of Horus, a mother-goddess. Temples were numerous and wealthy, though never the central economic institution of the community.

Probably the most striking feature of Egyptian religion was its focus on the afterlife. Unlike the Mesopotamians, the Egyptians believed that death could be an extremely pleasant continuation of life on earth. Hence, they actively sought immortality. The wealthy placed great emphasis on building tombs, decorating them with paintings and inscriptions, and stocking them with cherished possessions for use in the other world. The most cherished possession of all, of course, was the body itself, and the Egyptians provided for its preservation through their mastery of the science of embalming—hence the Egyptian mummies. The Egyptians distinguished between soul and body and believed that part of the soul, the *ka*, was immortal. Unlike later civilizations, however, they

Miniature Coffin of Tutankhamon This miniature coffin (8⅞ inches long) is one of four containing the internal organs of the king (r. 1336–1327 B.C.) removed during the embalming process. Made of gold inlaid with colored glass and carnelian, the coffin is typical of the splendor and luxury of the objects discovered in the substantially intact royal tomb. Note the hieroglyphic inscription offering divine protection to the remains. *(Egyptian Museum, Cairo)*

were not prepared to jettison the body altogether, believing instead that from time to time the soul desired to return to the body after death. That belief made mummification necessary.

Reserved for the king and his officials in the Old Kingdom, by the Middle Kingdom the afterlife became, as it were, democratized. In the wake of political and social change, Egyptian ideology changed. The Middle Kingdom and the First and Second Intermediate Periods were in many ways an inward-looking and reflective era, one in which materialism was de-emphasized and a sense of common humanity appears. "Even the timid fish shall come to thee," says one text of a First Intermediate Period ruler, " . . . because thou art the father of the orphan, the husband of the widow, the brother of the divorcee, and the apron of him that is motherless, . . . a leader free from covetousness, a great man free from wrongdoing, one who destroys falsehood and brings *ma'at* into being, and who comes at the cry of him who gives voice."[6] (See the box, "Humane Values.")

By the Middle Kingdom, even ordinary Egyptians could live in the afterlife as gods, as long as they could purchase for their graves funerary texts containing the relevant rituals and prayers. The texts emphasize ritual—incantations, magic spells, prayers—as the key to eternal life. Yet from time to time, especially during the Middle Kingdom, there is an impressive insistence on ethical behavior. Created in the likeness of god, men and women must worship the gods and provide for their fellows. A dead person has to appear before the court of a god, usually Osiris, for judgment on his or her life. Before forty-two judges of the underworld, the dead person declares his or her innocence of a variety of sins. The judges then weigh the dead person's heart in the balance against a feather, symbol of *ma'at*, or truth. The sinless are admitted into eternal life in the kingdom of the blessed; the guilty are wiped out.

Such absolute judgments were not found in daily life. Consider relations between the sexes. Egyptian women did not enjoy equal status with men, but they had a considerably greater measure of equality than women in other ancient societies, particularly in legal matters. As in Mesopotamia, so in Egypt a woman could buy or sell, bequeath or inherit, sue or testify in court, but an Egyptian woman, unlike her eastern sisters, could do so without a male guardian's approval. A married woman in Egypt retained the status of complete legal independence; she could even own property without her husband's involvement. But how often did women exercise such privileges? For example, relatively little evidence of female property owners survives from Egypt. Although Egyptian women could work outside the home in a variety of enterprises, they were rarely managers and rarely received the same pay as men. There were women workers in agriculture and trade, in the textile and perfume industries, in dining halls, and in entertainment, and women served as priestesses of various kinds. Yet in Egypt, as elsewhere, women were expected to make the home the focus of their activities. So, although the status of Egyptian women was high by ancient standards, nothing like modern conditions of relative equality between the sexes obtained.

The humane attitudes of the Middle Kingdom were founded on restored order. They were swept away in the period from about 1700 to 1570 B.C., when Semitic-speaking immigrants from Palestine—"Princes of Foreign Uplands," as they were called in Egyptian, or Hyksos, to employ the commonly used Greek term—settled in the delta region and then conquered and ruled much of Egypt. In many ways gentle conquerors, the Hyksos worshiped Egyptian gods, built and restored Egyptian temples, and intermarried with natives. As foreigners, however, the Hyksos were unpopular. Eventually a war launched from Upper Egypt, which had retained a loose independence, drove the Hyksos out.

Ahmose I (r. 1550–1525 B.C.) was the first restored Egyptian ruler of the New Kingdom. His proved to be a new Egypt indeed. The Hyksos had brought advanced military technology to Egypt, including the horse-drawn war chariot, new kinds of daggers and swords, and the composite bow. Made of laminated materials including wood, leather, and horn, the composite bow could hit a target at six hundred yards. Having once tasted foreign occupation, Egypt's new rulers made up their minds to use such weapons in aggressive military campaigns abroad.

Expansion and Reform, 1540–1293 B.C.

Warlike, expansionist, and marked by a daring attempt at religious reform, the New Kingdom's Eighteenth Dynasty (1540–1293 B.C.) has long held

Humane Values

Compilations of wise sayings were popular in Egypt. This text, preserved on a papyrus of around 1450 B.C. and composed at least as early as the Twelfth Dynasty (ca. 1991–1785 B.C.), claims to be the advice of a king of the First Intermediate Period (ca. 2075 B.C.) for his son and successor, Merikare. The text reflects the humane and sober values of that era.

Copy thy fathers and thy ancestors. . . . Behold, their words remain in writing. Open, that thou mayest read and copy their wisdom. Thus the skilled man becomes learned. . . .

Mayest thou speak justice in thy own house, that the great ones who are on earth may fear thee. Uprightness of heart is fitting for the lord. It is the forepart of the house [the master's quarters] that inspires respect in the back [the servants' quarters]. . . .

Do not distinguish the son of a man from a poor man, but take to thyself a man because of the work of his hands. Every skilled work should be practised according to the . . . of the lord of a strong arm. Protect thy frontier and build thy fortresses, for troops are of advantage to their lord. . . .

Generation passes generation among men, and the god, who knows men's characters, has hidden himself. But there is none who can withstand the Lord of the Hand: he is the one who attacks what the eyes can see. Revere the god upon his way, made of costly stones and fashioned of metal, like a flood replaced by another flood. . . . Enrich thy house of the West; embellish thy place of the necropolis, as an upright man and as one who executes the justice upon which men's hearts rely. More acceptable is the character of one upright of heart than the ox of the evildoer. Act for the god, that he may act similarly for thee, with oblations which make the offering-table flourish and with a carved inscription—that is what bears witness to thy name. The god is aware of him who acts for him.

Well directed are men, the cattle of the god. He made heaven and earth according to their desire, and he repelled the water-monster. He made the breath of life for the nostrils. They who have issued from his body are his images. He arises in heaven according to their desire. He made for them plants, animals, fowl, and fish to feed them. He slew his enemies and injured even his own children because they thought of making rebellion. He makes the light of day according to their desire, and he sails by in order to see them. . . . For the god knows every name.

Source: James B. Pritchard, ed., *Ancient Near Eastern Texts Relating to the Old Testament*, 3d ed., with Supplement (Princeton: Princeton University Press, 1969), pp. 415–417.

a special fascination for historians. The great warrior-pharaoh Thutmose III (r. 1479–1425 B.C.) symbolizes the dynasty's armed expansion into Nubia and Syria. He fought for twenty years in Syria and Palestine and established Egyptian predominance in the region. Thutmose won his greatest victory during his first campaign, at the Battle of Megiddo in 1457 B.C. (see Map 1.2), when Egypt completely defeated the attempt of the Hurrian kingdom of Mitanni to expand southward (see page 35).

Before Thutmose had reached adulthood, his stepmother, Queen Hatshepsut, served as regent and then assumed the kingship herself (r. 1479–1457 B.C.). Hatshepsut's was the most successful female reign in Egypt until the reign of Cleopatra (r. 51–30 B.C.). Although she led Egyptian armies on campaign to Nubia, Hatshepsut is best known for her less warlike works: at home, public works and temple rebuilding; abroad, a commercial expedition over the Red Sea to the "Land of Punt"

Egyptian Queen This elegant, red-granite statue of the pharaoh Hatshepsut (r. 1479–1457 B.C.) is one of the few to depict her as a woman. She is usually shown as a man, complete with beard, to symbolize her royal power. Centuries later the proportions and carving techniques of Egyptian stone sculpture would influence the Greeks, although Greek artists chose less to copy the Egyptians than to try to outdo them (see the photo on page 93). *(Brian Brake/Photo Researchers, Inc.)*

(perhaps modern Somalia, in eastern Africa). As illustrated in words and pictures on the wall of Hatshepsut's splendid, terraced, funerary temple at Deir el-Bahri, the expedition to Punt brought home such exotic objects as incense-bearing trees, ebony, perfume, panther skins, baboons, monkeys, and greyhounds.

As an imperial power, New Kingdom Egypt required an expanded government. There were more officials, more military officers, and more priests than ever before. It was a time of opportunity and of conflict. Consider the so-called Amarna reform, named for a major archaeological site at the modern town of Amarna.

Undertaken by Thutmose III's great-great-grandson, pharaoh Amenhotep IV (r. 1352–1336 B.C.), the Amarna reform was a struggle of power and faith. The god Amon-Re had become the chief deity of the New Kingdom. As supporters of the ideology of imperialism, his temple priests were rewarded with land and wealth until their power rivaled pharaoh's own. Amenhotep IV's dramatic response was to forbid the worship of Amon-Re and replace him with the god Aton, the solar disk. Changing his own name to Akhenaton ("pleasing to Aton"), the king ordered the erasure of Amon-Re's name from monuments throughout Egypt. As a further step, Akhenaton created a new capital city in central Egypt at an uninhabited site at the desert's edge: Akhetaton (modern Amarna). The new town had a distinctive culture. Akhenaton's wife, Nefertiti, figures prominently in Amarna art, and she too may have played an important role in the reform.

The reform shifted power away from the priests and toward the king, but we need not doubt the reformers' sincerity. Contemporary literature suggests intense religious conviction in Aton as a benevolent god and one who nurtured not only Egypt but all countries. Although the Aton cult focuses on one god, it was not monotheistic but henotheistic. The reformers recognized Re and Akhenaton himself as gods in addition to Aton. Indeed, only Akhenaton and his family were permitted to worship Aton directly; the rest of the Egyptian population was expected to worship the god through pharaoh.

Bold as the reform was, sustaining so dramatic a break with tradition proved impossible. After Akhenaton's death his son-in-law and successor, Tutankhaton (r. 1336–1327 B.C.) made a rapprochement with the priests of Amon-Re, which he signaled by changing his name to Tutankhamon. The Amon-Re cult was revived, the Aton cult was abolished, and the city of Akhetaton was abandoned. The priesthood had expanded its power permanently; henceforth, pharaoh's absolutism was not so great as previously.

Arts and Sciences

The Egyptians were superb builders, architects, and engineers. In addition to pyramids and irrigation works, they constructed numerous other monumental structures: royal tombs, palaces, forts, temples, and obelisks. At their best, Egyptian architects designed buildings in harmony with the unique landscape—one of the reasons for the structures' lasting appeal. Their most original and their most enduring work was done in stone. Stone temples, for example, culminated in the great pillared and monumental structures of the New Kingdom. That period also saw the construction of rock-cut temples, the most famous of which is Ramesses II's (r. 1279–1213 B.C.) project at Abu Simbel (see Map 1.2): Two chambers were carved out of rock, and in front of the larger chamber were four seated colossal statues of Ramesses, also carved out of rock. Obelisks were slender, tapering pillars carved of a single piece of stone. Inscribed with figures and hieroglyphs ("sacred carvings"), and usually erected in pairs in front of a temple, obelisks were meant to glorify the sun.

Throughout history, royal courts have excelled as patrons of the arts; the Egyptian court was one of the first and greatest. Egyptian craftsmen were masters of gold jewelry-work, glassmaking, and woodworking. The major arts are well represented in tombs, which were decorated with rich, multicolored wall paintings, the first narrative painting. There are scenes of the gods, court ceremony, ordinary life, war, and recreation amid the crocodiles and hippopotamuses of the Nile Valley. Like so much else in Egypt, painting had a religious purpose. Representations of living people were meant to perpetuate them in the afterlife.

Sculpture was another art form in which Egyptians excelled. Carved in stone, wood, or metal, Egyptian sculpture is a study in contrasts. The body posture is usually rigid and stiff, the musculature only sketchy; the face, in contrast, is often individualistic, the expression full of character and drawn from life. Statues represent kings and queens, gods and goddesses, husbands and wives, adults and children, officials, priests, scribes, animals. Mirroring broader cultural trends, statues of pharaohs undergo a stylistic change from the Old Kingdom, where the royal expression is usually one of majesty and power, to the Middle Kingdom, where the king's face often seems more human and weak. Statues of New Kingdom pharaohs often suggest imperial power, but Amarna sculpture places an unusual emphasis on introspective gazes, and it experiments with the grotesque. Eighteenth Dynasty sculpture often shows a striking interest in feminine beauty and grace.

Ancient Egyptian literature is notable for its variety. Religious subjects, historical and commemorative records, technical treatises in mathematics and medicine, and secular stories survive alongside business contracts and royal proclamations. A good example of Egyptian writing is *The Story of Sinuhe*, a Middle Kingdom prose tale. *Sinuhe* reveals both the charm of ancient Egyptian literature and its cultural chauvinism. (See the box, "Encounters with the West: Egyptian Attitudes Toward Foreigners.")

Egyptian literature is as important for its tools as for its substance. The discovery that the fibers of the papyrus plant could be made into writing material—the word *paper* comes from *papyrus*—would prove to be fundamental for ancient Mediterranean literature. Not only the Egyptians but later the Greeks and Romans and many other ancient peoples wrote on scrolls of papyrus sheets joined together—the precursors of books. Egyptian writing is best known for hieroglyphics, a system of pictures and abstract signs that represent sounds or ideas. Elaborate and formal, hieroglyphics were used only for monuments and ornamentation. Two simplified scripts served for everyday use.

The people who built the pyramids were skilled at arithmetic and geometry. Although not as sophisticated as later mathematicians, Egyptians were able to approximate *pi* (the ratio of the circumference of a circle to its diameter) and to solve equations containing one or two unknowns. Mathematical astronomy never reached the heights in Egypt that it reached in Babylon (see page 48), but the Egyptian calendar was a notable achievement. Based on observation of the star Sirius, the Egyptian calendar, with its 365-day year, approximates the solar calendar. Julius Caesar brought the Egyptian calendar to Rome. Corrected to 365¼ days, it survives to this day (in adjusted form) as the calendar of Europe, the Americas, and much of the rest of the world.

Egyptian medical doctors were admired in antiquity and were in demand abroad. They could set a dislocated shoulder. They had a full battery of splints, sutures, adhesive plasters, elementary

∼ ENCOUNTERS WITH THE WEST ∼
Egyptian Attitudes Toward Foreigners

The story of Sinuhe is a well-known piece of Middle Kingdom prose literature. A court official, Sinuhe fled Egypt for Syria-Palestine after the assassination of the king. There he married the daughter of a tribal chief and became a successful chief himself. In his old age he received permission to return home. The tale demonstrates Egyptian curiosity about Palestine and Syria while it reveals Egyptian cultural snobbery toward what another Egyptian text calls "the miserable Asiatic."

This decree of the King: . . . Come back to Egypt! See the residence in which you lived! Kiss the ground at the great portals, mingle with the courtiers! For today you have begun to age. You have lost a man's strength. Think of the day of burial, the passing into reveredness.

A night is made for you with ointments and wrappings from the hand of Tait [goddess of weaving]. A funeral procession is made for you on the day of burial; the mummy case is of gold, its head of lapis lazuli. . . . You shall not die abroad! Nor shall Asiatics inter you. You shall not be wrapped in the skin of a ram to serve as your coffin. Too long a roaming of the earth! Think of your corpse, come back! . . .

Copy of the reply to this decree:

The servant of the Palace, Sinuhe, says: In very good peace! . . . May the fear of you resound in lowlands and highlands, for you have subdued all that the sun encircles! . . .

Re [the sun-god] has set the fear of you throughout the land, the dread of you in every foreign country. Whether I am at the residence, whether I am in this place, it is you who cover this horizon. The sun rises at your pleasure. The water in the river is drunk when you wish. The air of heaven is breathed at your bidding. . . . This servant has been sent for!

Your Majesty will do as he wishes! One lives by the breath which you give.

[Sinuhe returns to Egypt and is brought into the king's presence.]

Then the royal daughters were brought in, and his majesty said to the queen: "Here is Sinuhe, come as an Asiatic, a product of nomads!" She uttered a very great cry, and the royal daughters shrieked all together. They said to his majesty: "Is it really he, O kings, our lord?" Said his majesty: "It is really he!" . . .

His majesty said: "He shall not fear, he shall not dread!" He shall be a Companion among the nobles. He shall be among the courtiers. Proceed to the robing-room to wait on him!"

I left the audience-hall, the royal daughters giving me their hands. We went through the great portals, and I was put in the house of a prince. In it were luxuries: a bathroom and mirrors. . . . Every servant was at his task. Years were removed from my body. I was shaved; my hair was combed. Thus was my squalor returned to the foreign land, my dress to the Sand-farers. I was clothed in fine linen; I was anointed with fine oil. I slept on a bed. I had returned the sand to those who dwell in it, the tree-oil to those who grease themselves with it.

Source: Miriam Lichtheim, *Ancient Egyptian Literature,* Volume 1: *The Old and Middle Kingdoms* (Berkeley: University of California Press, 1973), pp. 229–233.

disinfectants (from tree leaves), and fatty substances to treat burns. A brilliant treatise, the so-called Edwin Smith Papyrus, demonstrates their sophistication and rationalism. Dating from around 1750 B.C., the document claims to be a copy of an original from 2700 B.C. (the veracity of that claim is uncertain). In this treatise physicians divide diseases into three categories: treatable, possibly treatable, and untreatable. There are signs of careful observation and tantalizing evidence of postmortem dissection.

Unfortunately, as in Mesopotamia, medical science (at least written medical science) seems to have stagnated after a promising beginning. Although Egyptian doctors distinguished between medicine and magic, they were happy to use magic when all else failed—but usually only then. In a letter of the thirteenth century B.C. to a Hittite king, Ramesses II declines the king's request for an Egyptian physician to treat the king's sister's infertility. A physician could do nothing, Ramesses explains, because the unfortunate woman was too old to bear children. He goes on to say, however, that an Egyptian magician might be perfect for the job and he has decided to send one.

WIDENING HORIZONS: ANATOLIA AND THE LEVANT

The literate river-valley civilizations tend to capture our attention in the third millennium B.C., but we know that city-states were flourishing elsewhere, particularly in the Levant.* The discovery in 1974 of a huge cuneiform archive at Ebla (modern Tell Mardikh) in northern Syria has revolutionized our knowledge of one such city-state in the mid-third millennium B.C. Another city-state, Ugarit (modern Ras Shamra), a cosmopolitan port, flourished in the second millennium B.C.

In the second millennium B.C. the civilized world grew wider and more thoroughly interconnected. New kingdoms appeared, among them the Kassites in Babylonia, the Hittites in Anatolia, and the Hurrians in northern Mesopotamia and Syria. Their expansionist ambitions and those of New Kingdom Egypt made the period from approximately 1500 to 1200 B.C. one of international conflict, both military and diplomatic (Map 1.3). It was not only an age of wars and treaties, however, but also one of cultural creativity marked by achievements such as international law, sophisticated historical analysis, and the first alphabet. New kingdoms on the island of Crete (at its height, ca.

---

*The term *Levant* can be used to refer generally to the territory on the eastern shore of the eastern Mediterranean or, more particularly, to the geographical region known today as Syria and Palestine. In this text, *Levant* is used in the latter sense.

ANATOLIA AND THE LEVANT	
2500–2350 B.C.	Cuneiform texts from Ebla
1650–1450 B.C.	Hittite Old Kingdom
1457 B.C.	Battle of Megiddo
1450–1380 B.C.	Hittite Middle Kingdom
1400–1200 B.C.	Height of prosperity at Ugarit
1380–1180 B.C.	Hittite New Kingdom (empire)
1274 B.C.	Battle of Kadesh
1250–1150 B.C.	Sea Peoples invade

1800–1550 B.C.) and on the mainland of Greece (at its height, ca. 1400–1200 B.C.) also became part of the international system (see pages 64 and 67). In the century from about 1250 to about 1150 B.C., however, an unexplained series of economic and demographic disruptions, resulting in invasions and piracy, brought both the international system and its component kingdoms to ruin.

The City-States of Syria-Palestine, ca. 2500–1200 B.C.

Most of the documents in Ebla's archive are fragmentary. Nevertheless, the sheer number of them—more than sixteen thousand tablets—has more than doubled the total of known cuneiform documents from the early era of writing (down to ca. 2350 B.C.). Among the writings are the world's earliest known dictionaries.

A prosperous city, Ebla was known for commerce and artisanry. Sometime between 2500 and 2300 B.C., Ebla ruled a large kingdom, extending over much of Syria, and possibly containing as many as 250,000 people, of whom perhaps 30,000 lived in the city (see Map 1.3). Ebla's government fostered trade by negotiating commercial treaties and arranging dynastic marriages. One such treaty between Ebla and Ashur, a city about 435 miles to the east, is the earliest known agreement between two states. When diplomacy failed, Ebla resorted to war, with great success. Ebla's most notable conquest was Mari, a commercial competitor 300 miles downstream on the Euphrates.

Ebla was ruled by an oligarchy (a small, elite group) headed by fourteen regional governors who were probably also clan elders. The king, a sort of first among equals, was chosen by election rather than inheritance; his power was limited by the oligarchic council. Eblaites seem to have conceived of the state as a large family, the "children of Ebla." The queen and queen mother had significant government authority. The queen had her own properties, administered by officials who answered to her. The queen mother, officially called "the honored mother of the king," had considerable say in the succession.

Attacked by Akkadians around 2300 B.C., Ebla fell to the Amorites around 2000 B.C. It remained a wealthy city, though much diminished in power. Our eyes might now turn to Ugarit (see Map 1.3), a thriving Mediterranean port of Syria around 1400–1200 B.C., as a wealth of documentation indicates. The keynote of Ugarit's history is its cosmopolitanism, a result of the cross-cultural opportunities created by its merchant elite. As a trading center it linked ships coming from the eastern Mediterranean island of Cyprus or the Anatolian ports with land caravans to Babylonia. Like the later Phoenician cities (see page 00), it was both a middleman and an exporter of its own products such as purple-dyed textiles and metals. The indigenous inhabitants of Ugarit spoke a Semitic language; their culture and that of large numbers of people in southern Syria and Palestine is called Canaanite (from the Hebrew Bible, which calls Palestine "the land of Canaan"). The merchant community in Ugarit, however, was polyglot, including not only the Canaanite majority but Babylonians, Egyptians, Moabites (a people from the region that is now Jordan), Hittites, and Hurrians, among others.

Canaanite religion in the second millennium B.C. is well attested to in Ugaritic art and texts. By far the most influential legacy of Ugaritic culture, however, is the creation of the world's oldest alphabet. Perhaps a wish to set religious documents in writing lay behind the invention of the Ugaritic alphabet; perhaps commercial efficiency was the driving motive. Whatever the cause, Ugaritic scribes in the fourteenth century B.C. invented thirty cuneiform signs as an alphabet to write their Semitic language. It was a true alphabet in that each sign stood for one and only one sound. Later adapted by the Phoenicians and, through

them, the Greeks, the Ugaritic alphabet is the source of the English alphabet and most other alphabets in the world today.

The Hittites

How and when the Hittites first came to Anatolia are obscure, but somewhat before 1800 B.C. Hittite personal names appear in contemporary texts. The Hittites spoke an Indo-European language. (Nearly half of the world's people today speak an Indo-European language—such as English, Spanish, French, Italian, German, Greek, Russian, Iranian, and Hindi.) Indo-European-speakers probably originated between 4500 and 2500 B.C. in southern Russia, in the region of the Dnieper and Volga Rivers. A warlike, mobile, horse-riding people, they emigrated east and west.

The Hittites were masters of the horse. They ruled Anatolia from their city of Hattusas (modern Boghazköy). Rich in minerals and in farmland, Anatolia provided a solid foundation for empire.

Hittite history is divided into an Old Kingdom (ca. 1650–1450 B.C.) marked by the conquest and consolidation of Anatolia; a Middle Kingdom (ca. 1450–1380 B.C.), a period of retrenchment and loss of territory; a New Kingdom (ca. 1380–1180 B.C.) characterized by intervention in international politics and then collapse; and finally a Neo-Hittite era (ca. 1180–700 B.C.) of small successor states. The Hittite empire reached its zenith in the New Kingdom, when it extended into Syria and northern Mesopotamia. This was a time of shifting empires. For instance, the Hurrians carved out the kingdom of Mitanni on the upper Euphrates around 1500 B.C. (see Map 1.3). Archaeologists have recently identified in northern Syria the long-lost site of the Hurrians' capital city, Urkesh.

During the Old Kingdom, the Hittites could be characterized as a warrior society, with a weak king, a strong and boisterous nobility, and even a measure of equality for forceful queens. The monarch was neither god nor god's representative but rather first among equals. He was supported by an armed, horse-riding nobility who, in return for land, supplied him with troops and mounts. The nobles met in assembly and rendered legal judgments. The power of the nobility spelled trouble for central authority in the sixteenth century B.C., when conspiracy, feud, and assassination came close to destroying the Hittite kingdom. The

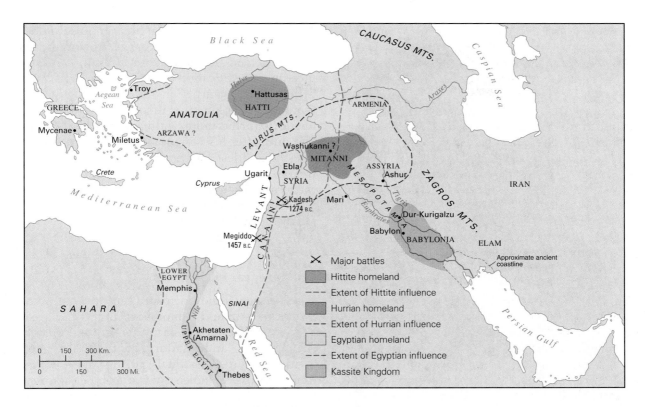

Map 1.3 The International System, ca. 1500–ca. 1200 B.C. In this era of competing kingdoms and city-states, the most dramatic conflict was that between Egypt and the Hittites for control of Syria and Palestine.

powerful King Telepinu finally established a secure hereditary succession to the throne around 1500 B.C. In the Hittite New Kingdom the balance of power swung further in favor of the king, who was now addressed as "my Sun" during his lifetime and was deified after death, as in Egypt or the Third Dynasty of Ur.

Hittite queens and queen mothers had strong and independent positions, as at Ebla. Puduhepa, wife of King Hattusilis III (r. 1278–1250 B.C.), played a memorable role in state affairs. Various evidence also suggests that Puduhepa was the prime mover in an important religious movement, whereby the Hurrian sun-goddess of Arinna (a shrine near Hattusas) became the chief deity of the Hittite state. The goddess was worshiped as "Queen of the Land of Hatti, Queen of Heaven and Earth, mistress of the kings and queens of the Land of Hatti, directing the government of the King and Queen of Hatti."[7]

Much of Hittite culture is derived from that of the pre-Hittite inhabitants of Anatolia (known as the Hattians) and from the Hurrians, who were in turn influenced by Mesopotamia. Most of the Hittites' gods and mythology were Hattian in origin until the Hittite New Kingdom, when Hurrian influence prevailed. Many scholars have been struck by the Hurrian-derived epic cycle of the god Kumarbi. Kumarbi, father of the gods, seizes power after castrating his father, Anu (heaven), and is then replaced by his own son, the weather-god Teshub. A Greek poem of about 700 B.C., Hesiod's *Theogony*, tells almost the same story, down to the details, about the three gods Ouranos (heaven), Kronos (father of the gods), and Zeus (the storm-god). It is likely that the story reached the Greeks by way of Phoenicia, where many Hurrians lived in the later second millennium B.C. Rarely can the historian so clearly trace cross-cultural influence at work.

Although Hittite religion is frequently derivative, the sophistication of Hittite political thought is quite original. Earlier peoples had kept lists and chronicles; Hittite annals are notably livelier,

A Hittite Warrior This 6½-foot-tall figure was carved on the wall of an entry gate to the city of Hattusas, the Hittite capital, during the New Kingdom Period (1380–1180 B.C.). Fierce-looking, vigorous, and outfitted with battle ax, sword, kilt, and possibly mail shirt, he is designed to frighten away both human and supernatural enemies. (*Ankara National Museum*)

better argued, and more conscious of cause and effect. The royal annals of King Hattusilis III, for example, read in parts like a lawsuit, carefully pleading a justification of the king's actions. Hattusilis excuses usurpation of the throne by stating that the former king had unjustly stripped him of territory; furthermore, Hattusilis rebelled openly, and only after his wife, Puduhepa, had dreamed that the goddess Ishtar was on their side. Hittite treaties with subordinate states similarly plead their case: They begin with an introduction providing historical background and justifying the relationship sworn to in the body of the text.

The First International System and Its Collapse, ca. 1500–1150 B.C.

The fourteenth and thirteenth centuries B.C. were an era of war and diplomacy among the great powers of western Asia and northeast Africa. Armies and ambassadors routinely traveled across the Syro-Palestinian corridor. For the first time a relatively stable system of competing international powers emerged (see Map 1.3). In the Old and Middle Kingdoms, the kings had entrusted the defense of Egypt to border fortifications and a small army. Pharaohs in New Kingdom Egypt, in contrast, pursued a forward defense policy, sending diplomats and, when necessary, large mobile armies into the Levant. Both for Egypt and for other large kingdoms such as that of the Hittites, Syria-Palestine became the battleground for power and influence.

War was one sign of the new international system. War consisted of skirmishes marked by an occasional dramatic battle, such as at Megiddo in 1457 B.C. (see page 29) and at Kadesh in 1274 B.C. The latter was a huge battle in northern Syria in which twenty thousand Egyptian troops faced seventeen thousand Hittites. Pharaoh Ramesses II failed to achieve his strategic goal of ending Hittite intervention in Egypt's Syrian sphere of influence. The two powers agreed to share control of Syria-Palestine, as a subsequent treaty attests.

Indeed, treaties are another sign of the international system. Quite a few treaties and letters between monarchs survive in cuneiform archives found at several locations, for example, Amarna. The texts reveal a system of gift exchange and commerce, politeness and formality, alliance and dynastic marriage, subjects and governors, rebels and garrisons. Kings of other great powers address pharaoh as "brother," while Canaanite princes call him "my lord and my Sun-god" and assure him that they are "thy servant and the dirt on which thou dost tread." Beneath the warm assurances, there is mundane and regular business: quarrels to be judged, rebellions to be squelched, and even the procurement of "fine concubines" for pharaoh in exchange for Egyptian products and manufactured goods.

As grand as the international system of the late second millennium B.C. was, it did not avoid a crashing end. From Mesopotamia to Greece, from Anatolia to Egypt, one state after another collapsed between about 1250 and 1150 B.C. Surviving evidence is fragmentary, but it suggests that both foreign and domestic problems led to the collapse. Raiders and invaders beset the eastern Mediterranean in this period. Called "Sea Peoples" by the Egyptians, they attacked both on land and at sea. We do not know precisely who they were. There is some evidence of famine and climatic change in some countries, leading to disruption and rebellion. Some states may have overextended themselves in war and thereby bred internal decay.

Whatever the cause, what followed would prove to be a different world. Yet the end of the state system did not result in the obliteration of ancient cultures. Considerable continuities reached into the first millennium B.C. (and beyond). Eventually, each of these cultures would flower anew.

SUMMARY

No other period in human history can match the contrasts encountered in this chapter, which ranges from the first hominids to the heirs of the great kingdoms of Egypt and western Asia after the collapse of the thirteenth century B.C. The achievements of this period may make it the most creative epoch in human history. First came the invention of human culture in the Upper Paleolithic era—that is, the development of communications to the degree that humans could exploit their natural environment by means of technology and social organization. Next came the move, in the Neolithic era, from a food-collecting to a food-producing economy. From its origins in the Fertile Crescent region of western Asia shortly after 10,000 B.C., food production spread throughout Africa, Asia, and Europe by 5000 B.C.

The next important development was the emergence of civilization in Mesopotamia after 3500 B.C. Complex though such large Neolithic towns as Çatal Hüyük or Jericho were, civilization marked a major step forward in sophistication and extent. Civilization brought cities commanding the manpower, technology, and degree of labor specialization needed to build a monumental urban architecture and reshape the agricultural hinterland; civilization brought governments and armies controlling wide areas; civilization brought, finally, writing. By 3000 B.C., civilization was present in Egypt and the Levant as well. Through trade networks, civilization affected a vast hinterland, including Europe. European societies, especially in southeastern Europe, were reshaped by trade with more advanced neighbors. European civilization emerged in the Aegean around 2000 B.C.

Mesopotamia and Egypt are the first and best remembered of the early civilizations. Their extraordinary achievements, later built on by the Greeks and Hebrews, laid the foundation for important Western concepts in government, religion, technology, art, and literature. It is hard to avoid the appearance of exaggeration when listing the inventions of Mesopotamia and Egypt, among them the first cities, kingdoms, and multi-ethnic empires; the first monumental architecture; the first advances in agriculture sweeping enough to support a large urban population; the first writing, and with it the first written attempts to explore the most profound subjects of life and death.

The second millennium B.C. was a period of competition, exchange, and warfare among the various civilizations of the eastern Mediterranean region. It was also an era of consolidation and further advance in literature and science, whose achievements were first written down in the third millennium. The great kingdoms of the second millennium collapsed, one after another, around 1250 to 1150 B.C. However disastrous that appeared at the time, in retrospect, the magnitude of human achievement to date promised even greater advances in the future.

It was not long before new states arose in Egypt and western Asia to replace those destroyed in the era of the Sea Peoples. In the first half of the first millennium B.C., new regions joined Egypt, Babylonia (southern Mesopotamia), and the Canaanite cities (known as Phoenicians in this later period) in making lasting contributions to the West: among them, Assyria (northern Mesopotamia), Persia, ancient Israel, and Greece.

NOTES

1. Samuel Noah Kramer, *History Begins at Sumer: Thirty-Nine Firsts in Man's Recorded History*, 3d ed. (Philadelphia: University of Pennsylvania Press, 1981), pp. 91, 94.
2. On the emergence of modern humans and the cultural revolution they effected, see Erik Trinkaus, ed., *The Emergence of Modern Humans. Biocultural Adaptations in the Later Pleistocene*. A School of American Research Book. (Cambridge, England: Cambridge University Press, 1989).
3. Meredith F. Small, *What's Love Got to Do with It? The Evolution of Human Mating* (New York: Anchor Books, Doubleday, 1995), pp. 12–22.
4. James B. Pritchard, ed., *Ancient Near Eastern Texts Relating to the Old Testament*, 3d ed. (Princeton: Princeton University Press, 1969), p. 107.
5. James H. Breasted, *The Conquest of Civilization* (New York: Harper & Bros., 1926), p. 112. Cited in Brian Tierney, Donald Kagan, and L. Pearce Williams, eds., *Great Issues in Western Civilization from Ancient Egypt Through Louis XIV* (New York: McGraw-Hill, 1992), pp. 68–69.
6. Pritchard, p. 408.
7. O. R. Gurney, *The Hittites*, 3d ed. (Harmondsworth, England: Penguin, 1975), p. 139.

SUGGESTED READING

General Surveys

Ferrill, Arther. *The Origins of War*. 1985. An excellent introduction to early warfare, though out of date on some points.

Frankfort, H., et al. *Before Philosophy: The Intellectual Adventure of Ancient Man. An Essay on Speculative Thought in the Ancient Near East*. 1946. Brilliant essays on the religious and political outlook of people in Mesopotamia and Egypt, contrasting them with the Hebrews and Greeks.

Gabriel, Richard A. *The Culture of War: Invention and Early Development*. 1990. Although marred by factual errors, the book is a thoughtful essay on the origins and nature of war from the Stone Age to Rome.

Knapp, A. Bernard. *The History and Culture of Ancient Western Asia and Egypt*. 1988. A clear, concise, and efficient introduction to the basic narrative.

Mallory, John. *In Search of the Indo-Europeans: Language, Archaeology, and Myth*. 1989. A general survey of the current consensus of opinion, arguing that the speakers of the original Indo-European language lived in southern Russia between the Dnieper and Volga Rivers around 4500 to 2500 B.C.

Moscati, Sabatino. *The Face of the Ancient Orient: A Panorama of Near Eastern Civilization in Pre-Classical Times*. Translated from the Italian original. 1962. Although somewhat out of date, an unusually lively and ambitious overview from Sumer to ancient Israel, emphasizing the balance of cultural change and continuities.

Neugebauer, Otto. *The Exact Sciences in Antiquity*. 1962. An introduction to ancient astronomy and mathematics.

Saggs, H. W. F. *Civilization Before Greece and Rome*. 1989. An extremely readable survey by a scholar of Babylonia and Assyria, with an emphasis on society and culture.

Seltzer, Robert M., ed. *Religions of Antiquity: Religion, History, and Culture. Selections from the Encyclopedia of Religion, Mircea Eliade, Editor in Chief*. 1989. The first five chapters are excellent introductions to the religions discussed in this chapter. They cover Mesopotamia, Egypt, the Hittites, Canaan, and goddess-worship.

Before Civilization

Cunliffe, Barry, ed. *The Oxford Illustrated Prehistory of Europe*. 1994. An introduction to European material culture from the Paleolithic era to the early medieval period, with chapters written by a dozen archaeologists. Especially valuable for its treatment of the early period and for its integration of Greco-Roman civilization and the wider continental context.

Gowlett, John A. J. *Ascent to Civilization: The Archaeology of Early Man*. 1984. A beautifully illustrated introduction to prehistory.

Lewin, Roger. *Human Evolution: An Illustrated Introduction*. 2d ed. 1989. A clear survey of a complex and rapidly changing field, with more charts but fewer photographs than the following book.

———. *In the Age of Mankind: A Smithsonian Book of Human Evolution*. 1988. Superb photographs and a readable scholarly text.

Mellaart, James. *The Neolithic of the Near East*. 1975. Though now out of date on some points, this remains a good introduction to the subject by the original excavator of Çatal Hüyük. Well illustrated.

Nissen, Hans J. *The Early History of the Ancient Near East, 9000–2000 B.C.* Translated by Elizabeth Lutzeier, with Kenneth Northcott. 1988. A scholarly introduction to the prehistory and the early history of western Asia, with an emphasis on archaeology.

Mesopotamia

Bottéro, Jean. *Mesopotamia: Writing, Reasoning, and the Gods*. Translated by Zainab Bahrani and Marc Van De Mierrop. 1992. A provocative collection of essays arguing that Western civilization began in Mesopotamia; contains a useful glossary.

Crawford, H. *The Sumerians*. 1991. An excellent introduction to the ways that recent archaeological excavation and survey have caused scholars to rethink many older ideas.

Jacobsen, Thorkild. *The Treasures of Darkness: A History of Mesopotamian Religion*. 1976. A rich and fundamental introduction.

Kramer, Samuel Noah. *History Begins at Sumer: Thirty-Nine Firsts in Man's Recorded History*. 3d ed. 1981. An engaging tribute to the achievements of early Mesopotamia, though at times perhaps exaggerated.

Lerner, Gerder. *The Creation of Patriarchy*. 1986. A theory of the origins of gender and class hierarchies in Mesopotamia, with developments in ancient Israel and classical Greece considered as well.

Oates, Joan. *Babylon*. Rev. ed. 1986. A well-illustrated introduction.

Oppenheim, A. L. *Ancient Mesopotamia: Portrait of a Dead Civilization*. Rev. ed. completed by E. Reiner. 1977. A difficult but rewarding introduction to Babylonian and Assyrian cultural history.

Postgate, J. N. *Early Mesopotamia: Society and Economy at the Dawn of History*. 1992. A detailed and perceptive introduction to the period from about 3000 to 1500 B.C., sensitive to the interaction of institutions and the environment and to the long-term patterns of change and continuity. A rich selection of translated texts and photos.

Roux, Georges. *Ancient Iraq*. 3d ed. 1992. An elegant and concise introduction to ancient Mesopotamia from the earliest times to the first millennium B.C.

Egypt

Bernal, Martin. *Black Athena: The Afro-Asiatic Roots of Classical Civilization*. Vol. 1: *The Fabrication of Ancient Greece 1785–1985*. Vol. 2: *The Archaeological Evidence*. 1987 and 1991. A stimulating but highly controversial argument for the influence of ancient Egypt on ancient Greece. Many scholars agree with the author's arguments on nineteenth-century historians, but few accept his reconstruction of ancient history.

Edwards, I. E. S. *The Pyramids of Egypt*. Rev. ed. 1986. A detailed and well-illustrated introduction, focusing on construction.

James, T. G. H. *Pharaoh's People: Scenes from Life in Imperial Egypt*. 1984. A discussion of Egyptian society in the mid-Eighteenth Dynasty (ca. 1500–1400 B.C.). Subjects include administration, justice, literacy, farming, household architecture, and the domestic economy.

Kemp, Barry J. *Ancient Egypt: Anatomy of a Civilization*. 1991. A sophisticated and up-to-date essay, focusing on archaeology and ideology, best read after a narrative introduction.

Lefkowitz, Mary, and Guy MacLean Rogers, eds. *Black Athena Revisited*. 1996. A lively and scholarly collection of essays challenging Bernal's theses.

Lichtheim, Miriam. *Ancient Egyptian Literature*. 3 vols. 1975–1980. A large selection of translations of Egyptian literary and religious texts.

Mokhtar, G., ed. *General History of Africa*. Vol. 2: *Ancient Civilizations of Africa*. Abridged ed. UNESCO General History of Africa. 1990. A good general introduction to the ancient cultures of Egypt, Nubia, Ethiopia, and Libya, among others.

Murnane, William J. *The Penguin Guide to Ancient Egypt*. 1983. Both a travel guide and a sound, basic introduction by a scholar; well illustrated.

Redford, Donald B. *Akhenaten: The Heretic King*. 1984. A highly readable and scholarly account.

———. *Egypt, Canaan, and Israel in Ancient Times*. 1992. A readable and scholarly overview of the relations between Egypt and western Asia down to 586 B.C., full of judicious discussion of a variety of individual issues.

Robins, Gay. *Women in Ancient Egypt*. 1993. A balanced introduction by an art historian, with many photographs.

Strouhal, Eugen. *Life of the Ancient Egyptians*. 1992. An excellent introduction to everyday life by an archaeologist who is also a physical anthropologist. Exceptional color photographs.

Trigger, B. G., B. J. Kemp, D. O'Conner, and A. B. Lloyd. *Ancient Egypt: A Social History*. 1983. A challenging introduction combining narrative with the analytic approach of the social sciences.

Wilson, John A. *The Burden of Egypt: An Interpretation of Ancient Egyptian Culture*. (Alternate title: *The Culture of Ancient Egypt*.) 1951. Out of date on some points, especially on Egypt's earliest history, but still a grand and beautifully written synthesis.

Anatolia and the Levant

Gurney, O. R. *The Hittites*. 3d ed. 1975. A sound introductory survey, with close attention to the sources of evidence.

Macqueen, J. G. *The Hittites and Their Contemporaries in Asia Minor*. 2d rev. ed. 1986. A well-illustrated, thematic discussion.

Pettinato, Giovanni. *Ebla: A New Look at History*. Translated by C. Faith Richardson. 1991. An introduction to the site and its historical significance by the scholar who deciphered Ebla's large royal archive of cuneiform tablets.

Sandars, N. K. *The Sea Peoples: Warriors of the Ancient Mediterranean, 1250–1150 B.C.* 1978. A logical and thorough discussion of the evidence for a complex subject, a case of archaeological detective work; beautifully illustrated.

THE ICEMAN AND HIS WORLD

On September 19, 1991, a German couple went hiking in the Italian Alps. At 10,530 feet above sea level, they thought they had left civilization and its problems behind until they stumbled on an unexpected sight: the body of a dead man lying in the melting ice. Nor was that their only surprise. At first they thought the corpse was the victim of a recent accident. When the authorities arrived, however, the body was discovered to be very old. A helicopter was ordered, and the body was brought to a research institute in Innsbruck, Austria. When the investigators were through, it was clear that the hikers had chanced upon one of the most remarkable archaeological discoveries of the century.*

He was 5300 years old. The Iceman—as the corpse has become known—is a natural mummy, preserved under the snow: the oldest known remains of human flesh. If that weren't striking enough, consider the clothes and extensive gear that survived with him—they are a window into the European world of about 3200 B.C. The most difficult and most fascinating question is this: Who was the Iceman?

His body offers an introduction. Genetic testing shows that he was a European, a close relative of modern northern and Alpine Europeans. Other tests indicate a difficult life. His growth was arrested by periods of illness, grave hunger, or metal poisoning. His teeth are badly worn, the result perhaps of chewing dried meat or, alternatively, of working leather. He may have undergone a kind of acupuncture; at any rate, he is tattooed, which in some cultures is a medical treatment rather than a form of decoration. He has several broken ribs, which indicates either damage under the ice, mishandling when the body was discovered, or an ancient accident or fight.

To get to know the Iceman better, however, we must go beyond his body to the artifacts found with it, which provide tantalizing clues to his social status. Look at the artist's drawing. A woven grass or reed cape lies over the Iceman's deerskin coat, which in turn covers a leather loincloth and garter, held in place by a leather belt. A fur hat, skin leggings, and calfskin shoes, stuffed with grass for insulation, complete his wardrobe. The Iceman and his contemporaries knew how to dress for the cold weather of the mountains.

The Iceman carries a rich tool kit. Notice his copper ax and six-foot-long bow. A quiver (arrow case), two birch bark containers, a waist pouch, and—probably part of a backpack—a frame hang from his body. Among his items of equipment are flint tools (including a knife, a retouching tool, and a scraper); a piece of net; two birch-fungus-like "polypores" threaded on a leather thong, probably used as a natural antibiotic; and fourteen arrows, all, oddly, broken. In short, it appears that the Iceman was equipped with a state-of-the-art mountain survival kit of his day.

What, however, was he doing on the mountain when he died? Scholars disagree. They all acknowledge that the Iceman probably reached the spot where he died from the south, since it is only from there—northern Italy—that the site was accessible in antiquity. What scholars differ about is the Iceman's occupation: Guesses range from a trader to hunter to metal prospector to shaman (a priest who uses magic).

Some argue that the Iceman was a refugee. His weapons point to violence, and so may his broken ribs. Perhaps he had retreated to the mountains from a fight. If so, it is not clear why he brought

*The best brief introduction to the Iceman is Lawrence Barfield's "The Iceman Reviewed," *Antiquity* 68 (1994): 10–26, on which this discussion relies. See also Konrad Spindler, *The Man in the Ice* (New York: Harmony Books, 1994).

broken arrows or how he had time to pack his goods so carefully before fleeing; nor could it have been a small feat to climb mountains with broken ribs.

Perhaps the most convincing theory is that the Iceman was a shepherd. Since ancient times it has been common for shepherds to move their flocks during the summer from the lowlands to greener pastures in the mountains, a pattern of migration known as *transhumance*. It has been suggested that the Iceman brought broken arrows with him to repair during his spare time. Perhaps he encountered a sudden snowstorm and died of exposure, perhaps after having broken his ribs in an accident.

If he was a shepherd, then the Iceman offers a rare illustration of the life of the kind of person who is not represented in most archaeological sites: a person at the margins of society. Tombs usually yield the skeletons and grave goods of the elite, especially the urban elite; they rarely illustrate the lives of ordinary countryfolk. The Iceman's equipment suggests that he was not poor, but only his copper ax might indicate unusual status—and it is not a decisive index. Were the copper ax a show item it might imply high status, but observe the Iceman's ax. It was set in a wooden handle and bound with leather, leaving little of the metal visible; it is, in short, a utensil rather than an ornament.

The copper ax is also the key to the Iceman's culture and its relationship with the wider world. Similar axes have been found in northern Italian tombs in Remedello, about 240 miles south of the Alps. Before the discovery of the Iceman, archaeologists believed that Italians learned the metalwork technology needed for such an ax from Anatolia, where similar pieces of metalwork are dated to approximately 2700–2400 B.C. Hence, the Remedello culture was usually also dated about 2700–2400 B.C. The discovery of the Iceman means that Remedello

Artist's Rendition of the Ice Man (*New York Times Photo Sales*)

must be backdated by about five hundred years. It is clear, then, that by about 3200 B.C. northern Italians not only borrowed from the more advanced eastern Mediterranean areas but also created their own original technology and culture. So a small object (a copper ax), placed within a larger body of evidence (Italian and Anatolian metalwork), permits broad generalization about the interaction and independence of ancient cultures. ✎

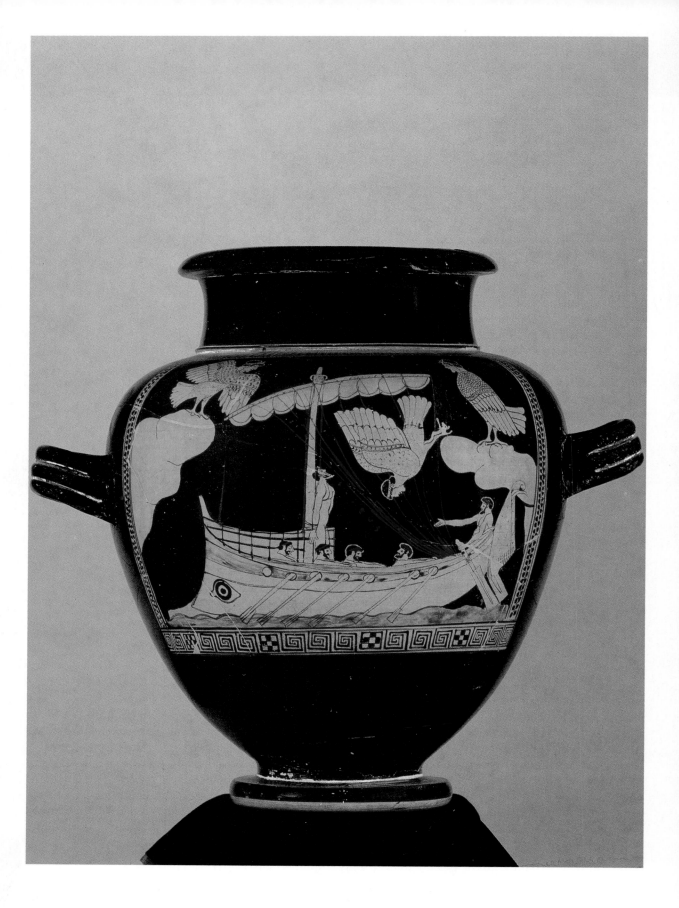

CHAPTER 2

The Book and the Myths: Western Asia and Early Greece

I n the sixth century B.C., an obscure prophet—we know him only as "Second Isaiah"—preached a bold message to his compatriots, a conquered people living in exile in Babylon. He told them that Yahweh, their god, was a god of justice and mercy—the one and only true god of the entire world—and that Yahweh had chosen the king of mountainous, backward Persia to conquer western Asia and redeem Yahweh's people. The Babylonians, imperialists who considered their city the center of the universe, might have laughed at the idea that two provincial peoples would divide spiritual and worldly rulership between them. Yet the Persians under Cyrus the Great conquered Babylon in 539 B.C. and a year later proclaimed the freedom of Yahweh's people—the Jews—to return to Palestine and re-establish the Temple to their god in the city of Jerusalem. They did so, and around this time they wrote down their religious and historical traditions in large sections of what would become the Hebrew Bible.

Also in the sixth century B.C., Peisistratus, the ambitious ruler of Athens, a tiny city-state a thousand miles northwest of Babylon, sponsored a literary project to preserve the religious and historical traditions of his people. The literary works whose texts were standardized under his patronage are the *Iliad* and *Odyssey*, the epic poems of Homer, who had composed them more than two centuries before.

Both the Hebrew Bible and the Homeric poems are deeply religious in outlook, but there the similarities end. The Hebrew Bible is monotheistic

Odysseus and the Sirens,
scene from Homer, *Odyssey*.
Early fifth century B.C.

WESTERN ASIA

ca. 1250–1150 B.C.	Sea Peoples
ca. 1200–1000 B.C.	Israelites settle Palestinian hill country
ca. 1050–750 B.C.	Height of Phoenician city-states
ca. 1020–1004 B.C.	Reign of first Israelite king, Saul
1004–965 B.C.	Reign of David
965–928 B.C.	Reign of Solomon
928–722 B.C.	Divided monarchy (Israel and Judah)
ca. 750–664 B.C.	Height of Assyrian Empire
722 B.C.	Assyrians conquer kingdom of Israel
622 B.C.	Judah accepts "Scroll of the Covenant"
612 B.C.	Conquest of Nineveh
598 B.C.	Neo-Babylonians conquer kingdom of Judah
559–530 B.C.	Reign of Cyrus
550–331 B.C.	Achaemenid Empire
539 B.C.	Cyrus conquers Babylon; permits Jews to return to Palestine
521–486 B.C.	Reign of Darius I
ca. 425 B.C.	Judean assembly accepts the Torah

that was harder and more durable than bronze. It was also easier to obtain, since iron ore is widespread—unlike tin, an essential element of bronze. Iron tools and weapons were often stronger and cheaper than their bronze predecessors, which opened up new technical and military possibilities.

The iron-clad soldiers of Assyria and Persia—to name the most successful examples—established empires that were more systematically organized than were the loose hegemonies of earlier imperialists such as the Akkadians, Hittites, and New Kingdom Egyptians. Guided by Zoroastrianism, a monotheistic and highly ethical religion, the Persian elite ruled a vast, multi-ethnic empire that stretched from Egypt to modern Pakistan. There was peaceful expansion, too, during the first millennium, through trade and colonization. Great shipbuilders, sailors, and merchants, the Phoenicians traveled as far as Britain and established colonies in the western Mediterranean.

ASSYRIANS, NEO-BABYLONIANS, PHOENICIANS, CA. 1200–CA. 500 B.C.

Ruthless soldiers, brutal conquerors, and innovative administrators, the Assyrians established an empire in western Asia and Egypt during the eighth and seventh centuries B.C. They were followed in turn by a Neo-Babylonian empire in the seventh and sixth centuries.

Few areas have changed hands more often than the hills and coastal plains south of Syria, the area of modern Lebanon, Israel, and Palestine. In the northern part of this region the Phoenicians created a vibrant culture of independent city-states. Neither the Egyptians nor the Hittites ever rebuilt the empires lost (1250–1150 B.C.), thereby making it possible for small states to carve out a sphere of independence, as the Phoenicians did. At the height of their prosperity (ca. 1050–750 B.C.), Phoenician merchants and colonizers spread the advanced civilization of western Asia westward across the Mediterranean.

The Roar of the Lions

The Assyrians, whose homeland was in what is today northern Iraq, spoke a Semitic language. For

and focuses on the individual's subordination to God. Homer is polytheistic and glorifies the hero, who, though doomed to fail, aspires to godlike achievement. For most scholars the Bible and Homer represent two poles of Western civilization: the sacred and the worldly, the reverent and the heroic, holy writ and poetic craftsmanship.

The first millennium B.C., therefore, was an era of new and divergent cultural creativity. It was also a period of material innovation. Scholars sometimes call the first millennium the "Iron Age." Thanks to new heating and cooling techniques, metalsmiths produced an alloy of carbon and iron

Map 2.1 The Assyrian and Persian Empires In the 660s B.C. the Assyrians ruled the largest empire the ancient world had seen yet, extending from the Tigris to the Nile. The Persian Empire was even greater. Around 500 B.C. it reached from its heartland in southwestern Iran westward to Macedonia and eastward to India.

most of the second millennium B.C., they were a military and mercantile power. Around 1200 B.C., the Assyrians' state collapsed during that era of international crisis (see page 36), but they held on to a small homeland of about 5000 square miles, roughly the size of the state of Connecticut. The toughened survivors emerged with an aggressive, expansionist ideology.

Assyria's greatest successes came in the eighth and seventh centuries. One by one, states large and small fell—Babylonia, Syria, the kingdom of Israel, Cilicia in southern Anatolia, even Egypt (though Assyrian rule there lasted only a generation). Assyria became the first state to rule the two great river valleys of the ancient Near East, the Nile and the Tigris-Euphrates (Map 2.1). Warrior-kings such as Tiglath-pileser III (r. 744–727 B.C.), Sargon II (r. 721–705 B.C.), Sennacherib (r. 704–681 B.C.), and Assurbanipal (r. 668–627 B.C.) became feared names everywhere.

The Assyrians were warriors. Asshur, their main deity, was a war-god. The key to Assyria's success was its army—from 100,000 to 200,000 men strong—which made an unforgettable impression on observers. The Israelite prophet Isaiah of Jerusalem ("First Isaiah") said of Assyrian soldiers: "[Their] arrows are sharpened, and all their bows bent, their horses' hoofs are like flint, their chariot wheels like the whirlwind. Their growling is like that of a lion" (Isaiah 5:28–29). He might have added that Assyrian spearmen, archers, and cavalrymen were equipped with iron weapons and armor. Assyria was the first major state to employ regular cavalry units (rather than charioteers) as the main strike force. The Assyrians were also excellent engineers, adept at taking walled cities by siege. (See the box, "An Assyrian King Attacks Phoenicia and Jerusalem.")

In addition, the Assyrians displayed superb organizational skills. The central, standing army

An Assyrian King Attacks Phoenicia and Jerusalem

In this inscription the warrior-king Sennacherib describes how he suppressed rebellions in the region of Syria-Palestine in 701 B.C. The king describes Assyrian methods of attacking walled cities and the harsh punishments meted out to the conquered. (The Hebrew Bible, in the Second Book of Kings 18:9–19, narrates the rebellion of Hezekiah, king of Judah, from the Israelite point of view.)

In my third campaign I marched against Hatti. Luli, king of Sidon, whom the terror-inspiring glamor of my lordship had overwhelmed, fled far overseas and perished. The awe-inspiring splendor of the "Weapon" of Ashur, my lord, overwhelmed his strong cities (such as) Great Sidon, Little Sidon, Bit-Zitti, Zaribtu, Mahalliba, Ushu (i.e., the mainland settlement of Tyre), Akzib (and) Akko, (all) his fortress cities, walled (and well) provided with feed and water for his garrisons, and they bowed in submission to my feet. I installed Ethba'al upon the throne to be their king and imposed upon him tribute (due) to me (as his) overlord (to be paid) annually without interruption. . . .

I assaulted Ekron [a city on Palestine's coastal plain] and killed the officials and patricians who had committed the crime [of rebelling] and hung their bodies on poles surrounding the city. . . .

As to Hezekiah, the Jew, he did not submit to my yoke. I laid siege to 46 of his strong cities, walled forts and to the countless small villages in their vicinity, and conquered (them) by means of well-stamped (earth-) ramps, and battering-rams brought (thus) near (to the walls) (combined with) the attack by foot-soldiers, (using) mines, breeches as well as sapper work. I drove out (of them) 200,150 people, young and old, male and female, horses, mules, donkeys, camels, big and small cattle beyond counting, and considered (them) booty. Himself I made a prisoner in Jerusalem, his royal residence, like a bird in a cage. I surrounded him with earthwork in order to molest those who were leaving his city's gate. His towns which I had plundered, I took away from his country and gave them . . . [to several Philistine kings]. Thus I reduced his country, but I still increased the tribute and the . . . presents (due) to me (as his) overlord which I imposed (later) upon him beyond the former tribute, to be delivered annually.

Source: James B. Pritchard, ed., *Ancient Near Eastern Texts Relating to the Old Testament*, 3d ed., with Supplement (Princeton: Princeton University Press, 1969), pp. 287–288.

was supplemented with draftees conscripted from around the empire. Provinces were kept small to prevent the emergence of separate power bases, and independent-minded nobles were regularly checked by the kings.

To control the restive subjects of their far-flung empire, the Assyrians met rebellion with ferocious reprisals. Disloyal cities were attacked and, if need be, destroyed. Sculptured reliefs and inscriptions were set up to show, often in gruesome detail, the fate awaiting Assyria's enemies. We see or read of cities burned to the ground; of men flayed alive, even though they had surrendered, and walls covered with their skin; and of piles of human skulls.

The Assyrians also engaged in mass deportation. They uprooted the people of a conquered country, resettled them far away—often in Assyria itself—and colonized their land with Assyrian loyalists. The so-called Ten Lost Tribes of Israel—the

Assyrian Art This sculptured relief from a royal palace depicts the king attacking a fortified city. A battering-ram and a mobile tower are the main weapons of assault. Notice the wheels of the battering ram, the archers on both the tower and the walls, and the damage done by the ram. *(Courtesy of the Trustees of the British Museum)*

people of the northern Israelite kingdom (see page 53)—were conquered by Assyria in 722 B.C. and transported to Mesopotamia, where they disappear from history.

Assyrian policy was the result of careful calculation. The political goal was to punish rebellion, the economic goal to create a varied labor force. For example, although it is estimated that the Assyrians deported several million people, they deported not whole populations but a carefully chosen cross section of professions. They also deported entire families together, to weaken deportees' emotional ties to their former homes.

There is another reason for Assyria's success: the relative weakness of other powers. Egypt, for example, was at the mercy of factions and invaders for much of the Third Intermediate Period (1075–656 B.C.). Between 1075 and about 950, the pharaohs ruled only the Nile Delta; the priests of Thebes controlled the Nile Valley. Around 950, the kingship came into the hands of Libyan mercenaries. Long settled in Egypt, these mercenaries represented a military elite. They retained Libyan names and some Libyan customs but had otherwise become Egyptian in culture. From the eighth

century on, their rule was challenged by invaders from the south, rulers of a new Nubian kingdom called Kush (see Map 1.2 on page 22). Around 719 the Kushites took Egypt from the Libyans, and Kushite pharaohs retained power until 656, when they withdrew back south. It was they who faced Assyrian attacks in 671 and 667.

The invasion of Egypt marked imperial Assyria's greatest extent—and its overextension (see Map 2.1). A coalition army consisting of soldiers from a revived Babylonian kingdom and of Medes (who had formed a powerful state in Iran; see page 59) conquered Nineveh, the Assyrian capital, in 612 B.C. and defeated the remnants of the Assyrian army in battles in 609 and 605. Few subjects mourned the empire's passing.

The destruction of Assyria led to a brief political and longer-lived cultural revival for Babylon, whose rulers attempted to revive the glories of Hammurabi's day (see page 16). For a short period, until the Persian conquest in 539 B.C., the Neo-Babylonian dynasty (founded in 626) and the Medes of Iran were the dominant military forces in western Asia. The Neo-Babylonian king Nebuchadrezzar II (Nebuchadnezzar in the Hebrew

Bible; r. 605–562 B.C.) conquered the kingdom of Judah (in central Palestine) in 598 and destroyed Jerusalem, its capital, in 586. He deported many thousands of Judeans to Babylon, an event remembered by Christians and Jews as the Babylonian Captivity. Most of the rest of western Asia also fell to Nebuchadrezzar's troops. His most enduring achievement was rebuilding Babylon on a grand scale. In addition to the city's numerous temples, shrines, and altars, he created the so-called Hanging Gardens, celebrated by Greek writers. They describe the structure as a large terraced complex that Nebuchadrezzar built for his queen, though it may have been a plant-covered ziggurat.

Following Mesopotamian tradition, the Neo-Babylonians had a great interest in astronomy, as indeed the Assyrians did as well. The prime motive of Babylonian astronomy was religious—that is, a belief in astrology (the prediction of the future by studying the movement of heavenly bodies). Astrology led to advances in the scientific observation of the heavens. By about 1000 B.C., Assyrians had produced relatively accurate circular diagrams (astrolabes) that showed the positions of the major constellations, stars, and planets over the course of the year. From about 800 B.C. on, Assyrian astronomical observations became particularly careful; by 600 B.C., Assyrian and Neo-Babylonian astronomers could predict solstices, equinoxes, and lunar eclipses.

Astronomy in Mesopotamia reached its heights in the centuries after 500 B.C. The zodiac, a diagram showing the movement of the sun and planets relative to the constellations, was invented in Persian-ruled Babylon in the fourth century B.C. In the third and second centuries B.C., when Babylonia was under Hellenistic Greek rule, native scientists made great advances in mathematical astronomy, composing tables that could be used to calculate movements of the moon and planets. More sophisticated mathematical astronomy was not produced in the West until the Scientific Revolution of the sixteenth century A.D.

Traders the World Honored

In the Hebrew Bible and in Homer the Phoenicians loom large as merchants and seamen, as "traders the world honored" (Isaiah 23:8).

Phoenicians were Canaanites, speakers of a Semitic language, and heirs to the civilization that had prospered in Ugarit around 1400 B.C. (see page 34). After the invasions of the Sea Peoples and others around 1200 B.C., the Canaanites' once large territory was reduced to a narrow strip along the Mediterranean in the area of modern Lebanon and northern Israel (see Map 2.1). Between 1050 and 750 B.C., the inhabitants of the area flourished; historians call them, as did the ancient Greeks, "Phoenicians." Their purple-dyed textiles gave the Greeks their word for the color purple: *Phoenician.*

Too little evidence survives to permit a detailed reconstruction of Phoenician civilization. What we can document, however, is the enormous role the Phoenicians played elsewhere in the Mediterranean. They played a major part in the spread of urbanism and literacy to both shores of that sea—in Europe and North Africa.

Like the Sumerians, the Phoenicians lived in independent and quarrelsome city-states. The most important and populous were Aradus, Byblos, Sidon, and Tyre, the greatest of all (see Map 2.2). Each city was typically governed by a king, who was advised by a council of elders that may have consisted of the leading merchants of the city.

Seafarers, merchants, and slave-traders, the Phoenicians served as middlemen between the Mediterranean lands and the caravan routes to Mesopotamia and points east. They were also important craftspeople in their own right. The Phoenicians were known for their use of hardwood and cedar, the latter often made into fine furniture; for purple dye, obtained from local shellfish and used to color textiles; for jewelry and other metalwork; for fine ivories and wooden carvings. They were renowned builders. Important trading partners included Egypt, Cyprus, Greece, Sicily, and Sardinia.

Great shipbuilders and sailors, the Phoenicians may have invented the trireme, an oared warship rowed by 170 men on three decks. Around 600 B.C., Phoenician ships accomplished the first known circumnavigation of Africa. Around 450 B.C., they made the first known commercial sailing trip to the British Isles. Some scholars think they even reached Brazil. The most lasting Phoenician achievement at sea, however, was the planting of

Ishtar Gate, Babylon Under Nebuchadrezzar II (r. 605–562 B.C.), Babylon received a double wall 10 miles long. The massive entryway, a restoration of which is illustrated here, was decorated with glazed, colored bricks showing bulls and dragons. *(Erich Lessing/Art Resource)*

colonies in the Mediterranean, probably beginning in the ninth century B.C.

Phoenicians established colonies for several reasons: to find precious metals, to siphon off excess population, to serve as a refuge. Unlike territory conquered by the Assyrians, Phoenician colonies were settled by people from the home country, who brought their language and customs with them. There were Phoenician colonies in Cyprus, Italy, southern France and Spain, and North Africa, as well as on central and western Mediterranean islands, including Malta and the Balearics. Many of the Phoenician colonies eventually became independent states. The greatest Phoenician colony was Carthage, founded by Tyre around 750 B.C. It was the major port city of the western Mediterranean for much of the next thousand years.

Around 750 B.C., the Phoenician city-states lost their independence to the Assyrians, and in later years Neo-Babylonians, Persians, and other foreign conquerors followed. But Phoenician culture survived: at home, in the colonies, and among the many Mediterranean peoples influenced by it. The result, though unintended, was that Phoenician colonists exported the civilization of western Asia to the western Mediterranean.

Between 1000 and 800 B.C., when the small towns of Greece were slowly developing into city-states, the sophisticated Phoenicians represented an important outside stimulus. Phoenician traders introduced advanced material goods, slaves, and possibly law codes to the Greeks. It was probably from the Phoenicians, whose alphabet derived from Ugarit, that the Greeks adapted their alphabet.

Closer to home, Phoenicians traded with their neighbor to the south, Israel. King Hiram of Tyre (r. 969–936 B.C.), for example, appears in the Hebrew Bible as an ally who provided King Solomon of Israel (r. 965–928 B.C.) with wood and workmen for building the Temple in Jerusalem. Phoenicians and Israelites spoke closely related Semitic languages, but they parted ways on matters of religion, for Israel broke dramatically with Canaanite polytheism.

ISRAEL, CA. 1500–400 B.C.

In the first millennium B.C. a small, often-conquered people turned imperialism on its head. Human achievement is meaningless, they argued; only the power of divinity matters. There is only one god, they said; all other gods are false. The one true god had revealed himself not to the imperialistic Assyrians but to the less powerful Hebrews—ancient Jews.

The Hebrews, also known as Israelites, had existed as a people since the late second millennium B.C. and perhaps for centuries earlier. Their enduring and influential religion gave rise to Christianity and Islam as well as to modern Judaism.

The Hebrew Bible

As literature and as religious teaching, the Bible is unquestionably the most important book in Western civilization. As a source of history, however, it presents difficulties. Much of the Hebrew Bible (called the "Old Testament" by Christians) is based on written sources that probably date back at least as far as the early Israelite monarchy of about 1000 B.C. Some scholars trace these written sources back several centuries earlier, to the religious leader Moses and the laws he is said to have promulgated. Other parts of the Hebrew Bible are probably the product of an oral tradition, and the nature, antiquity, and reliability of that tradition are also the subject of much scholarly debate.

A century or two before the birth of Christ, the Hebrew Bible reached something close to its current form. It consists of three main sections: (1) the Torah (literally, "teaching"), also known as the Pentateuch, or five books of Moses; (2) the Prophets, that is, the "historical" books of the early prophets (Joshua, Judges, Kings, and Chronicles) and the books of the later prophets (Isaiah, Jeremiah, Ezekiel, and the twelve "minor prophets"); and (3) the Writings, various books of poetry, proverbs, and wisdom literature.

The books of the Hebrew (and Christian) Bible are canonical: One by one, each was accepted by established authority as sacred. Two key dates stand out in the canonization of the Hebrew Bible: 622 B.C. and about 425 B.C. On the first date, Josiah, king of Judah (see page 53), assembled "the entire population, high and low," to swear to obey "the scroll of the covenant which had been discovered in the house of the Lord" (the scroll probably was Deuteronomy, now the fifth book of the Torah). On the second date, a similar assembly of the people, called by the religious leader Ezra (see page 56), swore to accept the five books of the Torah that had by then been assembled. The introduction of the Torah made its worshipers into what they have been ever since, "a people of the Book," as the Muslims would put it many years later. The written tradition and literacy became central to the Hebrews.

The Hebrews are the first people we know of to have a single national history book. That book was written not as secular history, however, but as sacred history. The Hebrew Bible is less the history of Israel than the story of the working out of God's pact, or covenant, with the Hebrews, his chosen people. The covenant, first made between God and Abraham, is reforged with Abraham's descendants at Mount Sinai (see page 52). Its purpose is to inspire faith, righteousness, and national solidarity, not to answer a modern researcher's questions.

Consider the fundamental significance of the covenant. All ancient peoples told stories of their semidivine foundation. Only the Hebrews, however, imagined the nation created by an actual treaty between the people and their god. When the Bible enjoins the Israelites to "love the Lord your God with all your heart and with all your soul" (Deuteronomy 6:5), it is using political language: In the international treaties of the second millennium B.C., *love* was a synonym for "exclusive loyalty."

The central fact of human existence in the Hebrew Bible is God's covenant with the Hebrews. Because of the covenant, history has meaning. History is the story of the success or failure of the Hebrew people in carrying out God's commandments. There is an emphatic focus on the individual: on individual characters taking actions that have moral consequences that unfold over time.

Many of the themes, narrative details, and styles of writing in the Hebrew Bible derive from earlier cultures. The biblical Flood story, for example, seems to be modeled on a similar flood in the *Epic of Gilgamesh* (see page 19). Biblical poems in praise of God are often similar to Egyptian poems in praise of pagan gods, and biblical wisdom literature often recalls Egyptian or Babylonian parallels. In spite of such borrowings, the Hebrew Bible is dramatically different from its predecessors because it subordinates everything to one central theme: God's plan for humanity and, in particular, for his chosen people—the Hebrews.

The Emergence of Monotheism, ca. 1500–600 B.C.

The earliest nonbiblical evidence of the Hebrews is an inscribed monument of the New Kingdom Egyptian pharaoh Merneptah (r. 1224–1214 B.C.). After a military expedition into Canaan, the pharaoh declared triumphantly that "Israel is laid waste." Scholars disagree about the historicity of the biblical account before this inscription and before archaeological evidence dating from approximately 1200 to 1000—evidence suggesting that Israelite invaders conquered the Canaanite towns of the highlands of Palestine.

Through a combination of the biblical narrative and archaeological evidence, Israelite history after 1200 B.C. is relatively easy to trace. A seminomadic people became settled farmers and shepherds in the hill country of Palestine and then, sometime after 1000 B.C., an urbanized elite slowly began to emerge. Governed at first by tribal leaders, the Hebrews soon adopted a centralized monarchy. Their state was superficially similar to other monarchies of the Levant but developed a unique religious and political ideology.

As for Israelite history before 1200 B.C., archaeology renders the biblical account credible but does not confirm it. If one follows the Bible, Hebrew history began sometime during the period 2000 to 1500 B.C. with the patriarchs, or founding fathers. Abraham, the first patriarch, decided to migrate to Canaan from the city of Harran in northern Mesopotamia. A seminomadic chieftain, Abraham settled on territory north and west of the Dead Sea, where he grazed his herds. His language, Hebrew, was one of the many Semitic tongues spoken between the Mediterranean Sea and the Euphrates River. Seminomadic clans in the region frequently made long migrations in antiquity, so the biblical account of Abraham and his descendants, Isaac and Jacob, is plausible.

The Bible, however, emphasizes the implausible: Abraham's extraordinary decision to give up Mesopotamian polytheism for belief in one god. This god commanded Abraham to leave Harran; indeed, he made a treaty, or covenant, with Abraham. In return for Abraham's faith, said the god, "As a possession for all time I shall give you and your descendants after you the land in which you are now aliens, the whole of Canaan, and I shall be their God" (Genesis 17:8). Strictly speaking, Abraham was a henotheist rather than a monotheist: Although he worshiped only one god, he did not deny the existence of other gods (see, for a comparison, the discussion of Akhenaten on page 30). Nevertheless, he took a giant step on the road to pure monotheism by coming to believe that only one god rules *all* peoples.

The god of Abraham had yet to become the god of all the Hebrews. According to the biblical account, that turning point came about several hundred years later, probably in the reign of pharaoh Ramesses II (r. 1290–1224 B.C.) or of Merneptah (r. 1224–1214 B.C.). In a time of famine, many of Abraham's descendants had left Canaan for prosperous Egypt. At first they thrived there, but in time they were enslaved and forced to build cities in the Nile Delta. Eventually, Moses, a divinely appointed leader, released the Hebrews from bondage in Egypt and led them back toward Canaan and freedom.

The Exodus ("journey out," in Greek), as this movement has been called, is a rare example of a successful national liberation movement in antiquity; it has served as a symbol of freedom ever since. Among those who accept its historicity, a date of approximately 1225 B.C. is frequently assigned to the Exodus. The Exodus is also one of the central events in the history of ancient Israel, because it marked another covenant, this time between the god of Abraham and the entire Israelite people. At Mount Sinai, traditionally located on the rugged Sinai Peninsula between Egypt and Palestine, the Israelites are said to have first accepted as their one god a deity whose name is represented in Hebrew by the letters corresponding to YHWH. YHWH is traditionally rendered in English as "Jehovah," but "Yahweh" is more likely to be accurate. The Israelites accepted Yahweh's laws, summarized by the Ten Commandments. In return for obedience to Yahweh's commandments, they would be God's chosen people, his "special possession; . . . a kingdom of priests, . . . [his] holy nation." The substance of the covenant is unique, but in form and style it bears a certain similarity to the treaties of international diplomacy of the period 1400–1200 B.C. This similarity suggests the genuine antiquity of the biblical tradition. (See the box, "The Covenant.")

The Ten Commandments are both more general and more personal than the laws of Hammurabi's Code. They are addressed to the individual, whom they commit to a universal standard. They emphasize prohibitions, saying more about what one should *not* do than about what one should do. The first three commandments establish Yahweh as the sole god of Israel, forbid misuse of the divine name, and prohibit any sculpture or image of God. The next two commandments are injunctions to honor one's parents and to observe the seventh day of the week (the Sabbath) as a day free of work. The next two commandments prohibit violent acts against neighbors, in particular adultery and killing. The final three commandments regulate community life by prohibiting stealing, testifying falsely, and coveting another man's wife or his goods.

Hebrew monotheism represents a new relationship between divinity and humanity. The other gods were part of nature, as powerful as the elements but as unpredictable. Israel's god transcended nature. He was the creator and master of nature; he was omnipotent. Whereas the pagan gods were often whimsical or cruel, Yahweh was ethical, just, and merciful. In his supreme and terrible power Israel's god was further removed

from human beings than other deities, but in his justice and mercy he was closer: He was both humane and unfathomably suprahuman.

Whether a visionary leader proclaimed monotheism to the Hebrews shortly before 1200 B.C. or whether monotheism emerged centuries later is a matter of scholarly debate. What is undebatable is that ordinary Hebrews had not committed themselves fully to monotheism in 1200 B.C. For centuries afterward, many Israelite worshipers deemed Yahweh their greatest god but not their only god. Unready for the radical innovation that monotheism represented, they carried out the rituals of various Canaanite deities, whom they worshiped on hilltop altars. Forging a national consensus for monotheism took centuries.

During the twelfth and eleventh centuries B.C., the Hebrews completed the conquest of the Palestinian hill country from the Canaanites. The Hebrews were governed in this period by a series of tribal leaders, or judges, but eventually the military threat posed by the Philistines forced the tribes to accept a centralized monarchy. The Philistines, one of the Sea Peoples, had captured the Palestinian coast in the twelfth and eleventh centuries and posed a serious threat to Israel. The first Israelite king, Saul (r. ca. 1020–1004 B.C.), had some success against them but eventually fell in battle with his son, Jonathan. The next king, David (r. 1004–965 B.C.), a former mercenary captain for the Philistines, defeated them decisively.

David was Israel's greatest king. He conquered an empire that extended into modern Jordan, Lebanon, and Syria. David, moreover, conquered the Canaanite city of Jerusalem, which he made into Israel's capital. David's son and successor, Solomon (r. 965–928 B.C.), was also a great king, a centralizer who moved from a loose kingship toward a tightly organized monarchy. His most famous act was to build in Jerusalem the Temple whose priesthood and sacrifices became the focus of the national cult of Yahweh. Previously, that focus had been a humble, movable wooden chest known as the Ark of the Covenant.

Solomon represented the high-water mark of the power of the Israelite monarchy. Under his successors the monarchy was split into a large northern kingdom of Israel with a capital at Samaria and a smaller southern kingdom of Judah centered on Jerusalem (Map 2.2). In 722 B.C., the

City of David When David conquered Jerusalem around 1000 B.C. and made it his capital, it was a small, 15-acre town on a steep hill above the valley of Kidron (foreground), outside the walls of today's Old City. His successors expanded the city to include the Temple Mount, once the site of Solomon's Temple, today crowned with the Dome of the Rock, an Islamic mosque. *(Zev Radovan, Jerusalem)*

Assyrians conquered the kingdom of Israel and deported its inhabitants. Judah survived, preserving its autonomy first as an Assyrian vassal and then as an independent power.

The religious history of the period of the two kingdoms (928–722 B.C.) and the Judean survivor-state (722–587 B.C.) is marked by an intense drive toward monotheism. The kings of Judah in the seventh century B.C., especially Hezekiah (r. 715–686 B.C.) and Josiah (r. 640–609 B.C.), aggressively attacked the worship of all gods other than Yahweh and all centers of Yahweh worship other than the Temple in Jerusalem. The kings acted both out of conviction and out of the desire to forge unity in the face of threatened outside conquest. They succeeded in making the Temple at Jerusalem the unquestioned religious center of the whole Israelite people, and they began the process of canonizing the Hebrew Bible.

The kings could not have succeeded without the help of the prophets, who were prominent from approximately 900 to 500 B.C. Seers uttering divinely inspired predictions were universal figures in ancient religion. No other culture of antiquity, however, has anything like the Hebrew prophets: charismatic, uncompromising, terrible figures of God's wrath and ultimate forgiveness. The prophets were a reminder of the most radical spiritual teachings of Israel: absolute monotheism, an insistence on righteousness, contempt for materialism and worldly power, love of the powerless. They often supported the kings but did not shrink from confronting authority and insisting on uncompromising justice. Among them were Amos, a humble shepherd who preached the superiority of righteousness to ritual; Jeremiah, who prophesied the destruction of Jerusalem as punishment for the people's worship of gods other than Yahweh; and Isaiah, who predicted a new day of universal peace and justice to be inaugurated by a savior.

A characteristic story of the prophets is the confrontation between Elijah, perhaps the most famous prophet, and Ahab, king of Israel (r. 871–852 B.C.). Ahab coveted the vineyard of one Naboth, but Naboth refused Ahab's offer to buy it. Spurred on by his wife, Jezebel, Ahab trumped up charges against Naboth, who was unjustly stoned to death; Ahab then confiscated the vineyard. God sent Elijah to declare to Ahab that, as punishment for committing murder, "dogs will lick [Ahab's] blood" and that of his family (1 Kings 21:19). In a remarkable scene we witness not only Elijah's courage in confronting the king but also the king's surrender and repentance before Elijah's spiritual authority. The Western tradition of civil disobedience owes much to the courage of the Hebrew prophets.

Exile and Return, 598–ca. 400 B.C.

The prophets prepared the people of Judah for survival by correctly predicting ruin and exile and promising that divine providence would guarantee return. The ability of the Judeans to absorb this message was remarkable. Indeed, it needed to be,

Map 2.2 Ancient Israel The Israelites settled in the Canaanite hill country west of the Jordan River and the Dead Sea after 1200 B.C. (top map). Control of Israelite territory after 928 B.C. was shared between two monarchies (bottom map): the kingdoms of Israel (conquered by the Assyrians in 722 B.C.) and Judah (conquered in 598 B.C.).

The Covenant

The central event in the history of ancient Israel was the covenant, or treaty, at Sinai between God and his chosen people. In this excerpt from the Book of Deuteronomy, Moses addresses the Israelites just before his death and reminds them of their obligations.

Moses summoned all Israel and said to them: Israel, listen to the statutes and the laws which I proclaim to you this day. Learn them, and be careful to observe them. The Lord our God made a covenant with us at Horeb [Sinai]. . . .

These are the commandments, statutes, and laws which the Lord your God commanded me to teach you to observe in the land to which you are crossing to occupy it, a land flowing with milk and honey, so that you may fear the Lord your God and keep all his statutes and commandments which I am giving to you, both you, your children, and your descendants all your days, that you may enjoy long life. If you listen, Israel, and are careful to observe them, you will prosper and increase greatly as the Lord the God of your forefathers promised you. . . .

What then, Israel, does the Lord your God ask of you? Only this: to fear the Lord your God, to conform to all his ways, to love him, and to serve him with all your heart and soul. This you will do by observing the commandments of the Lord and his statutes which I give you this day for your good. To the Lord your God belong heaven itself, the highest heaven, the earth and everything in it; yet the Lord was attached to your forefathers by his love for them, and he chose their descendants after them. Out of all nations you were his chosen people, as you are this day. So now you must circumcise your hearts and not be stubborn any more, for the Lord your God is God of gods and Lord of lords, the great, mighty, and terrible God. He is no respecter of persons; he is not to be bribed; he secures justice for the fatherless and the widow, and he shows love towards the alien who lives among you, giving him food and clothing. You too must show love towards the alien, for you once lived as aliens in Egypt.

Source: Deuteronomy 5:1–2, 6:1–3, 10:12–19, in *The Oxford Study Bible: Revised English Bible with the Apocrypha* (New York: Oxford University Press, 1992).

for between 598 and 586 B.C., the Neo-Babylonians conquered Judah, destroying Jerusalem and the Temple. The cultural, political, and economic elite was deported to Babylon. Those who could, fled for Egypt. The dispirited remnant in Palestine shared their land with colonists from neighboring regions, with whom they intermarried and among whom their religion all but disappeared.

And that, given the usual fate of exiled and uprooted peoples in antiquity, should have been that. Yet not only did Judeans in the Babylonian Captivity persevere in their religious loyalty; they actually returned to Palestine in large numbers. The Temple was rebuilt around 515 B.C., only seventy years after its destruction. This success was due in part to the Persians, who conquered Babylon in 539 B.C. and proclaimed the freedom of the Jews[*] to rebuild the Temple in Jerusalem. Still, Persian benevolence would have availed little if not for the ability of the Judean elite to keep the faith burning among the exiles.

The Neo-Babylonian rulers allowed Jewish deportees to continue to practice their religion. Jews in Babylon were not slaves; rather they rented land on royal estates, and some became quite prosperous. Although some Babylonian Jews assimi-

[*]Strictly speaking, the terms *Jew* and *Jewish* are anachronistic before the fifth century B.C.

lated to local ways, many continued a Jewish religious life. Communal worship was observed in open places, perhaps with associated buildings. Some scholars argue that synagogues ("gatherings" in Greek), modest centers of prayer and study that have been the focus of Jewish worship ever since, first emerged in Babylon. It is also possible that the exiles put together the Torah in something like its current form. Elders led the community while prophets continued to speak out: Two examples are Ezekiel, who preached the restoration of the Temple, and the man known to us only as "Second Isaiah" (Isaiah 40–66). Second Isaiah emphasized the universal aspect of the god of Israel, who could make empires rise and fall and bring the exiles home from far-off Babylon.

Second Isaiah's message points to a second important development among the exiles of Judah. As striking as the return to Palestine is the survival of large numbers of Judeans as an unassimilated people outside of Judah—in other words, as Jews. For the first time, membership in a community of worship was divorced from residence. Jewish communities flourished in Babylon, Persia, and Egypt, but the members often chose not to become Babylonians, Persians, or Egyptians. From the sixth century B.C. on, a majority of Jews lived outside Palestine, and the Jewish Diaspora ("dispersion") became a permanent part of Western history.

Restoring the Jewish community in Judea (the Persian province corresponding to the former kingdom of Judah) did not prove easy. After many difficult years, however, that community was established on a firm footing under the leadership of two men: the Persian Jewish governor Nehemiah, who arrived in Judea in 445 B.C., and the Babylonian Jew Ezra, who probably arrived a generation later. Nehemiah overcame local and imperial opposition and built a new city wall for Jerusalem, which rendered the capital secure. A priest and scribe, Ezra oversaw the adoption of the Torah by the Judean community (see page 50).

The People of the Covenant

A rough equality, limited government, and the rule of law under God were all fundamental Israelite political notions. According to Israelite belief, humans were made in God's image. Thus, all individuals were equal in a fundamental sense; all were bound by God's law. A king who disobeyed this law was illegitimate. Indeed, Israel was ambivalent at best about the institution of kingship, which was tolerated as an evil made necessary only by the country's many armed enemies. God's covenant with the Hebrews was a religious contract with political consequences, rendering God the only true king of Israel. Far from being gods themselves or even God's representatives, Israel's kings were merely the humble servants.

Israelite egalitarianism was restricted to males. Israelite women usually could not own or inherit property, as women could in Hammurabi's Babylon; or sue in court, as women could in pharaonic Egypt; or initiate a divorce, as women could in Athens (see page 100). The rise of monotheism meant that the powerful goddesses of other ancient cultures were absent in Israel. Women participated in the rituals of early Israelite religion and the original Temple (ca. 940–586 B.C.) but were segregated in a separate women's courtyard in the rebuilt Temple (ca. 515 B.C.–A.D. 79) and did not take part in temple ritual. Indeed, the perspective of the Hebrew Bible is predominantly male. Consider just two examples. First, of the 1426 names in the Hebrew Bible, 1315 are male; only 111 women's names appear, about 9 percent of the total.[1] Second, only males can bear the sign of the Lord's covenant with Israel—that is, circumcision.

Nevertheless, Israelite women enjoyed honor as mothers and partners in running the household. The Hebrew Bible states that woman (as exemplified by Eve, the first woman) was created as "a suitable partner" for man (Genesis 2:18, 20). Reproduction and hence motherhood assume great importance in the Hebrew Bible; the Lord enjoins humans to "be fruitful and multiply" (Genesis 1:28). The Bible also commands that children honor both their father and their mother: The two parents are equal in parental authority (Exodus 20:12).

The Hebrew Bible sometimes displays sympathy for and insights into the strategies that women used to counter the abuses of male power. Rebecca, for instance, thwarts her husband Isaac's plan to give his blessing to their son Esau; she sees to it that their son Jacob, whom she prefers, obtains her husband's blessing.

Only about a half-dozen women in the Hebrew Bible serve as leaders of Israel, but that is more than in the literature of most other ancient cultures. Deborah (ca. 1125 B.C.), for example, a charismatic Israelite preacher, organizes an army that destroys the forces of a Canaanite commander. Centuries later Esther, a Hebrew woman, becomes the wife of a Persian king whom the Bible calls Ahasuerus, who is probably Xerxes (r. 485–465 B.C.). Esther works ferociously at the Persian court to defeat a conspiracy to wipe out her people, and she saves them. The Book of Ruth (date uncertain) tells the story of a selfless and loyal woman, Ruth, who saves her mother-in-law, Naomi, from ruin and poverty. The Bible celebrates Ruth as Naomi's "devoted daughter-in-law, who has proved better to you [Naomi] than seven sons." (See the box, "Ruth.")

Israelite culture prized women for their cunning, courage, and perseverance—qualities that allowed the people to survive. Military prowess was highly valued in men, but there was appreciation for their inner qualities as well. Schooled in defeat and exile, many Israelites came to the conclusion that "wisdom is better than weapons of war" (Ecclesiastes 9:18). Thus, the Hebrew Bible stresses God's primary interest in goodness of soul: "The Lord seeth not as man seeth; for man looketh on the outward appearance, but the Lord looketh on the heart" (1 Samuel 16:7). The god of Israel prizes righteousness above military prowess, sacrifice, or ritual.

One might say that Israelite law reflects a similar tension between power and righteousness. On the one hand, just as Israel's god was omnipotent and jealous, so the law of Israel was meant to be comprehensive and forceful. Capital punishment existed for murder, rape, incorrigible rebelliousness of a son against his parents, adultery by a married woman (both she and her lover were to be executed), a woman's loss of her virginity before marriage, and other offenses. Harsh punishment was mandated for Canaanite towns taken by siege: The entire population was to be killed so as not to corrupt Israel with its religious practices.

On the other hand, by taking intention into account, Israelite law echoes a note already present in Mesopotamia. The so-called Law of the Goring Ox, for instance, allows someone to go unpunished for owning an ox that gores a person to death, unless the owner knew beforehand that the animal was dangerous. If the owner did know, then the owner must be put to death. Israelite law, moreover, demonstrates a belief in the sanctity of human life by prohibiting human sacrifice. An Israelite had to be ready in his or her heart (but *only* in his or her heart) to sacrifice his or her child to Yahweh, as Abraham was willing to sacrifice Isaac when Yahweh so commanded. After ascertaining Abraham's willingness to sacrifice his son, Yahweh freed Isaac from the altar and took a ram as a substitute offering. Western monotheism thus rejected human sacrifice.

PERSIA, CA. 1000–330 B.C.

Further east, the first millennium B.C. witnessed another civilization that experimented with monotheism: Persia. In Persia, however, a very different ruling ideology than Israel's emerged. At its height the empire of the Persians stretched from central Asia and northwest India in the east to Macedon and Libya in the west (see Map 2.1). Persia's vast empire was loosely governed by a Persian ruling elite and its native helpers. Unlike the iron-fisted Assyrians, the Persians were relatively tolerant and respectful of their subjects' customs. Many of Persia's kings were followers of Zoroastrianism, an ethical religion with monotheistic tendencies. A period of relative peace in most of Persia's domains from the 530s to the 330s B.C. fostered economic prosperity.

The Persians absorbed much of the culture of the peoples they conquered. Borrowing the administrative methods of the Assyrians and Medes and the long-established officialdom of Babylon, the Persians built a new and durable imperial government. Their official art stressed the unity of the peoples of the empire under Persian leadership. Persian rule represented the greatest success yet in implementing notions of universal kingship dating back to Sargon of Agade (r. 2371–2316 B.C.; see page 15). In turn, Persia transmitted the trappings of absolute kingship to later ambitious rulers, from Alexander the Great to the Caesars of Rome and from the Byzantine emperors to the Muslim caliphs.

Ruth

Some parts of the Hebrew Bible prohibit intermarriage. The Book of Ruth, however, praises marriage between Judean men and women from neighboring Moab (modern Jordan). This excerpt illustrates such unions, as it does the problem of food shortages, which were a special burden for widows.

Once, in the time of the Judges when there was a famine in the land, a man [Elimelech] from Bethlehem in Judah went with his wife [Naomi] to live in Moabite territory. . . .

Elimelech died, and Naomi was left a widow with her two sons. The sons married Moabite women, one of whom was called Orpah and the other Ruth. [After ten years the sons died.] . . . Then Naomi, bereaved of her two sons as well as of her husband, got ready to return to her own country with her daughters-in-law, because she had heard in Moab that the LORD had shown his care for his people by giving them food. . . .

Naomi said to her daughters-in-law, "Go back, both of you, home to your own mothers. May the LORD keep faith with you, as you have kept faith with the dead and with me; and may he grant each of you the security of a home with a new husband." . . . Then Orpah kissed her mother-in-law and took her leave, but Ruth clung to her.

"Look," said Naomi, "your sister-in-law has gone back to her people and her God. Go, follow her." Ruth answered, "Do not urge me to go back and desert you. Where you go, I shall go, and where you stay, I shall stay. Your people will be my people, and your God my God. Where you die, I shall die, and there be buried. I solemnly declare before the LORD that nothing but death will part me from you." When Naomi saw that Ruth was determined to go with her, she said no more.

 . . . [They go to Judah.]

Naomi had a relative on her husband's side, a prominent and well-to-do . . . [man named] Boaz. One day Ruth the Moabite asked Naomi, "May I go to the harvest fields and glean [that is, collect excess grain] behind anyone who will allow me?" "Yes, go my daughter," she replied. So Ruth went gleaning in the fields behind the reapers. [She met Boaz in his fields.] . . .

Boaz said to Ruth, "Listen, my daughter: do not go to glean in any other field. Do not look any farther, but stay close to my servant-girls. Watch where the men reap, and follow the gleaners; I have told the men not to molest you. Any time you are thirsty, go and drink from the jars they have filled." She bowed to the ground and said, "Why are you so kind as to take notice of me, when I am just a foreigner?" Boaz answered, "I have been told the whole story of what you have done for your mother-in-law since the death of your husband, how you left father and mother and homeland and came among a people you didn't know before. The LORD reward you for what you have done. . . ."

[Eventually, Boaz marries Ruth.]

Source: Ruth 1:1, 3–6, 8–9, 14–18; 2:1–3, 8–12, in *The Oxford Study Bible: Revised English Bible with the Apocrypha* (New York: Oxford University Press, 1992).

Building an Empire

Indo-European-speaking peoples, the Medes and the Persians arrived in western Iran around 900 B.C. and perhaps as early as 1500 B.C. The two peoples were closely related in language and customs. The Medes lived in the central Zagros Mountains. The Persians made their homeland farther south in Persis (modern Anshan). At first the Medes ruled the Persians, but in 550 B.C., the tables were turned when the Medes were suddenly conquered by the young Persian king Cyrus the Great (r. 559–530 B.C.).

It took Cyrus only twenty years to conquer most of western Asia and much of central Asia. Within five years of his death in 530 B.C., his son and successor, Cambyses (r. 530–525 B.C.), added Egypt and Libya. Cambyses's successor, Darius (r. 521–486 B.C.), added northwestern India and Thrace. The frontier regions, especially Egypt, were often in revolt, and the attempt of Darius and his successor, Xerxes (r. 486–465 B.C.), to extend Persian rule to Greece ended in failure (see pages 100–101). The Achaemenid Persian Empire (named after a legendary founder, Achaemenes), nonetheless, survived for two hundred years, until a Greco-Macedonian army under Alexander the Great, king of Macedon (r. 336–323 B.C.), destroyed it. Even then, Persia was only temporarily removed from power. By 246 B.C. a new empire under the dynasty of the Parthians, a northeastern Iranian people, was on the rise, eventually to rule the area extending from Mesopotamia to Bactria (modern Afghanistan).

Let us consider several reasons for the success of Achaemenid Persia. The first was military prowess. A warrior aristocracy ruled Persia, whose traditional values, according to the Greek historian Herodotus, were "riding, hunting, and telling the truth." The state was able to field a huge conscript army of about 300,000 men. Although the resultant hodgepodge of peoples from across the empire did not always fight as a unit, a crack infantry group, the 10,000 Immortals, provided a solid core. The Persians excelled as bowmen and cavalrymen. They made a final break with chariotry and turned the cavalry into the decisive strike force of the battlefield. Persia was equally innovative at sea, where its subjects built the first great navy. Although Persians served as marines and sometimes as commanders, the rowers and seamen were usually Phoenicians or Greeks.

The second reason for Persia's success was political. Unlike the Assyrians, the Persians considered generosity and tolerance to be more effective than terrorism and brutality. As Cyrus prepared to attack Babylon, for example, he portrayed himself as the champion of the traditional Babylonian deity Marduk, the power of whose priesthood had been challenged by the Neo-Babylonian kings. As

Achaemenid Persian Silver This silver rhyton (drinking vessel) is in the shape of a griffin, a mythological animal that is part lion and part eagle. Persian rulers commanded the talents of western Asia's best artists and craftsmen, silversmiths among them. *(Courtesy of the Trustees of the British Museum)*

a result, the Babylonians opened the city gates to the Persian army, allowing Cyrus to achieve that greatest measure of military success: victory without a battle. Cyrus's departure from Assyrian and Neo-Babylonian imperial policies is remembered today in his edict of 539 B.C. permitting the Jewish exiles in Babylon to return to Judea. (See the box, "Cyrus and His Subjects' Gods.")

The third reason for Persia's success was its skill at administration and organization. Darius played a crucial role in reorganizing the imperial administration and finances (military-minded Persians sneered at him as a "shopkeeper"). Like the Assyrian Empire, the Persian domain was divided into provinces, called *satrapies*. Each of the twenty satrapies was a unit of administration and tax collection. For the first time, taxes could be paid with a stable, official coinage: the gold daric (named after Darius) and the silver shekel. Coins had been invented in the kingdom of Lydia in western Asia Minor in the seventh century B.C. Croesus (r. 560–547 B.C.), Lydia's king, was known for his wealth—hence the expression "rich as Croesus"—before Cyrus conquered him in 547 B.C.

The provincial governors, or *satraps,* were powerful, often quasi-independent figures. The empire had many centralizing forces to oppose them, however. Each province had a royal secretary and was visited regularly by traveling inspectors known as "the king's eyes." A network of good roads radiated from the main capital city of Susa and from Persepolis, the capital in Persis proper. The most famous road, the so-called Royal Road, stretched 1600 miles from western Iran to western Anatolia (see Map 2.1). Covering the whole distance took most travelers three months, but the king's relay messenger corps, for whom a series of staging posts with fresh horse mounts was built along the way, could make the trip in a week.

Another unifying element was prosperity and stability. Darius proclaimed in an inscription that he had fostered the rule of law: "These countries [of the empire] showed respect toward my law; as was said to them by me, thus it was done." Although some scholars suggest that Darius turned the great body of traditional Babylonian case law into a new Persian code for the whole empire, evidence survives only for Egypt, where Darius ordered a codification of Egyptian law. Darius and other Persian kings helped create the conditions

for law-abidingness by taking an interest in the economy. For example, they opened to commercial traffic Persian roads and a canal connecting the Red Sea and the Nile.

Language, too, built unity. Aramaic, a Semitic language related to Hebrew, was the empire's basic language of commerce and administration. The language was first used by the Aramaeans, a nomadic people who settled in northern Syria about 1100 B.C. and ruled an area extending into Mesopotamia before succumbing to Assyrian conquest about 725 B.C. The Aramaeans dominated the overland trade routes, which, combined with the simple and easily learned Aramaic alphabet, contributed to the spread of their language. Aramaic facilitated the development of literacy and recordkeeping. Indeed, Aramaic would become the common language of western Asia for over a thousand years, until Arabic replaced it; Jesus Christ was to be its most famous native speaker.

Despite its success, Persia's empire faced several weaknesses. First, Cyrus had bequeathed a legacy as a charismatic war leader. Feeling the need to live up to his example, his successors sometimes undertook ambitious and expensive expeditions that failed, such as wars with the Scythians (a tough nomadic people in the Ukraine) and the Greeks. Second, however mild Persian rule, however peaceful and prosperous, it was still rule by foreigners and it still involved taxation. Persian officials, military garrisons, and colonists were found—and were resented—in every corner of the empire. Native resentment, particularly in Egypt, and the independence of certain satraps led to intermittent provincial revolts.

The King of Kings

The exaltation of the Persian king served as a counterweight to rebellious tendencies. From Darius on, the Persian monarch tried to overawe his officials with his despotic splendor.

The "King of Kings," as the monarch called himself, sat on a high, gold and blue throne, dressed in purple, decked out in gold jewelry, wearing fragrant oils and cosmetics, and attended by corps of slaves and eunuchs (castrated men employed in high positions). Although he was not

Cyrus and His Subjects' Gods

Although the Persians sometimes used brutal tactics, they preferred to win their subjects' loyalty by gestures of goodwill, such as winning the favor of the religious leaders. Excerpt (a), a Babylonian inscription, demonstrates the political skill by which Cyrus the Great secured the surrender of Babylon in 539 B.C. without a battle. Excerpt (b), from the Hebrew Bible, records the favor that Cyrus showed to the Jewish exiles in Babylon.

(a)

He [Marduk] scanned and looked (through) all the countries, searching for a righteous ruler willing to lead him (i.e., Marduk) (in the annual procession). (Then) he pronounced the name of Cyrus, king of Anshan, declared him to be(come) the ruler of all the world. . . . And he (Cyrus) did always endeavor to treat according to justice the black-headed whom he (Marduk) has made him conquer. Marduk, the great lord, a protector of his people/worshippers, beheld with pleasure his (i.e., Cyrus's) good deeds and his upright mind (and therefore) ordered him to march against his city Babylon. . . .

I am Cyrus, king of the world, great king, legitimate king, king of Babylon, king of Sumer and Akkad, king of the four rims (of the earth), son of Cambyses. . . .

When I entered Babylon as a friend and (when) I established the seat of the government in the palace of the ruler under jubilation and rejoicing, Marduk, the great lord, [induced] the magnanimous inhabitants of Babylon [to love me], and I was daily endeavoring to worship him. My numerous troops walked around in Babylon in peace, I did not allow anybody to terrorize (any place) of the [country of Sumer] and Akkad. I strove for peace in Babylon and in all his other sacred cities.

(b)

In the first year of King Cyrus of Persia [539 B.C.] the Lord, to fulfill his word spoken through Jeremiah, inspired the king to issue throughout his kingdom the following proclamation, which he also put in writing: The decree of King Cyrus of Persia. The Lord the God of the heavens has given me all the kingdoms of the earth, and he himself has charged me to build him a house at Jerusalem in Judah. Whoever among you belongs to his people, may his God be with him; and let him go up to Jerusalem in Judah, and build the house of the Lord the God of Israel, the God who is in Jerusalem. Let every Jew left among us, wherever he is settled throughout the country, be helped by his neighbours with silver and gold, goods and livestock, in addition to the voluntary offerings for the house of God in Jerusalem.

Sources: Excerpt (a): James B. Pritchard, ed., *Ancient Near Eastern Texts Relating to the Old Testament*, 3d ed. (Princeton: Princeton University Press, 1969), pp. 315–316. Excerpt (b): Ezra 1:1–3, in *The Oxford Study Bible: Revised English Bible with the Apocrypha* (New York: Oxford University Press, 1992).

considered a god, he had to be treated worshipfully. Persians spoke of the king's *khvarna*, his "kingly glory," a mysterious aura of power. Anyone who came into the royal presence had to approach him with a bow to the ground, face down. Even when entertaining dinner guests, the king normally ate alone in a separate room, looking at the guests through a curtain. If, after dinner, the king wished to drink with his guests, he would sit on a golden-footed couch while they sat on the floor, and of course he and they would drink wine from separate casks.

Impressive as the court ceremonial was, Persian kings were not all-powerful. They were bound by the rule of law and by the considerable power of Persia's proud nobility, on whom they relied to fill the top administrative positions. Competing factions of ministers, wives, concubines, eunuchs, and sons often brought intrigue and discord to court, especially in the fourth century B.C., a time of frequent rebellion. The kings were nonetheless accustomed to giving commands, and they could act with capriciousness and cruelty when thwarted.

Darius I, for example, proudly proclaimed in an inscription that he punished the chief of a rebellion by the Medes with mutilation and impalement and had the other ringleaders flayed.

Royal authority was symbolized in the decoration of the great palaces at Susa and Persepolis, a project begun by Darius I and completed by his son and successor, Xerxes. The Susa palace, the larger of the two, denoted the universality of the empire by the variety of hands that built it. In an inscription, Darius points out that the cedar for

Frieze at Persepolis This sculptured relief lines the stairway to the audience hall of King Darius (r. 521–486 B.C.). It depicts Persian nobles, well-groomed and formally dressed, carrying flowers for the New Year's Feast. *(Rony Jaques/Photo Researchers)*

the palace came from Lebanon, brought by Assyrians to Babylon and from there by Carians and Ionians (two peoples inhabiting western Anatolia; Ionians were Greek) to Susa; the gold came from Sardis (western Anatolia) and Bactria; the silver and ebony from Egypt; the ivory from Ethiopia, India, and central Asia. Craftsmen from east and west took part in the construction. The Persepolis palace, too, displayed the heterogeneity of the empire in its architecture. The palace was placed on a terrace, as in Mesopotamia, but contained columned halls as in Egypt, with Assyrian-style column capitals. Persepolis emphasized the king's vast power by means of a frieze of sculpted relief panels that lined a monumental stairway leading to the palace. The subject is an endless procession of the peoples of the world to do homage to the King of Kings: from the nobility to the Immortals to Median and Persian soldiers to tribute-bearing subjects from the ends of the earth. The overall feeling of the scene is static, as if the Persian Empire would last forever.

Zoroastrianism

One of ancient Persia's most original contributions to civilization is religious. From obscure beginnings, Zoroastrianism became the religion of Persia until the Muslim conquest in the seventh century A.D. Although largely extinct in today's Iran, an overwhelmingly Islamic country, Zoroastrianism still survives in small communities elsewhere, primarily in India. Basic Zoroastrian notions include *dualism* (the notion of a grand conflict between good and evil), *eschatology* (interest in the end of the world), and *soteriology* (belief in a savior). Some scholars argue that these Zoroastrian beliefs influenced similar beliefs in Judaism and Christianity, as well as Roman paganism and Indian Buddhism.

It is easier to describe ancient Zoroastrianism in broad strokes than in detail, partly because the religion changed radically over the course of its ancient history, partly because relatively little information survives before A.D. 300. This much is clear: The religion was founded by a great reformer and prophet named Zarathustra (Zoroaster in Greek). Zarathustra lived in eastern Iran. His teachings survive in the Gathas ("Songs"), a portion of the

Zoroastrian holy book called the Avesta. Some scholars date Zarathustra as late as 550 B.C.; others prefer an earlier date, 750 or even 1000 B.C.

Zarathustra's society was dominated by warriors whose religion consisted of blood cults, violent gods, animal sacrifice, and ecstatic rituals in which hallucinogens were eaten. Zarathustra rejected such violent practices in favor of an inward-looking, intellectual, and ethical religion. He favored ceremonies involving fire, considered a symbol of purity. Like the Jews, Zarathustra was a monotheist, believing in only one god for all people, the supremely good and wise creator of the universe, whom he called Ahura Mazda ("Wise Lord"). Unlike the Jews, however, Zarathustra considered the problem of evil to be virtually the central question of religion. If god was one, good, and omnipotent, how could evil exist?

Zarathustra's answer might be called *ethical dualism*. Ahura Mazda had twin children: the Beneficent Spirit and the Hostile Spirit. Each spirit had made a free choice: one for the "truth" and the other for the "lie"—that is, one for good and the other for evil. Every human being faces a similar moral choice between good and evil. "Reflect with a clear mind—man by man for himself—upon the two choices of decision, being aware to declare yourselves to Him before the great retribution," says Zarathustra.[2] Indeed, humanity is caught in a great cosmic struggle in which individuals are free to make a momentous choice. Zarathustra thus endowed humanity with great freedom and dignity. He distinguished between two states of being: the spiritual and the material. The more a person pursued spiritual purity, the greater was the person's ability to choose good rather than evil.

Zarathustra held a linear conception of history, similar to that in the Hebrew Bible. He believed that one day, through an ordeal by fire, Ahura Mazda would judge all the people who had ever lived. Those who had chosen good would be rewarded, and those who had chosen evil would be punished. Then would follow a Last Judgment in which the dead would be transfigured and restored to a glorious bodily existence. There would be, Zarathustra promised, "long destruction for the deceitful but salvation for the truthful." The notion of a savior who would initiate the Last Judgment is an early Zoroastrian belief, if perhaps not a doctrine of Zarathustra himself.

GREECE AND THE AEGEAN

2300 B.C.	Greek-speakers enter Greek mainland
2000 B.C.	First Minoan palaces on Crete
1800–1550 B.C.	Height of Minoan civilization
1626 B.C.	Eruption of Thera volcano
1550 B.C.	Most Minoan palaces destroyed
1375 B.C.	Palace at Knossos destroyed
1400–1200 B.C.	Height of Mycenaean civilization
1200 B.C.	Mycenaean palaces destroyed
1100–800 B.C.	Greek "Dark Ages"
800–750 B.C.	Homer
700 B.C.	Hesiod

Zarathustra's followers eased his uncompromising rejection of Iranian paganism. Under the leadership of priests, known as *magi* in western Iran, the religion evolved and changed considerably. Lesser deities beneath Ahura Mazda were added to the Zoroastrian pantheon, in part to suit the religion to the needs of the huge, multicultural Persian Empire.

It is tempting to attribute Cyrus's policy of toleration to the ethical teachings of Zarathustra, but it is uncertain whether Cyrus was Zoroastrian. We are on firmer ground with later Persian kings, particularly Darius I, who had an image of himself alongside Ahura Mazda carved on the face of an Iranian cliff. In an accompanying inscription Darius announces: "For this reason Ahura Mazda bore aid, and the other gods who are, because I was not hostile, I was not a Lie-follower, I was not a doer of wrong—neither I nor my family. According to righteousness I conducted myself."[3]

EARLY GREECE, TO CA. 750 B.C.

To most people, "ancient Greece" generally means either the city-states (ca. 700–300 B.C.) or the heroes portrayed in the *Iliad* and the *Odyssey*, the epic poems of Homer (ca. 750 B.C.). Both are products of the first millennium B.C. Civilization, however, flourished in Greece throughout the second millennium B.C., and Homer's works have roots in this earlier era. Most of what we know of this earlier period, called "Aegean Greece" by scholars, is the discovery of archaeologists. In particular, archaeology illustrates the rise and fall of two monument-building, literate civilizations: the Minoans on the island of Crete and the Mycenaeans on the Greek mainland (Map 2.3).

The Minoans and Early Greece, 3000–1375 B.C.

Greece is not an easy land. Mountainous, it contains little cultivable farmland. Although pastureland and forest are more abundant, one-third of the country is entirely unproductive. Most of the farmland, moreover, is to be found in upland plains, which are divided by mountains, making it difficult to concentrate a large labor force to work the land efficiently. There are few rivers. The south enjoys a mild, Mediterranean climate but is quite dry. The north has a Balkan climate of hot summers and cold winters. The indented seacoast provides Greece with many harbors. Greece's geography suggests several recurring features of its history: contrasts between seafarers and mountaineers and between north and south, and the difficulty of unifying so mountainous a terrain.

Archaeologists have discovered milestones in the emergence of civilization in Greece. The first agricultural villages appeared shortly after 7000 B.C., bronze-making skills after 3000. After 3500 B.C., Greece became a supplier of raw materials for the new cities of western Asia, and was changed in turn. Both on the islands and the mainland there appeared small towns, sometimes fortified with stone walls, occasionally containing substantial stone and mud-brick structures. Between 3000 and 2400 B.C., people living on the Cycladic islands of the Aegean Sea produced exquisite marble sculptures and incised terra-cotta dishes.

Europe's first monumental, literate civilization originated on the Aegean island of Crete around 2000 B.C. Its origins are hotly debated, but we know that it was literate because Cretan writing, a syllabary (a system of simple syllables that form words) called "Linear A," has survived (we

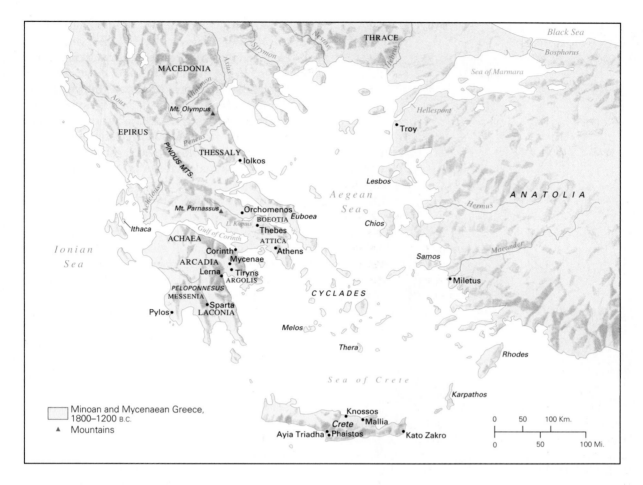

Map 2.3 Aegean Greece The Minoan civilization (height: ca. 1800–1550 B.C.) and the Mycenaean civilization (height: ca. 1400–1200 B.C.) flourished in turn in the second millennium B.C. Aegean region. The center of Minoan civilization was the island of Crete. A mainland people, the Mycenaeans conquered Minoan Crete around 1550 B.C.

know its language is not Greek, but we do not know what it is). The island of Crete is located on the sea routes between the Greek mainland, Egypt, and Anatolia. The archaeological record contains many signs of trade and cultural contact between Cretans and nearby peoples, from one of whom, perhaps, the Minoans were descended. The evidence is concentrated in Crete's palaces—monumental structures that first appeared at various locations on the island around 2000 B.C. After destruction by earthquake, the palaces were rebuilt on a grand scale, to flourish especially during the period from 1800 to 1550 B.C. Scholars call

the palace-builders and their civilization "Minoan," after King Minos of later Greek myth. He was supposed to have ruled a great sea empire from his palace at Knossos.

The Minoan palaces were not merely royal residences but centers of administration, religion, politics, and economics. Minoan palace bureaucrats supervised a large sector of the economy, just as their counterparts did in Ugarit, Egypt, the Hittite kingdom, and other ancient societies. The largest Cretan palace, as well as the first to be excavated, Knossos offers a striking example of Minoan civilization. The main building at Knossos

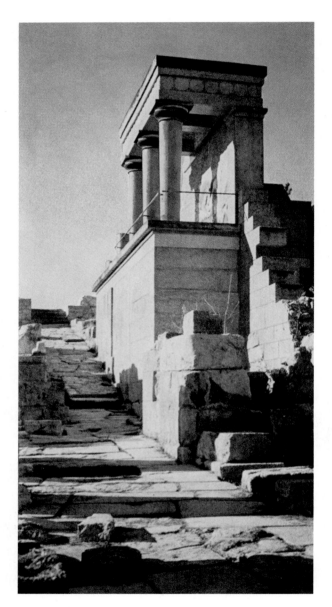

Palace of Knossos A paved ramp and (partially restored) portico are part of an entranceway to the palace. The tapered columns and combination of stone and timber are characteristic features of Minoan architecture. *(Dmitrio Harissiadis)*

palace had large staterooms, residence quarters, storage rooms, artisans' workshops, and bathrooms, interconnected by corridors, ramps, and stairways. Light wells admitted daylight, and brightly colored frescoes decorated the walls. Cretan architects were aware of palace architecture elsewhere in the eastern Mediterranean and may have borrowed from it, but precisely who influenced whom remains an open question.

The palaces make clear that the Minoans exploited Crete's considerable natural wealth in agriculture and timber. The stunning artwork, often in precious metal; the sophisticated frescoes; and the vast and elaborate architecture all testify to prosperity. Archaeological and linguistic evidence indicates a widespread Minoan trading network from the Levant to Sicily. A Minoan settlement flourished on the Aegean island of Thera, 70 miles north of Crete (see Map 2.3). This settlement was destroyed in 1626 (or possibly 1628) B.C. by one of the most violent volcanic eruptions in history. So huge an eruption produced climate changes for several years. The changes are visible in the pattern of tree rings in ancient wood; that is why scholars can offer so specific a date for Thera's eruption.

From the lack of fortifications around Cretan palaces and the small amount of arms and armor found in burial sites, it appears that the Minoans lived in relative peace. They worshiped a variety of gods and goddesses, often represented in Minoan art, but we do not know their names and functions. Minoan frescoes show that women as well as men played important roles in cult and ritual. The women portrayed by Cretan artists are often beautiful, bejeweled, and elegant, the men often graceful and athletic. Landscapes and animals are frequently illustrated. In short, Minoan civilization gives an impression of peace, prosperity, and happiness. There is thus a lost-Eden quality about the violent destruction of Minoan civilization. All of the palaces except Knossos were destroyed around 1550 B.C.; Knossos fell around 1375 B.C.

There has been no shortage of theories about the cause of the destruction, but the archaeological evidence strongly supports the notion of an invasion. But by whom? To find the answer, let us look to the Greek mainland.

covers three acres, the associated structures an additional two acres. The palace was built around a large central court, 180 feet long by 82 feet wide, that probably was used for public ceremonies. A mazelike structure surrounded the court. The

Fresco at Thera This detail of the so-called Fresco of the Ladies shows one of a pair of murals from a shrine. We see a festively costumed woman carrying clothes and ornaments. She is bringing them to a seated woman (not shown), perhaps a goddess. *(The Ancient Art & Architecture Collection)*

The Mycenaeans, to ca. 1200 B.C.

A wave of destruction put an end to the Greek mainland's Copper Age prosperity around 2300 B.C. Centuries of relative poverty followed until, around 1700 B.C., signs of power and prosperity appear at a series of burial sites in central Greece and the Peloponnesus. The most dramatic are at Mycenae (see Map 2.3). The royal burials at the site known as Grave Circle B (shafts sunk around 1700 B.C. into the rock of the slope of the citadel hill) contain pottery, weapons, vessels in precious stone, and a death mask made from an alloy of gold and silver. At Grave Circle A (ca. 1700–1600 B.C.) the burials are a treasure house of objects in gold and other precious metals.

How is this dramatic wealth to be explained? The inhabitants of Mycenae, unlike the earlier inhabitants of the Greek peninsula, were Greek-speakers. They and the wider civilization they represent are called Mycenaean. Just when and how the Mycenaeans got to Greece are tangled questions. Some scholars imagine migration, others invasion; some believe the Mycenaeans' ancestors arrived as early as 2300 B.C., whereas others think it was not until 1700.

Archaeology shows that the Mycenaeans adopted and adapted technology, ideas, and art from their advanced neighbors in Crete, Egypt, Anatolia, and Syria-Palestine. The Mycenaeans traded with these neighbors. They also fought with them, for Mycenaean society was dominated by warrior-kings, raiders who exchanged booty with one another in competitive displays of wealth.

Around 1550 B.C., the mainland warriors achieved their greatest feat: the conquest of Crete. Mycenaean-style artifacts dating from this period have been found in graves on Crete, and thousands of tablets inscribed mostly in an early form of Greek have been discovered in the remains of the final stage of the palace at Knossos. The warlike Mycenaeans had conquered the sophisticated Minoans. As a result, the Mycenaeans adopted a Minoan-style palace economy.

Between about 1400 and 1200 B.C., Mycenaean civilization was at its height. Kings lived in palaces whose storerooms were crammed with treasures. They traveled through their kingdoms on a network of good roads and could muster rowers and ships. Mycenaean artists excelled at pottery-making and fresco-painting, metal inlay work and ivory-carving. Mycenaean builders constructed

palaces, fortifications, bridges, huge vaulted tombs, and sophisticated drainage works.

Palace officials supervised considerable economic activity, often in minute detail, including agriculture, pasturage, and artisanry. Women and children as well as men were included in the labor force. Our knowledge of the palace economy comes primarily from thousands of clay tablets inscribed by palace scribes around 1200 B.C. They are inscribed in Linear B, mostly an early form of Greek consisting of a combination of syllabary and ideograms (a system of symbols that stand for words or for ideas).

Abroad, Mycenaean merchants replaced Minoans. They exported wine and scented oils from

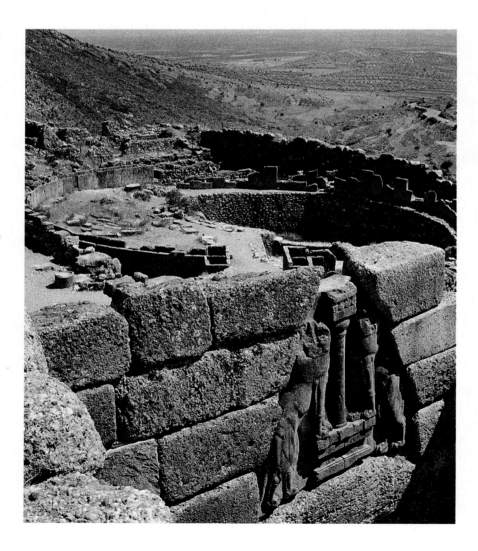

Lion Gate at Mycenae Carved about 1250 B.C. above the main gate of the citadel's massive walls, the lions—flanking a column, their front paws resting on altars—probably represent royal authority. Inside the walls is Grave Circle B, a royal burial site. *(Dmitrio Harissiadis)*

Sicily to the Levant and brought back metals, ivory, and perhaps slaves. Mycenaean warriors engaged in activities ranging from raids and skirmishes to formal battles.

In the thirteenth century B.C., at the height of Mycenaean power, trouble was brewing for the Mycenaean kings. Palaces at Mycenae and elsewhere were given strong fortification walls. By 1200 B.C., most of the fortified sites had been destroyed. Pylos, which had no walls, was destroyed by fire earlier. Occupation continued on a reduced scale. It appears likely that Mycenaean Greece suffered from a combination of internal weakness and invasion from abroad similar to that of most of the eastern Mediterranean around 1250–1150 B.C., the era of the Sea Peoples (see page 37).

Between Mycenae and the City-States, ca. 1100–800 B.C.

The term "Greek Dark Ages" is becoming a misnomer as archaeology increases our knowledge of the period from roughly 1100 to 800 B.C. The evidence does, however, suggest a considerable depopulation in Greece from the twelfth through the ninth centuries B.C. It seems that rich and poor alike were worse off than in Mycenaean times.

After the destruction of the palaces around 1200 B.C., Mycenaean culture continued to flicker before finally fading in the early eleventh century. New peoples began to move into central and southern Greece around this time. They probably were the Dorians, speakers of a Greek dialect who came from northern Greece. Their material culture was rougher and ruder than that of Mycenae's descendants; there is little distinctive about it besides the iron slashing sword and the long bronze fastener. The Dorians drove out or dominated the Mycenaean Greeks, turning much of central and southern Greece, including Crete, into Dorian centers. Among major settlements, only Athens maintained its independence. The city served as an asylum for Mycenaean refugees, many of whom migrated eastward around 1000 B.C. to the Aegean coast of Anatolia, which was destined to become an important center of Greek culture.

Greece from roughly 1100 to 800 B.C. was largely a poor and illiterate society of small towns and low-level agriculture and trade. Nevertheless, it produced notable painted pottery and pre-served an oral tradition of poetry handed down from the Mycenaean era. By the end of this period, the Greeks were poised to reach a milestone in narrative artistry in a literary genre: the epic poetry of Homer.

Homer and History

Had there been a Bible in ancient Greece, the *Iliad* and *Odyssey* of Homer would have been its two Testaments. Only Hesiod, a poet who lived around 700 B.C. and composed two shorter and more didactic poems in the epic tradition (*Theogony* and *Works and Days*), enjoyed a comparable influence on later generations. But Greece did not have a Bible. Homer and Hesiod were poets, not priests. (As far as we know, the Greek world never had a priestly class comparable to that of Egypt or western Asia.) Although their poems inspired, moved, and educated the Greeks—a large part of a Greek boy's education consisted of learning to recite Homer—they were not divine writ.

The Greeks were polytheists, their gods anthropomorphic. The gods of Greece are similar in many ways to the gods of Sumer. They share the foibles and foolishness of humanity but are immortal and far more powerful than humans. The gods figure prominently in early Greek poetry, but they are less powerful than Yahweh, less immediate, and less interested in the inner life of humans. Already, at the beginning of the Greek cultural tradition, there is a tendency toward the belief that became the hallmark of ancient Greece: that "man is the measure of all things," as the thinker Protagoras would say in the fifth century B.C.

The Greek gods of the first millennium B.C. existed in Mycenaean times—offerings to them are recorded on Linear B tablets. Because they were thought to live on Mount Olympus, a 9500-foot-high peak in northern Greece, the gods were called the Olympians. Hesiod's *Theogony* tells the story of the Olympians' birth and their triumph over an older generation of deities. The "household" of the Olympians—the early Greek pantheon was conceived of as a noble's household—included Zeus, a sky-god and the "father of gods and men," and his consort, Hera; Zeus's brother, Poseidon, god of the sea, earthquakes, and horses; Ares, god of war; and Aphrodite, goddess of love. Also in the "household" were Zeus's children: Athena, goddess of wisdom and cunning; Hephaestus, god of craftsmen; Hermes, god of travelers and thieves; Apollo, god of disease and healing; and Artemis, goddess of the hunt, of maidens, and of childbirth.

Flawed and sometimes unpredictable, the Greek gods often seem childish, but the natural world symbolized by the gods seemed equally inconstant to the ancients. The gods embody the values of a warrior society that put a premium on *aretê*, or excellence in battle. The heroes in the *Iliad* and the *Odyssey* seek glory through military exploits. They assume that the gods want precisely the same thing and that they will help those mortals whose achievements are most promising. Yet the gods want more. As Homer and Hesiod insist, Zeus, king of the gods, wants justice. Zeus punishes those who do evil—those who, for example, break oaths or give false judgments or violate the laws of hospitality. In the *Iliad*, a Trojan prince named Paris sparks the Trojan War by abducting the beautiful Helen from her husband, the Greek king Menelaus, while he is a guest in Menelaus's household. In return, the Greeks attack Troy. The gods destroy Troy as punishment for Paris's crime. (See the feature, "Weighing the Evidence: The Trojan War," on pages 76–77.)

The *Iliad* and the *Odyssey* focus on the Trojan War and its aftermath. The *Iliad* is set in the tenth year of the conflict. The strain of fighting leads to a quarrel between Greek chieftains: Agamemnon, king of Mycenae and the leader of the expedition, and Achilles, the greatest Greek warrior. The most prominent Trojans, King Priam and his eldest son, Hector, are less petty but will suffer the greater ruin. The *Odyssey* tells the story of the struggle of the Greek hero Odysseus to return home to Ithaca and to regain his kingship after a twenty-year absence, ten years in the war at Troy and ten years wandering homeward. It also focuses on the loyalty and ingenuity of Odysseus's wife, Penelope, who saves the household in her husband's absence, and the maturation of their son, Telemachus, who helps his father regain his kingdom.

Homer puts as much emphasis on brains as on brawn; Odysseus, for example, is a man of intelligence and cunning. Homer argues, moreover, that the gods hold human beings to a code of justice, hospitality, and respect for parents. Finally, although the Homeric poems focus on the upper classes—and primarily on men—the poems have a strain of sympathy for ordinary people and for women. Indeed, they have a general sympathy for failure. Homer's heroes court death and often obtain it. Unlike the psalmist of the Hebrew Bible, a Homeric hero walks alone "through the valley of the shadow of death" (Psalm 23:4); he has no god to redeem him. He knows that the gods ordain human life to be difficult and full of suffering. Human frailty, however, ennobles Homer's heroes.

Homer's nobles are proud and jealous. In the *Iliad*, for example, when Agamemnon is forced by divine command to return his "prize"—a girl captured in a raid—he viciously demands that he take the "prize" of Achilles, his greatest warrior—that is, Achilles' girl. Achilles' response is to sulk in his tent while the Trojans drive his fellow Greeks to near-defeat. In the *Odyssey*, a group of nobles lives off Odysseus's estate in his absence while they wait to see which of them Odysseus's wife (and ostensible widow) might marry. Odysseus's honor demands that he punish them by killing every last one. In both cases, Homer recognizes that the hero goes too far: Achilles' inaction leads to the death of his best friend, and ultimately to his own death; Odysseus's thirst for revenge leads to civil war.

Although Homer was aware of the societal consequences of such actions, he was not a historian. He was a bard, a professional singer of heroic poetry—of songs praising the deeds of the great. Heroic poetry consciously glorifies and magnifies the actions of its subjects. In all likelihood, there is a great deal of tall tale in Homer's stories of Achilles and Odysseus, of Helen and Penelope. We cannot even be sure that these men and women ever really existed.

Indeed, Homer lived neither in the age he sings about nor on the Greek mainland. Homer lived in Ionia (a region of the central western coast of Anatolia), perhaps in the city of Smyrna. Although we do not know just when he lived, it was not until centuries after the Trojan War. Most scholars today would date Homer to about 750 B.C., a period of increasing change, growth, and ferment in Greece. Some scholars doubt whether there was just *one* Homer and argue that the *Iliad* and *Odyssey* are the works of two different poets.

All would agree that the author of the poems worked in a bardic tradition going back to the

Mycenaean Age, from which he took stories, details, and language. Most scholars accept the theory that this tradition was oral, not written. Like oral poets elsewhere, Homer and his predecessors composed their poems as they sang them, making use of a stock of stories and formulaic expressions (such as the Greek equivalents of "swift-footed Achilles" and "grey-eyed goddess Athena"). In fact, Homer may have been illiterate.

The oral tradition gave Homer knowledge of a past society that was long gone by his day. Although Homer studs his poems with details of Mycenaean palace life, the ideology of his characters generally reflects the beliefs of his own, post-Mycenaean society.

World of the Heroes

Historians must distinguish between ideology and reality in Homer's poems. Homer focuses on the elite. Homeric warriors and their women hold aristocratic values and tend to look down on ordinary people. Scholarship shows, however, that the reality of society in Homer's day was more level and undifferentiated. Except for a small number of traders and craft specialists who lived in towns, most people in the Greece of 750 B.C. lived in villages and hamlets. Most farmed or herded pigs, goats, or sheep, and most were free. In each community the people were called the *demos;* the leading men were called *basileis. Basileis* means "kings," but it is more accurate to understand them as chiefs. No great difference of wealth existed between the basileis and ordinary free farmers.

We must, likewise, not exaggerate the difference between the roles in government and war played by basileis and ordinary men. To be sure, basileis took the lead in both spheres, but the demos was not excluded entirely. In war, for example, Homer emphasizes heroic contests between aristocratic champions on each side, just as epic convention demanded. Yet his battle scenes also include descriptions of a large number of ordinary men fighting in mass combat in close formation. Likewise, Homeric government is dominated by the basileis, but the demos also played a part.[4]

The basic instruments of government that would exist for centuries in Greece appear in the *Iliad* and the *Odyssey*: generals, orators, judges, a council, and an assembly. When making decisions about war and peace, a council of elder basileis consulted an assembly of the warriors. In this arrangement we see a fundamental principle of Greek government: The political community should be composed of the warriors. The younger basileis dominated the assembly, but the demos was present and its leaders sometimes spoke.

Let us turn now to the ideology of Homer's basileis, which would greatly influence later generations in antiquity. The chiefs formed an international network. Leading Greeks, for example, respected their Trojan counterparts more than fellow Greeks who belonged to the demos. Greek and Trojan chiefs killed each other on the battlefield but rarely hated each other. Indeed, some were bound by hereditary ties of guest-friendship and so declined to fight each other. (See the box, "Encounters with the West: Greeks and Trojans.")

The main activity of Homer's basileis is warfare. The *Iliad* consists largely of a series of battlefield contests. Homer's heroes are competitive and fearless. Yet society pays a price for their exploits. There is a tension in the *Iliad* and the *Odyssey* between the hero as family man and the hero as independent, adventurous, and dangerous youth: between Hector and Achilles, between Odysseus's wanderlust and his need to return home. Indeed, this tension continues as a central theme in ancient Greek culture. In spite of their respect for the power of the father, the Greeks display an ambiguous admiration for youths who assert themselves in the face of patriarchal authority.

Homer does not present women on an equal footing with men but is less misogynistic than the classical culture of the city-states would turn out to be. He shows considerable sympathy for women, particularly in the *Odyssey*. Homer's women are weaker than men, but they are neither timid nor helpless. Penelope, for example, personifies female resourcefulness: By drawing out interminably her weaving of a shroud for Odysseus's elderly father, she puts the noble suitors off for years. She is as concerned with honor as any Homeric man. By refusing to accept an offer of marriage while Odysseus might still be alive, Penelope does honor to her own good name and to her husband's.

~ ENCOUNTERS WITH THE WEST ~

Greeks and Trojans

For Homer's aristocratic heroes, war was a struggle not of nations but of individual loyalties. Friendship and family ties mattered more than patriotism. As these excerpts from the Iliad *show, individual Greeks sometimes considered their enemies, the Trojans (and Trojan allies), to be respected rivals or even honored friends.*

(a) Achilles and Agamemnon

Then looking darkly at him [Agamemnon] Achilles of the swift feet spoke:

"O wrapped in shamelessness, with your mind forever on profit, how shall any one of the Achaians [Greeks] readily obey you either to go on a journey or to fight men strongly in battle? I for my part did not come here for the sake of the Trojan spearmen to fight against them, since to me they have done nothing. Never yet have they driven away my cattle or my horses, never in Phthia where the soil is rich and men grow great did they spoil my harvest, since indeed there is much that lies between us, the shadowy mountains and the echoing sea; but for your sake, o great shamelessness, we followed, to do you favour, you with the dog's eyes, to win your honour and Menalos' from the Trojans."

(b) Glaukos and Diomedes

Now Glaukos, sprung of Hippolochos, and [Diomedes,] the son of Tydeus came together in the space between the two armies, battle-bent. Now as these advancing came to one place and encountered, first to speak was Diomedes of the great war cry: "Who among mortal men are you, good friend? . . . unhappy are those whose sons match warcraft against me."

Then in turn the shining son of Hippolochos answered: ". . . Hippolochos begot me, and I claim that he is my father; he sent me to Troy, and urged upon me repeated injunctions, to be always among the bravest, and hold my head above others, not shaming the generation of my fathers, who were the greatest men in Ephyre and again in wide Lykia. Such is my generation and the blood I claim to be born from."

He spoke, and Diomedes of the great war cry was gladdened. He drove his spear deep into the prospering earth, and in winning words of friendliness he spoke to the shepherd of the people [Glaukos]: "See now, you are my guest friend from far in the time of our fathers. . . . Let us avoid each other's spears, even in the close fighting. There are plenty of Trojans and famed companions in battle for me to kill, whom the god sends me, or those I run down with my swift feet, many Achaians for you to slaughter, if you can do it. But let us exchange our armour, so that these others may know how we claim to be guests and friends from the days of our fathers."

So they spoke, and both springing down from behind their horses gripped each other's hands and exchanged the promise of friendship; but Zeus the son of Kronos stole away the wits of Glaukos who exchanged with Diomedes the son of Tydeus armour of gold for bronze, for nine oxen's worth the worth of a hundred.

Source: The Iliad of Homer, trans. Richmond Lattimore (Chicago: University of Chicago Press, 1951), pp. 63, 156–159.

Homeric women play important roles in encouraging men or, in a more complex psychological process, in bolstering a man's courage by playing the foil to his doubts and fears. In the *Iliad*, Hector is emboldened to fight after his wife, Andromache, begs him not to fight, for her sake and that of their infant son. Moreover, by taking the burden of hearth and home on herself, Andromache allows Hector to define masculinity as making war. Achilles enjoys a similar relationship with his mother, Thetis, as does Odysseus's diffident son, Telemachus, with Penelope.

Loyalty to the family played an important role in social relations. A person's obligations to kin included the duty to avenge crime or murder. Friendship, cemented by an exchange of gifts, was another important social institution. Even humble peasants prided themselves on hospitality.

Such values served Homeric society well. Although they would survive in later centuries, they would be challenged after 700 B.C. by the emergence of the Greek city-state, which tended to challenge the family as a focus of loyalty.

SUMMARY

The first half of the first millennium B.C. was a time of dramatic change. Iron replaced bronze as the primary metal of work and war. New military technology, the frank adoption of brutal and inhumane methods, and improvements in administration led to the creation of the Assyrian Empire, stretching from western Iran to Palestine and briefly even to Egypt. After short-lived hegemonies by Neo-Babylonians and Medes, the Persians established an empire that was larger, better organized, and more tolerant than the empire of the Assyrians. Heirs to Canaanite civilization of the second millennium B.C., the Phoenician city-states expanded across the Mediterranean Sea, less by military conquest than by trade and colonization.

The most important developments of the era, however, were not in commerce, metallurgy, or imperialism but in new conceptions of the nature and meaning of human life. The Persians developed a new religion, Zoroastrianism, that emphasized ethics, the triumph of good over evil, and redemption through a divine savior. The Israelites conquered Palestine and, even after losing it, held on to their identity by means of a tenacious belief in one god. Like Zarathustra, they broke with tradition by insisting that their god was one, merciful, and just. Omnipotent, God gave history purpose and meaning. The purpose of life, in the Israelite view, was to serve God by acting righteously. The new religion eventually became Judaism. The Jews wrote down their religious and historical traditions in a book that, along with the Christian New Testament, proved to be the most influential single text in the history of the West: the Hebrew Bible.

We know little of the ideologies of the Minoan and Mycenaean civilizations of the second millennium B.C., but their economies and governments seem to be similar to those of the other palace-run states of the eastern Mediterranean. By the first millennium B.C., the Greeks, like the Persians and the Hebrews, had broken with tradition, but with a greater emphasis on the human than on the divine. Homer's epic poems, which had taken shape by the eighth century B.C., focus on the fragile dignity of heroic human actions. Homer idealizes a society of aristocratic warriors seeking honor and glory. Although the Greek gods show favor to heroes, they display no transcendent interest in redeeming human souls. Men and women were doomed to die. Homer's legacy, therefore, was to glorify human heroism while recognizing its fragility. It was a legacy that raised as many questions as answers. In the middle centuries of the first millennium B.C., the Greeks would attempt to provide new solutions to Homer's problems. Their successes and failures in such diverse activities as politics and philosophy, war and art, literature and history, still influence the West.

NOTES

1. Carol L. Meyers, "Everyday Life: Women in the Period of the Hebrew Bible," in Carol A. Newsom and Sharon H. Ringe, eds., *The Women's Bible Commentary* (Louisville, Ky.: Westminster/John Knox Press, 1992), p. 245.
2. S. Insler, *The Gāthās of Zarathustra: Acta Iranica*, 8 (Leiden: E. J. Brill, 1975), p. 33.
3. Roland G. Kent, *Old Persian: Grammar, Texts, Lexicon* (New Haven, Conn.: American Oriental Society, 1950), p. 132.

4. Kurt A. Raaflaub, "Homer to Solon. The Rise of the *Polis*: The Written Sources," in Mogens Herman Hansen, ed., *The Ancient Greek City-State. Symposium on the Occasion of the 250th Anniversary of the Royal Danish Academy of Science and Letters, July 1–4, 1992*, Historisk-filosofiske Meddelelser 67, The Royal Danish Academy of Sciences and Letters (Copenhagen: Munksgaard, 1993), pp. 41–105.

SUGGESTED READING

General Surveys

Ferrill, Arther. *The Origins of War.* 1985. "Assyria and Persia: The Age of Iron" (pages 65–89) offers a good analytic overview of warfare in the first millennium B.C., before the Greeks.

Knapp, A. Bernard. *The History and Culture of Ancient Western Asia and Egypt.* 1988. Chapters 4 and 5 (pages 135–267) are a clear and concise introduction to the subjects discussed here.

Knox, Bernard. "Myth and Attic Tragedy." In *Word and Action: Essays in the Ancient Theater* (pages 1–24). 1979. In this stimulating essay, the author discusses the notion of the Jews as a people of the book and the Greeks as a people of myths.

Seltzer, Robert M., ed. *Religions of Antiquity: Religion, History, and Culture. Selections from the Encyclopedia of Religion.* Mircea Eliade, Editor in Chief. 1989. Chapters 6 through 9 are good introductions to Israelite, Iranian, and Aegean religions as well as to Zoroastrianism.

Yadin, Yigael. *The Art of Warfare in Biblical Lands in the Light of Archaeological Study.* 2 vols. 1963. A survey of weapons, armor, fortified sites, strategy, and tactics from the Sumerians on, with an emphasis on Palestine. Superb illustrations.

Assyrians, Neo-Babylonians, and Phoenicians

Moscati, Sabatino. *The World of the Phoenicians.* Translated by Alastair Hamilton. 1968. A general survey of politics, society, and culture, with more emphasis on the western than on the eastern Mediterranean.

Muhly, James D. "Phoenicia and the Phoenicians." In *Biblical Archaeology Today: Proceedings of the International Congress on Biblical Archaeology. Jerusalem, April 1984* (pages 177–191). 1985. The author argues that although trade flourished among Greece, Cyprus, and Phoenicia between approximately 1050 and 850 B.C., the Phoenicians did not engage in trade in or colonize the western Mediterranean before 800 B.C. In a scholarly reply (pages 221–223; compare with pages 226–229), Ora Negbi argues that the Phoenicians were in the western Mediterranean as early as 1100–1000 B.C.

Oates, J. *Babylon.* Rev. ed. 1986. A well-illustrated survey, from the period of Sargon to the Hellenistic Greeks, with a section on Babylon's cultural legacy.

Oded, Bustenay. *Mass Deportations and Deportees in the Neo-Assyrian Empire.* 1979. A detailed study of an appalling practice.

Saggs, H. W. F. *The Might That Was Assyria.* 1984. A readable introductory history celebrating the Assyrians' achievements.

Israel

Alter, Robert. *The Art of Biblical Narrative.* 1981. By applying the techniques of literary criticism to the Hebrew Bible, the author argues for a much more complex and psychologically subtle world-view in that book than is usually thought.

de Vaux, Roland. *Ancient Israel.* Vol. 1, *Social Institutions.* Vol. 2, *Religious Institutions.* Translated 1961. A thorough and judicious survey of the literary evidence. Subjects include the family, the state, economics, law, the military, religious sanctions, priests, ritual, and festivals.

Drane, John. *Introducing the Old Testament.* 1987. An excellent introduction to the archaeology, history, and religion of biblical Israel. Very good illustrations and charts, with a thorough discussion of scholarly controversies.

Halpern, Baruch. *The First Historians: The Hebrew Bible and History.* 1988. A scholarly but readable introduction to the Hebrew Bible's contribution to the Western tradition of historiography.

Johnson, Paul. *A History of the Jews.* 1987. A marvelously readable though at times idealized account by a journalist. The first two chapters treat ancient Judaism.

Meyers, Carol. *Discovering Eve: Ancient Israelite Women in Context.* 1988. A sophisticated analysis combining archaeology, biblical scholarship, feminist theory, and comparative anthropology. The author argues for the existence of a tradition of powerful women in the Hebrew Bible, dating back to the gender equality of early Israelite peasant society.

Negev, Avraham. *The Archaeological Encyclopedia of the Holy Land.* 3d ed. 1990. A valuable and well-illustrated reference book.

Shanks, H., ed. *Ancient Israel. A Short History from Abraham to the Roman Destruction of the Temple.* 1988. Short, readable essays by scholars offering up-to-date introductions to the subject.

Persia

Boardman, John, N. G. L. Hammond, D. M. Lewis, and M. Ostwald, eds. *The Cambridge Ancient History.* 2d ed. Vol. 4, *Persia, Greece and the Western Medi-*

terranean, c. 525 to 479 B.C. 1988. Part 1, "The Persian Empire" (pages 1–286), is an excellent, detailed, scholarly survey of the rise of Achaemenid Persia and the condition of its main provinces.

Cook, J. M. *The Persian Empire.* 1983. A clear and readable introduction, updating Olmstead's book (see below) in the light of recent archaeological discoveries, particularly inscriptions.

Gershevitch, I., ed. *The Cambridge History of Iran.* Vol. 2, *The Median and Achaemenid Periods.* 1985. Contains detailed and scholarly chapters on, among other subjects, the rise of the Achaemenids, Cyrus, the Medes, sources of evidence, art, architecture, and religion.

Olmstead, A. T. *History of the Persian Empire.* 1948. Out of date in some of its findings but still an ambitious narrative history. The prose style is majestic.

Strauss, Barry, and Josiah Ober. *The Anatomy of Error: Ancient Military Disasters and Their Lessons for Modern Strategists.* 1990. An analysis of eight case studies from the ancient world. Several chapters (especially Chapters 1 and 4) discuss Achaemenid Persia.

Early Greece

Barber, R. L. N. *The Cyclades in the Bronze Age.* 1987. A thorough survey of the archaeological evidence.

Beye, C. R. *Ancient Greek Literature and Society.* 2d ed. Chapters 2 and 3 offer a good, brief introduction to Homer.

Chadwick, John. *The Mycenaean World.* 1976. A well-illustrated overview of Greek society around 1400 to 1200 B.C. emphasizing the evidence of Linear B texts. The author was one of the original decipherers of those texts.

Coldstream, N. *Geometric Greece.* 1977. A close examination of the art and archaeology of the period from roughly 900 to 700 B.C.

Desborough, V. *The Greek Dark Ages.* 1972. A thorough and detailed survey of the archaeological evidence for the period between approximately 1125 and 900 B.C.

Drews, R. *The Coming of the Greeks: Indo-European Conquests in the Aegean and the Near East.* 1988. A good introduction to a complex subject, although the author's argument that the Greeks arrived in Greece by invasion around 1600 B.C. does not close the case.

Finley, M. I. *The World of Odysseus.* Rev. ed. 1978. Essential introductory reading on the historicity, society, and ideology of the Homeric poems.

Graham, J. Walter. *The Palaces of Crete.* Rev. ed. 1986. A detailed analysis of the sites of Minoan Crete, with an emphasis on architecture. Well illustrated with a good comparative discussion of Egypt and western Asia.

Griffin, Jasper. *Homer on Life and Death.* 1980. Discusses religion in the epics, with particular attention to Homer's relationship to the literatures of Egypt and western Asia.

Hurwit, J. *Art and Culture of Early Greece, 1100–480 B.C.* 1985. The first two chapters offer a fascinating study of the light that vase-painting and Homeric poetry throw on each other and on early Greek culture.

Myers, J. W., E. E. Myers, and G. Cadogan. *The Aerial Atlas of Ancient Crete.* 1992. A well-illustrated introduction to the ancient sites, with a guide to earlier scholarship.

Starr, Chester. *The Origins of Greek Civilization, 1100–650 B.C.* 1961. Though out of date on some points, the book continues to offer a valuable overview, including a provocative discussion of the cultural significance of early Greek vase-painting.

Taylour, Lord William. *The Mycenaeans.* Rev. ed. 1983. A well-illustrated discussion of pottery and chronology, written sources, religion, architecture, art, daily life, war and trade, and the rise and fall of the Mycenaeans.

Traill, David A. *Schliemann of Troy: Treasure and Deceit.* 1995. A lively, readable discussion of Schliemann's pioneering but sometimes suspect methods of archaeology.

Vermeule, Emily. *Greece in the Bronze Age.* 1964, new preface 1972. Though written before some important excavations and discoveries of the past thirty years, this is still the best and most thorough overview of Greece from the beginnings to around 1100 B.C.

THE TROJAN WAR

It is one of the best-known events of antiquity. It is commemorated in works ranging from the *Iliad* and *Odyssey* of Homer to television documentaries. It is recalled in stone, in the ruins of Troy in northwestern Anatolia (see Map 2.3)—one of the most important sites in Mediterranean archaeology. Yet the Trojan War is still mysterious. We are unsure not only when or why it happened but whether it happened at all.

According to Homer, Troy was a prosperous and fortified city ruled by a king, Priam, and engaged in a war against a coalition of warriors from mainland Greece. Ten years of hard fighting ended in the sack and destruction of the city, a scene etched in the Greek imagination. Look at this vase painting, a work from about 490 B.C. by an Athenian artist known today as the Brygos painter. It is a detail of a larger illustration of the sack of Troy. Over a fallen, wounded Trojan man stands a Greek warrior, his sword ready to deliver the death blow. To the Greek's right, a Trojan woman, her hair disheveled, is running away.

The ancients had few doubts about the reality of such scenes or about the actual existence of Troy. Alexander the Great, for instance, in 334 B.C. visited the Greek polis of Troy, which claimed to sit on the site of Priam's city. The Greek scholar Eratosthenes (active 225 B.C.) dated the Trojan War to 1184–1183 B.C. By modern times, however, the city had disappeared, and the Trojan War was considered to be merely the stuff of legend.

Then, in 1829, a 7-year-old German boy received a history book from his father with a picture of Troy in flames. He conceived the lifelong conviction that the Trojan War was a genuine historical fact. Eventually he decided that his mission was to prove it true. By then an adult and a wealthy businessman, he fulfilled his ambition by excavating in Anatolia beginning in 1871. His name was Heinrich Schliemann.

A colorful and stormy man, Schliemann (1822–1890) was to be one of the founders of modern archaeology. Troy, he believed, was located within a large man-made mound about three miles from the Hellespont and about four miles from the Aegean Sea. There, he and several successors excavated. Few scholars doubt that Schliemann discovered Troy. The case of the Trojan War, however, is not so easily settled.

For one thing, the excavators discovered nine principal levels of occupation at the site, dating from approximately 3000 B.C. to around A.D. 500.

Troy VIIA, House
(Courtesy Archives & Rare Books Department, University of Cincinnati)

Sack of Troy (detail), Brygos Painter, ca. 490 B.C. *(Erich Lessing/Art Resource, NY)*

Most archaeologists assign Priam's Troy to the level known as Troy VIIA. This level was destroyed sometime between 1250 and 1225 B.C., which accords with chronological hints in the *Iliad* of a Late Mycenaean context. Also, Troy VIIA was destroyed by fire, which is consistent with a sack by Greek armies. But questions remain: Was the fire caused by war? Did the war last ten years? We have no way of knowing.

Troy VIIA was not the grand city of the *Iliad* but a relatively small and unimpressive place with simple architecture and few signs of luxuries. Look at the photograph of a house in Troy VIIA, one of numerous structures crowded into the space inside the walls. They indicate an impoverished population, perhaps under siege—at least that is what American scholars who excavated at Troy in the 1930s thought. Look at the jars sunk into the floor of the house. The excavators argued that they provided storage for supplies during wartime. Crowded housing and sunken jars are found at other ancient sites, however, and are not proof of war.

Yet few scholars are willing to leave the matter on so uncertain a note. Some historians have pointed out, for example, that Troy VIIA represents a rebuilding of Troy VI after an earthquake and fire. Troy VI seems to have been a large and impressive city. If war destroyed Troy VIIA, perhaps that war began a generation or two earlier, in the heyday of Troy VI—a theory that might explain why Homer describes Troy as being large and splendid. Another theory stems from an archaeo-logical survey in 1992, which found evidence that Troy VIIA was a much bigger city than earlier archaeologists had thought. What they had considered the city wall seems to have enclosed only the acropolis. The outer perimeter of the city was another 1300 feet farther away.

There is much archaeological evidence of Mycenaean Greek trade and settlement in western Anatolia, including Mycenaean pottery at Troy. Perhaps the Greeks did fight a war there, though perhaps the prize was Trojan booty rather than Helen, the kidnapped wife of the Greek king Menelaus. Troy's location might have allowed it to dominate maritime trade. Perhaps the destruction of Troy VIIA was one of countless similar destructions around the eastern Mediterranean in the era of the Sea Peoples (see page 00).

Scholars from other fields are also examining the question. Geologists and hydrologists (students of water and its underground sources) are surveying the Trojan plain to consider the accuracy of Homer's geographic references. Hittite experts point to references in a text from around 1400 B.C. to places called Taruisa and Wilusiya and to a man named Alaksandus—perhaps to be identified as Troy, Ilion (a variant name for Troy), and Alexander (a Trojan prince) and to be taken as suggesting an earlier date for the war.

The facts of the Trojan War are still unverified. We *can* say, though, that as long as Homer's poems survive, the Trojan War will continue to fascinate and intrigue us. ❧

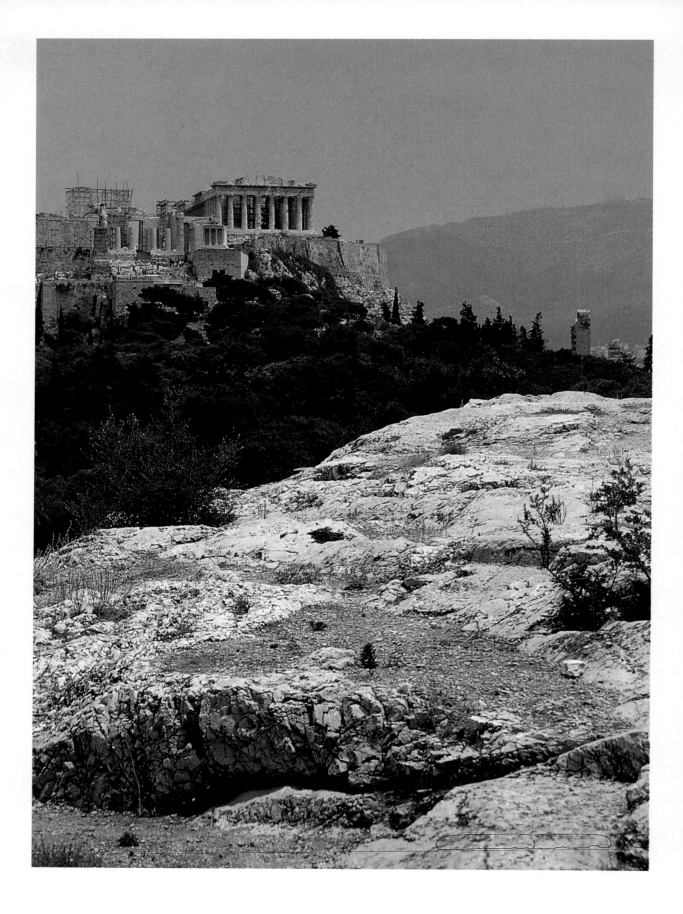

CHAPTER 3

The Age of the Polis: Greece, ca. 750–350 B.C.

I t is dawn. The light reveals a hillside in the city of Athens: a natural auditorium. Its rocky slopes, visible in the photo opposite, would have been covered, in the mid-first millennium B.C., with wooden benches facing a platform cut into the rock. The six thousand men gathered there constitute a heterogeneous group, ranging from farmers to philosophers, from dockyard workers to aristocrats. As they take their seats, these, the citizens of Athens, watch priests conducting prayers and a sacrifice. Then, all eyes turn to the individual who mounts the platform— a herald. His booming voice asks the question that marks the start of business: "Who wishes to speak?" And someone rises to address the assembly. It is the first democracy in history—and this is the central laboratory in this great experiment in participation.

The assembly meeting encapsulates the defining features of what was, in its era, the characteristic political institution in much of Greece: the *polis* (plural, *poleis*). Usually translated as "city-state," the polis is better understood as "citizen-state." The polis was the product of communal activities, whether in the assembly or the military or the theater, undertaken by its members—its citizens. Not every polis was a democracy, to be sure, but every polis emphasized cooperative activities whose participants enjoyed at least a measure of equality. Every polis also sought a balance between the group and the individual, be he the man on the speaker's platform or a military hero or a freethinker.

Balance is a difficult state to achieve, however, and the history of the polis is frequently one of tension and exclusion. Paradox marked the polis. Greek democracy, for example, failed to grant equal rights to women,

Athenian Acropolis, with Pnyx Hill in foreground.

THRACE

Byzantium•

Sea of Marmara

ANATOLIA

Hellespont

Troy•

Lesbos

Chios

LYDIA

Hermus

Sardis•

Smyrna•

IONIA

Ephesus•

Maeander

Miletus•

Mycale
479 B.C. ⚔

Halicarnassus•

Cos

Rhodes

Samos

Aegean Sea

Lemnos

Andros

Naxos

Paros

CYCLADES

Delos ⛩

Sea of Crete

Melos

Cythera

Knossos•

Crete

Gortyn•

Amphipolis•

CHALCIDICE

Potidaea•

▲Mt. Ossa

▲Mt. Pelion

Strymon

Axius

MACEDONIA

Pella•

▲Mt. Olympus

THESSALY

Peneus

PINDUS MTS.

AETOLIA

Thasos

Artemisium ⚔
480 B.C.

Thermopylae ⚔
480 B.C.

▲Mt. Parnassus
Delphi ⛩
▲Mt. Helicon
Chaeronea•
Leuctra•
BOEOTIA
Thebes•
Plataea•
479 B.C. ⚔

Euboea
Chalcis•
Eretria•

Mt. Parnes
Eleusis ⛩ ⚔ Marathon
Athens• 490 B.C.
Megara•   ATTICA
479 B.C. ⚔
Salamis 480 B.C.
Aegina

Saronic
Gulf

Gulf of Corinth

Sicyon•
Corinth•
Nemea•
Mycenae•
Argos•

ACHAEA

Elis•

ELIS

Olympia ⛩

ARCADIA

Mantinea•
Tegea•

PELOPONNESUS

▲Mt. Ithome

MESSENIA

Pylos•

Sparta•

TAYGETOS MTS.

LACONIA

ACARNANIA

Ithaca

EPIRUS
Dodona ⛩

Corcyra

Achelous

Ionian
Sea

Mediterranean Sea

Ancient Greece
Major battles of
the Persian Wars ✗
Mountains ▲
Sanctuaries ⛩

0   50   100 Km.
0   50   100 Mi.

immigrants, or slaves. Relations among poleis were less often a matter of cooperation than of war. Although the Greeks created magnificent religious architecture, a portion of their intellectual elite came to the conclusion that the gods were of little importance in explaining the universe. Although one leading polis, Sparta, was a paragon of militarism, obedience, and austerity, scorning the life of the mind, another, Athens, prided itself on freedom and cultural attainments. Yet the Greeks made the most even of such tensions, exploring them in literary genres—tragedy, comedy, history, and philosophy—that focused on the polis as a central theme. Creative tensions also marked Greek achievements in sculpture, painting, and architecture.

The era of the polis proved to be a defining moment in Western history. Although the Greeks of this era borrowed much from neighboring cultures, they were remarkably original. In the mid-first millennium B.C., while the monotheistic religious heritage of the West was first crystallizing in Israel, its philosophical and political heritage was first crystallizing in Greece.

SOCIETY AND POLITICS IN ARCHAIC GREECE, ca. 750–500 B.C.

Historians usually call the era in Greek history from roughly 750 to 500 B.C. the "Archaic period." In this context *archaic* refers to the style of sculpture in the two centuries before the "Classical period" (480–323 B.C.). Archaic Greece was a patchwork of hundreds of separate city-states, tribal leagues, and monarchies (Map 3.1). Nevertheless, it displayed a distinctive style and outlook not only in art but also in politics, military arrangements, technology, economics, literature, and religion.

The Archaic period was an era of paradoxes: the simultaneous growth of individualism and a tight community spirit, the emergence of social cohesion despite a continual state of war, the coexistence of deep religious piety and the West's first

Map 3.1 Archaic and Classical Greece The region of the Aegean Sea was the heartland of Greek civilization around 750–350 B.C. The mountainous terrain, rugged coastline, and large number of islands encouraged political fragmentation.

SOCIETY AND POLITICS IN ARCHAIC GREECE

ca. 750 B.C.	Greek colonization of Magna Graecia begins
ca. 725 B.C.	Sparta conquers Messenia
ca. 675 B.C.	Pheidon becomes tyrant of Argos
594 B.C.	Solon is archon in Athens
ca. 560 B.C.	Peisistratus becomes tyrant of Athens
508 B.C.	Cleisthenes begins reforms in Athens

nontheistic philosophy. The Archaic period was also the point of origin of now-familiar types of governmental regimes—tyranny, oligarchy, and the first steps toward democracy—and of fundamental notions of citizenship and the rule of law.

Eighth-Century B.C. Revival and Expansion

An observer of ninth-century B.C. Greece would not have predicted the great achievements that would arise from this poor, illiterate society of small settlements and low-level trade. Yet everything began to change in the eighth century. Peace contributed to a sharp population rise, and the economy shifted from herding to farming, a more efficient source of food.

Greek commerce, too, was expanding. Shortly before 800 B.C., men from the Greek island of Euboea, perhaps following the example of Phoenician merchants and seafarers who had been casual traders in Greece for a century (see page 48), established a trading post in Syria, at Al-Mina on the mouth of the Orontes River (near the modern border between Turkey and Syria; see Map 3.2). Al-Mina, at the terminus of the chief caravan route from Mesopotamia, was to become the major center of Greek trade with the east for two hundred years. Within a generation, by 775 B.C., Euboeans also established a settlement in the west, on the Bay of Naples in Italy. In both east and west, Greek merchants sought iron and luxury goods; what they offered in return was probably silver (of which ancient Greece had rich deposits) and slaves.

From establishing trading posts for commercial purposes, it was but a short step to founding colonies that siphoned off the extra mouths created by population growth. In colonization as in trade the Greeks may have followed the example of the Phoenicians, who had begun establishing colonies probably in the ninth century B.C. Between about 750 and 500 B.C., the Greeks founded colonies throughout the Mediterranean and the Black Sea, establishing nearly as many cities as already existed in Greece (Map 3.2). Colonization in Italy and Sicily began in earnest around 750 B.C., in the Chalcidice in the northeast Aegean perhaps a generation later, in the Sea of Marmara about 680, in North Africa around 630, and in the Black Sea about 610. In the far west, Massalia (modern Marseille) was established about 600. Southern Italy and Sicily, whose climate and landscape recalled the Aegean, were especially intense areas of Greek settlement, so much so that the Romans later called the region *Magna Graecia* ("Great Greece"). In the long run, Greek colonization proved to be of great importance for the spread of urban civilization westward, especially into Italy.

Motives for colonization ranged from wanderlust to profit seeking, but the main motive was land hunger. The typical colonist was young; the typical colony was small, consisting of a few hundred settlers. Colonists had to be prepared to fight, for colonies were frequently planted on land belonging to natives. Greek attitudes toward native peoples were complex. Though convinced of their own superiority, the Greeks were happy to trade and intermarry with natives once they had killed or enslaved some and carved out a colony on their land. It is usually assumed that most Greek colonists were male; if so, then the rate of Greek intermarriage with native females must have been high.

Trade and colonization inspired change at home. They made increasing numbers of Greeks into seafarers. This was a critical development, for as the historian Thucydides (ca. 455–ca. 399 B.C.) argues, a sea power tends to be more dynamic and innovative than a land power. Seafarers tend to come into contact with new ideas and institutions. In antiquity, ships moved more quickly and cheaply than land transport; thus, seapower tended to accelerate the rate of change.

One important consequence of foreign contact was the introduction to Greece of the alphabet, borrowed from the Phoenicians (who had adapted the Ugaritic alphabet; see page 48). The first datable examples of the Greek alphabet were inscribed on pots in about 750 B.C. The alphabet spread rapidly and widely in the next century. Literacy underlay the achievements in poetry, philosophy, and the law that Archaic Greece has left behind. We must remember, however, how few people at the time could read and write well. Ancient Greek culture remained primarily oral culture.

Demographic, social, cultural, and economic changes eventually led to political changes. Around 700 B.C. the *basileis*, the elite of landowning families, still held the upper hand over the *demos*, or ordinary people. Hesiod, in his poem *Works and Days*, calls them "gift-eating basileis," an indication of the bribes they demanded in return for protection or justice. Yet Hesiod also witnesses the growing size and prosperity of the class of free farmers. In the changing society of Greece around 700 B.C., such men were poised to break the power of the basileis.

Emergence of the Polis

What made the Greek city-state unique was social cohesion, military technology and formations, and above all, the practice and ideology of citizenship. *Polis* came to denote not just a city but the community as a whole, corresponding roughly to a country or nation. One crude gauge of the centrality of the polis is the words the Greeks derived from it: among them, *polites* (citizen), *politeia* (constitution), *politeô* (to govern), *ta politika* (politics), and *politikos* (politician).

Historians continue to debate the date of the emergence of the polis. In considering this question, one must distinguish between the physical and the ideological community. In physical terms, the polis existed as early as the ninth or even the tenth century B.C. The intense communal ideology of the polis, however, did not emerge until around 700 B.C.

Most poleis were small, many less than a hundred square miles in size. Athens was one of the largest. Its territory, known as Attica (see Map 3.3), covered a thousand square miles (approximately the size of the state of Rhode Island). It included many villages that had once been autonomous but had come under the authority of the city of Athens, perhaps around 800 B.C. At its

Map 3.2 Phoenician and Greek Colonization Both the Phoenicians (beginning perhaps after 900 B.C.) and the Greeks (beginning around 750 B.C.) established numerous colonies on the coasts of the Mediterranean and Black Seas.

height (ca. 430 B.C.) the population of Athens was about 400,000 (a typical polis contained between 5000 and 10,000 people). The philosopher Aristotle (384–322 B.C.) wrote that an ideal polis should be small enough that the citizens know one another personally.

The polis consisted of two parts: the urban area, which usually was tiny, and the surrounding countryside, where most people lived. From the earliest times, the urban public space included both a defensible hill (preferably with a water supply), called a "high city" (*acropolis*), and a "gathering place" (*agora*) used as a marketplace and for meetings. There was usually at least one temple. After around 500 B.C. stone buildings, including council houses, theaters, covered porticoes, gymnasia, and baths, became increasingly common.

What distinguished the early polis, however, was not its buildings but its ideology. As the poet Alcaeus (b. ca. 630 B.C.) puts it, "Not houses finely roofed or the stones of walls well-built, nay nor canals and dockyards, make the polis, but

men able to use their opportunity." The cultural and political framework of the polis was in large part the result of a military improvement: the hoplite phalanx.

The Hoplite Phalanx and the Community

The hoplite phalanx was a tightly ordered unit of heavily armed, pike-bearing infantrymen. The phalanx not only became the dominant military force in Archaic Greece, but, with relatively few changes in equipment and tactics, it remained supreme on land in Greece, western Asia, and other Mediterranean regions until its defeat by a Roman army in 197 B.C. Yet in spite of its importance, the phalanx is an enigma. Questions abound—above all, why men should fight in so uncomfortable and unsophisticated a manner, tightly massed in heavy armor that suited neither Greece's Mediterranean climate nor its mountainous terrain. The key may lie as much in social and cultural history as in military history.

Hoplites A detail from a Corinthian vase of 625–600 B.C. shows pike-wielding hoplites closed in battle over a fallen comrade. In this image as elsewhere, Greek artists rendered warriors seminude and fighting in small groups, but in reality hoplites went into battle wearing heavy armor and fought in large units. *(Louvre © R. M. N.)*

The phalanx emerged through a process of evolution rather than in a revolutionary leap. Before 800 B.C., single combat among the basileis appears to have decided battles. Around 800–750 B.C., armies began to include more men, fighting in close formation. Around 700 B.C., changes in society and technology improved armaments and allowed even more men than before to be able to afford to buy them: The result was the phalanx. The heavily armed infantryman (hoplite) of the fighting unit (phalanx) wore bronze armor on his shins and chest and a bronze helmet with only a narrow opening for eyes and mouth. He carried a heavy wooden shield rimmed with bronze, holding it in his left hand. His weapons were a pike—a heavy wooden thrusting spear with iron tip, at least nine feet long—and a short, iron stabbing sword.

An individual hoplite could accomplish little, but when he fought in a phalanx, he was formidable. The men of the phalanx were arranged in close ranks, normally four to eight deep. Soldiers stood together in line, each man's shield overlapping his neighbor's. Hoplite battles were set battles: head-to-head, army against army, all-or-nothing affairs, rather than individual skirmishes or guerrilla raids.

Too unwieldy for Greece's mountains, the phalanx fought only in the plains. Battle usually consisted of an initial charge, followed by a grueling contest. The men in the front line pounded the enemy with their pikes while the men in the rear pushed forward. Finally one side would give way. Most of the defeated would escape by running away. The winning phalanx would stake its claim to the field by erecting a trophy. By increasing the pool of warriors, the phalanx made warfare more common. For centuries, hoplite battle was virtually an annual occurrence in Greece. War became a way of life.

Aretê, now lamely translated as "excellence" or "virtue" but originally meaning "warrior prowess," was a central concept for the Greeks. In Homer, a warrior fought mainly for personal and familial honor (see page 70). By around 650 B.C., aretê referred also to the community. According to the poet Tyrtaeus (ca. 650 B.C.), the ideal soldier not only fights bravely but "heartens his neighbor by his words." Should he die, his death brings glory not only to his father but also to his city and his countrymen. Although the battlefield remained the favored arena for displays of aretê, the assembly or the council house became increasingly acceptable as an alternative.

Aretê inspired both competition and community. The Greeks came to call the polis a "common thing" (*koinon*). It was a commonwealth. It belonged to its people, not to a few nobles or to a king or a god. As early as about 700 B.C., important public documents were inscribed on stone. Acts of state are attributed not to a personified polis but to the community—for example, not to Thera but to "the Thereans," not to Sybaris but to "the Sybarites." The emphasis is on the plurality.

Hoplites were amateur soldiers. Most were full-time farmers outside of the fighting season, which lasted only for the summer months. The notion of the farmer-soldier, important in later political theory, had an immediate, practical effect: Those who fought for society soon demanded a say in governing it.

Tyranny in the Polis

The first political development in the wake of the hoplite phalanx was not democracy, however, but tyranny. *Tyrant,* a term borrowed from the East, possibly from Lydia (a wealthy kingdom in Anatolia), originally referred not to an arbitrary and oppressive ruler but rather to a champion of the people. Having overthrown a narrow and entrenched aristocracy, tyrants were popular at first. *Tyrant* did not become a pejorative word before roughly 550 B.C., when the people soured on the second and third generation of tyrants.

Greek tyranny began in Argos, a polis in the northeastern Peloponnesus, around 675 B.C. (see Map 3.1). The first tyrant was an Argive named Pheidon. By 660 tyranny had spread to nearby Corinth. Over the course of the seventh and sixth centuries B.C., all the major Greek poleis except Sparta became tyrannies.

Sources of evidence for the first tyrannies are poor. How and why the tyrants came to power, whom they represented, and what their historical significance is, are all much-debated questions. The most convincing explanation connects tyranny to the phalanx. At the introduction of the phalanx, most poleis were ruled by the basileis, grown arrogant during their long tenure of power. Hoplites resented their exclusion from office, and once they bore arms, they were in a position to act.

In the seventh century B.C., therefore, men who had been denied political power rose on the shoulders of the hoplites and overthrew a narrow elite. They set up one-man rule, but they did so in the name of a group much broader than the basileis: the prosperous farmers who fought in the phalanx.

Much of what the tyrants did, especially in the first generation, was popular and progressive. They stimulated the economy by founding colonies on trade routes, standardizing weights and measures, and encouraging the immigration of skilled craftsmen from other poleis. Corinth under the tyrant Cypselus (r. ca. 657–625 B.C.), for example, became the wealthiest city in Greece by exporting agricultural produce. Tyrants built temples and instituted festivals, providing both jobs and leisure-time activities.

When tyrants passed power on to their sons, however, the second generation tended to rule oppressively. Buoyed by the discontent of the demos, the basileis regrouped and tried to take back power. Thraysbulus of Miletus (ca. 600 B.C.), one second-generation tyrant, advised accordingly: To maintain power, a tyrant should "lop off the tallest ears of grain"—that is, execute or exile aristocrats in order to deny leaders to the opposition. But the tide of discontent was not to be stopped. Few tyrannies lasted beyond the third generation, when they were overthrown and replaced by oligarchy (literally, "rule by the few") or, less often, by democracy (literally, "power of the people"). By 500 B.C. tyranny had disappeared from most of Greece.

Sparta

Located in Laconia, a fertile valley in the south-central Peloponnesus, in the southern part of mainland Greece, Sparta seemed destined by geography for prosperity but not for glory. It was situated not at a crossroads or beside a great harbor but rather by rugged, isolating mountains (see Map 3.1). Yet Sparta proved to be an influential model of citizenship and constitutionalism, virtue and community, austerity and militarism.

The history of Sparta is not easy to write. Sparta was a closed, military society, contemptuous of book learning, suspicious of foreigners, and secretive toward the outside world. Careful scholarship has lifted the veil, however. For example, Spartans believed that their unique system had been created at one stroke, by the legendary law-giver Lycurgus, who is supposed to have lived (according to the most common version) in the eighth century B.C. and whose charter for Sparta was a divine command. Nowadays, scholars argue for gradual innovations in Sparta rather than revolutionary change, for a process beginning around 650 B.C. and continuing for generations. And it is by no means clear that there ever was a Lycurgus. Let us consider the question of origins.

The foundations of Spartan society were laid around 650 B.C., when a three-part class system emerged. Helots, unfree laborers who worked the land for their masters, were at the lowest level. *Perioikoi* (roughly, "neighbors"), who were free and locally autonomous but subordinate to the highest class, were above the helots. Similars, males who monopolized political power and were the only full citizens were above the perioikoi. We do not know the number of helots, but we do know that they vastly outnumbered the other two classes. When the system began around 650 B.C., there were about nine thousand Similars. Each Similar had the right, after reaching age 30, to attend a legislative and deliberative assembly and to hold public office. Each, moreover, was given a minimum land allotment that was worked by helots, thereby freeing the Similar to fight. As the name implies, Similars were alike but not equal. Wealthy Similars owned more land than the minimum allotment.

Although Sparta is remembered as a conservative society, the idea of sharing power among some nine thousand Similars was radical in its day. In contrast to tyranny or to the rule of the basileis, the nine thousand Spartan Similars shared a measure of equality. What gave them the clout and prestige to do so? Undoubtedly, the Similars were hoplites, the backbone of Sparta's army.

In the mid-seventh century B.C., Sparta was even more dependent on its army than was the average polis: The reason is the helots. Most helots were Messenians, whose fertile territory had been conquered by Sparta in about 725 B.C. Although the Messenians were Greeks, they were forced to labor for the conquerors. Sparta profited, but it now faced a security problem. The restive Messenian helots had to be policed, and a dramatic revolt sometime between 675 and 650 B.C. almost succeeded in expelling the Spartans. To keep Messenia, Sparta needed a crack army; to get that, Sparta

needed to train, nourish, and glorify its soldiers. The political and economic result was to make all Spartan hoplites into Similars.

Sparta was no democracy, however. The ancients classified the Spartan government as "mixed" because it combined elements of monarchy, rule by an elite few, and popular government. The assembly of Similars constituted the popular element in the regime, but its powers were limited. Ordinary Similars, for instance, were not encouraged to speak, and voting was conducted by shouting, a far more subjective measure than the show of hands used in the democratic assembly of Athens. Real power was shared among the kings, elders, and ephors (overseers), men generally belonging to a few wealthy families. The two kings (why two is unclear) were less monarchs than commanders of the army and chief priests. A Council of Elders (twenty-eight men plus the kings, for a total of thirty) and a board of five ephors represented the elite few. The assembly approved laws, but only after prior approval by the Council of Elders; only an ephor could propose a law. In reality, Sparta was an oligarchy, ruled by a few powerful men.

The oligarchs did not lead lives of luxury, however, at least not after around 550 B.C., when austerity became the order of the day. Society was re-ordered to ensure discipline, obedience, preparedness, and loyalty: the qualities needed to maintain control of the helots. For example, Spartans' diet was famous for its simplicity. The preferred food was a black broth of pork cooked in its own blood and spiced with salt and vinegar. To discourage consumption, Sparta issued no coins; the official "currency" consisted of heavy and unwieldy iron skewers. Since the outside world was considered corrupt, Sparta engaged in little trade and admitted few foreigners to its territory—and they were subject to periodic expulsion.

Other poleis offered little or no formal public education, but Sparta schooled its sons from childhood to be soldiers: a system known as the *agoge* ("upbringing"). Limited to male Similars, the agoge created a life cycle unique in Greece. At birth, babies were examined by public inspectors. Those who were considered deformed or unfit were "exposed"—that is, abandoned without food or shelter. The victims might die, but they might also be sold into slavery or even secretly adopted. (Other Greeks also practiced exposure of infants but left the matter up to private families.) Surviving children were raised at home up to the age of 7, at which point boys left the family to be boarded with a "herd" of their age mates. Girls did not leave home for barracks. Unlike most Greek girls, they received a public education—limited, however, to physical training, which was thought to strengthen females for childbearing. For the eleven years from age 7 to age 18, a boy went through the rigorous training of the agoge. On the theory that good soldiers should be strong and silent, boys learned only enough reading and writing for practical ends—for example, for messages to or from military headquarters.

Many boys between the ages of 18 and 20 served in the *krypteia* (secret service), an institution that combined the common Greek practice of initiatory service for young warriors with Sparta's security needs. Boys in the krypteia lived in the hills of Messenia, where they survived by hunting, foraging, and stealing. They spied on the ever-rebellious Messenian helots, whom they could kill with impunity because every year the Spartan state declared war on them. By age 20, all Similars had become hoplites, and they continued to serve in the army until age 60. Supported by helot labor, they devoted full time to fighting and training the next generation.

Men married around age 30, women around 20. Newlyweds were supposed to spend only enough time together to produce offspring. Spartan women were relatively more independent than women elsewhere in Greece. Often neglected by their husbands, and having been schooled to assertiveness by youthful physical training outdoors, Spartan women also had the advantage of being able to inherit property, unlike Athenian women. (See the box, "Spartan Women.")

The aims of the agoge were limited, and it achieved them. Other Greek hoplites were amateurs. Spartan soldiers, in contrast, were effective professionals, dominating land warfare in Greece for several hundred years. Unlike most of the other poleis, Sparta had no walls; the inhabitants claimed that Spartan men were all the defense that was necessary.

Beginning around 550 B.C., Sparta used its military might to build up a network of alliances (dubbed the "Peloponnesian League" by scholars) in the Peloponnesus and central Greece. It may seem paradoxical that a xenophobic society like Sparta became the *hegemon* (literally, "leader") of

an extensive alliance system, but in fact Sparta's fear of foreigners may account for its hegemony. Sparta intervened in the wider world only to prevent threats from arising on the horizon. It used its power abroad when need be, but usually only after cautious debate.

By around 500 B.C., all of the Peloponnesian poleis except Argos had alliances with Sparta, and Thebes came aboard shortly afterward. Allies swore "to follow Sparta wherever it may lead and to have the same friends and enemies." Sparta dominated most of the allies, but Corinth and Thebes, both military and economic powers in their own right, often engaged in independent policies. Until its breakup in the aftermath of the Peloponnesian War (431–404 B.C.; see page 103), the Peloponnesian League was the dominant land

Spartan Woman This bronze statuette (4¾ inches tall) from Laconia (ca. 530 B.C.) shows a woman running. Unlike other Greek women, elite Spartan women underwent physical education. Although personal freedom was limited in Sparta, women suffered fewer restrictions than their counterparts in democratic Athens did. *(National Archaeological Museum, Athens/TAP Service)*

Spartan Women

Spartan women were famous in antiquity for their remarkable freedom, but male observers differed as to whether the results were good or bad. In the following excerpts, Aristotle (384–322 B.C.) criticizes Spartan women while Plutarch (ca. A.D. 50–120), a Greek scholar living in the Roman Empire, praises them.

(a) Aristotle

. . . the legislator [Lycurgus] wished the city as a whole to be hardy, and this is manifest in terms of the men; but he thoroughly neglected it in the case of the women, who live licentiously in every respect and in luxury. Wealth will necessarily be honored in a regime of this sort, particularly if they are dominated by women, as is the case of most stocks that are fond of soldiering and war. . . . This was the case with the Spartans, and many matters were administered by the women during the period of their [imperial] rule [405–371 B.C.]. And yet what difference is there between women ruling and rulers who are ruled by women? For the result is the same. . . .

Now this laxness concerning women appears to have arisen among the Spartans in a way that is quite reasonable. They spent much time away from their own land when they were at war. . . . As for the women, they say Lycurgus attempted to lead them toward the laws, but they were resistant, and he gave it up. . . . That what is connected with the women is not finely handled would seem not only to create an inappropriateness in the regime in its own terms, as was said earlier, but to contribute to their greed. For next to what has just been said, one must censure what pertains to the disparity in possessions. For it has happened that some of them possess too much property, and others very little; hence the territory has come into the hands of a few. . . . Indeed, nearly two-fifths of the entire territory belongs to women, both because many have become heiresses and because large dowries are given.

(b) Plutarch

Aristotle claims wrongly that he [Lycurgus] tried to discipline the women but gave up when he could not control the considerable degree of license and power attained by women because of their husbands' frequent campaigning. . . . Lycurgus rather showed all possible concern for . . . [women] too. First he toughened the girls physically by making them run and wrestle and throw the discus and javelin. Thereby their children in embryo would make a strong start in strong bodies and would develop better, while the women themselves would also bear their pregnancies with vigour and would meet the challenge of childbirth in a successful, relaxed

way. He did away with prudery, sheltered upbringing and effeminacy of any kind. He made young girls no less than young men grow used to walking nude in processions, as well as to dancing and singing at certain festivals with the young men present and looking on. . . .

There was nothing disreputable about the girls' nudity. It was altogether modest, and there was no hint of immorality. Instead it encouraged simple habits and an enthusiasm for physical fitness, as well as giving the female sex a taste of masculine gallantry, since it too was granted equal participation in both excellence and ambition.

Sources: Aristotle, *The Politics,* trans. Carnes Lord (Chicago: University of Chicago Press, 1984), pp. 74–75; Plutarch, "Life of Lycurgus," in Richard J. A. Talbert, trans., *Plutarch on Sparta* (Harmondsworth, England: Penguin, 1988), p. 24.

Map 3.3 Attica Mountains and plains alternate in the 1000-square-mile area of ancient Attica. The Long Walls connecting Athens and the port city of Piraeus were built around 450 B.C.

power in Greece and, after defeating Persia in 480 B.C., in the entire eastern Mediterranean.

Sparta exemplified community spirit and respect for law. The people of Sparta, as the historian Herodotus (ca. 485–ca. 425 B.C.) reports a Spartan king as saying, "are free . . . , but not entirely free; for they have a master, and that master is Law, which they fear." Sparta was also an exemplar of equality—limited equality, to be sure, but equality extended to a wider group than ever before in Greece. The notion of the Similars, moreover, contains the germ of the idea of the citizen: a free member of the political community who, unlike a subject, has rights as well as duties. Few other poleis could match the stability and sense of civic duty fostered by Sparta. In the realms of equality and citizenship, however, Sparta was eventually

outstripped by Athens. In the realm of liberty, Athens wrote a new chapter in Western history.

Early Athens

Around 650 B.C., the basileis of the Attic Plain (Map 3.3), who proudly called themselves the Eupatrids ("well-fathered men"), ruled Athens. Nine archons, or magistrates, ran the administration. Each was chosen for a one-year term, after which he became a life member of the Areopagus, a council of elders named for its meeting place on the "hill of Ares." By its prestige, this aristocratic council held the lion's share of power, both in politics and in justice, for it also served as a court. The demos met in an assembly. Probably from early times on, the assembly had, in theory, supreme lawmaking power, but voting was by shouting, and few people challenged Eupatrid wishes. Athenian society was loosely organized in various groups: "comradeships" (aristocratic clubs), neighborhood associations, burial societies, organizations arranging religious sacrifices, and four so-called tribes based on kinship or residence.

By 632 B.C. the aristocrats faced trouble in Athens as elsewhere, because of corruption, economic change, and assertive hoplites. In that year one Cylon attempted to establish a tyranny. He failed, but the forces of change kept pressing. In 621 B.C. a loose coalition opposed to Eupatrid rule forced a codification of the laws, which were then issued in writing. This Code of Draco, named for its main drafter, was famous for its harsh provisions (hence the adjective *draconian*); it was written, as a later commentator observed, "not in ink but blood." Some of its provisions can be reconstructed, but only its homicide law has survived in detail.

Yet Draco's Code seems only to have whetted an appetite for change. A wealthy non-Eupatrid elite of hoplites was emerging, grown rich exporting olive oil. Some were merchants; most were prosperous farmers. They now wanted political power. As for ordinary Athenians, they typically worked small family farms. Over the years, bad harvests and soil exhaustion had sent many into debt. Those who had pledged their land as collateral became known as *hektemoroi* ("sixth-parters"), probably because they owed one-sixth of their crop to their creditors. Other farmers sank even further into debt and had only themselves or their children as collateral. Some ended up as slaves, sometimes sold abroad.

Because both rich and poor Athenians had grievances against the Eupatrids, revolution was in the air. Enter Solon (ca. 630–ca. 560 B.C.), who was appointed to the emergency position of sole archon for one year, probably 594 B.C. A Eupatrid who had become a merchant, Solon understood both the old and the new elite, and he was sympathetic too to ordinary Athenians. As his surviving writings show, Solon was a moderate. He could

Banqueting Scene This Corinthian wine bowl (ca. 600 B.C.) depicts a mythological banquet. The men recline on couches, waited upon by the woman. Banquets and symposia (drinking parties) were among the favorite recreations of Greek aristocrats. *(Louvre © Photo R.M.N.)*

have become tyrant, but he preferred to be a mediator; as such, he said, he "stood with a strong shield before both parties [the common people and the powerful] and allowed neither one to win an unfair victory."[1]

Solon's reforms were comprehensive, spanning both economics and politics. He helped ordinary people by the "shaking off of burdens," measures that abolished the institution of hektemorage and probably canceled some debts; he also abolished the practice of making loans on personal surety and set up a fund to redeem Athenians who had been sold into slavery abroad. Solon disappointed many poor people by refusing to confiscate and redistribute land, but by freeing the hektemoroi, Solon ensured Athens a large class of independent small farmers.

Solon's other economic reforms were aimed at encouraging Athenian trade. To foster production of olive oil, a cash crop, he restricted all other agricultural exports. He changed Athenian weights, measures, and perhaps coins to conform with the most common Greek standard. The result was a trade boom.

Solon made fundamental changes in Athenian government, too. He changed qualifications for office from birth to wealth, a boon to the non-Eupatrid elite. He established four census classes based on agricultural production. Most offices were reserved for men of property, but the poorest class, known as *thetes,* could participate in the assembly and courts. Thanks to Solon, such participation became a more valuable privilege. Solon probably established a Council of 400, which prepared the assembly's agenda. He probably also regularized council and assembly meetings and established the principle that the assembly vote be by the counting of hands, not shouting.

Solon's moderation, respect for law, and liberation of the poor and downtrodden are milestones in Greek history. Yet neither Eupatrids nor champions of the poor were satisfied with Solon's middle way. After years of conflict, around 560 B.C. advocates of radical reform established a tyranny under Peisistratus (ca. 600–528 B.C.). He and his sons held power for forty of the next fifty years.

Supported by the thetes, the Peisistratids exiled many Eupatrids and confiscated and redistributed their land. Peisistratus kept the façade of Solon's reforms while ensuring that loyal supporters held all key offices. Itinerant judges were appointed to administer justice in the villages of Attica.

A stable regime, the tyranny witnessed prosperity at home and the expansion of Athenian influence abroad. When the Persians conquered the Greek cities of western Anatolia in 547 B.C., Peisistratus welcomed refugees, thus bolstering Athenian claims to Hellenic leadership and adding skilled workers to the economy.

Peisistratus's dynasty lasted only two generations. A steadfast opponent of tyrants, Sparta deposed his son, Hippias, in 510 B.C. Athens's elites by birth and wealth were ready to establish an oligarchy, but the way was open for an unexpected development: the emergence of popular government.

THE CULTURE OF ARCHAIC GREECE

If one trend in Archaic culture was communal solidarity, as reflected in the hoplite phalanx, another was quite opposite: a growing sense of individualism. Increased prosperity and mobility (social, geographical, and political) during the Archaic period encouraged the breakdown of old ties and left some people with a sense of their uniqueness. An important manifestation of this new consciousness of the self is present in poetry and sculpture.

Archaic religion and thought, too, underwent superficially opposite trends. While monumental stone temples were being erected and international centers for divination were being built up, Greek thinkers were beginning to move away from divine and toward abstract and mechanistic explanations of the universe.

Revealing the Self: Lyric Poetry and Sculpture

Between approximately 675 and 500 B.C., the dominant Greek literary form was lyric poetry. This form consisted of short poems written in a variety of styles but sharing a willingness to experiment, sometimes by revealing private feelings, sometimes by commenting on contemporary politics (as in the poetry of Tyrtaeus). Epic poetry, by contrast, was longer, grander in theme and tone, and less personal.

Homer never speaks directly about himself, and Hesiod reveals only a few personal details. In contrast, Archilochus of Paros (ca. 700–ca. 650 B.C.), the earliest known of the lyric poets, flaunts the self. Born on the Cycladic island of Paros, Archilochus was the son, perhaps the illegitimate son, of a noble. He was a mercenary soldier (that is, he fought for pay for a foreign country) and a colonist before returning home and dying in a hoplite battle against a neighboring island. The varied subjects of Archilochus's poetry include love, travels, and war. Much of his poetry is satire, sometimes mocking and ironic, sometimes vicious and abusive. He often sets a mood of privacy. Consider, for example, a lonely mercenary described by Archilochus as using his spear to knead bread and to lean on while drinking wine. Archilochus takes an ironic and detached view of hoplite ideals, freely admitting that he once tossed away his shield to escape the battlefield: "And that shield, to hell with it! Tomorrow I'll get me another one no worse."[2]

Sappho of Lesbos (ca. 625 B.C.) is also famous as a private poet, one who composed unmatched descriptions of intimate feelings, among them love for other women. Sappho is one of the few women poets of antiquity whose work has survived—very little, unfortunately, but enough to show that she was educated, worldly, and versed in politics. Like a modern experimental poet, she uses language self-consciously. Sappho's sensuality comes through in a description of her feelings at seeing a woman whose company she wants, talking with a man: Her heart shakes, her tongue is stuck, her eyes cannot see, her skin is on fire. "I am greener than grass," Sappho writes, "I feel nearly as if I could die."[3]

Sappho discusses female sexuality, a subject that Greek elite culture, dominated by males, tended to ignore. We know little about the sexuality of Greek women or of nonelite males. Among the male elite, romantic love in Archaic and Classical Greece was homosexual love or, to be precise, pederasty ("boy love"). The ideal relationship was supposed to involve a man in his twenties and a boy in his teens. The male elite was, strictly speaking, bisexual. By age 30 a man was expected to marry and raise a family. Perhaps bisexuality prevailed among elite females as well; Sappho, for example, eventually married and had a child.

Another sign of Archaic Greece's interest in the personal is the growing attention paid to the depiction of the human body, both in painting (most of the surviving examples are painted pottery) and in sculpture. Archaic artists displayed increasing skill and sensitivity in depicting the human form. The rich marble deposits in Greek soil gave sculptors promising material; baked clay (terra cotta) and bronze were other common sculptural media.

Early Archaic marble sculpture (seventh century B.C.) was strongly influenced by the way Egyptian sculpture represented the human body. Like Egyptian statuary, early Greek sculpture tended to be formal and frontal. But over the course of the seventh and sixth centuries B.C., Greek sculptors experimented with a greater variety of poses and with increasing realism in showing musculature and motion. This realism, however, was within limits, for the favorite subject of Archaic sculptors was not ordinary people but idealized, beautiful, young people. Typical sculptural forms were the naked young man (*kouros*) and clothed young woman (*kore*), which often served as grave markers or monuments. The goal was to show people not as they were but as they might be.

Religious Faith and Practice

Civilizations came and went in Greece, but the Olympian gods survived, adapted by successive ages to fit their political and social structures. In the Archaic period, accordingly, the Olympian gods became gods of the polis.

Although the Olympians were worshiped throughout Greece, each polis had its patron deity: Apollo at Corinth, Hera at Argos and Samos, Athena at Athens and Sparta. Each polis also had its favorite heroes or demigods: Theseus, the legendary founder of Athens; Heracles (Hercules), a favorite of Dorian cities such as Sparta and Thebes. It was considered important to build a "house"—that is, a temple—for the patron god or at least for his or her statue. The first temples were built of wood; the earliest stone temple, a temple of Apollo at Corinth, was built around 550 B.C.

Temples were rectangular structures with long sides on the north and south, short sides on the east and west, a colonnade around all four sides, and a pitched roof. The columns were modeled on those of Egyptian architecture. Greek temples faced east to catch the sunlight to illuminate the interior, which consisted of two rooms: a small treasury, open to the west, and a larger main chamber, in which a statue of the deity stood. The interior decoration of the temple was simple. Outside, however, brownish-red roof tiles, painted sculpture above the colonnade and in the pediments (the area between the gables and the front and rear doorways), and terra-cotta roof ornaments created a festive and lively effect. The bare, white ruins seen today are misleading.

The emphasis on exterior rather than interior decoration in a Greek temple reflects the way the building was used. The main ceremony took place outside. A long altar stood in front of the temple and parallel to it. On feast days—and under the tyrants the number of such days was increased greatly, as a sop to the common people—temple priests would sacrifice animals (pigs, goats, lambs, and, less often, bulls) on the altar. Only the thighs would be burned for the gods. The rest of the meat would be boiled and distributed to worshipers.

As in other ancient cultures, so in Greece divination was an important element of religion. Divination was institutionalized in *oracles*, places where, it was believed, one could go to consult a god or hero for advice. The deity was thought to speak through the agency of his human servants, the priests and priestesses who tended the oracles. Of the various Greek oracles, that of Apollo at Delphi (in central Greece) became the most prestigious and respected. The utterances of Apollo of Delphi were famous among the Greeks for being ambiguous. Different people might interpret them in different ways, and Apollo could always be absolved after the fact if things did not turn out as the listener expected.

The priests of Delphi were regularly consulted by poleis wishing to establish colonies. The priests gave advice about the choice of location and the appropriate patron god or goddess, as well as helped settlers to draft new law codes for the colonies. Delphi was also active in the search for new constitutions in the old poleis of Greece. Tradition says that Sparta based its government on a pronouncement of the Delphic oracle.

Archaic thinkers pondered the theme of divine justice. In Archaic literature one sees less of the squabblings among the gods than in Homer and more of Zeus's majesty and justice. Although the wicked might seem to prosper, Zeus eventually punishes them or their descendants. "It never escapes him all the way when a man has a sinful

Athenian Kore This statue of a young woman *(kore)* exemplifies Archaic Greek sculpture's interest in the idealized human form. Note the slight smile, the carefully coiffed hair, and the elaborate clothes. Influenced by contemporary Egyptian statues, the Greek sculptors nonetheless created a new and original style. *(Robert Frerck/Odyssey Productions)*

spirit; and always, in the end, his judgment is plain," says Solon.[4]

Archaic writers delighted in portraying human emotions, but they had no confidence about the human ability to master emotions. In Archaic literature, people are weak and insignificant; their fortune is uncertain and mutable. The gods are jealous of human success. People who aim too high are guilty of *hybris*—that is, arrogance with overtones of violence and transgression. Hybris brings *nemesis*, "punishment" or "allotment." The safest course is for a person to be pious and humble.

So Archaic religion taught a humbling, even pessimistic, lesson. Yet religious teachings were not always heeded; the pages of Archaic history are full of examples of politicians, generals, athletes, merchants, and artists who aimed high and sought success with seemingly little worry. In Ionia (the territory of the Greek cities along the central western Anatolian coast), one group of Greek thinkers made a radical break with Archaic religion and invented speculative philosophy.

The Origins of Western Philosophy

Abstract, rationalistic, speculative thinking emerged in Greece during the sixth century B.C. The first developments took place in Miletus, an Ionian city (see Map 3.2). It is often said that the thinkers of Miletus (the Milesians) and their followers in other parts of Ionia invented philosophy. So they did, but we must be precise about what this means.

The Ionians were not the first to ask questions or tell stories about the nature and origins of the universe; virtually every ancient people did so. Nor did the Ionians invent science. They themselves conducted no experiments. By 600 B.C., moreover, science—including mathematics, astronomy, medicine, and engineering—had been thriving for over two thousand years in Egypt and Mesopotamia, a heritage with which the Ionians were familiar and from which they borrowed.

The real importance of the Ionians is as pioneers of rationalism. They began the movement away from anthropomorphic or divine explanations and toward an abstract and mechanistic explanation of the universe. They themselves did not make a clear distinction between reason and revelation, but they made it possible for later Greek thinkers to do so. Later Greek philosophers were rarely (if ever) atheists, but they took for granted what the Ionians labored to establish: the primacy of human reason.

The Ionians saw themselves as students of nature—*physis* (from which the word *physics* is derived). Although they also commented on morality and politics, their interest in natural phenomena is what makes the Ionians significant. In their own day, the Ionians were called "wise men" (*sophoi*); to a later generation, they were "lovers of wisdom," *philosophoi* (from which *philosopher* comes).

Thales, the first Milesian thinker, made a name for himself by successfully predicting a solar eclipse in 585 B.C. He is credited with founding Greek geometry and astronomy. Little survives of his writings or those of the other Milesians, but it is clear that he created the first general and systematic theory about the nature of the universe. According to Thales, the primary substance, the element from which all of nature was created, was water. He emphasized the mobility of water and its ability to nourish life.

A reply was not long in coming. Around 550 B.C., Anaximander of Miletus wrote the first known book of prose in Greek, expounding his own philosophy of nature. He attacked Thales for oversimplifying and for failing to do justice to the dynamism of nature. Anaximander accepted Thales' monist assumption—that there was only one primary substance—but he called the substance "the unlimited" or "the undefined" rather than water. According to Anaximander, the universe was in eternal motion, characterized by a conflict of opposites. A third Milesian, Anaximenes, replied that the primary substance might be unlimited but it was not undefined. It was air, whose properties of condensation and rarefaction symbolized the dynamic and changing nature of things.

Humble as these theories might seem today, they represent a dramatic development: an open and critical debate among thinkers, each of whom was proposing an abstract and rational model of the universe. Many scholars have speculated about the origins of this development. Why Miletus? Why the sixth century B.C.? There are no sure answers, although certain influences have been suggested. Among them are Miletus's contacts on the trade routes with sophisticated Babylon, the proximity of Ionia to non-Greek peoples and the resulting Milesian appreciation of variety and complexity, and the search for law and order in contemporary Greek political life and its extension to the philosophical plane.

Early Greek philosophy in its second generation moved to other Ionian cities and then migrated westward across the Mediterranean. Heracleitus of Ephesus (ca. 500 B.C.) proposed fire as the primary substance. Although fire was ever changing, it had an underlying coherence. According to Heracleitus, this paradox nicely symbolized the nature of the universe. He summed up the importance of change by the aphorisms "All things flow" and "You cannot step into the same river twice." The universe witnessed a constant struggle of opposites, yet an essential unity and order prevailed. To describe this order, Heracleitus used the term *logos*. This key concept of Greek philosophy is difficult to translate. Among other definitions, *logos* can mean "word," "thought," "reason," "story," or "calculation."

Heracleitus's contemporary, Pythagoras of Samos, was both a rationalist and a religious thinker. On the one hand, Pythagoras was a mathematician who discovered the numerical ratios determining the major intervals of the musical scale: that is, the range of sound between high and low. It is less certain if, as tradition has it, he discovered the so-called Pythagorean theorem—that in a right triangle the hypotenuse squared is equal to the sum of the squares of the other two sides.

On the other hand, Pythagoras believed that the purity of mathematics would improve the human soul. Just as he had imposed numerical order on the musical scale, so could philosophers understand the entire universe through number and proportion. The resulting knowledge was no mere academic exercise but a way of life. He devoted himself to "observation" or "contemplation"—to *theoria* (from which *theory* comes).

In Croton in Magna Graecia, Pythagoras founded a religious community. A strict rule of secrecy governed its members. Judging from the little reliable evidence that survives, they abstained from meat and paid much attention to ritual purity. They believed in the kinship of all living things. They also believed in the reincarnation of the human soul, though not necessarily into a human body. According to an anecdote, Pythagoras once stopped a man from beating a dog because he recognized from the barking that the dog was the reincarnation of a friend who had died.

The early Greek philosopher whose work is most fully preserved is Parmenides of Elea in Magna Graecia. Parmenides (b. ca. 515 B.C.) completely distrusted the senses. He believed that reality was a world of pure being: eternal, unchanging, and indivisible, comparable to a sphere. The change that Heracleitus had seen was, to Parmenides, a mere illusion. Parmenides, therefore, is the first Western philosopher to propose a radical difference between the world of the senses and re-

ality. This fundamental strain of Western thought would be taken up by Plato and his followers and then passed to Christianity.

To sum up, in philosophy as in so many other endeavors, the Archaic Greeks were great borrowers and even greater innovators, who left a profound mark on later ages. By the late sixth century B.C., Archaic Greece was poised on the brink of revolution that would give birth to the Classical period of Greek civilization.

CLASSICAL ATHENS

The word *democracy* comes from the Greek word *demokratia,* coined in Athens early in the fifth century B.C. *Demokratia* literally means "the power (*kratos*) of the people (*demos*)." A modern democracy is characterized by mass citizenship, elections, and representative government. Athenian demokratia, in contrast, was a direct democracy in which elections mattered less than direct participation; citizenship was narrowly restricted; women were excluded from politics; resident aliens could almost never become citizens; and citizens owned slaves and ruled an empire. Modern democracies may cover a huge territory, but Athens was only a thousand square miles in size. Modern democracies tend to emphasize individual rights. Athens, in contrast, often placed the community first. In spite of the differences, Athenian demokratia established principles that are enshrined in democracy today: freedom, equality, citizenship without property qualifications, the right of most citizens to hold public office, and the rule of law.

The Development of Demokratia, 508–321 B.C.

Tyranny often gave way to oligarchy—to government by wealthy men, both Eupatrids and non-Eupatrids. In Athens after Peisistratid rule, however, conditions were ripe for revolution. Solon had left a society of independent small farmers, while the Peisistratids had strengthened the ranks of immigrants and weakened the Eupatrids. Elite leaders nonetheless tried to establish an Athenian oligarchy. We may imagine strong popular opposition.

Ironically, a Eupatrid, a member of the Alcmeonid clan by the name of Cleisthenes (d. ca. 500 B.C.), led the revolution. Originally Cleisthenes aimed to head the oligarchy, but his rivals shut him out of power. He turned then to the demos, whose leader he became. Frightened by the assertive populace, the oligarchs called for Spartan military assistance, but to no avail: Cleisthenes rallied the people to victory. The Athenian triumph proved, in Herodotus's opinion, "that equality is an excellent thing, not in one way only but in many. For while they were under a tyranny, [Athenians] were no better at fighting than any of their neighbors, but once they were rid of tyrants they became by far the best."[5]

Cleisthenes' definition of demos was not all-inclusive. He meant mainly owners of medium-size farms, artisans, and merchants. The poorest Athenians, the thetes, were largely left out. Nevertheless, Cleisthenes laid the foundation for demokratia by establishing the principle that the demos controlled politics. The watchwords of the day were *equality* and *mixing*.

Cleisthenes undermined Eupatrid power once and for all by attacking its local bases of support. For example, he abolished the four traditional tribes and apportioned the people among ten new tribes. Immigrants or their descendants, who had been excluded from the old tribes, now joined natives in the new tribes. Every Athenian hoplite fought with fellow tribesmen in an army now divided into ten tribal units. The tribes also formed the basis of a new Council of 500 to replace Solon's Council of 400. Like the army, the council was divided into ten tribal units, each serving as a kind of executive committee for one of the ten months of the civic year. Each tribe chose its fifty councilmen, who served for annual terms.

The centerpiece of the government was the assembly, some of whose members, emboldened by the new spirit of equality, now spoke up for the first time. The new Council of 500, like the old Council of 400, prepared the assembly's agenda, but assemblymen felt free to amend it. Only the Areopagus council remained a privileged preserve.

The last and most unusual part of the Cleisthenic system was ostracism, a sort of annual *un*popularity contest that received its name from the pieces of broken pottery (*ostraka*) on which the names of victims were inscribed. The "winner" was forced into ten years of exile, although his property would not be confiscated. Ostracism was meant to protect the regime by defusing factionalism and discouraging tyrants; judging by Athens's consequent political stability, it worked.

In 508 B.C. the poorest Athenians had relatively little power in Cleisthenic government. They lacked the financial means, the political consciousness, and the self-confidence needed to engage in politics. These conditions changed by the 450s, rendering Athens a full demokratia. They changed because the oldest principle of Greek politics came to the fore: Whoever fights for the state governs it. To counter the Persian threat against Greece in the 480s (see page 101), Athens built a great navy. Athenian warships were oared ships, triremes, and the core of the rowers consisted of Athenian thetes. Just as hoplites supported new regimes in Greece after 700 B.C., so rowers supported new regimes in Greece after 500 B.C.

The Athenian government remained unchanged until 461 B.C. Then setbacks in foreign affairs under conservative leadership gave the leaders of the demos an opening for reform. Ephialtes (d. ca. 460 B.C.) and his young associate, Pericles (ca. 495–429 B.C.), turned to the last bulwark of privilege, the Areopagus. They stripped away the council's long-standing supervisory powers over the regime and redistributed those powers to the Council of 500 and the people's court. The decade of the 450s saw another innovation: payment for public service, specifically for jurors, who received a half-drachma (perhaps a half-day's wages) for a day of jury duty. Eventually other public servants also received pay. Conservatives complained bitterly, because they perceived, rightly, that state pay made political activity by poor people possible. State pay was, an Athenian said, "the glue of demokratia."

Demokratia became closely connected with Pericles, who inherited the constituency of Ephialtes after his assassination around 460 B.C. For much of the next thirty years, Pericles dominated Athenian politics. An aristocrat who respected the common people, an excellent orator who benefited from an education in philosophy, an honest and tireless worker, a war leader and a builder in peacetime, Pericles was a political giant. Under his leadership, demokratia became firmly entrenched as the government and way of life in Athens—so much so that Athenians would shortly speak of demokratia as their "ancestral constitution"

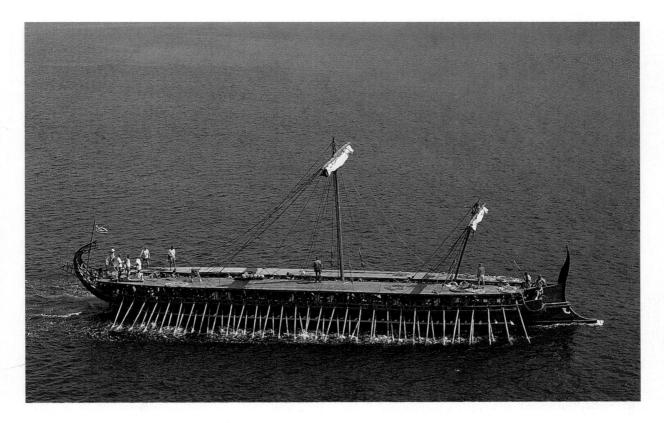

Greek Trireme The *Olympias* is a hypothetical reconstruction of an Athenian war galley of about 400 B.C. Rowed by 170 oarsmen arranged on three decks, the trireme fought by ramming an enemy ship with the bronze ram attached to its bow. *(Courtesy of the Trireme Trust)*

and modern scholars would speak of "Periclean democracy."

In truth, demokratia was neither ancestral nor limited to Pericles. Athenian democracy survived, with occasional oligarchic intrusions, for 150 years after Pericles' death. During those years it became more institutionalized and cautious, but it also became more thoroughly egalitarian.

How Demokratia Worked

Unlike most modern democracies, Athenian demokratia was direct and participatory. Pericles once claimed that in Athens "people pay attention both to their own household and to politics. Even those occupied with other activities are no less knowledgeable about politics."[6] This is part boast, but only part. Large numbers of ordinary citizens attended the assembly from time to time and held public office or served on the Council of 500 for a year or two. In addition, military service from ages 18 to 59 was universal for men. (See the box, "The Debate on Democracy.")

The instruments of government are easily sketched. The central and commanding institution was the assembly. Open to all male citizens over age 20, assembly meetings were held in the open air, on a hillside seating several thousand on benches (see the illustration on page 78). In the fourth century B.C. there was a minimum of forty meetings per year, one about every ten days.

The assembly heard the great debates of the day. It made decisions about war and peace, alliance and friendship; it granted honors and condemnations; it passed decrees relating to current issues and set up commissions to revise fundamental laws. In the assembly great orators addressed the people, but everyone, however humble, was theoretically entitled to speak.

The Debate on Democracy

Characters in Greek drama often discuss general principles. In this excerpt from Euripides'
tragedy **The Suppliant Women** *(ca. 420 B.C.), Theseus, legendary king of Athens, and a herald*
from Creon, tyrant of Thebes, debate the merits of democracy.

Herald

What man is tyrant in this land? To whom/
Must I give the word I bring from Creon,
ruler/In Cadmus' country [Thebes] . . . ?

Theseus

One moment, stranger./Your start was wrong,
seeking a tyrant here./This city is free, and
ruled by no one man./The people reign, in annual succession./They do not yield the power
to the rich;/The poor man has an equal share
in it.

Herald

That one point gives the better of the game/To
me. The town I come from is controlled/By one
man, not a mob. And there is no one/To puff it
up with words, for private gain,/Swaying it
this way, that way. . . . /The people is no right
judge of arguments./Then how can it give
right guidance to a city?/A poor man, working
hard, could not attend/To public matters, even

if ignorance/Were not his birthright. When a
wretch, a nothing,/Obtains respect and power
from the people/By talk, his betters sicken at
the sight.

Theseus

. . . Nothing/Is worse for a city than a
tyrant./In earliest days, before the laws are
common,/One man has power and makes the
law his own:/Equality is not yet. With written
laws,/People of small resources and the
rich/Both have the same recourse to justice.
Now/A man of means, if badly spoken of,/
Will have no better standing than the weak;/
And if the little man is right, he wins/Against
the great. This is the call of freedom:/"What
man has good advice to give the city,/And
wishes to make it known?" He who re-
sponds/Gains glory; the reluctant hold their
peace./For the city, what can be more fair than
that?

Source: Adapted from Euripides, *The Suppliant Women,* trans. Frank Jones, in *Euripides IV: The Complete Greek
Tragedies,* ed. David Grene and Richmond Lattimore (Chicago: University of Chicago Press, 1958), pp. 73–74.

The judicial branch consisted of courts, which, with a few exceptions, were open to all citizens, no matter how poor. Aristotle comments that "when the people have the right to vote in the courts, they control the constitution." Juries were large, commonly consisting of several hundred men chosen by lottery; small juries, it was felt, were easily bribed. After a preliminary hearing, cases were decided in a single day.

The executive consisted of the Council of 500 and some 700 public officials (also, under Athens's empire in the fifth century B.C., several hundred others living abroad). All citizens over age 30 were

eligible to serve. Most public officials were chosen by lottery, which put rich and poor, talented and untalented, on an equal footing. To guard against incompetents or criminals, all officials had to undergo a scrutiny by the council before taking office and an audit after the term. Most magistracies, moreover, were boards, usually of ten men, so even if a bad man managed to pass his scrutiny, he would be counterbalanced by his colleagues. Only generals and treasurers were chosen by election.

Athens had a relatively weak executive. There was no office like president or prime minister. Generals and orators led assembly debates, but ordinary people set the agenda and made the decisions by taking votes at each assembly meeting. On the local level, every deme (county) had an annually chosen executive and a deme assembly of all citizens. To a peasant in far-off Marathon (26 miles away), the Athenian assembly might have seemed remote, but his right to speak up in his deme assembly made demokratia real and vivid.

So novel and populist a system of government has not been without critics, either in antiquity or today. Some have charged that the Athenian people were uneducated, emotional, and easily swayed by oratorical tricks. Others say that demokratia degenerated into mob rule after the death of Pericles. Others complain about the lack of a system of formal public education, which denied many citizens equality of opportunity.

The copybook of Athenian democracy does have some blots in its history, particularly in the heat of wartime. The Peloponnesian War (431–404 B.C.; see page 103) witnessed several Athenian atrocities and judicial murders. Yet these were exceptions: In its roughly two hundred years of existence, Athenian demokratia was generally stable, law-abiding, and fair-minded.

Metics, Women, Slaves

Another charge against Athenian demokratia is more serious: that it was democracy for a small elite only. There were never more than approximately 40,000 adult male citizens out of a total population—men, women and children, resident aliens, and slaves—of about 400,000. To become a citizen, at age 18 a boy had to prove that he was the legitimate son of a citizen father and a citizen maternal grandfather. Girls were never officially registered as citizens; although the term *citizeness* existed, Athenian citizen women were usually referred to as "city women." As for resident aliens, whether male or female, they rarely attained citizenship. Athenian ideology emphasized the genetic homogeneity of Athenian citizens; they were, it was claimed, natives from time immemorial, "sprung from the soil itself." In reality, many had ancestors who had immigrated to Athens before 500 B.C., but this fact was glossed over.

In the fifth and fourth centuries B.C., Athens had a large population of foreigners. Some were transient. Others were officially registered resident aliens, or *metics*. Metics came by the thousands from all over the Greek world and beyond. Some, like Aristotle (a native of a Greek colony in Macedonia), were attracted by Athens's schools of philosophy, but most came because of its unparalleled economic opportunities. Metics could not own land in Athens, and they had to pay extra taxes and serve in the Athenian military. Nevertheless, they prospered in Athenian commerce and crafts.

Athenian women were excluded from politics and played only a humble role in commerce as small retailers. Women rarely received an education, even in physical activity. In legal and contractual matters they were almost always required to be represented by a male guardian. They did not have the legal rights of women in Egypt or Mesopotamia or the honor as mothers and household partners of women in Israel. Athenian women generally led restricted lives, but perhaps less restricted than it might seem. Let us distinguish between ideology and practice.

Paradoxically, the more power was distributed among the male citizenry, the more hostile to women's freedom did Athens's citizen ideology become. Greek males believed that the more honor a woman brought the man who won her, the more danger she might bring by tempting outsiders to seduce her. Hence demokratia promulgated an ideology of seclusion for women.

Practice, however, was another matter. As Aristotle asks rhetorically, "How is it possible to prevent the wives of the poor from going out?" "Poor" is a synonym for "ordinary" in ancient Greek. Ordinary women could not stay at home because they had to run errands, draw water, and sometimes even help make ends meet. Ordinary houses, moreover, were small and cramped, and in the Mediterranean heat women could not stay inside all the time.

Women played a large role in Athenian religion. They were priestesses in more than forty major cults. They participated each year in many festivals, including several reserved for women only. One such festival, the Thesmophoria, a celebration of fertility held each autumn, featured a three-day encampment of women on a hillside in the city, just beside the place where the Athenian assembly met. Women attended public funeral orations in honor of soldiers who had died fighting for Athens. Women probably attended the theater.

We occasionally get glimpses, sometimes more, of Athenian women resisting or working behind the scenes to rectify male mistakes. An inheritance case reveals a woman go-between interceding among her quarreling male relations. Greek comedy shows women mocking male pretensions and establishing friendships with each other. A woman who brought a large dowry into a marriage could use it and the threat of divorce to influence her husband (the dowry had to be returned to the woman's father or guardian if there was a divorce). In short, Athenian women had some access to the world outside the household and some influence within the household. There existed, nonetheless, a real disparity in power between men and women.

Slavery was widespread in democratic Athens. Some slaves served in agriculture, some labored under miserable conditions in Athenian silver mines, and some were engaged in commerce or the military (where some rowers were slaves). Most, however, worked as domestics or in small workshops as, for example, metalworkers or furniture makers. The vast majority of slaves were non-Greek. Most were prisoners of war; some were victims of pirates or debtors from states where, unlike Athens, citizens might still end up in debt-slavery. Thrace (roughly, modern Bulgaria) and Anatolia were the main sources of slaves, but some slaves came from North Africa and other Mediterranean regions.

The living conditions of slaves were usually poor and in the silver mines abysmal. Emancipation, however, was more common in Athens than in the American South before 1865. A few ex-slaves rose to positions of wealth and power in Athens. A striking and unusual case is that of Pasion (d. 370 B.C.). Originally a slave employee of a banking firm, he bought his freedom and became the wealthiest Athenian banker of his day, as well as an Athenian citizen.

Athenian demokratia lacked many features of modern democracy: a notion of universal human rights, the possibility for immigrants to become citizens, gender equality, the abolition of slavery, and public education. To its small citizen body, however, Athenian demokratia offered extraordinary freedom, equality, and responsibility, and a degree of participation in public life seldom equaled. Demokratia was a model of what democracy could be, but not of whom it could be for.

STRUGGLES FOR HEGEMONY

The polis generated community spirit, but that spirit had to compete with a strong passion for personal glory. The citizen was often unwilling to make compromises for the public good; the polis recoiled at the thought of sacrificing its honor for the sake of other poleis. The result was a constant struggle in diplomacy and war among city-states, often arranged in leagues under hegemons.

In 500 B.C., Sparta, hegemon of the Peloponnesian League, was the most prominent power of the Greek mainland. Across the Aegean Sea in Anatolia, the Greek city-states had been under Persian rule for two generations, since conquest in the 540s. In 499 B.C., however, events began to unfold that not only would revolutionize that balance of power but would throw the entire eastern Mediterranean into two hundred years of turmoil.

The Persian Wars, 499–479 B.C.

Led by Miletus, the Ionian Greek city-states rose in revolt against Persia in 499 B.C. Athens sent troops to help, but despite initial successes Athens lacked the will for a long war and its troops soon departed. The Ionian coalition broke down thereafter, and in 494 B.C. the Persian fleet crushed the Ionian navy. Miletus was besieged and destroyed, but otherwise Persia was relatively lenient in Ionia.

Upstart Athens, however, could not go unpunished. In 492 B.C., Darius I sent a large naval expedition to Athens. It was destroyed by a storm, but in 490 he sent a second Persian force of about 25,000 infantrymen and 1200 cavalrymen (with horses) to Marathon, some 26 miles from the city of Athens (see Map 3.3). Athens sent 10,000 men (including 1000 allies) to defend Marathon. A great battle ensued.

Under the general Miltiades (550–489 B.C.), the Greeks attacked. Persian overconfidence and the superiority of the Greek phalanx over Persia's loosely organized infantrymen won Athens a smashing victory: Persia suffered 6400 casualties, Athens only 192. (The story, unconfirmed, that a messenger ran the 26 miles to the city of Athens with the news, "Rejoice, we conquer!" is the basis for the modern marathon race.) After the battle, Athens experienced a burst of confidence that propelled it to power and glory. If Persia had won, Athens would have acquired neither wealth nor empire, demokratia never would have advanced, and the greatness of the Classical period never would have come about.

Persia sought a rematch. After Darius's death in 486, his son and successor, Xerxes, decided on a joint land-sea expedition against Athens. He amassed a huge force of several hundred ships and several hundred thousand soldiers and rowers, vastly outnumbering potential Greek opposition. Athens, under the leadership of Themistocles (ca. 525–460 B.C.), prepared by building a fleet of 200 ships. Athens joined Sparta and twenty-nine other Peloponnesian poleis in a Hellenic League of defense, with Sparta in overall command. Most poleis either stayed neutral or, like Thebes and Argos, collaborated with Persia. The Greeks had over 300 ships and about 50,000 infantrymen.

Persia invaded Greece in 480 B.C. and won the opening moves. A small Spartan army under King Leonidas held the narrow pass of Thermopylae in central Greece (see Map 3.1). With local help, however, the Persians found a way to outflank Leonidas and take both ends of the pass. They crushed the Spartans, who died fighting to the last man (thereby adding to their reputation for courage). After winning a naval victory near Thermopylae, the Persians marched on Athens. Abandoned by its defenders, it was sacked.

The tide then turned. The Greeks lured the Persian fleet into the narrow straits between Athens and Salamis. The Persians could not use their numerical superiority in this closed space, and the Greeks had the home-base advantage. The result was a crushing Persian defeat under the eyes of Xerxes himself, who watched the battle from a throne on a hillside near the shore.

Because their sea links to the Levant had been cut, Xerxes and the remainder of the Persian fleet left for home. Soon afterward the united Greek army under Spartan leadership defeated Persian forces on land at Plataea (just north of Attica; see Map 3.1) in 479 B.C. At about the same time, the Greek fleet defeated a reorganized Persian fleet off the Anatolian coast near Mycale. The victorious Greeks sailed the coast and liberated the Ionians. Not only did Persia fail to conquer the Greek mainland, but it also lost its eastern Aegean empire.

Greeks did not remember the invader fondly. After 480 they thought of Persians not merely as enemies but as barbarians—that is, cultural inferiors. (See the box, "Encounters with the West: The En-

WAR AND DIPLOMACY IN CLASSICAL GREECE

499 B.C.	Ionians revolt against Persia
490 B.C.	Battle of Marathon
480–479 B.C.	Persian invasion of Greece
477 B.C.	Delian League founded
431–404 B.C.	Peloponnesian War
395–386 B.C.	Corinthian War
371 B.C.	Battle of Leuctra

emy as Barbarian.") At the same time, Greeks became more conscious of their own common culture.

The Rise of the Athenian Empire

Sparta and Athens shared most of the credit for victory: Sparta had made the main contribution on land, Athens at sea. The two powers might have jointly stepped into the vacuum left by Persia's retreat, but Sparta let Athens have the field to itself. In 477 B.C., Athens became the hegemon of a new security organization, founded on the island of Delos in the Aegean Sea. The dual purpose of the so-called Delian League was to protect Greek lands and to attack and plunder Persian territory. Commander of the league fleet, Athens provided most of the ships and the core of the rowers (the rest were mercenaries or slaves). Salaries for the rowers, as well as the cost of building and repairing ships, came from an annual tribute levied on the allies. The number of allies grew from about 150 in 477 B.C. to about 250 in 431 B.C. at the height of the league.

Fearful as ever of entanglements outside the Peloponnesus, Sparta preferred to leave the Aegean to Athens. Many Spartans nonetheless watched with unease and jealousy as Athenian power boomed.

Athens, meanwhile, transformed its pride to arrogance. Within a generation, by the 450s, the Delian League was becoming an Athenian empire. In 454 B.C. the treasury was transferred from Delos to Athens on the excuse that it would be safer there. In the following decades, the allies were

∼ ENCOUNTERS WITH THE WEST ∼

The Enemy as Barbarian

Classical Greeks no longer regarded the enemy as honored rivals, as Homer's heroes regarded Trojans. (See the box, "Encounters with the West: Greeks and Trojans," in Chapter 2.) Rather, they looked down on the enemy as a barbarian. Their archenemies, the Persians, were often portrayed as indulgent, effeminate, emotional, slavish, cruel, and dangerous. Consider the portrait of Persian arrogance and Greek solidarity that emerges from these excerpts, drawn from the historian Herodotus's account of Persia's invasion of Greece in 480 B.C.

(a)

He [King Xerxes of Persia] then prepared to move forward to Abydos, where a bridge had already been constructed across the Hellespont from Europe to Asia. . . . It was here not long afterwards that the Greeks under Xanthippus the son of Ariphron took Artayctes the Persian governor of Sestos, and nailed him alive to a plank—he was the man who collected women in the temple of Protesilaus at Elaeus and committed various acts of sacrilege. This headland was the point to which Xerxes' engineers carried their two bridges from Abydos—a distance of seven furlongs. . . . The work was successfully completed, but a subsequent storm of great violence smashed it up and carried everything away. Xerxes was very angry when he learned of the disaster, and gave orders that the Hellespont should receive three hundred lashes and have a pair of fetters thrown into it. And I have heard before now that he also sent people to brand it with hot irons. He certainly instructed the men with the whips to utter, as they wielded them, the following words: "You salt and bitter stream, your master lays this punishment upon you for injuring him, who never injured you. But Xerxes the King will cross you, with or without your permission. No man sacrifices to you, and you deserve the neglect by your acrid and muddy waters"— a highly presumptuous way of addressing the Hellespont, and typical of a barbarous nation. In addition to punishing the Hellespont Xerxes gave orders that the men responsible for building the bridge should have their heads cut off. This unseemly order was duly carried out. . . .

(b)

To the Spartan envoys . . . [the Athenians] said: "No doubt it was natural that the Lacedaemonians should dread the possibility of our making terms with Persia; nonetheless it shows a poor estimate of the spirit of Athens. Were we offered all the gold in the world, and the fairest and richest country the earth contains, we should never consent to join the common enemy and bring Greece into submission. There are many compelling reasons to prevent our taking such a course, even if we wish to do so: the first and greatest is the burning of the temples and images of our gods—now mere heaps of rubble. It is our bounden duty to avenge this desecration with all the power we possess—not to clasp in friendship the hand that wrought it. Again, there is the Greek nation—the common blood, the common language; the temples and religious ritual; the whole way of life we understand and share together—indeed, if Athens were to betray all this it would not be well done. We would have you know, therefore, if you did not already know it, that we will never make peace with Xerxes so long as a single Athenian remains alive."

Source: Herodotus, *The Histories*, trans. Aubrey de Sélincourt (Baltimore: Penguin, 1954), pp. 429, 550.

compelled to send delegations to Athenian festivals, to use Athenian weights, measures, and coinage, and to refer major court cases to Athenian juries.

One by one, beginning with Thasos in 465 B.C., the major allied states rebelled, but Athens crushed each rebellion. Sometimes, after surrender, rebels were executed and their wives and children were sold into slavery. Allied complaints began to stir Sparta. A conflict between Greece's greatest land power, Sparta, and Greece's greatest seapower, Athens, started to look all but inevitable.

The Peloponnesian War, 431–404 B.C.

When it came, the conflict between Athens and Sparta proved exceptionally bloody and bitter. Battles between huge fleets, economic warfare, protracted sieges, epidemic disease, and ideological struggle produced a devastating war. It was clear that the Greeks could not maintain their unity against Persia; indeed, they appeared to be destroying themselves.

In the era of the Peloponnesian War, both democratic Athens and oligarchic Sparta sought to promote their respective ideologies. Some unfortunate states became ideological battlegrounds (Map 3.4). In Corcyra (modern Corfu), for example, bloody civil war marked a series of coups and countercoups in the 420s B.C. Athens itself was not immune from dissension and violence. A minority of oligarchs had never been reconciled to demokratia. When Athens began to falter in the Peloponnesian War after 413 B.C., they seized the opportunity and twice installed oligarchy in Athens: first in 411 and again in 404. Each time, the democrats came back to power, the second time only after foreign intervention and civil war.

Given Spartan supremacy on land and Athenian mastery of the sea, it is not surprising that the Peloponnesian War remained undecided for a decade and a half. The balance of power shifted only after an Athenian blunder. In 415 B.C., Athens adopted the bold plan of attacking Sparta indirectly by a quick raid on Sicily, whose fabled wealth the Athenians hoped to use to reshape the Greek balance of power in Athens's favor. Unfortunately for Athens, Sicily, led by Syracuse, proved to be a formidable foe. The raid became a quagmire and then a disaster, leading to total defeat and thousands of Athenian casualties.

By 412 B.C., most of the Athenian empire was in revolt, and Persia had intervened on Sparta's side—in return for Sparta's restoration of Ionia to Persia, an ironic counterpoint to Sparta's role in driving Persia from Greece in 479. Athens, nevertheless, was sufficiently wealthy and plucky to hold out until 405 B.C., when the Spartans, led by the shrewd and aggressive Lysander (d. 395 B.C.), finally captured almost the entire Athenian fleet in the Hellespont (see Map 3.4). Athens surrendered the next year.

The Fruitless Wars of the Fourth Century B.C.

Sparta won the Peloponnesian War, but establishing a new Greek order proved beyond its grasp. Trained as soldiers, not as diplomats, never fully reconciled to using seapower, lacking the oratorical skills valued by other Greeks, sure of themselves and contemptuous of others, Spartans made poor leaders. Sparta took over Athens's former empire and quickly had a falling-out with its allies. Corinth and Thebes were offended by Spartan heavy-handedness. Persia, meanwhile, faced repeated Spartan invasions of Anatolia to liberate the Ionian Greeks, whose surrender Spartans now regretted. United by a common enemy, an alliance of Athens, Corinth, Thebes, and Persia turned on Sparta in 395 B.C. After the indecisive Corinthian War (395–386 B.C.), so named because most of the fighting took place around Corinth (see Map 3.4), Sparta gave up Anatolia but held its own on the Greek mainland.

Thebes then emerged as Sparta's main rival. Over Spartan opposition, and inspired by brilliant Theban leaders like Epaminondas (d. 362 B.C.) and Pelopidas (403–364 B.C.), Thebes united the separate city-states of Boeotia under its rule.

In the meantime, Sparta was suffering from exhaustion and a vast decline in the number of citizens. The original nine thousand Similars of the seventh century B.C. had declined to about only fifteen hundred in 371 B.C. The main problem seems to have been greed. Rich Spartans preferred to get richer by concentrating wealth in fewer hands rather than open the elite to new blood. Thousands of men could no longer afford to live as elite soldiers. The result was military disaster. In 371 B.C., the Boeotian army crushed the Spartans at the battle of Leuctra, killing a

Map 3.4 Greece in the Peloponnesian War During the long and bloody Peloponnesian War (431–404 B.C.), much of the Greek world was divided in two camps: one led by Sparta, the other by Athens.

thousand men (including four hundred Similars) and a Spartan king. In the next few years Boeotia invaded the Peloponnesus, freed the Messenian helots, and restored Messenia to independence, after some 350 years of bondage. It was a fatal blow to Spartan power, but Boeotia, too, was exhausted and its main leaders, Epaminondas and Pelopidas, were dead. None of the Greek city-states had been able to maintain hegemony.

Nothing better demonstrates the fatal excess of individualism in classical Greece and the absence of cooperative virtues than the wars of the city-states in the fourth century B.C. They accomplished nothing but leaving Greece prey to outsiders.

THE PUBLIC CULTURE OF CLASSICAL GREECE

Classical Greek culture was public culture, whether in democratic Athens, with its emphasis on public speaking, or in oligarchic Sparta, with its public education. Poets, for example, were not introspective or alienated figures. Rather, to quote the Athenian playwright Aristophanes (ca. 455–ca. 385 B.C.), they were "the teachers of men" who commented on contemporary public debate. (As the quotation might also suggest, males, especially citizens, dominated public life.) Tragedy was performed in a state theater at a state religious festival. Private individuals competed to spend money on productions in order to win public glory. The philosopher Socrates (469–399 B.C.) discussed philosophy in marketplaces and gymnasia. It was the public, not private individuals, that was the major patron of sculpture and architecture.

Public life, accordingly, is the central theme of Classical Greek art and literature. Of tragedy, for example, one might be able to say that regardless of the particular hero or plot, the same character always looms in the background: the polis. The Classical historians Herodotus, Xenophon, and especially Thucydides do not have much to say about private life, focusing instead on public affairs. Classical philosophy ranged from biology to metaphysics; however, it made politics its central focus.

Religion and Art

A hallmark of Classical culture is the tension between the religious heritage of the Archaic period and the worldly spirit of the Classical period. The Classical period was a time of prosperity, political debate, and military conflict. "Wonders are many on earth, and none more wondrous than man," said the Athenian tragedian Sophocles (ca. 495–406 B.C.). Yet Sophocles was a deeply religious man who also believed that people were doomed to disaster unless they obeyed the laws of the gods. Sophocles mirrored a widespread debate, for he knew his countrymen well. He was not only a popular playwright but a general, state treasurer, priest, and intimate of Pericles.

Classical religion was less sure of itself than its Archaic predecessor. A few people even ques-

The Parthenon The temple of Athena Parthenos ("the Maiden") on the Athenian Acropolis, the Parthenon was dedicated in 438 B.C. One of the largest and most complex Greek temples, it was built of fine marble. The partially restored ruins symbolize the wealth, power, and greatness of classical Greece. (*William Katz/Photo Researchers*)

tioned the very existence of the gods, although most Greeks wanted religion to be adapted to the new age, not discarded altogether. Thus, Athenian religion was tailored to the needs of a democratic and imperial city. In the 440s B.C., under Pericles' leadership, Athens embarked on a vast, ambitious, and expensive temple-building project, using Delian League funds and serving as a large public employment program. Temples were built in and around the city, most notably on the Athenian Acropolis. (See the feature, "Weighing the Evidence: The Parthenon," on pages 116–117.)

Classical sculptors completed the process begun by their Archaic predecessors of mastering the accurate representation of the human body. In anatomical precision, Classical Greek sculpture was the most technically proficient sculpture the world had seen. Like Archaic sculpture, it was not, however, an attempt to portray humans "warts and all," but an idealization of the human form.

To adapt religion to a new age, new cults were introduced. The most popular was the worship of Aesclipius, god of healing. Traditionally a minor figure and considered a son of Apollo, Aesclipius became enormously popular in his own right beginning in the late fifth century B.C., perhaps in response to the high mortality of the Peloponnesian War. Outside Athens, large shrines to Aesclipius at Epidauros (in the Peloponnesus) and Cos (an island off the Anatolian coast) became pilgrimage centers in the fourth century B.C. for ailing people in search of a cure.

Another religious innovation was the deification of living humans. Greek religion had always recognized heroes as demigods, but nobody had ever seen a hero in the flesh; they had lived, if at all, centuries earlier. At the end of the Peloponnesian War in 404 B.C., however, Sparta's Ionian allies began worshiping the victor Lysander as a god. A decade later, when Athens's power was on the rise again and Sparta's was declining, the same Ionians began worshiping an Athenian admiral instead! Many Greeks were shocked by these cults, deeming it hybris to equate a mortal human with a god.

The Sophists and Socrates

Success in democratic politics required a knowledge of oratory. This demand was met in the late fifth century B.C. by the arrival in Athens of itiner-

ant professional teachers of *rhetoric*, the art of speaking. They were known as Sophists (from a word meaning "to instruct" or "make wise"). Sicilian Greeks invented rhetoric around 465 B.C. by drawing up the rules of argument. For a fee —rarely small and sometimes astronomical— Sophists taught young Athenians the art of speaking. Their curriculum consisted not only of rhetoric but also of the rudiments of linguistics, ethics, psychology, history, and anthropology—in other words, any aspect of "human nature" that might help an aspiring politician. Within a few years most ambitious young Athenians of prosperous families were studying with Sophists.

At their best, Sophists sharpened young minds. Athenian tragedians, historians, and philosophers all benefited from sophistic teaching. Protagoras (b. ca. 485 B.C.), perhaps the best-known Sophist, summed up the spirit of the age in his famous dictum "Man is the measure of all things"—an appropriate credo for the interest in all things human that is apparent in Classical literature and art. There is, however, a more troubling side to the Sophists. As teachers of rhetoric, they taught respect for success, not for truth. Thus, they acquired a reputation as word-twisters who taught men how to make "the weaker argument defeat the stronger."

Much to the distress of conservatives, Sophists drew a distinction between *nomos,* a word that means "law" or "convention," and *physis,* which means "nature." The distinction had revolutionary potential. In general, Sophists had little respect for the established order, or nomos. They considered it mere convention. A great man trained by a Sophist might rise above convention to realize the limitless potentialities of his nature, or physis: If he overturned democracy to establish a tyranny, so much the worse for democracy. Indeed, the Sophists trained both unscrupulous democratic politicians and many of the oligarchs who launched coups d'état against Athenian democracy at the end of the fifth century B.C. As a result, *sophist* became a term of abuse in Athens and remains so to this day.

Classical Greek advances in rhetoric, therefore, were as problematic as they were brilliant. The Sophists had a wide-ranging effect on many different branches of thought. Consider, for example, the work of Democritus (b. ca. 460 B.C.), a native of the northern Greek polis of Abdera but a visitor to Athens. Like many Sophists, Democritus believed that the reality of nature was far more radical than conventional opinion thought. He concluded that all things consisted of tiny, indivisible particles, which could be arranged and rearranged in an infinite variety of configurations. He called these particles *atoma,* "the uncuttable" (from which the word *atom* is derived).

The physicians of the Aegean island of Cos are known as Hippocratics, from Hippocrates (b. ca. 460 B.C.), the first great thinker of their school. If they were not directly influenced by the Sophists, they shared many similar habits of thought. Like the Sophists, the Hippocratics were religious skeptics. They considered disease to be strictly a natural phenomenon in which the gods played no part. Hippocratic medicine was noteworthy for its methodology, which emphasized observation and prognosis (the reasoned prediction of future developments). The Hippocratics were the most rigorously naturalistic physicians to date, although no more successful in curing illness than earlier practitioners.

In the fifth century B.C. not all thinkers welcomed the conclusions of the Sophists. Perhaps their most notable critic, and the greatest of all fifth-century philosophers, was Socrates (469–399 B.C.). Mistakenly considered a Sophist by the public, in 399 Socrates was tried, convicted, and executed by an Athenian court for alleged atheism and "corrupting the young." The Athenian public soon had second thoughts, and the trial of Socrates is usually considered one of history's great miscarriages of justice, as well as one of Athenian democracy's greatest blunders. (See the box, "Socrates' Defense.")

Socrates, in any case, was not a Sophist. He charged no fees, had no formal students, and did not claim to teach any positive body of knowledge. In fact, his basic thesis was negative: the radical ignorance of most people, including himself. His only superiority, he believed, was his awareness of his ignorance. Unlike the Sophists, most of whom were metics, Socrates was an Athenian citizen.

Socrates, however, resembled the Sophists in his intense interest in political theory. Like any good Athenian citizen, Socrates served in the military—as a hoplite during the Peloponnesian War. He had his doubts about democracy, which he criticized for inefficiency and for giving an equal voice to the uneducated. He preferred rule by a wise elite. Nonetheless, Socrates was too loyal an Athenian to

advocate revolution. What probably got him into the most trouble was his role as a self-styled "gadfly": Socrates stung the pride of Athens's leaders by demonstrating their ignorance.

Socrates was trained in the Ionian natural philosophy tradition. He went beyond it, as the Roman thinker Cicero later said, by bringing philosophy "down from the heavens into the streets"; he changed the emphasis from the natural world to human ethics. Like most Greeks, Socrates believed that the purpose of life was the pursuit of aretê. Unlike his contemporaries, however, he did not consider aretê to be primarily excellence in battle or in public life but, rather, excellence in philosophy. One became good by studying the truth, which is part of what Socrates meant by his saying "Virtue (aretê) is knowledge." He also meant that no one who truly understood goodness would ever do evil.

Such an outlook downgrades the importance of willpower or the emotions in shaping action, but it makes education into the cornerstone of society. Teach people well, according to Socrates, and they will behave morally. Socrates has gone down in history as an inspiring teacher, despite his protestations of not teaching anything. His emphasis was not on research or writing—Socrates refused to write anything down. He believed that truth could be found only in person, not through books; that philosophy requires a verbal give-and-take. His favorite technique was to ask people difficult questions. Pedagogy that relies on questioning is still called the "Socratic method."

Plato and Aristotle

Because Socrates never wrote anything down, we are dependent on others for our knowledge of him. Fortunately, he inspired many students who committed his thoughts to paper. Socrates' most distinguished student, and our most important source for his thought, was Plato (427–348 B.C.), who in turn was the teacher of Aristotle (384–322 B.C.). Together, these three men laid the foundations of the Western philosophical tradition. They were thinkers for the ages, but each was also a man of his times.

Socrates grew up in confident Periclean days. Plato came of age during the Peloponnesian War, a period culminating in the execution of Socrates. Shocked and disillusioned, Plato turned his back

Socrates' Defense

In 399 B.C., Socrates was tried on a charge of corrupting the youth of Athens and of believing in deities of his own invention instead of the state gods of Athens. Socrates' defense, as preserved by his pupil Plato, is a stirring description of philosophy as a way of life. His uncompromising stand did not persuade the jury, which voted for his conviction and execution, but his words convey why he was considered an inspiring teacher.

Suppose, then, that you acquit me. . . . Suppose that . . . you said to me, "Socrates, . . . we shall . . . acquit you, but only on one condition, that you give up spending your time on this quest and stop philosophizing. If we catch you going on in the same way, you shall be put to death.". . . I should reply, "Gentlemen, I am your very grateful and devoted servant, but I owe a greater obedience to God than to you; and so long as I draw breath and have my faculties, I shall never stop practising philosophy and exhorting you and elucidating the truth for everyone that I meet. I shall go on saying, in my usual way, 'My very good friend, you are an Athenian and belong to a city which is the greatest and most famous in the world for its wisdom and strength. Are you not ashamed that you give your attention to acquiring as much money as possible, and similarly with reputation and honor, and give no attention or thought to truth and understanding and the perfection of your soul?' And if any of you disputes this and professes to care about these things, I shall not at once let him go or leave him; no, I shall question him and examine him and test him; and if it appears that in spite of his profession he has made no real progress towards goodness, I shall reprove him for neglecting what is of supreme importance, and giving his attention to trivialities. I shall do this to everyone that I meet, young or old, foreigner or fellow-citizen; but especially to you my fellow-citizens, inasmuch as you are closer to me in kinship."

Source: Plato, *The Apology of Socrates,* in Plato, *The Last Days of Socrates,* trans. Hugh Tredennick (Harmondsworth, England: Penguin, 1969), p. 61.

on public life, although he was an Athenian citizen. Instead of discussing philosophy in public, Plato founded a private school in an Athenian suburb, the Academy. Plato held a low opinion of democracy, and when he did intervene in politics, it was not in Athens but in far-off Syracuse (in Sicily). Syracuse was governed by a tyranny, and Plato hoped to educate the tyrant's heir in philosophy—a vain hope, as it turned out.

In an attempt to recapture the stimulating give-and-take of a conversation with Socrates, Plato did not write straightforward philosophical treatises but, rather, dialogues or speeches. All of Plato's dialogues have more than one speaker, and in most the main speaker is named "Socrates": sometimes the historical Socrates, sometimes merely a mouthpiece for ideas Plato wished to explore.

A voluminous writer, Plato is not easily summarized. The word that best characterizes his legacy, though, is *idealism,* of which Plato is one of Western philosophy's greatest exponents. Like Parmenides, Plato believed that the senses are misleading. Truth exists but is attained only by training the mind to overcome common-sense evidence. The model for Plato's philosophical method is geometry. Just as geometry deals not with this or that triangle or rectangle but with ideal forms—with a pure triangle, a pure rectangle—so the philosopher could learn to recognize purity. A philosopher would not be misled by, for example, comparing aretê in Athens, Sparta, and Persia; a philosopher would understand the meaning of pure, ideal aretê. No relativist, Plato believed in absolute good and evil.

Philosophy is not for everyone, according to Plato; only a few people have the requisite intelligence and discipline. In the *Republic*, a dialogue that is perhaps his best-known work, Plato demonstrates the nature of his idealism and its political consequences. He envisioned a society whose elite would study philosophy and attain enlightenment. They would understand the vanity of political ambition but would nonetheless accept the responsibility of governing the masses. Plato never makes clear precisely the reason they should accept this responsibility. It is possible he was enough of a traditionalist, in spite of himself, to consider one's responsibility to one's polis to be obvious. In any case, Plato's ideal state was one where philosophers would rule as kings, benevolently and unselfishly.

Plato explored the details of such a state in the *Republic* and in other dialogues, particularly the *Laws*. It is not clear how wedded he was to individual details; indeed, some of them may have been meant merely to shock or to satirize. An overall picture emerges, however. The ideal state would be like a small polis: self-sufficient and closed to outside corrupt influences like Sparta but committed to the pursuit of things intellectual like Athens. Society would be sharply divided into three classes—philosophers, soldiers, and farmers—with admission to each class based on merit rather than heredity. Poetry and drama would be strictly censored. Plato advocated public education and toyed with more radical notions: not only gender equality but the abolition of the family and private property, institutions that he felt led to disunity and dissension.

Plato's ideas have always been controversial but almost never ignored. Even in his own day, most people considered Plato far too radical. The writings of his great student Aristotle were more to contemporary tastes. Originally from Macedonia, Aristotle spent most of his life in Athens, first as a student at the Academy, then as the founder of his own school, the Lyceum. Like Plato, Aristotle wrote dialogues, but none has survived. His main extant works are treatises, largely compilations by students of his lecture notes. One of the most wide ranging of intellectuals, Aristotle had a voracious appetite for knowledge and for writing. His treatises embrace politics, ethics, poetry, botany, physics, metaphysics, astronomy, rhetoric, zoology, logic, and psychology.

Aristotle This bronze bust, found in a Roman-era villa in the Italian city of Herculaneum, is said to represent the great Classical philosopher. The statue has the dignified and pensive look betokening one of the giants of ancient Greek thought. *(Alinari/Art Resource, NY)*

Although influenced by Plato's idealism, Aristotle was a far more practical, down-to-earth thinker. His father had been a doctor, which may account for Aristotle's interest in applied science and in biology and biological method. Unlike Plato, Aristotle placed great emphasis on observation and fieldwork and on classification and systemization. (See the box, "Man Is a Political Animal.")

Aristotle agreed with Plato about the existence of absolute standards of good and evil, but he emphasized the relevance of such standards to everyday life. Unlike Plato, Aristotle considered the senses important guides; change, he believed, was not an illusion but rather an important phenomenon. Aristotle's view of change was teleological—that is, he emphasized the goal (*telos* in Greek) of

"Man Is a Political Animal"

This excerpt from the **Politics** *(ca. 325 B.C.) reveals certain basic features of Aristotle's method. An expert logician, Aristotle is a clear and straightforward writer. He is fond of biological analogies, and he believes that each of the parts of nature, like each of the parts of the body, serves a function for the greater whole.*

Man is by nature an animal intended to live in a polis [literally, "a political animal"]. . . .

Nature, according to our theory, makes nothing in vain; and a human being alone of the animals is furnished with the faculty of language. The mere making of sounds serves to indicate pleasure and pain, and is thus a faculty that belongs to animals in general. . . . But language serves to declare what is advantageous and what is just and what is unjust. It is the peculiarity of man, in comparison with the rest of the animal world, that he alone possesses a perception of good and evil, of the just and the unjust, and of other similar qualities; it is association in these things which makes a family and a polis.

We may now proceed to add that [though the individual and the family are prior in the order of time] the polis is prior in the order of nature to the family and the individual. The reason for this is that the whole is necessarily prior to the part. If the whole body be destroyed, there will not be a foot or a hand. . . .

We thus see that the polis exists by nature and that it is prior to the individual. Not being self-sufficient when they are isolated, all individuals are so many parts all equally depending on the whole. The human being who is isolated—who is unable to share in the benefits of political association, or has no need to share because he is already self-sufficient—is no part of the polis, and must therefore be either a beast or a god. . . . A human being, when perfected, is the best of animals; but if he be isolated from law and justice he is the worst of all.

Source: Adapted from Ernest Barker, ed. and trans., *The Politics of Aristotle* (London: Oxford University Press, 1946), pp. 5–6.

change. According to Aristotle, every organism changes and grows toward a particular end and is an integral and harmonious part of a larger whole. The entire cosmos is teleological, and each and every one of its parts has a purpose. Behind the cosmos was a principle that Aristotle called "the unmoved mover," the supreme cause of existence.

Aristotle defined *aretê* as the fulfillment of one's function in the cosmos. The aretê of a horse, for example, was to be strong, fast, and obedient; the aretê of a rose was to look pretty and smell sweet. As for the aretê of a human being, Aristotle agreed with Plato: only the philosopher achieved true aretê. As a pragmatist, however, Aristotle did not imagine philosophers becoming kings. Not that he advocated democracy, which he considered mob rule. Instead, Aristotle advocated a gov-

ernment of wealthy gentlemen who had been trained by philosophers—not the best regime imaginable but, in Aristotle's opinion, the best one possible.

Aristotle believed that men had stronger capacities to make judgments than women and so should rule over them. He condemned states like Sparta that accorded power to women. (See the box, "Spartan Women," on page 88.) Hence, Aristotle would be cited in later centuries to justify male dominance. Ironically, however, Aristotle was more enlightened on gender issues than most contemporaries; for example, he believed that since women played a crucial role in the family, they should receive education in morality.

Aristotle may be the single most influential thinker in Western history. His scientific writings were not only the most influential philosophical classics of Greek civilization, and of Roman civilization as well, but remained so during the Middle Ages in the Arabic and Latin worlds. For more than two thousand years there were no serious challenges to Aristotle's intellectual supremacy.

Athenian Drama

Perhaps the greatest art form that emerged in the polis was drama. Modern comedy and tragedy find distant ancestors in the productions of Athens's theater of Dionysus, named for the god of unrestraint, liberation, and wine (also known as Bacchus). Comedy and tragedy began in religious festivals honoring the god but quickly became an independent forum for comment on public life.

Ancient drama was poetry, not prose. Because it highlighted the relation of the individual to the community, drama proved to be the most suitable poetic medium for the ideology of the polis.

According to ancient tradition, tragedy was first presented at the Dionysia festival in Athens by one Thespis in the 530s B.C. (hence the word *thespian* for "actor"). The first surviving tragedy dates from the 470s, the first surviving comedy from the 420s. A play in the fifth century B.C. consisted of a chorus (a group of performers working in unison) and three individual actors who played all the various individual speaking parts. Plays were performed in an open-air theater on the south hillside of the Acropolis. Enormously popular, drama spread all over Greece, and eventually most poleis had a theater.

Theater at Delphi Open to the air, an ancient Greek theater contained tiers of stone benches above a circular area where the action took place, behind which backdrops could be erected. The audience often had a view of stirring scenery that, at Delphi, included the temple of Apollo and the valley below. *(Art Resource)*

Classical Athenian tragedy was performed at the annual Dionysia in March. Each playwright would submit a trilogy of plays on a central theme, plus a raucous farce to break the tension afterward. Comedies, which were independent plays rather than trilogies, were performed both at the Dionysia and at a separate festival held in winter. Wealthy producers competed to outfit the most lavish and impressive productions. Judges would award prizes for the best plays: a typical reflection of Greek competitiveness.

Tragedy is not easy to define, except generally: a serious play with an unhappy ending. Perhaps a short tag from the playwright Aeschylus can be said to sum up tragedy if anything can: *pathos mathei*, "suffering teaches." The essence of tragedy is what has been called the tragic sense of life: the nobility in the spectacle of a great man or woman failing but learning from failure. In *Oedipus the Tyrant* (ca. 428 B.C.) by Sophocles, for example, the hero kills his father and unknowingly marries his mother. Oedipus cannot escape the consequences of his deeds, but he can react to his fate with dignity and heroism; he can try to understand it. Oedipus loses his power as tyrant and goes into exile, but he retains a degree of honor. He executes his own punishment by blinding himself. As Aristotle observed, tragedy derives its emotional power from the fear and pity that it evokes and from the purification (*katharsis*) of the senses that it leaves in its aftermath.

The great period of Attic tragedy began and ended in the fifth century B.C. Aeschylus (525–456 B.C.), Sophocles (ca. 495–406 B.C.), and Euripides (ca. 485–406 B.C.) were and are considered the three giant playwrights. Although there were other tragedians, only the works of these three men (or, rather, a small fraction of their works) have survived. Aeschylus was perhaps the most pious of the three. His plays—notably the trilogy of the *Oresteia* (the *Agamemnon,* the *Libation Bearers,* and the *Eumenides*), the only surviving tragic trilogy, dating from 458 B.C.—take as their central question the justice of Zeus. The subject is the myth of the house of Atreus—in particular, the murder of King Agamemnon by his much-wronged wife, Clytemnestra, and her murder in turn by their son, Orestes, avenger of his father. Aeschylus casts this primitive saga into an epic of the discovery of justice. Zeus puts an end to revenge killings and institutes the supposed first court of law: the court of the Areopagus in Athens.

Sophocles, too, was interested in divine justice; he focuses on the relationship between the individual and the community. Heroic individuals have a spark of the divine in them, but by towering over ordinary people, they threaten them. In *Antigone* (ca. 442 B.C.), for example, the heroine refuses to compromise with injustice. Her late brother had committed treason, for which his corpse is denied burial—the standard Greek punishment. Antigone, however, insists on following a higher law, Zeus's law, which demands that all bodies be buried. Turmoil, disorder, and death ensue, but Antigone stays true to principle.

Of the three tragedians, Euripides is the least traditional and the most influenced by the Sophists. His plays reflect the disillusionment of the Peloponnesian War era. Euripides was more impressed by divine power than by divine justice. The central gods of Aeschylean drama are Zeus the father and Apollo the lawgiver, while Sophocles focuses on semidivine heroes, but Euripides' major deities are Dionysus and Aphrodite, goddess of erotic passion. In *Medea* (431 B.C.), for example, Euripides dissects the feelings of love, jealousy, and revenge that drive a woman to murder her own children in order to avenge herself on her faithless husband (the children's father). In the *Bacchae* (406 B.C.), an arrogant young king named Pentheus is punished for refusing to recognize the power of Dionysus (Bacchus). When he goes to the hills to spy on drunken women called Bacchae who are worshiping the god, he ends up as their prisoner. Driven to frenzy by Dionysus, the women do not recognize the king; Pentheus's own mother, one of the Bacchae, mistakes him for an animal and kills him.

The changes in tragedy from Aeschylus to Euripides reflect the changes in Athens as first imperial arrogance and then the Peloponnesian War took their moral toll. Aeschylus's confidence in the goodness of the community gives way first to a focus on the individual and then to a fundamental doubt about the possibility of goodness. The civic order, celebrated so confidently at the end of the *Oresteia* (458 B.C.), looks less certain in Sophocles' *Oedipus* (ca. 428 B.C.) and by the time of Euripides' *Bacchae* (406 B.C.) seems terrifyingly weak.

Comedy, too, was invented in Athens in the Classical period. Like tragedy, comedy offers a moral commentary on contemporary Athenian life. Unlike tragedy, which is usually set in the past and takes its characters from mythology, Athenian comedy (the so-called Old Comedy) is set in the present and pokes fun at politicians and public figures. Whereas tragedy is generally serious and sad, comedy is humorous.

The greatest writer of comedy in the fifth century B.C. was Aristophanes (ca. 455–385 B.C.). His extant plays are lively, ribald, even scatological, and full of allusions to contemporary politics. Aristophanes loved to show the "little guy" getting the better of the powerful and women deflating the pretensions of men. In *Lysistrata* (411 B.C.), his best-known play, he imagines the women of Greece stopping the Peloponnesian War by going on a sex strike, which forces the men to make peace.

Historical Thought and Writing

Like drama, history flourished in the exciting intellectual atmosphere of classical Athens. Indeed, its two greatest historians, Herodotus (ca. 485–ca. 425 B.C.) and Thucydides (ca. 455–ca. 399 B.C.), are among the founders of history-writing in the West. This is not to discount the contributions of, for example, the Hittites or Hebrews, or the chronicles, inventories, and genealogies of early Greece. Herodotus and Thucydides, however, are more rationalistic than their predecessors, and their subject matter was war, politics, peoples, and customs—what we think of as the stuff of history-writing today. Indeed, the word *history* comes from a word used by Herodotus, *historiai,* meaning "inquiries" or "research."

The works of Herodotus (*The Histories*) and Thucydides (*The Peloponnesian War*) have unifying themes. The theme of Herodotus's *Histories* is the rise and fall of empires. Herodotus sees the Persian Wars as merely one episode in a vast historical drama. Again and again, hardy, disciplined peoples conquered their neighbors, grew wealthy, were corrupted by a life of luxury, and were eventually conquered in turn. Success made people arrogant, driving them to commit injustices, which were eventually punished by Zeus. The breadth of Herodotus's vision is noteworthy. A native of Hali-

carnassus (a polis on the southwestern coast of Anatolia), Herodotus traveled widely, eventually settling in Athens. He wrote not only about Greeks but also about Persians, Egyptians, and a host of other peoples in Europe, Asia, and Africa. (See the box, "Encounters with the West: The Enemy as Barbarian," on page 102.)

Only a child at the time of the Persian Wars, Herodotus gathered information by interviewing older people in various countries as well as by checking what limited written public records existed. Herodotus also wrote about previous centuries and places he had not visited, but with uneven accuracy. He could rarely resist a good story, and alongside solid research are tall tales, unconfirmed accounts, and myths.

Thucydides, however, by contrast, prided himself on accuracy. He confined himself mainly to writing about an event that he had lived through and participated in: the Peloponnesian War. A failed Athenian general, Thucydides spent most of the Peloponnesian War in exile, carefully observing, taking notes, and writing.

Like Herodotus, Thucydides was influenced by the grandeur of tragedy; he also shows the signs of the sophistic movement, especially in the finely crafted speeches he includes. Thucydides' great theme is the disastrous effect of war on the human soul. He believed that the Peloponnesian War proved that war is a harsh teacher that strips away the veneer of civilization and reveals the savagery of human nature. In Thucydides' opinion, Pericles' Athens had been a high point in the history of civilization. The strain of prolonged war, however, destroyed Athens's moral fiber as well as its empire.

SUMMARY

Western philosophy, science, politics, sculpture, painting, and literary genres such as comedy, tragedy, and history all crystallized in Archaic and Classical Greece. The focus of Greek life was the city-state, or polis. Though small, exclusive, often factionalized, and rarely capable of achieving unity in a large area, the polis may be unparalleled in its ability to foster individual creative genius. At the same time, the polis promoted the idea that public duty is more important than private advantage.

Paradox was the hallmark of the polis, tension a theme in Greek civilization. The Greeks invented democracy while at the same time limiting the freedom of women and immigrants, oppressing slaves, and engaging in imperialism. Although the Greeks originated the concept that natural phenomena have natural causes, they nonetheless recognized the power of the irrational—be it divine whims or human emotions. With its democracy, freedom, and high culture, Athens stands for one aspect of the achievement of the polis while, with its hierarchy, militarism, and austerity, Sparta stands for another.

Athens reached its peak under Pericles, whose leadership in the mid-fifth century B.C. ushered in a time of empire, prosperity, and cultural greatness. The major tragedians were all active, and the sophistic movement was at its most optimistic and progressive. Periclean Athens was unique, if not for the sheer concentration of talent, then for the sense that the state, the cultural elite, and the people were united in a common pursuit.

If later times witnessed a fall from that state of grace, they did not suffer any decline in creative achievement. The Peloponnesian War (431–404 B.C.) marked the beginning of a century in which Greek warfare was more brutal than before. Yet this century also witnessed, among other cultural achievements, the comedies of Aristophanes, the history-writing of Herodotus and Thucydides, and the philosophy of Socrates, Plato, and Aristotle.

By the end of the fourth century the polis was to lose its independence to a powerful monarchy. In succeeding years, new cities in western Asia and Egypt would have the wealth and power to challenge such old centers as Athens as cultural capitals. Yet the culture that flourished in the new sites was Greek culture. The polis lost its freedom but it gained a central place in the legacy of the West.

NOTES

1. Excerpt from a poem by Solon, cited in Aristotle, *Constitution of Athens*, trans. Barry S. Strauss.
2. Charles Rowan Beye, *Ancient Greek Literature and Society*, 2d ed., rev. (Ithaca, N.Y.: Cornell University Press, 1987), p. 78.
3. Ibid., p. 79.

4. Adapted from Richmond Lattimore, trans., *Greek Lyrics*, 2d ed. (Chicago: University of Chicago Press, 1960), p. 19.
5. Herodotus, *The Histories*, trans. Barry S. Strauss.
6. Thucydides, *The Peloponnesian War*, trans. Barry S. Strauss.

SUGGESTED READING

General Surveys

Beye, C. R. *Ancient Greek Literature and Society.* 2d ed. 1987. A witty and readable analysis from Homer to the Hellenistic era.

Biers, W. *The Archaeology of Ancient Greece: An Introduction.* Rev. ed. 1987. A clear presentation of the achievements and variety of archaeological excavation of Greece.

Cartledge, Paul. *The Greeks. Self and Other.* 1993. A challenging but rewarding introduction to the impact of Continental social-scientific theory on the study of ancient Greek history.

Finley, M. I. *The Ancient Economy.* 1973. A broad and insightful comparison of Greece and Rome and an excellent introduction to the subject.

Forrest, W. G. *The Emergence of Greek Democracy.* 1966. A well-illustrated and vivid introduction to the mainstream interpretation of Greek politics and society from around 800 to 400 B.C.

Green, Peter. *Ancient Greece: An Illustrated History.* 1973. Concise, useful, readable, and beautifully illustrated.

Murray, Oswyn. *Early Greece.* 1980. The best one-volume introduction to the Archaic era, with an emphasis on society and culture.

Pomeroy, S. *Goddesses, Whores, Wives, and Slaves: Women in Classical Antiquity.* 1975. An overview of women in politics and society in Greece, the Hellenistic world, and Rome.

Athens and Sparta

Cartledge, Paul. *Agesilaos and the Crisis of Sparta.* 1987. An introduction to classical Spartan society and politics as well as a specialized study and biography.

de Ste. Croix, G. E. M. *The Origins of the Peloponnesian War.* 1972. A wide-ranging analysis laying blame for the war squarely on Sparta's shoulders.

Hansen, Mogens Herman. *Athenian Democracy in the Age of Demosthenes.* 1991. A survey that places the political system in its social context.

Humphreys, S. C. *The Family, Women and Death: Comparative Studies.* 2d ed. 1993. Provocative and stimulating essays, influenced by anthropology, on classical Athenian society.

Just, Roger. *Women in Athenian Law and Life*. 1989. A careful examination of the evidence to reconstruct the reality and ideology of women in Athens in the fifth and fourth centuries B.C.

Kagan, Donald. *The Outbreak of the Peloponnesian War*. 1969. The first of a four-volume history of the war, this readable and stimulating book argues, against Thucydides, that the war could have been avoided.

Manville, P. B. *The Origins of Citizenship in Ancient Athens*. 1990. A thoughtful discussion based on comparative anthropology as well as close reading of Greek sources.

Ober, Josiah. *Mass and Elite in Democratic Athens: Rhetoric, Ideology, and the Power of the People*. 1989. A thorough and eloquent argument that Athens was a genuine democracy, in which the people ruled by ensuring that politicians listened to them.

Powell, Anton. *Athens and Sparta: Constructing Greek Political and Social History from 478 B.C.* 1988. A lively and scholarly introduction to the social and political history of the two most prominent Greek city-states of the fifth century B.C.

Strauss, Barry S. *Athens After the Peloponnesian War: Class, Faction, and Policy 403–386 B.C.* 1987. A case study of the interaction of politics and society and of war and peace in classical Athens.

———. *Fathers and Sons in Athens: Ideology and Society in the Era of the Peloponnesian War*. 1993. An examination of the degree to which Athenians imagined the Peloponnesian War as a metaphorical conflict of the generations.

Other City-States and Regions

Legon, Ronald P. *Megara: The Political History of a Greek City-State to 336 B.C.* 1981. An alternative to the usual emphasis on Athens and Sparta, this book examines the fortunes of a small polis astride the land route between Peloponnesus and central Greece.

Salmon, J. B. *Wealthy Corinth*. 1984. An examination of the history of what was perhaps the third most powerful Greek city-state, after Sparta and Athens.

Shipley, Graham. *A History of Samos, 800–188 B.C.* 1987. A political, sociological, and archaeological study of one of the most important of the Greek city-states, an island off the coast of Anatolia.

Society and Culture

Burkert, Walter. *Greek Religion*. 1985. A thorough and logical introduction.

Connor, W. R. *Thucydides*. 1984. A sophisticated and rewarding analysis of an ancient historian using the techniques of literary criticism.

Dover, K. J. *Greek Homosexuality*. Updated ed. 1989. A judicious introduction, with emphases on Athens, oratory, and vase-painting.

Fantham, Elaine, Helene Peet Foley, et al. *Women in the Classical World: Text and Image*. 1995. A scholarly and readable introduction, up to date and well illustrated.

Gould, John. *Herodotus*. 1989. A short and lively essay on the mind of the historian; a fine introduction.

Hall, Edith. *Inventing the Barbarian: Greek Self-Definition Through Tragedy*. 1989. Discusses the appearance, for the first time in the West, of the notion of the enemy as barbarian as it emerges in fifth-century B.C. Athenian literature.

Hanson, Victor Davis. *The Western Way of War: Infantry Battle in Classical Greece*. 1989. This well-written book evokes what fighting in a hoplite phalanx might have felt like.

———. *The Other Greeks: The Agricultural Roots of Western Civilization*. 1995. An argument for the importance of the independent small farmer to the creation of the Greek and hence Western ideals of freedom and equality.

Hurwit, J. *Art and Culture of Early Greece, 1100–480 B.C.* 1985. A discussion that places art in its societal context.

Irwin, T. *Classical Thought*. 1989. A reliable sketch of the outlines of ancient Greek philosophy.

Lloyd, G. E. R. *Early Greek Science: Thales to Aristotle*. 1971. A thoughtful and readable discussion of science in its social and cultural context.

Morgan, Catherine. *Athletes and Oracles: The Transformation of Olympia and Delphi in the Eighth Century B.C.* 1990. An archaeological and historical study of the role of religious sanctuaries and athletic games in the rise of the Greek polis.

Morris, Ian. *Burial and Ancient Society: The Rise of the Greek City-State*. 1987. A sophisticated analysis of gravesites and what they indicate about the origins of the polis.

Pollitt, J. J. *Art and Experience in Classical Greece*. 1972. An essay on the interrelationship of art, society, and culture in the fifth and fourth centuries B.C.

Starr, Chester. *The Influence of Seapower on Ancient History*. 1989. A concise overview, written with a sense of antiquity's importance in the larger scheme of naval history.

Thomas, Rosalind. *Literacy and Orality in Ancient Greece*. 1992. A demonstration that ancient culture was primarily oral rather than written.

Wiedemann, Thomas, ed. *Greek and Roman Slavery*. 1981. A collection of translated ancient sources, with commentary.

THE PARTHENON

The Parthenon, completed in 432 B.C., dominates both the skyline of Athens and the historical imagination of the West. The building's fine marble and classical proportions seem to bespeak the free, confident, and united society that one might expect of Periclean Athens, the world's first democracy (see illustration, page 105). A close look, however, suggests a more complex story. The Parthenon's sculpture offers glimpses of the tensions behind the classical façade.

The temple of Athena Parthenos ("the Maiden"), as the Parthenon is formally known, was a public project of Greece's wealthiest city-state, leading naval power, and premier democracy. Athenians spared no expense on its construction. Sculpture included a gold-and-ivory statue of the goddess Athena inside the temple and, on the outside, statuary in each pediment (the triangular space under the eaves) and sculptured reliefs running around the building above the exterior and interior colonnades.

So lavish a program of art demonstrated Athenian wealth but also served an educational purpose: to illustrate basic Athenian values. Because every Athenian male was expected to fight for the city when called on, militant competition is a central theme. Above the exterior colonnade, for example, ninety-two separate panels of relief sculpture depict gods and heroes fighting such foes as giants and centaurs. The sculpture above the interior colonnade is not so easily characterized, however.

The interior sculpture forms a continuous band, or frieze, around the four sides of the building. There are warriors aplenty, primarily cavalrymen but also hoplites and charioteers. See the detail from the west wall. Two riders are illustrated here: one turning and signaling, the other taking

The Parthenon Frieze, Detail from West Wall (*Courtesy of the Trustees of the British Museum*)

The Parthenon Frieze, Detail from East Wall (*The Louvre*)

control of a rearing horse. Naked youths, they embody the ideal of strong bodies in the service of the polis. The long hair worn by the first rider was popular among the upper classes, a reminder that Athenian cavalrymen were aristocrats.

Not all of the men in the interior frieze are warriors, though, and women, too, are depicted. See the detail from the east wall. Look at the four women shown here. Like the riders, they are young and in pairs, but there the similarity ends. The women are on foot, clothed, and in solemn procession. The heavy folds of their robes, the hands held at the side, and the expression on the one face that is visible, all suggest calm and decorum.

From both of these pieces we may detect Athenian commonplaces about gender. Young women were expected to be maidenly, reserved, and modest. Their bodies were to be kept private. Young men were expected to be outgoing and assertive. Although men wore clothes in public, they exercised naked in gymnasia, wrestling-grounds, and stadiums, competing in a healthy activity considered to be good preparation for war.

The historian finds subtler messages in the two scenes. For example, however constrained the role of women, their very presence in the frieze is significant. Women were not permitted to attend the Athenian assembly, but they participated in the rituals and festivals that played so large a role in Athenian public life. Notice, for instance, the two girls shown in the back who are carrying ritual vessels.

One group of people is notably absent from the frieze: Athenian rowers. The rowers who manned Athens's warships were poor men and the most loyal supporters of democracy. Why are they not depicted on a temple built by vote of Athens's popular assembly, the disbursements for whose construction were inscribed in stone and posted nearby so that any citizen could inspect the way public funds were handled?

The answer depends on knowing precisely what the frieze as a whole depicts, but that knowledge—despite the fame of the Parthenon and the relative wealth of documentation from Periclean Athens—is embarrassingly shaky. Most scholars argue that the subject is the Pan-Athenaic procession, held once every four years to honor Athena. The people depicted are said to be the people of Athens—a daring novelty, considering that all previous Greek temple sculpture was restricted to gods, heroes, and mythological figures.

Yet if the scene is the Pan-Athenaic procession, how are we to explain the absence of certain well-known features of that procession—for instance, a large ship model? Some scholars prefer to view the scene as an illustration of a legend from the early history of Athens, a period in which rowers played little role in the Athenian military. Still, there are many nautical motifs in Athenian myth, motifs the Athenians could have chosen to illustrate if they had wished to celebrate the rowers.

Clearly, the Athenians preferred to depict hoplites and horsemen. Some might conclude that Athens was not as democratic as it claimed to be. Another explanation is that Athenian rowers, despite all their political assertiveness, admired the ideal of the hoplite and appreciated good horsemanship, and that conservative traditions died hard even in democratic Athens. ✎

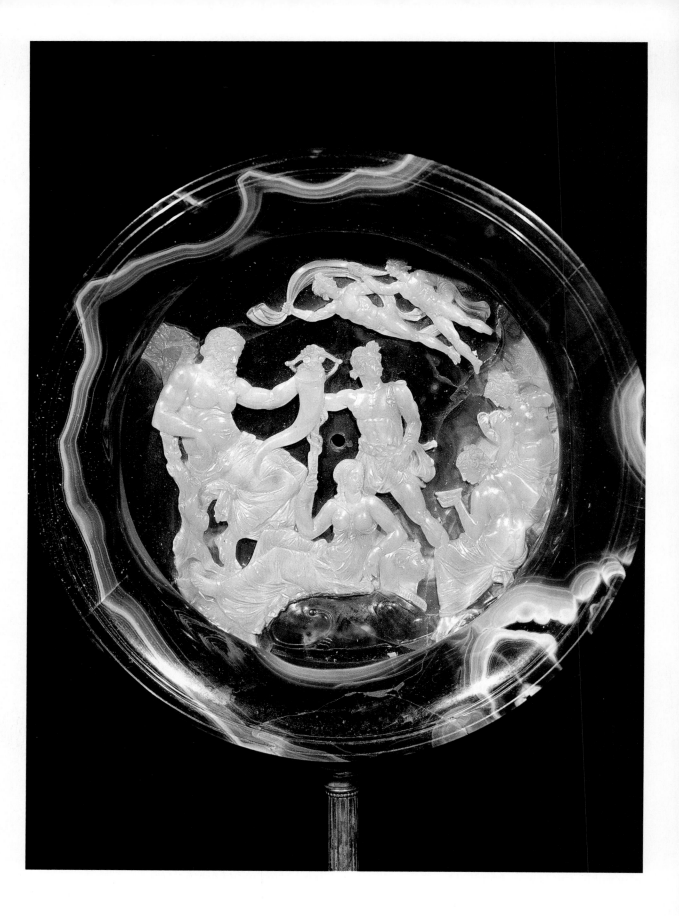

CHAPTER 4

The Hellenistic World, 323–30 B.C.

Around 270 B.C., a grand procession made its way along the broad avenues of Alexandria, the capital city of Egypt. The attractions included exotic animals from Ethiopia, Arabia, India, and Greece; floats carrying statues of gods, kings, and personifications of cities; soldiers in armor and women in finery; and gold and silver everywhere: in crowns, cups, and jewelry. The parade, and the festival of which it was a part, advertised the ruling dynasty, the Ptolemies: their authority, their wealth, and their empire. More important, it demonstrated the new realities of power established in the preceding half-century: The Greek world had expanded into Egypt and across western and central Asia as far as the Indian border.

Achieved by military conquest, that expansion was led by Macedon. A northeastern Greek kingdom that had previously been only a fringe power, Macedon rose meteorically under King Philip II (r. 359–336 B.C.) until it became the leader of Greece. Philip was a brilliant and ambitious general, but his son and successor, Alexander the Great (r. 336–323 B.C.), outstripped him.

In barely a dozen years, Alexander laid the foundations of a new Greek world: the world of the Hellenistic period (323–30 B.C.), in which Hellenic, or Greek, language and civilization spread and were transformed. This era was distinct in many ways from the preceding Hellenic period (ca. 750–323 B.C.). In Hellenistic times, Macedonians and Greeks replaced Persians as the ruling people of Egypt and western Asia. Large numbers of Greek-speaking colonists moved south and east. Governed by Macedonian dynasties, Egypt and the Levant became integral parts of the Greek world and remained so until the Arab conquest in the seventh century A.D. Greek-speaking kingdoms thrived briefly as far from mainland Greece as modern Afghanistan

The Nile (far left) and other figures symbolizing agricultural fertility: the "Farnese Plate" cameo.

119

and Pakistan. At times the new ruling elite was open to natives who learned Greek and adopted Greek ways, but more often the natives were excluded and exploited.

Conquest put huge amounts of wealth into Greek hands. Great new cities were built: Antioch in Syria, Pergamum in Anatolia, Seleucia in Mesopotamia, and, greatest of all, Alexandria in Egypt. Trade increased and expanded southward and eastward. The scale of political life expanded as well. Federal leagues replaced cities in importance in much of south and central Greece, while monarchies ruled most of the rest of the Greek-speaking world.

Material and political expansion led to unanticipated cultural changes. Hellenistic Greeks were as likely to be subjects of a king or members of a federation as they were to be citizens of an independent city-state. Frequently finding themselves among strange peoples, the Greeks sought comfort in new philosophies, religions, and modes of literary and artistic expression. Science flourished under royal patronage, as did the emerging discipline of literary criticism. The prestige of royal women tended to promote improvements in the overall status of Greek women.

Hellenistic Greeks boasted of having created one world, a common or ecumenical region (from the Greek *oikoumene*, "inhabited [area]"). In truth, that world was multiplex. The Greeks dominated government, but not without native assistance. Meanwhile, native cultures flourished. Greeks adapted and Hellenized a number of Egyptian and Asian deities. The seeds were sown in this era, moreover, for a momentous cross-fertilization between native and Greek religion: Christianity, which emerged from the contacts between Greeks and Jews in Hellenistic times.

PHILIP AND ALEXANDER

The Hellenistic world was founded by two conquerors: Philip II of Macedon (382–336 B.C.) and his son, Alexander III, known as Alexander the Great (356–323 B.C.). After a century of indecisive warfare among the Greek city-states, Philip conquered them in twenty years; in even less time Alexander conquered Egypt and all of western

Asia as far east as modern Pakistan. The legacy of these impressive conquests was a revolution in the history of the Mediterranean.

The Rise of Macedon

Macedon was a border state, long weaker than its more advanced neighbors but capable of learning from them and ultimately of conquering them. Though rich in resources and manpower, Macedon lacked the relatively efficient organization of the polis. It included both tribal groups and cities. Several dialects of Greek were spoken, some unintelligible to southern Greeks, who considered Macedonians "barbarians" (from the Greek *barbaros*, meaning "a person who does not speak Greek"). Ordinary Macedonians lived rough, sturdy lives, while the king and the royal court inhabited a sophisticated capital city: at Pella they sponsored visits by leading Greek artists and writers. Philip confounded Greek stereotypes of Macedonian barbarism by turning out to be a brilliant soldier and statesman—a man of vast ambition, appetite, and energy. A hard drinker, vain, and a man with numerous wives and lovers, he was also an excellent orator and general. Philip's goals were to make himself dominant in Macedon and then, after neutralizing opposition in Greece, to conquer the Persian Empire, or at least its holdings in Anatolia. He accomplished all but the last.

The instrument of Philip's success was his army, a well-trained, professional, year-round force. Macedon, with its plains and horses, was cavalry country, and Philip made cavalry his main attack weapon. The Macedonian phalanx was meant to hold the enemy phalanx until the cavalry could find a weak spot and attack. Accordingly, Macedonian hoplites carried extra-long pikes to stop the enemy at a distance without engaging him head on. Philip also mastered the technology of siegecraft, raising it to a level unseen since Assyrian days (see page 46).

Philip used his army effectively. After capturing the lucrative gold mine of Mount Pangaeum in Thrace (the region east of Macedon), he turned to the Greek city-states nearby. Olynthus, the most important, fell in 348 B.C. Led by the Athenian Demosthenes (ca. 385–322 B.C.), the main Greek city-states prepared to make a stand. Demosthenes was a superb orator, but his attempts to forge a unified force came too late. By 338 B.C., when an Atheno-Theban army met the Macedonians, Philip had already won over much of the Greek world (see Map 4.1). His complete military victory at Chaeronea in Boeotia was followed up with a lenient settlement in which all the Greeks except Sparta acknowledged Philip's hegemony. The Greeks would rebel against Macedon more than once, but always in vain, until they fell under the even greater power of Rome. The day was over when the polis could decide the fate of the eastern Mediterranean.

In 336 B.C., Philip was murdered by a disgruntled courtier, and the invasion of the Persian Empire fell to his 20-year-old son, Alexander, the new king.

FOUNDATIONS OF THE HELLENISTIC WORLD

359–336 B.C.	Reign of Philip II of Macedon
338 B.C.	Battle of Chaeronea
336–323 B.C.	Reign of Alexander the Great
331 B.C.	Battle of Gaugamela
322–275 B.C.	Wars of the Successors
312 B.C.	Seleucus I conquers Babylon
304 B.C.	Ptolemy I king of Egypt
276 B.C.	Antigonus Gonatas king of Macedon

Alexander the Conqueror

Alexander III of Macedon (r. 336–323 B.C.) is as famous in art as in literature, in romance as in history, in Iran or India as in Europe or America. Yet the evidence for the historical Alexander is almost as problematic as that for the historical Socrates or Jesus. After Alexander's untimely death at age 32, contemporaries wrote histories and memoirs, but none has survived. Several good historical accounts, based on earlier texts, are extant, but none was written less than three hundred years after Alexander's day. (See the box, "Virtues and Vices of Alexander the Great.") Alexander, moreover, was not only a legend in his own time but a master propagandist. Many of the incidents of his life took place in remote regions or among a few individuals, and they tended to grow with the telling.

Still, Alexander's virtues are clear. He was charismatic, handsome, intelligent, and well educated; as a teenager he had Aristotle himself as a private tutor. Alexander was ruthless as well as cultured. He began his reign with a massacre of his male relatives, but he brought a team of Greek scientists along with him on his expedition through the Persian Empire. Although he destroyed peoples and places, Alexander founded twenty cities, one of which, Alexandria in Egypt, later grew into the largest city in the Mediterranean. For all his varied interests, however, Alexander was first and foremost a warrior. Battlefield commander of the Mace-

donian cavalry at age 18, he devoted most of the rest of his life to warfare.

As a leader of men, Alexander was popular and inspiring, and he shared risks with the troops. He knew the value of propaganda and took pains to depict his expedition to the Greek city-states as a war of revenge for Persia's invasion of Greece in 480 B.C. instead of what it actually was: an act of Macedonian imperialism. He loved the colorful gesture. He began his expedition to conquer Persia in 334 B.C. by sacrificing animals to the gods at Troy, a site evoking Homer's heroes.

On the eve of invasion, Persia vastly outnumbered Macedon on both land and sea. Darius III of Persia was rich, but Alexander's treasury was virtually empty. The Macedonian expeditionary force was short on supplies. The peoples in Persia's multi-ethnic empire were restive, but so too were Alexander's Greek allies, the mainstay of his fleet. One of Darius's advisers proposed a naval campaign to raise a revolt in Greece and force the Macedonians home. How then did Alexander propose to conquer Persia?

The answer was the Macedonian army. Although Alexander invaded Anatolia with only about 35,000 men, they were the fastest marching, most experienced, and most skilled army in the eastern Mediterranean. If Persia would fight the Macedonians in a set battle, Alexander might be confident of victory—and it appeared that Persia

Alexander Mosaic This detail of a Roman-era mosaic from Pompeii shows Alexander the Great in battle, probably at Issus. Shining in his battle armor, Alexander is bareheaded, with a wide-eyed, intense gaze betokening his power. The larger scene includes the Persian king Darius, fleeing in his chariot. *(Scala/Art Resource, NY)*

would indeed fight. Persian elite ideology impelled the army to face the enemy head-on. Darius, moreover, was a new monarch and a usurper and so under pressure to prove himself in the field. As expected, Macedon crushed the enemy. The war was decided in three great battles (Map 4.1): at the Granicus River in Anatolia (334 B.C.), at Issus in Syria (333 B.C.), and at Gaugamela in Mesopotamia (331 B.C.). Darius fled into Iran and was deposed, assassinated, and replaced by a man whom Alexander captured and executed. By 328, Alexander's claim to be king of Persia was sealed with blood and iron.

Having conquered the Persian heartland, Alexander turned eastward. The last seven years of his career are marked by three themes. First is the continuing and, in Alexander's mind, apparently open-ended military campaign. He pushed his army not only into the eastern parts of the Per-

sian Empire but beyond, into modern Pakistan, which had not been controlled by Persia since the early fifth century B.C. The Macedonians won a major victory there in 326 B.C. near the Hydaspes River (modern Jhelum River) over the army of King Porus, a force employing as many as two hundred elephants (see Map 4.1). Alexander's infantry suffered considerable casualties before inflicting enough wounds on the elephants to make them uncontrollable. Alexander prepared to continue eastward, perhaps as far as the Bay of Bengal, but his exhausted and homesick men had other plans. They mutinied beside the Hyphasis River (modern Beas River, near the modern Indo-Pakistani border) and forced Alexander finally to turn back. He reached Persia in late 325 B.C.

The second theme of Alexander's later career is his increasing despotism. After conquering Persia, Alexander turned on the Macedonian nobility,

Virtues and Vices of Alexander the Great

Writing in the second century A.D., the historian Arrian composed from earlier accounts what is now the best surviving history of Alexander. A military man himself, Arrian keenly appreciated Alexander's practical skills but was not blind to his flaws.

Alexander died in the 114th Olympiad, in the archonship of Hegesias at Athens [June 323 B.C.]. . . . He had great personal beauty, invincible power of endurance, and a keen intellect; he was brave and adventurous, strict in the observance of his religious duties, and hungry for fame. Most temperate in the pleasures of the body, his passion was for glory only, and in that he was insatiable. He had an uncanny instinct for the right course in a difficult and complex situation, and was most happy in his deductions from observed facts. In arming and equipping troops and in his military dispositions he was always masterly. Noble indeed was his power of inspiring his men, of filling them with confidence, and, in the moment of danger, of sweeping away their fear by the spectacle of his own fearlessness. When risks had to be taken, he took them with the utmost boldness, and his ability to seize the moment for a swift blow, before the enemy had any suspicion of what was coming, was beyond praise.

Doubtless, in the passion of the moment Alexander sometimes erred; it is true he took some steps towards the pomp and arrogance of the Asiatic kings: but I, at least, cannot feel that such errors were very heinous, if the circumstances are taken fairly into consideration. For, after all, he was young; the chain of his successes was unbroken, and, like all kings, past, present, and to come, he was surrounded by courtiers who spoke to please, regardless of what evil their word might do. On the other hand, I do indeed know that Alexander, of all the monarchs of old, was the only one who had the nobility of heart to be sorry for his mistakes.

Source: Arrian, *The Campaigns of Alexander,* trans. Aubrey de Sélincourt. Rev. J. R. Hamilton. (Harmondsworth, England: Penguin, 1971), pp. 395–396.

among whom he feared potential rivals, for Macedonian nobles had a tradition of rebelling against strong kings. The years after 330 B.C. are marked by conspiracy trials, purges, and assassinations. The most spectacular took place in 328 in Marakanda (modern Samarkand, located in Uzbekistan) when, after a drunken quarrel, Alexander himself murdered Cleitus, one of his senior commanders.

Another sign of Alexander's growing despotism was his demand for the trappings of Persian kingship. After conquering Persia, for example, he made independent-minded Greeks and Macedonians bow down before him. He required that the Greek city-states deify him. "If Alexander wishes to be a god, let him be," was the laconic reply of the Spartans, but Alexander had now set a prece- dent for both Hellenistic monarchs and Roman emperors.

The third theme of Alexander's later career is his novel policy of fusion. After returning from the Indian subcontinent, Alexander began training an army of 30,000 Iranians and dismissed a large number of Macedonian troops. He forced his main commanders to marry Iranian women, just as he did himself. In 324 B.C., Alexander staged a grand banquet in Mesopotamia for 9000, at which he prayed for "concord and a partnership in rule between Greeks and Persians." Such actions were a sharp break with traditional Greek ethnocentrism. Aristotle, for example, had referred to the peoples of western Asia as fit only to be slaves. Alexander's policy probably owed less to idealism

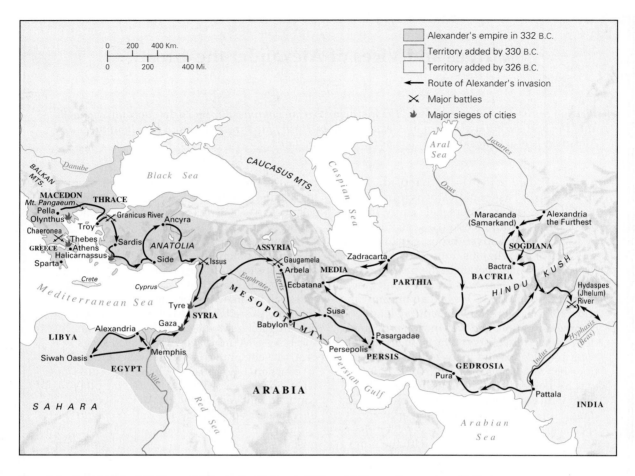

Map 4.1. Conquests of Philip and Alexander　Between 359 and 323 B.C., the armies of Macedon conquered first the Greek city-states and then the Persian Empire. Macedonian power extended from Greece and Egypt eastward to modern Pakistan.

than to a desire for a new power base independent of the Macedonian nobility.

Alexander died in Babylon in June of 323 B.C., a month before he turned 33, probably of malarial fever, although some contemporaries suspected poison and some historians have suggested drunkenness. Alexander did not designate a successor. His wife, pregnant at his death, would give birth to a son and heir, but he was shunted aside by the Macedonian generals, who began a long and bloody round of wars over the spoils of empire. It took approximately fifty years of fighting, from 322 to 275 B.C., to make clear that three large kingdoms—Macedon, Ptolemaic Egypt, and the Seleucid realm—would inherit most of Alexan-

der's empire. The rest was divided among small kingdoms, federal leagues, and independent city-states (see Map 4.2).

In the long run, Alexander's life was far more influential than his death. His conquests did nothing less than lay the foundations of the Hellenistic world. It is ironic to measure in such impersonal terms the achievements of one who, more than most people in history, exemplifies individual success. Whether it was exalting a savior or debunking a hero, much of Hellenistic culture centered on the myth of heroism that Alexander had engendered. Historians who believe the individual is insignificant will rarely have a more challenging counterexample than Alexander.

Map 4.2. Hellenistic Kingdoms, Leagues, and City-States, ca. 240 B.C. After Alexander's death, his empire lost its political unity. Great new cities and kingdoms arose in the lands he had conquered.

THE VARIETY OF THE HELLENISTIC KINGDOMS

Hellenistic political units ranged from multi-ethnic kingdoms to small, ethnically homogeneous city-states (Map 4.2). The history of the Greek peninsula was marked by a monarchy with republican pretensions and by experiments in federalism and in social revolution. In Asia and Egypt, Alexander's successors created a new ruling elite consisting both of Greeks and Macedonians and of natives. Although the first group tended to dominate high administrative and military office, natives were by no means excluded. The immigrants wanted land, wealth, or adventure. Their paths were smoothed by a new ideology that identified being Greek less with loyalty to an individual city than with participation in a common Greek civilization.

Although the Hellenistic world became relatively peaceful after 275 B.C., conflict among the kingdoms continued. Generally waged at a low level of intensity, with bribes and diplomacy as weapons, the conflict nonetheless sometimes broke out into major battles. Palestine and the southern Greek mainland and Aegean islands were chronic bones of contention among the large kingdoms. A number of small states emerged in Anatolia, notably Pergamum, whose wealthy rulers were patrons of literature and art, and Galatia, carved out by Celtic invaders from Europe.

Hellenism Redefined

The city-state of the Classical period was localistic: To be, say, a Theban, one had to be of Theban descent, live in Theban territory, and follow the Theban way of life. Disappointed by the endless wars and fragmentation of the fourth century B.C., however, Greek intellectuals moved away from particularism. A harbinger of things to come was Isocrates (428–338 B.C.), an Athenian teacher of rhetoric. Isocrates redefined the meaning of Greek identity. He promoted the idea that Greece was not a collection of city-states but, rather, a civilization. "The people we call Greeks," he wrote, "are those who have the same culture as us, not the same blood."[1]

By demoting the city, Isocrates promoted Pan-Hellenism, the ideal of Greek unity. Accordingly, he did not hesitate to support Philip of Macedon against his native Athens. Disillusioned by incessant warfare and disdainful of ordinary people, Isocrates rejected democracy, aiming instead to create a governing elite of educated gentlemen. Isocrates' ideas fell on ready ears, particularly after his death. Macedon, the dominant power in Greece, disliked democracy and preferred oligarchy, a regime closer to its own monarchy. Macedonian intervention in Greece contributed greatly to a general decline of democracy in the century following Alexander's death.

In the fourth century B.C., redefinition of Hellenism as a common culture made it easier for mainland Greeks to emigrate to far-off places and still consider themselves Greek. Finally, it was now possible for foreigners to become Greek by learning the Greek language and literature. The number of Hellenized foreigners was relatively small, yet their very existence marked a break from the Classical polis, where even a genius like Aristotle could not obtain Athenian citizenship because he was not of Athenian descent.

In the Hellenistic age, Greek competed with Aramaic to be the dominant language of the cities and of trade in the eastern Mediterranean. One obtains a sense of the importance of Isocrates' redefinition of Hellenism by considering that one of the most famous Greek-speakers of all antiquity was Paul, the Christian apostle who was born a Jew in Tarsus, a city in southern Anatolia.

Colonialism, Greek Style

Many Greeks and Macedonians emigrated south or east, especially during the fourth and third centuries B.C., but we do not know how many. The few surviving statistics indicate a significant migration but not a mass exodus. By the second century B.C., the colonizing impulse had diminished in Greece and Macedon, but there was a corresponding increase in Jewish emigration. The second century B.C. was a turbulent period in Palestine, and large numbers of Jews left, particularly for Egypt. Ptolemaic Egypt and the Seleucid realm were also the most common destinations for Greek and Macedonian migrants.

Immigrants sought to realize dreams of prosperity or adventure. Although agriculture was the main economic pursuit, trade, industry, finance, administration, and military service also offered opportunities. The large Ptolemaic bureaucracy offered numerous jobs in administration or tax collection.

In the Ptolemaic and Seleucid realms, administration was a joint effort of both immigrants and natives. The Macedonian conquerors might have preferred to rely on Macedonian and Greek administrators and soldiers, but there were never enough immigrants to make that possible. Besides the new rulers needed both the goodwill and the local knowledge of the people whom they had conquered. Thus, the upper echelons of government were dominated by Greek and Macedonian immigrants and their descendants, but native elites held governmental positions as well. Some natives served the new rulers as administrators or soldiers, usually in low- or mid-level positions but sometimes in high office. Others worked in the traditional native administrative structures that survived largely intact in the new kingdoms: They were judges or village headmen or priests.

Consider, for example, soldiers. To create a permanent, hereditary military group living in the countryside, Ptolemy I settled his soldiers on land allotments. Native Egyptians served as policemen. By the second century B.C., the dynasty turned to them as a new source of soldiers. In return for military service, natives now received land, tax breaks, and the right to call themselves Hellenes. Their Hellenism sometimes merely scratched the surface, but sometimes it entailed considerable cultural cross-fertilization.

An Egyptian named Plenis, a villager in middle Egypt in the late second century B.C., is a good example of this cross-fertilization. Plenis was a tenant farmer on a royal estate and a priest in a local Egyptian cult. His horizon was not narrow, however; like his father before him, Plenis served as a soldier in the Ptolemaic army. Plenis, moreover, could write Greek as well as Egyptian, and he even used a Greek name: Dionysius, son of Kephalas.

Temples, which often administered large estates, represented important sources of native power. Priests shaped local opinion and were in a position, therefore, both to enjoy considerable independence and to demand royal patronage. Both Ptolemies and Seleucids complied: From Babylon to Edfu, money poured into temple-building and renovation.

The Seleucids addressed the security needs of their far-flung realms by establishing over seventy colonies extending to central Asia. Some colonies were civilian, but most were military, composed of retired or reserve soldiers, mostly Greeks or Macedonians, but also including Jews and other non-Greek peoples. Colonists received land allotments. Greek-style public buildings were erected, and some cities were laid out according to a rectilinear grid plan reminiscent of the Classical polis. The gymnasium attained a great practical and symbolic importance as both the center of Greek culture and the preparatory school for entry into the elite. The Hellenistic gymnasium offered education in literature, philosophy, and oratory as well as athletics.

Some Seleucid colonies developed into flourishing cities. For example, Greek cities dominated the Syrian coastline and much of Anatolia until the coming of Islam in the seventh century A.D. Greek urbanization should not create the false impression, however, that the Seleucids were motivated by some civilizing mission. They were not. They established colonies to increase their power.

Immigration and colonization were not the only sources of new economic opportunities. At the beginning of the Hellenistic era, Alexander turned the huge gold and silver reserves of Persia into coinage and released it onto the market virtu-

Singing African This Hellenistic bronze figurine shows a black African, perhaps an Ethiopian, playing a musical instrument (now missing). The lithe body and emotionalism of the work are typically Hellenistic. Africans were a common subject for the sculptors of Alexandria, whence this piece may have come. *(Bibliothèque Nationale)*

ally all at once. Although Alexander's action stimulated a rapid inflation lasting about seventy-five years, it also had the positive effect of greatly stimulating commerce. In particular the economy of Hellenistic Egypt became highly monetarized, even on the village level. Barter continued to exist in Egypt, but the widespread presence of money served to stimulate the production and circulation of goods, helping to render Egypt an economic powerhouse. Another stimulus to trade was the creation of large, new Hellenistic cities, especially Alexandria with its great harbors, canals, marketplaces, and infrastructure of banks, inns, courts, and shipbuilding facilities.

During Hellenistic times, trade and commerce tended to shift from Greece proper to Anatolia and Egypt (see Map 4.3). The island of Rhodes, located off the southwest tip of Anatolia, grew into a major trading center, especially for grain. This development was the result of excellent harbors; a location on the merchant routes between Asia, Africa, and southeastern Europe; and a superb fleet. The Rhodian aristocracy grew rich off taxes and duties, wisely reinvesting a portion of the profits in naval infrastructure (such as arsenals and dockyards) and in campaigns against pirates. Egypt had many products to trade. Grain was the most important, but textiles, glass, papyrus (from which a kind of paper was produced), and luxury goods were also significant. Egyptian goods were sold throughout the Mediterranean. A network of canals connecting Alexandria to the Nile and the Red Sea beyond also made possible active trading with Sudan, Arabia, and India.

The Seleucid kingdoms controlled rich trade routes to Arabia, India, and central Asia. Commerce was facilitated by good roads, sea travel between the Persian Gulf and India, and a unified royal coinage. The Seleucids traded agricultural goods and manufactured products like textiles, glassware, and metalwork for spices from India and Arabia. In the first century B.C. they even had trade contacts with China, whose silk garments reached the Mediterranean. The kingdom of Pergamum, which stretched inland from Anatolia's northwest coast, exported the agricultural products of the rich hinterland it controlled, as well as the local gray-blue building stone and, as an alternative to Egyptian papyrus, parchment.

Slavery was an important part of the Hellenistic social and economic scene. Although war and piracy were the main sources of enslavement, some people were born into slavery. In Sicily and southern Italy, slaves worked huge plantations, but eastern Mediterranean slaves were commonly found in the household or in administration and in cities rather than in the countryside. Many unfree laborers worked on farms in Egypt and western Asia. Following the pre-Greek traditions of those regions, they were generally tenant farmers tied to kings or potentates rather than outright slaves.

On some plantations, conditions for slaves were bad enough to lead to mass uprisings. It was not unusual, however, for domestic or administrative slaves to buy their freedom, sometimes using savings they were allowed to keep, sometimes borrowing money from the master or from friends. Greeks enslaved fellow Greeks, but often, it seems, with guilty consciences; they frequently made special efforts to help Greek slaves win their freedom. Even as slaves, therefore, Greeks had special privileges.

Macedon and Greece

Macedon was the last of the three great Hellenistic kingdoms to emerge from civil war after Alexander's death. Not until 276 B.C. was Antigonus Gonatas, grandson of Alexander's general Antigonus the One-Eyed, established firmly on the throne. His Antigonid dynasty lasted about 140 years, until the Roman conquest.

True to the traditions of Macedon, the Antigonids projected an image of simplicity and toughness. Like Philip II and Alexander the Great, Antigonus immersed himself in the culture of the Greek city-states, partly because he admired it, partly because it brought him prestige. As a young man, Antigonus had studied the new school of Stoic philosophy in Athens (see page 142). As king, he devoted himself to the Stoic dictates of duty, describing his office as "noble servitude" and his diadem as a mere "rag." Antigonus shared the traditional Macedonian ambition to dominate the Greek city-states, but he faced rival powers (see Map 4.2). Besides Ptolemaic Egypt, there was the kingdom of Epirus in northwestern Greece and two new federal leagues in the south, the Aetolians (north of the Corinthian Gulf) and the Achaeans (in the Peloponnesus).

The federal leagues were more tightly organized than Classical Greek military leagues (such as the Peloponnesian League) and larger than the Boeotian League, a fourth-century B.C. federal league that had covered a relatively small territory. The new leagues permitted some participation by ordinary men but were dominated by the wealthy; they were not democracies.

Yet the leagues interest us as models of federalism that would one day influence the founders of the United States. The Aetolians, for example, practiced proportional representation by population in a federal council for constituent cities. The Achaeans successfully balanced local and federal authorities. Constituent cities kept their own constitutions while recognizing federal jurisdiction. The federal government consisted of a governing general (both president and commander-in-chief) and ten subordinate magistrates, an executive council and a general assembly. Assembly meetings alternated from city to city.

Athens, less successful than Sparta in maintaining independence, underwent frequent periods of Macedonian rule. Through a combination of war and diplomacy, however, Athens won periods of freedom from the late fourth to the mid-second century B.C., when all Greece came under Roman rule. Athens remained a vibrant democracy until the late third century B.C., when the oligarchic upper classes finally won the upper hand for good.

Extremes of wealth and poverty, problems of debt, and class conflict challenged Hellenistic Greece. The decline of democracy enabled the wealthy to contribute less to the public good in taxes and to amass private fortunes. The result was sometimes class conflict. Full-scale revolution, however, rarely occurred—in part because the elite sometimes bought off the poor with grain distributions and philanthropy, in part because poor citizens were unwilling to make common cause with slaves, whom they looked down on.

Revolution did briefly show its face in Sparta, thanks to the efforts of two great leaders. After defeat in the fourth century B.C., Sparta became impoverished (see page 103). In the late third century B.C., however, a social revolution was launched from above by Agis and Cleomenes, two Spartan kings working together. Their program included debt relief, a redistribution of land, and a restoration of classical Spartan austerity and equality. Popular in Sparta, the revolution threatened to spread elsewhere. Peloponnesian oligarchs called in Macedonian forces, which crushed Sparta in 222 B.C. and ended the revolution.

Ptolemaic Egypt

The wealthiest, the most sophisticated, and the longest lasting of the Hellenistic kingdoms was Ptolemaic Egypt. One of Alexander's great generals, Ptolemy, son of Lagus (d. 283 B.C.), became governor of Egypt in 323 B.C. and proclaimed himself king in 304. His dynasty lasted until Rome annexed Egypt in 30 B.C., after the suicide of the last of the line, Queen Cleopatra (see page 140). By contrast, Macedon was absorbed by Rome a century earlier, in 146; Pergamum was annexed in 133; the Seleucid kingdom was annexed in 64.

Unlike the Antigonids, the Ptolemies did not emulate the simple virtues but rather gloried in wealth and grandeur. Ptolemy I showed the way to his successors when he had Alexander's funeral procession hijacked on its way to Macedonia and established a tomb and regular cult in the capital city, Alexandria—a Greek hero-shrine in the land of the pyramids. Ptolemy I made arrangements to have himself proclaimed "Savior God" after his death; his successors, less reticent, took divine honors while still alive. Another legitimizing tool was the staging of splendid processions in Alexandria.

The most important Ptolemaic borrowing, however, was the pharaonic tradition of royal intervention in the economy, which the Ptolemies combined with Greek customs of literacy and the use of money rather than barter. The result was a highly complex and profitable economy. Putting to use the science of the Museum, the great institute in Alexandria (see page 135), the Ptolemies sponsored irrigation and land reclamation projects, the addition of new crops (for example, new varieties of wheat), and the greatly expanded cultivation of old ones (such as grapes for wine).

Most of the people of Egypt made their living in agriculture, either as independent small farmers or as tenants on large estates. Government enriched itself through taxes, rents, demands for compulsory labor, state monopolies (on such diverse items as oils, textiles, and beer), and various internal tolls and customs duties. The result was boom times under strong kings and queens in the third century B.C. Egypt became the most prosperous part of the Hellenistic world, and Alexandria became the most populous and wealthiest city in the Mediterranean, as well as its literary capital (Map 4.3). In the second century B.C., however, continued economic prosperity was offset by decline. Weak kings, bureaucratic corruption, inflation of the currency, and the end of Greek immigration created conditions for revolt.

Since pharaonic times tendencies toward regional independence had bedeviled Egypt's government. The Ptolemaic period was no exception. Regional unrest stirred in the 240s and then

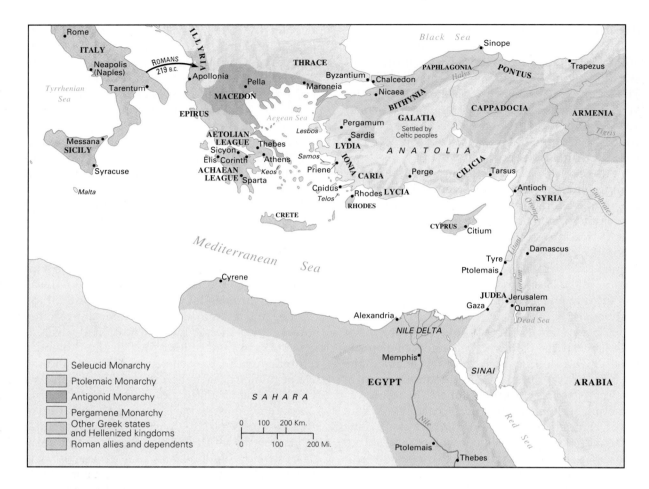

Map 4.3. The Eastern Mediterranean, ca. 200 B.C. The great Hellenistic powers contended for control of this vibrant, turbulent, and prosperous region. Conflict centered on Palestine and the Aegean islands, the rulership of which frequently changed hands.

burgeoned after the Battle of Raphia in 217 B.C., a struggle in Gaza between the Ptolemies and Seleucids for control of Palestine. The Ptolemies won, but only by enrolling thousands of Egyptians in the Macedonian phalanx, responding to a shortage of Greek mercenaries. Emboldened by their new military power, people in Upper Egypt soon broke into armed revolt against the government in far-off Alexandria. Rival kings appeared in the south, and unrest continued for about a century.

To advance their cause, the rebels inflamed anti-Greek sentiment. (See the box, "Encounters with the West: The Oracle of the Potter.") High taxes and regional rivalries, however, probably weighed more than nationalism in the minds of most people. Although friction between immigrants and natives sparked from time to time, most Egyptians readily accepted the Ptolemies as pharaohs as long as they brought peace and prosperity.

Nor did the Ptolemies allow national sentiment to stand in the way of reasserting their power. In 196 B.C., for example, Ptolemy V Epiphanes celebrated his coronation in full pharaonic ceremonial in Memphis. The occasion was recorded in Egypt's traditional language of kingship in a trilingual inscription (Greek, hieroglyphic, and demotic—ordinary—Egyptian). This inscription, discovered by Frenchmen in 1798 and dubbed the Rosetta Stone (named for the place where it was found), led to the modern European deciphering of hieroglyphics.

Despite the frictions, there is evidence of native-settler cooperation, especially in the countryside, where intermarriage and bilingualism became

∼ ENCOUNTERS WITH THE WEST ∼

The Oracle of the Potter

This document, from a Roman-era papyrus, is a version of a text first written about 130 B.C. Written in Greek, the papyrus is probably translated from an Egyptian original. It claims to be a prophecy from pharaonic times in which a potter predicts that Egypt will one day suffer under foreign rule until a savior-king rises, drives out the enemy, and restores prosperity. In fact, the text uses a traditional Egyptian literary form, prophecy, to support a revolt in Upper Egypt against Alexandria. Note the Egyptians' hostility to Alexandria and foreigners.

For in the time of the Typhonians [followers of the Egyptian god of the desert, storm, and foreigners] people will say "Wretched Egypt, you have been maltreated by the terrible malefactors who have committed evil against you." And the sun will darken as it will not be willing to observe the evils in Egypt. The earth will not respond to seeds. These will be part of its blight. The farmer will be dunned for taxes for what he did not plant. There will be fighting in Egypt because people will be in need of food. What one plants, another will reap and carry off. When this happens, there will be war and slaughter which will kill brothers and wives. For these things will happen when the great god Hephaistos [Ptah, patron god of Memphis, the largest native Egyptian city] will desire to return to the city [Memphis] and the Girdlewearers [the Greeks and Macedonians] will kill each other as they are Typhonians. . . .

Then the Good Daimon [the patron god of Alexandria] will abandon the city that had been founded and enter Memphis, and the city of foreigners [Alexandria], which had been founded, will be deserted. This will happen at the end of the evils of the time when there came to Egypt a crowd of foreigners. The city of the Girdlewearers [Alexandria] will be abandoned like my kiln because of the crimes which they committed against Egypt. The cult images, which had been transported there, will be brought back again to Egypt [from Alexandria], and the city by the sea [Alexandria] will be a refuge for fishermen because the Good Daimon and Knephis [an Egyptian god] will have gone to Memphis, so that passersby will say "All-nurturing was this city in which every race of men settled." Then will Egypt flourish when the generous fifty-five year ruler appears, the king descended from Helios, the giver of good things, the one installed by the greatest (Isis), so that the living will pray that the dead might arise to share the prosperity. Finally the leaves will fall. The Nile, which had never lacked water, will be full and winter, which had changed its orderly ways, will run its proper course and then summer will resume its own track, and normal will be the wind's breezes which previously had been weak.

Source: Stanley M. Burstein, ed. and trans. *The Hellenistic Age from the Battle of Ipsos to the Death of Kleopatra VII* (Cambridge, England: Cambridge University Press, 1985), pp. 136–137.

common. Many an ordinary Greek became fully assimilated to Egyptian ways. Over the centuries even wealthy, sophisticated, urban Greeks adopted a smattering of Egyptian customs. The Egyptian calendar, Egyptian names, and mummification were all in use. Certain Egyptian literary genres were translated into Greek and became popular: mimes (farces mimicking people and events), folktales, and romances. Around 280 B.C., Manetho, a native Egyptian priest, wrote a guide in Greek to Egyptian history and religion, establishing the standard division of ancient Egypt's dynasties. By 98 B.C., assimilation was evident in the cultural hybrid of a group of 18- and 19-year-old male youths

A Cretan Dream Interpreter in Egypt A painted stele (ca. 200 B.C.) advertises the services of a Greek in Memphis near the temple of Serapis, a Greco-Egyptian god. The inscription and pediment are Greek, while the pilasters, women, and sacred bull (facing an altar) are Egyptian. (*Egyptian Museum, Cairo*)

who received traditional Greek military and literary training but prayed to Egypt's crocodile-god.

Seleucids and Attalids

The kingdom founded by Alexander's general Seleucus (ca. 358–281 B.C.) experienced shifting borders and inhabitants. The Seleucid kingdom began when Seleucus took Babylon in 312 B.C. and ended in 64 B.C. when Syria became a Roman province. There were many territorial changes in between. The first three kings ruled a domain stretching from the Aegean to Bactria (modern Afghanistan), but by the early second century B.C. most of the Iranian Plateau and lands eastward

had been lost. At its height, in the third century B.C., the Seleucid kingdom had three nerve centers: Ionia (in western Anatolia), with a capital at Sardis; Syria, with a capital at Antioch; and Babylonia, whose capital was Seleucia-on-the-Tigris (near modern Baghdad; see Map 4.2).

Unlike the compact Nile Valley with its relatively homogeneous population, the far-flung and multi-ethnic Seleucid lands presented an enormous administrative challenge. To govern such a conglomerate, the kings took over the Persian system of satraps (provincial governors), taxes, and royal roads and post (see page 60), to which they added an excellent army trained according to Macedonian traditions, a common coinage, and a Hellenistic ruler cult. The chief Seleucid innovation was the establishment of colonies. Greek and Macedonian soldiers and administrators dominated, but the Seleucids also employed natives. Although Greek was the language of the court, Aramaic and Akkadian were frequently used for administration. There even exists an official Seleucid royal seal stamped in cuneiform.

Babylonia, an area of agricultural wealth, cultural sophistication, and strategic significance, was of great importance to the Seleucids. Archaeological evidence suggests that native Babylonian culture flourished and that traditional styles in art and architecture remained strong. The kings encouraged Greek settlement in this important region. In addition to the Greek city of Seleucia-on-the-Tigris, nearby Babylon had a Greek community, complete with gymnasium, agora, and theater, and was probably organized as a polis.

The greatest Seleucid city was Antioch, which became one of the wealthiest and most luxurious of all eastern Mediterranean cities; only Ptolemaic Alexandria outstripped it. The intellectual and artistic capital of Greek Asia in Hellenistic times, however, was not Antioch but Pergamum, in northwestern Anatolia (see Map 4.3).

The rulers of Pergamum, the Attalid dynasty of kings, carved out a small kingdom that became independent of the Seleucids in 263 B.C. and came into Roman hands in 133 B.C. The Attalids made Pergamum into a showplace of Greek civilization, a would-be second Athens. As in Athens, public building was focused on a steep acropolis. The upper city of Pergamum was laid out on hillside terraces rising to a palace and fortified citadel. One of the terraces housed the famous Pergamum Altar, a huge monument to an Attalid victory over the Celts, who first invaded Anatolia in 278 B.C. and whose advance the Attalids checked. They could not, however, stop the Celts from settling in central Anatolia, where they created their kingdom of Galatia.

Pergamum was famous for its sculptors and for a library second only to Alexandria's. Pergamene writers focused on scholarship to the exclusion of poetry, perhaps as a result of the influence of Stoic philosophers, who disapproved of poetry's emotionalism.

The Greco-Indian Interaction

The Seleucids could not hold on to Alexander's vast eastern domains in the long term. A new Persian dynasty, the Parthians, achieved independence in the mid-third century B.C. and over the

REBELLION AND REFORM	
263 B.C.	Kingdom of Pergamum founded
ca. 246 B.C.	Parthia revolts from Seleucids
ca. 245 B.C.	Bactria gains independence
244–222 B.C.	Reforms of Agis and Cleomenes in Sparta
217 B.C.	Battle of Raphia
167–142 B.C.	Maccabean revolt in Judea

next century carved out an empire extending westward into Mesopotamia. But to the east, Bactria remained Greek, if not Seleucid. From the mid-third century B.C., an independent Greek Bactria prospered (see Map 4.2).

Panel from Pergamum Altar This frieze (ca. 180–150 B.C.) decorating the podium of the altar of Zeus illustrates the war of the gods and the giants, imparting a heroic dimension to the battles of the Attalid kings and the Celts. The theme of Greeks and barbarians recalls the sculpture of Athens's Parthenon, suggesting that Pergamum was the successor to Athens as the champion of Greek civilization. *(Art Resource, NY)*

Vivid evidence of Greek colonization in Bactria comes from the site of Aï Khanum (its ancient name is unknown) in northern Afghanistan. This prosperous and populous city contained many reminders of Greece, among them a gymnasium, theater, and library. A pillar in the gymnasium was inscribed in the mid-third century B.C. with 140 moral maxims from Delphi in Greece, over 3000 miles away.

In the second century B.C., Bactrian kings extended their rule into the Indus River Valley and the Punjab, a region with a modest Greek presence since the fifth century B.C., when the Persians settled Greek mercenaries there. Virtually no literary evidence survives, but monuments and, particularly, coins demonstrate Greco-Indian cultural interaction. For example, some coins from the second century B.C. show bilingual inscriptions in Greek and Indian languages. Their designs include a variety of Indian religious motifs, such as the lotus plant, symbol of Lakshmi, goddess of wealth and good fortune. Indians admired Hellenistic astronomy; one text goes so far as to say that Greek scientists should be "reverenced like gods."

There is evidence of interest in the Hellenistic world on the part of King Asoka (r. ca. 270–230 B.C.), who ruled almost the entire subcontinent, the largest empire in India to date. Asoka is best remembered as a religious reformer. A convert to Buddhism, he played a major role in its spread, which proceeded under the slogan of *dhamma*, that is, morality or righteousness. One of his inscriptions records "victory" by dhamma, "where reigns the Greek king named Antiochus, and beyond the realm of Antiochus in the lands of the four kings named Ptolemy, Antigonus, Magas, and Alexander," which is generally thought to refer to embassies to the Hellenistic kingdoms.[2]

The envoys apparently found few converts, for it is difficult to find any trace of Buddhism in Hellenistic Greek culture, at least outside the Greco-Indian kingdoms. There, one of the most powerful Greek rulers, Menander Soter Dikaios (r. ca. 155–130 B.C.), may have converted to Buddhism in the mid-second century B.C. But Indian religion more generally did interest Greek intellectuals around the Mediterranean in Hellenistic and Roman times, especially India's powerful currents of asceticism, mysticism, and monasticism. Observers on Alexander's expedition, Hellenistic envoys, merchants, and philosophers in search of Eastern wisdom—all served as conduits between East and West. One of the most influential was Megasthenes, a Seleucid ambassador to the court of Asoka's grandfather, who published his *Indika*, a description of India, ca. 300 B.C.

Yet the degree to which this interest influenced Greek and Roman culture is debatable. Although ancient writers mention Greek or Roman philosophers who were attracted by Indian culture, modern scholars tend to be cautious. The ancients had a weakness for tall tales and stories of exotic inspiration. Consider, for example, the following reports. Pyrrho of Elis, founder of the Hellenistic philosophical school of skepticism (see page 144), supposedly based his notion of the imperturbable sage on one Calanos, an Indian whom Pyrrho saw step calmly on a funeral pyre when Pyrrho was part of Alexander's expedition. Around A.D. 40, one Apollonius of Tyana, a pagan religious thinker, is supposed to have traveled to India to study with its sages. Two centuries later the great Neo-Platonic philosopher Plotinus (A.D. 235–270) is reported to have traveled with the Roman emperor Gordian's army eastward, hoping in vain to get to India. Some scholars see Indian influence in Plotinus's mysticism and pantheism, but others dismiss these various reports.

Bactria was conquered by central Asian nomads in the late second century B.C. The Hellenistic kingdoms of India and Pakistan, however, survived until about the time of Christ, and some Greek communities lasted until the fifth century A.D. The Gandharan sculptors who flourished in a formerly Greek-ruled region in about A.D. 200 used Greek artistic techniques to depict Buddhist subjects, which might suggest the impact of Indian culture on the remaining Greek population.

THE ALEXANDRIAN MOMENT

In 331 B.C., at the site of a fishing village in the northwestern part of the Nile Delta, Alexander and his advisers marked out the ground plan of a new city. They planned a great eastern Mediterranean trading center to replace Tyre, whose inhabitants had been killed or enslaved by the

Macedonians who stormed the town in 332 B.C. The new city, called Alexandria, did not disappoint its founders. Grown to a population of a half-million or more by the first century B.C., it was one of the largest, wealthiest, and most important cities in the world. Greeks, Egyptians, and Jews were the largest groups in its cosmopolitan population, but no one would have been surprised to see an Indian or a Celt, an Italian or a Persian.

Under the Ptolemies, Alexandria became one of the great cultural centers of Hellenism, alongside Athens, Pergamum, and Antioch. Alexandria deserves close attention, not least because of the poignance with which its literature portrays social change in the elite. Other sources round out the picture, attesting to an increase in leisure time, a growth in educational opportunities for both sexes, royal patronage of culture, and the value of even a limited knowledge of Greek literature as the ticket to advancement.

The Anti-Epic Temperament

In 294 B.C. King Ptolemy I invited the deposed tyrant of Athens, Demetrius of Phalerum, to found an institution of culture in Alexandria. A writer himself, Ptolemy was no less sincere because the new foundation would bring him prestige and keep his engineers up to date on new technology for warfare and agriculture. Demetrius had studied with Aristotle's successor at the Lyceum, Theophrastus (ca. 370–288 B.C.), a pragmatist interested in compiling and cataloging knowledge.

The new institution was called the Museum (literally, "House of the Muses," the home of the female deities who inspired creativity). The Museum was a residence, study, and lecture hall for scholars, scientists, and poets. One of its key components was the Library, in its day the largest repository of Greek writing in the world. In the third century B.C.—at the height of the Ptolemaic kingdom—the Library contained 700,000 papyrus rolls, the equivalent of roughly 50,000 modern books. Its nearest competitor, at Pergamum, contained less than a third as many rolls.

The Library is one of several indicators of an increase in the size of the Hellenistic reading and writing public. As independence vanished, city-states changed their military training programs

A Greek-Influenced Indian Statue This figure of a *bodhisattva* ("enlightened one") belongs to the Gandharan school, which was heavily influenced by Hellenistic sculpture. The statue's proportions, facial features, and the drapery of its clothing particularly recall Hellenistic motifs and may be the work of a Greek sculptor. *(Royal Ontario Museum)*

for 18- and 19-year-old men into educational programs in literature and philosophy. The names of over a thousand writers of the Hellenistic era survive, and after 300 B.C., anthologies, abridgments, and school texts proliferated.

Dionysus on a Panther This rich mosaic of about 100 B.C. comes from the Aegean island of Delos, a thriving port in Hellenistic times. In this theatrical scene, the artist contrasts the ferocity of the panther with the calm and composure of the god. Dionysus holds a cymbal, recalling his patronage of music, dance, and drama. *(House of Masks, Delos/Archaeological Receipts Fund, Athens)*

Although modeled on Athens's Lyceum, the Museum represented a departure from the public culture of the Classical period. The denizens of the Museum were an elite, dependent on royal patronage and self-consciously Greek, as if to set up a barrier against Egyptians. At the Museum, culture was an object of study, not a part of civic life as it had been in Classical Athens. A witticism of Timon, a philosopher from the Peloponnesus who lived in the third century B.C., rings true: "In Egypt, land of diverse tribes, graze many pedants, fatted fowls that quarrel without end in the hen coop of the Muses."

Before we examine Alexandrian literature further, it is worth noting how greatly Hellenistic Athenian literature diverged from Classical culture. The greatest Hellenistic Athenian writer, and

a figure of international renown, was Menander (ca. 342–292 B.C.). He was the master of a style of comedy called "New Comedy," as distinguished from the "Old Comedy" of Aristophanes, which had flourished a century earlier (see page 113). Where Old Comedy was raucous and ribald, New Comedy was restrained; where Old Comedy focused on public matters like war and politics, New Comedy was domestic and private. New Comedy symbolized the turning away from public life in Hellenistic times.

Menander wrote over seventy plays, but only one complete play has survived, *Dyskolos* (*The Grouch*). There are also substantial excerpts from several other comedies as well as Roman imitations. The elements of Menander's skill and popularity shine through. Witty and fluent, he favored stock plots and stock characters: the boastful soldier, the clever slave, the dashing but inept young man, the sweet maiden, and the old miser. Within those limitations, Menander created realistic and idiosyncratic characters. As a Hellenistic critic asked rhetorically: "O Menander and Life, which of you imitated the other?"

Like Menander, Alexandrian writers turned from public themes, but in Alexandria the quintessential literary figure was not the playwright but the critic. He was a professional man of letters, as likely to write literary history as poetry. His works tended to be scholarly, even pedantic; they were refined, erudite, subtle—in a word, courtly. Critics prized diversity, novelty, and the exotic over the practical. Prime concerns of the critics were establishing a literary canon and standardizing the texts of the canonical authors. Adopted by the Romans, Alexandrian critical standards have influenced the West to this day.

Of the three greatest Alexandrian writers, two—Callimachus (305–240 B.C.) and Apollonius of Rhodes (b. ca. 295 B.C.)—worked at the Library; the third, Theocritus (ca. 300–ca. 260 B.C.), probably lived on a stipend from the Ptolemies. Popular for centuries, Callimachus was probably the most influential, the complete Hellenistic poet. A native of Cyrene who came to Alexandria as a schoolteacher, Callimachus found a position in the Library. There he composed a virtually universal history of all recorded Greek (and much non-Greek) knowledge.

A prolific writer, Callimachus generally preferred short to long poems: "Big book, big evil," he writes. Earlier Greek poets were usually austere and public minded; Callimachus preferred the private, the light, and the exotic. "Don't expect from me a big-sounding poem," he writes; "Zeus thunders, not I."[3] Callimachus was expert at the pithy statement in verse, the epigram.

The Causes, Callimachus's masterwork (of which little survives), is at seven thousand lines his one long poem, but it is a collection of brief vignettes rather than a unified narrative. The central theme is the origins of festivals, customs, institutions, and names, many of them obscure. Arcane diction and complex allusions abound. Only an elite could understand such writing, but Callimachus was an elitist. "I detest all common things," he states.

Another major Alexandrian writer was Callimachus's student, Apollonius of Rhodes. Tradition claims that Apollonius retired to Rhodes after his masterwork, the epic poem *Argonautica* (*Voyage of the Argo*), was poorly received. The subject is the legend of Jason and the heroes who travel on the ship *Argo* to Colchis, at the far end of the Black Sea, in pursuit of the Golden Fleece (the skin of a winged ram). With the help of the Colchian princess Medea, who falls in love with Jason, the heroes succeed and return home safely after numerous adventures.

Apollonius devotes much of the poem to a discussion of the roots of various names, cults, and customs. The main novelty, however, is a fundamental and pervading doubt about the very possibility of heroism. Apollonius's Jason is no Achilles, no Odysseus. Homer describes Odysseus as "never at a loss"; Apollonius describes Jason as "helpless." Men move the action in the *Iliad* and the *Odyssey*; Jason depends on a woman, Medea, for his success. Indeed, much of the *Argonautica* focuses on Medea and in particular on her love for Jason. With the exception of the works of Sappho, previous Greek poetry generally either ignored female eroticism or presented it in a hostile light. Apollonius's work illustrates both the improved status of women in Hellenistic ideology and the great interest of the age in the inner life of the emotions. All in all the *Argonautica* is less a traditional epic than an anti-epic.

Like Callimachus, Theocritus, a native of Syracuse, wrote short, polished poetry. He composed thirty-one subtle and refined poems, conventionally known as idylls. The best-known of the poems focus on country life. They are the first known pastoral poems; indeed, Theocritus probably invented the genre. Theocritus's pastorals explore nature, but always self-consciously, always with the city in mind. His peasants and shepherds are marvelously cultured; they seem more like townspeople on an excursion than true rustics. Through his Roman admirers, Theocritus's love of nature has exerted a powerful hold on the Western literary imagination.

Outside the Museum, Alexandria had a lively popular culture, much of it Egyptian or influenced by Egyptian models. A glimpse of it is afforded in the seven surviving mimes, or farces, of an obscure writer named Herondas or Herodas.

Although written in literary Greek, they discuss commonplace subjects such as shopping for shoes, tourism, lawsuits, and beatings at school, and titillating themes like adultery and prostitution. Lively, bawdy, and funny, filled with the grit of everyday life in the third century B.C., they are a reminder of just how specialized the culture of the Museum was.

Advances in Science and Medicine

The Ptolemies not only reaped practical benefits in military and agricultural technology from their Museum, but they became the patrons of a flourishing period in the history of Greek pure scientific inquiry. They also unwittingly promoted a split between philosophy and science that has characterized much of Western culture since. Antigonid patronage of ethical and political philosophy helped keep Athens pre-eminent in those fields. The study of science, in contrast, tended to move to Alexandria. The rulers of Pergamum and, far to the west, Syracuse, a flourishing Hellenistic city in Sicily, were great patrons of science as well. Wealth, improved communications and literacy, continued warfare, and cross-fertilization between Greek and non-Greek traditions, especially Greek and Babylonian astronomy, were all stimuli of Hellenistic science.

Some of the best-known figures of Hellenistic science were mathematicians. In his *Elements*, the Alexandrian Euclid (active ca. 300 B.C.) produced a systematic exposition of geometry, hugely influential in both Western and Islamic civilizations. Apollonius of Perge in Anatolia (active ca. 210 B.C.) did brilliant research on conic sections. A Sicilian Greek, Archimedes of Syracuse (287–212 B.C.), did original work on the geometry of spheres and cylinders, calculated the approximate value of pi (the ratio of a circle's circumference to its diameter), and made important discoveries in astronomy, engineering, optics, and other fields. Archimedes was as great an inventor as he was a theoretician. One of the most important of his inventions was the water snail, also known as Archimedes' screw: a screwlike device to raise water for irrigation. Invented by Archimedes during a stay in Egypt, the screw made it possible to irrigate previously bar-

ren land, as did the ox-driven water wheel, another Ptolemaic invention.

Advances in mathematics promoted advances in astronomy. Aristarchus of Samos (active ca. 275 B.C.) is known for his heliocentric hypothesis, which confounded tradition by having the earth revolve around the sun, instead of the sun around the earth. He was right, but Hellenistic astronomy lacked the data to prove his theory, so it was not unreasonable for Hipparchus of Nicaea (active ca. 135 B.C.) to insist on the centrality of the earth. A great researcher, Hipparchus also discovered the procession of the equinoxes—that is, the slight annual shift in the time of the occurrence of the autumn and spring equinoxes. Eratosthenes of Cyrene (active ca. 225 B.C.) was saddled with the frustrating nickname of "Beta" (the second letter of the Greek alphabet) because he was considered second best in every branch of study. This "second best" nonetheless calculated through simple geometry an extraordinarily accurate measurement of the earth's circumference.

Hellenistic medicine thrived in Alexandria. Both Greece and Egypt had long-established medical traditions. Greek medicine was more rationalistic, but Egyptian drugs, and possibly Egyptian doctors' knowledge of the eye as well as their emphasis on measuring, helped stimulate Alexandrian medical progress, as no doubt the mere fact of cross-fertilization did. The key to medical advance, however, was the dissection of human cadavers in Alexandria, a first in the history of science. In Greece, as in many ancient societies, religious tradition demanded that dead bodies not be mutilated; but in the frontier atmosphere of early Alexandria, tradition lost much of its force. Although Egyptians did not practice dissection, they did practice embalming, which may have helped Alexandrian Greeks overcome the taboo against cutting open the human body. Ever supportive of research, the Ptolemies provided corpses to Greek scientists for dissection; indeed, they had condemned criminals sent from prison for dissection while still alive by scientists. The practice, only a temporary one in the early third century B.C., outraged many writers in antiquity, just as today it would be considered an atrocity.

The leading scientific beneficiary was Herophilus of Chalcedon (ca. 320–250 B.C.), a practicing physician in Alexandria. Among his achievements was the recognition (against Aristotle) that the brain is the center of the nervous system, a careful dissection of the eye, the discovery of the ovaries, and the description of the duodenum, which he named (*duodenum* is a Latin translation of a Greek word meaning "twelve fingers," describing the organ's length). In addition, Herophilus developed a detailed theory of the diagnostic value of measuring pulse rates. His contemporary, Erasistratus of Ceos (ca. 330–255 B.C.), was another brilliant physician who worked either in Alexandria or in Seleucia (the sources are contradictory). His great achievement was a mechanical theory of organic processes such as digestion and of the workings of the vascular system, which he described in impressive detail.

Hellenistic technology has long fascinated and frustrated scholars. The great engineers invented both numerous engines of war and various "wonderworks" to amuse the royal court; among the latter were mechanical puppets and steam-run toys. Given these advances, why did the Greeks achieve neither an industrial transformation, such as was ushered in by the steam engine around A.D. 1800, nor a scientific revolution along the lines of the one begun in the early modern era by such thinkers as Copernicus and Galileo? Historians are not entirely sure but can venture a guess. Greek machine-making technology was not as sophisticated as that of eighteenth-century Europe. The prevalence of slavery in antiquity, moreover, discouraged the invention of labor-saving machines; steam was used only for playthings and gadgets. A related point is the elitist bias of Greek intellectual life. After Archimedes' death, for example, it was claimed that although he had written copiously on theoretical matters, he never bothered to write about his mechanical inventions because he considered them "ignoble and vulgar."

Perhaps the most important point is the Greek attitude toward nature. Whereas Jews and Christians learned from the Bible that human beings have dominion over nature, thereby making possible the conclusion that it is appropriate to conquer nature, the Greeks thought in more restricted terms. They believed that nature set limits, that a virtuous person tried to follow nature, not conquer it. Thus, Greek engineers were not inclined to make the revolutionary changes that their modern counterparts have promoted.

Men and Women in Art and Society

Like Hellenistic literature, Hellenistic art attests to changing male attitudes toward women and toward gender issues. The portrait of Jason and Medea in Apollonius's *Argonautica* makes fun of masculine pretensions and celebrates the triumph of female intelligence. It also presents a sympathetic portrait of a woman's romantic desire for a man, as does Theocritus's work. In the Classical period, depictions of romantic love were generally restricted to male homoeroticism. Accordingly, statues of naked males were common, but women were usually depicted clothed. Hellenistic sculpture, by contrast, affords many erotic examples of the female nude.

There are indications that the Hellenistic Greek male of the elite was much more willing than his Classical predecessor to see lovemaking as a matter of mutuality and respect. Classical vase-painting often depicts heterosexual lovemaking with the mood lusty and explicit. In Hellenistic vase-painting, in contrast, the emphasis is more often on tenderness and domesticity. Hellenistic males wrote with sensitivity about satisfying a woman's needs and desires. The vogue in Hellenistic art for representations of Hermaphrodite, the mythical creature who was half female and half male, may suggest a belief that the feminine was as important a part of human nature as the masculine.

Many a Hellenistic artist or writer seems to be as interested in emotion as in action and to focus on the inner as much as on the outer life. Callimachus's poem *Hecale,* for instance, ostensibly about the hero Theseus's defeat of the Bull of Marathon (near Athens), actually focuses on Hecale, an old woman who feeds Theseus in her cottage on his way to and from the battle. Hellenistic art often depicts women, children, and domestic scenes; representations of warriors may focus on their unrestrained emotions rather than on their soldierly self-control.

Hellenistic women enjoyed small improvements in political and legal status and considerable improvements in economic and ideological

Aphrodite of Cnidos This 7½-foot-tall marble statue is a Roman copy of an original by Praxiteles (ca. 350–330 B.C.). Perhaps the most famous of Hellenistic female nudes, the statue was housed in a special shrine where it could be viewed in the round to accommodate all the interest it generated. *(Vatican Museums)*

the loyal and prosperous subject replaced that of the independent citizen-warrior. Citizens in the Classical polis had been encouraged to be aggressive and exaggeratedly masculine to the point of misogyny. Subjects in Hellenistic monarchies were meant to cultivate the more passive and reflective virtues of legalism, obedience, and economic enterprise. Because Greek men associated these virtues with women, their respect for female qualities tended to increase. Too, in the new cities, as in many a frontier society, women more often were permitted to inherit and use property than in old Greece.

It was an era of powerful queens: Olympias, Alexander the Great's mother, played kingmaker after her son's death. Arsinoe II Philadelphus was co-ruler of Egypt with her husband (who was also her brother) for five years at the height of Ptolemaic prosperity around 275 B.C. The most famous Hellenistic woman, Cleopatra VII, was queen of Egypt from 51 to 30 B.C. Although she was the lover of two of the most powerful men in the world, the Romans Julius Caesar and Mark Antony, Cleopatra was no exotic plaything. Rather, she was a brilliant and ambitious strategist who nearly succeeded in winning a world empire for her family. (See the feature, "Weighing the Evidence: Images of Cleopatra" on pages 150–151.)

Writers in the new Hellenistic cities often described freedom of movement for women. Theocritus and Herondas, for example, show women visiting a temple or a show. Nor did Hellenistic men, even in Athens, obey Pericles' injunction not to speak of good women. In Hellenistic Athens, aristocratic fathers put up inscriptions in honor of their daughters who had participated in the cult of Athena. Although women generally continued to need a male guardian to represent them in public, in some situations, at least in Egypt (where the evidence is most plentiful), a woman could represent herself. A woman could petition the government on her own behalf. Widows and mothers of illegitimate children could give their daughters in marriage or apprentice their sons. A few cities granted women citizenship or even permitted them to hold public office. (See the box, "A Seleucid Queen Helps the City of Iasos.")

Some Hellenistic cities admitted women to the gymnasium, previously a male preserve. Heretofore only Sparta had promoted physical education

status. A number of reasons explain these changes. First, Greek women, particularly in the elite, benefited from the spread of monarchy. For one thing, queens and princesses in royal courts had power and prestige that had been denied women in city-states. For another, under monarchy the notion of

A Seleucid Queen Helps the City of Iasos

This letter from Queen Laodike III, wife of Antiochus III (r. 223–187 B.C.), was inscribed on a marble stele in Iasos (in southern Anatolia) around 197 B.C. It sheds interesting light on contemporary politics and society.

Queen Laodike to the Council and the people of the Iasians, greeting. Having heard often from my brother [Antiochus, actually her cousin and husband] both what concern he continues to show his friends and allies and how, on regaining your city which had met with unexpected mishaps, he returned freedom to you, and how he introduced laws and other measures to improve your government and bring it to a better condition, I, desiring also to act in conformity with his earnestness and zeal, and for this reason, to institute some benefaction for the poorer citizens but of general utility to the whole people, have written to Strouthion, the administrator, that yearly for ten years he should have brought into the city one thousand measures of wheat and turn them over to (representatives) of the people. You will, therefore, do well by instructing both the treasurers that, on receiving it, they should sell a set amount, and the presidents and whoever else you may designate, that they are to see that the money realized from these (sales) be assigned to dowries for the daughters of the poorer citizens, giving not more than three hundred Antiochene drachmas to each of those to be married; and as for you, should you act toward my brother and our house in general as is proper and be mindful of all our benefactions, I shall gladly endeavor to arrange also other (benefits) which I may think of.

Source: Adapted from Stanley M. Burstein, ed. and trans., The Hellenistic Age from the Battle of Ipsos to the Death of Kleopatra VII (Cambridge, England: Cambridge University Press, 1985), pp. 47–48.

for women, but by the first century A.D., women were even competing in the great Pan-Hellenic games. Gymnasia were also centers of education in music and reading; one consequence of growing literacy was the re-emergence of women poets and the first appearance of women philosophers in the West. Before dying at age 19, Erinna, who lived on the Aegean island of Telos during the late fourth century B.C., wrote the *Distaff*, a poem in memory of her childhood friend Baucis. This 300-line poem, famous in antiquity, described the shared experiences of girlhood. Hipparchia of Maroneia (b. ca. 350 B.C.), like her husband Crates of Thebes, studied Cynic philosophy. The Cynics, like another philosophical school, the Epicureans, supported a measure of equality between women and men. Hipparchia and Crates led an itinerant life, as popular teachers and the Hellenistic equivalent of counselors or psychologists.

Much of the explanation for the relative freedom of elite women lies in the new economic power of this group. There was probably a connection between one Phile's ability to hold a magistracy in Priene (in Anatolia) in the first century B.C. and her control of the financial resources to build the town a reservoir and an aqueduct. The new cities generally imposed fewer restrictions on women's economic role than had Classical poleis like Athens. In many cities women could sell land, borrow money, and decide whether their husbands could make loans or contracts on the strength of their dowry. Free women could manumit slaves as well.

The role reversals of male and female in Hellenistic art and literature, therefore, are indicators of genuine social change. Hellenistic women never attained the equality that sometimes exists between men and women today, but they did enjoy genuine though limited improvements in status. Men and women played new roles in a changed, complex world. The new Hellenistic philosophies and religions attempted to address that complexity.

THE TURN INWARD: NEW PHILOSOPHIES, NEW FAITHS

The events of the Hellenistic era generated uncertainty: emigration, a trend from independent city-states to monarchies and federal leagues, new extremes of wealth and poverty, and contact with foreign peoples and customs. As literacy expanded, more Greeks than ever before could participate in cultural debate. New philosophies and religions arose to meet new spiritual concerns, generating ideas that would be influential for centuries.

The meeting of Jews and Greeks proved to be just as significant. Challenged by Greek conquest, Greek colonization, and by their own immigration to Greek lands, Jews alternately embraced Hellenism and engaged in resistance, both cultural and armed. In the process, first Judaism and then Hellenism, through the agency of Christianity, were changed forever.

Stoics, Skeptics, Cynics, and Epicureans

Although the polis lost its military and political pre-eminence in the fourth century B.C., philosophy continued to thrive. It was, however, much changed. With the city-state losing significance as a focus of loyalty, and with the Greek-reading public growing in size and geographic extent, Hellenistic philosophy paid less attention than ever before to politics. Moreover, as we have seen, Hellenistic science tended to become a separate discipline from philosophy. What was left as the prime subject of philosophy was ethics, the discovery of the best way to live one's life. The essence of the good life, most philosophers agreed, was finding peace of mind, or freedom from troubles. Hellenistic philosophers won wide followings; indeed, for many people, primarily in the elite, philosophy became a way of life, even a religion.

Several competing philosophical schools emerged. The most popular was Stoicism, with Epicureanism second. Cynicism, never as wide-spread, was an important precursor of these two doctrines. Skepticism rejected the main philosophies as mere dogmatism and proposed instead a commonsense attitude toward ethics.

The first Cynic was Diogenes of Sinope (ca. 400–ca. 325 B.C.). An exile in Athens, Diogenes developed a philosophy that rejected all conventions. Happiness, he decided, would be found by satisfying one's natural needs with simplicity. Accordingly, Diogenes chose a life of poverty. A beggar in rags, he delighted in shocking conventional morality. Famous for wit and shamelessness, he was nicknamed "Dog" (*kuon*) because the Greeks considered dogs to be shameless animals; his followers were called "Doglike" (*kunikoi*, whence the name *Cynic*).

Although he founded no school, Diogenes had followers. One of them, Crates of Thebes (ca. 365–285 B.C.), was the teacher of Zeno (335–263 B.C.), who began one of the most important philosophical systems of antiquity: Stoicism. Zeno came to Athens in 313 B.C. from Citium in Cyprus, a multi-ethnic city; he was possibly of Phoenician origin. Influenced both by Cynicism and by Socratic philosophy, Zeno developed his own doctrines, which he taught in the Stoa Poikile ("Painted Porch," whence the name *Stoic*), a public building.

Like Plato and Aristotle, Zeno sought an absolute standard of good on which to base philosophical decisions. He found it in the divine reason (*logos*), which he considered the organizing principle of the universe and the guide to human behavior. The best life was a life in pursuit of wisdom—that is, a life of philosophy. Only that rare and forbidding figure, the Sage, could truly attain wisdom; ordinary people could merely progress toward it. What was required was study and the attempt to free oneself from all passion.

Stoicism may seem harsh; it is not surprising that *stoical* has come to describe austere indifference to pain. In some ways, however, Stoicism was comforting. First, freedom from passion was meant to bring peace of mind and happiness. Second, unlike Plato, the Stoics were empiricists—that is, they trusted the evidence of the senses, an attitude that they thought would inspire confidence and security. Third, the common share in divine logos entailed a common human brotherhood—led, to be sure, by a Greek-speaking elite. Fourth, because brothers have a duty to each other,

Early Stoic Ethics and Politics

The Roman Marcus Tullius Cicero (100–44 B.C.) studied Greek philosophy in Athens and was influenced by Stoicism, on whose basic ethical and political teachings he sheds light here.

In the case of all the philosophers mentioned, their End of Goods logically follows: with Aristippus [a philosopher from Cyrene, date uncertain], it is simply pleasure; with the Stoics, harmony with nature, which they interpret as meaning virtuous living, i.e., the morally good life, and further explain this as meaning to live with an understanding of the natural course of events, selecting things that are in accordance with nature and rejecting the opposite. . . .

They [the Stoics] hold that the universe is governed by divine will; it is a city or state of which both men and gods are members, and each one of us is a part of this universe; from which it is a natural consequence that we should prefer the common advantage to our own. For just as the laws set the safety of all above the safety of individuals, so a good, wise and law-abiding man, conscious of his duty to the state, studies the advantage of all more than that of himself or of any single individual. The traitor to his country does not deserve greater reprobation than the man who betrays the common advantage or security for the sake of his own advantage or security. This explains why praise is owed to one who dies for the commonwealth, because it becomes us to love our country more than ourselves.

Source: Jason L. Saunders, ed., *Greek and Roman Philosophy After Aristotle* (New York: Free Press, 1966), pp. 113, 125–126.

---

the Stoics argued that a good person should play an active role in public life. (See the box, "Early Stoic Ethics and Politics.")

Like Hellenistic poets or portraitists, the Stoics emphasized the inner life. They believed that intentions matter. This belief was an important Stoic departure from Greek tradition, which tended to emphasize the outcome of an action, whether intended or not. Stoicism also departed from traditional Greek localism, embracing a more cosmopolitan outlook. "This world is a great city, [and] has one constitution and one law," wrote Philo of Alexandria (30 B.C.–A.D. 45), a Stoic and a Jew. Many Stoics believed in a natural law or law of nations—overarching and common principles to govern international relations.

With its emphasis on duty and order, Stoicism became popular with Greek ruling elites, both Macedonian kings and their opponents in city-states and leagues. Stoicism would enjoy even greater success with the Romans, who found its strictures congenial to their own stern morality and who used its concept of a universal state to justify their empire. A great deal of Stoicism was later embraced by early Christian writers.

Epicurus (341–270 B.C.), an Athenian citizen, founded his philosophical school at around the same time as Zeno founded Stoicism. There were other similarities: Both schools were empiricist and materialist (that is, they tended to trust the evidence of the senses), both sought peace of mind, and both inspired widespread followings. Epicurus, however, taught not in a public place but in a private garden. Whereas the Stoics encouraged political participation, Epicureans counseled withdrawal from the rough and tumble of public life. "Calm" and "Live in hiding" are famous Epicurean maxims.

Epicurus's materialism is based on the atomic theory of Democritus (see page 106); it envisions a thoroughly mechanistic universe. The gods exist but play no active role in events. One need fear neither capricious deities nor an unhappy after-life, because the soul is merely a combination of atoms that ceases to exist after death. What might be the purpose of life in such an unheroic universe? The answer was the avoidance of pain and pursuit of pleasure. The latter was called "hedonism" (*pleasure* is *hedone* in Greek), but Epicureans meant intellectual pleasure, not the pursuit of food, drink, or sex. Friendship and fraternity were Epicurean ideals—the private analogs, as it were, of Stoic brotherhood.

The Epicureans raised eyebrows and sometimes ire, occasionally coming in for persecution by the state. They were accused of atheism and sensuality; to this day, *epicurean* is used to mean fond of luxury and pleasure. Classical Greek philosophy defined virtue as the highest good. The Epicurean emphasis on pleasure, even spiritual pleasure, seemed perverse to some. Yet Epicureanism was simple, sure of itself, practical, and offered both friendship and a sense of community. It became a popular philosophy, especially among the wealthy.

Skepticism was founded by Pyrrho of Elis (ca. 360–ca. 270 B.C.), a Greek who traveled with Alexander to India. Like Stoics and Epicureans, Skeptics sought peace of mind. They rejected those thinkers' conclusions, however, on the grounds that they were dogmatic—that is, based not on positive proof but merely on opinion (*doxa*). Considering the senses unreliable, Skeptics rejected the commonsense approach of Stoics and Epicureans. In their opinion, one had to suspend judgment on the great philosophical questions (hence our term *skepticism* for a doubting state of mind). Having done so, a person could accept the customs of the community, avoid politics, and thereby obtain peace of mind. Such a doctrine might appeal to practical people, and, indeed, the main source of Skeptic philosophy is the writing of a Greek physician, Sextus Empiricus (active ca. A.D. 200).

The Mystery Religions

The traditional Greek religion of the Olympian gods came under attack on every front in the Hellenistic era. First, the newly divinized kings stole the spotlight. Second, Hellenistic philosophers, like their Archaic and Classical predecessors, criticized the Olympians as primitive, unsophisticated, and immoral; their critique reached an ever widening audience. A third attack came from science and scholarship. Around 300 B.C., Euhemerus of Messene wrote in his *Sacred Scripture* that Zeus, Ouranos, and Kronos were not divine beings but merely great kings of the past who were rewarded with divinization, much like a Hellenistic monarch. Debunking the Olympians became a popular literary pastime. For instance, Poseidon was said to be worshiped as the sea-god because he had been the first shipbuilder, and Hades, god of the dead, was said to have invented burial rites.

The Olympians retained their temples, but the rituals seemed hollow and antiquarian. What was to replace them? Of the several new religious movements that marked the age, three stand out: the divinization of kings, the cult of Tyche (Fortune), and the mystery religions.

Under the Ptolemies and Seleucids, the ruler-worship that Alexander had demanded became standard procedure. Many subjects no doubt considered the divinity of their king or queen merely a patriotic formality; others treated the divinized monarch as something like a patron saint who could intercede in heaven. The old Greek city-states, especially the democracies, bristled at ruler-worship. "To transfer to men the honor due to the gods," the Athenian playwright Philippides (active ca. 300 B.C.) wrote, "is to dissolve the democracy."

He might have said much the same about the Hellenistic cult of Tyche (Fortune or Luck), often worshiped as a goddess, sometimes as the protector of a particular city. The most famous example was the Tyche of Antioch, personified as a statue of a woman wearing the battlements of the city on her head as a kind of crown—a very popular statue, to judge by the many copies found around the Hellenistic world. In the often-confusing expanse of that world, many people felt that only luck could help them.

The third major Hellenistic trend, the mystery religions, offered similar solace to that of the philosophical schools: ethical guidance, comfort, release from worries, reassurance about death, and a sense of unity. Unlike philosophies, however, they achieved their goals through the revelation of secret doctrines, or "mysteries," into which worshipers were initiated. Long a feature of Greek religion, mystery cults grew in popularity during Hellenistic times. Consider the cult of Demeter at

Eleusis, a town just outside the city of Athens. Demeter was the goddess of fertility. Her daughter, Persephone, supposedly spent half of the year in the underworld, among the dead, but came back to earth each spring. As told to initiates, the myth symbolized the promise of a blessed afterlife. The precise details of the ritual remain unknown to this day. What is clear is that they included fasting, ritual bathing in the sea, a procession, and a torch-lit ceremony in the great hall at Eleusis.

Various new mystery religions from outside Greece became more popular, particularly the Hellenized Egyptian cults of Serapis and of Isis. Created under Ptolemy I, Serapis was meant to combine Osiris, the Egyptian god of the afterlife, with Pluto, the Greek god of the underworld. Hence, it is an early example of the common Hellenistic practice of religious syncretism, or fusion. Despite its roots, Serapis-worship had little appeal to native Egyptians, but the god became popular in the Greek world as patron of healing and sailing.

Another traditional Egyptian deity, Osiris's wife, Isis, also became a popular Greek and, later, Roman goddess. Called the "Goddess of Ten Thousand Names," Isis was said to symbolize all the female deities of antiquity. Hers was a cult of the afterlife and of the suffering but tender and loving mother; she was particularly popular among women. Thus, under Ptolemaic sponsorship, ancient Egyptian cults were recast and spread throughout the Greek-speaking world, circulating such notions as the suffering mother, the Last Judgment, and blessed eternal life after death. Early Christianity was much influenced by such Greco-Egyptian religious notions, but it was more directly the product of debate and ferment within Hellenistic Judaism.

Hellenistic Judaism

Few consequences of Alexander's conquests had so lasting an impact as the mixing of Greeks and Jews. Even before Alexander took Judea from the Persians in 332 B.C., the two peoples were in contact, but it was little compared to what followed in the Hellenistic era, when their fates became intertwined. The Greeks governed Judea and then lost it to a Jewish independence movement; meanwhile millions of Jews settled in Egypt, Syria, Anatolia, and Greece. When the "people of the

Bronze Coin with Menorah This issue of Mattathias Antigone (r. 40–37 B.C.), the last Hasmonean king, is an early example of the use of the seven-branched candelabrum as the symbol of the Jewish people. A similar candelabrum was used in the Temple of Jerusalem. *(Erich Lessing/Art Resource, NY)*

book" met the people of myth and philosophy, the resulting relationship was one of fascination and hatred, assimilation and violence, conversion and apostasy, Hellenophilia and anti-Semitism. In the end the Romans, successors to the Greeks, destroyed the Jewish state, but the Jewish religion and the Jewish people survived. One might say, moreover, that the Jews forever changed the Greco-Roman soul through Christianity, which had roots in Judaism although it went its own way. Ethical monotheism and a moral code based on intentions and guilt, rather than on actions and shame, triumphed.

Hellenistic Judea was governed first by the Ptolemies until 200 B.C., afterward by the Seleucids, until the establishment of an independent Jewish state in 142 B.C., which came under Roman suzerainty in 63 B.C. The Greeks were not absentee rulers. Rather, they established a large number of Greek colonies in and around Judea, especially under the Seleucids. For many in the Jewish upper classes, the prestige of the dominant culture was irresistible. They abandoned Jewish customs for

The Jews Struggle over Hellenism

Greek colonists introduced Hellenic customs to Palestine in the second century B.C. The Jewish response varied greatly, from eager assimilation to violent resistance, as is demonstrated by the following selections from the First Book of Maccabees, written around 100 B.C.

At that time, lawless men arose in Israel and seduced many with their plea, "Come, let us make a covenant with the gentiles around us, because ever since we have kept ourselves separated from them we have suffered many evils." The plea got so favorable a reception that some of the people took it upon themselves to apply to the king, who granted them liberty to follow the practices of the gentiles. Thereupon they built a gymnasium in Jerusalem according to the customs of the gentiles. . . . They joined themselves to the gentiles and became willing slaves to evildoing. . . .

The king [Antiochus IV] wrote to all his kingdom, for all to become one people and for each to abandon his own customs. All the gentiles agreed to the terms of the king's proclamation. Many Israelites, too, accepted his religion and sacrificed to idols and violated the Sabbath. . . .

Many Israelites strongly and steadfastly refused to eat forbidden food. They chose death in order to escape defilement by foods and in order to keep from violating the Holy Covenant, and they were put to death. Indeed, very great wrath had struck Israel. . . .

[An Israelite sacrifices to Zeus.] When [the Jewish priest] Mattathias saw this, he was filled with zeal and trembled with rage and let his anger rise, as was fitting; he ran and slew him upon the altar. At the same time he also killed the king's official in charge of enforcing sacrifices, and he destroyed the altar.

Source: The First Book of Maccabees 1:11–15, 41–43, 62–64; 2:24–25, in *The Anchor Bible,* vol. 41 (New York: Doubleday, 1976).

the Greek gymnasium, theater, and political institutions. With the help of the Seleucid king Antiochus IV Epiphanes (r. 175–163 B.C.), Jewish Hellenizers in 175 B.C. had Jerusalem proclaimed a Greek polis, renamed Antioch, like many a Seleucid city; they even built a gymnasium at the foot of the Temple Mount. In 167 B.C. they went further by in effect abolishing Judaism. They outlawed Sabbath observance, prohibited circumcision, and rededicated the Temple to Olympian Zeus.

The traditionalists, however, resisted; aided by the political ineptitude of their opponents, who raised taxes, they rallied the Jewish masses into opposition. Soon a guerrilla revolt began in the countryside, led by the Hasmonean family, also known as the Maccabees, whose successes are still celebrated by Jews during the religious holiday of Hanukkah. (See the box, "The Jews Struggle over Hellenism.")

The guerrilla movement developed into a disciplined armed uprising, which forced the Seleucids to tolerate an independent state under the Hasmonean dynasty. Religiously conservative at home, the state was expansionist abroad, conquering nearby territories such as the Galilee and forcing their inhabitants to convert to Judaism.

During the struggle over Hellenism, new elements of lasting significance became part of Judaism. First, the Jews developed a literature of spiritual resistance to the foreigner. This literature was apocalyptic—that is, it claimed to reveal dramatic, heretofore secret truths. Drawing on both biblical and Mesopotamian traditions, Jewish apocalyptic writing predicted a future cataclysm, when a royal redeemer would evict the foreigner and establish a new kingdom of Israel. The redeemer was often identified with another notion that first became popular in this era: the Messiah (literally, "anointed one"), someone anointed with oil signifying his election as king, a descendant of King David, who would save Israel. Another new aspect of Hellenistic Judaism was martyrdom, the notion of the holy sacrifice of one's life for a religious cause. There was also a growing belief in a final judgment day and resurrection, when God would raise the meritorious dead to live again on earth in their own bodies.

Hellenistic Judaism was far from monolithic. Various sects each proposed its own version of Judaism. Among these sects were the Sadducees ("righteous ones"), a wealthy establishment group for whom the rituals of the Jerusalem Temple were the heart of Judaism. Their opponents, the Pharisees ("those who separated themselves"), insisted on the validity of the oral tradition of interpretation alongside the written law of the Hebrew Bible and the Temple rituals. The Pharisees proposed a kind of democratization of Judaism, emphasizing study and prayer in small groups. A third group was the Essenes, probably to be identified with the Qumran community in the Judean desert (see page 215). As for the Hellenizers, although some were merely place-seekers, others sincerely wished to combine Jewish ethical monotheism with the cosmopolitan spirit of Hellenistic civilization. They wanted, in short, to bring Jewish teachings to non-Jews, or Gentiles ("the nations").

Greek was the common tongue of Diaspora Jews, replacing Hebrew and Aramaic. Most Jews of the Hellenistic era lived outside Judea. The Diaspora had spread into (among other places) Syria, Anatolia, the Greek mainland, and Egypt, where a strong Jewish presence during the Persian period grew even greater, particularly in Alexandria. It is estimated that Jews made up 40 percent of the population of Alexandria at the height of Jewish prosperity, in the first century A.D., and tensions simmered between the large Jewish minority and the Greek majority. Greeks found the presence of so considerable a competing community threatening, and they looked down on Jewish dietary laws, circumcision, and other customs. Such attitudes spawned the first anti-Semitic literature as well as sporadic violence that at times broke into riots and persecution.

Foreign conversions and immigration into the Diaspora began to change the meaning of the word *Jew*. The word came to mean less "inhabitant of Judea" than "practitioner of Judaism." In short, *Jew* came to denote as much a religion as a nation.

SUMMARY

Histories of the Hellenistic world tend to be organized thematically rather than chronologically, a reflection of a period whose individual political actors appear dwarfed by the broad societal trends. The major legacy of the Hellenistic age was its culture. This Greek-speaking culture was dominated by inhabitants of or immigrants from old Greece and their descendants. The farsighted Pan-Hellenic ideas of Isocrates smoothed the way for the Greeks of different city-states to unite in kingdoms but offered less hope to others. We must not lose sight, however, of the continued flourishing of native cultures in the multi-ethnic kingdoms of the Ptolemies and Seleucids. Although Greeks and Macedonians dominated these regimes, they never imposed homogeneity, either in politics or in culture.

The most important Greek cultural development of the age was a retreat from a complex of values associated with the citizen-warrior ideal of the Classical city-state. The polis came under the shadow of federal leagues and kingdoms; philosophers questioned the very point of political activity. The hero gave way to the antihero, often a man whose success was dependent on the kindness and love of a woman. The female nude became as important a subject for sculptors as the male nude. Hellenistic women were freer than their predecessors in their movement and their ability to hold property and have some say in public life.

Stoic philosophers were far more interested in intention than were their Classical predecessors. Yet their interest in the subject pales before that of the Jews, new actors on the Greek stage. Judaism placed an emphasis on the interior dialogue between humans and the divine that was more radical than anything in the Greek tradition. Some

Greeks admired Jewish ethics, but few were willing to accept Jewish laws and rituals. Greeks did, however, borrow from other native religions. Hellenistic religion, therefore, was an exception to the general Greek indifference to native culture. The common denominator of the new religious teachings was a close, personal relationship with a savior-god who would guarantee comfort, peace, and eternal life after death.

Ironically, these very doctrines brought their Greek adherents closer to Hellenistic Judaism, which preached righteousness and justice in this life and the hereafter through subordination to the truth of the one and only God. The Jewish doctrine of messianic kingship might even have reminded Greeks of their own ruler cults. Imperceptibly, Hellenic and Hebraic were drawing closer. Under the Roman successor state, Hellenism and Judaism would be combined in a new and powerful form: Christianity.

NOTES

1. Isocrates, "Panegyricus," trans. H. I. Marrou, in *A History of Education in Antiquity*, trans. George Lamb (New York: Mentor Books/New American Library, 1956), p. 130.
2. Romila Thapar, *Aśoka and the Decline of the Mauryas* (Oxford: Oxford University Press, 1961), p. 256.
3. Quoted in Charles Rowan Beye, *Ancient Greek Literature and Society*, 2d ed., rev. (Ithaca, N.Y.: Cornell University Press, 1987), p. 265.

SUGGESTED READING

General Surveys

Grant, Michael. *From Alexander to Cleopatra: The Hellenistic World*. 1982. A lively and readable introduction, at its best on cultural history.

Green, P. *Alexander to Actium: An Essay in the Historical Evolution of the Hellenistic Age*. 1989. A collection of elegant essays synthesizing scholarship on a wide variety of topics in political, cultural, and social history.

Walbank, F. W. *The Hellenistic World*. Rev. ed. 1993. Fine introduction, especially to political history, by a leading scholar of Polybius.

Walbank, F. W., et al., eds. *The Cambridge Ancient History*, 2d ed. Vol. VII, Pt. 1, *The Hellenistic World*. 1984. Vol. VIIA, *Plates to Volume VII, Part 1*. New ed. 1984. An advanced-level survey from Alexander's death in 323 B.C. to the Battle of Raphia in 217 B.C.

Philip and Alexander

Badian, E. "Alexander the Great and the Loneliness of Power." In Badian, *Studies in Greek and Roman History*. 1964. A brilliant though speculative analysis of the moral costs of Alexander's success.

Cawkwell, G. *Philip of Macedon*. 1978. A short and lively introduction, written in an engaging prose style.

Ellis, J. R. *Philip II and Macedonian Imperialism*. 1976. An incisive analysis emphasizing the systemic factors shaping international relations in the mid-fourth century B.C. Aegean.

Green, P. *Alexander of Macedon, 356–323 B.C.: A Historical Biography*. 1991. A longer, more detailed study than Hamilton's, written in a polished style.

Hamilton, J. R. *Alexander the Great*. 1973. A reliable and remarkably concise introduction.

States and Regions

Bar-Kochva, Bezalel. *Judas Maccabeus. The Jewish Struggle Against the Seleucids*. 1989. A thorough introduction with an emphasis on military history.

Bowman, Alan K. *Egypt After the Pharaohs*. 1986. An excellent and highly readable introduction to the social history of the Ptolemaic and later periods.

Cohen, Shaye. *From the Maccabees to the Mishnah*. 1987. An excellent introduction by a distinguished scholar of Second Temple Judaism.

Ferguson, W. S. *Hellenistic Athens*. 1911. An older book but still a thoughtful, thorough, and delightful narrative account.

Kuhrt, Amélie, and Susan Sherwin-White. *From Samarkhand to Sardis: A New Approach to the Seleucid Empire*. 1993. An important and controversial book, full of challenges to conventional interpretations. The authors argue that Seleucid rule was more multicultural than is usually thought.

———, eds. *Hellenism in the East: The Interaction of Greek and Non-Greek Civilizations from Syria to Central Asia After Alexander*. 1987. An important collection of essays emphasizing the importance of Mesopotamia to the Seleucid kings and the importance of native elites in Seleucid administration.

Lewis, N. *Greeks in Ptolemaic Egypt*. 1986. An innovative reconstruction of the history of several families, some native and some Greek, across the span of the Ptolemaic period.

Samuel, A. E. *The Shifting Sands of History: Interpretations of Ptolemaic Egypt*. 1989. An extremely useful guide to the variety of modern scholarly appraisals.

Schürer, Emil. *History of the Jewish People in the Age of Jesus Christ (175 B.C.–A.D. 135)*. Rev. ed. 3 vols. 1973–1978. A classic and fundamental study, updated by Geza Vermes and Fergus Millar.

Sedlar, Jean W. *India and the Greek World: A Study in the Transmission of Culture*. 1980. A thoughtful and readable study, emphasizing philosophy and religion.

Shimron, Benjamin. *Late Sparta: The Spartan Revolution, 243–146 B.C.* 1972. A detailed, analytical narrative.

Society

Crawford, Dorothy J. *Kerkeosiris: An Egyptian Village in the Ptolemaic Period*. 1971. A fascinating glimpse of local social history.

Grant, Michael. *Cleopatra*. 1972. A very readable biography, well documented and nicely illustrated.

Griffith, G. T. *Mercenaries of the Hellenistic World*. 1935. A lively study of mercenaries as a fighting force and of their background and way of life.

Modrzejewski, Joseph Mélèze. *The Jews of Egypt: From Rameses II to Emperor Hadrian*. 1995. A good overview by an expert in Ptolemaic legal history.

Pomeroy, Sarah B. *Goddesses, Whores, Wives, and Slaves: Women in Classical Antiquity*. 1975. Chap. 7, "Hellenistic Women," is a sound introductory survey of the Hellenistic era.

———. *Women in Hellenistic Egypt from Alexander to Cleopatra*. 1984. A social history that documents women's growing autonomy.

Rostovtzeff, M. I. *Social and Economic History of the Hellenistic World*. 2d ed. 3 vols. 1953. An exhaustive survey by a great and original historian, although many of the conclusions are no longer accepted.

Thompson, Dorothy. *Memphis Under the Ptolemies*. 1988. A rich introduction to Ptolemaic Egypt's largest native city, which was also a significant site of foreign settlement.

Science, Literature, Religion, and Art

Beye, C. R. *Ancient Greek Literature and Society*. 2d ed. 1987. The last chapter, "The New Athens," is a succinct and lively introduction to the cultural and social trends found in Alexandrian poetry.

Bickerman, Elias J. "The Historical Foundations of Postbiblical Judaism." In Louis Finkelstein, ed., *The Jews: Their History*. 4th ed. 1970. A sound, succinct, and stimulating survey of Jewish religion and history from the return from Babylon to the Maccabees.

Ferguson, J. *Callimachus*. 1980. A brief survey of the evidence for Callimachus's works, as well as a discussion of Alexandrian culture and of Callimachus's long-term literary importance.

Hutchinson, G. O. *Hellenistic Poetry*. 1988. A good introduction, with an emphasis on the third century B.C.

Lloyd, G. E. R. *Greek Science After Aristotle*. 1973. An excellent introduction to science and society, with a discussion of philosophy and scientific culture and institutions as well as the specific achievements of mathematics and science. Many helpful diagrams.

Long, A. A. *Hellenistic Philosophy: Stoics, Epicureans, Sceptics*. 2d ed. 1986. A concise critical analysis of the main ideas and methods of thought of the major Hellenistic philosophers.

Momigliano, A. D. *Alien Wisdom: The Limits of Hellenization*. 1975. A brilliant, influential, and challenging essay on the interaction of Greeks with other cultures.

Onians, J. *Art and Thought in the Hellenistic Age: The Greek World View, 350–50 B.C.* 1979. An account that emphasizes the reshaping of the Classical Greek artistic heritage in a new age.

Von Staden, Heinrich. *Herophilus: The Art of Medicine in Early Alexandria*. 1989. A detailed, scholarly account. The first chapter ("Alexandrian and Egyptian Medicine") is a balanced discussion of the relative importance (or lack thereof) of Egyptian medicine for the early Greek physicians of Alexandria.

IMAGES OF CLEOPATRA

"Cleopatra's nose: if it had been shorter, the whole face of the earth would have changed," wrote the French philosopher Blaise Pascal (1623–1662). He does Cleopatra an injustice. It was not a pretty face and classical features that enabled her to win the throne of Egypt (r. 51–30 B.C.), to obtain first Julius Caesar and then Mark Antony as ally and lover, and finally to come close to gaining control of the Roman Empire. Intelligence, daring, charm, and extraordinary diplomatic skill account for Cleopatra's success.

Let us consider the queen's manipulation of her public image: no mean task, given the fragility of Ptolemaic power in the first century B.C. Within Egypt, the monarch had to satisfy several different ethnic groups. Most important were the Greeks and Macedonians—who dominated government, the military, and the economy—and the native

Bronze Coin of Cleopatra (*Courtesy of the Trustees of the British Museum*)

Egyptian majority. Daughter of Ptolemy XII (r. 80–51 B.C.), Cleopatra was supposed to rule jointly with her brother, but they had a falling-out. She wrested the throne from him and then from another brother and thus had to assert her legitimacy. Also, Ptolemaic Egypt had to project an image of unity to the Romans, who were threatening to annex it as they had the other Hellenistic monarchies.

Cleopatra, like earlier Ptolemaic monarchs, met these challenges by presenting two faces to the world. To the Greeks and Romans she was a Hellenistic monarch; to the Egyptians she was an ancient queen. Look first at the bronze coin of Cleopatra issued at Alexandria probably in the 30s B.C. The queen is shown as a young woman. Her hair, tied in a bun at the nape of her neck, is in the so-called melon style often seen in Hellenistic female portraits. She wears a diadem (royal headband), its ends hanging behind her neck. More commonly worn by Hellenistic kings than by queens, the diadem signifies Cleopatra's claim to authority.

So does the queen's profile. She is portrayed with a prominent chin, a large mouth, and a rugged nose. These features may not be the standard attributes of beauty, but they are precisely the features of coin portraits of Cleopatra's father. By emphasizing Cleopatra's physical similarity to her father, the portrait artist perhaps subtly suggests her right to sit on his throne.

The side of the coin not shown here is far from subtle: Its legend states clearly in Greek, "Queen Cleopatra." The illustration is of an eagle and thunderbolt and a double cornucopia (horn of plenty) entwined with a diadem. The eagle and thunderbolt recall the Greek god Zeus, and the two cornucopias suggest fertility and prosperity. All are recurrent symbols of Ptolemaic royalty. The coin thus portrays Cleopatra as a Greek monarch, the worthy heir of her father. It would have been an effective image in Alexandria, a city dominated by the Greeks and visited by Romans, but not in the countryside, especially south of

150

Relief of Cleopatra and Caesarion *(Erich Lessing/Art Resource, NY)*

the Nile Delta, in Upper Egypt, an area that was primarily Egyptian. Following dynastic custom, Cleopatra changed her image there.

In Upper Egypt, earlier Ptolemies frequently had been represented in stone in traditional pharaonic style, and they were great restorers of ancient Egyptian temples and builders of new ones. Look at the sculptural relief from the temple of the Egyptian cow-goddess Hathor at Dendera in Upper Egypt. The temple was a monumental structure to whose construction Ptolemy XII had contributed. Cleopatra, his daughter, added an enormous relief on the outside of the rear wall. Carved into the stone are two persons carrying offerings for Egyptian deities. The persons are Cleopatra (left) and her son Ptolemy XV Caesar, who ruled with his mother from 44 to 30 B.C. Alleged to be the illegitimate son of Julius Caesar, Ptolemy XV was commonly known as Caesarion or "little Caesar." At Dendera, however, he and his mother are shown neither as Romans nor as Greeks but as Egyptians.

Look closely at Cleopatra. She wears a long body-hugging robe. On her head is a royal headdress with symbols of the Egyptian gods: the lyre-shaped cow horns and sun-disk of Hathor, the tall plumes of Isis, and the ram's horn of Amon. Caesarion is shown as a pharaoh, wearing the double crown of Upper and Lower Egypt. Mother and son offer incense to the local deities. The small figure between Caesarion and Cleopatra is his *ka*, or soul.

Cleopatra's face is in profile but otherwise has very little in common with her portrait on the Alexandrian coin. Although the features are stylized pharaonic commonplaces, the shape of her head perhaps echoes the elegant and graceful relief portraits of Hatshepsut (r. 1479–1457 B.C.), the most famous female pharaoh before Cleopatra.

Cleopatra commissioned other artworks and monuments in the native style in the Nile Valley. This was the custom of her dynasty, and Cleopatra had absorbed its traditions, but she stands second to none of the Ptolemies in shrewdness and subtlety. She was the only Ptolemaic monarch to learn to speak Egyptian, and she was the only one to come even close to gaining the upper hand over Rome. As the artifacts shown here indicate, she was able to put on an Egyptian face as easily as a Greek one, but she never lost sight of her true interests. ✜

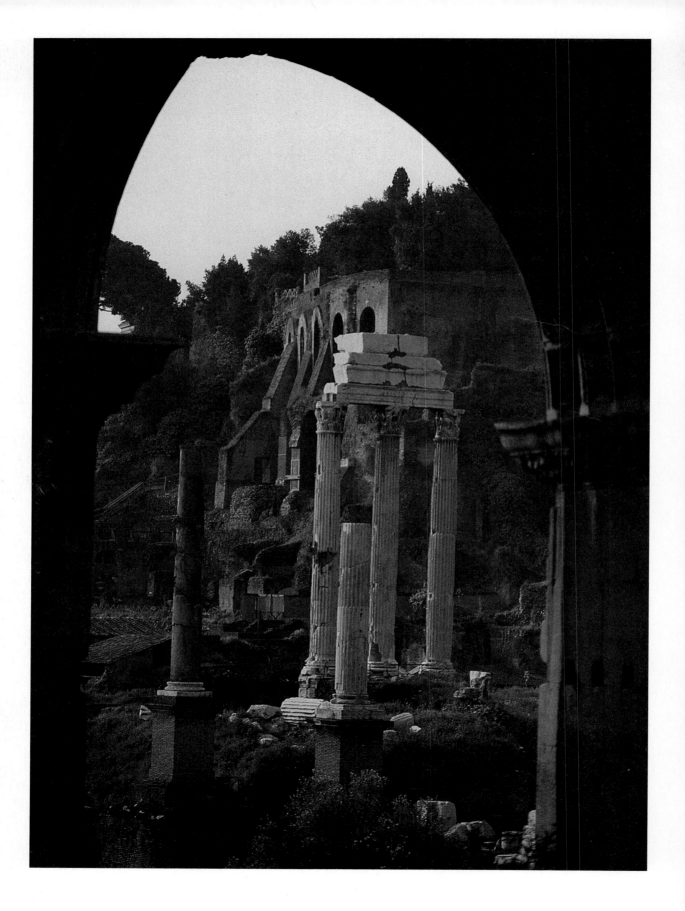

CHAPTER 5

Rome: From Republic to Empire, ca. 509–44 B.C.

There are many monuments to the ancient Romans, ranging from amphitheaters and aqueducts to law codes to Spanish, French, and the other languages derived from Latin, the language of the Romans. Practical monuments all, but that is appropriate, for the Romans were a practical people. Virgil (70–19 B.C.), for example, the greatest Roman poet (see pages 200–201), celebrates not his countrymen's artistry or cultivation but rather their pragmatic accomplishments:

> For other peoples will, I do not doubt,
> still cast their bronze to breathe with softer features,
> or draw out of the marble living lines,
> plead causes better, trace the ways of heaven
> with wands and tell the rising constellations;
> but yours will be the rulership of nations,
> remember, Romans, these will be your arts:
> to teach the ways of peace to those you conquer,
> to spare defeated peoples, tame the proud.[1]

The Romans were innovators in legal science and masters of political mythmaking and propaganda, but they are best known as imperialists who turned an Italian city-state into one of the largest empires in history, comprising all the countries of the Mediterranean as well as substantial parts of western Asia and of northern and central Europe. By holding this empire for centuries and by fostering prosperity, Rome planted in what would become Britain, France, Germany, and Spain (among other places) the seeds of the advanced civilizations of the Mediterranean.

Rome is no less important for its influence on the Western civic tradition. Much of the modern vocabulary of politics, from *president* to *inauguration* to

The Forum,
Rome.

forum, can be traced back to Rome. After an early period of monarchy, Rome was for centuries a republic (Latin, *res publica*, literally "public business") before essentially becoming a monarchy again under the Caesars. The Roman Republic was far more hierarchical than Greek democracy. Greek democrats governed themselves; Romans elected their leaders, aristocrats with wide powers of office. To create an effective and stable regime, the elite divided power among separate government bodies, creating a system of checks and balances that tended toward consensus. The elite also manipulated with skill the symbols of authority.

Roman elite politicians sought to control ordinary citizens but in some ways were more flexible than Greek democrats: Unlike Greece, Rome extended its citizenship to a large population, first throughout Italy and then across its entire empire. The modern nation-state with its mass citizenship owes much to Rome. Indeed, although Rome was not democratic, modern democracy—that is, popular government with a large population, whose officials are elected by the people—has roots in the Roman Republic as well as in the Greek city-state.

Fueled by fear, ambition, and greed, Roman expansion generated its own momentum. In tracing it, one shudders at the parallel paths of Roman success and arrogance: at the consolidation of power over huge territories alongside the mounting number of war atrocities, peoples enslaved, and cities destroyed with but little provocation. One also marvels at the irony of the process by which success slowly undermined both the solidarity of Rome's governing elite and the socioeconomic basis of the Roman army. Masters of war and diplomacy, the Romans unknowingly weakened their society with every brick they added to the edifice of the empire. One marvels too at the open-mindedness with which Romans borrowed from other societies, in particular from the Greeks, to whom the Republic owed great cultural debts. Also fascinating is the shrewdness and generosity with which the Romans shared their citizenship with the elites whom they had conquered, thereby winning their loyalty and strengthening Rome's grip on their territory.

Historians conventionally divide the Republic into three periods: Early (509–287 B.C.), Middle (287–133 B.C.), and Late (133–31 B.C.). This chapter

begins with the origins of the city of Rome in the early first millennium B.C. and then traces the Republic from its foundation to its imperial conquests to its collapse under their weight. Success spoiled Rome. The unintended consequences of conquest on Rome's society, politics, and culture led to a revolution which, in the century beginning in 133 B.C., saw the Republic's downfall.

BEFORE THE REPUBLIC

Romans in the third century B.C. believed that their city was founded by Romulus, the descendant of immigrants to Italy from far-off Troy. In the first century B.C., a Roman scholar even supplied a precise date for the founding: April 27, 753 B.C., by our reckoning.

Although the name "Romulus" supplies a convenient etymology for "Rome," little stock can be placed in this story. No history of Rome was written before the late third century B.C., and no history survives before the mid-second century (five and six hundred years after 753 B.C., respectively). In the third century B.C., however, Rome conquered the Greek cities of southern Italy and was captivated by their cultural richness. The Trojan connection was probably invented to give educated Romans a prestigious pedigree that recalled Greek epic but was nonetheless non-Greek.

Nevertheless, archaeology provides some confirmation of Roman tradition. Tombs as early as the tenth century B.C. have been found in Rome, but the first evidence of buildings comes from the eighth century B.C. A simple village of farmers and shepherds—a collection of huts—was established then on the Palatine Hill, one of the seven hills of what would be Rome and the place where tradition puts the settlement of 753. Other, similar settlements followed on two or three of Rome's other hills (see inset, Map 5.2).

Archaeological evidence does not mean that we have to accept mythology as history, but it does revive basic questions: What were Rome's origins and how did it grow? By examining the data of archaeology and of those elements in ancient historiography that seem to be based on accurate tradition, we can answer these questions, at least in outline.

Archaic Rome and Its Neighbors

Italy is a long peninsula, shaped roughly like a boot, extending about 750 miles from the Alps into the Mediterranean (Map 5.1). In the far north, the high Alps provide a barrier, though not an impenetrable one, to the rest of Europe. The Adriatic Sea to the east separates Italy from modern Slovenia and Croatia; to the west, the Tyrrhenian Sea faces the large islands of Sardinia and Corsica (and the smaller but iron-rich island of Elba) and the coasts of France and Spain beyond. Across from the "toe" of the Italian boot, and separated from the mainland by a narrow, 3-mile strait of water, is the island of Sicily, large and in antiquity agriculturally rich. Sicily is only 90 miles from North Africa. In short, Italy is centrally located in the Mediterranean and was thus both a tempting target for conquerors and a useful springboard for conquest.

Italy's distinct geographic regions comprise some of the ancient Mediterranean's most fertile and metal-rich land. In the north is the alluvial plain of the Padus (modern Po) and Adige Rivers. Traveling south along the west coast of Italy, one enters in turn the lowland alluvial plains of Etruria (modern Tuscany), Latium (the region of Rome), and Campania (the region of Naples). Although the Apennine mountains run southward along most of the Italian peninsula, they are low compared with the Alps and contain many passes, permitting the movement of armies.

In the first millennium B.C., Italy represented a complex mix of peoples and languages. They included the Etruscans in the north, Greek colonists along the southern Italian coasts and in Sicily, and such Apennine peoples as the Sabines, northeast of Rome, and the Samnites to the south. Latium was home to a number of small Latin-speaking towns, one of them Rome. In the fifth century B.C. another important people arrived on the Italian scene: Celts (called Gauls by the Romans), large numbers of whom crossed the Alps and settled in northern Italy after roughly 500 B.C. Most of these various peoples spoke Indo-European languages, of which Latin, the language of the Romans (among other peoples of Latium), was one.

Rome's location in Latium gave it a central and strategic position in the Italian peninsula. Located 15 miles inland on the Tiber, the largest river on Italy's west coast, Rome was near the sea but far enough away to be safe from sea raiders. The seven hills of the city also offered defensive protection. A midstream island makes Rome the first crossing place upstream from the Tiber's mouth, offering the Romans access north and south.

In the seventh century B.C., Archaic Rome (as the pre-Republican period is called) began to be transformed from a large village into a city. Signs of urbanization included Rome's first stone houses, first public building, and the first forum, or civic center. In the sixth century, streets, walls, drains, temples, and a racetrack followed. What caused the transformation? Probably the most important cause was contact with Magna Graecia, the Greek colonies to the south (see Map 5.1). Established in the eighth and seventh centuries B.C., the colonies transported westward the sophisticated urban civilization of the eastern Mediterranean.

More controversial is the impact of Rome on its neighbors to the north, the Etruscans. The twelve Etruscan city-states were organized in a loose confederation centered in Etruria. They grew wealthy from the mining of iron, copper, and silver, from piracy, from trade, and from a network of influential Etruscan emigrants throughout central Italy, possibly including Rome's last three kings (traditionally dated 616–509 B.C.).

Most scholars argue that the Etruscans conquered Rome and left a significant cultural and material legacy. Recent work, however, suggests a pattern of cross-fertilization and emigration rather than conquest; it argues that the Etruscan legacy in Rome was superficial. According to this view, to the extent that any outside culture influenced Archaic Rome, it was the Greeks—who also influenced the Etruscans and other central Italian peoples, for that matter. The Etruscan city-states were similar to Rome; they were its peer, not its elder sibling.

The new theory seems more plausible than the traditional one, given what we know of other ancient societies, but since so little evidence survives from Archaic Rome, we must be cautious. Likewise, our inability to decipher the Etruscan language (which is neither Indo-European nor Semitic) also dictates caution. There is no need to be wary about noting the Etruscans' rich artistic legacy, however, or the high status of Etruscan elite women compared to their Greek or Roman

Etruscan Tomb Painting This wall painting from Tarquinia shows a married aristocratic couple at a banquet. The style of the figures is derived from Greek art, but the depiction of husband and wife dining on the same couch is characteristically Etruscan. *(National Museum, Tarquinia/Scala/Art Resource, NY)*

counterparts. Etruscan women kept their own names, and Etruscan children bore the names of both parents. In addition, Etruscan elite women were permitted to attend athletic contests in spite of the presence of naked male athletes.

The Roman Monarchy

Tradition says that Rome was ruled by seven kings before the foundation of the Republic. Although the number of kings may be a later inven-

Map 5.1 Early Italy and Region of City of Rome. Early Italy comprised a variety of terrain and peoples. Rome was located in the central Italian region of Latium. The Alps separate Italy from northern Europe. The Apennine mountain range runs almost the entire length of the Italian peninsula. Much of the rest of Italy is fertile plain.

tion, there is no doubt about the existence of the monarchy, which leaves its traces in Republican institutions. A form of the Latin word *rex* ("king"), moreover, has been found inscribed on a Roman monument from the early sixth century B.C. The king's power, called *imperium* (from *imperare*, "to command"), was very great, embracing religious, military, and judicial affairs.

The king was advised by a council of elders, called the "fathers" (*patres* in Latin) or the "senate" (*senatus*, from *senex*, "old man"). In theory the senate was primarily an advisory body, but in practice it was quite powerful. Senators were often the heads of the most important families in Rome, so the king rejected their advice at his peril. Romans spoke of the senate's *auctoritas*, a quasi-religious prestige. Most senators were patricians, as early Rome's hereditary aristocracy was known. The rest of the people, the bulk of Roman society, were called plebeians. Plebeians were free; most were ordinary people, though some were wealthy. Patricians monopolized the senate and priesthoods, and they did not intermarry with plebeians.

The whole people, probably both patricians and plebeians, met in an assembly organized in thirty local units, or *curiae*, hence the name *curiate assembly*. The assembly's powers were limited. Before becoming law, resolutions of the assembly required approval by the senate.

Early Rome was a class-based society, but it was not closed to foreigners. Among others, Etruscans, Sabines, and Latins—as the inhabitants of other Latin-speaking towns are called—came to Rome. Unlike Athenians, who tried to hide the presence of immigrants in their country by a myth of indigenous origins, Romans openly discussed their mixed roots. Foreigners at first had a subordinate status but gained equality around 550 B.C. Military pressure made it necessary to expand the body of loyal infantrymen, so native Romans decided to incorporate the immigrants into their community—a reform traditionally associated with King Servius Tullius (578–535 B.C.). Servius probably introduced to Rome the hoplite phalanx (see page 84). Any man with enough property to afford the necessary training and equipment could serve as a hoplite or cavalryman.

In short, like the early Greeks, the Romans moved toward a notion of citizenship based on military service. As in early Greece so in Rome military change bred political upheaval. Within several generations of Servius's reform, Rome went from monarchy to republic.

FOUNDING THE ROMAN REPUBLIC

The traditional date of the overthrow of the kings and the establishment of the Republic is 509 B.C. A symbol of revolution in modern times, this event was in fact probably part of a long process rather than a dramatic upheaval. The institutions of the new Republic were not put in place at once but developed slowly by trial and error. Some scholars reject the date of 509 and put the transition years later. The traditional story is nonetheless revealing. Let us consider a foundation myth of the Re-

public and then turn to early Republican society and culture.

A few inscriptions and temple dedications, as well as lists of public officeholders, survive as documents of the Early Republic. For a coherent account, however, it is necessary to turn to the works of Roman historians. Written centuries after the events described, these works also tend to embroider the evidence, so we must be cautious.

A Foundation Myth of the Roman Republic

According to the historian Livy (59 B.C.–A.D. 17), the overthrow of the monarchy was prompted by the rape of Lucretia, wife of the aristocrat Tarquinius Collatinus, by Sextus, son of King Tarquinius Superbus (r. ca. 534–509 B.C.). (See the box, "The Rape of Lucretia.") Livy embellished the details of the story, which had been preserved for centuries in oral tradition before being written down, yet his version is nonetheless revealing of Roman mores. Livy claims that Sextus was attracted to Lucretia by her modesty: While other Roman wives made merry in their husbands' absence, Lucretia sat home spinning wool. Taking advantage of Collatinus's absence, Sextus entered the house as a guest. He then forced himself on Lucretia by threatening to kill her because, he would claim, he had found her in bed with a slave. Ashamed in spite of her innocence, Lucretia incited her husband and his kinsman, Lucius Junius Brutus, by revealing Sextus's crime and then killing herself with her own dagger. To avenge her, Collatinus and Brutus drove out the Tarquin kings and established the Republic.

That Rome's mythmakers should found the Republic on the need to avenge a rape may seem strange, but only at first. The main elements of the tale—violence, honor, and family—proved to be of permanent fascination to the Roman elite. Lucretia's honor was literally more important to her than her life. Centuries later, when Julius Caesar (100–44 B.C.) was asked why he preferred civil war to compromise, he too said that his honor was dearer to him than his life. The defining feature of Caesar's honor was political prestige, of Lucretia's chastity, but they shared a devotion to dignity and reputation—fundamental values for both sexes in Rome. The Lucretia story offers other insights into Roman elite mores: the expectation of hospitality among aristocrats, the class bias (adultery by a

The Rape of Lucretia

The historian Livy attributes the founding of the Roman Republic to outrage over the rape of the aristocratic woman Lucretia by Sextus Tarquinius, son of King Tarquinius Superbus. Though of dubious historicity, the story reveals a great deal about Roman attitudes toward gender, honor, and their political implications.

[A guest in Lucretia's house in her husband's absence, Sextus Tarquinius demands that she sleep with him.] But all in vain; not even the fear of death could bend her will. "If death will not move you," Sextus cried, "dishonor shall. I will kiss you first, then cut the throat of a slave and lay his naked body by your side. Will they not believe that you have been caught in adultery with a servant—and paid the price?" Even the most resolute chastity could not have stood against this dreadful threat.

[After being violated by Sextus Tarquinius, Lucretia summons her husband and father.] "In your bed, Collatinus, is the impress of another man. My body only has been violated. My heart is innocent, and death will be my witness. Give me your solemn promise that the adulterer shall be punished—he is Sextus Tarquinius. He it was who last night came as my enemy disguised as my guest, and took his pleasure of me. . . .

"What is due to *him*," Lucretia said, "is for you to decide. As for me, I am innocent of fault, but I will take my punishment. Never shall Lucretia provide a precedent for unchaste women to escape what they deserve." With these words she drew a knife from under her robe, drove it into her heart, and fell forward, dead.

Her father and husband were overwhelmed with grief. While they stood weeping helplessly, Brutus [aristocrat and family friend] drew the bloody knife from Lucretia's body, and holding it before him cried: "By this girl's blood—none more chaste till a tyrant wronged her—and by the gods, I swear that with sword and fire, and whatever else can lend strength to my arm, I will pursue Lucius Tarquinius Superbus, his wicked wife, and all his children, and never again will I let them or any other man be King in Rome."

Source: Livy, *The Early History of Rome*, trans. Aubrey de Sélincourt (Harmondsworth, England: Penguin, 1971), pp. 98–99.

noble woman was bad enough, but adultery by a noble woman with a slave was unthinkable), and the alleged antithesis between modest Romans and profligate Etruscans.

Lucretia's fate indicates the premium put by Roman nobles on defending family honor and avenging it when necessary. Indeed, the family holds many keys to understanding Rome.

The Roman Household

The Latin word *familia* is broader than the English word *family*: Better translated as "household," it connotes slaves, animals, and property, as well as the members of a nuclear family and their ancestors or descendants. The familia was the basic unit of Roman society. A center of both production and consumption, it was also a model of political authority. In theory, though not always in practice, the Roman household was an authoritarian institution governed by a male; thus, the familia is an example of patriarchy.

The legal head of the familia was the *paterfamilias*, the oldest living male—usually the father in a nuclear family, though occasionally the grandfather or, in cases of unusual longevity, the great-grandfather. According to Roman law, the pater-familias had supreme power within the household. Although he was supposed to call a council of senior male relatives to consult on big decisions, he was not required to follow their advice. He had the right to sell family members into slavery and the rarely used power to kill an errant wife or child. A son, no matter how old, was always legally subject to the authority of a living pater-familias. Only the paterfamilias, moreover, could own property free and clear. Thus, a 30-year-old man might be under the authority of his pater-familias and dependent on him for an allowance.

Roman respect for the paterfamilias stemmed from Roman esteem for ancestors, who were far more important than in Greek culture. All patricians and some plebeians belonged to a *gens* (plural, *gentes*), a kinship group that traced its ancestry back to a purported common ancestor. All Roman males had a personal and family name, and patricians and elite plebeians also had a third (middle) name, indicating their gens: for example, Gaius Julius Caesar, whose personal name Gaius was followed by the gens name Julius and the familia name Caesar.

In theory, the paterfamilias was the focus of power in the household, but practice was more complex. The sources are full of indications of fathers' affection, love, and even indulgence for their children. Moreover, Roman women usually married in their late teens and men in their late twenties. Given the low life expectancies, it was common for a man of 25 to have already buried his father. Many, perhaps even most, adult males were independent of a paterfamilias.

Unlike men, Roman women never became legally independent, even on the death of a pater-familias. Instead of receiving a personal name, a daughter was called by the name of her father's gens. For example, Gaius Julius Caesar's daughter was called Julia; if Caesar had had a second daughter, she would have been Julia Secunda ("Julia the Second"). Although fathers were expected to support all male children, they had to support only the first of their daughters. In other words, they were free to "expose" additional daughters—that is, leave them in the open to die or, as was perhaps more likely, to be adopted or raised as a slave. A father also arranged a daughter's marriage and provided her with a dowry. In theory, again, they

had a most severe relationship, but the evidence suggests considerable father-daughter affection, including married daughters who sought advice or aid from their fathers.

Most women in early Rome married *cum manu* (literally, "with hand")—that is, they were "handed over" to their husbands, who became their new paterfamilias. Even so, Roman wives and mothers had more prestige and freedom than their counterparts in Classical Greece. Legends of early Rome mention some who were peacemakers, negotiators, or (like Lucretia) catalysts of quarrels among men. Roman women regularly shared meals and social activities with their parents and were expected to take an interest in their husband's political life.

The hierarchy of the household was applied to Roman society and politics. Romans conceived of the state as a collection of heads of household, each head competing for honor for his own familia and gens. The imperium (power) of the chief magistrates (a Republican adaptation of the imperium of the king) was analogous to the supreme power of the paterfamilias. An ordinary Roman was expected to obey the magistrates, just as he would obey his paterfamilias.

Patrons and Clients

Patron (derived from *pater*, "father") means "defender" or "protector." *Client* means "dependent." Roman society consisted of pyramidlike patron-client networks. Most patrons were in turn clients of someone more powerful; only a very few men stood at the top of the pyramid. In the Roman imagination, justice required not equality between patron and client but mutual respect and obligation.

Various paths led to the status of client. A peasant in need of help on his farm might ask a wealthy neighbor to become his patron. A manumitted slave became the client of his former owner. A conquered foe became the client of the victorious general. The status of client or patron was hereditary.

Patron and client might help each other in various ways. A patron might provide a client with food or with property for a dowry. He might settle disputes or provide legal assistance. In return, a client owed his patron respect and service.

Shrine of a Wealthy Household This painting from Pompeii shows the spirit of the paterfamilias in a toga, which is wrapped around his head in keeping with Roman procedures of sacrifice. He is flanked by the spirits of departed ancestors. A snake symbolizes fertility. *(Alinari/Art Resource, NY)*

He escorted his patron in public on important occasions—possession of a large clientele signified prestige and power. If his patron sought political office, the client voted for him. If his patron needed money, the client was obligated to contribute, perhaps to an election campaign or to pay fines or ransoms.

Cloaked in an elaborate language of goodwill, the patron-client relationship was considered a matter of *fides* ("good faith" or "trustworthiness"). Romans spoke not of a client submitting to a patron's power but rather of a client "commending himself" to the patron's fides. A patron spoke not of his clients but of his "friends," especially if they were men of standing or substance.

A patron was supposed to put his clients before kin by marriage; only blood or adoptive rela-

tions were to take precedence. The Twelve Tables, a Roman law code of the mid-fifth century B.C. (see page 166), declares that a patron who defrauds his client is accursed and may be killed with impunity.

Patronage undergirded Roman domestic politics and foreign relations. Although Republican political institutions appeared to work through free elections and popular choice, the obligations of humble clients to wealthy patrons took precedence. If a man's clients grew discontented, another ambitious politician might offer himself as their new patron, leading in turn to political change. As for foreign affairs, experience as patrons schooled Roman leaders in treating the peoples they conquered as clients, often as personal clients. Moreover, the Roman state sometimes took foreign countries into its collective fides—much as a patron did a client—thus allowing Rome to extend its influence without the constraints of a formal alliance.

Religion and World-View

If we knew nothing about early Roman religion, we could deduce much about it from the familia and patronage. We could expect to find elements of patriarchy and contractualism, and both are indeed present. The task of a Roman priest, whether an official of the state or an individual paterfamilias, was to establish what the Romans called the "peace of the gods." Roman cults aimed at obtaining the gods' agreement to human requests, at "binding" the gods—the Latin term for which is *religio.*

The earliest Roman religion was animistic; that is, it centered on the spirits that, the Romans believed, haunted the household and the fields and forests and determined the weather. The Lares, the spirits of departed ancestors, guarded the house, and the Penates watched over stored grain. The spirit of the hearth was Vesta; of the door, Janus; of the rain and sun, Jupiter (later identified with the Greek sky-god and the father-god Zeus); of the crops and vegetation, Mars (later identified with the Greek war-god Ares). The Romans believed that these spirits needed to be appeased—hence the contractual nature of their prayers and offerings. Over the years, as a result of Greek influence, anthropomorphism (that is, the worship of humanlike gods and goddesses) supplanted Roman animism.

Roman state religion grew out of house religion. Vesta, the hearth-goddess, became goddess of the civic hearth; Janus, the door-god, became god of the city's gates; Jupiter became the general overseer of the gods; and Mars became the god of war. When trade and conquest brought the Romans into contact with foreign religions, the Romans tended to absorb them. The senate screened and sometimes rejected new gods, but by and large Roman polytheism was tolerant.

The Republic sponsored numerous priestly committees, or colleges, to secure the peace of the gods. Originally restricted to patricians, most of the highest priesthoods were opened to plebeians

by law in 300 B.C. Although some priesthoods were full-time jobs, most left the officeholder free to pursue a concurrent career as a magistrate or a senator. The two most important priestly colleges were the augurs, who were in charge of divination, and the pontiffs, who exercised a general supervisory function over Rome's numerous rituals, sacrifices, offerings, prayers, temples, and festivals. The chief pontiff, the *pontifex maximus,* was the head of the state clergy. The pontiffs alone controlled the interpretation of the law until the fourth century B.C. The Romans allowed priests to interpret the law on the theory that an offense against humans was also an offense against the gods.

There were only two colleges of priestesses: those of Ceres, goddess of fertility and death, and those of the Vestal Virgins. The six Vestals tended the civic hearth and made sure that its fire never went out. They served, as it were, as wives of the whole community, as guardians of the civil household. The Vestals were the only Roman women not under the authority of a paterfamilias. Chosen between the ages of 6 and 10 by the pontifex maximus, they had to remain virgins for thirty years or face death. The Vestals' virtue, like Lucretia's, was considered an index of male honor and so was watched closely.

By the Early Republic, class distinctions abounded in Rome. The elite papered over such differences by sponsoring an ideology of simple and austere farmers' virtues—discipline, hard work, frugality, temperance, and the avoidance of public displays of affection even between spouses. The supreme value of the household was *pietas*—devotion and loyalty to the familia, the gods, and the state. Household duties and gender obligations were defined clearly. Women were to be chaste, modest, and practical. Men were to project *gravitas* (weight, seriousness), never lightness or levity. A serious man would display self-control and constancy, the ability to persevere against difficult odds. The masculine ideal was *virtus* (literally, "manliness"), which indicated excellence in war and government.

Roman men who attained virtus considered themselves entitled to the reward of *dignitas,* meaning not only public esteem but the tangible possession of a dignified position and official rank—in short, public office. The ultimate test of virtus, however, was war. Let us turn to politics and the military.

GOVERNMENT AND SOCIETY IN THE EARLY AND MIDDLE REPUBLIC, CA. 509–133 B.C.

The history of Republican politics is both as simple as the patriarchal framework of the Roman household and as complex as the crosscurrents of affection and manipulation that ran through it. Although Rome had no written constitution, a hierarchical arrangement of public officials and popular assemblies emerged by the third century B.C. Documentation is poor for the earlier period, but later survivals shed some light on earlier practice. Much remains obscure, however, for several reasons. Rome's constitutional forms often mask the realities of elite power and manipulation. Furthermore, perhaps the best source for the mid-Republican constitution, the historian Polybius (ca. 200–ca. 118 B.C.), a Greek and former hostage who lived in Rome, used Greek categories to analyze the Roman government, thereby producing considerable distortion.

Political Institutions

Ancient theorists divided Roman political institutions into three branches: executive, deliberative, and legislative. Influenced by the Romans, the American founders adopted a similar division, but with the legislative and deliberative functions combined and a judicial branch added. In Rome, various magistrates of the executive branch administered justice, in addition to their other responsibilities. The Roman senate, which made up the deliberative branch, was far more powerful than the U.S. senate. The Roman legislative branch consisted of several popular assemblies.

The three parts of the Roman constitution, then, were the magistrates, the senate, and the people. Polybius describes the Middle Republic as a "mixed constitution": the assemblies, a democratic element; the senate, an oligarchic element; and the magistrates, a royal element. Polybius's

ROMAN GOVERNMENT AND SOCIETY	
753–509 B.C.	Monarchy (traditional dates)
509–287 B.C.	Early Republic
449 B.C.	Law of the Twelve Tables
445 B.C.	Plebeian-patrician intermarriage permitted
367 B.C.	Consulship opened to plebeians
300 B.C.	Highest priesthoods opened to plebeians
287 B.C.	Hortensian Law makes decisions of plebs legally binding
287–133 B.C.	Middle Republic
133–31 B.C.	Late Republic

model of power-sharing is elegant but wrong. Hierarchy characterized Roman government, just as it did Roman society and the household. Power flowed *away* from the people, at first to the magistrates, who were very strong in the Early Republic, and then to the senate, the dominant power in the government of the Middle Republic.

Executive power lay in the hands of the magistrates. They were more powerful and more elite figures than their counterparts in Greek democracies. Magistrates were elected to office by the Roman people rather than chosen by lottery, as in Greek democracy. Election required extensive campaigning, which in turn necessitated many clients. Magistracies were time-consuming jobs, but offered no salary, unlike public office in Greek democracy. Thus, only a wealthy, elite few could afford to be magistrates; almost all magistrates came from senatorial families. Because the number of magistracies was limited, competition for office among the elite was intense. Most magistracies required a minimum age of late thirties or early forties.

Eager for strong, effective magistrates but ever fearful that power might lead to corruption, Rome imposed the principles of collegiality and annuality on its officials. Every magistrate had one or more colleagues, and the tenure of office was only one year. The chief magistrates were eventually

A Clear Sign of Power The lictor of this bronze statuette (ca. first century A.D.) accompanied Roman magistrates, who had *imperium*, the power to issue punishments resulting in execution. That power is visible in the fasces he holds—an ax in a bundle of wooden rods bound with straps. (*Courtesy of the Trustees of the British Museum*)

called consuls, of which there were two. Each consul had the power to veto the other's actions. Like the former king, each consul had imperium, the power to issue commands and order punishments, including execution.

From about 500 B.C. to about 300 B.C., other magistracies emerged to assist the consul as administration grew more complex. In addition to those annual magistrates were two censors, older men elected once every four or five years for eighteen-month terms. At first their job was to supervise the census, the military register of citizens that recorded each man's property class. Later the censors began to punish those they considered bad citizens by consigning them to a lower census class. Censors could also expel bad citizens from the senate. The censors became, as it were, supervisors of public morals.

The Republic's government adapted flexibly to emergencies and to changing borders. In times of emergency the Republic turned power over to a single magistrate. The dictator, as he was called, held imperium, and his decisions were beyond appeal; but he held office for only six months. Another sign of flexibility was the practice of promagistracy—that is, of extending a magistrate's imperium past the normal term of office or of temporarily investing a private citizen with imperium. First employed in the fourth century B.C., promagistracy met Rome's needs as a conquering power by greatly expanding the pool of leaders able to serve as administrators and commanders away from home.

The deliberative branch of the Roman constitution consisted of the senate, which guided and advised the magistrates. During most of the Republic the senate consisted of three hundred men. In the third century B.C. and later, one became a senator after holding a magistracy. Senators served for life. As former magistrates and as members of a time-honored institution, senators possessed great authority. The senate sent and received ambassadors and supervised expenditures. Although the people formally declared war and ratified treaties, the senate was for all practical purposes in charge of foreign policy.

The legislative branch of the constitution consisted of four popular assemblies: the curiate assembly, the centuriate assembly, the council of the plebs, and the tribal assembly. Roman assemblies were not democratic. In contrast to Greece, in Rome assembly participants stood rather than sat down and received no salary for attendance. The ordinary Roman was unlikely to speak in the assembly, if he participated at all. Discussion was limited, and the patron-client system greatly constrained a client's voting freedom.

Although the curiate assembly of the monarchy survived, it held a largely ceremonial role. The centuriate assembly better suited the military oligarchy of the Republic. Based on a military formation (the century was the smallest unit of the Roman army), this assembly offered the façade of popular participation but the reality of control by the wealthy. The centuriate assembly elected consuls and lesser magistrates (and, when needed, dictators), voted on laws and treaties, accepted declarations of war and peace, and acted as a court in cases of treason, homicide, and appeals from the magistrates' decisions. The assembly, summoned by a trumpet call, met outside the city at dawn on a military parade ground. No discussion was permitted. The assembly was divided according to wealth into census classes of fighting men. The centuries voted in order of wealth. First came the equestrians, or cavalrymen, then five classes of infantrymen, and finally the *proletarii* ("breeders"), men too poor to provide their own arms. Because the equestrians and the first class of infantry—the wealthiest men—constituted a majority, in many elections the four remaining classes of infantry and the proletarii did not vote at all.

There were two other assemblies: the council of the plebs and the tribal assembly. The latter supplanted the former, becoming Rome's main legislative body in the third century B.C. To understand its evolution and workings, we turn now to the class conflicts in Rome during the fifth through third centuries B.C.

Conflict of the Orders

The Early Republic was a crucible. Social and political conflict, usually considered a struggle between the patrician and plebeian orders, tested the Roman state between 494 and 287 B.C. As in Archaic Greece, a relatively stable regime emerged: oligarchies and democracies in Greece, the Republic in Rome. As Rome reached a domestic political consensus, it presented an ever stronger military front to its external opponents. By 300 B.C., Rome was ready to grow from local power to dominance in Italy and then the Mediterranean.

Tradition gives Rome only 136 patrician families in 509 B.C., but they dominated the Early Republic. The plebs, in contrast, comprised masses of poor peasants and a tiny number of men who, though wealthy, were not patricians; there were plebeian artisans, traders, and shopkeepers, but they were only a small part of the population. In their own ways the various plebeian groups each wanted to break patrician power. Wealthy plebeians wanted unrestricted access to high office, from which they had been largely excluded. Ordinary plebeians demanded relief from debt, redistribution of land, and codification and publication of the law. For a century and a half, the two groups of plebeians made common cause, writing an important chapter in the history of political resistance.

Debt and hunger loomed large in the Early Republic. A form of debt-bondage called *nexum* forced a free man who defaulted on a loan to work off what he owed, often for the rest of his life. Plebeians wanted nexum abolished. The average peasant farm was too small to feed a family, rendering most peasants dependent on public land for farming and grazing. Time and again throughout Republican history, however, public land was occupied by the wealthy, who denied or restricted access to the poor. Their only hope was change.

The story of the plebs in the fifth century B.C. was one of solidarity. They organized themselves as kind of a state within the state, complete with their own assembly (the council of the plebs) and officials (the tribunes of the plebs). The decisions of the council of the plebs, called *plebiscita* (from which *plebiscite* comes), were binding only on the plebs; they did not receive the full force of law for over two hundred years. Yet the plebs did not retreat. On several occasions during the Early Republic they resorted to secession: The plebs as a whole left the city for the Aventine Hill, where they stayed until their grievances were addressed (see inset, Map 5.2).

The ten tribunes, elected annually by the plebs, were the people's champions. A tribune's house stood always open to any plebeian who needed him, and he could not leave the city limits. Inside the city of Rome, a tribune also had the right to veto any act of the magistrates, assembly, or senate that harmed plebeians. In return, the plebs swore to treat the tribunes as sacrosanct and to lynch anyone who harmed them.

Impressive as plebeian activity was, the patricians had formidable resources. Patricians dominated important priesthoods. Thanks to patrician financial aid, patricians' many clients could afford to serve as heavy infantrymen and thereby render support for continued patrician rule. Furthermore, patricians exercised great power in the new tribal assembly, created around the same time as the council of the plebs. The system of representation in the assembly heavily favored landowners. The tribal assembly elected lower magistrates and, in the same way as the centuriate assembly, voted on laws and acted as a court of appeals.

Nevertheless, the plebeians pressed onward, wringing concession after concession from the patricians, until finally the patricians retreated: They decided to neutralize the opposition by meeting the main demands of the plebeian elite. The outcome was a new, combined patrician-plebeian nobility. The patricians had wisely decided to compromise to preserve most of their privileges. The personnel changed, but the elite continued to rule Rome.

The specific events in the patrician-plebeian conflict follow two lines of development: major concessions to wealthy plebeians and small concessions to poor ones. For example, the year 449 B.C. witnessed publication of the law code known as the "Twelve Tables," eventually, if not at first, on twelve bronze tablets in the Forum. By modern standards, the code was primitive and severe, but its very existence was a plebeian victory, because published law became accessible and dependable. Unfortunately, the complex legal procedure remained a secret of the pontiffs for another 150 years, which ensured that no poor man could go to court without the help of a patron.

Around 445 B.C., the patricians accepted a law that permitted patrician-plebeian intermarriage, a victory for wealthy plebeians. Rather than endure plebeians as consuls, however, patricians suspended the consulship altogether for about eighty years, sharing the consuls' powers among a group of military officers, most of them patricians. In 367 B.C., a compromise was reached: The consulship was re-established and every year one of the two consuls had to be a plebeian. The same year a measure was passed for short-term debt relief, a problem worsened by the depredations of the Gauls

around 390 B.C. After 367 B.C., additional laws tried to reduce or abolish the rate of interest; nexum was finally abolished in 326 B.C.

After 367 B.C., integration of the patrician and plebeian elites proceeded despite conservative opposition. In 287 B.C., the merging of the orders culminated in a law that made decisions of the council of the plebs and the tribal assembly binding, so the year 287 B.C. has become the conventional starting date of the Middle Republic. Although the patriciate survived and remained prestigious, its importance gradually lessened. The new elite was based on wealth, not heredity. Its members were known as equestrians—men wealthy enough to serve as cavalrymen. The overwhelming majority of Romans remained excluded, as they had been from the patriciate. Equestrians who served in the senate formed the senatorial order, the inner circle of which comprised those who possessed an ancestor who had been consul.

Although ordinary plebeians improved their lot by their exertions, they still faced the twin problems of debt and land-hunger in the Middle Republic. No longer could they depend on wealthy plebeians as champions. Although their problems would come back with a vengeance to haunt the Late Republic, plebeians found temporary relief in the new land that Rome acquired through conquest.

FROM ITALIAN CITY-STATE TO WORLD EMPIRE

At the beginning of the Republic (ca. 509 B.C.), Roman territory comprised about 500 square miles, about half the size of the state of Rhode Island. By 338 B.C., Rome controlled the 2000 square miles of Latium and was moving north into Etruria and south into Samnite country. Three-quarters of a century later, in 265 B.C., Rome controlled all of the Italian peninsula south of an imaginary line from Pisae (modern Pisa) to Ariminum (modern Rimini), an area of about 50,000 square miles (Map 5.2).

Map 5.2 Roman Italy, ca. 265 B.C. Rome controlled a patchwork of conquered territory, colonies, and allied states in Italy, held together by a network of treaties and of roads. The city of Rome (inset) was built on seven hills beside the Tiber River.

Rome

0   500   1000 M.
0   1500   3000 Ft.

FIELD OF MARS

QUIRINAL HILL

VIMINAL HILL

ESQUILINE MT.

CAPITOLINE MT.

Senate House

Forum

Regia

Temple of Jupiter

Tiber Island

Tiber

PALATINE MT.

CAELIAN MT.

Circus Maximus

AVENTINE MT.

Servian Wall

☐ Hills of Rome

A L P S

Extent of Roman Italy by 218 B.C.

Aquileia

Verona

Adige

Cremona

Po

Placentia

CISALPINE GAUL

Genua

Bononia

Ariminum (Rimini)

Fanum Fortunae

Pisae (Pisa)

Arno

Florentia

Ancona

Ligurian Sea

Arretium

UMBRIA

Castrum Truentinum

Populonia

ETRURIA

PICENUM

ILLYRIA

Elba

Saturnia

Castrum Novum

Corsica

Aleria

Tiber

Reate

A d r i a t i c   S e a

Veii Rome

Corfinium

SAMNIUM

Appian Way

LATIUM

APULIA

Barium

Tarracina

CAMPANIA

Beneventum

Venusia

Appian Way

Brundisium

Capua

CALABRIA

Misenum

Tarentum

Neapolis (Naples)

LUCANIA

Paestum

Sardinia

Gulf of Tarentum

Neapolis

Tyrrhenian Sea

Thurii

Carales

Croton

BRUTTIUM

Messana

Locri

Rhegium

M e d i t e r r a n e a n   S e a

Lilybaeum

Sicily

Utica

Cape Bon

Syracuse

Carthage

Hippo Regius

NORTH AFRICA

Malta

0   50   100 Km.
0   50   100 Mi.

■ Roman territory (full citizens)
■ Roman territory (citizens without suffrage)
■ Roman allies
■ Latin colonies
■ Carthaginian possessions
■ Greek cities
— Major roads by 100 B.C.

By 146 B.C., Roman provinces included Sicily, Cisalpine Gaul (northernmost Italy), Sardinia, Corsica, and Spain (divided into two provinces). Once-great Carthage was the Roman province of Africa (roughly, modern Tunisia), and once-mighty Macedon was the province of Macedonia, whose governor was also effectively in charge of Greece. The Seleucid kingdom was free but fatally weakened. Rome was the supreme power between Gibraltar and the Levant. How and why had Rome reached this height from its humble beginnings as a local power in Italy?

Republican Expansion: The Conquest of Italy, ca. 509–265 B.C.

Romans maintain that they conquered an empire without ever committing an act of aggression. When war was declared, a special college of priests informed the gods that Rome was merely retaliating for foreign injury. True, the Romans were frequently attacked by others, but often only after provocative behavior by Rome had left its rivals little choice.

Rome's early conquests reveal many of its lasting motives for expansion. No doubt lust for conquest played a part, as did fear and hatred of outsiders, but self-control and shrewdness were stronger Roman characteristics. Greed, particularly land-hunger, was a perennial theme. Sometimes a domestic political motive was at work, for foreign adventure was a convenient way of deflecting plebeian energies. Perhaps the most significant factors, however, were the personal ambitions of a warrior elite and the presence of conflict in early Italy.

Victory in battle promised both a reputation for virtus and the booty with which to reward clients; moreover, it cleared the road to success in a public career. Military achievement brought unique acclaim. For example, certain victorious generals were allowed to celebrate a triumph; there was no such triumph for peacemakers or distinguished judges or other public benefactors. The triumphant general rode a chariot through the city to the temple of Jupiter on the Capitoline Hill. He was accompanied by his troops, by the spoils of victory including famous captives, and by the magistrates and senators. (See the box, "A Roman Triumph.")

The harsh reality of Italian politics also ruled against pacifism. Without the willingness to fight, Rome could neither have won its freedom from the Etruscans nor have maintained that freedom. Yet what began as a pragmatic response to present dangers hardened into a habit of meeting even remote threats with force. In the fourth century B.C., having gained control of Latium, Rome considered the Samnites of central and southern Italy to be a potential threat. In the third century B.C., once Rome controlled Italy, it felt threatened by the powerful Carthage. After Carthage, there was the threat of Macedon, and after Macedon, Seleucid Syria, and so on.

Though flexible and far-reaching, Roman diplomacy sometimes resulted in military engagement. Rome made formal alliances with some states, granting good relations and protection in return for obedience and the supplying of armies or navies when needed by Rome. Short of a formal commitment, however, Rome might accept a state "into its fides"—that is, treat the state as a client. The result was only a moral, and not a legal, commitment, which sometimes sufficed to frighten any would-be aggressor from Rome's new friend. If not, Rome found itself embroiled in war to prove its trustworthiness as a patron.

Military success requires tenacity, discipline, and flexibility: all qualities that Rome cultivated. Roman ideology prized toughness, the Roman social system instilled obedience, and the competitive ethos raised the stakes for Roman generals. Roman organizational ability and love of order made the Roman military camp a much more regular and systematic place than its Greek counterpart. Beginning in the fourth century B.C., Rome began to reward its soldiers with regular pay; this and the distribution of conquered land improved morale. Two other points are even more significant: the willingness to adopt foreign military technology and the combination of generosity and firmness with which Rome treated its allies.

Adopted by Rome in the sixth century B.C., the hoplite phalanx suited the relatively level ground of Latium but fared poorly in the rugged Apennines against the Samnites. Following a major defeat in 321 B.C., the Romans adopted with great success the Samnites' equipment and tactics.

Unlike the hoplite, the legionnaire, as the Roman soldier was now called, carried a long, oval body-shield; most legionnaires carried a throwing spear (javelin) instead of a pike, as well as a short sword. Unlike the phalanx, a Roman legion did not fight and maneuver as one thickly massed unit; rather, it contained a loose set of subunits. Legions were drawn up into three horizontal lines, organized according to age, experience, and equipment. The tactical unit was the maniple ("handful"), of which there were ten to each line, and thirty to a legion. Each maniple consisted of two centuries (literally "hundreds," although the number of men per century varied), and each century was commanded by a centurion. Legions also contained light-armed troops and cavalry.

A legion marched in a checkerboard pattern, leaving gaps in the lines. In battle each line closed its gaps as it attacked in turn. Unlike hoplites, who engaged the enemy at short range, legionnaires first threw their javelins at long range. Then, having broken the enemy's order, they charged and fought with sword and shield. The semi-independence of the maniples, each with its own commander and banner, created a more maneuverable army than that of the phalanx and one better suited for mountain fighting. When Rome's legions beat the Macedonian phalanx decisively in 197 B.C., military history entered a new era.

Rome was the leading power among the Latins, whom it led in an alliance known as the Latin League. Rome was first among equals, but the citizens of even the humblest Latin state had reciprocal rights of intermarriage and commerce with Romans and the right to become a citizen of another state by migrating there. Under Roman leadership the Latin League successfully defended Latium's borders against a series of enemies during the fourth and fifth centuries B.C. Sensing the wisdom of a policy of divide and conquer, the Romans deftly maneuvered their enemies into fighting Rome one by one. But eventually Rome had to confront a bitter two-year-long Latin revolt (340–338 B.C.).

The year 338 B.C. marked a turning point. Defeated peoples in the ancient world were often executed, deported, or enslaved. Victorious against the Latins, Rome, by contrast, pursued generosity. The Latin League was dissolved. Some of its member states were annexed, and their inhabitants became Roman citizens; others retained independence and alliance with Rome though no longer

Plaque of a Soldier This ivory, one of a pair from Latium dated about 250–200 B.C., provides the best evidence for the dress of a Roman legionnaire of the Middle Republic. *(Alinari/Art Resource, NY)*

A Roman Triumph

The Roman triumph symbolizes the prestige flowing from military success in Rome; it also demonstrates the senate's attempt to control victorious generals. This description is drawn from the Epitome *of Zonaras, a Byzantine historian of the twelfth century* A.D. *Zonaras drew his material on Rome from Plutarch (ca.* A.D. *50–120) and Dio Cassius (second–third century* A.D.*).*

When any great success worthy of a triumph had been gained, the general was immediately saluted as *imperator* by the soldiers, and he would bind sprigs of laurel upon the *fasces* and deliver them to the messengers who announced the victory to the city. On arriving home he would assemble the senate and ask to have the triumph voted him. And if he obtained a vote from the senate and from the people, his title of *imperator* was confirmed. . . .

Arrayed in the triumphal dress and wearing armlets, with a laurel crown upon his head, and holding a branch in his right hand, he called together the people. After praising collectively the troops who had served with him, and some of them individually, he presented them with money and honored them also with decorations. . . . A large part of the spoils also was assigned to the soldiers who had taken part in the campaign. . . .

After these ceremonies the triumphant general would mount his chariot [with his children and relatives]. . . . A public slave . . . rode with the victor in the chariot itself, holding over him the crown of precious stones set in gold, and kept saying to him, "Look behind!" . . . Thus arrayed, they entered the city, having at the head of the procession the spoils and trophies and figures representing the captured forts, cities, mountains, rivers, lakes, and seas—everything, in fact, that they had taken. . . . When these adjuncts had gone on their way, the victorious general arrived at the Roman Forum, and after commanding that some of the captives be led to prison and put to death, he rode up to the Capitol. There he performed certain rites and made offerings and dined in the porticoes up there, after which he departed homewards towards evening, accompanied by flutes and pipes.

Source: From Naphtali Lewis and Meyer Reinhold, eds., *Roman Civilization: Selected Readings*, vol. 1, *The Republic and the Augustan Age*, 3d ed. (New York: Columbia University Press, 1990), pp. 230–231.

---

with one another. The non-Latin allies of the former rebels were also annexed by Rome, but they received the unique halfway status of "citizenship without suffrage." They shared the financial and military burdens of Roman citizenship but also all the rights, except the vote; they also retained the right of local self-government. The settlement of 338 B.C. broke new ground by making it possible for Rome and its former allies and enemies to live together on the basis of relative equality.

The settlement also set a precedent for future Roman expansion. As Rome conquered Italy, a number of privileged Italian cities (called *municipia*) received the status of citizenship without suffrage. Others remained independent but were tied to Rome by perpetual alliance. Rome encouraged oligarchy in conquered towns, fostering a community of interests between the provincial and Roman elite.

If municipia were the carrots of Roman imperialism, the stick was a network of military roads and colonies crisscrossing Italy, allowing Rome to keep an eye on potential rebels. Roman roads allowed the swift movement of troops and linked the growing network of colonies. Colonies were established in strategically vital areas and were

The Appian Way Named for the censor Appius Claudius Caecus, who proposed its construction, Rome's first great road was built in 312 B.C., during the Samnite Wars. It originally ran 132 miles from Rome to Capua and was extended an additional 234 miles, probably by 234 B.C., to Brundisium, on Italy's southern Adriatic coast. (*F. H. C. Birch/Sonia Halliday Photographs*)

built with military discipline. The inhabitants, Roman and Latin, owed military service to Rome.

In later years, Italians would complain about treatment by Rome, but compared to inhabitants of Roman provinces outside Italy, they had a privileged status. Romans too would complain about allied demands for equality, but Rome received from its allies a huge and seemingly inexhaustible pool of military manpower. The allies staffed Roman armies that conquered Samnites, Etruscans, and Gauls, all of whom came into the Roman orbit by the early third century B.C. Manpower abundance won Rome's war (280–276 B.C.) against the Greek general Pyrrhus of Epirus (319–272 B.C.), an

adventurer who intervened in southern Italy. Although Pyrrhus won battle after battle, he was unable to match Roman willingness to sustain thousands of casualties time and again. Pyrrhus's seeming victories, therefore, turned out to be defeats, which sent him home to Greece disappointed and left us with the expression "Pyrrhic victory."

As for Rome, by 265 B.C. it emerged as the ruler of all of Italy south of the Pisae-Ariminum line (see Map 5.2). One might say that Rome unified Italy, although Italy was less a unity than a patchwork of Roman territory and colonies and of diverse cities, states, and peoples each allied to Rome by separate treaty.

ROMAN EXPANSION

494 B.C.	Latin League formed
338 B.C.	Latin League dissolved; Roman citizenship extended
312 B.C.	Appian Way constructed
264–146 B.C.	Punic Wars
197 B.C.	Rome defeats Macedonian phalanx
146 B.C.	Rome destroys Carthage and Corinth
112–105 B.C.	War in Numidia
91–89 B.C.	Social War
88–84 B.C.	First Mithridatic War
66–62 B.C.	Pompey's eastern campaigns
58–50 B.C.	Caesar conquers Gaul

Rome Versus Carthage: The Punic Wars, 264–146 B.C.

The conquest of Italy made Rome one of two great powers in the central Mediterranean. The other was Carthage. Founded around 750 B.C. by Phoenicians from Tyre, Carthage controlled an empire in North Africa, Sicily, Corsica, Sardinia, Malta, the Balearic Islands, and southern Spain. (The adjective *Phoenician* is *Punicus* in Latin, hence the term *Punic* for Carthaginian.) Like Rome, Carthage was run by an oligarchy, but its elite were mercantile rather than agrarian. Rome was a land power, Carthage a sea power. Rome had virtually no navy, but Carthage had a great war fleet, a mercantile monopoly of the western Mediterranean, and a major commercial presence in the East.

Carthage was an economic powerhouse. Carthaginian ships traveled to the eastern Mediterranean with minerals from Spanish mines, as well as from far-off West Africa and Britain. The Carthaginians were the first Mediterranean people to organize large-scale plantations of slaves for the production of single crops. Even though they zealously wiped out most of Carthaginian elite culture, the Romans did make sure to preserve one Carthaginian classic: a multivolume work on agriculture by Mago. Translated from Punic into Latin by order of the senate, Mago's treatise had enormous impact on Roman landowners, who, with the importation of massive numbers of slaves, adopted the plantation system in Italy (see page 176).

Carthage boasted brilliant generals, especially in the Barca family, whose most famous member was Hannibal (247–183 B.C.). Carthage might have been a handicapper's favorite at the outbreak of its long wars with Rome in 264 B.C., yet the end result was disaster for Carthage. A combination of Carthaginian weaknesses and Roman strengths accounts for the outcome.

Unlike Rome, Carthage did not have a citizen army. The commanders were Carthaginian, but most of the soldiers were mercenaries and so of questionable loyalty. A second difference in the two states lay in the treatment of allies. Rome treated the Italians with considerable respect and tolerance. Carthage showed contempt for its allies, who repaid the favor by revolting whenever they had the chance. Third, although Carthage's military manpower resources were considerable, they were not as great as Rome's.

At the start of the Punic Wars, Rome had no navy or commanders to match the Barca family but it proved adaptable, tenacious, and ruthless. The First Punic War (264–241 B.C.) took place almost entirely in Sicily. After initial success, Rome realized that it could not win the war without building a fleet. Rome's solution was to capture a Carthaginian warship and use it as a prototype for the Roman navy.

The long and bloody war exhausted both sides. In the end Rome won only because the Carthaginian government had had enough. Rome triumphed at sea, but the Carthaginian army in western Sicily under Hannibal's father, Hamilcar Barca (d. 229 B.C.), was still undefeated. At first Rome granted a mild peace treaty, requiring only that Carthage evacuate Sicily and pay an indemnity. Several years later, however, when Carthage was immersed in a mercenaries' revolt, Rome seized Corsica and Sardinia and demanded an additional indemnity.

Forced to give in to these treacherous exactions, Carthage decided to build a new and bigger empire in Spain, beginning in 237 B.C., under Barca family leadership. With Spain's rich deposits of silver and copper at its disposal, Carthage once again posed a credible threat to Rome. In the mid-220s, an ever watchful Rome negotiated that the Ebro River in northeastern Spain be the boundary of Carthaginian territory. Rome itself felt free to intervene south of the Ebro, where, through a Roman client, it challenged Carthaginian power, in effect by proxy. When Carthage responded with force, Rome threatened war. The new Carthaginian commander, 27-year-old Hannibal Barca, was not to be cowed, however, and the Second Punic War ensued (218–201 B.C.).

Carthage was willing to risk war because Hannibal promised a quick, cheap, and easy victory. Because Carthage no longer had a fleet, the Romans felt secure in Italy; Hannibal surprised them by marching overland to Italy, making a dangerous passage across the Alps. A tactical genius, Hannibal reckoned that with his superior generalship he could defeat the Romans in battle and cause them enormous casualties, and he was right. Hannibal's forces dominated the battlefield. Among his victories was the Battle of Cannae in Apulia (southeastern Italy) where, in 216 B.C., Carthage gave Rome the bloodiest defeat in its history, killing perhaps 30,000 Romans.

A crushing success, but huge casualties alone could not bring the Roman elite to its knees. Nor did Rome's allies revolt en masse, as Hannibal had hoped. Most stood by Rome, partly out of loyalty and partly out of fear of Roman reprisals. Roman pragmatism, moreover, showed itself able to deal with crisis. After Cannae, Rome's leadership accepted a cautious strategy of harassment, delay, refusal to fight, and attrition. Hannibal was stymied by an enemy who lost battles but refused to surrender.

In the meantime, Rome had bought valuable time to regroup. A new military star emerged: Publius Cornelius Scipio (236–183 B.C.), a Roman who finally understood Hannibal's tactics and matched them. First Scipio conquered Carthage's Spanish dominions and then he forced Hannibal back to North Africa for a final battle in 202 B.C. near Zama (in modern Tunisia). It was a hard-fought fight, but Carthage lost because of weak cavalry and fickle mercenaries. The conqueror of North Africa, Scipio was now surnamed Africanus. As for Hannibal, he played a prominent role in Carthaginian politics for

The Nurturing Goddess This terra-cotta statuette (late second or first century B.C.) may represent a Carthaginian goddess of fertility worshiped both in Punic and Roman Africa. The scene of mother and infant suggests later imagery of the Virgin Mary and Christ. *(Martha Cooper)*

about a decade, until Rome forced him into exile in Syria. In about 183 B.C., after taking part in the Seleucids' unsuccessful war against Rome, he committed suicide rather than face extradition to Rome.

The peace settlement of 201 B.C. stripped Carthage of its empire. Yet soon its economy rebounded, reviving old Roman fears of Carthage's

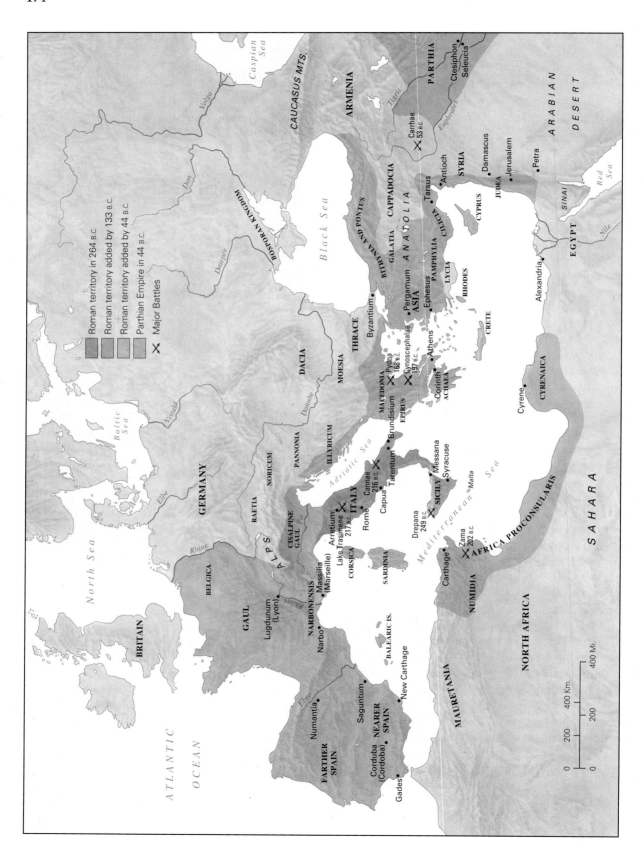

political ambitions. In the Third Punic War (149–146 B.C.) Rome mounted a three-year siege under the leadership of Scipio Aemilianus (185–129 B.C.), finally destroying the city of Carthage in 146 B.C. Approximately a century later, Carthage was refounded as a Roman colony and became one of the empire's greatest cities. In the meantime, it was left desolate, its people killed or enslaved.

Rome emerged from the Punic Wars as the greatest power in the Mediterranean. It had acquired new provinces in Sicily, Sardinia, Corsica, Spain, and North Africa (where Carthage's former territory was annexed as the province of Africa). The road to further conquest seemed to lead in all directions.

Victories in the Hellenistic East, ca. 200–133 B.C.

Most countries would have savored peace after such an ordeal as the Punic Wars, but Rome immediately leaped into a long conflict in Greece and Anatolia. The ostensible origin of the war was the alliance that Philip V of Macedon (r. 221–179 B.C.) had forged with Hannibal after Cannae. Several smaller Greek states, moreover, had asked Rome to declare war against Macedon in 200 B.C., on the grounds that Macedonian ambitions threatened their security. Such an invitation flattered the Roman elite; besides, Rome expected a relatively quick and easy victory. It was not disappointed; in 197 B.C. the legions crushed the Macedonian phalanx at Cynoscephalae in central Greece (see Map 5.3).

Rome had hoped to impose a patron-client relationship on Greece and Macedon, thereby avoiding a permanent military presence, but that hope failed. The independent-minded Greeks chafed at Roman domination. Several years of miscommunication and intrigue followed, only to lead to renewed wars. First the Seleucids, under the ambitious king Antiochus III (r. 223–187 B.C.), challenged Rome for hegemony in the Greek peninsula. It was in this war that Hannibal took a small part. Roman forces made short work of the enemy. Driven out

Map 5.3 Roman Expansion, 264–44 B.C. Wars against Carthage, the major Greco-Macedonian powers, Gauls, Germans, North Africans, and other peoples brought Rome an empire on three continents.

not only from Greece but from Anatolia as well, the Seleucids in effect recognized Roman supremacy in the Mediterranean (188 B.C.).

Then came another war between Rome and Macedon (171–167 B.C.), settled by a complete Roman victory at Pydna in northern Greece (168 B.C.). Two decades later, after additional revolts by Macedonians and Greeks, Macedon became a Roman province in 148 B.C. Greece, not formally a separate province until 27 B.C., was under the thumb of the Roman governor of Macedonia. Wherever democracy had survived in Greece, it was replaced with oligarchy. In 146 B.C., Rome destroyed Corinth, one of Greece's wealthiest cities, as a warning against further rebellion. Greece then suffered Roman neglect and taxation for nearly two hundred years.

By annexing Carthage, Macedon, and Greece in the mid-second century B.C., Rome created a dynamic for expansion around the entire Mediterranean. Before the century was over, southern Gaul was annexed, and Rome had gained a foothold in Asia. The kingdom of Pergamum (northwestern Anatolia) had supported Rome throughout Rome's wars in the east. When Attalus III of Pergamum died without an heir in 133 B.C., he surrendered his kingdom to the Roman people, who made it into a province of Asia.

Two great Hellenistic states remained independent: the Seleucid kingdom and Ptolemaic Egypt (Map 5.3). Roman ambassadors and generals frequently interfered in their affairs, however, and no one was surprised when, in the first century B.C., they too were annexed by Rome.

The Socioeconomic Consequences of Expansion

Expansion led to enormous and unintended changes in Rome's society, economy, and culture. Already wealthy, the Roman elite now came into fabulous riches. Huge profits awaited the generals, patrons, diplomats, magistrates, tax collectors, and businessmen who followed Rome's armies. In Italy, most profits were in the form of land; in the provinces, not only in land, but in slaves, booty, and graft. One of the worst grafters, Gaius Verres, governor of Sicily from 73 to 71 B.C., was prosecuted by Cicero (see page 185), then beginning his oratorical career, for allegedly extorting tens of thousands of pounds of silver from his province. But even Cicero skimmed off several thousand pounds of silver as governor of the province of Cilicia (southern Anatolia) from 51 to 50 B.C.

The first Roman coinage, traditionally dated to 289 B.C., facilitated commercial transactions. Previously, the Romans had made do with barter, uncoined bronze, and cast bronze bars, but now they imitated the workmanship and style of Greek coins. Equally prominent in the homes of wealthy Romans were Greek metalwork, jewelry, art objects, and other luxury goods. Conservatives bemoaned the decline of traditional Roman austerity, but they fought a rear-guard action. (See the feature, "Weighing the Evidence: Luxury Goods and Gender Wars in Rome," on pages 190–191.)

Ordinary Romans needed no reminder of the virtues of austerity, for they did not share in the elite's profit from Roman expansion. Indeed, a century of intensive warfare—from the outbreak of the Punic Wars in 264 B.C. to the destruction of Carthage and Corinth in 146 B.C.—strained the lot of the Roman people to the breaking point. Hannibal's invasion left much of the farmland of southern Italy devastated and Italian manpower considerably reduced. Yet most people might have rebounded from these problems within a generation or two, if they had not faced other serious troubles.

Conscription had become the norm. The average term of military service between ages 17 and 46 was six years; the maximum term was twenty years. Because experienced legionnaires were at a premium, commanders were loath to release them from service. But the longer a man was away in the army, the harder it was for his wife and children to keep the family farm running. With help from a patron, they might be able to make do, though most patrons in fact added to the problem through the introduction to Italy of large-scale agricultural entrepreneurship. Those who sought wealth monopolized Italian farmland, imported huge numbers of slaves, and brought ruin on the free peasantry of Italy.

The last two centuries B.C. witnessed the transformation of Roman rural society from a society of independent farmers to one in which slave labor played a major role. By the end of the first century B.C. there were, it is estimated, 2 to 3 million slaves in Italy, about a third of the peninsula's total population. Prisoners of war and conquered civilians provided a ready supply of slaves. Most worked in agriculture or mining, and their treatment was often abominable; the fewer house slaves were usually better off.

Wealthy Romans wanted to invest in large landed estates, or *latifundia*, worked by slaves. These estates were either mixed farms (most often devoted to cultivating vines, olives, and grain) or ranches (establishments where animals were raised for meat, milk, and wool). One devotee of the latter was the prominent conservative Marcus Porcius Cato (234–149 B.C.), known as Cato the Censor. Cato argued that there were only three ways to get rich: "pasturage, pasturage, and pasturage." All a would-be entrepreneur needed was land. Conquests had gained Rome a plenitude of land in Italy. Called public land, it belonged to the Roman people, but an individual was legally entitled to claim about 320 acres as his own. Many entrepreneurs flouted the law, however, and grabbed large chunks of public land for pasturage. They often forced families of absent soldiers off private land, either by debt foreclosure or by outright violence. Sometimes families would leave the land for the city, but usually they stayed as tenants.

Before about 170 B.C., poor Romans were sometimes able to find land in colonies. By 170 B.C., however, Rome had established all the colonies in Italy that its security demanded, so this avenue of escape from poverty was closed. A displaced farmer who wanted to compete in the labor market would have found it difficult to underbid cheap slave labor; in any case, Roman ideology frowned on wage labor by citizens. Nor was it practical for a poor farmer to sue a wealthy patron who seized his land, because a plaintiff himself had to bring the accused into court.

The situation of the Italian peasantry was becoming increasingly miserable by the mid-second century B.C. As one modern scholar has put it, "In conquering what they were pleased to call the world the Romans ruined a great part of the Italian people."[2]

The Impact of Greece on Rome and Its Empire

Rome learned much from its new encounters with foreign peoples—and from none more than the Greeks. Wealthy Romans cultivated interests in Greek art, literature, rhetoric, and speculative

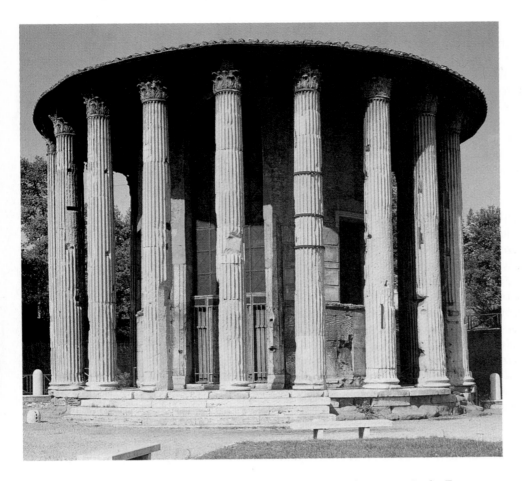

The Round Temple This elegant, circular, Corinthian-columned structure in the Forum Boarium in Rome, built around 150–100 B.C., is the oldest surviving marble temple in the city. Greek in style, it is an example of Roman borrowing from sophisticated Hellenistic culture. *(Scala/Art Resource, NY)*

thought; poor and rich alike enjoyed Greek drama. Before the mid-third century B.C., there was virtually no Roman literature. An oral tradition of songs, ballads, and funeral oratory kept alive the deeds of the famous, for writing was generally restricted to commercial and government records and inscriptions. In short, the Romans conquered Italy without writing about it.

Contact with the Greek cities brought changes. Large numbers of Roman soldiers in Magna Graecia (southern Italy and Sicily) were introduced to comedy, tragedy, mimes, and sophisticated song lyrics, and many developed a permanent taste for them. It is no accident that the first production of a drama at Rome took place in 240 B.C., the year after the end of the First Punic War. Afterward, the an-

nual production of such dramas became standard procedure.

No one could accuse the Romans of rushing headlong into a new age, however. The authorities continued to have their doubts about theater, which seemed excessively emotional and probably corrupt. They did not allow the building of a permanent theater in Rome until 55 B.C., insisting that the wealthiest city in the Mediterranean make do with makeshift wooden structures. Nor did the Roman elite readily become playwrights or poets. The first gentleman-poet in Rome, Lucilius (180–102 B.C.), did not arrive until the second century B.C., and he was a Latin, not a Roman.

His predecessors, the founders of Latin literature, were all of low social status; little of their work survives. Livius Andronicus (ca. 284–204 B.C.), the first person to translate tragedy and comedy from Greek into Latin, was a Greek freedman (a former slave) from Tarentum. He also translated Homer's *Odyssey* into Latin. His contemporary Gnaeus Naevius (ca. 270–201 B.C.), an Italian from the region of Capua, was a prolific writer whose most important work was an epic account of the First Punic War. This poem, which makes much of the myth tracing Rome's origins to Troy, demonstrates the Roman taste for a sophisticated, Greek-derived foundation myth. Naevius's career also demonstrates the perils of literature, for his lampoon of an aristocratic household is supposed to have earned him prison, then self-exile.

The two great early Latin playwrights are Titus Maccius Plautus (ca. 254–184 B.C.) and Publius Terentius Afer, today known as Terence (ca. 195–159 B.C.). Both of them wrote comedies on the model of the great Greek comic playwright Menander (see page 136). Plautus was an Umbrian and a poor man who learned his Latin in Rome; Terence was a North African slave, educated and freed in Rome. Twenty-one plays by Plautus and six by Terence survive. Plautus's plays are generally earthy slapstick farces. They are invariably set in Greece, not Rome, in part out of escapism (many were written during the Second Punic War), in part out of the censorial demands of the Roman authorities. They nonetheless reveal much about Roman society. Terence's plays are more subtle than Plautus's, indicating the growing sophistication of Roman theatergoers.

Latin prose developed more slowly than did poetry and drama. The first histories by Romans, composed after the Second Punic War, were written in Greek, for Latin lacked the vocabulary or the audience for history. The works (now mostly lost) of Quintus Fabius Pictor and Lucius Cincius Alimentus, both Roman senators of the late third century B.C., took the history of Rome down through the Punic Wars. Cato the Censor was the first historian of Rome to write in Latin. His *Origines*, of which little survives, recounted Roman history from the origin of the city to about 150 B.C. The earliest surviving Latin prose work is Cato's *On Agriculture.*

In the traditional education of a Roman aristocrat, parents and close family friends played the primary role. Although this practice continued, in the second century B.C., wealthy Romans began acquiring Greek slaves to educate their sons in Greek language and literature. Soon Greek freedmen began setting up schools offering the same subjects; it was not long before similar Latin grammar schools also opened.

One of the forms of Greek literature that appealed most to the practical-minded Romans was rhetoric. Roman orators studied Greek models, and many would say that they eventually outdid the Greeks. Cato was the first Roman to publish his speeches, and he also wrote a book on rhetoric. Both gave impetus to the spread of sophisticated rhetoric in Rome.

Scipio Aemilianus, conqueror of Carthage in 146 B.C., had a distinguished political and military career. He was also patron of a group of prominent statesmen and soldiers who shared his love of Hellenism. Among the writers whom they supported were the playwright Terence, the poet Lucilius, the historian Polybius, and the Stoic philosopher Panaetius (ca. 185–109 B.C.). The Stoic emphases on duty, wisdom, and world brotherhood appealed both to Rome's traditional ideology and to its more recent acquisition of empire. Yet not all Romans shared Scipio's admiration of Greek culture: Cato, for example, was famously ambivalent. (See the box, "Encounters with the West: Roman Attitudes Toward the Conquered.")

Cornelia, Scipio Aemilianus's mother-in-law, was an educated lover of Hellenism who wrote letters that existed several hundred years later as examples of elegant Latin prose. Her villa in the resort of Misenum on the bay of Naples was well known for the distinguished guests whom she received there. When her husband, an outstanding statesman and general, died, Cornelia chose to remain a widow. One of the men who tried to change her mind was no less a figure than the king of Egypt. The widow spent her time managing her own estate and supervising the education of her two sons, the future tribunes Tiberius and Gaius Gracchus (see page 180).

Although Cornelia's privileges were extraordinary, she is nonetheless a reminder of the opportunities that imperial expansion offered to wealthy Roman women. Marriage practices offer one example of change. Few women were married *cum manu* anymore, that is, handed over to their husband by their father. A woman's father or nearest male relative, not her husband, was most

∼ ENCOUNTERS WITH THE WEST ∼

Roman Attitudes Toward the Conquered

The Romans mainly expressed contempt and hatred for the Carthaginians, while admiring their military prowess. Roman attitudes toward the Greeks, however, were more complex, mixing admiration for Greek culture with fear of its corrosive effect on loyalty to the Roman state. In the first selection, the Roman historian Livy (59 B.C.–A.D. 17) cites the legend of Hannibal's oath; in the second, the Greek writer Plutarch (ca. A.D. 50–ca. 120) discusses Greek philosophy in Rome.

(a)

. . . High passions were at work throughout, and mutual hatred was hardly less sharp a weapon than the sword; on the Roman side there was rage at the unprovoked attack by a previously beaten enemy; on the Carthaginian, the bitter resentment at what was felt to be the grasping and tyrannical attitude of their conquerors. The intensity of the feeling is illustrated by an anecdote of Hannibal's boyhood: his father, Hamilcar, after the campaign in Africa, was about to carry his troops over into Spain, when Hannibal, then about nine years old, begged, with all the childish arts he could muster, to be allowed to accompany him; whereupon Hamilcar, who was preparing to offer sacrifice for a successful outcome, led the boy to the altar and made him solemnly swear, with his hand upon the sacred victim, that as soon as he was old enough he would be the enemy of the Roman people. . . .

Reckless in courting danger, he [Hannibal] showed superb tactical ability once it was upon him. . . . Mounted or unmounted he was unequaled as a fighting man, always the first to attack, the last to leave a field. So much for his virtues—and they were great; but no less great than his faults; inhuman cruelty, a more than Punic perfidy, a total disregard of truth, honor, and religion, of the sanctity of an oath and of all that other men held sacred.

(b)

Carneades the Academic and Diogenes the Stoic came as envoys from Athens to Rome [in 155 B.C.]. . . . The most studious of the youth at once went to wait upon these men, and frequently heard them speak with admiration. . . . The report spread far and wide that a Greek [Carneades] of amazing talent, who charmed and disarmed everybody, had infused a powerful passion into the young men, so that forsaking their other pleasures and pursuits, they were in ecstasies about philosophy. This pleased the other Romans, and they were glad to see the youth participating in Greek culture and consorting with such remarkable men. But Cato, when this passion for discussion came flowing into the city, from the beginning was distressed, fearing lest the youth, by diverting their ambitions in this direction, should prefer a reputation for speaking well before that of deeds and military campaigns. . . . Cato determined, under a specious pretext, to have all the philosophers cleared out of the city. And coming into the senate he blamed the magistrates for letting the envoys stay so long a time without settling the matter, though they were such persuasive persons that they could easily secure anything they wished; that therefore a decision should be made and a vote taken on the embassy as soon as possible, so that they might go home again to their own schools and lecture to the sons of the Greeks, while the Roman youth listened, as hitherto, to their own laws and magistrates.

Sources: Excerpt (a): Livy, *The War with Hannibal,* Books XXI–XXX of *The History of Rome from Its Foundation,* trans. Aubrey de Sélincourt, ed. Betty Radice (Harmondsworth, England: Penguin, 1965), pp. 23, 26. Excerpt (b): Plutarch, *Life of Cato the Elder,* in Naphtali Lewis and Meyer Reinhold, eds., *Roman Civilization: Selected Readings,* vol. 1, *The Republic and the Augustan Age,* 3d ed. (New York: Columbia University Press, 1990), pp. 528–529.

likely to be her paterfamilias, which meant that a husband's control over his wife's dowry was limited. The result was more freedom, at least for wealthy women.

Cornelia is also a reminder of the fundamental conservatism of Roman society. Although we know the years of birth and death of numerous elite Roman males of the second century B.C., we do not know Cornelia's. Nor did her literary interests entail any neglect of home and family. Cornelia bore twelve children, though only three of them lived to adulthood (such was the reality of infant mortality even for the wealthiest Romans).

THE REVOLUTION FROM THE GRACCHI TO CAESAR, 133–44 B.C.

After 350 years of expansion, a citizen of the Roman Republic in the mid-second century B.C. might have looked forward to a long and happy future for his country, unaware that the Republic was about to begin a century of domestic and foreign unrest that would bring down the whole system. In retrospect, the causes of this revolution are not hard to find. More than a century of warfare weighed heavily on the ordinary people of Italy— the Romans and allied peasants whose farms were ruined while they were off fighting. The Roman elite was bitterly divided over what to do about the problems of the peasants. One group wanted to redistribute land on behalf of the poor; another group had no sympathy for them. Both groups were willing to exploit the poor for their own ends.

By the Late Republic the city of Rome was crowded and populous: Scholars estimate the number of inhabitants to be between 750,000 and 1 million. The government had to take charge of the grain supply. But elite politicians exploited the issue for partisan purposes. Once before, during the struggle between the patrician and plebeian orders in the Early Republic, the elite had been similarly divided and had resolved its differences through compromise (see page 166). The Late Republic, however, was an age of individualism, sophistication, and cynicism; ambitious nobles were no longer willing to subordinate themselves to the community. It was not long before competing armies of land-hungry peasants were marching across Italy.

The Gracchi

Many in the Roman elite fretted over the military dimension of the agrarian crisis. In modern societies, draftees are often the poorest people. In Rome, military service was a prestigious activity, and putting weapons in the hands of the poor was considered unwise. Therefore, a property qualification was imposed on conscripts. As fewer and fewer potential soldiers could afford to own property, however, during the second century it became necessary to reduce the property qualification several times. By 150 B.C., a conscript had to own property worth only 400 denarii—roughly a small house, a garden, and some personal belongings. If the peasantry continued its decline, Rome would either have to drop the property qualification for the military altogether or stop fielding armies. Clearly, something had to be done.

Into the breach stepped Tiberius Sempronius Gracchus (d. 133 B.C.), one of the ten tribunes for the year 133 B.C. (See the box, "Tiberius Gracchus on Rome's Plight.") The son of Cornelia and a distinguished general and ambassador (whose name Tiberius shared), Tiberius seemed an excellent spokesperson for a group of prominent senators who backed land reform. He proved, however, to be arrogant and overly ambitious. In pursuit of his goals he deposed one of his fellow tribunes, Octavius, an opponent of reform, and thereby shocked and angered conservatives.

Tiberius's proposed law restored the roughly 320-acre limit to the amount of public land a person could own. A commission was to be set up to repossess excess land and redistribute it to the poor, in small lots that were to be inalienable— that is, the wealthy could not buy them back. The former landowners would be reimbursed for improvements they had made, such as buildings or plantings.

The proposal was moderate, but wealthy landowners attempted to quash it. Many senators suspected that Tiberius wanted to set himself up as a kind of superpatron, buoyed by peasant supporters. Tiberius's methods disturbed the senate even more than the substance of his proposed law.

Tiberius Gracchus on Rome's Plight

In 133 B.C. Tiberius Gracchus proposed to confiscate from wealthy landowners public land possessed in excess of the legal limit, and to redistribute it to poor Roman citizens. The proposal, and Tiberius's unorthodox methods of getting it passed into law, raised a controversy that led to his murder. Plutarch (ca. A.D. 50–ca. 120) discusses Tiberius's motives and paraphrases one of his speeches.

His brother Gaius recorded in one of his writings that when Tiberius on his way to Numantia [in Spain] passed through Etruria and found the country almost depopulated and its husbandmen and shepherds imported barbarian slaves, he [Tiberius] first conceived the policy which was to be the source of countless ills to himself and to his brother. But it was the people themselves who chiefly excited his zeal and determination with writings on the porticoes, walls, and monuments, calling on him to retrieve the public land for the poor.

. . . Tiberius, fighting for an honorable and just cause with an eloquence that would have dignified even a meaner cause, was formidable and invincible whenever, with the people crowding around . . . , he took his place and spoke in behalf of the poor. "The wild beasts that roam over Italy," he said, "have their dens, each has a place of repose and refuge. But the men who fight and die for Italy enjoy nothing but the air and light; without house or home they wander about with their wives and children. Their commanders lie when they exhort the soldiers in battle to defend sepulchers and shrines from the enemy, for not one of these many Romans has either hereditary altar or ancestral tomb; they fight and die to protect the wealth and luxury of others; they are styled masters of the world, and have not a clod of earth they can call their own."

Source: Plutarch, *Life of Tiberius Gracchus,* in Naphtali Lewis and Meyer Reinhold, eds., *Roman Civilization: Selected Readings,* vol. 1, *The Republic and the Augustan Age,* 3d ed. (New York: Columbia University Press, 1990), pp. 251–252.

In addition to deposing Octavius, Tiberius, when the bill became law, intervened in the senate's bailiwicks of foreign affairs and finances by earmarking tax receipts from the new province of Asia to finance land purchases. Finally, Tiberius availed himself of the expedient, of dubious legality, of running for a second consecutive term as tribune. While the tribal assembly prepared to vote on the new tribunes, some senators led a mob to the Forum and had Tiberius and three hundred of his followers clubbed to death.

This shocking event marked the first time in the Republic that a political debate was settled by bloodshed in Rome itself. The ancient sources agree that it was the beginning of a century of revolution. Tiberius's killers had not merely committed murder, but attacked the traditional inviolability of the tribunes. Yet over the next century public violence grew as a weapon of politics in the Republic. The land commission went ahead with its work, even without Tiberius. His younger brother, Gaius (d. 121 B.C.), ready to continue Tiberius's work, became tribune himself in 123 B.C. Gaius expanded Tiberius's coalition, adding to it supporters from the equestrian order and the urban populace, mainly composed of slaves and freedmen. He gave the plebs cheap grain at subsidized prices. The equestrians were wealthy, landed gentry, similar to senators in most respects except for their failure to have reached the senate; they yearned for political power. A small but important group of equestrians was engaged in commerce and tax collection in the provinces. The senate regulated their activities through the so-called extortion courts, which tried corruption cases. Gaius staffed those courts with equestrians. Alluding to the new equestrian power, Gaius remarked, "I have left a sword in the ribs of the senate."

Gaius's ultimate aims are unclear, but one thing is certain: the threat he posed to the senate's power. He sponsored an extension of his brother's agrarian law, new colonies, public works, and relief for poor soldiers. Eventually Gaius ran aground on a plan to include the Italian allies as beneficiaries of agrarian reform—a farsighted notion but one unpopular with the Roman people, who were jealous of their privileges. Gaius was denied a third term as tribune in 121 B.C. (he had won a second the previous year). Soon his supporters engaged in violent scuffling with their opponents. The senate responded to his action by passing a declaration of public emergency, empowering the magistrates to use whatever means necessary to protect the state.

One of the consuls had Gaius and 250 of his followers killed. Another 3000 Gracchans were executed soon thereafter. Within a few years, the Gracchan land commission was abolished. It is estimated that approximately 75,000 citizens had been given land. The law, however, was amended to permit the resale of redistributed land, and with the wealthy poised to buy land, the settlers' future was uncertain. The senatorial oligarchy was back in control.

Or so it seemed. In fact, Roman politics had become an unstable brew. In time, it became clear that the Gracchi had divided the political community into two loose groupings. On one side were the *optimates* ("the best people"), conservatives who asserted the rule of the senate against popular tribunes and the maintenance of the estates of the wealthy in spite of the agrarian crisis. On the other side were the *populares* ("men of the people"), who challenged the rule of the senate in the name of relief of the poor. The populares were not democrats. Like the optimates, they were Roman nobles who believed in hierarchy, but they advocated the redistribution of wealth and power as a way of restoring stability and strengthening the military.

Marius and Sulla

By 100 B.C., Rome's agrarian crisis had become a full-scale military crisis, too. Roman armies under senatorial commanders fared poorly, both in Numidia (modern Algeria) and in southern Gaul against Germanic invaders (see Map 5.3). The situation was saved by an outsider to established privilege, an equestrian named Gaius Marius (157–86 B.C.), the first member of his family to be elected consul, for 107 B.C. This "new man" proved to be a military reformer and a popularis. Marius streamlined the Roman army: Camp followers were reduced in number, and individual soldiers were made to carry their own equipment. To meet the Germans, who attacked in overwhelming waves, maniples—the tactical subunits of a legion—were reorganized and combined into larger units called cohorts, rendering the army firmer and more cohesive. Most important, Marius abandoned altogether the property qualification for the military. As a result, Roman soldiers were no longer peasants doing part-time military service but rather were landless men making a profession of the military.

Marius won battles in North Africa and Gaul. As a politician, he broke with oligarchic solidarity, demanding and receiving six elections to the consulship, unconstitutional though they were. Furthermore, after restoring peace, Marius championed his soldiers by asking in 100 B.C. that land be distributed to them. Violent senatorial opposition made him back down, but only at the cost of revealing the senate's unpopularity. The land-hungry poor recognized that only military leaders like Marius offered to meet their military needs. As a result, ordinary Romans, to all of whom the army lay open, transferred their loyalty from the senate to their commander.

The Republic was weak, and it became weaker still as a result of two new wars. First, its Italian allies rose against Rome in a bloody and bitter struggle from 91 to 89 B.C. known as the "Social War"—that is, war with the *socii* ("allies"). The allies fought hard, and Rome, in order to prevail, had to concede to them what they had demanded at the outset: full Roman citizenship. The war wrought devastation in the countryside, further destabilizing the Republic. The other conflict of this period pitted Rome against Mithridates (120–63 B.C.), king of Pontus (northern Anatolia). Mithridates conquered the Roman province of Asia (western Anatolia) and slaughtered the numerous Italian businessmen and tax collectors there. Once again a military man rose to save the day for Rome: Marius's rival and former lieutenant, Lucius Cornelius Sulla Felix (ca. 138–78 B.C.), consul for the year 88 B.C., patrician and optimas.

The senate assigned Sulla the command against Mithridates, but Marius, though elderly, wanted it for himself. The troops decided the issue: first Sulla's, which marched on Rome and confirmed their leader's authority, then Marius's, which recaptured the city after Sulla's departure for the East. Victorious over Mithridates, Sulla returned to Italy in 83 B.C., eager to settle scores. Marius had died in 86, but his allies took up the challenge of civil war. Sulla won, then sealed his victory with proscription: He had posted the names of his political opponents, as many as 2000 men. Their land was confiscated, their sons disenfranchised, and they were executed. Sulla settled his veterans, about 80,000 men, on land in Italy from which he had expelled entire communities that had opposed him.

Having assumed the long-dormant office of dictatorship—now, unconstitutionally, for life—Sulla attempted to reform the constitution. He aimed to restore the senatorial oligarchy of pre-Gracchan days. To this end, he greatly weakened the tribunate and strengthened the senate. By adding several hundred equestrians, Sulla doubled the size of the senate, from about 300 to about 600 members. The move added both equestrians and Italians to the pool of potential leaders.

The most long-lasting of Sulla's measures was his reform of the courts. He abolished trials before popular assemblies and equestrian-staffed courts. Criminal cases were now heard before one of seven standing courts, whose juries were composed of senators. Although later Roman criminal law evolved considerably, it was founded on Sulla's actions. Generally only wealthy people had access to the standing courts; alleged crimes involving ordinary people were heard before lesser magistrates.

Sulla retired in 79 B.C. and died a year later. His hope of restoring law and order under the senate died with him. Discontent smoldered among the men whose land he had confiscated. Equally serious, many senators, aspiring to what Sulla had done and not to what he had said, pursued personal power, not the collective interests of the senate.

Pompey and Caesar

New, would-be Mariuses or Sullas now arose. The dominant leader of the seventies and sixties B.C. was the optimas Pompey the Great (106–48 B.C.), a brilliant general and a supporter of Sulla. Young Pompey went from command to command: He put down an agrarian rebellion in Italy and a rebellion in Spain, cleared the Mediterranean of pirates, defeated Mithridates again, and added rich conquests to the empire in Anatolia, Syria, Phoenicia, and Palestine. In the fifties B.C. the tide began turning in favor of Gaius Julius Caesar (100–44 B.C.), an even more gifted general and politician—indeed, perhaps one of history's greatest. A popularis, Caesar had family connections to Marius and his supporters. Caesar's career depended on his dazzling oratory, his boldness, and his sheer talent at war and politics. Caesar conquered Gaul and gained a foothold in Britain and laid the foundations of Roman rule in Egypt (see Map 5.3).

While the elite of the Late Republic struggled to maintain order, ordinary people struggled for survival itself. Violence had become endemic to rural Italy. Many once-prosperous farmers, dispossessed peasants, and runaway slaves ended up as brigands or highwaymen. It was also an era of slave revolts, the most serious of which was led by the Thracian Spartacus from 73 to 71 B.C., at a time when Rome also faced major wars in Spain and Anatolia. An able commander, Spartacus beat nine separate Roman armies in two years before finally suffering defeat.

Roman women were sometimes pawns, sometimes partners in the political careers of Pompey and Caesar. In 80 B.C., for example, Pompey divorced his first wife to advance his career by marrying Aemilia, Sulla's stepdaughter. Aemilia was not only married at the time but pregnant by her first husband. Soon after her divorce and remarriage, she died in childbirth. Caesar took many mistresses, among whom was the queen of Egypt,

Coin of Julius Caesar Caesar was the first living Roman to be represented on a coin, a sign both of his power and of the break with tradition that he marked. *(Cabinet des Médailles, Bibliothèque Nationale/Editions Arnaud)*

Cleopatra (see pages 150–151). Caesar had a penchant for certain Egyptian institutions, such as the Egyptian calendar, and he toyed with becoming a monarch himself, an inclination that Cleopatra perhaps encouraged. Another of Caesar's mistresses was Servilia, stepsister of Marcus Porcius Cato (Cato the Younger, 95–46 B.C.), great-grandson of the famous censor (see page 176). She was also mother of Brutus, the man who would eventually help murder Caesar.

Pompey was an optimas, Caesar a popularis, but the two of them agreed that they, not the senate or the assemblies, should dominate Rome. In 60 B.C. they entered into a pact with a third ambitious noble, Marcus Licinius Crassus (d. 53 B.C.). Known today as the "First Triumvirate," this coalition amounted to a conspiracy to run the state. Their individual ambitions rebuffed by the senate, each man had an agenda that pooling resources in the triumvirate permitted him to fulfill: for Pompey, ratification of his acts in the East and land for his veterans; for Caesar, who became consul for 59 B.C., a long command with a free hand in Gaul; for Crassus, a rebate for the tax collectors of Roman Asia, whom he championed, and eventu-

ally a command in Syria to make war on Parthia (the revived Persian Empire).

Having achieved its goal, the triumvirate did not long survive, but its very existence bespeaks the demise of the Republic. Crassus died in an inglorious defeat at Carrhae in Syria in 53 B.C., made symbolically worse by the Parthians' successful capture of Roman legionary standards (see Map 5.3). Frightened by Caesar's stunning victories in Gaul, Pompey returned to the senatorial fold, now led by Cato the Younger. Cato and his supporters stood for the traditional rule of the senatorial oligarchy. In 49 B.C. they ordered Caesar to give up his command in Gaul, but instead Caesar marched on Italy with his army. Italy's northern boundary was marked by a tiny stream called Rubicon; when Caesar crossed it, he declared, "The die is cast." Indeed it was, for civil war. Caesar swept to victory against the senate's army, led by Pompey, at Pharsalus in Greece in 48 B.C. Pompey fled but was assassinated. The complete destruction of the senate's forces took until 45 B.C.

The years of civil war brought Caesar from Spain to Anatolia. During the fighting he showed the qualities that made him great: speed, adaptability, endurance, and intelligence. He also revealed diplomatic adeptness, offering clemency to any of his enemies who joined him. A talented writer, Caesar published two commentaries on his military campaigns: *On the Gallic War* and *On the Civil War*, the latter appearing after his death. These works sought to glorify Caesar's conquests and justify his decision to wage a bloody civil war.

Back in Rome, Caesar sponsored a vast number of reforms. His political goal was to elevate Italians and others at the expense of old Roman families. To achieve it, Caesar conferred Roman citizenship liberally, on all of Cisalpine Gaul (northernmost Italy) as well as on certain provincial towns. He enlarged the senate from six hundred to nine hundred, adding his supporters, including some Gauls, to the membership. Caesar's social and economic reforms included reducing debts and founding the first colonies outside Italy, where veterans and poor citizens were settled. He undertook an ambitious public building program in the city of Rome. Caesar's most long-lasting act was to introduce the calendar of 365¼ days, on January 1, 45 B.C. Derived from the calendar of Egypt, it is known as the Julian calendar.

Caesar often flaunted his contempt for Republican constitutional formalities. His acceptance of a dictatorship for life offended the old guard, his flirtation with the notion of a monarchy even more so. With one eye toward avenging Crassus and another toward equaling the achievements of Alexander the Great, Caesar made preparations for a war against Parthia, but in vain. His ascendancy ended abruptly on March 15, 44 B.C. (the Ides of March by the Roman calendar), when sixty senators stabbed him to death. The assassination took place in the portico attached to the Theater of Pompey, in front of a statue of Pompey himself, where the senate was meeting that day. It had been eighty-nine years since the murder of Tiberius Gracchus.

The assassins called themselves Liberators, believing that they were freeing themselves from tyranny just as the founders of the Republic had done centuries before. Indeed, one of the chief conspirators, Marcus Junius Brutus (ca. 85–42 B.C.), claimed descent from Lucius Junius Brutus, traditional leader of the revolt against the Tarquins that had established the Republic. Like his co-conspirator Gaius Longinus Cassius (d. 42 B.C.), Brutus had been a magistrate, military officer, and provincial administrator. Both men thought Caesar's murder justified by the public interest, but the assassination led only to more years of disorder, renewed civil war, and the threat of tyranny far more severe than Caesar's.

The World of Cicero

Marcus Tullius Cicero (106–43 B.C.) is one of the best-known figures of all antiquity. Like Marius, he was a wealthy equestrian from the central Italian town of Arpinum who, as consul (in 63 B.C.), became a "new man." Cicero was an optimas and defender of the senate, though ready for compromise with the equestrians, from whose ranks he himself had arisen. He made his name by successfully leading the opposition to Lucius Sergius Catilina, a down-and-out patrician who organized a debtors' revolt in Etruria; the army smashed the rebellion.

His intelligence, ambition, literary talents, and study of philosophy and oratory in Greece as a young man enabled Cicero to produce elevated and serious writings. Never as original as Plato or Aristotle, Cicero nonetheless was crucial in making the Latin language a vessel for the heritage of Greek thought. A prolific writer, Cicero produced over a hundred orations, of which about sixty survive; several treatises on oratory; philosophical writings on politics, ethics, epistemology, and theology; poetry (of which little survives); and numerous letters. After his death in 43 B.C., his voluminous correspondence was published with little expurgation. The letters and speeches provide a vivid, detailed, and sometimes damning picture of politics.

Politics in the Late Republic was loud and boisterous. The elite prided itself on free speech and open debate. In the senate, assemblies, and court cases, oratory—sometimes great oratory—was common. Few orators in history have matched Cicero's ability to lead and mislead an audience by playing on its feelings. He knew every rhetorical trick and precisely when each was appropriate. His orations are masterpieces of technique, famous for polish, wit, long, rolling sentences, and, above all, emotional power. (See the box, "Cicero in Defense of Milo.")

Because of increased freedom and greater educational opportunities, during the Late Republic it was possible for elite women as well as men to study oratory. Private tutors were common among the aristocracy, and girls often received lessons alongside their brothers. Girls sometimes also profited from a father's expertise. A particularly dramatic case is that of Hortensia, daughter of Quintus Hortensius Hortalus (114–50 B.C.), a famous orator and rival of Cicero. An excellent speaker herself, Hortensia defied tradition by arguing successfully in the Roman Forum in 42 B.C. against a proposed war tax on wealthy women.

Cicero pilloried one elite woman who enjoyed considerable freedom: Clodia (b. ca. 95 B.C.). Sister of the notorious populist gang leader Clodius and wife of optimas politician Metellus Celer (d. 59 B.C.), Clodia moved in Rome's highest circles. Cicero accused her of poisoning her husband. (The charge was unprovable.) She is better remembered from the poems of Catullus (ca. 85–54 B.C.), where she is called Lesbia. In passionate and psychologically complex verse, Catullus describes the ups and downs of their affair, which Clodia eventually ended.

Ordinary people lacked the education or the freedom to express themselves in the manner of a

Cicero in Defense of Milo

On January 18, 53 B.C., a brawl between the rival gangs of Clodius and Milo on the Appian Way left Clodius dead. Cicero himself defended Milo, a fellow optimas, but Milo was convicted and exiled. As this excerpt shows, Cicero's speech to the jury reveals both the violence of late Republican life and the elegance of his rhetoric.

As subsequent events demonstrated, his [Clodius's] plan was to take up a position in front of his own country manor, and set an ambush for Milo on the spot. . . .

Meanwhile, Milo . . . attended the Senate on that day, until the meeting was concluded. Then he proceeded to his home, changed his shoes and his clothes, waited for the usual period when his wife got ready, and then started off at just about the time when Clodius could have got back to Rome if it had been his intention to return at all on the day in question. But instead he encountered Clodius in the country. . . .

And so at about five in the afternoon, or thereabouts, he found himself confronted by Clodius before the gates of the latter's house. Milo was instantly set upon by a crowd of armed men who charged down from the higher ground; while, simultaneously, others rushed up from in front and killed the driver of the coach. Milo flung back his cloak, leapt out of the vehicle, and defended himself with energy. But meanwhile the people with Clodius were brandishing their drawn swords, and while some of them ran towards the coach in order to fall upon Milo from the rear, others believed he was already slain and began to attack his slaves who had been following behind him. A number of those slaves of Milo's lost their lives defending their master with loyal determination. Others, however, who could

see the fight round the coach but were unable to get to their master's help, heard from Clodius' own lips that Milo was slain, and believed the report. And so these slaves, without the orders or knowledge or presence of their master—and I am going to speak quite frankly, and not with any aim of denying the charge but just exactly as the situation developed— did what every man would have wished his own slaves to do in similar circumstances.

The incident, gentlemen, took place exactly as I have described it. The attacker was defeated. Force was frustrated by force; or, to put the matter more accurately, evil was overcome by good. Of the gain to our country and yourselves and all loyal citizens, I say nothing. It is not my intention to urge that the deed be counted in favor of Milo—the man whose self-preservation was destined to mean the preservation of the Republic and yourselves. No, my defense is that he was justified in acting to save his life. Civilized people are taught this by logic, barbarians by necessity, communities by tradition; and the lesson is inculcated even in wild beasts by nature itself. . . . That being so, if you come to the conclusion that this particular action was criminal, you are in the same breath deciding that every other man in the history of the world who has ever fought back against a robber deserves nothing better than death. . . .

Source: Cicero, "In Defense of Titus Annius Milo," in *Selected Political Speeches of Cicero,* trans. Michael Grant (Harmondsworth, England: Penguin, 1969), pp. 232–234.

Catullus or Hortensia, but a less civilized means of expression was open to them: the political gang. Brawls and violence between the rival groups of Clodius, a supporter of Caesar, and Milo, a sup-

porter of the senate, became increasingly common in the fifties B.C. As dictator, Caesar abolished the gangs. Meanwhile, among the elite, as Cicero's letters indicate, free speech gave way to gossip, plotting, factionalism, and flattery of Pompey and Caesar.

Cicero's works provide evidence of a crucial development in the practice of Roman law. Often unheralded, it was nonetheless of historical importance, for Cicero's contemporaries invented the very notion of the legal expert, a person devoted to explaining and interpreting the law. Complex and intricate, Roman law needed interpretation. Much of it was the work not of legislators but of magistrates, who issued annual edicts setting forth how their courts would work. In the Early Republic the pontiffs alone had the right to interpret the law (see page 162), but in the third and second centuries B.C. a group of lay legal interpreters known as jurisconsults emerged. In the first century they became true jurists; their interpretations began to be considered authoritative. Two outstanding jurists of this period were Quintus Mucius Scaevola (d. 82 B.C.), who wrote on the civil law, and Servius Sulpicius Rufus (d. 43 B.C.), who was an expert on the law of the magistrates. No earlier Mediterranean society had a professional class of legal experts, but no earlier society had faced issues as complex and turbulent nor had 3 million citizens, as the Roman Republic did in the mid-first century B.C. The Western tradition of legal science has its roots in Rome.

Rome's political system, unlike its legal system, did not adapt flexibly to changing circumstances. The disenfranchised of the Late Republic had reasonable goals: land for those who had fought for their country and admission to the senate of a wider group. Yet the old elite resisted both. Cicero's proposed solution was to build on Sulla's reforms by uniting the senatorial and equestrian orders and by widening the Roman ruling class to include the elite of all Italy. The newly widened ruling class could close ranks and establish *otium cum dignitate*, "peace with respect for rank." Cicero's new order was distinctly hierarchical.

In the turbulent times of the Late Republic, the Roman elite often turned to the Hellenistic philosophers. The poet Lucretius (ca. 94–ca. 55 B.C.) describes the Epicurean ideal of withdrawal into the contemplative life in a long didactic epic called *On the Nature of Things*. Most elite Romans, however, including Cicero, preferred the activist philosophy of Stoicism (see page 142). Cicero put forth a generous view of human brotherhood. He

argued that all people share a spark of divinity and are protected by natural law. Consequently, all persons have value and importance and should treat others generously. Such ideas would be influential in the new Roman Empire when, under the leadership of Augustus, fair treatment of provincials was a major theme. For Cicero, however, these ideas existed more as theory than as practice.

Cicero did not hide his lack of sympathy for his fellow citizens who were poor. In one speech he castigated "artisans and shopkeepers and all that kind of scum"; in a letter he complained about "the wretched half-starved populace, which attends mass meetings and sucks the blood of the treasury." Cicero also made his disdain for democracy clear: "The greatest number," he said, "should not have the greatest power."

Elitist as Cicero's views were, they were by no means extremist. Cassius, Brutus, and the other Liberators had little interest in even Cicero's limited compromises. Their stubbornness proved to be their downfall, for dispossessed peasants and ambitious equestrians transferred their loyalties to Julius Caesar, and, later, to Augustus. One of Caesar's supporters, Sallust (86–ca. 34 B.C.), wrote biting and bitter works of history that indicted the greed and corruption of the optimates, whom he blamed for the decline of the Republic. In any case, peace was not restored, for the generation of Liberators was wiped out in renewed civil war and a new generation emerged, weary for peace.

SUMMARY

From modest beginnings as a central Italian village urbanized after contact with more sophisticated neighbors, Rome became a monarchy and then a republic. It practiced imperialism with almost unlimited success, but ultimately the weight of empire brought down first the social system and then the political regime.

In the first centuries of its existence, the Republican oligarchy displayed a remarkable combination of flexibility and stability. It proved able to accommodate not only the competitive instincts of the aristocracy and the newly rich but the land-hunger of the people. The old aristocracy of the patricians opened its ranks to the newly ambitious leaders of the plebeians and also made room in the government for popular representation. The engrained hierarchy of the Roman social and cultural system helped keep politics stable.

The elite channeled popular energies into protecting the young republic from its numerous rivals in central Italy. Rome consolidated its control of that region by wisely treating its allies with a mixture of firmness and generosity. By extending Roman citizenship, Rome gave them a stake in continued Roman hegemony. Having disposed of its nearest enemies, Rome mounted a quest for absolute security, a quest that led to conquest in Italy and the rest of the Mediterranean. Greed and ambition, as well as fear, were powerful motives of expansion.

Having defeated all opponents near and far, Rome seemed to have won absolute security by the mid-second century B.C. Yet its strength was deceptive. Contact with Greek culture liberated the Romans from ruder, peasant ways but also loosened previous restraints. A huge influx of slaves made acquisition of large estates profitable. The Italian peasantry was already weakened by conscription and the devastation of farmland, and the elite was arrogant from its military success. Thus, it became easy for the strong to confiscate the land of the weak. The result was a growing and dangerous social instability with military and political ramifications. At the very moment of triumph, the Republic was in grave danger.

Members of the Roman elite, rather than displaying that talent for compromise that had made the Republic great, refused to share their wealth with the poor. The poor, however, got their revenge by throwing their support to new patrons, military leaders who raised private armies to win land for their followers and glory for themselves. By the first century B.C., the Republic had collapsed under the weight of political maneuvering, judicial murders, gang warfare, and civil war. The time was right for the last of the private commanders to recreate the Roman state under his leadership as Augustus, first of the emperors.

NOTES

1. *The Aeneid of Virgil*, trans. Allen Mandelbaum (Berkeley: University of California Press, 1971), pp. 160–161.

2. P. A. Brunt, *Social Conflicts in the Roman Republic* (New York: W. W. Norton, 1971), p. 17.

SUGGESTED READING

General Surveys

Brunt, P. A. *Social Conflicts in the Roman Republic*. 1971. A fine, non-Marxist view of the importance of class conflict throughout Republican history.

Cornell, T. J., and J. Matthews. *Atlas of the Roman World*. 1982. A readable introduction to Roman history written by two scholars. The maps and photos are beautiful, among the best available.

Crawford, Michael. *The Roman Republic*. 1982. The best short introduction, sophisticated, lively, and concise.

Heichelheim, F. M., C. A. Yeo, and A. M. Ward. *A History of the Roman People*. 2d ed. 1984. The best introductory textbook, readable and based on up-to-date scholarship.

Kunkel, Wolfgang. *An Introduction to Roman Legal and Constitutional History*. 2d ed. 1973. A survey of the evolution of Roman law in its social and political context from the earliest times to the early Byzantine era.

Early Italy and Early Rome

Bonfante, Larissa, ed. *Etruscan Life and Afterlife: A Handbook of Etruscan Studies*. 1986. A well-illustrated collection of essays on history, economy, art, architecture, coinage, language, daily life, and religion.

Cornell, T. J. *The Beginnings of Rome: Italy and Rome from the Bronze Age to the Punic Wars (c. 1000–264 B.C.)*. 1995. A readable and ambitious survey combining archaeological and literary evidence, often in support of iconoclastic conclusions.

Pallottino, M. *A History of Earliest Italy*. Translated by Martin Ryle and Kate Soper. 1991. Discusses the current state of the evidence, focusing on 900 to 300 B.C.

———. *The Etruscans*. 1975. An even-handed, well-illustrated introduction.

Government and Society in the Early and Middle Republic, ca. 509–133 B.C.

Dixon, Suzanne. *The Roman Mother*. 1988. A thoughtful and sophisticated interpretation of the evidence.

Gruen, E. S. *Culture and National Identity in Republican Rome*. 1992. A complex account of the ways in which Rome admired, distrusted, and finally absorbed Greek culture.

Nicolet, C. *The World of the Citizen in Republican Rome*. 1980. An innovative study of civil life focusing on patterns of behavior and structures of thought.

Pomeroy, S. B. *Goddesses, Whores, Wives, and Slaves: Women in Classical Antiquity*. 1976. Chapter VII offers a lively introduction to the women of the Republic.

Saller, Richard P. *Patriarchy, Property, and Death in the Roman Family.* 1994. A sophisticated yet readable study of the interplay of authority, mutual obligation, and affection in the Roman family.

Sutherland, C. H. V. *Roman Coins.* 1974. A readable and well-illustrated discussion from the Middle Republic to Late Antiquity.

Watson, A. *Rome of the Twelve Tables.* 1975. An attempt to reconstruct law and society in the Republic of the fifth century B.C.

From Italian City-State to World Empire

Badian, E. *Foreign Clientelae (264–70 B.C.).* 1958. A classic study, vigorously written, of the ways in which the Roman elite transferred its domestic patron-client system to Rome's foreign conquests.

Caven, B. *The Punic Wars.* 1980. A fluent and readable account, emphasizing military history.

Errington, R. M. *The Dawn of Empire: Rome's Rise to World Power.* 1973. A readable and reliable narrative of Rome's expansion.

Gruen, E. *The Hellenistic World and the Coming of Rome.* 1984. Attuned to the ironies of international affairs, this thoughtful and groundbreaking book argues that the Romans were drawn into domination of the Greek world by the Greeks themselves, not by any grand Roman imperial design.

Keppie, L. *The Making of the Roman Army: From Republic to Empire.* 1984. A sensible and readable reconstruction of the evidence, with particular attention to tactics and organization.

Scullard, H. H. *Roman Politics, 220–150 B.C.* 2d ed. 1973. A good example of the prosopographical approach to Roman politics, a methodology that emphasizes marriage and kinship ties.

Sherwin-White, A. N. *The Roman Citizenship.* 2d ed. 1973. An authoritative work on the varieties of citizenship and their political significance from the earliest times to the Late Empire.

Rome and Its Empire

Brunt, P. A. *Italian Manpower, 225 B.C.–A.D. 14.* 1971. A meticulous and authoritative study of the surviving manpower statistics, most of which are the product of military censuses.

Hopkins, Keith. *Conquerors and Slaves: Sociological Studies in Roman History.* Vol. 1. 1978. A wide-ranging and influential work applying sociological method to history. An excellent study of the impact of empire on the political economy of Italy.

Salmon, E. T. *The Making of Roman Italy.* 1982. A summary of recent research on the peoples of Italy conquered by Rome and of the impact on them of Roman hegemony.

Literature, Religion, Art

Ogilvie, R. M. *Roman Literature and Society.* 1980. A survey of literature in its social context from the Early Republic to the Early Empire. Good bibliographies.

———. *The Romans and Their Gods in the Age of Augustus.* 1970. A good general introduction to Republican religion and its legacy.

Ramage, A., and N. Ramage. *Roman Art: Romulus to Constantine.* 1991. A thorough, readable, and well-illustrated introductory textbook.

Wardham, A. *Rome's Debt to Greece.* 1976. An outline of opinions in Roman literature (from the first century B.C. to the second century A.D.) about Greeks and Greek thought.

From the Gracchi to Caesar, 133–44 B.C.

Badian, E. *Roman Imperialism in the Late Republic.* 2d ed. 1969. An argument against the economic motivation of Roman imperialism.

Beard, Mary, and Michael Crawford. *Rome in the Late Republic.* 1985. An unusual and innovative approach to the subject, emphasizing sociocultural and institutional analysis more than narrative.

Bernstein, Alvin H. *Tiberius Gracchus: Tradition and Apostasy.* 1978. A biography that sees Tiberius as a traditional member of the Roman aristocracy, disaffected by failures in his career prior to 133 B.C. and primarily interested in reform because of Rome's military problems.

Frier, Bruce. *The Rise of the Roman Jurists: Studies in Cicero's pro Caecina.* 1985. A thoughtful analysis of the professionalization of law in the Late Republic and its historical consequences.

Gelzer, M. *Caesar, Politician and Statesman.* 6th ed. Translated by P. Needham. 1968. An incisive, short treatment.

Gruen, Erich S. *The Last Generation of the Roman Republic.* 1974. A detailed analysis of the structure and practices of Roman politics in Cicero's day, arguing against the inevitability of the collapse of the Republic.

Hopkins, Keith. *Death and Renewal: Sociological Studies in Roman History.* Vol. 2. 1983. An argument, against an older view, that the senatorial elite of the Late Republic and Early Empire was surprisingly open to outsiders. Also discusses gladiatorial shows, funerals, mourning, and wills.

Rawson, Elizabeth. *Cicero: A Portrait.* 1975. A sensible, reliable, and readable introduction.

Scullard, H. H. *From the Gracchi to Nero.* 5th ed. 1982. A concise and reliable introduction, with an emphasis on political history.

Treggiari, Susan. *Roman Freedmen During the Late Republic.* 1969. An introduction to a fascinating but often overlooked segment of Roman society, including discussions of legal status, careers, political activity, religion, and the family.

LUXURY GOODS AND GENDER WARS IN ROME

The carefully wrought gold earrings shown here represent the height of fashion in the central Mediterranean around 200 B.C. Hellenistic taste favored such gold hoop earrings embellished with inlaid colored glass. This set, moreover, displays one of the favorite decorative motifs of the goldsmiths of Magna Graecia in southern Italy during this period: the dove. The artist has crafted the doves as pendants: Note how each dove hangs from the earring and stands on a small base trimmed with a garland. Two inches tall, the earrings are miniature sculptures. A Roman woman might wear such jewelry proudly, certain that it bespoke not only good taste and wealth but also the power of her city to command the best artistry of the Greek world.

Not all Romans, however, looked with favor on such finery. Some said it represented not Roman success but decadence. While some observers saw, reflected in the gold, the sight of Greek craftsmen dancing to Roman tunes, others perceived a scene of corruption and wastefulness. Both men and women in the Roman elite began to indulge a taste for luxury in the third century B.C., but women came in for special criticism.

Conservatives considered women's luxuries to pose a special threat to society, because they represented not only foreign influence but a threat to right order in the household. If women controlled the economic power to purchase luxury goods, where, then, was the authority of the paterfamilias? More open-minded Romans defended women's contributions to society and their right to the recognition that luxury goods betokened. A debate on women's luxuries raged in Rome around 200 B.C. Let us examine both its historical background and the position of its most famous participant, the conservative champion Marcus Porcius Cato (234-149 B.C.), known as Cato the Censor.

From their first conquest in Magna Graecia in the third century B.C., Romans began to bring home Greek artists and craftsmen and their works. The trickle of art flowing toward Rome is said to have become a flood when Roman armies entered Greece and Anatolia. The simple and frugal elite of traditional Roman ideology began to give way in the third century B.C. to lovers of the good life.

The new wealth and new tastes created a luxury-goods industry in Rome. Traditionalist opinion was shocked. Not that Rome lacked wealthy households before 300 B.C. Rather, before then Republican ideology had successfully frowned on conspicuous consumption and display. Now it became common for elite men to wear rings and for elite women to wear jewelry as well as fine clothes and cosmetics and—a particular sign of wealth and honor—to ride in carriages. Hannibal's invasion of Italy put the brakes on luxury, however, because it forced Romans to adopt austerity for the duration of the war. In 215 B.C., the Oppian Law put limits on the gold and fine clothing women could own and on their privilege of riding in carriages.

Twenty years later, in 195 B.C., when the emergency had passed, a proposal was made to repeal the law. Elite women demonstrated in favor of repeal. According to the historian Livy, Valerius (one of the consuls for 195) supported their position:

Women cannot claim magistracies or priesthoods or triumphs or military decorations or awards or the spoils of war. Cosmetics and adornments are women's decorations. They delight and boast of them and this is what our ancestors called women's estate.*

Enter Cato, the other consul for 195 and an advocate of traditional Roman values of austerity. Livy has Cato criticize luxury goods as signs of Greek

---

*Trans. E. Fantham in Elaine Fantham, Helene Peet Foley, Natalie Boymel Kampen, Sarah B. Pomeroy, and H. A. Shapiro, *Women in the Classical World: Image and Text* (New York: Oxford University Press, 1994), p. 261.

Hellenistic Earrings, Gold and Inlaid Glass *(Courtesy of the Museum of Fine Arts, Boston)*

corruption and women's license, even perhaps of women's eventual equality. Although some scholars doubt whether Cato ever so criticized the Greeks, there is no doubt about his hostility to luxury. As censor in 184 B.C., he assessed taxes on luxury goods and slaves at ten times their market value, in order to discourage their use.

Nor is there any doubt about the degree of male worry about women's wealth in Cato's Rome—even though the repeal of the Oppian Law eventually passed in 195 B.C., over Cato's opposition. For example, Cato's contemporary Plautus has a character in his play, *Pot of Gold*, condemn wealthy wives with their "fine clothes and jewelry . . . and maids and mules and coachmen and footmen and pages and private carriages."** In 186 B.C., nine years after the repeal of the Oppian Law, some elite women were found guilty of participation in alleged orgies of the god Bacchus (the Greek Dionysus). Seventeen years later, in 169 B.C., a law was passed to prevent the wealthiest Roman men from leaving more than half of their property

to a daughter, in order to prevent the loss through marriage of most of a family's wealth.

How can we explain such attention by the government to the behavior of elite women? The answer in large part is that war and empire had brought such women new power, power that elite men feared. While those men had often spent years abroad fighting Rome's wars, their wives had learned how to run households. The enormous wealth brought home from those wars often ended up as women's dowries. Women had the right to retain control of part of their dowries, which sometimes made them wealthier than their husbands. Cato complained that some wives went so far as to lend money to their husbands and then send a slave to reclaim the interest.

So the museum-piece earrings that now win our admiration as works of art once stirred up gender wars that rocked the Roman elite. They remind us how rich in unanticipated consequences was Rome's imperial success. Nonetheless, they must not blind us to the imbalance of wealth in Rome. As the carriages of wealthy women went by, the vast majority of Roman women could only stand and watch, hoping to catch a glimpse of gold. ✤

**Ibid.

CHAPTER 6

Imperial Rome, 27 B.C.– A.D. 284

The imperial family of Rome walks in stately procession to a sacrifice: Augustus, first of the emperors; his wife, Livia; his daughter, Julia; Julia's husband, Agrippa; and various cousins and in-laws and their children. They are formally dressed in togas and gowns, heads wreathed. The men and women gaze seriously; the boys and girls have impish looks, betraying stray thoughts of disobedience as they hold their parents' hands. They are all carved in stone, one of several sculptured reliefs decorating the walls of a public monument in Rome. Dedicated on Livia's birthday in 9 B.C., the monument shown here illustrates the propaganda themes of the new regime, among them the happy family as symbol of the restoration of harmony in the state after generations of civil war. The senate, which had commissioned the monument, called it the Ara Pacis Augustae, or Altar of Augustan Peace.

Having made peace was no idle boast on Augustus's part. Not only did he end the Roman revolution, but he laid the foundation of a regime that would bring prosperity and stability to the Roman Empire for two hundred years. Augustus took advantage of Rome's war-weariness and of his own superb political instincts to create a new government out of the ruins of the Republic. Like the builders of the Early Republic's constitution, Augustus displayed the Roman genius for compromise. Although he retained the final say, he shared a degree of power with the senate. He made financial sacrifices to feed the urban poor and distribute farms to landless peasants. He ended Rome's seemingly limitless expansion and stabilized the borders of the empire. He began to raise the provinces to a status of equality with Italy.

Ara Pacis, Rome
(detail).

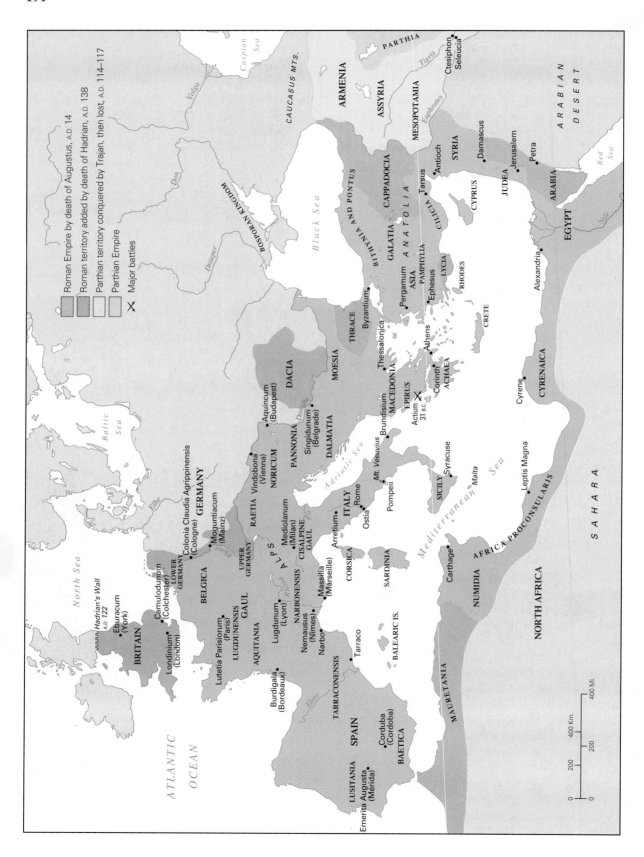

Roman Empire by death of Augustus, A.D. 14

Roman territory added by death of Hadrian, A.D. 138

Parthian territory conquered by Trajan, then lost, A.D. 114–117

Parthian Empire

X Major battles

PARTHIA

ARMENIA

ASSYRIA

MESOPOTAMIA

Ctesiphon
Seleucia

CAUCASUS MTS.

Caspian Sea

Volga

Don

Dnieper

BOSPORAN KINGDOM

Black Sea

Tigris

Euphrates

BITHYNIA AND PONTUS

CAPPADOCIA

GALATIA

ANATOLIA

CILICIA

Pergamum

ASIA

PAMPHYLIA

LYCIA

Ephesus

CYPRUS

RHODES

Tarsus

Antioch

SYRIA

Damascus

Jerusalem

JUDEA

Petra

ARABIA

A R A B I A N   D E S E R T

EGYPT

Red Sea

Nile

Alexandria

Baltic Sea

Elbe

Rhine

Danube

DACIA

Aquincum
(Budapest)

PANNONIA

Vindobona
(Vienna)

NORICUM

Singidunum
(Belgrade)

DALMATIA

MOESIA

THRACE

Byzantium

MACEDONIA

Thessalonica

EPIRUS

Actium
31 B.C. X

Brundisium

ACHAEA

Athens

Corinth

CRETE

Adriatic Sea

RAETIA

Moguntiacum
(Mainz)

Colonia Claudia Agrippinensis
(Cologne)

GERMANY

UPPER
GERMANY

LOWER
GERMANY

BELGICA

A L P S

Mediolanum
(Milan)

CISALPINE
GAUL

Po

Arretium

ITALY

Rome

Ostia

Pompeii

Mt. Vesuvius

CORSICA

SARDINIA

SICILY

Syracuse

Malta

Mediterranean Sea

Leptis Magna

CYRENAICA

Cyrene

AFRICA PROCONSULARIS

Carthage

NUMIDIA

NORTH AFRICA

MAURETANIA

S A H A R A

GAUL

LUGDUNENSIS

Lugdunum
(Lyon)

Lutetia Parisiorum
(Paris)

NARBONENSIS

Nemausus
(Nîmes)

Massilia
(Marseille)

Narbo

AQUITANIA

Burdigala
(Bordeaux)

Tarraco

TARRACONENSIS

BALEARIC IS.

Ebro

SPAIN

Corduba
(Cordoba)

BAETICA

LUSITANIA

Emerita Augusta
(Mérida)

North Sea

Hadrian's Wall
A.D. 122

Eburacum
(York)

Camulodunum
(Colchester)

Londinium
(London)

BRITAIN

A T L A N T I C   O C E A N

400 Mi.

400 Km.

200

200

0

0

The pax Romana ("Roman peace"), at its height between A.D. 96 and 180, was an era of enlightened emperors, thriving cities, intellectual vitality, and artistic and architectural achievement in an empire of 50 million or more people. The Roman peace was also an era of considerable spirituality. In the peaceful and diverse empire, ideas traveled from people to people, and the religious beliefs of an obscure sect from western Asia began to spread around the Mediterranean and into northern Europe. The new religion was Christianity.

After 180, Rome slowly passed into a grim period marked in turn by bad emperors, civil war, inflation, plague, invasion, and defeat. After reaching a nadir around 235–253, Rome's fortunes began to improve under a series of reforming emperors. Their works culminated in the reigns of Diocletian (r. 284–305) and Constantine (r. 312–337), who would forge a stronger and vastly different empire (see Chapter 7).

AUGUSTUS AND THE PRINCIPATE, 27 B.C.–A.D. 68

The assassination of Caesar threw Rome back into turmoil. Civil war followed for the next thirteen years, first between the Liberators and Caesar's partisans and then between the two leading Caesarians. The final struggle pitted Mark Antony (Marcus Antonius, ca. 83–30 B.C.), Caesar's chief lieutenant and successor to the affections of Cleopatra, against Octavian (Gaius Julius Caesar Octavianus, 63 B.C.–A.D. 14), Caesar's grandnephew and adopted son and heir. Although Octavian was younger than Antony, was not a general, and was cursed with poor health, he was a man of unusual cunning and prudence. His forces defeated Antony and Cleopatra at the naval battle of Actium (northwestern Greece) in 31 B.C.; their suicides followed shortly. Octavian spent the next forty-five years healing the wounds of a century of revolution. He did nothing less than lay the foundations of the prosperous two centuries of the Roman peace (Map 6.1).

Map 6.1 The Roman World in the Early Empire
Many modern cities are built on the site of Roman foundations, evidence of the immense extent of the Roman Empire at its height.

The Political Settlement

Octavian was both an astute politician and a lucky one. He was lucky in the length and violence of the civil wars. After Actium, most of his enemies were dead, so establishing the one-man rule that he claimed was necessary to restore stability was relatively easy. He was also lucky to live to be nearly 80—he had plenty of time to consolidate his rule. Octavian astutely learned the lesson of Caesar's mistake. He was a cagey man, a careful planner who loved to gamble with dice but never

Augustus of Prima Porta Named for the place where it was found, this statue (early first century A.D.) depicts an idealized and heroic Augustus. Scenes of victory, peace, and prosperity—symbols of the principate—decorate his breastplate. Riding a dolphin, the Cupid at Augustus's feet recalls the Julian family's claim of descent from the goddess Venus. *(Alinari/Art Resource, NY)*

Augustus: The Official Story

Not long before his death in A.D. 14, the emperor Augustus arranged for the display in Rome of two bronze tablets containing a record of his achievements. Copies of "the achievements of the Divine Augustus, by which he brought the world under the empire of the Roman people, and of the expenses which he bore for the state and people of Rome" were displayed around the empire. A complete copy survived in the Roman city of Ancyra in Anatolia (modern Ankara, Turkey).

1. At the age of nineteen on my own responsibility and at my own expense I raised an army, with which I successfully championed the liberty of the republic when it was oppressed by the tyranny of a faction. . . .

3. I undertook many civil and foreign wars by land and sea throughout the world, and as victor I spared the lives of all citizens who asked for mercy. 2. [*sic*] When foreign peoples could safely be pardoned I preferred to preserve rather than eliminate them. 3. The Roman citizens who took the soldier's oath of obedience to me numbered about 500,000. I settled rather more than 300,000 of these in colonies or sent them back to their home towns after a period of service; to all these I assigned lands or gave money as rewards for their military service. . . .

20. I restored the Capitol and the theatre of Pompey, both works at great expense without inscribing my name on either. 2. I restored the channels of the aqueducts, which in several places were falling into disrepair through age, and I brought water from a new spring into the aqueduct called Marcia, doubling the sup-

ply. . . . 4. In my sixth consulship I restored eighty-two temples of the gods in the city on the authority of the senate, neglecting none that required restoration at the time. . . .

26. I extended the territory of all those provinces of the Roman people on whose borders lay peoples not subject to our government. . . .

27. I added Egypt to the empire of the Roman people. . . .

28. . . . I compelled the Parthians to restore to me the spoils and standards of three Roman armies and to ask as suppliants for the friendship of the Roman people. Those standards I deposited in the innermost shrine of the temple of Mars the Avenger. . . .

35. In my thirteenth consulship the senate, the equestrian order and the whole people of Rome gave me the title of Father of my Country, and resolved that this should be inscribed in the porch of my house and in the Curia Julia and in the Forum Augustum below the chariot which had been set there in my honor by decree of the senate. 2. At the time of writing I am in my seventy-sixth year.

Source: P. A. Brunt and J. M. Moore, eds., *Res Gestae Divi Augusti: The Achievements of the Divine Augustus* (New York: Oxford University Press, 1967), pp. 19–37.

took chances in the game of power. He understood that the Roman elite, however weakened, was still strong enough to oppose a ruler who flaunted monarchial power. To avoid a second Ides of March, therefore, Octavian was infinitely diplomatic, aware that a cooperative senate could aid his rule greatly.

Rather than call himself Dictator, Octavian took the title of *Princeps* ("First Citizen"). From

princeps comes *principate,* a term often used to describe the constitutional monarchy of the "Early Empire," the name that historians have given to the period from 27 B.C. to A.D. 192. Four years after Actium, in 27 B.C. the senate granted Octavian the honorific title *augustus,* derived from the verb *augeo,* meaning "to grow." The name suggested prosperity and growth. Another appellation, *imperator* ("commander" and, later, "emperor"), recalled the military might that Augustus (as we shall henceforth call him) could call on if needed.

In 27 B.C., Augustus proclaimed "the transfer of the state to the free disposal of the senate and the people"—that is, the restoration of the Republic. Remembering similar claims by Sulla and Caesar, few Romans were likely to believe this, and few would have wanted the Republic restored in any case. They no doubt appreciated their ruler's tact, however. (See the box, "Augustus: The Official Story.") The new government that emerged, after trial and error, was a partnership between Augustus and the senate—an unequal partnership, in which Augustus held the upper hand, but a partnership nonetheless.

Several things made it work. First, Augustus deftly claimed both consular imperium and tribunician authority without constant election as consul and tribune, thereby separating his military and civil powers from Republican offices. Second, Augustus dispersed administrative authority to appease various groups and to foster efficient government. An example is his division of the provinces into two categories. To check any new would-be Caesar, he kept for himself the frontier provinces, with the main concentration of armies, as well as grain-rich Egypt. The local commanders were loyal equestrians who owed their success to Augustus. Most of the other provinces continued to be ruled as before by the senate and its promagistrates.

A third and crucial point is that Augustus's senators hardly resembled their predecessors. Unsavory senators enrolled during the civil wars were purged, and the membership of the senate was reduced to about six hundred. The princeps reshaped the Roman ruling class by elevating to the senate large numbers of equestrians, particularly Italians. Where once optimates had monopolized power, now the wealthy classes of Italy eagerly administered the government of the man who had championed their cause.

In order to use the senate as a sounding board, Augustus created a standing committee of magistrates and senators that evolved into an advisory group called the council of the princeps. In ordinary senate meetings, however, the old freedom of speech was gone. What with informers and secret agents, a senator might think twice before speaking.

The popular assemblies fared even worse. To remove all sources of instability, Augustus clamped down on their already limited powers; even these were gradually assumed, in later times, by the senate. In other moves against potential instability, Augustus established the city of Rome's first police force and also stationed there his own personal guard. Called the praetorians, or Praetorian Guard, the name used for a Roman general's bodyguard, the guard would play a role in future imperial politics.

More important for the public good, Augustus established the first civil service for Rome, Italy, and the provinces, embodied in a series of prefectures—or departments—supervising, for example, the city watch, the grain supply, the water supply, the building of roads and bridges, tax collection, and the provisioning of the armies. Equestrians were prominent in these prefectures and in the government of the imperial provinces, so they enthusiastically supported the Principate. Freedmen, too, rose rapidly in the imperial service.

Although one may speak loosely of "imperial bureaucracy," in truth neither Augustus nor his successors ever established a tight administrative grip on their far-flung empire. As in all ancient empires, Roman government tended to be decentralized and limited. In an age in which few public officials received a salary, bribes were accepted, nor was corruption uncommon.

The Economic and Social Settlement

The old Roman ruling class made its peace with Augustus, but some never forgave him for ending their ancient privileges. Although Augustus was generally a mild ruler, several of his successors made into the order of the day treason trials, judicial murder, witch-hunts for alleged conspirators, and *damnatio memoriae,* the erasure from the public record of a condemned man's existence. The conservative historian Tacitus (A.D. 55–ca. 117) looked back wistfully to the Late Republic as a golden era of freedom, eloquence, and "the old sound morality." (See the box, "Augustus: A Skeptical View.") Even Tacitus, however, was forced to admit the reality that the Principate was enormously popular with the vast majority of the inhabitants of the Roman world. The reason is simple: Augustus and his successors brought an age

Augustus: A Skeptical View

Tacitus, a member of the senatorial elite of the Early Empire, looked back to the freedom of the Roman Republic. His Annals *offer a scathing view of the early emperors, beginning with Augustus, whose reign he discusses briefly.*

Famous writers have recorded Rome's early glories and disasters. The Augustan Age, too, had its distinguished historians. But then the rising tide of flattery exercised a deterrent effect. The reigns of Tiberius, Gaius, Claudius, and Nero were described during their lifetimes in fictitious terms, for fear of the consequences; whereas the accounts written after their deaths were influenced by still raging animosities. So I have decided to say a little about Augustus, with special attention to his last period, and then go on to the reign of Tiberius and what followed. I shall write without indignation or partisanship: in my case the customary incentives to these are lacking.

The violent deaths of Brutus and Cassius left no Republican forces in the field. Defeat came to Sextus Pompeius in Sicily, Lepidus was dropped, Antony killed. So even the Caesarian party had no leader left except the "Caesar" himself, Octavian. He gave up the title of Triumvir emphasizing instead his position as consul; and the powers of a tribune, he proclaimed, were good enough for him—powers for the protection of ordinary people.

He seduced the army with bonuses, and his cheap food policy was successful bait for civilians. Indeed, he attracted everybody's goodwill by the enjoyable gift of peace. Then he gradually pushed ahead and absorbed the functions of the senate, the officials, and even the law. Opposition did not exist. War or judicial murder had disposed of all men of spirit. Upper-class survivors found that slavish obedience was the way to succeed, both politically and financially. They had profited from revolution, and so now they liked the security of the existing arrangement better than the dangerous uncertainties of the old regime. Besides, the new order was popular in the provinces. There, government by Senate and People was looked upon skeptically as a matter of sparring dignitaries and extortionate officials. The legal system had provided no remedy against these, since it was wholly incapacitated by violence, favoritism, and—most of all—bribery.

Source: Tacitus, *The Annals of Imperial Rome*, rev. ed., trans. Michael Grant (Harmondsworth, England: Penguin, 1988), p. 32.

of peace and prosperity after a century of disasters under the Late Republic. The sternness of the emperor Tiberius, the decadence of Caligula, and the excesses of Nero affected only a tiny minority in the elite; the ordinary person prized the Principate's stability.

The Augustan period was one of affluence, especially in Italy; the other provinces caught up with Italy by the second century A.D. Agriculture flourished with the end of civil war. Italian industries became leaders in exports, among them glass bowls and window panes, iron arms and tools, fancy silver eating utensils and candlesticks, and bronze statues and pots. Italian goods circulated from Britain and Norway to Sudan and eastward to south and central Asia. Augustus stimulated trade by creating the first stable imperial coinage. Brass and copper coins served everyday needs, and there were also gold and silver issues.

The perennial problem of the Late Republic had been land-hunger, which drove peasants into the hands of ambitious generals. Augustus ensured his troops' contentment by compensating 300,000 loyal veterans with land, money, or both, often in new overseas colonies. At first he paid from his own private sources; after A.D. 6, he supported the army from new taxes on the rich. In other words, Augustus made the elite part of a property transfer that they had resisted since the time of the Gracchi. Nevertheless, it should be noted, rural poverty and slavery continued in Italy. In the countryside, only the condition of soldiers and their families was ameliorated, but this improvement was enough to ensure peace.

To end the problem of renegade commanders that had so bedeviled the Late Republic, Augustus reduced the size of the army greatly, gradually cutting the number of legions from over sixty to twenty-eight, around 140,000 men. About the same number of men served as light infantry or cavalry in the auxiliaries, for a total army of about 300,000. This reduction freed the Roman economy of a considerable tax burden but left Augustus with only limited opportunity for expanding the empire. In A.D. 9, Rome lost three legions to a native revolt aimed at preventing the consolidation of Roman rule in Germany as far east as the Elbe River. Augustus had to accept the Rhine River as Rome's new German frontier (see Map 6.1).

Imperial defense remained a major issue. The European frontier, with its hostile populations and lack of central authorities to negotiate with, required strong armies. In the more favorable condimions of western Asia and northern Africa, in contrast, Augustus and his immediate successors avoided border conflict by setting up client kingdoms, such as Judea and Armenia, to protect Rome's provinces. With Parthia, Augustus negotiated a compromise settlement that failed to expand Roman territory but did achieve the symbolic victory of a return of the legionary standards lost by Crassus at Carrhae in 53 B.C.

The urban poor, many of them freedmen, also benefited under Augustus from a more efficient system of free grain distribution and a large increase in regularly held games and public spectacles—the imperial policy of "bread and circuses" designed to keep the masses content. Augustus also instituted a vast public works program, which provided jobs for the poor. He prided himself on having found Rome "a city of brick" and having left it "a city of marble."

To promote his ideology of renewal, Augustus sponsored social legislation embodying the old Republican virtues. He passed a series of laws encouraging marriage and childbearing and discouraging promiscuity and adultery. Such legislation was widely disobeyed. In 2 B.C., Augustus felt compelled to make an example of his own daughter, Julia (39 B.C.–A.D. 14), his only child, whose adulteries were the talk of Rome. As punishment she was banished to a barren islet.

Augustus's era marks the beginning of the classical period of Roman jurisprudence, during which the professionalism that had begun to mark Roman law in the Late Republic became a permanent fact. It was probably Augustus who established the practice, followed by later emperors, of granting a few distinguished jurists the exclusive right to issue legal opinions "on behalf of the princeps." He ensured, therefore, that experts guided the administration of justice. The first law school was opened in Rome under Augustus. Roman jurists, many of them provincials, adapted Roman law to the practices of the provinces. Although various provincial legal systems remained in use, the international system of Roman law was also used widely in the provinces.

In religion, too, Augustus was a legislator and reformer. Many traditional Roman cults had been neglected during the Late Republic. Augustus restored their rituals and priesthoods; he also claimed to have restored all of the eighty-two temples in Rome. The restoration of cults and temples was intended to publicize Augustus as Rome's savior.

The Romans deified Augustus after his death, just as Augustus and Antony had Julius Caesar deified after his death. The provinces worshiped Augustus as a god even while he was still alive—both the East, where the cult of Roma and Augustus grew in popularity, and the West, where centers of emperor-worship were established at the sites of Lyon and Cologne (see Map 6.1). Meanwhile, in Italy, associations of freedmen called *augustales* worshiped Augustus's *genius* (spirit), and the civic calendar grew crowded with various festival days celebrating Augustus. The imperial cult of Augustus, an important part of state propaganda until the empire became Christian in the fourth century A.D., was well underway.

Deification, whether formal or informal, was a heady brew, but Augustus deserved it more than most. He not only ended the Late Republican era of civil wars, but established the Roman Empire on a completely new footing. Republican institutions lost their old freedoms, but the emperor and bureaucrats brought stability. The peace of the Augustan Principate would last, with few interruptions, for two hundred years. Few people in history have created order so successfully.

The Culture of the Augustan Age

Like *Periclean*, the adjective *Augustan* has come to signify an era of literary and artistic flowering. In both periods there were strong elements of classicism in the arts—that is, an attempt to project fundamental, heroic, and idealized values, the values that the self-confident rulers of each epoch wished to promote. Both prose and poetry flour-

ished in Augustus's empire. The emperor and his close adviser Maecenas (d. 8 B.C.) were patrons of a number of important poets, chief among them Virgil (70–19 B.C.) and Horace (65–8 B.C.). The historian Livy (59 B.C.–A.D. 17), who wrote his history of Rome from the founding of the city to 9 B.C. under Augustus, also elicited the princeps's interest in his work. All three men contributed in their writings to the Augustan renewal and rededication of Rome.

In many ways, Virgil speaks for his contemporaries. In the *Eclogues*, poems that, following an Alexandrian model (see page 137), have rustic settings, Virgil describes the miseries of the civil wars and the blessings of peace under Augustus. "A god created this peace for us; for he will always be a god to me," as one character says. In the Fourth

Ara Pacis Augustae The Altar of Augustan Peace, contained in a square enclosure about 34 feet by 38 feet and about 23 feet high, and built 13–9 B.C., was reconstructed in the twentieth century. The relief sculpture of the marble walls depicts Augustus's family and mythological symbols of prosperity. *(Art Resource, NY)*

Eclogue, Virgil gives vent to messianic sentiments: A child will be born to usher in a restored Golden Age. At the church Council of Nicaea in A.D. 325 (see page 235), and later, this poem was given a Christian interpretation. In the *Georgics,* Virgil describes the glories of Italian agriculture, which, thanks to Augustus, could be practiced peacefully again.

Virgil's masterpiece is an epic poem, the *Aeneid,* "the story of Aeneas," the legendary Trojan founder of Rome, or at least of the Latin town from which Rome's founders eventually came. Legend also makes Aeneas the ancestor of Augustus. Thus the *Aeneid* indirectly celebrates Augustus, often considered Rome's second founder (if Virgil had written an epic directly about Augustus, he would have been constrained in what he could say). The poem explores the pain and burden as well as the glory of empire.

If Virgil's work has the grandeur of marble, Horace's poems—*Odes, Epodes, Satires, Epistles,* and *Ars Poetica (Art of Poetry)*—are more like finely cut gems. They tend to be polished, highly complex, and less emotional than the *Aeneid.* Like Virgil, Horace explores the themes of war and peace and praises Augustus. "With Caesar [Augustus] holding the lands, I shall fear neither turmoil nor violent death," declares one of the *Odes.* Both Horace and Virgil successfully adapted Greek models and, in the process, created something new. Few writers have had a greater influence on the later Western literary tradition.

Only 35 of the original 142 books of Livy's ambitious history have survived. Livy is both a master storyteller and an ironist. His anecdotes of Roman history are vivid and told in a grand rhetorical style. Livy is our major source of evidence for the Roman monarchy and Early Republic, but by modern historiographical standards, he is often found wanting. His account of early Rome is long on myth and short on fact. Nevertheless, Livy is not merely an entertaining stylist but a profound thinker on the meaning of history. He embroiders the facts and engages in frank, subjective judgments intended both to inspire patriotism and to inspire reflection on the ironies of history.

Another patron of writers in Augustus's circle was Messalla, himself an orator as well as a statesman. Love poetry was his special interest. Among the poets Messalla supported were Ovid, best

known for works on love and mythology; Tibullus, an eligist; and his ward, Sulpicia. Although little survives of Sulpicia's work, she is the only Roman woman of whose poetry there exists more than fragments. She describes her passion for one Cerinthus: "a worthy man . . . at last a love . . . of such a kind that my shame, Gossip, would be greater if I kept it covered than if I laid it bare."[1]

Augustus and his entourage were also great patrons of the arts and of architecture, which they considered propaganda tools. They sponsored many major building projects in Rome, from temples to a new Forum of Augustus, the Theater of Marcellus, the Baths of Agrippa, the Pantheon, and the Mausoleum of Augustus. The Augustan era also marked a great period of building activity in the provinces, including such monuments as the temple at Nemausus (modern Nîmes), known today as the Maison Carrée, and possibly the Pont du Gard aqueduct, both in southern France.

Augustan sculpture also manifests the themes of peace and plenty. The most common subject is Augustus himself; his statues were ubiquitous throughout the empire. Over the years sculptors experimented with a variety of images, perhaps at Augustus's command. Sometimes he is depicted as an idealized heroic youth, sometimes as a mature soldier in armor, sometimes as a pious Roman priest. Gems, coins, and relief sculpture also celebrated Augustus and his family.

The Julio-Claudians

Augustus and his successors presented the imperial household to the world as the model family, the very likeness of filial piety and marital fidelity and harmony: a paradigm of social order. The emperor's servants sowed the image throughout the empire on works of art and architecture, in inscriptions, and in rituals and ceremonies. Behind the walls of the palace, however, dwelled a troubled and sordid reality.

Augustus had only one child, Julia, from his first marriage, which ended in divorce. In 38 B.C., Augustus took as his second wife Livia (58 B.C.– A.D. 29), who divorced her husband to marry Augustus even though she was pregnant with their second son. She did not bear Augustus children. Seeking a male successor, Augustus used Julia as a pawn in a game of dynastic marriage, divorce,

Julio-Claudian Cameo
Known as the Grand Camée de France, this superb gem depicts the imperial family in its glory. The central scene shows Tiberius, Livia, and, among others, the child Caligula (extreme left). The deified Augustus hovers above them while barbarian captives are below.
(Giraudon/Art Resource, NY)

and remarriage, but to no avail. Julia's first two husbands both predeceased her, as did two sons, each of whom Augustus had adopted. In the end, Augustus was forced to choose as successor and as adopted son a man he disliked, Tiberius (42 B.C.–A.D. 37), Livia's elder son.

Livia was among the most powerful women of Roman history. One of Augustus's main advisers, she developed a reputation for intrigue, aimed, so gossip had it, at securing the succession for Tiberius. Livia's enemies accused her of poisoning Julia's husbands and sons; her own grandson, Germanicus (a brilliant general whose popularity threatened Tiberius's); and even Augustus himself, who died in bed after a short illness in A.D. 14. Yet when Tiberius finally became emperor, he resented Livia's influence; furthermore, when she died, he refused to execute her will or to permit her deification.

From A.D. 14 to 68, Rome was ruled by other emperors from Augustus's family. The dynasty, known as the Julio-Claudians, consisted of Augustus's stepson Tiberius, great-grandson Caligula, grandnephew Claudius, and great-great-grandson Nero. For many elite Romans, this era was one of decadence and scandal and oppression of the old nobility. The main trends of the period were more prosaic. An effective imperial administration grew. Equestrians and freedmen gained an increasing governmental role, while the senate's power declined. Treatment of the provinces improved, and imperial expansion was generally avoided.

The reign of Tiberius (r. 14–37) was marked by intrigue, treason trials, murders, and an increase of the power of the princeps at the expense of the senate. Unpopular with both the masses and the elite because he cut back on games and building projects, Tiberius was nevertheless a skilled and prudent administrator. He wisely drew back from war in Germany and Parthia, preferring diplomatic solutions. He reduced taxes and expenditures and promoted honesty among provincial governors.

His successor, his nephew Gaius (r. 37–41), nicknamed Caligula ("Baby Boots," after the boots he wore as a little boy in his father's army camp), attempted to elevate himself to the status of a god and to humiliate the senate. He made scandalous behavior into an art form. For example, he appointed his favorite horse not only high priest of a new cult in honor of Caligula the god but also a member of the senate. Caligula raised taxes and trumped up charges of treason in order to confiscate property. He wanted to have his statue erected in the Temple at Jerusalem. He would have had his way, but he was assassinated first, the victim of a high-level Roman conspiracy. After his death the senate debated restoring the Republic, but the imperial family made quite clear the realities of power.

Backed by the Praetorian Guard, Caligula's uncle, Claudius, forced the senate into naming him princeps. Lame and cursed with a speech impediment, Claudius (r. 41–54) was often the butt of jokes, but beyond that he was a historian, politician, and priest and was fully versed in the cunning ways of his family. An activist emperor, he expanded the imperial offices with their powerful freedmen; oversaw the construction of an artificial harbor at Rome's silt-clogged port of Ostia; and conquered Britain, where Roman arms had not intervened since Julius Caesar's forays in 55–54 B.C.

Claudius's death may have been the result of poisoning by his wife and niece, Agrippina the Younger (A.D. 15–59); in any case, her son by a previous marriage, Nero, became emperor (r. 54–68). As princeps, Nero's scandalous behavior rivaled Caligula's, and his treason trials outdid Tiberius's. A great fire in 64 destroyed half of Rome. Nero mounted an extravagant rebuilding program afterward, although he was accused of having started the fire so that he could become famous as a builder. Nero found a scapegoat for the fire in the members of a small and relatively new religious sect, the Christians, whom he persecuted.

In contrast to such behavior, Nero provided generally good government for the ordinary people of the empire, and they rewarded him with support. He was unpopular with the senatorial elite, however, and, more serious, he failed to pay all his troops promptly. Confronted with a major revolt in 68, Nero committed suicide. The next year, 69, witnessed Rome's first civil war in about a century. Three men each claimed the imperial purple after Nero. Finally, a fourth, Vespasian (Titus Flavius Vespasianus, r. 69–79), commander of the army quelling revolt in the province of Judea, was able to make his claim stick. Peace was restored, but not the rule of Augustus's family. Vespasian founded a new dynasty, the Flavians (r. 69–96), which was followed in turn by the Nervo-Trajanic (r. 96–138) and Antonine (r. 138–192) dynasties. The ultimate tribute to Augustus may be that his regime was stable enough to survive the extinction of his family.

THE ROMAN PEACE, A.D. 69–180

Much about Rome in the second century A.D. appears attractive today. Within the multi-ethnic empire, opportunities for inhabitants to become part of the elite were increasing. The central government was on its way to granting Roman citizenship to nearly every free person in the empire, a process completed in 212. The emperors emphasized sharing prosperity and spreading it through the provinces. Italy was no longer the tyrant of the Mediterranean, but merely first among equals. This period, the Roman peace, seems particularly golden in contrast with what followed: the disastrous and disordered third century A.D., in which the empire came close to collapse but survived because of a radical and rigid transformation.

The Flavians and the "Good Emperors"

The Flavian dynasty of Vespasian (r. 69–79) and his sons Titus (r. 79–81) and Domitian (r. 81–96) offered good government, and their successors built on their achievements. Unlike the Julio-Claudians,

Vespasian hailed not from the old Roman nobility but from an Italian propertied family. A man of rough-and-ready character, Vespasian is supposed to have replied when Titus complained that a new latrine tax was beneath the dignity of the Roman government, "Son, money has no smell." Unlike his father and brother, Domitian reverted to frequent treason trials and persecution of the aristocracy, which earned him assassination in 96, although the empire as a whole enjoyed peace and good administration under his reign.

The so-called Five Good Emperors are Nerva (r. 96–98), Trajan (r. 98–117), Hadrian (r. 117–138), and the first two Antonines, Antoninus Pius (r. 138–161) and Marcus Aurelius (r. 161–180). They are in several ways examples of the principle of merit. Trajan, a Roman citizen born in Spain, was Rome's first emperor from outside Italy. Hadrian and Marcus Aurelius also came from Spain, and Antoninus Pius from Gaul. Each of the Five Good Emperors except Marcus Aurelius adopted the most competent person, rather than the closest blood relative, as his son and successor, thus elevating duty over sentiment. Marcus Aurelius, a deeply committed Stoic, gave full vent to his sense of duty in his *Meditations,* which he wrote in Greek while living in a tent on the Danube frontier, where he fought long and hard against German raids. Antoninus was surnamed "Pius" ("Dutiful") because he was devoted to his country, the gods, and his adoptive father, Hadrian.

The Five Good Emperors made humaneness and generosity a theme of their reigns. Trajan, for example, founded a program of financial aid for the poor children of Italy. They also went to great lengths to care for the provinces. Hadrian, a noted lover of Hellenism, lavished attention on Greece, particularly Athens. Both Hadrian and Antoninus Pius contributed generously to buildings in Roman Carthage. These emperors not only commonly received petitions from cities, associations, and individuals in far-off provinces but answered them.

Like the Julio-Claudians, the Five Good Emperors advertised their wives to the world as exemplars of traditional modesty, self-effacement, and domesticity. In fact, they were often worldly, educated, and influential. Trajan's wife, Plotina,

for example (d. A.D. 121 or 123), acted as patron of the Epicurean school at Athens, whose philosophy she claimed to follow. She advised her husband on provincial administration as well as dynastic matchmaking. Hadrian's wife, Sabina, traveled in her husband's entourage to Egypt (A.D. 130), where her aristocratic Greek friend, Julia Balbilla, commemorated the trip by writing Greek poetry, which she had inscribed alongside other tourists' writings on the leg of the colossal statue of Memnon. Balbilla cites her own "noble blood" and identifies Sabina as "the august wife of the Lord Hadrian."

A darker leitmotif in the reign of the second-century emperors was the ever present problem of border defense. Augustus and the Julio-Claudians had established client kingdoms where possible, to avoid the expense and political dangers of raising armies. Later emperors were inclined to be more aggressive. A new border policy begun under the Flavians was in full operation in the second century A.D.: stationary frontier defense. Expensive fortification systems of walls, watchtowers, and trenches were erected along the perimeter of the empire's border and manned with guards. A prominent example is Hadrian's Wall, which separated Roman Britain from the enemy tribes to the north. Stretching 80 miles, the wall required 15,000 defense troops.

The most ambitious policy was that of Trajan, who crossed the Danube to carve out the new province of Dacia (modern Romania) and who seized on a pretext to invade Parthian Mesopotamia. Although Trajan swept all before him and reached the Persian Gulf, his Parthian campaign was ultimately a disaster. As soon as his army withdrew, Mesopotamia rose in a general revolt, and the Germans followed suit. Trajan's reign marked the empire's greatest geographic extent, but Trajan had overextended Rome's resources. When he died, his successor, Hadrian, had to abandon Trajan's province of Mesopotamia (see Map 6.1).

Prosperity and Romanization in the Provinces

Compared to a modern economy, the Roman economy was underdeveloped. Most people worked in agriculture, employed primitive technology, and

Double Portrait, Pompeii
This wall painting from a house joined to a bakery depicts a married couple, possibly the wealthy baker P. Paquius Proculus and his wife. The portraiture is realistic. The couple carry symbols of education: She holds wax tablets and a stylus (pen), while he grasps a sealed scroll. *(Scala/Art Resource, NY)*

lived at a subsistence level. Even so, the Roman Empire experienced modest economic growth during the first two centuries A.D. The chief beneficiaries were the wealthy few, but ordinary people shared in the economic expansion as well. (See the box, "Ordinary People.") In addition to stability and peace, several other factors encouraged economic development. The western provinces witnessed the opening of new lands to agriculture, where improved techniques were applied. The growth of cities increased agricultural demand. Changes in Roman law aided commerce by making it easier to employ middlemen in business transactions. Travel and communications were relatively easy and inexpensive.

The second century A.D., like the Principate generally, was a great age of city life. New cities were founded far from the Mediterranean. Many would be of permanent importance in European history: Cologne (Colonia Claudia Agrippensis), Paris (Lutetia Parisiorum), Lyon (Lugdunum), London (Londinium), Mérida (Emerita Augusta), Vienna (Vindobona), and Budapest (Aquincum). Some of the new cities were veterans' colonies. Some were army camps that grew into towns. Some were market towns that grew by slow accretion.

Whether old or new, cities attracted a large elite population. The Principate was not a domain of country gentry, but rather one in which ambitious people wanted to live in great cities, in emulation of the greatest city of the empire, Rome, which was by Augustus's day a city of perhaps a million people. In cities men competed with each other for positions as magistrates, in imitation of

Ordinary People

These funerary inscriptions, chosen from different parts of the empire, are just a few of the tens of thousands of surviving epitaphs that shed light on the plain folk of the Roman world. They illustrate a variety of levels of success, ranging from a slave's poverty to a craftsman's prosperity to a boxing champion's money.

(a)

[Rome]   To the spirits of the departed. [Remains of] Marcus Canuleius Zosimus; he lived twenty-eight years; his patron erected this to a well-deserving freedman. In his lifetime he spoke ill of no one; he did nothing without his patron's consent; there was always a great weight of gold and silver in his possession, and he never coveted any of it; in his craft, Clodian [silver] engraving, he excelled everybody.

(b)

[Macedonia]   Here lies Vitalis, slave of Gaius Lavius Faustus and also his [adopted] son, a slave born in his home. He lived sixteen years, [was] a clerk at the Aprian shop, popular with the public, but snatched away by the gods. I beg your pardon, wayfarers, if I ever gave short measure to make more profit for my father. I beg you by the gods above and below to take good care of my father and mother. And farewell.

(c)

[Puteoli, Italy]   To Grania Clara, freedwoman of Aulus, a worthy freedwoman; she lived twenty-three years and never caused me any vexation, save by her death.

(d)

[Pompeii]   Laturnia Januaria, lime burner, lived 45 years.

(e)

[Anatolia]   You see me a corpse, passers-by. My . . . name was Apollonis, my native town Apamea, but now in the soil of Nicomedia the thread of destiny spun by the Fates holds me fast to the ground. Eight times he won in athletic games, but in the ninth boxing match he met his fated end. Play, laugh, passer-by, knowing that you too must die. His wife Alexandria erected this memorial out of his money as a remembrance. If anyone dares to disturb this monument, he shall pay a fine of 2,500 *denarii* to the fisc.

(f)

[Rome]   To the spirits of the departed. You wanted to precede me, most sainted wife, and you have left me behind in tears. If there is anything good in the regions below—as for me, I lead a worthless life without you—be happy there too, sweetest Thalassia, nurse of a *vir clarissimus* and married to me for forty years. Paprius Vitalis, of the painters' craft, her husband, built this for his incomparable wife, himself, and their family.

(g)

Sacred to the gods of the dead. To Hapate, a Greek stenographer [slave], who lived 25 years. Pittosus put this up for his sweetest wife.

(h)

To the gods of the dead. [The tomb] of Irene the wool-weigher. She lived 28 years. Olympus put this up [for] his well-deserving wife.

Sources: Inscriptions (a)–(f): Naphtali Lewis and Meyer Reinhold, *Roman Civilization. Sourcebook II: The Empire* (New York: Columbia University Press, 1966), pp. 261, 266, 284–285. Inscriptions (g)–(h): Mary R. Lefkowitz and Maureen B. Fant, trans., in their *Women's Life in Greece & Rome: A Source Book in Translation*, 2d ed. (Baltimore: Johns Hopkins University Press, 1992), p. 223.

the two consuls, or on the local town council, often called a *curia*, like the senate in Rome; town councilors were called *decurions* and known collectively as the *curial order*. Decurions further competed with each other in lavish expenditures on public buildings in the Roman style, one man endowing a new forum, another a triumphal arch, a third a library, a fourth public baths, and so on. From Ephesus in Anatolia to Colchester in Britain, from Mainz in Germany to Leptis Magna in Libya, a Roman could find familiar government institutions, architecture, and street plans. (See the feature, "Weighing the Evidence: Pompeii," on pages 224–225.)

Unlike men, women did not usually hold magistracies, but wealthy women of the empire could and did lavish money on public benefactions. Women endowed temples and synagogues, amphitheaters and monumental gateways, games and ceremonies. They were rewarded with wreaths, front-row seats, statues, priesthoods, and inscriptions honoring them as "most distinguished lady," "patron," and even as "father of the city," to cite an extraordinary case from Roman Egypt.

The buildings were visible examples of Romanization, although the Romans did not use the term. Roman officials frequently established Roman buildings and monuments or Latin schools for the children of a conquered local elite, but the emperors did not attempt to impose uniformity on their subjects. Even if they had aspired to do so, uniformity would have been out of reach, given the size of the empire and the low state of ancient technology. Scholarly estimates of the total population of the empire range between 50 and 100 million people, most of whom lived in the countryside. The

Leptis Magna A wealthy coastal city in what is today Libya, Leptis Magna shows the impact of Romanization in its splendidly preserved architecture. The Severans were special patrons of their ancestral town. The image shows the theater, with the rows of columns of an architectural façade and a portico-enclosed square beyond. *(Roger Wood/Corbis)*

ROMAN PEACE AND THIRD-CENTURY CRISIS

44 B.C.	Caesar assassinated
31 B.C.	Octavian defeats Antony at Actium
27 B.C.	Augustus establishes principate
ca. A.D. 27–30	Ministry of Jesus
ca. A.D. 67	Death of Paul of Tarsus
79	Eruption of Vesuvius
96–180	The "Five Good Emperors"
212	Almost all free inhabitants awarded Roman citizenship
235–283	Period of military anarchy

small and largely urbanized Roman administration had little direct contact with most people. So, for example, only a minority of the inhabitants of the empire spoke Latin; in the East, Greek was the more common language of administration. Millions of people spoke neither Greek nor Latin. Celtic, Germanic, Punic, Berber, Coptic, Aramaic, and Syriac were other languages commonly spoken in Roman domains. In short, the empire lacked the unity of a modern nation-state.

What, then, might one mean by Romanization, besides buildings and language? One index has already been suggested: the participation of provincials in the central government, even as emperor. By around A.D. 200, about 15 percent of the known Roman equestrians and senators came from North Africa. By this time, the senate was no longer dominated by Italians but was representative of the empire as a whole.

Participation in government implies another index of Romanization, the extension of Roman citizenship. Pompey and Caesar began the process of enfranchising individuals and communities outside the old borders of Roman Italy. The process continued under the Julio-Claudians and Flavians and flourished under the second-century emperors, who gave magistrates, decurions, or

whole cities the privilege of citizenship. Citizens took Roman names reflecting the emperor or promagistrate who had enfranchised them. Thus the provinces were full of Julii, Claudii, and Flavii, among others. They also afford many examples of the juxtaposition of Roman names. The existence of a Roman citizen named Gaius Julius Hannibal, for instance, says something about both the extent and the limits of Romanization.

Finally, in A.D. 212, in a law known as the *Constitutio Antoniana*, the emperor Caracalla (r. 211–217) rendered nearly all of the free inhabitants of the empire Roman citizens. This law was probably less an expression of a yearning for universal brotherhood than of a more prosaic desire to collect increased taxes, for citizens had a heavier tax burden than noncitizens. Nor did near-universal citizenship mean an end to ingrained social inequality. Rather, privileges previously inherent in citizenship, such as exemption from flogging by officials, now tended to be based on a class distinction, enshrined in private and criminal law: a distinction between *honestiores* (in general, the curial order) and *humiliores* (everyone else). However limited the privileges of citizenship, Caracalla's law was nevertheless a landmark act. Near-universal Roman citizenship was a kind of halfway point between ancient empire and modern mass democracy.

Two other institutions were crucial in Romanization: Roman law, with which local elites became familiar, and the Roman army. In antiquity as today, military service had an egalitarian and educational function. The legions were restricted to citizens; non-Romans served as auxiliaries. They received Roman citizenship after completing their regular term of service, twenty-five years. A Syrian or Gallic peasant who served in the Roman military would experience a way of life rooted in central Italy nearly a millennium before. Soldiers often formed liaisons with local women, and so passed on Roman mores to them and their children. Beginning in the reign of Septimius Severus (r. 193–211), soldiers were permitted to marry a woman formally after twenty-five years of service.

Non-Italians had, and took, the opportunity to rise high in the army or government. This was all to Rome's credit; yet as Italians became a minority in the Roman army, and as ever larger numbers of frontier peoples were recruited, it became conceivable that someday the army might give up its loyalty to Rome.

The Culture of the Roman Peace

In Latin poetry the century or so after the death of Augustus is often referred to as the "Silver Age," a term sometimes applied to prose as well. The implication is that this period fell short of the golden Augustan era. It might be fairer to say that the self-confidence of the Augustan writers did not last. As the permanence of monarchy became clear, many in the elite looked back to the Republic with nostalgia and bitterness. Silver Age writing often takes refuge in irony and satire, in epigrammatic pithiness, or in formality or rhetorical flourish. Writing under Trajan, for example, the historian Tacitus pours detailed scorn on the Julio-Claudians and Flavians. Other Silver Age writers indulged in flattery and obsequiousness toward the emperor.

The Silver Age was an era of interest in antiquities and in compiling handbooks and encyclopedias, an era of self-consciousness and literary criticism. In the first two centuries A.D., Roman writers came from an ever greater diversity of backgrounds and wrote for an ever wider audience, as prosperity and educational opportunities increased. Consider Lucian (ca. A.D. 115–ca. 185), an essayist and satirist. A native of Syria who probably spoke Aramaic before learning Greek, he served as an administrator in Roman Egypt.

Many writers of the era pursued public careers, which offered access to patronage. Tacitus, for instance, rose as high as proconsul of the province of Asia. Prominent literary families emerged, such as that of Pliny the Elder (A.D. 23–79), an encyclopedic author on natural science, geography, history, and art; and his nephew, Pliny the Younger (ca. A.D. 62–ca. 113), orator and letter writer. The most notable literary family is that of Seneca the Elder (ca. 55 B.C.–ca. A.D. 40), a historian and scholar of rhetoric; his son, Seneca the Younger (ca. 4 B.C.–A.D. 65); and Seneca the Younger's nephew, the epic poet Lucan (A.D. 39–65).

The family came from Cordoba in Spain; the younger Seneca moved at an early age to Rome, where he became a successful lawyer and wealthy investor. He was well connected enough to be banished in A.D. 41 for alleged adultery with a sister of Caligula. Recalled in 49, he became tutor to the young Nero. When Nero became emperor in 54, Seneca and the commander of the praetorians, Burrus, became his two chief advisers and between the two of them brought good government to the empire. When Burrus died in 62, however, Nero came under the influence of bad advisers, and Seneca was forced into retirement. Three years later Seneca was accused of conspiracy and forced into suicide, as was Lucan.

Seneca the Younger was the major literary figure of his age, a jack-of-all-trades: playwright, essayist, pamphleteer, student of science, and noted Stoic philosopher. Some have criticized his work as lively but insubstantial. Seneca's personal life, in contrast, was made of sterner stuff. He is known for his courageous suicide, in which he opened his veins and bled to death while calmly discussing philosophy. Seneca's wife, Pompeia Paulina, insisted on dying with him, in the tradition of the courageous Roman matron. Nero, however, had her arms bandaged and saved her life. He was thinking of his own reputation, which was already stained with enough cruelty, but gossip accused Paulina of betraying her husband.

A literary career was safer under the Five Good Emperors. Consider Tacitus and his contemporary, the poet Juvenal (ca. A.D. 55–130). Juvenal's *Satires* are bitter and brilliant poems offering social commentary. He lamented the past, when poverty and war had supposedly kept Romans chaste and virtuous. Amid "the woes of long peace," luxury and foreign ways had corrupted Rome, in his opinion. Critics often blame society's woes on marginal groups. Juvenal, for example, launches harsh attacks on women and foreigners. Tacitus, too, is sometimes scornful of women. He notes, for example, the charge that Livia had "a woman's lack of self-control."

Tacitus, if biased on matters of gender, was far from ethnocentric. Few historians have expressed graver doubts about the value of their country's alleged success. For example, Tacitus highlighted the simple virtues of the German tribes, so different from the sophisticated decadence of contemporary Rome. Nostalgia for the Republic pervades his two greatest works, *The Histories*, which covers the civil wars of A.D. 69, and *The Annals* (only parts of which survive), chronicling the emperors from Tiberius through Nero. A masterpiece of irony and pithiness, Tacitus's style makes an unforgettable impression on the reader. (See the box on page 198.)

Plutarch (ca. A.D. 50–ca. 120), whose *Parallel Lives of Noble Greeks and Romans* later captured the imagination of Shakespeare, is probably the best-known pagan Greek writer of the first two centuries A.D. Like Livy, Plutarch emphasized the moral and political lessons of history. A careful scholar, Plutarch found his true calling in rhetorical craftsmanship—polished speeches and carefully chosen anecdotes. As in Rome, rhetoric was the basis of much of Greek literary culture in this period.

Head of Trebonianus Gallus This is a detail of a full-length bronze statue that probably depicts Trebonianus Gallus, emperor for only two years (A.D. 251–253) in the troubled third century A.D. The stern gaze and harsh features are often found in the sculpture of the period. *(The Metropolitan Museum of Art [05.30])*

THE CRISIS OF THE THIRD CENTURY, A.D. 180–284

The portrait sculpture of the Antonine era (A.D. 138–192) differs significantly from the portrait sculpture of the third century A.D. Antonine sculpture recalls Augustan classicism: busts of the imperial family, for instance, show good-looking, hard-working men and women with regular, often idealized features and thoughtful expressions. In third-century imperial portrait busts, physical features are sharper, chisel work is coarser, and the uniformities of Greco-Roman classicism give way to diverse local styles. Third-century emperors are sometimes shown scowling or even looking anxiously into the distance.

The emperors had reason to be anxious. Leaving the relative calm of the second century A.D. behind, the third-century Roman Empire descended into an ever widening spiral of crisis. Barbarian invasions, domestic economic woes, plague, assassinations, brigandage, urban decline: the list of Rome's problems is dramatic. The empire went "from a kingdom of gold to one of iron and rust," as Dio Cassius put it, summing up Roman history after the death of Marcus Aurelius in A.D. 180.

Severan Ambitions

Stability first began to slip away during the reign of the last of the Antonines, Marcus Aurelius's birth-son, Commodus (r. 180–192), a man with Nero's taste for decadence and penchant for terrorizing the senatorial elite. Dressed like Hercules, he appeared in the amphitheater, where he shot animals in the morning and fought as a gladiator in the afternoon. Ever suspicious of enemies, Commodus planned to kill both new consuls on New Year's Day 193, but they beat him to the punch on New Year's Eve by having him murdered: his training partner, a professional athlete named Narcissus, strangled Commodus in his bath. After several years of civil war, Septimius Severus, commander of the Danube armies, emerged as the unchallenged emperor (r. 193–211); he founded the Severan dynasty, which survived until 235.

Septimius and his family illustrate the decentralization of the Roman elite. Septimius was born in Roman Libya, into one of the leading families of the city of Leptis Magna, an old Phoenician city. Though his family was of Phoenician descent, they were Roman citizens—his grandfather had been educated in Italy. Septimius spoke Latin with a provincial accent; he knew Greek, too, but not as well as Punic, which he needed to know when out in the family estates in the Libyan countryside. His wife, Julia Domna, was a Syrian from the city of Emesa, where Aramaic and Greek were the main languages. Her father, Julius Bassianus, was a priest of the main local god, Elegabal, and descended from royalty. She was a powerful woman in a family of powerful women. Indeed, the reigns of the last two Severan emperors (218–235), Julia's two grand-nephews, were dominated by first her sister and then her niece.

Severan reformers attempted to re-establish the empire on a firmer footing, but they only brought the day of crisis nearer. Septimius financed great building programs in Rome and in his native Leptis, but the main theme of his reign was the transfer of power—from the senate to the army and from Italy to the provinces. Septimius believed that security demanded an extension of the Roman frontier in North Africa and western Asia. To achieve this goal, he expanded the army and improved the pay and conditions of service. "Give the soldiers money and despise everyone else": so Dio Cassius reports his dying words to his son. Traditionalists decried the transformation of the Principate into a military monarchy, whose great marshals elbowed aside civilian officals. The traditionalists were right, yet in an age of increasing border challenges, the empire could hardly continue to afford constitutional niceties. Septimius's great mistake was indulging in war with Parthia (197–199)—unnecessary war, because the crumbling Parthian kingdom was too weak to threaten Rome. What the war *did* accomplish, however, was to inspire the enemy's rejuvenation under a new dynasty, the Sassanids.

Shock and Recovery

With the assassination of the last Severan emperor, Severus Alexander, in 235, the empire began a half-century of one shock after another. The main problem was increased pressure on Rome's frontiers. The Sassanid Persians overran Rome's east-

ern provinces and captured the emperor Valerian himself in 260. (See the box, "Encounters with the West: Syria Between Rome and Persia.") The caravan city of Palmyra (in modern Jordan) took advantage of Rome's weakness to establish independence; its most famous leader was the queen Zenobia. Meanwhile, two Germanic tribes, the Franks and the Goths, hammered the empire from the northwest and northeast.

Ever since the time of Augustus, financial restraint and political prudence had kept Rome's military manpower limited. The result of that limitation, plus fierce resistance by Germans, Britons, and Persians, was little overall expansion of Rome's borders during the Early Empire. The invasions of Roman territory in the third century stretched the system to the breaking point and beyond. To pay for defense, the emperors devalued the currency. The result was massive inflation. As if this were not bad enough, a plague broke out in Egypt in midcentury and raged through the empire for fifteen years, compounding Rome's military manpower problems.

Assassinations and civil wars shook the stability of the government. Between 235 and 284, twenty men were emperor, however briefly in some cases. Civilians suffered. Pretenders to the purple needed to raise armies, and therefore taxes. To keep one step ahead of the tax collector and military recruiter, some civilians fled cities for the countryside, where some of them turned to brigandage. Those who remained in town faced greater financial burdens. Recognizing a shortage of potential benefactors and decurions, the emperors decreed that membership in the curial order become hereditary and that decurions be responsible for financing public services. Such decrees were easier to promulgate than to enforce.

The ability of the empire to rebound from such problems is a tribute to Roman resilience and a sign of the disunity and lack of staying power among the empire's enemies. Recovery began during the reign of Gallienus (r. 253–268), who ended the Frankish threat and nearly polished off the Goths. By 275, the Goths were defeated and the eastern provinces, including Palmyra, were reconquered. Gallienus excluded senators from high military commands and replaced them with professionals. Moreover, he began a new, more modest policy of border defense. The Romans now

⁓ ENCOUNTERS WITH THE WEST ⁓

Syria Between Rome and Persia

Rome and Persia fought three great battles in western Asia in A.D. *244, 252, and 260, all resulting in resounding victories for Persia under King Shapur I (r. ca. 241–272). In the first selection Shapur celebrates his success in an inscription carved in rock near Persepolis. The second selection provides a Greek view of what Syria's inhabitants endured when Shapur "burned, ruined and pillaged" in* A.D. *252. The selection comes from the* **Thirteenth Sibylline Oracle,** *a verse commentary on contemporary events, purporting to be ancient prophecy.*

(a)

I, the Mazda worshipping lord Shapur, king of kings of Iran and non-Iran, whose lineage is from the Gods. . . .

When at first we had become established in the empire, Gordian Caesar raised in all of the Roman Empire a force from the Goth and German realms and marched on Babylonia against the Empire of Iran and against us. On the border of Babylonia at Misikhe, a great "frontal" battle occurred. Gordian Caesar was killed and the Roman force was destroyed. And the Romans made Philip Caesar. Then Philip Caesar came to us for terms, and to ransom their lives, gave us 500,000 *denars,* and became tributary to us. . . .

And Caesar lied again and did wrong to Armenia. Then we attacked the Roman Empire and annihilated at Barbalissos a Roman force of 60,000 and Syria and the environs of Syria we burned, ruined and pillaged all. In this one campaign we conquered of the Roman Empire fortresses and towns . . . a total of 37 towns with surroundings.

In the third campaign when we attacked Carrhae and Urhai [Edessa] and were besieging Carrhae and Edessa Valerian Caesar marched against us. He had with him a force of 70,000. . . .

And beyond Carrhae and Edessa we had a great battle with Valerian Caesar. We made prisoner ourselves with our own hands Valerian Caesar and the others, chiefs of that army, the praetorian prefect, senators; we made all prisoners and deported them to Persis.

And Syria, Cilicia and Cappadocia we burned, ruined and pillaged. . . .

And men of the Roman Empire, of non-Iranians, we deported. We settled them in the Empire of Iran. . . .

We searched out for conquest many other lands, and we acquired fame for heroism, which we have not engraved here, except for the preceding. We ordered it written so that whoever comes after us may know this fame, heroism, and power of us.

(b)

. . . the evil Persians . . .
. . . the Persians, arrogant men . . .
. . . the arrow-shooting Persians . . .

Now for you, wretched Syria, I have lately been piteously lamenting; a blow will befall you from the arrow-shooting men, terrible, which you never thought would come to you. The fugitive of Rome will come, waving a great spear; crossing the Euphrates with many myriads, he will burn you, he will dispose all things

evilly. Alas, Antioch, they will never call you a city when you have fallen under the spear in your folly; he will leave you entirely ruined and naked, houseless, uninhabited; anyone seeing you will suddenly break out weeping. . . . Alas . . . they will leave ruin as far as the borders of Asia, stripping the cities, taking the statues of all and razing the temples down to the all-nourishing earth.

Sources: Excerpt (a): Richard N. Frye, trans., in his *History of Ancient Iran* (Munich: C. H. Beck'sche Verlagsbuch-handlung, 1984), pp. 371–372. Excerpt (b): D. S. Potter, trans., in his *Prophecy and History in the Crisis of the Roman Empire* (Oxford: Clarendon Press, 1990), p. 175.

conceded much of the frontier to the enemy. They instead used fortified cities near the frontier as bases from which to prevent deeper enemy penetration into Roman territory. They also concentrated mobile armies at strategic points in the rear, moving them where needed.

Gallienus's reforms pointed the way to imperial reorganization, but they remained to be completed by the two great reforming emperors at the end of the third century and the beginning of the fourth: Diocletian (r. 284–305) and Constantine (r. 306–337), subjects of the next chapter. When their work was done, the new Roman Empire of Late Antiquity might have barely been recognizable to a citizen of the Principate.

EARLY CHRISTIANITY

Increasing contact between Rome and its western provinces served to plant Roman cities, Roman law, and the Latin language (or its derivatives) in western Europe. As Rome in turn owed much to other Mediterranean peoples, it may be said that the Roman Empire was a vessel that transported ancient Mediterranean civilization to northern and western Europe. No feature of that civilization was to have a greater historical impact than the religion born in Tiberius's reign: Christianity.

Christianity began in the provincial backwater of Palestine among the Jews, whose language, Aramaic, was understood by few in Rome. It immediately spread to speakers of the two main languages of the empire, Greek and Latin, and the new movement addressed the common spiritual needs of the Roman world. By the reign of Diocletian, Christians had grown from the twelve apostles, Jesus's original disciples, to millions, despite government persecution (Map 6.2). In the fourth century A.D., Christianity unexpectedly became the official religion of the entire Roman Empire, replacing paganism—one of the most momentous changes in Mediterranean history. We turn to that change in the next chapter; here we consider the career of Jesus and the early spread of the Christian Gospel (literally, "Good Tidings").

Jesus of Nazareth

Christianity begins with Jesus. For all its historical importance, Jesus's life is poorly documented. The main source of information about it is the New Testament books of Matthew, Mark, Luke, and John. Jesus left no writings of his own. Early Christians, however, wrote a great deal. Between the second and fourth centuries A.D., Christians settled on a holy book consisting of both the Hebrew Bible, called the "Old Testament" by Christians, and a collection of writings about Jesus and his followers, called the "New Testament." The account of the Gospel According to Mark, probably the earliest Gospel, was most likely written about forty years after Jesus's crucifixion; several of the letters written by Paul of Tarsus (see page 216) date from the 40s A.D.; earliest pagan sources date from the early second century A.D. and are scanty.

No personality has generated as much discussion among Western scholars as has Jesus. Many would distinguish the Jesus of theology, the object of faith, from the Jesus of history, the figure who really lived in first-century Palestine. Recent work argues that the historical Jesus must be understood within the Judaism of his day. He was a product of the popular culture of the Palestinian countryside, a culture that was peasant and oral. Much of what the Gospels have to say about Jesus, some argue, must be rejected as later invention. These are controversial points, but many scholars would agree with one thing: We must be careful to avoid anachronism. By A.D. 200, there had emerged two new religions, orthodox Christianity and rabbinic Judaism (see page 217). Both groups claimed to be the rightful heir of the biblical Covenant. They engendered new perspectives that have colored the way Christians and Jews envisage the past before 200. The following account of Jesus seeks a middle ground among today's schools of interpretation.

Jesus was born a Jew. A speaker of Aramaic, he may have also known at least some Greek, widely spoken by both Jews and non-Jews in the several Hellenized cities of Palestine. To his followers, Jesus was Christ—"the anointed one" (from Greek *Christos*), the man anointed with oil and thus marked as the king of Israel. They considered him, that is, the Messiah (from the Hebrew for "anointed one") foretold in the Hebrew Bible who would redeem the children of Israel and initiate the kingdom of heaven. The dynamism and popularity of his teachings led to a clash with Jewish and Roman authorities in Jerusalem, the capital city of Judea, and to his

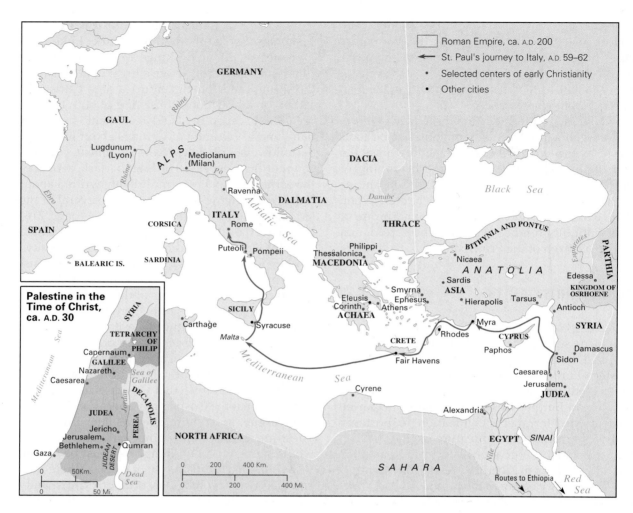

Map 6.2 The Expansion of Christianity to A.D. 200 After its origin in Palestine, early Christianity found its main centers in the Greek-speaking cities of the Roman East. Missionaries like Paul also brought the new faith to the Latin-speaking West, as well as to Ethiopia and Mesopotamia.

crucifixion. His mission began, however, in a corner of the Jewish world, in the northern region of Galilee, where he lived in the town of Nazareth (see inset, Map 6.2).

Jesus was probably born not long before the death in 4 B.C. of Herod, the Roman-installed client-king of Judea. (The date of 1 A.D. for Jesus's birth, a mistaken calculation of Late Antiquity, does not accord with the data of the New Testament.) At around age 30, Jesus was baptized by the mysterious preacher John the Baptist; soon afterward Herod Antipas, the Romans' client-king

of Galilee, ordered the execution of John. John preached the imminence of God's kingdom, a time of universal perfection and an end of misery. In preparation, sinful humankind needed to repent. Precisely how much influence John had on Jesus is a matter of debate, as is the question of John's relationship to the religious community of the Essenes. Judaism in the first century A.D. was in a state of creative and turbulent ferment, of which the Essenes are but one example. Indeed, in this era there was no one normative Judaism, but rather a variety of Judaisms.

The Good Shepherd This ceiling painting comes from a Christian catacomb in Rome dating before A.D. 284. The pastoral image, common in the early church, recalls Christ's ministry. It symbolizes both his beneficence and his sacrifice, as well as his closeness to ordinary people. *(Scala/Art Resource, NY)*

The Essenes lived apart from society in pursuit of a new covenant with God. The community at Qumran in the Judean desert, whose history is documented in the Dead Sea Scrolls, ancient texts discovered in 1947, was probably Essene. The tenets of Qumran included frugality, sharing, participating in a sacred communal meal, and avoiding oath-taking. Adherents anticipated the coming of the Messiah and an end of days in which God would punish the wicked. Although Essene doctrine has much in common with early Christianity, early Christians did not withdraw from the world as the Essenes did, but faced it.

There are both similarities and differences between Jesus's teaching and contemporary doctrines of Palestinian Judaism. The most popular group among Palestinian Jews, the Pharisees, focused on the spiritual needs of ordinary folk (see page 147). Pharisees believed that law was central to Judaism but argued that it could be interpreted flexibly, in light of the oral tradition that had grown up alongside the Hebrew Bible. The Pharisees believed in the superiority of spiritual to political matters. They emphasized charity toward the poor. They spoke in parables, vivid allegories that made their teaching accessible.

Jesus argued similarly. Like the Pharisees, moreover, he strongly criticized the pillar of the Jewish establishment, the Sadducees, a small group of priests and wealthy men who saw the

Jerusalem Temple and its rites as the heart of Judaism. Like the Pharisees, Jesus rejected the growing movement of the Zealots, advocates of revolt against Roman rule, although there were Zealots among his followers. Yet Jesus was neither a Pharisee nor an Essene. His teaching went further than the Pharisees in rejecting the need to follow the letter of biblical law. Inward purity became the key principle, as reflected in Jesus's statement to his disciples: "Whoever does not accept the kingdom of God like a child will never enter it" (Mark 10:15). Only an adult could become expert in biblical law, but it is probably easier for a child than for an adult to attain spiritual innocence.

Jesus argued that the kingdom of God, which John the Baptist had said was imminent, was actually already beginning to arrive. Jesus, moreover, said that he himself, acting through the direct order of God, could forgive sins. He emphasized the notion of God as a loving and forgiving father. Jesus often spoke in parables and announced himself through miracles, particularly faith healing. He welcomed marginalized groups, including such sinners as prostitutes and tax collectors. As a result, he won a wide following.

Jesus's teaching is typified in the Sermon on the Mount, addressed to his followers in Galilee. He praised the poor and the humble and scorned the pursuit of wealth instead of righteousness. He called for generosity and forgiveness, recalling the traditional Jewish Golden Rule—to treat others as one would like to be treated. He said that prayer, fasting, and acts of charity should be conducted in private, not in public, in order to emphasize purity of motive. He called on his followers to endure persecution in order to spread his teachings: "You are light for all the world," he said.

Jesus spoke with conviction and persuasiveness—with "authority," as his followers said. In Galilee they greeted him as king. For some this was a purely spiritual designation; others planned an overthrow of Roman rule, although Jesus rejected that course of action. In any case, his teachings won him hostility from some Pharisees, who considered blasphemous his claim to be able to forgive sins, and from Sadducees stung by his criticisms. Neither group accepted Jesus as the Messiah.

Jesus challenged central authority by going to Jerusalem and teaching and healing in the Temple under the eyes of the priests whom he criticized. Nor did he confine his opposition to words: He drove merchants and moneychangers away from the Temple precincts by overturning their tables and perhaps even threatening them with a whip. Jesus attracted large crowds of followers, at least some of whom were armed. Sadducee authorities feared trouble, and so did the overlords of Judea, the Romans. The governor, Pilate (Pontius Pilatus), had already endured vehement Jewish objections to the display in Jerusalem of an imperial medallion and of an inscription that seems to have asserted Augustus's divinity. Pilate had no need of further uproar. Temple police and Roman soldiers were called on to arrest Jesus quietly.

Jesus's subsequent trial and execution have always been controversial. The New Testament emphasizes the role of the Jewish leadership and the Jerusalem mob in Jesus's death. Written after the First Jewish Revolt (A.D. 66–77), however, the Gospels may reflect anti-Jewish sentiment in the empire. Crucifixion, the method used to execute Jesus, was a Roman penalty (the traditional Jewish method was stoning) imposed and carried out by Romans. Jesus probably appeared in informal and hurried proceedings before both the Jewish Council and Pilate. He suffered slow death by crucifixion on Golgotha (Calvary) Hill just outside the city. It was a spring Friday, on the eve of the Passover festival, around A.D. 30.

Paul of Tarsus

According to the Gospel writers, Jesus died on a Friday and rose from the dead on Sunday, an event commemorated at Easter. He is said to have then spent forty days on earth, cheering his disciples in Galilee and working miracles, before finally ascending to heaven. Heartened, the disciples returned to Jerusalem and spread Jesus's teachings. They preached in synagogues, private households, and even the Temple, and to Greek-speaking as well as Palestinian Jews. Their movement spread in the thirties and forties A.D. throughout Palestine and into Syria. In Jerusalem Christians were known as Nazarenes—that is, followers of Jesus of Nazareth; it was at Antioch that they were first called "men of Christ" (*christianoi*).

It was not clear at first that Christians would form a new religion separate from Judaism. Although Sadducees and Jewish civil officials were hostile, Christians found much support among Pharisees. Some Christians, however, contemplated a radical break; among them no one was more important than Paul of Tarsus (d. A.D. 67?).

Only Jesus himself played a greater role than Paul in the foundation of Christianity. A remarkable figure, Paul embodied three different and interlocking worlds. Born with the name of Saul, he was a Jew of the Diaspora from the southern Anatolian city of Tarsus. A learned Pharisee, Paul was a native speaker of Aramaic and knew Hebrew and Greek. His father was one of the few Jews to attain Roman citizenship, a privilege that Paul inherited. Paul's heritage speaks volumes about the variety of the Roman peace, and his religious odyssey speaks volumes more (see Map 6.2).

At first Paul joined in the persecution of the Christians, whom he considered blasphemous. Around A.D. 36, however, he claimed to see a blinding light on the road to Damascus, a vision of Jesus that convinced him to change from persecutor to believer. It was a complete turnaround, a *conversio* ("conversion"), to use the Latin word that would grow so important in years to come. Saul changed his name to Paul and became a Christian.

He also changed what being a Christian meant. The key to Paul's faith was not so much Jesus's life, although that was a model for Christian ethics, as it was Jesus's death and resurrection. Jesus's fate, Paul wrote, offered all humanity the hope of resurrection, redemption, and salvation. Paul retained his belief in Jewish morality and ethics but not in the rules of Jewish law. Following the law, no matter how carefully, would not lead to salvation; only faith in Jesus as Messiah would.

Such doctrines bespoke a break with Judaism, as did Paul's attitudes toward converts. Hellenistic Judaism had long reached out to Gentiles. Some became Jews. Others, scattered throughout the cities of the Roman Empire, were known as "God-fearers"—that is, they accepted the moral teachings of Judaism but refrained from following strict dietary laws, circumcision, and other Jewish rituals. Seneca the Younger, writing in the sixties, complains about the spread of Judaism: "The customs of this accursed race have gained such influence that they are now received throughout the world."[2]

The Jerusalem church baptized converts and considered them Jews, but Paul considered them not Jews but converts in Christ. For Pauline Christians there was no circumcision, no dietary laws, no strict observance of the Sabbath. From the late forties to the early sixties A.D., Paul tirelessly undertook missionary journeys through the cities of the Roman East and to Rome itself. He aimed to convert Gentiles, and so he did; but many of his followers were Hellenized Jews and "God-fearers." (See the box, "Christian Community and Christian Relationships.")

Paul started Christianity on the road to complete separation from Judaism. Events over the next century widened the division. First, while Pauline churches prospered, departing ever more from Jewish customs, the Jerusalem church was decimated. Jewish authorities persecuted its leaders and, after Rome's suppression of the First Jewish Revolt in A.D. 70, the rank and file of Palestinian Jews rallied to the Pharisees. Second, Jews and Christians competing for converts emphasized their respective differences. Third, although many Jews made their peace with Rome in A.D. 70, enough Jewish-Roman hostility remained to lead to uprisings in the Diaspora in 115 and to the Second Jewish Revolt in 132–135. Both were suppressed by Rome, and Judaism became ever more stigmatized among Gentiles.

Bereft of the Temple at Jerusalem, Judaism nonetheless continued to prosper as a religion. Indeed, Jewish missionary activities continued, although they did not keep pace with the number of converts gained by Christianity. More striking is the emergence of the rabbis (the religious leaders of the Pharisees) as the mentors of Judaism. Popular among Jews, the rabbis also attracted the Romans, because most rabbis opposed revolt. After both A.D. 70 and 135, the Romans made the rabbis responsible for Jewish self-government in Palestine. The rabbis left their mark on history, however, in an intellectual movement and not administration. Continuing in the tradition of the Pharisees, the rabbis amplified the oral law, that is, they wrote interpretations of the Hebrew Bible that clarified the practice of Judaism. They developed the notion of the "dual Torah," that is, the divine authority of the

Christian Community and Christian Relationships

Traditionally considered a letter of Paul to the church of Ephesus, "Ephesians" is perhaps rather the work of a Pauline Christian in about A.D. 100. As in undisputed letters of Paul, the text emphasizes the union of Jew and Gentile in the new Christian community: a community of spiritual equality but physical hierarchy by age, class, and gender.

(a)

Remember then your former condition, Gentiles as you are by birth, "the uncircumcised" as you are called by those who call themselves "the circumcised" because of a physical rite. You were at that time separate from Christ, excluded from the community of Israel, strangers to God's covenants and the promise that goes with them. Yours was a world without hope and without God. Once you were far off, but now in union with Christ Jesus you have been brought near through the shedding of Christ's blood. For he is himself our peace. Gentiles and Jews, he has made the two one, and in his own body of flesh and blood has broken down the barrier of enmity which separated them; for he annulled the law with its rules and regulations, so as to create out of the two a single new humanity in himself, thereby making peace. This was his purpose, to reconcile the two in a single body to God through the cross, by which he killed the enmity. So he came and proclaimed the good news: peace to you who were far off, and peace to those who were near; for through him we both alike have access to the Father in the one Spirit.

(b)

Be subject to one another out of reverence for Christ.

Wives, be subject to your husband as though to the Lord; for the man is the head of the woman, just as Christ is the head of the church. Christ is, indeed, the saviour of the body; but just as the church is subject to Christ, so must women be subject to their husbands in everything.

Husbands, love your wives, as Christ loved the church and gave himself up for it, to consecrate and cleanse it by water and word, so that he might present the church to himself all glorious, with no stain or wrinkle or anything of the sort, but holy and without blemish. In the same way men ought to love their wives, as they love their own bodies. In loving his wife a man loves himself. For no one ever hated his own body . . . the husband must love his wife as his very self, and the wife must show reverence for her husband.

Children, obey your parents; for it is only right that you should. . . .

Fathers, do not goad your children to resentment, but bring them up in the discipline and instruction of the Lord.

Slaves, give single-minded obedience to your earthly masters with fear and trembling, as if to Christ. Give cheerful service, as slaves of the Lord rather than of men. You know that whatever good anyone may do, slave or free, will be repaid by the Lord.

Masters, treat your slaves in the same spirit: give up using threats, and remember that you both have the same Master in heaven; there is no favouritism with him.

Source: The Letter of Paul to the Ephesians 2:11–17, 5:21–6:9, in *The Oxford Study Bible: Revised English Bible with the Apocrypha* (New York: Oxford University Press, 1992).

oral law as well as of written law of the Hebrew Bible. The notion legitimized the rabbis' enterprise, which made it possible for Judaism to evolve flexibly. The basic text of rabbinic Judaism is the Mishnah (ca. A.D. 200), a study of Jewish law. In rabbinic Judaism lies the basis of the medieval and modern forms of the Jewish religion.[3]

Expansion, Divergence, Persecution

Although Jesus's mission was mainly in the countryside, early Christianity quickly became primarily an urban movement. Through missionary activity and word of mouth, the religion slowly spread. It was concentrated in the Greek-speaking East, but by the second century A.D. there were churches in North Africa and Gaul and, beyond Roman boundaries, in Parthian Iraq and in Ethiopia (see Map 6.2).

By around A.D. 200, an orthodox (Greek for "right-thinking") Christianity had emerged. Rooted in Judaism, it was nonetheless a distinct and separate religion that found most of its supporters among Gentiles. A simple "rule of faith," emphasizing belief in one God and the mission of his son, Jesus, as savior, united Christians from one end of the empire to the other. Christianity attracted both rich and poor, male and female; its primary appeal was to ordinary, moderately prosperous city folk. Believers could take comfort from the prospect of salvation in the next world and in a caring community in the here-and-now. Christians emphasized charity and help for the needy, qualities all too often absent in Greco-Roman society. A Christian writer justly described a pagan's amazed comment on Christian behavior: "Look how they love each other." Most early Christians expected Christ's return to be imminent, upon which he would inaugurate the heavenly kingdom. This belief imparted urgency and excitement to their message.

Early churches were simple and relatively informal congregations that gathered for regular meetings. The liturgy, or service, consisted of readings from the Scriptures (the Old and New Testaments), teaching, praying, and singing hymns. Baptism was used to initiate converts. The Lord's Supper, a communal meal in memory of Jesus, was

a major ritual. The most important parts of the meal were the breaking and distribution of bread at the beginning and the passing of a cup of wine at the end; these recalled the body and blood of Christ. As organizational structures emerged (see page 233), churches in different cities were in frequent contact with each other, discussing common concerns and coordinating doctrine and practice.

Just as Jewish women were not rabbis, so early Christian women did not hold the priesthood. Jewish women, however, did hold office in the synagogue, and Christian women likewise served as deaconesses. Both endowed buildings and institutions. For example, consider the Italian Jewish woman Caelia Paterna, an officeholder honored by her congregation as "mother of the synagogue of the people of Brescia." Or the two Christian deaconesses, both slaves, whom Pliny the Younger had tortured during his governorship of the Anatolian province of Bithynia (ca. A.D. 110) in an attempt to extract information about the worrisome new cult. Deaconesses played an active part in church charities and counseling and now and then gave sermons.

As Christianity spread, its troubles with the authorities deepened. For one thing, Christians met in small groups, a kind of assembly that conservative Romans had long suspected as a potential source of sedition. More troubling, however, was Christians' refusal to make sacrifices to the emperor. The Romans expected all subjects to make such sacrifices as a sign of patriotism. The only exception was the Jews, who were permitted to forgo the imperial cult because their ancestral religion prohibited them from worshiping idols. The Christians, however, were a new group, and Romans distrusted novelty.

As a result, the emperors considered Christianity at best a nuisance and at worst a threat. Christians were tested from time to time by being asked to sacrifice to the emperor; those who failed to do so might be executed. At times of stress when scapegoats were needed, Christians were sometimes brought to the arena to be fed to the animals. More often, however, Romans tacitly tolerated Christians as long as they kept their religion private. Christians could not proselytize in public places, put up inscriptions or monuments, or build churches. Christianity thus spread under severe restrictions, but spread it did, particularly in the cities of the East. The willingness of martyrs to die for the faith made a strong impression on potential converts. Although the number of Christians in the empire is not known, it is clear that by the late third century they were, although a minority, a significant and growing one.

Mystery Religions

Roman policy toward Christianity by no means reflected an attempt to impose a single, unified relig-

Mithraeum This sculpted relief comes from an underground sanctuary along the Rhine frontier. It shows the hero-god Mithras sacrificing a bull, the central symbol of Mithraism. Actual bull sacrifices were carried out in Mithraea. *(Hildesheim Museum/Richard Erdoes)*

ion on the empire. Polytheists, Romans were usually willing to admit new gods to their pantheon, as long as their worshipers took part in the patriotic emperor cult. Roman conservatism, moreover, engendered respect for other peoples' traditional faiths. Although from time to time during Roman history the authorities had tried to expel these faiths from the city of Rome itself, the spread of new religions during the first three centuries A.D. proved irresistible. Besides Christianity and Judaism, the most important were Greek mystery cults, the cults of Isis and Mithras, and Manichaeism. These religions displayed a tendency toward syncretism, often borrowing rites, doctrines, and symbols from one another.

Greek mystery cults included cults of Dionysus, the god of wine, and of Demeter, goddess of grain, who was worshiped at annual ceremonies at Eleusis, a town outside Athens. The "mystery" consisted of secret rites revealed only to initiates. In the case of Demeter, the rites apparently had something to do with the promise of eternal life.

The cult of Isis derived from the ancient Egyptian cult of Isis (see page 145), her brother and husband, Osiris, and their son, Horus. Its central theme, too, was eternal life, through the promise of resurrection achieved by moral behavior in this life. Isis, the "Goddess of Ten Thousand Names," was portrayed as a loving mother caring for her son; elements of Isis were later syncretized in the cult of the Virgin Mary. Followers of Isis marched in colorful and at times terrifying parades through the streets of Roman cities, flagellating themselves as a sign of penitence.

Although men joined in the worship of Isis, the cult appealed particularly to women. The goddess's popularity crossed class lines; devotees ranged from slaves to one Julia Felix, whose estate at Pompeii included a garden shrine to Isis and Egyptian statuettes. By contrast with the followers of Isis, men, especially soldiers, dominated the worship of Mithras. Mithras, a heroic Persian god of light and truth, also promised eternal life. His worshipers believed that Mithras had captured and killed a sacred bull whose blood and body were the source of life. Accordingly, Mithraism focused on bull sacrifice carried out in a vaulted, cavelike temple called a *Mithraeum*. Initiates were baptized with bull blood and participated in various other rituals, among them a sacramental meal. Their moral code advised a life led in imitation of their hero.

Manichaeism also originated in Persia, but later, in the third century A.D. The founder, the Persian priest Mani, was martyred by conservative religious authorities. Mani is said to have traveled to India. His cult recognized not only Jesus but Zoroaster and Buddha as prophets. Manichaeism was characterized by philosophical dualism, which emphasized the universal struggle between good (Light) and evil (Darkness). According to believers, the world had been corrupted by Darkness, but eventually the Light would return. In the meantime, good Manichaeans were to attempt to lead pure lives. Much attention, for instance, was placed on proper diet. Manichaeism was a powerful religious force for two centuries; the great theologian Augustine flirted with it before becoming a Christian.

SUMMARY

Between the first century B.C. and the third century A.D., the Romans changed from a people who had come to destroy into a people who had come to fulfill. At the beginning of this period, the conquered provinces were oppressed by greedy bureaucrats and tax collectors, and Rome's imperial victories had nearly ruined the Italian peasantry, who lost their farms while fighting in the Roman army. Members of the Roman elite raised private armies to win land for their followers and glory for themselves. The Republic collapsed under the weight of political maneuvering, judicial murders, gang warfare, and civil war.

A shrewd and sickly outsider, Octavian, confounded expectations by creating a new empire that would enjoy two centuries of stability; as Augustus, he served as its first emperor. Augustus reconciled the senatorial class by sharing a degree of power, but he guaranteed peace by keeping most of the armies in his own hand. He wisely accepted compromise with Parthia and defeat in Germany, reduced military spending, and stabilized the frontiers. He solved the problem of the landless peasantry by raising taxes to provide farms for all veterans. Perhaps most important, he began a new policy toward the provinces, which

were slowly raised to equality with Italy. In short, Augustus initiated the prosperous Roman peace, an era lasting until the third century A.D. To survive the crises of that century, it was necessary for Rome to have a bigger army supported by higher taxes collected by a larger bureaucracy, requirements that would shake the social, political, and cultural foundations of the empire, as Chapter 7 discusses.

Literature and the arts flourished in the peaceful period of the Early Empire. In the provinces, the Roman peace made possible an era of architectural and literary flowering. Rome was a multiethnic empire whose inhabitants increasingly mixed with each other and exchanged ideas. None of these exchanges was more momentous than the emergence of several new religions, one of which would become in Late Antiquity the main religion of the Roman world: Christianity. Without the Roman peace of the Caesars, the Christian Gospel could not have been spread.

NOTES

1. Mary R. Lefkowitz and Maureen B. Fant, trans., in their *Women's Life in Greece & Rome. A Source Book in Translation*, 2d ed. (Baltimore: Johns Hopkins University Press, 1992), p. 9.
2. Seneca, *De Superstitione*, trans. Menachem Stern, in *Greek and Latin Authors on Jews and Judaism*, vol. 1 (Jerusalem: The Israel Academy of Sciences and Humanities, 1976), p. 431.
3. On these points, see Lawrence H. Schiffman, *From Text to Tradition: A History of Second Temple and Rabbinic Judaism* (Hoboken, N.J.: Ktav Publishing House, 1991), pp. 1–16.

SUGGESTED READING

See also the suggested readings for Chapter 5; several of the works cited there cover the period of Chapter 6 as well.

General Surveys

Gardner, Jane F. *Women in Roman Law and Society*. 1986. A straightforward survey concentrating on the Late Republic and Early Empire.

Garnsey, Peter, and Richard Saller. *The Roman Empire: Economy, Society, and Culture*. 1987. A thematic rather than chronological introduction by two distinguished social historians.

MacMullen, Ramsay. *Roman Social Relations 50 B.C.–A.D. 284.* 1981. A wide-ranging essay in social history that moves between anecdote and general trend.

Scullard, H. H. *From the Gracchi to Nero.* 5th ed. 1982. A concise and reliable introduction, with an emphasis on political history. Excellent bibliographies.

Augustus and the Principate

Earl, D. C. *The Age of Augustus.* 1968. A beautifully illustrated introduction to government, society, and religion.

Raaflaub, K., and M. Toher, eds. *Between Republic and Empire: Interpretations of Augustus and His Principate.* 1990. A good selection of the latest scholarly theories and controversies.

Syme, Sir Ronald. *The Roman Revolution.* Rev. ed. 1960. A classic and controversial analysis of Augustus, who, Syme thinks, never seriously shared power with the senate. A work of remarkable literary style.

Wirszubski, C. *Libertas as a Political Idea at Rome During the Late Republic and Early Principate.* 1960. An essay on ideology and practice, with an eye toward the uniqueness of Roman notions of liberty and their difference from modern notions.

The Roman Peace

Carcopino, J. *Daily Life in Ancient Rome: The People and the City at the Height of the Empire.* 1940. Somewhat out of date but a scholarly introduction that is both informative and a pleasure to read.

Luttwak, E. N. *The Grand Strategy of the Roman Empire from the First Century A.D. to the Third.* 1976. A perceptive overview by a nonspecialist of the evolution of strategies of imperial defense from Augustus to the Late Empire.

Millar, F. G. B. *The Emperor in the Roman World, 31 B.C.– A.D. 337.* 1977. A detailed and informative study of the duties and entourage of the emperor as well as a more general discussion of the Roman imperial government.

———. *The Roman Near East, 31 B.C.–A.D. 337.* 1993. A thoughtful, meticulous, and important study of ethnicity and empire, making special use of inscriptions.

Rostovtzeff, Michael I. *Social and Economic History of the Roman Empire.* 2d ed. 1971. A brilliant, ambitious, and original account, although out of date and its analysis of the third-century crisis is no longer convincing.

Saller, Richard. *Patriarchy, Property, and Death in the Roman Family.* 1994. A groundbreaking study of the demographic roots of familial sentiments.

Stambaugh, John E. *The Ancient Roman City.* 1988. A synthesis of archaeology and social history to illustrate the fabric of urban life.

Thompson, Lloyd A. *Romans and Blacks.* 1989. A fascinating study of black Africans and the Roman Empire. Discusses Roman categories of race and ethnicity and contrasts stereotypes and the reality of social relations.

Treggiari, Susan. *Roman Marriage: Iusti Coniuges from the Time of Cicero to the Time of Ulpian.* 1991. An up-to-date and thorough discussion.

Third-Century Crisis

Birley, Anthony. *Septimius Severus: The African Emperor.* Rev. ed. 1988. Lively and scholarly, this biography seamlessly blends narrative and analysis.

MacMullen, Ramsay. *Roman Government's Response to Crisis.* 1976. An analytical overview of the third century A.D. with special attention to institutions and society.

Potter, D. S. *Prophecy and History in the Crisis of the Roman Empire.* 1990. A detailed historical study of the *Thirteenth Sybilline Oracle* as a contemporary comment on the troubles of the third-century empire.

Religion

Chadwick, Henry. *The Early Church.* 1967. An account that covers approximately the same period as Frend's book (see below) but is briefer and more concise and emphasizes theology.

Cohen, Shaye J. D. *From the Maccabees to the Mishnah.* 1987. An excellent synthesis of recent work that sites the origins of both Christianity and rabbinic Judaism in the turbulent history of Judaism in this era.

Crossan, John Dominic. *The Historical Jesus: The Life of a Mediterranean Jewish Peasant.* 1991. Innovative and controversial, the book presents Jesus as a Jew and an agrarian rebel, and questions the authenticity of much of what the Gospels report that he said.

Fantham, Elaine, Helene Peet Foley, Natalie Boymel Kampen, Sarah B. Pomeroy, and H. A. Shapiro. *Women in the Classical World: Image and Text.* 1994. Chapters 10–13 provide an excellent introduction to the social and cultural history of women in the Roman Empire.

Ferguson, John. *The Religions of the Roman Empire.* 1970. A thorough introductory survey of pagan religions based on both archaeological and literary evidence. Illustrated.

Frend, W. H. C. *The Rise of Christianity.* 1984. A thorough and detailed account from the first century B.C. to the sixth century A.D., emphasizing religion in its social context.

Goodman, Martin. *The Ruling Class of Roman Judaea: The Origins of the Jewish Revolt Against Rome, A.D. 66–70.* An interpretation of the revolt in terms of elite politics in a book that opens a window onto Roman-native relations.

Grant, Michael. *The Jews in the Roman World.* 1973. A good survey of Jews, Romans, and Christians, including a succinct and balanced account of the life and trial of Jesus.

Johnson, Luke Timothy. *The Real Jesus: The Misguided Quest for the Historical Jesus and the Truth of the Traditional Gospels.* 1996. Well written, carefully argued, conservative, and cautious, this book offers a good introduction to the question of the historicity of Jesus.

Kraemer, Ross. *Her Share of the Blessings: Women's Religions Among Pagans, Jews, and Christians in the Greco-Roman World.* 1992. A readable and thoughtful synthesis of important recent work emphasizing the prominence of women in ancient religion; uses a mixture of archaeological and literary sources.

Meeks, Wayne A. *The First Urban Christians: The Social World of the Apostle Paul.* 1983. A social description of early Christianity, very readable and clear.

Shanks, Herschel, ed. *Understanding the Dead Sea Scrolls.* 1992. A very useful collection of introductory essays on a fascinating, much-debated subject.

Literature and Art

Henig, M., ed. *Handbook of Roman Art.* 1983. A well-illustrated collection of essays by various authors, written for the beginner.

Laistner, M. L. W. *The Greater Roman Historians.* 1963. A good, brief, general survey.

Russell, Donald. "The Arts of Prose: The Early Empire." In John Boardman, Jasper Griffin, and Oswyn Murray, eds., *The Roman World,* 243–266. 1988. A witty, perceptive, and concise treatment of Greek and Latin prose, excluding history writing, in the first two centuries A.D.

Zanker, Paul. *The Power of Images in the Age of Augustus.* 1988. An incisive study of Augustus's use of visual propaganda.

POMPEII

We enter their houses uninvited. We retrace their steps as they went about daily chores or stopped to gossip or dodged traffic or worshiped or made love. We even deprive them of the privacy of death. They are the people of Pompeii, famous even two thousand years after they lived—unenviably famous, for they were the victims of a great natural disaster that destroyed nine cities and towns in Roman Campania, of which Pompeii and nearby Herculaneum are the best known. Although most residents escaped, there were deaths, and many tens of thousands of people lost their homes and source of livelihood.

On August 23, A.D. 79, Pompeii and Herculaneum were thriving cities. The next day the volcano of Mount Vesuvius, several miles away, erupted. By August 25 the two towns no longer existed: Pompeii had been buried under more than 17 feet of volcanic ash and pumice stone, Herculaneum under more than 65 feet. Excavations at the two sites, beginning in the 1700s, have unearthed streets and buildings, fine statuary and painting, fresh-baked loaves of bread in the oven and a dining room table laden with fish and eggs, and the remains of humans and animals. To many visitors, these sites are a cross between an open-air museum and a graveyard on Halloween. They allow us almost to relive city life in the early years of the Roman Empire, as we may see in two scenes from Pompeii, the more fully excavated of the two cities.

Let us imagine ourselves first near the center of Pompeii, a city spread over 160 acres, surrounded by a wall about 2 miles in circumference. We are at the corner of Stabia and Nola Streets, looking north. A thriving center of cloth manufacture and of trade in wine and olive oil, Pompeii was home to about 10,000 people, with another 20,000 in the surrounding countryside. It is not difficult to see in the mind's eye pedestrians hurrying along the raised, curbed sidewalks visible here. A slave might bring textiles to the cloth-working shop in the house of Vesonius Primus, located up Stabia Street on the west side. A sculptor might bring a bronze family bust to the house of

Corner of Stabia and Nola Streets, Pompeii (*Scala/Art Resource, NY*)

the wealthy banker Lucius Caecilius Iucundus on the east side of the same street.

Steps at the corner provided convenient access to vehicles. Pedestrians crossed the street by means of the large steppingstones visible in the foreground, because stepping into the roadway meant risking an encounter with sewage and flowing water. The crossing stones also slowed wheeled vehicles. Without these "speed bumps," they might have moved rapidly along these streets, which, like all of Pompeii's main thoroughfares, were well paved with large stones.

The busy intersection of Stabia and Nola also provides evidence about two other important features of Pompeiian life: water and religion. Numerous public and private wells are found in Pompeii, and an aqueduct brought water to a reservoir inside the walls. Many homes had running water, but the poor depended on the public fountains found at many a corner. Look at the northwest corner of this intersection, where the four stone slabs of such a fountain are visible. Water poured into the basin from the raised stone block in the rear carved with a drunken Silenus, an attendant of the god Dionysus.

Behind the fountain we can see a tall brick tower, one of many neighborhood water towers. The central groove held a pipe bringing water from the reservoir. Smaller pipes carried water to the buildings that stretch northward along Stabia Street. Lining the street are buildings of either brick or rubble masonry, plus a small amount of plaster and wood. Marble was reserved for the wealthy and for public buildings.

Between the fountain and the tower we see a gabled shrine to the gods of the crossroads. Shrines may be found at major corners throughout the city. To Romans, street crossings meant transition. Corners were the home of spirits who, if propitiated, might grant luck and success.

Many Pompeiians no doubt prayed to the gods as they ran in flight from the city on August 24, but not all of their prayers were answered. Day turned into night, as the air filled with hot ash and poisonous gases. Many people died of asphyxiation before they could escape.

Consider our second scene, a room from the house of Marcus Fabius Rufus, located not far from

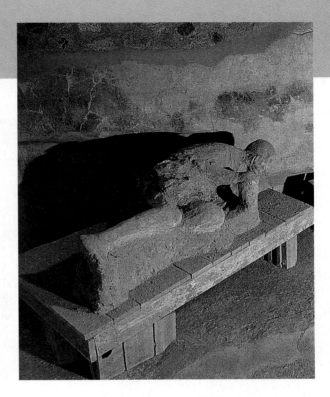

Plaster Cast of Skeleton, House of Fabius Rufus, Pompeii
(Alinari/Art Resource, NY)

Stabia and Nola Streets. Here excavators found examples of what is a common sight for modern visitors: the outline, in hardened ash, of people who died in flight from Vesuvius's eruption. We see them where they fell. Look at the figure shown here, struggling in vain to get up.

Although the bodies and clothing of the victims eventually decomposed, the moist ash hardened and preserved their shapes, down to the details. By pouring liquid plaster into the cavities where the bodies lay, archaeologists obtained fascinating and grotesque casts. The plaster casts show a virtual cross section of Pompeii: men and women, young and old, gladiators, slaves, priests, soldiers, rich people (evident from their clothes and jewelry), a beggar holding an alms sack, merchants, farmers, a goat. There are poignant scenes such as a young couple, a mother and child, and two children holding hands on the road where they lost their way forever. In the atrium of Vesonius Primus's house lies a dog, abandoned by the servants and struggling against its chain. At Herculaneum, skeletons of more than 150 human beings have been found on the beach, waiting, like Vesonius's dog, for help that never came. ❧

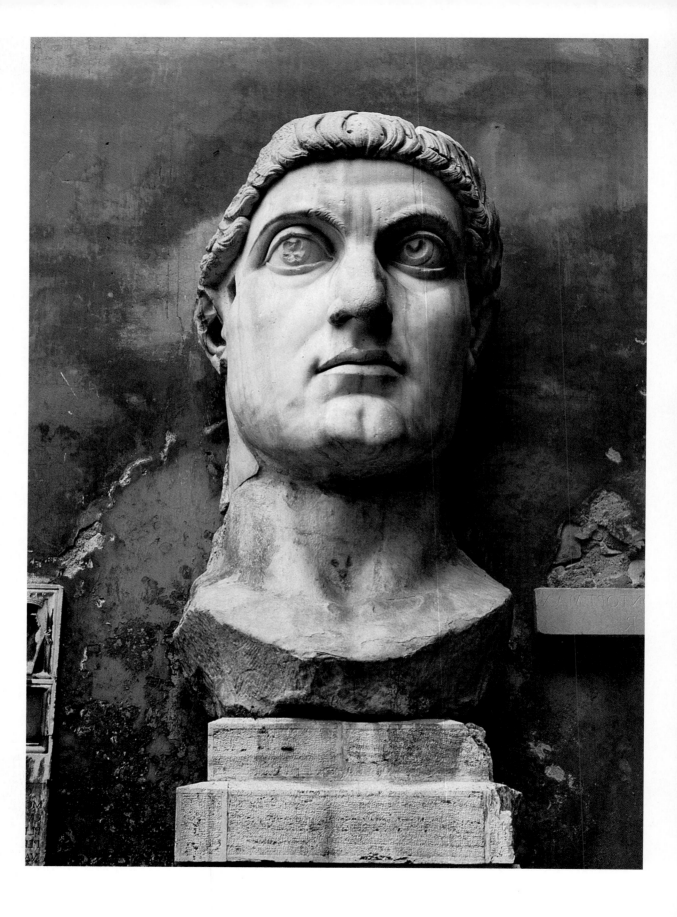

The World of Late Antiquity, ca. 300–600

Visitors to Rome's Capitoline museum can see the fragments of a colossal statue of Flavius Valerius Constantinus, known to history as Constantine the Great (r. 306–337). The head of this statue, itself more than 8 feet tall, is depicted to the left. Statues of earlier Roman emperors tended to be life-size or just a little larger, but Constantine's statue defies all human scale. His expressionless face did not meet the gaze of his subjects. He cared, it seems, nothing for them. His immense size proclaims imperial majesty in the abstract, not the visible presence of a human magistrate.

The scale of Constantine's statue is proportionate to this emperor's place in Roman history. Calling himself "the restorer of the Roman Empire," Constantine struggled mightily to solve some of that empire's most pressing problems. He put an end to the persecution of Christianity, granted important privileges to the Christian church, and became a Christian himself—the first Roman emperor to do so. He instituted military reforms that paved the way to a massive militarization of public life in the Roman world. And he contracted treaties with various barbarian peoples that, in the long run, provided those peoples with a stable framework for incorporating themselves into, and finally radically transforming, the Roman Empire itself. When Constantine died the Roman Empire was stronger than it had been in generations. But it was also very different.

The reigns of Constantine and of his immediate predecessor, Diocletian (r. 284–305), inaugurate a period that scholars now label "Late Antiquity." For a long time educated people, often taking their lead from the elegant and influential *The Decline and Fall of the Roman Empire* by the

Colossal statue
of Constantine.

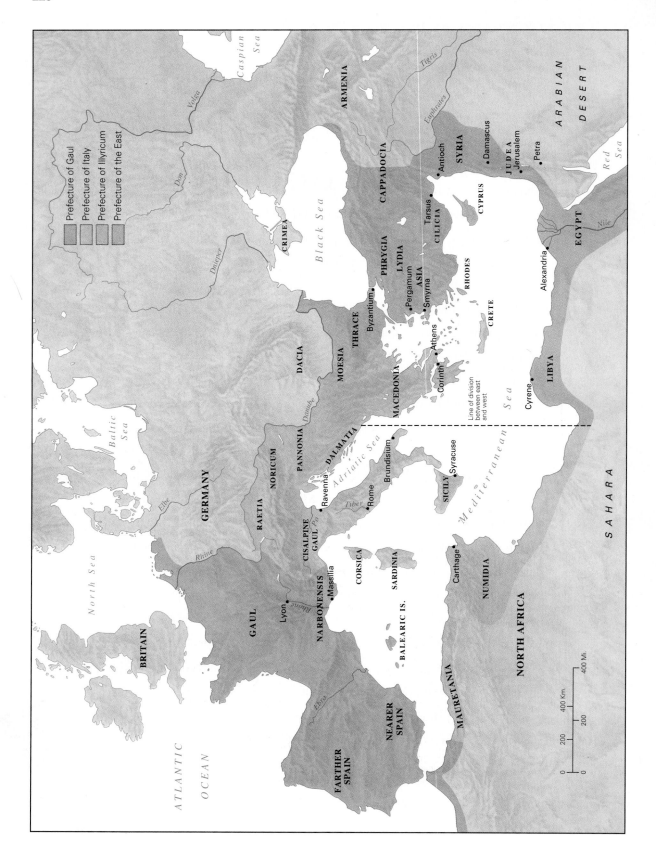

Prefecture of Gaul
Prefecture of Italy
Prefecture of Illyricum
Prefecture of the East

Caspian Sea

ARMENIA

Tigris

Volta

Don

Euphrates

ARABIAN DESERT

SYRIA
• Damascus
JUDEA
Antioch •
• Petra
Jerusalem

CAPPADOCIA

Red Sea

CYPRUS

Dnieper

Black Sea

CRIMEA

Tarsus •
CILICIA

EGYPT

Nile

PHRYGIA
LYDIA
ASIA
Pergamum •
Smyrna •

RHODES

• Alexandria

CRETE

THRACE

Byzantium •

Athens •

LIBYA

MOESIA

DACIA

Corinth •

MACEDONIA

Mediterranean Sea

Cyrene •

Line of division
between east
and west

Baltic Sea

PANNONIA

DALMATIA
Ravenna •

Adriatic Sea

Brundisium •

Syracuse •

NORICUM

GERMANY

RAETIA

Elbe

CISALPINE
GAUL
Po

Rome •

Tiber

SICILY

Carthage •

NUMIDIA

North Sea

Rhine

NARBONENSIS
• Massilia

CORSICA

SARDINIA

NORTH AFRICA

GAUL

Lyon •

Rhône

BALEARIC IS.

BRITAIN

Ebro

MAURETANIA

SAHARA

NEARER
SPAIN

400 Mi.
400

ATLANTIC OCEAN

FARTHER
SPAIN

200
200
0
0

British historian Edward Gibbon (1737–1794), believed that, beset by insurmountable problems, the Roman Empire "fell" in the fifth century. With that fall, such a view insisted, the glories of classical civilization gave way to the gloom of the "Dark Ages." Today, on the contrary, specialists in the period from roughly A.D. 300 to 600 see vigor and achievement. Above all they see coherence, not tumult and collapse. No one denies that the Roman world in 600 was different from the Roman world in 300. But recent writing tends to emphasize that continuity and change were twin dynamics in the late Roman world.

Let us remember that the Roman Empire had suffered from severe political, military, and economic problems in the third century. Keep in mind, too, that it was almost unimaginably vast, extending from the modern border between England and Scotland to Mesopotamia, from the North Sea to the Sahara. It numbered perhaps 50 million people whose languages, customs, and histories differed hugely. In such a threatened and complex world, changes were inevitable. The only matters in suspense were what forms those changes would take and who would direct them.

This chapter will attempt to answer those questions. In describing the forms the changes would take, we will pursue two themes. On the one hand, we will see that the fundamental structure of the imperial regime was militarized, that new peoples—the Germanic barbarians—were incorporated into the Roman system, and that gradually the western provinces of the empire turned into a series of kingdoms allied with but basically independent of Rome. At the same time, Christianity developed an empire-wide organizational structure, a sophisticated intellectual tradition, and an art, architecture, and literature that made it first a competitor and then the successor to the classical culture that had dominated the Mediterranean world for over a millennium. On the other hand, our discussion will reveal the remarkable extent to which the traditional Roman elite maintained itself

Map 7.1 Diocletian's Division of the Roman Empire
Corresponding to the tetrarchy, the empire was divided into eastern and western halves, and each half was divided into prefectures. Four regions, rulers, and bureaucratic administrations replaced the ineffective rule of one man.

in spite of the impressive changes that we will be chronicling. The Germanic warlords who replaced Roman administrators were tutored by the Romans themselves. The most prominent Christian clergy descended, in town after town, from the same powerful local families that had ruled for centuries. Christian culture borrowed not only the languages of the Roman Empire—Greek and Latin—but also the empire's philosophical traditions, learned vocabulary, legal customs, and art forms. The Roman Empire did not fall. It evolved. The crucible in which that evolution took shape was the world of Late Antiquity.

REBUILDING THE ROMAN EMPIRE

As we learned in Chapter 6, the third-century Roman Empire lurched from crisis to crisis. Swift and decisive action was needed if Rome were to survive. In particular, three somewhat interrelated sets of problems demanded attention. First, the constant civil wars of the years between 235 and 284 had to be stopped and a stable form of transition from one reign to another had to be found. Second, with the frontiers threatened in many sectors, the army needed to be expanded in size and deployed more effectively. Third, the economy had to be stabilized and its resources more efficiently tapped by the government to pay for administrative and military reforms. Rome was fortunate in raising up two rulers, with more than fifty years of rule between them, who understood the empire's problems and legislated energetically to correct them.

The Reforms of Diocletian (r. 284–305)

Diocletian put in place by 293 a regime that historians call the "tetrarchy," or rule by four (Map 7.1). Diocletian first selected an imperial colleague for himself, and then he and his colleague each selected a subordinate official. Diocletian and his colleague were called *augusti*, and the two subordinates were designated *caesares*. The names came from *Caesar*, which was both a family name and a general term for a ruler, and from the special title of *Augustus Caesar*. Diocletian retained the position of senior augustus and concentrated his efforts in the wealthy and populous eastern half of the empire. His aim was to provide colleagues, not

Tetrarchy Ideal and reality are both evident in this sculpture of the tetrarchy. The rulers, depicted equal in size, embrace one another but also bare their weapons—to one another and to the world. *(Scala/Art Resource, NY)*

equals. The system intended to provide four men of imperial rank who could lead armies and make decisions in political and administrative matters. Each augustus was to adopt his caesar as his son and heir. In this way, the tetrarchy was intended to provide for orderly succession to the imperial office and to promote experienced, respected men.

Diocletian also addressed an ideological flaw in the Roman imperial system. Ever since the Principate, emperors pretended to be lineal descendants of the Republican magistrates, but their real power was based on the military. Diocletian abandoned the pretense that he was an elected officer of the Roman people. He was addressed as *Dominus,* or "Lord and Master." He adopted Eastern, especially Persian, habits, such as wearing gorgeous clothes and a jeweled diadem, sitting on an elevated throne, rarely appearing in public and then only amid awe-inspiring ceremony, and requiring those who approached to undergo the ritual humiliation of prostration before him.

The Roman Empire was too vast for a single ruler to deal with its many problems. When Diocletian ascended the throne, the empire had some fifty provinces, which differed greatly in size, population, wealth, strategic importance, and degree of Romanization. Rome had traditionally asked for relatively little from its empire, primarily taxes, military recruits, and loyalty. Local authorities generally did the tax collecting and military recruiting, with little interference by imperial agents. The imperial administration, made up largely of aristocratic amateurs, numbered only a few hundred men on Diocletian's accession. The Roman Empire was dramatically undergoverned, given its size and problems.

Diocletian expanded the imperial administration by doubling the number of provinces and increasing the number of officials. Instead of adding new territories, he divided old, large provinces into smaller ones. He then organized groups of provinces into thirteen dioceses and joined the dioceses into four prefectures. To help the augusti and the caesares govern the prefectures, Diocletian equipped each of them with an entourage of military, legal, financial, and secretarial officials headed by a praetorian prefect. By 350 the number of officers from the provincial to the prefectorial level had risen from a few hundred to thirty-five or forty thousand. Diocletian wished to fill the bureaucracy with trained administrators instead of with wealthy senators and equestrians who viewed government service as a means of enriching themselves and enhancing the prestige of their families.

Diocletian also attended to Rome's military problems. His major initiative was an attempt to double the size of the army from about 300,000 to 600,000 men, although the final total ended up being only around 450,000. Diocletian also built new forts along the frontiers and improved the roads that supplied frontier defenders. The emperor raised conscription levels and began the systematic incorporation of Germans into the army. Military careers had once provided Roman citizenship as well as a secure and decent income. After 212, however, when citizenship was granted to almost everyone in the empire, the dangers of military life far exceeded the attractions. But noncitizen Germans living along the frontiers, whose only hope of citizenship was military service, found the army attractive.

These administrative and military reforms were expensive and required a predictable income. Thus, Diocletian attempted to regularize the tax system in the empire. A census was held to identify all taxpayers, and the productive value of land was assessed. Each praetorian prefect had to estimate his annual administrative costs; to raise the necessary funds, he assigned a tax assessment to the men and land in his prefecture. Tax reform was not enough to pay for all of Diocletian's new measures, however. To address the rampant inflation of the third century and to get control of skyrocketing prices, Diocletian issued in 302 the Edict of Maximum Prices, which froze prices and (largely to keep people from fleeing the countryside) made many occupations hereditary. Senators had long been exempt from taxes, and the taxation of business ventures never brought in much revenue. Because more than 80 percent of the population lived outside cities and towns, virtually the whole cost of the Roman system fell on agriculture, in particular on small farmers. Diocletian's routinization of the tax structure brought in more revenue, but it also caused hardships. A rising tax burden threatened those who were most vulnerable. And with more officials handling vastly greater sums of money, corruption ran rampant. Tax increases and dishonest officials loosened the bonds between subject and emperor. Most people never saw an emperor, but they saw too much of his tax-gouging local minions. (See the box, "A Contemporary View of Diocletian's Reforms.")

Diocletian's reforms were sensible in principle but costly in three respects: moral, social, and economic. The emperors had always been military dictators, but Diocletian removed all pretense that they served at the behest of the Roman people. His frankness may have enhanced the prestige of the imperial office, but it also loosened the ties between the ruler and his subjects. By stripping the senatorial order of military and civic responsibilities, Diocletian alienated a small but influential group numbering about two thousand. During the Principate, senators had gained enormous wealth, powerful offices, and personal prestige in return for their support of the imperial regime. That wealth, power, and prestige translated into immense private, local influence that endured long after the senators' official power ceased. Moreover, the enlarged imperial administration necessarily reduced the autonomy of cities and their local leaders, which for three centuries had been the key components of the imperial system. Civic loyalty to Rome was called into question. Finally, the expanded administration and army cost dearly in real cash. That cash had to be extracted from an empire that was in serious economic distress.

The Reforms of Constantine (r. 306–337)

Diocletian's careful plans for the imperial succession collapsed almost immediately after his voluntary retirement in 305. When Constantius,

A Contemporary View of Diocletian's Reforms

Historians usually praise Diocletian's reforms, but this passage, from a bitterly hostile Christian writer who hated Diocletian as a persecutor, may actually give the view of the ordinary person.

While Diocletian, who was the inventor of wicked deeds and the contriver of evil, was ruining everything, he could not keep his hands even from God. This man, through both avarice and cowardice, overturned the whole world. For he made three men sharers in his rule; the world was divided into four parts, and armies were multiplied, each of the rulers striving to have a far larger number of soldiers than the emperors had had when the state was ruled by single emperors. The number of those receiving pay from the state was so much larger than the number of those paying taxes that, because of the enormous size of the assessments, the resources of the tenant farmers were exhausted, fields were abandoned, and cultivated areas were transformed into wildernesses. And to fill everything with fear, provinces were cut into bits; many governors and more minor offices lay like incubi over each region and every municipality, likewise many procurators of revenues, administrators, and deputy prefects. Very few civil cases came before all of these, but only condemnations and frequent confiscations, and there were not merely frequent but perpetual exactions of innumerable things, and in the process of exaction intolerable wrongs.

Whatever was imposed to maintain the soldiery might have been endured, but Diocletian, with insatiable avarice, would never permit the treasury to be diminished. . . . When by various iniquities he brought about enormously high prices, he attempted to legislate the price of commodities. Thus much blood was spilled, and nothing appeared on the market, and prices soared still higher. . . . In addition he had a certain endless passion for building, and made no small exactions from the provinces for maintaining laborers and artisans and for supplying wagons and whatever else was necessary for the construction of public works. Here basilicas, there a circus, here a mint, there a shop for making weapons, here a house for his wife, there one for his daughter.

Source: Lactantius, On the Deaths of the Persecutors, vii, in Roman Civilization. Sourcebook II: The Empire, Naphtali Lewis and Meyer Reinhold, ed. and trans. (New York: Harper and Row, 1966), pp. 458–459.

Diocletian's western colleague as augustus, died in 306, his troops reverted to the hereditary principle and declared his son, Constantine, augustus. From 306 to 313 as many as six men claimed to be augustus somewhere in the empire. From 313 to 324, Constantine shared rule with one man, and from 324 to 337 he ruled alone, with his sons as caesars in various parts of the empire. This compromise between the hereditary and tetrarchal systems persisted for the next two centuries.

For Constantine, consistency with the basic policies of his predecessor was the rule. He had entered the imperial court as a young man in 293, when his father was made augustus, and he later served with his father in Britain and Gaul. He knew the system and maintained the administrative structure that Diocletian introduced. Constantine continued the eastward shift of power begun under the tetrarchy by creating a second imperial capital in the east. He selected an old Greek city, Byzantium, and renamed it after himself, "Constantine's polis" or Constantinople (modern Istanbul). Byzantium's location more than its size, wealth, or fame recommended it. The city straddled military roads between the eastern and western halves of the empire, overlooked crucial trade lanes to and from the Black Sea region, and was well sited to respond to threats along both the Balkan and the eastern frontiers (see Map 7.1).

In financial affairs, too, Constantine's work echoed his predecessor's. He issued a new gold *solidus*, the principal money of account in the Roman world. This coin achieved, and held for nearly a thousand years, monetary stability in the Mediterranean world. Unfortunately, a stable currency braked but could not stop the headlong rush of inflation.

In military affairs, Constantine believed that the long frontiers were too exposed to unpredictable attacks to be held securely, and he expanded the use of mobile field armies. These armies, recruited largely (as under Diocletian) from Germans living along or beyond the frontiers, were stationed well behind the frontiers so that they could be mobilized and moved quickly. They were given their own command structures, under officers whom the Romans called "Masters of the Soldiers." The praetorian prefects were deprived of their military responsibilities and became exclusively civilian officials. The separation of civilian and military command made sense administratively and politically, because it meant that no individual could combine the command of an army with one of the new and powerful government posts.

Scholars have long debated the strategic and political wisdom of Constantine's arrangements. Moving experienced troops from the frontiers may have invited attacks. Recruiting Germans into the field armies and leaving frontier defenses to German auxiliaries may have created divided loyalties and conflicts of interest. Most Roman provincials had not lived near soldiers. Now the soldiers and the veterans of the field armies became daily companions. One certain result of the reforms of Diocletian and Constantine was the militarization of Roman society, the transformation of the Roman Empire into a vast, armed camp. The financial resources of that empire were now largely devoted to maintaining a military establishment that was expensive, socially diverse, and potentially politically volatile.

Diocletian and Constantine responded with imagination to the third-century crisis. They also created a new kind of rulership in which a particular style of emperorship was replacing the rule of particular emperors. The statue of Constantine

THE EVOLUTION OF THE ROMAN EMPIRE

284–337	Reforms of Diocletian and Constantine
313	Edict of Milan grants toleration to Christianity
324–330	Founding of Constantinople
361–363	Pagan reaction of Julian the Apostate
378	Valens defeated by Visigoths at Adrianople
379–395	Reign of Theodosius the Great
408–450	Theodosius II consolidates eastern Roman Empire
410	Visigoths sack Rome
476	Deposition of last Roman emperor in the West
527–565	Reign of Justinian I

with which this chapter begins is an indicator of the late antique imperial ideology. Constantine's size serves to emphasize a distance that the viewer cannot articulate but cannot help feeling. The huge statue does not so much depict Constantine as proclaim emperorship. The majesty of Constantine and his long, successful reign, in conjunction with Diocletian's success and longevity, stand in stark contrast to the troubles of the third century.

The Legalization of Christianity

Since the first century, Christianity had been making steady progress throughout the Roman world, and by 300 there were Christians in every province. Also, Christianity won converts for many reasons. Basic teachings were important. Also, Christianity's strong appeal to women drew many adherents. Another factor in the expansion of Christianity was a structure that from humble beginnings grew into a vast hierarchical organization. The Roman Empire was rich in varieties of religious experience, but no pagan cult combined compelling teachings with a sophisticated institutional foundation.

The earliest communities of Christians had three kinds of officials, whose customary titles in English are *bishop, priest,* and *deacon.* Deacons were clearly subordinate to the other two. They were responsible for charitable works and for arranging meetings. Bishops and priests presided at celebrations, preached, and taught. Distinctions between bishops and priests developed over time. Within towns, the eldest priest was gradually accorded precedence and designated "overseer," the literal meaning of *bishop.* As more people converted, as the church acquired property, and as doctrinal quarrels began to cause divisions among the faithful, bishops began to be influential local officials. By the fourth century, even modest towns had bishops. There were more than eighty in Italy alone. By the late fourth century, the bishops in the major cities of the empire were called *metropolitan bishops,* or sometimes *archbishops,* and they had responsibility for territories often called *dioceses.* The Christian church was adapting to its own purposes the administrative geography of the Roman Empire.

Diocletian will always be remembered for undertaking the last persecution of Christianity, between 303 and 305. We shall never know exactly why he did it. He was a man of conventional piety, and it may be, as even Christian writers later said, that he was truly convinced that the presence of Christians in his army offended his ancestral gods. Whatever its cause, the persecution was harsh and well planned. Churches were closed, and the Scriptures were collected. Decrees demanded the arrest of the clergy and required citizens to present themselves at a temple for some act of sacrifice. Diocletian's agents had difficulty enforcing his decrees, and many people had no stomach for an organized reign of terror, and so gauging the effect of the persecution is difficult. It certainly did not eradicate Christianity, and it may have drawn favorable attention to the faith by making heroes of its victims, the martyrs whose blood, according to a contemporary, was "the seed of the church."

Constantine was just as interested as Diocletian in promoting the unity of the empire, but he took a different approach. Whereas Diocletian persecuted Christianity, Constantine embraced it. While marching toward Rome to fight for the imperial office to which his father's troops had elected him, Constantine believed that he saw in the sky a cross emblazoned on the sun and accom-

panied by the words, "In this sign you shall conquer." No full explanation has ever been found for the source or depth of Constantine's Christianity or for the actions he took after seeing this vision. Constantine's mother, Helena, was a Christian. She surely exposed her son to the new faith, but the young Constantine was raised at the court of Diocletian, where he received a traditional pagan upbringing.

Constantine put chi-rho monograms (from the first two letters of *Christos,* "Christ" in Greek) on his soldiers' uniforms and then defeated his rival Maxentius at the Milvian Bridge near Rome in 312. Constantine attributed his victory to the God of the Christians. Although Christian writers attributed to Constantine alone the Edict of Milan, which in 313 made Christianity a legal religion in the empire, the western augustus actually joined his eastern colleague in issuing the decree. In the years ahead, Constantine did more than just treat Christianity as the equal of all other religions. He promoted the Christian church, granting it tax immunities and relieving the clergy of military service. He provided money to replace the books and buildings that had been seized or destroyed in persecutions. He and his mother sponsored vast church-building projects in Rome, Constantinople, and Jerusalem.

Constantine soon discovered that supporting the church could involve considerable risk and distractions. Many quarrels among Christians had gone almost unnoticed when the church and its members could not practice their faith publicly. The Edict of Milan changed all that. Christian heresies almost immediately came to the emperor's attention. *Heresy* comes from a Greek word meaning "to choose." Heretics are persons who choose teachings or practices that persons in positions of authority deem wrong. In Egypt first, but eventually in much of the empire as well, a dispute arose that turned around the central mystery of Christianity itself: the divinity of Jesus Christ. Christian belief holds that God exists as three distinct but equal persons: Father, Son, and Holy Spirit.

A priest of Alexandria, Arius (ca. 250–ca. 336), began teaching that Jesus was the "first born of all creation"—that he was conceived by the Holy Spirit, was born of Mary, and was later than the Father in time. Christians had long been stung by the charge that their monotheism was a sham, that they really worshiped three gods. Arianism,

Santa Costanza, Rome, ca. 350 The overall decoration and the modeling of figures in this mosaic are fundamentally classical, but the theme is Christian: Christ hands a scroll of the law, signifying both the Hebrew law and the church, to Saint Peter in the presence of Saint Paul. The mosaic illustrates well the blending of classical and Christian cultures. *(Scala/Art Resource, NY)*

as the faith of Arius and his followers is called, sought to preserve monotheism by making Jesus slightly subordinate to the Father. Arianism won many adherents.

Constantine dealt with religious controversies by summoning theologians to guide him and by assembling church councils to debate issues and promulgate solutions. In 325 at Nicaea, near Constantinople (see Map 7.2), the emperor convened a council of more than three hundred bishops, who condemned Arius and his teaching. The bishops maintained that Christ was "one in being with the Father," as the words of the Nicene Creed still have it. Arianism did not die at Nicaea, however, and Late Antiquity was never free of doctrinal disputes.

Constantine claimed to be the specially chosen agent of God. Individual Christians did not object to this because the emperor did not ask to be worshiped, which earlier emperors had done. The Christian clergy was happy to have the awesome power of the state applied in favor of the church, as long as the emperor left precise doctrinal formulations to clerics. Constantine's acts nevertheless entangled the church with the government just as divisions among Christians were coming into view.

THE FOURTH-CENTURY EMPIRE: AN ILLUSORY STABILITY

By 337 stability and good government had replaced the turmoil of 284. Reforms had addressed every aspect of the third-century crisis. The key question now was whether the progress achieved by Diocletian and Constantine could be maintained or even advanced. The answer is somewhat surprising. The reforms did not stabilize the empire so much as they provided a stable framework for its gradual transformation.

Imperial Politics: Families and Armies

Constantine had employed a combination of the tetrarchal and dynastic systems. Under him were three caesars, but they were all his sons, and they succeeded him when he died. Constantine's sons had no heirs, and they did not appoint subordinate caesars. When the last of them died in 361, the army turned to Julian (331–363), a nephew of Constantine. Julian was known as a great leader and as a man who looked out for his troops. An attempt was being made to find a legitimate heir to Constantine, not merely a general who would reward the army. Familial and military politics were combining to secure the empire.

Julian ruled for only two years before he was killed fighting in Mesopotamia. He had no heirs and, acting on a long-standing precedent, the army controlled the succession. The choice fell on Valentinian (r. 364–375) and his brother, Valens (r. 364–378), who came from the frontier province of Pannonia (roughly, modern Hungary). Valentinian ruled in the west, his brother in the east. Although no one could have predicted it, Valentinian established a dynasty that ruled the Roman world for ninety-one years (364–455). In 378, when Valens was killed in battle, Valentinian's sons sent their brother-in-law, Theodosius I (r. 379–395), who had risen through the military ranks in Spain, to the east to maintain order.

Until his own death in 395, Theodosius was the most powerful man in the Roman world, and after his last brother-in-law died in 392, he was Rome's only ruler. He enjoyed the confidence of the people and the army—the former because he was exceptionally competent and honest and the latter because he was an old military man and a superb general. He divided the empire between his two sons without dynastic or military challenge. His branch of the family lived on until the deaths of Theodosius II in the east in 450 and of Valentinian III in the west in 455. Later rulers of the dynasty sometimes ruled alone, sometimes with chosen colleagues or subordinates. Dynastic and tetrarchal systems were blended effectively. Yet the army's influence was a troubling reminder of the third century.

The army was supposed to protect the empire, not play a role in Roman politics: The military reforms of Diocletian and Constantine had been designed to secure effective protection along the frontiers. In the 340s the Romans faced a renewed threat in the east from Persia, where an ambitious shah sought to revive the glories of his ancestors. The Romans did not take this Persian threat lightly, for they knew that in the Persians they faced an old and formidable foe. In the west, Rome faced no single enemy of such proportions, but a lot of relatively minor provocations hastened the army's rise to public prominence.

One serious challenge arose in the Balkans. The Visigoths lived just across the Danube from imperial territory. Since the reign of Constantine they had been "federates" (from *foedus*, meaning "treaty") and had been defending a section of the frontier as auxiliary troops. In 376 the Visigoths requested permission to enter the empire, cross the Danube, and settle in the Balkans. They were alarmed about the movement into the Danube basin of the Huns, Asiatic marauders who for some decades had been tormenting the Black Sea region.

Recent years had been difficult for the empire. The Persians had killed Julian in 363, and familial quarrels were disturbing the west. The Romans thus delayed responding to the Visigothic request. Fearful of the Huns, the Visigoths crossed the Danube on their own and then requested permission to settle in the Balkans. Reluctantly, Valens granted permission and said that permanent arrangements would have to be postponed. When the emperor made no progress on settlements, and when local officials began to extort money from the Visigoths, the latter revolted. Valens foolishly marched north to meet them with a small force and was defeated and killed at Adrianople in 378. Theodosius marched east, pacified the situation, and began the process of incorporating the Visigoths into the empire.

Two emperors had been killed in a short time and a third drawn into a frontier dispute. Rulers could not devise a strategy that precluded trouble from Rome's neighbors and enemies. Military provocations inevitably enhanced the role of the army in public life and gave military concerns precedence over civilian ones.

Administrative Successes and Failures

After Constantine there were no major administrative reforms. The province-diocese-prefecture structure continued to be refined, the number of imperial bureaucrats grew, and the new military organization was maintained. However, the futility of trying to achieve unity in such a diverse empire became ever more apparent. One example is particularly telling.

During his reign, Valentinian, a soldier raised to the imperial office by the army, wanted to make military careers more attractive and soldiers' lives more comfortable. To achieve these ends, Valentinian proposed to provide soldiers with plots of land and with seed grain. He aimed to supplement soldiers' pay, to tie them more securely to a particular region, and to make them more loyal to him. This creative idea complemented earlier military reforms.

Nonetheless, Valentinian's program angered the senators, who were still rich and influential. They agitated against the reform because, they said, the emperor was spending too much time worrying about the army, and he was depriving them of lands they desired. The senators also complained that the new program was expensive, and they were absolutely right. To pay for land and seed, Valentinian had to raise taxes.

Higher taxes were unpopular all around but especially in the cities, where the burden of collecting them fell on the decurions, the main local officials who composed the town councils. From the time of Valentinian in the late fourth century, it becomes possible to trace a steadily declining loyalty to Rome among these provincial urban elites. Part of Rome's success under the Principate had been directly tied to the regime's ability to win over local elites all over the empire. Now, a military reform that was perfectly sensible actually provoked suspicion and disloyalty among senators and decurions.

From the time of Augustus, the Roman regime had attempted to promote unity around the cult of the emperor, loyalty to the government, and a common culture. As we saw in Chapter 6 (pages 204–208), however, the Roman world was huge and diverse. In the time of Constantine, the empire may have numbered some 50 or 60 million inhabitants. Of these, not more than 5 to 10 million lived in towns. Because Roman government was based on towns, the actual capacity of the Roman administration to keep track of, to tax, to coerce, and to Romanize the population as a whole was limited.

Religious unity was also elusive. The Council of Nicaea (325) had tried in vain to eliminate Arianism. But Constantine's own son and successor, Constantius II (r. 337–361), was an avowed Arian, as was Valens later. For more than forty years, some of Rome's rulers embraced a faith that had been declared heretical. During this time, a Visigothic priest named Ulfilas entered the empire, was converted to Arian Christianity, and returned to spread this faith among his people. When the Visigoths entered the empire in 376, they were considered heretics; however, when they converted, in the 340s, the senior Roman ruler was an Arian.

Constantine's nephew, Julian, was called "the Apostate" by his Christian opponents because during his short reign (361–363) he attempted to restore paganism. He forbade Christians to hold most government or military positions or to teach in any school. He did not resort to persecution, however, believing that Christianity could be eradicated by appeals to tradition and by reasoned argument. Obviously, he was wrong, and his efforts died with him.

Julian's abortive pagan restoration was echoed a few years later in the affair of the victory altar. Emperor Gratian (r. 375–383), a Christian, removed the altar of victory from the Roman senate. This was a statue of the goddess of victory before which senators usually burned a bit of incense as they passed. Tradition held that this homage to victory had for centuries assured the success of Rome's armies. The removal of the altar provoked a cry of anguish from a number of prominent Roman senators, most of whom were still pagan and deeply respectful of Rome's ancient customs. To them, Gratian's act was not so much religious as ideological. He seemed to be turning his back on Roman tradition. Julian's failure, coupled with the senators' inability to get Gratian to change his mind, shows that Christianity in some form was winning over paganism. But in what form? Official policy in this area wavered during the fourth century.

The Development of the Catholic Church

After the Edict of Milan granted toleration of Christians, the Catholic church attracted a clear majority of the empire's population (Map 7.2). The Catholic church was Trinitarian in theology, usually aligned with the imperial government, and hierarchically organized under the bishops of Rome. The continuing appeal of Christianity's basic

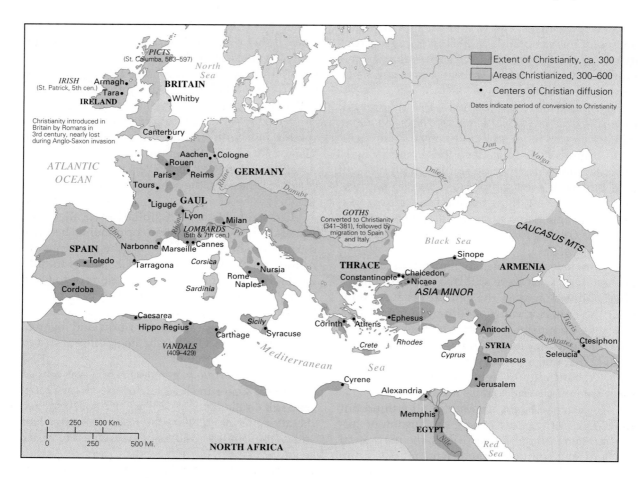

Map 7.2 The Spread of Christianity to A.D. **600** From its beginnings in Palestine (see Map 6.2 on page 214), Christianity, while still illegal, spread mainly in heavily urbanized regions. After Constantine legalized Christianity, the faith spread into every corner of the Roman world.

doctrines was key to its growth, but so too were imperial patronage and the increasing prominence of the Christian clergy. The rising significance of the clergy, particularly the bishops of Rome, eventually effected significant changes in the social and intellectual life, and even in the topography, of late antique towns.

All Christian bishops were understood to be the successors of the apostles. Because Jesus had told the original apostles to "Go forth and teach," it was believed that bishops, as the unique successors to the apostles, continued to possess the teaching authority, the guardianship of doctrine, assigned by Jesus to his original followers. The bishops of Rome coupled this general doctrine of apostolic succession with a particular emphasis on

the primacy of Peter (d. A.D. 67?) and created in the fourth and fifth centuries a new, dynamic institution in the Roman world: the papacy.

The New Testament accords a certain precedence to Peter among the apostles but provides no clear evidence that he possessed formal leadership. Around the time the church gained freedom in the Roman world, the bishops of Rome began to advance the idea that Peter had been the official leader of the apostles. Therefore, the bishop who was Peter's successor continued to have leadership of the whole Christian church. By 380 the bishop of Rome, by then regularly addressed as *papa*, or "pope" in English, had become so prominent that Emperor Theodosius required all Christians to believe as the pope did.

rsion.

Just as a council had been called at Nicaea to address the problem of Arianism, there continued to be church councils. Two principal issues attracted the attention of Christian thinkers and authorities. One of these concerned Trinitarian theology, the branch of theology that tries to explain how God can be triune (three in one). Arianism was the major Trinitarian heresy of antiquity, and the councils of Nicaea and Constantinople (381) pronounced against it. The second struggle concerned Christology, the branch of theology that attempts to understand how Jesus Christ can be both true God and true man. Catholic teaching held that Jesus had two distinct natures. The great Christological heresy of antiquity, monophysitism (literally "one nature-ism"), maintained that although Jesus appeared as a human, he had only one, divine nature. The Council of Chalcedon (451) condemned monophysitism.

In the later fourth century, and throughout the fifth, popes attempted to impose doctrinal decisions on the councils. Pope Leo I (r. 440–461) was the great theoretician of papal power. His ideas constitute the Petrine theory of papal primacy. According to this doctrine, Peter had not just a moral precedence but a legal primacy among the apostles, and that primacy was explicitly given to him by Jesus. What is more, Leo interpreted apostolic succession as a legal inheritance by the pope of Peter's jurisdictional primacy: As the apostles were teachers, so the pope was the greatest teacher; as the apostles had been the overseers of the early church, so the pope was the overseer of the whole church. It took centuries for the popes to translate their theoretical claims into real power.

The rise of the pope in the church as a whole was paralleled by the rise of bishops throughout the empire. By the last years of the fourth century, various ranking members of the social elite were everywhere entering the clergy and rising to its highest offices. This capture of the elite was the final, decisive factor in the triumph of Christianity.

The clergy was an outlet for the talents and ambitions of the elite. For some time, senators had been excluded from military offices and reduced in civilian influence, and decurions were growing dissatisfied with public service. The *episcopal* office (that is, the office of bishop) was desirable to prominent men for many reasons. It was prestigious. Bishops wore distinctive clothing when officiating and were addressed by special titles—

THE DEVELOPMENT OF CATHOLIC CHRISTIANITY

ca. 300	Emergence of Christian monasticism
313	The Edict of Milan
325	Council of Nicaea condemns Arian heresy
350–450	Age of the major Church Fathers
380	Theodosius requires Christians to believe as the pope does
382–392	Jerome prepares Vulgate Bible
451	Council of Chalcedon condemns monophysite heresy
440–461	Pope Leo I elaborates doctrine of papal primacy
492–496	Pope Gelasius delineates papal and imperial rule

traditional Roman marks of respect. They had opportunities to control patronage in the way that prominent Romans always had done. They could intervene on behalf of individuals at the imperial court. They came to control vast wealth, as the generosity of pious Christians put more resources at their disposal. By the middle of the fifth century, the dominant person in most towns was the bishop, not a civilian official. The bishops, however, were the same persons, from the same families, who had once dominated local society through civic service. In some ways the structure of Roman elite society was changing dramatically, but in other ways it was very stable.

One gauge of these changes relates to the topography of late antique towns. The elite had always been responsible for financing most local building projects, such as temples, basilicas, forums, and amphitheaters. Such benefactions declined sharply during the third century because of the uncertainty of the times. The fourth century at first saw little building on private initiative, but then came the construction of Christian cathedrals (a bishop's church, from *cathedra*, the chair or seat of the bishop's authority), episcopal residences, baptisteries, and local parish churches. Such buildings as a rule were not placed in the old city centers, which had associations with the pagan

Santa Maria Maggiore Imagine away the altar canopy and some of the decoration, and this church in Rome is a splendid example of a fifth-century basilica. Note its elegant, harmonious design. Secular buildings of the same time were no longer being built on this scale. *(Alinari/Art Resource, NY)*

past. Instead, they were placed away from town centers and on the edges of populated districts. In the future, these Christian centers served as poles around which ancient towns were reconfigured. As the imperial government became less important locally, the existence of an episcopal see (place of a bishop's authority) and building complex usually dictated whether a city survived. The Roman elites built to show pride in their cities and to promote themselves. This did not change in Late Antiquity, but this time the elites were bishops or rich Christians, and the buildings were cathedrals.

Shifting Social Hierarchies

Roman society was hierarchical. From Republican times, Rome had been governed by a hereditary class. Although the members of this class affected a style of life that set them apart, they were never a closed caste. First, they did not reproduce themselves very effectively. About two-thirds of the Roman aristocracy was replaced every century—a typical pattern in premodern societies. This meant that there were significant opportunities for social mobility. Second, just as the empire had been born in a social transformation that brought the Italian aristocracy into the Roman governing class, so Late Antiquity was characterized by a transformation that brought provincial elites and Germans into the framework of power. Social change was always masked as social continuity because when new men reached the top, they tried to embrace the culture and values of those whom they had replaced.

We can characterize the elite by means of three ideals: *otium, amicitia,* and *officium. Otium,* leisure, meant that the only life worth living was one of retreat and composure in which the finer things of life—literature, especially—could be cultivated. *Amicitia,* friendship, implied several things. It could mean the kinds of literary contacts that the thousands of surviving letters from Late Antiquity reveal. Friendship could also mean patronage. The doorstep of every noble household was crowded every morning with a gang of hangers-on who awaited their small offerings and any commands as to how they might do their patron's will. *Officium*, duty, was the sense of civic obligation that the Romans managed to communicate to the provincial upper classes.

Aristocrats governed in both public and private ways, which are almost impossible to differentiate. Though gradually excluded from key military and administrative posts, nobles did not lose their influence. They used their wealth to win or reward followers, bribe officials, and buy verdicts. Decurions in towns controlled local market privileges, building trades, police forces, fire brigades, and charitable associations. Their public and private means of persuasion and intimidation were immense. In the West, in the growing absence of an imperial administration, Roman public power did not so much "decline and fall" as find itself privatized and localized. Patronage and clientage in Roman society had a benevolent dimension, but they also revealed the raw realities of power.

There was in antiquity an implicit recognition that power was everything and that those who lacked power, whether they lacked money or not, were "poor." On this reckoning, much of the urban population was poor because it lacked access to the official means of coercion and security that the notables enjoyed. Merchants, artisans, teachers, and others were continuously vulnerable because their social, political, or economic position could change drastically at a moment's notice. They lacked the influence to protect themselves.

Most citizens of the late antique world can be classed as farmers, but this categorization is not very helpful because it lumps together the greatest landowners and the poorest peasants. Late Antiquity saw a trend in the countryside that continued into the Middle Ages: Freedom and slavery declined simultaneously. Many small, independent farmers, probably people who had long been the clients of local grandees, were actually handing over their possessions—*commending* them is the technical term—and receiving back the use of their former possessions in return for annual rents in money or in kind. They were becoming *coloni*, tenants. Their patrons promised to protect them from lawsuits or from severe economic hardship. More and more, these coloni, formerly clients, were bound to their places of residence and were forced to perform labors or to pay fees that marked their status as less than fully free even

though they had not been reduced to slavery. At the same time, many landlords were finding it economically unprofitable to house, feed, care for, and equip slaves. As a result they were manumitting their slaves and elevating them to the status of coloni. Probably there was very little change in the day-to-day lives of the great mass of the rural population, and their position at the bottom of the social hierarchy did not alter.

Women's lives are not as well known to us as men's. "Nature produced women for this very purpose," says a Roman legal text, "that they might bear children and this is their greatest desire." Ancient philosophy held that women were intellectually inferior to men, science said they were physically weaker, and law maintained that they were naturally dependent. In the Roman world women could not enter professions, and they had limited rights in legal matters. Christianity offered women conflicting models. There was Eve, the eternal temptress through whom sin had fallen upon humanity, and then there was Mary, the immaculate, virginal Mother of God. The Bible also presented readers with powerful, active women, such as Deborah and Ruth, and loyal steadfast ones, such as Jesus's female disciples. (See the box, "The Valor of a Woman." For an illuminating comparison, see also the box, "Ruth," on page 58.) Amid this varied popular and learned opinion, we can still detect some possibilities for independent and influential activity on the part of women.

Girls usually did not choose their marriage partners. Betrothals could take place as early as age 7 and lawful marriages at 12. Most marriages took place around 16. A daughter could reject her father's choice only if the intended man were unworthy in status and behavior. Women could inherit property from their fathers, and they retained some control over their marital dowry. Divorce was possible but only in restricted cases. A divorced woman was at a distinct disadvantage legally and economically unless she had great wealth.

Christianity brought some interesting changes in marriage practices. The new faith prized virginity and celibacy and, thus, gave women the viable option of declining marriage. The church at Antioch, for example, supported three thousand virgins and widows. Christianity also taught that both men and women were to be faithful, whereas Roman custom permitted men, but not women, recourse to lovers, prostitutes, and concubines.

The Valor of a Woman

This passage comes from a treatise by Saint Ambrose entitled **On Widows.** *Ambrose takes as his source the story of Deborah in the Old Testament* **Book of Judges.** *Deborah, a widow, raised an army of 10,000 men that defeated a Canaanite king. This passage is a good example of how the Church Fathers applied biblical teachings to their own times, and it reveals current attitudes about both men and women.*

She showed not only that widows have no need of the help of a man, but that they can be reinforcements for men. Without being at all restrained by the weakness of her sex, she undertook to perform the duties of a man—and she did even more than she had undertaken. And at last, when the Jews were being ruled under the leadership of the judges, because these could not govern them with manly justice or defend them with manly strength, so that wars broke out on all sides, they chose Deborah, to be ruled by her judgement. And so one widow both ruled many thousands of men in peace and defended them from the enemy.

There were many judges in Israel, but no woman before was a judge; just as, after Joshua, there were many judges but none of them was a prophet. And I think that her career as a judge has been narrated, and her deeds described, so that women should not be restrained from valorous actions by the weakness of their sex. A widow, she governed the people; a widow, she led armies; a widow, she chose generals; a widow, she made military decisions and had charge of triumphs. Evidently it is not nature which is answerable for the fault or subject to weakness. It is not sex, but valour which gives strength.

Source: Alcuin Blamires, ed., *Woman Defamed and Woman Defended: An Anthology of Medieval Texts* (Oxford: Oxford University Press, 1992), p. 60.

Further, Christianity frowned on divorce. This may have accorded women greater financial and social security, although at the cost of staying with abusive or unloved husbands.

Traditionally, women were not permitted to teach in the ancient world, though we do hear of women teachers such as Hypatia of Alexandria (355–415), renowned for her knowledge of both philosophy and mathematics. Some Christian women, such as Melania (see page 257), were formidably learned. Until at least the sixth century the Christian church had deaconesses who had important responsibilities in the instruction of women and girls. Medical knowledge was often the preserve of women, particularly in areas such as childbirth, sexual problems, and "female complaints." Perhaps because of women's practical contributions, medical theory came to regard men and women as essentially alike.

Jewish thought held that women could grind corn, bake, launder, prepare meals, nurse children, make beds, and work wool. If a woman brought slaves into her marriage, then she could escape one of these tasks for each such slave. Not surprisingly, Christian writers tried to attract women to the celibate life by emphasizing that housework was drudgery. Although the church won only some women away from the domestic realm, Christianity also affected daily life. Teaching on modesty demanded that clothing expose less skin, that hair be veiled, and that jewelry and cosmetics be used in moderation. Women were warned against using the public baths and latrines: Churchmen were concerned that women not be seen as sex objects.

Male or female, Christians thought and lived in distinctive new ways. All Christians were sinners, and so all were equal in God's eyes and equally in need of God's grace. Neither birth nor wealth nor status was supposed to matter in this democracy of sin, but Christianity did have hierarchies of its own. The basic offices of the church were hierarchical: popes, patriarchs, archbishops, bishops, priests, deacons. At councils a hierarchy of seniority was observed. In these respects, the structure of the church was very much like that of the secular world.

The church also introduced some novel status distinctions. Holiness, rather than office or achievement, became a badge of honor. Here was a kind of status that could be neither conferred nor withdrawn by anything in this world. And it was not exactly confined to this world. The holy dead were thought to be as present in Christian society as the holy or sinful living. Sanctuaries were dedicated to saints, and people visited the tombs of the saints to pray and to seek healing from physical and spiritual ailments. Miracle stories became popular. Many wanted to be buried near saints' tombs. Thus, in some ways Christianity produced a society that the ancient world had never known, a society where the living and the dead jockeyed for place in a hierarchy that was at once earthly and celestial. But in other ways, Christianity reoriented traditional Roman patron-client relations so that the bonds joined client sinners in this world to sanctified patrons in heaven.

FROM EMPIRE TO KINGDOMS: THE ASCENDANCY OF THE GERMANIC PEOPLES

The years from the 370s to the 530s were decisive in the history of the Roman Empire in the west. When this period opened, the dynasty of Valentinian was firmly in control. When it closed, the former western provinces of the empire had become a number of Germanic kingdoms, most of which maintained some formal relationship with the eastern Roman Empire. The process that brought the Germanic barbarians into contact with the Romans was an intricate one. Roman policies played as great a role in it as barbarian plans. Many barbarians were peacefully accommodated into the Roman system on essentially Roman terms. The settlement of the Germans thus illustrates the paradox of continuity and change evident in so many aspects of late antique life.

Invasions and Migrations

Few images of the ancient world are more fixed in the popular imagination than the overrunning of the Roman Empire by hordes of savages who ushered in a dark age. For centuries people have spoken of the "barbarian invasions." The Romans inherited the word *barbarian* from the Greeks, who had divided the world between Hellenes, who spoke Greek, and non-Hellenes, who did not speak Greek. Barbarians were literally babblers, foreigners who spoke an unknown language. After the Romans granted citizenship to virtually everyone in the empire in 212, they adopted a Greek-style differentiation between Romans and barbarians. Technically, the latter were just foreigners, but in practice Romans thought barbarians inferior to themselves.

Individual groups of barbarians did invade the empire in various places at different times, but there was never a single, coordinated barbarian invasion of the Roman world that had well-formulated objectives. The Romans and barbarians did not face one another as declared enemies. Violent confrontations between them occurred, but peaceful encounters were just as common. The Romans had long traded with the Germanic peoples, carried out complicated diplomacy with them, and recruited them into their armies. German veterans were settled in most provinces of the empire.

The idea of barbarian migrations is sometimes offered as an alternative to invasions. It is equally imprecise. The best source for the early Germans is archaeology. The evidence collected to date makes it clear that the Germans were settled agriculturalists. They lived in villages, farmed the surrounding country, and raised livestock. If barbarians moved from one place to another, this movement cannot be attributed to migratory habits.

Who were the barbarians? Linguists classify them as belonging to the Germanic branches of the Indo-European family of languages. The Germans can be differentiated from the Celtic and Slavic peoples with whom they shared much of central and eastern Europe, but apart from some minor linguistic variations, it is difficult to distinguish Germans from one another. What are we to make of the profusion of names offered to us by our sources: Franks, Alemans, Saxons, Gepids, Heruls, Vandals, Alans, Visigoths, Ostrogoths, Lombards, Burgundians? These were not discrete

Fifth-Century Looped Fibulae These garment clasps are from a Gothic tomb in what is now Austria, but they illustrate well the craftsmanship and artistic taste of the barbarians with whom the Roman world interacted. *(Kunsthistorisches Museum, Vienna)*

ethnic communities. The Romans referred to the German peoples as tribes, but that does not mean that they were actually groups of related people. Every Germanic tribe was a confederation, and these confederations formed, dissolved, and re-formed many times. For example, the so-called Visigoths who crossed the Danube in 376 were made up of Visigoths and more than a half-dozen other peoples. The confederations were formed either by powerful leaders who coerced less powerful people to join them or by groups of villages that banded together to protect themselves from aggressive neighbors. In addition to following a leader, confederations—tribes—intermarried and adopted common languages, laws, and lifestyles.

Incorporating the Barbarians

The transformation of the western Roman Empire began as a result of an unexpected set of events involving the Huns, a people from the steppes of central Asia. Classical sources first mention these nomadic warriors in 172, but for the next two centuries they confined themselves to plundering the frontiers of Persia and China. Then, by the middle of the fourth century, they encountered formidable opposition and moved west in search of booty and tribute. In 374 or 375 they fell on the Ostrogoths, who lived near the Black Sea. At this juncture, as was discussed earlier (see page 236), the Visigoths requested permission to enter the Balkans. The

Huns continued moving west and finally began settling in the Pannonian plain in the 390s (see Map 7.3).

Until the 420s, the rulers in the east saw the Visigoths as the greater menace; but then the Huns began raiding in the Balkans, preying on trade routes that crossed the region, and demanding tribute from the eastern emperor. At the same time, a Roman general in Gaul concluded an alliance with the Huns in an attempt to use them as a check on the Burgundians, a federate people who lived in the central Rhineland and were expanding their territories.

In 434 the Huns chose Attila as their king. In return for a huge imperial subsidy, he agreed to cease raiding in the Balkans, and he marched west, having accepted the alliance against the Burgundians. Attila and the Romans together dealt the Burgundians a severe defeat, but Attila saw the weakness of the Roman position and attacked Gaul in 451. The Roman leaders then defeated Attila with a vast network of alliances made up of Romans, Visigoths, Burgundians, and Franks. Attila turned to Italy in 452, even approaching Rome, where Pope Leo I, not the emperor, convinced him to withdraw. Moral preaching and bags of gold from the church's deep coffers were equally persuasive to Attila—plus, although he was a brilliant battlefield commander, he did not have the forces to lay siege to Rome. After returning to Pannonia, Attila died in 454. Before another year was out, the short-lived Hunnic kingdom, largely Attila's personal creation, had vanished. (See the box, "Encounters with the West: Two Views of the Huns.")

The history of the Visigoths presents another instructive example of Romano-Germanic relations. They had served as auxiliary troops along the Danube for a long time when they requested permission to cross the frontier in 376. While the central government considered how to deal with them, local authorities sold them food at exorbitant prices and even traded dog meat for Gothic children, who were then enslaved. Barbarians had no monopoly on barbarity. It took until 382 for Theodosius to grant the Visigoths what they had been demanding: land to settle on and a Roman military title—that is, official status—for their king. A spokesman for Theodosius captured the emperor's hope that the Visigoths could be useful to the Romans: "Which is better: To fill Thrace with corpses or with farmers? To fill it with graves or with people? To travel through wilderness or cultivated land? To count those who have perished or those who are ploughing?" For decades, barbarians had been settling inside the Roman frontiers, and they had served loyally in the army. Beginning in the fourth century, most high military officers in the Roman world were barbarians. The only peculiar thing about the Visigoths' situation was that never before had the Romans admitted a whole people, as a people.

For about thirty years the Visigoths struggled to improve the terms of their settlements in the Balkans. Alaric, the Visigothic king after 395, grew tired of unfulfilled promises and of being a pawn in other people's games. He forced matters by attacking Italy.

The Visigothic sack of Rome in 410 was a psychological shock to contemporaries, and it has loomed large for centuries in people's ideas about the "fall" of the Roman Empire. Actually, it was a ploy by Alaric to adjust the terms of his already official status. Alaric died in 410, and his brother took over leadership of the Visigoths. He marched the barbarians north, from Italy into southern Gaul. For good measure, the new Visigothic king captured the western emperor's sister, Galla Placidia, and forcibly married her. However objectionable this act must seem, the Visigoths viewed it as a further demonstration of their loyalty to Rome and their desire to effect a satisfactory new treaty.

THE BARBARIANS

284–337	Military reforms incorporate more barbarians in army
360s	Appearance of Huns in Black Sea region
376–378	Visigoths enter Balkans and defeat Valens
410	Visigoths sack Rome
411–418	Settlement of Visigoths in Gaul
430	Vandals seize North Africa
450–550	Angles, Saxons, and Jutes enter Britain
451	Romans, Franks, and Visigoths defeat Huns
481–511	Reign of Clovis: consolidation of Frankish kingdom
507	Franks defeat Visigoths and drive them into Spain
532–534	Justinian's forces defeat Vandals
535–555	Justinian's forces defeat Ostrogoths

In 418 the Roman government gave in. A new treaty permitted the Visigoths to settle in southern Gaul, with Toulouse as their base of operations. They were assigned the task of protecting the area from marauding bands of brigands. In return for their service, the Visigoths were given land on which to settle and a portion of Roman tax receipts as pay.

The Visigoths' treaty with Rome made theirs the first Germanic kingdom on Roman soil. From 418 to 451 the Visigoths' king, Theodoric I, served Rome loyally and earned the respect and admiration of the Gallo-Roman aristocrats among whom he lived. He died fighting against Attila in 451. Between 466 and 484, the Visigothic kingdom in Gaul reached its high point and continued to receive official recognition from Roman rulers. Southern Gaul, one of Rome's oldest and richest provinces, passed from the hands of the Roman bureaucracy and the local nobility into the control of the Visigoths. Nevertheless, from Constantine's first treaty with the Visigoths through the continuing recognition by the Romans of Visigothic kings in the fifth and sixth centuries, it was Roman policy more

～ ENCOUNTERS WITH THE WEST ～

Two Views of the Huns

The dread and disgust inspired by the Huns is well captured in the first passage, from the Roman historian Ammianus Marcellinus, while the second passage, from a surviving fragment of the history of Priscus, shows the Huns in quite a different light.

(a)

From the moment of their birth they make deep gashes in their children's cheeks, so that when in due course hair appears its growth is checked by the wrinkled scars; as they grow older this gives them the unlovely appearance of beardless eunuchs. They have squat bodies, strong limbs, and thick necks, and are so prodigiously ugly and bent that they might be two-legged animals. Their shape, however disagreeable, is human. They have no use for seasoned food, but live on the roots of wild plants and the half-raw flesh of any animal, which they warm a little by placing it between their thighs and the backs of their horses. They have no buildings to shelter them. They wear garments of linen or of the skins of field-mice stitched together. Once they have put their necks into some dingy shirt they never take it off or change it until it rots and falls to pieces. They have round caps of fur on their heads, and protect their hairy legs with goatskins. They are ill-fitted to fight on foot, and remain glued to their horses, hardy but ugly beasts, on which they sometimes sit like women to perform their everyday business and they even bow forward over their beasts' narrow necks to enjoy a deep and dreamy sleep.

(b)

[The Roman ambassadors] came upon a very large village in which the dwelling of Attila was said to be more notable than those elsewhere. It had been fitted together with highly polished timbers and encircled with a wooden palisade, conceived not for safety but for beauty. Next to the king's dwelling that of Onegisus [chief minister to Attila] was outstanding, and it also had a circuit of timbers but was not embellished with towers in the same way as Attila's. Not far from the enclosure was a large bath. . . . Maidens came to meet Attila as he entered this village, advancing before him in rows under fine white linen cloths stretched out to such a length that under each cloth, which was held up by the hands of the women along either side, seven or even more girls walked. There were many such formations of women under the linen cloths, and they sang Scythian songs. When he [Attila] came near the house of Onegisus, the wife of Onegisus came out with a host of servants, some bearing dainties and others wine, greeted him and asked him to partake of the food which she had brought for him with friendly hospitality. To gratify the wife of his intimate friend, he ate sitting on his horse, the barbarians accompanying him having raised the silver platter up to him. Having also tasted the wine, he went on to the palace, which was higher than the other houses and situated on a high place.

Sources: Excerpt (a): Ammianus Marcellinus, *The Later Roman Empire (A.D. 354–378)*, ed. and trans. Walter Hamilton (Harmondsworth, England: Penguin, 1986), 31.2, pp. 411–412. Excerpt (b): Priscus, Fragment 8, in C. D. Gordon, *The Age of Attila: Fifth-Century Byzantium and the Barbarians* (Ann Arbor: University of Michigan Press, 1961), pp. 84–85.

than Visigothic policy that determined the accommodation of this first Germanic kingdom within the framework of the western Roman Empire.

More Kingdoms: The End of Direct Roman Rule in the West

Valentinian III (r. 425–455) was born in 419 and succeeded to the throne as a 6-year-old. Until he came of age, his court was weakened by factional strife, and his regime, confined to the west, was dominated by military men. After Valentinian the western empire saw a succession of nonentities, the last of whom was deposed in 476 by Odoacer, a Germanic general, who simply sent the imperial regalia to Constantinople and declared that the West no longer needed an emperor. This is all that happened in 476, the traditional date for the "fall" of the Roman Empire.

Important events continued to unfold in Gaul. A vast coalition of Romans, Visigoths, Burgundians, and Franks had defeated the Huns. No sooner were the Huns beaten than Roman authorities in the Paris region discovered that the Visigoths were expanding north of the Loire River into central Gaul. To check this advance, the Roman commander in Paris forged an alliance with the Franks. The Franks, long Roman federates, had been expanding their settlements from the mouth of the Rhine southward across modern Holland and Belgium since the third century. Occasionally the Romans had halted their advance, but usually they had left the Franks alone. They now enlisted the Franks to help stop the Visigoths.

The fortunes of the Frankish kingdom, indeed of all of Gaul, rested with Clovis. He became king of one group of Franks in 481 and spent the years until his death in 511 subjecting all the other bands of Franks to his rule. He gained the allegiance of the Frankish people by leading them to constant military victories that brought territorial gains, plunder, and tribute. The greatest of Clovis's successes came in 507, when he defeated the Visigoths at Vouillé and drove them over the Pyrenees into Spain.

Clovis was popular not only with the Franks but also with the Gallo-Roman population. There were three reasons for his popularity. First, Clovis and the Romans had common enemies: Germanic tribes still living beyond the Rhine and pirates who raided the coast of Gaul. Second, whereas most of the Germanic peoples were Arian Christians, the majority of the Franks passed directly from paganism to Catholicism (see page 255). Thus, Clovis and the Gallo-Romans had a shared faith that permitted Clovis to portray his war against the Visigoths as, at least in part, a crusade against heresy. Third, Clovis eagerly sought from Constantinople formal recognition and titles, appeared publicly in the dress of a Roman official, and practiced such imperial rituals as distributing gold coins while riding through crowds of people. The Frankish kingdom under Clovis's family—called "Merovingian" from the name of one of his semilegendary ancestors—became the most successful of all the Germanic realms.

To meet threats elsewhere, the Romans had begun pulling troops out of Britain in the fourth century and abandoned the island to its own defense in 410. Thereafter, raiding parties from Scotland and Ireland, as well as seaborne attackers—called "Saxons" by contemporaries because some of them came from Saxony in northern Germany—ravaged Britain. Down to the 450s the British continually appealed to the military authorities in Gaul for aid, but to no avail. Some people in Britain resorted to hiring gangs of "Saxons" to defend them, but they could not stem the tide of new settlers. Between 450 and 600, much of southern and eastern Britain was taken over by diverse peoples whom we call the "Anglo-Saxons." The newcomers jostled for position with the Celtic Britons, who were increasingly confined to the north and west of the island. Gradually several small, impermanent kindgoms emerged. Although Britain retained contacts with Gaul, the island had virtually no Roman inheritance.

There were several unsuccessful kingdoms. The Burgundian kingdom that had once prompted the Romans to ally with the Huns was swallowed up by the more powerful Franks in the 530s. The Vandals, who crossed the Rhine in 406 and headed for Spain, crossed to North Africa in 429 (see Map 7.3). They were ardent Arians who persecuted the Catholic population. They refused imperial offers of a treaty on terms like those accepted by other Germanic peoples. And they constantly plundered the islands of the western Mediterranean and the Italian coast, even sacking Rome in 455. The Romans eliminated the Vandals in 534.

The Ostrogoths had been living in Pannonia since the 370s, subjects of the Huns for much of

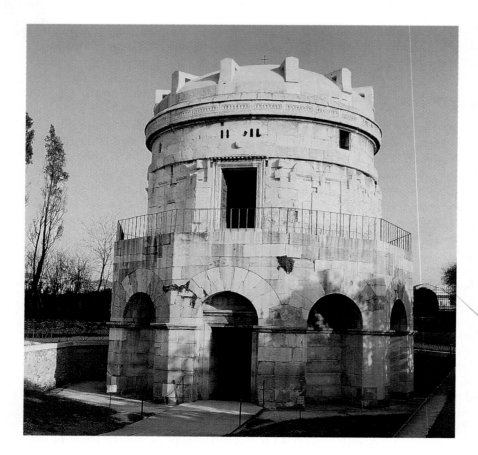

Mausoleum of Theodoric The deeply Romanized Ostrogoth Theodoric designed this classically inspired tomb for himself in Ravenna. The building displays the mixture of the Roman and the Germanic that is prevalent in Late Antiquity. *(C. M. Dixon Colour Photo Library)*

that time. They were sent to Italy in 493 by the Romans to remove Odoacer, the man who had deposed the last western emperor in 476. Odoacer had earned the displeasure of the Roman administration by laying hands on the sentimentally significant land of Italy—and by doing so on his own initiative, instead of by Roman directive. The government at Constantinople was familiar with the Ostrogoths' king, Theodoric, because he had been a hostage there for several years. The emperor also wished to remove the Ostrogoths from the Danube basin, where they were a potential threat. Sending Theodoric to Italy seemed like a way to solve two problems simultaneously.

Theodoric got rid of Odoacer quickly enough and set up his capital in Ravenna, the swamp-surrounded and virtually impregnable city that had sheltered the imperial administration for much of the fifth century after the Visigothic attack had exposed the weakness of Rome's defenses. Through the force of his personality, and by a series of marriage alliances, Theodoric became the dominant person in western Europe. In Italy he promoted peace, stability, and good government. He won to his service some of the leading men of the time. Still, Theodoric had two strikes against him. One, he and his people were Arians. Two, although the population of Italy was accustomed to having an imperial court dominated by Germans and to having Germanic military men in Gaul as the real powers in the state, they had never been directly ruled by a German, and some of them could not accept Theodoric. By the 520s Theodoric grew increasingly suspicious and dictatorial. After he died in 526, the government in Constantinople launched an attack on Italy that put an end to the Ostrogothic kingdom but also devastated Italy in twenty years of brutal warfare.

By the 530s the western Roman Empire had vanished after a process initiated by the entry of the Visigoths into the Balkans in 376. Of all the peoples who had contested for a share of Rome's legacy, only the Franks in Gaul, the Visigoths in Spain, and the Anglo-Saxons in Britain had cre-

Map 7.3 The Germanic Kingdoms in the Sixth Century By the late sixth century, the western provinces of the Roman Empire (compare Map 6.1 on page 194) had evolved into Germanic kingdoms. Just as provincial boundaries had changed numerous times, the existence and extent of kingdoms were also not permanent.

ated stable political entities. In some respects the map of the western Roman world was tidier in the middle of the sixth century than it had been at any time since the second (Map 7.3).

Several factors contributed to this outcome. Beginning with Constantine, Rome's best rulers were resident in and concerned mainly about the East. The Visigoths and other peoples were settled in their own kingdoms on Roman soil, instead of being enrolled in and dispersed among Roman army units. Beginning with Diocletian, the army was increasingly Germanized, and Germanic military men gained high offices in the state. Those leaders often dominated imperial courts and negotiated the series of treaties that submitted former provinces to barbarian peoples. Provincial elites had long been accustomed to having prominent Germans in their midst. The new situation

was not unusual to them. Churchmen readily embraced the Catholic Franks and tolerated Arians, such as the Visigoths, who promoted peace and good government without abusing the Catholic population.

The New Old West

The Germanic kingdoms had a great deal in common with one another and were very much like the late Roman Empire, which had been their common tutor. Each realm was led by a king who usually appeared in two distinct guises. To his people, the king was the military leader. The essential bond of unity among each Germanic people was loyalty to the leader, who repaid his followers in booty, tribute, land, judicial protection, and military security. To the Romans, the king appeared as an ally and magistrate. Almost all Germanic kings bore such Roman titles as *consul* or *patrician,* and in these officially conferred titles resided the authority necessary to govern Roman populations. The kings also succeeded to a long line of German Masters of the Soldiers, the title of the highest military officers in a prefecture. Each monarchy was led by a dynasty—for example, the Merovingians among the Franks—that was preeminent in wealth and possessed a sacral aura not unlike that of the Roman emperors. Among the Germans, as among the Romans, the dynasties provided both strength through continuity and tension as family members competed with one another and with envious outsiders.

The most common local officials were counts, a combined civilian-military position that made its first appearance in the fifth century. Initially a direct representative of the central government, a count had financial, judicial, and military responsibilities. Local notables, still usually great landowners, resented counts until the government's ability to manage local affairs declined and they themselves became counts. Kings were careful to promote important locals to the office of count.

Local administration continued to be based in cities and towns. Taxes continued to be paid to royal governments throughout the sixth century. Provincial populations did not find this policy odd or unjust. Their taxes had always gone primarily to pay for the Roman military establishment, and the monarchies were the heirs of that establishment. Latin continued to be the language of administration. Until the end of Late Antiquity, notaries continued to draw up wills, records of land transactions, and legal documents of all kinds. Major law codes were issued by the Germanic kingdoms, including the Salic Law of the Franks (511), two versions of the Burgundian Code, and several revisions of the Visigoths' laws. These were local adaptations of Roman provincial law. In other words, the legal conditions under which most people lived changed little. It is difficult to find convincing evidence that people's daily lives changed much as a result of the replacement of Roman provinces by Germanic kingdoms.

The Germans generally shared the Christian faith with the provincial populations, but here there were complications. A number of the Germans, chief among them the Vandals, Visigoths, and Ostrogoths, were Arians. Heresy was far from the worst of the Vandals' problems, but there can be no doubt that religious differences were damaging to the Ostrogoths and Visigoths. Cooperation between the Franks and the Gallo-Romans derived from many sources, but one of the strongest was a shared faith.

THE ROMAN EMPIRE IN THE EAST

The creation of the tetrarchy separated the eastern and western halves of the Roman Empire administratively. In theory there was only one empire, ruled by one senior augustus. The reality was different, however. The Eastern and Western courts followed different policies toward the Germans, for example. Eastern rulers, who ushered the Germans through the Balkans and into the West, lost virtually no territory to them. There were also fundamental differences between East and West. The East was more populous, more heavily urbanized, and more prosperous. The eastern Mediterranean was Greek in culture and livelier intellectually than the West. From Constantine in the fourth century to Justinian in the sixth, there emerged an eastern Roman Empire that, as the western empire was being parceled out into kingdoms, became the sole heir of the imperial tradition.

Constantinople and Its Rulers

Constantius II (r. 337–361), Constantine's son and successor, began making Constantinople a truly imperial city. He gave "New Rome" a senate and a set of urban magistrates of its own, placing the city on an equal constitutional footing with old Rome. Constantinople did not have an ancient aristocracy, so Constantius had to create a senatorial order. This he did by promoting prominent and cultivated persons from cities in the eastern half of the empire. Almost immediately rivalries arose between the senates of East and West. From the emperor's point of view, the new situation was satisfactory because there was in Constantinople a harmony of aristocratic and imperial interests.

With the exception of the founder, the ablest members of the dynasty of Valentinian ruled in the East. The greatest of these was Theodosius II (r. 408–450), who enjoyed the longest imperial reign in Roman history. Through skillful diplomacy and the occasional application of force, he managed to keep the eastern empire free of serious Germanic incursions and the Persians at bay in Mesopotamia. To protect his capital city, he built on the landward side massive walls whose ruins are impressive even today. He, along with his wife and his sister, promoted learning in the city and both added and beautified important buildings. Theodosius and his family made the new capital a real intellectual center.

Theodosius's greatest achievement was the law code that he issued in 438. The most comprehensive collection of Roman law yet produced, this code brought together all Roman laws issued since Constantine and arranged them in systematic fashion. The principal Germanic kingdoms were established just after the Theodosian code was issued. From this text, and from the Roman institutional structures that employed it, the Germans were taught the rule of law and regulations for the conduct of daily affairs.

The Emperor Justinian (r. 527–565)

After Theodosius II died in 450, the Eastern empire endured seventy-seven years of rule by military men who lacked the culture, vision, or administrative capacity of their predecessors. But they preserved the empire and kept its government functioning. It was from these rough soldiers that Justinian arose. Until his death in 565, he worked tirelessly in many fields, earning the nickname of "the emperor who never sleeps." He was the greatest ruler of Late Antiquity, one of the greatest of all Rome's emperors. (See the feature, "Weighing the Evidence: The Ravenna Mosaics," on pages 264–265.)

Justinian rose from the Illyrian (Croatian today) peasantry through the military to the imperial throne. Despite growing up in rural military camps, Justinian showed a wide range of interests and abilities. He surrounded himself with remarkable people and gave them considerable latitude. He flouted convention by marrying an actress named Theodora (d. 548). A woman of intelligence, imagination, and great courage, Theodora was one of Justinian's key advisers. Justinian identified and promoted such previously obscure figures as the gifted general Belisarius, the administrative genius John the Cappadocian, and the greatest legal mind of the age, Tribonian. He entrusted two famous mathematicians, Anthemius

of Tralles and Isidore of Miletus, with the task of designing the church of Hagia Sophia, which remains his principal monument.

Almost immediately on assuming the throne, Justinian put John the Cappadocian to work reforming an administration that had been little altered in two centuries despite vast changes in the scope of the empire. John worked particularly to secure tighter control of provincial administrators, to ensure a steady flow of tax revenue, and to eliminate official corruption. Tribonian and a commission were assigned the task of producing the first comprehensive review of Roman law since that of Theodosius II in 438. Between 529 and 533, Justinian's code was issued in three parts. The *Code* was a systematically organized collection of all imperial legislation. The *Digest* was a collection of the writings of the classical Roman jurists, the legal philosophers of the Early Empire. The *Institutes* was a textbook for law students. (See the box, "Basic Principles of Roman Law.") Justinian's code is the most influential legal collection in human history. It summarized a thousand years of legal work, reigned in the Eastern empire for another thousand years, and has affected almost every state and legal system in the modern world.

Not long after undertaking his legal and administrative reforms, Justinian launched an attempt to reconquer the empire's lost western provinces. Belisarius retook Africa from the Vandals and Italy from the Ostrogoths. Justinian also landed an army in Spain to attempt the reconquest of Iberia from the Visigoths. However, he never had the resources to carry out this task successfully.

Although he enjoyed some military successes in the west, Justinian faced constant threats in the Balkans from Bulgars and Slavs and in Mesopotamia from Persians. Costly treaties and humiliating subsidies bought a string of cease-fires but no definitive settlements in these areas. The emperor's campaigns were so expensive that his administrative reforms wound up looking like contrivances to make more money for the emperor to waste. Resentment flared in Constantinople in 532 in violent riots in which mobs coursed through the city demanding the dismissal of John the Cappadocian and other imperial agents. In 542, moreover, the Mediterranean world was visited by plague, one more blow to the empire.

Justinian's religious policy also met with sharp opposition. A genuinely pious man, Justinian

Theodora This magnificent sixth-century mosaic from Ravenna (it is one of a pair; see page 265) depicts Empress Theodora in all her power and majesty. *(Scala/Art Resource, NY)*

legislated frequently on behalf of the church and practiced, along with Theodora, generous charitable benefactions. Still, by both personal conviction and a sense of official duty, Justinian desired religious unity. Although the Council of Chalcedon had condemned monophysitism in 451, Justinian was mildly monophysite, and his wife was enthusiastically so. Justinian tried again and again to find a compromise that would bring all parties together. His church council of 553 assembled amid high hopes but in the end alienated the clergy in Syria, Egypt, and Rome.

Justinian had visions of grandeur, and to give them concrete expression he sought out Anthemius and Isidore. He wished for these great mathematicians to design a church that would be not merely impressive but magnificent. It was to represent the place where heaven and earth touched, the vestibule of heaven. Its symbolic role was to be given regular confirmation by the meeting in this place of the emperor, the patriarch (the archbishop of Constantinople), and the people. There is no evidence that Justinian dictated the form of his church—the church of Hagia Sophia ("Holy Wisdom")—but the fact that he did not turn to any of the city's regular builders suggests that he was not looking for a traditional basilica.

He got the largest Christian church ever built, but its size is almost the least of its qualities. Hagia Sophia starts from a square just over 100 feet on a side, 70 feet above which are four great arches. Two of the arches are solid and form the nave walls of the church; the other two give way to semicircular continuations of the nave. Above the main square

Basic Principles of Roman Law

Roman law is distinguished not only by its particular rules but also by its approach to the subject of law as a whole. These words are from the beginning of Justinian's Institutes, *his lawbook for students.*

Justice is an unswerving and perpetual determination to acknowledge all men's rights. Learning in the law entails knowledge of God and man, and mastery of the difference between justice and injustice. . . . The commandments of the law are these: live honorably; harm nobody; give everyone his due. There are two aspects to the subject: public and private. Public law is concerned with the organization of the Roman state, while private is about the well-being of individuals. [Private law] has three parts, in that it is derived from the law of nature, of all peoples, or of the state. The law of nature is the law instilled by nature in all creatures. It is not merely for mankind but for all creatures of the sky, earth and sea. From it comes intercourse between male and female, which we call marriage; also the bearing and bringing up of children. Observation shows that other animals also acknowledge its force. The law of all peoples and the law of the state are distinguished as follows. All peoples with laws and customs apply law which is partly theirs alone and partly shared by all mankind. The law which each people makes for itself is special to its own state. It is called "state law," the law peculiar to that state. But the law which natural reason makes for all mankind is applied the same everywhere. It is called the "law of all peoples" because it is common to every nation. The law of the Roman people is also partly its own and partly common to all mankind. . . . The name of a particular state, Athens for example, is used to identify its state law. Similarly we refer to the law of the Roman people as the Roman state law. By contrast, the law of all peoples is common to all mankind. The reality of the human condition led the peoples of the world to introduce certain institutions. Wars broke out. People were captured and made slaves contrary to the law of nature. By the law of nature all men were initially born free. Nearly all the contracts come from this law of all peoples: sale, hire, partnership, deposit, loan, and many others. Next, our law is either written or unwritten. . . . Written law includes acts, plebeian statutes, resolutions of the senate, imperial pronouncements, magistrates' edicts, and answers given by jurists. . . . Law comes into being without writing when a rule is approved by use. Long standing custom founded on the consent of those who follow it is just like legislation. . . . The law of nature, which is observed uniformly by all peoples, is sanctioned by divine providence and lasts forever, strong and unchangeable. The law which each state establishes for itself is often changed either by tacit consent of the people or by later legislation.

Source: Peter Birks and Grant McLeod, ed. and trans., *Justinian's Institutes,* 1.1–2 (Ithaca, N.Y.: Cornell University Press, 1987), pp. 37–39.

is a dome that seems to float on a blaze of light. The inside is a riot of color achieved by marble fittings in almost every imaginable hue, by mosaics and frescoes of indescribable beauty, and by the mysterious play of light and shadow. The effect of the whole is disorienting. Space in most basilicas is ordered, controlled, elegant. Space in Hagia Sophia is horizontal and vertical, straight and curved, square and round. The inside is by turns dark and light, purple and green, red and blue. It is indeed as if one has entered a realm that is anchored to this world but that gives access to another one. When Justinian first saw his church in its completed state, he said, "Solomon, I have outdone thee."

It is appropriate that in inspecting his great church Justinian should have looked backward to

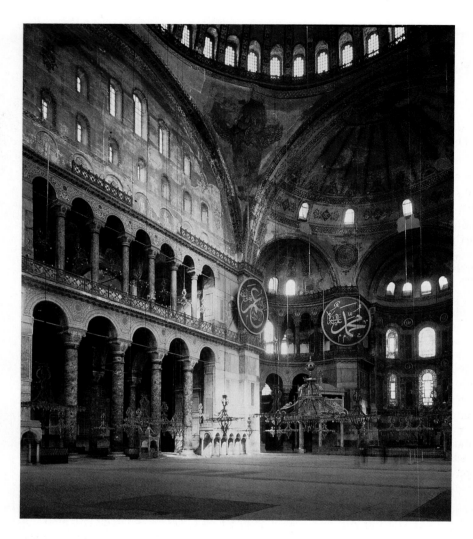

Hagia Sophia This interior view of Hagia Sophia conveys some sense of the dazzling complexity of this greatest of all late antique buildings. Compare it to Santa Maria Maggiore (page 240). *(Giraudon/Art Resource, NY)*

Solomon, the Hebrew king who built Jerusalem's Temple. In almost all respects Justinian was a traditional, backward-looking ruler. His concern for the administrative minutiae of his empire would have made perfect sense to Diocletian, and his combination of military and diplomatic initiatives would have been understood by Theodosius I, whose namesake, Theodosius II, would have admired Justinian's legal code. In his religious policies, especially in his quest for unity, Justinian drew from a deep well of imperial precedent. Even in his attempt to restore direct rule in Rome's former western provinces, Justinian showed himself a traditionalist.

CHRISTIAN CULTURE AND LIFE

Christian culture involved institutions that claimed people's allegiance, communities that nurtured them, ideas that inspired them, and a history that defined them. Christianity grew and spread in the Roman world. It spoke that world's languages, borrowed its philosophical and legal terminology, adapted its administrative structures, reinterpreted its celebrations, and recruited its ablest citizens. The French have a saying: "Plus ça change, plus c'est la même chose"—"The more things change, the more they remain the same." So it was in Late Antiquity, in the realms of both government and religion.

The True Church: Competing Visions

Around 450 a Christian writer said that the Catholic faith was the one believed "everywhere, all the time, by everyone." That is a good, working definition of *Catholicism*, a religious tradition that takes its name from a Greek word meaning "universal." It is no accident that a Catholic church grew up in a Roman world steeped in ideas of universality. The most deeply held tenet of Roman ideology maintained that Rome's mission was to civilize the whole world and bend it to Roman ways.

The Catholic church, in seeking to assume that mission, met opposition on at least two fronts. As a first case, let us look at a quarrel between an emperor and a pope. The popes had been working to gain leadership in the church and to make themselves final arbiters of doctrine. When Emperor Anastasius (r. 491–518) intervened in a quarrel between the Catholics and the monophysites, Pope Gelasius I (r. 492–496) sent him a harsh letter in which he protested the emperor's intervention. Gelasius told the emperor that the world was governed by the "power" of kings and by the "authority" of priests. Ordinarily, the pope said, the jurisdictions of kings and priests are distinct. In a controversy between them, however, priestly authority must have precedence because priests are concerned with the salvation of immortal souls but kings rule only mortal bodies. Gelasius was telling the emperor to stay out of theology, but he was implying much more. His opposition of the words *power*—meaning mere police power, the application of brute force—and *authority*—legitimacy, superior right—was of great importance. Gelasius elevated the church, with the pope at its head, above the whole secular regime with the emperor at its head.

Gelasius could take this position because he was in Rome, where there was no longer an emperor. The pope could also be confident of the unity of the church in the western Mediterranean; in contrast, the East was still riven by controversies. The emperor took sharp exception to Gelasius's arguments, but more pressing business faced him. He could not achieve unity among warring Christian factions, and he had to think about his frontiers more than about the writings of a troublesome priest in old Rome. Christians in the East agreed with Gelasius's views on priestly authority and kingly power only to the extent that they were already opposed to the emperor's theological pronouncements.

This controversy reveals several conflicting visions. Was the church a branch of the state and thus subject to imperial command? The emperor thought so, but the pope denied it. Was the pope the final arbiter of doctrine? Neither the emperor nor the pope's theological opponents were prepared to admit this. Would the pope actually have any real influence in the East? It seemed unlikely. But could the emperor impose his will in matters of religion, in the East or the West, as a practical matter of power or as a theoretical dimension of his office? This seemed unlikely too.

The second case concerns several broad patterns of Christian experience that emerged in Late Antiquity and survive to this day. One of the interesting developments is the emergence of several Christian communities claiming fidelity to a universal—a catholic—tradition. The Latin Christian church in the West was staunchly Nicene and Chalcedonian and took its bearings from Latin church writers. The Orthodox church in the East centered primarily on the emperors and patriarchs, used Greek, and followed Greek Christian writers. The Coptic church in Egypt was monophysite, followed the teachings of the patriarchs of Alexandria, and used the Coptic language. The Jacobite church, a mildly monophysite, Syriac-speaking group, was originally strong in Syria, from where it spread to Mesopotamia and beyond. Each of these churches produced a literature, an art, and a way of life that marked its members as a distinct community. These traditions did not reflect the emergence of something new in Late Antiquity so much as a Christian reinterpretation of very old cultures and ideals.

The Rise of Christian Monasticism

For some people the call of the Gospel was positively revolutionary. They did not wish to work to change this world for the better. They wished to escape this world in order to avoid all that might come between them and the God who was both the source and the goal of human existence. These people were monks who developed a theology and an institution that were among the most creative and long-lived of all the achievements of Late Antiquity. Christian monasticism emerged in Egypt in the last decades of the third century, but the forces that combined to produce monasticism are ancient and universal.

The practice of rigorous self-denial (*askesis*) was common to several religious and philosophical sects in antiquity—for example, the Pythagoreans and the Stoics—and was well known among the Jews in the time of Christ, as the Essenes show (see page 215). Widespread opinion held that if one could conquer the desires of the body, one could unite with those beings who were greater and purer than humans encumbered by their lusts for food, drink, knowledge, sex, and adventure. Sometimes ascetic practices were adopted by tightly knit groups, sometimes by heroic solitaries.

These traditions met in Egypt in the person of Anthony (d. 356). He was a man who, at about age 20, gave away all his possessions and took up in the Egyptian desert a life of prayer and renunciation. In the desert, Anthony sought to imitate the life of Christ. His spiritual quest became famous, and many disciples flocked to him. Finally, he decided to organize them into a very loose community. Anthony's form of monasticism is called *eremitic,* from the Greek *heremos* for "desert." The name *eremitic,* signifying extreme asceticism and individualism, gives us the word *hermit.*

Pachomius (290–346) created a second form of monastic life. He was a Roman soldier who left the service in 313, was baptized a Christian, and retired to the Egyptian desert, where he studied with a hermit. Eventually Pachomius founded a community of ascetics, and before long his community, and dozens like it, had thousands of members. An anomalous situation had arisen: Literally thousands of people were living alone but together in veritable cities out in the desert. Pachomius wrote the first Rule, or code for daily living, for a monastic community. He organized most aspects of the life of his community by designing a common life based on routines of private prayer, group worship, and work. Pachomius's pattern of monasticism is called *cenobitic,* from the Greek for "common life." People living this common life were called *monks,* and the place where they lived this life was called a *monastery.* The head of the community was designated *abbot,* a word meaning "father."

Monasticism spread from Egypt by means of texts such as the *Life of Anthony* (a late antique "bestseller"), collections of the wise sayings of famous desert abbots, and books written by persons who went to Egypt seeking a more perfect life—among whom were several prominent women, such as Melania. (See the box, "Melania the Younger: The Appeal of Monasticism to Women.") The appeal of monasticism grew greater after Christianity gained official status. Those who were attracted to monasticism saw it as a purer form of Christian life, uncorrupted by the wealth, power, and controversy of the hierarchical church. The ascetic life was popular with women for personal reasons and because offices in the church hierarchy were denied to women, whereas positions in monasteries, including that of abbess, provided outlets for female talent. Monasticism gave women a chance to choose a kind of family life different from the one available in households dominated by fathers and husbands.

As monasticism spread from Egypt, it adopted the two basic patterns. In the East, the eremitic pattern was prominent in Palestine and Syria and eventually throughout the Greek-speaking world. Eastern monasticism produced a great legislator in Basil (330–379), who wrote the most influential Rule in the Orthodox church. Generally these monks assembled only for weekly worship and otherwise ate, prayed, and worked alone.

Eremitic monasticism arrived in the West in the person of Martin of Tours (336–397). Like Pachomius, Martin was a pagan Roman soldier who, after his military service ended, embraced both Christianity and asceticism. Even though he was elected bishop of Tours, Martin kept to his rigid life of denial.

An admiring biography kept Martin's memory alive for centuries, but in the West the cenobitic pattern proved more successful than the eremitic. The first great center from which cenobitic monasticism spread was Lérins in the south of Gaul, where a community was founded in 410. The fame of Lérins spread rapidly throughout the western Roman Empire, and men came to it from all over. Lérins attracted many aristocrats, some of whom went on to become bishops and promoters of monasticism.

The most famous monastic founder in the West was Benedict of Nursia (480–545), a middle-class Roman who abandoned legal studies and a potential government career to pursue a life of prayer. Benedict's fame grew so great that he attracted a crowd of followers, and in about 520, at Monte Cassino—80 miles south of Rome—he drew

Melania the Younger: The Appeal of Monasticism to Women

The appeal of monasticism was great for men and women, rich and poor, as the career of Melania (383–438) shows. She came from a wealthy Roman family but renounced her possessions and traveled widely in Italy, North Africa, Egypt, and Palestine, visiting holy men and women. These selected passages from her biography provide glimpses of her life.

Melania was foremost among the Romans of senatorial rank. Wounded by divine love, she had from earliest youth yearned for Christ, and longed for bodily chastity. Her parents, because they were illustrious members of the Roman senate and expected that through her they would have a succession of the family line, forcibly united her in marriage . . . when she was fourteen and her husband, seventeen. [After having two children, Melania persuaded her husband to join her in renouncing the world.] She bridled nature and delivered herself to death daily, demonstrating to everyone that woman is not surpassed by man in anything that pertains to virtue, if her decision is strong. She was by nature a gifted writer and wrote without mistakes in notebooks. She decided for herself how much she should write every day, and how much she should read in the canonical books and in the collections of homilies. Then she would go through the Lives of the fathers as if she were eating dessert. The blessed woman read the Old and New Testaments three or four times a year. The most holy fathers [Egyptian abbots] received her as if she were a man. In truth, she had been detached from the female nature, and had acquired a masculine disposition, or rather, a heavenly one.

Source: Elizabeth A. Clark, ed. and trans., *The Life of Melania the Younger,* cc. 1, 12, 23, 26, 39, *Studies in Women and Religion,* vol. 14 (New York: Edwin Mellen Press, 1984), pp. 27–28, 35, 46, 53–54.

up a Rule. This Rule is marked by shrewd insights into the human personality. It emphasizes the bond of mutual love among the monks and obedience to the abbot. The abbot is assigned wide powers but is told to exercise them gently. Monks are permitted a reasonable diet and decent, though modest, clothing. Although punishment is provided for, loving correction is preferred. In Late Antiquity the monks of Lérins were the monastic elite of the West, but in later centuries Benedict's Rule came to dominate monastic life.

Eremitic or cenobitic, East or West, male or female monasticism represented an explicit challenge and a conscious alternative to the civic world of classical antiquity. Monks were assuredly not people who sought to give their lives meaning by service within cities. They went into deserts to serve God and one another. They sought not to acquire but to abandon. Spiritual wisdom counted for more than secular learning, and acknowledgment of their holiness was more important than recognition of their social status.

The Quest for a Catholic Tradition

The Christian clergy attracted not only talented administrators but also gifted intellectuals. As the church became first free and then triumphant, those intellectuals were able to reflect publicly on their faith and its place in the ancient world. The results of their labors produced a coherent tradition that can be called *Catholic.*

Christianity drew much from the pagan and Jewish environments within which it grew, but its fundamental inspiration was the collection of writings called in modern times the *Bible.* In antiquity this material was called *ta hagia biblia* or *sacra biblia,* meaning "the holy books." It was

The Temptation of Joseph by Potiphar's Wife (Genesis 39:11–20) This illumination (a painting that illustrates the accompanying text) is from a fifth- or sixth-century manuscript of the Old Testament. Compare the figures and the scene to the mosaic from Santa Costanza on page 235. (*Österreichische Nationalbibliothek*)

understood to be a collection of sacred writings, and the individual items in that collection had different meanings. From the second century, Christian writers began trying to define a canon, a definitive list of genuine Old and New Testament scriptures. It was widely recognized that until a standard set of Christian sources was defined, there could be no hope of uniformity of Christian belief. This process was not completed until the middle of the fifth century.

While the search was under way for an authoritative list of books, it was also necessary to try to get uniform versions of the books that were being pronounced canonical. The Greek East used the Greek version of the Old Testament and the Greek New Testament; but that version was unsuitable in the West, where Latin was the principal tongue. Late in the fourth century, Pope Damasus commissioned Jerome (331–420), a wealthy man who abandoned his luxury for a life of monasticism and scholarship, to prepare a Latin version based on a new translation of the Hebrew Scriptures and Greek New Testament. Jerome's version was called the "Vulgate" because it was the Bible for the "people" (*vulgus*) who knew Latin.

Once a scriptural canon had been identified, there was also a need for a creedal statement that

would set down precisely what Christians believed. The councils of Nicaea and Constantinople defined the nature of the Trinity, and Chalcedon formulated the relationship between the human and divine natures of Christ. These central dogmas, or teachings, of the Christian faith were not the only theological issues that arose, however. There were debates about the priesthood, the church, and the problem of human free will. Practical questions came up, too. How could Christians fulfill the moral demands of their faith while living in a world whose values were often at odds with church teachings?

Answers to these kinds of questions were provided by a group of Greek and Latin writers who are called the "Church Fathers" and whose era is called "patristic" (from *patres*, the Latin word for *fathers*). In versatility and sheer output they have few rivals at any time. Their intellectual breadth was matched by their elegant style and trenchant reasoning.

Many Christian writers addressed themselves to the problems of moral living in the world. Ambrose of Milan wrote *On Duties*, a treatise that attempted to Christianize the public ethos that Cicero had spelled out many years before in his book *On Duties*. Cicero talked of citizens' obligations to one another and to the law. He stressed the need for those in places of power and responsibility to be above reproach in the conduct of their personal lives. Ambrose reinterpreted these ideas as duties that Christians owed to one another because of their common worship of God. At about the same time the patriarch of Constantinople, John Chrysostom (347–407), one of the most popular and gifted preachers of Late Antiquity (his name means "golden tongued"), bitterly castigated the immorality of the imperial court and aristocracy because by setting a bad example they endangered the souls of their subjects.

No set of thematic categories could be drawn broadly enough to encompass Augustine (354–430). A later Spanish Father, Isidore of Seville, once said that if anyone tells you he has read all of Augustine's books you know he is a liar. It is difficult to capture the message and the genius of the most influential Christian thinker after Saint Paul. Augustine was born in North Africa to a family of modest means, and he received, at great sacrifice, the best education available. He embarked on a career as a professor of rhetoric. Once he had established himself, he moved on to Rome and then to Milan, which in the fourth century was the unofficial western capital. Augustine fell under the spell of Ambrose and embraced the Christianity that his mother had been urging on him throughout his life. Later Augustine chronicled his quest for truth and spiritual fulfillment in his *Confessions,* a classic of Western literature. (See the box, "The Moment of Augustine's Spiritual Awakening.") In 395, Augustine became a bishop and until his death served the North African community at Hippo, and the wider Christian world, with a torrent of writings.

Not a systematic thinker, Augustine never set out to provide a comprehensive exposition of the whole of Christian doctrine but instead responded to problems as they arose. Living in times of constant turmoil, he had opportunities to speak on a wide array of issues, crucial among which were the relationship between God and humans, the nature of the church, and the overall plan of God's creation.

In the early fifth century some people believed that they could achieve salvation by the unaided operation of their own will. Augustine responded that although God did indeed endow humankind with free will, Adam and Eve had abused their will to rebel against God. Ever since that first act of rebellion there was a taint, called by theologians "original sin," that predisposed humans to continual rebellion, or sin, against God. Only divine grace can overcome sin, and only by calling on God can people receive grace. Here was a decisive break with the classical idea of humanity as good in itself and capable of self-improvement, perhaps even perfection, in this world. According to Augustine, all people were flawed, were sinners, were in need of God's redemption.

Some North African heretics said that sacraments celebrated by unworthy priests were invalid. Augustine believed that the efficacy of the church's sacraments—those ritual celebrations that were considered to be channels for the communication of grace, of God's special aid and comfort to the faithful—did not depend on the personal merit of the minister. A priest or a bishop acted in God's place and through divine grace. Therefore, faith in God was paramount. The church, in this reckoning, was a community of acknowledged sinners that was being led by its clergy in a quest for eternal salvation. To Augustine, God alone was perfect. As in his view of humanity itself, so also in his view of the clergy and of the church, Augustine was emphasizing the almost unbridgeable chasm that separated God from creation. Only God was truly good, and God was a purely spiritual being. Clergy, rulers, churches: These were all human institutions, all more or less good in particular circumstances.

The sack of Rome by the Visigoths in 410 distressed many people in the Roman world. Some argued that Alaric's seizure of Rome was repayment for Rome's abandonment of its traditional gods. To refute them, Augustine took up his pen to write the most brilliant and difficult of all his works, *The City of God.* This book is a theology of history. It sees time not as cyclical, the traditional classical view, but as linear. There has been a plan in operation, God's plan, since the creation of the world, and that plan will govern all human activity until the end of time. On earth there will always be a struggle between those who call on divine grace, who are redeemed, who are citizens of the City of God, and those who keep to the ways of the world, who persist in sin, who live in the earthly city. One may observe the unfolding of the divine plan by seeing how much of the earthly city has been redeemed at any given time.

The Moment of Augustine's Spiritual Awakening

In this passage Augustine relates the moment of his conversion and abandonment of his former life. Notice the roles of God, books, his old friend Alypius, and his devoted mother, Monica.

So that I might pour out all these tears and speak the words that came with them I rose up from Alypius and went further away that I might not be embarrassed even by his presence. This was how I felt and he realized it. No doubt I had said something or other, and he could feel the weight of my tears in the sound of my voice. And so I rose to my feet, and he, in a state of utter amazement, remained in the place where we had been sitting. I flung myself down on the ground somehow under a fig tree and gave free rein to my tears; they streamed and flooded from my eyes. . . . And in my misery I would exclaim: "How long, how long this 'tomorrow and tomorrow'? Why not now? Why not finish this very hour with my uncleanness?"

So I spoke, weeping in the bitter contrition of my heart. Suddenly a voice reaches my ears from a nearby house. It is the voice of a boy or a girl (I don't know which) and in a kind of singsong the words are constantly repeated: "Take it and read it. Take it and read it." At once my face changed and I began to think carefully of whether the singing of words like these came into any kind of game which children play, and I could not remember that I had ever heard anything like it before. I checked the force of my tears and rose to my feet, being quite certain that I must interpret this as a divine command to me to open the book and to read the first passage which I should come upon. For I had heard this about Anthony: He had happened to come in when the Gospel was being read, and as though the words read were spoken directly to himself, he had re-

ceived the admonition: "Go, sell your possessions, and give to the poor. You will then have treasure in heaven. Afterward, come back and follow me" [Matthew 19:21]. And by such an oracle he had been converted to you.

So I went eagerly back to the place where Alypius was sitting, since it was there that I had left the book of the Apostle [Paul] when I rose to my feet. I snatched up the book, opened it, and read in silence the passage on which my eyes first fell: "Not in carousing and drunkenness, not in sexual excess and lust, not in quarreling and jealousy. Rather, put on the Lord Jesus Christ and make no provisions for the desires of the flesh" [Romans 13:13–14]. I had no wish to read further; there was no need to. For immediately I had reached the end of this sentence, it was as though my heart was filled with a light of confidence and all the shadows of my doubt were swept away.

Before shutting the book I put my finger or some other marker in the place and told Alypius what had happened. By now my face was perfectly calm. Alypius in his turn told me what had been going on in himself. He asked me to see that passage which I had read. . . . He was strengthened by the admonition. . . . The next thing we do is go inside and tell my mother. How happy she is! We describe to her how it all took place, and there is no limit to her joy and triumph . . . for she saw that with regard to me you had given her so much more than she used to ask for when she wept so pitifully before you. . . . I was now standing on that rule of faith just as you had shown me to her in a vision so many years before.

Source: St. Augustine, *The Confessions of St. Augustine*, trans. Rex Warner (New York: Mentor, 1963), pp. 182–183.

Even though the Roman Empire was officially Christian, Augustine refused to identify his City of God with it. Nor would he say that the church and the City of God were identical. What he did

say was that the sack of Rome was a great irrelevance because many kingdoms and empires had come and gone and would continue to do so, but only the kingdom of God was eternal and, in the long run, important. To a Roman people whose most cherished belief held that the world would last exactly as long as Rome's dominion, Augustine's dismissal of Rome's destiny sounded the death knell of the classical world view.

Augustine also addressed the problem of education. His was a world where salvation was to be the goal of life, but where people did have to carry on with their ordinary occupations, and where almost the entire educational establishment was pagan in design and content. Education was confined mainly to the elite, who sought schooling partly to orient themselves within their cultural tradition and partly to gain employment, often in the imperial or urban service. This education had three mainstays. Latin or Greek grammar—rarely both—was the first. Augustine, for instance, knew little Greek, and by the sixth century few people in the East knew Latin. The second was rhetoric, once the art of public speaking but now, increasingly, literary criticism. The third was dialectic, or the art of right reasoning. In Late Antiquity public schools were fast disappearing as the need for them slipped away. The imperial service, at least in the West, was all but gone by the sixth century, and the Church Fathers were generally dismissive of the Roman heritage. But the church still needed educated persons, so it provided schools in cathedrals and monasteries.

In a treatise entitled *On Christian Doctrine* Augustine expressed some ideas about education that proved influential for a millennium. He said that everything that one needs to know, not to get or do a job but for salvation, is contained in the Bible. But the Bible, written in learned language, is full of difficult images and allusions. How is an ordinary person to learn what he or she needs to know in order to master this great book? Augustine used the expressive image of "spoiling the Egyptians," borrowed from the account of the Hebrews' Exodus from Egypt, when they took with them whatever they could use. Augustine's attitude toward classical learning was that it was useful to the extent that it taught the things one needed to know in order to read the Bible, to understand it, and to seek salvation. Classical culture had no intrinsic merit. It might give pleasure, but it was equally likely to be a distraction or a temptation to immorality. In education as in all else, Augustine was a realist. He once said, "What we teach is one thing, what we tolerate is another."

Highly influential as well was the treatise *On Divine and Human Readings* by the Italian writer Cassiodorus (ca. 485–580), who had been a loyal servant of Theodoric in Italy. After the fall of the Ostrogothic kingdom, Cassiodorus retired and set up a school of Christian studies. His treatise served as a kind of annotated bibliography of the major writings on school subjects such as grammar, rhetoric, and dialectic, and on biblical commentary.

Cassiodorus agreed with Augustine's idea of "spoiling the Egyptians." He saw that there were no Christian grammars to teach the Latin language, no Christian rhetorical manuals to teach the finer points of writing and speaking, and no Christian dialectics to show how to prove or disprove an argument. These subjects had always formed the core of classical education, and they must still do so in the new Christian world of Late Antiquity. Secular grammars and the like formed Cassiodorus's human readings. These books were preparatory to divine readings, which consisted of the Bible, the commentaries on it, and the writings of the Church Fathers. For centuries schools organized on Augustine's and Cassiodorus's model did an estimable job of preparing the clergy to carry out their functions.

SUMMARY

The paradox of Late Antiquity, the years from around 300 to around 600, is the nearly invisible boundary between change and continuity. When the period opened, Rome's vast and diverse empire was beset with innumerable political, military, and economic problems. The classical culture that had evolved over more than a millennium in the Mediterranean world seemed to have lost much of its vigor and appeal. But energetic rulers such as Diocletian and Constantine undertook a half-century of intense military, economic, and administrative reform that put the empire on firm footings while simultaneously changing forever the basic nature of the Roman state.

To address pressing military threats, the empire's army was expanded and reorganized. This sensible reform had the unintended result of militarizing many aspects of public life. Traditional civilian government receded slowly into the background. To pay for the larger army, the Roman economy was harnessed to the needs of the military. Tax burdens pressed harder and harder on every level of society and called into question the cost of Roman leadership. To administer the empire more efficiently, the small, amateur government of the Early Empire was transformed into an omnipresent bureaucratic system that stripped local elites of much of their traditional autonomy. To put a halt to the endemic civil war of the third century, a tetrarchal system of imperial rule was installed, and enhanced imperial ceremony exalted the office and person of the emperor. Yet these measures could not permanently dampen the desire of the army to influence the choice of rulers or lessen the tendency for sons, brothers, or nephews of reigning emperors to attempt to succeed them. Every reform made sense. Every reform attained only limited success. And every reform contributed to altering the basic nature of the traditional Roman system.

Finally, the Roman Empire itself survived only in the east. Despite obvious changes in geographic shape and public forms, one senses that Diocletian or Constantine would have felt at home in the age of Justinian. But neither of those rulers could easily have recognized the kingdoms that stood on the soil of Rome's former western provinces. Over a long time, and facilitated by Roman policies, Germanic peoples, especially the Franks and the Visigoths, took over key military and administrative positions, building kingdoms that were, as far as possible, small imitations of the late Roman state.

The rise of a Mediterranean-wide Christian ecclesiastical structure parallels in some ways the elaboration of the late Roman government after Diocletian. In 303, Christianity, still a minority religion almost everywhere, endured severe persecution. A decade later, it was made legal. Within seventy-five years, it was made official. Within two centuries, popes declared that the Christian priesthood was morally superior to the imperial office itself. This remarkable transformation was made possible by the conversion of the emperor Constantine and by the patronage of the church by his successors and by the social elites. Once it could function openly, the church developed a sophisticated system of officials and governing bodies. No pagan cult had ever had such a structure, and it was crucial to the success of Christianity.

But Christianity was more than just an institutional network. Slowly a Catholic tradition emerged around the Bible, the creeds—especially the Nicene—and the patristic writings. That Catholic tradition used Greek and Latin, interpreted fundamental Christian ideas in light of centuries-old pagan philosophical ideas, and appropriated traditional literary and artistic forms. Beyond institutions and ideas, Christianity was also a community of believers. Its leading officials, bishops, usually came from the same local families that had been prominent for years. Its ordinary believers were the people who looked to earthly patrons such as bishops and to heavenly ones such as saints for guidance and protection. These people had always looked to their "betters" for assistance.

By 600, then, new elites (or reorganized old elites), the Catholic church, and the Christian faith were poised to refashion the world that would succeed Rome. Not surprisingly, the Roman world of Justinian in the East and the Germanic world of the West were going to look very different in the future. They had, after all, assembled quite different structures from the common quarry of Late Antiquity. But Rome was to have a third heir, too, after the followers of the Prophet Muhammad entered the quarry and hewed their own stones. In the next chapter we will observe how ancient Mediterranean traditions, Jewish and Christian religious beliefs, Roman structures and ideologies, and new ethnic communities formed three great civilizations—European, Byzantine, and Islamic—that for nearly a thousand years dominated the age we call "medieval."

SUGGESTED READING

General Surveys

Brown, Peter. *The World of Late Antiquity.* 1971. A sprightly and beautifully illustrated interpretation of cultural cross-currents by the most gifted interpreter of Late Antiquity.

Cameron, Averil. *The Mediterranean World in Late Antiquity, A.D. 395–600.* 1993. A superb and readable survey of all the major problems and interpretations.

Clark, Gillian. *Women in Late Antiquity: Pagan and Christian Lifestyles.* 1993. A first-ever attempt to capture the lives of late antique women in all respects.

Holum, Kenneth G. *Theodosian Empresses: Women and Imperial Dominion in Late Antiquity.* 1982. A fascinating account of the behind-the-scenes roles played by female members of the imperial family in the fifth century.

Jones, A. H. M. *The Later Roman Empire, 284–602*. 2 vols. 1964. Despite its age, this massive work remains the best history of the Roman Empire. Its great strength is its detailed treatment of the Roman government.

MacMullen, Ramsay. *Corruption and the Decline of Rome*. 1988. A fascinating assessment of the boundaries between public and private conduct, between legal and illegal behavior.

Matthews, John. *Western Aristocracies and Imperial Court, 364–425*. 1975. A detailed, challenging treatment of the social changes in the western empire in the age of Valentinian and Theodosius.

Williams, Stephen, and Gerard Friell. *Theodosius: The Empire at Bay*. 1995. An exciting account of the reign of one of Rome's greatest emperors. Strong on currents in scholarly interpretation.

The Barbarians

Goffart, Walter. *Barbarians and Romans, A.D. 418–584: The Techniques of Accommodation*. 1980. An important, stimulating, and controversial book on how the barbarians were actually integrated into the Roman system on essentially Roman terms.

Heather, Peter. *Goths and Romans, 332–489*. 1991. Less detailed than Wolfram (see below), this book stresses the complexity of Gothic social and political organization in the context of Gothic relations with different Roman authorities.

Musset, Lucien. *The Germanic Invasions: The Making of Europe, A.D. 400–600*. Translated by Edward and Columba James. 1975. Since its first appearance in 1965, this book has become the standard narrative treatment of the movement of the barbarians into the Roman world.

Thompson, E. A. *The Huns*. 1996. A revised and updated version of a classic study that presents a sympathetic portrait of this feared people.

Todd, Malcolm. *The Northern Barbarians, 100 B.C.–A.D. 300*. Rev. ed. 1987. An interesting account of what archaeologists have learned about the barbarians before their entry into the empire. Stresses daily life.

Wolfram, Herwig. *History of the Goths*. Translated by Thomas J. Dunlap. 1988. Not only a history of the Goths, this brilliant book explains current ethnographic thinking about the barbarians.

The Roman Empire in the East

Browning, Robert. *Justinian and Theodora*. Rev. ed. 1987. A readable, reliable, and well-illustrated account of two fascinating people and a remarkable period.

Cameron, Averil. *Procopius*. 1985. The subject of this book was the last great ancient historian. His own tale is interesting, as are his unique perspectives on his world.

Honoré, Tony. *Tribonian*. 1978. This difficult book repays close study by showing how legal thinkers in Justinian's world actually worked. One learns from it a great deal about law in general.

The Development of Christian Culture

Brown, Peter. *Augustine of Hippo: A Biography*. 1969. A penetrating account of the life and world of a man described by the author as possessing "a mind of terrifying acuteness."

———. *The Cult of the Saints: Its Rise and Function in Latin Christianity*. 1981. A lively, imaginative discussion of holy men and women and of their places in this world and the next.

———. *Power and Persuasion in Late Antiquity: Toward a Christian Empire*. 1992. A brilliant account of the emergence of the Christian bishops as a dominant force.

Chitty, Derwas J. *The Desert a City*. 1966. A comprehensive, readable account of monastic origins in Egypt and dissemination to the east.

Cochrane, Charles Norris. *Christianity and Classical Culture*. Rev. ed. 1944. This classic book explains both the borrowings and the oppositions between classical and Christian culture.

Elm, Susanna. *Virgins of God: The Making of Asceticism in Late Antiquity*. 1994. A fascinating and challenging discussion of the role of women in the making of late antique monastic culture.

Harries, Jill. *Sidonius Apollinaris and the Fall of Rome*. 1994. A difficult but rewarding study of a major Gallic aristocrat who became a bishop and whose letters are a key source.

Kelly, J. N. D. *Jerome*. 1975. A solid account of the life and work of the Church Father best known for the Vulgate Bible.

McLynn, Neil B. *Ambrose of Milan: Church and Court in a Christian Capital*. 1994. An accessible treatment of a major Church Father and his time.

Markus, Robert. *The End of Ancient Christianity*. 1990. This stimulating and beautifully written book explores the changing meanings of sacred and secular in the period from 400 to 600.

O'Donnell, James J. *Cassiodorus*. 1979. A solid treatment of the man whose educational ideas heavily influenced the next several centuries.

Pagels, Elaine. *Adam, Eve, and the Serpent*. 1988. A fascinating but controversial assessment of the evolution of attitudes toward women by the clergy.

Rousseau, Philip. *Pachomius: The Making of a Community in Fourth-Century Egypt*. 1985. A brilliant evocation of the social connections of the early monastic world.

Stancliffe, Claire. *St. Martin and His Hagiographer: History and Miracle in Sulpicius Severus*. 1983. Simultaneously an account of early Western eremitic monasticism and of how we know about it.

Wilken, Robert. *The Christians as the Romans Saw Them*. 1984. This well-written, interesting book gathers the evidence for the pagan reaction to Christianity.

THE RAVENNA MOSAICS

Propaganda. The word has unsavory connotations. It suggests that someone is trying to convince someone else to do or to believe what is wrong. Actually, the word means only "things to be propagated," a message to be gotten out. The message itself may be good or bad.

When we think of propaganda, we must consider both the message and the medium in which it is conveyed. In antiquity, governments had several means of getting their messages out. Almost all the means were public, visible, striking.

Mosaics are among the most spectacular art forms of Late Antiquity, and in the churches of Ravenna they attained the summit of their propagandistic power. A mosaic is a picture formed by the intricate arrangement of thousands of tiny bits (called *tesserae*) of glass, stone, or metal. An artist created a rough sketch of the intended picture and then laid out the tesserae to conform to the sketch. Next the artist applied wet plaster to a small section of the surface, usually a wall or a floor, that was to receive the picture and then embedded that section's tesserae into the plaster. This process was repeated until the whole mosaic was completed. The result was a durable art form of great beauty and visual interest. In the picture on the opposite page you can see the tesserae and even some of the sparkle produced by the effect of sunlight and candlelight reflecting off the mosaic.

Mosaics were sometimes placed in private homes by the very wealthy, but more often they were put in conspicuous public places. Churches commonly received them in Late Antiquity. As more of society became Christian, aristocrats in particular were happy to spend lavishly to adorn their places of worship with beautiful decorations. Masses of people saw those decorations, reflected on who had financed them, and pondered the meaning of the image itself.

The greatest patron of all was the emperor. By putting up any work of art, the emperor proclaimed his power and influence. His reach was vast even if he never left Constantinople. Nothing shows this better than the Ravenna mosaics erected by Justinian.

Let us recall the situation. The Arian Ostrogoths had taken over Italy in 493. Ruling from Ravenna, they claimed to be imperial allies and representatives. Down to 535 there were always strains between Ravenna and Constantinople, and in that year Justinian launched the twenty-year-long Gothic War. During and after the war churches were erected as symbols of the imperial restoration.

The mosaic pictured here is located on the left-hand side of the apse, above and behind the altar, in the church of San Vitale in Ravenna. Its central figure is the emperor Justinian. Immediately opposite it is another mosaic (partially reproduced on page 252) focusing on Empress Theodora. San Vitale was a monument to the defeat of the Arian Goths. Any worshiper who raised his or her eyes from the altar saw immediately both Justinian and Theodora. These images made a powerful statement in a city that had been ruled by a Gothic king for thirty-three years. Justinian was leaving no doubt about who was now in charge. Consider, too, the prominence accorded to Theodora. Justinian really did view her as a partner in his rule.

That the emperor and empress were in charge is indicated in several distinct ways. They are slightly larger and are standing in front of their attendants. They are not quite like the other humans shown in the mosaic. They wear crowns and rich purple—that is to say, imperial—garments. They present gifts: he a gold paten holding the eucharistic bread and she a golden chalice containing the eucharistic wine. Thus the emperor and empress are represented as the donors of the church and as the guarantors of authentic worship.

Justinian tried throughout his reign to promote *homonoia* ("concord"). He tried to reconcile many political and religious factions. Notice the figure to Justinian's left (your right), over whose bald head you can read "MAXIMIANUS." This man

Justinian and His Courtiers, Apse Mosaic, San Vitale, Ravenna *(Scala/Art Resource, NY)*

was the archbishop of Ravenna, a close ally of the emperor and the person responsible both for eradicating Arianism and for reconciling Arians. His prominent position next to the emperor, and the fact that he alone is named, assured everyone of the correct doctrinal position. And in case anyone needed a further reminder, Maximianus holds in his hand the cross of Christ: There would be no more Arian subordination of the second person of the Trinity to the first.

We may note one more piece of propaganda. Look at the man standing to the left of Justinian and slightly behind him—between Justinian and Maximianus. This is Julianus Argentarius, a wealthy layman who was in all things the emperor's agent in Ravenna. He helped to finance and oversaw the construction of not only San Vitale but also several other churches in Ravenna. His presence signifies homonoia again, this time the traditional concord between the emperor and the elite throughout the empire. Relations between the court

and the Italian elite had been very strained under the Ostrogoths. Julianus's presence signaled that all was well once again. Vanity played a role too. Julianus paid for the art, so he had himself included in it.

The church of San Vitale was itself a propaganda statement. Theodoric was buried in a grand octagonal tomb. Justinian's builders chose an octagonal form for San Vitale. This church, too, is a sepulchre—a shrine for the remains of Saint Vitalis, an early Ravenna Christian who was martyred for the true faith.

In a world without the modern mass media, the media of antiquity served well to broadcast messages to people who understood their real and symbolic language. Recall the image on a Hellenistic coin (page 150). Look again at the statue of the tetrarchs (page 230) and the massive statue of Constantine (page 226). Cassiodorus once said that Rome was "a forest of statues." Every one of them was a propaganda statement. ✑

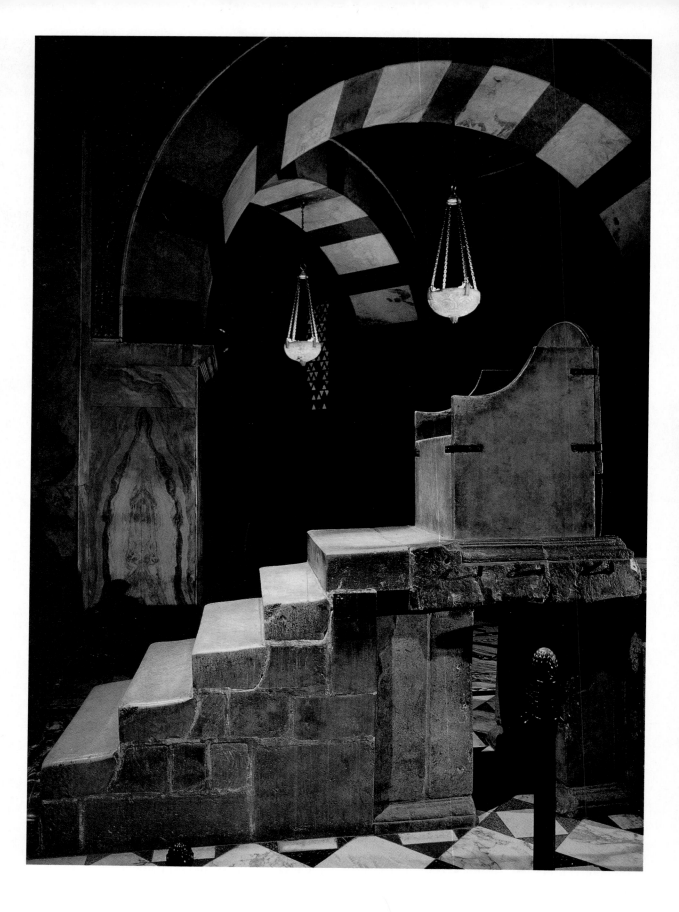

CHAPTER 8

Early Medieval Civilizations, ca. 600–900

An empty throne: grand, majestic, imperial perhaps, and a little mysterious. The photo to the left is of Charlemagne's throne, modeled on that of King Solomon and placed in a setting rich with Roman architectural reminiscences. There had been no emperors in the West since 476 but on Christmas Day in 800, Pope Leo III placed a crown on the head of Charles, the king of the Franks. One of Charles's closest friends called him "the Father of Europe," and in truth the last decades of the eighth century and the first decades of the ninth witnessed the birth of something new in the lands that had once been Rome's western provinces. Charles did not rule from Rome, however. After his coronation he trekked far to the north to his palace and chapel, where this throne is found—to Aachen, a small town near the modern border between Holland and Germany.

A time traveler transported to the Mediterranean world of 600 would almost certainly predict only two heirs to antiquity: the Roman East and the barbarian West. It is extremely unlikely that our intrepid wanderer would foresee one of the most dynamic developments in the history of Western civilization: the meteoric rise of Islam as a faith and of the Muslims as a people. In this chapter, three areas and histories, not just two, engage our attention. Remarkable similarities mark their historical development. For each, the seventh century was an era of dramatic change, the eighth century an era of reform and consolidation, and the ninth century a time of upheaval. The similarities are not merely chronological. A new imperial tradition developed in each area, a tradition rooted in a particular territory whose people believed themselves to be specially chosen

The throne of
Charlemagne, Aachen
Palace chapel.

by God and whose rulers defined themselves as God's earthly agents. In all three realms the interaction of local traditions with the Roman past produced new forms of central government that would prove influential for centuries. Commercial ties began to transform the Mediterranean world into a community of peoples who needed to balance mutual interests with bitter rivalries.

We begin by introducing the Arab peoples, their new religious faith—Islam—and the immense imperial realm—the caliphate—they created. Then we turn to the continuously evolving eastern Roman empire, which henceforth we will call the Byzantine Empire. This new name is meant to point to the dramatically reduced geographic shape of the empire, to its adjusted institutional forms, and to its increasingly Greek culture and distinctive religious traditions. Finally, we look at the Germanic West to see what happened to the kingdoms that succeeded to the western Roman Empire and to understand how and why the Frankish kingdom proved strong and confident enough to initiate a new Western imperial tradition in the person and achievements of Charlemagne.

The formative period from 600 to 900 is commonly called the "early Middle Ages" or "early medieval period." What do these terms mean? In the seventeenth century a Dutch scholar wrote of the *Medii Aevi*, the "Middle Times" that lay between antiquity and the dawning modern world. The name stuck. As a label for the post-Roman world, "Middle Ages" (whose adjectival form is "medieval") has become traditional. The fact that we no longer talk of an abrupt and catastrophic "fall" of the Roman Empire means that we no longer use the word *medieval* in exclusively pejorative ways.

THE ISLAMIC EAST

The Arabs, who inhabited much of the area from the Arabian peninsula to the Euphrates River, played a small role in the history of antiquity, and ancient writers took little notice of them. Shortly after 600, a prophet appeared among them preaching a faith old in its basic elements but new in its formulation. Converts to that new faith burst forth with unprecedented spiritual and military fervor, and they conquered territories from Spain to the

frontiers of China. Slowly, those lands were gathered into an imperial system with a coherent ideology and government apparatus. Even more slowly, political and cultural elites began forging out of the ethnic, religious, and historical diversity of that vast realm a common culture that was grounded in the teachings of the prophet Muhammad (570–632).

Arabia Before Muhammad

The Arab world in the early seventh century was large and turbulent. Long dominated by the Roman and Persian empires, the region had no stable, large-scale political entities. People belonged to close-knit clans, or extended families, that in varying associations formed tribes. The key element in Arab society, a tribe was in theory a group of people tracing descent from a known ancestor. In reality—in this Arab and Germanic peoples were alike—tribes were complex groups of relatives, allies, and political or economic clients.

As complex as its political situation was the region's ethnic and religious composition. The Roman world was overwhelmingly Christian, though there were many kinds of Christians. The Persian realm was officially Zoroastrian, but it had Jewish, Christian, Manichaean, and Buddhist minorities. The Arabs themselves were generally pagans, but Arabia had Jewish and Christian minorities.

The Arab East was also economically intricate and fragile. Bedouins (Arabs who were nomadic pastoralists) provided for their own needs from their herds of sheep and goats, from small-scale trading in towns, and from regular raids on one another and on caravans. There were some farmers, but in many areas soils were too poor and rain too infrequent to support agriculture. Cities supported traders who moved luxury goods, such as spices, incense, and perfumes, from the Indian Ocean region and southern Arabia up along caravan routes to the cities of the eastern Mediterranean. These traders formed the economic and political elite of Arabia, and they led the tribes. Mecca, dominated by the powerful tribe of the Quraysh, was the foremost city of Arabia, but competition among cities and tribes was fierce.

A solution to the competition among tribes and towns for control of trade routes was the institution of *harams*, or sanctuaries—places where contending parties could settle disputes peacefully. Usually the founding of a haram was attributed to a holy man whose prestige added to the sanctity of the spot. Mecca was one of the chief harams in Arabia, and its founding was attributed to the Israelite patriarch Abraham and one of his sons, Ishmael. The focus of the sanctuary was the black stone shrine known as the Kaaba. For centuries people from all over Arabia had made pilgrimages to Mecca, to the Kaaba.

The Prophet and His Faith

Muhammad was born in 570 to a respectable though not wealthy or powerful clan of the Quraysh tribe. His father died before he was born, his mother shortly afterward, leaving Muhammad under the care of his grandparents and an uncle. Like many young Meccans he entered the caravan trade. By the time he was 20, Muhammad held such a reputation for competence and moral uprightness that he became financial adviser to a wealthy Quraysh widow, Khadija (555–619). Although older than Muhammad, she became his wife in 595, and they had a loving marriage until her death.

From his youth Muhammad was a man of spiritual insight. He went into the desert or to caves near Mecca to fast and contemplate (see Map 8.1). In 610 he received the first of many revelations that commanded him to teach all people a new faith that called for an unquestioned belief in one god, Allah, and an uncompromised commitment to social justice for believers. Muhammad began teaching in Mecca, but he converted few people outside his own circle—his wife was his first convert. Some Meccans were envious of Muhammad. Others feared that his new faith and new god might call into question the legitimacy of the shrines in Mecca and jeopardize the traditional pilgrimages to the Kaaba and the trade that accompanied them. By 619, Muhammad's well-connected wife and uncle were dead, and his position was precarious.

At this juncture citizens from Medina, a smaller trading community wracked by dissension among pagan Arabs, Jews, and followers of Muhammad, asked Muhammad to establish a haram there. In the summer of 622, small groups of Muhammad's disciples made their way to Medina, and in September Muhammad joined them. His journey from

THE ISLAMIC WORLD	
570–632	The life of Muhammad
622	The hijra
632	Election of Abu-Bakr as caliph
632–634	Islamic conquest of Arabia
634	Beginning of Islamic expansion outside Arabia
661–750	Umayyad dynasty of caliphs
750	Abbassid dynasty of caliphs

Mecca to Medina, the *hijra*, marks the beginning of a new era, symbolized to this day in the Arab world by a calendar that dates "In the year of the Hijra."

Although Muhammad was fully in control in Medina, Mecca remained the focus of his attention. He had a sentimental attachment to Mecca, but its political and economic importance were critical to his emerging desire to convert all of Arabia. His followers began attacking Meccan caravans and battled with the Meccans several times in the 620s. In 630, Muhammad and many of his followers returned to Mecca in triumph. Muhammad left the Quraysh in control, and he retained the Kaaba as a focus of piety. After making local arrangements, he returned to Medina and set about winning over the Bedouins of the Arabian desert. When Muhammad died in 632, he had converted most of Arabia (Map 8.1).

To what, exactly, had Muhammad and his followers converted? At the most basic level, people were asked to surrender completely to Allah, the one, true God—that is, they were asked to make *al-Islam*, "the surrender." Those who surrendered became *Muslims* and joined the *umma muslima*, a completely new kind of community in which membership depended only on belief in Allah and acceptance of Muhammad as Allah's prophet. All members of the umma were understood to have personal and communal responsibility for all other members. No longer were one's duties confined to a particular clan, tribe, or town. Because of the experience of the hijra, Islam was a religion of exile, of total separation from the ordinary world, and of total dependence on God.

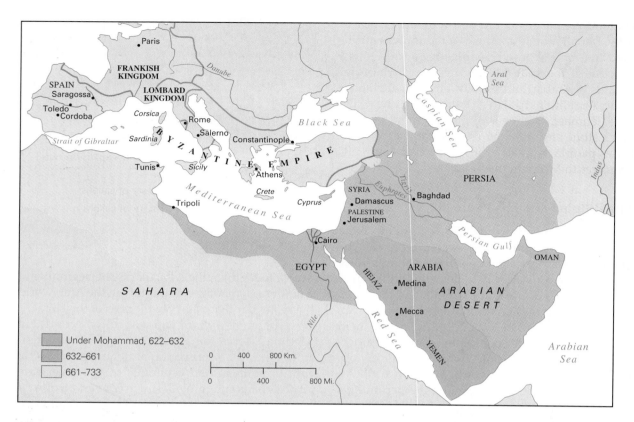

Map 8.1 The Expansion of Islam to 732 This map vividly illustrates the spectacular gains by Islam in the time of Muhammad, under the first caliphs, and under the Umayyads. Later there were slow, steady gains in Africa, central Asia, and India.

The basic teachings of Islam are traditionally described as "Five Pillars": (1) the profession of faith, "There is no God but Allah and Muhammad is His Prophet"; (2) individual prayer five times daily, plus group prayers at noon on Friday in a *mosque*, a Muslim house of prayer; (3) the sunup-to-sundown fast for one month per year; (4) the giving of alms amounting to 10 percent of a person's income to the poor; (5) pilgrimage to Mecca at least once in a person's lifetime. These pillars are still the central requirements of Islam.

The pillars sustained a faith that laid great stress on simple, uncompromising belief and on practices that affirmed that belief and built up a sense of community. At certain times of the day all Muslims everywhere bowed in prayer, with their heads facing toward Mecca. Everyone paid alms, creating thereby a feeling of solidarity among all members of the umma. Mecca itself and the experience of pilgrimage were central to all Muslims.

There was no elaborate theology, no intricate doctrinal mysteries, and no creed. There was no clergy. Men called *imams* led the Friday prayers in the mosque and usually offered sermons that applied Muslim teaching to the issues of the day, but there was no ordained priesthood as in Judaism or Christianity and no hierarchy as in the Christian churches.

Muhammad himself communicated God's teaching to his followers, always insisting that he was transmitting a direct, verbal revelation and not offering his own interpretations. That revelation came in the form of "recitations" that make up the *Quran*, the scriptures of Islam. Not long after Muhammad's death his closest followers arranged the recitations into 114 *Suras*, or chapters. The Quran contains legal and wisdom literature like the Hebrew Scriptures and moral teaching like the Christian New Testament. It also prescribes regulations for diet and for personal conduct. For example, the Quran forbids alcohol and gambling, censures luxury and ostentation, and imposes extreme sexual restraints on both men and women. Indeed, women are expected to remain shut away indoors or to shroud all but their eyes if they appear in public—a custom adopted from traditional Arab society. (See the box, "The Message of the Quran.")

Initially the Quran was interpreted rather freely within the umma, doubtless because there was no clergy to impose a uniform interpretation. After the prophet's death, some people felt the need for an authoritative teaching—as early Christians had felt the need for a canon of Christian scripture and teaching—and their efforts resulted in two important collections. One of these was the *sunna*, which means roughly the "good

practice"—that is, the customs and habits of Muhammad himself. The second was the *hadith*, the "sayings" of the prophet, presumably the comments he made at different times about how God's revelation was to be understood and applied. Extant compilations of the sunna and hadith date from the ninth century, and scholars are not sure what portion of them derives authentically from the age of the prophet. Quran, sunna, and hadith form the core of a dynamic spiritual message.

The Expansion of Islam

Muhammad's death brought a crisis. Who or what was to succeed him? In 632 the Meccan elite chose Abu Bakr as *caliph*, or "successor to the prophet." Abu Bakr was elderly, an early convert to Islam,

Dome of the Rock This magnificent mosque in Jerusalem (built in 691–692) is the second holiest shrine of Islam—after the Kaaba in Mecca. Muslims believe that Muhammad ascended to heaven from this spot. (*Michael Holford*)

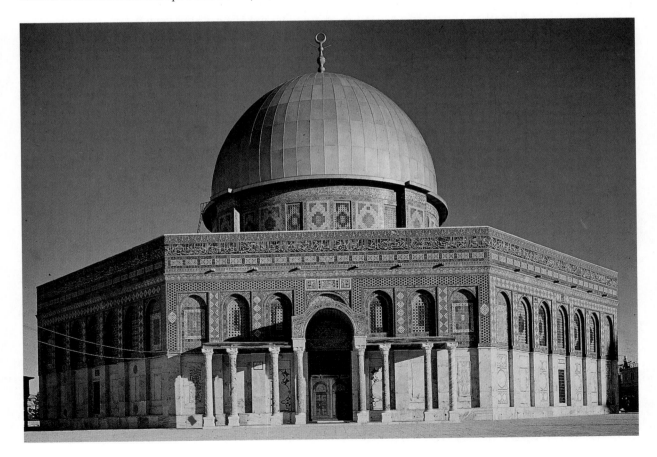

The Message of the Quran

The Quran consists of 104 Suras, literally the "steps" by which one rises to knowledge of Allah. The first two extracts below, from Suras 1 and 4, illustrate the simplicity and elegance of Muslim prayer and the absolute transcendance of Allah. The second extract, from Sura 2, demonstrates the profound sense of religious continuity that marked Muhammad's teaching.

Sura 1: In the name of Allah, Most Gracious, Most Merciful./Praise be to Allah, the Cherisher and Sustainer of worlds;/ Most Gracious, Most Merciful. / Master of the Day of Judgment./ Thee do we worship and thine aid we seek. Show us the straight way, the way of those on whom Thou hast bestowed Thy grace, Thou whose portion is not wrath, and who do not go astray.

Sura 4: O People of the Book! Commit no excesses in your religion, nor say of Allah anything but truth. Christ Jesus the son of Mary was an apostle of Allah . . . so believe in Allah and in his apostles. Say not "Trinity" . . . for Allah is one Allah. Glory be to Him for He is exalted above having a son. To him belong all things in the heavens and on earth.

Sura 2: Say ye: We believe in Allah, and the revelation given to us, and to Abraham, Ismail, Issac, Jacob and the tribes, and that given to Moses and to Jesus and that given to all prophets, but we make no difference between one and another of them, and we bow to Allah. . . . We gave Moses the book and followed him up with a succession of Apostles; We gave Jesus the son of Mary clear signs and strengthened him with the Holy Spirit. . . . If the People of the Book rely upon Abraham, let them study his history. His posterity included both Israel and Ismail. Abraham was a righteous man of Allah, a Muslim, and so were his children. Abraham and Ismail built the Kaaba as the house of Allah and purified it, to be a centre of worship for all the world: For Allah is the Allah of all peoples. . . . God's truth is continuous, and His Apostles from Adam, through Noah and Abraham, down to the last of the prophets, Muhammad, form one brotherhood. Of Imran father of Moses and Aaron sprang a woman, who devoted her unborn offspring to God. That child was Mary the mother of Jesus. Her cousin was the wife of the priest Zakariya, who took charge of Mary. To Zakariya, in his old age was born a son Yahya, amid prodigies: Yahya was the herald of Jesus the son of Mary and was known as John the Baptist.

Source: The Holy Qur-an, text, translation, and commentary by Abdullah Yusuf Ali (Lahore, Pakistan: Muhammad Ashrat, 1981), pp. 14–15, 40–41, 51,130–131, 233–234.

and a former secretary to Muhammad. He and his three successors down to 661 (Umar, Uthman, and Ali) were all Meccans, relatives of the prophet by marriage, and early converts. Islamic tradition calls them the "Rightly Guided Caliphs."

Abu Bakr left his successor, Umar, a united Arabia (see Map 8.1), no small feat in that fractious world. Umar began the lightning conquests by the Muslims of much of the Roman and Persian empires. He began the policy of granting choice positions in the expanding caliphate, the Muslim empire, to old converts and of ranking them according to precedence in conversion. As the old elite divided up the new provinces of the caliphate, some of them became *emirs* (governors), and others became lesser administrators. Muslim administrators then collected from all conquered people personal taxes and land taxes. Converts to

Islam paid only land taxes. Arab settlers paid no taxes and received salaries from the taxes paid by others. Numerous Arabs profited handsomely from the Muslim conquests.

Umar was murdered by a slave in 644, leaving his successor, Uthman, a huge empire to administer. A great centralizer, Uthman chose emirs, regulated the finances of the provinces, and authorized the preparation of the definitive text of the Quran. In attempting to preserve the advantages of the old Meccan elite, Uthman alienated many people, particularly in Egypt, Syria, and Iraq, who had benefited from conquest and who guarded jealously their newfound local wealth and power. Uthman was murdered in 656 and replaced by Ali, whose goal was to create a truly Islamic government by emphasizing the religious side of the caliph's office as the leader of the umma. Ali was in turn killed by a disillusioned follower in 661. Years later some Muslims looked back to Ali as the true model for the caliph because he was the prophet's son-in-law, committed to the essential equality of all believers, and strict in his view of Islam. These Muslims formed the *Shi'a*, the "Party of Ali."

When Ali was killed, the caliphate passed to Mu'awiya, a Meccan whose family had been highly favored since Uthman. He was the governor of Syria and commanded the finest army in the Muslim world. That army assured Mu'awiya's position. From 661 to 750 the Umayyads, as Mu'awiya's family is called, built many of the institutions that characterized the caliphate until the tenth century.

Greater centralization was instituted. This involved the introduction of a unified coinage, the Arabization of the administration—granting all key positions to Arabs—and taking tight control of provincial governors and taxes. The Umayyads moved the capital of the caliphate to Damascus in their own power base of Syria, more centrally located than the old towns of Mecca and Medina and closer to the militarily active zones in eastern Iran and along the Byzantine frontier in Syria. In addition, the Umayyads presided over the final territorial expansion of the caliphate (see Map 8.1). To the west, North Africa and Spain were taken, and raids were conducted deep into Gaul. In the east, after unsuccessful sieges against Constantinople, the frontier against the Byzantine

Empire was moved into the mountains of southern Anatolia and, farther east, campaigns established nominal authority as far as the Indus River valley.

How can we account for the astonishingly rapid creation of such a vast empire? Rome's empire expanded for 350 years, but the caliphate reached its zenith in scarcely 100. External factors were important. Byzantium and Persia had financially and militarily weakened themselves in a series of wars that ended just as the caliphate of Umar commenced. Moreover, those two states were exceedingly diverse, and the Muslim armies dismantled them piecemeal. Both old empires, but especially the Byzantine, had deep religious divisions. Coptic Egypt and Jacobite Syria, for example, willingly yielded to the Muslims, who demanded taxes and submission but otherwise left them alone. The Byzantines and Persians tended to depend on static frontier garrisons and large armies that could not be quickly mobilized and moved long distances. The Muslims rarely risked great pitched battles. They preferred a gradually expanding military frontier gained by numerous lightning strikes.

Internal factors were more significant, however. For centuries, raiding and plundering had been a way of life in Arabia, but because Islam forbade Muslims from raiding other Muslims, a new outlet for traditional violence was needed. The prophet himself had believed firmly in the need to expand the faith, and his successors shared that belief. Muslim ideology quickly divided the world into the "House of Islam" and the "House of War." In the House of Islam, the justice of Allah reigned supreme. In the House of War, *jihad*, holy war, was the rule. Christians and Jews, as fellow "Peoples of the Book"—sharers in a scriptural tradition reaching back to Abraham—were spared the choice of conversion or death, but "infidels" were expected to submit and convert. The simple, uncompromising teachings of Islam were attractive, but self-preservation and a desire to join in the material advantages of the new regime were also potent inducements. The Muslim conquests were carefully planned and directed to channel violence out of Arabia, to populate much of western Asia with loyal Muslims, and to permit members of the umma to enjoy vast rewards.

The Abbassid Revolution

The Umayyads were not popular, despite their military and administrative successes. Many resented their bureaucratic centralization. Such resentment was acute in areas heavily populated by recent converts, who had always disliked the old Arabian elites, and in frontier provinces, where Arab immigrants along with local converts desired autonomy. The secular nature of Umayyad rule also offended those pious Muslims who expected a high standard of personal morality from their rulers. The opposition came to a head in a series of rebellions that culminated in the naming of a rival caliph, Abu'l Abbas, in 749. In 750 he defeated his Umayyad rival.

The Abbassids reigned until the thirteenth century. In their earliest phases, especially in the caliphate of Harun al-Raschid (r. 786–809), they brought the Islamic world its first golden age. Harun's reign was marked by political stability, economic prosperity, and cultural achievements. Abbassid successes are attributable to political acumen and ideological restructuring.

With their frontier origins, the Abbassids always understood the concerns of the caliphate's provincial populations. Thus, they created a more international regime. Provincials, especially non-Arabs and recent converts, had for Islam, the prophet, and the prophet's family a loyalty that they could not grant to the old Arabian potentates who had led and initially benefited from the Arab conquests. The Abbassid polity was based on the idea of the fundamental equality of all believers, the common bond of Islam.

Key government posts were given to Iranians and other non-Arabs. Some provincial posts went to members of the Abbassid family, persons who had a certain aura of political and spiritual legitimacy, rather than to Meccan or Syrian aristocrats. Local persons, however, always got some choice positions. The capital of the caliphate was moved from Syria to Iraq, but to avoid favoring any existing group or region, the Abbassids built a new city, Baghdad. By addressing regional and ethnic sensitivities in an effective way, they were able to maintain, even extend, the centralized state of the Umayyad period.

The caliphs did not rule the Muslim world by themselves. The daily business of governing was usually in the hands of the *wazir,* who headed the administration, advised the caliph, and often exercised a powerful formative influence on the caliph's children and heirs. The first caliphs chose administrators from loyal Arabs and from experienced Christian subjects. Under the Umayyads the regime was Arabized. Then under Harun al-Raschid the government became international, professional, and hereditary. The chief agency of government was the treasury, which had separate branches dealing with the Muslim alms, with the land and poll taxes paid by subjects, and with the land taxes paid by converts. So sophisticated was this financial machinery that alone among early medieval governments the caliphate could draw up annual budgets. There was also an influential group of palace servants. They did not hold important public positions, but their informal influence on the caliph and his family was great. The army was another prominent body within the state.

The central government was linked to the provinces in several ways. In addition to controlling the army and provincial governorships, the caliph employed a network of regular envoys and spies. The court, especially under the Abbassids, drew able young men from all over into the service of the caliph and created hopes among provincial elites that they too might be chosen. In every district and city there were judges, *qadi,* to oversee the application of Islamic law. Qadi were under the authority of the caliph.

The death of Harun in 809 sparked a century of problems. Intense family rivalries touched both the succession to the caliphate and the possession of key provincial positions. The bureaucracy became an increasingly influential pressure group, and the palace servants began to foment intrigues. The army became more and more a professional body comprising non-Arabs, especially Turks, hired from the frontiers and beyond because Arabs, enjoying their salaries, declined to serve. The parallel with the Germanization of the late Roman army is striking. The army, the bureaucracy, and the courtiers all had different and conflicting interests and did not hesitate to press their own advantages. Religious divisions persisted, even intensified. Many felt the Abbassids had not gone far enough in erecting a truly Islamic regime. Whole regions took advantage of Abbassid leniency in granting local autonomy and began to fall away. Spain had actually been lost at the time of the Abbassid takeover in 750, when an Umayyad, Abd al-Rahman, erected an independent emirate at Cordoba. North Africa fell away in the mid-ninth century, and by the middle of the tenth century Abbassid power in southern Iraq, Syria, Egypt, and Arabia was negligible. After the early tenth century the Abbassid caliphs had little effective power.

The Emergence of Islamic Culture

Two currents are apparent in the culture of the Islamic East. One is the religious thought associated with the Quran; the other is the assimilation of the Greek heritage. Both were influenced by the eastward spread of Islam that mixed Iranian, Turkish, and even Hindu elements into a culture already rich with Arab, Christian, and Jewish ingredients.

Muslims assembled for prayer in mosques, the often beautiful buildings usually modeled on the original mosque in Medina. The worshipers—with men and women in separate areas—arrayed themselves in parallel rows and were led in prayer by an imam. In time the imams started offering interpretations of the Quran, and collections of these interpretations began to circulate. Similarly, Muslim judges began to issue opinions on how the Quran, sunna, and hadith might be applied to the daily lives of believers. Teachers in mosque schools were also influential. Together these authority figures, collectively the *ulama*, developed a body of religious thought. Lacking elaborate theology and creeds, Islamic religious thought pertains to practice and allegiance more than ideas. The point is not to *know* Islam but to *live* it.

The late ninth and early tenth centuries saw the emergence of a deep religious split in the Islamic world that persists to this day. The opposing groups were Shi'ite and Sunni Muslims. Shi'ites believed that caliphs should be chosen only according to strict standards of moral and spiritual worthiness. They further believed that the only way to assure such worthiness was to choose caliphs from the line of Ali, the caliph murdered in 661 who had been the husband of Muhammad's daughter Fatima. Moreover, they believed that the whole ulama should measure up to Shi'ite standards. Sunni Muslims, always the vast majority, proclaimed that only they adhered to the sunna, the "good practice" of Muhammad himself. Sunnis accept the legiti-

THE BYZANTINE EMPIRE	
610–641	Reign of Heraclius
622–629	Successful wars against Persians
634–640	Territorial losses to Muslims
674–678, 716–718	Arab sieges of Constantinople
717–741	Reign of Leo III
726–787	Iconoclastic controversy
797–802	Reign of Irene
843	Final restoration of icons
867–886	Reign of Basil I

macy of the whole line of Umayyad and Abbassid caliphs and the teachings of the ulama.

In 832 an Abbassid caliph endowed the "House of Wisdom," an academy for scholars in Baghdad, and from this point on Muslim scholars had the leisure and wherewithal to begin tackling the corpus of Greek thought, especially the scientific writers. Muslims actually showed little interest in the *literary* heritage of antiquity, the ancient legacy that was so important and controversial to Christian scholars. The earliest Arab scholars sought mainly to master the learning of the past. They tended to be encyclopedic—that is, to collect and to assimilate huge amounts of information. Works were collected and translated, manuscripts were copied, and libraries were built.

THE BYZANTINE EMPIRE

The century after Justinian's death in 565 was difficult for the eastern Roman Empire. Attacks by Persians, Bulgars, and Muslims, riots and rebellions, and plagues and famines left the empire in a perilous position. In 610 a process of reform and recovery began that had the long-term effect of transforming the eastern Roman regime into one that we call "Byzantine," from Byzantium, the ancient Greek name for the capital city, Constantinople. Before those reforms took hold, however, the eastern Roman state had to fight for its survival.

From the Eastern Roman Empire to the Byzantine Empire

In 610 Heraclius, a gifted, experienced ruler, ascended the throne. He ruled until 641 and set the basic pattern for the rest of the seventh century. That pattern emphasized the Eastern, Greek nature of the empire, abandoned military entanglements in the west in favor of security in the east, and initiated institutional reforms designed to take account of new cultural, political, and diplomatic realities.

Heraclius and his successors faced military challenges on two fronts. In the east, Byzantium was the victim of a cruel irony. Between 612 and 619, the Persians conquered Syria, Palestine, Mesopotamia, and Egypt. Heraclius reorganized his military and finances and between 622 and 629 fought a series of campaigns that recovered almost everything. When the unexpected Muslim challenge appeared in 634, an exhausted Byzantium had no effective response. In the Balkans, the Byzantines enjoyed some successes against Slavs, who had been pushing south for years, and against Avars and Bulgars (peoples related to the Huns), who had settled in the northwestern and northeastern Balkans, respectively. In the west, Spain and North Africa were abandoned to Muslims. In Italy and Sicily, effective imperial authority was minimal, confined to some outposts around Ravenna, Rome, Naples, and Sicily. The west was distant, divided, and distracting. It was clear that the east and the Balkans were critical. The change from the days of Justinian could not be more apparent.

Several cultural indicators point to the emergence of a regime that laid increasing stress on its Greek and Christian roots. For example, the emperors used Greek to call themselves "Emperor of the Romans." As Justinian had looked to his Latin and Roman roots, so Heraclius and his successors were unashamedly Greek and Eastern in their outlook. The emperor saw himself as God's specially chosen and protected agent with full authority over the church and over the religious life of all Christian people. To emphasize the religious foundations of their imperial office, the emperors began putting images of Christ on their coins. In one of his official titles the emperor was "The Thirteenth Apostle." As in the past, the emperors continued trying to solve the age-old Christological and Trinitarian problems (see pages 238–239).

The emperor's authority and prestige were great within his shrinking empire but negligible in most of Rome's former territories. Heraclius sought religious unity, but his efforts met opposition. For instance, the popes objected to Heraclius's policies, as did most Coptic and Jacobite Christians, who, as noted, offered little resistance to Muslim conquerors who did not interfere with their beliefs. The differences between Orthodox and other Christians were ever more visible.

The Eighth-Century Recovery

In 717, Leo III became emperor in a moment of acute crisis. Muslim armies had seized most of Anatolia and had laid siege to Constantinople itself. The city would surely have fallen had it not been for the "Greek fire" that made it impossible for the Muslim navy to operate beneath the seaward walls. Leo ruled until 741 and was followed until 775 by his able son, Constantine V. Together they extended the seventh-century focus on the eastern frontiers and on the Greek and Orthodox empire. Although official ideology in the eighth century claimed that the Roman Empire of Augustus was still in existence, under Leo and Constantine a new regime, the Byzantine, was consolidated.

After a century of military reverses, Leo III and Constantine V were often victorious (Map 8.2). They defended Constantinople, recovered Anatolian territory from the Muslims, and checked the advance of the Bulgars. Their successes stemmed from military reforms that amounted to a major administrative reorganization of the empire. For centuries the Romans had recruited, paid, and equipped soldiers out of tax revenues. In this way Rome procured standing armies along with frontier auxiliaries. Leo and Constantine, in contrast, brought to completion a system that began emerging in the sixth century.

Men from frontier regions were recruited and then settled on farms in military districts called *themes*. All themes, whether sea-based naval ones or land-based army ones, stood under a commander who was simultaneously the civil and military chief of his theme. The farmer-soldiers did not pay

Greek Fire Invented in the seventh century by Callimachus, a Syrian engineer, Greek fire was a mixture formed from petroleum, sulfur, saltpeter, and lime that ignited on contact with water. It was first used to repel the Muslim siege of Constantinople in 678. *(MAS, Barcelona)*

tax on their lands but discharged their obligations to the state by personal service. Some standing troops were retained, but several thematic armies now constituted the backbone of the Byzantine military.

The system worked for several reasons. It was less of a drain on the state treasury than the old one. Lower taxes could be levied and a smaller bureaucracy employed to secure revenues. The Byzantine Empire had to defend less territory than Rome had once defended, so armies could be mobilized and deployed locally, rather than moved long distances. The joining of civilian and military rule in a single hierarchy dependent on the emperor made sense in a state that was continually threatened on all sides.

Leo and Constantine did more than just reform military structures. In 726, Leo issued the *Ecloga,* the first major revision of Roman law since Justinian's. Issuing a law code was a matter of dynastic pride and self-assertion. But where Justinian's *Code* was beyond the capacity of all but the most sophisticated lawyers in Constantinople, the *Ecloga* was "a selection of laws," "an abridgment" whose purpose was to provide a simplified, unified body of law for provincial judges in the Byzantine Empire.

Leo and Constantine initiated far-reaching reforms in an imperial administration little changed since Late Antiquity. Roman administration had consisted of a few very large departments headed by officials with immense responsibilities and power. The new Byzantine system was characterized by a profusion of departments under officers who had more prestige than actual power and who were more heavily dependent on the emperor. The bureaucracy usually was not a breeding ground for factional squabbles, as in the caliphate. The emperors neutralized the bureaucrats by drawing them by merit from all social classes, paying them well, giving them fancy titles and public recognition, but dividing their responsibilities and curtailing their actual power.

The rulers also promoted religious and cultural unity. The so-called iconoclastic controversy serves as an example of Leo's and Constantine's policies. It was a dispute over icons—paintings of Christ, Mary, and saints. *Iconoclasts* are those who wish to destroy such images. For a while the emperors themselves were the leading iconoclasts.

Icons began to play a prominent role in Orthodox devotions in the fifth century. Some *iconodules*—defenders of icons—said that icons served to bring to mind the person depicted and thus helped indi-

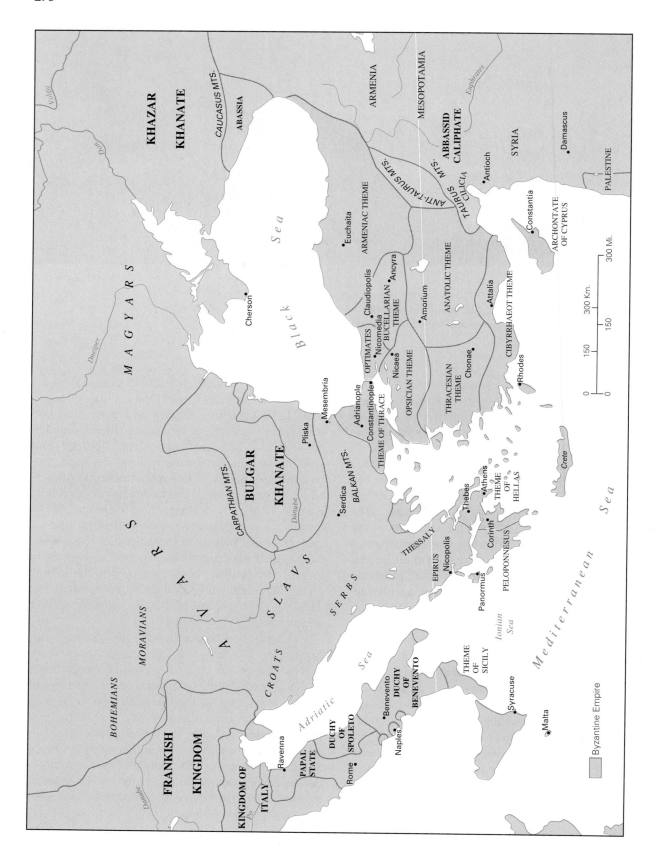

viduals in their spiritual life. Other iconodules felt that icons had theological significance by, for example, affirming the humanity of Christ: If Christ was truly human, then he could be depicted like any other human. By contrast the Jewish and Muslim traditions considered any attempt to depict God as idolatry, as sinful. Some influential Christian voices also said that any icon was really an idol.

In 726, Leo removed an icon of Christ from the gate of one of the imperial palaces, and for several years he and like-minded clergy agitated against icons. In 731, an imperial decree banned images of Christ or the saints, and thus the iconoclastic controversy arose. Why did an emperor faced with so many threats devote so much energy to this issue?

In the preface to the *Ecloga* Leo portrays himself as an Old Testament king who has a duty to lead his people in the path of righteousness. He seems to have believed quite sincerely that icons were idols and that they provoked God so strongly that God had permitted Byzantium's enemies to prosper. Constantine V, who was much better educated than his father, was opposed to icons for theological reasons. To him, icons laid excessive emphasis on the humanity of Christ—Christological quarrels had not disappeared.

Personal convictions played a role, but public issues were important, too. Many famous icons were housed in monasteries. Many monasteries were the object of generous gifts by pious laymen, and many extremely talented people embraced the monastic life rather than serving the state. The emperors had for a long time exercised control over the patriarchs, but they had never really gotten control of the monastic clergy. Attacking icons was in some ways an attempt to make complete the emperor's control of the church.

Iconoclasm had limited success. Many ordinary people cherished icons and ignored imperial policy. The emperors occasionally made an example of prominent iconophiles by exiling or executing them, but most people were left alone. Monks were popular, in some areas as popular as the em-

Saint Peter A rare pre-iconoclastic icon from Mt. Sinai: Peter is depicted as a late antique magistrate—wise and distinguished—not as a simple fisherman. The medallions depict Christ in the center, Mary on the right, and John the Evangelist on the left. In a late antique depiction of a consul, the images would have had the emperor in the center, the empress on the right, and the co-consul on the left. (*Alexandria-Michigan-Princeton Archeological Expedition to Mount Sinai/Roger Wood/Corbis-Bettmann*)

Map 8.2 The Byzantine Empire in the Eighth and Ninth Centuries After suffering tremendous territorial losses to barbarians and Muslims, the Byzantine Empire transformed its military, institutional, and cultural structures to create a regime that survived until it was conquered by Crusaders in 1204.

peror himself. Thus, attacks on monasteries sometimes backfired. Christians in Egypt or Syria, to the extent they knew about iconoclastic policies, regarded the emperor as a heretic. In Rome, a succession of popes rejected iconoclasm itself and, like their predecessors, wrote to the emperor to tell him that he had no business interfering in church doctrines. Unity based on religion remained as elusive for emperors as it was for caliphs.

Ninth-Century Problems

The dynasty of Leo III might have continued indefinitely but for a rapid accumulation of misfortunes in the last decades of the eighth century. Constantine V's promising son, Leo IV, died suddenly in 780, leaving a 6-year-old son, Constantine VI, and a remarkable widow, Irene (753–803). Shortly after assuming the regency for her son, Irene began planning the restoration of icons. This was a matter of personal conviction with her, but it also owed a lot to an awareness that the controversy over icons had not brought religious or political unity to the empire but had isolated the Byzantine church from all other Christian communities and the Byzantine Empire from all potential allies against Muslims and Bulgars. In 787, Irene convened a church council at Nicaea that pronounced against the iconoclastic decrees.

What Irene could not do was control her frivolous son, who refused to attend to the business of state and trysted with girls who served in his mother's chamber. Exasperated, she blinded him in the very room in which he had been born. Because any physical deformity rendered a person unfit for rule, Irene intended merely to disqualify her son and then to succeed in her own right. Instead, he died from his wounds, and she incurred the name of murderess. From 797 to 802, Irene ruled the empire, but her authority was never really accepted. Many people were horrified at her treatment of her son; others were simply unprepared to accept a woman as ruler. (See the box, "Encounters with the West: Muslim and Byzantine 'Diplomacy'?") Finally, however, she was the victim of a coup d'état because she could not retain the loyalty of the army or the bureaucracy. The irony in all this is that Irene was able, intelligent, resourceful, and, in truth, the real heir to Leo III.

From the deposition of Irene in 802 until the accession of Basil I (r. 867–886), the history of the Byzantine Empire is a study in contradictions. There were assassinations and usurpations but also effective rulers. Military successes were recorded but also defeats. The state was often short of cash, and its attempts to raise money angered many people. Religious policy shifted several times, too. For example, icons were again outlawed from 815 to 842, with no more effect than in the first period of iconoclasm.

Basil, himself a usurper, was a great soldier, a gifted administrator, and a hard-headed ruler who brooked no opposition. His dynasty, the Macedonian, reigned for two centuries and eventually won great victories in the Balkans and in Anatolia. Macedonian rulers were sometimes scholars themselves and usually patrons of learning. They promoted but also controlled the church and went far to soothe the divisions of the iconoclastic era.

The cultural life of early Byzantium is also riddled with contradictions and ironies. Initially the iconoclastic era was damaging. For obvious reasons, artists could find no patrons, and much of the physical inheritance of the past was destroyed. Architecture fared no better than art. There was too little money or security to finance the building of palaces and churches. The last of the Greek Church Fathers, John of Damascus (ca. 650–ca. 750), ended his career with passionate defenses of icons, but the early iconoclasts produced no distinguished theologians. In the ninth century, the renewal of iconoclasm sharpened the quality of intellectual discussion on both sides of the issue and gave churchmen a renewed prominence in the state until Basil I achieved peace and order.

CHRISTIAN KINGDOMS IN THE WEST

In the West, the seventh century was full of challenges, the eighth century was marked by innovation and accomplishment, and the ninth century was characterized by new challenges and in some areas near collapse. Parallels with the Islamic and Byzantine worlds are striking. There are other parallels, too. The social and political heritages of both the German and the Roman past interacted with Christianity and the Catholic church to produce Christian Europe. Crucial to these developments were the evangelization of the countryside, the spread of an ecclesiastical hierarchy, the shift of papal interests away from the Mediterranean world toward western Europe, and the evolving relationship between royal governments and the Catholic church.

≈ **ENCOUNTERS WITH THE WEST** ≈

Muslim and Byzantine "Diplomacy"?

This excerpt from an Arabic chronicle reveals something of the attitudes of Muslims and Byzantines toward each other. Notice the mistakes and misunderstandings.

A woman [Irene] came to rule over the Romans because at the time she was the only one of their royal house who remained. She wrote to the Caliphs with respect and deference and showered them with gifts. When her son [Constantine VI] grew up and came to the throne in her place, he brought trouble and disorder and provoked [Harun] al-Raschid. The empress, who knew al-Raschid and feared his power, was afraid lest the kingdom of the Romans pass away and their country be ruined. She therefore overcame her son by cunning and put out his eyes so that the kingdom was taken from him and returned to her. But the people disapproved of this and hated her for it. Therefore Nicephorus [emperor, 802–811] rose against her. . . . He wrote to al-Raschid, "From Nicephorus, the king of the Romans, to al-Raschid, the king of the Arabs" as follows: "That woman [Irene] put you in the place of kings and put herself in the place of a commoner. I put you in a different place and am preparing to invade your lands and attack your cities unless you repay me what that woman paid you. Farewell." Al-Raschid replied, "In the name of God, the Merciful, the Compassionate, from the servant of God, Harun, Commander of the faithful, to Nicephorus, dog of the Romans" as follows: "I have understood your letter, and I have your answer. You will see it with your eye, not hear it." Then he sent an army against the land of the Romans.

Source: Abu'l-Faraj al-Isfahani, *Al-Aghani*, in Bernard Lewis, ed., *Islam from the Prophet Muhammad to the Conquest of Constantinople*, vol. 1 (New York: Harper & Row, 1974), pp. 27–28.

The Struggles of Christian Spain

After Clovis's victory over them in 507, the Visigoths were never able to re-establish dynastic continuity. As a result, Spain witnessed rebellions and usurpations more frequently than any other early medieval area in the West. In addition to internal struggles, Spain faced external threats from the Franks, the Ostrogoths in Italy, the Byzantines, and finally the Muslims.

The accomplishments of the Visigothic king Leovigild (r. 568–586) seem remarkable given the state of Spain on his accession. He nearly unified the country, and he established a capital (Toledo) and a seat of government—which the Visigoths had been lacking since they lost Toulouse in 507. Leovigild was a good general and a charismatic leader who understood the value of enhancing the royal office. He wore royal vestments, sat on a throne, and issued coins with his own image and name. Leovigild's greatest problem was the Arianism of the Visigothic minority in the midst of the Catholic Hispano-Roman population. An Arian himself, he tried hard to convert Catholics to Arianism but failed. In 589, under King Reccared (r. 586–601), the Visigoths officially embraced Roman Catholicism.

The conversion of the Visigoths permitted close cooperation between the church and the monarchy and placed the human and material resources of the church at the disposal of the king as he attempted to unite and govern the country. The career of Archbishop Isidore of Seville (560–636) is a prime indicator of those resources. He came from an old Hispano-Roman family, received a fine education, and wrote histories, biblical commentaries, and a learned encyclopedia. By the mid-seventh century, economic prosperity, a high degree of assimilation between Goths and Hispano-Romans, and a brilliant culture marked the high point of Visigothic Spain. The succession problem, however, was never overcome, and a stable central government was beyond reach.

In 710, Muslims from North Africa invaded Spain. Within five years Berbers (native North Africans and recent converts to Islam who were led by Arabs) completed the conquest of much of the Iberian Peninsula, except for the northwest. In 716, the caliph at Damascus introduced an emir who ruled from Cordoba. The emirate of Cordoba struggled to make good its authority over all of Spain but failed to do so. Christians in the rugged mountains of the northwest—the region called Asturias—could not be dislodged, and the Muslims' part of Spain—known as al-Andalus—was plagued by the same divisions as the Islamic East: Arab factions against other Arab factions, Arabs against non-Arab Muslims, and Muslims against non-Muslims. Secure in mountainous Asturias (see Map 8.3), Christian kings built a capital at Oviedo and, in the ninth century, launched attacks against al-Andalus. For six hundred years this conflict between Christians and Muslims was the chief dynamic of Spanish history.

Italy and the Papal State

In 600 the Italian political scene was crowded. Several Germanic groups, four Byzantine outposts, and the popes were all contending for power. By the late eighth century, the Franks dominated northern Italy, the popes had created a state in the center, and the Byzantines clung to Naples and Sicily. That basic pattern then persisted for hundreds of years.

After defeating the Ostrogoths, the Romans were in principle masters of Italy, but their attempts to restore order were thwarted by the Lombards, who invaded in 568. These people had long lived in the Pannonian plain, and some of them had served in the Roman armies that defeated the Goths. The Lombard invasion caused the Byzantines to introduce a largely military regime under officers called *exarchs*. Stationed at Ravenna, exarchs appointed civilian and military officers.

The exarchate of Ravenna was weakened by the unwillingness of its population to pay heavy taxes to Constantinople when the receipts were spent in the Balkans and the east instead of against the Lombards. Moreover, Catholic Italy rejected Byzantine Christology and iconoclasm. Gradually the popes organized the defense of central Italy against the Lombards, stood up for the oppressed locals against Byzantine tax collectors, and led the opposition to unpopular theologies. In 751, the Lombard king conquered Ravenna. Muslims conquered Sicily in the ninth century, and Byzantine possessions in Italy were confined to the region around Naples.

Neither numerous nor united, the Lombards were also Arians. The Lombard kings had not systematically organized the conquest of Italy. From their capital at Pavia, the kings dominated the Po Valley, but other Lombards settled elsewhere and created independent duchies. Although the Lombard kings converted to Catholicism by 680, formed a strong government, and issued the most sophisticated Germanic law code, they always faced a dilemma. They were weakened because they did not control the duchies.

The strongest Lombard king of the eighth century, Aistulf (r. 749–757), decided to risk the consequences of attacking Ravenna and Rome. He conquered the former but caused the pope to turn to Pepin III, the king of the Franks, for aid and protection. Pepin came to Italy in 755 and 756, defeated Aistulf, and forced him to give to the pope all the lands he had taken from Rome and from Ravenna. A few years later Aistulf's successor reopened hostilities in central Italy. In 774, Charlemagne, Pepin's son and successor, defeated the Lombards, deposed their king, and took the Lombard crown for himself.

The Franks guaranteed to the popes undisputed possession of a substantial territory in central Italy. This first papal state was the culmination of three processes. First, as Roman imperial power declined in Late Antiquity, bishops often became the effective leaders of their towns. This position brought them power and prestige but also burdens. The popes found themselves responsible for Rome's food and water supply, the

A Mother Hen and Seven Chicks This delightfully frivolous object may have been a gift from Pope Gregory I to the Lombard queen Theudelinda. It helps us to appreciate the aesthetic tastes of the barbarians. *(Cathedral Treasure, Monza/Scala/Art Resource, NY)*

upkeep of its public buildings, and local charitable services. To pay for these functions, the popes began to organize the efficient bureaucratic administration of the patrimonies, the lands of the Roman church. Long before the 750s, the popes had been the landlords and patrons of many people in Italy, providing essential services formerly handled by the Roman state.

Second, the popes took the lead in protecting many people in central Italy, whether they lived on papal estates or not, from Byzantine taxes and heresy. This effort, too, forged bonds between the popes and the Italians. Third, eighth-century Rome spawned a justification for papal temporal rule. According to the *Donation of Constantine*, a document written in Rome (probably in the 760s), when Constantine departed Rome for the East in the 320s, he allegedly gave to the pope the authority to rule Rome and the whole West. In reality, no pope ever made such grandiose claims, and no concrete claims were ever based on the *Donation*. But the existence of the document signals a crucial progression from notions of landlordship and protection to direct rule. Thus, while kingdoms and exarchates were collapsing, a papal state was created that survives to this day as Vatican City.

The medieval popes who were simultaneously head of a church and of a state were the heirs of Pope Gregory I (r. 590–604). Scion of a Roman senatorial family, he held important secular offices before deciding to sell off all his properties and become a monk. His reputation for piety and integrity was so great, however, that the people and clergy of Rome elected him pope. Although Gregory would have preferred a life of monastic retreat, he threw himself into his new responsibilities. He negotiated with emperors and kings, disciplined churches and clerics in the whole West, and began creating and refining the bureaucratic apparatus by means of which popes for centuries would manage their city and patrimonies and later the papal state. Gregory was also a theologian of genius, the last of the Latin Church Fathers. He wrote biblical commentaries, books on moral living, and the *Pastoral Rule*, which circulated for a thousand years as a guide to how bishops should discharge their duties. Gregory was the founder of the medieval papacy.

The Fate of the British Isles

Britain was less thoroughly Romanized, more quickly abandoned by the Romans, and more deeply influenced by Germanic peoples than any other locality in the west. Around 600, the small Anglo-Saxon kingdoms created in the sixth century took the first steps toward converting to Christianity, transforming Britain into England, and joining England inseparably to the European world (see Map 8.3). But there was another history unfolding in the British Isles, that of the Celtic peoples in the north and west of Britain itself and in Ireland.

The Celts were the people who inhabited Britain before the Romans invaded in the first century. They were related to peoples who lived in a broad band from Anatolia to Ireland and Spain. The Anglo-Saxons confined the British Celts to the western regions of Cornwall and Wales and to the northern area of Scotland. Ireland had almost no Roman or Anglo-Saxon imprint.

The period between 600 and 900 saw only the faint beginnings of consolidation in the Celtic realms where the development of the Catholic church preceded political organization. Each Celtic region produced an elaborate mythology connected with heroic missionaries who supposedly brought the Christian faith in Late Antiquity. The best-known stories swirl around Ireland's Saint Patrick (390?–461?). The son of a minor Roman official in the north of Britian, Patrick was captured by pirates, enslaved in Ireland, freed, made a priest, and then returned to Ireland as a missionary. From his base at Armagh, Ireland's first bishopric, Patrick and his successors spread Christianity, and a vigorous monasticism, throughout the island. Historical too is the Irish aristocrat Columba (521–597) who, after his family lost a great battle, immigrated in 563 to the isle of Iona off the coast of Scotland. From his monastery on Iona, Columba and his successors began the evangelization of the Picts in Scotland.

Among the most successful Anglo-Saxon kingdoms were Wessex, Northumbria, and Mercia. Each had a reasonably large population and territory and opportunities for expansion. Wessex, for example, spread south and west into Devon, Cornwall, and Wales; Northumbria, which began on the North Sea coast, spread west to the Irish Sea and north into lowland Scotland (see Map 8.3). These kingdoms had ambitious rulers whose wars provided booty, land, and glory for old followers and new recruits.

Foreign connections played a role, too. Kent and East Anglia had diplomatic connections with the Franks, and Aethelbert (561–616), the greatest Kentish king, married Bertha, the daughter of a Frankish king. East Anglia's far-flung connections are revealed by a ship burial unearthed near Sutton Hoo in 1939. The ship, either a grave for or a memorial to an unknown king, had been hauled up onto the land, filled with treasures, and buried. The array of goods that was found at Sutton Hoo is astonishing. There is Byzantine silver, represented by spoons and a large dish; Frankish gold, in the form of dozens of coins, jewelry, and personal adornments from many places; and pots, beakers, and other domestic items of varied provenance. The artistic decorations on these items demonstrate influences ranging from the Mediterranean to the Rhineland, Scandinavia, and Ireland.

English kings quickly adopted symbolic aspects of rule to legitimize their authority and enhance their prestige. A fine scepter was found at Sutton Hoo, and Northumbrian kings were preceded by banners and a royal standard. Most kings issued coins in their own name. The kings of Northumbria presided in a magnificent wooden hall.

Relations with the church were important also. Two issues proved crucial: the conversion to Christianity and the development of an ecclesiastical hierarchy. In 597, Pope Gregory I sent a small band of missionaries under a Roman monk named Augustine (d. 604) to King Aethelbert of Kent, whose Christian wife, Bertha, had prepared the ground for the newcomers. From their base of operations at Canterbury in southeastern England, Augustine and his successors had limited success spreading Christianity, but a new field of influence was opened to them when Aethelbert's daughter married a king of Northumbria and took missionaries to her new home. Monks from Iona, as noted, were already spreading Christianity in central and lowland Scotland. When later Northumbrian kings turned to Iona for missionaries and bishops, Roman and Celtic Christianity came face to face in Northumbria.

The Christianity brought from Ireland did not differ in fundamental ways from the Roman Christianity imported at Canterbury. Indeed, the Irish were Roman Catholics. But Ireland had been isolated from the centers of Christian life since Late Antiquity, and its church had developed a number of distinctive local customs. For example, the two traditions used different calendars and thus celebrated Easter—the commemoration of the resurrection of Jesus Christ and the central celebration of the Christian year—on different days. In 664, the Northumbrian king Oswy called a synod, a church council, at the monastery of Whitby, whose abbess was the former royal princess Hilda (614–680), a champion of Celtic customs. (See the box, "Two English Holy Women: Hilda and Leoba.") At Whitby, Roman and Irish representatives debated their positions. Oswy, choosing the universal over the particular, decided for Rome.

In 668 the pope sent to England a new archbishop of Canterbury, Theodore (r. 668–690). He was a Syrian monk who had traveled widely in the East, lived for a time in Rome, gained great experience in church administration, and acquired a reputation for both learning and discretion. He came from Rome but was in many ways an outsider; neither the "Romans" nor the "Irish" in England could easily view him as a partisan. Lacking firm traditions, the church in England was in an administrative shambles. Working tirelessly, Theodore reconciled the conflicting parties, built up a typical Roman ecclesiastical structure, introduced authoritative Roman canon law for the church, and promoted Christian education. Theodore laid the foundations for a unified English church that contributed to the eventual political unification of England.

Ecclesiastical peace led to the flourishing of monastic life. Monasteries played two important roles in this period. First, they led the way in bringing Christianity to ordinary people. Despite early gains among kings and nobles, Christianity had barely begun to penetrate the countryside. Second, monks maintained international connections, ranging from Ireland to Rome, that attached England to the major intellectual currents of the day and enabled the English to make their own contributions.

After Theodore's school at Canterbury, the most important early center of learning was in

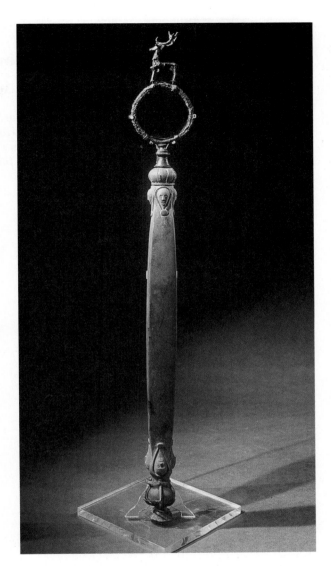

Whetstone from Sutton Hoo This whetstone, the traditional implement for sharpening knives, is surmounted by a stag, a symbol of virility and rulership among northern peoples. It was surely a symbol of the authority of the person commemorated at Sutton Hoo. (*Courtesy of the Trustees of the British Museum*)

Northumbria. There English, Irish, Frankish, and Roman currents flowed together in the monasteries of Lindisfarne, Wearmouth, and Jarrow and in the cathedral school of York. The schools of Canterbury, Lindisfarne, and Jarrow produced some of the most beautiful illuminated manuscripts—

Two English Holy Women: Hilda and Leoba

In these passages we can see some of the opportunities available to highborn women who embraced the religious life. Hilda, abbess of Whitby, was of royal descent and involved herself in many of the great events of her day. Leoba, of noble birth, joined a significant monastery in Wessex but later, and quite unusually, migrated to the Continent, where she joined forces with the famous missionary Boniface.

[Hilda] led her life in two equal parts, the first thirty-three years devoted to secular occupations and the second even more nobly devoted to the Lord in monastic life. She was indeed nobly born, the daughter of Hereric, a nephew of King Edwin. . . . When, having abandoned her secular garb, she decided to serve God alone, she went away to the land of the East Angles, whose king was a relative, from where she aimed to travel to Gaul and live as an exile for the Lord's sake where her sister Hereswith, mother of King Aldwith of the East Angles, was already living. But Bishop Aidan called her home and gave her land for a monastery. . . . Later she undertook to found a monastery at Whitby . . . and there she taught righteousness, mercy, purity, and other virtues, but above all peace and charity. . . . So great was her discretion that not only common people but even kings and princes used to come and ask her advice. . . . Those who submitted to her leadership had to study the scriptures . . . and five men from this monastery became bishops.

[Leoba's] mother consecrated her and handed her to Mother Tetta [abbess of Wimbourne and sister of an English king] to be taught the sacred sciences. . . . The girl, therefore, grew up and was taught with such care by the abbess

and all the nuns that she had no interests other than the monastery and the pursuit of sacred knowledge. She took no pleasure in aimless jests and wasted no time on girlish romances but, fired by the love of Christ, fixed her mind always on reading or hearing the Word of God. Whatever she heard or read she committed to memory, and put all that she learned into practice. . . . Boniface sent messengers to Tetta asking him to send Leoba . . . for Leoba's reputation for learning and holiness had spread far and wide and her praise was on everyone's lips. . . . When she came, the man of God [Boniface] received her with the deepest reverence, holding her in great affection, not so much because she was related to him on his mother's side as because he knew that by her holiness and wisdom she would confer many benefits by her word and example. . . . He gave her the monastery at a place called Bischofsheim, where there was a large community of nuns. These were trained according to her principles in the discipline of monastic life and made such progress in her teaching that many of them became superiors of others, so that there was hardly a convent of nuns in that part that did not have one of her disciples as abbess.

Sources: (Hilda): Venerabilis Baedae, *Historiam Ecclesiasticam Gentis Anglorum*, 4.21, ed. Charles Plummer (Oxford, England: Oxford University Press, 1896), pp. 252–254 (translated and adapted by T. Noble); (Leoba): Thomas F. X. Noble and Thomas Head, eds., *Soldiers of Christ: Saints and Saints' Lives from Late Antiquity and the Early Middle Ages* (University Park, Pa.: Pennsylvania State University Press, 1995), pp. 264–266.

books whose texts are adorned with gorgeous paintings—of the early Middle Ages.

The greatest product of this intellectual tradition was Bede (673–735). When he was 7, his parents placed him in the monastery at Wearmouth. He soon transferred to neighboring Jarrow and spent the rest of his life there. Bede was a teacher of genius, an erudite scholar, and a superb Latin stylist. His *Ecclesiastical History of the English People,* the most important source for English history from the fifth century to the eighth, did much to identify the Anglo-Saxons as a single English people. His biblical commentaries remained influential all over Europe for centuries. His studies of temporal reckoning popularized the use of A.D. dating, which replaced a bewildering array of local systems.

The career of King Offa of Mercia (r. 757–796) shows the trends in early Britain. His ancestors were pagans, but he was a patron of the church, convener of synods, and recipient of papal envoys. He dominated all of Britain and was the first to call himself "King of the English." He issued a law code, reformed Mercia's institutions, and signed England's first international trade agreement—with Charlemagne. After Offa's death, however, Viking raiders destroyed whatever unity had been achieved.

The kingdom of Wessex then struggled to maintain some semblance of leadership but faced a potent threat from Vikings, who, beginning in 865, conquered most of eastern and central England and began threatening the south. In 871, Alfred the Great (r. 871–899) ascended the throne, won a series of military victories, rallied the English, and began the slow reconquest of the rest of England from the Vikings. Alfred promoted intellectual recovery, church reform, and political stability. After two generations of chaos, Alfred revived the centralizing and unifying work of his eighth-century predecessors and laid the foundations for the English state of the tenth and eleventh centuries.

THE WORLD OF CHARLEMAGNE

Clovis and the Franks created the most effective of the early Germanic kingdoms. During the seventh century that kingdom, too, experienced difficulties but did not disappear. Just as Roman aristocrats had borne the ancient heritage into the Middle Ages, so now a Frankish family, called "Car-

THE GERMANIC WEST	
Sixth Century	Franks drive Visigoths into Spain
	Lombards enter Italy
	Franks and then Visigoths convert to Catholicism
	Irish and Roman missionaries initiate conversion of Britain
	Consolidation of Lombard, Visigothic, Frankish kingdoms
	Pontificate of Gregory I
Seventh Century	Political struggles in Frankish, Visigothic, and Anglo-Saxon kingdoms
	Lombards fight with popes and Byzantines
	England chooses Roman over Celtic Christianity
Eighth Century	Spain conquered by Muslims
	Carolingians become kings in Frankish world
	Emergence of papal state
	Offa of Mercia greatest early Anglo-Saxon ruler (757–796)
	Reign of Charlemagne (768–814)
	Imperial coronation of Charlemagne (800)
	Lombard kingdom conquered by Charlemagne
Ninth Century	Carolingian Renaissance
	Divisions of the Carolingian Empire
	Attacks of Muslims, Magyars, and Vikings

olingian" from the name of its greatest member, Charlemagne, assembled the talent and resources of the Frankish realm in a new way. Charlemagne reformed his government and church, patronized learning, and resurrected the western empire.

The Rise of the Carolingian Family

When Clovis died in 511, he divided his realm among his sons, and it soon became clear that several kingdoms would coexist. The Merovingian royal families feuded constantly, sought to expand at one another's expense, and drew local aristocracies into their battles. Trade and intellectual life declined, and some regions that had been conquered in the sixth century slipped away.

Nevertheless, the *idea* of a single kingdom of the Franks persisted. Kings and aristocrats in the small kingdoms competed for leadership of the realm as a whole. When the king in a region was weak, local nobles struggled to defend the kingdom or to hold it until a minor heir came of age. The flourishing, classicizing culture of late antique Gaul was largely gone, but a creative Christian monastic culture was growing up in all parts of the Frankish kingdom. Monks from the monasteries were accomplishing the difficult task of converting the countryside to Christianity. The seventh century, in other words, was a time when the late antique regime was slowly changing into the medieval regime.

Central to this development was the rise to prominence of the Carolingians. The family appeared in history just after 600 and thereafter monopolized the office of mayor of the palace (sort of a prime minister) to the king in Austrasia (the easternmost kingdom; see Map 8.3). The Carolingians were the boldest and wealthiest family in Austrasia, perhaps in the Frankish world. Within two generations they unified the Frankish realm and increased their own power.

The Carolingians used several methods to accomplish their ends. They formed alliances with powerful noble families in many regions. They waged war against the enemies of the Franks to restore the territorial integrity of the kingdom. Charles Martel (d. 741), Charlemagne's grandfather, led the Frankish forces that put an end to Arab raiding in Gaul, defeating a large force near Poitiers in 733. With booty from their wars, tribute from conquered peoples, spoils taken from recalcitrant opponents, and even lands seized from the church, the Carolingians attracted and rewarded more and more followers until no one, not even the Merovingians, was a match for them. The Carolingians also allied themselves very early with leading churchmen, both episcopal and monastic. They aided missionaries in the work of converting central Germany, thereby expanding Frankish influence in that area.

For years the Carolingians were content with the office of mayor of the palace. Then in 749,

Pepin III (son of Charles Martel) decided to send envoys to the pope to ask whether it was right that the person who had all the power in the land of the Franks was not the king. The pope responded that this situation contravened the divine plan. Accordingly, in 751, the last Merovingian king was deposed, and Pepin was elected in his place (r. 751–768). Pepin had prepared his usurpation very carefully with his Frankish supporters, but he appealed to the pope to make it appear that he had become king with divine approval and not by crude usurpation. Hard-pressed by the Lombards in Italy, the pope probably gave Pepin the answer he wanted to enlist him as an ally. Three years later the pope visited the Frankish kingdom, where he crowned and anointed Pepin and his sons, including Charlemagne. (The practice of anointing the head of a ruler with holy oil, which renders the recipient sacred, dates back to the kings of Israel. The head and hands of Catholic bishops were also anointed. The anointing of rulers and churchmen persisted throughout the Middle Ages and into the modern world.) The pope also forbade the Franks ever to choose a king from a family other than the Carolingians and received a promise of aid in Italy. The Merovingians, after nearly three centuries of rule, had yielded to a new royal dynasty that would last for more than two centuries.

The Empire of Charlemagne

Charlemagne (Carolus Magnus, "Charles the Great," in Latin) was a huge man, and his stature has grown in European history and legend. (See the box, "A Contemporary Portrait of Charlemagne.") Like all great leaders, Charlemagne (r. 768–814) was complex. He spoke and read Frankish, Latin, and some Greek but never learned to write. He promoted Christian morality but perpetrated unspeakable brutalities on his enemies and enjoyed several concubines. Many battles were fought in his name, but he rarely accompanied his armies and fought no campaigns that are remembered for strategic brilliance. Determination and organization were the hallmarks of his forty-six-year reign.

It took until the mid-780s for Charlemagne to assess and understand his world (Map 8.3). His first major achievement was the articulation of a

A Contemporary Portrait of Charlemagne

Einhard (770–840), a friend and adviser of Charlemagne, wrote his Life *in the 820s. Einhard selected suitable passages from* Lives of the Caesars, *by the first-century Roman historian Suetonius, to create a picture of Charlemagne that accords well with what is otherwise known about him.*

He loved foreigners and took great pains in receiving them, so much so that their vast numbers seemed an unwelcome burden not only for his palace but even for his kingdom. On account of his magnanimity he was scarcely troubled by his burden for the praise of his liberality and of his good name more than compensated for this considerable inconvenience. His body was full and strong, very tall but not more than was fitting, for his height was seven times the length of his feet. His head was round and his eyes, large and piercing. His nose was longer than normal, his white hair was beautiful, and his expression was happy, even joyful. The power and dignity of his form were very great when he was sitting or standing. His neck was short and thick and his belly stuck out a bit, but the overall fineness of his form veiled these features, indeed his step was firm and all his bearing was manly. His voice was clear but too high for so great a body. His health was good until fevers struck him in the last four years of his life, and at the end he was lame in one foot. Even then he acted more on his own than on the advice of his doctors, whom he practically considered to be enemies because they tried to convince him to give up the roasted foods to which he was accustomed and to live on boiled dishes. He always exerted himself vigorously in riding and hunting which came naturally to him—indeed you cannot find any race on earth that equals the Franks in this activity. He loved the hot-steam baths at Aachen—they were his reason for his constructing his palace there—and he exercised in the water when he could. No one could beat him in swimming. . . . Sometimes he invited his sons, nobles, and as many as a hundred men into the baths with him. . . . He dressed in the Frankish style. Next to his body he put on a linen shirt and drawers, then hose and a tunic with a silk border. He wore shoes and strips of cloth wound around his legs. In winter he protected his chest and shoulders with a jacket of otter or ermine. He wrapped himself in a blue cloak and wore a sword with hilt and belt of gold and silver. On festive days or to receive ambassadors, he wore a jewelled sword. The clothes of other peoples, however beautiful, he hated and would never have endured to put them on except at Rome, once when Pope Hadrian asked him to and again when his successor Leo requested it at Rome. Then he dressed in a long tunic and a heavy cloak and wore shoes made in the Roman style. On feast days he wore clothing woven with gold, jewelled shoes, a golden brooch to fasten his cloak, and crown with gold and gems. On other days his clothing hardly differed from that of the ordinary people. He was temperate in eating and drinking, particularly in drinking, for he hated drunkenness in anyone and especially in himself or in his own men.

Source: Einhard, *Vie de Charlemagne*, 4th ed., ed. Louis Halphen (Paris: Société d'Edition 'Les Belles Lettres,' 1967), cc. 21–23, pp. 64–70. Translated and adapted by Thomas Noble.

0 150 300 Km.

0 150 300 Mi.

Asturias Kingdom
Frankish Kingdom, 768
Areas conquered by Charlemagne
Tributary peoples
Byzantine territories

TREATY OF VERDUN, 843

Aachen
Paris •Verdun
Strasbourg

KINGDOM OF LOUIS THE GERMAN

TRIBUTARY PEOPLES

KINGDOM OF CHARLES THE BALD

KINGDOM OF LOTHAIR

PAPAL STATES

Rome

0 200 400 Km.

0 200 400 Mi.

Iona

SCOTLAND

Armagh•
IRELAND Dublin•

Jarrow•
NORTHUMBRIA
York•

DANISH MARCH

WALES
MERCIA
EAST ANGLIA

SAXONY 804

CORNWALL WESSEX ESSEX
Canterbury
KENT
SUSSEX
DEVON

•Utrecht

FLANDERS

Aachen•
AUSTRASIA
•Fulda

TRIBUTARY

Rouen•
Echternach• •Mainz

BRITTANY
Paris•

Rhine

NEUSTRIA Orléans•

ALEMANNIA

BAVARIA 788

Danube

SLAVIC

•Tours
Poitiers•

BURGUNDY

PEOPLES

AQUITAINE
Lyon•

•Bordeaux

GASCONY

VENETIA
Milan• Venice•
Pavia•

ISTRIA

Oviedo•

ASTURIAS Roncesvalles•

Aniane•

Rhône

Ebro

LOMBARDY Ravenna•

DALMATIA

SPANISH MARCH 811

Marseille• •Lérins

PAPAL STATES

UMAYYAD KINGDOM OF SPAIN

Toledo•

•Barcelona

CORSICA

Spoleto•

DUCHY OF SPOLETO

Rome•

•Monte Cassino

DUCHY OF BENEVENTO

•Salerno

•Cordoba

BALEARIC IS.

SARDINIA

BYZANTINE EMPIRE

SICILY

new ruling ideology in the Latin west. In capitularies—royal executive orders—of 789, Charlemagne required all males to swear an oath of allegiance to him, and he compared himself to a biblical king in his responsibility to admonish, to teach, and to set an example for his people. He referred to the people of his realm as a "New Israel," a new chosen people. Interestingly, this chosen people was not exclusively Frankish. No distinctions were to be made among Franks or Bavarians or Saxons. Everyone was to be equal in allegiance to the king and in membership in a sort of Augustinian City of God.

Einhard (ca. 770–840), Charlemagne's friend and biographer, said that Augustine's *City of God* (see page 259) was the king's favorite book. The king understood it to mean that there was a City of God consisting of all right-thinking Christians—the "New Israel"—and a City of Man consisting of pagans, heretics, and infidels. This idea is similar to the Islamic umma (see page 269). To Charlemagne and his advisers, it was obvious that as God was the sole legitimate ruler in heaven, Charlemagne was the sole legitimate and divinely appointed ruler on earth.

Modern readers may think that Charlemagne had crossed a boundary between church and state. It is crucial to understand that to Charlemagne, as to his Muslim and Byzantine contemporaries, no such boundary existed. Church (or religion) and state were complementary attributes of a polity whose end was salvation, not victory in war, domestic security, or personal fulfillment. Charlemagne's ideological legacy was twofold. On the one hand, it created possibilities for bitter struggles later in the Middle Ages between secular rulers and ecclesiastical powers about the leadership of Christian society. On the other hand, it made it hard to define the state and its essential purposes in other than religious terms.

The most disputed event in the reign of Charlemagne was his imperial coronation in Rome on Christmas in 800. It is important to separate how this event happened from what it meant to the participants. In April 799, some disgruntled papal bureaucrats and their supporters attacked Pope Leo III (r. 795–816) in an attempt to depose him. Leo was saved by an ally of Charlemagne and then traveled all the way to Saxony, where the king was with his army. Charlemagne agreed to restore the pope to Rome and, as his ally and protector, to investigate those who had attacked him. No real offenses could be proved against the pope, who appeared publicly in Rome to swear that he had done nothing wrong. Everything was handled to avoid any hint that the pope had been put on trial. When Charlemagne went to Saint Peter's Basilica on Christmas Day, he prayed before the main altar. As he rose from prayer, Pope Leo placed a crown on his head, and the assembled Romans acclaimed him as emperor.

Debate over this coronation arises from a remark of Einhard, who said that if Charlemagne had known what was going to happen he would not have gone to church that day, even though it was Christmas. Einhard's point was not that Charlemagne did not wish to be emperor. For at least fifteen years prominent people at the Carolingian court had been addressing Charlemagne in imperial terms in letters, treatises, and poems. What Einhard did mean was that Charlemagne saw himself as a Frankish and Christian emperor, not as a *Roman* emperor. The imperial office dignified his position as leader of the Frankish "Israel." Charlemagne did not wish to be beholden to the pope or to the Romans.

Charlemagne's policies did not change after his coronation. He continued his program of legal and ecclesiastical reform and put the finishing touches on some military and diplomatic campaigns. In 806 he divided his empire among his three legitimate sons; but then two of them died, so in 813 he made Louis his sole heir and successor. Charlemagne outlived most of the friends and companions of his youth and middle age. He outlived four wives and many of his children. Old and alone, ill and lame, he died in early 814.

Charlemagne's legacy was great. He brought together the lands that would become France,

Map 8.3 The Carolingian World The area over which Charlemagne exerted direct or indirect control was vast. The areas beyond the Rhine and Danube had never been part of the Roman Empire. The Franks made these regions part of European civilization. The Treaty of Verdun (see inset), signed by Charlemagne's grandsons in 843, was the first and most important of several divisions of the Carolingian Empire that resulted in the emergence of France and Germany. The kingdom of Italy and many small territories evolved from the kingdom of Lothair.

Germany, and northern Italy and endowed them with a common ideology, government, and culture. He provided a model that Europeans would look back to for centuries as a kind of golden age. His vast supraregional and supra-ethnic entity, gradually called "Christendom," drew deeply on the universalizing ideals of its Roman, Christian, and Jewish antecedents but was, nevertheless, original. In one sense the Carolingian Empire represented the final stage in the evolution of the Roman Empire of Late Antiquity, but in another sense the Carolingian Empire was a new kind of regime that pointed to the future.

Carolingian Government

Charlemagne accomplished much through the sheer force of his personality and his boundless energy. But he also reformed and created institutional structures. These helped him to carry out his tasks, guaranteed a measure of permanence to his reforms, and created government patterns that lasted in many parts of Europe until the twelfth century.

The king (or emperor—the offices differed little in practical importance) was the heart of the system. In theory, the king ruled by God's grace and did not have to answer for his conduct to any person. In reality, the king necessarily sought consensus through a variety of means. The king controlled vast lands, which gave him great wealth of his own and also the means to reward loyal followers. By controlling appointments to key positions, the king required men to come to him for power, wealth, and prestige.

The eastern contemporaries of the Carolingians relied on large numbers of carefully trained, paid civil servants. In contrast, the Carolingians employed a limited number of men who were tied to them by bonds of familial and personal allegiance. At the Carolingian court there were several ceremonial officers and a domestic staff. For example, the constable, an officer in charge of transporting the royal entourage, was usually a great aristocrat; the real work of the office was carried out by others. The treasurer was the keeper of the king's bedchamber, where the royal treasure chest was kept. Several chaplains, whose primary duty was to see to the spiritual needs of the court, kept official records. The queen controlled the domestic staff and the stewards who managed the royal estates. (See the box, "Carolingian Women and the Great Estate.")

Local government was mainly entrusted to counts. There were about six hundred counts in the empire and several times that number of minor officials. As in Merovingian times, the counts were at once administrative, judicial, and military officials. Most came from prominent families, and the office increased the wealth and importance of its holders. Counts had to promulgate and enforce royal orders and to preside in regular sessions of local courts. They got one-third of the fines so the zealous pursuit of justice was in their interest.

The royal court and the localities were linked in several ways. Under Charlemagne and his successors it became usual for all major officers, whether secular (counts and their subordinates) or ecclesiastical (bishops, abbots), to be *vassals* of the king. In return for their offices and grants of land called *benefices*, vassals solemnly pledged loyalty and service to the king. Vassalage drew on both Roman and Germanic customs. Patron-client ties had always been socially and politically important among the Romans, and the allegiance of warriors to a chief was a key bond among the Germans. But by connecting personal loyalty with public office and material reward, Charlemagne created something essentially new. Only a few thousand men, a tiny fraction of the total population, were vassals at any time. They constituted the political and social elite.

Another connection between the king and his local agents was the assembly that met in various places once or twice a year. In theory, all free men were to assemble at these gatherings, which sometimes had separate secular and ecclesiastical sessions, to advise the king on matters of great importance, such as war and peace or legal reforms. In practice only the vassals had the means or the interest to ensure their attendance. Most of the great Carolingian reforms were formulated in these assemblies by cooperation between the king and his most important subjects. The assemblies served to defuse dissension, but the king also brought his power to bear locally by traveling. The monarchy possessed estates all over the heartlands of the kingdom, and the royal entourage often moved from one place to another. Monasteries and cathedrals had to provide hospitality to the

Carolingian Women and the Great Estate

*These chapters (*capitula, *whence* capitulary) *from the capitulary* De Villis *("Concerning the Estates") reveal some of the roles that women played on large estates. Note that those roles ranged from management to production and involved women of different classes.*

16. It is our [the "royal we" means the king himself] wish that whatever we or the queen may order any steward, or whatever our officials, the seneschal or the butler, may order them in our name or in the name of the queen, they shall carry out in full as they are instructed. And whoever falls short in this through negligence, let him abstain from drinking from the moment he is told to do so until he shall come into our presence or the presence of the queen and seek forgiveness.

27. Our [i.e., the king's and queen's] houses are to have continuous watch-fires and guards to keep them safe. And when our *missi* and their retinues are on their way to or from the palace, they shall under no circumstances take lodging in the royal manor houses, except on our express orders or those of the queen.

31. They [the queen] shall set aside what is necessary for the household workers and for the women's workshops.

43. They are to supply the women's workshops with materials at the appropriate times . . . that is, linen, wool, woad, vermilion, madder, wool-combs, teazles, soap, oil, vessels, and the other small things that are needed there.

47. That our hunters and falconers, and the other servants who are in permanent attendance on us at the palace, shall throughout our estates be given such assistance as we or the queen may command in our letters.

49. That our women's quarters shall be properly arranged—that is, with houses, heated rooms and living rooms; and let them have good fences all around, and strong doors, so that they can do our work well.

58. When our puppies are entrusted to the stewards they are to feed them at their own expense . . . unless there should be an order from ourselves or the queen that they are to be fed at our expense.

Source: H. R. Loyn and J. Percival, *The Reign of Charlemagne: Documents on Carolingian Government and Administration* (London: Edward Arnold, 1975), pp. 67–71.

king. As the royal party traveled about the realm, they were able to check on local conditions and to compel local officials to comply with royal wishes.

In 788, Charlemagne began to build a palace at Aachen, and in the last twenty years of his life he was usually in residence there (see Map 8.3). The later Carolingian rulers all tended to have fixed residences, as did the Byzantines and the Abbassids. In adopting fixed residences and elaborate court rituals, the Carolingians may have been returning to Roman precedents or copying their contemporaries to appear as sophisticated as they. Elegant courts and intricate rituals project an aura of grandeur that enhances people's respect

for their rulers. It is no coincidence that a key innovation of Charlemagne's reign coincided with his permanent residence in Aachen. In the late 780s he began to send out pairs of roving inspectors, *missi dominici*, envoys of the lord king, to see that royal orders were being observed, that counts were dispensing justice honestly, and that persons of power were not oppressing the powerless.

The Carolingian Renaissance

Charlemagne's reforms culminated in a revival of learning that scholars have named the "Carolingian Renaissance" (from *renaissance*, French for

Charlemagne's Palace at Aachen In the foreground is the octagonal chapel and throne room of Charlemagne's palace at Aachen. It is joined by galleries to the residential quarters in the background. Construction was begun in 788. The models for these buildings were found in Rome and Ravenna. *(Römisch-Germanisches Zentralmuseum)*

"rebirth"). Charlemagne's fundamental ideas are revealed well by the constant use in contemporary sources of words such as *rebirth, renewal, reform,* and *restoration.* Charlemagne, his advisers, and his successors looked back for inspiration to Christian and papal Rome, to Saint Peter and Constantine, and to the Church Fathers. To them, the rebirth of Western society as a "New Israel" was equivalent to the theological rebirth of an individual in baptism. The Carolingians were the driving force behind intellectual growth in their era, and in all areas they subordinated learning to their ideological program.

To accomplish his objectives, Charlemagne required every cathedral and monastery to establish a school. To set up and run those schools he summoned to his court many of the most able and influential intellectual figures of the day, among them Franks, such as his biographer Einhard, grammar teachers from Italy, and Visigothic theologians from the Spanish border. His most famous recruit was the Anglo-Saxon Alcuin (735–804), the most learned man of his day and the heir of Bede and of the dynamic culture of Northumbria.

Much of the work of Alcuin and his associates was devoted to the production of textbooks and to the teaching of elementary knowledge. Charlemagne was convinced that people needed to be taught, accurately and intelligibly, the basic truths of Christianity, if he were to accomplish his task of leading them to salvation. A massive effort was undertaken to copy manuscripts of the Bible and of the writings of the Latin Church Fathers. These books, the essential sources for the whole program, needed to be disseminated as widely as possible. The process of copying was facilitated by a new script, Caroline minuscule. (See the feature, "Weighing the Evidence: The Manuscript Book," on pages 304–305.)

It is significant that Charlemagne could attract Alcuin from York, the most renowned school in the West, to head his palace school, just then forming.

Charlemagne could place more resources at Alcuin's disposal than anyone else, and he had the will to do so. Alcuin also saw the long-term benefits that would come from his work. Alcuin's pupils spread out in the next generation to create a network of schools that went right on multiplying across the ninth century. That is a powerful legacy. And Alcuin did more than just teach. He wrote learned works and poetry and was for twenty years Charlemagne's most trusted adviser.

With this plan, personnel, and schools in place, Charlemagne took many concrete steps. He got from Rome a copy of the then-authoritative canon law of the church. In 789, after some years of study by his court scholars, this law was issued for his whole kingdom. In about 786, Charlemagne got from the pope a sacramentary, a service book for worship in cathedral churches, and, again after a period of study, this was imposed throughout the kingdom. Charlemagne sought an authoritative copy of the *Rule of St. Benedict,* and after study and commentary, this Rule was imposed on all monasteries in the kingdom.

Secular reforms mirrored religious ones. Orders regularized the management of all royal estates. Charlemagne attempted to update local law codes and to make them as similar as possible. Not since Rome had governments possessed either the interest in or the means to promote such centralization. It is striking that in the eighth century the caliphate, the Byzantine Empire, and the Carolingian Empire were engaged in similar centralizing activities.

Versatility was a hallmark of Carolingian learning. There were figures who excelled at poetry, history, and biography. Biblical studies and theology attracted a lot of attention. One figure who personifies the "Carolingian Renaissance" is the Visigoth Theodulf. He came to court in about 785 and served thereafter as a missus, royal adviser, abbot of several monasteries, and bishop of Orléans. He issued important legislation for his diocese. He was the foremost Old Testament scholar of his day and the only one who knew Hebrew. In the *Caroline Books,* he offered the Frankish response to Byzantine iconoclasm. He wrote theological treatises, many letters, and dozens of poems. At Germigny he designed a church that is a masterpiece of early Carolingian architecture.

Carolingian art is a crowning glory of the age. The manuscripts decorated under Charlemagne's

Maiestas Domini (The Lord in Majesty) An ivory book cover from Charlemagne's court or a closely associated workshop, this image shows the enthroned Christ trampling beasts and encircled by scenes from his life. The image is an excellent Carolingian adaption of late antique themes and styles. *(Stiftsbibliothek, St. Gallen)*

patronage and then, for three generations, under the patronage of his descendants and of prominent churchmen show versatility, respect but not awe for the past, and innovation. Several distinct currents produced Carolingian art. Most prominent were the animal and geometric decorative motifs of Irish and Anglo-Saxon art, the elegance, formality, and sense of composition of classical art, basic elements of style from Byzantine painting, actual scenes from papal Rome, and the mysteries of Christian theology. Every element was borrowed, but the finished product was new.

Architecture shows the same trends. Charlemagne's palace complex at Aachen has parallels in imperial Constantinople, papal Rome, and Ostrogothic Ravenna. Workers and building materials were fetched from all over the empire. From 768 to 855, 27 cathedrals were built along with 417 monasteries and 100 royal residences. For basic buildings the Carolingians adapted the basilica. The basilica was fundamentally a horizontal building, but the Carolingians, by altering the western end and façade, added the dimension of verticality. In Romanesque and Gothic architecture this innovation would have a brilliant career (see pages 343–344 and 381–384).

THE FRAGMENTATION OF THE CAROLINGIAN EMPIRE

The Carolingian Empire itself did not outlive the ninth century. Rome's empire lasted much longer, as did Byzantium's and Islam's. All of these realms were fatally weakened by similar problems, but those problems arose more quickly and acutely in the Carolingian world than elsewhere. Both internal and external factors contributed to the breakup, and by the end of the ninth century a profusion of small political entities replaced the Carolingian Empire.

Internal Factors in the Carolingian Decline

Size and ethnic complexity contributed to the disintegration of the Carolingian Empire. The empire included many small regions—Saxony, Bavaria, Brittany, and Lombardy, for example—that had their own resident elites, linguistic traditions, and distinctive cultures, which had existed before the Carolingians came on the scene and persist to this day. The Merovingian and Carolingian periods were basically a unifying intrusion into a history characterized by regional diversity. The Carolingians made heroic efforts to build a common culture and to forge bonds of unity, but the obstacles were insuperable.

Another key issue in the breakup of the Carolingian Empire was political and dynastic. The Carolingians regularly tried to create subking-

doms for all their legitimate sons while preserving the imperial title for one of them. This was a creative attempt to concede limited autonomy to particular regions by means of local kingships—for instance in Bavaria, Italy, and Aquitaine—while preserving the "Augustinian" unity of the empire as a whole. Unfortunately, younger sons rarely yielded to their older brothers, and the bonds of loyalty among cousins, nephews, and grandchildren grew slender. Frequent divisions of the empire, or of segments of it, placed local nobilities in the difficult position of changing their allegiance frequently and of jeopardizing their offices and landholdings.

In the Treaty of Verdun in 843 (see the inset of Map 8.3) the three grandsons of Charlemagne—Charles the Bald, Louis the German, and Lothair—divided the empire into three realms: the West Frankish, the East Frankish, and the Middle Kingdom. After fierce battles among the brothers, each appointed forty members to a study commission that traversed the whole empire to identify royal properties, fortifications, monasteries, and cathedrals so that an equitable division could be made of these valuable resources. Each brother needed adequate resources to solidify his rule and to attract or hold followers. The lines drawn on the map at Verdun did not last even for a generation.

Slowly large west Frankish and east Frankish kingdoms emerged and created a framework for the future France and Germany. But they had to compete with many smaller entities. Some of these, in Italy, in the Rhineland, and in southern France, were old and distinctive regions that recaptured their former independence. Other areas were essentially new creations, born in the absence of firm Carolingian control. There were also newcomers on the scene, most prominently Scandinavian and Slavic principalities.

Before the ninth century, Scandinavia knew only small-scale political units under local chieftains and their trusted followers. Economic and political pressure from the Carolingians gradually began to push both Denmark and Norway in the direction of greater political consolidation. A single Danish monarchy has a continuous history from the late ninth century, and Norway's monarchy dates from the early tenth.

To the east of the Carolingian Empire lay a vast swath of Slavic lands. The Carolingians fought, allied, and traded with these peoples for

decades. Charlemagne destroyed the Avar kingdom in the Danube basin in campaigns between
788 and 804, and by the middle of the ninth century a cluster of Slavic states emerged in the region. Among these was Moravia, whose princes
played a complicated diplomatic game between
the east Frankish rulers and the Byzantine emperors. To the east of the Moravians, the Bulgarians
profited from the Avar and then the Carolingian
collapse to expand their kingdom. For two centuries the Bulgars dominated eastern Europe and
threatened Byzantium.

The most durable consequence of this political
restructuring along the eastern frontier of the
Frankish world was religious. In 863, on an invitation from Moravia and in hopes of countering the
Franks, the Byzantine emperor sent the missionaries Cyril (826–869) and Methodius (805–884) into
eastern Europe. The emperor hoped to erect an Orthodox union of his own realm, the southern Slavs,
and the newly converted Bulgars. Likewise he was
seeking a diplomatic bulwark between the Bulgars
in the east and the Franks in the west. Unfortunately for Byzantium, Cyril and Methodius agreed
with the pope to introduce Roman Catholic Christianity in return for the pope's permission to use
the Slavonic language in worship. Cyril and
Methodius were formidable linguists who created
a religious literature in "Church Slavonic" that
went far toward creating a new cultural realm in
central Europe.

Charles the Bald From a Bible dedicated to Charles the
Bald in about 846, this picture illustrates Carolingian art
and ideology. Charles the Bald is depicted with Roman
attributes of rule. He is clearly above his clerical advisers.
And the hand of God points at him. *(Bibliothèque Nationale)*

New Waves of Invasions

The external cause of the Carolingian Empire's fragmentation was a new wave of attacks. In the middle
decades of the ninth century, Arabs, Vikings, and
Magyars wreaked havoc on the Franks.

Based in North Africa and the islands of the
western Mediterranean, Arabs attacked Italy and
southern France. The Byzantines lost Sicily to Muslim raiders from North Africa in 827 and found
themselves seriously challenged in southern Italy.
In the 840s, Muslims raided the city of Rome.
These same brigands preyed on trade in the western Mediterranean and even set up camps in the
Alps to rob traders passing back and forth over
the mountains.

"From the fury of the Northmen, O Lord, deliver us," was a plaintive cry heard often in ninth-
century Europe. Those Northmen were Vikings,

mainly Danes and Norwegians, seeking booty,
glory, and political opportunity. Most Viking
bands were formed by leaders and their men who
had lost out in the dawning institutional consolidation of the northern world. Some were opportunists who sought to profit from the weakness
of Carolingian, Anglo-Saxon, and Irish rule. By the
mid-ninth century, Vikings settled and began their
own state-building activities in Ireland, England,
northwestern France ("Normandy"—the region of
the Northmen), and Russia.

Magyars, relatives of the Huns and Avars who
had preceded them into eastern Europe, were accomplished horsemen whose lightning raids, beginning in 889, hit Italy, Germany, and even France.
East Frankish Carolingians tried to use the Magyars as mercenaries against the troublesome Mora-

vians. In the end, the Magyars destroyed the incipient Moravian state and raided with impunity.

All of these attacks were unpredictable and caused local regions to fall back on their own resources rather than look to the central government. Commerce was disrupted everywhere. Schools, based in ecclesiastical institutions, suffered severe decline. The raids represented a thousand pinpricks, not a single, deadly sword stroke. Yet their collective effect amounted to despair and disruption on a massive scale.

Even though the Carolingian Empire itself disintegrated, the idea of Europe as "Christendom," as a single political-cultural entity, persisted. The Latin Christian culture promoted by Carolingian schools and rulers set the tone for intellectual life until the twelfth century. Likewise, Carolingian governing structures were inherited and adapted by all of the successor states that emerged in the ninth and tenth centuries. In these respects the Carolingian experience paralleled the Roman, and the Islamic and Byzantine, too: A potent, centralizing regime disappeared but left a profound imprint on its heirs.

EARLY MEDIEVAL ECONOMIES AND SOCIETIES

In economic and social history, the early Middle Ages provides additional evidence of continuity and change. The world remained rural, society was hierarchical, and women were excluded from public power. In rough terms, the Islamic world changed the most, the Byzantine the least, and the West fell somewhere between.

Trade and Commerce

Trade is a mechanism of exchange between producers and consumers that depends to some extent on markets. There are other exchange mechanisms. The Roman government, for example, moved large amounts of goods from the center of the empire to the frontiers to supply its armies. Roman, Byzantine, and Islamic governments raised taxes in one place, bought goods in another, and then consumed their purchases someplace else. Tribute and plunder were also effective exchange mechanisms—the Franks collected tributes in cows from the Saxons.

There were also diplomatic gifts: A caliph sent Charlemagne an elephant.

The commonest exchanges were intensely local, but several major trading networks operated during the early Middle Ages. Mesopotamia was linked by rivers to the Persian Gulf and to both east Africa and south Asia, by land and sea to Byzantium, and by land and rivers to the Black Sea region, Slavic Europe, and the Baltic. Byzantines traded mainly by sea. The whole Mediterranean was open to them, and from the Black Sea they received the products of the Danube basin. The Muslim world was fundamentally a land empire that had relatively poor roads and primitive wheeled vehicles, so transport considerations were crucial: A caravan of some five hundred camels could move only one-fourth to one-half of the cargo of a normal Byzantine ship.

The west had many trade routes. The Rhône-Saône river system moved goods, as did the land routes through the Alpine passes. The North and Baltic seas were the hubs of a network that linked the British Isles, the whole of the Frankish north—by means of its rivers—the Rhineland, Slavic Europe, Byzantium, and the Muslim world. The Danube was also a major highway. The major trade networks intersected at many points. Despite religious and ideological differences, Rome's three heirs regularly traded with one another.

Food and other bulk goods never traveled very far because the cost was prohibitive. Most towns were supplied with foodstuffs by their immediate hinterlands, so the goods that moved over long distances were portable and valuable. Cotton and raw silk were moved to the Mediterranean, where they were made into cloth in, respectively, Egypt and Byzantium. Paper and pottery were moved around the caliphate. Asian spices and perfumes were avidly sought everywhere. The Byzantines traded in silk cloth, fine ivories, delicate products of the gold- and silver-smiths' art, slaves, and naval stores. Byzantium, with its large fleet, usually controlled the Black and Mediterranean Seas but found trade relations difficult to sustain. Reduced in prosperity, the empire could no longer dictate trade terms to subject peoples and competed badly with the Muslims. Trade in the west was partly in high-value luxury goods but mainly in ordinary items such as plain pottery, raw wool, wool cloth, millstones, weapons, and slaves.

Town and Countryside

To think of the ancient world is to think of cities. Thinking of the medieval world brings to mind forests and fields. Actually, from 80 to 90 percent of people in antiquity lived in rural settings, and in the early Middle Ages the percentage was not much higher. What changed was the place occupied by towns in the totality of human life. Fewer government functions were based in towns, cultural life was less bound to the urban environment, and trade in luxuries, which depended on towns, declined.

Towns in the west lost Roman governmental significance but often survived as focal points of royal or, more often, ecclesiastical administration. A cathedral church required a large corps of administrators. Western towns were everywhere attracting *burgs*, new settlements of merchants, just outside their centers. Because Vikings frequently raided these burgs, their existence was precarious. Few western towns were impressive in size or population. Rome may have numbered a million people in the time of Augustus, but it had only about 25,000—one-fortieth of that amount—in 800. Paris had perhaps 20,000 inhabitants before the Vikings arrived. These were the largest cities by far in Christian Europe.

In the Byzantine East, apart from Constantinople, the empire had a more rural aspect after the Muslims took control of the heavily urbanized regions of Syria, Egypt, and parts of Anatolia in the seventh century. The weakening of the caliphate in the second half of the ninth century was a spur to urban growth in the Byzantine Empire. In provincial cities, population growth and urban reconstruction depended heavily on military conditions: Cities threatened by Muslims or Bulgars declined.

The Muslims were great city-builders. Baghdad—four times larger in area than Constantinople, with a million residents to the latter's 400,000—was created from scratch. The most magnificent city in the West was Cordoba, the capital of Muslim Spain. Its population may have reached 400,000, and its great mosque, begun in 785, held 5500 worshipers, more than any Latin church except St. Peter's. The city had 900 baths, 1600 mosques (Rome had about 200 churches), 60,000 mansions, and perhaps 100,000 shops. Its libraries held thousands of books when the largest Carolingian book collections numbered a few hundred.

Agriculture nevertheless remained the most important element in the economy and in the daily lives of most people in all three realms. Farming primarily meant the production of cereal grains, which provided diet staples such as bread, porridge, and beer. Regions tended to specialize in the crops that grew most abundantly in local circumstances. For example, olives and grapes were common in the Mediterranean area whereas cereals predominated around the Black Sea and in central Gaul. Animal husbandry was always a major part of the rural regime. English sheep provided wool and meat. In Frankish and Byzantine regions pigs, which were cheap to raise, supplied meat, but for religious reasons—Islam took over the Jewish prohibition against eating pork—pork was almost absent in the Muslim East.

A key development in the Frankish West was the appearance of a bipartite estate, sometimes called a "manor." On a bipartite estate, one part of the land was set aside as a reserve (or demesne), and the rest was divided into tenancies. The reserve, consuming from one quarter to one half of the total territory of the estate, was exploited directly for the benefit of the landlord. The tenancies were generally worked by the peasants for their own support. The bipartite estate provided the aristocrats with a livelihood while freeing them for military and government service.

Estates were run in different ways. A landlord might hire laborers to farm his reserve, paying them with money exacted as fees from his tenants. Or he might require the tenants to work a certain number of days per week or weeks per year in his fields. The produce of the estate might be gathered into barns and consumed locally or hauled to local markets. The reserve might be a separate part of the estate, a proportion of common fields, or a percentage of the harvest. The tenants might have individual farms or work in common fields. Although the manor is one of the most familiar aspects of European life throughout the Middle Ages, large estates with dependent tenants were also evolving in the Byzantine and Islamic worlds.

Social Patterns

Most of the surviving records were written by elite members of society and reveal little about the middle and lower orders of society. Nevertheless, certain similarities are evident in the social structures

Labors of the Months From a ninth-century West Frankish manuscript, this picture illustrates the labors of the various months of the year. How many of them can you figure out? How do these compare with farm labors where you live? *(Österreichische Nationalbibliothek)*

of all levels in all three societies. The elites tended to be large landholders, to control dependent populations, and to have access to government offices. There were regional differences, too. Scholars had more social rank in Byzantium than they had anywhere else; and churchmen, especially bishops, were powerful in Christian societies but had no counterparts in Muslim ones. Literature, surely reflecting social realities, portrays the cultivated Muslim gentleman in the Abbassid period. This social type, marked by learning, good manners, and a taste for fine things, does not appear in Byzantium or in the West until the twelfth century.

The middling classes show some disparities among the regions. Merchants, for example, often rose through the social ranks to become great aristocrats in Muslim societies. Islamic society often evinced great mobility, because of its restless, expanding nature and because Islamic ideology rejected distinctions in the umma. In Byzantium, traditional Roman prejudices against merchants and moneymaking activities persisted. Thus, there were rich merchants whose wealth gave them private power and influence but who lacked public power and recognition. In the West, merchants were neither numerous nor powerful in the Carolingian period. In some towns, moreover, commerce was in the hands of Jews, always outsiders in a militantly Christian society.

Merchants were not the only people occupying the middle rungs of the social ladder. All three societies, in fact, possessed both central elites and provincial elites. Service at the Carolingian, Byzantine, or Abbassid court counted for more than service in a provincial outpost. It was one thing to be abbot of a great monastery and quite a different thing to preside over a poor, tiny house. The thematic generals in Byzantium were lofty personages; their subordinates held inferior positions. The vassals of a Carolingian king formed a real aristocracy; vassals' vassals were of decidedly lower rank.

Degrees of freedom and local economic and political conditions shaped the lives of peasants. In all three societies some farmers were personally free and owed no cash or labor services to anyone but the central government. In areas such as Abbassid Iraq, ordinary free farmers led a comfortable life. In the Frankish world, most peasants existed outside the dawning manorial system. They were free, and if they lived in areas of good land and political security, such as the Paris basin, their lives most likely were congenial. Byzantine peasants, though free, often lived in areas of military danger, and in some parts of the Balkans they eked a living from poor soils. They were highly taxed, and their freedom was small compensation for their economic and personal insecurity. All peasants were alike in their subjection to political forces over which they had no control.

At the bottom of the social scale everywhere were slaves. Christianity did not object to slavery itself but forbade the enslavement of Christians. Islam was similar, forbidding Muslims to enslave other Muslims. Slaves therefore tended to be commonest in still-pagan societies—Scandinavia, for example—or in frontier regions where neighboring pagans could be captured and sold. There were more slaves in the Muslim world than in Byzantium, which had, in turn, more than the West.

Women were bound to the same social hierarchies as men. Predictably enough, women had few formal, public roles to play. Their influence, however great, tended to function in the private sphere, rarely revealed to us by sources that stem from the public realm of powerful men. Aristocratic women had opportunities and power that were denied ordinary women. Irene ruled at Byzantium as empress. Frankish and Anglo-Saxon queens were formidable figures in the life of their realms. Carolingian queens managed the landed patrimony of the dynasty, dozens of huge estates with tens of thousands of dependents. A lack of evidence and the rigorous exclusion of women from public life in the Islamic world means that virtually no Muslim women emerge as distinct personalities in the early Middle Ages.

The conversion of England to Christianity was fostered by women. Most convents of nuns had aristocratic abbesses who presided over complex enterprises and, often, schools. In the Frankish world aristocratic women secured some learning, and one, Dhuoda, wrote in 841 a manual of advice for her son that conveys biblical and patristic teachings as well as practical wisdom. The Frankish convent at Chelles was a renowned center for the copying of manuscripts. Some Anglo-Saxon nuns owned ships and invested in commercial activities to support their convent. Almost all aspects of the cloth industry were in women's hands.

One example of the problems in the evidence concerning women is church roles. Women could not hold priestly office; and although there were deaconesses at Hagia Sophia in the sixth century, they disappeared soon after and had long ago vanished in the West. Religious power could come from personal sanctity as well as holding office. One study of some 2200 saints from the early Middle Ages finds only about 300 females. It was hard for women to gain recognition as saints. And if a woman became a saint, her holiness was inevitably described either as "manly"—an extreme ascetic was praised for having the strength and courage of a man—or as beautiful, virginal, and domestic, in other words, with female stereotypes.

The domestic sphere is another difficult realm to enter. The Quran permitted a man up to four wives, if he could care for them and would treat them equitably. A Muslim woman, however, was given her dowry outright, and multiple marriages may have meant that relatively more Muslim women could gain a measure of security. In Byzantium and the West, families rarely arranged marriages for more than one or two daughters. Others remained single or entered convents. Women at all social levels tended to pass from the tutelage of their fathers to that of their husbands. In antiquity a suitor usually paid a fee, a "bride price," to his prospective wife's father and then endowed his wife with "bridewealth," money or possessions of her own. Gradually this practice changed to a system whereby a bride's father paid a dowry to her future husband. Thus, a wife who was cast aside could be left impoverished, for in most places the law did not permit her to inherit land if she had brothers. Females were such valuable property in the marriage market that rape was an offense not against a girl but against her father. A man could divorce, even kill, his wife for adultery, witchcraft, or grave robbing, and then marry again. A woman could usually gain a divorce only for adultery, and she could not remarry. For the vast majority of women, daily life was hedged about with legal limitations and personal indignities.

SUMMARY

We have traced three parallel trajectories in the history of the early Middle Ages. The first one is chronological. In the Islamic, Byzantine, and Frankish worlds, the seventh century was an age of rapid, dynamic change, the eighth century a time of consolidation and reform, and the ninth century a period of renewed challenges.

The second trajectory is political, religious, and ideological. Three large imperial states were created out of diverse peoples and territories. Each state developed a central government that focused on a powerful leader who was seen as a specially chosen agent of God. Each state erected a system of rule that tied a government capital to its outlying regions. In the Muslim and Byzantine worlds, that system was highly bureaucratic; in the Frankish world, the system was more amateur and personal. A religion—Islam, Orthodox Catholicism, or Roman Catholicism—provided the social glue that held each society together and defined the mission of its government. The cultural life of each area was inspired mainly by an attempt to integrate a powerful religious message with older intellectual traditions.

The third trajectory concerns results. In the Islamic and Frankish worlds, large states broke down to leave many smaller heirs. In each instance, changes in the caliber of leadership, unpredictable foreign attacks, and the sheer diversity of the polity pulled the large state apart. The Byzantine Empire, much smaller than the Roman Empire had been, managed to defend its territory. A sense of common and present danger probably helped to preserve the Byzantine state even in the face of severe foreign threats and domestic disputes. Byzantium was not much less complex than the Islamic or Frankish realms, but it was centuries older, and from tradition came strength and confidence.

We began this chapter by imagining what Rome's legacy might be. Islam and the caliphate emerged as surprising elements, while Byzantium and the Frankish world followed more predictable courses. In the next chapter, we shall have to ask what happened after about 900. This time the surprising element will be found in the West. Although battered in 900, Europe was on the verge of an astonishing period of growth and development.

SUGGESTED READING

General Surveys

Brown, Peter. *The Rise of Western Christendom*. 1996. A verbal feast, this book presents a stimulating assessment of the place of Christianity in the rise of Western culture.

Collins, Roger. *Early Medieval Europe, 300–1000*. 1991. A balanced and comprehensive narrative stressing political history. Includes a valuable bibliography.

Hodgson, Marshall G. S. *The Venture of Islam: Conscience and History in a World Civilization*. Vol. 1, *The Classical Age of Islam*. 1958. A stimulating, sympathetic interpretation of Islamic origins.

Kennedy, Hugh. *The Prophet and the Age of the Caliphates: The Islamic Near East from the Sixth to the Eleventh Century*. 1986. Detailed but readable, this is the best modern introduction to the emergence and spread of Islam.

McKitterick, Rosamond. *The New Cambridge Medieval History*, vol. II. 1995. Thirty well-written, comprehensive essays by experts covering the period 700 to 900.

Ostrogorsky, George. *History of the Byzantine State*. Rev. ed. Translated by Joan Hussey. 1969. Massive and detailed, this remains the preferred general history.

Randsborg, Klaus. *The First Millennium in Europe and the Mediterranean: An Archaeological Essay*. 1991. A remarkable account of the slow transformation of material life and the environment.

Whittow, Mark. *The Making of Orthodox Byzantium, 600–1025*. 1996. Lively, readable, controversial, engaging, this book will become the standard against which others on Byzantium are judged.

The Islamic East

Andrae, Tor. *Mohammed: The Man and His Faith*. 1960. First published in 1936, this brief, engaging book remains the best introduction.

Crone, Patricia, and Martin Hinds. *God's Caliph: Religious Authority in the First Centuries of Islam*. 1986. A sensitive discussion of the emergence of the Islamic polity and of the position of the caliphs.

Rahman, Fazlur. *Islam.* 2d ed. 1979. A thoughtful, readable account of the essentials of Islam from Muhammad's time to our own.

The Byzantine Empire

Hussey, J. M. *The Orthodox Church in the Byzantine Empire.* 1986. By a great authority, this text provides not so much a thorough survey as a series of reflections by the author.

Kaegi, Walter. *Byzantium and the Early Islamic Conquests.* 1992. A readable account of military and institutional problems at a decisive moment in Byzantine history.

Kazhdan, A. P., and Giles Constable. *People and Power in Byzantium: An Introduction to Modern Byzantine Studies.* 1982. A series of penetrating essays on politics, ideology, religion, and culture across the whole Byzantine period.

Mango, Cyril. *Byzantium: The Empire of New Rome.* 1980. By a brilliant art historian, this book is especially strong on cultural history.

The Western Kingdoms

Campbell, James, ed. *The Anglo-Saxons.* 1982. Brilliant essays and beautiful illustrations.

Collins, Roger. *Early Medieval Spain.* 2d ed. 1994. An intelligent, comprehensive history by a leading authority.

Fell, Christine. *Women in Anglo-Saxon England.* 1984. Interesting and readable, this book concentrates on depictions of women in literature.

Geary, Patrick J. *Before France and Germany: The Creation and Transformation of the Merovingian World.* 1988. A readable narrative, this book makes accessible the best French and German scholarship.

James, Edward. *The Franks.* 1988. By an archaeologist, this wide-ranging study combines the written and material evidence in the best introduction to Merovingian Gaul.

Mayr-Harting, Henry. *The Coming of Christianity to Anglo-Saxon England.* 3d ed. 1991. A fascinating, challenging interpretation of the English and Irish missions and of their impact on English society and culture.

Noble, Thomas F. X. *The Republic of St. Peter: The Birth of the Papal State, 680–825.* 1984. Detailed analysis of the emergence of papal temporal rule, the Franko-papal alliance, and the papal bureaucracy.

Ó Cróinín, Dáibhí. *Early Medieval Ireland, 400–1200.* 1995. Detailed and comprehensive but very readable and interesting, this is the best history of early Ireland ever written.

Smyth, Alfred P. *King Alfred the Great.* 1995. Massive yet readable, challenging and controversial.

Webster, Leslie, and Janet Backhouse, eds. *The Making of England: Anglo-Saxon Art and Culture,* A.D. *600–900.*

1991. A breathtaking and magnificently illustrated survey published to accompany a major British Museum exhibition in 1991–1992.

Wickham, Chris. *Early Medieval Italy: Central Power and Local Society, 400–1000.* 1981. A careful reading of the evidence and scholarship as they relate to both public and private power. Difficult but rewarding.

Wood, Ian. *The Merovingian Kingdoms, 450–751.* 1994. A penetrating analysis and narrative by the finest contemporary scholar of the Merovingians.

The World of Charlemagne

Bowlus, Charles. *Franks, Moravians, and Magyars: The Struggles for the Middle Danube, 788–907.* 1995. Though difficult, this important, learned book treats a misunderstood time and region.

Ganshof, François Louis. *Frankish Institutions Under Charlemagne.* Translated by Bryce and Mary Lyon. 1970. A technical yet readable account of the Carolingian government and army by the twentieth century's greatest historian of Charlemagne.

Hodges, Richard, and David Whitehouse. *Mohammed, Charlemagne and the Origins of Europe.* 1983. A stimulating reassessment, from archaeological and anthropological perspectives, of many controversial views concerning the end of the ancient world.

Mütherich, Florentine, and Joachim Gaehde. *Carolingian Painting.* 1976. A fine introduction, with beautiful plates, for the student without a substantial background in art history.

Riché, Pierre. *Daily Life in the World of Charlemagne.* Translated by Jo Ann McNamara. 1978. A highly readable account of how people lived—from what they ate, to their clothing and dwellings, to their customary beliefs and superstitions.

———. *The Carolingians: A Family Who Forged Europe.* 1993. A solid, readable, interesting account by a great French scholar.

Roesdahl, Else. *The Vikings.* 1991. A brief yet thorough discussion of all aspects of Viking culture and society in and after the age of invasions.

Stafford, Pauline. *Queens, Concubines, and Dowagers: The King's Wife in the Early Middle Ages.* 1983. Entertaining and informative, this book reveals much about the informal channels of power and influence open to women.

Sullivan, Richard, ed. *"The Gentle Voices of Teachers": Aspects of Learning in the Carolingian Age.* 1995. Eight intriguing essays that explore Carolingian culture from many vantage points. Massive bibliography.

Wemple, Suzanne. *Women in Frankish Society: Marriage and the Cloister, 500 to 900.* 1981. A pioneering study, this book is not easy to read but contains much valuable information and interesting interpretations.

THE MANUSCRIPT BOOK

How long would it take you to copy this whole textbook by hand? We know that it took about a year for two skilled monastic scribes to copy a Bible. Every medieval book was literally a manuscript (from *manuscriptum*, "written by hand"). Manuscripts contain important texts but are also revealing artifacts in their own right.

Codicology and paleography are the sciences of manuscript study. Codicology, the study of books as physical objects, investigates the materials and techniques used to make them. Paleography, the study of handwriting, seeks to read texts and to date and localize surviving books.

Depicted here is a folio (a page) of the Dagulf Psalter, named for the Carolingian scribe who wrote it in 795 on Charlemagne's orders as a gift for Pope Hadrian I (r. 772–795). The rich and powerful often used books as gifts. A psalter is a collection of the 150 biblical psalms and other canticles—songs or prayers derived from the Bible and used for worship. Can you make out the letters INCIPIUNT CANTICI, at the very top of the page? They mean "Here begin the canticles." The text is the Canticle of Isaiah (Isaiah 12:1–6). Its title is CANTICUM ESAIE PROP[H].

Cathedrals and monasteries usually had *scriptoria*, "writing offices," where scribes and illuminators worked with bookmakers to produce manuscripts. Manuscripts were made from parchment. To make parchment, an animal skin—preferably sheepskin or calfskin—was soaked in a caustic lye solution to remove hair and blemishes, scraped until it was smooth, and then dried on a stretching rack. After drying, the skin was cut to the desired size. The smallest surviving manuscript is 2 inches by 3 inches; the largest is about 36 by 19. The larger the pages, the more costly was the book. One huge Bible produced in Bede's Northumbria required the hides of 500 sheep.

After the parchment was cut and lined—notice how straight and even the lines are on the psalter folio—the bookmaker took four sheets, or folios, of parchment, laid them down together, and folded them, placing the fold at the left, to form a booklet of sixteen pages called a quire—see the drawing. Because the two sides of a piece of parchment differ in color—the "hair side," or outside, is usually darker than the "flesh side," or inside—the quires were arranged so that hair sides faced hair sides and flesh sides faced flesh sides. A manuscript consisted of many quires sewn together.

The first page of the first quire was numbered 1[r] and 1[v], or 1 recto and 1 verso, meaning 1 "right side" and 1 "turned side." The second sheet was numbered 2[r] and 2[v]. Today, book pages are numbered 1, 2, 3, and so on, and books always start with an odd-numbered page on the right side—an inheritance from medieval manuscripts.

Scribes and illuminators received the prepared quires. Scribes wrote text onto the parchment. Illuminators painted beautiful pictures or designs. You have on pages 297, 300, 322, and 324 examples of the magnificent illuminations that were put into medieval books. Most books, however, had no such images at all.

Now you are ready to learn some paleography. We have already deciphered the first two lines of the folio shown here. These lines are written in a "display script." For visual appeal and to facilitate reference, scribes often used different handwritings, colors, or both to highlight first letters, first words, or first lines. Books, like the one you are reading, maintain this tradition. The huge writing—can you make out CONFITE?—marks the begin-

A Quire

The Dagulf Psalter *(Österreichische Nationalbibliothek)*

ning of Isaiah's text. It continues, on line four, with *bor tibi dne qnm ira*. Line five carries on with *tus es mihi conversus*. Look at line six: *est furor tuus&consolatusesme*. Can you make out the letters yourself?

Several things bear notice here. First, the main script is Caroline minuscule, the new script that accompanied Charlemagne's educational reforms. Because of its clarity, it is the basis for many modern typefaces. Compare the letters in the picture with the ones you are reading.

Second, notice the frequent recourse to abbreviation. Writing was time- and space-consuming, prompting the development of elaborate systems of abbreviation. Can you see, in line four, the letters *dne* with a strike over them, and then the letters *qnm*, also with a strike? In this case the words expand to *domine* and *quoniam*. Look at line two, where you see *prop^h*, shorthand for *Prophetae* ("Prophet"). Also notice the ampersands in line six, eight, nine, and ten. They stand for *et*, Latin for "and." Note, too, how the last words in line six run together.

Third, in antiquity, texts had neither breaks between words nor punctuation. As non–Latin-speakers learned to write the language, however, they usually put breaks between the words to facilitate understanding. You can see that most of this text has breaks, except in line six. In lines one, eight, and ten, you can also see a rather curious symbol: ;. It is a full stop, or period.

What else might you learn from a manuscript? Handwriting and systems of abbreviation are distinctive, and specialists use them to date and localize manuscripts. Because parchment was prepared in different ways, some manuscripts can be dated or placed by an analysis of their parchment. Inks differed in chemistry and in appearance and thus help to date and localize books. Styles of illumination and forms of images can also be localized or traced from one scriptorium to another. By knowing when, where, and by whom books were written or illuminated, historians can reconstruct the life and work of intellectual centers that were scattered long ago.

It is estimated that a medieval manuscript without illuminations was worth one year's wages for an ordinary working person. Would you spend a year's wages for a book? ✎

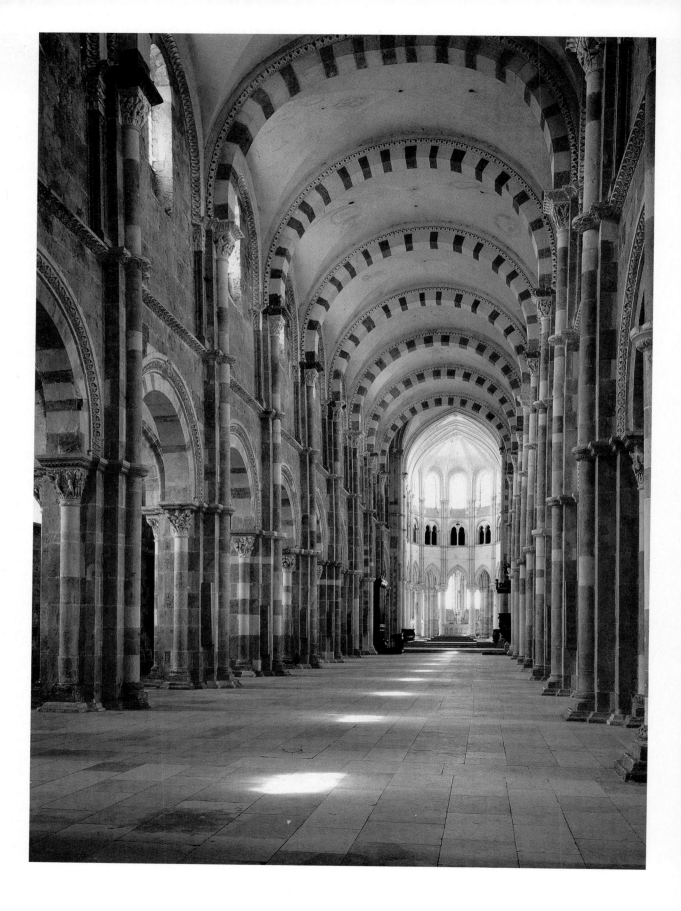

The Expansion of Europe, ca. 900–1150

L ooking down the nave of Burgundy's beautiful Vezelay basilica, one can almost hear the words of Ralph Glaber, that region's most famous chronicler: "Churches were to be seen being rebuilt all over the earth, but especially in Italy and Gaul; although most churches were very well constructed and had no need of rebuilding, each Christian community was driven by a true rivalry to have a finer church than that of its neighbors. It looked as though the very world was shaking itself to take off its old age and to reclothe itself all over in a white cloak of churches."[1] Glaber's words signal hope, optimism, progress, achievement. They seem remarkable when we remember that in the late ninth century, western Europe was suffering from Magyar, Muslim, and Viking attacks and from political dislocation.

Nevertheless, between about 900 and 1150, Europe's population began one of its longest periods of sustained growth. People brought more land under cultivation, introduced new crops, and made agriculture more efficient. Villages, towns, and cities grew in number and size. The tenth century saw the emergence of myriad local communities that were stable and creative. By the twelfth century, Europe witnessed the re-emergence of centralizing monarchies in France, England, and Spain, and a veritable explosion of new states along the frontiers of Carolingian Europe. Germany, Europe's most powerful state in 950, endured a tumultuous struggle with the papacy and found itself weakened and divided by 1150.

The church experienced several waves of reform activity. Monastic reformers attempted to improve the education, morals, and spiritual life of religious communities. Other reformers refined ecclesiastical law and

Monastic basilica of
Mary Magdalene, Vezelay,
CA. 1120–1140.

institutions. Still others engaged in sometimes bitter ideological controversies with kings and emperors over the respective powers of secular and ecclesiastical rulers.

Ecclesiastical schools and Latin letters remained important, but a superb vernacular literature began to appear all over Europe, not to challenge but to complement the Latin letters of the schools. "Romanesque" painting, sculpture, and architecture, of which Vezelay is a fine example, grew from Carolingian inspiration to triumphal realization.

Europeans spread aggressively in every direction. Normans conquered both England and southern Italy. Germans marched east into Slavic Europe. Spanish Christians pushed back the Muslims in the Iberian Peninsula. Armies of adventurers headed east in those remarkable expeditions, the Crusades.

Glaber's words evoke much of this: the energy, rivalry, religious zeal, economic growth, swelling population. *Expansion,* in both the literal and the figurative sense, captures the spirit of the West in the tenth, eleventh, and early twelfth centuries.

SIGNS OF EXPANSION

Medieval people did not keep the kinds of records of births, deaths, population, or business activity that modern states routinely accumulate. Evidence for the economic expansion of Europe abounds but is more often qualitative than quantitative. Literary anecdotes can be revealing of course, but they are no substitute for hard data. Hence our interpretations are usually based on inference and deduction.

The Growing Population

The population of Europe began rising slowly in the Carolingian period and may have doubled between 1000 and 1200. Scattered bits of evidence suggest that the total population of western Europe grew from around 30 million in 1000 to 55 or 60 million in 1200.

In a few regions where family size can be estimated, fertile marriages were producing on the average 3.5 children in the tenth century and from 6 to 7 in the twelfth. All families continued to experience the loss of children. Three queens—those of William "the Conqueror" and John of England, and

of Louis VIII of France—lost, respectively, 4 of 10, 6 of 14, and 7 of 12 children. The key change is that more babies were being born. People were also living longer than their forebears. Studies of aristocrats, high clergy, and soldiers show that a surprising 40 percent of them were over 40 years old. Male life expectancy was surely longer than female because of the dangers of childbirth, always the great killer of women in the premodern world. The general trend is clear: more babies being born, more infants living into adulthood, more adults living longer.

Everywhere in Europe, new land was brought into cultivation. More than half of the French documents relating to land in the twelfth century mention *assarting,* the bringing of new land under the plow. Literary texts often tell about knights wandering in a dense forest and suddenly entering a meadow. Those meadows did not get there by accident. Thousands of acres of forest were felled. Marshes were reclaimed from the sea. Some 380,000 acres were drained along the western coast of France and probably twice that amount in both Flanders and England. This activity is inexplicable without assuming a growing number of mouths to feed.

Agriculture benefited from a warmer and drier climate through the whole of this period. Not a single vegetable blight was recorded. There was more and also more nutritious food. Animals were increasingly reared for their meat, and higher meat consumption meant more protein in the diet. Beans and other legumes, also rich in protein, were more widely cultivated. Fine grains such as wheat replaced poorer cereals, ryes and spelts, in many areas. People of every class and region were almost certainly eating better and living longer and healthier lives.

Technological Gains

The eleventh century was a decisive period in the spread of new technologies in Europe. Innovations occurred in agriculture, transportation, mining, and manufacturing. Agricultural changes came first as a rising population created an increased demand for food that could be met only by new practices. Improvements in agriculture, coupled with others in transport, freed large numbers of persons not engaged in agriculture—urban dwellers, mainly—for other pursuits.

In the Carolingian period, the return on seed—the amount of seed realized for each seed sewn—is estimated at about 3 or 4 to 1. By the late twelfth century this ratio had risen in many areas to 8 or 10 to 1. Given that more land came under cultivation, the overall gains in the food supply were enormous.

The increases can be accounted for in several ways. Horses were more frequently used as draft animals. They were more expensive to acquire than oxen but no more costly to feed, and they did, in a day, a third or half again as much work. For much less "fuel," horses could haul loads farther and faster than oxen or mules. Thus, fewer men could, with horses, cultivate more land than their predecessors managed with oxen. In addition, they could cultivate the land more frequently and in-

crease yields because more seed would fall on more finely plowed soil. The more widespread use of horses was made possible by the dissemination of the horse collar—older forms of harness suitable for the low-slung, broad-shouldered ox would have choked a horse.

Plows also improved. The light wooden scratch plow used by the Romans was satisfactory for the thin soils of the Mediterranean region but barely disturbed the heavy soils of northern Europe. The invention of a heavy wheeled plow with an iron coulter (or plowshare) and a moldboard was a real breakthrough. The iron plowshare cut deeply into the soil, and then the moldboard turned and aerated the soil. This heavy plow made it possible for farmers to exploit good soils more fully without exhausting the ground too

Heavy Wheeled Plow This picture shows the improved plow, the horse collar, and the cooperative labors of many peasants in preparing the fields. *(Bibliothèque Nationale)*

rapidly. This plow seems to have been introduced in Carolingian Europe, but it was not widely adopted before the eleventh century.

Wider adoption of nitrogen-fixing crops, such as peas and some kinds of beans, retarded soil exhaustion—and also put more protein in the diet. Leaving land fallow was another means of avoiding soil exhaustion. In the early Middle Ages this meant setting aside about half of the arable land every year (the two-field system) or working the land intensively for a few years and then moving on. By the twelfth century three-field schemes of crop rotation were common.

Under the three-field system, two-thirds of the arable land saw nearly constant use. The amount of an estate under cultivation rose from 50 to 67 percent. Crop rotation brought other benefits as well. Horses ate oats, but (except in a few places like Scotland) medieval people generally did not. If farmers wished to use horses, they had to dedicate some of their land to growing oats. A three-field rotation allowed some flexibility. Finally, the alternation of winter crops (wheat and rye), spring crops (oats, barley, and legumes), and fallow ensured against a single season of unusually harsh weather.

Surplus produce was intended mainly for the growing towns. To supply that market, improvements in transportation were necessary. Kings often passed laws to secure the safety of highways, and popes three times (in 1097, 1132, and 1179) threatened highwaymen with excommunication. Landlords required their dependents to maintain roads and bridges. Many stone bridges were constructed in France between 1130 and 1170 because wooden bridges were so vulnerable to fire. Indeed, fire destroyed the bridge at Angers (in western France) five times between 1032 and 1167.

Transport improved because of safer roads and better vehicles. Documents and works of art agree that the old two-wheeled cart, drawn by oxen or mules, began giving way to the sturdy four-wheeled, horse-drawn wagon. As the horse collar aided agriculture, so too new systems of tandem harnessing aided transport. The fact that greater quantities of foodstuffs could be moved farther and faster meant that urban communities could be supplied from larger areas. This was a crucial factor in enabling cities to grow and in providing urban residents with a predictable and diverse range of foods.

Transport also moved grain to mills. By the mid-twelfth century no sizable village anywhere would have been without a mill to process grains. The construction of elaborate schemes of gearing and of water courses to shoot water over or under the wheels that turned the millstones grew more sophisticated all over Europe.

Evidence from various parts of Europe points to the years after 925 as the beginning of real growth in the mining industry. Notable improvements occurred in both the quarrying of stone and the extraction of metals. Mines were not deep because people lacked the means to keep the shafts and galleries free of water. Still, the exploitation of surface and near-surface veins of ore—principally iron but also tin and silver—intensified, to supply the increased demand for plowshares, tools, weapons, construction fittings, and coins. Stone quarrying, the commonest form of mining in the Middle Ages, benefited directly from more efficient stone saws and indirectly from improvements in transport. Better techniques in stone cutting, construction, and transport help to explain, for example, the increase in the number of England's stone religious buildings from sixty to nearly five hundred in the century after 1050.

Forms of Enterprise

Agricultural specialization became common. Instead of relying on estates or regions to provide for all of their needs, people began to cultivate intensively those crops that were best suited to local conditions. The area around Toulouse, for example, concentrated on herbs from which blue and yellow dyes were made. The central regions of France focused on cereal grains, while the Bordeaux and Burgundy regions turned to viticulture (cultivation of grapevines). Northern Germany specialized in cattle raising; northern England favored sheep.

Agricultural specialization helps to explain the growth in trade that is discernible everywhere. Local trade continued to flourish. Italian wines and olive oil, for example, were not produced for far-off markets; they tended to move from countryside to town within a region. The same was true of French or English grains. French wines were much prized, however, especially in England; and certain products, such as English wool and Flemish cloth, were carried far and wide. Salt fish from the Baltic found its way all over Europe. Lumber was routinely traded across the Mediterranean to the wood-poor Muslim world. Spain was a source of warhorses. Southern Europe supplied the northern demand for spices, oranges, raisins, figs, almonds, and other exotic foodstuffs. Caen, in Normandy, shipped stone, whose color and texture were admired, to England for the construction of churches and monasteries. Rising population, higher productivity, and greater prosperity added up to a larger volume of goods moving farther and more frequently.

The lumber industry reveals many facets of medieval economic activity. Before the twelfth century, wood was the main building material, and even after that time it yielded to stone mainly for the church and aristocracy. But wood could be used for things other than buildings—for example, ships. The Venetian shipyards needed about twenty oaks, twenty good-size pines, and fifty or so beeches to make a ship. In the early twelfth century the Venetians were making about ten vessels a year, twice the number they had been building two centuries earlier. Whether for shipping or for housing, there was a steadily growing demand for wood. In England, to take another example, about 500 cords (a cord is a stack measuring 128 cubic feet) of wood, nearly ten acres' worth, were needed to prepare one ton of silver. Under King Ethelred II (r. 978–1016) alone moneyers coined thirty tons of silver, consuming in the process some 15,000 cords of wood. Better mining and increased trade played complementary roles in increasing the demand for lumber.

Wood exemplifies the expansion and interconnectedness of the medieval economy and society. Forests were an important part of daily life, providing the wood for houses, fences, and fuel in villages and towns. Animals, especially pigs, were grazed at the edges of the forest to permit as much land as possible to be dedicated to food crops. Wild animals were hunted in the forest. For aristocrats hunting was partly for sport and partly for food. For poorer rural people, however, wild meat made up a significant part of the regular diet. The forest was also a plentiful source of fruits, nuts, and honey. If the peasants in a given place decided to cut some timber to smelt the king's silver, or to build a wooden wall around their village, or to dispatch masts to Venice or the Baltic, they had some critical choices to make. After the trees were gone, where would they hunt, or graze their ani-

Twelfth-Century Timbered House, Rouen, France The house at the center of this picture was destroyed in World War II after holding its place for nearly eight hundred years. It shows one of the many uses of timber, and its narrow street gives an authentic feel of a medieval town. (*Bibliothèque Municipale, Rouen*)

mals, or gather their berries? In the very early Middle Ages such choices imposed themselves with little urgency. In Ralph Glaber's world, the urgency was increasingly felt.

THE TRADITIONAL ORDER OF SOCIETY

Alfred the Great (r. 871–899) of England once said that a kingdom needed "men of prayer, men of war, and men of work." This division reveals the way the elite looked at the world. It provided neat places for warrior-aristocrats, for the clergy, and for the peasantry on whose labors the other two groups depended. The clergy and the nobility agreed that they were superior to the "workers," but fierce controversies raged over whether leadership in society belonged to the "fighters" or to the "prayers." This tripartite view of society may seem comprehensive at first, but it was not. It excluded townspeople, who were becoming ever more important. Town residents worked for a living, of course, but only farmers were considered "workers." And where, we may ask, did women fit in Alfred's tripartite scheme? Or Jews, who were becoming increasingly important in Europe's rising towns yet whose religion marked them off sharply from the overwhelmingly Christian environment?

Those Who Fight: The Nobility

The nobility of the eleventh and twelfth centuries constituted an increasingly closed and well-defined class. Carolingian families had been large, amorphous groupings of people who traced their descent on both the male and the female sides. Such families tended to dominate public and church offices, to hold vast landed possessions, to have regular access to the royal court, and to be fairly open to newcomers. From about the middle of the eleventh century, however, important changes appeared in the structure and behavior of noble families.

Loose groupings of relatives began to think of themselves as lineages, the descendants of one male ancestor. Such families began to practice primogeniture—the transmittal of all family lands, offices, and titles to the eldest male heir. By purchase, exchange, theft, and intimidation, lineages consolidated their landholdings into compact lordships. At the center of these lands was a castle, and from that castle the family took its name. (See the feature, "Weighing the Evidence: The Medieval Castle," on pages 350–351.) The sudden emergence in the eleventh century of abundant genealogical writings shows that noble families had a keen sense of their own identity.

The nobility was not yet closed or homogeneous. Fortunes and titles could be acquired quickly in politically volatile areas such as Spain, Norman England, Sicily, and along Germany's eastern frontier. In central France and Germany,

however, conditions were more stable, and three levels of nobility can often be discerned.

In the first level were the truly great: kings and other members of royal families, dukes, counts, and frontier lords. In the second were the direct vassals of the great. Many of these people were *castellans*, persons who built castles of their own and contested the great for power in particular regions. Some of them rose to the rank of the great; others were reduced in power and made dependent on their stronger neighbors. In the third level was a vast and growing class of ordinary knights. These were either the sons of the other two classes or else ordinary free men who owed no service or payments to anyone and were faring badly in the power contests of the age. The consolidation of lineages and of territorial lordships produced large numbers of men who had noble blood and upbringings, lofty ambitions, but limited prospects. These men, called in contemporary sources "the young," followed adventurers to every corner of the medieval world in search of glory and a livelihood. Some of them joined the retinue of a more powerful man, received cash support and sometimes a fief, and awaited a chance to find an heiress, through whose inheritance a new lineage might be established. These "young" men were often over 40.

Mentioning lords, vassals, and fiefs brings up the subject of feudalism. Charlemagne (see page 288), as one feature of his governing system, had connected personal loyalty (vassalage) with public office and material reward (the benefice or fief). In the tenth and eleventh centuries, versions of this arrangement spread all over Europe and to almost all levels of society. The result is sometimes, but misleadingly, called the "feudal system."

Feudalism may be defined as a social and political system wherein public responsibilities and powers that had fallen into the hands of private individuals were fulfilled by men who had sworn personal fidelity to one another. By solemn acts of homage and fealty, a vassal pledged never to do anything that would damage his lord or his lord's interests and also undertook to perform certain services—usually military service and appearance at the lord's court, the site of important judicial and political decisions. In return, the lord provided protection—physical, legal, or political—and gave the vassal something of value. From the tenth century, the lord's gift was usually a landed

Feudal Bonds and Obligations

Duke William of Aquitaine in 1020 asked Bishop Fulbert of Chartres to explain the nature of fealty. The first document is the bishop's idealized view of the mutual obligations of lords and vassals. The second text is a depiction from 1127 of the actual public ceremonies surrounding the feudal bond.

He who swears fealty to his lord ought always to have these six things in mind: what is harmless, safe, honorable, useful, easy, practicable. *Harmless,* that is to say, that he should not injure his lord in his body; *safe,* that he should not injure him by betraying his secrets or the defenses on which he relies for his safety; *honorable,* that he should not injure him in his justice or in other matters that pertain to his honor; *useful,* that he should not injure him in his possessions; *easy,* that he should not make difficult that which his lord can do easily; and *practicable,* that he should not make impossible for the lord that which is possible.

That the faithful vassal should avoid these injuries is proper, it is not for this alone that he deserves his holding; for it is not enough to abstain from evil, unless what is good is done also. He should faithfully aid and counsel his lord, if he wishes to be looked on as worthy of his benefice and to be safe concerning the fealty he has sworn.

The lord ought also to act toward his faithful vassal reciprocally in all these things for if he does not do these things he shall rightly be considered guilty of bad faith.

Through the whole remaining part of the day those who had been previously enfeoffed by the most pious Count Charles did homage to the new count, taking up now again their fiefs and offices and whatever they had before rightfully obtained.

First, they did their homage thus. The count asked the vassal if he were willing to become completely his man, and the other replied "I am willing"; and with hands clasped, placed between the hands of the count, they were bound together by a kiss. Secondly, he who had done homage gave his fealty to a representative of the count in these words: "I promise on my faith that I will be faithful to Count William, and will observe my homage to him completely against all persons, in good faith and without deceit." He took his oath on the relics of the saints.

Source: James Harvey Robinson, *Readings in European History,* vol. 1 (Boston: Ginn, 1904), pp. 184–185, 179–180 (slightly adapted).

estate, called by modern scholars a *fief* and by medieval texts a *feudum* (whence *feudalism*). (See the box, "Feudal Bonds and Obligations.")

Today many historians prefer to speak of "lordship." *Feudalism* is a lawyers' term. Although it has the virtue of precision, it also masks an amazing array of local variations in a "system" that was never systematic, not even in northern France and southern England, feudalism's classical regions. *Lordship* is more vague, but it usefully evokes the diversity of personal, political, legal, social, and economic ties that bound together members of the European elite from the Carolingian period to the dawn of modern times.

The retinues of noblemen spawned by the lordship system formed a kind of substitute kinship, especially for the "young," who had been cut loose from family ties. Noble groupings often joined in supporting a local monastery or in promoting the cult of a local patron saint. Noblemen frequently fought together and thought of themselves as comrades in arms. Their familiarity with weapons and horses, their clothing, diet, and dwellings—all were similar enough to give them a sense of group solidarity.

A specific ethos, chivalry, belonged to the nobility. Chivalry was a code of conduct for a warrior-aristocracy. Its very name derives from *cheval,* French for *horse,* the classic conveyance of a knight. Today, chivalry is often thought of as either a code of conduct regulating relations between the sexes or the value system behind the romantic image of dashing knights in shining armor saving damsels in distress from fire-breathing dragons. Actually, it prized most highly certain male and militant qualities. Military prowess was the most highly esteemed of chivalric virtues. A knight who was not a great warrior was useless. Literature of the time is full of accounts of battles with immense beasts or of hand-to-hand combat between a single hero and impossible numbers of the enemy.

Open-handed generosity was another key virtue. The truly noble person engaged in sumptuous display to manifest his power, to show concern for his dependents, and to attract even more followers. Medieval literature is full of rich banquets and stunning presents. In Anglo-Saxon England the king was called "the giver of rings." Knights were obsessed with their honor, their reputation. They sought glory, the better to win a lord or a bride.

There was also loyalty, the glue that held feudal society together. But what are we to make of statements such as the following one by William of Malmesbury? William, a twelfth-century English historian, wrote: "They [knights] are faithful to their lords, but swift to break faith. A breath of ill fortune and they are plotting treachery, a bag of money and their mind is changed." Knights, especially the "young," were loyal to their lords when they could be, but fundamentally they were loyal to themselves.

The nobility governed medieval society. Some nobles held public offices delegated to them by emperors or kings. Virtually all governed also in private capacities, ruling as direct lords over their landed patrimonies and over the people who lived on their lands. Their retinues served as guarantees of their power on the local scene, enabled them to extend their authority at the expense of their neighbors, and protected their lands from attack. The nobility, leaders and followers alike, were supported by the exertions of a vast number of dependents. These people paid rents and fees in both cash and kind and also performed labor services. Their labor freed the nobility for its military, government, and social diversions.

What role was left to noble women in a world of chivalry and lordship? Convents of aristocratic nuns remained places where women could be highly educated and almost entirely in control of their own affairs. Matilda, daughter of the German empress Adelaide, was abbess of Quedlinburg, mistress of vast estates in northern Germany, and a dominant figure in German politics. Less predictably, Gaita, wife of a Norman prince in Italy, fought in helmet and armor alongside her husband, as did Duchess Agnes of Burgundy. All over France, in the fluid political climate of the tenth and eleventh centuries, women were mistresses of castles and real powers in local politics.

By the late eleventh century, however, three developments adversely affected the position of aristocratic women. First, the elaboration of the chivalric ethos defined most key social and political roles as "manly" and thereby excluded women from them. By the middle of the twelfth century it was rare for a woman to hold a castle and unheard-of for one to ride to arms. Second, the consolidation of lineages by aristocratic families accompanied a moral campaign by the church to promote monogamous, unbreakable marriages. This situation subordinated women's freedom in the marriage market to the dynastic and patrimonial demands of great families. Third, the spread of lordship, with its intricate network of personal and proprietary relationships based on military service, tended to deprive women of independent rights over land.

Those Who Pray: The Clergy

Members of the clergy were overwhelmingly noble, but they may be differentiated from lay nobles by virtue of their priestly or monastic offices. As the church promoted its own vision of the tripartite ordering of society, it assigned primacy to the "prayers," to its own leaders. Within the clergy, however, sharp disagreements arose over whether the leading "prayers" were the monks in their monasteries or the bishops who conducted the public business of the church. Whereas in the Carolingian world, the clergy served occasionally as an avenue of upward social mobility for talented outsiders, the later consolidation of families began to confine church offices to the younger sons of the nobility. The church, always hierarchical, became in medieval society even more aristocratic in membership and outlook.

In the aftermath of the Carolingian collapse (see page 296), a great spiritual reform swept Europe. It began in 910 when Duke William of Aquitaine founded the monastery of Cluny in Burgundy on lands that he freely donated (see Map 9.2). At a time when powerful local families dominated almost all monasteries, Cluny was a rarity because it was freed of all lay and episcopal control and placed under the direct authority of the pope. Cluny's abbots were among the greatest European statesmen of their day and became influential advisers to popes, French kings, German emperors, and aristocratic families.

In the tradition of the Carolingian monastic reforms, Cluny placed great emphasis on liturgical prayer. The monks spent long hours in solemn devotions and did little manual work. Because Cluniac prayer was thought to be especially efficacious, noblemen all over Europe donated land to Cluny and placed local monasteries under Cluniac control. Many independent monasteries also appealed to Cluny for spiritual reform. By the twelfth century, hundreds of monasteries had joined in a Cluniac order. Individual houses were under the authority of the abbot of Cluny, and their priors had to attend an annual assembly. Although the majority of houses reformed by Cluny were male, many convents of nuns also adopted Cluniac practices.

Cluny promoted two powerful ideas. One was that the role of the church was to pray for the world, not to be implicated deeply in it. The other was that freedom from lay control was important if churches were not to be diverted from their spiritual tasks.

The same spiritual forces that drove the Cluniacs inspired Bishop Adalbero of Metz in 933 to assist in the restoration of Benedictine usages in the dilapidated Lorraine monastery of Gorze. Customs at Gorze resembled those at Cluny, and they spread widely in Lorraine, Germany, and England. The Gorze reform was well received by kings and nobles; its aim was not so much to withdraw from the world as to improve it. Monks from the Gorze and Cluniac traditions bitterly criticized clerical immorality and inappropriate lay interference in the church. They preached against clerical marriage and simony, the buying and selling of church offices.

Reformers in the eremitic tradition (see page 256) desired more profound changes. They criticized the monastery at Cluny, saying that it had become too opulent and successful, and the monastery at Gorze because it seemed too immersed in worldly affairs. A few were driven by a desire to recapture what they believed to be the way of life of the original apostolic community—a life of poverty, self-denial, and seclusion. Thus, the eleventh and early twelfth centuries saw a proliferation of both male and female experiments in eremitic monasticism. Other Europeans believed that the apostolic life demanded not only an austere regimen of personal renunciation but also an active life of Christian ministry. Cathedral clergy, called canons, in particular, adapted the rule of Saint Augustine so that they could live a communal life and carry out priestly duties.

The greatest critics of the Cluniac tradition, and the real monastic elite of the early twelfth century, were the Cistercians. In 1098, Abbot Robert left his Burgundian monastery of Molesme because he believed it had abandoned the strict teachings of Saint Benedict. He founded a new monastery at Cîteaux in Burgundy. This house was to follow the Benedictine Rule literally and to refuse all secular entanglements: lands, rents, and servile dependents. So rigorous and poor was the community that it struggled until a charismatic young Burgundian nobleman named Bernard (1090–1153) joined in 1112. Three years later Bernard left to found a daughter house at Clairvaux, of which he remained abbot for the rest of his life. Through his writing, preaching, and personal example Bernard dominated the religious life of Europe in his lifetime. By the end of the twelfth century there were about 500 Cistercian (from the Latin for *Cîteaux*) monasteries in Europe, and Bernard's own Clairvaux had 700 monks. A dedicated order of adult males, the Cistercians were unusual in refusing to accept boys and distinctive in denying access to women.

With the monastic clergy gaining so much in prestige and visibility, the episcopal clergy countered with its own view of society. Surely, the bishops agreed, spiritual, moral, and intellectual improvement were desirable. Likewise, it was time to end the grossest examples of lay interference in the church. But precisely because so many bishops came from great families and were so well connected, they were less inclined to be rigid about the line of demarcation between lay and clerical responsibilities. In Germany, for example, the king's chapel recruited young noblemen to train them as clerics and to inculcate in them the policies and ethos of the court. Many of these chaplains were appointed to bishoprics and then advanced the king's interests in their new areas of authority. But they were often men of spiritual depth, and they resented what they regarded as monastic carping about their worldliness. By the middle of the twelfth century, bishops, and finally popes, too, had imposed on the church a view that

monks belonged in their monasteries and that bishops should lead society.

It was always the special responsibility of the clergy to look after the moral order of society. In the turbulent world of gentlemen warriors, the church had its own ideas about what a perfect knight should do. The English bishop and scholar John of Salisbury (d. 1180), reflecting on knighthood in the twelfth century, concluded that it existed "to protect the church, to attack infidelity, to reverence the priesthood, to protect the poor, to keep the peace, to shed one's blood and, if necessary, to lay down one's life for one's brethren."

Turning large numbers of violent young men into servants of the church was a tall order for the

The Knight at Prayer This stained glass window from Chartres depicts the church's idealized conception of one of God's warriors: His sword and pious disposition combat the enemies of religion. *(Sonia Halliday Photographs)*

clergy, and they had only limited success. One example of the church's success is the military orders. The Knights of St. John, or Hospitallers, and the Knights of the Temple, or Templars, are the major examples, but others existed in Spain and Germany. The Hospitallers started near Jerusalem as a foundation under Benedictine auspices dedicated to charitable works and care of the sick. They evolved into a monastic order using a version of the Rule of Saint Benedict and devoted themselves to the defense of pilgrims to the Holy Land. The Templars were men living under religious rule and dedicated to protecting the small states created by the Crusaders (see page 346). These military orders measured up very well to the clergy's idea of what a perfect knight should be.

The clergy could also regulate disputes in society. For example, when a community was divided by a difficult conflict that demanded resolution, it might turn to the ordeal—a judicial procedure that sought divine judgment by subjecting the accused to a physically painful or dangerous test. An accused person might walk a certain distance carrying hot iron or plunge a hand into a boiling cauldron to pluck out a pebble. The resulting wounds would be bandaged for a set time and then examined. If they were healing, the person was considered innocent; if festering, guilty. The clergy officiated at ordeals before their participation was forbidden by the papacy in 1215.

Clergymen were also the conservators of the relics and shrines where people gained special access to the holiness of the saints. The clergy wrote and preached about the miracles of the saints. Stories told about relics kept in certain places brought people as pilgrims to often far-off shrines to seek healing from illness, injury, or misfortune. The clergy played unique roles in forming and nurturing communities in the world and in interceding for this world with God in the next.

Those Who Work: The Peasants

The peasants were the "workers" in the tripartite model. An extremely diverse segment of society, "peasants" ranged from slaves to free persons of some means. Except in frontier zones, where victims were available and religious scruples diminished, slaves declined dramatically in numbers during the tenth and eleventh centuries (as illustrated by the shift in meaning of the classical Latin

servus from "slave" to "serf"). Serfs, persons bound to the soil, everywhere constituted the majority of the peasants, although their legal and social status differed considerably from place to place. Serfdom was a mixture of economic, legal, and personal statuses. The serf could be flogged in public, could be set upon by dogs, was excluded from many judicial proceedings, required approval to contract a marriage, and was denied the right to bear arms.

The tenth and eleventh centuries were a decisive period in the reshaping of rural society. As lordships of all kinds and sizes formed in the countryside, they drew communities of people. Castles were critical. Powerful men generally sited their castles in close proximity to wood, water, and iron. Sometimes a monastery, rural church, or graveyard also attracted a castle or else grew up near one and helped to anchor a site. (See the feature "Weighing the Evidence: The Medieval Castle," on pages 350–351.)

People from a fairly wide area settled in the vicinity of the castle. Many, originally free, commended themselves to the local lord by handing over their properties and receiving them back in return for rents or personal services. Other people fell into dependent status through military or economic misfortune. What eventually emerged was the manor, an institution wherein a powerful lord controlled the lives of an often large number of dependents. He required payments and services from them and regulated their ordinary disputes. His control was simultaneously public and private.

A minor castellan, or lord of a castle, might control only a small manor and would probably be the vassal of a great lord. A powerful landed lord would generally control many manors and would often give some of them to retainers as fiefs. In other words, the reorganization of the countryside affected the nobility and the peasantry and created parallel sets of vertical bonds of association: Feudal lords and vassals entered into political bonds; lords and peasants entered into economic bonds.

The structure of individual manors, and the dues owed by peasants, varied tremendously across Europe. Certain trends were fairly consistent, however. As the economy expanded, as trade brought more and different products into Europe, and as a more consciously aristocratic lifestyle spread, the nobility began to want disposable cash. Thus, in many places corvées (labor services) were commuted into cash payments. Peasants were required to pay rent from their own holdings instead of working on the lord's lands. But lords still needed provisions, so they sometimes split peasant payments into cash and kind. Old forms of service could be wholly retained, involving many days per year of work on the lord's demesne, the portion of the manor set aside for the sole benefit of the lord. In such cases, the lord could still extract money from his peasants by requiring them to use his mill and oven and charging them fees.

The trend everywhere, however, was for labor services to diminish. In one region in northern France, twelfth-century peasants owed only three corvées of two days' each for harvesting and haymaking. Elsewhere, peasants might still be required to haul crops to market or to keep roads, bridges, and buildings in repair. On many estates where the menfolk had been largely freed from corvées, the women might still have to work in the lord's house washing laundry, sewing, plucking chickens and geese, cooking, minding dogs, and tending to other household chores.

In the expanding economy of the eleventh and twelfth centuries, the peasants grew more prosperous, and their lords constantly sought new ways to extract the fruits of that prosperity. Peasants thus began to band together to demand that "customs" be observed. These customs were more-or-less formal agreements spelling out the terms under which work and fees would be arranged. In general, life improved for the peasants in both legal status and living conditions.

The European village was a key product of the tenth and eleventh centuries. People who originally gathered together around a castle began to form a durable human community. Their church and graveyard helped to form a community by tying together the living and the dead and by giving the village a sense of memory and continuity. Peasants generally worked only 250 to 270 days per year, so they had a good deal of time for festivals and celebrations. Births, baptisms, betrothals, and deaths provided opportunities for the community to come together and affirm its mutual ties. Market days and sessions of the lord's court also assembled the village. Villagers needed to cooperate in many of the operations of daily life. They shared tools, plow teams, and wagons. They performed their corvées together. There was much

less social differentiation among the peasants than among the nobility, and so less tension.

The status of women in peasant society tended to be, in legal theory and in daily reality, the same as that of men at a time when the status of aristocratic women was declining. Marriage contracts from northern Italy show that brides often entered marriages with a complement of valuable tools. This suggests that peasant women retained some control over their own personal property and also reminds us that the huge gains in rural productivity are almost certainly attributable in part to the work and ingenuity of women. (See the box "Furnishings of a Welsh Household.")

Those Left Out: Townspeople and Jews

The tripartite model excluded two important groups of people. In the first group were the increasingly numerous citizens of Europe's growing towns. Obviously people in towns worked; but the prejudices of the aristocracy were rural, so the "workers" deemed necessary to the smooth functioning of the social order were farmers. In the second group were Europe's principal religious minority, the Jews. Jews could be found almost everywhere, although they constituted only about 1 percent of the population as a whole and had, outside Rome and parts of Spain, no single community numbering more than 1500.

The central factor in the growth of towns was the rise in the productivity and profitability of medieval agriculture. For the first time there was a regular and substantial surplus that could support an urban population that did not produce its own food. Increased local exchange, coupled with the relentless growth of a money economy, meant there were fortunes to be made and cash to be spent. Some of that cash was spent on luxury and exotic products that increasingly became the objects of far-flung commercial networks. A good part of the cash was spent by rural nobles, who earned it from rents, booty, and the profits of the private exercise of public power. When those nobles moved into towns, they created opportunities for merchants, craftsmen, day laborers, domestic servants, and professional people such as notaries and lawyers. This was particularly true in Europe's most heavily urbanized regions: Flanders, southern France, and northern Italy. The key point is that the growth of

Furnishings of a Welsh Household

This passage from the laws of Howell the Good concerns the distribution of household property in case of divorce. The aim was to achieve a nearly even split. Notice the kinds of things a house might hold and who got what.

The husband shall have all the pigs, the wife the sheep. The husband shall have all the horses and mares, the oxen and cows, bullocks and heifers; the wife shall have the goats. . . . All the vessels for milk, except one pail, are the wife's; all the dishes, except one meat dish, are the husband's. One cart and yoke are the wife's. All the jars and drinking vessels are the husband's. Of the bedding, the husband shall have all the bedclothes which are beneath, the wife those which are above. The husband shall have the cauldron, the pillow, the winnowing sheet, the coulter, the wood axe, the gimlet [hole-borer], the fire dog, all the sickles except one, and the gridiron. The wife shall have the pan and the tripod, the broadaxe and the sieve, the ploughshare, the flax and the seed of the flax, and the precious things except gold and silver. If there are any of these (gold or silver) they are to be divided in two equal parts. The products of the loom shall be divided in two equal parts, both linens and woolens. The husband shall have the barn and the grain and whatever is above or in the ground, and the hens and the geese and one cat. The wife shall have the meat that is salted and the cheese that is fresh . . . and the vessel of butter . . . and the ham . . . and as much of the flour as she can carry. Each of them shall have his or her personal clothing, except the cloaks which shall be divided.

Source: Ian F. Fletcher, ed. and trans., *Latin Redaction A of the Law of Hywel* (Aberystwyth, Wales: Center for Advanced Welsh and Celtic Studies, 1986), pp. 58–59.

the medieval city and of its human community began in the medieval countryside.

Town society was hierarchical, but its structures were new, ill defined, and flexible. Rich men built up bands of followers who supported them in urban politics, protected their neighborhoods, and occasionally raided the houses of their enemies in the next neighborhood. Relatives, friends, neighbors, people from a common rural district, or those engaged in similar trades tended to worship together in particular churches, observe certain festivals, and look after one another's families.

In the rapidly changing world of the tenth and eleventh centuries, towns provided numerous opportunities for women. In urban industries such as cloth making, tanning, laundering, and brewing there is evidence of women managing and even owning enterprises. Apart, perhaps, from finance and the law, distinctions between male and female roles were not as sharp in towns as in rural areas.

If urban men and all women stood in an ambiguous relationship to the ideals of the male, rural, aristocratic elite, we can hardly imagine what it must have been like for Jews. Because the Byzantine and Islamic worlds vacillated between persecution and toleration, many Jews migrated to western Europe. Some laymen and many members of the clergy were bitterly hostile to the Jews, but from the time of Gregory I (r. 590–604) the papacy urged peaceful coexistence and prayers for Jewish conversion. The Carolingians protected the Jews, as did some kings in succeeding centuries. Although some Jews in Italy, Spain, and Germany owned farms and vineyards, most Jews settled in cities, where they could live and worship in community with other Jews. There was also strength in numbers for people who could at any moment fall victim to persecution and whose power was not based on landholding.

Jews frequently served as royal advisers in Spain and were often entrusted with sensitive diplomatic missions elsewhere. This service earned them the envy of some Christians, as did their prominence in banking and moneylending. During the tenth century numerous Italian Jews crossed the Alps and settled in the growing towns of the German Rhineland. Attacks on Jews increased in the eleventh century, and laws were passed in Spain (1053) and Germany (1084) that took them under royal protection. The religious frenzy unleashed by the First Crusade brought savage attacks on the Jewish communities of Germany and induced many Jews to move to northern France and England. Twelfth-century Europe became increasingly dangerous for Jews.

GERMANY AND THE EMPIRE

In 950, Germany was the most powerful state in western Europe (Map 9.1) but by 1150 it lay on the brink of collapse. That radical transformation is the most significant political fact in European history in the period from 900 to 1150.

In the face of Viking and Magyar attacks, a series of resolute Saxon dukes built a kingdom, allied with the church, and revived the imperial title. German dynasties proved disastrously short-lived, however, and the monarchy's alliance with the church helped to precipitate the investiture controversy, a crisis in church-state relations. Promising beginnings for the German kingdom yielded meager results.

Unifying the Realm: The Saxon and Salian Rulers

After the Treaty of Verdun in 843 (see page 296), Louis the German and his successors managed to preserve the East Frankish Kingdom and created the possibility of an independent German kingdom. What lands that kingdom would possess was not yet clear. The Rhine has sometimes been Germany's river, sometimes its western boundary. Germany has no natural frontiers to the east, and incipient Slavic states resented German advances into their territories.

Germany consisted of several large duchies. Saxony, Franconia, Lorraine, Swabia, and Bavaria—the most important—had a dual historical origin. They were formed of people with distinctive historical traditions, although their leaders, or dukes, were usually Frankish aristocrats appointed by the Carolingians. As the monarchy weakened amid Carolingian political struggles and foreign invasions, the dukes became the bearers of the German political destiny. In 911 the last legitimate Carolingian of the East Frankish line died, and in 919 the dukes elected Duke Henry of Saxony as his successor.

Henry was the most powerful and the richest of the German dukes. He was chosen precisely because he offered the greatest hope of dealing decisively with the Viking threats in the north and the Magyar attacks in the east and south. Henry I (r. 919–936) ruled for nearly two decades and was then succeeded by his son, grandson, and great-grandson, all named Otto. These Saxon rulers created a solid German kingdom by consistently pursuing a few basic policies: warfare, control of Saxony and of the other duchies, domination of the church, and the acquisition of prestige.

The Saxon dukes had vassals of their own in Saxony, men to whom they had given lands or cash, from their control of the silver mines in the Hartz Mountains of Saxony, in return for military or administrative service. Henry I fought victoriously against the Vikings who were raiding northern Germany, and he initiated Saxony's eastern push into the Slavic lands along the Baltic coast. Otto I (r. 936–973) continued Henry's policies but also raised a pan-German army to meet the Magyar threat. At Lechfeld, near Augsburg, Otto won a decisive victory over the Magyars in 955, which removed a serious threat to Germany and vastly enhanced Otto's prestige. Otto II (r. 973–983) and Otto III (r. 983–1002) continued the German drive to the east into Slavic lands. The Ottonians' successful campaigns attracted more and more followers, who shared in the booty and received land.

In addition to building up a secure power base in Saxony, the Saxon dukes always tried to control one or more of the other German duchies. The German duchies had emerged together out of the late Carolingian world, and the Saxon dukes had not appointed and thus could not legally remove any of the other dukes. Sometimes, the Saxons managed to get one or more dukes to swear

Map 9.1 Germany and Its Duchies Throughout the Middle Ages, the chief dynamic in German history was a contest for power between the kings and the dukes.

homage to them as kings of Germany, but this oath was largely symbolic because the other dukes did not owe any specific services to the king. There was feudalism in Germany in the sense that all the dukes had vassals, but Germany was not a feudal monarchy because the dukes did not hold their duchies as fiefs granted by the king. The king's inability to control on a permanent basis any region but his own was a continuing weakness in Germany.

Control of the church partly compensated for the absence of central institutions or a hierarchy of vassalic bonds. Bishops and abbots remembered the Carolingian past when crown and church had

Otto III These beautiful examples of early Romanesque painting show Otto III enthroned with crown, scepter, and orb. He is receiving the homage of the four parts of his empire: Slavinia, Germania, Gallia, and Roma. *(Bayerische Staatsbibliotek, München)*

worked harmoniously for the reform of the kingdom. They willingly supported the king and provided him with able, educated advisers. Many of them, in good Carolingian fashion, saw the king as God's specially chosen agent and believed that it was their responsibility to aid him in the task of governing. The royal chapel, basically the office where documents were prepared and spiritual services were provided for the court, recruited capable, ambitious men from all over Germany, trained them, and then sent them back out as bishops or abbots. If the king could not appoint officials in Bavaria, for example, he could nevertheless name Bavaria's four bishops.

Finally, the Saxon rulers had a keen awareness of the value of prestige. Symbolic power substituted only partially for the lack of central institutions, capitularies, taxes, and other aspects of Carolingian rule, but the Saxons used it for all it was worth. The monarchy was itinerant; it moved about the country. One reason for this mobility was to consume on the spot the resources of various royal estates; another was to make a grand display of the king and his entourage, which

sometimes numbered from three to four hundred people. One German nobleman, on his deathbed, warned his son that the quickest way to impoverish himself was to host the king. A royal account says that the court daily consumed 100 pigs and sheep, 100 bushels of wheat, 8 oxen, 10 barrels of wine, and 10 barrels of beer. Otto I enjoyed great banquets where he mixed freely and drank liberally with his guests. Otto III dined alone at an elevated table, in the imperial style. Otto I secured a real prize when he won the hand of a Byzantine princess for his son, Otto II. The Saxon rulers attracted learned men to their court and trumpeted their close association with the abbots of Cluny. Cultural monuments, ranging from beautiful manuscripts to the dawning Romanesque architecture (see page 343), were all patronized by the Saxons. The greatest enhancement of the prestige of the Saxon monarchy, however, came with the restoration of the imperial title by Otto I in 962.

From the middle of the ninth century, Carolingian aristocrats occasionally made themselves kings of Italy, but no one was able to protect or to rule Rome. When Muslims began attacking the city in 844, the popes themselves had to defend Rome. In the tenth century the papacy fell into its darkest period. It became the prize in the game of local Roman politics. One remarkable woman, Marozia (d. ca. 945), was at different times mother, wife, and mistress of various popes. During these difficult circumstances, Otto I went to Italy in 952. He made himself king of Italy and protector of the papacy. Ten years later he returned and prevailed on the pope to crown him emperor. Few concrete rights came to Otto as a result of his coronation. He got to name some counts and bishops in Italy, to raise some taxes, and to keep south German nobles from meddling in Italy themselves. Mainly, Otto gained immensely in prestige, throughout Germany and the rest of Europe.

What the Saxons could not do was produce a long-lived dynasty. Otto III died without an heir. In 1002 and 1024, distant relatives of the Saxons were elected kings, and the Salian dynasty came to the throne. Based in Bavaria, the Salians often exercised some control of Swabia, but they rarely had any real power in the north, just as the Saxons had usually lacked power in the south (see Map 9.1). Henry III (r. 1039–1056) was a ruler of real ability and of deep religious piety. Viking and Magyar threats were long past, and the consolidation of the Slavic kingdoms had put a temporary end to Germany's eastward expansion. Lacking military opportunities, and having no more control over the German duchies than his predecessors had won, Henry focused even more than they on control of the church.

Henry saw himself as the church's protector. He also felt that, as God's anointed ruler, he had a duty to control, even to purify, the church. That duty extended all the way to Rome, to which the emperors had paid little attention in recent years. In 1046, Henry was confronted with the scandal of three men claiming to be the legitimate pope. Deeply offended, he removed them all and replaced them with the first of several ardent German reformers. Henry's reign marked the high point of the so-called German imperial church.

The Investiture Controversy

When Henry died in 1056, his son, Henry IV, was a child; and until he came of age in 1066, anarchy reigned in Germany. Moreover, at Rome the reformers introduced by Henry III objected to lay in-vestiture (the appointment of church officers by laymen) and to outside interference in the election of popes. Their concerns challenged the basis of the German imperial church and attacked a major source of Saxon-Salian prestige. They also signaled that Rome was now taking the lead in church reform. Ironically the reformers promoted by the Salians threatened to wreck the Salian system.

When Henry IV came of age, he controlled no duchies, faced a Saxony in open revolt, confronted bishops who had freed themselves of royal power, and had little idea of how the papacy would react to him. Henry had a high sense of his royal dignity and a burning desire to restore royal authority. He put down the revolt in Saxony, outmaneuvered most of the aristocrats who opposed him, and restored some control over the German church.

In 1072 the reformers in Rome elected as pope Cardinal Hildebrand, one of the reformers prominent since the 1050s. He took the name Gregory VII to cover himself with the mantle of spiritual authority possessed by Gregory the Great (see page 283). Gregory (r. 1073–1085) was a proud, brilliant, inflexible, self-righteous man who thought he understood perfectly well what was wrong with society in his day: Laymen were in control of too many church offices, and rulers ought to defer to the pope. Gregory and Henry IV fell into the life-and-death struggle that is usually called the "investiture controversy." The struggle concerned the legitimacy of royal and papal rule and the nature of German political and constitutional life.

By 1075, Henry decided to make a show of his restored power by intervening in the selection of a bishop at Milan. His decision came even though the papal court for some two decades had openly opposed such lay interference, and Gregory VII had made a series of strong claims about papal rights and powers. Gregory's view was that God had assigned leadership of the whole Christian world to the pope, and that kings, emperors, and ordinary officials existed only to do the bidding of the church, led by the pope.

During more than a century of strife among aristocratic factions, the territorial power of the popes had been shattered. But the popes in the eleventh and twelfth centuries, unlike their eighth-century predecessors, did not concentrate on territorial rule. Instead, they turned to tightening the control exercised by the pope within the church. They used the weapon of excommunication—

excluding a person from the sacraments and thus effectively expelling him or her from the church and denying forever the hope of salvation—to coerce persons whom they believed to have violated canon law. They used papal legates, official envoys, to tie the pope to the Western church. The college of cardinals was slowly evolving into a kind of senate for the church. The power of the papacy was expanding as never before.

Henry's view was that he was king by descent from his ancestors and by the election of God and thus had a perfect right—indeed, a profound duty—to supervise the church. But more than principle was at stake for Henry. The German kings had always ruled with the support and cooperation of the church. To ensure that support and cooperation, they had always played a key role in selecting bishops, and they had usually required those bishops to be their vassals. Given Henry's perilous position, he simply could not allow the church to slip from his control. (See the box, "The Issues in the Investiture Controversy.")

Gregory's response to Henry's action in Milan was to excommunicate him in 1076 and to release his subjects from their oaths of allegiance. Many churchmen and aristocrats abandoned Henry, not so much because they agreed with Gregory but because they relished the opportunity to weaken the king. A meeting of German nobles and papal representatives was arranged to investigate Henry's fitness for royal office. To forestall the meeting, Henry left Germany and met Gregory at Canossa in Tuscany in January 1077. The king stood in the snow before the castle where the pope was staying and begged his forgiveness. As a priest, Gregory could not refuse to forgive Henry, and that forgiveness restored the king to the church's good graces and restored his subjects' duty of allegiance.

In Germany, the nobles felt betrayed by Gregory and proceeded to elect a new king. This ac-

Henry IV, Duchess Matilda of Tuscany, and Abbot Hugh of Cluny The embattled Henry IV here implores Matilda, a tremendously wealthy landowner and ally of Pope Gregory VII, to intercede with the pope. The powerful abbot of Cluny looks over the scene protectively. Written documents do not portray women's power as vividly as this image does. *(Vatican Library, Rome)*

The Issues in the Investiture Controversy

These two documents illustrate the range of issues involved in the conflict between Pope Gregory VII and Henry IV. The first excerpt is from a long letter written by Henry in 1076. The second is a decree issued by Gregory in 1078.

Henry, king not by usurpation but by the holy ordination of God, to Hildebrand, not now pope but false monk:

Such greeting as this you have merited through your disturbances, for there is no rank in the church on which you have brought, not honor but disgrace, not blessing but curse. To mention only a few notable cases, you have dared to assail the holy rulers of the church, archbishops, bishops, and priests, and you have trodden them underfoot like slaves ignorant of what their master is doing; . . . you have regarded them as knowing nothing, yourself as knowing all things. . . .

We have endured all this in our anxiety to save the honor of the apostolic see, but you have mistaken our humility for fear and have ventured to attack the royal power conferred on us by God, and threatened to divest us of it. As if we had received our kingdom from you! As if the kingdom and empire were in your hands, not God's! For our Lord Jesus Christ did call us to the kingdom. . . . You have assailed me who, though unworthy of anointing, have nevertheless been anointed to the kingdom and who, according to the traditions of the holy fa-

thers, are subject to the judgment of God alone. . . . The true pope Peter exclaims "Fear God, honor the king." But you, who do not fear God, dishonor me, His appointed one. . . .

You, therefore, damned by this curse and by the judgment of all our bishops and ourselves, come down and relinquish the apostolic chair which you have usurped. I, Henry, king by the grace of God, together with all our bishops, say to you: "Come down, come down, to be damned throughout all eternity."

Inasmuch as we have learned that, contrary to the ordinances of the holy fathers, the investiture of churches is, in many places, performed by lay persons, and that from this cause many disturbances arise in the church by which the Christian religion is degraded, we decree that no one of the clergy shall receive the investiture of a bishopric, abbey, or church from the hand of an emperor, or king, or of any layperson, male or female. If anyone shall presume to do so, let him know that such investiture is void by apostolic authority, and that he himself shall lie under excommunication until fitting satisfaction shall have been made.

Source: James Harvey Robinson, *Readings in European History,* vol. 1 (Boston: Ginn, 1904), pp. 279–281, 275 (slightly adapted).

tion enraged Henry, whose ire increased when Gregory said that he would in due course decide between the claims of Henry and his rival. In addition, in 1078 Gregory issued a definitive (earlier pronouncements possessed moral, not legal, force) decree against lay investiture. In response, Henry's propagandists unleashed a torrent of bitterly antipapal writing, the first such campaign in European history, to discredit Gregory. In 1080 the pope excommunicated the king once again, and Henry responded by marching to Rome, chasing Gregory

out of the city, and installing a pope of his own, who promptly crowned him emperor (which Gregory had refused to do). Gregory, uncompromising to the end, died in exile.

Henry never recovered his position in Germany. Both the material and the moral bases of the German crown were destroyed. In 1106, Henry V actually deposed his pitiable father, who died within a few months. The reign of Henry IV exposed the flaws in the German system. If the king tightly controlled one or more duchies and the

KINGS AND WARRIORS

862	Foundation of Kiev
955	Battle of Lechfeld
962	Imperial coronation of Otto I
987	Accession of Hugh Capet in France
972–1015	Reign of Vladimir in Russia
1016	Conquest of England by Cnut
1059	Papal-Norman alliance in Italy
1066	Conquest of England by William of Normandy
1072–1085	Pontificate of Gregory VII
1077	Emperor Henry IV at Canossa
1078	Papal decree against lay investiture
1085	Spanish reconquest of Toledo
1086	Domesday Book
1095	First Crusade proclaimed
1122	Concordat of Worms

church, and if there was a credible foreign threat, the king could be very powerful indeed. But if one or more of these props were kicked out from under the king, the monarchy threatened to fall. It was unfortunate for Henry IV that, at a particularly difficult moment in German politics, militant churchmen decided to contest royal power and influence in ecclesiastical affairs.

Henry V (r. 1106–1125) struggled on for a generation trying to bring the investiture controversy to an end. In 1122 the Concordat of Worms between Henry V and Pope Calixtus II (r. 1119–1124) settled the matter. According to the concordat, Henry agreed that episcopal elections would be free and canonical (carried out according to canon law), and he surrendered investiture with ring and staff, the symbols of the bishop's religious office. Elections were to take place in the royal presence, however, and after the election the king could invest the new bishop with purely secular offices. The concordat was a compromise; but, insofar as it spelled the end of the German imperial church system, it was a victory for the papacy.

Henry V died without heirs in 1125 and was followed by the dukes of Saxony and of Swabia in succession. The nobles elected these men precisely because they were not powerful. In the early tenth century, the nobles had affirmed the royal principle by electing the most powerful of the dukes as kings. For nearly two centuries, when there were legitimate heirs of suitable age, the nobles had assented to their succession. Now, after three-quarters of a century of turmoil, the nobles elected weak men as kings. Those kings had slender material resources, limited control of the church, and jealous nobles on every side. By the middle of the twelfth century, Germany was weak and disunited.

SHAPING THE KINGDOM

Whereas the German Empire's trajectory in the period 900–1150 took it from strength to weakness, the course almost everywhere else was just the opposite. Both the variety of Europe's government patterns and the size of the individual governments expanded. Before about 1050, the majority of Europe's population was ruled, or misruled, by dukes and counts, by bishops and abbots, or by various petty magnates. After the middle of the eleventh century, kingdoms began to have a measurable effect on the lives of most people. Amid great local variety, one trend was constant: Personal bonds rather than bureaucratic administrations or abstract notions of allegiance to a state held the kingdoms together. By the middle of the twelfth century the units of rule were larger, and central governments were becoming more important. In many places the decade of the 1150s marked a major turning point.

The Rise of Capetian France

When the Treaty of Verdun created the West Frankish Kingdom, no one knew what the future France might be like. The twentieth-century French leader Charles de Gaulle once quipped, "It is impossible to govern a country with 325 kinds of cheese." He was referring to France's tremendous diversity.

During the late ninth century and much of the tenth, however, the area suffered cruelly from constant waves of Viking attacks and from repeated failures of the Carolingian family to produce adult heirs to the throne. Chroniclers often quoted the

Map 9.2 French Territorial Principalities As the Carolingian West Frankish kingdom
(see Map 8.3, inset) broke down, and as feudal bonds proliferated, many territories
arose under counts and dukes whose struggles to fight off royal control animated
French history.

lament of King Solomon: "Woe to thee, O land, whose king is a child."

Royal authority declined sharply because of the weakness of the later Carolingians, but what really damaged the royal office was the emergence of territorial principalities. Whereas Germany pro-

duced five major duchies, France saw the appearance of more than a dozen principalities (Map 9.2). Some of them had existed before the Carolingians came on the scene: Celtic Brittany in the west, Basque Gascony in the southwest, and Burgundy (formerly a kingdom) in the east. They re-emerged, not unlike the German duchies, as districts with some sense of ethnic cohesion and of historical tradition. Normandy, Anjou, Blois, Champagne, and other principalities were products of the years from 850 to 950. Confined largely to the Paris region, the king himself was a territorial prince.

Territorial princes built up their power by taking "bannal" (from the "ban," the king's right to command) rights of the king into their own hands: the rights to raise armies, hold courts, collect taxes, mint coins, and protect churches. The most successful of these territorial princes then reduced their less powerful neighbors to dependent status by making them swear homage and fealty and perform various services. Many formerly free men sought security in the entourage of powerful neighbors by handing over their possessions and then receiving them back in return for homage and service. France was becoming feudal.

Territorial princes ruled with little reference to the king, and the king had little power over them, but France was not anarchical. Feudalism was a creative response to, more than a cause of, the political disorder of the late Carolingian world. Feudal principalities, when they worked well, as in Normandy and Anjou, were models of effective local government.

Where did this leave the French crown? The Merovingian and Carolingian tradition was so strong that it never occurred to the French nobles to dispense with the monarchy. In 987, the nobles ignored the only legitimate Carolingian and turned to a family from Paris that had three times provided kings since 888. The man chosen was Hugh Capet (r. 987–996). No one could have known it at the time, but the Capetian family would rule France in the direct line until the fourteenth century.

The kings had a few real advantages. They possessed a landed patrimony—a demesne—that was minute if compared to the once-vast Carolingian demesne but about equal to the personal demesne of any of the other great nobles. The Capetian demesne, moreover, was situated strategically in the centrally located Paris basin. In theory all the territorial princes were the king's vassals, and the king received oaths of fidelity from most important noblemen. The early Capetians usually could not force their nominal vassals to

perform specific services for them, but no other nobleman could take up the oaths of his peers.

Powerful nobles, both secular and clerical, often had recourse to the royal court for arbitration of their disputes. Although the king could not demand that cases be brought to his court, he gained in prestige and political leverage whenever a case was heard there. In this way, kings created legal precedents for the later extension of their authority.

The kings also controlled about two dozen bishoprics and around fifty monasteries in northern France. The kings got great material support from the church and, through their right to appoint bishops and abbots, inserted their influence into many of the territorial principalities. As in Carolingian times, churchmen were enthusiastic supporters of and propagandists for the monarchy. To bishops, the king was the greatest of the "fighters."

The first four Capetian kings (987–1108) maintained the throne and enhanced royal power, even if only in small ways. Hugh Capet's son, Robert, called "the Pious" (r. 996–1030), acquired a reputation for sanctity and got along especially well with the clergy and with the most distinguished religious reformers of his day. He also was the first French king to display the "royal touch," a ceremony in which the king was believed to cure people of scrofula (a common respiratory ailment) by touching them. This particular type of royal charisma sharply separated the king from any ordinary nobleman.

The early Capetians also began the practice of having their sons crowned and anointed during their own lifetime. When one king died, another one was ready to take over. The role of the nobility in electing kings, very great in the ninth and tenth centuries, had almost disappeared by the twelfth century. In this regard, France and Germany were quite different. In Germany, dynastic failure and papal excommunications afforded the nobility repeated opportunities to engage in king-making.

Finally, the turmoil of the German investiture controversy was not visited on France. The king of France depended much less on his control of the church than the German ruler did, and the French king had less to lose by compromising with Rome, which he did more than a decade before the Germans. Several times when the popes were struggling with the emperors, they found refuge in France, and Pope Urban II (r. 1088–1099), the key successor of Gregory VII, was a Frenchman.

In the twelfth century, France had two gifted kings in succession: Louis VI (r. 1108–1137) and Louis VII (r. 1137–1180). Louis VI suppressed the minor nobility in the royal demesne and turned his own principality into one of the best governed and most efficient in France. He made extensive use of the royal touch as a means of focusing loyalty on the king. He promoted Saint Denis (the legendary first bishop of Paris) as a patron saint for France, as well as his shrine in Paris (the Capetian capital), as a way of creating unity throughout the kingdom. The number of important men who appeared in his court grew steadily, and his coins had a wider circulation than those of any king since the ninth century.

Louis VII began making ceremonial visitations around the kingdom, drawing attention away from the king's lack of real power by focusing attention on the monarchy's grandeur. Capetians and Saxons were alike in this regard. He began to hold larger and more impressive assemblies than any that had met since Carolingian times, and he got some of the greatest lords of France to perform ceremonial duties in his court. Louis also initiated the policy of allying the monarchy with the growing towns of France.

However, aristocratic, dynastic societies occasionally produce shocking transformations in the political landscape. Louis VII, for example, married the heiress of Aquitaine and thereby multiplied by several times the amount of land under his direct control. But his new bride, Eleanor of Aquitaine, disliked her pious, abstemious husband almost as much as he disliked her strong, independent temperament. Compliant clerics annulled their marriage and Louis lost all the lands he had gained. Then Eleanor married Henry of Anjou, who was about to inherit Anjou, Maine, and Touraine from his father (and who in two years would be crowned King Henry II of England). From his mother Henry would inherit Normandy. Through Eleanor, Henry got Poitou and Aquitaine. Thus, Louis VII was faced with a vassal who controlled about three-fifths of France. What was going to happen to all the patient work of the Capetian kings of France? No one could well have predicted in 1154.

Anglo-Saxon England and the Norman Conquest

At the very time when continental kingdoms were collapsing in the late ninth century, Alfred the Great rallied the English. In the tenth century his successors constructed a peaceful, well-governed kingdom. All men in the land owed allegiance to the king, and the king could summon all free men to the *fyrd*, the militia. The great men of the realm routinely attended meetings of the *witan*, the royal council that was partly a court of law and partly a political body that resolved disputes among the mighty. The king could issue writs, which were executive orders rather like the Carolingian capitularies. Only the king could issue coins.

All of England was divided into administrative districts called *shires*, and each shire had a royally appointed representative, the shire-reeve, or sheriff. A tax, the Danegeld, first levied on the whole kingdom in times of Viking danger, began turning into a routine source of royal income. Deliberate royal policy transformed Alfred's burghs, originally defensive positions in the struggle against the Vikings, into towns with markets and merchants.

English kings commanded at times the allegiance of various Welsh princes and of the kings in Scotland. Their international position can be seen in their marriages into French princely houses and even into the German imperial family. These kings corresponded with popes, promoted learning, and shared in the spiritual reforms that were sweeping Europe. England's future could not have looked brighter.

Then in 978, Ethelred II, a boy of about 10, rose to the throne. He has become known as "Ethelred the Unready" (more accurately, Ethelred "of no counsel"), but this label is unfair. Shortly after his accession, England was drawn into the world of northern politics. King Harald Bluetooth of Denmark was seeking to unify his country and to impose Christianity on the Danes. His methods were brutal, and after 980 gangs of Danish malcontents began raiding the English coast. In 988 Harald's son, Swein, a leader of the raiders, deposed his father and took over the kingdom. But he kept on raiding England.

Many people in northern and eastern England, the Danelaw, were of Scandinavian extraction.

Their loyalty to Ethelred may have been no stronger than their potential loyalty to Swein, who was no mere Viking adventurer but a crowned king. Ethelred was not much of a soldier at a time when military gifts were needed, and his heavy Danegelds were unpopular. The threat he faced was so great that he fled to Normandy in 1013.

England fell to Swein in 1014, but his sudden death left the consolidation of the conquest to his son, Cnut. Cnut ruled England from 1016 to 1035, and his sons after him ruled to 1042. No Viking savage, Cnut was one of the most powerful and capable men of his age. King of Denmark and England and briefly of Norway too, he wed his daughter to Emperor Henry III, and later married Emma, Ethelred's widow. He was a Christian and had visited the pope in Rome. England had long enjoyed good government, and Cnut saw no reason to change things. He added a few Scandinavian earls, high-ranking aristocrats owing allegiance to the king, but did not purge the Anglo-Saxon aristocracy. Far from being disruptive, this first "Norman Conquest" actually benefited England.

Cnut's sons having died without heirs, the Anglo-Saxons invited the son of Ethelred and Emma, Edward, known as "the Confessor," to become their king and to preserve the monarchy. Edward was pious and well intentioned, but he had taken a vow of chastity and would leave no heir. The jostling for position among the Anglo-Saxon nobles began almost immediately, intensified by Edward's penchant for promoting Normans to high position in England (he had spent most of his life in Normandy). What particularly angered some prominent Anglo-Saxons was Edward's promise of his throne to Duke William of Normandy.

When Edward died in 1066, the witan met and elected Harold of Wessex, the most powerful of the Anglo-Saxon nobles, as their king. Norman writers regarded this action as especially vicious because, in their telling, Harold had some years before promised to support William's claim. William began to make preparations to fight for the English throne. Harold, meanwhile, had another challenger in the king of Norway and Denmark, Harald Hardrada, who, as king of Denmark, claimed England in succession to Cnut. Harold of Wessex marched north to defeat Harald Hardrada, only to learn that William had landed in the south. Impulsively, he rushed south with a weary army and met William at Hastings. After

one day's fighting, England was conquered for the second time in fifty years.

William "the Conqueror" ruled from 1066 to 1087. Although his power was based on conquest and on a brutal pacification campaign carried out between 1066 and 1071, William always claimed to be the legitimate heir of Edward. Conquest gave William an opportunity to do almost anything he could get away with, but English and Norman government provided plenty of precedents for effective rule.

William maintained the traditional prerogatives of the Anglo-Saxon kings. He brought to England Lanfranc, a Norman abbot, and named him to England's primary archbishopric, Canterbury. Lanfranc, an ardent reformer, instituted changes designed to bring the church in England up to contemporary standards in administration and canon law. William controlled his church with an iron hand, but his relations with Pope Gregory VII were generally cordial. Gregory probably did not wish to pick any more fights, and William was a great supporter of Lanfranc's reforms. In many ways, William's takeover, like Cnut's, was purely traditional.

In one critical area, William innovated. He turned most of the estates in England into fiefs and distributed them among the 180 or so greatest of his followers. Each of these vassals held his fief in return for a fixed quota of knights for the royal army. To raise the five thousand total knights required by William, his own vassals had to create vassals of their own. The technical name for this process of vassals creating vassals to help them to perform their service is *subinfeudation*. William exacted in 1087 the Salisbury Oath, thereby establishing the principle of liege homage, according to which the king was final lord of all vassals. To avoid territorial principalities on the French model, William did not give his vassals compact blocks of land. By scattering his vassals' holdings around the kingdom, he kept the vassals from becoming too powerful in any one place.

William's keen sense of administrative order, along with his desire to know the value of his realm as a whole and the value of the individual segments of it that he had assigned to his vassals, led to the Domesday Book (named later by critics of the monarchy for the Day of Judgment against which there was no appeal) of 1086. Inspectors were sent throughout the country to take the

Bayeux Tapestry Anglo-Saxon nobles and Archbishop Stigand crown Harold of Wessex as king of England. This tapestry, 70 meters long, was made in Canterbury, England, shortly after the Norman conquest to tell the Norman side of the story. (*Tapissérie de la Reine Mathilde, Ville de Bayeux*)

sworn testimony of people everywhere. William sought an enumeration of people, buildings, animals, mills, and anything else of significant value. No comparable undertaking was attempted again until the American census of 1790.

William was succeeded by two of his sons, William II (r. 1087–1100) and Henry I (r. 1100–1135), who kept most of their father's system intact while adding some features. In particular, Henry streamlined the financial branch of the monarchy, the Exchequer (named from the checkerboard table on which accounts were reckoned). He introduced itinerant justices who traveled about the kingdom

on regular tours of judicial business. These justices in eyre (a judicial circuit) made it hard for feudal lords to take royal justice into their own hands as their counterparts in France often did. Circumventing the feudal nobility introduced by his father, Henry deftly appointed new men as sheriffs and judges.

England, like France, was spared a crisis in relations between monarchy and church. In Lanfranc's successor, Anselm, Henry I faced a determined reformer who refused to tolerate lay investiture. Down to 1107, Anselm spent a good deal of time in exile, but in that year he and

Henry effected a compromise that anticipated the provisions of the Concordat of Worms.

Henry's only legitimate heir drowned in the English Channel; so when the king died, the barons elected Stephen of Blois (r. 1135–1154), a grandson of William the Conqueror. Henry had tried in vain to convince the barons to accept his daughter Matilda as queen. Some barons simply refused to be ruled by a woman, but many also feared Matilda's husband, the formidable Count Geoffrey of Anjou. Most English baronial families still had holdings in Normandy, and the Angevins were old enemies of the Normans. Begun in inauspicious circumstances, Stephen's reign was marked by factional strife and by constant plotting by Matilda and her supporters.

In 1153 Matilda's son, Henry of Anjou, prevailed on Stephen to recognize him as his heir. What would this turn of events mean for England? Would Angevin and Norman factions carry on their squabbling? Would King Henry II be drawn by his vast French holdings to ignore England? It is striking how the decade of the 1150s emerged as a turning point for Germany, France, and England.

The Progress of the Reconquista in Spain

Spain, too, faced a crisis in the 1150s. Historians perceive two driving forces in the rich and colorful history of medieval Spain. One is the constant interplay within the Iberian Peninsula of three vibrant cultures: Christian, Jewish, and Muslim. The other is the bloody experience of several centuries of war along an expanding frontier.

The caliphate of Cordoba (see page 282) began breaking up after 1002, and the emergence of tiny Muslim realms afforded an unprecedented opportunity to the Christians living in the north of the peninsula. King Sancho I (r. 1000–1035) of Navarre launched an offensive against the Muslims. This war, carried on intermittently until the fifteenth century, came to be called the *Reconquista*, the Reconquest.

Before he died, Sancho divided his realm among his sons; thus, the kingdoms of Aragon and Castile arose alongside Navarre. It was Alfonso I (r. 1065–1109) of Castile who really advanced the Reconquista. In 1085 his forces captured the Muslim stronghold and old Visigothic capital of Toledo, an important moral and strategic victory. Alfonso's military successes owed much to the dashing warrior Rodrigo Díaz de Vivar, known as "El Cid" ("the Lord" from the Arabic *sayyid*). Rodrigo, a gifted but slightly unprincipled mercenary, fought for both Muslims and Christians. His career shows just how turbulent Spain then was. Rodrigo's successes, and the reconquest of Toledo, led the retreating Muslims to summon from North Africa militant Muslims, who temporarily halted the Christian advance.

Throughout the twelfth century, the Christian states of Spain pressed slowly but relentlessly forward (Map 9.3). The kings, especially the kings of Castile, managed to impose hereditary rule and to exact oaths of allegiance from all their free subjects. As the kingdoms grew and consolidated, the kings tried to force powerful nobles to become their vassals. They were more successful on the expanding frontier with Muslim Spain than at home. On the frontier, warriors could be given newly conquered fiefs in return for future military service. At home, in the old kingdoms, the local notables viewed their lands and rights as being independent of royal control.

Through the twelfth century, kings succeeded in getting their vassals to perform military service. A royal council and judicial institutions also helped to unify the kingdom. To rally the Christians and give them a sense of belonging to a single country, the kings promoted the cult of Saint James of Compostella, Jesus's brother who allegedly preached Christianity in Spain. In the end, however, it was the Reconquista that made the Spanish monarchy strong.

Down to the 1150s the Reconquista proceeded along three fronts. In the east, the emerging kingdom of Aragon-Catalonia advanced along the Mediterranean coast. In the center, León-Castile pressed hard against al-Andalus. In the west, the nascent kingdom of Portugal became a factor in Iberian politics. In the 1150s the Muslims of Spain once again turned to North Africa for assistance. Help arrived, and the Reconquista was halted again.

Kingdoms and Cities in Italy

Unlike its European neighbors, Italy did not suffer a crisis in the mid-twelfth century. Rather, its history during the period from 900 to 1150 is characterized by three important trends. First, as we

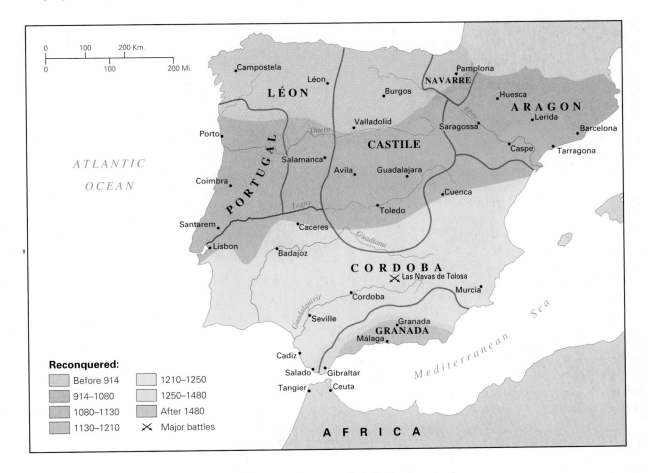

Map 9.3 The Christian Reconquista of Muslim Spain From slow beginnings in the ninth century to the epochal battle of Las Navas de Tolosa (1212), the Christians in Spain pushed back the Muslim frontier and built durable states behind it. (*Source:* David Nicholas, *The Evolution of the Medieval World.* Copyright © 1992. Used by permission of Longman Group UK.)

have seen, the Germans involved themselves in the affairs of Italy, Rome, and the papacy. Second, even before the Norman conquests of England, bands of Norman adventurers began a conquest of southern Italy and Sicily that would result in one of the most dynamic states of medieval Europe. Third, in northern and central Italy in the eleventh century a distinctive type of urban institution began to appear: the commune.

Since the ninth century, the whole region south of Rome had been contested among the Byzantines, the Muslims of North Africa, and local potentates. In 1026, Norman pilgrims bound for the Holy Land landed in southern Italy, where local people invited them to enlist in the fight against

the Muslims. By the 1040s the original Normans had been joined by many more who were seeking land and adventure. Initially opposed to the Normans, the papacy later allied with their leader, Robert Guiscard (d. 1085), as a counterweight against the Germans.

From his capital at Palermo, Roger II "the Great" (r. 1130-1154) ruled a complex state that blended Byzantine and Lombard administrative structures with Norman feudalism. In Italy, as in England, the Normans showed a genius for adaptation. Perched advantageously at the juncture of the Latin, Greek, and Arab worlds, the Norman court was more advanced in finance and bureaucratic administration than any of its European

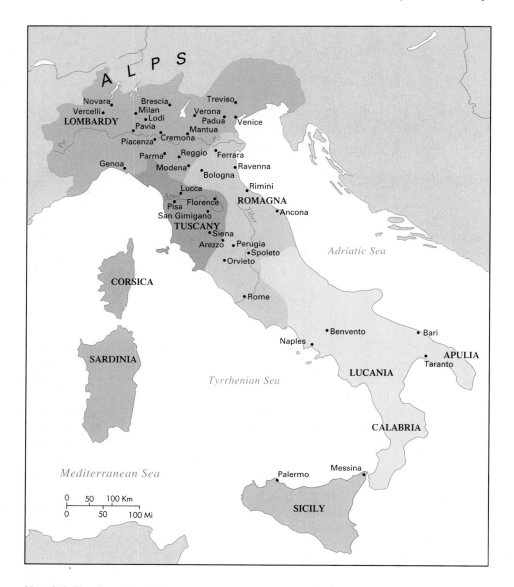

Map 9.4 The Communal Movement in Italy Beginning in the last decades of the eleventh century, towns all over northern and central Italy instituted communal forms of government. In northern Europe, comparable movements existed only in Flanders and parts of northern France.

contemporaries. No one forgot for a moment, however, that the Normans were primarily great warriors. Robert Guiscard's epitaph pronounced him "The terror of the world," and a chronicler said of the Normans, "They delight in arms and horses."

The most dynamic element on the Italian scene was the communal movement (Map 9.4). Two pieces of information help to explain the rise of communes. The first relates to economic expan-

sion. In 1015, Pisa and Genoa undertook a joint attack on Muslim pirates operating from Sardinia. Beginning in the 1060s, the Normans cleared the central Mediterranean of Muslim pirates. Venice was always looking for commercial advantages in the eastern Mediterranean. By 1100 the Mediterranean was a Latin lake, and Italian merchants were the primary beneficiaries.

The second piece of background relates to political developments in Italian towns. Carolingian towns had been governed by resident counts, and the German emperors tried to maintain this system. The powers of the counts tended to be weak, however, so the Germans also relied on bishops, who were, in Italy as in Germany, key props to the system of imperial rule. But bishops and counts were not alone in holding urban power. Since the late tenth century both bishops and counts had been granting fiefs to local men in order to strengthen their own authority and to procure defense for the town. Gradually these men, whose lands made them wealthy in the expanding economy, moved into the towns and, in turn, enfeoffed other men in the countryside. These lesser vassals were also growing in wealth and moving into towns, where they joined their lords in volatile political factions.

Communes were sworn associations of the local nobility—the vassals of the bishops and counts—and their vassals. The desire for reconciliation among violent and competing noble factions at a time of German and papal distraction was a key factor in the rise of communes. Commune members swore to uphold one another's rights and called themselves the *popolo,* the "people," although the people as a whole had nothing to do with the early communes. The commune accorded a high degree of participation to its members in choosing leaders and in coming together in an assembly that voted on matters of common concern. The leaders of the early communes were usually called *consuls.* The number of consuls varied from four to twenty in different cities. They were usually elected for a single year. The consuls proposed matters to an assembly that then voted "yes" or "no" on the matters presented to it. By the 1140s every significant city in northern and central Italy had a commune.

The communes did not necessarily originate as attempts to make cities independent. Frequently, however, as communal governments became more established and confident, that is what they did. One by one cities either refused to recognize papal or imperial overlordship or else renegotiated the terms under which they would acknowledge the rule of their historic masters. The working out of this ongoing relationship was a major development in the history of the Italian cities in the twelfth century.

The Italian commune was a radical political experiment. Everywhere else in medieval Europe, power was thought to radiate downward—from God, the clergy, the emperor, the king. In a commune, power radiated upward from the popolo to its leaders. For several centuries, the Italian city was arguably the most creative institution in the Western world.

THE GROWTH OF NEW STATES

By 1150, a band of new states surrounded the old Carolingian core of Europe (Map 9.5). In the Celtic, Scandinavian, and Slavic worlds one new kingdom or principality after another emerged and attained a measure of stability. No previous period in European history had seen comparable political expansion. Moreover, political, religious, and cultural ties between the new states and their neighbors assured that they were "Europeanized."

The Celtic Realms

When the Romans appeared on the scene, Celtic peoples could be found in virtually every region from Ireland to Anatolia. Eventually most Celts were submerged by more powerful Germanic and Slavic peoples. It was in the British Isles that the most durable and distinctive Celtic regions evolved into Ireland, Wales, and Scotland. There were three essential dynamics in each of these regions. First, tiny political entities gradually turned into larger kingdoms. Second, relations between England and the Celtic realms were everywhere decisive in the historical development of the latter. Third, the Celtic lands had complex relations with the wider European world.

In each of the Celtic realms the movement toward greater unity was opened by the efforts of powerful, ambitious leaders to subjugate numerous well-entrenched local potentates, many of whom had expanded their power during the period of Viking invasions. In Ireland, Brian Boru (r. 976–1014) became the first ruler to exercise real authority over most of the island. In Wales, Rhodri the Great (d. 898) and Howell the Good (d. 950) were the first rulers to gain at least nominal authority over the whole of the land. Although disunity is a continuous theme of Scottish history, the centuries after the reign of Kenneth MacAlpin (r. 843–858) give evidence for the slow creation of a national tradition.

The course of development in the Celtic lands was disrupted by the English in the eleventh and

Map 9.5 The States of an Expanding Europe The core states of Europe appeared inside the frontiers of the Roman Empire or just along them. After 900, new states, ranging from the Celtic realms in the west to Scandinavia in the north to Slavic regions in the east, surrounded and joined with the old core in a vastly larger, more diverse Europe.

especially in the twelfth century. The Norman Conquest of England brought adventurers to the frontiers of Wales and Scotland. Sometimes these continental knights advanced with the support of William the Conqueror and his sons, but more often they looked to wild frontier regions for opportunities to escape tight control. In Wales some Normans allied with various local princes who resented the growing power of the Welsh kings. Prince Grufydd ap Cynan (d. 1137) then turned to King Henry I in 1114 and promised allegiance if Henry would aid him in his quest to establish his authority all over Wales. From that time forward the actual power of Welsh rulers varied greatly, and English kings usually claimed some authority over the region. Scottish kings managed to enlist a good many Norman knights into their service, but this process angered the English kings and clouded the lines of allegiance in Northumbria, where many of those Norman knights had been

sent in the first place. Civil disturbances in Ireland induced King Rory O'Connor to turn to King Henry II of England for mercenaries to help him establish his power, but by 1171 Henry had invaded Ireland himself and inaugurated the complicated English involvement in the affairs of Ireland that persists to this day.

The Celtic realms participated vigorously in the European culture of the period. The coming of Christianity in the fifth century had introduced Mediterranean culture to the "end of the earth," as the Romans had dubbed Ireland. Irish schools had a high reputation, and both English and continental students went there. But Irish teachers and missionaries could also be found throughout Europe. Carolingian schools had prominent Irish teachers, as did twelfth-century schools. Celtic art forms, characterized by exuberantly intricate tracery, contributed to English, Carolingian, and Ottonian art. People told stories about King Arthur in Welsh and Irish long before Arthur became the common inheritance of much of Europe. In addition, the Irish Sea was a lively commercial basin linking the Celtic lands with England, Scandinavia, the Low Countries, and France. Finally, Cluniac and Cistercian monasticism struck deep roots in Ireland. Each of the Celtic regions experienced ecclesiastical reforms that resulted in hierarchical and territorial churches but none endured a bitter investiture controversy.

Scandinavia

Another group of new states emerged in this period in Scandinavia, the Roman name for the lands that became Denmark, Norway, and Sweden. Although the faint beginnings of political consolidation in Denmark can be traced to the Carolingian period, the effective development of the states of Scandinavia dates from the tenth and eleventh centuries. Overseas relations played one key role in northern political development. Another was the slow achievement of political unity by kings who had to break down powerful local interests.

The sea, not the land, is the great fact of Scandinavian history. Norway has more than one thousand miles of coastline, and no point in Denmark is more than 35 miles from the sea. Scandinavia did not offer opportunities for large, land-based kingdoms or empires, but the sea provided Scandinavians with a wide scope for activities.

We have mentioned Viking raiders several times already. It is important to recognize that along with raiders there were also many settlers. Much of northeastern England, the Danelaw, was settled by Northmen. In 911 the Norwegian Rollo and his followers settled what became Normandy in northern France. Between 870 and 930 many Norwegians and some Danes settled Iceland and a little later established bases in Greenland. In 862 a Swedish force, accustomed to raiding and trading along the rivers of later Russia, established a base at Kiev from which the first Russian state developed.

Raiders, traders, and settlers, the Scandinavians fostered the expansion of Europe. They aided in the creation of trade routes that stretched from Byzantium and the Islamic world to the remotest reaches of the north Atlantic. Roman Christianity and Latin culture entered Scandinavia through both individual and state-sponsored missionary efforts. Germany, in particular, sought to expand its influence in the north through the church.

Because the sea made exit from Scandinavia so easy, and because the whole region had absolutely no tradition of unified government, kings had a hard time establishing their power. Essentially kings were war-leaders with loyal bands of followers. Territorial states were thus built up as powerful leaders persuaded or forced more and more men to join them. Denmark's was the first of the northern monarchies to emerge in the early tenth century. Norway's monarchy arose a little later in the tenth century, but for much of the eleventh century Norway was under Danish control. As the Danes fell more and more under German influence in the eleventh century, Norway managed to break free. Sweden's monarchy was the last to emerge in the northern world; it was not fully stable until the twelfth century, but by 1300, it became the most powerful.

The Slavic World

A dozen or more loosely related groups of peoples make up the Slavs of eastern Europe. Rome neither conquered nor allied with these peoples, who, like the early Celts and Scandinavians, had no tradition of unified rule. As Slavic states began to emerge they had two features in common. First, they had the advantages and disadvantages of many powerful neighbors: Byzantines, Muslims, and Germans. Second, they were all fragile.

For geographical and linguistic reasons, historians divide the Slavs into Western, Southern, and Eastern categories. The Western Slavs included those peoples living from the Baltic Sea to Moravia, whose earliest organized existence makes occasional appearances in Carolingian sources (see Map 9.5). The most important of the west Slavic states were Bohemia, Poland, and Hungary. Bohemia emerged in the late ninth century when a powerful local duke forged an alliance of the Czech people of Bohemia proper and the Slovak peoples to the east. Early in the tenth century a Polish duke laid the foundations for the kingdom of Poland. Poland might have become the most powerful of the west Slavic states had not a twelfth-century king divided his kingdom among his four sons. The origins of the Hungarian kingdom trace to the defeat of the Magyars by the

Germans in 955. The Magyar leadership settled down in the Pannonian basin and ruled, as a minority, in conjunction with a large Slavic population. In the eleventh century the Hungarian kings profited from troubles in the German and Byzantine empires to build an effective state.

The Southern Slavs created a band of states reaching across the northern Balkans from the Adriatic to the Black Sea. In the extreme west the little states of Croatia, Slovenia, and Serbia appeared in the tenth and eleventh centuries. Croatia and Slovenia, although dominated by Hungary, managed to maintain their existence. The same is true of Serbia, except that the Serbs fell, at different times, under Byzantine or Bulgarian influence. The greatest of the south Slavic states was Bulgaria. Like the Magyars, the Bulgars were a minority ruling over a numerically superior Slavic population. Bulgaria was the oldest of the Slavic states, reaching back to the seventh century. Under Khan Symeon (r. 893–927) the Bulgars made war on Byzantium and controlled trans-Balkan trade routes. Symeon even dreamed of making himself emperor. The Byzantines so feared the Bulgars that they waged relentless war on them from 967 to 1018 and eventually destroyed the first Bulgar state.

The greatest of the east Slavic states was Russia. Swedes laid the foundation for the Russian state when they built a permanent trading station at Kiev in 862. Kiev lay near the junction of several major trade routes based on the Volga and Dneiper Rivers. These river valleys were full of Slavic farmers. Russia emerged as warrior-merchants and Slavic farmers made common cause against the untamed peoples of the Russian steppes. The ruling Swedish minority, in the early days, is comparable to the Magyar and Bulgar elites in Hungary and Bulgaria.

In 882, Prince Oleg of Novgorod, a northern Swedish station, extended his rule all the way to Kiev and became the first grand prince of Russia. A century later Vladimir (r. 978–1015) consolidated his power by neutralizing or exiling powerful nobles, converted to Orthodox Christianity, defended Kiev by means of fortifications, and went on the offensive against the steppe peoples. Despite Vladimir's efforts, Kiev did not remain in control of the young Russian state. Rule slowly passed to towns such as Novgorod and Vladimir-Suzdal that enjoyed favorable commercial locations while also lying deep enough in the Russian forests to ensure some protection from the steppe nomads who continually harassed Kiev.

The sixth-century Roman writer Procopius once spoke of "Slavic democracy." He might have had in mind either of two somewhat contradictory developments. First, in every Slavic area rulers

Twelfth-Century Polish Castle
This reconstruction of a castle shows it to have been a combination of earthworks and wooden stockades. Such castles, common in western Europe in the tenth and eleventh centuries, afforded protection to people from a wide area and permanent dwellings to a few. *(CAF Warsaw/Sovfoto)*

had to take seriously into account the views of a powerful, vocal nobility. Second, every Slavic realm had some version of the *zadruga*, the "great family." This was a group of people, not necessarily related, who had common responsibility for an agricultural community. The zadruga tended to moderate social distinctions at the local level and to facilitate ethnic assimilation. As everywhere else in tenth- to twelfth-century Europe, central governments grew only by a slow process of compromise between local and royal powers.

Merchants were obviously one major source of outside influence in the Slavic world. This is most evident in Russia but prominent too in Bulgaria, where the local rulers sought to minimize Byzantine and German economic influence. Aggression by powerful neighbors was another important path of influence. Byzantium constantly threatened Bulgaria and Serbia, while Germany pressed hard against Hungary, Bohemia, and Poland. The greatest outside force for internal change in the Slavic world, however, was Christianity. Regions such as Poland, Hungary, Bohemia, and Croatia that accepted Roman Catholicism nevertheless tried hard to escape German or Italian cultural suffocation. Areas that embraced Orthodox Christianity—Serbia, Bulgaria, and Russia—sometimes did so to avoid Roman Catholic and German influence but then faced the formidable task of eluding Byzantine domination. Even though Christianity took many forms in the Slavic world, the faith was a powerfully integrative force in the process of European expansion.

CULTURAL LIFE IN AN AGE OF EXPANSION

As in the late antique and Carolingian periods, courts and churches were the great patrons of artists and authors. But in this age of expansion the number and geographic spread of such patrons increased dramatically. By 1150 there were half again as many bishoprics and about three times as many monasteries as there had been in 900. In 1150 there were monarchies in many places—Scandinavia, Russia, and Sicily, for example—where none had existed in 900. In addition to an increase in the sheer amount of cultural activity, the years between 900 and 1150 also witnessed

innovations. Logic replaced grammar at the heart of the school curriculum. Latin letters remained ascendant, but literature in many vernacular (native) languages began to appear in quantity and quality. Romanesque art and architecture were fresh and original despite being lineal descendants of Carolingian ancestors. Europe's incipient urbanization produced the first stirrings of a distinctively urban culture. The dynamism so evident in the economic, social, and political life of Europe is just as apparent in cultural life.

Schools and Latin Letters

The breakup of the Carolingian Empire deprived schools and masters of the patronage that they had enjoyed for a century or more. Therefore, the tenth century was marked more by individual genius than by a program of learning.

Gerbert of Aurillac (940–1003) was the most distinguished intellect of his age. He left his home in Aquitaine to study in Spain and Italy before settling in Reims, in northern France, where he was a teacher and then briefly a bishop. He attracted the attention of the emperor Otto III and spent some time at the German court, earning appointments as abbot of Bobbio, bishop of Ravenna, and, finally, pope. Gerbert followed Carolingian tradition in being a collector of manuscripts and critic of texts, but he departed from older traditions in his interest in mathematics and in his study of logic, the formal rules of reasoning that, in the Western tradition, trace back over many thinkers to Aristotle (see page 109).

Fulbert of Chartres (960–1028), Gerbert's finest pupil, elevated the cathedral school of Chartres to the paramount place in Europe. Fulbert wrote letters in elegant Latin and fine poems. He carried on his master's literary interests more than his scientific ones, and well into the twelfth century Chartres remained a major center of literary studies.

Another figure of interest is the aristocratic German nun Roswitha of Gandersheim (d. 970). She wrote poems on saints and martyrs, as well as a story about a priest who sold his soul to the devil. In her mature years, Roswitha wrote Latin plays in rhymed verse based on the Roman writer Terence. In these plays she took tales from Roman and biblical history and used them to convey moral truths.

MONKS AND WRITERS

ca. 900	*Beowulf*
910	Foundation of Cluny
940–1003	Gerbert of Aurillac
960–1028	Fulbert of Chartres
d. 970	Roswitha of Gandersheim
1000–1088	Berengar of Tours
ca. 1033–1109	Anselm of Canterbury
ca. 1050–1150	Emergence of the Romanesque
1079–1142	Peter Abelard
1090–1153	Bernard of Clairvaux
1098	Foundation of Cîteaux
1098–1179	Hildegard of Bingen
ca. 1100	*The Song of Roland*
1140	Gratian's *Decretum*

The eleventh century, more settled and prosperous than the tenth, was more diverse culturally, though it is still hard to detect any coherent program such as the one that characterized the Carolingian Renaissance (see page 293). Law was a field of major innovation. The increasing sophistication of urban life demanded a better understanding of law. The growing responsibilities of the church called for orderly rules, and the church's frequent quarrels with secular rulers demanded careful delineations of rights and responsibilities.

In about 1012, Burchard, bishop of Worms, produced a collection of canon law that was influential for more than a century and heightened reformers' awareness of the law of the church. By midcentury scholars studying canon law in Italy and France helped to promote the papal view of reform. In Bologna, Irnerius (d. ca. 1130), a transplanted German and protégé of Emperor Henry V, began teaching Roman law from the law code of Justinian (see page 251). This legal work culminated in the publication in 1140 of the *Decretum* of the Bolognese monk Gratian. The most comprehensive and systematic book of canon law ever written, Gratian's work remained authoritative for centuries.

One of the chief accomplishments of the age came about almost by accident. Berengar (ca. 1000–ca. 1088), master of the school of Tours, wrote a treatise that denied Christ's presence in the Eucharist—the Holy Communion received by Catholics in the celebration of the mass. This position was heretical. Ordinarily, churchmen would have refuted it by simply quoting to Berengar various passages from the Scriptures or from the writings of the Church Fathers along with conciliar pronouncements. The evidence, however, was ambiguous. Berengar was finally refuted, at least to the satisfaction of his opponents, by Lanfranc, archbishop of Canterbury during the reign of William the Conqueror. Lanfranc used precise logical argumentation to dispose of Berengar's heretical arguments.

Carolingian schools had focused on grammar, on the basic foundations of language. Now that logic had come to the aid of the faith in one critical case, people began using it widely to solve intellectual problems. Anselm (ca. 1033–1109), Lanfranc's successor as archbishop of Canterbury, developed an ingenious proof for the existence of God. (See the box, "Saint Anselm on the Existence of God.") The French theologian and philosopher Peter Abelard (1079–1142) used logic to reconcile apparent contradictions in the Scriptures and in the writings of the Church Fathers. A logical cast of mind is also clearly apparent behind the legal work of Gratian and behind the tightly organized biblical commentaries of the age.

We must not suppose that Anselm and Abelard were skeptics. Anselm's motto was "Faith seeking understanding." Logic was for him the handmaiden of divine truth. He would have agreed completely with Abelard, who said that "Faith has no merit with God when it is not the testimony of divine truth that leads us to it, but the evidence of human reason." For conservatives like Bernard of Clairvaux (1090–1153), as for Hildegard of Bingen (1098-1179), faith and immediate divine inspiration were primary. To them, logical approaches to divine truth were the height of arrogance. Hildegard, well educated, gifted musically, knowledgeable in medical matters, was perhaps the most profound psychological thinker of her age. More than anyone before her, Hildegard opened up for discussion the feminine aspects of divinity. She, like Bernard, believed that God was to be found deep within the human spirit, not in

Saint Anselm on the Existence of God

In his **Proslogion,** *a work on logic, Anselm attempted to prove the existence of God. He was contemplating the fool in Psalm 14 who said, "There is no God," and he wondered if it were possible for something to exist in the mind and not also in reality. The fool must have had the idea of God in mind in order to deny God's existence. And if God existed in the mind of even this fool, must not God exist in reality, too?*

Lord, . . . give me to understand, as far as you can explain, that you exist as we believe, and that you are what we believe. And indeed we believe that you are the greatest thing imaginable. Or is there some other nature? For the fool has said in his heart: "There is no God." But surely that very same fool, hearing what I say: "the greatest thing imaginable," understands what he hears, and what he understands is in his mind, even if he does not understand that it exists. For the existence of the thing in the mind, and understanding that the thing exists, are two different concepts. For when an artist plans what he is going to do, he has it in his mind, but he does not yet understand what he has not yet consummated. But when he has finished the painting, he has it in his mind and also understands that what he has done exists. Therefore, even the fool is convinced that there is something in the mind, than which nothing greater is imaginable, because he understands this, when he hears it, and whatever is understood is in the mind. And surely the greatest thing imaginable cannot be in the mind only, or that very thing, than which a greater cannot be conceived, is a thing than which a greater can be conceived. But that is impossible. There exists therefore, without question, something than which a greater is inconceivable, both in the mind and in reality.

Source: Putnam's Dark and Middle Ages Reader, ed. Harry E. Wedeck (New York: Capricorn, 1965), p. 220.

books full of academic wrangling. (See the box, "The Making of a Saint and Scholar: Hildegard of Bingen.")

The future lay with Anselm and Abelard, however. Anselm was the most gifted Christian thinker since Augustine. He wrote distinguished works on logic, and his theological treatise *Why God Became Man* (c. 1100) served for three hundred years as a philosophical and theological explanation of the incarnation of Christ, the central mystery of the Christian faith.

Peter Abelard was a more colorful figure. He argued rudely and violently with all his teachers, though in the end he was probably more intelligent than any of them. He rose to a keener understanding of Aristotle than anyone in centuries, and he developed a sharper sense of both the power and the limitations of language than anyone since the Greeks. He concerned himself with ethics, too, and was one of the first writers to see intention as more important than simple action.

Abelard seduced and then secretly married Heloise, one of his pupils and the daughter of an influential Paris churchman. Heloise's relatives castrated Abelard for his refusal to live openly with his wife. Abelard then arranged for Heloise to enter a convent, and he joined a monastic community, where he continued writing and teaching. The two carried on a voluminous correspondence that reveals Heloise herself as a first-rate philosophical thinker. Some of Abelard's more imaginative ideas earned him formal ecclesiastical condemnations in 1121 and 1140. He popularized the schools of Paris, however, and attracted to them promising scholars from all over Europe. Once patronage alone had promoted learning, but now equally important was the sheer excitement of the expanding intellectual horizon.

The Making of a Saint and Scholar: Hildegard of Bingen

Although Hildegard was a great scholar, her biographers stressed her native intelligence and divine inspiration more than her formal education.

When Henry IV was the king of the Holy Roman Empire, there lived in Rhenish Franconia a maiden lady well known because of her aristocratic background as well as her holiness. Her name was Hildegard. Although her parents were involved in the cares of the world and were richly blessed with temporal goods, they were thankful for the gifts of their creator, and they consecrated their daughter to the service of God. Even in her early years the young lady showed signs of virginity since she appeared to withhold consent to desires of the flesh. When she was hardly able to utter her first words, she made those around her understand through her words and signs that she was conscious of an exceptional gift of visions.

When she was eight years old, she entered the monastery on the mountain of St. Disibod in order to be buried with Christ and to rise with him to immortality. She was under the care of the pious, consecrated Jutta. It was this lady who carefully trained her in the virtues of humility and chastity, and superbly trained her in learning and singing the sacred songs of David. Except for simple instruction in the psalms, she received no other schooling, either in reading or in music. Still, she left behind not a small, but rather a significant legacy of writings. It is worthwhile to explain this by using her own words: "When I was twenty-four years and seven months old, I saw an extremely strong, sparkling, fiery light coming from the open heavens. It pierced my brain, my heart, and my breast through and through like a flame which did not burn; however, it warmed me. It heated me up very much like the sun warms an object on which it is pouring its rays. And suddenly I had an insight into the meaning and interpretation of the psalter, the Gospel, and the other Catholic writings of the Old and New Testaments, but not into the meaning of the sentence structure and the hyphenation; also I had no understanding of events and times."

Source: Gottfried and Theodoric, *The Life of the Holy Hildegard*, 1.1, trans. James McGrath (Collegeville, Minn.: The Liturgical Press, 1995), pp. 35–36.

The Rise of Vernacular Culture

"Clericus, id est litteratus" ("A cleric, that is a literate person") ran a medieval motto. To know French or to write English did not give one "letters," did not make one a member of the community of scholars. Yet in the period 900–1150 many writers, most of them unknown to us by name, began to write in their native tongues. Everywhere on the frontiers of Latin Europe people embraced Roman or Orthodox Christianity, confronted Greek or Latin letters, and developed settled patterns of political existence. These encounters unlocked vernacular muses whose achievement is one of the most important legacies of the age.

The epic poem *Beowulf* is the first classic of English literature. We do not know who wrote it or when it was written. Scholars formerly assigned it to the eighth century, but they now usually place it later, in the ninth or possibly in the tenth century. The story focuses on three great battles fought by the hero, Beowulf. The first two are against the monster Grendel and Grendel's mother, who have been harrying the kingdom of an old ally of Beowulf's family. The third is against a dragon. *Beowulf* is a poem of adventure and of heroism, of loyalty and of treachery. It treats lordship, friendship, and kinship. Themes of good and evil are sounded throughout. The poem is barely Christian but nevertheless deeply moral. It speaks, in a mature, vigorous, and moving language, to and for the heart of a warrior society.

Beowulf is the best-known Anglo-Saxon work but by no means the only one. One of the Viking attacks that led to the undoing of Ethelred II was commemorated in *The Battle of Maldon*. There also survive several volumes of elegiac and lyric poetry, mostly on religious themes. Also written in Anglo-Saxon were chronicles, legal materials and charters, and at least one large collection of homilies.

France produced a number of *chansons de gestes*, "songs of deeds," or celebrations of the great. The best is the *Song of Roland*, written around 1100. In 778 as Charlemagne's army was returning from Spain, Basques raided the baggage train and killed Count Roland. By 1100 this obscure event, long kept alive in oral traditions, had been transformed into a heroic struggle between Charlemagne and his retinue and an army of countless thousands of "paynim," who are crude caricatures of Muslims.

Like *Beowulf*, *Roland* is a story about loyalty and treachery, about bravery in the face of insuperable odds, about the kindness and generosity of leaders. They take us into a man's chivalric world. Females are all but absent. The two works do not show us personal hopes, fears, or motivations. Everything that we think should be private is made public. What pours forth is the communal ethos and the dominant values of the elite, male social group. Although *Beowulf* is lightly clothed in Christianity, *Roland* is thickly vested in the faith. These texts are eloquent testimony to the literary attainments of the "illiterate." And by choosing for discussion one English and one French example, we risk concealing that similar attainments could be chronicled for peoples and languages extending from Ireland to Russia.

The Romanesque Achievement

Romanesque, "in the Roman style," is a term coined in the nineteenth century to characterize the architecture and, to a lesser extent, the painting of the period from the end of Carolingian art to the full emergence of Gothic art in the late twelfth century. Today scholars define the Ro-

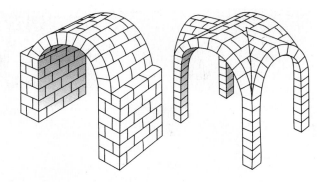

Figure 9.1 The Structure of Romanesque Architecture
The basic structural element of Romanesque architecture was the barrel vault, which, when two were joined at right angles, formed a groin vault. These vaults produced great height and strength but gave buildings a massive, fortresslike appearance. (*Source:* Anne Shaver-Crandell, *The Middle Ages* [Cambridge, England: Cambridge University Press, 1982], p. 4. Used by permission.)

manesque period as extending from roughly 1050 to 1150 and view the Romanesque style as transitional between Carolingian and Gothic.

At several places in Ottonian Germany a return of political stability led to the construction of churches. Ducal dynasties and women of the imperial family were among the most generous patrons. Pride in their Carolingian inheritance and their new imperial dignity led the Germans to a distinctive architectural style marked by very thick walls, alternating piers and columns in the nave, and galleries. As this architectural style spread all over Europe in the eleventh century, it produced true Romanesque, a style that differed from Roman and Carolingian styles mainly in the greater internal height and space made possible by vaulting (Figure 9.1). To the rectangular elegance of the classical basilica and the height of the Carolingian westworks (see page 296), Romanesque builders added a refined verticality.

Among the distinctive features of Romanesque churches were their wall paintings and frescoes, their sculpture, reliquaries, pulpits, and baptisteries—in short, their exuberant decoration and ornament. Europe's growing wealth and sophistication, and the self-conscious feelings of the church's aristocratic patrons, are very much in evidence. Especially in the south of France, the façades of Romanesque churches provided space for sculpture.

Saint Sernin, Toulouse This fortresslike church (ca. 1080–1120) was paid for by the offerings
of pilgrims on their way to shrines in Spain. Its massive walls and numerous colonnades are
typical of Romanesque architecture. The form of the building suggests the cross of Christ.
For the interior of a Romanesque church (Vezelay) see page 306. *(Jean Dieuzaid, Toulouse)*

The tympanum above doors, a space seen by all
who entered, was a favored location. Large-scale
sculpture had made a comeback after its almost total absence in the early Middle Ages.

A CLASH OF CULTURES:
THE FIRST CRUSADE

In 1096 an army of Christian knights who called
themselves pilgrims left Europe to liberate the
Holy Land from the Muslim "infidel." This was
the first of many Crusades, so called because the
warriors were *crucesignati,* "signed by the cross."

In the early tenth century, Europe was still reeling from a ceaseless round of attacks and from the
near collapse of its central governing structures. By
the late eleventh century, Europe would be an im-

pregnable fortress that had marshaled its resources
for an attack on the world around it. Europe's expanding population, economic dynamism, political
consolidation, and buoyant optimism made the
First Crusade possible. This crusade gathers together many of the themes of this chapter.

The Eastern Mediterranean Background

With the accession in 867 of the Macedonian dynasty in the person of Basil I, the Byzantine Empire experienced a period of vigorous, successful
rule that lasted until 1025. Although they fostered
impressive cultural achievements, carried out significant administrative reforms, and achieved the
kind of tight control of the church that had been so
elusive in the iconoclastic era (see page 279), the

Macedonians were primarily great soldiers. Along the Balkan frontier the Macedonian rulers managed to keep both the Bulgars and the incipient Russian state at bay while also neutralizing many smaller Slavic principalities. Basil II (r. 976–1025), called "the Bulgar Slayer," wore down Bulgaria in a series of relentless campaigns. In the west, the Macedonians maintained an effective diplomacy with Venice that permitted lucrative commercial opportunities in the Adriatic. In the east, the Macedonian rulers profited from the gradual dissolution of the Abbassid caliphate by expanding their frontier in Anatolia.

By contrast, throughout the ninth and tenth centuries the ability of the caliphs in Baghdad to control their vast empire declined precipitously. Egypt and North Africa escaped Baghdad's control almost completely, and religious strife between Sunni and Shi'ite Muslims further destabilized the Islamic state. Although Byzantium at first profited from this situation by expanding its holdings in Anatolia, in the long run the inability of the caliphate to control its frontiers led to serious challenges for the Byzantines.

In the years after Basil II's death in 1025, Byzantium suffered a long period of short reigns and abrupt changes in policy. Great aristocratic families in Anatolia slipped from imperial control. In the capital, factional squabbling swirled around the imperial court, and in the person of Patriarch Michael Cerularius (r. 1043–1058) the church sought to break out from two centuries of domination. When in 1054 Cerularius and Pope Leo IX quarreled so bitterly over ecclesiastical customs that they excommunicated each other, the traditionally cooperative papal-Byzantine religious diplomacy gave way to a deep schism between the Roman and Orthodox churches that still exists. Religious tensions were complicated when the bitterly anti-Byzantine Normans began creating their kingdom in southern Italy.

It was in these divisive circumstances that the Seljuk Turks appeared on the eastern frontier of Anatolia. Bands of Turks, peoples from central Asia, had been serving the caliphs as mercenaries since the ninth century. With new leaders at their head, and with both the caliphate and the empire distracted, the Turks broke into Anatolia with a vengeance. In 1071 at Manzikert a skirmish between Byzantine and Turkish soldiers turned into a rout in which Byzantium lost an army, an emperor, and the Macedonian reputation for military prowess.

Ever since the emergence of the Turkish threat in the early eleventh century, the Byzantines had been seeking mercenary help. The imperial defeat at Manzikert made their search more urgent and led to appeals to the West. Some troops were rounded up but not enough, so in 1095 Emperor Alexius Comnenus (r. 1081–1118) sent envoys to ask Pope Urban II to lend his support to an appeal for mercenary help against the Turks.

The Western Background

To most westerners the Turkish threat to Byzantium was a matter of little consequence. What mattered to them was Turkish attacks on pilgrims to Jerusalem. The popes saw in the plight of the Byzantines and of Western pilgrims some opportunities to manifest their leadership of the church. The papacy also wanted very much to heal the Roman-Orthodox rift. The popes placed a high value on aiding the Byzantines.

Moreover, the crusade was perfectly consonant with the ethos of the knights of western Europe. Knights were born and trained to fight. The vernacular literature of the age glorified war and warriors. But churchmen had for some years been advancing an ideal of Christian knighthood that stressed fighting God's enemies and aiding God's people. In the late tenth century there arose, first in France and then in many other places, peace movements called the "Peace of God" or the "Truce of God." These movements sought to prevent war in certain seasons, such as around Christmas and Easter, and on certain days of the week, chiefly Sundays. Peace movements also attempted to outlaw fighting near churches, protect noncombatants, and ameliorate the treatment of enemies and captives. Together the movements induced knights to fight non-Christians outside Europe.

As we noted earlier, the simultaneous rise in population and consolidation of family lineages was producing, especially in France, large numbers of restless, landless "young." These young knights viewed the crusade as an opportunity to do what they did best: fight. In addition to adventure, the crusade provided an opportunity for military glory that might procure advancement back home or a chance to acquire lands and titles far from Europe's highly competitive aristocratic milieu.

The "Pilgrimage" to Jerusalem

Pope Urban II received Alexius's envoys in 1095 and then left Italy for France. He was actually a fugitive because Henry IV controlled Rome. In November at Clermont, Urban delivered a rousing speech to a vast Christian assembly. He ignored the Eastern emperor's appeal for aid and instead promised salvation to soldiers who would enlist in a great struggle to free the Holy Land. The crowd acclaimed his words with a shout of "God wills it."

By 1096 four large armies, which eventually swelled to perhaps 100,000 men—mostly French knights with a smattering of troops from other parts of Europe—assembled under the leadership of the pope's legate. The forces were to rendezvous at the Byzantine capital of Constantinople, where they seem to have expected a cordial imperial welcome and all necessary assistance. Alexius, however, took a rather different view. A ragtag band of ordinary people preceding the Crusaders had torn through the Balkans like a plague of locusts. Then, the crusading armies themselves sorely taxed the imperial authorities who spent a lot of time and money arranging their passage from the frontier of Hungary to the gates of Constantinople. Finally, Alexius wanted mercenaries to fight Turks in Anatolia, not armed pilgrims intent on liberating Palestine.

After receiving nominal promises of loyalty and the return or donation of any lands captured, Alexius moved the Crusaders into Anatolia. Almost immediately the Latin army defeated a Turkish force, thus earning a valuable, though short-lived, reputation for invincibility. (See the box, "Encounters with the West: An Arab Perspective on the First Crusade.") The troops then entered Syria and laid siege to Antioch, which did not fall until 1098. At this point, rivalries among the Crusaders came into the open. One force went to the frontier of Armenia and carved out a principality. One of the ubiquitous Normans kept Antioch for himself. The main army pressed on to Jerusalem and, after a short but fierce siege, conquered it in July 1099. A Muslim historian described the scene:

In the Masjid [Mosque] al-Aqsa the Franks slaughtered more than 70,000 people, among them a large number of Imams and Muslim scholars, devout and ascetic men who had left their homelands to live lives of pious seclusion in the Holy Place. The Franks stripped the Dome of the Rock [the Mosque of Umar, near the al-Aqsa mosque] of more than forty silver candelabra, each of them weighing 3,600 drams [almost 40 pounds], and a great silver lamp weighing forty-four Syrian pounds, as well as a hundred and fifty smaller candelabra and more than twenty gold ones, and a great deal more booty.[2]

Godfrey of Bouillon, leader of the troops that had "liberated" Jerusalem, was named "Advocate of the Holy Sepulcher" and became ruler of the Christians in the East. He lived only a short time, however, and was replaced by his brother, Baldwin, as king of Jerusalem in 1100. The tiny "crusader states" created in the East were reinforced by soldiers and settlers in 1100 and 1101.

Judged on its own terms, the First Crusade was a success. The Holy Land was retaken from the infidel, and the pilgrim routes were passable once more. Entirely uncertain, however, were the prospects of the crusader states, the future course of Western relations with Byzantium, and the reaction of the Islamic world once it recovered from its initial shock.

SUMMARY

In 900, the survival of Europe's political, social, and intellectual order was in question. By 1150, Europe was prosperous, confident, and expansive.

Population rose steadily. People everywhere brought new land under cultivation, adopted better agricultural techniques, and improved transportation. Agricultural gains promoted urban growth as some people were freed from farming to undertake commercial and artisanal pursuits. Never before had Europe's economy improved so rapidly.

European society assumed between 900 and 1150 many of the distinctive features that it would bear until the modern period. A landed aristocracy competed with lesser nobles and with urban potentates for power and rank. In a militantly Christian society the clergy had great power and prestige, but it had to struggle continually with envious nobilities and governments in order to maintain its privileged status. Peasants gained ground economically and legally, but their position was always precarious.

Except in Germany, governments grew in power, scope, and sophistication. The Roman church expanded its governing structures. England, France, and Spain drew on both precedent

ENCOUNTERS WITH THE WEST

An Arab Perspective on the First Crusade

The Muslim historian Ibn al-Athir (1160–1233) provides in his **Perfect History** *several interesting perspectives on the First Crusade. The Baldwin with whom his account opens is not historical; or perhaps he is a composite of the many Baldwins then active in the West. Nevertheless, al-Athir's depiction of the crudeness of Roger of Sicily is interesting, as are his incidental revelations of Christian-Muslim cooperation and of divisions in the Islamic world.*

Baldwin, their king, assembled a great army and sent word to Roger [of Sicily] saying: "I have assembled a great army and now I am on my way to you, to use your bases for my conquest of the African coast. Thus you and I shall become neighbors." Roger called together his companions and consulted them about these proposals. "This will be a fine thing for them and for us!" they declared, "for by this means these lands will be converted to the Faith." At this Roger raised one leg and farted loudly, and swore that it was of more use than their advice. "Why?" "Because if this army comes here it will need quantities of provisions and fleets of ships to transport it to Africa, as well as reinforcements from my own troops. Then, if the Franks succeed in conquering this territory they will take it over and will need provisioning from Sicily. This will cost me my annual profit from the harvest. If they fail they will return here and be an embarrassment to me here in my own domain. As well as this Tamim [the emir of Tunisia in North Africa] will say that I

have broken faith with him and violated our treaty, and friendly relations and communications between us will be disrupted. As far as we are concerned, Africa is always there. When we are strong enough we will take it."

He summoned Baldwin's messenger and said to him: "If you have decided to make war on the Muslims your best course will be to free Jerusalem from their rule and thereby win great honour. I am bound by certain treaties and promises of allegiance with the rulers of Africa." So the Franks made ready to attack Syria.

Another story is that the Fatimids [local rulers] of Egypt were afraid when they saw the Seljuqids extending their empire through Syria as far as Gaza, until they reached the Egyptian border and Atziz [a general] invaded Egypt itself. They therefore sent to invite the Franks to invade Syria and so to protect Egypt from the Muslims [the Fatimids, although militantly Muslim, were regarded as heretics by other Muslims]. But God knows best.

Source: Francesco Gabrieli, *Arab Historians of the Crusades* (Berkeley: University of California Press, 1969), pp. 3–4.

and the innovative spirit of the present to create effective centralized institutions. In the Celtic, Scandinavian, and Slavic worlds dynamic new states emerged. Indeed, there were striking similarities among all the increasingly numerous states of post-Carolingian Europe.

Cultural horizons expanded, too. There were more and better schools than at any time since the Carolingian Renaissance. The curriculum moved beyond an elementary focus on grammar to logic.

Vernacular languages began taking their place alongside Latin as sophisticated tools for the expression of complex stories and ideas. Romanesque art represented richness, growth, and novelty.

But everything was fragile. No one in 1150 could have predicted whether the European economy would go on expanding. Cities and their residents might well have taken the lead in social and political life away from kings and landed nobles. Latin letters might have yielded their place to

French or English. The death of Bernard of Clairvaux in 1153 might have signaled the end of traditional monasticism or an opening for new forms of religious expression. Political crises in England, France, Germany, Sicily, Spain, Ireland, Poland, Russia, and Byzantium in the 1150s might have brought a return of political fragmentation, or they might have strengthened the centralizing tendencies in evidence since about 1000. The years after 1150 would be creative, but in ways quite different from those between 900 and 1150.

NOTES

1. Rodulfus Glaber, *Historiarum Libri Quinque*, 3.4.13, ed. and trans. John France (Oxford, England: Oxford University Press, 1989), pp. 114–116 (slightly adapted).
2. From the Gesta Francorum, trans. August C. Krey, in *The First Crusade* (Princeton, N.J.: Princeton University Press, 1921), p. 257 (slightly adapted).

SUGGESTED READING

General Surveys

Bartlett, Robert. *The Making of Europe: Conquest, Colonization and Cultural Change, 950–1350.* 1993. An engaging account of the expansion and "Europeanization" of Europe.

Brooke, Christopher. *Europe in the Central Middle Ages.* 1975. This somewhat dated book remains the best introduction in English to a period that has been heavily studied by European scholars.

Fichtenau, Heinrich. *Living in the Tenth Century: Mentalities and Social Orders.* Translated by Patrick Geary. 1991. Wide-ranging, readable, fascinating, this is the best introduction to the post-Carolingian world.

Le Goff, Jacques. *Medieval Civilization.* Translated by Julia Barrow. 1988. Le Goff, one of France's leading and most original medievalists, offers a comprehensive look at medieval civilization in all its aspects. Fascinating and challenging.

Southern, Richard W. *The Making of the Middle Ages.* 1953. Since its appearance this elegant, brilliant, stimulating book has become a classic. It evokes the mentality, society, and politics of Europe from the tenth century to the twelfth.

Society and Economy

Bisson, Thomas, ed. *Cultures of Power: Lordship, Status, and Process in Twelfth-Century Europe.* 1995. The thirteen sparkling essays in this book cover much of Europe and attempt to explain how power was wielded in an essentially "stateless" society.

Bloch, Marc. *Feudal Society.* Translated by L. A. Manyon. 2 vols. 1964. This is the best-known book by one of this century's greatest historians. Bloch seeks to explain the total history of the post-Carolingian world in terms of the ideals and practices of feudalism.

Duby, Georges. *The Three Orders: Feudal Society Imagined.* Translated by Arthur Goldhammer. 1980. A remarkable exploration of the dissemination and influence of social ideas.

———. *The Early Growth of the European Economy: Warriors and Peasants from the Seventh to the Twelfth Century.* Translated by Howard B. Clarke. 1974. Especially strong on the workings of rural society, this is another introduction to medieval economic history and to the thought of an important, original historian.

Fossier, Robert. *Peasant Life in the Medieval West.* Translated by Juliet Vale. 1988. This is the best introduction to "those who work." Although emphasizing France, the book contributes usefully to an understanding of wider European phenomena.

Ganshof, François-Louis. *Feudalism.* 2d ed. Translated by Philip Grierson. 1964. For almost fifty years, Ganshof's clear, concise, readable book has been the standard introduction to the essential personal and proprietary aspects of the feudal bond.

Herlihy, David. *Medieval Households.* 1985. Stretching from Late Antiquity to the fifteenth century, this engaging book by a master historian treats almost every aspect of the family in its social, domestic, and economic settings.

———. *Opera Muliebria: Women and Work in Medieval Europe.* 1990. This brief and nontechnical book covers most of Europe in the thousand years after about 500. It is full of interesting and sometimes surprising information.

Poly, Jean-Pierre, and Eric Bournazel. *The Feudal Transformation, 900–1200.* Translated by Caroline Higgett. 1991. This extraordinarily important book presents a synthesis of all the best French thinking in the past generation or two on social and institutional development, mainly in France.

Reynolds, Susan. *Fiefs and Vassals.* 1994. Brilliant, controversial, and difficult, this massive book challenges many long-standing ideas about feudalism.

———. *Kingdoms and Communities in Western Europe, 900–1300.* 1984. After exploring the kinds of legal notions that guided community building, this lively book turns to actual communities, ranging from the parish to the kingdom.

National and Regional Histories

Angold, Michael. *The Byzantine Empire, 1025–1204.* 1984. Dense and detailed, this book will reward the serious reader.

Chibnall, Marjorie. *Anglo-Norman England, 1066–1166.* 1986. Focusing on government, institutions, and society, this book is a remarkably effective introduction to a tumultuous century of English history.

Douglas, David C. *William the Conqueror.* 1967. Long, detailed, and challenging, Douglas's book remains the standard against which all biographies of William will be judged.

Duby, Georges. *Medieval France.* 1991. The author of this original and entertaining book is France's leading medievalist. This book is an especially good introduction to his many distinctive ideas about the shaping of French society in the eleventh and twelfth centuries.

Dunbabin, Jean. *France in the Making, 843–1180.* 1985. Readable and interesting, this book describes the making of France's territorial principalities and then shows how a centralized kingdom slowly superseded them.

Fine, John V. A. *The Early Medieval Balkans: A Critical Survey from the Sixth to the Late Twelfth Century.* 1983. Learned and comprehensive, this book does what its title says.

Fletcher, Richard. *The Quest for El Cid.* 1990. As entertaining and engaging as a detective novel, Fletcher's book seeks both to recapture the historical Cid and to explain literary and historical accounts about him.

Fuhrmann, Horst. *Germany in the High Middle Ages, c. 1050–1200.* Translated by Timothy Reuter. 1986. Beautifully written and translated, this book presents the thought of Germany's leading medievalist.

Gerber, Jane S. *The Jews of Spain: A History of the Sephardic Experience.* 1992. Interesting, lively, and comprehensive—though stronger on cultural than on political developments—this book presents a history that is too often lost in accounts of Christian and Muslim Spain.

Hyde, J. K. *Society and Politics in Medieval Italy: The Evolution of the Civil Life, 1000–1350.* 1973. More difficult than Waley (see below), this book is a sophisticated introduction to the social complexity and institutional creativity of Italian towns.

Martin, Janet. *Medieval Russia, 980-1584.* 1995. Nicely written and very current, this is the place to start on Russian history.

Matthew, Donald. *The Norman Kingdom of Sicily.* 1992. This interesting book treats the fascinating personalities and remarkable historical circumstances that made Norman south Italy so distinctive.

Reilly, Bernard F. *The Medieval Spains.* 1993. A concise, effective account of Christian and Muslim Spain.

Reuter, Timothy. *Germany in the Early Middle Ages, 800–1056.* 1991. This welcome, albeit dense, book covers comprehensively a period never before well treated in English.

Sedlar, Jean W. *East Central Europe in the Middle Ages.* 1994. Although difficult and confusingly organized, this book is as good an introduction as exists to central and eastern Europe.

Stafford, Pauline. *Unification and Conquest: A Political and Social History of England in the Tenth and Eleventh Centuries.* 1989. The subtitle of this well-written book accurately describes its scope and contents.

Waley, Daniel. *The Italian City-Republics.* 3d ed. 1988. This balanced, nicely written, readily understood book continues to be the best introduction to the incredibly complicated world of Italian urban politics.

Religion and the Church

Blumenthal, Uta-Renate. *The Investiture Controversy: Church and Monarchy from the Ninth to the Twelfth Century.* 1988. Brief, readable, and remarkably comprehensive, this book is the best introduction in any language to the great upheaval.

Constable, Giles. *The Reformation of the Twelfth Century.* 1996. Long awaited, this is the culmination of life's work for America's most distinguished medievalist.

Head, Thomas, and Richard Landes, eds. *The Peace of God: Social Violence and Religious Response in France Around the Year 1000.* 1992. The dozen essays in this book admirably survey religious thought and feeling among the French laity.

Lawrence, C. H. *Medieval Monasticism: Forms of Religious Life in Western Europe in the Middle Ages.* 2d ed. 1989. The chapters in this comprehensive, readable book treating Cluny, eleventh-century monastic innovations, and the Cistercians are relevant to this chapter.

Leyser, Henrietta. *Hermits and the New Monasticism: A Study of Religious Communities in Western Europe, 1000–1150.* 1984. Brief, lively, and informative, this book explains the sources and history of the many religious movements that spread throughout medieval Europe, emphasizing the eremitic ideal.

Newman, Barbara. *Sister of Wisdom: St. Hildegard's Theology of the Feminine.* 1987. Interesting and readable, this path-breaking study not only introduces Hildegard but also opens up wholly new ways of thinking about twelfth-century spiritual culture.

Southern, Richard W. *Saint Anselm: A Portrait in a Landscape.* 1990. The distillation of a life's work by a master historian, this wonderful book introduces not only Anselm but also the intellectual and spiritual life of his world.

Art and Architecture

Demus, Otto. *Romanesque Wall Painting.* 1970. Although the commentary in this book is a little challenging, the pictures are numerous and superb.

Kubach, Hans Erich. *Romanesque Architecture.* 1988. This is a standard introduction to a vast subject by an acknowledged authority. Comprehensive and accessible to nonspecialists.

Zarnecki, George. *Romanesque Art.* 1971. This clearly written, well-illustrated book introduces the reader to the rich, complex world of the Romanesque.

THE MEDIEVAL CASTLE

Storybook castles—think of Camelot—figure prominently in almost everyone's idea of the Middle Ages, but the reality was different. Medieval castles were generally small, homely, stark, and uncomfortable. Though not beautiful and romantic, castles were still important.

Castles represent a stage in the history of fortifications. Castles proper were private, residential, and military. A consideration of these three elements will place the castle in historical context and illustrate what historians learn from the impressive ruins that dot the landscape of Europe and the crusader states.

The medieval castle, at its rise in the tenth century, was a private creation. Powerful aristocrats erected castles as their principal dwellings and as a means to secure and extend their political influence. From his castle a lord could dominate a region. The castle also sheltered the lord's immediate dependents temporarily in the event of an attack, and his military retainers more or less permanently.

By the late twelfth and early thirteenth centuries, states, beginning with the French and English monarchies, began to monopolize the possession of castles. Cerreg Cennen, below, was built by a Welsh prince, Lord Rhys (d. 1197), and then seized from his descendants by Edward I of England. Château d'Angers, opposite, was erected by the counts of Anjou but became a garrison of the French monarchy in the thirteenth century. The French word *château* (from the Latin *castellum*) means "great house," signifying the castle's residential purpose. In later centuries, the castle (as château) retained its private and residential nature but lost its military character.

Castles of the tenth, eleventh, and twelfth centuries symbolize well the extreme localization and privatization of power then characterizing Europe. Not surprisingly, as European governments

Cerreg Cennen Castle, Wales *(Michael Holford)*

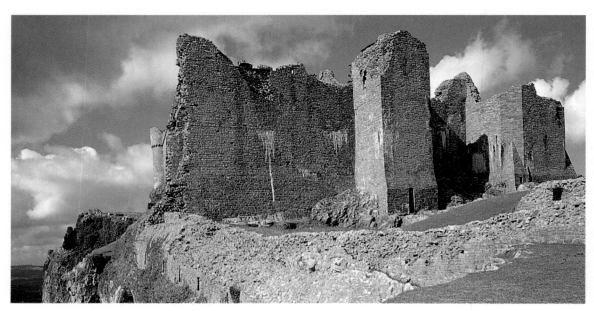

grew stronger in the twelfth century, they suppressed private castles as military entities. Thereafter, as in Roman times, fortresses served essentially public and military purposes. They had resident garrisons, but their purpose was not to be the private residence of a landed lord.

Castles could take many forms. From 900 to 1200 the "Motte and Bailey" form was the most common. A lord commanded his dependents to dig a circular ditch and to heap the dirt into a mound (the motte). The ditch, together with a wooden palisade—a fencelike wall—was the bailey. A wooden tower was often built atop the mound. Sometimes there was an elaborate series of mounds, ditches, and wooden walls—look at the picture of the Polish Motte and Bailey castle on page 338—but usually these structures were quite simple.

As siege techniques improved (catapults could hurl projectiles weighing 600 pounds) the wooden building(s) of the bailey began to be replaced by stone. By 1150 or 1200 stone towers (*donjons*, from the Latin *dominium* for "lordship") began to form only the inside portion—the "keep"—of a more complicated structure consisting of walls, towers, and gates. It was not unusual for walls to be 75 or 100 feet high. Because of the growing power of bombarding engines, castle walls had to be thickened often. Towers built at 40- or 50-foot intervals projected beyond the walls so that defenders armed with bows and arrows could fire at attackers along the length of a castle wall. Look at the spacing of the towers in the castles pictured here. Initially towers were square or rectangular, but defenders discovered that round towers—compare those of Cerreg Cennen and Angers—were preferable because projectiles were likely to glance off them.

People needed to enter and leave castles for both hostile and peaceful purposes. Thus castles had gate towers, usually with two gates, one on the outside and one on the inside. Intricate systems of winches, cranks, and counterweights regulated the raising and lowering of the gates. Speedy operation was essential. Some castles had small "sally-ports" from which soldiers could make a rapid dash to attack a besieging enemy.

When possible, lords sited their castles on cliffs, because fewer sides could be attacked and a garrison of modest size could defend the remain-

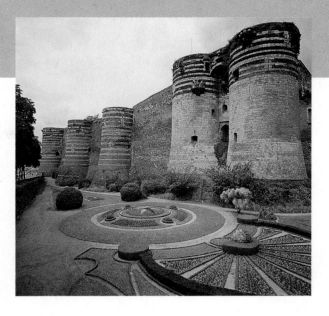

Château d'Angers, France (*Michael Holford*)

ing walls. Cerreg Cennen stands 300 feet above a gorge, as you can see from the left side of the picture. The bases of walls or towers were sometimes strengthened by embankments that sloped gently outward. Embankments made the castle walls hard to climb. You can see the embankments at Angers clearly in the photo.

Many things can be learned from the castle: the presence of numerous small castles across the countryside would reveal an extreme decentralization of power in a given place and time—remains of several hundred have been found in France alone; and in England in 1100, there was a castle every 10 miles. The existence of a few large, strategically sited castles would point to greater central control. Careful mapping of the known locations of castles can tell historians a great deal about the structure of social and political relationships. Castles both contributed and responded to developments in military technology such as more powerful catapults. Stone castles proliferated as Europe grew wealthier and as quarrying technology improved. Castles grew larger as monarchies rather than private individuals built them. Like cathedrals, large, state-funded castles tended to be built by professionals rather than by local laborers.

Both fortifications and magnificent dwellings have existed in Western civilization for millennia. The castle, however, met the needs of a politically dominant warrior-aristocracy for a private residence with military significance. &

CHAPTER 10

Medieval Civilization at Its Height, ca. 1150–1300

B ecause he hated war and violence, Saint Francis of Assisi, the most charismatic religious figure of the High Middle Ages, set out in 1219 for Egypt, where a crusading army was encamped.

He aimed to convert Malik al-Kamil, the sultan of Egypt, to Catholicism and thereby put an end to the Crusades. Captured by Muslim soldiers, Francis demanded to be taken before their leader. Here is an almost contemporary version of the encounter between the saint and the sultan:

> When they had dragged him before the sultan, the cruel beast was turned to gentleness by the expression on the face of the man of God, so that for several days he listened most attentively to his preaching to them the faith of Christ. At length, fearing lest some of his people should be converted to the Lord by the power of his words, and so go over to the Christian army, he ordered him, with all reverence and every safeguard, to return to our camp, saying to him at the last: "Pray for me that God may reveal to me that law and that faith which is to him most pleasing."[1]

The most remarkable aspect of this story is the sheer audacity of Francis. That a poor, humble man would think that he alone could, by power of persuasion, convert the mighty sultan of Egypt is astonishing. Yet audacious is in many ways a perfect description of many endeavors in late twelfth- and thirteenth-century Europe.

The papacy reached the high point of its institutional and ideological power, brought down kings and emperors, and yet was humiliated in a devastating conflict with France. The German Empire rebuilt its fortunes on the basis of an attempt to use Italy to control Germany, but ultimately the attempt failed. French and English kings refined their institutions as never before but emptied their treasuries in military adventures and infuriated their nobilities by constant attempts to neutralize them.

Saint Francis amid scenes from his life. Italian altarpiece (1235), one of the first dedicated to a saint.

354

CASPIAN SEA

ABBASID CALIPHATE

ARABIA

GEORGIA

SULTANATE OF SALADIN AND THE AYYUBIDS

Antioch

TRIPOLI

Jerusalem

LESSER ARMENIA

EMPIRE OF TREBIZOND

Trebizond

KINGDOM OF RUM

EMPIRE OF NICAEA

LATIN EMPIRE

Black Sea

Constantinople

R U S S I A

Kiev

BULGARIA

EPIRUS

SERBIA

HUNGARY

ESTONIA

LITHUANIA

POLAND

Cracow

BOHEMIA

Danube

Vienna

Mediterranean Sea

Melfi

KINGDOM OF THE TWO SICILIES

Assisi

Naples

Palermo

NORWAY

SWEDEN

DENMARK

Baltic Sea

Elbe

SAXONY

HOLY

Brunswick

ROMAN

EMPIRE

Venice

Bologna

BAVARIA

Florence

Siena

TUSCANY

Rome

PAPAL STATES

Corsica

Sardinia

Antwerp

Ghent

Bruges

Liège

Cologne

Rhine

Worms

Milan

LOMBARDY

Legnano

Pisa

A L P S

Constance

SWABIA

CHAMPAGNE

BURGUNDY

North Sea

SCOTLAND

Nottingham

London

IRELAND

WALES

Canterbury

ENGLAND

Thames

Bouvines

Paris

NORMANDY

Orléans

ANJOU

Loire

FRANCE

AQUITAINE

Lyon

Marseille

Rhône

Albi

Bordeaux

Garonne

Toulouse

NAVARRE

ARAGON

Las Navas de Tolosa

VALENCIA

DOMINIONS OF THE ALMOHADES

CASTILE

LEON

PORTUGAL

Cordoba

GRANADA

ATLANTIC OCEAN

X Major battles

— Boundary of the Holy Roman Empire

400 Mi.

400 Km.

200

200

0

0

Spanish rulers turned from wars of reconquest to struggles for political consolidation. Italian cities sought, with varying degrees of success, to attain a stability equal to their prosperity. Impressive political achievements in Europe's most easterly regions were cut short by the Mongols, the "Devil's Horsemen."

Towns continued to grow during this period. Urban institutions grew more numerous and sophisticated but began to limit opportunities for foreigners, women, and Jews. Trade routes continued to expand but shifted focus more than once. Agricultural innovation had fueled Europe's expansion before 1150, but urban and commercial development became decisive after that date. Particularly in the towns of high medieval Europe, social and religious movements, larger in scale than any seen previously, added to the dynamism and tension of the age.

Another innovation, the university, regularized and professionalized intellectual life. The early twelfth century's interest in logic grew into a rigorous and formal style of reasoning, Scholasticism. Inspired by Aristotle, theologians defined religious concepts and practices in terms drawn from antique and Arab science. One thinker, Thomas Aquinas, dreamed that he could explicate the totality of divine and human wisdom. Yet the end of the thirteenth century witnessed fierce intellectual struggles and a major crisis between church and state.

Gothic architecture is one of the most familiar achievements of the period. Viewed as a series of meditations on geometric themes, the architecture accords well with the rationalism of Scholasticism. Viewed as an attempt to break all the earthly bonds, to spring to the heavens, the architecture calls to mind the intense religious stirrings of the age. Latin continued to be the language of intellectual life and of law, but the vernaculars claimed a growing share of cultural life. The late twelfth century witnessed the emergence of the romance, and the late thirteenth saw the exquisite poetry of Dante.

In thinking about the period from 1150 to 1300, it is well to keep in mind the scene of Francis

Map 10.1 Europe, ca. 1220 By the early thirteenth century the European states that would exist into modern times were clearly visible, although each would continue to undergo changes. To gain a sense of the evolution of Europe, compare this map with Maps 6.1, 7.3, and 8.3.

before the sultan. It reminds us of people's lofty aspirations in high medieval Europe.

THE EMPIRE AND THE PAPACY

The century between 1152, when Frederick I ascended the German throne, and 1250, when Frederick II died, was decisive for both Germany and the papacy. Under its new Staufen dynasty, Germany at first recovered from its early-twelfth-century malaise and then collapsed as its rulers became more interested in Italy than in Germany itself. The papacy battled the German kings on a wide range of issues and had the satisfaction of seeing an excommunicated Frederick II die without a successor. Meanwhile, unprecedented legal and institutional growth led to the elaboration of the papal monarchy.

Revival of the Empire, 1152–1190

After years of near anarchy, many parties in Germany desired a return to stability. In an act of genuine statesmanship, Conrad III in 1152 designated as his successor the powerful Duke Frederick of Swabia instead of his own young son. The dukes concurred. Frederick I (r. 1152–1190), known as Barbarossa ("red-bearded"), achieved a remarkable restoration of the fortunes of the German and imperial crowns. Frederick—strong, athletic, handsome, chivalrous, and intelligent—was the grandest ruler of his generation.

Frederick controlled extensive territories in Swabia and, through his beloved wife Beatrice, in Burgundy (Map 10.1). He was related to the family that controlled Bavaria and Saxony. The German bishops had begun to regret the liberation they had achieved at Worms in 1122 (see page 326), because ducal domination more than compensated for freedom from royal interference. Frederick usually had the support of the most important members of the clergy.

Inside Germany, Frederick pursued one basic policy. He supported the dukes in their attempts to achieve peace and control in their own domains, as long as they agreed to swear homage and fealty to him. Frederick attempted to create a network of vassalic bonds throughout Germany. Vassalic bonds were no substitute for solid institutional control, but they were a start. The best evidence for this is that in 1180 Frederick was able to crush Duke Henry "the Lion" of Saxony, his most formidable opponent in Germany. Henry had failed to answer a royal summons to serve in the army, and Frederick ordered him to court to answer for this failure to live up to the most basic of a vassal's duties. A century earlier, when Henry IV had tried to establish his authority on firm foundations, shifting coalitions of dukes, bishops, peasants, townsmen, and popes opposed him. This time, such parties either stood aside or actively supported Frederick.

Frederick did face problems in Germany, however. He made little headway in getting control of his vassals' vassals. When Frederick brought down a rebellious subject, such as Henry the Lion, he could not routinely claim that subject's fiefs for himself, as often happened in France and England. He had to grant those fiefs to others as the price of their support. Having been elected himself, Frederick had only partial success in getting the German nobles to concede early recognition to his son as his successor.

It was in Italy that Frederick's regime nearly came to ruin. After three years spent gaining control of Germany, Frederick went to Italy in 1155 to help the pope crush a communal movement in Rome. As a reward for his trouble, the pope crowned Frederick emperor. In 1158, Frederick summoned representatives of the major northern and central Italian cities to demand full recognition of his regalian, or ruler's, rights. Even a partial listing of these rights shows the marked difference between the powers of a feudal king and of an emperor. Regalian rights included, in theory, military service; control of roads, ports and waterways, tolls, minting, fines, vacant fiefs, and confiscated properties; appointment of magistrates; construction of palaces; and control of mines, fisheries, and saltworks. Frederick's plans included an extension to Germany of this type of imperial control.

The Italians had no desire to be dominated anew by their northern neighbors, and the popes feared Frederick's growing power in Italy. For nearly twenty years Frederick and the papacy carried on a running battle. In 1157 a papal representative infuriated Frederick by telling him that the empire was a "benefice" held of the pope. Although the word could have a range of meanings, Frederick chose to interpret it as "fief." Recent popes had occasionally received vassals' oaths

from kings of Norway, Poland, Bohemia, Bulgaria, England, parts of Spain, Sicily, and Jerusalem. Papal writings frequently used metaphors to describe the relationship between secular and ecclesiastical powers. According to one, pope and emperor were like sun and moon—that is, the emperor derived his legitimacy from the pope. Frederick rejected the idea that his imperial dignity came from Rome. He believed that his imperial authority came directly from God and that his actual office was an inheritance from the ancient Romans and from Charlemagne.

More serious for Frederick was the formation in 1167 of the Lombard League, an association of Italian towns under Milan's leadership that opposed the emperor at every turn. In 1176, Frederick led an army to Italy, but he suffered a devastating defeat at Legnano (see Map 10.1). In 1183 the Peace of Constance finally resolved the most serious outstanding issues. Frederick and the papacy were reconciled when the emperor gave up his support for an antipope—a pope elected and acknowledged by Frederick and his supporters—and renounced direct control of Rome. The Lombard towns acknowledged a vague imperial suzerainty and paid some fees in recognition but were left largely independent in the conduct of their own affairs.

Despite his troubles in Italy, Frederick was a ruler of real stature. In German legend he is believed to be sleeping under a mountain, to awaken when Germany needs him. Frederick's accidental drowning in Turkey on the Third Crusade was a blow to Germany.

Imperial Authority and the Papal Challenge, 1190–1272

Henry VI (r. 1190–1197), Frederick's son, was promptly accepted as king in Germany, so he headed for Sicily, whose Norman heiress, Constance, he had married some years before. Since the 950s, German rulers had sought in Italy both prestige and resources to apply north of the Alps. But because the Peace of Constance had made Lombardy and Rome difficult to dominate, it made sense for Henry VI to attempt to make Sicily a base for his Italian policy.

It took Henry several years to gain recognition of his authority in Sicily. Then, before the pope

Innocent III In this wall painting, the pope wears a tiara, the triple crown that symbolizes his universal episcopate, supremacy of jurisdiction, and temporal rule. Though the greatest of popes, Innocent was also a friend of monks. This painting comes from the Holy Cave at Subiaco near Rome, where Benedict began his monastic life. *(Scala/Art Resource, NY)*

would crown him emperor, he had to give assurances that he would not try to control both northern and southern Italy. To buy time for his schemes in Italy, Henry gave the German princes virtual free rein. Suddenly, in 1197, Henry died without having consolidated imperial rule in Italy or royal rule in Germany.

The legitimate heir, Frederick II, was a 3-year-old whose mother, Constance of Sicily, had no standing in Germany and considerable opposition in Sicily from those who thought that she had sold out to the Germans. Shortly before her own death in 1198, Constance made her son the ward of Pope Innocent III (r. 1198–1216). In Germany, counsels were divided. One party favored Staufen claims and wished to avoid anarchy. Another party preferred ducal rights over Staufen power.

Once again dynastic instability threatened Germany, affording Innocent an unprecedented opportunity to intervene. The pope wished both to arbitrate the imperial office and to limit German power in Italy. In Germany, Frederick's uncle, Duke Philip of Swabia, planned to support his nephew's claim to the throne and to continue the family policy of

strong interests in Italy. Innocent had grave reservations about him. Meanwhile, Otto of Brunswick (son of Henry the Lion) emerged as leader of the anti-Staufen party and was crowned king in 1198. In return for papal recognition and imperial coronation, Otto was prepared to confine himself to Germany. In 1208, Philip, who had responded to Otto's challenge by having himself crowned king in 1198, was murdered. Accordingly, in 1209, Otto was crowned emperor in Rome, but he immediately invaded Sicily, hoping to secure its riches for himself. Innocent responded to this betrayal by excommunicating Otto in 1211 and by crowning his ward, Frederick, as emperor in 1212. (See the box, "Innocent III on His Rights and Powers.")

Innocent got Frederick II (r. 1212–1250) to swear that he would not attempt to unite Italy and Germany. In 1220, Frederick issued the Statute in Favor of the Princes, which almost totally abandoned regalian rights north of the Alps. Born in Sicily, Frederick loved the warm climate and cosmopolitan society of the south. All he wanted from the north was a vague recognition of his legitimacy. Frederick's actions stood the old Italian

Innocent III on His Rights and Powers

In this authoritative papal pronouncement from 1202, Innocent explains why he believes the pope has a right and duty to decide who is fit to be emperor. It would be instructive to compare this document with the box, "Issues in the Investiture Controversy" on page 325.

Among other things certain princes urge this objection particularly, that our venerable brother the bishop of Palestrina, legate of the apostolic see, acted as either an elector [of the emperor] or as a judge of the election. If as an elector, he put his sickle in a stranger's harvest and, by intervening in the election, detracted from the dignity of the princes; if as a judge, he seems to have proceeded incorrectly since one of the parties was absent. . . . We indeed by virtue of our office of apostolic service owe justice to each man and, just as we do not want our justice to be usurped by others, so too we do not want to claim for ourselves the rights of princes. We do indeed acknowledge, as we should, that the princes have by ancient custom the right and power to elect a king who is afterwards to be promoted emperor; and especially so since this right and power came to them from the apostolic see which transferred the Roman empire from the Greeks to the Germans in the person of the great Charles. But the princes should acknowledge, and indeed they do acknowledge, that the right and authority to examine the person elected as king, who is to be promoted to the imperial dignity, belong to us who anoint, consecrate and crown him; for it is regularly and generally observed that the examination of a person belongs to the one to whom the laying-on of hands belongs. If the princes elected as king a sacrilegious man or an excommunicate, a tyrant, a fool or a heretic, and that not just by divided vote but unanimously, ought we to anoint, consecrate and crown such a man? Of course not. Therefore, . . . we maintain that our legate the bishop of Palestrina . . . did not act as either an elector . . . or as a judge when he approved King Otto and rejected Duke Philip. And so he in no way usurped the right of the princes or acted against it. . . . Rather he exercised the office of one who declared that the king was personally worthy and the duke personally unworthy to obtain the imperial dignity, not considering so much the zeal of the electors as the merits of those elected.

Source: Brian Tierney, *The Crisis of Church and State, 1050–1300* (Englewood Cliffs, N.J.: Prentice-Hall, 1964), pp. 133–134.

policy of the German rulers since the tenth century on its head. Now an essentially Italian ruler had a German policy.

Frederick's Constitutions of Melfi, based on Norman precedents and issued for Sicily and southern Italy in 1231, shows what he aimed to do everywhere. Determined to unite almost all of Italy, Frederick planned to institute imperial vicars in all major regions. These were salaried officials appointed and removed at the emperor's will. Under them were to be staffs of experienced officers. Wandering inspectors would supervise the whole system. Unity and uniformity were Frederick's goals. Until death in 1250, Frederick was hounded by opposition from popes, who excommunicated him several times, and from urban Italians, who resented his challenges to their local autonomy.

Frederick has sometimes been seen as a very modern man: secular, rational, calculating. Actually, he was a man of his time. He was devoted to both astrology and the cult of saints. He wondered about the immortality of the soul but was no more skeptical than others. His bureaucratic reforms were based on Norman, papal, and Byzantine precedents. Jews, Arabs, and a troupe of dancing girls could be found at his court, for he lived in the most culturally diverse place in Europe, but he remained conventionally Christian.

Frederick's death created different problems in Italy and in Germany. His surviving legitimate son, Conrad IV, died in 1254 ignored by all parties. Manfred (d. 1268), one of Frederick's many illegitimate sons, tried to continue his father's Italian policies but could not overcome Italian and papal opposition. In Germany the period from 1250 to 1273 is called the "Great Interregnum" (the time "between the reigns"). For years the princes could not agree on the promotion of one of their own number until in 1273 they elected Rudolf of Habsburg king of Germany. He failed initially to establish a dynasty, although his family would be prominent in European politics until 1918. The powerful German state of the Saxons, and the revived state of the Staufen, had vanished.

Medieval Germany's failure was in some ways more apparent than real. It has never been easy to say just where or what Germany is. Through most of its history, Germany has been both an idea and a confederation of peoples and lands. Even today, German speakers and German lands are scattered all over the map of central Europe. Germany's medieval failure was really a failure of monarchy. Frederick Barbarossa built up his monarchy in ways very similar to those being used in France and England. What destroyed the medieval German monarchy were the Italian and papal entanglements and the inability of the German royal dynasties to produce heirs.

The Papal Monarchy

The papacy's ability to arbitrate the imperial succession and to break the Staufen rested on two foundations: ideology and institutions. We can summarize the ideological foundation, discussed here and in preceding chapters, in this way: Clerical and governmental elites elaborated a tripartite theory of social organization that assigned everyone a role in the construction of a Christian commonwealth. All legitimate power and authority in that society came from God. Battles raged over whether kings and emperors (on the one hand) or the priestly hierarchy with the pope at its head (on the other hand) stood nearer to God in a great chain of power. The legacy of the investiture controversy, of the Crusades, and of generations of spiritual reform had given the lead to the priestly power.

The second foundation was institutional. The twelfth-century popes turned resolutely to the refinement of their central government, which grew as never before. The ability of the Roman church to coerce secular rulers and to control local churches reached a high point. The canon law of the church surpassed all other contemporary legal systems in sophistication.

The papacy was an elective monarchy, but electoral procedures were a persistent problem. In 1059 an election decree had attempted to confine electoral participation to the cardinals but had not specified how many votes were necessary for election. The twelfth and thirteenth centuries were thus filled with contested elections. In 1179 a council decreed that a two-thirds majority was required for election. One problem was solved, but another arose.

Between 1241 and 1305, the papacy was vacant for almost ten years altogether, and once there was no pope for nearly three years. Groups of cardinals sometimes refused to show up for elections, or left Rome if events proceeded in a direction they disliked, or could not even get to Rome because of political struggles. In 1271 a conclave (shutting the cardinals in a room until they elected a pope) was used for the first time.

Who were the popes? What were they like? Most of them had been cardinals and had long experience in the government of the church. Many of the twelfth- and thirteenth-century popes were lawyers, which may explain, in part, their dedication to institutional and legal reforms. Not a single pope from this period has been canonized as a saint. One Englishman was elected; the rest were Roman, Italian, or French. Most were noblemen.

In Rome, the pope presided over the *curia*, the papal court. By the late twelfth century, the cardinals, who were increasingly drawn from all over Europe, were the key officers in that court. They sat with the pope in consistory, a small quasi-legislative meeting, and, again with the concurrence of the pope, issued decretals, or binding decrees. The cardinals headed the major branches of the papal administration and served as papal legates. In the thirteenth century these princes of the church began to wear their distinctive red hats.

The curia presided over both financial and judicial institutions. Revenues came from the papal lands in Italy, from diverse fees from all over Europe, and from the pious offerings of pilgrims. The judicial institutions administered the rulings of the papal government, heard appeals for dispensations from the ordinary operations of canon law (such as requests for permission to marry from two persons who were closely related), and heard appeals against decisions made by local ecclesiastical courts.

The hearing of appeals from lower courts points to another growing area of activity by the papal government: control of the church throughout Europe. The pope and cardinals had numerous means to work their will. Beginning in 1123, and then again in 1179, 1215, 1245, and 1274, the popes summoned a series of Lateran Councils, the largest since the councils of Late Antiquity. Now the great prelates of Europe met on a regular basis. Legates, often cardinals, were regarded as plenipotentiaries—that is, they could act as if they were the pope himself. "Papal provisions" enabled the pope to appoint bishops, and sometimes abbots and cathedral canons, all over Europe. In the past, such officers had been elected locally and merely confirmed by Rome. Rome demanded more fees, partly for economic reasons and partly as symbols of central papal authority. Popes promoted the continuous revision and updating of the canon law of the church and shaped that law to emphasize papal prerogatives.

The Roman church also sharpened the tools that it used to make its will felt. Since the early days of Christianity, churchmen could excommunicate a member of the faithful for some grievous offense. Separation from the sacraments of the church was always a serious punishment. In the Christian Middle Ages, its severity increased because the excommunicated person was forbidden *all* social intercourse. Excommunication thus could be politically, socially, and economically disastrous. Another tool was the interdict—a decree that might be directed at a person but more often fell on a region. The interdict brought to a halt the celebration of most sacraments. Its aim was to generate a popular outcry for a particular outcome or remedy.

Gregory IX (r. 1227–1241) sought to bring a measure of order and legality to the process of identifying and punishing heretics. Just as governments of all kinds had begun to employ wandering inquisitors to investigate a variety of issues, he began sending out teams of carefully trained inquisitors to take testimony according to precisely

defined rules. The work of these inquisitors laid the foundation for the later courts of inquisition.

In medieval society a person's religious faith was not a private matter of conscience but a public affair. The aim of the inquisitors was to reconcile the wayward, not to punish or execute them. The church could not administer corporal punishment or shed blood, so anyone found guilty in an inquisitorial proceeding was handed over to a secular court. Executions for heresy were comparatively rare. Of 945 cases heard in the south of France in 1246, not one resulted in a death penalty; ten years later, about 21 of 306 accused heretics were executed.

This ever more bureaucratic and intrusive church related to the laity—to its members—in a variety of ways. The line between the clergy and the laity was drawn more sharply than ever before. Members of the clergy could not be notaries, secular lawyers, or doctors. Lay people were denied any right to preach, to expound on the Scriptures, or to stand in judgment of any offense that a cleric might commit. In the writings of thirteenth-century ecclesiastics, the word *church* usually referred to the institutional entity, to the clergy, and not, as before, to the body of all believers. Believers were expected to submit to the clergy in all respects, which effective institutions enforced.

Ideology and institutions were important, but personalities mattered, too. Innocent III (r. 1198–1216), for example, was the most powerful man ever to hold the papal office. He came from a minor Italian noble family, received early training in theology and law, and entered the papal administration while in his twenties. His entire life was dedicated to promoting the legal prerogatives of the papacy and the moral improvement of Christian society. As a young man Innocent wrote a book, *On the Contempt of the World*, in which he expressed his hope for a life of peace and private contemplation. As an older man he hurled legal thunderbolts at the greatest public figures of the day.

THE EVOLUTION OF CENTRAL GOVERNMENTS

Just as the succession of Frederick I in 1152 was a harbinger of change for Germany, so too the decade of the 1150s opened new opportunities all over Europe. Five problems faced in varying degrees by every medieval government can serve to organize our discussion of the successes and failures of the major states of Europe: (1) Frontier problems: In no part of Europe was the exact geographic shape of the eventual state evident. (2) The expanding role of central governments: One constant of the age was a growth in the size, sophistication, and effectiveness of institutions. (3) Relations between rulers and their people: Growing government power often meant that traditional nobilities lost power while obscure men rose to prominence in the service of kings. New representative institutions gave power and voice either to people previously without them or to the formerly powerful in new ways. (4) Relations with the church: This was an old medieval problem, as noted in our discussion of the empire, but the growing competence of governments along with local traditions posed it in new ways. (5) Economic issues: Governments found themselves needing more resources at a time when the great expansion of the eleventh and twelfth centuries began to slow.

France

France in 1154 had a king, Louis VII (r. 1137–1180), who had built on the solid work of his predecessors but faced a single vassal, Henry II of England, who controlled more of France than he did. Welsh humorist Walter Map (1140–1209) provides this assessment of the scene:

> The emperor of Byzantium and the king of Sicily may boast about their gold and silken cloth, but they have no men who can do more than talk, men incapable of war. The Roman emperor or, as they say, the emperor of the Germans, has men apt in arms and warlike horses, but no gold, silk or any other wealth. . . .The king of England lacks nothing and possesses everything, men, horses, gold, silk, jewels, fruits and wild beasts. And we in France have nothing except bread, wine and joy.[2]

This passage reveals much about twelfth-century life and attitudes but somewhat underestimates the resources of the French.

Some of the "joy" that French people felt arose from their increasing domination of European culture. The First Crusade was widely seen as a French enterprise. The greatest twelfth-century monastic order, the Cistercian, was French. There were French quarters in almost all large towns out-

THE DEVELOPMENT OF STATES, 1150–1300	
1154–1189	Reign of Henry II of England
1155	Imperial coronation of Frederick Barbarossa
1167	Formation of the Lombard League
1170	Murder of Thomas Becket
1176	Battle of Legnano
1183	Peace of Constance
1198–1216	Pontificate of Innocent III
1204	Fourth Crusade
1208	Albigensian Crusade
1212	Imperial coronation of Frederick II
1212	Battle of Las Navas de Tolosa
1214	Battle of Bouvines
1215	Magna Carta
1215	Fourth Lateran Council
1226–1270	Reign of Saint Louis (Louis IX)
1272–1307	Reign of Edward I of England
1285–1314	Reign of Philip IV (the Fair)
1294–1303	Pontificate of Boniface VIII
1295	First meeting of Parliament

side France. The aristocracy of England conversed in French. French was the premier literary language after Latin, and French manners, style, and elegance were admired and emulated everywhere. The architecture that we know as Gothic was then called "the French style."

Although these resources were real, they were also evanescent. Louis VII and his son and successor, Philip II (r. 1180–1223)—usually called Philip Augustus—had sturdier bases on which to build, however. They carried on the traditional Capetian policy of controlling the centrally located royal demesne. They continued to associate their sons in their reigns in order to train the heir for rule and stifle any electoral pretensions among the nobility. The "Most Christian Kings of France," as their titles designated them, supported the church and

Twelfth-Century Paris This drawing was done by Sebastian Munster in 1550 from older sources. Note *B*, Sainte-Chapelle, built by Saint Louis to hold the "Crown of Thorns," and *D*, the Cathedral of Notre-Dame (see page 383). At the upper right, notice the colleges *(collegia)*, which became the University of Paris (see page 379). *(Courtesy, Jean-Claude Paissel)*

were supported by it in turn. Louis VII began the policy of granting both tangible and moral support to the emerging towns of France.

Louis and Philip even managed to turn the Angevin colossus to their own advantage. They became masters at fomenting trouble in Henry's vast continental holdings, usually by setting the Angevin sons against their father and against one another. France's greatest gains came at the expense of King John of England.

John (r. 1199–1216), son and successor to Henry II, was a vassal of the king of France for all of his father's vast continental holdings. He imprudently ran off with the fiancée of a French nobleman, who sued him in the court of Philip Augustus, feudal lord to them both. Philip summoned John to answer for his conduct. When John refused to answer the summons, Philip declared him "contumacious" and his fiefs "escheat" (meaning that

the fiefs were to revert to their lord). War ensued, and Philip won a resounding victory in 1204.

A decade later Philip confirmed his paramount position by defeating at Bouvines a joint attack on his kingdom by John and Otto IV of Germany, who were both trying to revive their sagging fortunes (see Map 10.1). One could say that the almost fastidious application of feudal laws had brought the king of France to an unmatched position in his own realm. One could also say that more than two centuries of patient, largely nonfeudal, Capetian policy had permitted the defeat of John of England and the seizure of a large piece of France.

French royal revenues at least doubled between 1180 and 1220. In this, France and Germany differed greatly. The French kings developed substantial revenues internally. When Philip seized the Angevin lands, he did not give them to anyone as fiefs. To govern his new possessions, Philip extended, with some modifications, the old institutions of the royal demesne. Estates on the demesne had been governed by minor noblemen called *provosts,* but after 1204 bailiffs became the overseers of the vastly expanded demesne. Bailiffs were non-noble officers, often trained in law, appointed for fixed terms. They had no property or family connections in the territories where they served, and at the end of their term they had to give an account of their work.

Philip was succeeded briefly by his son, Louis VIII, and then for more than four decades by Louis IX, known as "Saint Louis." Right away it is worth remarking that the prestige of the Capetian dynasty was enough to produce a saint. But if the Capetians had one eye on heaven, they had the other one firmly fixed on France.

Louis VIII (r. 1223–1226) hit on a means of simultaneously governing the old Angevin lands and providing for junior members of the royal family. He divided up some of the former Angevin lands into *apanages*—coherent blocks of land assigned to junior members of the royal family. In this way he kept land out of the hands of the nobility and provided resources and responsibility to persons who might otherwise have spent their time plotting against the king.

Louis IX (r. 1226–1270) believed that the king's highest duty was the promotion of peace and justice. He revived the Carolingian practice of sending wandering officials around the kingdom to check on the work of the bailiffs. He also issued *ordonnances,* the first systematic royal edicts of general application since the Carolingian capitularies. Saint Louis abolished serfdom and suppressed private warfare on royal lands. His reforms made people all over France look to the king rather than to local notables. (See the box, "A Contemporary View of Saint Louis.")

Before the reign of Louis VIII the French monarchy confined its activities to the regions north of the Loire River. There were temptations in the south. By the year 1200 the Cathar heresy (see page 373) was attracting attention from religious orders who rushed south to preach against the threat, from French noblemen who went adventuring where the royal reach did not yet extend, and from the papacy, who preached a crusade. But the Crown refused to be distracted until

it had defeated John and digested the Angevin lands that had been swallowed in one gulp. Louis VIII and Louis IX, however, sensing political opportunities and religious duties, finally entered the fray. By the 1250s the Albigensians—as the Cathars are usually called (the name derives from Albi, a Cathar stronghold; see Map 10.1)—were beaten. More important, the region of Langue d'Oc (see Map 9.2) was taken over by the Crown and submitted to royal administration. The Albigensian wars also served the kings of France as a kind of safety valve by draining off some of the land-lust and violence of the nobility.

Saint Louis was succeeded by his son, Philip III (r. 1270–1285), and then by his famous grandson, Philip IV (r. 1285–1314), "the Fair." Philip IV began a series of dangerous military and diplomatic gambles to extend his power into Flanders and Gascony.

Flanders was rich and had always been under the authority of the German Empire, which by now lay in shambles. It looked ripe for plucking. Gascony was a major wine-producing region and the last significant part of France not under royal control; treaties had left it under English authority. Philip's quarrels with England's Edward I (r. 1272–1307), involving issues ranging from the obligations of vassals to fishing rights to trading concessions, were costly to both kings and secured a permanent advantage for neither. They disrupted cross-Channel trade, however, and the Flemish depended on that trade for English wool to supply their cloth industry. Thus, the Flemish rose against Philip in 1302 and humiliated him by defeating the army he sent against them.

Philip's constant need for money to pay for his wars engendered resentment among various groups in France. He even resorted to seizing the property of the Jews of France and to repudiating his debts to Italian bankers. He died broke in 1314, but there was no reason to think that the impressive gains won by three centuries of Capetian policy would be lost. The kings of France were powerful and respected figures. France itself was paramount in Europe. Paris was evolving into a real capital with commercial interests, government offices, the royal court, and a university (see page 379). Despite the Crown's debt and noble resentment, prospects certainly looked brighter in 1314 than they had seemed in 1154.

A Contemporary View of Saint Louis

Jean, Sire de Joinville (ca. 1224–1319), accompanied Louis IX on crusade, served as a royal official, and gave evidence in the case for Louis's canonization. In 1309, at the request of Joan of Navarre, wife of Philip IV, he wrote the late king's **Life,** *from which this excerpt is taken.*

God, in whom he put his trust, preserved him ever from his infancy to the very last. As for his soul, God preserved it through the pious instructions of his mother [Blanche of Castile], who taught him to believe in God and to love Him, and place about him none but ministers of religion. And she made him, while he was yet a child, attend to all his prayers and to listen to all the sermons on saints' days. He remembered that his mother used sometimes to tell him that she would rather he were dead than that he should commit a deadly sin.

Sore need of God's help had he in his youth, for his mother, who came of Spain, had neither friends nor relatives in all the realm of France. Because the barons of France saw that the king was an infant, and the queen, his mother, a foreigner, they made the count of Boulogne, the king's uncle, their chief lord and they looked up to him. After the king was crowned, some of the barons asked the queen to bestow upon them large domains and because she would not the barons assembled at Corbie [north of Paris]. Neither the king nor his mother dared to return to Paris until the citizens of Paris came, with arms in their hands, to escort them. The road was filled with people, some with arms some not, and all cried to our Lord to give him a long and happy life, and to defend him from his enemies. . . .

Many a time it happened that in the summer he would go down and sit in the wood at Vincennes [just east of Paris] with his back to an oak, and make us take seats around him. And all who had complaints to make came to him without hindrance. Then he asked them himself: "Is there anyone here who has a cause?" Those who had a cause stood up, and he would say: "Silence all, and you shall be dispatched one after another."

Source: Frederic Austin Ogg, *A Source Book of Medieval History* (New York: American Book Co., 1908), pp. 313–314, 323 (slightly adapted).

England

Henry II (r. 1154–1189) promptly made it clear that he meant to rule England and also to retain control of his vast continental inheritances. Henry also introduced English rule in Ireland and reestablished at least a measure of English authority over Wales and Scotland. Within England, Henry made major changes in the scope and administration of English law.

The Continent proved to be a constant irritant for Henry. In anticipation of the later Capetian apanage system, Henry sought to provide from the Angevin lands individual holdings for his four sons. The boys, however, abetted by their mother, Eleanor of Aquitaine (see page 329), and by Louis VII and Philip II of France, plotted against their father and against one another. Henry never was able to unify law, institutions, economic practices, or culture in his far-flung "Angevin Empire." Although he was first a French prince, and although he spent more time in France than in England, his greatest contributions were in his island kingdom.

By returning to the practices of the Norman kings and by innovating, Henry fashioned the institutions that turned England into the best-governed kingdom in Europe. Like his contemporaries, he used men of low or modest means but of great intelligence and careful training to staff government offices. He supported, and usually was supported by, towns and the church in an effort to circumvent the nobility and to expand centers of royal influence. He also kept a sharp eye out for possible sources of revenue.

Henry expanded both the size and the competence of the English government. In the tradition of the Domesday investigators, he carried out two great inquests, one of knight's service and one of sheriffs. The former resulted in a detailed listing of the fiefs of England and of what was owed to the king by them. The latter resulted in the replacement of many of England's sheriffs, the key royal officers in the shires, with men who were more efficient and loyal to the king. It was from about this time that the Robin Hood stories arose, with their evocation of the evil, heartless sheriff of Nottingham. In fact, the sheriffs were neither more nor less evil than other men. They were just effective in doing the king's business.

Henry used judicial institutions to expand royal power and the central government. His objectives were to bring as much judicial activity as possible into royal courts and to diminish the role of the nobles. Through a series of enactments, Henry made it possible for almost anyone to secure a writ that would move a case into a royal court. Henry also developed rules for handling disputes over the possession of land, one of the commonest areas of legal activity. To handle this business, Henry expanded the system of permanent royal courts and attracted more judicial activity to Westminster, just outside London and the usual site of the royal court. Since not everyone could go to Westminster, Henry expanded the use of justices in eyre, who went four times a year through every shire to hear cases.

The justice dispensed in Henry's courts was swift and fair, and his courts were popular. Those who felt abused by powerful noble neighbors discovered that by having recourse to royal courts they could get real justice. With royal courts consistently applying a single law in all their sittings, a common law began to grow up throughout the country. No other realm in Europe advanced so far so early on the road to legal unification.

Henry II, ever tidy of mind, desired to bring "criminous clerks"—that is, members of the clergy who had committed crimes—into the royal courts. This policy provoked a howl of protest from Thomas Becket (c. 1118–1170), the archbishop of Canterbury. Thomas served loyally as Henry's chancellor—chief royal official—from 1155 to 1162, when the king instigated his election to the see of Canterbury in hopes of using his friend to secure tighter control over the English church. As archbishop, however, Thomas held to the traditional church teaching that only members of the clergy could judge other clerics. When in 1164 Henry passed regulations on criminous clerks with which Becket could not agree, the archbishop fled to France. Intense international efforts produced a reconciliation between Thomas and Henry in 1170. When he finally returned to England, Thomas was murdered before the altar of his cathedral by four knights who thought they were doing the bidding of their king, who was furious because Becket would not forgive some English bishops who had compromised with Henry. Becket was soon canonized as a saint, and Henry had to back down on criminous clerks. The church was still powerful enough to defeat any attempt to diminish its prerogatives.

In 1189, Henry's charismatic, crusading son, Richard "the Lionheart," became king and proved—in an ironic way—the strength of the foundations that his father had laid. Richard (r. 1189–1199) resided less than ten months in England during his ten-year reign. Mainly, he spent his time in France struggling with Philip II and going on the Third Crusade. Back in England the system put into place by Henry II functioned well in Richard's absence.

When John (r. 1199–1216) succeeded his brother Richard, he inherited some problems and created many of his own. Many English nobles were angry at having been circumvented by Henry II. The royal treasury was empty. A king's ransom, literally, had been raised to redeem Richard, who had been kidnapped on his way home from the Third Crusade.

John might have stabilized his position, but his loss of Normandy in 1204 (see page 362) was a financial and moral disaster. Still, English institutions were flexible enough that John went right back to work raising money and managed to forge an alliance with Otto IV of Germany. The two rulers planned to attack and divide France. As we have seen, Philip Augustus defeated his enemies at Bouvines in 1214, and John was humiliated yet again.

Like his father before him, John had severe run-ins with the church. To the intense displeasure of the clergy, John routinely abused episcopal vacancies. When a bishop died, John often withheld permission to proceed to an election and kept the income of the diocese. What really got him in trouble, though, was his refusal to accept Pope Innocent's candidate for the archbishopric of Canterbury. The pope placed England under interdict and excommunicated John. Despite widespread anger and embarrassment, John might have let this quarrel go on indefinitely, but he decided to capitulate in order to win support for the ultimately unsuccessful Bouvines campaign.

In June 1215 some English barons, supported by townspeople and members of the clergy, forced John to sign the Magna Carta, the "Great Charter" (the "great" referring to its large size). Its sixty-three clauses spelled out in traditional ways royal prerogatives vis-à-vis vassals, towns, the church, and courts of law. The barons were trying to get the king to admit that he had to obey certain rules, not to destroy the monarchy. The Magna Carta's central premise was that everyone, even the king, was under the law.

Under John's son, Henry III (r. 1216–1272), and grandson, Edward I (r. 1272–1307), certain problems recurred in England. The king wished to choose his own advisers, but the barons insisted on having some influence in the choices. The king demanded a wide array of taxes and revenues, but barons and townspeople withheld monies except on their explicit approval. The king sought money for an aggressive foreign policy, but people were reluctant to pay. It was clear to everyone that continuous rebellion served the long-term interests of no party. However, until 1295 there was no mechanism for the arbitration of disputes.

As early as 1236 a meeting of the English royal council was called a *Parliament,* from a French word that means "talking together." Down to 1265 and 1295, when the first Parliaments in the modern sense met, many different kinds of meetings bore this name. By 1295, Edward I needed money for his wars with Philip IV and with the Welsh and Scots. He also needed a secure means of gaining assent to his statutes, enactments that bear comparison with the ordonnances of Louis IX. The king therefore summoned the barons, bishops and abbots, the knights of the shires, and the burgesses (leading citizens of the towns) to a meeting.

As yet this Parliament had no defined role, no procedures, no fixed membership, and no set times for meetings. Moreover, it was viewed differently by its various attendees. The king saw it as something of a rubber stamp. The barons viewed it as a means of controlling royal excess. The knights and townsmen thought they had gained a means of making permanent the loose alliance that they had enjoyed with the Crown since the twelfth century. Even though no one realized it at the time, the political quarrels of the thirteenth century had resulted in the creation of an institution that would eventually become dominant in the governance of England.

Edward needed political cooperation in order to pursue his numerous military ventures. We have already encountered his struggles with France. Closer to home, Edward intervened repeatedly in the Celtic world. In 1277 he invaded Wales with the intention of totally subduing the Welsh. He built immense castles whose ruins are impressive today. Edward also made his son the Prince of Wales—still the title of the heir to the British throne. Between 1100 and 1260, England and Scotland went to war four times, and Edward resolved in the 1280s to put an end to this struggle by annexing Scotland. The Scots, however, rallied to the standard of Robert Bruce (r. 1306–1328), a dashing knight who was, ironically, of Norman extraction. Robert managed to free Scotland for centuries.

Like Philip IV, Edward I died nearly penniless in 1307. But his family was securely in power, and his country was effectively governed. In Parliament the English had created a potentially national institution. The common law, too, was a bond that Englishmen shared. Although the aristocracy still spoke French, virtually everyone in the country could speak English. Edward's England had lost many of Henry's overseas holdings and had created war zones in the Celtic world but was reasonably stable and well governed at home.

Spain

By around 1150 the Reconquista in Spain had stalled, not to resume until the early thirteenth century, when Pope Innocent III stirred up crusading zeal. The pope lent encouragement to clerics and nobles in Spain who wished to reopen hostilities against the Muslims. In 1212 a combined Castilian-Aragonese army won a decisive victory at Las Navas de Tolosa, south of Toledo (see Map

Alfonso X "the Wise" The Spanish king, depicted here in a thirteenth-century manuscript from Spain, is judging his Muslim and Christian subjects. Alfonso's reputation for impartiality was important in his culturally diverse realm. *(Biblioteca Nacional, Madrid)*

9.3). The victory of Las Navas de Tolosa was a great turning point in Spanish history. The outcome of the Reconquista, which did not conclude until the fifteenth century, was never again in doubt.

In the thirteenth century Spain produced kings of genius, especially James I of Aragon (r. 1213–1276) and Ferdinand III (r. 1217–1252) and Alfonso X (r. 1252–1284) of Castile. These rulers were pious men, genuinely inspired by the ideal of the Crusades, zealous in the promotion of the church. They were also hard-headed rulers. James turned Aragon-Catalonia into the greatest naval power of the western Mediterranean and a formidable economic power, too. Ferdinand and Alfonso derived great prestige from their successful wars. Those wars also provided a flow of booty and a supply of lands to reward the Castilian nobles who spent their energy on the frontier, rather than using it to attack the king. Strong central institutions were created. Increasingly professional officers were employed in key government posts,

and wandering officials were sent out from the court to inspect the work of local officials. Alfonso issued a major law book, the *Siete Partidas*, for the whole of Castile. These laws were based on Roman law and emphasized royal power. The Cortes, a representative assembly made up primarily of urban notables, began forging an alliance between the king and the towns. Spain was not united in the thirteenth century, but it had evolved into four coherent blocks: a small and impotent Muslim region in Valencia and Granada and three vibrant kingdoms centered on Portugal, Castile, and Aragon.

Italy

When Frederick Barbarossa crossed the Alps in 1155 (see page 355), the future of northern and central Italy hung in the balance. If his attempt to introduce tight control had succeeded, the subsequent development of the Italian communes might have been very different. But Frederick's defeat at Legnano in 1176 and the Peace of Constance in 1183 left the Italian cities free to continue their distinctive political evolution.

Although each Italian commune constituted an entity unto itself, a fairly coherent evolution is evident. By the late twelfth century, the consular communes were still governed by oligarchies of men whose wealth and power came from land, trade, and industry. Merchant interests, however, gained in prominence at the expense of the landed groups among whom the communal movement had arisen, and ordinary workers began to clamor for participation. The communes were becoming increasingly volatile and violent.

One solution to this potential crisis was the introduction of the *podestà*, a sort of city manager chosen by the local oligarchy. The podestà often came from the outside, served for a set period (usually six months or a year), and underwent a careful scrutiny at the conclusion of his term. He was expected to be competent not only at ordinary administration but also at military leadership, so that he could police the city as well as defend it. He brought with him a group of seasoned officials as subordinates. Normally, he could not be a property owner in the town, marry into local society, or dine privately with any citizen. By the middle of the thirteenth century, some podestàs were becoming virtual professionals. One man, for example, was elected sixteen times in nine cities over a period of thirty-four years, four times in Bologna alone. It is ironic that the Italian cities that had been feudal or episcopal principalities before the rise of the communes passed through a republican phase of wider and wider political participation, only to wind up under single rulers again.

We have already discussed the changing fortunes of the papal states in central Italy, but a few developments in the south are worthy of note. Once the popes had defeated Frederick II, they decided to look for more pliant allies in the south. In 1266 the papacy called in Charles of Anjou (r. 1226–1285) as king of Sicily and Naples. Charles, a brother of Saint Louis, had received a Capetian apanage in France but longed for greater adventures. He had gone on crusade and had also helped the papacy in its wars against the Staufen. Charles enjoyed the confidence of the popes, but as an outsider he had little support among any of the diverse ethnic groups of his kingdom. When he moved the capital from Palermo to Naples, he pro-

voked a rebellion in Sicily in 1282. By 1284 he had to flee. To stop Charles from regaining his power, some Sicilians turned to the increasingly powerful Aragonese for assistance. For a long time southern Italy was contested between French and Spanish interests, successors to earlier combatants: Byzantines, Muslims, Normans, and Germans.

Russia

In 1150 Russia's future was hard to predict. From their capital at Kiev, Russia's rulers had made some headway against both lawless nobles and the raids of frontier peoples. A flourishing church, deeply influenced by Byzantium, contributed to Russian unity. Commerce prospered.

How Russia's development might have proceeded is anybody's guess, but in the early thirteenth century Russia faced a grave new threat from the Mongols. These were a loose coalition of pastoral nomads from Mongolia (lands east of the Caspian Sea and north of China) and Turkic soldiers. The charismatic leader Jenghiz Khan (1154–1227) turned the Mongols into an invincible fighting force and eventually built an empire reaching from China's frontier to Germany's. (See the box, "Encounters with the West: William of Rubruck Reports on the Mongols.")

In 1221 the Mongols attacked Suzdal and in 1240 sacked Kiev (see Map 9.5). Jenghiz Khan died in 1227, and his successors divided his vast empire into several khanates. One of these, called the "Golden Horde" (from the splendid tent in which the khan presided), dominated Russia until the fifteenth century. The Mongols granted the Russians considerable local autonomy, but they demanded heavy taxes and occasionally carried out brutal raids to remind the Russians who was in control. Taxes fell most heavily on Russian peasants, who saw their status decline while that of Western peasants was rising. The Mongols also dominated trade and produced a weakening of both urbanization and the merchant classes.

A lasting consequence of the Mongol attack was the definitive shift of Russia's political center of gravity from Kiev and Suzdal to Moscow, a town far to the north and blanketed by deep forests, which afforded some protection from the Mongols. The Germans and Swedes profited from the Mongol attack by sacking Novgorod, Russia's remaining trading center. Prince Alexander Nev-

> ≈ **ENCOUNTERS WITH THE WEST** ≈
>
> # William of Rubruck Reports on the Mongols
>
> *Mongol attacks deep into eastern Europe prompted the papacy to try to convert the Mongols to Catholicism in hopes of using them in a grand crusade against the Muslims. Several Western clerics traveled to the Mongols to try to convert their khan. Here are extracts from the report of William of Rubruck, a Franciscan missionary, who visited the khan Baatu, the grandson of Jenghiz Khan and the founder of the Golden Horde, between 1253 and 1255. He was particularly struck by domestic arrangements. It is interesting to compare William's impressions with the boxes, "Two Views of the Huns" (page 246) and "Furnishings of a Welsh Household" (page 319), which are also concerned with daily life.*
>
> The dwelling in which they sleep has as its base a circle of interlaced sticks, and is made of the same material; these sticks converge into a little circle at the top and from this a neck juts up like a chimney; they cover it with white felt . . . the felt around the top they decorate with lovely and varied paintings. Before the doorway they also hang felt worked in multicolored designs. . . . The married women make for themselves really beautiful carts. . . . A wealthy Mongol may well have a hundred such carts with chests. Baatu has twenty-six wives and each of these has a large house . . . belonging to each house a good two hundred carts. When they pitch their houses the wife places her dwelling at the extreme west end and after her the others according to their rank, so that the last wife will be at the far east end, and there will be the space of a stone's throw between the establishment of one wife and another. . . . The camp of a rich Mongol will look like a large town and yet there will be very few men in it. One woman will drive twenty or thirty carts, for the country is flat. They tie together the carts, which are drawn by oxen or camels, one after the other, and the woman will sit on the front one driving the ox. . . . When they have pitched their houses with the door facing south, they arrange the master's couch at the northern end. The women's place is always on the east side . . . and the men's place is on the west side. On entering the house the men would by no means hang up their quivers in the women's section. Over the head of the master there is always an idol like a doll or little image of felt which they call the master's brother, and a similar one over the head of the mistress, and this they call the mistress's brother. . . . In the winter they make an excellent drink from rice, millet, wheat, and honey . . . in the summer they do not bother about anything but *cosmos* [fermented mare's milk]. *Cosmos* is always to be found inside the house before the entrance door, and near it stands a musician with his instruments. Our lutes and viols I did not see but many other instruments that are not known among us. When the master begins to drink, then one of his attendants cries out in a loud voice "Ha!" and the musician strikes his instrument. When it is a big feast they are holding they all clap their hands and also dance to the sound of the instrument, the men before the master and the women before the mistress. . . . Then they drink all around, the men and the women, and sometimes they vie with each other in drinking in a really disgusting and gluttonous manner. . . .
>
> *Source:* Christopher Dawson, ed., *The Mongol Mission* (New York: Sheed and Ward, 1953), pp. 93–98, 103–104, passim.

sky (1220–1263), whose father had been prince of Novgorod, rallied the Russians, defeated the Germans and Swedes, and made a treaty with the Mongols. Years later, from their base in the Grand Duchy of Moscow, Alexander's successors liberated Russia from the Mongols. Centuries of Mongol domination initiated Russia's subsequently ambivalent relations with both Europe and Asia.

Table 10.1 Population Increases in Italian Cities, 1200–1300

City	1200	1300	Percentage of increase
Florence	15,000	96,000	+640%
Siena	19,000	52,000	+274%
Pisa	20,000	38,000	+190%

Source: Adapted from Malcolm Barber, *The Two Cities: Medieval Europe, 1050–1320* (London: Routledge, 1992), p. 270.

ECONOMIC LIFE

In 1150 the European economy was in full expansion. By 1300 that expansion had begun to moderate and, in some areas, to reverse. Decline, however, is not the central theme of economic life in this period. It is more accurate to speak of innovation and adaptation. Urban dynamism supplanted rural creativity. Economic institutions in Europe grew more complex, interdependent, and sophisticated. People began to think in new ways about economic behavior.

The Roles of Cities and Towns

The key population trend was not overall growth but reorganization. Although the vast majority of people still lived in the country, cities were growing as never before. Table 10.1 shows the growth of three Italian cities. Such growth also occurred in cities in Flanders, such as Bruges and Ghent, and in Paris, London, and other cities that were evolving into national capitals. Ghent expanded its city walls five times between 1160 and 1300, a sure sign of growth even in the absence of population figures. Similar forces were operating in the countryside, too. In 1100 there were about 11 fortified villages outside Florence, but by 1200 there were 205.

Cities were becoming centers for many activities. Governments, which required larger and larger staffs of trained personnel, settled in towns, even when kings continued to ride about the countryside or go off on crusade. The towns of Italy and Flanders, though not national capitals, ruled over extensive hinterlands. Schools and eventually universities (see pages 379–380) were urban institutions. Mercantile, industrial, and legal organizations were based in towns. Ecclesiastical organization was always urban based. Towns began to compete with royal and aristocratic courts as literary centers, and cathedrals, the great buildings of the age, were exclusively urban.

One distinctive urban phenomenon was the rise of guilds. In 1200, for example, Paris had one guild of merchants and four or five craft or trade associations. By 1270 the city had 101 craft or trade guilds, and by 1292 the number had risen to 130.

The guilds had many functions. Mainly they were meant to regulate standards of production, to fix prices, and to control membership in their respective trades. But as towns grew larger and more impersonal, these associations of people engaged in similar occupations fostered a sense of belonging, a feeling of community. Members tended to live in the same areas and to worship together in a parish church. Growing wealth in general, coupled with fierce local pride, produced building competitions whose results are still visible in the huge neighborhood churches that survive in most European towns. The guilds indulged in elaborate festivals and celebrations, which sometimes turned into drunken debauches that hardly pleased the saints in whose honor they were held. The guilds were also mutual assurance societies. They saw to the funeral expenses of members and provided for widows and orphans.

The guilds played important roles in the political life of the towns. The older merchant guilds counted in their membership the urban elite. The newer craft guilds incorporated the workers in the industries that were growing up in cities. The former group had erected the first communes and reserved communal magistracies and council spots for itself. From the late twelfth century, masters in the craft guilds, or their elected representatives, began to demand positions on the city councils. Guilds contributed simultaneously to stability and to tension in cities. They controlled ever more tightly the economic, social, and political life of their members. That was stabilizing. But the old merchant elites shared power grudgingly with even the most prominent of the workers. That made for trouble.

The guilds had a damaging impact on women. As more economic activity came under the umbrella of the guild structures, women were more systematically excluded from guild membership. Usually women could become guild members only as wives or widows. They could not open economic enterprises of their own, although they were workers in many trades. Despite a growing, diversifying economy, women were increasingly denied opportunities, although later centuries would find women establishing their own guilds.

Commercial Growth and Innovation

Towns were focal points in commercial networks. The basic trade routes and networks had existed since Carolingian times, but a novelty of the twelfth century was the emergence of the Champagne fairs as a meeting point for the commerce of north and south (see Map 10.1). Since the early Middle Ages there had been permanent fairs in a few locations and occasional fairs in many places. By the middle of the twelfth century, however, the spices, silks, and dyes of the Mediterranean, the wool of England, the furs and linens of Germany, and the leather products of Spain began to be sold in a series of six fairs in the Champagne region of France that lasted seven weeks each from spring to autumn.

At any time of year, travel was difficult and costly. Few dared to venture across the Alps in the winter, and the northern seas, especially the passage around Denmark, were treacherous in cold weather. Even in the relatively calm Mediterranean, the Venetians refused to send out their trading fleet between November and March. Overland trade was impeded by snow, rain, mud, and highwaymen. Governments tried to restrain robbers, but no one could change the weather. After the road between Pisa and Florence was paved in 1286, it was passable most of the time, but there were not many like it. Because overland trade was so expensive, often multiplying the cost of goods tenfold, transport by water was preferred wherever possible.

Seaborne trade expanded. The stern rudder, better sails, the compass (in use by 1180), and better navigational charts facilitated sea travel, as did the growing use of larger ships. An Italian fleet sailed to Flanders in 1277, and within a few years the old overland trade routes, and with them the Champagne fairs, began a decline that was not reversed until the invention of the railroad in the nineteenth century.

Changing Economic Attitudes

As medieval society generated more wealth and populations concentrated in cities, people who were relatively well-off became more conscious of those who were less fortunate. Moralists began to argue that the poor were a special gift of God to the rich, who could redeem their own souls by generous charitable benefactions. Most towns established schemes of poor relief. But the numbers of poor people grew so rapidly, particularly in large towns, that they could not be dealt with. Some hospitals, for example, began to refuse abandoned babies for fear that they would be deluged with them.

Efforts to alleviate the condition of the poor constituted one ethical concern of medieval thinkers, but two issues attracted even more attention. First, theologians and lawyers alike discussed the "just price," the price at which goods should be bought and sold. Christian teaching had long held that it was immoral to hoard food during a famine or knowingly to sell a damaged item. But what was the correct price in ordinary circumstances? A theological view, often dismissed as unrealistic, held that items could be sold for only the cost of the materials in them and the labor absolutely necessary to produce them. A commercial view, often dismissed as immoral, insisted that a fair price was whatever the market would bear, regardless of consequences. A working consensus held that a just price was one arrived at by bargaining between free and knowledgeable parties.

The other ethical issue concerned usury, the lending of money at interest. Christian writers were always hostile to commercial enterprise, and they had plenty of scriptural warrant for their view. Psalm 15 warned that no one can be blameless "who lends his money at usury." The Gospel According to Luke said to "give without expecting to be repaid in full." Luke actually forbade the profit that makes most commercial enterprises possible. In the twelfth century, churchmen began to be much more assiduous in their condemnations of usury, a practice that had been winked at for centuries.

Prohibitions against usury in twelfth-century Europe—a society in full economic expansion—produced some remarkably inventive ways to get around the prohibitions. One person might agree to sell another person an item at a certain price and then buy it back on a fixed date at a higher price. Exchange rates between currencies could be manipulated to mask usurious transactions. Gradually thinkers began to defend usury on the grounds that a person who lent money incurred a risk and deserved to be compensated for that risk.

Investment demands credit, and credit requires some recompense for the lender. Even in the face of deep hostility, credit mechanisms spread in thirteenth-century Europe. They were held up to minute scrutiny by theologians and popular preachers and were found to be evidence of man's sinfulness, acquisitiveness, greed. But all these practices persisted, fueled by the expansion of the European economy, and began putting individual profit alongside community interest at the heart of social and economic thought.

SOCIAL AND RELIGIOUS MOVEMENTS

Twelfth- and thirteenth-century Europe witnessed several social movements unlike any that had occurred before. Spurred by increasingly intrusive governments, economic dislocation, and spiritual turmoil, they involved large numbers of people, cut across lines of gender, wealth, status, and occupation, and appeared in many places. Most of these movements had cohesive beliefs, even ideologies, and well-determined goals. They are the first large-scale social movements in European history.

Heretics and Dissidents

The canon lawyer Gratian (see page 340) defined heresy as a situation where "each man chooses for himself the teaching he believes to be the better one"; that is, he ignores official doctrines. For Gratian and his like-minded contemporaries, faith was not an individual matter. Unity of belief was crucial in a Catholic ("universal") Christian Europe. In the twelfth century, the church reacted ever more strictly to challenges to its teachings or to its exclusive right to teach. The effort by the church to define its law, theology, and bureaucratic procedures with greater precision drew lines more sharply than ever before between what was and was not acceptable.

Heretics did not see themselves as secessionists from the true church. They saw themselves as

its only representatives. Church teachings always encountered a degree of popular skepticism. Not everyone believed, for example, that Jesus was born of a virgin or that he was true God and true man. But such doubts had not previously led to mass defections. Before the middle of the twelfth century, challenges to the church came from men—as far as we can tell the ringleaders were all men—who saw themselves as inspired reformers. Their ideas were sometimes in line with those of more traditional reformers and sometimes radical extensions of those reformers' ideas. Some criticized the wealth and immorality of the clergy, while others attacked the priesthood itself and the sacraments.

Coherent movements of much larger proportions emerged later in the century. In 1173 Waldo, a rich merchant of Lyon, decided to sell all his property, give the proceeds to the poor, and embrace a life of poverty and preaching. Waldo was motivated by the same quest for the apostolic life that had animated the eremitical movement of the eleventh century. But there was a difference: He was a layman. Waldo attracted many followers (known as Waldensians), and in 1179 Pope Alexander III (r. 1159–1181) scrutinized him closely, found his beliefs to be essentially correct, and approved his vow of poverty. But the pope commanded Waldo to preach only when invited to do so by bishops. The bishops, jealous about their own power, extended no such invitations.

Waldo and his "Poor Men of Lyon" went right on preaching and in 1184 were formally declared heretics. Until this point it was not their ideas so much as their appropriation of a clerical duty, preaching, that had gotten them into trouble. From this time on, however, the Waldensians became more radical in their attacks on the church. In about 1204 one group of Waldensians was reconciled to the Catholic church; but the majority, which had spread all over southern France and Italy, into Germany, and as far away as Poland, was not reconciled. Waldensian communities exist to this day.

The most serious of the popular heretical movements was Catharism (from the Greek *katharos*, meaning "pure"). Because there were numerous Cathars near Albi, the whole movement is sometimes called "Albigensian" (see Map 10.1). In fact, there were Cathars all over Europe, although they did cluster in northern Italy and southern

France. Cathars were the religious descendants of Mani (see page 221), a third-century Persian who taught an extreme dualism that featured polarities in almost all things: good-evil, love-hate, flesh-spirit. Extreme Cathars abstained from flesh in all ways: They were vegetarians and renounced sexual intercourse so as not to produce offspring—that is, more flesh. Probably radiating from Bulgaria, Cathar ideas had spread widely in the West by the 1140s. Catharism attracted many converts when Nicetas, the Cathar bishop of Constantinople, visited Lombardy and Langue d'Oc between 1166 and 1176. People of every station joined the new church, which, in its own view, was the only true church.

The Catholic church sent isolated preachers against the Cathars, but with little success. In 1198 and 1203, Pope Innocent III organized systematic preaching tours in southern France, but these too lacked solid results, and in 1208 the pope's legate was murdered by a supporter of the count of Toulouse, who was sympathetic to the Cathars. The killing led to the launching of the Albigensian Crusade, a loosely structured movement that lasted into the 1260s. Although the crusade itself was largely over by the 1220s, there was a massacre of Albigensians in 1244, and inquisitorial campaigns in 1246 and again in 1256–1257. Isolated resisters struggled on into the fourteenth century.

Albigensians were staunchly opposed to the clergy of their day, seeing them as rich and corrupt. These teachings helped to draw to the Albigensian cause urban dwellers who resented the wealth and pretensions of the clergy—the same people who followed Waldo. Nobles may have been drawn to the movement because it gave them opportunities to take possession of extensive tracts of church lands, something the investiture controversy (see page 323) had denied them. Embracing Catharism may also have been a way for nobles to resist the increasing encroachment of the government of far-off Paris.

The Albigensians, like a number of other heretical sects, attracted many women. Unlike the Catholic church, which denied clerical, preaching, and teaching offices to women, the heretical sects tended to permit women to hold leading roles. But the Albigensians, like the Waldensians, were also driven by the same spiritual zeal and desire for ecclesiastical reform that moved many of their contemporaries. They differed from other would-be

The Expulsion of the Albigensians from Carcassone in 1209 This picture from a fourteenth-century manuscript depicts the grim realities of the Albigensian Crusade launched in 1208. But the Cathars of Carcassone fared less badly than those of Beziers, who were massacred. *(British Library)*

reformers in that they did not seek to reform the Catholic church from within but departed from it or insisted that they alone represented it. These heretical movements marked the first serious challenge to the ideology of a uniformly Catholic Christendom.

Reform from Within: The Mendicant Orders

Traditional monastic orders continued to win adherents, but their interpretation of the apostolic life meant ascetic withdrawal from the world, not pastoral work and preaching. Laymen who wished both to embrace poverty and to preach fell under the suspicion of the ecclesiastical authorities. Early in the thirteenth century a new movement arose, the mendicants (literally, beggars). Mendicants were men who aimed to preach, to be poor, and to create formal but noncloistered religious orders. Though similar to the heretics in many ways, they submitted willingly to ecclesiastical authority.

The mendicant phenomenon began when Francis of Assisi (1181–1226), the son of a rich Italian merchant, decided to renounce the wealth and status that were his birthright. He carried out his renunciation in a most public display before the bishop of Assisi in 1206. Francis had gradually grown tired of a life of ease and luxury, but he also experienced a blinding moment of spiritual insight when, by chance, his eyes fell on the passage in the Scriptures where Christ said, "Go, sell all you have, and follow me." He stripped himself naked so "that naked he might follow the naked Christ."

For a few years Francis wandered about Italy begging for his meager sustenance, repairing churches, caring for the sick, and preaching repentance to all who would listen. By 1210 he had attracted many followers, and together they set out to see Innocent III to win approval. After considering the matter for a while, Innocent decided to approve the new order of friars (that is "brothers," from the Latin *fratres*) as long as they would accept monastic tonsure—a ritual haircut signifying submission—profess obedience to the pope, and swear obedience to Francis. The pope was genuinely won over by Francis himself, but he also sensed that by permitting the formation of the Franciscan order he could create a legitimate and controllable repository for the explosive spiritual forces of the age.

Francis prepared a simple rule based on his understanding of the scriptural ideals of poverty, preaching, and service. Alarmed by the vagueness of the first rule and by the extraordinary influx of new members, the papal curia in 1223 prevailed on Francis to write a new rule that stressed order, a hierarchy of officials, and a novitiate—a regularized period of training for new members. Somewhat disappointed by this regulated formality, Francis withdrew more and more from the world and lived reclusively in the hills near Assisi.

After the death of Francis, his order (usually called "Franciscan," though it is technically the

"Friars Minor") split over the issues of property, power, education, and ordination. The movement had begun among laymen, but over time more Franciscans were ordained. Franciscans established schools in most great cities, and by the middle of the thirteenth century some of Europe's greatest intellects were Franciscans. This prominence, like the sacramental power of ordination, was a kind of wealth that Francis had wished to avoid. The real issue of wealth, however, turned on the possession of property. Francis had aimed for both personal and corporate poverty. In the 1230s papal legislation had alleviated strict poverty by permitting the order to acquire property to support its work. Nevertheless, the issue of property continued to spark controversy among the Franciscans.

The other major mendicant order, the Dominican, was the product of very different experiences. Its founder, Dominic de Guzman (1170–1221), was the son of a Spanish nobleman. He became a priest and later a cathedral canon. While traveling, he saw firsthand the Albigensian heresy in southern France, and in 1206 he went to Rome to seek permission to preach against the heretics. The Albigensian Crusade began in 1208, but Dominic's methods were those of persuasion, not coercion.

Albigensian criticisms of the ignorance, indifference, and personal failings of the clergy could never be applied to Dominic and his fellow preachers. Dominic and his followers were supported enthusiastically by the bishop of Toulouse, who saw how useful these zealous preachers of unblemished life could be. In 1215 Dominic, with his bishop's assistance, attempted to form a new order, but by that time Rome had forbidden the creation of new orders for fear of heresy or uncontrollable diversity. Thus, Dominic's "Order of Preachers" (the proper name for the Dominicans) adopted the Rule of Saint Augustine, which many communities of cathedral canons had been using since the eleventh century.

In 1217, Dominic presided at the first general meeting of the order. The Dominicans decided to disperse, some going to Paris, some (including Dominic) to Rome, some to other cities in Europe. Henceforth, the order saw its mission as serving the whole church. Dominican schools were set up all over Europe, and the order acquired a reputation for learning and scholarship. The Dominicans were voluntarily poor, but the order was never rent by a controversy over property as the Franciscans were. Dominic's was a vision of personal, not corporate, poverty. Likewise, as a preaching order, the Dominicans had to be learned and ordained. Franciscan misgivings on these issues did not touch them.

Both the Franciscan and Dominican orders reflected a widespread desire to emulate the apostolic life of the early church by poverty and preaching. Both submitted to legitimate authority. Francis's religious vision of charity and service was the product of a heartfelt need for repentance and renewal. Franciscans often served as missionaries: Think of Francis and the sultan or of William of Rubruck and the khan. Dominic set out to save the church from its enemies. He desired preachers who were sufficiently learned that they could combat the errors of heretics. Both men saw the need for exemplary lives. Francis was a more charismatic figure than Dominic, and his apostolate to the urban poor was

more compelling. By 1300 Franciscan houses outnumbered Dominican by 3 to 1. The mendicants were the greatest spiritual force in high medieval Europe.

Communities of Women

The religious forces that attracted men drew women as well. Traditional orders tended to be hostile to women. There was only one Cluniac house for women, and the Cistercians struggled to keep women out of their ranks. The wandering preachers of the twelfth century, without exception, acquired women as followers, but the usual results were either segregation of the women in cloisters or condemnation of the whole movement.

In 1212, Francis attracted the aristocrat Clare of Assisi (1194–1253), who was fleeing from an arranged marriage. She wanted to live the friars'

Francis and Clare of Assisi
This beautiful, moving Gothic painting by Giotto (late thirteenth century) depicts Francis's funeral cortege passing by Clare's church of San Damiano. Compare this Italian Gothic façade with the French ones on pages 384 and 391.
(Scala/Art Resource, NY)

New Orders for Women: Clares and Beguines

These documents, from the prologue to Clare's Rule (a) and from a document detailing the origins of the Beguines (b), illustrate the initiative women took in forming new religious communities. Observe, too, how the women's submission to authority relieved them from suspicion of heresy or insubordination.

(a)

Clare, the unworthy servant of Christ and the little plant of the most blessed Francis, promises obedience and reverence to the Lord Pope Innocent [III] and his canonically elected successors, and to the Roman Church. And, just as at the beginning of her conversion, together with her sisters she promised obedience to the Blessed Francis, so now she promises his successors to observe that same obedience inviolably, and the other sisters shall always be obliged to obey the successors of Blessed Francis and Sister Clare and other canonically elected abbesses who succeed her.

(b)

Those ladies of good memory, Joanna and her sister Margaret, successive countesses of Flanders and Hainault, noticed that the region was greatly abounding in women for whom, because of their own position or that of their friends, suitable marriages were not possible, and they saw that the daughters of respectable men, both nobles and commoners, wished to live chastely, but could not easily enter a monastery because of the great number of these girls and the poverty of their parents, and that respectable and noble but impoverished damsels had to go begging or shamefully support themselves or seek support from their friends, unless some solution could be found. Then by divine inspiration, as it is piously believed, having first obtained the advice and consent of respectable men of the diocese and elsewhere, in various parts of Flanders they set up certain spacious places which are called Beguinages, in which the aforesaid women, girls, and damsels were received, so that living in common therein, they might preserve their chastity, with or without taking vows, and where they might support and clothe themselves by suitable work, without shaming themselves or their friends.

Source: Emilie Amt, *Women's Lives in Medieval Europe* (New York: Routledge, 1993), pp. 236, 264.

life of poverty and preaching, and Francis wanted to assist her. Aware that the sight of women begging or preaching would be shocking, in 1215 he gave Clare and his other female followers their own rule. Clare became abbess of the first community of the "Poor Clares." Although cloistered and forbidden to preach, the Clares lived lives of exemplary austerity and attracted many adherents.

Beguines were communities of women who lived together, devoted themselves to charitable works, but did not take vows as nuns. The Beguine movement grew from the work in Nivelles, near Liège (see Map 10.1), of Mary of Oignies (ca. 1177–1213). She was drawn to the ideals of voluntary poverty and service to others. So strong was the pull that she renounced her marriage, gave away all her goods, worked for a while in a leper colony, and thought of preaching against the Cathars. Instead she formed a community.

Groups of Beguines appeared all over the Low Countries, western Germany, and northern France. This was the first exclusively women's movement in the history of Christianity. Beguines sometimes vowed poverty and sometimes did not. They sometimes cloistered themselves into communities and sometimes taught and served the poor and outcast. They neither challenged the officials and teachings of the church nor demanded a right to preach. As laywomen, they did not give rise to scandal as noncloistered nuns would have. They were content to have power over their own lives and communities but not over the wider world around them. (See the box, "New Orders for Women: Clares and Beguines.")

Thirteenth-century Europe knew more female than male mystics, and female mysticism tended to focus on Jesus, especially on His presence in the Eucharist. This is the first religious devotion that can be shown to have been more common to women than to men. Most of the mystics were either nuns or Beguines. As the clergy was defining its own prerogatives more tightly, and excluding women more completely from the exercise of formal public power, female communities provided a different locus for women's activity.

Women who spent their lives in community with other women reveal, in their writings and in writings about them, none of the sense of moral and intellectual inferiority that was routinely attributed to women by men and often by women themselves. Women who were in direct spiritual communion with God acquired, as teachers, mediators, and counselors in their communities, power that they simply could not have had outside those settings.

The Later Crusades

The factors that produced the First Crusade—papal leadership, a more militant Christianity, religious zeal, surplus soldiers, a spirit of adventure—persisted through the thirteenth century. Crusading continued to be a popular social movement. Men from all over Europe and every social class participated in the Crusades. By 1300, however, the energies long channeled into crusading were being diverted elsewhere, though there was still talk of crusading in Europe after 1500 (Map 10.2).

Crusading was intended to protect the Holy Land and keep open the pilgrim routes to Jerusalem. The creation of the small crusader states in the hostile environment of Syria and Palestine had made continued crusading almost inevitable. In 1144 the tiny crusader state at Edessa on the Armenian frontier fell to a Muslim army. Although the news saddened Europeans, it took the efforts of the pope and Bernard of Clairvaux to launch another crusade. They persuaded Conrad III of Germany and Louis VII of France to lead it. Neither Conrad nor Louis would willingly submit to the other's leadership, and the Second Crusade accomplished little. Its one achievement was an accident. In 1147 an army of English, French, and Flemish soldiers who were proceeding to the Holy Land by sea put in on the Iberian coast and captured Lisbon. This opened a new front in the Reconquista and laid the foundations for the later kingdom of Portugal.

The papacy called for the Third Crusade when Saladin (1138–1193), a powerful local leader typical of the disintegrating Abbassid caliphate, captured Jerusalem in 1187. It is a measure of the force of the crusading ideal that the greatest crowned heads of the day—Frederick Barbarossa, Philip II, and Richard the Lionheart—answered the call. It must be said, however, that only Frederick did so enthusiastically. Frederick died en route in 1190, while Philip returned home in 1191 and Richard in 1192. Because neither Richard nor Philip would stay in the East to fight Saladin, this crusade merely won access to Jerusalem for pilgrims.

Disappointed with the results of the Third Crusade, Innocent III began calling for another crusade immediately on his election in 1198. Popular preachers summoned an army, once again largely French, and the pope and the Fourth Crusade's military leaders engaged the Venetians to construct a fleet of war and transport ships. In less than eighteen months they produced 50 galleys and 450 transports, a tribute to the awesome capabilities of the Venetian shipyards.

Ships, however, were expensive, and the Venetians drove hard bargains. When too few Crusaders and too little money appeared, the Venetians suggested that the Crusaders could discharge some of their debt by recapturing from the Hungarians the formerly Venetian port of Zara on the Dalmatian coast (see Map 10.2). This idea outraged the pope, but he could do little about it. Then into the camp of the Crusaders came a pretender to the Byzantine throne, who promised that if the Crusaders would help him to claim his patrimony, he would contribute to the cost of the crusade. The Venetians urged the Crusaders to accept

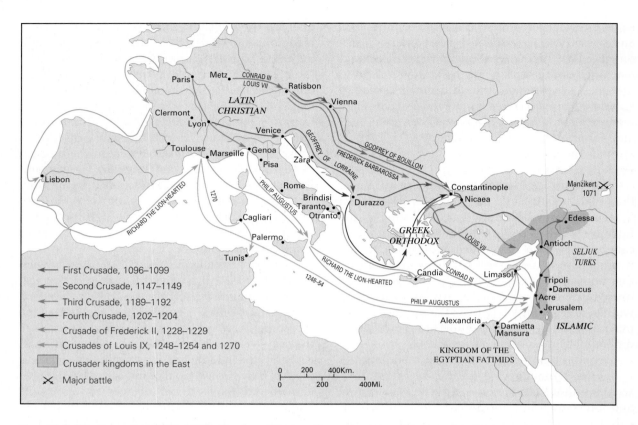

Map 10.2 The Crusades, 1095–1270 The long Western European interest in securing the Holy Land is illustrated by the repeated Crusades. Note the numerous routes taken, lands traversed, destinations attained, and points of cultural encounter.

this offer, and, to the horror of Innocent III, the Fourth Crusade turned to Constantinople.

Once in Constantinople, the Crusaders learned that their new ally had few friends in the Byzantine capital. The Venetians saw an opportunity to expand business opportunities in the East, and the soldiers welcomed a chance to plunder the Mediterranean's greatest city and to avenge what they regarded as a century of Byzantine perfidy. Thus, the Fourth Crusade captured not Jerusalem but Constantinople. Until 1261, the Eastern and Western churches were reunited under papal leadership, and substantial tracts of the Balkans fell to Western knights under a "Latin emperor" of Constantinople.

In later decades, popes began to take a more active role in planning Crusades. No pope wanted to lose control of a crusade as Innocent had done, and all popes saw that the liberation of Jerusalem required a solid base of operations in the eastern Mediterranean. Egypt was the objective of the Fifth

Crusade (1218–1221)—when, incidentally, Saint Francis visited the sultan—and the Sixth Crusade (1248–1250). Despite a few victories, the Crusaders could not win a secure base. No further crusades to the East were organized in the thirteenth century. In 1291 Acre, the last Crusader stronghold, fell and the original crusading era ended.

During the crusading period, the Holy Land was not the sole object of Crusaders' attentions. In about 1140 the pope preached a crusade against the Normans in southern Italy, and several popes in the thirteenth century, fearful of imperial encroachment, preached crusades against the Staufen in Italy. In 1147 the papacy authorized a crusade in the Baltic that opened nearly four centuries of German expansion into the pagan Slavic lands to the east of Saxony. In 1208, Innocent III proclaimed a crusade against the Albigensians.

Why did the Crusades end? There are several reasons. By the late thirteenth century, more violence was being directed inward against heretics and political foes of the papacy than outward against the alleged enemies of Christendom itself. As governments became more sophisticated and controlled more of their territories, they had less interest in the intangible benefits of crusading. The commercial cities of Italy now needed not so much to open up the Muslim East as to secure comparative advantage over one another. The Christian ideals of poverty, charity, and service, as embodied in the mendicants, were incompatible with warfare. Literary images provide another insight into the decline of the Crusades. After 1300, we are less likely to read about a Christian knight fighting honorably for God and king than about a gentleman of manners seeking the favor of a fair lady.

A balance sheet for the crusading movement as a whole reveals more losses than gains. The Crusades exported many violent men from Europe, but it is not clear that Europe became a less violent place. Relations between Christian Europe and the Muslim world grew more bitter as a result of the Crusades. The Fourth Crusade mortally wounded Byzantium and worsened the already tense relations between the Catholic and Orthodox churches. Crusading zeal was directed deliberately against heretics and coincidentally against Jews. The Crusades did not create anti-Semitism, but they worsened it. Some women, particularly in France, from which the majority of all Crusaders came, may have enjoyed momentary benefits in terms of control of land, wealth, and people while their husbands were away. But the long-term trend in feudal society was disadvantageous to women, and the Crusades did not change that. Finally, the Crusades may have done as much to disrupt Mediterranean trade as to promote it. Italian urban rivalries took the place of Latin-Muslim-Byzantine ones. That a single new product, the apricot, entered Europe in the crusading era seems small recompense for such huge effort.

THE HEIGHT OF MEDIEVAL CULTURE

Between 1150 and 1300 theologians grappled with the totality of divine and human wisdom, architects in the new Gothic style created some of the world's most beautiful buildings, and Dante Alighieri wrote poetry of unmatched spiritual power and linguistic beauty. New academic institutions, universities, which adorned some of Europe's major cities,

SPIRITUAL AND INTELLECTUAL LEADERS OF HIGH MEDIEVAL EUROPE

1135–1183	Chrétien de Troyes
1170–1221	Dominic
ca. 1177–1213	Mary of Oignies
1181–1226	Francis of Assisi
1194–1253	Clare of Assisi
1210–1280	Mechtild of Madgeburg
1225–1274	Thomas Aquinas
1265–1321	Dante Alighieri

brought a new rigor and precision to intellectual life. But even as traditional Latin letters reached new heights of erudition, the vernacular languages brought forth countless original and inspiring works, not least those of Dante himself.

The University

In the early decades of the twelfth century, students gathered wherever there were famous teachers. Such teachers—figures like Peter Abelard (see page 341)—clustered in a few centers, and the students congregated there as well. The last decades of the twelfth century saw a swarm of masters and students in Paris. Like members of secular guilds, the masters organized. The University of Paris was the result of their efforts. By 1300 there were universities elsewhere in France, as well as in Italy, England, and western Germany.

Several forces drove masters to organize. They wanted to negotiate with the bishop's chancellor, the traditional head of all schools in an episcopal city. They wanted to regulate the curriculum that students followed and to prescribe the requirements for entry into their own ranks. They also desired to set the fees to be charged for instruction. By 1209 the bishop of Paris, the pope, and the king of France had granted formal recognition to the university.

In Bologna, the university developed a little differently. Here the students came primarily to study law, after acquiring a basic education elsewhere. These law students were usually older and more affluent than students elsewhere, and foreign to Bologna. Consequently, in Bologna the university arose from a guild of students who united to set standards in fees and studies and to protect themselves against unscrupulous masters.

Universities were known for certain specializations: Paris for arts and theology, Bologna for law, Salerno in Italy and Montpellier in France for medicine, Oxford for mathematical and scientific subjects. Still, the basic course of study was similar. At Paris, a young scholar came to the city, found lodgings where he could, and attempted to find a master who would guide him through the arts curriculum. These boys might be in their early teens or several years older, depending on their earlier education and financial resources. The arts course, which was the prerequisite to all higher faculties, usually lasted from four to six years. The bachelor's degree was a license to teach, but a bachelor who wished to teach in a university needed to go on for a master's degree. The master's degree required at least eight years of study (including the baccalaureate years), which culminated in a public, oral examination. Some masters went on to become doctors in theology, law, or medicine. A doctorate required ten to fifteen years of study. Medieval academicians were immensely learned.

Student life was difficult. In many ways, students were always foreigners. Although their presence in a town enhanced its prestige, townspeople exploited them by charging exorbitant prices for food and rent. Students' own behavior was not always above reproach. There was surely some truth in the frequently lodged charge that students were noisy, quarrelsome, given to drinking, and excessively fond of prostitutes. England's Oxford and Cambridge were unique in always having residential colleges for students; Paris got one later and the mendicants often established houses of study. Typically, students were on their own.

Students had to work very hard. The arts curriculum demanded a thorough acquaintance with all the famous texts of grammar, logic, and rhetoric. Higher studies added more of Aristotle, particularly his philosophical writings. In theology, the students had to master the Scriptures, the principal biblical commentaries from patristic times to the present, and the *Book of Sentences,* a theology textbook (ca. 1160) by the Italian Peter Lombard. In medicine, the ancient writings of Galen and Hippocrates were supplemented by Arab texts as well as by observation and experimentation.

The basic method of teaching consisted of the recitation by the teacher of a short piece of a set text, followed by the presentation and discussion of many authoritative commentaries on that text, and concluded by the explanations of the teacher himself. Then another passage of the set text was presented and the whole process repeated. This education focused on standard books and received opinions and required students to remember large amounts of material. The curriculum nevertheless produced thinkers of prodigious originality.

In principle, universities were open to all males, but in practice they were restricted to those who had the means to attend them. Women were not accepted at universities, either as students or as teachers. It was generally thought, by men, that learning made women insubordinate. Lacking the required formal education, women were furthermore denied entry into the learned professions of theology, law, and medicine, despite the fact that many rural and some urban medical practitioners were women—it was common for women to possess and transmit massive knowledge of folk remedies. But not just folk remedies. Trotula of Salerno, who probably lived in the twelfth century, wrote a learned treatise, *On the Diseases of Women.* Naples documents record the names of twenty-four women surgeons between 1273 and 1410. How these women were educated is not known.

Scholasticism

Scholasticism, the intellectual outlook of the medieval schools, was the product of several related forces. Most important was the Christian tradition. Other forces were the quickening pace of intellectual life occasioned by Latin Europe's encounter with the worlds of Arab and Jewish learning in the era of the Crusades; the need to reconcile natural philosophy, or the claims of reason, with revealed religion, or the realm of faith; and the style of intellectual life that resulted from the twelfth-century fascination with logic.

By 1150, the Christian tradition had a well-defined set of basic sources—the Scriptures and the authoritative commentators—and two different approaches to the sources. One approach was to rely on divine inspiration, on mystical illumination. This approach to the biblical text was often learned but tended toward the allegorical. The other approach was more concrete and rationalistic and got a potent impetus from the development of logical studies in the twelfth century. The old intellectual struggle within Christian circles between faith and reason was made more acute by the dawning awareness of just how much the ancient Greeks had actually written and by the simultaneous discovery that Arab and Jewish scholars were also struggling to come to grips with that intellectual heritage.

Among many possible problems, we will mention two. First, Aristotle had taught that the universe was eternal and mechanistic. In his thinking there was no room for creation or for a benevolent deity who intervened to alter the course of events. Greek science, so obviously right about many things, seemed in this area to contradict fundamental Christian teachings. Second, as Arab and Jewish thinkers looked at natural philosophy and at their own religious traditions, some of them suggested that the Quran and the Hebrew Scriptures contained approximations to truth that were suitable only for persons of limited intellectual ability. Once again, the question was posed to Christians: Were the Scriptures true?

The answer of Thomas Aquinas (1225–1274) seemed most effectively to respond to the question. A Dominican friar, Thomas was educated at Naples, Cologne, and Paris. Apart from brief service at the papal court, he spent the years after 1252 teaching and writing in Paris. A prolific author, his two most famous works are the *Summa Contra Gentiles* and the *Summa Theologiae*. A *summa* was an encyclopedic compendium of carefully arrayed knowledge on a particular subject. Thomas's first summa was addressed to natural truth—that is, to the kinds of things that any person could know through the operation of reason. His second summa was a summation of the revealed truths of the Christian faith.

Thomas's works are distinctive for two reasons. First, no one before him had so rigorously followed the dialectical method of reasoning through the whole of a field of knowledge, not just a particular problem. For thousands of pages, Thomas poses a question, suggests answers, confronts the answers with objections, refutes the objections, and then draws a conclusion. Then he repeats the process. Second, Thomas carefully distinguished between two kinds of truths. On the one hand were *natural truths,* truths (even theological ones) that anyone can know (or so Thomas thought)—for example, that God exists. On the other hand were *revealed truths,* truths that can be known only through faith in God's revelation—for example, the Trinity or the incarnation of Christ. Thomas maintained that natural and revealed truths simply could not contradict one another because God was ultimately the source of both. If natural truth—for example, Aristotle's contention that the world is eternal—appeared to contradict a revealed truth, then Aristotle was wrong. Thomas was accused by some contemporaries of applying reason too widely, and after his death some of his ideas were condemned by the church. But he actually steered a middle path between intellectual extremes. (See the box, "Thomas Aquinas's Proof for the Existence of God.")

The Gothic Image

It is surely no coincidence that Gothic art and architecture emerged just as the West was absorbing the recovery of Euclid's mathematical writings and applying the intensely ordered logic of Aristotle to everything from legal problems to theological mysteries. One of the most familiar images of the Middle Ages is the inspiring beauty of the Gothic cathedral. It is thus ironic that the word *Gothic* first appeared in the sixteenth century as a term of derision for what was then regarded as an outmoded style so ugly that only the horrible conquerors of Rome, the Goths, could have been responsible for it. The name stuck, but today it simply identifies a period in European architecture, sculpture, and painting that lasted from the middle of the twelfth century to the early sixteenth century.

Gothic is a French invention. It was Abbot Suger (1085–1151) of St.-Denis, a monastery outside Paris, who, in rebuilding his basilica beginning in 1135, consciously sought a new style. He desired to achieve effects of lightness, almost weightlessness, in the stonework of his church and to admit large amounts of light to create a dazzling and mysterious aura on the inside. The Bible often uses images of light to refer to God, and Suger wished to give expression to those images in the house of God for which he was responsible. (See

Thomas Aquinas's Proof for the Existence of God

*This abbreviated account of Thomas's proofs for God's existence illustrates both the working methods of Scholasticism and the character of the **Summa Theologiae**. Aristotelian logic, formal reasoning through syllogisms, is the framework behind the whole system of Scholasticism.*

[Thomas responds to Anselm.]

Perhaps not everyone who hears this name *God* understands it to signify something than which nothing greater can be thought, seeing that some have believed God to be a body. Yet, granted that everyone understands that by this name *God* is signified something than which nothing greater can be thought, nevertheless, it does not therefore follow that he understands that what the name signifies exists actually, but only that it exists mentally. Nor can it be argued that there actually exists something than which nothing greater can be thought; and this precisely is not admitted by those who hold that God does not exist.

[Then Thomas takes another approach.]

It seems that the existence of God cannot be demonstrated. For it is an article of faith that God exists. But what is of faith cannot be demonstrated, because a demonstration produces scientific knowledge, whereas faith is of the unseen. Therefore it cannot be demonstrated that God exists.

[To this, Thomas poses several objections.]

If the existence of God were demonstrated, this could only be from His effects. But His effects are not proportionate to Him, since He is infinite, and between the infinite and the finite there is no proportion. Therefore, since a cause cannot be demonstrated by an effect not proportioned to it, it seems that the existence of God cannot be demonstrated.

[Through complex logical reasoning, Thomas refutes this objection, thus proving that God does indeed exist, and then he turns to another argument.]

It seems that God does not exist; because if one of two contraries be infinite, the other would be altogether destroyed. But the name of *God* means that he is infinite goodness. If, therefore, God existed, there would be no evil discoverable; but there is evil in the world. Therefore, God does not exist.

I answer that the existence of God can be proved in five ways. The first and most manifest way is the argument from motion. It is certain, and evident to our senses, that in the world some things are in motion. Now whatever is moved is moved by another. . . . Therefore it is necessary to arrive at a prime mover, moved by no other. The second way is from the nature of efficient cause. There is no case known in which a thing is found to be the efficient cause of itself; for so it would be prior to itself which is impossible. Therefore it is necessary to admit a first efficient cause, to which everyone gives the name of God. The third way is from possibility and necessity. If at one time there was nothing in existence, it would have been impossible for anything to have begun to exist; and thus even now nothing would be in existence—which is absurd. Therefore, not all beings are merely possible, but there must exist something the existence of which is necessary. This all men speak of as God. [He continues with ways four and five, and then turns to detailed explanations of all five.]

Source: Anton C. Pegis, *An Introduction to St. Thomas Aquinas* (New York: Random House, Modern Library, 1945), pp. 22–27.

the feature, "Weighing the Evidence: The Arts of Chartres Cathedral," on pages 390–391.)

Suger combined a number of elements that had long existed and produced something original. A *pointed arch* is more elegant than a round one; and it permits the joining of two arches of identical height but different widths, which, in turn, permits complex shapes and sizes. The *ribbed vault* is lighter and more graceful than the groin vaults characteristic of Romanesque architecture; it also exerts less stress and facilitates experimentation with shapes (Figure 10.1). Finally, *point support*—basically, the support of structural elements at only certain points—permitted the replacement of heavy, stress-bearing walls with curtains of stained glass. The points of support might be massive internal piers or intricate skeletal frameworks, called *buttresses*, on the outside of the church.

These three elements—pointed arch, ribbed vault, point support—produce a building that is characterized by verticality and translucency. Everything seems to spring upward, and stone surfaces appear so frequently punctured by light as almost to disappear altogether. The desired, and achieved, effect is one of harmony, order, and mathematical precision.

The Gothic style soon spread in central and northern France. The cathedral of Notre-Dame of Paris was built beginning in the 1150s, and the royal portal at Chartres Cathedral was reconstructed after 1145. Gothic churches could be huge. The interior of Notre-Dame, for example, is 493 feet long and 107 feet high. To avoid a sense of sheer mass, Gothic builders used triple or quadruple elevations inside the buildings and took advantage of point support to pierce the walls at frequent intervals with stained-glass windows. Exterior surfaces were broken up with windows, sculptures, colonnades, and towers. No opportunity was missed to create visual interest and complexity.

The thirteenth century was the most mature period for French Gothic architecture and also the

Figure 10.1 The Structure of Gothic Architecture The adoption of pointed arches, an import from the Islamic world, let Gothic builders join structures of identical heights but different widths (something that barrel and groin vaulting could not do; see Figure 9.1 on page 343). The resulting structures were high, light, airy, and visually interesting. (*Source:* Anne Shaver-Crandell, *The Middle Ages* [Cambridge, England: Cambridge University Press, 1982], p. 34. Used by permission.)

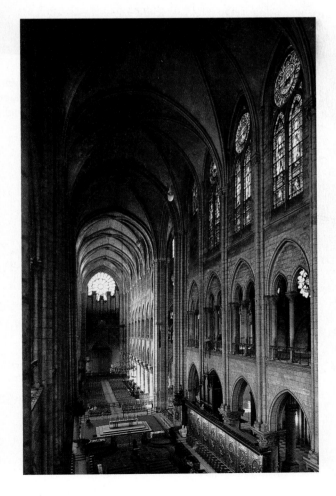

Interior of Notre-Dame, Paris The pointed vaults of the nave produce a verticality that is different in "feel" from the Romanesque (compare page 306). Note the triple elevation, the pointed arches, the ribbed vaulting, the ubiquitous glass that admits streams of multicolored light. The building can hold 10,000 people. (*Scala/Art Resource, NY*)

Exterior of Notre-Dame, Paris This most famous of cathedrals (1163–1220) shows all the classic elements of the Gothic style: highly decorated western end, cross shape formed by the nave and transept, flying buttresses to support the walls and roof, side walls that seem like curtains of glass. *(Altitude, Paris)*

time when Gothic spread most widely throughout Europe. This spread may be attributed to the superiority of French masons and stonecutters and also to the tremendous prestige of French culture. By 1300 there were distinctive Gothic traditions in almost all parts of Europe from Iceland to Poland.

Latin and Vernacular Culture

The prestige of French culture also points to the growing significance of vernacular literature. Nevertheless, many writers continued to use Latin. University scholars, for example, composed their learned treatises in the ancient tongue, but often in a style that was less rhetorically ornate than that of the classics. Most law books and public documents were still written in Latin, but in a "vulgar" Latin that was reasonably close to the vernacular in areas where Romance languages (derived from Latin) were spoken. Technical manuals, on farming and

animal husbandry, on warfare and armaments, or on law and government were prepared in Latin, too, but again in a style that was far more accessible than that of their ancient models. What is most striking, however, is that Latin was rarely used, after about 1200, as the language for serious, original literary compositions.

Here the change from the twelfth century could not be more drastic. Then, theology and poetry, history and biography, and romance and adventure had been written in Latin. Some of this material was serious, but some breathed a light and carefree spirit. The anonymous German known as the Archpoet (d. 1165) wrote poems about drinking and womanizing. These lines are typical of his work:

In the public house to die
Is my resolution;
Let wine to my lips be nigh
At life's dissolution:

That will make the angels cry,
With glad elocution
"Grant this toper, God on high,
Grace and Absolution!"[3]

No less insouciant were the authors of biting satires such as the anonymous *The Gospel According to the Silver Marks*, which excoriated the wealth and greed of the papal curia. But this fresh spirit was now largely confined to writings in the vernacular.

The heroic, epic tradition that *Beowulf* and the *Song of Roland* represent did not disappear, but literary energies were applied in new directions. Southern France, in the middle and last decades of the twelfth century, added something new to Western literature: the love lyrics of the troubadours. This poetry, composed by both men and women, profoundly influenced an age and created the literary movement that has long been called "courtly love." Chivalry was initially a code for men interacting with other men. In the world of courtly love, chivalry became an elaborate set of rules governing relations between men and women.

Courtly love had several sources. The classical poet Ovid (43 B.C.–?A.D. 17), who wrote *The Art of Love*, a manual of seduction, was one. Another was the lyrical poetry of Muslim Spain. Ironically, feudal values such as loyalty and service played a critical role as men became, in effect, love vassals. There was some contribution, too, from Platonic ideas, particularly the notion that any love in this world could be only a pale imitation of real love. The courtly poets sung of *fin'amours*, a pure love in contrast to the mere lust of the masses. A lover cherished an unattainable lady. He would do anything for the merest display of pleasure or gratitude on her part, as we see in these lines from Bernart de Ventadorn, court poet of the counts of Toulouse in the late twelfth century:

Down there, around Ventadorn, all my friends
have lost me, because my lady does not love me;
and so, it is right that I never go back there again,
because always she is wild and morose with me.
Now here is why the face she shows me is gloomy and
full of anger:
because my pleasure is in loving her and I have settled
down to it.
She is resentful and complains for no other reason.[4]

Male troubadours placed women on pedestals and worshiped them from afar. Women troubadours took a different line. Women's poems were more realistic, more human, more emotionally satisfying. Castellozza (b. ca. 1200), the southern French wife of a Crusader, idealized not at all when she wrote these lines:

Friend, if you had shown consideration,
meekness, candor and humanity,
I'd have loved you without hesitation,
but you were mean and sly and villainous.

And she did not assign the active role exclusively to the man:

Handsome friend, as a lover true
I loved you, for you pleased me,
But now I see I was a fool,
for I've barely seen you since.[5]

Count William IX of Poitou (1071–1127) was among the first of the troubadours, and his daughter, Eleanor of Aquitaine, brought the conventions of this poetry and point of view to the French and Angevin courts. She and her daughters were the greatest literary patrons of the late twelfth century. The wives of kings and nobles who were frequently away from home maintained stunning courts and cultivated vernacular literature.

The courtly literature of northern France owed much to the troubadour tradition of the south but broke new ground in both forms and content. The romance and the lay were the chief new forms. Both drew on classical literature, the heroic Germanic past, and the Arthurian legends of the Celtic world to create stories of love and adventure. The romance usually develops a complex narrative involving several major characters over a long time. The lay is brief and focuses on a single incident. The most famous twelfth-century writer of romance was Chrétien de Troyes (1135–1183), the court writer of Marie of Champagne, a daughter of Eleanor of Aquitaine. The greatest writer of lays was Marie de France, who wrote at the Angevin court in the 1170s.

The romances and lays explore the contradictions and tensions in a variety of human relationships. Loyalty and honor make frequent appearances. Lancelot, a paragon of knightly virtue, desperately loves his lord Arthur's wife, Guinivere. What is he to do? How can he be loyal to his lord, to his love, and to himself? What will he do when a single course of action brings both honor and dishonor? In the epics, speeches are made to swords, to horses, or sometimes to no one in particular; the points being made are universalized. In the romances, credible human beings struggle against powerful and conflicting emotional and moral ties.

Although the romances and lays were by no means the preserve of the elite, very little is known about popular literature. Two exceptions are the mystery play and women's devotional writing. Mystery plays made their first appearance in the eleventh century. The liturgy of the church, which formally re-enacted the life of Christ, was confined to the clergy. But this limitation did not prevent troupes of actors from staging, on church porches or village greens, scenes from the life of Christ in simple, direct language. By the twelfth and thirteenth centuries, guilds in many towns sponsored the production of plays commemorating the Christian mysteries. Such plays served as both a form of popular entertainment and a device for teaching elementary Christian ideas. The female religious movements of the age gave rise to prose and verse works in various vernaculars. Mechtild of Magdeburg (1210–1280), a German Beguine, wrote *The Flowering Light of Divinity*, a mystical, allegorical account of the marriage between God and a spiritual woman. The vernaculars opened avenues of expression to women, who were normally denied Latin learning.

France led the way in the production of vernacular literature, but by the early thirteenth century centers of romantic poetry flourished in Germany and Italy. That French models did not inspire slavish imitation is proved by the master of all vernacular writers, Dante Alighieri (1265–1321).

Dante began as a poet in *la dolce stil nuova*, "the sweet new style" that came from France and captivated Italians. But he moved beyond it in many ways. Dante was a man of extraordinarily wide learning and reading. He served Florence in public capacities and became an exile amid political strife. He wrote a long treatise in defense of the empire—or, really, against the secular rule of the church. But he is best known for one of the masterpieces of world literature, the *Divine Comedy*.

The secret of the *Comedy*'s success is not easy to grasp. It is a long and difficult poem. But it is also humorous, instructive, and moving. In an exquisitely beautiful Italian, Dante took the most advanced theology and philosophy of his time, the richest poetic traditions, a huge hoard of stories, many contemporary events, and a lot of common

sense and wove them into an allegorical presentation of the journey of the whole human race and of all people in their own lives.

Accompanied by the Roman poet Virgil (see page 200), Dante travels through Hell and Purgatory, commenting along the way on the condition of the people he meets. Then, because Virgil is a pagan and only Dante's true love can accompany Dante into paradise, Beatrice, the love of Dante's youth, joins him for a visit to Heaven. The poet's central metaphor is love; the love he feels for Beatrice stands metaphorically for the love God feels for the world. Dante canvasses humanity from the pits of hell, which he reserved for deceivers, to the summit of paradise, where a man inspired by pure love might, despite his sinfulness, dare to look into the face of God.

BONIFACE VIII AND PHILIP IV: CRISIS OF CHURCH AND STATE, 1294–1302

Even as Dante's poems transported their audience above the realm of daily affairs, the years around 1300 were disturbed by an all-too-earthly controversy between the king of France and the pope. This dispute encapsulates the major themes and particular issues that are discussed in this chapter.

The Issues

In 1294, Philip IV of France and Edward I of England both attempted to collect taxes from the clergy of their respective countries. They were at war in both Flanders and Gascony, their treasuries empty, and their nobilities hostile. In 1296, Pope Boniface VIII (r. 1294–1303) issued the bull (letter) *Clericis laicos* forbidding the taxation of the clergy without explicit papal permission, thereby repeating a decree of the Fourth Lateran Council of 1215. Edward I complied, but Philip responded with a propaganda campaign against the pope in France that was designed to rally popular support for the monarchy. He also issued an edict that forbade the export to Rome of bullion, coin, and valuables from France, an act meant to pressure Boniface by depriving him of vast ecclesiastical revenues.

The king felt he could not permit any power outside France to dictate when he could go to war by denying him valuable sources of income. In 1297, Boniface backed down. In the bull *Etsi de statu* he said that in a dire emergency "the conscience of the king" could decide whether or not to tax the clergy without papal permission.

Philip's edict had affected Rome immediately because the greatest share of papal revenues came from France. Its impact was made all the greater by the precariousness of Boniface's position. An able, intelligent, experienced man, Boniface as pope carried out many important reforms. But the circumstances surrounding his election were questionable, because his predecessor, Celestine V (r. 1294), had resigned to return to a monastery. No other pope had ever resigned (and none has since), and it was not clear whether doing so was strictly legal. Moreover, although Boniface came from an old, rich, powerful Roman family, he was the mortal enemy of several equally well-placed families. Roman factions saw in the dispute with France a fine opportunity to attack the pope.

In 1297, Boniface canonized as a saint Philip's grandfather, Louis IX, implying a reconciliation between Paris and Rome. In 1300, Boniface declared a jubilee year, a year of spiritual praise and thanksgiving, and Rome was filled with pilgrims, many of them French, and with joyous celebrations. The pope was working hard all the while to heal the rift between France and England so that the resources and energies of Europe could once again be directed against the Muslims. Boniface still envisioned a militant and unified Christian Europe, with him at its head, going forth against the enemies of the faith.

In these circumstances, in 1301, Philip IV hauled a minor French bishop before the royal court on charges of heresy, blasphemy, and treason. Perhaps naively, he asked Boniface to concur. Instead, the pope sent the bull *Ausculta, fili carissime* to France. Its language was conciliatory but its message firm: No layman, not even the king of France, should dare to sit in judgment of a prelate of the church. In addition, Boniface summoned the bishops of France to a council to investigate the whole matter. Boniface's actions challenged Philip's authority in two ways. They implied that a power outside France could judge the actions of the French king and limit what he could do inside France. Philip's actions threatened the plenitude of papal power in the church and in Western society.

Pope Boniface VIII This contemporary statue of Boniface by the sculptor and architect Arnolfo di Cambio (d. ca. 1302), who did the original design for Florence's cathedral, depicts this most troubled of popes in majesty. Boniface had enemies, but admirers, too. (*Alinari/Mansell/Time Inc.*)

Philip mounted another propaganda campaign. One of his publicists wrote, "You, noble king, by inheritance above all other princes defender of the faith and destroyer of heretics, can, ought, and are obliged to require and so arrange that the said Boniface be held and judged as a heretic."[6] The spread of lay literacy gave more people access to, and an understanding of, the issues involved in this controversy. Philip called a council of his own to decide if the pope was a heretic. Meanwhile, the pope's enemies in Rome, and also some clergy, were accusing the pope of heresy and questioning the legitimacy of his election.

The Outcome

Boniface pressed ahead and held his council in 1302. Few French bishops, and none from the north of France, attended. The council issued the bull *Unam sanctam.* Though fully rooted in the statements of popes going back to Gregory VII, *Unam sanctam* is the most blatant manifesto of papal triumphalism ever issued. Its argument was quite simple. Church and society are one, and the pope is the sole head. Philip responded by sending royal officials to Rome in 1303. They joined forces with Boniface's Roman foes and a gang of thugs and then seized and beat the pope at Anagni, his summer residence. Boniface died three weeks later.

Comparisons are telling. Think of England's Henry II backing down, finally, in the Becket controversy. Or think of Germany's Henry IV, shivering in the snow beneath the walls of Canossa castle, begging forgiveness from Gregory VII. Then think of a Roman mob and of the minions of the king of France physically abusing an 80-year-old pope. All of our sources for the earlier events are in Latin and were written by clerics. Many sources for the events of 1302 are in French and Italian and were written by laymen. Henry II and Henry IV were advised by noble companions and relatives. Philip IV was counseled by trained lawyers.

SUMMARY

Comparisons between the Europe of 1150 and that of 1300 are instructive both as reminders of what had happened and as suggestions of what was to come. In 1150, Germany was promising, but troubled. It reaped only the trouble. France and England showed great promise, too, and they realized much of it. France produced a strong government, a royal saint, and European cultural leadership. England developed a strong monarchy, a superb legal system, and a significant new institution, Parliament. But England and France were bitter rivals and had risked financial ruin to pursue their struggle. Foreign conflicts and the quest for funds threatened the position of the monarchy in each country. In Catalonia and Aragon, and to a degree in Portugal, the Iberian Peninsula witnessed the steady growth of monarchies with ideals and institutions much like those in France and England. The long Reconquista was not over, but its outcome seemed assured. Italian cities, as different from one another as they all were from the royal states of northern Europe, continued to be politically daring and socially volatile. Russia, despite promising beginnings and impressive resources, had been devastated by the Mongols. Recovery in this easternmost European region was anything but assured.

The papacy entered the thirteenth century with the powerful Innocent III and departed with the humiliated Boniface VIII. The church was still a formidable institution with the pope as its head, yet popes had lost the power to dictate to secular rulers as they had once done. But if the church was more unified than ever before as an institution, it was more diverse than at any time since Late Antiquity as a set of competing spiritualities. Traditional monastic orders, the new communities of mendicants, and dynamic women's orders competed for places within the church, while growing numbers of heretics challenged the church from the outside. Along with the Crusades, these religious currents added up to Europe's first large-scale social movements.

For centuries the countryside had driven economic change, but momentum shifted during this period to cities. Universities, fundamentally urban institutions, became dominant as centers of learning in England, France, Italy, and the Rhineland. The Gothic style, initially an urban architecture, barely existed in 1150, yet by 1300 it was about to develop a series of national forms. Scholasticism was just visible in the work of Anselm and Abelard but ascendant in Thomas Aquinas.

As the fourteenth century dawned, people all over Europe had reasons to be both hopeful and anxious. They were, in fact, at the start of one of the most turbulent and creative periods in Western history, the period of transformation to which we now turn.

NOTES

1. Jacques de Vitry, *Historia Orientalis*, quoted in John R. H. Moorman, *The Sources for the Life of St. Francis of Assisi* (Manchester: Manchester University Press, 1940), p. 56.
2. Walter Map, *De Nugis Curialium*, 5.5, in John H. Mundy, *Europe in the High Middle Ages* (London: Longman, 1973), p. 387.
3. John Addington Symonds, *Wine, Women and Song: Medieval Latin Students' Songs* (reprint, New York: Cooper Square, 1966), p. 69.
4. Frederick Goldin, *Lyrics of the Troubadours and Trouvères: An Anthology and a History* (New York: Doubleday, 1973), p. 135.
5. Meg Bogin, *The Women Troubadours* (New York: Norton, 1976), p. 69.
6. Mundy, *Europe in the High Middle Ages*, p. 585.

SUGGESTED READING

General Surveys
Barber, Malcolm. *The Two Cities: Medieval Europe, 1050–1320.* 1992. Readable, comprehensive, and reliable, this book is an excellent starting point for further explorations.
Mundy, John H. *Europe in the High Middle Ages, 1150–1309.* 1973. A detailed and comprehensive introduction that is readable, witty, and sophisticated.

National Histories
Abulafia, David. *Frederick II: A Medieval Emperor.* 1988. The author's intention is to replace the mythical Frederick with a credible, medieval character.
Arnold, Benjamin. *Count and Bishop in Medieval Germany.* 1991. An exceptionally readable book that gets right to the heart of German local politics and of why it was so hard for kings to build up centralized rule.
Baldwin, John W. *The Government of Philip Augustus: Foundations of French Royal Power in the Middle Ages.* 1986. Massive and detailed yet readable and interesting, this book lays bare how the Capetian system really worked.
Brentano, Robert. *Rome Before Avignon: A Social History of Thirteenth-Century Rome.* 1974. Beautifully written, this book makes the reader feel as if he or she were walking the streets of Rome.
Haverkamp, Alfred. *Medieval Germany, 1056–1273.* 2d ed. 1992. Covering every aspect of German life, this book is the best introduction in English to the complex history of Germany.
Holt, J. C. *Magna Carta.* 2d ed. 1992. Since its appearance, this has been the standard introduction to the charter and all its problems.
Munz, Peter. *Frederick Barbarossa: A Study in Medieval Politics.* 1969. An entertaining book that is sensitive more to political realities than to abstract theoretical problems.
Nicholas, David. *Medieval Flanders.* 1992. Detailed and comprehensive, this authoritative book introduces a region often mentioned but usually not studied in detail. Offers striking contrasts with Italian developments.
Richard, Jean. *Saint Louis: Crusader King of France.* 1992. The fruit of a lifetime's work by a leading French medievalist, this book is both a detailed account of Louis's life and a compelling introduction to his age.
Strayer, Joseph R. *The Reign of Philip the Fair.* 1980. A half-century in the making, this book is part biography and part analytical history of an age.
Turner, Ralph V. *Men Raised from the Dust: Administrative Service and Upward Mobility in Angevin England.* 1988. A set of six biographies of royal officials, this book provides an interesting explanation of who made the English government work.
VanCaenegem, R. C. *The Birth of the English Common Law.* 2d ed. 1989. Written by a legal historian with a gift for clarity of presentation, this book provides immediate access to perhaps England's greatest legacy to the West.
Warren, W. L. *Henry II.* 1973. The standard biography of the great Angevin, this book is comprehensive, detailed, readable, and entertaining.

Society and Economy
Epstein, Steven A. *Wage Labor and Guilds in Medieval Europe.* 1991. Readable, interesting, and wide-ranging, this book teaches much about both guilds and urban life.
Keen, Maurice. *Chivalry.* 1984. Among many, many books on this subject, Keen's can be recommended for its balance, readability, and reliability.
Le Goff, Jacques, ed. *Medieval Callings.* 1990. This exceptionally interesting book has chapters on, among others, peasants, townfolk, merchants, monks, artists, and intellectuals.
Mollat, Michel. *The Poor in the Middle Ages: An Essay in Social History.* 1986. A nice mix of social analysis and theoretical observation, Mollat's book is engaging and instructive.
Paterson, Linda M. *The World of the Troubadours: Medieval Occitan Society, c. 1100-1300.* 1993. A wonderfully evocative account of the history and culture of southern France.

(continued on page 392)

THE ARTS OF CHARTRES CATHEDRAL

"Images exist so that the unlettered may read in pictures what the lettered read in books." These words of Pope Gregory I provided for a thousand years one justification for Christian representational art. Remember that the Hebrews, and the Muslims after them, forbade such representations. And the Byzantine world suffered through a tumultuous quarrel over sacred art. Nevertheless, Christian art was one of the crowning achievements of the Middle Ages.

Medieval artists attempted to portray biblical stories and theological ideas in paintings, glass, and stone. Before the thirteenth century, paintings were usually confined to books and were seen by very few people. Glass existed in early medieval and Romanesque churches but came into its own in Gothic churches. Sculpture began to appear on the façades of Romanesque churches but achieved unprecedented harmony and beauty on Gothic cathedrals. Unlike manuscript paintings, cathedral arts were public and visible to everyone. They were indeed "Bibles for the poor," as many have called them from the Middle Ages to the present.

But, despite Gregory's assurances, can we actually believe that ordinary, uneducated people—or even professional people who lacked theological training—"read" the statues on the front of a building like Chartres Cathedral, whose western portals are shown here? Probably not. In fact, art historians believe that the arts of a cathedral functioned as just one part of a cycle of local teaching, preaching, and celebrating that, taken as a whole, communicated fundamental Christian truths to people and then reaffirmed those truths every time the artistic representations were viewed. Thus the modern historian who wishes to understand the arts of a medieval building must research what was known and taught in a given place at a given time. Some themes are consistent from one place or time to another, but often we find significant differences.

The west front of the cathedral of Notre-Dame ("Our Lady") of Chartres, called the "Royal Portal" because Christ in majesty appears over the central door and because Chartres had associations with the kings of France, tells the story of Christ and his redemption of humanity. The story must be read as a whole and then in detail—right, left, and center.

Notice the twenty-four columnlike figures adjoining the three doors. Representations of kings and prophets of the Old Testament, they symbolize the human and spiritual ancestors of Christ. Over the heads of these figures you can see a continuous frieze that tells the Gospel story of the life of Christ.

Now look at the tympanum (large panel) over the door on the right. It shows Mary giving birth, Mary presenting Jesus in the temple, and Mary sitting on a throne with the baby Jesus on her lap. The archivolts—the rows of sculpture surrounding the tympanum—portray figures representing the seven liberal arts. Thus the incarnation of Christ is depicted and interpreted as something that not even all the wisdom of the world is able to grasp.

Turn now to the left door, where Christ is shown ascending to heaven. Beneath him, angels bring promise of a final judgment to the apostles waiting below. The archivolts around Christ contain signs of the zodiac and the labors of the months. The scene on the left door teaches that Christ left behind the world of human activity and even the fixed universe created by God, his father. The promise of salvation is offered to humans because Christ suffered and died to redeem them.

Now look at the central door. Here you see Christ in majesty—a representation that art historians call a "Maiestas." The apostles, who teach about Christ, are below him, and figures from the Book of Revelation surround him. This scene provides a glimpse of heaven while reminding people of the judgment they will face.

Chartres Cathedral, Western Façade (*Sonia Halliday*)

Historians can connect cathedrals to major cultural trends. For example, written sources tell us that a dramatic upswing in popular devotion to Mary occurred in the twelfth and thirteenth centuries. Artwork devoted to Mary confirms this. These Marian devotions probably reflect women's increasing participation in the spiritual life of the High Middle Ages. By holding up to women the image of pure, maternal, submissive Mary, the church may have been trying to control the excesses of female piety.

Historians also learn about social and economic realities from a study of cathedrals and their arts. The years after about 1140 saw tremendous competition among towns to build larger, finer, more elaborately decorated churches. Chartres sat in the middle of France's greatest grain-growing region, and the rising town had important textile, weapons, and harness manufacturers. It could well afford to rebuild and redecorate the west front in the 1140s and 1150s, and then rebuild the rest of the church after a fire destroyed it in 1194.

The sculpted stone of Chartres can even reveal its secrets to chemists. Specialists can test the stone of Chartres to see where it was quarried. This leads to research into stone-quarrying techniques and into the methods and finances of transport.

The arts of Chartres also show the interconnectedness of medieval culture. At least three sculptors worked on the western front. One of them also worked at St.-Denis in Paris and another at Étampes in Normandy. The artistic models for Chartres are to be sought in Provence, Burgundy, and Paris.

Look at other examples of medieval art in this book, and see what you can make of them. Do you know enough of biblical history and Christian theology to "read" these images? Can you think of connections between Chartres and medieval France beyond those cited here? ✑

Shahar, Shulamith. *The Fourth Estate: A History of Women in the Middle Ages.* 1983. Comprehensive and detailed but less interesting than its subject would suggest, this book slights the early Middle Ages but is solid on the high and late periods.

Religion and the Church

Brundage, James A. *Medieval Canon Law.* 1995. Learned but accessible, this book opens up the world of law and lawyers.

Bynum, Caroline Walker. *Jesus as Mother: Studies in the Spirituality of the High Middle Ages.* 1982. A collection of sparkling essays by a major historian that makes the feminine in religious thought accessible, even central, to any discussion of medieval religion.

Grundmann, Herbert. *Religious Movements in the Middle Ages.* 1995. Translated into English sixty years after its appearance in German, this book has lost none of its interest or explanatory power.

Lambert, Malcolm. *Medieval Heresy: Popular Movements from the Gregorian Reform to the Reformation.* 2d ed. 1992. Brilliant and readable, this book is the best history of medieval heresy ever written and one of the best books on medieval religion generally.

Little, Lester K. *Religious Poverty and the Profit Economy in Medieval Europe.* 1978. Readable and entertaining, this book seeks to connect religious, social, and economic ideas ranging from poverty to usury to anti-Semitism.

Moore, R. I. *The Origins of European Dissent.* 1985. A stimulating and sympathetic account of the origins and nature of heretical movements.

Morris, Colin. *The Papal Monarchy: The Western Church from 1050 to 1250.* 1989. Very thorough and detailed, this up-to-date history by a mature scholar is a good starting point for almost any inquiry into ecclesiastical history. Useful bibliography.

Riley-Smith, Jonathan. *The Crusades: A Short History.* 1987. The Crusades have spawned a massive literature. This is by far the best introduction, and its useful bibliography points to the detailed works.

Strayer, Joseph R. *The Albigensian Crusades.* 1992. A helpful 64-page "epilogue" by Carol Lansing updates this 1971 work.

Art and Ideas

Bony, Jean. *French Gothic Architecture of the Twelfth and Thirteenth Centuries.* 1983. Huge, clearly presented, and magnificently illustrated, this is a browser's book as well as a sustained essay by a master of his subject.

Jantzen, Hans. *High Gothic: The Classic Cathedrals of Chartres, Reims and Amiens.* 1984. In the voluminous and technically daunting literature on Gothic, this short book can be recommended for clarity, readability, and reliability.

Le Goff, Jacques. *The Medieval Imagination.* 1985. Challenging but rewarding, these essays by a leading historian try to evoke the mental world of a wide array of medieval people.

Mâle, Emile. *The Gothic Image: Religious Art in the France of the Thirteenth Century.* 1958. Since its publication in 1913, this book has attracted admirers and critics. No one doubts its brilliance, readability, or enduring value.

Morris, Colin. *The Discovery of the Individual, 1050–1200.* 1972. Brief and readable, Morris's book has set off much controversy about the definition of individualism and the time of its first appearance in Europe.

Price, Betsy Barker. *Medieval Thought: An Introduction.* 1992. Comprehensive yet brief, readable, and nontechnical, this book is an excellent introduction to Christian philosophy and theology that acknowledges and explains Jewish and Arab contributions.

Shaver-Crandell, Anne. *Cambridge Introduction to the History of Art: The Middle Ages.* 1982. Brief, carefully illustrated, and clearly written for the nonspecialist, this is an excellent starting point for the student of medieval art and architecture.

Zink, Michel. *Medieval French Literature: An Introduction.* 1995. Free of jargon, clear, and readable, this book does for the beginner what its title promises.

Questa e lentrata et luscita della generale biccherna del
di siena fatta attempo de sani huomini thomme di nof
a chamarlengho per uno anno chominando adi p̄imo digiēnai

CHAPTER II

The Transformation of Medieval Civilization, 1300–1500

I n the fourteenth century, Europeans sang an old Franciscan hymn, "Day of Wrath, Day of Burning," which described the fear and disorder that would accompany the end of the world and God's judgment of the saved and the damned. Images of God's judgment and the terrible fates awaiting sinners were constantly on the minds of Christians. As we see in the facing illustration, sinners, like these gamblers, fell victim to deadly plague carried by arrows shot by the winged angel of death. The flood, fire, and pestilence that ravaged late medieval Europe were thought to be premonitions of coming judgment.

The late Middle Ages (ca. 1300–1500) is often described as a period of continued crisis and decline that saw the end of the growth and expansion of the previous three centuries. In truth, however, this period was an age of transformation, of both crisis and recovery, that witnessed not only dislocation but also growth. In this chapter we discuss the roots of the crisis and the later economic, social, and political recovery in the fifteenth century. The cultural and intellectual changes that accompanied the crisis and recovery are the focus of Chapter 12, "The Renaissance."

Military, political, religious, economic, and social crises burdened Europe in the fourteenth and early fifteenth centuries. Between 1337 and 1453, France and England fought what was in effect a world war. The Hundred Years' War, as it has come to be known, was primarily fought over English

Painted cover for a fifteenth-century government account book from Siena, Italy, showing symbols of death—arrows, a scythe, and a horse—to carry the angel of death from place to place.

claims to traditionally French lands. Social and political disruptions and the economic burdens of the war allowed the nobles of England and France to limit royal power and made local administration more difficult. Both monarchies transformed themselves in the aftermath of political strife, however, in ways that preserved and even increased royal power.

Problems were not confined to England and France. Although by 1300 the monarchies, the city-states of Italy, and the papacy had the legal systems, tax structures, and traditions of representation that were to be the foundations of modern European government and representative institutions, aristocrats in many parts of Europe challenged the hereditary rights of their rulers. In the towns of Germany and Italy, patrician classes moved to reduce the influence of artisans and laborers in government, instituting oligarchies or even aristocratic dictatorships in place of more democratic governments.

Questions of power and representation also affected the Christian church as ecclesiastical claims to authority came under attack. Secular governments challenged church jurisdictions. Disputed papal elections led to the so-called Great Schism, a split between rival centers of control in Rome and Avignon (a city in what is now the south of France). In dealing with the schism and with more general problems of moral reform, the church hierarchy was challenged by those who argued that authority resided in the whole church and not just with its head, the pope. In the aftermath of the crisis, the papacy was forced to redefine its place in both the religious and the political life of Europe.

A series of economic and demographic shocks worsened these political and religious difficulties. Part of the problem was structural: The population of Europe grew too large to be supported by the resources available. Famine and the return of the bubonic plague in 1348 sent the economy into long-term decline. In almost every aspect of political, religious, and social life, then, the fourteenth and early fifteenth centuries marked a pause in the expansion and consolidation that had characterized the previous century and a half and the growth that was to mark the sixteenth century.

Yet some of the seeds of that future growth were planted during this period. Two empires quite unlike the monarchical states of the twelfth and thirteenth centuries appeared in the fifteenth century. The marriage of the sovereigns of Aragon and Castile formed a new Spanish Empire that would become the most powerful government in sixteenth-century Europe, while at the other end of the Mediterranean, a new Muslim Turkish empire replaced the weakened Byzantine Empire. Neither state had existed in 1300, and the future seemed to belong to them.

THE CRISIS OF THE WESTERN CHRISTIAN CHURCH

Early in the fourteenth century, the Christian church endured a series of shocks that began a debate about the nature of church government and the role of the church in society. First, the popes moved from their traditional seat of authority in central Italy to Avignon. Then, in the wake of a disputed election, two and later three rivals claimed the papal throne. Simultaneously, the church hierarchy faced challenges from radical reformers who wished to change it. At various times all the European powers got involved in the problems of the church. By the mid-fifteenth century, the papacy realized that it needed a stronger, independent base. In response it transformed itself into a major political power in central Italy.

The French attack on Pope Boniface VIII in 1303 (see page 387) had exposed the weakness of the papacy as a political power and also revealed the deep splits within the Christian community. Although Philip IV's agents were excommunicated for their deeds, Boniface's successors, many of whom were from French-speaking lands, tried to reach an accommodation with the king. It was, in fact, largely because of Philip that the French archbishop of Bordeaux was elected Pope Clement V (r. 1305–1314). Clement chose to remain north of the Alps in order to seek an end to warfare between France and England and to protect, to the extent possible, the wealthy religious order of the Templars, which Philip was in the process of suppressing (see page 317). He hoped also to prevent the king from carrying through his threatened posthumous heresy trial of Boniface. After the death of Boniface, it was clear that the governments of Europe had no intention of recognizing papal authority as absolute.

The Babylonian Captivity, 1309–1377

Clement's pontificate marked the beginning of the so-called Babylonian Captivity, a period during which the pope resided almost continuously in what is now the south of France. In 1309, Clement moved the papal court to Avignon, on the Rhône River in a region that was technically part of the Holy Roman Empire (the name that by the fourteenth century was given to the medieval empire whose origin reached back to Charlemagne). Initially there had been no plan to remain outside of Italy, but by the 1330s the popes had created a large and brilliant court in Avignon, perhaps the largest in Europe. Pope John XXII (r. 1316–1334) set the tone for the court. To celebrate the marriage of his grandniece in 1324, for example, he ordered a wedding feast during which numerous guests consumed 4012 loaves of bread, 8¾ oxen, 55¼ sheep, 8 pigs, 4 boars, and vast quantities of fish,

capons, chickens, partridges, rabbits, ducks, and chickens. The repast was topped off with 300 pounds of cheese, 3000 eggs, and assorted fruits. The guests washed down this feast with about 450 liters of wine.

It is indicative of the changed circumstances of the popes that although the thirteenth-century papal administration required only two hundred or so officials, the bureaucracy grew to about six hundred in Avignon. It was not just the pope's immediate circle that expanded the population of Avignon. Artists, writers, lawyers, and merchants from across Europe were drawn to the new center of administration and patronage. Kings, princes, towns, and ecclesiastical institutions needed representatives at the papal court. Papal administrators continued to intervene actively in local ecclesiastical affairs, and revenues that the popes claimed in the form of annates (generally a portion of the first year's revenues from an ecclesiastical office

Papal Avignon During the pontificate of Benedict XII the papal palace was begun in Avignon. It became the center of the most brilliant and politically important court in fourteenth-century Europe. *(Altitude, Paris)*

THE CRISIS OF THE WESTERN CHURCH

1302	Boniface VIII issues *Unam sanctam*
1303	Boniface VIII is attacked at Anagni and dies
1305	Election of Clement V
1309	Clement V moves the papal court to Avignon; beginning of the Babylonian Captivity
1377	End of the Babylonian Captivity
1378	Death of Gregory XI in Rome
1378	Elections of rival popes: Urban VI and Clement VII; start of the Great Schism
1409	Council of Pisa elects a third pope
1414–1417	Council of Constance deposes all three papal claimants
1415	Council of Constance condemns and executes John Hus
1417	Election of Martin V by the Council of Constance; end of the Great Schism
1438	Pragmatic Sanction of Bourges gives French kings influence in the French church

granted by papal letter), court fees, and provisioning fees continued to grow.

Not everyone approved of this situation. It was the Italian poet and philosopher Francesco Petrarch (1304–1374) who first referred to a "Babylonian Captivity of the papacy." Recalling the exile of the Israelites and the image of Babylon as a center of sin and immorality, he complained of

[an] unholy Babylon, Hell on Earth, a sink of iniquity, the cesspool of the world. There is neither faith, nor charity, nor religion, nor fear of God, nor shame, nor truth, nor holiness, albeit the residence . . . of the supreme pontiff should have made it a shrine and the very stronghold of religion.[1]

To Petrarch and to others, the exile of the papacy from its traditional see in Rome stood as an example of all that was wrong with the church.

Those who came to the court were practical and worldly. Many people renowned for their piety, like Saint Catherine of Siena and Saint Bridget of Sweden, appealed to the pope to return to simpler ways and to Rome, his episcopal city. (See the box, "Saint Catherine and the Avignon Papacy.")

Late in 1377, Pope Gregory XI (r. 1370–1378) did return to Rome. He found churches and palaces in ruin and the city violent and dangerous. He would have retreated to Avignon had he not died a few months later. In a tumultuous election during which the Roman populace threatened to break into the conclave, the cardinals finally elected a compromise candidate acceptable both to the French cardinals and to the Roman mob. Urban VI (r. 1378–1389) was an Italian cleric from a French-controlled part of Italy. He was also violent, intemperate, and eager to reduce the privileges of the clerical hierarchy. Many cardinals soon feared for their own safety. Some immediately questioned the legitimacy of the election, which they believed had been conducted under duress. Within months they deposed Urban and elected in his place a French cardinal who took the name Clement VII (r. 1378–1394). Urban responded by denouncing the cardinals and continuing to rule in Rome. There were now two popes.

After some hesitation, Western Christians divided into two camps, initiating the Great Schism, a period of almost forty years during which no one knew for sure who was the true pope. Each side found ready supporters among the states of Europe; however, support for one pope or the other often had more to do with political rivalries than with religious conviction. The French supported Clement, who eventually resettled in Avignon. The English, together with the Italians and most of the German Empire, supported Urban, the pope in Rome. Scotland, a mortal enemy of the English, and Castile sided with the French.

The crisis gave impetus to new discussions about church government: Should the pope be considered the sole head of the church? Debates within the church followed lines of thought already expressed in the towns and kingdoms of Europe. Representative bodies—the English Parliament, the French Estates General, the Swedish Riksdag—already claimed the right to act for the realm, and in the city-states of Italy ultimate authority was thought to reside in the body of citizens. Canon lawyers and theologians similarly ar-

Saint Catherine and the Avignon Papacy

Like most of her female contemporaries, Catherine Benincasa (1347–1380) was given no formal education. Nonetheless, because of her piety and spirituality, she was named a "Doctor of the Church"—a title granted only to the most important and influential theologians. Catherine surrounded herself with a "spiritual family" of men and women from many parts of Italy and used her influence to pressure the popes to return to Rome and to reform the church. She was also more than willing to use her influence to bring about political reconciliation between the papacy and Italian governments. This letter to Pope Gregory XI was probably dictated (Catherine was illiterate) in 1376. It was instrumental in his decision to return to Rome.

My soul longs with inestimable love that God in His infinite mercy will take from you each passion and all tepidity of heart and will reform you into another man by rekindling in you an ardent and burning desire, for in no other way can you fulfill the will of God and the desires of all His servants. Alas, my sweetest Babbo [literally "Daddy"], pardon my presumption in what I have said and am saying—the sweet and primal Truth forces me. This is His will, Father; He demands this of you. He demands that you require justice in the multitude of iniquities committed by those nourished and sheltered in the garden of the Holy Church; He declares that beasts should not receive men's food. Because He has given you authority and because you have accepted it, you ought to use your virtue and power. If you

do not wish to use it, it might be better for you to resign what you have accepted; it would give more honor to God and health to your soul.

In addition, His will demands that you make peace with all Tuscany where now you have strife. Receive all your wicked and rebellious sons whenever you can peacefully do so—but punish them as a father would an offending son. . . . [T]hat which appears impossible to you is possible to the sweet goodness of God who has ordained and willed that it be so. Beware, as you hold your life dear, that you are not negligent in this nor treat lightly the works of the Holy Spirit. . . . You can have peace by avoiding the perverse pomps and delights of the world and by preserving God's honor and the Holy Church's rights.

Source: Robert Coogan, *Babylon on the Rhone: A Translation of Letters by Dante, Petrarch, and Catherine of Siena on the Avignon Papacy* (Potomac, Md.: Studia Humanitatis, 1983), p. 115.

gued that authority resided in the whole church, which had the right and duty to come together in council to correct and reform the church hierarchy. The most conservative of these "conciliarists" said merely that although the pope normally ruled the church on earth, the "Universal Church" had the right to respond in periods of heresy or schism. More radical conciliarists argued that the pope as bishop of Rome was merely the first among equals in the church hierarchy and he, like any other bishop, could be corrected by a gathering of his peers—that is, by a general council of the church.

As more and more churchmen assumed one or another of the conciliarist positions, the rival popes found themselves under increased pressure to end the schism. The issue seemed on its way to resolution when the two parties agreed to meet in northern Italy in 1408. In the end, though, the meeting never took place, and in retrospect many doubted whether either party had been negotiating in good faith. In exasperation the cardinals, the main ecclesiastical supporters of the rival popes, agreed to call a general council of the church. Meeting in Pisa in 1409, the council deposed both popes and elected a new pope. The council, however, lacked the power to force the rivals to accept deposition, and so the only result was that three men now claimed to be the rightful successor of Saint Peter and the Vicar of Christ. The outcome of the Council of Pisa demonstrated that the conciliarists, by themselves, could not heal the split in the church. A workable solution would not come until secular rulers were willing to enforce it.

Heresy, Reunion, and Reform

The Holy Roman emperor, Sigismund (r. 1411–1437), vigorously lobbied the other European powers to support a call for a council. When the other rulers agreed, the rival popes had to accept. The third papal claimant, John XXIII (r. 1410–1415), even felt compelled to call a general council of the church. Resolution of the schism was but one of the items on the agenda of the churchmen attending the council, which met from 1414 to 1417 in the German imperial city of Constance under the auspices of Sigismund.

Sigismund needed a council because he faced a religious civil war in Bohemia, the most important part of his family's traditional lands (see Map 11.3). Bohemia and its capital, Prague, were Czech-speaking. But Prague was also the seat of the Luxembourg dynasty of German emperors and the site of the first university in the German world. The issue centered on the preaching of Czech reformer John Hus (ca. 1370–1415). As preacher in the Bethlehem Chapel in Prague and theologian at the university, Hus was the natural spokesman for the non-German townsmen in Prague and the Czech minority at the university. His criticisms of the church hierarchy, which in Prague was primarily German, fanned the flames of Czech national feeling. It was Sigismund's hope that a council might heal the rift within the church of Bohemia.

The council's response to the issue of heresy was based on the church's experience with heresy over the previous forty years. In the 1370s, John Wyclif (1329–1384), an Oxford theologian and parish priest, began to criticize in increasingly vitriolic terms the state of the clergy and the depredations of the church hierarchy. By 1387, Wyclif's ideas had been declared heretical and his followers suffered ecclesiastical persecution. Wyclif's criticisms had been especially dangerous because he denied the position of the priest as an intermediary between God and believers. Wyclif believed that the church could be at once a divine institution and an earthly gathering of individuals. Thus, in his opinion, the pronouncements of the church hierarchy had no magisterial status. Wyclif gave that special status to Scripture, to the Bible. Wyclif once claimed that he had a number of "poor priests" spreading his doctrines in the countryside. He did gather about himself followers called Lollards, who emphasized Bible-reading and popular piety and supported public preaching by women. According to one, "every true man and woman being in charity is a priest."[2] Because of their attacks on the ecclesiastical hierarchy, Lollards were popular among the nobility of England, and especially at the court of Richard II during the 1390s. In the first two decades of the fifteenth century, however, their influence waned.

Wyclif's most lasting impact was probably his influence on John Hus and the Husite movement that he inspired. Following the teachings of Wyclif, Hus attacked clerical power and privileges. By 1403 the German majority in the university had condemned Hus's teaching as Wyclifite, thus initiating almost a decade of struggle between Czechs and Germans, Husites and Catholics. In an effort to break the impasse, Sigismund offered Hus a safe-conduct pass to attend the Council of Constance. The emperor fully expected some sort of reconciliation that would absolve Hus and thus reduce the possibility of civil war in Bohemia. As matters progressed, however, it became clear that the councilors and Hus himself were in no mood to compromise. The council revoked the pledge of safe conduct and ordered Hus to recant his beliefs. He refused. The council condemned him as a heretic and burned him at the stake on July 6, 1415.

Far from ending Sigismund's problems with the Bohemians, the actions of the council provided the Czechs with a martyr and hero. The Husite movement continued to gather strength. Radical Husites argued that the true church was the community of spiritual men and women. They had no use for ecclesiastical hierarchy of any kind. The German emperors were unable to defeat a united Husite movement. So from 1430 to 1433 the emperor and moderate Husites negotiated an agreement that allowed the Husites to continue some of their practices while returning to the church. The Husite war engulfed all of Bohemia and dragged on until 1436. Bohemia remained a center of religious dissent, and the memory of the execution of Hus at a church council would have a chilling effect on discussions of church reform during the Reformation in the sixteenth century.

The council was more successful in dealing with the schism, which to most Europeans seemed the most pressing issue before it. Gregory XII (r. 1406–1415), the Roman pope, soon realized that he had lost all his support. Although Pope John had convened the council, Gregory was allowed to issue a new call for the council (as a rightful pope should do). His call was immediately followed by his letter of resignation. John still hoped to survive as the one legitimately elected pope, but the council deposed him on May 29, 1415. The council also deposed Benedict III (r. 1394–1417), the pope in Avignon, in 1417. The council justified its actions in what was perhaps its most important decree, *Haec sancta synodus* (This sacred synod):

This sacred synod of Constance . . . declares . . . that it has its power immediately from Christ, and that all men, of every rank and position, including even the pope himself are bound to obey it in those matters that pertain to the faith.[3]

The Great Schism had ended. In the final sessions of the Council of Constance, Odo of Colonna, member of an old Roman noble family, was elected pope of the newly reunified church. Taking the name of Martin V (r. 1417–1431), he presided over an institution that had changed dramatically since the papacy of Boniface VIII a hundred years earlier. Popes could no longer expect to remain unchallenged if they made claims of absolute dominion similar to those made by Boniface in *Unam sanctam* (see page 388). And ecclesiastical rights and jurisdictions increasingly were matters for negotiation between popes and the governments of Europe. As we will see in Chapter 12 (see page 466) popes depended on their Italian lands for wealth and on the image of Rome for a historical explanation for their status and authority.

The Reformed Papacy

The issue of papal reform was complex. Critics agreed that the pope no longer behaved like the "Servant of the Servants of Christ" but instead acted like the "Lord of Lords." Cardinals claimed to represent the church at large as counterweights

Pope Martin Receiving the Crown from a Council Delegates to the Council of Constance stated that even the pope had to accept the decrees of a council sitting for the whole church. *(From* Chronik des Konstanzen Konzils, *1414–1418. Courtesy, Rosgartenmuseum, Constance)*

to papal abuse, but as the nobility of the church, they and other members of the hierarchy required multiple benefices to maintain their presence at the papal court. Both the cardinals and the popes viewed any reforms to the present system as potential threats to their ability to function. The council, however, recognized the need for further reforms. In the decree *Frequens* (Frequently), the council mandated that reform councils be called regularly, and a reform council met at Basel from 1431 to 1449, but with little success. It tried again to reduce papal power, but it received no support from European governments.

Because of the continuing conciliarist threat, the papacy was forced to accept compromises on the issues of reform, ecclesiastical jurisdictions and immunities, and rights to papal revenues. It continued to claim highest jurisdiction, but lay rulers viewed their own religious role as special. Various governments argued that it was they, and not the pope, who should be responsible for ecclesiastical institutions and jurisdictions within their territories.

Lay rulers focused on several issues. They wanted church officials in their territories to be from local families. They wanted ecclesiastical institutions to be subject to local laws and administration. And by the 1470s, it was clear that they wanted to have local prelates named as cardinal-protectors, churchmen who could serve as mediators between local government and the papacy. The most famous of these new political cardinals is Cardinal Thomas Wolsey of England (ca. 1470–1530), who was an important supporter of King Henry VII and chancellor of England under Henry VIII.

One of the most important compromises between the papacy and the monarchs was the Pragmatic Sanction of Bourges of 1438, by which the French crown established a claim to a church largely independent of papal influence. The agreement abolished papal rights to annates, limited appeals to the papal court, and reduced papal rights to appoint clergy within France without the approval of the local clergy or the Crown. The Pragmatic Sanction was the first of a number of claims for a unique "Gallican church," a national church free from outside interference. There were similar treaties throughout Europe. Perhaps the most momentous was a bull issued in 1478 by Pope Sixtus IV (r. 1471–1484) that allowed Ferdinand and Isabella of Aragon and Castile to institute a church court, the Spanish Inquisition, under their own authority (see page 430).

The papal concessions signaled a changed relationship between the papacy and the governments of Europe. With reduced revenues from jurisdictions, annates, and appointments, the papacy of the fifteenth century was forced to derive more and more of its revenue and influence from its traditional Papal States in central Italy. By the late 1420s, the Papal States produced about half of the annual income of the papacy. Papal interests increasingly centered on protecting the papacy's influence among the Italian states. Thus, the papacy had to deal with many of the jurisdictional, diplomatic, and military challenges that faced medieval governments.

THE CHALLENGE TO MEDIEVAL GOVERNMENTS

A lawyer who served King Philip IV of France (r. 1285–1314) observed that "everything within the limits of his kingdom belongs to the lord king, especially protection, high justice and dominion."[4] Royal officials in England and France generally believed that "liberties"—that is, individual rights to local jurisdictions—originated with the king. At almost the same time, however, an English noble challenged royal claims on his lands, saying, "Here, my lords, is my warrant," as he brandished a rusty longsword. "My ancestors came with William the Bastard [that is, with William the Conqueror in 1066] and conquered their lands with the sword, and by the sword I will defend them against anyone who tries to usurp them."[5] The old earl clearly believed that the rights and traditions of the aristocracy limited even royal attempts to centralize authority.

The issue throughout Europe in the late Middle Ages was whether central, regional, or even local authorities should dominate political and social life. In England and France traditional elites initially limited royal power, but by 1500 it was firmly re-established. From Italy through central Europe and into Scandinavia, however, late medieval monarchies found themselves hard-pressed to dominate political life. Yet as the development of the grand duchy of Tuscany, the independent feeling of the Swiss states, the free peasantry of Scandinavia, and the rise of Moscovy demonstrate, political order and stability may characterize territorial states as well as centralized monarchies.

England, France, and the Hundred Years' War

In the twelfth and thirteenth centuries, as we have seen, centralization of royal power proceeded almost without interruption. In the fourteenth century, matters changed. Charles IV of France died in 1328 without heirs, and his successor soon faced a long war that brought into question the king's control of most of France. And in England after the death of Edward I in 1307, monarchs found their power limited by forces largely beyond their control.

Fears arising from the growing power of the Crown and the weakness of an easily influenced king brought issues to a head during the reign of Edward II (r. 1307–1327). By the early fourteenth century, resident justices of the peace were replacing the expensive and inefficient eyre system of traveling justices (see page 365). In theory, they were royal officials doing the king's bidding. In reality, these unpaid local officials were modestly well-to-do gentry who were often clients of local magnates. Justices were known to use their office to carry out local vendettas and feuds and to protect the interests of the wealthy and powerful.

The barons, the titled lords of England, were interested in controlling more than just local justices. Fearing that Edward II would continue many of the centralizing policies of his father and ignore what the barons considered their traditional place as the king's natural advisers, the barons forced the king to accept the Ordinances of 1311. These statutes required a greatly expanded role for Parliament, and especially for the barons sitting in Parliament. According to the ordinances, the king could no longer wage war, leave the realm, grant lands or castles, or appoint chief justices and chancellors without the approval of the barons in Parliament. All funds raised by special taxes or subsidies were to be paid to the public Exchequer rather than into the king's private household treasury. Some of the ordinances were later voided, but the basic principle of parliamentary consent remained central to English constitutional history. In spite of Parliament's power to limit royal acts, kings used Parliament because it had the power to vote new taxes and generally did so when funds were necessary for the defense of the realm—a common occurrence during these centuries. Thus, Parliament grew in power because it usually did what the monarchy asked.

The baronial influence grew because Edward II was a weak and naive king, easily influenced by his court favorites. He suffered a humiliating defeat at the hands of the Scots at the Battle of Banockburn (1314), and his position steadily deteriorated until he was deposed in 1327 by a coalition of barons led by Queen Isabella. After a short regency, his son, Edward III (r. 1327–1377), assumed the throne. He was a cautious king, ever aware of the volatility of the baronage.

Observing the civil strife and open rebellion that characterized England in the early fourteenth century, French thinkers prided themselves on the stability of the French monarchy. "The government of the earth," the royal lawyer Jean of Jandun proclaimed, "belongs rightly to the august and sovereign House of France." Nonetheless, the French monarchy in the early fourteenth century also found its prerogatives limited. As in England, there were institutional limits to the power of the kings; and again, as in England, these limits were compounded by events that were to lead to virtual civil war within the kingdom.

A series of relatively weak kings during the fourteenth century made clear the limits of French

ENGLAND AND FRANCE IN THE LATE MIDDLE AGES

1259	Treaty of Paris grants Aquitaine to Henry III of England as a French fief
1311	English barons force Edward II to accept the Ordinances of 1311
1327	Parliament deposes Edward II
1328	The last Capetian king dies; French nobles elect Philip of Valois king of France (Philip VI)
1340	Edward III of England formally claims the French crown
1346	Battle of Crécy
1356	Battle of Poitiers
1399	Abdication of Richard II; accession of Henry IV
1415	Battle of Agincourt
1420	Treaty of Troyes
1422	Charles VI of France and Henry V of England die
1431	Joan of Arc is tried and executed
1453	The last battle of the Hundred Years' War
1483	Death of Edward IV; death of Edward V and his brother in the Tower of London
1485	Death of Richard III at the battle of Bosworth Fields
1491	Charles VIII reclaims French control of Brittany by marrying Anne of Brittany
1494	Charles VIII invades Italy

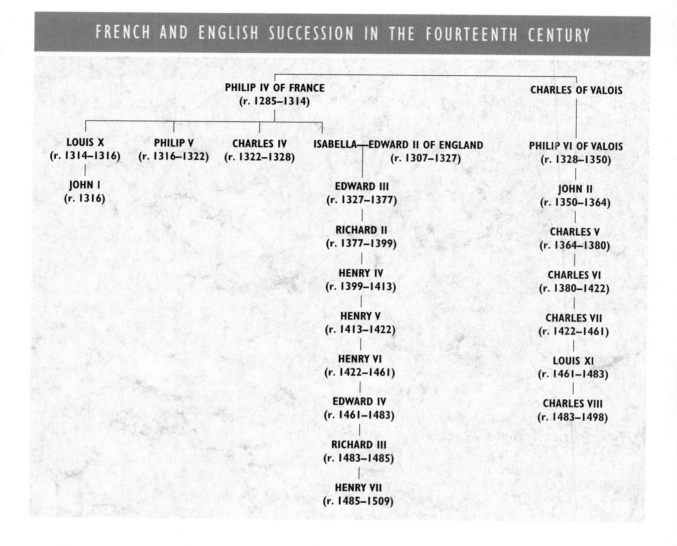

FRENCH AND ENGLISH SUCCESSION IN THE FOURTEENTH CENTURY

kingship. Philip IV was succeeded by his three sons, each of whom died without a legitimate male heir. In 1328 the direct Capetian line, which had provided the kings of France since the election of Hugh Capet in 987, finally died out. The last Capetians did produce daughters, but since the fourteenth century it was customary that the French crown should pass through the male line only. Thus, the French nobility selected as king Philip of Valois (Philip VI; r. 1328–1350), a cousin of the last king through the male line. He was chosen in preference to the daughters of the last kings and, more significantly, in preference to King Edward III of England, whose mother was the daughter of the late king Philip IV.

In 1340, Edward III of England formally claimed the title "king of France." As a grandson of Philip IV, he claimed he was the rightful heir of the last Capetian king. Although Edward's claim to the French throne was certainly part of the reason for the Hundred Years' War, the issue of the crown merely worsened diplomatic and political tensions between the two monarchies. There were numerous other problems: the long-standing claims of the English kings to territories in France, the fragmented nature of the French monarchy itself, and the volatile nature of international politics.

Since the mid-thirteenth century Treaty of Paris, the French had recognized English control of the duchy of Aquitaine, which the English king

Ransoming Captives One English strategy during the first stages of the Hundred Years' War was seizing and ransoming French knights such as Charles of Blois, whose capture is illustrated here. *(Bibliothèque Nationale)*

was to hold as a vassal of the French king (see Map 11.1). This created two insoluble problems. First, the French kings claimed that as dukes of Aquitaine, the English kings owed *liege homage*—that is, while kneeling before the French king, they had to swear to provide military aid whenever the French king asked for it. The French king could use liege homage to humiliate the English king and to limit English diplomatic relations with other kingdoms. Second, the treaty implied French sovereignty over Aquitaine, an area in which the French previously had enjoyed little influence. French kings claimed the rights to hear judicial appeals from the area. To the French kings, these appeals were a normal part of the process of judicial centralization. To the English kings, they were an unacceptable subversion of English jurisdiction and a sign that acknowledging French claims in Aquitaine had been a mistake. In frustration, Edward finally made his fateful claim to the French throne, thus igniting the war.

The Hundred Years' War was a series of short raids and expeditions punctuated by a few major battles and marked off by truces or ineffective treaties. The relative strengths of the two kingdoms dictated the sporadic nature of the struggle.

With a population of about sixteen million, France was far richer and more populous than England. On at least one occasion the French managed to field an army of over 50,000; at most the English mustered only 32,000. These armies were easily the largest ever assembled by a medieval kingdom. In almost every engagement the English were outnumbered. The most successful English strategy was to avoid pitched battles and engage in a series of quick, profitable raids during which they stole what they could, destroyed what they could not steal, and captured enemy knights to hold for ransom.

The war can be divided into four stages (Map 11.1). The first stage, from 1337 to 1360, was characterized by English raids led by the crown prince Edward, later called "the Black Prince" because of the black armor he once wore. The few pitched battles, Crécy (1346) and Poitiers (1356), for example, were resounding victories for the English, who took advantage of an individualistic French chivalric ethos according to which, in the words of one knight, "Who does the most is worth the most." In both battles, smaller English armies in excellent defensive positions used longbowmen to

406

English Channel

ENGLAND

Southampton · Calais
FLANDERS
PONTHIEU

NORMANDY
Paris · CHAMPAGNE
Seine

HOLY
ROMAN
EMPIRE

BRITTANY
MAINE
ANJOU
Loire
TOURAINE
BURGUNDY

POITOU

AUVERGNE
AQUITAINE
Bordeaux ·
Garonne
DAUPHINÉ
Rhône

0   100 Km.
0   100 Mi.
GASCONY
· Saint-Sardos
LANGUEDOC
· Toulouse

1337
(before the Battle of Crécy)

☐ English holdings
☐ French holdings
— Extent of English holdings
    after Treaty of Paris, 1259

SPAIN

Mediterranean
Sea

ENGLAND

English Channel

Calais
FLANDERS
Crécy ✕
1346
· Rouen

NORMANDY
Paris · CHAMPAGNE
Seine

HOLY
ROMAN
EMPIRE

BRITTANY
MAINE
ANJOU
Loire
TOURAINE
Poitiers ✕
1356
POITOU

BURGUNDY

AUVERGNE
AQUITAINE
Bordeaux ·
Garonne
DAUPHINÉ
Rhône

0   100 Km.
0   100 Mi.
GASCONY
LANGUEDOC
· Toulouse

1360
(after the Battle of Poitiers)

☐ English holdings
☐ French holdings
✕ Major battles

SPAIN

Mediterranean
Sea

ENGLAND

HOLY
ROMAN
EMPIRE

Calais
FLANDERS
Agincourt ✕
1415

English Channel

· Rouen
Reims ·
NORMANDY
Paris · CHAMPAGNE
Domrémy ·
Seine
· Orléans
BRITTANY
MAINE
ANJOU
Loire
· Bourges
DUCHY OF
BURGUNDY
COUNTY OF
BURGUNDY
TOURAINE

POITOU

AUVERGNE
AQUITAINE
Bordeaux ·
Garonne
DAUPHINÉ
Rhône

0   100 Km.
0   100 Mi.
GASCONY
LANGUEDOC
· Toulouse

SPAIN

ca. 1429
(after the siege of Orléans)

☐ English holdings
☐ French holdings
☐ Burgundian lands allied
    with England to 1435
✕ Major battle

Mediterranean
Sea

ENGLAND

Calais
FLANDERS
BRABANT

English Channel

LUXEMBOURG
HOLY
ROMAN
EMPIRE

NORMANDY
Paris · CHAMPAGNE
Seine

BRITTANY
MAINE
ANJOU
Loire
DUCHY OF
BURGUNDY
COUNTY OF
BURGUNDY
TOURAINE

POITOU

AQUITAINE
AUVERGNE
Bordeaux ✕ Castillon-sur-Dordogne
1453
Garonne
DAUPHINÉ
Rhône

0   100 Km.
0   100 Mi.
GASCONY
LANGUEDOC
· Toulouse

1453
(end of war)
SPAIN

☐ English holdings
☐ French holdings
☐ Burgundian lands reconciled
    with France after 1435
✕ Last battle

Mediterranean
Sea

their best advantage. In the second phase of the war, from 1360 to 1396, careful French leaders managed to regain control of much of the land they had lost. Edward III's grandson, Richard II (r. 1377–1399), could not afford the expensive French war and in 1396 signed an unpopular truce. Three years later he was forced to abdicate; he died, probably murdered, a year later.

The most fateful shift occurred in the third stage, from 1396 to 1422. Because King Charles VI (r. 1380–1422) of France suffered bouts of insanity throughout his long reign, effective French resistance to the English was almost impossible. Political power fell into the hands of dukes of Burgundy and of Orléans, whose political maneuvering led to civil war in France. With the aid of the Burgundian factions, the English king Henry V (r. 1413–1422) renewed his family's claim to the French throne. At Agincourt in 1415, the English (led this time by Henry) again enticed a larger French army into attacking a fortified English position, and again a hail of arrows from English longbows shattered the advance. With Burgundian aid, Henry gained control over Normandy, Paris, and much of northern France. By the terms of the Treaty of Troyes (1420), Henry married Catherine, the daughter of Charles VI, and became the heir to the French throne. A final English victory seemed assured, but both Charles VI and Henry V died in 1422, leaving the infant Henry VI with claims to both kingdoms.

The kings' deaths ushered in the final stage of the war, the French reconquest, from 1422 to 1453. In 1428, military and political power seemed firmly in the hands of the English and the great aristocrats. Charles VI's successor, the dauphin (or crown prince) Charles VII (r. 1422–1461), was derisively called "the king of Bourges," after the town south of the Loire where he remained under the protection and virtual control of a court faction. Yet in a stunning series of events, the French were able to reverse the situation.

In 1429, with the aid of the mysterious Joan of Arc (d. 1431), the king was able to raise the Eng-

lish siege of Orléans and begin the reconquest of the north of France. Joan was the daughter of prosperous peasants. Like other late medieval mystics she reported regular visions of divine revelation. Her "voices" told her to go to the king and aid him in driving out the English. Dressed as a man, she was Charles's most charismatic and feared military leader. With Joan's aid the king was crowned in the cathedral at Reims, the traditional site of French coronations. Joan was captured during an audacious attack on Paris itself. Charles, however, refused to ransom "the Maid," as she was known, and eventually she fell into English hands. Because of her "unnatural dress" and her claim to divine illumination, she was condemned and burned as a heretic in 1431. A heretic only to the English and their supporters, Joan almost instantly became a symbol of French resistance. Pope Calixtus III reversed the condemnation in 1456, and in 1920 she was canonized. (See the box, "The Inquisition of Joan of Arc.") The heretic became Saint Joan, patron of France.

Despite Joan's capture, the French advance continued. By 1450 the English had lost all their major centers except Calais. In 1453, the French armies captured the fortress of Castillon-sur-Dordogne in what was to be the last battle of the war (see Map 11.1). There was no treaty, only a cessation of hostilities.

The Results of the War

The war touched almost every aspect of life in late medieval Europe: political, religious, economic, and social. It ranged beyond the borders of France as Scotland, Castile, Aragon, and German principalities were drawn at various times into the struggle. French and English support for rival popes prevented early settlement of the Great Schism in the papacy (see page 398). Further, the war caused a general rise in the level of violence in society. As Henry V casually observed, "War without fire is as bland as sausages without mustard."[6] And because of the highly profitable quick raids, the war was never bland. Soldiers regularly stole or ransomed all they could take. What could not be carried was burned. During periods of truce soldiers went in search of work as mercenaries in other parts of Europe. The English mercenary Sir John Hawkwood (d. 1394), for example, finished his life as "ser Giovanni Acuto," a heralded military

Map 11.1 England and France in the Hundred Years' War The succession of maps depicts both why hit-and-run tactics worked for the English early in the war and why the English were ultimately unable to defeat the French and take control of all of France.

The Inquisition of Joan of Arc

Between January and May 1431, Joan of Arc was investigated by an inquisitorial commission. The minutes of the trial were later translated into Latin and copies were retained by the king of England and the Dominican inquisitor, among others. An important question was whether Joan's acts had any authoritative value: Were her voices from God or the Devil? The judges wanted to demonstrate to their own satisfaction that Joan was one of "the sowers of deceitful inventions" of which the Gospels warned. They fully expected that external signs could indicate internal dispositions. She was found guilty and burned alive as a heretic.

The following memorandum is a summation of the commission's case against the maid.

You said that you wore and still wear man's dress at God's command and to His good pleasure, for you had instruction from God to wear this dress, and so you put on a short tunic, jerkin, and hose with many points. You even wear your hair cut above the ears, without keeping about you anything to denote your sex, save what nature has given you. . . . The clergy declare that you blaspheme against God, despising Him and His sacraments, that you transgress divine law, Holy Scripture and the canons of the Church, that you think evil and err from the faith, that you are full of vain boasting, that you are given to idolatry and worship of yourself and your clothes, according to the customs of the heathen.

You have declared that you know well that God loves certain living persons better than you, and that you learned this by revelation from St. Catherine and St. Margaret; also that those saints speak French, not English, as they are not on the side of the English. And since you knew that your voices were for your king, you began to dislike the Burgundians.

Such matters the clergy pronounce to be a rash and presumptuous assertion, a superstitious divination, a blasphemy uttered against St. Catherine and St. Margaret, and a transgression of the commandment to love our neighbors.

And you have said . . . that you know that all the deeds of which you have been accused in your trial were wrought according to the command of God and that it was impossible for you to do otherwise. . . . Wherefore the clergy declare you to be schismatic, an unbeliever in the unity and authority of the Church, apostate and obstinately erring from the faith. . . . [The inquisitor admonished her,] "You have believed in apparitions lightly, instead of turning to God in devout prayer to grant you certainty; and you have not consulted prelates or learned ecclesiastics to enlighten yourself: although, considering your condition and the simplicity of your knowledge, you ought to have done so."

Source: The Trial of Jeanne d'Arc, trans. W. P. Barrett (New York: Gotham House, 1932), pp. 331–338.

captain for the Italian city of Florence. Other mercenary captains pillaged freely across Europe, kidnapping municipal officials and even laying siege to entire towns in order to extort money. Truces did not necessarily mean peace in fourteenth-century Europe.

The war also helped consolidate the French monarchy's power. A key to French military successes had been the creation of a paid professional army, which replaced the feudal host and mercenary companies of the fourteenth century. Charles VII created Europe's first standing army, a cavalry of about 8000 nobles under the direct control of royal commanders. Charles also expanded his judicial claims. He and his son, Louis XI (r. 1461–1483), created new provincial parlements, or law courts, at Toulouse, Grenoble, Bordeaux, and Dijon. They also required that local laws and customs be registered and approved by these local parlements.

French kings attacked the power of the great aristocratic families in two ways. First, ducal power was based on land. In 1477, when Charles the Bold of Burgundy was killed, Louis quickly seized his duchy, ridding himself of the greatest independent power in the kingdom. The process of consolidation was completed in 1491 when Charles VIII (r. 1483–1498), Louis's son, married Anne of Brittany, the heiress of the last independent duke of Brittany.

A second key to maintaining royal influence was the rise of the French court as a political and financial center. Through careful appointments and judicious offers of annuities and honors, Charles VII and Louis XI drew the nobility to the royal court and made the nobles dependent on it. "The court," complained a frustrated noble, "is an assembly of people who, under the pretense of acting for the good of all, come together to diddle each other; for there's scarcely anyone who isn't engaged in buying and selling and exchanging . . . and sometimes for their money we sell them our . . . humanity."[7] One of Louis XI's advisers noted that Charles VII never had revenues greater than 18,000 francs in a single year but that Louis collected 4.7 million. By the end of the fifteenth century, France had recovered from the crisis of war. It was once again a strong and influential state.

In England during the fifteenth century, the Hundred Years' War became the backdrop for a series of struggles over royal power. Although the English generally agreed that the king could institute new taxes to pay for foreign wars, theorists and parliamentary leaders alike held that the king should live off the income of his traditional rights and properties and honor the influence of the aristocracy.

It was fear of the king's power that contributed to the downfall of King Richard II in 1399. Recognizing the dangers of noble influence, Richard tried to insulate himself from the peers of the realm by choosing advisers from the lesser nobility and the middle classes as well as from the peerage. Simmering unrest overflowed, and leaders of the peers captured and forced Richard to abdicate. Parliament then elected as king Henry IV (r. 1399–1413), the first of the Lancastrian line.

In the beginning the Lancastrians were quite successful. Henry IV avoided war taxes and was

careful not to alienate the magnates. Henry V, perhaps the most charismatic of the late medieval English kings, gave the Lancastrians their greatest moments: the victory at Agincourt in 1415 and the Treaty of Troyes in 1420, designed to unify the French and English crowns. Within a decade, however, the French were beginning to force the English out of France, and Henry VI (r. 1422–1461) turned out to be weak-willed, immature, and prone to bouts of insanity.

The infirmity of Henry VI and the loss of virtually all French territories in 1453 led to factional battles called the Wars of the Roses—the red rose was the symbol of the Lancastrian dynasty and the white rose signified the Yorkist opposition. Edward of York eventually deposed Henry and claimed the crown for himself as Edward IV (r. 1461–1483). He faced little opposition because there seemed to be few alternatives. English public life was again thrown into confusion, however, at the death of Edward IV. The late king's brother, Richard, duke of Gloucester, claimed the protectorship over the 13-year-old king, Edward V (r. April–June 1483), and his brother. He seized the boys, who were placed in the Tower of London and never seen again. An Italian diplomat reported what little was known:

All the attendants who waited upon the king were debarred access to him. He and his brother were withdrawn into the inner apartments of the Tower proper, and day by day began to be seen more rarely behind the bars and windows till at length they ceased to appear altogether. . . . Whether, however, [the king] has been done away with, and by what manner of death, so far I have not at all discovered.[8]

Richard proclaimed himself king and was crowned Richard III (r. 1483–1485). The new king attempted to consolidate his control at the local level. He withstood early challenges to his authority but in 1485 was killed in the battle of Bosworth Fields, near Coventry, by Henry Tudor, a leader of the Lancastrian faction. Henry married Elizabeth, the surviving child of the late Edward IV. Symbolically at least, the struggle between the rival claimants to the crown appeared over.

Like his predecessor, Edward IV, Henry VII (r. 1485–1509) recognized the importance of avoiding war and taxation. Like the French kings, he created a patronage network of local officials to secure allies for his dynasty. Royal power, however, was not based on a transformation of the institutions of government. Following Edward IV's example, Henry VII controlled local affairs through the traditional system of royal patronage. He also imitated Edward in emphasizing the dignity of the royal office. Though careful with his funds, he was willing to buy jewels and clothing if they added to the brilliance of his court. As one courtier summed up his reign, "His hospitality was splendidly generous. . . . He knew well how to maintain his majesty and all which pertains to kingship." Henry's skill in marriage politics gave England ties with Scotland and Spain. He arranged the marriage of his daughter, Margaret Tudor, to James IV of Scotland and the marriage of his sons, Arthur and (after Arthur's death) Henry, to Catherine of Aragon, daughter of the Spanish rulers Ferdinand and Isabella.

The English monarchy of the late fifteenth century was not a new departure. The success of Henry VII was based on several factors: the absence of powerful opponents; lowered taxation, the result of twenty-five years of peace under Henry VII; and the desire, shared by ruler and ruled alike, for an orderly realm built on the assured succession of a single dynasty.

Italy

Compared to France and England, fourteenth- and fifteenth-century Italy was a land of cities. In northern Europe a town of over 20,000 or 30,000 people was unusual. The 100,000 or more people who lived in London or Paris in the fourteenth century made these capitals unlike any other cities north of the Alps. Yet at one time or another in the late Middle Ages, Milan, Venice, Florence, and Naples all had populations near or exceeding 100,000, and countless other Italian towns boasted populations of over 20,000. In comparison to northern Europe, however, the Italian peninsula seemed a power vacuum. The northern and central provinces largely belonged to the kingdom of Italy and thus were part of the Holy Roman Empire. Most of central Italy was part of the Papal States. Actual power, however, was most often located in Italy's flourishing towns. Political life revolved around the twin issues of who should dominate town governments and how could they learn to coexist peacefully.

By the late thirteenth century, political power in most Italian towns was divided among three major groups. The first was an old urban nobility that could trace its wealth back to grants of property and rights from kings, emperors, and bishops in the tenth and eleventh centuries. They were joined by a second group, the merchant families who enriched themselves in the twelfth and thirteenth centuries as Italians led the European economic expansion into the Mediterranean. These old urban groups were challenged in the first decades of the thirteenth century by modest artisans and merchants who had organized trade, neighborhood, or militia groups and referred to themselves as the *popolo*, that is, "the people" (see page 335). In many towns they elected a virtual parallel government headed by their own small council of elders, or *Anziani*. As early as 1198, the popolo of Milan had elected their own Captain of the People—an officer who served much as did the podestà, except in the interest of the people. The rise of the popolo brought little peace, however. "War and hatred have so multiplied among the Italians," observed one Florentine, "that in every town there is a division and enmity between two parties of citizens." It was not simply a fight divided along class lines. Townsmen gathered themselves together in factions based on wealth, family, profession, neighborhood, and even systems of clientage that reached back into the villages from which many of the townsmen had come. In times of unrest, urban nobles who held fortresses and even whole districts in the countryside often called on their peasants to form a band that might rival the town's own militia.

Riven with factions, townsmen would often turn control of their governments over to a *signor*, that is a "lord," or "tyrant," often a local noble with a private army. In 1264, for example, Obizzo d'Este took control of the town of Ferrara. In a carefully managed assembly of the people of Ferrara, Obizzo was proclaimed to be "Governor and Ruler and General and permanent Lord of the City of Ferrara." The rise of the Este lords of Ferrara seemed peaceful, but the force on which the transformation rested was clearer in Mantua. "[Pinamonte Bonacolsi (d. 1293)] usurped the lordship of his city and expelled his fellow-citizens and occupied their property," according to a chronicler. "And he was feared like the devil."[9] Once firmly in power, tyrants often allowed the town's government to continue to function as it had, requiring only that they should control all major political appointments.

The great republics of Venice and Florence escaped domination by signori, but only by undertaking significant constitutional change. In both republics political life was disrupted by large numbers of new citizens—immigrants drawn by the relatively greater economic opportunities in the towns and recently enriched merchants and speculators who demanded a voice in government. In 1297, reacting to increased competition for influence, the Venetian government enacted the so-called Closing of the Grand Council. The act guaranteed the political rights of the patriciate, the families who had held office during the late thirteenth century. Although the act initially enlarged to about 1100 the number of families eligible for public office, its ultimate effect was to freeze out subsequent arrivals. The Venetian patriciate became a closed urban nobility. Political tensions were hidden beneath a veneer of serenity as Venetians developed a myth of public-spirited patricians who governed in the interests of all the peoples, leaving others free to enrich themselves in trade and manufacture.

In Florence, by contrast, political life was convulsed by the issue of citizenship. Violent noble families, immigrants, and artisans of modest backgrounds found themselves cut off from civic participation by the passage of a series of reforms that culminated in the Ordinances of Justice of 1293–1295. These reforms, largely promoted by wealthy guildsmen, restricted political participation in Florence to members in good standing of certain merchant and artisan guilds. Further, members of violence-prone families were defined as "Magnate" (literally "the powerful") and therefore disqualified from holding public office. The Florentine system guaranteed that real political power remained concentrated in the hands of the great families, whose wealth was based primarily on banking and mercantile investments. Political power increasingly passed to individuals who used their family, neighbors, and political clients to dominate public life. After a political and diplomatic crisis in 1434 brought on by war and high taxes, virtual control of Florentine politics fell into the hands of Cosimo de' Medici, the wealthiest banker in the city. From 1434 to 1494, Cosimo; his son, Piero; his grandson, Lorenzo; and Lorenzo's son dominated the government in Florence. Al-

The Journey of the Magi The story of the journey of the Magi to Bethlehem to find the baby Jesus seemed a perfect image of the power and wisdom of rulers. This painting of the Magi was commissioned for the private chapel of Cosimo de' Medici, the de facto ruler of Florence. *(Palazzo Medici Riccardi, Florence/Art Resource, NY)*

ways careful to appease Florentine republican traditions, Medici control was virtually as complete as that of the lords of towns like Ferrara or Milan.

In the fifteenth century, the great towns of Italy dominated their lesser neighbors. The aristocratic Visconti family had taken control of Milan by the early fourteenth century and secured the title of duke. In the late fourteenth and fifteenth centuries the Viscontis and later their Sforza successors made marriage alliances with the French crown and created a splendid court culture in Milan. In a series of wars between the 1370s and 1450s, the dukes of Milan expanded their political control throughout most of Lombardy, Liguria, and, temporarily, Tuscany—the environs of Florence itself. It seemed to many that the Milanese were poised to unify all Italy under their control.

Republican Florence and Venice followed similar policies in dealing with warfare and competition with other states. Although Florentines maintained that they were protecting Florentine and Tuscan "liberty" against the Milanese invaders, their interests went beyond simple defense. Relations among Milan, Venice, Florence, Rome, and Naples were stabilized by the Peace of Lodi and the creation of the Italian League in 1454. In response to endemic warfare in Italy and the looming threat of the Ottoman Turks in the eastern Mediterranean (see page 423), the five powers agreed to the creation of spheres of influence that would prevent any one of them from expanding at the expense of the others. Despite several short wars, the league managed to avoid large-scale territorial changes from 1454 until 1494. Venice, Milan, and Florence were thus free to integrate much of northern and central Italy into what would become the Venetian republic and the duchies of Lombardy and Tuscany.

The limits of these territorial states of Italy became clear when King Charles VIII of France invaded Italy in 1494. French kings had hereditary claims to the duchy of Milan and to the kingdom of Naples, but an invitation from Ludovico Sforza of Milan finally enticed Charles to claim Naples.

The French invasion devastated Italy by touching off a series of wars called the Habsburg-Valois Wars. French control was immediately challenged by the Spanish, who themselves made claims on the south and much of Lombardy. The cost of warfare kept almost all governments in a state of crisis. Unrest brought on by the invasion allowed Pope Alexander VI (r. 1492–1503) to attempt to create a state for his son, Cesare Borgia (1475–1507), in central Italy.

In Florence, the wars destroyed the old Medici-dominated republic and brought in a new republican constitution. Fearing the French invaders, Piero de' Medici illegally surrendered key fortresses to Charles's army. Angry Florentines considered Piero's acts treasonous. Piero had little choice but to leave in order to avoid prosecution.

Anti-Medici republicans realized that their previous government had been a sham, with elections manipulated by the Medicis and their party. Reformers were initially led by the popular Dominican preacher Girolamo Savonarola (1452–1498). In the constitutional debates after 1494, Savonarola argued that true republican reform required a thoroughgoing religious reform of society. Gangs of youth flocked to his cause, attacking prostitutes and homosexuals. Many of his followers held "bonfires of vanities," burning wigs, silks, and other luxuries. In 1498, when his followers had lost influence in the government, Savonarola was arrested, tortured, and executed.

In spite of reforms, new fortresses, and a citizen militia, the Florentine government was unable to save itself from papal and imperial opposition. In 1512 the Medicis returned under papal and imperial protection. First treated as the leading citizens of Florence and as the emperor's allies in central Italy, the Medicis were later named dukes and then grand dukes of Tuscany. The grand duchy of Tuscany remained an independent, integrated, and well-governed state until the French Revolution of 1789. Venice also managed to maintain its republican form of government and its territorial state until the French Revolution; but, like the dukes of Tuscany, the governors of Venice were no longer able to act independently of the larger European powers.

The Habsburg-Valois Wars continued for over a half-century, ending with the Treaty of Cateau-Cambrésis in 1559, which left the Spanish kings in control of Milan, Naples, Sardinia, and Sicily. Thus, war and the political integration of the fifteenth century destroyed the tiny city-republics and left the remaining territorial states in a position where they could no longer act independently of foreign powers.

Germany and Switzerland

The issue of central versus local control played a key role in German affairs as well. The kingdom of Germany, or the Holy Roman Empire, of the late Middle Ages was dramatically different from the empire of the early thirteenth century (see pages 356–359). Emperors were unable to make claims to lands and jurisdictions outside Germany. And within Germany, power shifted to the east. Imperial power had previously rested on lands and castles in southwestern Germany. These strongholds melted away as emperors willingly pawned and sold the traditional crown lands in order to build up the holdings of their own families. Emperor Henry VII (r. 1308–1313) and his grandson, Charles IV (r. 1347–1378), for example, pawned and sold imperial lands west of the Rhine in order to secure the house of Luxemburg's claims to the crown of Bohemia and other lands in the east. The Habsburgs in Austria, the Wittelsbachs in Bavaria, and a host of lesser families staked out claims to power and influence in separate parts of the empire. As a result, Germany was becoming a loose collection of territories.

The local power of regional authorities in the empire was further cemented by the so-called Golden Bull of 1356, the most important constitutional document of late medieval German history. In it, Emperor Charles IV declared that henceforth the archbishops of Cologne, Mainz, and Trier plus the secular rulers of the Rhenish Palatinate, Saxony, Brandenburg, and Bohemia would be the seven electors responsible for the choice of a new emperor. The proclamation recognized the major political powers and defined a procedure for election. But it did not solve the inherent weakness of an electoral monarchy. Between the election of Rudolph of Habsburg in 1273 and 1519, there were fourteen emperors from six different dynasties, and only once, in 1378, did a son follow his father. The contrast between Germany and the monarchies of Iberia, France, and England is striking. By 1350, Germany had no hereditary monarchy, no common legal system, no common coinage, and no representative assembly. Political power rested in the hands of the territorial princes.

Territorial integration was least effective in what is now Switzerland, where a league of towns, provincial knights, and peasant villages successfully resisted a territorial prince. The Swiss Confederation began modestly enough in 1291 as a voluntary association to promote regional peace. In 1386 forces of the confederation defeated and killed Duke Leopold of Austria, who had claimed jurisdiction over the area governed by the confederation. By 1410, the confederation had conquered most of the traditionally Habsburg lands in the Swiss areas. By the 1470s the Swiss had invented the myth of William Tell, the fearless woodsman who refused to bow his head to a Habsburg official, as a justification for their independent and anti-aristocratic traditions. Their expansion culminated with the Battle of Nancy in Lorraine in 1477, when the Swiss infantry defeated a Burgundian army and killed Charles the Bold, the duke of Burgundy. From then on, the Swiss maintained their independence, and "Turning Swiss" became a battle cry for German towns and individuals who hoped to slow territorial integration.

Scandinavia and Eastern Europe

As in the rest of Europe, public authority in Scandinavia and eastern Europe depended to a large extent on relations among kings, their wealthy elites, and their powerful neighbors. In the fifteenth century, the Scandinavian kingdoms of Denmark, Sweden, and Norway—like the Swiss Confederation—lay open to economic and political influences from Germany. German merchants traded throughout the area, and German nobles sought to influence political life in the kingdoms. The Scandinavian aristocracy, however, especially in Denmark, remained wary of German interests. Scandinavian elites tended to intermarry and arrange themselves against the Germans.

In Denmark, rulers sought accommodations with the nobles and powerful cities of northern Germany. In Sweden and Norway, the situation was complicated by the fact that there was no nobility in the feudal sense of a class of vassals bound to a lord by an oath of homage. Aristocrats were merely leading landowners. Both they and the peasantry were traditionally represented in the Riksdag in Sweden and the Storting in Norway, popular assemblies that had the right to elect kings, authorize taxes, and make laws. The elites of Scandinavia spoke similar Germanic languages and had close social and economic ties with each other. Thus, it is not surprising that the crowns of the three kingdoms were joined during short periods of crisis. In 1397, the dowager Queen Margaret of Denmark was able to unite the Scandinavian crowns by the Union of Kalmar, which would nominally endure until 1523.

The political fluidity of Scandinavia was also typical of the Slavic East. German Teutonic knights controlled Prussia and, under the pretext of converting their pagan neighbors to Christianity, sought to expand eastward against the kingdom of Poland and the Lithuanian state. The conversion of the Lithuanian rulers to Christianity slowed and finally halted the German advance to the east. More serious for the knights was their defeat in 1410 at Tannenberg Forest in Prussia by a Polish-Lithuanian army led by Prince Vytautus (r. 1392–1439) of Lithuania. The reign of Prince Vytautus represented the high point of Lithuanian dominion. He ruled much of modern Poland and western Russia as well as modern Lithuania.

During the fifteenth century, Lithuania faced a formidable new opponent, the grand duchy of Moscow. Since the Mongol invasions in the thirteenth century, various Russian towns and principalities had been part of a Mongolian sphere of influence. With the waning of Mongol control, however, the Muscovites annexed other Russian territories. By 1478, Ivan III (r. 1462–1505), called "the Great," had taken control of the famed trading center of Novgorod. Two years later he was powerful enough to renounce Mongol overlordship and refuse further payments of tribute. After marriage to an émigré Byzantine princess living in Rome, Ivan began to call himself "Tsar" (Russian for "Caesar"), implying that in the wake of the Muslim conquest of Constantinople, Moscow had become the new Rome.

The stability resulting from the rise of Moscow enabled itinerant Russian warriors called *boyars* to transform themselves into landed aristocrats. The boyars came to play a dominant political, institutional, and legal role in provincial society through their control of provincial assemblies, or dumas. They used their political power to dominate the countryside and force formerly free peasants into a harsh serfdom from which the Russian peasantry would not emerge until the nineteenth century. It is too early to speak of a Russian national state, yet by 1500 the seeds of Russian dominion were clearly sown.

By 1500 it did seem that the French king's lawyer's claim that all within the kingdom belonged to the king was finally accepted. With the exception of Italy and Germany, central monarchies emerged from the wars of the fourteenth and fifteenth centuries much stronger. The Hundred Years' War and the resulting disorganization and unrest in France and England seemed to strike at the heart of the monarchies. But through the foundation of standing armies and the careful consolidation of power in the royal court, both countries seemed stronger and more able to defend themselves after the war. And as the Italians learned

in the wars following the French invasion of 1494, small regional states were no match for the monarchies. In part, Italians found that the economic and social changes of the late Middle Ages favored northern Europe rather than the regional governments of Italy.

ECONOMY AND SOCIETY

After nearly three centuries of dramatic growth, European society in 1300 was overpopulated and threatened by drastic economic and social problems. Estimates of Europe's population in 1300 have ranged from about 80 million to as high as 100 million. Levels would not be this high again for over two hundred years. Opportunities dwindled because of overpopulation, war, and epidemics. These shocks brought changes in trade and commerce. Lowered population, deflation, and transformed patterns of consumption also altered the nature of agriculture, which was still the foundation of the European economy. Changes brought on by wars, plagues, and religious controversy affected the structure and dynamics of families, the organization of work, and the culture in many parts of Europe.

The Black Death and Demographic Crisis

People in many parts of Europe were living on the edge of disaster in 1300. Given the low level of agricultural technology and the limited resources available, it became increasingly difficult for the towns and countryside to feed and support the growing population. The nature of the problem varied from place to place. There is evidence of a crisis of both births and deaths.

Growing numbers of people competed for land to farm and for jobs. Farm size declined throughout Europe as parents divided their land among their children. Rents for farmland increased as landlords found they could play one land-hungry farmer off against another. Competition for jobs kept wages low, and when taxes were added to high rents and low wages, many peasants and artisans found it difficult to marry and raise families. Thus, because of reduced opportunities brought on by overpopulation, poor townsmen and peasants tended to marry late and have small families.

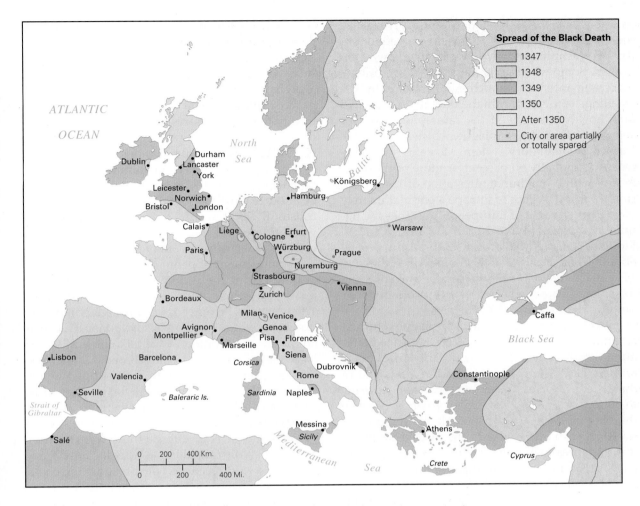

Map 11.2 The Progress of the Black Death The Black Death did not advance evenly across Europe; rather, as is clear from the dates at which it struck various regions, it followed the main lines of trade and communication.

More dramatic than this crisis of births were the famines that occurred in years of bad harvests. The great famine of 1315–1322 marks a turning point in the economic history of Europe. Wet and cold weather ruined crops in much of northern Europe. Food stocks were quickly exhausted, and mass starvation followed. People died so quickly, English chroniclers reported, that no one could keep up with the burials. At Ypres, in Flanders, 2800 people (about 10 percent of the population) died in just six months. And shortages continued. Seven other severe famines were reported in the south of France during the fourteenth century.

If Europe's problem had merely been one of famine brought on by overpopulation, recovery should have been possible. But, because of the return of a deadly epidemic disease, the economy did not recover. In 1348 bubonic plague returned to western Europe for the first time in six hundred years. Genoese traders contracted the plague in Caffa on the Black Sea coast. Infected sailors carried the disease south into Egypt and west to Sicily and then on to Genoa and Venice. From there it followed established trade routes first into central Italy and later to the south of France, the Low Countries, England, and finally through the North and Baltic Seas into Germany and the Slavic lands to the east (Map 11.2).

The bacillus that caused "the great Mortality," as contemporaries called it, was *Yersinia pestis*. In its bubonic form, the plague attacks the lymphatic system, bringing painful, discolored swelling under the armpits and in the groin or lower abdomen. Some who survived the first days of high fever and internal hemorrhaging caused by the swellings recovered from the bubonic plague. No one, however, survived the rarer pneumonic or septicemic forms of the plague, which attacked the lungs and circulatory system. Mortality rates varied, but generally 60 percent or more of those infected died. In the initial infestation of 1348–1351, from 25 to 35 percent of Europe's population may have died. In some of Europe's larger cities the figures may have risen to as high as 60 percent. In Florence, the population probably declined from about 90,000 to 50,000 or even less. (See the box, "The Black Death.") And the nearby town of Siena likely fared even worse, with a total mortality of 55 percent in the town and its suburbs.

After the initial outbreak, the plague returned again in 1363, and then for three centuries thereafter almost no generation could avoid it. Less is known about the plague in Muslim lands and in the eastern Mediterranean, but the situation seems to be similar to the European experience. Because the plague tended to carry off the young, the almost generational return of the disease accounts for the depressed population levels found in many parts of Europe and western Asia until the late seventeenth or eighteenth century.

Lacking an understanding of either contagion or infection, fourteenth-century doctors depended on traditional theories inherited from the Greeks, especially the work of Galen. In Galenic medicine good health was a condition that depended on the proper balance of hot and cold, moist and dry bodily fluids, or humors. It was believed that this balance could be upset by corrupt air, the movements of planets, and even violent shifts in emotions. Without a clear understanding of the biological nature of the disease and lacking modern antibiotics, Europeans were unable to treat plague effectively. Yet in the fifteenth and sixteenth centuries, as the rhythms of the plague infestations became clearer, towns and, later, territorial governments perceived the contagious nature of the disease. Officials instituted increasingly effective quarantines and embargoes to restrict the movement of goods and people from areas where the plague was raging.

Alongside medical theory, however, another class of explanations developed. Taking a lead from miracle stories in which Jesus linked illness and sin, many Christians considered the "great Mortality" a signal of the end of the world or at least a sign of the severe judgment of God on a sinful world. A traditional religious response was to urge various moral reforms or penitential acts—charitable gifts, special prayers, processions. (See the feature, "Weighing the Evidence: A Painting of the Plague," on pages 434–435.) Women were often thought to be a source of moral pollution and hence one of the causes of God's wrath. In Muslim Egypt women were ordered off the streets; in Christian Europe prostitutes were driven out of towns.

A movement of penitents called "flagellants" arose in Hungary and spread quickly into Germany and across France and the Low Countries. These men and women moved from town to town urging repentance and social and political reconciliation. In an imitation of Christ's life and sufferings, they ritually beat ("flagellated") themselves between the shoulders with metal-tipped whips. The flagellants, in their quest for a purer, truly Christian society, brought suspicion on all those who were not Christian or were otherwise suspect.

In some parts of Europe there were murderous attacks on outsiders, especially lepers and Jews, who were suspected of spreading the contagion in an attempt to bring down Latin Christian civilization. Like many of the anti-Semitic myths, the stories of Jewish poisoners seemed to arise in the south of France and spread in their most virulent forms to German towns along the Rhine. In many Rhineland towns, the entire Jewish population was put to the sword. In Strasbourg, attacks on Jews even preceded the arrival of plague. Except in a few districts, officials opposed attacks on Jews, lepers, and heretics. After a few months of violence, the flagellants and the leaders of the religious riots were driven from towns.

It was a commonplace among contemporary chroniclers that "so many did die that everyone thought it was the end of the world." Yet it was the young, the elderly, and the poor—those least likely to pay taxes, own shops, or produce new children—who were the most common victims. Even in towns like Florence, however, where mortality rates were so high, recovery was rapid. Government offices were closed at most for only a few

The Black Death

The plague of 1348 in Florence dominates the popular tales that form the bulk of the **Decameron.** *Giovanni Boccaccio (1313–1375) probably described the plague to emphasize how unusual and irresponsible his protagonists—young men and women who fled Florence, abandoning family and friends—really were. If so, Boccaccio failed miserably. Readers celebrate the fresh and lively irony of the tales. Moreover, Boccaccio's description fits with everything scholars have since discovered about the first infestation of the plague in Italy. Boccaccio's descriptions make clear not just what happened, but how the events affected the sensibilities of the people.*

This pestilence was so powerful that it was transmitted to the healthy by contact with the sick, the way a fire close to dry or oily things will set them aflame. And the evil of the plague went even further: not only did talking to or being around the sick bring infection and a common death, but also touching the clothes of the sick or anything touched or used by them seemed to communicate this very disease to the person involved. . . . There came about such fear and such fantastic notions among those who remained alive that almost all of them took a very cruel attitude in the matter; that is, they completely avoided the sick and their possessions; and in so doing, each one believed that he was protecting his good health.

There were some people who thought that living moderately and avoiding any excess might help a great deal in resisting this disease, so they gathered in small groups and lived entirely apart from everyone else. . . . Others thought the opposite: they believed that drinking excessively, enjoying life, going about singing and celebrating, and satisfying in every way the appetites as best one could, laughing, and making light of everything that happened was the best medicine for such a dis-

ease. . . . And in this great affliction and misery of our city the revered authority of the laws, both divine and human, had fallen and almost completely disappeared, for like other men, the ministers and executors of the laws were either dead or sick or so short of help that it was impossible for them to fulfill their duties. . . .

Others were of a crueler opinion (though it was, perhaps, a safer one): they maintained that there was no better medicine against the plague than to flee from it. . . . This disaster had struck such fear into the hearts of men and women that brother abandoned brother, uncle abandoned nephew, sister left brother, and very often wife abandoned husband and—even worse, almost unbelievable—fathers and mothers neglected to tend and care for their children as if they were not their own. . . . And since the sick were abandoned by their neighbors, their parents, and their friends and there was a scarcity of servants, a practice almost unheard of before spread through the city: when a woman fell sick, . . . she did not mind having a manservant (whoever he might be, no matter how young or old he was), and she had no shame whatsoever in revealing any part of her body to him. . . .

Source: Giovanni Boccaccio, *The Decameron*, trans. Mark Musa and Peter Bondanella (New York: New American Library, 1982), pp. 6–10.

weeks; markets reopened as soon as the death rate began to decline. And within two years tax receipts were back at preplague levels. Below the surface, however, plague, population decline, and religious unrest fueled the economic and social transformations of the late Middle Ages.

Patterns of Economic Change

In the aftermath of plague, the economy of Europe changed in a number of profound ways. As we will see, Italy's domination of the European economy was challenged by the growth of trade and manufacturing in many parts of Europe. Further, Italian bankers came to face competition from equally astute local bankers. These changes in the structure of economic life were accompanied by other economic disruptions brought on by plague and population decline.

Discussions of the economy must begin with Italy. It was the fulcrum of the international economy in 1300. Italian merchants sold woolens produced in Flanders and Italy to Arab traders in North Africa, who sold them along the African coast and as far south as the Niger Delta. The Italians used the gold that they collected in payment to buy spices and raw materials in the East, which they resold at the regional fairs of northern Europe.

Because of their expertise in moving bullion and goods and their ready sources of capital, Italian merchants like the Ricciardis of Lucca were ideal bankers and financial advisers to the papacy and European kings, who often needed immediate sources of capital. Kings normally were expected to live off their own estates or a series of traditional tolls and duties. They had few cash reserves. In time of war, when they needed money quickly, they tended to trade the rights to various revenues to Italian bankers, who had cash at hand.

Merchants from Cremona, Genoa, Florence, and Siena also forged commercial agreements with the kings of France, Aragon, and Castile and with the papacy. The great merchant-banking houses consisted of loose associations with agents in most of the cities of Europe. In the course of their operations they developed a network of couriers to move business mail, as well as bookkeeping procedures and techniques for the quick transfer of funds over long distances.

The most powerful bank in fifteenth-century Europe was the Medici bank of Florence. Founded in 1397 by Giovanni de' Medici (1360–1429), the bank grew quickly because of its role as papal banker. Medici agents transferred papal revenues from all parts of Europe to Rome and managed papal alum mines, which provided an essential mineral to the growing cloth industry. Cosimo de' Medici (1389–1464), son and successor of Giovanni, formed his bank as a series of bilateral partnerships with easily controlled junior partners in other parts of Europe.

The dramatic career of the Frenchman Jacques Coeur (1395?–1456) demonstrated that by the mid-fifteenth century, Italian merchants were not the only ones who understood international trade. Af-

The Feast of Saint John the Baptist John the Baptist was the patron saint of Florence. Each year a procession in his honor included government officials, the great associations and guilds in the city, and representatives from surrounding villages. *(Scala/Art Resource, NY)*

ter making a fortune trading in southern France, Coeur managed the French royal mint and became the financial adviser of King Charles VII (r. 1422–1461). He put the French monarchy back on a solid financial footing after the Hundred Years' War, becoming in the process the wealthiest individual in France. Unsurprisingly, his wealth and influence earned him jealous enemies: He was accused of murdering the king's mistress, trading with Muslims, and stealing royal funds. In 1451 his property was confiscated, and he was jailed for a short time. He later led a papal expedition against the Turks in the Aegean, where he died.

International trade flourished in other areas besides Italy and France. By the end of the fifteenth century, Italians faced increased competition from local merchants and never managed to penetrate beyond the Rhine in Germany. Italian expertise was least influential in those regions of Europe touching the North and Baltic Seas, areas most noted for fishing (a critical source of protein for much of Europe), salt, grain, and furs. The Hanseatic League, an association of over a hundred trading cities centered on the German city of Lübeck, dominated northern commerce. By 1358 it was referred to as a "League of German Cities," and individual merchants could participate only if they were citizens of one of the member towns. In the late fourteenth and early fifteenth centuries the Hansa towns controlled grain shipments from eastern Europe to England and Scandinavia. The league's domination waned in the second half of the fifteenth century, however, as trade diversified. Dutch, English, and even south German merchants took shares of the wool, grain, and fur trades. Towns in the eastern Baltic found that their interests no longer coincided with those of the Rhineland towns that made up the Hanseatic League. Wroclaw (in modern Poland) signaled the nature of the change when it resigned from the league in 1474 to expand trade connections with the south German towns.

In contrast to Hanseatic merchants, south Germans adopted Italian techniques of trade, manufacture, and finance to expand their influence throughout central Europe. Their favored trade routes ran through Nuremberg and farther east to Wroclaw and into Lithuania and were as important as the northern routes controlled by the Hanseatic League. German merchants regularly bought spices in the markets of Venice and distrib-uted them in central and eastern Europe. By the fifteenth century, the townsmen of south Germany also produced linen and cotton cloth, which found ready markets in central and eastern Europe.

The Fugger family of Augsburg in southern Germany, the most prosperous of the German commercial families, exemplifies this economic transformation. Hans Fugger (1348–1409) moved to Augsburg from a nearby village in the 1360s and quickly established himself as a weaver and wool merchant. By the 1470s, Hans's grandson, Jacob Fugger (1459–1525), was a dominant figure in the spice trade and also participated in a number of unusually large loans to a succession of German princes. They became leaders in the Tyrolean silver-mining industry, which expanded dramatically in the late fifteenth century. And in the early sixteenth century they handled all transfers of money from Germany to the papacy. Jacob Fugger's wealth increased fourfold between 1470 and 1500. The Fuggers were indispensable allies of the German emperors. Jacob himself ensured the election of Charles V as Holy Roman emperor in 1519, making a series of loans that allowed Charles to buy the influence that he needed to win election.

As wealthy as the great merchants were, in most parts of Europe, prosperity was still tied to agriculture and the production of food grains. In northern and western Europe, foodstuffs were produced on the manorial estates of great churchmen and nobles. These estates were worked by a combination of serfs who owed a variety of labor services and day laborers who were hired during planting and harvesting. In the aftermath of plague and population decline, landlords and employers found themselves competing for the reduced number of laborers who had survived the plague. In 1351 the English crown issued the Statute of Laborers, which pegged wages and the prices of commodities at preplague levels. According to the statute, regulation was necessary because laborers "withdrew themselves from serving great men and others unless they have living [in food] and wages double or treble of what they were [before the plague]." Government attempts to stabilize prices and control wages had little effect, however. Many large landowners gave up direct farming of their estates and instead leased out lands to independent peasant farmers, who, for the most part, worked their lands with family labor. In southwest Germany some landowners reforested their lands, hoping to take advantage of rising prices for timber and charcoal. In both cases, landlords reduced their dependence on laborers.

Cloth manufacture, not agriculture, was the part of the European economy that changed most dramatically in the late Middle Ages. First in Flanders, then later in Italy, England, and the rest of Europe, production shifted from urban workshops to the countryside. Industries in rural areas tended to be free of controls on quality or techniques. As a result, the production of light, cheap woolens, for which there was a significant demand, moved out of the cities and into the countryside. Rural production, whether in Flanders, Lombardy, or England, became the most dynamic part of the industry.

Rural cloth production, especially in southwest Germany and parts of England, was organized through the putting-out system. Merchants who owned the raw wool contracted with various artisans in the city, suburbs, or countryside—wherever the work could be done most cheaply—to process the wool into cloth. Rural manufacture was least expensive because it could be done as occasional or part-time labor by farmers, their wives, or children during slack times of the day or season. Because production was likely to be finished in the countryside (beyond guild supervision), the merchant was free to move the cloth to wherever it could most easily and profitably be sold; guild masters had no control over price or quality.

Two other developments also changed the woolen trade of the fifteenth century: the rise of Spain as an exporter of unprocessed wool and the emergence of England, long recognized as a source of prime wool, as a significant producer of finished cloth. Spain was an ideal region for the pasturing of livestock. Flocks of sheep regularly moved from mountainous summer pastures onto the plain in the late fall and winter. By the fifteenth century, highly prized Spanish wool from merino sheep was regularly exported to Italy, Flanders, and England. By 1500 there were over 3 million sheep in Castile alone, and revenues from duties on wool formed the backbone of royal finance.

In England, in contrast, economic transformation was tied to cloth production. Over the course of the late fourteenth and fifteenth centuries, wool exports declined as cloth exports rose. In 1350 the English exported just over 5000 bolts of cloth. By the 1470s exports had risen to 63,000 bolts, and

they doubled again by the 1520s. The growth of cloth exports contributed to the expansion of London. Located on the Thames River and easily reached by sea, the city was ideally placed to serve as both a political and an economic capital. During the fourteenth and fifteenth centuries, English commerce became increasingly controlled by London merchant-adventurers. Soon after 1500, over 80 percent of the cloth for export passed through the hands of the Londoners. This development, coupled with the rise of London as a center of administration and consumption, laid the foundation for the economic and demographic growth that would make London the largest and most prosperous city in western Europe by the eighteenth century.

All these patterns of economic change in the fifteenth century challenged customs and institutions by allowing new entrepreneurs into the marketplace. Patricians in many European towns, however, acted to dampen competition and preserve traditional values. Great banking families like the Medicis of Florence tended to avoid competition and concentrations of capital, because the leaders of rival banks were political and social peers. Not even the Medicis used political influence to create advantages for their own businesses. In northern Europe, governments in towns like Leiden restricted the concentration of resources in the hands of the town's leading cloth merchants. Their aim was to ensure full employment for the town's laborers, political power for the guild masters, and social stability in the town.

Full employment was the goal for men only, however. Opportunities for women declined significantly in the fifteenth century. Although men had controlled the guilds and most crafts in the thirteenth and early fourteenth centuries, women in England and many other parts of northern Europe had been actively involved in the local economy. Unlike southern Europe, where women had no public roles, some northern towns apparently even had women's guilds to protect their members' activities as artisans and even peddlers. Because they often worked before marriage, townswomen in northern Europe tended to marry at a later age than did women in Italy. Many women even earned their own marriage dowries. Since they had their own sources of income and often managed the shop of a deceased husband, women could be surprisingly independent. They were un-

Women at Work Although guild records tended to ignore the contributions of women, many women worked in their husband's shop. In this miniature, a woman is selling jewelry. Widows often managed the shops they inherited. (*Bibliothèque Nationale*)

der less pressure to remarry at the death of a spouse. Although their economic circumstances varied considerably, up to a quarter of the households in northern towns like Bern or Zurich were headed by women—almost entirely independent widows.

The fifteenth century brought new restrictions into women's lives. In England, for example, brewing ale had been a highly profitable part-time activity that women often combined with the running of a household. Ale was usually produced in small batches for household use and whatever went unconsumed would be sold. The introduction of beer changed matters. Because hops were added to beer as a preservative, it was easier to produce, store, and transport in large batches. Beer brewing became a highly profitable full-time trade, reducing the demand for the alewife's product and providing work for men as beer-makers.

At the same time the rights of women to work in urban crafts and industries were reduced. Wealthy fathers became less inclined to allow wives and daughters to work outside the home. Guilds banned the use of female laborers in many trades and severely limited the right of a widow to supervise her spouse's shop. For reasons that are not entirely clear, journeymen objected to working alongside women—perhaps because they now saw their status as employees as permanent instead of temporary. By the early sixteenth century, journeymen in Germany considered it "dishonorable" for a woman to work in a shop, even the daughter or wife of the master.

Despite the narrowing of economic opportunities for women, the overall economic prospects of peasants and laborers improved. Lowered rents and increased wages in the wake of plague meant a higher standard of living for small farmers and laborers. Before the plague struck in 1348, when grain prices were high and wages relatively low, most poor Europeans had subsisted on bread or grain-based gruel, consuming meat, fish, and cheese only a few times a week. A well-off peasant in England had lived on a daily ration of about two pounds of bread and a cup or two of oatmeal porridge washed down with three or four pints of ale; poorer peasants generally drank water except on very special occasions. After the plague, laborers were more prosperous. Adults in parts of Germany may have consumed nearly a liter of wine and a third of a pound of meat along with a pound or more of bread each day. Elsewhere people could substitute an equivalent portion of beer, ale, or cider for the wine. Hard times for landlords were good times for peasants and day laborers.

Landlords in England responded to their economic difficulties by converting their lands to grazing in order to produce for the growing woolen market and to reduce their need for labor. In parts of Italy, they invested in canals, irrigation, and new crops in order to increase profits. In eastern Europe, where landlords were able to take advantage of political and social unrest to force tenants into semi-free servile status, there was increased emphasis on commercial grain farming. This so-called second serfdom created an impoverished work force whose primary economic activity was in the lord's fields. Increasingly in the second half of the century, grains raised in Poland and Prussia found their way to markets in England and the Low Countries. Europe east of the Elbe River became a major producer of grain, but at a heavy social cost.

The loss of perhaps a third of the urban population due to the plague had serious consequences in the towns of Europe. Because of lower birthrates and higher death rates, late medieval towns needed a constant influx of immigrants in order to expand or even to maintain their population. Citizenship in most towns was restricted to masters in the most important guilds, and it was they who controlled government. In many towns, citizens constructed a system of taxation that worked to their own economic advantage and fell heavily on artisans and peasants. It was the masters of the most important guilds who were able to define working conditions in the industrialized trades, fields like metalworking and cloth production. Unskilled laborers and members of craft guilds depended for their economic well-being on personal relationships with powerful citizens who controlled the government and the markets. Peace and order in towns and in the countryside depended on a delicate balance of the interests of the well-to-do and the more humble—a balance easily destroyed by war, plague, and economic depression.

The Popular Revolts

The balance first broke in the 1330s, unleashing a wave of violence across Europe radically different from the violence of previous centuries. Private wars, vendettas, and popular outbursts had erupted in other times, but the violence, drama, and impact of the risings of the fourteenth century remain unique. Some of the revolts seemed directed at the remnants of the old feudal and manorial elites. In that respect they were, as some historians have maintained, merely "a high point in the struggle between landlords and tenants that had been going on at a local and uncoordinated level for at least two hundred years."[10] Urban revolts, however, often seemed to be popular revolutions against exploitation by the patricians and guild masters who dominated local politics and controlled the local economy. In nearly all cases, the popular risings against authorities seem to have been triggered by the breakdown of the traditional bonds that had been holding society together.

The first disturbances occurred in the industrial towns of Flanders during the 1330s. Flemish wealth was based on the manufacture of woolen cloth, which was dominated by the weavers of the towns of Ghent, Bruges, and Ypres. In 1338, just as the first battles of the Hundred Years' War were being waged, James van Artevelde was elected "captain," or emergency leader, of Ghent through the support of laborers and artisans who feared the weavers. Faced with the opposition of the local count, hostility from the other towns, and rising discontent in Ghent itself, van Artevelde found himself increasingly isolated. He was assassinated in July 1345 by local faction leaders, in an act that was as much a personal vendetta as a political statement. Politics in Ghent quickly reverted to its traditional pattern: The well-to-do were again in control.

In the aftermath of war and plague, urban and rural risings also broke out in France. Following the French disaster at Poitiers in 1356, Étienne Marcel, provost or director of the merchants of Paris, mobilized a protest movement. He advocated ordinances that resembled a French Magna Carta, providing that royal officials should be subject to the Estates General and that the Estates should control taxation. This revolution seemed too radical to conservative townsmen in the provinces. Marcel's only allies were bands of rebellious countrymen roaming the region around Paris. The rural movement, or *jacquerie* (the name comes from *jacque*, French for the "jacket" typically worn by peasants), began in response to long-standing economic and political grievances in the countryside that had been worsened by warfare. The rebels and eventually Marcel himself were isolated and then defeated by aristocratic armies.

Two decades after the defeat of the French rebels, Europe again experienced insurrections. But the risings of the 1370s and 1380s differed from the previous revolts in several significant ways. Political unrest now was much more broadly based than it had been. There were political revolutions in many German towns as members of lowly artisan guilds claimed the right to sit alongside patricians in urban governments.

In 1378 a dramatic revolt occurred in central Italy. In reaction to a costly Florentine war with the papacy, the Ciompi, unskilled workers in the woolen industry, led a popular revolution hoping to expand participation in government and limit the authority of the guild masters over semiskilled artisans and day laborers. Barely six weeks after the Ciompi risings, however, wealthy conservatives quashed the new guilds and exiled or executed the leaders of the movement, leaving political and economic power even more firmly in the hands of the patricians.

Not long after the destruction of the Ciompi, England was rocked by the Rising of 1381, often called the Peasants' Revolt despite the fact that townsmen as well as peasants participated. England seethed with unrest as a result of plague, landlord claims for traditional dues, and finally a poll tax that placed a heavy burden on the common people. To most, it seemed that England's fiscal and political problems were the responsibility of the king's evil advisers, who the poor believed supported the ambitions of the wealthy. The heart of

the uprising was a revolt by rural peasants and artisans in the southeast, primarily in Kent and Essex. Popular armies led by Wat Tyler (d. 1381), who may have had some military experience, converged on London in June 1381. Tyler was murdered during a dramatic meeting with Richard II outside London, and a reaction against the rebels quickly ensued. (See the box, "The Rising of 1381.")

Most of the revolts had few lasting consequences, for the elites quickly regained control. A series of revolts in Spain, however, had long-lasting and unfortunate effects on Iberian society. In 1391 an attack on the Jews of Seville led to murders, forced conversions, and suppression of synagogues throughout Spain. In the aftermath large portions of the urban Jewish population either converted to Christianity or moved into villages away from the large commercial cities. The Jewish population in Castile may have declined by a fourth. Although the anti-Jewish feelings were expressed in religious terms, the underlying cause was anger over the economic prominence of some Jewish or *converso* (recently converted Jewish-Christian) families. After 1391, anti-Jewish feeling increasingly became racial. As one rebel said, "The converso remains a Jew and therefore should be barred from public office."[11] Antagonism against Jews and conversos continued to build until the expulsion of the Jews from Spain in 1492 (see page 429).

FORMATION OF THE OTTOMAN AND SPANISH EMPIRES

In both Iberia and the eastern Mediterranean, political integration in the fifteenth century occurred because of political changes undreamed in previous centuries. The rise of the Ottoman Empire and the unification of Spain created the two powers around which politics and diplomacy would revolve in sixteenth-century Europe.

The Ottoman Turks

In 1453, the Muslim Ottoman Turks breached the walls of Constantinople, killed Emperor Constantine XI (r. 1448–1453), and destroyed the last vestiges of the Byzantine Empire and the Roman imperial tradition that reached back to the emperor

The Rising of 1381

The author of this chronicle—probably the most complete account of the English revolt of 1381— seems to have been an eyewitness to the dramatic events in London. Like most literate writers, the chronicler seems more at home with the attitudes and opinions of civil officials and landlords than with the concerns of the "rabble."

Wherefore the commons rose against [the royal] commissioner sent to investigate [rebellious acts in the region] and came before him to tell him that he was a traitor to the king and the kingdom and was maliciously proposing to undo them by the use of false inquests taken before him. Accordingly they made him swear on the Bible that never again would he hold such sessions nor act as a justice in such inquests. . . . They proposed to kill all the lawyers, jurors and royal servants they could find. . . .

[The rebels came to London, where they executed several royal servants. They, and possibly their leader, Wat Tyler, forced the king to agree to allow them to deal "with all the traitors against him."] And they required that henceforth no man should be a serf nor make homage or any type of service to any lord, but should give four pence for an acre of land. They asked also that no one should serve any man except at his own will and by means of a regular covenant. . . .

[In a confused melee during meeting with King Richard, Tyler was stabbed.] Wat spurred his horse, crying to the commons to avenge him, and the horse carried him some four score paces and then he fell to the ground half dead. And when the commons saw him fall, and did not know for certain how it happened, they began to bend their bows and to shoot. Therefore the king himself spurred his horse, and rode out to them, commanding them that they should all come before him at the field of St. John of Clerkenwell [a few hundred yards from where Tyler was wounded]. . . .

Afterwards, when the king had reached the open fields, he made the commons array themselves on the west side. . . . [The mayor of London had Wat Tyler] carried out to the middle of Smithfield [a market area on the edge of town] . . . and had him beheaded. . . . And so ended his wretched life. But the mayor had his head set on a pole and carried before him to the king, who still remained on the field. . . . And when the commons saw that their chieftain, Wat Tyler, was dead in such a manner, they fell to the ground there among the corn, like beaten men, imploring the king for mercy for their misdeeds. And the king benevolently granted them mercy.

Source: The Anonimalle Chronicle, in R. B. Dobson, *The Peasant's Revolt of 1381* (New York: St. Martin's Press, 1970), pp. 123, 125, 128, 161, 166–167.

Augustus. The sack of Constantinople sent shock waves through Christian Europe and brought forth calls for new crusades to liberate the East from the evils of Islam. It also stirred anti-Christian feelings among the Turks. The leader of the Turkish army, Sultan Mehmed II the Conqueror (r. 1451–1481), was acclaimed the greatest of all *ghazi*—that is, a crusading warrior who was, according to a Turkish poet, "the instrument of Allah, a servant of God, who purifies the earth from the filth of polytheism [i.e., the Christian Trinity]." The rise of the Ottoman Turks led to a profound clash between Christian and Muslim civilizations.

Turks had been invited into the Balkans as allies of the Byzantine emperors. Early in the fifteenth century, they were only one, and perhaps

The Siege of Constantinople
The siege of Constantinople by the Turks required the attackers to isolate the city both by sea and by land. This miniature from the fifteenth century shows the Turkish camps, as well as the movements of Turkish boats, completing the isolation of the city. *(Bibliothèque Nationale)*

not even the greatest, of the Balkan issues that concerned Christian Europe (Map 11.3). As the power of the Turks advanced, it became clear that a variety of other factors were at play. Hungarians, Venetians, and Germans also threatened the independence of local rulers. In the 1420s, for example, as the Turks and the Hungarians fought for control of Serbia, the Serbian king moved easily from alliance with one to alliance with the other. By changing religion, rulers often retained their political and economic influence. The Christian aristocracy of late-fifteenth-century Bosnia, for example, was welcomed into Islam and instantly created a cohesive elite fighting force for the Turks. Conversely,

Map 11.3 Turkey and Eastern Europe With the conquest of Constantinople, Syria, and Palestine, the Ottoman Turks controlled the eastern Mediterranean and dominated Europe below the Danube River. The Holy Roman emperors, rulers of Italy, and kings of Spain had to be concerned about potential invasions by land or by sea.

as Turkish power in Albania grew, one noble, George Castriota (d. 1467), known by his Turkish name Skanderbeg, reconverted to Christianity and became a leading figure in the resistance to the Turks. Only after his death were the Turks able to fully integrate Albania into their empire.

The defeat of a Christian crusading army at Varna on the Black Sea coast in 1444 virtually sealed the fate of Constantinople. It was only a matter of time before the Turks took the city. When Mehmed II finally turned his attention to Constantinople in 1453, the siege of the city took only fifty-three days. Turkish artillery breached the walls before a Venetian navy or a Hungarian army could come to the city's defense.

After the fall of Constantinople, the Turks worked to consolidate their new conquests. Ana-

tolia was the heart of the Ottoman Empire. Through alliance and conquest, Ottoman domination extended through Syria and Palestine and by 1517 to Egypt. Even the Muslim powers of North Africa were nominally under Turkish control. To the west and north of Constantinople, the Turks dominated Croatia, Bosnia, Dalmatia, Albania, eastern Hungary, Moldava, Bulgaria, and Greece. Turkish strength was based on a number of factors. The first was the loyalty and efficiency of the sultan's crack troops, the Janissaries. These troops were young boys forcibly taken from the subject Christian populations, trained in Turkish language and customs, and converted to Islam. Although they functioned as special protectors of the Christian community from which they were drawn, they were separated from it by their new faith. Because the Turkish population viewed them as outsiders, they were particularly loyal to the sultan.

The situation of the Janissaries underlines a secondary explanation for Ottoman strength: the unusually tolerant attitudes of Mehmed, who saw himself not only as the greatest of the ghazi but also as emperor, heir to Byzantine and ancient imperial traditions. Immediately after the conquest of Constantinople, he repopulated the city with Greeks, Armenians, Jews, and Muslims. Religious groups lived in separate districts centered on a church or synagogue, but each religious community retained the right to select its own leaders. Mehmed transferred the capital of the Turkish state to Constantinople. And by building mosques, hospitals, hostels, and bridges, he breathed new life into the city, which he referred to as Istanbul—that is, "the city." In the fifty years following the conquest, the population of the city grew an extraordinary 500 percent, from about 40,000 to over 200,000, making it the largest city in Europe, as it had been in antiquity. (See the box, "Encounters with the West: A European View of Constantinople.")

At a time when Christian Europe seemed less and less willing to deal with non-Christian minorities, the Ottoman Empire was truly exceptional. Christians and Jews were tolerated as long as they paid a special poll tax and accepted some Turkish supervision. Christian and Jewish leaders supervised the internal affairs of their respective communities. Muslims and non-Muslims belonged to the same trade associations and traveled throughout the empire. Mehmed quickly made trade agreements with the Italian powers in an attempt to consolidate his power. And in Serbia, Bulgaria, Macedonia, and Albania, he left in place previous social and political institutions, requiring only loyalty to his new empire.

Mehmed had to tread carefully because the Turks had a number of powerful enemies. The problems that the Ottoman Empire faced were most clear during the reign of Mehmed's son, Bayazid (r. 1481–1512). Following Turkish tradition, Mehmed had not chosen a successor but let his sons fight for control. Normally, the successful claimant achieved the throne by doing away with his closest relatives. Bayazid's brother, Jem, however, fled into the protective custody of Christian powers, where he spent the rest of his life. In times of crisis, kings and popes would threaten to fo-

ment rebellion in Ottoman lands by releasing him. Bayazid also had to worry about the Mamluk Turks, who controlled Egypt and Syria, and the new Safavid dynasty in Persia. Although both were Muslim, they were willing to join with various Christian states to reduce the power of the Ottomans. Only in the second decade of the sixteenth century, after Bayazid's son, Selim (r. 1512–1520), had defeated the Persians and the Mamluks, were the Ottomans finally safe from attack from the east or south.

The Union of Crowns in Spain

While expanding across the Mediterranean, the Turks came in contact with the other new state of the fifteenth century, the newly unified kingdom of Spain. In 1469, Ferdinand, heir to the kingdom of Aragon and Catalonia, married Isabella, daughter of the king of Castile. Five years later Isabella became queen of Castile, and in 1479, Ferdinand took control of the kingdom of Aragon (see Map 10.1 on page 354). This union of crowns would lead to the creation of a united Spain.

The permanence of the union was surprising because the two kingdoms were so different. Castile was a much larger and more populous state. It had taken the lead in the fight to reconquer Iberia and end Muslim rule (see page 332). As a result, economic power within Castile was divided among those groups most responsible for the Reconquista: military orders and nobles. The military orders of Calatrava, Santiago, and Alcantara were militias formed by men who had taken a religious vow similar to the vow taken by a monk, with an added vow to fight against the enemies of Christianity. In the course of the Reconquista the military orders assumed control of vast districts. Lay nobles who aided in the Reconquista also held large tracts of land and were very proud of their independence.

Castile's power stemmed from its agrarian wealth. During the Reconquista, Castilians took control of large regions and turned them into ranges for grazing merino sheep, producers of the prized merino wool exported to the woolen markets of Flanders and Italy. To maximize the profits from wool production, the kings authorized the creation of the Mesta, a brotherhood of sheep producers. The pastoral economy grew to the point that by the early sixteenth century there were

∼ ENCOUNTERS WITH THE WEST ∼

A European View of Constantinople

In the late fifteenth century, Italian governments began to send permanent ambassadors to foreign courts. They were the first governments to do so. Venetian ambassadors quickly earned an international reputation as careful observers of the countries to which they had been assigned. The following evaluation of the Ottoman Empire was written in 1585 by the Venetian ambassador Gianfrancesco Morosini. It is a combination of shrewd observation and praise of an alien civilization that was meant to highlight the limits of European values.

[The Turks] were organized as military squadrons or commando units until 1300 A.D., when one of their number, named Ottoman, a man of low birth, began to build a reputation as a strong and spirited leader. Shrewd and clever, he took advantage of rivalries among his people, attracted many of them to him, and led them in war and conquest, making himself master of various towns and provinces of both the Turks and their neighbors. . . .

They succeed to the throne without any kind of ceremony of election or coronation. According to Turkish law of succession, which resembles most countries' laws in this respect, the oldest son should succeed to the throne as soon as the father dies. But in fact, whichever of the sons can first enter the royal compound in Constantinople is called the sultan and is obeyed by the people and by the army. Since he has control of his father's treasure he can easily gain the favor of the janissaries and with their help the rest of the army and the civilians. . . .

The security of the empire depends more than anything else on the large numbers of land and sea forces which the Turks keep continually under arms. These are what make them feared throughout the world. The sultan always has about 280,000 well-paid men in his service. . . . These include roughly 16,000 janissaries who form the Grand Signor's advanced guard. . . .

The whole empire is inhabited by three groups of people: Turks, Moors [non-Turkish Muslims], and Christians. In Asia and Africa the Moors are more numerous than the Turks, while in Europe the largest number are Christians, almost all of whom practice the Greek rite. There are also many Jews since that is really their homeland, even though they live in it like strangers rather than natives.

In appearance they are very pious adherents of their false religion. . . . They are very regular in observing the hours of prayer and they always have the name of God on their lips, but never blaspheme. Every wealthy Turk builds a mosque, making it as splendid as he can, and provides a rich endowment for its upkeep. As a result, the mosques are kept so clean and orderly that they put us Christians to shame. . . . In addition to the mosques they also build asylums more pleasing than their own houses, and in many of these they will give food for three days to anyone who asks for it—not only Turks, but also Christians and Jews.

Source: J. C. Davis, *Pursuit of Power: Venetian Ambassadors' Reports on Spain, Turkey, and France in the Age of Philip II, 1560–1600* (New York: Harper & Row, 1970), pp. 126, 127, 129, 134–135.

nearly 3.5 million sheep in Castile. So great were the profits accruing to the Crown from the exporting of wool that all other aspects of the economy were sacrificed to the needs of the Mesta. Farmers who lived along the routes by which the vast flocks moved from mountains to the plains often lost their crops to the hungry animals. The agricultural economy was virtually extinguished in some areas.

Economic power in Castile lay with the nobility, but political power rested with the monarch. Because the nobility was largely exempt from taxation, nobles ignored the cortes, the popular assembly, which could do little more than approve royal demands. The towns of Castile were important only as fortresses and staging points for militias rather than as centers of trade and commerce. No force was capable of opposing the will of the monarch. As John II of Castile (r. 1406–1454) explained,

> All my vassals, subjects, and people, whatever their estate, . . . are, according to all divine, human, . . . and even natural law, compelled and bound . . . to my word and deed. . . . The king holds this position not from men but from God, whose place he holds in temporal matters.[12]

The kingdom of Aragon was dramatically different. The center of the kingdom was Barcelona, an important trading center in the Mediterranean. In the fourteenth and fifteenth centuries the kings of Aragon concentrated their efforts on expanding their influence in the Mediterranean, south of France and Italy. By the middle of the fifteenth century the Aragonese empire included the kingdom of Naples, Sicily, the Balearic Islands, and Sardinia.

The power of the Aragonese king, in sharp contrast to the Castilian monarchy, was limited because the Crown was not unified. The ruler was king in Aragon and Navarre but was count in Catalonia. Aragon, Catalonia, and Valencia each maintained its own cortes. In each area the traditional nobility and the towns had a great deal more influence than they had in Castile. The power of the cortes is clear in the coronation oath taken by the Aragonese nobility: "We who are as good as you and together are more powerful than you, make you our king and lord, provided that you observe our laws and liberties, and if not, not."[13] The distinction with Castile could not be stronger.

The union of the crowns of Aragon and Castile did little to unify the two monarchies. By 1474, Castile and Aragon already had a long history of warfare and mutual distrust. Nobles fought over disputed boundaries, and Castilian nobles felt exploited by Aragonese merchants. Trade duties and internal boundaries continued to separate the two. The two realms even lacked a treaty to allow for the extradition of criminals from one kingdom to the other. Castilians never accepted Ferdinand as more than their queen's consort. After the death of Isabella in 1504, he ruled in Castile only as regent for his infant grand-

THE UNION OF CROWNS IN SPAIN

1469	Ferdinand of Aragon marries Isabella of Castile
1474	Isabella becomes queen of Castile
1478	Spanish Inquisition is established
1479	Ferdinand becomes king of Aragon
1492	Conquest of Granada; Columbus's first voyage; expulsion of Jews from Spain
1496	Joanna of Castile marries Philip of Habsburg
1501	Catherine of Aragon marries Arthur Tudor of England
1504	Expulsion of Muslims from Spain; death of Isabella; Ferdinand rules Castile as regent for his grandson, Charles I

son, Charles I (r. 1516–1556). "Spain" would not emerge in an institutional sense until the late sixteenth century.

Nonetheless, the reign of Isabella and Ferdinand marked a profound change in politics and society in the Iberian kingdoms. The monarchs visited all parts of their realm, reorganized municipal governments, took control of the powerful military orders, strengthened the power of royal law courts, and extended the international influence of the monarchies. Many of their actions were designed to advance the interests of Aragon in the Mediterranean. Ferdinand and Isabella married their daughter, Joanna, to Philip of Habsburg in 1496 to draw the Holy Roman Empire into the Italian wars brought on by the French invasion (see page 412). The marriage of their daughter, Catherine of Aragon, to Prince Arthur of England in 1501 was designed to obtain yet another ally against the French. Those two marriages would have momentous consequences for European history in the sixteenth century.

The reign of Ferdinand and Isabella is especially memorable because of the events of 1492. In January of that year, a crusading army conquered Granada, the last Muslim stronghold in Iberia. In March, Ferdinand and Isabella ordered the Jews of Castile and Aragon to convert or leave the kingdom within four months. In April, Isabella issued

Ferdinand and Isabella Interrogating a Jew Jews in Spain and many other parts of Europe were considered to be under the specific jurisdiction of local rulers. Jews and their converso relatives turned to the king and queen in 1492 when Jews faced the order to convert or leave the kingdom. *(Museo de Zaragoza)*

perhaps 2 percent of the population of Iberia was Jewish, and the Muslim population may have been as high as 50 percent. The various groups were inextricably mixed. The statutes of the Jewish community in Barcelona were written in Catalan rather than Hebrew. *Maranos,* Jewish converts to Christianity, and *moriscos,* Muslim converts, mixed continuously with Christians and with members of their former religions. It was difficult at times to know which religion these converts, or conversos, actually practiced. One surprised northern visitor to Spain remarked that one noble's circle was filled with "Christians, Moors, and Jews and he lets them live in peace in their faith."

This tolerant mingling of Christians, Muslims, and Jews came under attack by 1400, however. Complaints arose from a variety of sources. Many of the most important financiers and courtiers were Jews or conversos, which increased tensions among the communities. The most conservative Christians desired a community free of non-Christian influences. All three religious communities thought that there should be distinct dress and behavior that would identify each group. Christians seemed concerned that many of the conversos were likely to reconvert to Judaism, and the fear of reconversion, or "judaizing," led many to advocate the institution of the Spanish Inquisition.

Inquisitions were well known in many parts of Europe, but the Spanish Inquisition was unique because in 1478 Pope Sixtus IV placed the grand inquisitor under the direct control of the monarchs. Like most Christian rulers, Ferdinand and Isabella believed that uniform Christian orthodoxy was the only firm basis for a strong kingdom. Inquisitors attacked those aspects of converso tradition that seemed to make the conversos less than fully Christian. They were concerned that many conversos and maranos had converted falsely and were continuing to follow Jewish or Muslim ritual. The "New Christians" tended to live near their Muslim or Jewish relatives, eat the foods enjoyed in their former communities, and observe holy days, such as Yom Kippur, the Jewish day of atonement. Over four thousand converso families fled from Andalusia in southern Spain in the wake of the arrival of an inquisitor in 1490.

Because its administration, finances, and appointments were in Spanish hands, the Spanish Inquisition quickly became an important instrument for the expansion of state power. Many inquisitors

her commission authorizing Christopher Columbus "to discover and acquire islands and mainland in the Ocean Sea" (see page 487).

The conquest of Granada and the expulsion of the Jews represented a radical shift in the Spanish mentality. Until the beginning of the fifteenth century, Spain maintained a level of religious tolerance unusual in Christendom. In the fourteenth century, used their offices to attack wealthy or politically important converso families both to drive them from public life and to fill the royal treasury, which was where the estates of those judged guilty wound up. "This inquisition is as much to take the conversos' estates as to exalt the faith," was the despairing conclusion of one conversa woman.[14]

Ferdinand and Isabella seem to have concluded that the only way to protect the "New Christians" was to order all Jews who would not convert to leave the kingdom within four months. The order was signed on March 31, 1492, and published in late April after an unsuccessful attempt by converso and Jewish leaders to persuade the monarchs not to implement it.

Many Jews could not dispose of their possessions in the four months allowed and so chose to convert and remain. But it is estimated that about ten thousand Jews left Aragon and that even more left Castile. Many moved to Portugal and then to North Africa. Some went east to Constantinople or north to the Low Countries. In 1504, the expulsion order was extended to include all Muslims.

The economic and social costs of the expulsion were profound. Not every Muslim or Jew was wealthy and cultured, but the exiles did include many doctors, bankers, and merchants. Spanish culture, which had been open to influences from Muslim and Jewish sources, became less so in later centuries. After the expulsion, there opened a chasm of distrust between the "Old Christians" and the "New." As early as the first decades of the fifteenth century, some religious orders had refused to accept "New Christians." They required that their members demonstrate *limpieza de sangre,* a purity of blood. By 1500 the same tests of blood purity were extended to a majority of religious and public offices. Thus, by the end of the fifteenth century, the Iberian kingdoms had created more powerful, unified governments, but at a terrible cost to the only area in Christendom that had ever practiced religious tolerance.

SUMMARY

Europe in 1500 was profoundly different from the Europe of two centuries earlier. The economy had grown more complex in the wake of plague and demographic change. New patterns of trade and banking and new manufacturing techniques spread throughout Europe. Along with economic

recovery came increased social and political consciousness, manifested in the urban and rural uprisings of the fourteenth century.

The kings of France and England, the princes and despots in Germany and Italy, and the papacy managed to overcome political and cultural crises. After the Hundred Years' War and challenges from aristocrats, townsmen, and peasants, governments grew stronger as kings, princes, and town patricians used royal courts and patronage to extend their control. Military advances in the fifteenth century, such as the institution of standing armies, gave advantages to larger governments, but the experiences of the Italian and German states demonstrated that regional powers, under certain circumstances, could remain virtually independent of royal control. Yet the strength of regional and local powers was largely overshadowed by the rise of the Turkish and Spanish empires. It was they who would dominate politics and diplomacy in the next century.

In the aftermath of schism and conciliar reform, the church also was transformed. Because of conciliar challenges to papal authority, popes had to deal much more carefully with the governments of Europe. The popes who returned to Rome from Avignon in the fifteenth century were adept at using art and literary culture to explain and magnify their court and their place in Christian history and society. Art and literature played an important role in the reform and expression of public life. It is to the role of culture that we turn in the next chapter.

NOTES

1. Quoted in Guillaume Mollat, *The Popes at Avignon, 1305–1378* (London: Thomas Nelson, 1963), p. 112.
2. Quoted in Mary Aston, *Lollards and Reformers: Images and Literacy in Late Medieval Religion* (Ronceverte, W.V.: 1984), p. 60.
3. Quoted in Francis Oakley, *The Western Church in the Later Middle Ages* (Ithaca, N.Y.: Cornell University Press, 1979), pp. 65–66.
4. Quoted in Charles T. Wood, *Joan of Arc and Richard III* (New York: Oxford University Press, 1988), pp. 56–57.
5. Quoted in Michael T. Clanchy, "Law, Government, and Society in Medieval England," *History* 59 (1974): 75.
6. A. Buchon, *Choix des Chroniques* (Paris, 1875), p. 565, as quoted in John Gillingham and J. C. Holt, eds.,

War and Government in the Middle Ages (Totowa, N.J.: Barnes & Noble, 1984), p. 85.

7. Quoted in Peter Shervey Lewis, *Later Medieval France: The Polity* (New York: Macmillan, 1968), p. 15.

8. Quoted in Jeffrey Richards, "The Riddle of Richard III," *History Today* 33 (August 1983): 20.

9. Salimbene de Adam, quoted in John Larner, *Italy in the Age of Dante and Petrarch, 1215–1380* (New York: Longman, 1980), p. 141.

10. Rodney Hilton in *The English Rising of 1381*, ed. R. H. Hilton and T. H. Aston (Cambridge, England: Cambridge University Press, 1984), p. 3.

11. Quoted in Angus MacKay, "Popular Movements and Pogroms, in Fifteenth-Century Spain," *Past & Present* 55 (1972): 52.

12. Quoted in Angus MacKay, *Spain in the Middle Ages: From Frontier to Empire, 1000–1500* (London: Macmillan, 1977), p. 137.

13. Ibid., p. 105.

14. Haim Beinart, ed., *Records of the Trials of the Spanish Inquisition in Ciudad Real*, vol. 1 (Jerusalem: The Israel Academy of Sciences and Humanities, 1974), p. 391. Trans. Duane Osheim.

SUGGESTED READING

General Surveys

Brady, Thomas A., Jr., Heiko A. Oberman, and James D. Tracy. *Handbook of European History, 1400–1600*. 2 vols. 1994–1996. An excellent collection of studies by leading scholars in Europe and North America on all aspects of the period.

Hay, Denys. *Europe in the Fourteenth and Fifteenth Centuries*. 1966. A well-written introductory survey of politics and society in Europe between 1300 and 1500; includes coverage of Scandinavia and the Slavic lands as well as the central areas of northwestern Europe.

War and Government

Allmand, Christopher. *The Hundred Years' War: England and France at War, 1300–1450*. 1988. A single-volume summary of the war and its impact on late medieval politics, government, military institutions, literature, and nationalism.

Du Boulay, F. R. H. *Germany in the Later Middle Ages*. 1983. This survey of German history designed for students emphasizes the growth of territorial governments at the expense of the central authorities.

Duby, G. *France in the Middle Ages, 987–1460*. Translated by Juliet Vale. 1991. In this general survey, France's most distinguished medievalist concentrates on social and cultural life. Includes excellent pictures, maps, and diagrams.

Goodman, A. *The New Monarchy: England, 1471–1534*. 1988. A short introduction to the changed nature of monarchy after the Wars of the Roses.

Guenée, B. *States and Rulers in Later Medieval Europe*. Trans. by Juliet Vale. 1985. The best general introduction to the nature of government in the late Middle Ages. It introduces recent trends in historical research.

Keen, Maurice H. *English Society in the Later Middle Ages, 1348–1500*. 1990. A recent general introduction to late medieval England that covers culture and religion as well as politics.

Larner, John. *Italy in the Age of Dante and Petrarch, 1215–1380*. 1980. A short introduction to the general developments in fourteenth-century Italy, treating but not concentrating on Florence and Venice.

Sumption, Jonathon. *The Hundred Years' War*. 1990. A projected multivolume history of the war. Vol. 1, *Trial by Battle*, is an excellent narrative of the background diplomacy and the first decades of the war.

Warner, Marina. *Joan of Arc: The Image of Female Heroism*. 1981. An excellent and quite readable book emphasizing the conflicting religious and political opinions about "the Maid."

Christianity and the Papacy

Cohen, J. *The Friars and the Jews: The Evolution of Medieval Anti-Judaism*. 1982. In a complex, closely argued study, Cohen describes the changed attitudes toward Jews in the thirteenth and fourteenth centuries.

Oakley, Francis. *The Western Church in the Later Middle Ages*. 1979. The best general history of the church in the late Middle Ages. Oakley gives superior treatments of the Great Schism and conciliarism.

Partner, Peter. *The Lands of St. Peter*. 1972. A thorough account of the political and diplomatic initiatives in the Papal States—the area that was the key to the practical power of the papacy.

Swanson, Ronald N. *Religion and Devotion in Europe, c. 1215–c. 1515*. 1995. A general introduction to the place of the church in social life in the late Middle Ages, with special attention to the connection of social and religious history.

Plague and Society

Abulafia, D. "Asia, Africa and the Trade of Medieval Europe." In *Cambridge Economic History*. 1987. A thorough introductory discussion of international trade in the late Middle Ages.

Carmichael, Ann G. *Plague and the Poor in Renaissance Florence*. 1985. A work directed at scholars that investigates the plague in a specific town, emphasizing the way in which the social and economic conditions that preceded the plague conditioned responses to the epidemic.

De Roover, R. A. *The Rise and Decline of the Medici Bank, 1397–1494.* 1966. Based largely on the family's business correspondence, this is a clear discussion of the business practices of this fifteenth-century bank.

Dyer, C. *Standards of Living in the Later Middle Ages: Social Change in England, c. 1200–1500.* 1989. An account that includes a sophisticated discussion of dietary changes in the wake of population decline and changed commodity prices in fifteenth-century England.

Hanawalt, Barbara, ed. *Women and Work in Pre-Industrial Europe.* 1986. Sophisticated case studies of the changing status of women's work in the late Middle Ages in England, France, and Germany.

Hatcher, J. *Plague, Population, and the English Economy, 1348–1530.* 1977. A clear discussion of the effect of declining population on the economy of England. This short introduction is designed for students.

Herlihy, David. *Women, Family and Society in Medieval Europe: Historical Essays, 1978–1991.* 1995. A collection of essays on late medieval European society. Extremely thoughtful and well written.

Howell, M. C. *Women, Production and Patriarchy in Late Medieval Cities.* 1986. After thoroughly reconstructing guild life in the Low Countries, the author argues that women were frozen out of the cloth industry. A difficult but important work.

Klapisch-Zuber, Christiane. *Women, Family, and Ritual in Renaissance Italy.* 1987. A collection of essays that make clear the contradictory pressures placed on women in late medieval Italy. Not always easy reading, but very rewarding.

Miskimin, Harry A. *The Economy of Early Renaissance Europe, 1300–1460.* 1975. An excellent, readable survey of how the economies of various parts of Europe responded to economic decline and plague.

Mollat, Michel, and Philippe Wolff. *The Popular Revolutions of the Late Middle Ages.* 1973. The best survey of the major revolutions of the fourteenth century, emphasizing the local political conditions that brought on the revolutions.

Ziegler, Philip. *The Black Death.* 1971. Although superseded on many specific points, this remains the best single volume on the plague in the fourteenth century.

The Ottoman and Spanish Empires

Holt, P. M., Ann Katharine Swynford Lambton, and Bernard Lewis, eds. *The Cambridge History of Islam.* 1970. The essays in this volume provide a general introduction for nonspecialists.

Housley, N. *The Later Crusades: From Lyons to Alcazar, 1274–1580.* 1992. This comprehensive account of crusading history includes an especially good consideration of Christian and Muslim relations in Iberia and the Balkans.

Inalcik, H. *The Ottoman Empire: The Classical Age, 1300–1600.* 1973. A general discussion of the growth of the Ottoman state by Turkey's best medieval historian.

Kamen, H. A. F. *The Spanish Inquisition.* 1966. This passionate introduction to Spain's most controversial institution demonstrates the truth of Lord Acton's observation that "Absolute power corrupts absolutely." Kamen gives an especially clear discussion of court procedures.

MacKay, A. *Spain in the Middle Ages: From Frontier to Empire, 1000–1500.* 1977. This short general introduction to Spain emphasizes the institutional changes that occurred in the late fourteenth and fifteenth centuries.

A PAINTING OF THE PLAGUE

Writers who survived the coming of bubonic plague in 1348 described a world of terror in which things seemed changed forever. Look at this painting, *St. Sebastian Interceding for the Plague-Stricken,* created by the Flemish artist Josse Lieferinxe between 1497 and 1499. One dying man seems to be falling terrified to the ground while a female bystander in the background screams in alarm. Images of Christ, Saint Sebastian (pierced by arrows), a devil, and a priest seem to indicate that something terrifying and undreamed-of is happening. But what exactly was the terror and what had changed?

The art of the later Middle Ages is an extremely valuable source for understanding social and religious values. As you look at *St. Sebastian Interceding for the Plague-Stricken,* the first step is to understand what men and women in the fourteenth and fifteenth centuries thought about death. After 1400, European Christians often depicted the universality of death in paintings showing the Dance of Death. The motif varies, but typically Death grasps the hands of men and women, rich and poor, noble and peasant, and leads them away. Deathbed scenes were another popular motif. In the late Middle Ages most people believed that at death the good and evil acts committed by an individual were tallied in the Book of Life and the person was granted either eternal life in Purgatory and then Paradise or consigned to eternal suffering in Hell. Judgment scenes often depict the Virgin Mary or another saint pleading before God or contending with the Devil or demons over the souls of the dying.

It was essential for people to prepare for a good death. Individuals studied the *artes moriendi,* the arts of dying. A lingering, painful illness was often interpreted as an opportunity for penitential suffering that would be good for the soul. At the point of death, the dying person could confess and receive both absolution for sins and the last sacraments of the church. From that moment on, he or she needed to maintain a calm faith, free from fear. Salvation and eternal life depended on avoiding further sin, especially the questioning of God's forgiveness and mercy. Death was a public event. Clergy, family, religious societies, even neighbors helped the dying person to keep hope. The person might pray, "Virgin Mary, Mother of God, I have placed my hope in you. Free my soul from care, and from Hell, and bitter death."*

The concept of a good death is critical to understanding the European response to bubonic plague. To be sure, individuals rarely look forward to death, now or in the Middle Ages. Boccaccio and numerous chroniclers remarked on the suddenness of death and on the lack of priests to hear confession. (See the box, "The Black Death" on page 417.) Individuals who were healthy in the morning might be dead by nightfall. The suddenness, the lack of preparation for a good death, heightened the dread that accompanied the onset of illness and death.

Medieval Christians turned to patron saints who could represent them before God at the point of death and to stop the onslaught of the plague. Three patron saints were especially popular. The Virgin Mary was often shown using her cloak to shelter towns and individuals from arrows carrying pestilence. Saint Roch, himself a victim of plague, was thought to intercede and protect those who prayed in his name. And Saint Sebastian, an early Christian martyr shot with arrows (later understood as symbols of death by plague), was thought to be an especially effective patron during epidemics. In times of plague, people went on pilgrimages to local shrines dedicated to these or local saints, carried images of the saints in processions, and built churches and chapels dedicated to the saints in thanks for deliverance from plague.

*Quoted in Philippe Ariès, *The Hour of Our Death* (New York: Knopf, 1981), p. 108.

Lieferinxe: St. Sebastian Interceding for the Plague-Stricken (*Walters Art Gallery, Baltimore*)

With these issues in mind, what do we see in Lieferinxe's painting? The painting portrays an outbreak of plague. We note first the body of the dead person, carefully shrouded. Ideally the dead, like the body in the foreground, were taken to a church and then given a Christian burial. But chroniclers often remarked that so many died, and died so quickly, that no one could be found to bury them properly. In many towns the dead were gathered on carts and hauled to large common graves outside the town. We can see one such cart leaving the castle in the background. In a series of images, then, Lieferinxe shows what mattered most to people. In the foreground is the shrouded body attended by a priest and by other clerics bearing a cross. This person experienced a good death. In contrast, the man

who has fallen behind the body is suffering a bad death, one that caught him unawares. He is the object of the concern and grief of those near him. In the sky just above the castle walls, a white-robed angel and a horned, ax-wielding demon contend over the souls of the dead and dying. At the top of the painting, Christ listens to the prayers of Saint Sebastian. The painting thus portrays the impact and horror of plague and also shows the way in which the epidemic might be ended.

Returning to our original question, we find that the terror of epidemic plague was not entirely like a modern panic. Medieval people understood the horror and panic as well as the solutions to the epidemic in terms of traditional religious values: The terror was to be caught unawares. ✜

CHAPTER 12

The Renaissance

I talians of the fourteenth and fifteenth centuries believed that the world needed to be dramatically reformed, and they were sure they knew why. "As the city of Rome had perished at the hands of perverse and tyrannical Emperors, so did Latin studies and literature undergo similar ruin and diminution. . . . And Italy was invaded by Goths and Lombards, barbarous, uncouth peoples, who practically extinguished all knowledge of literature."[1] This extinction of knowledge, according to Leonardo Bruni, a writer and later chancelor in fifteenth-century Florence, was responsible for the moral and political decay he feared had weakened Italian public life. The only answer, he was sure, was to change the way Italians were educated and how they thought about their past.

Bruni's feelings were common among artists and writers. Paolo Ucello's painting of the Battle of San Romano is an example of what had changed. The vivid colors and the realistic use of perspective to arrange the figures make it seem that we are present at the battle itself. This was a new kind of painting. Renaissance Italians wrote of themselves and their contemporaries as having "revived" arts, "rescued" painting, and "rediscovered" classical authors. They even coined the phrases "Dark Ages" and "Middle Ages" to describe the period that separated classical antiquity from the culture of their own times. In the sixteenth century the painter and art historian Giorgio Vasari described the revival as a *rinascità*, an Italian word meaning "rebirth." And to this day we use the French translation of that word, *renaissance,* to describe the period between 1300 and 1600.

We also use *renaissance* to describe any time of intense creativity and change that differs dramatically from what has gone before. This particular

Ucello's *The Battle of San Romano* (detail), ca. 1450, showing a complex, realistic scene—a Renaissance innovation.

definition of the word comes to us primarily from the work of the Swiss historian Jacob Burckhardt. In his book *The Civilization of the Renaissance in Italy* (1860), Burckhardt argued that the creativity and cultural brilliance of the period resulted when Italians suddenly found themselves freed from the medieval restraints of religion, guild, community, and family. Renaissance Italians, he believed, were the first individuals to recognize the state as an autonomous moral structure free from the strictures of religious or philosophical traditions. During the time of the Renaissance, an individual's success or failure in all matters depended on personal qualities of creative brilliance rather than on status in a family, religion, or guild. What Burckhardt thought he saw in Renaissance Italy were the first signs of the romantic individualism and the nationalism that characterized his own society.

Both Leonardo Bruni and Jacob Burckhardt misunderstood the relationship between the Renaissance and the period that preceded it. There was no "Dark Age." The culture of Renaissance Europe was in no way superior to the religious, philosophical, and literary culture that preceded or followed it. Although the culture of Renaissance Europe was in many aspects new and innovative, it had close ties both to the ideas of the High Middle Ages and to traditional Christian values.

We cannot answer aesthetic questions of whether Renaissance architecture, literature, and philosophy were actually superior to the culture out of which they grew. We can, however, describe the Renaissance in Europe as an important cultural movement that aimed to reform and renew by making art, education, religion, and political life congruent with the reformers' conception of classical and early Christian traditions. As we will see, Italians, and then other Europeans, came to believe that the social and moral values as well as the literature of classical Rome offered the best chance to change their own society for the better. This enthusiasm for a past culture became the measure for changes in literature, education, and art that established cultural standards that were to hold for the next five hundred years. Renaissance men and women misunderstood important aspects of classical culture; nevertheless, their attempts at reform had a profound effect on the development of European culture.

HUMANISM AND CULTURE IN ITALY, 1300–1500

Logic and Scholastic philosophy (see page 380) dominated university education in northern Europe in the fourteenth and fifteenth centuries, but had less influence in Italy, where education focused on the practical issues of town life rather than on theological speculation. Educated Italians of this period were interested in the *studia humanitatis*, which we now call humanism. By *humanism*, Italians meant rhetoric and literature—the arts of persuasion—not an ideological or a moral program based on philosophical arguments or religious assumptions about human nature. Poetry, history, letter writing, and oratory based on forms and aesthetic values consciously borrowed from ancient Greece and Rome formed the center of intellectual life.

Humanistic thought in the Renaissance was very much a product of the urban milieu of fourteenth- and fifteenth-century Italy. Italians turned to models from classical antiquity in an attempt to deal with current issues of cultural, political, and educational reform. The humanistic movement began as a belief in the superiority of the literature and history of the past. As humanists discovered more about ancient culture, they were able to understand more clearly the historical context in which Roman and Greek writers and thinkers lived. And by the early sixteenth century, their debates on learning, civic duty, and the classical legacy had led them to a new vision of the past and a new appreciation of the nature of politics.

The Emergence of Humanism

Humanism initially held greater appeal in Italy than elsewhere in Europe because the culture in central and northern Italy was significantly more secular and more urban than the culture of much of the rest of Europe. Members of the clergy were not likely to dominate government and education in Italy. Quite the reverse: Boards dominated by laymen had built and were administering the great urban churches of Italy. Religious hospitals and charities were often reorganized and centralized under government control. In 1300, four cities in Italy had populations of about 100,000 (Milan, Venice, Florence, and Naples), and countless others had populations of 40,000 or more. By contrast, London, which may have had a population of 100,000, was the only city in England with more than 40,000 inhabitants. Even the powerful Italian aristocracy tended to live at least part of the year in towns and conform to urban social and legal practices.

Differences between Italy and northern Europe are apparent in the structure of local education. In northern Europe, education was organized to provide clergy for local churches. In the towns of Italy, education was much more likely to be supervised by town governments to provide training in accounting, arithmetic, and the composition of business letters. In Italy it was common for town governments to hire lay grammar masters to teach in free public schools. They competed with numerous private masters and individual tutors who were prepared to teach all subjects. Giovanni Villani, a fourteenth-century merchant and historian, described Florence in 1338 as a city of about 100,000 people in which perhaps as many as 10,000 young girls and boys completed elementary education and 1000 continued their studies to prepare for careers in commerce. Compared to education in the towns of northern Europe, education in Villani's Florence seems broad based and practical. This may have been typical of education in the commercial towns of central and northern Italy.

Italian towns were also the focus of theorizing about towns as moral, religious, and political communities. Writers wanted to define the nature of the commune—the town government. Moralists often used "the common good" and "the good of the commune" as synonyms. By 1300 it was usual for towns to celebrate the feast day of their patron saint as a major political as well as religious festival. And town governments often supervised the construction and expansion of cathedrals, churches, and hospitals as a sign of their wealth and prestige. Literature of the early fourteenth century tended to emphasize the culture of towns. Italian historians chose to write the histories of their hometowns. Most, like Giovanni Villani of Florence, were convinced that their towns could rival ancient Rome. The majority of educated Italians in the early fourteenth century, however, were not captivated by thoughts of ancient Rome. Theirs was a practical world in which most intellectuals were men trained in notarial arts—the everyday skills of oratory, letter writing, and the recording of legal documents.

Vernacular Literatures

The humanistic movement, however, was not simply a continuation of practical and literary movements. The extent of its innovation will be clearer if we look briefly at the vernacular literatures (that is, written in native languages, rather than Latin) of the fourteenth and fifteenth centuries. Vernacular literatures continued to treat traditional Christian moral and ethical concerns with reference to traditional values and ideas. Even the most famous and most innovative work of the fourteenth century, *The Decameron* by Giovanni Boccaccio (1313–1375), was, in certain respects, traditional. Boccaccio hoped the lively and irreverent descriptions of contemporary Italians, which make his *Decameron* a classic of European literature, would also lead individuals to understand both what it is that makes them human and the folly of human desires. The tale describes a group of privileged young people who abandon friends and family during the plague of 1348 (see pages 414–417) to go into the country, where on successive days they mix feasting, dancing, and song with one hundred tales of love, intrigue, and gaiety. With its mix of traditional and contemporary images, Boccaccio's book spawned numerous imitators in Italy and elsewhere. But the point too often missed by Boccaccio's imitators was, as he himself said, that "to have compassion for those who suffer is a human quality which everyone should possess. . . ."

Boccaccio's work influenced another vernacular writer, Geoffrey Chaucer (ca. 1343–1400), the son of a London burgher, who served as a diplomat, courtier, and member of Parliament. In addition to the pervasive French influence, Chaucer read and studied Boccaccio. Chaucer's most well-known work, *The Canterbury Tales,* consists of stories told by a group of thirty pilgrims who left the London suburbs on a pilgrimage to the shrine of Saint Thomas à Becket at Canterbury. The narrators and the stories themselves allow Chaucer to describe a variety of moral and social types, creating an acute, sometimes bitter, portrait of English life. The Wife of Bath is typical of Chaucer's pilgrims: "She was a worthy woman all her life, husbands at the churchdoor she had five." After describing her own five marriages, she makes the point that marriage is a proper way to achieve moral perfection, but it can be so only if the woman is master.

Although Chaucer's characters have an ironic view of the good and evil that abound in society, Chaucer's contemporary, William Langland (ca. 1330–ca. 1400), takes a decidedly more serious view of the ills of English life. Whereas Dante, Boccaccio, and Chaucer all told realistic tales about life as it really seemed to be, Langland used the traditional allegorical language (that is, symbolic language where a place or person represents an idea) of medieval Europe. In *Piers Plowman* he writes of people caught between the "Valley of Death" and the "Tower of Truth." In his visions Langland describes the seven deadly sins that threaten all of society and follows with an exhortation to do better. Both Chaucer and Langland expected their audience to immediately recognize commonly held ideas and values.

Women and Culture Christine de Pizan objected to male denigration of the moral and cultural value of women. This illumination from her *City of the Ladies* shows her ideal society, a place where women, like men, are allowed to study and create. *(Bibliothèque Nationale)*

Despite the persistence of old forms of literature, new vernacular styles arose, although they still dealt with traditional values and ideas. Throughout Europe many writers directly addressed their cares and concerns. Some collected letters or wrote short works of piety, like *The Mirror for Simple Souls* of Marguerite of Porete (d. 1310). Though Marguerite was ultimately executed as a heretic, her work continued to circulate anonymously. Her frank description of love and God's love for humans inspired many other writers in the fourteenth and fifteenth centuries. Less erotic but equally riveting is the memoir of Margery Kempe, an alewife from England. She describes how she left her husband and family, dressed in white (symbolic of virginity), and joined with other pilgrims on trips to Spain, Italy, and Jerusalem.

One of the most unusual of the new vernacular writers was Christine de Pizan (1369–1430), the daughter of an Italian physician at the court of Charles V of France. Her father and later her husband had encouraged her to learn languages and to write. When the deaths of both of these men left her with responsibility for her children and little money, she turned to writing. From 1389 until her death, she lived and wrote at the French court. She composed a short life of Joan of Arc and an instructional book for the education of the crown prince, but she is perhaps best known for *The Book of the City of the Ladies* (1405). In it she added her own voice to what is known as the *querelle des femmes,* the "argument over women." Christine wrote to counter the many writings that characterized women as inferior to men and incapable of moral judgments. She argued that the problem was education: "If it were customary to send daughters to school like sons, and if they were then taught the natural sciences, they would learn as thoroughly and understand the subtleties of all the arts and sciences as well as sons." Christine described in her book an ideal city of ladies in which prudence, justice, and reason would protect women from ignorant male critics.

All these vernacular writings built on popular tales and sayings as well as traditional moral and religious writings. Unlike the early humanists, the vernacular writers saw little need for new cultural and intellectual models. The humanists' need for new models seems to have developed out of particular Italian political and social needs.

Early Humanism

The first Italians who looked back consciously to the literary and historical examples of ancient Rome were a group of northern Italian lawyers and notaries who imitated Roman authors. These practical men found Roman history and literature more stimulating and useful than medieval philosophy. Writers like Albertino Mussato of Padua (1262–1329) adopted classical styles in their poetry and histories. Albertino used his play *The Ecerinis* (1315) to tell of the fall of Can Grande della Scala, the tyrannical ruler of Verona (d. 1329) and to warn his neighbors of the dangers of tyranny. He celebrated the independent city-states and urged a renewal of republican values in the cities of the Po Valley. "The rule of justice lasts forever," Albertino concluded. "Virtue soars to heavenly joys."[2] From its earliest, the classical revival in Italy was tied to issues of moral and political reform.

This largely emotional fascination for the ancient world was transformed into a literary movement for reform by Francesco Petrarch (1304–1374), who popularized the idea of mixing classical moral and literary ideas with the concerns of the fourteenth century. Petrarch was the son of an exiled Florentine notary living at the papal court in Avignon. His father sent him to study law at the University of Bologna, but Petrarch had little interest in the law. After his father's death he quickly abandoned law for literature. Repelled by the urban violence and wars he had experienced, Petrarch was highly critical of his contemporaries: "I never liked this age," he once confessed. He criticized the "Babylonian Captivity" of the papacy in Avignon, as he named it (see page 397); he supported an attempt to resurrect a republican government in Rome; and he believed that imitation of the actions, values, and culture of the ancient Romans was the only way to reform his world.

Petrarch believed that an age of darkness—he coined the expression "Dark Ages"—separated the Roman world from his own time and that the separation could be overcome only through a study and reconstruction of classical values: "Once the darkness has been broken, our descendants will perhaps be able to return to the pure, pristine radiance."[3] A brilliant poet and linguist and a tireless self-promoter, he lived his entire life as an example of the way in which classical values could serve as a vehicle for moral and intellectual reform. Petrarch's program, and in many respects the entire Renaissance, involved first of all a reconstruction of classical culture, then a careful study and imitation of the classical heritage, and finally a series of moral and cultural changes that went beyond the mere copying of ancient values and styles.

Petrarch labored throughout his life to reconstruct the history and literature of Rome. He learned to read and write classical Latin. While still in his twenties, he discovered fragments of Livy's *Roman History*, an important source for the history of Republican Rome. He annotated and reorganized the fragments in an attempt to reconstruct the form Livy himself had intended. His work on Livy was merely the first step. In the 1330s he discovered a number of classical works, including orations by Cicero, the great philosopher, statesman, and opponent of Julius Caesar (see page 185). In 1345 he found the collection of letters that Cicero, while in exile, had written to his friend Atticus. These letters, filled with gossip, questions about politics in Rome, and complaints about his forced withdrawal from public life, created the portrait of an individual who was much more complex than the austere philosopher of medieval legend.

Petrarch was and remained a committed Christian. He recognized the tension between the Christian present and pagan antiquity. "My wishes fluctuate and my desires conflict, and in their struggle they tear me apart," he said.[4] Yet he prized the beauty and moral value of ancient learning. He wrote *The Lives of Illustrious Men*, biographies of men from antiquity whose lives he thought were worthy of emulation. He composed an epic Latin poem, *Africa*, about the Roman patrician Scipio Africanus. To spread humanistic values, he issued collections of his letters, written in classically inspired Latin, and his Italian poems. He believed that study and memorization of the writings of classical authors could lead to the internalization of the ideas and values expressed in those works, just as a honeybee drinks nectar to create honey. He argued that the ancient moral philosophers were superior to the Scholastic philosophers, whose work ended with the determination of truth, or correct responses. "The true moral philosophers and useful teachers of the virtues," he concluded, "are those whose first and last intention is to make hearer and reader good, those who do not merely teach what virtue and vice are but sow into our hearts love of the best . . . and hatred of the worst."[5] (See the box, "Petrarch Responds to His Critics.")

Humanistic Studies

Petrarch's belief in humanism inspired a broad-based transformation of Italian intellectual life that affected discussions of politics, education, literature, and philosophy. Wherever he traveled in Italy, numerous young scholars flocked to him. His style of historical and literary investigation of the past became the basis for a new appreciation of the present.

Petrarch's program of humanistic studies became especially popular with the wealthy oligarchy that dominated political life in Florence. The Florentine chancellor Coluccio Salutati (1331–1406) and a generation of young intellectuals who formed his circle evolved an ideology of civic humanism. Civic humanists wrote letters, orations, and histories praising their city's classical virtues and history. In the process they gave a practical and public meaning to the Petrarchan program. Civic humanists argued, like Cicero himself, that there was a moral and ethical value intrinsic to public life. In a letter to a friend, Coluccio Salutati wrote that public life is "something holy and holier than idleness in [religious] solitude." To another he added, "The active life you flee is to be followed both as an exercise in virtue and because of the necessity of brotherly love."[6]

More than Petrarch himself, civic humanists viewed their task as the creation of men of virtue who could take the lead in government and protect their fellow citizens from lawlessness and tyranny. In the early years of the fifteenth century, civic humanists praised Florence for remaining a republic of free citizens rather than falling under the control of a lord, like the people of Milan, whose government was dominated by the Viscontis (see page 411). In his *Panegyric on the City of Florence* (ca. 1400), Leonardo Bruni (ca. 1370–1444) recalled the history of the Roman Republic and suggested that Florence could recreate the virtues of the Roman state. To civic humanists, the study of Rome and its virtues was the key to the continued prosperity of Florence and similar Italian republics.

One of Petrarch's most enthusiastic followers was Guarino of Verona (1374–1460), who became the leading advocate of educational reform in Renaissance Italy. After spending five years in Constantinople learning Greek and collecting classical manuscripts, he became the most successful teacher and translator of Greek literature in Italy. There had been previously a widespread interest in Greek literature—Petrarch owned a copy of the *Iliad*, though he never managed to learn to read it—and Greek studies had been advanced by Manuel Chrysoloras (1350–1415), who, after his arrival from Constantinople in 1397, taught Greek for three years in Florence. Chrysoloras was later joined by other Greek intellectuals, especially after the fall of Constantinople to the Turks in 1453. Throughout the fifteenth century there was enthusiasm for Greek philosophy and theology. Guarino built on this interest.

Guarino emphasized careful study of grammar and memorization of large bodies of classical history and poetry. He coached students to write orations in the style of Cicero. Guarino believed that through a profound understanding of Greek and Latin literature and a careful imitation of the style of the great authors, a person could come to exhibit the moral and ethical values for which Cicero, Seneca, and Plutarch were justly famous. Although it is unclear that Guarino's style of education delivered the moral training he advocated, it did provide a thorough education in literature and oratory. In an age that admired the ability to speak and write persuasively, the new style of humanistic education pioneered by Guarino spread quickly throughout Europe. The elegy spoken at Guarino's funeral sums up Italian views of humanistic education as well as the contribution of Guarino himself: "No one was considered noble, as leading a blameless life, unless he had followed Guarino's courses."

Guarino's authority spread quickly. One of his early students, Vittorino da Feltre (1378–1446), was appointed tutor to the Gonzaga dukes of Mantua. Like Guarino, he emphasized close literary study and careful imitation of classical authors. But the school he founded, the Villa Giocosa, was innovative because he advocated games and exercises as well as formal study. In addition, Vittorino required that bright young boys from poor families be included among the seventy students normally resident in his school. Vittorino

Petrarch Responds to His Critics

Many traditional philosophers and theologians criticized humanists as "pagans" because of their lack of interest in discovering logical and theological truths and their love of non-Christian writers. In this excerpt from "On My Own Ignorance and That of Many Others," a letter written to defend humanistic studies, Petrarch discusses Cicero and explains the value of his work to Christians.

[Cicero] points out the miraculously coherent structure and disposition of the body, sense and limbs, and finally reason and sedulous activity. . . . And all this he does merely to lead us to this conclusion: whatever we behold with our eyes or perceive with our intellect is made by God for the well-being of man and governed by divine providence and counsel. . . . [In response to his critics who argued for the superiority of philosophy he adds] I have read all of Aristotle's moral books. . . . Sometimes I have become more learned through them when I went home, but not better, not so good as I ought to be; and I often complained to myself, occasionally to others too, that by no facts was the promise fulfilled which the philosopher makes at the beginning of the first book of his *Ethics*, namely, that "we learn this part of philosophy not with the purpose of gaining knowledge but of becoming better." . . . However, what is the use of knowing what virtue is if it is not loved when known? What is the use of knowing sin if it is not abhorred when it is known? However, everyone who has become thoroughly familiar with our Latin authors knows that they stamp and drive deep into the heart the sharpest and most ardent stings of speech by which . . . those who stick to the ground [are] lifted up to the highest thoughts and to honest desire. . . .

Cicero, read with a pious and modest attitude, . . . was profitable to everybody, so far as eloquence is concerned, to many others as regards living. This was especially true in [Saint] Augustine's case. . . . I confess, I admire Cicero as much or even more than all whoever wrote a line in any nation. . . . If to admire Cicero means to be a Ciceronian, I am a Ciceronian. I admire him so much that I wonder at people who do not admire him. . . . However, when we come to think or speak of religion, that is, of supreme truth and true happiness, and of eternal salvation, then I am certainly not a Ciceronian, or a Platonist, but a Christian. I even feel sure that Cicero himself would have been a Christian if he had been able to see Christ and to comprehend His doctrine.

Source: Petrarch, "On His Own Ignorance and That of Many Others," in *The Renaissance Philosophy of Man*, ed. Ernst Cassirer, Paul Oskar Kristeller, and John H. Randall (Chicago: University of Chicago Press, 1948), pp. 86, 103, 104, 114, 115.

was so renowned that noblemen from across Italy sent their sons to be educated at the Villa Giocosa.

Humanistic education had its limits, however. Leonardo Bruni of Florence once composed a curriculum for a young woman to follow. He urged her to learn literature and moral philosophy as well as to read religious writers. But, he suggested, there was no reason to study rhetoric: "For why should the subtleties of . . . rhetorical conundrums consume the powers of a woman, who never sees the forum? . . . The contests of the forum, like those of warfare and battle, are the sphere of men."[7] To what extent did women participate in the cultural and artistic movements of the fourteenth and fifteenth centuries? Was the position of women better than it had been previously? The current of misogyny, the assumption that women were intellectually and morally weaker than men, continued during the Renaissance, but it was not unopposed.

Isabella d'Este As part of the program to revive ancient Roman practices, Italian rulers had medals struck containing their own images. This image of Isabella was meant to celebrate the woman herself and the fact that her husband held the imperial office of duke. (*Kunsthistorisches Museum, Vienna*)

During the fifteenth century many women did learn to read and even to write. Religious women and wives of merchants read educational and spiritual literature. Some women needed to write in order to manage the economic and political interests of the family. Alessandra Macinghi-Strozzi of Florence (1407–1471), for example, wrote numerous letters to her sons in exile describing her efforts to find spouses for her children and to influence the government to end their exile. Yet many men were suspicious of literate women. Just how suspicious is evident in the career of Isotta Nogarola (b. 1418) of Verona, one of a number of fifteenth- and sixteenth-century Italian women whose literary abilities equaled those of male humanists. Isotta quickly became known as a gifted writer, but men's response to her work was mixed. One anonymous critic suggested that it was unnatural for a woman to have such scholarly interests and accused her of equally unnatural sexual interests. Guarino of Verona himself wrote to her saying that if she was truly to be edu-

cated she must put off female sensibilities and find "a man within the woman."[8]

The problem for humanistically educated women was that there was no acceptable role for them. A noblewoman like Isabella d'Este (see page 464), wife of the duke of Mantua, might gather humanists and painters around her at court, but it was not generally believed that women could create literary works of true merit. When women tried, they were usually rebuffed and urged to reject the values of civic humanism and to hold instead to traditional Christian virtues of rejection of the world. A woman who had literary or cultural interests was expected to enter a convent. Isotta Nogarola was given this advice when she informed a male humanist friend that she was contemplating marriage. It was wrong, he said, "that a virgin should consider marriage, or even think about that liberty of lascivious morals."[9] Throughout the fifteenth and early sixteenth centuries some women in Italy and the rest of Europe learned classical languages and philosophy, but they became rarer as time passed. The virtues of humanism were public virtues, and Europeans of the Renaissance remained uncomfortable with the idea that women might act directly and publicly. (See the box, "Cassandra Fedele Defends Liberal Arts for Women.")

The Transformation of Humanism

The fascination with education based on ancient authorities was heightened by the discovery in 1416 in the Monastery of Saint Gall in Switzerland of a complete manuscript of Quintilian's *Institutes of Oratory*, a first-century treatise on the proper education for a young Roman patrician. It was found by Poggio Bracciolini (1380–1459), who had been part of the humanist circle in Florence. The discovery was hardly accidental. Like Petrarch himself, the humanists of the fifteenth century scoured Europe looking for ancient texts to read and study. In searching out the knowledge of the past, these fifteenth-century humanists made a series of discoveries that changed their understanding of language, philosophy, and religion. Their desire to imitate led to a profound transformation of knowledge.

A Florentine antiquary, Niccolò Niccoli, coordinated and paid for much of the search for new manuscripts. A wealthy bachelor, Niccolò (1364–1437) spent the fortune he had inherited from his

Cassandra Fedele Defends Liberal Arts for Women

Cassandra Fedele (1465–1558) by the age of 12 had learned Latin and later learned Greek, rhetoric, and history. The Venetian senate praised her as an ornament of learning in the city, but there was no place for an educated woman. She eventually married a provincial physician and was unable to maintain her early prominence, although she occasionally wrote letters and orations. In this oration, which is in the form of a typical defense of liberal studies, she adds her own plea for education for women.

Aware of the weakness of my sex and the paucity of my talent, blushing, I decided to honor and obey [those who have urged me to consider how women could profit from assiduous study] . . . in order that the common crowd may be ashamed of itself and stop being offensive to me, devoted as I am to the liberal arts. . . . What woman, I ask, has such force and ability of mind and speech that she could adequately meet the standard of the greatness of letters or your learned ears? Thus daunted by the difficulty of the task and conscious of my weakness, I might easily have shirked this opportunity to speak, if your well-known kindness and clemency had not urged me to it. For I am not unaware that you are not in the habit of demanding or expecting from anyone more than the nature of the subject itself allows, or the person's own strength can promise of them.

Even an ignorant man—not only a philosopher—sees and admits that man is rightly distinguished from a beast above all by [the capacity of] reason. For what else so greatly delights, enriches and honors both of them than the teaching and understanding of letters and the liberal arts? . . . Moreover, simple men, ignorant of literature, even if they have by nature this potential seed of genius and reason, leave it alone and uncultivated throughout their whole lives, stifle it with neglect and sloth, and render themselves unfit for greatness. . . . But learned men, filled with a rich knowledge of divine and human things, turn all their thoughts and motions of the mind toward the goal of reason and thus free the mind, [otherwise] subject to so many anxieties, from all infirmity. . . . States and princes, moreover, who favor and cultivate these studies become much more humane, pleasing, and noble, and purely [through liberal studies] win for themselves a sweet reputation for humanity. . . . For this reason the ancients rightfully judged all leaders deficient in letters, however skillful in military affairs, to be crude and ignorant. As for the utility of letters, enough said. . . . Of these fruits I myself have tasted a little and [have esteemed myself in that enterprise] more than abject and hopeless; and armed with distaff and needle—woman's weapons—I march forth [to defend] the belief that even though the study of letters promises and offers no reward for women and no dignity, every woman ought to seek and embrace these studies for that pleasure and delight alone that [comes] from them.

Source: M. L. King and A. Rabil, *Her Immaculate Hand: Selected Works by and About the Women Humanists of Quattrocento Italy* (Binghamton, N.Y.: Center for Medieval and Early Renaissance Studies, State University of New York, 1983), pp. 74–77.

father by collecting ancient statuary, reliefs, and, most of all, books. When he died, his collection of more than eight hundred volumes of Latin and Greek texts was taken over by Cosimo de' Medici. It became the foundation of the humanist library housed in the Monastery of San Marco in Florence. Niccolò specified that all his books "should be accessible to everyone," and humanists from across Italy and the rest of Europe came to Florence to study his collection. It would be difficult to overemphasize the importance of the ancient texts collected and copied in Florence. Niccolò's library prompted Pope Nicholas V (r. 1447–1455) to begin the collection that is now the Apostolic Library of the Vatican in Rome. The Vatican library became a lending library, serving the humanist community in Rome. Similar collections were made in Venice, Milan, and Urbino. The Greek and Latin sources collected in these libraries allowed humanists to study classical languages in a way not possible before.

The career of Lorenzo Valla (1407–1457) illustrates the transformation that took place in the fifteenth century. Valla was born near Rome and received a traditional humanistic education in Greek and Latin studies. He spent the rest of his life at universities and courts lecturing on philosophy and literature. Valla was convinced that the key to philosophical and legal problems lay in historical-textual research. Valla's studies had led him to understand that language changes—that it, too, has a life and a history. In 1440 he published a work called *On the Donation of Constantine*. The *Donation of Constantine* purported to record the gift by the emperor Constantine (r. 311–337) of jurisdiction over Rome to the pope when the capital of the empire was moved to Constantinople (see page 283). In the high and late Middle Ages, the papacy used the document to defend its right to political dominion in central Italy. The donation had long been criticized by legal theorists, who argued that Constantine had no right to make it. Valla attacked the legitimacy of the document itself. Because of its language and form, he argued, it could not have been written at the time of Constantine:

Through his [the writer's] babbling, he reveals his most impudent forgery himself. . . . Where he deals with the gifts he says "a diadem . . . made of pure gold and precious jewels." The ignoramus did not know that the diadem was made of cloth, probably silk. . . . He thinks it had to be made of gold, since nowadays kings usually wear a circle of gold set with jewels.[10]

Valla was correct. The *Donation* was a forgery written in the eighth century.

Valla later turned his attention to the New Testament. Jerome (331–420) had put together the Vulgate edition of the Bible in an attempt to create a single accepted Latin version of the Old and New Testaments (see page 258). In 1444 Valla published his *Annotations on the New Testament*. In this

work he used his training in classical languages to correct the standard Latin text and to show numerous examples of mistranslations by Jerome and his contemporaries. Valla believed that true understanding of Christian theology depended on clear knowledge of the past. His annotations on the New Testament were of critical importance to humanists outside Italy and were highly influential during the Protestant Reformation.

The transformation of humanism exemplified by Valla was fully expected by some Florentines. They anticipated that literary studies would lead eventually to philosophy. In 1456, a young Florentine began studying Greek with just such a change in mind. Supported by the Medici rulers of Florence, Marsilio Ficino (1433–1499) began a project to translate the works of Plato into Latin and to interpret Plato in the light of Christian tradition. Between 1463 and 1469 he translated all of the Platonic dialogues. He was at the center of a circle of humanists who were interested in Platonism and its role in art and society. In 1469 he published the first versions of his *Platonic Theology*.

Ficino believed that Platonism, like Christianity, demonstrated the dignity of humanity. He wrote that everything was connected along a hierarchy ranging from the lowliest matter to the person of God. The human soul was located at the midpoint of this hierarchy and was a bridge between matter and God. True wisdom, and especially experience of the divine, could be gained only through contemplation and love. According to Ficino, logic and scientific observation did not lead to true understanding, for humans know logically only that which they can define in human language; they can, however, love things, such as God, that they are not fully able to comprehend.

Ficino's belief in the dignity of man was shared by Giovanni Pico della Mirandola (1463–1494), who proposed to debate with other philosophers nine hundred theses dealing with the nature of man, the origins of knowledge, and the uses of philosophy. Pico extended Ficino's idea of the hierarchy of being, arguing that humans surpassed even the angels in dignity. Angels held a fixed position in the hierarchy, just below God. In contrast, humans could either move up or move down in the hierarchy, depending on the extent to which they embraced spiritual or worldly interests. Pico further believed that he had proved that there was truth in all philosophies. He was one of the first

∼ ENCOUNTERS WITH THE WEST ∼

Rabbi Mordecai Dato Criticizes the Humanists

Until the Renaissance, Europeans exhibited little interest in Jewish learning. But beginning with Giovanni Pico della Mirandola, many Christian humanists became convinced that the Jewish Cabala shared an original wisdom with Egyptian magic, Greek mystical philosophy, and Christianity. And they enthusiastically studied Jewish literature in order to combine it with other traditions. Jews, however, worried that knowledge of their philosophy and theology would be used in an attempt to convert them. In this selection, Rabbi Mordecai Dato (1525–ca. 1591), who lived in northern Italy, protests to a Jewish colleague that in trying to combine so many traditions, humanists misunderstand them.

Let me inform you of two things: first . . . that whatever is said by one of the sages of the *Safed* [the original Cabala mystics] . . . in the introduction to the works of Truth and Justice [i.e., Cabala] is based upon the words of the Book of Splendor [Zahor, a thirteenth-century book of mysticism]; their words are its words; they emerge from its radiance, and without them no man might raise his hands or feet . . . in learning or in criticism, to speak about this wisdom, for they fear the great fire which consumes that man who makes things up from his heart, who has not heard [them] from his teacher as required in the Book of Splendor. . . . They ought not to rely upon their understanding or their dialectics, [though] they are very great, save in the interpretation of some few sayings of the Book of Splendor which seem to contradict one another . . . and even this only under certain conditions stated in the book itself. Secondly, that the words of the Book of Splendor are based upon tradition, and that one may not question them.

Everything which is probable ought to be accepted graciously—and that which is without reason ought to be confirmed by reason. [However], one is not obligated to find a rational explanation of the kind which I have mentioned for all the words of the Book of Wisdom, for many have fallen [in the attempt]. Go and see how one of the sages of the [gentile] nations, Johannes Reuchlin, made himself wise in one work which he made, which I saw many years ago, bringing selection after selection, at random . . . to find words of favor and natural philosophic reason in the words of the Book of Wisdom. And in his many clever words, albeit he avoided corporealization, he compared the Creator to his form, and the servant to his master [that is, he made critical logical errors] . . . heaven forbid.

Dato's letter is partially translated in Robert Bonfil, *Rabbis and Jewish Communities in Renaissance Italy* (Oxford and New York: Oxford University Press for The Littman Library, 1990), pp. 295–296.

humanists to learn Hebrew and to argue that divine wisdom could be found in Jewish mystical literature. Along with others, he studied the Jewish Cabala, a collection of mystical and occult writings that humanists believed dated from the time of Moses. Pico's adoption of the Hebrew mystical writings was often controversial in the Jewish community as well as among Christians.

(See the box, "Encounters with the West: Rabbi Mordecai Dato Criticizes the Humanists.")

Pico's ideas were shared by other humanists, who argued that there was an original divine illumination—a "Pristine Theology," they called it— that preceded both Moses and Plato. These humanists found theological truth in what they believed was ancient Egyptian, Greek, and Jewish magic. Ficino himself popularized the *Corpus Hermeticum* (the Hermetic collection), an amalgam of magical texts of the first century A.D. that was mistakenly assumed to date from the age of Moses and Pythagoras. Like the writings of Plato and his followers, Hermetic texts explained how the mind could influence and be influenced by the material and celestial worlds.

Along with Hermetic magic many humanists of the fifteenth and sixteenth centuries investigated astrology and alchemy. Hermetic magic, astrology, and alchemy posit the existence of a direct, reciprocal connection between the cosmos and the natural world. In the late medieval and Renaissance world, astrological and alchemical theories seemed reasonable. By the late fifteenth century many humanists assumed that personality as well as the ability to respond to certain crises was profoundly affected by the stars. It was not by accident that for a century or more after 1500, astrologers were official or unofficial members of most European courts. Belief in astrology was not universal, however. Some humanists, like Pico, opposed it because it seemed to deny that humans had free will.

Interest in alchemy was equally widespread though more controversial. Alchemists believed that everything was made of a primary material and that it was possible to transmute one substance into another. The most popular version, and the most open to hucksters and frauds, was the belief that base metals could be turned into gold. The hopes of most alchemists, however, were more profound. They were convinced that they could unlock the explanation of the properties of the whole cosmos. On a personal and religious level as well as on a material level, practitioners hoped to take the impure and make it pure. The interest in understanding and manipulating nature that lay at the heart of Hermetic magic, astrology, and alchemy was an important stimulus to scientific investigations and, ultimately, to the rise of modern scientific thought.

Humanism and Political Thought

The humanists' plan to rediscover classical sources fit well with their political interests. "One can say," observed Leonardo Bruni, "that letters and the study of the Latin language went hand in hand

with the condition of the Roman republic." Petrarch and the civic humanists believed that rulers, whether in a republic or a principality, should exhibit all the classical and Christian virtues of faith, hope, love, prudence, temperance, fortitude, and justice. Those qualities were the key to good government and good law. A virtuous ruler would be loved and obeyed. Those virtues were also the key to the preservation of government. The civic humanists viewed governments and laws as essentially unchanging and static. They believed that when change did occur, it most likely happened by chance—that is, because of fortune (the Roman goddess Fortuna). Humanists believed that the only protection against chance was true virtue, for the virtuous would never be dominated by fortune. Thus, beginning with Petrarch, humanists advised rulers to love their subjects, to be magnanimous with their possessions, and to maintain the rule of law. Humanistic tracts of the fourteenth and fifteenth centuries were full of classical and Christian examples of virtuous actions by moral rulers.

The French invasions of Italy in 1494 (see page 412) and the warfare that followed called into question many of the humanists' assumptions about the lessons and virtues of classical civilization. Francesco Guicciardini (1483–1540), a Florentine patrician who had served in papal armies, suggested that history held no clear lessons. Unless the causes of two different events were identical down to the smallest detail, he said, the results could be radically different. An even more thorough critique was offered by Guicciardini's friend and fellow Florentine, Niccolò Machiavelli (1469–1527). After a humanistic education and service from 1494 to 1512 in the anti-Medicean republican government of Florence, Machiavelli was forced by the Medici to abandon public life and leave Florence. While living on his farm outside Florence, Machiavelli developed in a series of writings what he believed was a new science of politics. He wrote *Discourses on Livy*, a treatise on military organization, a history of Florence, and even a Renaissance play entitled *The Mandrake Root*. He is best remembered, however, for *The Prince* (1513), a small tract numbering less than a hundred pages.

Machiavelli felt that his contemporaries paid too little heed to the lessons to be learned from history. Thus, in his discourses on Livy he comments on Roman government, the role of religion, and the nature of political virtue, emphasizing the sophisticated Roman analysis of political and military situations. A shortcoming more serious than ignorance of history, Machiavelli believed, was his contemporaries' ignorance of the true motivations for people's actions. His play *The Mandrake Root* is a comedy about the ruses used to seduce a young woman. In truth, however, none of the characters is fooled. All of them, from the young woman being seduced to her husband, realize what is happening but use the seduction to their own advantage. In the play Machiavelli implicitly challenges the humanistic assumption that educated individuals will naturally choose virtue over vice. He explicitly criticizes these same assumptions in *The Prince*. He rejects the humanistic belief that human nature is essentially good and that individuals, given an opportunity, will naturally be helpful and honorable. Machiavelli holds the contrary view, that individuals are much more likely to respond to fear and that power rather than the arts of rhetoric makes for good government.

Machiavelli's use of the Italian word *virtù* led him to be vilified as amoral. Machiavelli deliberately chose a word that meant both "manliness" or "ability" and "virtue as a moral quality." Earlier humanists had restricted *virtù* to the second meaning, using the word to refer to virtues like prudence, magnanimity, and love. Machiavelli tried to show that in some situations these "virtues" could have violent, even evil, consequences. If, for example, a prince was so magnanimous in giving away his wealth that he was forced to raise taxes, his subjects might come to hate him. Conversely, a prince who, through cruelty to the enemies of his state, brought peace and stability to his subjects might be obeyed and perhaps even loved by them. A virtuous ruler must be mindful of the goals to be achieved—that is what Machiavelli really meant by the phrase often translated as "the ends justify the means."

Machiavelli expected his readers to be aware of the ambiguous nature of virtue—whether understood as ability or as moral behavior. "One will discover," he concludes, "that something which appears to be a virtue, if pursued, will end in his destruction; while some other thing which seems to be a vice, if pursued, will result in his safety and his well-being."[11]

Like Guicciardini, Machiavelli rejected earlier humanistic assumptions that one needed merely

Machiavelli In this portrait Machiavelli is dressed as a government official. He wrote to a friend during his exile that each night when he returned from the fields he dressed again in his curial robes and pondered the behavior of governments and princes. *(Scala/Art Resource, NY)*

to imitate the great leaders of the past. Governing is a process that requires different skills at different times, he warned: "The man who adapts his course of action to the nature of the times will succeed and, likewise, the man who sets his course of action out of tune with the times will come to grief."[12] The abilities that allow a prince to gain power may not be the abilities that will allow him to maintain it.

With the writings of Machiavelli, humanistic ideas of intellectual, moral, and political reform came to maturation. Petrarch and the early humanists believed fully in the powers of classical wisdom to transform society. Machiavelli and his contemporaries admitted the importance of classical wisdom but also recognized the ambiguity of any application of classical learning to contemporary life.

THE ARTS IN ITALY, 1250–1550

Townsmen and artists in Renaissance Italy shared the humanists' perception of the importance of classical antiquity. Filippo Villani (d. 1405), a wealthy Florentine from an important business family, wrote that artists had recently "reawakened a lifeless and almost extinct art." In the middle of the fifteenth century the sculptor Lorenzo Ghiberti concluded that with the rise of Christianity "not only statues and paintings [were destroyed], but the books and commentaries and handbooks and rules on which men relied for their training." Italian writers and painters themselves recognized that the literary recovery of past practices was essential. The Renaissance of the arts can be divided into three periods. In the early Renaissance artists first imitated nature. In the middle period artists rediscovered classical ideas of proportion. In the High Renaissance, artists were "superior to nature but also to the artists of the ancient world," according to the artist and architect Giorgio Vasari (1511–1574), who wrote a famous history of the eminent artists of his day.

The Artistic Renaissance

The first stirrings of the new styles can be found in the late thirteenth century. The greatest innovator of the era was Giotto di Bondone of Florence (ca. 1266–1337). Although Giotto had a modest background, his fellow citizens, popes, and patrons

Giotto's Naturalism   Later painters praised the naturalistic emotion of Giotto's painting. In this detail from the Arena Chapel, Giotto portrays the kiss of Judas, one of the most dramatic moments in Christian history. *(Scala/Art Resource, NY)*

throughout Italy quickly recognized his skill. He traveled as far south as Rome and as far north as Padua painting churches and chapels. According to later artists and commentators, Giotto broke with the prevailing stiff, highly symbolic style and introduced lifelike portrayals of living persons. He produced paintings of dramatic situations, showing events located in a specific time and place. The frescoes of the Arena Chapel in Padua (1304–1314), for example, recount episodes in the life of Christ. In a series of scenes leading from Christ's birth to his crucifixion, Giotto situates his actors in towns and countryside in what appears to be actual space. More significantly, Giotto manages to capture the drama of key events, like Judas's kiss of betrayal in the Garden of Gethsemane. Even Michelangelo, the master of the High Renaissance, studied Giotto's painting. Giotto was in such demand throughout Italy that his native Florence gave him a public appointment so that he would be required by law to remain in the city.

Early in the fifteenth century, Florentine artists devised new ways to represent nature that surpassed even the innovations of Giotto. The revolutionary nature of these artistic developments is evident from the careers of Lorenzo Ghiberti (1378–1455), Filippo Brunelleschi (1377–1446), and Masaccio (born Tomasso di ser Giovanni di Mone, 1401–ca. 1428). Their sculpture, architecture, and painting began an ongoing series of experiments with the representation of space through linear perspective. Perspective is a system for representing three-dimensional objects on a two-dimensional plane. It is based on two observations: (1) As parallel lines recede into the distance, they seem to converge; and (2) there is a geometrical relationship that regulates the relative size of objects at various distances from the viewer. Painters of the Renaissance literally found themselves looking at their world from a new perspective.

In 1401 Ghiberti won a commission to design door panels for the baptistery of San Giovanni in Florence. He was to spend the rest of his life working on two sets of bronze doors. The reliefs he created told the stories of the New Testament (the north doors) and the Old Testament (the east doors). In the commissions for the Old Testament scenes, Ghiberti used the new techniques of linear perspective to create a sense of space into which he placed his classically inspired figures. His work made him instantly famous throughout Italy. Later

The Doors of Paradise Ghiberti worked on panels for the baptistery from 1403 to 1453. In his representations of scenes from the Old Testament he combined a love of ancient statuary with the new Florentine interest in linear perspective. (*Alinari/Art Resource, NY*)

in the sixteenth century Michelangelo remarked that the east doors were worthy to be the "Doors of Paradise," and so they have since been known.

In the competition for the baptistery commission, Ghiberti had beaten the young Filippo Brunelleschi, who, as a result, gave up sculpture for architecture and later left Florence to study in Rome. While in Rome he is said to have visited and measured surviving examples of classical architecture—the artistic equivalent of humanistic literary research. When he returned to Florence, he had a firm sense of the nature of Roman architecture and how its forms could be adapted for Florentine life. According to Vasari, he was capable of "visualizing Rome as it was before the fall." Brunelleschi's debt to Rome is evident in his masterpiece, Florence's foundling hospital. Built as a

Leonardo da Vinci's Anatomical Drawings Leonardo studied carefully to record as accurately as possible the appearance of the human body. He was convinced that his keen observations made him the equal of any humanist. *(The Royal Collection © Her Majesty Queen Elizabeth II)*

of Santa Maria Novella. Masaccio built on experiments in linear perspective to create a painting in which a flat wall seems to become a recessed chapel. The space created is filled with the images of Christ crucified, the Father, and the Holy Spirit.

In the middle years of the fifteenth century, artists came to terms with the innovations of the earlier period. In the second half of the fifteenth century, however, artists like the Florentine Sandro Botticelli (1445–1510) added a profound understanding of classical symbolism to the technical interests of Masaccio and Brunelleschi. Botticelli's famous *Birth of Venus* and *Primavera* (*Spring,* 1478), both painted for Medici houses, are filled with Neo-Platonic symbolism concerning truth, beauty, and the virtues of humanity. (See the feature, "Weighing the Evidence: The Art of Renaissance Florence," on pages 470–471.)

The high point in the development of Renaissance art came at the beginning of the sixteenth century in the work of several artists throughout Italy. Artists in Venice learned perspective from the Florentines and added their own tradition of subtle coloring in oils. Raphael Sanzio (1483–1520), who arrived in Rome from his native Urbino in 1508, demonstrated that artistic brilliance was not simply a Florentine monopoly. His decorations of the Vatican palaces in Rome included his *School of Athens,* a painting that literally shows the debt of the Renaissance to past learning by portraying the great philosophers of the past as well as contemporary artists. It is in effect the synthesis of the classical learning and artistic innovation for which the Renaissance is famous.

The work of two Florentines, Leonardo da Vinci (1452–1519) and Michelangelo Buonarroti (1475–1564), best exemplifies the sophisticated heights that art achieved early in the sixteenth century. Leonardo, the bastard son of a notary, was raised in the village of Vinci outside of Florence. Cut off from the humanistic milieu of the city, he desired above all else to prove that his artistry was the equal of the formal learning of his social superiors. In his notebooks he confessed, "I am fully conscious that, not being a literary man, certain presumptuous persons will think they may reasonably blame me, alleging that I am not a man of letters."[13] But he defended his lack of classical education by arguing that all the best writing, like the best painting and invention, is based on the close observation of nature. Close

combination of hemispheres and cubes and resembling a Greek stoa or an arcaded Roman basilica, the long, low structure is an example of how profoundly different Renaissance architecture was from the towering Gothic of the Middle Ages.

In the first decade of the fifteenth century, many commentators believed that painting would never be as innovative as either sculpture or architecture. They knew of no classical models that had survived for imitation. Yet the possibilities in painting became apparent in 1427 with the unveiling of Masaccio's *Trinity* in the Florentine church observation and scientific analysis made Leonardo's work uniquely creative in all these fields. Leonardo is famous for his plans for bridges, airships, submarines, and fortresses. There seemed to be no branch of learning in which he was not interested. In painting he developed chiaroscuro, a technique for showing aerial perspective. He painted horizons as shaded zones rather than as sharp lines. "I know," he said, "that the greater or less quantity of air that lies between the eye and the object makes the outlines of that object more or less distinct."[14] It was his analytical observation that made Leonardo so influential on his contemporaries.

Michelangelo, however, was widely hailed as the capstone of Renaissance art. In the words of a contemporary, "He alone has triumphed over ancient artists, modern artists and over Nature itself." In his career we can follow the rise of Renaissance artists from the ranks of mere craftsmen to honored creators, courtiers who were the equals of the humanists—in fact, Michelangelo shared Petrarch's concern for reform and renewal in Italian society. We can also discern the synthesis of the artistic and intellectual transformations of the Renaissance with a profound religious sensitivity.

The importance of Michelangelo's contribution is obvious in two of his most important works: the statue *David* in Florence and his commissions in the Sistine Chapel of the Vatican in Rome. From his youth Michelangelo had studied and imitated antique sculpture, to the point that some of his creations were thought by many actually to be antique. He used his understanding of classical art in *David* (1501). Artists and citizens of Florence alike hailed the mammoth statue as a masterpiece. Citizens recalled David's defeat of the giant Goliath, saving Israel from almost certain conquest by the Philistines. *David* thus became a symbol of the youthful Florentine republic struggling to maintain its freedom against great odds. The statue was moved to a place of honor before the Palazzo Vecchio, Florence's city hall, signifying, as Vasari noted, that "just as David had protected his people and governed them justly, so whoever ruled Florence should vigorously defend the city and govern it with justice."[15]

Michelangelo was a committed republican and Florentine, but he spent much of his life working in Rome on a series of papal commissions. In 1508 he was called to Rome to work on the ceiling of the Sistine Chapel. Michelangelo spent four years decorating the ceiling with hundreds of figures and with nine scenes from the book of Genesis, including the famous *Creation of Adam*. In the late 1530s, he completed painting *The Last Judgment* on the wall above the altar. In that painting the techniques of perspective and the conscious recognition of debts to classical culture recede into the background as the artist surrounds Christ in judgment with saints and sinners, including in the hollow, empty skin of Saint Bartholomew a psychological self-portrait of an artist increasingly concerned with his own spiritual shortcomings.

Michelangelo's self-portrait reminds us that the intellectual content of the artist's work is one of its most enduring traits. He was a Platonist who believed that the form and beauty of a statue were contained in the stone itself. The artist's job was to peel away excess material and reveal the beauty within. As he noted in one of his poems, it was a process like that of religious salvation:

Just as by carving . . . we set
Into hard mountain rock
A living figure
Which grows most where the stone is most removed;
In like manner, some good works . . .
Are concealed by the excess of my very flesh.[16]

Art and Patronage

The religious passion of Michelangelo's poetry indicates one of the reasons that art was so popular in Renaissance Italy. Art, like poetry, provided symbols and images through which Italians could reason about the most important issues of their communities. Italians willingly spent vast sums on art because of its ability to communicate social, political, and spiritual values.

Italy in the fourteenth and fifteenth centuries was unusually wealthy relative to the towns and principalities of northern Europe. Despite the population decline caused by plague and the accompanying economic dislocations, per person wealth in Italy remained quite high. Because of banking, international trade, and even service as mercenaries, Italians, and particularly Florentines, had money to spend on arts and luxuries. Thus, the Italians of the Renaissance, whether as public or private patrons, could afford to use consumption of art as a form of competition for social and

The Sistine Chapel Painted from 1508 to 1512, the ceiling of the Sistine Chapel is Michelangelo's most famous work. Powerfully summarizing Renaissance faith in the unity of Christian faith and pagan wisdom, Michelangelo illustrated God's giving life to Adam (among other biblical scenes), while around the ceiling's border he placed *sibyls,* classical symbols of knowledge. *(Vatican Museums. Photo: A. Bracchetti/P. Zigrossi)*

political status. Increasingly in the fourteenth and fifteenth centuries there was a market for luxuries, including art, and there were numerous shops in which artists could be trained.

Artists in the modern world are accustomed to standing outside society as critics of commonly held ideas. In the late Middle Ages and Renaissance, artists were not alienated commentators. In 1300 most art was religious in subject and was created to be displayed in public. Throughout Europe art fulfilled a devotional function. Painted crucifixes, altar paintings, and banners were often endowed as devotional or penitential objects. The Arena Chapel in Padua, with its frescoes by Giotto, was built and endowed by a merchant anxious to pay for some of his sins.

In the late Middle Ages and Renaissance, numerous paintings and statues throughout Italy (and much of the rest of Europe) were revered for their miraculous powers. During plague, drought, and times of war, people had recourse to the sacred power of the saints represented in these works of art. (See the feature, "Weighing the Evidence: A Painting of the Plague," on pages 434–435.) The construction of the great churches of the period was often a community project that lasted for decades, even centuries. These gigantic structures were mixtures of piety, civic pride, and religious patronage. The city council of Siena, for example, voted to rebuild its Gothic cathedral of Saint Mary, saying that the blessed Virgin "was, is and will be in the future the head of this city" and that through veneration of her "Siena may be protected from harm." Accordingly, it is clear that although the subject of art was primarily religious, the message was bound up in the civic values and ideas of the fourteenth and fifteenth centuries.

The first burst of artistic creativity in the fourteenth century was paid for by public institutions. Communal governments built and redecorated city halls to house government and to promote civic pride. These buildings contained the jail, the mint, law courts, assembly rooms, and even living quarters for administrators. Towns also reorganized streets, public squares, and the myriad hospitals and lodgings for travelers that dotted the city. In most towns there was a remarkable emphasis on the beauty of the work. Civic officials often named special commissions to consult with a variety of artists and architects before approving building projects. Governments, with an eye to the appearance of public areas, legislated the width of streets, height limits, and even the style of façades on houses.

The series of paintings called the *Good Government of Siena* illustrates how Italians used art to communicate political ideas. Painted in the first half of the fourteenth century by Ambrogio Lorenzetti (ca. 1300–1348), *Good Government* combined allegorical representations of Wisdom and the cardinal virtues on one wall with realistic street scenes of a well-ordered Siena on an adjacent wall. Across from the scenes of good government are its opposite, graphic representations of murder, rape, and general injustice and disorder. In this work the government sent a clear political message in a realistic painting that reminded viewers of specific events, times, places, and people. The popular preacher San Bernardino of Siena (1380–1444) made clear the message of Lorenzetti's painting: "To see Peace depicted is a delight and so it is a shame to see War painted on the other wall." And Bernardino's sermon reminded listeners of the conclusions they should draw: "Oh my brothers and fathers, love and embrace each other . . . give your aid to this toil which I have undertaken so gladly, to bring about love and peace among you."[17]

In Florence public art was often organized and paid for by various guild organizations. Guild membership was a prerequisite for citizenship, so guildsmen set the tone in politics as well as in the commercial life of the city. Most major guilds commissioned sculpture for the Chapel of Or San Michele, a famous shrine in the grain market (its painting of the Virgin was popularly thought to have wonder-working powers) and seat of the Guelf party, the city's most powerful political organization. Guilds took responsibility for the

building and maintenance of other structures in the city as well. The guild of the cloth merchants paid for the frescoes in the baptistery of Saint John the Baptist (the city's patron saint) and commissioned the bronze doors by Lorenzo Ghiberti. The guild of the silk merchants oversaw the selection of Filippo Brunelleschi to design the foundling hospital. Guildsmen took pride in the creation of a beautiful environment, but as the cloth makers made clear in their decision to supervise the baptistery, the work reflected not only on the city and its patron saint but also on the power and influence of the guild itself.

The princes who ruled outside the republics of Italy often had similarly precise messages that they wished to communicate. Renaissance popes embarked on a quite specific ideological program in the late fifteenth century to assert their role as both spiritual leaders of Christendom and temporal lords of a central Italian state (see page 466). Rulers like the Este dukes of Ferrara and the Sforza dukes of Milan constructed castles within their cities or hunting lodges and villas in the countryside and decorated them with pictures of the hunt or knights in combat, scenes that emphasized their noble virtues and their natural right to rule.

By the mid-fifteenth century, patrons of art works in Florence and most other regions of Italy were more and more likely to be wealthy individuals. Republics, where all families were in principle equal, initially displayed a great suspicion of elaborate city palaces and rural villas. By the middle of the fifteenth century, however, such reserve was found in none but the most conservative republics, like Venice or Lucca.

Palaces, gardens, and villas became the settings in which the wealthy could entertain their peers, receive clients, and debate the political issues of the day. The public rooms of these palaces were decorated with portraits, gem collections, books, ceramics, and statuary. Many villas and palaces included private chapels. In the Medici palace in Florence, for example, the chapel is the setting for a painting of the Magi (the three Wise Men who came to worship the infant Jesus) in which the artist, Benozzo Gozzoli (1420–1498), used faces of members of the Medici family for the portraits of the Wise Men and their entourage. The Magi, known to be wise and virtuous rulers, were an apt symbol for the family that had come to dominate the city.

Artists at princely courts were expected to work for the glory of their lord. Often the genre of choice was the portrait. Perhaps the most successful portraitists of the sixteenth century were Sofonisba Anguissola (1532–1625) and her five sisters, all of whom were well-known painters. Anguissola won renown as a prodigy; one of her paintings was sent to Michelangelo, who forwarded it to the Medici in Florence. Later she was called to the Spanish court, where she produced portraits of the king, queen, and their daughter. She continued to paint after her marriage and return to Italy. Even in her nineties, painters from all parts of Europe visited her to talk about techniques of portraiture.

THE SPREAD OF THE RENAISSANCE, 1350–1536

By 1500, the Renaissance had spread from Italy to the rest of Europe. Even in the Slavic East, beyond the borders of the old Roman Empire, in Prague and Wroclaw one could find a renewed interest in classical ideas about art and literature. As ideas about the past and its relevance to contemporary life spread, however, the message was transformed in several important ways. Outside of Italy, Rome and its history did not play the dominant role they played in Italy. Humanists were interested more in religious than in political reform, and they responded to a number of important local interests. Yet the Renaissance idea of renewal based on a deep understanding and imitation of the past remained at the center of the movement. The key to the spread of humanistic culture was the rise of printing, which allowed for the distribution of texts that previously had been available only in Italy.

The Impact of Printing

In the fifteenth century the desire to have and to read complete texts of classical works was widespread, but the number of copies was severely limited by the time and expense of hand-copying, collating, and checking manuscripts. Poggio Bracciolini's letters are punctuated with remarks about the time and expense of reproducing the various

classical manuscripts he had discovered. One copy he had commissioned was so inaccurate and illegible as to be nearly unusable. Traveling to repositories and libraries was often easier than creating a personal library. It was rarely possible for someone who read a manuscript once to keep a complete copy to compare with other works.

The invention of printing with movable lead type changed things dramatically. Although block printing had long been known in China and was a popular way to produce playing cards and small woodcuts in Europe, only with the creation of movable type in the 1450s did printing become a practical way to produce books. Johann Gutenberg (d. 1468) in the German city of Mainz produced between 180 and 200 copies of the so-called Gutenberg Bible in 1452–1453. It was followed shortly by editions of the Psalms. German printers spread their techniques rapidly. As early as 1460, there were printing presses in Rome and Venice, and by 1470 the technique had spread to the Low Countries, France, and England. It has been estimated that by 1500 there were a thousand presses in 265 towns (Map 12.1). The output of the early presses in the first century of their existence was extremely varied. Gutenberg's first mass printing, for example, was of a thousand copies of a letter of indulgence, a remission of penance, for participation in a crusade. Early printers also produced highly popular and profitable small devotional books, abridged collections of saints' lives, and other popular literature, as well as the complete editions of classical authors and their humanistic and theological texts.

There has been a long and complex debate over the impact of printing, but there is general agreement on a number of points. An unexpected aspect of print culture was the rise of the printshop as a center of culture and communication. The printers Aldus Manutius (1450–1515) in Venice and Johannes Froben (d. 1527) in Basel were humanists. Both invited humanists to work in their shops as they edited their texts and corrected the proofs before printing. Printshops became a natural gathering place for clerics and laymen. Thus, they were natural sources of humanist ideas and later, in the sixteenth century, of Protestant religious programs. Printing allowed for the creation of agreed-upon standard editions of works in law, theology, philosophy, and science. Scholars in various parts of the

Map 12.1 The Spread of Printing Printing technology moved rapidly along major trade routes to the most populous and prosperous areas of Europe. The technology was rapidly adopted in highly literate centers such as the Low Countries, the Rhine Valley, and northern Italy.

world could feel fairly confident that they and their colleagues were analyzing identical texts. Similarly, producing accurate medical and herbal diagrams, maps, and even reproductions of art and architecture was easier. Multiple copies of texts also made possible the study of rare and esoteric literary, philosophical, and scientific texts in all parts of the world. Scholars studied standard editions of important texts like the Bible thoroughly and systematically.

Humanism Outside Italy

As the influence of the humanist movement extended beyond Italy, the interests of the humanists changed. Although there was a strong religious strain in Italian humanism, public life lay at the center of Italian programs of education and reform. Outside Italy, however, moral and religious reform formed the heart of the movement. Northern humanists wanted to reform and renew Christian life. In the aftermath of the Great Schism (see pages 398–401), Christians continued to desire reform within the church. Critics complained that the clergy was wealthy and ignorant and that the laity was uneducated and superstitious. Northern humanists were involved in the building of educational institutions, in the search for and publication of texts by Church Fathers, and in the writing of local customs and history. In the work of the two best-known humanists, Thomas More and Desiderius Erasmus, there is a sharp critique of contemporary behavior and, in the case of Erasmus, a call to a new sense of piety. The religious views of Erasmus were so influential that northern humanism has generally come to be known as "Christian humanism."

The intellectual environment of the northern Europe into which humanism spread had changed significantly since the thirteenth century. The universities of Paris and Oxford retained the status they had acquired earlier but found themselves competing with a host of new foundations. Most of these universities aspired, as the charter of Heidelburg (1386) noted, "to imitate Paris in all things." Like Paris, almost all had theological faculties dominated by scholastically trained theologians. Nevertheless, the new foundations often had chairs of rhetoric, or "eloquence," which left considerable scope for those who advocated humanistic learning. These new universities, from Bratislava in Slovakia (1465) to Uppsala in Sweden (1477), also reflected the increased national feeling in various regions of Europe. The earliest university in German-speaking lands, the Charles University in Prague (1348), was founded at the request of Emperor Charles IV of Luxembourg, whose court was in Prague. Vienna (1365), Aix (1409), Louvain (1425), and numerous other universities owed their foundation to the pride and ambition of local rulers.

Humanists on faculties of law in French universities practiced the historical study of jurisprudence. Like Lorenzo Valla, they believed that historical and linguistic studies were the best way to learn the law. Italian-trained French lawyers introduced what came to be called the "Gallican style" of jurisprudence. Because legal ideas, like language, changed over time, they argued that Roman law had to be studied as a historically created system and not as an abstract and unchanging structure. Humanists like Guillaume Budé (1468–

1540) moved from the study of law to considerations of Roman coinage, religion, and economic life in order to better understand the formation of Roman law. The desire to understand the law led other humanist-legists to add the study of society in ancient Gaul to their work on Rome and then the law of other societies as well.

The new universities often became centers of linguistic studies. Humanistic interest in language inspired the foundation of "trilingual" colleges in Spain, France, and the Low Countries to foster serious study of Hebrew, Greek, and Latin. Like Italian humanists, other humanists believed that knowledge of languages would allow students to understand more clearly the truths of Christianity. Typical of this movement was the archbishop of Toledo, Francisco Jiménez de Cisneros (1436–1517), who founded the University of Alcalá in 1508 with chairs of Latin, Greek, and Hebrew. He began the publication of a vast new edition of the Bible, called the "Polyglot Bible" (1522) because it had parallel columns in Latin, Greek, and, where appropriate, Hebrew. Unlike Valla, Jiménez did not intend to challenge the Vulgate (see page 446). Rather, he expected to clear up any confusion about its meaning. The university and the Bible were part of an effort to complete the conversion of Muslims and Jews and reform religious practices among the old Christians.

To the northern humanists, the discovery and publication of early Christian authors seemed critical to any reform within the church. Jacques Lefèvre d'Étaples (1455–1529) of France was one of the most famous of these humanistic editors of early Christian texts. He initially gained fame for his textual work on Aristotle. But after 1500 he concentrated on the edition of texts by the early Church Fathers. The true spirit of Christianity, he believed, would be most clear in the works and lives of those who lived closest to the age of the apostles. Christian humanists inspired by Lefèvre became key players in the later Reformation movements in France. Lefèvre's faith in the value of classical languages was shared by John Colet (1467–1519) of England, founder of St. Paul's School in London. He instituted a thorough program of teaching Latin and Greek aimed at creating scholars who would have access to the earliest Christian writings.

Tensions between the humanists and the advocates of Scholastic methods broke out over the cultural and linguistic studies that formed the heart of the humanist program. Humanists like Pico della Mirandola (see page 446) believed that there were universal moral and spiritual truths in other philosophies and religions. Following Pico's lead, Johannes Reuchlin (1455–1522) of Württemberg embarked on a study of the Cabala. Johannes Pfefferkorn, a Dominican priest and recent convert from Judaism, attacked Reuchlin's use of Jewish traditions in the study of Christian theology. Sides were quickly drawn. The theological faculties of the German universities generally supported the Dominican. The humanists supported Reuchlin. In his own defense Reuchlin issued *The Letters of Illustrious Men*, a volume of letters that he had received in support of his position. This work gave rise to one of the great satires of the Renaissance, *The Letters of Obscure Men* (1516), written by anonymous authors and purporting to be letters from various narrow-minded Scholastics in defense of the Dominican. Although the debate arose over the validity of Hebraic studies for Christian theology and not over humanistic ideas of reform or wisdom, it indicates the tension and divisions between the humanists and much of the Scholastic community. The early controversies of the Protestant Reformation were initially misunderstood by many as a continuation of the conflicts between humanists and Scholastic theologians over the uses of Hebrew learning.

Thomas More and Desiderius Erasmus

The careers of two humanists exemplified both the strength and the limits of the humanistic movement outside Italy: Sir Thomas More (1478–1535) of London and Desiderius Erasmus (1466–1536) of Rotterdam. After becoming close friends during one of Erasmus's visits to England, the two developed their careers along very different paths. More had been educated at St. Anthony's school in London and became a lawyer. A friend of John Colet, he translated Lucan and wrote a humanistic history of Richard III while pursuing his public career. He is most famous for his work *Utopia* (1516), the description of an ideal society located on the island of Utopia (literally "nowhere") in the newly explored oceans. This powerful and contradictory work is written in two books. Book I is a debate over the moral value of public service between Morus, a well-intentioned but practical politician, and

Hythloday, a widely traveled idealist. Morus tries to make the bureaucrat's argument about working for change from within the system. Hythloday rejects the argument out of hand. Thomas More himself seems to have been unsure at that time about the virtues of public service. He was of two minds, and the debate between Morus and Hythloday reflects his indecision. As part of his critique of justice and politics in Europe, Hythloday describes in Book II the commonwealth of Utopia, in which there is no private property but strict equality of possessions, and, as a result, harmony, tolerance, and little or no violence.

Since the publication of *Utopia*, debates have raged about whether More, or we, could ever really hope to live in such a society. Some scholars have questioned how seriously More took this work—he seems to have written the initial sections merely to amuse friends. Yet whatever More's intentions, Utopia's society of equality, cooperation, and tolerance continues to inspire social commentators.

Ironically, More himself, like his creation Morus, soon found himself trying to work for justice within precisely the sort of autocratic court that Hythloday criticized. Not long after the completion of *Utopia*, More entered the service of King Henry VIII (r. 1509–1547), eventually serving as chancellor of England. As a staunch Catholic and royal official, More never acted on utopian principles of peace and toleration. He was, in fact, responsible for persecution of English Protestants in the years before Henry VIII's break with Rome (see pages 527–529). More's opposition to Henry's break with the papacy and divorce and his refusal to acknowledge Henry as the head of the English church led him to resign his offices. He was eventually imprisoned and executed. More's writing was a stinging critique of political values. He implied that society could be reformed, yet in the period after 1521, his humanism and the ideas of Utopia had no influence on his own public life.

Unlike More, who was drawn to the power of king and pope, Erasmus always avoided working for authorities. Often called the "Prince of Humanists," he was easily the best-known humanist of the early sixteenth century. He was born the illegitimate son of a priest in the Low Countries. Forced by relatives into a monastery, he disliked the conservative piety and authoritarian discipline of traditional monastic life. Once allowed out of the monastery to serve as an episcopal secretary, he never returned. He lived and taught in France, England, Italy, and Switzerland. Of all the humanists it was Erasmus who most benefited from the printing revolution. The printer Aldus Manutius invited him to live and work in Venice, and he spent the last productive years of his life at Johannes Froben's press in Basel. He left the city only when Protestant reformers took control of the city government.

Over a long career Erasmus brought out repeated editions of works designed to educate Christians. His *Adages*, first published in 1500, was a collection of proverbs from Greek and Roman sources. The work was immensely popular, and Erasmus repeatedly brought out expanded edi-

Van Eyck: The Arnolfini Wedding Careful observation of people and places was typical of the new art of both the north and the south. Van Eyck seems to have recreated this scene to the smallest detail. His own image appears in the mirror on the wall. *(Reproduced by Courtesy of the Trustees, The National Gallery, London)*

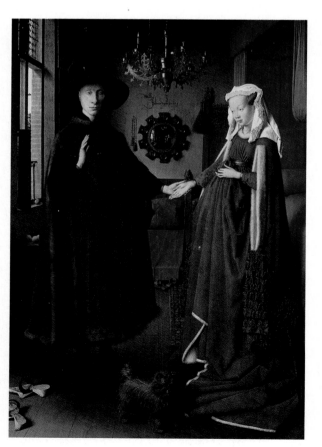

tions. He tried to present Greek and Roman wisdom that would illuminate everyday problems. *The Colloquies* was a collection of popular stories, designed as primers for students, that taught moral lessons even as they served as examples of good language. His ironic *Praise of Folly* (1511) was dedicated to Thomas More. An oration by Folly in praise of folly, it was satire of a type unknown since antiquity. Folly's catalog of vices includes everyone from the ignoramus to the scholar. But more seriously, Erasmus believed, as Saint Paul had said, that Christians must be "fools for Christ." In effect, human existence is folly. Erasmus's Folly first made an observation that Shakespeare would refine and make famous: "Now the whole life of mortal men, what is it but a sort of play in which . . . [each person] plays his own part until the director gives him his cue to leave the stage."[18]

Erasmus's greatest contributions to European intellectual life were his edition of and commentaries on the New Testament. After finding and publishing in 1505 Lorenzo Valla's *Annotations on the New Testament*, Erasmus embarked on creating a critical edition of the Greek text and a Latin translation independent of the fourth-century Latin Vulgate of Jerome. Like Valla, and unlike Jiménez, Erasmus corrected parts of the Vulgate. He rejected the authority of tradition, saying, "The sin of corruption is greater, and the need for careful revision by scholars is greater also, where the source of corruption was ignorance."[19] What was revolutionary in his edition was his commentary, which emphasized the literal and historical recounting of human experiences. This edition was the basis of later vernacular translations of the Bible during the Reformation.

Underlying Erasmus's scholarly output was what he called his "Philosophy of Christ." Erasmus was convinced that the true essence of Christianity was to be found in the life and actions of Christ. Reasonable, self-reliant, truly Christian people did not need superstitious rituals or magic. In his *Colloquies* he gives the example of a terrified priest who during a shipwreck promised everything to the Virgin Mary in order to be saved from drowning. But, Erasmus observed, it would have been more practical to start swimming!

Erasmus believed that classical and Christian wisdom could wipe away violence, superstition, and ignorance. Unlike More, Erasmus never abandoned the humanistic program. Yet his philosophy of Christ, based on faith in the goodness and educability of the individual, was swamped in the 1520s and 1530s by the sectarian claims of both Protestants and Catholics. Although Erasmus's New Testament was influential in the Reformation, his calls for reforms based on tolerance and reason were not.

Renaissance Art in the North

In the early fifteenth century, while Brunelleschi and Masaccio were revolutionizing the ways in which Italian artists viewed their world, artists north of the Alps, especially in Flanders, were making equally striking advances in the way they painted and sculpted. Artistic innovation in the North began with changes tied closely to the world of northern courts; only later did artists take up the styles of the Italian Renaissance. Northerners took Italian Renaissance art and fit it to a new environment.

Northern art of the late fourteenth and fifteenth centuries changed in two significant ways. In sculpture, the long, austere, unbroken vertical lines typical of Gothic sculpture gave way to a much more complex and emotional sculpture. In painting, Flemish artists moved from ornate, vividly colored paintings to experiments with ways to create a sense of depth. Artists strove to paint and sculpt works that more faithfully represented reality. The sculptures of Claus Sluter (1350–1406), created for a family chapel of the Burgundian dukes at Champmol, held a lifelike drama unlike the previous Gothic sculpture. Court painters like Jan van Eyck (c. 1390–1441) in miniatures, portraits, and altar paintings also moved away from a highly formalized style to a careful representation of specific places. In Van Eyck's portrait of the Italian banker and courtier Giovanni Arnolfini and his bride, the image of the painter is reflected in a small mirror behind the couple, and above the mirror is written, "Jan van Eyck was here, 1434." Where Italians of the early fifteenth century tried to recreate space through linear perspective, the Flemish used aerial perspective, softening colors and tones to create the illusion of depth.

The influence of Renaissance styles in the north of Europe dates from the reign of the French king Francis I (r. 1515–1547), when Italian artists in

Portrait of a Black Man Albrect Dürer sketched this portrait in the early sixteenth century, most likely in a commercial center such as Venice or Nuremberg. By that time it was common to show one of the Three Wise Men as black, but such depictions, unlike Dürer's drawing here, were rarely based on portrait studies. (*Graphische Sammlung, Albertina*)

significant numbers traveled north. Francis invited Italian artists to his court—most notably Leonardo da Vinci, who spent the last years of his life in France. The most influential of the Italian-style creations in France was doubtless Francis's château Fontainebleau, whose decorations contained mythologies, histories, and allegories of the kind found in the Italian courts. Throughout the sixteenth century, Italianate buildings and paintings sprang up throughout Europe.

Perhaps the most famous artist who traveled to Italy, learned Italian techniques, and then transformed them to fit the environment of northern Europe was Albrecht Dürer of Nuremberg (1471–1528). Son of a well-known goldsmith,

Dürer became a painter and traveled first through France and Flanders learning the techniques popular in northern Europe. Then in 1494 he left Nuremberg on the first of two trips to Italy, during which he sketched Italian landscapes and studied the work of Italian artists, especially in Venice. What he learned in Italy, combined with the friendship of some of Germany's leading humanists, formed the basis of Dürer's works, which combined northern humanistic interests with the Italian techniques of composition and linear perspective. Dürer worked in charcoal, watercolors, and paints, but his influence was most widely spread through the numerous woodcuts that he produced on classical and contemporary themes. His woodcut *Whore of Babylon*, prepared in the context of the debate over the reform of the church, is based on sketches of Venetian prostitutes completed during his first visit to Italy.

Numerous other artists and engravers traveled south to see the great works of Italian artists. The engravings they produced and distributed back home made the innovations of the Italians available to those who were unable to travel to the south. In fact, some now lost or destroyed creations are known only through the engravings produced by northern artists eager to learn about Italian techniques.

THE RENAISSANCE AND COURT SOCIETY

The educational programs of the humanists and innovations in the arts between 1300 and 1550 provided an opportunity for rulers and popes alike to use culture to define and celebrate their power. Art, literature, and politics merged in the brilliant life of the Renaissance Italian courts, both secular and papal. To understand fully the Renaissance and its importance in the history of Europe, we need to examine the uses of culture by governments, specifically investigating the transformation of European ideas about service at court during the fourteenth and fifteenth centuries. We will take as a model the politics and cultural life at one noble court: the court of the Gonzaga family of Mantua. We will also discuss the development of the idea of the Renaissance gentleman and courtier made famous by Baldassare Castiglione, who was reared at the Gonzaga court. Finally, we will see how the Renaissance papacy melded the

secular and religious aspects of art, culture, and politics in its glittering court in Rome.

The Elaboration of the Court

The courts of northern Italy interested themselves in the cultural and artistic innovations of the Renaissance artists and humanists inspired by classical civilization, and they closely imitated many of the values and new styles that were developing in the courts of northern Europe, such as the court of Burgundy. Throughout Europe, attendance at court became increasingly important to members of the nobility as a source of revenue and influence. Kings and the great territorial lords were equally interested in drawing people to their courts as a way to influence and control the noble and the powerful.

Rulers in most parts of Europe instituted monarchical orders of knighthood to reward allies and followers. The most famous in the English-speaking world was the Order of the Garter, founded in 1349 by King Edward III. The orders were but one of the innovations in the organization of the court during the fourteenth and fifteenth centuries. The numbers of cooks, servants, huntsmen, musicians, and artists employed at court jumped dramatically in the late Middle Ages. In this the papal court itself was a model for the rest of Europe. The popes at Avignon in the fourteenth century already had a household of nearly six hundred persons. If one included all the bureaucrats, merchants, local officials, and visitors who continually swarmed around the elaborate papal court, the number grew even larger.

Courts were becoming theaters built around a series of widely understood signs and images that the ruler could manipulate. Culture was meant to reflect the image of the ruler. On important political or personal occasions, rulers organized jousts or tournaments around themes drawn from mythology. The dukes of Milan indicated the relative status of courtiers by inviting them to participate in particular hunts or jousts. They similarly organized their courtiers during feasts or elaborate entries into the towns and cities of their realms.

The late fourteenth and fifteenth centuries were periods of growth in the political and bureaucratic power of European rulers. The increasingly elaborate and sumptuous courts were one of the tools that rulers used to create a unified culture and ideology. At the court of the Gonzagas in Mantua, one of the most widely known of the fifteenth-century courts, the manipulation of Renaissance culture for political purposes was most complete. Aristocratic values, humanism, and art all played a part in the creation of the Gonzaga reputation.

The Court of Mantua

The city of Mantua, with perhaps 25,000 inhabitants in 1500, was small in comparison with Milan or Venice—the two cities with which it was most commonly allied. Located in a rich farming region along the Po River, Mantua did not have a large merchant or manufacturing class. Most Mantuans were involved in agriculture and regional trade in foodstuffs. The town had been a typical medieval Italian city-state until its government was overthrown by the noble Bonacolsi family in the thirteenth century. Members of the family took control of most of the important communal offices, and friends of the Bonacolsis filled the representative assemblies. The Bonacolsis, in turn, were ousted from the city in 1328 by their erstwhile comrades, the Gonzagas, who ruled the city until 1627.

The Gonzagas faced a problem typical of many of the families who took control of towns in northern Italy. The state they were creating was relatively small, their right to rule was not very widely recognized, and their control over the area was weak. The first step for the Gonzagas was the creation of fortresses and fortified towns that could withstand foreign enemies. The second step was to gain recognition of their right to rule. They had, after all, taken power in a palace revolution. In 1329 they were named imperial vicars, or representatives in the region. Later, in 1432, they bought the title "marquis" from Emperor Sigismund for the relatively low price of £12,000—equivalent to a year's pay for their courtiers. By 1500 they had exchanged that title for "duke."

Merely buying the title, however, did little to improve the status of the family. The family's reputation was enhanced by Gianfrancesco (d. 1444) and Lodovico (d. 1478), who brought the Renaissance and the new court style to Mantua. Located in a strategic area between the Milanese and Venetian states, the Gonzagas maintained themselves through astute diplomatic connections with other Italian and European courts and through

service as well-paid mercenaries in the Italian wars of the fifteenth and sixteenth centuries. Lodovico served the Venetians, the Milanese, the Florentines, and even the far-off Neapolitans. With considerable understatement Lodovico concluded, "We have worn armor for a long time."

The creation of a brilliant court was an essential part of the Gonzaga program. By 1500 there may have been eight hundred or more nobles, cooks, maids, and horsemen gathered in the court. Critics called them idlers "who have no other function but to cater to the tastes of the Duke." Early in the Renaissance the Gonzagas involved themselves in the cultural movement of humanism. It was under the tutelage of the Gonzagas that Vittorino da Feltre created his educational experiment in Villa Giocosa, which drew noble pupils from throughout Italy. It would be hard to overestimate the value for the Gonzagas of a school that attracted sons of the dukes of Urbino, Ferrara, and Milan and numerous lesser nobles. The family also called numerous artists to Mantua. Lodovico invited Antonio Pisano, called Pisanello (ca. 1415–ca. 1456), probably the most famous court artist of the fifteenth century. Pisanello created a series of frescoes on Arthurian themes for the Gonzaga palace. In these frescoes Lodovico is portrayed as a hero of King Arthur's roundtable.

Although the Gonzagas never lost interest in the chivalric values of Arthurian romances, they are much better known for their patronage of art with classical themes. Leon Battista Alberti redesigned the façade of the church of Sant'Andrea for the Gonzagas in the form of a Roman triumphal arch. The church, which long had been associated with the family, became a monument to the Gonzaga court just as the Arch of Constantine celebrated imperial power. In the 1460s Lodovico invited Andrea Mantegna (1441–1506) to his court. Trained in Padua and Venice, Mantegna was at that time the leading painter in northern Italy. His masterwork is the *Camera degli Sposi* (literally, the "room of the spouses"), completed in 1474. It features family portraits of Lodovico Gonzaga and his family framed in imitation of Roman imperial portrait medallions. One scene shows Lodovico welcoming his son, a newly appointed cardinal, back from Rome—proof to all of the new status of the Gonzagas.

The Gonzaga court, like most other courts, was both public and private. Finances for the city, appointments to public offices, and important political decisions were made by the men who dominated the court. On the other hand, as the prince's domestic setting, it was both a place where women were expected to be seen and a place where they had influence. Women were actively involved in creating the ideology of the court. Through the patronage of classical paintings, often with moral and political messages, wives of princes helped make the court better known and more widely accepted throughout Italy and Europe.

The arrival of Isabella d'Este (1494–1539) at court as the wife of Franceso Gonzaga marked the high point of the Renaissance in Mantua. Isabella had been classically educated at Ferrara by the son of Guarino of Verona. She maintained an interest in art, architecture, and music. As a patron of the arts, she knew what she wanted. In one commission she specified the themes and the balance of the work and told the artist to "add nothing." (See the box, "Isabella d'Este Orders Art.") Isabella was also an accomplished musician, playing a variety of string and keyboard instruments. She and others of the Gonzaga family recruited musicians from Flanders as well as Italians to their court. By the end of the sixteenth century, Mantua was the most important musical center of Europe. One festival brought 12,000 visitors to the city. It was in Mantua that Claudio Monteverdi (1567–1643) wrote works that established the genre of opera.

In the fourteenth century Petrarch had complained that however enjoyable feasting in Mantua might be, the place was dusty, plagued by mosquitoes, and overrun with frogs. By the end of the fifteenth century, the Gonzagas had secured for themselves a prominent place on the Italian, and the European, stage.

Castiglione and the European Gentleman

Renaissance ideas did not just spread in intellectual circles. They also were part of the transformation of the medieval knight into the early modern "gentleman." In 1528, Baldassare Castiglione (1478–1529) published *The Book of the Courtier*, a work in which he distilled what he had learned in his years at the various courts of Italy. Castiglione was born in Mantua, distantly related to the ruling Gonzaga family. He grew up at court and was sent to the Sforza court in Milan to finish his education. He returned home in 1499 to begin a career that

would include service in Mantua, Urbino, and Rome. During his career Castiglione met the greatest lights of the Renaissance. While he was in Rome, he became friends with Michelangelo and Raphael as well as with numerous humanistic writers. He died in Spain while on a mission for Pope Clement VII. When informed of his death, the emperor Charles V remarked, "One of the greatest knights in the world has died!" In his life and in his book Castiglione summed up the great changes that had transformed the nature of late medieval chivalry.

The Book of the Courtier reports a series of fictional discussions at the court of Urbino held over the course of four nights in March 1507. Among the participants are the duchess of Urbino, Elizabeth Gonzaga; her lady-in-waiting; and a group of humanists, men of action, and courtiers. In four evenings, members of the circle try to describe the perfect gentleman of court. In the process they debate the nature of nobility, humor, women, and love.

It was in many respects a typical gathering at court and it reflects contemporary views of relations between men and women. The wives of princes were expected to be organizers of life at court, but still paragons of domestic virtues. The women organize the discussion, which is carried on by men. They direct and influence the talk by jokes and short intervention but cannot afford to dominate discussion. "[Women] must be more circumspect, and more careful not to give occasion for evil being said of them . . . for a woman has not so many ways of defending herself against false calumnies as a man has."[20]

The topics were not randomly chosen. Castiglione explained that he wished "to describe the form of courtiership most appropriate for a gentleman living at the courts of princes." Castiglione's popularity was based on his deliberate joining of humanistic ideas and traditional chivalric values. Although his topic was the court with all its trappings, Castiglione tells his readers that his models for the discussion are Greek and Latin dialogues, especially those of Cicero and Plato. He was a Platonist. He believed that there was an inborn quality of "grace" that all truly noble gentlemen had. It had to be brought out, however, just as Michelangelo freed his figures from stone. Castiglione held that all moral and courtly virtues existed in tension with their opposites: "no magnanimity without

Isabella d'Este Orders Art

In addition to her literary and musical interests, Isabella d'Este, the marchioness of Mantua, managed to create one of the foremost collections of Renaissance art in sixteenth-century Italy. In her quest to get representative works by the leading artists of the period, she has left an unparalleled collection of letters. In the following letter to Pietro Perugino she describes what she expects from a painting she had asked him to complete.

Master Perugino, painter, [shall] make a painting on canvas 2½ braccia high and 3 braccia wide, and the said Pietro, the contractor, is obliged to paint on it a certain work of Lasciviousness and Modesty (in conflict) with these and many other embellishments, transmitted in this instruction to the said Pietro by the said Marchioness of Mantua, the copy of which is as follows:

Our poetic invention, which we greatly want to see painted by you, is the battle of Chastity against Lasciviousness, that is to say, Pallas and Diana fighting vigorously against Venus and Cupid. And Pallas should seem almost to have vanquished Cupid, having broken his golden arrow and cast his silver bow underfoot; with one hand she is holding him by the bandage which the blind boy has before his eyes, and with the other she is lifting her lance and about to kill him. . . . And to give more expression and decoration to the picture, beside Pallas I want to have the olive tree sacred to her, with a shield leaning against it bearing the head of Medusa, and with the owl, the bird peculiar to Pallas, perched among the branches. And beside Venus I want her favorite tree, the myrtle, to be placed, but to enhance the beauty of the fount of water mist be included, such as a river or the sea, where fauns, satyrs and more cupids will be seen, hastening to the help of Cupid, some swimming through the river, some flying, and some riding upon white swans, coming to join such an amorous battle. . . .

I am sending you all these details in a small drawing so that with both the written description and the drawing you will be able to consider my wishes in this matter. But if you think that perhaps there are too many figures in this for one picture, it is left to you to reduce them as you please, provided that you do not remove the principal basis, which consists of the four figures of Pallas, Diana, Venus and Cupid. If no inconvenience occurs I shall consider myself well satisfied; you are free to reduce them, but not to add anything else. Please be content with this arrangement.

Source: David S. Chambers, *Patrons and Artists in the Italian Renaissance* (London and New York: Macmillan, 1970), pp. 136–138.

pusillanimity." With numerous examples of good and bad in the world, wisdom could be revealed only through careful imitation, for like the classical authors favored by humanists, Castiglione advises that "He who lacks wisdom and knowledge will have nothing to say or do."[21]

But what Castiglione's readers recalled most clearly was his advice about behavior. Francesco Guicciardini of Florence once remarked that "When I was young, I used to scoff at knowing how to play, dance, and sing, and other such frivolities. . . . I have nevertheless seen from experience that these ornaments and accomplishments lend dignity and reputation even to men of good rank."[22] Guicciardini's comment underlines the value that readers found in Castiglione's work. Grace may be inbred, but it needed to be brought to the attention of those who controlled the court. Courtiers should first of all study the military arts. They had to fight, but only in situations where their prowess would be noticed. Castiglione adds practical advice about how to dress, talk, and participate in music and dancing: Never leap about wildly when dancing as peasants might, but dance only with an air of dignity and decorum. Castiglione further urges the courtier to be careful in dress: The French are "overdressed"; the Italians too quickly adopt the most recent and colorful styles. Reflecting political as well as social realities, Castiglione advises black or dark colors, which "reflect the sobriety of the Spaniards, since external appearances often bear witness to what is within."

The courtier always must be at pains "to earn that universal regard which everyone covets." Too much imitation and obvious study, however, lead to affectation. Castiglione counseled courtiers to carry themselves with a certain diffidence or unstudied naturalness (*sprezzatura*) covering their artifice. If courtiers are successful, they will exhibit "that graceful and nonchalant spontaneity (as it is often called) . . . so that those who are watching them imagine that they couldn't and wouldn't even know how to make a mistake." Thus, Castiglione's courtier walked a fine line between clearly imitated and apparently natural grace.

Castiglione's book was an immediate success and widely followed even by those who claimed to have rejected it. By 1561 it was available in Spanish, French, and English translations. The reasons are not difficult to find. It was critical for the courtier "to win for himself the mind and favour of the prince." And even those who disliked music, dancing, and light conversation learned Castiglione's arts "to open the way to the favour of princes." Many of the court arts that Castiglione preached had been traditional for centuries. Yet Castiglione's humanistic explanations and emphasis on form, control, and fashion had never seemed so essential as they did to the cultured gentlemen of the courts of the Renaissance and early modern Europe. (See the box, "Giovanni della Casa on the Perfect Gentleman.")

The Renaissance Papacy

The issues of power and how it is displayed had religious as well as secular dimensions. After its fourteenth- and fifteenth-century struggles over jurisdiction, the Renaissance papacy found itself in need of a political and ideological counterweight to the centrifugal forces of conciliarism, reform, and local feeling. Popes needed to defend

their primacy within the church from conciliarists who had argued that all Christians, including the pope, were bound to obey the commands of general councils. The ideological focus of the revived papacy was Rome.

The first step in the creation of a new Rome was taken by Pope Nicholas V (r. 1446–1455), a cleric who had spent many years in the cultural environment of Renaissance Florence. Hoping to restore Rome and its church to their former glory, Nicholas and his successors patronized the arts, established a lively court culture, and sponsored numerous building projects. Nicholas was an avid collector of ancient manuscripts that seemed to demonstrate the intellectual and religious primacy of Rome. He invited numerous artists and intellectuals to the papal court, including the Florentine architect and writer Leon Battista Alberti (1404–1472). On the basis of his research in topography and reading done in Rome, Alberti wrote his treatise *On Architecture* (1452), the most important work on architecture produced during the Renaissance. It was probably under Alberti's influence that Nicholas embarked on a series of ambitious urban renewal projects in Rome, which included the construction of bridges, rebuilding of roads, and even plans for the rebuilding of Saint Peter's Basilica.

The transformation of Rome had an ideological purpose. As one orator proclaimed, "Illuminated by the light of faith and Christian truth, [Rome] is destined to be the firmament of religion . . . , the secure haven for Christians."[23] Thus, the papal response to critics was to note that Rome and its government were central to political and religious life in Christendom. By reviving the style and organization of classical antiquity, the church sought to link papal Rome to an imperial tradition reaching back to Augustus and even to Alexander the Great. Papal restorers rebuilt the earliest Christian churches of the city, emphasizing the literal continuity of imperial authority and apostolic tradition. To papal supporters, there could be only one authority in the church. Early tradition and the continuity of the city itself, they assumed, demonstrated papal primacy.

One particular monument in Rome captures especially vividly the cultural, religious, and ideological program of the papacy: the Sistine Chapel in the Vatican Palace. The chapel is best known for the decoration of the ceiling by the Florentine

Giovanni della Casa on the Perfect Gentleman

Giovanni della Casa (1503–1556), bishop of Benevento and a papal bureaucrat, wrote a book about how to get on at court. Il Galateo (Sir Galahad) *was a practical book of manners, concluding that the courtier should adopt not the most virtuous customs but the customs typical of the court.*

You must understand it behooves you to frame and order your manners and doings . . . to please those with whom you live. . . . For you must not only refrain from such things as being foul, filthy, loathsome, and nasty, but we must not so much as name them. . . . It is an ill-favoured fashion that some men use, openly to thrust their hands in what part of their body they like.

Likewise, I like it ill to see a gentleman settle himself to do the needs of nature in the presence of men, and after he had done to truss himself again before them. Neither would I have him (if I may give him counsel), when he comes from such an occupation, so much as wash his hands in the sight of honest company, for that the cause of his washing puts them in mind of some filthy matter that has been done apart. . . .

Besides, let not a man sit so that he turn his tail to him that sits next to him, nor lie tottering with one leg so high above the other that a man may see all bare that his clothes would cover. For such parts be never [dis]played but amongst those to whom a man need use no reverence. It is very true that if a gentleman should use such fashions before his servants, or in the presence of some friend of meaner condition than himself, it would betoken no pride, but a love and familiarity. . . .

We say that those be good manners and fashions which bring a delight or at least offend not their senses, their minds and conceits with whom we live. . . . It is not enough for a man to do things that be good, but he must also have a care he does them with a good grace. And good grace is nothing else but such a manner of light (as I may call it) as shines in the aptness of things. . . . Without which even proportion and measure, even that which is good is not fair.

Source: James Bruce Ross and Mary Martin McLaughlin, eds., *The Portable Renaissance Reader* (New York: Viking, 1953), pp. 340–347, from the 1576 translation by Robert Peterson.

artist Michelangelo (see page 452) and for the striking images of his painting of the Last Judgment. The chapel, however, was begun by Pope Sixtus IV in 1475. It was to be an audience chamber in which an enthroned pope could meet the representatives of other states. In addition it was thought that the college of cardinals would gather in the chapel for the election of new popes.

The decorations done before Michelangelo painted the ceiling reflect the intellectual and ideological values that Sixtus hoped to transmit to the churches and governments of Christendom. Along the lower sidewalls of the chapel are portraits of earlier popes, a feature typical of early Roman churches. More significant are two cycles of paintings of the lives of Moses and Christ, drawing parallels between them. To execute the scenes, Sixtus called to Rome some of the greatest artists of the late fifteenth century: Sandro Botticelli, Domenico Ghirlandaio, Luca Signorelli, and Pietro Perugino. The works illustrate the continuity of the Old Testament and New Testament and emphasize the importance of obedience to the authority of God. The meaning is most obvious in Perugino's painting of Saint Peter receiving the keys to the Kingdom of Heaven from Christ. The allusion is to Matthew 16:18: "Thou art Peter and upon this rock I shall build my church." The keys are the symbol of the

Giving of the Keys to Saint Peter Pietro Perugino's painting of Saint Peter's receiving from Christ the keys to "bind and loose" on earth and in heaven illustrates the basis of papal claims to authority within the Christian church. This is the central message of the decorative plan of the Sistine Chapel. *(Scala/Art Resource, NY)*

claim of the pope, as successor of Saint Peter, to have the power to bind and loose sinners and their punishments.

Directly across from Perugino's painting is Botticelli's *The Judgment of Corah,* which portrays the story of Corah, who challenged the leadership of Moses and Aaron while the Israelites wandered in the wilderness. Corah and his supporters, according to Numbers 16:33, were carried live into Hell. Various popes had cited the implications of the judgment of Corah. Eugenius IV (r. 1431–1437), for example, recalled the fate of Corah when he refused to acknowledge the power of the councils. The pope was bound to oppose the council, he argued, "to save the people entrusted to his care, lest together with those who hold the power of the council above that of the papacy they suffer a punishment even more dire than that which befell Corah."[24]

The effects of Renaissance revival were profound. Rome grew from a modest population of about 17,000 in 1400 to 35,000 in 1450. By 1517 the city had a population of over 85,000, five times its population at the end of the Great Schism. The papal program was a success. Rome was transformed from a provincial town to a major European capital, perhaps the most important artistic and cultural center of the sixteenth century. Visitors to the Sistine Chapel, like visitors to the papal city itself, were expected to leave with a more profound sense of the antiquity of the papal office and of the continuity of papal exercise of religious

authority. Because the building and decorating were being completed as the Protestant Reformation was beginning in Germany, some historians have criticized the expense of the political and cultural program undertaken by the Renaissance popes. But to contemporaries on the scene the work was a logical and necessary attempt to strengthen the church's standing in Christendom.

SUMMARY

Neither the world of Petrarch nor the world of courts described by Castiglione brought the beginning of modern individualism or a culture radically different from the medieval past. Between 1300 and 1600, however, Europe experienced profound cultural innovation in literature, political and social thought, and art. The attitudes toward the past and ideas about education formed in this period became the model of European cultural life for the next two hundred years. The cultural values of modern Europe were those inherited from the Renaissance.

The impulse for change arose from the belief, shared by thinkers from Petrarch to Machiavelli, that there was a great deal to be learned from study of the Roman past. This was the basis for humanistic innovations in language, history, and politics. Even revolutionary thinkers like Lorenzo Valla and Niccolò Machiavelli began with the study of classical literature and history. The same transformation is evident among the artists. Early in the fifteenth century, Florentines who experimented with perspective were intent on recovering lost Roman knowledge, and Michelangelo was praised not only for mastering but for going beyond Roman norms.

Issues of reform and renewal were less tied to public life in the monarchies of northern Europe. Moral and spiritual issues were more important. Yet the same movement from imitation to transformation is evident. Erasmus and Dürer assimilated the best of the new art and culture from Italy, but in the *Praise of Folly* and in Dürer's woodcuts, the use of past ideas and models was neither simple nor direct.

The integration of art, literature, and public life was most evident in the ways that art was used by governments. The Gonzaga court and the papacy clearly recognized the value of artistic and literary works as a way to explain and justify power and influence. The beauty of Mantegna's painting or the power of Michelangelo's vision does not obscure the message about power and authority.

Innovation depended on the study of the past. As humanists came to know more fully the art and history of Greece and Rome, they recognized the extent to which classical culture represented only one source of legal, historical, or moral understanding. Europeans' recognition of other, often competing, traditions would be tested in the sixteenth century, when they came face to face with a previously unknown world. It is to the geographic discoveries and European expansion that we now turn.

NOTES

1. Quoted in Federico Chabod, *Machiavelli and the Renaissance* (New York: Harper & Row, 1958), p. 153.
2. Albertino Mussato, *The Ecerinis*, trans. Joseph R. Berrigan. As quoted in Berrigan, "A Tale of Two Cities: Verona and Padua in the Late Middle Ages," in *Art and Politics in Late Medieval and Renaissance Italy, 1250–1500*, ed. Charles M. Rosenberg (Notre Dame, Ind.: University of Notre Dame Press, 1990), p. 77.
3. Quoted in J. B. Trapp, ed., *Background to the English Renaissance* (London: Gray-Mills Publishing, 1974), p. 11.
4. Quoted in N. Mann, *Petrarch* (Oxford: Oxford University Press), p. 67.
5. Petrarch, "On His Own Ignorance and That of Many Others," in *The Renaissance Philosophy of Man*, ed. Ernst Cassirer, Paul Oskar Kristeller, and John H. Randall (Chicago: University of Chicago Press, 1948), p. 105.
6. Quoted in Benjamin G. Kohl and Ronald G. Witt, *The Earthly Republic* (Philadelphia: University of Pennsylvania Press, 1978), p. 11.
7. Quoted in M. L. King, *Women of the Renaissance* (Chicago: University of Chicago Press, 1991), p. 194.
8. Quoted ibid., p. 222.
9. Quoted ibid., p. 198.
10. K. R. Bartlett, *The Civilization of the Italian Renaissance* (Lexington, Mass.: D. C. Heath, 1992), p. 314.
11. Quoted in *The Portable Machiavelli*, ed. and trans. Peter Bondanella and Mark Musa (New York: Penguin Books, 1979), p. 128.
12. Quoted ibid., p. 160.
13. Quoted in *The Notebooks of Leonardo da Vinci*, ed. J. P. Richter, vol. 1 (New York: Dover, 1883 and 1970), p. 14.
14. Quoted ibid., p. 129.
15. Giorgio Vasari, *The Lives of the Artists*, trans. George Bull (Baltimore: Penguin, 1965), p. 338.
16. Julia Bondanella and Mark Musa, eds., *The Italian Renaissance Reader* (New York: Meridian Books, 1987), p. 377.
17. I. Origo, *The Merchant of Prato: Francesco di Marco Datini*, 1335–1410 (New York: Knopf, 1957), pp. 155–156.
18. Quoted in A. Rabil, Jr., *Renaissance Humanism: Foundations, Forms, and Legacy*, vol. 2 (Philadelphia: University of Pennsylvania Press, 1988), p. 236.
19. Quoted ibid., p. 229.
20. Quoted in R. M. San Juan, "The Court Lady's Dilemma: Isabella d'Este and Art Collecting in the Renaissance," *Oxford Art Journal* 14 (1991): 71.
21. Unless otherwise noted, quotes of Castiglione are from Baldassare Castiglione, *The Book of the Courtier*, trans. George Bull (Baltimore: Penguin Books, 1967).
22. Quoted in R. W. Hanning and D. Rosand, eds., *Castiglione: The Ideal and the Real in Renaissance Culture* (New Haven, Conn.: Yale University Press, 1983), p. 17.
23. Raffaele Brandolini, as quoted in Charles L. Stinger, *The Renaissance in Rome* (Bloomington: Indiana University Press, 1985), p. 156.
24. Quoted in Leopold D. Ettlinger, *The Sistine Chapel Before Michelangelo* (Oxford: Oxford University Press, 1965), p. 105.

SUGGESTED READING

General Surveys

Brown, Alison. *The Renaissance.* 1988. An excellent short introduction to Renaissance art and culture designed for those with little or no background in the field.

(continued on page 472)

THE ART OF RENAISSANCE FLORENCE

In 1478 or shortly thereafter a member of the Medici family probably commissioned Sandro Botticelli to create the painting *Primavera (Spring)*. Since its completion, critics have been fascinated by its composition and lyrical qualities. Notice the figures who make up the picture. At the center is Venus, goddess of love. The group to Venus's left tells the classical myth of the return of spring. Zephyrus, the west wind, who brings the fertility and growth of springtime, pursues Chloris, a goddess of fertility. Flowers flow from Chloris's mouth as Zephyrus changes her into Flora, the flower-covered goddess of spring, who stands to her right. These figures are balanced by the group to Venus's right—the three Graces, who are dancing beside the figure of Mercury, the messenger and in this context the god of May. We can easily agree with the critics and connoisseurs who praise the grace and enchantment of Botticelli's mysterious wood filled with dark trees loaded with oranges and his meadow covered with flowers. The work demonstrates Botticelli's great artistic skill and the sophisticated knowledge of classical mythology current in Florence in the last quarter of the fifteenth century. But, you might ask, how much more can it tell us about the culture of Renaissance Florence?

Historians and art historians have struggled to find the best way to use art as a tool in historical studies. In the late nineteenth and early twentieth centuries, art connoisseurs carefully studied brush strokes and coloring so that they could understand and immediately recognize the techniques of the great masters. They believed that knowledge of an artist's technique would allow them to understand why the works of that artist were so widely popular. Modern historians, however, usually approach a work of art in other ways. We can ask, "What did the artist mean to paint?" Or we can ask, "How does Botticelli's *Primavera* compare to other great works of art, such as Pablo Picasso's *Guernica*?" But the most fruitful inquiry is, "What might Botticelli's contemporaries have noticed in the work?"

To consider what that last question implies, it becomes important to know the social and artistic conventions that might illuminate the meanings in the work, where the work was intended to be displayed, and, finally, how the work comments on the social and cultural interests of the people whom the artist expected to view it.

Contemporaries valued Botticelli's brush stroke—that is, his artistic touch. But, surprisingly, they valued just as highly the materials in which he worked. One of the few contracts we have for a work by Botticelli notes carefully the cost and quantities of gold foil and aquamarine blue paint (an expensive and precious color). From this we can see that Botticelli's contemporaries were very aware of color. As Leon Battista Alberti observed critically of fifteenth-century Italians, most people associate gold leaf and deep blue colors with sumptuousness and majesty. Florentines were also very aware of the writings of contemporary humanists—and especially of the humanist belief that classical and Christian wisdom were basically one. Imbuing classical images with contemporary meanings did not seem odd to them. Botticelli's great popularity in Florence actually rested in part on his sophisticated use of classically inspired figures to comment on contemporary issues.

Primavera was meant to decorate the palace of a relative of Lorenzo de' Medici. It was probably designed to be seen by Lorenzo "the Magnificent" himself, who not only held a position of political and economic importance in the city but was a gifted poet and leader of a *brigata,* or company of poets and humanists. The brigata, in fact, was the primary audience for Botticelli's work. Lorenzo and the poets of his circle were actively combining what they believed was the best of their Tuscan culture with the classical philosophy and literature revived by the humanists. Lorenzo once wore on his armor the motto *Le Tems revient*, which

Botticelli: Primavera *(Art Resource, NY)*

loosely translated means "The ages shall be renewed." As we have seen, this renewal was an idea popular among the artists and humanists of Renaissance Italy. In *Primavera* Botticelli uses a number of symbols meant to remind viewers of Lorenzo de' Medici and his cultural interests. Look at the oranges in the trees, for example. They resemble the three balls on the Medici crest. The coming of spring in the person of Flora is precisely the sort of image with which Lorenzo wanted to be associated.

But what of the three Graces? How do they fit into a picture meant to celebrate the merging of old and new in Medicean Florence? For Lorenzo's contemporaries, they may have been the best possible image of the marriage of classical and Tuscan traditions. Lorenzo and his friends knew of the Graces and their association with spring from a variety of classical sources. These particular Graces, however, are Tuscan. The cut of their gowns and their dance would have been recognizable to Lorenzo's friends as typically Florentine. Lorenzo

himself had earlier composed a dance, "A Simple Dance Called Venus," which could easily be the dance that they are doing. Next to them stands Venus, the goddess of love. But here she represents spring, flowering (Flora is, after all, the root of the name Florence), and renewal. Her arm is raised in a gesture of invitation. She is inviting us, or, more accurately, the Florentines of Lorenzo's time, to join in a dance of celebration and renewal.

What do we finally see in Botticelli's *Primavera*? It is not simply an imitation of either a classical text or any known classical figure. It seems instead that Botticelli created a sort of visual poem that incorporated numerous themes of classical learning and cultural renewal that were, by the late 1460s and 1470s, widely associated with Lorenzo de' Medici, the cultural and political master of Florentine life. The historian finds in the art of the Renaissance works of great beauty that convey through their materials, composition, and symbols a sense of the values and ideas that animated contemporary politics and culture.

Hale, John R. *The Civilization of Europe in the Renaissance.* 1994. A beautifully written survey of the culture of Europe from the fifteenth to the seventeenth century.

Kelly, Joan. *Women, History & Theory.* 1984. Includes Kelly's famous "Did Women Have a Renaissance?" as well as an essay on the *querelle des femmes.*

King, M. L. *Women of the Renaissance.* 1991. A survey of the social, economic, and cultural experience of women during the Renaissance.

Nauert, Charles G., Jr. *Humanism and the Culture of Renaissance Europe.* 1995. An excellent short survey of European thought in the Renaissance.

Rabil, Albert, Jr. *Renaissance Humanism: Foundations, Forms and Legacy.* 3 vols. 1988. An excellent and quite accessible introduction to Renaissance humanism.

Humanism

Kohn, Benjamin, and Ronald Witt, eds. *The Earthly Republic.* 1978. An important anthology of writings by fourteenth- and fifteenth-century civic humanists. The general introduction is an especially clear discussion of the rise of civic humanism.

Mann, N. *Petrarch.* 1984. An excellent introduction to Petrarch's life and thought, designed for readers with little prior experience with Renaissance thought.

Skinner, Q. *The Foundations of Modern Political Thought.* Vol. 1. *The Renaissance.* 1978. A survey of political thought that attempts to place thinkers in their social and political context.

Woodward, W. H., ed. *Vittorino da Feltre and Other Humanist Educators: Essays and Versions. An Introduction to the History of Classical Education.* 1897. A volume of essays and documents that are excellent introductions to the Renaissance educational program.

Art and Society in Renaissance Italy

Baxendall, Michael. *Painting and Experience in Fifteenth-Century Italy.* 1972. A volume that helps the reader see the art of the Renaissance as it would have been seen in the period.

Dempsey, Charles. *The Portrayal of Love: Botticelli's Primavera and Humanist Culture at the time of Lorenzo the Magnificent.* 1992. A complex but rewarding demonstration of how artistic and literary culture are combined in a single work. Essential for our discussion of Botticelli's *Primavera.*

Goldthwaite, Richard. *Wealth and the Demand for Art in Italy, 1300–1600.* 1993. A thoughtful essay about the social and economic influences on the creation and patronage of art.

Hartt, F. *History of Italian Renaissance Art: Painting, Sculpture, Architecture.* 1987. A comprehensive and lavishly illustrated survey of Renaissance art that is sensitive to the social and political milieu in which artists worked.

Letts, R. M. *The Renaissance.* 1992. An excellent introductory essay on the art of Renaissance Italy. Especially good on the innovations of the early fifteenth century.

Panofsky, E. *Renaissance and Renascences in Western Art.* 1969. A difficult but important essay on the concept of Renaissance and on the nature of the differences between the Renaissance and previous periods of creative innovation.

Humanism and Culture Outside Italy

Eisenstein, E. L. *The Printing Press as an Agent of Change: Communications and Cultural Transformations in Early Modern Europe.* 1979. A discussion of the ways in which print culture changed social and intellectual life, rather than of the technology of print itself.

Goodman, A., and A. Mackay, eds. *The Impact of Humanism.* 1990. A volume of basic surveys of the arrival of Italian humanistic ideas in the various lands of Europe.

Marius, R. *Thomas More: A Biography.* 1984. A beautifully written biography that questions More's humanistic interests and looks particularly at his divided feelings about religion and the state.

Murray, Linda. *The Late Renaissance and Mannerism.* 1967. An introductory survey that traces Renaissance themes as they move out of Italy, especially through France, Germany, and Flanders.

Panofsky, E. *Albrecht Dürer.* 1948. The best study of the life and work of Germany's greatest Renaissance artist.

Courts and Castiglione

Burke, Peter. *The Fortunes of the Courtier: The European Reception of Castiglione's Cortegiano.* 1995. A well-written survey of the influence of Castiglione's ideas.

Dickens, A. G., ed. *The Courts of Europe.* 1977. A well-illustrated collection of essays for the general reader on courts from the Middle Ages to the eighteenth century.

Elias, N. *The Civilizing Process.* 1978. A classic discussion of the transformation of manners and behavior at the courts of Renaissance Europe. Contains difficult analysis but lively descriptions.

Ettlinger, Leopold. *The Sistine Chapel before Michelangelo.* 1965. A scholarly discussion of the images and papal ideology discussed in this chapter.

Keen, Maurice. *Chivalry.* 1984. A well-written survey of chivalry that includes discussion on its transformation at the end of the Middle Ages.

Stinger, Charles L. *The Renaissance in Rome.* 1985. An engaging survey of the vibrant cultural life at the papal court and in the city during the Renaissance.

Woods-Marsden, J. *The Gonzaga of Mantua and Pisanello's Arthurian Frescoes.* 1988. A broad and well-illustrated discussion of how the artistic interests of the Gonzagas served their social and political needs.

CHAPTER 13

Europe, the Old World and the New

In the spring of 1493, Christopher Columbus wrote to a friend and supporter at the court of Ferdinand and Isabella, reporting the glorious discoveries he had recently made during his successful trip to the Indies. "I found very many islands filled with people innumerable, and of them all I have taken possession for their Highnesses, by proclamation made and with the royal standard unfurled, and no opposition was offered to me."[1] His actions, as reported in the letter, seemed to establish beyond question Spanish claims to these new lands. Columbus went on to enumerate the wealth, rivers, natural resources, and marvels to be found in this new world. He concluded by promising he could send the monarchs "as much gold as they need" and "a thousand other things of value." This letter, rather than a more sober report sent to the monarchs themselves, was almost instantly printed and reprinted throughout Europe.

Columbus soon arrived at the Spanish court himself, accompanied by seven natives from the Caribbean and countless green parrots. His initial enthusiasm—and awards—were great, but neither lasted particularly long. Columbus's voyage was both a capstone of previous contacts with non-European societies and a prelude to dramatic, often tragic encounters between Europe and the rest of the world. As we shall see, Europeans tended to respond to the challenges of this new world according to their view of themselves and the old world they had known.

Columbus's adventure was part of a series of voyages begun in the last decade of the fifteenth century that eventually carried Europeans to most parts of the world, unifying the "Old World" continents of Asia, Africa,

French map of
the New World,
ca. 1550.

and Europe with a "New World": the Americas and the islands of the Pacific. The story of the first navigators, their technological advances, and the colonies they established may seem straightforward, but scholars interested in the discoveries and expansion that occurred during the late fifteenth and sixteenth centuries have viewed these events in vastly different ways. Accounts of the meeting of the Old World and the New, perhaps more than any other episode of Western history, have been shaded by the perspectives of both the writer and the reader.

Those who wanted to focus on the transfer of European religion and culture to new lands have viewed Christopher Columbus and the other early explorers as important symbols of the creation of a New World with new values. Those who sought the origins of modern scientific rationalism have believed that Columbus's voyage across the Atlantic Ocean proves that he was a "Renaissance man" who saw through the myths and superstitions of the Middle Ages. However, the descendants of the native peoples who greeted the newly arriving Europeans—the Amerindians, Aborigines, Maori, and Polynesians who lived in North and South America, Australia, New Zealand, and the islands of the Pacific—remind us that the outsiders brought slavery, modern warfare, and epidemic diseases that virtually destroyed indigenous cultures.

Spain commissioned Columbus to sail west because the Portuguese already controlled eastern routes to Asia around the African coast and because certain technological innovations made long open-sea voyages possible. Thus, as those who celebrate Columbus's achievements have said, the story includes national competition, the development of navigational techniques, and strategic choices. Another aspect of the story, however, is the political, cultural, and military clash that took place in the Atlantic, the Caribbean, and Central and South America. The Europeans overthrew the great empires of the Aztecs and Incas, but the transfer of European culture was never as complete as the Europeans thought or expected. The language and customs of the conquered peoples, blanketed by European language and law, survived, though the lands colonized by the Europeans would never again be as they had been before their encounter with the Old World.

THE EUROPEAN BACKGROUND, 1250–1492

Over the course of the late Middle Ages, Europeans developed the desire and the ability to reach distant lands in Africa and Asia. Three critical factors for the exploratory voyages of the fifteenth and early sixteenth centuries were technology, curiosity and interest, and geographic knowledge. A series of technological innovations made sailing far out into the ocean less risky and more predictable than it had been. The writings of classical geographers, myths and traditional tales, and merchants' accounts of their travels fueled popular interest in the East and made ocean routes to the East seem safe and reasonable alternatives to overland travel.

Navigational Innovations

The invention of several navigational aids in the fourteenth and fifteenth centuries made sailing in open waters easier and more predictable. Especially important was the fly compass, consisting of a magnetic needle attached to a paper disk (or "fly"). The simple compass had been invented in China and was known in Europe by the late twelfth century, but it was not initially marked off in degrees so was only a rudimentary aid to navigation. By 1500, astrolabes and other devices enabling sailors to use the position of the sun and stars to assist in navigation were also available. An astrolabe allowed sailors to measure the altitude of the polestar in the sky and thereby calculate the latitude, or distance from the equator, at which their ship was sailing. Still, until the general adoption of charts marked with degrees of latitude, most navigators relied on the compass, experience, and instinct.

The most common Mediterranean ship of the late Middle Ages was a galley powered by a combination of sails and oars; such a vessel was able to travel quickly and easily along the coast. Because of limited space and the need for a large crew of rowers, galleys were not ideal for long-distance travel or transport of bulky materials. Throughout the Mediterranean, shipbuilders experimented with new designs, and during the fifteenth century the Portuguese and Spanish perfected the caravel. Large, square sails efficiently caught the wind and propelled the caravel forward, and smaller triangular sails (lateens) allowed the caravel to tack diagonally across a headwind, virtually sailing into the wind. The caravel was larger and needed a smaller crew than the galley, and it was more maneuverable than ships with only square sails.

By the 1490s the Portuguese and Spanish had developed the ships and techniques that would make long open-sea voyages possible. What remained was for Europeans, especially the Portuguese and Spanish, to conclude that such voyages were both possible and profitable.

Lands Beyond Christendom

The Greeks and Romans had contacts with the civilizations of Asia and Africa, and in the Middle Ages interest in the lands beyond Christendom had never been lost. In the thirteenth and fourteenth centuries, European economic and cultural contacts with these lands greatly increased. The rising volume of trade between Europe and North Africa brought with it information about the wealthy African kingdoms of the Niger Delta. The Mongols in the thirteenth century allowed European merchants and missionaries to travel along trade routes extending all the way to China, opening regions formerly closed to them by hostile Muslim governments.

Trade in the Mediterranean also kept Christians and Muslims, Europeans and North Africans in close contact. Europeans sold textiles to Arab traders, who carried them across the Sahara to Timbuktu, where they were sold for gold bullion from the ancient African kingdoms of Ghana and Mali located just above the Niger River. European chroniclers recorded the pilgrimage to Mecca of Mansa Musa, the fabulously wealthy fourteenth-century emperor of Mali. Italian merchants tried unsuccessfully to trade directly with the African kingdoms, but Muslim merchants prevented any permanent contact.

Europeans enjoyed more successful trade connections farther east. The discovery in London of a brass shard inscribed with a Japanese character attests to the breadth of connections in the early fourteenth century. After the rise of the Mongols, Italian merchants regularly traveled east through Constantinople and on to India and China. By the fourteenth century, they knew how long travel to China might take and the probable expenses along the way.

European intellectuals also maintained an interest in the lands beyond Christendom. They had

The World Beyond Christendom
Medieval Christians believed that wondrous peoples lived beyond the borders of Christendom. Images of headless or one-legged men were usually included in travel accounts. This picture from Marco Polo's *Travels* shows what many Europeans expected to find when they traveled.
(Bibliothèque Nationale)

read the late classical and early medieval authors who described Africa, the Indies, and China. The work of the greatest of the classical geographers, Ptolemy of Alexandria (ca. A.D. 127–145), was known only indirectly until the early fifteenth century, but medieval thinkers read avidly and speculated endlessly about the information contained in the works of authors from Late Antiquity, such as Martianus Capella, who lived in the fifth century A.D. Martianus preserved fantastic myths and tales along with geographic observations that he had gathered from the writings of Ptolemy and others. He reported, for example, that there were snakes in Calabria, in isolated southern Italy, that sucked milk from cows and men who became wolves—the earliest mention of werewolves. Martianus assumed that a person who traveled to the south and east of Europe was more and more likely to find wonders. Moreover, it seemed to early geographers that the heat at the equator must be so intense that it would be impossible for life to exist there. By the twelfth century, fictitious reports circulated widely in the West of a wealthy Christian country in the East or possibly in Africa. The fictitious kingdom of Prester John was often associated with the Christian groups living near the shrine of Saint Thomas in India or the kingdom of Ethiopia. In the fifteenth century, European Christians looked to Prester John and eventually to the Christians of Ethiopia for aid against the Muslims.

Tales of geographic marvels are epitomized by the *Travels of Sir John Mandeville*, a book probably written in France but purporting to be the observations of a knight from St. Albans, just north of London. Mandeville says that he left England in 1322 or 1323 and traveled to Constantinople, Jerusalem, Egypt, India, China, Persia, and Turkey. In the first half of the book he describes what seems to be a typical pilgrimage to the Holy Land. As the author's travels continue eastward, however, the narrative shifts dramatically. Sir John describes the islands of wonders, inhabited by dog-headed men, one-eyed giants, headless men, and hermaphrodites. Not only does he describe his discovery of the lost tribes of Israel but he also records the location of Paradise. Less fantastically, Mandeville reports that the world could be, and in fact has been, circumnavigated. He adds that the lands south of the equator, the Antipodes, are habitable.

Mandeville's *Travels* and similar fantastic tales kept alive geographic speculation. They also raised expectations in travelers who actually did venture to the East. Thirteenth-century visitors to central Asia carefully asked their Mongol hosts about the exact locations of these wonders. Columbus, in his dispatches, included reports he had received of an island of Amazons in the Caribbean, and he believed that he had found the rivers flowing from Paradise along the coast of Venezuela.

More reliable information became available in the thirteenth century largely because of the arrival of the Mongols. Jenghiz Khan and his descendants created an empire that reached from eastern Hungary to China (see page 368). This *pax Mongolica*, or area of Mongol-enforced peace, was a region tolerant of racial and cultural differences. In the 1240s and 1250s a series of papal representatives traveled to the Mongol capital at Karakorum near Lake Baikal in Siberia. The letters of these papal ambassadors, who worked extensively to gain converts and allies for a crusade against the Turks, were widely read and greatly increased accurate knowledge about Asia. Other missionaries and diplomats journeyed to the Mongol court and some continued farther east to India and China. By the early fourteenth century, the church had established a bishop in Beijing.

Italian merchants followed closely on the heels of the churchmen and diplomats. The pax Mongolica offered the chance to trade directly in Asia and the adventure of visiting lands known only from travel literature. In 1262, Niccolò and Maffeo Polo left on their first trip to China. On a later journey the two Venetians took Niccolò's son, Marco (1255–1324), who remained in China for sixteen or seventeen years. Marco dictated an account of his travels to a Pisan as they both sat as prisoners of war in a Genoese jail in 1298. It is difficult to know how much of the text really represents Marco's own observations and how much is chivalric invention by the Pisan. Some even suggest that Marco himself never traveled to China. His contemporaries, however, seem to have had few doubts. The book was widely known. Columbus himself owned and extensively annotated a copy of Marco Polo's *Travels*.

In his account Marco claims that he was an influential official in China; and he may, in fact, be the "Po-Lo" mentioned in Chinese sources as a low-level imperial bureaucrat of the emperor

Pegalotti on Travel to the East

In his **Handbook for Merchants**, *Francesco Pegalotti describes travel to Asia and the commercial customs of the area, demonstrating how usual such travel had become by 1340, when his work was published.*

First [of all] it is advisable for him [the traveler] to let his beard grow long and not shave. And at Tana [on the Black Sea coast] he should furnish himself with guide-interpreters, and he should not try to save by hiring a poor one instead of a good one. . . . And besides interpreters he ought to take along at least two good manservants who know the Cumanic [Mongol] tongue well. And if the merchant wishes to take along from Tana any woman with him, he may do so— and if he does not wish to take one, there is no obligation; yet if he takes one, he will be regarded as a man of higher condition than if he does not take one. . . . And [for the stretch] from Tana to Astrakhan he ought to furnish himself with food for twenty-five days—that is with flour and salt and fish, for you find meat in sufficiency in every locality along the road. . . . The road leading from Tana to Cathay is quite safe both by day and by night, according to what the merchants report who have used it—except that if he should die along the road, when going or returning, everything would go to the lord of the country where the merchant dies. . . .

All silver which the merchants carry with them when going to Cathay, the lord of Cathay causes to be withdrawn and placed in his treasury; and to the merchants who bring it he gives paper money, that is, yellow paper stamped with the seal of the said lord, that money being called *balisci*. And with the said money you may and can purchase silk and any other merchandise or foods you may wish to buy. And all the people of the country are bound to accept it, and yet people do not pay more for merchandise although it is paper money.

Source: R. S. Lopez and I. Raymond, eds., *Medieval Trade in the Mediterranean World* (New York: Columbia University Press, 1955), pp. 356, 357, 358.

Kublai Khan. Marco describes the long, difficult trip to China, his equally arduous return, and the cities and industries he found. He was most impressed by the trade of Ch'nan (modern Hangzhou on the central coast of China)—one hundred times greater, he thought, than the trade of Alexandria in Egypt, a renowned port on the Mediterranean. Marco also visited modern Sri Lanka, Java, and Sumatra. His tales mix a merchant's observations of ports, markets, and trade with myths and marvels—tales of dog-headed men and the kingdom of Prester John.

By 1300 there seems to have been a modest community of Italians in China. By the late thirteenth and fourteenth centuries, Italian traders were traveling directly to the East in search of Asian silks, spices, pearls, and ivory. They and other European merchants could consult the *Handbook for Merchants* (1340) by the Florentine Francesco Pegalotti, which described the best roads, likely stopping points, and the appropriate freight animals for a trip to the East. (See the box, "Pegalotti on Travel to the East.") These merchants found that they had cheap access to spices, silks, and even porcelains, which they shipped back to the West. Fragmentary reports of Europeans in the Spice Islands (also known as the Moluccas), Japan, and India indicate that many Europeans in addition to merchants traveled simply for the adventure of visiting new lands.

The Revolution in Geography

The situation changed significantly over the course of the fourteenth century. With the conversion of the Mongols to Islam, the breakdown of

Mongol unity, and the subsequent rise of the Ottoman Turks in the fourteenth century, the highly integrated and unusually open trade network fell apart. The caravan routes across southern Russia, Persia, and Afghanistan were closed to Europeans. Western merchants once again became dependent on Muslim middlemen.

The reports of travelers, however, continued to circulate long after the closing of the trade routes. This new information was avidly followed by Western geographers anxious to assimilate it. Marco Polo's *Travels* and the classical geographic theories of Ptolemy contributed to a veritable revolution in geography in the decades before the Portuguese and Spanish voyages.

In 1375, Abraham Cresques, a Jewish mathematician from the Mediterranean island of Majorca, produced what has come to be known as the *Catalan World Atlas*. He combined the traditional medieval *mappamundi* (or world map) with a Mediterranean portolan. The mappamundi attempted to show both spatial and theological relationships. It often followed the O-T form—that is, a circle divided into three parts (⊤) representing Europe, Africa, and Asia, the lands of the descendants of Noah. Jerusalem—the symbolic center of the Christian religion—is always at the center of the map. The portolan, in contrast, was entirely practical. From the late thirteenth century, mariners had been developing atlases that included sailing instructions and accurate portrayals of ports, islands, and shallows along with general compass readings. The *Catalan World Atlas* largely holds to the portolan tradition but has more accurate representations of the lands surrounding the Mediterranean.

In the fifteenth century, following Ptolemy's suggestions, mapmakers began to divide their maps into squares marking lines of longitude and latitude. This format made it possible to accurately show the contours of various lands and the relationship of one landmass to another. Numerous maps of the world were produced in this period. The culmination of this cartography was a globe constructed for the city of Nuremberg in 1492, the very year Columbus set sail. From these increasingly accurate maps, it has become possible to document the first exploration of the Azores, the Cape Verde Islands, and the western coast of Africa.

The Florentine mathematician Paolo Toscanelli, in a letter of 1474 to the king of Portugal, included a map demonstrating, he believed, the short distance to be covered if one were to sail straight west first to Japan and then on to China. Columbus knew the letter and some think he may have corresponded with the Florentine. Not surprisingly, Columbus, after his voyages, observed that maps had been of no use to him. True enough. But without the accumulation of knowledge by travelers and the mingling of that knowledge with classical ideas about geography, it is doubtful whether Columbus or the Portuguese Vasco da Gama would have undertaken or could have found governments willing to support the voyages that so dramatically changed the relations between Europe and the rest of the world.

PORTUGUESE VOYAGES OF DISCOVERY, 1350–1515

Portugal, a tiny country on the edge of Europe, for a short time led the European expansion. Portuguese sailors were the first Europeans to perfect the complex techniques of using the winds and currents of the south Atlantic, especially along the western coast of Africa (Map 13.1). Portugal's experience gives a good indication of the options open to the Europeans as they extended their influence into new areas. As the Portuguese moved down the African coast and later as they tried to compete commercially in Asia, they found that they could not automatically transfer European economic and commercial traditions into new environments. In each new location, they faced new challenges. Solutions varied from place to place. In some areas the Portuguese created a network of relatively isolated naval and trading stations to control the movement of goods. In other areas they attempted to create large, dominant Portuguese colonies. In still other areas they used plantation slavery to create commercial products for the international market. The other European states would use these same strategies in Asia and in the New World as they too extended their economic and political interests beyond continental Europe.

The Early Voyages

Portugal, like other late medieval European states, hoped that exploration and expansion would lead to "gold and Christians." The search for Christians

**Winter
Wind Patterns**

Ocean Currents

Map 13.1 Winds and Currents Winds and ocean currents move in giant clockwise and counterclockwise circles that limit the directions in which ships can sail efficiently. It was impossible, for example, for the explorers to sail directly south along the entire western coast of Africa.

was accelerated in the fifteenth century by the growing power of the Ottoman Turks. After the conquest of Constantinople in 1453 (see page 426), Turkish expansion into Syria and Palestine, and Turkish raids reaching into Austria and northeastern Italy, Europeans increasingly hoped for an alliance with the mythical Christian kingdoms of the East to open a second front against the Turks.

For the Portuguese, facing the Atlantic and in-sulated from the direct Turkish threat, the promise of gold was no doubt more alluring than the search for Christians. The nearest source of gold was well known to late medieval Christians: the African kingdoms of the Niger Delta. The problem for European traders and their governments was that commercial contacts with this wealthy region remained controlled by the Muslim Berber merchants of North Africa. The Portuguese and Spanish hoped to break the monopoly by taking control of the North African coast or by means of a flanking movement along the western coast of Africa.

Actual exploration of the Atlantic had begun long before Europeans recognized the extent of the Turkish threat. By 1350, the Madeiras and the Canaries, groups of islands off the western coast of Africa, regularly were included on European maps. By about 1365, Portuguese, Spanish, and probably French sailors were visiting the Canary Islands. By 1400, the Azores, one-third of the way across the Atlantic, were known and from early in the fifteenth century were regular ports of call for Portuguese ships. These voyages were no mean feat, calling for sophisticated ocean sailing out of sight of land for weeks at a time.

In the second decade of the fifteenth century the Portuguese expansion began in earnest with the capture of the Muslim port of Ceuta on the coast of Morocco (see Map 13.2). From then on, the Portuguese, led by Prince Henry "the Navigator" (1394–1460), younger son of King John I (r. 1385–1433), moved steadily down the western coast of Africa. Contemporaries reported that Prince Henry was intent on reaching the "River of Gold"—that is, the Gold Coast of Africa and the Niger Delta. To accomplish this, he directed efforts to colonize the Canaries (which eventually were lost to the Spanish), the Azores, and Madeira, the largest of the Madeira Islands. He also sponsored a series of expeditions down the African coast, reaching Senegal and the Cape Verde Islands by 1444. The Portuguese quickly established trading stations in the region and soon were exporting gold and slaves to Lisbon.

Prince Henry is often credited with creating a virtual school of seamanship in his court at Sagres on the coast of Portugal, but his efforts at colonization may have had more importance for Portuguese expansion. The islands off the coast of Africa were uninhabited, except for the Canaries, which the Portuguese tried unsuccessfully to wrest

from the Spanish. Thus, the Portuguese could not merely establish trading communities within a larger population, for on the Azores and Madeira there was no native population. As a result, by the early 1440s the Portuguese were bringing sheep, seed, and peasants to the hitherto uninhabited Azores and Madeira, and the Crown was forced to grant extensive lordships to nobles to encourage immigration to the Azores. The islanders survived largely by exporting sheep and grain to Iberia.

A significant transformation occurred on Madeira in the 1440s, when the Portuguese introduced sugar cane to the island. Within a decade sugar dominated the island's economy. By 1452, there was a water mill for processing the cane, and in the 1470s sugar revenues from Madeira constituted nearly 2 percent of the Crown's total income.

Sugar production was capital- and labor-intensive. A great many workers were needed to cut the cane, and expensive mills and lengthy processing were needed to extract and to produce sugar. On Madeira most of the work was done by Portuguese peasants. But when the Portuguese extended sugar cultivation to the newly discovered and colonized Cape Verde Islands in the 1460s, they found that Portuguese peasants would not work voluntarily in the sultry equatorial climate. Soon the Portuguese introduced a slave-based plantation system to produce sugar.

Slaves imported from the Black Sea areas had been used in agriculture since the introduction of sugar cultivation into the Mediterranean in the thirteenth century. The Portuguese had been trading in slaves along the western coast of Africa since the late 1440s—the date from which black slaves appear in Lisbon. African slaves along with slaves from the East could be found in Italy and throughout the Mediterranean in the fifteenth century, most often as domestics or laborers in small enterprises. Since Roman times, however, there had been no slave-based industries on the scale of the Portuguese sugar plantations. Sugar production in the New World would be modeled on the slave-based plantation system perfected by the Portuguese in their island colonies in the Atlantic.

The Search for a Sea Route to Asia

Until the middle of the fifteenth century, the Niger Delta remained the focus of Portuguese interest. Only after securing control of the western coast of

Africa through the extension of sugar cultivation to Madeira and the Cape Verdes, developing the gold and slave trade in Senegal, and constructing a fortress to control the Volta River (in modern Ghana) and secure access to most gold-producing areas of West Africa did the Portuguese look seriously at sailing around Africa and discovering a sea route to Asia.

The fifteenth-century sailors who first tried to sail down the coast of Africa faced enormous difficulties. Water and wind currents tend to move in clockwise and counterclockwise circles against which it is difficult for a sail-powered ship to make progress (see Map 13.1). Winds near the equator generally blow from the east, and farther to the north and south the westerlies prevail. In some zones and at certain times there are pockets of stillness with few breezes to propel ships. A navigator had to find winds and currents moving in the direction he wished to travel. Sailing directly to and from a port was virtually impossible.

By the second half of the fifteenth century, Portuguese sailors had learned to tack along a course, searching for favorable winds and currents. Knowledge of winds and currents allowed Bartholomeu Dias (1450?–1500) in 1487 to explore the coast of southern Africa (Map 13.2). He followed the traditional Portuguese routes until southeasterly winds forced him to sail south and west, almost to the Brazilian and Argentine coasts. Then he was able to ride the westerlies well past the southern tip of Africa, where he turned north. On his return he sighted what he called "the Cape of Storms," later renamed "the Cape of Good Hope" by the Portuguese king. Dias had perfected the techniques for searching out currents in the Southern Hemisphere and opened the way to India.

A decade after Dias's return from the Cape of Good Hope, Vasco da Gama (1460?–1524) set sail on a voyage that would take him to Calicut on the western coast of India. Using the information gathered from countless navigators and travelers, da Gama set sail in 1497 with four square-rigged, armed caravels and over 170 men. He had been provided with maps and reports that indicated what he might expect to find along the eastern coast of Africa. He also carried textiles and metal utensils, merchandise of the type usually traded along the western coast of Africa. This was a trade mission and not really a voyage exploring the unknown.

Da Gama followed established routes beyond the Cape of Good Hope and into the Indian Ocean. He traveled up the coast until he reached Malindi in Mozambique, where he hired an Arab pilot who taught him the route to Calicut. Although the goods the Portuguese traders presented were not appropriate for the sophisticated Asian market, da Gama did manage to collect a cargo of Indian spices, which he brought back to Portugal, arriving in 1499. From 1500 until the Portuguese lost their last colonies in the twentieth century (Goa, 1961; Mozambique, 1975), Portugal remained a presence in the Indian Ocean.

The Portuguese in Asia

Trade in the Indian Ocean was nominally controlled by Muslims, but in fact a mixture of ethnic and religious groups—including Muslims, Hindus, and Nestorian Christians—participated in the movement of cottons, silks, and spices throughout the region. The mixture of trade reflected the political situation. Vasco da Gama's arrival coincided with the rise of the Moguls, Muslim descendants of Jenghiz Khan. By 1530, they had gained control of most of northern India and during the sixteenth century, Mogul influence increased in the south. Throughout the sixteenth century the Moguls remained tolerant of the religious, cultural, and economic diversity found in India. Neither Muslim nor Hindu powers initially recognized the threat the Portuguese represented.

The Portuguese probably encountered some hostility, but there is no reason to believe that they could not have joined this complex mixture of traders. Local rulers collected taxes and ensured political control but otherwise left the various ethnic and religious communities to manage their own trade and manufacture. The problem for the Portuguese was that the products they brought from Europe had little value in sophisticated, highly developed Asian markets. In response to this difficult situation, they created a "Trading-Post Empire," an empire based on control of trade rather than on colonization.

Portugal's commercial empire in the East was based on fortified, strategically placed naval bases. As early as Vasco da Gama's second expedition in 1502, Portuguese bombarded Calicut and defeated an Arab fleet off the coast of India. This encounter set the stage for Portugal's most

Albuquerque Defends the Portuguese Empire

In this letter of 1512 to the king of Portugal, Alfonso d' Albuquerque, the governor-general of Portugal's colonies in India, informs the king of conditions in the East, explains his strategy, and defends himself against his critics.

The first time the Muslims entered Goa, we killed one of their captains. They were greatly grieved by the [Portuguese] capture of Goa and there is great fear of Your Highness among them. You must reduce the power of [the Muslim] rulers, take their coastal territories from them and build good fortresses in their principal places. Otherwise you will not be able to set India on the right path and you will always have to have a large body of troops there to keep it pacified. Any alliance which you may agree with one or other Indian king or lord must be secured, Sire, because otherwise you may be certain that, the moment your back is turned, they will at once become your enemies.

What I am describing has now become quite usual among them. In India there is not the same punctiliousness as in Portugal about keeping truth, friendship and trust, for nobody here has any of these qualities. Therefore, Sire, put your faith in good fortresses and order them to be built; gain control over India in time and do not place any confidence in the friendship of the kings and lords of this region because you did not arrive here with a just cause to gain domination of their trade with blandishments and peace treaties. Do not let anybody in Portugal make you think that this is a very hard thing to achieve and that, once achieved, it will place you under great obligation. I tell you this, Sire, because I am still in India and I would like people to sell their property and take part in this enterprise that is so much to your advantage, so great, so lucrative and so valuable. . . .

In a place where there is merchandise to be had and the Muslim traders will not let us have precious stones or spices by fair dealing, and we want to take these foods by force, then we must fight the Muslims for them. . . . If, on the other hand, they see us with a large body of troops, they do us honor, and no thought of deceit or trickery enters their heads. They exchange their goods for ours without fighting and they will abandon the delusion that they will expel us from India.

Source: T. F. Earle and J. Villiers, eds., *Albuquerque: Caesar of the East* (Warminster, England: Aris and Phillips, 1990), p. 109.

important strategist of empire, Alfonso d'Albuquerque (1453–1515), governor-general of Portuguese colonies in India. He convinced the monarchy that the key to dominance in the region was the creation of fortified naval bases designed to permit the Portuguese to dominate the Bay of Bengal and thereby control access to the spices in the Spice Islands. (See the box, "Albuquerque Defends the Portuguese Empire.") By 1510, Albuquerque had captured Goa (on the Indian coast south of Bombay) and Hormuz (controlling access to the Persian Gulf). Later he conquered the sultanate of Malacca on the Malay Peninsula, winning control of the straits that run from the Bay of Bengal to the Spice Islands. By 1600, the Portuguese had created a network of naval bases that reached from Mozambique and Mombasa on the eastern coast of Africa to Goa on the western coast of India and to the island of Macao off the southeastern coast of China (see Map 13.2).

The Portuguese established a royal trading firm, the Casa da India, to control the trade in

Map 13.2 World Exploration The voyages of Columbus, da Gama, and Magellan charted the major sea-lanes that became essential for communication, trade, and warfare for the next three hundred years.

Portuguese in India This watercolor by a Portuguese traveler shows the varied people and customs and the great wealth to be found in India. Europeans were fascinated by all that seemed different from their own world. *(Biblioteca Casanatense)*

cinnamon, ginger, cloves, mace, and a variety of peppers. Although their control was far from total, the Portuguese did become significant exporters of spices to Europe. More significant was the creation of the Portuguese Estado da India, or India office, to control Portuguese naval forces, administer ports, and regulate maritime trade. Under the Portuguese system all merchants were expected to acquire export licenses and to ship products through Portuguese ports.

Both the casa and the estado depended on naval power for their influence. Local boats were no match for the well-built Portuguese ships armed with cannon. Although the Portuguese navy was too small to enforce a complete blockade of clandestine trade, the Portuguese did manage to change the patterns of commerce in the area. Many Asians found it convenient to pay for export licenses and to trade through Portuguese ports. They even found it convenient to ship in European-style vessels and to use Portuguese as the language of commerce.

SPANISH VOYAGES OF DISCOVERY, 1492–1522

As early as 1479 the Spanish kingdoms had agreed to leave the exploration and colonization of the African coast to the Portuguese, yet they watched nervously as the Portuguese expanded their African contacts. The Castilians concentrated their efforts on what came to be called the "Enterprise of the Indies."

The sailing and exploration necessary to compete with the Portuguese produced critical information about winds and currents around the world and facilitated later voyages. They also established the basic approaches that the Spanish would follow in their exploration, conquest, and colonization of the lands to which they came.

The Role of Columbus

The story of the enterprise begins with Christopher Columbus (1451–1506), a brilliant seaman, courtier, and self-promoter who has become a symbol of European expansion. During the nineteenth century, patriots of the newly created United States of America celebrated Columbus as proof that the discovery and development of North America was not dependent on the British. By the early twentieth century, Italian immigrants to North America regarded him as a symbol of Italy's important role in the history of the Americas. And finally, modern historians have celebrated Columbus as one of the great men of the Renaissance who managed to break with medieval myth and superstition. The voyages of Columbus, they have argued, shattered the isolation and parochial vision of the Europeans. Columbus, however, was not a "Renaissance man" of vision, the harbinger of a new, more rational world. And he certainly was not a bold pioneer who fearlessly did what no others could conceive of doing.

Columbus was born into a modest family in Genoa and spent his early years in travel and in the service of the Castilian and Portuguese crowns. He apparently first put his plans to sail west to Asia before King John II (r. 1481–1495) of Portugal. Only after Portuguese rejection did he approach the Spanish monarchs, Ferdinand and Isabella. His vision seems to have been thoroughly traditional and medieval. Studying information in *Imago Mundi* (*Image of the World*, 1410), by the French philosopher Pierre d'Ailly (1350–1420), he convinced himself that the distance between the coast of Europe and Asia was much less than it actually is. Pierre d'Ailly had estimated that water covered only about one-quarter of the globe. This estimate put the east coast of Asia within easy reach of the western edge of Europe. "This sea is navigable in a few days if the wind is favorable," was d'Ailly's conclusion.

D'Ailly's theories seemed to be confirmed by the work of the Florentine mathematician Paolo Toscanelli (see page 480). Columbus knew of Toscanelli's calculations and even revised them downward. From his own reading of an apocryphal book of the Bible (Esdras 6:42) that reported that only one-seventh of the world was covered with water, Columbus concluded that the distance from the west coast of Europe to the east coast of Asia was about 5000 miles instead of the actual 12,000. Columbus's reading of traditional sources put Japan in the approximate location of the Virgin Islands. (It is not surprising that Columbus remained convinced that the Bahamas were islands just off the coast of Asia.)

Like Marco Polo before him, Columbus expected to find the marvels reported in the classical sources. In his own journals he recorded reports of islands where women avoided domestic responsibilities and instead hunted with bow and arrow. And he interpreted what he was told in the context of his assumptions. When Amerindians told him of Cuba, he concluded that it "must be Japan according to the indications that these people give of its size and wealth."[2] And on the basis of first-century descriptions, he assured Spanish authori-

OVERSEAS EXPLORATION AND CONQUEST

ca. 1350	The Madeira and Canary Islands are charted
ca. 1400	The Azores are charted
1444	Cape Verde Islands are discovered by Prince Henry the Navigator
1487	Dias is the first European to sail around the Cape of Good Hope
1492	Columbus sails from Spain and discovers the New World
1494	Treaty of Tordesillas
1497	Da Gama sails around the Cape of Good Hope and arrives in India; Cabot sights Newfoundland
1501	Vespucci sails along the coast of Brazil and concludes that Columbus had discovered a new continent
1507	Waldseemüller issues the first map showing "America"
1510	Portuguese capture Goa
1513	Balboa crosses the Isthmus of Panama and is the first European to see the Pacific Ocean
1519–1522	Magellan's expedition sails around the world from east to west
1519–1523	Cortés lands in Mexico, conquers the Aztecs, and destroys Tenochtitlán
1533	Pizarro conquers Cuzco, the Incas' capital
1534	Cartier discovers the St. Lawrence River
1542	Charles V issues the New Laws
1545	The Spanish discover the silver mines at Potosí

ties that King Solomon's mines were only a short distance west of his newly discovered islands. In addition to finding the gold of Solomon, Columbus also expected that by sailing west he could fulfill a series of medieval prophecies that would lead to the conversion of the whole world to Christianity. This conversion, he believed, would shortly precede the second coming of Christ. In Columbus's own view, then, his voyages were epochal not because they were ushering in a newer, more empirical world but because they signaled the completion of the long history of the creation and redemption.

Columbus's enthusiasm for the venture was only partially shared by Ferdinand and Isabella. Vasco da Gama was well supplied with large ships and a crew of over 170 men, but Columbus sailed in 1492 with three small ships and a crew of 90. Da Gama carried extra supplies and materials for trade and letters for the rulers he knew he would meet. Columbus had nothing similar. His commission did authorize him as "Admiral of Spain" to take possession of all he should find, but royal expectations do not seem to have been great.

After a stop in the Canary Islands, the small fleet sailed west. Columbus assumed that he would find the islands of Japan after sailing about 3000 miles. On October 12, about ten days later than he had calculated, he reached landfall on what he believed were small islands in the Japanese chain. He had actually landed in the Bahamas

(see Map 13.2). Because Columbus announced to the world he had arrived in the Indies, the indigenous populations have since been called "Indians" and the islands are called the "West Indies." (See the box, "Christopher Columbus Describes His Discoveries.")

Columbus returned to the New World three more times—in 1493, 1498, and 1502—exploring extensively in the Bahamas and along the coast of Panama and Venezuela, 800 miles to the south and east of the island of Hispaniola. The enthusiasm his discoveries raised was evident on his second voyage. He oversaw a fleet of seventeen ships with 1500 sailors, churchmen, and adventurers. And Columbus's initial rewards were great. He was granted a hereditary title, a governorship of the new lands, and one-tenth of all the wealth he had discovered.

Columbus reported to the Spanish monarchs that the "Indians" on the islands were friendly and open to the new arrivals. He described simple, naked people, eager, he believed, to learn of Christianity and European ways. The Taínos, or Arawaks, whom he had misidentified, did live

Cosa's Columbian Map Juan de la Cosa traveled with Columbus. His map of 1500 shows what was known of the New World and how it was connected to the Old. The western portions seem to be as accurate as he could make them; the east still holds traditional images such as the three kings. (*Museo Naval de Madrid*)

Christopher Columbus Describes His Discoveries

Columbus's hopes for wealth and titles for himself depended on getting and maintaining the goodwill of Ferdinand and Isabella. After each of his voyages he emphasized his accomplishments and their potential to enrich the Spanish monarchs. Columbus wrote this letter toward the conclusion of the first voyage, which he believed might secure his rights to lordship over all the new territories he found. He took pains to make clear that what he had found was what one would expect to find on the edge of Asia. In that respect this document deserves to be compared to the later observations of Friar Bernardino de Sahagún on page 503.

In conclusion, to speak only of what has been accomplished on this voyage, which was so hasty, their highnesses can see that I give them as much gold as they may need, if their highnesses will render me very slight assistance; moreover, spice and cotton, as much as their highnesses shall command; and mastic [yellow resin necessary for various adhesives], as much as they shall order to be shipped and which, up to now, has been found only in Greece, in the island of Chios, and the Seignory [of Venice] sells it for what it pleases; and also wood, as much as they shall order to be shipped, and slaves, as many as they shall order to be shipped and who will be from the idolaters. And I believe that I have found rhubarb and cinnamon [both were considered essential for medicine], and I shall find a thousand other things of value, which people I have left here will have discovered, for I have not delayed at any point . . . and in truth I shall have done more, if the ships had served me as reason demanded.

Source: C. Columbus, A. Bernáldez, et al., eds., *The Voyages of Christopher Columbus*, part 1 (London: Argonaut Press, 1930), p. 16.

simple, uncomplicated lives. The islands easily produced sweet potatoes, maize, beans, and squash, which along with fish provided an abundant diet. Initially these peoples shared their food and knowledge with the newcomers, who they seem to have thought were sky-visitors.

The Spanish, for their part, praised this smiling and happy people. Visitors commonly believed they had discovered a simple, virtuous people who, if converted, would be exemplars of Christian virtues to the Europeans. Columbus himself observed that

they are very gentle and do not know what evil is; nor do they kill others, nor steal; and they are without weapons. . . . They say very quickly any prayer that we tell them to say, and they make the sign of the cross, †. So your Highnesses ought to resolve to make them Christians.[3]

The Spanish authorities changed their opinion quickly. The settlers Columbus left at his fortress set an unfortunate example. They seized foodstocks, kidnapped women, and embarked on a frenzied search for gold. Those who did not kill one another were killed by the Taínos.

During succeeding voyages, Columbus struggled to make his discoveries the financial windfall he had promised the monarchs. He was unable to administer this vast new land. He quickly lost control of the colonists and was forced to allow the vicious exploitation of the island population. He and other Spanish settlers claimed larger and larger portions of the land and required the Indians to work it. Islands that easily supported a population of perhaps a million natives could not support those indigenous peoples and the Spanish newcomers and still provide exports to Spain. Largely because of diseases (see page 501), scholars have estimated that the native population of the islands may have fallen to little more than 30,000 by 1520. By the middle of the sixteenth century, the native population had virtually disappeared.

Columbus remained convinced that he would find vast fortunes just over the horizon. But he found neither the great quantities of gold he promised nor a sea passage to Asia. Even in the face of mounting evidence to the contrary, Columbus maintained that Asia must be just beyond the lands he was exploring. With the islands in revolt and his explorations seemingly going nowhere, the Spanish monarchs stripped Columbus of his titles and commands. Once he was returned to Spain in chains. After his final trip he maintained that he had finally found either the Ganges River of India or one of the rivers that flow out of the earthly paradise. Although Columbus died in 1506, rich and honored for his discoveries, he never gained all the power and wealth he had expected. He remained frustrated and embittered by the Crown's refusal to support one more voyage during which he expected to find the mainland of Asia.

In 1501, after sailing along the coast of Brazil, the Florentine geographer Amerigo Vespucci (1451–1512) drew the obvious conclusion from the information collected by Columbus's explorations. He argued that Columbus had discovered a new continent unknown to the classical world. These claims were accepted by the German mapmaker Martin Waldseemüller, who in 1507 honored Amerigo's claim by publishing the first map showing "America."

Columbus's Successors

Columbus's discoveries set off a debate over which nations had the right to be involved in trade and exploration. Portuguese claims were based on a papal bull of 1481, issued by Pope Sixtus IV (r. 1471–1484), that granted Portugal rights to discoveries south of the Canaries and west of Africa. After Columbus's return, the Spaniards lobbied one of Sixtus's successors, Alexander VI (r. 1492–1503), whose family, the Borgias, was from the kingdom of Aragon. In a series of bulls, Pope Alexander allowed the Spanish to claim all lands lying 400 miles or more west of the Azores. Finally, in the Treaty of Tordesillas (1494), Spain and Portugal agreed that the line of demarcation between their two areas should be drawn 1480 miles west of the Azores. The treaty was signed just six years before Petro Alvares Cabral (1467–1520) discovered the coast of Brazil. Thus the Spanish unwittingly granted the Portuguese rights to Brazil.

Adventurers and explorers worried little about the legality of exploration. Even as Columbus lay dying in 1506, others, some without royal permission, sailed up and down the eastern coasts of North and South America. Amerigo Vespucci traveled on Spanish vessels as far as Argentina, while Spanish explorers sailed among the islands of the Caribbean and along the coast of the Yucatán Peninsula. Vasco Nuñez de Balboa crossed the Isthmus of Panama in 1513 and found the Pacific Ocean where the natives living in the region said it would be.

The most important of the explorations that Columbus inspired was the voyage undertaken by Ferdinand Magellan in 1519 (see Map 13.2). Although his motives are unclear, Magellan (1480?–1521) may have planned to complete Columbus's dream of sailing to the Indies. By the 1510s mariners and others understood that the Americas were a new and hitherto unknown land, but they did not know what lay beyond them or what the distance was from the Americas to the Spice Islands of Asia. After sailing along the well-known coastal regions of South America, Magellan continued south, charting currents and looking for a passage into the Pacific. Early in 1520 he made the passage through the dangerous straits (now the Strait of Magellan) separating Tierra del Fuego from the mainland. The turbulent waters of the straits marked the boundary of the Atlantic and the Pacific Oceans. Once into the Pacific, Magellan sailed north and west to escape the cold and to find winds and currents that would allow him to continue to Asia. It took almost four months to travel from the straits to the Philippines. During that time, a crew member reported, "We ate biscuit, which was no longer biscuit, but powder of biscuit swarming with worms, for they had eaten the good."[4] The crew suffered greatly from scurvy and a shortage of water and at times had to eat the rats aboard ship to survive. Nevertheless, Magellan managed to reach the Philippines by March 1521. A month later, he was killed by natives.

Spanish survivors in two remaining ships continued west, reaching the Moluccas, where they traded merchandise that they had carried along for a small cargo of cloves. The Portuguese captured one of the ships as it tried to return to the Americas. The other proceeded on through the Indian Ocean, avoiding Portuguese patrols. It continued around Africa and back to Spain, landing with a crew of 15 at Cádiz in September 1522 after a voyage of three years and the loss of four ships and 245 men. No cargo of spices could have been worth the sacrifices. But the significance of the voyage was not the spices but the route established from South America to the Spice Islands. Further, Magellan completed and confirmed the knowledge of wind and ocean currents that European sailors had been accumulating. One of his sailors wrote of him: "More accurately than any man in the world did he understand sea charts and navigation."[5] The way was open for the vast movement of Europeans and European culture into all parts of the world.

Spanish adventurers were not the only ones to follow in Columbus's wake. The French and the English, however, concentrated their explorations further to the north. Building on a tradition of fishing off the coast of Newfoundland, English sailors under the command of John Cabot (1450?–1499?) sighted Newfoundland in 1497, and later voyages explored the coast as far south as New England. Cabot initiated an intense period of English exploration that would lead to an unsuccessful attempt to found a colony on Roanoke Island in 1587 and eventually to permanent settlement at Jamestown in 1607. French explorers followed Cabot to the north. In 1534, Jacques Cartier (1491–1557) received a royal commission to look for a passage to the East. He discovered the St. Lawrence River and began the process of exploration and trading that would lead to permanent settlements in Canada beginning in the early seventeenth century. But British and French settlements in the New World came later. The sixteenth century belonged to the Spanish.

Spanish penetration of the New World was not simply built on the model of the Portuguese in Asia. The Spaniards established no complex network of trade and commerce, and no strong states opposed their interests. A "Trading-Post Empire" could not have worked in the New World. To succeed, the Spaniards needed to colonize and reorganize the lands they had discovered.

SPAIN'S COLONIAL EMPIRE, 1492–1600

Between 1492 and 1600, almost 200,000 Spaniards immigrated to the New World. New Spain, as they called these newly claimed lands, was neither the old society transported across the ocean nor Amerindian society with a thin patina of Spanish and European culture. To understand the history of New Spain, we will discuss the two major civilizations the Spaniards overthrew, the conquests themselves, and the institutions the Spaniards created in the wake of conquest. We will also discuss the attempts by many of the Spanish to secure fair treatment of the indigenous peoples who had been made part of the Spanish Empire.

The Americas Before the European Invasion

The Spaniards and later their European peers entered a world vastly different from their own. It was a world formed by two momentous events. The first was the creation of the continents of North and South America. North and South America, along with Africa and the Eurasian landmass, were once part of a single supercontinent. The breakup of this supercontinent left the Americas, Africa, and Eurasia free to evolve in dramatically different ways. From one continent to another, the differences in plants and animals were so dramatic that one eighteenth-century naturalist confessed, "I was seized with terror at the thought of ranging to many new and unknown parts of natural history."[6] The continental breakup occurred millions of years ago, long before the appearance of human beings and many other forms of mammalian life.

The second momentous event was the temporary rejoining of the Americas to the Eurasian landmass by land and ice bridges that allowed Asians to cross over the Bering Strait to the Americas in the period between 30,000 and 10,000 B.C. Their arrival and its timing were important for two reasons. These hunter-gatherers seem to have played a significant role in the extinction of several large mammals—mastodons, mammoths, giant buffalo, and even early camels and horses. No easily domesticable large animals remained on the continent. These peoples also arrived in the Americas long before the beginnings of the Neolithic agricultural revolution, which involved the domestication of numerous plants and animals. The agricultural revolution in the Americas occurred around 3000 B.C., perhaps six thousand years after similar developments in the Old World (see page 7). The peoples of the Americas created complex societies, but those societies lacked large domesticated meat or pack animals (the llama was the largest), iron and other hard metals, and the wheel.

By the time of Columbus's arrival, relatively populous societies were living throughout North and South America. Population estimates for the two continents range from 30 million to 100 million—the lower figure is probably more correct. There were complex mound-builder societies in eastern North America and along the Mississippi River and pueblo societies in the deserts of the American Southwest, but the greatest centers of Amerindian civilization were in central and coastal Mexico and in the mountains of Peru.

In the late fifteenth century the two most powerful centers were the empires of the Aztecs and the Incas. When the collection of tribes now known as the "Aztec" (or Mexican) peoples appeared in central Mexico in the early fourteenth century, they found a flourishing civilization centered on the

cities and towns dotting the Valley of Mexico. Through conquest, the Aztecs united the many Nahuatl-speaking groups living in the valley into a confederation centered on the Aztec capital of Tenochtitlán, a city of perhaps 200,000 people built on an island in Lake Texcoco (Map 13.3). In early-sixteenth-century Europe, only London, Constantinople, and Naples would have been as large as the Aztec capital. The Spanish conqueror Hernán Cortés (see pages 494–497) described Aztec cities "that seemed like an enchanted vision" and that literally rose out of the water of Lake Texcoco. Only Venice could have equaled the sight. The whole valley supported an unusually high population of about a million, fed by farmers who raised a wide variety of crops on farms carefully formed beside canals and in the marshes on the edge of Lake Texcoco. Using canals along the edge of the lake and other canals in Tenochtitlán itself, mer-

Tenochtitlán The Aztec capital was built on an island. Its central temples and markets were connected to the rest of the city and the suburbs on the lake shore by numerous canals. The city and its surrounding market gardens seemed to the Spanish to be floating on water. *(The Newberry Library, Chicago)*

Map 13.3 Mexico and Central America The Valley of Mexico was a populous region of scattered towns, most of which were part of the Aztec Empire. As Cortés marched inland from Vera Cruz toward the valley, he passed through lands that had been in an almost constant state of war with the Aztecs.

chants easily moved food, textiles, gold and silver ornaments, jewels, and ceremonial feathered capes into the city markets. Spaniards later estimated that 50,000 or more people shopped in the city on market days.

Religion was integral to the Aztecs' understanding of their empire. They believed that the world was finite and that they lived in the last of five empires. It was only continued human sacrifice to Huitzilopochtli that allowed the world to continue. The Aztecs believed that the hearts of sacrificial victims were necessary to sustain their god, to ensure that the sun would rise again each morning. Thus, the Aztecs believed that their continued sacrifice to their god was essential for the continuation of life.

Tenochtitlán was the center of an imperial culture based on tribute. Towns and villages under Aztec control paid tribute in food and precious metals. To emphasize that Aztec power and dominance were complete, the Aztecs not only collected vast quantities of maize, beans, squash, and textiles but demanded tribute in everything down to centipedes and snakes. The most chilling tribute, however, was in humans for sacrifice. When there were no longer wars of expansion to provide prisoners, the Aztecs and their neighbors fought "flower wars"—highly ritualized battles to provide prisoners to be sacrificed. Five thousand victims were sacrificed at the coronation of Moctezuma II (r. 1502–1520) in 1502. Even more, reportedly twenty thousand, were sacrificed at the dedication of the great temple of Huitzilopochtli in Tenochtitlán.

Aztec society was a warrior society that maintained a perpetual state of war with the peoples beyond the mountains that ringed the Valley of Mexico—especially the people along the Caribbean

Map 13.4 Peru and Central America The Inca Empire was accessible to the Spaniards only by sea. Spanish exploration and domination brought the destruction of Inca mountain citadels and the transfer of administrative power to the new Spanish city of Lima on the coast.

coast. Given this state of war, plus the heavy burdens in tribute placed on the nearby subject cities, it is no small wonder that the Aztecs were obsessed by the contingencies of life. At the end of each calendar cycle of fifty-two years, all fires in the empire were extinguished until fire-priests ascertained that the world would continue. And the Aztec world did continue until August 1523 (see page 497).

The other great Amerindian empire of the fifteenth century, the empire of the Incas, was also of recent origin. During the fifteenth century the Incas formed efficient armies and expanded their control beyond the central highlands of Peru. Fifteen thousand miles of road and a sophisticated administrative system allowed the Incas to create a state that extended from Ecuador to Chile (Map

13.4). As they expanded, they demanded political control and tribute but seem to have been tolerant of local traditions and language. The Incas perfected systems of irrigation and bridge-building initiated by earlier inhabitants of the region. The empire, centered on the city of Cuzco high in the mountains of Peru, was able to sustain a population that may have reached 10 million by the end of the fifteenth century. (See the box, "Encounters with the West: An Inca Nobleman Defends His Civilization.")

Human sacrifice, though not unknown to the Incas, was not an essential part of their religious life. Their state was unsettled, however, by increasingly harsh tax exactions. Under the Inca system, the title Paca Inca, or "Great Inca," was inherited by the eldest son of the ruler's principal wife. The ruler's wealth, however, was retained by the rest of his family, who maintained the court as if the ruler still lived. Thus, each new ruler needed money to finance the creation of an entirely new court, and taxes were not only high but continuously increasing.

Both great Amerindian empires, despite their brilliance, rested on uneasy conquests. Subject groups would be willing allies for any invader.

The Spanish Conquests

Hernán Cortés (1485–1546) was ambitious to make something of himself in the New World. Of a poor but aristocratic background from the Extremadura region of southwest Spain, he had gone to the West Indies in 1504 to seek his fortune in the service of the governor of Cuba. The governor gave him a commission to lead an expeditionary force to investigate reports of a wealthy and prosperous Indian civilization. From the very beginning, Spanish authorities seem to have distrusted his aims. He was forced to depart hastily from Cuba to evade formal notification that the governor of Cuba had revoked his commission because of insubordination.

Cortés landed in Mexico at the site of the city he would name Vera Cruz ("True Cross") early in 1519 with a tiny command of 500 men, 16 horses, 11 ships, and some artillery. Aided by a devastating outbreak of smallpox and Amerindian peoples happy to overthrow Aztec control, Cortés and his troops managed to destroy the network of city-states dominated by the Aztecs of Tenochtitlán in

~ **ENCOUNTERS WITH THE WEST** ~

An Inca Nobleman Defends His Civilization

Huamán Poma was born into a noble Inca family with a long history of service first to the Inca kings and later to the Spanish administrators. Although Huamán Poma became a Christian and adapted to Spanish rule, he wrote this letter to the king of Spain in 1613 explaining the great merits of the Inca civilization that he feared would be lost. In the excerpt included here, he describes the Inca understanding of the origins of the world. His "traditional world" is, however, one heavily influenced by his new Christian faith.

The first white people in the world were brought by God to this country. They were descended from those who survived the flood in Noah's Ark. It is said that they were born in pairs, male and female, and therefore they multiplied rapidly.

These people were incapable of useful work. They could not make proper clothes so they wore garments of leaves and straw. Not knowing how to build houses, they lived in caves and under rocks. They worshipped God with a constant outpouring of sound like the twitter of birds, saying: "Lord how long shall I cry and not be heard?" . . .

In their turn these first people were succeeded by the two castes: the great lords, who were the ancestors of our Incas, and the common people, who were descended from bastards and multiplied rapidly in number.

However barbarous they may have been, our ancestors had some glimmer of understanding of God. Even the mere saying of [God's name] is a sign of faith and an important step forward. Christians have much to learn from our people's good way of life. . . .

Their usual diet consisted of maize, potatoes and other tubers; cress, sorrel, and lupin; pond-weed, laver and a grass with yellow flowers; leaves for chewing; mushrooms, edible grubs, shells, shrimps, crab and various sorts of fish. . . . The burial of the dead was conducted with dignity, but without undue ceremony in vaults constructed for the purpose. There were separate vaults, which were whitewashed and painted, for people of high rank. The Indians believed that after death they would have to endure hard labor, torture, hunger, thirst and fire. Thus they had their own conception of Hell, which they called the place under the earth or the abode of demons.

Source: Huamán Poma, *Letter to a King: A Picture History of the Inca Civilization* (New York: E. P. Dutton, 1978), pp. 24–25, 30.

two years and lay claim to the Valley of Mexico for the king of Spain. The manner in which Cortés explained and justified his mission can serve as a model against which to measure the adventures of other sixteenth-century Europeans in the Americas.

Cortés, like Machiavelli, believed in the power of truly able leaders (men of virtú) to overcome chance through bold acts. Even so, an attempt to capture a city of 200,000 with an army of 500 seems more foolhardy than bold. Cortés seems to have attempted it simply because he found himself with

very little choice. With his commission revoked by the governor of Cuba, Cortés arrived on the mainland as a rebel against both the governor of Cuba and the king of Spain. Much of what he did and said concerning the great Aztec Empire was an attempt to justify his initial act of insubordination and win back royal support. Cortés burned his ships so that his troops were forced to go with him. Then he founded the city of Vera Cruz, whose town government, which was his own creation, offered him a new commission to proceed inland to

Cortés and Doña Marina
Doña Marina was the critical mediator in gathering Amerindian allies and negotiating with local leaders. In this illustration from a sixteenth-century codex, Cortés—shown with Doña Marina and his army, which includes Amerindian allies—is greeted by local leaders during the march to Tenochtitlán. *(Trans. no. V/C 31(2). Courtesy Department of Library Sciences, American Museum of Natural History)*

Tenochtitlán. He quickly found allies among native groups that for their own reasons wished to see the Aztec Empire destroyed. The allied forces moved toward Tenochtitlán.

Cortés was greatly aided by fortune in the form of Malintzin, a Mexican woman who after her conversion called herself Doña Marina (ca. 1501–1550). Malintzin was Cortés's interpreter and, later, his mistress. Without her, one of Cortés's followers recalled, "We could not have understood the language of New Spain and Mexico." Her story illustrates many of the complex interactions at play in sixteenth-century Mexico. Born an Aztec, she was given away, ending up in the hands of Mayans, who gave her, along with twenty other women, to Cortés. Knowing the languages of the Mayans and Mexicans, and quickly learning Spanish, she was the one person who could mediate between Spaniard and native. She became Christian and after bearing Cortés a son, she finished her life in Spain as the wife of a Span-

ish gentleman. Like many of the natives who felt no affection for the Aztecs of Tenochtitlán, she did not find it difficult to aid the Spaniard.

Despite the help of Malintzin and Spaniards who had previously lived with the natives, the meeting of Aztecs and Spaniards demonstrated the breadth of the chasm separating the Old World and the New as well as the difficulty the one had in understanding the other. At first the Aztec king Moctezuma was unconcerned about the coming of the Spaniards. Later he seems to have attempted to buy them off. And finally he and his successors fought desperately to drive them out of Tenochtitlán. The Aztecs' indecision was caused in large part by the fact that in neither words nor gestures did the two groups speak the same language. Hearing that the Spaniards were marching toward Tenochtitlán, Moctezuma sent ambassadors bearing gold, silver, and other costly gifts, which they presented in a most humble fashion to the Spaniards. To a modern ear the gifts sound like (and have often been interpreted to be) desperate attempts to buy off the invaders. To Cortés, or any European or Asian resident of the Old World, such gifts were a sign of submission. But to Moctezuma and most Amerindians, the giving of gifts with great humility by otherwise powerful and proud people could be a sign of wealth and status. Seen in that light, Moctezuma's lavish gifts and apparent humility probably demonstrated to the Aztecs' own satisfaction the superiority of their civilization, and Cortés's acceptance of the gifts seemed to indicate his recognition of his own inferior status.

Spaniards later claimed that Moctezuma was confounded by the sudden appearance of these peoples from the East. Cortés reported to the king of Spain that when he first met Moctezuma, the Aztec leader said, "We have always held that those who descended from [the god Quetzalcoatl] would come and conquer this land and take us as his vassals." Later Spaniards explained that the Aztecs believed that Quetzalcoatl, the serpent-god symbolically conquered by Huitzilopochtli, had traveled to the East, promising one day to return and reclaim his lands, thus ending Aztec rule. The Spaniards believed that Moctezuma had been so ambivalent toward them because of his belief in that myth.

There seems, however, to be little truth in either of those stories. Cortés was simply attempting to justify his conquest. There is no surviving pre-conquest source for Moctezuma's supposed confession, and the myth of the return of Quetzalcoatl was first recorded in Spanish, not Indian, sources long after the conquest. In truth, neither Cortés nor historians can satisfactorily explain in Western terms Moctezuma's initial response to the Spaniards. Cortés took the Aztec leader captive in 1521 and began what would be a two-year battle to take control of the city and its empire. Although weakened by the arrival of virulent Old World diseases, the Aztecs continued to fight even as more and more of the subject peoples joined the Spanish forces. The Spaniards cut off food and water to the capital, but still the Aztecs fought.

Different understandings of the rules of war, different traditions of diplomacy, and different cultures prevented the Aztecs and Cortés from reaching any understanding. The peoples of the Valley of Mexico tried to take captives to be sacrificed in temples. The Spaniards, to Aztec eyes, killed indiscriminately and needlessly on the bat-

tlefield. Cortés later complained of the Aztecs' refusal to negotiate: "We showed them more signs of peace than have ever been shown to a vanquished people." Thus, to end a war that neither side could resolve in any other way, in August 1523 Cortés and his allies completely destroyed Tenochtitlán.

Cortés's insubordination was a model for other adventurers. His own lieutenants later rebelled against his control and attempted to create their own governments as they searched for riches and Eldorado, a mythical city of gold. Later adventurers marched throughout the North American Southwest and Central and South America following rumors of hidden riches. Using private armies and torturing native peoples, veterans of Cortés's army and newly arrived speculators hoped to find wealth that would allow them to live like nobles on their return to Spain. Like

Aztec Warrior This watercolor, by a Mexican artist who was trained in European painting, depicts a pre-Aztec ruler. But the dress and the stone-edged sword would have been typical of the Aztecs, too. *(Bibliothèque Nationale)*

Cortés, they claimed that they were acting for the monarchy and for Christianity, but in fact they expected that success would justify their most vicious acts.

Francisco Pizarro (1470–1541) was the most successful of the private adventurers. Poor, illegitimate at birth, he arrived in the Americas ambitious for riches and power. After serving in Balboa's army, participating in several slaving expeditions, and helping to found Panama City, Pizarro was prosperous but still not wealthy. Rumors of Inca wealth filtered through to Central America. Pizarro and a partner resolved in 1530 to lead an expedition down the west coast of South America in search of the Inca capital. Benefiting from disorganization caused by a smallpox epidemic and ensuing civil war, Pizarro was able to find local allies. Like Cortés, he used numerous Indian allies in his most important battles. Aided by Amerindians eager to throw off Inca domination, he captured and executed the Paca Inca and conquered the capital of Cuzco by 1533. He later built a new capital on the coast at Lima (see Map 13.4) from where he worked to extend his control over all of the old Inca Empire. Pizarro and his Spanish partners seized vast amounts of gold and silver from the Incas. The Spanish eventually discovered silver mines at Potosí, which would be a critical source of revenue for the Spanish monarchy. Resistance to Spanish rule continued into the 1570s, when the last of the independent Inca strongholds was finally destroyed.

Colonial Organization

The Spanish crown needed to create a colonial government that could control the actions of the numerous adventurers and create an orderly economy. Although the Spaniards proclaimed that they would "give to those strange lands the form of our own [land]," the resulting political and economic organization of the new Spanish possessions was a curious mixture of the Old World and the New.

The head of the administration was the monarchy. As early as the reigns of Ferdinand and Isabella, Spanish monarchs had tried to curb the excesses of the explorers and conquerors who traveled in their name. Isabella initially opposed the enslavement of Amerindians and any slave trade in the new lands. Further, they promoted a broad-

based debate about the rights of Amerindians and the nature of religious conversion. Royal influence, however, was limited by the sheer distance between the court and the new provinces. It could easily take two years for a royal response to a question to arrive at its destination. Things moved so slowly that as one viceroy ruefully noted, "If death came from Madrid, we should all live to a very old age." Given the difficulties of communication, the powers of local administrators had to be very broad.

By 1535, Spanish colonial administration was firmly established in the form it would retain for the next two hundred years. The king created a Council of the Indies located at court, eventually in Madrid, which saw to all legal and administrative issues pertaining to the new possessions. The new territories themselves were eventually divided into the viceroyalty of Mexico (primarily Central America and part of Venezuela) and the viceroyalty of Peru.

In Spain, Castilian conquerors completely dominated newly won lands, but in New Spain, royal administrators created Indian municipalities, or districts, in which Spaniards had no formal right to live or work. Government in these municipalities remained largely in the hands of preconquest native elites. Throughout the sixteenth century, official documents in these communities continued to be written in Nahuatl, the Aztec language. As long as taxes or tribute was paid and missionaries were allowed to circulate, the Spanish government tolerated considerable autonomy in the Indian municipalities.

The problem that most plagued the government was the conquerors' desire for laborers to work on the lands and in the mines that they had seized. From Columbus's first visit, the Spanish adopted a system of forced labor developed in Spain. A colonist called an *encomendero* was offered a grant, or *encomienda*, of a certain number of people or tribes who were required to work under his direction. In theory, the encomendero was to be a protector of the conquered peoples, someone who would Christianize and civilize them. In theory, Indians who voluntarily agreed to listen to missionaries or to convert to Christianity could not be put under the control of an encomendero. If they refused, however, the Spaniards believed they had the right of conquest. In fact, the conquerors assumed that they were entitled to encomiendas. Cortés himself claimed 115,000 people in Mexico, and Pizarro claimed 20,000 in Peru. In many areas encomenderos simply collected the traditional payments that the pre-conquest elites had claimed. In cases where the subject peoples were forced into mining districts, however, the conditions were brutal.

The pressures exerted by the encomenderos were worsened by the precipitous fall in the indigenous population. Old World diseases such as smallpox and measles swept through populations with no previous exposure to them (see page 501). In central Mexico, where we know most about population movements, the pre-conquest population was at least 10 or 12 million and may have been twice that. By the mid-sixteenth century, the native population may have fallen to just over 6 million, and it probably declined to less than 1 million early in the seventeenth century before beginning to grow again.

A large population was essential to the Spanish and the Portuguese when they introduced the Old World plantation system to the New World. The Caribbean islands and Brazil were ideal for the production of sugar—a commercial crop in great demand throughout Europe. At first, plantations and mines were worked by Amerindians, but when their numbers declined, the Spanish and Portuguese imported large numbers of slaves from Africa.

Africans had participated in the initial stages of the conquest. Some had lived in Spain and become Christian; indeed, Amerindians called them "black whitemen." Most Africans, however, were enslaved laborers. African slaves were in Cuba by 1518; they labored in the mines of Honduras by the 1540s. After the 1560s the Portuguese began importing large numbers of African slaves into Brazil to work on the sugar plantations. It has been estimated that 62,500 slaves were imported into Spanish America and 50,000 into Brazil during the sixteenth century. By 1810, when the movement to abolish the slave trade began to grow, almost 10 million Africans had been involuntarily transported to the New World.

The conquerors had hoped to find vast quantities of wealth that they could take back to the Old World. In the viceroyalty of Mexico the search for Eldorado remained unsuccessful. The discovery in 1545 of the silver mines at Potosí in Peru, however, fulfilled the Spaniards' wildest dreams.

Between 1550 and 1650, the Spanish probably sent back to Spain 181 tons of gold and 16,000 tons of silver, one-fifth of which was paid directly into the royal treasury. The tonnage of precious metals seemed so great to the French scholar Jean Bodin (see page 581) that he held this infusion of wealth responsible for the great inflation that was disrupting the European economy in the late sixteenth century. Bodin overestimated the European-wide impact of the precious metals, but they did represent one-quarter of the income of King Philip II of Spain in the 1560s and made him the richest monarch in Europe.

The Debate over Indian Rights

To most conquerors the opportunities for wealth and power need little justification, but the more thoughtful among the Spaniards were uneasy. "Tell me," demanded Friar Antonio Montesinos in 1511, "by what right or justice do you hold these Indians in such cruel and horrible slavery? By what right do you wage such detestable wars on these people who lived idly and peacefully in their own lands?"[7]

Initially the conquerors claimed the right to wage a just war of conquest if Amerindians refused to allow missionaries to live and work among them. Later, based on reports of human sacrifice and cannibalism written by Columbus and other early explorers, Europeans concluded that the inhabitants of the New World rejected basic natural laws. Juan Ginés de Sepulveda, chaplain of Holy Roman Emperor Charles V, argued in 1544 that the idolatry and cannibalism of the Indians made them, in Aristotle's terms, natural slaves—"barbarous and inhuman peoples abhorring all civil life, customs and virtue" was how he put it. People lacking "civil life" and "virtue" clearly could not be allowed self-government. Other writers commented that nakedness and cannibalism were both signs of the lack of "civility" among the Amerindians. Sepulveda implied that Indians were merely "humanlike," not necessarily human.

Franciscan and Dominican missionaries were especially vocal opponents of views like Sepulveda's. To these missionaries, the Indians initially seemed innocent and ideal subjects for conversion to the simple piety of Christ and his first apostles. In their eyes, Indians were like children who could be converted and led by example and, where

Crusade for Justice The criticisms of Bartolomé de Las Casas were published widely and accompanied by woodcuts like this one showing the cruelty of the conquerors toward the Amerindians. In response to Las Casas, Charles V passed laws protecting the rights of the indigenous peoples. (*The John Carter Brown Library at Brown University, Providence*)

necessary, by stern discipline. These mendicants saw themselves as advocates for Indians; they desired to protect the natives from the depredations of the Spanish conquerors and the corruptions of European civilization. The most eloquent defender of Indian rights was Bartolomé de Las Casas (1474–1566), a former encomendero who became a Dominican missionary and eventually bishop of Chiapas in southern Mexico. Las Casas passionately condemned the violence and brutality of the Spanish conquests. As part of a famous debate with Sepulveda, Las Casas rejected the "humanlike" argument. "All races of the world are men," he declared. All are evolving along a historical continuum. It was wrong, he added, to dismiss any culture or society as outside of natural law. Like all other peoples, Indians had reason. That being the case, even the most brutal could be civilized and Christianized. There was, in the view of Las Casas, no argument for natural slavery.

Charles V (who was king of Spain as well as Holy Roman emperor) accepted Las Casas's criticisms of the colonial administration. In 1542 he issued "New Laws" aimed at ending the virtual independence of the most adventurous of the encomenderos. He further abolished Indian slavery

and greatly restricted the transfer of encomiendas. At first the European conquerors in Mexico and Peru rejected royal attempts to restrict their rights in the New World, but from the 1540s Indians were protected from the most extreme exploitation.

We should have no illusion, however, that these measures reflected some acceptance of cultural pluralism. The very mendicants who protected Indians assumed that Westernization and Christianization would quickly follow. And in some cases when it did not, as during revolts in the 1560s, the mendicants themselves reacted with a puzzled sense of anger, frustration, and betrayal.

THE COLUMBIAN EXCHANGE

The conquerors, adventurers, and traders who followed in the wake of Christopher Columbus and Vasco da Gama profoundly altered the Old World and the New. Before 1492 there had been a system of world trade, but now, as the Spanish proclaimed, Europe and especially Spain were at the center of economic and political life. As the Spanish and other Europeans moved throughout the world, they carried with them religions, ideas, diseases, people, plants, and animals—forever uniting the Old World and the New. This amalgamation of culture is known as the "Columbian Exchange."

Disease

Columbus and those who followed him brought not only people to the New World but also numerous Old World diseases. "Virgin-soil" epidemics—that is, epidemics of previously unknown diseases—are invariably fierce. Although the New World may have passed syphilis to Spain, from which it quickly spread throughout the Old World, diseases transferred from the Old World to the New were much more virulent than syphilis. Smallpox spread from Cuba to Mexico as early as 1519. It was soon followed by diphtheria, measles, trachoma, whooping cough, chickenpox, bubonic plague, malaria, typhoid fever, cholera, yellow fever, scarlet fever, amoebic dysentery, influenza, and some varieties of tuberculosis. Disease served as the silent ally of the conquerors. During critical points in the conquest of Tenochtitlán, smallpox was raging in the Aztec population. The disease later moved along traditional trade networks. An epidemic shortly before Pizarro's expedition to Peru carried off the Paca Inca and may have contributed to the unrest and civil war that worked to the advantage of the invaders.

Lacking sources, historians cannot trace accurately the movement of epidemic disease or its effect on the New World populations, yet many archaeologists and historians remain convinced that Old World diseases moved north from Mexico and ravaged and disrupted Amerindian populations in eastern North America long before the arrival of European immigrants. In most of the New World, 90 percent or more of the native population was destroyed by wave after wave of previously unknown diseases. Explorers and colonists did not so much enter an empty land as an "emptied" one.

It was at least partially because of disease that both the Spanish and the Portuguese needed to import large numbers of African slaves to work their plantations and mines (see page 499). With the settlement of southeastern North America, plantation agriculture was extended to include the production of tobacco and later cotton. As a result of the needs of plantation economies and the labor shortage caused by disease, African slaves were

brought in large numbers. In the Caribbean and along the coasts of Central and South America the Africans created an African-Caribbean or African American culture that amalgamated African, European, and American civilizations.

Plants and Animals

It became increasingly clear to the Spaniards that the New World had been completely isolated from the Old. (See the box, "The New World and the

Old World in the New This painting of "traditional" Amerindian culture shows animals brought by the Spaniards to the New World. The lives of the Amerindians were changed forever by the introduction of horses, sheep, chickens, and cows, as well as apples, peaches, wheat, and oats. *(From Martínez Compañon, Trujillo del Peru, vol. II, plate 77. Courtesy, Harvard College Library)*

Old.") The impact of Old World peoples on native populations was immediately evident to all. But scholars have recently argued that the importation of plants and animals had an even more profound effect than the arrival of Europeans. The changes that began in 1492 created "Neo-Europes" in what are now Canada, the United States, Mexico, Argentina, Australia, and New Zealand. The flora and fauna of the Old World, accustomed to a relatively harsh, competitive environment, found ideal conditions in the new lands. Like the rabbits carried to the Canary Islands and to Australia, plants and animals alike multiplied.

The most important meat and dairy animals in the New World—cattle, sheep, goats, and pigs—are imports from the Old World. Sailors initially brought pigs or goats aboard ship because they were easily transportable sources of protein. When let loose on the Caribbean islands, they quickly took over. The spread of horses through what is now Mexico, Brazil, Argentina, the United States, and Canada was equally dramatic. To the list of domesticated animals can be added donkeys, dogs, cats, and chickens. The changes these animals brought were profound. Cattle, pigs, and chickens quickly became staples of the New World diet. Horses enabled Amerindians and Europeans to travel across and settle on the vast plains of both North and South America.

The flora of the New World was equally changed. Even contemporaries noted how Old World plants flourished in the New. Because Old World plants came from a more hostile, more competitive environment, they were able to drive out their New World competitors. By 1555, European clover was widely distributed in Mexico—Aztecs called it "Castilian grass." Other Old World grasses, as well as weeds like dandelion, quickly followed. Domesticated plants like apples, peaches, and artichokes spread rapidly and naturally in the new environment. Early in the twentieth century it was estimated that only one-quarter of the grasses found on the broad prairies of the Argentine pampas were native before the arrival of Columbus. Studies of plant life in California, Australia, and New Zealand offer much the same results. The Old World also provided new and widely grown small grains like oats, barley, and wheat.

The exchange went both ways. Crops from the New World also had an effect on the Old World.

By the seventeenth century, maize (or American corn), potatoes, and sweet potatoes had significantly altered the diets of Europe and Asia. It was the addition of maize and potatoes that supported the dramatic population growth in areas like Italy, Ireland, and Scandinavia. With the addition of the tomato in the nineteenth century, much of the modern European diet became dependent on New World foods.

The new plants and new animals, as well as the social and political changes initiated by the Europeans, pulled the Old World and the New more closely together.

Culture

One reason for the accommodation between the Old World and the New was that the Europeans and Amerindians tended to interpret conquest and cultural transformation in the same way. The peoples living in the Valley of Mexico believed that their conquest was fated by the gods and would bring in new gods. The Spaniards' beliefs were strikingly similar, based on the revelation of divine will and the omnipotence of the Christian God. Cortés, by whitewashing former Aztec temples and converting native priests into white-clad Christian priests, was in a way fulfilling the Aztecs' expectations about their conqueror.

Acculturation was also facilitated by the Spanish tendency to place churches and shrines at the sites of former Aztec temples. The shrine of the Virgin of Guadalupe (north of modern Mexico City), for example, was located on the site of the temple of the goddess Tonantzin, an Aztec fertility-goddess of childbirth and midwives. (See the feature, "Weighing the Evidence: A Mexican Shrine," on pages 506–507.) Early missionaries reported that Indians quickly took to Christianity, although investigations later in the sixteenth century raised questions about the depth of their belief. Nonetheless, Christianity quickly became the dominant religion of the peoples of the New World.

The colonists tended to view their domination of the New World as a divine vindication of their own culture and civilization. During the sixteenth century, they set about remaking the world they had found. In the century after the conquest of Mexico, Spaniards founded 190 new cities in the Americas. Lima, Bogotá, and many others were

The New World and the Old

In an effort to understand the New World, the Spanish friar Bernardino de Sahagún (1499?–1590) interviewed Mexicans about their way of life before the arrival of the Europeans. The resulting volume, called the **Florentine Codex** *because it now reposes in Florence, is a valuable source on life and religion in Mexico before the Spanish conquests. In this excerpt from the* **Codex,** *the friar reflects on the relation of the New World and the Old.*

It occurred to me to write here that in the diversity of foods there are scarcely any which resemble ours. It seems that this people had never been discovered until these times, because, of the foods which we enjoy and are enjoying in the regions whence we came, we find none here. We do not even find here the domesticated animals which those of us who came from Spain and all Europe use, from which it appears that [the people] did not come from those regions. Nor had men from those regions come to discover this land, for if they had come from there, they would have come to make them known in other times; from them we would find wheat, barley, or rye, or chicken from there, or horses, or bulls, or donkeys, or sheep, or goats, or other domesticated animals which we utilize, whence it appears that only in these times have these lands been discovered and not before.

As to the preaching of the Gospel in these regions, there has been much doubt as to whether or not it has been preached before now. . . . Two trusted religious assured me that in Oaxaca, . . . they have some very ancient paintings, painted on deerskin, which contained many things alluded to in the preaching of the Gospel. Among others was one where there were three women dressed as Indian women. . . . And on the ground before them was a naked man, legs and arms stretched on a cross, arms and legs tied to the cross with cords. This seems to me to allude to Our Lady [the Virgin Mary] and her two sisters and to our crucified Redeemer, which they must have derived from ancient sermons.

So in conclusion I say it is possible that they were preached to and that they completely lost the Faith which was preached to them and returned to the ancient idolatries. And now it seems to me that our Lord God . . . has desired to give [them] the Spanish nation to be as a fountain from which flows the doctrine of the Catholic Faith.

Source: Reprinted by permission from B. de Sahagún, *The Florentine Codex: General History of the Things of New Spain,* part 1, ed. and trans. Arthur J. O. Anderson and Charles E. Dibble (Santa Fe, N.M.: School of American Research, 1950), pp. 96–97. Copyright 1982 by the School of American Research, Santa Fe, and the University of Utah.

proudly modeled on and compared to the cities of Spain. In 1573, King Philip II (r. 1556–1598) established ordinances requiring all new cities to be based on a uniform grid with a main plaza, market, and religious center. The new cities became hubs of social and political life in the colonies. In these cities, religious orders founded colleges for basic education much like the universities they had organized in the Old World. And by mid-century, the Crown had authorized the foundation of universities in Mexico City and Lima modeled after the great Spanish university of Salamanca.

Colonists attempted to recreate in all essentials the society of Spain.

The experience of the Spanish and the Portuguese in the sixteenth century seemed confirmed by the later experiences of the French and English in the seventeenth century. In seventeenth-century New England, the English Puritan John Winthrop concluded, "For the natives, they are nearly all dead of smallpox, so as the Lord hath cleared our title to what we possess."[8] A seventeenth-century French observer came to a similar conclusion: "Touching these savages, there is a thing that I cannot omit to remark to you, it is that it appears visibly that God wishes that they yield their place to new peoples."[9] Political philosophers believed that if there was no evidence that a land was being cultivated by the indigenous people, the rights to that land passed to those who would use and improve it. Thus, colonists believed that they had divine and legal sanction to take and to remake these new lands in a European image.

SUMMARY

Modern historians considering decolonization, economic revolutions in many parts of Asia, and multiculturalism have been changing their ways of thinking about European expansion in the fifteenth century. The expansion of Europe was not the movement of highly developed commercial economies into underdeveloped areas. In Asia, the Portuguese and later the Dutch and English were a military presence long before they were an economic one. In the New World, even as the Spanish conquered people and changed their language, government, and religion, many aspects of Amerindian culture survived in the local Indian municipalities.

The economic, political, and cultural changes brought about by the conquest created a hybrid culture. It is impossible to say whether the economic and technical benefits of the amalgamation of the Old World and the New outweigh the costs. But even those who celebrate the transformation of the New World would probably agree with the conclusions of a native American in the Pacific Northwest: "I am not sorry the missionaries came. But I wish they had known how to let their news change people's lives from the inside, without imposing their culture over our ways."[10] Tolerance, however, was not yet a hallmark of Western societies. Europeans were incapable of allowing others to change "from the inside." The inability to understand and tolerate others was to be a key to the strife created by the other great event of the sixteenth century, the movement to reform church and society.

NOTES

1. Quoted in John H. Parry and Robert G. Keith, eds., *The New Iberian World: A Documentary History of the Discovery and Settlement of Latin America to the Early Seventeenth Century*, vol. 2 (New York: Times Books, 1984), p. 59.
2. Quoted in William D. Phillips, Jr., and Carla Rahn Phillips, *The Worlds of Christopher Columbus* (Cambridge, England: Cambridge University Press, 1992), p. 163.
3. Quoted ibid., p. 166.
4. Quoted in J. H. Parry, ed., *The European Reconnaissance: Selected Documents* (New York: Harper & Row, 1968), p. 242.
5. Quoted in Alfred W. Crosby, *Ecological Imperialism: The Biological Expansion of Europe, 900–1900* (Cambridge, England: Cambridge University Press, 1986), p. 125.
6. Quoted ibid., p. 11.
7. Quoted in Mark A. Burkholder and Lyman L. Johnson, *Colonial Latin America* (Oxford: Oxford University Press, 1990), p. 29.
8. Quoted in Crosby, p. 208.
9. Quoted ibid., p. 215.
10. Quoted in Maria Parker Pascua, "Ozette: A Makah Village in 1491," *National Geographic* (October 1991), p. 53.

SUGGESTED READING

General Surveys

Bethell, Leslie, ed., *The Cambridge History of Latin America*. Vol 1. 1984. A standard work with excellent discussions of America before the conquest as well as discussions of colonial life.

Crosby, Alfred W. *The Columbian Voyages, the Columbian Exchange, and Their Historians*. 1988. A short pamphlet about historical writing on Columbus and the expansion of Europeans; an excellent place for a beginning student to start.

Curtin, P. *The Tropical Atlantic in the Age of the Slave Trade*. 1991. An introductory pamphlet that is an excellent first work for students interested in the history of slavery and the movement of peoples from Africa to the New World.

Levenson, J. A., ed. *Circa 1492: Art in the Age of Exploration*. 1991. A museum catalog showing art from Asia, Africa, America, and Europe at the time of Columbus; it includes essays on politics and culture aimed at a general audience.

Parry, J. H. *The Age of Reconnaissance*. 1981. A classic introductory survey of Portuguese, Spanish, English, and French exploration and conquest to the end of the seventeenth century.

Scammell, Geoffrey. *The First Imperial Age: European Overseas Expansion, 1400–1715*. 1989. As the title implies, this is an introductory survey of European colonial interests through the early eighteenth century. The author puts the Spanish and Portuguese explorations in the context of later French and English experiences.

The European Background

Campbell, Mary B. *The Witness and the Other World: Exotic European Travel Writing, 400–1600*. 1988. A literary study of the narratives written by or about travelers, emphasizing especially the interest Columbus had in the reports of previous travelers.

Fernandez-Armesto, Felipe. *Before Columbus: Exploration and Colonization from the Mediterranean to the Atlantic, 1229–1492*. 1987. A well-written and accessible political and institutional narrative, especially valuable on the early Portuguese voyages.

Phillips, J. R. S. *The Medieval Expansion of Europe*. 1988. The best survey of European interest in and knowledge of the world beyond Christendom; especially good on European travelers to the East in the thirteenth century.

Exploration and Empire

Boxer, C. R. *The Portuguese Seaborne Empire, 1415–1825*. 1977. A classic political and institutional narrative of the Portuguese empire; detailed but accessible even to those with little background.

Burkholder, Mark A., and Lyman L. Johnson. *Colonial Latin America*. 1990. A thorough introduction to the conquest and colonization of Central and South America by the Spanish and Portuguese.

Clendinnen, Inga. *Ambivalent Conquests: Maya and Spaniard in Yucatan, 1517–1570*. 1987. A skillful, ironic study of the attempts of Maya and Spaniard to understand each other. It concentrates on the way in which Mayans transform European Christianity, including many of their pre-conquest beliefs and practices.

———. *Aztecs: An Interpretation*. 1991. A dramatic, beautifully written essay on the Aztecs that shows how daily life, religion, and imperialism were linked.

Elliott, John H. *The Old World and the New, 1492–1650*. 1970. Besides supplying the title for this chapter, these essays are excellent considerations of the reciprocal relations between the colonies and the kingdoms of Spain.

———. *Spain and Its World, 1500–1700: Selected Essays*. 1989. Essays by the greatest living historian of Spain and the New World. The essay on the mental world of Cortés is especially important.

Fuentes, Carlos. *The Buried Mirror: Reflections on Spain and the New World*. 1992. An essay with numerous illustrations, many in color, on the melding of the cultures of Spain and the New World, by one of Mexico's greatest writers. The author's reflections on the merging of Christianity and indigenous religions are particularly valuable.

Hale, John R. *Renaissance Exploration*. 1968. A broad-based introductory survey that emphasizes the technological and geographic innovations that were part of the early voyages.

Moseley, M. E. *The Incas and Their Ancestors: The Archaeology of Peru*. 1992. This general introduction to the Incas includes excellent maps and illustrations.

Phillips, W. D., Jr., and C. R. Phillips. *The Worlds of Christopher Columbus*. 1992. Though written for a popular audience, this is an excellent survey of Columbus and his voyages and an up-to-date summary of recent work on Columbus, maritime technology, and Spanish colonial interests.

Cultural Exchange

Crosby, A. W. *Ecological Imperialism: The Biological Expansion of Europe, 900–1900*. 1986. A discussion of how migrating peoples carried with them plants, animals, and diseases; has an excellent collection of maps and illustrations.

Hanke, L. *Aristotle and the American Indians: A Study in Race Prejudice in the Modern World*. 1959. The most general of Hanke's books about race and prejudice in the Old and New Worlds. Hanke states clearly the philosophical basis of debates over equality from classical Greece to the nineteenth century.

Pagden, Anthony. *The Fall of Natural Man: The American Indian and the Origin of Comparative Ethnology*. 1982. A brilliant, difficult, and rewarding book on the debate over Indians' rights in the sixteenth century.

Smithsonian Institution. *Seeds of Change*. 1991. This museum catalog has excellent illustrations and introductory essays on the transfer of diseases and plants between the Old World and the New. There is an especially good chapter on religion in the period before the arrival of the Spaniards.

A MEXICAN SHRINE

The shrine of the Virgin of Guadalupe lies on a slight hill on the edge of Mexico City, a bare three miles from the center of what was the Aztec city of Tenochtitlán. It is likely the holiest shrine in the Americas, visited by perhaps 15,000 pilgrims and tourists daily. Singing and prayer begin as pilgrims come in sight of the shrine; people fall to their knees in penance and devotion as they approach the church; and the pious hang homemade and commercially purchased *ex votos* (votive medals) along the walls. Pilgrim groups often break into traditional chants praising God for the dawn and concluding, "God bless you, Mary."*

The image the pilgrims venerate is a painting of a dark-skinned woman. We see her standing in the shimmering light of the moon seeming to combine Aztec and Spanish elements. According to later chronicles, the painting was found in 1531 by Juan Diego, an Aztec convert to Christianity, whose story was first told in Nahuatl, the Aztec language, rather than in Spanish. The pious Indian reported meeting a dark-skinned woman who identified herself as Mary, the Mother of God. She told him where to find the image and required that a shrine be built in her honor because she was the merciful mother of this land. Juan Diego eventually presented the painting of the Virgin carefully wrapped in his cloak to the bishop of Mexico City.

First a simple chapel and by the eighteenth century the magnificent church we see here, this shrine quickly became the most popular Mexican shrine and a symbol of Indian integration into the Christian world. The historian, however, wishes to know how such a shrine developed and how it came to possess such powerful associations for the people of Mexico. Who were the original worshipers? What was the connection of the Spanish to the shrine? And finally, what can this shrine tell us about the colonial experience in Mexico?

The shrine had a complex history during Mexico's colonial period—it was not simply a Christian center of Amerindian devotion. The shrine itself is located on the site of the pre-conquest shrine of Tonantzin, an Aztec fertility-goddess. Spanish priests who troubled to learn Nahuatl reported that Tonantzin's shrine was popular throughout the region. By the middle of the sixteenth century, Franciscan missionaries had managed to substitute the veneration of the Virgin Mary, whom they called "the good little grandmother,"** for worship of Tonantzin, "Our Mother." The adoption of Guadalupe by all Mexicans was not, however, a simple process.

The Virgin of Guadalupe *(Enrique Franco-Torrijos)*

*Quoted from a 1940 report in Victor and Edith Turner, *Image and Pilgrimage in Christian Culture, Anthropological Perspectives* (New York: Columbia University Press, 1978), p. 96.
**Quoted in William B. Taylor, "The Virgin of Guadalupe in New Spain: An Inquiry into the Social History of Marian Devotion," *American Ethnologist* 14 (1987): 11.

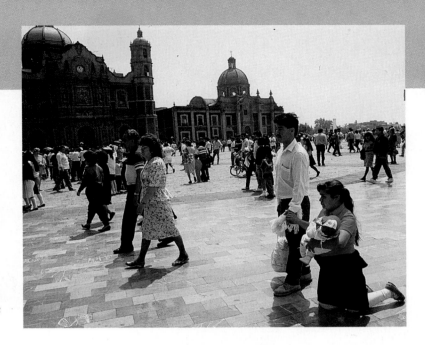

Pilgrims Approaching the Shrine of the Virgin of Guadalupe *(Alyx Kellington/DDB Stock Photo)*

As historians quickly learn, narratives may not necessarily be composed when they claim they were. Although the shrine to the Virgin is known to have existed in the sixteenth century, the story of Juan Diego's discovery of the painting cannot be shown to have circulated before the seventeenth century, perhaps not before the 1660s. This time sequence is very significant since it is Juan Diego who clearly identifies Guadalupe as a special Indian shrine. And that identification raises a further question: If Guadalupe appealed only to local Indians, who popularized the shrine? The answer seems to be that Guadalupe was most popular with the residents of Mexico City and with priests and clergy who were creole (people of mixed Spanish and Indian parentage)—individuals who did not fit easily in either the Spanish or the Indian communities. By the mid-sixteenth century, the shrine had come to mark the edge of Mexico City. An Englishman remarked that Spaniards could not pass the shrine without stopping and praying for protection from evil. If the shrine was primarily of interest to creoles and to residents of Mexico City, how did it come to represent all of Mexico, especially the Indian population of Mexico?

The Virgin of Guadalupe seems to have become popular with the Indians of Mexico only over the course of the late seventeenth and the eighteenth centuries. Veneration of her expanded as part of a general social and cultural transformation. The spread of the cult seems to have been the work of creole priests who celebrated the Feast of the Apparition, when the Virgin appeared to the humble Indian convert. There were reports of miracles by the Virgin of Guadalupe in various parts of Mexico. And by the late eighteenth century, an English traveler reported:

> If you travel through the *ranchos* of the entire kingdom you will find that two things are rarely lacking: an image of Nuestra Señora de Guadalupe and a poor school master who teaches reading and Christian doctrine.[†]

Mexicans seem to have embraced the cult of the Virgin for a variety of reasons. To many she was the "little grandmother," the mediator between humble people and the authorities. Yet in some cases, when the bonds between the authorities and the more humble people were broken, the Indians often took comfort in their belief that "Most Holy Mary is praying for us." And finally, during the revolutions of the nineteenth century, for those who understood themselves to be Mexican, separated from the Spanish government, the Virgin became a powerful symbol of independence and justice for Indians and common people.

What can historians learn from such a shrine? First, that symbols have many meanings. Depending on time and place, the Virgin of Guadalupe appealed to the religious and social concerns of Spaniards, creoles, and Indians. Second, and perhaps as important, the history of the shrine of Guadalupe shows us that religious symbols, ideas, and traditions may evolve over time. ✑

[†]Ibid., p. 15.

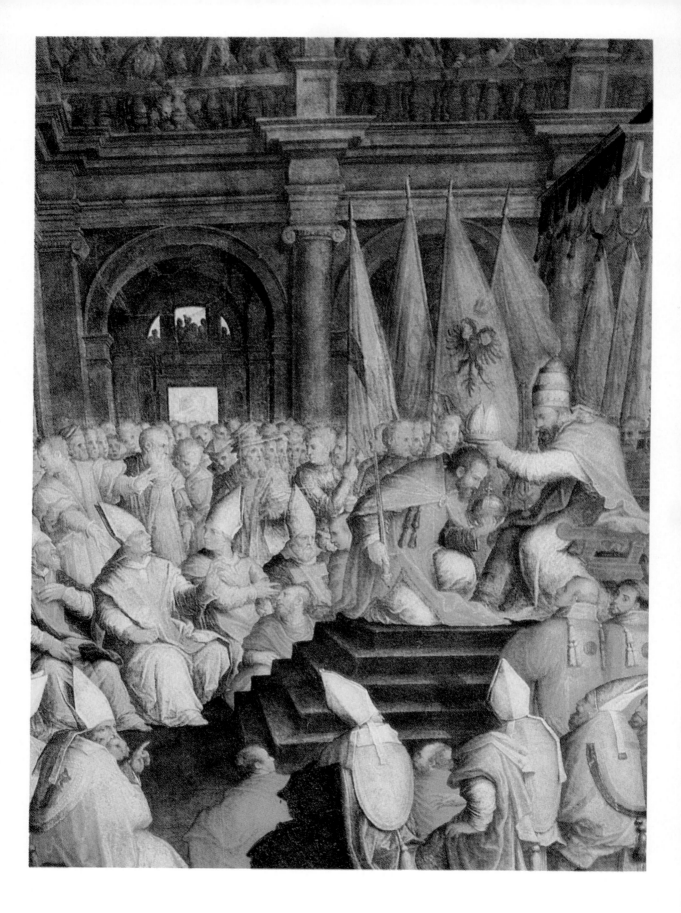

CHAPTER 14

The Age of the Reformation

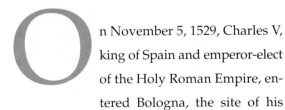

On November 5, 1529, Charles V, king of Spain and emperor-elect of the Holy Roman Empire, entered Bologna, the site of his coronation. He was met by twenty cardinals, four hundred papal guards, and a host of other papal and imperial soldiers. As he moved through the city, Charles's heralds tossed eight thousand ducats of gold and silver into the waiting crowds. Gates and streets were decorated with medallions of emperors and statues of patricians recalling ancient virtues and reminding the emperor-elect of his duties to preserve the law and defend Christendom.

Charles and his advisers believed that God had selected him to reestablish the power of the empire and to cement the special relationship between emperor and pope. But by the end of Charles's reign in 1556, less than thirty years after his triumphant entry into Bologna, just the opposite had occurred. The empire had become little more than a German state. And the coronation of Charles by Pope Leo X in Bologna was, in fact, the last papal coronation of an emperor.

This dramatic reversal resulted from a series of political, diplomatic, and religious crises that changed forever the face of Europe. The key issue was the sixteenth-century movement known as the Reformation, an ever widening controversy over the nature of Christianity, the relationship between the individual and God, and the role of government in society. The struggle began as an apparently minor theological controversy in Germany—a "quarrel between monks," as the papacy saw it. Debates about salvation quickly widened into arguments about the sacraments—that is, the means by which individuals receive God's grace. By the middle of the century, disagreements had expanded to the point that both the

Charles V and Clement VII entering Bologna, 1530.

509

Christian religion and politics were changed forever. As the controversy continued, issues spread from questions of theology to those of ecclesiastical and political organization. In the heat of this religious crisis the modern Christian churches, both Protestant and Catholic, were formed.

The Roman Catholic, Lutheran, Calvinist, and Anglican churches all came into being in the sixteenth century. But to speak of "Lutheran" or "Roman Catholic" during the first decades of the Reformation is to ignore the fluidity of the situation in which Europeans found themselves. At first, no one foresaw that the result of the controversies would be separate churches. The reformers of the first half of the sixteenth century shared many characteristics. Most had been influenced by the cultural and literary interests of the humanists. Many had received a humanistic education, with its emphasis on literary studies and the study of Latin, Greek, and Hebrew. Although most reformers eventually rejected the general humanistic assumption of the dignity and essential goodness of individuals, they shared with the humanists a faith in linguistic studies of Christian traditions, especially of the Bible. Almost all emphasized the Bible as the unique source of religious authority and rejected the medieval church's complex view of salvation. Initially, they all rejected any claim of special status or authority for the priesthood. And because of increasingly violent debates over theology and church government, the idea of a single Christendom did not survive the century.

The debates over religion and the power and authority of the church that raged during this period did not occur in a political vacuum. Supporters of the church, like Emperor Charles V, would gladly have used force to suppress the new theology, but events conspired to make such a response unrealistic. In Germany, the emperor faced hostile towns and princes as well as French and Turkish military threats—all of which made action against religious dissidents impossible. In England and Scandinavia, in contrast, monarchs viewed the church as an illegitimate political power and a threat to strong royal government, and reformers soon found themselves with royal patrons. Elsewhere, especially in eastern Europe, there was no strong central government to enforce religious unity, and a variety of Christian traditions coexisted.

By the second half of the sixteenth century it was clear that there would never again be a single

Christian church in western Europe. Political and religious powers concentrated their energies on a process of theological definition and institutionalization that historians call the "Second Reformation," or "Confessionalization." With the changes of the late sixteenth century it becomes appropriate to speak of Roman Catholic, Anglican, and Lutheran as clearly defined confessions, or systems of religious beliefs and practices.

In Protestant and Catholic churches the changes in religion increased the importance of the moral control exercised by religious authorities. Far from freeing the individual, the Christian churches of the late sixteenth century all emphasized correct doctrine and orderliness in personal behavior. The early Protestants may have rejected a sacramental system that they thought oppressed the individual, but the institutions that replaced the old church developed their own traditions of control. The increased moral control by churches accompanied and even fostered the growth in state power that would characterize the late sixteenth and seventeenth centuries.

THE REFORMATION MOVEMENTS, CA. 1517–1545

In 1517 a little-known professor of theology at the University of Wittenberg in Saxony began a protest against practices in the late medieval church. Martin Luther had no carefully worked-out idea about the nature of the church and salvation, but his theology struck a responsive chord with many of his contemporaries. Although the various protests resulted in the creation of separate and well-defined religious traditions, the differences among the reformers were not initially as clear as they became in the second half of the sixteenth century. Thus, it is appropriate to speak of "reformation movements" because all the reformers, even the most radical, shared with Luther a sense that the essential sacramental and priestly powers claimed by the medieval church were illegitimate.

"Protestant" is the label we now use to describe the churches that arose in opposition to the medieval Christian church. It is important to understand, however, that the word *Protestant* was originally a political term used to describe German princes who opposed imperial attempts to end a truce between supporters and opponents of the religious reformers in the 1530s. Only later was *Protestant* applied to the resulting churches. The reformers tended to think of themselves as "evangelical reformed Christians." They were evangelical in the sense that they believed that authority derived from the Word of God, the Bible. They were reformed Christians because their aim was merely to restore Christianity to the form they believed it exhibited in the first centuries of its existence.

The Late Medieval Context

Questions of an individual's salvation and personal relationship to God and to the Christian community remained at the heart of religious practice and theological speculation in the sixteenth as in previous centuries. Nominalist theologians, the leading thinkers of the late Middle Ages, rejected the key assumption of previous Scholastics —that there were universal ideas and generally applicable rules of order for moral life (see page 380). In the words of William of Ockham (ca. 1285–1347), "No universal really exists outside the mind." Truth was to be found in daily experience or in revealed scripture, not in complex logical systems. At the heart is Ockham's method—known as Ockham's razor—that what can be explained with only a few logical speculations "is vainly explained by assuming more."

Nominalist theologians rejected vast logical systems, but they held on to the traditional rituals and beliefs that tied together the Christian community. They believed in a holy covenant in which God would save those Christians who, by means of the church's sacraments and through penitential acts, were partners in their own salvation. Foremost among the penitential acts was the feeding of "Christ's Poor," especially on important feast days. The pious constructed and supported hospices for travelers and hospitals for the sick. Christians went on pilgrimages to shrines like the tomb of Saint Thomas à Becket in Canterbury or the church of Saint James of Compostela in Spain. They also built small chapels, called chantry chapels, for the sake of their own souls. To moralists, work itself was in some sense a penitential and ennobling act.

The most common religious practice of the late Middle Ages was participation in religious brotherhoods. Members vowed to attend monthly meetings, to participate in processions on feast days, and to maintain peaceful and charitable relations with fellow members. Religious brotherhoods often played a political role as well. In the south of France, for example, city governments often met in the chapels of the Brotherhoods of the Holy Spirit.

The most typical religious feast was that of *Corpus Christi* (the "Body of Christ"). The feast celebrated and venerated the sacrament of the mass and the ritual by which the bread offered to the laity became the actual body of Christ. Corpus Christi was popular with the church hierarchy because it emphasized the role of the priest in the central ritual of Christianity. The laity, however, equated Corpus Christi with the body of citizens who made up the civic community.

Kingdoms, provinces, and towns all had patron saints who, believers thought, offered protection from natural as well as political disasters. There were royal saints like Edward of England, Louis of France, and Olaf of Norway. Festivals in honor of the saints were a major event in the town or kingdom. The most revered saint in the late Middle Ages was the Virgin Mary, the mother of Jesus. The most popular new pilgrimage shrines in the north of Europe were dedicated to the Virgin. It was she, the Sienese maintained, who protected them from their Florentine rivals. As the veneration of the Virgin Mary shows, in the late Middle Ages it was not possible to distinguish between religion and society, church and state.

Women played a prominent role in late medieval religious life. Holy women who claimed any sort of moral standing often did so because of visions or prophetic gifts such as knowledge of future events or of the status of souls in Purgatory. Reputations for sanctity provided a profound moral authority. The Italian Blessed Angela of Foligno (ca. 1248–1309) had several visions and became the object of a large circle of devoted followers. She was typical of a number of late medieval female religious figures who on the death of a spouse turned to religion. Like Angela, these women tended to gather "families" around them, people whom they described as their spiritual "fathers" or "children." They offered moral counsel and warned businessmen and politicians of the dangers of lying and sharp dealings. "Oh my sons, fathers, and brothers," counseled Angela, "see that you love one another amongst your-selves . . . [and] likewise unto all people."[1]

In the late Middle Ages religious houses for women probably outnumbered those for men. For unmarried or unmarriageable (because of disabilities) daughters, convents were an economical, safe, and controlled environment. Moralists denounced the dumping of women in convents: "They give [unmarriageable daughters] to a convent, as if they were the scum and vomit of the world," was the conclusion of Saint Bernardino of Siena (1380–1444). The general public, however, believed that well-run communities of women promoted the spiritual and physical health of the community. In a society in which women were not allowed to control their own property and in which women outside the nobility lacked a visible role in political and intellectual life, a religious vocation may have appealed to women because it allowed them to define their own religious and social relationships. A religious vocation offered other advantages, too. Well-to-do or aristocratic parents appreciated the fact that the traditional gift that accompanied a daughter entering a religious house was much smaller than a dowry.

Some women declined to join convents, which required vows of chastity and obedience to a rule and close male supervision. Margery Kempe (ca. 1373–1439) of Lynn, England, traveled throughout Christendom on a variety of pilgrimages. She left her husband and family, dressed in white (symbolic of virginity), and joined with other pilgrims on trips to Spain, Italy, and Jerusalem. Many other women chose to live as anchoresses, or recluses, in closed cells beside churches and hospitals or in rooms in private houses. Men and women traveled from all parts of England seeking the counsel of the Blessed Julian of Norwich (d. after 1413), who lived in a tiny cell built into the wall of a parish church.

The most controversial group of religious women were the Beguines, who lived in communities without taking formal vows and often with minimal connections to the local church hierarchy (see page 376). By the early fifteenth century, Beguines were suspect because clerics believed that these independent women rejected traditional religious cloistering and the moral leadership of male clergy and were particularly susceptible to heresy. Critics maintained that unsupervised Beguines held to what was called the "Heresy of the Free

Spirit," a belief that one who had achieved spiritual perfection was no longer capable of sin. Rumors of sexual orgies, spread by fearful clerical critics, quickly brought suspect women before local inquisitors. Although some Beguines may have held such a belief in spiritual perfection, the majority certainly did not. But they were feared by an ecclesiastical hierarchy that distrusted independence.

A more conservative movement for renewal in the church was the Brothers and Sisters of the Common Life founded by the Dutchman Geert Groote (1340–1384). A popular preacher and reformer, Groote gathered male and female followers into quasi-monastic communities at Deventer in the Low Countries. Eventually a community of Augustinian canons was added at Windesheim. Brothers and Sisters of the Common Life supported themselves as book-copyists and teachers in small religious schools in the Low Countries. Members of these communities followed a strict, conservative spirituality that has come to be known as the *devotio moderna,* or "modern devotion." Although they called themselves "modern," their piety was traditional. Their ideas are encapsulated in *The Imitation of Christ,* a popular work advocating a traditional sort of monastic spirituality written by Thomas à Kempis (ca. 1380–1471), a canon of Windesheim. They advocated the contrary ideals of fourteenth-century religious life: broader participation by the laity and strict control by clerical authorities.

Religious life in the late medieval period was broadly based and vigorous. Theologians, lay women and men, and popular preachers could take heart they were furthering their own salvation and that of their neighbors. Thus, if reform was to be radically new, it would have to involve more than simple moral change.

Martin Luther and the New Theology

Martin Luther (1483–1546) eventually challenged many of the assumptions of late medieval Christians. He seemed to burst onto the scene in 1517, when he objected to the way in which papal indulgences—that is, the remission of penalties owed for sins—were being bought and sold in the bishopric of Brandenburg. Luther's father, a miner from the small town of Mansfeld, had hoped that his son would take a degree in law and become a wealthy and prestigious lawyer. Luther chose in-

Cranach: The True Church and the False This woodcut was designed to make clear the distinction between the evangelical church and the papacy. On one side Christ and his sacrifice are clearly at the center; on the other the pope and innumerable church officials are caught in the flames of Hell. *(Staatliche Kunstsammlungen Dresden)*

stead to enter a monastery and eventually become a priest.

Throughout his life, Martin Luther seems to have been troubled by a sense of his own sinfulness and unworthiness. According to late medieval theology, the life of a Christian was a continuing cycle of sin, confession, contrition, and penance, and the only way to achieve salvation was to have confessed all one's sins and at least begun a cycle of penance at the time of one's death. Christians lived in fear of dying suddenly without having any chance to confess. The purchase of indulgences, membership in penitential brotherhoods, ritualized charity, and veneration of popular saints were seen as ways to acquire merit and salvation in the eyes of God.

Luther came to believe that the church's requirement that believers achieve salvation by means of confession, contrition, and penance made too great a demand on the faithful. Instead, Luther said, citing the New Testament, salvation

(or justification) was God's gift to the faithful. Luther's belief is known as "justification by faith." Acts of charity were important products of God's love, but in Luther's opinion, they were not necessary for salvation. Late in his life, Luther explained how he came by these ideas:

Though I lived as a monk without reproach, I felt that I was a sinner before God with an extremely disturbed conscience. I could not believe that he was placated by my [acts of penance]. I did not love, yes, I hated the righteous God who punishes sinners. . . . At last, by the mercy of God, . . . I gave context to the words, namely, "In it the righteousness of God is revealed, as it is written, 'He who through faith is righteous shall live.'" There I began to understand that . . . the righteous lives by a gift of God, namely by faith. . . . Here I felt that I was altogether born again and had entered paradise itself through open gates.[2]

Although Luther recalled a sudden, dramatic revelation, it now seems clear that his insight developed slowly over the course of his academic career and during his defense of his teachings. Nonetheless, his recollection conveys a sense of the novelty of his theology and the reasons why his attack on the late medieval church proved to be so much more devastating than the complaints of earlier critics.

Other critics had complained of impious priests, an unresponsive bureaucracy, and a church too much involved in matters of government, but the theology that Luther developed struck at the very structure of the church itself. Luther separated justification from acts of sanctification—from the good works or charity expected of all Christians. In Luther's theology the acts of piety so typical of the medieval church were quite unnecessary for salvation, because Christ's sacrifice had brought justification once and for all. Justification came entirely from God and was independent of human acts. Luther argued that the Christian was at the same time sinner and saved, so the penitential cycle and careful preparation for a "good death" were, in his opinion, unnecessary.

Luther also attacked the place of the priesthood in the sacramental life of the church. The church taught that, through the actions of ordained priests, Christ was really present in the bread and wine of the sacrament of Holy Communion. Luther agreed that the sacrament transformed the bread and wine into the body and blood of Christ, but he denied that priests had a role in the transformation. Priests distributed only the bread to the laity, reserving the consecrated wine for themselves—further emphasizing their own special status. Priests, in Luther's view, were not mediators between God and individual Christians. John Wyclif and John Hus (see page 400) had argued against the spiritual authority of unworthy priests. Luther, however, directly challenged the role of the clergy and the institutional church in the attainment of salvation. Thus he argued for a "priesthood of all believers."

In the years before 1517, Luther's views on salvation and his reservations about the traditional ways of teaching theology attracted little interest outside his own university. Matters changed, however, when he challenged the sale of indulgences. Indulgences were often granted because of pilgrimages, or great acts of charity or sacrifice. The papacy frequently authorized the sale of indulgences to pay various expenses. Unscrupulous

priests often left the impression that purchase of an indulgence freed a soul from purgatory. After getting no response to his initial complaints, Luther made public his "Ninety-five Theses." Luther probably posted these theses on indulgences on the door of the Wittenberg Castle church, the usual way to announce topics for theological discussion about the interpretation of the Scriptures and the nature of penance. Luther's text created a firestorm when it was quickly translated and printed throughout German-speaking lands. His complaints about the sale of indulgences encapsulated German feelings about unworthy priests and economic abuses by the clergy. Luther was acclaimed as the spokesman of the German people.

In a debate with a papal representative in Leipzig in 1519, Luther was forced to admit that in some of his positions he agreed with the Czech heretic John Hus. In the Leipzig debate and in the following year Luther responded to his critics and tried to explain more fully the nature of the changes he advocated. Three tracts were especially important. In *Address to the Christian Nobility of the German Nation,* Luther urged the princes to reject papal claims of temporal and spiritual authority. (See the box, "Martin Luther's Address to the Christian Nobility of the German Nation.") In *On the Babylonian Captivity of the Church,* he argued for the principle of *sola scriptura*—that is, authority in the church had to be based on teachings found in the Bible. In *On Christian Freedom,* he explained clearly his understanding of salvation: "A Christian has all he needs in faith and needs no works to justify him." Luther was speaking of spiritual freedom from unnecessary ritual, not social or political freedom. This distinction would later be crucial to Luther's opposition to political and economic protests by peasants and artisans.

In 1520, Pope Leo X (r. 1513–1521) condemned Luther's teachings and gave him sixty days to recant. Luther refused to do so and publically burned the papal letter. In 1521, Emperor Charles V called an imperial diet, or parliament, at Worms to deal with the religious crisis. Charles demanded that Luther submit to papal authority. Luther, however, explained that religious decisions must be based on personal experience and conscience:

Unless I am convicted by the testimony of Scripture or by clear reason, for I do not trust either in the Pope or in

Martin Luther's Address to the Christian Nobility of the German Nation

Luther wrote this tract to the rulers of Germany to explain the nature of his conflict with the church over ecclesiastical authority. In this excerpt, he makes clear his disagreements with the system of clerical status and immunities that had grown throughout the Middle Ages. Compare his statements with those in the box, "Ignatius Loyola's Spiritual Exercises" on page 537.

The Romanists have very cleverly built three walls around themselves. In the first place, when pressed by the temporal power, they have made decrees and declared that the temporal power had no jurisdiction over them, but that on the contrary, the spiritual power is above the temporal. In the second place, when the attempt is made to reprove them with the Scriptures, they raise the objection that only the pope may interpret the Scriptures. In the third place if threatened with a council, their story is that no one may summon a council but the Pope.

Let us begin by attacking the first wall. It is pure invention that the Pope, bishops, priests, and monks are called the spiritual estate while princes, lords, craftsmen, and peasants are the temporal estate. This is indeed a piece of deceit and hypocrisy: . . . all Christians are truly of the spiritual estate. . . . The Pope or bishop anoints, shaves heads, ordains, consecrates, and prescribes garb different from that of the laity, but he can never make a man into a Christian or into a spiritual man by so doing. He might well make a man into a hypo-crite or a humbug and a blockhead, but never a Christian or a spiritual man. . . . Therefore a priest in Christendom is nothing else but an officeholder. As long as he holds his office, he takes precedence; where he is deposed, he is a peasant or a townsman like anybody else. . . .

The second wall is still more loosely built and less substantial. The Romanists want to be the only masters of Holy Scripture, although they never learn a thing from the Bible their life long. . . . Besides, if we are all priests, . . . and all have one faith, one gospel, one sacrament, why should we not also have the power to test and judge what is right or wrong in matters of faith?

The third wall falls of itself, when the first two are down. When the Pope acts contrary to the Scriptures, it is our duty to stand by the Scriptures and to reprove him and to constrain him, according to the word of Christ. . . . The Romanists have no basis in Scripture for their claim that the Pope alone was right to call or to confirm a council. This is just their own ruling, and it is only valid so long as it is not harmful to Christendom or contrary to the laws of God.

Source: Martin Luther, *Three Treatises,* in *The American Edition of Luther's Works* (Philadelphia: Fortress Press, 1970), pp. 10–22.

councils alone, since it is well known that they have often erred and contradicted themselves, . . . I cannot and will not retract anything, for it is neither safe nor right to go against conscience. I cannot do otherwise, here I stand, may God help me. Amen.[3]

The emperor and his allies, however, stayed firmly in the papal camp. The excommunicated Luther was placed under an imperial ban—that is, declared an outlaw. As Luther left the Diet of Worms, friendly princes took him to Wartburg Castle in Saxony, where they could protect him. During a year of isolation at Wartburg, Luther used Erasmus's edition of the Greek New Testament as the basis of a translation into German of the New Testament, which became an influential literary as well as religious work.

THE REFORMATION AND COUNTER-REFORMATION

1513–1517	Fifth Lateran Council meets to consider reform of the Catholic church
1517	Luther makes public his "Ninety-five Theses"
1518	Zwingli is appointed people's priest of Zurich
1520	Pope Leo X condemns Luther's teachings
1521	Luther appears at the Diet of Worms
1524–1525	Peasant revolts in Germany
1527	Imperial troops sack Rome
1530	Melanchthon composes the Augsburg Confession summarizing Lutheran belief
1534	Calvin flees from Paris; Loyola founds the Society of Jesus
1535	The Anabaptist community of Münster is destroyed
1536	Calvin arrives in Geneva and publishes the first edition of *Institutes of the Christian Religion*
1545–1563	Council of Trent meets to reform the Catholic church
1555	Emperor Charles V accepts the Peace of Augsburg

The Reformation of the Communities

Luther challenged the authority of the clerical hierarchy and called on lay people to take responsibility for their own salvation. His ideas spread rapidly in the towns and countryside of Germany because he and his followers took advantage of the new technology of printing. (See the feature, "Weighing the Evidence: A Reformation Woodcut," on pages 542–543.) Perhaps 300,000 copies of his early tracts were published in the first years of the protest. Luther's claim that the Scriptures must be the basis of all life and his appeal to the

judgment of the laity seem to have struck a responsive chord in towns and villages, where councils of local people were accustomed to making decisions based on ideas of the common good. It is also true that townsmen and villagers saw religious and civic life as being inextricably interconnected. For them, there was no such thing as a religiously neutral act.

The impact of Luther's ideas quickly became evident. If the active intercession of the clergy was not necessary for the salvation of individuals, then, according to Luther's followers, there was no reason for the clergy to remain unmarried and celibate, and there was no reason for men or women to cloister themselves in monasteries or convents. Also, maintained Luther's partisans, there was no need to restrict the laity's participation in the sacrament of the Eucharist. Thus, the priest must distribute wine to the laity along with the bread. With the spread of Luther's ideas came the end of a very visual part of the clerical monopoly. Because Luther's followers believed that penitential acts were not prerequisites for salvation, they tended to set aside the veneration of saints and not to make pilgrimages to the shrines and holy places all over Europe.

Many historians have referred to the spread of these reform ideas as "the Reformation of the Common Man." In Strasbourg, Nuremberg, Zurich, and other towns, ideas about the primacy of the Bible and attacks on clerical privilege were spread by "people's priests," preachers hired by the town government to see to preaching and the care of souls in the community. Many of the most famous reformers initially gained a following through preaching. The message then seems to have spread especially quickly among artisan and mercantile groups, which put pressure on town governments to press for reform. Agitation was often riotous. One resident of Augsburg exposed himself during a church service to protest what he believed was an evil and idolatrous service.

To quell disturbances and to arrive at a consensus within the community, cautious town councils often set up debates between reformers and church representatives. Because the church hierarchy rarely approved of such debates, traditional views were often poorly represented, giving a great advantage to the reformers. The two sides argued over the authority of the church hierarchy, the nature of salvation, and whether papal authority and the seven sacraments could be demonstrated in the Bible. At the conclusion of such a debate, many town governments ordered that preaching and practice in the town should be according to the "Word of God"—a code for reformed practice. In reformed towns, the city council became a council of elders for the church. Thus, civil government came to play an important role in the local organization of the church.

The case of Zurich is instructive. In 1519 the people's priest of Zurich was Huldrych Zwingli (1484–1531), son of a rural official from a nearby village. After a university education, he became a typical late medieval country priest, right down to his numerous mistresses. Yet after experiences as a military chaplain and an acquaintance with the humanist writings of Erasmus, Zwingli began to preach strongly biblical sermons. In 1522 he defended a group of laymen who broke a required Lenten fast to show their disapproval of what they saw as useless ritual. Later in the same year he requested episcopal permission to marry. Early in 1523, he led a group of reformers in a public debate over the nature of the church. The city council declared in favor of the reformers, and Zurich became, in effect, a Protestant city.

Unlike Luther, Zwingli believed that reform should be a communal movement—that town governments should take the lead in bringing reform to the community. Zwingli explained that moral regeneration of individuals was an essential precondition for God's gift of grace. In the years following 1523, the reformers restructured church services, abolishing mass; they also removed religious images from churches and suppressed monastic institutions. Zwingli further disagreed with Luther about the nature of the sacrament of Holy Communion. Whereas Luther, like Catholic theologians, accepted that Christ was truly present in the bread and wine, Zwingli argued that Christ's presence was merely spiritual—the bread and wine merely signified Christ. This disagreement created within the movement for reform a division that made a common response to papal or imperial pressure difficult (Map 14.1).

The reform message spread from towns into the countryside, but often with effects that the reformers did not expect or desire. Luther thought his message was a spiritual and theological one.

Many peasants and modest artisans, however, believed Luther's message of biblical freedom carried material as well as theological meaning.

In many parts of Germany villagers and peasants found themselves under increasing pressure from landlords and territorial princes. Taking advantage of changed economic and political conditions, these lords were intent on regaining claims to ancient manorial rights, on suppressing peasant claims to use common lands, and on imposing new taxes and tithes. Like townsmen, peasants saw religious and material life as closely connected. They argued that new tithes and taxes did not just go against tradition but violated the Word of God. Using Luther's argument that authority should be based on the Scriptures, peasants from the district of Zurich, for example, petitioned the town council in 1523–1524, claiming that they

Peasant Freedom The German peasants believed Luther's call for individual freedom of conscience included economic and political freedom. Their revolt of 1524–1525 struck terror in the hearts of German rulers. As this woodcut indicates, the peasant army was lightly armed. Many carried only tools, pitchforks, flails, and scythes. (*Title page of an anonymous pamphlet from the Peasants' War, 1525*)

Map 14.1 Reform in Germany The pattern of religious reform in Germany was complex. Although some territorial princes, such as the dukes of Bavaria, rejected the reform, most free towns, particularly those in the southwest, adopted it.

should not be required to pay tithes on their produce because there was no biblical justification for doing so. Townsmen rejected the peasants' demand, noting that the Bible did not forbid such payments and saying that the peasants should make them out of love.

Demands that landlords and magistrates give up human ordinances and follow "Godly Law" soon turned to violence. Peasants, miners, and villagers in 1524 and 1525 participated in a series of uprisings that began on the borderlands between Switzerland and Germany and spread throughout southwest Germany, upper Austria, and even into

northern Italy. Bands of peasants and villagers, perhaps a total of 300,000 in the empire, revolted against their seigneurial lords or even their territorial overlords.

Luther initially counseled landlords and princes to redress the just grievances. As reports of riots and increased violence continued to reach Wittenberg, however, Luther condemned the rebels as "mad dogs" and urged that they be destroyed. Territorial princes and large cities quickly raised armies to meet the threat. The peasants were defeated and destroyed in a series of battles in April 1525. It seems likely that, in response to these rebellions, lords lived in fear of another revolt and were careful not to overburden their tenants. But when it became clear that the reformers were unwilling to follow the implications of their own theology, villagers and peasants lost interest in the progress of the reform. As a townsman of Zurich commented, "Many came to a great hatred of the preachers, where before they would have bitten off their feet for the Gospel."[4]

John Calvin and the Reformed Tradition

The revolts of 1524 and 1525 demonstrated the mixed messages traveling under the rubric "true, or biblical religion." In the 1530s, the theological arguments of the reformers began to take on a greater clarity, mostly because of the Franco-Swiss reformer John Calvin (1509–1564). Calvin had a humanistic education in Paris and became a lawyer before coming under the influence of reform-minded thinkers in France. In 1534 he fled from Paris as royal pressures against reformers increased. He arrived in Geneva in 1536, where he would remain, except for a short exile, until the end of his life.

Because of the central location of Geneva and the power of Calvin's theology, Geneva quickly replaced Wittenberg as the source of Protestant thought and became a haven for many of Europe's religious refugees. Calvin's ideas about salvation and the godly community rapidly spread to France, the Low Countries, Scotland, and England. Until the end of his life, Calvin was a magnet drawing people interested in reform.

The heart of Calvin's appeal lay in his formal theological writings. In 1536 he published the first of many editions of *Institutes of the Christian Religion*, which was to become the summa of reform theology. In it Calvin laid out a doctrine of the absolute power of God and the complete depravity and powerlessness of humanity.

Calvin believed in predestination, that "the word of God takes root and grows only in those whom the Lord, by his eternal election, has predestined to be his children." Like Luther, Calvin viewed salvation as a mysterious gift of God.

Calvin believed that from the beginning of time God had elected those to be saved and those to be damned and that human actions play no part in the divine plan. The elect—that is, the people to whom God graciously grants salvation—freely do

John Calvin This image of Calvin in his study is similar to countless pictures of Saint Jerome and Erasmus at work and reminds viewers of Calvin's humanistic education and the role of Christian and classical learning in his theology. *(Lauros/Giraudon/Art Resource, NY)*

good works in response to "God's benevolence." Further, Calvin suggested, the elect would benefit from "signs of divine benevolence," an idea that would have a profound impact on the Calvinist understanding of the relationship of wealth to spiritual life. Calvin believed that good works and a well-ordered society were the result of God's grace. By the seventeenth century, followers of Calvin widely believed that the elect had a duty to work in the secular world and that wealth accumulated in business was a sign of God's favor. It was an idea nicely adapted to the increasingly wealthy world of early modern Europe.

That connection between salvation and material life, however, lay in the future. The aspect of election that most interested Calvin was the creation of a truly Christian community by the elect. To accomplish this, Calvinist Christians, later to be known as members of the Reformed church, purged their churches of any manifestation of "superstition." Like Zwingli they rejected the idea that Christ was really present in the sacrament of Holy Communion. They rejected the role of saints. They removed from their churches and destroyed paintings and statuary that they believed were indications of idolatry.

Public officials were to be "vicars of God." They had the power to lead and correct both the faithful and the unregenerate sinners who lived in Christian communities. In his years in Geneva, Calvin tried to create a "Christian Commonwealth," but Geneva was far from a theocracy. Calvin's initial attempts to create a Christian community by requiring public confession and allowing church leaders to discipline sinners were rejected by Geneva's city council, which exiled Calvin in 1538.

On his return in 1541 he sought to institute church reforms modeled on those he had observed in the Protestant city of Strasbourg. Calvin's Reformed church hierarchy was made up of four offices: preachers, teachers, deacons, and elders. Preachers and teachers saw to the care and education of the faithful. Deacons, as in the early church, were charged with attending to the material needs of the congregation. The elders—the true leaders of the Genevan church—were selected from the patriciate that dominated the civil government of the city. Thus, it makes as much sense to speak of a church governed by the town as a town dominated by the church. The elders actively intervened in education, charity, and attempts to regulate prostitution. Consistories, or church courts, made up of community elders who enforced community moral and religious values, became one of the most important characteristics of Reformed (Calvinist) communities.

Reformed churchmen reacted promptly and harshly to events that seemed to threaten either church or state. The most famous event was the capture, trial, and execution of Michael Servetus (1511–1553), a Spanish physician and radical theologian who rejected generally accepted doctrines like the Trinity and specifically criticized many of Calvin's teachings in the *Institutes*. After corresponding with Servetus for a time, Calvin remarked that if Servetus were in Geneva, "I would not suffer him to get out alive." After living in various parts of Europe, Servetus eventually did anonymously come to Geneva. He was recognized

and arrested. Calvin was as good as his word. After a public debate and trial, Servetus was burned at the stake for blaspheming the Trinity and the Christian religion. Calvin's condemnation of Servetus was all too typical of Christians in the sixteenth century. Lutherans, Calvinists, and Catholics all believed that protection of true religion required harsh measures. All too few could have said, as the humanist reformer Sebastion Castellio did, "To burn a heretic is not to defend a doctrine, but to burn a man."[5]

The Radical Reform of the Anabaptists

Michael Servetus was but one of a number of extremists who claimed to be carrying out the full reform implied in the teachings of Luther, Zwingli, and Calvin. Called "Anabaptists" (or "rebaptizers" because of their rejection of infant baptism), or simply "radicals," they tended to take biblical commands more literally than the mainline reformers. They rejected infant baptism as unbiblical, and they refused to take civil oaths or hold public office, for to do so would be to compromise with unreformed civil society.

The earliest of the radicals allied themselves with the rebels of 1525. Thomas Müntzer (1490–1525) was an influential preacher who believed in divine revelation through visions and dreams. His own visions told him that the poor were the true elect and that the end of the world was at hand. An active participant in the revolts of 1525, Müntzer called on the elect to drive out the ungodly. After the defeat of the rebels, he was captured and executed by the German princes.

Other radicals, such as the revolutionaries who took control of the north German city of Münster, rejected infant baptism, adopted polygamy, and proclaimed a new "Kingdom of Righteousness." The reformers of Münster instituted the new kingdom in the city by rebaptizing those who joined their cause and driving out those who opposed them. They abolished private property rights in Münster and instituted new laws concerning morality and behavior. Leadership in the city eventually passed to a tailor, Jan of Leiden (d. 1535), who proclaimed himself the new messiah and lord of the world. The Anabaptists were opposed by the prince-bishop of Münster, the political and religious lord of the city. After a sixteen-month siege, the bishop and his allies recaptured

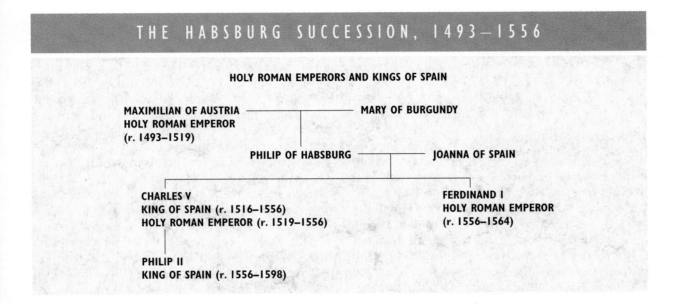

THE HABSBURG SUCCESSION, 1493–1556

HOLY ROMAN EMPERORS AND KINGS OF SPAIN

MAXIMILIAN OF AUSTRIA ———————— MARY OF BURGUNDY
HOLY ROMAN EMPEROR
(r. 1493–1519)

PHILIP OF HABSBURG ———————— JOANNA OF SPAIN

CHARLES V   FERDINAND I
KING OF SPAIN (r. 1516–1556)   HOLY ROMAN EMPEROR
HOLY ROMAN EMPEROR (r. 1519–1556)   (r. 1556–1564)

PHILIP II
KING OF SPAIN (r. 1556–1598)

the city from the Anabaptists in 1535. Besieging forces massacred men, women, and children. Jan of Leiden was captured and executed by mutilation with red-hot tongs.

With the destruction of the Münster revolutionaries in 1535, the Anabaptist movement turned inward. Under leaders like Menno Simons (1495–1561), who founded the Mennonites, and Jakob Hutter (d. 1536), who founded the Moravian Societies, the radicals rejected the violent establishment of truly holy cities. To varying degrees they also rejected connections with civil society, military service, even civil courts. They did, however, believe that their own communities were communities of the elect. They tended to close themselves off from outsiders and enforce a strict discipline over their members. The elders of these communities were empowered to excommunicate or "shun" those who violated the community's precepts. Anabaptist communities have proved unusually durable. Moravian and Mennonite communities continue to exist in western Europe, North America, and even in parts of what used to be the Soviet Union.

Like Luther, all of the early reformers appealed to the authority of the Bible in their attacks on church tradition. Yet in the villages and towns of Germany and Switzerland, many radicals were prepared to move far beyond the positions Luther had advocated. When they did so, Luther found himself in the odd position of appealing for vigorous action to the very imperial authorities whose inaction had allowed his own protest to survive.

THE EMPIRE OF CHARLES V (r. 1519–1556)

Luther believed that secular authorities should be benevolently neutral in religious matters. In his eyes, the success of the early Reformation was simply God's will:

I simply taught, preached and wrote God's Word; otherwise I did nothing. And while I slept or drank Wittenberg beer with my friends . . . , the Word so greatly weakened the Papacy that no prince or emperor ever inflicted such losses on it. I did nothing; the Word did everything.[6]

As great as the word of God was, Luther must have known that even as he drank his beer, the Holy Roman emperor could have crushed the reform movement if he had chosen to enforce imperial decrees. But attempts to resolve religious conflict became entangled with attempts to hold together the family lands of the Habsburg emperor and with political rivalries among the various German princes. The eventual religious settlement required a constitutional compromise that preserved the virtual autonomy of the great princes of Germany. The political realities of sixteenth-century Europe were that political leaders were afraid of the emperor even when he tried to preserve the essential unity of the Christian church.

Imperial Challenges

Emperor Charles V (r. 1519–1556) was the beneficiary of a series of marriages that, in the words of his courtiers, seemed to re-create the empire of Charlemagne. From his father, Philip of Habsburg, he inherited claims to Austria, the imperial crown, and Burgundian lands that included the Low Countries and the county of Burgundy. Through his mother, Joanna, the daughter of Ferdinand and Isabella of Spain, Charles became heir to the kingdoms of Castile, Aragon, Sicily, Naples, and Spanish America. During the Italian wars of the early sixteenth century, Charles's holdings in Italy expanded to include the duchy of Milan and most of the rest of Lombardy. By 1506 he was duke in the Burgundian lands; in 1516 he became king of Aragon and Castile; and in 1519 he was elected Holy Roman emperor. Every government in Europe had to deal with one part or another of Charles's empire. His chancellor enthused, "[God] has set you on the way towards a world monarchy, towards the gathering of all Christendom under a single shepherd."

Charles seems to have sincerely desired such a world monarchy, but each of the areas under his control challenged his authority. In Castile, for example, grandees, townsmen, and peasants felt they had grounds for complaint. They objected that taxes were too heavy and that Charles disregarded the Cortes and his natural advisers, the old nobility. But most of all they complained that too many of his officials were foreigners whom he had brought with him from his home in Flanders. Protests festered in the towns and villages of Castile and finally broke out into a revolt called the Comunero (townsmen's or citizens') movement. Between 1517 and 1522, when religious reform was making dramatic advances in Germany, many of the most important towns of Spain were in open rebellion against the Crown. Charles's forces eventually took control of the situation, and by 1522 he had crushed the Comuneros. Between 1522 and 1530, he was careful to spend much of his time in his Spanish kingdoms.

Charles's claims in Italy, as well as his claims to lands in the Pyrenees and in the Low Countries, brought him into direct conflict with the Valois kings of France. Again in the critical 1520s, the Habsburgs and the Valois fought a series of wars (see page 412). Charles dramatically defeated the French at Pavia in northern Italy in 1525, sacked and occupied Rome in 1527, and became the virtual arbitrator of Italian politics. In the course of the struggle, the Catholic Francis I of France, whose title was "the Most Christian king," found it to his advantage to ally himself with Charles's most serious opponents, the Protestants and the Turks. Francis demonstrated the truth of Machiavelli's dictum that private virtues very often play a small role in political and diplomatic life. The Habsburg-Valois Wars dragged on until, in exhaustion, the French king Henry II (r. 1547–1559) and the Spanish king Philip II (r. 1556–1598) signed the Treaty of Cateau-Cambrésis in 1559.

Charles was not the only ruler to claim the title "emperor" and a succession reaching back to the Roman Empire. After the conquest of Constantinople in 1453, the sultan of the Ottoman Turks began to refer to himself as "the Emperor." After consolidating control of Constantinople and the Balkans, Turkish armies under the command of Emperor Suleiman (r. 1520–1566), known as "the Magnificent," resumed their expansion to the north and west. After capturing Belgrade, Turkish forces soundly defeated a Hungarian army at the Battle of Mohács in 1526. Charles appealed for unity within Christendom against the threat. Even Martin Luther agreed that Christians should unite during invasion.

Suleiman's army besieged Vienna in 1529 before being forced to retreat. Turks also created a navy in the Mediterranean and, with French encouragement, began a series of raids along the coasts of Italy and Spain. The Turkish fleet remained a threat throughout the sixteenth century. The reign of Suleiman in many respects marked the permanent entry of Turkey into the European military and diplomatic system. Turkish pressure was yet another reason why Charles was unable to deal with German Protestants in a direct and uncompromising way. (See the box, "Encounters

The Capture of Belgrade During the sixteenth century Ottoman Turks dominated the Balkans militarily and were a significant force in European diplomacy. They were masters of coordinated attacks combining artillery and infantry. *(Österreichische Nationalbibliothek)*

with the West: Duels Among Europeans and Turks.")

German Politics

The political configuration of Germany had an ongoing influence on the course of the religious reform. In 1500, Germany was much less centralized than France or England. Since 1495, seven electoral princes (three archbishops and four lay princes) and a larger circle of imperial princes had claimed the right to representation in the imperial council, and nearly three hundred other towns or principalities demanded various exemptions from imperial control. The emperor's claims in most areas amounted to the right to collect modest taxes on households and individuals, a court of high justice, and the right to proclaim imperial truces. Yet the empire lacked a unified legal system, and the emperor himself had only one vote on the imperial council. In many respects political central-

ization and innovation were characteristics of individual territories, not of the empire as a whole. The power of the emperor depended on his relations with the towns and princes of Germany.

In the first years after Luther issued his "Ninety-five Theses," he was defended by the elector Frederick of Saxony, who held a key vote in Charles's quest for election as Holy Roman emperor. As long as Frederick protected Luther, imperial officials had to proceed against him with caution. When Luther was outlawed by the imperial Diet of Worms in 1521, Frederick and many other princes and towns refused to enforce the edict against him and his followers unless their own grievances with the emperor and their complaints about the church were taken up at the same time. In 1522 and 1526 the emperor again tried to enforce the ban, but imperial officials were bluntly informed that the towns were unable to conform. At the Diet of Speyer in 1526, delegates passed a resolution empowering princes and

∼ ENCOUNTERS WITH THE WEST ∼

Duels Among Europeans and Turks

A Flemish diplomat in the service of Ferdinand I of Austria (who became Emperor Ferdinand I after the abdication of Charles V), Augier Ghislain De Busbecq (1522–1592) was twice sent to Constantinople as ambassador. Understanding the Turks and their interests was critical for the Germans as attacks by the Turks in eastern Europe prevented the empire from either suppressing the German Protestants or pressing German claims against the French. The following selection is part of a letter written from Constantinople in 1560. In it, Busbecq discusses violence among the Turks and contrasts it with Europeans' behavior.

The mention I made a while ago of matters in the confines of Hungary, gives me occasion to tell you, what the Turks think of duels, which among Christians are accounted a singular badge of personal valor. There was one Arstambey, a sanjack [district official], who lived on the frontier of Hungary, who was very much famed as a robust person [Arsta signifies a lion in Turkey]. He was an expert with the bow; no man brandished his sword with more strength; none was more terrible to his enemy. Not far from his district there also dwelt one Ulybey, also a sanjack, who was jealous of the same praise. And this jealousy (initiated perhaps by other occasions) at length occasioned hatred and many bloody combats between them. It happened thus, Ulybey was sent for to Constantinople, upon what occasion I know not. When he arrived there, the Pashas [governors] had asked many questions of him in the Divan [court] concerning other matters. At last they demanded how it was that he and Arstambey came to fall out? . . . To put his own cause in the best light, he said that once Arstambey had laid an ambush and wounded him treacherously.

Which he said, Arstambey need not have done, if he would have shown himself worthy of the name he bears because Ulybey often challenged him to fight hand to hand and never refused to meet him on the field. The Pashas, taking great offense, replied, "How dare you challenge a fellow soldier to a duel? What? Was there no Christian to fight with? Do both of you eat your emperor's bread? And yet, you attempt to take one another's life? What precedent did you have for this? Don't you know that whichever of you had died, the emperor would have lost a subject?" Whereupon, by their command, he was carried off to prison where he lay pining for many months. And at last, with difficulty, he was released, but with the loss of his reputation.

It is quite different among us Christians. Our people will draw their swords many times against each other before they ever come in sight of a public enemy, and unfortunately, they count it a brave and honorable thing to do. What should one do in such a case? Vice has usurped the seat of virtue and that which is worthy of punishment is counted noble and glorious.

Source: The Four Epistles of A. G. Busbequius Concerning His Embassy to Turkey (London: J. Taylor & J. Wyat, 1694), pp. 196–198.

towns to settle religious matters in their territories as they saw fit. In effect, this resolution legitimated the reform in territories where authorities chose to follow the new teachings and presaged the eventual shape of the final religious settlement in Germany.

German princes took advantage of the emperor's relative powerlessness and made choices reflecting a complex of religious, political, and diplomatic issues. Electoral Saxony and ducal Saxony, the two parts of the province of Saxony, split over the issue of reform. Electoral Saxony, Luther's homeland, was Lutheran. Ducal Saxony was strongly Catholic. Especially in the autonomous towns, many decisions about religion were often made with an eye on the choices made by neighbors and competitors.

Some rulers made decisions that were even more consciously cynical. The Grand Master of the religious order of the Teutonic Knights, Albrecht von Hohenzollern (1490–1568), who controlled the duchy of Prussia, renounced his monastic vows. Then, at the urging of Luther and other reformers, he secularized the order's estates (that is, he transferred them from church to private ownership), which then became East Prussia, hereditary lands of the Hohenzollern family. In other territories, rulers managed to claim the properties of suppressed religious orders. Even when, as in the case of Count Philip of Hesse (1504–1567), much of the revenue from secularization was used to create

hospitals and an organized system of charity, the reforming prince was still enriched.

Some rulers found their personal reservations about Luther reinforced by their fears of popular unrest. Luther's call for decisions based on personal conscience seemed to the dukes of Bavaria, for example, to be a call for attacks on princely authority and even anarchy. In the confused and fluid situation of the 1520s and 1530s, imperial interests were never the primary issue.

The Religious Settlement

With the fading of the Turkish threat on Vienna in 1529, Charles V renewed his pressure on the German principalities at a meeting of the imperial diet at Augsburg in 1530. It was for this diet that Philip Melanchthon (1497–1560), Luther's closest adviser, prepared the Augsburg Confession, which would

The Augsburg Confession In this woodcut of the Augsburg Confession being read to Charles V, the artist has included in the background text and images of the Lutheran teachings on the sacraments and the nature of salvation. In contrast are the images on the left of a papal ceremony and court hierarchy in which, the artist implies, Christ is not present. *(Kunstsammlung Veste Coburg)*

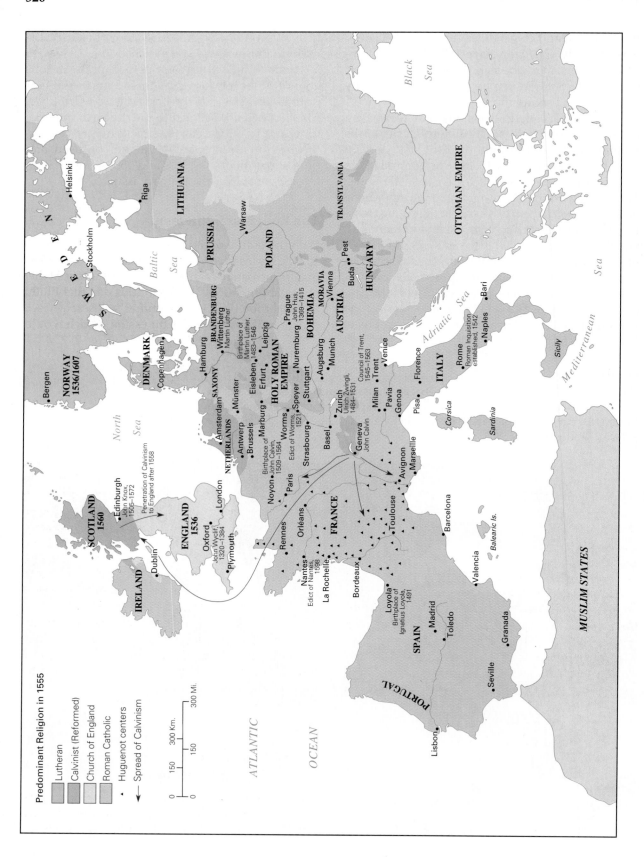

Predominant Religion in 1555

- Lutheran
- Calvinist (Reformed)
- Church of England
- Roman Catholic
- ▲ Huguenot centers
- → Spread of Calvinism

0   150   300 Km.
0   150   300 Mi.

ATLANTIC

OCEAN

North Sea

Baltic Sea

Black Sea

Adriatic Sea

Mediterranean Sea

MUSLIM STATES

OTTOMAN EMPIRE

SWEDEN
Stockholm
Helsinki
Riga
LITHUANIA
Warsaw
PRUSSIA
POLAND
TRANSYLVANIA

NORWAY
1536/1607
Bergen

DENMARK
Copenhagen

BRANDENBURG
Hamburg
Wittenberg
Birthplace of
Martin Luther
SAXONY
Leipzig
Eisleben, 1483–1546
Erfurt
Münster
Amsterdam
NETHERLANDS
Antwerp
Brussels
HOLY ROMAN
EMPIRE
Nuremburg
Speyer
Worms
Edict of Worms,
1521
Strasbourg
Birthplace of
John Calvin,
1509–1564
Noyon
Paris

Prague
John Hus,
1369–1415
BOHEMIA
MORAVIA
Vienna
AUSTRIA
Munich
Augsburg
Stuttgart

HUNGARY
Buda
Pest

Zurich
Ulrich Zwingli,
1484–1531
Basel
Geneva
John Calvin
Milan
Pavia
Genoa
Trent
Venice
Council of Trent,
1545–1563
Florence
Pisa
ITALY
Rome
Roman Inquisition
established, 1542
Naples
Bari
Corsica
Sardinia
Sicily

SCOTLAND
1560
Edinburgh
John Knox,
1505–1572
Penetration of Calvinism
to England after 1558

ENGLAND
1536
Oxford
London
John Wyclif,
1320–1384
Plymouth

IRELAND
Dublin

FRANCE
Rennes
Orléans
Nantes
Edict of Nantes,
1598
La Rochelle
Bordeaux
Toulouse
Avignon
Marseille

Loyola
Birthplace of
Ignatius Loyola,
1491
Madrid
Toledo
Barcelona
Valencia
Granada
Seville
SPAIN
PORTUGAL
Lisbon
Balearic Is.

become the basic statement of the Lutheran faith. Melanchthon hoped that the document would form the basis of compromise with Catholic powers, but the possibility was rejected out of hand by the imperial party. Charles aimed to affirm his strength in Germany by forcing the princes to end the reform movement and enforce the papal and imperial bans on Luther's teachings.

The Protestant princes responded by forming the League of Schmalkalden. At first, the founders of the league claimed that they were interested in protecting Reformed preaching, but the league quickly developed as a center of opposition to imperial influence in general. Eventually Charles and a group of allied princes managed to defeat the league at the Battle of Mühlberg in 1547. The emperor was unable to continue pressure on the Protestants, however, because he had depended on the support of some Protestant princes in his battles with the league. As a result, even after military defeat the Protestant princes were able to maintain religious autonomy. In the Religious Peace of Augsburg of 1555 the emperor formally acknowledged the principle that sovereign princes could choose the religion to be practiced in their territories, *cuius regio, eius religio* ("whose territory, his religion"). There were limits, however, for leaders could only remain under papal authority or adopt the Augsburg Confession outlined by Melanchthon. Reformed churches associated with Zwingli or Calvin were not legally recognized (Map 14.2).

Shortly after the settlement, Charles abdicated his Spanish and imperial titles. Exhausted by years of political and religious struggle, he ceded the imperial crown to his brother, Ferdinand (r. 1556–1564). His possessions in the Low Countries, Spain, Italy, and the New World he ceded to his son, Philip II (r. 1556–1598). Charles had believed his courtiers who compared his empire to that of the ancient Romans. He had believed that his duty as emperor was to unite Christendom under one

law and one church. But in no part of his empire did he ever command the authority that would have allowed him to unite his lands politically, let alone to re-establish religious unity. Following his abdication, Charles retired to a monastery in Spain, where he died in 1558.

THE ENGLISH REFORMATION, 1520–1603

England was closely tied to Germany. Since the twelfth century, large numbers of German merchants had lived and traded in England, and there was a major English community in Cologne. Anglo-German connections became especially significant during the Reformation. Reformers from Wittenberg and other Protestant towns had contact with English merchants from London who traded and traveled on the Continent. One reformer, William Tyndale (ca. 1494–1536), served as a bridge between the Continent and England. He had a humanistic education in classical languages and began working on a translation of the Bible in the 1520s. Forced to flee London by the church hierarchy, he visited Luther in Wittenberg before settling in Antwerp, where he completed his translation of the New Testament. By 1526, copies of his translation and his religious tracts flooded into England. By the 1520s, Lutheran influence was noticeable in London and Cambridge. To some extent the ground may have been prepared for the reformers by the few surviving Lollards, the followers of Wyclif, who had argued for church reform in the late fourteenth and fifteenth centuries (see page 400). Lollards, who tended to be literate, were an ideal market for Tyndale's English Bible and his numerous tracts.

As in Germany, institutional change in the church followed from both secular issues and reform ideas. In England, an initially hostile monarch began to tolerate reform ideas when he perceived the papacy as an unbiblical, tyrannical force blocking essential state policy.

Map 14.2 Protestants and Catholics in 1555
Christendom in western Europe was divided into three major groups. Lutheran influence was largely confined to parts of Germany and Scandinavia, while Calvinist influence spread from Switzerland into Scotland, the Low Countries, and parts of France. Most of the West, however, remained within the Roman Church.

Henry VIII and the Monarchical Reformation

Henry VIII (r. 1509–1547) began his reign as a popular and powerful king. Handsome, athletic, and artistic, he seemed to be the ideal ruler. Henry took an interest in theology and humanistic culture. At first, he was quite hostile to Luther's reform ideas and wrote *Defense of the Seven Sacraments,* which earned him the title "Defender of the Faith" from a grateful Pope Leo X. Throughout his life Henry remained suspicious of many Protestant ideas, but he led the initial phase of the break between the English church and the papacy because of his political problems with the highly orthodox Holy Roman emperor Charles V. The first phase of the English Reformation was thus a monarchical reformation.

Henry VII had initiated closer relations with Spain when he married his eldest son, Arthur, prince of Wales, to Ferdinand of Aragon's daughter, Catherine. After Arthur's death the future Henry VIII was married to Catherine in 1509. Henry VIII later tried to further the Anglo-imperial alliance when he arranged a treaty by which the emperor Charles V, who was Catherine of Aragon's nephew, agreed to marry Henry's daughter, Mary Tudor. But by the late 1520s the Anglo-imperial alliance fell apart when Charles, responding to Spanish pressures, renounced the proposed marriage and instead married a Portuguese princess.

Henry's relations with Charles were further weakened by what the English called "The King's Great Matter," that is, his determination to divorce Catherine of Aragon. Recalling the unrest of the Wars of the Roses, Henry believed that he needed a son to ensure that the Tudors could maintain control of the English crown. By 1527, Henry and Catherine had a daughter, Mary, but no living sons. Henry became convinced that he remained without a male heir because, by biblical standards, he had committed incest by marrying his brother's widow. As Leviticus 20:21 says, "If a man takes his brother's wife, it is impurity; . . . they shall remain childless." Henry desired an annulment. Unfortunately for him, Leo X's successor, Pope Clement VII (r. 1523–1534), was a virtual prisoner of imperial troops who had recently sacked Rome and taken control of most of Italy. As long as Charles supported Catherine of Aragon and his forces occupied Rome, there would be no possibility of a papally sanctioned annulment of the marriage.

The king's advisers quickly divided into two camps. Sir Thomas More, the royal chancellor and a staunch Catholic, urged the king to continue his policy of negotiation with the papacy and his efforts to destroy the growing Protestant party. Until his resignation in 1532, More led royal authorities in a vigorous campaign against the dissemination of the newly translated Tyndale Bible and against the spread of Protestant ideas. More was opposed and eventually ousted by a radical party of Protestants led by Thomas Cranmer (1489–1556) and Thomas Cromwell (1485?–1540), who saw in the king's desire for a divorce an effective wedge to pry Henry out of the papal camp. Cromwell, who eventually replaced More as chancellor, advised the king that the marriage problem could be solved by the English clergy without papal interference.

Between 1532 and 1535, Henry and Parliament took a number of steps that effectively left the king in control of the English church. Early in 1533, Cranmer was named archbishop of Canterbury. Later in the year Parliament ruled that appeals of cases concerning wills, marriages, and ecclesiastical grants had to be heard in England. In May an English court annulled the king's marriage to Catherine. Four months later, Henry's new queen, Anne Boleyn, gave birth to a daughter, Elizabeth.

Even before Cromwell became chancellor, Henry had attacked absentee clergy, restricted church courts, and prohibited the payment of certain papal taxes. After the split began, the king started to seize church properties. Parliamentary action culminated in the passage of the Act of Supremacy in 1534, which declared the king to be "the Protector and only Supreme Head of the Church and the Clergy of England." (See the box, "The Act of Supremacy.") Henry meant to enforce his control by requiring a public oath supporting the act. Sir Thomas More refused to take the oath and was arrested, tried, and executed for treason. In some respects, Parliament had acted as an instrument of reform, much like the town councils of the German and Swiss towns that moderated debates over the reform of the church. In England, however, Parliament and perhaps a majority of the laity perceived this reformation primarily as a political issue.

Cromwell and Cranmer had hoped to use the "King's Great Matter" as a way to begin a Lutheran-style reform of the church. But, though separated from the papal party, Henry remained suspicious of religious changes. Although he continued to object to the parts of the older tradition that he called "idolatry and other evil and naughty ceremonies," he rejected the Protestant under-

The Act of Supremacy

The Act of Supremacy makes clear what issues Henry VIII considered essential in the correction of the English church. Issued in 1534, it is the constitutional basis for the subsequent development of the Church of England. As befits a document dealing with the "King's Great Matter," the Act of Supremacy is entirely practical. This excerpt makes an interesting comparison with Luther's discussion of clerical authority in his "Address to the Christian Nobility" (see the box on page 515).

Albeit the King's Majesty justly and rightfully is and ought to be the supreme head of the Church of England, and so is recognized by the clergy of this realm in their Convocations; yet nevertheless for the corroboration and confirmation thereof, and for the increase of virtue in Christ's religion within this realm of England, and to repress and extirpate all errors, heresies and other enormities and abuses heretofore used in the same, Be it enacted by the authority of this present Parliament that the King our sovereign lord, his heirs and successor kings of this realm, shall be taken, accepted, and reputed the only supreme head in earth of the Church of England. . . . And that our said sovereign lord, his heirs, and successor kings of this realm, shall have full power and authority from time to time to visit, repress, redress, reform, order, correct, restrain and amend all such errors, heresies, abuses, offenses, contempts and enormities, whatsoever they be, which by any manner spiritual authority or jurisdiction ought or may lawfully be reformed, repressed, ordered . . . most to the pleasure of Almighty God, the increase of virtue in Christ's religion, and for the conservation of the peace, unity and tranquillity of this realm.

Source: David Englander, Diana Norman, Rosemary O'Day, and W. R. Owens, eds., *Culture and Belief in Europe, 1450–1600: An Anthology of Sources* (Oxford, England: Basil Blackwell in association with the Open University, 1990), pp. 442–443.

standing of justification and what anti-Protestant critics called "bibliolatry." He complained of radicals who "do wrest and interpret and so untruly allege [novel understandings of Scripture] to subvert and overturn as well the sacraments of Holy Church as the power and authority of princes and magistrates." Between 1534 and Henry's death in 1547, neither the Protestant nor the Catholic party was able to gain the upper hand at court or in the English church. Substantive changes in the English church would be made by Henry's children.

Reform and Counter-Reform Under Edward and Mary

Prince Edward, Henry's only surviving son in 1547, was born to Henry's third wife, Jane Seymour. He was only 10 years old at his father's death. By chance, Edward Seymour, who was Prince Edward's uncle, and the Protestant faction were in favor at the time of Henry's death. Seymour was named duke of Somerset and Lord Protector of the young king Edward VI (r. 1547–1553). Under Somerset, the Protestants were able to make significant changes in religious life in England. The Protestant party quickly changed the nature of the Eucharist, allowing the laity to take both bread and wine in the Protestant manner. The process of confiscating properties belonging to chapels and shrines was completed under Edward. In an act of great symbolic meaning, priests were legally allowed to marry; many had already done so. Finally, Archbishop Cranmer introduced the first edition of the English *Book of Common Prayer* in 1549. The book updated some late medieval English prayers and combined them with liturgical and theological ideas taken from Luther, Zwingli, and Calvin. In its beautifully expressive English, it provided the laity with a primer on how to combine English religious traditions with reform theology. Later, continental Protestants were named to teach theology at Oxford and Cambridge. If Edward had not died of tuberculosis in 1553, England's reform would have looked very much like the changes that occurred in Switzerland and southern Germany.

Protestant reformers attempted to prevent Mary Tudor (r. 1553–1558), Henry's Catholic daughter, from claiming the throne, but Mary and the Catholic party quickly moved into control of the court and the church. Mary immediately

The Queen in Parliament This image was meant to show the willingness of the Commons to support the queen, a key element of the Elizabethan Settlement. *(Bibliothèque Nationale)*

declared previous reform decrees to be void. Cardinal Reginald Pole (1500–1558), who had advocated reform within the Catholic church, became the center of the Catholic restoration party in Mary's England. Pole rooted out Protestants within the church. More than eight hundred gentlemen, clerics, and students fled England for the Protestant parts of the Continent. Three hundred mostly humble artisans and laborers were tried and executed by church courts, earning the queen her nickname, "Bloody Mary."

The policies of the queen brought about an abrupt return of the English church to papal authority. Most of the English quickly and easily returned to traditional religious practices. Statues were removed from hiding and restored to places of honor in churches and chapels. Although there is no conclusive evidence, the queen's initial successes may indicate that the Reformation was not broadly supported by the people. In fact, the restoration of Catholicism by Mary might have worked if the queen had not died after little more than six years on the throne. At her death there was still no clear indication of what the final settlement of the reform would be in England.

The Elizabethan Settlement

Queen Elizabeth (r. 1558–1603), daughter of Anne Boleyn, succeeded to the throne at the death of her half-sister. The reign of Elizabeth was one of the most enigmatic and successful of English history. She managed to gain control of the various political and religious factions in the country and play off a variety of international powers against each other. She seems to have understood well the necessity of striking a balance between opposing forces.

Her first great problem was a religious settlement. Early in her reign she twice left church services at the elevation of the bread by the priest. Since in Catholic thought it was the action of the priest that made Christ present in the bread, she was indicating symbolically her opposition to a purely Catholic understanding of the sacraments. In the next few years she continued to work for the restoration of many features of her father's and her half-brother's reforms. In 1559 the new Act of Supremacy and an Act of Uniformity reinstituted royal control of the English church and reestablished uniform liturgical and doctrinal standards. The *Book of Common Prayer* composed by

Cranmer was brought back, and final changes were made in the liturgy of the church.

Protestants had hoped for a complete victory, but the "Elizabethan Settlement" was considerably less than that. Although figures are lacking, it is likely that a large portion of the English population did not support a return to Henry's and Edward's reforms. After making clear her significant differences with Rome, Elizabeth confounded her most fervent Protestant supporters by offering a number of concessions to Anglo-Catholics. She herself remained celibate, and she ordered the Anglican clergy to do the same—although there was little she could do to prevent clerical marriage. More important, she and her closest advisers allowed a great variety of customs and practices favored by Anglo-Catholics. These matters, the queen's supporters argued, were not essential to salvation, and thus individuals could be allowed to choose. Many of the prayers in the *Book of Common Prayer*, for example, seemed "papist" to the most radical Protestants. Similarly, many of the traditional clerical vestments and altar furnishings remained unchanged. Elizabeth probably knew that the Protestants had no alternative to supporting her and thus felt free to win back the support of the Anglo-Catholics.

In fact, from the 1570s Elizabeth seems to have been especially concerned to regain control of insubordinate clerics. In these years the main outlines of her religious settlement became clear. She created a reformed liturgy that seemed acceptable to both Protestants and Catholics. At the same time she retained the parish and diocesan structure of the medieval church. She seems to have been most careful to restrict theological debate to the universities.

Toward the end of Elizabeth's reign, Richard Hooker (1554–1600) published his *Laws of Ecclesiastical Polity*, which provides an excellent description of the Anglican (English) church born of the Elizabethan Settlement. England, Hooker maintains, has its own way of handling religious affairs. Theologically it represents a middle way between the traditions cultivated by the Roman church and the more radically biblical religion favored by the Lutherans of Germany and the Calvinists of Switzerland. The Church of England moderated Luther's and Calvin's absolute reliance on Scriptures with history and tradition. In areas where tradition was strong, processions and other pre-Reformation traditions continued to animate village life. In other areas, more austere reformed practices were likely to predominate.

REFORM IN OTHER STATES, 1523–1560

In England and in the empire of Charles V the success of the new religious ideas depended greatly on the political situation. It would be naive to conclude, as Luther claimed, that "the Word did everything." Yet this complex religious reform movement cannot be reduced to the politics of kings and princes. The issues will be clearer if we survey politics and reform in the rest of Europe, noting whether and to what extent the new ideas took root. In France, for example, the widespread, popular support of the old religion limited the options of the country's political leaders. Similarly, in northern Europe religious reform was an issue both of popular feeling and of royal politics.

France

Luther's work, and later the ideas of the urban reformers of southwestern Germany and Switzerland, passed quickly and easily into France. Geneva is in a French-speaking area close to the French border. It, like Strasbourg, was easy for French Protestants to reach. Perhaps because of France's proximity to the Calvinists in French-speaking Switzerland or because of the clarity and power of Calvin's *Institutes*, French Protestants, known as Huguenots, were tied more closely to the Calvinists of Geneva than to the Lutherans of Germany.

It is difficult, however, to know how many French Christians were Protestants. At the height of the Reformation's popularity, Protestants probably represented no more than 10 percent of the total population of France. It has been estimated that there were about 2100 Protestant congregations in the 1560s—in a country that had perhaps 32,000 traditional parish congregations. Protestants seem to have been a diverse mix that included two of the three most important noble families at court: the Bourbon and the Montmorency families. Clerics interested in moral reform and artisans who worked at new trades, like the printing industry, also made up a significant portion of the converts. As a group Protestants tended to be of

higher-than-average literacy even if they were not
necessarily among the most prestigious lords in
French society. The Protestant population was
spread throughout the country. Protestants were
well represented in towns; they were probably a
numerical majority in the southern and western
towns of La Rochelle, Montpellier, and Nîmes.
Paris was the one part of the realm in which they
had little influence, and their absence in the capital may have been their undoing.

The conservative theologians of the Sorbonne
in Paris were some of Luther's earliest opponents.
They complained that many masters at the University of Paris were "Lutheran." As early as 1523,
Parisian authorities seized and burned books said
to be by Luther. But as in Germany, there was no
clear understanding of who or what a Lutheran
was. The Sorbonne theologians were suspicious of
a number of "pre-reformers," including Jacques
Lefèvre d'Étaples (1450–1537), who late in life had
come to an understanding of justification quite
like Luther's. Others were clerics who were intent
on religious reform within the traditional structures. Unlike Luther and the French Protestants,
these pre-reformers did not challenge the priests'
relationship to the sacraments. They were interested in the piety and behavior of churchmen.
They never challenged the role of the clergy in salvation. King Francis's own sister, Margaret of Angoulême (1492–1549), gathered a group of religious persons at her court, even including several
reformers. (See the box, "The Conversion of
Jeanne d'Albret.") But Margaret herself urged that
theology be left to scholars; she believed that the
laity should stick to simple pieties. Like Margaret,
most French Christians had no clear sense that
Protestant teachings required a complete break
with medieval Christian traditions.

Like previous French kings, Francis I (r. 1515–
1547) hoped to extend royal jurisdictions in France
and make France an international power. Engaged
in the seemingly intractable wars with the Habsburgs, Francis generally ignored religious questions. In 1525, he was taken captive in the wake of
a military disaster at Pavia in Lombardy. He was
held prisoner for nearly a year, during which time
conservatives at the Sorbonne and in Paris moved
actively against suspected Protestants. Francis was
not initially opposed to what seemed to be moral
reform within the church. His own view was that

the king's duty was to preserve order and prevent
scandal, and at first carrying out that duty meant
protecting reformers whom the conservative militants persecuted. The king feared disorder more
than he feared religious reform.

On October 18, 1534, however, Francis's attitude changed when he and all Paris awoke to find
the city covered with anti-Catholic placards containing, in the words of the writers, "true articles
on the horrible, great and insufferable abuses of
the Papal Mass." The response of the Parisians
was immediate and hostile. They attacked foreigners, especially those who by dress or speech
seemed "Lutheran"—that is, German or Flemish.
Several months later Francis himself led a religious procession through Paris in honor of the
Blessed Sacrament. The "Affair of the Placards"
changed Francis's ideas about the sources of disorder. Opposition to traditional religious practices
became more difficult and more dangerous. John
Calvin himself was forced to leave Paris and eventually France because he feared persecution. Between 1534 and 1560, some ten thousand Protestants fled France, many joining Calvin in Geneva.

By the middle of the sixteenth century it was
clear that neither Protestant nor Catholic factions
would be able to control religious and political life
in France. Francis I died in 1547, and the stage was
set for a series of destructive factional struggles
over religion and political power that would continue for the rest of the century. In Chapter 15 we
will examine this struggle known as the "French
Religious Wars."

Eastern Europe

In some respects, a political vacuum in eastern Europe allowed for the expansion of Protestantism.
The church hierarchy was not in a position to enforce orthodoxy. Some rulers were indifferent to
religious debates, as were the Muslim Ottoman
Turks, who controlled much of eastern Hungary
and what is now Romania. Other rulers offered
toleration because they could ill afford to alienate
any portion of their subject populations.

Protestant ideas initially passed through the
German communities of Poland and the trading
towns along the Baltic coast. But in the 1540s,
Calvinist ideas spread quickly among the Polish
nobles, especially those at the royal court. Given

The Conversion of Jeanne d'Albret

Jeanne d'Albret was the niece of King Francis I and mother of Henry of Navarre, the future Henry IV. In this letter, written in 1555 to Viscount Gourdon, a Huguenot supporter, she explains the pressures to remain Catholic and why she chose to become Protestant. After her conversion, her court became a center of the Huguenot movement.

I am writing to tell you that up to now I have followed in the footsteps of the deceased Queen, my most honored mother—whom God forgive—in the matter of hesitation between the two religions. The said Queen [was] warned by her late brother the King, François I of good and glorious memory, my much honored uncle, not to get new doctrines in her head so that from then on she confined herself to amusing stories. . . . Besides, I well remember how long ago, the late King, my most honored father . . . surprised the said Queen when she was praying in her rooms with the ministers Roussel and Farel, and how with great annoyance he slapped her right cheek and forbade her sharply to meddle in matters of doctrine. He shook a stick at me which cost me many bitter tears and has kept me fearful and compliant until after they had both died. Now that I am freed by the death of my said father two months ago . . . a reform seems so right and so necessary that, for my part, I consider that it would be disloyalty and cowardice to God, to my conscience and to my people to remain any longer in a state of suspense and indecision. . . . It is necessary for sincere persons to take counsel together to decide how to proceed, both now and in the future. Knowing that you are noble and courageous and that you have learned persons about you, I beg you to meet me.

Source: Nancy L. Roelker, trans., *Queen of Navarre: Jeanne d'Albret, 1528–1572* (Cambridge, Mass.: Harvard University Press, 1968), p. 127 (slightly adapted).

the power and influence of some of the noble families, Catholics were unable to suppress the various secret Calvinist congregations. During the first half of the sixteenth century, Protestantism became so well established in Poland that it could not be rooted out. Throughout the sixteenth century, Protestantism remained one of the rallying points for those opposed to the expansion of royal power.

The situation was much the same in Hungary and Romania. Among German colonists, Magyars, and ethnic Romanians there were numerous individuals who were interested first in Luther's message and later in Calvinist revisions of the reformed theology. Because no one could hope to enforce uniformity, some cities adopted a moderate Lutheran theology, and others followed a Calvinist confession. By the 1560s the Estates (representative assemblies) of Transylvania had decreed that both religions were to be tolerated. Further, when various radical groups migrated from the west in search of toleration, they too were able to create their own communities in Slavic and Magyar areas.

The Reformation was to have virtually no influence farther to the east, in Russia. The Orthodox church in Russia was much more firmly under control than was the church in the West. The Russian church followed the traditions of the Greek church, and Western arguments over justification made little sense in Orthodox churches. Given the historic suspicion of the Orthodox for Rome, the Russians were more tolerant of contacts with the Protestants of northern Europe. But there would be no theological innovation or reform in Russia.

Scandinavia

All of Scandinavia became Lutheran. Initial influences drifted north from Germany, carried by Hanseatic merchants and students who had studied at the universities of northern Germany. Yet the reform in Sweden and Denmark even more than in England was a monarchical reformation. In both Scandinavian kingdoms the kings began with an attack on the temporal rights and properties of the church. Changes in liturgy and practice came later as reformers gained the protection of the kings.

Since 1397 all Scandinavia had been united in theory in the Union of Kalmar (see page 413). But early in the sixteenth century the last pretenses of unity were shattered. Christian I of Denmark (r. 1513–1523) invaded Sweden and captured Stockholm, the capital. So great was his brutality that within a few years Gustav Vasa, a leading noble, was able to secure the loyalty of most of the Swedes and in 1523 was elected king of Sweden. Gustav's motto was "All power is of God." Like Henry VIII of England, Gustav (r. 1523–1560) moved carefully in an attempt to retain the loyalty of as many groups as possible. Although he never formally adopted a national confession of faith, the church and Swedish state gradually took on a more Lutheran character. In an effort to secure royal finances, the Riksdag, or parliament, passed the Västerås Ordinances, which secularized ecclesiastical lands and authorized the preaching of the "Pure Word of God." Olaus Petri (1493–1552), Sweden's principal reform preacher, was installed by royal order in the cathedral of Stockholm.

In Denmark the reformers also moved cautiously. Frederick I (r. 1523–1533) and his son, Christian III (r. 1534–1559), continued the policy of secularization and control that Christian I had initiated. Danish kings seemed interested in reform as a diplomatic means of attack on the Roman church. It seems that in Denmark the old religion simply suffered from a sort of royal indifference. The kings tended to support reformers as a way to attack the political power of the bishops. The Danes finally accepted the Augsburg Confession, which was becoming the most widely accepted explanation of Lutheran belief, in 1538. The transformation of practice proceeded slowly over the next decades.

In the frontier regions of Scandinavia—Finland, Iceland, and Norway—the reform was undertaken as a matter of royal policy. Initially there were only a few local reformers to introduce the new theology and practice. In many regions resistance to the Reformation continued for several generations. One valley hidden in the mountains of western Norway continued to follow the old religion for three centuries after its contacts with Rome had been severed.

THE LATE REFORMATION, CA. 1545–1600

In the first half of the sixteenth century, the term *Lutheran* applied to anyone who was anticlerical. As Francesco Guicciardini (1483–1540), a papal governor in central Italy, remarked:

> I know of no one who loathes the ambition, the avarice, and the sensuality of the clergy more than I. . . . In spite of all this, the positions I have held under several popes have forced me, for my own good, to further their interests. Were it not for that, I should have loved Martin Luther as much as myself—not so that I might be free of the laws based on Christian religion as it is generally interpreted and understood; but to see this bunch of rascals get their just deserts, that is, to be without vices or without authority.[7]

Guicciardini's remarks catch both the frustration many Christians felt with the traditional church and also the very real confusion over just what it was that Luther had said. In parts of Germany by the late 1520s and across Europe by the 1550s, political and religious leaders attempted to make clearer to the peoples of Europe just what *Lutheran, Calvinist,* and *Catholic* had come to mean. Historians term the process of defining and explaining what each group believed, or confessed, the "Second Reformation," or "Confessionalization." After the middle of the sixteenth century, it was true that along with theological and political changes, the Reformation represented a broad cultural movement.

The profound changes that began in the sixteenth century continued into the seventeenth. People began to sort out what it meant to belong to one church instead of to another. Central governments supported religious authorities who desired religious uniformity and control over individual Christians. In all parts of Europe, religious behavior changed. Both Protestants and Catholics became more concerned with the personal rather than the communal aspects of Christianity. After the sixteenth century, the nature of Christianity and its place in public life, whether in Protestant or in Catholic countries, differed profoundly from what it had been in the Middle Ages.

Catholic Reform

Historians commonly speak of both a movement for traditional reform and renewal within the Catholic church and a "Counter-Reformation," which was a direct response to and rejection of the theological positions championed by the Protestants. It is certainly true that one can categorize certain acts as clearly challenging the Protestants, but to do so is to miss the point that the energetic actions of the Roman church during the sixteenth century both affirmed traditional teachings and created new institutions better fitted to the early modern world.

The idea of purer, earlier church practices to which the "modern" church should return had been a commonplace for centuries. The great ecumenical Council of Constance early in the fifteenth century had called for "reform in head and members" (see page 400). In 1512, five years before Luther made his public protests, Pope Julius II (r. 1503–1513) convened another ecumenical council, the Fifth Lateran Council (1513–1517), which was expected to look into the problems of nonresident clergy, multiple benefices, and a host of other issues. This tradition of moral reform was especially strong in Spain, Portugal, and Italy, lands where political rulers were either indifferent or opposed to Protestant reforms.

The desire for reform along traditional lines was deeply felt within the church. In the wake of the sack of Rome by imperial troops in 1527, one Roman cardinal, Bishop Gian Matteo Giberti of Verona (1495–1543), returned to his diocese and began a thoroughgoing reform. He conducted visitations of the churches and other religious institutions in Verona, preached tirelessly, worked hard to raise the educational level of his clergy, and required that priests live within their parishes. Giberti believed that morally rigorous traditional reform and renewal could counter the malaise he perceived. Other reforming bishops could be found throughout Catholic Europe.

New religious foundations sprang up to renew the church. The Spanish mystic Teresa of Avila (1515–1582) reflected the thinking of many

A Counter-Reformation Saint Saint Teresa of Avila came from a converso family. She believed that renewal within the Christian church would come through mysticism, prayer, and a return to traditional religious practices. She founded a reformed Carmelite order of nuns to further religious renewal in Spain. *(MAS Barcelona)*

when she complained, "No wonder the Church is as it is, when the religious live as they do." Members of the new orders set out to change the church through example. The Florentine Filippo Neri (1515–1595) founded the Oratorian order, so named because of the monks' habit of leading the laity in prayer services. Filippo was joined in his work by Giovanni Palestrina (ca. 1525–1594), who composed music for the modest but moving prayer gatherings in Rome. Palestrina's music combined medieval plainchants with newer styles of polyphony, creating complex harmonies without obscuring the words and meaning of the text. The popularity of the Oratorians and their services can be measured in part by the fact that oratories, small chapels modeled on those favored by Filippo, remain to this day important centers of the musical life in the city of Rome.

The Catholic reform of the sixteenth century, however, was better known for its mystical theology than for its music. In Italy and France, but especially in Spain, a profusion of reformers chose to reform the church through austere prayer and contemplation. Teresa of Avila, who belonged to a wealthy converso family, led a movement to reform the lax practices within the religious houses of Spain. Famed for her rigorous religious life, her trances, and her raptures, Teresa animated a movement to reform the order of Carmelite nuns in Spain. Because of her writings about her mystical experiences she was named a "Doctor of the Church," a title reserved for the greatest of the church's theologians.

The most important of the new religious orders was the Society of Jesus, or Jesuits, founded in 1534 by Ignatius Loyola (1491–1556). A conservative Spanish nobleman, Loyola was wounded and nearly killed in battle. During a long and painful rehabilitation, he continuously read accounts of lives of the saints. After recovering, he went on a pilgrimage and experienced a profound conversion.

Loyola initially meant to organize a missionary order directed at the Muslims. The structure of his order reflected his military experience. It had a well-defined chain of command leading to the general of the order and then to the pope. To educate and discipline the members, Loyola composed *Spiritual Exercises,* emphasizing the importance of obedience. (See the box, "Ignatius Loyola's Spiritual Exercises.") He prohibited Jesuits from holding any ecclesiastical office that might compromise their autonomy. After papal approval of the order in 1540, the Jesuits directed their activities primarily to education in Catholic areas and reconversion of Protestants.

Throughout Europe, Jesuits gained fame for their work as educators of the laity and as spiritual advisers to the political leaders of Catholic Europe. In the late sixteenth and early seventeenth centuries they were responsible for a number of famous conversions, including that of Christina (1626–1689), the Lutheran queen of Sweden, who abdicated her throne in 1654 and spent the rest of her life in Rome. Jesuits were especially successful in bringing many parts of the Holy Roman Empire back into communion with the papacy. They have rightly been called the vanguard of the Catholic reform movement.

Catholic reformers were convinced that one of the reasons for the success of the Protestants was that faithful Christians had no clear guide about

what were and what were not orthodox teachings. The first Catholic response to the reformers was to try to separate ideas they held to be correct from those they held to be incorrect. Successive popes made public lists of books and ideas that they considered to be in error. The lists were combined into the *Index of Prohibited Books* in 1559. The climate of suspicion was such that the works of humanists like Erasmus were prohibited alongside the works of Protestants like Martin Luther. The *Index* continued to be revised into the twentieth century. It was finally suppressed in 1966.

During the first half of the sixteenth century, Catholics joined Protestants in calls for an ecumenical council that all believed would solve the problems dogging the Christian church. But in the unsettled political and diplomatic atmosphere that lasted into the 1540s, it was impossible to find any agreement about where or when a universal council should meet. Finally, in 1545, at a time when the hostilities between the Valois and Habsburgs had cooled, Pope Paul III (r. 1534–1549) was able to open an ecumenical council in the city of Trent, a German imperial city located on the Italian side of the Alps.

It is difficult to overemphasize the importance of the Council of Trent. It marked and defined the Roman Catholic church for the next four hundred years. Reformers within the Catholic church hoped that it would be possible to create a broadly based reform party within the church and that the council would define theological positions acceptable to the Protestants, making reunion possible. Unfortunately for the reformers, conservatives quickly took over the Italian-controlled council.

The Council of Trent sat in three sessions between 1545 and 1563. The initial debates were clearly meant to mark the boundaries between Protestant heresy and the orthodox positions of the Catholic church. In response to the Protestant emphasis on the Scriptures, the council said that the church always recognized the validity of traditional teaching and understanding. Delegates rejected the humanists' work on the text of the Bible, declaring that the Latin Vulgate edition compiled by Jerome was the authorized text. In response to the widely held Protestant belief that salvation came through faith alone, the council declared that good works were not merely the outcome of faith but were prerequisites to salvation. The council rejected Protes-

Ignatius Loyola's Spiritual Exercises

Loyola intended the spiritual exercises to be a tool for meditation and prayer by which members of the Society of Jesus would grow in faith, understanding, and obedience. Loyola sets out a series of meditations that are to continue over the course of a month, which reflect his views on the relations of individual Jesuits to the Catholic church.

The following rules are to be observed in order that we might hold the opinions we should hold in the Church militant.

We should put away completely our own opinion and keep our minds ready and eager to give our entire obedience to our holy Mother the hierarchical Church, Christ our Lord's undoubted spouse.

We should speak with approval of confession to a priest, of the reception of Holy Communion once a year, still more once a month, most of all once a week, the requisite conditions being duly fulfilled.

We should openly approve of the frequent hearing of Mass, and also of hymns, psalms and lengthy prayers, both inside and outside the church. . . .

We should speak with approval of religious orders, and the states of virginity and celibacy, not rating matrimony as high as any of these.

We should approve of relics of the saints, showing reverence for them and praying to the saints themselves. . . .

We should approve of the laws of fasting and abstinence in Lent . . . as well as mortifications both interior and exterior.

We should praise church decoration and architecture, as well as statues, which we should venerate in view of what they portray.

Finally, all the Church's commandments should be spoken of favorably, our minds always being eager to find arguments in her defense, never in criticism.

We should be inclined to approve and speak well of the regulations and instructions as well as the personal conduct of our superiors. It may well be that these are not or have not been always praiseworthy; but to criticize them, whether in public utterances or in dealings with ordinary people, is likely to give rise to complaint and scandal rather than to do good. . . .

To arrive at complete certainty, this is the attitude of mind we should maintain: I will believe that the white object I see is black if that should be the decision of the hierarchical Church, for I believe that between Christ our Lord the Bridegroom and His Bride the Church, there is one and the same Spirit, ruling and guiding us for our soul's good. For our Holy Mother the Church is guided and ruled by the same Spirit, the Lord who gave the Ten Commandments.

Source: David Englander, Diana Norman, Rosemary O'Day, and W. R. Owens, eds., *Culture and Belief in Europe, 1450–1600: An Anthology of Sources* (Oxford, England: Basil Blackwell in association with the Open University, 1990), pp. 241–242.

tant positions on the sacraments, the giving of wine to the laity during Holy Communion, the marriage of clergy, and the granting of indulgences.

Protestant critics often list these positions and conclude that the work of the council was merely negative. To do so, however, is to ignore the many ways in which the decrees of the council were an

essential part of the creation of the Roman Catholic church that would function for the next four centuries. The delegates at Trent generally felt that the real cause of the Protestant movement was the lack of leadership and supervision within the church. Many of the acts of the council dealt with that issue. First, the council affirmed apostolic succession—

the idea that the authority of a bishop is transmitted through a succession of bishops, ultimately leading back through the popes to Saint Peter. Thus, the council underlined the ultimate authority of the pope in administrative as well as theological matters. The council ordered that local bishops should reside in their dioceses, that they should establish seminaries to see to the education of parish clergy, and that, through regular visitation and supervision, they should make certain that the laity participated in the sacramental life of the church. At the final sessions of the council the nature of the Roman Catholic church was summed up in the Creed of Pius IV, which like the Lutheran Augsburg Confession summarized the basic position of the church.

Confessionalization

The labors of the Jesuits and the deliberations of the Council of Trent at midcentury made clear that reconciliation between the Protestant reformers and the Catholic church was not possible. Signs of the recognition of the permanence of the separation include the flight of several important Protestant religious leaders from Italy in the late 1540s and the wholesale migration of Protestant communities from Modena, Lucca, and other Italian towns to Switzerland. These actions signify the beginnings of the theological, political, and social separation of "Protestant" and "Catholic" in European society.

The theological separation was marked in a number of visual and symbolic ways. Churches in which both bread and wine were distributed to the laity during the sacrament of Holy Communion passed from Catholic to Protestant. Churches in which the altar was moved forward to face the congregation but the statuary was retained were likely to be Lutheran. Churches in which statues were destroyed and all other forms of art were removed were likely to be Reformed (Calvinist), for Calvin had advised that "only those things are to be sculpted or painted which the eye is capable of seeing; let not God's majesty, which is far above the perception of the eyes, be debased through unseemly representations."[8] Even matters like singing differentiated the churches. Although the Calvinist tradition tended to believe that music,

like art, drew the Christian away from consideration of the word, Luther believed that "next to the Word of God, music deserves the highest praise." Lutherans emphasized congregational singing and the use of music within the worship service. Countless pastors in the sixteenth and seventeenth centuries followed Luther in composing hymns and even theoretical tracts on music. This tradition would reach its zenith in the church music of Johann Sebastian Bach (1685–1750), most of whose choral works were composed to be part of the normal worship service.

Music had played an important role in Catholic services since well before the Reformation; it was really architecture that distinguished Catholic churches from Protestant churches in the late sixteenth and seventeenth centuries. In Rome, the great religious orders built new churches in the baroque style (see page 582). Baroque artists and architects absorbed all the classical lessons of the Renaissance and then went beyond them, sometimes deliberately violating them. Baroque art celebrates the supernatural, the ways in which God is not bound by the laws of nature. Where Renaissance art was meant to depict nature, baroque paintings and sculpture seemed to defy gravity. The work celebrated the supernatural power and splendor of the papacy. This drama and power are clear in the construction of the Jesuit Church of the Jesù in Rome and especially in Gianlorenzo Bernini's (1598–1680) throne of Saint Peter made for the church of St. Peter in the Vatican. The construction of baroque churches, first in Spain and Italy but especially in the Catholic parts of Germany, created yet another boundary between an austere Protestantism and a visual and mystical Catholicism.

The Regulation of Religious Life

Because of the continuing religious confusion and political disorder brought on by the reforms, churchmen, like state officials, were intent on enforcing what they understood to be true Christianity. Yet this true religion was much less a public and communal religion than medieval Christianity had been. Medieval Christians had worried greatly about public sins that complicated life in a community. In the age of confessionalization, the-

The Jesù in Rome This church is the center of the Jesuit Order and the burial place of Saint Ignatius Loyola. Its baroque architecture set the tone for many later buildings in Rome and for many new Catholic churches elsewhere. (*Scala/Art Resource, NY*)

ologians—both Protestant and Catholic—worried about the moral status and interior life of individuals. Sexual sins and gluttony now seemed more dangerous than economic sins like avarice or usury. Even penance was understood as less a "restitution" that would reintegrate one into the Christian community than a process of coming to feel a true sense of contrition for sins.

The changed attitude toward penance made the sense of Christian community less important and left individuals isolated and more subject to the influence of the church authorities. In all parts of Europe officials became preoccupied with the control and supervision of the laity.

All of the major religious groups in the late sixteenth century emphasized education, right doctrine, and social control. In Catholic areas there was renewed emphasis on private confession by the laity to ensure a proper understanding of doctrine. During this period Charles Borromeo, archbishop of Milan (1538–1584), introduced the private confessional box, which isolated priest and penitent from the prying ears of the community. This allowed confessors time and opportunity to carefully instruct individual consciences. As early as the 1520s some Lutheran princes had begun visitations to ensure that the laity understood basic doctrine. Churchmen in both Protestant and Catholic areas used catechisms, handbooks containing instruction for the laity. The first and most famous was by Luther himself. Luther's *Small Catechism* includes the Lord's Prayer, Ten Commandments, and Apostles' Creed along with simple, clear explanations of what they mean. More than Catholic rulers, Protestant rulers used church courts to enforce discipline within the community.

Churchmen began to criticize semireligious popular celebrations such as May Day, harvest feasts, and the Feast of Fools, whose origins lay in popular myths and practices that preceded Christianity, because they seemed to encourage superstition and because they mocked the social and political order with, for example, parodies of fat or ignorant clergy and foolish magistrates.

Religious authorities also were concerned by what seemed to be out-of-control mysticism and dangerous religious practices, especially among women. The impact of the Reformation on the status of women has often been debated. The Protestant position is that the Reformation freed women from the cloistered control of traditional convents. Further, the Protestant attack on state-controlled prostitution reduced one of the basest forms of exploitation. To the realists who argued that young, unmarried men would always need sexual outlets, Luther replied that one cannot merely substitute one evil practice for another. Critics of the Reformation counter that a convent was one of very few organizations that a woman could administer and direct. Women who took religious vows, Catholics point out, could engage in intellectual and religious pursuits similar to those enjoyed by men. The destruction of religious houses for women, Catholics argued, destroyed one of the few alternatives that women had to life in an authoritarian, patriarchal society.

In fact, in the late sixteenth and early seventeenth centuries, both Protestant and Catholic authorities viewed with suspicion any signs of religious independence by women. In the first years of the Reformation, some women did leave convents, eager to participate in the reform of the church. Early in the 1520s some women wrote tracts concerning the morality of the clergy. And there was for a time a tradition of women deacons in some Calvinist churches. Yet like the female witches discussed in Chapter 15, these religious women seemed to be dangerous. Lutheran and Calvinist theologians argued that a woman's religious vocation should be in the Christian care and education of her family. And even the most famous of the sixteenth- and seventeenth-century female Catholic mystics were greeted with suspicion and some hostility. Religious women in Catholic convents were required to subordinate their mysticism to the guidance they received

from male spiritual advisers. Calvinist theologians exhibited similar suspicions toward the theological and spiritual insights of Protestant women. For the laity in general and for women in particular, the late Reformation brought increased control by religious authorities.

SUMMARY

During the age of the Reformation, Europe experienced a number of profound shocks. The medieval assumption that there was a unified Christendom in the West was shattered. No longer could Europeans assume that at heart they held similar views of the world and the place of individuals in it. Charles V had begun his reign with the hope that there would be one law and one empire. He ended it by dividing his empire and retiring to a monastery.

The Protestant challenge did not simply attack the institutional structure or the moral lapses as previous heretical movements had done. The early Protestant reformers rejected the very nature of the medieval church. Peasants and artisans argued that Luther's message of Christian freedom liberated them from both economic and spiritual oppression. Both Protestant and peasant rejected the traditions of the late Middle Ages.

Monarchies and republics throughout Europe came to view religious institutions and religious choices as matters of state. When faced by theological challenges and cries for moral reform, governments reacted in ways that offered religious change and bolstered the claims of secular government. In England and Sweden, calls for reform resulted in the secularization of church property, which put vast new sources of wealth in the hands of the kings. In the towns of Germany and Switzerland, governments redoubled their efforts to regulate religion and moral life. Thus, both Reformation and Counter-Reformation brought about a significant strengthening of religious and secular authorities.

Ironically, the reforms that Luther and other Protestants advocated on the basis of clear, incontrovertible religious truths eventually led to the suspicion that no truths could be known with certainty. Religious strife led some to conclude that in matters of religion toleration was the only appropriate option. Others concluded that if the truth could not be known, the state must be allowed to make the big decisions. And the states of the seventeenth century were quite willing to do so.

NOTES

1. Angela of Foligno, *The Book of Divine Consolation of the Blessed Angel of Foligno,* trans. Mary G. Steegmann (New York: Cooper Square Publishers, 1966), p. 260.
2. Martin Luther, *Works,* vol. 34 (Philadelphia: Fortress Press, 1955; St. Louis: Concordia Publishing House, 1986), pp. 336–337.
3. Quoted in Steven Ozment, *The Age of Reform, 1250–1550* (New Haven: Yale University Press, 1980), p. 245.
4. Quoted in Robert W. Scribner, *The German Reformation* (London: Macmillan, 1986), p. 32.
5. Quoted in Carter Lindberg, *The European Reformations* (New York: Blackwell Publishers, 1996), p. 269.
6. Quoted in Euan Cameron, *The European Reformation* (Oxford, England: Clarendon Press, 1991), pp. 106–107.
7. Francesco Guicciardini, *Maxims and Reflections (Ricordi),* trans. Mario Domandi (Philadelphia: University of Pennsylvania Press, 1965), p. 48.
8. Quoted in Lindberg, *European Reformations,* p. 375.

SUGGESTED READING

General Surveys

Bossy, John. *Christianity in the West, 1400–1700.* 1985. A subtle, important essay arguing that the Reformation ended communal Christianity and created in its place a more personal religion emphasizing individual self-control.

Cameron, Euan. *The European Reformation.* 1991. The best recent history of the Reformation, emphasizing the common principles of the major reformers.

Chatellier, Louis. *The Europe of the Devout: The Catholic Reformation and the Formation of a New Society.* 1989. An important study of the reconstruction of Catholic Christianity in the late sixteenth century.

Chaunu, Pierre, ed. *The Reformation.* 1989. A colorfully illustrated general history of the Reformation containing essays on the major events.

Davidson, Nicholas S. *The Counter Reformation.* 1987. A short introduction emphasizing how the accomplishments of the Council of Trent laid the basis for a Catholic revival.

Dickens, Arthur G., and John Tonkin. *The Reformation in Historical Thought.* 1985. A comprehensive survey of debates over the meanings of the Reformation, beginning with the earliest historians and continuing into the twentieth century.

Eisenstein, Elizabeth. *The Printing Revolution in Early Modern Europe.* 1983. A general study of the printing revolution that includes a chapter on the importance of printing in the spread of reform.

Englander, David, Diana Norman, Rosemary O'Day, and W. R. Owens, eds. *Culture and Belief in Europe, 1450–1600: An Anthology of Sources.* 1990. A collection of documents illustrating religious and social values and giving an excellent overview of popular reform.

Lindberg, Carter. *The European Reformations.* 1996. A very balanced introduction that tries to give serious coverage to northern and eastern Europe.

Oberman, Heiko, Thomas Brady, and James Tracy, eds. *Handbook of European History, 1400–1600: Late Middle Ages, Renaissance, and Reformation.* 1994–1995. A collection of excellent introductory studies of political, religious, and social life.

O'Connell, Marvin R. *The Counter Reformation, 1559–1610.* 1974. A very good general introduction to the theology and politics of reform in Catholic Europe.

Ozment, Steven. *The Age of Reform, 1250–1550.* 1980. A clear, well-written introduction to late medieval and Reformation religious ideas, emphasizing the ways in which reformers transformed medieval theological debates.

Schilling, Heinz, ed. *Religion, Political Culture, and the Emergence of Early Modern Society.* 1992. A demanding collection of essays on the organization and regulation of Protestant churches in Germany and the Netherlands, making clear the way in which the new churches disciplined their members.

The Reformers

Bainton, Roland H. *Here I Stand: A Life of Martin Luther.* 1978. First published in 1950 but still an excellent introduction to the life of the reformer.

Bouwsma, William. *John Calvin: A Sixteenth-Century Portrait.* 1987. An important but demanding book on Calvin, emphasizing his debt to the humanist movements of the fifteenth and sixteenth centuries.

Dillenberger, John, ed. *Martin Luther: Selections from His Writings.* 1961. An excellent collection of writings that allows readers to follow the evolution of Luther's thought.

McGrath, Alister E. *A Life of John Calvin: A Study in the Shaping of Western Culture.* 1990. An excellent biography emphasizing the definitive role of Calvin's religious thought.

Oberman, Heiko. *Luther: Man Between God and the Devil.* 1989. A brilliant, beautifully written essay connecting Luther to prevailing late medieval ideas about sin, death, and the devil.

(continued on page 544)

A REFORMATION WOODCUT

Erhard Schön's 1533 woodcut "There Is No Greater Treasure Here on Earth Than an Obedient Wife Who Desires Honor" and other broadsheets like it informed and amused Europeans of all walks of life in the late fifteenth and sixteenth centuries. Schön's image of a henpecked husband and his wife followed by others would have been instantly recognizable to most people. Accompanying texts made clear the message implied in the woodcut itself. But how may we, centuries later, "read" this message? How does the modern historian analyze Schön's broadsheet to investigate popular ideas about social roles, religion, and politics? What do it and similar broadsheets tell us about popular responses to the social and religious tumults of the sixteenth century?

Look at the simple and clear lines of the woodcut. They give a clue about the popularity of broadsheets. They were cheap and easy to produce and were printed on inexpensive paper. Artists would sketch an image that an artisan would later carve onto a block. A printer could produce a thousand or more copies from a single block. Even famous artists like Albrecht Dürer (see page 461) sold highly profitable prints on religious, political, and cultural themes.

Almost anyone could afford broadsheets. Laborers and modest merchants decorated their houses with pictures on popular themes. In the middle of the fifteenth century, before the Reformation, most images were of saints. It was widely believed, for example, that anyone who looked at an image of Saint Christopher would not die on that day.

During the political and religious unrest of the sixteenth century, artists increasingly produced images that referred to the debates over religion. Schön himself made his living in Nuremberg producing and selling woodcuts. He and other artists in the city were closely tuned to the attitudes of the local population. One popular image was entitled "The Roman Clergy's Procession into Hell."

Schön's image reproduced here reflected a worry shared by both Protestants and Catholics: the rebellious nature of women. Evidence suggests that women in the late fifteenth and sixteenth centuries may have been marrying at a later age and thus were likely to be more independent-minded than their younger sisters. The ranks of single women were swollen by widows and by former nuns who had left convents and liberated themselves from male supervision. Thus, it was not difficult for men in the sixteenth century to spot women who seemed unnecessarily independent of male control.

Let us turn again to the woodcut, to see what worried villagers and townsmen and how Schön visualized their fears. Notice the henpecked husband. He is harnessed to a cart carrying laundry. Both the harness and the laundry were popular images associated with women's duties. During popular festivals, German villagers often harnessed unmarried women to a plow to signify that they were shirking their duty by not marrying and raising children. Doing the laundry was popularly thought to be the first duty that a powerful wife would force on her weak-kneed husband. Countless other images show women, whip in hand, supervising foolish husbands as they pound diapers with a laundry flail. "Woe is me," says the poor man, all this because "I took a wife." As if the message were not clear enough, look at what the woman carries in her left hand: his purse, his sword, and his pants. (The question "Who wears the pants in the family?" was as familiar then as now.) But the woman responds that he is in this position not because of marriage but because he has been carousing: "If you will not work to support me, then you must wash, spin, and draw the cart."*

*Keith Moxey, *Peasants, Warriors and Wives: Popular Imagery in the Reformation* (Chicago: University of Chicago Press, 1989), pp. 108–109; includes a translation of portions of the texts in the broadsheet.

Schön: There Is No Greater Treasure Here on Earth Than an Obedient Wife Who Desires Honor *(Gotha, Schlossmuseum)*

The figures following the cart are commenting on the situation. The young journeyman is asking the young maiden at his side, "What do you say about this?" She responds, "I have no desire for such power." The woman dressed as a fool counsels the young man never to marry and thus to avoid anxiety and suffering. But an old man, identified as "the wise man," closes the procession and ends the debate over marriage. "Do not listen to this foolish woman," he counsels. "God determines how your life together will be, so stay with her in love and suffering and always be patient."

If we think about this woodcut's images and texts, we can understand the contrary hopes and fears in sixteenth-century Germany. Like the young woman, the Christian wife was expected to avoid claiming power either inside or outside the home. Martin Luther concluded that "the husband is the head of the wife even as Christ is head of the Church. . . . Therefore as the Church is subject to Christ, so let wives be subject to their husbands in everything."** Authority was to be in the hands of husbands and fathers. But if the good wife was required to avoid power, the good husband was also expected to follow Luther's precepts for the Christian family. As the wise old man observes, the husband must be a loving and forgiving master.

Schön's woodcut and others similar to it should remind you of the "argument over women" discussed in Chapter 12 (see page 440). The words of the wise man and the young maid bring to mind Christine de Pizan's *City of the Ladies* when they urge love and understanding, but their hopefulness is undercut by the power and immediacy of the image. As the broadsheet makes clear, suspicion of women characterized even the most simple literature of Reformation Europe. ✑

**Ephesians 5:23–24.

Potter, George R., and Mark Greengrass, eds. *John Calvin*. 1983. Selections from Calvin's most important works, along with short introductions.

Reformation in Specific Countries

Brady, Thomas A. *Turning Swiss: Cities and Empire, 1450–1550*. 1985. A masterful history of the political and ideological concerns of the townsmen of southwestern Germany.

Collinson, Patrick. *The Birthpangs of Protestant England: Religious and Cultural Change in the Sixteenth and Seventeenth Centuries*. 1988. A series of lectures describing the process by which the Protestant religion was established in England.

Dickens, Arthur G. *The English Reformation*. 1964. A classic, clear discussion of English religion, emphasizing the popular enthusiasm for reform, which Dickens believes is connected to the earlier Lollard movements.

Fenlon, Dermot. *Heresy and Obedience in Tridentine Italy: Cardinal Pole and the Counter Reformation*. 1972. A complex book that argues that there was a strong interest in church reform in papal circles until the middle of the sixteenth century.

Greengrass, Mark. *The French Reformation*. 1987. A short pamphlet to introduce students to the political and religious development of the Reformation in France.

Haigh, Christopher, ed. *The English Reformation Revised*. 1987. A collection of essays criticizing Dickens's thesis on the popular basis of reform in England; the introduction is especially useful for following what is still an important debate over reform.

Hsia, R. Po-Chia, ed. *German People and the Reformation*. 1988. A collection of essays that introduce and comment on the various currents of research on the German Reformation.

Moeller, Bernt. *Imperial Cities and the Reformation*. 1972. Three classic essays on why townsmen responded so enthusiastically to the reform message.

Monter, E. William. *Calvin's Geneva*. 1967. A fascinating introduction to life in Geneva during the Reformation, emphasizing that the city was not a theocracy controlled by Calvin.

Moxey, Keith. *Peasants, Warriors, and Wives: Popular Imagery in the Reformation*. 1989. A study of social and religious ideas spread throughout Germany by means of woodcuts; it contains numerous illustrations.

Roper, Lyndal. *The Holy Household: Women and Morals in Reformation Augsburg*. 1990. A study of domestic values in a Protestant city, demonstrating the ways in which reform ideas limited women's religious role to instruction within the family.

Scarisbrick, J. J. *The Reformation and the English People*. 1984. An excellent, clearly written survey of religious practice in England, emphasizing the vitality and popularity of the church on the eve of the Reformation.

Scribner, Robert W. *The German Reformation*. 1986. A short introduction for students to the reform in Germany; it has excellent summaries of social and political issues in Germany.

———. *For the Sake of Simple Folk: Popular Propaganda for the German Reformation*. 1981. A study, illustrated with contemporary woodcuts, that shows how reformers used the new technology of printing to spread popular ideas about reform.

CHAPTER 15

Europe in the Age of Religious War, 1555–1648

In the early hours of a sultry summer morning—August 24, 1572—armed noblemen accompanied by the personal guard of the king of France hunted out about one hundred other nobles, asleep in their lodgings in and around the royal palace in Paris, and murdered them in cold blood. The attackers were Catholic, their victims were Protestant— but all were French nobles, many of them related to one another. The king and his counselors had planned the murders as a preemptive political strike because they feared that other Protestant noblemen were gathering an army outside of Paris. But the calculated strike became a general massacre when ordinary Parisians learned that their king had authorized the murders of Protestant leaders. Believing they were acting in the king's name, these Parisians, who were overwhelmingly Catholic, turned on their neighbors. About three thousand Protestants were murdered in Paris over the next three days.

This massacre came to be called the Saint Bartholomew's Day Massacre for the Catholic saint on whose feast day it fell. Though particularly horrible in its scope (indeed, thousands more people were murdered in the French provinces as word of events in Paris spread), the massacres were not unusual in the deadly combination of religious and political antagonisms they reflected. Throughout Europe ordinary people took religious conflict into their own hands as rulers, for their part, tried to enforce religious uniformity, or at least religious peace. Religious conflicts were by definition intractable political conflicts, since virtually every religious group felt that all others were heretics who must not be tolerated, and rulers of all stripes looked to religious authority and institutions to uphold their own power.

The Saint Bartholomew's Day Massacre.

In addition, existing political tensions contributed to instability and violence, especially when reinforced by religious difference. Royal governments continued to consolidate authority, but resistance to royal power by provinces, nobles, or towns accustomed to independence now might have religious sanction. Tensions everywhere were also worsened by the rise of prices and unemployment as the sixteenth century wore on. Economic stress was heightened because changes in military technology and tactics made warfare itself more destructive than ever before.

A period of tension, even extraordinary violence, in political and social life, the late sixteenth and early seventeenth centuries were also distinguished by great creativity in some areas of cultural and intellectual life. The plays of Shakespeare, for example, mirrored the passions but also reflected on the tensions of the day and helped to analyze Europeans' circumstances with a new degree of sophistication.

SOCIETY AND THE STATE

Religious strife, warfare, and economic change disrupted the lives of whole communities as well as individuals in the late sixteenth and early seventeenth centuries. The sixteenth century, especially, saw profound economic transformation that, by the end of the century, altered power relations in cities, in the countryside, and in the relationship of both to central governments.

The most obvious economic change was a steady rise in prices, which resulted in the concentration of wealth in fewer hands. Economic change by itself, however, did not spawn all of this era's social and political change. States made war for religious and dynastic reasons more than for calculated economic advantage. Nevertheless, together, the movements of the economy and the policies of governments created notable shifts in centers of wealth and power.

Economic Transformation and the New Elites

Sixteenth-century observers attributed rising prices to the inflationary effects of the influx of precious metals from Spanish territories in the New World. Historians now believe that there

were also European causes for this "price revolution." Steady population growth caused a relative shortage of goods, particularly food, and the result was a rise in prices. Both the amount and the effect of price changes were highly localized, depending on factors such as the structure of local economies and the success of harvests. Between 1550 and 1600, however, the price of grain may have risen between 50 and 100 percent, and sometimes more, in cities throughout Europe—including eastern Europe, the breadbasket for growing urban areas to the west. Where we have data about wages, we can estimate that wages lost between one-tenth and one-fourth of their value by the end of the century. The political and religious struggles of the era thus took place against a background of increasing want, and economic distress was often expressed in both political and religious terms.

These economic changes affected the wealthy as well as the poor. During this period, monarchs were making new accommodations with the hereditary aristocracy—with the Crown usually emerging stronger, if only through concessions to aristocrats' economic interests. Underlying this new symbiosis of monarchy and traditional warrior-nobles were the effects of economic changes that would eventually blur lines between these noble families and new elites and simplify power relationships within the state. Conditions in the countryside, where there were fewer resources to feed more mouths, grew less favorable. But at the same time more capital became available to wealthy urban or landholding families to invest in the countryside, by buying land outright on which to live like gentry or by making loans to desperate peasants. This capital came from profits from expanded production and trade and was also an effect of the scarcity of land as population and prices rose. Enterprising landholders raised ground rents wherever they could, or they converted land to the production of wool, grain, and other cash crops destined for distant markets.

As a result, a stratum of wealthy, educated, and socially ambitious "new gentry," as these families were called in England, began growing and solidifying. Many of the men of these families were royal officeholders, and they held on to their offices, confident of their wealth and the leisure it made possible. Where the practice existed, many bought titles outright or were granted nobility as a benefit of their offices. They often lent money to royal governments. The monumental expense of wars made becoming a lender to government, as well as to individuals, an attractive way to live off one's capital.

No one would have confused these up-and-coming families with warrior-aristocrats from old families, but the social distinctions between them are less important (to us) than what they had in common: legal privilege, the security of landownership, a cooperative relationship with the monarchy. Monarchs deliberately favored the new gentry as counterweights to independent aristocrats.

City governments also changed character as wealth accumulated in the hands of formerly commercial families. By the beginning of the seventeenth century, traditional guild control of government had been subverted in many places. Town councils became dominated by successive generations of privileged families, now more likely to live from landed than from commercial wealth. Towns became more closely tied to royal interests by means of the mutual interests of Crown and town elites. The long medieval tradition of towns serving as independent corporate bodies had come to an end.

Economic Change and the Common People

The growth of markets around Europe and in Spanish possessions overseas had a profound effect on urban producers in western Europe. Production of cloth on a large scale for export, for example, now required huge amounts of capital—much more than a typical guild craftsman could amass. In many regions, guild members lost political power in towns as the relative importance of their limited scale of production declined, and the guild structure itself began to break down. The decline in market size for traditional artisans meant that fewer and fewer apprentices and journeymen could expect to become master artisans. The masters began to treat apprentices virtually as wage laborers, at times letting them go when there was not enough work. The household mode of production, in which apprentices and journeymen had worked and lived side by side with the master's family, also began to break down, with profound economic, social, and political consequences.

Effects on women workers were particularly dramatic. One of the first reflections of the dire circumstances faced by artisans was an attempt to lessen competition at the expense of the artisans' own mothers, sisters, daughters, and sons. Increasingly, widows were forbidden to continue practicing their husband's trade, though they headed from 10 to 15 percent of households in many trades. Women had traditionally learned and practiced many trades but rarely followed the formal progress from apprenticeship to master status. A woman usually combined work of this kind with household production, with selling her products and those of her husband, and with bearing and nursing children. Outright exclusion of women from guild organization appears as early as the thirteenth century but now began regularly to appear in guild statutes. In addition, town governments tried to restrict women's participation in work such as selling in markets, which they had long dominated. Even midwives had to defend their practices, even though as part of housewifery women were expected to know about herbal remedies and practical medicine. (See the box, "A Woman Defends Her Right to Practice Healing.") Working women thus began to have difficulty supporting themselves if single or widowed and difficulty supporting their children. In the changing position of such women, we can see the distress of the entire stratum of society that they represent.

Many women worked in cloth production, for spinning was a life skill that women learned as a matter of course. Cloth production was changing, too; it became increasingly controlled by new investor-producers with large amounts of capital and access to distant markets. These entrepreneurs bought up large amounts of wool and hired it out to be cleaned, spun into thread, and woven into cloth by wage laborers in urban workshops or by pieceworkers in their homes. Thousands of women and men in the countryside helped to support themselves and families in this way.

Wealth in the countryside was also becoming more stratified, creating more families that could not adequately support themselves on the land. In western Europe, the most dramatic impact came from the investment in land by wealthy elites. Countless peasants lost their lands to these "rentiers," who lent them money and reclaimed the land when the money was not repaid. Other peasants were unable to rent land as rents rose, or they were unable to make a secure living because of the higher cost of land. To survive, some sought work

A Woman Defends Her Right to Practice Healing

In this document, Katharine Carberiner testifies to the city council of Munich that she does not deliberately compete with male doctors but has skills that might lead other women to choose her rather than male medical practitioners.

I use my feminine skills, given by the grace of God, only when someone entreats me earnestly, and never advertise myself, but only when someone has been left for lost. . . . I do whatever I can possibly do . . . using only simple and allowable means that should not be forbidden or proscribed in the least. Not one person who has come under my care has a complaint or grievance against me. If the doctors, apothecaries or barber-surgeons have claimed this, it is solely out of spite.

At all times, as is natural, women have more trust in other women to discover their se-crets, problems and illnesses, than they have in men—but perhaps this jealousy came from that. Undoubtedly as well, husbands who love and cherish their wives will seek any help and assistance they can, even that from women, if the wives have been given up (by the doctors) or otherwise come into great danger.

Because I know that I can help in my own small way, I will do all I can, even, as according to the Gospel, we should help pull an ox out of a well it has fallen into on Sunday.

Source: Merry Wiesner, "Women's Defense of Their Public Role," in Mary Beth Rose, ed., *Women in the Middle Ages and the Renaissance* (Syracuse: Syracuse University Press, 1986), p. 9.

as day laborers on the land of rich landlords or more prosperous farmers. But with the demise of so many opportunities for farming, there was not enough work. Many found their way to cities, where they swelled the ranks of the poor. Others, like some of their urban counterparts, coped by becoming part of the newly expanding network of cloth production, combining spinning and weaving with subsistence farming. However, one bad harvest might send them out on the roads begging or odd-jobbing; many did not long survive such a life.

In eastern Europe, peasants faced other dilemmas, for their lands had a different relationship to the wider European economy. The more densely urbanized western Europe, whose wealth controlled the patterns of trade, sought bulk goods, particularly grain, from eastern Germany, Poland, and Lithuania. Thus, there was an economic incentive for landowners in eastern Europe to bind peasants to the land just as the desire of their rulers for greater cooperation had granted the landlords more power. Serfdom now spread in eastern Europe when precisely the opposite conditions prevailed in the West.

Coping with Poverty and Violence

The common people of Europe did not submit passively either to economic difficulties or to the religious and political crises of their day. The townspeople of France and the Netherlands, for example, played a significant role in the establishment and defense of their "reformed" as well as Catholic religions. Whether Catholic or Protestant, common people took the initiative in attacking members of the other faith to rid their communities of them. At the community level, heretics were considered to be spiritual pollution that might provoke God's wrath. Thus, ordinary citizens believed that they had to eliminate heretics if the state failed to do so. Both elites and common people were responsible for the violence that sometimes occurred in the name of religion.

Ordinary people fought in wars from conviction but also from the need for self-defense. Indeed, although nobles remained military leaders, armies consisted mostly of infantry made up of common people, not mounted knights. It was ordinary people who defended the walls of towns, dug siege works, and manned artillery batteries. Women were part of armies, too. Much of the day-to-day work of finding food and firewood, cleaning guns, and endlessly repairing inadequate clothing was handled individually by women looking after their husbands and lovers among the troops.

Many men joined the armies and navies of their rulers because the military seemed a reasonable way of life, given their options. Landless farm hands, day laborers, and out-of-work artisans found the prospect of employment in the army attractive enough to outweigh the dangers of military life. Desertion was common, since joining up represented a choice, even if a choice among evils. Nothing more than the rumor that a soldier's home village was threatened might prompt a man to abandon his post. Battle-hardened troops could threaten their commanders not only with desertion but with mutiny. A mutiny of Spanish troops in 1574 was a well-organized affair, some-

what like a strike. Whole units of the army mutinied together and found ways to defend themselves while they negotiated with the Spanish command. Occasionally, mutinies were brutally suppressed; more often, they were successful and troops received some of their back wages.

Townspeople and countrypeople participated in riots and rebellions to protest their circumstances when the situation was particularly dire or when other means of action had failed. The devastation of civil war in France, for example, led to a number of peasant rebellions and urban uprisings. Former soldiers, prosperous farmers, or even noble landlords whose economic fortunes were tied to peasant profits might lead rural revolts. If they succeeded, it would be only to relieve a local problem, such as a local tax burden. Urban protests could begin spontaneously when new grievances worsened existing problems. In a town in central France in 1594, for example, the execution for thievery of a servant whose master was believed to be a thief became the occasion for a demonstration to protest the privilege of the well-to-do. In Naples, in 1585, food riots were provoked not

Food and Clothing Distributed by Government Officials In this rendering, a poor woman receives bread and a destitute man, clothing. Wealthy citizens' wills began to reflect the new definition of charity: Bequests to institutions increased and personal donations to the poor dwindled. *(The British Library)*

simply by a shortage of grain but by a government decision to raise the price of bread during the shortage. The property of the privileged was sometimes seized, and city leaders were sometimes killed, but these protests rarely generated lasting political change and were usually brutally quashed.

Governments at all levels tried to cope with the increasing problem of poverty by changing the administration and scale of poor relief. In both Catholic and Protestant Europe, caring for the poor became more institutionalized and systematic and more removed from religious impulses. In traditional Catholic doctrine, charity had been considered one of the many random ways by which an individual could merit grace and move toward eternal life. Such ideas were anathema to Protestant doctrine, but, interestingly, official Catholic practice concerning charity began to change early in the sixteenth century, before the pressure of Protestantism. Official Protestant attitudes toward charity, when they later came into being, closely resembled Catholic ones.

In the second half of the sixteenth century, public almshouses and poorhouses to distribute food or to care for orphans or the destitute sprang up in towns throughout Catholic and Protestant Europe. In certain ways, these institutions reflected an optimistic vision, drawn from humanism, of an ideal Christian community attentive to material want. But by the end of the century, the distribution of food was accompanied by attempts to distinguish "deserving" from "undeserving" poor, by an insistence that the poor be forced to work to receive their ration of food, and even by an effort to compel the poor to live in almshouses and poorhouses.

These efforts were not uniformly successful. Begging was outlawed by Catholic and Protestant city governments alike, but never thoroughly suppressed. Catholic religious orders and parishes often resisted efforts at rationalizing their charitable work imposed from above—even by Catholic governments. Nonetheless, the trend was clear. From viewing the poor as a fact of life and as an occasional lesson in Christian humility, European elites were beginning to view them collectively as a social problem and individual poor people as problems too, in need of collective control and institutional discipline. The establishment of centralized poor relief thus reflected a vision of Christian community in which the relationship between religious belief and community order, at least for elites, became increasingly direct.

The Hunt for Witches and the Illusion of Order

Between approximately 1550 and 1650, Europe saw a dramatic increase in the persecution of women and men for alleged witchcraft. Approximately one hundred thousand people were tried and about sixty thousand executed. The surge in witch-hunting was closely linked to the aftermath of the Protestant Reformation.

Certain kinds of witchcraft had long existed in Europe. So-called black magic of various kinds—one peasant casting a spell on another peasant's cow—had been common since the Middle Ages and continued to be a routine and favored means of coping with personal difficulty. What began to make black magic seem menacing to magistrates, judges, and other authorities were theories linking black magic to Devil worship. Catholic leaders and legal scholars first began to advance such theories in the fifteenth century. By the late sixteenth century, both Catholic and Protestant elites viewed a witch not only as someone who might cast harmful spells but also as a heretic. Persecution for witchcraft rose dramatically after the initial phases of the Reformation ended, reflecting a continuation of reforming zeal directed at the traditional forms of folk religion and magic.

As far as we can tell, no proof that an accused person ever attended a Devil-worshiping "black" Sabbath was ever produced in any witch trial. Nevertheless, authorities were certain that Devil worship occurred, so convinced were they that Satan was in their midst and that the folkways of common people were somehow threatening.

Contemporary legal procedures allowed the use of torture to extract confessions. Torture or the threat of torture led most of those accused of witchcraft to "confess." Probably willing to say what they thought their captors wanted to hear, many named accomplices or others who were also "witches." In this way, a single initial accusation could lead to dozens of prosecutions. In regions where procedures for appealing convictions and sentences were fragile or nonexistent, prosecutions were pursued with zeal. They were widespread, for example, in the small principalities and imperial cities of the Holy Roman Empire, which were virtually independent of all higher authority.

Prosecutions also numbered in the thousands in Switzerland, Poland, France, and Scotland. The majority—perhaps 80 percent—of those convicted and executed in all areas of Europe were women. Lacking legal, social, and political resources, women may have been more likely than men to use black magic for self-protection or advancement and hence were accused more often than men by their neighbors. Community fear and guilt may account for the fact that many of the accused women were poor. The marked increase in poverty during the late sixteenth and early seventeenth centuries made poor women particularly vulnerable to accusations of witchcraft. It was easier to find such a person menacing—and to accuse her of something—than to feel guilty because of her evident need. The modern stereotype that depicts the witch as an ugly old crone dates from this period.

Christian dogma and classically inspired humanistic writing portrayed women as morally weaker than men and thus as more susceptible to the Devil's enticements. Devil worship was described in sexual terms, and the prosecution of witches had a voyeuristic, sexual dimension. The bodies of accused witches were searched for the "Devil's mark"—a blemish thought to be the imprint of the Devil. Both Protestantism and Catholicism taught that sexual lust was evil. One theory is that women accused of being witches were victims of the guilt that elite men felt because of the latter's own sexual longings, which they believed were sinful and might be evidence of damnation. These men sought to lay blame elsewhere.

The witch-hunts virtually ended by the late seventeenth century, as intellectual energies shifted from religious to scientific thought. (See Chapter 17.) Reflecting religious fear, guilt, and class divisions, the witch-hunts are central to understanding European life in this period. They are both the last chapter in the history of the Reformation and a first chapter in the history of the modern state.

IMPERIAL SPAIN AND THE LIMITS OF POWER

To contemporary observers, no political fact of the late sixteenth century was more obvious than the ascendancy of Spain. Philip II (r. 1556–1598) even-tually ruled Portugal as well as Spain, plus the Netherlands, parts of Italy, and Spanish territories in the Americas (Map 15.1). Yet imperial Spain did not escape the political, social, and religious turmoil of the era. Explosive combinations of religious dissent and political disaffection led to revolt against Spain in the Netherlands. This conflict highlights the tensions of sixteenth-century political life: towns, provinces, and nobles trying to safeguard medieval liberties against efforts at greater centralization, with the added complications of economic strain and religious division. The revolt also demonstrated the material limits of royal power, since even with gold and silver from the American colonies pouring in, Philip could at times barely afford to keep armies in the field. As American resources dwindled in the seventeenth century, Philip's successors faced severe financial and political strains even in their Spanish homelands.

The Revolt of the Netherlands

Philip II's power stemmed in part from the far-flung territories he inherited from his father, the Habsburg Holy Roman emperor Charles V: Spain, the Low Countries (the Netherlands), the duchy of Milan, the kingdom of Naples, and the conquered lands in the Americas. (Control of Charles's Austrian lands had passed to his brother, Philip's uncle.) Treasure fleets bearing precious metals from the New World began to reach Spain regularly during Philip's reign. In addition, Spain now belonged to an expanding trading economy unlike any that had existed in Europe before. To supply its colonies, Spain needed timber and other shipbuilding materials from the hinterlands of the Baltic Sea. Grain from the Baltic fed the urban populations of Spain (where wool was the principal cash crop) and the Netherlands, while the Netherlands, in turn, was a source of finished goods, such as cloth. The major exchange point for all of these goods was the city of Antwerp in the Netherlands, the leading trading center of all of Europe.

Thus, Spain's expanding trading network necessitated tight links with the Netherlands, the real jewel among Philip's European possessions. These seventeen provinces (constituting mostly the modern nations of Belgium and the Netherlands) had been centers of trade and manufacture since the twelfth century and, in the fourteenth

The City of Antwerp Antwerp, in the southern Netherlands, was the point of sale for Portuguese spices brought from around Africa, the selling and transshipping center for Baltic goods, including timber, fur, and grain, and the source for manufactured goods such as cloth. *(Musées royaux des Beaux-Arts de Belgique)*

and fifteenth centuries, had enjoyed political importance and a period of cultural innovation under the control of the dukes of Burgundy. By the time Philip inherited the provinces from his father, a sort of federal system of government had evolved to accommodate the various regional centers of power there. Each province had a representative assembly (Estates) that controlled taxation, but each also acknowledged a central administrative authority in the form of a governing council sitting in Brussels. Heading the principal council of state was a governor-general, typically, like Philip, a member of the Habsburg family.

Map 15.1 The Spanish Habsburgs and Europe Philip II's control of territories in northern Italy permitted the overland access of Spanish troops to the Netherlands and heightened the Spanish threat to France. Lands bordering the western Mediterranean made the sea a natural sphere of Spanish influence as well. Habsburg lands in central Europe were controlled after 1556 by Charles V's brother Ferdinand and his descendants.

Yet the revolt in the Netherlands that began early in Philip's reign clearly showed the limits to dynastic rule in such diverse territories (Map 15.2). Political power, here and elsewhere, was still highly decentralized, and Philip, like other rulers, could rule effectively only with the cooperation of local elites. Clumsy efforts to adjust this distribution of power in his favor caused Philip to push his subjects in the Netherlands into revolt.

Economic, political, and religious tensions began to strain the relationship between Philip and his subjects in the Netherlands early in his reign. Tensions arose partly over taxation and partly over Spanish insistence on maintaining tight control. Although taxes paid, in effect, to Spain were always resented, bad harvests and commercial disruptions occasioned by wars in the Baltic region in the 1560s depressed the Netherlands' economy and made it difficult for the provinces to afford higher taxes. When the Peace of Cateau-Cambrésis of 1559 brought an end to the long struggle over territory between the Habsburgs

Map 15.2 The Netherlands, 1559–1609 The seventeen provinces of the Netherlands were strikingly diverse politically, economically, and culturally. Like his father, Philip was, technically, the ruler of each province separately: He was count of Flanders, duke of Brabant, and so forth.

and the Valois kings of France, the people of the Netherlands had reason to hope for lower tax burdens and reduced levels of Spanish control.

Philip, born and raised in Spain, had little real familiarity with the densely populated, linguistically diverse Netherlands and never visited there after 1559. To assist the governor-general, his half-sister, Margaret of Parma, he left in place a council composed of ministers and secretaries who either were Spanish themselves or had close ties to the Spanish court. These arrangements affronted local nobles who had fought for Philip and his father before 1559 and who were accustomed to positions of influence in the council of state.

To economic and political tensions were added severe religious problems created by the

policies of Philip II. These policies addressed both heresy and ecclesiastical administration. Unlike his father, Philip directed the hunt for heretics not just at lower-class dissenters but also at well-to-do Calvinists—followers of the French Protestant religious reformer John Calvin—who now existed in increasing numbers. Punishment for heresy now included confiscation of family property as well as execution of the individual.

To ensure a high degree of religious control, Philip proposed in 1561 to add fourteen new bishoprics to the Netherlands' traditional four. Local nobles feared their family members would be passed over for appointment to these new church offices in favor of Spaniards or locals sympathetic to Spain. Moreover, each new bishopric was to have inquisitors to root out heretics. By 1565, municipal councils in the Netherlands routinely refused to enforce Philip's religious policies, believing that urban prosperity—as well as their personal security—depended on relative restraint in the prosecution of heresy. Leading nobles stopped enforcing the policies on their estates.

During the spring and summer of 1566, religious dissension in the Netherlands grew dramatically. Encouraged by greater tolerance, Protestants began to hold open-air meetings, and in many towns ordinary people began to embrace Protestantism for the first time. In a series of actions called the "iconoclastic fury," townsfolk stripped Catholic churches of the relics and statues deemed idolatrous by Calvinist doctrine. Reflecting the economic strain of these years, food riots also occurred. Both Spanish authorities and local elites feared the outbreak of general unrest. (See the box, "Elite Fears of Popular Religious Unrest in the Netherlands.")

By early 1567 Calvinist insurgents had seized two towns in the southern Netherlands by force of arms in hopes of stirring a general revolt that would secure freedom of worship. Nobles in various areas also supported a widening rebellion, for their own religious and political reasons. Margaret of Parma successfully quelled the uprisings by rallying city governments and loyal nobles, now alarmed for their own power and property. But she then learned that far away in Spain a decision had been made to send in the Spanish duke of Alba with an army of ten thousand men.

Alba arrived in August 1567 and, to bolster his own shaky standing at the Spanish court, acted more like a conqueror than a peacemaker. He bil-

Elite Fears of Popular Religious Unrest in the Netherlands

In 1566, Calvinists in the Netherlands, urged to action by their preachers, plundered Catholic churches and defied local authorities by holding large public worship services. In document (a), a government agent in a small city reports on the iconoclasm he has witnessed. In document (b), a member of Margaret of Parma's government, writing to a friend in Spain, describes his fears about the effects of the Calvinists' activities.

(a)

The audacity of the Calvinist preachers in this area has grown so great that in their sermons they admonish the people that it is not enough to remove all idolatry from their hearts; they must also remove it from their sight. Little by little, it seems, they are trying to impress upon their hearers the need to pillage the churches and abolish all images.

(b)

The town of Ypres, among others, is in turmoil on account of the daring of the populace inside and outside who go to the open-air services in the thousands, armed and defended as if they were going off to perform some great exploit of war. It is to be feared that the first blow will fall on the monasteries and clergy and that the fire, once lit, will spread, and that, since trade is beginning to cease on account of these troubles, several working folk—constrained by hunger—will join in, waiting for the opportunity to acquire a share of the property of the rich.

Source: Geoffrey Parker, *The Dutch Revolt* (London: Penguin, 1985), pp. 75–76.

---

leted troops in friendly cities, established new courts to try rebels, arrested thousands of people, executed about a thousand rebels (including Catholics as well as prominent Protestants), and imposed onerous taxes to support his own army. Thus, Alba repeated every mistake of Spanish policy that had triggered rebellion in the first place.

Margaret of Parma resigned in disgust and left the Netherlands. Protestants from rebellious towns escaped into exile and were joined by nobles who had been declared treasonous for minor lapses of loyalty. The most important of these was William of Nassau, prince of Orange (1533–1584), whose lands outside of the Netherlands, in France and the empire, lay out of Spanish reach and so could be used to finance continued warfare against Spain. Thus, a significant community with military capability began to grow in exile.

In 1572, ships of exiled Calvinist privateers known as the "Sea Beggars" captured some fifty towns in the northern provinces. The towns' impoverished inhabitants—eager to strike a blow at expensive Spanish rule—welcomed the exiles. Shortly thereafter, noble armies led by William of Orange invaded the southern provinces but were forced by Alba to withdraw when promised French help did not arrive. For the rest of the century, the northern provinces became increasingly Calvinist strongholds and were the center of opposition to the Spanish, who concentrated their efforts against rebellion in the wealthier southern provinces. Occasionally the French and English lent aid to the rebels.

The Spanish never had the resources to crush the rebellion. The war in the Netherlands exemplifies many of the tensions of the era—such as ones arising from aristocratic privilege, dynastic right, regionalism, and religion. The revolt was also a stage for the destructive and costly technology of warfare in this period. In an attempt to supply the

Netherlands with seasoned veterans and materiel from Spain and Spanish territories in Italy, the Spanish developed the "Spanish Road," an innovative string of supply depots where provisions could be gathered in advance of troops sent along the "Road" to the Netherlands (see Map 15.1).

Spanish supply efforts came partly in response to improved fortifications in the Netherlands' cities, some of which were equipped with new defensive works known as "bastions"; such cities could not be taken by storm but had to be besieged for long periods. Military campaigns in the Netherlands now consisted of grueling sieges, skirmishes in a city's surrounding area for control of villages' supplies, and occasional pitched battles between besiegers and forces attempting to break the siege. Vast numbers of men were required both for an effective besieging force and for garrisoning the fortresses that controlled farmlands and defended major towns. Inevitably, the army put a great strain on the countryside, and both soldiers and civilians suffered great privations. On occasion, Spanish troops reacted violently to difficult conditions and to delayed pay (American treasure dwindled badly between 1572 and 1578). In 1576, Spanish troops sacked the hitherto loyal southern city of Antwerp and massacred about eight thousand people. This event was remembered in the Netherlands as the "Spanish Fury."

Angered by the massacre, leaders in the southern provinces now raised money for citizen armies to protect themselves against the Spanish. In late 1576 the southern leaders concluded the Pacification of Ghent, an alliance with William of Orange and the northern rebels. The terms of the agreement called for nonbelligerence on religious grounds and cooperation to drive the Spanish out. This treaty might have initiated a self-governing United Netherlands were it not for old divisions and Spanish recovery.

The northern and southern provinces were increasingly divided by religion. When Calvinist artisans now seized control of several cities in the southern provinces, city leaders and nobles there grew frightened on political and religious grounds at the same time. Philip's new commander in the Netherlands, Margaret's son Alexander, duke of Parma, was skilled as both a negotiator and a soldier, and by 1578 had renewed shipments of American treasure to help him. He wooed the Catholic elites of the southern provinces back into

REVOLT OF THE NETHERLANDS

1559	Peace of Cateau-Cambrésis
1561	Philip II attempts to place fourteen new bishoprics in the Netherlands
1564	Netherlands city councils and nobility ignore Philip's law against heresy
1566	Calvinist "iconoclastic fury" begins
1567	Duke of Alba arrives in the Netherlands; Margaret of Parma resigns her duties as governor-general
1572	"Second Revolt" of the Netherlands, led by William of Orange, begins
1573	Alba is relieved of his command
1576	Sack of Antwerp / Pacification of Ghent
1579	Union of Utrecht
1609	Truce is declared between Spain and the Netherlands

loyalty to Philip, in return for promises to respect their provincial liberties and to safeguard their property from troops.

By 1579 the northern provinces concluded a defensive alliance, the Union of Utrecht, against the increasingly unified south. Parma could not cope with the geographic barrier of four rivers that bisect the Low Countries (see Map 15.2), and he faced declining resources as Spain diverted money to conflicts with England in 1588 and in France after 1589. In 1609 a truce was finally concluded between Spain and the northern provinces. This truce did not formally recognize the "United Provinces" as an independent entity, though in fact they were. The modern nations of Belgium and the Netherlands are the distant result of this truce.

The independent United Provinces (usually called, simply, the Netherlands) was a fragile state, an accident of warfare at first. But commercial prosperity had begun to emerge as its greatest strength. Much of the economic activity of Antwerp had shifted north to Amsterdam in the province of Holland because of fighting in the south and a naval

The Bastion Seen here in an example from an Italian fortress, the bastion was the triangular projection from the fortress wall. It enabled defenders to fire on the flanks of besieging forces; lower than medieval fortress walls and reinforced with earth, walls built in this manner were also less vulnerable to artillery blasts. (*Universitäts und Stadtbibliothek Cologne*)

blockade of Antwerp by rebel ships. Philip's policies had created a new enemy nation and had enriched it at his expense.

The Failure of the Invincible Armada

The political and economic importance of the Netherlands lured Spain into wider strategic involvement, most notably against England. England and Spain had long maintained cordial relations. They had a common foe in France and common economic interests. Philip's marriage to Mary Tudor, the Catholic queen of England (r. 1553–1558), had been a logical step in that relationship, though the opportunity to return England to Catholicism was an added inducement to maintaining close ties. Even after the accession of the Protestant queen Elizabeth (r. 1558-1603), Spanish-English relations initially remained cordial.

Relations started to sour, however, when Elizabeth began tolerating the use of English ports by the rebel Sea Beggars and authorizing English attacks on Spanish treasure fleets. In response, Spain supported Catholic resistance to Elizabeth within England, including a series of plots to replace Elizabeth on the throne with Mary, Queen of Scots. Greater Spanish success in the Netherlands, raids by the Spanish and English on each other's shipping, and Elizabeth's execution of Mary in 1587 prompted Philip to order an invasion of England. A fleet (*armada*) of Spanish warships sailed in 1588.

"The enterprise of England," as the plan was called in Spain, represented an astounding logistical effort. The Spanish Armada was supposed to clear the English Channel of English ships in order to permit an invading force—troops under Parma in the Netherlands—to cross the Channel on barges. The fleet of about 130 ships also carried troops from Spain to supplement Parma's force, as well as large quantities of supplies for the invasion. The sheer number of ships required for the undertaking meant that some, inevitably, were slower supply ships, or naval vessels designed for the more protected waters of the Mediterranean. The fleet as a whole was slower and less maneuverable than the English force it faced. The English also had the advantage in arms, since they had better long-range artillery and better-trained gunners.

When the Armada entered the Channel on July 29, the English fleet fell in behind them, with the westerly wind and current in their favor. They could harass the Spanish with artillery from a distance without sustaining much damage themselves. The logistical problems of the Spanish plan, given the technologies of the day, then became apparent: Parma could not get his men readied on their barges quickly enough once the fleet's presence in the Channel had been confirmed by messenger. Nor could the fleet protect itself while waiting offshore, since no friendly harbor was available. On the night of August 7, the English launched eight fireships into the anchored Spanish fleet; at dawn on August 8, they attacked the disorganized enemy off Gravelines, and their advantage in arms was decisive (see Map 15.1).

The Battle at Gravelines was the first major gun battle by sailing ships and helped set the future course of naval warfare. For the Spanish, it was a disaster. Many ships were sunk at Gravelines. Many more sank in bad weather, or were forced into hostile harbors, as the Spanish rounded the northern tip of the British Isles and sailed for home along the west coast of Ireland. Fifteen thousand sailors and soldiers—half of all on board—died in battle or on the return journey. Less than half of Philip's great fleet made it back to Spain.

Successes at Home and Around the Mediterranean

Many of Philip's interests still centered on the Mediterranean, despite the new overseas empire and his preoccupation with the Netherlands. Spain and the kingdom of Naples had exchanged trade for centuries. Newer ties had been forged with the duchy of Milan and the city-state of Genoa, whose bankers were financiers to the Spanish monarchy. Charles V had tried to secure the western Mediterranean against the Turks and their client states along the African coast, but it was under Philip that the Turkish threat in the western Mediterranean receded.

The years of the greatest Turkish threat coincided with the beginning of the Netherlands' revolt. To Philip and his advisers, the Turks represented a potential internal threat to Spain as well. Philip thus inaugurated a new wave of persecution of his Muslim subjects, eventually provoking a major rebellion in Granada between 1568 and 1571. After this revolt was crushed, the Muslim inhabitants of Granada were forcibly exiled farther north in Spain. The Spanish allied temporarily with the papacy and Venice—both were concerned with the Turkish advances in the Mediter-

ranean—and their combined navies inflicted a massive defeat on the Turkish navy at Lepanto, off the coast of Greece, in October 1571 (see Map 15.1). The Turks remained a power in the eastern Mediterranean, but their ability to threaten Spain and Spanish possessions in the west was over.

Philip's powers in each of his Spanish kingdoms were circumscribed by the traditional privileges of towns, nobility, and clergy. In Aragon, for example, he could raise revenues only by appealing to local assemblies, the Cortes. In Castile, the arid kingdom in the center of the Iberian Peninsula, the king was able to levy taxes with greater ease but only because of concessions that allowed nobles undisputed authority over their peasants. Philip established his permanent capital, Madrid, and his principal residence, the Escorial, there. The Spanish Empire became more and more Castilian as the reign progressed, with royal advisers and counselors increasingly drawn only from the Castilian elite. Yet the rural economy of Castile was stunted by the dual oppression of landholders and royal tax collectors.

Philip made significant inroads into Aragonese independence by the end of his reign. Noble feuds and peasant rebellions had combined to create virtual anarchy in some areas of Aragon by the 1580s, and in 1591 Philip sent in veteran troops from the Netherlands campaigns to establish firmer royal control. Philip was successful in the long run in Aragon because he used adequate force but tempered it afterward with constitutional changes that were cleverly moderate. Finally, he cemented the peace by doing what he had failed to do in the Netherlands. He appeared in Aragon in person, in the words of a contemporary, "like a rainbow at the end of a storm."[1]

Philip also invaded and successfully annexed Portugal in 1580, thus completing the unification of the Iberian Peninsula. The annexation was ensured by armed force but had been preceded by careful negotiation to guarantee that Philip's claim to the throne—through his mother—would find some support within the country. This was old-fashioned dynastic politics at its best. When Philip died in 1598, he was old and ill, a man for whom daily life had become a painful burden. His Armada had been crushed; he had never quelled the Netherlands' revolt. Yet he had been more successful, by his own standards, in other regions that he ruled.

Spain in Decline

Spain steadily lost ground economically and strategically after the turn of the century. Imports of silver declined. The American mines were exhausted and the natives forced to work in them were decimated by European diseases and brutal treatment. Spain's economic health was further threatened by the very success of its colonies: Local industries in the Americas began to produce goods formerly obtained from Spain. The increasing presence of English, French, and Dutch shipping in the Americas provided colonists with rival sources for the goods they needed. Often, these competitors could offer their goods more cheaply than Spaniards could, for Spanish productivity was low and prices were high because of the inflationary effects of the influx of precious metals.

Spain renewed hostilities with the United Provinces in 1621, after the truce of 1609 had expired. Philip IV (r. 1621–1645) also aided his Habsburg cousins in the Thirty Years' War in the Holy Roman Empire (see page 571). Squeezed for troops and revenue for these commitments, other Spanish territories revolted. The uprisings reflected both economic distress and unresolved issues of regional autonomy. The government of Spain was Castilian, and Castile bore the brunt of the financial support of the state. The chief minister to Philip IV, Gaspar de Guzmán, Count Olivares (1587–1645), was an energetic Castilian aristocrat determined to distribute the burdens of government more equitably among the various regions of Spain. His policies provoked rebellions in Catalonia and Portugal.

In Catalonia, a province of the kingdom of Aragon, the revolt began as a popular uprising against the billeting of troops. At one point Catalan leaders invited French troops south to defend them and solemnly transferred their loyalty to the French king in the hope that he would respect their autonomy. Spain resumed control only in 1652, after years of military struggle and promises to respect Catalan liberties.

In Portugal, a war of independence began in 1640, also with a popular revolt. The Spanish government tried to restore order with troops under the command of a leading Portuguese prince, John, duke of Braganza. The duke, however, was the nearest living relative to the last king of Portugal, and he seized this opportunity to claim the

Philip II in 1583 Dressed in the austere black in fashion at the Spanish court, Philip holds a rosary and wears the Order of the Golden Fleece, an order of knighthood, around his neck. At age 56 Philip has outlived four wives and most of his children. *(Museo del Prado, Madrid)*

crown of Portugal for himself and lead a fight for independence. Although war dragged on until 1668, the Portuguese under John IV (r. 1640–1656) succeeded in winning independence from Spain.

As a result of these uprisings, Count Olivares resigned in disgrace in 1643. In 1647 there would also be upheaval in Spain's Italian possessions of Sicily and Naples. By midcentury, Spain had lost its position as the preeminent state in Europe.

RELIGIOUS AND POLITICAL CRISIS IN FRANCE AND ENGLAND

Civil war wracked France from 1562 until 1598. As in the Netherlands, the conflicts in France had religious and political origins as well as international implications, and political and religious questions became entangled in ways that made the conflicts almost impossible to resolve. Though a temporary resolution was achieved by 1598, religious division still existed, and conflict over the legitimate nature and extent of royal power remained. England, in contrast, was spared dramatic political and religious upheaval in the second half of the sixteenth century, in part because of the talents—and long life—of its ruler. But in the seventeenth century, constitutional and religious dissent began to reinforce each other in new and dramatic ways and threaten the stability of the realm.

The French Religious Wars

The king of France, Henry II (r. 1547–1559), had concluded the Peace of Cateau-Cambrésis with Philip II in 1559, ending the Habsburg-Valois Wars, but had died in July of that year from wounds suffered at a tournament held to celebrate the new treaty. His death was a political disaster. Great noble families vied for influence over his 15-year-old son, Francis II (r. 1559–1560). Two brothers of the house of Guise were related to the young king by marriage and succeeded in dominating him. But the Guises faced continual challenges from members of the Bourbon family, who claimed the right to influence the king because they were princes of royal blood and stood next in line to the throne after Henry II's sons.

The queen mother, Catherine de' Medici (1519–1589), worked carefully and intelligently to balance the nobles' interests. She gained greater authority when, in late 1560, the sickly Francis died and was succeeded by his brother, Charles IX—a 10-year-old for whom Catherine was officially the regent. But keeping the conflicts among the great courtiers from boiling over into civil war proved impossible.

In France, as elsewhere, noble conflict invariably had a violent component. Noble men went about armed and accompanied by armed entourages. Although they relied on patronage and army commands from the Crown, the Crown depended on their services. Provincial landholdings afforded enough resources to support private warfare, and the nobles assumed a right to wage it.

In addition, religious tension was rising throughout France. (Henry II had welcomed the 1559 treaty in part because he wanted to turn his attention to "heresy.") Public preaching by, and secret meetings of, Protestants (known as "Huguenots" in France) were causing unrest in towns. At court, members of the Bourbon family and other leading nobles had converted to Protestantism and worshiped openly in their rooms in the palace. In 1561 Catherine convened a national religious council, known as the Colloquy of Poissy, to reconcile the two faiths. When it failed, she decided that the only practical course was at least provisional religious toleration, so she issued a limited edict of toleration in the name of the king in January 1562.

The edict, however, led only to further unrest. Ignoring its restrictions, Protestants armed themselves, while townspeople of both faiths insulted and attacked one another at worship sites and religious festivals. Then in March 1562, at Vassy, the duke of Guise's men killed a few dozen Protestants gathered in worship near one of the duke's estates.

The killing at Vassy began the first of six civil wars because it brought together the military power of the nobility with the broader problem of religious division. In some ways, the initial conflict was decisive. The Protestant army lost the principal pitched battle of the war, near Dreux, west of Paris, in December. This defeat ultimately checked the growth of the Protestant movement. It reduced the appeal of the movement to nobles, and the limited rights granted to Protestants in the Crown's peace edict made it difficult for Protestant townspeople to worship, particularly in areas where they were not a majority. But if the Protestants were not powerful enough to win, neither could the Crown decisively beat them.

The turning point most obvious to contemporaries came a decade later. The Protestant faction was still well represented at court by the Bourbon princes and by the very able and influential nobleman Gaspard de Coligny, related to the Bourbons by marriage. Coligny pressed for a war against Spain in aid of Protestant rebels in the Netherlands. Alarmed by this pressure and by rumors of Protestant armies outside of Paris, Charles IX (r. 1560–1574) and his mother authorized royal guards to murder Coligny and other Protestant leaders on August 24, 1572—Saint Bartholomew's Day. Coligny's murder touched off a massacre of

THE FRENCH SUCCESSION, 1515–1715

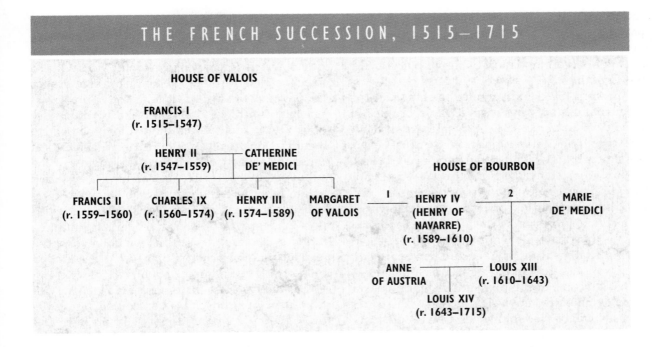

HOUSE OF VALOIS

FRANCIS I
(r. 1515–1547)

HENRY II ——— CATHERINE
(r. 1547–1559)   DE' MEDICI

HOUSE OF BOURBON

FRANCIS II   CHARLES IX   HENRY III   MARGARET   1   HENRY IV   2   MARIE
(r. 1559–1560)   (r. 1560–1574)   (r. 1574–1589)   OF VALOIS   (HENRY OF   DE' MEDICI
                                                                          NAVARRE)
                                                                          (r. 1589–1610)

                                                         ANNE ——————— LOUIS XIII
                                                         OF AUSTRIA   (r. 1610–1643)

                                                              LOUIS XIV
                                                              (r. 1643–1715)

Protestants throughout Paris and, once news from Paris had spread, throughout the kingdom.

The Saint Bartholomew's Day Massacre revealed the degree to which religious differences had strained the fabric of community life. Neighbor murdered neighbor, in an effort to rid the community of heretical pollution; bodies of the dead, including Coligny's, were torn apart, mutilated. Gathered in the south of France, the remaining Huguenot forces vowed "never [to] trust those who have so often and so treacherously broken faith and the public peace."[2] Many Catholics also renounced reconciliation. When further war produced the inevitable truces and limited toleration, some noblemen formed a Catholic league to fight in place of the vacillating monarchy.

Another impetus to the breakdown of royal authority by the 1580s was the accession to the throne of Charles's brother, Henry III (r. 1574–1589), another king of limited abilities. Middle-aged, Henry had no children. The heir to his throne was the Protestant Henry of Navarre, and the assumption of the throne by a Protestant was unimaginable to the zealous Catholic faction at court and to thousands of ordinary Catholics besides. By the end of Henry III's reign, the king had almost no royal authority left to wield. He was forced to cooperate with first one of the warring parties and then with

another. In December 1588, he resorted to murdering two members of the Guise family who led the ultra-Catholic faction, and, in turn, he was murdered by a priest in early 1589.

Henry of Navarre, who became Henry IV (r. 1589–1610), had to fight for his throne. Facing him were Catholic armies now subsidized by Philip II of Spain, an extremist Catholic city government in Paris, a kingdom of subjects who were tired of war but mainly Catholic, and only meager support from Protestants abroad. Given these obstacles, Henry was able to force acceptance of his rule only after agreeing to return to Catholicism himself.

After his conversion in 1593, the wars continued for a time, but, after thirty years of civil war, many of his subjects realized that only rallying to the monarchy could save France from chaos. Catholic nobility and townspeople fought among themselves over the direction to take. The nobility favored acceptance of Henry IV and imposed its will on the citizens of Paris and other cities.

The civil wars had demonstrated the power of the warrior-nobility to disrupt the state. But now nobles grew increasingly disposed, for both psychological and practical reasons, to cooperate with the Crown. Service to a successful king could be a source of glory, and Henry was personally esteemed because he was a talented general and brave, gregarious, and charming. The civil war period thus proved to be an important phase in the continual accommodation of the nobility to the power of the state.

In April 1598 Henry granted toleration for the Huguenot minority in a royal edict proclaimed in the city of Nantes. The Edict of Nantes was primarily a repetition of provisions from the most generous edicts that had ended the various civil wars. Nobles were allowed to practice the Protestant faith on their estates; townspeople were granted more limited rights to worship in selected towns in each region. Protestants were guaranteed access to schools, hospitals, royal appointments, and separate judicial institutions to ensure fair treatment. They were also guaranteed rights of self-defense—specifically, the right to maintain garrisons in about two hundred towns. About half of these garrisons would be paid for by the Crown.

The problem was that the Edict of Nantes, like any royal edict, could be revoked by the king at any time. Moreover, the provision allowing Protestants to keep garrisoned towns reflected concessions to powerful nobles who could support their followers by paid garrison duty. These concessions also meant that living peacefully with religious diversity was not yet thought to be possible. Thus, although Henry IV successfully ended the French religious wars, the problem of religious and political division within France had not been solved.

The Consolidation of Royal Authority in France, 1610–1643

During Henry IV's reign, France recovered from the long years of civil war. Population and productivity began to grow; the Crown encouraged internal improvements to facilitate commerce. Henry's chief minister, Maximilien de Béthune, duke of Sully (1560–1641), increased royal revenue by nibbling away at traditional local self-government and control of taxation. He succeeded in creating a budget surplus and in extending mechanisms of centralized government.

Yet Henry's regime was stable only in comparison with the preceding years of civil war. The power of the great nobility had not been definitively broken. Several leading nobles plotted with foreign powers, including Spain, to influence French policy and gain materially themselves.

Moreover, the king had agreed to a provision, known as the *paulette* (named for the functionary who first administered it), that allowed royal officeholders not merely to own their offices but also to bequeath those offices to their heirs in return for the payment of an annual fee. It was, primarily, a financial expedient to raise revenue after decades of civil war. In addition, the paulette helped cement the loyalty of royal bureaucrats at a critical time, particularly that of the royal judges of the supreme law court, the Parlement of Paris, who had recently agreed to register the Edict of Nantes only under duress. However, that privileged position made royal officeholders largely immune from royal control since a position in the royal bureaucracy now became property, like the landed property of the traditional nobility.

A fanatical Catholic assassinated Henry IV in 1610. Henry's death left his son, Louis XIII (r. 1610–1643), only 9 years old, to face the challenges of governing as well as a return of religious conflict. Louis's mother, Marie de' Medici, acted ably as regent, but was temporarily disgraced when her unpopular leading minister was assassinated in 1617. This courtier was an Italian, and hence doubly resented for being a foreigner as well as for his crass ambition. His rise and fall was typical of the volatile court life of the period, as great aristocrats vied to control and profit from royal policies.

Soon after Louis took control of government from his mother, he faced a major rebellion by his Huguenot subjects in southwestern France. Huguenots felt threatened by the recent marriage of the king to a Spanish princess and by Louis's reintroduction of Catholic institutions in nearby Navarre (see Map 15.1). Louis's ancestors had themselves established Protestantism in this small kingdom bordering Spain, now united to the French crown. Certain Huguenot nobles, afraid that royal support of toleration was wavering, initiated fighting in 1621 as a show of force against the king.

These religious wars persisted, on and off, until 1629. They reflected not only the continuing power of great nobles to wield independent military might, but also the importance of fortifications in warfare: The Crown had difficulty successfully besieging even small fortress towns. The course of the wars also reflected the ascendancy of the western port city of La Rochelle—well-fortified, Protestant-controlled, and wealthy from mounting overseas and European trade. Not until the king took the city, after a siege lasting more than a year and costing thousands of lives, did the Protestants accept a peace on royal terms.

The Peace of Alais (1629) was a political triumph for the Crown because it broke the connection between religious dissent and political upheaval. The treaty reaffirmed the policy of religious toleration but rescinded the Protestants' military and political privileges. It thus deprived French Protestants of the means for further rebellion while reinforcing their dependence on the Crown for religious toleration. Most of the remaining great noble leaders began to convert to Catholicism.

The Peace of Alais was also a personal triumph for the king's leading minister, who crafted the treaty and who had directed the bloody siege that made it possible: Armand-Jean du Plessis (1585–1642), Cardinal Richelieu. From a provincial noble family, Richelieu had risen in the service of the queen mother. His enormous intelligence was apparent to everyone at court; he was admired and feared for his skill in the political game of seeking and bestowing patronage—a crucial skill in an age when elites received offices and honor through carefully cultivated links with the court. His control of many lucrative church offices gave him the resources to build up a large network of clients. He and the king—whose sensitive temperament Richelieu handled adeptly—formed a lasting partnership from this point on that had a decisive impact not only on French policy but also on the entire shape of the French state. (See the box, "Richelieu Supports the Authority of the State.")

Richelieu favored an aggressive foreign policy to counter what he believed still to be the greatest threat to the French crown: the Spanish Habsburgs. War had resumed between the Netherlands and Spain when their truce expired in 1621 (see page 561); since then, Richelieu had used his growing power to direct limited military campaigns against Spanish power in Italy. After 1630, with the king's full confidence, he superintended large-scale fighting against Spain in the Netherlands itself, as well as in Italy, and subsidized armies fighting the Spanish and Austrian Habsburgs in Germany.

Richelieu's policies were opposed by many people, who saw taxes double, then triple, in just a few years. Many courtiers and provincial elites had favored the tenuous peace with a fellow Catholic state and objected to alliances with German Protestants. They were alarmed by the increasing taxes and by the famine, disease, and, above all, the revolts that accompanied the peasants' distress. Their own power was also directly threatened by Richelieu's monopoly of royal patronage and by his creation of new mechanisms of government to manage his policies, which bypassed their offices. In 1632, for example, Richelieu created the office of *intendant*. Intendants had wide powers for defense and administration in the provinces that overrode the established bureaucracy.

By 1640 Richelieu's ambitious foreign policy seemed to be bearing fruit. The French had won territory along their northern and eastern borders by their successes against Habsburg forces. But when Richelieu and Louis XIII died within five months of each other, in December 1642 and May 1643, Richelieu's legacy was tested. Louis XIII was succeeded by his 5-year-old son, and the warrior-nobility as well as royal bureaucrats would dramatically challenge the Crown's new authority.

England: Precarious Stability, 1558–1603

England experienced no civil wars during the second half of the sixteenth century, but religious dissent challenged the stability of the monarchy. In Elizabeth I (r. 1558–1603), England—in stark contrast to France—possessed an able and long-lived ruler. Elizabeth was well educated in the humanistic tradition and was already an astute politician at the age of 25, when she acceded to the throne. Religious, political, and constitutional disputes existed in England as elsewhere, but they would not provoke violence on anything like the continental scale.

Elizabeth came to the throne at the death of her Catholic half-sister, Mary Tudor (r. 1553–1558), wife of Philip II. Elizabeth faced the urgent problem of reaching a policy of consensus in religious matters—a consensus that could embrace the two extremes of the Catholic-like doctrine and practice of Anglicanism, which had prevailed under her father, Henry VIII (r. 1509–1547), and Calvinist-inspired Protestantism, which had developed under her half-brother, Edward VI (r. 1547–1553). True Catholicism, such as Mary had tried to reimpose, was out of the question. The Roman church had never recognized Henry VIII's self-made di-

Richelieu Supports the Authority of the State

In this excerpt from his Political Testament *(assembled from his notes after his death by loyal secretaries), Richelieu justifies methods for ensuring obedience to the Crown. Notice his pessimistic view of human rationality; rewards (such as patronage) but also severity are both necessary to ensure obedience.*

It is a common but nevertheless true saying which has long been repeated by intelligent men that punishments and rewards are the two most important instruments of government in a realm. It is certain that whatever else one may do in governing states, one must be inflexible in punishing those who fail to obey, and religiously scrupulous in rewarding those who perform notable services. In other words, one would not govern badly if guided by this precept since most people can be held to their duty through either fear or hope. I rate punishments, I must say, higher than rewards, because if it were necessary to dispense with one of these, it would be better to give up the latter than the former. The good ought to be adhered to for its own sake, and in all justice no one should be rewarded for this. But there is no crime which does not violate those precepts men are obligated to obey, so that punishment to be expected for disobedience of this sort is therefore justified, and this obligation is so direct in many cases that to let the act go unpunished is to commit further error.

I speak here of things which injure the state and which have been premeditated, and not of those lesser offenses which result from chance or misfortune, toward which princes may and should often show indulgence. But while in matters of this sort it can be praise-worthy to pardon, it is a criminal omission not to punish breaches which open the door to licentious abandon. Both theologians and political experts agree that on special occasions it would be an error not to pardon certain individuals, but it would be inexcusable for those charged with public responsibilities to substitute indulgence for severe punishment. Experience teaches those who have had long practice in this world that men easily lose the memory of rewards and, when they are heaped with them, they expect even more, and become both ambitious and ungrateful at the same time. This teaches us to realize that punishments are a surer means of holding a person to his duty, since people are less likely to forget what has made an impression on their emotions. This is more persuasive for most men than reason, which has little power over many minds.

To be severe in dealing with private individuals who glory in disobeying the laws and orders of the state makes a good impression on the people, and one can commit no greater crime against the public interest than to be indulgent toward those who violate them. In thinking over the many cabals, factions, and plottings which have occurred in this realm in my time, I can recall none in which leniency induced any person with evil inclinations to rectify the error of his ways.

Source: Henry Bertram Hill, ed. and trans., *The Political Testament of Cardinal Richelieu* (Madison: University of Wisconsin Press, 1965), pp. 84–86.

vorce and thus regarded Elizabeth as a bastard with no right to the throne.

Most important to Elizabeth was a new Act of Supremacy (1559), intended to restore the monarch as head of the Church of England. Elizabeth and most of her ministers were willing to accept some room for maneuver between liturgical practice and personal belief for the sake of defeating the common enemy, Roman Catholicism. For example, a new prayer book, the *Book of Common Prayer,* incorporated, side by side, elements of both traditional and radical interpretations of

Elizabeth I: The Armada Portrait Both serene and resolute, Elizabeth is flanked by "before" and "after" glimpses of the Spanish fleet; her hand rests on the globe in a gesture of dominion that also memorializes the circumnavigation of the globe by her famous captain, Sir Francis Drake, some years before. *(By kind permission of Marquess of Tavistock and Trustees of Bedford Estate)*

communion. Church liturgy, clerical vestments, and, above all, the hierarchical structure of the clergy closely resembled Catholicism, however. Elizabeth firmly handled resistance to the Act of Supremacy. She simply arrested bishops and lords whose votes would have blocked its passage by Parliament.

The problem of religious dissent, however, was not definitively solved. Catholicism continued to be practiced. Loyal nobility and gentry in the north of England practiced it with discretion. But priests returning from exile beginning in the 1570s, most newly imbued with the proselytizing zeal of the Counter-Reformation (the Catholic response to the Protestant Reformation), practiced it more visibly. In the last twenty years of Elizabeth's reign, approximately 180 Catholics were executed for treason; two-thirds of them were priests. (By 1585, being a priest in itself was a crime.)

In the long run, however, the greater threat to the English crown came from growing tensions with the most radical Protestants in the realm, known (by their enemies initially) as Puritans. Puritanism was a broad movement for reform of church practice along familiar Protestant lines: emphasis on Bible reading, preaching, private scrutiny of conscience, and a de-emphasis on institutional ritual and clerical authority. Most Puritans had accepted Elizabeth's religious compromise for practical reasons but grew increasingly alienated by her insistence on clerical authority. A significant Presbyterian underground movement began to form among them. Presbyterians wanted to dismantle the episcopacy, the hierarchy of priests and bishops, and govern the church instead with councils, called "presbyterys," that included lay members of the congregation. Laws were passed late in the reign to enable the Crown more easily to prosecute, and even to force into exile, anyone who attended "nonconformist" (non-Anglican) services.

The greatest challenge Elizabeth faced from Puritans came in Parliament, where they were well represented by many literate gentry. Parliament met only when called by the monarch, and in theory could merely voice opinions and complaints; it could not initiate legislation or demand changes in royal policy. However, only Parliament could vote taxes, and, since its authority had, in effect, helped constitute royal authority by means of the Acts of Supremacy, Parliament's supposedly consultative role had been expanded by the monarchy itself. During Elizabeth's reign, Puritans used meetings of Parliament to press their cause of further religious reform. In 1586, they went so far as to introduce bills calling for an end to the episcopacy and the Anglican prayer book. Elizabeth had to resort to imprisoning one Puritan leader to end debate on the issue and on Parliament's right to address it.

Elizabeth's reign saw the beginnings of English expansion overseas, but great interest in overseas possessions lay in the future; Elizabeth, like all her forebears, felt her interests tightly linked to affairs on the European continent. Her prime interest lay in safeguarding the independence of the Netherlands. Philip II's policy in the Netherlands increasingly alarmed her, especially in view of France's weakness. She began to send small sums of money to the rebels and allowed their ships access to southern English ports, from which they could raid Spanish-held towns on the Netherlands' coast. In 1585, in the wake of the duke of Parma's successes against the rebellions, she committed troops to help the rebels.

Her decision was a reaction not only to the threat of a single continental power dominating the Netherlands but also to the threat of Catholicism. Spain had threatened her interests, and even her throne, in other ways. From 1579 to 1583, the Spanish had helped the Irish fight English domination and were involved in several plots to replace Elizabeth with her Catholic cousin, Mary, Queen of Scots. These threats occurred at the height of the return of Catholic exiles to England.

Eventually, in 1588, the English faced the Spanish Armada and the threat of invasion that it brought. The defeat of the Armada was by no means certain for the English. They did not know, for example, how poorly prepared Parma actually was to cross the Channel. Thus, in the wake of victory, a mythology quickly built that portrayed Spain as an aggressive Goliath confronting the tiny David of England. The victory over the Spanish fleet was quite rightly celebrated, for it ended any Catholic threat to Elizabeth's rule.

The success against the Armada has tended to overshadow other aims and outcomes of Elizabeth's foreign policy. In the case of Ireland, England was Goliath to Ireland's David. Since the twelfth century, an Anglo-Irish state dominated by great princely families had been loosely supervised from England, but most of Ireland remained under the control of Gaelic chieftains. Just as Charles V and Philip II attempted to tighten their governing mechanisms in the Netherlands, so in England did Henry VIII's minister, Thomas Cromwell, streamline control of outlying areas such as Wales and Anglo-Ireland. Cromwell proposed that the whole of Ireland be brought under English control partly by the established mechanism of feudal ties: The Irish chieftains were to do homage as vassals to the king of England.

Under Elizabeth, this legalistic approach gave way to virtual conquest. Elizabeth's governor, Sir Henry Sidney, appointed in 1565, inaugurated a policy whereby Gaelic lords, by means of various technicalities, could be entirely dispossessed of their land. Any Englishman capable of raising a private force could help enforce these dispossessions and settle his conquered lands as he saw fit. This policy provoked stiff Irish resistance, which was viewed as rebellion and provided the excuse for further military action, more confiscations of land, and more new English settlers. Eventually, the Irish, with Spanish assistance, mounted a major rebellion, consciously Catholic and aimed against the "heretic" queen. The rebellion gave the English an excuse for brutal suppression and massive transfers of land to English control. The political domination of the Irish was complete with the defeat, in 1601, of the able Gaelic chieftain Hugh O'Neill, lord of Tyrone, who controlled most of the northern quarter of the island. Although the English were unable to impose their Protestantism on the conquered Irish, to Elizabeth and her English subjects the conquests in Ireland seemed as successful as the victory over the Spanish Armada.

The English enjoyed remarkable peace at home during Elizabeth's reign. However, her reign ended on a note of strain. The foreign involvements, particularly in Ireland, had been very expensive. Taxation granted by Parliament more than doubled during her reign, and local taxes further burdened the people. Price inflation caused by government spending, social problems caused by returned, unemployed soldiers, and a series of bad harvests heightened popular resentment against taxation. Despite her achievements, therefore, Elizabeth passed two potential problems on to her successors: unresolved religious tensions and financial instability. Elizabeth's successors would also find in Parliament an increasing focus of opposition to their policies.

Rising Tensions in England, 1603–1642

In 1603 Queen Elizabeth died and James VI of Scotland acceded to the English throne as James I (r. 1603–1625). Religious tensions between Anglicans and Puritans were temporarily quieted under James because of a plot, in 1605, by Catholic dissenters. The Gunpowder Plot, as it was called, was a conspiracy to blow up the palace housing both king and Parliament at Westminster. The attention of Protestants of all stripes once again became focused not on their differences but on their common enemy, Catholicism.

Financial problems were James's most pressing concern. Court life became more elaborate and an increasing drain on the monarchy's resources. James's own leanings toward extravagance were partly to blame for his financial problems, but so were pressures for patronage from elites. There were considerable debts left from the Irish conflicts and wars with Spain. Moreover, as the reign progressed, James was forced into further foreign involvement. His daughter and her husband, a German prince, were trying to defend their claim to rule Bohemia against the powerful Austrian Habsburgs (see page 573).

To raise revenue without Parliament's consent, James, like Elizabeth, relied on sources of revenue that the Crown had enjoyed since medieval times: customs duties granted to the monarch for life, wardship (the right to manage and liberally borrow from the estates of minor nobles), and the sale of monopolies, which conveyed the right to be sole agent for a particular kind of goods. James increased the number of monopolies sold and added other measures, such as the sale of Crown lands and of noble titles, to increase royal revenue.

These expanded financial expedients were resented: Merchants opposed monopolies' arbitrary restriction of production and trade; common people found that the prices of certain ordinary commodities, like soap, rose prohibitively. Resentments among the nobility were sharpened, and general criticism of the court heightened, by James's favoritism of certain courtiers and their families. The chief beneficiary of patronage and the most influential adviser to the king was George Villiers (1592–1628), duke of Buckingham, a powerful but corrupt and inadequate first minister.

When James summoned Parliament for funds in 1621, Parliament used the occasion to protest court corruption and the king's financial expedients. The members impeached and removed from office two royal ministers. In 1624, still faced with expensive commitments to Protestants abroad and in failing health, James again called Parliament, which voted new taxes but also openly debated the king's foreign policy.

Under James's son, Charles I (r. 1625–1649), tensions between Crown and Parliament rose. One reason was the growing financial strain of foreign policy as well as the policies themselves. Retaining the unpopular duke of Buckingham as chief courtier and adviser, Charles declared war on Spain and pursued an indecisive but costly foreign policy in France in support of the Huguenot rebels there. Many wealthy merchants opposed this aggressive foreign policy, which disrupted trading relationships. In 1626, Parliament was dissolved without granting any monies in order to stifle its objections to royal policies. The Crown's reliance on unpopular financial expedients thus of necessity continued and reached a new level of coercion. In 1627, Charles imprisoned certain gentry who refused to lend money to the government.

Above all, Charles's religious policies were a source of controversy. Charles was personally inclined toward "high church" practices: an emphasis on ceremony and sacrament reminiscent of Catholic ritual. He also was a believer in Arminianism, a school of thought that justified the emphasis on sacrament and ritual by denying the Calvinist notion that God's grace cannot be earned. These emphases highlighted the authority of clerics instead of lay control over religion. Charles was intent on fashioning an official religion that would better reflect and justify royal claims to power but found himself on a collision course with gentry and aristocrats who leaned toward Puritanism.

Charles's views were supported by William Laud (1573–1645), archbishop of Canterbury from 1633 and thus leader of the Church of England. He tried to impose ritual changes in worship, spread Arminian ideas, and censor opposing views. He also challenged the redistribution of church property, which had occurred in the Reformation of the sixteenth century, and thereby alienated the gentry on economic as well as religious grounds.

Charles's style of rule worsened religious, political, and economic tensions. Cold and intensely private, he was not a man to build confidence or smooth over tensions with charm or dexterous political maneuvering. His court was ruled by formal protocol, and access to the king himself was highly restricted—a serious problem in an age when personal access to the monarch was the guarantee of political power.

Struggle over issues of revenue and religion dominated debate in the Parliament of 1628–1629, which Charles had called, once again, to get funds for his foreign policy. In 1628 the members of Parliament presented the king with a document called the Petition of Right, which protested his financial policies as well as arbitrary imprisonment. (Seventeen of Parliament's members had been imprisoned for refusing loans to the Crown.) Though couched conservatively as a restatement of cus-

Criticism of Monopolies Holders of royally granted monopolies were bitterly resented by English consumers and tradespeople alike, as this contemporary print reveals. The greedy beast pictured here controls even ordinary commodities such as pins, soap, and butter. *(Courtesy of the Trustees of the British Museum)*

tomary practice, the petition was in fact a bold claim to a tradition of parliamentary participation in the government of the realm. It reflected Parliament's growing determination to check arbitrary royal actions. Charles dissolved the Parliament in March 1629, having decided that the money he might extract was not worth the risk.

For eleven years, Charles ruled without Parliament. When he was forced to call Parliament again, in 1640, not only were royal finances in desperate straits but political tension had risen markedly on many fronts. In the intervening eleven years, Archbishop Laud's religious policies had raised concern and opposition among a wide spectrum of elites, not just radical Puritans, as well as among ordinary citizens of London, where his clerical influence was greatest. Moreover, Charles had pressed collection of revenues far beyond traditional bounds. In 1634, for example, he revived annual collection of "ship money"—a medieval tax levied on coastal districts to help support the navy during war. England, however, was not at war, and the tax was levied not only on seaports but on inland areas, too. Resistance to the collection of various customs duties and taxes grew; some gentry refused outright to pay them.

In addition, Charles also faced a rebellion by his Scottish subjects, which had occasioned his now desperate need for money. Like Philip II in the Netherlands, Charles tried to rule in Scotland through a small council of men who did not represent the local elite. He also tried to force the Scots, most of whom practiced Presbyterianism, to adopt Anglican liturgy and ritual. In 1639, Charles had started a war against them but, lacking men and money, was forced to agree to a peace treaty. Intent on renewing the war, he was forced to summon Parliament to obtain funds.

Thus, in the spring of 1640, Charles faced Parliament further weakened by military failure. His political skills were far too limited for him to reestablish a workable relationship with Parliament under the circumstances; indeed, he compounded his own difficulties. Charles dissolved this body, which is now known as the "Short Parliament," after just three weeks, when members questioned the war with the Scots and other royal policies. More politically risky even than dissolving the Parliament at this juncture was the lack of respect Charles had shown the members: A number of them were harassed or arrested. Mistrust fomented by the eleven years in which Charles had ruled without Parliament thus increased.

Another humiliating and decisive defeat at the hands of the Scots later in 1640 made summoning another Parliament imperative. Members of Parliament could now exploit the king's predicament. This Parliament is known as the "Long Parliament" because it sat from 1640 to 1653. Charles was forced to agree not to dissolve or adjourn Parliament without the members' own consent and to summon Parliament at least every three years. Parliament abolished many of his unorthodox and traditional sources of revenue and impeached and removed from office his leading ministers, including Archbishop Laud. The royal commander deemed responsible for the Scottish fiasco, Thomas Wentworth, earl of Strafford, was executed without trial in May 1641.

The execution of Strafford shocked many aristocrats in the House of Lords as well as some moderate members of the House of Commons. Meanwhile, Parliament began debating the perennially thorny religious question. A bare majority of members favored abolition of Anglican bishops as a first step in thoroughgoing religious reform. Working people in London, kept apprised of the issues by the regular publication of parliamentary debates, demonstrated in support of that majority. Moderate members of Parliament, in contrast, favored checking the king's power but not upsetting the Elizabethan religious compromise.

An event that unified public and parliamentary opinion at a crucial time—a revolt against English rule in Ireland in October 1641—temporarily eclipsed these divisions and once again focused suspicion on the king. The broad consensus of anti-Catholicism once again became the temporary driving force in politics. Few trusted the king with the troops necessary to quash the rebellion, however. It was even widely rumored that Charles would use Irish soldiers against his English subjects. Parliament demanded control of the army to put down the rebellion, and in November the Puritan majority introduced a document known as the "Grand Remonstrance," an appeal to the people and a long catalog of parliamentary grievances against the king. By a narrow margin it was passed, further setting public opinion in London against Charles. The king's remaining support in Parliament eroded in January 1642, when he attempted to arrest five leading members on charges of treason. The five escaped, but the attempt set the stage for wider violence. The king withdrew from London, unsure he could defend himself there, and began to raise an army. In mid-1642 the kingdom stood at the brink of civil war.

THE HOLY ROMAN EMPIRE AND THE THIRTY YEARS' WAR

The Holy Roman Empire enjoyed a period of comparative quiet after the Peace of Augsburg halted religious and political wars in 1555. By the early seventeenth century, however, fresh causes of instability brought about renewed fighting. Especially destabilizing was the drive by the Habsburgs, as emperors and territorial princes, to reverse the successes of Protestantism both in their own lands and in the empire at large and to consolidate their rule in their diverse personal territories.

In the Thirty Years' War (1618–1648), as it is now called, we can see the continuation of conflicts from the sixteenth century—religious tensions, regionalism versus centralizing forces, dynastic and strategic rivalries between rulers. The war was particularly destructive because of the size of the armies, the burden they imposed on civilian populations, and the degree to which army commanders evaded control by the states for which they fought. Some areas of the empire suffered catastrophic losses in population and productive capacity. As a result of the war, the empire was eclipsed as a political unit by the regional powers within it.

Peace Through Diversity, 1555–ca. 1618

Through most of the second half of the sixteenth century, the Holy Roman Empire enjoyed an uneasy peace. The Peace of Augsburg (1555) permitted rulers of the various states to impose either Lutheranism or Catholicism in their lands and, for a time, proved to be a workable enough solution to the problem of religious division. Complicating matters, however, was the rise of Calvinism, for which no provision had been necessary in 1555. A number of rulers adopted this newest religion, but the impact of their choices was felt more directly outside the empire than within it because they chose to support French Huguenots and the Dutch

THE THIRTY YEARS' WAR, 1618–1648

1618	Bohemian revolt against Habsburg rule Defenestration of Prague
1619	Ferdinand II is elected Holy Roman emperor
	Frederick, elector of the Palatinate, is elected king of Bohemia
1620	Catholic victory at Battle of White Mountain
1621	Truce between Spain and the Netherlands expires; war between Spain and the Netherlands begins
1626	Imperial forces defeat armies of Christian IV of Denmark
1629	Peace of Lübeck
1631	Swedes under Gustav Adolf defeat imperial forces at Breitenfeld
	Catholic forces sack Magdeburg
1632	Death of Gustav Adolf
1635	Peace of Prague
1643	French defeat Spanish in the Netherlands
1648	Peace of Westphalia

rebels but not to disturb the peace within the empire. For the most part, there was not a second wave of reforming zeal among the population.

The Habsburgs ruled over a diverse group of territories. Most lay within the boundaries of the empire, but many were not German (Map 15.3). Though largely contiguous, the territories comprised independent duchies and kingdoms, each with its own institutional structure. Habsburg lands included speakers of Italian, German, and Czech, as well as other languages. The non-German lands of Bohemia and Hungary had been distinct kingdoms since the High Middle Ages. Most of Hungary was now under Ottoman domination, but Bohemia, with its rich capital, Prague, was a wealthy center of population and culture in central Europe.

Unlike the Netherlands, these linguistically and culturally diverse lands were still governed by highly decentralized institutions. The Habsburg family often divided rule of the various territories among themselves. For example, during the lifetime of Holy Roman Emperor Charles V, his brother Ferdinand (d. 1564) was more active than he in governing these family lands. At Ferdinand's death, as he wished, rule of the various provinces and kingdoms was split among his three sons. One member of the family was routinely elected Holy Roman emperor.

Moreover, the Habsburgs, unlike most of their contemporaries, made no attempt to impose religious uniformity in this period. Ferdinand was firmly Catholic but tolerant of diverse reform efforts within the church, including clerical marriage and allowing the laity to receive both wine and bread at communion. His son, Emperor Maximilian II (r. 1564–1576), granted limited rights of worship to Protestant subjects within his lands and kept his distance from policies pursued by Catholic rulers elsewhere—most notably, those of his cousin, Philip II, in the Netherlands. During Maximilian's reign, partly because of his positive leadership and partly because of a lack of persecution, a variety of faiths flourished side by side in Habsburg lands. In this tolerant atmosphere, education, printing, and humanistic intellectual life flourished.

But, given the course of events elsewhere in Europe, this late Renaissance was unlikely to last. The balance began to shift under Maximilian's son, Rudolf II (r. 1576–1612). Rudolf shared the religious style of his father and grandfather. He was an energetic patron of the arts and sponsored the work of scientists. Yet he was virtually a recluse at his court, pursuing an eccentric intellectual life, and he did not attend carefully to the routine problems of governing.

In any case, the religious balance began to shift on its own in the second half of the century in the wake of the appearance of resurgent Catholicism. Members of the Jesuit order began to appear in Habsburg lands in the reign of Maximilian. Tough-minded and well trained, they established Catholic schools and became confessors and preachers to the upper classes. Self-confident Catholicism emerged as one form of cultural identity among the German-speaking ruling classes and thus as a religious impetus to further political consolidation of all these Habsburg territories. Ferdinand II (r. 1619–1637) was raised in the atmosphere of reformed Catholicism. He was committed both to tighter rule and to uniformity in matters of relig-

Map 15.3 Territories of the Austrian Habsburgs In addition to the lands constituting modern Austria, Austrian Habsburg lands comprised the Tyrol (modern west Austria and northeast Italy), Carniola (modern Slovenia), part of Croatia, Bohemia (the core of the modern Czech Republic and southern Poland), and Hungary. Most of Hungary had been in Ottoman hands since the Battle of Mohács in 1527.

ion. Like the English under Elizabeth, Habsburg subjects had enjoyed a period of relative peace in political and religious matters. Now, as in England, the stage was set for conflict of both kinds.

The Thirty Years' War, 1618–1648

Both political and religious problems surfaced early in the seventeenth century. In one incident, in 1606, the aggressively Catholic prince of Bavaria seized an imperial free city in north central Germany, in the wake of religious in-fighting there—a city theoretically subject to no one but the emperor himself. Tensions between Catholic and Protestant states (and among Protestants, for Calvinists and Lutherans were not necessarily allies) were further heightened by a succession crisis. The childless emperor Rudolf II was aging, and factions of the Habsburg family sought allies among the German states to promote their various candidates for the imperial crown.

In 1618 a revolt against Habsburg rule in the kingdom of Bohemia touched off widespread warfare. Bohemia (the core of the modern Czech Republic) was populous and prosperous and had a large Protestant population. Rudolf II had used Prague, its bustling capital, as an imperial capital. Although Catholicism was reclaiming lost ground,

RUSSIA

POLAND

Black Sea

CRIMEA

FINLAND

ESTONIA

LIVONIA

SWEDEN

Vilna

Warsaw

PRUSSIA

MOLDAVIA

WALLACHIA

TRANSYLVANIA

HUNGARY

Belgrade

Constantinople

Athens

CRETE
(To Rep. of Venice)

NORWAY

Baltic Sea

Copenhagen

Gdansk
(Danzig)

POMERANIA

MECKLENBURG

BRANDENBURG

Berlin

Breitenfeld
1631

SAXONY

Lübeck

SILESIA

White Mountain 1620

Prague

BOHEMIA

MORAVIA

Vienna

STYRIA

Pest

Buda

CROATIA

CARNIOLA

Naples

Palermo

SICILY

See Inset

DENMARK

JUTLAND

SCHLESWIG

Hamburg

Magdeburg

Lützen 1632

Elbe

LOWER
PALATINATE

Nördlingen 1634

BAVARIA

Augsburg

REPUBLIC OF VENICE

PAPAL
STATES

Rome

FLORENCE

NORTH Sea

Essen

UNITED
PROVINCES

Amsterdam

Antwerp

SPANISH
NETHERLANDS

Cologne

Rhine

UPPER
PALATINATE

Metz

FRANCHE-
COMTÉ

Zurich

SWITZERLAND

Geneva

SAVOY

PIEDMONT

MILAN

GENOA

CORSICA
(To Genoa)

SARDINIA

Edinburgh

SCOTLAND

ENGLAND

London

IRELAND

Dublin

Rocroi
1643

Paris

Nantes

Loire

FRANCE

BALEARIC IS.

ATLANTIC
OCEAN

SPAIN

Madrid

PORTUGAL

Tagus

Lisbon

Dnieper

SWEDEN

POMERANIA

WISMAR

VERDEN

BREMEN

DENMARK

Austrian Habsburg lands

Spanish Habsburg lands

Other German states

Swedish lands by 1648

Boundary of Holy Roman Empire

✕ Major battles

300 Mi.

300 Km.

150

150

0

0

Protestants had been confirmed in their rights to worship in the early seventeenth century both by Rudolf and by his younger brother, Matthias, who hoped to succeed Rudolf as king of Bohemia and as Holy Roman emperor. The crown of Bohemia was bestowed by election, so rival claimants to this wealthy throne needed the acquiescence of the ruling elites, both Protestant and Catholic, of the kingdom.

When Matthias did become king of Bohemia and Holy Roman emperor (r. 1612–1619), he reneged on his promise to the Protestants. The Habsburg succession to the Bohemian throne seemed secure, and concessions to Protestant elites seemed less necessary. As in the Netherlands, there was in Bohemia a delicate balance between regional integrity and Bohemia's expectation of sharing its ruler with other regions. As Philip II had done, Matthias appointed a council of regents that enforced unpopular policies, particularly with regard to religion. The right to build new Protestant churches was denied. Bohemian crown lands were given to the Catholic church.

On May 23, 1618, delegates to a Protestant assembly that had unsuccessfully petitioned Matthias to end these policies marched to the palace in Prague where the hated royal officials met. After a confrontation over their demands, the delegates "tried" the officials on the spot for treason and, literally, threw them out the window of the palace. The incident became known as the Defenestration of Prague (from the Latin, *fenestra*, "window"). (The officials' lives were saved only because they fell into a pile of manure.) The rebels proceeded to set up their own government.

The new Bohemian government deposed Matthias's successor as king, his Catholic cousin, Ferdinand, and elected a new king in 1619. Ferdinand, however, ruled as Holy Roman emperor until 1637. The direct challenge to Habsburg control in Bohemia had implications for the empire as a whole because the new king of Bohemia was a Protestant, Frederick, elector of the Palatinate. Frederick was a Calvinist prince. His territories in

Map 15.4 Europe in the Thirty Years' War The Thirty Years' War was fought largely within the borders of the Holy Roman Empire. It was the result of conflicts within the empire as well as the meddling of neighbors for their own strategic advantage.

west central Germany (called the Lower Palatinate and the Upper Palatinate) carried with them the right to be one of the seven electors who chose the emperor.

Encouraged by these events, Protestant subjects in other Habsburg lands asked for guarantees of freedom of worship like those enjoyed by Protestants in Bohemia. This new Protestant success seemed to threaten the religious balance of power in the empire. Other princes saw their chance to make political gains. Rival claimants to Habsburg rule in Hungary took up arms. The Protestant king of Denmark, Christian IV (r. 1588-1648), who was also duke of Holstein in northern Germany, sought to take advantage of the situation and conquer more German territory.

Foreign powers were also interested in these events. England practiced a pro-Protestant foreign policy, and the English king, James I, was Frederick's father-in-law. Spain's supply routes north from Italy to the Netherlands passed next to Frederick's lands in western Germany. France's first interest was its rivalry with Spain; thus, France kept its eye on the border principalities that were strategically important to Spain. In addition, it was in France's interest, much to the disgust of the devout Catholic faction at the French court, to keep Protestant as well as Catholic rulers in the empire strong enough to thwart Austrian Habsburg ambitions.

The revolt in Bohemia thus triggered a widespread war because it challenged Habsburg control in a direct and undeniable fashion and because other princes felt their interests to be involved. From the outset, the war was not only a conflict over the Habsburgs' power in their own lands but also a conflict over the balance of power in the empire and in Europe (Map 15.4).

By the fall of 1620 a Catholic army was closing in on Bohemia; the army was supported by the duke of Bavaria, who had been offered the Palatinate as a victory prize. On November 8, on a hillside west of Prague, the Catholic force faced a Bohemian army that had not garnered much concrete aid from Protestant allies. The resulting Battle of White Mountain was a complete Catholic victory.

Fighting then became more widespread. The truce between Spain and the Netherlands, established in 1609, expired in 1621, and the nearby Lower Palatinate, now in Catholic hands, offered a staging point for Spanish forces. At this point,

Christian IV, the Protestant king of Denmark, decided to seize more territory, both to give himself greater control over profitable German Baltic seaports and to defend himself against any Catholic attempt to seize northern German territory. Christian received little help from Protestant allies, however; the Dutch were busy with Spain, the English were still wary of continental entanglements, and Denmark's regional rivals, the Swedish, were uninterested in furthering Danish ambitions in the Baltic.

The confusing blend of politics and religion that motivated the Protestant rulers was also evident on the Catholic side. Imperial forces defeated Christian's armies in 1626. Alarmed at the possibility of greater imperial control in northern Germany, Catholic princes led by the duke of Bavaria arranged a truce that led to the Peace of Lübeck in 1629—and to Denmark's withdrawal from the fighting on relatively generous terms.

Christian's rival, Gustav Adolf, king of Sweden (r. 1611–1632), immediately assumed the role of Protestant champion. A brilliant and innovative military leader, Gustav Adolf hoped to gain territory along the Baltic seacoast, but personal aggrandizement also was one of his goals. His campaigns were capped by a victory over an imperial army at Breitenfeld in Saxony in 1631. The tide turned in the favor of imperial forces, however, after Gustav Adolf was killed at the Battle of Lützen in late 1632. A decisive imperial victory over a combined Swedish and German Protestant army, at Nördlingen in 1634, led to a general peace treaty favorable to the Catholics: the Peace of Prague (1635).

The Peace of Prague brought only a temporary peace, however, because French involvement increased, now that other anti-Habsburg forces had been eclipsed. France tried to seize imperial territory along its own eastern border and generously subsidized continued fighting within the empire by channeling monies to Protestant mercenaries there. Fighting dragged on. The Swedes reentered the war, hoping to obtain territory on the northern coast. In the south, rivals to the Habsburgs in Hungary tried to seize territory. By the end of the war, order had disintegrated so completely in the wake of the marauding armies that both staunchly Catholic rulers and firmly Protestant ones made alliances with religious enemies to safeguard their states.

A comprehensive peace treaty did not become possible until France withdrew its sponsorship of continued fighting. There were domestic reasons for France's withdrawal. Louis XIII (r. 1610–1643), the king of France, had died, leaving a minor child to rule and to face the burden of war debt. France wanted only a workable balance of power in the empire; more important to France was the continued rivalry with the Spanish Habsburgs for control of territory along France's eastern and northern borders and in Italy. A defeat by France in the Spanish Netherlands in 1643 had convinced Spain to concentrate on that rivalry too, and fighting between them continued until 1659.

The Effects of the War

The Thirty Years' War caused economic devastation and population decline in many parts of the empire and had long-term political consequences for the empire as a whole. One reason for the war's devastation was a further step in the application of firepower to warfare that increased both the size of armies and their deadly force in battle. This was the use of volley fire, the arrangement of foot soldiers in parallel lines so that one line of men could fire while another reloaded. This tactic, pioneered in the Netherlands around the turn of the century, was further refined by Gustav Adolf of Sweden. Gustav Adolf amassed large numbers of troops and increased the rate of fire so that a virtually continuous barrage was maintained; he also used maneuverable field artillery to protect the massed troops from cavalry charges.

Following Gustav Adolf's lead, armies of all the major states adopted these tactics. Despite these new offensive tactics, defensive tactics—such as holding fortresses—remained important, and pitched battles, such as at Nördlingen in 1634, still tended to be part of sieges. The costs in resources and human life of this kind of warfare reached unheard-of dimensions. Popular printed literature and court drama both condemned the seeming irrationality of the war.

Where fighting had been concentrated, such as in parts of Saxony, between a third and half of the inhabitants of rural villages and major towns may have disappeared. Many starved, were caught in the fighting, or were killed by marauding soldiers. The most notorious atrocity occurred

Gustav Adolf at the Battle of Lützen In this detail of Jan Asselyn's *Charge by the Swedish Cavalry*, the Swedish king (in the plumed hat with raised sword) leads a successful cavalry charge, a tactic he had helped to refine. Leading advancing infantry later in the battle, Gustav Adolf was shot and killed. *(Herzog Anton Ulrich—Museum Braunschweig)*

in the aftermath of the siege of Magdeburg in 1631. After the city surrendered to besieging Catholic forces, long-deprived soldiers ate and drank themselves into a frenzy, raped and killed indiscriminately, and set fires that destroyed the town (killing some of their own ranks in the process). Some victims of war migrated to other regions in search of peaceful conditions and work. Some joined the armies in order to survive. Others formed their own armed bands to fight off the soldiers or to steal back enough goods to live on.

Compounding these effects of war were the actions of armies hired by enterprising mercenary generals for whom loyalty to the princes who paid them took a back seat to personal advancement. They contracted to provide, supply, and lead troops and thus were more willing than the princes would have been to allow troops to live "economically" on plunder. All states and commanders strained to pay and supply their troops, but mercenary armies, and their generals, were especially difficult to control.

A series of treaties known as the Peace of Westphalia (1648) finally ended fighting in the empire. The treaties recognized Calvinism as a tolerated religion within the empire. The requirement that

all subjects must follow their rulers' faith was retained, but some leeway was allowed for those who now found themselves under new rulers. The property of those who decided to move elsewhere for religious reasons was protected. In its recognition of religious plurality, the Peace of Westphalia effectively put an end to religious war in the empire. The rights of states, however, were still enforced over the desires of individuals.

In political matters, the treaties reflected some of the recent successes of the Swedish by granting them Baltic coast territory. France gained the important towns of Metz, Toul, and Verdun on its eastern border. Most of the major Catholic and Protestant rulers in the empire, such as the dukes of Bavaria and Saxony, extended their territories at the expense of smaller principalities and cities. The son of Frederick, king of Bohemia, was given the smaller of the two Palatine territories that his father had held. The Upper Palatinate—as well as the right to be a new elector of the emperor—was given to the powerful duke of Bavaria.

The most important political outcomes of the war were not explicitly mentioned in the peace treaties because no one needed to have them spelled out. One outcome was that the states within the empire would henceforth be virtually autonomous. From this point forward, each major state of the empire would conduct its own foreign policy; the Holy Roman Empire was no longer a meaningful political entity. Another outcome was that the Habsburgs, though weakened as emperors, were strengthened as rulers of their own hereditary lands on the eastern fringes of the empire. They moved their capital from Prague to Vienna, and the government of Habsburg lands gained in importance as administration of the empire waned.

SOCIETY AND CULTURE

Both imaginative literature and speculative writing, such as political theory, bear the stamp of their times. In the late sixteenth and early seventeenth centuries, political speculation often concerned questions of the legitimacy of rulers and of the relationship of political power to divine authority—urgent problems in an age when religious division threatened the very foundations of political order. The form as well as the content of thought reflected its context. Authors and rulers alike often relied on still-prevalent oral modes of communication. Indeed, some of the greatest literature of the period and some of the most effective political statements were presented as drama and not conveyed in print. Nevertheless, literacy continued to spread and led to greater opportunities for knowledge and reflection. The medium of print became increasingly important to political life. In the visual arts, the dramatic impulse was wedded to religious purposes to create works that conveyed both power and emotion.

Literacy and Literature

Traditional oral culture changed slowly under the impact of the spread of printing, education, and literacy. (See the feature, "Weighing the Evidence: Signatures," on pages 586–587.) Works of literature from the late sixteenth and early seventeenth century incorporate material from traditional folktales, consciously reflecting the coexistence of oral and literature culture. In *Don Quixote*, by Spain's Miguel de Cervantes (1547–1616), the title character and his companion, Sancho Panza, have a long discussion about the subject. The squire Panza

speaks in the style that was customary in oral culture—a rather roundabout and repetitive style, by our standards, that enabled the speaker and listener to remember what was said. Much of the richness of *Don Quixote* is due to the interweaving of prose styles and topical concerns from throughout Cervantes' culture—from the oral world of peasants to the refined world of court life. The detachment that enabled Cervantes to accomplish this rich portrayal came about from highly developed literacy and the awareness of language that literacy made possible.

The spread of education and literacy in the late sixteenth century had a dramatic impact on attitudes toward literature and on literature itself. The value of education—particularly of the continuing humanist recovery of ancient wisdom—was reflected in much literature of the period. Writers found in humanistic education a vision of what it meant to be cultivated and disciplined men of the world. This vision provided the beginnings of a new self-image for members of the warrior class.

Certain elite women who were able to secure a humanistic education were moved to reflect on their own situation in society. The French poet Louise Labé (1526–1566), writing in 1555, described the benefits of education for women but exaggerated its availability:

Since the time has come . . . when the severe laws of men no longer prevent women from applying themselves to the sciences and other disciplines, it seems to me that those of us who can should use this long-craved freedom to study and let men see how greatly they wronged us when depriving us of its honor and advantages. . . . Apart from the good name our sex will acquire thereby, we shall have caused men to devote more time and effort in the public good to virtuous studies.[3]

It is customary to regard the French author Michel de Montaigne (1533–1592) as the epitome of the reflective and—most important—*self*-reflective gentleman. Montaigne had trained for the law and became a judge in the Parlement of Bordeaux; he resigned from the court in 1570, however, and retired to his small chateau, where he wrote his *Essais* (from which we derive the word *essays*), a collection of short reflections that were revolutionary in both form and content. Montaigne invented writing in the form of a sketch, a "try" (the literal meaning of *essai*), which enabled him to combine self-reflection with formal analysis.

~ **ENCOUNTERS WITH THE WEST** ~

Montaigne Discusses Barbarity in the New World and the Old

In one of his most famous essays, Michel de Montaigne ironically compares the customs of Native Americans, about whom he has heard, with the customs of his own society.

They have their wars with [other] nations, to which they go quite naked, with no other arms than bows or wooden spears. . . . It is astonishing that firmness they show in their combats, which never end but in slaughter and bloodshed; for, as to routs and terror, they know nothing of either.

Each man brings back as his trophy the head of the enemy he has killed. . . . After they have treated their prisoners well for a long time with all the hospitality they can think of . . . they kill him with their swords. This done, they roast him and eat him in common and send some pieces to their absent friends.

I am not sorry that we notice the barbarous horror of such acts, but am heartily sorry that . . . we should be so blind to our own. I think there is more barbarity . . . in tearing by tortures and the rack a body still full of feeling, in roasting a man bit by bit, having him bitten and mangled by dogs (as we have not only read but seen within fresh memory . . . among neighbors and fellow citizens, and what is worse, on the pretext of piety and religion).

Three of these men (were brought to France) . . . and [someone] wanted to know what they had found most amazing. . . . They said that in the first place they thought it very strange that so many grown men, bearded, strong and armed who were around the king . . . should submit to obey a child. . . . Second (they have a way in their language of speaking of men as halves of one another), they had noticed that there were among us men full and gorged with all sorts of good things, and that their other halves were beggars at their doors, emaciated with hunger and poverty; and they thought it strange that these needy halves could endure such injustice.

Source: Donald M. Frame, trans., *The Complete Essays of Montaigne* (Stanford, Calif.: Stanford University Press, 1948), pp. 153, 155–159.

Montaigne's reflections ranged from the destructiveness of the French civil wars to the consequences of European exploration of the New World. Toward all of these events and circumstances, Montaigne was able to achieve an analytic detachment remarkable for his day. For example, he noted an irony in Europeans labeling New World peoples "savage," given Europeans' seemingly endless and wanton violence against those "savages" and against each other. (See the box, "Encounters with the West: Montaigne Discusses Barbarity in the New World and the Old.") He deflated pretensions to superiority in his own class of Frenchmen by noting "however high the chair, one is still sitting on one's own behind."

Montaigne's greatest achievement was the deep exploration of his own private moral and intellectual life, detached from any vocation or social role (though not detached, of course, from the leisure that his status made possible). Owing to the spread of printing and literacy, Montaigne had—in addition to his own effort and the resources of leisure—a virtually unparalleled opportunity to reflect on the world through reading the wide variety of printed texts available to him. For the first time, it was possible for the leisured lay reader to juxtapose different events, values, and cultures. Montaigne's writings thus reflect a distancing from his own society and a tolerance of others.

His essays also reveal a distancing from himself, and this distancing is another result of literacy—not simply the ability to read and write but the ability to put literacy to use so that one might enjoy long periods of solitude and reflection in the company of other solitary voices contained in books. Montaigne's works mark the beginning of what we know as the "invention" of private life, in which an individual is known more by internal character and personality traits than by social role and past behavior.

Dramatists, poets, and prose writers like Montaigne generally ask profound and in some ways timeless questions about the meaning of human experience; however, the kinds of questions thought important change as society changes. The works of the great English poet and playwright William Shakespeare (1564–1616) are still compelling to us because of the profundity of the questions he asked about love, honor, and political legitimacy, but he asked these questions in terms appropriate to his own day. One of his favorite themes—evident in *Hamlet* and *Macbeth*—is the legitimacy of rulers. He was at his most skilled, perhaps, when exploring the contradictions in values between the growing commercial world he saw around him and the older, seemingly more stable world of feudal society. Subtle political commentary distinguishes Shakespeare's later plays, written near and shortly after the death of Queen Elizabeth in 1603, when political and economic problems were becoming increasingly visible. Shakespeare explored not only the duties of rulers but also the rights of their subjects. In *Coriolanus,* he portrays commoners as poor but as neither ignorant nor wretched; they are in fact fully rational and capable of analyzing their situation—perhaps more capable, Shakespeare hints, than their ruler is. The play is safely set in ancient Rome, but the social and political tensions it depicts clearly referred to the Elizabethan present.

Shakespeare, Cervantes, and other writers of their day were also representatives of what were starting to be self-consciously distinct national literatures. The spread of humanism added a historical dimension to their awareness of their own languages and to their subject matter: their own society and its past. This kind of self-consciousness is evident in Shakespeare's play *Richard II.* The playwright depicts the kingdom of England, which King Richard is destroying, in terms that reflect the Elizabethan sense of England as a separate and self-contained nation:

This royal throne of kings, this sceptred isle,
This earth of majesty, this seat of Mars,
This other Eden, demi-paradise,
This fortress built by Nature for herself
Against infection and the hand of war,
This happy breed of men, this little world,
This precious stone set in the silver sea,
Which serves it in the office of a wall,
Or as [a] moat defensive to a house,
Against the envy of less happier lands;
This blessed plot, this earth, this realm, this England . . .
(*Richard II,* act 2, sc. 1, lines 40–50)[4]

The Great Age of Theater

Shakespeare's career was possible because his life coincided with the rise of professional theater. In the capitals of both England and Spain, professional theaters first opened in the 1570s. Some drama was produced at court or in aristocratic households, but most public theaters drew large and very mixed audiences, including the poorest city dwellers. Playwrights, including Shakespeare, often wrote in teams under great pressure to keep acting companies supplied with material. The best-known dramatist in Spain in this period, Lope de Vega (1562–1635), wrote more than fifteen hundred works with a wide range of topics. Although religious themes remained popular in Spanish theater, as an echo of medieval drama, most plays in England and Spain treated secular subjects and, as in *Coriolanus,* safely disguised political commentary.

Over time, theater became increasingly restricted to aristocratic circles. In England, Puritan criticism of the "immorality" of public performance drove actors and playwrights to seek royal patronage. The first professional theater to open in Paris, in 1629, as political and religious turmoil quieted, quickly became dependent on Cardinal Richelieu's patronage. Inevitably, as court patronage grew in importance, the wide range of subject matter treated in plays began to narrow to those of aristocratic concern, such as family honor and martial glory. These themes were depicted in the work of the Spaniard Pedro Calderón (1600–1681), who wrote for his enthusiastic patron, Philip IV, and in that of the Frenchman Pierre Corneille (1606–1684), whose great tragedy of aristocratic life, *Le Cid*, was one of the early successes of the seventeenth-century French theater.

That drama was one of the most important art forms of the late sixteenth and early seventeenth centuries is reflected in its impact on the development of music: The opera, which weds drama to music, was invented in Italy in the early seventeenth century. The first great work in this genre is generally acknowledged to be *Orfeo* (*Orpheus*, 1607) by Claudio Monteverdi (1567–1643). Opera, like drama, reflected the influence of humanism in its secular themes as well as a desire more precisely to emulate Greek drama, which had used both words and music. The practice of music itself changed under the dramatic impulse. Monteverdi was the first master of a new musical style known as monody, which emphasized the progression of chords. Monodic music was inherently dramatic, creating a sense of forward movement, expectation, and resolution.

Sovereignty in Ceremony, Image, and Word

Whether produced formally on a stage or in some less structured setting, drama was a favored method of communication in this era because people responded to and made extensive use of oral communication. Dramatic gesture and storytelling to get a message across were commonplace and were important components of politics.

What we might call "street drama" was an ordinary occurrence: When great noble governors entered major towns, such as when Margaret of Parma entered Brussels, a solemn yet ostentatious formal "entry" was often staged. The dignitary would ride into the town through its main gate, usually beneath a canopy made of luxurious cloth. The event might include staged tableaux in the town's streets, with costumed townspeople acting in brief symbolic dramas such as David and Goliath, and it might end in an elaborate banquet. A remnant of these proceedings survives today in the ceremony by which distinguished visitors are given "the keys to the city," which, in the sixteenth century, really were useful.

Royalty made deliberate and careful use of dramatic ceremony. Royal entries into towns took on an added weight, as did royal funerals and other occasions. These dramas reinforced political and constitutional assumptions in the minds of witnesses and participants. Thus, over time, we can see changes in the representations of royal power. In France, for example, the ritual entry of the king into Paris had originally stressed the participation of elites such as the leading guilds, judges, and administrators and had symbolized their active part in governing the city and the kingdom. But in the last half of the sixteenth century, the procession began to glorify the king alone.

The very fact that rulers experimented self-consciously with self-representation suggests that issues pertaining to the nature and extent of royal power were profoundly important and far from settled. Queen Elizabeth had the particular burden of assuming the throne in a period of great instability. Hence, she paid a great deal of attention to the image of herself that she fashioned in words and authorized to be fashioned in painting. Elizabeth styled herself variously as mother to her people and as a warrior-queen (drawing on ancient myths of Amazon women). She made artful use of the image of her virginity to buttress each of these images—as the wholly devoted, self-sacrificing mother (which, of course, had religious tradition behind it) or as an androgynous ruler, woman but doing the bodily work of man. (See the box, "Elizabeth I Addresses Her Troops.")

More formal speculation about constitutional matters also resulted from the tumult of the sixteenth and seventeenth centuries. The civil wars in France provided the impetus for energetic reconsideration of the principles and theories underlying royal government. The Huguenot party advanced an elaborate argument for the limitation of royal power, particularly after the Saint Bartholomew's Day Massacre. The best-known Huguenot tract (probably authored by the well-educated nobleman Philippe Duplessis-Mornay), *Defense of Liberty Against Tyrants* (1579), advanced the notion of a contract between the king and the people. Under the terms of this contract, obedience to the king was conditional, dependent on his acting for the common good—above all, maintaining and protecting God's true church.

Alternative theories enhancing royal authority were offered, principally in support of the Catholic position though also simply to buttress the beleaguered monarchy itself. The most famous of these appeared in *The Six Books of the Republic* (1576), by the legal scholar Jean Bodin (1530–1596). Bodin was a Catholic but offered a fundamentally secular perspective on the purposes and source of power

Elizabeth I Addresses Her Troops

The day after English ships dispersed the Spanish Armada in 1588, Elizabeth addressed a contingent of her troops. She used the opportunity to fashion an image of herself as a warrior above all but also as the beloved familiar of her people, unafraid of potential plots against her.

My loving people, we have been persuaded by some that are careful of our safety, to take heed how we commit ourselves to armed multitudes, for fear of treachery. But I assure you, I do not desire to live to distrust my faithful and loving people. Let tyrants fear. I have always so behaved myself that, under God, I have placed my chiefest strength in the loyal hearts and good will of my subjects; and therefore I am come amongst you, as you see, at this time, not for my reaction or disport, but being resolved, in the midst and heat of the battle, to live or die amongst you all, to lay down for my God, and for my kingdom, and for my people, my honor and my blood, even in the dust. I know I have the body of a weak and feeble woman, but I have the heart and the stomach of a king, and of a king of England too, and think foul scorn that Parma or Spain, or any prince of Europe should dare to invade the borders of my realm; to which, rather than any dishonor shall grow by me, I myself will take up arms, I myself will be your general, judge, and rewarder of every one of your virtues in the field.

Source: J. E. Neale, *Queen Elizabeth I* (New York: Anchor, 1957), pp. 308–309.

---

within a state. His special contribution was a vision of a truly sovereign monarch. Bodin offered theoretical understanding that is essential to states today and is the ground on which people can claim rights and protection from the state—namely, that there is a final sovereign authority. For Bodin that authority was the king. He recognized that in practice there were limitations to royal power, but it was the theoretical grounding for royal authority that interested Bodin.

French contract theory legitimized resistance to the Catholic monarchy but had to be abandoned when Henry IV granted toleration in 1598. In England, theoretical justification of resistance to Charles I was initially limited to invoking tradition and precedent; contract theory as well as other sweeping claims regarding subjects' rights would be more fully developed later in the century.

Bodin's theory of sovereignty, however, was immediately echoed in other theoretical works, most notably that of Hugo Grotius (1583–1645). A Dutch jurist and diplomat, Grotius developed the first principles of modern international law. He accepted the existence of sovereign states who owed no loyalty to higher authority (such as the papacy) and thus needed new principles to govern their interactions. His major work, *De Jure Belli ac Pacis (On the Law of War and Peace)* (1625), was written in response to the turmoil of the Thirty Years' War. Grotius argued that relations between states could be based on respect for treaties voluntarily reached between them. In perhaps his boldest move he argued that war must be justified and developed criteria to distinguish just wars.

Baroque Art and Architecture

Speculation about and celebration of power, as well as of dramatic emotion, also occurred in the visual arts—most notably in painting and architecture, in the style now known as "baroque." The word *baroque* comes from the Portuguese *barroco*, used to describe irregularly shaped pearls; the term as applied to the arts was initially derogatory, describing illogic and irregularity. Baroque architecture modified the precision, symmetry, and orderliness of Renaissance architecture to produce a sense of greater dynamism in space. Façades and

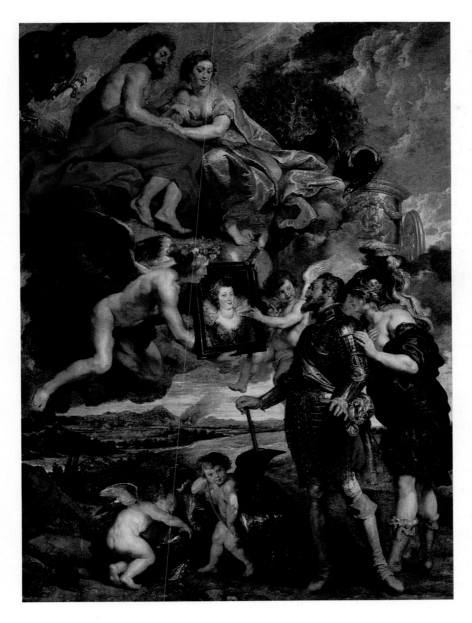

The Political Uses of Baroque Art This 1633 painting by Rubens was one of twenty-one commissioned by Marie de' Medici to celebrate her life and reign, after she was eclipsed as a power at her son's court. It commemorates the moment more than thirty years before when Henry IV first saw a likeness of Marie, his bride-to-be. The image is extravagant and fanciful by our standards, but also very engaging in its use of rich colors and flowing drapery, and in the beautifully executed figures of Jupiter and Juno, gazing down on Henry below them. *(Louvre/Giraudon/Art Resource, NY)*

interiors were both massive and, through clever use of architectural and decorative components, suggestive of movement. Hence baroque churches, for example, were impressively grand and emotionally engaging at the same time. Baroque techniques were pioneered in Italy, first in church design, in the late sixteenth century and spread slowly, with many regional variations, especially throughout Catholic Europe, during the seventeenth century.

One of the primary purposes of baroque architecture and painting was to encourage piety that was emotionally involved but also capable of inspiring awe. Italian baroque painting made use of the realism developed in Renaissance art but added dynamism and emotional energy—such as by painting throngs of people or by using light to create direction and energy in the scene portrayed. Dramatic illusion was also a common device, such as painting a chapel ceiling with receding figures apparently ascending to heaven.

The most influential baroque painter in northern Europe was Peter Paul Rubens (1577–1640), a native of Flanders in the southern Netherlands.

His early career in Italy, from 1600 to 1608, was profoundly important both in shaping him as an artist and in establishing his secondary career as a diplomat, trusted by his princely patrons. Throughout his life, he undertook diplomatic missions, on behalf of the viceroys in the Spanish Netherlands, to Spain, France, and England, where he also gained artistic commissions. He simultaneously maintained a large studio in Antwerp where he could train students. Rubens's subject matter varied widely. It included church design and decoration as well as portraiture and landscapes. His technique was distinguished by the brilliant use of color and by the dynamic energy of his figures, often executed on a very large scale.

SUMMARY

The late sixteenth and early seventeenth centuries were an era of intense struggle over political and religious authority. Rulers everywhere, through a variety of expedients, tried to buttress and expand royal power. They were resisted by traditional centers of power, such as independent-minded nobles. But they were also resisted by the novel challenge of religious dissent, which empowered subjects both to claim a greater right to question authority and to risk more in their attempts to oppose it. In some areas of Europe, such as the Holy Roman Empire, the struggles reached some resolution. In other areas, such as England, decades of bloody conflict still lay ahead.

On the whole, these conflicts did not result in victories for ordinary people, since for the most part it was victorious elites who decided matters of religion and governance in their own interests. In addition, the difficult economic circumstances of these decades meant that working people, desperate for a secure livelihood, rioted or took up arms out of economic as well as religious concern.

Yet however grim the circumstances people faced, the technology of print and the spread of literacy helped spur speculative and creative works by providing the means for reflection and the audiences to receive it. Ironically, the increased importance of court life, although a cause of political strain, was also a source of patronage for art, literature, and drama. Some of the works we still value, such as Rubens's paintings, portray the splendor and power of court life. Other works, such as Shakespeare's plays, both reflect and re-

flect on the tensions and contradictions in the society of the day: for example, the importance of the stability provided by royal authority and the dignity and wisdom of ordinary people, who had no claim to power at all.

NOTES

1. Quoted in A. W. Lovett, *Early Habsburg Spain, 1517–1598* (Oxford, England: Oxford University Press, 1986), p. 212.
2. Quoted in R. J. Knecht, *The French Wars of Religion, 1559–1598* (London: Longman, 1989), p. 109.
3. Quoted in Ann Rosalind Jones, "City Women and Their Audiences: Louise Labé and Veronica Franco," in Margaret W. Ferguson et al., *Rewriting the Renaissance: The Discourses of Sexual Difference in Early Modern Europe* (Chicago: University of Chicago Press, 1986), p. 307.
4. From *The Riverside Shakespeare*, 2d ed. (Boston: Houghton Mifflin, 1997), p. 855.

SUGGESTED READING

General Surveys

Bonney, Richard. *The European Dynastic States, 1494–1660.* 1991. A recent, rich survey of the period. Good on eastern as well as western Europe but written from an English point of view; thus, it does not consider England as part of Europe.

Elliott, J. H. *Europe Divided, 1559–1598.* 1968. An older but still reliable and readable survey by a leading scholar of Spanish history.

Hale, J. R. *War and Society in Renaissance Europe.* 1985. An analysis of war as a function of government and as a part of social, economic, and intellectual life through the sixteenth century.

Parker, Geoffrey. *The Military Revolution.* 1988; and Black, Jeremy. *A Military Revolution?* 1991. Two works that disagree about the nature and extent of the changes in military practices and their significance for military, political, and social history. Black tries to refute claims for a dramatic military "revolution."

Society and Economy

Braudel, Fernand. *The Perspective of the World.* Vol. 3, *Civilization and Capitalism, 15th to 18th Century.* Translated by S. Reynolds. 1984. A particularly useful volume by this celebrated author of economic history concerning overall patterns in the European and international economies.

Gutman, Myron P. *Toward the Modern Economy.* 1988. An account of the development of cloth production and the decline of guild manufacture through the early modern period.

Huppert, George. *After the Black Death: A Social History of Early Modern Europe.* 1986. A survey of developments in social and economic history throughout Europe from the fifteenth through the seventeenth centuries. A brief but very usable bibliography will guide further reading.

Jütte, Robert. *Poverty and Deviance in Early Modern Europe.* 1994. Discusses poverty, poor relief, and peasant rebellion.

Klaits, Joseph. *Servants of Satan.* 1985.

Levack, Brian P. *The Witch-Hunt in Early Modern Europe.* 1987. Two surveys of witch-hunting in the sixteenth and seventeenth centuries. Levack synthesizes the work of various historians with particular care; Klaits's work is more interpretive.

Wiesner, Merry. *Women and Gender in Early Modern Europe.* 1993. Discusses all aspects of women's experience, including their working lives.

Spain and the Dutch

Elliott, J. H. *Imperial Spain, 1469–1716.* 1963.

Lynch, John. *Spain, 1516–1598: From Nation-State to World Empire.* 1991. Two excellent surveys.

Parker, Geoffrey. *The Army of Flanders and the Spanish Road.* 1972. A detailed study of Spanish innovations in supplying its armies during the Netherlands' revolt.

———. *The Dutch Revolt.* 2d ed. 1985. The best survey of the revolt available in English.

Wedgewood, C. V. *William the Silent.* 1968. A sympathetic biography of the aristocratic leader of the Dutch revolt, which portrays him as a man ahead of his time in his acceptance of religious diversity. Useful for capturing the flavor of the period, though not for its interpretation.

France and England

Bercé, Yves-Marie. *The Birth of Absolutism: A History of France, 1598–1661.* 1992. A readable recent interpretation of the foundations of absolutism in France.

Diefendorf, Barbara. *Beneath the Cross: Catholics and Huguenots in Sixteenth-Century Paris.* 1991. Traces the intersection of political and religious conflict in the French capital during the religious wars. Excellent bibliography.

Hirst, Derek. *Authority and Conflict: England, 1603–1658.* 1986. A thorough study of political and social conditions in England.

Holt, Mack P. *The French Wars of Religion, 1562–1629.* 1995. An up-to-date synthesis that evaluates social and political context while not slighting the importance of religion.

Mattingly, Garrett. *The Armada.* 1959. A well-crafted and gripping narrative of the sailing of the Armada and all the interrelated events in France, the Netherlands, England, and Spain, told from a decidedly English perspective.

Smith, A. G. R. *The Emergence of a Nation-State: The Commonwealth of England, 1529–1660.* 1984. A good place to start through the immense bibliography on the Elizabethan period.

The Thirty Years' War and Its Aftermath

Evans, R. J. W. *The Making of the Hapsburg Monarchy.* 1979. A thorough survey of the rise of the Austrian Habsburg state from the breakup of Charles V's empire, emphasizing the importance of the ideology and institutions of Catholicism in shaping the identity and guaranteeing the coherence of the Habsburg state.

Parker, Geoffrey. *The Thirty Years' War.* 2d ed. 1987. A readable general history by one of the best-known military historians.

Literacy, Literature, and Political Theory

Church, William F. *Constitutional Thought in Sixteenth-Century France.* 1969. A survey of sixteenth-century political theory in France.

Eagleton, Terry. *William Shakespeare.* 1986. A brief and highly readable interpretation of Shakespeare that emphasizes the tensions in the plays caused by language and by ideas from the new world of bourgeois, commercial life.

Giesey, Ralph E. *The Royal Funeral Ceremony in Renaissance France.* 1960. One of the earliest studies of royal ceremony in the period.

Greenblatt, Stephen. *Renaissance Self-Fashioning.* 1979. An interpretation of sixteenth-century literature and culture that emphasizes the "invention" of interior self-reflection and self-awareness.

Houston, R. A. *Literacy in Early Modern Europe.* 1988. A general introduction to the issues of the spread of education and the impact of literacy in Europe.

Kamen, Henry. *The Rise of Toleration.* 1967. This older and rather optimistic study chronicles the slow emergence of secularism and toleration during and after the Reformation.

Kelley, Donald R. *The Beginnings of Ideology: Consciousness and Society in the French Reformation.* 1981. A study of political thought, including but not limited to formal theory, as inspired by the experience of the wars of religion.

Ong, Walter J. *Orality and Literacy: The Technologizing of the Word.* 1982. A synthesis of scholarship that concentrates on the psychological and cultural impact of literacy.

Patterson, Annabel. *Shakespeare and the Popular Voice.* 1989. An interpretation of Shakespeare's work that emphasizes his connection to the complex political and social milieu of his day.

Regosin, J. *The Matter of My Book: Montaigne's "Essais" as the Book of the Self.* 1977. One of the leading scholarly treatments of Montaigne's work.

Weighing the Evidence

SIGNATURES

Right now you are staring at words printed on the page of a book. We are so dependent on written communication that we cannot imagine functioning without these symbols. The often-heard warning "Don't believe everything you read" reflects our habit of trusting written information. But what might it be like if words were only fleeting events—spoken and heard in moments of personal interaction—and not things, objects gazed at in silence, easily saved and retrieved?

Let us consider what evidence we have about the spread of literacy in the sixteenth century. Historians have gained a rough idea about what portion of the population was literate in the sixteenth century by counting the signatures on representative samples of legal documents such as wills and marriage contracts. The ability to sign one's name is a fairly reliable indication of literacy in the sixteenth century because then, unlike today, writing was taught in schools only *after* reading was already mastered. For this reason, however, the *lack* of a signature may mask considerable reading ability, for no special significance was attached to learning to write one's name. Sixteenth-century documents are filled with signatures like those reproduced here: the scissors, for a tailor; the arrow, for a fletcher (arrow-maker). Both of the men who made these marks may well have been able to read.

Where documentation is dense, such as in towns, and where the evidence of signatures has been collected, we have profiles of the literacy rates of selected communities. Literacy rates var-

ied widely according to the location of a particular community (remote ones had fewer literate inhabitants) and its economy (certain trades favored literacy; poverty generally worked against it). Overall, men were more literate than women, and western and northern Europeans were more literate than southern and eastern Europeans. In prosperous regions of western Europe, where literacy rates were highest, there was nearly 100 percent literacy, as one might predict, among bureaucrats, officials, and well-to-do townsmen. Among artisans, the rate neared 50 percent. Among peasants, it could be 10 percent or lower.

If we suppose these figures to be accurate, what can we conclude about the impact of literacy on people's lives? Our own reliance on literacy once led us to assume that people in the past would naturally use these skills if they knew how and that literate knowledge—gleaned from books—would quickly replace folk traditions and knowledge communicated orally. But the "signatures" of the tailor, the fletcher, and thousands of others imply that many Europeans lived with partial literacy. And we now realize that the spread of literacy only slowly changed Europeans' reliance on oral communication. Reading and writing supplemented but initially did not replace traditional ways of learning and communicating.

Aristocrats, for example, usually learned to read and write and occasionally were highly educated. But they learned their most valued skills, such as estate management and military expertise, from their older peers, rather as artisan children learned their skills through apprenticeship. Nobles kept copious written records about their landed property but often relied on memory instead of documents to settle disputes. At all levels of society, most reading was done in a group. It was integrated into the common entertainment of storytelling, illustrated in the drawing reproduced here. An evening's storytelling in a household or tavern might include reading aloud but was not fundamentally changed by the inclusion of reading.

Signatures from English Court Depositions *(Adapted from David Cressy,* Literacy and the Social Order *[Cambridge, England: Cambridge University Press, 1980], p. 60.)*

Tailor   Fletcher

586

Joseph Anton Koch: Shepherds Around the Fire *(Staatliche Kunstsammlungen Dresden/Kupferstich-Kabinett)*

There is evidence that people who could read still trusted written material less than, or at least no more than, spoken information. A literate peasant would consult a farmer's almanac, but more for entertainment than for information. His first-hand knowledge of the local climate, crops, and animal husbandry seemed more reliable to him—and was likely to be more reliable—than any text that a distant publisher might provide. Nobles frequently wrote brief letters to each other in which they said little other than "Please trust X, the bearer of this letter." The real message was imparted orally. It was face-to-face communication, built on a personal relationship, that was trusted.

Some of the most dramatic evidence of the persistence of oral culture is in the use of language that is preserved in informal documents such as long letters or the relatively rare memoir. Most people still relied on the repetitive phrasing that is common when language is wholly oral. Thus, even when they wrote words down, they were "thinking" without literacy.

Although we have learned that evidence of literacy does not mean that sixteenth-century people relied on reading and writing the way we do, we are just beginning to understand what their limited reliance on it really meant for their lives and their society. Access to literacy and the use of documents were tools of power and control. Our tailor might be at a disadvantage in a transaction if he could not read the document he signed. But unlike us, he did not need documents to establish his identity. And with virtually none of his past recorded in writing, he and other sixteenth-century people were free in ways that we are not.

Consider also the tenacity of oral communication. Let us set aside our assumption that written information is superior and try to imagine how powerful oral communication can be. Look carefully at the evidence supplied in the drawing of shepherds gathered around a fire. It dates from the late eighteenth century, when literacy was increasingly widespread and when the persistent oral culture of lower-class people was beginning to be derided in the way that illiteracy is derided today. The cultural gap between literate and illiterate is reflected here in the somewhat derisive representations of the subjects: They are made to seem uncouth. Yet still captured is something of the power of speech and of hearing. Words are events here, and speaker and listeners are active in their parts. The speaker gestures while his companions lean forward attentively to hear and perhaps to argue with him.

In an oral culture, information always is accompanied by sensory input: the sights, smells, and sounds of the person conveying it. And you always know your source. Is it any wonder that common people resisted the "authority" of book learning? ✎

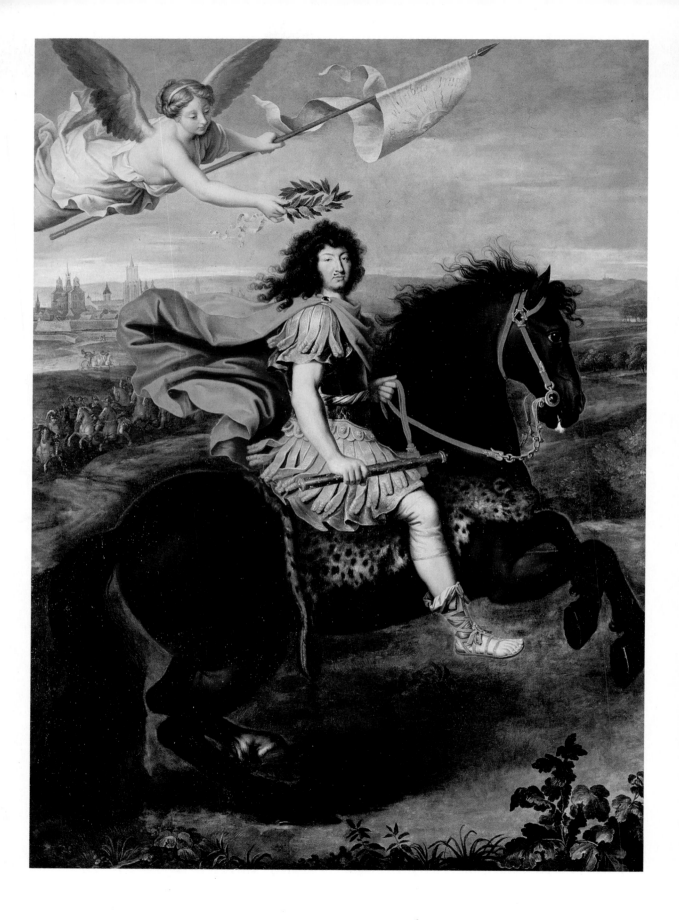

CHAPTER 16

Europe in the Age of Louis XIV, ca. 1610–1715

Toward the end of his reign, the subjects of Louis XIV of France began to grumble that he had lived too long. In fact, he outlived his own son and grandson and was followed on the throne by a great-grandson when he died in 1715. In his prime, Louis symbolized the success of royal power in surmounting the challenges of warrior-nobles, in suppressing religious dissent, in tapping the wealth of the nation's population, and in waging war. A period of cultural brilliance early in his reign and the spectacle of an elaborate court life crowned his achievements. By the end of his reign, however, France was struggling under economic distress brought on by the many wars fought for his glory. Although Louis outlived his welcome, he was then, and is for us now, a symbol of the age that ended with his death.

In England, by contrast, the Crown was not as successful in overcoming political and religious challenges to its authority. Resistance to the king, led by Parliament, resulted in a revolutionary overturning of royal authority that was temporary but had long-term consequences. In central and eastern Europe, a period of state building in the aftermath of the Thirty Years' War led to the dominance in the region of Austria, Brandenburg-Prussia, and Russia. The power of these states derived, in part, from the economic relationship of their lands to the wider European economy.

The seventeenth century also witnessed a dynamic phase of European overseas expansion, following on the successes of the Portuguese and the Spanish in the fifteenth and sixteenth centuries. Eager migrants settled in the Americas in ever increasing numbers, while forced migrants—enslaved Africans—were transported by the thousands to work on the

The king in martial glory: Louis XIV in Roman armor, by the contemporary painter Charles Le Brun.

profitable plantations of European colonizers. Aristocrats, merchants, and peasants back in Europe jockeyed to take advantage of—or to mitigate the effects of—the local political and economic impact of Europe's expansion.

FRANCE IN THE AGE OF ABSOLUTISM

Absolutism describes the extraordinary concentration of power in royal hands achieved by the kings of France, most notably Louis XIV (r. 1643–1715), in the seventeenth century. Louis continued the expansion of state power begun by his father's minister, Cardinal Richelieu (see page 565). The extension of royal power, under Louis as well as his predecessor, was accelerated by the desire to sustain an expensive and aggressive foreign policy. The policy itself was a traditional one: fighting the familiar Habsburg enemy and seeking military glory more generally. Louis XIV's successes in these undertakings made him both envied and emulated by other rulers; the French court became a model of culture and refinement. But increased royal authority was not accepted without protest either by common French people or by elites.

The Last Challenge to Absolutism

Louis came to the throne as a 5-year-old child in 1643. Acting as his regent, his mother, Anne of Austria (1601–1666), had to defuse a serious challenge to royal authority during her son's minority. Together with her chief minister and personal friend, Cardinal Jules Mazarin (1602–1666), she faced opposition from royal bureaucrats and the traditional nobility as well as the common people.

Revolts against the concentration of power in royal hands and against high taxation that had prevailed under Louis's father began immediately. In one province, a group of armed peasants cornered the intendant and forced him to agree to lower taxes; elsewhere, provincial parlements tried to abolish special ranks of officials created by Richelieu. In 1648, after several more years of foreign war and of financial expedients to sustain it, the most serious revolt began, led by the Parlement and the other sovereign law courts in Paris.

The source of the Parlement's leverage over the monarchy was its traditional right to register laws and edicts, which amounted to a right of judicial review. Now, the Parlement, as the legitimate guardian of royal authority, attempted to extend this power by debating and even initiating government policy: The courts sitting together drew up a reform program abolishing most of the machinery of government established under Richelieu and calling for consent to future taxation. The citizens of Paris rose to defend the courts when royal troops were sent against them in October. In the countryside, the machinery of government, particularly tax collection, virtually ceased to function.

Mazarin was forced to accept the proposed reform of government, at least in theory. He also had to avert challenges by great nobles for control of the young king's council. Civil war waxed and waned around France from 1648 until 1653. The main combatants were conventionally ambitious great nobles, but reform-minded urban dwellers often had to make common cause with them, to benefit from their military power. Meanwhile, middling nobles in the region around Paris began to meet on their own to plan a thoroughgoing reform program and to prepare for a meeting of the Estates General to enact it.

These revolts, begun in 1648, were derided with the name "Fronde," which was a children's game of the time. However, the Fronde was a serious challenge to the legacy of royal government as it had developed under Richelieu. It ended without a noteworthy impact on the growth of royal power for several reasons. First, Mazarin methodically regained control of the kingdom through armed force and by making concessions to win the loyalty of individual aristocrats, always eager for the fruits of royal service. Meanwhile, the Parlement of Paris, as well as many citizens of the capital, welcomed a return to royal authority when civil war caused starvation as well as political unrest.

Moreover, the Parlement of Paris was a law court, not a representative assembly. Its legitimacy derived from its role as upholder of royal law, and it could not, over time, challenge the king on the pretext of upholding royal tradition in his name. Parlementaires tended to see the Estates General as a rival institution and helped quash the proposed meeting of an Estates General. Above all, they did not want reforms to include measures like the abolition of the paulette, a fee guaranteeing the hereditary right to royal office (see page 564), which were against their own self-interest.

Unlike in England, there was in France no single institutional focus for resistance to royal power. A strong-willed and able ruler, such as Louis XIV proved to be, could eclipse challenges to royal power, particularly when he satisfied the ambitions of aristocrats and those bureaucrats who profited from the expansion of royal authority.

France Under Louis XIV, 1661–1715

Louis XIV fully assumed control of government at Mazarin's death in 1661. It was a propitious moment. The Peace of the Pyrenees in 1659 had ended in France's favor the wars with Spain that had dragged on since the end of the Thirty Years' War. As part of the peace agreement, Louis married a Spanish princess, Maria Theresa. Louis had been called *le Dieudonné*, "the gift of God," when he was born in 1638, twenty years after his parents' marriage. He was physically attractive and extremely vigorous; he had been carefully and lovingly coached in his duties by Mazarin and by his mother, Queen Anne. Louis XIV proved a diligent king. He put in hours a day at a desk while sustaining the ceremonial life of the court with its elaborate hunts, balls, and other public events.

In the first ten years of his active reign, Louis achieved a degree of control over the mechanisms of government unparalleled in the history of monarchy in France or anywhere else in Europe. He did not invent any new bureaucratic devices but rather used existing ranks of officials in new ways that increased government efficiency and the centralization of control. He radically reduced the number of men in his High Council, the advisory body closest to the king, to include only three or four great ministers of state affairs. This intimate group, with Louis's active participation, handled all policymaking. The ministers of state, war, and finance were chosen exclusively from men of modest backgrounds whose training and experience fitted them for such positions. Jean-Baptiste Colbert (1619–1683), perhaps the greatest of them, served as minister of finance and of most domestic policy from 1665 until his death; he was from a merchant family and had served for years under Mazarin.

Several dozen other officials, picked from the ranks of up-and-coming lawyers and administrators, drew up laws and regulations and passed them to the intendants for execution at the provincial level. These officials at the center were often sent to the provinces as short-term intendants on special supervisory missions. The effect of this system was largely to bypass many entrenched provincial officials, particularly many responsible for tax collecting. The money saved by the more efficient collection of taxes enabled the government to streamline the bureaucracy: Dozens of the offices created to bring cash to the Crown were bought back by the Crown from their owners.

The system still relied on the bonds of patronage and personal service, however. Officials rose through the ranks by means of service to the great, and family connection and personal loyalty still were essential. Of the seventeen different men who were part of Louis XIV's High Council during his reign, five were members of the Colbert family, for example. In the provinces, important local families vied for minor posts, which at least provided prestige and some income.

Some of the benefits of centralized administration can be seen in certain achievements of the early years of Louis's regime. Colbert actively encouraged France's economic development. He reduced internal tolls and customs barriers, relics of medieval decentralization. He encouraged industry with state subsidies and protective tariffs. He set up state-sponsored trading companies—the two most important being the East India Company and the West India Company, established in 1664.

Mercantilism, the philosophy behind Colbert's efforts, stressed self-sufficiency in manufactured goods, tight control of trade to foster the domestic economy, and the absolute value of bullion. Capital for development—bullion—was presumed to be limited in quantity. Protectionist policies were believed necessary to guarantee a favorable balance of payments.

This static model of national wealth did not wholly fit the facts of growing international trade in the seventeenth century. Nevertheless, mercantilist philosophy was helpful to France. France became self-sufficient in the all-important production of woolen cloth, and French industry expanded notably in other sectors. Colbert's greatest success was the deliberate expansion of the navy and merchant marine. By 1677 the size of the navy had increased almost six times, to 144 ships. By the end of Louis XIV's reign, the French navy was virtually the equal of the English navy.

A general determination to manage national resources distinguished Louis's regime. Colbert and the other ministers began to develop the kind of planned government policymaking that we now take for granted. Partly by means of their itinerant supervisory officials, they tried to formulate and execute policy based on carefully collected information. How many men of military age were available? How abundant was the harvest? Answers to such questions enabled not only the formulation of sound economic policy but the deliberate management of production and services to achieve certain goals, such as the recruitment and supply of the king's vast armies.

Beginning in 1673, Louis tried to bring the religious life of the realm more fully under royal control by claiming for himself some of the church revenues and powers of appointment in France that still remained to the pope. Partly to bolster his position with the pope, he also began to attack the Huguenot community in France. He offered financial inducements for conversions to Catholicism, then quartered troops in Huguenots' households to force them to convert. In 1685 he declared that there was no longer any Protestant community, and he officially revoked the Edict of Nantes. A hundred thousand Protestant subjects who refused even nominal conversion to Catholicism chose to emigrate.

Despite the achievement of unprecedented centralized control, Louis's regime is poorly described by the term *absolutism,* which historians often apply to it. By modern standards, the power of the Crown was still greatly limited. Neither Louis nor his chief apologists claimed that he was all-powerful, in the sense of being above the law. Louis's foremost apologist, Bishop Jacques Bossuet (1627–1704), asserted that although the king was guided only by fear of God and his own reason in his application and interpretation of law, he was obligated to act within the law. The "divine right" of kingship, effectively claimed by Louis, did not mean unlimited power to rule; rather it meant that hereditary monarchy was the divinely ordained form of government, best suited to human needs.

Absolutism meant not iron-fisted control of the realm but rather the successful focusing of energy and loyalties on the Crown, in the absence of alternative institutions. The government functioned well in the opening decades of Louis's reign because his role as the focal point of power and loyalty was both logical, after the preceding years of

unrest, and skillfully exploited. Much of the glue holding together the absolutist state lay in informal mechanisms such as patronage and court life, as well as in the traditional hunt for military glory—all of which Louis amply supplied.

The Life of the Court

An observer comparing the way prominent noble families in the mid-sixteenth and mid-seventeenth centuries lived would have noticed striking differences. By the second half of the seventeenth century, most sovereigns or territorial princes had the power to crush revolts, and the heirs of the feudal nobility had to accommodate themselves to the increased power of the Crown. The nobility relinquished its former independence but retained economic and social supremacy and, as a consequence, considerable political clout. Nobles also developed new ways to safeguard their privilege by means of cultural distinctions. This process was particularly dramatic in France as a strong Crown won out over an independent and powerful nobility.

A sign of Louis's success in marshaling the loyalty of the aristocracy was the brilliant court life that his regime sustained. No longer able to wield independent political power, aristocrats lived at court whenever they could, where they could participate in the endless jostling for patronage and prestige—for commands in the royal army and for offices and honorific positions at court itself. Both women and men struggled to secure royal favor for themselves, their relations, and their clients. (See the box, "Politics and Ritual at the Court of Louis XIV.") In this environment, new codes of behavior were used to ensure their political and social distinctiveness. Elaborate rules of courtesy and etiquette regulated court life. Instead of safeguarding one's status with a code of honor backed up by force of arms, the seventeenth-century courtier relied on elegant ceremonial, precise etiquette, and clever conversation. (See the feature, "Weighing the Evidence: Table Manners," on pages 622–623.)

As literacy became more widespread, and the power of educated bureaucrats of humble origin became more obvious, more and more nobles from the traditional aristocracy began to use reading and writing as a means to think critically about their behavior—in the case of men, to reimagine them-

Politics and Ritual at the Court of Louis XIV

This document is from the memoirs of Louis de Rouvroy, duke of Saint-Simon (1675–1755), a favored courtier but one critical of Louis's power over the nobility. Notice his descriptions of court ceremony focusing on the most private moments of the king—an example of Louis's deliberate and exaggerated use of tradition, in this case of personal familiarity among warriors.

The frequent fetes, the . . . promenades at Versailles, the journeys, were means on which the king seized in order to distinguish or mortify courtiers, and thus render them more assiduous in pleasing him. He felt that of real favors he had not enough to bestow. . . . He therefore unceasingly invented all sorts of ideal ones, little preferences and petty distinctions, which answered his purpose as well.

He was exceedingly jealous of the attention paid him. . . . He looked to the right and to the left, not only upon rising but upon going to bed, at his meals, in passing through his apartments, or his gardens of Versailles . . . ; not one escaped him, not even those who hoped to remain unnoticed. He marked well all absences from court. . . .

At eight o'clock [every morning] the chief valet . . . woke the king. At the quarter [hour] the grand chamberlain was called, and those who had what was called the *grandes entrées*. The chamberlain or chief gentleman drew back the [bed] curtains and presented holy water from the vase. . . . The same officer gave [the king] his dressing gown; immediately after, other privileged courtiers entered, and then everybody, in time to find the king putting on his shoes and stockings. . . . Every other day we saw him shave himself; . . . he often spoke of [hunting] and sometimes said a word to somebody.

Source: Bayle St. John, trans., *The Memoirs of the Duke of Saint-Simon on the Reign of Louis XIV and the Regency*, 8th ed. (London: George Allen, 1913); quoted in Merry Wiesner et al., eds., *Discovering the Western Past*, 3d ed., vol. 2 (Boston: Houghton Mifflin, 1997), pp. 37–38.

selves as gentlemen rather than primarily as warriors. Noble women and men alike began to reflect on their new roles by means of writing—in letters, memoirs, and the first novels. A prominent theme of these works is the increasing necessity for a truly private life of affection and trust, with which to counterbalance the public façade necessary to an aspiring courtier. The most influential early French novel was *The Princess of Cleves* by Marie-Madeleine Pioche de la Vergne (1634–1693), best known by her title, Madame de Lafayette. Mme. de Lafayette's novel treats the particular difficulties faced by aristocratic women who, without military careers to buttress their honor, were more vulnerable than men to gossip and slander at court.

Louis XIV's court is usually associated with the palace he built at Versailles, southwest of Paris.

Some of the greatest talent of the day worked on the design and construction of Versailles from 1670 through the 1680s. It became a masterpiece of luxurious but restrained baroque styling—a model for royal and aristocratic palaces throughout Europe for the next one hundred years.

Before Louis's court settled in at Versailles, it traveled among the king's several chateaux in the countryside and in Paris, and in this period of the reign, court life was actually at its most creative and productive. These early years of Louis's personal reign were the heyday of French drama. The comedian Jean-Baptiste Poquelin, known as Molière (1622–1673), impressed the young Louis with his productions in the late 1650s and was rewarded with the use of a theater in the main royal palace in Paris. Like Shakespeare earlier in the

Louis at Versailles Louis XIV (center, on horseback) is pictured among a throng of courtiers at a grotto in the gardens of Versailles. The symbol of the sun appeared throughout the palace; the image of Louis as the "Sun King" further enchanced his authority. *(Château de Versailles/Art Resource, NY)*

century, Molière explored the social and political tensions of his day. He satirized the pretensions of the aristocracy, the social climbing of the bourgeoisie, the self-righteous piety of clerics. Some of his plays were banned from performance, but most not only were tolerated but were extremely popular with the elite audiences they mocked—their popularity is testimony to the confidence of Louis's regime in its early days.

Also popular at court were the tragedies of Jean Racine (1639–1699), who was for French theater what Shakespeare was to the English: the master of the poetic use of language. His plays, which treated familiar classical stories, focused on the emotional and psychological life of the characters and tended to stress the limits that fate places even on royal persons. The pessimism in Racine foreshadowed the less successful second half of Louis's reign.

Louis XIV and a Half-Century of War

Wars initiated by Louis XIV dominated the attention of most European states in the second half of the seventeenth century. Louis's wars sprang from traditional causes: the importance of the glory and dynastic aggrandizement of the king and the preoccupation of the aristocracy with military life.

But if Louis's wars were spurred by familiar concerns about territorial and economic advantage, they were more demanding on state resources than any previous wars.

In France and elsewhere, the size of armies and the need for greater state management of them grew markedly. The new offensive tactics developed during the Thirty Years' War (see page 576) changed the character of armies and hence the demands on governments to provide for them. A higher proportion of soldiers became gunners, and their effectiveness lay in how well they operated as a unit. Armies began to train seriously off the field of battle because drill and discipline were vital to success. The numbers of men on the battlefield increased somewhat, but the total numbers of men in arms supported by the state at any time increased dramatically once the organization to support them was in place. Late in the century, France kept about 400,000 men in arms when at war (which was most of the time).

Ironically, battles were not necessarily made more decisive by the great augmentation in army size. Most wars were still won by destroying enemy resources and by wearing down enemy forces. States that tended to matters off the battlefield such as recruitment and supply were most likely to be successful. Louis XIV's victories in the second half of the century are partly traceable to his regime's attention to such concerns.

Louis's first war reflected the continuing French preoccupation with Spanish power. The goal was territory along France's eastern border to add to the land recently gained by the Peace of Westphalia (1648) and the Peace of the Pyrenees (1659). Louis invoked rather dubious dynastic claims to demand, from Spain, lands in the Spanish Netherlands and the large independent county on France's eastern border called the Franche-Comté (Map 16.1).

War began in 1667. French troops first seized a wedge of territory in the Spanish Netherlands without difficulty and then, in early 1668, occupied the Franche-Comté. But the French retained only some towns in the Spanish Netherlands by the Treaty of Aix-la-Chapelle, which ended the brief conflict later that year. Louis had already begun to negotiate with the Austrian Habsburgs over the eventual division of Spanish Habsburg lands, for it seemed likely that the Spanish king, Charles II (r. 1665–1700), would die without heirs. So, for the moment, Louis was content to return the Franche-

Comté, confident that he would get it back, and much more, in the future.

Louis's focus then shifted from Spain to a new enemy: the Dutch. The Dutch had been allied with France since the beginning of their existence as provinces in rebellion against Spain. The French now turned against the Dutch for reasons that reflect the growth of the international trading economy—specifically, the Dutch dominance of seaborne trade. The French at first tried to lessen the Dutch advantage in trade with tariff barriers against Dutch goods. But, after the easy victories of 1667–1668, Louis's generals urged action against the vulnerable Dutch lands. "It is impossible that his Majesty should tolerate any longer the insolence and arrogance of that nation," added the pragmatic Colbert in 1670.[1]

The Dutch War began in 1672, with Louis personally leading one of the largest armies ever fielded in Europe—perhaps 120,000 men. At the same time, the Dutch were challenged at sea by England. The English had fought the Dutch over these same issues, such as trade, in the 1650s; now Louis secretly sent the English king a pension to ensure his alliance with the French.

At first, the French were spectacularly successful against the tiny Dutch army. Louis, however, presumptuously overrode a plan to move decisively on Amsterdam so that he could preside at the solemn reinstatement of Catholic worship in one of the Dutch provincial cathedrals. The Dutch opened dikes and flooded the countryside to protect their capital, and what had begun as a French rout became a stalemate. Moreover, the Dutch were beating combined English and French forces at sea and were gathering allies who felt threatened by Louis's aggression. The French soon faced German and Austrian forces along their frontier, and, by 1674, the English had joined the alliance against France as well.

Nonetheless, the French managed to hold their own, and the Peace of Nijmegen, in 1678, gave the illusion of a French victory. Not only had the French met the challenge of an alliance against them, but Spain ceded them further border areas in the Spanish Netherlands as well as control of the Franche-Comté.

Ensconced at Versailles since 1682, Louis seemed to be at the height of his powers. Yet the Dutch War had in fact cost him more than he had gained. Meeting the alliance against him had meant

Map 16.1 Territorial Gains of Louis XIV, 1667–1715 Louis's wars, though enormously expensive for France, produced only modest gains of territory along France's eastern and northern frontiers.

fielding ever-increasing numbers of men—more than 200,000 in arms at one time. Internal reforms in government and finance ended under the pressure of paying for war, and old financial expedients of borrowing money and selling privileges were revived. Other government obligations, such as encouraging overseas trade, were neglected. Colbert's death in 1683 dramatically symbolized the end of an era of innovation in the French regime.

Louis's unforgiving Dutch opponent, William of Orange, king of England from 1689 to 1702, renewed former alliances against him. The war, now known as the Nine Years' War, or King William's War, was touched off late in 1688 by French aggression—an invasion of Germany to claim an in-

heritance there. In his ongoing dispute with the pope, Louis seized the papal territory of Avignon in southern France. Boldest of all, he helped the exiled Catholic claimant to the English crown mount an invasion to reclaim his throne.

A widespread war began with all the major powers—Spain, the Netherlands, England, Austria, the major German states—ranged against France. The French also carried the fighting abroad by seizing English territory in Canada. As with the Dutch War, the Nine Years' War was costly but had indecisive results on most fronts. And this time there was no illusion of victory for Louis. In the Treaty of Ryswick (1697), Louis had to give up most of the territories in Germany, the

Spanish Netherlands, and northern Spain that he managed to occupy by war's end. Avignon went back to the pope, and Louis gave up his contentious claim to papal revenues. The terrible burden of taxes to pay for the wars combined with crop failures in 1693 and 1694 caused widespread starvation in the countryside. French courtiers began to criticize Louis openly.

The final major war of Louis's reign, now called the War of Spanish Succession, broke out in 1702. In some ways it was a straightforward dynastic war in which France and its perennial Habsburg opponent had an equal interest. Both Louis and Holy Roman Emperor Leopold I (r. 1657–1705) hoped to claim for their heirs the throne of Spain, left open at the death in 1700 of the Spanish king, Charles II. A will of Charles II gave the throne to Louis's grandson, Philip of Anjou, who quickly proceeded to enter Spain and claim his new kingdom. War was made inevitable when Louis renounced one of the conditions of Charles's will by insisting that Philip's accession to the throne of Spain did not mean that he had abandoned his rights to the throne of France. This declaration was an act of sheer belligerence, for Philip was only third in line for the French throne. The Dutch and the English responded to the prospect of a Frenchman on the throne of Spain and the consequent disruption of the balance of power in Europe by joining the emperor in a formal Great Alliance in 1701. The Dutch and English also wanted to defend their colonial interests, since the French had already begun to profit from new trading opportunities with the Spanish colonies.

Again the French fought a major war on several fronts on land and at sea. Again the people of France felt the cost in crushing taxes worsened by harvest failures. Major revolts inside France forced Louis to divert troops from the war. For a time it seemed that the French would be soundly defeated, but they were saved by the superior organization of their forces and by dynastic accident: Unexpected deaths in the Habsburg family meant that the Austrian claimant to the Spanish throne suddenly was poised to inherit rule of Austria and the empire as well. The English, who were more afraid of a revival of unified Habsburg control of Spain and Austria than of French domination of Spain, began peace negotiations with France.

The Peace of Utrecht in 1713 resolved long-standing political conflicts and helped to set the agenda of European politics for the eighteenth century. Philip of Anjou became Philip V of Spain, but on the condition that the Spanish and French crowns would never be worn by the same monarch. To maintain the balance of power against French interests, the Spanish Netherlands and Spanish territories in Italy were ceded to Austria, which for many decades would be France's major continental rival. The Peace of Utrecht also marked the beginning of England's dominance of overseas trade and colonization. The French gave to England lands in Canada and the Caribbean and renounced any privileged relationship with Spanish colonies. England was allowed to control the highly profitable slave trade with Spanish colonies.

Louis XIV had added small amounts of strategically valuable territory along France's eastern border (see Map 16.1), and a Bourbon ruled in Spain. But the costs in human life and resources were great for the slim results achieved. Moreover, the army and navy had swallowed up capital for investment and trade; strategic opportunities overseas were lost, never to be regained. Louis's government had been innovative in its early years but remained constrained by traditional ways of imagining the interest of the state.

THE ENGLISH REVOLUTION

In England, unlike in France, a representative institution—Parliament—became an effective, permanent brake on royal authority. The process by which Parliament gained a secure role in governing the kingdom was neither easy nor peaceful, however. As we saw in Chapter 15, conflicts between the English crown and its subjects, focused in the Crown-Parliament conflict, concerned control over taxation and the direction of religious reform. Beginning in 1642, England was beset by civil war between royal and parliamentary forces. The king was eventually defeated and executed, and there followed a period when the monarchy was abolished altogether. The monarchy was restored in 1660, but Parliament retained a crucial role in governing the kingdom, a role that was confirmed when, in 1688, it again deposed a monarch whose fiscal and religious policies became unacceptable to its members.

Civil War and Revolution, 1642–1649

Fighting broke between Charles I and parliamentary armies in the late summer of 1642. The Long Parliament (see page 571) continued to represent a broad coalition of critics and opponents of the monarchy, ranging from aristocrats concerned primarily with the abuses of royal prerogative to radical Puritans eager for thorough religious reform and determined to defeat the king. Fighting was halfhearted, initially, and the tide of war at first favored Charles.

In 1643, however, the scope of the war broadened. Charles made peace with Irish rebels and brought Irish troops to England to help his cause. Parliament, in turn, sought military aid from the Scots in exchange for promises that Presbyterianism would become the religion of England. Meanwhile, Oliver Cromwell (1599–1658), a Puritan member of the Long Parliament and a cavalry officer, helped reorganize parliamentary forces in order to defeat the king's forces. The eleven-hundred-man cavalry trained by Cromwell and known as the "Ironsides" helped parliamentary and Scottish infantry defeat the king's troops at Marston Moor in July 1644. The victory made Cromwell famous.

Shortly afterward, Parliament reorganized its forces to create the New Model Army, rigorously trained like Cromwell's Ironsides. Sitting members of Parliament were barred from commanding troops, hence upper-class control of the army was reduced. This army played a decisive role not only in the war but also in the political settlement that followed the fighting.

The New Model Army won a convincing victory over royal forces at Naseby in 1645. In the spring of 1646, Charles surrendered to a Scottish army in the north. In January 1647, Parliament paid the Scots for their services in the war and took the king into custody. In the negotiations that followed, Charles tried to play his opponents off against each other, and, as he hoped, divisions among them widened.

Most members of Parliament were Presbyterians, Puritans who favored a strongly unified and controlled state church along Calvinist lines. They wanted peace with the king in return for acceptance of the new church structure and parliamentary control of standing militias for a specified pe-

riod. They did not favor expanding the right to vote or other dramatic constitutional or legal change. These men were increasingly alarmed by the rise of sectarian differences and the actual religious freedom that many ordinary people were claiming for themselves. With the weakening of royal authority and the disruption of civil war, censorship was relaxed and public preaching by ordinary women and men who felt a religious inspiration was becoming commonplace.

Above all, Presbyterian gentry in Parliament feared more radical groups in the army and in London that had supported them up to this point but favored more thoroughgoing reform. Most officers of the New Model Army, such as Cromwell, were Independents, Puritans who favored a decentralized church, a degree of religious toleration, and a wider sharing of political power among men of property, not just among the very wealthy gentry. In London, a well-organized artisans' movement known as the Levelers favored universal manhood suffrage, reform of law, and better access to education in addition to decentralized churches—in short, the separation of political power from wealth and virtual freedom of religion. Many of the rank and file of the army were deeply influenced by Leveler ideas.

In May 1647 the majority in Parliament voted to disband the New Model Army without first paying most of the soldiers' back wages and to offer terms to the king. This move provoked the first direct intervention by the army in politics. Representatives of the soldiers were chosen to present grievances to Parliament but, when this failed, the army seized the king and, in August, occupied Westminster, Parliament's meeting place. Independent and Leveler elements in the army debated the direction of possible reform to be imposed on Parliament. (See the box, "The Putney Debates.")

However, in November, Charles escaped from his captors and raised a new army among his erstwhile enemies, the Scots, who were also alarmed by the growing radicalism in England. Civil war began again early in 1648. Although it ended quickly with a victory by Cromwell and the New Model Army in August, the renewed war further hardened political divisions and enhanced the power of the army. The king was widely blamed for the renewed bloodshed, and the army did not

The Putney Debates

In October 1647, representatives of the Leveler movement in the army ranks confronted Independents—largely comprising the officer corps—in formally staged debates in a church at Putney, outside London. The debates reflected the importance of the army in deciding the shape of change. Reproduced here is one exchange between the Leveler representative, Thomas Rainsborough, advocating universal manhood suffrage, and Cromwell's fellow officer, Henry Ireton, who argues for a franchise more restricted to men of some means.

Rainsborough: . . . Really I think that the poorest he that is in England hath a life to live as the greatest he; and therefore truly, sir, I think it's clear, that every man that is to live under a government ought first by his own consent to put himself under that government; and I do think that the poorest man in England is not at all bound in a strict sense to that government that he hath not had a voice to put himself under; and I am confident that, when I have heard the reasons against it, that something will be said to answer those reasons, insomuch that I should doubt whether I was an Englishman or no, that should doubt of these things.

Ireton: That's this.

Give me leave to tell you, that if you make this the rule, I think you must fly for refuge to an absolute natural right, and you must deny all civil right; and I am sure it will come to that in the consequence. . . . I think that no person hath a right to an interest or share in the disposing of the affairs of the kingdom, and in determining or choosing those that shall determine what laws we shall be ruled by here, no person hath a right to this that hath not a permanent fixed interest in this kingdom, and those persons together are properly the represented of this kingdom, who taken together, and consequently are to make up the representers of this kingdom, are the representers, who taken together do comprehend whatsoever is of real or permanent interest in the kingdom, and I am sure there is otherwise (I cannot tell what), otherwise any man can say why a foreigner coming in amongst us, or as many as

will be coming in amongst us, or by force or otherwise settling themselves here, or at least by our permission having a being here, why they should not as well lay claim to it as any other. We talk of birthright. Truly birthright there is thus much claim: men may justly have by birthright, by their very being born in England, that we should not seclude them out of England. That we should not refuse to give them air and place and ground, and the freedom of the highways and other things, to live amongst us, not any man that is born here, though he in birth, or by his birth there come nothing at all that is part of the permanent interest of this kingdom to him. That I think is due to a man by birth. But that by a man's being born here he shall have a share in that power that shall dispose of the lands here, and of all things here, I do not think it a sufficient ground, but I am sure if we look upon that which is the utmost, within man's view, of what was originally the constitution of this kingdom, upon that which is most radical and fundamental, and which if you take away, there is no man hath any land, any goods, you take away any civil interest, and that is this: that those that choose the representers for the making of laws by which this state and kingdom are to be governed, are the persons who taken together, do comprehend the local interest of this kingdom; that is, the persons in whom all land lies, and those in corporations in whom all trading lies. This is the most fundamental constitution of this kingdom, and which if you do not allow, you allow none at all.

Source: G. E. Aylmer, ed., *The Levellers in the English Revolution* (Ithaca: Cornell University Press, 1975), pp. 100–101.

trust him to keep any agreement he might now sign. When Parliament, still dominated by Presbyterians, once again voted to negotiate with the king, army troops under a Colonel Thomas Pride prevented members who favored Presbyterianism or the king from attending sessions. The "Rump" Parliament that remained after "Pride's Purge" voted to try the king. Charles I was executed for "treason, tyranny and bloodshed" against his people on January 30, 1649.

The Interregnum, 1649–1660

A Commonwealth—a republic—was declared. Executive power resided in a council of state. Legislative power resided in a one-chamber Parliament, the Rump Parliament (the House of Lords was abolished). Declaring a republic proved far easier than running one, however. The execution of the king shocked most English and Scots people and alienated many elites from the new regime.

The legitimacy of the Commonwealth government would always be in question.

The tasks of making and implementing policy were made difficult by the narrow political base on which the government now rested. Excluded were the majority of the reformist gentry who had been purged from Parliament. Also excluded were the more radical Levelers; Leveler leaders in London were arrested when they published tracts critical of the new government. Within a few years, many disillusioned Levelers would join a new religious movement called the Society of Friends, or Quakers, which espoused complete religious autonomy. Quakers refused all oaths or service to the state, and they refused to acknowledge social rank.

Above all, the new government was vulnerable to the power of the army, which had created it. In 1649 and 1650 Cromwell led expeditions to Ireland and Scotland, partly for sheer revenge and partly to put down resistance to the new English government. In Ireland, Cromwell's forces acted with great ruthlessness. English control there was

Popular Preaching in England Many women took advantage of the collapse of royal authority to preach in public—a radical activity for women at the time. This print satirizes the Quakers, a religious movement that attracted many women. *(Mary Evans Picture Library)*

furthered by more dispossession of Irish land-holders, which also served to pay off the army's wages. Meanwhile, Parliament could not agree on systematic reforms, particularly the one reform Independents in the army insisted on: more broadly based elections for a new Parliament. Fresh from his victories in the north, Cromwell led his armies to London and dissolved Parliament in the spring of 1652.

In 1653 some army officers drew up the "Instrument of Government," England's first and only written constitution. It provided for an executive, the Lord Protector, and a Parliament to be based on somewhat wider male suffrage. Cromwell was the natural choice for Lord Protector, and whatever success the government of the Protectorate had was largely due to him.

Cromwell was an extremely able leader who was not averse to compromise. Although he had used the army against Parliament in 1648, he had worked hard to reconcile the Rump Parliament and the army before marching on London in 1652. He believed in a state church, but one that allowed for control, including choice of minister, by local congregations. He also believed in toleration for other Protestant sects, as well as for Catholics and Jews, as long as no one disturbed the peace.

As Lord Protector, Cromwell oversaw impressive reforms in law that testify to his belief in the limits of governing authority. For example, contrary to the practice of his day, he opposed capital punishment for petty crimes. The government of the Protectorate, however, accomplished little because Parliament remained internally divided and opposed to Cromwell's initiatives. Cromwell was challenged by radical republicans in Parliament who thought the Protectorate represented a step backward, away from republican government. In the population at large, there were still royalist sympathizers, and a royalist uprising in 1655 forced the temporary division of England into military districts administered by generals.

In the end, the Protectorate could not survive the strains over policy and the challenges to its legitimacy. When Cromwell died of a sudden illness in September 1658, the Protectorate did not long survive him. In February 1660, the decisive action of one army general seeking a solution to the chaos enabled all the surviving members of the Long Parliament to rejoin the Rump. The Parliament summarily dissolved itself and called for new elections.

Oliver Cromwell Cromwell had seen his family's income decline under the weight of Charles I's exactions. Elected to Parliament in 1628 and again in 1640, he also brought a long-standing religious zeal to his public life. His opposition to the "tyranny and usurpation" of the Anglican church hierarchy first prompted him to criticize royal government. *(In the collection of the Duke of Buccleuch and Queensberry KT)*

The newly elected Parliament recalled Charles II, son of Charles I, from exile abroad and restored the monarchy. The chaos and radicalism of the late civil war and interregnum—the period between reigns, as the years from 1649 to 1660 came to be called—now spawned a conservative reaction.

The Restoration, 1660–1685

Charles II (r. 1660–1685) claimed his throne at the age of 30. He had learned from his years of uncertain exile and from the fate of his father. He did not seek retribution but rather offered a general pardon to all but a few rebels (mostly those who had signed his father's death warrant), and he suggested to Parliament a relatively tolerant religious settlement that would include Anglicans as well as

Presbyterians. He was far more politically adept than his father and far more willing to compromise.

That the re-established royal government was not more tolerant than it turned out to be was not Charles's doing but Parliament's. During the 1660s, the "Cavalier" Parliament, named for royalists in the civil war, passed harsh laws aimed at religious dissenters. Anglican orthodoxy was reimposed, including the re-establishment of bishops and the Anglican *Book of Common Prayer*. All officeholders and clergy were required to swear oaths of obedience to the king and to the established church. As a result, hundreds of them were forced out of office. Holding nonconformist religious services became illegal, and Parliament passed a "five-mile" act to prevent dissenting ministers from traveling near their former congregations. Property laws were strengthened and the criminal codes made more severe.

The king's behavior began to mimic prerevolutionary royalist positions. Charles II began to flirt with Catholicism, and his brother and heir, James, openly converted. Charles promulgated a declaration of tolerance that would have included Catholics as well as nonconformist Protestants, but Parliament would not accept it. When Parliament moved to exclude the Catholic James from succession to the throne, Charles dissolved it. A subsequent Parliament, cowed by fears of a new civil war, backed down. By the end of his reign, Charles was financially independent of Parliament thanks to increased revenue from overseas trade and to secret subsidies from France, his recent ally against Dutch trading rivals.

Underneath this seeming return to a prerevolutionary status quo were conditions that reflected the legacy of the revolution that had cost Charles I his head. First, despite the harsh laws, to silence all dissent was not possible. After two decades of religious pluralism and broadly based political activity it was impossible to reimpose conformity; there were well-established communities of various sects and a self-confidence that bred vigorous resistance. Also, anti-Catholic feeling still united all Protestants. In 1678 Charles's secret treaties with the French became known, and rumors of a Catholic plot to murder Charles and reimpose Catholicism became widespread. No evidence of any plot was ever unearthed, though thirty-five people were executed for alleged participation. Parliament focused its attention on anti-Catholicism, passing an act barring all but Anglicans from Parliament itself.

The clearest reflection of the regime's revolutionary background was the power of Parliament: It was able to assert its policies against the desires of the king. Nevertheless, financial independence and firm political tactics enabled Charles to retain a great deal of power. If he had been followed by an able successor, Parliament might have lost a good measure of its confidence and independence. But his brother James's reign and its aftermath further enhanced Parliament's power.

The Glorious Revolution, 1688

When James II (r. 1685–1689) succeeded Charles, Parliament's royalist leanings were at first evident. James was granted customs duties for life and was also given funds to suppress a rebellion by one of Charles's illegitimate sons. James did not try to impose Catholicism on England, but he did try to achieve toleration for Catholics in two declarations of indulgence in 1687 and 1688. His efforts were undermined by his heavy-handed tactics. When several leading Anglican bishops refused to read the declarations from their pulpits, he had them imprisoned and tried for seditious libel. The jury, however, acquitted them.

James also failed because of the coincidence of other events. In 1685, at the outset of James's reign, Louis XIV in France had revoked the Edict of Nantes. The possibility that subjects and monarchs in France and, by extension, elsewhere could be of different faiths seemed increasingly unlikely. Popular fears of James's Catholicism were thus heightened early in his reign, and his later declarations of tolerance, though benefiting Protestant dissenters, were viewed with suspicion. In 1688, not only were the Anglican bishops acquitted but the king's second wife, who was Catholic, gave birth to a son. The birth raised the specter of a Catholic succession.

In June 1688, to put pressure on James, leading members of Parliament invited William of Orange, husband of James's Protestant daughter, Mary, to come to England. William mounted an invasion that became a rout when James refused to defend his throne. James simply abandoned England and went to France. William called Parliament, which declared James to have abdicated and offered the throne to him and to Mary. James eventually invaded Ireland in 1690 with French support but was defeated by William at the Battle of Boyne that year.

The substitution of William (r. 1689–1702) and Mary (r. 1689–1694) for James, known as the "Glorious Revolution," was engineered by Parliament and confirmed its power. Parliament presented the new sovereigns with a Declaration of Rights upon their accession and, later that year, with a Bill of Rights that defended freedom of speech, called for frequent Parliaments, and required subsequent monarchs to be Protestant. The effectiveness of these documents was reinforced by Parliament's power of the purse. Parliament's role in the political process was ensured by William's interests in funding his ambitious military efforts, particularly to support the Netherlands' ongoing wars with France.

The issues that had faced the English since the beginning of the century were common to all European states: religious division and elite power, fiscal strains and resistance to taxation. Yet events in England had so far set it apart from the experience of other states in that the incremental assumption of authority by a well-established institution, Parliament, made challenge of the monarchy more legitimate and more effective. Political participation also developed more broadly in England than in other states. In the long run, the strength of Parliament would make easier the task of permanently broadening participation in government.

NEW POWERS IN CENTRAL AND EASTERN EUROPE

By the end of the seventeenth century, three states dominated central and eastern Europe: Austria, Brandenburg-Prussia, and Russia. After the Thirty Years' War, the Habsburgs' power as emperors waned, and their interest in the coherence of their own territories, which centered on Austria, grew. Brandenburg-Prussia, in northeastern Germany, grew to a position of power rivaling that of the Habsburg state. The rulers of Brandenburg-Prussia had gained lands in the Peace of Westphalia, and astute management transformed their relatively small and scattered holdings into one of the most powerful states in Europe. Russia's new stature in eastern Europe resulted in part from the weakness of its greatest rival, Poland, and the determination of one leader, Peter the Great, to as-

sume a major role in European affairs. Sweden controlled valuable Baltic territory through much of the century but by the end of the century was also eclipsed by Russia as a power in the region.

The development of and the competition among states in central and eastern Europe was closely linked to developments in western Europe. This was true politically and strategically as well as economically. One of the most important factors influencing the internal political development of these states was their relationship to the wider European economy: They were sources of grain and raw materials for the more densely urbanized west.

The Consolidation of Austria

The Thirty Years' War (see pages 571–577) weakened the Habsburgs as emperors but strengthened them in their own lands. The main Habsburg lands in 1648 were a collection of principalities comprising modern Austria, the kingdom of Hungary (largely in Turkish hands), and the kingdom of Bohemia (see Map 16.2). In 1713 the Peace of Utrecht ceded the Spanish Netherlands to Austria and renamed them the "Austrian Netherlands." Although language and ethnic differences prevented an absolutist state along French lines, Leopold I (r. 1657–1705) instituted political and institutional changes that enabled the Habsburg state to become one of the most powerful states in Europe through the eighteenth century.

Much of the coherence that already existed in Leopold's lands had been achieved by his predecessors in the wake of the Thirty Years' War. The lands of rebels in Bohemia had been confiscated and redistributed among loyal, mostly Austrian, families. In return for political and military support for the emperor, these families were given the right to exploit their newly acquired land and the peasants who worked it. The desire to recover population and productivity after the destruction of the Thirty Years' War gave landlords further incentive to curtail peasants' autonomy sharply, particularly in devastated Bohemia. Austrian landlords throughout the Habsburg domains provided grain and timber for the export market and grain and other foodstuffs for the Austrian armies, and elite families provided the army with officers. This political-economic arrangement provoked numerous serious peasant revolts, but the peasants were not able to force changes in a system that suited both the elites and the central authority.

Although Leopold had lost much influence within the empire itself, an imperial government made up of various councils, a war ministry, financial officials, and the like still functioned in his capital, Vienna. Leopold worked to extricate the government of his own lands from the apparatus of imperial institutions, which were staffed largely by Germans more loyal to imperial than to Habsburg interests. In addition, Leopold used the Catholic church as an institutional and ideological support for the Habsburg state.

Leopold's personal preoccupation was the reestablishment of zealous Catholicism throughout his territories. Acceptance of Catholicism became the litmus test of loyalty to the Habsburg regime,

Celebrating Habsburg Power Leopold I is depicted here trampling a Turkish soldier, wearing armor and a medieval order of knighthood around his neck—appropriate garb with which to represent a victory over "the Infidel." Compare this illustration with the painting of Louis XIV in Roman armor on page 588. (*Kunsthistorisches Museum, Vienna*)

and Protestantism vanished among elites. Leopold encouraged the work of Jesuit teachers and members of other Catholic orders. These men and women helped staff his government and administered religious life down to the most local levels.

Leopold's most dramatic success, as a Habsburg and as a religious leader, was his reconquest of the kingdom of Hungary from the Ottoman Empire. Since the mid-sixteenth century, the Habsburgs had controlled only a narrow strip of the kingdom. Preoccupied with countering Louis XIV's aggression, Leopold did not himself choose to begin a reconquest. His centralizing policies, however, alienated nobles and townspeople in the portion of Hungary he did control, as did his repression of Protestantism, which had flourished in Hungary. Hungarian nobles began a revolt, aided by the Turks, aiming for a reunited Hungary under Ottoman protection.

The Habsburgs emerged victorious in part because they received help from, among others, the talented Polish king, Jan Sobieski, whose own lands in Ukraine were threatened by the Turks. The Turks overreached their supply lines to besiege Vienna in 1683. After the siege failed, Habsburg armies slowly pressed east and south, recovering Buda, the capital of Hungary, in 1686 and Belgrade in 1688. The Danube basin lay once again in Christian hands.

Leopold gave land in the reclaimed kingdom to Austrian officers whom he believed were loyal to him. The traditions of Hungarian separatism, however, were strong, and the great magnates—whether they had defended the Habsburgs against Turkish encroachment or guarded the frontier for Turkish overlords—retained their independence. The peasantry, as elsewhere, suffered a decline in status as a result of the Crown's efforts to ensure the loyalty of elites. In the long run, Hungarian independence weakened the Habsburg state, but in the short run Leopold's victory over the Turks and the recovery of Hungary itself were momentous events, confirming the Habsburgs as the preeminent power in central Europe.

The Rise of Brandenburg-Prussia

Three German states, in addition to Austria, gained territory and stature after the Thirty Years' War: Bavaria, Saxony, and Brandenburg-Prussia. By the end of the seventeenth century, the strongest was

Brandenburg-Prussia, a conglomeration of small territories held, by dynastic accident, by the Hohenzollern family. The two principal territories were electoral Brandenburg, in northeastern Germany, with its capital, Berlin, and the duchy of Prussia, a fief of the Polish crown along the Baltic coast east of Poland proper (see Map 16.2). In addition there was a handful of small principalities near the Netherlands. The manipulation of resources and power that enabled these unpromising lands to become a powerful state was primarily the work of Frederick William, known as "the Great Elector" (r. 1640–1688).

Frederick William used the occasion of a war to effect a permanent change in the structure of government. He took advantage of a war between Poland and its rivals, Sweden and Russia (the First Great Northern War, described in the next section), to win independence for the duchy of Prussia from Polish overlordship. When his involvement in the war ended in 1657, he kept intact the general war commissariat, a combined civilian and military body that had efficiently directed the war effort; he thus bypassed traditional councils and representative bodies. He also used the standing army to force the payment of high taxes. Most significantly, he established a positive relationship with the *Junkers,* hereditary landholders, which assured him both revenue and loyalty. He agreed to allow the Junkers virtually total control of their own lands in return for their agreement to support his government—in short, to surrender their accustomed political independence.

Peasants and townspeople were taxed, but nobles were not. The freedom to control their estates led many nobles to invest in profitable agriculture for the export market. The peasants were serfs who received no benefits from the increased productivity of the land. Frederick William further enhanced his state's power by sponsoring state industries. These industries did not have to fear competition from urban producers because the towns had been frozen out of the political process and saddled with heavy taxes. Although an oppressive place for many Germans, Brandenburg-Prussia attracted many skilled refugees, such as Huguenot artisans fleeing Louis XIV.

Bavaria and Saxony, in contrast to Brandenburg-Prussia, had vibrant towns, largely free peasantries, and weaker aristocracies but were less powerful in international affairs. Power on the European stage depended on military force. Such power, whether in a large state like France or in a small one like Brandenburg-Prussia, usually came at the expense of the state's inhabitants.

Competition Around the Baltic: The Demise of the Polish State and the Zenith of Swedish Power

The rivers and port cities of the Baltic coast were conduits for the growing trade between the Baltic hinterland and the rest of Europe; tolls assessed on the passage of timber, grain, and naval stores were an important source of local income, and the commodities themselves brought profits to their producers. This trading system had profound social and political consequences for all of the states bordering the Baltic Sea in the seventeenth century.

First, it was a spur to war: Sweden and Denmark fought over control of the sea-lanes connecting the Baltic and North Seas. Sweden, Poland, and Russia fought for control of the eastern Baltic coastline in the sixteenth and seventeenth centuries. In the seventeenth century, Poland and Russia fought over grain- and timber-producing lands comprising modern Belarus, parts of modern Russia, and Ukraine. Second, profits from the production of grain for export in such volume reinforced the power of large landholders, particularly within Poland, where most of the grain was produced.

In 1600 a large portion of the Baltic hinterland lay under the control of Poland-Lithuania, a dual kingdom at the height of its power (Map 16.2). A marriage in 1386 had brought the duchy of Lithuania under a joint ruler with Poland; earlier in the fourteenth century, Lithuania had conquered Belarus and Ukraine. Poland-Lithuania commanded considerable resources, including the Vistula and Niemen Rivers and the ports of Gdansk and Riga on the Baltic coast. Like the neighboring Habsburg lands, it was a multi-ethnic state, particularly in the huge duchy of Lithuania, where Russian-speakers predominated. Poland was Catholic but had a large minority of Protestants and Jews. Owing to ties with Poland, Lithuanians themselves were mostly Catholic (and some were Protestant), but Russian-speakers were Orthodox. German-speaking families dominated trade in most coastal cities.

Internal strains and external challenges began to mount in Poland-Lithuania in the late sixteenth century. The economic power of Polish landlords

Prussian territory in 1640

Prussian acquisitions in 1688

Russian territory in 1693

Seized by Peter the Great from Sweden, 1694-1725

Austrian territory by 1699

Ottoman Empire in 1699

Boundary of the Holy Roman Empire

Map 16.2 New Powers in Central and Eastern Europe The balance of power in central and eastern Europe shifted with the strengthening of Austria, the rise of Brandenburg-Prussia, and the expansion of Russia at the expense of Poland and Sweden.

gave them considerable political clout; the king was forced to grant concessions that weakened urban freedoms and bound peasants to the nobles' estates. In 1572 the sudden death of the very able but childless king, Sigismund II (r. 1548–1572), only enhanced the nobles' power. Sigismund's successors would be elected, would have no voice in the succession, and would be closely supervised by noble counselors.

The spread of the Counter-Reformation, encouraged by the Crown, created tensions with both Protestant and Orthodox subjects in the diverse kingdom. In Ukraine, communities of Cossacks, nomadic farmer-warriors, grew as Polish and Lithuanian peasants fled harsh conditions to join them. The Cossacks had long been tolerated because they were a military buffer against the Ottoman Turks to the south, but now Polish landlords wanted to reincorporate the Cossacks into the profitable political-economic system that they controlled. Meanwhile, the Crown was involved in several wars. From 1609 to 1612 Polish armies tried but failed to impose a Polish king on the Russians during a dispute over the succession. While aiding Austria in the Thirty Years' War against the Turks, their common enemy, the Poles lost Livonia (modern Latvia) and other bits of northern territory to the aggressive Gustav Adolf of Sweden.

In 1648 the Polish crown faced revolt and invasion that it could not counter. The Cossacks, with the Crimean Tatars and their Ottoman overlords as allies, staged a major revolt, defeated Polish armies, and established an independent state. In 1654 the Cossacks transferred their allegiance to Moscow and became part of a Russian invasion of Poland that, by the next year, had engulfed much of the eastern half of the dual kingdom. At the same time, the Swedes seized central Poland and competed with the Russians for control elsewhere; the Swedes were helped by Polish and Lithuanian aristocrats acting like independent warlords.

Often called the First Great Northern War, this war is remembered in Poland as "the Deluge." Polish royal armies managed to recover much territory—most important, the western half of Ukraine. But the invasions and subsequent fighting were disastrous. The population of Poland may have declined by as much as 40 percent, and vital urban economies were in ruins. The Catholic identity of the Polish heartland had been a rallying point for resistance to the Protestant Swedes and the Ortho-dox Russians, but the religious tolerance that had distinguished the Polish kingdom and had been mandated in its constitution was thereafter abandoned. In addition, much of its recovery of territory was only nominal. In parts of Lithuania inhabited by Russian-speaking peoples, the Russian presence during the wars had achieved local transfers of power from Lithuanian to Russian landlords loyal to Moscow.

The elective Polish crown passed in 1674 to the brilliant military commander Jan Sobieski (r. 1674–1696), known as "Vanquisher of the Turks" for his victory in raising the siege of Vienna. Given Poland's internal weakness, however, Sobieski's victories in the long run helped the Austrian and Russian rivals of the Turks more than they helped the Poles. His successor, Augustus II of Saxony (r. 1697–1704, 1709–1733), dragged Poland back into war, from which Russia would emerge the obvious winner in the power struggle in eastern Europe.

On the Baltic coast, however, Sweden remained the dominant power through most of the seventeenth century. Swedish efforts to control Baltic territory began in the sixteenth century, first to counter the power of its perennial rival, Denmark, in the western Baltic. It then competed with Poland to control Livonia, whose principal city, Riga, was an important trading center for goods from both Lithuania and Russia. By 1617, under Gustav Adolf, the Swedes gained the lands to the north surrounding the Gulf of Finland (the most direct outlet for Russian goods) and in 1621 displaced the Poles in Livonia itself. Swedish intervention in the Thirty Years' War came when imperial successes against Denmark both threatened the Baltic coast and created an opportunity to strike at Sweden's old enemy. The Treaty of Westphalia (1648) confirmed Sweden's earlier gains and added control of further coastal territory, mostly at Denmark's expense.

The port cities held by Sweden were indeed profitable but simply served to pay for the costly wars necessary to seize and defend them. All of these efforts to hold Baltic territory were driven by dynastic and strategic needs as much as economic rationales. The ruling dynasty struggled against Denmark's control of western Baltic territory in order to safeguard its independence from the Danes, who had ruled the combined kingdoms until 1523. Similarly, competition with Poland for the east Baltic was part of a dynastic struggle after

War for the Baltic Control of the Baltic littoral was hotly contested throughout the seventeenth century. While fighting in Poland during the First Great Northern War, the Swedes were attacked, in turn, by their longstanding rivals, the Danes. The Swedish king, Karl Gustav, marched his army over frozen sea lanes and beat the Danes at the Battle of Ifveros, depicted here, in the winter of 1658. *(National Museum of Stockholm)*

1592. Sigismund Vasa, son of the king of Sweden, had been elected king of Poland in 1587 but also inherited the Swedish throne in 1592. Other members of the ruling Swedish Vasa family fought him successfully to regain rule over Sweden and extricate Swedish interests from Poland's continental preoccupations. Sigismund ruled Poland until his death in 1632 but was replaced on the Swedish throne by an uncle in 1604.

The one permanent gain that Sweden realized from its aggression in the First Great Northern War was the renunciation of the Polish Vasa line to any claim to the Swedish crown. Owing to its earlier gains, Sweden remained the dominant power on the Baltic coast until the end of the century, when it was supplanted by the powerful Russian state.

The Expansion of Russia: From Ivan "the Terrible" Through Peter "the Great"

The Russian state expanded dramatically through the sixteenth century. Ivan IV (r. 1533–1584) was proclaimed "Tsar [Russian for "Caesar"] of All the Russias" in 1547. This act was the culmination of the accumulation of land and authority by the princes of Moscow through the late Middle Ages, when Moscow had vied for pre-eminence with other Russian principalities. Ivan IV's grandfather, Ivan III (r. 1462–1505), the first to use the title *tsar,* had absorbed neighboring Russian principalities and ended Moscow's subservience to Mongol overlords.

Ivan IV, also known as Ivan "the Terrible," was the first actually to be crowned tsar and routinely to use the title. His use of the title aptly reflected his imperial intentions, as he continued Moscow's push westward and, especially, eastward against the Mongol states of central Asia. Two of the three Mongol states to the east and south fell, and the Russians pushed eastward over the Ural Mountains to Siberia for the first time.

Within this expanding empire, Ivan IV ruled as an autocrat. Part of his authority stemmed from his own personality. He was willing—perhaps because of mental imbalance—to use ruthless methods, including the torture and murder of thousands of subjects, to enforce his will. The practice of gathering tribute for Mongol overlords had put many resources in the hands of Muscovite princes. Ivan IV was able to bypass noble participation and intensify the centralization of government by creating ranks of officials, known as the service gentry, loyal only to him. The name "the Terrible" comes from the Russian word *groznyi*, which is better translated as "awe-inspiring."

A period of disputed succession known as the Time of Troubles followed Ivan's death in 1584, not unlike similar crises in other European states, where jealous aristocrats vied for power during periods of royal weakness. In this case, aristocratic factions fought among themselves as well as against armies of Cossacks and other common people who disputed nobles' ambitions and wanted less oppressive government. Nonetheless, the foundations of the large and cohesive state laid by Ivan enabled Michael Romanov to rebuild autocratic government readily after being chosen tsar in 1613.

The Romanovs were an eminent aristocratic family related to Ivan's. Michael (r. 1613–1645) was chosen to rule by an assembly of aristocrats, gentry, and commoners who were more alarmed at the civil wars and recent Polish incursions than at the prospect of a return to strong tsarist rule. Michael was succeeded by his son, Alexis (r. 1645–1676), who presided over the extension of Russian control to Ukraine in 1654 and developed interest in further relationships with the West.

Shifting the balance of power in eastern Europe and the Baltic in Russia's favor was also the work of Alexis's son, Peter I, "the Great" (r. 1682–1725). Peter accomplished this by military successes against his enemies and by forcibly reorienting Russian government and society toward involvement with the rest of Europe.

Peter was almost literally larger than life. Nearly 7 feet tall, he towered over most of his contemporaries and had physical and mental energy to match his size. He set himself to learning trades and studied soldiering by rising in the ranks of the military like any common soldier. He traveled abroad to learn as much as he could about other states' economies and government. He wanted the revenue, manufacturing output, technology and trade, and, above all, the up-to-date army and navy that other rulers enjoyed. In short, Peter sought for Russia a more evolved state system because of the strength it would give him.

Peter initiated a bold and even brutal series of changes in Russian society upon his accession to power. Peasants already were bearing the brunt of taxation, but their tax burden worsened when they were assessed arbitrarily by head and not by output of the land. Peter noticed that European monarchs coexisted with a privileged but educated aristocracy and that a brilliant court life symbolized and reinforced the rulers' authority.

Peter the Great This portrait by a Dutch artist shows Peter in military dress according to European fashions of the day. *(Rijksmuseum-Stichting, Amsterdam)*

Peter the Great Changes Russia

Peter the Great's reforms included not only monumental building and a new relationship with elites but also practical changes in education, technology, and administration. Writing about a hundred years after the end of Peter's reign, the Russian historian Mikhail Pogodin (1800–1875) reflected on all the changes Peter had introduced, perhaps exaggerating only the respect Peter earned in foreign eyes in his lifetime.

Yes, Peter the Great did much for Russia. . . . One keeps adding and one cannot reach the sum. We cannot open our eyes, cannot make a move, cannot turn in any direction without encountering him everywhere, at home, in the streets, in church, in school, in court, in the regiment. . . .

We wake up. What day is it today? . . . Peter ordered us to count the years from the birth of Christ; Peter ordered us to count the months from January.

It is time to dress—our clothing is made according to the fashion established by Peter the First, our uniform according to his model. The cloth is woven in a factory which he created. . . .

Newspapers are brought in—Peter the Great introduced them.

You must buy different things—they all, from the silk neckerchief to the sole of your shoe, will remind you of Peter. . . . Some were ordered by him . . . or improved by him, carried on his ships, into his harbors, on his canals, on his roads.

Let us go to the university—the first secular school was founded by Peter the Great.

You decide to travel abroad—following [his] example; you will be received well—Peter the Great placed Russia among the European states and began to instill respect for her; and so on and so on.

Source: Nicholas V. Riasanovsky, *A History of Russia*, 2d ed. (London: Oxford University Press, 1969), pp. 266–267.

So he set out to refashion Russian society in what amounted to an enforced cultural revolution. (See the box, "Peter the Great Changes Russia.") He provoked a direct confrontation with Russia's traditional aristocracy over everything from education to matters of dress. He elevated numerous new families to the ranks of gentry and created an official ranking system for the nobility to encourage and reward service to his government.

Peter's effort to reorient his nation culturally, economically, and politically toward Europe was most apparent in the construction of the city of St. Petersburg on the Gulf of Finland, which provided access to the Baltic Sea (see Map 16.2). In stark contrast to Moscow, dominated by the medieval fortress of the Kremlin and churches in the traditional Russian style, St. Petersburg was a modern European city with wide avenues and palaces designed for a sophisticated court life.

But although Peter was highly intelligent, practical, and determined to create a more productive and better governed society, he was also cruel, ruthless, and authoritarian. The building of St. Petersburg cost staggering sums in money and in workers' lives. Peter's entire reform system was carried out autocratically; resistance was brutally suppressed. Victims of Peter's oppression included his son, Alexis, who died after torture while awaiting execution for questioning his father's policies.

Peter faced elite as well as populist rebellions against the exactions and the cultural changes of his regime. The most serious challenge, in 1707, was a revolt of Cossacks of the Don River region against the regime's tightened controls. The primary reason for the high cost of Peter's government to the Russian people was not the tsar's determination to increase his internal power but rather his ambition for territorial gain—hence Peter's emphasis on an improved, and costly, army and navy. Working side by side with workers and technicians, many of whom he had recruited while abroad, Peter created the Russian navy from scratch. At first, ships were built in the south to contest Turkish control of the Black Sea; later, they were built in the north to contest the Baltic. Peter also modernized the Russian army by employing tactics, training, and discipline he had observed in the West. He introduced military conscription. By 1709, Russia was able to manufacture most of the up-to-date firearms its army needed.

Russia waged war virtually throughout Peter's reign. Initially with some success, he struck at the Ottomans and their client state in the Crimea. Later phases of these conflicts brought reverses, however. Peter was spectacularly successful against his northern competitor, Sweden, for control of the weakened Polish state and the Baltic Sea. The conflicts between Sweden and Russia, known as the Second Great Northern War, raged from 1700 to 1709 and, in a less intense phase, lasted until 1721. By the Treaty of Nystadt in 1721, Russia gained the territory in the Gulf of Finland near St. Petersburg that it now has, plus Livonia and Estonia. These acquisitions gave Russia a secure window on the Baltic and, in combination with its gains of Lithuanian territory earlier in the century, made Russia the pre-eminent Baltic power at Sweden's and Poland's expense.

THE RISE OF OVERSEAS TRADE

By the beginning of the seventeenth century, competition from the Dutch, French, and English was disrupting the Spanish and Portuguese trading empires in Asia and the New World. During the seventeenth century, European trade and colonization expanded and changed dramatically. The Dutch not only became masters of the spice trade but led the expansion of that trade to include many other commodities. In the Americas, a new trading system linking Europe, Africa, and the New World came into being with the expansion of sugar and tobacco production. French and English colonists began settling in North America in increasing numbers. By the end of the century, trading and colonial outposts around the world figured regularly as bargaining chips in disagreements be-

tween European states. More importantly, overseas trade had a dramatic impact on life within Europe: on patterns of production and consumption, on social stratification, and the distribution of wealth.

The Growth of Trading Empires: The Success of the Dutch

By the end of the sixteenth century, the Dutch and the English were trying to make incursions into the Portuguese-controlled spice trade with areas of India, Ceylon, and the East Indies. Spain had annexed Portugal in 1580, but the drain on Spain's resources from its wars with the Dutch and French prevented Spain from adequately defending its enlarged trading empire in Asia. The Dutch and, to a lesser degree, the English rapidly supplanted Portuguese control of this lucrative trade (Map 16.3).

The Dutch were particularly well placed to be successful competitors in overseas trade. They already dominated seaborne trade within Europe, including the most important long-distance trade, which linked Spain and Portugal—with their wine and salt, as well as spices, hides, and gold from abroad—with the Baltic seacoast, where these products were sold for grain and timber produced in Germany, Poland-Lithuania, and Scandinavia. The geographic position of the Netherlands and the fact that the Dutch consumed more Baltic grain than any other area, because of their densely urbanized economy, help to explain their dominance of this trade. In addition, the Dutch had improved the design of their merchant ships to enhance their profits. By 1600 they were building the *fluitschip* (flyship) to transport cargo economically; it was a vessel with a long, flat hull and simple rigging and made from cheap materials.

The Dutch were successful in Asia because of institutional as well as technological innovations. In 1602 the Dutch East India Company was formed. The company combined the government management of trade, typical of the period, with both public and private investment. In the past, groups of investors had funded single voyages or small numbers of ships on a one-time basis. The formation of the Dutch East India Company created a permanent pool of capital to sustain trade. After 1612 investments in the company were negotiable as stock. The enlarged pool of capital meant the risks and delays of longer voyages

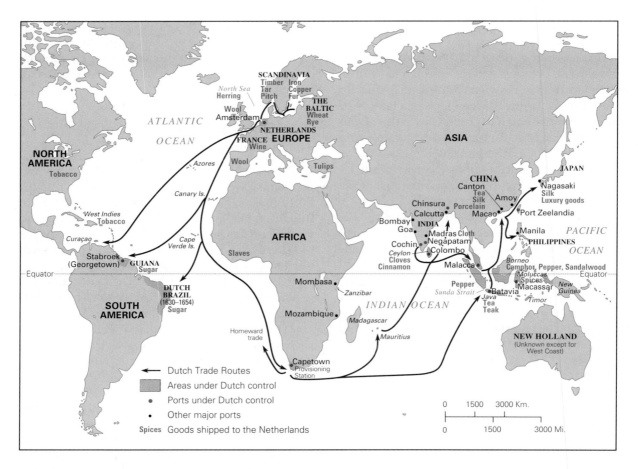

Map 16.3 Dutch Commerce in the Seventeenth Century The Dutch supplanted Portuguese control of trade with Asia and dominated seaborne trade within Europe.

could be spread among larger numbers of investors. In addition, more money was available for warehouses, docks, and ships. The English East India Company, founded in 1607, also supported trade, but more modestly. It had one-tenth the capital of the Dutch company and did not use the same system of permanent capital held as stock by investors until 1657. The Bank of Amsterdam, founded in 1609, became the depository for the bullion that flowed into the Netherlands with trade. The bank established currency-exchange rates and issued paper money and instruments of credit to facilitate commerce.

A dramatic expansion of trade with Asia resulted from the Dutch innovations, so much so that by 1650 the European market for spices was glutted, and traders' profits had begun to fall. To control the supply of spices, the Dutch seized some of the areas where they were produced.

Control of supply helped prop up prices, but these gains were somewhat offset by greater military and administrative costs.

The Dutch and English further responded to the oversupply of spices by diversifying their trade. The proportion of spices in cargoes from the East fell from about 70 percent at midcentury to just over 20 percent by the century's end. New consumer goods such as tea, coffee, silks, and cotton fabrics took their place. The demand of ordinary people for inexpensive yet serviceable Indian cottons grew steadily. Eventually, the Dutch and the English diversified their trade in Asia even more by entering the local carrying trade among Asian states. Doing so enabled them to make profits without purchasing goods, and it slowed the drain of hard currency from Europe—currency in increasingly short supply as silver mines in the Americas were worked out. (See the box, "En-

The Grain Market in Amsterdam Though the Dutch had spectacular success overseas in the seventeenth century, dominance of the carrying trade within Europe, particularly with the Baltic, remained a foundation of its prosperity. Grain exported from the Baltic was the single most important commodity traded in Amsterdam. (*British Library*)

counters with the West: Agents of the Dutch East India Company Confront Asian Powers.")

The "Golden Age" of the Netherlands

The prosperity occasioned by the Netherlands' "mother trade" within Europe and its burgeoning overseas commerce helped to foster social and political conditions unique within Europe. The concentration of trade and shipping sustained a large merchant oligarchy but also an extensive and prosperous artisanal sector. Disparities of wealth were smaller here than anywhere else in Europe. The shipbuilding and fishing trades, among others, supported large numbers of workers with a high standard of living for the age.

Political decentralization in the Netherlands persisted: Each of the seven provinces retained considerable autonomy. However, merchant oligarchs in the Estates of the province of Holland in fact constituted the government for the whole for long periods because of Holland's economic dominance. The head of government was the pensionary (executive secretary) of Holland's Estates. An Estates General existed but had no independent powers of taxation.

The only competition in the running of affairs came from the House of Orange, aristocratic leaders of the revolt against Spain (see pages 553–558). They exercised what control they had by means of the office of *stadholder*— a kind of military governorship—to which they were elected in individual provinces. Their principal interest was the traditional one of military glory and self-promotion. Therein lay a portion of their influence, for they continued to lead the defense of the Netherlands against Spanish attempts at reconquest until the Peace of Westphalia in 1648. Their power also came from the fact that they represented the only possible counterweight within the Netherlands to the dominance of Amsterdam merchant interests. Small towns dependent on land-based trade or rural areas dominated by farmers and gentry looked to the stadholders of the Orange family to defend their interests.

As elsewhere, religion was a source of political conflict. The stadholders and the leading families of Holland, known as regents, vied for control of the state church; the pensionaries and regents of Holland generally favored less rigid and austere Calvinism than the stadholders' faction. This view reflected the needs of the diverse mercantile com-

∼ ENCOUNTERS WITH THE WEST ∼

Agents of the Dutch East India Company Confront Asian Powers

This 1655 letter from a local agent of the Dutch East India Company to its board of directors (the "Seventeen") shows that the Dutch had to maintain good working relationships with local powers in Asia, in this case, with the king of Siam (modern Thailand). The letter discusses the Dutch blockade of Tennasserim, a major port under Siamese control, and the promises of help the Dutch, via their local agents, had made the king for some of his military ventures.

It appears that the merchant Hendrich Craijer Zalr had promised, so they [the Siamese] say, 20 ships, which was a very rash proceeding on his part, and thereupon they made the above-mentioned expedition, which they said, if our support did not appear, would be obliged to return unsuccessful and with shame and dishonor to the crown, as was actually the case. Moreover, it happened that a writing had come unexpectedly from the governor of Tennasserim that two Dutch ships had held the harbor there for 2 months, and had prevented the entrance and departure of foreign traders, which caused great annoyance in Siam, especially at Court, and embittered everyone against us. This gave the [English] Companies very favorable opportunity to blacken us and to make us odious to everyone, and to change the King's feeble opposition into open enmity, the more so since the news has from time to time been confirmed and assured, and no one there doubts it any longer.

Wherefore the resident Westerwolt, who was convinced of the contrary, since he would certainly have been informed before any such action was taken, finally found himself obliged to ask that certain persons, on the King's behalf and on his own, should be deputed and sent overland to Tennasserim, in order to discover on the spot the truth of the case, which request was granted by the King, and on our behalf the junior merchant, Hugo van Crujlenburgh was sent.

Meanwhile the aforementioned resident Westerwolt had on various occasions made complaint of the bad and unreasonable treatment received, . . . so that the resident was in very great embarrassment and did not know whether even his life was any longer safe. These questions were for the most part on the subject of the help asked for against Singgora, the Siamese professing to have gone to war with the Spanish on our account, and to have suffered much damage in the same, and that we now refused to assist his Majesty against the rebels with ships and men; whereas the beforementioned merchant, Hendrich Craijer, had definitely made him such promises.

Source: Records of the Relations Between Siam and Foreign Countries in the Seventeenth Century (Bangkok: Council of the Vajiranana National Library, 1916), vol. 2. Quoted in Alfred J. Andrea and James H. Overfield, The Human Record: Sources of Global History, 2d ed., vol. 2: Since 1500 (Boston: Houghton Mifflin, 1994), pp. 134–135.

munities of Holland, where thousands of Jews as well as Catholics and various kinds of Protestants lived. Foreign policy also turned on Holland's desire for peace in order to foster commerce versus the stadholder's greater willingness to engage in warfare for territory and dynastic advantage.

These differences notwithstanding, Dutch commercial dominance involved them in costly wars throughout the second half of the century. Between 1657 and 1660 the Dutch defended Denmark against Swedish ambitions in order to safeguard the sea-lanes and port cities of the Baltic.

Other, more costly, conflicts arose simply because of rivalry with other states, notably England and France. Under Cromwell, the English attempted to close their ports to the Dutch carrying trade. In 1672 the English under Charles II allied with the French, assuming that together they could destroy Dutch power and perhaps even divide the Netherlands' territory between them. The Dutch navy, rebuilt since Cromwell's challenge, soon forced England out of the alliance.

Owing largely to the land war with France, the Estates in Holland lost control of policy to William of Nassau (d. 1702), prince of Orange after 1672. William drew the Netherlands into his family's long-standing close relationship with England. Like other members of his family before him, William had married into the English royal family: His wife was Mary, daughter of James II.

Ironically, after he and Mary assumed the English throne in 1689 (see page 602), Dutch commerce suffered more in alliance with England than in its previous rivalry. William used Dutch re-

sources for the land war against Louis XIV and reserved for the English navy the fight at sea. Dutch maritime strength was being eclipsed by English seapower by the end of the century.

The Netherlands was controlled by a privileged few for most of the seventeenth century and was virtually a monarchy led from abroad by the end of the century. Nevertheless, the Netherlands appeared to contemporaries to be an astonishing exception to the normal structures of politics. In France and most other states in Europe, political life was dominated by a court where aristocrats and ministers mingled and conspired and an elaborate ritual of honor and deference glorified the king. The princes of Orange surrounded themselves with splendid trappings, but their court was not the sole focus of political life in the Netherlands. The portraits of the Dutch painter Rembrandt van Rijn (1606–1667) portray the austerity of the merchant oligarchs; theirs was a novel kind of power that could be symbolized with ostentatious simplicity.

Rembrandt: The Syndics of the Cloth Drapers' Guild (1662) In this painting, the last group portrait of his career, Rembrandt depicts the guild members with artful, stylized simplicity. It was Rembrandt's genius also to be able to convey a sense of personality and drama in such commissioned portraits. *(Rijksmuseum-Stichting, Amsterdam)*

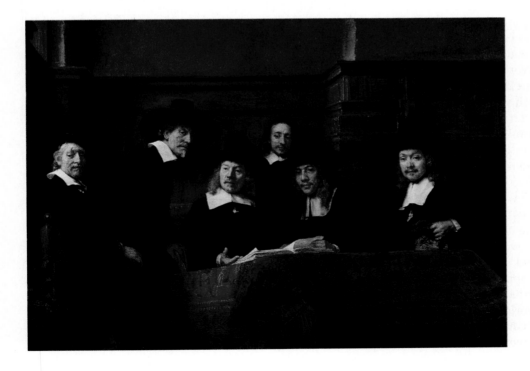

The Growth of Atlantic Colonies and Commerce

In the seventeenth century, the Dutch, the English, and the French joined the Spanish as colonial and commercial powers in the Americas. The Spanish colonial empire, in theory a trading system closed to outsiders, was in fact vulnerable to incursion by other European traders. Spanish treasure fleets themselves were an attraction. In 1628, for example, a Dutch captain seized the entire fleet. But by then Spain's goals and those of its competitors had begun to shift; the limits of an economy based on the extraction of wealth rather than on the production of wealth became clear with the declining output of the Spanish silver mines during the 1620s. In response, the Spanish and their Dutch, French, and English competitors expanded the production of the cash crops of sugar and tobacco.

The European demand for sugar and tobacco, both addictive substances, grew steadily in the seventeenth century. The plantation system—the use of forced labor to work large tracts of land—had been developed on Mediterranean islands in the Middle Ages by European entrepreneurs who used slaves from the Black Sea region as well as local labor. Sugar production by this system was established on Atlantic Islands, using African labor, and then in the Americas by the Spanish and Portuguese. The French, English, and Dutch followed their lead and established sugar plantations on the Caribbean islands they held. Sugar production in the New World grew from about 20,000 tons in 1600 to about 200,000 tons by 1770.

While the Dutch were exploiting Portuguese weakness in the eastern spice trade, they were also seizing sugar regions in Brazil and replacing the Portuguese in slaving ports in Africa. The Portuguese were able to retake some of their Brazilian territory, but because the Dutch monopolized the carrying trade, they were able to become the official supplier of slaves to Spanish plantations in the New World and the chief supplier to most other regions. The Dutch were able to make handsome profits until the end of the seventeenth century, when they were supplanted by the British.

Aware of the great Spanish territorial advantage in the New World, and hoping for treasures such as the Spanish had found, the English, French, and Dutch were also ambitious to explore and settle North America. From the early six-teenth century, French, Dutch, English, and Portuguese seamen had fished and traded off New-foundland. By 1630, small French and Scottish settlements in Acadia (near modern Nova Scotia) and on the St. Lawrence River and English settlements in Newfoundland were established to systematically exploit the timber, fish, and fur of the north Atlantic coasts.

In England population growth and consequent unemployment, as well as religious discontent, created a large pool of potential colonists. The first of the English settlements to endure in what was to become the United States was established at Jamestown, named for James I, in Virginia in 1607. ("Virginia," named for Elizabeth I, the "virgin" queen, was an extremely vague designation for the Atlantic coast of North America and its hinterland.)

The Crown encouraged colonization, but a private company similar to the companies that financed long-distance trade was established actually to organize the enterprise. The directors of the Virginia Company were London businessmen. Investors and would-be colonists purchased shares. Shareholders among the colonists could participate in a colonial assembly, though the governor appointed by the company was the final authority.

The colonists arrived in Virginia with ambitious and optimistic instructions. They were to open mines, establish profitable cultivation, and search for sea routes to Asia. However, the colonists struggled at first merely to survive. (See the box, "The Disappointments of the Virginia Colony.") The indigenous peoples in Virginia, unlike those in Spanish-held territory, were not organized in urbanized, rigidly hierarchical societies that, after conquest, could provide the invaders with a labor force. Indeed, the native Americans in this region were quickly wiped out by European diseases. The introduction of tobacco as a cash crop a few years later saved the colonists economically—though the Virginia Company had already gone bankrupt and the Crown had assumed control of the colony. With the cultivation of tobacco, the Virginia colony, like the Caribbean islands, became dependent on forced, eventually slave, labor.

Among the Virginia colonists were impoverished men and women who came as servants indentured to those who had paid their passage. Colonies established to the north, in what was called "New England," also drew people from the

The Disappointments of the Virginia Colony

In this letter sent to the Virginia Company in 1608, Captain John Smith (1580–1631) explains somewhat angrily that the colony cannot produce the profits that the investors were hoping for. He notes the folly of carrying boats west over the fall line of the Virginia rivers—where, it had been assumed, they might sight the Pacific Ocean as the Spaniards had done in Panama. He reports no sign of the colony of Sir Walter Raleigh, which vanished after settlement in North Carolina in 1587. He also notes the difficulties of extracting wealth and the difficulties of mere survival.

I have received your letter, wherein you write that . . . we feed you but with ifs and ands and hopes, and some few proofs . . . and that we must expressly follow your instructions sent by Captain Newport [the commander of the supply ship], the charge of whose voyage . . . we cannot defray.

For the quartered boat to be borne by the soldiers over the falls, Newport had 120 of the best men. . . . If he had burned her to ashes, one might have carried her in a bag, but as she is, five hundred cannot, to a navigable place above the falls. And for him, at that time to find in the South Sea a mine of gold, or any of them sent by Sir Walter Raleigh, at our consultation I told them was as likely as the rest. . . . In their absence I followed the new begun works of pitch and tar, glass, [potash, and lumber], whereof some small quantities we have sent you. But if you rightly consider, what an infinite toil it is in Russia and [Sweden], where the woods are proper for naught else [and where] there be the help of both man and beast . . . yet thousands of those poor people can scarce get necessaries to live. . . .

From your ship we had not provision in victuals worth twenty pound, and we are more than two hundred to live upon this. . . . Though there be fish in the sea, fowls in the air, and beasts in the woods . . . they are so wild and we so weak and ignorant, we cannot much trouble them.

Source: Philip L. Barbour, ed., *The Complete Works of Captain John Smith (1580–1631)*, vol. 2 (Chapel Hill: University of North Carolina Press, 1986), pp. 187–189.

margins of English society: Early settlers there were religious dissidents. The first to arrive were the Pilgrims, who arrived at New Plymouth (modern Massachusetts) in 1620. They were a community of religious separatists who had originally immigrated to the Netherlands from England for freedom of conscience.

Following the Pilgrims came Puritans escaping escalating persecution under Charles I. The first, in 1629, settled under the auspices of another royally chartered company, the Massachusetts Bay Company. Among their number were many prosperous Puritan merchants and landholders. Independence from investors in London allowed them an unprecedented degree of self-government once the Massachusetts Bay colony was established.

Nevertheless, the colonies in North America were disappointments to England because they generated much less wealth than expected. Shipping timber back to Europe proved too expensive, though New England timber did supply some of the Caribbean colonists' needs. The fur trade became less lucrative as English settlement pushed westward the native Americans who did most of the trapping and as French trappers to the north encroached on the trade. Certain colonists profited enormously from the tobacco economy, but the mother country did so only moderately because the demand in Europe for tobacco never grew as quickly as the demand for sugar.

The colonies' greatest strength, from the English viewpoint, was that the settlements continued

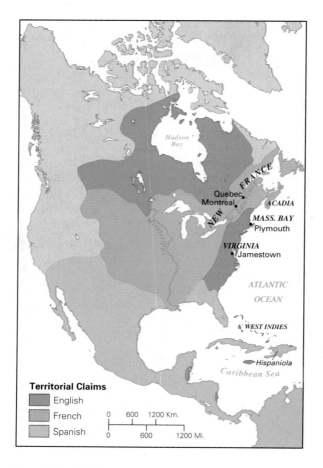

Map 16.4 British and French in North America, ca. 1700 By 1700 a veritable ring of French-claimed territory encircled the coastal colonies of England. English-claimed areas, however, were more densely settled and more economically viable.

partly to the sites of their settlements but mostly to the relationship between the mother country and the colonies. The French hold on territory was always tenuous because of the scant number of colonists from France. There seems to have been less economic impetus for colonization from France than from England. And, after the French crown took over the colonies, there was no religious impetus, for only Catholics were allowed to settle in New France. Moreover, control by the Crown forced a traditional hierarchical political organization on the French colonies. There was a royal governor, and large tracts of land were set aside for privileged investors. Thus, there was little in North America to tempt people of modest means who were seeking a better life.

The first successful French colony was established in Acadia in 1605. This settlement was an exception among the French efforts because it was founded by Huguenots, not by Catholics. A few years later, the intrepid explorer Samuel de Champlain (1567?–1635) navigated the St. Lawrence River and founded Quebec City. He convinced the royal government, emerging from its preoccupations with religious wars at home, to promote the development of the colony. French explorers went on to establish Montreal, farther inland on the St. Lawrence (1642), and to explore the Great Lakes and the Mississippi River basin (see Map 16.4).

Such investment as the French crown was able to attract went into profitable trade, mainly in furs, and not into the difficult business of colonization. French trappers and traders who ventured into wilderness areas were renowned for their hardiness and adaptability, but it was not their business to establish European-style communities. Quebec remained more of a trading station, dependent on shipments of food from France, than a growing urban community. Much of the energy of French colonization was expended by men and women of religious orders bringing their zeal to new frontiers. By the middle of the seventeenth century, all of New France had only about three thousand European inhabitants.

The seeming weakness of the French colonial effort in North America was not much noticed at the time. French and English fishermen, trappers, and traders competed intensely with each other, and there were outright battles between English and French settlements. But for both England and

to attract migrants. By 1640 Massachusetts had some 14,000 European inhabitants. Through most of the next century, the growth of colonial populations in North America would result in an English advantage over the French in control of territory. In the long run, however, the size of the colonial communities, their degree of routine political independence from the mother country, and their loose economic ties to England led them to seek independence.

The French began their settlement of North America at the same time as the English, in the same push to compensate for their mutual weakness vis-à-vis the Spanish (Map 16.4). The French efforts, however, had very different results, owing

France the major profits and strategic interests in the New World lay to the south, in the Caribbean. The Dutch experience in North America reveals the degree to which North America was of secondary importance, for all colonial powers, to the plantation profits farther south. In 1624 the Dutch founded a trading center, New Amsterdam, at the site of modern New York City. In 1674 they relinquished it to the English in return for recognition of the Dutch claims to sugar-producing Guiana (modern Suriname) in South America. Consequently, by far the largest group of migrants to European-held territories in the Americas were forced migrants: African men and women sold into slavery and transported across the Atlantic. A conservative estimate is that approximately 1,350,000 Africans were forcibly transported as slave labor to the New World during the seventeenth century.

The Beginning of the End of Traditional Society

Within Europe, the economic impact of overseas trade was profound. Merchants and investors in a few of Europe's largest cities reaped great profits. Mediterranean trading centers such as Venice and Genoa, once the heart of European trade, did not share in the profits generated by goods now being shipped to and from the New World. Atlantic ports such as Seville, through which most Spanish commerce with the New World flowed, and, above all, Amsterdam began to flourish. The population of Amsterdam increased from about 30,000 to 200,000 in the course of the seventeenth century.

All capital cities, however, not just seaports, grew substantially in the seventeenth century. Increasing numbers of government functionaries, courtiers and their hangers-on, and people involved in trade lived and worked in capital cities. These cities also grew indirectly from the demand such people generated for services and products, ranging from fashionable clothing to exotic foodstuffs. For the first time, cities employed vast numbers of country people. Perhaps as much as one-fifth of the population of England passed through London at one time or another, creating the mobile, volatile community so active in the English civil war and its aftermath.

The economy became more productive and flexible as it expanded, but social stratification in-

Marie de l'Incarnation, Colonial Settler Marie Guyart (1599–1672), as she was known in lay life, was an Ursuline nun who abandoned her own family in France to help found a convent and school for girls in Quebec, Canada. She welcomed both settlers' daughters and Native American girls to the school; she also learned several Amerindian languages during her life. *(Thomas Fisher Rare Book Library, University of Toronto)*

creased. Patterns of consumption in cities reflected the economic gulfs between residents. Most people could not afford to buy imported pepper or sugar. Poverty increased in cities, even in vibrant Amsterdam, because they attracted people fleeing rural unemployment. As growing central governments increased their tax burdens on peasants, many rural people were caught in a cycle of debt; they abandoned farming and made their way to cities.

Many such people on the margins of economic life were innovative in their efforts to survive, but they were increasingly vulnerable to both economic forces and state power. Thousands of rural people, particularly those close to thriving urban centers, supplemented their farm income by means of the putting-out system, or cottage industry. An entrepreneur loaned, or "put out," raw materials to rural workers, who processed them at home and returned a finished product to the entrepreneur. For example, the rural workers might receive wool to be spun and woven into cloth. The entrepreneur would pay the workers by the piece and then sell the finished product. In the long run, the putting-out system left workers open to economic vulnerability of a new, more modern, sort. A local harvest failure might still endanger them, and so might a foreign war or disaster at sea that affected the long-distance trade for their product.

Peasant rebellions occurred throughout the century as a result of depressed economic conditions and heavy taxation. Some of the revolts were extremely localized and involved limited direct action, such as seizing the tax collector's grain or stopping the movement of grain to the great cities. Urban demand for grain often caused severe shortages in rural areas in western Europe, despite the booming trade in grain with eastern Europe via the Baltic.

The typical peasant revolt in western Europe during the seventeenth century, however, was directed against escalating taxation. Tax rebellions often formed spontaneously, perhaps as tax officials passed through a village, but they were not mere chaotic gatherings of rabble. Countryfolk were accustomed to defending themselves as communities—against brigands and marauding soldiers, for example. Local gentry and even prosperous peasants might ordinarily fulfill the function of local constable or other lowly state office and generally be interested in maintaining order; yet they led such revolts from time to time, convinced that they represented the legitimate interests of the community against rapacious officials higher up. The scale of peasant violence meant that thousands of troops at times had to be diverted from a state's foreign wars; as a matter of routine, soldiers accompanied tax officials and enforced collection all over Europe. Thus, as the ambitions of rulers grew, so too did resistance of ordinary people to the exactions of the state.

SUMMARY

The beginning of the seventeenth century was marked by religious turmoil and by social and political upheaval. By the end of the century, the former had faded as a source of collective anxiety, and the latter was largely resolved. Nascent political configurations in the Low Countries, in the Holy Roman Empire, and on the frontiers of eastern Europe had evolved into new centers of power: the Netherlands, Brandenburg-Prussia, and the newly powerful Russia of Peter the Great. Most European states had moved from internal division—with independent provinces and aristocrats going their own way—to relative stability. This internal stability was both cause and consequence of rulers' desire to make war on an ever larger scale. By the end of the century, only those states able to field large armies were competitive on the European stage.

At the beginning of the century, overseas trade and colonization had been the near monopoly of Spain and Portugal; at the century's end, the English, French, and Dutch controlled much of the trade with Asia and were reaping many profits in the Americas. Beneath all these developments lay subtle but significant economic, social, and cultural shifts. One effect of the increased wealth generated by overseas trade and the increased power of governments to tax their subjects was a widening of the gulf between poor and rich. New styles of behavior and patterns of consumption highlighted differences between social classes. Long-term effects of overseas voyages on European attitudes, as well as fundamental change in viewing the world culminating in the development of modern science, would have revolutionary effects on Europeans and their cultures.

NOTES

1. Quoted in D. H. Pennington, *Europe in the Seventeenth Century,* 2d ed. (London: Longman, 1989), p. 508.

SUGGESTED READING

General Surveys
Howard, Michael. *War in European History.* 1976. A general study of warfare emphasizing the relationship between war making and state development.

Pennington, D. H. *Europe in the Seventeenth Century.* 2d ed. 1989; and Bonney, Richard. *The European Dynastic*

States, 1494–1660. 1991. Two general histories covering various portions of the century.

France

Beik, William. *Absolutism and Society in Seventeenth-Century France.* 1984. A case study focusing on a province in southern France but nevertheless an important interpretation of the nature and functioning of the absolutist state; has an extensive bibliography.

Collins, James B. *The State in Early Modern France.* 1995. An up-to-date synthesis by one of the leading scholars of French absolutism.

Goubert, Pierre. *The French Peasantry in the Seventeeth Century.* 1986.

———. *Louis XIV and Twenty Million Frenchmen.* 1970. Two works that consider political and social history from a broad analytic framework that includes long-term economic, demographic, and cultural data.

England

Aylmer, G. E. *Rebellion or Revolution? England from Civil War to Restoration.* 1987. A useful work that summarizes the important studies on each facet of the revolution; has an extensive bibliography.

Hill, Christopher. *A Century of Revolution, 1603–1714.* Rev. ed. 1980.

———. *The World Turned Upside Down.* 1972. The first work is a general history, the second an exploration of Levelers, Diggers, and other groups of lower-class participants in the English revolution.

Stone, Lawrence. *The Causes of the English Revolution, 1529–1642.* 1972. A brief and clear introduction.

Central and Eastern Europe

Bérenger, Jean. *A History of the Hapsburg Empire, 1273–1700.* 1990. A detailed and nuanced history of all the Habsburg domains and of the Habsburgs' relationship to Europe as a whole.

Kirby, David. *Northern Europe in the Early Modern Period, 1492–1772.* 1990.

Oakley, Stewart P. *War and Peace in the Baltic, 1560–1790.* 1992. Two excellent surveys of the Baltic region in the early modern period.

Riasanovsky, Nicolas V. *A History of Russia.* 2d ed. 1969. A reliable and readable survey of Russian history from medieval times; has an extensive bibliography of major works available in English.

Vierhaus, Rudolf. *Germany in the Age of Absolutism.* 1988. A concise survey of the development of German states from the end of the Thirty Years' War through the eighteenth century.

Wandycz, Piotr. *The Price of Freedom: A History of East Central Europe from the Middle Ages to the Present.* 1992.

A lively survey of the histories of Poland, Hungary, and Bohemia.

Early Modern Economy, Society, and Culture

Alpers, Svetlana. *The Art of Describing: Dutch Art in the Seventeenth Century.* 1983. An innovative approach to Dutch art, considering it in its social and broader cultural context.

Bercé, Yves-Marie. *Revolt and Revolution in Early Modern Europe.* Translated by Joseph Bergin. 1987.

———. *History of Peasant Revolts.* Translated by A. Whitmore. 1990. The first work is a general, comparative survey of revolts and revolutionary movements of all sorts across Europe between 1500 and 1800; the second is a more intensive study of French peasant movements.

Blum, Jerome. *Lord and Peasant in Russia.* 1961. A work that highlights the extension of serfdom in Russia fostered by Peter the Great and other tsars.

Boxer, C. R. *The Dutch Seaborne Empire.* 1965. The standard work detailing the development of the Dutch empire.

Curtin, Philip D. *The Rise and Fall of the Plantation Complex.* 1990. A good starting place for understanding the reasons behind and the significance of Europeans' establishment of plantation agriculture in the New World.

De Vries, Jan. *The Economy of Europe in an Age of Crisis, 1600–1750.* 1976. The single most important work on the development of the European economy in this period, integrating developments within and around Europe with the growth of overseas empires.

Parry, J. H. *The Establishment of European Hegemony, 1415–1715.* 1961. A brief introduction to the motives, means, and results of European expansion through the seventeenth century; somewhat dated in its overemphasis on the English in North America but nevertheless a useful overview.

Ritchie, Robert C. *Captain Kidd and the War Against the Pirates.* 1986. An interesting work on the communities of castoffs and adventurers that grew up in the Caribbean during European expansion and their place in the Atlantic economic and political worlds.

Sabean, David Warren. *Power in the Blood.* 1984. An innovative series of essays about life in German villages from the sixteenth through the eighteenth centuries; raises questions about the increasing efforts of the state to control village life and the resistance mounted by villagers to these efforts.

Wolf, Eric R. *Europe and the People Without History.* 1982. A survey of European contact with and conquest of peoples after 1400; includes extensive treatments of non-European societies and detailed explanation of the economic and political interests of the Europeans.

TABLE MANNERS

If you were to sit down in a fancy restaurant, order a juicy steak, and then eat it with your bare hands, other diners would undoubtedly stare and think what bad manners you have. It has not always been the case that table manners meant very much—were able to signal social status, for example. It was not always the case that table manners existed at all in the sense that we know them. How did they evolve? How did they come to have the importance that they do? And why should historians pay any attention to them?

Imagine that you have been invited to dinner at a noble estate in the year 1500. As you sit down, you notice that there are no knives, forks, and spoons at your place at the table, and no napkins either. A servant (a young girl from a neighboring village) sets a roast of meat in front of you and your fellow diners. The lords and ladies on either side of you hack off pieces of meat with the knives that they always carry with them, and then they eat the meat with their fingers. Hunks of bread on the table in front of them catch the dripping juices.

One hundred fifty years later, in 1650, dinner is a much more "civilized" meal. Notice the well-to-do women dining in this engraving by the French artist Abraham Bosse (1602–1676). The table setting, with tablecloths, napkins, plates, and silverware, is recognizable to us. The lady at the extreme right holds up her fork and napkin in a somewhat forced and obvious gesture. These diners have the utensils that we take for granted, but the artist does not take them for granted: They are intended to be noticed by Bosse's elite audience.

In the seventeenth century, aristocrats and gentry signaled their political and social privilege with behavior that distinguished them from the lower classes in ways their more powerful ancestors had felt no need for. Historians have called this the invention of civility. As we have seen, proper courtesy to one's superiors at court was considered essential. It marked the fact that rituals of honor and deference were increasingly taking the place of armed conflict as the routine behavior of the upper classes. Also essential, however, were certain standards of physical privacy and delicacy. Something as seemingly trivial as the use of a fork became charged with symbolic significance. As the actual power of the aristocrats was circumscribed by the state, they found new expressions of status. Since the sixteenth century, new kinds of manners had been touted in handbooks, reflecting changes that already had occurred at Italian courts. During the seventeenth century, these practices became more widespread and opened up a gulf of behavior between upper and lower classes.

Some of the new behaviors concerned bodily privacy and discretion. A nobleman now used a handkerchief instead of his fingers or coat sleeve, and he did not urinate in public. The new "rules" about eating are particularly interesting. Why did eating with a fork seem refined and desirable to aristocrats trying to buttress their own self-image? As any 3-year-old knows, eating with a fork is remarkably inefficient.

Using a fork kept you at a distance—literal and symbolic—from the animal you were eating. Napkins wiped away all trace of bloody juices from your lips. Interestingly, as diners began to use utensils, other eating arrangements changed in parallel ways. Sideboards had been in use for a long time, but pieces of meat were now discreetly carved on the sideboard and presented to diners in individual portions. The carcass was brought to the sideboard cut into roasts instead of unmistakably whole, and it was often decorated—as it is today—to further disguise it.

The new aristocrat was increasingly separated from the world of brute physical force, both in daily life and on the battlefield. In warfare, brute force was no longer adequate. Training, discipline, and tactical knowledge were more important and heightened the significance of rank,

Table Manners of the Upper Class in the Seventeenth Century *(Courtesy of the Trustees of the British Museum)*

which separated officers from the vast numbers of common soldiers (see page 595). Aristocrats now lived in a privileged world where violence was no longer a fact of life. Their new behavior codes signaled their new invulnerability to others. Above all, they worked to transform a loss—of the independence that had gone hand in hand with a more violent life—into a gain: a privileged immunity to violence.

Specific manners became important, then, because they were symbols of power. The symbolic distance between the powerful and the humble was reinforced by other changes in habits and behavior. A sixteenth-century warrior customarily traveled on horseback and often went from place to place within a city on foot, attended by his ret-

inue. A seventeenth-century aristocrat was more likely to travel in a horsedrawn carriage. The presence of special commodities from abroad—such as sugar—in the seventeenth century created further possibilities for signaling status.

It is interesting to note that other personal habits still diverged dramatically from what we would consider acceptable today. Notice the large, stately bed in the same room as the dining table in Bosse's engraving. Interior space was still undifferentiated by our standards, and it was common for eating, talking, sleeping, and estate management all to go on in a single room. The grand bed is in the picture because, like the fork, it is a mark of status. Like virtually everything else, what is "proper" varies with historical circumstance. ✎

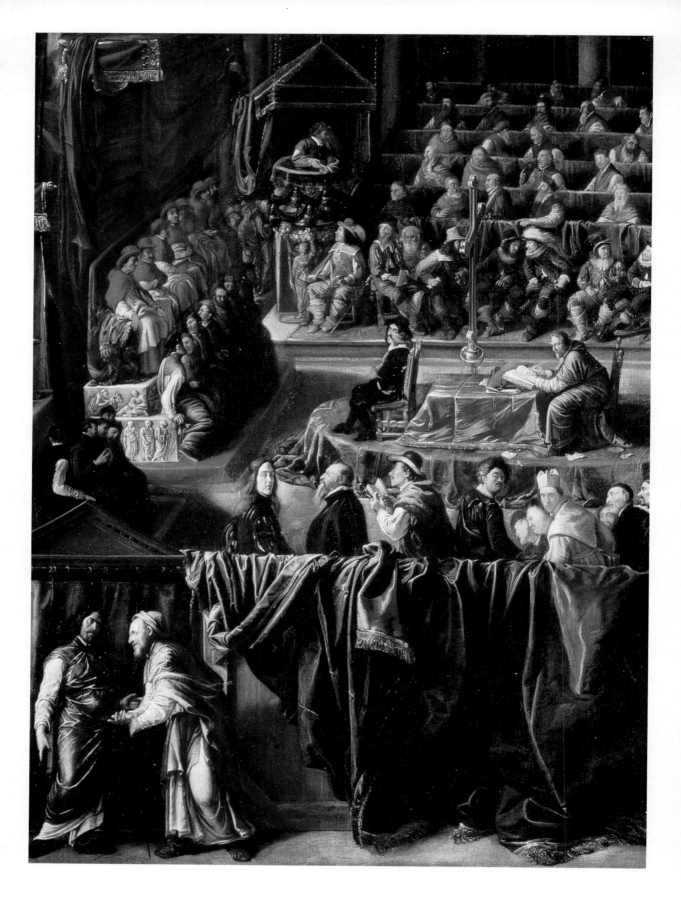

CHAPTER 17

A Revolution in World-View

As famous as the confrontation between the religious rebel Martin Luther and Holy Roman Emperor Charles V at Worms in 1521 is the confrontation between the astronomer Galileo and the judges of the papal inquisition that ended on June 22, 1633. On that day, Galileo knelt before the seven cardinals who represented the inquisition to renounce his errors and to receive his punishment. His "errors" included publishing scientific propositions that disagreed with views accepted by the church—particularly the view that the earth is stationary and does not spin on its axis and orbit the sun. As Galileo left the cardinals' presence, he is supposed to have muttered, "Eppur si muove" ("But it *does* move").

This seems a wonderful moment of historical drama, but we should be suspicious of it because it oversimplifies historical circumstances. The changes that we know as "the Reformation" and "the Scientific Revolution" were far more complex than the actions of a few individuals whose deeds now seem heroic and larger than life. Galileo, in fact, never made the defiant statement he is credited with.

Moreover, just as we cannot simply credit "heroes" with causing a revolution in scientific understanding, we cannot treat their new scientific views simply as truth finally overcoming ignorance and error. The history of scientific thought is not merely a history of discovery about the world; it is also a history of explanations of the world. From its beginnings the Scientific Revolution was a broad cultural movement. Copernicus, Galileo, and others contributed important new data to the pool of knowledge, but even more important was their collective contribution to a fundamentally

Trial of Galileo before
the inquisition, 1633.
(Anonymous, 17th century.)

new view of the universe and of the place of the earth and human beings in it.

By the end of the seventeenth century, a vision of an infinite but orderly cosmos appealing to human reason had largely replaced the medieval vision of a closed universe centered on earth and suffused with Christian purpose. Religion became an increasingly subordinate ally of science as confidence in an open-ended, experimental approach to knowledge came to be as strongly held as religious conviction. It is because of this larger shift in world-view, not because of particular scientific discoveries, that the seventeenth century may be labeled the era of the scientific *revolution*.

THE REVOLUTION IN ASTRONOMY

Because the Scientific Revolution was a revolution within science itself as well as a revolution in intellectual life more generally, we must seek its causes within the history of science as well as in the broader historical context. Many of the causes are familiar. They include the intellectual achievements of the Renaissance, the challenges that were posed by the discovery of the New World, the expansion of trade and production, the spread of literacy and access to books, and the increasing power of princes and monarchs.

The scientific origins of the seventeenth-century revolution in thought lie, for the most part, in developments in astronomy. Various advances in astronomy spurred dramatic intellectual transformation because of astronomy's role in the explanations of the world and of human life that had been devised by ancient and medieval scientists and philosophers. By the early part of the seventeenth century, fundamental astronomical tenets were successfully challenged. The consequence was the undermining of both the material explanation of the world (physics) and the philosophical explanation of the world (metaphysics) that had been standing for centuries.

The Inherited World-View and the Sixteenth-Century Context

Ancient and medieval astronomy accepted the perspective on the universe that unaided human senses support—namely, that the earth is at the center of the universe, and the celestial bodies ro-

tate around the earth. The intellectual and psychological journey from the notion of a closed world centered on the earth to an infinitely large universe of undifferentiated matter with no apparent place for humans was an immense process with complex causes.

The regular movements of heavenly bodies and the obvious importance of the sun for life on earth made astronomy a vital undertaking for both scientific and religious purposes in many ancient societies. Astronomers in ancient Greece carefully observed the heavens and learned to calculate and to predict the seemingly circular motion of the stars and the sun about the earth. The orbits of the planets were more difficult to explain, for the planets seemed to travel both east and west across the sky at various times and with no regularity that could be mathematically understood. Indeed, the very word *planet* comes from a Greek word meaning "wanderer."

We now know that all the planets simultaneously orbit the sun at different speeds and are at different distances from the sun. The relative positions of the planets thus constantly change; sometimes other planets are "ahead" of the earth and sometimes "behind." In the second century A.D. the Greek astronomer Ptolemy attempted to explain the planets' occasional "backward" motion by attributing it to "epicycles"—small circular orbits within the larger orbit. Ptolemy's mathematical explanations of the imagined epicycles were extremely complex, but neither Ptolemy nor medieval mathematicians and astronomers were ever able fully to account for planetary motion.

Ancient physics, most notably the work of Aristotle (384–322 B.C.), explained the fact that some objects (such as cannonballs) fall to earth but others (stars and planets) seem weightless relative to the earth by presuming that objects are made up of different sorts of matter. Aristotle thought that different kinds of matter had different inherent tendencies and properties. In this view, all earthbound matter (like cannonballs) falls because it is naturally attracted to earth—heaviness being a property of earthbound things.

In the Christian era, the Aristotelian explanation of the universe was infused with Christian meaning and purpose. The heavens were said to be made of different, pure matter because they were the abode of the angels. Both earth and the humans who inhabited it were changeable and

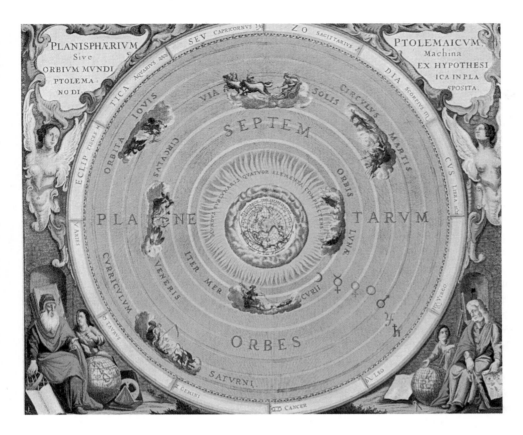

The Traditional Universe In this print from around 1600, heavenly bodies are depicted orbiting the earth in perfectly circular paths. In fact, the ancient astronomer Ptolemy believed that the planets followed complex orbits-within-orbits, known as *epicycles,* moving around the stationary earth. *(Hulton-Getty/Tony Stone Images)*

corruptible. Yet God had given human beings a unique and special place in the universe. The universe was thought to be literally a closed world with the stationary earth at the center. Revolving around the earth in circular orbits were the sun, the moon, the stars, and the planets. The motion of all lesser bodies was caused by the rotation of all the stars together in the crystal-like sphere in which they were embedded.

A few ancient astronomers theorized that the earth moved about the sun. Some medieval philosophers also adopted this heliocentric thesis (*helios* is the Greek word for "sun"), but it remained a minority view because it seemed to contradict both common sense and observed data. The sun and stars *appeared* to move around the earth with great regularity. Moreover, how could objects fall to earth if the earth was moving beneath them? Also, astronomers detected no difference in angles from which observers on earth viewed the stars at different times. Such differences would exist, they thought, if the earth changed positions by moving around the sun. It was inconceivable that the universe could be so large and the stars so distant that the earth's movement would produce no measurable change in the earth's position with respect to the stars.

Several conditions of intellectual life in the sixteenth century encouraged new work in astronomy and led to revision of the earth-centered world-view. The most important was the humanists' recovery of and commentary on ancient texts. Now able to work with new Greek versions of Ptolemy, mathematicians and astronomers noted that his explanations for the motions of the planets were imperfect and not simply inadequately transmitted, as they had long believed. Also, the discovery of the New World dramatically undercut the assumption that ancient knowledge was superior and specifically undermined Ptolemy's authority once again, for it disproved many of his assertions about geography.

The desire to explain heavenly motions better was still loaded with religious significance in the sixteenth century and was heightened by the immediate need for reform of the Julian calendar (named for Julius Caesar). Ancient observations of the movement of the sun, though remarkably accurate, could not measure the precise length of the solar year. By the sixteenth century, the cumulative error of this calendar had resulted in a change of ten days: The spring equinox fell on March 11 instead of March 21. An accurate and uniform system of dating was necessary for all rulers and their tax collectors and recordkeepers but was the particular project of the church, because the calculation of the date of Easter was at stake.

Impetus for new and better astronomical observations and calculations arose from other features of the intellectual and political landscape as well. Increasingly as the century went on, princely courts became important sources of patronage for and sites of scientific activity. Rulers eager to buttress their own power by symbolically linking it to dominion over nature sponsored investigations of the world, as Ferdinand and Isabella had so successfully done, and displayed the marvels of nature at their courts. Sponsoring scientific inquiry also yielded practical benefits: better mapping of the ruler's domains and better technology for mining, gunnery, and navigation.

Finally, schools of thought fashionable at the time, encouraged by the humanists' critique of Scholastic tradition, hinted at the possibilities of alternative physical and metaphysical systems. The first was Paracelsianism, named for the Swiss physician Philippus von Hohenheim (1493–1541), known as Paracelsus. Paracelsus offered an alternative to the theory, put forth by the ancient master, Galen (ca. 131–ca. 201), that the imbalance of bodily "humors" caused illness. He substituted a theory of chemical imbalance.

Neo-Platonism, the second school of thought, had a more systematic and far-reaching impact. Neo-Platonism, a revival primarily in Italian humanist circles of certain aspects of Plato's thought, contributed directly to innovation in science because it emphasized the abstract nature of true knowledge and thus encouraged mathematical investigation. This provided a spur to astronomical studies, which, since ancient times, had been con-

cerned more with mathematical analysis of heavenly movements than with physical explanations for them. Also, like Paracelsianism, Neo-Platonism had a mystical dimension that encouraged creative speculation about the nature of matter and the organization of the universe. Neo-Platonists were particularly fascinated by the sun as a symbol of the one divine mind or soul at the heart of all creation.

The Copernican Challenge

Nicolaus Copernicus (1473–1543), son of a prosperous Polish merchant, pursued wide-ranging university studies in philosophy, law, astronomy, and mathematics—first in Cracow in Poland and then in Bologna and Padua in Italy. In Italy he was exposed to Neo-Platonic ideas. He took a degree in canon law in 1503 and became a cathedral canon in the city of Frauenburg in East Prussia (modern Poland), where he pursued his own interests in astronomy while carrying out administrative duties for the cathedral. When the pope asked Copernicus to assist with the reform of the Julian calendar, he replied that reform of the calendar required reform in astronomy. His major work, *De Revolutionibus Orbium Caelestium* (*On the Revolution of Heavenly Bodies*, 1543), was dedicated to the pope in the hopes that it would help with the task of calendar reform—as indeed it did. The Gregorian calendar, issued in 1582 during the pontificate of Gregory XIII (r. 1572–1585), was based on Copernicus's calculations.

Copernicus postulated that the earth and all the other planets orbit the sun. He did not assert that the earth does in fact move around the sun but offered the heliocentric system as a mathematical construct, useful for predicting the movements of planets, stars, and the sun. However, he walked a thin line between making claims for mathematical and physical reality. He had searched in ancient sources for thinkers who believed the earth did move. Other astronomers familiar with his work and reputation urged him to publish the results of his calculations. But not until 1542, twelve years after finishing the work, did he send *De Revolutionibus* to be published; he received a copy just before his death the next year. (See the box, "Copernicus's Preface to *On the Revolution of Heavenly Bodies*.")

Copernicus's colleagues were right: His work was immediately useful. Copernicus's schema

Copernicus's Preface to *On the Revolution of Heavenly Bodies*

In this dedicatory letter to the pope, Copernicus explains his desire to assist with calendar reform. Principally, however, he seeks to justify his novel conclusions. He not only cites ancient authority for the movement of the earth but also stresses the mathematical nature of the problem and of his solution.

To the Most Holy Lord, Pope Paul III

I may well presume, most Holy Father, that certain people, as soon as they hear that in this book about the Revolutions of the Spheres of the Universe I ascribe movement to the earthly globe, will cry out that, holding such views, I should at once be hissed off the stage. . . . How I came to dare to conceive such motion of the Earth, contrary to the received opinion of the Mathematicians and indeed contrary to the impression of the senses, is what your Holiness will rather expect to hear. So I should like your Holiness to know that I was induced to think of a method of computing the motions of the spheres by nothing else than the knowledge that the Mathematicians are inconsistent in these investigations. . . . Mathematicians are so unsure of the movements of the Sun and the Moon that they cannot even explain . . . the constant length of the seasonal year.

. . . I pondered long upon this uncertainty of mathematical tradition. I . . . read again the works of all the philosophers on whom I could lay a hand to seek out whether any of them had ever supposed that the motions of the spheres were other[wise]. I found first in Cicero that Hicetas [of Syracuse, fifth century B.C.] had realized that the earth moved. . . . Mathematics are for mathematicians, and they, if I be not wholly deceived, will hold that my labors contribute somewhat . . . to the Church. . . . For under Leo X, the question of correcting the ecclesiastical calendar was . . . left undecided.

Source: Thomas S. Kuhn, *The Copernican Revolution* (Cambridge, Mass.: Harvard University Press, 1985), pp. 137–143.

made possible a simpler explanation of all planetary motion. For example, he accounted for most backward motion without resorting to epicycles. But Copernicus still assumed that the planets traveled in circular orbits, so he retained some epicycles to account for the circular motion.

By positing the earth's movement around the sun but also retaining features of the old system, such as circular orbits, Copernicus faced burdens of explanation not faced by Ptolemy. In general, however, the Copernican account of planetary motion was simpler than the Ptolemaic account. It appealed to other astronomers of the age because it was useful and because it highlighted the harmony of heavenly motion, which remained a fundamental physical and metaphysical principle. Accessible only to other astronomers, Copernicus's work only slowly led to conceptual revolution, as astronomers worked with his calculations and assembled other evidence to support the heliocentric theory.

The most important reason that Copernican theory only gradually led to fundamental conceptual change was that Copernicus did not resolve the physical problems his theory raised. If Copernicus were right, the earth would have to be made of the same stuff as other planets. How, then, would Copernicus explain the motion of objects on earth—the fact that they fall to the earth—if it was not in their nature to fall toward the heavy, stationary earth? In Copernicus's system, the movement of the earth caused the *apparent* motion of the stars. But if the stars did not rotate in their crystalline sphere, what made all other heavenly bodies move?

Copernicus was not as troubled by these questions as we might expect him to be. Since ancient

MILESTONES OF THE SCIENTIFIC REVOLUTION

1543	Copernicus, *On the Revolution of Heavenly Bodies*
	Vesalius, *On the Fabric of the Human Body*
1576	Construction of Brahe's observatory begins
1591	Galileo's law of falling bodies
1609	Kepler's third law of motion
1610	Galileo, *The Starry Messenger*
1620	Bacon, *Novum Organum*
1628	Harvey, *On the Motion of the Heart*
1632	Galileo, *Dialogue on the Two Chief Systems of the World*
1637	Descartes, *Discourse on Method*
1660	Boyle, *New Experiments Physico-Mechanical*
1668	Cavendish, *Grounds of Natural Philosophy*
1687	Newton, *Principia*

times, mathematical astronomy—the science of measuring and predicting the movement of heavenly bodies—had been far more important than, and had proceeded independently of, physical explanations for observed motion. Nevertheless, as Copernicus's own efforts to buttress his notion that the earth moves reveal, his theories directly contradicted many of the supposed laws of motion. The usefulness of his theories to other astronomers meant that the contradictions between mathematical and physical models for the universe would have to be resolved. Copernicus himself might be best understood as the last Ptolemaic astronomer, working within inherited questions and with known tools. His work itself did not constitute a revolution, but it did initiate one.

The First Copernican Astronomers

In the first generation of astronomers after the publication of *De Revolutionibus* in 1543 we can see the effects of Copernicus's work. His impressive computations rapidly won converts among fellow astronomers. Several particularly gifted astronomers

continued to develop the Copernican system. Thus, by the second quarter of the seventeenth century, they and many others accepted the heliocentric theory as a reality and not just as a useful mathematical fiction. The three most important astronomers to build on Copernican assumptions, and on the work of each other, were the Dane Tycho Brahe (1546–1601), the German Johannes Kepler (1571–1630), and the Italian Galileo Galilei (1564–1642).

Like generations of observers before him, Tycho Brahe had been stirred by the majesty of the regular movements of heavenly bodies. After witnessing a partial eclipse of the sun, he abandoned a career in government and became an astronomer. Brahe was the first truly post-Ptolemaic astronomer because he was the first to improve on the data that the ancients and all subsequent astronomers had used. Ironically, *no* theory of planetary motion or mathematics to explain it could have reconciled the data that Copernicus had used: They were simply too inaccurate, based as they were on naked-eye observations, even when errors of translation and copying, accumulated over centuries, had been corrected.

In 1576 the king of Denmark showered Brahe with properties and pensions enabling him to build an observatory, Uraniborg, on an island near Copenhagen. At Uraniborg, Brahe improved on ancient observations with large and very finely calibrated instruments that permitted precise measurements of celestial movements by the naked eye. His attention to precision and frequency of observation produced results that were twice as accurate as any previous data had been.

As a result of his observations, Brahe agreed with Copernicus that the various planets did rotate around the sun, not around the earth. He still could not be persuaded that the earth itself moved, for none of his data supported such a notion. Brahe's lasting and crucial contribution was his astronomical data. They would become obsolete as soon as data from use of the telescope were accumulated about a century later. But in the meantime, they were used by Johannes Kepler to further develop Copernicus's model and arrive at a more accurate heliocentric theory.

Kepler was young enough to be exposed to Copernican ideas from the outset of his training, and he quickly recognized in Brahe's data the means of resolving the problems in Copernican analysis. Though trained in his native Germany,

STELLÆBURGUM sive OBSERVATORIUM SUBTERRANEUM, A TYCHONE BRAHE Nobili Dano
IN INSULA HVÆNA, EXTRA ARCEM URANIAM, EXTRVCTVM CIRCA ANNVM M D LXXXIIII.

Tycho Brahe's Observatory Brahe's fame was initially established by his observation and measurement of a new star in 1572, but his enduring contribution to astronomy was the meticulous collection of data by means of the instruments assembled at Uraniborg. *(The Fotomas Index)*

Kepler went to Prague, where Brahe spent the last years of his life after a quarrel with the Danish king, and became something of an apprentice to Brahe. After Brahe's death in 1601, Kepler kept his mentor's records of astronomical observation and continued to work at the imperial court as Rudolf II's court mathematician.

Kepler's contribution to the new astronomy, like that of Copernicus, was fundamentally mathematical. In it, we can see the stamp of the Neo-Platonic conviction about the purity of mathematical explanation. Kepler spent ten years working to apply Brahe's data to the most intricate of all the celestial motions—the movement of the planet Mars—as a key to explaining all planetary motion. Mars is close to the earth but farther from the sun than is the earth. This combination produces very puzzling and dramatic variations in the apparent movement of Mars to an earthly observer.

The result of Kepler's work was laws of planetary motion that, in the main, are still in use.

First, Kepler eliminated the need for epicycles by correctly asserting that planets follow elliptical and not circular orbits. Elliptical orbits could account, both mathematically and visually, for the motions of the planets when combined with Kepler's second law, which described the *rate* of a planet's motion around its orbital path. Kepler noted that the speed of a planet in its orbit slows proportionally as the planet's distance from the sun increases. A third law demonstrated that the distance of each planet from the sun and the time it takes each planet to orbit the sun are in a constant ratio.

Kepler's work was a breakthrough because it mathematically confirmed the Copernican heliocentric hypothesis. In so doing, the work directly challenged the ancient world-view, in which heavenly bodies constantly moved in circular orbits around a stationary earth. Hence, Kepler's laws invited speculation about the properties and motion of heavenly and terrestrial bodies alike. A new physics would be required to explain the novel motions that Kepler had posited. Kepler himself, in Neo-Platonic fashion, attributed planetary motion to the sun:

[The sun] is a fountain of light, rich in fruitful heat, most fair, limpid and pure . . . called king of the planets for his motion, heart of the world for his power. . . . Who would hesitate to confer the votes of the celestial motions on him who has been administering all other movements and changes by the benefit of the light which is entirely his possession?[1]

Galileo and the Triumph of Copernicanism

Galileo Galilei holds a pre-eminent position in the development of astronomy for several reasons. He provided compelling new evidence to support Copernican theory, and he contributed to the development of a new physics—or, more precisely, mechanics—that could account for the movement of bodies in new terms. Just as important, his efforts to publicize his findings and his condemnation by the church spurred popular debate about Copernican ideas in literate society and helped to determine the course science would take.

Born to a minor Florentine noble family, Galileo studied medicine and mathematics at the University of Pisa and became professor of mathematics there in 1589 at the age of 25. He had already completed important work on mechanics and within three years was given a chair at the University of Padua, where Copernicus had once studied. He continued work in mechanics during the 1590s but did not publish the results of his experiments until much later. Instead, he became famous for the results of his astronomical observations, which he began in 1609 and first published the next year. *Sidereus Nuncius* (*The Starry Messenger,* 1610) described in lay language the results of his scrutiny of the heavens with a telescope that he had built.

Galileo was the first person that we know who used a telescope to look at the sky. In *The Starry Messenger,* he documented sighting new (previously invisible) stars, another blow to the authority of ancient descriptions of the universe. He also noted craters and other "imperfections" on the surface of the moon as well as the existence of moons orbiting the planet Jupiter. Three years later he published his observations of sunspots in *Letters on Sunspots.* Sunspots are regions of relatively cool

gaseous material that appear as dark spots on the sun's surface. For Galileo the sunspots and the craters of the moon constituted proof that the heavens were not perfect and changeless but rather were like the supposedly "corrupt" and changeable earth. His telescopic observations also provided further support for Copernican heliocentrism because they revealed that each heavenly body rotated on its axis: Sunspots, for example, could be tracked across the visible surface of the sun as the sun rotated.

Galileo's principal contribution to mechanics lay in his working out of an early theory of inertia. As a result of a number of experiments with falling bodies (balls rolling on carefully constructed inclines—not free-falling objects that, according to myth, he dropped from the Leaning Tower of Pisa), Galileo ventured a new view of what is "natural" to bodies. Galileo's view was that uniform motion is as natural as a state of rest. In the ancient and medieval universe, all motion needed a cause, and all motion could be explained in terms of purpose. "I hold," Galileo countered, "that there exists nothing in external bodies . . . but size, shape, quantity and motion."[2] Galileo retained the old assumption that motion was somehow naturally circular. Nevertheless, his theory was a crucial step in explaining motion according to new principles and in fashioning a world-view that accepted a mechanical universe devoid of metaphysical purpose. These theories were published only toward the end of his life. His astronomical theories were more influential at the time.

Galileo's works were widely read, and his work became common currency in the scientific societies already flourishing in his lifetime and in courtly circles where science was encouraged. In 1610 Galileo became court mathematician to Cosimo de' Medici, the grand duke of Tuscany (r. 1609–1620), as a result of the fame brought by *The Starry Messenger.* Soon after his arrival, however, rumors that "Galileists" were openly promulgating heliocentrism led to an investigation and, in 1616, the official condemnation of Copernicus's works by the inquisition in Rome. This condemnation allowed room for maneuver. After meeting personally with the pope, Galileo was assured that he could continue to use Copernican theory, but only as a theory.

In 1632 Galileo issued a bold response to that limitation. *Dialogue on the Two Chief Systems of*

Galileo Confronts the Church

His work increasingly under attack after the publication of **Letters on Sunspots** *(1613), Galileo defended himself by criticizing the claim that biblical authority could decide matters of astronomy. This dangerous line of argument not only argued for a separation of theology and science but also presumed to evaluate the work of theologians and even offered an interpretation of biblical passages. In this document, from a 1615 essay couched as a letter to his patron Christina of Lorraine, Galileo broaches these ideas.*

But I do not feel obliged to believe that . . . God who has endowed us with senses, reason and intellect has intended to forgo their use and by some other means to give us knowledge which we can attain by them. . . . This must be especially true in those sciences of which but the faintest trace . . . is to be found in the Bible. Of astronomy, for instance, so little is found that none of the planets except Venus are so much as mentioned. . . .

Now, if the Holy Spirit has purposely neglected to teach us propositions of this sort as irrelevant to the highest goal (that is, to our salvation), how can anyone affirm that it is obligatory to take sides on them, and that one belief is required by faith, while another side is erroneous? . . . I would assert here something that was heard from [a respected cleric]: . . . "the intention of the Holy Ghost is to teach us how to go to heaven, not how heaven goes."

Moreover, we are unable to affirm that all interpreters of the Bible speak with divine inspiration, for if that were so there would exist no differences between them about the sense of a given passage. Hence [it would be wise] not to permit anyone to usurp scriptural texts and force them in some way to maintain any physical conclusion to be true, when at some future time the senses . . . may show the contrary. Who . . . will set bounds to human ingenuity? Who will assert that everything in the universe capable of being perceived is already . . . known?

Source: Stillman Drake, *The Discoveries and Opinions of Galileo* (New York: Doubleday, 1957), pp. 183–187.

the World was perhaps the most important single source for the popularization of Copernican theory. The work consists of a dialogue among three characters supposedly debating the merits of Copernican theory. Simplicio, the character representing the old world-view, was, as his name suggests, an example of ignorance, not wisdom. In this work, Galileo expresses his supreme confidence—bordering on arrogance—in his own powers and in human power generally to use the senses and reason to understand the physical world.

By publishing the *Dialogue*, Galileo was defying the papal ban on advocating Copernicanism. In an earlier work, *Letter to the Grand Duchess Christina* (1615), Galileo had also been impolitic. In the *Letter,* he had trespassed on the church's authority to interpret the Scriptures. (See the box, "Galileo Confronts the Church.") He was tried for heresy and forced to condemn his "errors" in 1633, though Pope Urban VIII (r. 1623–1644) intervened to give him the light sentence of house arrest at his villa in Tuscany. There, until his death in 1642, Galileo continued his investigations of mechanics.

THE SCIENTIFIC REVOLUTION GENERALIZED

Galileo's work found such a willing audience because Galileo, like Kepler and Brahe, was not working alone. Dozens of other scientists were working energetically on old problems from the fresh perspective offered by the breakthroughs in astronomy. Some were analyzing the nature of matter, now that it was supposed that all matter in the universe was somehow the same despite its varying appearances. Many of these thinkers addressed the metaphysical issues that their investigations inevitably raised.

The Promise of the New Science

No less a man than Francis Bacon (1561–1626), lord chancellor of England during the reign of James I, wrote a utopian essay extolling the benefits of science for a peaceful society and for human happiness. In *New Atlantis,* published one year after his death, Bacon argued that science would produce "things of use and practice for man's life."[3] In *New Atlantis* and in *Novum Organum* (1620), Bacon revealed his faith in science by advocating patient, systematic observation and experimentation to accumulate knowledge about the world. He argued that the proper method of investigation "derives axioms from . . . particulars, rising by gradual and unbroken ascent, so that it arrives at the most general axioms of all. This is the true way but untried."[4]

Bacon himself did not undertake experiments, though his widely read works were influential in encouraging both the empirical method (relying on observation and experimentation) and inductive reasoning (deriving general principles from particular facts). Indeed, Bacon was a visionary. Given the early date of his writings, it might even seem difficult to account for his enthusiasm and confidence. In fact, Bacon's writings reflect the widespread interest and confidence in science within his elite milieu, an interest actively encouraged by the state. In another of his writings he argued that a successful state should concentrate on effective "rule in religion *and nature,* as well as civil administration."[5]

Bacon's writing reflected the fact that an interest in exploring nature's secrets and exercising "dominion over nature" had become an indispensable part of princely rule. Princely courts were the main source of financial support for science and a primary site of scientific work during Bacon's lifetime. Part of the impetus for this development had come from the civic humanism of the Italian Renaissance, which had celebrated the state and service to it and had provided models both for educated rulers and for cultivated courtiers. The specific turning of the rulers' attention to science

and to its benefits for the state also reflected the scope of princely resources and ambitions: the desire of rulers for technical expertise in armaments, fortification, building projects in general, navigation, and mapmaking. (See the feature, "Weighing the Evidence: Modern Maps," on pages 654–655.)

The promise of the New World and the drive for overseas trade and exploration especially encouraged princely support of scientific investigation. A renowned patron of geographic investigation, from mapmaking to navigation, was Henry, prince of Wales (d. 1612), son of James I. Prince Henry patronized technical experts such as experienced gunners and seamen as well as those with broader and more theoretical expertise. One geographer at his court worked on the vital problem of calculating longitude, sketched the moon after reading and emulating Galileo's work with the telescope, and—in a spirit of empiricism often associated with Bacon—compiled information about the new territory Virginia, including the first dictionary of any Native American language.

Science was an ideological as well as a practical tool for power. Most courts housed collections of marvels, specimens of exotic plants and animals, and mechanical contrivances. These demonstrated the ruler's interest in investigation of the world—his or her status, in other words, as an educated person. These collections and the work of court experts also enhanced the ruler's reputation as a patron and the image of the ruler's power. Galileo was playing off such expectations when he named some of his newly discovered bodies "Medician Stars."

Exploring the secrets of nature became a tool for rulers and an honorable activity for scholars and courtiers. By the beginning of the seventeenth century, private salons and academies where investigators might meet on their own were another major site of scientific investigation. These, too, had their roots in the humanist culture of Italy, where circles of scholars without university affiliations had formed. They were an important alternative to princely patronage, since a ruler's funds might wax and wane according to his or her other commitments. Also, private organizations could avoid the hierarchical distinctions that were inevitable at court.

The earliest academy dedicated to scientific study was the Accadèmia Segreta (Secret Academy) founded in Naples in the 1540s. The members pur-

A Collection of Naturalia Displays of exotica, such as these specimens in Naples, symbolized the ruler's authority by suggesting his or her power over nature. *(From Ferrante Imperato,* Dell' Historia Naturale *[Naples, 1599]. By permission of the Houghton Library, Harvard University)*

sued experiments together, in order, in the words of one member, "to make a true anatomy of the things and operations of nature itself."[6] During the remainder of the sixteenth century and on into the seventeenth, such academies sprang up in many cities. The most celebrated was the Accadèmia dei Lincei, founded in Rome by an aristocrat in 1603. Its most famous member, Galileo, joined in 1611. The name "Lincei," from *lynx*, was chosen because of the legendary keen sight of that animal, an appropriate mascot for "searchers of secrets."

Galileo's notoriety and the importance of his discoveries forced acceptance or rejection of Copernicanism on all communities. Throughout the seventeenth century, specific investigation of natural phenomena would continue in increasingly sophisticated institutional settings. The flowering of scientific thought in the seventeenth century occurred because of the specific innovations in astronomy and the general spread of scientific investigation that had been achieved by the end of Bacon's life.

Scientific Thought in France: Descartes and a New Cosmology

Philosophers, mathematicians, and educated elites engaged in lively debate and practical investigation throughout Europe in the first half of the seventeenth century, but in France questions about cosmic order were being posed at a time of political disorder. The years following the religious wars

René Descartes had been given the best of traditional educations. From the Jesuits he had learned not only scholastic logic and rhetoric but also, perhaps for purposes of debate, Galileo's new discoveries. *(Royal Museum of Fine Arts, Copenhagen)*

saw the murder of Henry IV, another regency, and further civil war in the 1620s (see pages 564–565). In this environment, questions about order in the universe and the possibilities of human knowledge took on particular urgency. It is not surprising that a Frenchman, René Descartes (1596–1650), created the first fully articulated alternative world-view.

Descartes's work emerged in dialogue with a circle of other French thinkers. His work became more influential among philosophers and lay people than the work of some of his equally talented contemporaries because of its thoroughness and rigor, grounded in Descartes's mathematical expertise, and because of his graceful, readable French. His system was fully presented in his *Discours de la méthode* (*Discourse on Method*, 1637). This work was intended to be the centerpiece of a series of scien-

tific treatises, including works on optics and geometry. Descartes described some of his intellectual crises in *Meditations* (1641).

Descartes accepted Galileo's conclusion that the heavens and the earth are made of the same elements. In his theorizing about the composition of matter, he drew on ancient atomic models that previously had not been generally accepted. His theory that all matter is made up of identical bits, which he named "corpuscles," is a forerunner of modern atomic and quantum theories. Descartes believed that all the different appearances and behaviors of matter (for example, why stone is always hard and water is always wet) could be explained solely by the size, shape, and motion of these "corpuscles." Descartes's was an extremely mechanistic explanation of the universe. It nevertheless permitted new, more specific observations and hypotheses and greater understanding of inertia. For example, because he reimagined the universe as being filled with "corpuscles" free to move in any direction, "natural" motion no longer seemed either circular (Galileo's idea) or toward the center of the earth (Aristotle's idea). The new understanding of motion would be crucial to Isaac Newton's formulations later in the century.

In his various works, Descartes depicts and then firmly resolves the crisis of confidence that the new discoveries about the universe had produced. The collapse of the old explanations about the world made Descartes and other investigators doubt not only what they knew but also their capacity to know anything at all. Their physical senses—which denied that the earth moved, for example—had been proved untrustworthy. Descartes's solution was to re-envision the human rational capacity, the mind, as completely distinct from the world—that is, as distinct from the human body—and the betraying sense data it offers. In a leap of faith, Descartes presumed that he could count on the fact that God would not have given humans a mind if that mind were to betray them. For Descartes, God became the guarantor of human reasoning capacity, and humans, in Descartes's view, were distinguished by that capacity. This is the significance of his famous claim "I think, therefore I am."

Descartes thus achieved a resolution of the terrifying doubt about the world, a resolution that exalted the role of the human knower. The Cartesian universe was one of mechanical motion, not purpose or mystical meaning, and the Cartesian human being was pre-eminently a mind that could apprehend that universe. In what came to be known as "Cartesian dualism," Descartes was proposing that humans are detached from the world yet at the same time can be objective observers of the world.

Important implications followed from Descartes's ambitious view of human reason. One was the emphasis on deductive reasoning (a process of reasoning in which the conclusion follows necessarily from the stated premises), which naturally followed from his philosophical rejection of sense data. In actuality, Descartes did rely on sense data; he did experiments and urged his readers to keep careful records of their thoughts, observations, and conclusions. But, like the mathematician he was, he urged that science "[keep] the right order for one thing to be deduced from that which precedes it."[7] In the short run, Descartes's embrace of absolute certainty proved very useful to the advancement of knowledge because with a positive sense of purpose—even within the limits of deductive reasoning—natural philosophers could tolerate enormous uncertainty and speculate fruitfully about specific problems.

Descartes's vision of the enhanced position of the individual knower, and of the power of the knower's reason, was attractive to philosophers. (Galileo's self-confidence comes to mind.) His views were also attractive to educated lay people who sought in science an affirmation of their own status in the world, which could now be expressed in terms of intellectual power and power over nature, rather than only as political power. Descartes was careful not to advocate the "madness" of applying reason to changing the state. The state alone had made humans civilized, he maintained; and although he and other thinkers had to rebuild knowledge of the universe from its foundations, he believed it was "unreasonable for an individual to conceive the plan of reforming a state by changing everything from the foundations."[8]

Similar possibilities for human perception were being suggested in other areas of creative endeavor. Renaissance painters, who utilized the principles of linear perspective, presented views of the world as detached still life—more distant and distinct than the world ever was in real life. A similar detachment was evident in the memoirs and essays of writers such as Michel de Montaigne (1533–1592; see page 578). Descartes's view of rationality, however, was the most radical detachment of all, for Descartes claimed objectivity for his perspective.

Though much of Cartesian physics would be surpassed by Newton at the end of the century, Descartes's assumption about the objectivity of the observer would become an enduring part of scientific practice. The sense of detachment from the world also fostered a belief in humans' ability to control nature. In our own time, we have become aware of the possible limits of our ability to control nature, as well as the arbitrariness of Descartes's distinction of mind and body. In Descartes's day, the most radical aspect of his thought was the reduction of God from being an active presence in the world to the position of guarantor of knowledge. Later generations of scientists would be fearful of Descartes's system because it seemed to encourage "atheism." In fact, a profound faith in God was necessary for Descartes's creativity in imagining his new world system—but the system did work without God. Although Descartes would have been surprised and offended by charges of atheism, he knew that his work would antagonize the church. He had moved to the Netherlands to study in 1628, and his *Discourse* was first published there.

A contemporary of Descartes, Blaise Pascal (1623–1662), drew attention in his writings and in his life to the limits of scientific knowledge. Son of a royal official, Pascal was perhaps the most brilliant mind of his generation. A mathematician like Descartes, he stressed the importance of mathematical representations of phenomena, built one of the first calculating machines, and invented probability theory. He also carried out experiments to investigate air pressure, the behavior of liquids, and the existence of vacuums.

Pascal's career alternated between periods of intense scientific work and religious retreat. Today he is well known for his writings that defended Jansenism, an austere strain of Catholicism, and explored the human soul and psyche. His *Pensées* (*Thoughts*, 1657) consists of the published fragments of his defense of Christian faith, which remained unfinished at the time of his early death. Pascal's appeal for generations after him may lie in his assumption that matters of faith and of feeling must also be open to investigation. His most famous statement, "The heart has its reasons which the reason knows not," can be read as a statement of the limits of the Cartesian world-view.

Science and Revolution in England

The new science had adherents and practitioners throughout Europe by 1650. Dutch scientists in the commercial milieu of the Netherlands, for example, had the freedom to pursue practical and experimental interests. The Dutch investigator Christiaan Huygens (1629–1695) worked on a great variety of problems, including air pressure and optics. He invented and patented the pendulum clock in 1657, the first device accurately to measure small units of time, essential for a variety of measurements.

England, however, because of the political revolution that occurred there, offered a unique environment for the development of science in the middle of the century. Religious and political struggle in England took place at a time when scientific questions were also to the fore. Thus, differing positions on science became part and parcel of differing positions on Puritanism, church hierarchy, and royal power. Scientific investigation and speculation were spurred by the urgency of religious and political agendas. Scientific, along with political and religious, debate was generally encouraged by the collapse of censorship beginning in the 1640s.

In the 1640s natural philosophers with Puritan leanings were encouraged in their investigations by dreams that science, of the practical Baconian sort, could be the means by which the perfection of life on earth could be brought about and the end of history, the reign of the saints preceding the return of Christ, accelerated. Their concerns ranged from improved production of gunpowder (for the armies fighting against Charles I) to surveying and mapmaking. Perhaps the best-known member of this group was Robert Boyle (1627–1691). In his career we can trace the evolution of English science through the second half of the seventeenth century.

Boyle and his colleagues were theoretically eclectic, drawing on Cartesian mechanics and even Paracelsian chemical theories. They attacked the university system, still under the sway of Aristotelianism, and proposed widespread reform of education. They were forced to moderate many of their positions, however, as the English revolution

proceeded. Radical groups such as the Levelers used Hermeticism and the related Paracelsianism as part of their political and religious tenets. The ancient doctrine of Hermeticism, revived since the Renaissance, claimed that matter is universally imbued with divine (or magical) spirit. The Levelers and others believed that each person was capable of a godly life and divine knowledge without the coercive hierarchy of officials of church and state.

Boyle and his colleagues responded to these challenges. They gained institutional power, accepting positions at Oxford and Cambridge. They formed the core of the Royal Society of London, which they persuaded Charles II to recognize and charter on his accession to the throne in 1660. They worked to articulate a theoretical position that combined the orderliness of mechanism, a continued divine presence in the world, and a Baconian emphasis on scientific progress. This unwieldy set of notions was attractive to the educated elite of their day who wanted the certainties of science without losing all of the authoritarian aspects of the old Christian world-view.

Their most creative contribution, both to their own cause and to the advancement of science, was their emphasis on and refinement of experimental philosophy and practice. In 1660, Boyle published *New Experiments Physico-Mechanical*. The work described the results of his experiments with an air pump that he had designed, and it laid out general rules for experimental procedure. Descartes had accounted for motion by postulating that "corpuscles" of matter act on each other, thereby eliminating the possibility of a vacuum in nature. Recent experiments on air pressure suggested otherwise, however, and Boyle tried to confirm their findings with his air pump.

Boyle's efforts to demonstrate that a vacuum could exist—by evacuating a sealed chamber with his pump—were not successes by modern standards because they could not readily be replicated. Boyle tied the validity of experimental results to the agreement of witnesses to the experiment—a problematic solution, for only investigators sympathetic to his hypothesis and convinced of his credibility usually witnessed the results. In response to a Cambridge scholar who criticized his interpretation of one of his experiments, Boyle replied that he could not understand his critic's objections, ". . . the experiment having been tried both before our whole society [the Royal Society of London], and very critically, by its royal founder, his majesty himself."[9] Rather than debate differing interpretations, Boyle chose to fall back on the authority and prestige of the participants themselves. In English science in the mid-seventeenth century, the various aspects of the modern scientific profession—the agreement on principles, the acceptance of experimental procedures, and the authority of practitioners—were all being worked out simultaneously.

The Newtonian Synthesis: The Copernican Revolution Completed

The Copernican revolution reached its high point with the work of the Englishman Isaac Newton (1642–1724), who was born the year Galileo died. Newton completed the new explanation for motion in the heavens and on earth that Copernicus's work had initiated and that Kepler, Galileo, and others had sought. In Newton's career, we can see how different was the climate for science by the second half of the seventeenth century. When Newton entered Cambridge University as a student in 1661, Copernicanism was studied, the benefits of scientific investigation were debated, and much attention was focused on the problems of Descartes's explanations of matter.

Like all the other natural philosophers before him, Newton was as concerned by questions of metaphysics as by physics. In the 1680s, he devoted himself primarily to the study of church history, theology, and alchemy. As a student at Cambridge he was strongly influenced by the work of a group of Neo-Platonists who were critical of Cartesian dualism, which posited God as a cause of all matter and motion but removed God as an explanation for the behavior of matter. Their concerns were both religious and scientific. As Newton says in some of his early writing while a student, "However we cast about we find almost no other reason for atheism than this [Cartesian] notion of bodies having . . . a complete, absolute and independent reality."[10] He reflected his mentors' concern to harmonize science with a securely Christian world-view following the "excesses" of the English revolution. Meanwhile, they were all uncertain how to account for motion in a world filled with matter, as Descartes had posited. The experiments of Robert Boyle in creating a vacuum shed further doubt on Descartes's schema.

Newton combined his scientific skepticism and his religious certainty to posit the existence of gravity—a mysterious force that accounts for the movement of heavenly bodies. Others had speculated about the existence of gravity, but Newton's extraordinary contribution was the mathematical computation of the laws of gravity and planetary motion, which he combined with a fully developed concept of inertia. The concept of inertia as so far elaborated by Galileo, Descartes, and others suggested the need for the concept of gravity. Otherwise, if a planet was "pushed" (say, in Kepler's view, by the "motive force" of the sun), it would

Isaac Newton Pictured here about fifteen years after the publication of the *Principia*, Newton was also one of the developers of calculus. The cumbersome mathematics he still relied on in the *Principia*, however, has led one scholar to ponder: "What manner of man he was who could use as a weapon what we can scarcely lift as a burden."[11] *(National Portrait Gallery, London)*

continue along that course forever unless "pulled back" by something else.

In 1687 Newton published *Philosophia Naturalis Principia Mathematica* (*Mathematical Principles of Natural Philosophy*). In this mathematical treatise—so intricate that it was inaccessible to lay people, even those able to read Latin—Newton lays out his laws of motion and expresses them as mathematical theorems that can be used to test future observations of moving bodies. Then he demonstrates that these laws also apply to the solar system, confirming the data already gathered about the planets and even predicting the existence of an as-yet-unseen planet. His supreme achievement was his law of gravitation, with which he could predict the discovery of the invisible planet. This law states that every body, indeed every bit of matter, in the universe exerts over every other body an attractive force proportional to the product of their masses and inversely proportional to the square of the distance between them. Newton not only accounted for motion but definitively united heaven and earth in a single scheme and created a convincing picture of an orderly nature.

Neither Newton nor anyone else claimed that his theorems resolved all questions about motion and matter. Exactly what gravity is and how it operates were not clear, as they still are not. Newton himself was troubled by his lack of understanding of gravity except in mathematical terms. He couched the *Principia* as a mathematical treatise rather than as a general treatise in philosophy because he felt he could make no systematic claims, as did Descartes, since the problem of gravity had not been solved. After its publication, he experienced periods of severe depression, leading to a nervous breakdown in 1693.

Newton's laws of motion are still taught because they still adequately account for most problems of motion. The fact that so fundamental a principle as gravity remains unexplained in no way diminishes Newton's achievement but is clear evidence about the nature of scientific understanding: Science provides explanatory schemas that account for many—but not all—observed phenomena. When a scientific explanation ceases to account satisfactorily for enough data, it collapses of its own weight. No schema explains everything, and each schema contains open doorways that lead to further discovery and blind alleys that lead to mistaken impressions. Newton, for example, also studied alchemy during his most productive years. He assumed that the spiritual forces that somehow accounted for gravity would mysteriously work on metals so that they might "quickly pass into gold."[12]

Other Branches of Science

The innovations in astronomy that led to the new mechanistic view of the behavior of matter did not automatically spill over to other branches of science. Developments in astronomy were very specific to that field; innovation came at the hands of skilled practitioners after the ancient and medieval inheritance had been fully assimilated and its errors made undeniable. Other branches of science followed their own paths, though all were strongly influenced by the mechanistic world-view.

In chemistry, the mechanistic assumption that all matter was composed of small, equivalent parts was crucial to understanding the properties and behavior of compounds (combinations of elements). But knowledge of these small units of matter was not yet detailed enough to be of much use in advancing chemistry conceptually. Nevertheless, the flawed conceptual schema did not hold back all chemical discovery and development. Lack of understanding of gases, and of the specific elements that make them up, for example, did not prevent the development and improvement of gunpowder. Indeed, unlike the innovations in astronomy, eventual conceptual innovation in chemistry and biology owed a great deal to the results of experiment and the slow accumulation of data.

A conceptual leap forward was made in biology in the sixteenth and seventeenth centuries. Because biological knowledge was mostly a byproduct of the practice of medicine, biological studies had been and remained very practical and experimental. But the discovery of *On Anatomical Procedures,* a treatise by Galen, encouraged dissection and other practical research. Andreas Vesalius (1514–1564), in particular, made important advances by following Galen's exhortation to anatomical research. Born in Brussels, Vesalius studied at the nearby University of Louvain, and then at Padua, where he was appointed professor of surgery. He ended his career as physician to Emperor Charles V and his son, Philip II of Spain. In his teaching at Padua he embodied newly discovered Galenic precepts by doing dissections himself rather than giving the work to technicians. In 1543 he published versions of his lectures as an illustrated compendium of anatomy, *De Humani Corporis Fabrica* (*On the Fabric of the Human Body*). The results of his dissections of human corpses, revealed in this work, demonstrated a number of errors in Galen's knowledge of human anatomy, much of which had been derived from dissection of animals. Neither Vesalius nor his immediate successors, however, questioned overall Galenic theory about the functioning of the human body, any more than Copernicus had utterly rejected Aristotelian physics.

The slow movement from new observation to changed explanation is clearly illustrated in the career of the Englishman William Harvey (1578–1657). Much like Vesalius, Harvey was educated first in his own land and then at Padua, where he benefited from the tradition of anatomical research. He also had a career as a practicing physician in London and at the courts of James I and Charles I.

Harvey postulated the circulation of the blood—postulated rather than discovered because, owing to the technology of the day, he could not observe the tiny capillaries where the movement of arterial blood into the veins occurs. After conducting on animals vivisectional experiments that revealed the actual functioning of the heart and lungs, he reasoned that circulation must occur. He carefully described his experiments and his conclusions in *Exercitatio Anatomica de Motu Cordis et Sanguinis in Animalibus* (1628), usually shortened to *De Motu Cordis* (*On the Motion of the Heart*).

Harvey's work challenged Galenic anatomy and, like Copernicus's discoveries, created new burdens of explanation. According to Galenic theory, the heart and the lungs helped each other to function. The heart sent nourishment to the lungs through the pulmonary artery, and the lungs provided raw material for the "vital spirit," which the heart gave to the blood to produce and sustain life. The lungs also helped the heart to sustain its "heat." Like "vital spirit," "heat" was considered necessary to living organisms. It was understood to be an innate property of organs, just as "heavi-

ness," in traditional physics, was considered to be an innate property of earthbound objects. One chamber of the heart was supposedly reserved for the cleansing of waste products from venous blood—which was thought to be entirely separate from the "nourishing" blood pumped out by the heart.

From his observations, Harvey came to think of the heart in terms consonant with the new mechanistic notions about nature: as a pump to circulate the blood. But to Harvey the heart was never only that. Harvey did not leap to a new conceptualization of the body's function. Rather, he adjusted but did not abandon Galenic theories, for example, concerning how "heat" and "vital spirit" were made. The lungs had been thought to "ventilate" the heart by providing air to maintain "heat" (like bellows on a fire) and by drawing off heat to cool the heart as necessary. In light of his discovery of the pulmonary transit (that all of the blood is pumped through the lungs and back through the heart), Harvey suggested that the lungs carried out some of these functions for the blood, helping it to concoct the "vital spirit." Only in this context could the heart be thought of as a machine, circulating this life-giving material around the body.

Harvey's explanation of bodily functions in light of his new knowledge thus did not constitute a rupture with Galenic tradition. But by the end of his life, Harvey's own adjustments of Galenic theory were suggesting new conceptual possibilities. His work inspired additional research in physiology, chemistry, and physics. Robert Boyle's efforts to understand vacuums can be traced in part to questions Harvey raised about the function of the lungs and the properties of air.

SCIENCE AND SOCIETY

Scientists wrestled with questions about God, human capacity, and the possibilities of understanding the world every bit as intently as they attempted to find new explanations for the behavior of matter and the motion of the heavens. Eventually, the profound implications of the new scientific posture would affect thought and behavior throughout society. Once people no longer thought of the universe in hierarchical terms, questioning the hierarchical organization of society became easier. Once all matter was thought of as equal, thinking of all people as equal became easier. Once people questioned the authority of traditional knowledge about the universe, the way was clear for them to begin to question traditional views of the state and social order.

Such profound changes of perspective happened gradually. In the short term, Louis XIV and other rulers actually welcomed the new science for its practical value, and the practice of science remained wedded to religion. The advances in science did lead to revolutionary cultural change; but, until the end of the seventeenth century, traditional institutions and ideologies circumscribed this change.

The Rise of Scientific Professionalism

Institutions both old and new supported the new science developing in the sixteenth and seventeenth centuries. Some universities were the setting for scientific breakthroughs, but court patronage, a well-established institution, also sponsored scientific activity. The development of the Accadèmia dei Lincei (see page 635), to which Galileo belonged, and other academies was a step toward modern professional societies of scholars, although these new organizations depended on patronage.

In both England and France, royally sponsored scientific societies were founded in the third quarter of the century. The Royal Society of London, inaugurated in 1660, received royal recognition but no money and remained an informal institution sponsoring amateur scientific interests as well as specialized independent research. The Académie Royale des Sciences in France, established in 1666 by Jean-Baptiste Colbert, Louis XIV's minister of finance (see page 591), sponsored research and supported chosen scientists with pensions. These associations were extensions to science of traditional kinds of royal recognition and patronage. Thus, the French Académie was well funded but tightly controlled by the government of Louis XIV, and the Royal Society of London received little of Charles II's precious resources or his scarce political capital.

One important role of academies and patrons was to support the publication of scientific work.

The Accadèmia dei Lincei published two of Galileo's best-known works. The Royal Society of London published its fellows' work in *Philosophical Transactions of the Royal Society*, beginning in 1665.

The practice of seventeenth-century science took place in so many diverse institutions—academies, universities, royal courts—that neither *science* nor *scientist* was rigorously defined. Science as a discipline was not yet detached from broad metaphysical questions. Boyle, Newton, Pascal, and Descartes all concerned themselves with questions of religion, and all thought of themselves not as scientists but, like their medieval forebears, as natural philosophers. These natural philosophers were among the elite who met in aristocratic salons to discuss literature, politics, or science with equal ease and interest. Nevertheless, the beginning of the narrowing of the practice of science to a tightly defined, truly professional community is evident. Robert Boyle and his fellow advocates of experimentalism, for example, claimed that their procedures alone constituted true science.

The importance of court life and patronage to the new science had at first enabled women to be actively involved. Women ran important salons in France, aristocratic women everywhere were important sources of patronage for scientists, and women themselves were scientists, combining, as did men, science with other pursuits.

Noblewomen and daughters of gentry families had access to education in their homes, and a number of such women were active scientists—astronomers, mathematicians, and botanists. The astronomer Maria Cunitz (1610–1664), from Silesia (a Habsburg-controlled province, now in modern Poland), learned six languages with the support and encouragement of her father, who was a medical doctor. Later, she published a useful simplification of some of Kepler's mathematical calculations. Women from artisanal families might also receive useful training at home. Such was the case of the German entomologist Maria Sibylla Merian (1647–1717). Merian learned the techniques of illustration in the workshop of her father, an artist in Frankfurt. Later, she used her artistic training and her refined powers of observation to study and record the lives of insects and plants.

Margaret Cavendish, duchess of Newcastle (1623–1673), wrote several major philosophical

Maria Merian, Entomologist Merian's scientific drawings of insect life in Europe and South America (where she traveled with her daughter) were widely used and reproduced until the nineteenth century. Eleven insect and six plant species, which she discovered and recorded, are named for her. *(Oeffentliche Kunstsammlung Basel)*

works, including *Grounds of Natural Philosophy* (1668). She was a Cartesian but was influenced by Neo-Platonism. She believed matter to have "intelligence" and thus disagreed with Cartesian dualism, but she criticized English philosophers with whom she agreed on some matters because, like Descartes, she distrusted sense knowledge as a guide to philosophy.

Women were proposed as members of and were accepted in Italian academies regularly but they were excluded from formal membership in the academies in London and Paris, though they could use the academies' facilities and received prizes from the societies for their work. One reason for the exclusion of women was the limited amount of patronage available: Coveted positions automatically went to men. Moreover, the hierarchical distinction signified by gender made the ex-

clusion of women a useful way to define the academies as special and privileged.

Margaret Cavendish was aware of the degree to which her participation in scientific life depended on informal networks and on the resources available to her because of her aristocratic status. (See the box, "Margaret Cavendish Challenges Male Scientists.") Women scientists from more modest backgrounds, without Cavendish's resources, had to fight for the right to employment as public institutions gained importance as settings for the pursuit of science. The German astronomer Maria Winkelman (1670–1720), for example, tried to succeed her late husband in an official position in the Berlin Academy of Sciences in 1710. She had worked as her husband's unofficial partner during his tenure as astronomer to the academy and now sought to continue her work to

Astronomers Elisabetha and Johannes Hevelius were one of many collaborating couples among the scientists of the seventeenth century. Women were usually denied pensions and support for their research when they worked alone, however. *(From Hevelius,* Machinae coelestis. *By permission of the Houghton Library, Harvard University)*

support her four children. The academy would not extend an official position to Winkelman after her husband's death, however, despite her experience and accomplishments (she had discovered a new comet, for example, in 1702). The secretary of the academy stated:

That she be kept on in an official capacity to work on the calendar or to continue with observations simply will not do. Already during her husband's lifetime the society was burdened with ridicule because its calendar was prepared by a woman. If she were now to be kept on in such a capacity, mouths would gape even wider.[13]

Winkelman worked in private observatories, but was able to return to the Berlin Academy only as the unofficial assistant to her own son, whose training she herself had supervised.

Margaret Cavendish Challenges Male Scientists

In her preface to her earliest scientific work, **The Philosophical and Physical Opinions (1655),** *Cavendish addresses scholars at Oxford and Cambridge universities with deceptive humility. She implies that the seeming limitations of women's abilities are in fact the consequence of their exclusion from education and from participation in affairs.*

Most Famously Learned,

I here present to you this philosophical work, not that I can hope wise school-men and industrious laborious students should value it for any worth, but to receive it without scorn, for the good encouragement of our sex, lest in time we should grow irrational as idiots, by the dejectedness of our spirits, through the careless neglects and despisements of the masculine sex to the female, thinking it impossible we should have either learning or understanding, wit or judgment, as if we had not rational souls as well as men, and we out of a custom of dejectedness think so too, which makes us quit all industry towards profitable knowledge, being imployed only in low and petty imployments which take away not only our abilities towards arts but higher capacities in speculations, so that we are become like worms, that only live in the dull earth of ignorance, winding ourselves sometimes out by the help of some refreshing rain of good education, which seldom is given us, for we are kept like birds in cages, to hop up and down in our houses . . . ; thus by an opinion, which I hope is but an erroneous one in men, we are shut out of all power and authority by reason we are never employed either in civil or martial affairs, our counsels are despised and laughed at and the best of our actions are trodden down with scorn, by the over-weening conceit men have of themselves and through a despisement of us.

Source: Moira Ferguson, ed., *First Feminists: British Women Writers, 1578–1799* (Bloomington and New York: Indiana University Press and The Feminist Press, 1985), pp. 85–86.

The New Science and the Needs of the State

The new natural philosophy had implications for traditional notions about the state. The new worldview that all matter was alike and answerable to discernible natural laws gradually undermined political systems resting on a belief in the inherent inequality of persons and on royal prerogative. By the middle of the eighteenth century, a fully formed alternative political philosophy would argue for more "rational" government in keeping with the rational, natural order of things. But the change came slowly, and while it was coming, the state of Louis XIV and other rulers found much to admire and make use of in the new science.

New technological possibilities were very attractive to governments and members of ruling elites. Experiments with vacuum pumps had important applications in the mining industry. The astronomy professor at Gresham College in London was required to teach navigation, and other professors at Gresham worked with naval architects to improve the design of ships.

Governments also sponsored purely scientific research. The French Académie des Sciences sponsored the construction of an astronomical observatory in Paris. A naval expedition to Cayenne, in French Guiana, led to refinements of the pendulum clock but had as its main purpose progressive observations of the sun to permit the calculation of the earth's distance from the sun.

The sponsorship of pure science is evidence of both the adaptability of institutions and the complexity of change. Members of the elite, such as

Colbert in France, saw the opportunity not only for practical advances but also for prestige and, most important, confirmation of the orderliness of nature. It is hard to overestimate the psychological impact and intellectual power of this fundamental tenet of the new science—namely, that nature is an inanimate machine that reflects God's design not through its purposes but simply by its orderliness. Human beings could now hope to dominate nature in ways not possible before. Dominion, order, control—these were the goals of ambitious and powerful rulers in the seventeenth century.

Thus, in the short run, the new science supported a vision of order that was very pleasing to a monarch of absolutist pretensions. Louis XIV, among others, energetically sponsored scientific investigation by the Académie des Sciences and reaped the benefits in improved ships, increasingly skillful military engineers, and new and improved industrial products.

Religion and the New Science

Because of Galileo's trial, the Catholic church is often seen as an opponent of scientific thought, and science and religion are often seen as antagonists. But this view is an oversimplification. Indeed, scientific thought remained closely tied to religion during the seventeenth century. Both religion and the Catholic church as an institution were involved with scientific advancement from the time of Copernicus. Copernicus himself was a cleric, as

Science and Royal Power This painting memorializes the founding of the French Académie des Sciences and the building of the royal observatory in Paris. This celebration of the institutions' openings reveals Louis XIV's belief in their importance, both symbolic and practical. *(Château de Versailles/Laurie Platt Winfrey, Inc.)*

were many philosophers and scientists active in the early seventeenth century. This is not surprising, for most research in the sciences to this point had occurred within universities sponsored and staffed by members of religious orders.

Moreover, religious and metaphysical concerns were central to the work of virtually every scientist. The entire Cartesian edifice of reasoning about the world, for example, was founded on Descartes's certainty about God. God's gift of the capacity to reason was the only certainty that Descartes claimed. Copernicus, Kepler, and other investigators perceived God's purpose in the mathematical regularity of nature. In addition, traditional Christian views of the operations and purpose of the universe were evident in the work of all scientists from Copernicus to Newton—from Galileo's acceptance of perfect circular motion to Newton's theological writings.

It is true that the new astronomy and mechanics challenged specific tenets of faith and the Catholic church's role in shaping and controlling matters of knowledge and faith. Adjusting to a new view of nature in which God was less immanently and obviously represented was not easy for the church, for several reasons. First of all, the church itself mirrored the hierarchy of the old view of the universe in its own hierarchy of believers, priests, bishops, popes, and saints. Moreover, in its sponsorship of institutions of higher learning, the church was the repository of the old view. In the inevitable scientific disagreements spawned by the new theories and discoveries, the church was both theoretically and literally invested in the old view.

Nevertheless, the church's condemnation of Galileo shocked many clerics, including a number of whom were scientists themselves, as well as three of Galileo's judges, who voted for leniency at his trial. Over the course of the centuries, several apparent conflicts between scientific arguments and sacred teachings had been resolved with great intelligence and flexibility. Many scientists who were also clerics continued to study and teach the new science when they could; for example, Copernicanism was taught by Catholic missionaries abroad. (See the box, "Encounters with the West: Jesuits and Astronomy in China.")

The rigid response of the church hierarchy to Galileo's challenge must be seen in the context of the Protestant Reformation, which, in the minds

of the pope and others, had demonstrated the need for a firm response to any challenge. Galileo seemed threatening because he was well known, wrote for a wide audience, and, like the Protestants, presumed on the church's right to interpret the Scriptures.

The condemnation of Galileo had a chilling effect on scientific investigators in most Catholic regions of Europe. They could and did continue their research, but many could publish results only by smuggling manuscripts to Protestant lands. Descartes, as we have seen, left France for the more tolerant Netherlands, where his *Discourse on Method* was first published; he also sojourned at the Swedish court at the invitation of Queen Christina. Many of the most important empirical and theoretical innovations in science occurred in Protestant regions after the middle of the seventeenth century.

Protestant leaders, however, at first were not receptive to Copernican ideas because they defied scriptural authority as well as common sense. In 1549 one of Martin Luther's associates wrote:

The eyes are witnesses that the heavens revolve in the space of twenty-four hours. But certain men, either from love of novelty or to make a display of ingenuity, have concluded that the earth moves. . . . Now it is want of honesty and decency to assert such notions publicly and the example is pernicious. It is part of a good mind to accept the truth as revealed by God and to acquiesce in it.[14]

Protestant thinkers were also as troubled as Catholics by the metaphysical problems that the new theories seemed to raise. In 1611, one year after the publication of Galileo's *Starry Messenger*, the English poet John Donne (1573–1631) reflected in "An Anatomie of the World" on the confusion about human capacities and social relationships that Copernican astronomy caused:

[The] new Philosophy calls all in doubt,
The Element of fire is quite put out;
The Sun is lost, and th'earth, and no man's wit
Can well direct him where to look for it.

.   .   .   .

Tis all in pieces, all coherence gone;
All just supply, and all Relation:
Prince, Subject, Father, Son, are things forgot,
For every man alone thinks he hath got
To be a Phoenix, and that then can be
None of that kinde, of which he is, but he.[15]

~ **ENCOUNTERS WITH THE WEST** ~

Jesuits and Astronomy in China

The Italian Matteo Ricci (1552–1610) was one of the first of a series of Jesuit missionaries to establish himself at the imperial court in China. He was appreciative as well as critical of Chinese science, but his remarks are more interesting to us because they reveal that Ricci himself regarded expertise in mathematics and astronomy as worthy of esteem. Ricci's own scientific knowledge was crucial to his acceptance at court; Jesuit missionaries who followed Ricci in the seventeenth century found their scientific expertise equally valued, and several openly taught Copernican theory there.

The Chinese have not only made considerable progress in moral philosophy but in astronomy and in many branches of mathematics as well. At one time they were quite proficient in arithmetic and geometry, but in the study and teaching of these branches of learning they labored with more or less confusion. They divide the heavens into constellations in a manner somewhat different from that which we employ. Their count of the stars outnumbers the calculations of our astronomers by fully four hundred, because they include in it many of the fainter stars which are not always visible. And yet with all this, the Chinese astronomers take no pains whatever to reduce the phenomena of celestial bodies to the discipline of mathematics. Much of their time is spent in determining the moment of eclipses and the mass of the planets and the stars, but here, too, their deductions are spoiled by innumerable errors. Finally they center their whole attention on that phase of astronomy which our scientists term astrology, which may be accounted for the fact that they believe that everything happening on this terrestrial globe of ours depends upon the stars.

Some knowledge of the science of mathematics was given to the Chinese by the Saracens [Mongols], who penetrated into their country from the West, but very little of this knowledge was based upon definite mathematical proofs. What the Saracens left them, for the most part, consisted of certain tables of rules by which the Chinese regulated their calendar and to which they reduced their calculations of planets and the movements of the heavenly bodies in general. The founder of the family which at present regulates the study of astrology prohibited anyone from indulging in the study of this science unless he were chosen for it by hereditary right. The prohibition was founded upon fear, lest he who should acquire a knowledge of the stars might become capable of disrupting the order of the empire and seek an opportunity to do so.

Source: Louis J. Gallagher, trans., *China in the Sixteenth Century: The Journals of Matthew Ricci: 1583–1610* (New York: Random House, 1953), pp. 30–31.

The dilemma of accounting in religious terms for the ideas of Copernicus and Descartes became more urgent for Protestants as the ideas acquired an anti-Catholic status after the trial of Galileo in 1633, and as they became common scientific currency by about 1640. The development of the new science in the mid-seventeenth century coincided with religious and political upheavals throughout Europe. Religious, political, and scientific view-points became inextricably mixed. A religious certainty about divine force that could account for the motion of bodies in a vacuum enabled Newton to develop his theories on motion and gravity. In short, religion did not merely remain in the scientists' panoply of explanations; it remained a fundamental building block of scientific thought, in the same way that it remained central to most scientists' lives.

The Mechanistic World Order and Human Affairs at the End of the Seventeenth Century

Traditional institutions and ideologies checked the potential effects of the new science for a time, but by the middle of the seventeenth century, political theory was beginning to show the impact of the mechanistic world-view. Political philosophers viewed neither the world nor human society as an organic whole in which each part was distinguished in nature and function from the rest. Thomas Hobbes, John Locke, and others reimagined the bonds that link citizens to each other and to their rulers.

Because of the political turmoil in England, Thomas Hobbes (1588–1679) spent much of his productive life on the Continent. After the beginnings of the parliamentary rebellion, he joined a group of royalist émigrés in France. He met Galileo and lived for extended periods in Paris, in contact with the circle of French thinkers that included Descartes. Like Descartes, he theorized about the nature and behavior of matter; he published a treatise on his views in 1655.

Hobbes is best known today for *Leviathan* (1651), his treatise on political philosophy. *Leviathan* applies to the world of human beings Hobbes's mostly Cartesian view of nature as composed of "self-motivated" atomlike structures. Hobbes viewed people as mechanistically as he viewed the rest of nature. In his view, people were made up of appetites of various sorts—the same kind of innate forces that drove all matter. The ideal state, concluded Hobbes, is one in which a strong sovereign controls the disorder that inevitably arises from the clash of desires. Unlike the medieval philosophers, Hobbes did not draw analogies between the state and the human body (the king as head, judges and magistrates as arms, and so forth). Instead, Hobbes compared the state to a machine that "ran" by means of laws and was kept in good working order by a skilled technician—the ruler.

Hobbes's pessimism about human behavior and his insistence on the need for order imposed from above reflect, like the work of Descartes, a concern for order in the wake of political turmoil. This concern was one reason he was welcomed into the community of French philosophers, who were naturally comfortable with royalty as a powerful guarantor of order. But Hobbes's work, like theirs, was a radical departure because it envisions citizens as potentially equal and constrained neither by morality nor by natural obedience to authority.

Another Englishman, John Locke (1632–1704), offered an entirely different vision of natural equality among people and of social order. Locke's major works, *Essay on Human Understanding* (1690) and *Two Treatises on Government* (1690), reflect the experimentalism of Robert Boyle, the systematizing rationality of Descartes, and other strands of the new scientific thought. In the *Essay*, Locke offers a view of human knowledge that is more pragmatic and utilitarian than the rigorous mathematical model of certainty used by many other philosophers. He argues that human knowledge is largely the product of experience. He agrees with Descartes that reason orders and explains human experience. But he thinks that reason does not necessarily perceive reality as it really is but rather perceives reality in a limited way that is nevertheless useful. Unlike Descartes, Locke thinks there are limits to what human reason can achieve, but Locke offers a more optimistic vision of the possible uses of human reason. Whereas Descartes was interested in mentally ordering and understanding the world, Locke was interested in humans' functioning in the world.

Locke's treatises on government reflect his notion of knowledge based on experience as well as his particular experiences as a member of elite circles in the aftermath of the English revolution. A trained physician, he served as personal physician and general political assistant to Anthony Ashley Cooper (1621–1683), Lord Shaftsbury, one of the members of Parliament most opposed to Charles II's pretensions to absolutist government. When James II acceded to the throne in 1685, Locke remained in the Netherlands, where he had fled to avoid prosecution for treason. He became an adviser to William of Orange and returned to England with William and Mary in 1688. Locke's view of the principles of good government, then, came to reflect the pro-parliamentary stance of his political milieu.

Unlike Hobbes, Locke argues that people are capable of restraint and mutual respect in their pursuit of self-interest. The state arises from a contract that individuals freely enter into to protect themselves, their property, and their happiness

Locke's View of the Purpose of Government

In this passage from the second of his treatises on government, Locke describes men as naturally free and willing to enter into communities only for the protection of property. Notice how Locke justifies private property as "natural" by linking it to an individual's labor.

Men being . . . by nature all free, equal, and independent, no one can be put out of this estate and subjected to the political power of another without his own consent. The only way whereby any one divests himself of his natural liberty and puts on the bonds of civil society is by agreeing with other men to join and unite into a community for their comfortable, safe, and peaceable living amongst one another, in a secure enjoyment of their properties and a greater security against any that are not of it. This any number of men may do, because it injures not the freedom of the rest; they are left as they were in the liberty of the state of nature. When any number of men have so consented to make one community or government, they are thereby presently incorporated and make one body politic wherein the majority have a right to act and conclude the rest. . . . And thus that which begins and acutally constitutes any political society is nothing but the consent of any number of freemen capable of a majority to unite and incorporate into such a society. And this is that, and that only, which did or could give beginning to any lawful government in the world.

If man in the state of nature be so free . . . , and if he be absolute lord of his own person and possessions, equal to the greatest, and

subject to nobody, why will he part with his freedom, why will he give up his empire and subject himself to the dominion and control of any other power?

The great and chief end, therefore, of men's uniting into commonwealths and putting themselves under government is the preservation of their property. . . . Though the earth and all inferior creatures be common to all men, yet every man has a property in his own person; this nobody has any right to but himself. The labor of his body and the work of his hands, we may say, are properly his. Whatsoever then he removes out of the state that nature has provided and left it in, he has mixed his labor with, and joined to it something that is his own, and thereby makes it his property. It being by him removed from the common state nature has placed it in, it has by this labor something annexed to it that excludes the common right of other men. For this labor being the unquestionable property of the laborer, no man but he can have a right to what that is once joined to, at least where there is enough and as good left in common for others. . . . As much land as a man tills, plants, improves, cultivates, and can use the product of, so much is his property. He by his labor does, as it were, enclose it from the common.

Source: Second Treatise, in John Locke, *Two Treatises of Civil Government* (London: G. Routledge & Sons, 1884).

from possible aggression by others. They can invest the executive and legislative authority to carry out this protection in monarchy or any other governing institution, though Locke believed the English Parliament was the best available model. Because sovereignty resides with the people who enter into the contract, rebellion against abuse of power is justified. Thus, Locke frees people from

arbitrary bonds of authority to the state and to each other.

Locke's experience as a member of the elite of his society is apparent in his emphasis on private property, which he considers one of the fundamental human rights. (See the box, "Locke's View of the Purpose of Government.") Indeed, there is no place in his political vision for serious disagree-

Science Gains an Audience This illustration from Bernard de Fontenelle's major work popularized the new science. It reveals the audience for which the work was intended. A gentleman, sitting with a lady in a formal garden, gestures to a depiction of the solar system as it was now understood; the lady is presumed to understand and to be interested in the information. *(By permission of Houghton Library, Harvard University)*

ment about the nature of property. Locke even found a justification for slavery. He also did not consider women to be political beings in the same way as men. The family, he felt, was a separate domain from the state, not bound by the same contractual obligations.

Locke's dismissal of women from the realm of politics and of questions of power and justice from the family was not an accident. The ability of Locke and many other seventeenth-century thinkers to imagine a new physical or political order was constrained by the prevailing view of gender as a "nat-

ural" principle of order and hierarchy. Gender distinctions are in the main socially ascribed roles that are easily misinterpreted as "natural" differences between women and men. Although Margaret Cavendish (see the box on page 645) and other women disputed the validity of such distinctions, men frequently used them. Locke's use of gender as an arbitrary organizing principle gave his bold new political vision a claim to being "natural." The use of gender-specific vocabulary to describe nature itself had the effect of making the new objective attitude toward the world seem "natural."

Works by seventeenth-century scientists are filled with references to nature as a woman who must be "conquered," "subdued," or "penetrated."

Traditional gender distinctions limited and buttressed most facets of political thought, but in other areas, the fact of uncertainty and the need for tolerance was embraced. Another of Locke's influential works was the impassioned *Letter on Toleration* (1689). In it he argues that religious belief is fundamentally private and that only the most basic Christian principles need be accepted by everyone. Others went further than Locke by entirely removing traditional religion as a fundamental guarantor of morality and order. Fostering this climate of religious skepticism were religious pluralism in England and the irrationality of religious intolerance—demonstrated by Louis XIV's persecution of Protestants.

Pierre Bayle (1647–1706), a Frenchman of Protestant origins, argued that morality can be wholly detached from traditional religion. Bayle cited as an example of morality the philosopher Baruch Spinoza (1632–1677). Spinoza believed the state to have a moral purpose and human happiness to have spiritual roots. Yet he was not a Christian at all but a Dutch Jew who had been ejected from his local synagogue for supposed atheism. One need hardly be a Christian of any sort in order to be a moral being, Bayle concluded.

Bayle's skepticism toward traditional knowledge was more wide ranging than his views on religion. His best-known work, *Dictionnaire historique et critique* (*Historical and Critical Dictionary*, 1702), was a compendium of observations about and criticisms of virtually every thinker whose works were known at the time, including recent and lionized figures such as Descartes and Newton. Bayle was the first systematic skeptic, and he relentlessly exposed errors and shortcomings in all received knowledge. His works were very popular with elite lay readers.

Bayle's fellow countryman Bernard de Fontenelle (1657–1757), secretary to the Académie des Sciences from 1699 to 1741, was the greatest popularizer of the new science of his time. His *Entretiens sur la Pluralités des Mondes* (*Conversations on the Plurality of Worlds,* 1686) was, as the title implies, an informally presented description of the infinite universe of matter. It went through numerous editions and translations. As secretary to the Académie, Fontenelle continued his work as popularizer by publishing descriptions of the work of the Académie's scientists. He died one month short of his hundredth birthday. At his death in 1757 it was said that "the Philosophic spirit, today so much in evidence, owes its beginnings to Monsieur de Fontenelle."[16]

SUMMARY

Fontenelle is a fitting figure with whom to end a discussion of the Scientific Revolution because he represents, and worked to accomplish, the transference of the new natural philosophy into political and social philosophy—a movement we know as the "Enlightenment." The Scientific Revolution began, as innovation in scientific thinking often does, with a specific research problem whose answer led in unexpected directions. Copernicus's response to traditional astronomical problems led to scientific and philosophical innovation because of his solution and because of the context into which it was received.

Other scientists, following Copernicus, built on his theories, culminating in the work of Galileo, who supported Copernican theory with additional data and widely published his findings. The Frenchman Descartes was the first to fashion a systematic explanation for the operations of nature to replace the medieval view. The political and intellectual climate in England, meanwhile, encouraged the development of experimental science and inductive reasoning. Isaac Newton provided new theories to explain the behavior of matter and expressed them in mathematical terms that could apply to either the earth or the cosmos; with his work, traditional astronomy and physics were overturned.

Rulers made use of the new science for the practical results it offered despite the ideological challenge it presented to their power. By the end of the seventeenth century, the hierarchical Christian world-view grounded in the old science was being challenged on many fronts. A fully articulated secular world-view would be the product of the Enlightenment.

NOTES

1. Quoted in Thomas S. Kuhn, *The Copernican Revolution* (Cambridge, Mass.: Harvard University Press, 1985), p. 131.
2. Quoted in Margaret C. Jacob, *The Cultural Meaning of the Scientific Revolution* (Philadelphia: Temple, 1988), p. 18.
3. Quoted ibid., p. 33.
4. Quoted in Alan G. R. Smith, *Science and Society in the Sixteenth and Seventeenth Centuries* (New York: Science History Publications, 1972), p. 72.
5. Quoted in Jacob, *Cultural Meaning*, p. 32 (emphasis added).
6. Quoted in Bruce T. Moran, ed., *Patronage and Institutions: Science, Technology and Medicine at the European Court* (Rochester: The Boyden Press, 1991), p. 43.
7. Quoted in Jacob, *Cultural Meaning*, p. 59.
8. Quoted ibid., p. 58.
9. Quoted in Steven Shapin, *A Social History of Truth* (Chicago: University of Chicago Press, 1994), p. 298.
10. Quoted in Jacob, *Cultural Meaning*, p. 89.
11. Quoted in Smith, *Science and Society*, p. 130.
12. Quoted in Jacob, *Cultural Meaning*, p. 25.
13. Quoted in Londa Schiebinger, *The Mind Has No Sex?* (Cambridge, Mass.: Harvard University Press, 1989), p. 92.
14. Quoted in Kuhn, *The Copernican Revolution*, p. 191.
15. *Complete Poetry and Selected Prose of John Donne*, ed. John Hayward (Bloomsbury, England: Nonesuch Press, 1929), p. 365; quoted in Kuhn, *The Copernican Revolution*, p. 194.
16. Quoted in Paul Edwards, ed., *The Encyclopedia of Philosophy*, vol. 3 (New York: Macmillan, 1967), p. 209.

SUGGESTED READING

General Surveys

Debus, Allen G. *Man and Nature in the Renaissance*. 1978. A survey of developments in science and medicine during the two centuries leading up to the seventeenth-century revolution; its special contribution stems from Debus's emphasis on Paracelsianism and alchemy.

Hall, A. Rupert. *The Revolution in Science, 1500–1800*. 1983. A thorough introduction to all scientific disciplines that de-emphasizes the larger context of scientific development but explains many of the innovations in detail.

Kearney, Hugh. *Science and Change*. 1971. A readable general introduction to the Scientific Revolution.

Kuhn, Thomas. *The Copernican Revolution*. 1985. A readable treatment of the revolution in astronomy that also lucidly explains the Aristotelian world-view; important for setting Copernicus's work in the context of the history of astronomy; the first thing to read to understand the Copernican revolution.

———. *The Structure of Scientific Revolutions*. 1970. A path-breaking work that argues that all scientific schemas are systems of explanation and that science progresses by shifting from one general paradigm to another, not from error to "truth."

Lindberg, D. C., and R. S. Westman. *Reappraisals of the Scientific Revolution*. 1990. Essays re-evaluating classic interpretations of the Scientific Revolution. Includes a rich bibliography.

Mandrou, Robert. *From Humanism to Science*. 1978. A general intellectual history of the period 1450–1650 that sets the Scientific Revolution in the context of broader intellectual, social, and economic currents.

Merchant, Carolyn. *The Death of Nature: Women, Ecology and the Scientific Revolution*. 1980. An important corrective interpretation that focuses on the changing definition of nature—particularly how nature became something to be dominated and consumed—and the way in which this definition reinforced negative cultural views of women.

Thomas, Keith. *Religion and the Decline of Magic*. 1971. An exploration of the changing character of religious belief and "superstitious" practice; finds roots outside of science for changing, increasingly secular world-views.

Westfall, Richard S. *The Construction of Modern Science: Mechanisms and Mechanics*. 1977. A general treatment of the Scientific Revolution that emphasizes and explains the mechanistic world-view.

Individual Scientists

Bordo, Susan R. *The Flight to Objectivity: Essays on Cartesianism and Culture*. 1987. A collection that studies Descartes's work as a metaphysical and psychological crisis and discusses implications of Cartesian mind-body dualism.

Cohen, I. Bernard. *The Newtonian Revolution*. 1987. A brief introduction to Newton and the meaning of his discoveries; a good place to start on Newton.

Drake, Stillman. *Galileo at Work: His Scientific Biography*. 1978. A detailed chronological study that reveals Galileo's character and illuminates his scientific achievements.

Frank, Robert G., Jr. *Harvey and the Oxford Physiologists*. 1980. An explanation of Harvey's work in the context of traditional Galenic medicine and a discussion of the community of scholars who accepted and built on Harvey's innovations.

Redondi, Pietro. *Galileo Heretic*. 1987. A careful account of Galileo's confrontation with the church.

(continued on page 656)

MODERN MAPS

We take for granted that contemporary maps will provide accurate representations of geography and present information in standardized ways we can easily read. But how did these standards of clarity and accuracy come about?

Modern mapping was developed during the Scientific Revolution. Like most of the changes we have labeled the "Scientific Revolution," changes in mapping were the result of several influences: innovations in Renaissance art, knowledge gleaned from voyages of exploration, the impact of new astronomical discoveries, and the interest and support of princely patrons.

Let us look at Christopher Saxton's map of Somerset, a county in England. This map was printed in 1579 in one of the first atlases ever published. We might be struck by how different this map appears from contemporary maps; many of its features seem decorative or even quaint. Ships, not drawn to scale, ride at anchor or sail off the coast. Towns are represented not by dots of various sizes but by miniature town buildings. Relief in the landscape is depicted with hills drawn, like the town buildings, from a side view inconsistent with the aerial perspective of the map as a whole. The large royal coat of arms that occupies the upper left quadrant of the map seems the most antiquated and irrelevant feature.

But is it irrelevant? Let us try to appreciate what a striking and powerful image this map must have been for its original viewers. Because the features are represented in ways that we consider decorative, it is easy for us to overlook the fact that this map illustrates a revolutionary method of depicting space. Saxton provides an aerial view of an entire county, with all locales arrayed in accurate spatial relationship to one another. This accurate rendering of space was, first, the result of the discovery of linear perspective by Renaissance artists. This discovery enabled space to be imagined from the perspective of a distanced observer. Saxton's maps—and the few others published at about the same time—represented the first time Europeans could take "visual possession" of the land they

Map of the County of Somerset, England, 1579
(British Library)

Map of the French Coastline, 1693 *(Bibliothèque Nationale)*

lived in, in the way we now take for granted whenever we buy a road map.*

Precise measurement of land forms—the location of hills in this map, for example—still relied on the established craft of systematic surveying. And here is where the royal coat of arms enters the picture, literally. Saxton's surveying and the production of his atlas were sponsored by the government of Queen Elizabeth. Thus, just as this map enabled contemporary observers to envision for the first time, in its entirety, the land they lived in, it simultaneously marked royal power over that land.

Now let us look at a 1693 map of the coastline of France. We immediately note that most decorative elements are gone: No ships sail the abundant seas, for example. The figure of a compass marks the Paris meridian—the site of the city, we are shown, has been precisely determined by means of its longitude and latitude. More accurate calculation of longitude had been made possible by the work of Kepler and Galileo, whose mapping of heavenly bodies provided known points in the night sky from which to calculate the longitude of the observer's position on earth. (Calculation of latitude had always been easier, since it involved

only determining the angle of the sun above the horizon, but it was also improved by better instrumentation in the seventeenth century.) After 1650, French cartographers, among others, systematically collected astronomical observations from around the world more precisely to map all known lands.

This map superimposes a corrected view of the coastline of France over an older rendering. The power of this coastline map, then, lies in the way it dramatically advertises the progress of mapmaking itself. Royal power remains connected to scientific effort: The title reads, "Map of France, corrected by order of the King by the observations of Messieurs of the Academy of Sciences."

Thus, both of these maps glorify royal power: one by linking it with a dramatically new visualization of the land it ruled, the other by presenting royalty as a patron and guarantor of knowledge. But in the second map, royal identity is no longer pictured along with the land it claims. Instead, the king is mentioned discreetly, in what is coming to be a standardized label.

Like all innovations of the Scientific Revolution, those in mapmaking had unintended consequences. Claims to royal power articulated on maps lost their force when placed next to the information the maps conveyed; royal power had many practical and ideological uses for the new science but, in the end, would be undermined by the world-view the new science made possible.

---

*Richard Helgerson, "The Land Speaks: Cartography, Chorography, and Subversion in Renaissance England," *Representations* 16 (Fall 1986): 51. This discussion of Saxton's map and the evolution of mapmaking is drawn from Helgerson and from Norman J. W. Thrower, *Maps and Civilization* (Chicago: University of Chicago Press, 1996), chaps. 5 and 6.

Shapin, Steven, and Simon Schaffer. *Leviathan and the Air-Pump.* 1985. One of the most important studies of seventeenth-century science: traces the conflict between Cartesian science, as represented by Hobbes, and experimental science, in the work of Boyle; and shows the relationship of Hobbes and Boyle to their respective contexts as well as some of the political, cultural, and philosophical implications of each school of thought.

Thoren, Victor E. *The Lord of Uraniborg: A Biography of Tycho Brahe.* 1990. An up-to-date study of the life and work of the Danish astronomer.

Political, Social, and Cultural Contexts for Science

Biagioli, Mario. *Galileo, Courtier.* 1993. A new study that stresses the power of patronage relations to shape scientific process.

Hunter, Michael. *Science and Society in Restoration England.* 1981. A study that sets English science in its political and cultural contexts; critical of Webster's classic study (see below).

Jacob, Margaret C. *The Cultural Meaning of the Scientific Revolution.* 1988. An account that moves from the Scientific Revolution through the industrial transformation of the nineteenth century, sketching the relationship of developments in science, metaphysics, and technology to the political and social history of the various eras.

————. *The Newtonians and the English Revolution.* 1976. A work that links the development of Newtonian science to its political and social context and examines the simultaneous evolution of religion that could accept the new science yet maintain traditional perspectives.

Moran, Bruce T., ed. *Patronage and Institutions: Science, Technology and Medicine at the European Court.* 1991. A work that looks at royal courts as shaping and sustaining institutions for science from the early sixteenth century onward.

Schiebinger, Londa. *The Mind Has No Sex?* 1989. An examination of the participation of women in the practice of science and an explanation of how science began to reflect the exclusion of women in its values and objects of study—above all, in its claims about scientific "facts" about women themselves.

Webster, Charles. *The Great Instauration.* 1975. A classic study that links the development of the modern scientific attitude to the Puritan revolution in England.

CHAPTER 18

Europe on the Threshold of Modernity, ca. 1715–1789

A customer in one of the growing number of cafés in Paris on February 10, 1778, might have wondered if the king himself was entering the city, such was the commotion as Parisians turned out to welcome a former resident. Now 84, this old man had journeyed to the city to preside at the opening of his latest play, but everyone realized that this most likely would be his last visit, and he was given a hero's welcome. The king himself would not receive the visitor, but literary and political elites clamored to be admitted to audiences with him. Benjamin Franklin brought his grandson to receive the old man's blessing. Though he was treated like royalty, the man was not a ruler, but a political thinker and writer: the philosopher Voltaire.

A prolific writer, critic, and reformer in his own country of France, Voltaire was lionized by elites everywhere, including the rulers of several European states. Voltaire is an apt symbol for the age not only because of his personal influence, but also because he was simply the best known of dozens of thinkers and writers who made up the philosophical movement we know as the Enlightenment. The Enlightenment constituted a revolution in political philosophy, but it was also much more: The era witnessed the emergence of an informed body of public opinion, critical of the prevailing political system, that existed outside the corridors of power. The relationship between governments and the governed had begun to change: Subjects of monarchs were becoming citizens of nations.

Frederick the Great of Prussia, Catherine the Great of Russia, and other rulers self-consciously tried to use Enlightenment precepts to guide

Voltaire, by Houdon.
In the foyer of the
Théâtre Français, Paris.

their efforts at governing. They had mixed success, however. Powerful interests opposed their efforts at reform, and their own hereditary and autocratic power was incompatible with Enlightenment perspectives. Elites still sure of their power, as well as the traditional interests of states, dominated eighteenth-century politics.

Nevertheless, profound changes in economic, social, and political life began in this period. Economic growth spurred population growth, which in turn stimulated industry and trade. The increasing economic and strategic importance of overseas colonies made them important focal points of international conflict. The dramatic political and social changes that began as the century closed had their roots in the intellectual, economic, and social ferment of eighteenth-century life.

THE ENLIGHTENMENT

One of Isaac Newton's countrymen wrote the following epitaph for the English scientist:

Nature and Nature's Laws lay hid in Night.
God said, "Let Newton be," and all was Light.

The most important works of Enlightenment philosophy reflected the intellectual confidence that Newton's work generated. The poet's assertion that "all was Light," however, requires scrutiny.

The phrase evokes the determination and confidence of an intellectual elite that felt it held a new key to truth. In this sense, the Enlightenment was nothing less than the transfer into general philosophy, particularly political and social thought, of the intellectual revolution that had already taken place within the physical sciences. But, like the Scientific Revolution, the Enlightenment was not only sweeping in its impact but specific in its content. In this so-called Age of Reason, *reason* had specific meanings, and philosophers' speculations had particular goals.

Enlightenment philosophy occurred in the context of increasingly widespread publications and new opportunities in literary societies, clubs, and salons for the exchange of views. This context shaped the outline of Enlightenment thought, which was for the most part an elite set of preoccupations. It also determined the radicalism of the Enlightenment, by helping to ensure that an entire

level of society would share in attitudes that were fundamentally critical of that society.

Voltaire and the Enlightenment

The Enlightenment was not so much a body of thought as it was an intellectual and social movement. Originating in France, it consisted, first, of the application to political and social thought of the confidence in the intelligibility of natural law that theoretical science had recently achieved. Enlightenment thinkers combined confidence in the intelligibility of the world and its laws with confidence in the human capacity to discern and work in concert with those laws. The former confidence was Newton's legacy; the latter was the legacy of Descartes and Locke. The most dramatic effect of confidence was the desacralizing of social and political bonds—a new belief that society can be grounded on rational foundations to be determined by humans, not arbitrary foundations determined by God.

A wide range of thinkers participated in the Enlightenment; in France, they were known as *philosophes,* a term meaning not a formal philosopher but rather a thinker and critic. To most philosophes, the main agenda was clear. For too long, humans had been mired in ignorance. Rather than regarding themselves as thinkers, they thought of themselves as sinners. Arbitrary laws and institutions oppressed them. Lack of proper education and the tyranny of the church condemned them to ignorance. French thinkers singled out the Catholic church as the archenemy because of its opposition to their positive views of human nature and because it controlled much education and was still a force in political life.

The following passage from Voltaire's *Dictionnaire philosophique* (*Philosophical Dictionary,* 1764) is typical of his work in its casual format and biting wit and is also typical of the venomous Enlightenment view of the church. The dictionary entry for "authority" is not about authority in general but focuses on the arbitrary authority of the church:

A hundred times [you clerics] have been spoken to of the insolent absurdity with which you condemned Galileo, and I shall speak to you for the hundred and first. . . . I desire that there be engraved on the door of your holy office: Here seven cardinals assisted by minor brethren had the master of thought of Italy thrown into prison at the age of seventy, made him fast on bread and water, because he instructed the human race.

The life of Voltaire (1694–1778), the most famous of the philosophes, spanned the century. Born François-Marie Arouet to a middle-class family, he took the pen name Voltaire in 1718, after one of his early plays was a critical success. He was educated by the Jesuits, whom he despised but admired for their teaching methods. He produced a vast array of written work: plays, epic poems, novelettes—some of which have explicit philosophical or political content—as well as philosophical tracts. Voltaire moved in courtly circles. Mockery of the regent, the duke of Orléans, led to a year's imprisonment in 1717, and an exchange of insults with a leading courtier some years later led to enforced exile in Great Britain for two years.

After returning from Britain, Voltaire published his first major philosophical work. *Lettres philosophiques* (*Philosophical Letters*, 1734) revealed the influence of his British sojourn and helped to popularize Newton's achievement. The empirical tradition in British philosophy profoundly influenced Voltaire. To his confidence in the laws governing nature he added cautious confidence in humans' attempts to establish truth. From Locke's work (see pages 649–651) he drew confidence in human educability tempered by awareness of the finite nature of the human mind. These elements gave Voltaire's philosophy both its passionate conviction and its practicality.

Voltaire portrayed Great Britain as a more rational society than France. He was particularly impressed with the religious and intellectual toleration evident there. The British government had a more workable set of institutions and the economy was less crippled by the remnants of feudal privilege, and education was not in the hands of the church. (See the box, "Voltaire on Britain's Commercial Success.")

After the publication of his audacious *Lettres*, Voltaire was again forced into exile from Paris, and he resided for some years in the country home of a woman with whom he shared a remarkable intellectual and emotional relationship: Emilie, marquise du Châtelet (1706–1749). Châtelet was a mathematician and a scientist. She set to work on a French translation of Newton's *Principia* while Voltaire worked at his accustomed variety of writing, which also included a commen-

Etablissement de la nouvelle Philosophie. Notre Berceau fut un Caffé.

Café Society The caption under this contemporary illustration reads: "Establishment of the new philosophy; our cradle was the café." Cafés were one of the new settings where literate elites could discuss the new philosophy and explore its implications for social and political life. (*Carnavalet Museum, Paris*)

tary on Newton's work. Because of Châtelet's tutelage, Voltaire became more knowledgeable about the sciences and more serious in his efforts to apply scientific rationality to human affairs. He was devastated by her sudden death in 1749.

Shortly afterward, he accepted the invitation of the king of Prussia, Frederick II, to visit Berlin. His stay was stormy and brief because of disagreements with other court philosophers. He resided

Voltaire on Britain's Commercial Success

In this excerpt from **Philosophical Letters,** *Voltaire compares British trade and seapower with the commercial activities of the German and French elites, who scorn trade in order to engage in aristocratic pretentiousness and court politics. Voltaire's admiration for England and his penchant for criticizing irrationalities of all sorts are evident, as is his famed wit. Wit and irony were important tools, enabling Voltaire to advance trenchant criticism when seeming only to poke fun.*

Commerce, which has brought wealth to the citizenry of England, has helped to make them free, and freedom has developed commerce in its turn. By means of it the nation has grown great; it is commerce that little by little has strengthened the naval forces that make the English the masters of the seas. . . . Posterity may learn with some surprise that a little island with nothing of its own but a bit of lead, tin . . . and coarse wool became, by means of its commerce, powerful enough to send three fleets at one time to three different ends of the earth.

All this makes the English merchant justly proud; moreover, the younger brother of a peer of the realm does not scorn to enter into trade. . . . [In Germany], they are unable to imagine how [an aristocrat could enter trade since they have] as many as thirty Highnesses of the same name, with nothing to show for it but pride and a coat of arms.

In France anybody who wants to can [act the part of marquis] and whoever arrives in Paris with money to spend and a [plausible name] may indulge in such phrases as "a man of my rank and quality" and with sovereign eye look down upon a wholesaler. . . . Yet I don't know which is the more useful to a state, a well-powdered lord who knows precisely what time the king gets up in the morning . . . and who gives himself airs of grandeur while playing the role of slave in a minister's antechamber, or a great merchant who enriches his country.

Source: Ernest Dilworth, trans. and ed., *Voltaire: Philosophical Letters* (New York: Bobbs-Merrill, 1961), pp. 39–40.

for a time in Geneva, until his criticisms of the city's moral codes forced yet another exile on him. He spent most of the last twenty years of his life at his estates on the Franco-Swiss border, where he could be relatively free from interference by any government. These were productive years. He produced his best-known satirical novelette, *Candide,* in 1758. It criticized aristocratic privilege and the power of clerics as well as the naiveté of philosophers who took "natural law" to mean that the world was already operating as it should.

Voltaire's belief that one must struggle to overturn the accumulated habits of centuries is also reflected in his political activity. Voltaire became involved in several celebrated legal cases in which individuals were pitted against the authority of the church, which was still backed by the authority of the state. The most famous case was that of Jean Calas (1698–1762), a Protestant from southern France who was accused of murdering his son, allegedly to prevent him from converting to Catholicism. Calas maintained his innocence until his execution in 1762. Voltaire saw in this case the worst aspects of religious prejudice and injustice and worked tirelessly to establish Calas's innocence as a matter of principle and so that his family could inherit his property. In pursuit of justice in these cases and in criticism of his archenemy the church, Voltaire added a stream of straightforward political pamphlets to his literary output. He also worked closer to home, initiating agricultural reform on his estates and working to improve the status of peasants in the vicinity.

Voltaire died in Paris in May 1778, shortly after his triumphal return there. By then, he was no longer leader of the Enlightenment in strictly intellectual terms. Thinkers and writers more radical than he had earned prominence during his long life and had dismissed some of his beliefs, such as the notion that reform could be introduced by a monarch. But Voltaire had provided a crucial stimulus to French thought with his *Lettres philosophiques*. His importance lies also in his embodiment of the critical spirit of eighteenth-century rationalism: its confidence, its increasingly practical bent, its wit and sophistication. Until the end of his life, Voltaire remained a bridge between the increasingly diverse body of Enlightenment thought and the literate elite audience.

The Variety of Enlightenment Thought

Differences among philosophes grew as the century progressed. In the matter of religion, for example, there was virtual unanimity of opposition to the Catholic church among French thinkers, but no unanimity about God. Voltaire was a theist—believing firmly in God, creator of the universe, but not a specifically Christian God. To some later thinkers, God was irrelevant—the creator of the world, but a world that ran continuously according to established laws. Some philosophes were atheists, arguing that a universe that ran according to discoverable laws needs no higher purpose and no divine presence to explain, run, or justify it. In Protestant areas of Europe, in contrast to France, Enlightenment thought was often less hostile to Christianity.

Questions about social and political order, as well as about human rationality itself, were also pondered. Charles de Secondat (1689–1755), baron of Montesquieu, a French judge and legal philosopher, combined the belief that human institutions must be rational with Locke's assumption of human educability. Montesquieu's treatise *De L'Esprit des lois* (*The Spirit of the Laws*, 1748) was published in twenty-two printings within two years. In it Montesquieu maintained that laws were not meant to be arbitrary rules but derived naturally from human society: The more evolved a society was, the

MAJOR WORKS OF THE ENLIGHTENMENT

Year	Work
1721	Montesquieu, *Persian Letters*
1734	Voltaire, *Philosophical Letters*
1748	Montesquieu, *The Spirit of the Laws* Hume, *Essay Concerning Human Understanding*
1758	Voltaire, *Candide*
1751–65	Diderot, *The Encyclopedia*
1762	Rousseau, *The Social Contract*
1764	Voltaire, *Philosophical Dictionary*
1776	Smith, *The Wealth of Nations*
1784	Kant, *What Is Enlightenment?*
1792	Wollstonecraft, *A Vindication of the Rights of Woman*
1795	Condorcet, *The Progress of the Human Mind*

more liberal were its laws. This notion provided a sense of the progress possible within society and government and deflated Europeans' pretensions in regard to other societies, for a variety of laws could equally be "rational" given differing conditions. Montesquieu is perhaps best known to Americans as the advocate of the separation of legislative, executive, and judicial powers that later became enshrined in the American Constitution. To Montesquieu, this scheme seemed to parallel in human government the balance of forces observable in nature and seemed best to guarantee liberty.

The "laws" of economic life were also investigated. In France, economic thinkers known as *physiocrats* proposed ending what they regarded as artificial control over land use in order to free productive capacity and permit the flow of produce to market. Their target was traditional forms of land tenure, including collective control of village lands by peasants and seigneurial rights over land and peasant labor by landlords. The freeing of restrictions on agriculture, manufacture, and trade was proposed by the Scotsman Adam Smith in his treatise *An Inquiry into the Nature and Causes of the Wealth of Nations* (1776).

Smith (1723–1790), a professor at the University of Glasgow, is best known in modern times as the originator of "laissez-faire" economics: the assumption that an economy will regulate itself without interference by government and, of more concern to Smith, without the monopolies and other economic privileges common in his day. Smith's schema for economic growth was not merely a rigid application to economics of faith in natural law. His ideas grew out of an optimistic view of human nature and human rationality that was heavily indebted to Locke. Humans, Smith believed, have drives and passions that they can direct and govern by means of reason and inherent sympathy for one another. Thus, Smith said, in seeking their own achievement and well-being, they are often "led by an invisible hand" to simultaneously benefit society as a whole.

Throughout the century, philosophers of various stripes disagreed about the nature and the limits of human reason. Smith's countryman and friend David Hume (1711–1776) was perhaps the most radical in his critique of the human capacity for knowing. He was the archskeptic, taking Locke's view of the limitations on pure reason to the point of doubting the efficacy of sense data. His major work in which he expounded these views, *Essay Concerning Human Understanding* (1748), led to important innovations later in the century in the work of the German philosopher Immanuel Kant but were, at the time, almost contrary to the prevailing spirit of confidence in empirical knowledge. Hume himself separated this work from his other efforts in moral, political, and economic philosophy, which were more in tune with the prevailing views of the day.

Mainstream confidence in empirical knowledge and in the intelligibility of the world is evident in the production of the *Encyclopédie* (*Encyclopedia*), a seventeen-volume compendium of knowledge, criticism, and philosophy assembled by leading philosophes in France and published there between 1751 and 1765. The volumes were designed to contain state-of-the-art knowledge about arts, sciences, technology, and philosophy. The guiding philosophy of the project, set forth by its chief editor, Denis Diderot (1713–1784), was a belief in the advance of human happiness through the advance of knowledge. The *Encyclopédie* was a kind of history of the advance of knowledge as

Diderot's Encyclopedia This illustration of typesetting at a newspaper printshop is one of many depicting industry and technology of the day in the multivolume *Encyclopedia*. Newspapers increased in size, number, and frequency of publication during the course of the eighteenth century. *(Division of Rare & Manuscript Collections, Cornell University Library)*

well as a compendium of known achievements. It was revolutionary in that it not only intrigued and inspired intellectuals but assisted thousands of government officials and professionals. Catherine the Great, empress of Russia, remarked in a letter that she consulted its pages to find guidance concerning one of her reform schemes.

The encyclopedia project illustrates the political context of Enlightenment thought as well as its philosophical premises. The Catholic church placed the work on the Index of prohibited books, and the French government might have barred its publication but for the fact that the official who would have made the decision was drawn to Enlightenment thinking. Many other officials, however, worked to suppress it. By the late 1750s, losses in wars overseas had made French officials highly sensitive to political challenges of any kind. Thus, like Voltaire, the major contributors to the *Encyclopédie* were lionized by certain segments of the elite and persecuted by others in their official functions.

The *Encyclopédie* reflects the complexities and limitations of Enlightenment thought on another score—the position of women. One might expect that the Enlightenment penchant for challenging received knowledge and traditional social and political hierarchies would lead to revised views of women's abilities and rights. Indeed, some contributors blamed women's inequality with men not on any deficiencies in women but rather on the customs and laws that had kept women from education and the development of their abilities. However, other contributors blamed women, and not society, for the inequality women suffered, or they argued that women had talents that fit them only for the domestic sphere.

Both positions were represented in Enlightenment thought as a whole. The assumption of the natural equality of all people provided a powerful ground for arguing the equality of women with men. Some thinkers, such as Mary Astell (1666–1731), challenged Locke's separation of family life from the public world of free, contractual relationships. (See the box, "An English Feminist Criticizes Unenlightened Views of Women.") Most advocated increased education for women, if only to make them more fit to raise enlightened children. By 1800 the most radical thinkers were advocating full citizenship rights for women and equal rights to property along with enhanced education.

The best-known proponent of those views was an English woman, Mary Wollstonecraft (1759–1797), who authored *A Vindication of the Rights of Woman* (1792). She assumed that most elite women would devote themselves to domestic duties, but she argued that without the responsibilities of citizenship, the leavening of education, and economic independence, women could be neither fully formed individuals nor worthy of their duties. Working women, she concluded, needed these rights simply to survive.

A more limited view of women's capacities was one element in the influential work of Jean-Jacques Rousseau (1712–1778). Like Locke, Rousseau could conceive of the free individual only as male, and he grounded his critique of the old order and his novel political ideas in an arbitrary division of gender roles. Rousseau's view of women was linked to a critique of the artificiality of elite, cosmopolitan society in which Enlightenment thought was then flourishing and in which aristocratic women were fully involved. Rousseau believed in the educability of men but was as concerned with issues of character and emotional life as with knowledge. Society—particularly the artificial courtly society—was corrupting. The true citizen had to cultivate virtue and sensibility, not manners, taste, or refinement. Rousseau designated women as guarantors of the "natural" virtues of children and as nurturers of the emotional life and character of men—but not as fully formed beings in their own right.

Rousseau's emphasis on the education and virtue of citizens was the underpinning of his larger political vision, set forth in *Du Contrat social* (*The Social Contract*, 1762). He imagined an egalitarian republic—possible particularly in small states such as his native Geneva—in which men would consent to be governed because the government would determine and act in accordance with the "general will" of the citizens. The "general will" was not majority opinion but rather what each citizen *would* want if he were fully informed and were acting in accordance with his highest nature. The "general will" became apparent whenever the citizens met as a body and made collective decisions, and it could be imposed on all inhabitants. (See the box, "Rousseau Discusses the Benefits of Submitting to the General Will.") This was a breathtaking vision of direct democracy—but one with ominous possibilities, for Rousseau

An English Feminist Criticizes Unenlightened Views of Women

Both male and female writers criticized the failure of some Enlightenment thinkers to view ideas about women with the same skepticism and rationalism that they brought to other subjects. One of the earliest was the Englishwoman Mary Astell (1666–1731). In this excerpt from Some Reflections on Marriage (1700), *Astell criticizes, in an ironic tone, negative assessments of women's capacities, Locke's separation of the public and private spheres, and the denial to women of the rights that men enjoy in public life.*

'Tis true, through want of learning, and that of superior genius which men, as men, lay claim to, she [the author] was ignorant of the natural inferiority of our sex, which our masters lay down as self-evident and fundamental truth. She saw nothing in the reason of things to make this either a principle or a conclusion, but much to the contrary.

If they mean that some men are superior to some women, this is no great discovery; had they turned the tables, they might have seen that some women are superior to some men. . . .

Again, if absolute sovereignty be not necessary in a state, how comes it to be so in a family? Or if in a family why not in a state, since no reason can be alleged for the one that will not hold more strongly for the other? If the authority of the husband, so far as it extends, is sacred and inalienable, why not that of the prince? The domestic sovereign is without dispute elected and the stipulations and contract are mutual; is it not then partial in men to the last degree to contend for and practice that arbitrary dominion in their families which they abhor and exclaim against in the state? For if arbitrary power is evil in itself, and an improper method of governing rational and free agents, it ought not to be practiced anywhere.

Source: Moira Ferguson, ed., *First Feminists* (Bloomington: Indiana University Press, 1985), pp. 191–193.

rejected the institutional brakes on state authority proposed by Locke and Montesquieu. Also, the demands of citizenship in such a political order, in contrast to simple obedience under a monarchy, necessitated, for Rousseau, the subordination of women's lives to those of male citizens.

Rousseau's emphasis on the private emotional life anticipates the romanticism of the early nineteenth century. It also reflects Rousseau's own experience as the son of a humble family, always sensing himself an outcast in the brilliant world of Parisian salons. He had a love-hate relationship with this life, remaining attached to several aristocratic women patrons even as he decried their influence. His own personal life did not match his prescriptions for others. He completely neglected to give his own four children the nurturing and education that he argued were vital; indeed, he abandoned all of them to a foundling home. He was nevertheless influential as a critic of an elite society still dominated by status, patronage, and privilege. Rousseau's work reflects to an extreme degree the tensions in Enlightenment thought generally: It was part of elite culture as well as its principal critic.

The Growth of Public Opinion

It is impossible to understand the significance of the Enlightenment without an analysis of how it was a part of public life. Most of the philosophes were of modest origin. They influenced the privileged elite of their day because of the social and political environment in which their ideas were elaborated. Indeed, the clearest distinguishing feature of the Enlightenment may be the creation of

Rousseau Discusses the Benefits of Submitting to the General Will

*In this excerpt from his **Social Contract**, Rousseau describes the relationship of individuals to the general will. Notice the wider-ranging benefits Rousseau believes men will enjoy in society as he envisions it; Rousseau is clearly interested in intellectual, moral, and emotional well-being.*

I assume that men reach a point where the obstacles to their preservation in a state of nature prove greater than the strength that each man has to preserve himself in that state. Beyond this point, the primitive condition cannot endure, for then the human race will perish if it does not change its mode of existence. . . .

"How to find a form of association which will defend the person and goods of each member with the collective force of all, and under which each individual, while uniting himself with the others, obeys no one but himself, and remains as free as before." This is the fundamental problem to which the social contract holds the solution. . . .

The passing from the state of nature to the civil society produces a remarkable change in man; it puts justice as a rule of conduct in the place of instinct, and gives his actions the moral quality they previously lacked. . . . And although in civil society man surrenders some of the advantages that belong to the state of nature, he gains in return far greater ones; his faculties are so exercised and developed, his mind is so enlarged, his sentiments so ennobled, and his whole spirit so elevated that . . . he should constantly bless the happy hour that lifted him for ever from the state of nature and from a stupid, limited animal made a creature of intelligence and a man. . . .

For every individual as a man may have a private will contrary to, or different from, the general will that he has as a citizen. His private interest may speak with a very different voice from that of the public interest; his absolute and naturally independent existence may make him regard what he owes to the common cause as a gratuitous contribution, the loss of which would be less painful for others than the payment is onerous for him; and fancying that the artificial person which constitutes the state is a mere fictitious entity (since it is not a man), he might seek to enjoy the rights of a citizen without doing the duties of a subject. The growth of this kind of injustice would bring about the ruin of the body politic.

Hence, in order that the social pact shall not be an empty formula, it is tacitly implied in that commitment—which alone can give force to all others—that whoever refuses to obey the general will shall be constrained to do so by the whole body, which means nothing other than that he shall be forced to be free; for this is the necessary condition which, by giving each citizen to the nation, secures him against all personal dependence, it is the condition which shapes both the design and the working of the political machine, and which alone bestows justice on civil contracts—without it, such contracts would be absurd, tyrannical and liable to the grossest abuse.

Source: Jean-Jacques Rousseau, *The Social Contract*, trans. Maurice Cranston (London: Penguin Books, 1968), pp. 59–60, 63–65.

an informed body of public opinion that stood apart from court society.

Increased literacy and access to books and other print media are an important part of the story. Perhaps more important, the kinds of reading that people favored began to change. We know from inventories made of people's belongings at the time of their death (required for inheritance laws) that books in the homes of ordinary people were no longer just traditional works such as devotional literature. Ordinary people now read secular and contemporary philosophical works. As the availability of such works increased, reading itself evolved from a reverential encounter with traditional material to a critical encounter with new material. Solitary reading for reflection and pleasure became more widespread.

Habits of reading and responding to written material changed not only because there were increased opportunities to read but also because there were changes in the social environment. In the eighteenth century, forerunners of the modern lending libraries made their debut. In Paris, for a fee, one could join a *salle de lecture* (literally, a "reading room") where the latest works were available to any member. Booksellers, whose numbers increased dramatically, found ways to meet readers' demands for inexpensive access to reading matter. One might pay for the right to read a book in the bookshop itself. In short, new venues encouraged people to see themselves not just as readers but as members of a reading public.

Among the most famous and most important of these venues were the Parisian salons, where Voltaire and others read their works in progress aloud and discussed them. Several Parisian women—mostly wealthy, but of modest social status—invited courtiers, bureaucrats, and intellectuals to meet in their homes at regular times each week. The *salonnières* (salon leaders) themselves read widely in order to facilitate the exchange of ideas among their guests. This mediating function was crucial to the success and the importance of the salons. Manners and polite conversation had been a defining feature of aristocratic life since the seventeenth century, but they had largely been means of displaying status and safeguarding honor. The leadership of the salonnières and the protected environment they provided away from court life enabled a further evolution of "polite society" to occur: Anyone with appropriate manners could participate in conversation as an equal. The assumption of equality, in turn, enabled conversation to turn away from maintaining the status quo to questioning it.

The influence of salons was extended by the wide networks of correspondence salonnières maintained. Perhaps the most famous salonnière in her day, Marie-Thérèse Geoffrin (1699–1777) corresponded with Catherine the Great, the reform-minded empress of Russia, as well as with philosophes outside of Paris and with interested would-be participants in her salon. The ambas-

sador of Naples regularly attended her salon before returning to his native city, from which he exchanged weekly letters with her. He reflected on the importance of salon leaders like Geoffrin when he wrote from Naples, lamenting,

[our gatherings here] are getting farther away from the character and tone of those of France, despite all [our] efforts. . . . There is no way to make Naples resemble Paris unless we find a woman to guide us, organize us, *Geoffrinise* us.[1]

Various clubs, local academies, and learned and secret societies copied some features of the salons of Paris. Hardly any municipality was without a private society that functioned both as a forum for political and philosophical discussion and as an elite social club. Here mingled doctors, lawyers, local officials—some of whom enjoyed the fruits of the political system in offices and patronage. In Scotland, universities were flourishing centers of Enlightenment thought, but political clubs in Glasgow and Edinburgh enriched debate and the development of ideas.

Ideas circulated beyond the membership of even the many far-flung clubs by means of print. Newsletters reporting the goings-on at salons in Paris were produced by some participants. Regularly published periodicals in Great Britain, France, and Italy also served as important means for the dissemination of enlightened opinion in the form of reviews, essays, and published correspondence. Some of these journals had been in existence since the second half of the seventeenth century, when they had begun as a means to circulate the new scientific work. Now, subscribers included Americans anxious to keep up with intellectual life in Europe. Europeans who could not afford the annual subscriptions could peruse the journals in the newly available reading rooms and libraries. In addition to newsletters and journals, newspapers, which were regularly published even in small cities throughout western and central Europe, circulated ideas.

In all these arenas, Enlightenment ideas became the encouragement for and the legitimation of a type of far-reaching political debate that had never before existed, except possibly in England during the seventeenth century. Understanding the Enlightenment involves understanding the milieu in which these ideas were received. The first and greatest impact of the Enlightenment,

The Growth of the Book Trade Book ownership dramatically increased in the eighteenth century, and a wide range of secular works—from racy novelettes to philosophical tracts—was available in print. In this rendering of a bookshop, shipments of books have arrived from around Europe. Notice the artist's optimism in the great variety of persons, from the peasant with a scythe to a white-robed cleric, who are drawn to the shop by "Minerva" (the Roman goddess of wisdom). *(Musée des Beaux-Arts de Dijon)*

particularly in France, was not the creation of a program for political or social change but the creation of a culture of politics that could generate change.

Art in the Age of Reason

The Enlightenment reverberated throughout all aspects of cultural life. Just as the market for books and the reading public expanded, so did the audience for works of art in the growing leisured urban circles of Paris and other great cities. The modern cultured public—a public of concertgoers and art-gallery enthusiasts—began to make its first appearance. The brilliant and sophisticated

courts around Europe continued to sponsor composers, musicians, and painters by providing both patronage and audiences. Yet some performances of concerts and operas began to take place in theaters and halls outside the courts and were more accessible to the public.

Beginning in 1737, one section of the Louvre palace in Paris was devoted annually to public exhibitions of painting and sculpture (though by royally sponsored and approved artists). In both France and Britain, public discussion of art began to take place in published reviews and criticisms: The role of art critic was born. Works of art were also sold by public means, such as auctions. As works became more available by such means, demand grew and production increased.

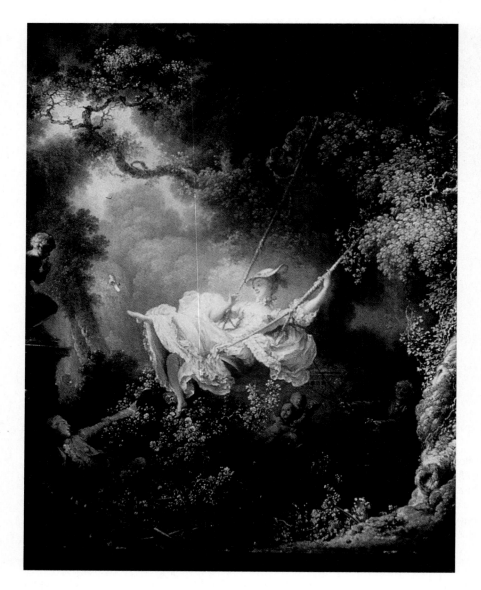

The Cult of Sensibility in Art
This painting, *The Swing*, by the Frenchman Fragonard, depicts a moment of playful and sensuous intimacy. This style of painting was an elaboration of baroque style known as *rococo*. It began to be considered too excessive and lighthearted and was replaced by the more serious neoclassical style as the century wore on. *(Wallace Collection/Bridgeman Art Library/Art Resource, NY)*

In subject matter and style these various art forms exhibited greater variety than works in preceding centuries had shown. We can nevertheless discern certain patterns and tendencies in both the content and the form of eighteenth-century European art. Late baroque painters contributed to an exploration of private life and emotion sometimes called the "cult of sensibility." Frequently, they depicted private scenes of upper-class life, especially moments of intimate conversation or flirtation.

The cult of sensibility was fostered by literature as well. The private life of emotion was nurtured by increased literacy, greater access to books, and the need to retreat from the elaborate artifice of court life. The novel became an increasingly important genre as a means of exploring human problems and relationships. In English literature the novels of Samuel Richardson (1689–1761)—*Pamela* (1740) and *Clarissa* (1747–1748)—explored personal psychology and passion. Rousseau followed Richardson's lead in structuring his own novels *La Nouvelle Héloïse* (1761) and *Emile* (1762). The cult of sensibility was not mere entertainment; it also carried the political and philosophical message that honest emotion was a "natural" virtue and that courtly manners, by contrast, were irrational and degrading. The enormous popularity of Rousseau's novels, for example, came from the fact that their intense emotional appeal was simultaneously felt to be uplifting.

A revival of classical subjects and styles after the middle of the century evoked what were thought to be the pure and timeless values of classical heroes. This revival revealed the influence of Enlightenment thought by assuming the educability of its audience by means of example. Classical revival architecture illustrated a belief in order, symmetry, and proportion. Americans are familiar with its evocations because it has been the architecture of their republic, but even churches were built in this style in eighteenth-century Europe. The classical movement in music reflected both the cult of sensibility and the classicizing styles in the visual arts. Embodied in the works of Austrians Franz Josef Haydn (1732–1809) and Wolfgang Amadeus Mozart (1756–1791), this movement saw the clarification of musical structures, such as the modern sonata and symphony, and enabled melody to take center stage.

Another trend in art and literature was a fascination with nature and with the seemingly "natural" in human culture—less "developed" or more historically distant societies. One of the most popular printed works in the middle of the century was the supposed translation of the poems of Ossian, a third-century Scots Highland poet. Early English, German, Norse, and other folktales were "discovered" (in some cases invented) and published. Many of these went through several editions during the century.

The fact that folk life, other cultures, and untamed nature itself began to be celebrated just when they were being more definitively conquered is very revealing. (See the feature, "Weighing the Evidence: Gardens," on pages 694–695.) The early poetry of Scotland, for example, was celebrated just as the Scottish Highlands were being punished and pacified by the English because of the clans' support for a rival claimant to the English throne. Once purged of any threat, the exotic image of another culture (even the folk culture of one's own society) could be a source of imagination and create a sense of distance from which to measure one's own sophistication. Thus, both ancient and exotic subjects reinforced a sense of dominance and control.

EUROPEAN RULERS AND EUROPEAN SOCIETY

Mindful of the lessons to be learned from the revolution in England and the achievements of Louis XIV, European rulers in the eighteenth century continued their efforts to govern with greater effectiveness. Some, like the rulers of Prussia and Russia, were encouraged in their efforts by Enlightenment ideas that stressed the need for reforms in law, economy, and government. In the main they, like Voltaire, believed that monarchs could be agents for change. In Austria, significant reforms, including the abolition of serfdom, were made. The changes were uneven, however, and at times owed as much to traditional efforts at better government as to enlightened persuasion.

In all cases, rulers' efforts to govern more effectively meant continual readjustments in relationships with traditional elites. Whether or not elites could formally participate in the governing process by means of established institutions such as the English Parliament, royal governments everywhere were still dependent on their participation. Enlightened monarchs were changing their view of themselves and their image from the diligent but self-aggrandizing image of Louis XIV to that of servant of the state. In this way, monarchs actually undermined the dynastic claim to rule by refounding it on a utilitarian basis. The state was increasingly seen as separate from the ruler.

France During the Enlightenment

It is one of the seeming paradoxes of the era of the Enlightenment that critical thought about society and politics flourished in France, an autocratic state with institutionally privileged elites. Yet in France there was a well-educated elite, a tradition of scientific inquiry, and a legacy of cultured court life that, since the early days of Louis XIV, had become the model for all Europe (see pages 592–594). French was the international intellectual language, and France was the most fertile center of elite cultural life. Both Adam Smith and David Hume, for example, spent portions of their careers in Paris and were welcomed into the salons. In fact, the French capital was an environment that encouraged debate and dissent precisely because of the juxtaposition of the new intellectual climate with the difficulties the French state was facing and the institutional rigidities of its political system—a system that excluded many talented and productive members of the elite from its privileged circles.

In the last decades of the reign of Louis XIV (d. 1715), many thoughtful French people criticized the direction the French state was taking. They began to question the point of foreign wars that yielded ever diminishing returns. The intoxicating blend of stability, effective government, national interest, and the personal glory of the monarch began to dissolve.

Louis XIV was followed on the throne by his 5-year-old great-grandson, Louis XV (r. 1715–1774). During the regency, nobles clamored for the establishment of councils so that they could become more active partners in government. Likewise, the supreme law courts, the parlements, reclaimed the right of remonstrance—the right to object to royal edicts and thus to exercise some control over the enactment of law. Throughout Louis XV's reign, his administration often locked horns with the parlements, particularly as royal ministers coped with France's financial crises. Louis XIV had exhausted the nation financially—in need of more money and of new and more reliable ways to get money. During Louis XV's reign the pressures of further wars intensified the need for wholesale reform.

Louis XV's government continued some of the rationalizing policies of Louis XIV by which relics of the decentralized medieval economy were abolished. Roads were improved and more and more internal customs barriers eliminated. The Crown did not challenge the Catholic church's privileged status or property, which would have been welcomed by many elites. Nor was Louis XV able, for most of his reign, to undercut the power of the parlements in order to reform the fiscal system.

By the late 1760s, the weight of government debt from foreign wars finally forced the king into action. He threw his support behind the reforming schemes of his chancellor, Nicolas de Maupeou. Maupeou dissolved the parlements early in 1771 and created new law courts whose judges would not enjoy independent power.

Public opinion was split over this conflict between the monarch and the parlements. A number of ministers under Louis XV and his successor, Louis XVI (r. 1774–1792), shared Enlightenment views of the efficiency of creating economic change from the top and the rationality of doing away with privileges such as the exemption of the nobility from taxation. However, the role of consultative bodies and the separation of powers beloved of Montesquieu, himself a parlementaire, were much prized, and the parlements were the only institutions that could legitimately check monarchical powers. Ordinary property holders, such as provincial nobles, who had little in common with privileged officeholders, might nevertheless see the parlementaires' privileges as the best guarantor of their own.

Further hampering reform efforts was the character of the king himself. Louis XV displayed none of the kingly qualities of his great-grandfather. He was not pleasant or affable, and he was lazy. By the end of his reign, he was roundly despised. He did not give the "rationality" of royal government a good name.

Not surprisingly, from about the middle of the century, enlightened public opinion, nurtured in salons and other new settings, began proposing a variety of ways to enhance representation, consultation, and reform. There were calls to revive the moribund Estates General, the cumbersome representative assembly last called in 1614, as well as for the establishment of new councils or local, decentralized representative assemblies. The workability of these proposals is less important than the simple fact that they were made.

The Crown lost control of reform in 1774, when Louis XV died. His grandson, Louis XVI, well meaning but insecure, allowed the complete restoration of the parlements. Further reform efforts, sponsored by the king and several talented ministers, came to naught because of parlementary opposition. The French crown had lost the chance to reform royal government from above. By the time an Estates General was finally called in the wake of further financial problems in 1788, the enlightened elites' habit of carrying on political analysis and criticism of government outside the actual corridors of power had given rise to a volatile situation.

Monarchy and Constitutional Government in Great Britain

After the deaths of William (d. 1702) and Mary (d. 1694), the British crown passed to Mary's sister, Anne (r. 1702–1714), and then to a collateral line descended from Elizabeth (d. 1662), sister of the beheaded Charles I. Elizabeth had married Frederick, elector of the Palatinate (and had reigned with him briefly in Bohemia at the outset of the Thirty Years' War; see page 575), and her descendants were Germans, now electors of Hanover. The new British sovereign in 1714, who reigned as George I (r. 1714–1727), was both a foreigner and a man of mediocre abilities. Moreover, his claim to the throne was immediately contested by Catholic descendants of James II, who attempted to depose him in 1715, and later his son, George II (r. 1727–1760), in 1745.

This second attempt to depose the Hanoverian kings in 1745 was more nearly successful. The son of the Stuart claimant to the throne, Charles (known in legend as Bonnie Prince Charlie), landed on the west coast of Scotland, with French assistance, and marched south into England with surprising ease. Most of the British army, and George II himself, was on the continent, fighting in the War of Austrian Succession (see page 682).

Scotland had been formally united with England in 1707 (hence the term *Great Britain* after that time), and Charles found some support among Scots dissatisfied with the economic and political results of that union.

But the vast majority of Britons did not want the civil war that Charles's challenge inevitably meant, especially on behalf of a Catholic pretender who relied on support from Britain's great commercial and political rival, France. Landholders and merchants in lowland Scotland and northern England gathered militia to oppose Charles until regular army units returned from abroad. Charles's army, made up mostly of poor Highland clansmen, was destroyed at the Battle of Culloden in April 1746. Charles fled back to France, and the British government used the failed uprising as justification for the brutal and forceful integration of the still-remote Highlands into the British state.

Traditional practices, from wearing tartans to carrying the accustomed personal daggers and

The Destruction of the Highlanders Although English rulers had previously attacked individual clans, Highland culture maintained its independence until the uprising of 1745. For the first time, clansmen were decisively beaten in battle by British troops, who used the tactics of volley fire and disciplined bayonet charge. *(The Royal Collection © 1993 Her Majesty Queen Elizabeth II)*

even playing bagpipes, were forbidden. Control of land was redistributed to break the social and economic bonds of clan society. Thousands of Highlanders died at the battle itself, in prisons or deportation ships, or by deliberate extermination by British troops in the aftermath of the battle.

Despite this serious challenge to the new dynasty and the brutal response it occasioned, the British state, overall, enjoyed a period of relative stability as well as innovation in the eighteenth century. The events of the seventeenth century had reaffirmed both the need for a strong monarchy and the role of Parliament in defending elite interests. The power of Parliament had recently been reinforced by the Act of Settlement, by which the Protestant heir to Queen Anne had been chosen in 1701. By excluding the Catholic Stuarts from the throne and establishing the line of succession, this document reasserted that Parliament determined the legitimacy of the monarchy. In addition, the act claimed greater parliamentary authority over foreign and domestic policy in the wake of the bellicose William's rule (see pages 602–603).

Noteworthy in the eighteenth century were the ways in which cooperation evolved between monarchy and Parliament as Parliament became a more sophisticated and secure institution. Political parties—that is, distinct groups within the elite favoring certain foreign and domestic policies—came into existence. Two groups, the Whigs and the Tories, had begun to form during the reign of Charles II (d. 1685). The Whigs (named derisively by their opponents with a Scottish term for horse thieves) had opposed Charles's pro-French policies and his efforts to tolerate Catholicism and had wholly opposed his brother and successor, James II. Initially, the Whigs favored an aggressive foreign policy against continental opponents, particularly France. The Tories (also derisively named—for Irish cattle rustlers) tended to be staunch Anglicans uninterested in Protestant anti-Catholic agitation. They tended to have a conservative view of their own role, favoring isolationism in foreign affairs and an attitude of deference toward monarchical authority. Whigs generally represented the interests of the great aristocrats or wealthy merchants or gentry. Tories tended to represent the interests of provincial gentry and the traditional concerns of landholding and local administration.

The Whigs were the dominant influence in government through most of the century to 1770. William and Mary as well as Queen Anne favored Whig religious and foreign policy interests. The loyalty of many Tories was called into question by their support for a Stuart, not Hanoverian, succession at Anne's death in 1714. The long Whig dominance of government was also ensured by the talents of Robert Walpole, a member of Parliament who functioned virtually as a prime minister from 1722 to 1742.

Walpole (1676–1745) was from a minor gentry family and was brought into government in 1714 with other Whig ministers in George I's new regime. An extremely talented politician, he took advantage of the mistakes of other ministers over the years and, in 1722, became both the first lord of the treasury and chancellor of the exchequer. There was not yet any official post or title of "prime minister," but the great contribution of Walpole's tenure was to create that office in fact, if not officially. He chose to maintain peace abroad where he could and thus presided over a period of recovery and relative prosperity that enhanced the stability of government.

Initially, Walpole was helped in his role as go-between for king and Parliament by George I's own limitations. The king rarely attended meetings of his own council of ministers and, in any case, was hampered by his limited command of English. Gradually, the Privy Council of the king became something resembling a modern Cabinet dominated by a prime minister. By the end of the century the notions of "loyal opposition" to the Crown within Parliament and parliamentary responsibility for policy had taken root.

In some respects, the maturation of political life in Parliament resembled the lively political debates in the salons of Paris. In both cases, political life was being legitimized on a new basis. In England, however, that legitimation was enshrined in a legislative institution, which made it especially effective and resilient.

Parliament was not yet in any sense representative of the British population, however. Because of strict property qualifications, only about 200,000 adult men could vote. In addition, representation was very uneven, heavily favoring traditional landed wealth. Some constituencies with only a few dozen voters sent members to Parliament.

Many of these "pocket boroughs" were under the control of (in the pockets of) powerful local families who could intimidate the local electorate, particularly in the absence of secret ballots.

Movements for reform of representation in Parliament began in the late 1760s as professionals, such as doctors and lawyers, with movable (as opposed to landed) property and merchants in booming but underrepresented cities began to demand the vote. As the burden of taxation grew—the result of the recently concluded Seven Years' War (see page 682)—these groups felt increasingly deprived of representation. Indeed, many felt kinship and sympathy with the American colonists who opposed increased taxation by the British government on these same grounds and began a revolt in 1775.

However, the reform movement faltered over the issue of religion. In 1780, a tentative effort by Parliament to extend some civil rights to British Catholics provoked rioting in London (known as the Gordon Riots, after one of the leaders). The riots lasted for eight days and claimed three hundred lives. Pressure for parliamentary reform had been building as Britain met with reversals in its war against the American rebels, but this specter of a popular movement out of control temporarily ended the drive for reform.

"Enlightened" Monarchy

Arbitrary monarchical power might seem antithetical to Enlightenment thought, which stressed the reasonableness of human beings and their capacity to discern and act in accord with natural law. Yet monarchy seemed an ideal instrument of reform to Voltaire and to many of his contemporaries. The work of curtailing the influence of the church, reforming legal codes, and eliminating barriers to economic activity might be done more efficiently by a powerful monarch than by other means then available, particularly because there was great confidence in the power of education to transform an individual (in this case, a ruler) and in the accessibility of the principles of reason. Historians have labeled a number of rulers of this era "enlightened despots" because of the arbitrary nature of their power and the enlightened or reformist uses to which they put it.

"Enlightened despotism" aptly describes certain developments in the Scandinavian kingdoms in the late eighteenth century. In Denmark, the Crown had governed without significant challenge from the landholding nobility since the mid-seventeenth century. The nobility, however, like its counterparts in eastern Europe, had guaranteed its supremacy by means of ironclad domination of the peasantry. In 1784, a reform-minded group of nobles, led by the young Crown Prince Frederick (governing on behalf of his mentally ill father), began to apply Enlightenment remedies to the kingdom's economic problems. The reformers encouraged freer trade and sought, above all, to improve agriculture by improving the status of the peasantry. With improved legal status and with land reform, which enabled some peasants to own the land they worked for the first time, agricultural productivity in Denmark rose dramatically. These reforms constitute some of the clearest achievements of any of the "enlightened" rulers.

In Sweden, in 1772, Gustav III (r. 1771–1796) staged a coup with army support that overturned the dominance of the Swedish parliament, the Riksdag. In contrast to Denmark, Sweden had a relatively unbroken tradition of noble involvement in government, stemming in part from its marginal economy and the consequent interest of the nobility in participation in the Crown's aggressive foreign policy. Since Sweden's eclipse as a major power after the Great Northern War (see pages 607–608), factions of the Riksdag, not unlike the rudimentary political parties in Great Britain, had fought over the reins of government. After reasserting his control, Gustav III began an ambitious program of reform of the government. Bureaucrats more loyal to parliamentary patrons than to the Crown were replaced, restrictions on trade in grain and other economic controls were liberalized, the legal system was rationalized, the death penalty was strictly limited, and legal torture was abolished.

Despite his abilities (and his charm), Gustav III suffered the consequences of the contradictory position of advancing reform by autocratic means in a kingdom with a strong tradition of representative government. Gustav eventually tried to deflect the criticisms of the nobility by reviving grandiose—but completely untenable—schemes for the reconquest of Baltic territory. However, in

Frederick the Great is pictured here returning from military maneuvers. Frederick's self-imposed work as king included arduous travel throughout his domains to check on local conditions and monitor local governments. *(Staatliches Schlösser und Gärten, Potsdam-Sans Souci)*

1796 he was mortally wounded by an assassin hired by disgruntled nobles.

Another claimant to the title "enlightened" monarch was Frederick II of Prussia (r. 1740–1786), "the Great." Much of the time, Frederick resided in his imperial electorate of Brandenburg, near his capital, Berlin. His scattered states, which he extended by seizing new lands, are referred to as "Prussia," rather than as "Brandenburg-Prussia," because members of his family were now kings of Prussia thanks to their ambitions and the weakness of the Polish state of which Prussia had once been a dependent duchy. In many ways, the Prussian state *was* its military victories, for Frederick's bold moves and the policies of his father, grandfather, and great-grandfather committed the state's resources to a military presence of dramatic proportions. Prussia was on the European stage only due to the degree of that commitment.

The institutions that constituted the state and linked the various provinces under one administration were dominated by the needs of the mili-

tary. Frederick II's father, Frederick William (r. 1713–1740), had added an efficient provincial recruiting system to the state's central institutions, which he also further consolidated. But in many other respects, the Prussian state was in its infancy. There was no tradition of political participation—even by elites—and little chance of cultivating any. Nor was there any political or social room for maneuver at the lower part of the social scale. The rulers of Prussia had long ago acceded to the aristocracy's demand for tighter control over peasant labor on their own lands in return for their support of the monarchy. The rulers relied on nobles for local administration and army commands. Thus, there was a stark limit to the kinds of social, judicial, or political reforms that Frederick could personally hope to carry out.

Frederick tried to introduce improved agricultural methods and simultaneously to improve the condition of peasants, but he met stiff resistance from noble landholders. He did succeed in abolishing serfdom in some regions. He tried to stimulate the economy by sponsoring state industries and trading monopolies, but there were not enough resources or initiative from the tightly controlled merchant communities to create much economic expansion. Simplifying and codifying the inherited jumble of local laws was a goal of every ruler. A law code published in 1794, after Frederick's death, was partly the product of his efforts.

Frederick's views of the role of Enlightenment thought reflect the limitations of his situation. One doesn't have to lead a frontal assault on prejudices consecrated by time, he thought; instead, one must be tolerant of superstition because it will always have a hold on the masses. Perhaps his most distinctive "enlightened" characteristic was the seriousness with which he took his task as ruler. He was energetic and disciplined to a fault. In his book *Anti-Machiavel* (1741) he argued that a ruler has a moral obligation to work for the betterment of the state. He styled himself as the "first servant" or steward of the state. However superficial this claim may appear, in his energy and diligence he compares favorably to Louis XV of France, who, having a much more wealthy and flexible society to work with, did much less.

Describing Frederick as "enlightened," however, masks the degree to which his activities reflected as much the traditional goals of security and prosperity as the impetus of "enlightened" thinking. Indeed, some of the most thoroughgoing administrative, legal, and economic reforms were accomplished in rival Austria entirely within such a traditional framework, during the reign of Maria Theresa (r. 1740–1780), the daughter of Emperor Charles VI (r. 1711–1740).

Maria Theresa was a remarkable ruler in her diligence and determination. She overcame difficulties that surrounded her accession, survived the near dismemberment of Austrian territories in the wars that marked her reign, and embarked on an energetic reform program to shore up the weaknesses in the state that the conflicts had revealed. The Austrian monarchy was still a highly decentralized state. Maria Theresa worked to streamline and centralize administration, finances, and defense. She created new centralized governing councils and, above all, reformed the assessment and collection of taxes so that the Crown could better tap the wealth of its subjects. She established new courts of justice and limited the exploitation of serfs by landlords. In general, she

presided over an effort to bypass many of the provincial and privatized controls on government still in the hands of great nobility. She accomplished all of this without being in any way "enlightened." For example, she had a traditional fear of freedom of the press and insisted on orthodoxy in religious matters.

Her son, Joseph, is an interesting contrast. Self-consciously "enlightened," Joseph II (r. 1780–1790) carried out a variety of reforms that his mother had not attempted, including freedom of the press and limited freedom of religion. Some of his reforms were particularly dramatic, such as drastic curtailment of the death penalty and encouragement of widespread literacy. Like Frederick the Great, Joseph regarded himself as a servant of the state. During his ten-year reign, the political climate in Vienna began to resemble that in Paris, London, and other capitals where political life was no longer confined to court life.

Many of Joseph's reforms, however, were simply extensions of his mother's. For example, he extended further legal protection to peasants and eventually abolished serfdom in all Habsburg lands. And in some ways he was less successful than Maria Theresa had been. Though persuaded of the benefits of enlightened government, he was by temperament an inflexible autocrat, whose methods antagonized many of his most powerful subjects. In the name of "rational" administration, he tried to extend Austrian institutions to the kingdom of Hungary—including the use of the German language for official business. He also tried to bypass the authority of the representative Estates in the Austrian Netherlands in order to achieve some of his aims. In this action reminiscent of his ancestor Philip II of Spain, Joseph II revealed that the curious blend of "enlightenment" and traditional absolutism was not greater than the sum of its parts. Joseph's policies provoked simmering opposition and open revolt in a number of his lands, and some of his reforms were repealed even before his death.

Catherine the Great and the Empire of Russia

Another ruler with a claim to the title "enlightened despot" was Catherine, empress of Russia (r. 1762–1796). Catherine was one of the ablest rulers in the eighteenth century and perhaps

Catherine the Great Catherine was a German princess who had been brought to Russia to marry another German, Peter of Holstein-Gottorp, who was being groomed as heir to the Russian throne. There had been several Russian monarchs of mixed Russian and German parentage since the time of Peter the Great's deliberate interest in and ties with other European states. *(The Luton Hoo Foundation)*

the single most able of all the rulers of imperial Russia. She combined intelligence with vision, diligence, and skill in handling people and choosing advisers. Her intelligence and political acumen were obvious early in her life in Russia simply from the fact that she survived at court. In 1745 she had been brought to Russia from her native Germany to marry the heir to the Russian throne. She was brutally treated by her husband, Tsar Peter III. In the summer of 1762, Catherine engineered a coup against him. Peter was overthrown and killed, and Catherine ruled alone as empress for most of the rest of the century.

Catherine the Great, as she came to be called, was the true heir of Peter the Great in her abilities,

policies, and ambitions. Under Catherine, Russia committed itself to general European affairs in addition to its traditional territorial ambitions. In situations involving the major European powers, Russia tended to ally with Britain (with which it had important trading connections, including the provision of timber for British shipbuilding) and with Austria (against their common nemesis, Turkey), and against France, Poland, and Prussia. In 1768, Catherine initiated a war against the Turks from which Russia gained much of the Crimean coast. She also continued Peter's efforts to dominate the weakened Poland. She was aided by Frederick the Great, who proposed the deliberate partitioning of Poland to satisfy his own territorial

Map 18.1 The Partition of Poland and the Expansion of Russia Catherine the Great
acquired modern Lithuania, Belarus, and Ukraine, which had once constituted the
duchy of Lithuania, part of the multi-ethnic Polish kingdom.

ambitions as well as those of Russia and Austria, with which he competed. In 1772, portions of Poland were gobbled up in the first of three successive "grabs" of territory (Map 18.1). Warsaw itself eventually landed in Prussian hands, but Catherine gained all of Belarus, Ukraine, and modern Lithuania—which had constituted the duchy of Lithuania. Thus, like any successful ruler of her age, Catherine counted territorial aggrandizement among her chief achievements.

Nevertheless, Catherine also counted herself a sincere follower of the Enlightenment. While young, she had received an education that bore the strong stamp of the Enlightenment. Like Frederick, she attempted to take an active role in the intellectual community, corresponding with Voltaire over the course of many years and acting as patron to Diderot. One of Catherine's boldest political moves was the secularization of church lands. Although Peter the Great had extended government control of the church, he had not touched church lands. Catherine also licensed private publishing houses and permitted a burgeoning periodical press. The number of books published in Russia tripled during her reign. This enriched cultural life was one of the principal causes of the flowering of Russian literature that began in the early nineteenth century.

The stamp of the Enlightenment on Catherine's policies is also clearly visible in her attempts at legal reform. In 1767 she convened a legislative commission and provided it with a guiding document, the *Instruction,* which she had authored. The commission was remarkable because it included representatives of all classes, including peasants, and provided a place for the airing of general grievances. Catherine hoped for a general codification of law as well as reforms such as the abolition of torture and capital punishment—reforms that made the *Instruction* radical enough to be banned from publication in other countries. She did not propose changing the legal status of serfs, however, and class differences made the commission unworkable in the end. Most legal reforms were accomplished piecemeal and favored the interests of landed gentry. Property rights were clarified and strengthened, and judicial procedures were streamlined but constructed to include legal privileges for the gentry.

Like the Austrian rulers, Catherine undertook far-reaching administrative reform to create more effective local units of government. Here again, political imperatives were fundamental, and reforms in local government strengthened the hand of the gentry. The legal subjection of peasants in serfdom was also extended as a matter of state policy to help win the allegiance of landholders in newly acquired areas—such as Ukrainian territory gained in the partition of Poland. Gentry in general and court favorites in particular, on whom the stability of her government depended, were rewarded with estates and serfs to work them.

In Russia as in Prussia and Austria, decline of the peasantry occurred because the monarch wanted to win the allegiance of the elites who lived from their labor. The cooperation of elites was particularly valued by Catherine because the Russian state was in a formative stage in another sense as well. It was trying to incorporate new peoples, such as the Tatars in the Crimea, and to manage its relationship with border peoples such

as the Cossacks. Catherine's reign was marked by one of the most massive and best-organized peasant rebellions of the century. Occurring in 1773, the rebellion expressed the grievances of the thousands of peasants who joined its ranks and called for the abolition of serfdom. The revolt took its name, however, from its Cossack leader, Emelian Pugachev (d. 1775), and reflected the dissatisfaction with the Russian government of this semi-autonomous people.

The dramatic dilemmas faced by Catherine illustrate both the promise and the costs of state formation throughout Europe. State consolidation permitted the imposition of internal peace, of coordinated economic policy, of reform of justice, but it came at the price of greater—in some cases much greater—control and coercion of the population. Thus, we can see from the alternative perspective of Russia the importance of the political sphere that was opening up in France and was being consolidated in England. It was in that environment, rather than in Russia, that the Enlightenment philosophy could find most fertile ground.

STATES IN CONFLICT

In the eighteenth century a new constellation of states emerged to dominate politics on the Continent. Along with the traditional powers of England, France, and Austria were Prussia in central Europe and Russia to the east (see Map 18.1). Certain characteristics common to all these states account for their dominance. None is more crucial than their various abilities to field effective armies. Traditional territorial ambitions accounted for many wars in the eighteenth century, but the increasing significance of overseas trade and colonization was the most important source of conflict between England and France.

A Century of Warfare: Circumstances and Rationales

The large and small states of Europe continued to make war on each other for both strategic and dynastic reasons. The expense of war, the number of powerful states involved, and the complexities of their interests meant that wars were preceded and carried out with complex systems of alliances and were followed by the adjustments of many borders and the changing control of many bits of territory. We can distinguish certain consistent interests of the major states, however, and some of the circumstances within which all of the states acted.

States fought over territory that had obvious economic and strategic value. A fight over the Baltic coastline, for example, absorbed Sweden and Russia early in the century (see pages 605–608). Often these conflicts were carried out in arbitrary ways that revealed the dynastic view of territory that still existed. Although rational and defensible "national" borders were important, collecting isolated bits of territory was also still the norm. The wars between European powers thus became extremely complex strategically. France, for example, might choose to strike a blow against Austria by invading an Italian state in order to use the conquered Italian territory as a bargaining chip in eventual negotiations.

Dynastic claims were not merely strategic ploys but also major causes of war. Indeed, the fundamental instability caused by hereditary rule accounts for many of the major wars of the eighteenth century. The century opened with the War of Spanish Succession, and later the succession of the Austrian Habsburgs would be the cause of a major continental war.

The state of military technology, tactics, and organization also shaped the outcomes of conflicts. In the eighteenth century, weapons and tactics became increasingly refined. More reliable muskets were used. A bayonet that could slip over a musket barrel without blocking the muzzle was invented. Coordinated use of bayonets required even more assured drill of troops than volley fire alone to ensure disciplined action in the face of enemy fire and charges. Artillery and cavalry forces were also subjected to greater standardization of training and discipline in action. Increased discipline of forces meant that commanders could exercise meaningful control over a battle for the first time, but such battles were not necessarily decisive, especially when waged against a comparable force.

One sure result of the new equipment and tactics was that war became a more expensive proposition than ever before and an ever greater burden on a state's resources and administration. It became increasingly difficult for small states such as

Sweden to compete with the forces that others could mount. Small and relatively poor states, such as Prussia, that did support large forces did so by means of an extraordinary bending of civil society to the economic and social needs of the army. In Prussia, twice as many people were in the armed forces, proportionally, as in other states, and a staggering 80 percent of meager state revenue went to support the army.

Most states introduced some form of conscription in the eighteenth century. In all regions, the very poor often volunteered for army service to improve their lives. However, conscription of peasants, throughout Europe but particularly in Prussia and Russia, imposed a significant burden on peasant communities and a sacrifice of productive members to the state. Governments everywhere supplemented volunteers and conscripts with mercenaries and even criminals, as necessary, to fill the ranks without tapping the wealthier elements of the community. Thus, common soldiers were increasingly seen not as members of society but as its rejects. Said Frederick II, "Useful hardworking people should [not be conscripted but rather] be guarded as the apple of one's eye," and a French war minister agreed that armies had to consist of the "scum of people and of all those for whom society has no use."[2] Brutality became an accepted tool for governments to use to manage such groups of men. From the eighteenth century, the army increasingly became an instrument of social control used to manage and make use of individuals who otherwise would have had no role in society.

But the costs of maintaining these forces had other outcomes as well. Wars could still be won or lost not on the battlefield but on the supply line. Incentive still existed to bleed civilian populations and to exploit the countryside. Moreover, when supply lines were disrupted and soldiers not equipped or fed, the armies of a major power could be vulnerable to the small and "unmodernized" armies of lesser states. Finally, neither good generalship nor the discipline of soldiers could be guaranteed, yet both were crucial to success. Culloden, in 1746 (see page 673), was the first battle in which the British army was able decisively to defeat the fierce charge and hand-to-hand fighting of Highland clansmen by holding its position and using disciplined volley fire. Warfare became increasingly professional but was still an uncertain business with unpredictable results.

The Power of Austria and Prussia

Major continental wars had a marked impact on the balance of power among states in western and central Europe. The first of these, now known as the War of Austrian Succession, began in 1740. Emperor Charles VI died that year without a male heir, and his daughter, Maria Theresa, succeeded him. Charles VI had worked to shore up his daughter's position as his heir by means of an act called the Pragmatic Sanction, first issued in 1713. He had negotiated carefully to persuade allies and potential opponents to accept it. The question was not whether a woman could rule, for many women had ruled and did rule other states. However, a new ruler about whom there was any doubt—a woman, child, or any distant relative—opened the door for rival dynastic claims. In 1740, Frederick II of Prussia took advantage of Habsburg vulnerability by invading the wealthy Habsburg province of Silesia (see Map 18.1), to which he had a hereditary claim of sorts.

Maria Theresa proved a much more tenacious opponent than Frederick had anticipated. In the end, he was lucky to be able to hold onto Silesia, which was at some distance from Maria Theresa's other territories. Although Austrian forces were never able to dislodge Frederick, they did best most of the forces ranged against them by their perpetual opponent, France, and by other German states allied with Frederick. In a preliminary peace signed in 1745, Frederick was confirmed in possession of Silesia, but the throne of the Holy Roman Empire was returned to the Habsburgs—given to Maria Theresa's husband, who reigned as Francis (Franz) I (r. 1745–1765). A final treaty in 1748 ended all the fighting that had continued since 1745, mostly by France on the Continent and simultaneous fighting by France and Britain overseas.

The gainers were Prussia and Austria. Austria came out ahead because its succession had not been disrupted and its lands had not been dismembered. Prussia, because of the annexation of Silesia and the psychological imprint of victory, emerged as a power of virtually equal rank to the Habsburgs in Germany. Frederick II was now well placed to make further territorial gains.

Not surprisingly, the power of Prussia provoked the outbreak of the next major war. Indeed, the unprecedented threat that Austria now felt from Prussia caused a veritable revolution in alliances across Europe. So great in Austrian minds was the change in the balance of power that Austria was willing to ally with France, its traditional enemy, in order to isolate Prussia. In the years before what would later be known as the Seven Years' War (1756–1763), Austrian officials began to approach France to propose a mutual defensive alliance—a move that became known as the Diplomatic Revolution. Sweden and Russia, with territory to gain at Prussia's expense, joined the alliance system. Sweden wanted to regain territory along the Baltic Sea, and Russia coveted East Prussia, which bordered Russian territory.

Frederick initiated hostilities in 1756, hoping, among other outcomes, to prevent consolidation of the new alliances. Instead, he found that he had started a war against overwhelming odds. What saved him was limited English aid. The English, engaged with France in the overseas conflict known as the French and Indian War, wanted France to be heavily committed on the Continent. Also helpful to Frederick was Russia's withdrawal from the alliance against him when a new ruler took the throne there in 1762. Prussia managed to emerge intact—though strained economically and demographically.

The results of the war confirmed Prussia and Austria as the two states of European rank in German-speaking Europe. Their rivalry would dominate German history until the late nineteenth century. The war also demonstrated how fragile even successful states could be and revealed something about what it took for them to be successful. Military victory and the reputation that went with it—even at great cost—could allow a ruler a place on the European stage. The nearness of Prussia's escape also revealed that fortune had a great deal to do with the rise of this state.

The Atlantic World: Trade, Colonization, Competition

The importance of international trade and colonial possessions to the states of western Europe grew dramatically in the eighteenth century. Between 1715 and 1785, Britain's trade with North America rose from 19 to 34 percent of its total trade, and its trade with Asia and Africa rose from 7 to 19 percent of the total. By the end of the century, more than half of all British trade was carried on outside of Europe; for France, the figure was more than a third.

European commercial and colonial energies were concentrated in the Atlantic world in the eighteenth century, because there the profits were greatest. The population of British North America grew from about 250,000 in 1700 to about 1.7 million by 1760. The densely settled New England colonies provided a market for manufactured goods from the mother country, though they produced little by way of raw materials or bulk goods on which traders could make a profit. The colonies of Maryland and Virginia produced tobacco, the Carolinas rice and indigo (a dyestuff). England re-exported all three throughout Europe at considerable profit.

The French in New France, numbering only 56,000 in 1740, were vastly outnumbered by the British colonists. Nevertheless, the French successfully expanded their control of territory in Canada. Settlements sprang up between the outposts of Montreal and Quebec on the St. Lawrence River. Despite resistance, the French extended their fur trapping—the source of most of the profits that New France generated—west and north along the Great Lakes, consolidating their hold as they went by building forts. They penetrated as far as the modern Canadian province of Manitoba, where they cut into the British trade run out of Hudson Bay to the north. The French also contested the mouth of the St. Lawrence River and the Gulf of St. Lawrence with the British. The British held Nova Scotia and Newfoundland, the French held parts of Cape Breton Island, and both states fished the surrounding waters.

The commercial importance of all of these holdings, as well as those in Asia, was dwarfed by the European states' Caribbean possessions, however. The British held Jamaica and Barbados; the French, Guadeloupe and Martinique; the Spanish, Cuba and San Domingo; and the Dutch, a few small islands. Sugar produced by slave labor was the major source of profits, along with other cash crops such as coffee, indigo, and cochineal (another dyestuff). The concentration of shipping to this region indicates the region's importance.

Tobbaco Label This shipping label for American-grown tobacco fancifully depicts slaves enjoying a smoke. *(The Granger Collection, New York)*

By the 1760s, the British China trade occupied seven or eight ships. In the 1730s, British trade with Jamaica alone drew three hundred ships. The tiny Dutch possession of Guiana on the South American coast required twice as many visits by Dutch ships as the Dutch East India Company sent into Asia.

The economic dependence of the colonies on slave labor meant that the colonies were tied to their home countries not with a two-way commercial exchange but with a three-way "triangle" trade (Map 18.2). Certain European manufactures were shipped to western ports in Africa, where they were traded for slaves. The enslaved Africans were then transported to South America, the Caribbean, or North America, where planters bought and paid for them with profits from their sugar and tobacco plantations. (See the box, "Encounters with the West: An African Recalls the Horrors of the Slave Ship.") Sugar and tobacco

Great Britain
France
Portugal
Spain
Netherlands

Hudson
Bay

LOUISIANA

MEXICO

NEW FRANCE
QUEBEC

NEWFOUNDLAND
(To Gr. Br., 1713)

GREAT
BRITAIN

NOVA SCOTIA
(ACADIA)
(To Gr. Br., 1713)

Furs

NETH.

FLORIDA

Tobacco

Colonial products

Mississippi

Silver

Manufactured goods

FRANCE

CUBA

Sugar

PORTUGAL   SPAIN

JAMAICA

HISPANIOLA

Porto
Bello

ATLANTIC   OCEAN

CANARY IS.
(Spain)

GUADELOUPE
(Fr.)

MARTINIQUE
(Fr.)

NEW GRANADA

BARBADOS
(Gr. Br.)

AFRICA

DUTCH
GUIANA

FRENCH
GUIANA

CAPE VERDE IS.
(Port.)

Cape
Verde

Amazon

PERU

Sugar

European forts and trading stations

Slaves

BRAZIL

ANGOLA

∾ ENCOUNTERS WITH THE WEST ∾

An African Recalls the Horrors of the Slave Ship

Olaudah Equiano (ca. 1750–1797) was one of the few Africans sold into slavery in the Americas to leave a written record of his experiences. An Ibo from the Niger region, he first experienced slavery as a boy when kidnapped from his village by other Africans. But nothing prepared him for the brutality of the Europeans who bought and shipped him to Barbados, in the British West Indies. He eventually regained his freedom and received an education.

The first object which saluted my eyes when I arrived on the [African] coast was the sea and a slaveship . . . waiting for its cargo. . . . When I was carried on board I was immediately handled, and tossed up, to see if I were sound, by some of the crew. . . . I was soon put down under the decks, and there I received such a salutation in the nostrils as I had never experienced in my life; so that, with the loathsomeness of the stench . . . I became so sick and low that I was not able to eat. . . . I now wished for the last friend, death, to relieve me; but soon, to my grief, two of the white men offered me eatables; and, on my refusing to eat, one of them held me fast by the hands and laid me across, I think, the windlass, and tied my feet while the other flogged me severely.

One day, when we had a smooth sea and a moderate wind, two of my wearied countrymen, who were chained together, preferring death to such a life of misery, somehow made through the nettings and jumped into the sea; immediately another dejected fellow who [was ill and so not in irons] followed their example. . . . Two of the wretches were drowned, but they got the other and afterwards flogged him unmercifully for thus attempting to prefer death to slavery. In this manner we continued to undergo more hardships than I can now relate. Many a time we were near suffocation for want of fresh air. . . . This, and the stench of the necessary tubs, carried off many.

Source: Philip D. Curtin, *Africa Remembered* (Madison: University of Wisconsin Press, 1967), pp. 92–96.

were then shipped back to the mother country to be re-exported at great profit throughout Europe. A variety of smaller exchanges also took place. For example, timber from British North America was traded in the Caribbean for sugar or its byproducts, molasses and rum. Individual planters in the colonies were not the only ones whose fortunes and status depended on these networks. Merchants in cities such as Bordeaux in France and

Map 18.2 The Atlantic Economy, ca. 1750 The "triangle trade" linked Europe, Africa, and European colonies in the Americas. The most important component of this trade for Europe was the profitable plantation agriculture that depended on enslaved Africans for labor.

Liverpool in England were also heavily invested in the slave trade and the re-export business.

The proximity and growth of French and British settlements in North America ensured conflict (see Map 18.3). The Caribbean and the coasts of Central and South America were strategic flashpoints as well. At the beginning of the eighteenth century, several substantial islands remained unclaimed by any power. The British were making incursions along the coastline claimed by Spain and were trying to break into the monopoly of trade between Spain and Spain's vast possessions in the region. Public opinion in both Britain and France became increasingly sensitive to colonial issues. For the first time, tensions abroad would fuel major conflicts between two European states.

Great Britain and France: Wars Overseas

In the eighteenth century, England became the dominant naval power in Europe. Its navy protected its far-flung trading networks, its merchant fleet, and the coast of England itself. England had strategic interests on the Continent as well, however. England's interest lay in promoting a variety of powers on the Continent, none of which (or no combination of which) posed too great a threat to England, to its coastline, or to its widespread trading system. From across the Channel, the French appeared a particular threat. They assembled a fleet on more than one occasion and actually dispatched one fleet to aid the cause of the Stuart claimants to the British throne (see page 673).

A second, dynastic consideration in continental affairs was the electorate of Hanover, the large principality in western Germany that was the native territory of the Hanoverian kings of England. Early in the century especially, the interests of this German territory were of importance to the Hanoverian kings and were a significant factor in British foreign policy. Unable to field a large army, given their maritime interests, the British sought protection for Hanover in alliances and subsidies for allies' armies on the Continent. The money for these ventures came from the profits on trade.

After the death of Louis XIV in 1715, England's energies centered on colonial rivalries with France, its greatest competitor overseas. There were three major phases of conflict between England and France in colonial regions. The first two were concurrent with the major land wars in Europe: the War of Austrian Succession (1740–1748) and the Seven Years' War (1756–1763). The third phase coincided with the rebellion of British colonies in North America—the American Revolution—beginning in the 1770s. France was inevitably more committed to affairs on the Continent than were the British. The French were able to hold their own successfully in both arenas during the 1740s, but by 1763, though pre-eminent on the Continent, they had lost many of their colonial possessions to the English.

In the 1740s, France was heavily involved in the War of Austrian Succession while Britain vied with Spain for certain Caribbean territories. Both France and England also tested each other's strength in scattered colonial fighting, which began in 1744 and produced a few well-balanced gains and losses. Their conquests were traded when peace was made in 1748.

Tension was renewed almost immediately at many of the strategic points in North America. French and British naval forces harassed each

French Fort Builders in North America
The French, whose settlements in North America were sparsely populated, tried to secure the vast territories they claimed with a series of strategically placed forts. The imagined fortifications in this contemporary engraving, which probably mocks the French effort, were far too elaborate for American conditions, where simple wooden palisades were the rule. *(Colonial Williamsburg Foundation)*

other's shipping in the Gulf of St. Lawrence. The French reinforced their encirclement of British colonies with more forts along the Great Lakes and the Ohio River. When British troops (at one point led by the colonial commander George Washington) attempted to strike at these forts, beginning in 1754, open fighting between the French and the English began.

In India, meanwhile, both the French and the British attempted to strengthen their commercial footholds by making military and political alliances with local Indian rulers. The disintegration of the Mogul Empire facilitated this move, heightening competition among Indian rulers, and sparked a new level of ambition on the part of the European powers in their struggle with each other. A British attack on a French convoy provoked a declaration of war by France in May 1756, three months before fighting in the Seven Years' War broke out in Europe. For the first time, a major war between European nations had started and would be fought in their empires, signifying a profound change in the relation of these nations to the world.

The French had already committed themselves to an alliance with Austria and were increasingly involved on the Continent after Frederick II initiated war there in August 1756. Slowly, the drain of sustaining war both on the Continent and abroad began to tell, and Britain scored major victories against French forces after an initial period of balanced successes and failures. The French lost a number of fortresses on the Mississippi and Ohio Rivers and on the Great Lakes and, finally, also lost the interior of Canada with the fall of Quebec and of Montreal in 1759 and 1760, respectively (Map 18.3).

In the Caribbean, the British seized Guadeloupe, the main French sugar-producing island. Superior resources in India enabled the British to take several French outposts there, including Pondicherry, the most important. The cost of involvement on so many fronts meant that French troops were short of money and supplies. They were particularly vulnerable to both supply and personnel shortages—especially in North America—not only because they were weaker than the British at sea but also because the territory they had occupied and fortified remained sparsely settled and dependent on the mother country for food.

By the terms of the Peace of Paris in 1763, France regained Guadeloupe. In India, France re-tained many of its trading stations but lost its political and military clout. British power in India was dramatically enhanced not only by French losses but also by victories over Indian rulers who had allied with the French. In the interior Britain now controlled lands that had never before been under the control of any European power; British political rule in India, as opposed to merely a mercantile presence, began at this time. The British now also held Canada. They emerged as the preeminent world power among European states.

ECONOMIC EXPANSION AND SOCIAL CHANGE

The eighteenth century was an era of dramatic change, though that change was not always apparent to those who lived through it. The intellectual and cultural ferment of the Enlightenment laid the groundwork for domestic political changes to come, just as British victories in the Seven Years' War shifted the balance of power abroad. More subtle and potentially more profound changes were occurring in the European countryside, however: Population, production, and consumption were beginning to grow beyond the bounds that all preceding generations had lived within and taken for granted.

More Food and More People

Throughout European history, there had been a delicate balance between available food and numbers of people to feed. Population growth had accompanied increases in the amount of land under cultivation. From time to time, however, population growth surpassed the ability of the land to produce food, and people became malnourished and prey to disease. In 1348 the epidemic outbreak of bubonic plague known as the Black Death struck just such a vulnerable population in decline.

There were few ways to increase the productivity of land. Peasants safeguarded its fertility by alternately cultivating some portions while letting others lie fallow or using them as pasture. Manure provided fertilizer, but during the winter months livestock could not be kept alive in large numbers. Limited food for livestock meant limited fertilizer, which in turn meant limited production of food for both humans and animals.

Map 18.3 British Gains in North America The British colonies on the Atlantic coast were effective staging posts for the armies that ousted the French from North America by 1763. However, taxes imposed on the colonies to pay the costs of the Seven Years' War helped spark revolt—the American Revolution—a decade later.

After devastating decline in the fourteenth century, the European population experienced a prolonged recovery, and in the eighteenth century the balance that had previously been reached began to be exceeded for the first time. Infant mortality remained as high as ever. No less privileged a person than Queen Anne of England outlived every one of the seventeen children she bore, and all but one of them died in infancy. Population growth occurred because of a decline in the death rate for adults and a simultaneous increase in the birthrate in some areas owing to earlier marriages.

Adults began to live longer partly because of a decline in the incidence of the plague. However, the primary reason adults were living longer, despite the presence of various epidemic diseases, was that they were better nourished and thus bet-

ter able to resist disease. More and different kinds of food began to be produced. The increase in the food supply also meant that more new families could be started.

Food production increased because of the introduction of new crops and other changes in agricultural practices. The cumulative effect of these changes was so dramatic that historians have called them an "agricultural revolution." The new crops included fodder, such as clover, legumes, and turnips, which did not deplete the soil and could be fed to livestock over the winter. The greater availability of animal manure, in turn, boosted grain production. The potato, introduced from the Americas in the sixteenth century, is nutrient-dense and can feed more people per acre than can grain. In certain areas, farming families produced potatoes to feed themselves while they grew grain to be sold and shipped elsewhere.

More food being produced meant more food available for purchase. The opportunity to buy food freed up land and labor. A family that could purchase food might decide to convert its farm into a dairy farm. In such a case, many families might be supported from a piece of land that had supported only one family when used for traditional agriculture. Over a generation or two, a number of children might share the inheritance of what had previously been a single farm, yet each could make a living from his or her share, and population could grow as it had not done before.

Farmers had known about and experimented with many of the crops used for fodder for centuries. However, the widespread planting of these crops, as well as other changes, was long in coming and happened in scattered areas. A farmer had to have control over land in order to institute change. In the traditional open-field system, peasants had split up all the land in each community so that each family might have a piece of each field. Making dramatic changes was hard when an entire community had to act together. Most important, changing agriculture required capital for seed and fertilizer and for the greater number of people and animals needed to cultivate the new crops. Only prosperous farmers had spare capital. Few were inclined to take risks with the production of food and trust the workings of the market. The bad condition of roads alone was reason enough not to rely on distant markets.

Yet where both decent roads and growing urban markets existed, some farmers—even entire villages working together—were willing to produce for urban populations. Capital cities, like London and Amsterdam, and trading centers such as Glasgow and Bordeaux were booming. These growing cities demanded not only grain but also specialized produce such as dairy products and fruits and vegetables. Thus, farmers had an incentive to make changes such as to dairy farming. Urbanization and improved transportation networks also encouraged agriculture because human waste produced by city dwellers—known as "night soil"—could be collected and distributed in the surrounding agricultural regions to further increase soil fertility. By the late eighteenth century, pockets of intensive, diversified agriculture existed in England, northern France, the Rhineland

in Germany, the Po Valley in Italy, and Catalonia in Spain.

In other areas, changes in agriculture were often accompanied by a shift in power in the countryside. Wealthy landlords began to invest in change in order to reap the profits of producing for the new markets. Where the traditional authority of the village to regulate agriculture was weak, peasants were vulnerable. In England, a combination of weak village structure and the attraction of urban markets created a climate that encouraged landlords to treat land speculatively. To make their holdings more profitable, they raised the rents that farmers paid. They changed cultivation patterns on the land that they controlled directly. They appropriated the village common lands, a process known as "enclosure," and used them for cash crops such as sheep (raised for their wool) or beef cattle. Among other ramifications, the clans of Scotland completely disintegrated as meaningful social units as markets for beef, wool, and other Highland commodities drew chieftains' resources and turned what remained of their traditional relationships with dependent clansmen into exploitative commercial ones.

Thus, although the agricultural revolution increased the food supply to sustain more people in Europe generally, it did not create general prosperity. The growth of population did not mean that most people were better off. Indeed, many rural people were driven off the land or made destitute by the loss of the resources of common lands. Peasants in eastern Europe produced grain for export to the growing urban centers in western Europe, but usually by traditional methods. In both eastern and western Europe, the power and profits of landlords were a major force in structuring the rural economy.

The Growth of Industry

Agricultural changes fostered change in other areas of economic and social life. As more food was grown with less labor, that labor was freed to do other productive work. If there was enough work to be had making other products that people needed, then the nonagricultural population could continue to grow. If population grew, more and more consumers would be born, and the demand for more goods would help continue the cycle of population growth, changes in production, and economic expansion. This is precisely what happened in the eighteenth century. A combination of forces increased the numbers of people who worked at producing a few essential materials and products (Map 18.4).

There was a dramatic expansion in the putting-out system, also known as cottage industry, in the eighteenth century, for reasons that were closely related to the changes in the agricultural economy (see page 620). All agricultural work was seasonal, demanding intensive effort and many hands at certain times but not at others. The labor demands of the new crops meant that an even larger number of people might periodically need nonfarm work in order to make ends meet. Rural poverty, whether as a result of traditional or new agricultural methods, made manufacturing work in the home attractive to more people.

Overseas trade stimulated the expansion of production by spurring the demand in Europe's colonies for cloth and other finished products and increasing the demand at home for manufactured items, such as nails to build the ships on which trade depended. The production of cloth expanded also because heightened demand led to changes in the way cloth was made. Wool was increasingly combined with other fibers to make less expensive fabrics. By the end of the century wholly cotton fabrics were being made cheaply in Europe from cotton grown in America by slave labor.

Steady innovation in production played an important part in the expansion of production because it meant that products were being aimed at a broad market. In the Middle Ages, weavers produced a luxury-quality cloth, and their profits came not from demand, which was relatively low, but from the high price that consumers paid. In the eighteenth century, cloth production became a spur to a transformed industrial economy because cheaper kinds of cloth were made for mass consumption. Producing more became important, and innovations that promoted productivity were soon introduced.

A crucial innovation was increased mechanization. The invention of machines to spin thread in the late eighteenth century brought a marked increase in the rate of production and profound changes to the lives of rural workers who had been juggling agricultural and textile work according to season and need. The selected areas of England, France, and the Low Countries where the new technologies were introduced stood, by the end of the century, on the verge of a massive industrial transformation that would have dramatic social consequences.

Control and Resistance

The economic changes of the century produced both resistance and adaptation by ordinary people and, at times, direct action by state authorities. Sometimes ordinary people coped in ways that revealed their desperation. In many cities, numbers of abandoned children rose greatly because urban families, particularly recent immigrants from the countryside, could not support their offspring. The major cities of Europe put increasing resources into police forces and city lighting schemes. Charitable institutions run by cities, churches, and central governments expanded. By 1789, for example, there were more than two thousand *hôpitaux*—poorhouses for the destitute and ill—in France. The poor received food and shelter but were forced to work for the city or to live in poorhouses against their will. Men were sometimes taken out of poorhouses and forced to become soldiers.

Resistance and adaptation were particularly visible wherever the needs of common people conflicted with the states' desire for order and for revenue. The states' desire for order and revenue on the high seas, for example, led to the suppression of piracy. Piracy had been a way of life for hundreds of Europeans and colonial settlers since the sixteenth century. From the earliest days of exploration, European rulers had authorized men known as privateers to commit acts of war against specific targets; the Crown took little risk and was spared the cost of arming the ships but shared in the plunder. True piracy—outright robbery on the high seas—was illegal, but in practice the difference between piracy and privateering was often small. As governments' and merchants' desire for regular trade began to outweigh that for the irregular profits of plunder, and as national navies developed in the late seventeenth century, a concerted effort to eliminate piracy began.

Life on the seas became an increasingly vital part of west European economic life in the eighteenth century, and it began to resemble life on land in the amount of compulsion it included. English-speaking seamen alone numbered about thirty thousand around the middle of the eighteenth

Map 18.4 Population and Production in Eighteenth-Century Europe The growth of cottage industry helped to support a growing population. With changes in agriculture, more land-poor workers were available in the countryside to accept work as spinners, knitters, and weavers.

century. Sailors in port were always vulnerable to forcible enlistment in the navy by impressment gangs, particularly during wartime. A drowsy sailor sleeping off a night of celebrating with new-gotten wages could wake up to find himself aboard a navy ship. Press gangs operated throughout England and not just in major ports, for authorities were as interested in controlling "vagrancy" as in staffing the navy. Merchant captains occasionally filled their crews by such means, particularly when sailing unpopular routes.

Like soldiers in the growing eighteenth-century armies, sailors in the merchant marine as well as the navy could be subjected to brutal disci-pline and appalling conditions. Merchant seamen attempted to improve their lot by trying to regulate their relationship with ships' captains. Contracts for pay on merchant ships were becoming more regularized, and seamen often negotiated their terms very carefully, including, for example, details about how rations were to be allotted. Sailors might even take bold collective action aboard ship. The English-language term for a collective job action, *strike*, comes from the sailing expression "to strike sail," meaning to lower the sails so that they cannot fill with wind. Its use dates from the eighteenth century, from "strikes" of sailors protesting unfair conditions.

An Idle Apprentice Is Sent to Sea, 1747 In one of a series of moralizing engravings by William Hogarth, the lazy apprentice, Tom, is sent away to a life at sea. The experienced seamen in the boat introduce him to some of its terrors: On the left dangles a cat-o'-nine-tails, and on the distant promontory is a gallows, where pirates and rebels meet their fate. *(From the Collections of Lauinger Library, Georgetown University)*

Seafaring men were an unusual group because they were a large and somewhat self-conscious community of workers for wages. Not until industrialization came into full swing a century later would a similar group of workers exist within Europe itself (see Chapter 21). But economic and political protest by ordinary people on the Continent also showed interesting parallel changes, even though strike activity itself would await the large wage labor force of industrialization. Peasant revolts in the past had ranged from small-scale actions against local tax officials to massive uprisings suppressed by an army. The immediate goals of the rebels were usually practical. They aimed not to eliminate taxation altogether but to limit its extent or to protest the collection of a particularly burdensome tax. The political rationale behind such actions was not a hope that the system could be eliminated but rather a hope that it could be adjusted to operate more fairly. Where there was a revolutionary vision, it was usually a utopian one—a political system with no kings, landlords, taxes, or state of any kind.

Peasant revolts continued to be commonplace and to follow those patterns in the eighteenth century. They were also driven by the localized unemployment caused by agricultural reforms or by objections to press gangs. In certain cases, however, peasants, like sailors, began to confront the state in new ways. Peasants often attacked not state power but the remnants of the various powers over them wielded by landlords, including forced labor and compulsory use of landlords' mills. They also increasingly marshaled whatever legal devices they could to keep control over their land and thwart landlords' efforts to enclose fields and cultivate cash crops. This change, though subtle, was important because it signaled an effort to bring permanent structural change to economic and legal relationships and was not simply a temporary redress of grievances. (See the box, "The Condition of Serfs in Russia.")

Both the old and the new approaches to resisting authority are evident in the Pugachev rebellion of 1773, during the reign of Catherine in Russia (see page 677). The movement began among the Ural Cossacks but eventually included thousands of people with traditional grievances against the regime: Cossacks resisting absorption by the state, miners and other poor workers, peasants, and rebellious dissidents. The rebels thus represented a mixture of traditional grievances and acted under the rubric of "tsarist" legitimacy. Pugachev, in fact, proclaimed himself the legitimate tsar and set up a quasi-imperial court. The rebels' demands were utopian—the elimination of all landlords, all state officials, and all taxation. Less idealistic and more modern were their de-

The Condition of Serfs in Russia

Generally, the condition of agricultural workers was worst in eastern Europe, where political and economic forces kept them bound in serfdom. In A Journey from St. Petersburg to Moscow *(1790), the reform-minded nobleman Alexander Radishchev (1749–1802) describes an encounter with a serf who, like most serfs, was forced to work the lord's lands at the expense of his own.*

A few steps from the road I saw a peasant plowing a field. It was now Sunday, [about midday]. The ploughing peasant, of course, belonged to a landed proprietor, who would not let him pay a commutation tax. The peasant was plowing very carefully. The field . . . was not part of the master's land. He turned the plow with astonishing ease.

"God help you," I said, walking up to the ploughman, who, without stopping, was finishing the furrow he had started. . . . "Have you no time to work during the week, then, and can you not have any rest on Sundays, in the hottest part of the day, at that?"

"In a week, sir, there are six days, and we go six times a week to work on the master's field; in the evening, if the weather is good, we haul to the master's house the hay that is left in the woods. . . . God grant that it rains this evening. If you have peasants of your own, sir, they are praying for the same thing."

"But how do you manage to get food enough [for your family] if you have only the holidays free?"

"Not only the holidays, the nights are ours too."

"Do you work the same way for your master?"

"No, sir, it would be a sin to work the same way. On his fields there are a hundred hands for one mouth, while I have two for seven mouths: you can figure it out for yourself."

Source: Alexander Radishchev, *A Journey from St. Petersburg to Moscow,* trans. Leo Wiener, ed. Roderick Page Thaler (Cambridge, Mass.: Harvard University Press, 1958); quoted in Robert and Elborg Forster, eds., *European Society in the Eighteenth Century* (New York: Harper and Row, 1969), pp. 136–139.

mands to end serfdom and their attempts to set up an alternative administration in the areas they controlled. They also tried to form a creditable army—inevitably the weak spot of popular uprisings.

SUMMARY

It is important not to exaggerate the degree to which circumstances of life changed in the eighteenth century. The economy was expanding and the population growing beyond previous limits, and the system of production was being restructured. But these changes happened incrementally over many decades and were not recognized for the fundamental changes they were.

Most of the long-familiar material constraints were still in place. Roads, on which much commerce depended, were generally impassable in bad weather. Shipping was relatively dependable and economical—but only relatively. Military life likewise reflected traditional constraints. Despite technological changes and developments of the administrative and economic resources of the state to equip, train, and enforce discipline, the conduct of war was still hampered by problems of transport and supply that would have been familiar to warriors two centuries before.

Similarly, though some rulers were inspired by precepts of the Enlightenment, all were guided by traditional concerns of dynastic aggrandizement and strategic advantage. One new dimension of relations between states was the importance of conflict over colonies abroad, but the full economic and strategic impact of British colonial gains would not be felt until the next century.

The most visible change would happen first in politics, where goals and expectations

(continued on page 696)

GARDENS

What is a garden? We first think of intensely culti-vated flower gardens, such as the famous Rose Garden at the White House. We usually don't think of the yards around houses as gardens, yet that is what they are. The landscaping around most ordinary American homes derives from Eng-lish landscape gardening of the eighteenth cen-tury and after—a fact that is reflected in the British custom of calling the "yards" around their homes "gardens." Like most of the art forms that we see habitually, the garden, reproduced in the Ameri-can backyard, is difficult to analyze or even to think of as an art form. Like the buildings they surround, however, gardens have much to tell us about human habits and values. Let us examine their eighteenth-century ancestors for evidence of contemporaries' attitudes toward nature and their relationship with it.

Look at the two English-style gardens illus-trated here. The first is next to the Governor's Mansion in Williamsburg, the capital of the Eng-lish colony of Virginia. Construction of this garden began at the end of the seventeenth century; the photograph shows the restored gardens that tourists may visit today. The second garden, from the private estate of West Wycombe in England, looks very different—much more like a natural landscape. The engraving reproduced here dates from the 1770s. The two gardens represent distinct epochs in the development of the garden, hence the differences between them. However, each of these gardens in its own way celebrates human domination of nature.

This symbolic domination of nature is more ob-vious to us in the Williamsburg garden. The lawns and hedges are trimmed in precise geometrical shapes and are laid out, with the walkways, in straight lines. This "palace garden" was a small English variant of the classical garden developed in France—most spectacularly at Versailles Palace—and then imitated throughout Europe during the seventeenth century. At Versailles, the garden is so vast that at many points all of nature visible to the eye is nature disciplined by humans.

We can think of such gardens as pieces of ar-chitecture, because that is how they were origi-nally conceived: The design originated in the en-closed courtyard gardens of the homes of classical antiquity. The straight lines and squared shapes of these gardens mimic the buildings they are at-

The Governor's Mansion and Formal Gardens at Williamsburg, Virginia *(© Robert Llewellyn)*

Landscape Garden at West Wycombe, England *(Courtesy of the Trustees of the British Museum)*

tached to. In fact, these seventeenth- and eighteenth-century gardens were usually laid out as an extension of the building itself. Notice the wide staircase that descends from the central axis of the Governor's Mansion into the central walkway of the garden. Other architectural details, such as the benches positioned at the ends of various walkways, add to the sense of the garden as an exterior room. Elsewhere, this sense was enhanced by the construction of devices such as grottoes, such as that at Versailles. The garden symbolizes the taming of nature into a pleasing vision of order and regularity.

The later, eighteenth-century garden represents even greater confidence in the human relationship with nature, although it does not appear to do so at first glance. The extensive gardens at first seem to be nature itself plus a few added details, such as the statuary, and a few improvements, such as the grass kept trim by the workers in the foreground. Our familiarity with such landscapes—in our own suburban yards—keeps us from immediately perceiving how contrived such a landscape is. Nature, however, does not intersperse dense stands of trees or clumps of shrubbery with green expanses of lawns. Nor does nature conveniently leave portions of a hillside bare of trees to provide a view of the water from the palatial house, to the left on the hill. Note also that the waterfall cascading over rocks and statuary flows from an artificial lake, neatly bordered by a path.

This kind of garden reflects Enlightenment optimism about humans' ability to understand and work with nature. Such gardens were asymmetrical: Paths were usually curved, and lakes and ponds were irregularly shaped, as they would be in nature. Trees and shrubs were allowed to maintain their natural form. Nevertheless, this landscaping conveys a powerful message of order. Humans cannot bend or distort nature to their own ends, but they can live in harmony with it as they manage it and enjoy its beneficence. People were freed from regarding nature as hostile and needing to be fought. In this garden, one lives with nature but improves upon it. The workers cutting the grass do not detract from the engraving but rather make the scene more compelling.

This brand of landscape gardening appeared in English colonies across the Atlantic by the end of the eighteenth century. One of the best examples is at Monticello, Thomas Jefferson's Virginia estate, first designed in the 1770s and constructed and improved over the remainder of Jefferson's life (1743–1826). If you tour Monticello, you will notice a curving garden path bordered by flowers in season, with mature trees scattered here and there. Jefferson, we know, planned every inch of this largely random-looking outdoor space, just as he planned the regimented fruit and vegetable garden that borders it. The older classical style of the Williamsburg garden is partly explained by its earlier date and also because this more aggressively controlling style lasted longer in the American colonies than in Europe, perhaps because "nature" seemed more wild and still more formidable in the New World. You might wish to consider the curious blend of "nature" and order that is evident in the landscapes we create and live with today.

nurtured by Enlightenment philosophy clashed with the rigid structure of the French state and triggered the French Revolution. The Enlightenment was not simply an intellectual movement that criticized society. It also encompassed the public and private settings where "enlightened" opinion flourished. The revolutionary potential of Enlightenment thought came from belief in its rationality and from the fact that it was both critical of its society and fashionable to practice.

NOTES

1. Quoted in M. S. Anderson, *Europe in the Eighteenth Century, 1713–1783*, 3d ed. (London: Longman, 1987), pp. 218–219.
2. Dena Goodman, *The Republic of Letters: A Cultural History of the French Enlightenment* (Ithaca: Cornell University Press, 1994), p. 89.

SUGGESTED READING

General Surveys

Anderson, M. S. *Europe in the Eighteenth Century, 1713–1783*. 3d ed. 1987.

Doyle, William. *The Old European Order, 1660–1800*. 1978.

Treasure, Geoffrey. *The Making of Modern Europe, 1648–1780*. 1985. Three general histories covering political, social, economic, and cultural developments; each has an extensive bibliography.

The Enlightenment

Chartier, Roger. *The Cultural Uses of Print in Early Modern France*. 1987. A discussion of changes in reading habits and in the uses of printed materials throughout the eighteenth century in France.

Darnton, Robert. *The Literary Underground of the Old Regime*. 1982. One of several important works by Darnton on the social history of print culture.

Gay, Peter. *The Enlightenment: An Interpretation*. 2 vols. 1966–1969. A detailed study of Enlightenment thought by one of its foremost modern interpreters.

———. *Voltaire's Politics*. 1959. A lively introduction to Voltaire's career as a political and social reformer.

Goodman, Dena. *The Republic of Letters: A Cultural History of the French Enlightenment*. 1994. Indispensable for understanding the social context of the enlightenment and the role of women.

Hampson, Norman. *The Enlightenment*. 1968. A useful general survey.

Hazard, Paul. *The European Mind*. 1935. An older but still useful interpretation that depicts a European intellectual crisis between 1680 and 1715.

State Building and Warfare

Carsten, F. L. *The Origins of Prussia*. 1982. An introduction to the growth of the Prussian state in the seventeenth and eighteenth centuries.

Colley, Linda. *Britons: Forging the Nation, 1707–1837*. 1992. A history of the British that emphasizes the interrelationships of political, social, and cultural history.

Devine, T. M. *Clanship to Crofters' War: The Social Transformation of the Scottish Highlands*. 1994. A brief and readable study that follows the destruction and transformation of Highland culture from the Late Middle Ages to the nineteenth century.

Ford, Franklin. *Robe and Sword*. 1953. A path-breaking though controversial study of the consolidation of aristocratic power in France in the eighteenth century.

Gagliardo, John. *Enlightened Despotism*. 1968. A general introduction to the concept and to the rulers of the era.

Hubatsch, Walter. *Frederick the Great*. 1981. A recent biography that illuminates Frederick's system of government.

Kennedy, Paul. *The Rise and Fall of British Naval Mastery*. 1976. The authoritative work on the rise of British seapower from the sixteenth century to modern times.

Madariaga, Isobel de. *Russia in the Age of Catherine the Great*. 1981. The best recent biography of Catherine.

See also the works by Evans, Howard, Parker, Riasanovsky, and Vierhaus cited in Chapters 15 and 16.

Early Modern Economy and Society

Cipolla, Carlo. *Before the Industrial Revolution*. 1976. The most comprehensive single treatment of the development of the European economy and technology through this period.

De Vries, Jan. *The Economy of Europe in an Age of Crisis, 1600–1750*. 1976. Essential reading for understanding the changes in Europe's economy and in its trade and colonial relationships throughout the world.

Gullickson, Gay. *Spinners and Weavers of Auffay*. 1986.

Gutman, Myron P. *Toward the Modern Economy*. 1988. Two works that focus on specific communities in western Europe and thus provide compelling, detailed analyses of the changes in the European economy in the seventeenth and eighteenth centuries.

Hufton, Olwen. *The Poor of Eighteenth-Century Paris*. 1974. An analysis of the lives of the poor and the responses of the state.

Laslett, Peter. *The World We Have Lost*. 1965. An innovative study of premodern society and culture, emphasizing the differences in habits and values that separate our society from preindustrial times.

Parry, J. H. *Trade and Dominion: The European Overseas Empires in the Eighteenth Century*. 1971. A reliable survey of developments.

CHAPTER 19

Revolutionary Europe, 1789–1815

One day in early July 1792, a troop of national guardsmen from the city of Marseille in southern France marched into Paris, singing as they came:

> Allons enfants de la patrie,
> Le jour de gloire est arrivé
> Contre nous de la tyrannie
> L'étendard sanglant est levé!

> (Come, children of the nation)
> (The day of glory is at hand)
> (Against us is raised)
> (The bloody standard of tyranny!)

Their song quickly became famous as the "Marseillaise," and three years later was officially declared the French national anthem. This choice is appropriate, for the French Revolution, which was unfolding that July, profoundly shaped the growth and character of modern France.

Today the Revolution is considered the initiation of modern European as well as modern French history. The "Marseillaise" had been composed some months earlier by a French army captain in Alsace, where French troops were facing Austrian and German forces. Events in France reverberated throughout Europe because the overthrow of absolute monarchy threatened other monarchs. Revolutionary fervor on the part of ordinary soldiers compensated for inexperience, and France's armies unexpectedly bested many of their opponents. By the late 1790s the armies of France would be led in outright conquest of other European states by one of the most talented generals in European history: Napoleon Bonaparte. What he brought to the continental European nations that his armies eventually conquered was a fascinating amalgam of imperial aggression and revolutionary fervor. Europe was transformed both by the changing balance of power and by the spread of revolutionary ideas.

Léon Cogniet, *The National Guard of Paris leaves to join the army in September 1792* (detail).

Understanding the French Revolution means understanding not only how it began but also the complicated course it took and why, together with the significance of those events. Part of the Revolution's importance lay in the power of symbols, such as the "Marseillaise," to challenge an old political order and to legitimate a new one. Challenges to the power of the king were not new, but the Revolution overthrew his right to rule at all. The notion that the people constituted the nation, were responsible as citizens, and had some right to representation in government replaced a system of government by inherited privilege. Louis XVI was transformed from the divinely appointed father of his people to an enemy of the people, worthy only of execution. But on the day in 1792 the men from Marseille marched into Paris, none of this was clear.

BACKGROUND TO REVOLUTION

"I am a citizen of the world," wrote John Paul Jones, a captain of the fledgling United States Navy, in 1778. He was writing to a Scottish aristocrat, apologizing for the conduct of men under his command who had raided the lord's estate while conducting coastal raids against the British Isles during the American Revolution. Jones (1747–1792) himself was a Scotsman, who had begun a life at sea as a boy. He was one of the thousands of cosmopolitan Europeans who were familiar with European cultures on both sides of the Atlantic. As a sailor, Jones literally knew his way around the Atlantic world. He was a "citizen of the world" in another sense as well. When the Scotsman, Lord Selkirk, wrote back to Jones, he expressed surprise that his home had been raided because he was sympathetic to the American colonists. Like Jones, he said, he was a man of "liberal sentiments."[1] Both Jones and Lord Selkirk felt they belonged to an international society of gentlemen who recognized certain principles regarding just and rational government that grew out of the Enlightenment.

In the Atlantic world of the late eighteenth century, both practical links of property and trade and shared ideals about "liberty" were important shaping forces. The strategic interests of the great European powers were also always involved. Thus, when the American colonists actively re-

sisted British rule and then in 1776 declared their independence from Britain, there were many consequences: British trading interests were challenged, French appetites for gains at British expense were whetted, and illusive notions of "liberty" seemed more plausible and desirable. The victory of the American colonies in 1783, followed by the creation of the United States Constitution in 1787, further heightened the appeal of liberal ideas elsewhere. There were attempts at liberal reform in several states, including Ireland, the Netherlands, and Poland. However, the American Revolution had the most direct impact on later events in France because the French had been directly involved in the American effort.

Revolutionary Movements Around Europe

While the British government was facing the revolt of the American colonies, it also confronted trouble closer to home. The war against the American colonies was not firmly supported by Britons. Like many Americans, many Britons had divided loyalties, and many others were convinced that the war was being mismanaged. The prosecution of the war against the American colonies proceeded amid calls for reform of the ministerial government. In this setting, a reform movement in Ireland began to spring up in 1779. The reformers demanded greater autonomy from Britain. Like the Americans, Irish elites felt like disadvantaged junior partners in the British Empire. They chafed over British policies that favored British imperial interests over those of the Irish ruling class: for example, the exclusion of Irish ports from much trade in favor of English and Scottish ports and the granting of political rights to Irish Catholics so that they might fight in Britain's overseas armies.

Protestant Irish landlords, threatened by such policies, expressed their opposition not only in parliamentary but also in military ways. Following the example of the American rebels, middle- and upper-class Anglo-Irish set up a system of locally sponsored voluntary militia to resist British troops if necessary. The Volunteer Movement was undercut when greater parliamentary autonomy for Ireland was granted in 1782, following the repeal of many restrictions on Irish commerce. Unlike the Americans, the Irish elites faced an internal challenge to their own authority—the Catholic population whom they had for centuries dominated. That challenge forced them to reach an accommodation with the British government.

Meanwhile, a political crisis with constitutional overtones was also brewing in the Netherlands. Tensions between the aristocratic stadtholders of the House of Orange and the merchant oligarchies of the major cities deepened during the American Revolution, because the Dutch were then engaged in a commercial war against the British, to whom the stadtholder was supposed to be sympathetic. The conflict ceased to be wholly traditional for two reasons. First, the representatives of the various cities, calling themselves the Dutch "Patriot" party, defended their position in the name of the traditional balance of powers within the Netherlands as well as with wider claims to "liberty," like those of the American revolutionaries. Second, the challenge to traditional political arrangements widened when middling urban dwellers, long disenfranchised by these oligarchies, demanded "liberty," too—that is, political enfranchisement within the cities—and briefly took over the Patriot movement. Just as many Irish rebels accepted the concessions of 1782, many "Patriot" oligarchs in the Netherlands did nothing to resist an invasion in 1787 that restored the power of the stadtholder, the prince of Orange, and thereby ended the challenge to their own control of urban government.

Both the Irish "volunteers" and the Dutch "Patriots," though members of very limited movements, echoed the American rebels in practical and ideological ways. Both were influenced by the economic and political consequences of Britain's relationship with its colonies. Both were inspired by the success of the American rebels and their thoroughgoing claims for political self-determination.

Desire for political reform flared in Poland as well during this period. Reform along lines suggested by Enlightenment precepts was accepted as a necessity by Polish leaders after the first partition of Poland in 1772 had left the remnant state without some of its wealthiest territories (see Map 18.1 on page 679). Beginning in 1788, however, reforming gentry in the *sejm* (representative assembly) went further; they established a commission to write a constitution, following the American example. The resulting document, known as the May 3 (1791) Constitution, was the first codified constitution in Europe; it was read and admired by George Washington.

The Constitution established a constitutional monarchy in which representatives of major towns as well as gentry and nobility could sit as deputies. The *liberum veto,* which had allowed great magnates to obstruct royal authority at will, was abolished. However, Catherine the Great, empress of Russia, would not tolerate a constitutional government in place so close to her own autocratic regime; she ordered an invasion of Poland in 1792. The unsuccessful defense of Poland was led by a veteran of the American Revolution, Tadeusz Kościuszko (1746–1817). The second, more extensive partition of Poland followed, to be followed in turn in 1794 by a widespread insurrection against Russian rule, again led by Kościuszko. The uprising was mercilessly suppressed by an alliance of Russian and Prussian troops. Unlike the Americans from whom they drew inspiration, the Poles' constitutional experiment was doomed by the power of its neighbor.

The American Revolution and the Kingdom of France

As one of Britain's greatest commercial and political rivals, France naturally was drawn into Britain's struggle with its North American colonies. The consequences for France were momentous for two reasons. First, the cost of French aid for the American rebels was so great that it helped accelerate a financial crisis in the French monarchy. Second, French involvement directly exposed many French aristocrats and common soldiers to the "enlightened" international community to which John Paul Jones felt he belonged, though the absolute monarchy of France turned a cold shoulder toward "liberal" ideas.

Rivalry with Great Britain gave France a special relationship with the American colonies and their fight for independence. In the Seven Years' War (1756–1763), the French had lost many of their colonial settlements and trading outposts to the English (see page 687). Stung by this outcome, certain courtiers and ministers pressed for an aggressive colonial policy that would regain for France some of the riches in trade that Britain was threatening to monopolize. The American Revolution seemed to offer the perfect opportunity. The French extended covert aid to the Americans from the very beginning of the conflict in 1775. After the first major defeat of British troops by the

Americans—at the Battle of Saratoga in 1777—France formally recognized the independent United States and established an alliance with them. The French then committed troops as well as monetary support for American forces. John Paul Jones's most famous ship, the *Bonhomme Richard*, was purchased and outfitted in France at French government expense, as were many other American naval vessels during the war. French support was decisive. In 1781 the French fleet kept reinforcements from reaching the British force besieged at Yorktown by George Washington. The American victory at Yorktown effectively ended the war; the colonies' independence was formally recognized by the Treaty of Paris in 1783.

The effect on France of the alliance with the American colonies was complicated. Aid for the Americans saddled France with a debt of about 1 million *livres* (pounds), which represented as much as one-quarter of the total debt that the French government was trying to service. A less tangible impact of the American Revolution was also important. About nine thousand French soldiers, sailors, and aristocrats participated in the war. The best known is the Marquis de Lafayette, who became an aide to George Washington and helped to command American troops. For many humble men, the war was simply employment. For others, it was a quest of sorts. For them, the promise of the Enlightenment—belief in the rationality of men, natural rights, and natural laws by which society should be organized—was brought to life in America.

Exposure to the American conflict occurred at the French court, too. Beginning in 1775, a permanent American mission to Versailles lobbied hard for aid and later managed the flow of that assistance. The chief emissary of the Americans was Benjamin Franklin (1706–1790), a philosophe by French standards, whose writings and scientific experiments were already known to French elites. His talents—among them, a skillful exploitation of a simple, Quaker-like demeanor—succeeded in promoting the idealization of America at the French court.

The United States Constitution and the various state constitutions and the debates surrounding them were all published in Paris and were much discussed in salons and at court, where lively debate about reform of French institutions had been going on for decades. America became the prototype of what Enlightenment philosophy

said was possible. It was hailed as the place where the irrationalities of inherited privilege did not prevail. A British observer, Arthur Young (1741–1820), believed that "the American revolution has laid the foundation of another in France, if [the French] government does not take care of itself."[2]

By the mid-1780s there was no longer a question of whether the French regime would experience reform but rather what form the reform would take. The royal government was almost bankrupt. A significant minority of the politically active elite was convinced of the fundamental irrationality of France's system of government. Nevertheless, the cataclysmic proportions that the French Revolution eventually reached raise questions about why less drastic change did not happen. A dissatisfied elite and a financial crisis—even with the encouragement of a successful revolt elsewhere—do not necessarily lead to revolution. Why did the French government—the *Ancien Régime*, or "Old Regime," as it became known after the Revolution—not take care of itself?

The Crisis of the Old Regime

The Old Regime was brought to the point of crisis in the late 1780s by three factors: (1) an antiquated system for collecting revenue, as well as old and recent debts; (2) institutional constraints on the monarchy that defended privileged interests; and (3) elite public opinion that envisioned thoroughgoing reform and pushed the monarchy in that direction. Another factor was the ineptitude of the king, Louis XVI (r. 1774–1793).

Louis came to the throne in 1774, a year before the American Revolution began. He was a kind, well-meaning man better suited to carry out the finite responsibilities of a petty bureaucrat than to be king. The queen, the Austrian Marie Antoinette (1755–1793), was unpopular. She was regarded with suspicion by those for whom the alliance with Austria had never felt natural. She, too, was politically inept, unable to negotiate the complexities of court life, and widely rumored to be selfishly wasteful of royal resources despite the realm's financial crises.

The fiscal crisis of the monarchy had been a long time in the making and was an outgrowth of the system in which the greatest wealth was protected by traditional privileges. At the top of the social and political pyramid were the nobles, a legal grouping that included warriors and royal officials. In France, nobility conferred exemption from much taxation. Thus, the royal government could not directly tax its wealthiest subjects.

This situation existed throughout much of Europe, a legacy of the individual contractual relationships that had formed the political and economic framework of medieval Europe. Unique to France, however, was the strength of the institutions that defended this system. Of particular importance were the royal law courts, the parlements, which claimed a right of judicial review over royal edicts. All the Parlementaires—well-educated lawyers and judges—were noble and loudly defended the traditional privileges of all nobles. Louis XV (d. 1774), near the end of his life, had successfully undermined the power of the parlements by a bold series of moves. Louis XVI, immediately after coming to the throne, buckled under pressure and restored the parlements to full power.

Deficit financing had been a way of life for the monarchy for centuries. After early efforts at reform, Louis XIV (d. 1715) had reverted to common fund-raising expedients such as selling offices, which only added to the weight of privileged investment in the old order. England had established a national bank to free its government from the problem, but the comparable French effort early in the century had been undercapitalized and had failed. Late in the 1780s, under Louis XVI, one-fourth of the annual operating expenses of the government was borrowed, and half of all government expenditure went to paying interest on its debt.

Short-term economic crises added to the cumulative problem of government finance. During Louis's reign there were several years of disastrously poor harvests, and throughout the reign there was a downturn in the economy. The weakness of the economy proved to be a crucial component in the failure of overall reform.

The king employed able finance ministers who tried to institute fundamental reforms, such as replacing the tangle of taxes with a simpler system in which all would pay and eliminating local tariffs, which were stifling commerce. The parlements and many courtiers and aristocrats, as well as ordinary people, resisted these policies. Ordinary people did not trust the "free market" (free from traditional trade controls) for grain; most feared that speculators would buy up the grain supply and people would starve. Trying

Criticism of Marie Antoinette In a satirical engraving from 1787, the queen toasts the dismissal of a reforming minister. She wears a famous diamond necklace that had caused scandal and widespread criticism of the monarchy two years before; it was a gift from a cardinal with whom the queen was wrongly accused of having an affair. (*Musée Carnavalet/Jean-Loup Charmet*)

to implement such reforms in a time of grain shortage almost guaranteed their failure. Moreover, many supported the parlements out of self-interest and because they were the only institution capable of standing up to the monarchy. Yet not all members of the elite joined the parlements in opposing reform. The imprint of "enlightened" public opinion shaped in salons and literary societies was apparent in the thinking of some aristocrats, who believed that the government and the economic system as a whole needed reform and debated the nature and extent of reform needed.

In 1787 the king called an "Assembly of Notables"—an ad hoc group of elites—to support him in facing down the parlements and proceeding with some reforms. He found little support even among men known to be sympathetic to reform. Some did not support particular reforms, and many were reluctant to allow the monarchy free rein. Others, reflecting the influence of the American Revolution, maintained that a "constitutional" body such as the Estates General, which had not been called since 1614, needed to make these decisions.

Ironically, nobles and clergy who were opposed to reform supported the call for the Estates General, for they assumed that they could control its deliberations. The three Estates met and voted separately by "order"—clergy (First Estate), nobles (Second Estate), and commoners (Third Estate). It was thus assumed that the votes of the clergy and nobles would nullify whatever the Third Estate might propose.

In 1788 popular resistance to reform in the streets of Paris and mounting pressure from his courtiers and bureaucrats induced Louis to summon the Estates General. On Louis's orders, deputies to the Estates General were elected by intermediate assemblies chosen by wide male suffrage. Louis assumed there was widespread loyalty to the monarchy in the provinces, and he wished to tap into it by means of this voting. Louis also agreed that the Third Estate should have twice as many deputies as the other two Estates, but he did not authorize voting by head rather than by order, which would have brought about the dominance of the Third Estate. Nevertheless, he hoped that the specter of drastic proposals put forth by the Third Estate would frighten the aristocrats and clergy into accepting some of his reforms.

Louis faced a critical situation when the Estates General convened in May 1789. As ever, he faced immediate financial crisis. He also faced a constitutional crisis. There was already a sense of legitimacy about the Estates General, about the role of the Third Estate, and about the authority of the Third Estate to enact change. Political pamphlets abounded arguing that the Third Estate deserved enhanced power because it carried the

mandate of the people. The most important of them was *What Is the Third Estate?* (1789) by Joseph Emmanuel Sieyès (1748–1836), a church official from the diocese of Chartres. The sympathies of Abbé Sieyès, as he was known, were with the Third Estate: His career had suffered because he was not noble. Sieyès argued that the Third Estate represented the nation because it did not reflect special privilege.

Among the deputies of the first two Estates—clergy and nobility—were men, like the Marquis de Lafayette (1757–1834), who were sympathetic to reform. More important, however, the elections had returned to the Third Estate a large majority of deputies who reflected the most radical political thought possible for men of their standing. Most were lawyers and other professionals who were functionaries in the government but, like Sieyès, of low social rank. They frequented provincial academies, salons, and political societies. They were convinced of their viewpoints and determined on reform and had little stake in the system as it was. When this group convened and met with resistance from the First and Second Estates and from Louis himself, they seized the reins of government and a revolution began.

1789: The Revolution Begins

The three Estates met at Versailles, but the opening of the Estates General was celebrated first in Paris with a solemn procession and religious services attended by all the participants—the last public ritual of the Old Regime. The three Estates marched separately—the clergy arrayed in magnificent vestments, the nobles decked out in furs and velvet, the "commoners" dressed in simple black, bringing up the rear. Neither this staged portrayal of social distinctions, nor the spectacularly presented king and queen, nor the religious symbolism that linked monarchy to divine order could conceal the political conflicts.

As soon as the three Estates began to meet, the conflicts surfaced. The ineptness of the Crown was immediately clear. On the first day of the meetings, Louis and his ministers failed to introduce a program of reforms for the deputies to consider. This failure raised doubt about the monarchy's commitment to reform. More important, it allowed the political initiative to pass to the Third Estate. The deputies challenged the Crown's insistence that the three Estates meet and vote separately. Deputies to the Third Estate refused to be certified (that is, to have their credentials officially recognized) as members of only the Third Estate rather than as members of the Estates General as a whole.

For six weeks the Estates General was unable to meet officially, and the king did nothing to break the impasse. During this interlude, the determination of the deputies of the Third Estate strengthened. More and more deputies were won over to the notion that the three Estates should meet together and that the reform process must begin in the most systematic way: France must have a written constitution.

By the middle of June, more than thirty reformist members of the clergy were sitting jointly with the Third Estate, which had invited all deputies from all three Estates to meet and be certified together. On June 17 the Third Estate simply declared itself the National Assembly of France. At first, the king did nothing, but when the deputies arrived to meet on the morning of June 20, they discovered they had been locked out of the hall. Undaunted, they assembled instead in a nearby indoor tennis court and produced the document that has come to be known as the "Tennis Court Oath." It was a collective pledge to meet until a written constitution had been achieved. Only one deputy refused to support it. Sure of their mandate, the deputies had assumed the reins of government.

The king continued to handle the situation with both ill-timed self-assertion and attempts at compromise. As more and more deputies from the First and Second Estates joined the National Assembly, Louis "ordered" the remaining loyal deputies to join it, too. Simultaneously, however, he ordered troops to come to Paris. He feared disorder in the wake of the recent disturbances throughout France and believed that any challenge to the legitimacy of arbitrary monarchical authority would be disastrous.

The Tennis Court Oath It was raining on June 20 when the deputies found themselves barred from their meeting hall and sought shelter in the royal tennis court. Their defiance created one of the turning points of the Revolution; the significance was recognized several years later by this painting's artist. *(Photographie Bulloz)*

Storming the Bastille The crowd was convinced that the Bastille held political prisoners as well as a large supply of arms. In fact, it held neither. Thousands of Parisians—including artisans and shopkeepers and not merely desperate rabble— surrounded the fortress and forced the garrison to surrender. *(Photographie Bulloz)*

This appeal for armed assistance stirred unrest in the capital. Paris, with a population of about 600,000 in 1789, was one of the largest cities in Europe. There were thousands of workers in all trades plus thousands more—perhaps one-tenth of the inhabitants—jobless recent immigrants from the countryside. Paris was the political nerve center of the nation; it was the site of the publishing industry, salons, the homes of Parlementaires and royal ministers. The city was both extremely volatile and extremely important to the stability of royal power. The king's call for troops aroused Parisians' suspicions. Some assumed that there was a plot afoot to

starve Paris and destroy the National Assembly. Already they considered the Assembly to be a guarantor of acceptable government.

It took little—the announcement of the dismissal of a reformist finance minister—for Paris to erupt in demonstrations and looting. Crowds besieged City Hall and the royal armory, where they seized thousands of weapons. A popular militia formed as citizens armed themselves. Armed crowds assailed other sites of royal authority, including the huge fortified prison, the Bastille, on the morning of July 14. The Bastille now held only a handful of petty criminals, but it still remained a

Declaration of the Rights of Man and the Citizen

Each of the articles of the 1789 Declaration was a response to some feature of Old Regime society or law that was now deemed unacceptable.

Preamble: The representatives of the French people, organized as a National Assembly, believing that the ignorance, neglect, or contempt of the rights of man are the sole cause of public calamities and the corruption of governments, have determined to set forth in a solemn declaration the natural, inalienable, and sacred rights of man. . . .

(1) Men are born and remain free and equal in rights. Social distinctions may be founded only upon the general good.

(2) The aim of all political association is the preservation of the natural and imprescriptible rights of man. These rights are liberty, property, security, and resistance to oppression.

(3) The principle of all sovereignty resides essentially in the nation. No body or individual may exercise any authority which does not proceed directly from the nation.

(6) Law is the expression of the general will. Every citizen has the right to participate personally, or through his representative, in its formation. It must be the same for all. . . . All citizens, being equal in the eyes of the law, are equally eligible to all dignities and to all public positions and occupations, according to their abilities, and without distinction except that of their virtues and talents.

(11) The free communication of ideas and opinions is one of the most precious rights of man. . . .

(13) A common contribution is essential for the maintenance of the public forces and for the cost of administration. This should be equitably distributed among all the citizens in proportion to their means.

Source: James Harvey Robinson, *Readings in European History* (Boston: Ginn, 1906), pp. 409–411.

potent symbol of royal power and, it was assumed, held large supplies of arms. Like the troops at the armory, the garrison at the Bastille had not been given firm orders to fire on the crowds if necessary. After leading a hesitant defense, the garrison commander decided to surrender after citizens managed to secure cannon and drag them to face the prison. Most of the garrison were allowed to go free, although several officers, including the commander, were murdered by the crowd.

The citizens' victory was a great embarrassment to royal authority. The king immediately had to embrace the popular movement. He came to Paris and in front of crowds at City Hall donned the red and blue cockade worn by the militia and ordinary folk as a badge of resolve and defiance. This symbolic action signaled the legitimation of politics based on new principles.

Encouraged by events in Paris, inhabitants of cities and towns around France staged similar uprisings. In many, the machinery of royal government completely broke down. City councils, officials, and even Parlementaires were thrown out of office. Popular militias took control of the streets. There was a simultaneous wave of uprisings in rural areas. Most of them were the result of food shortages, but their timing added momentum to the more strictly political protests in urban areas. These events forced the members of the National Assembly to work energetically on the constitution and to pass legislation to satisfy popular protests against economic and political privileges.

On August 4 the Assembly issued a set of decrees abolishing the remnants of powers that landlords had enjoyed since the Middle Ages, including the right to compel peasants to labor for them and the bondage of serfdom itself. Although largely symbolic, because serfdom and forced labor had been eliminated in much of France, these changes represented a dramatic inroad into the property rights of the elite as they had been traditionally construed. They were hailed as the "end of feudalism." A blow was also struck at established religion by abolishing the tithe. At the end of August, the Assembly issued a Declaration of the Rights of Man and the Citizen. It was a bold assertion of principles condemning the old order. (See the box, "Declaration of the Rights of Man and the Citizen.")

In September, the deputies debated the king's role in a new constitutional government. Deputies known as "monarchists" favored a government rather like England's, with a two-house legislature, including an upper house representing the hereditary aristocracy and a royal right to veto legislation. More radical deputies favored a single legislative chamber and no veto power for the king. After deliberation, the Assembly reached a compromise. The king was given a three-year suspensive veto—the power to suspend legislation for the sitting of two legislatures. This was still a

formidable amount of power but a drastic limitation of the king's formerly absolute sovereignty.

Again, Louis resorted to troops. This time, he called them directly to Versailles, where the Assembly sat. News of the troops' arrival provoked outrage, which heightened with the threat of another grain shortage. Women in street markets in Paris, early on the morning of October 5, noticed food shortages and took immediate collective action. "We want bread!" they shouted at the steps of City Hall. Women often led protests over bread shortages, because they procured food for their families. This protest, however, went far beyond the ordinary. A crowd of thousands gathered and decided to go all the way to Versailles, accompanied by the popular militia (now called the "National Guard"), to petition the king directly for sustenance.

At Versailles, they presented a delegation to the National Assembly, and a joint delegation of the women and deputies was dispatched to see the king. Some of the women fell at the feet of the king with their tales of hardship, convinced that the "father of the people" would alleviate their suffering. He did order stored grain supplies distributed in Paris, and he also agreed to accept the

Women's March on Versailles The Parisian marketwomen marched the twelve miles to Versailles, some provisioning themselves with tools, stolen firearms, and horses as they left the capital. *(Jean-Loup Charmet)*

A Young Woman Recounts the March to Versailles

In the months after the women's march of October 1789, the municipal council in Paris, suspicious of such popular action, questioned some of the participants. These depositions present problems as historical sources because the witnesses' words were not recorded verbatim and, in any case, each witness would have been very careful in her testimony. The following document comes from the questioning of a 20-year-old Marie-Rose Barré, a lace worker.

[Marie-Rose Barré] . . . [d]eposes that on October 5 last, at about eight o'clock in the morning, going to take back some work, she was stopped at the Pont Notre Dame by about a hundred women who told her that it was necessary for her to go with them to Versailles to ask for bread there. Not being able to resist this great number of women, she decided to go with them. At the hamlet at the Point-du-Jour, two young men, unknown to her, who were on foot and going their way, told them that they were running a great risk, that there were cannon mounted at the bridge at Saint-Cloud. This did not prevent them from continuing on their way. . . . The two young men of whom she spoke met them near Viroflay and told them that they had escaped at Saint-Cloud but that at Versailles they would be fired on. But they continued on their way. At Versailles they found the King's Guards lined up in three ranks before the palace. A gentleman dressed in the uniform of the King's Guard . . . came to ask them what they wanted of the King, recommending peaceful behavior on their part. They answered that they were coming to ask him for bread. This gentleman was absent for a few minutes and then returned to take four of them to introduce them to the King. The deponent was one of the four. . . .

They spoke first to M. de Saint-Priest, and then to His Majesty, whom they asked for bread. His Majesty answered them that he was suffering at least as much as they were, to see them lacking it, and that so far as he was able he had taken care to prevent them from experiencing a dearth. Upon the King's response, they begged him to be so good as to arrange escorts for the flour transports intended for the provisioning of Paris, because according to what they had been told at the bridge in Sèvres by the two young men of whom she spoke earlier, only two wagons out of seventy intended for Paris actually arrived there. The King promised them to have the flour escorted and said that if it depended on him, they would have bread then and there. They took leave of His Majesty and were led, by a gentleman in a blue uniform with red piping, into the apartments and courts of the palace to the ranks of the Flanders regiment, to which they called out, "Vive Le Roi!" It was then about nine o'clock. After this, they retired into a house on Rue Satory and went to bed in a stable.

Source: Philip Dawson, ed., *The French Revolution* (Englewood Cliffs, N.J.: Prentice-Hall, Inc., 1967), pp. 66–67.

constitutional role that the Assembly had voted for him. (See the box, "A Young Woman Recounts the March to Versailles.")

The march ended on an odd note as the National Guard replaced much of the royal guard around the person of the king. That night the National Guard saved the king's life when members of the crowd broke into the palace and managed to kill two members of the royal guard still in atten-

dance outside the queen's chamber. The king agreed to return to Paris, so that he could reassure the people. But the procession back to the city was a curious one. The entire royal family was escorted by militia and city people, and the severed heads of the killed guardsmen were carried on pikes.

The king was now in the hands of his people. Already, dramatic change had occurred as a result of a complex dynamic among the three Estates, the

Crown, and the people of Paris. The king was still assumed to be the fatherly guardian of his people's well-being; but his powers were now limited, and his authority was badly shaken. The Assembly had begun to govern in the name of the "nation" and, so far, had the support of the people.

THE FRENCH REVOLUTIONS

The French Revolution was a complicated affair. It was a series of changes, in a sense a series of revolutions, driven not by one group of people but by several groups. Even among elites convinced of the need for reform there was a wide range of opinion. The people of Paris continued to be an important force for change. Country people also became active, primarily in resisting changes forced on them by the central government.

All of the wrangling within France was complicated by foreign reaction. Managing foreign war soon became a routine burden for the fragile revolutionary governments. In addition, there were the continuing problems that had precipitated the Revolution in the first place: the indebtedness of the government, economic difficulties, and recurrent shortages of grain. Finally, the Revolution itself was an issue in that momentum for further change was created once the traditional arrangements of royal government had been altered.

The First Phase Completed, 1789–1791

At the end of 1789, Paris was in ferment, but for a time the forward progress of change blunted the threat of disastrous divisions between king and Assembly and between either of those and the people of Paris. The capital continued to be the center of lively political debate. Salons continued to meet; academies and private societies proliferated. Deputies to the Assembly swelled the ranks of these societies or helped to found new ones. Several would be important throughout the Revolution—particularly the Jacobin Club, named for the monastic order whose buildings the members used as a meeting hall.

These clubs represented a wide range of revolutionary opinion. Some, in which ordinary Parisians were well represented, focused on economic policies that would directly benefit common people. Women were active in a few of the more

radical groups. Monarchists dominated other clubs. At first similar to the salons and debating societies of the Enlightenment era, the clubs increasingly became both sites of political action and sources of political pressure on the government. A bevy of popular newspapers also contributed to the vigorous political life in the capital.

The broad front of revolutionary consensus began to break apart as the Assembly forged ahead with decisions about the constitution and with policies necessary to remedy France's still-desperate financial situation. The largest portion of the untapped wealth of the nation lay with the Catholic church, an obvious target for anticlerical reformers. The deputies did not propose to dismantle the church, but they did make sweeping changes. They kept church buildings intact and retained the clergy as salaried officials of the state. They abolished all monasteries and pensioned the monks and nuns to permit them to continue as nurses and teachers where possible. The Assembly seized most of the vast properties of the church and declared them national property (*biens nationaux*) to be sold for revenue.

Economic and political problems ensued. Revenue was needed faster than the property could be inventoried and sold, so government bonds (*assignats*) were issued against the eventual sale of church properties. Unfortunately, in the cash-strapped economy, the bonds were treated like money, their value became inflated, and the government never realized the hoped-for profits. A greater problem was the political divisiveness generated by the restructuring of the church. Many members of the lower clergy, living as they did near ordinary citizens, were among the most reform-minded of the deputies. These clergy were willing to go along with many changes, but the required oath of loyalty to the state challenged clerical identity and seemed overly intrusive.

The Civil Constitution of the Clergy, as these measures were called, was passed by the Assembly in July 1790 because the clerical deputies opposing it were outvoted. More than half of the clergy did take the oath of loyalty. Those who refused, concentrated among the higher clergy, were in theory thrown out of their offices. A year later (April 1791) the pope declared that clergy who had taken the oath were suspended from their offices. Antirevolutionary sentiment grew among thousands of French people, particularly among rural people, to whom the church was still important. This religious opposition helped to undermine the legitimacy of the new government.

Meanwhile, the Assembly proceeded with administrative and judicial reform. The deputies abolished the medieval provinces as administrative districts and replaced them with uniform *départements* (departments). They declared that local officials would be elected—a revolutionary dispersal of power that had previously belonged to the king.

As work on the constitution drew to a close in the spring of 1791, the king decided that he had had enough. Royal authority and government had been virtually dismantled. Louis had always lived in splendid isolation in Versailles, but he now was a virtual prisoner in the Tuileries Palace in the very heart of Paris. Afraid for himself and his family, he and a few loyal aides worked out a plan to flee France. The king and the members of his immediate family set out incognito on June 20, 1791. However, the royal party missed a rendezvous with a troop escort and was stopped along the way—and recognized—in the town of Varennes, near the eastern border of the kingdom.

Louis and his family were returned to Paris and now lived under lightly disguised house arrest. The circumstances of his flight were quickly discovered. He had intended to invade France with Austrian troops if necessary. He and the queen had sent money abroad ahead of themselves. He had left behind a document condemning the constitution. Thus, in July 1791, just as the Assembly was completing its proposal for a constitutional monarchy, the constitution it had created began to seem unworkable because the king was not trustworthy.

Editorials and popular demonstrations against the monarchy echoed these sentiments. In an incident known as the Massacre of the Champ (Field) de Mars, government troops led by Lafayette charged citizens gathered in a public demonstration organized by certain clubs against the monarchy. The government of the National Assembly fired on the demonstrators, and about fifty men and women died. This incident both reflected and heightened tensions between moderate reformers satisfied with the constitutional monarchy, such as Lafayette, and those, including increasing numbers of Parisian citizens, who were openly republican and hoping to eliminate the monarchy.

THE FRENCH REVOLUTION, 1789–1791

May 5, 1789	Meeting of Estates General
June 17, 1789	Third Estate declares itself the National Assembly
June 20, 1789	Tennis Court Oath
July–August 1789	Storming of the Bastille (July 14); abolition of feudalism (August 4); Declaration of the Rights of Man and of the Citizen (August 27)
October 5–6, 1789	Women's march on Versailles; Louis XVI's return to Paris
July 1790	Civil Constitution of the Clergy
June 1791	Louis XVI attempts to flee Paris; is captured and returned
September 1791	New constitution is implemented; Girondins dominate newly formed Legislative Assembly

On September 14 the king swore to uphold the constitution. He had no choice. The event became an occasion for celebration, but the tension between the interests of the Parisians and the provisions of the new constitution could not be glossed over. Though a liberal document for its day, the constitution reflected the views of the elite deputies who had created it. The right to vote, based on a minimal property qualification, was given to about half of all adult men. However, these men only chose electors, for whom the property qualifications were higher. The electors in turn chose deputies to national bodies and also local officials. Although in theory any eligible voter could be an elected deputy or official, the fact that elite electors voted candidates into office reduced the likelihood that ordinary citizens would be national deputies or local officials. The Declaration

Declaration of the Rights of Woman

Authored in 1791 by Olympe de Gouges (1748?–1793), a butcher's daughter from southwestern France, this document and its author's career reflect the complexity of political life during the Revolution. Gouges's advocacy of women's rights represents the extension to women of the broad-based challenge to tradition that the Revolution embodied. Gouges dedicates the Declaration to the queen, drawing on the tradition of aristocratic patronage. Ironically, given Article 10, Gouges died on the scaffold for her revolutionary sympathies.

Man, Are you capable of being just? It is a woman who poses the question; you will not deprive her of that right at least. Tell me, what gives you sovereign empire to oppress my sex? . . . Bizarre, blind, bloated with science and degenerated—in a century of enlightenment and wisdom—into the crassest ignorance, he wants to command as a despot a sex which is in full possession of its intellectual faculties; he pretends to enjoy the Revolution and to claim his rights to equality in order to say nothing more about it.

(1) Woman is born free and lives equal to man in her rights. Social distinctions can be based only on the common utility.

(2) The purpose of any political association is the conservation of the natural and imprescriptible rights of woman and man; these rights are liberty, property, security, and especially resistance to oppression.

(4) Liberty and justice consist of restoring all that belongs to others; thus, the only limits on the exercise of the natural rights of woman are perpetual male tyranny; these limits are to be reformed by the laws of nature and reason.

(10) No one is to be disquieted for his very basic opinions; woman has the right to mount the scaffold; she must equally have the right to mount the rostrum. . . .

Source: Darlene Gay Levy, Harriet Branson Applewhite, and Mary Durham Johnson, *Women in Revolutionary Paris, 1789–1795* (Urbana: University of Illinois Press, 1979), pp. 87–91.

of Rights that accompanied the constitution reflected a fear of the masses that had not existed when the Declaration of the Rights of Man and the Citizen was promulgated in 1789. Freedom of the press and freedom of assembly, for example, were not fully guaranteed.

Further, no political rights were accorded to women. Educated women had joined Parisian clubs such as the Cercle sociale (Social Circle), where opinion favored extending rights to women. Through such clubs, these women had tried to influence the National Assembly. But the Assembly granted neither political rights nor legal equality to women, nor did it pass other laws beneficial to women such as legalizing divorce or mandating female education. The prevailing view of women

among deputies seemed to reflect those of the Enlightenment philosophe Rousseau, who imagined women's competence to be entirely circumscribed within the family. A Declaration of the Rights of Woman was drafted by a woman named Olympe de Gouges to draw attention to the treatment of women in the constitution. (See the box, "Declaration of the Rights of Woman.")

Very soon after the constitution was implemented, the fragility of the new system became clear. The National Assembly declared that its members could not serve in the first assembly to be elected under the constitution. Thus, the members of the newly elected Legislative Assembly, which began to meet in October 1791, lacked any of the cohesiveness that would have come from collective experience. Also, unlike the previous National Assembly, they did not represent a broad range of opinion but were mostly republicans.

In fact, the Legislative Assembly was dominated by republican members of the Jacobin Club. They were known as Girondins, after the region in southwestern France from which many of the club's leaders came. The policies of these new deputies and continued pressure from the ordinary citizens of Paris would cause the constitutional monarchy to collapse in less than a year.

The Second Revolution and Foreign War, 1791–1793

An additional pressure on the new regime soon arose: a threat from outside France and a war to counter the threat. Antirevolutionary aristocratic émigrés, including the king's brothers, had taken refuge in nearby German states and were planning to invade France. The emperor and other German rulers did little actively to aid the émigrés. Austria and Prussia, however, in the Declaration of Pilnitz of August 1791, declared, as a concession to the émigrés, that they would intervene if necessary to support the monarchy in France.

The threat of invasion, when coupled with distrust of the royal family, seemed more real to the revolutionaries in Paris than it actually was. Many deputies actively wanted war. They assumed that the outcome would be a French defeat, which would lead to a popular uprising that would rid them, at last, of the monarchy. In April 1792, under pressure from the Assembly, Louis XVI declared war against Austria. From this point, foreign war would be an ongoing factor in France's revolution—not only because of the threat of foreign invasion but also because of deliberate decisions to take war abroad in order to safeguard the revolution at home.

At first, the war was a disaster for France. The army had not been reorganized into an effective fighting force after the loss of many aristocratic officers and the addition of newly self-aware citizens. On one occasion, troops insisted on putting an officer's command to a vote. The French lost early battles in the Austrian Netherlands, but the Austrians did not press their advantage and invade France because they were preoccupied with problems in eastern Europe.

THE FRENCH REVOLUTION, 1792–1793	
April 1792	France declares war on Austria
August 10, 1792	Storming of the Tuileries; Louis XVI arrested
September 21, 1792	National Convention declares France a republic
January 21, 1793	Louis XVI is guillotined

Louis XVI in 1792 The king, though a kindly man, had neither the character nor the convictions necessary to refashion royal authority symbolically as the Revolution proceeded. When Parisian crowds forced him to wear the "liberty cap," the monarchy was close to collapse. *(Metropolitan Museum of Art, The Elisha Whittelsey Collection, The Elisha Whittelsey Fund, 1962)*

The defeats heightened criticism of the monarchy and pressure for dramatic change. Under the direction of the Girondins, the Legislative Assembly began to press for the deportation of priests who had been leading demonstrations against the government. The Assembly abolished the personal guard of the king and ordered provincial national guardsmen, including those from Marseille, to come to Paris. The king's resistance to these measures, as well as fears of acute grain shortages owing to a poor harvest and the needs of the armies, created further unrest. Crowds staged dramatic marches near the king's palace, physically confronted him, and forced him to don the "liberty cap," a symbol of republicanism. The king's authority and prestige were now thoroughly undermined.

By July 1792, tensions had become acute. The grain shortage was severe, Austrian and Prussian troops committed to saving the royal family were threatening to invade, and, most important, the populace was better organized and more determined than ever before. In each of the forty-eight "sections"—administrative wards—of Paris a miniature popular assembly thrashed out all the events and issues of the day just as deputies in the nationwide Legislative Assembly did. Derisively called *sans-culottes*, "without knee pants," because they could not afford elite fashions, the ordinary Parisians in the section assemblies included shopkeepers, artisans, and laborers. Their political organization enhanced their influence with the Assembly, the clubs, and the newspapers in the capital. By late July most sections of the city had approved a petition calling for the exile of the king, the election of new city officials, the exemption of the poor from taxation, and other radical measures.

10 August 1792 One of the turning points of the Revolution is captured by the contemporary painter François Gérard. The Parisian crowds have just successfully stormed the Tuileries Palace and now confront members of the Legislative Assembly. Notice the sympathetic portrayal of the people, accomplished in part by the inclusion of figures of children. The royal family, having just taken refuge in the Assembly's meeting hall, is visible behind the grille. *(Louvre © R.M.N.)*

In August they took matters into their own hands. On the night of August 9, after careful preparations, the section assemblies sent representatives who constituted themselves as a new city government with the aim of "saving the state." They then proceeded with an organized assault on the Tuileries Palace, where the royal family was living. In the bloody confrontation, hundreds of royal guards and citizens died. After briefly taking refuge in the Legislative Assembly itself, the king and his family were imprisoned in one of the fortified towers in the city, under guard of the popularly controlled city government.

The storming of the Tuileries inaugurated the second major phase of the Revolution: the establishment of republican government in place of the monarchy. The people of Paris now physically dominated the Legislative Assembly. Some deputies had fled. Those who remained agreed under pressure to dissolve the Assembly and make way for another body to be elected by universal manhood suffrage. On September 20, that assembly—known as the National Convention— began to meet. The next day, the Convention declared the end of the monarchy and began to work on a constitution for the new republic.

Coincidentally, on the same day French forces won their first real victory over the allied Austrian and Prussian forces that had attempted to invade France. Though not a decisive battle, it was a profound psychological victory. A citizen army had defeated the professional force of a ruling prince. The victory bolstered the republican government and encouraged it to put more energy into the wars. Indeed, maintaining armies in the field became increasingly a factor in the delicate equilibrium of revolutionary government. The new republican regime let it be known that its armies were not merely for self-defense but for the liberation of all peoples in the "name of the French Nation."

The Convention faced the divisive issue of what to do with the king. Louis had not done anything truly treasonous, but some of the king's correspondence, discovered after the storming of the Tuileries, provided the pretext for charges of treason. The Convention held a trial for him, lasting from December 11, 1792, through January 15, 1793. He was found guilty of treason by an overwhelming vote (683 to 39), reflecting the fact that the republican government would not compromise with monarchy. Less certain was the sentence:

THE FRENCH REVOLUTION, 1793–1794

February 1793	France declares war on Britain, Spain, and the Netherlands
June 1793	Radical Jacobins purge Girondins from the Convention
July 1793	Robespierre assumes leadership of Committee of Public Safety
July 1793–July 1794	Reign of Terror
July 1794	Robespierre is guillotined

Louis was condemned to death by a narrow majority, 387 to 334.

The consequences for the king were immediate. On January 21, 1793, Louis mounted the scaffold in a public square near the Tuileries and was beheaded. The execution split the ranks of the Convention and soon resulted in the breakdown of the institution itself.

The Faltering Republic and the Terror, 1793–1794

In February 1793, the republic was at war with virtually every state in Europe, except the Scandinavian kingdoms and Russia. Moreover, the regime faced massive and widespread counterrevolutionary uprisings within France. Vigilance against internal as well as external enemies seemed necessary. Nevertheless, for a time, the republican government functioned adequately. In May 1793, for example, it passed the first Law of the Maximum, which tried to fix the price of grain and ensure adequate supplies of bread flour, so that urban people could afford their staple food.

The Convention established an executive body, the Committee of Public Safety. In theory, this executive council was answerable to the Convention as a whole. As the months passed, however, it acted with greater and greater autonomy not only to institute various policies but also to

Robespierre Justifies the Terror

In this excerpt from a speech before the Convention in December 1793, Robespierre justifies the revolutionary government's need to act in an extraconstitutional manner. He echoes Rousseau's notion of a highly abstract sense of the public good. He also warns against challenges to the Revolution within France posed by foreign powers.

The defenders of the Republic must adopt Caesar's maxim, for they believe that "nothing has been done so long as anything remains to be done." Enough dangers still face us to engage all our efforts. It has not fully extended the valor of our Republican soldiers to conquer a few Englishmen and a few traitors. A task no less important, and one more difficult, now awaits us: to sustain an energy sufficient to defeat the constant intrigues of all the enemies of our freedom and to bring to a triumphant realization the principles that must be the cornerstone of public welfare. . . . Revolution is the war waged by liberty against its enemies; a constitution . . . crowns the edifice of freedom once victory has been won and the nation is at peace. . . . The principal concern of a constitutional government is civil liberty; that of a revolutionary government, public liberty. [A] revolutionary government is obliged to defend the state itself against the factions that assail it from every quarter. To good citizens revolutionary government owes the full protection of the state; to the enemies of the people it owes only death.

Is a revolutionary government the less just and the less legitimate because it must be more vigorous in its actions and freer in its movement than ordinary government? . . . It also has its rules, all based on justice and public order. . . . It has nothing in common with arbitrary rule; it is public interest which governs it and not the whims of private individuals.

Thanks to five years of treason and tyranny, thanks to our credulity and lack of foresight . . . Austria and England, Russia, Prussia, and Italy had time to set up in our country a secret government to challenge the authority of our own. . . . We shall strike terror, not in the hearts of patriots, but in the haunts of foreign brigands.

Source: George Rudé, ed., *Robespierre* (Englewood Cliffs, N.J.: Prentice-Hall, 1967), pp. 58–63.

eradicate internal and external enemies. The broadly based republican government represented by the Convention began to disintegrate.

The first major narrowing of control came in June 1793. Pushed by the Parisian sections, a group of extreme Jacobins purged the Girondin deputies from the Convention and arrested many of them. The Girondins were republicans who favored an activist government in the people's behalf, but they were less radical than the Jacobins, less insistent on central control of the Revolution, and less willing to share power with the citizens of Paris. After the purge, the Convention still met, but most authority was held by the Committee of Public Safety.

New uprisings against the regime began. Added to counterrevolutionary revolts by peasants and aristocrats were new revolts by Girondin sympathizers. As resistance to the government mounted and the foreign threat continued, a dramatic event in Paris led the Committee of Public Safety officially to adopt a policy of political repression. A well-known figure of the Revolution, Jean Paul Marat (1743–1793), publisher of a radical republican newspaper very popular with ordinary Parisians, was murdered on July 13 by Charlotte Corday (1768–1793), a young aristocratic woman who had asked to meet with him. Shortly afterward, a long-time member of the Jacobin Club, Maximilien Robespierre (1758–1794), joined the

A Citizen of Paris Suffers Under the Terror

The apparatus of the Terror meant that ordinary citizens could be arrested for the slightest offense. Here, a woman describes her arrest, which led to months of grim imprisonment. (She was eventually released only because she persuaded the authorities that she was pregnant.)

For a long time I have had to feed the members of my household on bread and cheese and . . . tired of complaints from my husband and my boys, I was compelled to go wait in line to get something to eat. For three days I had been going to the same market without being able to get anything, despite the fact that I waited [all day]. After the distribution of butter on the twenty-second, . . . a citizen came over to me and said I was in a very delicate condition [and I answered] "You can't be delicate and be on your legs for so long . . ." He replied that I needed to drink milk. I answered that I had men in my house and couldn't nourish them on milk [and that] if he . . . was sensitive to the difficulty of obtaining food, he would not vex me so, and that he was an imbecile and wanted to play despot, and no one had that right.

I was arrested [on the spot and] was led to the Revolutionary Committee [of the section] where I was called a counterrevolutionary and was told I was asking for the guillotine because I told them I preferred death to being treated ignominiously. . . . I was asked if I knew whom I had called a despot . . . and I was told that he was the commander of the post. I said he was more [a commander] beneath his own roof than anyone, given that he was there to maintain order and not to provoke bad feelings. For [these] answers, I was told that I had done three times more than was needed to get the guillotine and that I would be explaining myself before the Revolutionary Tribunal.

Source: Darlene Gay Levy, Harriet Branson Applewhite, and Mary Durham Johnson, *Women in Revolutionary Paris, 1789–1795* (Urbana: University of Illinois Press, 1979), pp. 267–268.

Committee and called for "Terror"—the systematic repression of internal enemies. He was not alone in his views. Radicals in the section assemblies of Paris led demonstrations to pressure the government into making Terror the order of the day.

Robespierre himself embodied all the contradiction of the policy of Terror. He was an austere, almost prim, man who lived very modestly—a model, of sorts, of the virtuous, disinterested citizen. The policies followed by the government during the year of his greatest influence, from July 1793 to July 1794, included generous, rational, and humane policies to benefit ordinary citizens as well as the policy of official Terror. (See the box, "Robespierre Justifies the Terror.")

Terror meant the use of intimidation to silence dissent. Since the previous autumn, the guillotine had been at work against identified enemies of the regime, but now a more energetic apparatus of terror was instituted. A Law of Suspects was passed that allowed citizens to be arrested simply on vague suspicion of counterrevolutionary sympathies. (See the box, "A Citizen of Paris Suffers Under the Terror.") Revolutionary tribunals and an oversight committee made arbitrary arrests and rendered summary judgment. In October a steady stream of executions began, beginning with the queen, imprisoned since the storming of the Tuileries the year before. The imprisoned Girondin deputies followed, and then the process continued relentlessly. In Paris there were about 2600 executions from 1793 to 1794.

Around France, approximately 14,000 executions were the result of verdicts from revolutionary tribunals. Another 10,000 to 12,000 people died in prison. Ten thousand or more were killed,

Robespierre the Incorruptible A lawyer who had often championed the poor, Robespierre was elected to the Estates General in 1789 and was a consistent advocate of republican government from the beginning of the Revolution. His unswerving loyalty to his political principles earned him the nickname "the Incorruptible." *(Musée des Beaux-Arts, Lille)*

usually by summary execution, after the defeat of counterrevolutionary uprisings. For example, 2000 people were summarily executed in Lyon when a Girondin revolt collapsed there in October. The repression in Paris, however, was unique because of the city's role in the nation's political life. The aim of the repression was not merely to stifle active resistance; it was also to stifle simple dissent. The victims in Paris included not merely aristocrats or former deputies but also sansculottes. The radical Jacobins wanted to seize control of the Revolution from the Parisian citizens who had helped them to power.

The Terror notwithstanding, the government of the Committee of Public Safety was effective in providing direction for the nation at a critical time. It instituted the first mass conscription of citizens into the army (*levée en masse*), and an effective popular army came into existence. In the autumn of 1793, this army won impressive victories. Accomplishments in domestic policy included an extended Law of the Maximum (September 1793) that applied to necessary commodities other than

bread. Extensive plans were made for a system of free and universal primary education. Slavery in the French colonies was abolished in February 1794. Divorce, first legalized in 1792, was made easier for women to obtain.

In the name of "reason," traditional rituals and rhythms of life were changed. One reform of long-term significance was the introduction of the metric system of weights and measures. Although people continued to use the old, familiar measures for a very long time, the change was eventually accomplished, leading the way for change throughout Europe. Equally "rational" but not as successful was the elimination of the traditional calendar. The traditional days, weeks, and months were replaced by forty-day months and *decadi* (ten-day weeks with one day of rest). All saints' days and Christian holidays were eliminated. The years had already been changed—Year I had been declared with the founding of the republic in the autumn of 1792.

Churches were rededicated as "temples of reason." Believing that outright atheism left people with no basis for personal or national morality, Robespierre sought instead to promote a cult of the Supreme Being. The public festivals organized around either principle were solemn civic ceremonies intended to ritualize and legitimize the new political order. These and other innovations of the regime were not necessarily welcomed. The French people generally resented the elimination of the traditional calendar. In the countryside, there were massive peasant uprisings over loss of poor relief, community life, and familiar ritual.

Divorce law and economic regulation were a boon, especially to urban women, but women's participation in sectional assemblies and in all organized political activity—which had been energetic and widespread—was banned in October 1793. The particular target of the regime was the Society of Revolutionary Republican Women, a powerful club representing the interests of female sans-culottes. By banning women from political life, the regime helped to ground its legitimacy, since the seemingly "natural" exclusion of women might make the new system of government appear part of the "natural" order. (See the feature, "Weighing the Evidence: Political Symbols," on pages 734–735.) Elimination of women's clubs and women's participation in section assemblies also eliminated a source of popular power, from which the regime was now trying to distance itself.

The Committee and the Convention were divided over religious and other policies, but the main policy differences concerned economic matters: how far to go to assist the poor, the unemployed, and the landless. Several of the temperate critics of Robespierre and his allies were guillotined because they differed with them on policy and on the continuing need for the Terror itself. Their deaths helped to precipitate the end of the Terror because Robespierre's power base shrank so much that it had no further legitimacy.

Deputies to the Convention finally dared to move against Robespierre in July 1794. French armies had scored a major victory over Austrian troops on June 26, so there was no longer any need for the emergency status that the Terror had thrived on. In late July (the month of Thermidor, according to the revolutionary calendar), the Convention voted to arrest Robespierre, the head of the Revolutionary Tribunal in Paris, and their closest associates and allies in the city government. On July 28 and 29, Robespierre and the others—

about a hundred in all—were guillotined, and the Terror ended.

Thermidorian Reaction and the Directory, 1794–1799

After the death of Robespierre, the Convention reclaimed many of the executive powers that the Committee of Public Safety had seized. The Convention dismantled the apparatus of the Terror, repealed the Law of Suspects, and forced the revolutionary tribunals to adopt ordinary legal procedures. The Convention also passed into law some initiatives, such as expanded public education, that had been proposed in the preceding year but not enacted. This phase of the Revolution that followed the Terror is called the "Thermidorian Reaction" because it began in the revolutionary month of Thermidor (July 19–August 17).

The stability of the government, however, was threatened from the outset. Counterrevolutionary uprisings in western France during the autumn of 1794 were joined by landings of émigré troops the following June. These challenges were put down. There were also popular uprisings against the Terror throughout France. Officials of the previous regime were lynched, and pro-revolutionary groups were massacred by their fellow citizens.

The people of Paris tried to retain influence with the new government. With the apparatus of Terror dismantled, the Convention was unable to enforce controls on the supply and price of bread. Thus, economic difficulties and a hard winter produced famine by the spring of 1795. In May crowds marched on the Convention, chanting "Bread and the Constitution of '93," referring to the republican constitution drafted by the Convention but never implemented because of the Terror. The demonstrations were met with force and were dispersed.

Fearful of a renewed, popularly supported Terror, or even of desperate popular support for a royalist uprising, the Convention drafted a new constitution that limited popular participation, as had the first constitution of 1791. The new plan allowed fairly widespread (but not universal) male suffrage, but only for electors, who would choose deputies for the two houses of the legislature. The property qualifications for being an elector were very high, so all but elite citizens were effectively disenfranchised.

THE FRENCH REVOLUTION, 1794–1799

August 1794	Thermidorian reaction begins
October 1795	Directory is established
November 1799	Napoleon seizes power

In the fall of 1795, as the Convention was preparing to dissolve so that new elections might proceed, a final popular uprising shook Paris. The Convention anticipated the trouble, and when a crowd of twenty thousand or more converged on the Tuileries Palace, the officer in charge ordered his troops to fire. Parisian crowds never again seriously threatened the government, although living conditions worsened as food prices soared. The army officer who issued the command to fire was Napoleon Bonaparte.

A new government began under the provisions of the new constitution. It was called the Directory for the executive council of five men chosen by the upper house of the new legislature. To avoid the concentration of authority that had produced the Terror, the members of the Convention had tried to enshrine separation of powers in the new system. However, because of unsettled conditions throughout France, the governments under the Directory were never stable and never free from attempted coups and extraconstitutional maneuvering.

The most spectacular challenge, the Conspiracy of Equals, was led by extreme Jacobins who wanted to restore popular government and aggressive economic and social policy on behalf of the common people. The conspiracy ended with arrests and executions in 1797. When elections in 1797 and 1798 returned many royalist as well as Jacobin deputies, the Directory resorted to force to forestall challenges to its authority: Many deputies were arrested, sent into exile, or denied seats.

By 1799, conditions had once again reached a critical juncture. France was again at war with a coalition of states and was faring badly in the fighting. The demands of the war effort, together with other economic woes, brought the govern-

ment again to the brink of bankruptcy. The government seemed to be losing control of the countryside; there were continued royalist uprisings and local political vendettas as well as outright banditry.

Members of the Directory had often turned to sympathetic army commanders to carry out the arrests and purge of the legislature. They now invited General Napoleon Bonaparte to help them form a government that they could more strictly control. Two members of the Directory plotted with Napoleon and his brother, Louis Bonaparte, to seize power on November 9, 1799.

THE NAPOLEONIC ERA

Napoleon Bonaparte (1769–1821) was the kind of person who gives rise to myths. He was talented, daring, and ruthless. He was also charming and charismatic. His audacity, determination, and personal magnetism enabled him to profit from the political instability and confusion in France and ensconce himself in power. Once in power, he stabilized the political scene by enshrining in law the more conservative gains of the Revolution. He also used his power and his abilities as a general to continue wars of conquest against France's neighbors.

Napoleon's troops, in effect, exported the Revolution when they conquered most of Europe. Law codes were reformed, governing elites were opened to talent, and public works were undertaken in most states under French control. Yet French conquest also meant domination, pure and simple, and involvement in France's rivalry with Britain. The Napoleonic era left Europe an ambiguous legacy—war and its complex aftermath yet also revolution and encouragement to further change.

Napoleon: From Soldier to Emperor, 1799–1804

Napoleon was from Corsica, a Mediterranean island that had passed from Genoese to French control in the eighteenth century. The second son of a large gentry family, he was educated at military academies in France, and he married the politically well-connected widow Joséphine de Beauharnais (1763–1814), whose aristocratic husband had been a victim of the Terror.

Napoleon Crossing the Great St. Bernard This stirring portrait by the great neoclassical painter Jacques-Louis David memorializes Napoleon's 1796 crossing of the Alps before his victorious Italian campaign, as a general under the Directory. The painting depicts the moment heroically rather than realistically (Napoleon wisely crossed the Alps on a sure-footed mule, not a stallion), in part because it was executed in 1801–1802. Napoleon, as First Consul, wanted images of himself that would justify his increasingly ambitious claims to power. *(Louvre © R.M.N.)*

Napoleon steered a careful course through the political turmoil of the Revolution. By 1799, however, he was well known and popular because of his military victories. He demonstrated his reliability and ruthlessness in 1795 when he ordered troops guarding the Convention to fire on the Parisian crowd, but his greatest victories had been against France's foreign opponents. In 1796 and 1797 he had conquered all of northern Italy, forcing Austria to relinquish that territory as well as to cede control of the Austrian Netherlands, which revolutionary armies had seized in 1795. He then commanded an invasion of Egypt in an attempt to strike at British influence and trade connections in the eastern Mediterranean. The Egyptian campaign failed in its goals, but individual spectacular victories during the campaign ensured Napoleon's military reputation. In addition, Napoleon had demonstrated his widening ambitions. He had taken leading scientists and skilled administrators with him to Egypt in order to export the seeming benefits of French civilization as well as to buttress military victory with more lasting military authority.

Napoleon's partners in the new government after the November coup in 1799 soon learned of his great political ambition and skill. In theory, the new system was to be a streamlined version of the Directory: Napoleon was to be first among equals in a three-man executive—First Consul, according to borrowed Roman terminology. But Napoleon soon asserted his primacy among them and began not only to dominate executive functions but also to bypass the authority of the various legislative bodies in the new regime.

Napoleon was careful to avoid heavy-handed displays of power. He cleverly sought ratification of each stage of his assumption of power through national plebiscites (national referendums in which all eligible voters could vote for or against proposals)—one plebiscite for a new constitution in 1800 and another when he claimed consulship for life in 1802. Perhaps most important to the success of his increasingly authoritarian regime was his effort to include, among his ministers, advisers, and bureaucrats, men of many political stripes—Jacobins, reforming liberals, even former Old Regime bureaucrats. He welcomed many exiles back to France, including all but the most ardent royalists. He thus stabilized his regime by healing some of the rifts among ruling elites.

Napoleon combined toleration with ruthlessness, however. Between 1800 and 1804 he imprisoned, executed, or exiled dozens of individuals for alleged Jacobin agitation or royalist sympathies. His final gesture to intimidate royalist opposition came in 1804 when he kidnapped and coldly murdered a Bourbon prince who had been in exile in Germany.

By the terms of the Treaty of Amiens in 1802, Napoleon made peace with Britain, France's one remaining enemy. The fragile and short-lived peace only papered over the two countries' commercial and strategic rivalries, but it gave Napoleon breathing room to establish his rule more securely in France. One of the most important steps had been accomplished a year earlier by means of the Concordat of 1801. The aim of this treaty with the pope was to solve the problem of church-state relations that for years had caused antirevolutionary rebellions. The agreement allowed for the resumption of Catholic worship and the continued support of the clergy by the state, but also accepted the more dramatic changes accomplished by the Revolution. Church lands that had been sold were guaranteed to their new owners. Protestant churches were also allowed and their clergy was paid, although Catholicism was recognized as the "religion of the majority of Frenchmen." Later, Napoleon granted new rights to Jews also. Nonetheless, the Concordat removed one of the most important grounds for counterrevolutionary upheaval in the countryside and undermined royalist resistance to the new regime from abroad.

The law code that Napoleon established in 1804 was much like his accommodation with the church in its limited acceptance of revolutionary gains. His Civil Code reflected the revolutionary legacy in its guarantee of equality before the law and its requirement for the taxation of all social classes; it also enshrined modern forms of property ownership and civil contracts.

But neither the code nor Napoleon's political regime fostered individual rights, especially for women. Women lost all of the rights they had gained during the Revolution. Fathers' control over their families was enhanced. Divorce was no longer permitted except in rare instances. Women lost all property rights when they married, and they generally faced legal domination by fathers and husbands.

Napoleon helped to put the regime on better financial footing by establishing a national bank. The Bank of France, modeled on the Bank of England, provided capital for investment and could help the state manage its money and return to a system of hard coinage. Napoleon also further streamlined and centralized the administrative system, set up by the first wave of revolutionaries in 1789, by establishing the office of prefect to govern the départements. All prefects and their subordinates were appointed by Napoleon.

Some of these legal and administrative changes occurred after the final political coup that Napoleon undertook—declaring himself emperor. This was a bold move, but Napoleon approached it dexterously. For example, long before he declared himself emperor, Napoleon had begun to sponsor an active court life appropriate to imperial pretensions. The empire was proclaimed in May 1804 with the approval of the Senate; it was also approved by another plebiscite. Members of Napoleon's family were given princely status, and a number of his favorites received various titles and honors. The titles brought no legal privilege but signaled social and political distinctions of great importance. Old nobles were allowed to use their titles on this basis.

Many members of the elite, whatever their persuasions, tolerated Napoleon's claims to power because he safeguarded a number of revolutionary gains and reconfirmed their own status. War soon resumed against political and economic enemies—principally Britain, Austria, and Russia—and, for a time, Napoleon's success in the field continued. Because military success was central to the political purpose and self-esteem of elites, Napoleon's early successes as emperor further enhanced his power.

Conquering Europe, 1805–1810

Napoleon maintained relatively peaceful relations with other nations while he consolidated power at home, but the truces did not last. Tensions with the British quickly re-escalated when Britain resumed aggression against French shipping in 1803, and Napoleon countered by seizing Hanover, the ancestral German home of the English king. Then Napoleon seized several Italian territories and extended his influence in other German states. By 1805, all the states of Europe were threatened. Austria was alarmed by his power in Italy. England was at war on the high seas with Spain and the Netherlands, which Napoleon had forced to enter the fray. Napoleon began to gather a large French force on the northern coast of France, with which he could invade England.

The British fleet, commanded by Horatio Nelson (1758–1805), intercepted the combined French and Spanish fleets that were to have been the invasion flotilla and inflicted a devastating defeat off Cape Trafalgar in southern Spain (see Map 19.1) on October 21, 1805. The victory ensured British mastery of the seas and, in the long run, contributed to Napoleon's defeat. In the short run, the defeat at Trafalgar paled for the French beside Napoleon's impressive victories on land. Even as the French admirals were preparing for battle, Napoleon had abandoned the plans to invade England and in August had begun to march his army east through Germany.

In December 1805, after some preliminary, small-scale victories, Napoleon's army confronted a Russian force near Austerlitz, which is north of Vienna (see Map 19.1). Tsar Alexander I (r. 1801–1825) led his own troops into a battle that he ought to have avoided. Austrian reinforcements could not reach him in time, and French armies shattered the Russian force. The Battle of Austerlitz was Napoleon's most spectacular victory. Austria sued for peace. In further battles in 1806, French forces defeated Prussia as well as Russian armies once again.

Prussia was virtually dismembered by the subsequent Treaty of Tilsit (1807), but Napoleon tried to work out terms to make Russia into a contented ally. His hold on central Europe would not be secure with a hostile Russia, nor would the anti-British economic system that he envisioned—the Continental System (see page 725)—be workable without Russian participation.

French forces were still trying to prevail in Spain, which had been a client state since its defeat by revolutionary armies in 1795 but was resisting outright rule by a French-imposed king. In 1808, however, Napoleon turned his attention to a more fully subduing Austria. Napoleon won the Battle of Wagram in July 1809 but did not totally defeat Austria. Like Russia, Austria accepted French political and economic hegemony in a sort of alliance. By 1810 Napoleon had transformed most of Europe into allied or dependent states (see Map 19.1). The only exceptions were Britain and the parts of Spain and Portugal that continued to resist France with British help.

The states least affected by French hegemony were its reluctant allies: Austria, Russia, and the Scandinavian countries. Denmark had allied with France in 1807 only for help in fending off British naval supremacy in the Baltic. Sweden had reluctantly made peace in 1810 after losing control of Finland to Napoleon's ally, Russia. Sweden only minimally participated in the Continental System. At the other extreme were territories that had been incorporated into France. These included the Austrian Netherlands, territory along the Rhineland, and territories in Italy that bordered France. These regions were occupied by French troops and were treated as though they were départements of France itself.

In most other regions, some form of French-controlled government was in place, usually headed by a member of Napoleon's family. In both northern Italy and, initially, the Netherlands, where "sister" republics had been established after French conquests under the Directory, Napoleon imposed monarchies. Rulers were also imposed in the kingdom of Naples and in Spain. Western German states of the Holy Roman Empire that had allied with Napoleon against Austria were organized into the Confederation of the Rhine, with Napoleon as its "Protector." After a thousand years, the Holy Roman Empire ceased to exist. Two further states were created, largely out of the defeated Prussia's territory: the kingdom of Westphalia in western Germany and the duchy of Warsaw in the east (see Map 19.1).

Napoleon's domination of these various regions had complex, and at times contradictory,

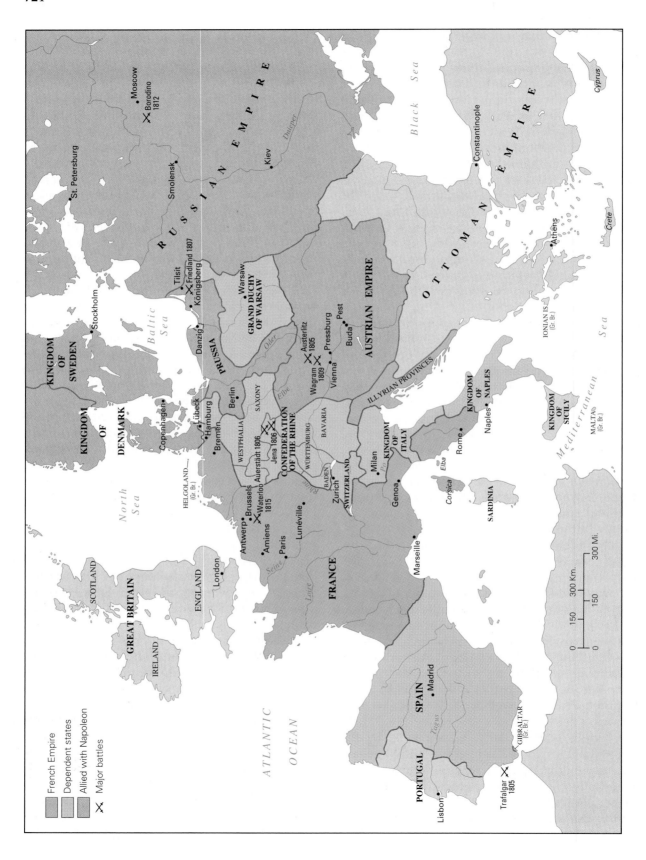

Moscow
• Borodino
1812

St. Petersburg

R U S S I A N   E M P I R E

Dnieper

Smolensk

Kiev

Black   Sea

Cyprus

O T T O M A N   E M P I R E

Constantinople

Tilsit
× Friedland 1807
Königsberg

GRAND DUCHY
OF WARSAW

Warsaw

Athens

Crete

Danzig

PRUSSIA

IONIAN IS.
(Gr. Br.)

Sea

Baltic
Sea

KINGDOM
OF
SWEDEN

Stockholm

Austerlitz
× 1805

Pressburg
Pest
• Buda

A U S T R I A N   E M P I R E

Copenhagen

Lübeck

Berlin

SAXONY

Oder

Wagram
× 1809
Vienna

ILLYRIAN PROVINCES

MALTA
(Gr. Br.)

KINGDOM
OF
DENMARK

Hamburg
Bremen

WESTPHALIA
Auerstädt 1806
× Jena 1806 ×

Elbe

CONFEDERATION
OF THE RHINE

BAVARIA

KINGDOM
OF
NAPLES

Naples

KINGDOM
OF
SICILY

Mediterranean

HELGOLAND
(Gr. Br.)

North
Sea

Brussels
Waterloo
Antwerp 1815 ×

Amiens Paris
Luneville

WÜRTTEMBERG

BADEN

Zurich
SWITZERLAND

Rhine

Milan

KINGDOM
OF
ITALY

Po

Genoa

Rome

Elba

Corsica

SARDINIA

SCOTLAND

London

GREAT BRITAIN

ENGLAND

IRELAND

Seine

Loire

FRANCE

Marseille

ATLANTIC

OCEAN

Madrid

SPAIN

Tagus

GIBRALTAR
(Gr. Br.)

300 Mi.

300 Km.

150

150

0

0

PORTUGAL

Lisbon

Trafalgar
× 1805

French Empire

Dependent states

Allied with Napoleon

× Major battles

consequences. On the one hand, Napoleonic armies literally exported the French Revolution, in that French domination brought with it political and economic reform akin to that of the early phases of the Revolution, now enshrined in the Napoleonic Civil Code. Equality before the law was decreed following the French example; this meant the end of noble exemption from taxation in the many areas, like France, where it existed. In general, the complex snarl of medieval taxes and tolls was replaced with straightforward property taxes from which no one was exempt. As a consequence, tax revenues rose dramatically—by 50 percent in the kingdom of Italy, for example. Serfdom and forced labor were also abolished, as they had been in France in August 1789.

In most Catholic regions, the church was subjected to the terms of the Concordat of 1801. The tithe was abolished, church property seized and sold, and religious orders dissolved. Though Catholicism remained the state-supported religion in these areas, Protestantism was tolerated and Jews were granted rights of citizenship. Secular education, at least for males, was encouraged.

On the other hand, Napoleon would countenance only those aspects of France's revolutionary legacy that he tolerated in France itself. Just as he had suppressed any meaningful participatory government in France, so too did he suppress it in conquered regions. This came as a blow in states like the Netherlands, which had experienced its own democratizing "Patriot" movement and which had enjoyed republican self-government after invasion by French armies during the Revolution itself. Throughout the Napoleonic Empire, many of the benefits of streamlined administration and taxation were offset by the drain of continual warfare; deficits rose three- and fourfold, despite increased revenues. In addition, one of the inevitable costs of empire was political compromise to secure allies. In the duchy of Warsaw, reconstituted from lands Prussia had seized in the eighteenth century, Napoleon tampered little with either noble privileges or the power of the church. And, throughout Europe, Napoleon randomly allotted lands to reward his greatest generals and ministers, thereby exempting those lands from taxation and control by his own bureaucracy.

If true self-government was not allowed, a broad segment of the elite in all regions was nevertheless won over to cooperation with Napoleon by being welcomed into his bureaucracy or into the large multinational army, called the Grande Armée. Their loyalty was cemented when they bought confiscated church lands.

The impact of Napoleon's Continental System was equally mixed. Under this system, the Continent was in theory closed to all British shipping and British goods. The effects were widespread but uneven, and smuggling to evade controls on British goods became a major enterprise. Regions heavily involved in trade with Britain or its colonies or dependent on British shipping suffered in the new system, as did overseas trade in general when Britain gained dominance of the seas after Trafalgar. Peasants and landlords in many regions that produced grain for export suffered, and some cities dependent on overseas trade experienced catastrophic decline. However, the closing of the Continent to British trade, combined with increases in demand resulting from the need to supply Napoleon's armies, spurred the development of continental industries, at least in the short run. This industrial growth, enhanced by the improvement of roads, canals, and the like, formed the basis for further industrial development.

Defeat and Abdication, 1812–1815

Whatever its achievements, Napoleon's empire was ultimately precarious because of the hostility of Austria and Russia, as well as the belligerence of Britain. Austria resented losing the former Austrian Netherlands and lands in northern Italy to the French. Russia was a particularly weak link in the chain of alliances and subject states because Russian landowners and merchants were angered when their vital trade in timber for the British navy was interrupted and when supplies of luxury goods, brought in British ships, began to dwindle. A century of close alliances with German ruling houses made alliance with a French ruler extremely difficult politically for Tsar Alexander I.

It was Napoleon, however, who ended the alliance by provoking a breach with Russia. He suddenly backed away from an arrangement to marry

Map 19.1 Napoleonic Europe, ca. 1810 France dominated continental Europe after Napoleon's victories. Though French control would collapse quickly after defeats in Russia and Spain in 1812, the effects of French domination were more long-lasting.

one of Alexander's younger sisters and accepted the Austrian princess Marie Louise instead. (He had reluctantly divorced Joséphine in 1809 because their marriage had not produced an heir.) In addition, he seized lands along the German Baltic seacoast belonging to a member of Alexander's family. When Alexander threatened rupture of the alliance if the lands were not returned, Napoleon mounted an invasion. Advisers warned him about the magnitude of the task he seemed so eager to undertake—particularly about the preparations needed for winter fighting in Russia—but their warnings went unheard.

Napoleon's previous military successes had stemmed from a combination of strategic innovations and audacity. Napoleon divided his forces into independent corps. Each corps included infantry, cavalry, and artillery. Organized in these workable units, his armies could travel quickly by several separate routes and converge in massive force to face the enemy. Numbers were important to success, but so were discipline, control of troop movements, and determination to follow up initial gains. Leadership on the battlefield came from a loyal and talented officer corps that Napoleon had fashioned by welcoming returning aristocrats and favoring rising new talent. The final ingredient in the success formula was the high morale of French troops under Napoleon. Napoleon's English nemesis, Arthur Wellesley (1769–1852), duke of Wellington, once remarked that Napoleon's presence on a battlefield was worth forty thousand men.

The campaign against Russia began in June 1812. It was a spectacular failure. Napoleon had gathered a force of about 700,000 men—about half from France and half from allied states—a force twice as large as Russia's. The strategy of quickly moving independent corps and assembling massive forces could not be implemented because simply assembling so many men along the border was already the equivalent of gathering them for battle. Also, sustaining them thereafter was beyond the capacity of the supply system, which had always been Napoleon's weakness. Bold victories had often enabled Napoleon's troops to live off the countryside while they waited for supplies to catch up with them. But when the enemy attacked supply lines, when the distances traveled were very great, when the countryside was impoverished, or when battles were not decisive, Napoleon's ambitious strategies proved unwork-able. In varying degrees, these conditions prevailed in Russia.

By the time the French faced the Russians in the principal battle of the Russian campaign—at Borodino, west of Moscow (see Map 19.1)—the Grande Armée had been on the march for two and a half months and stood at less than half its original strength. After the indecisive but bloody battle, the French occupied and pillaged Moscow but found scarcely enough food and supplies to sustain them. When Napoleon finally led his troops out of Moscow late in October, after an uncharacteristic period of indecisiveness, the fate of the French forces was all but sealed. The army marched south to reach the warmer and better-provisioned Ukraine but was turned back by Russian forces. The French then retreated north and west out of Russia, the way they had come. French soldiers who had not died in battle died of exposure or starvation or were killed by Russian peasants when they wandered away from their units. Of the original 700,000 French and allied troops, fewer than 100,000 made it out of Russia.

Napoleon left his army before it was fully out of Russia. A coup attempt in Paris prompted him to return to his governing duties before the French people realized the extent of the disaster in Russia. The collapse of his reign had begun, spurred by a coincidental defeat in Spain. Since 1808, Spain had been largely under French domination, with Napoleon's brother, Joseph, as king. A rebel Cortes (assembly), however, continued to meet in territory that the French did not control, and British troops were never expelled from the Iberian Peninsula. In 1812, as Napoleon was beginning his move against Russia, the collapse of French control accelerated. By the time Napoleon got back to Paris at the turn of the new year, Joseph had been expelled from Spain, and an Anglo-Spanish force led by the duke of Wellington was poised to invade France.

Napoleon's most able generals rallied what remained of his troops and held off Prussian and Russian forces in the east until he returned from France in April 1813 with a new army of raw recruits. Napoleon lost his last chance to stave off a coalition of all major powers against him when he refused an Austrian offer of peace for the return of conquered Austrian territories. With Britain willing to subsidize the allied armies, Tsar Alexander determined to destroy Napoleon, and the Austrians now anxious to share the spoils, Napoleon's empire

The French Army Flees Russia Napoleon's engineers built bridges for a night crossing of the Berezina River (in Belarus), which blocked the French retreat. The remainder of the army was saved from annihilation, but as in the rest of the Russian campaign, the cost was high: wagons and provisions, as well as thousands of wounded soldiers, were abandoned on the Russian side. Many of the engineers died of exposure. *(Musée de l'Armée)*

began to crumble. Napoleon's forces were crushed in a massive "Battle of Nations" near Leipzig in October, during which some of his troops from German satellite states deserted him on the battlefield. The allies were able to invade France and forced Napoleon to abdicate on April 6, 1814.

Napoleon was exiled to the island of Elba, off France's Mediterranean coast, but was still treated somewhat royally. He was installed as the island's ruler and was given an income drawn on the French treasury. Meanwhile, however, the restored French king was having his own troubles. Louis XVIII (r. 1814–1824) was the brother of the executed Louis XVI; he took the number eighteen out of respect for Louis XVI's son, who had died in prison in 1795. He had been out of the country and out of touch with its circumstances since the

beginning of the Revolution. In addition to the delicate task of establishing his own legitimacy, he faced enormous practical problems, including pensioning off thousands of soldiers now unemployed and still loyal to Napoleon.

Napoleon, bored and almost penniless on his island kingdom (the promised French pension never materialized), took advantage of the circumstances and returned surreptitiously to France on February 26, 1815. His small band of attendants was joined by the soldiers sent by the king to prevent him from advancing to Paris. Louis XVIII abandoned Paris to the returned emperor.

Napoleon's triumphant return lasted only one hundred days, however. Though many soldiers welcomed his return, many members of the elite were reluctant to throw in their lot with Napoleon again. Many ordinary French citizens had also become disenchanted with him since the defeat in Russia, and with the high costs, in conscription and taxation, of raising new armies. In any case, Napoleon's reappearance galvanized the divided allies, who had been haggling over a peace settlement, into unity. Napoleon tried to strike first, but he lost against English and Prussian troops in his first major battle, at Waterloo (in modern Belgium; see Map 19.1) on June 18, 1815. When Napoleon reached Paris after the defeat, he discovered the government in the hands of an ad hoc committee that included the Marquis de Lafayette. Under pressure, he abdicated once again. He was exiled to the tiny, remote island of St. Helena in the South Atlantic, from which escape would be impossible. He died there in 1821.

THE IMPACT OF REVOLUTION ON FRANCE AND THE WORLD

The process of change in France between 1789 and 1815 was so complex that it is easy to overlook the overall impact of the Revolution. Superficially, the changes seemed to come full circle—with first Louis XVI on the throne, then Napoleon as emperor, and then Louis XVIII on the throne. Even though the monarchy was restored, however, the Revolution changed the fundamental premises of political life in France and served to catalyze challenges to the existing order elsewhere.

The Significance of Revolution in France

The French monarchy was restored in 1815, but the Revolution had discredited absolute monarchy in theory and practice. The restored constitutional monarchy governed with only a small group of representatives of the elite, but their participation slowly widened during the nineteenth century. An important legacy of the Revolution was thus new principles on which to base a government: the right of "the people," however narrowly defined, to participate in government and to enjoy due process of law.

There was fundamental disagreement, however, about which people were worthy of inclusion in the political process and the degree to which the government might govern in their interests. There was a significant philosophical differ-

ence between many republicans and the reformers who had supported the Revolution in its initial stages. The latter argued for access to government only by the politically sophisticated elite and for the freeing of the economy from traditional constraints. The more inclusive view and the more activist posture regarding the appropriate role of government would be reinstated by revolutionary action later in the nineteenth century (see Chapter 20). Neither notion included a vision of women as citizens coequal with men.

Other legacies of the Revolution and the Napoleonic era included a centralized political system. The nation was divided into départements rather than provinces. For the first time, a single code of law applied to all French people. Most officials—from département administrators to city mayors—were appointed by the central government until the late twentieth century. The conscientious attention of the government, at various stages of the Revolution, to advances for France generally reflects the positive side of this centralization. The government sponsored national scientific societies, a national library and archives, and a system of teachers' colleges and universities. Particularly under Napoleon, there was a spate of canal- and road-building.

Napoleon's legacy, like that of the Revolution itself, was mixed. His self-serving reconciliation of aristocratic pretensions with the opening of careers to men of talent helped to ensure the long-term success of revolutionary principles from which the elite as a whole profited. His reconciliation of the state with the Catholic church helped to stabilize his regime and to ensure some revolutionary gains. The restored monarchy could not renege on these gains. But Napoleon could not eliminate the antirevolutionary bent of the church as a whole, and the church continued to be a reactionary force in France. The Napoleonic Code was a uniform system of law for the nation. But although it guaranteed equality under the law for men, it enshrined political and legal inferiority for women.

Whatever the concrete gains of the Revolution and Napoleon's rule, Napoleon's overthrow of constitutional principles worsened the problem of political instability. Napoleon's return to power in 1815, though brief, was nevertheless important. It reflects the degree to which his power was always rooted in military adventurism and in the loyalty of soldiers and officers. His bravado suggests the importance of personal qualities to the success of an authoritarian regime. But the swiftness of his collapse suggests that although the empire under Napoleon may have seemed an enduring solution to the political instability of the late 1790s, its legitimacy and security were as uncertain as the legitimacy and security of the revolutionary governments.

Although Louis XVIII acknowledged the principle of constitutionalism at the end of the Revolution, it rested on fragile footing. Indeed, the fragility of new political systems was one of the most profound lessons of the Revolution. There was division over policies, but even greater division over legitimacy—that is, the acceptance by a significant portion of the politically active citizenry of a particular system or of a particular government's right to rule.

Politics, the Revolution revealed, takes place in part on a symbolic level. What is acceptable and what is legitimate are expressed not only in words but also symbolically. The symbols are effective because they link a specific political system to a broader, fundamental system of values. The religious symbolism used by the monarchy, for example, linked royal government to divine order. Similarly, the public cults of reason and of the Supreme Being that Robespierre promoted during the Terror were attempts to link patriotism and support of the government to universal principles. Other, more limited, symbols were constantly in use: the red and blue cockades that supporters of the National Assembly put in their caps; the "liberty cap" that Louis XVI donned on one occasion; various representations of the abstract notion of "Liberty" in newspapers and journals widely available at the time.

Before the Revolution started, there was a significant shift in notions about political legitimacy. The deputies who declared themselves to be the National Assembly in June 1789 already believed that they had a right to do so. In their view, they represented "the nation," and their voice had legitimacy for that reason. The shift reflects not the innate power of ideas but the power of ideas in context. The deputies brought to Versailles not only their individual convictions that "reason" should be applied to the political system but also their experience in social settings where those ideas were well received. In their salons, clubs, and literary societies, they had experienced the familiarity, trust, and sense of community that are essential to effective political action.

The deputies' attempt to transplant their sense of community into national politics was not wholly successful. Factions, competing interests, and clashes of personality can be fatal to an insecure system. The National Assembly had scarcely inaugurated a secure system when its deputies undermined its workability by making themselves ineligible to hold office under the new constitution. The king also actively undermined the system because he disagreed with it in principle. The British parliamentary system, by comparison, though every bit as elitist as the narrowest of the representative systems during the French Revolution, had a long history as a workable institution for lords, commoners, and rulers. This shared experience was an important counterweight to differences over fundamental issues, so that Parliament as an institution both survived political crises and helped solve them.

The Revolution thus left a powerful yet ambiguous legacy for France. Politics was established on a new footing, yet still lacking were the practical means to achieve the promise inherent in the new principles.

The Impact of the Revolution Overseas

Throughout Europe and overseas, the Revolution left a powerful and complex legacy. French conquests in Europe were the least enduring of the dramatic changes of the revolutionary era. Nevertheless, French domination had certain lasting effects: Elites were exposed to modern bureaucratic management, and equality under the law transformed social and political relationships. Although national self-determination had an enemy in Napoleon, the breaking down of ancient political divisions provided important practical grounding for later cooperation among elites in nationalist movements. In Napoleon's kingdom of Italy, for example, a tax collector from Florence for the first time worked side by side with one from Milan. The example of the Revolution also helped inspire the uprising against Russian domination of Poland in 1794 (see page 701). This insurrection included not only educated elites, such as its leader Kościuszko, but also artisans and peasants; indeed, Catherine the Great was appalled when the rebels hanged members of a Russian-supported puppet government and vowed to crush the Polish "Jacobins."

European colonies overseas felt the impact of the Revolution and subsequent European wars in several ways. The British tried to take advantage of Napoleon's preoccupation with continental affairs by seizing French colonies and the colonies of the French-dominated Dutch. They were largely successful. In 1806 they seized the Dutch colony of Capetown—crucial for support of trade around Africa—as well as French bases along the African coast. In 1811 they grabbed the island of Java. In the Americas, French sugar colonies in the Caribbean were particularly vulnerable to English seapower. The British readily seized Martinique, Guadeloupe, and other islands while Napoleon was executing his brilliant victories on the Continent after 1805. The sugar island of Haiti was an exception to this pattern of French losses because British aggression there occurred in the context of a local revolution.

In Haiti the Revolution itself, and not merely the strategic moves of great powers, had an impact. The National Assembly in Paris delayed abolishing slavery in French colonies, despite the moral appeal of such a move, because of pressure from the white planters on Haiti and out of fear that the financially strapped French government would lose some of its profitable sugar trade. But the example of revolutionary daring in Paris and confusion about ruling authority that occurred as the Assembly and the king wrangled invited challenges to authority in the colonies.

Many white planters hoped to seize the opportunity the Revolution provided to gain political and economic independence from France. White planter rule in Haiti was challenged, in turn, by wealthy people of mixed European and African descent and then by a full-fledged slave rebellion, beginning in 1791. (See the box, "Encounters with the West: A Planter's Wife on the Haitian Slave Revolt.") Britain sent aid to the rebels when it went to war against the French revolutionary government in 1793. Only when the republic was declared in Paris and the Convention abolished slavery did the Haitian rebels abandon alliances with France's enemies and attempt to govern in concert with the mother country.

France, however, never regained control of Haiti. Led by a former slave, François Dominique Toussaint-Louverture (1743–1803), the new government of Haiti tried to run its own affairs, though without formally declaring independence from France. Napoleon, early in his rule, decided to tighten control of the profitable colonies by reinstituting slavery and ousting the independent government of Haiti. In 1802 French forces fought their way onto the island. They captured Toussaint-Louverture, who died shortly thereafter in prison. But in 1803 they were forced to leave by another rebellion prompted by the threat of renewed slavery.

The French Revolution and Napoleonic rule had a great impact on Spanish colonies in the Americas also, and for many of the same reasons as in Haiti. The confusion of authority in Spain enabled some Spanish colonies to govern themselves independently in all but name. Like the British North American colonies, the Spanish colonies wanted freedom from the closed economic ties the mother country tried to impose.

The liberal ideas that had helped spawn the French Revolution spurred moves toward independence in Spanish America. There were also echoes of radical republican ideology in some of the events in Spanish America. For example, participants in two major rebellions in Mexico espoused the end of slavery and generally championed the interests of the poor against local and Spanish elites. The leaders of these self-declared revolutions were executed (in 1811 and 1815), and their movements were crushed by local elites in alliance with Spanish troops. The efforts of local elites to become self-governing—the attempted liberal revolutions—were little more successful. Only Argentina and Paraguay broke away from Spain at this time. But as in Europe, a legacy remained of both limited and more radical revolutionary activity.

The View from Britain

Today the city of Paris is dotted with public monuments that celebrate Napoleon's victories. One of the main train stations is the Gare (Station) d'Austerlitz. A column in a city square, crowned with a statue of Napoleon, was made from the metal of enemy cannon captured at Austerlitz.

In London, another set of events and another hero is celebrated. In Trafalgar Square stands a statue of Lord Nelson, the British naval commander whose fleet destroyed a combined French and

~ **ENCOUNTERS WITH THE WEST** ~

A Planter's Wife on the Haitian Slave Revolt

The following are excerpts from two letters of Madame de Rouvray, a wealthy planter's wife living in the French colony of Saint-Domingue (the western half of the island of Hispaniola), to her married daughter in France. The decree of May 15, 1791, that Madame de Rouvray mentions in her first letter granted civil rights to free persons of mixed race. The decree affected only a few hundred persons on Saint-Domingue (many of whom themselves owned slaves), but white planters feared any breach in the barriers between the races. Tensions between white planters, on the one hand, and mulattos and modest white settlers who favored revolutionary changes, on the other, enabled the well-organized slave rebellion to be dramatically successful. It began in late August 1791 and is the backdrop to Madame de Rouvray's second letter. Madame de Rouvray and her husband fled the island—renamed Haiti, the Native American term for Hispaniola, after the revolt—for the United States in 1793.

July 30, 1791   I am writing to you from Cap [a city on the island] where I came to find out what the general mood is here. . . . All the deputies who make up the general assembly [of the colony] left here the day before yesterday to gather at Léogane [another city]. If they conduct themselves wisely their first action should be to send emissaries to all the powers who have colonies with slaves in order to tell them of the decree [of May 15] and of the consequences that will follow from it, and ask for help from them in case it happens that the National Assembly actually abolishes slavery too, which they will surely do. After their decree of May 15, one cannot doubt that that is their plan. And you understand that all the powers who have slave colonies have a common interest in opposing such a crazy plan because the contagion of liberty will soon infect their colonies too, especially in nearby Jamaica. It is said that [the English] will send a ship and troops [which] would be wonderful for us. Your father thinks it won't be long before the English take control here.

September 4, 1791   If news of the horrors that have happened here since the 23rd of last month have reached you, you must have been very worried. Luckily, we are all safe. We can't say whether our fortunes are also safe because we are still at war with the slaves who revolted [and] who have slaughtered and torched much of the countryside hereabouts. . . . All of this will gravely damage our revenues for this year and for the future, because how can we stay in a country where slaves have raised their hands against their masters? . . . You have no idea, my dear, of the state of this colony; it would make you tremble. Don't breathe a word of this to anyone but your father is determined, once the rebels have been defeated, to take refuge in Havanna.

Source: M. E. McIntosh and B. C. Weber, *Une Correspondance familiale au temps des troubles de Saint-Domingue* (Paris: Société de l'Histoire des Colonies Françaises et Librairie Larose, 1959), pp. 22–23, 26–28. Trans. by Kristen B. Neuschel.

Spanish fleet in 1805. Horatio Nelson was a brilliant tactician, whose innovations in maneuvering ships in the battle line resulted in stunning victories at Trafalgar and, in 1798, at the Nile Delta, which limited French ambitions in Egypt and the eastern Mediterranean.

Trafalgar looms large in British history in part because Nelson was mortally wounded during the battle. More significant, the battle ensured British mastery of the seas, which then forced Napoleon into economic policies that strained French ties to France's allies and satellites. Virtually

The Funeral of Lord Nelson, January 8, 1806 Nelson had been mortally wounded on the deck of his flagship at the Battle of Trafalgar in October. Rather than being buried at sea, as was the custom, his body was returned to London for an impressive state funeral, commemorated here in a contemporary engraving. *(National Maritime Museum, London)*

unchallenged seapower enabled the British to seize colonies formerly ruled by France and its allies.

Britain's seizure of French possessions expanded British trading networks overseas. The struggles against Napoleon also enhanced British trading networks and strategic dominance closer to home, particularly in the Mediterranean. As long as the British had been involved in trade with India, the Mediterranean had been important for economic and strategic reasons: It marked the end of the land route for trade from the Indian Ocean. Especially after Napoleon's aggression in Egypt, the British redoubled their efforts to control important strategic outposts in the Mediterranean, such as ports in southern Italy and on the island of Malta.

Since the late eighteenth century, the British had steadily made other gains abroad. In 1783, Britain had lost control of thirteen of its North American colonies; however, it had more successfully resolved the Irish rebellions. Similarly, in the Caribbean, British planter families, like Irish elites, were willing to accept tighter rule from the mother country in return for greater security against their subject population. In regions of India, the East India Company was increasing its political domination, and hence its economic stranglehold on Indian manufacture and trade.

The British economy would expand dramatically in the nineteenth century as industrial production expanded. The roots for that expansion were laid in this period in the countryside of Britain, where changes in agriculture and in production were occurring. These roots were also laid in Britain's overseas possessions by the profits made there and also, increasingly, by the control of sources of raw materials, notably raw cotton raised in India. The export of Indian cotton expanded significantly during the revolutionary period as part of an expanding trading system that included China, the source of tea.

However, economic expansion was not the sole motive for British aggression. In fact, economic expansion was often the product of increased British control of particular regions or sealanes, and the reasons for it were as much strategic as economic. Not every conquest had direct economic payoffs, but British elites were sure that strategic domination was a desirable step, wherever it could be managed. One Scottish landholder, writing in the opening years of the nineteenth century, spoke for many when he said that Britain needed an empire to ensure its greatness and that an empire of the sea was an effective counterweight to Napoleon's empire on land. Much as the French were at that moment exporting features of their own political system, the British, he said, could export their constitution wherever they conquered territory.

Thus, England and France were in fact engaged in similar phases of expansion in this period. In both, the desire for power and profit drove policy. In each, myths about heroes and about the supposed benefits of domination masked the state's self-interest. In both, the effects of conquest would become a fundamental shaping force in the nineteenth century.

SUMMARY

The French Revolution was a watershed in European history because it successfully challenged the principles of hereditary rule and political privilege by which all European states had hitherto been governed. The Revolution began when a financial crisis forced the monarchy to confront the desire for political reform by a segment of the French elite. Political philosophy emerging from the Enlightenment and the example of the American Revolution moved the French reformers to action. In its initial phase, the French Revolution established the principle of constitutional government and ended many of the traditional political privileges of the Old Regime.

The Revolution moved in more radical directions because of the intransigence of the king, the threat of foreign invasion, and the actions of republican legislators and Parisian citizens. Its most radical phase, the Terror, produced the most effective legislation for ordinary citizens but also the worst violence of the Revolution. A period of unstable conservative rule that followed the Terror ended when Napoleon seized power.

Though Napoleonic rule enshrined some of the gains of the Revolution, it also subjected France and most of Europe to the great costs of wars of conquest. After Napoleon, the French monarchy was restored but forced to accept many limitations on its power as a result of the Revolution. Indeed, hereditary rule and traditional social hierarchies remained in place in much of Europe, but they would not be secure in the future. The legacy of revolutionary change would prove impossible to contain in France or anywhere else.

NOTES

1. Quoted in Samuel Eliot Morison, *John Paul Jones: A Sailor's Biography* (Boston: Little, Brown, 1959), pp. 149–154.
2. Quoted in Owen Connelly, *The French Revolution and Napoleonic Era* (New York: Holt, Rinehart and Winston, 1979), p. 32.

SUGGESTED READING

General Surveys
Connelly, Owen. *French Revolution/Napoleonic Era*. 1979. A clear and readable survey that devotes equal time to the Revolution and to Napoleon.
Sutherland, D. M. G. *France, 1789–1815*. 1986. A dense and detailed treatment, with extensive bibliography, that emphasizes the revolutionary over the Napoleonic period.
Thompson, John. *The French Revolution*. 1951. A classic liberal interpretation of the Revolution, useful for its clarity and detail.

Recent Interpretations of the Revolution
Baker, Keith Michael, ed. *The French Revolution and the Creation of Modern Political Culture*. 1987. A collection of essays by diverse scholars emphasizing the Revolution as a period of change in political culture.
Furet, François. *Interpreting the French Revolution*. 1981. The major work by the outstanding French scholar of the Revolution of the current generation, written in reaction to liberal and Marxist interpretations.
Hufton, Olwen. *Women and the Limits of Citizenship in the French Revolution*. 1992. A series of essays by the leading scholar on the history of women in the Revolution.
Hunt, Lynn. *The Family Romance of the French Revolution*. 1992. A study of political ideology and symbolic politics emphasizing the vast cultural consequences of killing the king and queen.
———. *Politics, Culture and Class in the French Revolution*. 1984. A survey and assessment of other interpretations of the Revolution, emphasizing the role of symbols and symbolic politics.
Kennedy, Emmet. *A Cultural History of the French Revolution*. 1989. An ambitious interpretation of the Revolution as a period of cultural change.

(continued on page 736)

POLITICAL SYMBOLS

During the French Revolution, thousands of illustrations in support of various revolutionary (or counterrevolutionary) ideas were reproduced on posters, on handbills, and in pamphlets. Some satirized their subjects, such as Marie Antoinette, or celebrated revolutionary milestones, such as the fall of the Bastille. The etching here of the woman armed with a pike, dating from 1792, falls into this category. Other pictures, such as the representation from 1795 of Liberty as a young woman wearing the liberty cap, symbolized or reinforced various revolutionary ideals.*

Political images like these are an invaluable though problematic source for historians. Let us examine these two images of women and consider how French people during the Revolution might have responded to them. To understand what they meant to contemporaries, we must know something about the other images that these would have been compared to. We must also view the images in the context of the events of the Revolution itself. Immediately, then, we are presented with an interpretive agenda. How ordinary and acceptable was this image of an armed woman? If women were not citizens coequal with men, how could a woman be a symbol of liberty? What, in short, do these political images reveal about the spectrum of political life in their society?

The woman holding the pike stares determinedly at the viewer. Many details confirm what the caption announces: This is a French woman who has become free. In her hat she wears one of the symbols of revolutionary nationhood: the tricolor cockade. The badge around her waist celebrates a defining moment for the revolutionary nation: the fall of the Bastille. Her pike itself is inscribed with the words "Liberty or death!"

The woman appears to be serving not merely as a symbol of free women. She comes close to being the generic image of a free citizen, willing and able to fight for liberty—an astonishing symbolic possibility in a time when women were not yet treated equally under the law or granted the same

An Armed Citizen, ca. 1792 *(Bibliothèque Nationale, Cabinet des estampes)*

*This discussion draws on the work of Joan Landes, "Representing the Body Politic: The Paradox of Gender in the Graphic Politics of the French Revolution," and Darlene Gay Levy and Harriet B. Applewhite, "Women and Militant Citizenship in Revolutionary Paris," in Sara E. Melzer and Leslie W. Rabine, eds., *Rebel Daughters: Women and the French Revolution* (New York: Oxford University Press, 1992), pp. 15–37, 79–101.

political rights as the men of their class. Other images prevalent at the time echo this possibility. Many contemporary representations of the women's march on Versailles in 1789 (see page 708) show women carrying arms, active in advancing the Revolution. By the time this image was created (most likely in 1792), many other demonstrations and violent confrontations by ordinary people had resulted in the creation of dozens of popular prints and engravings that showed women acting in the same ways as men.

Repeatedly during 1792, women proposed to the revolutionary government that they be granted the right to bear arms. Their request was denied, but it was not dismissed out of hand. There was debate, and the issue was in effect tabled. Nevertheless, women's actions in the Revolution had created at least the possibility of envisaging citizenship with a female face.

The image of liberty from 1795 does not reflect the actions of women but rather represents their exclusion from political participation. It is one of a number of images of Liberty that portray this ideal as a passive, innocent woman, here garbed in ancient dress, surrounded by a glow that in the past had been reserved for saints. Liberty here is envisaged as a pure and lofty goal, symbolized as a pure young woman.

Late in 1793, during the Terror, women were excluded from formal participation in politics with the disbanding of women's organizations. Nor did they gain political rights under the Directory, which re-established some of the limited gains of the first phase of the Revolution. The justification offered for their exclusion in 1793 was borrowed from Rousseau: It is contrary to nature for women to be in public life (see page 665). Women "belong" in the private world of the family, where they will nurture male citizens. Women embody ideal qualities such as patience and self-sacrifice; they are not fully formed beings capable of action in their own right.

"Liberty" as a Young Woman, ca. 1795 (S. P. Avery Collection, Miriam and Ira D. Wallach Division of Art, Prints, and Photographs, The New York Public Library, Astor, Lenox, and Tilden Foundations)

Such notions made it easy to use images of women to embody ideals for public purposes. A woman could represent Liberty precisely because actual women were not able to be political players.

The two images shown here thus demonstrate that political symbols can have varying relationships to "reality." The pike-bearing citizen is the more "real." Her image reflects the way actual women acted, and it represents a way of thinking about politics that became possible for the first time because of their actions. The other woman reflects not the attributes of actual women but an ideal type spawned by the use of arbitrary gender distinctions to legitimize political power. In these images we can see modern political life taking shape: the sophistication of its symbolic language, the importance of abstract ideas such as liberty and nationhood—as well as the grounding of much political life in rigid distinctions between public and private, male and female. ✑

Landes, Joan. *Women and the Public Sphere in the Age of the French Revolution.* 1988. An analysis of the uses of gender ideology to fashion the new political world of the revolutionaries.

Manceron, Claude. *The Age of the French Revolution.* 1986. An innovative, multivolume study of the experience of the Revolution, beginning in the 1770s, told by means of biographical vignettes.

Origins and Preconditions of the Revolution

Censer, Jack, and Jeremy D. Popkin. *Press and Politics in Pre-Revolutionary France.* 1987. A work that is helpful in understanding the context of opposition to the monarchy before the outbreak of the Revolution.

Chartier, Roger. *The Cultural Origins of the French Revolution.* 1991. An interpretation of intellectual and cultural life in the eighteenth century with a view to explaining its revolutionary results; has a good bibliography.

Lefebvre, Georges. *The Coming of the French Revolution.* Translated by R. R. Palmer. 1947. The greatest of several works by this French historian; a readable Marxist interpretation that remains useful.

Palmer, R. R. *The Age of Democratic Revolution.* 2 vols. 1959. A study of the American and European revolutionary movements and their reciprocal influences; detailed, erudite, but immensely readable.

The Phases of Revolution, 1789–1791

Godeschot, J. *The Taking of the Bastille, July 14, 1789.* 1970. An explanation of the circumstances and significance of the seizure of the Bastille.

Rudé, George. *The Crowd in the French Revolution.* 1959. A classic Marxist assessment of the importance of common people to the progress of the Revolution.

Tackett, Timothy. *Priest and Paris in Eighteenth-Century France.* 1977. A study of rural Catholic life before the Revolution and after the impact of the Civil Constitution of the Clergy.

The Phases of Revolution, 1791–1794

Jordan, D. P. *The King's Trial.* 1979. A thorough and readable study of Louis XVI's trial and its importance.

Palmer, R. R. *Twelve Who Ruled.* 1941. A study of the principal figures of the Terror by one of the greatest American historians of the French Revolution.

Patrick, A. *The Men of the First French Republic.* 1972. A study of the Girondins—their identity and their coherence as a political faction.

Soboul, Albert. *The Sans-Culottes.* 1972. A study of the workers of Paris who were active in the Revolution, by Georges Lefebvre's successor as the foremost Marxist historian of the Revolution.

The Phases of Revolution, 1795–1799

Barton, H. Arnold. *Scandinavia in the Revolutionary Era, 1760–1815.* 1986. Treats the Scandinavian countries' response to and involvement in revolutionary movements and the Napoleonic wars.

James, C. L. R. *The Black Jacobins.* 1938. The classic study of the Haitian revolution in the context of events in Europe.

Sydenham, M. *The First French Republic, 1792–1804.* 1974. A useful survey of the relatively neglected phases of the Revolution.

Napoleon and Napoleonic Europe

Bayly, C. A. *Imperial Meridian.* 1989. A new study of the developing British Empire in the context of both European and world affairs; has an extensive bibliography.

Connelly, Owen. *Blundering to Glory: The Campaigns of Napoleon.* 1992. A new assessment of Napoleon's military achievements by an expert on Napoleonic warfare.

Lyons, Martyn. *Napoleon Bonaparte and the Legacy of the French Revolution.* 1994. A clear, readable, and up-to-date synthesis of scholarship on Napoleon.

Markham, Felix. *Napoleon.* 1963. The best biography in English of Napoleon.

CHAPTER 20

Restoration, Reform, and Revolution, 1814–1848

I n 1791 in the midst of revolution the comte de Provence had fled his homeland, disguised as a foreign merchant. Shunted from country to country he lived in exile, depending upon subsidies of foreign courts. Since the revolutionaries had beheaded his brother, Louis XVI, and a nephew had died in captivity, when he returned to France after twenty-three years abroad, he did so as king of France, Louis XVIII (r. 1814–1824).

With Louis's return to French soil in April 1814, the Bourbons were restored. In many other states, too, with the fall of Napoleon, monarchy and aristocracy attempted to reassert, to "restore," their authority. Historians often call the period from 1814 to 1832 in Europe the "restoration." Yet the old world could not be entirely re-created—from the beginning efforts to restore it were challenged by forces that had appeared during the revolutionary years.

The Great Powers tried to re-establish as much of the old European state system as possible. The international arrangements of the victorious powers—Austria, Great Britain, Prussia, and Russia—were soon shaken by outbreaks of nationalist fervor. Nationalists aimed either to create larger political units, as in Italy and Germany, or to win independence from foreign rule, as in Greece.

Domestically, the attempt to set the clock back was of limited success. The conservatism of European rulers and their opposition to change were at odds with the new dynamism of European society. Between 1800 and 1850, Europe's population increased by nearly 50 percent, from around 190 million to 280 million. Population growth and the development of

Celebrating the revolution of 1848 in Vienna. Anton Ziegler, *The Barricade at Michaelerplatz on the Evening of 26th May* (1848).

739

industry created large cities where there had been small towns or rural areas. Factory manufacturing was on the rise, promising to reshape class structures and the lives of workers. Romanticism, liberalism, and other systems of thought were redefining the relationship of the individual to society.

European statesmen in 1814 consciously tried to forestall revolution, but in less than a generation they were challenged by waves of protest and violence, most notably in the revolutions of 1848. Revolutionaries did not win all their goals, and in many cases the forces of order crushed them. Yet major intellectual, social, and political changes had occurred by midcentury.

THE SEARCH FOR STABILITY: THE CONGRESS OF VIENNA

The defeat of Napoleon put an end to French dominance in Europe. In September 1814 the victorious Great Powers—Austria, Great Britain, Prussia, and Russia—convened an international conference in Vienna to negotiate the terms of peace. The victors sought to draw territorial boundaries advantageous to themselves and to provide long-term stability on the European continent.

Although many small powers attended the Congress of Vienna, their role was reduced to ratifying the large states' decisions. Having faced a powerful France, which had mobilized popular forces with revolutionary principles, the victors decided to erect an international system that would remove such threats. One method was to restore the European order that had existed before the French Revolution. Thus, following principles of "legitimacy and compensation," they redrew the map of Europe (Map 20.1). Rulers who had been overthrown were restored to their thrones. As we have seen, the eldest surviving brother of Louis XVI of France became King Louis XVIII. In Spain, Ferdinand VII was restored to the throne from which Napoleon had toppled him and his father. The restoration, however, was not so complete as its proponents claimed. Since the French Revolution, certain new realities had to be recog-

Map 20.1 Europe in 1815 The map of Europe was redrawn at the Congress of Vienna.

nized. For example, Napoleon had consolidated the German and Italian states; the process was acknowledged in the former with the creation of a loose German Confederation.

Negotiations at the Congress of Vienna strengthened the territories bordering France, enlarged Prussia, created the kingdom of Piedmont-Sardinia, joined Belgium to Holland, and provided the victors with spoils and compensation for territories bartered away. Russia's reward for its contribution to the war effort was most of Poland and all of Finland, which had belonged to Sweden. Sweden's king was compensated for the loss of Finland by being permitted to rule in a joint union over Norway, formerly under the Danish crown. Denmark was thus punished for adhering to the Napoleonic alliance longer than the victorious Great Powers thought was appropriate. Austria received Venetia and Lombardy in northern Italy to compensate for the loss of Belgium and the loss of parts of Poland to Russia and to strengthen its position in general. Prussia was also allowed annexations in compensation for giving up parts of Poland. England acquired a number of colonies and naval outposts. Thus, even as they proclaimed their loyalty to the prerevolutionary past, conservative statesmen changed the map of Europe.

The leading personality at the Congress of Vienna was the Austrian foreign minister, Prince Clemens von Metternich (1773–1859), who presided over the meetings. An aristocrat in exile from the Rhineland, which had been annexed by revolutionary France, he had gone into the service of the Habsburg empire and risen to become its highest official. Personal charm, tact, and representation of a state that for the time being was satisfied with its territories made Metternich seem a disinterested statesman. His influence at the Congress was great.

Made wary by their long war against France, the four powers of the Quadruple Alliance—Austria, Great Britain, Prussia, and Russia—had pledged before the Congress of Vienna to cooperate to prevent any future French aggression. They also planned to meet periodically to resolve all European issues, creating what was known as the "Concert of Europe." Yet at Vienna the wily French foreign minister, Count Charles Talleyrand (1754–1838), was able to insinuate himself into the councils of the Great Powers. The desire of Russia and Prussia for sizable territorial gains alarmed both

Conservatism

The architects of the restoration justified their policies with doctrines based on the ideology of conservatism, emphasizing the need to preserve the existing order. As a coherent movement, conservatism sprang up during and after the French Revolution to resist the forces of change. When the old order faced serious challenges in the late eighteenth and early nineteenth centuries, an ideology justifying traditional authority emerged. Before the American and French Revolutions, the existing political institutions appeared to be permanent.

Edmund Burke (1729–1797), a British statesman and political theorist, launched one of the first intellectual assaults on the French Revolution. The revolutionary National Assembly had asserted that ancient prerogatives were superseded by the rights of man and principles of human equality based on appeals to natural law. In *Reflections on the Revolution in France* (1790), Burke said that such claims were abstract and dangerous and that the belief in human equality undermined the social order. Government should be anchored in tradition, he argued. No matter how poorly the French monarchy and its institutions had served the nation, they should be preserved; their very longevity proved their usefulness. Burke's writings were widely read and influential on the Continent.

In the English-speaking world, one of the most popular writers, Hannah More (1745–1833), who with her four sisters ran a prosperous school, saw piety as a rampart against rebellion. In a series of moral tracts entitled *Cheap Repository Tracts*, she advocated the acceptance of the existing order and the solace of religious faith. Costing but a penny, the tracts were often handed out by the rich together with alms or food to the poor. More was the first writer in history to sell over a million copies; within three years the sales doubled. Conservative values thus spread to a very large audience in both Britain and the United States, where one of her works appeared in thirty editions.

A more extreme version of conservatism was the counterrevolutionary or ultra-royalist ideology. Unlike Burke, who was willing to tolerate some change, counterrevolutionaries wanted to restore society to its prerevolutionary condition. The most extreme counterrevolutionaries were those with personal experience of the upheavals of the Revolution. Count Joseph de Maistre (1753–1821), a

Metternich The consummate statesman and aristocrat, Metternich tried to quell revolution at home and abroad. Some called his era the Metternichean age. *(The Royal Collection © 1993 Her Majesty Queen Elizabeth II)*

Austria and Great Britain, and France joined them in limiting Russian and Prussian ambitions. At Talleyrand's insistence, France was counted as one of the five Great Powers.

The Concert of Europe, including France, continued to function, and met several times to try to resolve subsequent crises. Underlying the states' cooperation was the principle of a common European destiny.

IDEOLOGICAL CONFRONTATIONS

The international and domestic political system established in 1815 was modified by a series of challenges, even revolts, culminating in revolutions throughout Europe in 1848. The order established in 1815 was inspired by conservatism. Its challengers advocated competing ideologies: romanticism, nationalism, liberalism, and socialism.

Savoyard (from the Franco-Italian border region) nobleman whose estates were occupied by the invading French, described monarchy as a God-given form of government in his *Considerations on France* in 1796. Any attempt to abolish or even limit it was a violation of divine law. According to de Maistre and his fellow reactionaries, the authority of church and state was necessary to prevent human beings from falling into evil ways. De Maistre advocated stern government control, including the generous use of the death penalty, to keep people loyal to throne and altar.

In Germany the influential thought of Georg Wilhelm Friedrich Hegel (1770–1831), philosophy professor at the University of Berlin, was interpreted by many of his disciples as a defense of the conservative order re-established by the restoration. In Hegel's view, history was propelled from one stage to another by the "world spirit" incarnate in the dominant power. Just as Rome had fulfilled divine plans by dominating the ancient world, so Napoleon, when he entered Jena in 1806, was hailed by Hegel as a "world soul." The emperor's fall, however, convinced Hegel that the true world soul was incarnate in the victorious allies, particularly Prussia. The state, Hegel said, showed "the march of God in the world"; the existing power, reactionary and authoritarian, was divinely ordained.

Conservatism was also influenced by romanticism, with its glorification of the past, taste for pageantry, and belief in the organic unity of society. But by no means were all conservatives romantics. Metternich, for instance, saw his work as the attempt of an enlightened mind to restore the world that had been undermined by the emotional turmoil of the French Revolution. (See the box, "Metternich's Cure for Europe.")

Romanticism

The long-lived romantic movement emerged in the 1760s as a rebellion against rationalism and persisted until the 1840s. It was primarily a movement in the arts. Writers, painters, composers, and others consciously rebelled against the Enlightenment and its values (see pages 660–671). In contrast to the philosophes with their emphasis on reason, romantics praised emotion and feeling. Jean-Jacques Rousseau's strong appeal to sentiment was taken up by the German writer Johann Wolfgang von Goethe (1749–1832), who declared that "Feeling is everything." Goethe's *Sorrows of Young Werther* (1774), the most widely read book of the era—Napoleon had a copy by his bedside—depicted the passions of the hero, who, depressed by unrequited love, kills himself. Many readers dressed in "Werther clothes"—tight black pants, blue vest, and an open yellow shirt—and in some cases emulated the tragic hero by committing suicide.

Whereas the Enlightenment had studied nature for the principles that it could impart, romantics worshiped nature for its inherent beauty. The German composer Ludwig van Beethoven (1770–1827) wrote his *Pastoral* Symphony in praise of nature. The English poets William Wordsworth (1770–1850) and Samuel Taylor Coleridge (1772–1834) treated untamed wilderness as a particular subject of wonder. Fellow Englishman Joseph Turner (1775–1851) displayed the raw passions of the sea in his paintings *Fire at Sea* (1834) and *Snowstorm, Steamboat off a Harbour's Mouth* (1842). To paint the latter, Turner is said to have tied himself to a ship's mast and braved a snowstorm for four hours.

In pursuit of the authentic and the ancient, and in pursuit of feeling rather than rationality, many romantics rediscovered religion. In some areas of Europe, popular religion had anticipated the artists' and intellectuals' romantic sensibilities. France experienced a revival of Catholicism. In the German states, pietism, which emerged in the seventeenth and eighteenth centuries, stressed the personal relationship of the individual to God, unimpeded by formal theology or religious authorities. The influence of pietism, with its emphasis on feeling and emotion, spread throughout central Europe in schools and churches.

In England emotionalism in religion expressed itself in the popularity of Methodism. Founded in the 1730s by the English preacher John Wesley (1703–1791), this movement emphasized salvation by faith. Appealing especially to the poor and desperate, Methodism by the 1790s had gained 70,000 members, and within a generation it quadrupled its flock.

The classicism of the Enlightenment had required an audience well versed in the traditional texts. Since the mid-eighteenth century, however, the reading public had grown to include people without access to elite culture. Appeals to emotion and sentiment were congenial to these new

Metternich's Cure for Europe

Metternich, Austria's foreign minister from 1809 to 1848, had an impact beyond his empire's borders, providing much of the leadership of the reactionary regimes of Europe between 1815 and 1848. In this secret letter to Russia's Tsar Alexander I, Metternich analyzed the current ailments of Europe and saw their cure in firm support for king and church.

Kings have to calculate the chances of their very existence in the immediate future; passions are let loose, and league together to overthrow everything which society respects as the basis of its existence; religion, public morality, laws, customs, rights, and duties all are attacked, confounded, overthrown, or called in question. . . .

Having now thrown a rapid glance over the first causes of the present state of society, it is necessary to point out in a more particular manner the evil which threatens to deprive it, at one blow, of the real blessings, the fruits of genuine civilisation, and to disturb it in the midst of its enjoyments. This evil may be described in one word—presumption; the natural effect of the rapid progression of the human mind towards the perfecting of so many things. This it is which at the present day leads so many individuals astray, for it has become an almost universal sentiment. . . .

The Governments, having lost their balance, are frightened, intimidated, and thrown into confusion, by the cries of the intermediary class of society, which, placed between the Kings and their subjects, breaks the sceptre of the monarch, and usurps the cry of the people. . . .

We are convinced that society can no longer be saved without strong and vigorous resolutions on the part of the Governments. . . . By this course the monarchs will fulfill the duties imposed upon them by Him who, by entrusting them with power, has charged them to watch over the maintenance of justice, and the rights of all, to avoid the paths of error and tread firmly in the way of truth. . . .

. . . [L]et the Governments govern. . . . Let them not encourage by their attitude or actions the suspicion of being favourable or indifferent to error: let them not allow it to be believed that experience has lost its rights to make way for experiments which at the least are dangerous.

Source: Metternich to Emperor Alexander, Troppau, December 15, 1820, in Prince Richard Metternich, ed., *Memoirs of Prince Metternich, 1815–1829,* vol. 3, trans. Mrs. Alexander Napier (New York: Scribner & Sons, 1881), pp. 455, 458–459, 468–470, 474.

---

audiences, and a new interest developed in folklore and rustic life. But where an earlier era had mythologized country life, the romantic in loving detail painted its realistic charms.

The philosophes had decried the Middle Ages, but romantics celebrated the medieval period. Sir Walter Scott (1771–1832) in Scotland and Victor Hugo (1802–1885) in France celebrated chivalry and the age of faith in such popular works as *Ivanhoe* (1819) and *The Hunchback of Notre Dame* (1831). Painters frequently had as their theme Gothic buildings or ruins. Architects imitated the Gothic style in both private and public buildings.

The romantics sought displacement not only in time but also in place. The exotic had great appeal to them. Recently conquered Algeria in North Africa provided exotic scenes for French painters, among them Eugène Delacroix (1798–1863) and Jean Ingrès (1780–1867). Senegal in West Africa, recovered by the French from the British in 1815, offered the setting for Théodore Géricault's powerful *Raft of the "Medusa."* (See the feature, "Weighing the Evidence: *Raft of the 'Medusa,'*" on pages 772–773.)

After the French Revolution, nobles and monarchs ceased sponsoring art on a grand scale and were expected to conduct their lives soberly. Cut

Turner: Snowstorm, Steamboat Off a Harbour's Mouth Completed in 1842, this painting powerfully displays one of the romantics' prime subjects—the force of raw nature. Although the steamship is one of the new wonders of human inventiveness, it is insignificant in the face of the storm. *(The Clore Collection, Tate Gallery, London/ Art Resource, NY)*

off from royal patronage, artists had to depend on members of the new middle classes to buy paintings and books and attend plays and musical performances. Earning a livelihood had often been difficult for artists in the past, but now it became even more so. Forced to live marginally, they cultivated the image of the artist as a bohemian—a gypsy. In their lifestyles and their work, they deliberately rejected the conventions of society. The romantic period gave rise to the notion of the starving genius, alienated from society, loyal only to art.

Romanticism exalted mythical figures as the embodiment of human energy and passion. In the dramatic poem *Faust*, Goethe retold the legend of a man who sold his soul to the devil in exchange for worldly success. In the poetic drama *Prometheus*

Unbound, the English romantic poet Percy Bysshe Shelley (1792–1822) celebrated Prometheus, who stole fire from the gods and gave it to human beings. In much the same spirit, many romantics exalted Napoleon, who had overthrown kings and states. Delacroix, who witnessed the July Revolution of 1830 in Paris, celebrated the heroism and passion of the revolutionaries in his huge canvas, *Liberty Leading the People* (1830).

Romantics often challenged existing power relations, including the relation of the sexes. The French writer Amandine-Aurore Dupin (1804–1876), better known by her pen name, George Sand, spoke for the emancipation of women from the close supervision of their husbands, fathers, and brothers. In her personal life, Sand practiced the freedom she preached, dressing like a man, smoking cigars, and openly pursuing affairs with the writer Prosper Mérimée (1803–1870), the poet Alfred de Musset (1810–1857), and the composer Frédéric Chopin (1810–1849). The English writer Mary Ann Evans (1819–1892), like George Sand, adopted a male pseudonym, George Eliot. She conducted her life in a nonconformist manner, living with a married man. The adoption of male pen names by both writers attests to the hostility that intellectual women still faced.

Romantics of many stripes declared their determination to overthrow the smug present and create a new world. Victor Hugo called for "no more rules, no more models" to constrain the human imagination. Romantic painters and musicians consciously turned their backs on the classical tradition in both subject matter and style. Old methods were discarded for new ones. The English poet George Gordon, Lord Byron (1788–1824), declared war on kings, on established religion, and on the international order; a nationalist as well as a romantic, he died while fighting for the independence of Greece.

Nationalism

The ideology of nationalism emerged in, and partly shaped, this era. Nationalism is the belief that people derive their identity from their nation and owe their nation their primary loyalty. A list of criteria for nationhood is likely to include a common language, religion, and political authority, as well as common traditions and shared historic experiences. Some nineteenth-century nationalists found any one of those criteria sufficient. Others insisted that all of them had to be present before a group could consider itself a nation.

In an era that saw the undermining of traditional religious values, nationalism offered a new locus of faith. To people who experienced the social turmoil brought about by the erosion of the old order, nationalism held out the promise of a new community. Nationalism became an ideal espoused as strongly as religion. The Italian nationalist Giuseppe Mazzini (1805–1872) declared that nationalism was "a faith and mission" ordained by God. The religious intensity of nationalism helps explain its widespread appeal.

Many forces shaped nationalism. Its earliest manifestation, cultural nationalism, had its origins in Rousseau's ideas of the organic nature of a people (see pages 665–666). Johann Gottfried Herder (1744–1833), Rousseau's German disciple, elaborated on Rousseau's ideas, declaring that every people has a "national spirit." To explore the unique nature of this spirit, intellectuals all over Europe began collecting folk poems, songs, and tales. In an effort to document the spirit of the German people, the Grimm brothers, Jacob (1785–1863) and Wilhelm (1786–1859), collected fairy tales and published them between 1812 and 1818; among the better known are "Little Red Riding Hood" and "Snow White."

Political nationalism, born in the era of the French Revolution, injected urgency and passion into the new ideology. In the 1770s, French aristocrats resisted attempts by the French monarchy to impose taxes, claiming that they embodied the rights of "the nation" and could not be taxed without its consent. Thus, the concept of nation was given general currency. When revolutionary France was attacked by neighboring countries, which were ruled by kings and dukes, the Legislative Assembly called on the French people to rise and save the nation. The realm of the king of France had become the French nation.

In reaction to the French threat, intellectuals in Germany and Italy embraced the spirit of nationalism. In Germany the philosopher Johann Gottlieb Fichte (1762–1814) delivered his series of *Addresses to the German Nation* after the Prussian defeat at Jena, calling on all Germans to rise up against Napoleon. He argued that Germans were endowed with a special genius that had to be safeguarded for the well-being of all humankind. In Italy, the writer Vittorio Alfieri (1749–1803) challenged France's claim to the right to lead the peoples of Europe. That right, Alfieri insisted, properly belonged to Italians, the descendants and heirs of ancient Rome.

Culture could also be invoked for the purpose of throwing off a foreign yoke and shaping a newly independent state. In the 1810s, as part of a campaign to free Greece from the Turks, Greek intellectuals reissued the classics of ancient Greek literature in "purified" language, ridding Greek of developments in popular speech that spanned two millennia, to make the language resemble more closely its classical antecedent. These intellectuals wanted to remind their fellow Greeks that they were the sons and daughters of Hellas.

For the most part, however, early-nineteenth-century nationalism was generous and cosmopolitan in its outlook—excepting the French Revolution and the Napoleonic era. Herder and Mazzini believed that each of Europe's peoples was destined to achieve nationhood and that the nations of Europe would then live peacefully side by side. The members of dedicated nationalist groups like Young Germany and Young Italy were also members of Young Europe. Many nationalists in the 1830s and 1840s were also committed to the ideal of a "Europe of free peoples." Victor Hugo even envisioned a "European republic" with its own parliament.

It is important to remember, however, that although many intellectuals found nationalism attractive, in the first half of the nineteenth century most people were likely to feel local and regional affinities more than national loyalties. Only as the result of several decades of propaganda by nationalists and governments was the ideology to win wide support, and only then did it become natural for Europeans to think of dying for their nation.

Liberalism

Liberalism was a direct descendant of the Enlightenment's critique of eighteenth-century absolutism. Nineteenth-century liberals believed that individual freedom was best safeguarded by the reduction of government powers to a minimum. They wanted to impose constitutional limits on government, to establish the rule of law, to sweep away all restrictions on individual enterprise—specifically, state regulation of the economy—and to ensure a voice in government for men of property and education. Liberalism was influenced by romanticism, with its emphasis on individual freedom and the imperative of the human personality to develop to its full potential. Liberalism was also affected by nationalism, especially in multinational autocratic states like Austria, Russia, and the Ottoman Empire, in which free institutions could be established only if political independence were wrested from, respectively, Vienna, St. Petersburg, and Constantinople.

Liberalism was both an economic and a political theory. In 1776 Adam Smith (1723–1790), the influential Scottish economist, published *An Inquiry into the Nature and Causes of the Wealth of Nations,* a

systematic study of the economic knowledge of his era. Smith advocated freeing national economies from the fetters of the state. (See the box, "Adam Smith Describes the Workings of the Market Economy.") Under the mercantilist system, prevalent throughout Europe until about 1800, the state regulated the prices and conditions of manufacture (see page 591). Smith argued for letting the free forces of the marketplace shape economic decisions. He was the founder of the classical school of economics; this school rested on the belief that economics was subject to basic unalterable laws, which could be discerned and applied in the same fashion as natural laws. Chief among them, in Smith's view, was the idea that economic self-interest was compatible with and even advantageous to the general interest. He argued that entrepreneurs who lower prices will sell more goods, thus increasing their own profits and providing the community with affordable goods. In this way, an individual's drive for profit benefits society as a whole. The economy is driven as if "by an invisible hand." This competitive drive for profits, Smith predicted, would expand the "wealth of nations." In France, advocates of nonintervention by government in the economy were called supporters of *laissez faire* (to leave alone, to let run on its own). Adam Smith was the most widely read and influential proponent of this policy.

Wages and employment were also seen as subject to the laws of supply and demand. Thomas Malthus (1766–1834), an Anglican minister, published in 1798 *An Essay on the Principle of Population.* Malthus posited that if employers paid their workers higher salaries, workers would be able to afford to marry earlier and have more children, thus glutting the labor market and driving wages down. He wanted wages to be kept at subsistence level. Workers, Malthus suggested, are "themselves the cause of their own poverty."

The third giant among the classical economists was the retired English stockbroker David Ricardo (1772–1823), who set forth his ideas in *Principles of Political Economy* (1817). Ricardo saw the capitalist system as typified by what he called the "iron law of wages." Capitalists' major expenses were wages, and to be competitive they had to keep depressing wages. According to the school of classical economics, the economy is driven by laws, and intervention of any sort will only worsen the situation.

Adam Smith Describes the Workings of the Market Economy

In **An Inquiry into the Nature and Causes of the Wealth of Nations,** *Adam Smith stressed how the economy can expand and society as a whole benefit if all participants try to maximize their own interests. Among the various economic activities, trade and specialization particularly contribute to the well-being of both society and the individual. Characterized by a mixture of theory and down-to-earth examples, his writings remain a pleasure to read.*

In almost every other race of animals each individual, when it is grown up to maturity, is entirely independent, and in its state has occasion for the assistance of no other living creature. But man has almost constant occasion for the help of his brethren, and it is in vain for him to expect it from their benevolence only. He will be more likely to prevail, if he can interest their self-love in his favour, and shew them that it is for their advantage to do for him what he requires of them. Whoever offers to another a bargain of any kind, proposes to do this. Give me that which I want, and you shall have this which you want, is the meaning of every such offer; and it is in this manner that we obtain from one another the far greater part of those good offices which we stand in need of. It is not from the benevolence of the butcher, the brewer, or the baker, that we expect our dinner, but from their regard to their own interest. We address ourselves, not to their humanity, but to their self-love, and never talk to them of our own necessities, but of their advantages. Nobody but a beggar chooses to depend chiefly upon the benevolence of his fellow-citizens. . . .

So it is this same trucking [trading] disposition which originally gives occasion to the division of labour. In a tribe of hunters or shepherds a particular person makes bows and arrows, for example, with more readiness and dexterity than any other. He frequently exchanges them for cattle or venison with his companions; and he finds at last that he can in this manner get more cattle and venison, than if he himself went to the field to catch them. From a regard to his own interest, therefore, the making of bows and arrows grows to be his chief business, and he becomes a sort of armourer. Another excels in making the frames and covers of their little huts or moveable houses. He is accustomed to be of use in this way to his neighbours, who reward him in the same manner with cattle and with venison, till at last he finds it in his interest to dedicate himself entirely to this employment, and to become a sort of house-carpenter. In the same manner a third becomes a smith or a brazier, a fourth a tanner or dresser of hides of skin, the principal part of the clothing of savages. And thus the certainty of being able to exchange all that surplus part of the produce of his own labour, which is over and above his own consumption, for such parts of the produce of other men's labour as he may have occasion for, encourages every man to apply himself to a particular occupation. . . .

Source: Adam Smith, *Inquiry into the Nature and Causes of the Wealth of Nations* (London: W. Strahan, 1776), pp. 17–18.

Liberals in the political realm argued that political power must be limited to prevent despotism. Enlightened eighteenth-century monarchs had declared that the purpose of their rule was to promote the public good. In even more ringing terms, the

French Revolution had proclaimed that the purpose of government is to ensure the happiness of humankind. As Thomas Jefferson (1743–1826), another child of the Enlightenment, asserted in the Declaration of Independence (1776), among the "unalienable rights" of individuals are "life, liberty, and the pursuit of happiness." The purpose of government is to safeguard and promote those rights.

The Enlightenment had posited natural law as the basis of government. French liberals in the nineteenth century continued to see human liberty as founded on natural law but their English counterparts were less theoretical in outlook. Jeremy Bentham (1748–1832) argued that the purpose of government is to provide "the greatest happiness of the greatest number" and that governments should be judged on that basis. Bentham and his disciples believed that the test of government is its usefulness; they were known as "utilitarians."

Democracy was implicit in Bentham's philosophy: The greatest number could ensure its own happiness only by voting for its rulers. John Stuart Mill (1803–1873), a disciple of Bentham, was the foremost proponent of liberalism, seeing it as ensuring the development of a free society. Individuals could best develop their talents if they were not hampered by the interference of the state. In his essay *On Liberty,* one of the fundamental documents of nineteenth-century liberalism, Mill argued for the free circulation of ideas—even false ideas. For in the free marketplace of ideas, false ideas will be defeated in open debate and truth will be vindicated. Mill also asserted that a free society should be free for all its members. Influenced by Harriet Taylor (1807–1856), who was to become his wife, he penned *On the Subjection of Women* (1861). Women should vote and have access to equal educational opportunities as well as to the professions. Such equality not only would be just but also would have the advantage of "doubling the mass of mental faculties available for the higher service of humanity." Mill, the foremost male proponent of women's rights in his generation, helped win a broader audience for the principle of equality between the sexes.

Despite Mill's influence, many liberals, especially in the early nineteenth century, feared the masses and therefore vigorously opposed democracy. The French liberal Benjamin Constant (1767–1836) denounced democracy as "the vulgarization of despotism"; the vote, he declared, should be reserved for the well-off and educated. When less fortunate Frenchmen denounced the property requirements that prevented them from voting, the liberal statesman François Guizot (1787–1874) smugly replied, "Get rich."

If unsympathetic to extending suffrage to the lower classes, the bourgeoisie championed liberalism, which justified its right to participate in governance. Economic liberalism was also congenial to merchants and manufacturers who wished to produce wealth without state interference.

In the second half of the century, however, many people came to believe that the laws of the marketplace could not be allowed to operate without intervention. Even Mill grew to accept that to protect workers and consumers, some controls on market forces were needed. In politics, however, the basic tenets of the liberal credo—the sanctity of human rights, freedom of speech and freedom to organize, the rule of law and equality before the law, and the abolition of torture—eventually became so widely accepted that even conservative and socialist opponents of liberalism accepted them as fundamental rights.

Socialism

The notion that human happiness can best be assured by the common ownership of property had been suggested in earlier times by individuals as different as the Greek philosopher Plato (427?–347 B.C.) and Sir Thomas More (1478–1535), English author of *Utopia.* Troubled by the condition of the working classes, thinkers in Britain and France came to espouse theories that, beginning in the 1820s, were called "socialist." Socialists believed that the "social" ownership of property, unlike private ownership, would benefit society as a whole. During the first half of the nineteenth century, most workers, even in industrializing England, were artisans. It was in a later era that socialism would address the issues raised by industry.

In 1796, during the French Revolution, Gracchus Babeuf (1760–1797), a minor civil servant, participated in the Conspiracy of Equals (see page 720). The Revolution, however haltingly, had proclaimed political equality for its citizens, but it had failed to bring economic equality. Babeuf decided to resort to revolution to bring about a "communist" society—a society in which all property would be owned in common and private property would be abolished. Work would be provided for everyone; medical services and education would be free to all. Babeuf's plot was discovered, and he was guillotined, but his theories and example of conspiratorial revolutionary action would influence later socialists.

Several other important French thinkers made contributions to European socialism. Curiously, a French aristocrat, Henri de Saint-Simon (1760–1825), emphasized the need "to ameliorate as promptly and as quickly as possible the moral and physical existence of the most numerous class." The proper role for the state, Saint-Simon declared, was to ensure the welfare of the masses. The course of history, he suggested, was in the direction of expertise. No longer could people rule on the basis of their birth. Rather, Europe should come to be governed by a council of artists and scientists who would oversee the economy and ensure that everyone enjoyed a minimum level of well-being.

Young intellectuals who gravitated to Saint-Simonism took on the master's faith in the capacity of technology to transform society. They became the dynamic entrepreneurs and engineers who in the 1850s would build up the French banking, investment, and rail systems. Still later, Saint-Simonism would inspire technocracy, the notion that social problems can be resolved by the application of technology.

Another vital contribution to socialist thought came from thinkers who tried to imagine an ideal world. They were later derisively dismissed as dreamers, as builders of utopias, fantasy worlds (the Greek word *utopia* means "no place"). Their schemes varied, but they shared the view that property should be owned in common and used for the common good. They also believed that society should rest on principles of cooperation rather than competitive individualism.

One of the earliest and most notable utopians was the Welsh mill-owner Robert Owen (1771–1859). In New Lanark, Scotland, beginning in 1800 he ran an economically successful cotton mill. He also provided generously for his workers, including guaranteeing them a job and a decent education for their children. In his writings Owen suggested the establishment of self-governing communes owning the means of production. Essentials would be distributed to all members according to their needs. Owen's ideas for the new society included equal rights for women.

Owen received little support from fellow manufacturers and political leaders. In 1824 he established in New Harmony, Indiana, an ideal new society that was to be a model for others. Within four years of its founding, New Harmony ran into economic difficulty and was torn by internal dissension. Disheartened, Owen abandoned the community and returned to Britain.

Another influential contributor to early socialist theory was the Frenchman Charles Fourier (1772–1837). A clerk and salesman, Fourier wrote out in great detail his vision of the ideal future society. It would consist of cooperative organizations called "phalanxes," each with 1600 inhabitants who would live in harmony with nature and with one another. Everyone would be assured gainful employment. Work would be made enjoyable by rotating jobs and by sharing pleasurable and unpleasurable tasks. Cooperative communes often faced the issue of who would carry out the unpleasant tasks. Fourier thought that because children enjoy playing with dirt, they should be put in charge of picking up garbage.

Fourier's belief in equality of the sexes gave him an important female following. In Belgium, the activist Zoé Gatti de Gamond (1806–1854) co-founded a phalanx for women. She believed that if women could be assured of economic well-being, other rights would follow. Inspired also by Fourier, Flora Tristan (1801–1844) was an effective advocate for workers' rights. In her book *Union Ouvrière (Workers' Union)*, she suggested that all workers should contribute to establish a "Worker's Palace" in every town. In the palace, the sick and disabled would have shelter and the workers' children could be given a free education. Crossing France on foot, she spread the word of workers' solidarity and self-help.

There were other approaches. The French socialist journalist Louis Blanc (1811–1882) saw in democracy the means of bringing into existence a socialist state. By securing the vote, the common people could win control over the state and have it serve their needs. The state could be induced to buy up banks, insurance companies, and railway systems and set up a commercial and retail chain that would provide jobs for workers and offer goods and services at prices unaffected by the search for profits. Once the workers controlled the state by the ballot, the state in turn would establish social workshops where the workers were responsible for production and supervision of business matters. Society should be established in such a way that it would be possible to "Let each produce according to his aptitudes and strength; let each consume according to his need."

Blanc's contemporary Louis Blanqui (1805–1882) suggested a more violent mode of action. He advocated seizure of the state by a small, dedicated band of men who were devoted to the welfare of the working class and who would install communism, for the equality of all. Blanqui was a perpetual conspirator, confined to state prisons for much of his long life. His ideas strengthened the notion of class warfare, and his own life served as a symbol of this struggle. The thought and example of Blanqui and the other socialists would play a major role in shaping the thinking of the most important socialist of the nineteenth century, Karl Marx (see pages 802–805).

RESTORATION AND REFORM

Despite the new ideologies that emerged to challenge the existing order, efforts at restoration appeared successful until at least 1830. Indeed in central and eastern Europe, from the German states to Russia and the Ottoman Empire, the political systems established in 1815 would persist virtually unchanged until midcentury. In western Europe, however, important transformations would occur by the 1830s as reaction gave way to reform. Then in 1848, widespread revolutions would break out on much of the Continent. The language of liberalism and nationalism and even the newer idiom of socialism would be heard on the barricades, in popular assemblies, and in parliamentary halls.

France

The most dramatic restoration was that of the Bourbons in France. The restoration turned the clock back, not to 1789 but closer to 1791, when the country had briefly enjoyed a constitutional monarchy, and it went beyond that in maintaining the Napoleonic Code with its provisions of legal equality.

Louis XVIII granted France a charter. Liberals considered such a grant ominous, for what the king gave he could presumably also revoke. Yet the charter had many reassuring provisions. Political and religious liberties and legal equality were confirmed. The new constitution provided for a parliament with an elected lower house, the

Chamber of Deputies, and an appointed upper house, the Chamber of Peers. Although suffrage to the Chamber of Deputies was limited to a small elite of men with landed property—100,000 voters, about 0.2 percent—it was a concession to representative government that had not existed in the Old Regime (see pages 702–704). Louis XVIII stands out among European rulers because he realized that it would be necessary to compromise on the principles of popular sovereignty proclaimed by the French Revolution. His intention was to "popularize the monarchy" and "royalize the nation." However, the exiled noblemen who returned with him thwarted this worthy goal. Opposed to new ideas, they were determined to restore all their old privileges and prerogatives.

In an effort to win over the people who had benefited from the sale of confiscated church and aristocratic property, Louis's charter guaranteed the ownership of property acquired during the Revolution. But the returned émigrés and spokesmen of the church challenged these terms, demanding the return of their lost properties. Returning aristocrats also reclaimed their previous positions in the army and administration from men identified with the revolutionary and Napoleonic regimes.

The most extreme reactionaries strengthened their position when liberals were blamed for the assassination in 1820 of the Duc de Berry (1778–1820), second in line to the throne. The press was fettered; suffrage, already limited, was further restricted, and a new law allowed the government to imprison without trial anyone suspected of conspiracy.

When Louis was succeeded by his ultra-reactionary brother, Charles X (r. 1824–1830), the reactionaries came into their own. The new king encouraged passage of an indemnity bill to pay the émigrés for property lost during the Revolution and Napoleon's regime. Bourgeois and lower-class taxpayers were outraged. Many of them resented the increased power granted the clergy and were shocked by the introduction of the death penalty for acts deemed sacrilegious. Charles X's dissolution of the National Guard, one of the bastions of the middle class, further alienated the bourgeoisie.

Frustration mounted with an economic downturn in 1827, marked by poor harvests and increased unemployment in the cities. Liberal

Louis XVIII as Military Leader The French king, returned to his throne by France's foreign enemies, had no military glory attached to his reign. But in 1823 France successfully invaded Spain, helping its reactionary king quell a liberal revolt. This painting celebrates the return of the victorious French troops. *(Château de Versailles/Laurie Platt Winfrey, Inc.)*

parliamentary majorities refused to accept the reactionary ministers the king appointed. On July 26, 1830, after the humiliating defeat of his party at the polls, the king issued a set of decrees suspending freedom of the press, dissolving the Chamber of Deputies, and stiffening property qualifications for voters in subsequent elections. The king appeared to be engineering a coup against the existing political system.

The first to protest were the Parisian journalists and typesetters, directly threatened by the censorship laws. On July 28, others joined the protest and began erecting barricades across many streets. After killing several hundred protesters, the king's forces lost control over the city. The uprising, known as "the three glorious days," drove the king into exile.

Alarmed by the crowds' clamor for a republic, the liberal opposition—consisting of some of the leading newspaper editors and liberal deputies—quickly drafted the duke of Orléans, Louis Philippe (1773–1850), known for his liberal opinions, to occupy the throne. The idea of a republic frightened the middle classes because it evoked memories of the Terror. A liberal constitutional monarchy was more in tune with their goals. They were better organized than the republicans and prevailed on the Chamber of Deputies to invite Louis Philippe to accept the throne.

Louis Philippe proclaimed himself "King of the French," thus acknowledging that he reigned at the behest of the people. Freedom of the press was reinstated, suffrage was extended to twice as many voters as before, 200,000 men. The July

Monarchy, named after the month in which it was established by revolution, legitimated itself by celebrating the great Revolution of 1789. Louis Philippe commissioned huge canvasses celebrating great moments of the Revolution, and on the site where the Bastille had been razed in 1789, the government erected a large column with the names of the victims of the July 1830 revolution, thus suggesting a continuity between those who had fought tyranny in 1789 and 1830.

Identification with the Revolution appeared to legitimate the regime, but could also subvert it. Fearful that the cult of revolution would encourage violence against the new monarchy, the regime censored artistic production, promoting only works that celebrated the period from 1789 to 1791, when the revolutionaries had attempted to found a constitutional monarchy. Now that the revolution of 1830 had established a constitutional monarchy, the regime was suggesting, any further uprisings were illegitimate.

But the July Monarchy was challenged from many quarters. As time passed, more people were nostalgic for the republic that had existed under the Revolution. Republicanism, the belief that France should have a republic rather than a monarchy, spread. The lackluster foreign policy of the July Monarchy made some long for the glories of the Napoleonic era. Shortly after the revolution of 1830, another downturn in the economy led to further unemployment. Then came an epidemic of cholera that affected most of Europe. Also contributing to the unsettled atmosphere was labor agitation. In the silk-producing city of Lyon, for instance, artisans who were exasperated by their worsening prospects staged bloody uprisings in 1831 and 1834. In the countryside there were rumors of mass arson. In the face of unrest, the monarchy often resorted to censorship and other forces of repression. Parliament became essentially a rubber stamp. The most advanced liberals demanded that suffrage be broadened, but the government was unyielding. Foreign visitors coming from more authoritarian societies were impressed by France's apparently liberal institutions (see the box, "Encounters with the West: A Moroccan Description of the French Freedom of the Press"), but many French liberals saw the regime as a travesty of the hopes and promises it had represented on coming to power in 1830. In-

augurated by revolution, in a few years it would face revolution.

Great Britain

In comparison to the rest of Europe, Great Britain enjoyed considerable constitutional guarantees and a parliamentary regime. Yet liberals and radicals found their government retrograde and repressive. Traumatized by the French Revolution, the ruling class clung to the past, certain that advocates for change were Jacobins in disguise. Change seemed to invite revolution.

Social unrest beset Britain as it faced serious economic dislocation. The arrival of peace in 1815 led to a sudden drop in government expenditures, the return into the economy of several hundred thousand men who had been away at war, financial disarray, and a drop in prices. There was much discontent among the poor and the middle classes, who were incensed by the clear economic advantages that the landed classes, dominating Parliament, had secured for themselves in 1815 in passing the Corn Law. This legislation imposed high tariffs on imported "corn"—that is, various forms of grain. It thus shielded the domestic market from international competition and allowed landowners to reap huge profits at the expense of consumers. All these issues were cause for demonstrations, petitions, protest marches, and other challenges to the authorities.

In August 1819, sixty thousand people gathered in St. Peter's Fields in Manchester to demand universal suffrage for men and women alike, an annual Parliament, and other democratic reforms. The crowd was peaceful and unarmed, but when a speaker whom the government considered a rabble-rouser took to the podium, mounted soldiers charged, attempting to arrest him. In the ensuing melee, eleven people were killed and four hundred wounded. The British public was shocked by this use of violence against peaceful demonstrators. Parliament responded in autumn 1819 by passing the Six Acts, which outlawed freedom of assembly and effectively imposed censorship.

While continuing conservative policies, the government began to embrace change in the 1820s. The provisions that prevented Catholics from holding any government position and from serving in Parliament were removed in 1829. In

~ **ENCOUNTERS WITH THE WEST** ~

A Moroccan Description of the French Freedom of the Press

In 1845–1846 a Moroccan diplomatic mission visited Paris; the ambassador's secretary, Muhammad as-Saffar (d. 1881), wrote an account of this visit. He was struck by many aspects of French society, and in the following passage he described France's press.

The people of Paris, like all the French—indeed, like all of [Europe]—are eager to know the latest news and events that are taking place in other parts [of the world]. For this purpose they have the gazette. [In] these papers . . . they write all the news that has reached them that day about events in their own country and in other lands both near and far.

This is the way it is done. The owner of a newspaper dispatches his people to collect everything they see or hear in the way of important events or unusual happenings. Among the places where they collect the news are the two Chambers, the Great and the Small, where they come together to make their laws. When the members of the Chamber meet to deliberate, the men of the gazette sit nearby and write down everything that is said, for all debating and ratifying of laws is matter for the gazette and is known to everyone. No one can prevent them from doing this. . . .

. . . [I]f someone has an idea about a subject but he is not a member of the press, he may write about it in the gazette and make it known to others, so that the leaders of opinion learn about it. If the idea is worthy they may

follow it, and if its author was out of favor it may bring him recognition.

No person in France is prohibited from expressing his opinion or from writing it and printing it, on condition that he does not violate the law. . . .

In the newspapers they write rejoinders to the men of the two Chambers about the laws they are making. If their Sultan demands gifts from the notables or goes against the law in any way, they write about that too, saying that he is a tyrant and in the wrong. He cannot confront them or cause them harm. Also, if someone behaves out of the ordinary, they write about that too, making it common knowledge among people of every rank. If his deeds were admirable, they praise and delight in him, lauding his example; but if he behaved badly, they revile him to discourage the like.

Moreover, if someone is being oppressed by another, they write about that too, so that everyone will know the story from both sides just as it happened, until it is decided in court. One can also read in it what their courts have decided.

Source: Susan Gilson Miller, ed. and trans., *Disorienting Encounters—Travels of a Moroccan Scholar in France in 1845–1846. The Voyage of Muhammad as-Saffar* (Berkeley: University of California Press, 1992), pp. 150–153.

other ways as well, a more just order was introduced. The number of crimes punishable by death was reduced to just one, homicide. Prison reforms were made. Sir Robert Peel (1788–1850), heir to a manufacturing fortune and an enthusiastic reader of Bentham's works, was the driving force behind many of these reforms. He became home secretary (with duties including internal security) in 1828,

and the following year he organized an efficient London police force, known ever after as "bobbies" in his honor, to control crime and contain popular protests.

The major political problem facing Britain in the early nineteenth century was the composition of Parliament. It did not reflect the dramatic population shifts that had occurred since the seventeenth century. Industrialization had transformed mere villages into major cities—Manchester, Birmingham, Leeds, Sheffield—but those cities had no representation in Parliament. Localities that had lost population, however, were still represented. In districts known as "pocket boroughs," single individuals owned the right to a seat in Parliament. In districts known as "the rotten boroughs," a handful of voters elected a representative.

News of the July 1830 revolution in Paris encouraged liberals to push for reform and made some conservatives reluctant to oppose reform for fear of suffering the same fate as the hapless Charles X. In 1831 the liberal Whig government of Earl Grey (1764–1845), a hereditary peer who nevertheless was well attuned to the demands of the middle classes, introduced a reform bill abolishing or reducing representation for sparsely populated areas while granting representation for the populous and unrepresented cities. The bill also widened the franchise by lowering property qualifications to include many middle-class men. Following a prolonged, bitter political battle between the government and middle classes on one side and aristocracy on the other, the House of Lords finally passed what came to be known as the "Great Reform Bill of 1832."

The reform was not particularly radical. Only the upper layers of the middle class were enfranchised, or one of seven adult males. The old franchise had not excluded women from the vote, but the new law did so. Yet despite its shortcomings, the reform demonstrated the willingness of the political leaders to acknowledge the increasing economic importance of manufacturing. Parliament became a more representative forum whose composition better reflected the shift of economic power from agricultural landowners to the industrial and commercial classes. The bill passed as a result of nationwide agitation; its passage revealed the ability of the political system to bring about reform peacefully.

Parliament justified the population's new-found faith in its efficacy by undertaking several more reforms. The Poor Law of 1834 had a mixed impact. The new law denied aid to the able-bodied, no matter how destitute, offering them only the option of entering workhouses, where prison-like conditions deterred all but the most desperate. This measure of the bill was severe, but another of its features potentially improved the lot of

"Peterloo" Massacre In August 1819 at St. Peter's Fields in Manchester, a crowd demanding parliamentary reform was charged by government troops, leading to bloodshed. Many English people derided the event and called it "Peterloo." (*Public Record Office*)

the poor. Previous poor laws had provided supplements to very low salaries, thus making it unnecessary for employers to pay workers a living wage; such measures depressed wages. The law of 1834 abolished this provision and may have played some role in raising wages. Though harsh toward the poor, the Poor Law was an acknowledgment of a national responsibility for the underprivileged. The following year Parliament passed the Municipal Corporation Act, which provided for more representative municipal councils with increased decision-making powers in local affairs.

A series of colonial reforms also showed a willingness to adapt to changing circumstances. In Britain opposition to slavery had been voiced since the 1780s. (See the box, "A Plea to Abolish Slavery in the British Colonies.") Slavery, the very opposite of human freedom, was an affront to liberal principles. Moreover, its persistence threatened the

A Plea to Abolish Slavery in the British Colonies

Among the causes that British reformers embraced was the abolition of slavery. The slave trade had been abolished in 1807; one more step was left—ending in the colonies the institution of slavery itself. In this petition to Parliament in 1823, the Society for the Mitigation and Gradual Abolition of Slavery Throughout the British Dominions explained the harsh and immoral nature of the institution. Under the pressure of this type of agitation, Parliament in 1833 abolished slavery in the British Empire.

In the colonies of Great Britain there are at this moment upwards of 800,000 human beings in a state of degrading personal slavery.

These unhappy persons, whether young or old, male or female, are the absolute property of their master, who may sell or transfer them at his pleasure, and who may also regulate according to his discretion (within certain limits) the measure of their labour, their food, and their punishment.

Many of the slaves are (and all may be) branded like cattle, by means of a hot iron, on the shoulder or other conspicuous part of the body, with the initials of their master's name; and thus bear about them in indelible characters the proof of their debased and servile state. . . .

It can hardly be alleged that any man can have a right to obtain his fellow creatures in a state so miserable and degrading as has been described. And the absence of such right will be still more apparent, if we consider how these slaves were originally obtained. They, or their parents, were the victims of the Slave Trade. They were obtained, not by lawful means, or under any colourable pretext, but by the most undisguised rapine, and the most atrocious fraud. Torn from their homes and from every dear relation in life, barbarously manacled, driven like herds of cattle to the sea-shore, crowded into the potential holds of slave-ships, they were transported to our colonies and there sold in bondage. . . .

The Government and Legislature of this country have on various occasions, and in the most solemn and unequivocal terms denounced the Slave Trade as immoral, inhuman, and unjust; but the legal perpetuation of that state of slavery, which has been produced by it, is surely, in its principle, no less immoral, inhuman and unjust, than the trade itself. . . .

Source: Reprinted in *Circular Letters of the Society for the Mitigation and Gradual Abolition of Slavery Throughout the British Dominions* (April 1823).

empire—in 1831, 60,000 slaves rebelled in Jamaica. Parliament took heed of the call for change and in 1833 abolished slavery in the British Empire.

In addition, the British began to review their imperial administration. Their control over Canada had been challenged in an uprising in 1837; London sent out a fact-finding mission headed by Lord Durham (1806–1848). As a result of the *Durham Report,* the British government promulgated self-government for Canada in 1839 and 1841; eventually all the British colonies with a majority of white settlers were given similar rights of self-rule.

Reforms solidified Britain's influence overseas. In Canada they reduced opposition to British rule.

The antislavery campaign led to the extension of British power into Africa. Having abolished the slave trade in 1807, the British worked to compel other nations to end the trade. With the largest navy in the world, Britain was well equipped to patrol the coast of West Africa, trying to suppress the traffic in humans and hinder its colonial rivals from benefiting from the trade. Needing bases for these patrols, the British established a number of minor settlements in West Africa, becoming the predominant European power along the coast. Although unimportant when acquired, these possessions foreshadowed the increasing European intrusion into African affairs.

Parliament's reforming zeal stimulated support for Chartism, a movement intended to transform Britain from essentially an oligarchy—rule by a few—into a democracy. In 1838 political radicals with working-class support drew up a "people's charter" calling for universal male suffrage, equal electoral districts, salaries and the abolition of property qualifications for members of Parliament, the secret ballot, and annual general elections. By giving workers the vote, Chartists hoped to end the dominance of narrow upper classes in Parliament and ensure an improvement in the workers' lot. Chartism won wide support among men and women in the working class, sparking demonstrations and petition drives of unprecedented size. Women participated to a larger extent than in any other political movement of the day, founding over a hundred female Chartist organizations. Some Chartists, especially female members, asked for women's suffrage; but this demand failed to gain overall adherence from the membership.

Winning mass support during particularly hard economic years, Chartism lost followers during a temporary economic upswing. The movement also fell under the sway of advocates of violence, who scared off many artisans and potential middle-class supporters. It lost credibility too by criticizing British institutions for being unresponsive to the needs of the working class, whereas in fact Parliament introduced a number of significant reforms. Lacking popular support, Chartism failed as a political movement; yet it drew public attention to an integrated democratic program whose main provisions (except for yearly elections) would be adopted piecemeal over the next half-century.

In 1839 urban businessmen founded the Anti–Corn Law League for the purpose of abolishing the Corn Law of 1815, which was increasing the price of grain. The Corn Law was unpopular with manufacturers, who knew that low food prices would allow them to pay low wages. It was also unpopular with workers, who wanted bread at a price they could afford. The anti–Corn Law movement proved more effective than Chartism because it had the support of the middle classes. Parliament, alarmed by the threat of famine due to the poor harvest of 1845, repealed the Corn Law in 1846.

In the end, repeal did not affect the price of grain. Nevertheless, repeal of the Corn Law was a milestone in British history, demonstrating the extent to which organized groups could bring about economic and social reform by putting pressure on Parliament. It also underscored what the Great Reform Act of 1832 had already revealed: Political and economic power was shifting away from the landed gentry to the urban industrial classes, and the British political system responded more flexibly to this change than did the political systems of the Continent. When revolution broke out on the Continent, it did not cross the English Channel.

Spain

The term *liberal* was first coined in Spain, where the fate of liberals prefigured what would happen elsewhere in continental Europe. In 1812 a national parliament, the Cortes, elected during the Napoleonic occupation, issued a democratic constitution that provided for universal manhood suffrage and a unicameral legislature with control over government policy. Supporters and admirers of the constitution in Spain and elsewhere were known as "liberals," or friends of liberty.

The Bourbon king Ferdinand VII (r. 1808, 1814–1833) was overthrown by Napoleon and replaced by the French emperor's brother, Joseph Bonaparte (r. 1808–1813). In 1814 Ferdinand returned to power, promising to respect the 1812 constitution. But Ferdinand was by temperament hostile to the new order, and he was a believer in the divine right of kings. He had no real intention of abiding by the constitution of 1812, a document drawn up by the educated middle classes and reflecting their anticlericalism and desire for power. Ferdinand drew his support from the aristocracy and from segments of the general population still loyal to the call of throne and altar. Liberals were arrested or driven into exile.

Ferdinand's plan to restore Spain to its earlier prominence included a reassertion of control over its American colonies. The Spanish dominions had grown restless in the eighteenth century, for they had witnessed the advent of an independent United States and the French occupation of Spain itself. The dominions refused to recognize the Napoleonic regime in Madrid and became increasingly self-reliant. Their attitude did not change when French control of Spain ended. Ferdinand refused to compromise with the overseas territories. Instead, he gathered an army to subdue them. Some liberal junior officers, declaring the army's

EUROPEAN REVOLUTIONS, 1820–1831

January 1820	Spain
July 1820	Naples
August 1820	Portugal
March 1821	Piedmont; Greece
December 1825	Russia
July 1830	France
August 1830	Belgium
September 1830	Brunswick; Saxony; Hesse-Cassel
November 1830	Poland
February 1831	Revolt in Piedmont, Modena, and Parma; revolt in Papal States

loyalty to the constitution of 1812, won support from the rank and file, who balked at going overseas. This military mutiny coincided with a sympathetic provincial uprising to produce the "revolution of 1820," the first major assault on the European order established in 1815 at the Congress of Vienna. Ferdinand appealed to the European powers for help. France intervened on his behalf and crushed the uprising.

Ferdinand restored his reactionary regime but could not regain Spain's American colonies. The British, sympathetic to the cause of Latin American independence and eager for commercial access to the region, opposed reconquest, and their naval dominance of the seas rendered Britain's opposition effective. The United States, meanwhile, had recognized the independence of the Latin American republics and wished to see their independence maintained. In 1823 President James Monroe issued the statement known as the Monroe Doctrine, proclaiming U.S. opposition to any European colonization or intervention in the affairs of independent republics in the Americas. The United States had no military power to back this proclamation, but the British navy effectively enforced it. By 1825 all Spain's colonies on the mainland in Central and South America had won their freedom.

The newly independent states patterned their regimes on models of Spanish liberalism; all of them had constitutions, separation of powers, and guaranteed human rights. Brazil, the Portuguese empire in the Americas, was a monarchy for most of the rest of the nineteenth century, as was Mexico for a short time, but all the other states became republics, opting for what was then an unusual form of government. Although most of the Latin regimes eventually became despotic, lip service continued to be paid to liberal values.

Upon Ferdinand's death in 1833, Spain was torn by competing claims to the succession. A civil war between liberal and conservative factions led to extreme cruelty on both sides. The moderates and liberals won, but the military gained the upper hand in governing. A Cortes and what appeared to be constitutional government were established, but real power lay in the hands of the army, representing a small oligarchy of the business and landowning classes. Several successive officers served as dictators of the country, replacing each other in a series of coups. One of them, General Ramón Narváez (1799–1868), brutally ran the country from 1844 to 1851. When he was on his deathbed, he was asked whether he forgave his enemies. He answered, "I have no enemies. I have shot them all!"

Austria and the German States

The Austrian empire's far-flung territories seemed to its Habsburg rulers to require a firm hand (see Map 20.1). Liberalism, which challenged imperial power, could not be countenanced. Nor, in this multinational empire, could nationalism be tolerated. The emperor, Francis I (r. 1806–1835), was opposed to any change; his motto was "Rule and change nothing." Prince Metternich, Francis's chief minister, viewed the French Revolution of 1789 and its aftermath as a disaster and believed his task was to hold the line against the threat of revolution. Quick to interpret protests or the desire for change as a threat to the fundamental order, Metternich established a network of secret police and informers to spy on the imperial subjects and keep them in check.

In most of the German states, the political order was authoritarian and inflexible. The states of Baden and Württemberg in the west and Bavaria in the south had been granted constitutions by their rulers, although effective power remained in the hands of the ruling houses. The king of Prussia had repeatedly promised a constitution, but none had materialized. A central, representative Diet would not meet until 1847. Prussia was ruled by an alliance of the king and the *Junkers*, the landowning aristocrats who staffed the officer corps and the bureaucracy. Both the officer corps and the bureaucracy were efficient enough to serve as models for the rest of Europe. Where Prussia lagged by liberal standards was in its political institutions.

Throughout the German states, the urban middle classes, intellectuals, journalists, university professors, and students were frustrated with the existing system. They were disappointed by the lack of free institutions and the failure of the patriotic wars against Napoleon to create a united Germany. University students formed *Burschenschaften*, or brotherhoods, whose slogan was "Honor, Liberty, Fatherland." Metternich imposed a policy of reaction on the German Confederation and had it adopt the Carlsbad Decrees in July 1819, establishing close supervision over the universities, censorship of the press, and dissolution of the youth groups. Wholesale persecution of liberals and nationalists followed. The Prussian king dismissed his more enlightened officials.

The outbreak of revolution in Paris in 1830 inspired further political agitation. The authoritarian ruler of the state of Brunswick was forced to resign. Under pressure, his successor and the rulers of Saxony, Hanover, and Hesse-Cassel promulgated new constitutions. Mounting opposition to local despots and agitation for national unity led to the prosecution of outspoken liberals. Many associated with the nationalist "Young Germany" movement fled abroad, particularly to Paris.

Renewed nationalist agitation swept the German states in the 1840s. In response to possible French ambitions on the Rhine during a diplomatic crisis in 1840, there was a mass outpouring of patriotic sentiment. Two patriotic songs were penned: "The Watch on the Rhine" and "Deutschland, Deutschland über alles" ("Germany, Germany above all"), the latter becoming Germany's national anthem half a century later. German rulers, who in the past had been reluctant to support the national idea, now attempted to co-opt it. In Bavaria King Ludwig II built the Walhalla, named after the hall where fallen heroes gather in

Germanic lore; Ludwig's Walhalla was to be a "sacred monument" to German unity adorned with statues of famous Germans. The Cologne Cathedral, unfinished in its construction, became a symbol of German enthusiasm; from all over Germany donations came in to finish it. Inaugurating the rebuilding, Prussia's King William Frederick IV (r. 1840–1861) declared it "the spirit of German unity and strength." These events suggested a broadening base for nationhood, which potentially could replace the existing system of a fragmented Germany.

Italy

Austria exercised considerable power over Italy through its possession of Italian territory. Some lands had been acquired in the eighteenth century; some, like Lombardy and Venetia, were acquired in 1815 (see Map 20.1). Austria had dynastic ties to several ruling houses in the central part of the peninsula and political alliances with others, including the papacy. The only ruling house free of Austrian ties—and hence eventually looked to by nationalists as a possible rallying point for the independence of the peninsula—was the Savoy dynasty of Piedmont-Sardinia.

Italy consisted of eight political states, and it was in Austria's interest to maintain disunity. Many Italian rulers—notably the papacy, the kingdom of Naples, and the central Italian duchies—imposed repressive policies, knowing that they could count on Austrian assistance in case of a popular uprising. Metternich's interventions to crush liberal rebellions generated hatred of Austria among Italian liberals and nationalists.

Political reaction in the Italian states cannot be wholly blamed on Austria, however. Piedmont, which was free of Austrian influence, nevertheless embraced restoration. When the royal house of Savoy returned to power in 1815, it nullified all laws passed during Napoleon's reign and banned from government service all officials who had served the French. The Jesuits were put in charge of education and censorship.

Throughout Italy, there was resistance to the restoration. Liberal journalists favored a constitutional system. The Carbonari (literally, "charcoal burners," suggestive of men of simple occupations), a nationalist conspiratorial group that had been formed to fight the French occupation, after

1815 targeted the restoration regimes. In March 1821, liberal-minded young army officers in Piedmont, inspired by recent events in Spain, proclaimed their support of a constitution and their desire to evict Austria from Italy. The movement, essentially military, did not win much popular support. With the help of Austria, Piedmontese loyal to the monarch Charles Felix (r. 1821–1831) crushed the uprising.

A decade later, catalyzed by the July revolution in Paris, the same forces came to the fore. An uprising broke out in Piedmont, then spread to the Papal States and Modena. The revolt was aimed at the authoritarian rulers of the various Italian states, but it was also in support of a united Italy. Led by intellectuals and some members of the middle classes, the uprisings lacked a popular base and were fragmented by the participants' primary loyalties to their individual states and cities. The Austrians promptly crushed hopes for the liberty and unity of Italy.

Russia

By far the most autocratic of the European states was tsarist Russia. Since 1801 it had been ruled by Alexander I (r. 1801–1825). An enigmatic character whose domestic policy vacillated between liberalism and reaction and whose foreign policy wavered between brutal power politics and apparently selfless idealism, Alexander puzzled his contemporaries. When the Congress of Vienna gave additional Polish lands to the tsar, he demonstrated his liberalism to the world (and curried favor with his new subjects) by granting Poland a liberal constitution. But he offered no such constitution to his own people. He and his council discussed terms for the abolition of serfdom in 1803 and again in 1812, but like so many of his plans this one was not implemented. Although he earnestly desired freedom for the serfs, the tsar was unwilling to impose any policy detrimental to the interests and privileges of the landed gentry.

Toward the end of his rule, Alexander became increasingly authoritarian and repressive, probably in response to growing opposition. Western liberal ideas, including constitutionalism, were adopted by Russian military officers who had served in western Europe, by Russian Freemasons who had corresponded with Masonic lodges in western Europe, and by Russian intellectuals who read Western liberal political tracts. These groups formed secret societies with varying programs. Some envisioned Russia as a republic, others as a constitutional monarchy, but all shared a commitment to the abolition of serfdom and the establishment of a freer society.

Alexander died in December 1825, leaving ambiguous which of his brothers would succeed him. Taking advantage of the confusion, the military conspirators declared in favor of the older brother, Constantine, in the belief that he favored a constitutional government. The younger brother, Nicholas, claimed to be the legal heir. The St. Petersburg garrison rallied to the conspirators' cause. The officers, taking their cue from the Spanish uprising of 1820, believed that the military could bring about change on its own in a country in which popular participation in governance was unknown.

The "Decembrist uprising," as it is known, quickly failed. The military revolt in the Russian capital was badly coordinated with uprisings planned in the countryside, and Nicholas moved quickly to crush the rebellion. He had the leaders executed, sent to Siberia, or sent into exile. In spite of its tragic end, throughout the nineteenth century the Decembrist uprising served as an inspiration to Russians resisting tsarist oppression.

Coming to the throne after crushing a revolt, Nicholas I (r. 1825–1855) was obsessed with the danger of revolution and determined to suppress all challenges to his authority. The declared goal of his rule was to uphold "orthodoxy, autocracy, and nationality." Nicholas created a stern, centralized bureaucracy to control all facets of Russian life. He originated the modern Russian secret police called the "Third Section"; it was above the law—a state within the state. Believing in the divine right of monarchs, Nicholas refused to accept limits to his imperial powers. The tsar supported the primacy of the Russian Orthodox church within Russian society; the church in turn upheld the powers of the state. Nicholas also used nationalism to strengthen the state, glorifying the country's past and trying to Russify non-Russian peoples, especially the Poles, by imposing the Russian language on them.

Russia's single most overwhelming problem was serfdom. Economically, serfdom had little to recommend it; free labor was far more efficient.

Moreover, public safety was threatened by the serfs' dissatisfaction with their lot. During Nicholas's thirty-year reign there were over six hundred peasant uprisings, half of them quelled by the military. Nicholas understood that serfdom had to be abolished for Russia's own good, but he could envision no clear alternative to it. Emancipation, he believed, would only sow further disorder. Except for a few minor reforms, he did nothing. Nicholas's death, followed by Russia's defeat in the Crimean War (see page 812), eventually brought to an end the institution that had held nearly half of the Russian people in bondage.

The Ottoman Empire

In its sheer mass, the Ottoman Empire continued to be a world empire. It extended over three continents. In Africa it ran across the whole North African coast. In Europe it stretched from Dalmatia (on the Adriatic coast) to Constantinople. In Asia it extended from Mesopotamia (present-day Iraq) to Anatolia (present-day Turkey). But it was an empire in decline, seriously challenged from within by nationalist movements and from outside by foreign threats.

The Ottoman bureaucracy, once the mainstay of the government, had fallen into decay. In the past, officials had been recruited and advanced by merit; now lacking funds, Constantinople sold government offices. Tax collectors ruthlessly squeezed the peasantry. The Janissaries, formerly an elite military force, by the eighteenth century had become an undisciplined band that menaced the peoples of the Ottoman Empire—especially those located at great distances from the close control of the capital. The reform-minded Sultan Selim III (r. 1789–1807) sought to curb the army, but he was killed by rebellious Janissaries, who forced the new ruler, Mahmud II (r. 1808–1839), to retract most of the previous improvements. The worst features of the declining empire were restored.

Most of the Ottoman Empire was inhabited by Muslims, but in the Balkans Christians were in the majority. Ottoman officials usually treated Christians no differently from their Muslim neighbors. But the Christian subject people found in their religion a means of collectively resisting a harsh and at times capricious rule. Some Christian peoples in the Balkans looked back nostalgically to earlier eras—the Greeks to when they had formed a great

Nicholas I, Emperor of Russia Acceding to the throne at the same time as the Decembrist uprising, Nicholas was haunted by the danger of revolution and ran a repressive regime. *(The Fotomas Index)*

civilization or the Serbs to when they had lived under Serb rule. The ideas of nationalism and liberty that triggered changes in western Europe also stirred the peoples of the Balkans.

The Serbs were the first people to revolt successfully against Ottoman rule. A poor, mountainous region, Serbia suffered greatly from the rapaciousness of the Janissaries. In protest a revolt broke out in 1804. At first the Ottomans were able to quell the uprising, but in 1815 they had to recognize one of its leaders, Milosh Obrenovich (r. 1815–1839), as governor and allow the formation of a national assembly. In 1830, under pressure from Russia, which took an interest in fellow Slavs and members of the Orthodox faith, Constantinople recognized Milosh as hereditary ruler over an autonomous Serbia.

The Greeks' struggle led to complete independence from Ottoman rule. Greeks served as administrators throughout the Ottoman lands and, as merchants and seafarers, traveled widely throughout the Mediterranean world and beyond. They had encountered the ideas of the French Revolution; wanting to revive their own homeland, they formed a conspiratorial group, the *Philike Hetairia* (Society of Friends), which was dedicated to restoring Greek independence.

Greek peasants were not particularly interested in politics, but they were hostile to the Turks, who had accumulated vast landholdings at their expense. This in part motivated Greek peasants to join the anti-Turkish revolt that began in 1821. Greeks killed large numbers of defenseless Turks in the Morea, in the Peloponnesus. The Turkish authorities hanged the Greek patriarch in Constantinople and massacred or sold into slavery the population of the Aegean island of Chios. The war continued fitfully. By 1827 the Ottomans, aided by their vassal Mehemet Ali (1769–1849) of Egypt, controlled most of the Balkan peninsula. The rest of Europe, excited by the idea of an independent Greece restored to its past greatness, widely supported the Greek movement for freedom. The Great Powers intervened in 1827, sending their navies to intercept supplies intended for the Ottoman forces. At Navarino Bay, in the southwest of the Peloponnesus, the Ottoman navy fired on the allies, who returned fire and sank the Turkish ships. With the destruction of Ottoman power, the independence of Greece was ensured. In 1830 an international agreement spelled out Greek independence.

In the 1820s and 1830s, local agitation and several Russian military interventions weakened Ottoman control over Wallachia and Moldavia (future Romania). Constantinople lost its right to name the governors of the provinces. It had to reduce its fortifications there, and from 1828 to 1834 Russian troops occupied the provinces.

Losing influence in the Balkans, the Ottoman Empire was also challenged elsewhere. In Egypt, Mehemet Ali modernized his army and used it to wrest Syria away in 1831. He threatened to march against his overlord, the sultan. Britain and Russia, concerned lest the Ottoman Empire collapse and thus threaten the region's balance of power, intervened on the empire's behalf. Constantinople won back Syria but in 1841 had to acknowledge Mehemet Ali as the hereditary ruler of Egypt. The

survival of the Ottoman Empire was beginning to depend on the goodwill of the Great Powers.

THE REVOLUTIONS OF 1848

From France in the west to Poland in the east, at least fifty separate revolts and uprisings shook the Continent in 1848, the most extensive outbreak of popular violence in nineteenth-century Europe (Map 20.2). The revolt had an impact far beyond Europe's borders. Brazilians, inspired by the example of the European revolutions, rose up against their government. In Bogota, Colombia, church bells rang to celebrate the announcement of a republic in France. And as a result of the Parisian revolution, slaves in French colonies were emancipated.

Roots of Rebellion

At no time since 1800 had so many Europeans been involved in collective action. There were many reasons for this outbreak of discontent. In the countryside, such changes in access to land as land enclosure (see page 689) frustrated peasants. Although in the past many had enjoyed free access to village commons, these were coming increasingly under private control, or there was competition for their use; formerly a peasant might have grazed his sheep in the commons, but now his two or three competed with herds of sometimes hundreds of sheep, owned by a rich farmer. Also, the poor once had relatively free access to forests to forage for firewood, but the limitation of this right now led to frequent conflicts in the countryside.

Points of friction were made worse by growing populations that put pressure on available resources. In the urban environment there was a crisis in the handicrafts industry, which dominated city economies. Urban artisans were being undercut by the putting-out system or cottage industry (see page 690), in which capitalists had goods produced in the countryside by cottagers—part-time artisans who supported themselves partly through agriculture and were thus willing to work for lower wages. Crises in the crafts hurt the journeymen who wanted to be masters; they had to serve far longer apprenticeships and in many cases could never expect promotion. Where the guild system still existed, it was in decline, unable

Map 20.2 Major Revolutions and Reforms, 1848–1849 In no other year had as many revolts broken out simultaneously; in many cases the revolutions led to reforms and new constitutions.

to protect the economic interests of artisans anxious about their future.

These developing concerns came to a crisis point as a result of the economic depression of 1845–1846. In 1845 there was a crop disaster, including the spread of potato blight, destroying the basic food of the poor in northern Europe. Wheat and rye production also plummeted. Food prices doubled from what they had been in the early 1840s. An industrial downturn accompanied these agricultural disasters, creating massive unemployment. Municipal and national governments seemed unable to deal with the crowding, disease, and unsanitary conditions that were worsening tensions running high in the cities, the sites of national governments. People were ready to heed

those who called for the overthrow of the existing regimes. The established political and administrative elites were disoriented and found they could not count on their traditional sources of support. Revolts were triggered by discontent, but also by the hope for change.

France

Once again the spark for revolution was ignited in Paris and spread from there to the rest of the Continent. Economic crisis had a severe impact in the French capital. In some occupations as many as half the people were out of work. The price of bread had shot up to over one franc a pound, which meant that the entire salary of the average male worker—a franc a day—would not even buy enough bread to sustain him. Thousands of workers were willing to pour into the streets to protest the government's seeming indifference to their desperation.

Meanwhile, liberals were agitating for the expansion of suffrage. When political meetings were forbidden in 1847, they resorted to banquets featuring long-winded toasts indistinguishable from political speeches. Such a banquet was scheduled for Paris on February 22, 1848, to celebrate the birthday of George Washington—an icon to French liberals. When the government banned the meeting, mass demonstrations by students and workers broke out. Unlike the British with their professional urban police, the French had no forces trained in crowd control. The government called in the military, whose tactics were more appropriate to engaging an enemy army than to containing civilian demonstrators. On February 23, soldiers guarding the Ministry of Foreign Affairs panicked and shot into a crowd; fifty-two people died.

Word spread that the government was shooting at the people. To protect themselves, residents of the traditionally revolutionary neighborhoods near the Bastille square erected barricades. On February 24, police and army posts were attacked, and the royal palace was surrounded. The National Guard, a civilian force recruited from the artisans and the middle class and charged with restoring order, had become sympathetic to the protesters and refused to fight the populace. Louis Philippe resigned as king and fled for London under the pseudonym "Mr. Smith." The royalists were clearly discredited.

The abruptness of the king's resignation left the opposition in disarray. The protesters shared one goal, the extension of suffrage, but otherwise diverged sharply. Liberals accepted the monarchy but were offended by its corruption, manipulation of elections, and restrictive suffrage. More radical elements favored a democratic republic. Socialists' prime goal was a government that would ensure social justice.

The new regime, hastily organized under the pressure of a mob invasion of the Chamber of Deputies, lacked uniformity in its makeup or ideas. The provisional government consisted of well-known liberal opponents of the July Monarchy such as the poet Alphonse de Lamartine (1790–1869) and the journalist Alexandre Ledru-Rollin (1807–1874). Under pressure from the radicals, socialist journalist Louis Blanc (see page 750) and a worker known only as Albert joined the government. At first, the liberal supporters of constitutional democracy and the radical republicans committed to economic justice for the underprivileged cooperated with each other. Under the strain of events, however, the coalition fell apart by late spring.

Bowing to pressure from the poor and unemployed of Paris, who resorted to demonstrations and occupied City Hall, the government established national workshops and a commission headed by Louis Blanc to study the problems of the poor. The national workshops were not a substitute for the capitalist order, as Louis Blanc had intended, but were a stopgap measure to enable the unemployed to earn a livelihood. They nevertheless represented the most ambitious plan that any French government had yet undertaken to combat the misery of the poor.

The new republic was quick to institute other reforms. It abolished slavery in the colonies and the death penalty for political crimes. Imprisonment for debt ceased, and the workday was limited to ten hours in Paris, eleven hours in the départements. The most radical move was the adoption of universal male suffrage. Men in 1789 had identified citizenship as a distinctly male prerogative, and they continued to do so.

In the general euphoria over human liberties, women asserted their rights. A new woman's newspaper, *La Voix des Femmes* (*The Voice of Women*), argued for equal pay, political rights, and educational opportunities. Many of the militants took their cue from the women who had fought for their rights in 1789 (see page 708). Women's political clubs flourished in the capital as well as in Lyon and lesser provincial towns. (See the box: "A Revolutionary of 1848 Calls for Women's Political Rights.") When women's political clubs petitioned for the vote, the revolutionary government abolished them. In light of women's active role at the barricades that had toppled the monarchy, this was a bitter disappointment.

The first universal-manhood elections took place in April. The results were surprising. Nearly everyone expected enfranchisement of the poor and uneducated to bring about the election of radicals and outsiders. Most of France's population, however, consisted of rural peasants. Although

Revolutionary Women In this cartoon, entitled "The Divorced Women," Daumier ridicules women who fought for their rights in the revolution of 1848. They are seen as divorced, deprived of male companionship, and probably therefore crazed. This kind of depiction was one of many ways in which women were discouraged from participating in politics. *(Jean-Loup Charmet)*

there were some radical peasants, particularly in the south, most peasants distrusted the radicalism of the capital and resented the tax increases needed to support social programs. At the polls, peasants tended to vote for their social superiors: the local landowner, notary, or lawyer. Even Paris elected mostly moderate deputies. The new National Assembly elected by popular vote did not look much different from that of the July Monarchy. Most members were landowners and lawyers; among the new deputies, there were only seventeen workers and no peasants.

The government was soon at loggerheads with the radical workers in Paris. Under conservative pressure, the Assembly in May disbanded the national workshops, which were expensive to run and—though they provided a livelihood for more than half of working-class males—were accomplishing little construction of buildings, roads, and the like. At the news of the closings, people who depended on the workshops rose up in de-

spair. After days of fighting in which 1500 were killed and 12,000 arrested, government forces regained control of the city. Passionate feelings on both sides led to savagery: Corpses were mutilated, and severed heads were paraded through the streets. Both the liberal Alexis de Tocqueville and the socialist Karl Marx called the June uprisings class warfare between the poor and the rich.

The defeat of the insurgents revealed that universal suffrage had enabled the government to mobilize moderate public opinion against radicalism in Paris. The advent of railroads had allowed the government to muster military support from outside the city. Thereafter, it would be far more difficult for radical Parisian crowds to dictate policies to the rest of the country.

People had entered into the revolution in February with confidence, but the June uprisings transformed the situation. The propertied classes, feeling menaced by the poor, looked to the authorities for security. Of the several candidates for

A Revolutionary of 1848 Calls for Women's Political Rights

Jeanne Deroin was a French advocate of women's suffrage who served as editor of the newspaper representing women, L'opinion des femmes, *during the revolution of 1848. Frustrated that women were denied a role in the political process, she tried to run for parliament in 1849. In an election poster and in correspondence with a socialist paper, which although socially radical was opposed to female suffrage, Deroin proclaimed the rights of women.*

I present myself for your votes, out of devotion to the consecration of a great principle: the civil and political equality of the sexes.

It is in the name of justice that I appeal to the sovereign people against negating the great principles that are the foundation for the future of our society.

If using your right, you call upon women to take part in the work of the Legislative Assembly, you will consecrate our republican dogmas in all their integrity: Liberty, Equality, Fraternity for all women as well as for all men.

A Legislative Assembly composed entirely of men is incompetent to make the laws that rule a society of men and women, as an assembly composed entirely of privileged people to debate the interests of workers, or an assembly of capitalists to sustain the honor of the country. . . .

It is precisely because woman is equal to man, and yet not identical to him, that she should take part in the work of social reform and incorporate in it those necessary elements that are lacking in man, so that the work can be complete.

Liberty for woman, as well as for man, is the right to utilize and to develop one's faculties freely.

Life's unity can be considered to be in three parts: individual life, family life, and social life; this is a complete life. To refuse woman the right to live the social life is to commit a crime against humanity.

. . . this is a holy and legitimate protest against the errors of the old society and against a clear violation of our sacred principles of liberty, equality, and fraternity.

Source: Election poster to the Electors of the Department of Seine, *L'opinion des femmes,* April 10, 1849; *La Démocratie pacifique,* April 13, 1849. Trans. K. Offen. Reprinted in Susan Groag Bell and Karen M. Offen, eds., *Women, the Family, and Freedom: The Debate in Documents,* vol. I (Stanford: Stanford University Press, 1983), pp. 280–281.

president in 1848, Louis Napoleon (1808–1873), a nephew of Napoleon Bonaparte, appealed to the largest cross section of the population. The bourgeoisie was attracted by the promise of authority and order. Peasants disillusioned by the tax policies of the republic remained loyal to the memory of Napoleonic glory. Workers embittered by the government's repression of the June uprisings were impressed by Louis Napoleon's vaguely socialistic program.

Louis Napoleon received nearly three times as many votes as all his opponents combined. His government was conservative, composed of men

of the old order. Three years later, Louis Napoleon dissolved the National Assembly by force and established a personal dictatorship. In 1852 he declared himself Emperor Napoleon III.

Austria

In Austria, news of the overthrow of Louis Philippe and of agitation in the German states prompted demonstrations and petitions calling for a constitution and the dismissal of Metternich, the symbol of the reactionary order. In the face of growing opposition, Metternich resigned, and the army withdrew from Vienna, which appeared to have fallen under the control of students and workers. On March 15, 1848, the imperial court, surrounded by crowds of students and workers, announced its willingness to issue a constitution. Even more important was the decision to abolish serfdom. There had been fear of a serf uprising, but the relatively generous terms of the emancipation mollified the peasantry.

The promised constitution was issued, but it was drafted by the emperor rather than by representatives of the people. It was probably acceptable to the male middle classes because it enfranchised them, but students and workers who favored popular sovereignty opposed it. Mass demonstrations and an invasion of the prime minister's office prompted the court to leave Vienna for Innsbruck on May 17.

The government also faced revolts in the non-German parts of the empire: in Italy, Hungary, the Czech lands, and Croatia. In March Vienna acquiesced to Hungary's demands; from that point on, Hungary was joined to the Austrian Empire by personal union to the emperor. Constitutional government was then established in Hungary, but participation in the political process was limited to Magyars, who were the single largest ethnic group but who made up only 40 percent of the population. The other peoples of Hungary—Romanians, Slovaks, Croats, and Slovenes—preferred the more distant rule of German Vienna to Magyar authority.

Many nationalities rallied to the Austrian Empire in 1848 for their own reasons—fear of falling under German rule in Bohemia, fear of Magyar rule in Hungary, fear of Polish rule in Galicia (the Austrian part of Poland)—and the empire survived. There was no solidarity among the various nationalities that rose up against Vienna's rule. The empire had been able to practice a policy of divide and rule, yet the dangers nationalism posed to its survival were also revealed.

The revolution in Austria and its possessions was suppressed as soon as the court was able to gather an army and send it against the rebels. Prague was bombarded into submission in June and Vienna in November 1848. By the following August, Austria had crushed the rebellious Hungarians with the help of Russia and suspended the liberal constitution it had previously granted. A reactionary regime under Prince Felix von Schwarzenberg (1800–1852) re-established absolutist rule over the empire.

Italy

In the years before 1848, the Italian peninsula was in the grip of economic hardship and social unrest; nationalists and liberals hoped somehow to see their program of a united and free Italy implemented. The election in 1846 of Pius IX (r. 1846–1878) was seen as a harbinger of change. The pope was not only a religious leader but also secular ruler of the Papal States. Pius appeared to be a liberal and a supporter of Italian unification. In January 1848, revolution forced the king of Sicily to grant a constitution to his subjects. The Sicilian revolution was the first to erupt in Europe, but it was news of the Paris uprising in February that stimulated revolutions elsewhere in Italy.

Italians under Austrian rule revolted, forcing the Austrians to evacuate their Italian possessions. The middle classes, though eager to be free of Austrian rule, saw working-class radicals as a threat. They believed that annexation to nearby Piedmont would provide security from both Austria and the lower classes. The king of Piedmont, Charles Albert (r. 1831–1849), reluctantly decided to unite Italy under his throne if doing so would prevent the spread of radicalism to his kingdom. On March 24, 1848, he declared war on Austria but was defeated in July and had to sue for an armistice.

The pope had expressed sympathy for Italian unification but provided no support for the cause. Republicans, disappointed by the pope's abandonment of the national cause and a liberal program, forced the pope to flee. In January 1849 they declared the Roman Republic. Hope ran high that it would become the capital of a united republican Italy. Giuseppe Mazzini was to be a member of the governing triumvirate.

In Piedmont, meanwhile, Charles Albert's desire to bring the radical movement under control by defeating the Austrians tempted him to declare war on Austria once again, in March 1849. The outcome for Piedmont was even worse than it had been a year earlier. Within six days its army was defeated. Humiliated, Charles Albert resigned his throne to his son, Victor Emmanuel II (r. 1849–1878).

The Austrians quickly reconquered their lost provinces and helped restore their puppet governments to power. Louis Napoleon, the newly elected president of France, eager to curry favor with Catholic voters, sent French troops to Rome, restoring the pope to power in July 1849. Nevertheless, profound liberal and even revolutionary ideas—constitutional government, universal suffrage, abolition of the remnants of the Old Regime—had been expressed and in some cases implemented, though briefly. Most reforms were rescinded, but Piedmont's liberal constitution, the *Statuto*, implemented in 1848, was retained and later became the constitution of a united Italy.

The German States

News of the February uprising in Paris also acted as a catalyst for change in the German states. In response to large public demonstrations in the grand duchy of Baden in southwestern Germany, the duke—reluctant to suffer the same fate as Louis Philippe—dismissed his conservative prime minister and installed in March 1848 a government sympathetic to the aspirations of middle-class liberals. The forces of change seemed irresistible. As the king of Württemberg observed, "I cannot mount on horseback against ideas." The wisest course appeared to be compromise. He and many of his fellow dukes and princes changed their governments, dismissing their cabinets and instituting constitutions. Bavaria's King Ludwig I (r. 1825–1848), who had scandalized the court by his public liaison with an exotic dancer, found himself without supporters when public demonstrations broke out. The only German monarch to lose his throne, he abdicated in favor of his son.

Up to this point Prussia was conspicuous for being untouched by the revolutionary wave. But when news of Metternich's fall reached Berlin on March 16, middle-class liberals and artisans demonstrated for reforms. To appease his subjects, King Frederick William IV appointed a liberal Rhenish businessman to head a new government. Representative government was introduced, and suffrage was extended, though it was still restricted to men of property. Government, no longer the exclusive preserve of the aristocracy, was opened to men from the liberal professions and the business classes.

The revolutionary outbreaks in the German states in 1848 were triggered by dissatisfaction with local economic and political conditions, not by agitation for German unification. But once the revolutions had taken hold, preoccupying the two largest states, Prussia and Austria—which both opposed unification lest it undermine their power—the question of a single Germany quickly came to the fore. In March 1848, a self-appointed national committee invited five hundred prominent German liberals to convene in Frankfurt to begin the process of national unification. In addition to fulfilling a long-standing liberal dream, a united nation would consolidate the liberal victory over absolutism.

The gathering called for suffrage based on property qualifications. The poor and the artisan classes were thus excluded from the political process and alienated from the evolving new order. The vast majority of those elected to the first all-German National Assembly in 1848 came from the liberal professions; one quarter were lawyers, only four were artisans, and one was a peasant. The liberals rejoiced that they controlled the new parliament, but it was unrepresentative and lacked broad popular support.

The first all-German elected legislature met in May 1848 in Frankfurt to pursue the unification of Germany. It faced the thorny issue of the shape of this new Germany: which regions should be included and which excluded? The most ambitious plan envisioned a *Grossdeutschland*, or large Germany, consisting of all the members of the German Confederation, including the German-speaking parts of Austria and the Germanized western parts of Bohemia. Such a solution would include many non-Germans, including Poles, Czechs, and Danes. The proponents of *Kleindeutschland*, or small Germany, which would exclude Austria and its possessions, saw their solution as a more likely scenario for national unity, although it would exclude many Germans. They succeeded in the end, largely because the reassertion of Austrian imperial power in the fall of 1848 made the areas under Vienna's control ineligible for inclusion.

The Frankfurt assembly formed a provisional government in June 1848. The individual states, however, including Prussia and Austria, did not recognize the assembly's authority, so it was utterly powerless. The minister of war could not raise any soldiers, and the minister of finance could not impose taxes. The United States, enthusiastic about a new republic consciously modeled

Constitutional Government in Denmark On March 21, 1848, 15,000 Danes, inspired by the example of Paris, marched on the palace to demand constitutional rights. Unlike in the French capital, however, this event was peaceful and led to the establishment of constitutional government. This painting honors the new parliament that came into being after the liberal constitution was adopted in 1849. *(Statens Museum for Kunst, Copenhagen)*

on its own, was one of the few nations to accept an ambassador from the all-German government.

The parliament also lacked the power to transfer authority from the individual states to itself. It might have succeeded if it had called for a national uprising against the princes, but the liberals in Frankfurt were loath to do so. They distrusted the populace and feared working-class opposition. Force was still in the hands of the traditional authorities. At one point, when the parliament was invaded by radicals, it survived only by calling on Prussia to restore order. Its longevity apparently depended on how long the king of Prussia would tolerate it.

By the fall of 1848, a royalist reaction had begun to take shape in Prussia. In October, facing a workers' uprising triggered by economic despair, the king brought soldiers into Berlin, declared a state of siege, and dissolved the Prussian assembly. The Prussian reassertion of royal power, though partial, was a signal for other German rulers in late 1848 to dismiss their liberal ministers.

The moment for liberalism and national unification to triumph had passed by the time the Frankfurt assembly drew up a constitution in the spring of 1849. Having opted for the *Kleindeutsch* solution, the parliament offered the throne to Frederick William IV, king of Prussia. Although the king was not a liberal, he ruled the largest state within the designated empire. If power had to be used to promote and protect German unity, he possessed it in the form of the Prussian army. But Frederick William feared that accepting the throne would lead to war with Austria. Believing in the principle of monarchy, he also did not want an office offered by representatives of the people.

Lacking an alternative plan in case their offer was refused, most members of the Frankfurt assembly went home. A rump parliament and a series of uprisings in favor of German unity were crushed by the Prussian army.

So German unification failed. Liberalism was unable to bring about German unity; other means would be required to do so.

SUMMARY

The revolutions of 1848 released many of the forces for change that had been gathering strength since 1815. In spite of the Congress of Vienna's effort to restore the old order after Napoleon's fall, the generation after 1815 established a new order. The ideas of change that had powered the French Revolution of 1789 continued to shape an era that claimed to be rolling history back to prerevolutionary times. Liberalism contested authoritarianism.

Reform-minded regimes in Europe improved the lives of people in colonies overseas, abolishing slavery in British and then French colonies and providing self-rule for Canada. Some states even turned away from monarchy and experimented with republicanism, a form of government that until then many had thought fit only for small states. All of the Latin American colonies except Mexico became republics on gaining independence from Spain. In Europe during 1848–1849 the French, German, Hungarian, and Roman republics were proclaimed. These experiments suggested new modes of political organization that were to become common in the following century.

The generation after 1815 experienced revolutions frequently and broadly. These uprisings usually failed, and the forces of order were able to recapture power. Yet the status quo was altered. In many cases absolutist rulers had to grant constitutions and accept ministers who were not their choice. Even though most of these arrangements were temporary, they established an important precedent. If unusual in the first half, constitutions became the norm in the second half of the century.

Nationalism arose in these years. The desire for national independence and unity was voiced in Italy, Germany, Hungary, Poland, and the land of the Czechs. The Spanish colonies in freeing themselves from Madrid's rule employed a nationalist discourse borrowed from Europe. Europe

in the second half of the century was to contend with the forces of nationalism that first appeared after 1814.

The middle classes found their position strengthened after 1848. They did not dominate the political system, but their influence was increasing with the growth of entrepreneurship. Middle-class professionals were recruited into the civil services of states determined to streamline their operation in order to withstand revolution more effectively. Revolutionary fervor waned after 1848, but the current of economic and social change continued to transform Europe.

SUGGESTED READING

General Surveys

Hobsbawm, E. J. *The Age of Revolution, 1789–1848*. 1962. A compellingly argued book that describes the era as being dominated by two simultaneous revolutions, the French Revolution and the industrial transformation.

Johnson, Paul. *The Birth of the Modern World Society, 1815–1830*. 1991. A weighty but readable book providing a panoramic view of the era. Particularly strong in providing biographical sketches of some of the major figures of the time.

Langer, William L. *Europe in Social Upheaval, 1832–1852*. 1969. Provides a strong emphasis on the social aspects of these years.

Kissinger, Henry. *A World Restored*. 1957. A study by a future U.S. secretary of state who emphasizes the efforts of diplomats to build an international order resistant to revolution.

Nicolson, Harold. *The Congress of Vienna*. 1946. An account by a prominent British diplomat who provides colorful sketches of the diplomats at Vienna.

Palmer, Alan. *Metternich*. 1972. The best one-volume life in English of the dominant statesman of the era.

Ideological Confrontations

Anderson, Benedict. *Imagined Communities*. 1983. A noted anthropologist underscores the extent to which a nation is an "imagined community."

Carlisle, Robert B. *The Proffered Crown: Saint-Simonianism and the Doctrine of Hope*. 1987. A work that shows the originality of Saint-Simonian thought and its continuity after the founder's death.

Grana, Cesar. *Bohemian vs. Bourgeois: French Society and the Man of Letters in the Nineteenth Century*. 1964. A consideration of the intellectual origins of the notion of artist as rebel.

Harrison, J. F. C. *Quest for the New Moral World: Robert Owen and the Owenites in Britain and America*. 1969. A good biography that views the movement as affected by contemporary religious notions of a coming millennium.

Kedourie, Elie. *Nationalism.* 1960. An account that describes the German romantics as developers of modern nationalism and creators of an essentially pernicious force.

Porter, Roy, and Mikulas Teich, eds. *Romanticism in National Context.* 1988. An up-to-date series of essays on romanticism in different national settings.

Restoration and Reform

Brock, Michael. *The Great Reform Act.* 1973. An account that emphasizes the sense of crisis on the eve of the Great Reform Act.

Bushnell, David, and Neill Macaulay. *The Emergence of Latin America in the Nineteenth Century.* 1988. A brief but suggestive synthesis.

Church, Clive. *Europe in 1830: Revolution and Political Change.* 1983. A view of the end of the restoration period, punctured by the revolutions of 1830, from a European-wide perspective.

Collingham, H. A. C. *The July Monarchy: A Political History of France.* 1988. An account of the divisions in France that continued in spite of the new king's well-meaning efforts.

Jardin, André, and André-Jean Tudesq. *Restoration and Reaction, 1815–1848.* 1988. A general survey of France.

Jones, Gareth Stedman. *The Languages of Class: Studies in English Working-Class History, 1832–1982.* 1983. A work that considers Chartism a movement of the politically disenfranchised seeking a voice within the political system.

Kann, Robert A. *A History of the Habsburg Empire, 1526–1918.* 1977. Examines the problems of maintaining the multinational empire.

Kirmmse, Bruce H. *Kierkegaard in Golden Age Denmark.* 1990. A rich survey of Danish society and politics in the first half of the nineteenth century.

Lincoln, W. Bruce. *Nicholas I: Emperor and Autocrat of All the Russias.* 1978. A biography of the tsar, revealing the ruler's dedication to preserve the autocratic regime and its values.

More, Charles. *The Industrial Age: Economy and Society in Britain, 1750–1985.* 1989. A survey of British economic and social history.

Pinkney, David H. *The French Revolution of 1830.* 1972. The standard work on the subject.

Sheehan, James J. *German History, 1770–1866.* 1989. A survey of the variety and contrast of the German experience.

Sked, Alan. *The Decline and Fall of the Habsburg Empire, 1815–1918.* 1989. A brief, clear study stressing the very real threat the revolutions of 1848 posed to imperial survival.

Woodward, Sir Llewellyn. *The Age of Reform, 1815–1870.* 2d ed. 1962. A strong political narrative of British history.

Woolf, Stuart Joseph. *A History of Italy, 1700–1860.* 1979. A consideration of the problems of political divisions in Italian life.

The Revolutions of 1848

Agulhon, Maurice. *The Republican Experiment.* 1983. A work that stresses how the splits between different political groups made it difficult for revolutionary goals to succeed.

Ginsborg, P. *Daniele Manin and the Venetian Revolution of 1848–1849.* 1979. An account portraying a heroic opponent of Habsburg rule as a representative of the local bourgeoisie.

Price, Roger. *The French Second Republic: A Social History.* 1972. An account suggesting that divisions in French society produced the revolution of 1848 and that local elites asserting their interests caused its demise.

———. *The Revolutions of 1848.* 1989. A general history of the European revolutions describing them as the result of discontent with an economic and political system out of tune with the needs and desires of most peoples.

Sheehan, James J. *German Liberalism in the Nineteenth Century.* 1978. The standard work revealing the difficulties that German liberals faced as early as the first half of the nineteenth century.

Snell, John L. *The Democratic Movement in Germany, 1789–1914.* 1976. A long and detailed work emphasizing the development of a democratic and liberal movement over more than a century.

Sperber, Jonathan. *The European Revolutions, 1848–1851.* 1994. The best up-to-date synthesis, which includes some new emphases, such as the role of rural and religious discontent in shaping the revolts.

Stadelmann, Rudolf. *Social and Political History of the German 1848 Revolution.* 1975. An account in which both the outbreak and the unraveling of the 1848 revolution are attributed to social and political forces.

RAFT OF THE "MEDUSA"

In September 1816 the French were shocked at the news of the disaster that had befallen the government ship, *Méduse* (Medusa), as it headed for Senegal in West Africa the previous July. Including the ship's crew, 400 passengers had boarded the vessel.

The captain of the ship was a nobleman, Duroys de Chaumareys, whom the restoration government had appointed solely on the basis of his family and political connections. Inexperienced as a seaman, the captain clumsily ran his ship aground on the Mauritanian coast, off West Africa, on July 2. The *Medusa* had only six lifeboats capable of carrying a total of 250 people; for the rest of the passengers a raft was rigged with planks, beams, and ropes. The captain and his officers forcefully took over the lifeboats, abandoning 150 passengers, including one woman, to the less secure raft. With no navigational tools and insufficient food and water, the passengers of the raft were at the mercy of stormy seas and a brutal sun. Anger at officers for having abandoned them led seamen on the raft to murder some of their superiors. By the third day, driven by thirst and hunger, some passengers ate their dead companions— killed by exposure or drowned by huge waves. On the sixth day, the strongest among the survivors, fearing that their rations were dwindling, banded together and murdered the weaker ones. On the thirteenth day, the French brig *Argus* spotted the raft and rescued fifteen survivors. Five died soon after, leaving only ten survivors out of the raft's original 150 passengers.

Although the government tried to suppress information about the event, the French press exposed the incompetence and cowardice of Captain de Chaumareys. The event was understood to reflect the weakness of the regime that had appointed him. The selfish act of the captain and his fellow officers suggested the narrow class interest of the restoration government, favoring aristocracy at the cost of the common people.

The French painter Théodore Géricault (1791– 1824) befriended the ship surgeon Henri Savigny,

one of the lucky ten who survived the harrowing experience on the raft of the *Medusa*. In addition to press reports, Géricault thus had a direct eyewitness account of the event. The painter shared Savigny's sense of outrage against the government for having appointed the incompetent captain and for having treated the survivors callously—at one point arresting Savigny for publicizing the tragedy. The light prison sentence imposed on the captain was another source of grievance.

Since 1815 the French government had sought to bring distinction to itself by displaying art in salon expositions. That of 1819 was intended to be larger, more glorious than any previous one. Among its paintings was Géricault's huge canvas—the largest in that year's exposition— measuring 16 feet high by 24 feet wide, innocently titled *Scene of Shipwreck*. Carelessly, the regime had wanted to gain glory for itself by exhibiting this impressive artwork, while at the same time keeping hidden its real subject. But the stratagem failed; everyone recognized the painting to be the *Raft of the "Medusa"* and an attack on the Bourbon regime.

The painting, reproduced here, depicts the moment the survivors have spotted the frigate, the *Argus,* barely visible in the horizon. Notice the figure of an African standing at the fore of the raft, waving a red-and-white cloth to attract the ship's attention. In this painting the nobility and symbol of hope the African symbolizes is an attack on the slave trade, which Britain had abolished but which France was still engaged in. And so by including the African, the painting is implicitly criticizing the restoration regime for sanctioning commerce in humans. Just as the *Argus* is coming to the rescue of the shipwrecked, the painting appears to suggest, so Africans will see the day when their enslavement will be ended.

Historians often regard the *Raft of the "Medusa"* as the most important painting of French romanticism, and it includes nearly all the major themes of the movement. By locating the scene off the coast of Africa, Géricault incorporates an element of ex-

Géricault: Raft of the "Medusa" *(Erich Lessing/Art Resource, NY)*

oticism. Nature—cruel and unforgiving—is central to the scene, reflected in the turbulent sea, dark clouds, and imperiled raft. The canvas includes an extraordinary range of passions: Observe, for example, the inconsolable grief of the figure at the bottom left, a father cradling the dead body of his son. Other figures express despair and terror, and still others limitless hope. The painting evokes the dark passions humans are capable of. Although it does not show the scenes of insanity, murder, and cannibalism that the survivors had witnessed, they undoubtedly came to the mind of the viewers, who were familiar with the tragic events. The painting was a powerful indictment of Enlightenment faith in humans as creatures of reason and balance.

Romantic artists wanted to engage the passions of those viewing, reading, or hearing their works. *Raft of the "Medusa"* purposely stages the events in the foreground in order to pull viewers into the picture and make them participants in the drama; they thus share in the alternating feelings of terror and hope that swept the raft.

The fate of the painting and the artist followed a romantic script. When Géricault started the painting, he intended it as an indictment of the restoration government. He poured energy into it in an effort to take his mind off a disastrous love affair, and as his work proceeded he came to see the painting as an allegory of larger human passions and concerns. Yet when it was displayed, much to his disappointment, the painting was mainly understood in political terms. Disillusioned by this reaction, Géricault thereafter painted no major works. He grew sickly, rarely bestirred himself, and died of bone tuberculosis in 1824, aged 33. He illustrated the romantics' view of a heroic life—the genius who performs a major feat and then dies young, before realizing his potential. To the romantics, human intent and effort often appeared thwarted by larger forces. This painting, originally meant to criticize the regime, was after Géricault's death purchased by the restoration government and hung in France's national museum, the Louvre. ❧

The Industrial Transformation of Europe

As his country was swept by economic and technological changes, the eighteenth-century English writer Samuel Johnson (1709–1784) remarked, "The age is running mad after innovation. All the business of the world is to be done in a new way." A generation later, in the 1830s, the French socialist Louis Blanqui (see page 751), struck by the dramatic transformations across the Channel, proposed a descriptive term for them, suggesting that just as France had experienced a political revolution, so Britain was undergoing an "industrial revolution." Eventually, that expression entered the general vocabulary to describe the advances in production that occurred first in England and were dominating most of western Europe by the end of the nineteenth century. Many economic historians now emphasize how gradual and cumulative the changes were and question the appropriateness of the term. Indeed, it seems best to discuss the changes not as an industrial revolution but as a continuous process of economic transformation.

Industrial development left its mark on just about every sphere of human activity. Scientific and rational methods altered production. Economic activity became increasingly specialized. The unit of production changed from the family to a larger and less personal group. Significant numbers of workers left farming to enter mining and manufacturing, and major portions of the population moved from a rural to an urban environment. Machines replaced or supplemented manual labor.[1]

The economic changes physically transformed Europe. Greater levels of production were achieved and more wealth was created than ever before. Factory chimneys belched soot into the air. Miners in search

The Nineteenth Century, Iron and Coal (detail), by William Bell Scott.

of coal, iron ore, and other minerals cut deep gashes into the earth. Cities, spurred by industrialization, grew quickly, and Europe became increasingly urban.

Industrialization simultaneously created unprecedented advancement and opportunity as well as unprecedented hardships and social problems. Different groups tried various strategies to strike a balance between the positive and negative effects. Many entrepreneurs and their sympathizers stood for liberal principles based on classical economics. Workers, with a growing sense of solidarity, struggled for their common interests. Out of the socialist ideologies of the early nineteenth century, Karl Marx forged a militant ideology to address the needs of the industrial working class.

SETTING THE STAGE FOR INDUSTRIALIZATION

No one can say with certainty which conditions were necessary for the industrialization of Europe. Nevertheless, we do know why industrialization did not spread widely to the rest of the world in the nineteenth century. A certain combination of conditions—geographic, cultural, economic, demographic—helped make industrialization possible in Europe.

Why Europe?

A fortunate set of circumstances seems to explain why Europe was the stage for industrial development. Since the Middle Ages, political transformations in western Europe reduced risk and uncertainty while encouraging productive investment. With the development of legal due process, rich merchants did not run the risk of having their wealth confiscated—as they did, for instance, in the Ottoman Empire. The unfolding of state power in Europe reduced the frequency of brigandage—still common in many parts of the world—and thus encouraged trade. Discrepancies in risk are apparent in the differences in interest rates on borrowing money in the eighteenth century: 3 percent in England, 36 percent in China.

In Europe, disparities of wealth, though serious, were less extreme than in other parts of the world; thus, there was a better market for goods. At the time western Europe industrialized, the average yearly income per person was equivalent to $500—more than the amount in many non-Western societies even today. And nearly half of the population was literate, again a very high proportion compared to non-Western societies.

Although population grew in Europe during the eighteenth century (see page 687), late marriages and limited family sizes kept its rise in check; hence European society was rarely overwhelmed by the pressures of population. In India and China, by contrast, population growth was so dramatic that society had to be fully engaged to feed the people and could not be readily mobilized for other production.

Europe enjoyed a measure of cultural, political, and social diversity unknown elsewhere. Challenges to dominant religious and political powers had brought some religious diversity—a rarity outside the West, where large territories tended to be dominated by a single ruler and faith. Diversity encouraged a culture that tolerated and eventually promoted innovation. Competitiveness drove states to try to catch up with each other. Governments actively encouraged industries and commerce to enrich a country and make it more powerful than its neighbors. None of these factors alone explains why industrialization occurred, but their combination seems to have facilitated the process when it did occur.[2]

The industrialization of Europe radically transformed power relationships between the industrial West and nonindustrial Africa, Asia, and South America. By 1900 the latter were overwhelmed by the economic and military power of the former. Within Europe, power shifted to the nations that were most industrial. Britain was the first to industrialize, and it was the dominant political power throughout the nineteenth century. Britain was widely admired and seen not only as an economic model but also as a political and cultural one. As France had been the dominant power in the eighteenth century, so Britain dominated the nineteenth, a stellar accomplishment for a small island nation.

Transformations Accompanying Industrialization

A number of transformations preceded or accompanied and helped define the industrializing era. Changes in commerce, agriculture, transportation,

~ ENCOUNTERS WITH THE WEST ~

A Persian Discovers the British Rail System

In 1836 a delegation of three Persian princes visited England. Traveling widely, they had the opportunity to meet important Englishmen and to inspect and experience some of the new technological advances, including the railroad. One of the princes, Najaf-Kuli Mirza, wrote down his observations. In this entry on the new British rail system, he attempts to describe its workings to fellow Persians.

All the wonderful arts which require strong power are carried on by means of steam, which has rendered immense profits and advantages. The English then began to think of steam coaches, which are especially applicable to their country, because it is small, but contains an enormous population. Therefore, in order to do away with the necessity for horses, and that the land which is sown with horse-corn [rye] should be cultivated with wheat, so as to cause it to become much more plentiful (as it is the most important article of food), and that England might thereby support a much greater population, they have with their ingenious skill invented this miraculous wonder, so as to have railroads from the capital to all parts of the kingdom.

Thus, by geometrical wisdom, they have made roads of iron, and where it was necessary these roads are elevated on arches. The roads on which the coaches are placed and fixed are made of iron bars. The coach is so fixed that no air or wind can do it any harm and twenty or thirty coaches may be fixed to the first in the train, and these one after the other.

All that seems to draw these coaches is a box of iron, in which they put water to boil, as in a fire-place; underneath this iron box is like an urn, and from it rises the steam which gives the wonderful force: when the steam rises up, the wheels take their motion, the coach spreads its wings, and the travellers become like birds. In this way these coaches go the incredible distance of forty miles an hour.

We actually travelled in this coach, and we found it very agreeable, and it does not give more but even less motion than horses; whenever we came to the sight of a distant place, in a second we passed it. The little steam engine possesses the power of eighteen horses.

Source: Najaf-Kuli Mirza, *Journal of a Residence in England and of a Journey to and from Syria* II (London, 1839, Reprinted, Farnborough, England: Gregg International Publishers, 1971), pp. 11–12.

and behavior of the population, if not always creating the preconditions of industrial development, were at least the major stimuli making them possible.

Changes in agriculture increased the productivity of the land. Farmers more frequently used fertilizer and improved the rotation of their crops, easing the exhaustion of the soil. New, more efficient plows enabled them to cultivate more land than ever before. In the eighteenth century, new crops that provided high yields even in poor soil were introduced into Europe: maize (corn) and potatoes from the Americas (see page 688). The wealth created by agriculture allowed for investment in industry and for expenditures on infrastructure, such as roads and canal systems, useful to industry. A wealthier landed class could purchase manufactured goods such as iron plows and even machine-woven textiles, thus providing an impetus for industry. Most important, the new crops and the more efficient cultivation of traditional ones increased the capacity to feed a growing population and freed many people to go to the city and work in the industries.

In the seventeenth and eighteenth centuries, European trade had increased significantly, enriching businessmen and making them aware of the fortunes to be made by marketing goods that were in demand not just locally but even far away. A new dynamic ethos took hold of businessmen eager to venture into untried fields of economic endeavor.

Population grew during the years of the industrial transformation. It was significant enough to promote industrialization, yet not so large as to put a brake on economic expansion. The first spurt in population growth occurred in the mid-eighteenth century, before the effects of industrialization could be widely felt. Thereafter the population of Europe increased dramatically throughout the industrial era: from 1750 to 1850 it grew by 100 percent.

The growth was largely due to a lowering of the death rate. Infant mortality had been very high from diseases such as smallpox and tuberculosis. Although none of these diseases had been medically conquered, improved standards of living after 1750, such as greater food intake, enabled children to better resist killer diseases. Better employment opportunities led to earlier marriages and thus higher fertility. Most of the population increase occurred in the countryside. This growing group of people supplied the labor force for the new industries and provided the large surge in consumers of various industrial goods.

In the countryside industrialization was foreshadowed by a form of production that had developed beginning in the seventeenth century—the putting-out system or cottage industry (see page 690). During the winter and at other slack times, peasants took in handwork such as spinning, weaving, or dyeing. Often they were marginal agriculturists, who on a part-time basis were able to augment their incomes. Entrepreneurs discovered that some individuals were better than others at specific tasks. Rather than have one household process the wool through all the steps of production until it was a finished piece, the entrepreneur would buy wool from one family, then take it to another to spin, a third to dye, a fourth to weave, and so on.

Some historians believe that this form of production, also called *protoindustrialization,* laid the basis for industrial manufacture. Like the latter it depended on specialization and supplied goods to a market beyond the producers' needs. In some areas, for instance, Flanders and northern Italy, protoindustry was followed by industrial manufacture; in other regions, such as western France, it became a substitute for industry. In still other areas, like Catalonia and the Ruhr region of western Germany, industry flourished without the previous development of cottage industries. Although cottage industry was an important contributor to industrialization in some regions, it did not play a role in every case.

A less ambiguous prerequisite for industry was a good transportation network. Transportation improved significantly in the eighteenth century. Better roads were built; coaches and carriages were constructed to travel faster and carry larger loads. Government and private companies built canals linking rivers to each other or to lakes. Road- and canal-building were important preconditions for industrialization, hastening and cheapening transportation and making possible the movement of raw materials to manufacture and from there to market without too great an increase in the price of the finished good. In Great Britain these transformations occurred simultaneously with industrialization; on the Continent they were actual precursors to economic change.

In Britain, industrialization preceded rail-building; yet once railroad expansion occurred, beginning in the 1830s, the order for iron rails, steam engines, and wagons sustained and advanced industrial growth. (See the box, "Encounters with the West: A Persian Discovers the British Rail System," on page 777.) On the Continent rail-building promoted industrialization, notably in Germany and later in Italy.

INDUSTRIALIZATION AND EUROPEAN PRODUCTION

Several important technological advances powered European industry, and breakthroughs in one field often led to breakthroughs in others. The first two industries to be affected by major technological breakthroughs were textiles and iron. New forms of energy drove the machinery; novel forms of directing labor and organizing management further enhanced production. At first limited to the British Isles, industry spread to the Continent, a development that occurred unevenly in various regions and at different times.

Advances in the Cotton Industry

A series of inventions in the eighteenth century led the way to the mass manufacture of textiles. One of the earliest was the flying shuttle, introduced in Britain in 1733 by John Kay (1704–1764). It accelerated the weaving process to such an extent that it increased the demand for thread. This need was met in the 1760s by James Hargreaves (d. 1778), who invented the spinning jenny, a device that spun thread from wool or cotton. Improved spinning machines, such as the "mule" of Samuel Crompton (1753–1827), made the spinning jenny increasingly efficient, and by 1812 one spinner could produce as much yarn as two hundred had made before the invention of the jenny. In 1769

Richard Arkwright (1732–1792), a barber and wig-maker, invented the water frame. This huge spinning machine drove two pairs of rollers, moving at different speeds. It was installed in a single establishment with three hundred employees, forming the first modern factory. The frame was originally powered by horses or by a waterfall, but in 1777 Arkwright had James Watt construct a steam engine to operate it. With these innovations, cotton manufacturing increased 130-fold between 1770 and 1841.

In the past, finished cloth had been soaked in buttermilk and spread out in the meadows to be bleached by the sun. That method was hardly practical for the unprecedented quantities of cloth rolling out of the factories. The introduction of

British Cotton Manufacture Machines simultaneously performed various functions. The carding machine (front left) separated cotton fibers, readying them for spinning. The roving machine (front right) wound the cotton onto spools. The drawing machine (rear left) wove patterns into the cloth. Rich in machines, this factory needed relatively few employees; most were women and children. (*The Granger Collection, New York*)

MAJOR INVENTIONS OF THE INDUSTRIAL TRANSFORMATION

1708	Use of coke in blast furnaces by Abraham Darby
1712	Steam-operated water pump by Thomas Newcomen
1733	Flying shuttle by John Kay
1764	Spinning jenny by James Hargreaves
1769	Water frame by Richard Arkwright
	Improved steam engine by James Watt
1776	Steam engine–operated machinery by James Watt
1779	The "mule" by Samuel Crompton
1784	Chlorine gas as a textile bleach by Claude Berthollet
1793	Cotton gin by Eli Whitney

sulfuric acid solved the problem. It was a far more economical bleach than buttermilk and sunlight, and it could be produced in commercial quantities. It in turn was replaced in the 1790s when the Frenchman C. L. Berthollet (1748–1822) discovered the bleaching powers of chlorine gas. Entrepreneurs or artisans made many of the other industrial inventions, but the breakthroughs in bleaching demonstrated that more and more, industry would be fueled by advances in scientific knowledge and training.

The cotton-manufacturing industry in Great Britain represented another important departure. For the first time in history a staple industry was based on a natural resource that was not domestically provided. Grown mainly in the U.S. South, cotton was transformed into cloth in Britain.

Manufactured cotton was comfortable to wear and easy to wash and became so cheap that it competed effectively with all handmade textiles. The popularity of cotton may have improved public health as well, for it enabled people to own several changes of clothing and keep them clean. Everyone was eager to buy British cottons. The higher demand for raw material put pressure on cotton growers in the U.S. South, who opened up new land.

In 1793, the American Eli Whitney (1765–1825) invented the cotton gin, a device that mechanically removed the seeds from cotton. The cotton gin meant that more cotton could be processed and thus more could be grown. It heightened the profitability of the United States's southern plantation economy, and that situation increased the attractiveness of slave labor. The second half of the eighteenth century marked the height of the slave trade. Between 1750 and 1800 approximately 3 million Africans were forcibly transported to the New World.

The cotton industry in Britain is an example of how local manufacturing may produce a ripple effect across the oceans. Among those benefiting overseas were American farmers, cotton traders, and merchants, as well as consumers of English cotton cloth around the world. Elsewhere, people were adversely affected—in Africa, where slaving raids increased, and in India, where local spinners were driven out of business.

In ways beneficial and not, people were interconnected by the cotton trade; later other products would also link the economies of various nations and peoples. No longer, as in preindustrial trade, were all goods locally made, nor did the consumer meet producers and buy from them. Increasingly, specialization became the norm. Those best fit performed a particular function efficiently and productively. The results were high production and low price for the finished product.

Iron, Steam, and Factories

Charcoal had traditionally fueled the smelting of iron. Britain, however, ran out of wood before other European countries did and needed an alternative source of fuel. There was plenty of coal, but it contained impurities, particularly sulfur, which contaminated the materials with which it came into contact. In 1708, Abraham Darby (1677–1717), an English ironmaster, discovered that coal in a blast furnace could smelt iron without these attending complications. His discovery triggered the iron industry's use of coal. In 1777, the introduction of a steam engine to operate the blast furnace considerably increased efficiency. In 1783, a steam engine was used to drive a forge hammer to shape the iron; three years later, steam-driven rollers rolled the iron into sheets. With these innovations, the output of the English iron industry doubled between 1788 and 1796 and again in the following eight years.

The greater supply of iron stimulated other changes. Relatively cheap and durable iron machines replaced wooden machines, which wore out rapidly. The new machines fueled further advances. Improvements in manufacturing methods and techniques led to the production of ever larger amounts of goods, usually at lower prices. Industrial change started with cotton but was continued and sustained by breakthroughs in the use of iron and coal.

Before the age of industry, the basic sources of power were humans, animals, wind, and water. Humans and animals were limited in their capacity to drive the large mills needed to grind corn or operate a sawmill. Wind was unreliable because it was not constant. Water-driven mills depended on the seasons—streams dried up in the summer and froze in the winter. And water mills could be placed only where there was a waterfall. Clearly what was needed was a power source that was constant and that could be located just about anywhere. The steam engine, invented and improved on in Britain, met that need and stoked the island's industrial growth. As late as the 1860s more than half of the energy needs of manufacturing in Great Britain and the United States were still supplied by people, animals, and wind- and water-operated machines. But the steam engine was clearly the wave of the future.

The steam engine was first used to pump out coal mines. As mining shafts were dug ever deeper, water in the mines became an increasing hindrance. In 1712 Thomas Newcomen (1663–1729) invented a steam-operated water pump. Its use spread rapidly. The first steam engine in the Americas was a Newcomen engine installed in New Jersey in 1753. James Watt (1736–1819) improved on the Newcomen engine considerably, making it twice as efficient in energy output. Eventually he made it capable of converting the reciprocating motion of the piston to rotary motion. This breakthrough enabled the steam engine to power a variety of machines. Thus, mills that had been powered by water or wind could be operated by steam engines. Further changes improved Watt's engines—most notably, the invention of the powerful and energy-efficient high-pressure steam engine. The use of steam engines spread in Britain, to the Continent, and to the United States.

Newcomen Engine Thomas Newcomen, an iron-monger, produced the first successful operating steam engine in 1712. Steam was introduced into a cylinder that was then cooled, creating a partial vacuum. The pressure of the atmosphere forced the piston down, pulling down one end of the beam, creating a pumping stroke. The engine could make as many as fourteen pumping strokes a minute. (*The Fotomas Index*)

The steam engine centralized the workplace. With the machine as a central power source, it became practical and commonplace to organize work in a central factory. The location of a factory where it was most convenient eliminated the expense of transporting raw materials to be worked on at a power source such as a waterfall. The central factory also reinforced work discipline. These factories were large, austere edifices inspired sometimes by military architecture and therefore resembling barracks. With the introduction of blast furnaces and other heat-producing manufacturing methods, the tall factory chimney became a common sight on the industrial landscape.

Factories ranged in size from small food-manufacturing operations to large textile mills. In the first half of the nineteenth century, the average number of employees in both English and French textile mills was between 200 and 300. Some plants were big, but by 1850 the small workshop, worked by the owner and his relatives or by a handful of employees, was still the most common site of manufacturing in Britain.

British production became truly industrial only after 1850. For decades industry coexisted with the artisan trades and other nonindustrial occupations, and indeed in a number of cases it aided their growth. Cheap industrially manufactured thread allowed handweaving to survive. Skilled craftsmen made by hand many of the machines and boilers used in factories. Income from the new industries created a wealthy middle class, which consumed more handmade goods and employed a great number of domestic servants; except for agriculture, domestic service was the single largest field of employment for women. By 1850 factory labor did not yet dominate the economy of western Europe, but it had become clear that the mechanized factory had overwhelming advantages and that it would be increasingly difficult for handmade products to compete.

The steam engine powered a dramatic growth in production. It increased the force of blast furnaces and the mechanical power of machinery used to forge iron and to produce equipment for spinning and weaving. In Britain cotton production grew 200-fold between 1740 and 1840, more than 400-fold between 1840 and 1860. Assisted by machines, workers were enormously more productive than when they depended on hand-operated tools. In 1700 spinning 100 pounds of cotton took 50,000 worker-hours; by 1825, it took only 135—a 370-fold increase in productivity capacity per worker.

Inventions and Entrepreneurs

The industrial age was triggered by inventions, and it was sustained by the continued flow of new ones. In the decade 1700–1709, 22 patents were issued in Britain; between 1840 and 1849, 4581 had been issued. Something revolutionary was occurring. People were seeing in their lifetime sizable growth in productivity, both in the factory and on the farm. Rather than cling to traditional methods, many entrepreneurs consciously and persistently challenged tradition and attempted to find new ways of improving production. In this age of invention, invention was prized as never before.

Most of the early industrialists belonged to merchant families. In Britain, very few were landed noblemen, industrial workers, or artisans. However, in the iron industry, it was not uncommon for metalworkers to build up a modest iron mill and then enlarge it. That was also the case with potters. Josiah Wedgwood (1730–1795), who pioneered the industrial manufacturing of china, came from a long line of artisan potters and is a good example of a self-made man. The thirteenth child of a potter, who died when Josiah was 9 years old, he went to work for his brother as an apprentice and gradually established himself on his own. Richard Arkwright was a barber before his invention of the water frame brought him a knighthood and a personal fortune of half a million pounds. Many entrepreneurs began as farmers, then became involved in the putting-out system, and then graduated to industrial manufacture. A disproportionate number of the early manufacturers were university educated, a fact suggesting that even in the early stages of industry, scientific knowledge was valuable. In fact, the self-made man was more the exception than the rule. Most entrepreneurs came from relatively privileged backgrounds.

Entrepreneurs such as Arkwright and Watt pioneered innovations and became famous, but most who advanced the cause of industrial production were not particularly inventive. They just replicated methods of production that had proved profitable to others. Truly successful entrepreneurs, however, seemed to share one attribute: They were driven by a nearly insatiable appetite for innovation, work, and profit. Near the mid-nineteenth century mark, one of the most successful French textile tycoons advised his son, "One seeks by means of imagination, by means of effort, to surpass one's neighbor; therefore, work, work, always work."

Entrepreneurs took the financial risk of investing in new types of enterprises. Most entrepreneurs by themselves or with a partner ran a single plant, but even in the early stages, some ran several plants. In 1788, Richard Arkwright and his partners ran eight mills. Some enterprises were vertically integrated, controlling production at the various stages. The Peels in Britain owned enterprises ranging from spinning to printing and even banking. The entrepreneurs' dynamism and boldness fostered the growth of the British industrial system, making the small nation the "workshop of the world."

Britain's Lead in Industrial Innovation

Britain led the way industrially for many reasons. It was the first European country to have a standard currency, tax, and tariff system. It enjoyed the most emancipated labor. Although Britain was by no means an egalitarian society, it accommodated some movement between the classes. Ideas and experiments were readily communicated among entrepreneurs, workers, and scientists. Although other countries had scientific societies, several societies in Britain brought together theoreticians and practical businessmen—for example, the Lunar Society in Birmingham and the Literary and Philosophical Society in Manchester.

Britain was far more open to dissent than were other European countries at the time. The lack of conformity was reflected in religion, and also in a willingness to try new methods of production. In fact, the two often went together. A large proportion of British entrepreneurs were Quakers or belonged to one of the dissenting (non-Anglican) religious groups—for instance, the ironmaking Darby family, the engineer of the steam engine James Watt, and the inventor of the "mule" Samuel Crompton. Perhaps they were accustomed to questioning authority and treading new paths. They were also well educated and, as a result of common religious bonds, inclined to provide mutual aid, including financial support.

England had gained an increasing share of international trade since the seventeenth century. This trade provided capital for investment in industrial plants. The world trade network also ensured that Britain had a market beyond its borders, and because aggregate demand was relatively high, mass manufacture was feasible. The international network built up by trade also enabled Britain to import raw materials for its industry, the most important of which was cotton.

Earlier than its competitors, Britain had a national banking system that could provide capital to industries in areas where it was needed. In addition to numerous London banks lending mainly in the capital, there were by 1810 six hundred pro-

Map 21.1 The Industrial Transformation in England, ca. 1850 Industry developed in the areas rich in coal and iron fields. Important cities sprang up nearby and were linked to each other by a growing rail network.

vincial banks. The banking system reflected the growth of the economy as much as it contributed to it. Banking could flourish because Britons had wide experience in trade, had accumulated considerable amounts of wealth, and had found a constant demand for credit.

Geographically, Britain was also fortunate. Coal and iron were located close to each other (Map 21.1). A relatively narrow island, Britain has easy access to the sea—no part of the country is more than 70 miles from a seacoast. This was a strategic advantage, for water was by far the cheapest means of transportation. Compared to the Continent, Britain had few tolls, and goods could move around easily.

On the whole, British workers were better off than their continental counterparts. They were more skilled, earned higher wages, and had discretionary income to spend on the manufactured goods now for sale. But because their wages were higher than wages on the Continent, there was an incentive for British business owners to find labor-saving devices and reduce the number of workers needed for production.

Population growth in Great Britain—in part the result of industrial growth—increased by 8 percent in each decade from 1750 to 1800. This swelling population expanded the market for goods. The most rapid growth occurred in the countryside, causing a steady movement of people from rural to urban areas. The presence of this work force was another contributing factor in Britain's readiness for change.

The timing of the industrial transformation in Britain was also influenced by plentiful harvests in the years 1715–1750, creating low food prices and thus making possible low industrial wages. The demand for industrial goods was reasonably high. Farmers with good earnings could afford to order the new iron manufactured plows. It is likely that the income from farming helped bring about changes associated with industrialization, such as population growth, improvements to the transportation system, and the growing availability of capital for investment. Thus, each change triggered more change, and the cumulative effect was staggering (see Map 21.1).

The Spread of Industry to the Continent

The ideas and methods that were changing industry in Britain spread to the Continent by direct contact and emulation. Visitors came to Britain, studied local methods of production, and returned home to set up blast furnaces and spinning works inspired by British design. The German engineer August Börsig (1804–1854), after studying steam engines in Britain, built the first German steam engine in 1825 and the first German locomotive in 1842. Some visitors even resorted to industrial espionage, smuggling blueprints of machines out of Britain. Although a British law forbade local artisans from emigrating, some did leave, including entrepreneurs who helped set up industrial plants in France and Belgium. By the 1820s British technicians were all over Europe—in Belgium, France, Germany, and as far east as Austria.

Belgium was the first country on the Continent to industrialize, perhaps because, like Britain, Belgium had iron and coal in proximity (Map 21.2). Belgium also had a long tradition of working cloth and iron and could readily adapt new methods to increase production of both. Belgium's location on the route between Britain and Germany fostered the development of railroads. And rail-building facilitated industrialization not only by providing fast and cheap transportation but also by stimulating the iron industry. In 1840, there were 200 miles of rail in Belgium; twenty years later, there were 1200 miles. Belgium was more densely equipped with railroads than any European country. The Belgian government encouraged industrial modernization by building railroads and investing in the shipping industry. In the early years it kept tariffs high to protect nascent industries; later it negotiated free-trade agreements providing expanded markets for its manufacturers.

In the eighteenth century France seemed a more likely candidate for economic growth than Britain. France's overseas trade was growing faster than Britain's. In 1780, France's industrial output was greater than Britain's, though production per person was less. In the nineteenth century, however, while Britain's industry boomed and it became the workshop of the world, France lagged behind. Why?

Historians have suggested several reasons. The war and revolutions of the late eighteenth century were certainly contributing factors. They slowed economic growth and cut France off from the flow of information and new techniques from Britain. Moreover, in the 1790s, when the French peasants pressured for legislation to ease their situation, the revolutionaries responded positively. Thus, the misery of the peasantry was somewhat relieved, and peasants were comfortable enough to feel no urgency to leave the land and provide the kind of cheap and ready labor that Britain had. Further, the Napoleonic Code of 1804 abolished primogeniture, so that when a peasant died, his younger sons were not forced off the land.

Population figures suggest another reason for France's relatively low economic growth. Between 1800 and 1914, the population of France grew at half the average rate of the rest of the Continent. In Britain during this period, much of the labor that left the land and worked the factories and mills came from the rural population explosion;

Map 21.2 Continental Industrialization, ca. 1850 Despite the fact that industry had begun on the Continent by the mid-nineteenth century, it was still sparse there, as was the rail network.

but no such phenomenon occurred in the French countryside, and thus the labor force in France was not as available for industrial growth.

Traditionally France had produced high-quality luxury goods, and French entrepreneurs who sought to emulate British accomplishments faced serious difficulties. Iron and coal in France were not close together (see Map 21.2). Labor was still quite cheap; there was no incentive to invest in labor-saving machines, because goods still could be manufactured inexpensively by hand. Soon, however, French manufacturers found themselves facing British competition. By being the first to industrialize, the British had the advantage of being able to manufacture goods and to corner markets efficiently and relatively cheaply. The French were

the first to feel the negative effects of being an industrial latecomer.

Although France's growth rate was lower than that of its neighbors, the French economy experienced slow but nearly constant growth throughout the nineteenth century. When population is taken into account, the French did better than Great Britain and only slightly less well than Germany. From 1810 to 1850, both the production of coal and the consumption of raw cotton quintupled. In 1830 France had 130 steam-driven machines; by 1852 it had 16,000. In ceramics, glass, porcelain, and paper manufacturing, France was a pioneer. Most French manufacturing, however, remained small; the typical firm had a handful of employees. Production by artisans, rather than by mass industrial production, continued longer there than in Britain or Germany.

The invasions of Germany by Napoleon caused considerable destruction, but they also brought some positive economic benefits. The example of the French Revolution led to important socioeconomic changes. Restrictive guilds declined. The French occupiers suppressed the small German states with their many tariffs and taxes, established a single unified legal system—which survived even after 1815—and introduced a single standard of measurement based on the metric system.

Government in Germany played an important role in the adoption of improved methods of manufacturing. The Prussian state, eager for industrial development, sent an official to Britain to observe the puddling process (the method by which iron is freed of carbon) and bring that know-how back to Prussia. The Prussian government promoted in-

dustrial growth by investing in a transportation network to carry raw materials for processing and finished goods to their markets. To spur both trade and industrial growth, Prussia took the lead in creating a customs union, the Zollverein, which abolished tariffs among its members. By 1834 a German market embracing eighteen German states with a population of 23 million had been created.

German industrial growth accelerated dramatically in the 1850s. Massive expenditures on railways created a large demand for metal, which pressured German manufacturers to enlarge their plant capacities and increase efficiency. Germany was not yet politically unified, but the German middle classes saw economic growth as the means by which their country could win a prominent place among Europe's nation-states. Germany's growth was phenomenal. It successfully emulated Britain, overtook France, and toward the end of

The Börsig Ironworks in the 1840s August Börsig, an artisan, founded these ironworks in Berlin. The factory expanded to meet the needs of the burgeoning German rail system. By the time of Börsig's death in 1854, his factory had built five hundred locomotives. *(Bildarchiv Preussischer Kulturbesitz)*

the nineteenth century served as a pioneer in the electrical engineering and chemical industries. If France experienced the disadvantages of being a latecomer, Germany reaped the benefits of that situation. The Germans were able to avoid costly and inefficient early experimentation and adapt the latest methods; moreover, Germany entered fields that Britain had neglected.

Even by the end of the century, however, progress remained slow in many areas of Europe. As long as Russia retained serfdom (until 1861), it would lack the mobile labor force needed for industrial growth. And until late in the century, the ruling Russian aristocracy hesitated to adopt an economic system in which wealth was not based on land. In Austria, Bohemia was the only important industrial center; otherwise, Austria was heavily agrarian (see Map 21.2).

The impoverished southern Mediterranean countries experienced little economic growth. With mostly poor soil, their agriculture yielded only a meager surplus. Spain, lacking coal and access to other energy sources, could not easily diversify its economic base. There was some industry in Catalonia, especially around Barcelona, but it was limited in scope and did not have much impact on the rest of the country. The Italian peninsula was still industrially underdeveloped in the middle of the nineteenth century. There were modest advances, but growth was too slow to have a measurable positive impact on the Italian economy. In 1871, 61 percent of the population of Italy was still agrarian.

Although by midcentury only a few European nations had experienced industrialization to any great extent, many more would do so by the end of the century, pressured by severe competition from their more advanced neighbors (Figure 21.1). The potential threat was political and military as well as economic, for the industrialized nations represented military might and superiority. As compared to the rest of the world, the European continent in the nineteenth century had acquired a distinct material culture that was increasingly based on machine manufacture or recognized to be in the process of becoming so. The possession of "skillful industry," one Victorian writer exulted, was "ever a proof of superior civilization." Although only some regions of Europe were industrialized, many Europeans came to view their continent as obviously "superior," while the

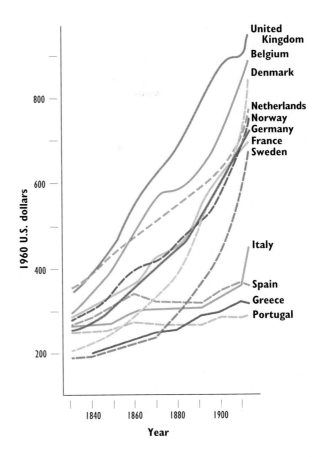

Figure 21.1 The Increase in Gross National Product per Capita in Principal European Countries, 1830–1913
The countries that industrialized rapidly—such as the United Kingdom in particular, and also Belgium, France, and Germany—experienced dramatic increase in per capita income during the nineteenth century. Other countries such as Greece and Portugal economically trailed the industrial leaders, and per capita income remained essentially flat. (*Source:* Norman J. G. Pounds, *An Historical Geography of Europe, 1800–1914* [New York: Cambridge University Press, 1985], p. 32. Used by permission of Cambridge University Press.)

other continents were in comparison deemed to be "inferior."

THE TRANSFORMATION OF EUROPE AND ITS ENVIRONMENT

Industry changed the traditional methods of agriculture, commerce, trade, and manufacture. It also transformed people's lives, individually and collectively. It altered how they made a livelihood, where and how they lived, and how they thought of themselves. Industry's need of people with specialized skills created new occupations. Because industry required specialization, the range of occupations that people adopted expanded dramatically.

The advent of industry transformed the way society functioned. Until the eighteenth century, the basis of influence and power was hereditary privilege, which meant aristocratic birth and land. The aristocracy did not disappear overnight. In the late eighteenth century, however, it was challenged by a rising class of people whose wealth was self-made and whose influence was based on economic contributions to society rather than on bloodlines. Increased social mobility opened opportunities even for some workers. Industrialization transformed both the social and the natural environment. Cities grew dramatically as a result of industrialization, and Europeans faced urban problems and the pollution of their air and water.

Urbanization and Its Discontents

A sociologist at the end of the nineteenth century observed, "The most remarkable social phenomenon of the present century is the concentration of population in cities."[3] The number and size of cities grew as never before. The major impetus for urban growth was the concentration of industry in cities and the resulting need of large numbers of urban workers and their families for goods and services (Map 21.3).

Industrialization was not the only stimulus. France provides many examples of urban growth with little industry. Increased commercial, trading, and administrative functions led to the growth of cities such as Toulouse, Bordeaux, and Nancy. Neither Holland, Italy, nor Switzerland experienced much industrial development in the first half of the nineteenth century, yet their cities grew. In general, however, industry transformed people from rural to urban inhabitants. People wanted to live near their work, and as industries concentrated in cities, so did populations.

Urban growth in some places was dramatic. In the entire eighteenth century, London grew by only 200,000; but in the first half of the nineteenth century, it grew by 1.4 million, more than doubling its size. Liverpool and Manchester experienced similar growth in the same period. Census figures show that by 1851 Britain was a predominantly urban society, the first country to have as many people living in cities as in the countryside. For Germany that date was 1891, and for France it was 1931. Although the proportion of people who were urban varied from place to place, the trend was clear and has continued.

In some cases factories were built in the countryside at a distance from towns, and as they prospered, cities grew up around them. The steelworks in Le Creusot, France, followed that pattern. In 1846 Le Creusot had 6000 inhabitants; in 1860, 16,000; by 1875, 25,000. In other cases industry gave rise to dramatic growth in once-modest towns—for instance, the west German town of Essen. In 1850 Essen had 9000 inhabitants; by 1900 its population had increased 30-fold. Occasionally, industry actually led to people leaving a city, when manufacturers located on the outskirts of urban areas or when subcontracting expanded the work of people involved in the putting-out system. But such an outward flow was unusual.

As the pace of industry governed in part urban growth, it was fueled in turn by urbanization. Large cities provided convenient markets for goods and a labor pool for manufacturing. The concentration of people encouraged the exchange of ideas. A large city was likely to have scientific societies and laboratories in which engineers and scientists could discuss new ideas and new inventions that would encourage industrial production. After midcentury, industrialization was driven more and more by scientific and technological breakthroughs made in urban environments.

Cities pulled in people from near and far. Usually, the larger the city, the stronger its ability to attract migrants from great distances. The medium-sized French town of Saint-Etienne drew migrants from the nearby mountains, while Paris drew from the entire country. Industrial centers attracted people from beyond the nation's borders. The Irish arrived in large numbers to work in the factories in Lancashire, Belgians came for mine work in northern France, and Poles sought employment in the Ruhr in western Germany. Industrial activity stimulated the growth of world trade and shipping across the seas, taking merchant sailors far from home. Africans and Asians inhabited port cities such as Amsterdam, Marseille, and Liverpool. Many large cities were marked by heterogeneous populations, which included people

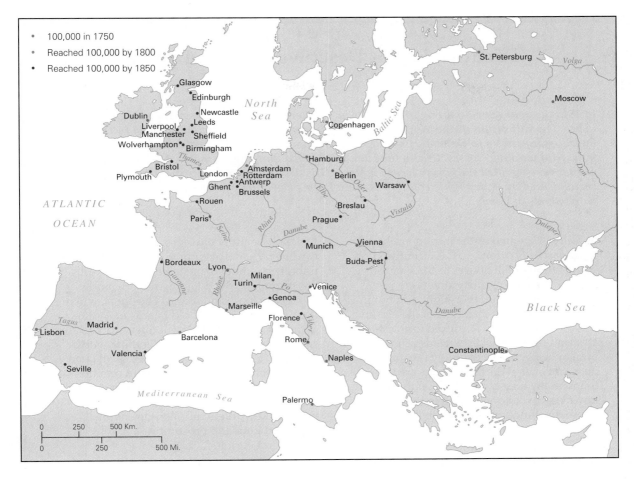

Map 21.3 Cities Reaching Population Level of 100,000 by 1750, 1800, and 1850 In 1750 the largest cities owed their existence to factors other than industry, but thereafter the development of industry often determined the growth of cities. England, the leading industrial nation, contained many of the largest cities. (*Source:* Data from Tertius Chandler, *Four Thousand Years of Urban Growth: An Historical Census* [Lewistown, N.Y.: St. David's University Press, 1987], pp. 22–24.)

with different native languages, religions, and national origins, as well as, in some cases, people of different races.

With the growth of cities came a multitude of urban ills. In the first half of the nineteenth century, mortality rates were higher in the cities than in the countryside. In the 1840s Britain as a whole had a death rate of 22 per thousand, but Liverpool averaged 39.2 and Manchester 33.1. In France national mortality rates were around 22 per thousand, but in some French cities the rate was as high as 35 per thousand. There was a dramatic social inequality in the face of death. Including the high child mortality rate, the average age at death for members of gentry families in Liverpool in 1842 was 35; for members of laborers's families it was 15. In 1800 boys living in urban slums were 8 inches shorter than their more fortunate contemporaries.

The rapid growth of the cities caught local authorities unprepared, and in the early stages of industrialization city life was particularly severe for the poor. Urban slums developed. The most notorious London slum was St. Giles, which became a tourist attraction because of its squalor. (See the box, "Friedrich Engels Describes an Urban Slum.") In many cities, large numbers of people were crammed into small areas. The houses were built back to back on small lots and had insufficient

Friedrich Engels Describes an Urban Slum

In 1845 the young socialist Friedrich Engels, who later became Karl Marx's literary partner, published **The Condition of the Working Class in England.** *Having lived in England in 1842–1844, Engels on his return to Germany provided a lively description of the hardships facing the English industrial working classes. Critics then and later noted that Engels, motivated by socialist zeal, at times exaggerated the misery he encountered. His description of the urban slum, however, was corroborated by many of his contemporaries. In this selection he describes St. Giles, one of the worst slums of London.*

St. Giles is situated in the most densely-populated part of London. . . . It is a confused conglomeration of tall houses of three or four stories. The narrow, dirty streets are just as crowded as the main thoroughfares, but in St. Giles one sees only members of the working classes. The houses are packed from cellar to attic and they are as dirty inside as outside. No human being would willingly inhabit such dens. Yet even worse conditions are to be found in the houses which lie off the main road down narrow alleys leading to the courts. These dwellings are approached by covered passages between the houses. The extent to which these filthy passages are falling into decay beggars all description. There is hardly an unbroken windowpane to be seen, the walls are crumbling, the door posts and window frames are loose and rotten. The doors, where they exist, are made of old boards nailed together. Indeed in this nest of thieves doors are superfluous, because there is nothing worth stealing. Piles of refuse and ashes lie all over the place and the slops thrown out into the street collect in pools which emit a foul stench. Here live the poorest of the poor. Here the worst-paid workers rub shoulders with thieves, rogues and prostitutes.

Source: Friedrich Engels, *The Condition of the Working Class in England,* trans. and ed. W. O. Henderson and W. H. Chaloner (Stanford, Calif.: Stanford University Press, 1968), pp. 33–34.

lighting and ventilation. Overcrowding was the norm. One study of a working-class parish in central London in midcentury showed three-quarters of the families living in single rooms. On one particular street, between twelve and twenty people were sleeping in each room. In Preston in 1842, 2400 persons slept three to a bed. The proximity of buildings blocked out sunlight. In the 1840s from 12 to 20 percent of people in Manchester and Liverpool were living in cellars.

Sanitation was rudimentary or nonexistent. A single privy in a courtyard was likely to serve dozens of tenants—in some notorious cases in Britain and France, a few hundred. Waste from the privy might drain through open sewers to a nearby river, which was likely to be the local source of drinking water. Or the privy might be connected to a cesspool from which wastewater would seep and contaminate nearby wells. Some tenants lacked toilets and relieved themselves in the street. In the 1830s people living in the poorest sections of Glasgow stored human waste in heaps along their houses and sold it as manure.

In the cities water was scarce and dirty. Piped water was reserved for the rich. The poor had to supply themselves from public fountains or wells and were often obliged to carry water a considerable distance. In Birmingham in the middle of the century, out of 40,000 houses only one-fifth had running water. French cities were usually worse; some of the major ones had only about two gallons of public water available per person a day.

In manufacturing towns factory chimneys spewed soot, and everything was covered with dirt and grime. Smoke and fog created the famous London fog, which not only reduced visibility but

St. Giles The most notorious London slum was St. Giles, whose human squalor made it a tourist attraction. *(From Thomas Beames,* The Rookeries of London. *Courtesy Harvard University Library)*

posed serious health risks. City streets were littered with refuse; rotting corpses of dogs and horses were common. In 1858 the stench from sewage and other rot was so severe that the British House of Commons was forced to suspend its sessions.

At midcentury the city fathers of Marseille described the center of their city as "covered with old, narrow houses that are in ruins, where air and light hardly reach, [and] infected sewers spread epidemics." It is not surprising that cholera, a highly infectious disease transmitted through contaminated water, swept the city and other European urban centers. In the 1830s one of the first epidemics of modern times struck Europe, killing 100,000 in France, 50,000 in Britain, and 238,000 in Russia. The cholera epidemic of 1854 killed 150,000 Frenchmen. Typhoid fever, also an acute infectious disease, hit mostly the poor but did not spare the privileged. Queen Victoria of Great Britain nearly died of it, and her husband, Prince Albert, did.

For most of its denizens, the city provided a crowded and squalid environment. Only in the second half of the nineteenth century would any attempts be made to bring order to the chaos of urban life.

The Working Classes and Their Lot

In 1842 a middle-class observer traveling in industrial Lancashire noted that around the mills and factories there had developed a "population [that] like the system to which it belongs is NEW . . . hourly increasing in breadth and strength."[4] A French countess, using the pen name Daniel Stern, wrote in her memoirs of France in the 1830s and 1840s of the emergence of "a class apart, as if it were a nation within the nation," working in factories and mines, called "by a new name: the industrial proletariat."[5]

As industry advanced and spread, more and more people depended on it for a livelihood. In the putting-out system, when there was an agricultural downturn, a cottager could spend more time on hand labor, and when there was a slack in demand for hand labor, the cottager could devote more time to the land. But people living in industrial cities were totally dependent on manufacturing. And neither skilled nor unskilled workers were assured of regular employment: Any downturn in the economy translated into layoffs or loss of jobs.

In addition, the introduction of new industries often devastated laborers in older forms of production. The mechanization of cotton production reduced the earning power of weavers in England and in Flanders, for instance. The production of linen was mechanized in Belgium by the 1840s, but cotton production was so much cheaper that in order to price their wares competitively, linen producers drastically reduced their workers' wages.

Most factory work was dirty and laborious, in grim plants with heavy machinery. Sixteen-hour days were common. Child labor was widespread. Because there were no safety provisions, the workers were prone to accidents—especially new workers unaccustomed to work routines, or experienced workers untrained on new machines. Few factory owners protected their workers against dangerous substances or circumstances. Mercury used in hat manufacturing gradually poisoned the hatmakers and often led to dementia. There were sound reasons to speak of "mad hatters." Lead used in paints and pottery also had a devastating impact on workers' health. Metal grinding caused serious health problems. In Sheffield in 1842, three-quarters of the cutlery workers had lung disease by the age of 40. In the 1840s the British military rejected four of ten rural volunteers because of some health deficiency; in the industrializing cities the rate of rejection was 90 percent. In the industrial area of Saint-Etienne in France from 1836 to 1847, the average life expectancy of a farmer was 59 years, but that of a miner was 37 years.

Usually physically lighter than boys and often underfed, young girls were faced with heavy labor that undermined their health. In 1842, 18-year-old Ann Eggley, a mineworker since the age of 7, hauled carriages loaded with ore weighing 800 pounds, for twelve hours a day. She testified to a parliamentary commission that she was so tired from her work that when she came home she often fell asleep before even going to bed. Isabel Wilson, another mineworker, testified that she had given birth to ten children and had suffered five miscarriages. These women—overworked, exhausted, vulnerable to disease, and especially endangered by complications from giving birth—faced premature death. The mortality rate for adult women during the era of industrial transformation was slightly higher than that for men. This situation changed only toward the end of the nineteenth century, and today women outlive men.

Did industrialization improve the workers' lot? Perhaps the question is best answered by an-

other question: What would the workers have done without industrial employment? A population explosion meant that many did not have enough land to make a living, and more efficient farming methods lessened the need for farm hands. It is not clear that these workers could have made a living if they had remained in the country.

Until the mid-nineteenth century, information on workers' income and expenses is incomplete. The best evidence comes from Britain, where an average family needed at least 21 shillings a week to escape from poverty. Skilled workers, who were in demand, might earn as much as 30 shillings a week, but most workers were unskilled. In Manchester in the mid-1830s, workmen producing coarse calicoes earned only between 6 and 8 shillings a week. And although a healthy, skilled male worker might earn 30 shillings, if he became less productive because of illness or old age, his wages fell. Thus, if women and children did not always need to work to help the family meet its minimum needs, at some point they usually did have to pitch in. Women who were the main breadwinners almost never received wages high enough to meet a family's total needs.

Incomes were so low that workers normally spent between two-thirds and three-fourths of their budget on food. Those who lived in rural areas might raise chickens or pigs or have a plot of potatoes. Bread was the largest single item consumed, varying between one and two pounds a day per person. In Britain and Germany people also ate a lot of potatoes. A little bacon or other meat gave flavor to the soup in which people dipped their bread or potatoes, but meat was rarely consumed as a main course. Because men were the chief breadwinners and tended to have the most strenuous occupation, they received the choice piece of meat and the largest amount of food. Women and children ate what was left.

Nevertheless, from the beginning, industrialization did increase wealth. "Optimist" historians argue that some of the new wealth trickled down to the lower levels of society. "Pessimist" historians say that a downward flow did not necessarily occur. Statistics suggest that by the 1840s workers' lives in Britain did improve. Their real income rose by 40 percent between 1800 and 1850. In part this advance was due to an increase in the numbers of skilled workers, who were paid more than their unskilled counterparts. And if factory workers' wages took time to improve, they were usually higher than wages in the handicrafts; in Lille, in northern France, in the 1830s women in spinning mills received wages one-quarter to one-half higher than those of lacemakers, whose work was done by hand.

Factory workers benefited not only from increased earnings but from the relatively low prices of many basic goods. In London, the price of 4 pounds of household bread fell from 15 pennies at the beginning of the nineteenth century to 8½ pennies in the 1830s. As the cost of cloth declined, there was a marked improvement in the dress of working-class people. On the Continent, the lot of workers improved a little later than in Britain, but the process followed the same pattern. In Germany workers' wages did not increase appreciably between 1800 and 1829, but by 1850 they had increased by 25 percent and by 1870 by another 50 percent. (See the feature, "Weighing the Evidence: Workers' Wages," on pages 808–809.)

Industrialization and the Family

Industrialization dramatically changed the character of the working-class family and household. Job segregation reserved the best-paying jobs for men; positions as foremen and the running of machinery such as the jenny were reserved for men. Especially in the textile industries, factory owners employed children and women in the lowliest positions. They were thought to be more pliable than men, and their wages were considerably lower. Women generally received from 30 to 50 percent of men's wages, children from 5 to 25 percent. In 1839 Thomas Heath, a weaver in Spitalfields, a London neighborhood, earned 15 shillings a week, his wife but 3 shillings.

Factory work often undermined the ability of women to take care of their children. As farmers or cottagers, women had been able simultaneously to work and to supervise their children; the factory, however, often separated mothers from their children. Many children were given heavy burdens at an early age, and it was not uncommon for an older child, sometimes only 5 or 6 years old, to be entrusted with the care of his or her sibling. Suzanne Monnier, the daughter of a French worker, described in her memoirs how her mother on giving birth had the 9-year-old Suzanne kiss her new sister and then told her, "This is not a sister I am giving you, but a daughter."

Other workers resorted to more dangerous methods of child care. They might send a newborn to a "babyfarm," to individuals in the countryside who were paid to take care of the child. Very often these babies were neglected, and their mortality rate was extremely high. In many cases, babyfarming was no more than a camouflaged form of infanticide. Mothers who kept their children but were obliged to leave them unwatched at home during factory hours sometimes pacified the children by drugging them with mixtures of opium, readily available from the local druggist.

Working-class women carried a heavy burden in the family. In addition to sometimes working outside the home, they were responsible for running the household, managing the family income, and taking care of the children, providing most of the nurture and supervision they required. Because of the many demands on married women, their employment pattern often was affected by the life cycle. Young women might work before marriage, or before giving birth, then stay home until the children were older, and then return to work. Factory work had a harsh impact on women's lives, but it should be remembered that relatively few women were in the wage market— by 1850 only about a quarter in both Britain and France. And of that quarter few worked in factories; far more were in agriculture, crafts industries (which still flourished despite poor working conditions), and domestic service, with many of these women working part-time while their children were small.

Some sectors of industry had a large proportion of women in them—for instance, textiles. Other sectors, such as the metal and mining industries, were heavily male-dominated. In Belgium, however, women represented 15 percent of miners.

The textile industry found employment for children once they were over the age of 5 or 6. Their size made them useful for certain jobs, such as reaching under machines to pick up loose cotton. Because of their small hands they were also hired as "doffers," taking bobbins off frames and replacing them. Elizabeth Bentley began work as a doffer in 1815 at the age of 6. At the age of 23, when she testified before a parliamentary commission, she was "considerably deformed . . . in consequence of this labor." (See the box, "The

The Young Girl in the Factory

Reformers in Parliament, among them Michael Sadler, denounced the appalling conditions in the factories. Sadler was appointed to head a commission to hold hearings; workers appeared before it giving vivid descriptions of their lot. Public and parliamentary outrage at the conditions revealed by these hearings led to the Factory Act of 1833. Among the witnesses was Elizabeth Bentley, a 23-year-old weaving machine operative, who gave the following testimony.

What age are you?—23 . . .

What time did you begin to work in a factory?—When I was 6 years old. . . .

What were your hours of labor? . . . —From 5 in the morning till 9 at night, when they were thronged.

For how long have you worked that excessive length of time?—For about half a year.

What were your usual hours of labor when they were not so thronged?—From 6 in the morning till 7 at night.

What time was allowed for your meals?—40 minutes at noon. . . .

Your labor is very excessive?—Yes, you have not time for anything.

Suppose you flagged a little, or were too late, what would they do?—Strap us. . . .

Girls as well as boys?—Yes.

Severely?—Yes.

Could you eat your food well in that factory? —No, indeed, I had not much to eat, and the little I had I could not eat it, my appetite was so poor, and being covered with dust; and it was no use taking it home, I could not eat it . . . .

Did you live far from the mill?—Yes, two miles.

Had you a clock?—No, we had not. . . .

Were you generally there in time?—Yes; my mother has been up at four o'clock in the morning and at two o'clock; the colliers used to go to their work at about three or four o'clock, and when she heard them stirring she has got up out of her warm bed, and gone out and asked them the time; and I have sometimes been at Hunslet Car at 2 o'clock when it was steaming down with rain, and we have had to stay till the mill was opened [at 5 A.M.].

Source: Great Britain, *Sessional Papers, House of Commons,* Hearing of June 4, 1832, vol. XV (1831–1832), pp. 195–197.

Young Girl in the Factory.") Child labor certainly did not start with the industrial transformation; it had always existed. What was new was the harsh industrial discipline imposed on the children.

Although children were common in British textile industries, overall less than 10 percent of working children were in industry. Most were in agriculture or the service sector. In the early stages of industrialization, children were primarily employed in textile mills to pick up waste and repair broken threads. As technological advances reduced both problems, the need for children lessened.

Improved technology and the growth of industries other than textiles increased the employment of adult men. In iron and later steel plants, physical strength was essential. Despite the higher labor costs that resulted when men were employed, managers had no choice but to hire them. However, in France, where textiles were still the predominant product after the turn of the nineteenth century, women made up two-thirds of the work force as late as 1906.

In some cases, industrialization meant a transformation in the authority structure of workers' households, undermining the influence of the male as head of the household. A woman could make a living independent of her spouse, and children at a reasonably early age could emancipate themselves from their parents and make a go of it working in a factory or a mine. These options were not possible in agriculture or in the putting-out system. As in the putting-out system, however, often whole families were hired as a group to perform a specific function. Contemporaries sometimes denounced industry for dissolving family bonds, but the family remained an effective work unit.

If not participating in the wage market, wives and children contributed in other ways to the household budget—by making clothes, raising a pig, tending a potato patch, and performing daily household chores. Grandparents often moved from the country to live with the family and take care of children. A study of Verviers, an industrial city in eastern Belgium, showed that at mid-nineteenth century a sizable number of children over the age of 20 continued to live with their parents and to contribute to the financial well-being of the family unit. (See the feature, "Weighing the Evidence: Workers' Wages," on pages 808–809.) In the steel-manufacturing city of Solingen in western Germany, a cutlery worker known as Fritz B., the subject of a sociological study in 1851, lived with his wife and four children. All were contributing either in cash or in labor to the family's well-being. When industrial workers married, they often settled with their spouses on the same street or in the same neighborhood where their parents lived. Although industry had the potential to undermine traditional family structures, the historical evidence is that the family adjusted and survived the challenges posed by the new economic system.

The Land, the Water, and the Air

Industrialization seriously challenged as well the environment, transforming the surface of the earth, the water, and the air. To run the new machinery, coal was mined in increasing amounts (Table 21.1). Iron and other minerals were also in great demand. The exploitation of coal ushered in the modern age of energy use, in which massive amounts of nonrenewable resources are consumed.

To extract coal and other minerals, miners dug deep tunnels. Millions of tons of earth, rock, and other debris were removed from underground.

Table 21.1 Coal Production in Industrializing Nations

	Millions of tons	Kilograms per inhabitant
1700	4	26
1750	7	16
1800	16	76
1830	30	120
1860	129	390

Source: Based on B. R. Mitchell, "Statistical Appendix, 1700–1914," in Carlo Cippola, ed., *The Fontana Economic History of Europe*, vol. 4 (London: Collins, 1973), pp. 747, 770; and Norman J. G. Pounds, *An Historical Geography of Europe, 1500–1840* (New York: Cambridge University Press, 1979), pp. 268–269.

This material, plus slag and other waste from the factories, was heaped up in mounds that at times covered acres of land, creating new geological formations. In one district in England in 1870, a million cubic yards of soda waste occupied 50 acres.

With axes and saws people cut down trees, depleting forests to supply the wood needed to build shafts for coal, iron, and tin mines, or to make the charcoal necessary for glassmaking. Between 1750 and 1900, industrial and agricultural needs led to the clearing of 50 percent of all the forests ever cleared. Many of Europe's major forests disappeared or were seriously diminished. Deforestation in turn sped up soil erosion.

Industry changed the physical environment in which people lived. Forests, lakes, rivers, and air—as well as people themselves—showed the harmful effects of industry. Centrifugal pumps drained large marshes in the Fenland in eastern England. A contemporary lamented, "The wind which, in the autumn of 1851 was curling the blue water of the lake, in the autumn of 1853 was blowing in the same place over fields of yellow corn." Factories dumped waste ash into rivers, changing their channels and making them considerably shallower. Because of pollution from industrial and human waste, by 1850 no fish could survive in the lower Thames River. Smoke and soot darkened the skies, intensifying the fog over London and other cities. Foul odors from factories could be detected at several miles' distance. Not merely

Manchester, England, 1851   A small, unimportant town of 20,000 in the 1750s, Manchester—as a result of industrialization—had 400,000 inhabitants in 1850. In this 1851 painting, the polluted industrial city is contrasted with its idealized rural suburb.
(The Royal Collection © 1993 Her Majesty Queen Elizabeth II)

unpleasant, various air pollutants caused cancer and lung disease.

RESPONSES TO INDUSTRIALIZATION

People in the new industrial classes living at subsistence levels were disquieting evidence of the impact of industrialization. What should be done about the working classes—or for them? These new classes developed their own sense of a common interest and fate. The result was a resounding cry for political and social democracy that began in the first half of the nineteenth century and became increasingly insistent. Many solutions were proffered. The proposals became powerful ideologies shaping the nineteenth and twentieth centuries, not only in Europe but also in most of the world.

Economic Liberalism

The classical economists of the late eighteenth and early nineteenth centuries (see page 747) argued in favor of laissez faire, the policy of nonintervention by the government in the economy. The laws of supply and demand, they contended, if allowed to operate unhindered, would provide for the well-being of both the individual and society. Their arguments formed the basis of what is known as "economic liberalism."

The classical economists' theories had a large audience. Popularizers spread the gospel of free enterprise, teaching the advantages of the capitalist system while justifying the conditions of the wealthy. They were particularly prevalent in Britain. Among them, Samuel Smiles (1812–1904) was widely read. Originally a physician, Smiles turned to popular education and in 1859 published *Self-Help,* one of the most influential books of the nineteenth century. In *Self-Help* he argued that the remedy for poverty lay in the hands of poor people themselves. If they lived thrifty, industrious lives, the good life would come to them. The improvement of the human condition was dependent not on society but on the character of the individual. Smiles's works sold a quarter million copies in Britain by the end of the century and were translated into many languages.

Building on earlier liberals' advocacy of laissez-faire policies, others more directly and even more uncompromisingly argued against any government action to improve the condition of the working classes. The British social theorist Herbert Spencer (1820–1903) took to extremes the lessons of classical economics. Although he lived on inherited money, he unabashedly asserted that wealth reflected innate virtue and poverty indicated innate vice. According to Spencer, the state should guarantee the right of everyone to pursue freedom as long as the pursuit did not infringe on others. In *Social Statics* (1851), Spencer opposed relief for the poor on the grounds that it unfairly deprived some—the rich—of their property. He also argued that schooling was outside the authority of the state.

Applying to human society Charles Darwin's principle of "natural selection" (see page 865), Spencer was a Social Darwinist. In 1864 he coined the expression "survival of the fittest." Society, he believed, should be established in such a way that the strongest and most resourceful would survive. The weak, poor, and improvident were not worthy of survival, and if the state helped them survive—such as by providing education—it would only perpetuate the unfit. Spencer's harsh doctrine was widely acclaimed.

Many of those who basically favored laissez-faire policies criticized some aspects of the market economy, however. In France in the first half of the nineteenth century, commentators on the factory system, including industrialists, expressed fear that factory work would undermine the stability of family life and hence of society itself. Philanthropic intervention, they hoped, would resolve the problems they had identified.

Even some of the British classical economists doubted the wisdom of allowing the market economy to operate entirely without regulation and of trusting it to provide for human happiness.

The Scottish economist Adam Smith (1723–1790) warned that the market tended to form monopolies, and he suggested that government intervene to prevent this situation. According to Smith, not all human needs could be provided by the marketplace; the government needed to supply education, road systems, and an equitable system of justice. The liberal thinker and government reformer Jeremy Bentham (1748–1832) was fearful of an overly intrusive government but also saw government as a possible force for good, to ensure the greatest happiness for the greatest number. Edwin Chadwick (1800–1895) advocated government intervention to ensure public sanitation and care for the poor; as a government official he worked to implement these twin goals.

John Stuart Mill (1806–1873), the leading British economic and political thinker at midcentury, in the first edition of his *Principles of Political Economy* (1848), voiced strong support for laissez-faire economics. The individual if left alone could carry on economic functions better than the government, Mill insisted. In subsequent editions, however, he remarked that the state had an obligation to intervene in the face of human misery. There were also many human needs that the free market could not address satisfactorily. Once wealth was produced, he noted, its distribution was subject to traditions and to decisions made by those in power. Thus, presumably, wealth could be shared by society as a whole. Toward the end of his life, Mill seemed to be leaning toward socialism.

The liberal economists' views on the virtues of laissez-faire policy gradually changed. In the face of unsanitary urban conditions, child labor, and other alarming results of industrialization, the state in many countries around midcentury began to intervene in areas of concern that would have been unthinkable a half-century earlier.

The Growth of Working-Class Solidarity

Hardest hit by economic changes, workers sought to improve their conditions by organizing and articulating their needs. In the preindustrial economy, artisans and craftsmen lived in an accepted hierarchy with prescribed rules. They began by serving for a certain number of years as apprentices to a master, next became journeymen, and finally with hard work and good fortune became masters of their trade. As tradesmen with common interests, they tended to band together into brotherhoods, promising one another help and trying to improve their working conditions.

With industrialization, guilds declined. Unlike the skilled handicrafts that required years of apprenticeship, much of industrial production did not require lengthy periods of training. The system of dependence between apprentice and master became irrelevant. Guilds trying to protect their members often resisted new technologies and came to be seen as a hindrance to economic development. Liberals viewed guilds as constraints on trade and the free flow of labor. In France, the revolutionaries abolished the guilds and all workers' coalitions. In Britain, Parliament throughout the eighteenth century passed various acts against "combinations" by workmen.

While guilds faded in importance, the solidarity and language born of the guild continued to shape workers' attitudes throughout much of the nineteenth century. New experiences also reinforced the sense of belonging to a group and sharing common aspirations.

Cultural forces fostered workers' sense of solidarity. The common language of religion and shared religious practice united workers, and many religious groups were born as a result. Religious sects flourished in an environment of despair punctuated by hopes of deliverance. Some historians believe that the growth of Methodism in England in the 1790s (see page 743) was a response to economic conditions. Emphasis on equality before God fueled the sense of injustice in a world where some were privileged and living in luxury while others were condemned to work along with their children for a pittance. Joanna, a self-proclaimed prophet active in the 1810s in England, announced both salvation and the coming of a new world of material well-being. In France, workers believed the new society would come about by their martyrdom; like Jesus, the workers would suffer, and from their suffering would emerge a new, better society. Ideas of social justice were linked in the countryside with religious broadsides speaking of "Jesus the worker." Religious themes and language continued to be important in labor organization for many years.

Other cultural and social factors created bonds among workers. Housing was increasingly segregated. Workers lived in low-rent areas—in slums in the center of cities or in outlying areas near the factories. Thus, urban workers lived close together, in similar conditions of squalor and hardship. Entrepreneurs who built factories or established mineworks in the countryside had to provide housing in order to attract and retain workers. Although this housing was sometimes better than the quarters of urban workers, it nevertheless reinforced the workers' solidarity and sense of commonality.

Workers grew close by spending their leisure time together, drinking in pubs, attending theaters and new forms of popular entertainment such as the circus, or watching traditional blood sports like boxing or cockfights. Popular sports emerged in the 1880s. In sports such as soccer, which developed in England at this time, both players and fans were drawn overwhelmingly from the working class.

Social institutions also encouraged class unity. In the eighteenth century both husband and wife were usually in the same craft. By 1900 it became more common for workers to marry across their crafts, thereby strengthening the sense of solidarity that encompassed the working classes as a whole.

Faced with the uncertainties of unemployment and job-related accidents, in addition to disease and other natural catastrophes, workers formed so-called friendly societies in which they pooled their resources to provide mutual aid. These societies, descendants of benefit organizations of the Middle Ages and Renaissance, combined business activity with feasts, drinking bouts, and other social functions.

Friendly societies had existed as early as the seventeenth century, but they became increasingly popular and important after industrialization. Their strength in a region often reflected the degree to which the area was industrialized. First started to provide aid for workers in a particular trade, they soon included members in several crafts. They federated into national organizations, so that a worker who moved to a new town could continue membership in the new locale. Connected by common membership in friendly societies, workers expressed a feeling of group solidarity beyond their individual occupations. Though far from accomplished, a working class was in the making.

Leisure Activity for the Working Poor Some harsh forms of entertainment turned up in the industrial period. Scores of working-class spectators came to see the celebrated dog "Billy" kill a hundred rats at one time at the Westminster Pit in London in 1822. *(The British Library)*

Collective Action

Militant and in some cases violent action strengthened workers' solidarity. In politics, workers expressed common grievances, and some of their disappointments in the political arena underscored their common situation.

In the face of hardships, artisans organized for collective action. In 1811–1812 British hand weavers, faced with competition from mechanized looms, organized in groups claiming to be led by a mythical General Ned Ludd. In the name of economic justice and to protect their livelihood, the "Luddites," as the general's followers were called, smashed machines or threatened to do so. To bring the Luddite riots under control, twelve thousand troops were dispatched, and in January 1813, British authorities executed ten people for Luddism. Similarly, in Saxony in eastern Germany in the 1830s and 1840s, weavers went on machine-

crushing campaigns. These movements revealed the militance of labor and its willingness to resort to violence.

In Lyon, France, in 1831 and 1834, workers led uprisings demanding fair wages for piecework. Angered when the silk merchants lowered the amount they would pay, the workers marched in the streets bearing banners proclaiming "Live Working or Die Fighting." Troops were brought in to restore order to the riot-torn city. Although conditions of the silk trade had been the immediate impetus for the uprising, the workers appealed for help to their fellow workers in other trades.

Labor agitation in much of Europe increased in the 1840s; a major strike wave involving twenty thousand workers broke out in Paris in 1840. In the summer of 1842, an industrial downturn in England led to massive unemployment and rioting. During the summer of 1844 in Silesia, in eastern Prussia, linen handloom weavers desperate because of worsening conditions brought on by competition from machine-made cotton fabrics, attacked the homes of the wealthy. In 1855 in Barcelona, the government tried to dissolve unions, and fifty thousand workers went on strike carrying banners that warned "Association or Death."

Many of the friendly societies struggled to improve their members' working conditions, acting very much as labor unions would. They organized strikes and provided support to members while they were on strike. Unions were illegal in Britain until 1825, in Prussia until 1859, and in France until the 1860s. The advantages offered by unions were well understood. As a French workers' paper declared in 1847, "If workers came together and organized . . . nothing would be able to stop them." An organized force could threaten to withhold labor if the employer did not grant decent wages and acceptable conditions. Unions made workers a countervailing force to the factory owners.

Discipline in the factory was often severe. (See the box, "The New Discipline of the Factory System.") Workers had to conform to rigid rules not only in the workplace but also away from it. Workers in some factories were forbidden to read certain newspapers, had to attend religious services, and could marry only with the owners' permission. Workers resisted these attempts at control and resented employers' intrusiveness. They wanted freedom from outside regulation, and unions provided a means to ensure that freedom.

The process of unionization was difficult. By 1850 many countries had passed laws supporting employers against the workers. Censorship and the use of force against organized strikes were not uncommon. Population growth made it difficult for workers to withhold labor lest they be replaced by others only too willing to take their place. Foreign workers—for example, the Irish who streamed into England and the Belgians and Italians who streamed into France—were often desperate for work and not well informed about local conditions.

In many countries, workers formed unions before unions were legalized. Most were centered around a single craft or a single industry. In Britain, however, there were early attempts to organize unions on a national basis. In 1834 Welsh

socialist Robert Owen (1771–1858) helped launch the Grand National Consolidated Trades Union. The organization's goal was to use the principles of cooperation to unite all of labor against the capitalist system. Internal strife and government repression kept this organization from succeeding. Not until 1860 was a federal structure created for the British unions—the Trade Union Congress.

In Germany in 1848 the General Workers' Brotherhood was founded. Its first members were people from many walks of life, but gradually its membership included workers only. Most of the members were craftsmen and artisans: skilled workers such as cigar makers, book printers, typesetters. The year after its founding, the General Workers' Brotherhood had 15,000 members and 170 locals. After 1859, when labor unions were legalized, they grew significantly.

The composition of union membership evolved over time. Because labor unions originated in the crafts tradition, the earliest members were skilled craftsmen who organized to protect their livelihood from the challenge that industrialization posed. These craftsmen were usually literate and long-time residents of their communities. They provided the labor movement with much of its leadership and organization. Skilled craft workers played a strong role in developing a sense of class consciousness. The language and institutions that they had developed over decades and sometimes over centuries became the common heritage of workers in general.

Workers looked to political action as the means to improve their situation. In the 1830s and 1840s English workers agitated for the right to vote; they saw voting as a way to put themselves on equal footing with the privileged and to win better conditions. The failure to win the vote in 1832 with the passage of the Great Reform Bill disappointed many workers, and they heavily backed the Chartist movement of the 1840s (see page 757). Symptomatically, Chartism won its greatest support in the industrial areas.

In France urban laborers who had played an important part in the various stages of the Revolution continued to shape political events. In July 1830 workers helped topple the Bourbon monarchy and bring Louis Philippe (r. 1830–1848) to the throne. They insisted that their labor had created the wealth of the nation and that their self-sacri-

The New Discipline of the Factory System

The new factories regimented the work force and were likely to impose stiff penalties for infractions of the rules. This document lists some of the regulations of the Berlin Foundry and Engineering Works of the Royal Overseas Trading Company of 1844.

The normal working day begins at all seasons at 6 A.M. precisely and ends, after the usual break of half an hour for breakfast, an hour for dinner, and half an hour for tea, at 7 P.M., and it shall be strictly observed.

Five minutes before the beginning of the stated hours of work until their actual commencement, a bell shall ring and indicate that every worker employed in the concern has to proceed to his place of work, in order to start as soon as the bell stops.

The doorkeeper shall lock the door punctually at 6 A.M., 8:30 A.M., 1 P.M., and 4:30 P.M.

Workers arriving 2 minutes late shall lose half an hour's wages; whoever is more than 2 minutes late may not start work until after the next break, or at least shall lose his wages until then.

Repeated irregular arrival at work shall lead to dismissal. This shall also apply to those who are found idling by an official or overseer, and refuse to obey their order to resume work. . . .

All conversation with fellow-workers is prohibited. . . .

Smoking in the workshops or in the yard is prohibited during working-hours; anyone caught smoking shall be fined five silver groschen for the sick fund.

Natural functions must be performed at the appropriate places. . . .

It goes without saying that all overseers and officials of the firm shall be obeyed without question, and shall be treated with due deference. Disobedience will be punished by dismissal.

Immediate dismissal shall also be the fate of anyone found drunk in any of the workshops. . . .

The gatekeeper and the watchman, as well as every official, are entitled to search the baskets, parcels, aprons, etc. of the women and children who are taking the dinners into the works, on their departure, as well as search any worker suspected of stealing any article whatever. . . .

A free copy of these rules is handed to every workman, but whoever loses it and requires a new one, or cannot produce it on leaving, shall be fined 2½ silver groschen.

Source: S. Pollard and C. Holmes, eds., *Documents of European Economic History*, vol. 1 (New York: St. Martin's Press, 1968), pp. 534–536.

fice had brought in a freer government. Workers were disappointed by their failure to win political representation under the July Monarchy, and their sense of betrayal strengthened their class solidarity vis-à-vis the wealthy, privileged upper classes.

Politically, workers played a major role in the European revolutions of 1848. They demonstrated and helped bring down the July Monarchy in France. In Germany and Austria, they participated as organized groups in the initial successful uprisings against the established orders. Workers also influenced the course of the revolutions. However vague their ideas, European workers showed that their organizations were legitimate representatives of the people and that the lot of the worker should be the concern of government. In general, workers upheld the ideal of a moral economy—one in which all who labored got a just wage and a minimum level of well-being was assured to all.

The working classes were never a monolithic group. They consisted of people with varying skills, responsibilities, and incomes. (See the feature, "Weighing the Evidence: Workers' Wages," on pages 808–809.) Craftsmen with valuable skills were the segment that employers most respected and favored in pay and in working conditions. In contrast, unskilled workers were poorly paid, harshly treated, and often given only temporary work. Many skilled workers looked with contempt on the unskilled.

If both sexes worked side by side, there was little solidarity between them. Men worried that women were undermining their earning power by accepting lower wages. They often excluded women from their unions. They even went on strike to force employers to discharge women. An exception to this practice was Belgium, where labor organizations were remarkably receptive to female members.

Nor was there solidarity across nationalities. Foreign workers were heartily despised. British workers were hostile to their Irish colleagues, the French to the Belgians and Italians in their midst. The hostility often led to fisticuffs. In London anti-Irish riots were common.

Thus, many forces fostered dissension among the working classes in the nineteenth century, and unity among workers was far from achieved. Nevertheless, various experiences, including the spread of industry, broadened and deepened workers' sense of a common fate and goal.

The middle classes came to believe that all workers formed a single class. By the mid-nineteenth century, they had developed a clear fear of workers, not only as individuals but as a group, as a class. It was not unusual for members of the elite to refer to workers as "the swinish multitude" or, as the title of a popular English book put it, *The Great Unwashed* (1868). In France reference was alternately made to "the dangerous classes" and "the laboring classes." Not just workers but even the privileged seemed to see relations between the groups as a form of class war.

Marx and Marxism

Socialism provided a powerful language for the expression of working-class interests. Many of the workers who were enfranchised in the latter part of the century joined political parties espousing this doctrine. As we have seen, socialism existed before Karl Marx came on the scene. Henri de Saint-Simon and Charles Fourier in France, and Robert Owen in Great Britain, were the foremost prophets of socialism (see page 750). Marx drew on their theories and gave them a very special twist, and in the end his became the dominant form of socialism.

Karl Marx (1818–1883), the son of a lawyer, grew up in the Rhineland, in western Germany, an industrializing area that was particularly open to political ideas and agitation. The Rhineland had been influenced by the ideas of the French Revolution and was primed for political radicalism. As a young man Marx studied philosophy at the University of Berlin and joined a group known as the "Young Hegelians," self-declared disciples of the idealist philosopher G. W. F. Hegel (1770–1831) (see page 743). Marx showed an early interest in political liberty and socialism. In 1842–1843 he edited a newspaper that spoke out for freedom and democracy in Germany. The following year in Paris, he met several of the French socialist writers. Even as a young man, he was perceived by his contemporaries as bright but unyielding in his determination.

Because of his radical journalism, he was exiled from the Rhineland and lived briefly in Paris, then Brussels. In 1849 he settled in London, where he lived for the rest of his life, dedicated to establishing his ideas on what he viewed as scientific bases. Deriving a modest income from writing for the *New York Daily Tribune* and from funds provided by his friend and collaborator Friedrich Engels (1820–1895), Marx was never able to provide well for his family, which constantly lived on the edge of poverty. Of the six children born to the Marx household, three died in infancy.

In 1848 Marx and Engels published the *Communist Manifesto*. (See the box, "The *Communist Manifesto*.") A pamphlet written for the Communist League, a group of Germans living in exile, the manifesto was an appeal to the working classes of the world. The league deliberately called itself "Communist" rather than "Socialist." Communism was a radical program, bent on changing property relations by violence; socialism was associated with more peaceful means of transformation. The pamphlet was too late and too obscure to influence the revolutions of 1848. However, it laid out Marx's basic ideas, calling on the proletariat to rise—"You have nothing to lose but your chains"—and create a society that would end the exploitation of man by man.

A number of political and polemical works flowed from Marx's pen, but most of them remained unpublished during his lifetime. The first volume of his major work, *Capital,* was published in 1867; subsequent volumes appeared posthumously. Marxism, the body of Marx's thought, is complex and sometimes contradictory. It is written in an obscure style, difficult to penetrate. But certain basic concepts resound throughout and were embraced by Marx's followers.

Marx agreed with Hegel and many of his contemporaries that human history has a goal. Hegel believed that the goal was the realization of the world spirit. Marx believed that it was the abolition of capitalism, the victory of the proletariat, the disappearance of the state, and the ultimate liberation of all humankind.

Whereas Hegel thought that ideas govern the world, Marx insisted that material conditions determine it. Hegel said that truth evolves by a "dialectic method": A person states a proposition and then states its opposite; from the clash of the two emerges a synthesis that leads to a higher truth. Marx called his philosophy "dialectic materialism." Following Hegel, he posited a world of change but said that it was embedded in material conditions, not in a clash of ideas. Ideas, to Marx, were but a reflection of the material world.

Marx grouped human beings into classes based on their relationship to factories and machines—the means of production. Capitalists were one class, because they owned the means of production. Workers were a separate class—the proletariat—because they did not own any of the means of production and their income came only from their own hands. Because these two classes had different relationships to the means of production, they had different—in fact, antagonistic—interests and were destined (Marx believed) to engage in a class struggle.

Some of Marx's contemporaries lamented the increasing hostility between workers and capitalists. Marx, however, saw the conflict as necessary to advance human history, and he sought to validate his thesis by the study of the past. In the Mid-

Karl Marx Through his writings and agitation, Marx transformed the socialism of his day and created an ideology that helped shape the nineteenth and twentieth centuries. *(Corbis-Bettmann)*

dle Ages, he pointed out, the feudal class dominated society but eventually lost the struggle to the commercial classes. Now, in turn, the capitalists were destined to be overwhelmed by the rising proletariat.

In the study of history and economics, Marx found not only justification for but irrefutable proof of the "scientific" basis of his ideas. Capitalism was itself creating the forces that would supplant it. The large industrial plants necessitated an ever greater work force with a growing sense of class interest. The inherently competitive nature of capitalism would inevitably drive an increasing number of enterprises out of business, and there would emerge a form of monopoly capitalism, abusive of both consumers and workers. As a result of ever more savage competition, more businesses would fail, and consequently more workers would become unemployed. Angered and frustrated by their lot, workers would overthrow the system that had abused them for so long: "The

The *Communist Manifesto*

The **Communist Manifesto** *provides a preview of the major themes that would inform Marx and Engels's later writings: the concept of class formation and class antagonism, the privileged role of the proletariat, and the inevitability of the proletariat's success.*

The history of all hitherto existing society is the history of class struggles.

Freeman and slave, patrician and plebeian, lord and serf, guild-master and journeyman, in a word, oppressor and oppressed, stood in constant opposition to one another, carried on an uninterrupted, now hidden, now open fight, that each time ended, either in a revolutionary reconstitution of society at large, or in the common ruin of the contending classes. . . .

In ancient Rome we have patricians, knights, plebeians, slaves; in the Middle Ages, feudal lords, vassals, guild-masters, journeymen, apprentices, serfs; in almost all of these classes, again, subordinate gradations.

The modern bourgeois society that has sprouted from the ruins of feudal society, has not done away with class antagonisms. It has but established new classes, new conditions of oppression, new forms of struggle in place of the old ones. . . .

Society as a whole is more and more splitting up into two great hostile camps, into two great classes directly facing each other: Bourgeoisie and Proletariat. . . .

With the development of industry the proletariat not only increases in number; it becomes concentrated in greater masses, its strength grows and it feels that strength more. . . . the collisions between individual workmen and individual bourgeois take more and more the character of collisions between two classes. . . .

Of all the classes that stand face to face with the bourgeoisie today, the proletariat alone is a really revolutionary class. The other classes decay and finally disappear in the face of modern industry; the proletariat is its special and essential product.

All previous historical movements were movements of minorities. The proletarian movement is the self-conscious, independent movement of the immense majority. The proletariat, the stratum of our present society, cannot stir, cannot raise itself up, without the whole superincumbent strata of official society being sprung into the air. . . .

. . . The development of modern industry, therefore, cuts from under its feet the very foundation on which the bourgeoisie produces and appropriates products. What the bourgeoisie therefore produces, above all, are its own grave-diggers. Its fall and the victory of the proletariat are equally inevitable.

Source: Karl Marx and Friedrich Engels, *Communist Manifesto* (1848; reprint, New York: International Publishers, 1948), pp. 9, 17, 20–21.

knell of private property has sounded. The expropriators will be expropriated." The proletariat would take power and to solidify its rule would temporarily exercise the "dictatorship of the proletariat." Once that had taken place, the state would wither away. With the coming to power of the proletariat, the history of class war would end and the ideal society would prevail. Ironically,

Marx, who spent his life writing about the nature and history of social change, envisaged a time when change would cease, when history, as it were, would stop.

Many protested the evils of industrialism but Marx described economic change in dramatic terms as a necessary stage for humankind to traverse on its way to liberation. The suffering of the workers was not in vain; rather, it was a necessary process, part of the drama that would finally lead to human emancipation. Unlike some of the utopians who deplored industrialism, Marx accepted it and saw it as part of the path that history was fated to take.

Marx's study of economics and history proved to him that the coming of socialism was not only desirable—as the utopians had thought—but inevitable. The laws of history dictated that capitalism would collapse, having created within itself the means of its own destruction—namely, the rising proletariat. By proclaiming his brand of socialism as scientific, Marx gave it the aura it needed to become the faith for millions of people. For to declare ideas scientific in the nineteenth century, when science was held in such high esteem, was a promising way of gaining a popular following for them.

SUMMARY

Its industrial transformation altered the face of Europe. The process, which started around 1750 in parts of England, spread by 1850 to other states of Europe. Material and cultural factors combined with a number of fortuitous circumstances explain why industrial production originated in England. The proximity of coal and iron, the relative ease of domestic transportation, a culture open to innovation and entrepreneurship, and the existence of an already relatively dynamic economy help explain why Britain was the first nation to industrialize.

Economies based on industry changed power relations within Europe and altered the relationship of Europe to the rest of the world. As a result of the transformation in its economy Britain became in the nineteenth century the most powerful nation in Europe and achieved worldwide influence. Although Europe was industrialized only in certain areas, many Europeans came to think of their continent as economically and technologically superior to the rest of the world. Being industrial became synonymous for many with Europe's identity.

Industry changed the nature of work for large numbers of Europeans. Machines replaced human energy in the workplace. By the application of science and technology, manufacturing productivity increased significantly. A decreasing number of people worked in agriculture, and more entered manufacturing. Population patterns changed; cities grew dramatically, and for the first time European cities had over a million inhabitants.

The massing of workers in factories and urban areas called attention to their misery and also to their potential power. Eager to improve their lives and working conditions, workers began to express their solidarity. They organized into groups that were more broadly based and therefore more powerful than workers' groups of the past. As workers began to think of themselves as a group, the dominant groups within society began to perceive them as such.

Confronted by the realities of industrialization, many people changed their intellectual convictions. It was obvious that the laissez-faire system could not meet many workers' needs. Classical liberal economists revised their orthodoxy; the state became more interventionist, trying to remove some of the worst abuses.

Drawing on earlier strands of socialism, Karl Marx articulated this ideology in a new and compelling way. Marxism gave a powerful voice to the new proletarian class that industrialization had created, and it was to cast a shadow far into the next century.

NOTES

1. Phyllis Deane, *The First Industrial Revolution* (Cambridge, England: Cambridge University Press, 1965), p. 1.
2. These ideas are provocatively developed by E. L. Jones, *The European Miracle: Environments, Economies and Geopolitics of Europe and Asia* (Cambridge, England: Cambridge University Press, 1981).
3. Adna Ferrin Weber, *The Growth of Cities in the Nineteenth Century: A Study in Statistics* (New York: Macmillan, 1899; Ithaca, N.Y.: Cornell University Press, 1963), p. 1.
4. W. Cooke Taylor, *Notes of a Tour in the Manufacturing Districts of Lancashire, in a Series of Letters to His Grace the Archbishop of Dublin* (London, 1842), pp. 4–6, quoted in E. P. Thompson, *The Making of the English Working Class* (New York: Vintage, 1963), p. 191.
5. Marie de Flavigny d'Agoult [Daniel Stern], *Histoire de la Révolution de 1848*, 2d ed., vol. 1 (Paris, 1862), p. 7, quoted in Theodore S. Hamerow, *The Birth of a New Europe: State and Society in the Nineteenth Century* (Chapel Hill: University of North Carolina Press, 1983), pp. 206–207.

SUGGESTED READING

General Surveys

Jones, E. L. *The European Miracle.* 1981. A broad comparative work considering the forces leading to the industrialization of the West.

Landes, David S. *Prometheus Unbound.* 1969. A standard work emphasizing technological and cultural factors as explanations for industry.

Mokyr, Joel. *The Lever of Riches: Technological Creativity and Economic Progress.* 1990. A work that provides a comparative study of Western and Chinese technology, emphasizing cultural elements as explanations for the industrialization of the West.

Industrialization of Britain

Brown, Richard. *Society and Economy in Modern Britain, 1700–1850.* 1991. A work pointing out that British development was gradual, varied regionally, and was unequally spread.

Mathias, Peter. *The First Industrial Nation: An Economic History of Britain, 1700–1914.* 1969. A consideration of the unique combination of factors that explain Britain's pioneering role as an industrializer.

O'Brien, Patrick K., and Roland Quinault, eds. *The Industrial Revolution and British Society.* 1993. A broad set of essays on the origins and impact of industry on British society.

The Spread of Industry to the Continent

Gullickson, Gay L. *Spinners and Weavers of Auffay: Rural Industry and the Sexual Division of Labor in a French Village, 1750–1850.* 1986. A very fine study of the long-term subsistence of rural industry in a rural environment.

Milward, A., and S. B. Saul. *The Development of the Economies of Continental Europe.* 1977. An examination of the relationship between the availability of capital, labor, and technology and the speed of industrial development.

Pollard, Sidney. *Peaceful Conquest.* 1981. A reminder that although industrialization started in England, it occurred not throughout the whole country but only in specific regions; likewise when industry spread to the Continent, it spread only to specific regions.

Pounds, Norman J. G. *An Historical Geography of Europe, 1800–1914.* 1985. A consideration of the impact of geographic factors in shaping industry and how industry changed the physical face of Europe.

Sylla, Richard, and Gianni Toniolo, eds. *Patterns of European Industrialization.* 1991. A volume describing the patterns of industrialization in a comparative perspective.

The Industrial Transformation of Society

Alter, George. *Family and the Female Life Course: The Women of Verviers, Belgium, 1849–80.* 1988. A reminder that women were usually not continuously in the industrial work force but entered and exited according to family needs.

Anderson, Michael S. *Family Structure in Nineteenth Century Lancashire.* 1971. A study of the industrial town of Preston, revealing a family system far more resilient than the system usually described by contemporaries.

Brimblecombe, Peter. *The Big Smoke: A History of Air Pollution in London Since Medieval Times.* 1987. An account of the causes of pollution and the attempts to control it.

Chinn, Carl. *Poverty Amidst Prosperity: The Urban Poor in England, 1834–1914.* 1995. Concentrates on the harsher aspects of industrialization.

Hilden, Patricia P. *Women, Work, and Politics: Belgium, 1830–1914.* 1993. Reveals the unique experience of women in the industrial work force in the first continental country to industrialize.

Hohenberg, Paul M., and Lynn Hollen Lees. *The Making of Urban Europe, 1000–1950.* 1985. A good general introduction to the impact of industry on urbanization, emphasizing less the pathology of cities and more their resilience.

Hopkins, Eric. *Birmingham: The First Manufacturing Town in the World, 1760–1840.* 1989. An account that emphasizes the extent to which the city and its industry depended on manufacture by hand rather than by machine.

Lawton, Richard, and Robert Lee. *Urban Population Development in Western Europe from the Late Eighteenth to the Early Twentieth Century.* 1989. A country-by-country study of urban growth.

Nardinelli, Clark. *Child Labor and the Industrial Revolution.* 1990. A work that represents child labor as less harsh than some contemporaries claimed and as a rational adjustment to existing economic conditions.

Ponting, Clive. *A Green History of the World.* 1991. A work that includes some remarks on the impact of early industry on the European environment.

Tilly, Louise, and Joan Scott. *Women, Work and Family.* 1978. A description of the family wage economy in which all members contributed to the economy of the family, especially in the early stages of industrialization.

Turner, B. L., et al. *The Earth as Transformed by Human Action: Global and Regional Changes in the Biosphere over the Past 300 Years.* 1990. A work that includes some information on the nineteenth-century impact of industry on the environment.

Responses to Industrialization

Furet, François. *Marx and the French Revolution.* 1988. A consideration of the impact of the French Revolution on Marx.

Himmelfarb, Gertrude. *The Idea of Poverty: England in the Early Industrial Age.* 1983. A work that describes the image of the poor among Victorian middle-class observers.

Kelly, Alfred, ed. *The German Worker: Working-Class Autobiographies from the Age of Industrialization.* 1987. A collection of workers' accounts of their lives.

Kolakowski, Leszek. *Main Currents of Marxism,* vol. 1, *The Founders.* 1978. A work that traces the intellectual background of Marx's thought and the nature of the original synthesis he created.

Lynch, Katherine A. *Family, Class, and Ideology in Early Industrial France: Social Policy and the Working-Class Family, 1825–1848.* 1988. A study of social concerns in France over the corrosive impact of industry on working-class families.

Maynes, Mary Jo. *Taking the Hard Road.* 1995. An analysis of French and German workers' experiences during industrialization.

Mazlish, Bruce. *The Meaning of Karl Marx.* 1984. An easy-to-read introduction to the man and his thought, em-phasizing the shaping of both by the era in which Marx lived.

Moss, Bernard H. *The Origins of the French Labor Movement, 1830–1914: The Socialism of Skilled Workers.* 1976. A work that traces the origins of labor militancy among artisans.

Sewell, William H., Jr. *Work and Revolution in France: The Language of Labor from the Old Regime to 1848.* 1980. An account that stresses continuity in the development of the French working class from the time of the Old Regime to the mid-nineteenth century.

Thompson, E. P. *The Making of the English Working Class.* 1963. A work that emphasizes cultural factors that encouraged the development of working-class consciousness in England.

Traugott, Mark, ed. *The French Worker: Autobiographies from the Early Industrial Era.* 1993. A collection of telling excerpts from workers' recollections.

WORKERS' WAGES

In 1869 the Chamber of Commerce of Verviers, a town in eastern Belgium, published a report on workers' wages. In the seventeenth century, Verviers, located on the Vesdre River, had become a major producer of woolens. The river provided water for power, for washing the cloth, and for carrying away industrial waste. Thus, the site was ideal for finishing textiles, and the merchants of Verviers drew upon the labor of spinners and weavers in the surrounding farm areas. With a population of 4500 in the mid-seventeenth century, Verviers had 10,000 inhabitants by the end of the eighteenth.

Two local entrepreneurs brought the Englishman John Cockerill to town. In 1802 he set up the first spinning machine on the Continent and in 1816 the first steam engine in Belgium. Thirty years later, Verviers boasted forty factories and the population had increased to 23,000.

Industrialization transformed the people's lives in many ways. The table of wages reveals the existence of a variegated, hierarchical work force with clear, separate functions and specified salaries. It indicates the uneven ways in which people benefited from industry, depending on their skills, age, and gender.

For example, this list allows us to compare the wages of industrial workers and artisans. Industry made it difficult for the artisans to survive; unable to compete with machine manufacture, many had to give up their trade or tighten their belts to make ends meet. The new machine age, however, created an increased demand for the services of some artisans. Early in the nineteenth century the new machines eliminated hand spinning, for example, but inexpensive yarn at first increased the demand for handloom weavers. Notice that handloom weavers ("hand weavers" in the table) were relatively well paid in 1836. This is due to the uneven introduction of mechanical production. Weaving of high-quality woolens proved to be more difficult to mechanize than cotton goods. Power looms did not become common in Verviers until the 1860s, and we see the relative wages of hand-

loom weavers decline in 1869. Joiners and ironsmiths not only did the work they had traditionally done but found new opportunities building and repairing machines. The ironsmiths, joiners, and carpenters of Verviers were all paid better than other workers.

We may note several things about the impact of industry on the labor force. Notice the specialized descriptions of occupations in the textile industry. Among the factory workers we find some significant wage discrepancies. Compare, for example, the wages of the nonspecialized laborer to the wages of the other industrial workers.

Changes in technology, productivity, labor supply, and market demand for certain goods increased the relative wages of workers. Thus the relative wages of jobs changed between 1836 and 1869. Notice that a wool washer in 1869 was making 174 percent more than a wool washer made in 1836, but in the same period the wages paid to a warper had increased by 300 percent.

Let us next consider women in the labor force. Notice that the list is divided into "male occupations," "female occupations," and finally "children's occupation." Work is divided according to gender and age. Look at the list of women's industrial occupations. The absence of spinning female occupations in this list is significant. Spinning had been a female occupation since antiquity, but the spinning machines in Verviers were tended by men. Notice how little differentiation is evident; far fewer industrial occupations are listed for women than for men. Also look at the wages. Women's wages were all equally depressed, with the one exception of menders' wages, hovering in 1836 around .7 francs but climbing by 1869 to 2.25 francs, an increase of over 300 percent. Among men's occupations the spread of salaries was far greater. In 1869 the highest-paid women (menders) received 40 percent more than the lowest-paid women in 1836 (scourers), but the highest-paid men (ironsmiths) received 138 percent more than the lowest-paid men (wool washers) in 1836. By 1869 the wage gap had somewhat dimin-

Wage Differentials in Verviers, Belgium, 1836–1869

		Wages (francs per day)				
		1836	1846	1856	1863	1869
Male Occupations	Ironsmith*	1.73	2.25	2.50	3.00	3.87
	Carpenter*	1.90	2.25	2.65	2.87	3.50
	Dyer	1.40	1.46	1.60	2.60	3.37
	Spinner	1.80	1.90	2.90	3.12	3.40
	Carder	1.47	1.75	2.30	3.25	3.30
	Tanner*	1.83	2.00	2.25	3.00	3.25
	Warper	0.80	0.95	1.57	1.65	3.25
	Hand weaver*	1.97	1.70	2.85	3.00	3.00
	Joiner*	1.98	2.00	2.25	2.75	3.00
	Tenterer	—	1.25	1.40	2.34	3.00
	Presser	1.47	1.78	1.78	2.15	3.00
	Machine weaver	—	—	—	—	2.75
	Comber	0.84	1.27	1.50	1.75	2.65
	Fuller	1.40	1.50	1.75	2.30	2.67
	Laborer	—	1.25	1.50	1.87	2.50
	Wool washer	1.15	1.25	1.40	1.75	2.25
Female Occupations	Mender	0.73	0.80	1.10	1.40	2.25
	Wool sorter	0.98	1.08	1.70	1.85	2.00
	Gigger	0.75	0.80	0.80	1.25	2.00
	Burler	0.77	1.00	1.20	1.70	1.80
	Seamstress*	0.73	0.80	1.10	1.40	—
	Scourer	0.70	0.75	0.85	1.35	1.62
Children's Occupation	Piecener	—	0.70	0.90	1.10	1.60

*Artisans. (Those not starred were industrial workers.)

Source: Chamber of Commerce of Verviers, *Rapport général sur la situation du commerce et de l'industrie en 1868* (Verviers, 1869), p. 69; repr. in George Alter, *Family and the Female Life Course—The Women of Verviers, Belgium, 1849–1880* (Madison: University of Wisconsin Press, 1988), p. 103. Used by permission.

ished for both men and women, but it was still far larger for men (72 percent) than for women (28 percent).

Some male artisans consistently received wages higher than the wages of many machine operators—consider the wages of carpenters, for example. But notice the one female artisan occupation: seamstress. Although a seamstress was probably quite skilled, she was paid no more than the women in the factories. Special crafts, still prized for some men, were not given much monetary value when practiced by women.

Note the wage differences overall between male and female workers. In 1836 the average female worker received wages equivalent to 53.2 percent of the average male worker's wages. By 1869, there was some improvement: The difference had declined by 11 percentage points; still, women earned 64 percent of men's pay.

The table lists only one occupation for children: piecener. Small and nimble, children were paid to fix broken threads. They worked in many other capacities as well. Some were paid wages by their employers; others helped their parents in a factory or workshop. The wages of some adults probably included compensation for their children's labor.

We can learn much from a statistical table such as this about the impact of industrialization on the labor force. Some workers benefited, and others were harmed by the adoption of industry; over time workers experienced changes in their circumstances. If statistical tables are informative on such issues, they also have their limits. They do not tell us how workers interpreted and understood their experience. As workers suffered daily hardships, they had to try to make sense of their changing world.

CHAPTER 22

New Powers and New Tensions, 1850–1880

I n 1866 when Prince Charles, a member of the Prussian royal family, was offered the throne of Romania, he reportedly had to look at a map to locate his future kingdom. His puzzlement was partly understandable, for a united Romania had existed for only five years. The prince and his contemporaries in the generation after 1848 witnessed the emergence of several new nation-states. And as the map of Europe changed, a much enlarged and more powerful United States also emerged.

The changing political scenery was accompanied by the development of new political institutions. To meet the demand for popular participation in government so dramatically expressed in 1848, every European state, except the Ottoman and Russian Empires, found it necessary to have a parliament. Rare before midcentury, such institutions became common thereafter. No longer was the demand for popular participation seen as a threat to the existing political and social order. In fact, popular participation, or the appearance of it, gave the existing order a legitimacy it had not enjoyed since the French Revolution. Nationalism flourished during this period, emerging as a decisive force in European affairs and in the United States, where it promoted territorial expansion and a determination to preserve the Union.

These political transformations occurred in an era of unprecedented economic growth and prosperity, touched off by the discovery of gold in California in 1848. The increased supply of gold allowed for the expansion of credit, which led to the founding of new banks and mass investments in growing industries. The iron output of Britain, France, and Germany tripled in the years between 1850 and 1880. During this same period the

William I is proclaimed ruler of the German Empire at Versailles, 1871.

standard of living of every class rose significantly in industrializing nations. The middle classes expanded dramatically, while the elites sought to reestablish their power in new ways.

In the first half of the century, international relations had been dominated by the congress system, in which representatives of the major European states met periodically to preserve the balance of power. This order disappeared in the second half of the century, as political leaders pursued the narrow interests of their state. Instead of negotiation, brute military force—or the threat of its use—was employed to resolve international conflict. The new age was dominated not by ideals but by force, announced Prussian chancellor Otto von Bismarck, the main practitioner of what became known as *Realpolitik*, a policy in which war became a regular instrument of statecraft.

Crimean War This photograph shows the interior of the Sevastapol fortress after it had been battered into surrender. The Crimean War was the first conflict to be documented by photographers. *(Courtesy of the Board of Trustees of the Victoria & Albert Museum)*

THE CHANGING SCOPE OF INTERNATIONAL RELATIONS

The Crimean War and its aftermath shaped European international relations for several decades. Rising mutual suspicion led nations to act in their own self-interest and ignore the concerns of the other major players in the international system.

The Crimean War as a Turning Point, 1854–1856

The Crimean War had many causes. Principally, however, it was ignited by the decision of French and British statesmen to contain Russian power in the Balkans and keep it from encroaching on the weakening Ottoman Empire. Russian claims to have the right to intervene on behalf of Ottoman Christians had led to war between the two states in October 1853. The defeat of the Ottoman navy at Sinope in November left the Ottoman Empire defenseless.

British and French statesmen had considerable interest in the conflict. Britain had long feared that the collapse of the Ottoman Empire would lead Russia to seek territorial gains in the Mediterranean. Such a move would challenge Britain's supremacy. An explosion of public sentiment against Russia also obliged the British government to take an aggressive stance. Meanwhile, the French emperor, Napoleon III, viewed defeat of Russia as a way to eclipse one of the states most dedicated to preserving the existing European borders. He wanted to undermine existing power relations, hoping that a new order would lead to increased French power and influence. Napoleon also imagined that fighting side by side with Britain could lay the foundation for Anglo-French friendship. And so England and France rushed to defend the Ottoman Empire and declared war on Russia in March 1854.

The war was poorly fought on all sides. Leadership was woefully inadequate, and there were five times more casualties from disease than from enemy fire. The Russians had a standing army of a million but never managed to use more than a fraction of that number due largely to poor communications and supply systems. In Britain, failures in military supplies and leadership were denounced in the press and in Parliament. For the first time the press played an active role in report-

Florence Nightingale in the Crimean War

Florence Nightingale used her influential family connections to win an appointment to the Crimean battlefield. Once there, she organized nursing for the wounded and was able to secure additional personnel and medical supplies for her hospital. In this letter, Nightingale describes the plight of the wounded in an army lacking sufficient supplies.

We have no room for corpses in the wards. The Surgeons pass on to the next, an excision of the shoulder-joint—beautifully performed and going on well—ball lodged just in the head of the joint, and fracture starred all round. The next poor fellow has two stumps for arms—and the next has lost an arm and leg. As for the balls, they go in where they like, and do as much harm as they can in passing. That is the only rule they have. The next case has one eye put out, and paralysis of the iris of the other. He can neither see nor understand. But all who can walk come into us for Tobacco, but I tell them that we have not a bit to put into our own mouths. Not a sponge, nor a rag of linen, not anything have I left. Everything is gone to make slings and stump pillows and shirts. These poor fellows have not had a clean shirt nor been washed for two months before they came here, and the state in which they arrive from the transport is literally *crawling*. I hope in a few days we shall establish a little cleanliness. But we have not a basin nor a towel nor a bit of soap nor a broom—I have ordered 300 scrubbing brushes. But one half the Barrack is so sadly out of repair that it is impossible to use a drop of water on the stone floors, which are all laid upon rotten wood, and would give our men fever in no time. . . .

I am getting a screen now for the Amputations, for when one poor fellow, who is to be amputated tomorrow, sees his comrade today die under the knife it makes impression—and diminishes his chance. But, anyway, among these exhausted frames the mortality of the operations is frightful.

Source: Letter to Dr. William Bowman, November 14, 1854, in Sue M. Goldie, ed., *"I Have Done My Duty": Florence Nightingale in the Crimean War, 1854–56* (Iowa City: University of Iowa Press, 1987), pp. 37–38.

ing war, and photography brought to readers at home the gruesome realities of battle.

One of the few heroic figures to emerge from this conflict was Florence Nightingale (1820–1910), who organized a nursing service to care for the British sick and wounded. Later, her wartime experience allowed her to pioneer nursing as a professional calling. (See the box, "Florence Nightingale in the Crimean War.")

The war ended in December 1855 when Russia surrendered the fortified port of Sevastopol after a long, bitter siege. The Russians were reluctant to admit defeat, but the threat of Austrian entry into the war on the side of the Western allies convinced them to sue for peace.

The Crimean War killed three-quarters of a million people—more than any European war be-tween the end of the Napoleonic Wars and World War I. The slowness with which each side mobilized, the lack of planning and foresight in staging battles, the large number of fatalities from causes other than enemy fire—all were reminiscent of hostilities from earlier eras. It was a particularly futile, senseless war whose most important consequence was political, for it unleashed dramatic new changes in the international order.

The Congress of Paris and Its Aftermath

The former combatants met in Paris in February 1856 to work out a peace treaty: Their decisions—which pleased no one—shaped relations among European states for the next half-century. Russian statesmen were especially discontented. The Congress of Paris forbade Russia from having a fleet in the Black Sea and forced it to withdraw from Moldavia and Wallachia, where it had enjoyed the right of intervention since the 1830s. Tsar Nicholas I had expected Austrian assistance in the war in return for his help in crushing the Hungarian rebellion in 1849. Instead, Austria's leaders had not only withheld aid but even threatened to join the Western alliance, and Russian officials denounced Austrian "betrayal." Nor did French leaders feel their nation had benefited. Although holding the congress in Paris flattered the emperor's pride, no other clear advantages emerged for France. The north Italian state of Piedmont, which had joined the allies, gained from the congress only a vague statement on the unsatisfactory nature of the existing situation in Italy. Prussia was invited to attend the congress only as an afterthought and hence also felt slighted.

Although the war seemed to have sustained the integrity of the Ottoman Empire, the peace settlement weakened it indirectly by dictating reforms in the treatment of its Christian populations. These reforms impaired the empire's ability to repress growing national movements and opened the door to the possibility of independent Balkan states. British political leaders, galled by the heavy sacrifices of the war, moved toward isolationism in foreign policy. Austrian policymakers, who hoped to gain the aid of Britain and France in preserving the Habsburg empire, found them hostile instead, thereby encouraging the forces undermining it. At the time the peace treaty was signed, few people foresaw the enormous results that would flow from it.

In the past the congress system had tried to ensure that no major power was dissatisfied enough to subvert the existing distribution of power, but the Crimean War and the peace treaty markedly changed that situation. For example, in the first half of the century the international order had been upheld in part by the cooperation of the rulers of the conservative Eastern powers: Russia, Austria, and Prussia. Now these powers were rivals, and their competition contributed to growing instability in the international system. By and large, the decisions reached in Paris were either disregarded or unilaterally revised. This new international climate also allowed the emergence of new states without international sanction.

ITALIAN UNIFICATION

In the words of Prince von Metternich of Austria, Italy at midcentury was nothing but a "geographic expression." The revolution of 1848 (see page 767) had revealed an interest in national unification, but the attempt had failed. Yet within a dozen years what many believed to be impossible would come to pass. Idealists like Giuseppe Mazzini (1805–1872) had preached that Italy would be unified by its people, who would rise and establish a free republic. Instead, it was unified by royalty, by war, and by the help of a foreign state. Although ideals were not absent from the process of unification, cynical manipulation and scheming also came into play.

After the failed 1848 revolution, various Italian rulers resorted to repression. In Modena, the Habsburg duke Francis V jailed liberals, closed the universities, and personally caned passersby who did not tip their hat to him. In the Papal States, men were imprisoned for "appearing inclined to novelty." Pope Pius IX, who first had appeared sympathetic to Italian unification, opposed it as soon as he realized it was attainable only by war against Catholic Austria. Italian nationalists viewed him as a traitor as he became a firm opponent of both liberalism and nationalism. In Naples, the government was so weak it established its authority by working with organized crime. In Parma, the duke was assassinated in 1854—to the relief of his people—and the uprising that accompanied this desperate act was suppressed by three thousand Austrian troops sent in by the duke's ally, the Habsburgs.

Compared to this dismal record, the kingdom of Piedmont in northern Italy appeared stable and successful. It was the only Italian state that kept the liberal constitution it had adopted during the 1848 revolution, and it welcomed political refugees from other Italian states. Economically, it was a beacon to the rest of Italy, establishing modern banks and laying half the rail lines on the peninsula.

Since the late eighteenth century, some Italians had called for a *risorgimento*, a political and cultural renewal of Italy. By the mid-nineteenth century the idea was actively supported by a small, elite group of the educated middle class, urban property owners, and members of the professional classes, who were open to nationalist arguments. For merchants, industrialists, and professionals, a unified state would provide a larger stage on which to pursue their ambitions. Members of these groups founded the National Society, a grassroots unification movement. This organization now looked to Piedmont to lead the peninsula toward national unity.

Cavour Plots Unification

The statesman who was to catapult Piedmont into a position of leadership in the dramatic events leading to Italian unification was Count Camillo di Cavour (1810–1861). The son of a Piedmontese nobleman and high government official, he grew up speaking French, the language of the court and of formal education in Piedmont, and mastered Italian only as an adult. Cosmopolitan in his interests, Cavour knew more about Britain and France than about Italy. He was sympathetic to the aspirations of the middle class and saw in Britain and France models of what Italy ought to become, a liberal and economically advanced society.

Short, fat, and near-sighted, Cavour hardly cut a heroic figure. Yet he was ambitious, hard-working, and driven to succeed. In 1850 he joined the government of Piedmont. Two years later he was appointed prime minister. He shared the general enthusiasm of the middle classes for an Italian nation, but his vision probably did not include the entire Italian peninsula, only its north and center, which then could dominate the rest of the peninsula in a loose federation. One fateful lesson he had learned from the failures of 1848 was that foreign help, especially French assistance, would be necessary to expel the Austrians from the peninsula.

When the Crimean War broke out in 1854, Cavour steered Piedmont to the allied side, hoping to advance his cause. He sent twenty thousand troops to the Crimea, one-tenth of whom died. This act gained him a seat at the Congress of Paris, where his presence boosted the kingdom's prestige—and where he and Napoleon III had an opportunity to meet and size up each other.

Napoleon III favored the cause of Italian liberation from Austrian rule and some form of unification of the peninsula. Austria had been France's traditional opponent; destroying Austria's power in Italy might strengthen France. Thus the French emperor and the Piedmontese prime minister, both desirous of changing the map of Europe,

each for his own reasons, secretly met in July 1858 at Plombières, a French spa, to discuss how Italian unity could be achieved. They agreed that Piedmont would stir up trouble in one of Austria's Italian territories in an effort to goad the Austrians into war. France would help the Piedmontese expel Austria from the peninsula, and the new Piedmont, doubled in size, would become part of a confederation under the papacy. In exchange, the French emperor demanded the cession of Nice and Savoy. (See the box, "Cavour and Napoleon III Plot War.")

This demand presented difficulties: Savoy was the heartland of the Piedmont kingdom, the area from which the royal house came; and the city of Nice was clearly Italian in nationality. France's other demand was that the king of Piedmont, who represented the House of Savoy, the oldest reigning house in Europe, allow his 15-year-old daughter to marry the emperor's 38-year-old dissipated cousin. To accept these terms seemed a betrayal of national honor and conventional morality. But such scruples gave way to political ambition, and Cavour assented.

War between Austria and Piedmont began in April 1859. By June the combined Piedmontese and French forces had routed the Austrians at Magenta and Solferino (Map 22.1). The bloodiness of these battles impressed contemporaries: The color magenta was named after the color of the blood flowing on the battlefield, and when a Swiss humanitarian, Henri Dunant (1828–1901), organized emergency services for both French and Austrians wounded at Solferino, he proposed the founding of voluntary relief societies in every nation, called the Red Cross.

Instead of pressing on after these two military victories, Napoleon III decided to end the fighting. Several developments motivated his decision. First, he was truly shocked by the bloodshed he had witnessed, and he was alarmed by the Prussian mobilization on the Rhine on behalf of Austria. Second, his plans for Italy threatened to develop in unforeseen directions. To the south of Piedmont, popular revolts in August and September had broken out against local rulers. Each side fearing victory by the other, both revolutionaries and the local officials appealed for annexation to Piedmont, which resulted in a larger independent state than Napoleon III had anticipated. These factors led Napoleon to sign an armistice with the

Cavour and Napoleon III Plot War

In July 1858 Cavour and Napoleon III met at Plombières in France to plot war against Austria with the intention of evicting it from Italy. Italy's borders were to be reorganized, giving Piedmont additional territory, and France was to receive compensation for its assistance. On July 24, Cavour outlined the contents of the agreement in a letter to the king of Piedmont, a cynical display of realpolitik.

. . . [T]ogether we began to go through the Italian States, in search of those grounds for war which were so difficult to find. After we had traveled the whole length of the peninsula without success, we came almost unawares upon Massa and Carrara, and there discovered what we had been trying so hard to find. When I had given the Emperor an exact description of that unfortunate country, of which he already had a pretty clear idea anyway, we agreed on getting in a petition from the inhabitants to Your Majesty asking for his protection and even requesting the annexation of these Duchies to Sardinia. Your Majesty would not accept the proposed surrender, but would support the cause of these oppressed populations by addressing a haughty and menacing note to the Duke of Modena. The Duke, confident of Austrian support, would reply in an impertinent manner. Thereupon, Your Majesty would occupy Massa, and the war would begin. . . .

What would be the aim of the war?

The Emperor freely agreed that the Austrians must be driven out of Italy altogether, leaving them not an inch of land this side of the Alps and the Isonzo. . . .

After we had settled the future fate of Italy, the Emperor asked me what France would get, and if Your Majesty would cede Savoy and the County of Nice.

Source: Cavour to Victor Emmanuel, July 24, 1858, in David Thomson, ed., *France: Empire and Republic, 1850–1940* (New York: Harper, 1968), pp. 322–324.

Austrians, allowing Austria to keep part of Lombardy and all of Venetia and to participate in an Italian Confederation. Cavour was outraged by Napoleon's betrayal of their agreement and resigned as prime minister; he returned to office, however, in January 1860.

Unification Achieved, 1860

The overthrow of the Austrian-backed rulers in Parma, Modena, and Tuscany led these areas in 1859 to vote in plebiscites to join Piedmont. Farther south, in central Italy, agitation against the papal misrule also inclined those regions toward the more enlightened Piedmont.

Cavour had envisioned no more than a united northern Italy. Unexpected events in the south, however, dramatically changed that vision. The centuries-old misgovernment of Naples led to an uprising, further abetted by the revolutionary firebrand Giuseppe Garibaldi (1807–1882), a rival of Cavour who favored unification and won a large popular following. In May 1860, with but a thousand poorly armed, red-shirted followers, he set sail for Sicily to help the island rise up against its Bourbon ruler. Winning that struggle, Garibaldi's forces crossed to the mainland. Victory followed victory, and enthusiasm for Garibaldi grew. His army swelled to 57,000 men, and he won the entire kingdom of Naples.

Threatened by the advance of Garibaldi's power and fearing its reach into the Papal States, Cavour sent his army into the area in September 1860. This action, a brutal attack on a weak state that had not harmed Piedmont, was viewed by many Catholics as aggression against the spiritual head of their church. However, as Cavour explained to his parliament, political necessity required it. The inter-

Map 22.1 The Unification of Italy, 1859–1870 Piedmontese leadership and nationalist fervor united Italy.

ests of the state of Piedmont and the about-to-be-born Italy superseded traditional morality.

Although Garibaldi was a republican, he was convinced that Italy could best achieve unity under the king of Piedmont, and he willingly submit-ted the southern part of Italy, which he controlled, to the king, Victor Emmanuel II (r. 1849–1878). Thus by November 1860, Italy lay united under Piedmontese rule (see Map 22.1). The territories that came under Piedmontese control affirmed

Garibaldi Leading His "Red Shirts" to Victory over the Neapolitan Army, May 1860
Garibaldi's successful conquests in the south and Cavour's in the north opened the way
for Italian unification. *(Museo di Risorgimento, Milan/Scala/Art Resource, NY)*

their desire to be part of the new Italy in plebiscites based on universal male suffrage. By huge majorities, the populations voted affirmatively. Undoubtedly there was pressure from the occupying army and from the upper classes, who marched the people dependent on them—workers, employees, tenant farmers—to the polls. Voting was not secret, and fraud was widespread. But in an age drawn to democracy, the plebiscite gave legitimacy to the new state and won sympathy from liberally inclined states abroad.

Still to be joined to the new state were Austrian-held Venetia in the northeast and Rome and its environs, held by the pope with the support of a French garrison. But within a decade, a propitious international situation enabled the fledgling country to acquire both key areas. After Austria was defeated in the Austro-Prussian War in 1866, Venetia was ceded to Italy. Then the Franco-Prussian War forced the French to evacuate Rome, which they had occupied since 1849. Rome was joined to Italy

and became its capital in 1870. With that event, unification was complete (see Map 22.1).

The Problems of Unified Italy

National unity had been achieved, but it was frail. The nation was divided between the modernizing north and the traditional south. The uprisings in the south that had led to its inclusion in a united Italy were motivated more by hatred of the Bourbons than by fervor for national union. And once the union occurred, the north behaved like a conquering state—sending its officials to the south, raising taxes, and imposing its laws. In 1861 an uprising of disbanded Neapolitan soldiers and brigands broke out. To crush the revolt, half the Italian army was sent south; the civil war lasted five years and produced more casualties than the entire effort of unification.

Other major divisions remained. In 1861 only 2.5 percent of the population spoke the national language, Florentine Italian. The economy also remained divided. The north was far more industrialized than the rural south. In the south, child mortality was higher, life expectancy was lower, and illiteracy reached the 90 percent mark. The two regions seemed to belong to two different nations.

Piedmont imposed strong central control, resolutely refusing a federal system of government, which many Italians in an earlier era had hoped for. This choice reflected the determination of Piedmont to project its power onto the rest of the peninsula, as well as fear that any other form of government might lead to disintegration of the new state. The United States, with a federal system of government, was wracked by secessionism leading in early 1861 to the Civil War (see page 831). Piedmont wanted to save the new Italian state from such a fate.

Piedmont imposed its constitution on unified Italy. This constitution limited suffrage to men of property and education, less than 2 percent of the population. Further, although parliamentarism was enshrined in the constitution, Cavour's maneuvering as prime minister had kept governments from being answerable to the parliament. Shifting majorities meant that the government could cajole and bribe the opposition, transforming previous foes into supporters. This system of manipulation, known as *trasformismo*, characterized Italian government for decades. However, although Italian parliamentarism was far from complete, a liberal state recognizing legal equality and freedom of association had been established, providing more freedom for its citizens than the peninsula had seen for centuries.

The new Italian state was weakened by the hostility the Catholic church directed against it. In the process of unifying Italy, Piedmont had seized the Papal States and finally in 1870 annexed Rome, leaving the pope to administer only a few square blocks around the papal palace, the Vatican. The popes considered themselves prisoners of the new Italian state and denounced it and all those supporting it, including those participating in elections. Thus the new state was contested by many Catholics, who refused to recognize it for decades, thwarting its claim to legitimacy.

In 1870 Italy, with its 27 million people, was the sixth-most-populated European nation. It was too small to be a great power and too large to accept being a small state. Italian statesmen found it difficult to define their country's role in interna-tional politics, and they lacked a firm consensus on Italy's future.

GERMAN UNIFICATION

Like Italy, Germany began as a collection of polities, first loosely united in the Holy Roman Empire and then, after 1815, equally loosely organized in the German Confederation. As did Piedmont in Italy, Prussia, the most powerful German state, led the unification movement. And just as Italy had in Cavour a strong leader who imposed his will, so did German unification have a ruthless and cunning leader: Otto von Bismarck, prime minister of Prussia.

In 1848 German unification under Prussian leadership had appeared likely, but the process ended quickly when the king of Prussia refused to accept a throne offered by an elected assembly. When national unity was ultimately achieved, it was not as a result of popular decision but by the use of military force and the imposition of Prussian absolutism over the whole country.

The Rise of Bismarck

Austria under Metternich had always treated Prussia as a privileged junior partner. After Metternich's fall in 1848, however, rivalry erupted between the two German states. Each tried to use for its own aggrandizement the desire for national unity that had become manifest during the revolution of 1848.

In March 1850, Prussia invited various German rulers to a meeting in Erfurt to consider possible unification under its sponsorship. Austria, which had been excluded, insisted that the "Erfurt Union" be dissolved and that Prussia remain in the German Confederation. Austrian leaders backed their demands with the threat of war; at a meeting in Olmütz in November, Prussia had to scuttle the Erfurt Union and accept Austrian leadership in Germany. The Prussians dubbed this event the "humiliation of Olmütz," and many were determined to regain the advantage in Germany. At that time, however, the Prussian military was not strong enough to challenge Austria. But this situation changed under the new Prussian king, William I (r. 1861–1888), who was committed to expanding the size and effectiveness of the army. He wanted to reduce the reserve army, increase the professional army, and expand the training period from two to three years. These measures needed parliamentary approval, but the parliament, which was dominated by the liberals, opposed the increased costs.

When the parliament refused to accept the king's proposals, he dissolved it. It was immediately re-elected, with an even stronger liberal majority. The issue was not purely military, but rather one of who should govern the country—the king or the elected representatives. To get his way, the king appointed Otto von Bismarck as prime minister to implement his program of reforms.

Bismarck was a Junker, a Prussian aristocrat known for his reactionary views, who had opposed the liberal movement in 1848. As Prussian emissary to the German Confederation, he had challenged Austrian primacy. Devoted to his monarch, Bismarck smarted at the humiliation of Olmütz and sought to heighten Prussian power in Germany and throughout Europe. He faced down the parliament, telling the Budget Commission in 1862, "The position of Prussia in Germany will be decided not by its liberalism but by its power . . . not through speeches and majority decisions are the great questions of the day decided—that was the mistake of 1848–49—but by 'iron and blood.'"[1]

Bismarck tried to win over the liberals by suggesting that with military force at its disposal, Prussia could lead German unification. But the liberals resisted, and the Parliament voted against the military reforms. Ignoring the elected assembly, Bismarck decided to carry out the military measures anyway and to collect the taxes that would make them possible. The citizens acquiesced and organized no resistance.

Several factors explain why Bismarck prevailed. The liberals who opposed him represented the business and professional classes who had received the vote as a result of the 1848 revolution. They had not implemented effective political or social programs, and they did not enjoy mass support. Had they wished to mobilize large segments of the population on behalf of their principles, they could not have done so.

Neither the Prussian king nor Bismarck's fellow aristocrats were nationalists. They believed in a strong Prussia, but they feared that a united Germany would dilute Prussian power and influence.

German unification had been part of the liberals' program, not the conservatives'.

German liberals were faced with a dilemma: Did they value nationhood or the principles of liberty more? Fellow liberals elsewhere lived in existing nation-states, where statehood had preceded the development of liberalism. Even in Italy, the liberals had been faced by a less harsh dilemma, for unification was led by the liberal state of Piedmont. That was not the case in Germany, where the natural leader, Prussia, had a long tradition of militarism and authoritarianism. To be effective in opposition to Bismarck, German liberals would have had to join with the working classes, but they feared them and held themselves aloof from such an alliance.

Bismarck's genius was to exploit a growing desire for German unification. During the Franco-Austrian War of 1859, which launched Italian unification, Germans had feared that the French would cross the Rhine River; only a strong, united Germany could give its inhabitants security. Professional and cultural organizations now often extended beyond a single state and were all German, for instance, the German Commercial Association, the Congress of German Jurists, and the German Sharpshooters League. Many individual German states, each calculating possible political gains, launched proposals for unification in the 1860s. Although it had yet to find much resonance among the lower classes, the idea of a united Germany was gaining a wider audience.

Prussian Wars and German Unity

Having established the supremacy of royal power in Prussia, Bismarck was ready to enlarge Prussia's role in Germany at the expense of Austria. The provocation was a crisis over Schleswig-Holstein (Map 22.2). These two provinces, ethnically and linguistically German (except for northern Schleswig), were ruled by Denmark. Historically and by previous treaty agreements Schleswig and Holstein were legally inseparable. When in 1863 the Danish king, contrary to earlier treaty obligations, attempted to connect Schleswig more closely to the Crown, Holstein, with a mainly German population, felt threatened. Although the latter was under Danish rule, it was also a member of the German Confederation, and it called on the Confederation for protection.

Map 22.2 The Unification of Germany A series of military victories made it possible for Prussia to unite Germany under its domain.

Acting on behalf of the Confederation, Prussia and Austria intervened, sending troops that won a quick, cheap victory. Prussia occupied Schleswig, and Austria took Holstein.

Joint military action in no way united Prussia and Austria, who continued to be bitter rivals for domination of Germany. Bismarck believed war was the only means to win this contest, and conflicts over the administration of Schleswig and Holstein served as a pretext. With no declaration of war, Prussia attacked Austrian-administered Holstein in June 1866 and defeated the Austrian

GERMAN UNIFICATION

1862	Bismarck appointed prime minister of Prussia
January 1864	Austria and Prussia attack Denmark and occupy Schleswig and Holstein
June 1866	Austro-Prussian War
July 3, 1866	Prussia wins Battle of Sadowa
1867	The North German Confederation
March–July 1870	Crisis over Hohenzollern candidacy for Spanish throne
July 13, 1870	Interview at Ems and publication of Ems dispatch
July 19, 1870	France declares war on Prussia
September 1, 1870	Prussia victorious at Battle of Sedan
January 18, 1871	The German Empire declared in the Hall of Mirrors in Versailles

army at Sadowa (Königgratz) on July 3. Austria sued for peace.

Prussia annexed its smaller neighbors who had supported Austria, thus creating a contiguous state linking Prussia with the Rhineland. This enlarged Prussia intended to dominate the newly formed North German Confederation, comprising all the states north of the Main River. Henceforth Austria was excluded from German affairs.

The triumph of Sadowa transformed Bismarck into a popular hero. Elections held on the day of the battle returned a conservative pro-Bismarck majority to the Prussian parliament. The legislature, including a large number of liberals mesmerized by the military victory, voted retroactively to legalize the illegal taxes that had been levied since 1862 for the purpose of upgrading the military. Enthusiastic at the prospect that Prussia might now successfully lead German unity, these liberals readily compromised their principles. They rational-

ized that national unity ought to be gained first, with liberal constitutional institutions secured later. They proved to be wrong.

The unification of Germany, like that of Italy, was facilitated by a favorable international situation. The Crimean War had estranged Russia from Austria. In 1850 Austrian resistance to Prussian attempts to lead Germany had been backed by Russia, but by the time the Austro-Prussian War broke out in 1866, Austria stood alone. Although it would have been opportune for France to intervene on the Austrian side, the French emperor was indecisive and in the end did nothing. He also had been lulled into security by vague Prussian promises of support for French plans to annex Luxembourg. Once the war was won, however, Bismarck reneged on these promises, and France was left with the problem of a strong, enlarged Prussia on its eastern border, which threatened France's position as a Great Power. British statesmen likewise did not intervene in the unification process. Disillusioned by the results of the Crimean War, they were in an isolationist mood. Moreover, Britain's government was sympathetic to the rise of a fellow Protestant power.

Bismarck hoped that the southern German states would eventually merge with the North German Confederation. For the time being, he allowed them to remain outside the new body, but he obliged them to sign a military treaty with Prussia. Economically, they continued to be dependent as a result of the *Zollverein* (the customs union). Many southerners favored unity, especially business people who saw in it the hope of an improved economy. And German nationalists, north and south, sought the realization of a decades-long dream.

The Franco-Prussian War and Unification, 1870–1871

French leaders, however, were determined to prevent German unity. They feared the loss of influence in the southern German states that had traditionally been France's allies. Moreover, since the mid-seventeenth century, French security had been linked to a weak and divided Germany.

Both Berlin and Paris anticipated war. And war came soon enough, precipitated by a crisis over the Spanish succession. In 1868, a military coup had overthrown the Spanish queen Isabella, and the new authorities offered the throne to a

The Battle of Sadowa, July 3, 1866 In this important battle, the Prussians defeated Austria, eclipsing it as a German power. Now the road to Prussian supremacy in Germany lay open. *(Giraudon/Art Resource, NY)*

Catholic member of the Hohenzollerns, the reigning Prussian monarch's family. The French viewed this candidacy as an unacceptable expansion of Prussian power and influence. Fearing a two-front war with Prussia in the east and Spain in the south, they insisted the Hohenzollerns refuse the proffered throne. As passions heated, Bismarck was elated at the prospect of war. But the Prussian king was not. On July 12, 1870, he withdrew the young prince's candidacy, removing the cause for war. Bismarck was bitterly disappointed.

Not content with the prestige they won with this diplomatic victory, the French pushed their luck further. On July 13 the French ambassador met the king of Prussia at Ems and demanded guarantees that no Hohenzollern would ever again be a candidate to the Spanish throne. Unable to provide any more concessions without a serious loss of prestige, the Prussian king refused the French demand.

William telegraphed an account of his meeting to Bismarck. The chancellor was heartened by the opportunity this message provided. He edited what became known as the Ems dispatch, making the exchange between king and ambassador seem more curt than it actually had been; then he re-

leased it to the press. As he hoped, the French interpreted the account as a deliberate snub to their ambassador. Faced by a flood of emotional demands for redress of the imagined slight to French national honor, Napoleon III declared war on July 15.

The Prussians led a well-planned campaign. An army of 384,000 Prussians was rushed by rail to confront a force of 270,000 Frenchmen. The French had the advantage of better rifles, but the Prussians were equipped with heavier guns, which at a distance could pulverize French positions. Within a few weeks, Prussia won a decisive victory at Sedan, taking the French emperor prisoner on September 2. The French continued the struggle, despite difficult odds. Infuriated by the continuation of the war, the Prussians resorted to extreme measures, even targeting civilians. They took hostages and burned down whole villages, and they laid siege to Paris, starving and bombarding its beleaguered population.

Throughout Germany the outbreak of the war was met with general enthusiasm for the Prussian cause. Exploiting this popular feeling, Bismarck called on the other German states to accept the unification of Germany under the Prussian king. Reluctant princes, such as the king of Bavaria, were bought off with bribes. On January 18, 1871, the German princes met in the hall of mirrors of the Versailles palace, symbol of past French greatness, and acclaimed William I as German emperor (see Map 22.2).

In May 1871 the Treaty of Frankfurt established the peace terms. France was forced to give up the provinces of Alsace and Lorraine and to pay a heavy indemnity of five billion francs. These harsh terms embittered the French, leading many to desire revenge and establishing a formidable barrier to future relations between France and Germany.

The Character of the New Germany

German unity had been forged by a series of wars—against Denmark in 1864, Austria in 1866, and France in 1870—and lacked the popular democratic base that had been present in Italy. Because the military had been instrumental in the formation of the new German state, it remained dominant in the new society that followed. Italian unity had been sanctioned by plebiscites and a vote by an elected assembly accepting the popular verdict. The founding act of the new German state was the meeting of the German rulers on the soil of a defeated neighbor. Thus the rulers placed themselves above elected assemblies and popular sanction. (See the box, "Bismarck Considers the Dynastic Role in German Unification.")

The constitution of the new Germany was remarkably democratic on the surface, however. It provided for an upper, appointed house, the Bundesrat, representing the individual German states, and a lower house, the Reichstag, which was elected by universal manhood suffrage. The latter seemed a surprising concession from Bismarck, the authoritarian aristocrat. But he knew the liberals lacked mass support and gambled that, with appropriate appeals, he would be able to create majorities that could be manipulated for his purposes.

The dominant state in the new Germany was, of course, Prussia, which also had two-thirds of its population. Within the Bundesrat, Prussia had 17 of the 43 seats and could block any legislation it opposed with the aid of only a few other states. The king of Prussia occupied the post of emperor, and the chancellor and other cabinet members were responsible not to parliament but to him. He alone could make foreign policy and war, com-

mand the army, and interpret the constitution. The authoritarianism of Prussia had been projected onto all of Germany.

The emergence of a strong, united Germany disrupted the European balance of power. In February 1871 the British political leader Benjamin Disraeli observed that the unification of Germany was "a greater political event than the French revolution of last century. . . . There is not a diplomatic tradition which has not been swept away. You have a new world. . . . The balance of power has been entirely destroyed."[2] Germany had become the dominant power on the Continent.

PRECARIOUS SUPRANATIONAL EMPIRES

In an age of nationalism that saw two new nation-states emerge—Italy and Germany—those European states that were multinational found themselves in a precarious position. The Habsburg and Ottoman Empires of central and eastern Europe consisted of numerous peoples speaking different languages, holding different religious beliefs, and having different historical traditions. In the past such multinational states had been quite normal in Europe, but in the nineteenth century they became increasingly anomalous. The peoples living under the authority of Vienna and Constantinople became more and more restive. Facing this severe challenge, the Austrian and Ottoman Empires attempted to strengthen themselves by restructuring their institutions.

The Dual Monarchy in Austria-Hungary

Austrian statesmen sensed the vulnerability of their empire. By 1860 they had lost much of their Italian possessions; they met with resistance in Hungary from the Magyars, a powerful minority still resentful they had not won independence in 1848; and they faced the bitter struggle for German supremacy with Prussia. To give his government credibility, in February 1861, Emperor Francis Joseph (r. 1848–1916) issued what were known as the February Patents, which liberalized the government, guaranteed civil liberties, and provided local self-government and an elected parliament.

The need to concentrate on safeguarding the remaining territories was clear. By 1866 the Austrian Habsburgs were no longer a German or Ital-

Bismarck Considers the Dynastic Role in German Unification

After leaving office in 1890, Bismarck wrote his **Memoirs.** *In this selection he examines the efforts of the various states in promoting national unification. He denounces many of them for having resisted this movement but emphasizes the importance of Prussia's role. The rulers, rather than the German people, he insists, formed the new united Germany. And only monarchy can guarantee national unity.*

Never, not even in Frankfurt [in 1848] did I doubt the key to German politics was to be found in princes and dynasties, not in publicists, whether in parliament and the press, or on the barricades. The opinion of the cultivated public as uttered in parliament and the press might promote and sustain the determination of the dynasties, but perhaps provoked their resistance more frequently than it urged them forward in the direction of national unity. . . . The Prussian dynasty might anticipate that the hegemony in the future German empire would eventually fall to it, with an increase of consideration and power. It could foresee its own advantage. . . .

The Gordian knot of German circumstances . . . could only be cut by the sword: it came to this, that the King of Prussia, conscious or unconscious, and with him the Prussian army, must be gained for the national cause, whether from the "Borussian" [Prussian] point of view one regarded the hegemony of Prussia or from the national point of view the unification of Germany as the main object; both aims were co-extensive. So much was clear to me. . . .

In order that German patriotism should be active and effective, it needs as a rule to hang on the peg of dependence upon a dynasty; independent of dynasty it rarely comes to the rising point, though in theory it daily does so in parliament, in the press, in public meeting. . . . The German's love of Fatherland has need of a prince on whom it can concentrate its attachment. . . .

The preponderance of dynastic attachment, and the use of a dynasty as the indispensable cement to hold together a definite portion of the nation calling itself by the name of the dynasty, is a specific peculiarity of the German empire.

Source: Otto von Bismarck, *The Man and the Statesman*, trans. A. J. Butler (London: Smith Elder & Co., 1898), vol. 1, pp. 318–321, 323–324.

---

ian power (Venetia had been handed over to a united Italy). The strongest challenge to Habsburg rule came from Hungary, where the Magyars insisted on self-rule, a claim based on age-old historic rights and Vienna's initial acceptance of autonomy in 1848. Since Magyar cooperation was crucial for the well-being of the Habsburg empire, the government entered into lengthy negotiations with Magyar leaders in 1867. The outcome was a compromise that created a new structure for the empire that lasted until 1918. The agreement divided the Habsburg holdings into Austria in the west and Hungary in the east (Map 22.3). Each was independent, but they were linked by the person of the emperor of Austria, Francis Joseph, who was also king of Hungary. Hungary had full internal autonomy and participated jointly in imperial affairs—state finance, defense, and foreign relations. The new state created by the compromise was known as the dual monarchy of Austria-Hungary.

The emperor of the new state of Austria-Hungary had come to the throne as an 18-year-old in that year of crisis, 1848. Francis Joseph was a well-meaning monarch who took his duties seriously. His upbringing was German, he lived in German-speaking Vienna, and he headed an

army and a bureaucracy that was mostly German, but Francis Joseph was markedly cosmopolitan. He spoke several of his subjects' languages and thought of himself as the emperor of all his peoples. In both halves of the empire, he was a much-loved, regal figure who provided a visible symbol of the state. He lacked imagination, however, and did little more than try to conserve a disintegrating empire coping with the modern forces of liberalism and nationalism.

The compromise confirmed Magyar dominance in Hungary. Although numerically a minority, Magyars controlled the Hungarian parliament, the army, the bureaucracy, and other state institutions. They opposed self-rule by the Croats, Serbs, Slovaks, Romanians, and others in the kingdom and attempted a policy of Magyarization—teaching only Magyar in the schools, conducting all government business in Magyar, and giving access to government positions only to those fully assimilated in Magyar culture. This arrangement created frustrations and resistance among the various nationalities under their rule.

The terms of the compromise also gave the Hungarians a voice in imperial foreign policy. Magyars feared that Slavic groups outside the empire, who planned to form independent states or had already done so, would inspire fellow Slavs in Austria-Hungary to revolt. To prevent that, the Hungarians favored an expansionist foreign policy in the Balkans, which the monarchy gladly embraced (see Map 22.3). Having lost its influence in Germany, Austria-Hungary found in the Balkans an area in which to assert itself. The policy was fraught with risks and, by bringing more discontented Slavs into the empire, led to hostility with other states.

The Ailing Ottoman Empire

At midcentury the Ottoman Empire was still one of the largest European powers, but it faced unrest within its borders and threats by the expansionist designs of its neighbors. The ailing empire was commonly referred to as "the sick man of Eu-

rope." Over the next twenty-five years, the empire shed some of its territory and modernized its government, but nothing could save it from decline in the face of nationalist uprisings in its Balkan possessions.

As early as the 1840s, the Ottoman Empire had begun various reform movements to bring more security to its subjects. Known as the *Tanzimat*, these changes were initiated by Sultan Abdul Mejid (r. 1839–1861), with the help of his able prime minister, Reshid Mustafa Pasha (1800–1858). Reshid had served as the Ottoman ambassador in London and Paris and was familiar with Western institutions, which he admired and wished to emulate. The reforms tightened control over the Janissaries, the traditional military elite that had become a marauding force in the countryside. They also introduced security of property, equality of taxation, and equality before the law regardless of religion. Government officials—who previously had been free to collect taxes arbitrarily, sending the required amount to the central government and keeping the rest—were given fixed salaries and subjected to regular inspections.

These reforms were strengthened after the Crimean War by further imperial edicts. Contacts with the West encouraged Turks to think of transforming their empire into a more modern, Westernized state. Many young intellectuals were impatient with the rate of change, however, and critical of the sultan. Unable freely to express their opinions at home, some went into exile in the late 1860s to Paris and London. Their hosts called them the "Young Turks," an expression that became synonymous with the desire for change and improvement.

Alarmed by challenges to its rule, the central government began to turn away from reform, and in 1871 the sultan decided to assert his personal rule. His inability successfully to wage war and hold onto the empire led to dissatisfaction, and in the spring of 1876 rioters demanded and won the establishment of constitutional government. Within less than a year, however, the new sultan, Abdul Hamid II (r. 1876–1909), dismissed the constitutional government and reverted to personal rule.

Part of the administration's problem was financial. The Crimean War had forced the empire to borrow money abroad. The easy terms of foreign credit lured the sultan into taking out huge

Map 22.3 Austria-Hungary in 1878 A multinational state, the Austro-Hungarian Empire acquired Bosnia in 1878, bringing more dissatisfied peoples under its rule. Tensions in the Balkans would lead to the outbreak of war in 1914.

loans to finance extravagant projects. By 1875 more than half the annual income of the empire went to pay the interest on the debt. In spite of a drought and famine, the authorities raised taxes, fostering discontent within the realm.

Opposition to the government increased, fueled by nationalist fervor. The empire tolerated religious diversity and did not persecute people because of their religion. But the central administration had lost control over its provincial officials, who were often corrupt and tyrannical. In particular, much of the Balkan region was isolated from any benign control Constantinople might have wished to exercise. Christians, the majority population in the Balkans, blamed their suffering on Islamic rule, and many were inspired by the 1821

Greek war of independence and the revolutions of 1848 to seek their own independence.

The Romanians, for example, who lived mainly in the adjoining provinces of Moldavia in the north and Wallachia in the south, began to express nationalist sentiments in the late eighteenth century. These sentiments were nurtured by Western-educated students, who claimed for their countrymen illustrious descent from Roman settlers of antiquity. News of revolution in Paris in 1848 helped trigger a revolt in both provinces demanding unification and independence. This uprising was quickly crushed by the Turks.

The 1856 Peace of Paris removed Russia's right of protection over Moldavia and Wallachia and provided for a referendum to determine their future. Forbidden by international agreement from uniting, the two provinces chose a local nobleman, Alexander Cuza (r. 1859–1866), as ruler of each territory. Thus they were separate legally but united under one ruler. In 1861, the Ottoman Empire under pressure from the Romanians recognized the union of the two principalities in the single, autonomous state of Romania, and in 1878, at the Congress of Berlin, full independence was granted. Thus, in less than a quarter-century, two provinces of the Ottoman Empire merged and gained full sovereignty.

The path to independence was much more violent for the Bulgars. Influenced by neighboring Serbia and encouraged by the Russians, revolutionary committees spread propaganda and agitated against Ottoman rule. An uprising in Bulgaria broke out in May 1876. The Christian rebels attacked not only symbols of Ottoman authority but also peaceable Turks living in their midst. The imperial army, aided by local Turk volunteers, quickly re-established Ottoman authority. Incensed by the massacre of fellow Muslims, the volunteers resorted to mass killing, looting, and burning of Christian villages. The "Bulgarian horrors" shocked Europe and made the continuation of Turkish rule unacceptable.

The Bulgar crisis was resolved by the Balkan wars of 1876–1878, which were provoked by the uprising of the westernmost Ottoman provinces of Bosnia and Herzegovina. Since many of the inhabitants of these two provinces were Serbs, they had the sympathy of Serbia, which believed it could unify the southern Slavs. Together with the neighboring mountain state of Montenegro, Serbia de-

Nationalistic Uprising in Bulgaria In this 1879 lithograph, Bulgaria is depicted in the form of a maiden—protected by the Russian eagle, breaking her chains, and winning liberty from the Ottoman Empire. *(St. Cyril and Methodius National Library, Sofia)*

clared war on the Ottoman Empire. They were savagely defeated by the Turks.

Russia, which saw itself as the protector of the Slavic peoples, reacted to the Bulgarian horrors by also declaring war on the empire, in April 1877. At first progress was slow, then the Russians broke through the Turkish lines and forced the sultan to sue for peace. The resulting Treaty of San Stefano, signed in March 1878, excluded the Ottoman Empire from Europe and created a huge, independent Bulgaria as essentially a Russian satellite.

The British, Austrians, and French were shocked at the extent to which the San Stefano treaty favored Russia. Under their pressure, the European powers met in Berlin in 1878 to reconsider the treaty. The Congress of Berlin reduced the size of the Bulgarian territory, allowing the rest to revert to Constantinople. Bosnia and Herzegovina were removed from Ottoman rule and put under that of Austria-Hungary (see Map 24.4 on page 911). Constantinople was forced to acknowledge the legal independence of Serbia, Montenegro, and Romania and the autonomy of Bulgaria. The British insisted on being given nearby Cyprus to administer, an outpost from which they might prevent further challenges to the existing balance of power.

Thus Turkey was plundered, not only by its enemies but also by powers that had intervened on its behalf. When France complained that it received no compensation, it was given the chance to grab Tunisia, another land under Ottoman rule. Russia, which had signed an alliance with Romania and promised to respect its territorial integrity, ignored its obligations and took southern Bessarabia from its ally. The work of the congress reflected the power politics that now characterized international affairs. Statesmen shamelessly used force against both foe and friend for the aggrandizement of their own state. Neither morality nor international law restrained ambition.

THE EMERGENCE OF A POWERFUL UNITED STATES, 1840–1880

Across the seas a new power emerged in these years, the United States. It enlarged its territories, strengthened its national government, and broadened its democracy by including a large category of people previously excluded from the political process—African Americans. But these achievements came at the expense of the bloodiest conflict in all of American history, the Civil War.

Territorial Expansion and Slavery

In the first few years of its existence, the United States was confined to the thirteen colonies, but in the nineteenth century it gained much territory through westward expansion (Map 22.4). In 1803 President Thomas Jefferson, negotiating with the French, secured the Louisiana Purchase, which nearly doubled the size of the United States. In 1819 most of Florida was acquired from Spain. Some Americans looked even farther, moving into Mexican-held territories in the southwest and British-held territories in the Pacific Northwest. The United States, some began to insist, was destined to occupy the whole North American continent from coast to coast; expansion would fulfill what was often called America's Manifest Destiny.

The U.S. government used the settlements of American citizens in Mexican- and British-held territories as pretexts for expansion. In 1845 Congress voted to annex Texas, which had gained independence from Mexico in 1836. Threats of war against Britain, if it did not hand over the Oregon territory, led the British government to abandon its claims to this region by treaty in 1846. Declaring war on Mexico in the same year, the United States won California and the southwest in 1848. Territorial growth in the 1840s increased the size of the country by about 60 percent. The Gadsden Purchase in 1853 rounded off the American gains. The United States now spanned the continent from the Atlantic to the Pacific.

The nature of the U.S. federal government was transformed in these years: From being a weak institution exercising authority only in a limited number of domains, the government in Washington, D.C., became a powerful authority. This change represented the only practical resolution of regional disagreements that threatened to tear the country apart in the mid-nineteenth century.

Beginning in the 1820s the United States saw serious sectional clashes between east and west as well as north and south. The latter were more important. Many issues divided the two regions, notably a conflict between the industrial interests of the North and the agrarian interests of the South. What particularly sharpened this divide, however,

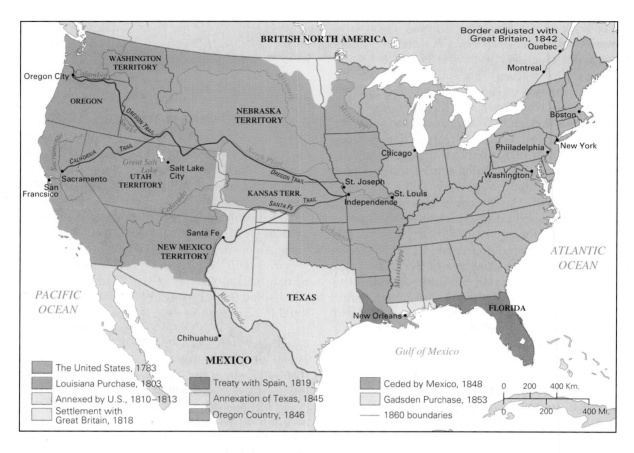

Map 22.4 U.S. Expansion Through 1853 In eight short years, from 1845 to 1853, the United States increased its territorial size by a third. The principle of Manifest Destiny appeared to be fulfilled, as the United States now stretched from the Atlantic to the Pacific.

was the issue of slavery. As the United States annexed new territories, the question of whether they would be slave or free divided the North and South, the North opposing the spread of the "peculiar institution," and much of the South, fearing isolation, favoring its spread. Southerners believed that if the new areas were closed to slavery, the institution would weaken in the South and eventually disappear. They would then be unable to withstand the political and economic pressure of an economically richer and more populous North, unsympathetic to slavery.

The issue of slavery was passionately debated for decades. Some Americans wanted slavery abolished thoughout the United States; if that could not be done, some of the most committed abolitionists, especially in New England, advocated the secession of free states from the Union. On the other side, southerners threatened that if their

way of life—meaning a society based upon slavery—were not assured, then the South would secede. The threat of secession was lightly and frequently made by partisans of various causes for many decades. Commitment to national unity was weak and underdeveloped.

The election in November 1860 of the Illinois Republican Abraham Lincoln (1809–1865) as president appeared to the South as a final blow. Lincoln opposed the spread of slavery beyond its existing borders and hence appeared to threaten the future of slavery. Within a few weeks, the South reacted to Lincoln's election.

Beginning in December 1860 a number of southern state legislatures voted to secede from the Union, forming in February 1861 the Confederate States of America. The South saw its cause as being one of states' rights, claiming that the people of each state had the right to determine their destiny, free from what they viewed as the tyranny of the national government. Southern states seized federal funds and property, and in April 1861 the Confederates bombarded federally held Fort Sumter. Lincoln, inaugurated in March 1861, was determined to preserve the Union and to put down the insurrection. A calamitous civil war (1861–1865) had begun.

Civil War and National Unity

The North had many advantages over the South. It was nearly three times more populous than the South, it had a strong industrial base that could supply an endless stream of manufactured weapons, and it had a more extensive rail system allowing for better transport of men and materiel to the front. Although there were a number of important military engagements between the two parties, the North essentially strangled the South, which toward the end of the war was short of men, money, and supplies.

During both the war and its aftermath, the government took measures that centralized power in the United States, changing the nation from a loose federation of states to a more centrally governed entity. As one historian has noted, the United States changed from "they" to "it." The federal government intruded into areas of life from which it had before been absent. Slaves, previously considered property, were declared by Lincoln to be free with the Emancipation Proclamation in 1863. In fighting the war, the Union imposed conscription, enrolling every young able-bodied male in the army. A federal income tax was instituted, and with the National Banking Act of 1863, state banks were driven out of business and replaced by a uniform national banking system. The federal government provided massive subsidies for a national railroad system, and with the Morrill Land Grant College Act of 1862, it created a national system of state universities. Lincoln established the National Academy of Sciences to advise him on scientific matters. The word *national* came into increasing use. Senator John Sherman of Ohio declared during the war that "the policy of this country ought to be to make everything national as far as possible."

The principle of state sovereignty, which the Southern states had espoused and which the North had tried to accommodate before the war, now lay defeated. The North occupied the South in an attempt to "reconstruct" it. Reconstruction included efforts to root out the Confederate leadership and to ensure full civil and political rights for the newly emancipated African Americans. The government also embarked on a short-lived campaign to provide freed slaves with enough land to ensure them of a livelihood—another example of federal authority at work. When the occupation of all the South ended in 1877, the supremacy of the national government over states was clearly established.

The Frontiers of Democracy

One of the major transformations in the United States that began in the 1820s and culminated in the 1860s was the inclusion of an ever greater number of people in the political process. By the late 1820s, under the impact of popular pressure, states abandoned restrictions on voting, and most adult white males received the vote. Symbolic of this new "age of the common man" was the election of Andrew Jackson as U.S. president in 1828. All his predecessors had been men of education and property—some were even described as "Virginia aristocrats"—but Jackson represented himself as a self-made man, a rugged frontiersman. State legislatures had in the past elected members to the presidential Electoral College, but in response to public calls for change, state legislatures altered the system so that Electoral College members were selected by direct popular vote.

National presidential campaigns became rough-and-tumble affairs, with emotional appeals to the public. Scurrilous attacks, many untrue, were mounted against opponents. In 1828, for instance, during President John Quincy Adams's reelection campaign, his opponents charged him with corruption, although once he was defeated, they admitted he had been one of the nation's most honest officeholders. Campaigns began to revolve around easily grasped symbols, and when William Henry Harrison ran for president in 1840 he was depicted as a simple frontiersman. His supporters wore log-cabin badges, sang log-cabin songs, and carried log-cabin replicas on floats in parades. Such paraphernalia became a common sight in American elections. If some contemporary observers, such as the Frenchman Alexis de Tocqueville (1805–1859), were disappointed at the

Bingham: The Verdict of the People In George Caleb Bingham's 1855 painting set in the American West, voters await election results. Unlike in Europe, where religious and property barriers to suffrage continued throughout the nineteenth century, many U.S. states had universal white male suffrage by the 1820s. *(From the Art Collection of NationsBank)*

lack of a thoughtful and deliberate process in choosing political leaders, they thought democracy was nowhere in the world as fully developed as in the United States, where it foreshadowed the future of other societies.

When Abraham Lincoln was elected U.S. president in 1860, nobody of his social standing occupied an equivalent position in Europe. At the news of his assassination in 1865, workmen and artisans, seeing in the dead president a kindred spirit, stood for hours in line outside the U.S. legation in London and the consul general's office in Lyon (France) to sign a book of condolence to express their sorrow. It was also a form of tribute to a nation that had elected a backwoodsman, born in a log cabin, to its highest office.

The frontiers of democracy appeared to have widened after the Civil War when amendments to the U. S. Constitution granted African Americans full equality with whites. Slavery was forbidden throughout the United States, and regardless of "race, color, or previous condition of servitude," all Americans were declared to be citizens and guaranteed the exercise of their rights. During the first few years of Reconstruction, whites who had supported the Confederacy were deprived of the right to vote, and African Americans represented a voting bloc in the South. As a result, for the first time the United States saw the election of a black governor as well as several lieutenant-governors, senators, congressmen, postmasters, and innumerable county and town officials who were black. After the end of military occupation of the south, however, local white power reasserted itself and the rights of African Americans were sharply curtailed. Yet, compared to the situation before the Civil War, African Americans had advanced significantly. They were no longer slaves but citizens, they were free to move where they wanted, and in some places they were able to participate in the political process.

By 1880 the United States not only had seen four decades of territorial expansion but had been transformed by the ordeal of the Civil War, which brought about the extension of federal authority and—however hesitatingly—of the rights of citi-

∼ ENCOUNTERS WITH THE WEST ∼

A Japanese View of the British Parliament

In 1862 the Japanese government sent its first diplomatic mission to Europe. Accompanying the delegation was its young translator, Fukuzawa Yukichi (1835–1901). Intrigued by what he saw and eager to interest his fellow Japanese in the West, Fukuzawa published several books. In fact, all books about the West in Japan came to be known as "Fukuzawa-bon." Toward the end of his life in his Autobiography he described how, while in London, he had tried to understand the workings of the British Parliament.

Of political situations at that time, I tried to learn as much as I could from various persons that I met in London . . . though it was often difficult to understand things clearly as I was as yet unfamiliar with the history of Europe. . . . A perplexing institution was representative government. When I asked a gentleman what the "election law" was and what kind of an institution the Parliament really was, he simply replied with a smile, meaning I suppose that no intelligent person was expected to ask such questions. But these were the things most difficult of all for me to understand. In this connection, I learned that there were different political parties—the Liberal and the Conservative— who were always "fighting" against each other in the government.

For some time it was beyond my comprehension to understand what they were "fighting" for, and what was meant, anyway, by "fighting" in peace time. "This man and that man are 'enemies' in the House," they would tell me. But these "enemies" were to be seen at the same table, eating and drinking with each other. I felt as if I could not make much out of this. It took me a long time, with some tedious thinking, before I could gather a general notion of these separate mysterious facts. In some of the more complicated matters, I might achieve an understanding five or ten days after they were explained to me. But all in all, I learned much from this initial tour of Europe.

Source: The Autobiography of Fukuzawa Yukichi, trans. Eiichi Kiyooka (Tokyo: Hokuseida Press, 1948), pp. 138, 143–144.

zenship to new groups. A large, powerful democracy had arisen in the North American continent.

STABILITY IN VICTORIAN BRITAIN

The mid-nineteenth century was a period of exceptional wealth and security for Britain as the population as a whole began to share in the economic benefits of industrialization. Britain enjoyed both social and political peace. The political system was not challenged as it had been in the generation after the Napoleonic wars. A self-assured, even smug, elite—merchants, industrialists, and landowners—developed a political system reflecting liberal values.

Parliamentary Government

Although suffrage was still very restricted, the parliamentary system became firmly established, with a government clearly responsible to the electorate. The importance of Parliament was symbolized by the new building in which it met, finished in 1850 on the site of previous parliamentary buildings but of a splendor and size that was unprecedented. The form of government developed in its halls after midcentury represented a model that aroused the curiosity and envy of much of the world. (See the box, "Encounters with the West: A Japanese View of the British Parliament.") Parliament consisted of an upper, hereditary House of Lords and a lower, elected House of Commons.

Increasingly, the royal cabinet became answerable to Parliament.

In the twenty years after 1846, five different parties vied for power. Depending on the issue, parties and factions coalesced to support particular policies. After 1867, however, a clear two-party system emerged: Liberal and Conservative (Tory), both with strong leadership. This development gave the electorate a distinct choice. The Conservatives were wedded to preserving traditional institutions and practices, while the Liberals tended to be open to change.

Gladstone, Disraeli, and the Two-Party System

Heading these parties were two strong-minded individuals who dominated British political life for over a generation: William E. Gladstone (1809–1898), a Liberal, and Benjamin Disraeli (1804–1881), a Conservative. Gladstone came from an industrial family and married into the aristocracy; Disraeli was the son of a Jewish man of letters who had converted to Christianity. His father's conversion made possible his career—before the 1850s Jews were barred from Parliament. Prior to heading their parties, Gladstone and Disraeli both served in important cabinet positions. They were master debaters; Parliament and the press hung on their every word. Each was capable of making speeches lasting five hours or more and of conducting debates that kept the house in session until 4 A.M. The rivalry between the two men thrilled the nation and made politics a popular pastime.

The Conservatives' electoral base came from the landed classes, Anglicans, and from England, rather than the rest of the United Kingdom. The Liberals' base came from the middle classes, Christian groups other than the Church of England, and from Scotland and Wales. In the House of Commons both parties had a large number of members from the landed aristocracy, but increasingly cabinet members were chosen for political competence rather than family background. Aristocratic birth was no longer a requirement for reaching the pinnacle of power, as Gladstone and Disraeli so clearly illustrated.

The competition for power between the Liberals and Conservatives led to an extension of suffrage in 1867. The Second Reform Bill lowered property qualifications, extending the vote from 1.4 to 2.5 million electors out of a population of 22 million, and gave new urban areas better representation by equalizing the electoral districts. Although some in Parliament feared that these changes would lead to the masses capturing political power—"a leap into the dark," one member called it—in fact no radical change ensued. Extending the vote to clerks, artisans, and other skilled workers made them feel more a part of society, and thus bolstered the existing system. John Stuart Mill, then a member of Parliament, championed the cause of women's suffrage, but he had few allies and that effort failed.

As the extension of voting rights increased the electorate, parties became larger and stronger. Strong party systems meant a clear alternation of power between the Liberals and the Conservatives. With an obvious majority and minority party, the monarch could no longer play favorites in choosing a prime minister. The leader of the majority party had to be asked to form a government. Thus, even though Queen Victoria (r. 1837–1901) detested Gladstone, she had to ask him to form governments when the Liberals won parliamentary elections. (See the feature, "Weighing the Evidence: An Engraving of the British Royal Family," on pages 842–843.)

The creation of a mass electorate also meant that politicians had to make clear appeals to the public and its interests. In the past, oratory had been limited to the halls of Parliament, but after the electoral reforms, it occurred in the public arena as well. Public election campaigns became part of the political scene in England. The democratic "American" style of campaigning appealed to the common man. Also borrowed from across the seas was the "Australian ballot"—the secret ballot—adopted in 1872. This protected lower-class voters from intimidation by their employers, landowners, or other social superiors. In 1874 the first two working-class members of Parliament were elected, sitting as Liberals. Although their victory represented a very modest gain for workers' representation, it presaged the increasingly democratic turn England was to take.

FRANCE: FROM EMPIRE TO REPUBLIC

Unlike Britain, which gradually transformed into a parliamentary democracy, France took a more tumultuous path. Revolutions and war overthrew existing political systems and inaugurated new ones. Each time the French seemed to have democracy within reach, the opportunity slipped away. At the same time, authoritarianism was equally elusive.

The People's Emperor, Napoleon III

The constitution of the Second French Republic provided for a single four-year presidential term. Frustrated by this limitation of power, Louis Napoleon by a coup d'état extended his presidency to a ten-year term in 1851. The following year, he called for a plebiscite to confirm him as Napoleon III (r. 1852–1870), emperor of the French. Both of these moves were resisted in the countryside, particularly in the south, but the resistance was put down by massive repression.

In the rest of the country, huge majorities of voters endorsed first the prolonged presidency and then the imperial title. The new emperor seemed different from his predecessors. He believed in the principle of popular sovereignty (he maintained universal male suffrage, introduced in 1848), he did not pretend to reign by divine grace, and he repeatedly tested his right to rule by an appeal to the popular vote. He seemed to combine order and authority with the promises of the Revolution—equality before the law, careers open to talent, and the abolition of hereditary rights.

The mid-nineteenth century was a period of prosperity for most Frenchmen, including urban workers and peasants. Louis Napoleon, in his youth the author of a book on pauperism, introduced government measures congenial to labor. On the one hand, workers were required to keep a booklet in which their conduct was to be recorded by their employers; on the other hand, they were granted limited rights to organize strikes, and labor unions were virtually legalized. The emperor expressed his desire to improve the workers' lot, and the government initiated a few concrete measures, such as providing some public housing. Although slum clearance during the rebuilding of Paris drove many from their homes to the outskirts of the city, it did provide healthier towns for those who stayed behind, and the ambitious urban projects provided work for many (see page 858). Other public works projects, such as ports, roads, railroads, and monumental public buildings, also created jobs. Railroads in France in-

Disraeli and Gladstone: Victorian Political Rivals This 1868 cartoon from *Punch* magazine captures the politians' personalities. Disraeli was known as vain and theatrical, while Gladstone was dour and moralistic. *(Mary Evans Picture Library)*

creased tenfold and provided the means for peasants to market their harvests more widely. If some peasants had initially opposed Louis Napoleon, most supported him once he was in power. Not only were they a cautious group, preferring stable authority, but they saw in the emperor—the heir to the great Napoleon—an incarnation of national glory.

Not all the French supported the emperor; many republicans could not forget that he had usurped the constitution of 1848. In protest, some had gone into exile, including the poet Victor Hugo. Trying to win over the opposition, Napoleon made some concessions in 1860, easing censorship and making his government more accountable to the parliament. Instead of winning him new support, however, this liberalization allowed the expression of mounting opposition. A coordinated republican opposition rebuked the economic policies of the empire, notably the decision to sign a free-trade treaty with England. Although this policy helped the wine and silk exporters, it left iron and textile manufacturers unprotected. Businessmen in these fields rallied their workers against the imperial regime.

A number of other issues—notably, widespread hostility to the influence of the Catholic church and the desire for more extensive freedoms of expression and assembly—also helped forge a republican alliance of the middle classes and workers. This alliance was particularly powerful in the large cities and in some southern regions notorious for their opposition to central government control. Republicanism was better organized than in earlier years and had a more explicit program, and its proponents were now better prepared to take over the government, if the opportunity arose.

By 1869 the regime, which declared itself a "liberal empire," had fully evolved into a constitutional monarchy, responsible to the Legislative Corps, the lower house of the parliament. In a plebiscite in May 1870, Frenchmen supported the liberal empire by a vote of five to one. It might have endured, but two months later Napoleon III rashly declared war against Prussia over the imagined slight to French national honor precipitated by the Ems dispatch (see page 823). Defeat brought down the empire. In September, at news of the emperor's capture, the republican opposition in the Legislative Corps declared a republic. It continued the war but had to sign an armistice in January 1871.

The leader of the new government was an old prime minister of Louis Philippe, Adolphe Thiers (1797–1877). To sign a definite peace, the provisional government held elections. The liberals, known as republicans since they favored a republic, were identified with continuing the war; the conservatives, mostly royalists, favored peace. Mainly because of their position on this issue, the royalists won a majority from a country discouraged by defeat.

The Paris Commune, 1871

The new regime had no time to establish itself before an uprising in the spring of 1871 shook France, while reminding the rest of Europe of revolutionary dangers. The uprising was called the Paris Commune, a name that harked back to 1792–1794, when the Paris crowds had dictated to the government. The Commune insisted on its right to home rule. It was greeted by both radicals and conservatives as a workers' revolt that sought to establish a workers' government. Marx described it as the "bold champion of the emancipation of labor."

Although labor discontent played a role in the Paris Commune, other forces also contributed to its outbreak. Primarily the uprising was triggered by the Prussian siege of Paris during the Franco-Prussian war. Paris had become radicalized during the siege: The rich had evacuated the city, leaving a power vacuum quickly filled by the lower classes. Parisians suffered much because of the siege, and angered at the lack of recognition for their economic needs and their courage in withstanding the Prussians, they rose up against the new French government. Under their pressure, the Commune, composed largely of artisans, began governing the city.

In March 1871 the Commune declared itself free to carry out policies without hindrance from the central government in Versailles. The government sent forces to crush the Commune, and they massacred 25,000 people, arrested 40,000, and deported several thousand more. Although the savagery of this repression indicated that the Commune was viewed as unacceptably radical, it was, in fact, quite moderate. It sought free universal education, a fairer taxation system, a minimum wage, and disestablishment of the official Catholic church.

Nonetheless, the crushing of the Paris Commune and some of its sister communes in southern France, which were also asserting local autonomy, signified the increasing power of the centralized state. The emerging modern state had the strength to squelch popular revolts that in the past had seriously threatened regimes. Western Europe would not again witness a popular uprising of this magnitude.

Creation of the Third Republic, 1871–1875

Despite its brutality, the crushing of the Commune by Thiers's new government reassured many Frenchmen. "The Republic will be conservative, or it will not be," declared Thiers. The question now at hand was what form the new government would

Manet: The Barricade In detail from this 1871 painting, Edouard Manet catches a scene from the Paris Commune of 1871. With barricades, the communards are trying to protect themselves from the onslaught of government troops. Although fewer than a thousand government soldiers died, over 25,000 communards were killed. *(Reproduced by courtesy of the Board of Directors of the Budapest Museum of Fine Arts)*

take. The monarchist majority was split between those favoring a restoration to the throne of the Bourbon heir, the grandson of Charles X, and those favoring the Orléanist heir, grandson of Louis Philippe. Partisans of both sides finally compromised on an offer of the throne to the elderly and childless Bourbon pretender. However, he insisted he would become king only if the *tricouleur*—the flag of the Revolution, which long since had become a cherished national symbol—were discarded and replaced by the white flag of the house of Bourbon. The monarchists realized their project was unfeasible; their plan was thus scuttled and France remained a republic. The republic, as Thiers put it, "is the regime which divides us the least."

By 1875 the parliament had approved a set of basic laws that became the constitution of the Third Republic. Ironically, a monarchist parliament had created a liberal, democratic parliamen-

tary regime. The parliament was to consist of two chambers: the Chamber of Deputies, elected by universal male suffrage, and the Senate, chosen indirectly by local officials. The two houses sitting jointly elected the president, who was to occupy essentially a ceremonial role as chief of state. The head of government—the premier—and his cabinet were responsible to the parliament. A century after the French Revolution, the republican system of government in France was firmly launched.

RUSSIA AND THE GREAT REFORMS

By the 1840s concern about the archaic nature and structure of Russian government was mounting. Many officials lamented the tendency of a timid bureaucracy to lie and mislead the public. Defeat in the Crimean War widened the critique of Russian institutions. Calls for *glasnost*—greater openess—became the leading motif in the great reforms of the 1860s.

The Abolition of Serfdom, 1861

The chief problem that needed resolution was serfdom. Educated opinion had long denounced serfdom as immoral, but this was not the principal reason for its abolition. Serfdom was abolished because it presented clear political disadvantages in both the domestic and international domains. The new tsar, Alexander II (r. 1855–1881), feared that if the abolition of serfdom was not mandated from above, it would occur from below—by a violent serf rebellion that would sweep away everything in its path, including the autocracy itself.

Serfdom was also linked to Russia's place in the world. Defeat in the Crimean War suggested that if Russia depended for its defense upon a soldiery of serfs rather than free men, it would be unable to survive in an increasingly competitive international situation. The Russian army would be more powerful if it consisted of soldiers with a stake in their society rather than men committed to lifetime servitude. In addition, the victorious Western states had won in part because their industrial might translated into more and better guns, ammunition, and transportation. Industrial progress required a mobile labor force, not one tied to the soil by serfdom. For many educated Russians, the defeat in the Crimea revealed general Russian backwardness. To catch up with the West, Russia needed to rid itself of its timeworn institutions, particularly serfdom.

In April 1861, the tsar issued a decree freeing the serfs. (See the box, "The Tsar Demands the Freeing of the Serfs.") It was a radical measure to emancipate 22 million people from a system that allowed them to be bought and sold, separated from their families, and treated in the cruelest ways imaginable. Emancipation represented a compromise with the gentry, which had reluctantly agreed to liberate its serfs but insisted on compensation. As a result, the newly liberated peasants had to reimburse the government with mortgage payments lasting fifty years. The peasants received some land, but its value was vastly overrated and its quantity insufficient for peasant families. To make ends meet, the freed peasants continued working for their former masters.

The mortgage payments and taxes imposed on the peasants by the central government were handled by the local commune, the *mir*. The mir determined how the land was to be used, and it paid collectively for the mortgage and taxes on the land. As a consequence, the commune was reluctant for the peasants to leave the land, and they could do so only with its permission. Freed from serfdom, the peasants still suffered many constraints. In fact, the emancipation declaration was accompanied by massive peasant uprisings that had to be put down by force.

The tsar and his advisers feared the large mass of uneducated peasants as a potential source of anarchy and rebellion. Thus they depended on the mir to preserve control even though the commune system had some inherent economic disadvantages. Increased productivity benefited the commune as much as the individual peasant; hence there was little incentive for land improvement, and yield remained low.

Reforms in Russian Institutions

Alexander was called the "tsar emancipator" by his contemporaries, but he was wedded to the principles of autocracy. His aim in abolishing serfdom and introducing other reforms was to modernize and strengthen Russia and stabilize his divinely mandated rule. Like most Russians, Alexander believed that only the firm hand of autocracy could hold together a large, ethnically diverse country. The peasant uprisings that accompanied emancipation only confirmed these beliefs.

Clearly, however, the sudden freedom of 22 million illiterate peasants threatened to overwhelm existing institutions, and some changes had to be made. Although he surrendered no powers, Alexander did promulgate a number of reforms, altering the government and the judicial and military systems so they could more effectively deal with all the changes in Russian society.

Government reform had paramount importance. Between about 1800 and 1850, the Russian population had increased from 36 to 59 million, and it had become more and more difficult to administer this vast country. Overcentralized, with a poorly trained civil service, the government was unable to cope effectively with the problems of its people. Emancipation of the serfs greatly exacerbated this situation; an enormous number of people, freed

The Tsar Demands the Freeing of the Serfs

In January 1861, Tsar Alexander II addressed the Council of State, an advisory body that he had asked four years earlier to prepare a draft law emancipating the serfs. After this forceful speech, a workable proposal emerged and was implemented six weeks later.

The matter of the liberation of the serfs, which has been submitted for the consideration of the State Council, I consider to be a vital question for Russia, upon which will depend the development of her strength and power. . . . [T]his matter cannot be postponed . . . I repeat—and this is my absolute will—that this matter should be finished right away.

. . . [Y]ou will assure yourselves that all that can be done for the protection of the interests of the nobility has been done . . . but I ask you only not to forget that the basis of the whole work must be the improvement of the life of the peasants—an improvement not in words alone or on paper but in actual fact. . . .

My predecessors felt all the evils of serfdom and continually endeavored, if not to destroy it completely, to work toward the gradual limitation of the arbitrary power of the estate owners.

Already in 1856, before the coronation, while in Moscow I called the attention of the leaders of the nobility of the Moscow guberniia to the necessity for them to occupy themselves with improving the life of the serfs, adding that serfdom could not continue forever and that it would therefore be better if the transformation took place from above rather than from below. . . .

I have the right to demand one thing from you: that you, putting aside all personal interests, act not like estate owners but like imperial statesmen invested with my trust. Approaching this important matter I have not concealed from myself all those difficulties that awaited us and I do not conceal them now.

Source: Speech of January 28, 1861, in George Vernadsky et al., eds., *A Sourcebook for Russian History from Early Times to 1917*, vol. 3. Copyright © 1972. Reprinted by permission of the publisher, Yale University Press.

from their owners' control, were abruptly in need of services. Thus in 1864 a law was passed providing for local governments, or *zemstvos*, at the village and regional level, giving Russians the authority and the opportunity to use initiative in local matters.

The zemstvos were largely controlled by the gentry and not particularly democratic. They were forbidden to debate political issues, and their decisions could be overridden or ignored by local officials appointed by the tsar. Some hoped that zemstvos could become the basis for self-government at the national level and looked for the creation of an all-Russian zemstvo, but such hopes were firmly squelched by the tsar, who jealously insisted on undivided and undiminished absolutism. Nonetheless, the zemstvos were an attempt to modernize an overburdened central government.

The tsar also created an independent judiciary that ensured equality before the law, public jury trials, and uniform sentences. Russian political leaders recognized that public confidence in the judiciary was a prerequisite for the development of commerce and industry. Businessmen would no longer fear arbitrary intervention by capricious officials and could develop enterprises in greater security.

In addition, censorship of the press was abolished. Under the previous tsar, Nicholas, all ideas that did not conform to government policy were censored. Such censorship prevented the central government from being well informed about public opinion or about the effects of its policies on the country. Under Alexander, openness in the press was viewed as a remedy for corruption and misuse of power. People could be punished only for specific violations after publication, and they would face trial in an independent court.

Reform also extended to the Russian army. Its structure and methods became more Western. Military service, previously limited to peasants, became the obligation of all Russians. All men submitted to a lottery, and those with an "unlucky" number entered the service. In an effort to make military service more attractive, however, the length of service was drastically cut and corporal punishment was abolished. Access to the officer corps was to be by merit rather than by social connection. The Ministry of War also improved the system of reserves, enabling Russia to mobilize a larger army with more modern weapons in case of war.

Although the tsarist regime remained autocratic and repressive, it did institute several key reforms. A new page had been turned in Russian history.

SUMMARY

Novel configurations of power appeared on the West's chessboard in the period from about 1850 to 1880 as new or enlarged states were created through warfare or the threat of force. Liberal nationalists in the early nineteenth century had believed that Europe would be freer and more peaceful if each people had a separate nation, but they were now proved wrong. The Crimean War and its aftermath replaced the congress system, which had sought a balance of power among partners, with a system of rival states in pursuit of their own self-interest. The international order was severely shaken as Italy and Germany emerged from the center of Europe and Romania and Bulgaria were carved out of the Ottoman Empire in the east.

Both new and existing states faced a choice between federalism and centralized rule. In the process of unification, Italy and Germany could have opted for a loose federal union, but both Piedmont and Prussia chose central control. And the crushing of the Paris Commune spelled the doom of those who wanted a France of decentralized self-governing units. Strong, centralized governments increasingly became the norm. That was also the case across the ocean in the United States, where North and South fought a bloody civil war over the issues of slavery and state sovereignty,

and the victorious federal government imposed its will on the rebellious states.

To achieve legitimacy, however, governments had to appear to be enjoying the consent of their peoples. Hence all European rulers except those of the Ottoman and Russian Empires found it necessary to have a parliament. France and Britain became increasingly democratic in these years, answerable to a growing electorate. In other states parliaments had only limited powers, but once they were in place, it could be argued—and was— that more power should be shifted toward them and that they should be chosen by an expanded electorate. In the United States whites already enjoyed freer and more open institutions than existed anywhere else, and the post–Civil War era marked a further enlargement of political participation when African Americans were granted the rights of citizenship.

Two major changes that liberals in 1848 had agitated for had become reality: freer political institutions and the organization of nation-states. Although neither of these was fully implemented everywhere, both appeared to have been successfully established. Many Europeans could easily believe they were living in an age of optimism.

NOTES

1. Quoted in Otto Pflanze, *Bismarck and the Development of Germany*, vol. 1 (Princeton: Princeton University Press, 1990), p. 184.
2. Quoted in William Flavelle Monypenny and George Earle Buckle, *The Life of Benjamin Disraeli: Earl of Beaconsfield*, vol. 2 (London: John Murray, 1929), pp. 473–474.

SUGGESTED READING

International Relations

Goldfrank, David M. *The Origins of the Crimean War.* 1994. Blames the Russian Tsar Nicholas I for irresponsibly launching the war.

Pearton, Maurice. *The Knowledgeable State: Diplomacy, War and Technology since 1830.* 1982. Emphasizes the contribution of breakthroughs in science, technology, and social organization to military matters.

Rich, Norman. *Why the Crimean War? A Cautionary Tale.* 1985. Argues that the war was caused by the Western powers' decision to eliminate the Russian threat to the Ottoman Empire.

Italian Unification

Coppa, Frank J. *The Wars of Italian Independence*. 1992. Views Italian unification within an international context.

Grew, Raymond. *A Sterner Plan for Italian Unity*. 1963. Studies the role of the National Society in advancing the cause of unification.

Hearder, H. *Italy in the Age of the Risorgimento, 1790–1870*. 1983. Considers regional differences in the peninsula and analyzes the debates among various protagonists of the risorgimento.

Smith, Dennis Mack. *Cavour and Garibaldi, 1860*. 1954. Contrasts the heroic, but sometimes naive, Garibaldi with the master manipulator, Cavour.

———. *The Making of Italy, 1796–1870*. 1968. Considers the long-term forces leading to Italian unity.

———. *Cavour*. 1985. Debunks the notion that the Italian statesman was a liberal nationalist who carried out a carefully planned strategy to unite the peninsula.

Woolf, Stuart. *A History of Italy, 1700–1860*. 1979. Provides a long-term view of the place of unification in Italian history.

German Unification

Carr, William. *The Wars of German Unification*. 1991. A careful examination of the three wars that led to unification.

Hamerow, Theodore S. *The Social Foundations of German Unification, 1858–1871*, 2 vols. 1969 and 1972. Reveals the essentially middle-class support for the program of German unification.

Howard, Michael. *The Franco-Prussian War: The German Invasion of France, 1870–71*. 1961. Reveals some of the more "modern" aspects of the war, including a willingness to target civilians.

Pflanze, Otto. *Bismarck and the Development of Germany. I: The Period of Unification, 1815–1871*. 1990. Emphasizes Bismarck's flexibility and ability to improvise to accomplish long-range goals.

Sheehan, James. *German Liberalism in the Nineteenth Century*. 1978. Emphasizes the environment that conditioned the shaping of liberalism in a country that unified late and had to deal with a fast-emerging working class.

The Ottoman and Habsburg Empires

Jelavich, Charles and Barbara. *The Establishment of the Balkan National States, 1804–1920*. 1977. Traces the emergence of independent states from the Ottoman Empire.

Shaw, Stanford J. *History of the Ottoman Empire and Modern Turkey. II: Reform, Revolution and Republic: The Rise of Modern Turkey, 1808–1975*. 1977. Emphasizes the success of reform in the Ottoman Empire and sees its decline as essentially due to foreign aggression.

Sked, Alan. *The Decline and Fall of the Habsburg Empire, 1815–1918*. 1989. Provides a revisionist interpretation, concentrating on the strengths of the empire.

The United States, 1840–1880

Bensel, Richard Franklin. *Yankee Leviathan: The Origins of Central State Authority in America, 1859–1877*. 1990. Emphasizes the extent to which the Civil War led to centralization of government in the United States.

Smith, Page. *The Nation Comes of Age: A People's History*, vol. 4. 1981. Describes the development of the United States from 1828 to 1860, in an account marked by vivid prose and strong narrative.

———. *Trial by Fire: A People's History*, vol. 5. 1982. Equally strong in analysis and narrative, it covers the Civil War and Reconstruction.

Victorian Britain

Blake, Robert. *Disraeli*. 1966. The authoritative biography of the Victorian statesman who helped shape the British parliamentary system.

Evans, Eric J. *The Forging of the Modern State: Early Industrial Britain, 1783–1870*. 1983. Considers the development of political parties for the period covered in this chapter.

Wilson, A. N. *Eminent Victorians*. 1990. Has a chapter devoted to Gladstone that emphasizes his idealism and devotion to great causes.

France, from Empire to Republic

Greenberg, Louis. *Sisters of Liberty: Marseilles, Lyon, Paris, and the Reaction to a Centralized State, 1868–1871*. 1971. Reminds us that the Commune did not break out only in Paris but also in several provincial French cities and insists that local self-government was at least as important a goal to the Communards as their social program.

Smith, William H. C. *Napoleon III*. 1972. Provides a sympathetic view of Napoleon III as a staunch believer in popular sovereignty who was devoted to the welfare of his people.

Williams, Roger L. *The French Revolution of 1870–1871*. 1969. Describes the Commune as the continuation of the French revolutionary tradition.

Russia and the Great Reforms

Kolchin, Peter. *Unfree Labor: American Slavery and Russian Serfdom*. 1987. The most recent study of Russian serfdom, of particular interest to American readers.

Lincoln, W. Bruce. "The Problem of Glasnost in Mid-Nineteenth-Century Russian Politics." *European Historical Quarterly*, 11 (April 1981): 171–188. Considers the origins of the concept in the Russian bureaucracy.

———. *In the Vanguard of Reform*. 1982. Argues that the great reforms originated in the 1840s.

———. *Great Reforms*. 1990. Shows the reforms to be part of a general program of modernization.

AN ENGRAVING OF THE BRITISH ROYAL FAMILY

Why were Queen Victoria and her family depicted in the manner shown in this popular engraving? The illustration might well have been of an upper-middle-class family. Note the family's attire. The queen is soberly dressed; her husband, Prince Albert, is wearing a dark business suit; the children are simply dressed. The image extends from the royal family to the rest of England, depicted as a simple farm, some cottages, and a grouping of common people. Notice the crown hovering over this idyllic scene. Victoria's reign was the longest of any British monarch; the manner in which she conducted herself, and her subjects' image of her, shaped the monarchy and people's expectations of it.

Illustrations of this type familiarized the British with their monarch. Surrounded by her husband and children, the queen seemed to have an endearing common touch. In the past representations of the monarchy had suggested power and intimidation. The aura of the close-knit, nuclear royal family, akin to the families of the queen's middle-class subjects, suggested a serenity that was reassuring to those subjects.

Victoria cultivated the image of herself as contented mother, but in reality she resented much about motherhood. She complained of the extent to which her pregnancies interfered with her daily routines, preventing her from traveling and being as much with her beloved Albert as she would have liked; she described childbearing as an "annoyance" that made her feel "so pinned down—one's wings clipped." She also refused to romanticize birthing, seeing it as an animal-like act, reducing a woman to "a cow or a dog." Biology put women in an inauspicious position; "I think our sex a most unenviable one," she lamented. And Victoria continued viewing the children, once they were no longer babies, as a burden, describing them as "an awful plague and anxiety for which they show one so little gratitude very often!" But such views were expressed strictly privately, and the public never suspected Victoria's ambivalence toward her role as mother.

Whatever her complaints about children, Victoria's family life was in strong contrast to that of her predecessors, projecting a new image of the monarchy. Her grandfather George III (r. 1760–1820) had bouts of insanity. Her uncle George IV (r. 1820–1830) was a notorious philanderer. George IV and his brothers, the Duke of Clarence (later to be William IV [r. 1830–1837]) and the Duke of Kent (Victoria's father), were bigamists. They fathered a large brood of illegitimate children and were involved in numerous public scandals.

The character of Victoria's three predecessors and of the various other men in line to the throne had strengthened opposition to the monarchy. Public outrage at their excesses had led to a call for the abolition of the institution. When the 18-year-old Victoria came to the throne, it would have been difficult to imagine that she would on her death leave the monarchy considerably strengthened.

The image of Victoria shown here intentionally contrasts her reign to the reigns of her predecessors. Victoria is surrounded by four of her children (eventually she would have nine). Her predecessors had died leaving no legitimate direct heirs and thus endangering the regular succession to the throne. The engraving announces that the royal line is assured. English people wary of a female ruler can find solace in knowing that Victoria would be succeeded by one of her sons. Later, Victoria's children and their progeny would intermarry with the rest of Europe's royalty, and by the end of her reign most of Europe's crowned heads would be related to one another.

Although Victoria's uncles and father were wastrels and bankrupts, the queen and her husband lived frugally by royal standards and conducted an exemplary family life. Under the wise administration of Prince Albert, royal wealth increased; he carefully administered various royal estates and investments. Instead of being subject to various debtors, the British royal house became one of the wealthiest landowners in Great Britain, achieving financial independence and winning social prestige. Among the large landowning mag-

THY CHOICEST GIFTS IN STORE, ON HER BE PLEASED TO POUR.

GOD SAVE THE QUEEN.

Illustration from *A Book of English Song*

nates of Britain, the royal house became the most prominent.

The model royal family appealed to the growing middle class of Victorian society. Consider how the simple terms in which the monarch is depicted here and in many other illustrations reflect the increasingly democratic spirit of the era. The ruler and her family appear in a common scene. Victoria is queen, but she also is a mother and wife. There is no sign here of pomp and ceremony.

Given the disrepute into which the monarchy had fallen and the rise of republican sentiment, the coming to the throne of a woman in 1837 may have substantially lessened antimonarchical sentiment. The last woman to rule England had been one of its greatest monarchs, Elizabeth I (r. 1558–1603), who had provided stability and brought glory to her kingdom. There also happened to be a certain gallantry toward a young, seemingly f ail woman coming to the throne. Also, because of her gender Victoria was seen as less of a threat to constitutional liberties.

Under Victoria's rule Britain completed the process of becoming a constitutional monarchy. Although Victoria's predecessors had been openly partisan, the queen cultivated the image of being above party, a symbol of national unity and the state. Fellow monarchs in central and eastern Europe exercised greater power, but after World War I they were toppled. In Britain, monarchy in its constitutional form endured. Victoria established a pattern of public and private behavior by which members of subsequent generations of the British royal family were to be judged. ❧

CHAPTER 23

The Age of Optimism, 1850–1880

The first department store in Paris, which served as a model for others in France and abroad, "Bon Marché" (the "good buy") opened its doors in the 1850s. The store bought goods in mass quantities and thus could sell them at low prices. Constructed of glass and iron, Bon Marché represented the new, modern age. It combined under one roof a large range of products that previously had been available only in separate specialty shops—a time-saving device in an increasingly harried age. The store also had a large catalog sales department for customers too busy or distant to shop in person. Filled with toys, bed linens, furniture, crystal, and other items, the department store was a symbol of the new opulence of the middle classes.

This new type of store would not have been possible in an earlier age. It serves as a summary of the various technological and social changes experienced by the more prosperous regions of the West as industrialization advanced in the second half of the nineteenth century. Industrial innovation had lowered the price of glass and steel, so that these new, huge commercial emporiums could be built at reasonable cost. Railroads brought customers from outside the city and trams and omnibuses from within it. The penny press provided advertising for the department store, which in turn supported the emergence of this new medium. The expansion of the postal system facilitated catalog sales and the mailing of goods to customers. And the higher incomes available to many people allowed them to purchase more than just the necessities. A phenomenon began that became predominant in the West a century later—the consumer society.

Felix Valloton,
Le bon marché.

As industrialization spread throughout western Europe, rising productivity brought greater wealth to many social groups and nations. This wealth not only led to more consumer spending but also contributed to a change in attitudes. The late nineteenth century was an era shaped to a large extent by the growing middle classes, who were filled with optimism and convinced they were living in an age of progress. The successful application of science and technology to social problems gave many men and women confidence in the human ability to improve the world. People controlled their environment to a degree never before possible. On farms they increased the fertility of the soil; to the burgeoning cities they brought greater order. Scientists used new methods to study and combat disease. Public authorities founded schools, trained teachers, and reduced illiteracy. Transportation and communication rapidly improved.

In fact, not all of society benefited from the fruits of progress. The new wealth was far from equally shared. Eastern and southern Europe changed little, and even in the western part a large group of the population still lived in great misery. If some cities carried out ambitious programs of urban renewal, others continued to neglect slums. Public sanitation programs did not affect the majority of Europeans who lived in rural areas. Despite spectacular advances in science, much of the population maintained a traditional belief in divine intervention. Many intellectuals strongly denounced the materialism and smugness of the age, stressing the meanness and ignorance that lay just beneath the surface.

Still, the tone of the age was set by the ascendant middle classes in western Europe, which embraced change and believed that the era was heading toward even more remarkable improvements. Their optimism was all the greater because the ultimate effects of the social and technological changes taking place in Europe were not yet known: The major processes discussed in this chapter occurred in the generation living between 1850 and 1880, but many were as yet incomplete by 1880.

INDUSTRIAL GROWTH AND ACCELERATION

Beginning in the 1850s, western Europe experienced an unprecedented level of economic expansion. Manufacturers created new products and employed new sources of energy. An enlarged banking system provided more abundant credit to fund the expansion. Scientific research was systematically employed to improve methods of manufacture. A revolution in transportation speedily delivered goods and services to distant places. For many Europeans, daily life was profoundly changed by technological innovations.

The "Second Industrial Revolution," 1850–1914

The interrelated cluster of economic changes that began in the generation after 1850 is often called the "second industrial revolution." It was characterized by a significant speedup in production and by the introduction of new materials such as mass-produced steel, synthetic dyes, and aluminum. Manufacturers replaced the traditional steam engine with stronger steam-powered turbines or with machines powered by new forms of energy—petroleum and electricity.

The invention of new products and methods of manufacture spurred this industrial expansion. The second half of the nineteenth century has often been called the "age of steel." Up to then, steel production had been limited by the expense involved in its manufacture, but in 1856, Sir Henry Bessemer (1813–1898) discovered a much cheaper method, which produced in twenty minutes the same amount of steel previously produced in twenty-four hours. Ten years later, William Siemens (1823–1883) in England and Pierre Martin (1824–1915) in France developed an even better technique of steel production, the open-hearth process. The Thomas-Gilchrist method, invented in 1878, made possible the use of phosphor-laden iron ore, which previously had been economically unfeasible.

The results were dramatic. In Great Britain, steel production increased fourfold, and the price of steel fell by more than 50 percent between the early 1870s and the following decade. Greater steel production made possible the expansion of the rail system, the creation of a steamship fleet, and an explosive growth in the building industry. No longer was steel a rare alloy used only for the finest swords and knives; it became the material that defined the age.

Significant changes in the supply of credit further stimulated economic expansion. Discovery of gold in California and Australia led to the inflow of huge amounts of the precious metal to Europe, expanding the supply of money and credit. This led to the establishment of the modern banking system.

Each advance made possible additional changes. Increased wealth and credit accelerated further expansion of industrial plants and the financing of an ambitious infrastructure of roads, railroads, and steamships, which in turn boosted trade. Between 1800 and 1840, the value of world trade had doubled. In the twenty years following 1850, it increased by 260 percent.

By the 1880s important scientific discoveries fueled industrial improvements. Electricity began to be more widely used, replacing coal as a source of energy. Synthetic dyes revolutionized the textile industry, as did alkali in the manufacture of soap and glass. Dynamite, invented by the Swedish chemist Alfred Nobel (1833–1896) in the 1860s, made it possible to level hills and blast tunnels through mountains, facilitating construction. Five years after Nobel's death, his will established a prestigious prize named after its donor, to honor significant contributions to science and peace.

Transportation and Communications

The rail system grew dramatically in the middle decades of the nineteenth century. When the English engineer Robert Stephenson (1803–1859) demonstrated the feasibility of the steam locomotive, the "Rocket," in 1829, it ran on a track that was one-and-a-half miles long. By 1880 the total European railroad mileage was 102,000 (Map 23.1). In 1888 the "Orient Express" line opened, linking Constantinople to Vienna and thus to the rest of Europe. Distance was conquered by speed as well: By midcentury trains ran 50 miles per hour, ten times as fast as when they were invented. The cost of rail transport steadily decreased, allowing for its greater use. Between 1850 and 1880 in Germany, the number of rail passengers increased tenfold and the volume of goods eightyfold. In France and Great Britain, the increases were nearly as impressive.

Ocean transportation also changed dramatically. In 1869 the French built the Suez Canal

IMPROVEMENTS IN COMMUNICATIONS AND TRANSPORTATION	
1820s	The omnibus is introduced in France
1829	Robert Stephenson runs the "Rocket"
1833	Invention of the telegraph
1840	Introduction of the penny stamp
1850s	Clipper ships
	Invention of the tramway
1863	Building of underground railroad in London
1865	Transoceanic telegraph cable installed
1869	Opening of Suez Canal
1875	Alexander Graham Bell invents the telephone

across Egyptian territory, linking the Mediterranean to the Red Sea and the Indian Ocean. It reduced by 40 percent the journey between London and Bombay. More efficient ships were developed; by midcentury the clipper ship could cross the Atlantic in fourteen days. Steamships were also built, although they did not dominate ocean traffic until the 1890s. By 1880 European shipping carried nearly three times the cargo it had thirty years earlier.

The optimism born of conquering vast distance was reflected in a popular novel by the French writer Jules Verne (1828–1905), *Around the World in Eighty Days* (1873). The hero, Phineas Fogg, traveled by balloon, llama, and ostrich, as well as by the modern steam locomotive and steamship to accomplish in eighty days a feat that, only thirty years earlier, would have taken at least eleven months. Such was the impact of the steamship, locomotive, and the Suez Canal.

Along with the new speed, advances in refrigeration changed food transport. Formerly, refrigeration could be achieved only with natural ice, cut from frozen ponds and lakes, but this changed in the 1870s with the introduction of mechanical ice-making machines. By the 1880s dairy products and meat were being transported vast distances by rail and even across the seas by ship. Thanks to

Map 23.1 European Rails, 1850 and 1880 During the mid-nineteenth century, European states built railroads at an increasing rate, creating a dense network by the 1880s. (*Adapted from Norman J. G. Pounds*, An Historical Geography of Europe, 1800–1914 *[New York: Cambridge University Press, 1985].*)

these advances, the surplus food of the Americas and Australia, rich in grasslands, could offer Europe a cheaper and far more varied diet.

Regular postal service was also a child of the new era of improved transportation. In 1840 Britain instituted a postage system based on standard rates. Replacing the earlier practice in which the recipient paid for the delivery of a letter, the British system enabled the sender to buy a stamp—priced at the low rate of one penny—and drop the letter

into a mailbox. It was collected, transported speedily by the new railroads, and delivered. The efficiency and low cost of mail led to a massive increase in its use. In Great Britain the number of letters mailed in a year increased from 7 per person per year in 1840 to 32 by 1880.

The post combined with transoceanic telegraphs and the invention of the telephone to transform the world of information. In the late 1830s the telegraph was invented, and by 1864,

The Suez Canal Opened in 1869, the canal significantly shortened the voyage by ship from Europe to East Asia. The Suez Canal exemplified the speeding up of transportation and communication in the second half of the nineteenth century. *(AKG London)*

80,000 miles of telegraph wire were laid on the European continent. By 1865 transoceanic cables connected the Americas to Europe. Suddenly news from distant parts of the globe—of earthquakes, revolutions, or the outbreak of war—could reach Europe within minutes. In 1875 American inventor Alexander Graham Bell (1847–1922) invented a machine capable of transmitting the human voice by electrical impulses; in 1879 the first telephones were installed in Germany; two years later they appeared in France.

The speedy linking of distant places called attention to the need to standardize time. Up to now, countries typically had innumerable time zones; each town established its time according to the location of the sun. Railroad traffic made these quaint differences a source of annoyance to travelers and railroad officials, and it became imperative to have a standard time for each nation. The electric telegraph made it possible to set that time to the second.

CHANGING CONDITIONS AMONG SOCIAL GROUPS

Industrial advances transformed the traditional structure of European society. Fewer people worked the land; more worked in industry. The social and political influence of the landed aristocracy waned as wealth became far less dependent on ownership of land. To varying degrees, this influence now had to be shared with the growing middle classes. Generally, life for both industrial and farm workers improved in this period. However, there were great disparities; many people continued to suffer from profound deprivation.

The Declining Aristocracy

Always a small, exclusive group, the European aristocracy in the nineteenth century represented less than 1 percent of the population. There were regional variations; in Bavaria and Bohemia, nobles accounted for less than one-tenth of 1 percent of the population, while in Hungary they represented 5 percent. Many of those of noble birth were quite poor and economically indistinguishable from their non-noble neighbors. Others owned vast estates and were fabulously wealthy. The duke of Sutherland in Britain and the Esterhazy family in Hungary owned over one million acres, Count Orloff in Russia half that amount.

Some ennoblements were of recent origin. In England, most titles were less than a hundred years old, having originally been conferred on individuals in recognition of service to the state, the arts, or the economy. In France both Napoleons had ennobled persons they wished to honor. In Germany, Bismarck ennobled the Jewish banker Gerson Bleichröder (1822–1893) for helping finance the wars of the Prussian state and for relieving the German chancellor of personal financial worries by making profitable investments for him.

Distinctions between aristocrats and members of the upper middle class became increasingly blurred; noble families in financial straits often married their children to the offspring of wealthy merchants. And many nobles who previously had shunned manufacture participated in the new economy by becoming industrialists and bankers. Idle members of the nobility were now somewhat rare. Although many aristocrats still enjoyed a lavish lifestyle, others had the habits of successful business people.

Despite the theories of egalitarianism sweeping Europe in the aftermath of the French Revolution and the rapidly changing social structure engendered by industrialization, the power of the aristocracy did not disappear. In Prussia, some of the wealthiest industrialists came from the highest

aristocracy—among them Prince Henckel von Donnersmarck and the duke of Utjest. The heavily aristocratic officer corps played an important role in running the Prussian state and unified Germany. In France about 20 to 25 percent of officers and many diplomats were aristocrats. In Britain officers, diplomats, and high-ranking civil servants were usually of noble birth. In Austria and Russia, aristocratic origin was the norm for government service.

Nonetheless, nobles no longer asserted privileges based exclusively on birth. In most European states, such a claim had become an anachronism.

The Expanding Middle Classes

Up to the eighteenth century, society had been divided by legally separate orders based on birth. In the nineteenth century, it became more customary to classify people by their economic function. The "middle class" belonged neither to the nobility nor to the peasantry nor to the industrial working class. It included such people as wealthy manufacturers, country physicians, and bank tellers. Given this diversity, it has become common to use the plural and think of all these people as forming the "middle classes." Another term frequently used to describe these people is *bourgeois*, which originated in the twelfth and thirteenth centuries when a new wealthy class based on urban occupations—whose members were called burghers, or bourgeois—emerged.

The nineteenth century has often been described as "the bourgeois century." Although such a label may be too broad, after the midcentury mark it is appropriate enough to use as a shorthand term to describe the dominance of the bourgeois elites. This situation was especially prevalent in western Europe, where the middle classes helped fashion much of society.

The middle classes expanded dramatically in the wake of industrialization. More trade and manufacture meant more entrepreneurs and managers, while the increasingly complex society called for more engineers, lawyers, accountants, and bankers. New standards of comfort and health demanded more merchants and doctors. Urban improvements in the generation after 1850 created a need for architects and contractors, among other professionals.

The middle and lower levels of middle-class society grew most rapidly as business, the professions, and government administration created more jobs. In the 1870s about 10 percent of urban working-class people reached lower-middle-class status by becoming storekeepers, lower civil servants, clerks, or salespeople. Faster growth occurred for white-collar workers than for their blue-collar counterparts. As industries matured, the increasing use of machinery and better industrial organization meant that fewer additional laborers and more clerks and bureaucrats were needed. Large import-export businesses, insurance companies, and department stores provided opportunities of this kind. So did the expansion of government services. In the second half of the nineteenth century, France increased its teacher corps by 80,000 and hired 50,000 more postal employees. In Britain the size of the postal staff grew by six times and the teaching corps by two-and-one-half times between 1851 and 1891.

The social impact of job growth was great. The men and women staffing these new positions often came from modest backgrounds. For the son or daughter of peasants to become village postmaster, schoolteacher, or clerk in a major firm signified social ascension, however modest. And for the family, such a position, even more than income, meant joining the lower stratum of the middle classes. Accessibility to its ranks was certainly one of the strengths of the bourgeoisie. It was an ever growing group whose promise of social respectability and material comfort exercised a compelling force of attraction over the lower classes. In midcentury Britain the middle classes represented 15 percent of the population; by 1881, 25 percent. Elsewhere, the proportion was lower, but it was growing in number and strength as the economy expanded.

A widening subgroup of the middle classes consisted of members of the professions, those whose prestige rested on the claim of exclusive expertise in a particular field. In the early nineteenth century, requirements for exercising a profession varied, depending on the country. In France and Prussia, for example, government regulation stipulated the necessary qualifications to practice medicine; in England anyone might practice it. As the professions attempted to create a monopoly for themselves and eliminate rivals, they established more standards. Medical doctors, for instance, began requiring specialized education to distinguish themselves from herbalists, midwives, bonesetters, healers, and other rivals, and they insisted on their exclusive right to exercise their profession.

Although the professionalization of medicine did not create better doctors immediately, as the science of medicine taught at universities improved, so did the preparation and expertise of doctors. Similarly, in other professions, such as law, architecture, and engineering, common standards and requirements encouraged professional practice. By midcentury either professional associations or the state itself accredited members of the professions. Women had limited access to these professions; typically their opportunities were confined to lower teaching positions. After the Crimean War, as a result of Florence Nightingale's efforts (see page 813), nursing became an increasingly popular profession for women.

The growing role of the state in society led to bureaucratic expansion. More and more, civil servants were selected by merit rather than through patronage. By the eighteenth century, Prussia had instituted a civil service examination system. After the Revolution, France instituted educational requirements for certain government corps, and by the 1880s it established civil service exams for the rest of government service. Beginning in 1870, Britain introduced the civil service examination and eliminated patronage.

Middle-Class Lifestyles

The standard of living of the growing middle classes varied considerably, from the wealthy entrepreneur who bought a château, or built one, to the bourgeois who dwelled in a modest apartment. But they all lived in new standards of comfort. Their homes had running water, upholstered furniture, and enough space to provide separate sleeping and living quarters. They had several changes of clothing and consumed a varied diet that included meat and dairy products, sugar, coffee, and tea. They read books and subscribed to newspapers and journals. Having at least one servant was a requisite for anyone who wished to be counted among the middle classes in the mid-nineteenth century.

By 1900 servants were still common among bourgeois households, but they were fewer in proportion to the population as a whole. In 1861 in Barmen, Germany (present-day Wuppertal), 16 percent of the population consisted of domestics; by 1911 the figure was 2.5 percent. As service industries developed, the need for servants decreased. With the growth of cab services, for instance, a family could dispense with a coachman and stable boy. And many families went without servants. Toward the end of the century, domestics' wages rose as competing forms of employment vied for their service, and only the upper layers of the bourgeoisie still employed domestic help.

In some areas suburban living became fashionable. The wealthy lived in large, imposing houses; the less well-off lived in smaller houses with a garden for privacy and quiet. Some owned two homes—one in the city and one in the countryside, providing respite from the rushed urban environment.

For further relief from the crowded cities, visits to resorts became popular. Throughout Europe, resort towns sprang up, devoted principally to the amusement of the well-off. It became fashionable to "take the waters"—bathing in hot springs and drinking the mineral waters thought to have special attributes—and gamble in resorts such as Baden-Baden in Germany and Vichy in France. For the first time, tourism became big business. Thomas Cook (1808–1892), an Englishman, organized tours to the Crystal Palace exhibition of 1851. (See the feature, "Weighing the Evidence: The Crystal Palace," on pages 876–877.) Discovering the large market for travel tours, he began running tours in England and on the Continent. In the eighteenth century the European tour had been a custom of the aristocracy, but now many members of the middle classes demanded this experience as well. Beginning in 1835, a German publisher, Karl Baedeker (1801–1859), issued a tourist guide to the Rhine, followed by guidebooks to various European countries and the Middle East. The Baedeker guides were eagerly purchased and provided the pattern for the multitude of guidebooks that followed.

New wealth and leisure time led as well to more hotels, restaurants, and cafés. In 1869 Paris had 20,000 cafés and 4000 hotels and lodging houses; the largest hotel had 700 well-appointed rooms. Vienna's National Hotel, with 300 rooms,

had steam heat, spring water on every floor, and an icehouse providing cool drinks. For the traveler's convenience, many hotels, such as the monumental Charing Cross Hotel in London, were located next to train stations. At home or away, the bourgeois valued comfort.

The middle classes shared certain attitudes about the conduct of their lives. They believed their successes were due not to birth but to talent and effort. They wanted to be judged by their merits, and they expected their members to abide by strict moral principles. Their lives were supposed to be disciplined, especially with regard to sex and drink. The age was called "Victorian" because the middle classes in Britain saw in the queen who reigned for two-thirds of the century a reflection of their own values. (See the feature, "Weighing the Evidence: An Engraving of the British Royal Family," on pages 842–843.) "Victorian morality," preached but not always practiced, was often viewed as hypocritical by social critics. Yet as the middle classes came to dominate society, their values became the social norms. Public drunkenness was discouraged, and anti-alcoholic movements vigorously campaigned against drinking. Public festivals were regulated, making them more respectable and less rowdy. In several countries, societies for the protection of animals agitated against blood sports such as cock-and-bull fights.

In spite of their differences in education, wealth, and social standing, most of the bourgeoisie resembled one another in dress, habits of speech, and deportment. Bourgeois men dressed somberly, in dark colors, avoiding any outward signs of luxury. Their clothing fit closely and eschewed decoration—an adjustment to the machine age, where elaborate dress hampered activity. It also reflected a conscious attempt to emphasize the frugal and achievement-oriented attitudes of the bourgeoisie in contrast to what was seen as the frivolous nobility.

Bourgeois conventions regarding women's dress were less reserved. Extravagant amounts of colorful cloth used to fashion huge, beribboned hoop dresses reflected the newfound wealth of the middle classes and confirmed their view of women as ornaments whose lives were to be limited to the home and made easier by servants. This era was dominated by domesticity, by the ideal of the home. The wife was to provide her family with

Advice on Running the Middle-Class Household

In 1861 Isabella Mary Mayson Beeton, a London housewife, published **Mrs. Beeton's Book of Household Management,** *which in Britain was outsold only by the Bible. Her popular book provided British middle-class women with advice on running their households and reflected their values concerning discipline, frugality, and cleanliness.*

As with the commander of an army, or the leader of an enterprise, so is it with the mistress of a house. Her spirit will be seen through the whole establishment; and just in proportion as she performs her duties intelligently and thoroughly, so will her domestics follow in her path. Of all those acquirements, which more particularly belong to the feminine character, there are none which take a higher rank, in our estimation, than such as enter into a knowledge of household duties; for on these are perpetually dependent the happiness, comfort, and well-being of a family. . . .

Early rising is one of the most essential qualities which enter into good Household Management, as it is not only the parent of health, but of innumerable other advantages. Indeed, when a mistress is an early riser, it is almost certain that her house will be orderly and well-managed. . . .

Cleanliness is indispensable to health, and must be studied both in regard to the person and the house, and all that it contains. . . .

Frugality and economy are home virtues, without which no household can prosper. . . .

Charity and benevolence are duties which a mistress owes to herself as well as to her fellow-creatures; and there is scarcely any income so small, but something may be spared from it. . . . Great advantages may result from visits paid the poor, for there being, unfortunately, much ignorance, generally amongst them with respect to all household knowledge, there will be opportunities for advising and instructing them in a pleasant and unobtrusive manner, in cleanliness, industry, cookery, and good management. . . .

A housekeeping account-book should invariably be kept, and kept punctually and precisely. . . .

. . . The treatment of servants is of the highest possible moment as well to the mistress as to the domestics themselves. On the head of the house the latter will naturally fix their attention; and if they perceive that the mistress's conduct is regulated by high and correct principles, they will not fail to respect her. If, also a benevolent desire is shown to promote their comfort, at the same time that a steady performance of their duty is exacted, then their respect will not be unmingled with affection, and they will be more solicitous to continue to deserve her favour.

Source: Isabella Mary Mayson Beeton, *Mrs. Beeton's Book of Household Management* (London: S. O. Beeton, 1861), pp. 1–6.

a shelter from the storms of daily life. (See the box, "Advice on Running the Middle-Class Household.") While the man was out in the secular world earning a living and advancing his career, the bourgeois woman was to run her household. She decorated the house, changed curtains with the seasons and the styles, supervised the servants, kept the accounts, oversaw the children's homework and religious education, and involved herself in charitable works. In the decades around midcentury, the assumption that there were two separate spheres—one male and public, the other female and private—reached its height.

In spite of the relatively passive role assigned to women, many bourgeois women were very active. Some took up philanthropic causes, helping

Josephine Grey Butler An important Victorian reformer, Butler agitated for several causes, most notably abolition of the Contagious Diseases Act. This act empowered the police to arrest any woman it suspected of prostitution and to force her to be examined for venereal disease. Largely as a result of Butler's efforts, this act was repealed in 1886. *(Fawcett Library/Mary Evans Picture Library)*

the sick and the poor. In England, Josephine Grey Butler (1828–1906), a member of a family of reformers, fought for the spread of education to impoverished women. She also waged a fierce battle against prostitution. Many bourgeois women helped their husbands or fathers in the office, the business, or the writing of scientific treatises. Others achieved success on their own terms, running their own businesses, writing, painting, teaching. Some took advantage of the very impediments placed in their way. Rosa Bonheur (1822–1899), who because of her gender was not allowed to attend sketching sessions of nudes at her art school, concentrated on painting animals and became the best-known painter of domestic animals in the nineteenth century.

The expectation that middle-class women would be married and taken care of by their husbands led to the provision of inferior education for girls and young women. Even bright and intellectually curious young girls could not receive as good an education as their brothers, nor as a consequence pursue as interesting a career—a situation that had prevailed for centuries. Proponents of women's rights protested against this situation, insisting on equal access to education and the professions. Slowly, secondary and university education was made available to young women. In Europe the first university to admit women was the University of Zurich in Switzerland in 1865. Although British universities admitted women, the University of London did not grant them degrees until after 1878, and the most prestigious British institutions, Oxford and Cambridge, did not grant degrees to women until after World War I. In spite of discriminatory laws, harassment by male students, and initial obstruction by professional and accrediting groups, a few female doctors and lawyers practiced in England by the 1870s and on the Continent in the following decades.

Women more easily penetrated lower levels of middle-class occupations. Expanding school systems, civil services, and businesses provided new employment opportunities for women. By the 1890s, two-thirds of primary school teachers in England and half the post office staff in France were women; by 1914 nearly half a million women worked as shop assistants in England. Some new technologies created jobs that were heavily feminized, such as the positions of typist and telephone operator.

The Workers' Lot

The increased prosperity and greater productivity of the period gradually improved the conditions of both female and male workers in the generation after 1850. Their wages and standard of living rose, and they enjoyed more job security. In Britain the earning power of the average worker rose by one-third between 1850 and 1875.

For the first time, workers were able to put money aside to tide them over in hard times. By 1870 two million Frenchmen had savings accounts. By the 1860s, one million people in England subscribed to post office savings accounts established especially for those of limited means.

The workers' increased income permitted a better diet. In France the average number of calories consumed per adult male increased by one-third between 1840 and 1890. In Britain, between 1844 and 1876, per capita consumption of tea tripled, and that of sugar quadrupled. The quality of food as well as the amount also improved; people consumed more meat, fish, eggs, and dairy products.

Legislation gradually reduced the length of the workweek. The British workweek, typically 73 hours in the 1840s, was reduced to 56 hours in 1874. In France it was reduced to 10 hours a day, in Germany to 11. But these improvements were accompanied by an increased emphasis on efficiency at the workplace. Fewer informal breaks were allowed as industrialists insisted on greater worker productivity. New machines increased the tempo of work, frequently leading to accidents and exhaustion.

As workers had more time and more money, their leisure patterns changed. Some leisure activities that previously had been limited to the upper classes became available to workers. The introduction of rail connections to resort towns such as Brighton in England or Trouville and Dieppe in France enabled workers to visit such places. New music and dance halls, popular theaters, and other forms of public entertainment sprang up to claim workers' increased spending money.

Although most workers believed their lot had improved, they were also aware that a vast gulf remained between them and the middle and upper classes. In the 1880s in the northern French industrial city of Lille, the combined estate of 20,000 workers equaled that of an average industrialist. In Paris the gluttonous rich ate multicourse meals; the leftover scraps from their plates found a ready market among the poor, who bought them for a few centimes from specialized vendors. Life expectancies still varied dramatically according to income; in Bordeaux in 1853 the life expectancy of a male bourgeois was twenty years greater than that of a male laborer.

The disparity between rich and poor was especially striking in the case of domestics. Most servants were female, and they led tiring and restricted lives under close supervision of their

Ladies' Bicycling Fashion This new mode of transportation suggested possibilities for female emancipation. Free, on her bicycle, the young woman is contrasted with a man, who rides only a tricycle. *(From Karin Helm (ed.),* Rosinen aus der Gartenlaube *[Gutersloh: Signum Verlag, n.d.]. Reproduced with permission.)*

employers. Their hours were overly long: A six-and-one-half-day week was not uncommon. Housed in either the basement or the attic, servants experienced extremes of cold, heat, and humidity. Sometimes they were subjected to physical or sexual abuse by the master of the house, his sons, or the head of the domestic staff. And yet, for impoverished rural women with little chance of finding better work, domestic service was a risky but often necessary option. It provided free housing, food, and clothing and allowed the servant to save an annual sum equivalent to an amount between one-third and one-half of a worker's yearly wages. These savings often served as a dowry and allowed the young woman to make an advantageous match. Two out of five female wage earners in England were in domestic employ in 1851.

Although a few members of the working class managed to enter the lower levels of the middle classes, most remained mired in the same profession as their grandparents. Poverty was still pervasive. In the 1880s about one-third of Londoners were living at or below the subsistence level. Industrial and urban diseases, such as tuberculosis, were common among workers. Compared to the healthier, better-fed, and better-housed middle classes, the workers continued living in shabby and limited circumstances.

The Transformation of the Countryside

Before the nineteenth century, the countryside had hardly changed at all, but beginning at midcentury it was radically transformed. Especially in western Europe, an increasing number of people left the land. In 1850, 20 percent of the population

of Britain were agricultural workers; by 1881 only 11 percent were. The decrease of the agricultural population led in many places to labor shortages and therefore higher wages for farm hands.

Agriculture became increasingly efficient, and the food supply grew significantly. More land was put under the plow. Sweden's acreage more than doubled, Italy's grew by more than one-half, Germany's and Hungary's by more than one-third. In Italy and Denmark, land was reclaimed from marshes, in Holland from the North Sea. Not only was more land cultivated but the yield per acre increased. In 1760 an agricultural worker in England could feed himself and one other person; by 1841 he could feed himself and 2.7 others. The population of Europe nearly doubled in the years between 1800 and 1880, and yet it was nourished better than ever before.

Higher yields were due to an increased use of manure, augmented in the 1870s by saltpeter imported from Chile and, beginning in the 1880s, by chemical fertilizers manufactured in Europe. Innovations in tools also improved productivity. The

Steam-Powered Thresher This image shows the thresher being operated in the French countryside in 1860. It would be decades before this kind of technology became a common sight in Europe, but it was a harbinger of the change coming to the rural world. *(Bibliothèque Nationale)*

sickle, which required the laborer to crouch to cut grass or wheat, was replaced by the long-handled scythe, which allowed the field hand to stand and use the full weight of the body to swing the instrument through the grain. This new method increased efficiency fourfold. And in the 1850s steam-driven threshing machinery was introduced in some parts of western Europe. Organizational techniques borrowed from industrial labor, including specialization and the insistence on regularity in the workplace, also contributed to greater productivity on the land.

Improved roads and dramatically expanded rail lines enabled farmers to extend their markets. No longer did they need to produce only for the local area; they could depend on a national market and beyond for customers. In Brittany, in western France, a rail line to Paris led to a boom in dairy farming. The demand for agricultural products rose, and so did the price on many items, thus improving the lot of the farmer.

While the prices of farm products rose, those of industrial products fell, allowing farmers to purchase machinery to work the land and items providing personal convenience such as cast-iron stoves. Owners of medium and large farms did particularly well. For the first time, many had credit available to them, and some of the vagaries of farming were buffered by the availability of fire and weather insurance.

Life in the countryside became less insular. Not only did rail lines connect farms to cities, but national school systems brought teachers into the villages. Local dialects and in some cases even distinct languages that peasants had spoken for generations were replaced by a standardized national language. Local provincial costumes became less common as styles adopted in the cities spread to the countryside via consumer catalogs. The farm girls who went to the cities as maids to work in middle-class homes returned to their villages with urban and middle-class ideals. The military draft brought the young men of the village into contact with urban folk and further spread urban values to the countryside.

Even so, the rural world remained very distinct from urban society. Many of the forces seen as contributing to modernity exacerbated rural conditions. The expansion of manufacturing in cities contributed to the decline of cottage indus-

try in rural areas, where agricultural workers had relied on the putting-out system to provide supplementary income; thus farm workers were idle during slack seasons, and rural unemployment grew. In many cases railroads bringing goods made elsewhere wiped out some of the local markets on which these cottage industries had depended. The steamship lowered the cost of transporting freight, including grain from distant Canada and Argentina, which often undersold wheat grown in Europe. The resultant crisis, worsened by a rural population explosion, led to the emigration of millions, who left the land for towns and cities or even migrated across the seas to the Americas and Australia (see pages 897–898). Although this process was painful for large segments of the rural population, the result was that for those who were able to remain on the land, the situation eventually improved.

These trends had a striking effect in the rural areas of western Europe. Eastern Europe, in contrast, was hardly touched by them. In Russia agriculture remained backward; the average yield per acre in 1880 was one-quarter that of Great Britain. The land sheltered a large surplus population that was underemployed and contributed little to the rural economy. In the Balkans, most peasants were landless and heavily indebted.

URBAN PROBLEMS AND SOLUTIONS

By 1851 the majority of English people lived in cities; by 1891 the majority of Germans did as well. To cope with urban growth and its attendant problems—epidemics, crowding, traffic jams—cities developed public health measures and introduced planning and rebuilding programs. They adapted the new technologies to provide such urban amenities as streetlights, public transportation, water and sewer systems, and police forces. Cities gradually became safer and more pleasant places to live, although for a long time city dwellers continued to suffer high mortality rates.

City Planning and Urban Renovation

Most of Europe's cities had begun as medieval walled cities and had grown haphazardly into major industrial centers. Their narrow, crooked streets

Pissarro: L' avenue de l' Opéra, Sunlight, Winter Morning Camille Pissarro, one of the leading impressionists, portrayed the broad new avenue designed by Baron Haussmann. The
avenue leads to the new opera, in background, also planned during the Second Empire.
(*Musée Saint-Denis, Reims/Giraudon/Art Resource, NY*)

could not accommodate the increased trade and
daily movement of goods and people, and traffic
snarls were common. City officials began to recognize that broad, straight avenues would resolve
the traffic problem and also bring sunlight and
fresh air into the narrow and perpetually dank
lanes and alleys. In the 1820s, London saw the first
ambitious street-widening initiative. On Regency
Street, old hovels were torn down and replaced
with fancy new houses; the poor were usually displaced. Later projects followed this pattern.

The most extensive program of urban rebuilding took place in midcentury Paris. Over a period
of eighteen years, Napoleon III and his aide, Baron
Georges Haussmann (1809–1891), transformed
Paris from a dirty medieval city to a beautiful
modern one (Map 23.2). Broad, straight avenues
were carved through what had been dingy slums.
The avenues were lined with trees and graced with
elegant houses. Enhancing the city were public
monuments and buildings, such as the new opera
house. The tremendous costs of this ambitious

Map 23.2 Haussmann's Paris, 1850–1870 During the reign of Napoleon III, Baron Georges Haussmann reshaped the city of Paris, replacing its narrow medieval streets with a system of broad avenues and public parks and encircling the city with a railway.

scheme kept the city of Paris in debt for decades. (See the box, "Haussmann Justifies the Rebuilding of Paris.") In addition, the slum-removal program drove tens of thousands of the poorest Parisians to the outskirts of the city, leading to greater social segregation than had previously existed.

Haussmann's extensive work in Paris served as a model for other cities, and although none was rebuilt as extensively, many underwent significant improvements. The cities of Europe began to display an expansive grace and sense of order, supporting the belief of the middle classes that theirs was an age of progress.

The Introduction of Public Services

Beginning at midcentury, government at the central and local level helped make cities more livable by

Haussmann Justifies the Rebuilding of Paris

Baron Georges Haussmann, whom Napoleon III had appointed to rebuild Paris, explained in his **Memoirs** *(published in 1890) what he had accomplished and why. Haussmann also justified the important role the central government played in the capital's transformation.*

The present generation does not know what this part [the center] of Paris was like, before its complete transformation between 1852 and 1854.

It ignores that the first section of Rue Rivoli, along the Tuileries Gardens, ended abruptly. . . . beyond was an unspeakably foul neighborhood, consisting of squalid houses. . . . the Place de la Colonnade was obstructed by wretched constructions and was connected to other neighborhoods which were equally obstructed and impassable to traffic. . . .

. . . This last named street was so narrow that the rotten front of a house which in vain was trying to topple over could not do so for it was leaning on the house across.

And what a population lived there!

Those who had not explored the Paris of that time in all directions would not have an idea of what it was like. . . . the narrow, crooked streets were nearly impenetrable to traffic, dirty, stinking, unhealthy. . . .

. . . Our widening of streets gave old and new neighborhoods air, light, green space and flowers—in a word everything needed to improve public health and to be pleasant to the eye. . . .

The splendor of this city reflects on the whole country; the well-being of its population is meaningful to nearly all families in France. . . . If Paris is a great city, the center of commercial and industrial activities, as well as specialized production, and the site of prodigious consumption and constant trade, it is the capital of a mighty Empire, the governmental seat of a glorious sovereign. . . . the world capital of letters, the sciences and the arts. . . .

The State must directly and constantly intervene in the city's affairs, for it contributes to its splendor, by the palaces and public buildings which it constructs, by its financial contribution to certain public services such as the police, the upkeep of the streets, street lighting, water services and public transportation. . . .

Source: Baron Georges Haussmann, *Mémoires*, 2d ed., vol. 2 (Paris: Victor-Havard, 1890), pp. 26–28, 197–198, 203. Trans. by William Cohen.

---

legislating sanitary reforms and providing public transportation and lighting. Medical practitioners in the 1820s had observed that disease and higher mortality were related to dirt and lack of clean air, water, and sunshine. Since diseases spreading from the poorer quarters of town threatened the rich and powerful, there was a general interest in improving public health by clearing slums, broadening streets, and supplying clean air and water to the cities.

Reform began in England, where the lawyer and civil servant Edwin Chadwick (1800–1895) drafted important plans for reform that became

the basis for legislation. The Public Health Bill of 1848 established national standards for urban sanitation and required cities to regulate the installation of sewers and the disposal of refuse. The 1875 Health Act required cities to maintain certain basic health standards such as water and drainage. Armed with these laws, cities and towns took the initiative: Birmingham cleared fifty acres of slums in the 1870s, for example.

London was also a leader in supplying public water, a service later adopted by Paris and many other cities. Berlin had a municipal water system in 1850, but it took several decades before clean water was available in every household. As late as the 1870s, Berlin's sewage was carried in open pipes. In Paris, which typically led France in innovations, 60 percent of the houses had running water in 1882. The French capital did not have a unitary sewer system until the 1890s, however.

As running water in the home became a standard rather than a luxury, bathing became more common. The English upper classes had learned the habit of daily baths from their colonial experience in India; on the Continent it was not the custom until about the third quarter of the nineteenth century. French artist Edgar Degas (1834–1917) frequently painted bath scenes portraying the new European habit.

All these changes had a direct impact on the lives of city dwellers. Life became healthier, more comfortable, and more orderly. Between the 1840s and 1880, London's death rate fell from 26 per thousand to 20 per thousand. In Paris for the same period the decline was from 29.3 to 23.7 per thousand. There was a more immediate decline in the incidence of diseases associated with filthy living conditions. Improved water supplies provided a cleaner environment and reduced the prevalence of water-borne diseases such as cholera and typhoid.

Other improvements also contributed to a better quality of life. With the introduction of urban transportation, city dwellers no longer had to live within walking distance of their work. Early public transportation was seen in the French omnibus service of the 1820s—a system of horse-drawn carriages available to the public on fixed routes. Other cities followed—Hamburg in 1843, Berlin in 1846. In the 1850s the tram was introduced. A carriage drawn on a rail line, it could pull larger loads of passengers faster than the omnibus. Because of the many rail stations in London and the difficulty of getting from one station to another in time to make a connection, London built an underground railway in 1863, the predecessor of the subway system. The bicycle also became a serious means of transportation for some city dwellers. By the mid-1880s, there were nearly 100,000 bicycles in Great Britain, and a decade later, 375,000 in France.

Improvements in public transportation enabled workers to move out of the inner city into the less dense and less expensive suburbs. This trend in turn led to a decrease in urban population

Public Transportation in Berlin A few years after this photograph was taken, horses were dispensed with, as trams were electrified and buses were motorized. (*Landesbildstelle, Berlin*)

density and eventually helped make the city a healthier place to live.

Gaslights also improved city life, making it easier and safer to move around at night. (Prior to gaslights, city dwellers depended mainly on moonlight or, rarely, expensive and time-consuming oil lamps for street lighting.) In 1813 London was the first city to be illuminated by gas; Berlin followed in 1816. By 1860, 250 German towns had some form of street illumination. The first gaslights appeared in Paris in the 1820s, and by 1844 the city had 65,000 gas lamps. Electrical lights were introduced in Paris in 1875, although they were not common until the end of the century.

Cities also significantly expanded police forces to impose order, to control criminal activity, and to discourage behavior deemed undesirable, such as dumping garbage on the street, relieving oneself in public, or singing loud, raucous songs late at night. In 1850 London was the best-policed city in Europe with a 5000-man force. Paris had around 3000 policemen. These numbers continued to increase: By 1870 the French capital had 6000 policemen and London about 8000.

SOCIAL AND POLITICAL INITIATIVES

New institutions and groups emerged to tackle the unequal wealth and critical urban problems that followed in the wake of economic growth. The state intervened in the economy in new ways. Private charitable groups sprang up. And socialist parties, exclusively dedicated to improving the lot of the worker, gained in numbers and strength.

State Intervention in Welfare

The difficult conditions industry imposed on workers led to debates in several countries about the need for the state to protect the workers. The growing militancy of organized labor also forced the established authority to consider ways to meet the workers' needs. While some rejected government intervention in the free operation of market forces, others argued that the laws of supply and demand had caused the exploitation of many who ought to have been protected—especially very young children and pregnant women.

To right some of these abuses, the Scottish philanthropist Robert Owen (1771–1858) agitated in Parliament for the first effective British factory act, which passed in 1819. This act forbade labor for children under the age of 9 and limited the workday of children over that age to twelve hours a day. Then, beginning in 1833, a series of factory acts further limited the work hours of children and women in factories and mines and funded inspections to enforce these laws. French laws for the protection of children were passed as early as 1841, but government funding for their enforcement was not approved until 1874. Confronted with a declining birthrate and the need to strengthen itself against rival Germany, France further limited the work hours of children and women in a series of laws between 1892 and 1905. In addition, workmen's compensation became law in 1898.

In Prussia an 1839 law prohibited factory work for children under the age of 9 and established the precedent for state intervention in the rest of Germany. Ten years later, legislation was passed to create a social security system to which workers and their employers were required to contribute. Beginning in the 1840s, Prussia limited a city's right to refuse welfare support to its poor. Laws passed in the 1890s protected workers from harsh conditions and limited the hours of women. In much of Europe, however, the state did little to improve the welfare of the working class. In eastern Europe, where industry was still in its infancy, there was no protection of workers.

Fear of social upheaval and the rising strength of socialist political parties prompted some governments to act. In France moderate bourgeois liberals attempted to defuse class war by advocating "Solidarism," insisting on the responsibility of each class and individual for its fellow citizens. In newly unified Germany, the government wanted to show workers the benefits they could gain from the state so they would abandon the growing Socialist party and back the kaiser's government. It embarked on a deliberate program to tame the workers and win their support for the existing political and economic institutions. Thus, in the 1880s the new German government provided a comprehensive welfare plan that included health insurance and old-age pensions. Although local governments in many European states had provided welfare services in various forms, Germany was the first to recognize a national responsibility, and German social programs became models for the rest of Europe.

In addition to the welfare initiatives by state and city governments, middle and upper classes worked to better the workers' lot. Concern among these groups and individuals arose from a mixture of pity for workers' conditions, religious teachings about their responsibilities for the less fortunate, and fear of the consequences of unrelieved misery. In Paris, for example, three thousand private charitable organizations were founded between 1840 and 1900; their combined outlay in aid equaled the public charity available. In London the sum of £6 million—more than the total budget of many European states—was employed on behalf of the poor in 1890.

Women participated heavily in volunteer charity work. By the end of the nineteenth century, as many as half a million English women contributed their time to provide charity to the less fortunate. In Sweden by the 1880s, women had founded refuges for the destitute, old-age homes, a children's hospital, an asylum for the mentally handicapped, and various societies to promote female industry. In Spain a number of religious orders devoted to providing free education to the poor flourished in the 1880s.

In Catholic and Protestant countries, the Christian churches traditionally had identified with the rights of employers and seemed to ignore the lot of the workers. However, a number of Christians, lay and clerical, began to emphasize the need to address social issues. In Germany, Bishop Wilhelm Von Ketteler (1811–1877) preached the need for the well-off to take responsibility for the less privileged. His message was taken up in France, Italy, and Spain among what became known as "social Catholics." In England, Protestants' concern for the poor was evidenced by the founding of the Salvation Army in 1878. Religious groups also hoped they could win converts among the less privileged by demonstrating concern for their plight.

Increasingly, states, municipalities, volunteer groups, and churches accepted responsibility for the well-being of others. This trend marked the beginning of an evolution that would eventually spread in scope and lead to the welfare state in much of twentieth-century Europe.

Educational and Cultural Opportunities

At the beginning of the nineteenth century, governments took little responsibility for providing education. The upper classes educated their children with private tutors, parents from more modest economic groups taught their children what they knew, and the poor attended the few schools—usually one-room schools—provided by charitable and religious groups. In England the education of the masses became a national responsibility after the Second Reform Bill of 1867. This legislation extended the vote to the artisan classes and prompted a movement to ensure that the new voters were educated. In 1870 the English government began to provide significant subsidies for education, to set educational standards, and to establish a national inspection system to enforce them. England and France initiated mandatory primary school education in the 1880s. In Britain, one million children attended school in 1865; by 1880 more than three million attended.

Public education included not only reading, writing, and arithmetic but other skills as well. By insisting on punctuality and obliging students to carry out repetitive skills such as copying letters, words, or sentences, schools encouraged people to fit into the emerging industrial society. Obedience and the respect for authority learned at school shaped the soldiers and factory workers of the future. And regardless of political inclination, each regime took advantage of its control of the educational system to inculcate in the young the love of country and of its form of government.

Secondary education was, on the whole, available only to the privileged few in the upper middle classes. It confirmed their social status and won them access to the universities and the professions. To a very small number from the lower middle classes, secondary school attendance provided the means to ascend socially. The lower middle class was sparsely represented in universities, and the children of workers and peasants were totally absent.

Public education spread from the schools to other institutions, which made culture available to the masses in new ways. Between 1840 and 1880, the number of large libraries in Europe increased from 40 to 500, and by the late 1870s England had over 66 public lending libraries. The French national public library, the Bibliothèque Nationale, was established in Paris in the 1860s. This iron-and-glass building, radical for its time, was an impressive monument to the desire to make reading available to an expanded public. Many provincial cities, as well as the glittering capitals of Europe, were endowed with new libraries. Less grandiose, but probably more important for mostly rural populations, were the traveling libraries.

Museums and art galleries, which in the previous century had been open to only a select few, gradually became accessible to the general public. The first museum to open to the public was the Louvre in Paris after the French Revolution. The rest of Europe lagged behind in making the cultural heritage available to the masses. The British Museum restricted entrance to the wealthy and the well connected, for there was widespread fear of the possible destruction that the "vulgar classes" might cause if they were allowed to visit. But the sedate manner in which the crowds behaved during the Crystal Palace exposition reassured British authorities, and finally in 1879 the museum was opened daily to the general public. (See the feature, "Weighing the Evidence: The Crystal Palace," on pages 876–877.)

CULTURE IN AN AGE OF OPTIMISM

The improving economic and material conditions of the second half of the nineteenth century buoyed European thinkers. Many believed that men and women were becoming more enlightened, and they expressed faith in humankind's ability to transform the world with new scientific and technological breakthroughs. The world seemed knowable and perfectible. This faith advanced secularism while it undermined the certainties of traditional religion. The arts reflected these new values, emphasizing realism and science—as well as an underlying foreboding of the dark side of this "age of optimism."

Darwin and the Doctrine of Evolution

By midcentury most thinkers accepted the notion of change and transformation of society—and by analogy of the natural environment. The French thinker Auguste Comte (1798–1857) championed

the notion that human progress proceeded by developmental stages. Human progress was a law of nature leading men and women irresistibly to the final and highest stage of development, the positive—or scientific—stage. Widely read throughout Europe and Latin America, Comte's writings helped gird the era's faith in science, and the very progress science made seemed to confirm its precepts. Comte's philosophy, known as *positivism*, dominated the era. While the romantics had emphasized feeling, positivists upheld the significance of the measurable, the palpable, that which could be scientifically understood. Their methods, they were confident, would assure the continued progress of humanity. Science had proved that the world was evolving to ever higher forms.

In the field of geology, the Englishman Charles Lyell (1797–1875) maintained that the earth was far older than the biblical story of Genesis suggested. He argued that its geological formations—the mountains, valleys, and seas—had been subject to natural forces that, over hundreds of thousands, even millions, of years, had transformed them. Most educated people accepted his theory, which led many to wonder if it might also be true that the animal kingdom had evolved gradually over long periods of time.

Although evolution in the biological realm had been suggested as early as the end of the eighteenth century, Charles Darwin (1809–1882) was the first to offer a plausible explanation of the process. As the naturalist on an official British scientific expedition in the 1830s, he had visited the Galápagos Islands off the coast of South America. On these islands he found species similar to but different from those on the mainland and even different from one another. Could they be the result of separate creation? Or was it more likely that in varying environments they had adapted differently? Darwin theorized that closely related species compete for food and living space. In this struggle, those in each species that are better adapted to the environment have the advantage over the others and are hence more likely to survive. These surviving members of the species, Darwin claimed, pass on their desirable adaptive traits to their offspring, while the others die off. Darwin described this continuous process as a "struggle for existence," in which only the fittest endure. He called the mechanism that explained the evolution and development of new species "natural selection," a process that was imperceptible but continuous. (See the box, "Darwin's Basic Laws of Evolution.")

Darwin's theory of the inevitability of evolution in nature echoed the era's confidence in change and its conviction that the present represented a more developed stage of the past. His work was seen as confirming the notion that societies—like species—were preordained to evolve toward progressively higher stages. Darwin at first avoided the question of whether human beings, too, were affected by the laws of evolution. To do so would be to question humanity's uniqueness, its separation from the rest of creation by its possession (in the Christian view) of a soul. But in *Descent of Man* (1871), Darwin did confront this issue, clearly stating his belief that humanity, too, was subject to these natural laws. The recognition that human beings were members of the animal kingdom like other species disturbed him, and the admission, he wrote, "is like confessing a murder." Nonetheless, for Darwin scientific evidence took precedence over all other considerations.

Many Christians were shocked by these assertions, and some denounced the new scientific findings. Some argued that science and faith belonged to two different worlds. Others claimed that there was no reason that God could not have created the world through natural forces. In the long run, however, Darwinism seemed to undermine the certainties of religious orthodoxies by showing their incompatibility with scientific discovery.

Physics, Chemistry, and Medicine

Dramatic scientific breakthroughs occurred in the nineteenth century, confirming the prevalent belief that human beings could understand and control nature. In physics, laws regarding electricity and magnetism were articulated by Michael Faraday (1791–1867) and James Clerk Maxwell (1831–1879) in the 1830s and 1850s, respectively. Their work established the field of electrical science. In the 1840s, Hermann von Helmholtz (1821–1894) in Germany and James Joule (1818–1889) in Great Britain defined the nature of energy in the laws of thermodynamics. In chemistry, new elements were discovered almost every year, and individual findings contributed to the under-

Darwin as an Ape This was one of many cartoons suggesting that if Darwin's theories on evolution were correct, then the great scientist must be descended from apes. (*From* The Hornet, *March 22, 1871*)

standing of larger patterns. In 1869 Russian chemist Dmitri Mendeleev (1834–1907) developed the periodic table, in which the elements are arranged by their atomic weight. He left blank spaces for elements still unknown but that he predicted would be discovered. Within ten years, three of these elements were discovered, affirming the belief that science is not only knowledge that can be experimentally tested but also knowledge that can have predictive value. Such triumphs further enhanced science's prestige.

Prolific research yielded discoveries in one field of knowledge that could be transferred to another. For example, chemists produced new dyes, enabling biologists to color slides of microorganisms and better study their evolution. Scientific breakthroughs also led to technical achievements that had industrial uses; for instance, inventions in

Darwin's Basic Laws of Evolution

In **On the Origin of Species by Means of Natural Selection** *(1859) Darwin explained his theories of evolution. Writing in an age of vast transformations, he could imagine the mutability of all nature, including species, over time. And, like his contemporaries, he could imagine that evolution would lead to improvement, to increasing "perfection" of various species.*

A religious man, who lost much of his faith as a result of his scientific work, he was anxious to reassure Christians that evolution could be seen as part of the divine plan.

Nothing at first can appear more difficult to believe than that the more complex organs and instincts have been perfected, not by means superior to, though analogous with, human reason, but by the accumulation of innumerable slight variations, each good for the individual possessor. Nevertheless, this difficulty, though appearing to our imagination insuperably great, cannot be considered real if we admit the following propositions, namely, that all parts of the organisation and instincts offer, at least, individual differences—that there is a struggle for existence leading to the preservation of profitable deviations of structure or instinct—and, lastly, that gradations in the state of perfection of each organ may have existed, each good of its kind. The truth of these propositions cannot, I think, be disputed. . . .

As geology plainly proclaims that each land has undergone great physical changes, we might have expected to find that organic beings have varied under nature, in the same way as they have varied under domestication. And if there has been any variability under nature, it would be an unaccountable fact if natural selection had not come into play. . . .

There is grandeur in this view of life, with its several powers, having been originally breathed by the Creator into a few forms or into one; and that, whilst this planet has gone cycling on according to the fixed law of gravity, from so simple a beginning endless forms most beautiful and most wonderful have been, and are being evolved.

Source: Charles Darwin, *On the Origin of Species by Means of Natural Selection*, 6th ed., vol. 2 (1872; reprint, New York: Appleton, 1923), pp. 267–268, 279, 305–306.

chemistry led to the development of the first artificial fertilizers in 1842 and to synthetic dyes in the 1850s.

Science also became increasingly specialized. In the eighteenth century, the scientist had been a learned amateur practicing a hobby. In the nineteenth century, as the state and industry became more involved in promoting scientific research, the scientist became a professional, employed by a university, a hospital, or some other institution. New theories and discoveries were disseminated by scientific journals and by meetings of scientific associations and congresses.

Internationally, scientific cooperation became common, but science also promoted international rivalry. The nationalism of the late nineteenth century spurred on scientific competition. When cholera broke out in Egypt in 1883, a French and a German team of scientists rushed to the area to discover its cause. The German team led by Robert Koch (1843–1910) uncovered the cholera bacillus as the source; on returning to his homeland he was feted as a national hero who had vindicated German superiority in science.

Around the midcentury mark, a number of important breakthroughs occurred in medicine.

Before the development of anesthesia, surgical intervention had been nearly impossible. With only alcohol to dull the patient's pain, even the swiftest surgeons could perform only modest surgical procedures. In the 1840s, however, the introduction of ether and then chloroform allowed people to undergo more extensive surgery. It also was used to quiet pain in more routine procedures such as childbirth; Queen Victoria asked for chloroform when giving birth.

Increasingly, the experimental method in science was applied to medicine, and as a result physicians became concerned not simply with treating diseases but with discovering their origins. Louis Pasteur (1822–1895) achieved notable breakthroughs when he discovered that microbes, small organisms invisible to the naked eye, cause various diseases. Pasteur found that heating milk to a certain temperature kills disease-carrying organisms. This process, called *pasteurization,* reduced the incidence of certain diseases that were particularly harmful to children. Pasteur initiated other advances as well in the prevention of disease. Vaccination against smallpox had started in England in the eighteenth century, but Pasteur invented vaccines for other diseases and was able to explain the process by which the body, inoculated with a weak form of bacilli, developed antibodies that successfully overcame more serious infections.

In England the surgeon John Lister (1827–1912) developed an effective disinfectant, carbolic acid, to kill the germs that caused gangrene and other infections in surgical patients. Eventually, midwives and doctors began to reduce the incidence of the puerperal fever that killed so many women after childbirth by washing their hands and sterilizing their instruments. Lister's development of germ-free procedures transformed the science of surgery. By reducing the patient's risk, more ambitious surgery could be attempted. The first surgical kidney removal took place in 1876; the first successful brain surgery in modern times was performed three years later.

The increasingly scientific base of medicine and its visible success in combating disease improved its reputation. The medical profession began to control access to its ranks by establishing powerful professional associations—for example, the British Medical Association (1832) and the German Medical Association (1872). In addition,

medical journals also emerged to spread scientific knowledge.

Science was fashionable. In 1869 Empress Eugénie in France had Louis Pasteur come to tea, draw blood from her finger, and examine it under a microscope, all to the astonishment of her guests. Some frogs, brought in for experimentation, escaped down palace corridors. The spectacle of science as the chic entertainment of an empress was a reminder of the increasing authority it commanded in the later nineteenth century.

Birth of the Social Sciences

The scientific method, so dramatically effective in uncovering the mysteries of nature, was also applied to the human enterprise. Just as the secrets of nature were unlocked, the workings of society, it was thought, could be understood in a scientific manner.

No field in the human sciences flourished as much in the nineteenth century as history. In an era undergoing vast transformations, many people became interested in change over time. They were eager to employ the methods of the scientist to explore their past. The father of modern historical writing is the German Leopold von Ranke (1795–1886). Departing from the tradition of earlier historians, who explained the past as the ongoing fulfillment of an overarching purpose—divine will, the liberation of humanity, or some other goal—Ranke insisted that the role of the historian was to "show how things actually were." Like a scientist, the historian must be objective and dispassionate. By viewing humankind of all eras and environments on their own terms, and not those of others, historians could arrive at a better understanding of humanity.

This perspective transformed the study of history into a discipline with recognizable common standards of evidence. Historians studied and interpreted original (or "primary") sources; they collected and published their findings; they founded professional organizations and published major journals.

Other social sciences also developed in this period. Anthropology, the comparative study of people in different societies, had been the subject of speculative literature for hundreds of years. Increased contacts with non-European societies in the nineteenth century as a result of dramatically increased trade, exploration, and missionary activities stimulated anthropological curiosity. In 1844 the Society of Ethnology was founded in Paris, followed by the Anthropological Society (1859). London, Berlin, and Vienna quickly followed suit, establishing similar societies in the 1860s. Consisting of medical doctors, biologists, and travelers, these societies speculated on the causes of the perceived differences among human races. The Paris Anthropological Society was dominated by the medical doctor Paul Broca (1824–1880) and other physicians, who saw in biological structure the explanation for differences among human groups, thus giving apparent "scientific" backing to the era's racism. They used their findings to demonstrate that non-Europeans were condemned to an existence inferior to the white races.

In Britain, the main anthropological theorist was Edward Tylor (1832–1917), the son of a brass manufacturer. Through his travels, Tylor came into contact with non-European peoples, who aroused his curiosity. Strongly influenced by the evolutionary doctrines of his day, Tylor believed that the various societies of humankind were subject to discoverable scientific laws. Just as if one could travel back in time, one would find humankind increasingly unsophisticated, so Tylor posited, the farther one became distanced from Europe, the more primitive humankind became. The contemporary African was at a level of development similar to that of Europeans in an earlier era.

Tylor was not technically a racist, since he argued that the conditions of non-Europeans were not due to biology but rather were a function of their institutions. Like racists, however, evolutionists believed in the superiority of the European over other races. Anthropology gave scientific sanction to the idea of a single European people, sharing either a similar biological structure or a common stage of social development, which distinguished them from non-Europeans.

Anthropology gradually gained recognition and legitimacy as a profession. In 1872 in France, Broca founded a journal emphasizing physical anthropology. In 1876 he founded a school of anthropology with six chaired professors. In Britain in 1884, Tylor—who was so closely identified with anthropology it was called "Mr Tylor's science"—

was appointed to the first university chair in anthropology in his country.

Sociology is a term originally coined by Auguste Comte. A number of ambitious thinkers, among them the English "social philosopher" Herbert Spencer (see page 797), had considered how individuals are affected by the society in which they live. In the 1840s various social reformers published detailed statistical investigations revealing relationships between, for instance, income and disease and death rates. A few decades later, the theoretical principles underlying sociology were spelled out. Among the first to do so was Emile Durkheim (1858–1917), who insisted that sociology was a verifiable science. He occupied the first chair of sociology at a French university in 1887. A few years later he founded a journal of sociology and gathered around him a coterie of disciples who ensured the success of sociology as a professionalized discipline.

Whereas in the past, history, anthropology, and sociology were the purview of amateurs, now professional historians, anthropologists, and sociologists were engaged full-time in research and teaching at universities or research institutes. The professionalization that had occurred in medicine and physics also transformed the social sciences. Professionalization and specialization led to significant advances in several disciplines, but it also led to the fragmentation and compartmentalization of knowledge. People of broad learning and expertise became far less common.

The Challenge to Religion

The scientific claims of the era seemed to clash with the traditions of religion. A number of scientists, including Darwin himself, found their Christian faith undermined by theories on evolution. Although most Europeans continued to be strongly influenced by traditional religious beliefs, they appeared less confident than in earlier eras.

After the revolutions of 1848, religion was seen as a bulwark of order. In France, Napoleon III gave the Catholic church new powers in education, and the bourgeoisie flocked to worship. In Spain, moderates who had been anticlerical began to support the church, and in 1851 they signed a concordat declaring Roman Catholicism "the only religion of the Spanish nation." In Austria in 1855, the state surrendered to the bishops full control over the clergy, the seminaries, and the administration of marriage laws.

In 1848 the papacy had been nearly overthrown by revolution, and in 1860 it lost most of its domains to Italy. Thus Pope Pius IX became a sworn enemy of liberalism, and in 1864, in the *Syllabus of Errors*, he condemned a long list of what he perceived to be modern errors, among them "progress," "liberalism," and "modern civilization." To establish full control over the clergy and believers, the Lateran Council in 1870 issued the controversial doctrine of infallibility, declaring that the pope, when speaking officially on faith and morals, was infallible. This doctrine became a target of anticlerical opinion.

The political alliance the Catholic church struck with reactionary forces meant that when new political groups came to power they moved against the church. In Italy, since the church had discouraged national unification, conflict raged between the church and the new state. In Germany, Catholics had either held on to their regional loyalties or favored unification under Austrian auspices. When Protestant Prussia unified Germany, Chancellor Bismarck viewed the Catholics with suspicion as unpatriotic and started a campaign against them, the *Kulturkampf* ("cultural struggle").

In France the republicans, who finally won the upper hand over monarchists in 1879, bitterly resented the church's support of the monarchist party. They were also strongly influenced by Comte's ideas of positivism, believing that France would not be a free country until the power of the church was diminished and its nonscientific or antiscientific disposition was overcome. The republican regime reduced the role of the church in education as well as some other clerical privileges.

Greater religious tolerance, or perhaps indifference to religion in general, led to more acceptance of religious diversity. In 1854 and 1871 England opened university admission and teaching posts at all universities to non-Anglicans. Anti-Catholicism, at times a popular and virulent movement, declined in the 1870s. In France, too, the position of religious minorities improved. Some of the highest officials of the Second Empire were Protestants, as were some early leaders of the Third Republic and some important business leaders and scientists.

Legal emancipation of Jews, started in France in 1791, subsequently spread to the rest of the Continent. England removed restrictions on Jews when the House of Commons, in 1858, and the House of Lords the following decade allowed Jews to hold a parliamentary seat. In the 1860s Germany and Austria-Hungary granted Jews the rights of citizenship. Social discrimination continued, however, and Jews were not accepted as social equals in most of European society. Although some Jews occupied high office in France and Italy, in Germany and Austria-Hungary they had to convert before they could aspire to such position. In other fields, access was easier. Some of the major banking houses were founded by Jews—the Rothschilds in France, Britain, and Germany, and the Warburgs in Germany, for instance.

In the expanding economy of western Europe, where the condition of most people was improving, the enhanced opportunity of a previously despised minority aroused relatively little attention. In other parts of Europe, Jews were not so fortunate. When they seized economic opportunities in eastern Europe and moved into commerce, industry, and the professions, they were resented. Rashes of violence against them, called *pogroms*, broke out in Bucharest, capital of Romania, in 1866 and in the Russian seaport of Odessa in 1871. Although economic rivalries may have fueled this anti-Semitism, they do not completely explain it. In most cases anti-Jewish sentiment occurred in the areas of Europe least exposed to liberal ideas of human equality and human rights.

The emphasis on science and reason transformed religion in the nineteenth century, but, as the continued anti-Semitism showed, it by no means always led to increased tolerance or weakened religious fervor. On the contrary, in certain cases religiosity grew. French people reported frequent sightings of the Virgin Mary. A shepherdess in 1858 claimed to have seen and spoken with her at Lourdes, which became an especially important shrine whose waters were reputed to heal the lame and the sick. In 1872 construction of a rail line allowed 100,000 people a year to visit the town.

Church attendance continued to be high, especially in rural areas. In England villagers usually attended church, many twice or more each Sunday. Children dutifully attended Sunday schools. Advances in printing made it possible to distribute large quantities of inexpensive religious tracts to a sizable and avid readership. The faithful eagerly engaged in proselytizing, sending large numbers of missionaries to all corners of the globe.

Art in the Age of Material Change

The new era of technology, science, and faith in progress was reflected in the arts. Some artists optimistically believed they could more accurately depict reality by adopting the methods of the scientist, cooly describing their subject. A minority, however, were disillusioned by the materialism of the age and warned against its loss of values.

Photography had a direct impact on painting. Various experiments in the late eighteenth century, plus the inventions of the Frenchman Louis Daguerre (1789–1851), made the camera relatively usable by the 1830s. It was still a large, cumbersome object, however, until the dry plate and miniature camera were introduced in the 1870s. Twenty years later, with the invention of celluloid film, it came into wide use—the best-known mass-produced camera being the Kodak camera invented by the American George Eastman (1854–1932). Unlike paintings and portraits, photography was accessible to the public. And photographic services were in high demand; by the 1860s, 30,000 people in Paris made a living from photography and allied fields. Many Europeans became amateur photographers—Queen Victoria and Prince Albert had a darkroom at Windsor Castle.

The ability of photography to depict a scene with exactitude had a significant impact on art. On the one hand, it encouraged many artists to be true to reality, to reproduce on the canvas a visual image akin to that of a photograph. On the other hand, other artists felt that such realism was now no longer necessary in their sphere. However, the great majority of the public, which now had wide access to museum exhibitions, was accustomed to photographic accuracy and desired art that was accessible and understandable. Realistic works of art met this need, at least superficially.

Discarding myths and symbols, many artists described the world as it actually was or appeared to them—a world without illusions, everyday life in all its grimness. The realist painter Gustave Courbet (1819–1877) proclaimed himself "without

ideals and without religion." His fellow Frenchman, Jean-François Millet (1814–1875), held a similar opinion. Instead of romanticizing peasants in the manner of earlier artists, he painted the harsh physical conditions under which they labored. In England the pre-Raphaelites took as their model the painters of Renaissance Italy prior to Raphael, who presumably had depicted the realistic simplicity of nature. In painting historical scenes, these artists emphasized meticulous research of the landscape, architecture, fauna, and costumes of their subjects. To paint the Dead Sea in *The Scapegoat,* English artist Holman Hunt (1827–1910) traveled all the way to Palestine to guarantee accurate portrayal of the site.

In the past, artists had been concerned about composition and perspective. But under the influence of photography, they began to paint incomplete, off-center pictures. *Orchestra of the Paris Opera* by French artist Edgar Degas looks as if it has been cropped, with only half of a musician showing on each edge and the top half of the ballet dancers missing.

On April 15, 1874, six French artists—Edgar Degas (1834–1917), Claude Monet (1840–1926), Camille Pissarro (1830–1903), Auguste Renoir (1840–1919), Alfred Sisley (1839–1899), and Berthe Morisot (1841–1895)—opened an exhibition in Paris that a critic disparagingly called "impressionist," after the title of one of Monet's paintings, *Impression: Sunrise.* The impressionists were influenced by new theories of physics that claimed images were transmitted to the brain as small light particles that the brain then reconstituted. The impressionists wanted their paintings to capture what things looked like before they had been "distorted" by the brain. In their search for realism, impressionist painters ceased painting in their studios and increasingly went outdoors to paint objects exactly as they looked when light hit them at a certain angle. Monet, for example, emphasized outdoor painting and the need for spontaneity—for reproducing subjects without the preconception of how they had been depicted in earlier work, and seeking to show exactly how the colors and shapes hit the eye. Monet was particularly interested in painting several views of the same object to underscore that there was no single correct depiction of a subject but that it depended on viewpoint, weather, and time of day.

Courbet: The Stone Breakers This realistic 1849 painting depicts the rough existence of manual laborers. The bleakness of the subject matter and the style in which it was carried out characterized much of the realistic school of art. *(Staatliche Kunstsammlungen, Dresden/The Bridgeman Art Library, London)*

The school of realism also influenced literature, especially the novel. In realist novels, life was not glorified or infused with mythical elements; the stark existence of daily life was seen as a suitable subject. Charles Dickens (1812–1870), who came from a poor background and had personally experienced the inhumanity of the London underworld, wrote novels depicting the lot of the poor with humor and sympathy. The appalling social conditions he described helped educate his large middle-class audience on the state of the poor. He also provided numerous examples of individuals who by hard work were able to rise above their circumstances. In fact, the income from Dickens' many novels provided him with a comfortable income; by the pen he was able to join the middle class himself.

Another realist, the French novelist Gustave Flaubert (1821–1880), consciously debunked the romanticism of his elders. His famous novel, *Madame Bovary*, describes middle-class life as bleak, boring, and meaningless. The heroine seeks to escape the narrow confines of provincial life by adulterous and disastrous affairs.

Emile Zola (1840–1902), another Frenchman, belonged to the naturalist school of literature. The writer, he declared, should be like a surgeon or chemist, providing a scientific cause and record of human behavior; his work, in Zola's words, is similar to "the analysis that surgeons make on cadavers." (See the box, "Emile Zola on the Novelist as Scientist.") In his Rougon-Macquart series, which describes in detail the experience of several generations of a family, Zola's major theme is the impact of environment and heredity on his characters' lives of degradation and vice. His characters seem locked in a Darwinian struggle for survival; some are doomed by the laws of biology to succeed and others to succumb.

Emile Zola on the Novelist as Scientist

Emile Zola believed that the novelist should act like a scientist, experimenting with characters' reactions to differing circumstances in order to determine the laws that govern thought and emotion. Zola wanted to be the literary equivalent of the great French scientist, Claude Bernard (1813–1878), one of the founders of experimental science. The title of this essay, "The Experimental Novel," published in 1880, echoes the title of Bernard's Introduction to Experimental Medicine *(1865).*

Here you have scientific progress. In the last century, a more exact application of the experimental method creates chemistry and physics which free themselves from the irrational and the supernatural. Profound studies lead to the discovery that there are established laws; phenomena are mastered. Then a fresh step is taken. Living bodies, in which the vitalists still admitted a mysterious influence, are in their turn reduced to the general mechanism of matter.

Science proves that the conditions of life of all phenomena are the same in matter and in living bodies; hence, physiology gradually acquires the same certitude as chemistry and physics. But will we stop at that? Evidently not.

When we have proved that the body of man is a machine, which we shall one day be able to take to pieces and put together again at the experimenter's will, then it will be time to pass on to the sentimental and intellectual activities of man. This means that we should enter a realm which, until now, belonged wholly to philosophy and literature; it will be the decisive victory of science over the hypotheses of philosophers and writers. We already have experimental chemistry and physics; we are going to have experimental physiology; and then, later, we shall have the experimental novel. This is a necessary progression, and one whose end can easily be foreseen today. Everything is related, one had to start from the determinism of matter to arrive at the determinism of living bodies. . . . The same determinism must rule the stones in the roadway and the brains of man. . . .

It follows that science already enters our domain—the domain of writers like us, who are at the moment the students of man in his private and social activities. By our observations, by our experiments, we carry forward the work of the physiologist who had continued that of physicists and chemists.

Source: Eugen Weber, ed. and trans., *Paths to the Present* (New York: Dodd, Mead & Co., 1960), p. 170.

The Russian novelist Leo Tolstoy (1828–1910) brought a new perspective to the historical novel in *War and Peace.* Instead of a heroic approach to battle, he showed the individual caught in forces beyond his control. Small and insignificant events, rather than major ones, seem to govern human destiny. Another Russian novelist often associated with the realist school, Feodor Dostoyevsky (1821–1881), aimed to portray realistically the psychological dimensions of his characters in novels such as *Crime and Punishment* (1866), *The Idiot* (1868), and *The Brothers Karamazov* (1879–1880).

Although material progress was generally celebrated in this era, a number of intellectuals reacted against it. They were alarmed by the prospect of the popular masses achieving political power by winning the vote and by mass production and consumption. They denounced the smug and the self-satisfied, who saw happiness in acquisition and consumption. Some condemned the age in severe terms. Dostoyevsky denounced the materialism and egotism of the West, describing its civilization as driven by "trade, shipping, markets, factories." In Britain—the nation that seemed to embody

~ **ENCOUNTERS WITH THE WEST** ~

A Chinese Official's Views of European Material Progress

Educated in European universities, Ku Hung-Ming rose to become a high official in the Chinese court. His essays were penned under the impact of the European military intervention in China during the Boxer Rebellion in 1900. Ku denounced European notions of superiority over Asia, arguing that material progress was an inappropriate measure of a civilization.

In order to estimate the value of a civilisation, it seems to me, the question we must finally ask is not what great cities, what magnificent houses, what fine roads it has built and is able to build; what beautiful and comfortable furniture, what clever and useful implements, tools and instruments it has made and is able to make; no, not even what institutions, what arts and sciences it has invested: the question we must ask, in order to estimate the value of a civilisation,—is, *what type of humanity, what kind of men and women it has been able to produce.* In fact, the man and woman,—the type of human beings—which a civilisation produces, it is this which shows the essence, the personality, so to speak, the soul of that civilisation. Now if the men and women of a civilisation show the essence, the personality and soul of that civilisation, the language which the men and women in that civilisation speak, shows the essence, the personality, the soul of the men and women of that civilisation. . . .

To Europeans, and especially to unthinking practical Englishmen, who are accustomed to take what modern political economists call "the standard of living" as the test of the moral culture of or civilisation of a people, the actual life of the Chinese and of the people of the East at the present day, will no doubt appear very sordid and undesirable. But the standard of living by itself is not a proper test of the civilisation of a people. The standard of living in America at the present day, is, I believe, much higher than it is in Germany. But although the son of an American millionaire, who regards the simple and comparatively low standard of living among the professors of a German University, may doubt the value of the education in such a University, yet no educated man, I believe, who has travelled in both countries, will admit that the Germans are a less civilised people than the Americans.

Source: Ku Hung-Ming, *The Spirit of the Chinese People,* 2d ed. (Beijing: Commercial Press, 1922), pp. 1, 144–145.

progress—the historian Thomas Carlyle (1795–1881) denounced his age as one not of progress but of selfishness. Parliamentarianism he saw as a sham, and he called for a strong leader to save the nation from endless palavers and compromises. Unlike most of his contemporaries, who saw in material plenty a sign of progress, Carlyle saw the era as one of decline, bereft of spiritual values.

Another Englishman, John Ruskin (1819–1900), looked back to the Middle Ages as an ideal era in human history. People then did not produce with machines, but exercised a fine sense of craftsmanship. People then supposedly had a better sense of community and labored for the common good. Ruskin was one of the founders of the arts and crafts movement, which emphasized the need to produce goods for daily use with an eye for beauty and originality. "Industry without art is brutality," Ruskin warned.

In France republicans saw in the ostentation of the Second Empire a sign of depravity and decline. Defeat in war in 1870 and the outbreak of the Commune furthered a mood of pessimism among many intellectuals. Flaubert detested his own age, seeing it as petty and mean. The characters in Zola's Rougon-Macquart novels are constantly headed downward in mental faculties, social position, and morality. And some abroad were also unimpressed. (See the box, "Encounters with the West: A Chinese Official's Views of European Material Progress.")

Thus, all was not optimistic in this age of optimism. If many people celebrated what they viewed as an age of progress, others claimed that under the outer trappings of material comfort lay a frightening ignorance of aesthetic, moral, and spiritual values.

SUMMARY

During the second half of the nineteenth century, advances in industry created for many westerners an era of material plenty, providing more riches and comforts to a larger population than ever before. It was a self-confident age that believed in progress and anticipated further improvements in its material and intellectual environment.

Economic changes transformed the class structure of many European countries, and middle-class values and tastes defined the second half of the century. The new wealth and technologies led to improvements in both the countryside and the cities; in both, life became more comfortable and safer. Governments provided new services such as public education, cultural facilities, and expanded welfare services.

The material changes in society were reflected in intellectual currents. Change and evolution were embraced as an explanation for the origin of species. A new confidence in scientific research led to many scientific and technological breakthroughs. Novelists and painters aimed to dissect as scientists the world around them, creating realism in the arts. Some intellectuals, however, revolted against a certain crass self-satisfaction that imbued the bourgeoisie, and they criticized an age that worshiped industry and materialism.

Progress, as Europeans were to learn in a later era, was two-edged: The very forces that improved life for many also threatened it. The same breakthroughs in chemistry that led to the development of artificial fertilizers also provided more

powerful military explosives. The expansion of education and reduction of illiteracy meant an end to ignorance but also the creation of a public that could more easily absorb messages of hate against a rival nation or against religious or ethnic minorities at home. Material progress and well-being continued, but there were new forces in the shadows that would ultimately undermine the comforts, self-assurance, and peace of this age.

SUGGESTED READING

General Surveys

Hearder, Harry. *Europe in the Nineteenth Century, 1830–1880.* 2d ed. 1988. A broad survey of this period.

Hobsbawm, Eric J. *The Age of Capital, 1848–1875.* 1979. Particularly strong on social and economic developments.

Rich, Norman. *The Age of Nationalism and Reform, 1850–1890.* 1970. Emphasizes the growing confidence in human progress in these years.

Economic Growth

Milward, A. S., and S. B. Saul. *The Development of the Economies of Continental Europe, 1850–1914.* 1977. Has good chapters on economic developments in the second half of the nineteenth century.

Ville, Simon P. *Transport and the Development of the European Economy, 1750–1918.* 1990. Describes the importance of transportation in the modernization of Europe.

Social Change

Blum, Jerome. *The End of the Old Order in Rural Europe.* 1978. A broad, comparative study of the position of the peasantry in nineteenth-century Europe.

Cocks, Geoffrey, and Konrad H. Jarausch, eds. *German Professions, 1800–1950.* 1990. Describes the relationship between the professions and the state.

Geison, Gerald L., ed. *Professions and the French State, 1700–1900.* 1984. Considers the development of the various professions in France.

Grew, Raymond, and Patrick J. Harrigan. *School, State and Society—The Growth of Elementary Schooling in Nineteenth-Century France.* 1991. Reveals the constantly growing demand for education throughout the nineteenth century and the spread of formal schooling to the whole country.

Hurt, J. S. *Elementary Schooling and the Working Classes, 1860–1918.* 1979. Studies the impact of compulsory education on the British working class.

Mayer, Arno. *The Persistence of the Old Regime—Europe to the Great War.* 1981. Argues for the persistence of the aristocracy throughout the nineteenth century.

Pilbeam, Pamela. *The Middle Classes in Europe, 1789–1914*. 1990. Reviews the formation and values of the bourgeoisie in four continental European nations.

Thompson, F. M. L. *The Rise of Respectable Society—A Social History of Victorian Britain, 1830–1910*. 1988. Depicts considerable social mobility and well-being in Britain in the second half of the nineteenth century.

Weber, Eugen. *Peasants into Frenchmen: The Modernization of Rural France, 1870–1914*. 1976. A lively description of the process by which the French peasantry was modernized.

Women's Experience

Adams, Carole Elizabeth. *Women Clerks in Wilhelmine Germany*. 1988. Provides a history of female store employees.

Holcombe, Lee. *Victorian Ladies at Work*. 1973. Considers the various forms of employment open to middle-class Victorian women.

Peterson, M. Jeanne. *Family, Love, and Work in the Lives of Victorian Gentlewomen*. 1989. Offers a revisionist examination of the view that women were passive in the Victorian era.

Prochaska, F. K. *Women and Philanthropy in Nineteenth-Century England*. 1980. Reveals the important role women played in charity work throughout the century.

Robertson, Priscilla. *An Experience of Women and Change in Nineteenth-Century Europe*. 1982. Describes the private lives of bourgeois women in the nineteenth century, emphasizing the differing cultural traditions of various nations.

Smith, Bonnie G. *Ladies of the Leisure Class—The Bourgeoises of Northern France in the Nineteenth Century*. 1981. Emphasizes the separate world of domesticity bourgeois women created and maintained.

Urban Development

Briggs, Asa. *Victorian Things*. 1989. Provides an amusing and instructive history of the various new objects that became part of consumer culture.

Lees, Andrew. *Cities Perceived: Urban Society in European and American Thought, 1820–1940*. 1985. Depicts how various writers in Europe and the United States perceived their cities.

Miller, Michael B. *The Bon Marché—Bourgeois Culture and the Department Store, 1869–1920*. 1981. Views the first and largest department store in Paris as both manifestation and promoter of bourgeois culture.

Olsen, Donald J. *The City as a Work of Art—London, Paris, Vienna*. 1986. Compares and contrasts how these cities evolved in the nineteenth century.

Pinkney, David. *Napoleon III and the Rebuilding of Paris*. 1958. The standard work on the urban renewal of Paris.

Science and Medicine

Bowler, Peter J. *Evolution—The History of an Idea*. Rev. ed. 1989. Written by a scientist, who examines the history and development of the concept while evaluating the scientific merit of the debates.

Burrow, J. W. *Evolution and Society: A Study in Victorian Social Theory*. 1966. Considers the impact of the evolutionary paradigm in the social sciences.

Chadwick, Owen. *The Secularization of the European Mind in the Nineteenth Century*. 1973. Considers the rise and spread of secular attitudes at the cost of religion.

Desmond, Adrian, and James Moore. *Darwin*. 1991. A lengthy and interesting biography of the great scientist.

Youngson, A. J. *The Scientific Revolution in Victorian Medicine*. 1979. A record of innovation in British medicine.

Art

Clark, T. J. *Image of the People: Gustave Courbet and the 1848 Revolution*. 1973. Explores the impact of the sociopolitical environment on Courbet's paintings and the audience's reactions to them.

Pool, Phoebe. *Impressionism*. 1985. Studies the origins, accomplishments, and legacies of impressionism.

Weisberg, Gabriel P., ed. *The European Realist Tradition*. 1982. A multinational study revealing the pervasiveness of realism in European art.

THE CRYSTAL PALACE

No construction summarized the aspirations and achievements of the mid-nineteenth century as well as the Crystal Palace, erected in London in 1851 to house the "Great Exhibition of the Works of Industry of all Nations." Presided over by Prince Albert, consort to Queen Victoria, the exhibition was the first of many international expositions proudly displaying the new world of invention and plenty.

The building, a major technological feat, was a product of the new age. Observe that the building is mainly made of two materials that as a result of industrialization could now be produced cheaply—steel and glass. They also could be produced rapidly, shortening the time between the design of the building and its erection. The structure was put up within six months; the secret of its speedy construction was that it consisted of standard interchangeable parts: 3300 iron columns, 2300 girders, and 293,655 glass panes.

The designer of the building was Joseph Paxton (1801–1856); his plan perhaps predictably resembled one of the greenhouses he had designed at the estate where he started his gardening career. Paxton's life and career exemplified the opportunities that at least some people could seize in an era of expanding wealth and possibilities. The son of a farmer, Paxton did not have even an elementary education. He took employ as a gardener and then became estate manager; investments in railways made him a wealthy man. Having already designed and constructed a number of important buildings—among them the duke of Devonshire's iron and glass conservatory at Chatsworth—he accepted the invitation to plan the exposition hall. His ingenious project provided for a light and airy structure with the added advantage, unlike some competing designs, of easy removal at the end of the exposition, planned to last only six months. The iron and glass structure provided a model for much industrial architecture in the nineteenth century, including the Victoria railroad station in London, department stores like the Bon Marché in Paris (see pages 844–845), and public libraries such as France's National Library.

The Crystal Palace was immense, 1848 feet long and 450 feet wide, or more than four times the size of a football field. Not wanting to cut down some elm trees on the planned site, the organizing committee decided to make the building tall enough to enclose them; it was 66 feet high, rising to 108 feet at the arched ceilings of its transepts. It was built to accommodate tens of thousands of people at once; in fact during peak attendance 110,000 men, women, and children fit inside the building at the same time. Just before the building was to open, sparrows invaded it and no stratagem seemed capable of dislodging them. Queen Victoria decided to call on the duke of Wellington, victor at Waterloo (see page 728), for advice. After a moment's reflection, he suggested, "Try sparrow-hawks, Ma'am." And that worked.

The "Great Exhibition of the Works of Industry of all Nations" displayed 100,000 objects from 14,000 exhibitors, half from Great Britain and its empire and the other half from foreign nations. Note the panels indicating the nation of origin of various booths—next to the Indian booth are the Persian and Russian ones. The Crystal Palace was a celebration of plenty and of a new form of globalism made possible by improved communications, transport, and imperialism. Never before had so many objects from so many different parts of the world been brought together in one place. The exposition represented a triumph of industry, wealth, and power.

Among the objects the Crystal Palace proudly displayed were some of the newest products of the industrial age—turbine engines and sophisticated printing presses. It celebrated ingenuity and inventions, some useful, others merely novel, such as the bed that could wake up sleepers at a predetermined time by dumping them on the floor. Luxuries available to the newly prosperous

The Crystal Palace
(Courtesy of the Trustees of the British Museum)

were also shown: elaborate vases, overstuffed furniture, grand pianos, reproductions—from the sublime to the garish—of various paintings and statuary from ancient and modern times. Many exhibitors showed consumer goods produced by artisans, such as glycerine soap, perfume, lace, porcelain, and glass.

Britain, with the most far-flung empire in the first half of the century, displayed an array of objects bound to strike visitors as exotic. A birch-bark canoe from Canada able to hold twenty people and a stuffed Indian elephant carrying a silk canopied seat reflected the rich diversity of the world's largest empire.

The exposition was the first in Great Britain intended for the masses; depending on the day, the entrance fee was as low as one shilling, thus accessible to the working classes. During the six months it was open the exposition attracted six million visitors, a feat possible only because of the development of railroads, which provided rapid and cheap access to nearly all Britons; without trains, only Londoners would have been able to attend. Members of the elite had voiced some apprehension about how the "public" would behave, fearing it might be rowdy and harm the objects on display. The crowd's collective good behavior was, however, reassuring and led to the opening of museums to the general public.

Most visitors to the Crystal Palace in 1851 left with a great sense of pride in their contemporaries' accomplishments, but there were also reasons for unease. Some noticed the crass materialism. Charles Dickens complained, "There's too much." The exposition included a number of cannon by the Prussian arms manufacturer Alfred Krupp, a grim reminder that industry was capable of producing instruments of death at record levels. Many of the exotic objects came from Europe's overseas possessions—an empire acquired and maintained by force. If the exposition showed Britain's global ascendancy, it also revealed that that ascendancy was ensured not only by Britain's economic prowess but also by its domination of other peoples.

The Crystal Palace was scheduled for demolition after the exposition ended its successful run in October 1851, but Joseph Paxton was able to save his creation by having it moved to Sydenham Hill near London. Rebuilt, the structure was even larger, and over the years a number of buildings such as an aquarium were added to it. A visible celebration of a great age of optimism, the Crystal Palace burned down at a time when prospects for the future appeared far less promising—in 1936, when Great Britain was mired in a worldwide economic depression and had to face an increasingly menacing Germany. ✍

Escalating Tensions, 1880–1914

I n the spring of 1914, U.S. President Woodrow Wilson, concerned over the growing international crisis, sent his aide, Colonel Edward House, to Europe. The colonel toured several capitals—Berlin, Paris, and London—and on May 29, 1914, he reported, "The situation is extraordinary. It is militarism run stark mad. Unless some one . . . can bring about a different understanding there is one day to be an awful cataclysm."[1] This prediction was far more accurate than the author could have imagined; nine weeks later Europe was at war. And in less than three years even the United States was swept into what became a world war.

Colonel House could imagine war breaking out in 1914, yet the preceding years in Europe had on the whole been peaceful and prosperous. Contemporaries often characterized the generation before the war as "la belle époque"—the beautiful era. A growing economy provided expanding opportunities for many. The arts flourished and were celebrated. Parliamentary government continued to spread, and more nations seemed to be adapting to democracy as suffrage was extended. Yet hand in hand with these trends of apparent progress came troubling new tendencies. Several developments in the generation before 1914 undermined and threatened all the accomplishments of these years.

In many societies, governing became more complex as populations increased. The population of Europe jumped from 330 million in 1880 to 460 million by 1914. A larger population coupled with extended suffrage meant that more people participated in the political system, but it became harder to find consensus. The example of democracy in some countries led to frustration in the autocratic ones at their failure to move toward freer

Arnold Bocklin,
The War (1896).

institutions. In the same way that prosperity and economic growth aroused resentment in those who did not share in the benefits, some groups were frustrated by their exclusion from the political system.

Intellectuals revolted against what they viewed as the smug self-assuredness of earlier years. They no longer felt certain that the world was knowable, stable, subject to comprehension and, ultimately, mastery by rational human beings. Some jettisoned rationality, imagining that they had made strides in sophistication by glorifying emotion, irrationality, and, in some cases, violence. The works of painters and writers seemed to anticipate the impending destruction of world order.

The anxieties and tensions that beset many Europeans took a variety of forms. Ethnic minorities became the target of hatreds. Overseas, non-Europeans were forcibly put under white domination as European states embarked on a race for empire throughout the world. On the European continent, states increasingly felt insecure, worried that they would be subject to attack. They established standing armies, shifted alliances, drafted war plans, and, ultimately, went to war.

FROM OPTIMISM TO ANXIETY: POLITICS AND CULTURE

Many of the beliefs and institutions that had seemed so solid in the "age of optimism" found themselves under attack in the next generation. Forces hostile to liberalism became increasingly vocal. In the arts and philosophy, the earlier confidence was replaced by doubt, relativism, and a desire to flee the routines of everyday life.

The Erosion of the Liberal Consensus

In 1850 liberalism appeared to be the ascendant ideology, and liberals assumed that with the passage of time more and more people would be won over to their world-view. By 1900, however, toward the end of the century, liberalism faced serious challenges. Principles eroded within the liberal camp, and in addition, various ideas and movements—some new, some rooted in the past—served to erode the liberal consensus. Prominent among these were socialism, anarchism, a new political right, racism, and anti-Semitism.

The undermining of the liberal consensus began among liberals themselves, who, in the face of changing circumstances, retreated from some of their basic tenets. For example, one of the principal emphases of liberalism had always been free trade. But under the pressure of economic competition, liberals supported tariffs at home and created closed markets for the mother country overseas in the empire.

Historically, liberals had typically stood for an expansion of civil liberties, yet several groups were denied their rights. Power remained an exclusively male domain, and liberal males saw nothing wrong or inconsistent in continuing to deny women both the vote and free access to education and professional advancement. In the face of labor agitation, many liberals no longer unconditionally supported civil liberties and favored instead the violent crushing of strikes.

Similarly, liberals had always upheld the sanctity of private property, but under the pressure of events, they abandoned this principle as an absolute goal. To ensure workers' safety, they placed limits on employers by passing legislation on working conditions. In some countries, they supported progressive income taxes, which many perceived as a serious invasion of private property. When it became clear that a free market was unable to meet many human needs, welfare programs were instituted in several countries. These reforms were intended to strengthen the state by winning support from the masses. But because they reflected the liberals' willingness to breach fundamental principles, these measures also revealed the apparent inability of liberal ideology to deal with the problems of the day.

The Growth of Socialism and Anarchism

Among the groups challenging the power and liberal ideology of the middle classes were the socialist parties, both Marxist and non-Marxist, whose goal was to win the support of workers by espousing their cause. Socialists varied in their notions of how their goals should be achieved; some thought they could be achieved gradually and peacefully; others were dedicated to a violent overthrow of capitalist society.

In Britain, where the Liberal party was more open to the needs of workers than in other European states, a separate socialist party, the Independent Labour party, was established relatively late, in 1893. It was not until the 1920s that this party gained any particular electoral success. More influential in the late nineteenth century was the Fabian Society, founded in 1884. The Fabians criticized the capitalist system as inefficient, wasteful, and unjust. They believed that by gradual, democratic means, factories and land could be transferred from the private sector to the state, which would employ them for the benefit of society as a whole. Socialism was a desirable system that would replace capitalism because it was more efficient and more just. It would come into being not through class war but through enlightened ideas. This gradualist approach became the hallmark of British socialism.

In Germany there were two socialist parties in the 1860s. The first, founded in 1863 by Ferdinand Lassalle (1825–1864), viewed universal suffrage as the means of assuring the workers' well-being. A competing party, formed in 1868 and influenced by Marx, called for a workers' revolution. In 1875 the two socialist parties united around a common program.

Unification did not prevent the German Social Democratic party from a bitter debate soon to be echoed in all European socialist parties. A German socialist leader, Eduard Bernstein (1850–1932), who had visited England and had soaked up the influence of the Fabians, argued in a book with the telling English title *Evolutionary Socialism* (1898) that Marx had been wrong to suggest that capitalism necessarily led to the increasing wretchedness of the working class. The capitalist economy had in fact expanded and been able to provide for steadily improved conditions. Workers would not need to seize power by some cataclysmic act. Rather, by piecemeal democratic action they could win more power and legislate on behalf of their interests. Since he argued for a revision of Marxist theory, Bernstein was labeled a "revisionist."

Opposing Bernstein in this great debate was the party theoretician Karl Kautsky (1854–1938). Although Kautsky agreed that in material terms the workers' lot had not worsened, he insisted that workers were worse off in political terms, as their rights were abridged and their hopes of having a voice in government grew fainter. In Germany, he argued, workers could come to power only if they first overthrew autocracy. A violent revolution would thus be necessary to institute socialism.

Although the party officially rejected revisionism and seemed to embrace the doctrine of a violent proletarian revolution, it in fact practiced the former. The German Social Democratic party had become a part of established society, with its newspapers, party bureaucracy, and headquarters; it had gained a vested interest in society and was not ready to overthrow it. Nevertheless, it continued to espouse a militant ideology of class war.

Similarly ambiguous developments occurred in neighboring France. One of Marx's French disciples, Jules Guesde (1845–1922), founded a socialist party with a strong working-class membership devoted to carrying on a workers' revolution. Opposing his brand of socialism was Jean Jaurès (1859–1914), an idealistic schoolteacher who saw socialism as an ethical system. Unlike the Marxists, he did not regard the advent of socialism as inevitable but rather as desirable to bring about a more equitable and just society. Jaurès believed that socialism could be achieved in cooperation with the more enlightened members of the middle

Jean Jaurès The leader of the French Socialist party, Jean Jaurès, addresses a meeting in 1913. A charismatic figure, he was one of France's greatest orators. *(Roger-Viollet)*

classes, and he abhorred the vocabulary of class warfare so frequently voiced by Guesde. In 1905 the socialist parties led by Guesde and Jaurès merged, and Jaurès became virtual party leader. Although Jaurès' brand of gradual democratic socialism influenced the daily functioning of the newly unified party, the French Socialist party formally continued to adhere to Guesde's doctrines of revolution and class war. In 1914, on the eve of the outbreak of war, a nationalist, incensed by Jaurès' call on his government to avoid war, assassinated him.

Another movement that sought to liberate the downtrodden was anarchism, which proclaimed that humans could be free only when the state had been abolished. According to anarchist theory, in a stateless society people would naturally join together in communes and share the fruits of their labor. Some anarchists believed their goal could be reached by educating people, but others were more impatient and hoped to speed up the process by making direct attacks on existing authority. The Russian nobleman Michael Bakunin (1814–1876), frustrated at the authoritarianism of his homeland, became a lifelong anarchist. He challenged tsarism at home and participated in the 1848 revolutions throughout Europe. He viewed all governments as repressive and declared war on them: "The passion for destruction is also a creative passion." His ideas were particularly influential in Italy, Spain, and parts of France, especially among the artisan classes.

Many anarchists of this period wanted to bring about the new society by "propaganda of the deed." An attack on the bastions of power, these anarchists believed, could bring about the dissolution of the state. They formed secret terrorist organizations that assassinated heads of state or those close to them. Between 1894 and 1901, the president of France, the prime minister of Spain, the empress of Austria, the king of Italy, and the president of the United States were killed by anarchists. These murders fixed the popular image of anarchism as a violence-prone ideology. More important, such manifestations of the "propaganda of the deed" produced no particular improvement in the lives of the working-class people, on whose behalf these campaigns were supposedly launched.

Without accepting the anarchists' methods, some in the labor movement shared their hostility toward parliamentary institutions. A working-class program, labor activists argued, could be implemented only by a pure workers' movement, such as unionization. Workers should eschew the political arena and concentrate on direct workers' action. According to this line of thought, known as *syndicalism* (after the French word for unions), workers should amass their power in unions, and at the right moment carry out a general strike, crippling capitalist society and bringing it down. Syndicalism was particularly popular in Mediterranean countries, where its more militant form, *anarchosyndicalism*, radicalized labor and made a sizable number of workers hostile to parliamentarism.

European socialism also attempted to have an international presence. In 1864 Marx had participated in the founding of the International Workers' Association, which fell prey to internal dissension and dissolved after a few years. Known as the First International, it was followed by a more robust organization, the Second International, in 1889. The International met yearly and debated issues of concern to socialists in general, including the worsening relations among European states. As early as 1893 the International called on European states to resolve their conflicts by mandatory arbitration.

In 1907, sensing impending war, the International called on the workers to strike and refuse military service in case of international conflict. The International saw itself as a bulwark of peace; it did not realize that once war broke out, Europeans, including socialists, would be swept up in nationalist fervor and would willingly go to war. Although most socialists advocated peace at home and abroad, many had contributed to a militant discourse by emphasizing class war.

The New Right, Racism, and Anti-Semitism

The traditional opponents of liberalism on the political right were the conservatives, wedded to preserving the existing order. Beginning in the 1880s, however, a "new right" emerged that was populist and demagogic. Although conservatives had been wary of nationalism, the new right embraced it. Alienated by industry, democracy, and social egalitarianism, many in this new right rejected doctrines of human equality and embraced racist ideologies.

Racist thinking was common in the nineteenth century. Many Europeans believed human races were not only different physiologically but also—as a result of these biological variations—differently endowed in intelligence and other qualities (see page 868). Europeans were often ethnocentric, convinced they were the epitome of humankind while members of other races belonged to lesser groups. In midcentury the Frenchman Arthur de Gobineau (1816–1882) published his *Essay on the Inequality of Human Races,* declaring that race "dominates all other problems and is the key to it." Biologists and early anthropologists made similar statements, thus giving racism a scientific aura. Throughout the second half of the nineteenth century, race was thought to be the principal explanation for the differences that were discovered among human groupings. Some races were relegated to near subhuman levels. For example, the British anatomist Robert Knox (1798–1862) declared that the Africans lacked the "grand qualities which distinguish man from animal."

These racist ideas helped fuel anti-Semitism. For centuries Jews had been the object of suspicion and bigotry. Originally, the basis of the prejudice was religious. As early as the Middle Ages, however, the argument emerged that "Jewish blood" was different. And with the popularization of pseudoscientific racist thinking in the nineteenth century, Jews were commonly viewed as a separate, inferior race, unworthy of the same rights as the majority of the population.

Historically, Christians had relegated the Jews in their midst to marginal positions. In the Middle Ages, when land was the basis of wealth and prestige, Jews had been confined to such urban trades as cattle trading and moneylending. They incurred high risks by lending money: They often were not paid back and faced unsympathetic courts when they tried to collect their due. To counteract these risks, Jewish moneylenders charged high interest rates that gave them the unpopular reputation as usurers.

The emancipation of the Jews, which began in France with the Revolution and spread to Germany and Austria by the 1860s, provided them opportunities they had not had before, and some members of society found it hard to adjust to the prominence a few Jews gained. Because their increased prominence and success occurred concur-rently with the wrenching social transformations brought by industrialization and urbanization, anti-Semites pointed to the Jews as the perpetrators of these unsettling changes.

Many people perceived Jews as prototypical of the new capitalist class. Although most Jews were of modest means, resentment of the rich often was aimed at Jews. Earlier in the century, many anti-Semites were socialists, speaking on behalf of the working class. Later they came from among the petty bourgeois, small shopkeepers and artisans, who felt threatened by economic change.

Political movements based on anti-Semitism were founded in the 1880s. They depicted Jews as dangerous and wicked and called for their exclusion from the political arena and from certain professions. In some cases they suggested that Jews be expelled from the state. The mayor of Vienna, Karl Lueger (1844–1928), was elected on an anti-Semitic platform. In Berlin the emperor's chaplain, Adolf Stöcker (1835–1909), founded an anti-Semitic party, hoping to make political inroads among the working-class supporters of socialism. In France Edouard Drumont (1844–1917) published one of the best-sellers of the second half of the nineteenth century, *Jewish France,* in which he attributed all the nation's misfortunes to the Jews.

In Russia organized pogroms, or mass attacks, on Jews killed two thousand in the 1880s and one thousand in 1905, frightening two million Jews into exile, mostly to the United States. Russian Jews lived under social as well as legal disabilities; condemned to second-class citizenship, they won full emancipation only with the Bolshevik Revolution of 1917.

In the face of growing hostility, some Jews speculated that they would be safe only in their own nation. The Austrian Jewish journalist Theodore Herzl (1860–1904), outraged by the Dreyfus affair in France, in which a Jewish officer was imprisoned on trumped-up charges of treason (see page 901), founded the Zionist movement. He advocated establishing a Jewish state in the Jews' ancient homeland of Israel. In the beginning, the Zionist movement won a following only in eastern Europe, where the Jews were particularly ill-treated, but by 1948, it led to the founding of the state of Israel.

Various manifestations of anti-Semitism revealed the vulnerability of the principle of toleration, one of the basic ideas of liberalism. It became eminently clear that racism, with its penchant for irrationality and violence, could easily be aroused.

Irrationality and Uncertainty

In contrast to the confidence in reason and science that prevailed at midcentury, the era starting in the 1880s wrestled with the issues of irrationality and uncertainty—in philosophy, in science, in the arts, even in religion. The positivism of the earlier era had emphasized surface reality but neglected inner meaning and ignored the emotive and intuitive aspects of life. By the 1890s a neoromantic mood, emphasizing emotion and feeling, stirred major intellectual movements.

The intellectuals who matured in the 1890s, and thus are known as "the generation of 1890," stressed the extent to which irrational forces guide human beings and their relation to one another. Nonetheless, they remained strongly affected by the positivists, adopting their scientific methods to study irrationality and hoping to find ways to make human beings more rational. Following this group came those intellectuals who matured around 1905, known as the "generation of 1905." Like their seniors, they believed human beings were irrational and the world was unknowable, but they did not express any regret at this condition. Rather, they glorified it.

The intellectual trends of the 1890s are exemplified in the work of the Austro-Hungarian Sigmund Freud (1856–1939), who founded psychoanalysis, a method of treating psychic disorders by exploring the unconscious. Freud believed that people were motivated not only by observed reality but also by their unconscious feelings and emotions. Whereas earlier physicians had described the mental condition of hysteria as a physical ailment, Freud saw its roots as psychological, the result of unresolved inner conflicts. Although Freud's work was influenced by rational methods, he stressed that irrational forces played a significant role in human behavior. Reflecting the concerns of his contemporaries, Freud hoped that understanding these forces would make people more rational.

In philosophy, the tension between reason and emotion was expressed in the work of the German philosopher Friedrich Nietzsche (1844–1900), who proclaimed that rationality had led humankind into a meaningless abyss. Reason would not resolve human problems, nor would any preconceived ideas. "God is dead," Nietzsche declared. With no God, humankind was free of all outside constraints, free to overthrow all conventions. Nietzsche admonished his readers to challenge existing institutions and accepted truths and create new ones. However, he realized that such nihilism offered great temptations to inflict unspeakable horrors. According to Nietzsche, only a "superman" could resist these temptations. Nietzsche's call for restraint reflected a hesitation to embrace the full implications of his philosophy. Unfortunately, his warnings were not always heeded. Nietzsche's ideas spread throughout Europe by the turn of the century and were reflected not only in philosophy but also in art and literature.

In contrast to Nietzsche, the French philosopher Henri Bergson (1859–1940) reflected the values of the generation of 1905. He argued that science—and indeed life—must be interpreted not rationally but intuitively. "Science," Bergson declared, "can teach us nothing of the truth; it can only serve as a rule of action." Meaningful truths could best be understood emotively, such as the truth of religion, literature, and art. (See the box, "The Limits of Intellect.")

The scientists of this period seemed to underscore the philosophers' conclusions. In 1905, Albert Einstein (1879–1955) proposed the theory of relativity, which undermined the certainties of Newtonian physics. Einstein's theory demonstrated that time and space are not absolute but exist relative to the observer. Much of the research in atomic theory also revealed variations and unexplained phenomena. For example, the work of German physicist Max Planck (1858–1947) in quantum theory showed that energy was not absorbed or emitted continuously, as previously assumed, but rather emitted discontinuously. Some scientists no longer shared the self-confidence that their colleagues had maintained half a century earlier, finding it increasingly difficult to believe in ultimate certainties.

In the arts, the idea of being *avant-garde*—French for "at the forefront"—took hold among creative people. Breaking the taboos of society and the conventions of one's craft seemed to be signs of artistic creativity. Artistic movements pro-

The Limits of Intellect

In Creative Evolution *(1907), a widely heralded work that influenced a whole generation of European intellectuals, the French philosopher Henri Bergson spearheaded the revolt against intellectualism, arguing that intuition was a far better guide.*

We see that the intellect, so skillful in dealing with the inert, is awkward the moment it touches the living. Whether it wants to treat the life of the body or the life of the mind, it proceeds with the rigor, the stiffness and the brutality of an instrument not designed for such use. . . . *The intellect is characterized by a natural inability to comprehend life. . . .*

Instinct, on the contrary, is molded on the very form of life. While intelligence treats everything mechanically, instinct proceeds, so to speak, organically. If the consciousness that slumbers in it should awake, if it were wound up into knowledge instead of being wound off into action, if we could ask and it could reply, it would give up to us the most intimate secrets of life. For it only carries out further the work by which life organizes matter—so that we cannot say, as has often been shown, where organization ends and where instinct begins. . . .

Our eye perceives the features of the living being, merely as assembled, not as mutually organized. The intention of life, the simple movement that runs through the lines, that binds them together and gives them significance, escapes it. This intention is just what the artist tries to regain, in placing himself back within the object by a kind of sympathy, in breaking down, by an effort of intuition, the barrier that space puts up between him and his model. It is true that this aesthetic intuition, like external perception, only attains the individual. But we can conceive an inquiry turned in the same direction as art, which would take life in *general* for its object, just as physical science, in following to the end the direction pointed out by external perception, prolongs the individual facts into general laws. . . .

. . . A complete and perfect humanity would be that in which these two forms of conscious activity [intuition and intellect] should attain their full development. . . . Intuition . . . is a lamp almost extinguished, which only glimmers now and then, for a few moments at most. But it glimmers wherever a vital interest is at stake. On our personality, on our liberty, on the place we occupy in the whole of nature, on our origin and perhaps also on our destiny, it throws a light feeble and vacillating, but which none the less pierces the darkness of the night in which the intellect leaves us.

Source: Henri Bergson, *Creative Evolution,* trans. Arthur Mitchell (New York: Holt Rinehart & Winston, 1911), pp. 165, 177, 267–268.

claimed idiosyncratic manifestos and constantly called for the rejection of existing forms of expression and the creation of new ones. The symbolists in France and Italy, the expressionists in Germany, the futurists in Italy, and the secessionists in Austria all reflected the sense that they were living through a fractured period.

In protest against the mass culture of their day, artists focused on images that were different and unique. Unlike earlier art, which had a clear message, the art of this era did not. Many artists no longer believed their role was to portray or spread ideals; rather, they tended to be introspective and even self-absorbed. The public at large found it difficult to decipher the meaning of the new art, but a number of patrons confirmed the avant-garde artists' talent and insight.

Unlike the realists who preceded them, artists in the 1890s surrendered to neoromanticism, trying to investigate and express inner forces. As French

Munch: The Scream Painted in 1893, this work reflects the fear and horror that some intellectuals experienced at the end of the nineteenth century. *(Edvard Munch,* The Scream, *1893. Tempera and oil pastel on cardboard. 91 × 73.5 cm. Photo: J. Lathion, Nasjonalgalleriet, Oslo. Copyright Munch Museum, Oslo, 1993)*

painter Paul Gauguin (1848–1903) noted, the purpose of painting was to communicate not how things looked but the emotions they conveyed. The Russian Wassily Kandinsky (1866–1944) asked viewers of his art to "look at the picture as a graphic representation of a mood and not as a representation of objects." Artists appeared to be examining the hidden anxieties of society. The Frenchman Gustave Moreau (1826–1898) displayed monsters, creations of nightmare, byproducts of the unconscious. The Austrian artist Egon Schiele (1890–1918) and the Norwegian painter Edvard Munch (1863–1944) emphasized scenes of violence, fear, and sheer horror.

Religion, too, felt the effects of these intellectual trends. Although large numbers of people still held traditional religious beliefs and followed traditional practices, indifference to organized religion spread. In urban areas of western Europe,

church attendance declined; as these regions urbanized, they became increasingly secular. But with the decline of traditional Christian practices, various forms of mysticism became more widespread. Some people were attracted to Eastern religions like Buddhism and Hinduism and to other mystical beliefs. These attitudes may have reflected a loss of faith in Western culture itself. As the century came to an end, a number of intellectuals argued that their culture, like the century, was destined for decline.

THE NEW IMPERIALISM

The age of empire building that started in Europe in the sixteenth century seemed to have ended by 1750. Then, in the 1880s, the European states launched a new era of expansionism and conquered an unprecedented amount of territory. In only twenty-five years, Europeans seized 10 million square miles and subjugated 500 million people—one half of the world's non-European population. European expansion was also manifest in a massive movement of people; between 1870 and 1914, 55 million Europeans moved overseas, mainly to Australia, the United States, Canada, and Argentina.

This era of ambitious conquest is often called the "new imperialism" to differentiate it from the earlier stage of empire building. Whereas the earlier imperialism focused on the Americas, nineteenth-century imperialism centered on Africa and Asia. And unlike the earlier period, the new imperialism occurred in an age of mass participation in politics and was accompanied by expressions of popular enthusiasm.

Economic and Social Motives

The hope of profit overseas was crucial in the dynamic of the new imperialism. When the English explorer Henry Stanley (1841–1904) returned from Africa in the late 1870s, he told the Manchester Chamber of Commerce, "There are forty million people beyond the gateway of Congo, and the cotton spinners of Manchester are waiting to clothe them." However, many Europeans had unrealistic notions of the potential markets that might be available to them. French explorers and statesmen spoke of a western Sudan inhabited by "two hundred million" people—a sixtyfold exaggeration of the real situation. Nonetheless, such illusions of huge markets were instrumental in stirring an interest in empire.

Certain economic anxieties beset European states, and colonization seemed to resolve them. An economic downturn in 1873 had led to a decade-long depression, and many political leaders worried about the economic and social repercussions of this economic crisis. Colonies, it was believed, would provide eager markets for European goods that would stimulate production at home. "Colonial policy is the daughter of industrial policy," declared French Prime Minister Jules Ferry (1832–1893). In the face of rising tariff walls, European nations sought to establish colonies that would provide reliable markets.

However, there is considerable evidence that colonies did not represent large markets for the mother countries. In 1914, France's colonies represented only 12 percent of its foreign trade. Great Britain's trade with its colonies represented one-third of its foreign trade, but most of that was with the settlement colonies and not those acquired through direct conquest. As for Germany, colonial trade represented less than 1 percent of its exports. Even when protective tariffs were imposed in colonies, monopoly of trade was by no means secured. Despite tariffs in Indochina, French exports represented only 40 percent of goods entering the Asian colony in 1914. And despite rising tariffs, France, Germany, and Great Britain continued as one another's main customers, rather than rely on their colonies.

Although export to the colonies proved to be economically unprofitable, many people agreed with those who contended that the colonies would turn out to be profitable in the long run. Though the colonies were not necessary to the capitalist system—as Marxist critics argued—the belief in colonial profitability was certainly present.

Some proponents of empire, known as social imperialists, argued that possession of an empire could resolve social as well as economic issues. It would give employment to the working classes and thus keep them satisfied with their lot. Joseph Chamberlain (1836–1914), a former mayor of Birmingham and British colonial secretary between 1895 and 1903, was a vigorous proponent of empire, asserting that its loss meant "half at least of our population would be starved." His fellow imperialist Cecil Rhodes (1853–1902) claimed that Britain's empire was saving the country "from a murderous civil war." In Belgium King Leopold II (r. 1865–1909) believed that the political strife between Catholics and liberals in his state could be overcome by territorial aquisition overseas.

An empire could be an outlet for a variety of domestic frustrations, especially for those nations concerned about overpopulation. German and Italian imperialists often argued that their nations needed colonies to settle their multiplying poor. Once the overseas territories were acquired, however, few found them attractive for settlement.

Nationalistic Motives

To a large extent, empire building was triggered by the desire to assert national power. At the end of the nineteenth century, two major powers emerged, Russia and the United States. Compared to them, western European nations seemed small and insignificant, and many of their leaders believed that to compete effectively on the world stage they needed to become large territorial entities. Empires would enable them to achieve that goal.

The British Empire, with India as its crown jewel, constituted the largest, most powerful, and apparently wealthiest of all the European domains. It was the envy of Europe. Although the real source of Britain's wealth and power was the country's industrial economy, many people believed possession of a vast empire explained Britain's success. And so the British example stimulated other nations to carve out empires.

Once the European states entered the fray, they excited mutual suspicion and fear. When the French appeared to be expanding in West Africa in the 1890s, the British, afraid they would be cut off from the trade of the Niger Valley, aggressively conquered huge tracts of land that previously had been ignored. And the French had begun their conquests believing that they needed to reach the Niger before the British did (see Map 24.1). Thus the scramble for Africa was triggered by European rivalries, by fear of missing an opportunity that would never return. Similarly in Asia, Britain annexed Burma in 1885 under the impression that France was about to annex it. And France expanded in Indochina in the 1880s and 1890s for fear the British would beat them to the punch (see Map 24.2).

France, defeated by Prussia in 1870, found in its colonies proof that it was still a Great Power. Germany and Italy, which formed their national identities relatively late, cast a jealous eye on the British and French empires and decided that if they were to be counted as Great Powers, they too

Queen Victoria Proclaimed Empress of India In 1877 British officials in the Indian capital, Delhi, conducted a *Durbar*, a large public festival, at which Victoria was declared empress of India. The new title was intended to impress Indians and the rest of the world with Britain's resolve to hold on to India permanently. *(The Illustrated London News Picture Library)*

would need overseas colonies. King Leopold II of Belgium spun out various plans to acquire colonies to compensate for his nation's small size. And Britain, anxious at the emergence of rival economic and political powers in the late nineteenth century, found in its colonies a guarantee for the future. Even colonies with no current value might come to possess some in the future; a British prime minister in the 1890s declared colonial acquisition important "in order to peg out claims for posterity."

In the race for colonies, worldwide strategic concerns stimulated expansion. Because the Suez Canal ensured the route to India, the British established a protectorate over Egypt in 1882. And then, in 1900, fearing that a rival power might threaten their position by encroaching on the Nile, they established control over the Nile Valley all the way south to Uganda. Russian expansion southward into central Asia toward Afghanistan was intended to avert a British takeover of this area, while the British movement northwestward to Afghanistan had the opposite intention—to prevent Russia from encroaching on India. The "great game" played by Russia and Britain in central Asia lasted the entire nineteenth century, ending only in 1907.

The strategic imperative also applied to areas contiguous to an acquired territory, which were viewed as vital for the protection of the original colony. European statesmen decided that these adjoining regions must not fall to rival powers or become staging areas for attacks by the local peoples on the colonial power. Such concerns help explain why France, after conquering Algeria in 1830, turned on Tunisia in 1881 and Morocco in 1911, and why Britain, wanting to safeguard its position in India, forcibly annexed Burma in 1885. In the second half of the nineteenth century, Russia steadily pushed southward and eastward, annexing much of central Asia and portions of China, creating a vast contiguous territory reaching to the Pacific (see Map 24.2).

Much of this expansion was due to the desire to control the often turbulent frontiers of newly acquired areas. Once these frontiers had been brought under control, there were, of course, again new frontiers that had to be subdued. As the Russian foreign minister said of such an incentive for expansion, "The chief difficulty is to know where to stop." The imperial powers rarely did.

The bitter rivalry among the Great Powers helps explain the division of the globe, but it also protected some regions from falling under European domination. In an effort to contain their rivalry in southeast Asia, Britain and France established Siam (Thailand) as a buffer state. China's sovereignty was seriously violated when Russia took large chunks of territory as it moved southward and eastward, and the Western powers seized "treaty ports" and insisted on the right of their merchants and missionaries to move freely. Yet most of China survived because the European powers held one another's ambitions in check. No state alone could conquer all of China; none would allow another to do so either.

Given all the arguments Europeans marshalled in favor of imperialism, one might assume that far-flung lands were acquired as a result of a policy determination in the capitals of Europe. However, that was not always the case. The local situation and "the man on the spot," the European official dispatched overseas, often determined the pace and direction of empire building. In 1883 British Prime Minister Gladstone sent General Charles Gordon (1833–1885) to the Sudan to supervise the withdrawal of British troops who had only temporarily entered the country. Gordon disregarded orders and tried to overthrow the local political and religious leader, the Mahdi, who counterattacked, laid siege to Khartoum, entered the city, and killed Gordon. In the face of public outrage over the killing, the British annexed the Sudan.

A parallel incident in Indochina also highlighted how disobedient officials, hungry for action, created unexpected opportunities for colonial annexation. In 1883 France dispatched Commander Henri Rivière (1827–1883) to the southern part of Vietnam, already under French authority. Exceeding his orders, Rivière marched northward and he and his troops were massacred. When news reached Paris, the National Assembly unanimously voted an expedition of 20,000 men, who more than avenged the hapless commander. They brought northern Vietnam under French control.

Other Ideological Motives

In addition to the search for profit and nationalistic pride, a strong sense of mission was used to rationalize imperialism. Because Europeans were endowed with technological and scientific know-how, many imperialists believed it was Europe's duty to develop Africa and Asia for the benefit of colonizer and colonized. Railroads, telegraphs, hospitals, and schools would transform colonial peoples by opening them to what were seen as the beneficent influences of Europe. If necessary, these changes would be realized by force.

Influenced by Darwin and his theory of the struggle for survival, many argued that just as competition among species existed in nature, so did groups of humans struggle for survival. Dubbed "Social Darwinists," these thinkers envisioned a world of fierce competition. They believed that the most serious struggle was among the races; and in this struggle the white race was destined to succeed, the nonwhites to succumb.

At the same time that Europeans were making substantial material progress as a result of industrialization, their wide-scale expansion overseas brought them into contact with Africans and Asians who had not created an industrial economy. They assumed that the dramatic disparity between their own material culture and that of colonial peoples was proof of their own innate superiority. Africans and Asians were seen as primitive, inferior peoples, still in their evolutionary "infancy." (See the feature, "Weighing the Evidence: The Layout of the British Museum," on pages 914–915.)

Social Darwinists claimed that the law of nature dictated the eclipse of weaker races and the victory of the stronger and presumably better race. Lord Salisbury (1830–1903), the British prime minister, declared that the nations of the world could be divided between "the living and the dying," the former replacing the latter. Others believed that the white man had an obligation to dominate and lead the "lesser breeds" to a "higher stage." The British bard of imperialism, Rudyard Kipling (1865–1936), celebrated this view in his poem "White Man's Burden" (1899):

Take up the White Man's burden—
Send forth the best ye breed—
Go bind your sons to exile
To serve your captives' need. . . .

Each nation was certain that providence had chosen it for a colonial mission. Cecil Rhodes declared that he thought God wanted him to "paint as much of the map of Africa British as possible." His superior, Secretary of Colonies Chamberlain,

exulted that "the British race is the greatest governing race the world has ever seen." France, its leaders announced, had a civilizing mission to fulfill in the world; Ferry, its prime minister, declared it the duty of his country "to civilize the inferior races." Although European states were colonial rivals, they also believed they were engaged in a joint mission overseas. Empire building underscored the belief in a common European destiny, as opposed to the ascribed savagery and backwardness of non-Europeans.

Pointing to historic antecedents, imperialists colored their activities with a hue of heroism. Many Europeans took satisfaction in the idea that their country performed feats akin to those of ancient Rome or the Crusaders, spreading "civilization" to far-flung empires. Colonial literature celebrated white men of action who, by their heroism, conquered and administered what had been large kingdoms or empires in Africa and Asia. Novelists like Kipling emphasized the superiority and heroism of white men over perfidious, cowardly "natives."

Missionary groups also were motivated by strong ideals favoring expansion. David Livingstone (1813–1873), a missionary doctor who had explored central and East Africa in the 1850s, had come across slave caravans and other practices that he found shocking. If the area were opened to commerce, he proclaimed, then Christianity and civilization would follow. His *Travels* and posthumous *Last Journals* were widely read by the British public, and they seemed to suggest that Africa would be vastly improved if it were "opened" to European contact. Missionaries were gripped by the notion of millions of "heathens" in Africa and Asia, and they welcomed European expansion to ensure the spread of Christianity.

Missionaries also unwittingly created conditions that invited European intervention. Often they went to lands that were inhospitable and even hostile. In societies where the indigenous religion sanctioned existing social and political structures, local leaders perceived European missionaries who preached a different religion as a threat. The execution of French missionaries in Vietnam in 1851 and 1852 led to reprisals by the French navy; Emperor Napoleon III saw this action as a convenient way to win support from Catholics at home. The killing of missionaries in China also brought intervention by Europe. In addition to demanding in 1860 the right of missionaries to travel freely in China, the European powers also demanded the right of traders to move about freely and forced the Chinese government to cede to them treaty ports. In 1886 the murder of British missionaries in the kingdom of Buganda, in East Africa, fixed British interest on the area and eventually led to its conquest. In Madagascar, competition between British Protestant and French Catholic missionaries for influence over the Malagasy queen precipitated French military intervention and conquest in 1896.

Colonial acquisitions triggered public support for further expansion of the empire—support that was expressed by the founding of various colonial societies. Britain's Primrose League, which supported empire as well as other patriotic goals, had one million members. In Germany, the German Colonial Society, founded in 1888, had 43,000 members by 1914. The French and Italian groups were limited in size but had influential contacts with policymakers. Colonial societies generally drew their membership from the professional middle classes, who were quite open to nationalist arguments—civil servants, professors, and journalists. These societies produced a steady stream of propaganda favoring empire building.

Much of the literature celebrating empire building described it in manly terms. European men were seen as proving their virility by going overseas, conquering, and running empires. Women were to stay home; if later they came overseas, it was as helpmates to male colonial officials. A few women heroically explored distant lands; Englishwoman Mary Kingsley (1862–1900) went on two exploration trips into Africa. (See the box, "Mary Kingsley on Africans and British Imperialism.") Her books were popular and focused British interest on overseas territories, but they in no way shook the established view that empire was a manly enterprise.

Conquest, Administration, and Westernization

Industrialization gave Europeans the means to conquer overseas territories. They manufactured rapid-fire weapons and had steam-driven gunboats and ocean-going vessels, effectively projecting power overseas. Telegraphic communications tied the whole world into a single network, allowing Europeans to gather information and coordinate military and political decision making. Such advantages made Europeans virtually invincible in a colonial conflict. One remarkable exception was the defeat of the Italians in Adowa in 1896, when the Italians faced an Ethiopian force that was not only superior in numbers but better armed.

Conquest was often brutal. In September 1898, British-led forces at the Battle of Omdurman slaughtered 20,000 Sudanese. From 1904 to 1908, an uprising in southwest Africa against German rule led to the killing of an estimated 60,000 of the Herero people; the German general, who had expressly given an order to exterminate the whole population, was awarded a medal by William II.

In many colonies resistance continued long after conquest had officially been declared. Continuous skirmishes, in some cases full-scale wars, were fought. Britain annexed Burma in 1886, but it then faced popular rebellion for five years. In Indochina, the French were confronted with the "Scholars' Revolt," led by mandarins who refused the protectorate; it took twenty years to defeat the uprising. In West Africa, France declared the Ivory Coast to be a French possession in the 1890s; it was 1916 before the whole territory was "pacified" (Map 24.1).

Colonial governments could be brutally insensitive to the needs of the indigenous peoples. (See the box, "Encounters with the West: Chief Montshiwa Petitions Queen Victoria.") To save money, France in the 1890s put large tracts of land in the French Congo under the administration of private rubber companies, which systematically and brutally coerced the local people to collect rubber. When the scandal broke in Paris, the concessionary companies were abolished and the French state re-established its control.

The most notorious example of exploitation, terror, and mass killings was connected with the Belgian Congo. Leopold II of Belgium had acquired it as a personal empire and mercilessly exploited it and its people. An international chorus of condemnation finally forced the king to surrender his empire and put it under the administration of the Belgian government, which abolished some of the worst features of Leopold's rule.

Brutal and exploitive, imperialism spread Western technologies, institutions, and values. By 1914 Great Britain had built 40,000 miles of rail in India—nearly twice as much as in Britain. In India

Mary Kingsley on Africans and British Imperialism

Mary Kingsley belonged to a small but hardy group of women who, despite the Victorian ideal of the woman as homebody, went exploring overseas. In two separate expeditions she visited the western part of Africa. Her observations of Africans represent a mixture of views: If she believes that Africans are different from Europeans, and even inferior in some aspects, she also sees them as excelling in other fields. Kingsley bases her views on differences of culture, rather than of biology. She suggests that because Africans are less developed than Europeans, Britain has a special duty and obligation to them.

I openly and honestly own I sincerely detest touching on this race question. For one thing, Science has not finished with it; for another, it belongs to a group of enormous magnitude, upon which I have no opinion, but merely feelings, and those of a nature which I am informed by superior people would barely be a credit to a cave man of the paleolithic period. . . . I am often cornered for the detail view, whether I can reconcile my admiration for Africans with my statement that they are a different kind of human being to white men. Naturally I can, to my own satisfaction, just as I can admire an oak tree or a palm; but it is an uncommonly difficult thing to explain. All that I can say is, that when I come back from a spell in Africa, the thing that makes me proud of being one of the English is not the manners of customs up here, certainly not the houses or the climate; but it is the thing embodied in a great railway engine. I once came home on a ship with an Englishman who had been in South West Africa, for seven unbroken years; he was sane and in his right mind. But no sooner did we get ashore at Liverpool, than he rushed at and threw his arms round a postman, to that official's embarrassment and surprise. Well, that is how I feel about the first magnifi-

cent bit of machinery I come across: it is the manifestation of the superiority of my race.

In philosophic moments I call superiority difference, from a feeling that it is not mine to judge the grade in these things. Careful scientific study has enforced on me, as it has on other students, the recognition that the African mind naturally approaches all things from a spiritual point of view. . . . [H]is mind works along the line that things happen because of the action of spirit upon spirit. . . . We think along the line that things happen from action of matter upon matter. . . . This steady sticking to the material side of things, I think, has given our race its dominion over matter; the want of it has caused the African to be notably behind us in this. . . .

This seems to me simply to lay upon us English for the sake of our honour that we keep clean hands and a cool head, and be careful of Justice; to do this we must know what there is we wish to wipe out of the African, and what there is we wish to put in, and so we must not content ourselves by relying materially on our superior wealth and power, and morally on catch phrases. All we need to look to is justice.

Source: Mary H. Kingsley, *West African Studies* (London: Macmillan, 1899), pp. 329–331.

and Egypt, the British erected hydraulic systems that irrigated previously arid lands. Colonials built cities often modeled on the European grid system. In some cases they were graced with large, tree-lined avenues, and some neighborhoods were equipped with running water and modern sanita-

tion. Schools, patterned after those in Europe, taught the imperial language and spread Western

Map 24.1 Africa in 1914 European powers in the late nineteenth century conquered most of Africa. Only Liberia and Ethiopia were left unoccupied by 1914.

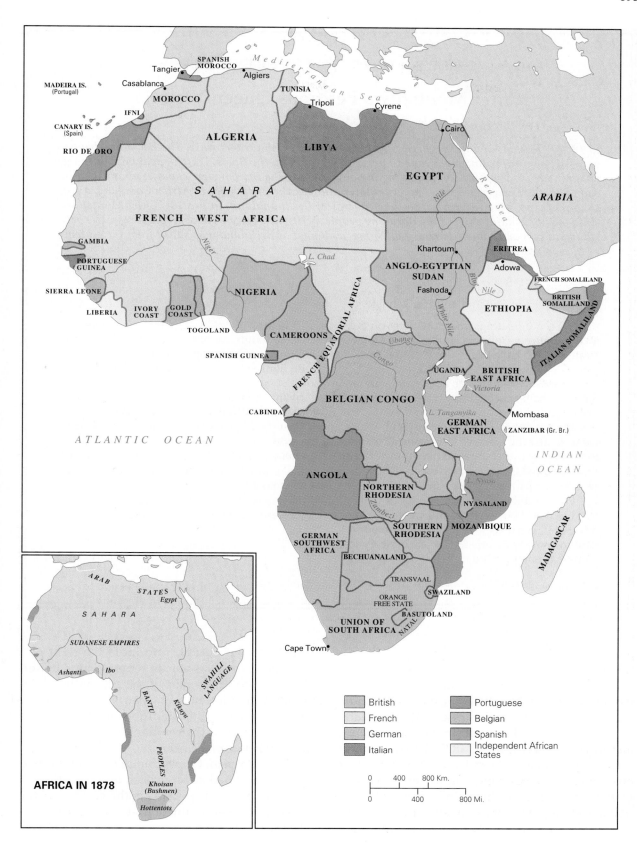

Tangier
SPANISH MOROCCO
Algiers
Mediterranean Sea
MADEIRA IS.
(Portugal)
Casablanca
TUNISIA
MOROCCO
Tripoli
Cyrene
IFNI
Cairo
CANARY IS.
(Spain)
ALGERIA
LIBYA
RIO DE ORO
EGYPT
SAHARA
Nile
Red Sea
ARABIA
FRENCH WEST AFRICA
GAMBIA
Niger
L. Chad
Khartoum
ERITREA
PORTUGUESE
GUINEA
ANGLO-EGYPTIAN
SUDAN
Adowa
FRENCH SOMALILAND
SIERRA LEONE
NIGERIA
Fashoda
Blue Nile
BRITISH
SOMALILAND
IVORY
COAST
GOLD
COAST
ETHIOPIA
LIBERIA
White Nile
TOGOLAND
Ubangi
ITALIAN SOMALILAND
CAMEROONS
FRENCH EQUATORIAL AFRICA
SPANISH GUINEA
Congo
UGANDA
BRITISH
EAST AFRICA
CABINDA
BELGIAN CONGO
L. Victoria
ATLANTIC OCEAN
L. Tanganyika
Mombasa
GERMAN
EAST AFRICA
ZANZIBAR (Gr. Br.)
INDIAN
OCEAN
ANGOLA
NORTHERN
RHODESIA
Nyasa
NYASALAND
Zambezi
MADAGASCAR
SOUTHERN
RHODESIA
MOZAMBIQUE
GERMAN
SOUTHWEST
AFRICA
BECHUANALAND
TRANSVAAL
SWAZILAND
ORANGE
FREE STATE
BASUTOLAND
UNION OF
SOUTH AFRICA
NATAL
Cape Town

AFRICA IN 1878

ARAB
STATES
Egypt
SAHARA
SUDANESE EMPIRES
SWAHILI
LANGUAGE
Ashanti
Ibo
BANTU
Kikoyu
PEOPLES
Khoisan
(Bushmen)
Hottentots

British	Portuguese
French	Belgian
German	Spanish
Italian	Independent African States

0   400   800 Km.

0   400   800 Mi.

~ **ENCOUNTERS WITH THE WEST** ~

Chief Montshiwa Petitions Queen Victoria

In 1885 Bechuanaland in southern Africa became a British protectorate. The Bechuana leaders saw British protection as a means to prevent takeover by the Boers, Dutch-speaking white settlers who were aggressively expanding in South Africa. The British were cavalier about their responsibilities, however, and a few years later allowed the British South Africa Company, a particularly exploitive enterprise, to take control of Bechuanaland. In protest, Chief Montshiwa (1815–1896), a major chief of the Baralong people, petitioned Queen Victoria for redress. His petition was supported by missionary lobbying, and most of Bechuana was saved from the clutches of the company.

Mafeking, 16 August, 1895

To the Queen of England and Her Ministers:

We send greetings and pray that you are all living nicely. You will know us; we are not strangers. We have been your children since 1885.

Your Government has been good, and under it we have received much blessing, prosperity, and peace. . . .

We Baralong are very astonished because we hear that the Queen's Government wants to give away our country in the Protectorate to the Chartered Company; we mean the B[ritish] S[outh] A[frica] Company.

Our land there is a good land, our fathers lived in it and buried in it, and we keep all our cattle in it. What will we do if you give our land away? My people are increasing very fast and are filling the land.

We keep all the laws of the great Queen; we have fought for her; we have always been the friends of her people; we are not idle; we build houses; we plough many gardens; we sow. . . .

Why are you tired of ruling us? Why do you want to throw us away? We do not fight against your laws. We keep them and are living nicely.

Our words are No: No. The Queen's Government must not give my people's land in the Protectorate to the Chartered Company. . . .

Peace to you all, we greet you;
Please send a good word back.

I am etc,

Montshiwa

Source: S. M. Molema, *Montshiwa, 1815–1896* (Cape Town: G. Struik, 1966), pp. 181–182.

ideas and scientific knowledge—though only to a small percentage of the local population.

Colonial rulers imposed laws and practices modeled after those of the home country. In India the colonial administration prided itself on safeguarding the condition of Indian women by, for instance, abolishing in 1829 the tradition of "suttee" whereby widows were burned on their husband's pyre. At times, however, European models reduced the rights of indigenous women. In Hindu law a wife could leave her husband, but

British law introduced into India the right of a husband to force his wife to return to him. In Kerala, in the southern part of the subcontinent, inheritance and descent were matrilineal; the British tried to legislate this tradition out of existence since it disturbed their notion of the proper relationship between the sexes.

The European empire builders created political units that had never existed before. Although there had been many efforts in the past to join the whole Indian subcontinent under a single author-

Victoria Terminus, Bombay Europeans' tendency to transfer values and institutions to their colonies included the export of architectural style. Various traditional European architectural styles, mainly the neo-Gothic that was so popular in nineteenth-century England, shaped this edifice, completed in 1888. *(The British Library, Oriental and India Office Collections)*

ity, the British were the first to accomplish this feat (Map 24.2). Through a common administration, rail network, and trade, Britain gave Indians the sense of a common condition, leading in 1885 to the founding of the India Congress party. Initially this party demanded reforms within the British colonial system; eventually it became the major nationalist group. The Congress party platform included the demand for constitutional government, representative assemblies, and the rule of law—concepts all based on Western theory and practice.

The transformations that Europeans wrought confirmed their sense of themselves as agents of progress, building a new and better world. Europeans arrogantly believed they knew what was best for other people; and they accepted force as a means of dealing with others. Such attitudes may have colored the increasingly caustic relations between European states.

The ties of empire affected metropolitan cultures. The Hindi word for bandit became the Eng-

lish word *thug;* the Hindi number five, denoting the five ingredients necessary for a particular drink, became *punch.* Scenes from the colonial world often were the themes of European art, such as Paul Gauguin's paintings of Tahiti and advertising posters for products as different as soap and whiskey. After the turn of the century Pablo Picasso's cubism reflected his growing familiarity with African art. In running the largest empire in the world, the British emphasized the need to develop masculine virtues; they cultivated competitive sports and stern schooling, which, they believed, would develop "character" and leadership. To administer their overseas colonies, Europeans developed sophisticated means of gathering and managing information that benefited metropolitan societies. A growing number of people from the colonies also came to live in European cities. By 1900 some former colonists, despite various forms of discrimination, had become full participants in the life of their host country; two East Indians won election to the British Parliament in the 1890s.

RUSSIAN EMPIRE

SIBERIA

Sea of Okhotsk

Sakhalin

KARAFUTO
(Jap. 1905)

JAPANESE EMPIRE

PACIFIC

OCEAN

AMUR DISTRICT
(1858)

Khabarovsk
(1858)

Vladivostok
(1860)

Sea of Japan

Tokyo

Harbin

MANCHURIA

Mukden

KOREA
(1905, 1910)
(1905) Jap. 1905)

New Guinea

(Port. 1859)
Timor
(Neth.)

INNER
MONGOLIA

Peking
Tientsin

Kiaochow
(Ger. 1898)

Port Arthur
(Rus. 1898; Jap. 1905)

Weihaiwei
(Gr. Br. 1898)

*East
China
Sea*

Pescadores
(Jap. 1895)

Formosa
(Jap. 1895)

PHILIPPINE IS.
(U.S. from Spain 1898)

Manila

L. Baikal

Chita

Irkutsk

OUTER MONGOLIA
(Autonomous, Russian sphere 1912)

Nanking

Shanghai
(Gr. Br. 1842)

Hankow

Foochow
Amoy
(Gr. Br. 1842)
Canton

Hong Kong
(Gr. Br. 1842)

Kwangshowan
(Fr. 1898)

*South
China
Sea*

BRITISH
NORTH BORNEO
(1888)

SARAWAK
(1888)

Borneo

Celebes

Omsk

Irtysh

CHINA

Chungking

Huang Ho

Yangtze

Macao
(Port. 1557)

FRENCH
INDOCHINA
(1859, 1907)

Saigon

MALAY STATES
(1874, 1909)

Singapore
(Gr. Br. 1819)

Java
(1619)

Sumatra

Tobolsk

L. Balkhash
(1854)

Tashkent
(1864)

SINKIANG

TIBET

Lhasa

HIMALAYAS

BHUTAN

NEPAL

BURMA
(1852, 1885)

Hanoi

SIAM

Bangkok

Rangoon

Andaman Is.
(Gr. Br.)

*Bay
of
Bengal*

Merv
(1884)

*Aral
Sea*
(1873)

AFGHANISTAN

KASHMIR
(1846)

PUNJAB

Delhi

BALUCHISTAN
(1883)

Indus

Karachi

BRITISH
SPHERE
(1907)

RUSSIAN SPHERE
(1907)

PERSIA

Teheran

Caspian Sea

BRITISH INDIA

INDIA

Bombay

Diu
(Port.)

Goa
(Port.)

Madras

Karikal
(Fr.)

Yanaon
(Fr.)

Pondichéry
(Fr.)

Calcutta

Ganges

Ceylon

*Arabian
Sea*

INDIAN   OCEAN

Territories held by:

Great Britain
Netherlands
France
United States
Russia
Japan
Railroads

1000 Mi.

1000 Km.

500

500

0

0

Overseas Migrations and the Spread of European Values

The nineteenth century saw a phenomenal expansion in European overseas migrations, adding to Europe's impact on other societies (Map 24.3). Europeans had always migrated. They left villages for towns, or in the case of migrant farm laborers, traveled from village to village as the seasons changed and different crops needed to be harvested. With the expansion of European power abroad beginning in the sixteenth century, Europeans migrated overseas; between the sixteenth and eighteenth centuries around six million people left Europe. These numbers pale in significance, however, in the nineteenth century. Between 1870 and 1914, 55 million Europeans left the Continent for the New World, Australia, and New Zealand.

As with the new imperialism migration was male dominated. As many as three-quarters of all immigrants to the United States were young males, and even though Brazil recruited whole families, the majority of immigrants were also male. There were, however, some notable exceptions to these rules; during some decades women dominated Irish immigration to the United States, arriving as domestics.

Changing social and technological forces account for migrations. Economic crises and over-population in rural Europe (see page 857) led many men and women to look overseas for new opportunities; they either settled there or labored as migrant workers to save money, which when brought home could pay the mortgage or buy more land for a family whose holdings were too small to sustain it. Advances in technology such as the steamship introduced cheap and rapid communications with other continents. A trans-Atlantic ticket did not cost much, and in many cases employers in the Americas advanced the price of a ticket in efforts to recruit labor. The trip was relatively short—a crossing from Liverpool to New York took no more than two weeks. If in the past people had trekked for weeks

Map 24.2 Asia in 1914 China, Siam (Thailand), and a portion of Persia were the only parts of Asia still independent after the great powers, including the United States and Japan, subjugated the Continent to alien rule.

from their village to the city in search of work, they could now in the same amount of time reach New York or Buenos Aires. And unlike overseas migrants of the seventeenth and eighteenth centuries, those of the nineteenth century could envision the move as temporary. In fact, of the 34 million migrants to the Americas, about a third returned to Europe. Many were truly seasonal workers, known as swallows in Italy, who every year went back and forth between Europe and the Americas.

Increased literacy, inexpensive printing, and the ease of correspondence with the outside world spread what was called "America fever." Many immigrants wrote back to their native villages; between 1900 and 1906 three million letters were sent to eastern Europe from the United States. Correspondence to relatives and friends boasted of the material advantages of life in the New World. A Swede who had settled in the United States wrote home, "And I can tell you that here we do not live frugally but here one has egg pancake and canned fish and fresh fish and fruits of all kinds, so it is different from you who have to sit and hold herring bones." Such letters, often reprinted in local newspapers or gathered in pamphlets, unleashed mass waves of migration.

Certain European groups migrated to specific areas. Scandinavians settled in the upper Midwest of the United States, Italians in Argentina, Germans in Paraguay, Britons in South Africa, Portuguese in Brazil, each group leaving its imprint on its adopted land. The upper Midwest was known as "the great desert," but Scandinavians used farm techniques from their homelands to cultivate these dry lands. German Mennonites settled in Kansas and brought with them a strain of wheat that became the basis of the state's prosperity. Immigrants also put their imprint on urban sites. Durban in South Africa looks like an English city, and some towns in Paraguay resemble Alpine villages of southern Germany. The Germans who came to Milwaukee, Wisconsin, made it a city of beer and strong socialist convictions.

Emigration scattered peoples and extended cultures overseas. By 1914 nearly half of all the Irish and the Portuguese lived outside Europe. The settlers consumed many European goods and in turn produced for the European market, increasing the centrality of Europe in the world market. The migrations across the globe were an added force to that of imperial conquest, further

Map 24.3 European Migrations, 1820–1910 Throughout the nineteenth century, millions of Europeans left home for overseas; most headed for the United States. *(Source:* Reproduced from *The Times Atlas of World History,* 3d ed., by kind permission of Times Books. Some data from Eric Hobsbawm, *The Age of Empire, 1875–1914* [New York: Pantheon, 1987].)

putting Europe's imprint on peoples and societies abroad.

THE DEMOCRATIC POWERS

By the end of the nineteenth century, most of Europe's political systems floundered in crisis. The major powers with democratic institutions—Great Britain, France, and Italy—confronted volatile public opinion and had difficulty winning broad consensus for their policies. They struggled with new challenges emerging from an expanded electorate that was at times frustrated by the failure of the system to resolve its demands. Turning away from the democratic precept to resolve differences through the ballot and legislation, many people—both in government and out—were willing to resort to extraparliamentary means, including violence, to see their interests prevail.

Petersen: Emigrants Preparing to Depart Edward Petersen's 1890 painting depicts Danish emigrants readying to leave their homeland. Between 1860 and 1914, 300,000 people emigrated from the small country of Denmark, most of them to the United States. (*Courtesy of the Aarhus Kunstmuseum. Reproduced with permission of Thomas, Poul, and Ole Hein Pedersen, Aarhus.*)

Great Britain

In Great Britain the Reform Bill of 1884 transformed the political landscape by doubling suffrage to five million—giving the vote to two of every three adult males. The appeal of this enlarged electorate tempted politicians to make demagogic promises, which were often broken later to the frustration of their constituents. It was also more difficult to establish compromise in a Parliament that no longer consisted of a fairly limited class of people with common interests and values. The British political system was faced with issues it was unable to resolve peacefully, and it was obliged—uncharacteristically—to resort to force or the threat of force.

As in earlier periods, Ireland proved to be a persistent problem. The political consciousness of the Irish had risen considerably, and they seethed

under alien rule. In an attempt to quell Irish opposition in 1886, Prime Minister Gladstone proposed autonomy, or "home rule," for Ireland. There were many objections to such a plan, the most serious being that if Ireland, a predominately Catholic country, ruled itself, the local Protestant majority in Ulster, the northeast part of the island, would be overwhelmed and likely to fall under Catholic control. "Home rule is Rome rule," chanted the supporters of Ulster Protestantism. Among Gladstone's own Liberals, many opposed changing the existing relationship between England and its possession. They seceded from the Liberals and formed the Unionist party, which, in coalition with the Conservatives, ruled the country from 1886 to 1905. When the Liberals returned to power in 1906, they again proposed home rule. In 1911, the House of Commons passed a home-rule bill, but it was obstructed in the House of Lords and was not slated to go into effect until September 1914.

In the process of debating the Irish issue, many segments of British society showed they were willing to resort to extralegal and even violent means. Fearing Catholic domination, Protestants in northern Ireland armed themselves, determined to resist home rule. In the rest of Ireland, Catholic groups armed, too, insisting on the unity of the island; they were ready to fight for home rule for the whole of Ireland. The Conservative party in Britain, which opposed home rule, called on Ulster to revolt. British officers threatened to resign their commissions, rather than fight Ulster. The behavior of the Conservatives and the army indicated a breakdown of order and authority, a disregard for tradition by two of its bulwarks. Only the outbreak of world war in 1914 delayed a showdown over Ireland, and then for only a few years.

Once back in power in 1906, the Liberals committed themselves to a vast array of social reforms but were frustrated by the difficulty of getting their program through the House of Lords. The feisty Liberal chancellor of the Exchequer, David Lloyd George (1863–1945), expressed his outrage that the will of the people was being thwarted by a handful of magnates in the House of Lords, sitting there not by election but by hereditary right.

The Liberals' social reform program included old-age pensions. To finance them, Lloyd George proposed raising income taxes and death duties and levying a tax on landed wealth. A bill with these measures easily passed the House of Commons in 1909 but was stymied in the upper chamber, where many members were prominent landowners. The House of Lords technically had the power to amend or reject a bill passed by Commons, but for nearly 250 years it had been understood that it did not have the right to reject a money bill. Nonetheless, motivated by economic self-interest and personal spite against the Liberals, a majority in the House of Lords disregarded convention and voted against the bill. This decision created a major constitutional crisis.

The Liberal government wanted not only to pass its bill but to reduce the power of the House of Lords. In 1911 it sponsored a bill, quickly passed by the House of Commons, to limit the House of Lords to a suspensive veto. This would mean that a bill defeated in the House of Lords could be prevented from going into effect for only a predetermined period—in this case, two years. The House of Lords refused at first to pass such a law. But at the request of the government, the king threatened to appoint four hundred new lords. Reluctantly, the House of Lords passed the bill.

During the debate over the bill, Conservatives—the representatives of British traditionalism and the upholders of decorum—resorted to brawling and refused to let the prime minister speak. It was the first time in British parliamentary history that such an act of defiance had occurred. The British Parliament, considered the model for supporters of free institutions, had shown itself unable to resolve issues in a reasoned manner.

Violence also appeared in another unlikely place: the women's suffrage movement. Most liberal males, when speaking of the need to extend human liberty, had excluded the female gender. Toward the end of the nineteenth century, that, too, was challenged. Women began to organize into groups devoted to winning the vote but had little initial success. In 1903 Emmeline Pankhurst (1858–1928) and her two daughters founded the Women's Social and Political Union, whose goal was immediate suffrage.

Angered and frustrated by their lack of progress, the suffragists (often referred to by contemporaries as "suffragettes"), led by the Pankhursts, began in 1906 a more militant program of protest—disturbing proceedings in Parliament, breaking windows at the prime minister's residence, slashing canvases at the National Gallery, burning down empty houses, dropping acid into mailboxes, and throwing bombs. There were even threats on the lives of the prime minister and the king. Suffragists who were arrested often engaged in hunger strikes. Fearing they would die, the authorities force-fed the women. Female protesters were also physically attacked by male thugs. (See the box, "Pankhurst on Women's Rights.") That women would resort to violence, and that men in and outside of the government would resort to force against them, seemed to show how widespread the cult of force had become.

France

The Third Republic, founded in 1870 after France's humiliating military defeat at the hands

A Suffragist Attempts to Chain Herself to the Gates of Buckingham Palace, 1914 In their effort to win the vote, women resorted to public protests and the police often violently intervened. *(Popperfoto/Archive Photos)*

of the Prussians, also continued to face an ongoing series of crises. Challenged by enemies on the political left and right who continually called for the abolition of democracy, the regime found itself buffeted from all sides.

The French government itself contributed to an unstable political situation by its lack of strong leadership. The need to build coalitions among the several parties in the parliament rewarded those politicians who had moderate programs and were flexible. Thus there was little premium on firm ideas and commitments, and the prime minister was often more a conciliator than a leader. Further, lackluster leadership appealed to republicans, who continued to fear that a popular leader might—as Louis Napoleon had in 1851—exploit his support to make himself dictator.

The regime seemed to lurch from scandal to scandal. The most notorious was the Dreyfus affair. In October 1894, Captain Alfred Dreyfus (1859–1935) of the French army was arrested and charged with passing military secrets to the German embassy. Dreyfus seems to have attracted suspicion because he was the only Jewish officer on the general staff. The evidence was flimsy—a letter written in a handwriting that some thought resembled that of Dreyfus, although other experts testified it was not that of the young officer.

This letter, and materials that later turned out to be forged, led the French army to court-martial Dreyfus and sentence him to life imprisonment on Devil's Island off the coast of South America. By March 1896, the general staff had evidence that it was another officer, Major Esterhazy, who was actually the spy. But to reopen the case would be to admit the army had made an error, and the general staff refused to do so.

By late 1897, when the apparent miscarriage of justice became widely known, French society split over "the affair." The political left, including many intellectuals, argued for reopening the case. For them it was crucial that justice be carried out.

Pankhurst on Women's Rights

In 1908 the suffragists, led by Emmeline Pankhurst, issued a handbill calling on the people of London to "rush" Parliament and win the vote for women. The legal authorities interpreted their action as a violation of the peace, and several suffragists, including Pankhurst, were put on trial. They put up a spirited defense, in which Pankhurst movingly explained her motives for leading the suffragist cause.

I want you to realise how we women feel; because we are women, because we are not men, we need some legitimate influence to bear upon our law-makers.

Now, we have tried every way. We have presented larger petitions than were ever presented for any other reform, we have succeeded in holding greater public meetings than men have ever had for any reform, in spite of the difficulty which women have in throwing off their natural diffidence, that desire to escape publicity which we have inherited from generations of our foremothers; we have broken through that. We have faced hostile mobs at street corners, because we were told that we could not have that representation for our taxes which men have won unless we converted the whole of the country to our side. Because we have done this, we have been misrepresented, we have been ridiculed, we have had contempt poured upon us. The ignorant mob at the street corner has been incited to offer us violence, which we have faced unarmed and unprotected by the safeguards which Cabinet Ministers have. We know that we need the protection of the vote even more than men have needed it. . . .

We believe that if we get the vote it will mean better conditions for our unfortunate sisters. We know what the condition of the woman worker is . . . and we have been driven to the conclusion that only through legislation can any improvement be effected, and that that legislation can never be effected until we have the same power as men have to bring pressure to bear upon our representatives and upon Governments to give us the necessary legislation. . . .

I should never be here if I had the same kind of power that the very meanest and commonest of men have—the same power that the wife-beater has, the same power that the drunkard has. I should never be here if I had that power, and I speak for all the women who have come before you and other magistrates. . . .

If you had power to send us to prison, not for six months, but for six years, for sixteen years, or for the whole of our lives, the Government must not think that they can stop this agitation. It will go on. . . .

We are here not because we are lawbreakers; we are here in our efforts to become lawmakers.

Source: F. W. Pethick Lawrence, ed. *The Trial of the Suffragette Leaders* (London: The Women's Press, 1909), pp. 21–24.

The army and its supporters, right-wing politicians, royalists, and Catholics, argued that the decision should not be changed. As the bulwark against internal and foreign threats, the army should be above challenge, and the fate of a single man—guilty or innocent—was immaterial.

The affair unleashed a swirl of controversy and rioting, which led the government to order a retrial in 1899. But the court again found Dreyfus guilty—this time with "extenuating circumstances" and the recommendation that he be pardoned. Finally, in 1906, Dreyfus was fully exonerated. He ended his days as a general in the army that had subjected him to so much suffering.

The strong encouragement Catholics gave to those who supported the original verdict confirmed the republicans' belief that the church was a menace to the regime. The Radical party, the staunchest backers of Dreyfus, won the elections in 1898. Despite its title, the Radical party favored moderate social reforms. It was uncompromising, however, in its anticlericalism, determined to wreak vengeance on Catholics and end the influence of the church once and for all. In 1905 the parliament passed a law separating church and state, thus ending the privileged position the Catholic church had enjoyed. Violent language and physical confrontations on both sides accompanied this separation. Catholics trying to prevent state officials from entering churches to take required inventories sometimes resorted to force, using weapons or, in one case, a bear chained to the church. Armed soldiers broke down church doors and dragged monks away.

Labor problems also triggered repeated confrontations with the government. Increased labor militancy produced long, drawn-out strikes, which in 1904 alone led to the loss of four million workdays. There was agitation in the countryside, too, particularly in 1907 in the Midi, the south of France. This region suffered from a crisis in the wine industry caused by disease, competition from cheap foreign wines, and fraud. More important, the region witnessed increased rural proletarianization as population grew and larger landholdings were concentrated under smaller numbers of owners. Rural militancy led to revolt in 1907. Troops were sent in, killing dozens and winning for the Radical government the title "government of assassins."

Italy

The third major power in Europe to adopt parliamentary government also had grave problems. Although unification took place in 1860, Italy found genuine unity elusive; the country was plagued by regionalism, social strife, and an unrepresentative political system. As in the past, the south especially challenged the central government. Assertive regionalism, brigandage, and poverty made the areas resistant to most government programs.

The parliamentary system established in 1860 was far from democratic. Property qualifications limited suffrage to less than 3 percent of the population. And as a result of the persistence of trasformismo—the practice by which government corrupted and co-opted the opposition—electoral choice was short-circuited.

Between 1870 and 1890 the Italian government introduced some important reforms, but it was difficult to improve the general standard of living for a people undergoing rapid population growth. In the fifty years after unification, population increased from 25 to 35 million, and the country had limited resources to deal with such growth. In the south, a few wealthy landowners held large latifundia, or private estates, while the majority of the peasants were landless and forced to work the land for minimum wages. In the north, industrialization had started, but the region was not rich in coal or iron. To be competitive, industry paid very low wages, and the workers lived in abject misery.

Conditions on the land and in the factory led to widespread protests, followed by stern government repression. In 1893 a Sicilian labor movement won the adherence of 300,000 members, who seized land and attacked government offices. The government responded with massive force and declared martial law. In 1896, with unrest spreading throughout the peninsula, the government placed half of the provinces under military rule. A cycle of violence and counterviolence gripped the nation. In May 1898 labor protests against government repression in the northern industrial city of Milan led to brutal retaliation. In this general atmosphere of violence, an anarchist killed King Umberto I on July 29, 1900.

After the turn of the century, a new prime minister, Giovanni Giolitti (1842–1928), tried to bring an end to the upheaval. He used government force more sparingly and showed a spirit of cooperation toward the workers. Seeking to broaden his popularity by an appeal to nationalist fervor, Giolitti launched an attack on Libya in 1911, wresting it from the ailing Ottoman Empire. The territory was arid and bereft of economic promise, but its conquest was championed as a test of national virility and the foundation of national greatness. The imperialists proudly proclaimed force the arbiter of the nation's future.

Domestically, the nation also returned to force. A wave of workers' discontent seized the nation again, and in June 1914 a national strike led to rioting and seizure of power in many municipalities, including Bologna. In the Romagna, an

William II The German emperor liked to be viewed in a heroic and military posture. His crippled left hand is turned away from the viewer. *(Landesbildstelle, Berlin)*

independent workers' republic was proclaimed. It took 100,000 government troops ten days to restore order. The workers' restlessness and the apparent difficulty of keeping them under control led some nationalist right-wing extremists to form "volunteers for the defense of order," anticipating the vigilante thugs who were to make up the early bands of Italian fascism.

THE AUTOCRACIES

Four major autocracies dominated central and eastern Europe: Germany, Austria-Hungary, the Ottoman Empire, and Russia. If the democracies were faced with difficulties in these years, the autocracies faced even more severe challenges. Although many groups in the parliamentary regimes grew impatient at the slowness of change, theoretically at least they could believe that someday their goals would be realized. Not so in the autocracies. The severity of autocratic rule varied

from state to state, ranging from the absolutism of the Ottoman Empire to the semiparliamentary regime of Germany, but the ruler had the final political say in all of them. Resistance to the autocracies included broad popular challenges to the German imperial system, the reduction of Austria-Hungary into a nearly ungovernable empire, and revolution in the Russian and Ottoman Empires.

Germany

Although Germany had a parliament, the government was answerable to the kaiser, not the people's electoral representatives. And in the late nineteenth century, Prussia, the most reactionary part of the country, continued to dominate.

To rule effectively, Chancellor Otto von Bismarck maneuvered and intrigued to quell opposition. In the face of socialist growth, he used an attempt to assassinate the emperor as the excuse to ban the Socialist party in 1879. He succeeded in simultaneously winning over conservative agrarian and liberal industrial interests by supporting tariffs on both imported foodstuffs and industrial goods. He also turned against the Catholics, who were lukewarm toward Protestant Prussia, persecuting them and their institutions. These measures, however, did not prevent the growth of the Socialist and Catholic Center parties.

Unfortunately for Bismarck, whose tenure in office depended on the goodwill of the emperor, William I died in 1888, to be succeeded first by his son Frederick, who ruled only a few months, and then by his grandson, William II (r. 1888–1918). The young Kaiser William intended to rule as well as reign, but he was ill fit to govern. Convinced of his own infallibility, he bothered to learn very little. Born with a crippled hand, William seemed to want to compensate for this infirmity by appearing forceful, even brutal. He hated any hints of limitation to his powers, announcing, "There is only one ruler in the Reich and I am he. I tolerate no other." A restless individual, William changed uniforms eight times daily and traveled ceaselessly among his seventy-five castles and palaces. Dismayed by Bismarck's proposals of reprisals against the Socialists and the chancellor's unwillingness to take on a clearly pro-Austrian and anti-Russian foreign policy, the kaiser dismissed him. But he also did so to rid himself of a formidable, intimidating individual.

The emperor was determined to make Germany a world power whose foreign policy would have a global impact. He wanted Germany to have colonies, a navy, and major influence among the Great Powers. This policy, *Weltpolitik,* or "world politics," greatly troubled Germany's neighbors, partly because they were already worried by a new, assertive power in central Europe and partly because German moves were accompanied by the kaiser's bombastic threats. Within Germany, however, *Weltpolitik* won support. Steel manufacturers and shipbuilders received lucrative contracts; workers seemed assured of employment.

Although the nationalist appeals impressed many Germans, the nation could not be easily managed. The emperor's autocratic style was challenged, and his behavior was increasingly viewed as irresponsible. In the elections of 1912, one-third of all Germans voted for the Socialist party. Thus the largest single party in the Reichstag was at least rhetorically committed to the downfall of the capitalist system and autocracy. Labor militancy also reached new heights. In 1912, one million workers—a record number—went on strike. More and more Germans pressed for a parliamentary system with a government accountable to the people's elected representatives.

The emperor could not tolerate criticism of his behavior. He had come to Bismarck's conclusions and frequently talked about using the military to crush socialists and the parliament. These thoughts were echoed in the officer corps and in government circles. To some observers it seemed likely that the days of German autocracy were numbered—or that there would be a violent confrontation between the army and the people.

Austria-Hungary

The neighboring Austro-Hungarian Empire also continued to face a series of crises. In an age of intense nationalism, a multinational empire was an anomaly, as the Emperor Francis Joseph (r. 1848–1916) himself acknowledged. Although the relationship between the two parts of the empire was regulated by the agreement of 1867 (see page 825), the agreement did not prevent conflict between Austria and Hungary, particularly over control of their joint army. The insistence on separate Hungarian interests had developed to such a degree that, had it not been for the outbreak of the world war, Hungary probably would have broken loose from the dual monarchy.

In the Hungarian half of the empire, the Magyars found it increasingly difficult to maintain control. Other nationalities opposed Magyarization—the imposition of the Magyar language and institutions—and insisted on the right to use their own languages in the schools and administration. The Hungarian government resorted to censorship and jailings to silence nationalist leaders. In the Austrian half of the empire, the treatment of nationalities was less harsh, but the government was equally strife-ridden.

There were no easy solutions to the many conflicts that the empire faced. Since much of the national agitation was led by middle-class intellectuals, the Habsburg government introduced universal male suffrage in 1907 in an effort to undercut their influence. However, the result was an empire even more difficult to govern. It became nearly impossible to find a workable majority within a parliament that included thirty ethnically based political parties.

The virulence of debate based on nationality and class divisions grew to unprecedented extremes. Within the parliament, deputies threw inkwells at each other, rang sleigh bells, and sounded bugles. Parliament ceased to be relevant. By 1914 it had been dissolved and so had several regional assemblies. Austria was being ruled by decree. Emperor Francis Joseph feared the empire would not survive him.

The Ottoman Empire

In the generation before 1914, no political system in Europe suffered from so advanced a case of dissolution as the Ottoman Empire, undermined by both secessionist movements within its own borders and aggression from other European powers. Sultan Abdul Hamid II (r. 1876–1909) ruled the country as a despot and authorized mass carnage against those who contested his rule, earning him the title of the "Great Assassin."

Young, Western-educated Turks—the "Young Turks"—dismayed at one-man rule and the continuing loss of territory and influence, overthrew Abdul Hamid in a coup in July 1908. They set up a government responsible to an elected parliament. The Young Turks hoped to stem the loss of territory by establishing firmer central control, but their efforts had the opposite effect. The various nationalities of the empire resented the attempts at "Turkification," the imposition of Turkish education and administration. Renewed agitation broke out in Macedonia, Albania, and among the Armenians. The government carried out severely repressive measures to end the unrest, killing thousands of Armenians.

For foreign powers, the moment seemed propitious to plunder the weakened empire. In 1911 Italy occupied Libya, an Ottoman province. Greece, Bulgaria, and Serbia—impatient to enlarge their territory—formed an alliance, the Balkan League, which in 1912 prosecuted a successful war against the empire. Albania became independent, and Macedonia was partitioned among members of the league. Thus the empire lost most of its European possessions, except for the capital, Constantinople, and a narrow strip of surrounding land.

Russia

Through the Great Reforms of the 1860s, the Russian autocracy had attempted to resolve many of the problems facing its empire and people. But the reforms and the major social changes of the period unleashed new forces, making it even more difficult for the tsars to rule.

The needs of a modernizing country led to an increase in the number of universities and students. However, the newly educated Russian youths began almost instantly an ardent, sustained critique of autocracy. In the absence of a large group upholding liberal, advanced ideas, university students and graduates, who came to be known as the intelligentsia, saw it as their mission to transform Russia. In the 1870s, university youths by the thousands organized a populist movement, hoping to bring change to the countryside.

These youthful idealists intended to educate the peasants and make them more politically aware. But they met with suspicion from the peasantry and repression by the government. Large numbers of populists were arrested and put on trial. Frustrated at the difficulty of bringing about change from below by transforming the people, disaffected young radicals formed the People's Will, which turned to murdering public officials to hasten the day of revolution.

Although the regime intensified repression, it also sought to broaden its public support. In 1881 Tsar Alexander II decided to create an advisory committee that some thought would eventually lead to a parliamentary form of government. In March 1881, as he was about to sign the decree establishing this committee, the tsar was assassinated by members of the People's Will.

The new ruler, Tsar Alexander III (r. 1881–1894), who had witnessed the assassination, blamed his father's leniency for his death. By contrast, he was determined to uphold autocracy firmly. He sought to weaken his father's reforms, reducing local self-rule in the process.

When Alexander's son, Nicholas II (r. 1894–1917), succeeded his father on the throne in 1894, he declared he would be as autocratic as his father. However, he lacked the methodical, consistent temperament such a pledge required. A pleasant man, he wanted to be liked, and he lacked the forcefulness to establish a coherent policy for his troubled country.

Since the Great Reforms, serious problems had accumulated that threatened the stability of the regime. In the countryside the situation worsened steadily as the population exploded and pressure on the land increased. The provisions that had accompanied the freeing of the serfs left considerable discontent. The peasants were not free to come and go as they pleased; they had to have the permission of the village council. Agriculture remained inefficient, far inferior to that of western Europe; hence the allotted land was insufficient to feed the peasants, creating a constant demand for more land.

The attempted modernization of Russia had changed it more dramatically and rapidly than any other central or eastern European state. In the 1890s the minister of finance, Sergei Witte (1849–1915), launched an ambitious railroad-expansion program, which triggered a broader program of industrial development. Although Russia remained largely agrarian, pockets of industrial growth were created. Some factories and mining concerns were unusually large, with as many as six thousand employees. When workers grew incensed at their condition and insistent on winning the same rights and protection that existed in western Europe, they engaged in massive strikes that crippled industry.

A Conspiratorial Revolutionary Party

The Russian Socialist party was racked by internal debates over the direction and means by which a socialist revolution could be created. The majority favored a broad-based Socialist party, but in his 1902 essay, "What Is to Be Done?" Lenin explained why revolution in Russia could succeed only if it were led by a cadre of professional revolutionaries, organized into a tightly knit conspiratorial group.

We must have a committee of professional *revolutionaries* . . . irrespective of whether they are students or working men. I assert: 1) That no movement can be durable without a stable organization of leaders to maintain continuity; 2) that the more widely the masses are drawn into the struggle and form the basis of the movement, the more necessary it is to have such an organization and the more stable it must be— otherwise it is much easier for demagogues to sidetrack the more backward sections of the masses; 3) that the organization must consist chiefly of persons engaged in revolution as a profession; 4) that in a country with a despotic government, the more we *restrict* the membership of this organization to persons who are engaged in revolution as a profession and who have been professionally trained in the art of combating the political police, the more difficult will it be to catch the organization; and

5) the *wider* will be the circle of men and women of the working class or of other classes of society able to join the movement and perform active work in it. . . .

It is . . . argued against us that the views on organization here expounded contradict the "principles of democracy."

Ponder a little over the real meaning of the high-sounding phrase . . . and you will realize that "broad democracy" in party organization, amidst the gloom of autocracy and the domination of the gendarmes, is nothing more than a *useless and harmful toy.* It is a useless toy, because as a matter of fact, no revolutionary organization has ever practiced *broad* democracy, nor could it, however much it desired to do so.

The only serious organizational principle the active workers of our movement can accept is: Strict secrecy, strict selection of members and the training of professional revolutionists.

Source: Lenin, "What Is to Be Done?" *Collected Works,* vol. 4 (New York: International Publishers, 1929), pp. 198–199, 210–213.

Political dissatisfaction with the autocracy grew. Members of the expanding middle classes began to clamor that, like their contemporaries in western Europe, they should be given the opportunity to participate in governance. Increasingly, aristocrats also demanded a right to political participation.

Various revolutionary groups committed to socialism continued to flourish. The heirs to the populists were the Social Revolutionaries, who emerged as a political force in the 1890s. They believed that the peasants would bring socialism to Russia. In 1898 the Russian Social Democratic

party was founded; a Marxist party, it promoted the industrial working class as the harbinger of socialism. In 1903 that party split between the Mensheviks and the Bolsheviks. The Mensheviks insisted that Russia had to go through the stages of history Marx had predicted—to witness the full development of capitalism and its subsequent collapse before socialism could come to power. The Bolsheviks, a minority group, were led by Vladimir Lenin (1870–1924), a zealous revolutionary and Marxist. Rather than wait for historic forces to undermine capitalism, he insisted that a revolutionary cadre could seize power on behalf

Workers' Demonstration in Moscow, 1905 In 1905 workers as well as peasants protested against the Russian autocracy. To bring the revolution under control, Nicholas II was obliged to grant several concessions. *(Novosti)*

of the working class. Lenin favored a small, disciplined, conspiratorial party, like the People's Will, while the Mensheviks favored a more open, democratic party. (See the box, "A Conspiratorial Revolutionary Party," on page 907.)

At the turn of the century these groups were still quite small and played a limited role in the mounting opposition to tsarism. But popular opposition soon grew in the face of Russian military ineptness in the war against Japan, which had broken out in February 1904 in a dispute over control of northern Korea. Antagonism to the tsarist regime escalated as a result of social tensions, heightened by an economic slowdown.

Beginning in January 1905, a series of demonstrations, strikes, and other acts of collective violence began. Together, they were dubbed "the revolution of 1905." One Sunday in January 1905, 400,000 workers seeking redress of their griev-

ances gathered in front of the tsar's palace. Rather than hear their protests, officials ordered soldiers to fire on them, resulting in 150 deaths and hundreds more wounded. "Bloody Sunday" angered the populace. The tsar, instead of being viewed as an understanding, paternal authority, had become the murderer of his people. Unrest spread to most of the country. As reports reached Russia of more defeats in the war with Japan, the regime's prestige was further undermined. By September 1905, Russia had to sue for peace and admit defeat. Challenged in the capital, where independent workers' councils called soviets had sprung up, the government also lost control over the countryside, the site of widespread peasant uprisings.

Fearing for his regime, Nicholas hoped to split the forces challenging tsarism by meeting the demands for parliamentary government and granting major constitutional and civil liberties, including freedom of religion, speech, assembly, and association. At the end of October, the tsar established an elective assembly, the Duma, with restricted male suffrage and limited political power. It was far from the Western-style parliament that Russian liberals had desired, but it quickly became the arena for criticism of autocracy. Anxious to create a more pliant instrument, the tsar suspended the assembly, changing its electoral base and its rules of operations. Even many conservatives were disillusioned with the tsar's backtracking and his breach of the promise he had made in 1905 to establish constitutionalism and parliamentarism.

A new prime minister, Peter Stolypin (1862–1911), tried to win support for the regime by a series of reforms, including improvement in the lot of the peasantry: The government reduced the peasants' financial obligations; the power of the commune was weakened; and local self-rule was extended to the peasants. But these changes did little to alleviate a worsening relationship between population and land. Between emancipation and 1914 the peasant population grew by 50 percent, but it acquired only ten percent more land. Rural poverty was widespread; in 1891 famine broke out in 20 provinces, killing a quarter of a million people. Rural discontent was widespread.

Labor unrest also mounted among industrial workers. In 1912 there were 725,000 strikers, but by the first half of 1914 there were twice that number. When the French president visited St. Petersburg on the eve of the outbreak of the war, barricades were rising in the workers' neighborhoods.

THE COMING WAR

Instability and upheaval characterized international relations in the years between 1880 and 1914. But the outbreak of war was not inevitable. Good common sense dictated against it, and some intelligent people predicted that in the new modern era, war had become so destructive that it was unthinkable. Finally, no European state wanted a war, although the Great Powers carried on policies that brought them to its brink.

Power Alignments

Germany enjoyed an unchallenged position in the international order of the 1870s and 1880s.

It was united in an alliance with the two other eastern conservative states—Russia and Austria-Hungary—in the Three Emperors' League, formed in 1873 and renewed by treaty in 1884. And it was part of the Triple Alliance with Austria and Italy. France was isolated, without allies. Britain, with little interest in continental affairs, appeared to be enjoying a "splendid isolation."

However, Germany's alliance system was not free from problems. Two of its allies, Austria-Hungary and Russia, were at loggerheads over control of the Balkans. How could Germany be the friend of both? To reassure the Russian government, wary of apparent German preference for Austria, Bismarck signed the Reinsurance Treaty in 1887, assuring Russia that Germany would not honor its alliance with Austria if the latter attacked Russia. After Bismarck's resignation in 1890, Emperor William allowed the Reinsurance Treaty to lapse. Alarmed, the Russians turned to France and, in January 1894, signed the Franco-Russian Alliance, by which each side pledged to help the other in case either was attacked by Germany.

The Great Powers on the Continent were now divided into two alliances, the Triple Alliance and the Franco-Russian Alliance. Britain formally belonged to neither. But if it favored any side, it would be the German-led alliance. Britain's strongest competitors in the 1880s and 1890s were France and Russia. Both rivaled Britain for influence in Asia, while France challenged Britain for control of Africa.

However, distrust of Germany, increasingly seen as a dangerous neighbor, led Britain and France to resolve their difficulties overseas. In 1904 Britain and France signed an understanding, or entente, resolving their rivalries in Egypt; and in 1907, Great Britain and Russia regulated their competition for influence in Persia (present-day Iran) with the Anglo-Russian Entente. Now Europe was loosely divided into two groups: the Triple Alliance of Germany, Austria-Hungary, and Italy, and the Triple Entente of Great Britain, France, and Russia.

The Momentum for War

Only through a series of crises did these alignments solidify to the point where their members were willing to go to war to save them. France's attempts to take over Morocco twice led to conflict with

MAJOR DIPLOMATIC ALLIANCES AND AGREEMENTS

1873	Three Emperors' League (Germany, Austria-Hungary, and Russia)
1879	Alliance between Germany and Austria
1882	Triple Alliance (Germany, Austria, and Italy)
1884	Renewal of Three Emperors' League
1887	Reinsurance Treaty (Germany and Russia)
1894	Franco-Russian Alliance
1904	Anglo-French Entente
1907	Anglo-Russian Entente

Germany. In 1905 Germany insisted that an international conference discuss the issue and deny France this kingdom adjacent to its colony of Algeria. In 1911, when France grabbed Morocco anyway, Germany accepted the situation only after extorting compensation from the French, who deeply resented what they viewed as German bullying.

Britain also began to view Germany as a serious international menace. Over the years, Britain had developed a navy equal to none. An island nation, dependent on international trade for its economic survival, Britain saw its navy as a necessity. Wishing to challenge Britain's supremacy on the seas, however, Germany began building its own navy in the 1890s.

The heightened international rivalry forced the European states to increase their arms expenditures, which added in turn to their sense of insecurity. The British had felt safe with a huge navy that none could equal. In 1906 they introduced a new class of ships with the launching of the *Dreadnought*. Powered by steam turbines, it was faster than any other ship; heavily armored, it could not be sunk easily; and its ten 12-inch guns made it a menace on the seas. The British thought Germany could not build equivalent ships, but it did, wiping out British supremacy—older British ships could easily be sunk by German dreadnoughts. No longer able to depend on its past supremacy, Britain was feeling less secure than at any time

since the Napoleonic Wars, and it continued an expensive and feverish naval race with Germany.

In Germany the changing military capacity of Russia created great anxieties. When Japan defeated the tsarist empire in 1905, the Russian military was revealed to be inferior and was thought of as a lumbering giant, slow to mobilize in case of war. As a result Germany was not particularly afraid of its eastern neighbor. But stung by its humiliation in 1905, Russia quickly rebuilt its army and planned to establish an extensive rail network in the west. Russia thus had a greater military capacity than ever. To many in Germany, their country appeared encircled by a hostile Russia in the east and an equally unfriendly France in the west. Germany became genuinely worried, and beginning in 1912 many in the military and within the government started thinking about a preventive war. If war was inevitable, it should, many Germans argued, occur before Russia became even stronger. Fear of the future military balance made some of the highest policymakers see the crisis that broke out in the summer of 1914 as an opportunity to go to war and throttle Russia.

Many political leaders viewed the escalating arms race as a form of madness. Between 1904 and 1913 French and Russian arms expenditures increased by 80 percent; that of Germany by 120 percent; Austria-Hungary by 50 percent; and Italy by 100 percent. British Foreign Secretary Sir Edward Grey (1862–1933) warned that if the arms race continued, "it will submerge civilization." But no way was found to stop it.

On the whole warfare was not feared. Except for short victorious colonial wars, the Western powers had not experienced a major conflict since the Crimean War. Russia had successfully warred against the Ottoman Empire in 1876. Its war against Japan in 1905 had been a calamity, but it could imagine that this was a nonreplicable disaster. Most policymakers believed that the next war would be short. The wars that had so dramatically changed the borders of European states in the second half of the nineteenth century, notably the Austro-Prussian War of 1866 and the Franco-Prussian War of 1870, had been decided within a few short weeks. Few imagined that the war, if it came, would be so brutal and lengthy. And therefore many of Europe's leaders did not dread war enough to make a major effort to prevent or avoid it.

It was the territorial rivalry between Austria and Russia that triggered international disaster. For decades there had been growing enmity between the two empires for control over the Balkans (Map 24.4). In 1903, following a bloody military coup that killed the king and queen of Serbia, a pro-Russian party took control of the Serbian government. It spread anti-Austrian propaganda and sought to unify under its banner the Slavs living in the Balkans, including those under Austrian rule. As a result, many Austrian officials were convinced that the survival of the Austro-Hungarian Empire required that Serbia be destroyed. Talk of an attack on Serbia filled the Austrian court in 1914.

On June 28, 1914, the heir to the Habsburg throne, Archduke Francis Ferdinand, visited Sarajevo in Austrian-ruled Bosnia. A young Bosnian-Serb nationalist, hostile to Austrian rule, who had been trained and armed by a Serb terrorist group called the Black Hand, assassinated the archduke and his wife.

The assassination of the heir to the throne provided Austria with an ideal pretext for military action. The German kaiser, fearing that failure to support Vienna would lead to Austrian collapse and a Germany bereft of any allies, urged Austria to attack Serbia. On July 23, Austria issued an ultimatum to Serbia, deliberately worded in such a way as to be unacceptable. When Serbia refused the ultimatum, Austria declared war on July 28.

Perceived self-interest motivated each state's behavior in the ensuing crisis. Although in the past Russia had failed to protect Serbia, now it was determined to help. Russia's status as a great power demanded that it not allow its client state to be humiliated, much less obliterated. In the past the French government had acted as a brake on Russian ambitions in the Balkans. On the very eve of the war in 1914 France counseled restraint, but it did not withhold its aid; increasingly after 1911, France feared isolation in the face of what it perceived as growing German aggressiveness. Its only ally on the continent was Russia. To remain a great power, France needed to preserve its friendship with Russia and help it maintain its own great power status.

Germany could not allow Austria, its only ally, to be destroyed. Its leaders may also have seen the crisis as a propitious moment to begin a war that was going to occur sooner or later any-

Map 24.4 The Balkans in 1914 By 1914 the Ottoman Empire was much diminished, containing virtually none of Europe. Political boundaries did not follow nationality lines. Serbia was committed to unite all Serbs at the expense of the Austro-Hungarian Empire.

way. Before the entente powers, especially Russia, became stronger, it appeared to be a good moment to strike. As the German prime minister put it, his country was about to take "a leap in the dark," and he declared war on Russia. Assuming that France would come to the aid of Russia, Germany invaded France through Belgium. The British, concerned by the threat to their ally France, and outraged by the violation of Belgian neutrality to which all the great powers had been signatories since 1839, declared war on Germany. Events had hurtled forward between the Austrian declaration of war on Serbia on July 28 and the British decision on August 4. Europe was at war. Eventually so would be much of the world.

SUMMARY

On the surface, the years from 1880 to 1914 seemed comfortable. More people than ever before enjoyed material advantages and an improved standard of living. Literacy spread. Death rates went down; life expectancy rose. But a revolution of rising expectations had been created, and people grew more demanding, insisting in sometimes violent ways on their political and economic rights. Although mass movements such as socialism and the women's suffragist movement generally made use of peaceful means in their campaigns to change society, some of their members advocated and employed force. Anarchism appeared to stalk Europe. And in turn, states did not hesitate to use force in efforts to quell various protest movements, even resorting to martial law.

Reflecting these trends, intellectuals like Freud and Bergson and artists like Munch and Moreau suggested that there was a hidden, irrational dimension of life beneath surface appearances. Behind the façade of security and conformity lay many disturbing impulses such as racism, anti-Semitism, and the desire to suppress the emerging democracies by violent means and replace them with dictatorships.

In their relations with Africa and Asia, Europeans to an unprecedented degree resorted to force, conquering most of the African and much of the Asian continents. The new empires were intended to benefit Europe by providing it with new sources of wealth, trade, and the trappings of power. Increasingly, Europeans found it natural to regard themselves as belonging to a master race, destined to dominate the world.

Although most Europeans were confident and optimistic about their future, such self-assuredness was not universally shared. Intellectuals spoke of decadence and decline. Statesmen, worried about the future of their countries and anxious to avoid the threat of decline, resorted to extreme measures such as empire building overseas and armed competition in Europe. Among European thinkers and statesmen, force had become widely accepted as the means to an end, and some leaders—notably those of Austria-Hungary and Germany—favored war over negotiation in July 1914.

The major powers—except Britain, confident in its naval dominance—built up large standing armies with millions of men and much modern equipment. Europe's network of alliances led inexorably to the larger conflict. If there were some leaders who feared war, more dreaded the consequences of not fighting, believing that war would save their regimes from the internal and external challenges they faced. Few could foresee the dire consequences of such a choice.

NOTES

1. Charles Seymour, ed. *The Intimate Papers of Colonel House,* vol. 1 (Boston: Houghton Mifflin, 1926), p. 249.

SUGGESTED READING

General Surveys

Gilbert, Felix. *The End of the European Era, 1890 to the Present.* 1979. Sees the years from 1890 to 1914 as helping to shape the rest of the twentieth century.

Hobsbawm, Eric. *The Age of Empire, 1875–1914.* 1987. A fine survey, emphasizing social change, by a leading British historian.

Romein, Jan. *The Watershed of Two Eras—Europe in 1900.* 1978. A long and at times challenging study of the generation straddling the turn of the century.

Politics and Culture

Gay, Peter. *Freud—A Life for Our Time.* 1988. An admiring study by a prominent historian and trained psychoanalyst.

Geary, Dick. *European Labor Protest, 1848–1939.* 1981. A brief, clearly written work that emphasizes the deradicalization of labor.

Hughes, H. Stuart. *Consciousness and Society: The Reorientation of European Social Thought, 1890–1930.* 1979. A classic on changes in European social thought.

Joll, James. *The Second International, 1889–1914.* 1955. A brief, well-written history of the successes and failures of the international socialist organization.

Katz, Jacob. *From Prejudice to Destruction, 1700–1933.* 1980. A survey of two centuries of European anti-Semitism.

Schorske, Carl E. *Fin de Siècle Vienna—Politics and Culture.* 1980. A critically acclaimed work on the arts and social and political thought in the Habsburg capital at the turn of the century.

Teich, Mikulas, and Roy Porter, eds. *Fin de Siècle and Its Legacy.* 1990. A collection of critical essays summarizing the cultural trends at the end of the century.

European Migration and Imperialism

Baumgart, Winfried. *Imperialism—The Idea and Reality of British and French Colonial Expansion, 1880–1914.* 1989.

A comparative study, emphasizing the political aspects of imperialism.

Betts, Raymond F. *The False Dawn—European Imperialism in the Nineteenth Century*. 1975. An elegantly written survey by one of the most authoritative historians of the subject.

Davis, Lance E., and Huttenback, Robert A. *Mammon and the Pursuit of Empire*. 1988. A careful statistical study that shows British imperialism overall not to have been a profitable venture.

Headrick, Daniel R. *The Tentacles of Progress—Technology Transfer in the Age of Imperialism, 1850–1940*. 1988. Considers the extent and limits of technology transfer from the West to its empire.

Hoerder, Dirk, and Leslie Page Moch, eds. *European Migrants—Global and Local Perspectives*. 1996. A collection of up-to-date articles on migrations of Europeans within their continent and overseas.

Pakenham, Thomas. *The Scramble for Africa*. 1991. A long but colorful narrative of the European conquest of Africa, emphasizing personalities.

Strobel, Margaret. *European Women and the Second British Empire*. 1991. Considers the role of women in the formation of the British Empire.

The Democratic Powers

Brédin, Jean-Denis. *The Affair: The Case of Alfred Dreyfus*. 1986. The most authoritative account, written by a prominent French lawyer, covers both the details of the affair and its context.

Clark, Martin. *Modern Italy, 1872–1982*. 1984. Contains some fine chapters on the decades before the war, emphasizing the difficulties of governing a society as divided and diverse as Italy.

Feuchtwanger, E. J. *Democracy and Empire, Britain, 1865–1914*. 1985. While describing the challenges to the existing order, emphasizes the resilience of British institutions.

Harrison, J. F. C. *Late Victorian Britain, 1875–1901*. 1990. Considers how different social classes experienced the social and economic transformations of the era.

Levine, Philippa. *Victorian Feminism*. 1987. Shows that Victorian women were involved in several campaigns for their rights, including the suffragist movement.

Mayeur, Jean-Marie, and Madeleine Réberioux. *The Third Republic—From Its Origins to the Great War, 1871–*

1914. 1987. The most up-to-date survey of France in these years, emphasizing the emergence of republican government and the challenges it faced.

Thayer, John A. *Italy and the Great War, Politics and Culture, 1870–1915*. 1964. Surveys Italy's political and cultural life in these years.

Townshend, Charles. *Political Violence in Ireland*. 1983. Concentrates on violence in Ireland since 1848, stressing its social and economic origins.

The Autocracies

Bridge, F. R. *The Habsburg Monarchy among the Great Powers, 1815–1918*. 1990. Contrary to most works on the Habsburg empire, praises Austrian leaders for preserving the empire as long as they did.

Kohut, Thomas A. *Wilhelm II and the Germans—A Study in Leadership*. 1991. A psychohistorical study, analyzing the German emperor's youth and unsatisfactory relations with his parents.

Lieven, Dominic. *Russia's Rulers under the Old Regime*. 1989. Presents a study of Russia's aristocracy and its attitudes toward most public issues in the nineteenth century.

Rogger, Hans. *Russia in the Age of Modernization, 1881–1917*. 1983. Concentrates on Russian institutions in the generation prior to the revolution.

Origins of World War I

Joll, James. *The Origins of the First World War*. 1984. A clear, concise, readable history emphasizing strategic interests and nationalist passions leading to the outbreak of the war.

Kennedy, Paul. *The Rise and Fall of the Great Powers, 1500 to 2000*. 1987. Masterfully summarizes the factors that led to the shifting fates of the Great Powers.

Massie, Robert K. *Dreadnought—Britain, Germany and the Coming of the Great War*. 1991. A very long but lively discussion of Anglo-German affairs in the generation leading up to the war. The author emphasizes the leading personalities involved.

Wilson, Keith, ed. *Decisions for War, 1914*. 1995. A collection of articles, based on the most recent scholarship, highlighting the actions of the major and some minor powers in the crises of July 1914.

THE LAYOUT OF THE BRITISH MUSEUM

The British Museum was founded in the mid-eighteenth century when the government acquired some private collections. The museum increased the size of its collections, largely through donations, bringing in objects from around the world. In its early years the museum was located in a converted private mansion; then in 1847, to house its growing collection, the museum moved into a monumental building with a neoclassical façade. Until the 1830s public access was limited to the upper classes, mainly the learned. By the mid-nineteenth century, however, a million people a year were visiting the museum. Displays of materials gathered from non-European cultures drew particularly large audiences.

Consider how the exhibits reflected British imperialism. In the first half of the nineteenth century, objects from Oceania, reflecting British activities in the Pacific, were acquired. African materials became more plentiful with the British conquest of much of Africa after the 1880s; the British military expedition to Nigeria in 1897 led to the acquisition of the fabulous Benin bronzes.

While imperial adventures were shaping the museum collection, the museum in turn was supporting imperialism. Museum officials declared that increased knowledge about regions overseas would fuel enthusiasm for the imperial venture and make the British people better fit to rule their new subjects.

The manner in which the British Museum displayed some of its possessions reflected the intellectual currents of the times. In the late eighteenth and early nineteenth centuries the museum grouped its non-European objects with "natural history"; non-Europeans were associated with nature, with the beasts of the earth. Running out of space, the museum moved the natural history collection to a separate Natural Museum in South Kensington, and in the 1880s ethnography, the branch of anthropology devoted to human cultures, constituted a separate collection.

The late-nineteenth-century plan of the upper floor of the museum shown here reflects the racial views of imperial Britain. After climbing the stairs from the ground floor, we start at the room labeled 1, the Anglo-Saxon Room, which celebrates England's early history. Then comes the Waddesdon Bequest Room, which houses various artifacts of ancient and medieval English and European history (the room is named after the Rothschild mansion where the collection was previously housed). Next we arrive at the Medieval Room itself. Using the route most visitors would then take, we come to the Asiatic Saloon, filled with pottery, porcelain, and other works of art from Japan, China, Persia, and India.

What is the significance of this juxtaposition of rooms? The British and other Europeans had developed an ethnocentric view of the human races, believing that the white race was by far superior to all others. This belief seemed confirmed by the material accomplishments of Europeans, especially impressive in the nineteenth century. Of the non-Europeans, Asians had won the grudging respect of the British and other Europeans. China, with its thousands of years of recorded history and sophisticated government structures, was one of several Asian societies that impressed them. Because many African societies lacked a written culture and had government and religious systems dramatically different from the Europeans', the British and other Europeans often considered Africans ignorant and primitive.

Biologists, anthropologists, and others speculating about the human races offered two different explanations for racial variations. These hypotheses competed with each other for public acceptance. According to the first, biology determined the level of civilization of each people. According to the second, different peoples were at different levels of development. In this view, Europeans were most developed, Africans least; but eventually Asians and Africans would progress and reach a level akin to that of Europeans. In the meantime non-Europeans illustrated European life at earlier stages of development.

It is interesting that the Asiatic Saloon, with its swords, shields, and other elaborate Asian objects, was next to the Medieval Room. The position-

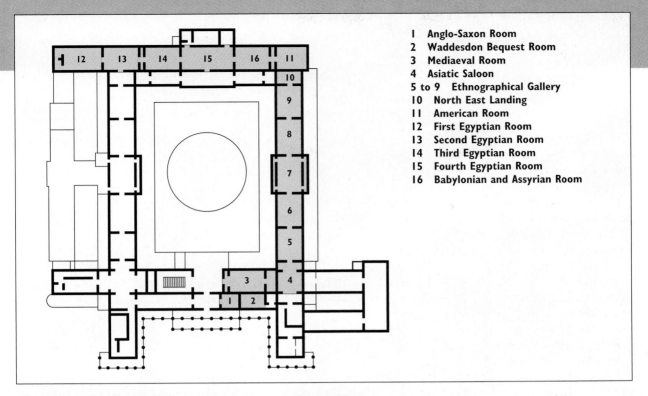

Plan of the Upper Floor of the British Museum, ca. 1880 *(Based on map in Henry C. Shelley,*
The British Museum: Its History and Treasures *[Boston: L. C. Page, 1911], pp. 274–275.)*

ing invites consideration that some nineteenth-century Asian societies were at a level of development akin to medieval England.

An empty corridor separated this part of the museum from the Ethnographic Gallery, giving visitors the sense that what they would view was separate from medieval England and selected Asian societies. The Ethnographic Gallery displayed objects from Asia, Oceania, Africa, and the Americas. They tended to be objects of daily life such as household wares, weapons, and clothing. The stress was on their simplicity and primitiveness—presumably reflections of the primitive culture of their makers. The objects were not differentiated chronologically; pre-Columbian artifacts from the Americas were displayed beside modern African crafts. Ethnographic items were seldom dated, implying that the peoples who created them did not develop and had no history. The museum guidebook invited nineteenth-century viewers to consider how close the development of these peoples was to that of the earliest Europeans.

After passing through the Ethnographic Gallery, a visitor would arrive at the North East Landing and then enter the American Room. It con-tained items from Eskimos, native Americans, and other peoples whom Victorians considered "primitives," but it also included artifacts from the Aztecs and Incas, whom the British considered to have been highly developed.

The Aztec and Inca collections abutted the room devoted to two ancient civilizations with monumental architecture, the Babylonian and Assyrian Room. Next came four Egyptian rooms. In the nineteenth century the greatness of ancient Egyptian culture was recognized. The British Museum allotted ancient Egypt ample space far removed from what were seen as the "primitive" peoples represented in the Ethnographic Gallery.

In 1972 the ethnographic collection was moved out of the British Museum and now constitutes a separate Museum of Mankind. With the loss of empire and the decline of confidence in the superiority of the white race, the old uses for the objects collected overseas had become obsolete.* ✂

*I am grateful to Thomas Prasch, Washburn University, for his help and advice and for making available to me two of his unpublished papers on this subject.

CHAPTER 25

War and Revolution, 1914–1919

As the European powers prepared for a military showdown, an Egyptian-Sudanese intellectual, Mohammed Ali Duse (1867–1944), contemplated the long-term consequences this war might have—both for the Europeans themselves and for the millions in the non-Western world caught up in the European orbit: "We can only watch and pray. Unarmed, undisciplined, disunited, we cannot strike a blow; we can only await the event. But whatever that may be, all the combatants, the conquerers and the conquered alike, will be exhausted by the struggle, and will require years for their recovery, and during that time much may be done. Watch and wait! It may be that the non-European races will profit by the European disaster. God's ways are mysterious."[1]

Duse was right. The fighting that began in August 1914 would become the first "world war"—a dramatic turning point in world history and the beginning of the end of European hegemony. The geographic reach of the war was unprecedented, especially after the intervention of the Ottoman Empire spread the war to the Middle East. But also because of the European colonial networks, the war directly involved non-Europeans, from Chinese to sub-Saharan Africans, in combat or support roles. Although the old colonialism continued into the postwar era, the war nourished the forces that would later overthrow it.

In Europe the overwhelming majority initially welcomed the war, but the eventual consequences for Europeans—from emperors to ordinary people—were often cataclysmic, most dramatically in the countries that met defeat. Long-standing empires and dynasties fell apart, so the political and territorial map had to be fundamentally redrawn after the war was over.

Paul Nash,
The Menin Road.

Coming after a century of relative peace and apparent progress, the war had an enduring impact partly because of the way it was fought, the experience it entailed; much about that experience was so new that it could scarcely have been imagined before 1914. A far wider and more destructive war would follow within a generation, but it was World War I, known to contemporaries as "the Great War," that shattered the old European order, with its comfortable assumptions of superiority, rationality, and progress. After this war, neither Westerners nor non-Westerners could still believe in the privileged place of Western civilization in quite the same way.

The war proved such a turning point because the fighting, which had been expected to produce a quick result, instead bogged down in a stalemate during the fall of 1914. By the time it finally ended, in November 1918, the war had strained the whole fabric of life, affecting everything from economic organization to literary vocabulary, from journalistic techniques to the role of women. And because of these unforeseen strains, the war ended up producing effects unrelated to its causes. Most notably, the difficulties of war led to a communist revolution in Russia that had an incalculable impact on the subsequent history of the twentieth century. So whereas the war solved some of the problems that had caused it, it introduced significant new problems and left much unresolved.

THE UNFORESEEN STALEMATE, 1914–1917

When the war began in August 1914, enthusiasm and high morale, based on expectations of quick victory, marked both sides. But fighting on the crucial western front led to a stalemate by the end of 1914, and the particularly brutal encounters of 1916 made it clear that this was not the sort of war most had expected at its start. By early 1917 the difficulties of the war experience brought to the surface underlying questions about what it was all for—and whether it was worth the price.

August 1914: The Domestic and Military Setting

Although some, like Helmuth von Moltke (1848–1916), chief of the German general staff, worried

that this would prove a long, destructive war testing the very fabric of Western civilization, the outbreak of fighting early in August produced a wave of euphoria and a remarkable degree of domestic unity. To many, war came almost as a relief; at last, the issues that had produced tension and intermittent crisis for the past decade would find a definitive solution. Especially among educated young people, this settling of accounts seemed to offer the prospect of renewal, even a kind of redemption, for themselves and their societies. The war promised an escape from the stiflingly respectable bourgeois world and, in response to the common danger, an end to the petty bickering and divisiveness of everyday politics.

An unexpected display of patriotism from the socialist left reinforced the sense of domestic unity and the high morale that went with it. Defying their long-standing rhetoric about international proletarian solidarity, members of the socialist parties of the Second International rallied to their respective national war efforts almost everywhere in Europe. To socialists and workers, national defense against a more backward aggressor seemed essential to the eventual creation of socialism. French socialists had to defend France's democratic republic against autocratic and militaristic Germany; German socialists had to defend German institutions, and the strong socialist organizations that had proven possible within them, against repressive tsarist Russia. The German Socialists' vote for war credits in the Reichstag on August 4 dramatically symbolized the failure of the Second International to prevent working-class involvement in a European war.

In France, the government had planned, as a precaution, to arrest roughly one thousand trade union and socialist leaders in the event of war, but no such arrests seemed necessary when the war began. Instead, the order of the day was "Sacred Union," which even entailed Socialist participation in the new government of national defense. Germany enjoyed a comparable "Fortress Truce," including an agreement to suspend labor conflict during the war, although here no Socialist was invited to join the war cabinet.

The high spirits of August were possible because so few Europeans could foresee what they were getting into. It would be "business as usual" as the British government put it—no shortages, no rationing, no massive government intervention.

There was little inkling of the total mobilization to come or of the eventual costs of the war.

Before the war began, the forces of the Triple Entente outnumbered those of Germany and Austria-Hungary. Russia had an army of over 1 million men, the largest in Europe, and France had 700,000. Britain, which did not introduce conscription until 1916, had about 250,000. Germany led the Central Powers with 850,000; Austria-Hungary contributed 450,000. Though outnumbered, the Central Powers had potential advantages in equipment, coordination, and speed over their more dispersed adversaries. Thus, the outcome was hardly a foregone conclusion in August 1914.

After the fighting began, a second tier of belligerents intervened one by one, expanding the war's scope and complicating the strategic alternatives. In November 1914 the Ottoman Empire, fearful of Russia, joined the Central Powers, thereby extending the war along the Russo-Turkish border and on to Mesopotamia and the approaches to the Suez Canal in the Middle East. For Arabs disaffected with Ottoman Turkish rule, the war presented an opportunity to take up arms—with the active support of Britain and France. Italy, after dickering with both sides, committed itself to join the Entente with the Treaty of London of April 1915. This secret agreement specified the territorial compensation Italy was to receive in the event of Entente victory—primarily the Italian-speaking areas still within Austria-Hungary. In September 1915 Bulgaria entered the war on the side of the Central Powers, seeking territorial advantages at the expense of Serbia, which had defeated Bulgaria in the Second Balkan War in 1913. In much the same way, Romania intervened on the side of the Entente, in August 1916, hoping to gain Transylvania, then part of Hungary.

Thus the war was fought on a variety of fronts (Map 25.1). This fact, combined with uncertainties about the role of sea power, led to ongoing debate among military decision makers about strategic priorities. Because of the antagonism that the prewar German naval buildup had caused, some expected that Britain and Germany would quickly be drawn into a decisive naval battle. Britain promptly instituted an effective naval blockade on imports to Germany, but the great showdown on the seas never materialized. Even the most significant naval encounter between them, the Battle of

No Trenches in Sight Spirits were high early in August 1914, as soldiers like these in Paris marched off to war. None foresaw what fighting this war would be like. None grasped the long-term impact the war would have. *(Archives Larousse-Giraudon)*

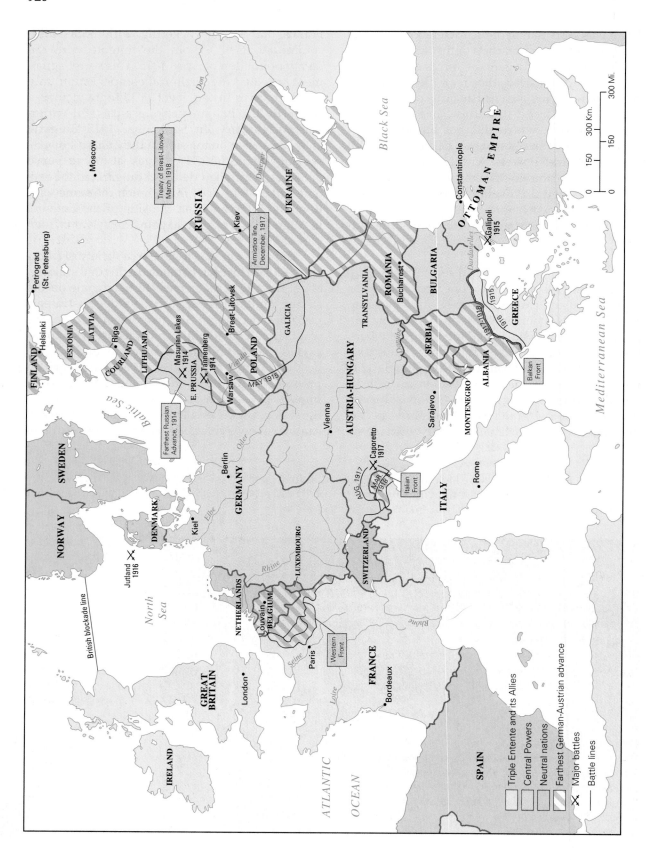

Moscow

Treaty of Brest-Litovsk, March 1918

RUSSIA

UKRAINE

Don

Dnieper

Kiev

Black Sea

OTTOMAN EMPIRE

Constantinople

Armistice line, December, 1917

Gallipoli 1915

Dardanelles

Petrograd (St. Petersburg)

ROMANIA

Bucharest

BULGARIA

1915

GREECE

Balkan Front 1917-1918

1916

FINLAND

Helsinki

ESTONIA

LATVIA

Riga

COURLAND

LITHUANIA

Vistula

Brest-Litovsk

TRANSYLVANIA

SERBIA

Farthest Russian Advance, 1914

Masurian Lakes 1914

Tannenberg 1914

E. PRUSSIA

POLAND

Warsaw

MAY 1915

GALICIA

AUSTRIA-HUNGARY

Sarajevo

MONTENEGRO

ALBANIA

Mediterranean Sea

Baltic Sea

SWEDEN

NORWAY

Vienna

Berlin

Oder

GERMANY

Caporetto 1917

AUG. 1917

MAR. 1918

Italian Front

Rome

ITALY

Jutland 1916

DENMARK

Kiel

Elbe

Rhine

LUXEMBOURG

SWITZERLAND

North Sea

British blockade line

NETHERLANDS

Louvain

BELGIUM

Western Front

Rhône

IRELAND

GREAT BRITAIN

London

Seine

Paris

FRANCE

Bordeaux

Loire

ATLANTIC OCEAN

SPAIN

300 Mi.

300 Km.

150

150

0

0

Triple Entente and its Allies

Central Powers

Neutral nations

Farthest German-Austrian advance

✕ Major battles

— Battle lines

Jutland in 1916, was indecisive. Despite the naval rivalry of the prewar years, World War I proved fundamentally a land war.

Germany faced not only the long-anticipated two-front war against Russia in the east and France and Britain in the west; it also had to look to the southeast, given the precarious situation of its ally Austria-Hungary, fighting Serbia and Russia, then also Italy and eventually Romania as well. On the eastern front, Germany managed decisive victories during 1917 and 1918, forcing first Russia, then Romania, to seek a separate peace. But it was the western front that proved decisive.

Into the Nightmare, 1914

With the lessons of the wars of German unification in mind, both sides had planned for a short war based on rapid offensives, a war of movement. According to the Schlieffen Plan, drafted in 1905, Germany would concentrate first on France, devoting but one-eighth of its forces to containing the Russians, who were bound to need longer to mobilize. After taking just six weeks to knock France out of the war, Germany would then concentrate on Russia. French strategy, crafted by General Joseph Joffre (1852–1931), similarly relied on rapid offensives. The boys would be home by Christmas—or so it was thought.

Although German troops encountered more opposition than expected from the formerly neutral Belgians, they moved rapidly through Belgium into northern France during August. By the first week of September they had reached the Marne River, threatening Paris and forcing the French government to retreat south to Bordeaux. But French and British troops under Joffre counterattacked September 6–10, forcing the Germans to fall back and begin digging in along the Aisne River. By holding off the German offensive at this first Battle of the Marne, the Entente had undercut the Schlieffen Plan—and with it, it turned out, any chance of a rapid victory by either side.

Map 25.1 Major Fronts of World War I Although World War I included engagements in East Asia and the Middle East, it was essentially a European conflict, encompassing fighting on a number of fronts. A vast territory was contested in the east, but on the western front, which proved decisive, fighting was concentrated in a relatively small area.

During the rest of the fall of 1914, each side tried—unsuccessfully—to outflank the other. When, by the end of November, active fighting ceased for the winter, a military front of about three hundred miles had been established, all the way from Switzerland to the coast of the North Sea in Belgium (Map 25.2). And this line failed to shift more than ten miles in either direction over the next three years. So the result of the first six weeks of fighting on the western front was not gallant victory by either side but a grim and unforeseen stalemate.

Virtually from the start, the war took a destructive turn that few had predicted. In northern France in September 1914, the Germans fired on the cathedral at Reims, severely damaging the roof and nave, because they believed—apparently correctly—that the French were using one of the cathedral's towers as an observation post. If this could happen, at the very outset, to one of the great Gothic monuments in Europe, who could say what else this war might bring?

The two sides were forced to settle into a war of attrition relying on an elaborate network of defensive trenches. Although separated by as much as five miles in some places, enemy trenches were sometimes within shouting distance, so there was occasionally banter back and forth, even attempts to entertain the other side. But the trenches quickly became almost unimaginably grim—filthy, ridden with rats and lice, noisy and smoky from artillery fire, and foul-smelling, partly from the odor of decaying bodies.

As defensive instruments, however, the trenches proved quite effective, especially because each side quickly learned to take advantage of barbed wire, mines, and especially machine guns to defend its positions. A mass of barbed wire, 3 to 5 feet high and 30 yards wide, guarded a typical trench. The machine gun had been developed before the war as an offensive weapon; few foresaw the decided advantage it would give the defense. But with machine guns, it proved possible to defend trenches even against massive assaults—and to impose heavy casualties on the attackers.

In 1916 the tank was introduced as an antidote to the machine gun, but, as skeptics had warned, tanks proved too ungainly and unreliable to be widely effective. Although the French used them to advantage in the decisive Allied offensive in 1918, tanks were not crucial to the outcome of the war.

Map 25.2 Stalemate and Decision on the Western Front On the western front, in northern France and Belgium, trench warfare developed and the most famous battles of the war were fought. Notable sites included Verdun, Passchendaele, and the Marne and Somme Rivers.

Though the defensive trenches had formidable advantages, neither side could give up the vision of a decisive offensive to break through on the western front. Thus the troops were periodically called on to go "over the top" and then across "no man's land" to assault the enemy trenches. Again and again, however, such offensives proved futile, producing incredibly heavy casualties: "Whole regiments gambled away eternity for ten yards of wasteland."[2]

For the soldiers on the western front the war became a nightmarish experience in a hellish landscape. Bombardment by new, heavier forms of artillery not only threatened the enemy more directly but devastated the terrain in the war zone with craters, which then became muddy, turning the landscape into a near swamp. (See the box, "Into the Trenches.") Beginning early in 1915, tear gas, chlorine gas, and finally mustard gas found use on both sides. Although the development of

gas masks significantly reduced the impact of this menacing new chemical warfare, the threat of poison gas added another nightmarish element to the experience of those who fought the war.

The notions of patriotism, comradeship, duty, and glory that had been prevalent in 1914 gradually dissolved as those in the trenches experienced the unforeseen horrors of warfare on the western front. A French soldier, questioning his own reactions after battle in 1916, responded with sarcasm and irony: "What sublime emotion inspires you at the moment of assault? I thought of nothing other than dragging my feet out of the mud encasing them. What did you feel after surviving the attack? I grumbled because I would have to remain several days more without *pinard* [wine]. Is not one's first act to kneel down and thank God? No. One relieves oneself."[3]

Although the Germans had been denied their quick victory in the west, by the end of 1914 they

Trench Warfare Grim though they were, the trenches proved effective for defensive purposes. Here a British soldier guards a trench at Ovillers, on the Somme, in July 1916. *(Trustees of the Imperial War Museum)*

occupied much of Belgium and almost one-tenth of France, including major industrial areas and mines producing most of France's coal and iron. On the eastern front, as well, the Germans won some substantial advantages in 1914—but not a decisive victory.

The first season of fighting in the east suggested that the pattern there would not be trench warfare but rapid movement across a vast but thinly held front. When the fighting began in August, the Russians came more quickly than anticipated, confronting an outnumbered German force in a menacing, if reckless, invasion of East Prussia. But by mid-September German forces under General Paul von Hindenburg (1847–1934) and his chief of staff General Erich Ludendorff (1865–1937) repelled the Russian advance, taking a huge number of prisoners and seriously demoralizing the Russians.

As a result of their victory in East Prussia, Hindenburg and Ludendorff emerged as heroes, and they would play major roles in German public life thereafter. Hindenburg, the senior partner, became chief of staff of the entire German army in August 1916, but the able and energetic Luden-

dorff remained at his side. Ludendorff proved to be the key figure as this powerful duo gradually assumed undisputed control of the whole German war effort, both military and domestic.

Seeking a Breakthrough, 1915–1917

After the campaigns of 1915 proved inconclusive, German leaders decided to concentrate in 1916 on a massive offensive against the great French fortress at Verdun, intending to inflict a definitive defeat on France. To assault the fortress, the Germans gathered 1220 pieces of artillery for attack along an 8-mile front. Included were thirteen "Big Bertha" siege guns, weapons so large that nine tractors were required to position each of them; a crane was necessary to insert the shell, which weighed over a ton. The level of heavy artillery firepower that the Germans applied at Verdun was unprecedented in the history of warfare.

German forces attacked on February 21, taking the outer defenses of the fortress, and appeared poised for victory. The tide turned, however, when General Philippe Pétain (1856–1951) assumed control of the French defense at Verdun.

Into the Trenches

As the initial offensives on the western front turned into stalemate, ordinary soldiers on both sides began to experience unprecedented forms of warfare in an eerie new landscape. Writing home to his family from France in November 1914, a young German soldier, Fritz Franke (1892–1915), sought to convey what this new war was like. He was killed six months later.

Yesterday we didn't feel sure that a single one of us would come through alive. You can't possibly picture to yourselves what such a battlefield looks like. It is impossible to describe it, and even now, when it is a day behind us, I myself can hardly believe that such bestial barbarity and unspeakable suffering are possible. Every foot of ground contested; every hundred yards another trench; and everywhere bodies—rows of them! All the trees shot to pieces; the whole ground churned up a yard deep by the heaviest shells; dead animals; houses and churches so utterly destroyed by shellfire that they can never be of the least use again. And every troop that advances in support must pass through a mile of this chaos, through this gigantic burial ground and the reek of corpses.

In this way we advanced on Tuesday, marching for three hours, a silent column, in the moonlight, toward the Front and into a trench as Reserve, two to three hundred yards from the English, close behind our own infantry.

There we lay the whole day, a yard and a half to two yards below the level of the ground, crouching in the narrow trench on a thin layer of straw, in an overpowering din which never ceased all day or the greater part of the night— the whole ground trembling and shaking! There is every variety of sound—whistling, whining, ringing, crashing, rolling . . . [ellipses in the original] the beastly things pitch right above one and burst and the fragments buzz in all directions, and the only question one asks is: "Why doesn't one get me?" Often the things land within a hand's breath and one just looks on. One gets so hardened to it that at the most one ducks one's head a little if a great, big naval-gun shell comes a bit too near and its grey-green stink is a bit too thick. Otherwise one soon just lies there and thinks of other things. . . .

One just lives from one hour to the next. For instance, if one starts to prepare some food, one never knows if one may'nt have to leave it behind within an hour. . . .

. . . Above all one acquires a knowledge of human nature! We all live so naturally and unconventionally here, every one according to his own instincts. That brings much that is good and much that is ugly to the surface.

Source: A. F. Wedd, ed., *German Students' War Letters,* translated and arranged from the original edition of Dr. Philipp Witkop (London: Methuen, 1929), pp. 123–125.

Pétain had the patience and skill necessary to organize supply for a long and difficult siege. Furthermore, he proved able, through considerate treatment, to inspire affection and confidence among his men. By mid-July the French army had repelled the German offensive, although only in December did the French retake the outer defenses of the fortress. The French had held firm in what would prove the war's longest, most trying battle—one that killed 600,000 men on both sides. For the French the Battle of Verdun would remain the epitome of the horrors of World War I.

Meanwhile, early in July 1916, the British led a major attack at the Somme River that was similarly bloody—and that affected Britain much as Verdun affected France. On the first day alone the British suffered 60,000 casualties, including 21,000 killed. Fighting continued into the fall, but the offensive proved futile in the end. One-third of those involved, or over 1 million soldiers, ended up dead, missing, or wounded.

Dominated by the devastating battles at Verdun and the Somme, the campaigns of 1916 marked the decisive end to the high spirits of the summer of 1914. Both sides suffered huge losses—and apparently for nothing. By the end of 1916, the front had shifted only a few miles from its location at the beginning of the year.

In light of the frustrating outcome so far, the French turned to new military leadership, replacing Joffre with Robert Nivelle (1856–1924), who promptly sought to prove himself with a new offensive during the spring of 1917. Persisting even as it became clear that this effort had no chance of success, Nivelle provoked increasing resistance among French soldiers, some of whom were simply refusing to follow orders by the end of May.

With the French war effort in danger of collapse, the French government replaced Nivelle with General Pétain, the hero of the defense of Verdun and the obvious person to restore morale. Pétain managed to re-establish discipline by adopting a conciliatory approach—improving food and rest, visiting the troops in the field, listening, offering encouragement, urging patience, even dealing relatively mercifully with most of the resisters themselves. To be sure, many of the soldiers who had participated in this near-mutiny were court-martialed, and over 3400 were convicted. But of the 554 sentenced to death, only 49 were actually executed.

After the failure of the Nivelle offensive, the initiative fell to the British under General Douglas Haig (1861–1928), who was convinced, despite skepticism in the British cabinet, that Nivelle's offensive had failed simply because of tactical mistakes. Beginning near Ypres in Belgium on July 31, 1917, and continuing until November, the British attacked, but, as before, the effort yielded only minimal territorial gains—about fifty square miles—at a horrifying cost, including 240,000 British casualties. Known as the Battle of Passchendaele, the British offensive of 1917 ranks with the Battles of Verdun and the Somme as the bloodiest of the war.

1917 as a Turning Point

Meanwhile, the Germans, feeling that the Russians could not hold out much longer, decided to

Paul von Hindenburg and Erich Ludendorff The talents of Hindenburg (left) and Ludendorff meshed effectively to carry them from success on the eastern front in 1914 to a predominant role in the German war effort. They are shown here at a reception in honor of Hindenburg's seventieth birthday in October 1917. (*AKG London*)

concentrate on the eastern front in 1917 in an effort to knock Russia out of the war at last. This intensified German military pressure helped spark revolution in Russia, and in December 1917 Russia's new revolutionary regime asked for a separate peace. The defeat of Russia freed the Germans at last to concentrate on the west, but by this time France and Britain had a new ally.

On April 6, 1917, the United States entered the war on the side of the Entente, in response to Germany's controversial use of submarines. Germany lacked sufficient strength in surface ships to respond to Britain's naval blockade, whether by attacking the British fleet directly or by mounting a comparable blockade of the British Isles. So the Germans decided to use submarines to interfere with shipping to Britain. Submarines, however, were too vulnerable to be able to surface and confiscate goods, so the Germans had to settle for sinking suspect ships with torpedoes. In February 1915 they declared the waters around the British Isles to be a war zone and served notice that they would torpedo not only enemy ships but also neutral ships carrying goods to Britain.

The German response was harsh, but so was the British blockade, which violated a number of earlier international agreements about the rights of neutral shipping and the scope of wartime blockades. The British had agreed that only military goods such as munitions and certain raw materials, not such everyday goods as food and clothing, were to be subject to confiscation. Yet in blockading Germany, the British refused to make this distinction, prompting the sarcastic German quip that Britannia not only rules the waves, but waives the rules.[4]

In May 1915 a German sub torpedoed the *Lusitania,* a British passenger liner, killing almost 1200 people and producing widespread indignation. Partly because 128 of those killed were Americans, U.S. President Woodrow Wilson issued a severe warning, which contributed to the German decision in September 1915 to pull back from unrestricted submarine warfare. But in this war of attrition, the flow of supplies became ever more critical. As German suffering under the British blockade increased, pressure steadily mounted within Germany to put the subs back into action.

The issue provoked bitter debate among German leaders. Chancellor Theobald von Bethmann-Hollweg and the civilian authorities opposed resumption out of fear it would provoke the United States to enter the war. But Ludendorff and the military finally prevailed, partly with the argument that even if the United States did intervene, U.S. troops could not get to Europe in sufficient numbers, and in sufficient haste, to have a major impact. Germany announced the resumption of unrestricted submarine warfare on January 31, 1917, and the United States responded with a declaration of war on April 6.

Many on both sides doubted that U.S. intervention would make a decisive difference; most assumed that it would take at least a year for the American presence to materialize in force—an assessment that proved accurate. Still, the entry of the United States gave the Entente at least the promise of more fighting power. And the United States seemed capable of renewing the sense of purpose on the Entente side, showing that the war had a meaning that could justify the unexpected costs and sacrifice.

THE EXPERIENCE OF TOTAL WAR

As the war dragged on, the distinction between the military and civilian spheres blurred. Suffering increased on the home front, and unprecedented governmental mobilization of society proved necessary to wage war on the scale that had come to be required. Because it became "total" in this way, the war affected not simply international relations and the power balance but also culture, society, and the patterns of everyday life.

Hardship on the Home Front

The war meant food shortages, and thus malnutrition, for ordinary people in the belligerent countries, although Britain and France, with their more favorable geographic positions, suffered considerably less than others. Germany was especially vulnerable and promptly began suffering under the British naval blockade. With military needs taking priority, the Germans encountered shortages of the chemical fertilizers, farm machinery, and draft animals necessary for agricultural production. The government began rationing bread, meat, and fats during 1915. The increasing scarcity of foodstuffs produced sharp increases in diseases like rickets and tuberculosis and in infant and childhood mortality rates in wartime Germany.

The need to pay for the war produced economic dislocations as well. Government borrowing covered some of the cost for the short term, but to cover the rest, governments all over Europe found it more palatable to inflate the currency, by printing more money, than to raise taxes. The notion that the enemy would be made to pay once victory had been won seemed to justify this decision. But this way of financing the war meant rising prices and severe erosion of purchasing power for ordinary people all over Europe. In both France and Germany, the labor truce of 1914 gave way to increasing strike activity during 1916.

With an especially severe winter in 1916–1917 adding to the misery, there were serious instances of domestic disorder, including strikes and food riots, in many parts of Europe during 1917. In Italy, major strikes developed in Turin and other cities over wages and access to foodstuffs. The revolution that overthrew the tsarist autocracy in Russia that same year began with comparable protests over wartime food shortages.

The strains of war even fanned the flames in Ireland, where an uneasy truce over the home-rule controversy accompanied the British decision for war in 1914. Partly because of German efforts to stir up domestic trouble for Britain, unrest built up again in Ireland, culminating in the Easter Rebellion in Dublin in 1916. The brutality with which British forces crushed the uprising intensified demands for full independence—precisely what Britain would be forced to yield to the Irish Republic shortly after the war.

Moreover, new technologies made civilians ever less immune to wartime violence. Most dramatically, an entirely new aspect of war-making, bombing from aircraft, directly assaulted civilians. Although bombing began with an immediate military aim—to destroy industrial targets or to provide tactical support for other military units—it quickly became clear that night bombing, especially, might demoralize civilian populations. As early as 1915, German airplanes were bombing English cities, provoking British retaliation against cities in the German Ruhr and Rhineland areas. These raids had little effect on the course of the war, but they showed that new technologies could make warfare more destructive even for civilians.

Domestic Mobilization

Once it became clear, by the end of 1914, that the war would not be over quickly, leaders on both sides began to realize that the outcome would not be determined on the battlefield alone. Victory required mobilizing all of the nation's resources and energies. So World War I became a total war, involving the whole society, not just the military.

The British naval blockade on Germany, which made no distinction between military and nonmilitary goods, was a stratagem characteristic of total war. The blockade would not affect Germany's immediate strength on the battlefield, but it could damage Germany's long-term war-making capacity. And the blockade did prove significant, partly because Germany had not made effective economic preparations—including stockpiling—for this long war of attrition.

In peacetime, Germany had depended on imports of food, fats, oils, and chemicals, including the nitrates needed for ammunition. With the onset of war, these commodities were immediately in short supply, as was labor. Thus Germany seemed to need stringent economic coordination and control. By the end of 1916, the country had developed a militarized economy, with all aspects of economic life coordinated for the war effort. Under the supervision of the military, state agencies, big business, and the trade unions were brought into close collaboration. The new system included rationing, price controls, and compulsory labor arbitration, as well as a national service law enabling the military to channel workers into jobs deemed vital to the war effort.

Forced to provide for an unexpectedly long war, the Germans did not hesitate to exploit the economy of occupied Belgium, requisitioning foodstuffs even to the point of causing starvation among the Belgians themselves. They forced 62,000 Belgians to work in German factories under conditions of virtual slave labor. Although this practice was stopped in February 1917, by then nearly a thousand Belgian workers had died in German labor camps.

The most influential feature of Germany's war economy was the Kriegsrohstoffabteilung (KRA), or war raw materials office, established under the authority of the War Ministry to provide the materials essential to the war effort. Led initially by the able Jewish industrialist Walther Rathenau (1867–1922), this agency came to symbolize the unprecedented coordination of the German economy for war. Recognizing as early as the fall of 1914 that Germany lacked the raw materials for a long war, Rathenau devised an imaginative program that included the development of synthetic substitute products and the creation of new mixed (private and government) companies to allocate raw materials. The KRA's effort was remarkably successful—a model for later economic planning and coordination.

Although Germany presented the most dramatic example of domestic coordination, the same pattern was evident everywhere, even in France, with its economic individualism and distrust of an

Domestic Mobilization and the Role of Women

Early in 1917, the British writer Gilbert Stone published a remarkable collection of statements intended to illuminate the new experiences that British women were encountering in the workplace. The following passage by Naomi Loughnan, a well-to-do woman who worked in a munitions factory, makes it clear that the new work experience during the war opened the way to new questions about both gender and class.

Engineering mankind is possessed of the unshakable opinion that no woman can have the mechanical sense. If one of us asks humbly why such and such an alteration is not made to prevent this or that drawback to a machine, she is told, with a superior smile, that a man has worked her machine before her for years, and that therefore if there were any improvement possible it would have been made. As long as we do exactly as we are told and do not attempt to use our brains, we give entire satisfaction, and are treated as nice, good children. Any swerving from the easy path prepared for us by our males arouses the most scathing contempt in their manly bosoms. . . . Women have, however, proved that their entry into the munitions world has increased the output. Employers who forget things personal in their patriotic desire for large results are enthusiastic over the success of women in the shops. But their workmen have to be handled with the utmost tenderness and caution lest they should actually imagine it was being suggested that women could do their work equally well, given equal conditions of training—at least where muscle is not the driving force. This undercurrent of jealousy rises to the surface rather often, but as a general rule the men behave with much kindness, and are ready to help with muscle and advice whenever called upon. If eyes are very bright and hair inclined to curl, the muscle and advice do not even wait for a call.

The coming of the mixed classes of women into the factory is slowly but surely having an educative effect upon the men. "Language" is almost unconsciously becoming subdued. There are fiery exceptions who make our hair stand up on end under our close-fitting caps, but a sharp rebuke or a look of horror will often bring to book the most truculent. . . . It is grievous to hear the girls also swearing and using disgusting language. Shoulder to shoulder with the children of the slums, the upper classes are having their eyes pried open at last to the awful conditions among which their sisters have dwelt. Foul language, immorality, and many other evils are but the natural outcome of overcrowding and bitter poverty. If some of us, still blind and ignorant of our responsibilities, shrink horrified and repelled from the rougher set, the compliment is returned with open derision and ribald laughter. . . . On the other hand, attempts at friendliness from the more understanding are treated with the utmost suspicion, though once that suspicion is overcome and friendship is established, it is unshakable.

Source: Naomi Loughnan, "Munition Work," in Gilbert Stone, ed., *Women War Workers: Accounts Contributed by Representative Workers of the Work Done by Women in the More Important Branches of War Employment* (New York: Thomas Y. Crowell, [1917]), pp. 35–38.

interventionist state. In Britain, the central figure proved to be David Lloyd George (1863–1945), appointed to the newly created post of minister of munitions in 1915. During his year in that office, ninety-five new factories opened, soon overcoming the shortage of guns and ammunition that had impeded the British war effort until then. In fact, types of ammunition that had formerly taken a year to manufacture were now being produced in weeks, even days. His performance as munitions minister made Lloyd George seem the one person who could organize Britain for victory. Succeeding

Herbert Asquith as prime minister in December 1916, he would direct the British war effort to its victorious conclusion.

Accelerating Socioeconomic Change

Everywhere the war effort quickened the long-term socioeconomic change associated with industrialization. Guaranteed government orders for war materiel fueled industrial expansion. In France, the Paris region now became a center of heavy industrial production for the first time. The needs of war spawned new technologies—advances in food processing and medical treatment, for example—that would carry over into peacetime.

With so many men needed for military service, women were called on to assume new economic roles—running farms in France, for example, or working in the new munitions factories in Britain. (See the box, "Domestic Mobilization and the Role of Women.") During the course of the war, the number of women employed in Britain rose from 3.25 million to 5 million. In Italy, 200,000 women had war-related jobs by 1917. Women also played indispensable roles at the front, especially in nursing units.

The expanded opportunities of wartime intensified the debate over the sociopolitical role of women that the movement for women's suffrage had stimulated. The outbreak of war led some antiwar feminists to argue that women would be better able than men to prevent wars, which were essentially masculine undertakings. Women should have full access to public life, not because they could be expected to respond as men did but because they had a distinctive—and valuable— role to play. At the same time, by giving women jobs and the opportunity to do many of the same things men had done, the war undermined the stereotypes that had long justified restrictions on women's political roles and life choices.

For many women, doing a difficult job well, serving their country in this emergency situation, afforded a new sense of accomplishment, as well as a new taste of independence. Freed from male domination, women were now much more likely to have their own residences, to go out in public on their own, eating in restaurants, even smoking and drinking. Yet while many seized new opportunities and learned new skills, women frequently had to combine paid employment with housework and child rearing, and those who left home—to serve in nursing units, for example—often felt guilty about neglecting traditional family roles.

Propaganda and the "Mobilization of Enthusiasm"

Because the domestic front was crucial to sustaining a long war of attrition, it became ever more important to shore up civilian morale as the war dragged on. The result was the "mobilization of enthusiasm"—the conscious manipulation of collective passions by national governments on

Mobilizing Women Responding to appeals like this, women quickly become prominent in the munitions industry in Britain as elsewhere. The chance to perform valued public roles during the wartime emergency proved a watershed for many women. *(Trustees of the Imperial War Museum)*

an unprecedented scale. Everywhere there was extensive censorship, even of soldiers' letters from the front. Because of concerns about civilian morale, the French press carried no news of the Battle of Verdun, with the horrifying number of casualties it involved. In addition, systematic propaganda included not only patriotic themes but also attempts to discredit the enemy, even through outright falsification of the news. British anti-German propaganda helped draw the United States into the war in 1917.

At the outset of the war, the brutal behavior of the German armies in Belgium made it easy for the French and the British to discredit the Germans. Having expected to pass through neutral Belgium unopposed, the Germans were infuriated by the Belgian resistance they encountered. At Louvain late in August 1914 they responded to alleged Belgian sniping by shooting a number of hostages and setting the town on fire, destroying the famous old library at the university. This noto-rious episode led the London *Times* to characterize the Germans as "Huns," a reference to the Mongolian tribe that began invading Europe in the fourth century. Stories about German soldiers eating Belgian babies began to circulate.

In October 1914 ninety-three important German intellectuals, artists, and scientists signed a manifesto, addressed to "the World of Culture," justifying Germany's conduct in Belgium and larger purposes in the war. To a point, such gestures stemmed from expected forms of patriotism, but as passions heated up, major intellectuals on both sides—from the German theologian Adolf von Harnack (1851–1930) to the French philosopher Henri Bergson (1859–1941)—began denigrating the culture of the enemy and claiming a monopoly of virtue for their own side.

This unprecedented propaganda combined with the unexpected destruction and loss of life to give the war an increasingly catastrophic aura. This was no mere adjustment in the traditional

Devastation at Louvain Unexpected destruction at the outset of the war fanned the flames of hatred and changed the stakes of the conflict. Located in the path of the first German advance, the Belgian city of Louvain was particularly hard hit. *(Trustees of the Imperial War Museum)*

balance of power; so great were the strains of war, in fact, that the sense of common involvement in a single civilization, or a single European state system based on an accepted set of rules, began to weaken. Some came to believe that real peace with an adversary so evil, so different, was simply not possible. Thus, there must be no compromise, but rather total victory, no matter what the cost.

At the same time, however, war-weariness produced a countervailing tendency to seek a "white peace," a peace without victory for either side. Both sets of impulses were at work as Europeans began debating war aims in earnest in 1917, at a time when dramatic events were changing the war's meaning for contemporaries. The most significant was the Russian Revolution, which developed from wartime difficulties and which then fundamentally affected the nature of the war.

TWO REVOLUTIONS IN RUSSIA: MARCH AND NOVEMBER 1917

Strained by war, the old European order finally cracked in Russia in 1917. Revolution against the tsarist autocracy seemed first to lay the foundations for parliamentary democracy. But by the end of the year, the Bolsheviks, the smallest and most extreme of Russia's major socialist parties, had taken power, an outcome that was hardly conceivable when the revolution began.

The Wartime Crisis of the Russian Autocracy

The Russian army performed better than many had expected during the first year of the war, and as late as June 1916, it was strong enough for a successful offensive against Austria-Hungary. Russia had industrialized sufficiently by 1914 to sustain a modern war, at least for a while, and the country's war production increased significantly by 1916. But Russia suffered from problems of leadership and organization—in transportation, for example—that made it less prepared for a long war than the other belligerents. Even early in 1915, perhaps a fourth of Russia's newly conscripted troops were sent to the front without weapons, instructed to pick up rifles and supplies from the dead.

As problems mounted, Tsar Nicholas II (1868–1918) assumed personal command of the army in August 1915, but his absence from the capital only accelerated the deterioration in government and deepened the bitter divisions within the ruling clique. With the tsar away, the illiterate but charismatic Siberian monk Grigori Rasputin (c. 1872–1916) emerged as the key political power within the circle of the German-born Empress Alexandra (1872–1918). He won her confidence because of his alleged ability to control the bleeding of her hemophiliac son, Alexis, the heir to the throne. Led by Rasputin, those around the empress made a shambles of the state administration. Many educated Russians, appalled at what was happening, assumed—incorrectly—that pro-German elements at court were responsible for the eclipse of the tsar and the resulting government chaos. Asked one Duma deputy of the government's performance, "Is this stupidity, or is it treason?"

Finally, late in December 1916, Rasputin was assassinated by aristocrats seeking to save the autocracy from these apparently pro-German influences. This act indicated how desperate the situation was becoming, but it made no decisive difference.

By the end of 1916, the immediate difficulties of war had combined with the strains of rapid wartime industrialization to produce a revolutionary situation in Russia. The country's urban population had increased rapidly, and now, partly because of transport problems, the cities faced severe food shortages. Strikes and demonstrations spread from Petrograd (the former St. Petersburg) to other cities during the first two months of 1917. In March renewed demonstrations in Petrograd, spearheaded by women protesting the lack of bread and coal, led to revolution.

The March Revolution and the Fate of the Provisional Government

At first, the agitation that began in Petrograd on March 8, 1917, appeared to be just another bread riot. Even when it turned into a wave of strikes, the revolutionary parties expected it to be crushed by the government troops stationed at the Petrograd garrison. But when called out to help the police break up the demonstrations, the soldiers generally avoided firing at the strikers. Within days, they were sharing weapons and ammunition with the workers; the garrison was going over to what was now becoming a revolution.

Late in the afternoon of March 12, leaders of the strike committees, delegates elected by factory workers, and representatives of the socialist parties formed a soviet, or council, following the example of the revolution of 1905, when such soviets had first appeared. Regiments of the Petrograd garrison also began electing representatives, soon to be admitted to the Petrograd Soviet, which officially became the Council of Workers' and Soldiers' Deputies. This soviet was now the ruling power in the Russian capital. It had been elected and was genuinely representative—though of a limited constituency of workers and soldiers. Following the lead of Petrograd, Russians elsewhere promptly began forming soviets, so that over 350 local units were represented when the first All-Russian Council of Soviets met in Petrograd in April. The overwhelming majority of their representatives were Mensheviks and Socialist Revolutionaries; only about one-sixth were Bolsheviks.

On March 14 a committee of the Duma, recognizing that the tsar's authority had been lost for good, persuaded Nicholas to abdicate, then formed a new provisional government. Particularly because it derived from the Duma elected in 1907, under extremely limited suffrage, this government was supposed to be temporary, to pave the way for an elected constituent assembly, which would establish fully legitimate governmental institutions.

Considering the strains in the autocratic system that had produced the revolution of 1905 after the Russo-Japanese War, it was hardly surprising that the system would shatter now, in light of this far more trying war and the resulting disarray within the tsarist government. Russia had apparently experienced, at last, the bourgeois political revolution necessary to develop a Western-style parliamentary democracy. Even from an orthodox Marxist perspective, this was the revolution to expect, and Marxists could only help consolidate bourgeois democracy. The longer-term pursuit of socialism could take place within that new political framework. These, however, were anything but orthodox times, and the March revolution proved only the beginning.

Although the fall of the tsarist order produced widespread relief, Russia's new leaders faced difficult questions about priorities. Many, both inside and outside Russia, believed that the revolution's immediate purpose was to revitalize the Russian war effort. Yet war-weariness was widespread,

and there were pressures to get on with domestic political change. Moreover, the provisional government had to operate with the potentially more radical Petrograd Soviet, the keystone of the network of soviets across the country, looking over its shoulder.

At first the Petrograd Soviet was perfectly willing to give the provisional government a chance to govern. In this bourgeois revolution, it was not up to socialists and workers to take responsibility by participating directly in government, though they could offer support, especially against any attempt at counterrevolution. Even among the Bolsheviks, there was widespread support for conciliation and at least short-term acceptance of the new government. Although the Bolshevik leader, Vladimir Lenin, took a different tack, he was in exile in Switzerland and could not yet make his will prevail.

Given its chance by the Petrograd Soviet, the provisional government took important steps toward Western-style liberal democracy, establishing universal suffrage, civil liberties, autonomy for ethnic minorities, and labor legislation, including provision for an eight-hour workday. But the government failed in two key areas, fostering discontents that the Bolsheviks soon exploited. First, the new government persisted in fighting the war. Second, it dragged its feet on agrarian reform.

The provisional government's determination to renew the war effort stemmed from genuine concern about Russia's obligations to its allies, about the country's national honor and position among the great powers. Moreover, the long-standing goal of Russian diplomacy—an outlet to the Mediterranean Sea through the Dardanelles Strait—seemed within reach if a revitalized Russia could continue the war, contributing to an Allied victory. The educated, well-to-do Russians who led the new government expected that ordinary citizens, now free, would fight with renewed enthusiasm, like the armies that had grown from the French Revolution over a century before. These leaders failed to grasp how desperate the situation of ordinary people had become.

The March revolution grew from unrest in the cities, but in the aftermath the peasantry moved into action as well, seizing land, sometimes burning the houses of their landlords. By midsummer, a full-scale peasant war seemed to be in the offing in the countryside, and calls for radical agrarian

Lenin as Leader Although he was in exile during much of 1917, Lenin's leadership was crucial to the Bolshevik success in Russia. He is shown here addressing a May Day rally in Red Square, Moscow, on May 1, 1919. *(ITAR-TASS/Sovfoto)*

reform became increasingly insistent. Partly from expediency, partly from genuine concern for social justice, the provisional government promised a major redistribution of land, but it insisted that the reform be carried out legally—not by the present provisional government, but by a duly elected constituent assembly.

Calling for elections would thus seem to have been the first priority. The new political leaders kept putting it off, however, waiting for the situation to cool before giving up power to a newly elected assembly. But the situation did not allow the luxury of playing for time. As unrest grew in the countryside, the authority of the provisional government diminished and the soviets gained in stature. But what role were the soviets to play?

The Bolsheviks Come to Power

In the immediate aftermath of the March revolution, the Bolsheviks had not seemed to differ substantially from their rivals within the socialist movement, at least on matters of most immediate concern—the war, land reform, and the character of the revolution itself. But the situation began to change in April when Lenin returned from exile in Switzerland, thanks partly to the help with transportation that the German military provided. The Germans assumed—correctly, it turned out—that the Bolsheviks would help undermine the Russian war effort. Largely through the force of Lenin's leadership, the Bolsheviks soon assumed the initiative.

Lenin (1870–1924), born Vladimir Ilich Ulianov, came from a comfortable upper-middle-class family and was university-educated and trained as a lawyer. But after an older brother was executed in 1887 for participating in a plot against the tsar's life, Lenin followed him into revolutionary activity. He was arrested for the first time in 1895, then exiled to Siberia. After his release in 1900, he made his way to western Europe, and there he remained, except for a brief return to Russia during the revolution of 1905, until the renewal of revolution in 1917.

The Bolshevik party was identified with Lenin from its beginning in 1903, when it emerged from the schism in Russian Marxist socialism. Because of his emphases, Bolshevism came to mean discipline, organization, and a special leadership role for a revolutionary vanguard. Lenin proved effective because he was a stern and somewhat forbidding figure, disciplined, fiercely intelligent, sometimes ruthless. As a Bolshevik colleague put it, Lenin was "the one indisputable leader . . . a man of iron will, inexhaustible energy, combining a fanatical faith in the movement, in the cause, with an equal faith in himself."[5]

Still, when Lenin began taking the initiative in 1917, his reading of the situation astonished even many Bolsheviks. He held that the revolution was about to pass from the present bourgeois-democratic stage to a socialist phase, involving dictatorship of the proletariat in the form of government by the soviets. It was time, then, for active opposition to the provisional government, and this meant both criticism of the war, as fundamentally imperialist, and calls for the distribution of land from the large estates to the peasants. This latter measure had long been identified with the Socialist Revolutionaries; most Bolsheviks had envisioned collectivization and nationalization instead.

But what Lenin envisioned was anything but "socialism in one country," with embattled, relatively backward Russia trying to create a socialist order on its own. Rather, a Bolshevik-led revolution in Russia would provide the spark to ignite the proletarian revolution smoldering elsewhere in Europe, especially in Germany. Although some remained skeptical, Lenin's strategic vision promptly won acceptance among most of his fellow Bolsheviks.

In April 1917 moderate socialists still had majority support in the soviets, so the Bolsheviks sought to build gradually, postponing any decisive test of strength. But events escaped the control of the Bolshevik leadership in mid-July when impatient workers, largely Bolshevik in sympathy, took to the streets of Petrograd on their own. The Petrograd Soviet refused to support the uprising, and the provisional government had no difficulty getting military units to put it down, killing two hundred in the process. Though the uprising had developed spontaneously, Bolshevik leaders felt compelled to offer public support, and this gave the government an excuse to crack down on the Bolshevik leadership in the aftermath. Lenin managed to escape to Finland as a number of his colleagues suffered arrest and imprisonment.

With the Bolsheviks on the defensive, counter-revolutionary elements in the Russian military decided to seize the initiative with a march on Petrograd in September. In resisting this attempted coup, the provisional government, now under the young, charismatic Socialist Revolutionary Alexander Kerensky (1881–1970), had to rely on whomever could offer help, including the Bolsheviks. Bolshevik propaganda led the soldiers under the command of the counterrevolutionaries to refuse to fight against the upholders of the revolution in Petrograd. Within days, the Bolsheviks won their first clear-cut majority in the Petrograd Soviet, then shortly gained majorities in most of the other soviets as well.

During the fall of 1917, the situation became increasingly volatile, eluding control by anyone. People looted food from shops; peasants seized land, sometimes murdering their landlords. Desertions and the murder of officers increased within the Russian military.

With the Bolsheviks at last the dominant power in the soviets, and with the government's control diminishing, Lenin, from his hideout in Finland, began urging the Bolshevik central committee to prepare for armed insurrection. Although some found this step unnecessarily risky, the majority accepted Lenin's argument that the provisional government would continue dragging its feet, inadvertently giving right-wing officer leagues time for another counterrevolutionary coup.

Because Lenin himself remained in hiding, the task of organizing the seizure of power fell to Leon Trotsky (1870–1940), who skillfully modified Lenin's aggressive strategy. Lenin wanted the Bolsheviks to rise in their own name, in opposition to the provisional government, but Trotsky linked the insurrection to the cause of the soviets and played up its defensive character, against the ongoing danger of a counterrevolutionary coup. With the political center at an impasse, the only alternative to such a coup seemed to be a Bolshevik initiative to preserve the Petrograd Soviet, by now the sole viable institutional embodiment of the revolution and its promise. Trotsky's interpretation led people who wanted simply to defend the Soviet to support the Bolsheviks' initiative.

During the night of November 9, armed Bolsheviks and regular army regiments occupied key points in Petrograd, including railroad stations, post offices, telephone exchanges, power stations, and the national bank. Able to muster only token resistance, the provisional government collapsed. Kerensky escaped by morning and mounted what quickly proved a futile effort to rally troops at the front for a counterattack against the Bolsheviks. In contrast to the March revolution, which had taken about a week, the Bolsheviks took over the capital, overthrowing the Kerensky government, literally overnight, and almost without bloodshed. A wave of popular euphoria followed. But though the Bolsheviks had taken Petrograd, they would need three more years and a civil war to extend their control across the whole Russian Empire. (See the box, "The Bolsheviks in Power, November 1917.")

However, the revolution's immediate prospects, and the wider impact it might have, were bound up with the course of the war. Would the Bolshevik Revolution in Russia prove the spark for revolution elsewhere in war-weary Europe, as Lenin anticipated? If not, could a Bolshevik regime survive in Russia on its own?

The Russian Revolution and the War

Having stood for peace throughout the revolution, the Bolsheviks promptly moved to get Russia out of the war, agreeing to an armistice with Germany in December 1917. They hoped that Russia's withdrawal would speed the collapse of the war effort on all sides and that this, in turn, would intensify the movement toward revolution elsewhere in Europe. The Russian Revolution, they believed, was but a chapter in a larger story, proceeding from war to wider revolution. As Lenin noted to Trotsky, "If it were necessary for us to go under to assure the success of the German revolution, we should have to do it. The German revolution is vastly more important than ours." Indeed, said Lenin to the Communist party congress of March 1918, "It is an absolute truth that we will go under without the German revolution."[6]

Still, the Bolsheviks did not have to wait passively for events elsewhere to unfold. They could help spark wider revolution by demonstrating the imperialist basis of the war. After assuming control in November, they published the tsarist government's secret documents concerning the war— the treaties and understandings specifying how the spoils were to be divided in the event of victory. In doing so, the Bolsheviks hoped to show ordinary people elsewhere that this had been, all along, a war on behalf of capitalist interests. This Bolshevik initiative added fuel to the controversy already developing in all the belligerent countries over the war's purpose and significance.

THE NEW WAR AND THE ENTENTE VICTORY, 1917–1918

Because the stakes of the war changed during 1917, the outcome, once the war finally ended in November 1918, included consequences that Europeans could not have foreseen in 1914. Thus German defeat brought revolution against the monarchy and the beginning of a new democracy. Thus grandiose new visions competed to shape the postwar world.

The Debate over War Aims

The French and British governments publicly welcomed the March revolution in Russia, partly because they expected Russia's military performance to improve under new leadership, but also because the change of regime seemed to have highly favorable psychological implications. With Russia no longer an autocracy, the war could be portrayed—and experienced—as a crusade for democracy. At the same time, the March revolution could only sow confusion among the many Germans who had understood their own war effort as a matter of self-defense against reactionary Russia. But the November revolution required a deeper reconsideration for all the belligerents.

Entente war aims agreements, like the secret Treaty of London that brought Italy into the war in 1915, had remained secret until the Bolsheviks published the tsarist documents. Products of old-style diplomacy, those agreements had been made by a restricted foreign policy elite within the governing circles of each country; not only the general public but also the elected parliaments were generally not aware of what they contained. The debate over war aims that developed in 1917 thus became a debate over decision making as well, stimulating calls for greater popular involvement, which seemed sure to diminish the possibility of such wars in the future. In addition, there were exhortations for all the parties in the present war to renounce annexations and settle for a white peace.

The Bolsheviks in Power, November 1917

John Reed (1887–1920), an American journalist and communist leader from Portland, Oregon, was in Russia during the fall of 1917, when the second revolution began. His enthusiastic first-hand account, which drew the praise of Lenin himself, conveys the drama and excitement of the revolution. In the following passage, Reed provides a sense of the combination of emergency, improvisation, and revolutionary enthusiasm that marked the Bolsheviks' first days in power.

Having settled the question of power, the Bolsheviki turned their attention to problems of practical administration. First of all the city, the country, the Army must be fed. Bands of sailors and Red Guards scoured the warehouses, the railway terminals, even the barges in the canals, unearthing and confiscating thousands of *poods* [a *pood* is thirty-six pounds] of food held by private speculators. Emissaries were sent to the provinces, where with the assistance of the Land Committees they seized the storehouses of the great grain dealers. Expeditions of sailors, heavily armed, were sent out in groups of five thousand to the South, to Siberia, with roving commissions to capture cities still held by the White Guards, establish order and *get food* [italics in the original]. . . .

Towards the end of November occurred the "wine-pogrom"—looting of the wine cellars—beginning with the plundering of the Winter Palace vaults. For days there were drunken soldiers on the streets. In all this was evident the hand of the counterrevolutionists, who distributed among the regiments plans showing the location of the stores of liquor. The Commissars of Smolny began by pleading and arguing, which did not stop the growing disorder, followed by pitched battles between soldiers and Red Guards. Finally the Military Revolutionary Committee sent out companies of sailors with machine-guns, who fired mercilessly upon the rioters, killing many; and by executive order the wine cellars were invaded by Committees with hatchets, who smashed the bottles—or blew them up with dynamite.

. . . In all quarters of the city small elective Revolutionary Tribunals were set up by the workers and soldiers to deal with petty crime. . . .

Alert and suspicious, the working class of the city constituted itself a vast spy system, through the servants prying into bourgeois households, and reporting all information to the Military Revolutionary Committee, which struck with an iron hand, unceasing. In this way was discovered the Monarchist plot led by a former Duma-member Purishkevich and a group of nobles and officers, who had planned an officers' uprising. . . .

Still the strike of the Ministries went on, still the sabotage of the old officials, the stoppage of normal economic life. Behind Smolny was only the will of the vast, unorganized popular masses; and with them the Council of People's Commissars dealt, directing revolutionary mass action against its enemies. In eloquent proclamations, couched in simple words and spread over Russia, Lenin explained the Revolution, urged the people to take the power into their own hands, by force to break down the resistance of the propertied classes, by force to take over the institutions of Government. Revolutionary order. Revolutionary discipline! Strict accounting and control! No strikes! No loafing!

Source: John Reed, *Ten Days That Shook the World* (London: Penguin, 1977), pp. 244–246.

It was time to call the whole thing off and bring the soldiers home.

Seeking to counter such sentiments, especially the Russian contention that the war was not worth

continuing, the idealistic U.S. president, Woodrow Wilson (1856–1924), insisted on the great potential significance of an Allied victory. First in his State of the Union speech of January 1918, and in several declarations thereafter, Wilson developed the "Fourteen Points" that he proposed should guide the new international order. (See the box, "A Meaning to the War: Wilson's Fourteen Points.") Notable among them were open diplomacy, free trade, reduced armaments, self-determination, a league of nations, and a recasting of the colonial system, recognizing that the indigenous populations had rights equal to those of the colonizers.

Lenin and Wilson, then, offered radically different interpretations of the war, with radically different implications for present priorities. Yet they had something in common compared to the old diplomacy. Together, they seemed to represent a whole new approach to international relations—and the possibility of a more peaceful world. Thus, they found an eager audience among the war-weary peoples of Europe.

Despite the unforeseen strains of the war, Sacred Union in France did not weaken substantially until April 1917, with General Nivelle's disastrous offensive. But then, as near-mutiny began to develop within the army, rank-and-file pressures forced Socialist leaders to demand clarification, then revision, of French war aims. Suddenly French government leaders found themselves under considerable pressure to endorse the notion that the war had idealistic and democratic purposes. Growing doubts about the government's goals threatened to turn into active opposition to the war.

The same pressures were at work in Germany, where antiwar sentiment grew within the Social Democratic party (SPD), finally leading the antiwar faction to split off and form the Independent Socialist party (USPD) in April 1917. A large-scale debate on war aims, linked to considerations of domestic political reform, developed in the Reichstag by the summer of 1917, culminating in the Reichstag war aims resolution of July 19. Affirming that Germany's purposes were solely defensive, the measure passed by a solid 60 percent majority. Germany too seemed open to a white peace.

But just as the dramatic events of 1917 interjected important new pressures for moderation and peace, pressures in the opposite direction also mounted as the war dragged on. The old European order seemed to have changed irrevocably; this war might prove only the beginning of a new era of intense international competition, in which the old rules would no longer apply. War aims grew more grandiose as it began to seem that this

WORLD WAR I AND ITS AFTERMATH	
August 1914	Fighting begins
September 1914	French forces hold off the German assault at the Marne
August–September 1914	German victories over the Russians in the Battles of Tannenberg and Masurian Lakes
May 1915	Italy declares war on Austria-Hungary
February–December 1916	Battle of Verdun
May 1916	Naval Battle of Jutland
July–November 1916	Battle of the Somme
January 1917	Germans resume unrestricted submarine warfare
March 1917	First Russian revolution: fall of the tsar
April 1917	U.S. declaration of war
July 1917	German Reichstag war-aims resolution
November 1917	Second Russian revolution: the Bolsheviks take power
March 1918	Treaty of Brest-Litovsk between Germany and Russia
March–July 1918	Germany's last western offensive
July 1918	Second Battle of the Marne
July–November 1918	French-led counter-offensive
November 1918	Armistice: fighting ends
January 1919	Peace congress convenes at Paris
June 1919	Victors impose Treaty of Versailles on Germany

war offered a precious opportunity to secure advantages for the more contentious world that would follow, and that would surely entail further war before long.

A Meaning to the War: Wilson's Fourteen Points

After the United States entered the war in April 1917, President Woodrow Wilson sought to play down conventional national interests and to emphasize wider, more idealistic purposes. His key statement proved to be his 1918 State of the Union address, during which he offered his famous Fourteen Points.

It will be our wish and purpose that the processes of peace, when they are begun, shall be absolutely open and that they shall involve and permit henceforth no secret understandings of any kind. The day of conquest and aggrandizement is gone by; so is also the day of secret covenants entered into in the interest of particular governments and likely at some unlooked-for moment to upset the peace of the world. . . .

. . . What we demand in this war, therefore, is nothing peculiar to ourselves. It is that the world be made fit and safe to live in; and particularly that it be made safe for every peace-loving nation which, like our own, wishes to live its own life, determine its own institutions, be assured of justice and fair dealing by the other peoples of the world as against force and selfish aggression. All the peoples of the world are in effect partners in this interest; and for our own part we see very clearly that unless justice be done to others it will not be done to us. The program of the world's peace, therefore, is our program; and that program, the only possible program, as we see it, is this:

I. Open covenants of peace, openly arrived at, after which there shall be no private international understandings of any kind but diplomacy shall proceed always frankly and in public view. . . .

IV. Adequate guarantees given and taken that national armaments will be reduced to the lowest point consistent with domestic safety.

V. A free, open-minded, and absolutely impartial adjustment of all colonial claims, based upon a strict observance of the principle that in determining all such questions of sovereignty the interests of the populations concerned must have equal weight with the equitable claims of the government whose title is to be determined. . . .

XII. The Turkish portions of the present Ottoman Empire should be assured a secure sovereignty, but the other nationalities which are now under Turkish rule should be assured an undoubted security of life and an absolutely unmolested opportunity of autonomous development. . . .

XIII. An independent Polish state should be erected which should include the territories inhabited by indisputably Polish populations, which should be assured a free and secure access to the sea, and whose political and economic independence and territorial integrity should be guaranteed by international covenant.

XIV. A general association of nations must be formed under specific covenants for the purpose of affording mutual guarantees of political independence and territorial integrity to great and small states alike. . . .

Source: The Public Papers of Woodrow Wilson, V. War and Peace: Presidential Messages, Addresses, and Public Papers (1917–1924) (New York: Harper & Brothers, 1927; New York: Kraus Reprint, 1970), vol. 1, pp. 158–161.

The shape of the present war convinced top German officials that Germany's geography and dependence on imports made it especially vulnerable in a long war. The purpose of the war for Germany increasingly seemed the conquest of the means to fight the next war on a more favorable footing. Responding in February 1918 to calls for a white peace, General Ludendorff stressed that "if Germany makes peace without profit, it has lost the war." Germany, insisted Ludendorff, must win the military and economic basis for future security—to "enable us to contemplate confidently some future defensive war."[7]

Many in German government circles felt that Germany had to win control of the Belgian coast to achieve the parity with Britain necessary for peace. German security seemed to require a more favorable situation in eastern Europe as well, including control over Russian Poland and over Lithuania and Courland (western Latvia) on the Baltic Sea.

When, in response to the Russian request for an armistice, Germany was able to establish the terms of peace with Russia, it became clear how radically annexationist Germany's war aims had become. The outcome of negotiations at Brest-Litovsk early in 1918 was a dictated peace that Russia finally had no choice but to accept. Germany was to annex 27 percent of Russia's European territory, including the agriculturally valuable Ukraine, 40 percent of its population, and 75 percent of its iron and coal. All the German Reichstag parties, except the Socialists, accepted the terms of the treaty, which, in fact, produced a new wave of enthusiasm for a victorious peace after the disillusionment that had led to the Reichstag war aims resolution of July 1917.

France, less vulnerable geographically than Germany, tended to be more modest. But news of the terms the Germans had imposed at Brest-Litovsk inflamed the French, supporting the notion that France must push on to definitive victory in order to secure substantial advantages against an ongoing German menace.

The Renewal of the French War Effort

The domestic division in France that followed the failure of Nivelle's offensive reached its peak during the fall of 1917. In November, with pressures for a white peace intensifying and France's ability to continue fighting in doubt, President Raymond Poincaré called on Georges Clemenceau (1841–1929) to lead a new government. The 76-year-old Clemenceau was already known as a "hawk"; his appointment portended a stepped-up prosecution of the war, using whatever measures were necessary to achieve a decisive victory. And his message was simple as he appeared before the Chamber of Deputies on November 20, 1917: "If you ask me about my war aims, I reply: my aim is to be victorious." For the remainder of the war, France

was under the virtual dictatorship of Clemenceau and his cabinet.

Clemenceau moved decisively on both the domestic and military levels. By cracking down on the antiwar movement—imprisoning antiwar leaders, suppressing defeatist newspapers—he produced an undeniable stiffening of morale. Choosing a new commander of all Allied forces in the west, Clemenceau bypassed Pétain and picked General Ferdinand Foch (1851–1929). From Clemenceau's perspective, Pétain was too passive, even defeatist. After some initial friction, Clemenceau let Foch have his way on the military level, and the two proved an effective leadership combination.

The German Gamble, 1918

As the campaign of 1918 began, Germany seemed in a relatively favorable military position: Russia had been knocked out at last, and American troops were yet to arrive. Moderates in Germany wanted to take advantage of the situation to work out a compromise peace while there was still a chance. But the military leadership persuaded Emperor William II that Germany could still win a definitive victory on the western front if it struck quickly, before U.S. help became significant. Germany would be out of reserves by summer, so the alternative to decisive victory in the west would be total German defeat.

The German gamble almost succeeded. From March to June 1918, German forces seized the initiative with four months of sustained and effective attacks. By May 30 they had again reached the Marne, where they had been held in 1914, and again Paris, only 37 miles away, had to be evacuated (see Map 25.2). Even as late as mid-July, Ludendorff remained confident of victory, but by mid-August it was becoming clear that Germany lacked the manpower to exploit the successes of the first several months of 1918.

Those successes had caused mutual suspicion between the French and the British at first, but under Foch's leadership the Western allies eventually managed fuller and more effective coordination. By mid-1918 American involvement was also becoming a factor. On June 4, over a year after the U.S. declaration of war, American troops went into action for the first time, bolstering French forces along the Marne. Even this was a small operation, in which the Americans' performance was amateurish when compared to that of their battle-seasoned allies. But as the Allied counterattack proceeded, 250,000 U.S. troops were arriving per month, considerably boosting Allied morale and battlefield strength.

Germany lost the initiative for good during the second Battle of the Marne, which began on July 15 with yet another German attack. Foch commenced a sustained counterattack on July 18, using tanks to good advantage, and never lost the initiative thereafter. By early August the whole western front began to roll back. With astonishing suddenness, the outcome was no longer in doubt, although most expected the war to drag on into 1919. Few realized how desperate Germany's situation had become.

Military Defeat and Political Change in Germany

By late September it was clear to Ludendorff that his armies could not stop the Allied advance, so he informed the government on September 29 that to avoid invasion, Germany had to seek an immediate armistice. Hoping to secure favorable peace terms and to make the parliamentary politicians take responsibility for the defeat, Hindenburg and Ludendorff asked that a government based on greater popular support be formed. A leading moderate, Prince Max von Baden (1867–1929), became chancellor, and the Reichstag again became significant after its eclipse during the virtual dictatorship of the military. Prince Max promptly replaced Ludendorff with General Wilhelm Groener (1867–1939), who seemed more democratic in orientation. By now it was clear that ending the war could not be separated from the push for political change in Germany.

After securing a written request for an armistice from Hindenburg, Prince Max sent a peace note to President Wilson early in October, asking for an armistice based on Wilson's Fourteen Points. During the month that followed, Prince Max engineered a series of measures, passed by the Reichstag and approved by the emperor, that reformed the constitution, abolishing the three-class voting system in Prussia and making the chancellor responsible to the Reichstag. At last Germany had a constitutional monarchy. But President Wilson encouraged speculation that Germany could expect better peace terms if William II

were to abdicate and Germany were to become a republic. If the emperor, and even the monarchy itself, could not survive, was Germany to become a parliamentary democracy on the Western model, or was there to be more radical change, perhaps inspired by the Russian example?

A radical outcome seemed a real possibility during late 1918 and early 1919. As negotiations for an armistice proceeded in October, the continuing war effort produced instances of mutiny in the navy and breaches of discipline in the army. By early November workers' and soldiers' councils were being formed all over the country, just as in Russia the year before. In Munich, on November 7, antiwar socialists led an uprising of workers and soldiers that expelled the king of Bavaria and proclaimed a new Bavarian republic, which sought its own peace negotiations with the Allies. In Berlin on November 9, thousands of workers took to the streets to demand immediate peace, and the authorities could not muster enough reliable military force to move against them.

The senior army leadership grew concerned that the collapse of governmental authority would undermine the ability of army officers even to march their troops home. So Hindenburg and Groener persuaded the emperor to abdicate. Having lost the support of the army, William II accepted the inevitable and left for exile in the Netherlands.

With the German right, including the military, in disarray, and with even the centrist parties discredited by their support for what had become an annexationist war, the initiative passed to the socialists. They, at least, had been in the forefront of the movement for peace. But the socialists had divided in 1917, mostly over the question of response to the war. To many leftist socialists, the fact that the reformist mainstream of the SPD had supported the war for so long had discredited the party irrevocably. The most militant of these leftist socialists, led by Karl Liebknecht (1871–1919) and Rosa Luxemburg (1870–1919), envisioned using the workers' and soldiers' councils as the basis for a full-scale revolution, more or less on the Bolshevik model.

The SPD, on the other hand, clung to its reformist heritage and insisted on working within parliamentary institutions. A Bolshevik-style revolution was neither appropriate nor necessary under the circumstances Germany faced. Partly to head off the extreme left, SPD moderates proclaimed a parliamentary republic on November 9, just hours before the revolutionaries proclaimed a soviet-style republic. The next day the soldiers' and workers' councils in Berlin elected a provisional executive committee, to be led by the moderate socialist Friedrich Ebert (1871–1925). As the new republic sought to consolidate itself, the radical leftists continued to promote further revolution. So the end of the war meant for Germany a leap into an unfamiliar democratic republic, which had to establish itself in conditions not only of military defeat and economic hardship but also of incipient revolution on the extreme left.

Birth from military defeat was especially disabling for this new republic because the German people were so little prepared for the defeat when it came. The vigorous censorship had kept the public from any grasp of Germany's real situation as the war sped to conclusion. Thus the request for an armistice early in October came as a shock. At no time during the war had Germany been invaded from the west, and by mid-1918 the German army had seemed on the brink of victory. It appeared inconceivable that Germany had lost a military decision, plain and simple. Thus the "stab in the back" myth, the notion that political intrigue and revolution at home had undermined the German military effort, developed to explain what otherwise seemed an inexplicable defeat. This notion would prove a heavy burden for Germany's new democracy to bear.

THE OUTCOME AND THE IMPACT

After the armistice officially ended the fighting on November 11, 1918, those responsible for a formal peace settlement faced unprecedented challenges. The war's casualties included the Habsburg and Ottoman Empires, as well as the Hohenzollern and Romanov dynasties, so the peacemakers had to deal not just with defeated adversaries but with a changed political and territorial order in much of Europe and beyond. And the volatile sociopolitical situation in the wake of war and revolution inevitably colored their deliberations.

To make peace was to restore order, though necessarily on a new basis. But the disintegration of the old order had produced a sense of vulnerability hard to overcome. The number of casualties,

the advent of terrifying new weapons, the destruction of famous monuments—all gave the war an apocalyptic aura that heightened its psychological impact. After all that had happened since August 1914, it was not clear what a restoration of peace and order would require.

The Costs of War

Raw casualty figures do not begin to convey the war's human toll, but they afford some sense of the magnitude of the catastrophe that had befallen Europe and much of the world. Estimates differ, but it is generally agreed that from 10 to 13 million military men lost their lives, with another 20 million wounded. In addition, between 7 and 10 million civilians died as a result of the war and its hardships. In the defeated countries, especially, food shortages and the resulting malnutrition continued well after the end of the fighting. Adding to the devastation in 1918 was a pandemic of influenza that killed 20 million people worldwide.

Germany suffered the highest number of military casualties, but France suffered the most in proportional terms. Two million Germans were killed, with another 4 million wounded. Military deaths per capita for France were roughly 15 percent higher than for Germany—and twice as severe as for Britain. Of 8 million Frenchmen mobilized, over 5 million were killed or wounded. Roughly 1.5 million French soldiers, or 10 percent of the active male population, were killed—and this in a country already concerned about demographic decline. The other belligerents suffered less, but still in great numbers. Among the military personnel killed were 2 million Russians, 500,000 Italians, and 114,000 Americans.

Especially in light of all the assumptions about European superiority and progress, this unprecedented bloodletting deeply affected the European self-image. It was the worst loss of life Europe had suffered since the Black Death of the fourteenth century. Although World War II would be far more destructive, its psychological impact was in some ways less, for the illusions had been shattered by World War I. (See the feature, "Weighing the Evidence: The Poetry of World War I," on pages 954–955.)

Economic costs were heavy as well. In addition to the privations suffered during the years of war, Europeans found themselves reeling from inflation and saddled with debt, especially to the United States, once the war was over. Although the immediate transition to a peacetime economy did not prove as difficult as many had feared, the war and its aftermath produced an economic disequilibrium that lingered, helping to produce a worldwide depression by the end of the 1920s.

The Search for Peace in a Revolutionary Era

The war had begun because of an unmanageable nationality problem in Austria-Hungary, and it led not simply to military defeat for Austria-Hungary but to the breakup of the Habsburg system. Thus, in east-central Europe, the end of the war brought bright hopes for self-determination to peoples like the Czechs, Slovaks, Poles, Serbs, and Croats. Even before the peacemakers began deliberating in January 1919, some of these ethnic groups had begun creating a new order on their own. For example, a popular movement of Czechs and Slovaks established a Czechoslovak republic on October 29, 1918, and a new Yugoslavia and an independent Hungary similarly emerged from indigenous movements. Some of these new nations were amalgams of different ethnic groups that found cooperation advantageous now, but that might disagree in the future. Moreover, many of these countries lacked traditions of self-government, and they had reason to feud among themselves. With the Habsburg system no longer imposing one form of stability, a power vacuum seemed likely in this potentially volatile part of Europe.

The triumph of a revolutionary regime in Russia immeasurably complicated the situation, because in the unsettled conditions of the former Habsburg territories, as in Germany, the revolution seemed poised to spread in the wake of defeat—precisely according to the script the Russian revolutionaries were reading to the world. Still a precarious minority within Russia in 1918, the Bolsheviks continued to bank on immediate revolution elsewhere in Europe until 1920. Shortly after taking power, they had rechristened themselves "Communists," partly to jettison the provincial Russian term *bolshevik,* but especially to underline their departure from the old reformist socialists of the Second International. Communism meant revolution along Russian

lines. The Russian Communists influenced revolutionaries elsewhere both by force of example and by actively seeking to spread the revolution.

Outside Russia, the greatest communist success in the wake of the war was in Hungary, where a communist regime under Béla Kun (1885–1937) governed Budapest and other parts of the country from March to August 1919, before it was put down by Allied-sponsored forces from Romania. At about the same time, separatist communist republics lasted for months in the Slovak part of Czechoslovakia and in the important German state of Bavaria. Even in Italy, which had shared in the victory, Socialists infatuated with the Bolshevik example claimed that the labor unrest of 1919–1920 was the beginning of full-scale revolution.

Fears that the Russian Revolution might spread fueled foreign intervention in Russia beginning in June 1918, when 24,000 French and British troops entered the country. As long as the war with Germany lasted, military concerns helped justify this course, but after the armistice of November 1918, the intervention became overtly anticommunist. A series of thrusts, involving troops from fourteen countries at one time or another, struck at Russia from diverse points on its huge border. That effort aided the counterrevolutionary Whites, especially members of the old elites dispossessed by the Bolsheviks, who challenged the communist control of the Russian Empire in what became a brutal civil war during 1918–1920. There was never a coordinated strategy between the Whites and the foreign troops, but foreign intervention was intended to help topple the new regime and undercut its effort to export revolution.

The fourth of the major prewar regimes to disappear with defeat was the Turkish Ottoman Empire, which had controlled much of the Middle East in 1914. The Arab revolt against the Turks that developed in the Arabian peninsula in 1916 did not achieve its major military aims, though it endured, causing some disruption to the Turkish war effort. Its success was due partly to the collaboration of a young British officer, T. E. Lawrence (1888–1935), who proved an effective military leader and an impassioned advocate of the Arab cause. The support that Britain, especially, had offered the Arabs suggested that independence, perhaps even a single Arab kingdom, might follow from a defeat of the Ottoman Empire.

But British policy toward the Arabs was uncertain and contradictory. Concerned about the Suez Canal, the British government sought to tighten its control in Egypt by declaring it a protectorate in 1914, causing increased anti-British sentiment. The secret Sykes-Picot Agreement of May 1916, named for the British and French diplomats who negotiated it, projected a division of the Ottoman territories of the Middle East into colonial spheres of influence. France would control Syria and Lebanon, while Britain would rule Palestine and Mesopotamia, or present-day Iraq.

Potentially complicating the situation in the region was Zionism, the movement to win a Jewish state in Palestine. Led by Chaim Weizmann (1874–1952), a remarkable Russian-born British chemist, the Zionists reached an important milestone when British foreign secretary Arthur Balfour (1848–1930) cautiously announced, in the Balfour Declaration of November 1917, that the British government "looked with favor" on the prospect of a "Jewish home" in Palestine. At this point, British leaders sympathetic to Zionism saw no conflict in embracing the cause of the Arabs against the Ottoman Turks at the same time; indeed, Arabs and Jews, each seeking self-determination, could be expected to collaborate.

In the heat of war, the British, especially, established their policy for the former Ottoman territories of the Middle East without careful study. Thus, they made promises and agreements that were not entirely compatible. After the war, the victors' effort to install a new order in the Middle East would create fresh conflicts.

The Peace Settlement

The peace conference took place in Paris, beginning in January 1919. Its labors led to five separate treaties, with each of the five defeated states, known collectively as the Paris peace settlement. The first and most significant was the Treaty of Versailles with Germany, signed in the Hall of Mirrors of the Versailles Palace on June 28, 1919. But treaties were also worked out, in turn, with Austria, Bulgaria, Hungary, and finally Turkey, in August 1920.

This was to be a dictated, not a negotiated, peace. Germany and its allies were excluded, as was renegade Russia. The passions unleashed by the long war had dissolved the possibility of a more conciliatory outcome, a genuinely negotiated peace. Having won the war, France, Britain, the United States, and Italy were to call the shots on their own, with the future of Europe and much of the world in the balance. However, spokesmen for many groups—from Slovaks and Croats to Arabs, Jews, and pan-Africanists—were in Paris as well, seeking a hearing for their respective causes. For example, both the Arab Prince Faisal (1885–1933), who would later become king of Iraq, and Colonel T. E. Lawrence were there to plead for an independent Arab kingdom. (See the box, "Encounters with the West: Prince Faisal at the Peace Conference.") The African American leader W. E. B. DuBois (1898–1963), who took his Ph.D. at Harvard in 1895, led a major pan-African congress in Paris concurrently with the peace conference.

The fundamental challenge for the peacemakers was to reconcile the conflicting visions of the postwar world that had emerged by the end of the war. U.S. President Wilson represented the promise of a new order that could give this terrible war a lasting meaning. As he toured parts of Europe en route to the peace conference, Wilson was greeted as a hero. Clemenceau, in contrast, was a hard-liner concerned with French security and dismissive of the new diplomacy. Since becoming prime minister in 1917, he had stressed that only a permanent preponderance of French military power over Germany, and not some utopian league of nations, could guarantee a lasting peace. The negotiations at Paris centered on this fundamental difference between Wilson and Clemenceau. Although Britain's Lloyd George took a hard line on certain issues, he also sought to mediate, helping engineer the somewhat awkward compromise that resulted. When, after the peace conference, he encountered criticism for the outcome, Lloyd George replied, "I think I did as well as might be expected, seated as I was between Jesus Christ and Napoleon Bonaparte."[8]

In Article 231 of the final treaty, the peacemakers sought to establish a moral basis for their treatment of Germany by assigning responsibility for the war to Germany and its allies. On this basis, the Germans would be made to pay reparations to reimburse the victors for the costs of the war. The determination to make Germany pay for what had become a fabulously expensive war was one of the factors militating against a compromise peace by 1917. Thus the peacemakers found it essential to fix a reparations responsibility, although the amount

∼ ENCOUNTERS WITH THE WEST ∼

Prince Faisal at the Peace Conference

With the war nearing its end in October 1918, British authorities, in line with provisions of the Sykes-Picot agreement, permitted Faisal ibn-Husayn (1885–1933) to set up a provisional Arab state, with its capital at Damascus. As head of a delegation from this area to the Paris Peace Conference, Faisal claimed to speak for all Arab Asia, but some in the Arabian peninsula challenged his claim. In the memorandum of January 1919 that follows, he outlined the Arab position, mixing pride and assertiveness with a recognition that the Arabs would continue to need the support and help of Western powers. After the peace was concluded, Faisal found himself caught up in British and French rivalries as he was installed as king first of Syria, then of Iraq, but his efforts were central to the eventual achievement of Arab independence in the Middle East.

We believe that our ideal of Arab unity in Asia is justified beyond need of argument. If argument is required, we would point to the general principles accepted by the Allies when the United States joined them, to our splendid past, to the tenacity with which our race has for 600 years resisted Turkish attempts to absorb us, and, in a lesser degree, to what we tried our best to do in this war as one of the Allies. . . .

The various provinces of Arab Asia—Syria, Irak, Jezireh, Hedjaz, Nejd, Yemen—are very different economically and socially, and it is impossible to constrain them into one frame of government.

We believe that Syria, an agricultural and industrial area thickly peopled with sedentary classes, is sufficiently advanced politically to manage her own internal affairs. We feel also that foreign technical advice and help will be a most valuable factor in our national growth. We are willing to pay for this help in cash; we cannot sacrifice for it any part of the freedom we have just won for ourselves by force of arms.

. . . The world wishes to exploit Mesopotamia rapidly, and we therefore believe that the system of government there will have to be buttressed by the men and material resources of a great foreign Power. We ask, however, that the Government be Arab, in principle and spirit, the selective rather than the elective

principle being necessarily followed in the neglected districts, until time makes the broader basis possible. . . .

In Palestine the enormous majority of the people are Arabs. The Jews are very close to the Arabs in blood, and there is no conflict of character between the two races. In principles we are absolutely at one. Nevertheless, the Arabs cannot risk assuming the responsibility of holding level the scales in the clash of races and religions that have, in this one province, so often involved the world in difficulties. They would wish for the effective super-position of a great trustee, so long as a representative local administration commended itself by actively promoting the material prosperity of the country. . . .

In our opinion, if our independence be conceded and our local competence established, the natural influences of race, language, and interest will soon draw us together into one people; but for this the Great Powers will have to ensure us open internal frontiers, common railways and telegraphs, and uniform systems of education. To achieve this they must lay aside the thought of individual profits, and of their old jealousies. In a word, we ask you not to force your whole civilisation upon us, but to help us to pick out what serves us from your experience. In return we can offer you little but gratitude.

Source: J. C. Hurewitz, *Diplomacy in the Near and Middle East: A Documentary Record: 1914–1956* (Princeton, N.J.: D. Van Nostrand, 1956), vol. 2, pp. 38–39.

An Arab in Paris Prince Faisal (foreground) attended the Paris Peace Conference, where he lobbied for the creation of an independent Arab kingdom from part of the former Ottoman Turkish holdings in the Middle East. Among his supporters was the British Officer T. E. Lawrence (middle row, second from the right), on his way to legend as "Lawrence of Arabia." *(Trustees of the Imperial War Museum)*

that Germany was to pay was not established until 1921.

In addition, Germany was forced to dismantle much of its military apparatus. For example, the army was to be limited to 100,000 men, all of whom would be volunteers. The treaty severely restricted the size of the German navy as well, and Germany was forbidden to manufacture or possess military aircraft, submarines, tanks, heavy artillery, or poison gas.

France took back Alsace and Lorraine, the provinces it had lost to Germany in 1871 (Map 25.3). But for France, the crucial security provision of the 1919 peace settlement was the treatment of the adjacent Rhineland section of Germany itself. For fifteen years Allied troops were to occupy the west bank of the Rhine River in Germany—the usual military occupation of a defeated adversary. But this would only be temporary. The long-term advantage for France was to be the permanent demilitarization of all German territory west of the Rhine and a strip of 50 kilometers along its east bank. Germany was to maintain no troops on this part of its own soil, so in the event of hostilities French forces could march unopposed into this economically vital area of Germany.

French interests also helped shape the settlement in east-central Europe. Wilsonian principles called for self-determination, but in this area of great ethnic complexity, ethnic differences were not readily sorted out geographically. Was it best to countenance proliferation and fragmentation of ethnic groups, or to foster consolidation in an effort to build larger states, which might have a better chance of maintaining their independence and succeeding economically?

Worrying little about the problematic principle of self-determination, the French approached the situation in east-central Europe in terms of their own strategic concerns. So that Germany would again face potential enemies from both east and west, the French envisioned building a network of allies starting with the new Poland, created from Polish territories formerly in the German, Russian, and Austro-Hungarian Empires. That network might come to include Czechoslovakia, Yugoslavia, and Romania as well. These states would be weak enough to remain under French influence but, taken together, strong enough to replace Russia as a force against Germany. Yet to maximize the strength of these countries often required combining more than one nationality grouping within

Boundaries of German, Russian, and
Austro-Hungarian empires in 1914
Areas lost by Austro-Hungarian Empire
Areas lost by Russian Empire
Areas lost by German Empire
Areas lost by Bulgaria
Areas lost by Ottoman Empire
Demilitarized Zones
Boundaries of 1926
Areas controlled under mandates from
the League of Nations, 1920

North
Sea

NORWAY
Oslo

SWEDEN

FINLAND

Helsinki

Stockholm

Tallinn

Leningrad
(St. Petersburg)

ESTONIA

Baltic Sea

GREAT
BRITAIN

DENMARK

Copenhagen

Riga LATVIA

Memel

LITHUANIA

Vilnius

RUSSIAN
EMPIRE
(Became Union of Soviet
Socialist Republics, 1922)

Volga

NETHERLANDS
Amsterdam

GERMANY

Danzig
POLISH
CORRIDOR

EAST
PRUSSIA

Brussels
BELGIUM

RUHR
Cologne

Berlin

POLAND

Warsaw

Ural

Paris
FRANCE
LORRAINE
ALSACE

LUX.

Weimar
Frankfurt

Elbe

Oder

Kiev

Seine

Rhine

Strasbourg

Prague

Vistula

GALICIA

Don

Dnieper

Geneva

Bern
SWITZ.

CZECHOSLOVAKIA

Locarno
Milan

S.
TYROL

Vienna
AUSTRIA

Budapest

Rhône

Po

Venice

HUNGARY

Trieste

BESSARABIA

Genoa
Rapallo

Zagreb
CROATIA

ROMANIA

Caspian
Sea

Corsica

ITALY

Belgrade

YUGOSLAVIA

Danube

Bucharest

Rome

MONTENEGRO
(To Yugoslavia 1921)

SERBIA

Black Sea

Batum

Naples

ALBANIA

BULGARIA
Sofia

Kars

Baku

Sardinia

GREECE

Istanbul
(Constantinople)

Ankara

TURKEY

Tabriz

Sicily

Athens

Izmir
(Smyrna)

PERSIA
(IRAN)

Crete

Cyprus
(Gr. Br.)

Annexed
by Turkey
1939

Aleppo

SYRIA
(French Mandate)

Euphrates

Tigris

Baghdad

IRAQ
(MESOPOTAMIA)
(British Mandate)

Kut el Amara

TUNISIA
(French)

Mediterranean

Beirut

Damascus

PALESTINE
(British Mandate)
Jerusalem

Amman

TRANSJORDAN
(British Mandate)

Basra

KUWAIT
(Gr. Br.)

Sea

NEUTRAL
ZONES

LIBYA
(Italian)

Cairo

Suez Canal

EGYPT
(Independent 1922)

NEJD
(SAUDI ARABIA)

Riyadh

0   200   400 Km.

Nile

Red
Sea

Medina

0   200   400 Mi.

The Victors and the Peace In June 1919 the leaders of the major victorious powers exude confidence after signing with Germany the Treaty of Versailles, the most important of the five treaties that resulted from the Paris Peace Conference. From the left are David Lloyd George of Britain, Georges Clemenceau of France, and Woodrow Wilson of the United States. *(Corbis-Bettmann)*

them; some of those national groups were more numerous and advantaged than others.

The new Czechoslovakia was not only an amalgam of Czechs and Slovaks but also included numerous Germans and Magyars. Indeed, Germans, mostly from the old Bohemia, made up 22 percent of the population of Czechoslovakia. Yugoslavia was even more complex, encompassing not only Serbs and Croats, but also Slovenes, Macedonians, Albanians, and other minorities.

Map 25.3 The Impact of the War: The Territorial Settlement in Europe and the Middle East The defeat of Russia, Austria-Hungary, Germany, and Ottoman Turkey opened the way to major changes in the map of east-central Europe and the Middle East. A number of new nations emerged in east-central Europe, while in the Arab world the end of Ottoman rule meant not independence but new roles for European powers.

But French policymakers were so determined to foster a strong Czechoslovakia and Yugoslavia that they ordered the French police to force the spokesmen for Slovak and Croat separatism to leave Paris as the conference deliberated.

Partly as a result of French priorities, Poland, Czechoslovakia, Yugoslavia, and Romania ended up as large as possible, either by the fusion of ethnic groups or by the incorporation of minorities that, on ethnic grounds, belonged with neighboring states. Austria, Hungary, and Bulgaria, on the other hand, found themselves diminished (Map 25.4). What remained of Austria, the German part of the old Habsburg empire, was prohibited from choosing to join Germany, an obvious violation of the Wilsonian principle of self-determination.

Concern to contain and weaken communist Russia was also at work in the settlement in east-central Europe. A band of states in east-central

Map 25.4 Ethnicity in East-Central Europe, 1919
Ethnic diversity made it hard to create homogeneous
nation-states in east-central Europe. The new states that
emerged after World War I mixed ethnic groups, and
ethnic tensions would contribute to future problems.

Europe, led by France, could serve not only as a
check to Germany but also as a shield against the
Russian threat. Romania's aggrandizement came
partly at the expense of the Russian Empire, as did
the creation of the new Poland. Finland, Latvia,
Estonia, and Lithuania, all part of the Russian Empire for over a century, now became independent
states (see Map 25.3).

    The overall territorial settlement cost Ger-
many almost 15 percent of its prewar territory, including major iron- and coal-producing regions,
as well as about 10 percent of its prewar population. But the great bitterness that developed in

Germany over the terms of the peace stemmed
above all from a sense of betrayal. In requesting an
armistice, German authorities had appealed to
Wilson, whose emphasis had not been on war
guilt and reparations. He seemed to be saying that
the whole prewar international system, not one
side or the other, had been to blame for the current conflict. In 1919, however, the peacemakers
treated Germany as the guilty party, so for Germans the terms of the peace greatly intensified the
sting of defeat.

    Wilson had been forced to compromise with
French interests in dealing with east-central Europe, but he achieved a potentially significant success in exchange—the establishment of a League
of Nations, embodying the widespread hope for a
new international order. According to the League
covenant worked out by April, disputes among
member states were no longer to be settled by war
but by mechanisms established by the League.
Other members were to participate in sanctions,
from economic blockade to military action, against
a member that went to war in violation of League
provisions.

    How could Wilsonian hopes for a new inter-
national order be squared with the imperialist system, which seemed utterly at odds with the ideal
of self-determination? As Mohammed Ali Duse
had anticipated in 1914, the war had sown the
seeds of dramatic change in those areas of the
world subject to European colonial rule. Elites
among the colonial peoples tended to support the
war efforts of their imperial rulers, but often in the
hope of winning greater autonomy or even independence. The Indian leader Mohandas Gandhi
(1869–1948), who had been educated in the West
and admitted to the English bar in 1889, actively
supported the British war effort, even helping recruit Indians to fight on the British side. But his
aim was to speed Indian independence, and he led
demonstrations that embarrassed the British during the war. (See the box, "Encounters with the
West: Gandhi on Nonviolence," on page 1001.) And
though most educated Indians, after over a century of British rule and Western influence, rallied
to the British side, the war unleashed expectations
and demands that led the British, in 1917, to
promise home rule for India.

    Colonial peoples participated directly in the
war on both sides. In sub-Saharan Africa, for example, German-led Africans fought—and fought

well—against Africans under British or French command. France brought colonial subjects from West and North Africa into front-line service during the war. But this experience expanded political consciousness—and raised expectations—among the peoples subject to European imperialism.

Duse's *African Times and Orient Review* found reason for optimism in March 1917: "[A] Franco-British success will mean a greater freedom of the peoples we represent than they have previously experienced. The once despised black man is coming to the front in the battle for freedom, and the freedom which he helps to win for the white man, must also be meted out to him when the day of reckoning arrives. In helping the British Empire and the French Republic in the hour of need you are helping yourselves to a freedom that cannot be denied to you."[9] The same line of thinking led China and Siam (now Thailand) to associate with the Allied side in 1917, in an effort to win international stature and thereby eventually to regain their lost sovereignty. China sent 200,000 people to work in France to help ease France's wartime labor shortage.

At the peace conference, spokesmen for the non-Western world tended to be moderate in their demands. Even DuBois, who was often more radical, called simply for colonial peoples to be given a voice in colonial governments. And the victors, prodded by Wilson, made some concessions.

German colonies and Ottoman territories were not simply taken over by the victors, in the old-fashioned way, but fell under the authority of the League, which then assigned them as mandates to one of the victorious powers, which was to report back to the League annually. There were various classes of mandates, based on how prepared for sovereignty the area was taken to be. In devising this system, the Western powers formally recognized for the first time that non-Western peoples under Western influence had rights and interests of their own and that, in principle, they were progressing toward independence.

Still, the mandate approach to the colonial question was a halting departure at best. Although Britain granted considerable sovereignty to Iraq in 1932, the victorious powers generally operated as before, assimilating the new territories into their existing systems of colonial possessions. After the hopes raised in the Arab world during the war, this outcome produced a sense of betrayal among Arab leaders, who had expected complete independence. Continuing Arab unrest provoked, most notably, a revolt against the French presence in Syria, put down only at heavy expense to the French during the mid-1920s.

The Chinese felt similarly betrayed. Despite China's contribution to the Allied war effort, the victors acquiesced in special rights for Japan in China, causing a renewed sense of humiliation among Chinese elites and provoking a wave of popular demonstrations and a boycott of Japanese goods. In this instance, Western leaders were allowing a non-Western power, Japan, access to the imperial club, but they were hardly departing from imperialism. For Chinese, Arabs, and others, the West appeared hypocritical. Those whose political consciousness had been raised by the war came to believe not only that colonialism should end, but that the colonial peoples would themselves have to take the lead in ending it.

The incongruities of the postwar settlement prompted Marshal Foch to proclaim, "This is not peace. It is an armistice for twenty years."[10] The most basic question was whether the three principal victors had the resolve, and the capacity, to preserve the new order they had solidified at Paris. Debate over the American role promptly developed in the United States as President Wilson sought Senate ratification of the peace treaty, which entailed U.S. membership in the League of Nations as well as commitments to France and Britain. Wilson's opponents worried especially that League membership would compromise U.S. sovereignty. Although it was not clear, at this point, how significant the departure from the old international system was to be, other nations proved more willing to ratify the treaty and join the League. U.S. reluctance stemmed especially from the isolationist backlash that developed as Americans increasingly questioned whether the United States had been wise to become involved, for the first time, in a war in Europe. Late in 1919, at the height of the debate, Wilson suffered a disabling stroke. The Senate then refused to ratify the peace treaty, thereby keeping the United States out of the League of Nations. By 1920 the United States seemed to be pulling back from the leadership role it had been poised to play in 1918.

American hesitation stemmed partly from the doubts about the wisdom of the peace settlement that quickly developed in both Britain and the United States. During the peace conference, a member of the British delegation, the economist

Beckmann: The Night In this painting from 1918–1919, the German expressionist Max Beckmann (1884–1950) drew on medieval art and a complex personal symbolism to convey the violence, insecurity, and hardship that surrounded Germany's defeat in 1918. *(Kunstsammlung Nordrhein-Westfalen)*

John Maynard Keynes (1883–1946), resigned to write *The Economic Consequences of the Peace* (1920), which helped undermine confidence in the whole settlement. Keynes charged that the shortsighted, vindictive policy of the French, by crippling Germany with a punishing reparations burden, threatened the European economy and thus the peace of Europe over the long term. For some, then, the challenge was not to enforce the Versailles treaty but to revise it. This lack of consensus about the legitimacy of the peace made it especially hard to predict what the longer-term outcome of the war would be.

SUMMARY

By destroying the Habsburg empire and the imperial regime in Germany, World War I seemed to

have solved the immediate problems that caused it. More generally, the war accelerated processes, involving everything from technological development to women's suffrage, that many deemed progressive.

Yet the war also produced new tensions and revealed possibilities that seemed considerably less benign. Despite all the hopes for a peaceful new order, the novel forms of warfare introduced during World War I portended a dangerous and even terrifying new era. A generation later, to be sure, the advent of the nuclear age occasioned a measure of terror hardly imaginable earlier, but the experience of World War I was the turning point, the end of an earlier innocence. Thanks to modern technology, which had been central to the West's confident belief in progress, Europeans had now experienced machine-gun fire, poison gas attacks, and the terror-bombing of civilians from airplanes.

The war touched virtually everyone, but it marked for life those who knew the nightmarish experience of the trenches. At first, traditional notions of glory, heroism, and patriotic duty combined with images of fellowship and regeneration to enable the soldiers to make a certain sense of their wartime experience. But as the war dragged on, such sentiments gradually eroded, giving way to resignation and cynicism. (See the feature, "Weighing the Evidence: The Poetry of World War I," on pages 954–955.)

After the war was over, many of those who had fought it felt a sense of ironic betrayal; their prewar upbringing, the values and assumptions they had inherited, had not equipped them to make sense of what they had lived through. But the quest for meaning continued, and beginning in the late 1920s a wave of writings about the war appeared. Many were memoirs, such as *Goodbye to All That* by the English writer Robert Graves (1895–1985) and *Testament of Youth* by Vera Brittain (1893–1970), who had served as a British army nurse at the front. The most famous exploration of the war was the antiwar novel *All Quiet on the Western Front* (1929) by German writer Erich Maria Remarque (1898–1970), which sold 2.5 million copies in twenty-five languages in its first eighteen months in print.

Although Remarque had seen front-line action, his novel said more about the growing feeling of disillusionment after the war than it did about the actual experience of those in the trenches. By the end of the 1920s an element of myth-making was creeping into these efforts to give meaning to the war experience. Still, there was something undeniably genuine in the laments of loss of innocence, in the sense of belonging to a "lost generation," that marked much of this writing. Not only were many friends dead or maimed for life, but all the sacrifices seemed to have been largely in vain, a sentiment that fueled determination to avoid another war in the future.

What followed from the war, most fundamentally, was a new sense that Western civilization was neither as secure nor as superior as it had seemed. The celebrated French poet Paul Valéry (1871–1945), speaking at Oxford shortly after the war, observed that "we modern civilizations have learned to recognize that we are mortal like the others. We had heard . . . of whole worlds vanished, of empires foundered. . . . Elam, Nineveh, Babylon were vague and splendid names; the total ruin of these worlds, for us, meant as little as did their existence. But France, England, Russia . . . these names, too, are splendid. . . . And now we see that the abyss of history is deep enough to bury all the world. We feel that a civilization is as fragile as a life."[11] Valéry went on to warn that the coming transition to peace would be even more difficult and disorienting than the war itself. So traumatic might be the convulsion that Europe might lose its leadership and be shown up for what it was in fact—a pathetically small corner of the world, a mere cape on the Asiatic landmass. Astounding words for a European, yet even Valéry, for all his foresight, could not anticipate what Europe would go through in the decades to follow.

NOTES

1. From *African Times and Orient Review*, August 4, 1914; quoted in Imanuel Geiss, *The Pan-African Movement*, translated by Ann Keep (London: Methuen & Co., 1974), pp. 229–230.

2. Thus wrote the German poet Ivan Goll in 1917; quoted in Modris Eksteins, *Rites of Spring: The Great War and the Birth of the Modern Age* (Boston: Houghton Mifflin, 1989), p. 144.

3. The remarks of Raymond Joubert, as quoted in John Ellis, *Eye-Deep in Hell: Trench Warfare in World War I* (Baltimore: Johns Hopkins University Press, 1989), p. 104.

4. Brian Bond, *War and Society in Europe, 1870–1970* (New York: Oxford University Press, 1986), p. 114.

5. By A. N. Potresov, as quoted in Richard Pipes, *The Russian Revolution* (New York: Random House, Vintage, 1991), p. 348.

6. Both statements are quoted in Koppel S. Pinson, *Modern Germany: Its History and Civilization*, 2d ed. (New York: Macmillan, 1966), p. 337.

7. Quoted in Arno J. Mayer, *Political Origins of the New Diplomacy, 1917–18* (New York: Random House, Vintage, 1970), p. 135.

8. Quoted in Walter Arnstein, *Britain Yesterday and Today: 1830 to the Present*, 6th ed. (Lexington, Mass.: D. C. Heath, 1992), p. 266.

9. Unsigned editorial, *African Times and Orient Review*, March 1917; quoted in Geiss, *The Pan-African Movement*, p. 479, n. 2.

10. Quoted in P. M. H. Bell, *The Origins of the Second World War* (London and New York: Longman, 1986), p. 14.

11. Paul Valéry, *Variety*, 1st series (New York: Harcourt, Brace, 1938), pp. 3–4.

SUGGESTED READING

General Surveys

Ferro, Marc. *The Great War, 1914–1918.* 1973. Combines a narrative of events with a feel for the war experience, based on the expectations and perceptions of those involved.

King, Jere Clemens, ed. *The First World War.* 1972. A superior documentary history, with selections on an array of topics, from military operations to trench life, from diplomacy and peacemaking to the role of women in the war.

Robbins, Keith. *The First World War.* 1985. An accessible, balanced, and comprehensive treatment, covering everything from military operations to the domestic impact of the war.

Winter, J. M. *The Experience of World War I.* 1989. An ideal introductory work that proceeds via concentric circles from politicians to generals to soldiers to civilians, then to the war's longer-term effects.

Fighting the War

Ellis, John. *Eye-Deep in Hell: Trench Warfare in World War I.* 1989. A compelling account of life and death in the trenches, covering topics from trench construction to eating, drinking, and sex. Includes striking photographs.

Hough, Richard. *The Great War at Sea, 1914–1918.* 1983. A survey of naval operations, featuring the British navy. Includes photographs.

Kennett, Lee. *The First Air War, 1914–1918.* 1991. A vivid account of the new flying machines, those who flew them, and their diverse wartime roles, from reconnaissance to combat.

Leed, Eric J. *No Man's Land: Combat and Identity in World War I.* 1979. A pioneering study of the experience of World War I, exploring its challenge to masculine identity.

War and Society

Becker, Jean-Jacques. *The Great War and the French People.* 1985. Landmark study of the relationship between battlefield fortunes and wider public responses as France bore the brunt of the fighting during World War I.

Bond, Brian. *War and Society in Europe, 1870–1970.* 1986. Lucid, well-balanced survey of the relationship between war and society, with particular attention to the two world wars.

Brayborn, Gail, and Penny Summerfield. *Out of the Cage: Women's Experiences in Two World Wars.* 1987. Comparative study of the impact of the two world wars on women, relying especially on direct testimony. Considers not only the workplace but also everyday experience, from home life and health to courtship and marriage.

Higonnet, Margaret Randolph, et al., eds. *Behind the Lines: Gender and the Two World Wars.* 1987. Varied essays on the role of women during the two world wars, concerned especially with the impact of war on gender definition.

Horne, John N. *Labour at War: France and Britain, 1914–1918.* 1991. A sophisticated study exploring the impact of wartime challenges on the evolution of the organized labor movement, with a useful comparative dimension.

Kocka, Jürgen. *Facing Total War: German Society, 1914–1918.* 1984. Using concepts of class and monopoly capitalism in a flexible way, a leading German historian analyzes the impact of the war on German society.

Marwick, Arthur. *The Deluge: British Society and the First World War.* 1970. A lively account by a leading British social historian, conveying what it was like to live in Britain during the war and tracing the enduring impact of wartime social changes.

Winter, Jay, and Jean-Louis Robert, eds. *Capital Cities at War: Paris, London, and Berlin, 1914–1919.* 1997. Assessing the war's impact on the lives of ordinary city dwellers, this collection of scholarly essays ranges from purchasing power to food supply to public health. Concludes with an effective synthesis by the editors.

The Russian Revolution

Fitzpatrick, Sheila. *The Russian Revolution, 1917–1932,* 2d ed. 1994. An ideal introductory work that places the events of 1917 in the sweep of Russian history.

Pipes, Richard. *The Russian Revolution.* 1991. A detailed, comprehensive study, critical of the Bolshevik takeover as a mere coup, as opposed to a genuinely revolutionary transformation. Argues that a tendency toward terror followed from the nature of the revolution itself.

Service, Robert. *Lenin: A Political Life,* 3 vols. 1985, 1991, 1995. Landmark, readable biography that does justice both to Lenin's ruthlessness and to the visionary purpose that made him one of the decisive actors of the twentieth century. The third volume, covering the years from 1918 until Lenin's death in 1924, takes advantage of newly available Russian sources.

Ulam, Adam B. *The Bolsheviks: The Intellectual, Personal and Political History of the Triumph of Communism in Russia.* 1968. Well-known study focusing on Lenin and his central role in shaping the strategy that brought the Bolsheviks to power.

Von Laue, Theodore H. *Why Lenin? Why Stalin? Why Gorbachev? The Rise and Fall of the Soviet System,* 3d ed. 1993. A widely used survey. Accents the larger context of international preoccupations and power relations that helped shape the revolution and the system that developed from it.

War Aims, Diplomacy, and Peacemaking

Fromkin, David. *A Peace to End All Peace: The Fall of the Ottoman Empire and the Creation of the Modern Middle East.* 1989. Detailed but gripping account of the role of the war and the peace process in transforming the lands of the Ottoman Empire.

Mayer, Arno J. *The Politics and Diplomacy of Peacemaking: Containment and Counterrevolution at Versailles, 1918–1919.* 1967. Emphasizes the impact of domestic political concerns and fears of spreading revolution on thinking about the end of the war and the aims of the peace.

———. *Political Origins of the New Diplomacy, 1917–18.* 1970; first pub. 1959. Influential account of the war-aims debate; analyzes the competing efforts of Wilson and Lenin to redefine the meaning of the war.

Nicolson, Harold. *Peacemaking 1919.* 1965. A classic account, critical of the treaty, by a junior member of the British delegation.

Rowland, Peter. *David Lloyd George: A Biography.* 1975. Lively, balanced—one of the best one-volume treatments of Lloyd George, including his role as a wartime leader and a major architect of the peace.

Sharp, Alan. *The Versailles Settlement: Peacemaking in Paris, 1919.* 1991. A brief, clear, and balanced overview that seeks to do justice to the magnitude of the task the peacemakers faced.

Memory and Cultural Impact

Eksteins, Modris. *Rites of Spring: The Great War and the Birth of the Modern Age.* 1989. Original and provocative exploration of the relationship between culture and the war experience. Good on the difference between the actual experience of the war and the memory fabricated after the fact.

Ellis, John. *The Social History of the Machine Gun.* 1986. A pioneering exploration of the wider impact of the new technologies that came of age during World War I.

Fussell, Paul. *The Great War and Modern Memory.* 1975. Widely admired study of the attempts to forge the new language, through literature, necessary to make sense of the British war experience.

Hanna, Martha. *The Mobilization of Intellect: French Scholars and Writers During the Great War.* 1996. Challenges the widespread notion that World War I galvanized a unified assault of French intellectuals against German culture. Traces the ongoing divisions in the French intellectual community during the war.

Mosse, George L. *Fallen Soldiers: Reshaping the Memory of the World Wars.* 1990. Shows how the encounter with mass death in World War I led to new ways of sanctifying and justifying war.

Winter, J. R. *Sites of Memory, Sites of Mourning.* 1995. Using an effective comparative approach, a leading authority argues that Europeans relied on relatively traditional means of making sense of the bloodletting of World War I.

Wohl, Robert. *The Generation of 1914.* 1979. Probes the common features in the experience of educated young people in France, Britain, Germany, Italy, and Spain.

———. *A Passion for Wings: Aviation and the Western Imagination, 1908–1918.* 1994. Engaging, handsomely illustrated exploration of the cultural impact of flight in the context of the rapid technological change surrounding World War I.

THE POETRY OF WORLD WAR I

We don't normally think of poetry and war together, and World War I, with its unexpected brutality and hardship, may seem the least poetic of wars. Yet even during the war, soldiers like the Englishmen Rupert Brooke (1887–1915) and Wilfred Owen (1893–1918) sought to shape their experiences into poetic imagery. What does such poetry tell us about what the war meant to those who fought it? How has poetic testimony affected our understanding of the place of World War I in the Western experience?

In Brooke's wartime poetry what strikes us first is his gratitude that his generation had come of age at this dramatic historical moment:

Now, God be thanked Who has matched us with His
    hour,
    And caught our youth, and wakened us from sleep-
        ing

But why would a young man like Brooke welcome war? He seemed to envision release, deliverance— but from what?

ANTHEM FOR DOOMED YOUTH

What passing-bells for these who die as cattle?
    —Only the monstrous anger of the guns.
    Only the stuttering rifles' rapid rattle
Can patter out their hasty orisons.
No mockeries now for them; no prayers nor
    bells;
    Nor any voice of mourning save the choirs,—
The shrill, demented choirs of wailing shells;
    And bugles calling for them from sad shires.

What candles may be held to speed them all?
    Not in the hands of boys but in their eyes
Shall shine the holy glimmers of goodbyes.
    The pallor of girls' brows shall be their pall;
Their flowers the tenderness of patient minds,
And each slow dusk a drawing-down of blinds.
                                    Wilfred Owen

When the war broke out, Brooke promptly volunteered, even pulling strings to get into a combat unit. Seeing action for the first time, in Belgium in October 1914, he was excited by the intensity of battle and pleased by his own calm self-control. Back in England for further training shortly thereafter, he wrote several sonnets, including "Peace," the one reproduced here, expressing his feelings about the war. But he died of blood poisoning on the way to battle in April 1915—without ever fully experiencing trench warfare.

Although most of the young Englishmen who took up arms with such enthusiasm in 1914 assumed that their country was in the right, that Germany was at fault, they did not worry much about the purposes of the war or the larger historical impact it might have. Brooke understood that the war would not accomplish all that was claimed for it, but he was grateful for the personal experience it made possible. Somehow it meant "peace," as the title of his sonnet suggests, and even cleanliness:

To turn, as swimmers into cleanness leaping,
Glad from a world grown old and cold and weary

Brooke's sense of deliverance responded to personal frustrations, yet he spoke for others of his generation who also were finding it difficult to assume a place in adult society at that particular time. Though they came from educated, upper-middle-class families, they were contemptuous of the routines and compromises of the respectable, everyday world to which they were expected to adjust. Thus Brooke welcomed the chance to

Leave the sick hearts that honour could not move,
And half-men, and their dirty songs and dreary

Yet those of Brooke's generation were equally troubled by their own uncertainty about values and commitments—to marriage, career, a place in society. Thanks to the overwhelming, inescapable reality of the war, values that had seemed empty— honor, country, duty, fellowship—now seemed

PEACE

Now, God be thanked Who has matched us with His hour,
  And caught our youth, and wakened us from sleeping,
With hand made sure, clear eye, and sharpened power,
  To turn, as swimmers into cleanness leaping,
Glad from a world grown old and cold and weary,
  Leave the sick hearts that honour could not move,
And half-men, and their dirty songs and dreary,
  And all the little emptiness of love!

Oh! we, who have known shame, we have found release there,
  Where there's no ill, no grief, but sleep has mending,
    Naught broken save this body, lost but breath;
Nothing to shake the laughing heart's long peace there
  But only agony, and that has ending;
    And the worst friend and enemy is but Death.

Rupert Brooke

Rupert Brooke (1887–1915)
(Mansell/ Time Inc.)

meaningful after all. To his surprise and relief, Brooke found that he himself was capable of courage, commitment, and sacrifice. With its promise of cleanliness and renewal, the war was worth even its highest price, which was merely death.

Unlike Brooke, Wilfred Owen hated the war from the start. He was quickly struck by its sheer ugliness, as manifested in the landscape, the noise, the language of the soldiers themselves. Yet he served with distinction, was decorated for bravery, and was killed by machine-gun fire just one week before the armistice in November 1918.

Owen, then, experienced the reality of World War I in a way that Brooke did not. The sonnet here, "Anthem for Doomed Youth," was written during September and October 1917, after the war had come to entail a terrible bloodletting. Thus Owen sought to shape sentiments very different from Brooke's—a sense of waste, of loss, of incongruity between suffering endured and results achieved. Whereas Brooke had brushed aside the possibility of death, Owen saw death as relentless, carrying off a generation of innocent youth, dying like cattle.

In a sense, even the dignity of death had become a casualty of the war. Thus Owen mixed funeral images with the new horror that this war had brought forth: The only mourning was "The shrill, demented choirs of wailing shells." Mock-ing the ongoing effort to sweeten the reality of death at the front through reference to nobility and sacrifice, Owen drowned out his initial suggestion of bells with the new and awful sounds of machine-gun fire:

—Only the monstrous anger of the guns.
Only the stuttering rifles' rapid rattle

Quite apart from its military and political outcome, World War I has assumed a particular place in our collective memory, thanks partly to those like Brooke and Owen who managed to frame their wartime experiences in the memorable language of poetry. At first, Brooke's poetry helped to justify the alarming slaughter to those who began questioning the war's purpose as it claimed the lives of their sons. Yet by now we find it hard to grasp the ideals that inspired his poetic testimony, for they were in one sense consumed by the war and the era of violence that it began. We still live in the world that emerged from that war, so Owen, with his cynicism and sense of tragedy, is far more our contemporary. Brooke may still reveal for us something of the innocence that was lost, but it is especially through Owen's way of conveying the tragedy, the sense of betrayal and lost innocence, that World War I has continued to haunt the memory of Western civilization.

CHAPTER 26

The Illusion of Stability, 1919–1930

I n 1925 Josephine Baker (1906–1975), a black entertainer from St. Louis, moved from the chorus lines of New York to Paris, where she quickly became a singing and dancing sensation. Also a favorite in Germany, she was the most famous of the African American entertainers who took the cultural capitals of Europe by storm during the 1920s. After the disillusioning experience of war, many Europeans found a valuable infusion of vitality in Baker's jazz music, exotic costumes, and "savage," uninhibited dancing.

The attraction to African Americans as primitive and savage, vital and sensual, reflected a good deal of racial stereotyping, and black performers like Baker sometimes played to these stereotypes. But there really was something fresh and uninhibited about American culture, especially its African American variant. African American entertainers in Europe had great fun ironically subverting racial stereotypes even as they played to them. And many realized they could enjoy opportunities in parts of Europe that were still denied them in the United States. Baker herself was a woman of great sophistication who became a French citizen in 1937, participated in progressive causes, and was decorated for her secret intelligence work in the anti-Nazi resistance during World War II.

The prominence of African Americans in European popular culture during the 1920s was part of a wider infatuation with things American as Europeans reached out to embrace the new. America was exciting because it seemed at once primitive and modern. Lacking the cultural baggage of Europe, Americans could help revitalize Europe and point the way to modernity at the same time. With so many old conventions shattered

Kees van Dongen,
Au cabaret nègre (detail).

The Sensational Josephine Baker A native of St. Louis, the African American Josephine Baker moved to Paris in 1925 and quickly created a sensation in both France and Germany as a cabaret dancer and singer. Playing on the European association of Africa with the wild and uninhibited, she featured unusual poses and exotic costumes. *(Hulton-Getty/Tony Stone Images)*

by the war, the ideal of being "modern" became widespread among Europeans, affecting everything from sex education to furniture design. "Modern" meant no-nonsense efficiency, mass production, and a vital popular culture, expressed in jazz, movies, sport, and even advertising.

Although the new infatuation with America made clear the depth of the change at work in European culture and society, Europeans themselves had pioneered modernism in many areas of the arts and sciences. During the 1920s, Paris held its own as an international cultural center, nurturing innovative artistic movements like surrealism, which drew on Freudian psychoanalysis, and hosting a decorative arts exhibition in 1925 that produced art deco, the sleek, "modernistic" style that helped

give the decade its distinctive flavor. And in the unsettled conditions of postwar Germany, Berlin emerged to rival Paris for cultural leadership during what Germans called "the Golden Twenties." Innovations ranged from avant-garde drama to a sophisticated cabaret scene with a prominent homosexual dimension.

But there was something dizzying, even unnerving, in the eager embrace of the new during the 1920s. Whereas many European cultural observers saw, in the vogue of black American entertainers like Josephine Baker, the revitalization needed to overcome European decadence and loss of confidence, others saw the African American influence as a symptom of that decadence. It could only undermine further the best of European civilization.

More generally, insecurity lurked beneath the quest for novelty and vitality during the 1920s. After the disruption of World War I, many wanted simply to return to normal. But so much had been changed in the crucible of war that the prewar European order was gone forever. And so attempts to find new bases of order, in everything from architecture to classical music to the international economy, were central to the decade.

Although the immediate disruptions of wartime carried over to 1923, a more hopeful era of relative prosperity and international conciliation followed, continuing until 1929. It seemed, briefly, that European civilization had managed to quell the disorder unleashed by the war. The new communist regime in the Soviet Union remained a potentially disruptive force, but it suspended its effort to lead a wider revolution. In Germany, where the new democracy got off to a rocky start, political stability seemed on its way by the later 1920s, as Germany gradually patched things up with the war's victors. Still, the victors' decreasing willingness to enforce the harsh and punitive peace, though helpful in one sense, could be destabilizing in another. And disillusionment at Western hypocrisy led colonial elites to question colonial rule more aggressively, which contributed, in turn, to serious if sporadic outbreaks of anticolonialist activity.

In Italy, the democracy that had emerged in the nineteenth century gave way to the first regime to call itself fascist, and some of the new democracies in east-central Europe did not survive the decade. Even in the more established democracies of Britain and France, tensions came close to the surface. When the Great Depression began at the end of the decade, serious sociopolitical strains became evident throughout most of the Western world. The restabilization of the 1920s proved only an illusion.

THE WEST AND THE WORLD AFTER THE GREAT WAR

Before 1914, the great powers had been the European powers, who had apportioned much of the non-Western world in imperial networks. But the war and the peace had weakened—and to some extent discredited—the belligerent countries of Europe, who now found themselves saddled with foreign debts and unbalanced economies. Though the United States had pulled back from a direct political role in Europe, it became far more active in world affairs, helping to engineer major conferences on arms limitation and international economic relations during the 1920s. But in crucial respects the shape of the postwar international order still depended on Europeans. Six European countries—Britain, France, the Netherlands, Belgium, Italy, and Portugal—had significant colonial possessions at a time when colonialism was under strain. And colonial concerns continued to affect the balance of power in Europe, where it fell to the two major victors in the war, France and Britain, to enforce the controversial peace settlement.

The Erosion of European Power

Emerging from the war as the principal power in East Asia was a non-Western country, Japan, whose claims to the German bases in the region and to special rights in China were formally recognized by the other victors at the Paris Peace Conference. With the Washington treaty of 1922, Japan won naval parity with Britain and the United States in the East Asian region. The Western nations were recognizing Japan as a peer, a great power—even a threat. Aspects of the Washington agreements were intended to block Japanese expansion in East Asia. If a new international system was to emerge, it would not be centered in Europe to the extent the old one had been.

The European colonial presence was as strong as ever, but after the slaughter of the war and the hypocrisy of the peace, Europeans could no longer claim to embody civilization with the same arrogance. But if the old Europe lost prestige, President Wilson's ideals of self-determination and democracy were greeted enthusiastically outside the West—in China, for example. At the same time, the Russian revolutionary model appealed to those in the colonial world seeking to understand the mainsprings of Western imperialism—and the means of overcoming colonial rule. To some Chinese intellectuals by the early 1920s, Leninism was attractive because it showed the scope for mass mobilization by a revolutionary vanguard.

Non-Western elites were learning to pick and choose from among the elements of the Western tradition. During the war and continuing into the 1920s, ever greater numbers of colonial subjects went to western Europe, often for education. Paris was a favored destination, partly because France made some genuine effort to assimilate colonial peoples. In one sense, those educated in Paris and elsewhere in the West were subject to Westernization, but that did not have to mean accepting Western rule. In fact, Western political education led many not only to question colonialism but to ask new questions about their own traditions—and how they might serve the quest for a postcolonial order.

By the 1920s, a generation of anticolonialist, nationalist intellectuals was emerging to lead the non-Western world. Some were more radical than others, but now began variations on themes that would be heard for decades—decades of struggle for independence, cultural confidence, and national self-respect. In response to imperial rule, the challenge was to learn from the West and to modernize, but without simply copying the West and losing one's own distinctive cultural identity. It was imperative to sift through tradition, asking what needed to be changed and what was worth preserving. The pioneering Chinese nationalist Sun Yixien (Sun Yat-sen, 1866–1925) was typical in recognizing the need to adopt the science and technology of the West. But China, he insisted, could do so in its own way, without sacrificing the distinctiveness of its cultural and political traditions. (See the box, "Encounters with the West: Sun Yixien on Chinese Nationalism.")

Britain had been the greatest imperial power, and as an island nation, it still emphasized its navy and its empire even after playing a major role on the Continent during World War I. But this meant Britain was especially vulnerable to the growing anticolonial sentiment. Although the British were comparatively sensitive and flexible in handling colonial pressures, they seem, in retrospect, to have faced a losing battle. Yet that battle drew British attention and energy away from the problems of Europe after the war and the peace settlement.

In light of the strong Indian support for the British war effort, in 1917 the British government promised to extend the scope for Indian involvement in the colonial administration in India. Growing expectations as the war was ending provoked episodes of violence against the British, whose troops retaliated brutally in April 1919, firing indiscriminately into an unarmed crowd. This Amritsar Massacre helped galvanize India's independence movement, even though the British,

seeking conciliation in the aftermath, extended self-rule by entrusting certain less essential government services to Indians. Another milestone was reached in 1921, when Mohandas Gandhi, the British-educated leader of the Indian independence movement, shed his European clothes in favor of simple Indian attire. But it was on the basis of Western egalitarianism, not some indigenous value, that he demanded political rights for the "untouchables," the lowest group in India's long-standing caste system.

In Egypt anticolonialist violence led to a full-scale anti-British insurrection in 1919. After the rebellion was suppressed by British troops, British authorities offered to grant moderate concessions in Egypt, as in India. Tensions remained, however, for Egyptian nationalists demanded more substantial concessions. Finally, in 1922, the British granted Egypt formal independence, to be followed over the next few years by representative government and universal suffrage under a constitutional monarchy. But Britain retained a predominant influence in Egypt until a nationalist revolution in 1952.

At the same time, nationalism was growing among West Africans studying in England. Even before the war, demands for representation in colonial government had been raised in the African press, and such demands were stepped up after the war. In March 1919 Western-educated Africans in the Gold Coast asked the British governor to establish representative institutions so that Africans could at least be consulted. The West African National Congress, formed in 1920, concentrated on the same demands. The British agreed to new constitutions for Nigeria in 1923 and the Gold Coast in 1925 that took significant steps in that direction. They also agreed to build more schools, though they tended to promote practical education, including African languages and agriculture, whereas the African leaders wanted room for the Western classics that "made gentlemen." Such differences in priorities indicate the complexities of the relationships at work between colonial rulers and the emerging elites among the colonized peoples.

Enforcing the Versailles Settlement

The strains that followed World War I were evident not only in the colonies but in Europe. It was up to France and Britain to make sure the new

∼ ENCOUNTERS WITH THE WEST ∼

Sun Yixien on Chinese Nationalism

Sun Yixien (Sun Yat-sen), widely regarded as the father of modern China, founded the Guomindang (Kuomintang), the Chinese nationalist movement, in 1912. Educated by Western missionaries in China, he lived in the United States for extended periods and came to admire the West in important respects. But he insisted that China, to make the best use of what the West offered, had to reconnect with its own unique traditions. Variations on this argument would be heard for decades as the rest of the world sought to come to terms with the apparently more advanced West. The following passages are from an influential series of lectures that Sun Yixien presented in China in the early 1920s.

What is the standing of our nation in the world? In comparison with other nations we have the greatest population and the oldest culture, of four thousand years' duration. We ought to be advancing in line with the nations of Europe and America. But the Chinese people have only family and clan groups; there is no national spirit. Consequently, in spite of four hundred million people gathered together in one China, we are in fact but a sheet of loose sand. We are the poorest and weakest state in the world, occupying the lowest position in international affairs; the rest of mankind is the carving knife and the serving dish, while we are the fish and the meat. Our position now is extremely perilous; if we do not earnestly promote nationalism and weld together our four hundred millions into a strong nation, we face a tragedy—the loss of our country and the destruction of our race. To ward off this danger, we must espouse Nationalism and employ the national spirit to save the country. . . .

But even if we succeed in reviving our ancient morality, learning, and powers, we will still not be able, in this modern world, to advance China to a first place among the nations. . . . [W]e will still need to learn the strong points of Europe and America before we can progress at an equal rate with them. Unless we do study the best from foreign countries, we will go backward. With our own fine foundation of knowledge and our age-long culture, with our own native intelligence besides, we should be able to acquire all the best things from abroad. The strongest point of the West is its science. . . .

As soon as we learn Western machinery we can use it anytime, anywhere; electric lights, for example, can be installed and used in any kind of Chinese house. But Western social customs and sentiments are different from ours in innumerable points; if, without regard to customs and popular feelings in China, we try to apply Western methods of social control as we would Western machinery—in a hard and fast way—we shall be making a serious mistake. . . .

. . . For the governmental machinery of the United States and France still has many defects, and does not satisfy the desires of the people nor give them a complete measure of happiness. So we in our proposed reconstruction must not think that if we imitate the West of to-day we shall reach the last stage of progress and be perfectly contented. . . .

Only in recent times has Western culture advanced beyond ours, and the passion for this new civilization has stimulated our revolution. Now that the revolution is a reality, we naturally desire to see China excel the West and build up the newest and most progressive state in the world. We certainly possess the qualifications necessary to reach this ideal, but we must not merely imitate the democratic systems of the West.

Source: Sun Yat-sen, *San Min Chu I: The Three Principles of the People* (Taipei, Taiwan: China Cultural Service, 1953), pp. 5, 46, 109–113, 136, 138–139.

international order worked, but it was not clear that either had the will and the resources to do so. Cooperation between them was essential, yet sometimes their differences—in geography, in values, and in perceptions—seemed to doom them to work at cross-purposes.

France was unquestionably the dominant power on the European continent after World War I, and until well into the 1930s it boasted the strongest army in the world. Yet even in the early 1920s there was something artificial about France's strength—thus the shrillness and the defensiveness that marked French thinking and French policy. To be sure, France seized the initiative and offered strong leadership at first, but contradictions, and resignation, gradually came to the fore.

In light of Germany's stronger demographic and industrial base, France's long-term security seemed to require certain measures to tip the scales in its favor. By imposing German disarmament and the demilitarization of the Rhineland, the Versailles treaty gave France immediate military advantages. Yet each of these measures was in some ways limited. How long could they be maintained, once the passions of war had died down and Germany no longer seemed such a threat? France had hoped for British help in enforcing the treaty, but during the 1920s, as after other major European wars, Britain pulled back from the Continent to concentrate on its empire.

At first, France felt confident enough to take strong steps even without British support. In response to German foot-dragging in paying reparations, Prime Minister Raymond Poincaré decided to get tough in January 1923. Declaring the Germans in default, he sent French troops at the head of an international force to occupy the Ruhr industrial area and force German compliance. But the move backfired. The costs of this military intervention more than offset the increase in reparations that France received, so the French government had to raise taxes to pay for the venture. Moreover, the move alienated the British, whose lack of support bordered on active hostility.

Quite apart from their imperial concerns, the British wanted to avoid getting dragged into the uncertain situation in east-central Europe, where vital national interests did not seem to be at stake. Yet the French, to replace their earlier link with Russia, promptly developed an alliance system with several of the new or expanded states of the

region, including Poland, Czechoslovakia, Romania, and Yugoslavia. France's ties to east-central Europe made the British especially wary of definitive agreements with the French.

Even when western Europe was at issue, Britain was reluctant to become closely allied with France, which seemed unnecessarily vindictive and bellicose. Indeed, the Versailles treaty increasingly seemed counterproductive to the British, who placed great store in the League of Nations and in the international arms reduction effort prominent by the later 1920s. So France found itself with ever less support from its wartime allies as it sought to enforce the peace settlement. The Ruhr occupation of 1923 proved the last time the French dared to go it alone.

From that point on, France lost the advantages it had gained by defeating Germany, and its veneer of self-confidence gradually peeled away to reveal defensiveness and resignation. The defensive mentality found physical embodiment in the Maginot Line, a system of fortifications on the country's eastern border. Remembering the defensive warfare of World War I, and determined to preclude the sort of invasion France had suffered in 1914, Marshal Pétain and the military convinced France's political leaders to adopt a defensive strategy based on a fortified line. The Maginot system was conceived in 1925, begun in 1929, and reached at least preliminary completion in 1935, when it extended along France's border with Germany from Switzerland to the Ardennes Forest at the border with Belgium.

Although this defensive system had some military justification, it was not consistent with the other major strands of French military and diplomatic policy, especially the alliances with several of the states between Germany and Russia in east-central Europe. If France emphasized defense behind an impregnable system of forts, what good were French security guarantees to such new allies as Poland and Czechoslovakia? French efforts to avoid another war by adopting a defensive strategy were not consistent with the role that France set out to play in Europe after its victory in 1918.

Still, the situation remained fluid during the 1920s. In France, as in Britain, national elections in 1924 produced a victory for the moderate left, ending a period of conservative nationalist dominance since the war. In each country, international relations was a major issue in the elections, and the

Cracks in Western Imperialism There was no return to normal in the areas subject to European imperial control after World War I. Here, in Cairo in 1919, British-led troops attempt to control rioting Egyptian nationalists protesting the banishment of a major nationalist leader. Such pressure continued, forcing the British not only to permit the leader to return but to allow Egypt greater autonomy. *(Hulton-Getty/Tony Stone Images)*

outcome forecast a more conciliatory tack, especially in relations with Germany. If democracy was taking root in the land of its old enemy, then perhaps France's fears about German aggressiveness and the European power balance were misplaced.

TOWARD MASS SOCIETY

As many had feared, the problems of readjustment to peace caused wild economic swings in the first few years after the war. The downturns were relatively short, however, and by the later 1920s, Europe was enjoying renewed prosperity. Common involvement in the war had blurred class lines and accelerated the trend toward what contemporaries began to call "mass society." As the new prosperity spread the fruits of industrialization more widely, ordinary people increasingly set the cultural tone, partly through new mass media like film and radio. To some, the advent of mass society portended a welcome revitalization of culture and a more authentic kind of democracy, while others saw only a debasement of cultural standards and a susceptibility to populist demagoguery. But though the contours of mass society now became evident, social change did not keep up with the promise of—and the requirements for—democratic politics.

The war was supposed to have paved the way for democracy, and the fall of the monarchies in Russia, Germany, and Austria-Hungary seemed especially to create opportunities. But where democracy was new, as in Poland and Germany, it often led a tortured existence and soon gave way to more authoritarian forms of government. Even in France and Britain, where victory in the war seemed to have confirmed democratic values and institutions, the new strains and missed opportunities of the 1920s stand out in retrospect. In Italy, hopes for democratic renewal gradually receded as a new regime, hostile to parliamentary democracy, triumphed by the middle of the decade. So despite the aspirations that had surrounded the end of the war, the decade that followed did not see the consolidation of the political democracy that optimistic observers had assumed would correspond with the emerging mass society.

Economic Readjustment and the New Prosperity

In their effort to return to normal, governments were quick to dismantle wartime planning and control mechanisms. But the needs of war had stimulated innovations that helped fuel the renewed economic growth of the 1920s. The civilian air industry, for example, developed rapidly during the decade by taking advantage of wartime work on aviation for military purposes. More generally, newer industries such as chemicals, electricity, and advanced machinery led the way to a new prosperity in the 1920s, which significantly altered patterns of life in the more industrialized parts of the West. The automobile, a luxury plaything for the wealthy before the war, began to be mass-produced in western Europe. In France, which had pioneered automotive manufacture, the production of automobiles shot up dramatically, from 40,000 in 1920 to 254,000 in 1929.

But the heady pace masked problems that lay beneath the relative prosperity of the 1920s, even in victorious Britain and France. If new industries prospered, old ones declined in the face of new technologies and stronger foreign competition. In Britain, the industries responsible for Britain's earlier industrial pre-eminence—textiles, coal, shipbuilding, and iron and steel—were now having trouble competing. Rather than investing in new technologies, companies in these older industries sought to survive by demanding government protection and by imposing lower wages and longer hours on their workers. At the same time, however, British labor unions resisted the mechanization necessary to make these older industries more competitive.

Rather than realistically assessing Britain's prospects in the more competitive international economy, British leaders sought to return to the prewar situation, based on the gold standard, with London the world's financial center. For many Britons, the government's announcement in 1925 that the British pound was again freely convertible to gold at 1914 exchange rates was the long-awaited indication that normality had returned at last. Yet the return to 1914 exchange rates overvalued the pound relative to the U.S. dollar, making British goods more expensive on export markets and making it still more difficult for aging British industries to compete. Further, Britain no longer had the capital to act as the world's banker. By trying to do so, Britain became all the more vulnerable when the international economy reached a crisis in 1929.

If the structural decline of older industries was clearest in Britain, inflation and its psychological impact was most prominent in Germany and France. By the summer of 1923, Germany's response to the French occupation of the Ruhr had transformed an already serious inflationary problem, stemming from wartime deficit spending, into one of the great hyperinflations in history. At its height, when it took 4.2 trillion marks to equal a dollar, Germans were forced to take wheelbarrows of paper money to buy ordinary grocery items. Simply printing the necessary currency was a severe strain for the government. By the end of 1923, the government managed to stabilize prices through currency reform and drastically reduced government spending—a combination that elicited greater cooperation from the victors. But the rampant inflation, and the readjustment necessary to control it, wiped out the life savings of ordinary people while profiting speculators and those in debt, including some large industrialists. This inequity left scars that remained even as Germany enjoyed a measure of prosperity in the years that followed.

Inflation was less dramatic in France, but it affected French perceptions and priorities in significant ways between the two world wars. For over a century, from the Napoleonic era to the outbreak of war in 1914, the value of the French franc had remained stable. But the war started France on an inflationary cycle that shattered the security of its many small savers—those, like teachers and shopkeepers, who had been the backbone of the Third Republic. To repay war debts and rebuild war-damaged industries, the French government continued to run budget deficits, and thereby cause inflation, even after 1918. Runaway inflation threatened during 1925 and 1926, but the franc was finally restabilized in 1928, though at only about one-fifth its prewar value.

On the international level, war debts and reparations strained the financial system, creating problems with the financing of trade. But in the course of the 1920s, experts made adjustments that seemed to be returning the international exchange system to equilibrium. Only in retrospect, after the international capitalist system fell into crisis late in 1929, did it become clear how potent those strains were—and how inadequate the efforts at readjustment.

Work, Leisure, and the New Popular Culture

The wartime spur to industrialization produced a large increase in the industrial labor force all over Europe, and a good deal of labor unrest accompanied the transition to peacetime. Some of that agitation challenged factory discipline and authority relationships. Seeking to re-establish authority on a new basis for the competitive postwar world, business leaders and publicists fostered a new cult of efficiency and productivity, partly by adapting Taylorism and Fordism, influential American ideas about mass production. On the basis of his "time-and-motion" studies of factory labor, Frederick W. Taylor (1856–1915) argued that breaking down assembly line production into small, repetitive tasks was the key to maximizing worker efficiency. In contrast, Henry Ford (1863–1947) linked the gospel of mass production to mass consumption. In exchange for accepting the discipline of the assembly line, the workers should be paid well enough to be able to buy the products they produced—even automobiles. Sharing in the prosperity that mass production made possible, factory workers would be loyal to the companies that employed them. Not all Europeans, however, welcomed the new ideas from America. In the new cult of efficiency and mass production, some saw an unwelcome sameness and a debasement of cultural standards. (See the box, "Doubts About Mass Society.")

In light of the major role women had played in the wartime labor force, the demand for women's suffrage proved irresistible in Britain, Germany, and much of Europe, though not yet in France or Italy. In Britain, where the call for women's suffrage had earlier met with controversy (see page 902), the right to vote was readily conceded in 1918, partly because women no longer seemed a threat to the political system. Once given the vote, British women simply flowed into the existing parties, dissolving earlier hopes—and fears—that a specifically feminist political agenda would follow from women's suffrage.

Although female employment remained higher than before the war, many women were willing to return home, yielding their jobs to the returning soldiers. The need to replace the men killed in the war lent renewed force to the traditional notion that women served society, and fulfilled themselves, by marrying and rearing families. This notion was symptomatic of the widespread desire to return to normal after the disruptions of the war years.

Still, the spirit of innovation brought into the public arena subjects with significant implications for gender roles—subjects largely taboo before the war. The desire to be "modern" produced a more open, unsentimental, even scientific discussion of sexuality and reproduction. Theodore Hendrik van de Velde's *Ideal Marriage* (1927) sold widely throughout the Western world for decades. Though van de Velde assumed male leadership in the sexual relationship, his study furthered the growing sense that sexual fulfillment was important to a healthy marriage—and required techniques that could be learned and discussed.

The new "rationalization of sexuality" fed demands that governments provide access to sex counseling, birth control, and even abortion as they assumed ever greater responsibilities for promoting social health. This direction was especially prominent in Germany, although German innovators learned from experiments in the new Soviet Union and from the birth control movement that Margaret Sanger (1883–1966) was spearheading in the United States. The more open and tolerant attitude toward sexuality fostered the development of a gay subculture, prominent in the vibrant cabaret scene that emerged in Berlin during the 1920s.

Innovation affected many reaches of everyday life. Mass consumption was the reverse side of the mass production that created the new prosperity of the 1920s. As it became possible to mass-produce

Doubts About Mass Society

The writer Stefan Zweig (1881–1942) was born in Vienna and traveled widely in America, Asia, and Europe. In an article for a Berlin newspaper in 1925, he expressed misgivings about the new sociocultural tendencies prominent after the war—tendencies that he, like many of his contemporaries, identified with Americanization. His thinking combined hyperbole with an acute sense that something valuable was being lost.

Everything is becoming more uniform in its outward manifestations, everything leveled into a uniform cultural schema. The characteristic habits of individual peoples are being worn away, native dress giving way to uniforms, customs becoming international. Countries seem increasingly to have slipped simultaneously into each other; people's activity and vitality follows a single schema; cities grow increasingly similar in appearance. Paris has been three-quarters Americanized, Vienna Budapested: more and more the fine aroma of the particular in cultures is evaporating, their colorful foliage being stripped with ever-increasing speed, rendering the steel-grey pistons of mechanical operation, of the modern world machine, visible beneath the cracked veneer. . . .

Two or three decades ago dance was still specific to nations and to the personal inclinations of the individual. One waltzed in Vienna, danced the csardas in Hungary, the bolero in Spain, all to the tune of countless different rhythms and melodies in which both the genius of an artist and the spirit of the nation took obvious form. Today millions of people, from Capetown to Stockholm, from Buenos Aires to Calcutta, dance the same dance to the same short-winded, impersonal melodies. . . .

A second example is fashion. Never before has such a striking uniformity developed in all countries as during our age. . . . New York decrees short hair for women: within a month, as if cut by the same scythe, 50 or 100 million female manes fall to the floor. . . .

A third example: cinema. Once again utter simultaneity in all countries and languages, the cultivation of the same performance, the same taste (or lack of it) in masses by the hundreds of millions. . . .

A fourth example is radio. All of these inventions have a single meaning: simultaneity. Londoners, Parisians, and Viennese listen at the same second to the same thing, and the supernatural proportions of this simultaneity, of this uniformity, are intoxicating. There is an intoxication, a stimulus for the masses, in all of these new technological miracles, and simultaneously an enormous sobriety of the soul, a dangerous seduction of the individual into passivity. Here too, as in dance, fashion, and the cinema, the individual acquiesces to a herdlike taste that is everywhere the same. . . .

America is the source of that terrible wave of uniformity. . . . From the other side of our world, from Russia, the same will to monotony presses ominously in a different form: the will to the compartmentalization of the individual, to uniformity in world views, the same dreadful will to monotony. Europe remains the last bulwark of individualism and, perhaps, of the overly taut cramp of peoples—our vigorous nationalism, despite all its senselessness, represents to some extent a fevered, unconscious rebellion, a last, desperate effort to defend ourselves against leveling. But precisely that cramped form of resistance betrays our weakness. . . .

. . . [I]n all of these new means for mechanizing humanity there is an enormous power that is not to be overcome. For they all fulfill the highest ideal of the average: to offer amusement without demanding exertion. . . . Autonomy in the conduct of one's life and even in the enjoyment of life has by now become a goal for so few people that most no longer feel how they are becoming particles, atoms in the wash of a gigantic power.

Source: Anton Kaes, Martin Jay, and Edward Dimendberg, eds., *The Weimar Republic Sourcebook* (Berkeley and Los Angeles: University of California Press, 1994), pp. 397–400.

the products of the second industrial transformation, more people could afford automobiles, electrical gadgets like the radio and phonograph, and clothing of synthetic fabrics, developed through innovations in chemistry. First came rayon, produced in small quantities since 1891 but mass-produced beginning in the 1920s. Its advent was of particular symbolic importance; in this new artificial form, silk, which had long been one of the trappings of wealth, was now within the means of ordinary people.

With the eight-hour day increasingly the norm, growing attention was devoted to leisure as a positive source of human fulfillment—for everyone, not just the wealthy. Ordinary people began to have the time, and the means, to take vacations. European beach resorts grew crowded. An explosion of interest in soccer among Europeans paralleled the growth of baseball and football in the United States. Huge stadiums were built across Europe.

The growth of leisure was linked to the development of mass media and mass culture. During the early 1920s radio became a commercial venture, reaching a mass audience in Europe, as in the United States. Although movies had begun to emerge as vehicles of popular entertainment even before the war, they came into their own during the 1920s, when the names of film stars became household words for the first time.

The rapid development of film showed that new, more accessible media could nurture extraordinary innovation. Germany led the way with such films as *The Cabinet of Dr. Caligari* (1920), *Metropolis* (1927), and *The Blue Angel* (1930), but the Russian Sergei Eisenstein (1898–1948) became perhaps the most admired film maker of the era with *Potemkin* (1925), his brilliant portrayal of the Russian revolution of 1905. In some spheres, however, America was beginning to outdo both Paris and Berlin. Marlene Dietrich (1901–1992), famous as Lola Lola in *The Blue Angel*, was among a number of German film celebrities who went to Hollywood.

Exploiting the new popular fascination with air travel, the American Charles Lindbergh (1902–1974) captured the European imagination in 1927 with the first solo flight across the Atlantic. Lindbergh's feat epitomized the affirmative side of the decade—the sense that there were new worlds to conquer and that there still were heroes, despite the ironies of the war and the ambiguities of the peace.

Weimar Cinema This poster advertises Fritz Lang's film *Metropolis*, which explored the dehumanization and exploitation of the modern city. *(Schulz-Neudamm, Metropolis, 1926. Lithograph, 83″ × 36½″. The Museum of Modern Art, New York. Gift of Universum Film Aktiengesellschaft.)*

Society and Politics in the Victorious Democracies

France and Britain seemed the best positioned of the major European countries to take advantage of renewed peace and stability to confront the sociopolitical challenges of the postwar era. And during the 1920s, each seemed to return to normal. But was normal good enough, in light of the rupture of the war and the challenges of the emerging mass society?

Victory in the Great War seemed to belie France's prewar concerns about decadence and decline. In the immediate aftermath of the war, French leaders were confident in dealing with radical labor unrest and aggressive in translating the battlefield victory into a dominant position on the European continent. But despite the victorious outcome, the war itself, with its tremendous loss of French lives, had produced a widespread conviction that France could not withstand another such challenge. The renewed confidence thus proved hollow.

Although some in prewar France had worried about falling behind rapidly industrializing Germany, the victory seemed to have vindicated France's more cautious, balanced economy, with its blend of industry and agriculture. Thus, the prewar mistrust of rapid industrial development continued. Rather than foster a program of economic modernization that might have afforded the basis for genuine security, the French pulled back even from the measure of state responsibility for the economy that had developed during the war.

To be sure, in France, as elsewhere, the 1920s were a decade of relative prosperity. Led by the oil and electricity industries, the economy grew at an annual rate of 4.6 percent between 1923 and 1929, double the prewar rate. Industrial production by 1929 was 40 percent higher than it had been in 1913. But, with the exception of Britain, other Western economies grew more rapidly during the 1920s, and the opportunity that growth afforded to modernize the French economy was not seized. Although government grants helped reconstruct almost eight thousand factories, most were simply rebuilt as they were before the war. Moreover, the working class benefited little from the relative prosperity of the 1920s. Housing remained poor, wages failed to keep up with inflation, and France continued to lag other countries in social legislation.

The British political system remained stable between the wars, although it opened up in one significant sense as the Labour party supplanted the Liberals to become the dominant alternative to the Conservatives by the early 1920s. The Labour party even got a brief taste of power when Ramsay MacDonald (1866–1937) formed Britain's first Labour government in January 1924. The coming of Labour to power wrought a significant expansion of the governmental elite to incorporate those, like MacDonald himself, with genuinely working-class backgrounds.

The rise of Labour was striking, but it was the Conservative leader, Stanley Baldwin (1867–1947), who set the tone for British politics between the wars in three stints as prime minister during the years from 1923 to 1937. Although the wealthy son of a steel manufacturer, Baldwin deliberately departed from the old aristocratic style of British conservative politics. More down-to-earth and pragmatic than his predecessors, he was the first British prime minister to use radio effectively, and he made an effort to foster good relations with the workers. Yet Baldwin's era was one of growing social tension.

With exports declining, unemployment remained high in Britain throughout the interwar period, never falling below 10 percent. The coal industry, though still the country's largest employer, had become a particular trouble spot in the British economy. As coal exports declined, British mine owners became ever more aggressive in their dealings with labor, finally, in 1926, insisting on a longer workday and a wage cut of 13 percent to restore competitiveness. The result was a coal miners' strike in May that promptly turned into a general strike, involving almost all of organized labor—about 4 million workers—in the most notable display of trade-union solidarity Britain had ever seen. For nine days the British economy stood at a virtual standstill. But threats of arrest and a growing public backlash forced the union leadership to back down, accepting a compromise. The miners continued the strike on their own, but they finally returned to work six months later at considerably lower wages.

Although for somewhat different reasons, Britain and France both failed during the 1920s to take advantage of what would soon seem, in retrospect, to have been a precious opportunity to adjust their economies, to heal social wounds, and thereby to create a deeper consensus and a more meaningful democracy. The lost opportunity would mean growing social tensions once the relative prosperity of the decade had ended.

Democracy Aborted

In east-central Europe, new democracies seemed to take root after the war, but except in Czechoslovakia and Finland the practice of parliamentary government did not match the promise of the immediate postwar period. Democracy seemed divisive and ineffective, so one country after another adopted a more authoritarian alternative during the 1920s and early 1930s.

Poland offers the most dramatic example. Although its democratic constitution of 1921 established a cabinet responsible to a parliamentary majority, the parliament fragmented into numerous parties so that instability proved endemic from the start. Indeed, Poland had fourteen different ministries from November 1918 to May 1926, when a coup d'état led by Marshal Josef Pilsudski replaced parliamentary government with an authoritarian regime stressing national unity. This suppression of democracy came as a relief to many Poles—and was even welcomed by the trade unions. After Pilsudski's death in 1935, a group of colonels ruled Poland until the country was invaded by Nazi Germany in 1939.

Democracy proved hard to manage in east-central Europe partly because of special economic difficulties resulting from the breakup of the Habsburg system. New national borders meant new economic barriers, disrupting long-standing economic relationships. Centers of relative industrial strength like Vienna and Budapest found themselves cut off from their traditional markets and sources of raw materials. In what was now Poland, Silesians had long been oriented toward Germany, Galicians toward Vienna, and those in eastern Poland toward Russia; the creation of the Polish nation-state was not in itself sufficient to form a cohesive economic unit.

The countries of east-central Europe remained overwhelmingly agrarian, and this, too, proved unconducive to democracy. Land reform that accompanied the transition to democracy made small properties the norm in much of the region. But these units were often too small to be efficient, so agricultural output actually decreased after

land was redistributed, most dramatically in Romania and Yugoslavia. When agricultural prices declined by the late 1920s, many of those peasants had no choice but to sell out to larger landowners. What had seemed a progressive and democratic reform thus failed to provide a stable agrarian smallholder base for democracy.

THE WEIMAR REPUBLIC IN GERMANY: A CANDLE BURNING AT BOTH ENDS

The trial of democracy in Poland and elsewhere in east-central Europe was important, but the venue for the most significant test was Germany, a large, dynamic, culturally sophisticated country where democracy had never taken firm root. With the Weimar Republic of 1918–1933, Germany experienced full-fledged parliamentary democracy for the first time, but this democracy had great difficulty establishing its legitimacy, and it reached an impasse when confronted with economic depression by 1930. As a result, the Nazi leader Adolf Hitler (1889–1945) got a chance to govern early in 1933. He immediately began creating a new regime, the Third Reich, intended as the antithesis of Weimar democracy.

Because its failure led to Nazism, the Weimar Republic has been much scrutinized. What might its leaders have done differently to produce a more viable democracy at this point in German history? Are the republic's immediate problems enough to explain its failure, or was some longer-term German aversion to democratic institutions crucial as well?

Germany's Cautious Revolution, 1919–1920

The Weimar Republic had two strikes against it virtually from the outset: It was born of national defeat, and it was forced to take responsibility for the harsh and dictated Treaty of Versailles in 1919. During its first years, moreover, the regime encountered severe economic dislocation, culminating in the hyperinflation of 1923, as well as ideological polarization that threatened to tear the country apart.

Although Germany had strong military and authoritarian traditions, the initial threat to the new democracy came not from the right, disoriented and discredited, but from the left, stimulated by the Russian example. Those seeking further revolution, and those who feared it, could easily equate the proclamation of a German republic in November 1918 with the first revolution in Russia; as in Russia, the new, more democratic order could prove a mere prelude to communist revolution.

Spearheaded by Karl Liebknecht and Rosa Luxemburg in Berlin, revolutionary unrest reached its peak in Germany during December 1918 and January 1919. But even after Liebknecht and Luxemburg were captured and murdered in January, there remained a serious chance of further revolution through May 1919, and communist revolutionary agitation continued to flare up until the end of 1923.

As it turned out, there was no further revolution, partly because the parallel between Germany and Russia carried only so far. The new German government had made peace, whereas the leaders of the provisional government in Russia had sought to continue the war. Furthermore, those who ended up controlling the councils that sprang up in Germany during the fall of 1918 favored political democracy, not communist revolution, and therefore they supported the provisional government.

Even so, the revolutionary minority constituted a credible threat. And the new government made repression of the extreme left a priority—even if it meant leaving in place some of the institutions and personnel of the old imperial system. In November 1918, at the birth of the new republic, the moderate socialist leader Friedrich Ebert had agreed with General Groener to preserve the old imperial officer corps to help prevent further revolution. But when the regular army, weakened by war and defeat, proved unable to control radical agitation in Berlin in December, it seemed the republic would have to take extraordinary measures to defend itself from the revolutionary left. With the support of Ebert and Groener, Gustav Noske (1868–1946), the minister of national defense, began to organize "Free Corps," irregular volunteer paramilitary groups to be used against the revolutionaries. Noske, who was a socialist, but one long supportive of the military, noted that "somebody will have to be the bloodhound—I won't shirk the responsibility."[1]

During the first five months of 1919, the government unleashed the Free Corps to crush leftist movements all over Germany, often with wanton brutality. In relying on right-wing paramilitary groups, the republic's leaders were playing with fire, but the immediate threat at this point came from the left. In 1920, however, the government faced a right-wing coup attempt, the Kapp Putsch. The army declined to defend the republic, but the government managed to survive thanks largely to a general strike by leftist workers. The republic's early leaders had to juggle both extremes because, as one of them put it, the Weimar Republic was "a candle burning at both ends."

Though sporadic street fighting by paramilitary groups continued, the republic survived its traumatic birth and by 1924 had achieved an uneasy stability. But Germany's postwar revolution had remained confined to the political level. There was no program to break up the cartels, with their concentrations of economic power. Even on the level of government personnel, continuity was more striking than change. There was no effort to build a loyal republican army, and no attempt to purge the bureaucracy and the judiciary of antidemocratic elements from the old imperial order. When right-wing extremists assassinated prominent leaders, such as the Jewish industrialist Walther Rathenau in 1922, the courts often proved unwilling to prosecute those responsible. In general, those who ran the new government day-to-day were often skeptical of democracy, even hostile to the new regime.

In light of the republic's eventual failure, the willingness of its early leaders to leave intact so much from the old order has made them easy targets for criticism. It can be argued, however, that the course they followed—heading off the extreme left, reassuring the established elites, and playing for time—was the republic's best chance of success. The new regime might establish its legitimacy by inertia, much like the Third Republic in France, which had similarly been born of defeat. Even lacking the sentimental fervor that had earlier surrounded democratic ideals, Germans might gradually become "republicans of reason," recognizing that this regime was the lesser of evils, that it could be a framework for prosperity and renewed German prominence in international affairs. In the event of an early crisis, however, a republic consolidating itself in this cautious way would be likely to find fewer active defenders than active opponents.

Elections in January 1919 produced a constituent assembly that convened in Weimar, seat of what seemed the best traditions of German culture, to draft a democratic constitution. The elections took place before the peace conference had produced the widely detested Treaty of Versailles. When the first regular parliamentary elections finally were held in June 1920, the three moderate parties that had led the new government and been forced to accept the treaty now suffered a major defeat, dropping from 76 to 47 percent of the seats. Those were the parties most committed to democratic institutions, but they were never again to achieve a parliamentary majority. The 1920 elections, like many of those that followed, revealed a lack of consensus and a tendency toward polarization and extremism in the German electorate.

The lack of consensus produced a multiparty system and a fragmented Reichstag. Indeed, no single party ever won an absolute majority during the Weimar years, so government was always by inherently unstable party coalition. Not only was the Weimar party system fragmented and complex, but it encompassed a wide ideological array, including extremes both of left and right that were interested not in consolidating but in sabotaging or at best exploiting the new democratic institutions. Polarization to the left favored the Communists, who constantly criticized the more moderate Socialists for supporting the republic. To the right, the situation was more complex. On the extreme right, the National Socialists, or Nazis, were noisy and often violent, but they did not attract much electoral support until 1930. More damaging to parliamentary democracy for most of the Weimar period was the right-wing Nationalist party (DNVP), which played on nationalist resentments and fears of socialism and offered only the most tenuous support for democratic institutions.

Gustav Stresemann and the Scope for Gradual Consolidation, 1920–1929

Still, all was not necessarily lost for the republic when the three moderate, pro-Weimar parties were defeated in 1920. Germans who were unsupportive or hostile at first might be gradually won over. After the death of President Ebert in 1925, Paul von Hindenburg, the emperor's field mar-

shal, was elected president. Depending on the circumstances, having a conservative military leader from the old order in this role could be advantageous, or damaging, for the future of democracy. As long as there remained scope for consolidation, Hindenburg's presidency suggested to skeptics that the new regime was legitimate and a worthy object of German patriotism. But when crisis came by 1930, Hindenburg was quick to give up on parliamentary government—with devastating results.

The individual who best exemplified the possibility of winning converts to the Weimar Republic in the early 1920s was Gustav Stresemann (1878–1929), the leader of the German People's Party (DVP), a conservative but relatively flexible party that offered at least the possibility of broadening the republic's base of support. As chancellor, and especially as foreign minister, Stresemann proved the republic's leading statesman.

Stresemann was conservative in background and instinct. Early in 1918, for example, he was among the many to applaud the annexationist treaty of Brest-Litovsk, and he was sufficiently frustrated with the new republic by 1920 tacitly to support a coup attempt, the Kapp Putsch. But the volatility that marked German politics in 1920 convinced Stresemann that the alternative to the new republic would not be the conservative monarchy he preferred in principle, but increasing polarization leading to the triumph of the extreme left. Moreover, it had become clear by 1920 that the new democratic republic was not likely to be revolutionary on the socioeconomic level. It made sense, then, to work actively to make the new regime succeed; the alternative could be much worse. Within the framework that the new republic afforded, Germany could pursue its international aims, negotiating modifications of the Versailles treaty and returning to great power status. So although Stresemann was never emotionally attached to democratic ideals, he came to accept the republic and did his best to make it work.

Stresemann became chancellor in August 1923, when inflation was raging out of control. Within months his government had Germany back on its feet, exporting more and again growing economically. Stresemann managed to surmount the inflationary crisis partly because the other powers were becoming more conciliatory. By November 1923 even the French agreed that an

Hopes for Peace Foreign ministers Aristide Briand (left) of France and Gustav Stresemann of Germany spearheaded the improved international relations that bred optimism during the later 1920s. *(Corbis-Bettmann)*

international commission should review the reparations question, specifying realistic amounts based on Germany's ability to pay. During the summer of 1924, a commission led by the American financier Charles G. Dawes produced the Dawes Plan, which remained in force until 1929. The plan worked well by pinpointing revenue sources, lowering payments, providing loans, and securing the stability of the German currency.

At the same time, Stresemann understood that better relations with the victors, starting with France, had to be a priority if Germany was not only to overcome the present crisis but also to return to the councils of the great powers. French foreign minister Aristide Briand (1862–1932) shared Stresemann's desire for improved relations, and together they engineered the new, more conciliatory spirit in international relations evident by 1924. Its most substantial fruit was the Locarno Agreement of October 1925. France and Germany accepted the postwar border between the two countries, which meant that Germany gave up any claim to Alsace-Lorraine. France, for

its part, renounced the sort of direct military intervention in Germany that it had attempted with the Ruhr invasion of 1923 and agreed to begin withdrawing troops from the Rhineland ahead of schedule. On the other hand, Germany freely accepted France's key advantage, the demilitarization of the Rhineland, and Britain and Italy now explicitly guaranteed the measure.

By acquiescing in the status quo in the west, Stresemann was freeing Germany to concentrate on eastern Europe, where he envisioned gradual but substantial revision in the territorial settlement that had resulted from the war. Especially with the creation of Poland, that settlement had come partly at Germany's expense. Stresemann, then, was pursuing German interests, not subordinating them to some larger European vision. But he was willing to compromise and, for the most part, to play by the rules as he did so.

With the Locarno treaty, the victors accepted Germany as a diplomatic equal for the first time since the war. Germany's return to good graces culminated in its entry into the League of Nations in 1926, further evidence of conciliation that was widely welcomed. Indeed, Stresemann and Briand were joint winners of the Nobel Peace Prize for 1926.

Still, Stresemann had already discovered that even successes in dealing with Germany's former enemies could prove costly to him and his party in the volatile German political climate. Beginning in 1924 the German Nationalist party continually exploited German resentments by criticizing Stresemann's compromises with the victors of 1918—in accepting the Dawes Plan, for example. Stresemann concluded that he could overcome this domestic political volatility only by completing the revision of the Versailles treaty as quickly as possible. But his negotiations continued to agitate the German electorate.

With the expiration of the Dawes Plan in 1929, the Young Plan, conceived by American businessman Owen D. Young, removed Allied controls over the German economy and specified that Germany pay reparations until 1988. The annual amount was less than Germany had been paying, so it was expected that this plan constituted a permanent, and reasonable, settlement. Nevertheless, the Young Plan produced considerable resentment in Germany, leading, yet again, to political gains on the right.

The political controversy that surrounded Stresemann, a German conservative pursuing conventional national interests, indicates how volatile the German political situation remained, even with the improved economic and diplomatic climate of the later 1920s. Still, Stresemann's diplomatic successes were considerable, and his death in October 1929, at the age of 51, was a severe blow to the republic.

The End of the Weimar Republic, 1929–1933

Although Weimar Germany was considerably better off in 1929 than it had been in 1923, the political consensus remained weak, the political party system remained fragmented, and unstable coalition government remained the rule. The onset of the economic depression by the end of 1929 produced problems that Germany's fragile new democracy proved unable to handle. The pivotal issue was unemployment insurance, which became a tremendous financial burden for the government as unemployment grew. As it happened, a Socialist chancellor, Hermann Müller (1876–1931), was leading the government when the Depression began, and as the crisis deepened, his party demanded increases in insurance coverage. When the Socialists failed to convince their coalition partners, the Müller government resigned in March 1930. That proved to be the end of normal parliamentary government in Weimar Germany.

By this point conservatives, including military leaders close to President Hindenburg, sensed the chance to replace the fragmented parliamentary system with a more authoritarian government that would attack the economic crisis head on. Upon the advice of these advisers, Hindenburg called on Heinrich Brüning (1885–1970), leader of the moderate, Catholic Center party, to replace Müller as chancellor. Brüning promptly proposed to the Reichstag a hard-nosed, deflationary economic program intended to stimulate exports by lowering prices. Like most of the German middle classes, Brüning feared inflation, disliked unemployment insurance, and believed that Germany could not afford public works projects to pump up demand—the obvious alternative to his deflationary policy.

Though able, upright, and sincere in his economic program, Brüning did not understand the risky political game in which he had become enmeshed. His program encountered opposition not only from socialists but also from conservatives, eager to undermine the republic altogether. As a result, Brüning could get no parliamentary majority. Rather than resigning or seeking a compromise, he invoked Article 48, the emergency provision of the Weimar constitution, which enabled him to govern under presidential decree.

When this expedient provoked strenuous protests, Brüning decided to dissolve the Reichstag and schedule new elections for September 1930. At this point there was still some chance that a more conciliatory tack would have enabled the chancellor to build a new parliamentary majority—and save parliamentary government. The Socialists were seeking to be more cooperative in the face of the deepening economic crisis and the prospect of new parliamentary elections, which, under these difficult circumstances, seemed to invite trouble. However, Brüning persisted, believing the electorate would vindicate him.

In fact, the outcome of the 1930 elections was disastrous—for Brüning, and ultimately for Germany as well. While two of the democratic, pro-Weimar parties lost heavily, the two extremes proved the big winners. The Communists gained 23 seats, for a total of 77 deputies in the Reichstag; the National Socialists did even better, climbing from the 12 seats they had garnered in 1928 to 107.

Brüning continued to govern, still relying on President Hindenburg and Article 48 rather than majority support in the Reichstag. His efforts climaxed in December 1931 with a series of deflationary measures that raised taxes and decreased government spending, even for unemployment benefits. But the impact on the economy was disappointing. Meanwhile, the growth of the political extremes helped fuel an intensification of the political violence and streetfighting that had bedeviled the Weimar Republic from the beginning. As scuffles between Nazis and Communists sometimes approached pitched battles, the inability of the government to keep order further damaged the prestige of the republic.

In May 1932 Hindenburg's advisers finally persuaded him to dump Brüning in favor of an antidemocratic conservative. By this point the republic was a mere shell covering the backroom manipulation and dealing in Hindenburg's circle. The results of the elections that followed in July 1932 proved the republic's death knell. The Nazis won 37.3 percent of the vote (230 seats), and the Communists 14.3 percent (89 seats). Together, the two extremes controlled a majority of the seats in the Reichstag, and each refused to work in coalition with any of the mainstream parties. Although he resisted for months, Hindenburg found it difficult not to give Adolf Hitler, as the leader of the largest party in the Reichstag, a chance to govern. He finally called upon Hitler to form a government in January 1933.

It became clear virtually at once that the outcome of the Weimar crisis was a dramatic change of regime, the triumph of Hitler and Nazism. But though the Nazis had always wanted to destroy the Weimar Republic, they were not directly responsible for overthrowing it. The Weimar Republic failed on its own—or collapsed from within—largely because the Germans disagreed fundamentally about problems and priorities after the war. The new democracy produced unstable government based on multiparty coalitions and encountered virtual paralysis by 1930, when Germany faced the crisis of the Depression.

During the brief and tortured history of the Weimar Republic, there were twenty different cabinets, lasting an average of eight and a half months each. The experience of instability, divisiveness, and finally paralysis reinforced the perception, long prominent in Germany, that parliamentary democracy was petty, divisive, and ineffective. By 1932, the majority of the German electorate had simply lost confidence in the institutions of parliamentary democracy. Even those who voted for the Nazis were not clear what they might be getting instead, but, in light of economic depression and political impasse, it seemed time to try something else.

It was also crucial that elements from Germany's traditional antidemocratic elites were eager to exploit the economic crisis and the political impasse to get rid of the democratic republic altogether. Even as the Socialists became more conciliatory in an effort to find a compromise, those around Hindenburg pushed toward an authoritarian alternative. They were not seeking what proved the outcome—a monopoly of power for Hitler and the Nazis. Indeed, they finally tried working with Hitler in 1933 only as a last resort. But they were quick to begin undercutting a democracy that they had never really embraced in the first place.

COMMUNISM, FASCISM, AND THE NEW POLITICAL SPECTRUM

The Weimar Republic encountered crisis by 1930 partly because of the strength of the new extremes of left and right that had emerged directly from World War I. In making their revolution in 1917, the Bolsheviks had expected to spark a series of revolutions elsewhere. The postwar period began in the context of hopes for—and fears of—further revolution all over Europe. The Russian communists initially enjoyed extraordinary prestige on the European left; but as the nature of Leninist communism became clearer, some Marxists grew skeptical or hostile, and so the Russian model eventually produced a damaging split in international socialism. By the end of the 1920s revolution elsewhere was nowhere in sight, and it seemed that, for the foreseeable future, the communist regime in Russia would have to go it alone.

By then, a new and unexpected political movement had developed in Italy, expanding the political spectrum in a different direction. This was fascism, which brought Benito Mussolini to power in 1922. Emerging directly from the war, the fascism movement was violent—and thus disturbing. The term *fascism* derived from the ancient Roman *fasces,* a bundle of rods surrounding an ax that guards carried at state occasions as a symbol of power and unity. Stressing national solidarity and discipline, the fascists were hostile not only to liberal individualism and multiparty parliamentary democracy, but also to Marxist socialism, with its emphasis on class struggle and the special role of the working class. Largely because of its hostility to Marxism, fascism is generally placed on the "right" of the political spectrum. But though conservatives sought to exploit it, fascism was not merely conservative. It claimed to be a third way—a new, specifically modern alternative to both liberal democracy and Marxist communism, based on values that the war had brought to the fore.

With its claim to offer a modern political alternative, Italian fascism quickly attracted the attention of those in other countries who were disillusioned with parliamentary politics and hostile to the Marxist left. And just as fascism was anti-Marxist, the communists eventually made struggle against fascism their top priority. The interplay of communism and fascism, as new political experiments, proved central to the whole interwar period.

Consolidating Communist Power in Russia, 1917–1921

Even after leading the revolution that toppled the provisional government in November 1917, the Bolsheviks could not claim majority support in Russia. When the long-delayed elections to select a constituent assembly were finally held a few weeks after the revolution, the Bolsheviks ended up with fewer than one-quarter of the seats, while the Socialist Revolutionaries won a clear majority. But over the next three years the Communists, as the Bolsheviks renamed themselves, gradually consolidated their power, establishing a centralized and nondemocratic communist regime. Power lay not with the soviets, and not with some coalition of socialist parties, but solely with the Communist party. The Communists also established centralized control of the economy, subjecting workers to more rigorous discipline.

During its first years, the new communist regime encountered a genuine emergency that seemed to require a monopoly of power. For over two years the communist "Reds" had to fight a brutal civil war against counter revolutionary "Whites," people who had been dispossessed by the revolution or who had grown disillusioned with the Communist party. The Whites drew support from foreign intervention and from separatist sentiment, as several of the non-Russian nationalities of the old Russian Empire sought to defect, freeing themselves from Russian and communist control.

The counterrevolutionary assault seriously threatened the young communist regime and the territorial basis of the state it had inherited from the Russian Empire. In the final analysis, however, the Whites proved unable to rally much popular support. Peasants feared, plausibly enough, that a White victory would mean a restoration of the old order, including the return of their newly won lands to their former landlords. By the end of active fighting in November 1920, the communist regime had not only survived but regained most of the territory it had lost early in the civil war (Map 26.1).

The need to launch the new communist regime in this way, fighting counterrevolutionaries sup-

ported by foreign troops, inevitably affected Communist perceptions and priorities. Separatist sentiment might continue to feed counterrevolutionary efforts, so the new regime exerted careful control over the non-Russian nationalities. Ukraine, for example, had been the base for anticommunist activity as an independent republic under Menshevik leadership beginning in 1918, so in retaking the area in 1920 the Communists sought to bury all hopes for Ukrainian self-determination.

Even after the end of active fighting, the communist government had trouble re-establishing control over Georgia, Azerbaijan, and Russian Armenia in light of the strong separatist sentiment in those areas. Thus, when the Union of Soviet Socialist Republics (U.S.S.R.) was organized in December 1922, it was only nominally a federation of autonomous republics; strong centralization from the Communists' new capital in Moscow was the rule from the start.

Although they had to concentrate on the civil war from 1918 to late 1920, the Russian communists founded the Third, or Communist, International—commonly known as the Comintern—in March 1919, to make clear their break with the seemingly discredited strategies of the Second International. Through the Comintern, the Russian communists expected to translate their success in Russia into leadership of the international socialist movement. At the same time, however, many old-line Marxists elsewhere found it hard to swallow the notion that the leadership of European socialism had passed to the Bolshevik leaders of backward Russia. (See the box, "A Marxist Critique of Communism.")

From its founding in March 1919 until the spring of 1920, as a wave of leftist political agitation and labor unrest swept Europe, the Comintern actively promoted the wider revolution that Lenin had originally envisioned. Seeking to win mass support, the organization accented leftist solidarity and reached out to the rank and file in the labor unions. By the spring of 1920, however, it seemed clear that further revolution was not imminent. Thus, Comintern leaders began concentrating on improving organization and discipline for a more protracted revolutionary struggle.

The Russians felt that poor organization and planning had undermined the wider revolutionary possibility in Europe during 1919 and 1920. The Comintern would therefore cut through all

Boundary of the Russian Empire 1914
Boundary of area controlled by the Bolsheviks August 1918
Boundary of area controlled by the Bolsheviks October 1919
Boundary of Soviet territory March 1921
Boundary of area controlled by the anti-Bolshevik forces May 1920
White Russian armies
Non-Russian anti-Bolshevik forces

NORWAY

SWEDEN

FINLAND
(Independent)
1917

Entente fleet

Murmansk
BRITISH
FRENCH
CANADIANS
ITALIANS
SERBS

CANADIANS
AMERICANS

Archangel

BRITISH
FRENCH

FINNS

Helsinki

Kronstadt

Petrograd (Leningrad)

Yudenich
1918–20

British fleet

ESTONIA

Baltic Sea

LETTS

Pskov

LATVIA
Riga

BALTIC
GERMANS

BOLSHEVIK RUSSIA

Volga

Perm

Kazan

CZECHS

Kolchak 1918–19

LITHUANIA

GERMANY
(E. PRUSSIA)

Minsk

Vistula

Warsaw

POLAND

Brest-
Litovsk

Smolensk

Mogilev

Kaluga

Moscow

Nizhniy-
Novgorod

Penza

Samara

Orenburg

Ural

POLES

Gomel

Orel

Voronezh

Tambov

Saratov

Zhitomir

Kiev

UKRAINE

Denikin
1919

Kharkov

Poltava

Don

Tsaritsyn
(Stalingrad)

COSSACKS
1918–20

CZECHOSLOVAKIA

HUNGARY

ROMANIANS

Dnieper

Dniester

BESSARABIA

Yekaterinoslav

Rostov-on-
Don

Novocherkassak

Volga

Astrakhan

ROMANIA

FRENCH

Odessa

Cossacks

YUGOSLAVIA

Danube

Simferopol
FRENCH

Novorossiysk
BRITISH

BRITISH
Batum

Tiflis

BRITISH

Baku

Krasnovodsk

BRITISH

BULGARIA

GREECE

Kars

TURKEY

Tabriz

1918-19

Entente fleet

0   200   400 Km.

0   200   400 Mi.

PERSIA

the revolutionary romanticism and rhetoric to show the others what the Leninist strategy, or communism, meant in fact. The Russians themselves would have to call the shots, because what communism meant, above all, was tight organization and discipline.

The second Comintern congress, during the summer of 1920, devised twenty-one points, or conditions, to be fulfilled by a socialist party seeking affiliation with the Comintern. Most notably, any such party had to accept the Comintern's authority, to adopt a centralized organization, and to purge its reformists. The result of the Comintern's aggressive claim to leadership was a lasting schism in the European socialist movement by early 1921, for the Comintern attracted some, but not all, of the members of the existing socialist parties. All over the world those parties split between "communists," who chose to affiliate with the Comintern, and "socialists," who rejected Comintern leadership. These socialists still claimed to be Marxists, but they were not Leninists; they rejected the Russian Bolshevik strategy for taking political power.

At first, many European socialists had difficulty assessing the Comintern objectively. The Russian communists enjoyed great prestige because they had made a real revolution, while elsewhere socialists had talked and compromised, even getting swept up in wartime patriotism. When, for example, the French socialist party considered the matter at its national congress in December 1920, about 70 percent of the delegates opted for the Comintern and the twenty-one points, while a minority walked out to form a new socialist party. But as the implications of Comintern membership became clearer over the next few years, the balance shifted to favor the social-

Tatlin: Monument to the Third International Vladimir Tatlin created this model for a monument to the Third International, or Comintern, during 1919 and 1920. He envisioned a revolving structure, made of glass and iron, and twice as tall as the later Empire State Building. Although the monument was never built, Tatlin's bold, dynamic form symbolized the utopian aspirations of the early years of the communist experiment in Russia. *(David King Collection)*

Map 26.1 Foreign Intervention and Civil War in Revolutionary Russia, 1918–1920 By mid-1918 the new communist regime was under attack from many sides, by both foreign troops and anticommunist Russians. Bolshevik-held territory shrank during 1919, but over the next year the Red Army managed to regain much of what had been lost and to secure the new communist state. Anton Deniken, Alexander Kolchak, and Nicholas Yudenich commanded the most significant counter-revolutionary forces. (*Source:* Adapted from *The Times Atlas of World History*, 3d ed., by kind permission of Times Books.)

ists. Membership in the French Communist party, which stood at 131,000 in 1921, declined to 28,000 by 1932.

Late in 1923 the Comintern finally concluded that revolution elsewhere could not be expected any time soon. The immediate enemy was not capitalism or the bourgeoisie, but the socialists, the communists' rivals for working-class support. The communists' incessant criticism of the socialists, whom they eventually dubbed "social fascists," demoralized and weakened the European left, especially in the face of the growing threat of fascism.

A Marxist Critique of Communism

Karl Kautsky (1854–1938) was the leading spokesman for orthodox Marxism within the German Social Democratic party, the most influential Marxist party in the world during the era of the Second International. Thus it is striking that he harshly criticized Leninist Bolshevism, or communism, as a heretical departure that could lead only to disaster. Kautsky's **Terrorism and Communism,** *written in 1919, was central to a volley of charges and counter-charges that pitted him first against Lenin, then against Trotsky.*

The hereditary sin of Bolshevism has been its suppression of democracy through a form of government, namely, the dictatorship, which has no meaning unless it represents the unlimited and despotic power, either of one single person, or of a small organization intimately bound together. . . . It is easy to begin a dictatorship as it is to begin war, if one has the State power under control. But when once such steps have been taken, it is as difficult at will to stop the one as the other. . . .

. . . [W]herever Socialism does not appear to be possible on a democratic basis, and where the majority of the population rejects it, its time has not yet fully come. Bolshevism, on the other hand, argues that Socialism can only be introduced by being forced on a majority by a minority. . . . The Bolsheviks are prepared, in order to maintain their position, to make all sorts of possible concessions to bureaucracy, to militarism, and to capitalism, whereas any concession to democracy seems to them to be sheer suicide. And yet that alone offers any

possibility . . . of leading Russia along paths of economic progress and prosperous development towards some higher form of existence. . . .

. . . [S]ince the rise of the Soviet Republic, a new wedge has been driven through the Socialist ranks of Germany by Bolshevik propaganda, which has demanded that our Party should relinquish the essential claims of democracy. . . .

. . . It was only after long and bitter struggle that the proletariat succeeded in acquiring universal and equal suffrage—a perfectly well-known fact, which, however, all communists and their friends seem to have completely forgotten. Democracy, with its universal equal suffrage, is the method to transform the class-struggle out of a hand-to-hand fight into a battle of intelligence, in which one particular class can triumph only if it is intellectually and morally on a level with its opponent. Democracy is the one and only method through which the higher form of life can be realised. . . .

Source: Karl Kautsky, *Terrorism and Communism: A Contribution to the Natural History of Revolution* (Westport, Conn.: Hyperion Press, 1973), pp. 217–218, 220–222, 226, 229, 231.

From Lenin to Stalin, 1921–1929

Although it managed to win the civil war, the communist regime was clearly in crisis by the beginning of 1921, partly because of "war communism," the rough-and-ready controlled economy that the war effort seemed to make necessary. With industrial production only about one-fifth the 1913 total, there were strikes in the factories, and peasants

were resisting further requisitions of grain. Finally, in March 1921, sailors at the Kronstadt naval base mutinied, suffering considerable loss of life as governmental control was re-established.

With the very survival of the revolution in question, Lenin replaced war communism with the New Economic Policy, or NEP, in March 1921. Although transport, banking, heavy industry, and wholesale commerce remained under state control, the NEP restored considerable scope for private enterprise, especially in the retail sector and in agriculture. The economy quickly began to revive and by 1927 was producing at prewar levels.

But what about the longer term? If revolution elsewhere was no longer on the immediate horizon, could the Soviet Union—relatively backward economically and scarred by over a decade of upheaval—build a genuinely socialist order on its own? Certain measures were obvious: The new regime engineered rapid improvements in literacy, for example. But the Marxist understanding of historical progress required industrialization, and so debate focused on industrial development—the scope for it under Soviet conditions and its relationship to the creation of socialism.

This debate about priorities became bound up with questions about the leadership of the new regime. Lenin suffered the first of a series of strokes in May 1922 and then died in January 1924, setting off a struggle among his possible succes-

sors. Leon Trotsky, a powerful thinker and architect of the Red Army, was by most measures Lenin's heir apparent. Although he favored tighter economic controls to speed industrial development, Trotsky insisted that the Soviet Union should continue to concentrate on spreading the revolution to other countries.

In contrast, Nikolai Bukharin wanted to concentrate on the gradual development of the Soviet Union, based on a more open and conciliatory strategy than Trotsky envisioned. The way to promote industrialization was not by tightening controls, squeezing a surplus from agricultural producers, as Trotsky proposed, but by allowing those producers to profit, thereby building up purchasing power. By the time of his death early in 1924, Lenin had apparently begun thinking along the same lines. And he had come to have considerable misgivings about the man who would win this struggle for direction within the fragile new Soviet regime.

Rivals for the Soviet Leadership In July 1926 in Moscow, Soviet leaders carry the coffin of Feliks Dzerzhinsky, the first head of the secret police. Among them are Trotsky (with glasses, center left), Stalin (right foreground), and Bukharin (with mustache, at far right), rivals for the Soviet leadership after Lenin's death. The winner, Stalin, would eventually have his two competitors killed. *(David King Collection)*

The victory of Joseph Stalin (1879–1953), born Josef Djugashvili into a lower-class family in Georgia, in the Caucasian region, proved crucial to twentieth-century history—and decisive for the fate of Soviet communism. From the position of party secretary that he had assumed in 1922, he established his control within the Soviet system by 1929. Though he lacked Trotsky's charisma and knew little of economics, Stalin proved a master of backstage political maneuvering, playing his rivals against each other and accusing his critics of lack of faith in the Soviet working class. He first outmaneuvered Trotsky and his allies, removing them from positions of power, and finally forcing Trotsky himself into exile in 1929. Bitterly critical of Stalin to the end, Trotsky was finally murdered by Stalin's agents in Mexico in 1940. Stalin's victory over those like Bukharin was more gradual, but ultimately just as decisive.

The key was the policy of crash industrialization, favoring heavy industry and based on forced agricultural collectivization, that Stalin had put in place by 1929. In embarking on this program, he played up the great historical drama surrounding the Soviet experiment, with its almost incredible targets and goals. Suggestions by some that the pace could not be maintained only proved grist for Stalin's mill: "No, comrades," he told a workers' conference early in 1931, "the tempo must not be reduced. On the contrary, we must increase it as much as is within our powers and capabilities. . . . To slow the tempo would mean falling behind. And those who fall behind get beaten. . . . Do you want our socialist fatherland to be beaten and to lose its independence? . . . We are fifty or a hundred years behind the advanced countries. We must make good this distance in ten years. Either we do this or they will crush us."[2]

Stalin's program of rapid industrialization called forth an attempt to mobilize and control society without precedent in Western history. Although the economic sphere was crucial, this mobilization affected the whole shape of the regime—including, for example, cultural and artistic policy. During the 1920s, the possibility of building a new socialist society in the Soviet Union had attracted a number of modernist artists, who assumed that artistic innovation went hand in hand with the radical socioeconomic transformation the communists were seeking to engineer. These artists wanted to make art more socially useful and more central to the lives of ordinary people. With Soviet cultural officials welcoming their experiments, such Soviet artists as Vladimir Tatlin (1885–1956) and Kasimir Malevich (1878–1935) developed striking new cultural forms between 1919 and 1929.

But in 1929 Soviet officials began mobilizing the cultural realm to serve the grandiose task of building socialism in one country. No longer welcoming experiment and innovation, they demanded "socialist realism," which portrayed the achievements of the ongoing Soviet revolution in an inspiring, heroic light. Modernism, in contrast, they denounced as decadent and counter-revolutionary.

In retrospect, it is clear that a Stalinist revolution within the Soviet regime began in 1929, but where it was to lead was by no means certain—not even to Stalin himself. Still, the Soviet Union was pulling back, going its own way, by the end of the 1920s. For the foreseeable future, the presence of a revolutionary regime in the old Russia would apparently be less disruptive for the rest of Europe than it had first appeared.

The Crisis of Liberal Italy and the Creation of Fascism, 1919–1925

Fascism emerged directly from the Italian experience of World War I, which proved especially controversial because the Italians could have avoided it altogether. No one attacked Italy in 1914, and the country could have received significant territorial benefits just by remaining neutral. Yet it seemed to many, including leading intellectuals and educated young people, that Italy could not stand idly by in a European war, especially one involving Austria-Hungary, which still controlled significant Italian-speaking areas. To participate in this major war would be the test of Italy's maturity as a nation. In May 1915, Italy finally intervened on the side of the Triple Entente. The government's decision stemmed not from vague visions of renewal but from the commitment of tangible territorial gains, primarily at the expense of Austria-Hungary, that France and Britain made to Italy with the secret Treaty of London in April.

Despite the near collapse of the Italian armies in October 1917, Italy lasted out the war and contributed to the victory over Austria-Hungary. Supporters of the war felt that this success could lead to a thoroughgoing renewal of Italian public life. Yet many Italians had been skeptical of claims for the war from the outset, and the fact that it proved so much more difficult than expected hardly won them over. To Socialists, Catholics, and those loyal to the long-time liberal political leader Giovanni Giolitti, intervention itself had been a tragic mistake. Thus, despite Italy's participation in the victory, division over the war's significance immensely complicated the Italian political situation after the war was over.

The situation became even more volatile when Italy did not manage all the gains expected at the Paris Peace Conference. Italy got most of what it had been promised in the Treaty of London, but appetites increased with the dissolution of the Austro-Hungarian Empire. To some Italians, the disappointing outcome of the peace conference simply confirmed that the war had been a mistake, its benefits not worth the costs. But others were outraged at what seemed a denigration of the Italian contribution by France, Britain, and the United States. Thus the outcome fanned resentment not only of Italy's allies but also of the country's political leaders, who seemed too weak to deliver on what they had promised.

Italy's established leaders also failed at the task of renewing the country's political system in light of the war experience. The last gasp of the old liberal politics was Giovanni Giolitti, who returned for a final stint as prime minister in 1920, at the age of 78. But Giolitti, who had been adept at piecing together parliamentary majorities before the war, found the situation much less manageable now. In 1919, in a spirit of democratic reform, Italy had adopted proportional representation to replace the old system of small, single-member constituencies. The new system meant a greater premium on mass parties and party discipline at the expense of the one-to-one bargaining at which Giolitti had excelled. But the new mass politics quickly reached an impasse—partly because of the stance of the Italian Socialist party.

In contrast to the French and German parties, the Italian Socialists had never supported the war, and they did not accept the notion that the war experience could yield political renewal in the aftermath. So rather than reaching out to discontented war veterans, Socialist leaders talked of imitating the Bolshevik Revolution. During 1919 and 1920, the Italian situation seemed at least potentially

revolutionary. A wave of quasi-revolutionary labor unrest included several national strikes and finally a series of factory occupations during September 1920. But despite their revolutionary rhetoric, Italian Socialist leaders did not understand what Leninism involved in practice, and they did not carry out the planning and organization that might have made an Italian revolution possible.

The established political system was at an impasse, and the Socialist party seemed at once too inflexible and too romantic to lead some sort of radical transformation. It was in this context that fascism emerged, claiming to offer a third way. It was bound to oppose the Socialists and the socialist working class because of conflict over the meaning of the war and the kind of transformation Italy needed. And this antisocialist posture made fascism open to exploitation by reactionary interests. By early 1921 landowners in northern and central Italy were footing the bill as bands of young fascists drove around the countryside in trucks, beating up workers and burning down socialist meeting halls. But fascist spokesmen claimed to offer something other than mere reaction, a new politics that would prove better than Marxist socialism at pursuing the long-term interests of the working class.

At the same time, important sectors of Italian industry, which had grown rapidly thanks to government orders during the war, looked with apprehension toward the more competitive international economy that loomed now that the war was over. With its relative lack of capital and raw materials, Italy seemed to face an especially difficult situation. Nationalist thinkers and business spokesmen questioned the capacity of the present parliamentary system to provide the vigorous leadership that Italy needed. Prone to short-term bickering and partisanship, ordinary politicians lacked both the vision to pursue Italy's long-term international economic interests and the will to impose the necessary discipline on the domestic level. Thus, the government had been relatively weak in responding to the labor unrest of 1919 and 1920. (See the box, "Toward Fascism: Alfredo Rocco on the Weakness of the Liberal Democratic State.")

In postwar Italy, then, there was widespread discontent with established forms of politics, but those discontented were socially disparate, and their aims were not entirely compatible. Some had

Toward Fascism: Alfredo Rocco on the Weakness of the Liberal Democratic State

As Italy's minister of justice from 1925 to 1932, the Italian legal scholar Alfredo Rocco (1875–1935) spearheaded the construction of the new fascist state. Speaking in November 1920, he revealed why he would seek to replace parliamentary democracy with a new, stronger form of government. Rocco was troubled, most immediately, by the apparent weakness of the liberal state in the face of strikes by unions, or syndicates, of public-service employees. But the deeper problem he saw was liberal individualism, linked to shortsighted pursuit of personal advantage.

There is a crisis within the state; day by day, the state is dissolving into a mass of small particles, parties, associations, groups and syndicates that are binding it in chains and paralysing and stifling its activity: one by one, with increasing speed, the state is losing its attributes of sovereignty. . . . The conflict of interests between groups and classes is now being settled by the use of private force alone. . . . The state stands by impassively watching these conflicts which involve countless violations of public and private rights. This neutrality which, in liberal doctrine, was intended to allow free play for economic law in the clash of interests between the classes is now being interpreted as allowing the state to abandon its essential function of guardian of public order and agent of justice. . . .

. . . The eighteenth-century reaction against the state . . . came to a head politically in the explosion of the French Revolution. . . . From that time onwards, the claims of individualism knew no bounds. The masses of individuals wanted to govern the state and govern it in accordance with their own individual interests.

The state, a living organism with a continuous existence over the centuries that extends beyond successive generations and as such the guardian of the immanent historical interests of the species, was turned into a monopoly to serve the individual interests of each separate generation. . . .

Now there can be no doubt that one of the most serious consequences of liberal agnosticism was the emergence of syndicalism, a syndicalism that was at once violent, subversive, and opposed to the state.

. . . The state must return to its traditions, interrupted by the triumph of liberal ideology, and treat the modern syndicates exactly as it treated the medieval corporations. It must absorb them and make them part of the state. . . . On the one hand, syndicates must be recognized as essential and on the other they must be placed firmly beneath the control of the state. . . . But above all, it is necessary to change them from aggressive bodies defending particular interests into a means of collaboration to achieve common aims.

Source: Adrian Lyttelton, ed., *Italian Fascisms from Pareto to Gentile* (New York: Harper & Row, Harper Torchbooks, 1975), pp. 269, 273–275, 278–280.

been socialists before the war, others nationalists hostile to socialism. While some envisioned a more intense kind of mass politics, others thought the masses already had too much power. Still, these discontented groups agreed on the need for an alternative to both conventional parliamentary politics and conventional Marxist socialism. It was

widely felt that the germs of that alternative could be found in the Italian war experience.

The one person who seemed able to translate these discontents and aspirations into a new political force was the one-time socialist, Benito Mussolini (1883–1945). Mussolini came from the Romagna region of central Italy, his father a

Benito Mussolini The founder of fascism is shown with other fascist leaders in 1922, as he becomes prime minister of Italy. Standing at Mussolini's right (with beard) is Italo Balbo, later a pioneering aviator and fascist Italy's air force minister. *(Corbis-Bettmann)*

blacksmith and a socialist, his mother a teacher. Moderately well educated, Mussolini taught French for a time, but he demonstrated such talent in socialist journalism that he became editor of the Socialist party's national newspaper, *Avanti!*, in 1912, when only 29 years old. At that point many saw him as the fresh face needed to revitalize Italian socialism.

His concern with renewal had made Mussolini an unorthodox socialist even before 1914, and when the European war broke out, he was prominent among those on the Italian left who began to call for Italian intervention. The fact that socialists in France, Germany, and elsewhere had immediately rallied to their respective national war efforts caused him to reconsider the old socialism, based on international proletarian solidarity. But the Socialist party refused to follow his call for intervention, remaining neutralist and aloof, so Mussolini found himself cut off from his earlier constituency.

Through his new newspaper, *Il popolo d'Italia (The People of Italy)*, however, Mussolini promptly emerged as a leading advocate of Italian participation in the war. He saw military service once Italy intervened, and after the war he sought to rally those who aspired to translate the war experience into a new form of politics. But after founding the *fasci di combattimento* in March 1919, Mussolini became embroiled in periodic disputes with important sectors of his movement, especially as fascism gathered force in violent reaction against the socialist labor movement by 1921. Although young fascist militants wanted to replace the established parliamentary system with a wholly new political order, Mussolini seemed ever more prone to use fascism simply as his personal instrument as he jockeyed for power within the existing system. When his maneuvering finally won him the prime minister's post in October 1922, it was not at all clear that a change of regime, or a one-party dictatorship, was in the offing.

At that point, Mussolini, like most Italians, emphasized normalization and legality. Fascism had apparently been absorbed within the political system, perhaps to provide an infusion of youthful vitality after the war. With Mussolini as prime minister, there would be changes, but not revolutionary changes. Government would become more vigorous and efficient; the swollen Italian bureaucracy would be streamlined; the trains would run on time. But those who had envisioned more sweeping change were frustrated that nothing more had come of fascism than this.

In June 1924 the murder of Giacomo Matteotti (1885–1924), a moderate socialist parliamentary deputy, sparked a crisis that forced fascism to begin replacing the existing political system with a regime of its own. Shortly after a speech denouncing fascist violence, Matteotti was killed by fascist thugs. A great public outcry followed, and the key question for Italians in the months that followed concerned the responsibility of the government— and especially Mussolini himself—for the crime. Many of those from the establishment who had tolerated Mussolini as the man who could keep order now deserted him. A growing chorus called for his resignation.

Mussolini sought at first to be conciliatory and reassuring, but more radical fascists saw the crisis as a precious opportunity for fascism to end the compromise with the old order and to commit itself to creating a whole new political system. The crisis came to a head on December 31, 1924, when thirty-three militants called on Mussolini to demand that he make up his mind. The way out of the crisis was not to delimit the scope of fascism but to expand it. And Mussolini himself would have to accept responsibility for the fascist revolution, including its violent excesses. He was not an ordinary prime minister but the leader of fascism, *Il Duce,* and in that role he would have to implement the fascist revolution.

Finally at a crossroads, Mussolini committed himself to a more radical course when he addressed the Chamber of Deputies a few days later, on January 3, 1925. Defiantly claiming the "full political, moral, and historical responsibility for all that has happened," including "all the acts of violence," he promised to accelerate the transformation that he claimed to have initiated with his agitation for intervention in 1914 and 1915.[3] And now began the creation of a new fascist state, although

the compromises continued and the direction was never as clear as committed fascists desired.

Innovation and Compromise in Fascist Italy, 1925–1930

Early in 1925, the fascist government began to undermine the existing liberal system by imprisoning or exiling opposition leaders and outlawing the other parties and the nonfascist labor unions. But fascism was not seeking simply a conventional monopoly of political power; the new fascist state was to be totalitarian, all-encompassing, limitless in its reach. Under the old liberal regime, the fascists charged, the state had been too weak to promote the national interest, and the society had been too fragmented to enable the Italian nation to achieve its potential. So Mussolini's regime expanded the state's sovereignty and mobilized the society to create a deeper sense of national identity and solidarity among Italians. Thus, for example, a new system of labor judges settled labor disputes, replacing the right to strike. And the Fascist party fostered new forms of participation in organizations it devised for youth, for women, for leisure-time activities, and the like.

The centerpiece of the new fascist state was corporativism, which entailed mobilizing people as producers, through organization of the workplace. Groupings based on occupation, or economic function, were gradually to replace parliament as the basis for political participation and decision making. Beginning in 1926, corporativist institutions were established in stages until a Chamber of Fasces and Corporations at last replaced the old Chamber of Deputies in 1939.

It was especially through this corporative state that the fascists claimed to be fulfilling their grandiose mission and providing the world with a third way beyond both outmoded democracy and misguided communism. The practice of corporativism during the 1930s never lived up to such rhetoric, but the effort to devise new forms of political participation and decision making, as an alternative to parliamentary democracy, was central to fascism's self-understanding and its quest for legitimacy. And that effort attracted much attention abroad, especially with the Great Depression of the 1930s.

Despite the commitment to a new regime, however, fascism continued to compromise with pre-existing elites and institutions. The accommodation was especially evident in the arrangements with the Catholic church that Mussolini worked out in 1929, formally ending the dispute between the church and the new Italian state that had resulted from national unification in the nineteenth century. With the Concordat and the Lateran Pact, Mussolini restored the sovereignty of the Vatican and conceded to the church autonomy in education and supremacy in marriage law. This settlement of an old and thorny dispute afforded Mussolini a good deal of prestige abroad, as well as among nonfascist Italians. At the same time, the compromise seemed to imply a kind of endorsement of Mussolini's government on the part of the church and the establishment in Italy.

But such a compromise with a traditional institution displeased many fascists, who complained that it undermined the totalitarian aspirations of fascism to give this powerful, nonfascist institution an autonomous role in Italian public life. Such complaints led to a partial crackdown on Catholic youth organizations in 1931, as Mussolini continued trying to juggle traditionalist compromise and revolutionary pretension.

By the end of the 1920s, then, it remained unclear whether Italian fascism was a form of revolution or a form of restoration. It could be violent and disruptive, dictatorial and repressive, but Mussolini seemed dynamic and creative. Fascism featured corporativist reconstruction during the later 1920s, but it might move in other directions, especially if a new international configuration should tempt its restless leader. Though its ultimate direction remained unclear, fascism attracted those discontented with liberal democracy and Marxist socialism all over Europe. It was thus a major source of the volatility and ideological polarization that marked the postwar European political order.

THE SEARCH FOR MEANING IN A DISORDERED WORLD

For all its vitality, the new culture of the 1920s had something brittle about it; the frenetic pace masked a deeper sense that things had started to come apart and might well get worse. The feeling of release and excitement combined with an anxious longing for stability, for a return to order. The war had accelerated the long-term "moderniza-

EVENTS OF THE 1920s

March 1919	Founding of the Italian fascist movement
November 1920	End of fighting in the Russian civil war
October 1922	Mussolini becomes Italian prime minister
January 1923	French-led occupation of the Ruhr
January 1924	First Labour government in Britain
	Death of Lenin
August 1924	Acceptance of the Dawes Plan on German reparations
October 1925	Locarno Agreement
May 1926	Pilsudski's coup d'état in Poland
	Beginning of general strike in Britain
August 1929	Acceptance of the Young Plan on German reparations
October 1929	Death of Stresemann

tion" process toward large industries, cities, and bureaucracies, and toward mass politics, society, and culture. That process was positive, even liberating, in certain respects, but it was also disruptive and disturbing. Thus the emphases of intellectuals and artists differed dramatically in the 1920s.

Anxiety, Alienation, and Disillusionment

Concern about the dangers of the emerging mass civilization was especially clear in the *Revolt of the Masses* (1930), by the influential Spanish thinker José Ortega y Gasset (1883–1955). Ortega concluded that contemporary experience showed that ordinary people were intolerant and illiberal, incapable of creating standards, and content with the least common denominator. Communism and fascism indicated the violent, intolerant, and ultimately barbaric quality of the new mass age. But Ortega found the same tendencies in American-style democracy. Much of Europe seemed to be moving toward the mass politics and culture of the United States, but, as far as Ortega was concerned, that was a symptom of the deeper problem, not a solution.

Concern with cultural decline was part of a wider pessimism about the condition of the West, which stood in stark contrast to the belief in progress, and the attendant confidence in Western superiority, that had been essential to Western self-understanding before 1914. The German thinker Oswald Spengler (1880–1936) made concern with decline almost fashionable with his bestseller of the immediate postwar years, *The Decline of the West* (1918), which offered a cyclical theory purporting to explain how spirituality and creativity were giving way to a materialistic mass-based culture in the West.

To Sigmund Freud, the eruption of violence and hatred during the war and after indicated a deep, instinctual problem in the human makeup. In his gloomy essay *Civilization and Its Discontents* (1930), he suggested that the progress of civilization entails the bottling up of aggressive instincts, which are directed inward as guilt, or left to erupt in violent outbursts. This notion raised fundamental questions not only about the scope for progress but also about the plausibility of the Wilsonian ideals that had surrounded the end of the war. Perhaps, with civilization growing more complex, the Great War had been only the beginning of a new era of hatred and violence.

The sense that there is something incomprehensible, even nightmarish, about modern civilization, with its ever more complex bureaucracies, technologies, and cities, found vivid expression in the works of the Czech Jewish writer Franz Kafka (1883–1924), most notably in the novels *The Trial* and *The Castle*, published posthumously in the mid-1920s. In a world that claimed to be increasingly rational, Kafka's individual is the lonely, fragile plaything of forces utterly beyond reason, comprehension, and control. In such a world, the quest for law, or meaning, or God is futile, ridiculous.

Especially in the unsettled conditions of Weimar Germany, the anxiety of the 1920s tended to take extreme forms, from irrational activism to a preoccupation with death. There was a striking increase in suicides among students, even before the Depression. Youthful alienation prompted the novelist Jakob Wassermann (1873–1934) to caution German young people in 1932 that not all action is

good simply because it is action, that feeling is not always better than reason and discipline, and that youth is not in itself a badge of superiority.

Recasting the Tradition

Expressions of disillusionment revealed something about human experience in the unsettled new world, but they were sometimes morbid and self-indulgent. Other cultural leaders sought to be more positive; the challenge was not to give vent to new anxieties but to find antidotes to them. One direction was to recast traditional categories—in the arts, in religion, in politics—to make them relevant to contemporary experience. Although not all were optimistic about human prospects, an array of figures found such a renewal of tradition to be the best hope for responding to the disarray of the postwar world.

Even modernist artists sought to consolidate earlier gains, to pull things back together after the headlong experiment of the years before 1914. In music, composers as different as Igor Stravinsky (1882–1971) and Paul Hindemith (1895–1963) adapted earlier styles, although often in a somewhat ironic spirit, as they sought to weave new means of expression into familiar forms. The overall tendency toward neoclassicism during the period was an effort to give musical composition a renewed basis of order.

One of the most striking responses to the anxieties of this increasingly secular age was a wave of neo-orthodox religious thinking, most prominent in Protestants like the Swiss theologian Karl Barth (1886–1968). In his *Epistle to the Romans* (1919), Barth reacted against the liberal theology, the attempt to marry religious categories to secular progress, that had become prominent by the later nineteenth century. The war, especially, had seemed to shatter the liberal notion that the hand of God was at work in history, and Barth emphasized the radical cleft between God and this, the human world of history, sunken in sin. Recalling the accents of Augustine and Luther, he portrayed humanity as utterly lost, capable only of a difficult relationship with God, through faith, grace, and revelation.

With democracy faring poorly in parts of Europe, and with fascism and communism claiming to offer superior alternatives, some sought to make new sense of the democratic tradition. In Italy, Benedetto Croce (1866–1952) agreed with critics that the old justifications for liberal democracy, based on natural law or utilitarianism, were deeply inadequate, but he also became one of Europe's most influential antifascists. He insisted that the most significant innovations in modern thought show us why democratic values, institutions, and practices are still appropriate. We human beings are free, creative agents of a history that we make as best we can, without quite understanding what will result from what we do. Humility, tolerance, and equal access to political participation are essential to the process whereby the world is endlessly remade.

The new political challenges also stimulated fresh thinking within the Marxist tradition. By showing that Marxism could encompass consciousness as well as economic relationships, the Hungarian Georg Lukács (1885–1971) invited a far more sophisticated Marxist analysis of capitalist culture than had been possible before. Lukács accented the progressive role of realistic fiction and attacked the disordered fictional world of Kafka, which seemed to abandon all hope for human understanding of the forces of history. Though more eclectic, the Institute for Social Research, founded in Frankfurt, Germany, in 1923, gave rise to an influential tradition of criticism of capitalist civilization in what came to be known as the Frankfurt School. These innovations helped give the Marxist tradition a new lease on life in the West, even as it was developing in unforeseen ways in the Soviet Union.

The Search for a New Tradition

While some sought renewal from within the tradition, others insisted that a more radical break was needed—but also that the elements for a viable new cultural tradition were available.

Reflecting on the situation of women writers in 1928, the British novelist Virginia Woolf (1882–1941) showed how women in the past had suffered from the absence of a tradition of writing by women. By the 1920s, women had made important strides, but Woolf suggested that further advance required a more self-conscious effort by women to develop their own tradition. Most basically, women needed greater financial indepen-

dence so that they could have the time for scholarship, the leisure of cultivated conversation, and the privacy of "a room of one's own." Woolf also envisioned a new sort of historical inquiry, focusing on how ordinary women lived their lives, that could show contemporary women where they have come from—and thus deepen their sense of who they are. (See the box, "Tradition and Women: The Conditions of Independence.")

A very different effort to establish a new tradition developed in Paris in the early 1920s as the poet André Breton (1896–1966) spearheaded the surrealist movement in literature and the visual arts. Surrealism grew directly from Dada, an artistic movement that had emerged in neutral Zurich and elsewhere during the war. Radically hostile to the war, Dada artists developed shocking, sometimes nihilistic forms to deal with a reality that now seemed senseless and out of control. Some made collages from gutter trash; others indulged in nonsense or relied on chance. By the early 1920s, however, the surrealists felt it was time to create a new and deeper basis of order after the willful disordering of Dada. Having learned from Sigmund Freud about the subconscious, they sought to adapt Dada's novel techniques—especially the use of chance—to gain access to the subconscious, which they believed contains a deeper truth, without the overlay of logic, reason, and conscious control.

But other artists, seeking to embrace the modern industrial world in a more positive spirit, found surrealism merely escapist. Among them was Walter Gropius (1883–1969), a pioneering modernist architect and leader of an influential German art school, the Bauhaus, during the 1920s. (See the feature, "Weighing the Evidence: Modern Design," on pages 992–993.) Gropius held that it was possible to establish new forms of culture, even a new tradition, that could be affirmative and reassuring in the face of the postwar cultural disarray. Rather than putting up familiar neoclassical or neo-Gothic buildings, "feigning a culture that has long since disappeared," we must face up to the kind of civilization we have become—industrial, technological, efficient, urban, democratic, mass-based. If we pick and choose from among the elements of our new machine-based civilization, we can again have a culture that works, an "integrated pattern for living."[4]

Tradition and Women: The Conditions of Independence

Speaking in 1928 about the situation of women writers, the British novelist Virginia Woolf raised questions that were relevant to all women seeking the opportunity to realize their potential. Indeed, her reflections about the value of difference, and the need for particular traditions, inspired those seeking equal opportunity for decades to come. And her question about why we know so little about women's lives in the past helped stimulate later historians to ask precisely the questions she envisioned about the experience of ordinary people.

Woman . . . pervades poetry from cover to cover; she is all but absent from history. . . .

Occasionally an individual woman is mentioned, an Elizabeth, or a Mary; a queen or a great lady. But by no possible means could middle-class women with nothing but brains and character at their command have taken part in any one of the great movements which, brought together, constitute the historian's view of the past. . . . What one wants . . . is a mass of information; at what age did she marry; how many children had she as a rule; what was her house like; had she a room to herself; did she do the cooking; would she be likely to have a servant? All these facts lie somewhere, presumably, in parish registers and account books; the life of the average Elizabethan woman must be scattered about somewhere, could one collect it and make a book of it. It would be ambitious beyond my daring, I thought, looking about the shelves for books that were not there, to suggest to the students of those famous colleges that they should rewrite history, though I own that it often seems a little queer as it is, unreal, lop-sided. . . .

But whatever effect discouragement and criticism had upon their writing—and I believe they had a very great effect—that was unimportant compared with the other difficulty which faced them (I was still considering those early nineteenth-century novelists) when they came to set their thoughts on paper—that is that they had no tradition behind them, or one so short and partial that it was of little help. For we think back through our mothers if we are women. It is useless to go to the great men writers for help, however much one may go to them for pleasure. . . .

. . . [W]omen have sat indoors all these millions of years, so that by this time the very walls are permeated by their creative force, which has, indeed, so overcharged the capacity of bricks and mortar that it must needs harness itself to pens and brushes and business and politics. But this creative power differs greatly from the creative power of men. And one must conclude that it would be a thousand pities if it were hindered or wasted, for it was won by centuries of the most drastic discipline, and there is nothing to take its place. It would be a thousand pities if women wrote like men, or lived like men, or looked like men. . . . Ought not education to bring out and fortify the differences rather than the similarities?

Source: Virginia Woolf, *A Room of One's Own* (San Diego: Harcourt Brace Jovanovich, Harvest/HBJ, 1989), pp. 43–45, 76, 87–88.

This "constructive," promodern impulse was particularly prominent in Germany, but it could be found all over—in the modernists of the Russian Revolution, in the French painter Fernand Léger (1881–1955), in the Swiss architect Le Corbusier (1887–1965). Whereas many of their contemporaries were at best ambivalent about the masses, these artists sought to bring high art and mass society together in the interests of both. And they welcomed the new patterns of life that seemed to be emerging in the new world of mass production and fast-paced cities.

Léger: Three Women With their sleekly impersonal forms, Fernand Léger's paintings suggested that human beings could fit comfortably into the mass machine age that was emerging. This work dates from 1921. (*Léger, Fernand,* Three Women [Le grand dejeuner], *1921. Oil on canvas, 6'¼" × 8'3". The Museum of Modern Art, New York. Mrs. Simon Guggenheim Fund.*)

SUMMARY

The 1920s proved a contradictory period of vitality and despair, pacifism and violence, restabilization and instability. The era began with bright hopes for democracy, yet the outcome of the democratic experiment in east-central Europe was disappointing. In Germany as well, the new democratic republic remained on the defensive, then failed to weather the economic depression that began in 1929. Even Italy, heir by the 1920s to a respectable tradition of democracy, gave rise to the troubling new phenomenon of fascism. A hopeful new spirit of international conciliation drew France and Germany closer together by the end of 1925, but France and Britain seemed to draw further apart as the British, preoccupied with colonial concerns, distanced themselves from politics on the Continent.

Despite tensions and doubts, however, in early 1929 restabilization seemed to have taken hold in Europe. Even Germany, Italy, and the Soviet Union, the most volatile and potentially disruptive of the major countries, seemed to be settling down. Still, it would all come apart over the next decade, leading to political extremism and another major war. In light of that outcome, the successes, even the vitality, of the 1920s appear superficial, and the unrecognized tensions stand out. When the decade is taken on its own terms, it is clear that the vitality, the renewed prosperity, and the diplomatic goodwill were all real, but so were the unresolved problems that made the 1920s a prelude to the more difficult 1930s, when the notion that Europe had returned to normal came to seem but a fairy tale.

NOTES

1. Quoted in Robert G. L. Waite, *Vanguard of Nazism: The Free Corps Movement in Postwar Germany, 1918–1923* (New York: W. W. Norton, 1969), pp. 14–15.
2. Quoted in Martin McCauley, *The Soviet Union Since 1917* (London and New York: Longman, 1981), pp. 72–73.
3. Benito Mussolini, speech to the Italian Chamber of Deputies, January 3, 1925, from Charles F. Delzell, ed., *Mediterranean Fascism, 1919–1945* (New York: Harper & Row, 1970), pp. 59–60.
4. Walter Gropius, *Scope of Total Architecture* (New York: Collier Books, 1962), pp. 15, 67.

SUGGESTED READING

General Surveys

Ansprenger, Franz. *The Dissolution of the Colonial Empires.* 1989. Covers the whole decolonization process but is stronger than most surveys on the impact of World War I and the events of the interwar period.

Kitchen, Martin. *Europe Between the Wars: A Political History.* 1988. A clear narrative of international and domestic political developments from a leftist perspective.

Sontag, Raymond J. *A Broken World, 1919–1939.* 1971. Comprehensive survey by a master historian. Concerned especially with domestic politics and international relations but includes developments in science and the arts.

Political Restoration

Carsten, F. L. *Revolution in Central Europe, 1918–1919.* 1972. A straightforward study emphasizing Germany, Austria, and Hungary. Accents the failure to overcome conservative forces and to lay the foundations for successful democracy.

Maier, Charles S. *Recasting Bourgeois Europe: Stabilization in France, Germany, and Italy in the Decade After World War I.* 1975. An important but somewhat difficult study showing how European elites sought new bases of stability, especially through new authority relationships in industry, during the 1920s.

Marquand, David. *Ramsay MacDonald.* 1977. Thorough and balanced account of the controversial career of Britain's first Labour prime minister.

Trachtenberg, Marc. *Reparation in World Politics: France and European Economic Diplomacy, 1916–1923.* 1980. A detailed but readable study questioning the widespread view that France imposed an unreasonable reparations burden on Germany after World War I.

The Soviet Union

Fitzpatrick, Sheila, Alexander Rabinowitch, and Richard Stites, eds. *Russia in the Era of NEP: Explorations in Soviet Society and Culture.* 1991. Illuminating scholarly essays accenting the ambiguities of the transitional 1920s, when class identity, economic activity, and gender roles had been radically disrupted but had not yet settled into the forms that, in the 1930s, came to characterize the Soviet experiment.

Lewin, M[oshe]. *Russian Peasants and Soviet Power: A Study of Collectivization.* 1975. A pioneering account of the process leading to the decision for forced collectivization by 1929.

———. *The Making of the Soviet System: Essays in the Social History of Interwar Russia.* 1985. Essays by a leading social historian. Especially strong on agriculture and the peasantry.

Stites, Richard. *Revolutionary Dreams: Utopian Visions and Experimental Life in the Russian Revolution.* 1989. A vivid account of the utopian aspirations that gave the new communist regime emotional force from 1917 to 1930.

Tucker, Robert C. *Stalin as Revolutionary, 1879–1929: A Study in History and Personality.* 1973. A pioneering account of Stalin's early years and rise to power, probing the sources of the elements of character and personality that helped shape his subsequent rule.

Fascism in Italy

De Grand, Alexander. *Italian Fascism: Its Origins and Development,* 2d ed. 1989. An accessible overview, providing a good sense of the heterogeneity of both the purposes and the policies of Italian fascism.

Forgacs, David, ed. *Rethinking Italian Fascism: Capitalism, Populism and Culture.* 1986. An important collection of essays, reflecting critical rethinking of conventional approaches and interpretations.

Gentile, Emilio. *The Sacralization of Politics in Fascist Italy.* 1996. Engaging account of the rituals, symbols, and myths that, in Italy during the 1920s, fed the first overtly totalitarian experiment.

Lyttelton, Adrian. *The Seizure of Power,* 2d ed. 1988. Based on pioneering archival research, this book offers a detailed dissection of the complex process through which the fascist movement took control of Italy.

Mack Smith, Denis. *Mussolini: A Biography.* 1983. A lively, critical account, and one of the most important biographies of Mussolini in English.

Sarti, Roland. *Fascism and the Industrial Leadership in Italy, 1919–1940: A Study in the Expansion of Private Power Under Fascism.* 1971. Carefully researched study demonstrating the cat-and-mouse relationship between the fascist regime and big business.

Segré, Claudio. *Italo Balbo: A Fascist Life.* 1987. A readable biography of one of the most colorful of Mussolini's lieutenants.

Tannenbaum, Edward. *The Fascist Experience: Italian Society and Culture, 1922–1945.* 1972. A comprehensive study of life in fascist Italy.

Weimar Germany

Diehl, James M. *Paramilitary Politics in Weimar Germany.* 1977. Probing account of the rise and normalization of political violence, showing how it helped undermine the Weimar Republic.

Gay, Peter. *Weimar Culture: The Outsider as Insider.* 1970. An influential study providing a good sense of the conflicting impulses—the embrace of modernity, the nostalgia for wholeness, the sense of foreboding—that made German culture so intense and vital during the 1920s.

Herf, Jeffrey. *Reactionary Modernism: Technology, Culture, and Politics in Weimar and the Third Reich.* 1984. Influential study showing how antimodern and technocratic themes could be fused in the special circumstances of interwar Germany.

Kolb, Eberhard. *The Weimar Republic.* 1988. Provides a good overall survey, then pinpoints the recent trends in research and the questions at issue among historians of the period.

Mommsen, Hans. *The Rise and Fall of Weimar Democracy.* 1996. A detailed political history identifying the social tensions that the democratic political process proved unable to handle.

Peukert, Detlev. *The Weimar Republic: The Crisis of Classical Modernity.* 1992. Accessible interpretive study, accenting the strains stemming from the rapid modernization of the 1920s. Stresses the loss of political legitimacy even before the onset of Depression.

Schrader, Bärbel, and Jürgen Schebera. *The "Golden" Twenties: Art and Literature in the Weimar Republic.* 1988. A superbly illustrated study that gives a good sense of complexity and contradiction of German culture in the 1920s.

Stern, Fritz. *The Politics of Cultural Despair: A Study in the Rise of the Germanic Ideology.* 1961. A classic work focusing on three thinkers of the German radical right; shows how their resentment of the modernization process fed antidemocratic sentiment in Germany.

Turner, Jr., Henry Ashby. *Stresemann and the Politics of the Weimar Republic.* 1963. A well-balanced study of the most important German statesman of the Weimar period.

Willett, John. *Art and Politics in the Weimar Period: The New Sobriety, 1917–1933.* 1978. A lively, complex study that plays up the effort of German cultural innovators to make art constructive by combining it with work, production, and everyday life.

Social Change and Gender Relations

Grossmann, Atina. *Reforming Sex: The German Movement for Birth Control and Abortion Reform, 1920-1950.* 1995. Innovative study tracing German debate and policy across three distinct political regimes.

Kent, Susan Kingsley. *Making Peace: The Reconstruction of Gender in Interwar Britain.* 1993. Concise and accessible work examining the use of traditionalist representations of gender roles in response to the anxieties unleashed in Britain by the war.

Nolan, Mary. *Visions of Modernity: American Business in the Modernization of Germany.* 1994. Examines the ambiguous impact of Americanism on Germany in the 1920s, when the United States seemed to stand both for economic success based on mass production and for an impersonal, alienating mass culture.

Pedersen, Susan. *Family, Dependence, and the Origins of the Welfare State: Britain and France, 1914–1945.* 1993. An effective comparative study showing how concerns about gender roles and family relations helped shape discussion and policy as government assumed greater responsibility for social welfare. Detailed but readable, a landmark in the new gender history.

Roberts, Mary Louise. *Civilization Without Sexes: Reconstructing Gender in Postwar France, 1917-1927.* 1994. Sophisticated study arguing that the anxieties accompanying dislocation and change in France after World War I were brought to the level of ordinary people through gender categories, which even came to shape the understanding and experience of change itself.

MODERN DESIGN

Led by Walter Gropius, the Bauhaus of Weimar Germany became the most influential art school of the twentieth century. As the incubator of modern architecture and design, it helped determine what the "modern world" would look like. And it did so consciously, believing it could help us embrace as our own the unnerving new world of machines, mass production, and rapid transit. But many, especially in the unsettled conditions of Weimar Germany, found the Bauhaus style alienating and threatening. Bauhaus artists seemed to foster all that was negative in the emerging world of industry and technology, impersonal cities, and large bureaucracies. When the Nazis came to power in 1933, they promptly closed the Bauhaus down.

Things made by the Bauhaus, from chairs to housing projects, still look "modern"—but why? How do they symbolize or manifest modernity? Do these new forms lead us to affirm the modern world, or are they alienating and repelling?

We note first that the Bauhaus stressed clean lines, simple and precise forms. In designing the chair shown here, Marcel Breuer tried to eliminate

Marcel Breuer, Chair, Tubular Steel and Black Fabric, 1925–1926 (*Bauhaus Archiv, Berlin*)

everything extraneous to the function of the chair as an object to sit in. The Bauhaus's own building, illustrated here, has none of the classical or Gothic ornament—the columns and pediments, the gargoyles and pointed arches—that had long seemed essential to architecture. Notice the extensive use of glass and steel. Bauhaus architects sought to use the new materials and construction techniques that industrialization made possible. On the one hand, Bauhaus design seems coolly impersonal, on the other utilitarian and functional.

In evaluating these pioneering modern forms, we must ask what the Bauhaus architects and designers were reacting against. In the nineteenth century, historical revivals dominated architecture, but by the 1920s such historical references seemed irrelevant, even dishonest. Why should banks look like Greek temples? Why should modern universities copy Gothic guild halls? According to the Bauhaus, it was time we faced up to the fact that the industrial age has cut us off from the old tradition. At first, the experience of disruption may be troubling, but we can develop an honest, satisfying, distinctively modern style based on the possibilities and patterns of the industrial world itself.

If the modern world is one of mass culture and mass society, perhaps even the best artists need to rethink the purpose of what they do. Students at the Bauhaus were taught that art was no longer something to be venerated in a museum or acquired by a cultivated and wealthy elite. Rather, art was to be socially useful. No longer was there to be a rigid distinction between art objects and utilitarian objects. Bauhaus artists placed great emphasis on the design of ordinary things for everyday use, from textiles to chairs to desk lamps. No longer was art to express the personality of the artist. Reacting against the romantic cult of individual self-expression, the Bauhaus stressed teamwork and impersonal design. Moreover, by using new materials, mass production, and even prefabrication, artists could play a newly democratic role—in designing, for example, housing projects that would give ordinary working people more light and fresh air than older urban buildings provided. Projects like the one shown here, built for employees of the Siemens electrical company, could be constructed affordably because they stressed the efficient use of materials and avoided irrelevant ornamentation.

Mass production, efficiency, and the purging of ornaments, however, did not have to undermine beauty. According to the Bauhaus, beauty in the modern world is to be found in clarity, in economy of means, in sleekly impersonal precision. From the Bauhaus perspective, Breuer's chair and the Siemens housing project are beautiful because they are efficient and functional.

Others, however, found the impersonal art of the Bauhaus to be cold and materialistic. Some, including the Nazis, labeled it "international" and "Bolshevik" as well. As far as such critics were concerned, the Bauhaus was simply giving in to the tyranny of the machine.

The cultural historian Peter Gay has argued that "what Gropius taught, and what most Germans did not want to learn, was . . . that . . . the cure for the ills of modernity is more, and the right kind of modernity."* Surely it is true that many Germans were particularly nostalgic and resistant to change during the 1920s. But perhaps the Bauhaus was too quick to assume that in the modern world we have no choice but to start over; perhaps it underestimated the need for continuity with our cultural traditions.

The kind of thinking nurtured at the Bauhaus led to the urban renewal and freeway projects that, by the end of the 1960s, had radically altered the face of many American cities, destroying much that had connected the present with the past. We continue to wrestle with what tradition means in the face of modernity and change, but

*Peter Gay, *Weimar Culture: The Outsider as Insider* (New York: Harper & Row, 1970), p. 101.

The Bauhaus Building, Dessau, 1925–1926 *(Vanni/Art Resource, NY)*

Housing Complex for Siemens Company Employees, Berlin, 1929 *(Bauhaus Archiv, Berlin)*

we are now less likely to assume that we can do without the old, the visible embodiments of a living tradition.

In the aftermath of World War I, however, Walter Gropius and his colleagues at the Bauhaus thought it would be healthier and more honest to make a clean break with the past. They set out with missionary fervor to derive a wholly new tradition from the modern industrial world. And controversial though they were, their designs were instrumental in giving "modern" its characteristic look. ✑

CHAPTER 27

The Tortured Decade, 1930–1939

"They shall not pass," proclaimed the charismatic Spanish communist Dolores Ibarruri (1895–1989), whose impassioned speeches and radio broadcasts helped inspire the heroic defense of Madrid during the civil war that gripped Spain, and captured the attention of the world, during the later 1930s. Known as La Pasionaria—the passion flower—Ibarruri became a living legend for her role in defending the new Spanish republic, formed in 1931, against the nationalist forces seeking to overthrow it. But the Republican side lost, and she spent 38 years in exile before returning to Spain in 1977, after the end of the military dictatorship that had resulted from the Spanish civil war.

In her effort to rally the Republican side, Ibarruri stressed the political power of women, and indeed women were prominent in the citizen militias defending Madrid and other Spanish cities. Women fought for the Spanish republic in part because it seemed to open new opportunities for them, especially as it became more radical by 1936. But just as some women welcomed the new direction, others became politically active on the opposing Nationalist side—to support the church, to combat divorce, to defend separate spheres for women as the guardians of private life and family values.

The ideological polarization that characterized the Spanish civil war reflected the expanding reach of politics in the 1930s, whenthe advent of economic depression and the challenge from new governmental systems immeasurably complicated the European situation. The intricate mechanisms used to realign the international economy after World War I had seemed effective for most of the 1920s, but by 1929, they were beginning

"¡No pasarán!" ("they shall not pass"):
Defending the democratic republic during the Spanish civil war.

to backfire, helping to trigger the Great Depression. During the early 1930s the economic crisis intensified sociopolitical strains all over the Western world and even beyond, intensifying anti-Western feeling and creating further opportunities for anticolonialists. In Germany, the Depression helped undermine the Weimar Republic and gave a major impetus to Nazism. The rise to power of the Nazi leader, Adolf Hitler, intensified the ideological polarization in Europe, and his policies produced a series of diplomatic crises that eventually led to a new European war.

German Nazism paralleled Italian fascism in its hostility to both parliamentary democracy and Marxist socialism, in its willingness to use violence, and in its reliance on a single charismatic leader. But Nazism emphasized racism and anti-Semitism in a way that Italian fascism did not, and it more radically transformed its society.

At about the same time, the direction of Stalin's communist regime in the Soviet Union seemed to converge, in some ways, with these new fascist regimes—especially with German Nazism. So though they expressed widely different aims, Stalinism and Nazism are sometimes lumped together as instances of totalitarianism. Both apparently sought total government control over all aspects of society, and in both secret police agencies came to play significant roles. But by the later 1930s the Soviet Union under Stalin experienced a form of police terror that not even Nazi Germany could match. Thus, although "totalitarianism" has become central to twentieth-century political language, it proves a tricky concept indeed, and whether it is correct to group Stalinist communism with Nazism remains controversial.

However they are to be classified, fascism, Nazism, and communism seemed able to sidestep—or surmount—the ills of the Depression, and they stood opposed to the parliamentary democracy that had established roots in Britain, France, Scandinavia, and elsewhere. Such liberal democracy had long seemed the direction of progressive political change, but in the face of the political and economic challenges of the 1930s the democratic movement appeared to lose its momentum. The defeat, by early 1939, of the democratic republic in Spain by the authoritarian Nationalists seemed to exemplify the political direction of the decade.

THE GREAT DEPRESSION

Although the stock market crash of October 1929 in the United States helped usher in the world economic crisis of the early 1930s, it had this effect only because the new international economic order after World War I was extremely fragile. By October 1929, in fact, production was already declining in all the major Western countries except France.

The economies of Germany and the states of east-central Europe remained particularly vulnerable after World War I, and in the increasingly interdependent economic world, their weaknesses magnified problems that started elsewhere. The crash of the U.S. stock market led to a restriction of credit in central Europe, which triggered a more general contraction in production and trade. Facing cruel dilemmas, policymakers proved unable to master the situation for the first few years of the crisis. The consequences—both human and political—were profound.

Sources of the Economic Contraction

Certain economic sectors, especially coal mining and agriculture, were already suffering severe problems by the mid-1920s, well before the stock market crash of 1929. British coal exports fell partly because oil and hydroelectricity were rapidly developing as alternatives. Unemployment in Britain was never less than 10 percent even in the best of times between the wars. In agriculture high prices worldwide during the war produced oversupply, which, in turn, led to a sharp drop in prices once the war was over. During the later 1920s, bumper harvests of grain and rice in many parts of the world renewed the downward pressure on prices. The result of low agricultural prices was a diminished demand for industrial goods, which impeded growth in the world economy.

Throughout the 1920s, finance ministers and central bankers had difficulty juggling the economic imbalances created by the war, centering on war debts to the United States and German reparations obligations to France, Britain, and Belgium. The strains in the system finally caught up with policymakers by 1929, when an international restriction of credit forced an end to the international economic cooperation that had been attempted in the past decade.

Unemployment in Britain
The Depression hit Britain hard—and its effects continued to be felt throughout the 1930s. These unemployed shipyard workers from Jarrow, in northeastern England, are marching to London in 1936 to present a protest petition. *(Hulton-Getty/Tony Stone Images)*

The shaky postwar economic system depended on U.S. bank loans to Germany, funneled partly by international agreements but also drawn by high interest rates. By 1928, however, U.S. investors were rapidly withdrawing their capital from Germany in search of the higher returns that could be made in the booming U.S. stock market. This tightened credit in Germany. And then the crash of the overpriced U.S. market in October 1929 deepened the problem by forcing suddenly strapped American investors to pull still more of their funds out of Germany. This process continued over the next two years, weakening the major banks in Germany and the other countries of central Europe, which were closely tied to the German economy. In May 1931 the bankruptcy of Vienna's most powerful bank, the Credit-Anstalt, made it clear that a crisis of potentially catastrophic proportions was in progress.

Despite attempts at adjustment on the international level, fears of bank failure or currency devaluation led to runs on the banks and currencies of Germany and east-central Europe. To maintain the value of the domestic currency in world markets, and thereby to resist the withdrawal of capital, government policymakers raised interest rates. This measure was not sufficient to stem the capital flight, but by restricting credit still more, it further dampened domestic economic activity.

Finally, the Germans seemed to have no choice but to freeze foreign assets—that is, to cease allowing conversion of assets held in German marks to other currencies. In this atmosphere, investors seeking the safest place for their capital tried to cash in currency for gold—or for British pounds, which could then be converted to gold. This flight to gold, however, soon put such pressure on the British currency that Britain was forced to devalue the pound and sever it from the gold standard in September 1931. This proved the definitive end of the worldwide system of economic exchange based on the gold standard that had gradually crystallized during the nineteenth century.

The absence of a single standard of exchange, combined with various currency restrictions, made foreign trade more difficult and uncertain, thereby diminishing it further. So did the scramble for tariff protection that proved a widespread response to the developing crisis. Crucial was the U.S. Smoot-Hawley Tariff Act of June 1930, which raised taxes on imports by 50 to 100 percent, forcing other nations to take comparable steps. Even Britain, long a bastion of free trade, adopted a peacetime tariff for the first time in nearly a century with the Import Duties Act of 1932, which imposed a 10 percent tax on most imports.

The decline of trade spread depression throughout the world economic system. By 1933 most major European countries were able to export no more than two-thirds, and in some cases as little as one-third, of the amount they had sold in 1929. At the same time, losses from international bank failures contracted credit and purchasing power and furthered the downward spiral, until by 1932 the European economies had shrunk to a little over half their 1929 size. This was the astonishing outcome of the short-lived prosperity of the 1920s.

Consequences and Responses

The Depression was essentially a radical contraction in economic activity; with less being produced and sold, demand for labor declined sharply. In Germany, industrial production by early 1933 was only half what it had been in 1929, and roughly 6 million Germans, or one-third of the labor force, were unemployed.

Although its timing and severity varied, the Depression profoundly affected the lives of ordinary people throughout the Western world and beyond. Unemployment produced widespread malnutrition, which led, in turn, to sharp increases in such diseases as tuberculosis, scarlet fever, and rickets. The decline in employment opportunities helped produce a backlash against the ideal of "the new woman," working outside the home, which had been a prominent aspect of the new freedom of the 1920s in Germany and elsewhere. (See the box, "Retreating from 'the New Woman.'") Even those men and women who hung on to jobs suffered from growing insecurity. In his aptly titled *Little Man, What Now?* (1932), the German novelist Hans Fallada (1893–1947) explored the effects of the Depression on members of the lower middle class—store clerks, shopowners, civil servants. Such people were first resentful, then resigned, as their dreams of security, of "order and cleanliness," fell apart.

During the first years of the Depression, central bankers everywhere sought to balance budgets in order to reassure investors and stabilize the currency. With economies contracting and tax revenues declining, the only way to balance the budget was to reduce sharply government spending. In addition, governments responded to the decline in exports by forcing wages down, seeking to enhance competitiveness abroad. But by cutting

purchasing power at home, both these measures reinforced the contraction in economic activity.

Economic policymakers based their responses on the "classical" economic model that had developed from the ideas of Adam Smith in the eighteenth century (see pages 747–748). According to this model, a benign "invisible hand" ensured that a free-market price for labor, for capital, and for goods and services would produce an ongoing tendency to economic equilibrium. A downward turn in the business cycle was a normal and necessary adjustment; government interference would only upset this self-adjusting mechanism.

By 1932, however, it was clear that the conventional response was not working, and governments began seeking more actively to stimulate the economy. Strategies varied widely. In the United States, Franklin D. Roosevelt (1882–1945) defeated the incumbent president, Herbert Hoover, in 1932 with the promise of a New Deal—a commitment to increase government spending to restore purchasing power. In fascist Italy, a state agency created to infuse capital into failing companies proved a reasonably effective basis for collaboration between government and business. In Germany, economics minister Hjalmar Schacht (1877–1970) mounted an energetic assault on the economic problem after Hitler came to power in 1933. Government measures sealed off the German mark from international fluctuations, stimulated public spending, partly on rearmament, and kept wages low. By 1935 Germany was back to full employment. This success added tremendously to Hitler's popularity.

High unemployment in Norway, Sweden, and Denmark helped social democrats win power in all three of these Scandinavian countries by the mid-1930s. The new left-leaning governments responded to the economic crisis not by a frontal assault on capitalism but by pioneering the "welfare state," providing such benefits as health care, unemployment insurance, and family allowances. To pay for the new welfare safety net, the Scandinavian countries adopted a high level of progressive taxation and pared military expenditures to a minimum. The turn to a welfare state in Scandinavia eased the immediate human costs of the Depression and helped restore production by stimulating demand. At the same time, the Scandinavian model attracted much admiration as a "third way"

Retreating from "the New Woman"

By the 1930s the ideal of "the new woman" was fading, partly because, with jobs scarce, women felt pressured to concentrate on home and family. But some women had already begun to question the ideal after encountering the disillusioning side of the new freedom, the "modernity," of the 1920s. In an essay entitled "Back to the Good Old Days?" published in Germany in January 1933, just as Hitler was coming to power, the leftist psychologist Alice Rühle-Gerstel (1894–1943) sought to make sense of the changes at work.

It began with a slight uneasiness; with a feeling that something was not right, was no longer right. About two or three years ago. Just at the time, incidentally, when the world crisis was first making itself known with the same slight, uneasy feeling. Gradually a few timid women's emancipationists retreated into the ranks of the opponents of women's emancipation, into the ranks of those who had always—already in 1870, already in 1920—said "that's as far as it can go" with the so-called liberation of women. It began, that is, as women began to cut an entirely new figure. A new economic figure who went out into public economic life as an independent worker or wage-earner entering the free market that had up until then been free only for men. A new political figure who appeared in the parties and parliaments, at demonstrations and gatherings. A new physical figure who not only cut her hair and shortened her skirts but began to emancipate herself altogether from the physical limitations of being female. Finally, a new intellectual-psychological figure who fought her way out of the fog of sentimental ideologies and strove toward a clear, objective knowledge of the world and the self.

This new figure never became average, never became the mass female. There was no time for that. Until today this new figure has remained a pioneer, the standard-bearer—no, the female standard-bearer—of something that had yet to develop. But before she could evolve into a type and expand into an average, she once again ran up against barriers. Her old womanly fate—motherhood, love, family—trailed after her into the spheres of the new womanliness, which immediately presented itself as a new objectivity. And she therefore found herself not liberated, as she had naively assumed, but now doubly bound: conflicts between work and marriage now appeared, between uninhibited drives and inhibited mores, conflicts between the public and private aspects of her life, which could not be synthesized. . . .

The emancipated woman, having emerged from the muddy pond (or, if you will, the clear lake) of her previous state, found herself on a bleak shore, surrounded here and there by skyscrapers that blocked her view. She simply noted: I have less time than my mother had; I have less money, less joy, less hope, less consolation. And thus did she too, with quiet disillusion defiantly concealed, begin her cautious return to the ranks of the backward-looking.

. . . [T]he ideology of the new womanliness hangs in the present vacuum, flat as yesterday's balloon.

Source: Anton Kaes, Martin Jay, and Edward Dimendberg, eds., *The Weimar Republic Sourcebook* (Berkeley and Los Angeles: University of California Press, 1994), pp. 218–219.

between free-market capitalism and the various dictatorial extremes.

In the other European democracies the Depression proved more intractable. Although Britain saw some recovery by the mid-1930s, it was especially the rearmament of the later 1930s, financed by borrowing, or deficit spending, that got the British economy growing again. France, less dependent on international trade, experienced the consequences of the world crisis only gradually. But by the early

~ **ENCOUNTERS WITH THE WEST** ~

Gandhi on Nonviolence

Mohandas Gandhi, a successful English-educated lawyer, emerged as a major force in the movement for Indian independence just after World War I. Calling first for a strategy of noncooperation with the British colonial overlords, Gandhi gradually developed a philosophy of nonviolent civil disobedience, which won widespread sympathy for the cause of Indian independence. The following excerpts from articles published in 1935 and 1939—years notable for outbreaks of violence elsewhere—explain the significance of nonviolence to Gandhi's overall strategy.

Non-violence to be a creed has to be all-pervasive. I cannot be non-violent about one activity of mine and violent about others. That would be a policy, not a life-force. That being so, I cannot be indifferent about the war that Italy is now waging against Abyssinia. . . . India had an unbroken tradition of non-violence from times immemorial. But at no time in her ancient history, as far as I know it, has it had complete non-violence in action pervading the whole land. Nevertheless, it is my unshakeable belief that her destiny is to deliver the message of non-violence to mankind. . . .

. . . India as a nation is not non-violent in the full sense of the term. . . . Her non-violence is that of the weak. . . . She lacks the ability to offer physical resistance. She has no consciousness of strength. She is conscious only of her weakness. If she were otherwise, there would be no communal problems, nor political. If she were non-violent in the consciousness of her strength, Englishmen would lose their role of distrustful conquerors. We may talk politically as we like and often legitimately blame the English rulers. But if we, as Indians, could but for a moment visualize ourselves as a strong people disdaining to strike, we should cease to fear Englishmen whether as soldiers, traders or administrators, and they to distrust us. Therefore if we became truly non-violent we should carry Englishmen with us in all we might do. In other words, we being millions would be the greatest moral force in the world, and Italy would listen to our friendly word. . . .

. . . [W]hen society is deliberately constructed in accordance with the law of non-violence, its structure will be different in material particulars from what it is today. But I cannot say in advance what the government based wholly on non-violence will be like.

What is happening today is disregard of the law of non-violence and enthronement of violence as if it were an eternal law. The democracies, therefore, that we see at work in England, America and France are only so called, because they are no less based on violence than Nazi Germany, Fascist Italy or even Soviet Russia. The only difference is that the violence of the last three is much better organized than that of the three democratic powers. Nevertheless we see today a mad race for outdoing one another in the matter of armaments. And if when the clash comes, as it is bound to come one day, the democracies win, they will do so only because they will have the backing of their peoples who imagine that they have a voice in their own government whereas in the other three cases the peoples might rebel against their own dictatorships.

Holding the view that without the recognition of non-violence on a national scale there is no such thing as a constitutional or democratic government, I devote my energy to the propagation of non-violence as the law of our life—individual, social, political, national and international. I fancy that I have seen the light, though dimly. I write cautiously, for I do not profess to know the whole of the Law. If I know the successes of my experiments, I know also my failures. But the successes are enough to fill me with undying hope.

I have often said that if one takes care of the means, the end will take care of itself. Non-violence is the means, the end for every nation is complete independence.

Source: Raghavan Iyer, ed., *The Essential Writings of Mahatma Gandhi* (Delhi: Oxford University Press, 1991), pp. 245–247, 262–263.

1930s, France, too, was suffering its effects, which lingered to the end of the decade, helping to poison the political atmosphere.

The Depression also had a major impact on the non-Western world and its relations with the West. The radical restriction of international trade meant a sharp decline in demand for the basic commodities that colonial and other regions exported to the industrialized West. The value of Latin American exports declined by half. With foreign exchange scarce, Latin Americans had to curtail imports and to intensify their efforts to industrialize on their own. This enterprise required a greater role for the state—and often entailed political change in an authoritarian direction.

In colonial nations, strains from the Depression further undermined the prestige of the liberal capitalist West, already shaken by World War I, and fed nationalist, anti-Western sentiments. In India, the increase in misery among rural villagers spread the movement for national independence from urban elites to the rural masses. In this context Mohandas Gandhi, who had become known by 1920 for advocating noncooperation with the British, became the first Indian leader to win a mass following throughout the Indian subcontinent. Encouraging villagers to boycott British goods, Gandhi accented simplicity, self-reliance, and an overall strategy of nonviolent civil disobedience based on Indian traditions. (See the box, "Encounters with the West: Gandhi on Nonviolence.")

In Japan, the strains of the Great Depression helped produce precisely the turn to imperialist violence that Gandhi sought to counter. Densely populated yet lacking raw materials, Japan was particularly dependent on international trade and thus reacted strongly as increasing tariffs elsewhere cut sharply into Japanese exports. Led by young army officers who were already eager for their country to embrace a less subservient form of Westernization, Japan turned to aggressive imperialism, seeking to justify its course by claiming to spearhead a wider struggle to free East Asia from Western imperialism. Attacking in 1931, Japanese forces quickly reduced Manchuria to a puppet state, but the Japanese met stubborn resistance when they began seeking to extend this conquest to the rest of China in 1937.

Japanese pressure indirectly furthered the rise of the Chinese communist movement, led by Mao Zedong (1893–1976). Securing a base in the Yanan district in 1936, Mao began seeking to apply Marxism-Leninism to China through land reform and other measures to link the communist elite to the Chinese peasantry. Mao was notable among those adapting Western ideas to build an indigenous movement that would at once overcome Western imperialism and create an alternative to Western liberal capitalism.

The Depression, and the halting responses of the democracies in dealing with it, enhanced the prestige of the new regimes in the Soviet Union, Italy, and Germany, which appeared either to have avoided the economic crisis or to be dealing with it more creatively. Capitalism seemed to be on trial—and so, increasingly, did parliamentary democracy.

THE STALINIST REVOLUTION IN THE SOVIET UNION

Seeking to build "socialism in one country," Joseph Stalin led the Soviet Union during the 1930s through one of the most astounding transformations the world had ever seen. It mixed change and achievement with brutality and terror in bizarre and often tragic ways. The resulting governmental system, which gave Stalin unprecedented power, proved crucial to the outcome of the great experiment that began with the Russian Revolution of 1917. But whether the fateful turn of the 1930s had been implicit in the Leninist revolutionary model all along, or stemmed mostly from unforeseen circumstances and Stalin's idiosyncratic personality, remains uncertain.

Crash Industrialization and Forced Collectivization, 1929–1933

Stalin's strategy entailed rapid industrialization accompanied by compulsory collectivization in agriculture. By forcing peasants into large, government-controlled farms, political leaders could control agricultural pricing and distribution. On that basis, the government could squeeze a surplus from agriculture to be sold abroad, earning money to buy the equipment needed to build factories, dams, and power plants.

Beginning in 1930, the peasants were forcibly herded into collectives. So unpopular was this measure that many peasants killed their livestock or smashed their farm implements rather than let

1002   *Chapter 27*   **The Tortured Decade, 1930–1939**

The Struggle for Socialism
The effort to create a socialist society in the Soviet Union required that Communist party activists educate the peasants in rural areas. As a result of the Stalinist strategy chosen by 1930, this process included touting the new collective farms and denouncing those peasants who had prospered in the relatively liberal economic climate after 1923. Here, a party activist (in dark shirt) leads a meeting of a rural committee in the Chuvash Republic of Russia during the early years of collectivization. *(Endeavour Group UK)*

them be collectivized. During the first two months of 1930, as many as 14 million head of cattle were slaughtered, resulting in an orgy of meat eating and a shortage of draft animals. In 1928, there had been 60 million cattle in the Soviet Union; by 1934 there were only 33.5 million.

Collectivization served, as intended, to squeeze from the peasantry the resources needed to finance industrialization. But it was carried out with extreme brutality. What was being squeezed was not merely a surplus—the state's extractions cut into subsistence. So while Soviet agricultural exports went up in the years after 1930, large numbers of peasants starved to death. The great famine that developed during 1932–1933 resulted in between 5 and 6 million deaths, over half of them in Ukraine. This "terror-famine" went unrecorded in the Soviet press. (See the box, "Carrying out the Stalinist Revolution.")

By 1937 almost all Soviet agriculture took place on collective farms—or on state farms set up in areas not previously under agriculture. However, restrictions on private plots and livestock ownership were eased slightly after 1933, and partly as a result agriculture rebounded and living standards began to rise. By the late 1930s, moreover, significant increases in industrial output had established solid foundations in heavy industry, including the bases for military production.

Soviet propaganda, including art in the official socialist realist style, glorified the achievements of the new Soviet industrial and agricultural workers. "Stakhanovism," named for a coal miner who had heroically exceeded his production quota, became the term for the prodigious economic achievements that the regime came to expect as it proclaimed the superiority of the communist system. Indeed, the fact that in the Soviet Union state management seemed to produce results while much of the world languished in depression helps explain the prestige that communism developed among intellectuals, in both the Western and non-Western worlds.

But, whatever its successes, this forced development program created many inefficiencies and entailed tremendous human costs. The Soviet Union could probably have done at least as well, with much less suffering, through other strategies of industrial development. Moreover, Stalin's program departed from certain socialist principles—egalitarianism in wages, for example—that the regime had taken very seriously during the late 1920s. By 1931, bureaucratic managers, concerned simply with maximizing output, were openly fa-

Carrying out the Stalinist Revolution

Lev Kopelev (b. 1912), who came from a middle-class Jewish family, was an enthusiastic Communist as a young man. Believing the Soviet Communist party embodied the progressive movement of history, he eagerly assisted in the forced collectivization drive of the early 1930s, which caused such suffering and death in his native Ukraine. But after World War II he became critical of Soviet communism, and he was finally exiled from the Soviet Union in 1980.

Our great goal was the universal triumph of Communism, and for the sake of that goal everything was permissible. . . . And to hesitate or doubt about all this was to give in to "intellectual squeamishness" and "stupid liberalism," the attributes of people who "could not see the forest for the trees."

. . . . I saw what "total collectivization" meant—how . . . mercilessly they stripped the peasants in the winter of 1932–33. I took part in this myself, scouring the countryside, searching for hidden grain, testing the earth with an iron rod for loose spots that might lead to buried grain. With the others, I emptied out the old folks' storage chests, stopping my ears to the children's crying and the women's wails. For I was convinced that I was accomplishing the great and necessary transformation of the countryside; that in the days to come the people who lived there would be better off for it; that their distress and suffering were a result of their own ignorance or the machinations of the class enemy; that those who sent me—and I myself—knew better than

the peasants how they should live, what they should sow and when they should plow.

In the terrible spring of 1933 I saw people dying from hunger. I saw women and children with distended bellies, turning blue, still breathing but with vacant, lifeless eyes. . . .

Nor did I lose my faith. As before, I believed because I wanted to believe. Thus from time immemorial men have believed when possessed by a desire to serve powers and values above and beyond humanity. . . .

That was how we thought and acted—we, the fanatical disciples of the all-saving ideals of communism. When we saw the base and cruel acts that were committed in the name of our exalted notions of good, and when we ourselves took part in those actions, what we feared most was to lose our heads, fall into doubt or heresy and forfeit our unbounded faith. . . .

. . . The concepts of conscience, honor, humaneness we dismissed as idealistic prejudices, "intellectual" or "bourgeois," and, hence, perverse.

Source: Lev Kopelev, *No Jail for Thought* (London: Secker & Warburg, 1977), pp. 11–13.

voring workers in certain industries. To ensure labor discipline, new labor laws established harsh punishments for absenteeism or tardiness and severely limited the freedom of workers to change jobs. There was no collective bargaining and no right to strike.

From Opposition to Terror, 1932–1938

Stalin's radical course, with its brutality and uncertain economic justification, quickly provoked opposition. During the summer of 1932, a group centered around M. N. Ryutin (1890–1937) circulated

among party leaders a two-hundred-page tract calling for a retreat from Stalin's economic program and a return to democracy within the party. It advocated readmitting those who had been expelled—including Stalin's archenemy, Leon Trotsky. Moreover, the document strongly condemned Stalin personally, describing him as "the evil genius of the Russian Revolution, who, motivated by a personal desire for power and revenge, brought the Revolution to the verge of ruin."[1]

Stalin promptly had Ryutin and his associates expelled from the party, then arrested and imprisoned. But especially as the international situation grew menacing during the 1930s, Stalin became ever more preoccupied with the scope for further opposition. Both Germany and Japan exhibited expansionist aims that might threaten Soviet territories. Trotsky from exile might work with foreign agents and Soviet dissidents to sabotage the Soviet development effort.

In 1934 the assassination of Sergei Kirov (1888–1934), party leader of Leningrad (the former Petrograd), gave Stalin an excuse to intensify the crackdown against actual and potential opponents. Though not conclusive, the evidence suggests that Stalin was himself responsible for killing Kirov, a popular moderate who seemed a plausible rival. In any case, the event served Stalin's interests by creating a sense of emergency justifying extraordinary measures. The eventual result was a series of bizarre show trials, deadly purges, and, ultimately, a kind of terror, with no one safe from arrest by the secret police.

Between 1936 and 1938, famed Bolshevik veterans like Nikolai Bukharin and major functionaries like Genrikh Yagoda (1891–1938), who had just been removed as chief of the secret police, confessed to a series of sensational trumped-up charges: that they had been behind the assassination of Kirov, that they would have killed Stalin if given the chance, that they constituted an "anti-Soviet, Trotskyite center," spying for Germany and Japan and preparing to sabotage Soviet industry in the event of war.

The authorities extracted these confessions partly through torture, partly through threats to the families of the accused. But some, at least, offered false confessions because they believed they were serving the revolution in doing so. All along, the revolution had required a willingness to compromise one's personal scruples, including concerns about personal honor and dignity. Even though they were false, these confessions could help the communist regime ward off the genuine dangers it faced. So in confessing, the accused would be serving the long-term cause, which they believed to be bigger than Stalin and the issues of the moment. What some could not see—or admit—was that the triumph of Stalinism was fatally compromising the original revolutionary vision.

Almost all the accused, including Bukharin and others who had been central to the revolution, were convicted and executed. Soviet authorities did not dare risk public trial for the few who refused, even in the face of torture, to play their assigned roles and confess. Among them was Ryutin, who was shot in secret early in 1937.

But the show trials were very public, surrounded by great propaganda. And the unending talk of foreign intrigues, assassination plots, and "wrecking"—all intended to undo the heroic achievements of the Soviet Union—shaped the perceptions of the Soviet people. There seemed a vast conspiracy at work, responsible, among other things, for the shortages and economic misfortunes that had accompanied the crash industrialization program.

Meanwhile, a purge of the army in 1937 wiped out its top ranks, with 35,000 officers—half the entire officer corps—shot or imprisoned in response to unfounded charges of spying and treason. The Communist party underwent several purges, culminating in the great purge of 1937 and 1938. Of the roughly two thousand delegates to the 1934 congress of the Communist party, over half were shot during the next few years. In particular, the purge of the party got rid of the remaining "old Bolsheviks," those who had been involved in the revolution in 1917 and who thus retained a certain independence. By 1939, Stalin loyalists constituted the entire party leadership.

Although it centered on the party, the purge process touched virtually everyone as the net widened by 1938. Everybody knew someone who had been implicated, so everyone felt some measure of vulnerability to arrest, which would be followed by execution or exile to forced-labor camps. Moreover, there was a random, arbitrary quality to the purges, so there was no way to be sure what was punishable or who was "guilty." Ordinary people were thus tempted to denounce others, if only to demonstrate their own loyalty and conscientiousness.

The final toll was staggering. Of the approximately 160 million people in the Soviet Union, something like 8.5 million were arrested during 1937 and 1938, and of these perhaps 1 million were executed by shooting. Half the total membership of the Communist party—1.2 million people—was arrested; of these, 600,000 were executed, and the vast majority of the rest died in forced-labor camps. Altogether, the several purges resulted in approximately 8 million deaths. The death toll from all of Stalin's peacetime policies between

1929 and 1939, including the forced collectivizations, was perhaps 20 million. Even Hitler and the Nazi regime did not match this appalling total.

Communism and Stalinism

This fateful turn in the development of the communist regime in the Soviet Union proved to be one of the pivotal events of modern history. Some insist that Stalin was pursuing a deliberate, coordinated policy, seeking to create an all-encompassing system of control. Others argue that though Stalin's ultimate responsibility is undeniable, he was simply responding on an improvised basis to a situation that became chaotic as the communists tried to carry through a revolution in a backward country.

Virtually from the beginning of its power, the Communist party had attracted careerists and opportunists, and thus there were bitter differences among party leaders over party membership. Was membership to be limited to a trained professional elite, which would need to purge the party of opportunists periodically, or was the party to be a mass-based vehicle for socialist education? The concern to root out potential opponents during the 1930s gave various factions an opportunity to have it out with their enemies. Stalin sometimes held back before lending his support to one side or the other. But even if the chain of events did not stem from a coherent policy, Stalin took advantage of it and, by 1939, had crushed all actual or potential opposition. In a sense, the outcome was the triumph of Stalin over the Communist party, which had held on to the original Bolshevik ideal of collective leadership by a revolutionary vanguard.

Obviously Stalinism was one possible outcome of Leninist communism, but was it the logical, even the inevitable, outcome? Leninism had accented centralized authority and the scope for human will to force events, so it may have created a framework in which Stalinism was likely to develop. Yet Stalin's personal idiosyncrasies and growing paranoia seem to have been crucial for the Soviet system to develop as it did by the end of the 1930s.

Stalin had won his position from within the Communist party, based on his backroom political skill, not his popular appeal. Although a special aura came to surround him by the end of the 1930s, he remained essentially the chief bureau-

crat, referring to the surviving fragments of the Marxist-Leninist blueprint as he oversaw the process of revolutionary implementation. So even as Stalin monopolized power, his style of leadership remained decidedly different from that of Mussolini and Hitler, who based their power on personal charisma and a direct relationship with the people.

HITLER AND NAZISM IN GERMANY

Beset with problems from the start, the Weimar Republic lay gravely wounded by 1932. Various antidemocratic groups competed to replace it. The winner was the Nazi movement, led by Adolf Hitler, who became chancellor in January 1933. Nazism took inspiration from Italian fascism, but Hitler's regime proved far more dynamic—and more troubling—than Mussolini's.

To understand where Nazism came from, it is necessary to distinguish among the motives and purposes that nourished it. For example, the substantial voting support the Nazis gained by 1932 was essential in giving Hitler a chance to govern. But to understand why so many Germans voted for the Nazis is not to understand why Hitler ended up using power as he did. Nor can we explain Nazism simply by invoking power and opportunism, because the most troubling aspects of Nazism, from personal dictatorship to the extermination of the Jews, stemmed from a wider vision of the world, radiating from Hitler himself.

Nazism was not conventionally revolutionary, in the sense of mounting a frontal challenge to the existing socioeconomic order. Some of its themes were traditionalist and even antimodernizing. But in the final analysis Nazism was anything but conservative. Indeed, it constituted a direct assault on what had long been held as the best of the Western tradition.

The Rise of Nazism, 1919–1933

The National Socialist German Workers' party (NSDAP), or Nazism, emerged from the turbulent situation of Munich just after the war. A center of leftist agitation, the city also became a hotbed of the radical right, nurturing a number of new nationalist, militantly anticommunist political groups. One of them, a workers' party founded

Early Nazism Although Nazism did poorly in national elections before the Depression, the movement attracted a loyal and militant membership, in which young people were especially numerous. Here young Nazis parade with banners in 1923. *(© Harlingue-Viollet)*

under the aegis of the right-wing Thule Society early in 1919, attracted the attention of Adolf Hitler, who soon gave it his personal stamp.

Adolf Hitler (1889–1945) had been born not German but Austrian, the son of a lower government official. As a young man he had gone to Vienna, hoping to become an artist, but he failed to gain admission to the Viennese Academy of Fine Arts. By 1913 he had become a German nationalist hostile to the multinational Habsburg empire, and he immigrated to Germany to escape service in the Austrian army. He was not opposed to military service per se, however, and when war broke out in 1914, he immediately volunteered for service in the German army.

Corporal Hitler experienced firsthand the fighting at the front and, as a courier, performed bravely and effectively. Indeed, he was in a field hospital being treated for gas poisoning when the war ended. Although his fellow soldiers considered him quirky and introverted, Hitler found the war experience crucial; it was during the war, he said later, that he "found himself."

Following his release from the hospital, Hitler worked for the army in routine surveillance of extremist groups in Munich. In this role he joined the infant German Workers' party late in 1919. When his first political speech at a rally in February 1920 proved a resounding success, Hitler began to believe he could play a special political role. From this point, he gradually developed the confidence to lead a new nationalist, anticommunist, and anti-Weimar movement.

But Hitler jumped the gun in November 1923 when, with Erich Ludendorff at his side, he led the Beer Hall Putsch in Munich, an abortive attempt to launch a march on Berlin to overthrow the Republic. On trial after this effort failed, Hitler gained greater national visibility as he denounced the Versailles treaty and the Weimar government. Still, *Mein Kampf* (My Battle), the political tract that he wrote while in prison during 1924, sold poorly. To most, Hitler was simply a right-wing rabble-rouser whose views were not worth taking seriously.

His failure in 1923 convinced Hitler that he should exploit the existing political system, but not challenge it directly, in his quest for power on the national level. Yet Hitler did not view the NSDAP as just another political party, playing by the same rules as the others within the Weimar system. Thus, most notably, the Nazi party maintained a paramilitary arm, the *Sturmabteilung* (SA), which provoked a good deal of antileftist street violence.

By 1928, the Nazis were still peripheral to national politics, attracting only 2.6 percent of the vote in the Reichstag elections of that year. However, in the elections of September 1930, the first since the onset of the Depression, they increased their share dramatically to 18.3 percent of the vote. When elections were held again in July 1932, their vote exploded to 37.3 percent, enough to make them the largest party in the Reichstag.

Both the Nazis and the Communists gained electoral support as unemployment grew, but the Germans voting for the Nazis were not simply those most threatened economically. Nor did the Nazi party appeal primarily to the uneducated or socially marginal. Rather, the party served as a focus of opposition for those now alienated from the

Weimar Republic itself. Although the Nazis did relatively poorly among Catholics and industrial workers, they put together a broad, fairly diverse base of electoral support, ranging from artisans and small shopkeepers to university students and civil servants. Still, that support was shallow. The Nazi vote in 1932 was largely a protest vote, reflecting the hope that Nazism, or Hitler himself, portended something new and more effective. Although Nazism was clearly anticommunist, anti-Weimar, and anti-Versailles, its positive program remained vague.

As the crisis of the Weimar Republic deepened in 1932, conservative fears of a Marxist outcome played into Hitler's hands. By May 1932, when Heinrich Brüning's government fell, President Hindenburg was relying heavily on a narrow circle of advisers who wanted to take advantage of the Nazis' mass support for conservative purposes. Two of those advisers, Franz von Papen (1878–1969) and General Kurt von Schleicher (1882–1934), each got a chance to govern, but neither succeeded. By January 1933, each had grown hostile to the other, and Papen lined up a new coalition that he proposed to Hindenburg to replace Schleicher's government. Hitler would be chancellor, Papen himself vice chancellor, and Alfred Hugenberg (1865–1951), the leader of the Nationalist party, finance minister. For months, Hindenburg had resisted giving Hitler a chance to govern. But he felt this combination might work to establish a parliamentary majority, box out the left, and contain Nazism. So Hindenburg turned to Hitler, who became chancellor at last on January 30, 1933.

The Consolidation of Hitler's Power, 1933–1934

When Hitler became chancellor, it was not obvious that a change of regime was beginning. Like his predecessors, he could govern only with the president's approval, and governmental institutions like the army, the judiciary, and the diplomatic corps, though hardly bastions of democracy, were not in the hands of committed Nazis. But although an element of caution and cultivated ambiguity remained, a revolution quickly began, creating a new regime, the Third Reich.

On February 23, just weeks after Hitler became chancellor, a fire engulfed the Reichstag building in Berlin. It was set by a young Dutch communist acting on his own, but it seemed to suggest that a communist uprising was imminent. This sense of emergency afforded the new Hitler government an excuse to restrict civil liberties and imprison leftist leaders, including the entire Communist parliamentary delegation. Even in this atmosphere of crisis the Nazis could not win a majority in the Reichstag elections of March 5. But support from the Nationalists and the Center party enabled the Nazis to win Reichstag approval for an enabling act granting Hitler the power to make laws on his own for the next four years, bypassing both the Reichstag and the president.

Although the Weimar Republic was never formally abolished, the laws that followed fundamentally altered government, politics, and public life in Germany. The other parties were either outlawed or persuaded to dissolve so that in July 1933 the Nazi party was declared the only legal party. When President Hindenburg died in August 1934, the offices of chancellor and president were merged, and Germany had just one leader, Adolf Hitler, with unprecedented power in his hands. Members of the German armed forces now swore loyalty to him personally.

During this period of power consolidation, Hitler acted decisively but carefully, generally accenting normalization. To be sure, his methods occasionally gave conservatives pause. In an especially dramatic episode, the "blood purge" of June 30, 1934, he had several hundred people murdered. Although Hitler used the occasion to settle a number of old scores, the purge was directed against the SA, led by Ernst Röhm (1887–1934). Because Röhm and the SA had had pretensions of controlling the army, his removal seemed evidence that Hitler was taming the radical elements in his own movement. In fact, however, this purge led to the ascendancy of the Schutzstaffel, or SS, the select Nazi elite, led by Heinrich Himmler (1900–1945). Linked to the Gestapo, the secret police apparatus, the SS became the institutional basis for the most troubling aspects of Nazism. The blood purge proved a step to radical measures barely conceivable in 1934.

Hitler's World-View

In achieving the chancellorship and in expanding his power thereafter, Hitler showed himself an

Hitler's World-View: Nature, Race, and Struggle

Hitler outlined his beliefs and aims in **Mein Kampf,** *which he wrote while in prison in 1924. The following passages reveal the racism, the anti-Semitism, and the emphasis on nature and struggle that formed the core of his world-view.*

No more than Nature desires the mating of weaker with stronger individuals, even less does she desire the blending of a higher with a lower race, since, if she did, her whole work of higher breeding, over perhaps hundreds of thousands of years, might be ruined with one blow.

Historical experience . . . shows with terrifying clarity that in every mingling of Aryan blood with that of lower peoples the result was the end of the cultured people. . . .

Here, of course, we encounter the objection of the modern pacifist, as truly Jewish in its effrontery as it is stupid! "Man's rôle is to overcome Nature!"

. . . [T]his planet once moved through the ether for millions of years without human beings and it can do so again some day if men forget that they owe their higher existence, not to the ideas of a few crazy ideologists, but to the knowledge and ruthless application of Nature's stern and rigid laws. . . .

In the Jewish people the will to self-sacrifice does not go beyond the individual's naked instinct of self-preservation. . . .

If the Jews were alone in the world, they would stifle in filth and offal; they would try to get ahead of one another in hate-filled struggle and exterminate one another. . . .

Source: Adolf Hitler, *Mein Kampf* (Boston: Houghton Mifflin, Sentry, 1943), pp. 286–289, 299, 301–302.

adept politician, but he was hardly a mere opportunist, seeking to amass power for its own sake. Power was only the instrument for the grandiose transformation he believed necessary.

Hitler acted on the basis of a world-view that coalesced by about 1924—and that remained extremely important to him. (See the box, "Hitler's World-View: Nature, Race, and Struggle.") This is not to say that he was an original thinker or that his ideas were true—or even plausible. But he sought to make systematic sense of things, and the most disturbing features of his political activity stemmed directly from the resulting world-view. His most committed followers shared certain of his ideas, although fanatical loyalty to Hitler himself was more important for some of them. The central components of Hitler's thinking—geopolitics, biological racism, anti-Semitism, and Social Darwinism—were by no means specifically German. They could be found all over the Western world by the early twentieth century.

Geopolitics claimed to offer a scientific understanding of world power relationships based on geographic determinism. In his writings of the 1920s, Hitler warned that Germany faced imminent decline unless it confronted its geopolitical limitations. To remain fully sovereign in the emerging new era of global superpowers like the United States, Germany would have to act quickly to expand its territory. Otherwise it would end up like Switzerland or the Netherlands.

For decades German imperialists had argued about whether Germany was better advised to seek overseas colonies or to expand its reach in Europe. As Hitler saw it, Germany's failure to make a clear choice had led to its defeat in World War I. Now choice was imperative, and current geopolitical thinking seemed to indicate the direction for expansion. Far-flung empires relying on naval support were said to be in decline. The future lay with land-based states—unified, geographically contiguous, with the space necessary for self-sufficiency. By expanding eastward, into Poland and the western part of the Soviet Union, including Ukraine especially, Germany could conquer the living space, or *Lebensraum*, necessary for agricultural-industrial balance—and ultimately for self-sufficiency.

Though limited and mechanistic, this geopolitical way of thinking is at least comprehensible, in light of the German vulnerabilities that had surfaced during the war. The other three strands of Hitler's world-view were much less plausible, though each had become prominent during the second half of the nineteenth century. Biological racism insisted that built-in racial characteristics determine what is most important about any individual. Anti-Semitism went beyond racism in claiming that Jews play a special and negative role. The fact that the Jews were dispersed and often landless indicated that they were different—and parasitical. Finally, Social Darwinism, especially in its German incarnation, accented the positive role of struggle—not among individuals, as in a prominent American strand, but among racial groups.

The dominant current of racist thinking labeled the "Aryans" as healthy, creative, superior. Originally the Sanskrit term for "noble," Aryan came to indicate the ancient language assumed to have been the common source of the modern Indo-European languages. An Aryan was simply a speaker of one of those languages. By the late nineteenth century, however, the term had become supremely ill defined. In much racist thinking, Germanic peoples were somehow especially Aryan, but race mixing had produced impurity—and thus degeneration. Success in struggle with the other races was the ultimate measure of vitality, the only proof of racial superiority for the future.

Hitler brought these themes together by emphasizing that humanity is not special, but simply part of nature, subject to the same laws of struggle and selection as the other animal species. Humanitarian ideals are thus dangerous illusions. As he put it to a group of officer cadets in 1944:

Nature is always teaching us . . . that she is governed by the principle of selection: that victory is to the strong and that the weak must go to the wall. She teaches us that what may seem cruel to us, because it affects us personally or because we have been brought up in ignorance of her laws, is nevertheless often essential if a higher way of life is to be attained. Nature . . . knows nothing of the notion of humanitarianism, which signifies that the weak must at all costs be protected and preserved even at the expense of the strong.

Nature does not see in weakness any extenuating reasons . . . on the contrary, weakness calls for condemnation.[2]

To Hitler, the Jews were not simply another of the races involved in this endless struggle. Rather, as landless parasites, they had played a special historical role, embodying the principles—from humanitarianism to class struggle—that were antithetical to the healthy natural struggle among unified racial groups. "Jewishness" was bound up with the negative, critical intellect that dared suggest things ought to be not natural but just, even that it was up to human beings to change the world and make it just. The Jews were the virus keeping the community from a healthy natural footing. Marxist communism, embodying divisive class struggle as well as utopian humanitarian ideals, was fundamentally Jewish.

The central features of Nazism in practice, from personal dictatorship to the extermination of the Jews, followed from Hitler's view of the world. First, the racial community must organize itself politically for this ceaseless struggle. Individuals are but instruments for the success of the racial community. Parliamentary democracy, reflecting short-term individual interests, fostered selfish materialism and division, thereby weakening that community. The political order must rest instead on a charismatic leader, united with the whole people through bonds of common blood.

Nazi Aims and German Society

Although Hitler's world-view provided the underlying momentum for the Nazi regime, it did not specify a consistent program that could be implemented all at once. Moreover, the regime sometimes found it necessary to adopt short-term expedients that conflicted with its long-term aims. Thus it was possible for Germans living under Nazi rule in the 1930s to embrace aspects of Nazism in practice without seeing where it was all leading.

Hitler's special leadership function was based on a charismatic relationship with the German people, a nonrational bond resting on common race. But to create a genuine racial community, or *Volksgemeinschaft*, it was necessary to unify society and instill Nazi values, thereby making the individual feel part of the whole—and ultimately an instrument to serve the whole. This entailed more or less forced participation in an array of Nazi organizations, from women's groups to the Hitler Youth, from the Labor Front to the Strength Through Joy leisure-time organization.

Common participation meant shared experiences such as weekend hikes and the weekly one-dish meal. Even the most ordinary, once-private activities took on a public or political dimension. Moreover, the Nazis devised unprecedented ways to stage-manage public life, using rituals like the Hitler salute, symbols like the swastika, new media like radio and film, and carefully orchestrated party rallies—all in an effort to foster this sense of belonging. (See the feature, "Weighing the Evidence: Film as Propaganda," on pages 1028–1029.)

Hitler and Children Adolf Hitler was often portrayed as the friend of children. This photograph accompanied a story for an elementary school reader that described how Hitler, told it was this young girl's birthday, picked her from a crowd of well-wishers to treat her "to cake and strawberries with thick, sweet cream." *(From* Jugend um Hitler, *Heinrich Hoffman © "Zeitgeschichte" Verlag und Vertriebs-Gesellschaft Berlin. Reproduced with permission. Photo courtesy Wiener Library, London)*

Did the Nazis succeed in drawing ordinary Germans into their orbit? The matter remains sensitive and difficult. Hitler's regime enjoyed considerable popular support, but even after Hitler was well entrenched in power, most Germans did not grasp the regime's deeper dynamic. Certainly some welcomed the sense of unity, the feeling of belonging and participation, especially after what had seemed the alienation and divisiveness of the Weimar years. Moreover, Hitler himself was immensely popular, partly because of his personal charisma, partly because his apparently decisive leadership was a welcome departure from the near paralysis of the Weimar parliamentary system. But most important, before the coming of war in 1939, he seemed to go from success to success, surmounting the Depression and repudiating the major terms of the hated Versailles treaty.

The skillful work of Hitler's propaganda minister, Joseph Goebbels (1897–1945), played on these successes to create a "Hitler myth," which made Hitler seem at once heroic and a man of the people, even the embodiment of healthy German ideals against the excesses and corruptions of the Nazi party. This myth became central to the Nazi regime, but it merely provided a façade behind which the real Hitler could pursue deeper, longer-term aims. These aims were not publicized directly, because the German people did not seem ready for them. In this sense, then, support for Hitler and his regime was broad but shallow during the 1930s.

Moreover, resistance increased as the regime became more intrusive. Youth gangs actively opposed the official Hitler Youth organization as it became more overbearing and militaristic by the late 1930s. But people resisted especially by minimizing their involvement with the regime, retreating into the private realm, in response to the Nazi attempt to make everything public.

Did such people feel constantly under threat of the Gestapo, the secret police? In principle, the Gestapo could interpret the will of the *Führer*, or leader, and decide whether any individual citizen was "guilty" or not. And the Gestapo was not concerned about due process; on occasion it simply bypassed the regular court system. But the Gestapo did not terrorize Germans at random. Its victims were generally members of specific groups, people suspected of active opposition, or people who protected those the Gestapo had targeted. It did not become as intrusive as its Soviet counterpart, the

NKVD, became during the height of the Stalinist terror in the late 1930s.

Moreover, changes and contradictions in Nazi goals allowed considerable space for personal choices. For example, the Nazis claimed to embrace traditional family values. During the 1920s they had emphasized the woman's role as wife and mother and deplored the ongoing emancipation of women. Once Hitler came to power, concerns about unemployment reinforced these views. During the summer of 1933, Hitler's government began offering interest-free loans to help couples set up house if the woman agreed to leave the labor force. Moreover, efforts to increase the German birthrate reinforced the emphasis on child rearing in Nazi women's organizations. Nonetheless, the size of the family continued to decrease in Germany as elsewhere in the industrialized world during the 1930s.

And beginning in 1936, when rapid rearmament began to produce labor shortages, the regime did an about-face and began seeking to attract women back to the workplace, especially into jobs central to military preparation. These efforts were not notably successful, and by 1940 the military was calling for conscription of women into war industries.

Further, the Nazis valued the family only insofar as it was congruent with the "health" of the racial community, so efforts to promote that health also compromised traditional family values. The regime regulated marriage and sought actively to eliminate the "unhealthy," those deemed unfit. Just months after coming to power in 1933, Hitler brushed aside the objections of Vice Chancellor Franz von Papen, a Catholic, and engineered a law mandating the compulsory sterilization of persons suffering from certain allegedly hereditary diseases. Medical personnel sterilized some 400,000, the vast majority of them "Aryan" Germans, during the Nazi years.

Hitler's regime also began immediately to single out the Jews, although Nazi Jewish policy remained an improvised hodgepodge prior to World War II. Within weeks after Hitler became chancellor in 1933, new restrictions limited Jewish participation in the civil service, in the professions, and in German cultural life—and quickly drew censure from the League of Nations. The Nuremberg Laws, announced at a party rally in 1935, included prohibition of sexual relations and marriage between Jews and non-Jewish Germans. Beginning in 1938, the Jews had to carry special identification cards and to add "Sarah" or "Israel" to their given names.

Although Hitler and other Nazi leaders claimed periodically to be seeking a definitive solution to Germany's "Jewish problem," this led during the 1930s only to sporadic attempts to force German Jews to emigrate. About 11 percent, or 60,000, of Germany's 550,000 Jews emigrated during 1933 and 1934, and perhaps 25 percent had gotten out by 1938. The fact that the regime stripped emigrating Jews of their assets made emigration more difficult, because other countries were unwilling to take in substantial numbers of penniless Jews.

On November 9, 1938, using the assassination of a German diplomat in Paris as a pretext, the Nazis staged the Kristallnacht (Crystal Night) pogrom, during which almost all the synagogues in Germany and about seven thousand Jewish-owned stores were destroyed. Between 30,000 and 50,000 relatively prosperous Jews were arrested and forced to emigrate after their property was confiscated. Although the German public had generally acquiesced in the earlier restrictions on Jews, this pogrom with its wanton violation of private property shocked many Germans.

Concentration camps—supplementary detention centers—had become a feature of the Nazi regime virtually at once, but prior to 1938 they were used primarily to hold political prisoners. As part of the Crystal Night pogrom, about 35,000 Jews were rounded up and sent to the camps, but most were soon released as long as they could document their intention to emigrate. When World War II began in 1939, the total camp population was about 25,000. The systematic physical extermination of the Jews began only during the war, in newly constructed death camps in Poland.

However, the killing of others deemed superfluous or threatening to the racial community began earlier, with the so-called euthanasia program initiated under volunteer medical teams in 1939. Its aim was to eliminate chronic mental patients, the incurably ill, and people with severe physical handicaps. Those subject to such treatment were primarily ethnic Germans, not Jews or foreigners. Although the regime did all it could to make it appear the victims had died naturally, a public outcry developed, especially among relatives and church leaders. Thus the program had to be discontinued in 1941, but by then it had claimed 100,000 lives.

The euthanasia program was based on the sense, fundamental to radical Nazism, that readiness for war was the real norm for society. In war, societies send individuals to their deaths and, on the battlefield, make difficult distinctions among the wounded, letting some die in order to save those most likely to survive and return to battle. Struggle necessitates selection, which requires overcoming humanitarian scruples—the notion that "weakness" calls for special societal protection. Thus it was desirable to kill even ethnic Germans who were deemed unfit, as "life unworthy of life."

Preparation for war was the core of Nazism in practice. The conquest of living space in the east would make possible a more advantageous agricultural-industrial balance, thereby providing not only the self-sufficiency necessary for sovereignty but also the land-rootedness necessary for racial health. Such a war of conquest would strike not only the Slavic peoples of the region but also communism, centered in the Soviet Union.

The point of domestic reorganization was to marshal the community's energies and resources for this war. Because business interests generally seemed congruent with Nazi purposes, Nazi aims did not appear to require some revolutionary assault on business elites or the capitalist economy. But the Nazis had their own road to travel, and beginning in 1936 they proved quite prepared to bend the economy, and to coordinate big business, to serve their longer-term aims of war-making.

The Nazi drive toward war during the 1930s transformed international relations in Europe. The other European powers sought to understand

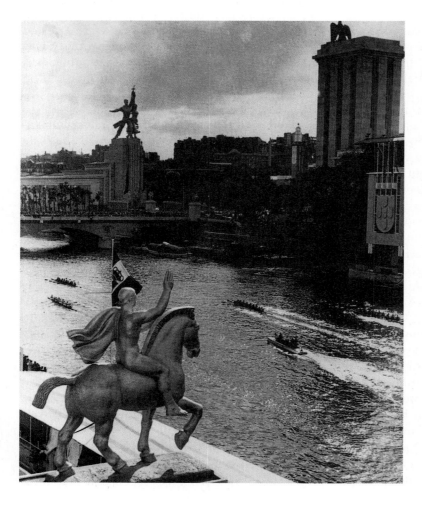

Ideological Confrontation At a major international exhibition in Paris in 1937, the new antidemocratic political regimes of the interwar period made bold propaganda statements. With a sculpture from fascist Italy's pavilion in the foreground, we look across the Seine River to a classic representation of the ideological warfare of the 1930s: the Soviet Pavilion, on the left, facing the German pavilion, on the right. *(Wide World Photos)*

Hitler's Germany in terms of the increasingly polarized political context of the period. Before considering the fortunes of Hitler's foreign policy, we must consider fascism as a wider phenomenon—and the efforts of the democracies, on the one hand, and the Soviet Union, on the other, to come to terms with it.

FASCIST CHALLENGE AND ANTIFASCIST RESPONSE

Communism, fascism, and Nazism departed from the parliamentary democracy that had been the West's political norm. Each seemed subject to violence and excess, yet each had features that some found attractive. In the difficult socioeconomic circumstances of the 1930s, the very presence of these new political systems caused polarization all over Europe.

Yet communists and adherents of the various forms of fascism were bitterly hostile to each other, and beginning in 1934 communists sought to join with anyone who would work with them to defend democracy against further fascist assaults. This effort led to new antifascist coalition governments in Spain and France. In each case, however, the Depression restricted maneuvering room, and these governments ended up furthering the polarization they were seeking to avoid. By mid-1940 democracy had fallen in Spain, after a brutal civil war, and even in France, in the wake of military defeat. Ideological polarization had weakened and then undermined democracy in much of Europe.

The Reorientation of Fascist Italy

Mussolini's regime in Italy continued to seek, through corporativism, to involve people in political decision making based on their roles in the national economy (see page 984). But though corporativist institutions were gradually constructed, with great rhetorical fanfare, fascism became bogged down in compromise with prefascist elites and institutions by the mid-1930s. Italian businessmen, cautious and suspicious of Mussolini, sought to maintain their autonomy against the fascist effort to subordinate business to the political sphere. And generally they succeeded. The corporative institutions never developed into genuine vehicles of mass participation through the workplace—if anything, in fact, they served simply to regiment the working class. Mussolini offered assurances that, despite the necessary compromises, fascism's corporativist revolution was continuing, but those seeking a corporative state were sharply critical of the inadequacies of the new system.

Mussolini was never merely the instrument of the established Italian elites, but neither was he a consistent ideologue like Hitler, forcing his regime in a certain direction. By the early 1930s, he sometimes seemed satisfied with his cult of power as he juggled the various contending forces in fascist Italy. But he was increasingly frustrated by the limitations he had encountered on the domestic level. On the international level, however, the new context after Hitler came to power offered him some welcome space for maneuver. So as the fascist revolution in Italy faltered, Mussolini began concentrating on foreign policy.

Though Italy, like Germany, remained dissatisfied with the territorial status quo, it was not obvious that fascist Italy and Nazi Germany had to end up in the same camp. For one thing, Italy was anxious to preserve an independent Austria as a buffer with Germany, whereas there was considerable sentiment among Germans and Austrians for the unification of the two countries. Such a greater Germany might then threaten the gains Italy had won at the peace conference at the expense of Austria. When, in 1934, Germany seemed poised to absorb Austria, Mussolini helped stiffen the resistance of Austria's leaders and played a part in forcing Hitler to back down. Mussolini even warned that Nazism, with its racist orientation, posed a significant threat to the best of European civilization.

As it began to appear that France and Britain might have to work with the Soviet Union to check Hitler's Germany, French and British conservatives pushed for good relations with Mussolini's Italy to provide ideological balance. So Italy was well positioned to play off both sides as Hitler began shaking things up on the international level after 1933. In 1935, just after Hitler announced significant rearmament measures, unilaterally repudiating provisions of the Versailles treaty for the first time, Mussolini hosted a meeting with the French and British prime ministers at Stresa, in northern Italy. In a move clearly intended to contain Germany, the three powers agreed to resist "any unilateral repudiation of treaties which may endanger the peace of Europe."

However, Mussolini was already preparing to extend Italy's possessions in East Africa to encompass Ethiopia (formerly called Abyssinia), assuming that the French and British, who needed his support against Hitler, would not offer significant opposition. Ethiopia had become a League of Nations member in 1923—sponsored by Italy, but opposed by Britain and France because it still practiced slavery. After a border incident in December 1934, Italian troops invaded in October 1935, prompting the League to announce sanctions against Italy.

These sanctions were applied haphazardly, largely because France and Britain wanted to avoid irreparable damage to their longer-term relations with Italy. In any case, the sanctions did not deter Mussolini, whose forces prevailed through the use of aircraft and poison gas by May 1936. But they did make Italy receptive to German overtures in the aftermath of its victory. And the victory made Mussolini more restless. Rather than seeking to play again the enviable role of European balancer, he began sending Italian troops and materiel to aid the antidemocratic Nationalists in the Spanish civil war, thereby further alienating democratic opinion elsewhere.

Conservatives in Britain and France continued to push for accommodation with Italy, hoping to revive the "Stresa Front" against Hitler. Some even defended Italian imperialism in East Africa. But Italy continued its drift toward Germany. Late in 1936 Mussolini spoke of a new Rome-Berlin axis for the first time. During 1937 and 1938 he and Hitler exchanged visits. Finally, in May 1939, Italy joined Germany in an open-ended military alliance, the Pact of Steel, but Mussolini made it clear that Italy could not be ready for a major European war before 1943.

To cement this developing relationship, fascist Italy adopted anti-Semitic racial laws modeled on Germany's, even though Italian fascism had not originally been anti-Semitic and indeed had attracted Jewish Italians to its membership in about the same proportion as non-Jews. Although the imperial venture in Ethiopia had been popular among the Italian people, the increasing subservience to Nazi Germany displeased even many committed fascists. Such opposition helped keep

Mussolini from immediate intervention when war broke out in September 1939.

But in the wake of stunning Nazi successes by May 1940, Italy finally intervened, expecting to gain territorial advantage at the expense of France at relatively low cost. Mussolini was not expecting a long war, for which he knew Italy was unprepared. But a long and difficult war was forthcoming, and in July 1943 the poor Italian performance led not only to military defeat but to the fall of Mussolini and the collapse of the fascist regime.

Fascism and the Popular Front Response

The influence of Hitler's regime extended far beyond fascist Italy. With its apparent dynamism and success, Nazi Germany stimulated interest in fascism among those elsewhere who were disaffected with democracy and hostile to communism. But the line between fascism and conservative authoritarianism blurred in the volatile political climate of the 1930s. To some, any retreat from democracy appeared a step toward fascism.

In east-central Europe, political distinctions became especially problematic. Movements like the Arrow Cross in Hungary and the Legion of the Archangel Michael in Romania modeled themselves on the Italian and German prototypes, but they never achieved political power. Those who controlled the antidemocratic governments in Hungary and Romania, as in Poland, Bulgaria, and Yugoslavia, were authoritarian traditionalist, not really fascist. Still, many government leaders welcomed the closer economic ties with Germany that Hitler's economics minister, Hjalmar Schacht, engineered. The difference between authoritarianism and fascism remained clearest in Austria, where Catholic conservatives undermined democracy during 1933 and 1934. They were actively hostile to the growing pro-Nazi agitation in Austria, partly because they wanted to keep Austria independent.

In France various nationalist, anticommunist, and anti-Semitic leagues gathered momentum during the early 1930s. They covered a spectrum from monarchism to outspoken profascism, but together they constituted at least a potential threat to French democracy. In February 1934, right-wing demonstrations against the Chamber of Deputies provoked a bloody clash with police and forced a change of ministry. As it began to seem that even France might be vulnerable to fascism, those from the center and left of the political spectrum began to think about working together to keep fascism from spreading further. The Communists, especially, took the initiative by promoting "popular fronts" of all those seeking to save democracy from fascism.

This was a dramatic change in strategy for international communism. Even as Hitler was closing in on the German chancellorship in the early 1930s, German Communists, following Comintern policy, continued to attack their socialist rivals rather than seek a unified response to Nazism. From the communist perspective, fascism represented the crisis phase of monopoly capitalism, so a Nazi government would actually be useful to strip away the democratic façade hiding class oppression in Germany. But when the new Hitler government promptly outlawed the German Communist party and arrested all the Communists it could find, and when the demonstrations in Paris in February 1934 made it seem that even France might "go fascist," the Comintern abruptly changed direction. The threat of fascism was so pressing that the Communists had to begin actively promoting electoral alliances and governing coalitions with Socialists and even liberal democrats to resist its further spread. From 1934 until 1939, Communists everywhere consistently pursued this "popular front" strategy.

But by the mid-1930s it was becoming ever harder to be sure what was fascist, what was dangerous, what might lead where. As fears intensified, perceptions became as important as realities. Popular front governments, intended to preserve democracy against what appeared to be fascism, could seem, to conservatives, to be leaning too far to the left. Ideological polarization made democracy extraordinarily difficult. The archetypal example proved to be Spain, where a tragedy of classical proportions was played out.

From Democracy to Civil War in Spain, 1931–1939

Spain became a center of attention in the 1930s, when its promising new parliamentary democracy, launched in 1931, led to civil war in 1936 and the triumph of a repressive authoritarian regime

THE DIPLOMATIC REVOLUTION OF THE 1930s	
January 1933	Hitler becomes German chancellor
October 1933	Germany withdraws from the League of Nations
March 1935	Hitler announces rearmament in defiance of the Versailles treaty
April 1935	Britain, France, and Italy meet at Stresa
October 1935	Italy invades Ethiopia
March 1936	Remilitarization of the Rhineland
July 1936	Beginning of the Spanish civil war
March 1938	The Anschluss: Germany absorbs Austria
September 1938	Munich conference ends Sudetenland crisis
March 1939	Dismemberment of Czechoslovakia
August 1939	Nazi-Soviet nonaggression pact
September 1, 1939	German invasion of Poland
September 3, 1939	Britain and France declare war on Germany

in 1939. The country's earlier effort at constitutional monarchy had fizzled by 1923, when King Alfonso XIII (1886–1941) supported a new military dictatorship. But growing opposition led first to the resignation of the dictator in 1930 and then, in April 1931, to the end of the monarchy and the proclamation of a republic. The elections for a constituent assembly that followed in June produced a solid victory for a coalition of liberal democrats and Socialists, as well as considerable hope and expectation.

The optimism began to break down first because the leaders of the new republic dragged their feet on land reform, which seemed necessary especially in southern Spain, where large estates

Map 27.1 The Spanish Civil War, 1936–1939 The Nationalist insurgents quickly took over most of northern and eastern Spain in 1936 and then gradually expanded their territory. The fall of Madrid early in 1939 marked the end of fighting. The revolutionary effort of 1936–1937 within the Republican zone was centered in Barcelona. (*Source:* Adapted from *The Times Atlas of World History*, 3d ed., by kind permission of Times Books.)

worked by landless day laborers remained the rule. A significant agrarian reform law was passed in 1932, but the new government was slow to implement it. Feeling betrayed, Socialists and agricultural workers became increasingly radical, producing growing upheaval in the countryside. Radicalism on the left made it harder for the moderates to govern and, at the same time, stimulated conservatives to become more politically active.

A conservative, or right-wing, coalition (the CEDA) under José Maria Gil Robles (1898–1980) grew in strength, becoming the largest party in parliament with the first regular elections, held in November 1933. In light of its parliamentary strength, the CEDA had a plausible claim to a government role, but it was kept from participation in government until October 1934. It seemed to the left, in the ideologically charged atmosphere of the time, that the growing role of the CEDA was

a prelude to fascism. To let the CEDA into the government would be to hand the republic over to its enemies.

A strong Catholic from the traditional Spanish right, Gil Robles refused to endorse the democratic republic as a form of government, but he and the CEDA were willing to work within it. So the Spanish left may have been too quick to see the CEDA as fascist—and to react when the CEDA finally got its government role. However, Mussolini and Hitler had each come to power more or less legally, from within parliamentary institutions. The German left has been criticized for its passive response to the advent of Hitler; the Spanish left wanted to avoid the same mistake.

Thus, during the fall of 1934 the left responded to the opening of the government to the CEDA with quasi-revolutionary uprisings in Catalonia and Asturias, where a miners' commune was put down only after two weeks of heavy fighting. In the aftermath, the right-leaning government of 1935 began undoing some of the reforms of the left-leaning government of 1931–1933, though still legally, within the framework of the parliamentary republic.

In February 1936 a popular front coalition to ward off fascism won a narrow electoral victory, sufficient for an absolute majority in parliament. As would be true in France a few months later, electoral victory produced popular expectations that went well beyond the essentially defensive purposes of the popular front. Hoping to win back the leftist rank and file and head off what seemed a dangerous attempt at revolution, the new popular front government began to implement a progressive program, now including the land reform that had been promised but not implemented earlier. But it was too late to undercut the growing radicalization of the masses.

A wave of land seizures began in March, followed by a quasi-insurrectionary strike movement, the most extensive in Spanish history, which took on a clearly revolutionary character during June and July. To many, the government's inability to keep order had become the immediate issue. By the early summer of 1936, leaders of the democratic republic had become isolated between the extremes of left and right, each preparing an extralegal solution.

Finally, in mid-July, several army officers initiated a military uprising intended as a coup to seize power. Soon led by General Francisco Franco (1892–1975), these Nationalist insurgents took control of substantial parts of Spain, but elsewhere they failed to overcome the resistance of the Republican Loyalists, those determined to defend the republic. So the result was not the intended military takeover but a brutal civil war (Map 27.1). The substantial Italian fascist and Nazi German intervention on the Nationalist side by the end of 1936 intensified the war's ideological ramifications. At the same time, the remarkable, often heroic resistance of the Loyalists captured the imagination of the world. Indeed, 40,000 volunteers came from abroad to fight to preserve the Spanish republic.

It proved a war of stunning brutality on both sides. Loyalist anticlericalism led to the murder of twelve bishops and perhaps one-eighth of the parish clergy in Spain. On the other side, the German bombing of the Basque town of Guernica on a crowded market day in April 1937, represented

Picasso: Guernica Created for the Spanish pavilion at the famed 1937 Paris Exhibition, Picasso's painting conveyed horror and outrage in response to the German bombing of Guernica on a crowded market day in 1937, during the Spanish civil war. Picasso's stark, elemental imagery helped define this era of violence and suffering for the generations that followed. (*Pablo Picasso,* Guernica *[1937, May–early June]. Oil on canvas. © SPADEM, Paris/ARS, New York*)

unforgettably in Pablo Picasso's painting, came to symbolize the violence and suffering of the whole era.

Republican Loyalists assumed that Franco and the Nationalists represented another instance of fascism. In fact, however, Franco was no fascist, but rather a traditional military man whose leadership role did not rest on personal charisma. He was an authoritarian emphasizing discipline, order, and Spain's Catholic traditions.

Still, in their effort to rally support during the civil war, Franco's forces found it expedient to take advantage of the appeal of the Falange, a genuinely fascist movement that had emerged under the leadership of the charismatic young José Antonio Primo de Rivera (1903–1936). Although extremely weak at the time of the election in February 1936, the Falange grew rapidly in opposition to the leftist radicalism that followed the popular front victory. As street fighting between left and right intensified that spring, the republic arrested José Antonio, as he was called, and thus he was in prison when the civil war began.

José Antonio decided his best hope was alliance with the military. Although he was contemptuous of their shortsighted conservatism, he felt their very absence of ideas, "their abysmal political mediocrity," afforded an opening for the Falange to provide direction, a genuine alternative. But it worked out the other way. In November 1936, José Antonio was tried and executed for conspiring to overthrow the republic, and the Nationalists promptly began using the trappings of the Falange, including the memory of José Antonio, to increase their popular appeal.

Meanwhile, the Republicans had to fight a civil war while dealing with continuing revolution in their own ranks. Developing especially in Catalonia from the uprisings of 1936, that revolution was not communist but anarchist and syndicalist in orientation. The Communists, true to popular front principles, insisted that this was no time for such "infantile leftist" revolutionary experiments. What mattered, throughout the Republican zone, was the factory discipline necessary to produce essential war materiel. So the Communists, under Stalin's orders, were instrumental in putting down the anarchist revolution in Catalonia in June 1937.

Under these extraordinary circumstances, the Communists, at first a distinct minority on the Spanish left, gradually gained the ascendancy on the Republican side, partly because they were disciplined and effective, partly because the assistance the Soviets offered enhanced their prestige. When all was said and done, however, this single-minded prosecution of the civil war did not prove enough to defeat the military insurgency, despite the considerable heroism on the Loyalist side. The war ended with the fall of Madrid to the Nationalists in March 1939. General Franco's authoritarian regime governed Spain until his death in 1975.

In Spain, as in Weimar Germany, the initial lack of consensus in a new republic made parliamentary democracy difficult, and the wider ideological framework magnified the difficulties. With the political boiling point so low, the left and the right each viewed the other in extreme terms and assumed that extraordinary responses to the other were necessary. Thus the tendency of the left to view even conservatives operating within a parliamentary framework as "fascist." And each side was relatively quick to give up on a democratic republic that seemed to be tilting too far in the other direction.

France in the Era of the Popular Front

In France, as in Spain, concern to arrest the spread of fascism led to a popular front coalition, here including Socialists, Communists, and Radicals, that governed the country from 1936 to 1938. Although it did not lead to civil war, the popular front was central to the French experience of the 1930s, producing polarization and resignation, and undermining confidence in the Third Republic.

Beginning in 1934, the French Communists took the initiative in approaching first the Socialists, then the Radicals, to develop a popular front coalition against fascism. In reaching out to the Radicals, the Communists stressed French patriotism and made no demand for significant economic reforms. Stalin gave this effort a major push in 1935 when, in a stunning change in the communist line, he stressed the legitimacy of national defense and explicitly approved of French rearmament.

In the elections of April and May 1936, the popular front won a sizable majority in the Chamber of Deputies, putting the Socialists' leader, Léon Blum (1872–1950), in line to become France's first socialist prime minister. The Communists pledged full support of the new Blum government but, to avoid fanning fears, they did not participate directly. However, despite the popular front's moderate and essentially defensive aims, the situation quickly began to polarize after the elections.

Fearing that the new Blum government would be forced to devalue the French currency, thereby diminishing the value of assets denominated in francs, French investors immediately began moving their capital abroad. At the same time, the popular front victory produced a wave of enthusiasm among workers that escaped the control of popular front leaders and culminated late in May in a spontaneous strike movement, the largest France had ever seen. By June 4 it had spread to all major industries nationwide. Although the workers' demands—for collective bargaining, a forty-hour week, and paid vacations—were not extraordinary, the movement involved sit-down strikes as well as the normal walk-out form and thus seemed quasi-revolutionary in character. The major trade union confederation, the Communists, and most Socialists, including Blum himself, saw the strikes as a danger to the popular front, with its more modest aims of defending the republic, and eagerly pursued a settlement.

That settlement, the Matignon Agreement of June 8, 1936, was a major victory for the French working class. Having been genuinely frightened by the strikes, and now reassured that the popular front government would at least uphold the law, French industrialists were willing to make significant concessions. So the workers got collective bargaining, elected shop stewards, and wage increases as a direct result of Matignon, then a forty-hour week and paid vacations in a reform package promptly passed by parliament.

In the enthusiasm of the summer of 1936, there were other reforms as well, but after that the popular front was forced onto the defensive. Two problems undermined its energy and cohesion: the noncooperation of French business and the Spanish civil war. The cautious response of Blum, the Socialist prime minister, is striking in each case, but he faced a situation with little maneuvering room in 1936.

From the outset Blum stressed that he had no mandate for revolution, and as France's first Socialist prime minister, he felt it essential to prove that a Socialist could govern responsibly. Thus, Blum did not respond energetically to the capital flight, even though it produced serious currency

Léon Blum The French Socialist leader appears in an enthusiastic moment after the popular front victory in 1936. He was about to become France's first socialist prime minister, but in that role he encountered one dilemma after another. By 1938, the high spirits of 1936 had dissolved. *(Archives Ringart)*

and budgetary difficulties. Instead of devaluing the franc or imposing exchange controls, he simply tried to persuade French capital holders to repatriate their assets. When this proved unsuccessful, he finally was forced to devalue in September 1936, but with only limited results. Perhaps, as critics suggest, he should have acted more aggressively to overhaul the French banking and credit system, but Blum shied away from any such drastic measures, both to prove he could be responsible and to avoid antagonizing business.

Blum was also uncertain as he faced the dilemmas surrounding the Spanish civil war. The key question was whether the French government should help the beleaguered Spanish republic, at least by sending supplies. Although he initially favored such help, Blum changed his mind under pressure from three sides. The Conservative government of Stanley Baldwin in Britain was against it. So was the French right; some even suggested that French intervention would provoke civil war in France as well. Moreover, the Radicals in his own coalition were generally opposed to helping the Spanish republic, so intervention would jeopardize the popular front itself. Thus, rather than help supply the Spanish republic, Blum promoted a nonintervention agreement among the major powers, including Italy and Germany. Many Socialists and Communists within the popular front disliked Blum's nonintervention policy, however, especially as it became clear that Mussolini and Hitler were violating the nonintervention agreement. As Blum stuck to nonintervention, the moral force of the popular front dissolved.

Blum's first government lasted about a year. He got a brief second chance in 1938, but by then the popular front was simply disintegrating. A new government under the Radical Edouard Daladier (1884–1970), still nominally a creature of the popular front, began dismantling some of the key gains of 1936, even attacking the forty-hour week. Citing productivity and national security concerns, Daladier adopted pro-business policies and succeeded in attracting capital back to France.

Daladier's policies produced a serious rift with Blum, however, and a sense of betrayal among the workers, who watched the gains they had won in 1936 gradually slip away. At the same time, businessmen and conservatives began blaming the workers' gains—like the five-day week—for slowing French rearmament. Rather than work shifts, the argument went, the workers insisted on a "double Sunday," or two-day weekend, so the provision for a five-day week cut into the production necessary for rearmament. Although such charges were not entirely fair, they indicated how poisoned the atmosphere in France had become in the wake of the popular front.

As France began to face the possibility of a new war, the popular front was widely blamed for French weakness. When war came at last, resignation and division were prevalent, in contrast with the patriotic unity and high spirits of 1914. It was partly for that reason that France was so easily defeated by Germany in 1940. And partly for the same reason, when France fell the democratic Third Republic fell with it, and the country opted for an authoritarian alternative.

THE COMING OF WORLD WAR II, 1935–1939

Still under the long shadow of World War I, most Western leaders were determined to preserve the peace during the two ensuing decades. But the peace settlement that had followed the war created new problems, many of which remained when Hitler came to power in 1933 despite promising adjustments during the 1920s. And Hitler had consistently trumpeted his intention to overturn that settlement. What scope was there for peaceful revision? Could Hitler be stopped by threat of war?

Restoring German Sovereignty, 1935–1936

During his first years in power, through 1936, Hitler could be understood as merely restoring German sovereignty, revising a postwar settlement that had been misconceived in the first place. However uncouth and abrasive he might seem, it was hard to find a basis for opposing him. Yet in commencing German rearmament in 1935, and especially in remilitarizing the Rhineland in March 1936, Hitler fundamentally reversed the power balance established in France's favor at the peace conference.

France's special advantage had been the demilitarization of the entire German territory west of the Rhine River and a 50-kilometer strip on the east bank. The measure had been reaffirmed at Locarno in 1925, now with Germany's free agreement, and it was guaranteed by Britain and Italy. Yet on a Saturday morning in March 1936, that advantage disappeared as German troops moved into the forbidden area. The French and British acquiesced, uncertain of what else to do. After all, Hitler was only restoring Germany to full sovereignty.

But Hitler was not likely to stop there. As a result of the war and the peace, three new countries—Austria, Czechoslovakia, and Poland—bordered Germany (see Map 27.2). In each, the peace settlement had left trouble spots involving the status of ethnic Germans; in each the status quo was open to question.

Austria, Czechoslovakia, and Appeasement

As early as 1934, Hitler had moved to encompass his homeland, Austria, but strenuous opposition from Italy led him to back down. The developing understanding with Italy by 1936 enabled Hitler to focus again on Austria—initiating the second, more radical phase of his prewar foreign policy. On a pretext in March 1938, German troops moved into Austria, which was promptly incorporated into Germany. This time Mussolini was willing to acquiesce, and Hitler was genuinely grateful.

The Treaty of Versailles had explicitly prohibited this *Anschluss,* or unity with Germany, though that prohibition violated the principle of self-determination. It was widely believed in the West that most Austrians favored unity with Germany—and this perception was no doubt correct. The Anschluss could be justified as revising a misconceived aspect of the peace settlement.

Czechoslovakia presented quite a different situation. Although it had preserved democratic institutions, the country suffered from nationality problems. It included restive minorities of Slovaks, Magyars, Ruthenians, Poles, and—concentrated especially in the Sudetenland, along the German and Austrian borders—about 3.25 million Germans. After having been part of the dominant nationality in the old Habsburg empire, those Germans were frustrated with their minority status in the new Czechoslovakia, especially because they seemed to suffer disproportionately from the Depression. Hitler's agents actively stirred up their resentments.

Leading the West's response, when Hitler began making an issue of Czechoslovakia, was Neville Chamberlain (1869–1940), who followed Stanley Baldwin as Britain's prime minister and foreign minister in May 1937. An intelligent, vigorous, and public-spirited man from the progressive wing of the Conservative party, Chamberlain has long been derided as the architect of the "appeasement" of Hitler at the Munich conference of 1938, which settled the crisis over Czechoslovakia. Trumpeted as the key to peace, the Munich agreement proved but a step to the war that broke out less than a year later. Yet though it failed, Chamberlain's policy of appeasement stemmed not from cowardice or mere drift and certainly not from some unspoken pro-Nazi sentiment.

Rather than let events spin out of control, as seemed to have happened in 1914, Chamberlain sought to master the difficult international situation through creative bargaining. The excesses of Hitler's policy resulted from the mistakes of

Versailles; redo the settlement on a more realistic basis, and Germany would behave responsibly. The key, Chamberlain felt, was to pinpoint the sources of Germany's frustrations and, as he put it, "to remove the danger spots one by one."

Moreover, in Britain as elsewhere, there were some who saw Hitler's resurgent Germany as a bulwark against communism, which might spread into east-central Europe—especially in the event of another war. Indeed, the victor in another war might well be the revolutionary left. To prevent such an outcome was worth a few concessions to Hitler.

Although the Czechs, led by Eduard Beneš (1884–1948), made some attempt to liberalize their nationality policy, by April 1938 they were becoming ever less sympathetic to Sudeten German demands for autonomy, especially because a threat of German intervention seemed to accompany them. Tensions between Czechoslovakia and Germany mounted, and by late September 1938 war

The Illusion of Peace Neville Chamberlain, returning home to Britain from Munich to a hero's welcome, waves the peace declaration that was supposed to have brought "peace in our time." This was late September 1938. Less than a year later, Europe was again at war. *(Hulton-Getty/Tony Stone Images)*

Toward Appeasement: The Longing for Peace

Late in September 1938, the crisis that developed over Germany's demands on Czechoslovakia produced an emotional roller coaster for Europeans. Central to the continuing effort to preserve the peace was the British prime minister, Neville Chamberlain, who flew to Germany twice to meet with Hitler before the crisis reached its climax. At first, Chamberlain thought he had found a formula for peace, but then Hitler upped his demands. Thus, Chamberlain's tone was somber when he addressed the British people by radio shortly after his second trip, on September 27, at what proved the height of the crisis.

First of all I must say something to those who have written to my wife or myself in these last weeks to tell us of their gratitude for my efforts and to assure us of their prayers for my success. Most of these letters have come from women— mothers or sisters of our own countrymen. But there are countless others besides—from France, from Belgium, from Italy, even from Germany, and it has been heartbreaking to read of the growing anxiety they reveal. . . .

If I felt my responsibility heavy before, to read such letters has made it seem almost overwhelming. How horrible, fantastic, incredible it is that we should be digging trenches and trying on gas masks here because of a quarrel in a far-away country between people of whom we know nothing. It seems still more impossible that a quarrel which has already been settled in principle should be the subject of war.

I can well understand the reasons why the Czech Government have felt unable to accept the terms which have been put before them in the German memorandum. Yet I believe after my talks with Herr Hitler that, if only time

were allowed, it ought to be possible for the arrangements for transferring the territory that the Czech government has agreed to give to Germany to be settled by agreement under conditions which would assure fair treatment to the population concerned. . . .

However much we may sympathise with a small nation confronted by a big and powerful neighbor, we cannot in all circumstances undertake to involve the whole British Empire in war simply on her account. If we have to fight it must be on larger issues than that. . . . [I]f I were convinced that any nation had made up its mind to dominate the world by fear of its force, I should feel that it must be resisted. . . . but war is a fearful thing, and we must be very clear, before we embark on it, that it is really the great issues that are at stake. . . .

For the present I ask you to await as calmly as you can the events of the next few days. As long as war has not begun, there is always hope that it may be prevented, and you know that I am going to work for peace to the last moment. Good night.

Source: Neville Chamberlain, *In Search of Peace: Speeches (1937–1938)* (London: Hutchinson, 1939), pp. 274–276.

appeared imminent, despite Chamberlain's efforts to mediate. (See the box, "Toward Appeasement: The Longing for Peace.") Both the French and the British began mobilizing, with French troops manning the Maginot Line for the first time.

A 1924 treaty bound France to come to the aid of Czechoslovakia in the event of aggression. Moreover, the Soviet Union, according to a treaty of 1935, was bound to assist Czechoslovakia if the French did so. And throughout the crisis, the Soviets pushed for a strong stand in defense of Czecho-

slovakia against German aggression. For both ideological and military reasons, however, the British and French were not anxious for a war on the side of the Soviet Union. The value of the Soviet military was uncertain, at best, at a time when the Soviet officer corps had just been purged.

By September, Hitler seemed eager to smash the Czechs by force, but when Mussolini proposed a four-power conference, he was persuaded to talk again. At Munich late in September, Britain, France, Italy, and Germany settled the matter, with Czechoslovakia—and the Soviet Union—excluded. Determined not to risk war over what seemed Czech intransigence, the British ended up agreeing to what Hitler had wanted all along—not merely autonomy for the Sudeten Germans but German annexation of the Sudetenland.

The Munich agreement specified that all Sudeten areas with German majorities be transferred to Germany; plebiscites were to be held in areas with large German minorities, and Hitler pledged to respect the sovereignty of the newly diminished Czechoslovak state. Chamberlain and his French counterpart, Edouard Daladier, each returned home to a hero's welcome, having transformed what had seemed certain war to, in Chamberlain's memorable phrase, "peace in our time."

Rather than settle the nationality questions bedeviling Czechoslovakia, the Munich agreement only provoked further unrest. First, disputed areas with large Polish and Hungarian populations fell to Poland and Hungary, respectively. Each proved eager to exploit the new weakness of Czechoslovakia. Then unrest stemming from Slovak separatism afforded a pretext for Germany to send troops into Prague in March 1939. The Slovak areas were spun off as a separate nation, while the Czech areas became the Protectorate of Bohemia and Moravia. Less than six months after the Munich conference, most of what had been Czechoslovakia had landed firmly within the Nazi orbit (Map 27.2). It was no longer possible to justify Hitler's actions as seeking to unite all Germans in one state.

Poland, the Nazi-Soviet Pact, and the Coming of War

With Poland, the German grievance was still more serious, for the new Polish state had been created partly at German expense. Especially galling to Germans was the Polish corridor, which cut off East Prussia from the bulk of Germany in order to give Poland access to the sea. The city of Danzig, historically Polish (Gdansk) but part of Germany before World War I, was left a "free city," supervised by the League of Nations.

Disillusioned by Hitler's dismemberment of Czechoslovakia, and angered by the Germans' menacing rhetoric regarding Poland, Chamberlain announced in the House of Commons on March 31, 1939, that Britain and France would intervene militarily in the event of a threat to Poland's independence. Chamberlain was not only abandoning the policy of appeasement; he was making a clear commitment to the Continent, of the sort that British governments had resisted since 1919. He could do so partly because Britain was rapidly rearming; by early 1940, in fact, Britain was spending nearly as large a share of its national income on the military as Germany was.

Chamberlain's assertive statement was not enough to deter Hitler, who seems to have been determined to settle the Polish question by force. Hitler continued, however, to stress how limited and reasonable German aims were in an effort to localize the conflict. Germany simply wanted Danzig and German transit across the corridor; it was the Polish stance that was rigid and unreasonable. Hitler seems to have believed that Polish intransigence would alienate the British and French, undercutting their support. And as the crisis developed by mid-1939, doubts were increasingly expressed, on all sides, that the British and French were really prepared to aid Poland militarily—that they had the will "to die for Danzig."

Although they had been lukewarm to Soviet proposals for a military alliance, Britain and France began to negotiate with the Soviet Union more seriously during the spring and summer of 1939. But doubts about the value of a Soviet alliance continued to gnaw at Western leaders. For one thing, Soviet troops could gain access to Germany only by moving through Poland or Romania, neither of which was willing to grant passage. Poland and Romania each had territory gained at the expense of Russia in the postwar settlement, so the British and French, suspicious of Soviet designs on both, were reluctant to insist that Soviet troops be allowed to pass through them.

Even as negotiations between the Soviet Union and the democracies seemed to continue, the Soviet Union came to its own agreement with Nazi Germany on August 22, 1939, in a pact that astonished the world. Each of them had been denouncing the other, and although Hitler had explored the possibility of Soviet neutrality in May, serious negotiations began only that August, when the Soviets got the clear signal that a German invasion of Poland was inevitable. It now appeared that no Soviet alliance with Britain and France could prevent war. Under these circumstances, a nonaggression pact with Germany

Map 27.2 The Expansion of Nazi Germany, 1936–1939 Especially with the remilitarization of the Rhineland in 1936, Hitler's Germany began moving, step by step, to alter the European power balance. In September 1939 the Soviet Union also began annexing territory, capitalizing on its agreement with Germany the month before.

seemed better to serve Soviet interests than a problematic war on the side of Britain and France. So the Soviets agreed with the Germans that each would remain neutral in the event that either became involved in a war with some other nation.

The Soviet flip-flop stemmed partly from disillusionment with the British and French response to the accelerating threat of Nazism. The democracies seemed no more trustworthy, and potentially no less hostile, than Nazi Germany. Moreover, a secret protocol to the Nazi-Soviet Pact apportioned major areas of east-central Europe between the Soviet Union and Germany. Thus the Soviets soon regained much of what they had lost after

World War I, when Poland, Finland, and other states had been created or aggrandized with territories that had been part of the Russian Empire.

The Nazi-Soviet Pact seemed to give Hitler the free hand he wanted in Poland. With the dramatic change in alignment, the democracies were surely much less likely to intervene. But Chamberlain, again determined to avoid the hesitations of 1914, publicly reaffirmed the British guarantee to Poland on August 25. Britain would indeed intervene in the event of a German attack. And after Hitler ordered the German invasion of Poland on September 1, the British and French responded with a declaration of war on September 3.

With each step on the path to war, Hitler had vacillated between apparent reasonableness and wanton aggressiveness. Sometimes he accented the plausibility of his demands in light of problems with the postwar settlement; sometimes he seemed to be actively seeking war. Even in invading Poland, he may still have been hoping to localize hostilities. But he was certainly willing to risk a more general European war, and the deepest thrust of his policy was toward a war of conquest—first against Poland, but ultimately against the Soviet Union. War was essential to the Nazi vision, and only when the assault on Poland became a full-scale war did the underlying purposes of Nazism become clear.

SUMMARY

The 1930s made a cruel mockery of the hopes for restabilization that had followed World War I. The Depression and the challenges from new political regimes called both capitalism and democracy into question. Hitler's Germany, especially, presented an unprecedented challenge to the European order, but the leading democracies, Britain and France, were slow to respond. Eagerness to avoid another war affected their reactions, as did the ideological polarization of the decade. Led by Britain, the democracies began unequivocally to resist the Nazi challenge only in 1939.

The most important new political systems of the interwar period—Italian fascism, German Nazism, and Stalinist communism—were dictatorial and hostile to liberal democracy, but they were not merely authoritarian in the old-fashioned, predemocratic sense. They were clearly novel, and they had some features in common. Their common direction is often summed up as *totalitarian*, a useful though problematic term. In each of the three regimes, the sovereignty of the state was to become all-encompassing, breaking down the distinction between public and private—thus Mussolini's boast that there was "nothing outside the state" in fascist Italy, and the proclamation of Robert Ley, head of the Nazi Labor Front, that "the private citizen has ceased to exist."

The common totalitarian direction is important, but it glosses over differences, especially in origins and purposes, that are at least as important. Racism and anti-Semitism, fundamental to radical Nazism, were not central to Italian fascism, which sought to respond to the apparent inadequacies of parliamentary democracy by constructing a new "corporative state." Though it never lived up to the rhetoric, Italian fascist corporativism produced a web of institutions that Nazi Germany did not duplicate.

In practice, Nazism and Stalinism were far more extreme than Italian fascism, so comparison of these two regimes is crucial to any attempt to understand the troubling political experience of the 1930s. Again, whatever the convergence in practice, the difference in origins and purposes must not be forgotten.

Twisted though it became, the Marxist vision of human liberation, based on long-standing Western values, was still manifest in the ongoing Soviet revolution during the 1930s. Committed communists believed that extreme measures were necessary if they were to carry out, in the difficult conditions the Soviet Union faced, a transformation that would eventually benefit all humanity. Nazism never claimed a comparably universal aim. Indeed, with its emphasis on racial determinism and natural struggle, Hitler's world-view was the antithesis of the humanistic tradition that found in Marxism one coherent, if extreme, manifestation. More generally, Hitler's radical Nazism was fundamentally antithetical to basic Western values, which emphasized the worth of human life and the dignity of every individual.

But whatever the differences in values and intentions, the final reckoning must rest on the results. Stalin's way of implementing the Marxist revolution made individual human lives expendable, just as they were for Hitler. The outcome of both Stalinism and Nazism was mass murder on a horrifying scale.

It was symptomatic that Hitler and Stalin came together with the cynical nonaggression pact of August 1939, the immediate prelude to war. Yet the underlying difference between the two became paramount in the life-and-death struggle that began in 1941, when Hitler betrayed Stalin and invaded the Soviet Union. If he could realize his long-standing aim of conquering the Soviet Union, Hitler could eradicate communism and provide Germany with essential living space at the same time. The four-year battle between Nazi Germany and the Soviet Union would be decisive to World War II, which proved the awful culmination of the destructiveness unleashed in the 1930s.

NOTES

1. Quoted in Robert Conquest, *The Great Terror: A Reassessment* (New York: Oxford University Press, 1990), p. 24.
2. Quoted in Helmut Krausnick et al., *Anatomy of the SS State* (New York: Walker, 1968), p. 13.

SUGGESTED READING

The Great Depression

Eichengreen, Barry. *Golden Fetters: The Gold Standard and the Great Depression, 1919–1939.* 1992. Accents the role of the gold standard both in intensifying the destabilizing process that led to the Depression and in limiting the responses of policymakers.

James, Harold. *The German Slump: Politics and Economics, 1924–1936.* 1986. Weaves economics and politics to explain the Depression in Germany and the economic recovery after Hitler came to power in 1933.

Kindleberger, Charles. *The World in Depression, 1929–1939.* Revised and enlarged ed. 1986. An important revisionist work arguing that the Depression stemmed from difficulties in the international exchange system rather than from problems and responses in the United States.

Skidelsky, Robert. *Politicians in the Slump: The Labour Government of 1929–1931.* 1967. Searching analysis of the inability of Britain's Labour government to respond effectively to the mass unemployment of the first years of the Depression.

Stalinism and the Soviet Union

Conquest, Robert. *The Harvest of Sorrow: Soviet Collectivization and the Terror-Famine.* 1986. Dramatic, pioneering account of the deportation and forced collec-

tivization of peasants that proved the cornerstone of the Stalinist revolution of 1929–1933.

———. *The Great Terror: A Reassessment.* 1990. Updated edition of an influential work first published in 1968. Offers a gripping account of the Stalinist purges of the 1930s, emphasizing Stalin's personal responsibility.

Fitzpatrick, Sheila. *Stalin's Peasants: Resistance and Survival in the Russian Village after Collectivization.* 1994. Probing study of the peasant response to the forced collectivization that inaugurated Stalin's rule in the Soviet Union.

Getty, J. Arch. *Origins of the Great Purges: The Soviet Communist Party Reconsidered, 1933–1938.* 1985. Challenges the notion that the purges, show trials, and terror of the 1930s were parts of a single totalitarian system orchestrated by Stalin. Argues that they were ad hoc responses to disparate pressures.

Rosenberg, William G., and Lewis H. Siegelbaum, eds. *Social Dimensions of Soviet Industrialization.* 1993. Important series of essays showing the impact of the crash industrialization program of the 1930s on the experience of ordinary people, from peasants to industrial workers to those responsible for factory discipline.

Thurston, Robert W. *Life and Terror in Stalin's Russia, 1934–1941.* 1996. Challenges the conventional understanding based on notions of terror and totalitarianism. Seeks to penetrate to the level of ordinary people and everyday life to understand the successes of the Stalinist regime during the pivotal 1930s.

Tucker, Robert C. *Stalin in Power: The Revolution from Above, 1928–1941.* 1990. The second volume of the author's acclaimed study of Stalin, but stands on its own. Provides a superb account of the crash industrialization and forced collectivization that led to the Stalinist regime.

Hitler and Nazism

Bessel, Richard, ed. *Life in the Third Reich.* 1987. Essays on the connections between the Nazi regime and German society. An ideal introductory work.

Bracher, Karl Dietrich. *The German Dictatorship: The Origins, Structure, and Effects of National Socialism.* 1970. A comprehensive synthesis by a major German authority.

Fest, Joachim C. *The Face of the Third Reich: Portraits of the Nazi Leadership.* 1970. Perceptive collective biography of the major Nazi hierarchs, highlighting common personal weaknesses.

Fischer, Klaus P. *Nazi Germany: A New History.* 1995. Comprehensive, well researched, and carefully balanced, this is perhaps the best one-volume treatment of Nazism in English.

Jaeckel, Eberhard. *Hitler's World View: A Blueprint for Power.* 1981. Influential account of the combination of racism, anti-Semitism, and Social Darwinism that structured Hitler's thinking—and ultimately the aspirations of the Nazi regime.

Kershaw, Ian. *The "Hitler Myth": Image and Reality in the Third Reich*. 1987. Explores the often contradictory image of Hitler created in Nazi propaganda.

———. *The Nazi Dictatorship: Problems and Perspectives of Interpretation*. 3rd ed. 1993. Excellent historiographical account of the major issues and recent controversies concerning the Nazi regime in practice.

Koonz, Claudia. *Mothers in the Fatherland: Women, the Family, and Nazi Politics*. 1987. Influential and accessible study of women in Nazism, accenting the active roles of women in implementing Nazism on the grassroots level in welfare, education, and leisure activities, while ultimately stressing the subordination of women within the wider Nazi universe.

Noakes, J[eremy], and G[eoffrey] Pridham, eds. *Nazism: A History in Documents and Eyewitness Accounts, 1919–1945*. 2 vols. 1990. An invaluable collection of documents on all aspects of Nazism, usefully arranged with running commentary by the editors.

Peukert, Detlev J. K. *Inside Nazi Germany: Conformity, Opposition, and Racism in Everyday Life*. 1987. Among the best of recent efforts to understand Nazi Germany by depicting how Nazism affected the everyday lives of ordinary people.

Stephenson, Jill. *Women in Nazi Society*. 1975. Pioneering work on what Nazism meant for women's status and opportunities. Shows that by the late 1930s, German women were neither better nor worse off than women elsewhere in the West.

Comparative Approaches to the Dictatorships

Bessel, Richard, ed. *Fascist Italy and Nazi Germany: Comparisons and Contrasts*. 1996. A well-selected series of essays by major experts on fascism.

Bullock, Alan. *Hitler and Stalin: Parallel Lives*. 1992. A lengthy yet gripping comparative account by a master of the biographical approach to history.

Griffin, Roger. *The Nature of Fascism*. 1991. Sophisticated but accessible effort to identify the core of aspirations, stemming especially from the new situation created by the war and the Russian Revolution, that led to the fascist movements of the interwar period.

Laqueur, Walter. *Fascism: Past, Present, Future*. 1996. Wide-ranging interpretative account, devoting much attention to recent "neofascism," including comparisons with religious extremism.

Payne, Stanley G. *A History of Fascism, 1914–1945*. 1995. A comprehensive account by a leading historian of twentieth-century Europe. Includes historical and interpretive sections, as well as an epilogue on the scope for neofascism.

France and Spain

Carr, Raymond. *The Spanish Tragedy: The Civil War in Perspective*. 1977. An accessible account, blending narrative with analysis and commentary. Particularly useful on the politics of the Nationalist zone.

Colton, Joel. *Leon Blum: Humanist in Politics*. 1987. First pub. 1966. Sympathetic but carefully balanced biography, featuring dilemmas stemming from Blum's background as a socialist intellectual.

Fraser, Ronald. *Blood of Spain: An Oral History of the Spanish Civil War*. 1986. Based on interviews with participants, this book provides a running history of the war and the revolutionary efforts that accompanied it.

Jackson, Julian. *The Popular Front in France: Defending Democracy, 1934–38*. 1988. Combines narrative with thematic chapters on the most controversial issues surrounding the popular front experience.

Payne, Stanley. *The Spanish Revolution*. 1970. Focuses on the disintegration of the second Spanish republic and the coming of the civil war.

Weber, Eugen. *The Hollow Years: France in the 1930s*. 1994. Lively account of French life and manners during a decade that led to humiliation and defeat.

Diplomacy and the Coming of War

Bell, P. M. H. *The Origins of the Second World War in Europe*. 1986. A well-organized and nicely balanced survey.

Cameron, Donald Watt. *How War Came: The Immediate Origins of the Second World War, 1938–1939*. 1989. Detailed but readable narrative account, based on thorough research.

Overy, R. J., and Andrew Wheatcroft. *The Road to War*. 1989. Without questioning Hitler's ruthlessness and ultimate responsibility, the authors challenge standard views of the causes of World War II by recreating the particular situations and perspectives of each country.

Weinberg, Gerhard L. *The Foreign Policy of Hitler's Germany*. Vol. 1, *Diplomatic Revolution in Europe, 1933–1936*, and Vol. 2, *Starting World War II, 1937–1939*. 1970, 1980. Comprehensive study focusing on the key decisions and those who made them. Emphasizes Hitler's aims and German initiatives in the process that led to war.

FILM AS PROPAGANDA

One of the extraordinary pieces of evidence from the Nazi period is *Triumph of the Will,* a documentary film on the sixth Nazi party rally, which took place September 4–10, 1934, in the historic city of Nuremberg, by this time the official site for such party rallies. Directed by a talented young woman, Leni Riefenstahl (b. 1902), *Triumph of the Will* has long been recognized as one of the most compelling propaganda films ever made. What can we learn from this film about how the Nazis understood and used propaganda? What was the Nazi regime trying to convey in sponsoring the film, with the particular images it contained?

A sense of the scope for political propaganda was one of the defining features of the Nazi movement virtually from its inception. In his quest for power Hitler allotted an especially significant role to his future propaganda minister, Joseph Goebbels. Both Hitler and Goebbels saw that new media and carefully orchestrated events might be used to shape the political views of masses of people.

The Nazi party held the first of what would become annual conventions in Nuremberg in 1927. From the start, these meetings were rallies of

As seen in *Triumph of the Will*, the Leader . . .

the faithful, intended to give the Nazi movement a sense of cohesion and common purpose; but they increasingly became carefully staged propaganda spectacles, with banners and searchlights, parades and speeches. When, by 1934, the regime had completed the task of immediate power consolidation, it seemed time to seize the potential of the film medium to carry the spectacle beyond those present in Nuremberg. The intention to make a film thus influenced the staging of the 1934 rally. Film would transform the six-day event into a single potent work of art.

When Hitler came to power, Goebbels, as propaganda minister, assumed control of the German film industry, and he was particularly jealous of his prerogatives in this sphere. If there was to be a film of one of the Nuremberg rallies, he assumed that he would be in charge. So he objected strenuously when Hitler decided that Riefenstahl, who was not even a party member, should film the 1934 rally.

Already popular as an actress, Riefenstahl had established her own film-making company in 1931, before she turned 30. Her first film won the admiration of Hitler, who sought her out and eventually proposed that she direct the film of the party rally. Although she was an artist with no special interest in politics, Riefenstahl, like many Germans, believed at this point that Hitler might be able to revive Germany's fortunes. So despite considerable reluctance, she bowed to Hitler's persistence and agreed to do the film—though only after she was guaranteed final control over editing. Her relations with Goebbels remained strained, but Hitler continued to support her as she made *Triumph of the Will.*

Riefenstahl developed the 107-minute film by editing sixty-one hours of footage that covered everything from Hitler's arrival and motorcade to the closing parades and speeches. As depicted on film, the party rally does not convey an overt ideological message. We hear Hitler not attacking Jews or glorifying conquest but simply trumpeting German renewal. What strikes us in Riefenstahl's portrayal are the unity and epic monumentality that

. . . and the Disciplined, Tightly Knit Community of Followers *(Both photos from the Museum of Modern Art/Film Stills Archive)*

Nazism had apparently brought to Germany thanks to Hitler's leadership.

The film opens as Hitler emerges from dramatic cloud formations to arrive by airplane, descending from the sky like a god. He appears throughout the film as an almost superhuman figure, even, as in the shot shown here, as inspired, possessed, uncanny. Above all, he is a creator who shapes reality by blending will and art, forging masses of anonymous individuals into one people, one racial community, ready for anything. Those individuals seem, from one perspective, to lose their individuality in a monolithic mass, as in the shot of the parade grounds. But their sense of involvement in grandiose purposes charges them emotionally, even gives them a kind of ecstasy. The symbols, the massed banners, the ritualistic show of conformity, all strengthened this sense of participation in the new people's community. But unity and community were not ends in themselves; the film exalted military values and depicted a disciplined society organized for war.

Triumph of the Will extended participation in the spectacle to those who were not actually present in Nuremberg. The film chiseled the sprawl-

ing event into a work of art, so seeing the film was in some ways more effective than being there. The Nazis looked for every means possible to involve the whole society in ritualistic spectacles that could promote a sense of belonging and unity. In addition to film, they made effective use of radio, even subsidizing the purchase of radio sets, or "people's receivers." Such new media were to help ordinary Germans feel a more meaningful kind of belonging than possible under the democracy of the Weimar Republic. But this was only an emotional involvement, not the active participation of free citizens invited to make rational choices.

Triumph of the Will had its premiere in March 1935, with Hitler in the audience. It won several prizes in Germany and abroad but enjoyed only mixed success with the German public, especially outside the large cities. For some, it was altogether too artistic, and the Nazi regime did not use it widely for overt propaganda purposes. Still, the Nazis commissioned no other film about Hitler, for *Triumph of the Will* captured the way he wanted to be seen. Indeed, Hitler praised the film as an "incomparable glorification of the power and beauty of our Movement." ✑

CHAPTER 28

The Era of the Second World War, 1939–1949

"The effects could well be called unprecedented, magnificent, beautiful, stupendous and terrifying. No man-made phenomenon of such tremendous power had ever occurred before. . . . Thirty seconds after the explosion came first, the air blast pressing hard against the people and things, to be followed almost immediately by the strong, sustained, awesome roar which warned of doomsday and made us feel that we puny things were blasphemous to dare tamper with the forces heretofore reserved to The Almighty."[1]

So wrote Brigadier General Thomas F. Farrell, who had just witnessed the birth of the atomic age. On July 16, 1945, watching from a control shelter 10,000 yards away, Farrell had seen the first explosion of an atomic bomb at a remote, top-secret U.S. government testing ground near Alamogordo, New Mexico. Such a weapon had been little more than a theoretical possibility when World War II began, and it required a remarkable concentration of effort, centered first in Britain, then in the United States, to make possible the awesome spectacle that confronted General Farrell. Exceeding most expectations, the test revealed a weapon of unprecedented power and destructiveness.

Within weeks, the United States dropped two other atomic bombs—first on Hiroshima, then on Nagasaki—to force the surrender of Japan. Thus ended the Second World War, the conflict that had begun six long years earlier with the German invasion of Poland. The atomic bomb was the awesome final step in an escalation of violence that made World War II the most destructive in history. In using the atomic bomb, the Americans not only ended the war but assured that a new set of anxieties would accompany the return to peace.

A new war,
a new age.

World War II proved more destructive than World War I, and more truly global in scope, partly because it grew from its European beginnings to encompass Japan late in 1941. In World War I, Japan had played only a secondary role, on the side of Britain. But now, allied with Germany and Italy, Japan was aggressively seeking an empire in East Asia and the Pacific. Japan's far greater involvement in World War II brought the full brunt of the war to that region and dramatically changed the geography and strategy of the war. Moreover, because the war expanded as it did, it profoundly affected the place of Western civilization in the world, speeding the dissolution of the Western colonial empires. Yet the Japanese dared to become fully involved in the war, attacking the United States late in 1941, only because of the outcome in Europe to that point. And ultimately it was the European theater that proved decisive.

The ironic outcome of the Second World War was a new cold war between the United States and the Soviet Union, allies in the victorious struggle against Germany, Italy, and Japan. Of the European states, only the Soviet Union emerged from the war with more territory and more power, thrust into a world role that would have been inconceivable just a few years before. But the wartime success of the United States had been even more dramatic, and the Americans were determined not to repeat what now seemed their mistaken return to isolationism in the aftermath of World War I. By the end of the 1940s, the United States and the Soviet Union had divided Europe into competing spheres of influence. Indeed, the competition between these two superpowers almost immediately became global in scope, creating a bipolar world. And the cold war between them was especially terrifying because, seeking military advantage, they raced to stockpile ever more destructive nuclear weapons. Thus the threat of nuclear annihilation helped define the cold war era.

World War II led to the defeat of the Axis powers—first Italy, then Germany, and finally Japan—and in this sense resolved the conflicts that had caused it. But the experience of this particular war changed the world forever. Before finally meeting defeat, the Nazis were sufficiently successful to begin implementing their "new order" in Europe, especially in the territories they conquered to the east of Germany. As part of this effort, in what has become known as the Holocaust, they began systematically murdering Jews in extermination camps, eventually killing as many as 6 million. The most destructive of the camps was at Auschwitz, in Poland. Often paired after the war, Auschwitz and Hiroshima came to stand for the incredible new forms of death and destruction that the war had spawned—and that continued to haunt the world long after it had ended, posing new questions about the meaning of Western civilization.

THE VICTORY OF NAZI GERMANY, 1939–1941

Instead of the enthusiasm evident in 1914, the German invasion of Poland on September 1, 1939, produced a grim sense of foreboding, even in Germany. Well-publicized incidents like the German bombing of civilians during the Spanish civil war and the Italian use of poison gas in Ethiopia suggested that the frightening new technologies introduced in World War I would now be used on a far greater scale, making the new conflict a much uglier war, more directly involving civilians.

Still, as in 1914, there were hopes that this war could be localized and brief—that it would not become a "world war." Hitler did not expect a protracted war with Britain. In light of the Nazi-Soviet Pact (see page 1023), war between Germany and the Soviet Union seemed unlikely. And isolationist sentiment in the United States made U.S. intervention doubtful.

Rather than a long war, Hitler and the Germans envisioned a *Blitzkrieg,* or "lightning war." At first events seemed to confirm German expectations. When Poland fell after just over a month, Hitler publicly offered peace to Britain and France, seriously thinking that might be the end of it. The British and French refused to call off the war, but from 1939 through 1941 the Nazis won victory after victory, establishing the foundation for their new order in Europe.

Initial Conquests and "Phony War"

The Polish army was large enough to have given the Germans a serious battle. But in adapting the technological innovations of World War I, Germany had developed a new military strategy based on rapid mobility. This Blitzkrieg strategy employed swift, highly concentrated offensives based on mobile tanks covered with concentrated air support, including dive-bombers that struck just ahead of the tanks. In Poland this strategy proved decisive. The French could offer only token help, and the last Polish unit surrendered on October 2, barely a month after the fighting had begun. The speed of the German victory stunned the world.

Meanwhile, the Soviets began cashing in on the pact they had made with Nazi Germany a few weeks before. It offered a precious opportunity to undo provisions of the World War I settlement that had significantly diminished the western territories of the former Russian Empire, thereby damaging the interests and defenses of the new Soviet state. On September 17, with the German victory in Poland assured, Stalin sent Soviet forces into Poland. Soon Poland was again divided between Germany and Russia, as it had been before 1914. Stalin looked next to the Baltic states of Estonia, Latvia, and Lithuania, which had been part of the Russian Empire before World War I. The Nazi-Soviet agreement had assigned Lithuania to the German orbit, but the Germans agreed to let the Soviets have it in exchange for an additional slice of Poland. Initially let off with treaties of mutual assistance, Estonia, Latvia, and Lithuania were incorporated as republics within the Soviet Union during the summer of 1940.

When Finland proved less pliable, the Soviets invaded in November 1939. In the ensuing "Winter War," the Finns held out bravely, and only by taking heavy casualties did the Soviets manage to prevail by March 1940. These difficulties seemed to confirm suspicions that Stalin's purge during the mid-1930s had substantially weakened the Soviet army. Still, by midsummer 1940 the Soviet Union had regained much of the territory it had lost during the upheavals surrounding the revolution of 1917.

In the West, little happened during the strained winter of 1939–1940, known as the "Phony War." Then, on April 9, 1940, the Germans attacked Norway and Denmark in a surprise move to preempt a British and French scheme to cut off the major route for the shipment of Swedish iron ore to Germany. Denmark fell almost at once, while the staunch resistance in Norway was effectively broken by the end of April. The stage was set for the German assault on France.

The Fall of France, 1940

The war in the West began in earnest on May 10, 1940, when the Germans attacked France and the Low Countries. They launched their assault on France through the Ardennes Forest, above the northern end of the Maginot Line—terrain so difficult the French had discounted the possibility of an enemy strike there (see page 962). As in 1914, northern France quickly became the focus of a major war pitting French forces and their British allies against invading Germans. But this time, in startling contrast to World War I, the Battle of France was over in less than six weeks, a humiliating defeat for the French. What had happened?

The problem for the French was not lack of men and materiel, but strategy: how men and materiel were used. For example, Germany had no more than a slight numerical advantage in tanks. But in France, as in Poland, Germany took advantage of mobile tanks and dive-bombers to mount rapid, highly concentrated offensives. Germany achieved the essential breakthrough partly because the French command underestimated the speed with which the German army could move through Belgium.

French strategy, in contrast, was based on lessons learned during World War I. Anticipating another long, defensive war, France dispersed its tanks among infantry units along a broad front. Once the German tank column broke through the French lines, it quickly cut through northern France toward the North Sea. France's poor showing convinced the British that rather than commit troops and planes to a hopeless battle in France, they should get out and regroup for a longer global war. Finally, 200,000 British troops—as well as 130,000 French—escaped German encirclement and capture through a difficult evacuation at Dunkirk early in June (see Map 28.1).

By mid-June, barely five weeks after the fighting began, France had been thoroughly defeated. As the French military collapsed, the French cabinet resigned, to be replaced by a new government under Marshal Philippe Pétain, who had led the successful French effort in the Battle of Verdun during World War I. Pétain's government first asked for an armistice and then engineered a change of regime. The French parliament voted by an overwhelming majority to give Pétain exceptional powers, including the power to draw up a new constitution. So ended the parliamentary democracy of the Third Republic, which seemed responsible for France's weakness. The republic gave way to the more authoritarian Vichy regime, named after the resort city to which the government retreated as the Germans moved into Paris. The end of the fighting in France resulted in a kind of antidemocratic revolution, but one in which the French people, stunned by military defeat, at first acquiesced.

According to the armistice agreement, the French government was not only to cease hostilities but also to collaborate with the victorious Germans. French resistance began immediately, however. In a radio broadcast from London on June 18, Charles de Gaulle (1890–1970), the youngest general in the French army, called on French forces to rally to him to continue the fight against Nazi Germany. The military forces stationed in the French colonies, as well as the French troops that had been evacuated at Dunkirk, could form the nucleus of a new French army. Under the circumstances of military defeat and political change, de Gaulle's appeal seemed quixotic at best, and most French colonies went along with what seemed the legitimate French government at Vichy. For the new Vichy government, de Gaulle was a traitor. Yet a new Free French force grew from de Gaulle's remarkable appeal, and its subsequent role in the war helped overcome the humiliation of France's quick defeat in 1940.

What next for Hitler and the Germans, who seemed virtually invincible after their conquest of France? Ultimately decisive would be the assault on the Soviet Union in June 1941, but two chains of events after the Battle of France influenced the timing of the assault—perhaps in crucial ways. Britain proved a more implacable foe, and Italy a more burdensome friend, than Hitler had expected.

Winston Churchill and the Battle of Britain

With the defeat of France, Hitler seems to have expected that Britain, now apparently vulnerable to German invasion, would come to terms. But the British, having none of it, found a new spokesman and leader in Winston Churchill (1874–1965), who had replaced Neville Chamberlain as prime minister when the German invasion of western Europe began on May 10. Although Churchill had been prominent in British public life for years, his career to this point had not been noteworthy

for either judgment or success. He was obstinate, difficult, something of a curmudgeon. Yet he rose to the wartime challenge, becoming one of the notable leaders of the modern era. In speeches to the House of Commons during the remainder of 1940, he uttered perhaps the most memorable words of the war as he sought to dramatize the situation and inspire his nation. Some Britons, hoping for a negotiated settlement with Germany as the Battle of France ended, objected to Churchill's rhetoric, but his dogged promise of "blood, toil, tears, and sweat" helped rally the British people, so that later he could say, without exaggeration, that "this was their finest hour."

After the fall of France, Britain moved to full mobilization for a protracted war. Churchill consolidated economic policy under a small committee that promptly gave Britain the most thoroughly coordinated war economy of all the belligerents. Between 1940 and 1942, Britain outstripped Germany in the production of tanks, aircraft, and machine guns. In 1941 Britain adopted a National Service Act that subjected men aged 18 to 50 and women aged 20 to 30 to military or civilian war service. The upper age limits were subsequently raised to meet the demand for labor. Almost 70 percent of the 3 million people added to the British work force during the war were women.

Britain, then, intended to continue the fight even after France fell. Hitler weighed his options and decided to attack. In light of British naval superiority, he hoped to rely on aerial bombardment to knock the British out of the war without an actual invasion. The ensuing Battle of Britain culminated in the nightly bombing of London from September 7 through November 2, 1940, killing 15,000 and destroying thousands of buildings. But the British held. Ordinary people holed up in cellars and subway stations, while the fighter planes of the Royal Air Force fought back effectively, inflicting heavy losses against German aircraft over Britain.

Although the bombing continued into 1941, the British had withstood the worst the Germans could deliver, and Hitler began looking to the east, his ultimate objective all along. In December 1940 he ordered preparations for Operation Barbarossa, the assault on the Soviet Union. Rather than continuing the attack on Britain directly, Germany would use submarines to cut off shipping—and thus the supplies the British needed for a long war. Once Germany had defeated the Soviet

British Resistance At the height of the German bombing of Britain in 1940, Winston Churchill surveys the damage in London. *(Hulton-Getty/Tony Stone Images)*

Union, it would enjoy the geopolitical basis for world power, while Britain, as an island nation relying on a dispersed empire, would sooner or later be forced to come to terms.

Italian Intervention and the Spread of the War

Lacking sufficient domestic support, and unready for a major war, Mussolini could only look on as the war began in 1939. But as the Battle of France neared its end, it seemed safe for Italy to intervene, sharing in the spoils of what appeared certain victory. Thus in June 1940 Italy entered the war, expecting to secure territorial advantages in the Mediterranean, starting with Corsica, Nice, and Tunisia at the expense of France. Italy also hoped eventually to supplant Britain in the region—and even to take the Suez Canal.

Although Hitler and Mussolini got along remarkably well, their relationship was sensitive. When Hitler seemed to be proceeding without Italy during the first year of the war, Mussolini grew determined to show his independence and finally, in October 1940, ordered Italian forces to attack Greece. But the Greeks mounted a strong

resistance, thanks partly to the help of British forces from North Africa.

Meanwhile, Germany had established its hegemony in much of east-central Europe without military force, often by exploiting grievances over the outcome of the peace conference in 1919. In November 1940 Romania and Hungary joined the Axis camp, and Bulgaria followed a few months later. But in March 1941, just after Yugoslavia had similarly committed to the Axis, a coup overthrew the pro-Axis government in Yugoslavia, and the new Yugoslav government prepared to aid the Allies.

By this point Hitler had decided it was expedient to push into the Balkans with German troops, both to reinforce the Italians and to consolidate Axis control of the area. As the war's geographic extent expanded, its stakes increased, yet the Germans continued to meet every challenge. By the end of May 1941 they had taken Yugoslavia and Greece (Map 28.1).

At the same time, the war was spreading to North Africa and the Middle East because of European colonial ties. The native peoples of the area sought to take advantage of the conflict among the Europeans to pursue their own independence. Iraq

Map labels:

SOVIET UNION

Baku

Russian front, Nov. 1942

Siege of Stalingrad, Aug. 21, 1942–Jan. 31 1943

Stalingrad

Russian front, Dec. 1941

Volga

SYRIA

TRANS-JORDAN (Br. Mandate)

PALESTINE (Br. Mandate)

Don

Suez Canal

Moscow

TURKEY

Nile

Cairo

Tula

Dnieper

Russian front, Spring 1944

Smolensk

Yalta

Black Sea

Ankara

CYPRUS

EGYPT

El Alamein, Summer 1942

Siege of Leningrad, Sept. 1941–Jan. 1944

Leningrad

Kiev

UKRAINE

FINLAND

Helsinki

Pinsk

BULGARIA

Sofia

ROMANIA

Bucharest

Danube

GREECE

Athens

Crete

Mediterranean Sea

LIBYA

Riga

Baltic Sea

Vistula

Posen

Warsaw

Cracow

SLOVAKIA

HUNGARY

Budapest

Vienna

YUGOSLAVIA

SERBIA

ALBANIA

Russian front, Feb. 1945

SWEDEN

Stockholm

Berlin

Elbe

GERMANY

Danube

CROATIA

Monte Cassino, May 1944

Salerno, Sept. 1943

Sicily, July 1943

Sicily

MALTA (Gr. Br.)

Rhine Crossing, March 7, 1945

Po

Bologna

Italian front, Feb. 1945

ITALY

Rome

Allies invade Sicily and Italy, July–Sept. 1943

NORWAY

Oslo

DENMARK

Copenhagen

Rhine

SWITZERLAND

German surrender: Reims, May 7, 1945 Berlin, May 8, 1945

NETHERLANDS

Dunkirk

BELGIUM

Battle of the Bulge, Dec. 1944

Western front, Feb. 1945

VICHY FRANCE (occupied Nov. 1942)

Allies land in Provence, Aug. 15, 1944

Rommel defeated in Tunisia; Axis troops evacuated, May 1943

TUNISIA

North Sea

Battle of Britain, Fall 1940

GREAT BRITAIN

London

Paris

FRANCE

Vichy

Invasion of Normandy, June 6, 1944

Axis troops occupy Vichy France, Nov. 10 and 11, 1942

Ebro

ALGERIA (Vichy France)

NORTHERN IRELAND

IRELAND

ATLANTIC OCEAN

Madrid

SPAIN

GIBRALTAR (Gr. Br.)

SP. MOROCCO

Casablanca, Nov. 1942

FRENCH MOROCCO

PORTUGAL

Lisbon

400 Mi.

400 Km.

200

200

0

0

Legend:

- Hitler's Greater Germany
- Allied with Germany
- Occupied by Germany and its allies
- Grand Alliance
- Neutral nations
- ✕ Major battles

and Syria became involved as Germans operating from Syria, administered by Vichy France, aided anti-British Arab nationalists in Iraq. But most important proved to be North Africa, where Libya, an Italian colony since 1912, lay adjacent to Egypt, where the British presence remained strong.

In September 1940 the Italian army drove 65 miles into Egypt, initiating almost three years of fighting across the North African desert. A British counteroffensive from December 1940 to February 1941 drove the Italians back 340 miles into Libya, prompting Germany to send some of its forces from the Balkans into North Africa. Under General Erwin Rommel (1891–1944), the famous "Desert Fox," Axis forces won remarkable successes in North Africa from February to May 1941. But successful though they had been by this point, the German forays into the Balkans and North Africa had delayed the crucial attack on the Soviet Union.

THE ASSAULT ON THE SOVIET UNION AND THE NAZI NEW ORDER

In ordering preparations for Operation Barbarossa in December 1940, Hitler decided to risk attacking the Soviet Union before knocking Britain out of the war. Then he invaded the Balkans and North Africa in what may have been an unnecessary diversion. In retrospect, it is easy to pinpoint that combination as his fatal mistake. But in light of the Soviet purges of the 1930s and the poor performance of the Soviet army in 1939 and 1940, Hitler had reason to believe the Soviet Union would crack relatively easily. Western military experts had come to similar conclusions, estimating that German forces would need but six weeks to take Moscow. And if Germany were to defeat the Soviet Union with another Blitzkrieg, it could gain control of the oil and other resources required for a longer war against Britain and, if necessary, the United States.

Map 28.1 World War II: European Theaters Much of Europe saw fighting during World War II, although different fronts were important at different times. What proved decisive was the fighting that ensued in the vast expanse of the Soviet Union after the Germans invaded in June 1941.

Forgive Me, Comrade . . . On June 23, 1941, the day after Nazi Germany attacked the Soviet Union, the London *Daily Mail* published this cartoon depicting Hitler's betrayal of his 1939 pact with Stalin. (Daily Mail, *London, 23 June 1941. Reprinted with permission*)

So the Nazi assault on the Soviet Union was not ill considered. Ultimately, however, it failed, and its failure was the decisive fact of World War II. Although supplies from its new Allies—Britain and eventually the United States—helped the Soviet forces to prevail, the most important factor was the unexpected strength of the Soviet military effort.

Before they were defeated, the Germans penetrated well into the Soviet Union, reaching the apex of their power in 1942. German conquests by that point enabled Hitler to begin constructing the new European order he had dreamed of. Although in western Europe the Nazis generally sought the collaboration of local leaders, in Poland and the Soviet Union the new order meant brutal subjugation of local populations. Now, and only now, did

EXTERMINATION AND CONCENTRATION CAMPS

REICHSKOMMISSARIAT OSTLAND

REICHSKOMMISSARIAT UKRAINE

TREWNIKI

BELZEC

GOVERNMENT GENERAL OF POLAND

SOBIBOR

MAJDANEK

PONIATOWA

AUSCHWITZ

TREBLINKA

SLOVAKIA

HUNGARY

CHELMNO

SACHSENHAUSEN

Berlin

GREATER GERMANY

PROTECTORATE OF BOHEMIA AND MORAVIA

MAUTHAUSEN

SWEDEN

DENMARK

BERGEN-BELSEN

BUCHENWALD

DACHAU

ITALY

CROATIA

SERBIA

ROMANIA

Poland before Sept. 1, 1939

◆ Extermination camps

■ Concentration camps

SOVIET UNION

Caspian Sea

Ural

Volga

Stalingrad

Don

Moscow

Volga

FINLAND

Helsinki

Leningrad

REICHSKOMMISSARIAT OSTLAND

Kiev

REICHSKOMMISSARIAT UKRAINE

Dnieper

Baltic Sea

Stockholm

SWEDEN

NORWAY

Oslo

DENMARK

Copenhagen

Warsaw

GOVERNMENT GENERAL OF POLAND

Bug

Vistula

Oder

Black Sea

Istanbul

TURKEY

Berlin

GREATER GERMANY

Prague

Elbe

SLOVAKIA

Budapest

HUNGARY

Vienna

Danube

ROMANIA

Bucharest

Belgrade

SERBIA

Sofia

BULGARIA

Athens

GREECE

Crete

Mediterranean Sea

LIBYA

Bonn

Luxembourg

PROTECTORATE OF BOHEMIA & MORAVIA

Rhine

SWITZ.

CROATIA

MONTENEGRO

ALBANIA

ITALY

Rome

Po

Sicily

Malta

Corsica

Sardinia

HOLLAND

Amsterdam

Brussels

BELGIUM

Paris

FRANCE

Seine

Loire

Vichy

VICHY FRANCE

GREAT BRITAIN

London

IRELAND

North Sea

SPAIN

Tagus

400 Km.

400 Mi.

200

200

0

0

Greater Germany

Italy, including occupied and annexed territories

Satellite states of Germany including annexed territory

Areas under direct German control in the east

Countries under German military occupation in the west

Vichy France, nominally sovereign

Area of German military operations

Neutral and non-belligerent states

Opponents of Germany

Boundary of Greater Germany

the Nazis begin physically exterminating the Jews of Europe in specially constructed death camps.

An Ambiguous Outcome, 1941–1942

Attacking the Soviet Union on June 22, 1941, German forces achieved notable successes during the first month of fighting, partly because Stalin was so unprepared for this German betrayal. Ignoring warnings of an impending German assault, he had continued to live up to his end of the 1939 bargain with Hitler, even supplying the Germans with oil and grain. After the attack, Russia's defenses were at first totally disorganized, and by late November, German forces were within 20 miles of Moscow.

But the Germans were ill equipped for Russian weather, and as an early and severe winter descended, the German offensive bogged down. In December, the Soviets mounted a formidable surprise counterattack near Moscow. The German Blitzkrieg, which had seemed a sure thing in July, had failed; Germany might still prevail, but a different strategy would be required.

Although their initial assault had stalled, the Germans still had the advantage. German forces failed to take the key city of Leningrad in 1941, but they cut it off by blockade and, until early 1944, kept it under siege with relentless bombing and shelling. And during the summer of 1942, they mounted another offensive, moving more deeply into the Soviet Union than before, reaching Stalingrad in November. But this proved the deepest penetration of German forces—and the zenith of Nazi power in Europe.

Hitler's New Order

By the summer of 1942, Nazi Germany dominated the European continent as no power ever had before (Map 28.2). German military successes allowed the Nazi regime to begin building a new order in the territories under German domination. Satellite states in Slovakia and Croatia, and client governments in Romania and Hungary, owed their existence to Nazi Germany and readily adapted themselves to the Nazi system. Elsewhere in the Nazi orbit, some countries proved eager collaborators; others did their best to resist; still others were given no opportunity to collaborate but were ruthlessly subjugated instead.

The Nazis' immediate aim was simply to exploit the conquered territories to serve the continuing war effort. Precisely as envisioned, access to the resources of so much of Europe made Germany considerably less vulnerable to naval blockade than it had been during World War I. France proved a particularly valuable source of raw materials; by 1943, for example, 75 percent of French iron ore went to German factories.

But the deeper purposes of the war were also clear in the way the Nazis treated the territories under their control, especially in the difference between east and west. In western Europe, there was plenty of brutality, but Nazi victory still led to something like conventional military occupation. The Germans tried to enlist the cooperation of local authorities in countries like Denmark, the Netherlands, and France, though with mixed results. And though the Nazis exploited the economy of France, for example, it never became clear what role France might play in Europe after a Nazi victory. However, in Poland and later in the conquered parts of the Soviet Union, there was no pretense of cooperation, and it at once became clear what the Nazi order would entail.

After the conquest of Poland, the Germans annexed the western part of the country outright and promptly executed, jailed, or expelled members of the Polish elite—professionals, journalists, business leaders, and priests. The Nazis prohibited the Poles from entering the professions and restricted even their right to marry. All the Polish schools and most of the churches were simply closed.

In the rest of Poland, administered by a German governor-general, Nazi policy was slightly less brutal at first. Most churches remained open, and Poles were allowed to practice the professions, but the Nazis closed most schools above the fourth grade, as well as libraries, theaters, and museums as they sought to root out every

Map 28.2 The Nazi New Order in Europe, 1942

At the zenith of its power in 1942, Nazi Germany controlled much of Europe. Concerned most immediately with winning the war, the Nazis sought to coordinate the economies of their satellite states and conquered territories. But they also began establishing what was supposed to be an enduring new order in eastern Europe. The inset shows the location of the major Nazi concentration camps and of the six extermination camps the Nazis constructed in what had been Poland.

expression of Polish culture. Whether the Poles in this area were to be exterminated, enslaved, or shipped off to Siberia was much debated, but the decision was postponed—to be made after the victory. (See the box, "Toward the Nazi New Order.")

With the conquest of Poland, Nazi leaders proclaimed that a new era of monumental resettlement in eastern Europe had begun for Germany. By mid-1941, 200,000 Germans, carefully selected for their racial characteristics, had been resettled—primarily on farms—in the part of Poland annexed to Germany. Many were ethnic Germans who had been living outside Germany. During the fall of 1942, the select Nazi elite, the Schutzstaffel (SS), under the leadership of Heinrich Himmler, began to arrest and expel peasants from the rest of Poland to make way for further German resettlement. By 1943 perhaps one million Germans had been moved into what had been Poland.

After the assault on the Soviet Union, Hitler made it clear that eastern Europe as far as the Ural Mountains was to be opened for German settlement. War veterans were to be given priority, partly because the German settlers would have to be tough to resist the Slavs, who would be concentrated east of the Urals. To prepare for German colonization, Himmler told SS leaders that Germany would have to exterminate 30 million Slavs in the Soviet Union. After the German invasion, the SS promptly began executing prisoners of war, as well as any Soviet leaders they could find. However, the Nazis expected that several generations would be required for the resettlement of European Russia, and here, in contrast to Poland, the program barely got started during the war years.

The Holocaust

Conquest of the east also gave the Nazis the opportunity for a more radical solution to the "Jewish problem" than they had attempted before. Under the cover of war, they began exterminating the Jews within their orbit. Thus began the process, and the experience, that has come to be known as the Holocaust.

When and why this policy was chosen remains controversial. Although prewar Nazi rhetoric occasionally suggested the possibility of actual physical destruction, the Nazi goal of a "final solution to the Jewish problem" seemed to mean simply forced emigration. The conquest of Poland, with a

Jewish population of 3 million, gave the Nazis control over a far greater number of Jews than ever before. In 1940, as part of their effort to create a new order, the Nazis began confining Polish Jews to ghettos set up in Warsaw and five other cities. No one knew what was to become of these Jews at first. Himmler and the SS were making tentative plans to develop, after the Nazi victory, a kind of superghetto for perhaps 4 million Jews on the island of Madagascar, at that point still a French colony. However, as the Polish ghettos grew more crowded and difficult to manage, Nazi officials in Poland began pressing for a more definitive policy.

In 1940 Hitler seemed to endorse the Madagascar plan, but he cultivated ambiguity on the operational level—and he left no paper trail. So the precise chain of events that led to a more radical approach will no doubt remain uncertain. The evidence suggests, however, that Hitler ordered the physical extermination of the Jews in the spring of 1941, before the German assault on the Soviet Union in June. By the fall, the Nazis were actively impeding further Jewish emigration from the occupied territories. And they were sending large numbers of German and Austrian Jews to the ghettos in Poland.

With the invasion of the Soviet Union, special SS "intervention squads" were assigned to get rid of Jews and Communist party officials. By late November, the Nazis had killed 136,000 Jews, most by shooting, in the invaded Soviet territories. But as it became obvious that mass shooting was impractical, Nazi leaders sought a more systematic and impersonal method of mass extermination. Late in July 1941, Reinhard Heydrich of the SS began developing a detailed plan, which he explained in January 1942 at a conference of high-ranking officials at Wannsee, a suburb of Berlin. The conference had been postponed from November, and by now the Nazis were already implementing Heydrich's plan for the extermination of the Jews.

The Nazis took advantage of the methods, and especially the deadly Zyklon-B gas, that had proven effective during the euthanasia campaign of 1939 through 1941 in Germany (see page 1011). By March 1942 they had constructed several large extermination camps with gas chambers and crematoria, intended to kill Jews and dispose of their bodies as quickly and efficiently as possible. And now they began the full-scale mass killing, target-

Toward the Nazi New Order

After Nazi Germany conquered much of Poland in 1939, the SS assumed major responsibility for creating a new Nazi order in the conquered territories. In a memorandum dated May 15, 1940, and endorsed by Hitler, the SS leader Heinrich Himmler offered "some thoughts on the treatment of the alien population in the east." The passages that follow make clear the racist basis of Nazi wartime policy.

In our treatment of the foreign ethnic groups in the east we must . . . fish out the racially valuable people from this mishmash, take them to Germany and assimilate them there.

. . . The non-German population of the eastern territories must not receive any education higher than that of elementary school with four forms. The objective of this elementary school must simply be to teach: simple arithmetic up to 500 at the most, how to write one's name, and to teach that it is God's commandment to be obedient to the Germans and to be honest, hard-working, and well-behaved. I consider it unnecessary to teach reading.

There must be no schools at all in the east apart from this type of school. Parents who wish to provide their children with a better education both in the elementary school and later in a secondary school, must make an application to the higher SS and Police Leader. . . . If we recognize such a child as being of our blood then the parents will be informed that the child will be placed in a school in Germany and will remain in Germany indefinitely. . . .

The parents of these children of good blood will be given the choice of either giving up their child . . . or they would have to agree to go to Germany and become loyal citizens there. . . .

Apart from the examination of the petitions which parents put forward for a better education, all 6–10 year olds will be sifted each year to sort out those with valuable blood and those with worthless blood. Those who are selected as valuable will be treated in the same way as the children who are admitted on the basis of the approval of the parents' petition.

. . . [T]he moment the children and parents arrive in Germany they should not be treated in school and life as outcasts but—after changing their names and despite being treated with vigilance—should be integrated into German life on the basis of trust. The children must not be made to feel rejected; for, after all, we believe in our own blood, which through the mistakes of German history has flowed into a foreign nation, and are convinced that our ideology and ideals will find an echo in the souls of these children which are racially identical to our own. . . . Abusive expressions such as "Polack" or "Ukrainian" and such like must be out of the question. . . .

After these measures have been systematically implemented during the next ten years, the population of the General Government will inevitably consist of an inferior remnant. . . . This population will be available as a leaderless laboring class and provide Germany with migrant and seasonal labor for special work projects (road-building, quarries, construction); even then they will get more to eat and have more from life than under Polish rule. . . .

Source: J. Noakes and G. Pridham, *Nazism: A History in Documents and Eyewitness Accounts, 1919–1945*, vol. 2 (New York: Schocken, 1990), pp. 932–934.

ing first the Polish Jews who had already been confined to ghettos. Once the apparatus for mass extermination had been constructed, the ghettos became mere way stations on the journey to the death camps. The Nazis brutally suppressed at-

tempts at resistance, like the Warsaw ghetto uprising of April and May 1943.

During the course of the war the Nazis constructed six full-scale death camps, although not all were operating at peak capacity at the same time. All six were located in what had been Poland (see inset, Map 28.2). Horrifying though they were, the concentration camps in Germany, such as Dachau, Buchenwald, and Bergen-Belsen, were not extermination camps, although many Jews died in them late in the war.

The largest of the six death camps was the Auschwitz-Birkenau complex, which became the principal extermination center in 1943. The Nazis shipped Jews from all over Europe to Auschwitz, which was killing about 12,000 people a day at the peak of its operation in 1944. Auschwitz was one of two extermination camps that included affili-

Children at Auschwitz Images from the Nazi camps haunted the decades that followed the Second World War. The Auschwitz-Birkenau complex proved the largest and most destructive of the camps that the Nazis created specifically for mass killing. The overwhelming majority of those sent to these camps were Jews, most of whom were killed by gassing shortly after their arrival. Those deemed fit for work might be spared, at least for a while, but children were typically killed at once. *(Hulton-Getty/Tony Stone Images)*

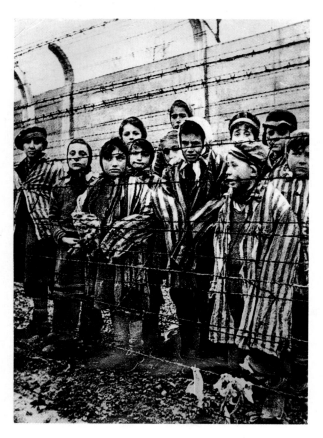

ated slave-labor factories, in which Jews most able to work were literally worked to death. Among the companies profiting from the arrangement were two of Germany's best-known, Krupp and IG Farben.

The Jews typically arrived at one of the camps crammed into cattle cars on special trains. Camp personnel, generally SS medical doctors, subjected new arrivals to "selection," picking some for labor assignments and sending the others, including most women and children, to the gas chambers. Camp personnel made every effort to deceive the Jews who were about to be killed, to lead them to believe they were to be showered and deloused. Even in camps without forced-labor factories, Jews were compelled to do much of the dirty work of the extermination operation. But under the brutal conditions of the camps, those initially assigned to work inevitably weakened; most were then deemed unfit and put to death.

The Nazis took every precaution to hide what was going on in the death camps. The SS personnel involved were sworn to silence. Himmler insisted that if secrecy was to be maintained, the operation would have to be quick—and total, to include women and children, "so that no Jews will remain to take revenge on our sons and grandsons." Indeed, Himmler constantly sought to accelerate the process, even though it required labor and transport facilities desperately needed for the war effort.

Himmler and the other major SS officials, such as Rudolf Höss, the commandant at Auschwitz, or Adolf Eichmann, who organized the transport of the Jews to the camps, cannot be understood simply as sadists who enjoyed humiliating their victims. Rather, they took satisfaction in doing what they believed was their duty without flinching, without signs of weakness. Addressing a group of SS members in 1943, Himmler portrayed the extermination of the Jews as a difficult "historical task" that they, the Nazi elite, must do for their racial community: "Most of you know what it means to see a hundred corpses piled up, or five hundred, or a thousand. To have gone through this and—except for cases of human weakness— to have remained decent, that has made us tough. This is an unwritten, never to be written, page of glory in our history."[2]

However, as Himmler's casual reference to "cases of human weakness" suggests, some among the SS camp guards failed to live up to this image and indulged in wanton cruelty, humiliating their helpless victims. For some, the extermination process became the occasion to act out sadistic fantasies. But though this dimension is surely horrifying, the bureaucratic, factory-like nature of the extermination process is in some ways more troubling.

Despite the overriding emphasis on secrecy, reports of the genocide reached the West almost immediately in 1942. Especially at first, however, most tended to discount them as wartime propaganda of the sort many had believed during World War I, when stories about Germans eating Belgian babies had circulated. Skepticism about extermination reports was easier because there were a few concentration camps, like Theresienstadt in the former Czechoslovakia, that housed Jews who had been selected for special treatment. These camps were not used for extermination and were not secret; the Red Cross was even allowed to inspect Theresienstadt several times. Those outside, and the German people as well, were led to believe that all the Jews were being interned, for the duration of the war, in camps like these, much as Japanese-Americans were being interned in camps in the western United States at the same time. But even as the evidence grew, Allied governments, citing military priorities, refused pleas from Jewish leaders in 1944 to bomb the rail line into Auschwitz.

The Nazis' policy of actually murdering persons deemed undesirable or superfluous did not start with, and was not limited to, the Jews. First came the euthanasia program in Germany, and the war afforded the Nazis the chance to do away with an array of other "undesirables," from communists and homosexuals to Gypsies and Poles. So the most radical and appalling aspect of Nazism did not stem from anti-Semitism alone. This must not be forgotten, but neither must the fact that the Jews constituted by far the largest group of victims—perhaps 5.7 to 6 million, almost two-thirds of the Jews in Europe. (See the feature, "Weighing the Evidence: Holocaust Testimony," on pages 1070–1071.)

Collaboration and Resistance

In rounding up Jews for extermination, and in establishing their new order in Europe, the Nazis found willing collaborators among some of the countries within their orbit. Croatia, the most pro-Nazi of the satellite states, was eager to round up Jews and Gypsies, as well as to attack Serbs, on its own. Romania, too, was happy to deliver foreign-born Jews to the Germans, though it dragged its feet when the Germans began demanding acculturated Romanian Jews.

But degrees of collaboration varied widely across Europe. In Denmark, Norway, and the Netherlands, the Nazis thought racial kinship would matter, but they never found sufficient support to make possible genuinely independent collaborationist governments. In Denmark and the Netherlands, governments put up a façade of cooperation but still managed to foster resistance. Denmark did especially well at resisting the German effort to round up Jews, as did Italy and Bulgaria.

Vichy France was somewhere in the middle, and thus it has remained particularly controversial. When the Vichy regime was launched during the summer of 1940, there was widespread support for Marshal Pétain, its 84-year-old chief of state. Pétain promised to maximize French sovereignty and shield his people from the worst aspects of Nazi occupation. At the same time, the Vichy government claimed to be implementing its own "national revolution," returning France to authority, discipline, and tradition after the shambles of the Third Republic. Vichy's revolution was anti-Semitic and hostile to the left, so it seemed compatible, up to a point, with Nazism. And at first Germany seemed likely to win the war. Thus, Pétain's second-in-command, Pierre Laval (1883–1945), was willing to collaborate actively with the Nazis. The Vichy regime ended up doing much of the Nazis' dirty work for them—rounding up workers for forced shipment to German factories, hunting down members of the anti-German resistance, and picking up Jews to be sent to the Nazi extermination camps.

After the war, Pétain, Laval, and others were found guilty of treason by the new French government. Because of his advanced age, Pétain was merely imprisoned, while Laval and others were executed. But the shame of Vichy collaboration continued to haunt the French, deepening the humiliation of the defeat in 1940.

Though the Nazis found some willing collaborators, the great majority of those living under German occupation came to despise the Nazis as their brutality became ever clearer. Nazi rule meant pillage; it meant rounding up workers for forced labor in Germany; it meant randomly killing hostages in reprisal for resistance activity. In one extreme case, the Germans destroyed the Czech village of Lidice, killing all its inhabitants, in retaliation for the assassination of SS security chief Reinhard Heydrich.

Clandestine movements of resistance to the occupying Nazi forces gradually developed all over Europe. In western Europe, resistance was especially prominent in France and, beginning in 1943, northern Italy, which was subjected to German occupation after the Allies defeated Mussolini's regime. But the anti-German resistance was strongest in Yugoslavia, Poland, and the occupied portions of the Soviet Union, where full-scale guerrilla war against the Germans and their collaborators produced the highest civilian casualties of World War II. The Polish resistance achieved some notable successes in sabotaging roads and railroads, although it met disastrous defeat when it sought to tackle the Germans head-on in Warsaw in 1944.

The role of the resistance proved most significant in Yugoslavia, where the Croatian Marxist Josip Broz, taking the pseudonym Tito (1892–1980), forged the opponents of the Axis powers into a broadly based guerrilla army. Its initial foe was the inflated Croatian state that the Germans, early in 1941, carved from Yugoslavia and entrusted to the pro-Axis Croatian separatist movement, the Ustashe. But Tito's forces soon came up against a rival resistance movement, led by Serb officers, that tended to be pro-Serb, monarchist, and anticommunist. By 1943 Tito led 250,000 men and women in what had become a brutal civil war, one that deepened ethnic divisions and left a legacy of bitterness. Tito's forces prevailed, enabling him to create a communist-led government in Yugoslavia late in the war.

In France and Italy as well, communists played a leading role in the wartime resistance movements. As a result, the Communist party in each country overcame the disarray that followed from the Nazi-Soviet Pact of 1939 and after the war enjoyed a level of prestige that would have been unthinkable earlier.

In the French case, there could have been conflict between the indigenous resistance, with its significant communist component, and the Free French under Charles de Gaulle, operating outside France until August 1944. But it is striking how well they were able to work together. Still, de Gaulle took pains to cement his own leadership in the overall struggle. Among the measures to this end, he decreed women's suffrage for France, partly because women were playing a major role in the resistance. After the liberation of France in 1944, he sought to control a potentially volatile situation by disarming the resistance as quickly as possible.

The western European resistance movements are easily romanticized, their extent and importance overstated. Compared to regular troops, resistance forces were poorly trained, equipped, and disciplined. In France, fewer than 30 percent of the nearly 400,000 active resisters had firearms in 1944. But though the Allies never tried to use them in a systematic way, the resistance movements made at least some military contribution, especially through sabotage. And they boosted national self-esteem for the longer term, helping countries humiliated by defeat and occupation make a fresh start after the war.

Toward the Soviet Triumph

The import of what happened elsewhere in Europe depended on the outcome of the main event, the German invasion of the Soviet Union. Although the German Sixth Army, numbering almost 300,000 men, reached Stalingrad by late 1942, the Germans could not achieve a knockout. (See the box, "Stalingrad: The Diary of a German Soldier.") The Soviets managed to defend the city in what was arguably the pivotal military engagement of World War II. While some Soviet troops fought street by street, house by house, others counterattacked, encircling the attacking German force. Hitler refused a strategic retreat, but his doggedness backfired. By the end of January 1943, the Soviets had captured what remained of the German force, about 100,000 men, very few of whom survived to return to Germany. Perhaps 240,000 German soldiers died in the Battle of Stalingrad or as prisoners afterward. But the price to the Soviets for their victory was far greater: A million Soviet soldiers and civilians died at Stalingrad.

Although the Germans resumed the offensive on several fronts during the summer of 1943, the Soviets won the tank battle of Kursk-Orel in July, and from then on Soviet troops relentlessly moved

Stalingrad: The Diary of a German Soldier

The following excerpts from the diary of a soldier named Wilhelm Hoffman reveal the changing German mood during 1942, as the Nazis penetrated deeply into the Soviet Union, then met disastrous defeat at Stalingrad. The writer himself did not survive the battle; his closing curse was his last diary entry.

July 29. The company commander says the Russian troops are completely broken, and cannot hold out any longer. To reach the Volga and take Stalingrad is not so difficult for us. The Führer knows where the Russians' weak point is. Victory is not far away. . . .

August 2. . . . What great spaces the Soviets occupy, what rich fields there are to be had here after the war's over!

August 17. The last few days our regiment has been in battle all the time. . . . The heat and the constant fighting are utterly exhausting. But we are all ready to advance quickly to the Volga. . . .

September 26. Our regiment is involved in constant heavy fighting. After the [grain storage] elevator was taken the Russians continued to defend themselves just as stubbornly. You don't see them at all, they have established themselves in houses and cellars and are firing on all sides, including from our rear—barbarians, they use gangster methods. . . .

October 14. It has been fantastic since morning: our aeroplanes and artillery have been hammering the Russian positions for hours on end; everything in sight is being blotted from the face of the earth. . . .

October 22. Our regiment has failed to break into the factory. We have lost many men;

every time you move you have to jump over bodies. . . . Who would have thought three months ago that instead of the joy of victory we would have to endure such sacrifice and torture, the end of which is nowhere in sight? . . .

The soldiers are calling Stalingrad the mass grave of the [German army]. . . .

October 27. Our troops have captured the whole of the Barrikady factory, but we cannot break through to the Volga. The Russians are not men, but some kind of cast-iron creatures; they never get tired and are not afraid of fire. We are absolutely exhausted; our regiment now has barely the strength of a company. . . .

November 21. The Russians have gone over to the offensive along the whole front. . . . So, there it is—the Volga, victory and soon home to our families! We shall obviously be seeing them next in the other world.

December 14. Everybody is racked with hunger. Frozen potatoes are the best meal, but to get them out of the ice-covered ground under fire from Russian bullets is not so easy.

December 26. . . . The soldiers look like corpses or lunatics, looking for something to put in their mouths. They no longer take cover from Russian shells; they haven't the strength to walk, run away and hide. A curse on this war!

Source: Vasili I. Chuikov, *The Battle for Stalingrad* (New York: Holt, Rinehart and Winston, 1964), pp. 248–254.

west, forcing the Germans to retreat. By February 1944 Soviet troops had pushed the Germans back to the Polish border, and the outcome of the war was no longer in doubt (see Map 28.1).

The Soviet victory in what proved the decisive front of World War II was incredible, in light of the upheavals of the 1930s and the low esteem in which most held the Soviet military in 1941. Portraying

the struggle as "the Great Patriotic War" for national defense, Stalin managed to rally the Soviet peoples as the Germans attacked. Rather than emphasize communist themes, he recalled the heroic defenses mounted against invaders in tsarist times, including the resistance to Napoleon in 1812. But though the Soviets ultimately prevailed, the cost in death, destruction, and suffering was almost unimaginable. For example, by the time Soviet forces finally broke the siege of Leningrad in January 1944, a million people in the city had died, most from starvation, freezing, or disease.

The invading Germans gained access to major areas of Soviet industry and oil supply, and by the end of 1941 the country's industrial output had been cut in half. Yet the Soviet Union was able to weather this blow and go on to triumph. Help from the outside contributed a little, but only 5 to 15 percent of Soviet supplies came from the West. Between 1939 and 1941, Soviet leaders had begun building a new industrial base east of the Urals. And when the Germans invaded in 1941, the plant and equipment of 1500 enterprises were dismantled and shipped by rail for reassembly farther east, out of reach of German attack. Then, beginning in 1942, thousands of brand-new factories were constructed in eastern regions as well.

Moreover, the earlier purges of the armed forces proved to have done less long-term damage than outside observers had expected. If anything, the removal of so many in the top ranks of the military hierarchy made it easier for talented young officers like Georgi Zhukov (1896–1974), who would become the country's top military commander, to move quickly into major leadership positions.

When the United States entered the war in December 1941, the Soviets were fighting for survival. They immediately began pressuring the United States and Britain to open another front in Europe, preferably by landing in northern France, where an Allied assault could be expected to have the greatest impact. But the Allies did not invade northern France and open a major second front until June 1944. By then the Soviets had turned the tide in Europe on their own.

A GLOBAL WAR, 1941–1944

European colonial links spread the war almost at once, most dramatically to North Africa but also to East Asia and the Pacific. The Soviet Union also had interests in Asia and the Pacific, where it had long bumped up against the Japanese. During the 1930s, the United States, too, had become involved in friction with Japan. By 1941 President Franklin Roosevelt was openly favoring the anti-Axis cause, though it took a surprise attack by the

Japanese in December 1941 finally to bring the United States into the war.

Japan and the Origins of the Pacific War

As a densely populated island nation lacking the raw materials essential for industry, Japan had been especially concerned about foreign trade and spheres of economic influence as it modernized after 1868. By the interwar period, the Japanese had become unusually reliant on exports of textiles and other products. During the Depression of the 1930s, when countries all over the world adopted protectionist policies, Japan suffered from increasing tariffs against its exports. This situation tilted the balance in Japanese ruling circles from free-trade proponents to those who favored a military-imperialist solution.

To gain economic hegemony by force, Japan could choose either of two directions. The northern strategy, concentrating on China, would risk Soviet opposition as well as strong local resistance. The southern strategy, focusing on southeast Asia and the East Indies, would encounter the imperial presence of Britain, France, the Netherlands, and the United States.

Japan opted for the northern strategy in 1931, when it took control of Manchuria, in northeastern China. But the Japanese attempt to conquer the rest of China, beginning in 1937, led only to an impasse by 1940. Japanese aggression in China drew the increasing hostility of the United States, a strong supporter of the Chinese nationalist leader Chiang Kai-shek (1887–1975), as well as the active opposition of the Soviet Union. Clashes with Soviet troops along the border between Mongolia and Manchuria led to significant defeats for the Japanese in 1938 and 1939. The combination of China and the Soviet Union seemed more than Japan could handle.

By 1941, however, Germany's victories in Europe had seriously weakened Britain, France, and the Netherlands, the major European colonial powers in southeast Asia and the East Indies. This seemed a precious opportunity for Japan to shift to a southern strategy. To keep the Soviets at bay, Japan agreed to a neutrality pact with the Soviet Union in April 1941. Rather than worry about China and the areas of dispute with the Soviet Union, the Japanese would seek control of south-

THE ERA OF WORLD WAR II

September 1, 1939	Germany invades Poland	June 6, 1944	D-Day: Allied landings in Normandy
May 10, 1940	Germany attacks the Netherlands, Belgium, and France	February 1945	Yalta conference
		April 30, 1945	Suicide of Adolf Hitler
June 22, 1941	Germany attacks the Soviet Union	May 7–8, 1945	German surrender
August 1941	Churchill and Roosevelt agree to the Atlantic Charter	June 1945	Founding of the United Nations
		July–August 1945	Potsdam conference
December 7, 1941	Japanese attack on Pearl Harbor	August 6, 1945	U.S. atomic bombing of Hiroshima
January 1942	Wannsee conference; Nazi plan for the extermination of the Jews	August 14, 1945	Japanese surrender
		March 1947	Truman Doctrine speech
August 1942–February 1943	Battle of Stalingrad	August 1947	India becomes independent
November 1942	Allied landings in North Africa	May 1948	Founding of Israel
		June 1948–May 1949	Berlin Blockade and airlift
January 1943	Casablanca conference	August 1949	First Soviet atomic bomb
April–May 1943	Warsaw Ghetto revolt		
July 1943	Soviet victory in Battle of Kursk-Orel	September 1949	Founding of the Federal Republic in West Germany
July 1943	Allied landings in Sicily; fall of Mussolini; Italy asks for an armistice	October 1949	Founding of the People's Republic of China
November 1943	Teheran conference		

east Asia, a region rich in such raw materials as oil, rubber, and tin—precisely what Japan lacked.

Japan had already joined with Nazi Germany and fascist Italy in an anticommunist agreement in 1936. In September 1940, the three agreed to a formal military alliance. For the Germans, alliance with Japan was useful to help discourage U.S. intervention in the European war. Japan, for its part, could expect the major share of the spoils of the European empires in Asia. However, diplomatic and military coordination between Germany and Japan remained minimal.

The United States began imposing embargoes on certain exports to Japan in 1938, in response to the Japanese aggression in China. After Japan had assumed control of Indochina, nominally held by Vichy France, by the summer of 1941, the United

States imposed total sanctions, and the British and Dutch followed, forcing Japan to begin rapidly drawing down its oil reserves. Conquest of the oil fields of the Dutch East Indies now seemed a matter of life and death to the Japanese.

These economic sanctions brought home how vulnerable Japan was and heightened its determination to press forward aggressively now, when its likely enemies were weakened or distracted. But the Japanese did not expect to achieve a definitive victory over the United States in a long, drawn-out war. Rather, Japanese policymakers anticipated, first, that their initial successes would enable them to grab the resources to sustain a longer war if necessary, and, second, that Germany would defeat Britain, leading the United States to accept a compromise peace allowing the Japanese what they wanted—a secure sphere of economic hegemony in southeast Asia.

Some Japanese leaders—diplomats, businessmen, naval officers, and even the emperor and some of his circle—were dismayed by the prospect of war with the United States. But as the influence of the military grew during the 1930s, it became ever more difficult for those opposing Japan's new imperialist direction to make themselves heard. By 1941, a conformist confidence in victory was demanded, and dissenters dared not speak out for fear of being labeled traitors.

The Japanese finally provoked a showdown on December 7, 1941, with a surprise attack on Pearl Harbor, a U.S. naval base in Hawaii. The next day, Japanese forces seized Hong Kong and Malaya, both British colonies, and Wake Island and the Philippines, both under U.S. control. The United States promptly declared war; in response, Hitler kept an earlier promise to Japan and declared war on the United States. World War II was now unprecedented in its geographic scope (see Map 28.3).

Much like their German counterparts, Japanese forces got off to a remarkably good start. By the summer of 1942, Japan had taken Thailand, the Dutch East Indies, the Philippines, and the Malay Peninsula. Having won much of what it had been seeking, it began devising the Greater East Asia Co-Prosperity Sphere, its own new order in the conquered territories. (See the box, "Encounters with the West: Japan's 'Pan-Asian' Mission.")

The United States in Europe and the Pacific

During the first years of the war in Europe, the United States under President Franklin Roosevelt had not been a disinterested bystander. At this point the United States did not have armed forces commensurate with its economic strength; in 1940, in fact, its army was smaller than the Belgian army. But the United States could be a supplier in the short term, and, if it chose to intervene, a major player over the longer term. With the Lend-Lease Act of March 1941, intended to provide war materiel without the economic dislocations of World War I, the United States lined up on the side of Britain against the Axis powers. In August 1941, a meeting between Churchill and Roosevelt aboard a cruiser off the coast of Newfoundland produced the Atlantic Charter, the first tentative agreement about the aims and ideals that were to guide the anti-Axis war effort. The Americans extended lend-lease to the Soviet Union the next month.

But though President Roosevelt was deeply committed to the anti-Axis cause, isolationist sentiment remained strong in the United States. It took the Japanese attack on Pearl Harbor in December to bring the United States into the war as an active belligerent. By May 1942 the United States had joined with Britain and the Soviet Union in a formal military alliance against the Axis powers.

The two democracies had joined with Stalin's Soviet Union in a marriage of expediency, and mutual suspicions marked the relationship from the start. Initially, Britain and the United States feared that the Soviet Union might even seek a separate peace, as Russia had in World War I. The Soviets, for their part, worried that these new-found allies, with their long-standing anticommunism, might hold back from full commitment, or even seek to undermine the Soviet Union.

In response to pressure from Stalin, Britain and the United States agreed to open a second front in Europe as soon as possible. But the Nazis dominated the Continent, so opening such a front required landing troops from the outside. It proved far more difficult to mount an effective assault on Europe than either Churchill or Roosevelt anticipated in 1942. The resulting delays furthered Stalin's suspicions that his allies were only too eager to have the Soviets do the bulk of the fighting against Nazi Germany—and weaken themselves in the process.

The United States agreed with its new allies to give priority to the war in Europe. But because it had to respond to the direct Japanese assault in the Pacific, the United States was not prepared to act militarily in Europe right away. However, it quickly played a major role in supplying the British with the ships needed to overcome German submarines, which seriously threatened shipping to Britain by 1942.

In the Pacific theater, in contrast, it was immediately clear that the United States would bear the brunt of the fighting against Japan. Although the Japanese went from one success to another during the first months of the war, they lacked the long-term resources to exploit their initial victories. In May 1942 the Battle of Coral Sea—off New Guinea, north of Australia—ended in a stalemate, stopping

≈ ENCOUNTERS WITH THE WEST ≈

Japan's "Pan-Asian" Mission

With the coming of war against the Western powers in 1941, the Japanese could claim to be free-ing Asians from Western imperialism and establishing a new economic order in East Asia and the Pacific. This selection from an essay entitled "Our Present War and Its Cultural Signifi-cance," written just after the bombing of Pearl Harbor by the well-known author Nagayo Yoshio (1888–1961), accents Japan's anti-Western mission in the region. Yoshio understood, especially from his country's recent experience in China, that Asians might find Japanese hegemony just as oppressive as Western domination. Although it served Japan's own economic interests and was often applied brutally, Japanese "Pan-Asianism" helped fuel the reaction against Western impe-rialism in Asia and the Pacific, with lasting results after the war.

Whenever Japan has faced a powerful enemy it has been the *yamato damashii* [Japanese na-tional spirit] which provided the basis of our courage. Now that we can talk in retrospect of the Sino-Japanese War, I am afraid our national spirit has not been given a proper chance to be aroused, due to the deplorable fact that we had to fight with China, our sister nation, with no foreseeable conclusion to look forward to. . . . While desperately fighting with a country which we made our enemy only reluctantly we were trying to find out a principle, an ethic based upon a new view of the world, which would justify our course of action. . . . The China incident was not only insufficient to ful-fill this goal but also met with insurmountable obstacles. Consequently, time and opportunity ripened to declare war against the United States and England. . . .

. . . We would have nothing to say for our-selves if we were merely to follow the exam-ples of the imperialistic and capitalistic ex-ploitation of Greater East-Asia by Europe and the United States. . . .

. . . It is true that the science of war is one manifestation of a nation's culture. But from this time on we have to realize the increasing responsibility on our part if we are to deserve the respect of the people of East-Asian coun-tries as their leaders, in the sphere of culture in general (not only the mere fusion and continu-ance of Western and Oriental cultures but some-thing surpassing and elevating them while making the most out of them) such as the for-mation of national character, refinement, intel-lect, training to become a world citizen, etc. . . .

The sense of awe and respect with which the Orientals have held the white race, espe-cially the Anglo-Saxons, for three hundred years is deep-rooted almost beyond our imagi-nation. It is our task to realize this fact and deal this servility at its root, find out why the white people became the objects of such rever-ence. It goes without saying that we cannot conclude simplemindedly that their shrewd-ness is the cause. Also we have to be very care-ful not to impose the *hakko ichiu* [the gathering of the whole world under one roof] spirit arbi-trarily upon the Asians. If we make this kind of mistake we might antagonize those who could have become our compatriots and thus might also blaspheme our Imperial rule. . . .

To sum up, we have finally witnessed the dawn of a new principle which we had been searching for over ten years. . . . [T]he phrase "Greater East-Asian Coprosperity Sphere" is no longer a mere abstract idea.

Source: William H. McNeill and Mitsuko Iriye, eds., *Modern Asia and Africa* (New York: Oxford University Press, 1971), pp. 232–236.

the string of impressive Japanese successes. Then in June, the United States defeated the Japanese navy for the first time in the Battle of Midway, northwest of Hawaii. After the United States stopped at-tempted Japanese advances in the Solomon Islands and New Guinea early in 1943, U.S. forces began steadily advancing across the islands of the Pacific toward Japan (Map 28.3).

Map 28.3 The War in East Asia and the Pacific After a series of conquests in 1941 and 1942, the Japanese were forced gradually to fall back before U.S. forces. When the war abruptly ended in August 1945, however, the Japanese still controlled much of the territory they had conquered.

The Search for a Second Front in Europe

As the Soviet army fought the Germans in the Soviet Union, the United States and Britain tried to determine how they could help tip the scales in Europe, now an almost impregnable German fortress. Stalin kept urging a direct assault across the English Channel, which, if successful, would have the greatest immediate impact. Churchill,

however, advocated attacking the underbelly of the Axis empire by way of the Mediterranean, which would first require winning control of North Africa. And it was that strategy that the Allies tried first, starting in 1942.

In North Africa the initial Italian assault on Egypt in 1940 led to eighteen months of attack and counterattack across the desert. But after Axis forces under Rommel pushed 570 miles east by

June 1942, the British held at El Alamein, in Egypt, and then began a counterattack that forced the Axis troops to begin what proved a definitive retreat. In November, as this British counterattack proceeded, American and additional British forces landed at several points on the coasts of Morocco and Algeria, weakly defended by Vichy France. Joined by Free French troops, they, too, steadily advanced, squeezing Rommel's Axis forces, until, by May 1943, the Allies had won control of North Africa (see Map 28.1).

But North Africa was valuable for the Allies only as a staging ground for an attempt to penetrate Europe from the south. Meeting at the Moroccan city of Casablanca in January 1943, Churchill and Roosevelt agreed that British and American forces would proceed from North Africa to Sicily and on up through Italy. The Soviets, still pushing for an invasion across the English Channel into France, objected that the Germans could easily block Allied advance through the long, mountainous Italian peninsula.

Crossing from North Africa, Allied troops landed in Sicily in July 1943, leading to the arrest of Mussolini and the collapse of the fascist regime. Supported by King Victor Emmanuel III, the Italian military commander, Pietro Badoglio, formed a new government to seek an armistice. Meanwhile, Allied forces moved on to the Italian mainland, but the Germans quickly occupied much of Italy in response. They even managed a daring rescue of Mussolini and promptly re-established him as puppet leader of a new rump republic in northern Italy, now under German control. Just as the Soviets had warned, the Germans sought to block the Italian peninsula, and it was only nine months later, in June 1944, that the Allies reached Rome. So Churchill's strategy of assaulting Europe from the south proved less than decisive.

Only when Churchill, Roosevelt, and Stalin met for the first time, at Teheran, Iran, in November 1943, did they agree that the next step would be to invade western Europe from Britain. Preparations had been underway since early 1942. Finally, Allied troops crossed the English Channel to make an amphibious landing on the beaches of Normandy, in northern France, on June 6, 1944, known to history as D-Day.

The success of the D-Day invasion opened a major second front in Europe at last. Now American-led forces from the west and Soviet forces from the east worked systematically toward Germany. The one substantial German counterattack in the west, the Battle of the Bulge in December 1944, slowed the Allies' advance, but on March 7, 1945, Allied troops crossed the Rhine River (see Map 28.1).

By June 1944, when Allied forces landed at Normandy, Soviet forces had already crossed the 1939 border with Poland as they moved steadily westward. But in August the Soviets stopped before reaching Warsaw, and the major Soviet thrust began cutting south, through Romania, which surrendered in August, and on into the Danube valley in Hungary and Yugoslavia during the fall. The Soviets resumed their advance westward through Poland and toward Germany only in January 1945.

Now, with the defeat of Germany simply a matter of time, Allied concern shifted to the postwar order. Churchill, especially, worried about the implications of the Soviet advances in east-central Europe and the Balkans. As a supplement to the D-Day landings, he wanted to strike from Italy through Yugoslavia into east-central Europe. But the Americans resisted; Churchill's priorities, they felt, reflected old-fashioned concerns over spheres of influence that were no longer appropriate. So the Allies concentrated instead on a secondary landing in southern France in August 1944. This assault, in which Free French forces were prominent, led quickly to the liberation of Paris. But because the Allies made both their landings in France, and not in southeastern Europe, the Western democracies were involved only in the liberation of western Europe. It was the Soviets who drove the Germans from east-central Europe and the Balkans. This fact, and the resulting geographic distribution of military strength, fundamentally affected the postwar order in Europe.

THE SHAPE OF THE ALLIED VICTORY, 1944–1945

The leaders of the Soviet Union, Britain, and the United States sought to mold that postwar order at two notable conferences in 1945. They brought different aspirations for the postwar world, but they also had to face the hard military realities that had resulted from the fighting so far: Each had armies in certain places, but not in others.

D-Day, 1944 Allied forces land at Normandy, early in the morning of June 6, 1944, at last opening a major second front in Europe. *(National Archives, Washington)*

Those military realities led to the informal division of Europe into spheres of influence among the victors.

The most serious question the Allies faced concerned Germany, which would soon be forced to surrender unconditionally. Germany was widely held responsible for the two world wars, as well as for Nazism with all its atrocities—including the concentration and extermination camps, discovered with shock and horror by the advancing Allied armies in 1945. How should Germany be treated?

In the Pacific theater, as in Europe, the way the war ended had major implications for the postwar world. The United States decided to use the atomic bomb, forcing Japan to surrender in a matter of days. The suddenness of the ending helped determine the fate of the European empires in Asia.

Yalta: Shaping the Postwar World

When Stalin, Roosevelt, and Churchill met at Yalta, a Soviet Black Sea resort, in February 1945, Allied victory was assured, and the three leaders accomplished a great deal. Yet the Yalta conference has long been surrounded by controversy. Western critics have charged that the concessions made there to Stalin consigned east-central Europe to communist domination and opened the way to the dangerous cold war of the next forty years. At the time, however, the anticipation of victory produced a relatively cooperative spirit among the Allies. Thus, they firmed up plans for military occupation of Germany in separate zones, for joint occupation of Berlin, and for an Allied Control Council, composed of the military commanders-in-chief, which would make policy for all of Germany by unanimous agreement.

Each of the Allies had special concerns, but each got much of what it was seeking at Yalta. Roosevelt was eager for Soviet help against Japan as soon as possible, and he won Soviet commitment to an agreement tentatively worked out earlier. In exchange for territorial concessions in Asia and the Pacific, Stalin agreed to declare war on Japan within three months of the German surrender.

Churchill, meanwhile, worried about the future of Europe in light of the American intention, which Roosevelt announced at Yalta, to maintain occupation troops in Europe for only two years after the war. To help balance Soviet power on the Continent, Churchill felt it essential to restore France as a great power. To this end, he urged that France be granted a share in the occupation of Germany and a permanent seat on the Security Council of the proposed new international organization, the United Nations (see page 1061). Roosevelt agreed, even though he had little use for

Charles de Gaulle or what he viewed as the pretensions of the French.

It seemed to the Americans that both Britain and the Soviet Union remained too wedded to traditional conceptions of national interest as they sought to shape the postwar world. Hence, one of Roosevelt's major priorities was to secure British and Soviet commitment to the United Nations before the three allies began to disagree over particular issues. He won that commitment at Yalta, but only by giving in to Churchill on the sensitive matter of British colonies.

Because anti-imperial sentiment had worked to Japan's advantage in Asia, the United States had pestered Britain on the colonial issue since early in the war. Roosevelt had even asked Churchill in 1941 about British intentions in India. So prickly was Churchill that he proclaimed in 1942, "I have not become the King's First Minister in order to preside over the liquidation of the

The Big Three at Yalta With victory over Nazi Germany assured, Churchill, Roosevelt, and Stalin were in reasonably good spirits when they met at Yalta, a Black Sea resort in the Soviet Union, in February 1945. Important sources of friction among them were evident at the meeting, but the differences that led to the cold war did not seem paramount at this point. The Yalta conference proved to be the last meeting of the three leaders. *(F.D.R. Library)*

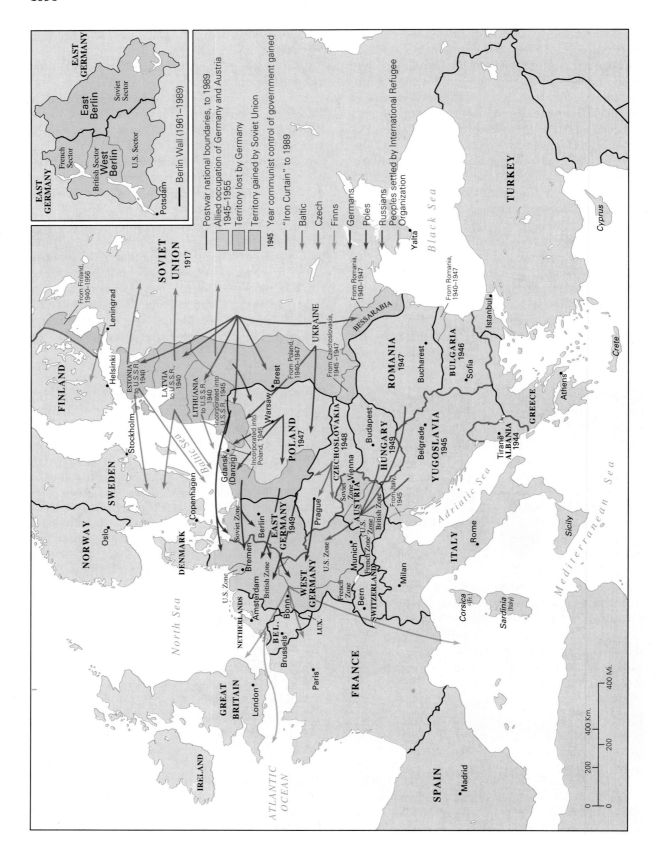

British Empire." It was agreed at Yalta that the British Empire would be exempt from an anticipated measure to bring former colonies under United Nations trusteeship after the war.

Although it was not the only question on the table, the future of the former Axis territories was central to the deliberations at Yalta. By the time of the conference, the division of former Axis territory into spheres of influence among the Allies was already becoming evident, and, in light of the location of Allied troops, the alignment was probably inevitable. In Italy, where U.S. and British troops held sway, the two democracies had successfully resisted Stalin's claim for a share in the administration. In east-central Europe, however, the Soviet army was in control. Still, the United States, with its vision of a new world order, objected to spheres of influence and insisted that democratic principles be applied everywhere. At Yalta this American priority led to an awkward compromise over east-central Europe; the new governments in the area were to be both democratic and friendly to the Soviet Union.

Most important to the Soviets was Poland, with its crucial location between Russia and Germany. Although the Soviets insisted that Communists lead the new Polish government at the outset, they compromised by allowing a role for the noncommunist Polish government-in-exile in London. They also promised free elections in Poland. The three Allies agreed that the Polish-Soviet border would be the line established after World War I. Poland would gain substantial German territory to its west to make up for what it would lose to the U.S.S.R. to its east (Map 28.4).

In addition, the United States and Britain were to have a role in committees set up to engineer the transition to democracy in the rest of east-central Europe. However, only the Soviets had troops in the area, and those committees proved essentially powerless. But though the sources of future tension were already at work at Yalta, they generally

Map 28.4 The Impact of World War II in Europe As a result of World War II the Soviet Union expanded its western borders and Poland shifted westward at the expense of Germany. Territorial changes added to the wartime disruption and produced a flood of refugees. The cold war division of Europe did not depend on immediate territorial changes, but soon Germany itself came to be divided along east-west lines.

remained hidden by the high spirits of approaching victory.

Victory in Europe

Although the tide had turned in 1943, Germany managed to continue the war by exploiting its conquered territories and by more effectively allocating its domestic resources for war production. Thanks partly to the efforts of armaments minister Albert Speer, war production grew sharply between 1941 and 1944, so Germany had plenty of weapons even as the war was ending. But Germany encountered two crucial bottlenecks that finally crippled its military effort: It was running out of military manpower, and it was running out of oil.

Despite making effective use of synthetics, the Nazi war machine depended heavily on oil from Romania. Late in August 1944, however, Soviet troops crossed into Romania, taking control of the oil fields. In addition, beginning in mid-1944, U.S. and British planes successfully bombed German oil installations.

From the start of the war, some, especially among British military leaders, insisted that bombing could destroy the economic and psychological basis of the enemy's ability to wage war. Beginning in 1942, British-led bombing attacks destroyed an average of half the built-up area of seventy German cities, sometimes producing huge firestorms. The bombing of the historic city of Dresden in February 1945 killed more than 135,000 civilians in the most destructive air assault of the war in Europe. But despite this widespread destruction, such bombing did not undermine morale or disrupt production and transport to the extent expected. In the face of steady Allied bombing, Germany increased its war production during 1943 and 1944.

The more precise targeting favored by U.S. strategists proved more effective. In May 1944, the United States began bombing oil fields in Romania and refineries and synthetic oil plants in Germany. Soon Germany lacked enough fuel even to train pilots; by 1945 German industry was producing more aircraft than the German air force could use. Though its proponents consistently overestimated its value, strategic bombing made a significant contribution to the Allied war effort by the end.

Soviet troops moving westward finally met U.S. troops moving eastward at the Elbe River in

Germany on April 26, 1945. With his regime now thoroughly defeated and much of his country in ruins, Hitler committed suicide in his underground military headquarters in Berlin on April 30, 1945. The war in Europe finally ended with the German surrender to General Dwight D. Eisenhower (1890–1969) at Reims, France, on May 7 and to Marshal Zhukov at Berlin on May 8. The world celebrated the end of the fighting in Europe, but an element of uncertainty surrounded the Allied victory because East-West differences were increasingly coming to the fore within the anti-German alliance.

The Potsdam Conference and the Question of Germany

The immediate question for the victorious allies was the fate of Germany, which was bound to be central to the shape of the postwar era. The leaders of the United States, Britain, and the Soviet Union confronted the question at the last of their notable wartime conferences, at Potsdam, just outside Berlin, from July 17 to August 2, 1945. The circumstances were dramatically different from those at Yalta just months before. With Hitler dead and Germany defeated, no common military aim provided unity. And of the three Allied leaders who had been at Yalta, only Stalin remained. President Roosevelt had died in April, so his successor, Harry Truman (1884–1972), represented the United States. In Britain, Churchill's Conservatives lost the general election during the first days of the conference, so Clement Attlee (1883–1967), the new Labour prime minister, assumed the leadership of the British delegation.

At Potsdam, the Allies had to determine how to implement their earlier agreements about Germany, which, devastated by bombing and left without a government, depended on the Allied occupying forces even for its day-to-day survival.

The Soviet Victory in Europe After forcing the Germans back for almost two years, Soviet troops reached Berlin in April 1945. Although it required a day of heavy fighting and bombardment, the Soviets took the Reichstag building, in the heart of the now devastated German capital, on April 30. Here two Soviet sergeants, Yegorov and Kantariya, plant the Soviet flag atop the Reichstag, symbolizing the Soviet victory in the decisive encounter of World War II in Europe. *(ITAR-TAS/Sovfoto)*

The Allies had agreed that Germany was to be forced to surrender unconditionally, but it was not yet clear what would be done with the country over the longer term. For a time U.S. policymakers had even considered destroying Germany's industrial capacity in perpetuity. However, cooler heads understood that the deindustrialization, or "pastoralization," of Germany would not be in anyone's economic interests. Moreover, as the democracies grew increasingly suspicious about Soviet intentions, an economically healthy Germany seemed necessary to help in the balance against the Soviet Union.

For their part, the Soviets had reason to take a much harder line against Germany. Having been invaded—and devastated—by German forces twice within living memory, the Soviet Union wanted to weaken Germany both territorially and economically. But of the three victors, the Soviets had suffered a greatly disproportionate share of the wartime destruction and economic loss, so they also sought to exploit the remaining resources of Germany by exacting heavy reparations. Moreover, the British and the Americans accepted the Soviet proposal that Germany's eastern border with Poland be shifted substantially westward, to the line formed by the Oder and Neisse Rivers. But just as Poland gained at the expense of Germany, the Soviet Union kept a substantial slice of what had been eastern Poland (see Map 28.4).

Each of the three Allies had responsibility for administering a particular zone of occupation, but they were supposed to coordinate their activities in a common policy toward Germany. This effort was to include de-Nazification, demilitarization, and an assault on concentrations of economic power—to root out what seemed the sources of Germany's antidemocratic and aggressive tendencies. But disagreements over economic policy soon undermined the pretense of joint government. Thus East-West differences, already influencing events in east-central Europe, came to affect the settlement in Germany as well.

The Atomic Bomb and the Capitulation of Japan

In the Pacific, Japan had been forced onto the defensive by September 1943, but during 1944 it mounted two major counterattacks to challenge the Americans' newly won naval supremacy. The Japanese wanted especially to prevent American reconquest of the Philippines, which would cut Japan off from its vital raw materials farther south. But the naval battles of 1944 led only to further Japanese defeat. The resulting losses of ships, coupled with increasing shortages of fuel, had virtually crippled the Japanese navy by the end of the year. U.S. forces encountered only token naval resistance when they invaded Okinawa in April 1945 (see Map 28.3).

However, as the situation grew more desperate for Japan, Japanese ground soldiers battled ever more fiercely, often fighting to the death, or taking their own lives, rather than surrendering. Beginning late in 1944, aircraft pilots practiced *kamikaze*, suicidally crashing planes filled with explosives into U.S. targets. The Japanese used this tactic especially as the Americans sought to take Okinawa in the spring of 1945; the U.S. forces finally prevailed in June, but only after the most bitter combat of the entire Pacific war.

In conquering Okinawa, American forces got close enough for air raids on the Japanese home islands. But though the United States was now clearly in control, it seemed likely that an actual invasion of Japan would be necessary to force a Japanese surrender. Some estimated that invasion might cost the United States as many as 1 million additional casualties, because the Japanese could be expected to fight even more desperately to defend their own soil. It was especially for this reason that the Americans decided to try to end the war in an altogether different way, by using an atomic bomb.

In 1939 scientists in several countries, including Germany, had started to advise their governments that new, immensely destructive weapons based on thermonuclear fission were theoretically possible. The German economics ministry began seeking uranium as early as 1939, but Hitler promoted jet- and rocket-propelled terror weaponry instead, especially the V-2 rocket bombs that the Germans began showering on England in the fall of 1944. Still, fear that the Nazis were developing atomic weapons lurked behind the Allied effort to produce an atomic bomb as quickly as possible.

Although the British were the first to initiate an atomic weapons program, by late 1941 the Americans were building on what they knew of British findings to develop their own crash program, known as the Manhattan Project. Constructing an atomic bomb proved far more difficult and costly than most had expected in 1941, and it took a concerted effort by the United States to have atomic weapons ready for use by mid-1945.

The U.S. decision actually to use the atomic bomb, dropping two of them on Japanese civilians, has been one of the most controversial of modern history. The decision fell to the new president, Harry Truman, who had known nothing of the bomb project when Roosevelt died in April 1945. During the next few months, Truman listened to spirited disagreement among American policymakers. Was it necessary actually to drop the bomb to force the Japanese to surrender? Especially because the ultimate victory of the United States was not in doubt, some argued that it would be enough simply to demonstrate the new weapon to the Japanese in a test firing.

By July, when the Allies met at Potsdam, the United States was prepared to use the bomb, but President Truman first warned Japan that if it did not surrender at once, it would be subjected to destruction immeasurably greater than Germany had just suffered. The Japanese decided to ignore the American warning, although the United States had begun area-bombing Japanese cities a few months before. The bombing of Tokyo in March produced a firestorm that gutted one-fourth of the city and killed over 80,000 people. In light of the Japanese refusal to surrender, the use of the atomic bomb could seem the logical next step.

At 8:15 on the morning of August 6, 1945, from a height of 32,000 feet above the Japanese city of Hiroshima, an American pilot released the first atomic bomb to be used against an enemy target. The bomb exploded after 45 seconds, 2000 feet above the ground, killing 80,000 people outright and leaving tens of thousands more to die in the aftermath. Three days later, on August 9, the Americans exploded a second atomic bomb over Nagasaki, killing perhaps 50,000 people. Although sectors of the Japanese military held out for continued resistance, Emperor Hirohito (1901–1989) finally surrendered on August 15. The bombing of civilians had discredited the Japanese military, which not only had proven unable to defend the country but had systematically misled the Japanese people about the country's prospects.

The war in the Pacific ended more suddenly than had seemed possible just a few months be-

fore (see Map 28.3). This proved advantageous to the various national liberation or decolonization movements that had developed in Asia during the war, for the Europeans had little opportunity to reassert their control in the colonial territories they had earlier lost to the Japanese.

In Burma and the Dutch East Indies, the Japanese had encouraged anticolonial sentiment, even helping local nationalists create patriotic militias. After the war, the Dutch were never able to reestablish their control against the Indonesian nationalist movement the Japanese had fostered in the East Indies. But even when its target was Japanese occupation, local resistance intensified nationalist feeling and produced hostility to the former colonial masters, as well as to the Japanese. British troops returned to Malaya and Singapore in time to accept the Japanese surrender, but they eventually came into conflict with local forces that they themselves had helped to develop against the Japanese.

Japanese pressure during the war also served the cause of Indian independence. Fearing a Japanese attack on India, the United States pressured Britain into a conciliatory stance toward the growing movement for Indian independence, directed by the charismatic spiritual leader Mohandas Gandhi (see page 1000). In March 1942 the British government pledged that as soon as the war was over, India would be granted independence under a constitution the Indians could devise for themselves. Still, Britain cracked down on Indian dissidents demanding immediate independence during the remainder of the war, so it was not clear what would happen to India once the war was over.

In Asia and the Pacific, then, Japanese occupation and pressure provoked resistance that fed anticolonialism. In 1945 Japan had been defeated, but the war had severely weakened the old Western imperialism in the region. What would follow remained unclear.

Death, Disruption, and the Question of Guilt

World War II left 50 to 60 million people dead—three times as many as World War I. About that same number were left homeless for some length of time, or found themselves forced onto the mercies of others as refugees. The Soviet Union and Germany suffered by far the highest casualty

Reconstruction Begins Shortly after the end of the war, women in Berlin pass pails of rubble along a line to a dump. Wartime bombing had severely damaged cities throughout much of Europe, although destruction was greatest in Germany. *(Hulton-Getty/Tony Stone Images)*

figures; for each, the figure was considerably higher than in World War I. An appalling 23 million Soviet citizens died, of whom 12 to 13 million were civilians. Germany lost 5 to 6 million, including perhaps 2 million civilians.

In contrast, casualty rates for Italy, Britain, and France were lower than in World War I. Italy suffered 200,000 military and 200,000 civilian deaths. Total British losses, including civilians, numbered 450,000, to which must be added 120,000 from the British Empire. Despite its quick defeat, France lost more lives than Britain because of the ravages of German occupation: The 350,000 deaths among French civilians considerably exceeded the British figure, closer to 100,000.

The United States lost 300,000 servicemen and 5,000 civilians. Figures for Japan are problematic, partly because the Japanese claim that 300,000 of those who surrendered to the Soviets in 1945 have remained unaccounted for. Apart from this number, 1,740,000 Japanese servicemen died from 1941 to 1945, more from hunger and disease than from

combat, and 300,000 civilians died in Japan, most from U.S. bombing.

But this war was not confined to the major powers. Armed forces in east-central Europe also suffered substantial losses, perhaps 300,000 to 400,000 each for Hungary, Yugoslavia, Poland, Austria, and Romania. In addition, up to 1.5 million from the Yugoslav resistance died in fighting that took on the dimensions of a civil war.

The bombing of Europe destroyed buildings and left huge areas of major cities in rubble by the end of the fighting. This destruction, in turn, left hundreds of thousands homeless and contributed to the unprecedented uprooting of peoples that marked the era of World War II.

During the war, Jews, Poles, and others deemed undesirable by the Nazis had been rounded up and shipped to ghettos or camps, where the great majority had died. Of those Jews who were still alive when the Nazi camps were liberated, almost half died within a few weeks. Even those who managed to return home sometimes faced pogroms when they arrived; forty Jews were killed in the worst of them, at Kielce, in Poland.

The redrawing of Germany's borders contributed to the huge wave of refugees just after the war. To guarantee the permanence of the new territorial configuration of Poland, the Soviets and Poles began expelling ethnic Germans from the historically German areas that were now to become Polish. They constituted the bulk of the estimated 7 million Germans who were rounded up for deportation from reconstituted Poland during the years 1945 and 1946 alone. These Germans were sometimes sent to detention camps, and when they were shipped out, it was often in cattle cars. Some 2 million died in the process. By 1958, perhaps 10 million Germans had been forced out of the new Poland, leaving only about 1 million Germans still living there. Similarly, the Czechs were expelling Germans from the Sudetenland area of Czechoslovakia by 1947. So a flood of German refugees was forced to move west after the war, into the shrunken territory of the new Germany. They were among the 16 million Europeans who were permanently uprooted and transplanted between 1939 and 1947.

As the war was ending, Europeans began attempting to assess guilt and punish those responsible for the disasters of the era. In the climate of violence, resistance forces in France, Italy, and elsewhere often subjected fascists and collaborators to summary justice, sometimes through quick trials in ad hoc courts. In Italy, this process led to 15,000 executions; in France, 10,000. French women accused of sleeping with German soldiers were shamed by having their heads shaved. After the war, governments sought to dispense justice in a more orderly way, but the results differed widely across Europe. In Belgium, 634,000 of a population of 8 million were prosecuted for collaborating with the Nazis, whereas in Austria, with a comparable population, only 9000 were brought to trial.

The most sensitive confrontation with the recent past took place in Germany, where the occupying powers imposed a program of de-Nazification. In the western zones, German citizens were required to attend lectures on the virtues of democracy and to view the corpses of the victims of Nazism. In this context, the allies determined to identify and bring to justice those responsible for the crimes of the Nazi regime. This effort led to the Nuremberg trials of 1945 to 1946, the most famous

of a number of war crimes trials held in Germany and the occupied countries after the war.

Although Hitler, Himmler, and Goebbels had committed suicide, the occupying authorities apprehended for trial twenty-four individuals who had played important but very different roles in Hitler's Third Reich. All but three were convicted of war crimes and "crimes against humanity." Twelve were sentenced to death; two of them committed suicide, and the other ten were executed.

Questions about their legitimacy dogged the Nuremberg trials from the start. To a considerable extent the accused were being judged according to law made after the fact. The notion of "crimes against humanity" remained vague. Moreover, even insofar as a measure of international law was in force, it was arguably binding only on states, not individuals. But in light of the unprecedented atrocities of the Nazi regime, there was widespread agreement among the victors that the Nazi leaders could not be treated simply as defeated adversaries.

The effort to apprehend the perpetrators of Nazi atrocities continued for over a half-century thereafter, resulting in a number of highly publicized trials. But even as the century drew to a close, there remained uncertainty about responsibility and guilt, and about what it would mean to come to terms with the brutality that had marked the era of World War II.

TOWARD THE POSTWAR WORLD

Even after the fighting stopped in 1945, remarkable changes continued as the forces unleashed by the war played themselves out. Most immediately, differences between the Soviets and the Western democracies soon undermined the wartime alliance, producing the division of Germany and a bipolar Europe. Thus the conclusion of World War II led directly to the danger of a third world war, which might involve nuclear weapons and threaten the very survival of life on earth.

In addition to the dramatic changes in Europe, the wider effects of the war brought to the forefront a whole new set of issues, from anticolonialism to the Arab-Israeli conflict to the spread of communism within the non-Western world. These issues would remain central for decades, but by 1949 it was possible to discern the contours of the new postwar world, a world with new sources of hope but also with conflicts and dangers hardly imaginable ten years earlier.

Conflicting Visions and the Coming of the Cold War

Starting with the Atlantic Charter conference of 1941, Roosevelt had sought to assure that the common effort against the Axis powers would lead to a firmer basis for peace, to be framed through a new international organization after the war. At a conference at Dumbarton Oaks in Washington in September 1944, the United States outlined the structure of a new United Nations. Seeking to design a more effective body than the discredited League of Nations, Roosevelt proposed that the United States, Britain, the Soviet Union, and China play a special collective role as permanent members of a Security Council, which would form a directing nucleus for the new international body. At Yalta a few months later, Churchill persuaded Roosevelt that France, too, should have a permanent seat on the Security Council.

By the end of the war, several international meetings had used the United Nations title. In July 1944 the United Nations Monetary and Financial Conference at Bretton Woods, New Hampshire, brought together delegates from forty-four nations to deal with problems of currency and exchange rates. Although it produced only recommendations subject to ratification by the individual states, the conference indicated a new determination to cooperate on the international level after the failures of the interwar period. And the outcome of the conference, the Bretton Woods Agreement, laid the foundation for international economic exchange in the noncommunist world for the crucial quarter-century of economic recovery after the war. In addition, the conference gave birth to the International Monetary Fund and the International Bank for Reconstruction and Development, which became pillars of the global economic order.

At a conference in San Francisco from April to June 1945, delegates from almost fifty anti-Axis countries translated the principles discussed at Dumbarton Oaks into a charter for the new United Nations. As Roosevelt had envisioned, the major powers were given a privileged position in the organization as permanent members of the Security Council, each with veto power. But it was hoped that the United Nations would institutionalize the spirit of cooperation that had developed among those who had struggled against the Axis during the war. To dramatize its departure from the Geneva-based League of Nations, which the United States had refused to join, the United Nations was headquartered in New York. In July 1945 the American Senate approved U.S. membership in the international body almost unanimously.

The creation of the United Nations afforded hope for the future, but the virtually simultaneous advent of the cold war soon cast a heavy shadow over the new organization. Whereas the United States envisioned a world order based on the ongoing cooperation of the three victors, the Soviet Union gave top priority to creating a buffer zone of friendly states in east-central Europe, especially as a bulwark against Germany. The Soviets were particularly determined to have their own way in Poland, with its central location between the Soviet Union and Germany.

While seeking this sphere of influence in east-central Europe, Stalin gave the British a free hand to settle the civil war between communists and anticommunists in Greece, and he did not push for revolution in western Europe. The strong communist parties that had emerged from the resistance movements in Italy and France were directed to work within broad-based democratic fronts rather than try to take power. Although no formal deal was made, Stalin saw this moderate position in western and southern Europe as a tacit exchange with the West for a free hand in east-central Europe.

The United States refused simply to acquiesce as the Soviets established this sphere of influence in east-central Europe. Whatever the realism of their alternative vision of the postwar world, the American reluctance to abandon the peoples of east-central Europe to unwelcome Soviet hegemony is understandable. But U.S. policymakers failed to grasp the historical and strategic basis for Soviet priorities and assumed the Soviets were trying to spread communism. The cleft between the emerging superpowers widened.

The Division of Germany

The area of greatest potential stress between the Soviets and the democracies was inevitably Germany. At first, the Western Allies were concerned especially to root out the sources of Germany's antidemocratic, aggressive behavior, but that concern faded as communism, not Nazism, came to seem the immediate menace. And it was especially conflict over Germany that cemented the division of Europe.

Disagreements over economic policy proved the major source of the split. Historians differ in apportioning the blame—and in assessing the inevitability of the outcome. Neither side lived up to all its agreements, but in light of the fundamental differences in priorities, cooperation between the democracies and the Soviets was bound to be difficult at best.

At Potsdam, the West had accepted Soviet demands for German reparations, but rather than wait for payment, the Soviets began removing German factories and equipment for reassembly in the Soviet Union. To assure that they got their due, the Soviets wanted access to the economic resources not simply of the Russian occupation zone but of the whole of Germany. The United States and Britain, in contrast, gave priority to economic reconstruction and quickly began integrating the economies of the Western zones for that purpose.

Friction developed from 1945 to 1948 as the West insisted on reduced reparations and a higher level of industrial production than the Soviets wanted. Finally, as part of their effort to spur economic recovery, the United States and Britain introduced a new currency without Soviet consent. Stalin's response, in June 1948, was to blockade the city of Berlin, cutting its western sectors off from the main Western occupation zones, almost two hundred miles west. The Western Allies responded with a massive airlift that kept their sectors of Berlin supplied for almost a year, until May 1949, when the Soviets finally backed down.

The fragile Potsdam agreement concerning Germany had gradually disintegrated. And the pretense of Allied collaboration, sustained for a while after 1945, disappeared altogether by 1948, when two separate states clearly began emerging from the Allied occupation zones. The growing split with the Soviet Union reinforced the determination of the United States and Britain to get the Western zones back on their feet as quickly as possible. Western Germany must become a viable state—economically, politically, and even militarily.

The Western occupying powers began restoring local government immediately after the war,

to create the administrative framework necessary to provide public utilities and food distribution. Gradually a governing structure was built from the ground up in the Western zones, which were increasingly coordinated. By 1949 it was possible to restore government on the national level.

With Allied support, a "parliamentary council" of German leaders met during 1948 and 1949 and produced a document that, when ratified in September 1949, became the "basic law" of a new Federal Republic of Germany. This founding document was termed simply the basic law, as opposed to the constitution, to emphasize the provisional character of the new West German state. For the same reason, the capital was placed in the small, provincial city of Bonn, which was obviously no substitute for Berlin (see Map 28.4). As far as many West Germans were concerned, the advent of a new state limited to the west did not foreclose the future reunification of Germany. But as it became clear that a new state was being created in the Western zones, and that Germany was thus to be at least temporarily divided, the Soviets settled for a new state in their zone, in eastern Germany. Thus the Communist-led German Democratic Republic, with its capital in East Berlin, was born in October 1949.

The "Iron Curtain" and the Emergence of a Bipolar World

In east-central Europe, only Yugoslavia and Albania had achieved liberation on their own, and the communist leaders of their resistance movements had a plausible claim to political power. Elsewhere, the Soviet army had provided liberation, and the Soviet military presence remained the decisive political fact as the war ended. In much of the region, authoritarianism and collaboration had been the rule for a decade or more, so there was no possibility of returning to a clearly legitimate prewar political order. To be sure, each country had local political groups, some representing former governments in exile, that now claimed a governing role, but their standing in relation to the Soviet army was uncertain.

Under these circumstances, the Soviets were able to work with local communists to install new communist-led regimes friendly to the Soviet Union in most of east-central Europe. But though Churchill warned as early as 1946 that "an iron curtain" was descending from the Baltic to the Adriatic, the process of Soviet power consolidation was not easy, and it took place gradually, in discrete steps over several years. (See the box, "Discerning the Iron Curtain.") The Communist-led government of Poland held elections in January 1947—but rigged them to guarantee a favorable outcome. In Czechoslovakia, the communists faced serious losses in upcoming elections and so finally took power outright in 1948. By 1949 there were communist governments, relying on Soviet support, in Poland, Czechoslovakia, East Germany, Hungary, Romania, and Bulgaria, with Yugoslavia and Albania also communist but capable of a more independent line.

Communism might have spread still farther in Europe, and perhaps beyond, but the West drew the line at Greece. There, as in Yugoslavia, an indigenous, communist-led resistance movement had become strong enough to contend for political power by late 1944. But when it sought to oust the monarchical government that had just returned to Greece from exile, the British intervened, helping the monarchy put down the communist uprising. Although Stalin gave the Greek communists little help, communist guerrilla activity continued, thanks partly to support from Tito's Yugoslavia. In 1946 a renewed communist uprising escalated into civil war.

As the cold war developed, both the Soviet Union and the United States began taking a more active interest in the Greek conflict. After the financially strapped Labour government in Britain reduced its involvement early in 1947, the United States stepped in to support the Greek monarchy against the communists. American policymakers feared that communism would progress from the Balkans through Greece to the Middle East. Greece seemed the place to draw the line. Thus, in March 1947, President Truman announced the Truman Doctrine, which committed the United States to the "containment" of communism throughout the world. American advisers now began re-equipping the anticommunist forces in Greece. Faced with this determined opposition from the West, Stalin pulled back, but the Greek communists, with their strong indigenous support, were not defeated until 1949.

Thus the wartime marriage of expediency between the Soviet Union and the Western democracies fell apart in the war's aftermath. Only in Austria, jointly occupied by the Soviets and the Western democracies, were the former Allies able to arrange the postwar transition in a reasonably amicable way. The Soviets acquiesced in the neutralization of a democratic Austria as the occupying powers left in 1954. Elsewhere, Europe was divided into two antagonistic power blocs. The antagonism between the two superpowers became more menacing when the Soviets exploded their first atomic bomb in August 1949, intensifying the postwar arms race. By then, in fact, the United States was on its way to the more destructive hydrogen bomb. The split between these two nations, unmistakable by 1949, established the framework for world affairs for the next forty years. (See the box, "The Soviet View of the Cold War.")

The West and the New World Agenda

At the same time, other dramatic changes around the world suggested that, with or without the cold war, the postwar political scene would be hard to manage. Events in India in 1947, in Israel in 1948, and in China in 1949 epitomized the new hopes and uncertainties that had emerged directly from World War II.

Although the British, under U.S. pressure, had reluctantly promised independence for India in order to elicit Indian support during the war, British authorities and Indian leaders had continued to skirmish. Mohandas Gandhi was twice jailed for resisting British demands and threatening a massive program of nonviolent resistance to British rule. But by 1946 the British lacked the will and the financial resources to maintain their control in India. Thus Britain acquiesced in Indian independence, proclaimed on August 15, 1947. Allowing independence to India, long the jewel of the British Empire, raised questions about Britain's role in the postwar world and portended a wider disintegration of the European colonial system. There would be new countries, many of them poor—and resentful of Western imperialism. What would that mean for the new world order, centering on the United Nations, that Roosevelt had envisioned?

Questions about the fate of the Jews, who had suffered so grievously during World War II, were inevitable as well. Almost two-thirds of the Jews of Europe had been killed, and many of the survivors either had no place to go or had concluded that they could never again live as a minority in

Discerning the Iron Curtain

Winston Churchill, out of office and touring the United States, sought to specify the contours of the postwar international situation in a speech at Westminster College in Fulton, Missouri, on March 5, 1946. To characterize the developing division of Europe, Churchill referred to "an iron curtain," a term that attracted immediate attention and dramatically affected public opinion in both the United States and western Europe. Soviet historians dated the beginning of the cold war from this speech.

A shadow has fallen upon the scenes so lately lighted by the Allied victory. Nobody knows what Soviet Russia and its Communist international organization intends to do in the immediate future, or what are the limits, if any, to their expansive and proselytizing tendencies. . . . We understand the Russian need to be secure on her western frontiers by the removal of all possibility of German aggression. We welcome her to her rightful place among the leading nations of the world. . . . It is my duty, however, to place before you certain facts. . . .

From Stettin in the Baltic to Trieste in the Adriatic, an iron curtain has descended across the Continent. Behind that line lie all the capitals of the ancient states of central and eastern Europe. Warsaw, Berlin, Prague, Vienna, Budapest, Belgrade, Bucharest, and Sofia, all these famous cities and the populations around them lie in what I must call the Soviet sphere, and all are subject in one form or another, not only to Soviet influence but to a very high and, in many cases, increasing measure of control from Moscow. Athens alone—Greece with its immortal glories—is free to decide its future at an election under British, American and French observation. The Russian-dominated Polish Government has been encouraged to make enormous and wrongful inroads upon Germany, and mass expulsions of millions of Germans on a scale grievous and undreamed-of

are now taking place. The Communist parties, which were very small in all these Eastern States of Europe, have been raised to pre-eminence and power far beyond their numbers and are seeking everywhere to obtain totalitarian control. . . .

If now the Soviet Government tries, by separate action, to build up a pro-Communist Germany in their areas, this will cause new serious difficulties in the British and American zones, and will give the defeated Germans the power of putting themselves up to auction between the Soviets and the Western Democracies. Whatever conclusions may be drawn from these facts—and facts they are—this is certainly not the Liberated Europe we fought to build up. Nor is it one which contains the essentials of permanent peace. . . .

. . . I do not believe that Soviet Russia desires war. What they desire is the fruits of war and the indefinite expansion of their power and doctrines. But what we have to consider here to-day while time remains, is the permanent prevention of war and the establishment of the conditions of freedom and democracy as rapidly as possible in all countries. . . .

From what I have seen of our Russian friends and allies during the war, I am convinced that there is nothing they admire so much as strength, and there is nothing for which they have less respect than for weakness, especially military weakness.

Source: Winston S. Churchill, *His Complete Speeches, 1897–1963*, vol. VII, *1943–1949*, ed. Robert Rhodes James (New York: Chelsea House, 1974), pp. 7290–7292.

Europe. Many insisted that they must have a homeland of their own. For decades such Zionist sentiment (see page 943) had centered on the biblical area of Israel, in what had become, after

World War I, the British mandate of Palestine. Jewish immigration to the area accelerated during the interwar period, but it caused increasing friction between Jews and the Palestinian Arabs.

The Soviet View of the Cold War

The first cold war document the Soviet government made available to Western scholars was a telegram that Nikolai Novikov, the Soviet ambassador to the United States, sent from Washington to Soviet Foreign Minister Vyacheslav Molotov on September 27, 1946. Novikov sought to pinpoint the essential features of the new foreign policy the United States seemed to be pursuing after its victory in World War II. In releasing the document in 1990, Soviet authorities contended it had been of central importance in the Soviet effort to understand postwar American intentions and to formulate their own policy in response.

The foreign policy of the United States, which reflects the imperialist tendencies of American monopolistic capital, is characterized in the postwar period by a striving for world supremacy. This is the real meaning of the many statements by President Truman and other representatives of American ruling circles: that the United States has the right to lead the world. All the forces of American diplomacy—the army, the air force, the navy, industry, and science— are enlisted in the service of this foreign policy. For this purpose broad plans for expansion have been developed and are being implemented through diplomacy and the establishment of a system of naval and air bases stretching far beyond the boundaries of the United States, through the arms race, and through the creation of ever newer types of weapons. . . .

. . . [W]e have seen a failure of calculations on the part of U.S. circles which assumed that the Soviet Union would be destroyed in the war or would come out of it so weakened that it would be forced to go begging to the United States for economic assistance. Had that happened, they would have been able to dictate conditions permitting the United States to carry out its expansion in Europe and Asia without hindrance from the USSR. . . .

One of the most important elements in the general policy of the United States, which is directed toward limiting the international role of the USSR in the postwar world, is the policy with regard to Germany. In Germany, the United States is taking measures to strengthen reactionary forces for the purpose of opposing democratic reconstruction. Furthermore, it displays special insistence on accompanying this policy with completely inadequate measures for the demilitarization of Germany. . . .

Careful note should be taken of the fact that the preparation by the United States for a future war is being conducted with the prospect of war against the Soviet Union, which in the eyes of American imperialists is the main obstacle in the path of the United States to world domination. This is indicated by facts such as the tactical training of the American army for war with the Soviet Union as the future opponent, the siting of American strategic bases in regions from which it is possible to launch strikes on Soviet territory, intensified training and strengthening of Arctic regions as close approaches to the USSR, and attempts to prepare Germany and Japan to use those countries in a war against the USSR.

Source: "The Novikov Telegram," *Diplomatic History,* vol. 15, no. 4 (Fall 1991), pp. 527–528, 536–537.

Concerned about access to Middle Eastern oil, the British sought to cultivate good relations with the Arab world after the war. Thus they opposed further immigration of Jews to Palestine, as well as proposals to carve an independent Jewish state from the area. The United States, however, was considerably more sympathetic to the Zionist cause. As tensions built, Jewish terrorists blew up the British headquarters in Jerusalem, and the British decided to abandon what seemed a no-win situation. In September 1947, they announced their intention to withdraw from Palestine, leaving its

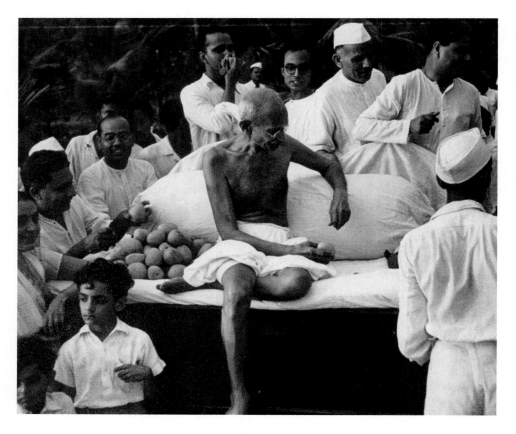

Gandhi and Indian Independence An apostle of nonviolence, Mohandas Gandhi inspired the movement that finally won India's independence from Britain in 1947. He is shown here distributing fruit to children near Bombay in 1944. *(Dinodia Picture Agency/Image Works)*

future to the United Nations. In November the UN voted to partition Palestine, creating both a Jewish and a new Arab Palestinian state (Map 28.5).

Skirmishing between Jews and Arabs became full-scale war in December, and in that context the Jews declared their independence as the new state of Israel on May 14, 1948. When fighting ended in 1949, the Israelis had conquered more territory than had been envisioned in the original partition plan, and the remaining Arab territories fell to Egypt and Jordan, rather than forming an independent Palestinian state. Thus was born the new state of Israel, partly a product of the assault on the Jews during World War II. Yet it was born amid Arab hostility and Western concerns about oil.

In 1949 the communist insurgency in China under Mao Zedong (Mao Tse-tung) (see page 1000) finally triumphed over the Chinese Nationalists under Chiang Kai-shek, who were forced to flee to the island of Taiwan. During the war, the Communists had done better than the Nationalists at identifying themselves with the Chinese cause against both Japanese and Western imperialism. And after their victory, the Chinese Communists enjoyed great prestige among other "national liberation" movements struggling against Western colonialists. To many in the West, however, the outcome in China by 1949 simply intensified fears that communism was poised to spread in the unsettled postwar world.

At the same time, the Chinese revolution undermined Roosevelt's conception of the United Nations. The United States had long supported Chiang Kai-shek as a bulwark against Japan and a source of stability in Asia. And at Roosevelt's insistence, China had been accorded a permanent seat on the UN Security Council as the war was ending. Even after being forced from the mainland in 1949, the militantly anticommunist Chinese Nationalists retained their permanent Security Council seat until 1971, when the communist People's Republic of China was admitted to the UN—and assumed China's seat on the Security Council. The obviously artificial role that the Nationalists played for so long damaged the credibility of the new United Nations.

SUMMARY

By 1949 the division of Europe, the advent of nuclear weapons, and the symptomatic events in India, Israel, and China made it clear that the world's agenda had been radically transformed in the ten years since the beginning of World War II. With the Soviet Union and United States emerging from the war as superpowers, and with the once-dominant European countries weakened and chastened, the center of gravity in the West changed dramatically. Thus the relationship between the West and the world was bound to be radically different. Such was the war's complex and often unexpected legacy.

Although the war opened a new universe of problems and possibilities, it brought to a close an era of European history dominated by fascism. As a result of the war, the two major fascist powers collapsed and fascist forms of politics, with their hostility to democracy and their tendencies toward violence and war, stood at least temporarily discredited. But Nazism and fascism continued to haunt the Western mind, especially with the discovery of the Nazi camps. It was not clear, moreover, whether Germany and Italy, and, for that matter, much of the rest of Europe, would be able to develop effective democratic political systems amid defeat and destruction.

The Soviets had borne the brunt of the war in Europe, and the Soviet Union—and its communist system—emerged with enhanced prestige. At the same time, an overseas war had again drawn the United States, which was prepared in the aftermath, as it had not been after World War I, to play an ongoing leadership role in world affairs. The Soviet Union and the United States offered competing visions of the future, and during the decades that followed their competition helped shape everything from Italian domestic politics to the decolonization struggle in Mozambique.

Map 28.5 The Partition of Palestine and the Birth of the State of Israel In November 1947 the United Nations offered a plan to partition the British mandate of Palestine, but complications immediately arose. The Jews of the area won their own state, Israel, but the Palestinian Arabs did not. Thus tensions continued in the area.

Dwarfed by the two new superpowers, the old European states seemed destined to play a diminished role in world affairs. It quickly became apparent that the costs of the war had left even Britain, a full partner in the Allied victory, too weak to remain a great power. Almost at once, the Europeans began retreating from their long-standing imperial roles, though not without resentment, resistance, and more bloodshed. By 1949 it was clear that non-Western nations would be playing a more prominent role in world affairs in the future.

Whereas there had been, for a while, some illusion of a "return to normal" after World War I, it was obvious after World War II that the old Europe was gone forever and that the relationship between the West and the rest of the world would never be the same. Indeed, much of Europe's proud culture, on the basis of which it had claimed to lead the world, lay in the ruins of war, apparently exhausted. What role could Europe play in Western civilization, and in the wider world, after all that had happened?

NOTES

1. From Farrell's full account as related by General Leslie Groves in his "Memorandum to the Secretary of War," dated July 18, 1945, in Philip L. Cantelon, Richard G. Hewlett, and Robert C. Williams, eds., *The American Atom: A Documentary History of Nuclear Policies from the Discovery of Fission to the Present*, 2d ed. (Philadelphia: University of Pennsylvania Press, 1991), pp. 56–57.
2. Quoted in Karl Dietrich Bracher, *The German Dictatorship: The Origins, Structure, and Effects of National Socialism*, trans. Jean Steinberg (New York: Praeger, 1970), p. 423.

SUGGESTED READING

General Surveys

Calvocoressi, Peter, Guy Wint, and John Pritchard. *Total War: Causes and Courses of the Second World War*, 2d ed., revised. 2 vols. 1989. New edition of a standard, readable work.

Campbell, John, ed. *The Experience of World War II*. 1989. Focusing on the experience of those touched by the war, this collaborative volume covers everything from prisoners of war to the uses of the arts for propaganda purposes. A handsome volume in a large format, with superb illustrations and maps.

Keegan, John. *The Second World War*. 1989. A detailed but readable study featuring military operations. Well illustrated.

Parker, R. A. C. *Struggle for Survival: The History of the Second World War*. 1990. An accessible, comprehensive, and well-balanced survey. Especially good on debates over strategy and the wider implications of the strategies chosen.

Weinberg, Gerhard L. *A World at Arms: A Global History of World War II*. 1994. An enlightening global approach by a leading historian of the period. Stresses the interrelationship among simultaneous events and decisions in the various theaters of the war around the world.

Wright, Gordon. *The Ordeal of Total War, 1939–1945*. 1968. Masterly synthesis of all aspects of the war experience, from the battlefield to the scientific labora-

tory, from the Nazi new order to the coming of the cold war.

Fighting the War

Ellis, John. *On the Front Lines: The Experience of War through the Eyes of the Allied Soldiers in World War II*. 1991. Based partly on oral testimony, a vivid account of the experiences of those who fought the war on the Allied side in Europe, Africa, and the Pacific.

Fussell, Paul. *Wartime: Understanding and Behavior in the Second World War*. 1989. Explores the rationalizations and euphemisms, the contempt and subversion, that enabled U.S. and British fighting men to deal with the horrors of World War II.

Glantz, David M., and Jonathan M. House. *When Titans Clashed: How the Red Army Stopped Hitler*. 1995. Detailed but compelling account of the decisive encounter in World War II, based partly on newly available materials from the former Soviet Union.

Overy, Richard J. *Why the Allies Won*. 1995. Denying that the sheer weight of numbers made the outcome inevitable, this account accents the differences in political, economic, and even moral mobilization to explain why the Allies defeated the Axis powers in World War II.

The Home Front

Harrison, Mark. *Soviet Planning in Peace and War, 1938–1945*. 1985. Shows how Soviet economic planners responded to invasion in 1941, enabling the Soviet Union to defeat Nazi Germany and emerge from the war as a great power.

Milward, Alan S. *War, Economy and Society, 1939–1945*. 1979. A detailed study of the economic adjustments that the war necessitated—and that sustained the long years of fighting.

Overy, R. J. *War and Economy in the Third Reich*. 1994. An important series of essays on the interpenetration of war and economy in Nazi Germany, from rearmament to surrender.

Pelling, Henry. *Winston Churchill*. 1974. Among the best single-volume biographies of Churchill. Balanced and readable.

Summerfield, Penny. *Women Workers in the Second World War: Production and Patriarchy in Conflict*. 1989. Shows how the disruptions of war affected women's opportunities and self-understanding.

Collaboration and Resistance

De Gaulle, Charles. *The Complete War Memoirs of Charles de Gaulle*. 3 vols. in one. 1955, 1959, 1960. Revealing personal account of de Gaulle's remarkable role as leader of the Free French forces during World War II.

Delzell, Charles F. *Mussolini's Enemies: The Italian Anti-Fascist Resistance*. 1961. An exhaustive account of Italian resistance activities, proceeding region by region.

Lacouture, Jean. *De Gaulle*. Vol. 1, *The Rebel, 1890–1944*. 1990. First volume of a standard biography, detailed but accessible. Shows how de Gaulle's maverick qualities enabled him to play his special role during the war.

Paxton, Robert O. *Vichy France: Old Guard and New Order*. 1975. A widely admired study that assesses Vichy claims to have shielded the French from the worst features of Nazi occupation.

The Holocaust

Friedländer, Saul, ed. *Probing the Limits of Representation: Nazism and the "Final Solution."* 1992. Searching essays on the enduring impact of the Holocaust and our uncertain attempts to make sense of it.

Gilbert, Martin. *The Holocaust: A History of the Jews of Europe During the Second World War*. 1986. A comprehensive but straightforward account, making effective use of the testimony of those involved.

Hilberg, Raul. *Perpetrators, Victims, Bystanders: The Jewish Catastrophe, 1933–1945*. 1992. The dean of Holocaust historians offers an accessible, compelling account by weaving capsule portraits delineating the many layers of involvement and responsibility at issue in the Holocaust.

———. *The Destruction of the European Jews*. Revised and definitive ed. 3 vols. 1985. Pioneering, detailed account of the Holocaust, based on exhaustive research. Especially revealing on the administrative mechanics of the process.

Laqueur, Walter. *The Terrible Secret: Suppression of the Truth about Hitler's "Final Solution."* 1982. Raises the gnawing questions about who knew what, and when, about the extermination of the Jews. Without exonerating policymakers who might have responded more effectively, the author shows how difficult it was to comprehend what seemed incomprehensible.

Lifton, Robert Jay. *The Nazi Doctors: Medical Killing and the Psychology of Genocide*. 1986. A major expert on the psychology of extreme situations seeks to understand the large number of German medical doctors who played central roles in Nazi programs of mass killing.

Marrus, Michael. *The Holocaust in History*. 1987. An ideal introduction to the major issues. Readable and balanced.

Yahil, Leni. *The Holocaust: The Fate of European Jewry*. 1990. A clear and comprehensive account that accents the underlying continuity in Nazi policy and assesses the Jewish response.

The Wider Impact of the War

Laqueur, Walter. *A History of Zionism*. 1989. Surveys the five decades of European Zionist activity that helped bring about the establishment of the state of Israel.

Marrus, Michael R. *The Unwanted: European Refugees in the Twentieth Century*. 1985. Pioneering account of the rise of the refugee phenomenon as a major but neglected aspect of modern political disruptions.

Rhodes, Richard. *The Making of the Atomic Bomb*. 1988. An acclaimed study that combines science, politics, and personality in an especially dramatic way.

The Coming of the Cold War

Eisenberg, Carolyn Woods. *Drawing the Line: The American Decision to Divide Germany, 1944–1949*. 1996. A detailed, scholarly account that uses newly available sources to accent the American role in the process that culminated in the division of Germany by 1949.

Gaddis, John Lewis. *We Now Know: Rethinking Cold War History*. 1997. Taking advantage of newly available Russian and Chinese documents, a leading authority reassesses the cold war, from its origins to the Cuban missile crisis of 1962.

Paterson, Thomas G. *On Every Front: The Making and Unmaking of the Cold War*. 1992. Updated edition of a highly regarded survey.

Reynolds, David, ed. *The Origins of the Cold War in Europe: International Perspectives*. 1994. With chapters devoted to individual countries, traces the origins of the cold war and its impact on subsequent development in western Europe. Includes a fine introduction by the editor.

Yergin, Daniel. *Shattered Peace: The Origins of the Cold War*. Revised ed. 1990. Readable, balanced narrative, focusing especially on the bases of American policy.

HOLOCAUST TESTIMONY

There were loud announcements, but it was all fairly restrained: nobody did anything to us. I followed the crowd: "Men to the right, women and children to the left," we had been told. The women and children disappeared into a barrack further to the left and we were told to undress. One of the SS men—later I knew his name, Küttner—told us in a chatty sort of tone that we were going into a disinfection bath and afterwards would be assigned work. Clothes, he said, could be left in a heap on the floor, and we'd find them again later. . . .

The queue began to move and I suddenly noticed several men fully dressed standing near another barrack further back, and I was wondering who they were. And just then another SS man (Miete was his name) came by me and said, "Come on, you, get back into your clothes, quick, special work." That was the first time I was frightened. Everything was very quiet, you know. And when he said that to me, the others turned around and looked at me—and I thought, my God, why me, why does he pick on me? When I had got back into my clothes, the line had moved on and I noticed that several other young men had also been picked out and were dressing. We were taken through to the "work-barrack," most of which was filled from floor to ceiling with clothes, stacked up in layers. . . . You understand, there was no time, not a moment between the instant we were taken in there and put to work, to talk to anyone, to take stock of what was happening . . . [ellipses in the original] and of course never forget that we had no idea at all what this whole installation was for. One saw these stacks of clothing—I suppose the thought must have entered our minds, where do they come from, what are they? We must have connected them with the clothes all of us had just taken off outside . . . [ellipses in the original] but I cannot remember doing that. I only remember starting work at once making bundles.*

*The testimony of Richard Glazar is from Gitta Sereny, *Into That Darkness: An Examination of Conscience* (New York: Random House, Vintage Books, 1983), pp. 176–179, 183.

This is the voice of Richard Glazar, recalling when, as a young Jewish student from Prague, he arrived at the Nazi extermination camp at Treblinka in October 1942. Glazar was telling his story in 1972 to the British journalist Gitta Sereny, who had been covering the trial in Germany of the commandant of the Treblinka camp, Franz Stangl. Seeking to understand Stangl, Sereny tracked down a number of those who had come into contact with him, including survivors like Glazar.

Glazar's recollections are part of a rich body of testimony by Jewish survivors of the Holocaust, testimony that is often moving, gripping, terrifying. Some accounts offer direct personal recollections. Others integrate personal remembrance into literature. Still others use the insights of social psychology in an effort to explain the special features of the camp experience.

Even with all this evidence, we wonder if we can ever really grasp what millions of Jews experienced at the hands of the Nazis in the extermination camps. But listening to witnesses like Glazar, we gain some sense of the uncertainty and fear, the suffering and humiliation, that helped define that experience. And we recognize the determination, the affirmation of life, that marked the Jewish response.

We may be surprised at Glazar's insistence that "we had no idea at all what this whole installation was for." Didn't the Jews understand what the camps held for them? In fact, some Jews had a better idea than others, but in most cases only through rumor, and no one could know the whole story as it was unfolding. Over a year before, Glazar's family had sent him to work in the country, where they assumed he would be safe, so he had been relatively isolated. But what one knew, or could surmise, also depended on what one was prepared to believe was possible, what the world could hold. Some simply could not believe the rumors.

Once they were in the camps, however, the Jews could only come to terms with the unprece-

Arrival at the Auschwitz Extermination Camp
(Corbis-Bettmann)

dented situation as best they could. Let us listen further to Glazar, whose insights into the minds of the SS overseers help us better to grasp the terrible capriciousness of the situation:

> One must not forget their incredible power, their autonomy within their narrow and yet, as far as we were concerned, unlimited field; but also the isolation created by their unique situation and by what they—and hardly anyone else even within the German or Nazi community—had in common. Perhaps if this isolation had been the result of good rather than evil deeds, their own relationship towards each other would have been different. As it was, most of them seemed to hate and despise each other and do anything—almost anything—to "get at" each other. Thus, if one of them selected a man out of a new transport for work, in other words to stay alive at least for a while, it could perfectly easily happen . . . that one of his rivals . . . would come along and kill that man just to spite him. . . . All this created a virtually indescribable atmosphere of fear. The most important thing for a prisoner at Treblinka, you see, was not to make himself conspicuous.

But what, then, can be said about the human attributes that such conditions called forth—and that enabled some, at least, to survive?

> Our daily life? It was in a way very directed, very specific. . . . [I]t was essential to fill oneself completely with a determination to survive; it was es-sential to create in oneself a capacity for dissociating oneself to some extent from Treblinka; it was important not to adapt completely to it. . . .
>
> It wasn't *ruthlessness* that enabled an individual to survive—it was an intangible quality, not peculiar to educated or sophisticated individuals. Anyone might have it. It is perhaps best described as an overriding thirst—perhaps, too, a talent for life, and a faith in life.

Glazar, of course, was speaking thirty years later, and despite the engaging spontaneity of his testimony, he may have forgotten things, or the experiences of the intervening years may have colored his memory. Moreover, he could only tell what he recalled through the categories of language, which may be inadequate to convey, to those who were not there, what it was like to be sent to the Nazi extermination camps. Perhaps survivors called upon, years later, to put their recollections into words are bound to impose too much order, even to romanticize, by using categories their listeners can understand—or want to hear. Glazar was clearly stretching to find the words. Does "talent for life" ring true? We will continue to wonder.

As for Glazar himself, he escaped from Treblinka in an uprising in August 1943, and then made his way to Germany, where he managed to survive the war disguised as a foreign laborer. When Sereny reached him in 1972, he was living in Switzerland, working as an engineer. ✎

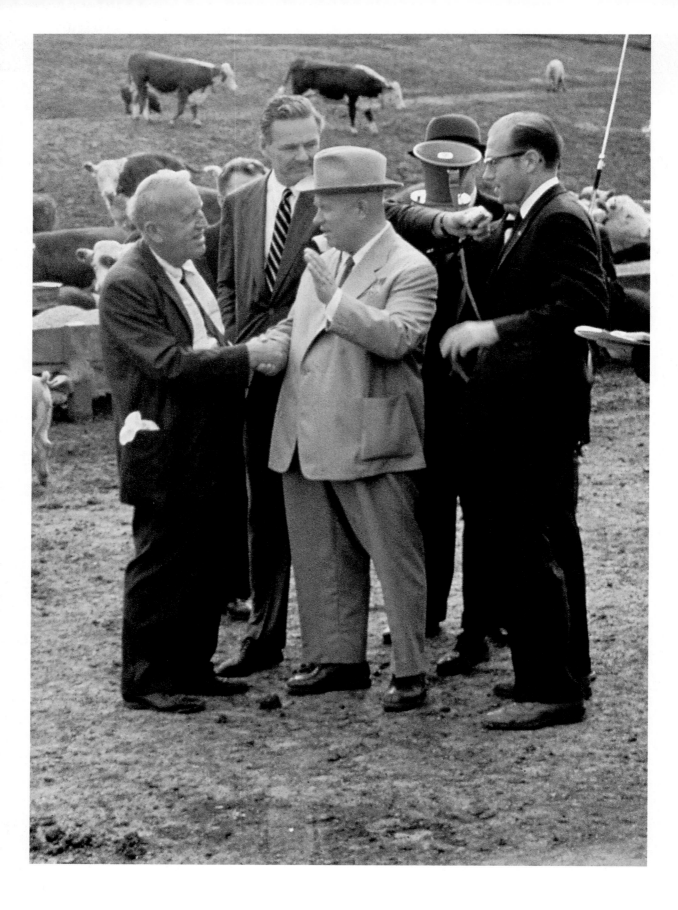

CHAPTER 29

An Anxious Stability: The Age of the Cold War, 1949–1985

Sampling an American hot dog at a meatpacking plant in Iowa in 1959, the leader of the Soviet Union, Nikita Khrushchev, wryly observed that "we have beaten you to the moon, but you have beaten us in sausage-making." Khrushchev was in the midst of a two-week visit to the United States in response to an invitation from President Dwight Eisenhower. Though the visit included the expected top-level talks and communiqués, it also gave Khrushchev a chance to witness American life, from a Manhattan nightclub to a southern California suburb to an Iowa farm. The Soviet leader grew peevish when, for security reasons, the American authorities would not let him visit recently opened Disneyland, but he found much to praise in American society, and he took every occasion to stress the possibility of "peaceful coexistence." Still, Khrushchev also took it for granted that, in virtually every sphere, competition would continue between the United States, leading the capitalist West, and the Soviet Union, leading the communist East.

Americans were not sure what to make of this robust, plain-spoken leader of the communist world. The large crowd that came out to see his motorcade in New York was, according to one account, "restrained and curious rather than hostile." Some of those who met him provoked heated exchanges by criticizing recent Soviet actions in east-central Europe, or by questioning the treatment of workers in the Soviet Union, or by harping on Khrushchev's remark, a few years earlier, about "burying" the United States. But Khrushchev sought seriously to avoid divisive issues and to

Soviet leader Nikita
Khrushchev (in hat) visiting
an Iowa farm in 1959.

find areas of common ground, even with respect to difficult international issues like the status of Germany.

It was time to recognize, Khrushchev insisted, that each side fervently believed in its own system; hence, there was no point in trying to convince the other. The two sides would simply compete—and the competition could be peaceful. Noting his own humble origins, Khrushchev stressed how far his country had come in its brief period under communism; indeed, it was remarkable that the Soviet Union could now stand head to head with an advanced country like the United States. And if they were not quite up to America in hot dogs and other consumer goods, the Soviets seemed to be setting the pace in significant areas of advanced technology. They had been first in space with an artificial satellite, *Sputnik I,* in 1957, and they had just sent the first unmanned rocket to the moon. Thus Khrushchev's confident appeal to the future: "Let us compete peacefully and let the people be the judges of which system provides greater possibilities." Everything that was not progressive would die away. The ongoing competition between the two superpowers, and the respective socioeconomic systems they represented, did not have to mean an endless arms race and the threat of nuclear annihilation.

But in 1960, less than a year after Khrushchev's visit, the Soviet military shot down a U.S. spy plane over the Soviet Union, partly, it seems, to undercut Khrushchev's effort at better relations with the United States. Soviet hawks found Khrushchev too trusting, too accommodating. The incident wrecked a previously planned summit meeting, and relations between the Soviet Union and the United States cooled. Although they would eventually warm again, ideological competition, mutual suspicion, and a costly and dangerous arms race continued to characterize the postwar era. It seemed possible that, virtually overnight, the cold war could develop into a hot war that could lead to nuclear annihilation. Only as it was ending, more than four decades after World War II, did it become clear that the anxious cold war era had been one of relative stability and peace.

Both halves of Europe had to operate within the bipolar framework, but the Western and Soviet blocs each confronted different challenges and evolved in very different ways. Dependent on U.S. leadership, unable to resist the tide of decoloniza-

tion, the countries of Western Europe adjusted to a diminished international role. The change in scale led many to advocate some form of European union, which might eventually enable the Western Europeans to deal with the superpowers on a more equal basis. On the domestic level, the postwar situation was so unsettled at first that no Western European country, not even victorious Britain, could simply apply a prewar model. Postwar reconstruction rested on a new consensus that government must play a more active role in promoting both economic growth and social welfare. By the 1960s the promise of shared prosperity was realized to a remarkable extent. But changing circumstances by the early 1970s threatened the consensus that postwar prosperity had made possible.

Although the Soviet Union had suffered immensely in winning World War II, the communist regime emerged from the war with renewed legitimacy. Having led the country to superpower status, it seemed to offer its citizens a better future, just as Khrushchev emphasized in 1959. During the 1950s and 1960s, the Soviet system achieved some significant successes, but its efforts to outgrow its Stalinist framework were halting. By 1980 the system was becoming rigid and stagnant. Still, it was not until the late 1980s that the terms of the long postwar settlement radically changed, bringing the cold war era to a dramatic close.

THE SEARCH FOR CULTURAL BEARINGS

The events from World War I to the cold war added up to an unprecedented period of disaster for Europe. Europeans were bound to ask what had gone wrong, and what could be salvaged from the ruins of a culture that had made possible the most destructive wars in history, as well as fascism, totalitarianism, and the Holocaust. The cold war framework inevitably affected the answers. Some embraced the Soviet Union or sought a renewed Marxism. Opposition to communism helped stimulate others to return to religious or classical traditions or to embrace new ideas associated with America's recent successes. In Western Europe, at least, this effort to take stock led promptly to the renewed determination and fresh ideas that helped produce the dramatically successful postwar reconstruction.

Absurdity and Commitment in Existentialism

The postwar mood of exhaustion and despair found classic expression in the work of the Irish-born writer Samuel Beckett (1906–1989), especially in his plays *Waiting for Godot* (1952) and *Endgame* (1957). Through Beckett's characters, we see ourselves going through the motions, with nothing worth saying or doing, ludicrously manipulating the husks of a worn-out culture. The only redeeming element is the comic pathos we feel as we watch ourselves.

The same sense of anxiety and despair led to the vogue of existentialism, a movement that marked philosophy, the arts, and popular culture from the later 1940s until well into the 1950s. Existentialism developed from the ideas of the German thinker Martin Heidegger (1889–1976), especially *Being and Time* (1927), one of the most influential philosophical works of the century. Though it was a philosophy of sorts, existentialism was most significant as a broader cultural tendency, finding expression in novels and films. The existentialists explored what it means to be a human being in a world cast adrift from its cultural moorings, with no mutually accepted guideposts, standards, or values.

The most influential postwar existentialists were the Frenchmen Albert Camus (1913–1960) and Jean Paul Sartre (1905–1980), each of whom had been involved in the French resistance, Camus in a particularly central role as editor of an underground newspaper. For both, an authentic human response to a world spinning out of control entailed engagement, commitment, responsibility—even though every action is fraught with risk for the individual. (See the box, "Existentialism and the Loss of Bearings.")

Rather than accept the bleak, ludicrously comic vision of Beckett's plays, Camus sought to show how we might go on living in a positive, affirmative spirit, even in an absurd world, even after all that had happened. Conventional values like friendship and tolerance could be made usable again, based on the simple fact that we human beings are all caught up in this unmasterable situation together. People suffer and die, but as we come together to help as best we can, we might at least learn to stop killing one another.

Camus split from Sartre in a disagreement over the ongoing value of Marxism and the communist experiment in the Soviet Union. Though never an orthodox communist, Sartre found potential for human liberation in the working class, in communist parties, even in the Soviet Union

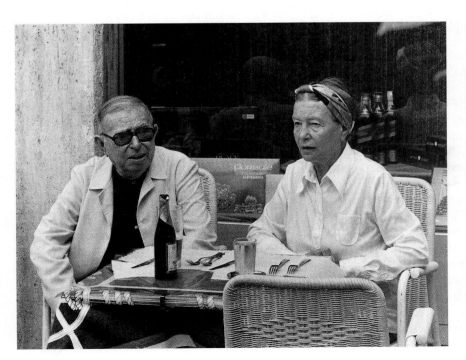

Sartre and de Beauvoir
Among the most influential intellectual couples of the century, Jean-Paul Sartre and Simone de Beauvoir emerged as leaders of French existentialism by the later 1940s. See the boxes on pages 1076 and 1083. *(Giansant/Sygma)*

Existentialism and the Loss of Bearings

In 1945, in a lecture entitled "Existentialism is a Humanism," Jean Paul Sartre offered the classic explanation of the fundamental existentialist tenet: "Existence precedes essence." In a world in which the traditional sources of order and direction appear to have dissolved, we human beings simply find ourselves existing, without some "human nature" that tells us what we are or might become. But then what?

What do we mean by saying that existence precedes essence? We mean that man first of all exists, encounters himself, surges up in the world—and defines himself afterwards. If man as the existentialist sees him is not definable, it is because to begin with he is nothing. He will not be anything until later, and then he will be what he makes of himself. . . . [M]an is, before all else, something which propels itself towards a future and is aware that it is doing so. . . . If . . . existence is prior to essence, man is responsible for what he is. Thus, the first effect of existentialism is that it puts every man in possession of himself as he is, and places the entire responsibility for his existence squarely upon his own shoulders. And, when we say that man is responsible for himself, we do not mean he is responsible only for his own individuality, but that he is responsible for all men. . . . [N]othing can be better for us unless it is better for all. . . . In fashioning myself I fashion man. . . .

. . . If a voice speaks to me, it is still I myself who must decide whether the voice is or is not that of an angel. If I regard a certain course of action as good, it is only I who choose to say that it is good and not bad. . . .

It is nowhere written that "the good" exists, that one must be honest or must not lie, since we are now upon the plane where there are only men. . . . [M]an . . . cannot find anything to depend upon either within or outside himself. He discovers forthwith, that he is without excuse. For if indeed existence precedes essence, one will never be able to explain one's actions by reference to a given and specific human nature; in other words, there is no determinism—man is free, man is freedom. [W]e have neither behind us, nor before us in a luminous realm of values, any means of justification or excuse. That is what I mean when I say that man is condemned to be free.

Source: Walter Kaufmann, ed., *Existentialism from Dostoevsky to Sartre* (Cleveland: World, Meridian Books, 1956), pp. 290–295. (First pub. in French in 1946; first English ed. 1948.)

---

itself, which he saw as the strongest alternative to U.S. imperialism. By the 1950s, he was portraying existentialism as fundamentally a way to revitalize Marxism.

By contrast, Camus, who had started as a communist in the 1930s, had grown disillusioned even before the war, and his major political tract, *The Rebel* (1951), was partly an attack on Marxism and communism. Establishing new bases for human happiness and solidarity meant recognizing limits to what human beings could accomplish, limits even to our demands for freedom and justice. These were precisely the limits that the new political movements of the century had so disas-

trously overstepped. Communism, like fascism, was part of the problem, not the solution.

Marxists and Traditionalists

Sartre was among the many European intellectuals who believed that Marxism had won a new lease on life from the wartime resistance. As they saw it, Marxism could be revamped for the West, without the Stalinist excesses of the Soviet Union. Marxism remained a significant strand in the political culture of the West during the cold war era, but it also attracted periodic waves of denunciation.

In Italy, as in France, the communists' major role in the resistance enhanced their prestige, preparing the way for the extraordinary posthumous influence of Antonio Gramsci (1891–1937), a founder of the Italian Communist party who had spent most of the fascist period in prison. His *Prison Notebooks*, published during the late 1940s, became influential throughout the world and helped make Marxism a powerful force in postwar Italian culture. Seeking to learn the lessons of the fascist triumph in Italy, Gramsci pointed Marxists toward a flexible political strategy, attuned to the special historical circumstances of each country.

Loosely Marxist ideas were central to the renewal of political activism in the West by the later 1960s, although Marxism proved more effective as a critique of capitalism than as a blueprint for change. The best-known spokesman for a renewed radicalism on both sides of the Atlantic during the late 1960s and early 1970s was the German-born social thinker Herbert Marcuse (1898–1979), who explored the cultural mechanisms through which capitalism perpetuates itself in *One-Dimensional Man* (1964).

Even during the late 1940s, however, others, like Camus, held that Marxism was inherently flawed and denied that any recasting could overcome its deficiencies. Damaging revelations about the excesses of Stalinism during the 1930s seemed to confirm this view. Such writers as the Hungarian-born Arthur Koestler (1905–1983) and the Italian Ignazio Silone (1900–1978), who had believed in communism during the 1930s, now denounced it as "the God that failed." Whatever its initial promise, Marxism would inevitably lead to the kind of tyranny that had developed in the Soviet Union. In his futuristic novel *Nineteen Eighty-Four*, published in 1949, the British intellectual George Orwell, long a partisan of leftist causes, chillingly portrayed the dehumanization that seemed to threaten from the totalitarian direction that many now associated with communism.

By the mid-1970s, the disturbing portrait of the Stalinist gulag, or forced-labor-camp system, by the exiled Soviet writer Alexander Solzhenitsyn (b. 1918) stimulated another wave of anticommunist thinking. And whether or not Marxism was necessarily Stalinist and repressive in implication, its relevance to the increasingly prosperous industrial democracies of Western Europe was open to question. Did the Marxist understanding of capitalism and class relations illuminate the core social problems and point the way to solutions, or had the progress of the capitalist West rendered Marxist categories irrelevant? By the early 1980s, many had come to believe that Marxism was simply passé.

Those hostile to Marxism often insisted that the West had to reconnect with older traditions if it were to avoid further horrors like those it had just been through. Especially in the first years after the war, many, like the French Catholic thinker Jacques Maritain (1882–1973), held that only a return to religious traditions would suffice. For the American-born British writer T. S. Eliot (1888–1965), the essential return to tradition had to embrace family and locality, as well as religion. Without a return to tradition, Eliot warned, the West could expect more excesses like fascism and totalitarianism in the future.

The Intellectual Migration and Americanism

The extraordinary migration of European artists and intellectuals to the United States to escape persecution during the 1930s and 1940s profoundly affected the cultural life of the postwar period. An array of luminaries arrived on American shores, from the composer Igor Stravinsky to the theoretical physicist Albert Einstein, from the architect Walter Gropius to the radical social theorist Herbert Marcuse.

Before this cross-fertilization, American culture had remained slightly provincial, sometimes proudly and self-consciously so. All the direct contact with the Europeans by the 1940s helped propel the United States into the Western cultural mainstream. No longer could "Western" culture be identified primarily with Europe. In some spheres—painting, for example—Americans were now confident enough to claim the leadership for the first time.

With the abstract expressionism of the later 1940s, American painters began creating visual images the like of which had never been seen in Europe. In comparison with the raw, energetic painting of Jackson Pollock (1912–1956), the work of the Europeans seemed merely "pretty"—and the newly brash Americans were not shy about telling them so. Now New York began to supplant Paris as the art capital of the Western world.

But the American achievement owed something to European existentialism, and it became possible only because so many of the most innovative European painters had come to New York, where the Americans had been able to learn their lessons at first hand. At the same time European painters like Jean Dubuffet (1901–1985) in France and Francis Bacon (1910–1992) in Britain created new forms of their own—sometimes playful, sometimes brutal—as they sought the startling new visual imagery that seemed appropriate to Western culture after the era of fascism and war. Even in the United States, artists began reacting against the deep seriousness of abstract expressionism during the mid-1950s. One new direction led by the early 1960s to "pop art," which was "American" in a different sense, featuring the ordinary objects and mass-produced images of modern consumerist culture. (See the feature, "Weighing the Evidence: Pop Art," on pages 1110–1111.)

Some Europeans were eager to embrace what seemed distinctively American, because America had remained relatively free of the political ideologies that seemed to have led Europe to totalitarianism and ruin. By the 1950s there was much talk of "the end of ideology," with America pointing the way to a healthier alternative, combining technology, value-free social science, and scientific management. Whereas the old European way led either to mere theorizing, to political extremism, or to polarization and impasse, the American approach got results by tackling problems one at a time, so that they could be solved by managerial or technical experts.

Such Americanism fed the notion that Europe needed a clean break based on technological values. If such a break was necessary, however, what was to become of the European tradition, for centuries the center of gravity of the West, and until recently dominant in the world? Did anything

Dubuffet: Spinning Round   Seeking to depart from the European tradition of sophisticated, well-made art, Jean Dubuffet developed imagery that was at once crude and primitive, playful and whimsical. *(Dubuffet, Jean, Spinning Round, 1961. ARS Tate Gallery, London, Great Britain)*

distinctively European remain, or was Europe doomed to lick its wounds in the shadow of America? These questions lurked in the background, but first Europeans faced the difficult task of economic and political restoration.

PROSPERITY, DEMOCRACY, AND THE NEW SOCIAL COMPACT IN WESTERN EUROPE

By 1941 democracy seemed to be dying on the European continent, yet in Western Europe it quickly revived after World War II, taking root more easily than most had thought possible. The bipolar international framework helped. The United States sought actively to encourage democracy, and Europeans nervous about communism and the Soviet Union were happy to follow the American lead. Success at economic reconstruction was important as well. Not only was there greater prosperity, but governments could afford to deliver on promises of enhanced security, social welfare, and equality of opportunity. It also mattered that Western Europeans learned from past mistakes.

From Economic Reconstruction to Economic Miracle

It is hard to imagine how desperate the situation in much of Western Europe had become by 1945. Major cities like Rotterdam, Hamburg, and Le Havre lay largely in ruins, and normal routines suffered radical disruption. Production had declined to perhaps 25 percent of the prewar level in Italy, to 20 percent in France, and to a mere 5 percent in southern Germany. Cigarettes, often gained through barter from American soldiers, served widely as a medium of exchange.

Although the U.S. commitment to help reconstruct Europe was not originally a cold war measure, the developing cold war context made it seem all the more necessary for the United States to help the Europeans get their economies running again as quickly as possible. The key was the Marshall Plan, which U.S. secretary of state General George Marshall outlined in 1947, and which channeled $13.5 billion in aid to Western Europe by 1951. The need to rebuild afforded Europeans a chance to start over, using the most up-to-date methods and technologies. Though rebuilding strategies dif-

fered, the Western European countries made remarkable recoveries.

The new German government cut state aid to business and limited the long-standing power of cartels. The state was permitted to intervene in the economy only to ensure free competition. In France, by contrast, many were determined to use government to modernize the country, thereby overcoming the weakness that had led to defeat. So virtually at once after the war, France adopted a flexible, pragmatic form of government-led economic planning.

In 1946 Jean Monnet (1888–1979) launched the first of the French postwar economic plans, which brought government and business leaders together to agree on production targets. Economic planning enabled France to make especially effec-

Architects of the New Europe Offering decisive leadership in the unsettled postwar world, Jean Monnet (left) spearheaded European economic integration, and Konrad Adenauer (right) guided the new West German democracy. The two greatly admired each other, and the cooperation they fostered between their two countries was crucial to the peace and prosperity in Western Europe after World War II. *(Eclair Mondial/Sipa Press)*

tive use of the capital that the Marshall Plan provided. French industrial production returned to its prewar peak by 1951, and by 1957 it had risen to twice the level of 1938.

Strong and sustained rates of economic growth were achieved throughout much of Western Europe through the mid-1960s. From 1953 to 1964, annual rates of growth averaged 6 percent in Germany, 5.6 percent in Italy, and 4.9 percent in France. Britain, however, lagged considerably, averaging only 2.7 percent growth annually during that same period.

As part of the new postwar consensus, labor was supposed to be brought more fully into economic decision making. Thus, for example, the trade unions participated in the planning process in France. In Germany the co-determination law of 1951 provided for labor participation in management decisions in heavy industry, and labor representatives were given access to company books and full voting memberships on boards of directors. This measure ultimately made little difference in the functioning of the affected firms, but it helped head off any return to trade-union radicalism.

During the first years of rapid economic growth, the labor movement remained fairly passive in Western Europe, even though wages stayed relatively low. After an era of depression, fascist repression, and war, workers were grateful simply to have jobs, free trade unions, and at least the promise of greater prosperity in the future. By the 1960s, however, it seemed time to redeem that promise; labor began demanding—generally with success—to share more fully in the new prosperity. Now, rather abruptly, much of Western Europe assumed the look of a consumer society, with widespread ownership of automobiles, televisions, and other household appliances.

Social Welfare and the Issue of Gender

Western governments began to adopt social welfare measures on a large scale late in the nineteenth century (see page 862), and by the 1940s some degree of governmental responsibility for unemployment insurance, workplace safety, and even old-age pensions was widely accepted. Some Europeans, seeking renewal after the war, found an attractive model in Sweden and Denmark, where the outlines of a welfare state had emerged by the 1930s. Sweden, especially, attracted attention as a "middle way" that avoided the extremes

of both Soviet Marxism, with its coercive statism, and American-style capitalism, with its brash commercialism and selfish individualism.

Sweden's economy remained fundamentally capitalist, based on private ownership; even after World War II, its nationalized, or government-run, sector was not large by European standards. But the system of social insurance in Sweden was the most extensive in Europe, and the government worked actively with business to promote full employment and to steer the economy in directions deemed socially desirable. Moreover, the welfare state came to mean a major role for the Swedish trade unions, which won relatively high wages for workers and even enjoyed a quasi-veto power over legislation.

At the same time, the Swedish government began playing a more active role in spheres of life that had formerly been private, from sexuality to child rearing. Thus, for example, drugstores were required to carry contraceptives beginning in 1946. Sweden was the first country to provide sex education in the public schools—on an optional basis beginning in 1942, then on a compulsory basis in 1955. By 1979 the Swedes were limiting corporal punishment—the right to spank—and prohibiting the sale of war toys. This deprivatization of the family stemmed from a sense, especially pronounced in Sweden, that society is collectively responsible for the well-being of its children.

Although Sweden and the other Scandinavian countries had pioneered the welfare state, Britain's decision to move in the same direction evidenced its widening appeal. Britain had been a major victor in the war and was apparently still a great imperial power. Yet it began constructing a welfare state just after the war, even dumping Winston Churchill in the process.

Churchill's inspired leadership of Britain during the darkest days of the war made him perhaps the most admired Western leader of the twentieth century. But when Britain held its first postwar elections, in July 1945, Churchill's Conservatives suffered a crushing loss to the Labour party, led by Clement Attlee (1883–1967). Even early in the war most Britons came to take it for granted that major socioeconomic changes would follow from victory, and Labour seemed better equipped to deliver on that promise.

Greater collective responsibility for the well-being of all British citizens seemed appropriate

Social Welfare in Sweden
With the state playing a major role, Sweden proved a pioneer in responding to the family and children's issues that became increasingly prominent after World War II. Here children play at a daycare center in Stockholm in 1953. *(Roland Janson/Pressens Bild, Stockholm)*

in light of the shared hardships the war had imposed. Moreover, the successes of government planning and control in response to the wartime emergency suggested that once the war was over, government could assume responsibility for the basic needs of the British people, guaranteeing full employment and providing a national health service. But only after the Labour victory in the 1945 elections did formal legislation begin putting these aspirations into practice, creating the British welfare state.

Although some expected, and others feared, that the result would be a form of socialism, establishing a welfare state did not undermine the capitalist economic system. The Labour government nationalized some key industries, but 80 percent of the British work force remained employed in private firms in 1948. Moreover, even under Labour, the British government did not seek the kind of economic planning role that government was playing in France. Much like the United States, Britain relied on monetary and fiscal policy to coordinate its economy.

The core of the British departure in 1945 was not nationalization but a set of social welfare measures that significantly affected the lives of ordinary people. These included old-age pensions; insurance against unemployment, sickness, and disability; and allowances for pregnancy, child rearing, widowhood, and burial. The heart of the system was free medical care, to be provided by a National Health Service, created in November 1946 and operating by 1948.

In Britain as elsewhere, gender roles were inevitably at issue as government welfare measures were debated and adopted. Were married women to have access to the welfare system as individual citizens, or as members of a family unit, with special responsibility for child rearing and dependent on their husbands as wage-earning breadwinners? Should government seek to enable women to be both mothers and workers, or should goverment help make it possible for mothers not to have to work outside the home? Women themselves did not always agree on priorities, and there were some instructive differences in accent across national boundaries.

As during the First World War, the percentage of women in the work force had increased significantly during World War II, but in the post–World War II period both women and men showed a more marked tendency to return to the security of traditional domestic patterns. So the war itself did not change gender patterns of work even to the extent that World War I had done. In Britain women made up about 30 percent of the labor force in 1931, 31 percent in 1951. The percentage of women in the U.S. work force increased from 26 to 36 percent during the war years, but by 1947 it had returned to 28 percent. Thus the embrace of welfare measures took place at a time of renewed conservatism in conceptions of gender roles.

British feminists at first welcomed provisions of the British welfare state recognizing the special role of women as mothers. The government was to ease burdens by providing family allowances, to be paid directly to mothers, for more than one child. This seemed a progressive step beyond the long-standing British trade union demand for a "family wage"—a wage high enough to enable the male breadwinner to support a family so that his wife would not have to work. Such a wage was to be paid to all workers, regardless of family status. The new provisions of the British welfare state singled out mothers for benefits and enabled them to stay home with their children. At the same time, however, those provisions reinforced both the traditional assumption that marriage meant economic dependence for women and the actual economic dependence of married British women on their husbands.

In France, which had refused even to grant women the vote after World War I, the very different situation after 1945 stimulated a more innovative response, which eventually made the French approach to gender and family issues a model for others. After the experience of defeat, collaboration, and resistance, the French were determined to pursue both economic dynamism and individual justice. But they also remained concerned with population growth, so they combined incentives to encourage large families with measures to promote equal opportunity and economic independence for women. Thus, as they expanded the role of government after the war, the French tended more than the British to assume that paid employment for women was healthy and desirable. The French did not, however, view work outside the home as incompatible with a special female role in child rearing. They recognized that women had special needs as mothers—even as they also recognized that, in crucial respects, husbands shared the responsibility for parenting. The challenge, then, was to combine equal treatment, including equal employment opportunities, with support for child rearing.

New laws gave French women equal access to civil service jobs and guaranteed equal pay for equal work. In addition, the French welfare system treated women as individual citizens, regardless of marital or economic status. Thus they were equally entitled to pensions, health services, and job-related benefits. Yet the French system also recognized a special motherhood role by providing benefits for women during and after pregnancy. However, there were also family allowances that treated the two parents as equally essential.

Although female participation in the paid labor force declined just after the war, it began rising throughout the West during the 1950s, then accelerated during the 1960s, reaching new highs in the 1970s and 1980s. Thanks partly to the expansion of government, the greatest job growth was in the service sector—in social work, health care, and education, for example—and many of these new jobs went to women. From about 1960 to 1988, the percentage of women aged 25 to 34 in the labor force rose from 38 to 67 in Britain, from 42 to 75 in France, and from 49 to 87 in Germany. These statistics reflected significant changes in women's lives, but even as their choices expanded in some respects, women became more deeply aware of enduring limits to their opportunities. Their awareness served to energize a new feminist movement by the later 1960s (see page 1107). That movement drew intellectual inspiration from *The Second Sex*, a pioneering work published in 1949 by the French existentialist Simone de Beauvoir (1908–1986), who started with the existentialist emphasis on human freedom to show how cultural conventions continued to restrict the range of choices for women. (See the box, "Human Freedom and the Origins of a New Feminism.")

Restoration of Democracy in Germany, France, and Italy

With its turn to a welfare state, Britain was seeking to renew a long-standing democracy after an arduous victory. Much of continental western Europe faced a deeper challenge—to rebuild democracy after defeat and humiliation. With the developing cold war complicating the situation, the outcome of the effort to restore democracy was by no means certain in the late 1940s. Although the division of Germany weakened communism in the new Federal Republic, in France and Italy strong Communist parties had emerged from the wartime resistance and claimed to point the way beyond conventional democracy altogether.

The new Federal Republic of Germany held its first election under the Basic Law in August

Human Freedom and the Origins of a New Feminism

The renewed feminism that became prominent during the later 1960s took inspiration from **The Second Sex,** *a pioneering work by the French existentialist Simone de Beauvoir that was first published in 1949. Even while valuing sexual difference, she showed the scope for opening the full range of human choices to women.*

[T]he nature of things is no more immutably given, once for all, than is historical reality. If woman seems to be the inessential which never becomes the essential, it is because she herself fails to bring about this change. . . .

To decline to be the Other, to refuse to be a party to the deal—this would be for women to renounce all the advantages conferred upon them by their alliance with the superior caste. Man-the-sovereign will provide woman-the-liege with material protection and will undertake the moral justification of her existence; thus she can evade at once both economic risk and the metaphysical risk of a liberty in which ends and aims must be contrived without assistance. Indeed, along with the ethical urge of each individual to affirm his subjective existence, there is also the temptation to forgo liberty and become a thing. . . .

If a caste is kept in a state of inferiority, no doubt it remains inferior; but liberty can break the circle. Let negroes vote, and they become worthy of having the vote; let woman be given responsibilities and she is able to assume them. . . .

. . . [T]here will be some to object that . . . when woman is "the same" as her male, life will lose its salt and spice. . . .

. . . And it is true that the evolution now in progress threatens more than feminine charm alone: in beginning to exist for herself, woman will relinquish the function as double and mediator to which she owes her privileged place in the masculine universe. . . . There is no

denying that feminine dependence, inferiority, woe, give women their special character; assuredly woman's autonomy, if it spares men many troubles, will also deny them many conveniences; assuredly there are certain forms of the sexual adventure which will be lost in the world of tomorrow. But this does not mean that love, happiness, poetry, dream, will be banished from it.

. . . New relations of flesh and sentiment of which we have no conception will arise between the sexes; already, indeed, there have appeared between men and women friendships, rivalries, complicities, comradeships—chaste or sensual—which past centuries could not have conceived. . . .

. . . [T]here will always be certain differences between man and woman; her eroticism, and therefore her sexual world, have a special form of their own and therefore cannot fail to engender a sensuality, a sensitivity, of a special nature. . . .

. . . To emancipate women is to refuse to confine her to the relations she bears to man, not to deny them to her; let her have her independent existence and she will continue none the less to exist for him *also:* mutually recognizing each other as subject, each will yet remain for the other an *other.* . . . [W]hen we abolish the slavery of half of humanity, together with the whole system of hypocrisy that it implies, then the "division" of humanity will reveal its genuine significance and the human couple will find its true form.

Source: Simone de Beauvoir, *The Second Sex* (New York: Random House, Vintage, 1989), pp. xxv, xxvii, 728–731.

1949, launching what proved a successful democracy. Partly to counter the Soviet Union but also to avoid what seemed the disastrous mistake of the harsh peace settlement after World War I, the victors sought to help get Germany back on its feet as

quickly as possible. At the same time, German political leaders, determined to avoid the mistakes of the Weimar years, now better understood the need to compromise, to take responsibility for governing the whole nation.

To prevent the instability that had plagued the Weimar Republic, the creators of the new government strengthened the chancellor in relation to the Bundestag, the lower house of parliament. In the same way, the Basic Law helped establish a stable party system by discouraging splinter parties and by allowing the courts to outlaw extremist parties. On that basis, the courts outlawed both the Communist party and a neo-Nazi party during the formative years of the new German democracy.

The new West German republic proved more stable than the earlier Weimar Republic partly because the political party system was now considerably simpler. Two mass parties, the Christian Democratic Union (CDU) and the Social Democratic party (SPD), were immediately predominant, although a third, the much smaller Free Democratic party (FDP), proved important for coalition purposes.

Konrad Adenauer (1876–1967), head of the CDU, the largest party in 1949, immediately emerged as postwar Germany's leading statesman. A Catholic who had been mayor of Cologne under Weimar, he had withdrawn from active politics during the Nazi period, but he re-emerged after the war to lead the council that drafted the Basic Law. As chancellor from 1949 until 1963, he oriented the new German democracy toward Western Europe and the Atlantic bloc, led by the United States.

The new bipolar world confronted West Germany with a cruel choice. By accepting the bipolar framework, the country could become a full partner within the Atlantic bloc. But by trying to straddle the fence instead, it could keep open the possibility that Germany could be reunified as a neutral and disarmed state. The choice was made in the early 1950s when the outbreak of war in Korea intensified the cold war, and the United States pressured West Germany to rearm and join the Western bloc.

Although some West Germans resisted, Adenauer led the Federal Republic into the Atlantic alliance in 1955. This was to accept not only U.S. leadership but also, for the foreseeable future, the division of Germany. Adenauer was eager to anchor the new Federal Republic to the West, partly to buttress the new democracy in West Germany, but also to cement U.S. support for Western Europe in the face of what seemed an ongoing Soviet threat to German security.

By the late 1950s the West German economy was recovering nicely, and the country was a valued member of the Western alliance. Adenauer's CDU seemed so potent that the other major party, the SPD, appeared to be consigned to permanent—and sterile—opposition. Frustrated with its outsider status, the SPD began to shed its Marxist trappings in an effort to widen its appeal. Prominent among those pushing in this direction was Willy Brandt (1913–1992), who became mayor of West Berlin in 1957, and who would become the party's leader in 1963. At its watershed national congress at Bad Godesberg in 1959, the party officially gave up talk of the class struggle and adopted a more moderate program.

Adenauer stepped down in 1963 at the age of 87, after fourteen years as chancellor. The contrast with Weimar, which had known twenty-one different cabinets in a comparable fourteen-year period, could not be more striking. The Adenauer years proved to Germans that liberal democracy could mean stable and effective government, economic prosperity, and foreign policy success. Still, Adenauer had become somewhat authoritarian by his later years, and it was arguable that West Germany had become overly reliant on him and his party.

During the years from 1963 to 1969, the CDU proved it could govern without Adenauer, and the SPD came to seem ever more respectable, even joining as junior partner in a government coalition with the CDU in 1966. Finally, in October 1969, new parliamentary elections brought Brandt to the chancellorship, and the SPD became responsible for governing West Germany for the first time since the war.

Brandt sought to provide a genuine alternative to the CDU without undermining the consensus that had developed around the new regime since 1949. He wanted especially to improve relations between West Germany and the Soviet bloc, but this required a more independent foreign policy than Germany had followed under Adenauer and his successors. Under Adenauer, the Federal Republic had refused to deal with East Germany at all. So for a socialist chancellor seeking to prove his respectability, Brandt's opening to the East, or *Ostpolitik*, was risky, but he pursued it with skill and success.

In treaties with the Soviet Union, Czechoslovakia, and Poland, West Germany accepted the main lines of the postwar settlement. This was to abandon any claim to the former German territory east of the Oder-Neisse line, now in Poland. Brandt also managed to improve relations with East Germany. After the two countries finally agreed to mutual diplomatic recognition, each was admitted to the United Nations in 1973. Brandt's overtures made possible closer economic ties between them, and even broader opportunities for ordinary citizens to interact across the east-west border. His *Ostpolitik* was widely popular and helped deepen the postwar consensus in West Germany.

In France and Italy, unlike West Germany, communists emerged powerful from major roles in wartime resistance movements. Indeed, in either nation they might conceivably have made a bid for power as the war was ending. But Moscow, concerned with the larger picture in Europe, called for the moderate route of participation in coalitions instead, at least partly because the presence of Western troops in these countries gave the leverage to noncommunists. And the United States intervened persistently to minimize the communists' role as new democracies took root in both nations after 1945.

When the first parliamentary elections were held in the new Fourth Republic in France in 1946, the Communists won the largest number of seats, and their support continued to rise until 1949. Partly because of pressure from the United States, however, they were forced out of the coalition government in 1947, and after 1949 their strength began leveling off. During the years that followed, the French Communist party proved particularly inflexible and unimaginative, maintaining strict subservience to the Soviet Union.

As the leader of the overall resistance effort, Charles de Gaulle immediately assumed the dominant political role after the liberation of France in August 1944. But he withdrew, disillusioned, from active politics early in 1946, as political life under the new Fourth Republic seemed to return to the patterns of the old Third Republic. As before, government depended on multiparty coalitions; it required considerable political energy simply to put together a stable majority. The Fourth Republic became something of a laughingstock as governments rose and fell every six months, on the average, over its twelve-year life. Still, governmental decision making changed significantly as the nonpolitical, technocratic side of the French state

The Return of de Gaulle Disillusioned with the political squabbles of the early Fourth Republic, General Charles de Gaulle retired from public life in 1946. But he believed his country would need his leadership again. He returned to power in 1958, with France in turmoil over the Algerian War, and spearheaded the creation of the Fifth Republic. *(Keystone/Sygma)*

gained power in areas such as economic planning. And government technocrats survived the fall of the Fourth Republic in 1958, when de Gaulle returned to politics at a moment of crisis, stemming from France's war to maintain control of Algeria (see page 1089).

Although de Gaulle became prime minister within the Fourth Republic, it was clear that his return signified a change of regime. The French legislature promptly gave his government full powers for six months, including a charge to draft a new constitution, which was then approved by referendum in the fall of 1958. The result was the new Fifth Republic, which featured a stronger executive—and soon a president elected directly by the people and not dependent on the Chamber of

Deputies. It was only in 1958, with the return of de Gaulle and the advent of the Fifth Republic, that government in postwar France began to assume definitive contours.

Italy's political challenge, after more than twenty years of fascism, was even more dramatic than France's. Shortly after the war, the Italians adopted a new democratic constitution and voted to end the monarchy, thereby making modern Italy a republic for the first time. But much depended on the balance of political forces, which quickly crystallized around the Christian Democratic party (DC), oriented toward the Catholic church, and the Communist and Socialist parties. The international context favored the Christian Democrats, who assumed the dominant political role. As the cold war developed, the United States intervened as necessary to support the Christian Democrats as the chief bulwark against the Communists. Many Italian moderates with little attachment to the church supported the DC for the same reason.

Well into the 1970s, the Christian Democrats' share of the vote remained relatively stable at around 40 percent in national parliamentary elections. The DC was invariably the largest single party, yet not a majority, so it was forced to work in coalition with smaller parties. Beginning in the early 1960s, with the much-trumpeted "opening to the left," this could even include the Socialist party (PSI), which typically won 10 to 15 percent of the vote in national elections. This total fell far behind that of the Communist party, which for decades remained the second largest at 25 to 35 percent. The relative strength of the political parties established the framework for the curious combination of surface instability and deeper stability—or immobility—that came to characterize the new Italian democracy. Domination by the Christian Democrats was the fundamental fact of Italian political life until the early 1990s.

Unlike their counterparts in France, the Italian Communists did not settle for a role of opposition and protest. Taking their cue from Gramsci's writings, they sought to make their presence felt in as many areas of Italian life as possible in order gradually to establish their legitimacy. And they had considerable success as they organized profit-making cooperatives for sharecroppers, won local and regional elections, and garnered the support of intellectuals, journalists, and publishers. At one

time or another, they ran many of Italy's local and regional governments, often for years at a time, and they generally did well at it. Heavily communist Bologna, for example, was one of the best-governed cities in Europe.

But as the years after World War II turned to decades, the Italian Communists' successes raised awkward questions. What were the Communists trying to accomplish on the national level, and how long was it supposed to take? Could a communist party function as a governing party within a democratic political system? Because the Italian Communists, unlike the German Social Democrats, never established their credibility as a national governing party, the Christian Democrats grew ever more entrenched, becoming increasingly arrogant and corrupt.

WESTERN EUROPE AND THE WORLD

By the early 1950s, the old Europe seemed dwarfed by the two global superpowers and, for the foreseeable future, divided by the conflict between them. The colonial networks that had symbolized European predominance unraveled rapidly at the same time. One obvious response was some form of European unity. A unified Europe might eventually have the clout to stand as a global superpower in its own right. Although the first steps toward European unity did not go so far as visionaries had hoped, they established lasting foundations by the late 1950s—and they served European prosperity and security well.

NATO and the Atlantic Orientation

As the Soviets tightened their grip on the satellite states of east-central Europe, fears of Soviet expansion into western Europe led to the creation of the North Atlantic Treaty Organization (NATO) under U.S. leadership in April 1949. In pooling the forces of its member countries under a unified command, NATO went beyond the usual peacetime military alliance. This Atlantic bloc assumed definitive shape only in 1955, when it encompassed the newly rearmed West Germany (see Map 29.2). The prospect of German rearmament made the French nervous at first, but by 1954 they had come to agree that the best course for French security was to integrate the western part of a divided Germany into the U.S.-led Western bloc.

NATO was intended specifically to prevent any Soviet expansion in Europe. Yet the Soviets had considerable superiority in conventional forces, which had ready access to western Europe. As a balance, the United States offered its nuclear superiority; indeed, the American nuclear guarantee was the cornerstone of the NATO alliance. Thus it seemed crucial for the United States to maintain its superiority in nuclear weapons, a fact that helped fuel the continuing arms race and nuclear buildup.

However, as the Soviet Union developed the capacity for a nuclear strike at the United States, Europeans began asking whether the Americans could be counted on to respond with nuclear weapons to a conventional Soviet attack on western Europe. The Americans might hesitate, now that the United States was vulnerable to Soviet nuclear retaliation. Did it make sense, then, for western Europeans to rely on the United States as the ultimate guarantor of their defense? Such doubts became especially widespread in France, where President de Gaulle, citing concerns for French sovereignty and security, accelerated the development of a French nuclear force during the 1960s.

The Varieties of Decolonization

The advent of a new world configuration, with a circumscribed place for Europe, found dramatic expression in the rapid disintegration of the European colonial empires after World War II (Map 29.1). The process of decolonization was varied and uneven, partly because the local independence movements differed but also because the interests of Europeans varied. Where there were large numbers of European settlers or their descendants, the remaining colonial powers— Britain, France, Belgium, the Netherlands, and Portugal—were reluctant to yield to independence forces. But everywhere they were more likely to yield if they could negotiate their withdrawal with local moderates, thereby preserving

Ban the Bomb As nuclear tension escalated during the 1950s, some built air-raid shelters; others took to the streets in antinuclear protest. The protest movement was especially prominent in Britain, where the noted philosopher Bertrand Russell (1872–1970) played a central role. Here, seated at right, he awaits arrest during a sit-in demonstration outside the British Defense Ministry. *(Hulton-Getty/Tony Stone Images)*

JAPAN

NORTH KOREA 1948
SOUTH KOREA 1948
From Japan

PACIFIC OCEAN

PHILIPPINES 1946

BRUNEI 1984 From Great Britain

INDONESIA 1949

NORTH VIETNAM 1954
Unified 1974
SOUTH VIETNAM 1954

CAMBODIA 1954

MALAYSIA 1963

SINGAPORE 1965

LAOS 1949
MYANMAR (BURMA) 1947

PAKISTAN 1947
BANGLADESH 1973

SRI LANKA (CEYLON) 1948

INDIA 1947

PAKISTAN 1947

Date is year independence was achieved.
Shading indicates former ruler.

	Belgium
Great Britain	Portugal
France	United States
Netherlands	
Italy	

INDIAN OCEAN

MAURITIUS 1968 From Great Britain

KUWAIT 1961
BAHRAIN 1971
QATAR 1971
UNITED ARAB EMIRATES 1971

P.D.R. OF YEMEN 1967
DJIBOUTI 1977

SOMALIA 1960

MADAGASCAR 1960

IRAQ 1932
JORDAN 1946

YEMEN 1967

ETHIOPIA 1941

KENYA 1963

MALAWI 1964

SWAZILAND 1968

LESOTHO 1966

SYRIA 1944
CYPRUS 1960
LEBANON 1944
ISRAEL 1948

EGYPT 1922

SUDAN 1956

UGANDA 1962
RWANDA 1962
BURUNDI 1962

TANZANIA 1964

MOZAMBIQUE 1974

ZIMBABWE 1980

MALTA 1964 From Great Britain
TUNISIA 1956

DEM. REP OF CONGO 1960

ZAMBIA 1964

BOTSWANA 1966

ITALY

LIBYA 1951

CHAD 1960

CENTRAL AFRICAN REPUBLIC 1960

ANGOLA 1975

NAMIBIA 1985 From South Africa

SOUTH AFRICA (Republic 1961)

NETHERLANDS
BELGIUM

NIGER 1960

CAMEROON 1960

GABON 1960

FRANCE

GREAT BRITAIN

ALGERIA 1962

NIGERIA 1960
BENIN 1960

REPUBLIC OF CONGO 1960

SPAIN

MALI 1960

BURKINA FASO 1960

TOGO 1960

EQUATORIAL GUINEA 1968 From Spain

PORTUGAL

MOROCCO 1956

MAURITANIA 1960

GUINEA 1958
CÔTE D'IVOIRE 1960
GHANA 1957

WESTERN SAHARA (Morocco) 1975 From Spain

SENEGAL 1960
GAMBIA 1965
GUINEA-BISSAU 1974
SIERRA LEONE 1961
LIBERIA 1820s

ATLANTIC OCEAN

| 0 | 500 | 1000 | 1500 Mi. |
| 0 | 500 | 1000 | 1500 Km. |

property rights and the possibility of continued influence.

The Second World War proved a major catalyst for anticolonialist independence movements throughout the world. In southeast Asia and the Pacific, quick Japanese conquests revealed the vulnerability of France, the Netherlands, and Britain. And it was not colonial reconquest that marked the end of the war, but the atomic bomb and the victory of the United States, which took a dim view of conventional European colonialism.

The effort of the Netherlands to regain control of the Dutch East Indies led to four years of military struggle against the Indonesian nationalist insurgency. Although most independent observers felt they could not win, the Dutch were reluctant to relinquish control of the East Indies, which had been in Dutch hands since the seventeenth century. Especially after the humiliations of defeat and occupation during World War II, the Dutch took pride in their imperial role. The struggle lasted from 1945 to 1949, when the Dutch finally had to yield as their former colony became independent Indonesia.

Unlike the Netherlands, Britain was still a great power in the twentieth century, and its empire had seemed essential to its stature. Although India, the crown jewel of the empire, had won full independence in 1947, many Britons still envisioned extending Commonwealth status to the former British colonies as a way of retaining economic ties and political influence. But the Commonwealth idea proved to have little appeal for Britain's former colonies; the British Commonwealth became little more than a voluntary cooperative association. Despite illusions and hesitations, however, Britain proved the most realistic of the European colonial powers, grasping the need to compromise and work with emerging national leaders.

Nevertheless, even Britain decided to resist in 1956, when it provoked an international crisis over the status of the Suez Canal in Egypt (see Map 28.1 on page 1036). Once a British protectorate, Egypt had remained under heavy British

influence even after nominally becoming sovereign in 1922. But a revolution in 1952 produced a new government of Arab nationalists, led by the able and charismatic Colonel Gamel Abdul Nasser (1918–1970). In 1954 Britain agreed with Egypt to leave the Suez Canal zone within twenty months, though the zone was to be international, not Egyptian, and Britain was to retain special rights there in the event of war. In 1956, however, Nasser announced the nationalization of the canal, partly so that Egypt could use its revenues to finance public works projects.

Led by the Conservative Anthony Eden (1897–1977), Britain decided on a showdown. Eden won the support of Israel and France, each of which had reason to fear the pan-Arab nationalism that Nasser's Egypt was now spearheading. Israel had remained at odds with its Arab neighbors since its founding in 1948, and Nasser was helping the Arabs who were beginning to take up arms against French rule in Algeria.

Late in 1956 Britain, Israel, and France orchestrated a surprise attack on Egypt. After the Israelis invaded, the British and French bombed military targets, then landed troops to take the canal. But the troops met stubborn Egyptian resistance, and the British and French encountered decisive defeat in the diplomatic maneuvering that accompanied the outbreak of fighting. Both the United States and the Soviet Union opposed the Anglo-French-Israeli move, as did world opinion. The old European powers had sought to act on their own, by the old rules, but the outcome of the Suez crisis demonstrated how limited the reach of the Western European states had become. Moreover, nations like Egypt, formerly subservient to Europeans, could be a factor in their own right within the new bipolar framework.

Still, the outcome in 1956 did not convince France to abandon its struggle to retain Algeria. And that struggle proved the most dramatic, wrenching experience that any European country was to have with decolonization. For the French the process started not in North Africa but in Indochina, in southeast Asia, during World War II.

Led by the communist Ho Chi Minh (1890–1969), the Indochinese anticolonialist movement gained strength resisting the Japanese during the war and then, before the French could return, established a political base in northern Vietnam in 1945. Although the French re-established control

Map 29.1 From Colonialism to Independence During a thirty-five-year period after World War II, the European empires in Africa, Asia, and the Pacific gradually came apart as the former colonies became independent nations.

in the south, negotiations between the French and the Vietnamese nationalists seemed at first to be moving toward some form of self-government for Vietnam. However, there was considerable opposition in France, especially within the army, to giving in to the Vietnamese independence movement. In 1946 French authorities in Indochina deliberately provoked an incident to undercut negotiations and start hostilities. Eight years of difficult guerrilla war followed, creating a major drain on the French economy.

With its strongly anticolonialist posture, the United States was unsympathetic to the French cause at first. But the communist takeover in China in 1949 and the outbreak of war in Korea in 1950 made the French struggle in Indochina seem a battle in a larger war against communism in Asia. By 1954 the United States was covering 75 percent of the cost of the French effort in Indochina. Nonetheless, when the fall of the fortified area at Dien Bien Phu in May 1954 signaled a decisive French defeat, the United States decided to pull back and accept a negotiated settlement. Partly at the urging of its European allies, the United States had concluded that the Soviet threat in Europe must remain its principal concern.

France worked out the terms of independence for Vietnam in 1955. The solution, however, entailed north-south partition to separate the communist and anticommunist forces, pending elections to unify the country. The anticommunist regime the United States sponsored in the south resisted holding the elections, so the country remained divided (see Map 29.1). Only in 1975, after a brutal war with the United States, would the communist heirs of those who had led the fight against the French assume the leadership of a unified Vietnam.

In France, the defeat in Indochina left a legacy of bitterness, especially among army officers, many of whom felt that French forces could have won had they not been undercut by politicians at home. When the outcome in Indochina emboldened Arab nationalists in North Africa to take up arms against the French colonial power, the French army was anxious for a second chance— and the French government was willing to give it to them. The French agreed to independence for Tunisia and Morocco by 1956, but only so that they could concentrate their military forces in Algeria, where the stakes seemed high enough for a

showdown. Algeria had been under French control since 1830, and it had a substantial minority of ethnic Europeans, totaling over a million, or 10 percent of the population.

Although France gradually committed 500,000 troops to Algeria, the war bogged down into what threatened to become a lengthy stalemate, with increasing brutality on both sides. As it drained French lives and resources, the war became a highly volatile political issue in France. The situation came to a head during the spring of 1958 when the advent of a new ministry, rumored to favor a compromise settlement, led to violent demonstrations, engineered by the sectors of the French army in Algeria. Military intervention in France itself seemed likely to follow—and with it the danger of civil war.

It was at this moment of genuine emergency that Charles de Gaulle returned to lead the change to the Fifth Republic. Those determined to hold Algeria welcomed de Gaulle as their savior. But de Gaulle fooled them, working out a compromise with the nationalist rebels that ended the war and made Algeria independent in 1962. No doubt only de Gaulle could have engineered this outcome without provoking still deeper political division in France.

The anticolonial movement in Algeria gave rise to a more radical new political order than had been the case in Tunisia and Morocco. The new Algerian government's policy of expropriation and nationalization led most of the French settlers to relocate to France.

All over Europe, the colonialist impulse, which had still been significant immediately after World War II, waned noticeably by the end of the 1950s. The economic successes of Germany and Italy, both free of colonialist expenses, suggested to other Europeans that they would be better off without colonies, particularly if maintaining them required a heavy military burden.

But there remained resistance, and considerable variation, as the colonies of sub-Saharan Africa moved toward independence in the decades following World War II. Outcomes depended on the number and intransigence of white settlers, on the extent to which local elites had emerged, and on the confidence of the Europeans that they could retain their influence if they agreed to independence. Of the major imperial powers in the region, Britain had done best at preparing local leaders and proved the most willing to work with indigenous elites. The two smaller countries, Belgium and Portugal, were less certain they could maintain their influence, and they proved the most reluctant to give up their imperial status.

The transition was smoothest in British West Africa, where the Gold Coast achieved independence as Ghana, first as a Commonwealth dominion in 1957, then as a fully independent republic in 1960. There were few British settlers in that part of Africa, and the small, relatively cohesive African elite favored a moderate transition, not revolution. Where British settlers were relatively numerous, however, as in Kenya or Rhodesia, the transition to independence proved much more difficult. The very presence of Europeans had impeded the development of cohesive local elites, so movements for independence in those areas tended to become more radical, threatening the expropriation of European-held property.

The British had to use 50,000 troops and police to put down a major rebellion in Kenya from 1951 to 1956. This episode helped convince the British that the cost of maintaining colonial rule was simply too high, and they gradually developed a compromise that led to independence for Kenya in 1963. In Southern Rhodesia, however, unyielding European settlers resisted the British government's effort to promote a comparable compromise. A white supremacist government declared its independence from Britain in 1965, fueling a guerrilla war. The Africans won independence as Zimbabwe only in 1980.

Nowhere was decolonization messier than in the two largest Portuguese colonies in Africa, Mozambique and Angola. Portugal had run the most repressive of the African colonial regimes, with elements of the earlier system of forced labor lingering into the 1960s. Portuguese intransigence radicalized the independence movement, which took advantage of help from the communist world to resist the colonizers militarily. Finally, by 1974, sectors of the Portuguese military, weary of a colonial war they lacked the resources to win, engineered a political coup at home. The new government promptly washed its hands of the debilitating colonialist struggle, granting independence to both Mozambique and Angola in 1975. In each of the new countries, communist-supported radicals had won the upper hand within divided anticolonialist movements, but the struggles themselves, and the

DECOLONIZATION	
1919	League of Nations mandate system
	Amritsar massacre in India
	Anti-British insurrection in Egypt
1921	Mohandas Gandhi adopts native Indian attire
1922	British grant formal independence to Egypt
1941	Japanese establish control in French Indochina
1947	India achieves independence from Britain
1949	Indonesia wins independence from the Netherlands
1954	Defeat of France in Vietnam
1955	Bandung conference of non-Western countries in Indonesia
1956	Peace terms in Vietnam yield north-south partition
	Suez crisis; defeat for Britain and France in Egypt
1957	Establishment of independent Ghana (from Gold Coast and British Togoland)
1962	Algerian War results in Algerian independence from France
1965	White supremacist government declares independence of Southern Rhodesia from Britain
1975	Independence of Mozambique and Angola from Portugal
	North Vietnamese defeat of South Vietnam and the United States leads to reunification of Vietnam
1980	End of guerrilla war in Southern Rhodesia; independence of Zimbabwe

sudden departure of the Portuguese, left considerable socioeconomic disarray.

The process of decolonization led to a remarkable transformation in the thirty-five years after World War II. Forms of colonial rule that had been taken for granted before World War I stood discredited, virtually without defenders, by the late twentieth century. But decolonization hardly offered a neat and definitive solution. In formerly

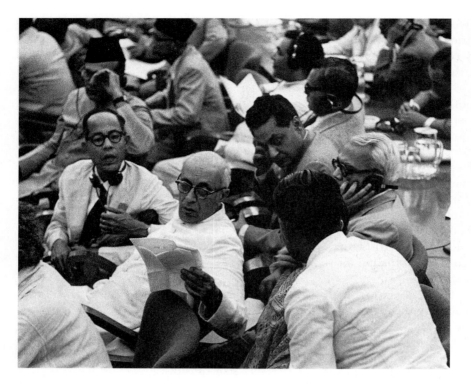

Nonalignment in a Bipolar World At a major conference of Asian and African leaders at Bandung, Indonesia, in 1955, India's Jawaharlal Nehru (center) advocated "nonalignment" for the nations outside the immediate orbits of the United States and the Soviet Union. Although its results were inconclusive, the Bandung conference marked a new level of awareness among Asians and Africans that their nations—many of them new—could work together to play a major role in world affairs. *(Wide World Photos)*

colonial territories, new political boundaries often stemmed from the way Europeans had carved things up, rather than from indigenous ethnic or national patterns. Moreover, questions remained about the longer-term economic relationships between the Europeans and their former colonies.

The leader of Ghana, Kwame Nkrumah (1909–1972), used the term *neocolonialism* to suggest that more subtle forms of Western exploitation had replaced direct colonial rule. But attempts by the former colonies to do without economic ties to the West often proved counterproductive, and in some areas reasonably good relations, compatible with Western economic interests, eventually developed. Generally, postcolonial leaders were highly ambivalent toward the West, where many of them had been educated. Nkrumah, for example, had studied in the United States and England during the 1930s and 1940s, and India's Jawaharlal Nehru had attended some of the best schools in England. These leaders understood the need to learn from the West, but at the same time they claimed their countries could "modernize" without losing the traditions that made them different from the West—and in some ways superior.

At the same time, the context of superpower rivalry afforded new challenges and opportunities for the postcolonial world. In April 1955 the leaders of twenty-nine Asian and African nations met at Bandung, Indonesia, in a conference that proved a watershed in the self-understanding of what was coming to be called the "Third World." The most influential, like Nehru, Nasser, and Indonesia's Achmed Sukarno (1901–1970), were charismatic nation-builders, at once anti-Western and Westernizing, who understood the scope for postcolonial countries to play major roles in global politics. Along with Tito of Yugoslavia, Nehru was the leading proponent of "nonalignment," of navigating an independent course between the Western and the Soviet blocs. And whether or not their countries were formally nonaligned, Third World leaders often found ways of exploiting the superpower rivalry to their own advantage.

The reaction against Eurocentrism that accompanied the turn from colonialism was not confined to those who had been subjected to European imperialism. It contributed to the vogue of "structuralism," as developed in anthropology by Claude Lévi-Strauss (b. 1908) in such works as *Tristes Tropiques* (1955). While raising deep questions about any notion of Western superiority, Lévi-Strauss also expressed a certain nostalgia for a world untouched by Western influence. There

~ ENCOUNTERS WITH THE WEST ~

The Legacy of European Colonialism

In the following passage from **The Wretched of the Earth** *(1961), Frantz Fanon probes the negative consequences of colonialism—for both colonizers and colonized—and tries to show why a radical, even violent break from colonialism was necessary.*

The violence which has ruled over the ordering of the colonial world, which has ceaselessly drummed the rhythm for the destruction of native social forms and broken up without reserve the systems of reference of the economy, the customs of dress and external life, that same violence will be claimed and taken over by the native at the moment when, deciding to embody history in his own person, he surges into the forbidden quarters. . . .

. . . In the colonial context the settler only ends his work of breaking in the native when the latter admits loudly and intelligibly the supremacy of the white man's values. In the period of decolonization, the colonized masses mock at these very values, insult them, and vomit them up.

. . . All that the native has seen in his country is that they can freely arrest him, beat him, starve him: and no professor of ethics, no priest has ever come to be beaten in his place, nor to share their bread with him. As far as the native is concerned, morality is very concrete; it is to silence the settler's defiance, to break his flaunting violence—in a word, to put him out of the picture. . . .

. . . The colonialist bourgeoisie, in its narcissistic dialogue, expounded by the members of its universities, had in fact deeply implanted in the minds of the colonized intellectual that the essential qualities remain eternal in spite of all the blunders men may make: the essential

qualities of the West, of course. . . . Now it so happens that during the struggle for liberation, at the moment that the native intellectual comes into touch again with his people, . . . [a]ll the Mediterranean values—the triumph of the human individual, of clarity, and of beauty—. . . are revealed as worthless, simply because they have nothing to do with the concrete conflict in which the people is engaged.

Individualism is the first to disappear. . . . The colonialist bourgeoisie had hammered into the native's mind the idea of a society of individuals where each person shuts himself up in his own subjectivity, and whose only wealth is individual thought. Now the native who has the opportunity to return to the people during the struggle for freedom will discover the falseness of this theory. The very forms of organization of the struggle will suggest to him a different vocabulary. Brother, sister, friend—these are words outlawed by the colonialist bourgeoisie, because for them my brother is my purse, my friend is part of my scheme for getting on. The native intellectual . . . will . . . discover the substance of village assemblies, the cohesion of people's committees, and the extraordinary fruitfulness of local meetings and groupments. Henceforward, the interests of one will be the interests of all, for in concrete fact *everyone* will be discovered by the troops, *everyone* will be massacred—or *everyone* will be saved.

Source: Frantz Fanon, *The Wretched of the Earth* (New York: Grove, 1968), pp. 40–47.

was also much interest among westerners in the work of Frantz Fanon (1925–1961), a black intellectual from Martinique who became identified especially with the cause of the Algerian rebels. In *The Wretched of the Earth* (1961), Fanon found the West

spiritually exhausted and called on the peoples of the non-Western world to go their own way, based on their own values and traditions. (See the box, "Encounters with the West: The Legacy of European Colonialism.")

Economic Integration and the Coming of the European Union

As the old colonialism increasingly fell into disrepute, many found in European unity the best prospect for the future. Although hopes for full-scale political unity were soon frustrated, the movement for European integration gradually achieved significant fruit in the economic sphere, especially through the European Economic Community (EEC), or Common Market, established in 1957.

The impetus for economic integration came especially from a new breed of "Eurocrats"—technocrats with a supranational, or pan-European, outlook. Two remarkable French leaders, Jean Monnet and Robert Schuman (1886–1963), set the pattern. Schuman came from Lorraine, which had passed between France and Germany four times between 1870 and 1945. After serving as a German officer in World War I, he was elected to the French Chamber of Deputies in 1919 as Lorraine was returned to France. Monnet, by contrast, served as an official of the League of Nations while a young man just after World War I. He quickly became convinced that the League was too much a collection of existing, unequal nations; peace and cooperation required stronger rules and institutions to transcend parochial national interests.

As French foreign minister after World War II, Schuman was responsible for a 1950 plan to coordinate French and German production of coal and steel. The Schuman Plan quickly encompassed Italy and the Benelux countries to become the European Coal and Steel Community (ECSC) in 1951. Monnet served as the ECSC's first president. From this position, he pushed for more thoroughgoing economic integration, and the successes of the ECSC led directly to the Common Market. (See the box, "Practical Thinking and European Integration.")

The quest for European integration was boosted by the 1956 Suez crisis, which dramatized Europe's dependence on Middle Eastern oil. In light of this long-term vulnerability, economic cooperation seemed essential to the very survival of Europe. It helped, too, that in 1957 the Soviet Union launched *Sputnik I,* the first artificial satellite, suggesting that unless the nations of Western Europe could work together, they were in danger of falling ever further behind the superpowers in advanced technology.

In March 1957, leaders of France, Germany, Italy, Belgium, the Netherlands, and Luxembourg signed the Treaty of Rome, establishing the Common Market, or EEC. Subsequently ratified by the parliaments of the member nations, the treaty took effect on January 1, 1958. Over the next four decades the EEC's membership gradually expanded, encompassing Denmark, Ireland, and Britain in 1973, Greece in 1981, Spain and Portugal in 1986, and Austria, Finland, and Sweden in 1995 (Map 29.2).

The immediate aim of the EEC was to facilitate trade by eliminating customs duties within the Common Market and establishing a common tariff on imports from the rest of the world. For each member of the EEC, tariff reduction entailed the advantage of access to wider markets abroad, but also the risks of new competition in its own domestic market. So it was hard to be sure who might gain and who might lose from the move toward a common market. However, the EEC proved advantageous to so many that tariff reduction proceeded well ahead of schedule. By 1968 the last internal tariffs had been eliminated.

With tariffs dropping, trade among the member countries nearly doubled between 1958 and 1962. French exports of automobiles and chemicals to Germany increased more than eightfold. Partly because the increasing competition stimulated initiative and productivity, industrial production within the EEC increased at a robust annual rate of 7.6 percent during those years.

After the merger of the governing institutions of the several European supranational organizations in 1967, the term *European Community* (EC) and later *European Union* (EU) came to replace the "Common Market" to indicate the institutional web that had emerged since the launching of the European Coal and Steel Community in 1951. This broadening of the EEC did not, however, occur without vigorous debate.

The goal of the Common Market—to enable goods, capital, and labor to move freely among the member countries—required some coordination of the social and economic policies of the member states. Thus state sovereignty became an important issue. To what extent was the Common Market to be a new whole, greater than the sum of

Practical Thinking and European Integration

Jean Monnet insisted that European unity would grow not from idealistic pronouncements but from technical solutions to specific problems, taken one at a time. In the following passages from his memoirs, he outlines the thinking that led him to help create the European Coal and Steel Community, which proved a springboard for the Common Market and, eventually, the European Union.

In places like London, New York, and Washington, where the big decisions are made, my first talks have always been with people who cannot afford to make mistakes—bankers, industrialists, lawyers, and newspapermen. What others say may be colored by imagination, ambition, or doctrine. I certainly respect their influence, but I base my judgement on the wisdom of practical men. . . .

By the end of 1949 . . . French production could look forward to a more settled future: but other problems would soon arise out of the very achievements that [the new French planning authority] had helped to make possible. It was at that time, I well remember, that I came to realize the limits of what any one nation could do. The French could not become modern or great by themselves. . . .

Looking back on this mid-century period, one can hardly fail to be struck by the extraordinary ferment in men's minds about the idea of European unity. . . . [I]ndeed, the vocabulary and arguments still used on the subject today were already current then. But they had nothing to do with action . . . , and I found it hard to take much interest. . . .

. . . Experience had taught me that one cannot act in general terms, starting from a vague concept, but that anything becomes possible as soon as one can concentrate on one precise point which leads on to everything else. . . . Unity would gradually be created by the momentum of a first achievement. Our efforts must therefore be concentrated on the very point about which disagreements had come to a head. . . .

If only the French could lose their fear of German industrial domination, then the greatest obstacle to a united Europe would be removed. A solution which would put French industry on the same footing as German industry, while freeing the latter from the discrimination born of defeat—that would restore the economic and political preconditions for the mutual understanding so vital to Europe as a whole. It could, in fact, become the germ of European unity. . . .

The joint resources of France and Germany lay essentially in their coal and steel, distributed unevenly but in complementary fashion over a triangular area artificially divided by historical frontiers. . . . Coal and steel were at once the key to economic power and the raw materials for forging weapons of war. This double role gave them immense symbolic significance. . . . To pool them across frontiers would reduce their malign prestige and turn them instead into a guarantee of peace.

Source: Jean Monnet, *Memoirs* (Garden City, N.Y.: Doubleday, 1978), pp. 271, 277, 282–283, 286, 292–293.

its parts, as opposed to a mere federation of existing states?

In the mid-1960s President de Gaulle of France forced some of the underlying uncertainties about the Common Market to the fore. Though he had willingly turned from the old colonialism, de Gaulle was not prepared to compromise French sovereignty, and he was not persuaded that supranational integration offered the best course for postwar Europe. With the end of the Algerian War in 1962, de Gaulle's France began playing an assertively independent role in international affairs. Thus, for example, de Gaulle developed an independent French nuclear force,

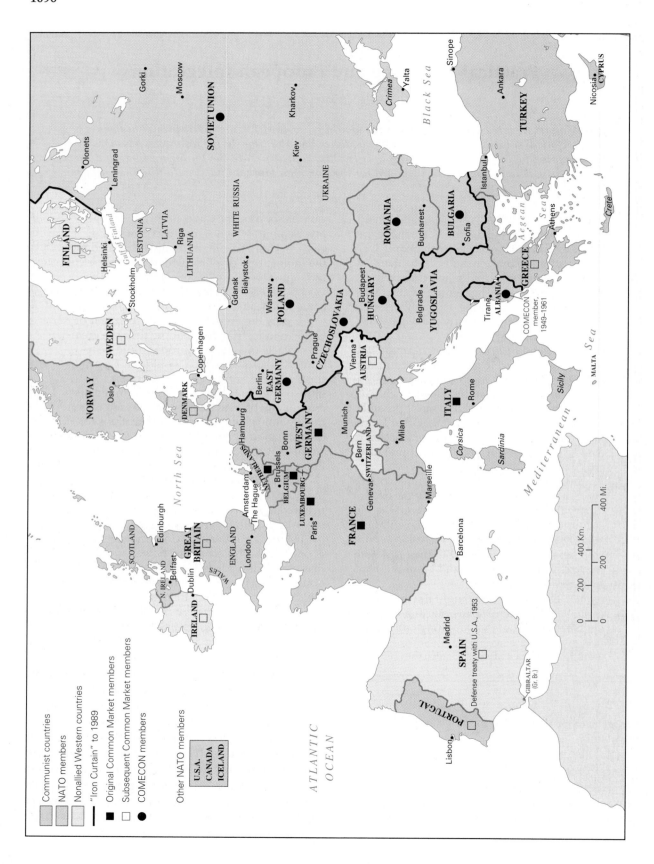

Communist countries

NATO members

Nonallied Western countries

"Iron Curtain" to 1989

Original Common Market members

Subsequent Common Market members

COMECON members

| U.S.A. | CANADA | ICELAND |

Other NATO members

■ □ ●

COMECON member, 1949–1961

Defense treaty with U.S.A. 1953

SOVIET UNION

Moscow •
Gorki •
Olonets •
Leningrad •
Kharkov •
Kiev •
WHITE RUSSIA
UKRAINE
Crimea
Yalta •
Sinope •
Black Sea

FINLAND
Helsinki •
Stockholm •
SWEDEN
NORWAY
Oslo •
Gulf of Finland
ESTONIA
LATVIA
Riga •
LITHUANIA

Copenhagen •
DENMARK
Hamburg •
Berlin •
EAST GERMANY
Gdansk •
Bialystok •
Warsaw •
POLAND
Prague •
CZECHOSLOVAKIA
Bonn •
WEST GERMANY
Munich •
Vienna •
AUSTRIA
Budapest •
HUNGARY
Bern •
SWITZERLAND
Belgrade •
YUGOSLAVIA
Bucharest •
ROMANIA
Sofia •
BULGARIA
Tiranë •
ALBANIA
GREECE
Athens •
Istanbul •
TURKEY
Ankara •
Nicosia •
CYPRUS
Aegean Sea
Crete

NETHERLANDS
Amsterdam •
The Hague •
Brussels •
BELGIUM
LUXEMBOURG
Paris •
FRANCE
Geneva •
Milan •
ITALY
Rome •
Marseille •
Corsica
Sardinia
Sicily
Mediterranean Sea
MALTA

North Sea
GREAT BRITAIN
SCOTLAND
Edinburgh •
ENGLAND
London •
WALES
N. IRELAND
Belfast •
Dublin •
IRELAND

ATLANTIC OCEAN

SPAIN
Madrid •
Barcelona •
GIBRALTAR (Gr. Br.)
PORTUGAL
Lisbon •

400 Mi.
400 Km.
200
200
0
0

curtailed the French role in NATO, and recognized the communist People's Republic of China.

This determination to assert France's sovereignty inevitably led to friction between de Gaulle and the supranational Eurocrats of the Common Market. Matters came to a head in 1965, when a confrontation developed over agricultural policy. The immediate result was a compromise, but de Gaulle's tough stance served to check the increasing supranationalism evident in the Common Market until then. As the economic context became more difficult during the 1970s, it became still harder to maintain the cohesion of the EEC. So though the Common Market proved an important departure, it did not overcome the older forms of national sovereignty or give Western Europe a new world role during the first decades after World War II.

THE SOVIET UNION AND THE COMMUNIST BLOC

By the late 1950s, there were increasing concerns in the West that the Soviet Union, though rigid and inhumane in important respects, might have significant advantages in the race with the capitalist democracies. While still making jokes about goods "made in Japan," Westerners worried about producing enough scientists and engineers to match the Soviets. With the Great Depression still in memory, some economists held that central planning might prove as efficient as capitalism.

Nonetheless, flaws in the political and economic system that had emerged under Stalin continued in the Soviet Union, and its system of satellites in east-central Europe presented new dilemmas. Efforts to make the Soviet system more flexible after Stalin's death in 1953 proved sporadic at best, and the Soviet suppression of the reform movement in Czechoslovakia during the "Prague Spring" of 1968 confirmed the rigidity of the Soviet system.

Dilemmas of the Soviet System in Postwar Europe

The Soviet Union had suffered enormously in leading the victory over Nazi Germany. Especially in the more developed western part of the country, thousands of factories and even whole towns lay destroyed, and there were severe shortages of everything from labor to housing. Yet the developing cold war seemed to require that military spending remain high.

At the same time, the Soviet Union faced the challenge of solidifying the new system of satellite states it had put together in east-central Europe. Most of the region had no desirable interwar past to try to reclaim, and thus there was widespread sentiment for significant change, including nationalization of industry. Even in Czechoslovakia, which had been the most prosperous and democratic state in the region, considerable nationalization was completed *before* the communist takeover in 1948. And whatever integration into the new Soviet bloc might mean politically, it was not clear in the late 1940s that it had to be economically disadvantageous over the long term. The Soviet system seemed to have proven itself in standing up to the Nazis, and many believed that a socialist economic system could be made to work. So a measure of idealism and enthusiasm surrounded postwar reconstruction even in the satellite states of east-central Europe.

Partly in response to U.S. initiatives in Western Europe, the Soviets sought to mold the new communist states into a secure, coordinated bloc of allies. In the economic sphere, the Soviets founded a new organization, COMECON, as part of their effort to lead the economies of the satellite states away from their earlier ties to the West and toward the Soviet Union (see Map 29.2). Thus, for example, whereas only 7 percent of Poland's foreign trade had been with the Soviet Union before the war, by 1951 the figure was 58 percent. Through such mechanisms as artificial pricing of imports and exports, these new economic relationships often entailed outright exploitation of the satellite states for the benefit of the Soviet Union.

Map 29.2 Military Alliances and Multinational Economic Groupings in the Era of the Cold War The cold war split was reflected especially in the two military alliances: NATO, formed in 1949, and the Warsaw Pact, formed in 1955. Each side also had its own multinational economic organization, but the membership of the EEC, or Common Market, was not identical to that of NATO. Although communist, Yugoslavia remained outside Soviet-led organizations, as did Albania for part of the period.

In the military-diplomatic sphere, the Soviets countered NATO in 1955 by bringing the Soviet bloc countries together in a formal alliance, the Warsaw Pact, which provided for a joint military command and mutual military assistance. The Warsaw Pact established a new basis for the continuing presence of Soviet troops in the satellite states, but the tensions within the Soviet-dominated system in east-central Europe soon raised questions about what the pact meant.

From the start, Yugoslavia had been a point of vulnerability for the Soviet system. Communist-led partisans under Tito had liberated Yugoslavia from the Axis on their own, and they had not needed the Red Army to begin constructing a new communist regime. Tito was willing to work with the Soviets, but because he had his own legitimacy, he could be considerably more independent than those elsewhere whose power rested on Soviet support. Thus the Soviets deemed it essential to bring Tito to heel, lest his example encourage too much independence in the other communist states. When Soviet demands, including control of the Yugoslav police and army, became intolerably meddlesome from the Yugoslav point of view, Tito broke with the Soviet Union altogether in 1948. Yugoslavia then began developing a more flexible socialist economic system, with greater scope for local initiatives. Soviet leaders worried that others, too, might seek their own directions, causing the Soviet satellite system to fall apart.

Stalin's initial response to Tito's defection in 1948 was a crackdown on potential opponents throughout the Soviet bloc. In the Soviet Union itself, a major target was the army, which enjoyed great prestige after its victory in World War II. Its top commander, Marshal Georgi Zhukov, was reassigned from Berlin to an obscure post. As during the 1930s, Stalin relied especially on the secret police, which executed those suspected of deviation, inspiring fear even among those closest to him.

As arrest and execution of communist leaders continued in the satellite states, opposition strikes and demonstrations developed as well, finally reaching a crisis point in East Germany in 1953. The East German communist leader, Walter Ulbricht (1893–1973), was worried that the cold war maneuvering of the two superpowers might undermine his regime. As the United States pressed West Germany to rearm and join NATO, some Soviet leaders concluded that Soviet interests would be better served by a reunified but strictly neutral and disarmed Germany than by the integration of West Germany into a military alliance against the Soviet Union. German reunification, however, would entail free elections, which the East German Communists could not hope to win. Seeking to head off any such scenario, Ulbricht intensified the industrial development of East Germany, to make his country too valuable an economic ally for the Soviet Union to sacrifice. The resulting pressure on labor produced growing opposition, which came dramatically to a head in East Berlin in June 1953.

A workers' protest against a provision to increase output or face wage cuts promptly led to political demands, including free elections and the withdrawal of Soviet troops. Disturbances spread from East Berlin to the other major East German cities. Though this spontaneous uprising was not well coordinated, Soviet troops and tanks had to intervene to put down the movement and save the Ulbricht government. The East German example helped stimulate strikes and antigovernment demonstrations elsewhere in the Soviet bloc, convincing Soviet leaders that something had to give. But at this point, shortly after Stalin's death, the leadership of the Soviet Union was still being sorted out.

De-Stalinization Under Khrushchev, 1955–1964

Although a struggle for succession followed Stalin's death, the nature of the struggle itself forecasted a turn from the extremes of Stalinism. The political infighting involved a reasonable degree of give and take, as opposed to terror and violence. To be sure, the contestants quickly ganged up on the hated secret police chief, Lavrenti Beria, who was tried and executed within months, but this was part of their agreed-upon effort to limit the role of the secret police. Moreover, although one of the eventual losers was sent to Siberia to run a power station and the other was made ambassador to Outer Mongolia, it was a major departure that the winner, Nikita Khrushchev (1894–1971), had neither of them exiled or executed.

Although he had not been Stalin's heir apparent, Khrushchev gradually established himself as the new leader by building up patronage networks and playing off factions. Slightly crude, even something of a buffoon, he won out by 1955 partly because his opponents repeatedly underestimated him. Although his period of leadership was brief, it was eventful indeed—and in some ways the Soviet system's best chance for renewal.

At a closed session of the Soviet Communist party's twentieth national congress in February 1956, Khrushchev made a dramatic late-night speech denouncing the criminal excesses of the Stalinist system and the "cult of personality" that had developed around Stalin himself. (See the box, "Denouncing the Crimes of Stalinism.") Khrushchev's immediate aim was to undercut his hard-line rivals, but he also insisted that key features of Stalinism had amounted to an unnecessary deviation from Marxism-Leninism. So the advent of Khrushchev suggested there might be liberalization and reform.

At the same time, however, the growing popular discontent in the satellite states placed the whole system in crisis. In the face of the East German uprising of 1953, the Soviets backed off from hard-line Stalinism, making room for more moderate communists they had previously shunned, like the Hungarian Imre Nagy (1896–1958) and the Pole Wladislaw Gomulka (1905–1982). Khrushchev even sought to patch things up with Tito, exchanging visits with him in 1955 and 1956. In his speech to the party congress in 1956, Khrushchev condemned Stalin's treatment of Tito and suggested that different countries might take different routes to communism.

To keep their new system together, the Soviets apparently had to allow greater flexibility among the satellite states. But could liberalization be contained within the larger framework of Soviet leadership, or were openness and innovation bound to threaten the system itself? In Poland beginning in June 1956, strikes against wage cuts took on a political character, finally provoking the intervention of Soviet troops by October. Nonetheless, the Soviets found they could work with the moderate communist Gomulka, who favored reform within Poland but was quite loyal to the Warsaw Pact as a bulwark against Germany. By the fall of 1956, however, the events in Poland had helped stimulate comparable demonstrations in Hungary, where reformers led by the moderate communist Nagy had taken advantage of the liberalizing atmosphere by mid-1956 to begin making dramatic changes.

THE ERA OF THE COLD WAR

Year	Event
1947	Marshall Plan announced
1949	Formation of NATO
1951	Formation of the European Coal and Steel Community
1953	Death of Stalin
	Workers' revolt in East Germany
1955	West Germany joins NATO
	Warsaw Pact
1956	Khrushchev speech to the twentieth party congress
1956	Suez crisis
	Hungarian reform movement crushed
1957	*Sputnik I* launched
	Treaty of Rome establishes Common Market
1958	Beginning of Fifth Republic under de Gaulle
1959	Bad Godesberg: reorientation of German socialism
1961	Berlin Wall erected
1962	Cuban missile crisis
1964	Ouster of Nikita Khrushchev
1968	Days of May uprising in France
	Prague Spring reform movement crushed
1969	Willy Brandt becomes West German chancellor
1973	First OPEC oil crisis begins
1978	Kidnapping and assassination of Aldo Moro in Italy
1981	François Mitterand elected French president

The Hungarians dismantled their collective farms and moved toward a multiparty system and democratic coalition government. Then they called for Soviet troops to withdraw, to enable Hungary to leave the Warsaw Pact and become neutral. These were not changes within the system, but changes that would undermine the system itself. So when a democratic coalition government was set up by November, the Soviets used tanks to

Denouncing the Crimes of Stalinism

In his speech to the Soviet Communist party's national congress in 1956, Nikita Khrushchev repeatedly contrasted Stalin with Lenin, seeking to show that Stalinism had been an unfortunate and unnecessary deviation, not the logical outcome of the communist revolution. Khrushchev's denunciation of Stalin produced considerable commotion in the hall.

[I]t is impermissible and foreign to the spirit of Marxism-Leninism to elevate one person, to transform him into a superman possessing supernatural characteristics akin to those of a god. . . .

Such a belief about a man, and specifically about Stalin, was cultivated among us for many years. . . .

While ascribing great importance to the role of the leaders and organizers of the masses, Lenin at the same time mercilessly stigmatized every manifestation of the cult of the individual. . . .

Stalin originated the concept "enemy of the people." This term . . . made possible the usage of the most cruel repression, violating all norms of revolutionary legality, against anyone who in any way disagreed with Stalin, against those who were only suspected of hostile intent, against those who had bad reputations. This concept, "enemy of the people," actually eliminated the possibility of any kind of ideological fight or the making of one's views known on this or that issue, even those of a practical character. In the main, and in actuality, the only proof of guilt used, against all norms of current legal science, was the "confession" of the accused himself; and, as subsequent probing proved, "confessions" were acquired through physical torture against the accused. . . .

Arbitrary behavior by one person encouraged and permitted arbitrariness in others. Mass arrests and deportations of many thousands of people, execution without trial and without normal investigation created conditions of insecurity, fear and even desperation. . . .

Lenin used severe methods only in the most necessary cases, when the exploiting classes were still in existence and were vigorously opposing the revolution, when the struggle for survival was decidedly assuming the sharpest forms, even including a civil war. Stalin, on the other hand, used extreme methods and mass repressions at a time when the revolution was already victorious, when the Soviet state was strengthened, when the exploiting classes were already liquidated. . . . It is clear that here Stalin showed in a whole series of cases his intolerance, his brutality and his abuse of power. . . .

Source: The Anti-Stalin Campaign and International Communism: A Selection of Documents, edited by the Russian Institute, Columbia University (New York: Columbia University Press, 1956), pp. 2, 4, 12–14, 17, 20–21.

crush the Hungarian reform movement. Thousands were killed during the fighting or were executed, and 200,000 Hungarians fled to the West.

Yet even the crackdown in Hungary did not mean a return to the old days of Stalinist rigidity throughout the Soviet bloc. The Soviets understood that the system had to become more palatable, but they had made it clear that liberalization was to be kept within certain limits. It could not challenge the system itself, especially communist monopoly rule and the Warsaw Pact.

Hungary's new leader, János Kádár (b. 1912), collectivized agriculture more fully than before, but he also engineered a measure of economic decentralization, allowing scope for local initiatives and market mechanisms. There was eventually an amnesty for political prisoners, as well as considerable liberalization in cultural life, so that Hungary came to enjoy freer contact with the West than the other satellites.

Even where hard-liners remained predominant, as in East Germany and Romania, differences

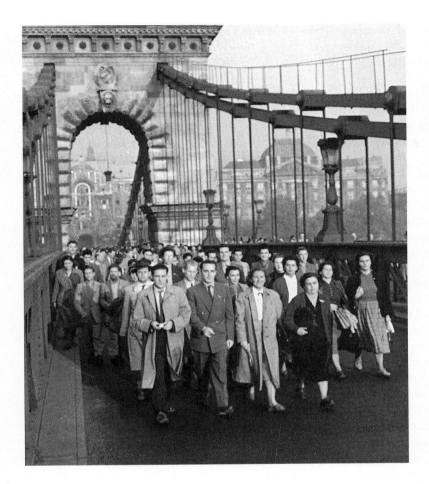

Revolution and Restoration in Hungary Led by students and faculty from the Karl Marx University of Economics, Hungarians march across the Chain Bridge in Budapest on October 23, 1956, initiating the revolutionary phase of the movement for change in communist Hungary. Within two weeks, a Soviet-led crackdown, including shelling by Soviet tanks, had crushed the revolution, inflicting 27,000 casualties on the Hungarians. *(MTI/Eastfoto/Sovfoto)*

arose. Although Romania under Nicolae Ceausescu (1918–1989) remained one of the most repressive communist states, it grew relatively independent from the Soviet Union in matters of foreign and economic policy. And Ceausescu fostered autonomy by playing up the ethnic difference between the Romanians, Latin in background, and the Slavic peoples of much of the Soviet bloc.

By contrast, East Germany's communist leaders had every reason *not* to try to distance themselves from the Soviets by playing up nationalism and distinctiveness. Walter Ulbricht, who remained in power until his retirement in 1971, concentrated on central planning and heavy industry in orthodox fashion, but he made the East German economy the most successful in the Soviet bloc.

Still, because that economic growth was built on low wages, East German workers were tempted to immigrate to West Germany as the West German economic miracle gleamed ever brighter during the 1950s. The special position of Berlin, in

the heart of East Germany yet still divided among the occupying powers, made such immigration relatively easy, and 2.6 million East Germans left for the west between 1950 and 1962. With a population of only 17.1 million, East Germany could not afford to let this hemorrhaging continue. Thus, in August 1961 the Ulbricht regime erected the Berlin Wall, which would long serve as a grim reminder that despite periodic thaws in East-West relations, the iron curtain remained in place.

From Liberalization to Stagnation

The most intense phase of the cold war ended with Stalin's death in 1953. In his speech to the twentieth party congress in 1956, Khrushchev repudiated the previous Soviet tenet that the very existence of Western capitalist imperialism made a military showdown with the communist world inevitable. During his visit to the United States in 1959, he stressed that the ongoing competition between the two sides could be peaceful. However, despite summit conferences and sporadic efforts at better relations, friction between the Soviet Union and the United States continued.

Indeed, a new peak of tension was reached in October 1962 when the Soviets placed missiles in Cuba, which had developed close ties with the Soviet Union after the 1959 revolution led by Fidel Castro (b. 1926). Although the United States had its own offensive missiles in Turkey, adjacent to the Soviet Union, the Soviet attempt to base missiles in Cuba seemed an intolerable challenge. For several days, military confrontation appeared a distinct possibility, but President John F. Kennedy (1917–1963) managed an effective combination of resistance and restraint in responding to the Soviet move. The Soviets withdrew their missiles in exchange for a U.S. promise not to seek to overthrow the communist government in Cuba. The outcome was essentially a victory for the United States, which retained its offensive missile capacity adjacent to the Soviet Union. The Cuban missile crisis was the closest the superpowers came to direct armed confrontation during the cold war period.

At the same time, it became increasingly clear that international communism was not the monolithic force it had once seemed. The most dramatic indication was the Sino-Soviet split, which developed during the 1950s as the communists under Mao Zedong solidified their regime in China. In the long struggle that led to their victory in 1949, the Chinese communists had often had no choice but to go their own way, and during the 1940s, especially, Stalin had been willing to subordinate any concern for their cause to Soviet national interests. After taking power in 1949, the Chinese communists pursued their own path to development without worrying about the Soviet model. With some justification, the Soviets feared that the independent, innovative Chinese might be prepared to challenge Soviet leadership in international communism. By the early 1960s, the communist Chinese path had become appealing especially in the non-Western world, though it attracted dissident communists in the West as well. The split within world communism, and the antagonism between China and the Soviet Union, added another layer of uncertainty to the cold war era.

As a domestic leader, Khrushchev proved mercurial and erratic, but he was an energetic innovator, willing to experiment. He jettisoned the worst features of the police state apparatus, including some of the infamous Siberian prison camps, and offered several amnesties for prisoners. He also liberalized cultural life and gave workers greater freedom to move from one job to another. The economic planning apparatus was decentralized somewhat, affording more scope for local initiatives and placing greater emphasis on consumer goods. The government expanded medical and educational facilities and, between 1955 and 1964, doubled the nation's housing stock, substantially alleviating a severe housing shortage.

As part of the domestic thaw in the Soviet Union after Stalin, divorce became easier and abortion was legalized. Women received liberal provisions for maternity leave as well as measures to ensure equal access to higher education and the professions. Still, women were concentrated in lower-paying occupations and rarely rose to the top echelons. To be sure, they were prominent in medicine in the Soviet Union, but Soviet doctors did not have the status—or the incomes—their counterparts enjoyed in the West.

Though living standards remained relatively low, Khrushchev's reforms helped improve the lives of ordinary people by the early 1960s. Even his claim in 1961 that the Soviet Union would surpass the Western standard of living within twenty years did not seem an idle boast. After all, the Soviets had launched *Sputnik I* in 1957, assuming the lead in the ensuing space race. They followed by putting the first human into space in 1961. Such achievements suggested that even ordinary Soviet citizens had reason for optimism. More generally, the communist regimes throughout the Soviet bloc entered the 1960s with confidence after having achieved excellent rates of economic growth during the 1950s.

Yet Khrushchev had made enemies with his erratic reform effort, and this led to his forced retirement in October 1964. After the unending experiment in the economy, his opponents wanted to consolidate, to return to stability and predictability. But not until 1968 did it become clear that the liberalization and innovation of the Khrushchev era were over.

By early 1968 a significant reform movement had developed within the Communist party in Prague, the capital of Czechoslovakia. Determined to avoid the fate of the Hungarian effort in 1956, the reformers emphasized that Czechoslovakia was to remain a communist state and a full member of the Warsaw Pact. But within that framework, they felt, it should be possible to invite freer cultural expression, to democratize the Communist party's procedures, and to broaden participation in public life.

However, efforts to reassure the Soviets about the limits of the movement's aims alienated some of its supporters, who stepped up their demands as a result. As earlier in Hungary, the demand for change seemed to outstrip the intentions of the movement's organizers. Finally, Soviet leaders in Moscow decided to crack down. In August 1968 Soviet tanks moved into Prague to crush the reform movement—precisely what its leaders had been seeking to avoid.

The end of the "Prague Spring" closed the era of relative flexibility and cautious innovation in the Soviet bloc that had begun as early as 1953. A period of relative stagnation followed under Leonid Brezhnev (1906–1982), a careful, consensus-seeking bureaucrat. Now setting the tone was the "Brezhnev doctrine," which specified that the Soviet Union would help established communist regimes remain in power against any "counter-revolutionary" threat. This blanket statement helped chill reform hopes during the years that followed. Even as efforts toward détente and arms control made news during the 1970s, this Soviet willingness to intervene, with military force when necessary, in the affairs of the satellite states suggested the ongoing fragility of the whole Soviet system.

Poland, too, experienced a reform effort in 1968, but it was initiated by students and failed to attract the support of workers, who were largely loyal to the communist regime. Though quick to infringe on "bourgeois" civil liberties, the Polish communist government—like others in the Soviet bloc—was eager for working-class support. Thus it provided subsidized food, housing, and medical care. But to pay the bill the government had to borrow from foreigners. The loans were ostensibly to help Poland modernize, and thereby to boost efficiency. But in fact the money was used for immediate consumption, for inefficient state-owned companies, and for bureaucratic graft. Despite the infusion of capital, productivity was actually declining in Poland by the end of the 1970s, and the problem was becoming clear to creditors. So even in Poland, where the communist regime seemed

generally to satisfy the workers, its way of doing so was increasingly artificial—and unsustainable.

After the successes of the 1950s and early 1960s, the Soviet Union was finding it ever harder to match the West in economic growth and technological innovation. And despite periodic efforts at economic reform, the satellite states did not do appreciably better with the central planning model. Ordinary people became increasingly frustrated as the communist economic system proved erratic in providing even the most basic consumer goods.

Frustration grew especially among women, who seemed to bear a disproportionate share of the burdens. Women were more likely to be employed outside the home in the Soviet bloc than in the West. For example, around 90 percent of adult women in the Soviet Union and East Germany had paid jobs outside the home by 1980. In 1984, 50 percent of the East German work force was female, compared with 39 percent in West Germany. Yet not only were women concentrated in jobs with low pay and prestige in the communist countries, but they also still bore the major responsibility for child care, housework, and shopping. They had few of the labor-saving devices available in the West, and they often had to spend hours in line to buy ordinary consumer items. Dissatisfaction among women fed a new underground protest movement that began developing in the Soviet bloc in the mid-1970s—a further indication of the growing strains in the overall system.

But what would it take for these strains to produce a full-scale crisis? Although often secretive and arrogant, the Soviet Union remained preoccupied with its place in the postwar international order. It had long wanted some sort of international conference that would regularize the status of East Germany and confirm the western border of Poland. When, in 1969, Willy Brandt became West Germany's chancellor and began pursuing his *Ostpolitik*, or opening to the East, the Soviets got their chance. But the eventual outcome was hardly what they envisioned.

In 1975, high-level representatives of thirty-five countries, including all of the Soviet bloc, came together in Helsinki, Finland, in the most prominent of the international meetings that Brandt's policy made possible. The parties recognized East Germany and all borders, precisely according to the Soviet script. But they also adopted a detailed agreement on human rights, which came to be known as the Helsinki Accords. And that agreement, merely symbolic in one sense, ended up providing a foundation for forces that would eventually bring the whole Soviet system crashing down.

DEMOCRACY AND ITS DISCONTENTS, 1968 AND AFTER

The year 1968, which saw the end of the "Prague Spring," proved a turning point in Western Europe as well. By this point, a generation after World War II, democracy seemed to have succeeded remarkably, and, indeed, it would win further successes in the 1970s as Greece, Spain, and Portugal turned from authoritarianism to democratic government. But during the late 1960s it became clear that, despite the economic prosperity and political stability, political alienation had been building in Western Europe. And though they came to be exaggerated, the dissatisfactions that began erupting in 1968 fundamentally changed the tone of politics in Europe and the West. The economic difficulties that began in 1973 only added fuel to an already smoldering fire.

Democratic Consolidation and Political Alienation

Observing the success of democracy in the most developed parts of Western Europe, Spain, Portugal, and Greece established workable democracies after periods of dictatorial rule. Following the death of Francisco Franco in 1975, almost forty years after his triumph in the Spanish civil war, democracy returned to Spain more smoothly than most had dared hope. Franco established that a restoration of the monarchy would follow his death, and King Juan Carlos (r. 1975–) served as an effective catalyst in the transition to democracy.

When the first democratic elections in Spain since the civil war were held in 1977, the extremes of both left and right did poorly. The big winners were a democratic centrist party and a moderate socialist party. The Socialists won a parliamentary majority in the next elections, in 1982, and a moderate Socialist replaced the centrist leader as prime minister. The transition suggested that Spain had quickly found its way to an effective two-party system. Meanwhile, the new constitution of 1978 dismantled what was left of the Franco system so

that, for example, Catholicism was no longer recognized as the official religion of the Spanish state.

A comparable transition from military rule to democracy took place in Portugal and Greece. Like Spain, each sought to help cement a long-term commitment to democracy by seeking entry into the European Economic Community, and each was accepted by the end of the 1970s. For all three, EEC membership became a pillar of the solidifying democratic consensus.

At the same time, however, political disaffection threatened the consensus in the more established democracies of the European continent. The most dramatic eruption of radical protest was the "Days of May" uprising that shook France during May 1968. The movement was partly a reaction against the priorities of de Gaulle's Fifth Republic—especially the preoccupation with France's international role. But it was also a response to the unevenness in the modernization effort that had seemed necessary to support that role. The commitment to technocratic values had produced impressive economic growth, but many ordinary people felt left out of France's economic success. Despite all the growth, public services had been neglected, and problems in such areas as housing and education continued—or even worsened.

Higher education in France affords a telling example. Enrollment in French universities more than doubled between 1939 and 1960, then more than doubled again between 1960 and 1967. Apart from a few highly selective *grandes écoles*, the institutions of the state-run university system were open to anyone who passed a standard examination, and it was not considered politically feasible to limit enrollments by restricting access. Instead, the government tried to build to keep up with demand—thereby creating vast, impersonal institutions with professors increasingly inaccessible to students. But overcrowding persisted, and the value of a university degree diminished, leaving graduates with uncertain job prospects.

The uprising of 1968 started with university students, who sought to reach out to others, especially industrial workers, by offering a broad critique of the present system. But union activists and workers generally declined to join the movement, and the students ended up settling for relatively limited concessions. Still, the uprising made it clear that the university system needed a complete overhaul—and that students and faculty had to be involved in the changes. Over the next several years, the Education Ministry carried out reforms, breaking existing institutions into smaller units, with more local control over budgets and instructional methods. At the same time, however, student and faculty participation in institutional governance tended to politicize French universities, some of which became communist strongholds, others bastions of the right. And this caused friction with the education bureaucrats in Paris.

At first glance, the parties of the Marxist left might appear the likely beneficiaries of the popular discontent that emerged during the late 1960s. But the effort to come to terms with the events of 1968 deepened divisions within the Communist party and initiated a renewed disenchantment with Marxism among French intellectuals. Unable to transcend long-standing class categories and to encompass the aspirations of those, like the students, who were newly disaffected, French communism increasingly seemed old and stale. However, the French Socialist party gained dramatically during the 1970s. Claiming the mantle of the new left that had emerged in 1968, the Socialists appealed to those, especially young people, who believed the promise of that year could still be translated into substantial change.

The Oil Crisis and the Changing Economic Framework

As the political situation in Western Europe became more volatile, events outside Europe made it clear how interdependent the world had become—and that the West did not hold all the trump cards. In the fall of 1973, Egypt and Syria attacked Israel, seeking to recover the losses they had suffered in a brief war in 1967. Although the assault failed, the Arab nations of the oil-rich Middle East came together in the aftermath to retaliate against the Western bloc for supporting Israel. By restricting the output and distribution of the oil its members controlled, the Arab-led Organization of Petroleum Exporting Countries (OPEC) produced a sharp increase in oil prices and a severe economic disruption all over the industrialized world. Western Europe, which was heavily dependent on Middle Eastern oil, was especially hard hit. By January 1975 the price of oil was six times what it had been in 1973, before the embargo, and this increase remained a source of inflationary pressure throughout the Western world until the early 1980s.

The immediate European response to the oil embargo dramatized the limits of the economic integration so far achieved through the Common Market. When OPEC imposed especially harsh measures on the Netherlands, which had taken a strong stand in support of Israel, the other nations of the Common Market dealt separately with the cartel rather than stand together.

The 1970s proved to be an unprecedented period of "stagflation"—sharply reduced rates of growth combined with inflation and rising unemployment. The economic miracle that had transformed much of Western Europe had clearly ended, partly because the European economies

Oil, the West, and the World
Led by several oil-rich Arab states, OPEC drove up world oil prices by restricting production during the 1970s. The power of the oil cartel made it clear that decisions by non-Westerners could vitally affect the industrialized West. OPEC delegates are shown here in Algiers in 1975. (*Sygma*)

were subject to growing competition from non-Western countries, most notably Japan. Everywhere the labor movement was suddenly on the defensive in light of increasing global competition, technological change, and high unemployment.

Strains in the Welfare State

A tighter economy made it harder for governments to afford the welfare measures that had helped establish the new political consensus in much of the West since World War II. Although much publicity surrounded the British welfare state, the percentage of the British economy devoted to public expenditure for welfare, housing, and education by the early 1970s—18.2 percent—was about average for the industrialized nations of the West. Sweden had the highest figure at 23.7 percent, and the Swedish case particularly dramatized the problems of managing a welfare state in conditions of economic stringency.

By the early 1970s, 40 percent of Sweden's national income went for taxes to finance the system—the highest rate of taxation in the world. At the same time, Sweden found itself less competitive, both because its wages were so high and because it was not keeping abreast of technological developments. In Sweden, as elsewhere, there were growing doubts that a welfare state could nurture the initiative and productivity needed for success in the increasingly competitive global economy. By 1980 unemployment and efforts to cut government spending led to the most severe labor unrest the country had experienced since the war. Even on the level of everyday life, it seemed that the Swedish model, with its emphasis on societal responsibility, entailed excessive governmental intrusion in the private sphere.

In Britain a dramatic assault on the welfare state began developing at the same time. Until the early 1970s, Britain retained the consensus on the government's role in social welfare that had emerged with the end of the war. But the British economy lagged the others of the industrialized West, then suffered especially during the 1970s. Between 1968 and 1976, the country lost 1 million manufacturing jobs. By the mid-1970s this economic decline threatened to shatter Britain's postwar settlement, because there was no consensus over how to apportion the pain of the necessary austerity measures.

During the 1970s each of Britain's two major political parties made a serious effort to deal with the situation, but neither succeeded, especially because neither could deal effectively with Britain's strong trade unions. The election of the militantly conservative Margaret Thatcher (b. 1925) as Conservative party leader in 1975 proved a turning point, however. When she became prime minister in 1979, it was clear that Britain was embarking on a radically different course.

The Democratic Consensus and Its Limitations

Even where the welfare state was not the immediate bone of contention, discontent with the political consensus led to a variety of new political alignments and expedients, some of them violent. In Italy the Communists responded to economic crisis and political alienation by offering to share power—and responsibility—with the Christian Democrats on the national level for the first time. In 1976, the Communist party's share of the vote in national elections reached an all-time high of 34.4 percent. By the end of the 1970s, however, the Communists' efforts had led nowhere; their share of the vote steadily declined, as did their support among younger people and intellectuals. But the Christian Democrats, too, were losing electoral support by the early 1980s. Their message seemed ever less relevant as Italy became a more secular society. And as the Italian Communists declined, many found it less important to support Christian Democracy as a bulwark against communism.

During the 1970s, frustration with the political immobility that seemed to have neutralized even the established left gave rise to a new wave of terrorism, prominent especially in Italy and Germany. Terrorists in such groups as the Red Brigades in Italy and the Baader-Meinhof gang in Germany assassinated a number of prominent public officials and businessmen, including the long-time Italian Christian Democratic leader Aldo Moro (1916–1978). By the late 1970s, left- and right-wing extremism fed each other, and it was right-wing extremists who were responsible for Italy's most deadly terrorist episode, a bombing in the railway station in Bologna that killed eighty-five people in August 1980.

But political frustration also found productive outlets, as new coalitions developed around newly politicized issues—from abortion to the environment—that had not been associated with the Marxist left. In Germany, the Green movement formed by peace and environmental activists during the late 1970s took pains to avoid acting like a conventional party. Concerned that Germany, with its central location, would end up the devastated battleground in any superpower confrontation, the Greens opposed deployment of additional U.S. missiles on German soil and called for an alternative to the endless arms race. The SPD, as the governing party in an important NATO state, seemed unable to confront this issue and lost members as a result.

Prominent among the new political currents that began emerging around 1968 was the feminist movement, comparable to the earlier movement for women's suffrage. This new movement for "women's liberation" sought equal opportunities for women in education and employment. It was striking, for example, that despite major steps toward equal educational opportunity in postwar France, the country's prestigious engineering schools were still not admitting women in the late 1960s—and would begin doing so only during the 1980s. But feminists also forced new issues onto the political stage, working, for example, to liberalize divorce and abortion laws throughout the Western world. At the same time, women faced new questions after a generation of experience with the activist postwar state. In Britain, where government had sought to free mothers from the necessity of employment outside the home, feminists increasingly saw the welfare state as a major source of what seemed their ongoing second-class status. But the tradeoffs were complex, and a deeper sense of gender issues would become central to public debate and personal choice all over the Western world during the last two decades of the century.

Although the timing varied greatly from country to country, the tendency throughout Western Europe after World War II was toward the consolidation of democracy in some form of two-party system. The domestication of the socialist left was essential to that process. After Willy Brandt became chancellor in 1969, the West German Socialists led the government for thirteen years, finally meeting electoral defeat in 1982. By that point, Socialists and Conservatives agreed on the essentials; there was disagreement only about degrees. The

Socialists had completed the turn to moderation that they began in the late 1950s, leaving Germany essentially with a two-party system. The strength of the Green party, which had first seemed to offer a new political direction, leveled off during the 1980s at 10 to 15 percent of the vote—significant, but hardly a breakthrough.

During the early 1980s, revitalized socialist parties in France, Spain, and Italy marginalized the communists and, for a time, even seemed poised to reorient government. In France François Mitterrand (1916–1996) was elected president in 1981, promising to create the first genuinely democratic socialism. But during the 1980s, he gradually abandoned his talk of socialism in the face of economic and political pressures. By the end of the decade, he was questioning the relevance of long-standing socialist tenets and playing up the virtues of entrepreneurship, the profit mechanism, and free-market competition. The key was that France, like the other industrial democracies, had to operate in an increasingly competitive international economy. The Socialists met defeat in the early 1990s, but they had proven they could work within the system, and, despite their immediate discredit, it seemed likely that they would eventually regain power, taking their turn in a two-party democracy.

SUMMARY

In the decades that followed World War II, a bipolar framework, dominated by the United States and the Soviet Union, shaped world affairs. The states of western and central Europe, dominant before 1914 but shaken by World War I, declined in influence, even losing their remaining colonial possessions. The new bipolar framework opened certain possibilities but also limited political options in both halves of newly divided Europe. The Western European states had to follow the U.S. lead, especially in matters of national security, though France under de Gaulle grew especially restive. But this framework enabled Western Europe to achieve remarkable prosperity and even to take significant steps toward multinational integration.

In the communist bloc, Stalin's death in 1953 ended the most repressive features of the Soviet regime, and under his successor, Nikita Khrushchev, the Soviet Union seemed able to compete with the United States in areas from education to economic growth to the exploration of outer space.

But the experiment with various forms of central planning in the Soviet bloc proved ever less successful. At the same time, the fate of a series of opposition and reform efforts, from East Berlin in 1953 to Prague in 1968, made it clear that the Soviets intended to keep their east-central European satellite states on a relatively tight leash. The degree of unity demanded by the Soviet system imposed stability in a potentially volatile part of Europe, keeping long-standing ethnic rivalries in check.

In Western Europe, the shared experience of wartime led to a new social compact based on greater government responsibility for economic well-being and social welfare. The implicit promise of growing prosperity for all made possible a measure of cooperation between business and labor that eroded earlier assumptions of irreconcilable class struggle. And the new consensus provided a foundation for democracy, which became solidly established in Western Europe during the first two decades after the war.

By 1968, however, strains began to appear in the Western democracies, and slower economic growth during the 1970s jeopardized the postwar settlement. Even in the context of increasing prosperity, a diffuse discontent developed among many Western Europeans, who felt left out as the most important decisions were made by party leaders, technocratic planners, EEC Eurocrats, or the executives of multinational corporations. Thus the quest for new forms of political participation that began in 1968 and continued throughout the 1970s.

The bipolar world rested on a kind of balance between the superpowers. And though significant political discontents surfaced in both halves of divided Europe in 1968, Western Europe came to take for granted a substantial measure of prosperity and political legitimacy, while Eastern Europe was not so fortunate. That imbalance threatened to undermine the anxious stability that characterized the era from 1949 to 1985.

SUGGESTED READING

General Surveys and the Cold War Framework

Crockatt, Richard. *The Fifty Years' War: The United States and the Soviet Union in World Politics, 1941–1991.* 1995. A balanced history of U.S.-Soviet relations, showing the global impact of their cold war rivalry.

Gleason, Abbott. *Totalitarianism: The Inner History of the Cold War.* 1995. A Soviet specialist examines the uses and misuses of the concept of totalitarianism, especially as it helped shape understanding in the West during the cold war period.

Hanrieder, Wolfram F. *Germany, America, Europe: Forty Years of German Foreign Policy.* Updated ed. 1991. A major work on the place of West Germany in the cold war era. Updated edition considers the import of German reunification.

Laqueur, Walter. *Europe in Our Time: A History, 1945–1992.* 1992. A comprehensive, well-balanced survey by a leading authority on twentieth-century Europe.

Maier, Charles S., ed. *The Cold War in Europe: Era of a Divided Continent,* 3d ed. 1996. A series of essays on the implications of the cold war framework for Western European development during the four decades after World War II.

Cultural and Intellectual History

Hughes, H. Stuart. *Between Commitment and Disillusion: The Obstructed Path and the Sea Change, 1930–1965.* 1987. Updated edition of two previously published works by an influential intellectual historian. *The Sea Change* covers the intellectual migration from Europe to America.

Judt, Tony. *Past Imperfect: French Intellectuals, 1944–1956.* 1992. A spirited critique of the apologies for communism that French intellectuals like Sartre and de Beauvoir offered in the years after World War II.

Stromberg, Roland N. *After Everything: Western Intellectual History Since 1945.* 1975. A survey, good on the 1940s and 1950s, less sympathetic on the innovations of the later 1960s and thereafter.

Restabilization, Economic Growth, and Social Change

Ellwood, David W. *Rebuilding Europe: Western Europe, America and Postwar Reconstruction.* 1992. Readable, well-balanced survey of the course of reconstruction in Western Europe in the decade after World War II.

Hogan, Michael J. *The Marshall Plan: America, Britain, and the Reconstruction of Western Europe, 1947–1952.* 1987. Concerned especially with U.S. policy toward Europe; emphasizes the American desire for a neo-capitalist world system based on free trade.

Kuisel, Richard F. *Capitalism and the State in Modern France: Renovation and Economic Management in the Twentieth Century.* 1981. A careful and thorough study tracing the emergence of economic planning and a technocratic ethos in France.

Maier, Charles S. *In Search of Stability.* 1987. Essays on the wider sociopolitical context of economic policies in the twentieth century. Several essays contrast the two postwar periods in illuminating ways.

Milward, Alan S. *The Reconstruction of Western Europe, 1945–51.* 1984. An influential account that emphasizes the importance of European initiatives, as opposed to

American help, in making the postwar economic boom so durable.

Ruggie, Mary. *The State and Working Women: A Comparative Study of Britain and Sweden.* 1984. A sophisticated study that seeks to explain why women achieved greater economic equality in Sweden than in Britain.

Postwar Government and Politics

Bark, Dennis L., and David R. Gress. *A History of West Germany.* Vol. 1, *From Shadow to Substance, 1945–1963,* and Vol. 2, *Democracy and Its Discontents, 1963–1988.* 1989. Offers a favorable account of West Germany's democracy and its Atlantic and European roles in the face of ongoing suspicion and criticism.

Ginsbourg, Paul. *A History of Contemporary Italy: Society and Politics, 1943–1988.* 1990. A comprehensive survey especially good on the radical postwar socioeconomic transformation in Italy.

Larkin, Maurice. *France Since the Popular Front: Government and People, 1936–1986.* 1988. A comprehensive survey that focuses on the interaction between political life and socioeconomic change.

Morgan, Kenneth O. *The People's Peace: British History 1945–1990.* 1992. A thorough survey that seeks to avoid overemphasis on decline and pessimism. Accents the relative peace and stability of the period.

Pulzer, Peter. *German Politics, 1945–1995.* 1995. Brief and clear yet probing account of political developments in both East and West Germany. Also good on the impact of reunification.

Sapelli, Giulio. *Southern Europe Since 1945: Tradition and Modernity in Portugal, Spain, Italy, Greece, and Turkey.* 1995. Using a regional and comparative approach, shows how industrialization led to social change and the consolidation of political democracy in the decades after World War II.

Turner, Henry Ashby, Jr. *Germany from Partition to Reunification.* 1992. A fair-minded treatment of both East and West Germany. Explains the collapse of communism in East Germany and the subsequent German reunification.

Williams, Charles. *The Last Great Frenchman: A Life of Charles de Gaulle.* 1993. Comprehensive, straightforward, balanced account of a remarkable career.

Decolonization

Holland, R. F. *European Decolonization, 1918–1981: An Introductory Survey.* 1985. A sensitive, comprehensive account that gives particular attention to the British experience.

Porter, Bernard. *The Lion's Share: A Short History of British Imperialism, 1850–1995.* 1996. Updated edition of a widely read survey of the British imperial experience, with effective chapters on decolonization and the Commonwealth system that Britain sought to foster as the empire came apart.

Mommsen, Wolfgang J., and Jürgen Osterhammel, eds. *Imperialism and After: Continuities and Discontinuities.* 1986. A collection of essays by leading scholars. Analyzes the informal means through which European influence continued even after the end of formal imperial control.

Von Laue, Theodore H. *The World Revolution of Westernization: The Twentieth Century in Global Perspective.* 1987. A comprehensive, readable, sometimes provocative survey, especially helpful on the transition from decolonization to the new global age.

European Integration and the Common Market

Brinkley, Douglas, and Clifford Hackett, eds. *Jean Monnet: The Path to European Unity.* 1991. A collection of essays on Monnet's central role in the movement toward European integration after World War II.

Dedman, Martin J. *The Origins and Development of the European Union, 1945–95: A History of European Integration.* 1996. A concise and accessible introductory work.

Duchêne, François. *Jean Monnet: The First Statesman of Interdependence.* 1994. A carefully researched and quite readable biography featuring Monnet's role as the architect of European integration.

Hackett, Clifford. *Cautious Revolution: The European Community Arrives,* 2d ed. 1995. An effective blend of history with prescription, suggesting how the European Community could become capable of unified political decision.

Pinder, John. *European Community: The Building of a Union.* 1991. Combines a historical account of the development of EC institutions with a balanced assessment of the prospects for European federation.

The Soviet Union and the Soviet Bloc

Hosking, Geoffrey. *The First Socialist Society: A History of the Soviet Union from Within.* Enlarged ed. 1990. Looks at family, religion, nationality, and the experience of factory workers in an effort to portray the lives of ordinary Soviet citizens.

Linden, Carl A. *Khrushchev and the Soviet Leadership: With an Epilogue on Gorbachev.* Updated ed. 1990. Especially good on the internal political maneuvering that eventually led to Khrushchev's ouster. Includes a useful epilogue on the course from Khrushchev's ambiguous legacy to Gorbachev's reform effort.

Rothschild, Joseph. *Return to Diversity: A Political History of East Central Europe Since World War II,* 2d ed. 1993. A straightforward survey that makes sense of the differences as well as the similarities among the Soviet bloc countries during the cold war.

Stokes, Gale, ed. *From Stalinism to Pluralism: A Documentary History of Eastern Europe Since 1945,* 2d ed. 1991. A collection of documents, with effective commentaries. Includes the disintegration of communism in 1989 and the immediate aftermath.

POP ART

Hamburgers, comic strips, soup-can labels, familiar images of entertainment icons—such was the stuff of "pop art," which burst onto the New York art scene in the early 1960s and came to exert a widespread cultural influence. Indeed, with their imaginative renderings of familiar images and whimsical sculptures of everyday objects, artists like Andy Warhol (1928–1987), Roy Lichtenstein (b. 1923), and Claes Oldenburg (b. 1929) helped shape the experience of the later twentieth century. But was this serious art—or a joke, a parody, a put-on? Were the pop artists poking fun at the triviality of modern society, or were they deepening our encounter with defining aspects of contemporary culture? And whatever their intent, what does the emergence of this striking new art form tell us about the direction of Western culture in the decades after World War II?

The term *pop art* was coined in England in the later 1950s, when a group of artists and critics became interested in bridging the cultural gap between "fine art" and the emerging popular culture of mass media and machine-produced images, of

Oldenburg: Floor Burger, 1962 (Claus Oldenburg [American, b. 1929], Floor Burger, 1962. Painted sailcloth stuffed with foam, 132.1 × 213.4 cm. Art Gallery of Ontario, Toronto.)

advertising and automobiles. Like everyone else, they associated that consumerist mass culture with America—the America of Hollywood, Detroit, and Madison Avenue. And they found it more vital than the conventional fine art of the period. The American pop artists were similarly fascinated by the impersonal, mass-produced, often expendable quality of the objects and images that have come to surround us.

Pop art was part of a wider reaction against the deeply serious abstract expressionist painting that emerged in New York just after the Second World War. By the early 1950s, abstract expressionists like Jackson Pollock and Mark Rothko had created images of unprecedented power, whether seeking to forge an artistic identity in the face of nothingness or to transcend selfhood in a cosmic wholeness (see page 1077). In the mid-1950s, however, younger artists "tired of the stink of artists' egos" began reacting against the self-importance of abstract expressionism. For these younger artists, art did not have to be a vehicle for the psychological expression of the artist or a quest for "the tragic and timeless." Although the reaction took several forms, pop art proved the most influential. The pop movement emerged especially in the United States, and it interested Europeans as typically American, fresh and fascinating or garish and vulgar, depending on one's point of view.

Whereas the abstract expressionists had sought to rise above the everyday world, Claes Oldenburg's sculptures played with the scale and context of the most ordinary objects—a mixer, a three-pronged plug, a lipstick, a hamburger—to deepen our involvement with the everyday things that surround us. In this sense, the aim of pop art was not simply to parody or satirize, but to affirm our relationship with the objects and images of ordinary life. Hollywood, Detroit, and Madison Avenue were all right after all; indeed, they had become the centers of Western culture by the later twentieth century.

Warhol: Marilyn Diptych, 1962 *(© Copyright ARS, NY. Tate Gallery, London/Art Resource, NY)*

Though anonymous and impersonal, the modern world of mass production, mass consumption, and mass media is "popular"—its images and objects are accessible to us all. In fact, they bombard us from all directions, giving shared shape and definition to our everyday lives. This is our world, the pop artists were saying, and they were creating the art appropriate to our time. They invite us to relax and enjoy that world, but they also enhance our experience by making art from it, thereby awakening us to its novelty and vitality.

But some viewers have found an element of melancholy, nostalgia, even tragedy just beneath the surface in pop art. In a world of mass media and reproduced images, more of our experience becomes secondhand and literally superficial, for pop subjects, from fast food to billboards, have no deeper meaning, no expressive personal trappings. With his multiplied image of Marilyn Monroe, Andy Warhol dealt not with the actress herself but with the obsessive familiarity of her image. He cultivated a deadpan, detached style that reflected the machine-made quality of his subject matter—the quality that made the images he started with so familiar in the first place. But even as, on one level, he embraced aspects of the new mass culture, Warhol was exploring precisely the emotional detachment—and the accompanying trivi-alization of emotion—at work in the culture that had produced the images he adapted. Especially in his paintings treating impersonal newspaper images of disaster and death, Warhol bore witness to our indifference—and perhaps to a cosmic meaninglessness as well. One expert has noted that "in Warhol's pictures of the material objects and other false idols that most of us worship, the pain lies just below the bright surfaces of the images and waits passively to engage us."*

The advent of pop art provoked a series of questions that remain without definitive answers. Is the embrace of the mass-produced and commercial, at the expense of traditional "fine-art" values, a symptom of exhaustion or a healthy affirmation of contemporary popular culture, so bound up with the commercial world? Or is pop art perhaps a valuable comment on the emptiness of that culture, with its impersonal conformity, garish commercialism, and mechanical repetition? In the final analysis, were the pop artists abandoning the artist's mission and giving in to the ordinary, or were they the first to show us what "Western civilization" had come to mean by the late twentieth century? ✄

*Eric Shanes, *Warhol* (New York: Portland House, 1991), p. 41.

CHAPTER 30

The West and the World in the Late Twentieth Century

During the fall of 1989, three teenaged Muslim girls were suspended from a public school near Paris because they insisted on wearing the headscarves traditional for Islamic women. School authorities cited a law barring religious displays in France's strictly secular state-run school system. The three girls, however, protested that Islamic teaching required women to cover their heads in public as a sign of modesty. Yet in the eyes of some Westerners, that practice simply reflected the second-class status of women in Islamic civilization. The leader of France's largest teachers' union contended that "this flaunting of a clear symbol of women's subordination negates the teaching of human rights in schools." Thus, when the French Minister of Education defended the students' right to wear the scarves, he was widely criticized for condoning the oppression of women in Islam.

In fact, the education minister was not seeking to defend Islamic tradition or cultural diversity, let alone the oppression of women. He wanted simply to keep these girls—and the many others like them—in France's state-run schools, to expose them to secular influence and thereby to promote their assimilation into French culture.

In 1989 Muslims totaled 5 percent of the French population, or 2.7 million people, and this episode prompted many of them to demonstrate for greater pluralism and tolerance in France. Some of France's non-Muslim majority joined in, even wearing scarves in solidarity. Others, in contrast, called for stepped-up efforts to assimilate immigrants and those with foreign backgrounds into the common French civilization.

"The hijab [headscarf] is our honor":
Muslim women and girls demonstrate
in Paris, October 1989.

France's prestigious Council of State soon ruled that the scarves did not violate the constitutional separation of church and state, as long as they were not worn in an effort to flaunt religion or to proselytize. The council left it to local school authorities to decide each case. But the riddles of multiculturalism at issue in this "affair of the scarves" kept coming up in France and elsewhere by the late twentieth century, as contact between the West and other parts of the world took new forms.

In an increasingly global age, traditional cultural boundaries were breaking down. Communications and flow of capital became instantaneous, products like Coca-Cola and McDonald's burgers and fries became familiar worldwide, and a common urban youth culture began to emerge. In spheres from popular music to food, elements from diverse societies seemed to be fusing. Talk of a single "global village" became commonplace. Yet, as the controversy over the Islamic scarves suggests, in some respects cultural boundaries loomed larger as cultural contact deepened.

Cultural convergence stemmed especially from the process known as modernization, or "Westernization," though it took varied forms in the non-Western world as it mixed with indigenous traditions. The process entailed, above all, participation in the competitive global market economy that had spread from Europe. Paradoxically, however, Westernization meant that "the West" was becoming less meaningful as a category or basis for distinction. Western Europe and the United States encountered formidable economic competition first from Japan, and later from other countries of the East Asian Pacific rim, such as Taiwan, Korea, Thailand, and Malaysia. What increasingly mattered, from this perspective, was the difference between the industrialized, relatively affluent "North" and the less developed "South," including much of Africa, Latin America, southern Asia, and the Middle East.

As the population exploded in the less developed world, the gap between rich and poor nations widened. The prosperous countries of the North were increasingly a magnet for the disadvantaged from around the world. The resulting immigration created new social and political pressures that raised questions about citizenship and assimilation, pluralism and diversity, identity and community.

Such questions came to center stage partly because of the end of the cold war, which had overshadowed all else for decades after World War II.

In 1989, precisely the year of the affair of the scarves in France, dramatic change in the Soviet bloc came to a head, leading to the end of communism and even the dissolution of the Soviet Union. The unraveling of the whole Soviet system brought an abrupt end to the postwar era, which had rested on a tense balance between the communist states and the capitalist democracies.

The former communist countries sought to follow the West in pluralistic liberal democracy, but the Western democracies were themselves facing unprecedented economic challenges in the late twentieth century. The pace of technological change, and related changes in the structure of international capitalism, seemed so rapid that no one could foresee the next stage—and thus no one could feel secure. Moreover, key decisions seemed to be made increasingly by multinational corporations or supranational organizations, beyond democratic control. Some looked to those organizations with hope, others with suspicion and resentment. By the early 1990s, the apparent limits of government power and, in some countries, the short-sightedness and corruption of politicians bred political disillusionment. Even in the democratic West a new set of anxieties and uncertainties quickly replaced those of the cold war era.

CHALLENGES OF AFFLUENCE IN THE WEST

After the economic dislocations of the 1970s, most of Western Europe again enjoyed strong economic growth by the early 1980s. In Italy a "second economic miracle" enabled the country to surpass Britain and become the world's fifth largest economy. But in Italy and elsewhere in Western Europe, growth was uneven, confined to certain sectors and regions. By the 1990s prosperity mixed with ongoing worries about international competition, technological unemployment, and environmental constraints in a small and crowded continent.

By the 1980s democracy had become the unchallenged norm in Western Europe, where the radical right was largely discredited and the Marxist left seemed to have been domesticated for good. In important respects, in fact, conservatives and social democrats sounded more and more alike. But at the same time there was a weakening of the postwar consensus about governmental responsibility for social and economic well-being, as

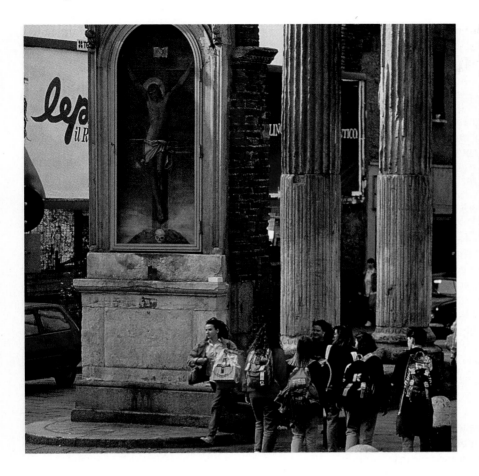

Old and New in Contemporary Europe Especially with the transformation of Europe since World War II, new styles of life intersect with living artifacts from the past to form sometimes ironic combinations. Here, in a neighborhood in Milan, Italy, teenagers wearing blue jeans and backpacks seem oblivious to the legacies of Roman antiquity and Christianity that are prominent around them. (© 1993 George Steinmetz)

new questions arose about the scope of the public sphere, the reach of the state.

Many of the trends important in Europe were visible in the United States as well. The widening gap between rich and poor, the weakening of organized labor, the growing prominence of women in the work force, the increasing concern about such family issues as child care—all were characteristic of Western civilization in general by the late twentieth century. But there were some instructive differences in the ways the different nations of the West dealt with these issues.

The Changing Economies: Prosperity, Imbalance, Limitation

By the 1980s there was greater prosperity in the Western democracies, but for a smaller proportion of the people. In Western Europe unemployment reached levels not seen since the Great Depression. Even after solid growth resumed by 1983, unemployment hovered stubbornly at around 10 percent throughout much of the region, with 13 percent the norm in some older industrial areas. These figures would have seemed unimaginable fifteen years before and were much higher than the rates of 5 to 7 percent typical of the United States during the same period. Yet unemployment persisted, even worsening in some areas. By the mid-1990s, it was highest in Spain, at 20 percent, followed by Finland at 17 percent.

This combination of prosperity and unemployment stemmed in part from the technological changes that, during the late twentieth century, produced a "third industrial revolution." (See the box, "Toward a Postindustrial Society.") Based most dramatically on the computer, it encompassed everything from robotics to fiber optics. The advent of new technologies in a context of increasing global competition produced new winners, but it also transformed the workplace and patterns of employment in worrisome ways.

Such technologies created opportunities for new firms able to start from scratch, without the

Toward a Postindustrial Society

The Canadian communications theorist Marshall McLuhan (1911–1980) offered pioneering analyses of the power of the mass media to shape the form, the scale, and even the content of human interaction in the emerging "global village." Writing in 1964, he also sought to outline what automation and the dawning of the computer age—the transition from the mechanical to the "electrical"—would mean for the future. In the offing was not merely the latest phase in the ongoing process of industrialization, but a deeper revolution, comparable to the advent of printing, which McLuhan identified with its fifteenth-century inventor, Johann Gutenberg.

The future of work consists of earning a living in the automation age. This is a familiar pattern in electric technology in general. It ends the old dichotomies between culture and technology, between art and commerce, and between work and leisure. Whereas in the mechanical age of fragmentation leisure had been the absence of work, or mere idleness, the reverse is true in the electric age. As the age of information demands the simultaneous use of all our faculties, we discover that we are most at leisure when we are most intensely involved, very much as with the artists in all ages.

. . . The new kind of interrelation in both industry and entertainment is the result of the electric instant speed. Our new electric technology now extends the instant processing of knowledge by interrelation that has long occurred within our central nervous system. It is that same speed that constitutes "organic unity" and ends the mechanical age that had gone into high gear with Gutenberg. Automation brings in real "mass production," not in terms of size, but of an instant inclusive embrace. Such is also the character of "mass media." They are an indication, not of the size of their audiences, but of the fact that everybody becomes involved in them at the same time. . . .

. . . With the electric technology, the new kinds of instant interdependence and interprocess that take over production also enter the market and social organizations. For this reason, markets and education designed to cope with the products of servile toil and mechanical production are no longer adequate. Our education has long ago acquired the fragmentary and piecemeal character of mechanism. It is now under increasing pressure to acquire the depth and interrelation that are indispensable in the all-at-once world of electric organization.

Paradoxically, automation makes liberal education mandatory. The electric age of servomechanisms suddenly releases men from the mechanical and specialist servitude of the preceding machine age. . . . We are suddenly threatened with a liberation that taxes our inner resources of self-employment and imaginative participation in society. This would seem to be a fate that calls men to the role of artist in society. It has the effect of making most people realize how much they had come to depend on the fragmentalized and repetitive routines of the mechanical era. . . . Men are suddenly nomadic gatherers of knowledge, nomadic as never before, informed as never before, free from fragmentary specialism as never before—but also involved in the total social process as never before; since with electricity we extend our central nervous system globally, instantly interrelating every human experience.

Source: Marshall McLuhan, *Understanding Media: The Extensions of Man* (Cambridge, Mass.: The MIT Press, 1994), pp. 346–347, 349, 357–358.

problems of redundant workers or outmoded plant and equipment that older competitors faced. A good example was Benetton, an Italian clothing firm founded in 1964 that quickly made effective use of computer technology in all aspects of its operation. But Benetton was so successful partly because it needed fewer workers. Manufacturing jobs tended to be lost as competition forced the industrial sector to become more efficient through computers and automation. In the German steel industry, which had spearheaded a remarkable industrial transformation a century before, over half the jobs disappeared during the 1970s and 1980s.

Changing labor patterns reinforced the decline of organized labor, which was decidedly on the defensive throughout Western Europe and the United States by the 1980s. In France, for example, the organized labor movement was at once divided and relatively small, with fewer than 10 percent of workers unionized. The increasing danger of unemployment undercut the leverage of the unions. And as the economy grew more complex, workers were ever less likely to understand themselves as members of a single, unified working class.

Affluence and Secularization

Postwar economic growth created a secular, consumerist society throughout much of Western Europe by the mid-1960s, establishing patterns that would continue into the less secure 1990s. Growing prosperity meant not only paid annual vacations of three to four weeks but also the luxury of spending them away from home, often at crowded beach resorts. Prosperity entailed the democratization of leisure, increasingly enjoyed in the privacy of the home rather than in a public café, pub, or theater. Television was virtually universal in households across Europe by the beginning of the 1980s. Still, spectator sports grew more popular at the same time, with soccer, the undisputed king, drawing rowdy and sometimes violent crowds.

In Western Europe, as in the United States, a remarkable baby boom had followed the end of the war and carried into the early 1960s. The birthrate declined rapidly thereafter, however, so that family size diminished markedly by 1990. In Italy, where changes in lifestyle accompanying the new prosperity were especially dramatic, the number of births in 1987 was barely half the number in 1964, when the postwar baby boom reached its peak. By 1995 the population was not sustaining itself in Italy or Spain.

Secularization diminished the once central role of the churches in popular culture, which had long revolved around religious festivals and holy days. Regular church attendance declined steadily. In assuming responsibility for social welfare, the state had taken over much of the charitable role that the churches had long played. Seeking to change with the times, the Catholic church undertook a notable modernization effort under the popular Pope John XXIII (r. 1958–1963). But under his more conservative successors, the church became caught up in controversy, especially over issues like abortion that women had forced to the fore. By the last decade of the century, its conservative social policy had put the Catholic church on the defensive.

In traditionally Catholic countries like France, Italy, and Spain, many people considered themselves "cultural Catholics" and ignored church rulings they found inappropriate, especially those concerning sexuality, marriage, and gender roles. The easier availability of contraception—especially the birth control pill, widely obtainable by the late 1960s—fostered a sexual revolution that was central to the new secular lifestyle. In referenda in 1974 and 1981, two-thirds of Italians defied the Vatican by voting to legalize divorce and approve abortion rights. Even in heavily Catholic Ireland, the electorate narrowly approved the legalization of divorce in 1995, after defeating it overwhelmingly in a referendum just nine years before. Controversy also developed over the possibility of ordaining women as priests.

Increasing affluence led to rising expectations and demands for still wider opportunity. Such pressure focused especially on access to government-supported higher education, the chief vehicle for upward mobility based on merit. In France, university admission required passing the *baccalauréat* exam at the end of secondary school. The percentage of the age group that reached this threshold grew from 1 percent in 1900 to 5 percent in 1949, then rose to 23 percent by 1974. In Italy the number of university students increased sixfold from the late 1930s to the late 1960s, partly the result of an open enrollment policy. In West Germany higher education was still restrictive, elitist, and authoritarian at the end of the 1960s, but under pressure from the left the university system quadrupled in size by 1975.

The development of a mass-based university system produced new dilemmas. In France, demands for reform of higher education had been central to the uprising of 1968, but subsequent government efforts to decentralize the system produced widespread opposition from students and faculty by the 1980s. The government's proposal to give individual universities the right to choose their own students provoked protests and strikes, the most notable of which, in 1986, involved 400,000 demonstrators and violent clashes with police. Such opposition forced the government to abandon much of its reform effort.

The resistance to reform reflected the reverse side of social mobility—the considerable status anxiety among students and faculty, especially those in the humanities and social sciences. As French universities had become institutions of mass education, the market value of the state diploma had declined substantially, as had the prestige of the faculty. For those who opposed reform, fear of loss outweighed the possibility of gain from a more competitive system. The French experience with university reform made it clear that mobility and security, equality and excellence, opportunity and merit meshed uneasily in the democratic societies of the West.

The Significance of Gender

As the cases of class and religion indicate, long-standing bases of identity were becoming less important as an affluent, secular society emerged. But new ones became central at the same time. A striking example by the 1980s was the growing preoccupation with gender, which, like the concern with higher education, stemmed from the ongoing quest for equality of opportunity to provide the basis for individual self-realization. In this area, too, the pursuit of equality of opportunity—now across gender lines—encountered tensions.

As it matured, the feminist movement that crystalized in the late 1960s found it necessary to expand its focus beyond the quest for equal opportunity. Examining subtle cultural obstacles to equality led feminists to the more general issue of gender—the way societies perceive sexual difference and thereby define social roles. There was much interest in the innovative ideas of the French existentialist Simone de Beauvoir, who had raised in 1949 precisely the issues that came to the fore during the 1980s. (See the box, "Human Freedom and the Origins of a New Feminism," on page 1083.) And as debate expanded from "women's issues" to gender roles, the self-understanding and often the immediate economic advantage of men were at issue as well.

Insofar as differentiated gender roles are "constructed" by particular societies, gender had been important throughout the long history of the West. Indeed, "gendering" had been central to the socialization process whereby young people learn how to function in their societies. But the gender roles dictated by society were usually taken as natural, so gender was only rarely as explicit and controversial an issue as it became in the late twentieth century. By the 1990s the gender issue was central not only to public policy but also to private relationships and to decisions about life choices in much of the Western world.

It was increasingly recognized that, at least implicitly, debates about the welfare state had often centered on gender from the beginning. After World War II, concerns about labor shortage in both East and West led to conflicting impulses in policy discussions and decisions. Should women be encouraged to work or to concentrate on rearing the children who would be the workers of the future? In Western Europe immigration helped ease the labor shortage, so it was especially in the Soviet bloc that this tension was evident in shifting public policy. In 1981, for example, the Soviet Union reversed course by increasing child care payments and adopting measures to reduce the hours that mothers worked outside the home.

With the dramatic slowdown in population growth in Western Europe after the mid-1960s, there was renewed fear about shortages of labor. At the same time, the feminist movement, seeking equal opportunity, sought measures like government-subsidized day care that would enable women to combine paid employment with raising a family. By the 1970s, these impulses had come together in much of Western Europe. Seeking to enhance both equality of opportunity and long-term economic productivity, governments assumed responsibility for combining productive working parents with effective childhood development.

Setting the pace was France, where the government began making quality day care available to all during the 1980s. Government subsidy kept costs within reach for ordinary working families. In addition, 95 percent of French children aged 3 to 6 were enrolled in the free public nursery schools available by the early 1990s. Comparable figures for Italy (85 percent) and Germany (65 to 70 percent) were also high, although Britain lagged at 35 to 40 percent.

The increasing reliance on child care both reflected and reinforced a decline in the socializing role of the traditional family. This trend prompted concern about the long-term consequences for the socialization of children—and thus for the future of society. At issue was the interaction of family roles, economic functions, individual self-realization, and the well-being of children. Even committed feminists disagreed about whether the undoubted biological difference in childbearing and nursing entailed a special role for women—and had implications for public policy. No one could be sure about the longer-term consequences of this departure from traditional family roles, which was a crucial phase of the ongoing experiment in the West.

Still, the French model seemed to work well in combining child support with equal opportunity for paid employment. Moreover, in France social services were delivered with less paperwork and intrusiveness than elsewhere. By the 1990s, the question was simply whether France could still afford such benefits. And this question reflected a wider set of concerns, becoming central everywhere, about the political order and the role of government.

Re-evaluating the Role of Government

Although the welfare state was in question everywhere by the 1980s, the most dramatic and single-minded assault came in Britain after Margaret Thatcher became prime minister in a new conservative government in 1979. Thatcher insisted that Britain could reverse its economic decline only by fostering a new "enterprise culture," restoring the individual initiative that had been sapped, as she saw it, by decades of dependence on government. Thatcher took it for granted that the free market, undistorted by government intervention, produced optimum economic efficiency and thus, in the long term, the greatest social benefit.

Abandoning its paternalistic tendencies and aristocratic vestiges, the Conservative party now appealed especially to the upwardly mobile, entrepreneurial middle class. But in light of the socioeconomic difficulties Britain faced by the late 1970s, Thatcher's message had broad appeal across the social spectrum. With Labour increasingly isolated, identified with decaying inner cities and old industrial regions, Thatcher easily won re-election in 1983 and 1987.

Three immediate priorities followed directly from Thatcher's overall strategy. First, her government made substantial cuts in taxes and corresponding cuts in spending for education, national health, and public housing. Second, the government fostered privatization, selling off an array of state-owned firms from Rolls Royce to British

Thatcher's Conservative Revolution As British prime minister from 1979 to 1990, Margaret Thatcher led an assault on the welfare state and a renewed embrace of free market economics in Britain. Together with U.S. president Ronald Reagan, who greatly admired her, she came to symbolize the retreat from government that marked the 1980s. Thatcher is shown here at a political rally in London in 1987. *(D. Hudson/Sygma)*

Airways. The government even sold public housing to tenants, at as much as 50 percent below market value, a measure that helped Thatcher win considerable working-class support. Third, Thatcher curbed the power of Britain's labor unions, which were already on the defensive in this period of high unemployment.

Several new laws curtailed trade-union power, and Thatcher refused to consult with union leaders as her predecessors had done since the war. A showdown was reached with the yearlong coal miners' strike of 1984 and 1985, one of the most bitter and violent European strikes of the twentieth century. The strike's failure in the face of government intransigence further discredited the labor movement and enhanced Thatcher's prestige. Still, the violent encounters between police and picketing strikers, carried nationwide on TV, indicated the cracks in the relative social harmony that Britain had long enjoyed.

In addition, riots by unemployed youths broke out in several major industrial cities in 1981 and again in 1985. On one issue, however, the Thatcher government managed a meeting of the minds with discontented city dwellers. Even before Thatcher took office, increasing immigration from Britain's former colonies was being blamed for a variety of social ills, from unemployment to urban crime. Taking a hard line on the immigration issue, Thatcher's Conservatives sponsored the Nationality Act of 1982, which restricted emigration from the former British colonies.

With her nationalist bent, Thatcher resisted the growing power of the multinational European Union. But her stance on this issue, coupled with what seemed an increasingly arrogant, strident tone, provoked growing opposition even within her own party, which finally ousted her as party leader, and thus as prime minister, in 1990.

Controversy over the significance of the Thatcher years mounted after her departure. On the plus side, her efforts helped boost the competitiveness of British industry. Productivity grew at an average annual rate of 4.5 percent in Britain from 1979 to 1988, 50 percent above the average of the other industrial democracies. This striking improvement stemmed partly from the attack on the trade unions, which had limited productivity by protecting redundant labor. Even critics admitted that Thatcher's policies, especially her willingness

to curb the unions, had produced a significant change in British attitudes in favor of enterprise and competition. Privatization found increasing approval, while the number of new businesses reflected a revival of entrepreneurship—apparently the basis for better economic performance over the longer term. Whatever the gains during the Thatcher years, however, the gap between rich and poor widened and the old industrial regions of the north were left ever further behind.

Although Thatcher's assault was unequaled, the social and economic role of the state came under scrutiny all over the Western world at the same time. Still, a renewed emphasis on market economics did not always produce a restriction of the welfare state. In Italy reforms during the 1970s made available a wider range of state services than ever before, from kindergarten and medical care to sports and recreational facilities. In France by the mid-1990s, five-week paid vacations were mandatory, with the government sometimes subsidizing the cost of transportation to seaside or mountain resorts. Comparable government subsidies kept the costs of cultural events affordable to ordinary workers. Accustomed to a strong government role in society, Europeans had difficulty understanding how measures like government-sponsored health care could cause such controversy among Americans.

Even as they prospered as never before, however, countries like France and Italy seemed unable to afford, at a time of intensifying economic competition, all the benefits their governments had gradually come to promise. But what the developed countries of the West could afford for pensions, education, welfare, or health care could not be established objectively; at issue, rather, were societal priorities, to be worked out through the political process. As the economy became more ruthlessly competitive and the gap in incomes widened, the winners, and even those holding their own, seemed ever more reluctant to pay for those who were less successful. The growing preoccupation with cost reflected an erosion of the sense of community and fairness that had been essential to the postwar consensus—and that had led to the expanded government role in the first place. That phenomenon raised questions about the long-term health of the democracies that had consolidated themselves after World War II.

ON THE RUINS OF THE COMMUNIST SYSTEM

By the early 1980s, the system hammered out by Stalin and his successors still seemed firmly entrenched in the Soviet Union and its satellites in east-central Europe, despite a lackluster period under the aging leadership of Leonid Brezhnev and his allies. Yet crises were building in both the Soviet Union and the satellite states, producing forces for change that finally engulfed the whole communist bloc. In one sense, the process began in Poland, Hungary, and Czechoslovakia, where new challenges to the communist system emerged during the 1970s. But no one had forgotten the fate of the earlier reform movements in Hungary and Prague; whatever pressures might develop in the satellite states, the outcome would depend on the Soviet response.

So in another sense, the death of Leonid Brezhnev in 1982 and the beginning of a concerted reform effort in the Soviet Union in 1985 were the decisive moments. By the end of the 1980s the forces for change in the Soviet Union and its satellites had intersected, leading the whole communist system to unravel. The dangerous but stable bipolar world that had emerged from World War II had suddenly vanished, and the countries of the former Soviet bloc began seeking to rejoin the rest of Europe.

BEYOND THE COLD WAR	
1979	Margaret Thatcher becomes prime minister of Britain
	First direct elections to European parliament
1980	Formation of Solidarity in Poland
1981	Mitterrand elected president of France
1982	Death of Leonid Brezhnev in the Soviet Union
1985	Gorbachev comes to power in the Soviet Union
1986	Explosion at Chernobyl nuclear power plant
1989	Collapse of communism in east-central Europe
1990	Reunification of Germany
	Persian Gulf War begins
1991	Collapse of communism in the Soviet Union; dissolution of the Soviet Union
	Beginning of fighting in Yugoslavia
	Maastrict agreement expanding scope of the European Union
1996	Peace in Bosnia
	Yeltsin re-elected as Russian president

Crisis and Innovation in the Soviet Bloc

The impressive rates of economic growth achieved in the Soviet Union and several of its satellite states after World War II continued into the 1960s. However, much of that success came from adding labor—women and underemployed peasants—to the industrial work force. By the end of the 1960s that process was reaching its limits, so increasingly the challenge for the Soviet bloc was to boost productivity through technological innovation.

Even compared to those elsewhere in the communist bloc, the command economy the Soviet Union had developed was particularly centralized and inflexible, involving methods of accounting and resource allocation that proved increasingly counterproductive as the economic challenge gradually changed. The results of the agriculture plan of 1976 to 1980 were especially disappointing. The persistent shortages of many consumer goods, understandable during the transformation to an industrial society, seemed less and less tolerable. And by the late 1970s the Soviet Union was falling behind in high technology, which required the freedom to experiment and exchange ideas that was notably lacking in the rigid Soviet system. As that system bogged down, the expense of the arms race with the United States dragged ever more seriously on the Soviet economy.

In satellite countries like Poland and Hungary, the communist governments managed for a while to win mass support by borrowing from foreign banks so that they could provide meat and other consumer goods at artificially low prices. "Sausage-stuffing," some called it. But as the lending banks came to realize, by the end of the 1970s, that such loans were not being used for their stated purpose of fostering modernization and productivity, these governments found it much harder to borrow. Thus they began having to impose greater austerity.

For all its terrible excesses, Stalin's regime had continued to inspire a measure of genuine idealism during his lifetime. But by the 1970s the Soviet system had settled into narrow routine or outright corruption. Its major functionaries were increasingly a class apart, enjoying access to special shops and other privileges. Brezhnev himself took enormous pleasure in his collection of expensive automobiles.

Brezhnev's death in 1982 made possible the rise of Mikhail Gorbachev (b. 1931), who became party secretary in 1985 and who represented a new generation, beyond those who had been groomed for party careers during the Stalinist 1930s. He quickly charted a reform course—and attracted the admiration of much of the world.

Gorbachev's effort encompassed four intersecting initiatives: arms reduction; liberalization in the satellite states; *glasnost*, or "openness" to discussion and criticism; and *perestroika*, or economic "restructuring." This was to be a reform within the Soviet system. There was no thought of giving up the Communist party's monopoly on power or embracing a free-market economy. The reformers still took it for granted that communism could point the way beyond Western capitalism, with its widespread crime, its illegal drugs, its shallow consumerism. So a measure of idealism guided the reformers' efforts. But they had to make communism work.

Gorbachev understood that "openness" was a prerequisite for "restructuring." The freedom to criticize was essential to check abuses of power, which, in turn, was necessary to overcome the cynicism of the workers and improve productivity. Openness was also imperative to gain the full participation of the country's most creative people, whose contribution was critical if the Soviet Union was to become competitive in advanced technology.

The main thrust of restructuring was to depart from the rigid economic planning mechanism by giving local managers more autonomy. The alternative did not have to entail privatization or a return to free-market capitalism. It could mean, for example, letting workers elect factory managers. But any restructuring was bound to encounter re-

sistance, especially from those with careers tied to the central planning apparatus.

The Crisis of Communism in the Satellite States

Meanwhile, in the Soviet satellites, opposition had continued beneath the surface even after the crushing of the Prague reform effort in 1968. Although the intellectual response in Czechoslovakia would prove significant, Hungary and Poland were the best positioned of the Soviet-bloc countries to respond to the fresh air from the Soviet Union.

For many intellectuals in the Soviet bloc, the Soviet suppression of the Prague Spring in 1968 ended any hope that communism could be made to work. The immediate outcome was a sense of hopelessness and resignation, but by the mid-1970s an opposition movement, centering on underground (or *samizdat*) publications, had begun to take shape in Hungary, Poland, and Czechoslovakia.

In one sense, these dissidents realized, the dominant condition of intellectuals and ordinary people alike was powerlessness in the face of heavy-handed communist government. But they came to argue that there was still scope for individual honesty, for "living the truth," by ceasing to participate in the empty rituals of communist rule. And simple honesty could have political potential, thanks especially to the Helsinki Accords on human rights that the Soviets had accepted in 1975 (see page 1103). By demanding that the communist governments live up to their pretensions, opposition intellectuals could begin to cast doubts upon the legitimacy of the communist regimes. Through various "Helsinki Watch" groups monitoring civil liberties, the opposition managed to assume the moral leadership.

The most significant such group was Charter 77 in Czechoslovakia, which grew from a movement of protest against the arrest of a rock group called "The Plastic People of the Universe." Long-haired and anti-establishment like their counterparts in the West, the Plastic People were deemed filthy, obscene, and disrespectful of society by the repressive Czechoslovak regime. In 1977, protesting the crackdown on the group, 243 individuals signed "Charter 77"—using their own names and addresses, living the truth, acting as if they were free to register such an opinion. Their point was not explicitly political or ideological; rather, in protest-

Power from Below: Living the Truth

Considering the scope for change in the communist world by the late 1970s, Václav Havel imagines a conformist grocer who routinely puts a sign in his window with the slogan "Workers of the world, unite!" simply because it is expected. That same grocer, says Havel, has the power to break the stifling sociopolitical system, which ultimately rests on those innumerable acts of everyday compliance.

[T]he real meaning of the greengrocer's slogan has nothing to do with what the text of the slogan actually says. Even so, this real meaning is quite clear and generally comprehensible because the code is so familiar: the greengrocer declares his loyalty . . . in the only way the regime is capable of hearing; that is, by accepting the prescribed *ritual,* by accepting appearances as reality, by accepting the given rules of the game. In doing so, however, he has himself become a player in the game, thus making it possible for the game to go on, for it to exist in the first place. . . .

Let us now imagine that one day something in our greengrocer snaps and he stops putting up the slogans merely to ingratiate himself. He stops voting in elections he knows are a farce. He begins to say what he really thinks at political meetings. . . . He rejects the ritual and breaks the rules of the game. He discovers once more his suppressed identity and dignity. . . .

. . . He has shown everyone that it *is* possible to live within the truth. Living within the lie can constitute the system only if it is universal.

The principle must embrace and permeate everything. There are no terms whatsoever on which it can coexist with living within the truth, and therefore everyone who steps out of line *denies it in principle and threatens it in its entirety.* . . .

And since all genuine problems and matters of critical importance are hidden beneath a thick crust of lies, it is never quite clear when the proverbial last straw will fall, or what that straw will be. This . . . is why the regime prosecutes, almost as a reflex action preventively, even the most modest attempts to live within the truth.

. . . [T]he crust presented by the life of lies is made of strange stuff. As long as it seals off hermetically the entire society, it appears to be made of stone. But the moment someone breaks through in one place, when one person cries out, "The emperor is naked!"—when a single person breaks the rules of the game, thus exposing it as a game—everything suddenly appears in another light and the whole crust seems then to be made of a tissue on the point of tearing and disintegrating uncontrollably.

Source: Václav Havel et al., *The Power of the Powerless: Citizens Against the State in Central-Eastern Europe* (Armonk, N.Y.: M. E. Sharpe, 1985), pp. 31, 37, 39–40, 42–43.

ing this violation of human rights they at once made clear the scope for basic honesty and called attention to the gulf between honesty and the communist regime.

A leader in Charter 77 was the writer Václav Havel (b. 1936), who noted that after 1968 there was no hope of reforming the state or the Communist party through direct political action. Hopes for change depended on people organizing themselves, outside the structures of the party-state, in diverse, independent social groupings. (See the box, "Power from Below: Living the Truth.") Havel

and a number of his associates were in and out of jail as the government sought to head off this protest movement.

Despite the efforts of Havel and his colleagues, government remained particularly repressive and unimaginative, and ordinary people remained relatively passive, in Czechoslovakia until the late 1980s. For quite different reasons, Hungary and Poland offered greater scope for change.

Even after the failed reform effort of 1956, Hungary proved the most innovative of the European communist countries. Partly because its government allowed small-scale initiatives outside the central planning apparatus, Hungary was relatively prosperous by the end of the 1970s. But like others in the Soviet bloc, it faced difficulties paying off its foreign debt. The Hungarians responded as nowhere else, however, committing the economy to the discipline of the world market by joining the International Monetary Fund and the World Bank in 1982. This move required economic austerity, and Hungarian living standards declined during the early 1980s. But it also entailed, first, some role for reformers within the Communist party and, second, further encouragement of the "second economy," the country's autonomous private sector. Thus, for example, small food-processing enterprises developed, and independent craftsmen began contracting with the state on their own. Even on the collective farms, agricultural workers were allowed to work their particular sector as a family unit. By the mid-1980s various alternative forms of ownership were responsible for one-third of Hungary's economic output.

This openness to experiment in the economy enabled reformers within the Hungarian Communist party to gain the upper hand. Amid growing talk of "socialist pluralism," the Hungarian elections of 1985 introduced an element of genuine democracy. Mikhail Gorbachev's visit to Budapest in 1986 helped embolden the reformers, but by then the course of change in Hungary had developed a momentum of its own. Finally, in 1988, communist reformers ousted the aging János Kádár, who lacked the vision for continued reform. Increasingly open to a variety of viewpoints, the Hungarian communists gradually pulled back from their long-standing claim to a monopoly of power.

With growing concern for the Hungarian minority in Romania helping to galvanize political consciousness, new political clubs proliferated in Hungary. Finally, in June 1989, popular pressure led to the ceremonial reburial of Imre Nagy, who had led the reform effort in 1956. After having been convicted of treason, executed, and buried in obscurity, Nagy had been derided as a counter-revolutionary traitor in official government pronouncements. The significance of his reburial indicated the importance of historical memory—and who controls it. With the reformers' victory in this battle, Hungarians no longer had to live with the official lie about what had happened in 1956.

The reform effort that built gradually in Hungary stemmed especially from reform aspirations within the governing elite. More dramatic was the course of change in Poland, where there was already a tradition of labor militancy, especially among shipyard workers on the Baltic coast. In fact, these workers' demands for independent, genuinely representative trade unions in 1970 had led to a violent crackdown by the government.

It was crucial that, whereas Polish workers had not supported dissident students and intellectuals who had demonstrated in 1968, the two sides managed to come together during the 1970s. When Polish workers struck again in 1976, in response to a cut in food subsidies, intellectuals formed a Committee for the Defense of the Workers, soon expanded to become the Social Self-Defense Committee (KOR). This alliance had become possible because dissident intellectuals in Poland, as in other Soviet-bloc countries, were coming to emphasize the importance of grassroots efforts that challenged the logic of the communist system without attacking it directly.

But an extra ingredient from an unexpected quarter also affected the situation in Poland, perhaps in a decisive way. In 1978 the College of Cardinals of the Roman Catholic church departed from long tradition and, for the first time since 1522, elected a non-Italian pope. But even more startling was the fact that the new pope was from Poland, behind the iron curtain. He was Karol Cardinal Wojtyla (b. 1920), the archbishop of Kracow, who took the name John Paul II.

After World War II, the Polish Catholic church had been unique among the major churches of east-central Europe in maintaining and even enhancing its position. It worked just enough with the ruling communists to be allowed to carve out a measure of autonomy. For many Poles, the church thus remained a tangible institutional alternative to communism and the focus of national self-consciousness in the face of Soviet domination. Thus the new pope's visit to Poland in 1979 had an electrifying effect on ordinary Poles, who took to the streets by the millions to greet him—and found they were not alone. This boost in self-confidence provided the catalyst for the founding of a new trade union, Solidarity, in August 1980.

Led by the remarkable shipyard electrician Lech Walesa (b. 1944), Solidarity emerged most

Lech Walesa and Solidarity A shipyard electrician, Walesa spearheaded the dissident Polish trade union, Solidarity, formed in 1980, and then emerged from prison to lead the movement that eventually toppled the communist regime in Poland in 1989. Here he addresses a rally during a strike at the Lenin shipyards in Gdansk in August 1988. *(Sygma)*

immediately in response to labor discontent in the vast Lenin shipyard in Gdansk, on the Baltic Sea (see Map 30.1). Demanding the right to form their own independent trade unions, 70,000 workers took over the shipyards, winning support both from their intellectual allies and from the Catholic church. Support for Solidarity grew partly because the government, facing the crisis of its "sausage-stuffing" strategy, was cutting subsidies and raising food prices. But the new union developed such force because it placed moral demands first—independent labor organizations, the right to strike, and freedom of expression. Reflecting the wider opposition thinking in east-central Europe, Solidarity was not to be bought off with lower meat prices, even had the government been able to deliver them.

After over a year of negotiation, compromise, and broken promises, the tense situation came to a head in December 1981, when the government under General Wojciech Jaruzelski (b. 1923) declared martial law and outlawed Solidarity, imprisoning its leaders. Strikes in protest were crushed by military force. Soviet intervention was a definite possibility—but proved unnecessary.

So much for that, it seemed. Another lost cause, another reform effort colliding with inflexible communist power in east-central Europe, as in 1953, 1956, and 1968. But this time, it was different.

The ideas of Solidarity continued to spread underground. Walesa remained a powerfully effective leader, able to keep the heterogeneous movement together. Then the advent of Gorbachev in 1985 changed the overall framework of the communist bloc, for Gorbachev was convinced that the essential restructuring of the Soviet system required reform in the satellites as well. So as the Polish economy, already in difficulty by 1980, reached a crisis in 1987, Solidarity began stepping up its efforts.

When proposed price increases were rejected in a referendum, the Polish government imposed them by fiat. Strikes demanding the relegalization of Solidarity followed during the spring of 1988. The government again responded with military force, but Solidarity-led strikes in August forced

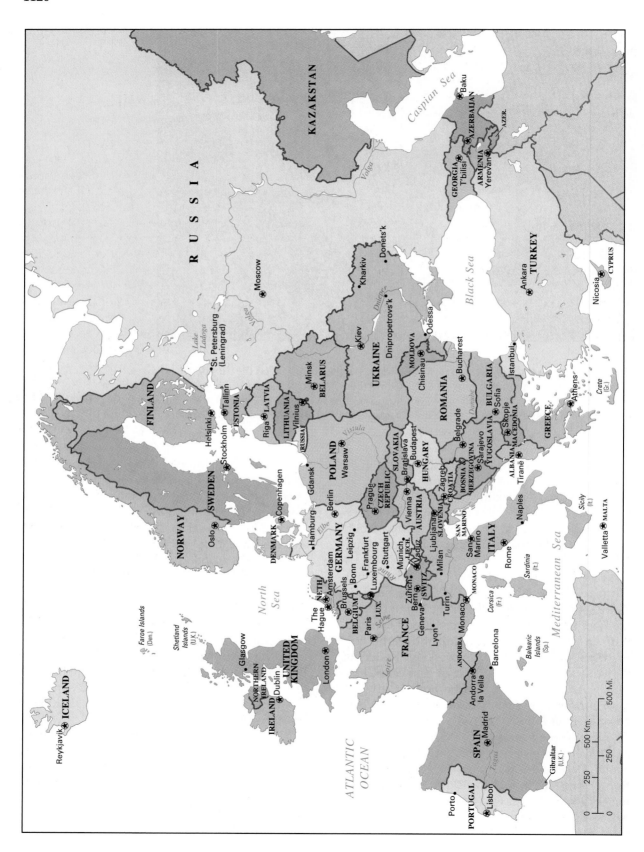

government leaders to send signals that they might be prepared to negotiate. With the economy nearing collapse, the government recognized that it could no longer govern on its own.

The negotiations that followed early in 1989 proved pivotal. When they began, Walesa and his advisers wanted primarily to regain legalization for Solidarity within the communist-dominated system, still under Jaruzelski. In exchange, they assumed they would have to help legitimate a rigged election to approve painful but necessary economic measures. But as these "Round Table" negotiations proceeded, the government gave ever more in exchange for Solidarity's cooperation. Not only did it consent to legalize Solidarity, but it agreed to make the forthcoming elections free enough for the opposition to participate genuinely.

The elections of June 1989 produced an overwhelming repudiation of Poland's communist government. Even government leaders running unopposed failed to win election as voters crossed out their names. In the aftermath of the elections, President Jaruzelski was forced to give Solidarity a chance to lead. Not all members of the opposition felt it wise to accept government responsibility under such difficult economic circumstances, but finally Tadeusz Mazowiecki (b. 1927), Walesa's choice and one of the movement's most distinguished intellectuals, agreed to form a government.

The chain of events in Poland culminated in one of the extraordinary events of modern history—the negotiated end of communist rule. That a communist government might give up power voluntarily had been utterly unforeseen. It happened partly because the Soviet Union under Gorbachev was seeking reform and thus had become much less likely to intervene militarily. It also mattered that the Polish Catholic church was available to act as mediator, hosting meetings, reminding both sides of their shared responsibilities in the difficult situation facing their country. By some accounts, General Jaruzelski, who seemed for most of the 1980s to be just another military strongman, willing to do the Soviets' bidding, had proven a national hero for his grace, perhaps even ingenu

ity, in yielding power to the opposition. But most important was the courage, the persistence, and the vision of Solidarity itself.

The Anticommunist Revolution, 1989–1991

Although the Hungarians were already breaking out of the communist mold, it was especially the Polish example that suggested to others in the Soviet bloc that the communist system was open to challenge. During 1989, demands for reform and, increasingly, for an end to communist rule spread through east-central Europe by means of the domino effect that had preoccupied the Soviets from the start. By the end of that year, the Soviet satellite system was in ruins (Map 30.1).

Though antigovernment strikes and demonstrations took place throughout the region, the end of the established communist order in Hungary, Czechoslovakia, East Germany, Bulgaria, and Albania was more peaceful than anyone would have dreamed possible a few years before. Starting with Hungary, these countries essentially followed the model established in Poland and negotiated the transfer of power from the Communists to opposition leaders. In Czechoslovakia, the transition was so peaceful that it was promptly dubbed the "Velvet Revolution." The signal exception was Romania, where the communist dictator Nicolae Ceausescu's bloody crackdown on the reform movement provoked an armed revolt that finally overthrew the government. The opposition executed Ceausescu and his wife on Christmas Day 1989.

Though the outcome was relatively peaceful, the possibility of violent repression was never far from the surface. Just months before, in June 1989, the communist leadership in China had used massive force to crush a comparable movement for democracy in Tiananmen Square in Beijing. As the opposition movement grew in East Germany early in the fall, with weekly demonstrations in Leipzig attracting 300,000 people, the East German communist leader Erich Honecker (1912–1994) began preparing for such a "Chinese solution" in his country. But a dramatic appeal for nonviolence by local opposition leaders in Leipzig helped persuade the police to hold off. At the same time, Gorbachev, visiting Honecker in October, called for moderation. Gorbachev still believed that reform offered the best hope for saving the system. Honecker was

Map 30.1 Europe After the Cold War The reunification of Germany and the breakup of the Soviet Union, Yugoslavia, and Czechoslovakia fundamentally altered the map of Europe by the early 1990s.

soon forced out of the East German leadership in favor of communists who desired reform.

A marked increase in illegal emigration from East Germany to the west had been one manifestation that the whole satellite system was starting to unravel. During 1989 the reform-minded Hungarian communists decided to stop impeding East Germans, many of whom vacationed in Hungary, from immigrating to the west at the Hungarian border with Austria. If the communist reformers in East Germany were to have any chance of turning the situation around, they had to relax restrictions on travel and even grant the right to emigrate. Thus they immediately began preparing legislation to both ends, amid a host of reforms intended to save the system. On November 9, 1989, the regime in East Germany did what had long seemed unthinkable: It opened the Berlin Wall, which was promptly dismantled altogether. Germans now traveled freely back and forth between east and west.

This liberalization effort proved too late, however, for by now discontented East Germans envi-

sioned not simply reforming the communist system but ending it altogether. As it became possible to contemplate even German reunification, the communist system in the east quickly dissolved. Decisive steps toward reunification followed almost immediately during 1990.

The opening of the Berlin Wall in November 1989 signaled the end of the cold war. The immediate result in the west was euphoria, but few failed to recognize that a still more difficult task lay ahead. To be sure, reformers in the former communist countries claimed to want individual freedom, political democracy, and free-market capitalism. But it would be necessary to build these on the ruins of the now-discredited communist system and its command economy, a task never confronted before.

Meanwhile, in the Soviet Union, what began as a restructuring of the communist system became a struggle for survival of the system itself. The much-trumpeted glasnost produced greater freedom in Soviet culture and politics, but Gorbachev sought to avoid alienating hard-line com-

The Fall of the Wall In November 1989 the dismantling of the Berlin Wall, erected in 1961, marked the dramatic end of the cold war era. Here crowds assemble at the Brandenburg gate in the heart of Berlin to be part of the action as history was made—live on television. *(Corbis-Bettmann)*

munists, so he compromised, watering down the economic reforms essential to perestroika. The result proved a set of half-measures that only made things worse. Because so little was done to force the entrenched Soviet bureaucracy to go along, the pace of economic reform was lethargic. The essential structures of the command economy weakened, but free-market forms of exchange among producers, distributors, and consumers did not emerge to replace them.

In 1986 an accidental explosion at the Soviet nuclear power plant at Chernobyl, in Ukraine, released 200 times as much radiation as the atomic bombs dropped on Hiroshima and Nagasaki combined. The accident contaminated food supplies and forced the abandonment of villages and thousands of square miles of formerly productive land. According to later estimates, the radioactivity released would eventually hasten the death of at least 100,000 Soviet citizens. Despite his commitment to openness, Gorbachev reverted to old-fashioned Soviet secrecy for several weeks after the accident, in an effort to minimize what had happened. As a result, the eventual toll was far greater than it need have been. The accident and its aftermath seemed stark manifestation of all that was wrong with the Soviet system—its arrogance and secrecy, its premium on cutting corners to achieve targets imposed from above.

By the end of the 1980s, Soviet citizens felt betrayed by their earlier faith that Soviet communism was leading to a better future. A popular slogan spoke sarcastically of "seventy years on the road to nowhere." The economic situation was deteriorating, yet people were free to discuss alternatives as never before. As the discussion came to include once unthinkable possibilities like privatization and a market economy, it became clear that the whole communist system was in jeopardy.

The Soviet Communist party began losing members—4 million from January 1990 to July 1991. By mid-1990, moreover, the union of Soviet republics itself tottered on the verge of collapse. Lithuania led the way in calling for outright independence. But the stakes were raised enormously in June 1990 when the Russian republic, the largest and most important in the U.S.S.R., followed Lithuania's lead.

In June 1990 the newly elected chairman of Russia's parliament, Boris Yeltsin (b. 1931), persuaded the Russian republic to declare its sovereignty. Yeltsin had grown impatient with the slow pace of economic and political change, and by threatening that Russia might go its own way, he hoped to force Gorbachev's reform effort beyond the present impasse. As a further challenge to Gorbachev, Yeltsin dramatically resigned from the Communist party during the televised twenty-eighth congress in July 1990. When, in June 1991, free elections in the Russian republic offered the first clear contest between communists determined to preserve the system and those seeking to replace it, the anticommunist Yeltsin was elected the republic's president by a surprising margin.

After tilting toward the hard-liners late in 1990, Gorbachev sought a return to reform after Yeltsin's dramatic election as president of Russia in June 1991. Late in July, Gorbachev prepared a new union treaty that would have given substantial powers, including authority over taxation, to the constituent republics. He also engineered a new party charter that jettisoned much of the Marxist-Leninist doctrine that had guided communist practice since the revolution.

These measures promised the radical undoing of the Soviet system, and now the hard-liners finally struck back, initiating a coup in August 1991. They managed to force Gorbachev from power—but only for a few days. As the world held its breath, Yeltsin, supported by ordinary people in Moscow, stood up to the conspirators. Key units of the secret police, charged to arrest Yeltsin and other opposition leaders, refused to follow orders, prompting the Soviet army, already divided, to back off from the conspirators' plan to take Moscow. The coup quickly fizzled, but the episode galvanized the anticommunist movement and radically accelerated the pace of change.

Although Gorbachev was restored as head of the Soviet Union, the winner was Yeltsin, who quickly mounted an effort to dismantle the party apparatus before it could regroup. Spontaneous anticommunist demonstrations across much of the Soviet Union toppled statues of Lenin and dissolved local party networks. In a referendum in December 1991, Ukraine, the second most populous Soviet republic, overwhelmingly voted for independence. Not only the communist system but the Soviet Union itself was simply disintegrating.

Liberating though it was, the dissolution of the Soviet empire brought a new set of problems. What was to become of the 27,000 nuclear

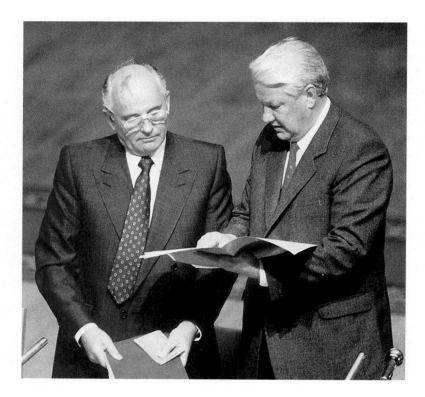

Gorbachev and Yeltsin The two leaders appear together in August 1991, just after the failure of an attempted coup by Soviet hard-liners. After the coup attempt, as it became clear that Gorbachev's effort to reform Soviet communism had stalled, the initiative passed to Yeltsin, who was determined to replace the communist system altogether. *(De Keerle/Grochowiak/Sygma)*

weapons stationed in four of the Soviet republics? Moreover, as the economic situation deteriorated, individual republics began setting up obstacles to economic exchange with the others, keeping what they produced for themselves. Some new form of coordination and unity seemed essential. Thus in December 1991, the leaders of Russia, Ukraine, and Belarus spearheaded the creation of a new Commonwealth of Independent States, which replaced the Soviet Union with a much looser confederation of eleven of the fifteen former Soviet republics. Late in December, Gorbachev finally resigned, paving the way for the official dissolution of the Soviet Union on January 1, 1992 (see Map 30.1).

Life After Communism

All over the formerly communist part of Europe, calls for Western-style democracy accompanied the end of the old order. But the area had little experience with the give and take of democratic politics, and the fragile new political systems found themselves responsible for the difficult transition from a command to a free-market economy. As economic hardship produced backlash and even

nostalgia for the certainties of communist rule, the key question was the staying power of the quest for democracy and a free-market economy in the former communist countries.

Political prospects rested in large part on the success of the economic transition. The economies in the former communist countries were close to chaos as the process began, and the attempt to construct a market economy brought on unemployment, inflation, and widespread corruption. No longer could ordinary people count on the subsidized consumer goods or the welfare safety net that the communist regimes, for all their inadequacies, had provided. While many ordinary citizens suffered great hardship, some former communist functionaries quickly got rich by taking over state-owned companies—and provoked widespread resentment. Still, the transition to a market economy seemed to be working by the mid-1990s, though the course of change varied considerably from one country to the next.

Some of the postcommunist governments concentrated on privatizing existing state-owned concerns while others sought especially to foster entrepreneurship and innovation. In Poland, privatization lagged, but a buoyant new private sector emerged as the Poles proved adept at starting new businesses. By the mid-1990s Poland had a reasonably stable, outward-looking market economy. Privatization, in contrast, was greatest in the Czech Republic under the forceful leadership of Václav Klaus, a passionate partisan of market economics. By the end of 1995, the Czechs had achieved a solid annual economic growth rate of 4 percent with low unemployment and relatively low inflation. But even in this, the most stable of the former communist countries, there was restiveness over corruption and problems in health care and other areas of the public sector.

Privatization was also rapid in Russia, where two-thirds of formerly state-owned industry had been redistributed by mid-1994. However, the fairness of the process was subject to much dispute. Optimists emphasized that thanks to this process, forty million Russians owned shares in newly privatized companies. But even the most optimistic could not deny that in certain sectors, especially natural resources and energy, the process included much insider dealing so that in Russia, more than anywhere else in the former communist world, privatization benefited former Communist party functionaries, some of whom became instant multimillionaires.

In Russia, too, the governmental weakness that accompanied the fall of communism yielded a chilling increase in lawlessness—from ordinary street crime like auto theft to sophisticated, organized crime with a significant role in the nation's economy. Thus in part the nostalgia for the stability of communism that led many Russians to vote Communist in 1995 and 1996. Despite the drama of the anticommunist revolution of 1989–1991, the postcommunist experience made it clear that to adopt democracy and a market economy were but tentative first steps.

In the political sphere, the former communist countries tended first toward political fragmentation—a multiplicity of parties in a weak, divided parliament—which in turn encouraged reliance on a strong leader. Postcommunist Poland's first parliamentary elections in October 1991 produced a parliament splintered among twenty parties, none strong enough to muster more than 12 percent of the vote. This situation seemed to open the way to an ever more authoritarian approach from the president, who, beginning in December 1990, was none other than Lech Walesa himself. Al-

though Walesa, during his five years as president, never became the authoritarian some feared, he was sometimes bullying and intolerant, and his dominant role reflected the wider tendency for a strong leader to emerge in the face of parliamentary fragmentation.

Throughout the formerly communist part of Europe, most were eager to jettison the communist label at first. But by 1992 those in power in Lithuania, Romania, Bulgaria, and the dominant Serbian part of Yugoslavia were former communists whose long-term commitment to democracy remained suspect. And by the mid-1990s, the shock of switching to a market economy was producing a growth in strength or return to power of former communists. Sometimes these communists worked in coalition with nationalists troubled by increasing Western economic penetration as their respective nations joined the international free-market economy. But some one-time communists were more reformed than others, and their electoral successes did not mean the same thing everywhere. Poland and Hungary experienced a tilt to the left by the mid-1990s, but these countries were maturing politically, and even the election of former communists did not mean undercutting democracy or the market economy.

When a charismatic young ex-communist, Alexander Kwasniewski, defeated Walesa in a watershed presidential election in Poland in 1995, it was not a repudiation of the anticommunist revolution that Walesa and Solidarity had spearheaded. By this point, in fact, Walesa was no longer a progressive force. His vote came largely from traditionalist, rural, strongly Catholic parts of Poland, while Kwasniewski attracted Poles interested in expanding the market economy and developing closer ties with Western Europe.

In Russia, communism had far deeper roots than elsewhere in the former Soviet bloc. It had not been imposed by foreigners, and it had been in power far longer than elsewhere. Communist or former communist hard-liners sought to oust not only Gorbachev in 1991 but also Yeltsin in 1993, when the elected parliament, which included many opposed to Yeltsin's free-market reforms, unsuccessfully challenged the president's authority within the new system. By late 1995, when Russia's second postcommunist parliamentary elections took place, the communists, led by Gennady Zyuganov, profited from the unpopularity of reform and the attendant backlash against Yeltsin to win a plurality of seats. Unlike the former communists who had won elections in Lithuania, Hungary, and Poland, these Russian communists had never dropped the communist label and had never fully embraced democratic principles.

When presidential elections followed in 1996, the communists exploited economic discontent and won support especially from workers and older pensioners. But the communist economic platform was riddled with contradictions, and it was hardly clear what a communist victory would have meant. Yeltsin, in contrast, enjoyed the support of Russia's powerful new entrepreneurial class, which opposed any retreat from free-market principles.

An astute, surprisingly resilient politician, Yeltsin capped a remarkable uphill struggle by defeating Zyuganov for president in July 1996. The campaign and election had given Russians their fullest experience of democracy to date, but it remained unclear whether the outcome would prove a turning point in the consolidation of a democratic order in postcommunist Russia.

Although economic reconstruction was paramount, the end of communism opened up divisive new questions across the former Soviet bloc. It quickly became clear that political freedom did not necessarily bring wider rights and liberties. For example, the eclipse of communism in Poland initially promised a major role for the Roman Catholic church, but angry debate followed when, in 1990, the government ordered that children be taught the Catholic religion in school and the head of the Polish church called for an end to the "communist-inspired" separation of church and state. An effort to pass a strong anti-abortion bill in time for a visit by Pope John Paul II in 1991 caused more heated debate; public opinion polls indicated that a majority of Poles favored abortion rights.

Abortion was similarly a major issue as, just after the fall of communism, the former East Germany was incorporated into the Federal Republic of Germany. Abortion law had been more liberal in the communist east than in the west. In the same way, East Germany was considerably more generous than the Federal Republic in providing maternity leaves, day care, and other measures to enable mothers to work outside the home. Though some East German feminists, by the mid-1980s, were accenting gender differences to enable

women to pull back from the workplace, they feared that the difficult transition to capitalism could mean diminished employment opportunities for women. Though a compromise was worked out on the abortion issue, the differences in priorities that surfaced between West and East German feminists made it clear that the end of communism was no panacea.

In the former satellite states, as in several of the republics of the former Soviet Union, autonomy and democracy quickly opened the way to ethnic tensions that occasionally led to outright rebellion. Ethnic repression and conflict were not new to the region, but within the Soviet bloc they had been kept largely submerged.

In Czechoslovakia, which had been widely admired for its peaceful, civilized departure from communism, the Slovak minority broke away to form an independent republic at the beginning of 1993. By 1995 the government was making Slovak the only official language, angering the large Hungarian minority in Slovakia and drawing protests from Hungary. The status of the Hungarian minority in Romania was an ongoing concern as well. But most dramatic—and tragic—was the situation in Yugoslavia, where ethnic and religious conflict produced not only the disintegration of the country but also a brutal, multisided war among Serbs, Croats, and Bosnian Muslims (see Map 30.2). One of the defining events of the 1990s, this war proved a major challenge for the new international order that had emerged from the cold war.

EUROPE AND THE WEST AFTER THE BIPOLAR PEACE

The dissolution of the Soviet system meant the swift, unexpected end of the cold war framework that had defined the era since World War II. Though it seemed only a balance of terror at the time, the cold war had provided a measure of order and security in the years from 1949 to 1989. What sort of international configuration was to follow? Though it could claim, in one sense, to have won the cold war, the United States had also declined in relative strength from the unprecedented pre-eminence it had enjoyed after World War II. Thus the end of the cold war meant not unchallenged U.S. hegemony but a new universe of uncertainties and possibilities.

The new framework seemed to invite Western Europe to become a superpower in its own right, so as the cold war ended, the ongoing push for European integration intensified, producing a more integrated union of fifteen members by the mid-1990s. But obstacles remained, stemming especially from traditional concerns about national sovereignty. And fighting in the former Yugoslavia raised questions about the ability of the European Union, or any international body, to assure stability in the chaotic world that seemed to be emerging after four decades of bipolar peace.

The Changing International Framework

As the potential threat from the Soviet Union dissolved, the United States lost some of its leverage in Europe because American support no longer seemed essential for European security. But despite a renewed military buildup during the 1980s, the Americans, by the early 1990s, could no longer claim the same kind of leadership in any case. The role of superpower had taken its toll on the United States, just as it had on the U.S.S.R. These two had been the big winners of World War II, yet the subsequent arms race burdened the budgets of both countries, while the war's major losers, Germany, Japan, and Italy, pulled back from any great power role to prosper as never before.

The ambiguities of the new international situation came to the fore during the first major international crisis of the post–cold war period, the Persian Gulf War, which the United States led against Iraq in 1990 and 1991. With superpower rivalry no longer an issue, the United States assembled a wide-ranging coalition that reversed an Iraqi takeover of neighboring, oil-rich Kuwait. Though the United States led successfully, it had to pass the hat among its prosperous allies to pay for the Gulf War, and those called on to contribute seemed unlikely to settle for such arrangements again. This was especially true of Japan and Germany, each of which was engaged in reassessing its international role.

The end of the cold war especially affected Germany because the collapse of communism in east-central Europe paved the way for German reunification in 1990. Despite some nervousness, the four postwar occupying powers—the United States, Britain, France, and the Soviet Union—gave their blessing as the Federal Republic simply incorporated the five states of the former East Germany. Although some in West Germany were hesitant about immediate reunification, especially because of the economic costs that seemed likely, West German Chancellor Helmut Kohl (b. 1930) sought to complete the process as quickly as possible. By early 1990 immigration of East Germans to the west had become a flood. West German law treated these Germans as citizens, entitled to social benefits, so their arrival in such numbers presented a considerable financial burden. It seemed imperative for West Germany to regularize the situation as quickly as possible, assuming responsibility for the east and restoring its economy.

Reunification prompted anxiety about the role the new Germany, already a major economic power, might seek to play in Europe and the world. Because 30 percent of the territory of present-day Poland had been taken from Germany after World War II, the Poles were especially concerned. Germany, however, remained eager to prove its good intentions by leading the continuing movement toward European integration. Some worried that the EU would itself become a vehicle for German domination, but the Germans took care to offer reasoned, cautious leadership, with no hint of bullying.

Reunified Germany also encountered new domestic problems that promoted caution. Because reunification proved far more costly than Kohl had expected, his government found it hard to keep some of the promises it had made, in the euphoria of reunification, to Germans in the east. When, in 1993, his government pulled back from its promise of wage equality between east and west, workers in the former East Germany mounted the most serious strikes the Federal Republic had experienced since World War II. Moreover, the strains and costs of reunification contributed to the growing controversy over the role of immigrants in Germany by the early 1990s.

The French were particularly restive about the reunification of Germany, which threatened the leading role on the western Europe continent that France had played since World War II. But France was still willing to act independently—and it could be influential in doing so. When the post–cold war international system fell into discredit with the multisided ethnic fighting in the former Yugoslavia, French pressure, late in 1995,

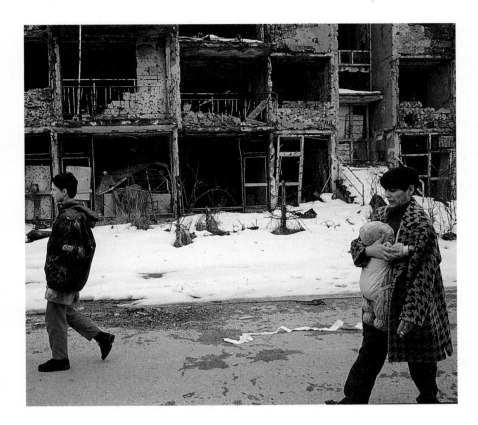

The Agony of Bosnia The wars that accompanied the breakup of Yugoslavia during the 1990s made it tragically clear that the end of the cold war was no guarantee of peace in Europe. The Serb shelling of the Bosnian capital, Sarajevo, from 1992 to 1996 caused widespread destruction and forced many to flee the city. Here Bosnian Muslims return to the Dobrinja area of Sarajevo in March 1996, just after the end of the Serb siege. (*Christopher Morris/Time/Black Star*)

helped bring the situation to a head. President Jacques Chirac's threat to pull France out of the multinational peacekeeping force in the region influenced U.S. President Bill Clinton to step up the U.S. role—with perhaps decisive results. The French initiative in this case manifested the new complexity in relations among the Western allies, but the outcome confirmed the centrality of U.S. leadership in a crucial sense.

The brutality that characterized the fighting in Bosnia, and the halting efforts of the international community in response, brought to an abrupt end the optimism that at first surrounded the end of the cold war. The Serbs, especially, were widely accused of "ethnic cleansing"—brutal forced relocation or killing to rid much of Bosnia of its Muslim inhabitants (Map 30.2). Muslim enclaves in

Map 30.2 Ethnic Conflict in East-Central Europe Much of east-central Europe, and particularly the Balkans, has long been an area of complex ethnic mixture. The end of communist rule opened the way to ethnic conflict, most tragically in what had been Yugoslavia. This map shows ethnic distribution in the region in the early 1990s.

Bosnia suffered grievously under Serb fire. In the Bosnian capital, Sarajevo, a culturally diverse city long known for its tolerant, cosmopolitan atmosphere, more than 10,000 civilians, including 1500 children, were killed by shelling and sniper fire during a Serb siege from 1992 to early 1996.

When a Serb mortar killed thirty-seven civilians in a marketplace in Sarajevo in August 1995, NATO forces responded with air strikes that led to peace accords and the end of four years of fighting by early 1996. The tide turned partly because a Western embargo had devastated the economy of what remained of Yugoslavia, forcing its Serb leader Slobodan Milosevic to cooperate with those seeking a peaceful solution.

But though the peace agreement envisioned a unified Bosnian state, the contending Serbs, Croats, and Bosnian Muslims quickly began carving out separate spheres, violating agreements about repatriation and the rights of minorities as they did so. Traditions of statehood were weak in this part of the Balkans, so it remained unclear whether the forces of disintegration at work in the former Yugoslavia were simply an anomaly in the greater scheme of twentieth-century Western history or an indication of potential, disintegrative forces at loose in Europe and the West. If every ethnic minority were to claim territorial autonomy, the future was uncertain indeed.

Although it was a NATO force that imposed peace in the former Yugoslavia, declining cohesion made NATO's future uncertain as well. The alliance had been formed to check Soviet expansion in Europe; with the apparent end of the Soviet threat, it made sense for its members to rethink their security needs and military priorities. This reconsideration led in several directions, not all of them compatible. Ten leading members of the European Union began developing a common defense mechanism, the Western European Union (WEU), but it remained tied to NATO. Some envisioned expanding NATO to encompass certain of the former Soviet bloc countries, starting with Hungary, Poland, and the Czech Republic. Others suggested that under the new circumstances, each nation would be well advised to look after its own defense. France resumed nuclear testing in the South Pacific in 1995, though in light of the international protest that resulted, it soon promised to cease such testing.

Postcommunist Russia was an especially uncertain player on the international scene. For many Russians, the collapse of communism brought national humiliation, in contrast to the renewed pride and independence to be found in the former satellite states. The role of the West in Bosnia and the prospect of NATO expansion eastward brought home Russia's sudden weakness—and led many Russians to insist that their country still be treated as a great power. Hard-liners began proposing that the now-collapsed "Soviet Union" be revived as a military alliance. Some even favored selling nuclear technology to such countries as Iran, Iraq, and Algeria—to put pressure on the West, especially the United States, which many Russians blamed for their problems. The danger of anti-Western extremism reinforced the support that Yeltsin enjoyed in the West even as it increased pressure at home to take an independent foreign policy line.

The European Union

The end of the cold war added urgency to the process of European integration. From the start, its proponents had hoped that the Common Market could promote greater uniformity in areas like tax policy and business law, in which national differences constituted barriers to economic activity across national borders. Although a full customs union had technically been achieved by the late 1960s, national governments continued to compromise the open market, especially by favoring certain companies to give them a competitive advantage in international competition. For domestic political reasons, governments sometimes confined their purchases to national firms or granted subsidies to domestic producers, thus enabling them to offer artificially lower prices to compete with foreign firms.

Still, movement toward the full-scale integration of the member economies continued by fits and starts. After another oil crisis in 1979, and amid increasing concern about "Eurosclerosis," or lack of innovation and competitiveness, the EEC's twelve members committed themselves in 1985 to the measures necessary to create a true single market with genuinely free competition by the end of 1992. Not only were goods, services, and money to circulate freely among the member countries, but there would be uniform product standards, as well as equal competition for the government contracts of each country.

By the late 1980s, the thrust toward economic integration increasingly assumed a political dimension. A European Parliament had developed from the assembly of the European Coal and Steel Community by 1962, though it had little importance at first. The provision for direct election to this body, which had formerly comprised delegations from the national parliaments, increased its stature when the first such elections were held in 1979. By the mid-1990s the European Union included a network of interlocking institutions, variously seated in Brussels, Strasbourg, and Luxembourg. Among them the European Parliament and the European Court of Justice played increasingly important roles.

Meeting at Maastrict, in the Netherlands, in 1991, the members of the European Union buttressed the powers of the European Parliament, agreed to move toward a common policy of workers' rights, and committed to a common currency and central banking structure by 1999. But this Maastrict agreement required the approval of the EU members, and in one country after another the ensuing debate over European integration proved more divisive than expected. In addition to the fear of German domination, some opponents of further integration saw it as a loss of sovereignty, which would mean entrusting vital decisions to faceless bureaucrats in foreign cities.

Moreover, the creation of an internal customs union, benign though it seemed, did not commit the EU to freer trade with nonmember countries like the United States and Japan. French farmers, especially, relied on a system of government supports that shielded them from U.S. competition. Conversely, high EU agricultural subsidies undercut the chance for Americans to sell their agricultural products in Europe. In 1992 the possibility that the French government would lower those supports, partly in response to pressures from the United States, caused massive demonstrations by French farmers.

Although the EU's members eventually ratified most of the Maastrict agreements, their implementation was not always smooth. Whereas Kohl's Germany continued to try to strengthen the European Commission and the European Parliament, even at the expense of national sovereignties, France and Britain dragged their feet. Citing the danger of terrorism and drug-smuggling, France essentially opted out of a provision to free the movement of people within Europe, whereas Germany found this provision indispensable.

Most controversial, however, was the provision for an Economic and Monetary Union (EMU), based on a common currency, to be in place by 1999. By eliminating the costs of currency exchange, this measure promised significantly to boost trade among the member countries. But to become part of the mechanism, countries had to maintain budget deficits no higher than 3 percent of gross domestic product; to reach that target, most of the member countries would have to decrease their deficits substantially. Governmental efforts to comply with this provision produced conflict on the domestic level, as the thrust toward European Union crashed against the social compact, already under pressure, that had produced high government spending for social welfare measures.

In a televised speech in 1995, President Chirac emphasized his determination to cut the government's budget deficit to enable France to meet the Maastrict criteria for economic and monetary union by 1999. The required austerity would include reducing welfare and pension payments

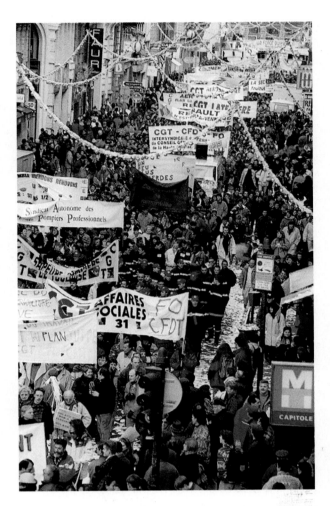

Protesting the New Austerity During the fall of 1995, widespread protest took place in France when the government announced new austerity measures, which it said were necessary to meet the budgetary requirements for membership in the European monetary union. Throughout the fifteen nations of the European Union, uncertainties about the role of government and the allure of further European integration meshed uneasily with the desire for the benefits that governments had come to provide since World War II. *(Wide World Photos)*

and restructuring the debt-plagued state railways. But Chirac's initiative prompted intense popular reaction during the fall of 1995. Railroad workers led the most serious wave of strikes that France had experienced in a decade, including periodic interruptions of public services. Students joined in, insisting that the university system needed more money, not less.

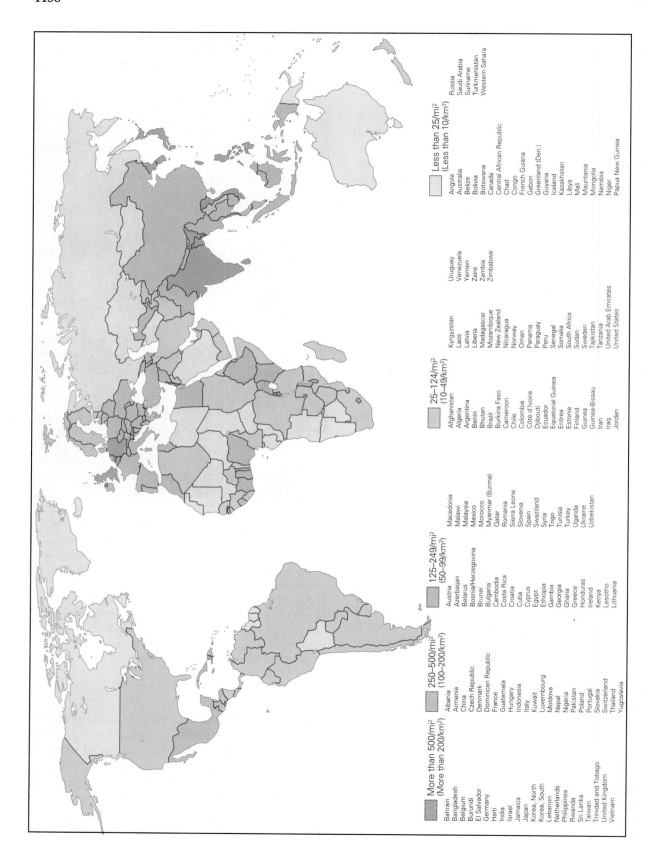

For many in France, embracing the EU seemed to jeopardize the egalitarianism that helped sustain social cohesion among the French. So even as the collapse of communism and the retreat from the interventionist state appeared to leave the field clear for free-market economics, the French response forced new questions about the relationship between social values and market forces. But the outcome of the strikes of 1995 was an awkward, provisional compromise. For France, and for the West, it was not clear how to arrive at a balance, in either economic or political terms.

Supranational Initiatives and Global Issues

Although less visible than the EU, other supranational entities also wielded increasing clout during the late twentieth century, making decisions that deeply affected the lives of ordinary people. Most obvious were multinational corporations, but the World Bank and the International Monetary Fund also played important roles, helping to keep the industrial economies synchronized and the less developed economies on a free-market path. These organizations could strongly influence domestic policies—by refusing, for example, to lend to countries spending heavily on defense. They were also major vehicles for the influence of the wealthy nations, centered in the West, on those from east-central Europe to south-central Africa that were trying to catch up.

At the same time, international cooperation took on greater urgency because growing concern with the global environment intensified the sense of world interdependence. Such problems as global warming, the destruction of rain forests, and the deterioration of the ozone layer were inherently supranational in scope. Yet environmental concerns complicated relations between the industrialized nations and the rest of the world. Countries seeking to industrialize encountered environmental constraints that had not been at issue

when the West industrialized. The challenge for the West was to foster protection of the environment in poorer regions of the globe without imposing unfair limitations on economic growth.

At the same time, changing demographic and economic patterns suggested that "North-South" tensions between the prosperous countries, concentrated in the northern hemisphere, and the poorer ones, more likely to be found farther south, might replace the East-West tensions of the cold war. World population reached 5.5 billion in 1993, having doubled in forty years. This was the fastest rate of world population growth ever, and by the 1990s virtually all of the growth was in Africa, Asia, and Latin America. The population of Europe was growing at only 0.2 percent per year, and in several countries, including Italy, Germany, and Spain, the population would actually have declined without the boost provided by immigration (Map 30.3).

Demographic pressure in the less developed countries contributed to the rising immigration to western Europe that made Africans selling hats, figurines, and sunglasses familiar in European cities by the early 1990s. But such immigration became a divisive political issue as Europeans faced the problems of an increasingly competitive world economy. In France the government's expulsion of illegal African immigrants sparked a major protest in 1996. The question of response to the needs of poorer countries with burgeoning populations had become central to the post–cold war agenda.

The combination of supranational organization, new technologies, and the global economy seemed to hold unprecedented promise, but startling scandals made clear the unprecedented scope for abuse it also allowed. When they came to light in 1991, the activities of the Bank of Credit and Commerce International (BCCI), a multinational bank nominally based in Luxembourg, brought home how vulnerable the world had become in an age of instant communications and global financial networks. For several years BCCI had dealt in drugs, illegal arms, terror, and money-laundering on a colossal international scale, corrupting prominent individuals throughout the world. Revelations of its operations suggested the need for more sophisticated forms of international regulation and accounting, but the pace of technological change seemed to outstrip the capacity of the international community to react.

Map 30.3 World Population Density, mid-1990s Most of Europe remains densely populated, but the explosive population growth of the late twentieth century took place especially in the poorer countries of Asia, Africa, and Latin America. (*Source:* Data from *1997 Information Please Almanac* (Boston: Houghton Mifflin, 1996), pp. 143 ff.)

Moreover, as the European Union and other supranational organizations became more prominent, forces in the opposite direction—subnational, religious, ethnic, tribal—simultaneously grew more powerful, producing conflict from Northern Ireland to Yugoslavia, from Spain to Lithuania. Such subgroup conflict was most tragic in east-central Europe (see Map 30.2), but it grew in western Europe as well, indicating that its sources were deep and widespread. Beginning in 1969, the British had to use troops in Northern Ireland to keep order in the face of ongoing threats from Irish Catholics seeking the end of British rule and unification with the Republic of Ireland. The result was polarization between Protestants and Catholics that defied solution. In Spain the restoration of democracy gave the long-restive Basque and Catalan minorities the chance to press openly for autonomy. Even in Belgium, there was growing antagonism between Flemish-speaking Flemings and French-speaking Walloons during the 1990s.

Immigration and Citizenship

With immigration growing sharply in Western Europe by the 1980s, questions about citizenship became politically central, giving a new twist to the interaction with the non-Western world that had helped define "the West" from the beginning. By 1995 there were 11 million legal resident immigrants living in the countries of the European Union—including, as the largest contingent, 2.6 million Turks. There were also as many as 4 million illegals. As economic pressures grew during the 1980s and 1990s, the tensions surrounding immigrants and foreigners threatened the political consensus in Western Europe.

At issue was not only new immigration, but the status of immigrant families already resident, in many cases for several generations since World War II. Some of those raising questions were not seeking simply to preserve economic advantages by limiting access. Rather, they were concerned about community, diversity, and national identity—about what it meant to belong. Because of differences in tradition, individual countries tended to conceive the alternatives differently.

Germany had actively recruited foreign workers during the decades of economic boom and labor shortage that followed the war. By 1973 non-citizens constituted 2.6 million workers, or 11.9

percent of the work force. At first these "guest workers" were viewed not as immigrants but as temporary, almost migrant, workers. But as they remained in Germany, their family patterns came to approximate those of the rest of the country, though their birthrates were considerably higher. By the 1980s, Germany had a large and increasingly settled population of non-Germans, many of them born and educated there.

In addition, the German Federal Republic had adopted a generous asylum law in an effort to atone for the crimes of the Nazi period. With the turmoil surrounding the end of communism in the Soviet bloc, the newly reunified Germany found 60,000 new arrivals seeking asylum every month by 1993. At that point Germany had a large foreign population of 6.4 million.

The law governing citizenship for immigrants and their descendants had originated in 1913 and reflected a long-standing German assumption that citizenship presupposed German ethnicity—or at least full assimilation. Thus ethnic Germans—over a million of whom moved to Germany from the former Soviet bloc between 1988 and 1991—were immediately accorded German citizenship. But there were many Turks, for example, who had been born in Germany but who could not become citizens. Precisely because citizenship entailed full assimilation, some Germans opposed citizenship for such "foreigners" or immigrants out of respect for cultural diversity.

But as the new wave of immigration from the east swelled the "foreign" population in Germany, more mundane motives came to the fore. Germans subject to economic pressures, especially, felt that foreigners and asylum-seekers were getting a better deal than ordinary citizens such as themselves. In 1992 alone, there were two thousand attacks on foreigners, some of them fatal. Those responsible were sometimes "skinheads," young people with uncertain economic prospects who claimed to admire Nazism. Their violence provoked massive counter-demonstrations by Germans eager to disavow any such ethnic hatred. But as reaction against refugees and foreign workers grew, the German parliament voted in 1993 to restrict the right of asylum.

These issues provoked particular controversy in Germany, but the claims of immigrants and refugees confronted all the Western democracies with difficult questions about the meaning of citizenship. In France the right-wing National Front, led by Jean-Marie LePen, forced the issue to center stage during the 1980s. Unlike the Germans, the French accorded citizenship automatically to second-generation immigrants, assuming that the offspring of immigrants would be readily assimilated into the national community. But as France began to attract rising numbers of immigrants, especially from Algeria and the other Islamic countries of North Africa, critics like LePen attacked the French citizenship law as too loose, charging that too many recent immigrants did not want to assimilate. Whereas the French left defended cultural diversity and its compatibility with citizenship, the right complained that citizenship was being devalued as a mere convenience, requiring no real commitment to the national community. This difference in perspective helps explain the controversy over the Muslim girls' headscarves that gripped France in 1989.

As these issues became ever more central in the West, representatives of twenty-seven Mediterranean countries—some European, some Middle-Eastern, some African—met in Barcelona in 1995 to seek common ground. The Europeans feared a continuing influx of immigrants fleeing poverty or the Islamic fundamentalism that was growing in the Islamic parts of the Mediterranean region. They also associated this wave of immigration with terrorism and illegal drug-dealing. For their part, the non-European countries of the Mediterranean feared that Europeans would begin expelling immigrants, thereby exacerbating the problems these immigrants had fled in the first place. To help limit the flow of immigrants, the Europeans pledged to help the other Mediterranean economies, but the need to protect competing EU agriculture made it hard to deliver. The Barcelona conference dramatized the web of interlocking difficulties that surrounded Western Europe's relations with its neighbors by the late twentieth century.

IN THE SHADOW OF HISTORY: THE EXPERIMENT CONTINUES

The rapid change of the later twentieth century raised new questions for Europeans about the meaning of their distinctive history and traditions. Some worried that prosperity necessarily entailed "Americanization," the unwelcome sameness of mass consumer culture. For the formerly communist countries of east-central Europe, the challenge was to find a positive way of reconnecting with their own national histories after decades of Soviet domination and communist ideology. In some cases, this return of history and memory contributed to the renewed emphasis on ethnic identity, which itself produced conflict and repression.

The collapse of communism in the Soviet bloc seemed to mean the triumph of democratic capitalism. But rapid economic and technological change introduced problems that proved hard to handle within the democratic political sphere. And during the 1990s, divisive issues all over the Western world—from the role of the state to environmental protection to immigration and cultural diversity—threatened to disrupt the political consensus that had crystallized since World War II.

Europe and America, Old and New

The center of gravity of Western civilization had changed before, gradually shifting from the eastern Mediterranean to the North Atlantic, but its location became especially uncertain with the dramatic changes surrounding World War II. Having weakened itself disastrously in the two world wars, Western Europe found itself dependent on the United States, first for its economic recovery, then for its defense. For decades after 1945, Europe seemed to have no choice but to follow the U.S. lead. Such subservience troubled some Europeans, and a kind of love-hate relationship with the United States developed in Western Europe during the later twentieth century.

Even after Europe's postwar economic recovery, the United States continued to set the pace in high-technology industries, prompting concerns that Europe would become a mere economic satellite of the United States. Europe seemed to be caught in a dilemma: To retain its distinctiveness over the long term, it apparently had to become more like America in the short term. The French writer Jean-Jacques Servan-Schreiber (b. 1924) made this case in his widely discussed book *The American Challenge*, first published in France in 1967 and quickly recognized as the classic statement of postwar Europe's ambivalent attitude toward Americanization. Haunted by the decline of earlier civilizations, Servan-Schreiber warned that if Europeans failed to become sufficiently

Kiefer: Osiris and Isis The German artist Anselm Kiefer combined unusual materials to create haunting images that often suggested the horrors of recent history. In this work from 1985 to 1987, the interpenetrating layers of human culture include images of ruin and death, hope and resurrection. *(Anselm Kiefer,* Osiris und Isis, *1985–87. Mixed media on canvas, 150″ × 220½″ × 6½″. San Francisco Museum of Modern Art. Purchased through a gift of Jean Stein by exchange, the Mrs. Paul L. Wattis Fund, and the Doris and Don Fisher Fund. Photo: Ben Blackwell)*

dynamic to compete with the Americans, Europe would gradually sink into decadence without ever understanding why it had happened. (See the box, "Europe and the American Challenge.")

By the 1980s much of Western Europe had caught up with the United States in standard of living, and the Western Europeans set the pace in confronting some of the new problems that resulted from ongoing socioeconomic change. The French day-care system was one prominent example. Nonetheless, concerns about Americanization deepened at the same time. By the late 1980s consumerism and the widening impact of American popular culture—from blue jeans and American TV to shopping malls and theme parks— suggested a growing homogenization in the capitalist democracies. A Euro-Disneyland opened in France in 1992 and, after a slow start, proved increasingly popular. Tangible reminders of Europe's distinctive past survived, but the growing "heritage industry" in Britain and elsewhere suggested that they were merely commodities to be packaged like any other.

Although the shadow of fascism and war remained, Europe had experienced a radical transformation in the half-century since World War II, a transformation that in some ways had cut Europeans off from their own tradition. Visible artifacts of Europe's history, including its difficult recent past, lurked as bits and pieces in present experience, and the contemporary relationship to the tradition grew increasingly uncertain, even ironic.

Europe and the American Challenge

Throughout the twentieth century, the complex relationship between Europe and the United States helped to define "the West." Writing in 1967, the French writer Jean-Jacques Servan-Schreiber worried that postwar Western Europe's dependence on America would deprive European civilization of its distinctiveness, vitality, and purpose.

Today's generation faces a . . . clear choice of building an independent Europe or letting it become an annex of the United States. The sheer weight of American power is pushing our hesitant countries along the path of annexation, and the point of no return may be reached before today's ten-year-olds are able to vote.

It is still possible for us to catch up, but there is a great deal of dead weight to overcome. . . . [P]erhaps it is asking too much of Europeans to adapt to global competition, shake themselves loose from entrenched national habits, pull together dispersed resources, adjust to severe new rules of management, and stop wasting precious men and capital. Is it reasonable to ask an old continent to show the vitality of a new nation—especially when the satellization of Europe is accompanied, at least initially, by a rising standard of living and by only a very gradual reduction in our freedom of thought? . . .

There is no way of leaving the "economic area" to the Americans so that we can get on with political, social, and cultural areas in our own way, as some people would like to believe. There is no such compartmentalization in the real world. . . .

A few leading firms, subsidiaries of American corporations, would decide how much European workers would earn and how they would live. . . . American capital and American management will not stop short at the gates of our society.

. . . [T]hese managers . . . will take a majority interest in, and then control, the firms that dominate the market in publishing, the press, phonograph recording, and television production. The formulas, if not all the details, of our cultural "messages" would be imported. . . .

Cairo and Venice were able to keep their social and cultural identities during centuries of economic decline. But it was not such a small world then, and the pace of change was infinitely slower. A dying civilization could linger for a long time on the fragrance left in an empty vase. We will not have that consolation. . . .

There is no excuse for Europeans to be passive or complacent, for they are free to examine the American experience critically. . . .

If Europe decides to do this, she would greatly improve the chances of building a decent world, one that could reconcile the unity of modern industrial society with the variety of national cultures that compose it. A polycentric world would ensure a growing exchange of goods and ideas, and the continuing competition between human societies that has always been the condition of human progress. Would an isolated Egypt, Greece, or Rome have done any better than the Mayas trapped in their jungle?

An independent Europe is essential for orderly world economic development. Is there any group of advanced nations—other than those of the Common Market, together with Britain—that could form a pole of attraction different from both America and Russia? A united Europe could bring about significant changes in the world power balance, and not only from the strength of her ideas. They would come, above all, from the very creation of a third great industrial power with no imperial pretensions—one whose only strategy is to help build a more unified international community.

Source: Jean-Jacques Servan-Schreiber, *The American Challenge* (New York: Avon, 1969), pp. 175–180.

This ambiguous relationship found striking expression in architecture and painting by the last decades of the century.

During the first two decades after World War II, modernist architecture, turning from tradition to embrace the modern industrial age, had triumphed at last, transforming cities throughout the world. By the 1980s, however, architects were turning from modernism to postmodernism, a glitzy way of building with ambiguous or ironic references to a tradition that was still present, even if those living within it were not quite sure what to make of it.

This uneasy contemporary relationship with the past, especially the traumatic past of the earlier twentieth century, took more pointed form in the neoexpressionism prominent in German and Italian painting during the 1980s. Artists like Anselm Kiefer (b. 1945) and Sandro Chia (b. 1946) created striking images that reflect the ongoing search for meaning in the context of an unmastered past.

Technology and the Fragile European Environment

With the disintegration of the Soviet bloc, it became clear that the years of communism had produced environmental degradation on an appalling scale. The Stalinist determination to industrialize quickly had combined with the Marxist faith in human mastery and progress to produce this result, and those who came after were left to clean up as best they could. But in Western Europe as well, the impact of rapid economic growth on the European landscape and cityscape continued to provoke concern.

The number of automobiles in Western Europe increased from 6 million in 1939 to 16 million by 1959 to 42 million by 1969. Almost overnight, traffic and air pollution fundamentally changed the face of Europe's old cities. In 1976 five statues that had supported the Eastern Portico of the Erectheum Temple on the Acropolis in Athens since the fifth century B.C. had to be replaced by replicas and put in a museum to save them from the rapid decay that air pollution was causing. There was talk of the "melancholy of progress" as the dimensions of the conflict between economic prosperity and the tangible monuments of Europe's history became clear.

The natural setting proved just as vulnerable. By the early 1980s acid rain had damaged one-third of the forests of West Germany, including the famous Black Forest of the southwest. Water pollution was a major problem from the Rhine to the Mediterranean to the Black Sea.

During much of the 1970s and 1980s, environmental concerns focused on the difficult question of nuclear power, which solved certain environmental problems while posing the risk of still more serious ones. By the 1990s the West's greatest proponent of nuclear power was France, which was getting 80 percent of its electricity from nuclear plants and was striving for 100 percent, whereas in the United States and Britain the comparable figure was only 20 percent—and shrinking. The French could boast that they had experienced no major safety problems and that by using nuclear power they were avoiding the hazards associated with fossil fuels, from acid rain to global warming. In much of Europe, however, there was decisive movement away from nuclear power, even before the Soviet nuclear accident at Chernobyl in 1986. In Germany the Greens led demonstrations in 1977 that forced the government drastically to decrease its plans for nuclear power. In Austria a referendum banned nuclear power altogether in 1978.

The Uncertain Triumph of Democratic Capitalism

The end of the cold war, the discrediting of communism, and the domestication of socialism all seemed to mean the triumph of political democracy and free-market capitalism. The superiority of both to the Soviet-style alternatives was all but universally recognized by the early 1990s. But though there was a good deal of self-congratulation in the West at first, what followed its victory was not a period of untroubled confidence but a deeper questioning of the capitalist democracy that had triumphed.

In light of the Western political experience so far, few denied that what worked best, and afforded the only basis for political legitimacy, was representative democracy based on universal suffrage within an open, pluralistic society guaranteeing individual freedom. There must be freedom not only to inquire and to criticize but also to pursue in dividual advantage within a market economy. At the same time, that free-market system had to be bounded by some measure of governmental responsibility—for education, for social welfare, for workplace and product safety, and for the environment. But there remained difficult questions about the proper role for government in coordinating, channeling, or balancing market forces. Some emphasized the contrast between the "social market economy" of Germany and the more unrestrained capitalism of the United States and Britain. (See the box, "The Varieties of Liberal Capitalism.")

As the former communist East struggled to catch up to the West, Western affluence increasingly seemed brittle and uncertain. It was largely economic insecurity that made immigration such a volatile issue all over the Western world by the 1990s. High unemployment, the result of technological change and increasing global competition, persisted in Western Europe, even afflicting Germany by the mid-1990s. In the United States, unemployment was considerably lower, but new jobs were often poorly paid, with few health and insurance benefits. Moreover, Americans did not have quite the safety net that the European welfare states provided—in health care, most notably. For most, real wages advanced little between the mid-1970s and the mid-1990s. The widening gap between the well-off and those barely getting by suggested the emergence of a "winner-take-all" society.[1]

Although the socialist left had won reforms that were now central to the consensus around democratic capitalism, it had abandoned much of what it had stood for—from class struggle and revolution to state ownership and a centrally planned economy. Socialism could apparently serve only as the mildly left-leaning party within the framework of capitalist democracy. In France the effort of Socialist President François Mitterrand to create a democratic socialist alternative bogged down by the later 1980s. As French socialism seemed to lose its sense of direction, some leading Socialists got caught up in corruption scandals, and the party met massive defeat at the polls in 1993 and 1995. In Italy, too, the Socialists were central to a corruption scandal that began convulsing the country in 1992, and that quickly spread to discredit the Christian Democrats as well—and indeed the whole entrenched Italian political class.

With the decline of socialism as a political alternative, the new right, which had been associated especially with anti-immigrant sentiment at first, grew in prominence by the mid-1990s as it sought to expand the range of political choices. Although differing considerably in priorities, respectability, and success, right-leaning political leaders—from LePen in France and José Maria Aznar in Spain to Jörg Haider in Austria and Gianfranco Fini in Italy—tapped into the growing political frustration and economic uncertainty.

But what did it mean to be "right wing" or conservative by the late twentieth century? In Italy and Austria, new right politicians criticized the prevailing understanding of the recent past—the era of fascism and the Second World War—playing up the patriotic, anticommunist thrust of the interwar right. But as far as present priorities were concerned, conservatives sometimes differed sharply among themselves. In Britain the Thatcher government had tamed the labor unions and sold state-owned industries, but conservative critics pointed out that it had expanded centralized control over local government, health care, and education. With its ideological agenda, the Thatcher government had been activist and interventionist, not cautious, gradualist, and pragmatic—not truly conservative. In addressing economic anxieties, the new right sometimes articulated problems that mainstream politicians ignored, but it seemed unable to propose viable solutions. Its proponents even disagreed over the relative merits of free trade and protectionism.

Extreme though it was, the Italian corruption scandal of the early 1990s dramatized troubling tendencies in the democratic political system of the later twentieth century. The need for money to finance electioneering and political patronage kept the whole system on the edge of corruption. Democracy seemed to place a premium on short-term advantage over vision and principle. By the early 1990s, declining voter turnout suggested growing political cynicism and disillusionment all over the Western world.

At the same time, participation in national politics came to seem less significant partly because key decisions were often made elsewhere, by multinational corporations or supranational organizations not directly subject to democratic control. As global competition intensified, the logic of capitalism, or the market, seemed increasingly to overwhelm the capacities of democratic politics.

The Varieties of Liberal Capitalism

The collapse of communism during 1989–1991 meant the triumph of capitalism, but it also brought to center stage the choices and trade-offs at work within the advanced capitalist world. Postwar West Germany had achieved remarkable success with its "social market economy," but as renewed under Ronald Reagan and Margaret Thatcher during the 1980s, the more individualistic, entrepreneurial capitalism of the United States and Britain attracted increasing support. Writing in 1991, the French industrialist and government leader Michel Albert offered a spirited critique of Anglo-American capitalism and advocated that France embrace the German "Rhine model" within a more fully integrated European Union.

The rich need no longer feel ashamed of their wealth. Where they once shunned any hint of ostentation, they now display it with an immodesty that the French used to consider shockingly vulgar when they witnessed it in Americans. And this wealth increasingly rubs shoulders with a new poverty of the kind that is flourishing in the USA. France, too, now has its zones of urban blight, dumping-grounds populated by a growing army of the unemployed, those whose benefit has run out, young people seeking their first job, and immigrants—illegal or otherwise. . . .

The Rhine model . . . embodies, on the one hand, capitalism which can provide social security, and on the other, a system in which the company is seen not just as a heap of capital but a group of people. This is exactly what France badly needs. . . .

. . . If the aim is to harness capitalism without impairing its efficiency, it is no longer to the nation state that we must look, but to Europe. And Europe must produce both powerful financial structures . . . and political institutions. . . .

. . . [A] whole new ideology of capitalism had come to power:

[T]he market is good, the state is bad; social welfare provision, once a sign of progress, is blamed for encouraging laziness; taxation, once an indispensable means for reconciling economic development and social justice, is accused (not without reason) of discouraging talent and initiative. . . . Where the nineteenth century saw capitalism challenge the state, but with no thought of replacing it in such areas as health, education or the media . . . , the late twentieth century now proposes to substitute market forces for the state. . . . [I]n the majority of developed countries, more and more services, from broadcasting to rubbish collection and from the water supply to the post office, are being transferred from the public to the private sector. . . .

We Europeans are, more than anyone else on the planet, faced with the question of which sacrifices we shall make, and for which gains. The European Community is the main battleground on which the conflict of capitalism against capitalism will be fought. . . .

1. Either Europeans will fail to understand what is really at stake, and so will not press their leaders to make the imaginative leap towards true political union: in which case, the Single Market will begin to fray and disintegrate before it has begun; the possibility of unity will recede ever further under a cloud of permanent Euro-pessimism; the slide towards the neo-American model will accelerate as the zones of decay and deprivation already staked out on the periphery of our cities continue to swell. . . .

2. Or we will actually begin to build the United States of Europe: in which case, we will have all the means at our disposal to choose the best possible socioeconomic system, that which has already proven its mettle within one part of the continent and which will become the "European model" of capitalism.

Source: Michel Albert, *Capitalism Against Capitalism* (London: Whurr, 1993), pp. 238–240, 244, 247, 253–254, 260.

CONCLUSION: WESTERN CIVILIZATION IN A GLOBAL AGE

By the late twentieth century, the West was part of a world that, in one sense, was dramatically less Eurocentric than it had been a century before, when European imperialism was at its peak. Events in the West competed for attention with OPEC meetings, Japanese economic decisions, or the struggle against apartheid in South Africa. Decisions vitally affecting Europeans or Americans might be made anywhere. A planetary culture, a threatened environment, and an interdependent international economy required people to think and react in global terms as never before.

One of the defining characteristics of the modern period in the West had been a "master narrative"—a conception of all human development—that took the European model as privileged and assumed everyone else to be trying to catch up. Such developmentalist assumptions were linked to the arrogant sense of superiority that had once seemed to justify Western imperialism. There was no question that capitalism had spread from Europe, but even as Westernization continued at the end of the twentieth century, it was increasingly recognized that the West was not necessarily the model, the standard of development.

Although as late as 1965 a distinguished British historian suggested that sub-Saharan Africa had no real history prior to the arrival of Europeans, there was growing interest in the non-Western world and increasing respect for its diverse traditions during the latter part of the century. At the same time, scholars like Edward Said, a Palestinian teaching in the United States, showed how Western images of the non-Western world had been constructed, and become stereotypes, reinforcing assumptions of Western superiority. (See the box, "Encounters with the West: The Case of 'Orientalism.'")

Such insights contributed to the "postmodern" departure from a Eurocentered master narrative as the basis of our historical self-understanding. This departure enabled the West to place cultural differences in more genuinely global, or human, perspective. At the same time, it led some to deny that Western civilization merited privilege as an object of study. After that civilization had been glorified for so long, this stance was no doubt understandable, though it also involved a measure of overreaction. The discussion gradually made it clearer that the point of such study was not to celebrate Western civilization but simply to understand it—as the matrix that continued to shape the West and, less directly, the world. That tradition included much that might be criticized, and its present outcome entailed much that might be changed. But understanding had to come first. The invitation to think freely about the Western tradition, to criticize it, and to build a better future on it rested on precisely that tradition—and remained perhaps its most fundamental legacy.

But as the end of the century approached, the concern about diversity and assimilation throughout much of the Western world suggested that controversy would continue over the significance of the Western tradition in contemporary life. (See the feature, "Weighing the Evidence: The Debate over Western Civilization," on pages 1150–1151.) Concern about immigration was one manifestation, as was the controversy over "multiculturalism" in the United States. There was little agreement even about what an educated person in the West ought to know about the cultures of the world—including the West. At issue was how to do justice to difference and diversity without forgetting the common humanity, the recognition of shared experience, that gives substance to the notion of "the humanities." On that basis, we seek to learn from others, even those, perhaps especially those, with different backgrounds and values, as we also seek to understand the complex, tension-ridden tradition of the West.

A question that dramatized some of the difficulties at work concerned the sources of jazz, the American musical form that moved up the Mississippi River from New Orleans early in the twentieth century and took Europe by storm in the 1920s. Jazz contributed to the more generic American popular music that, in turn, helped nourish the worldwide popular culture emerging by the end of the century. Yet during the mid-1990s there was a divisive debate in the United States over the "ownership" of jazz. Was it a cultural blend, confirming the long-cherished notion that America had been a melting pot, or was it an African creation that the dominant, European-derived culture sought to expropriate? Each side appealed to history to justify its interpretation.

Debate about cultural contributions, even about fusion and expropriation, seems likely to continue. And it invites some measure of ideologi-

∽ ENCOUNTERS WITH THE WEST ∽

The Case of "Orientalism"

In his influential book Orientalism, *published in 1978, the Palestinian-American scholar Edward Said explored the process through which Westerners had constructed the "Middle East"—as different from the West. Though critical of the West, Said appealed to our common humanity in an effort to overcome the ongoing tendency, which was not confined to the West, to understand oneself as superior by stereotyping others. In the final analysis, he suggested, we all need to learn from one another.*

The Orient is not only adjacent to Europe; it is also the place of Europe's greatest and richest and oldest colonies, the source of its civilizations and languages, its cultural contestant, and one of its deepest and most recurring images of the Other. In addition, the Orient has helped to define Europe (or the West) as its contrasting image, idea, personality, experience. . . .

. . . The relationship between Occident and Orient is a relationship of power, of domination, of varying degrees of a complex hegemony. . . . There is very little consent to be found, for example, in the fact that Flaubert's encounter with an Egyptian courtesan produced a widely influential model of the Oriental woman; she never spoke of herself, she never represented her emotions, presence, or history. *He* spoke for and represented her. He was foreign, comparatively wealthy, male, and these were historical facts of domination that allowed him not only to possess Kuchuk Hanem physically but to speak for her and tell his readers in what way she was "typically Oriental." . . .

. . . [T]here is no avoiding the fact that even if we disregard the Orientalist distinctions between "them" and "us," a powerful series of political and ultimately ideological realities inform scholarship today. No one can escape dealing with, if not the East/West division, then the North/South one, the have/have-not one, the imperialist/anti-imperialist one, the white/colored one. We cannot get around them all by pretending they do not exist; on the contrary, contemporary Orientalism teaches us a great deal about the intellectual dishonesty of dissembling on that score, the result of which is to intensify the divisions and make them both vicious and permanent. Yet an openly polemical and right-minded "progressive" scholarship can very easily degenerate into dogmatic slumber, a prospect that is not edifying either.

. . . [E]nough is being done today in the human sciences to provide the contemporary scholar with insights, methods, and ideas that could dispense with racial, ideological, and imperialist stereotypes of the sort provided during its historical ascendancy by Orientalism. I consider Orientalism's failure to have been a human as much as an intellectual one; for in having to take up a position of irreducible opposition to a region of the world it considered alien to its own, Orientalism failed to identify with human experience, failed also to see it as human experience. . . . I hope to have shown my reader that the answer to Orientalism is not Occidentalism. No former "Oriental" will be comforted by the thought that having been an Oriental himself he is likely—too likely—to study new "Orientals"—or "Occidentals"—of his own making. If the knowledge of Orientalism has any meaning, it is in being a reminder of the seductive degradation of knowledge, of any knowledge, anywhere, at any time. Now perhaps more than before.

Source: Edward W. Said, *Orientalism* (New York: Random House, Vintage, 1979), pp. 1–2, 4–8, 327–328.

cal or political distortion, from whichever side. Such debate makes it clear that historical study has become more relevant than ever in this era of rapid cultural cross-fertilization, yet history is also more contested, as the ultimate court of appeal. So the danger is not indifference to history but the opposite—that historical inquiry will become too politicized to allow us genuinely to learn from it.

Such learning is crucial not to enable us to celebrate "who we are," but to deepen our understanding, even to make us more self-critical, so that, continuing the experiment, we may act more effectively—and thereby create a better future.

NOTES

1. Robert H. Frank and Philip J. Cook, *The Winner-Take-All Society* (New York: Free Press, 1995).

SUGGESTED READING

Western Society in the Late Twentieth Century

Ardagh, John. *France Today*, revised ed. 1988. Updated edition of a lively, perceptive survey of the remarkable changes in French life since World War II.

Barkan, Joanne. *Visions of Emancipation: The Italian Workers' Movement Since 1945.* 1984. A sympathetic account of the influential postwar Italian labor movement. Provides a good feel for the experience of factory workers and makes sense of their demands for autonomy.

Bridenthal, Renate, et al., eds. *Becoming Visible: Women in European History.* 1987. A major collection of essays on women's history, including seven that deal with twentieth-century topics. Jane Jenson's "Both Friend and Foe: Women and State Welfare" offers an illuminating comparative study of women and the welfare systems in Britain and France in the post–World War II period.

Brubaker, Rogers. *Citizenship and Nationhood in France and Germany.* 1992. Lucid comparative study showing how very different conceptions of citizenship emerged in these two countries as a result of their contrasting historical experiences over the past two centuries.

Hollifield, James F., and George Ross, eds. *Searching for the New France.* 1991. A collection of essays on topics from political structure and foreign policy to immigration and higher education.

Marwick, Arthur. *British Society Since 1945.* 1990. A lively, comprehensive survey, accenting the change to a consumer culture in the 1960s, but with due emphasis on the conservative transformation of the 1980s.

Mosse, George L. *The Image of Man: The Creation of Modern Masculinity.* 1996. Traces the idea and image of the masculine from the advent of nineteenth century bourgeois society to the late twentieth century, when gender roles were open to discussion as rarely before in the West.

Sorlin, Pierre. *European Cinemas, European Societies 1939–1990.* 1991. Emphasizes the themes of urbanization, immigration, and gender. Contrasts European with U.S. film making.

Questioning the Role of Government

Cheles, Luciano, et al., eds. *The Far Right in Western and Eastern Europe,* 2d ed. 1995. A superior collection of essays on the revival of the extreme right in the 1980s and 1990s.

Jenkins, Simon. *Accountable to None: The Tory Nationalisation of Britain.* 1995. Provocative conservative critique of Margaret Thatcher's revolution in Britain. Argues that Thatcher increased centralization even as she fostered privatization.

Maier, Charles, ed. *Changing Boundaries of the Political: Essays on the Evolving Balance Between the State and Society, Public and Private in Europe.* 1987. Though uneven and sometimes difficult, this is a useful collection of essays on an important and elusive topic. Good, for example, on the changing politics of health care.

Pierson, Paul. *Dismantling the Welfare State? Reagan, Thatcher, and the Politics of Retrenchment.* 1994. A comparative analysis of what worked and what did not in the conservative effort at retreat from the welfare state in the 1980s. Concludes that because of the high political costs of retrenchment, the welfare state remained essentially intact.

Young, Hugo. *The Iron Lady: A Biography of Margaret Thatcher.* 1989. A full-scale, readable biography that challenges Thatcher's consistency and questions her achievement.

The Transformation in Eastern and East-Central Europe

Elster, Jon, ed. *The Roundtable Talks and the Breakdown of Communism.* 1996. Separate essays on the negotiated end to communist rule in five east-central European countries, with an additional essay on the contrasting case of China.

Funk, Nanette, and Magda Mueller, eds. *Gender Politics and Post-Communism: Reflections from Eastern Europe and the Former Soviet Union.* 1993. Country-by-country analysis and critique by feminist scholars from the region, with an effective mixture of outside perspectives.

Garton Ash, Timothy. *The Magic Lantern: The Revolution of '89 Witnessed in Warsaw, Budapest, Berlin, and Prague.* 1990. Firsthand testimony on the fall of communism by a British intellectual with close contacts among anticommunists in east-central Europe.

Goldman, Marshall I. *What Went Wrong with Perestroika.* 1991. Focuses on the incongruity between the successful political restructuring, which went beyond what Gorbachev intended, and the inadequate economic reform.

Havel, Václav. *Disturbing the Peace: A Conversation with Karel Hvížďala.* 1991. Part autobiography, part history, part philosophy, part personal testimony. Demonstrates the moral vision that made Havel so effective as a leader in the Czech opposition to communism.

(continued on page 1152)

THE DEBATE OVER WESTERN CIVILIZATION

A striking theme in Western civilization during the last third of the twentieth century has been the intense debate that has erupted over "Western civilization" itself—its significance, and even its legitimacy as a concept. Why have the points at issue been contested so passionately at this moment in history, and what can we learn from this ongoing debate? The following testimony, from four very different thinkers, raises the central questions.

Jacques Ellul Writing in 1975, this influential French intellectual sought to counter the overreaction that he believed marked the increasing tendency—even in the West—to idealize non-Western cultures and denigrate Western civilization.

I admit, then, all the accusations leveled at the West for its colonialism and imperialism. . . .

Am I therefore to become a masochist and reject everything western, deny all the values of our world? No! . . . I accept responsibility for the evil that has been done, but I deny that only evil has been done. I know our civilization is built on bloodshed and robbery, but I also know that every civilization is built on bloodshed and robbery. . . .

. . . [W]e cannot expect to find justice and innocence "somewhere else." The Chinese and the Africans are not free of the sin we acknowledge in ourselves; they have been colonialists no less than we. . . .

. . . If the Chinese have done away with binding the feet of women, and if the Moroccans, Turks, and Algerians have begun to liberate their women, whence did the impulse to these moves come from? From the West, and nowhere else! Who invented the "rights of man"? The same holds for the elimination of exploitation. . . . The whole of the modern world, for better or for worse, is following a western model; no one imposed it on others, they have adopted it themselves, and enthusiastically. (*Source:* Jacques Ellul, *The Betrayal of the West,* trans. Matthew J. O'Connell [New York: Seabury Press (Continuum), 1978], pp. 7, 9, 11–12, 16–17.)

Silvia Federici Twenty years after Ellul expressed his views, this Italian-American scholar questioned the whole concept of "Western civilization" and the purposes that, over the past two centuries, led some to place such emphasis on it.

[T]he concept of "the West" is highly problematic, since it pretends to be constructed by reference to conven-

tional geographical coordinates and yet maps the world in ways that defy "common sense," leaving entire regions in limbo. . . . Worse yet, a genealogy of "Western Civilization" demonstrates that this concept has historically developed in the context of military and ideological warfare, as the label for a political reality that could be conceived as unified only by reference to perceived enemies and contenders. . . .

Only in the aftermath of the nineteenth-century colonial penetration of India, China, and the Middle East did "the West" take on a more prominent political role, as the signifier of Europe's imperial project. It was at this time that it began . . . to merge with the concept of "civilization." . . .

As a synonym for social progress, "civilization" remained throughout the nineteenth century the prime signifier in the anthropological self-presentation of the European elites. Thus, the "civilized"/"savage" ("primitive," "backward") contrast became a standard element in European literature. (*Source:* Silvia Federici, ed., *Enduring Western Civilization: The Construction of the Concept of Western Civilization and Its "Others"* [Westport, Conn.: Praeger, 1995], pp. 65–66.)

Jean Dubuffet Writing in the early 1980s, this well-known French artist did not deny that there is a recognizable Western cultural tradition, but he found it elitist, limiting, even "asphyxiating."

It is naive to think that the few meager deeds and few meager works that happened to be preserved from the past are necessarily the best and most important of the thoughts of these times. Their preservation results only from that fact that a small coterie chose and applauded them, while eliminating all others. Those who celebrate culture do not think enough about the great number of humans and the innumerable character of productions of the mind. . . . The Westerner's idea that culture is the business of books, paintings and monuments is childish. . . .

When I think of these nations that had only an oral culture, and which left us no trace of their thought, it strikes me that the same is true of our nation. For we cannot call the works that form our scholastic material the work of a nation, all of which—writings, paintings, monuments—are products of a very restricted circle—the caste of lords—and of a handful of scholars who work for them. (*Source:* Jean Dubuffet, *Asphyxiating Culture,* trans. Carol Volk (New York: Four Walls Eight Windows, 1988), pp. 17-19.)

V. S. Naipaul Speaking in New York in 1990 on the universal significance of the Western tradition, this influential novelist, born and raised in Trinidad, began by reflecting on his own Indian Hindu family background.

We were a people of ritual and sacred texts. . . . But . . . [o]ur literature, our texts, didn't commit us to an exploration of our world; rather they were cultural markers, giving us a sense of the wholeness of our world, and the alienness of what lay outside. I don't believe that, in his family, anyone before my father would have thought of original literary composition. That idea came to my father in Trinidad with the English language . . . in spite of the colonial discouragements of the place. . . .

The universal civilization . . . wasn't always as attractive as it is today. The expansion of Europe gave it for at least three centuries a racial tint, which still causes pain. In Trinidad I grew up in the last days of that kind of racialism. And that, perhaps, has given me a greater appreciation of the immense changes that have taken place since the end of [World War II], the extraordinary attempt of this civilization to accommodate the rest of the world. . . .

. . . [T]he idea of the pursuit of happiness . . . is at the heart of the attractiveness of the civilization to so many outside it or on its periphery. . . . It implies a certain kind of society, a certain kind of awakened spirit. I don't imagine my father's parents would have been able to understand the idea. So much is contained in it: the idea of the individual, responsibility, choice, the life of the intellect, the idea of vocation and perfectibility and achievement. It is an immense human idea. (*Source:* V. S. Naipaul, "Our Universal Civilization," reprinted in *The New York Review of Books*, January 31, 1991, pp. 22, 25.)

Whether or not we find Federici's critique convincing, she formulated the most basic questions—is it legitimate to speak of "the West" at all, and what purposes were at work as the notion of "Western civilization" evolved? Most agree that there is a distinctive cultural tradition in what, despite the obvious geographical imprecision, is usefully termed "the West," though the questions about its value, and the uses or misuses that have been made of it, remain. Dubuffet recognized a coherent Western cultural tradition, but he found it so limited, reflecting the interests of the winners—the powerful—and their intellectual allies, as to be a problem, not a source of sustenance.

Despite his claim to strike a balance, Ellul was perhaps too eager to have it both ways as he denied the uniqueness of the West's crimes while crediting the West for the values of individualism and freedom. At the very least, his argument suggests the need for cross-cultural historical comparisons. It is striking, however, that Naipaul, from his cross-cultural perspective, associated the West with essentially the same values Ellul emphasized—and similarly found them at once uniquely Western in origin and universal in appeal and significance.

It first seems ironic that this debate would come to the fore during the decades after World War II, when, according to Naipaul, Western civilization became more open and began more genuinely living up to its ideals. But this was also the period of decolonization and the quantum leap in "globalization," trends that were bound to raise new questions as the West pulled back from the pretense of cultural superiority. The democratization of the era similarly prompted the new line of questioning that we find in the passage from Dubuffet.

Even those most skeptical, like Federici and Dubuffet, do not simply turn from the Western tradition but invite us to question it afresh, thereby expanding our sense of what it includes and deepening our relationship with it. In the same way, even defenders like Ellul and Naipaul lead us to ask what, in the wider globalization, is best understood as "Westernization"—as opposed to cultural fusion, or ongoing diversity, or renewed exploitation. Moreover, Ellul and Naipaul stress that the contemporary democratic impulse itself grew from within the Western tradition. That impulse has prompted historians to expand their focus to ordinary people and, in the realm of "high" culture, to expand the "canon"—the body of works considered worthy of our attention. The Western tradition has proven flexible enough even to accommodate changes in our understanding of the West's past.

The debate over Western civilization is itself testimony to the openness and freedom of that tradition. For all of us, the Western tradition entails an invitation, and a responsibility, to question "Western civilization" as part of our effort to learn from the whole human experience. ✀

Hosking, Geoffrey. *The Awakening of the Soviet Union.* Enlarged ed. 1991. Seeks to understand the Gorbachev reform effort from the perspective of ordinary people. Accents the potential for autonomy and initiative that would enable Soviet citizens to carry the reform effort beyond the intent of its leaders.

Laba, Roman. *The Roots of Solidarity.* 1991. Seeks to show that workers, as opposed to the Polish intelligentsia, were the driving force behind the Solidarity movement.

Malia, Martin. *The Soviet Tragedy: A History of Socialism in Russia, 1917–1991.* 1994. A deeply critical assessment of the course of the Soviet experiment from the perspective of its failure by the early 1990s.

Remnick, David. *Lenin's Tomb: The Last Days of the Soviet Empire.* 1994. Acclaimed and compelling account of the fall of the communist regime. Makes effective use of oral testimony.

Skidelsky, Robert. *The Road from Serfdom: The Economic and Political Consequences of the End of Communism.* 1996. Using the collapse of communism as a starting point, a leading economic historian accents the global dimensions of the shift to liberal capitalism in the 1980s and outlines a cautiously optimistic scenario for the future.

Steele, Jonathan. *Eternal Russia: Yeltsin, Gorbachev, and the Mirage of Democracy.* 1994. Places events before and after the fall of communism in useful historical perspective, while criticizing the preoccupation with privatization and the corresponding failure to foster a culture of democracy.

Stokes, Gale. *The Walls Came Tumbling Down: The Collapse of Communism in Eastern Europe.* 1993. Dramatic and comprehensive, the first standard account of the dissolution of communism in east-central Europe.

The New International Situation

Caplan, Richard, and John Feffer, eds. *Europe's New Nationalism: States and Minorities in Conflict.* 1996. Sophisticated essays by international scholars on the renewal of nationalism in Europe after the end of the cold war.

Donia, Robert J., and John V. A. Fine, Jr. *Bosnia and Hercegovina: A Tradition Betrayed.* 1994. Accessible, well-illustrated historical overview leading up to the region's central place in the Wars of Yugoslav Seces-sion, which helped redefine international politics after the end of the cold war. Accenting the long tradition of ethnic and religious toleration in the area, insists that the conflict stemmed from contemporary political and territorial ambitions, not historically rooted ethnic or religious tensions.

Garton Ash, Timothy. *In Europe's Name: Germany and the Divided Continent.* 1993. A searching essay on Germany's place in Europe and the world, from the years of division, to reunification, to the post–cold war order.

Glenny, Misha. *The Fall of Yugoslavia: The Third Balkan War.* 3d revised edition. 1996. Influential account of the disintegration of Yugoslavia, combining historical analysis with dramatic treatment of the multisided ethnic fighting of the 1990s.

Jarausch, Konrad H. *The Rush to German Unity.* 1994. A clear and compelling account of the process of German reunification after the fall of communism in the east, with a careful assessment of the outcome.

Treverton, Gregory. *America, Germany, and the Future of Europe.* 1992. Treats the historical background of European-American relations after the cold war and shows why the United States seems bound to play a diminished role in Europe.

Europeans and Americans

Dean, John, and Jean-Paul Gabillet, eds. *European Readings of American Popular Culture.* 1996. Varied essays by European scholars assessing the impact of American popular culture in postwar Europe.

Diner, Dan. *America in the Eyes of the Germans: An Essay on Anti-Americanism.* 1996. A German-Israeli historian offers a provocative, critical look at the tendency of Germans—and Europeans more generally—to use America as a metaphor for the dark side of modernism.

Kroes, Rob. *If You've Seen One, You've Seen the Mall: Europeans and American Mass Culture.* 1996. Lively, sophisticated essay on the European way of transforming themes from American popular culture.

Kuisel, Richard F. *Seducing the French: The Dilemmas of Americanization.* 1993. Illuminating study of the French response to all things American in the half-century of American hegemony that followed World War II.

Chapter Opener Credits

Text Credits

Chapter 4: Page 123: "Virtues and Vices of Alexander the Great" from *The Campaigns of Alexander* by Arrian, translated by Aubrey de Sélincourt. (Penguin Classics, 1958). Copyright © 1958 by the Estate of Aubrey de Sélincourt. Reprinted by permission of Frederick Warne & Co. (Penguin Books UK). **Page 131:** "The Oracle of the Potter" from *The Hellenistic Age: From the Battle of Ipsos to the Death of Kleopatra VII*, Stanley M. Burstein, editor and translator. Copyright © 1985 by Cambridge University Press. Reprinted by permission. **Page 141:** "A Seleucid Queen Helps the City of Iasos" from *The Hellenistic World from Alexander to the Roman Conquest: A Selection of Ancient Sources in Translation* by M. M. Austin. Copyright © 1981 by Cambridge University Press. Reprinted by permission. **Page 143:** "Early Stoic Ethics and Politics" from *Greek and Roman Philosophy After Aristotle* by Jason L. Saunders. Copyright © 1966 by Jason L. Saunders. Reprinted by permission of The Free Press, a division of Simon & Schuster. **Page 146:** "The Jews Struggle Over Hellenism" from I Maccabees, *The Anchor Bible*, Vol. 41, Translation notes and commentary by Jonathan A. Goldstein. Copyright © 1976 by Jonathan A. Goldstein. Reprinted by permission of Doubleday, a division of Bantam Doubleday Dell Publishing Group, Inc.

Chapter 5: Page 153: From *The Aeneid of Virgil*, translated by Allen Mandelbaum. Copyright © 1971 by Allen Mandelbaum. Reprinted by permission of Bantam Books, a division of Bantam, Doubleday, Dell Publishing Group, Inc. **Page 159:** "The Rape of Lucretia" from *The Early History of Rome* by Livy, translated by Aubrey de Sélincourt (Penguin Classics, 1960). Copyright © 1960 by the Estate of Aubrey de Sélincourt. Reprinted by permission of Frederick Warne & Co. (Penguin Books UK). **Pages 170, 179, 181:** "A Roman Triumph," "Roman Attitudes Toward the Conquered," "Tiberius Gracchus on Rome's Plight" from *Roman Civilization, Sourcebook I: The Republic*, third edition, edited by Naphtali Lewis and Meyer Reinhold. Copyright © 1951 by Columbia University Press. Reprinted by permission of the publisher. **Page 186:** "Cicero in Defense of Milo" from *Cicero: Selected Political Speeches* translated by Michael Grant. (Penguin Classics, 1969). Copyright © 1969 by Michael Grant Publications Ltd. Reprinted by permission of Frederick Warne & Co. (Penguin Books UK).

Chapter 6: Page 196: "Augustus: The Official Story" from *Res Gestae Divi Augusti: The Achievements of the Divine Augustus*, edited by P. A. Brunt and J. M. Moore. Copyright © 1967. Reprinted by permission of Oxford University Press. **Page 198:** "Augustus: A Skeptical View" from *The Annals of Imperial Rome* by Tacitus, translated by Michael Grant. (Penguin Classics, 1951, revised edition 1971). Copyright © 1956, 1959, 1971 by Michael Grant Publications Ltd. Reprinted by permission of Frederick Warne & Co. (Penguin Books UK). **Page 206:** "Ordinary People" from *Roman Civilization* by Naphtali Lewis and Meyer Reinhold. Copyright 1951 by Columbia University. Reprinted by permission of the publisher. **Page 212:** "Syria Between Rome and Persia" from *History of Ancient Iran*, translated by Richard N. Frye, Emeritus Professor of Iranian History, Harvard University (Munich: C. H. Beck'sche Verlagsbuchhandlung, 1984). Reprinted by permission of Richard N. Frye.

Chapter 7: Page 232: "A Contemporary View of Diocletian's Reforms" from *Roman Civilization* by Naphtali Lewis and Meyer Reinhold. Copyright © 1951 by Columbia University Press. Reprinted by permission of the publisher. **Page 253:** "Basic Principles of Roman Law" from *Justinian's Institutes* 1.1–2 edited and translated by Peter Birks and Grant McLeod. Cornell University Press, 1987. Reprinted by permission of the

publisher. **Page 257:** "Melania the Younger: The Appeal of Monasticism to Women" from *The Life of Melania the Younger: Studies in Women and Religion*, Vol. 14, edited and translated by Elizabeth A. Clark. (New York: Edwin Mellen Press, 1984). Reprinted by permission of Edwin Mellen Press. **Page 260:** "The Moment of Augustine's Spiritual Awakening" from *The Confessions of St. Augustine*. Translation by Rex Warner, renewed 1991 by F. C. Warner. Introduction Copyright © 1963, renewed 1991 by Vernon J. Bourke. Reprinted by permission of Dutton Signet, a division of Penguin Books USA.

Chapter 9: Page 347: "An Arab Perspective on the First Crusade" from *Arab Historians of the Crusades* by Francesco Gabrieli. Selected and Translated from the Arabic Sources by E. J. Costello. Copyright © 1969 by the University of California Press. Reprinted by permission of the Regents of the University of California and the University of California Press.

Chapter 10: Page 358: "Innocent III on His Rights and Powers" from *The Crisis of Church and State, 1050–1300* by Brian Tierney. Copyright © 1964 by Prentice Hall, Inc., renewed 1992 by Brian Tierney. Reprinted by permission of Simon & Schuster. **Page 369:** "William of Rubruck Reports on the Mongols" from *The Mongol Mission*, edited by Christopher Dawson. New York: Sheed and Ward, 1953. Introduction Copyright by the Estate of Christopher Dawson. Reprinted by permission of Sheed and Ward. **Page 382:** "Thomas Aquinas's Proof for the Existence of God" from *An Introduction to St. Thomas Aquinas* by Anton C. Pegis (Random House, Modern Library, 1945). Reprinted by permission of the Estate of Anton Pegis. **Page 385:** From *The Lyrics of the Troubadour, Trouveres* by Frederick Goldin. Copyright © 1973 by Frederick Goldin. Reprinted by permission of Doubleday, a division of Bantam Doubleday Dell Publishing Group, Inc. From lyrics by Castellozza in *The Women Troubadours* by Meg Bogin, (W. W. Norton, 1976). Copyright 1976 by Magda Bogin. Reprinted by permission of Magda Bogin.

Chapter 11: Page 399: "Saint Catherine and The Avignon Papacy" from *Babylon on the Rhone: A Translation of Letters by Dante, Petrarch, and Catherine of Siena on the Avignon Papacy* by Robert Coogan. Copyright © 1983 by Robert Coogan. Reprinted by permission of the author. **Page 417:** "The Black Death" from *The Decameron* by Giovanni Boccaccio, translated by Mark Musa and Peter Bondanella. Translation copyright © 1982 by Mark Musa and Peter Bondanella. Reprinted by permission of Dutton Signet, a Division of Penguin Books USA Inc. **Page 424:** "The Rising of 1381" from *Peasant's Revolt of 1381, The Anoniimalle Chronicle* by R. B. Dobson. Copyright © 1970 by The Macmillan Press Ltd. Reprinted by permission of Macmillan Press Ltd. **Page 428:** "A European View of Constantinople" from *Pursuit of Power* by James C. Davis. English translation copyright © 1970 by James C. Davis. Reprinted by permission of HarperCollins Publishers, Inc.

Chapter 12: Page 453: Poem by Michelangelo from *The Italian Renaissance Reader* by Julia Bondanella and Mark Musa. Copyright © 1987 by Julia Conaway Bondanella and Mark Musa. Reprinted by permission of Dutton Signet, a division of Penguin Books USA Inc. **Page 443:** "Petrarch Responds to His Critics" from *The Renaissance Philosophy of Man* by Ernst Cassirer, Paul Oskar Kristeller, and John H. Randall. Copyright 1948 The University of Chicago Press. Reprinted by permission of the publisher. **Page 445:** "Cassandra Fedele Defends Liberal Arts for Women" from *Her Immaculate Hand: Selected Works By and About the Women Humanists of Quattrocento Italy*

(Binghamton, N.Y.: Center for Medieval and Early Renaissance Studies, State University of New York, 1983). Reprinted by permission. **Page 447:** "Rabbi Mordecai Dato Criticizes the Humanists" from *Rabbi's and Jewish Communities in Renaissance Italy* edited and translated by Robert Bonfil, Oxford University Press 1990. Reprinted by permission of Oxford University Press: England. **Page 465:** "Isabella d'Este Orders Art" from *Patrons and Artists in the Italian Renaissance* by David S. Chambers. Copyright 1970 by Macmillan Ltd. Reprinted by permission of the publisher. **Page 467:** "Giovanni della Casa on the Perfect Gentleman" from *The Portable Renaissance Reader* edited by James Bruce Ross and Mary Martin McLaughlin. Copyright 1953, renewed © 1981 by Viking Penguin Inc. Reprinted by permission of Viking Penguin, a division of Penguin Books USA Inc.

Chapter 13: Page 479: "Pegalotti on Travel to the East" from *Medieval Trade in the Mediterranean World,* edited by Robert S. Lopez and Irving W. Raymond. Copyright © 1990 by Columbia University Press. Reprinted by permission of the publisher. **Page 485:** "Albuquerque Defends the Portugese Empire" from *Albuquerque: Caesar of the East.* Copyright © 1990 by Aris and Phillips. Reprinted by permission of the publisher. **Page 495:** "An Inca Nobleman Defends His Civilization" from *Letter to a King, a Picture History of the Inca Civilization* by Huáman Poma. Originally published by Unwin Hyman Ltd., a division of HarperCollins Ltd.: London 1978. **Page 503:** "The New World and the Old" from *The Florentine Codex: General History of the Things of New Spain* by Fray Bernardino de Sahagún. Introductory Volume, pp. 96–97. Translated by Arthur J. O. Anderson and Charles E. Dibble. Copyright 1982 by the School of American Research, Santa Fe and The University of Utah, Salt Lake City. Reprinted by permission of the School of American Research.

Chapter 14: Page 515: "Martin Luther's Address to the Christian Nobility of the German Nation" from *The American Edition of Luther's Works.* Copyright © 1943 Muhlenberg Press. Reprinted by permission of Augsburg Fortress. **Page 537:** "Ignatius Loyola's Spiritual Exercises" from *Culture and Belief in Europe, 1450–1600: An Anthology of Sources,* edited by David Englander, Diana Norman, Rosemary O'Day, and W. R. Owens. (Basil Blackwell in association the Open University, 1990). Reprinted by permission of Blackwell Publishers.

Chapter 15: Page 566: "Richelieu Supports the Authority of the State" from *The Political Testament of Cardinal Richelieu: The Significant Chapters and Supporting Selections* edited and translated by Henry Bertram Hill. Copyright 1961. Reprinted by permission of The University of Wisconsin Press. **Page 579:** "Montaigne Discusses Barbarity in the New World and the Old" from *The Complete Essays of Montaigne,* translated by Donald M. Frame. Stanford University Press 1948. Reprinted by permission of the publisher. **Page 580:** Lines 40–50 from *Richard II,* Act 2, Scene 1, in *The Riverside Shakespeare,* edited by G. Blakemore Evans. Copyright © 1997 by Houghton Mifflin Company. Reprinted by permission of the publisher.

Chapter 16: Page 599: "The Putney Debates" from "The Levellers" in *The English Revolution,* edited by G. E. Aylmer (Cornell University Press 1975). Copyright Thames & Hudson Ltd. Reprinted by permission of Thames & Hudson Ltd.

Chapter 17: Page 633: "Galileo Confronts the Church" from *The Discoveries and Opinions of Galileo* by Stillman Drake. Copy-

right © 1957 by Doubleday. Reprinted by permission of Doubleday, a division of Bantam, Doubleday, Dell Publishing Group, Inc. **Page 648:** "Jesuits and Astronomy in China" from *China in the Sixteenth Century: The Journals of Matthew Ricci: 1583–1610* translated by Louis J. Gallagher, S. J. Copyright 1953 by Louis J. Gallagher. Reprinted by permission of Random House Inc.

Chapter 18: Page 662: "Voltaire on Britain's Commercial Success" from *Philosophical Letters: Voltaire* by Ernest Dilworth. Copyright © 1961. Reprinted by permission of Prentice-Hall, Inc., Upper Saddle River, NJ. **Page 667:** "Rousseau Discusses the Benefits of Submitting to the General Will" from *The Social Contract* by Jean-Jaques Rousseau, translated and introduced by Maurice Cranston. Copyright 1968 by Maurice Cranston. Reprinted by permission of the Peters Fraser and Dunlop Group Ltd. on behalf of the estate of Maurice Cranston.

Chapter 19: Page 709: "A Young Woman Recounts the March to Versailles" from *The French Revolution,* edited by Philip Dawson. Copyright © 1967 by Prentice-Hall, Inc., renewed 1995 by Philip Dawson. Reprinted by permission of Simon & Schuster. **Pages 712, 717:** "Declaration of the Rights of Woman" and "A Citizen of Paris Suffers Under the Terror" from *Women in Revolutionary Paris, 1789–1795* translated by Darline Gay Levy, Harriet Branson Applewhite, and Mary Durham Johnson. Copyright 1979 by the Board of Trustees of the University of Illinois. Reprinted by permission of the University of Illinois Press. **Page 716:** "Robespierre Justifies the Terror" from *Robespierre,* edited by George Rude. Copyright © 1967 by Prentice-Hall, Inc., renewed 1995 by George Rude. Reprinted by permission of Simon & Schuster.

Chapter 20: Page 754: "A Moroccan Description of the French Freedom of the Press" from *Disorienting Encounters: Travels of a Moroccan Scholar in France in 1845–1846* by Muhammad As-Saffar, translated and edited by Susan Miller (Berkeley, 1992). Reprinted by permission of the Regents of California and the University of California Press.

Chapter 21: Page 790: "Friedrich Engels Describes an Urban Slum" from *The Condition of The Working Class in England* by Friedrich Engels, translated and edited by W. O. Henderson and W. H. Chaloner, 1968. Reprinted by permission of Stanford University Press and Basil Blackwell Publishers. **Page 801:** "The New Discipline of the Factory System" from *Documents of European Economic History* by Holmes & Pollard. Reprinted by permission of St. Martin's Press, and Hodder & Stoughton Ltd.

Chapter 22: Page 816: "Cavour and Napoleon III Plot War" from *France: Empire and Republic, 1850–1940: Historical Documents,* selected and introduced by David Thomson. Copyright © 1968 by David Thomson. Reprinted by permission of HarperCollins Publishers, Inc. **Page 839:** "The Tsar Demands the Freeing of the Serfs" from *A Sourcebook for Russian History from Early Times to 1917,* Volume 3, edited by George Vernadsky et al. Copyright 1972 by Yale University Press. Reprinted by permission of the publisher.

Chapter 23: Page 872: "Emile Zola on the Novelist as Scientist" from *Movements, Currents, Trends: Aspects of European Thought in the Nineteenth and Twentieth Centuries* by Eugen Weber. Copyright © 1992 by D.C. Heath and Company. Reprinted by permission of Houghton Mifflin Company.

Chapter 24: **Page 907:** "A Conspiratorial Revolutionary Party" from *Collected Works of Lenin, 1929*. Reprinted by permission of International Publishers.

Chapter 25: **Page 924:** "Into the Trenches" from *German Students' War Letters*, edited by A. F. Wedd, translated and arranged from the original edition of Dr. Philipp Witkop. London: Methuen 1929. **Page 936:** "The Bolsheviks in Power, November 1917" from *Ten Days that Shook the World* by John Reed. (London: Penguin 1977).

Chapter 26: **Page 966:** "Doubts About Mass Society" from *The Weimar Republic Sourcebook* by Anton Kaes, Martin Jay, and Ed Dimendberg. Copyright © 1994 by the University of California Press. Reprinted by permission of the Regents of the University of California and the University of California Press. **Page 988:** "Tradition and Women: The Conditions of Independence" from *A Room of One's Own* by Virginia Woolf. Copyright 1929 by Harcourt Brace & Company and renewed 1957 by Leonard Woolf. Reprinted by permission of Harcourt Brace & Company and the Society of Authors as the literary representative of the estate of Virginia Woolf.

Chapter 27: **Page 999:** "Retreating from 'The New Woman'" in *The Weimar Republic Sourcebook*, edited by Anton Kaes, Martin Jay, and Edward Dimendberg. Copyright © 1994 by the University of California Press. Reprinted by permission of the Regents of the University of California and the University of California Press. **Page 1001:** "Gandhi on Nonviolence" from *The Essential Writings of Mahatma Gandhi*, edited by Raghavan Iyer (Delhi: Oxford University Press, 1991). Copyright 1991 by the Navajivan Trust. Reprinted by permission of the Navajivan Trust. **Page 1003:** "Carrying Out the Stalinist Revolution" from *No Jail for Thought* by Lev Kopelev (London: Secker & Warburg Ltd., 1977. An imprint of Reed Consumer Books). **Page 1008:** "Hitler's World-View: Nature, Race, and Struggle" from *Mein Kampf* by Adolf Hitler, translated by Ralph Manheim. Copyright 1943, renewed 1971 by Houghton Mifflin. Reprinted by permission of Houghton Mifflin Company and Random Century Group UK. All rights reserved.

Chapter 28: **Page 1041:** "Toward the Nazi New Order" from *Nazism: A History in Documents and Eyewitness Accounts*, edited by Jeremy Noakes and G. Pridham. Copyright © 1988 by Department of History and Archaeology, University of Exeter. Reprinted by permission of Jeremy Noakes. **Page 1045:** "Stalingrad: The Diary of a German Soldier" from *The Battle of Stalingrad* by Vasili I. Chuikov. Copyright © 1964 by HarperCollins Publishers Ltd. Reprinted by permission. **Page 1049:** "Japan's 'Pan-Asian' Mission" from Nagayo Yoshiu, "Our Present War and the Cultural Significance," translated by Mitsuko Iriye in *Modern Asia and Africa*, edited by William H. McNeill and Mitsuko Iriye (Oxford University Press, 1971). Reprinted by permission of William H. McNeill. **Page 1065:** "The Soviet View of the Cold War" from "The Novikov Telegram" in *Diplomatic History*, Vol. 15, No. 4 (Fall 1991). Reprinted by permission of Blackwell Publishers.

Chapter 29: **Page 1083:** "Human Freedom and the Origins of a New Feminism" from *The Second Sex* by Simone de Beauvoir, translated by H. M. Parshley. Copyright 1952 and renewed 1980 by Alfred A. Knopf Inc. Reprinted by permission of Alfred A. Knopf, the Estate of Simone de Beauvoir, and Jonathan Cape. **Page 1093:** "Legacy of European Colonialism" from *The Wretched of the Earth* by Frantz Fanon, translated by Constance Farrington. Copyright © 1963 by Presence Africaine. Reprinted by permission of Grove/Atlantic, Inc. **Page 1095:** "Practical Thinking and European Integration" from *Memoirs* by Jean Monnet, Introduction by George W. Ball, translated by Richard Mayne. Translation copyright © 1978 by Doubleday, a division of Bantam Doubleday Dell Publishing Group, Inc. Reprinted by permission of the publisher. **Page 1100:** "Denouncing the Crimes of Stalinism" from *The Anti-Stalin Campaign and International Communism*, edited by the Russian Institute. Copyright © 1956 by Columbia University Press. Reprinted by permission of the publisher.

Chapter 30: **Page 1116:** "Toward a Postindustrial Society" from *Understanding Media: The Extensions of Man* by Marshall McLuhan. Copyright © 1994 by Marshall McLuhan. Reprinted by permission of the MIT Press. **Page 1143:** "Europe and the American Challenge" from *The American Challenge* by Jean-Jacques Servan-Schreiber. Copyright © 1975 by Éditions Denoël. English translation copyright © 1968 by Atheneum House, Inc. Reprinted by permission of Georges Borchardt, Inc., and Éditions Denoël. **Page 1146:** "The Varieties of Liberal Capitalism" from *Capitalism Against Capitalism* by Michel Albert (London: Whurr, 1993). Reprinted by permission of Whurr Publishers Limited. **Page 1148:** "The Case of 'Orientalism'" from *Orientalism* by Edward W. Said. Copyright © 1978 by Edward W. Said. Reprinted by permission of Pantheon Books, a division of Random House, Inc. **Page 1151:** From "Our Universal Civilization" by V. S. Naipul in *New York Review of Books*, January 31, 1991. Copyright © 1991 by V. S. Naipaul. Reprinted by permission of Aitken & Stone Ltd.

Index

Aachen, 293, 294(illus.), 296
Abbas, Abu'l, 274
Abbassids, 274–275, 345
Abby, *see* Cluny monastery; Monasteries and monasticism
Abdul Hamid II (Ottoman Empire), 827, 905
Abdul Mejid (Ottoman Empire), 827
Abelard, Peter, 340, 341, 379
Abolition: of slavery (U.S.), 831; of serfdom (Russia), 838. *See also* Serfs and serfdom; Slaves and slavery
Abortion rights, 1107, 1132
Abraham (patriarch), 51
Absolutism, 590–597
Absurdity (intellectual thought), 1075–1076
Abu Bakr, 271–272
Abu Simbel, 31
Abyssinia, *see* Ethiopia
Académie Royal des Sciences, 642–643, 646
Academies, 108, 634–635, 643. *See also* Scientific societies
Acadia, 618
Accadèmia dei Lincei, 635, 642, 643
Accadèmia Segreta, 634–635
Acculturation, in New World, 502
Achaean league, 128, 129
Achaemenid Persian Empire, 59 and *illus.*
See also Persia and Persian Empire
Acropolis, 78(illus.), 83, 105(illus.). *See also* Parthenon
Actium, Battle of, 195
Act of Settlement, 674
Act of Uniformity, 530
Acts of Supremacy, 528, 529(box), 530, 566, 567
A.D. (*anno Domini*), 4n, 214
Adages (Erasmus), 460
Adalbero of Metz, 315
Adams, John Quincy, 831
Adaptation, human, 5
Addresses to the German Nation (Fichte), 746
Address to the Christian Nobility of the German Nation (Luther), 514, 515(box)
Adenauer, Konrad, 1079, 1084
Administration: Persian, 60; Roman, 197, 230–231, 236–237; Germanic, 250; under Justinian, 251; of Islam, 272, 274; in Byzantine Empire, 277–279; Carolingian, 292–293; of England, 329, 330–331; in German Empire, 355–356; of papacy, 359–360; French, 363, 722, 729; in Italy, 368; of colonies, 498–499, 891–895; of Netherlands, 556
Adriatic region, 155, 338
Adventurers, *see* Americas; Exploration; specific adventurers and explorers

Aegean Greece, 64, 65(map). *See also* Greece
Aegean region, 80(map). *See also* Aegean Greece; Anatolia; Greece
Aeneid (Virgil), 201
Aereopagus council, 96
Aeschylus, 112
Aesclipius (god), 106
Aethelbert (Kent), 284
Aetolian league, 128–129
Afer, Publius Terentius, *see* Terence
"Affair of the Placards" (France), 532
Afghanistan, 889. *See also* Bactria
Africa (Petrarch), 441
Africa and Africans, 4; Egypt and, 23; Hellenistic sculpture and, 127(illus.); trade and, 477, 482, 683; slavery and, 482, 499, 501, 619, 773 and *illus.*; Portugal and, 482–483; British power in, 756; imperialism in, 888, 889, 890, 891; Kingsley on, 892(box); in 1914, 893(map); Bechuanaland and, 894(box); World War I and, 948–949; nationalism and, 960; Mussolini and, 1014; independence movements and, 1090–1092. *See also* Egypt; Nile River region; North Africa; Slaves and slavery
African Americans, 832, 957–958
African Times and Orient Review (Duse), 949
Africanus, *see* Scipio Africanus, Publius Cornelius
Afterlife (Egypt), 24, 28
Agamemnon (Aeschylus), 112
Age of Optimism, 845–874, 876–877
Age of Reason, 660. *See also* Enlightenment
Agga of Kish, 14
Agincourt, Battle at, 407, 409
Agis (Sparta), 129
Agoge, 87
Agora, 83
Agrarian crisis, in Rome, 180–182
Agriculture, 7, 8, 419; Egyptian, 21, 129; Athenian, 90, 91; in Rome, 198, 205; in Middle Ages, 299, 355; technology and, 308–310, 309(illus.), 856–857, 856(illus.); economic decline and, 414, 422; in Americas, 491–492; revolution in, 687–689; in Britain, 732, 784; industrialization and, 777; Great Depression and, 996; Soviet collectivization and, 1000–1002; in Hungary, 1100. *See also* Animals; Farms and farming; Plants
Agrippa, 193
Agrippina the Younger, 203
Ahab (Israelite king), 54
Ahasuerus, 57
Ahmose I (Egyptian king), 28

Ailly, Pierre d', 487
Airlift, *see* Berlin
Airplanes, 927, 967
Air quality, 795–796. *See also* Environment
Aistulf, 282
Aix-la-Chapelle: university at, 458; Treaty of, 595. *See also* Aachen
Akhenaton, *see* Amenhotep IV
Akhetaton (Egyptian city), 30
Akkadian empire and language, 14, 15–16
Alais, *see* Peace of Alais
Alamogordo, New Mexico, 1031
Alaric (Visigoth), 245
Alba, Duke of (Fernando Álvarez de Toledo), 556–557
Albania, 906, 1096(map), 1127
Albert (England), 791, 842
Albert, Michel, 1146(box)
Alberti, Leon Battista, 463, 466
Albigensians, 363, 372–373 and *illus.*, 378
Albret, Jeanne d', 533(box)
Albuquerque, Alfonso d', 485 and *box*
Alcaeus, 83
Alchemy, 448
Alcuin, 294–295
Alexander I (Russia), 723, 725–726, 760
Alexander II (Russia), 838–839 and *box*
Alexander III (Pope), 372
Alexander III (Russia), 906
Alexander VI (Pope), 412, 490
Alexander Nevsky, 368–369
Alexander the Great (Macedon), 59, 119, 120, 121–124, 122(illus.), 123(box), 124(map), 134–135
Alexandra (Russia), 931
Alexandria, Egypt, 119, 120, 130, 131(box), 137–139, 147
Alexandrian movement, 134–142
Alexis (Russia), 609, 610
Alexius Comnenus (Byzantine), 345, 346
Alfieri, Vittorio, 746
Alfonso I (Castile), 332
Alfonso X (Castile), 367 and *illus.*
Alfonso XIII (Spain), 1015
Alfred the Great (England), 287, 311
Algebra, 20
Algeria, 889, 910, 1089, 1090
Ali (caliph), 272, 273, 275
Ali, Mehemet, 762
Alienation (intellectual), 985–988
Alimentus, Lucius Cincius, 178
Allah, 272. *See also* Islam; Quran
Allegory, 440
Alliances: of Sparta, 87; of Carolingians, 288; Quadruple, 741; Balkan League, 906; World War I and, 909, 919;

Alliances (cont.): German-Italian, 1014; Japanese, 1046–1047; Allies (World War II), 1048, 1051–1060; military, 1096(map); after collapse of Soviet Union, 1136. See also Blocs; Congress of Vienna; Defense; Treaties
Allied Control Council, 1052
Allies, 1051–1060. See also Triple Entente; World War I; World War II
All Quiet on the Western Front (Remarque), 951
All-Russian Council of Soviets, 932
Al-Mina, 81
Alphabet, 11–12, 34, 50, 82. See also Language; Writing
Alps region, 9, 40–41 and illus., 157(map), 367–368
Alsace and Lorraine, 945, 972
Altamira caves, 6
Amarna, 30, 31. See also Akhetaton
Ambrose of Milan, 258
Amenhotep II (Egyptian king), 26(box)
Amenhotep III (Egyptian king), 24–25
Amenhotep IV (Egyptian king Akhenaton), 30
American Challenge, The (Servan-Schreiber), 1141–1142, 1143(box)
American Indians, see Amerindians
Americanization, 1141
American Revolution, 686, 700, 701–702
Americas, 4, 474(map), 475–476; exploration of, 486–491, 494–498; naming of, 490; before European invasion, 491–494; colonization of, 498–500; Columbian Exchange and, 500–504; Old World and, 503(box); trade with, 611; immigration to, 897. See also Central America; Colonies and colonization; Columbus, Christopher; Exploration; North America; South America; specific countries
Amerindians, 487; Columbus and, 488–489; Inca as, 492, 494; Aztecs as, 492–494; Cortés and, 499, 501; rights of, 499–500
Amiens, Treaty of, 722
Amon-Re (god), 30
Amorites, 16, 34
Amos (prophet), 54
Amritsar Massacre, 960
Amsterdam, 612, 613 and illus. See also Netherlands
Anabaptists, 520–521
Anarchism and anarchists, 882, 903
Anarchosyndicalism, 882
Anastasius (Roman Empire), 255
Anatolia, 7, 33, 34–36, 69, 100, 103, 127, 175, 276, 345, 346, 426
Anatomy, 641–642
Anaximander of Miletus, 94
Anaximenes, 94
Ancien Régime (Old Regime, France), 702–704, 751
Ancient Greece, see Greece
Ancient world, 3–4, 5–9
al-Andalus, 282, 332
Anesthetics, 867
Angela of Foligno, 511–512

Angel of death, 395(illus.)
Angevins, 332, 362–363, 364
Anglicans, 569, 602
Anglo-Russian Entente, 909
Anglo-Saxons, 247, 284, 329–330
Angola, 1091
Anguissola, Sofonisba, 456
Animals, 310; Columbian Exchange and, 501–502, 501(illus.)
Animistic religion, 162
Anjou, 328
Annals, The (Tacitus), 210
Annates, 397–398
Anne (England), 672, 674
Anne (France), 591
Anne of Austria, 590
Anne of Brittany, 409
Annotations on the New Testament (Valla), 460
Annulment, Henry VIII and, 528
Anschluss, 1021
Anselm, 331–332, 340, 341 and box
Anthemius of Tralles, 251, 252
Anthony, 256
Anthropology, 867–868, 1092–1093
Anticolonialism, 960, 1058; structuralism and, 1092–1093; new issues in, 1107; in France, 1141, 1145. See also Decolonization; Democracies (nations); Power (authority)
Anti-Corn Law League (Britain), 757
Antigone (Sophocles), 112
Antigonid dynasty, 128
Antigonus Gonatas, 128
Anti-Machiavel (Frederick II, Prussia), 677
Antinuclear protests, 1087(illus.). See also Nuclear weapons
Antioch, 120, 132, 146
Antiochus III, 175; wife of, 141(box)
Antiochus IV Epiphanes (Seleucid), 146
Antipodes, 478
Antipope, 356, 400
Anti-Semitism, 147, 379, 869, 883–884, 901–903, 1014. See also Hitler, Adolf; Jews and Judaism; Nazis and Nazism
Antonine dynasty, 203, 210
Antoninus Pius (Rome), 204
Antony, Mark, 140, 150, 195
Antwerp, 553, 555(illus.), 558
Anxiety (intellectual): between world wars, 985–988. See also Culture
Apanage system, 364
Apennines: peoples, 155; mountains, 157(map)
Aphrodite of Cnidos (Praxiteles), 140(illus.)
Apocalyptic writings, 146–147
Apollo, oracle of, 93
Apollonius of Perge, 138
Apollonius of Rhodes, 137
Apollonius of Tyana, 134
Apostles, 213, 226, 238, 239
Apostolic Library, 446
Apostolic succession, 537–538
Appeasement, 1022–1023, 1022(box)
Appian Way, 171(illus.)

Aqueducts, 225
Aquitaine region, 329, 404–405. See also Eleanor of Aquitaine; Henry II (England)
Arabia, uniting of, 272
Arabic language, 15, 60
Arab-Israeli conflicts, 1060
Arabs and Arab world: Islam and, 268, 275; trade in, 268–269, 477; First Crusade and, 346, 347(box); World War I and, 919; revolt by, 942; at peace conference, 943, 944(box); unrest of, 949; in Palestine, 1064–1066; oil crisis and, 1105. See also Egypt; Islam; Israel; Middle East; Muslims; Palestine
Aragon, 332, 367, 396, 427–431, 560
Aramaeans, 60
Aramaic language, 60, 126, 213
Ara Pacis Augustae, 192(illus.), 193
Arawaks, 488
Archaeology, 5–6
Archaic Greece, 81–95. See also Greece
Archaic Period (Egypt), 23
Archaic Rome, 155–157. See also Rome
Archbishop of Canterbury, 330, 331–332, 340, 341 and box, 365
Archbishops, Christian, 234
Archers, 8–9
Archilochus of Paros, 92
Archimedes of Syracuse, 138
Architecture: Mesopotamian, 11; Egyptian, 31; at Knossos, 65–66 and illus.; in Greece, 83, 92–93; Roman, 177(illus.); Augustan, 201; in Late Antiquity, 248(illus.); of Hagia Sophia, 252–254; Carolingian, 296; Romanesque, 322, 343–344 and illus., 343(illus.); Gothic, 355, 375(illus.), 381–384, 383(illus.); in Renaissance, 451–452, 454, 455, 466; Jesù (church), 538, 539(illus.); baroque, 582–584; gardens as, 694–695 and illus., 694(illus.); industrial, 876; western, in Bombay, 895(illus.); between world wars, 987; Bauhaus and, 992, 993(illus.); postmodernism and, 1144. See also Temples
Archpoet, 384–385
Ardennes Forest, 1033
Arena Chapel (Padua), 454
Aretê concept, 84–85, 108, 110
Argentina, 730
Argonautica (Apollonius of Rhodes), 137, 139
Arians and Arianism, 234–235, 237, 239, 247, 248, 250, 282
Aristarchus of Samos, 138
Aristocracy, 301, 549; Roman, 157, 240–241; French, 409; in Scandinavia, 413; decline in, 850. See also Elites; Nobility
Aristophanes, 104, 113
Aristotle, 99, 107, 109–111, 109(illus.), 626; on Spartan women, 88; truths and, 381
Arithmetic, 20
Ark of the Covenant, 52
Arkwright, Richard, 779, 782
Armada, see Spanish Armada
Armed forces, see Military
Armenia, 199
Armenians, 906

Armistice, German, 940

Arms and armaments, *see* Weapons and weaponry

Arms race, 910

Arnolfini Wedding, The (Van Eyck), 460(illus.), 461

Arnolfo di Cambio, 387(illus.)

Around the World in Eighty Days (Verne), 847

Arsinoe II Philadelphus (Egyptian queen), 140

Ars Poetica (Horace), 201

Art(s): cave painting and, 5, 6 and *illus.*; stone engravings, 6–7; Neolithic and Copper Age, 8, 9–10 and *illus.*; in Mesopotamia, 19; in Egypt, 22–23, 31; in Assyria, 47(illus.); in Crete, 66 and *illus.*; Mycenaean, 68 and *illus.*; in classical Greece, 106; Hellenistic, 127(illus.), 139–142; of Germanic peoples, 244(illus.); Ravenna mosaics and, 264–265 and *illus.*; Carolingian, 295–296; Celtic, 336; in Middle Ages, 339, 390; Romanesque, 343–344 and *illus.*, 343(illus.); Gothic, 381–384; in Renaissance Italy, 450–456, 461–462, 463–464, 470–471; patronage and, 453–456; baroque, 538, 582–584, 583(illus.); religion and, 542–543 and *illus.*; Rembrandt and, 615 and *illus.*; in Enlightenment, 669–671; cult of sensibility in, 670(illus.); romanticism in, 743; women in, 854; realism in, 870–874; avant-garde, 884–885; expressionism in, 950(illus.); Dada in, 987; surrealism in, 987; between world wars, 987–988, 989(illus.); American leadership in, 1077–1079; pop art and, 1110–1111 and *illus.*, 1110(illus.); postmodernism in, 1144. *See also* Architecture; Design; Drama; Literature; Music; Painting; Poets and poetry; Sculpture

Arthur (England), 410, 429, 528

Arthurian legend, 336–337, 385–386

Art of Love, The (Ovid), 385

Aryans, Hitler and, 1009, 1011

Ascetic practices, 256

Asia: Rome and, 175; Huns from, 236, 244; sea route to, 482–483; Portuguese in, 483–486; Russia and, 609; trade with, 611–613, 683; imperialism in, 889; in 1914, 896(map); in World War I, 920(map); after World War I, 959–960; World War II and, 1046–1048, 1050(map). *See also* East Asia; Japan; Western Asia

Asoka (India), 134

Asquith, Herbert, 929

Assassinations: of Caesar, 185; in Roman Empire, 211; Umberto I, 903; Alexander II, 906; of Francis Ferdinand, 911; terrorist, 1106

Asselyn, Jan, 577(illus.)

Assembly: in Athens, 97; in Rome, 158, 163, 164–165, 197; in Scandinavia, 413; in Netherlands, 555; in Poland, 701; of Notables (France), 704; sans-culottes (France), 714. *See also* Council of 400; Council of 500; Legislative Assembly (France)

Assembly lines, 965

Assimilation: Akkadian, 15–16; in Ptolemaic Egypt, 131–132 and *illus.*

Associations, 867, 868. *See also* specific international organizations

Assurbanipal (Assyria), 45

Assyrian Empire, 44–48, 45(map), 47(illus.)

Astell, Mary, 665, 666(box)

Astrolabe, 48, 476

Astrology, 48, 448

Astronomy, 19, 20–21, 138, 626–633; in Egypt, 31; Neo-Babylonians and, 48; Greek, 94; Scientific Revolution and, 626–633; Copernicus and, 628–630; Jesuits and, in China, 648(box)

Asturias, 282, 1016

Asylums, 863

Atheism, 637, 663

Athenian Empire, 101–103

Athens, 43, 82; Acropolis in, 78(illus.); early period in, 89–91; classical, 95–100; Persia and, 100–101; Peloponnesian War and, 103, 104(map); religion in, 106; Plato and, 107–108; drama and writing of, 111–113, 111(illus.); in Hellenistic world, 129. *See also* Attica; Parthenon; Philosophy

Atlantic bloc, 1084, 1086–1087

Atlantic Charter, 1048

Atlantic region, 482, 616–619, 682–685, 700

Atomic bomb, 1030(illus.), 1031, 1057–1058. *See also* Nuclear weapons

Atomic theory, 107, 636

Aton (god), 30

Attalid dynasty, 132

Attalus III of Pergamum, 175

Attica, 82, 89(map). *See also* Athens

Attila (Hun), 244

Attlee, Clement, 1056, 1080

Augsburg, Peace of, 527

Augsburg Confession, 525–527, 525 (illus.), 534

Augustine (archbishop of Canterbury), 284

Augustine of Hippo, 259, 260(box)

Augustus (Octavian, Gaius Julius Caesar Octavianus), 187, 193, 195–197, 195(illus.), 196(box); Tacitus on, 198(box); deification of, 199–200; Roman culture under, 200–201; Altar of Augustan Peace and, 200(illus.)

Augustus II (Saxony), 607

Augustus Caesar, use of term, 229

Auschwitz, 1032, 1042 and *illus.*, 1071(illus.)

Austerlitz, Battle at, 723, 730

Australia, 847, 897

Australian ballot, 834

Austrasia, 288

Austria, 677, 814, 821, 943, 947; Holy Roman Empire and, 522; Habsburg territories in, 573(map); Spanish throne and, 597; consolidation of, 603–604; power of, 682; France and, 687, 713–714; Napoleon and, 723, 726–727; Congress of Vienna and, 741; reform in, 758–759; Italy and, 759, 767; revolutions of 1848 and, 766–767; industrialization and, 787;

Italian liberation from, 815; war with Piedmont, 815, 817(map); French treaty with, 815–816; Germany and, 819–820; rivalry with Russia, 910; Germany and, 1013, 1020–1021; after World War II, 1063. *See also* Austria-Hungary; Metternich, Clemens von; Papal states; Renaissance; Roman Empire; Rome

Austria-Hungary, 824–827, 826(map); autocracy in, 905; alliances of, 909; Balkan rivalries and, 911; states made from, 945–948. *See also* Austria; Hungary

Austrian Empire, 758, 767. *See also* Austria; Austria-Hungary

Austrian Netherlands, 603. *See also* Netherlands

Austro-Prussian War, 818, 822, 910

Authoritarianism, 963, 969, 974–985; German Nazism and, 973–974; Russia and, 975–980; Italian fascism and, 980–985. *See also* Napoleon I

Authority, *see* Power (authority)

Autocratic governments, 904–909, 931

Automobiles, 964

Avant-garde, 884–885

Avanti! (newspaper), 983

Avars, 276, 297

Avesta, 63

Avignon, 597; Great Schism and, 396, 397–401, 399(box)

Axis powers, 1014, 1035

Aznar, José Maria, 1145

Azores, 482

Aztecs, 492–494, 497(illus.); Cortés and, 494–498

Baader-Meinhof gang, 1106

Baatu, 369(box)

Babeuf, Gracchus, 749

Baby boom, 1117

Babylon, 47, 132; Hammurabi and, 16–17; arts and sciences of, 19–21; Jews and, 43; Nebuchadrezzar II and, 48. *See also* Mesopotamia

Babylonia, Kassites in, 33

Babylonian Captivity, 55, 397–400

Babylonian creation epic, 19

Bacchae (Euripides), 112

Bacchus, 191

Bach, Johann Sebastian, 538

Bacon, Francis (painter), 1078

Bacon, Francis (philosopher), 634

Bactria (Afghanistan), 132, 133–134

Baden, Max von, 940

Baden-Baden, 852

Bad Godesberg conference, 1084

Badoglio, Pietro, 1051

Baedeker, Karl, 852

Baghdad, 275, 299

Bahamas, 488

Bailiffs, demesne and, 363

Baker, Josephine, 957, 958 and *illus.*

Bakunin, Michael, 882

Balance of power, 1053

Balbilla, Julia, 204

Balboa, Vasco Nuñez de, 490

Baldwin, Stanley, 968, 1020

Balfour Declaration, 943
Balkan League, 906
Balkan region, 338, 1037; Romans and, 236; Huns and, 244; Visigoths and, 244, 248–249; First Crusade and, 346; Ottomans, 424–425, 828; nationalism in, 761–762; Austria-Hungary and, 827; peasants in, 857; rivalries in, 910 and map; World War I and, World War II and, 1051; ethnic conflict in, 1132, 1134(map), 1135–1136. See also specific countries
Baltic region, 419, 576, 605; crusade in, 378; power in, 605–608; war over, 608(illus.); Russia and, 609, 610, 611; Napoleon and, 726; in World War II, 1033. See also specific countries
Bandung conference, 1092
Bank of Amsterdam, 612
Bank of Credit and Commerce International (BCCI), 1139
Bank of France, 722
Banks and banking: in Italy, 418; families in, 420; British, 783; in U.S., 831; in Great Depression, 997, 998
Bannal rights, in France, 328
Banockburn, Battle of, 403
Baptism, 219
Barbarians, 102(box), 120, 229, 243–247
Barca family, 172
Barcelona conference, 1141
Barons (England), 366, 403. See also Magna Carta
Baroque arts, 538, 582–584, 583(illus.), 670. See also Art(s)
Barré, Marie-Rose, 709(box)
Barth, Karl, 986
Basic Law (Germany), 1082, 1084
Basil (Saint), 256
Basil I (Byzantine Emperor), 280, 344–345
Basil II (Byzantine Empire), 345
Basilicas: Santa Maria Maggiore, 240(illus.); Carolingian, 292–293; Gothic style in, 381–384, 383(illus.); Chartres, 390–391 and illus. See also Architecture; Cathedrals
Basque peoples, 1140
Bastille (Paris), 706–707, 706(illus.)
Bastions, 558, 559(illus.)
Bathing, 861
Battle of Britain, 1034–1035 and illus.
Battle of Maldon, The (epic poem), 343
Battle of San Romano, The (Ucello), 436(illus.), 437
Battles, see Wars and warfare; specific battles
Battles of Nations, 727
Bauhaus, 987, 992–993 and illus., 992(illus.)
Bavaria, 320, 323, 604, 605, 759, 768
Bayazid (Ottoman emperor), 427
Bayeux tapestry, 331(illus.)
Bayle, Pierre, 652
Beatrice (German Empire), 355
Beauvoir, Simone de, 1075(illus.), 1083(box), 1118
Bechuanaland, 894(box)
Becket, Thomas, 365, 511
Beckett, Samuel, 1075
Beckmann, Max, 950(illus.)

Bede, 287
Bedouins, 268
Beer Hall Putsch, 1006
Beethoven, Ludwig van, 743
Beguines, 375, 377, 512
Being and Time (Heidegger), 1075
Belarus, 605, 1130
Belgian Congo, 891
Belgium, 553, 927; United Provinces and, 558–559; Congress of Vienna and, 741; industrialization in, 784; workers in, 792; wages in, 809(illus.); imperialism of, 889; Germany and, 911; in World War I, 923; conflict in, 1140. See also Low countries; Netherlands; World War I
Belgrade, 523(illus.)
Belisarius, 251
Bell, Alexander Graham, 849
Belle époque, la, 879
Benedict III (Pope), 401
Benedict XII (Pope), 397(illus.)
Benedictines, 315
Benedict of Nursia, 256–257
Benefices, 292, 356
Benelux countries, 1094
Benes, Eduard, 1021
Benetton, 1116–1117
Bentham, Jeremy, 749, 797
Beowulf, 342–343, 385
Berbers, 282
Berengar, 340
Bergen-Belsen, 1042
Bergson, Henri, 884, 885(box), 930
Beria, Lavrenti, 1098
Bering Strait, land bridge across, 491
Berlin, 605, 860–861; blockade and airlift in, 1062
Berlin Wall, 1101, 1128 and illus.
Bernardino of Siena, 512
Bernard of Clairvaux, 315, 340, 348, 377
Bernart de Ventadorn, 385
Bernini, Gianlorenzo, 538
Bernstein, Eduard, 881
Berry, Duc de, 751
Bertha (Franks), 284
Berthollet, C. L., 780
Bessemer, Henry, 846
Bethmann-Hollweg, Theobald von, 926
Béthune, Maximilien de (duke of Sully), 564
Bible, 258, 268, 511; Hebrew, 19, 43–44, 50–57; Old and New Testaments, 213; women in, 241; Quran and, 270; Valla's annotations on, 446; Gutenberg, 456; "Polyglot," 458; Catholic, 536
Bibliothèque Nationale, 864
Bicycling, 855(illus.), 861
Big Bertha guns, 923
Bingham, George Caleb, 832(illus.)
Biology, 640–641, 885
Bipartite estate, 299
Bipolar world, 1084. See also Cold War
Birmingham, 790, 860
Birth control movement, 965
Birth of Venus (Botticelli), 452
Birthrate, 308, 863
Bisexuality, 92

Bishops, 234, 238, 314. See also Apostolic succession; Catholicism and Catholic church
Bismarck, Otto von, 819–820, 825(box), 904. See also Germany
Black Death (plague), 395(illus.), 396, 415–417 and box, 415(illus.), 434–435 and illus.
Black Hand, 911
Black magic, 552
Black Prince, see Edward IV (England)
Black Sea region, 82, 83(map), 236, 298, 338, 426. See also Constantinople
Black slaves, see Slaves and slavery
Blanc, Louis, 750, 764
Blanqui, Louis-Auguste, 751, 775
Blast furnace, 780, 781
Bleichröder, Gerson, 850
Blitzkrieg (lightning war), 1032, 1039
Blockades, 925
Blocs: Atlantic, 1084, 1086–1087; communist, 1097–1104
"Blood purge," in Germany, 1007
Blood purity, Spanish tests of, 431
"Bloody Sunday" (Russia), 908
Blum, Léon, 1018–1020, 1019(illus.)
Boccaccio, Giovanni, 417(box), 439
Bodhisattva, 135(illus.)
Bodin, Jean, 499, 581–582
Boeotia, 103
Bohemia, 337, 400–401, 413, 569, 573–574, 603, 767, 787
Boleyn, Anne, 528, 530
Bologna, 340, 379
Bolsheviks (Russia), 907, 932, 933–935, 936(box), 974–980. See also Communism; Lenin, Vladimir; Russia
Bombay, 895(illus.)
Bombs and bombings: in World War I, 927; Battle of Britain and, 1034–1035 and illus., 1057; of Germany, 1055, 1059(illus.); antinuclear protests and, 1087(illus.). See also Atomic bomb
Bonacolsi family, 463; Pinamone, 410
Bonaparte family: Louis, 720; Napoleon I, 720–728; Joseph, 726; Louis Napoleon (Napoleon III), 766. See also Napoleon I; Napoleon III
"Bonfires of vanities," 412
Bonheur, Rosa, 854
Boniface VIII (Pope), 386–388, 387(illus.), 396
Bon Marché department store, 844(illus.), 845, 876
Bonn, 1062
Book of Common Prayer, 529–530, 531, 566–567, 602
Book of Sciences (Lombard), 380
Book of the City of the Ladies (Christine de Pizan), 440 and illus., 543
Book of the Courtier (Castiglione), 464
Books, 294, 667–668, 669(illus.); Maiestas Domini, 295(illus.); manuscript, 304–305 and illus., 304(illus.); printing and, 456–457; literacy and, 586–587 and illus. See also Bible; Printing
Borders: Roman policy and, 204; in World War I, 919; Maginot Line and, 962;

Borders *(cont.)*: between France and Germany, 972; German, 1020–1022; buffer zone and, 1061. *See also* Defense; specific borders and regions
Borgia family, 490; Cesare, 412
Borodino, Battle of, 726
Borromeo, Charles, 539
Börsig, August, 786(illus.)
Boru, Brian, 335
Bosnia, 828, 829; war in, 1132, 1134(map), 1135–1136, 1135(illus.)
Bosse, Abraham, 622, 623(illus.)
Bossuet, Jacques, 592
Bosworth Field, Battle of, 409
Botticelli, Sandro, 452, 467, 468, 470–471
Boundaries, *see* Borders; Frontier regions; specific boundaries
Bourbon family, 531, 562, 597, 757, 800, 837
Bourgeoisie, *see* Middle class
Bourges, *see* Pragmatic Sanction of Bourges
Bouvines, Battle at, 362
Boyars, 414
Boyle, Robert, 638, 643
Boyne, Battle of, 603
Bracciolini, Poggio, 444
Brahe, Tycho, 630, 631(illus.)
Brandenburg-Prussia, 603, 604–605
Brandt, Willy, 1084, 1103, 1107
Bratislava, 458
Brazil, 499, 616
"Bread and circuses" policy, 199
Brest-Litovsk, Treaty of, 939
Breton, André, 987
Bretton Woods Agreement, 1061
Breuer, Marcel, 992 and illus., 993
Brezhnev, Leonid, 1103, 1122
Briand, Aristide, 972 and illus.
Bridges, 310. *See also* Land bridge
Bridget of Sweden, 398
British Empire, 888. *See also* England (Britain); North America
British Museum, 914–915 and illus.
Brittain, Vera, 951
Brittany, 327
Broca, Paul, 868
Bronze and Bronze Age, 12, 44. *See also* Sumer
Brooke, Rupert, 954–955 and illus.
Brotherhoods, religious, 511
Brothers and Sisters of the Common Life, 512
Brothers Karamazov, The (Dostoyevsky), 872
Bruce, Robert, 366
Bruges, 370, 422
Brunelleschi, Filippo, 451–452, 455
Bruni, Leonardo, 438, 442, 443, 448
Brunswick, 759
Brutus, Marcus Junius, 184, 185
Bubonic plague, *see* Black Death (plague)
Buchenwald, 1042
Buckingham, duke of (George Villiers), 569
Buddhism, 134
Budé, Guillaume, 458
Buffer zone, 1061
Buganda, 891
Building(s), Roman, 201, 207, 211. *See also* Architecture

Bukharin, Nikolai, 979(illus.), 1004
Bulgaria, 338, 828–829, 906, 919, 943, 1127
Bulgars, 276, 297
Bulge, Battle of the, 1051
Bullion, 591
Bulls, *see* Papal bulls
Bundesrat (Germany), 824
Burchard (bishop of Worms), 340
Burckhardt, Jacob, 438
Bureaucracy: in Roman Empire, 237; Renaissance courts and, 462–468; in France under Louis XIV, 591; in Russia, 760; in Soviet Union, 1002–1003. *See also* Government
Burgs, 299
Burgundian Code, 250
Burgundians, 244, 247
Burgundy, 327
Burials: sites of, 9; in Mesopotamia, 19; at Grave Circle B, 67
Burke, Edmund, 742
Burma, 888, 889, 891
Business, 310–311, 851. *See also* Commerce; Economy
Butler, Josephine Grey, 854(illus.)
Byron, Lord (George Gordon), 746
Byzantine Empire, 273, 275–280, 279(map), 297; and Constantinople, 232; frontiers of, 273, 276; Macedonian dynasty in, 280; First Crusade and, 344–345; destruction of, 423–424
Byzantium, 379

Cabinet, Privy Council as, 674
Cabot, John, 491
Cabral, Petro Alvares, 490
Caesar, Julius, 140, 150, 158, 160, 183–185, 184(illus.); calendar and, 31, 184
Caesar, use of term, 229
Caesarion, 151 and illus.
Café society, 661(illus.)
Calais, 407
Calas, Jean, 662
Calderón, Pedro, 580
Calendar: in Egypt, 31; Julian, 31, 184; in Arab world, 269; astronomy and, 628; Gregorian, 628; in France, 718, 719
California, 811, 847
Caligula, 202, 203
Caliphs and caliphate, 268, 271–272, 274, 332
Calixtus II (Pope), 326
Callimachus (writer), 137
Calvin, John, 519–520, 519(illus.); France and, 531
Calvinism and Calvinists, 526(map), 556, 557(box)
Cambyses (Persia), 59
Camera degli Sposi (Mantegna), 463
Camus, Albert, 1075–1076
Canaanites, 34, 48, 52
Canada, 596, 597, 616, 683, 687, 756
Canals, 778. *See also* Suez Canal
Canary Islands, 482, 488
Cannae, Battle of, 173
Canonical elections, 326
Canon law, 295, 340

Canons, 315
Canterbury, 330
Canterbury Tales, The (Chaucer), 439–440
Cape of Good Hope, 483
Capetian kings (France), 326–329, 361–362, 404
Cape Verde Islands, 482
Capital, 418, 689
Capitalism, 1144–1145, 1146(box); liberal economists on, 747; Marx on, 803–804; socialism and, 881; imperialism and, 887; in 1920s, 965; intellectual criticism of, 987. *See also* Economics; Economy; Great Depression; Market economy
Caracalla (Rome), 208
Caravans and caravan routes, 48, 81, 298, 480
Caravels, 477, 483
Carbonari, 759–760
Cardinals, 359
Careers, of middle-class women, 854
Caribbean region, 597, 683, 687, 730, 732
Carlsbad Decrees, 759
Carlyle, Thomas, 873
Carmelite nuns, 535(illus.), 536
Caroline Books (Theodulf), 295
Caroline minuscule (script), 294, 304–305
Carolingian dynasty, 320
Carolingian Empire, 287–296, 290(map)
Cartel, oil, 1105(illus.)
Cartesian dualism, 639
Cartesian universe, 636–637
Carthage and Carthaginians, 49, 172–175, 179(box)
Cartier, Jacques, 491
Cartography, 480
Casa, Giovanni della, 467(box)
Casablanca meeting, 1051
Casa da India, 485–486
Cassiodorus, 261
Cassius, Gaius Longinus, 185
Castellans, 312, 317
Castellio, Sebastion, 520
Castellozza, 385
Castiglione, Baldassare, 464–466
Castile, 332, 367, 396, 427–431, 560, 561
Castillon-sur-Dordogne, Battle at, 407
Castle, The (Kafka), 986
Castles, 312, 317, 350–351, 350(illus.), 351(illus.). *See also* Bastions; Defense; Forts
Castriota, George (Skanderbeg), 426
Castro, Fidel, 1102
Casualties: at Somme River, 924–925; of Napoleon's Russian campaign, 726; in Crimean War, 813; of World War I, 941; of World War II, 1058–1059
Catalan peoples, 1140
Catalan World Atlas (Cresques), 480
Çatal Hüyük, 8, 13
Catalonia, 427, 561, 1016
Cateau-Cambrésis, Treaty of, 412, 522, 555–556, 562
Cathar heresy, 363, 372–373
Cathedrals, 239–240. *See also* Architecture; Basilicas
Catherine II (the Great, Russia), 665, 668, 677–680, 678(illus.), 692, 701, 729

Catherine de' Medici, *see* Medici family
Catherine of Aragon, 410, 429, 528
Catherine of Siena, 398, 399(box)
Catholicism and Catholic church, 237–240, 255, 526(map); pope and, 239, 323–324; Franks and, 247; traditions of, 257–261; in Spain, 281–282; in Italy, 282; Britain and, 284–287, 365–366; reform in, 307–308; in Germany, 321–322, 323; investiture controversy and, 323–326; in France, 328; Crusades and, 344–346, 377–379; heretics and dissidents in, 372–373; mendicant orders in, 373–375; Babylonian Captivity and, 397–400; Great Schism in, 398–399; Council of Constance and, 400; modern, 510; in 1555, 526(map); Mary Tudor and, 530; Counter-Reformation and, 535–538; Saint Bartholomew's Day Massacre and, 546(illus.), 547, 562–563; Netherlands and, 556; France and, 562–565, 722, 728, 836; England and, 565–567, 569–571, 602, 753; in Austria, 604; Galileo and, 632–633 and *box*; science and, 646, 648; Diderot and, 665; in Ireland, 700–701, 899, 900; Italy and, 819; challenges to, 868–869; in Germany, 904; Mussolini and, 985; modernization and, 1117; in Poland, 1124, 1132. *See also* Christianity; Clergy; Heresy; Monasteries and monasticism; Popes and papacy; Religion
Cato the Censor (Marcus Porcius Cato), 176, 178, 190
Cato the Younger, 184
Catullus, 185
Causes, The (Callimachus), 137
Cavalier Parliament, 602
Cavemen, 6
Cavendish, Margaret, 643, 645(box), 651
Cave paintings, 5, 6 and *illus.*
Cavour, Camillo di, 815, 816–817, 816(box)
Çayönü Tepesi, 7
C.E. (of the common era), 4n
Ceausescu, Nicolae, 1101, 1127
CEDA (Spain), 1016
Celtic peoples, 247, 284, 335–336, 366
Celts (Gauls), 155
Cenobitic monasticism, 256
Censorship, 743, 751–752, 759, 835, 839–840
Census, 365, 788. *See also* Domesday Book
Central America, 685; Mexico and, 493(map); Peru and, 494(map); Old World diseases in, 499. *See also* Americas; Aztecs; Incas; North America; South America
Central Europe: Christianity in, 297; new powers in, 603–605, 606 (map); autocracies in, 904–905; self-determination in, 942; after World War I, 945–948 and *map*. *See also* East-central Europe; Eastern Europe; Europe; specific countries
Central government, 359, 360–369. *See also* Government
Centralization: in Islam, 273; of royal power, 402–403; in France, 409, 722
Central Powers, 919
Centuriate assembly, 164, 165
Ceremonies, sovereignty and, 581

Cerreg Cennen Castle (Wales), 350(illus.), 351
Cerularius, Michael (Patriarch), 345
Cervantes, Miguel de, 578, 580
Chadwick, Edwin, 797, 860
Chaeronea, Boeotia, 121
Chalcedon, *see* Council of Chalcedon
Chamberlain, Joseph, 887
Chamberlain, Neville, 1021–1022, 1021(illus.)
Chamber of Deputies (France), 751, 752, 837, 1018
Chamber of Deputies (Italy), 984
Chamber of Fasces and Corporations (Italy), 984
Champagne, 328, 371
Champlain, Samuel, 618
Charities, 690, 863
Charlemagne, 287–296, 289(box); throne of, 266(illus.), 267; in Italy, 282; palace at Aachen, 293, 294(illus.); vassalage, fiefs, and, 312
Charles (Franks), *see* Charlemagne
Charles (Scotland, Bonnie Prince Charlie), 673
Charles I (England), 569–570, 582, 598, 600, 638
Charles I (Spain), 429
Charles II (England), 601, 638
Charles II (Spain), 595, 597
Charles IV (Holy Roman emperor), 413
Charles IV (Luxembourg), 458
Charles V (Holy Roman emperor), 419, 500, 508(illus.), 509, 514, 515, 521–527, 553, 572
Charles VI (Austria), 677, 682
Charles VI (France), 407
Charles VII (France), 407, 408, 419
Charles VIII (France), 409, 412
Charles IX (France), 562–563
Charles X (France), 751–752, 837
Charles Albert (Piedmont), 767
Charles Felix (Italy), 760
Charles of Anjou, 368
Charles of Blois, 405(illus.)
Charles the Bald (emperor), 296, 297(illus.)
Charles the Bold (France), 409, 413
Charles University (Prague), 458
Charter, in France, 751
Charter 77 (Czechoslovakia), 1122–1123
Chartism, 757, 800
Chartres cathedral, 316(illus.), 390–391 and *illus.*
Château, 350, 351(illus.)
Châtelet, Emilie, marquise du, 661
Chaucer, Geoffrey, 439–440
Chaumareys, Duroys de, 772
Chauvet cave art, 6 and *illus.*
Cheap Repository Tracts (More), 742
Chemistry, 640, 865–866. *See also* Science
Cheops, *see* Khufu
Chernobyl nuclear accident, 1129, 1144
Chia, Sandro, 1144
Chiang Kai-shek, 1046, 1066
Childbirth, 308, 867
Child labor, 792, 793–794 and *box*, 862
Children, 6, 793, 808, 1009, 1010(illus.), 1118–1119. *See also* Child labor; Families and family life

China, 4, 949, 959; Mongols and, 368; trade with, 478–479, 683; Jesuits and science in, 648(box); European material progress and, 873(box); imperialism in, 889; nationalism in, 960, 961(box); Mao Zedong in, 1000; World War II and, 1046, 1047; communism in, 1066–1067; split with Soviet Union, 1102; anticommunism in, 1127
China (pottery), 782
Chirac, Jacques, 1135
Chivalry, 314, 385
Cholera, 753, 791, 866
Chopin, Frédéric, 746
Chosen people, 50. *See also* Hebrews; Jews and Judaism
Chrétien de Troyes, 385
Christ, Jesus, *see* Jesus Christ
Christendom, 298, 477–479, 477(illus.); division of (1555), 526(map). *See also* Christianity
Christian I (Denmark), 534
Christian III (Denmark), 534
Christian IV (Denmark), 575, 576
Christianity, 213–221, 218(box), 233–235, 237–239, 1116; dating methods and, 4; Hellenism, Jews, and, 142; Nero and, 203; expansion of, 214(map), 219–220; legalization of, 233–235; Arianism in, 234–235, 237; Catholic church and, 237–240; spread of, 238(map); culture and life under, 241–243, 258–261; of Germanic peoples, 250; Justinian and, 251–252; Ravenna mosaics and, 264–265 and *illus.*; Byzantine Empire and, 276; iconoclastic controversy and, 278–280; in Spain, 281–282, 332; in Italy, 282–283; in Britain, 284–287; and Ireland, 285; Carolingians and, 288, 297; Charlemagne's society and, 294; military orders in, 317; Reconquista and, 332, 333(map); expansion of, 336, 337; First Crusade and, 344–346; usury and, 371; in Lithuania, 413–414; Muslim Turks and, 425–426; Spanish Inquisition and, 430–431; concept of death in, 434–435 and *illus.*; Valla and, 446; reform and, 457–459; Erasmus on, 460–461; exploration, missionaries, and, 480–481, 487–488, 499–500, 502; Holy Roman Empire and, 509, 521–527; Protestantism and, 510–511; lay reform and, 516–519; types of, 534–535; religious life in, 538–540; universe and, 626–627; science and, 646–648; in Ottoman Empire, 761; public welfare and, 863; missionaries and, 890; neo-orthodox thinking and, 986. *See also* Apostles; Catholicism and Catholic church; Heresy; Monasteries and monasticism; Popes and papacy; Protestantism; Reformation; specific popes and saints
Christina (Sweden), 536
Christine de Pisan, 440 and *illus.*, 543
Christology, 239, 276
Chrysoloras, Manuel, 442

Church and state, 255, 291, 315–316; investiture controversy and, 323–326; in France, 328–329; in England, 331–332; in German Empire, 356; crisis between, 386–388; conservative views on, 743; in France, 903; in Germany, 904; in Italy, 985

Churches: true vs. false, 513(illus.). *See also* Christianity; Church and state; Clergy; Power; Religion; specific countries and religions

Church Fathers, 258

Churchill, Winston, 1034–1035 and *illus.*, 1048, 1051, 1052–1055, 1053(illus.), 1062–1063, 1064(box)

Church of England, 528, 566

Church Slavonic, 297

Cicero, 175–176, 185–187, 186(box), 258–259, 441

Cid, Le (Corneille), 581

Ciompi revolt, 423

Cisneros, Francisco Jiménez de, 458

Cistercians, 315, 361

Cîteaux, monastery at, 315

Cities and towns, 790–791; in Mesopotamia, 10; in Hellenistic world, 120, 140–141; cathedrals in, 239–240; medieval, 299; townspeople and Jews in, 318–320; in Italy, 334–335, 368, 410, 438–439; in Middle Ages, 354; economic life in, 370–371; population of, 422, 789(map); in New World, 502–503; governments of, 549; growth of, 689; planning and renovation of, 857–859, 860(box); public services in, 859–862. *See also* City-states; Villages; specific cities and towns

Citizens and citizenship: derivation of term, 82; in Athens, 97, 99; Roman, 170, 180, 208, 241; in Italy, 410–411; in France, 764; in U.S., 832–833; immigration and, 1140–1141

Citizen-warrior concept, 147. *See also* Hoplite phalanx

City of God, The (Augustine), 259, 291

City of the Ladies, see Book of the City of the Ladies (Pizan)

City planning, 857–859, 860(box)

City-states, 35(map); Syro-Palestinian, 4, 33–34; of Sumer, 12–14; in Levant, 33–34, 36–37; Phoenician, 48; Greek, 64, 79, 120–121; Etruscan, 155. *See also* Greece; Polis

Civic life, 442, 448

Civil Code (Napoleon), 722, 723

Civil Constitution of the Clergy, 710

Civilization, 3, 4–10, 22–23; emergence of, 10–12; in Anatolia and Levant, 33–37; early Greek, 64–73; early medieval, 267–268; Islamic East as, 268–275; Christian kingdoms in West, 280–287; British Museum exhibits on, 914–915 and *illus.*; critiques of, 985–986; debate over Western, 1150–1151. *See also* Colonies and colonization; Culture; Empires; Society; specific civilizations

Civilization and Its Discontents (Freud), 986

Civilization of the Renaissance in Italy, The (Burckhardt), 438

Civil liberties, 1122

Civil service, 851

Civil wars: in Rome, 184, 195, 203, 211; in France, 561–565, 590; in England, 598–600; in United States, 831; in Russia, 942, 975, 976(map); in Spain, 994(illus.), 995, 996, 1015–1018, 1016(map)

Clairvaux, monastery at, 315

Clarence, Duke of, *see* William IV (England)

Clare of Assisi, 375–376, 375(illus.)

Clare's Rule, 376(box)

Clarissa (Richardson), 670

Classes (economic and social), 963; in Sumer, 14; in Mesopotamia, 16–17; in Athens, 90, 99; in Rome, 158, 165–166, 208; medieval, 300–301, 311–320; suffrage and, 749; workers as, 803; conditions among, 849–857; education, social mobility, and, 1117–1118. *See also* Aristocracy; Elites; Estates General; Hierarchical society; Middle class; Workers

Classical culture, 81, 104–114, 261; renewed interest in, 441–442, 448, 671

Classical economics, 797, 998

Classical languages, 458

Claudius, 202, 203

Cleisthenes, 96

Clemenceau, Georges, 939, 943

Clement V (Pope), 396, 397

Clement VII (Pope), 398, 508(illus.), 528

Cleomenes (Sparta), 129

Cleopatra, 140, 150–151, 150(illus.), 151(illus.), 183–184, 195

Clergy, 239, 255, 300; position of, 312; in Middle Ages, 314–317; laity and, 360; Henry II (England) and, 365; Albigensians and, 373; taxation of, 386–387; privileges of, 516; in France, 704, 710–711

Clericis laicos (Boniface VIII), 386

Clermont, 346

Client kingdoms, 199, 204

Clients, in Rome, 160–162

Climate, of Greece, 64

Clinton, Bill, 1135

Clipper ship, 847

Clodia (Rome), 185

Clodius, 185, 186(box)

Closing of the Grand Council (Venice), 411

Cloth and clothing, 7, 363, 420, 549, 551(illus.), 690, 779–780, 852, 967

Clovis, 247, 287

Cluny monastery, 315, 324(illus.)

Cnut, 330

Coal and coal industry, 780–781, 795(illus.), 996

Codes: of Hammurabi, 16–17 and *box*; of Draco, 90; Twelve Tables, 161, 166; Burgundian, 250; Justinian, 251; Theodosian, 251; Napoleonic, 722, 725. *See also* Law(s)

Codicology (manuscript study), 304

Coeur, Jacques, 418–419

Coins, Roman, 176

Colbert, Jean-Baptiste, 591–592, 642

Cold War, 1061, 1065(box), 1072(illus.), 1073–1107

Coleridge, Samuel Taylor, 743

Colet, John, 458

Coligny, Gaspard de, 562

Collective action, 799–802

Collectivization (Soviet), 1000–1003

College of cardinals, 324

Colloquy of Poissy, 562

Cologne, 199

Colonies and colonization: Phoenician, 49, 83(map); Greek, 82, 83(map), 126–128; Seleucid, 132; Roman, 170–171; Portuguese, 482; British, 491, 683; Spain and, 498–499, 561, 758; trade and, 611; in Atlantic region, 616–619; American Revolution and, 700, 701–702; after French Revolution, 730; in Africa, 756; new imperialism and, 886–898; administration and, 891–895; in Middle East, 943; colonial peoples and, 948–949; European power and, 959–960; anticolonialism and, 960; decolonization and, 1087–1093; independence and, 1088(map); neocolonialism and, 1092; legacy of, 1093 (box). *See also* Empires; Imperialism

Columba (Ireland), 284

Columbian Exchange, 500–504

Columbus, Christopher, 430, 475–476, 480, 484(map), 486–490, 489(box)

COMECON, 1097

Comedy, 113

Comintern (Third International), 975–977 and *illus.*, 1015

Commandments, *see* Ten Commandments

Commerce, 310–311; Greek, 81; Hellenistic, 127–128; medieval, 298–299, 371; Italian, 418; Dutch, 611–613, 612(map). *See also* Trade

Committee of Public Safety (France), 715–716, 718, 719

Commodus, 210

Common law (England), 366

Common Market, 1094–1095 and *box*, 1104, 1136. *See also* European Union (EU)

Common people: Reformation and, 516–519; economic change and, 549–550; poverty, violence, and, 550–552; in France, 704. *See also* Estates General (France); French Revolution; Peasants; Workers

Commonwealth of Independent States, 1130

Commonwealths, 85, 600–601

Communal movement, 334(map), 335, 356, 368, 370

Communication, 587, 848–849. *See also* Transportation

Communion, 514

Communism, 942; Marx and, 802, 978(box); in Germany, 970, 973; fascism and, 974–975; in Russia, 975–980; popular fronts and, 1015, 1018–1020; Spanish civil war and, 1018; resistance movements and, 1044; in non-Western world, 1060; in Germany, 1062; in east-central Europe, 1062–1063, 1121–1132; containment policy and, 1063; in Greece, 1063;

Communism (cont.), in China, 1066–1067; in postwar France, 1085; in Italy, 1086, 1106; twentieth national congress and, 1099; splits in, 1102–1104; democracies and, 1114; anticommunist revolution and, 1127–1132; dissolution of Soviet Union and, 1129. See also Internationals
Communist bloc, 1097–1104, 1121–1127
Communist Manifesto (Marx and Engels), 802, 803(box)
Community of the elect, 519–520
Compass, 476
Competition (economic), 1120
Computer, impact of, 1115–1117
Comte, Auguste, 864, 868
Comunero, 522
Concentration camps, 1011. See also Extermination camps; Holocaust
Concert of Europe, 742
Conciliarists, 399–400, 402
Concordat of Worms, 326, 355
Confederate States of America, 830–831
Confederation of the Rhine, 723
Confederations, 244, 413
Confessionalization, 538
Confessions (Augustine), 259
Congo, 891
Congress of Berlin (1878), 828, 829
Congress of Paris, 813–814
Congress of Vienna, 741–742
Conrad III (German Empire), 355, 377
Conrad IV (German Empire), 356
Conscription, 176, 231, 681, 718
Conservatism, 742–743; new right and, 882; in Britain, 1119–1120. See also Right (political)
Conservatives (Britain), 899, 900, 968
Considerations on France (Maistre), 743
Conspiracy of Equals, 720, 749
Constance, Council of, see Council of Constance
Constance, Peace of, see Peace of Constance
Constance of Sicily, 356, 357
Constant, Benjamin, 749
Constantine (the Great, Rome), 195, 213, 226(illus.), 227–229; reforms of, 231–233; military and, 233; Christianity and, 234, 237; Nicene Creed and, 235
Constantine V (Byzantine Empire), 276–277, 279, 280
Constantine XI (Byzantine emperor), 423
Constantinople, 232, 250, 275, 276; Ottoman Turks and, 424, 425(illus.), 426, 427; European view of, 428(box). See also Council of Constantinople; Istanbul
Constantius I (Rome), 231
Constantius II (Rome), 237, 250
Constitutio Antoniana, 208
Constitution: royal government and, 581; of United States, 700, 702; in Poland, 701; in France, 711–713, 719, 751; in German states, 758–759; in Austria, 767; in Piedmont, 768; in Denmark, 769(illus.); of Italy, 819; of Germany, 824; in Ottoman Empire, 827
Constitutional monarchy, 701, 753, 836, 940

Constitutions of Melfi, 358
Consuls and consulship (Rome), 164, 166
Consumer goods, 612, 845
Consumerism: in 1920s, 965–967; pop art and, 1078
Consumer society, 845
Containment policy, 1063
Continent (Europe), 364, 784–787, 785(map), 824. See also Europe
Continental System, 723, 725
Contract: between king and people, 581; between state and people, 649–650. See also Social Contract, The (Rousseau)
Convents, 301, 512, 540
Conversations on the Plurality of Worlds (Fontenelle), 652
Conversion: of Paul of Tarsus, 217; of Constantine, 234; to Islam, 269; of Spanish Jews, 423, 429; of Amerindians, 499–500
Converso, 423
Cook, Thomas, 852
Cooperative communes, 750
Copernicus, Nicolaus, 628–630, 629(box), 632–633, 639, 646–647
Copper Age, 9–10
Coptic church, 255
Coptic Egypt, 273
Coral Sea, Battle of, 1048
Corday, Charlotte, 716
Cordoba, 275, 282, 299, 332
Corinth, 85, 87, 103, 175
Corinthian War, 103
Coriolanus (Shakespeare), 580
Corneille, Pierre, 580–581
Cornelia (Rome), 178–180. See also Gracchus family
Corn Law (Britain), 753, 757
Cornwall, 284
Corporativism (Italy), 984
Corpus Christi feast, 511
Corpus Hermeticum, 448
Cortes (Spanish parliament), 757, 758
Cortés, Hernán, 492, 493(map), 494–498
Corvées (labor services), 317–318
Cos (island), 106, 107
Cosa, Juan de la, map of, 488(illus.)
Cosimo de' Medici, see Medici family
Cosmology, 635–638
Cossacks, 607, 610–611, 692
Cottage industry, 690, 762, 778, 857
Cotton and cotton industry, 298, 690, 732, 779–780, 779(illus.)
Council of 400 (Athens), 91
Council of 500 (Athens), 96, 98
Council of Chalcedon, 239, 252
Council of Constance, 400, 401 and illus., 535
Council of Constantinople, 239
Council of Nicaea, 201, 235, 237, 239, 280
Council of Pisa, 399–400
Council of the Indies, 498
Council of the plebs, 165
Council of Trent, 536, 537–538
Counter-Reformation, 535–538, 567, 607. See also Reformation
Counterrevolution (Russia), 975, 976(map). See also Civil wars, in Russia
Counterrevolutionary ideology, 742–743

Countryside, see Rural society
Courbet, Gustave, 870, 871(illus.)
Courtiers and court life, 292, 293, 300–301, 462–468, 464, 592–594, 593(box)
Courtly literature, 385
Courtly love, 385
Courts (judicial), 98; Roman, 183; ecclesiastical, 360; English, 365; French parlements as, 408–409; depositions in, 586
Covenants (with God), 50–51, 52, 55(box), 56–57
Crafts, 7, 762
Cranmer, Thomas, 528
Crassus, Marcus Licinius, 184, 185
Crates of Thebes, 142
Creation epic, 19
Creation of Adam (Michelangelo), 453
Creative Evolution (Bergson), 885(box)
Creativity, in Renaissance, 437–438
Crécy, Battle at, 405
Credit, 372, 847
Cresques, Abraham, 480
Crete, 33, 64–66, 65(map), 67–68
Crime, in Mesopotamia, 16–17
Crime and Punishment (Dostoyevsky), 872
Crimean region, 680
Crimean War, 812–813, 812(illus.), 813 and box, 837, 838
Croatia, 338
Croats, Bosnian war and, 1132, 1134(map), 1135–1136
Croce, Benedetto, 987
Crompton, Samuel, 779, 783
Cromwell, Oliver, 598, 600–601 and illus., 615
Cromwell, Thomas, 528, 568
Crops, 299, 310, 502, 683, 688–689. See also Agriculture
Cross-cultural fertilization, 1147–1149
Croton, Magna Graecia, 95
Crucifixion, 216
Crusades, 377–379, 378(map); military orders and, 317; Jews and, 320; First, 344–346; Louis IX and, 364; Third, 365; Spain and, 366; Albigensians and, 373, 378; in Baltic region, 378
Crystal Palace exhibition, 852, 864, 876–877 and illus.
Cuba, 487, 494, 495
Cuban missile crisis, 1102
Culloden, Battle of, 673, 681
Cult of personality, Stalin and, 1099
Cult of sensibility, 670–671, 670(illus.)
Cults, 30, 106, 144, 145, 199, 220
Culture, 5, 863–874, 866(box), 880–886; Egyptian, 22–23; Hittite, 35–36; of Iceman, 41; Dorian, 69; of archaic Greece, 91–95; of classical Greece, 102(box), 104–113; Hellenistic, 120, 126–128; Greco-Indian interaction, 133–134; Alexandrian movement and, 134–142; of Hellenistic Jews, 145–147, 146(box); impact of Greece on Rome, 176–180; of Rome, 200–201, 209–210, 213; classical and Christian, 235(illus.); Christian, 254–261; Islamic, 275; in Byzantine Empire, 280; Carolingian Renaissance and, 293–296; in Middle Ages, 332, 339–344, 355, 379–386; vernacular

Culture (cont.), and, 342–343, 384–386; French, 361; Italian humanism and, 438–449; women and, 440(illus.); New World and, 476; indigenous American, 492–494; Columbian Exchange and, 502–504; society and, 578–584; in Russia, 610; nationalism and, 746; of India, 895; in Tahiti, 895; anxiety and, 985–988; after World War II, 1074–1079; impact of American, 1077–1079, 1141; pop art and, 1110–1111; assimilation and, 1113–1114; religion and, 1117; European, 1141–1144; global, 1147–1149, 1148(box). See also Americanization; Art(s); Civilization; Popular culture; Westernization
Cuneiform, 11–12 and illus., 16
Cunitz, Maria, 643
Curia, 207, 359
Curiate assembly, 158, 164
Currency, 612–613, 997, 1137
Currents (ocean), 481(map), 483
Customs union, of EU, 1137
Cuza, Alexander, 828
Cuzco, 494, 498
Cylon, 90
Cynic philosophy, 141, 142
Cynoscephalae, Battle at, 175
Cyprus, 34, 829
Cypselus (tyrant), 85
Cyril, 297
Cyrus the Great (Persia), 59–60, 61(box), 64
Czechoslovakia, 942, 945, 1060, 1063; Hitler and, 1021–1023; reform movement in, 1102–1103; Charter 77 in, 1122–1123; anticommunist revolution in, 1127; ethnic groups in, 1132. See also Bohemia; Prague Spring; Sudetenland
Czech people and language, 337, 400
Czech Republic, 1131

Dachau, 1042
Dacia (Romania), 204
Dada, in arts, 987
Da Gama, Vasco, 480, 483, 484(map), 488
Dagulf Psalter, 304–305 and illus., 304(illus.)
Daily life, see Lifestyle
Daladier, Edouard, 1020
Damasus (Pope), 258
Danegeld, 320
Danelaw, 329–330, 337
Dante Alighieri, 355, 379, 386
Danube region, 236, 298, 604
Darby, Abraham, 780
Darius I (Persia), 59, 60, 62, 100
Darius III (Persia), 121, 122
Dark Ages, 229, 437, 438, 441; Greek, 69
Darwin, Charles, 797, 864–865 and illus., 866(box)
Dating methods, 4, 214, 287
Daughters, see Women, in Rome
Daumier, Honoré, 765(illus.)
David, Jacques-Louis, 721(illus.)
David (Israelite king), 52, 53(illus.)
David (Michelangelo), 453
Dawes Plan, 972
Day care, 1118
Days of May uprising, 1104

D-Day landings, 1051
Dead Sea Scrolls, 215
Death, 19, 24, 27–28; Christian concept of, 434–435 and illus.
Death camps, see Extermination camps; Holocaust
Deborah (Old Testament), 242(box)
Debt, in France, 672
Decameron (Boccaccio), 417(box), 439
Decembrist uprising, 760
Decimal system, 20
Declaration of Independence, 748–749
Declaration of Pilnitz, 713
"Declaration of the Rights of Man and the Citizen," 707(box), 708, 711–712
"Declaration of the Rights of Woman," 712(box)
Decline and Fall of the Roman Empire, The (Gibbon), 227–229
Decline of the West, The (Spengler), 986
Decretum (Gratian), 340
Decurions, 207
Deductive reasoning, 637
Defenestration of Prague, 575
Defense: of Roman Empire, 199, 204, 211, 231; medieval, 350–351, 350(illus.), 351(illus.); Maginot Line as, 962; EU and, 1136. See also Alliances; North Atlantic Treaty Organization (NATO); Treaties
Defense of Liberty Against Tyrants, 581
Defense of the Seven Sacraments (Henry VIII), 528
Deficits, see Economy; Inflation
Degas, Edgar, 861, 870
De Gaulle, Charles, 326, 1034, 1044, 1053, 1085–1086, 1085(illus.), 1090, 1095
Deification, of Augustus, 199–200
Deities, see Gods and goddesses
Delacroix, Eugène, 744, 745
Delian League, 101–103
Delphi, 93, 111(illus.)
Delta, see Nile River region
Demesne, 299, 328, 329, 363
Demeter, cult at Eleusis, 144–145
Demetrius of Phalerum, 135
Democracies (nations), 898–904, 968–969, 982(box), 1114, 1115–1117, 1144–1145, 1146(box)
Democracy: in Greece, 79–81, 129; Athenian, 96–99; debate over, 98(box); in U.S., 831–833; mass society and, 963–964; in east-central Europe, 969, 1055; in Western Europe, 1079; in West Germany, 1082–1085; in 1960s and 1970s, 1104–1107; in Hungary, 1124. See also Democracies (nations)
Democritus, 106–107, 143
Demography, in Europe, 414–417, 879
Demos (people), 71, 89–90, 96
Demosthenes, 120–121
De Motu Cordis (On the Motion of the Heart) (Harvey), 641
De-Nazification policy, 1060
Deniken, Anton, 976(map)
Denmark, 337, 413, 605, 607, 675; Carolingian Empire and, 296; monarchy in, 296;

England and, 330; Reformation and, 534; Dutch and, 614–615; Napoleon and, 723; Congress of Vienna and, 741; constitutional government in, 769(illus.). See also Christian IV (Denmark); Scandinavia
Départements (departments), in France, 711
Department stores, 844(illus.), 845, 876
Depression, 763. See also Great Depression
De Revolutionibus Orbium Caelestium, see On the Revolution of Heavenly Bodies
Deroin, Jeanne, 766(box)
Descartes, René, 636–637, 636(illus.), 647
Descent of Man (Darwin), 865
Desert Fox, see Rommel, Erwin
Design, 987, 992–993 and illus., 992(illus.). See also Architecture; Art(s)
Despotism, 122–123. See also Enlightened despotism
De-Stalinization, 1098–1101, 1100(box)
Deuteronomy, 55(box)
Developed countries (North), 1114
Devil, see Witch-hunts
Dhuoda, 301
Dialectic materialism, 803
Dialogue on the Two Chief Systems of the World (Copernicus), 632–633
Dialogues (Plato), 108
Dias, Bartholomeu, 483
Diaspora, 56, 147
Díaz de Vivar, Rodrigo ("El Cid"), 332
Dickens, Charles, 871, 877
Dictatorship, 183, 758, 983. See also Authoritarianism; specific dictators
Diderot, Denis, 664–665, 664(illus.)
Diego, Juan, 506
Dien Bien Phu, 1090
Diet (nutrition), 422, 759, 851, 855
Diet of Augsburg, 525–527
Diet of Speyer, 523–524
Diet of Worms, 514, 515
Dietrich, Marlene, 967
Diocletian (Rome), 195, 213, 227, 228(map), 229–231, 232(box), 234
Diogenes of Sinope, 142
Dionysus (god), 111
Diplomacy, 36–37, 52, 281(box), 935–939. See also International relations
Direct democracy, 97
Directory (France), 720
Disarmament, 1087(illus.)
Discourse on Method (Descartes), 636, 647
Discourses on Livy (Machiavelli), 448
Discoveries, see Exploration
Disease: Black Death, 415–417, 415(illus.); smallpox, 494; in Central America, 499; Columbian Exchange of, 501; cholera, 753; urbanization and, 791; urban improvements and, 861; medicine and, 866–867; pasteurization and, 867; influenza pandemic and, 941. See also specific diseases
Disraeli, Benjamin, 834, 835(illus.)
Dissection, 138
Distaff (Erinna), 141
Diversity: of Roman world, 204–208, 237; in Holy Roman Empire, 571–573; religious, 869

Divination, in Greece, 93
Divine Comedy (Dante Alighieri), 386
Divine kingship, in Egypt, 23–25
Divine right of kings, 592
Divinity, *see* Gods and goddesses; Religion
Divorce, 242, 302, 528–529, 718, 719
Doctors, *see* Medicine
Dome of the Rock, 53(illus.), 271(illus.)
Domesday Book, 330
Domestic mobilization, 927–929, 928(box)
Domestic plants and animals, 7, 491–492; Columbian Exchange and, 502
Dominicans, 374–375, 499–500
Dominic de Guzman, 374–375
Domitian (Rome), 203, 204
Domna, Julia, 211
Donation of Constantine, 283, 446
Donne, John, 647
Donnersmarck, Henckel von, 850
Don Quixote (Cervantes), 578
"Doors of Paradise," 451 and *illus.*
Dorians, 69
Dostoyevsky, Feodor, 872
Dowry, 100, 301–302
Draco's Code, 90
Draft (military), *see* Conscription
Drake, Francis, 567(illus.)
Drama, 104–105, 111–113, 111(illus.), 177, 178, 386. *See also* specific dramatists
Dreadnought (ship), 910
Dresden bombing, 1055
Dreux, Battle at, 562
Dreyfus, Alfred, 901–903
Drug-dealing, 1141
Drumont, Edouard, 883
Dualism, 63, 639
Dual monarchy (Austria-Hungary), 824–827, 826(map)
Du Bois, W.E.B., 949
Dubuffet, Jean, 1078 and *illus.*, 1150–1151
Duchies, 320–321 and *illus.*, *map*, 412
Duchy of Milan, 553
Duels, among Europeans and Turks, 524(box)
Du Jure Belli ac Pacis (Grotius), 582
Dukes, in Germany, 320
Duma (Russia), 909, 932
Dumbarton Oaks conference, 1061
Dunant, Henri, 815
Dunkirk evacuation, 1034
Duplessis-Mornay, Philippe, 581
Dürer, Albrecht, 461–462, 461(illus.), 542
Durham, Lord, 756
Durham Report, 756
Durkheim, Emile, 868
Duse, Muhammed Ali, 917, 948, 949
Dutch, *see* Netherlands
Dutch East India Company, 611–613, 614(box)
Dutch East Indies, 1047, 1089
Dutch War (1672), 595–596
Dynamite, 847
Dynasties: in Sumer, 14; of Sargon, 15; Egyptian, 131; in Roman Empire, 203; of Germanic kingdoms, 250; Macedonian (Byzantine Empire), 280; Carolingian,

288–297; Safavid, 427; wars among, 681, 686. *See also* specific dynasties and rulers
Dyskolos (Menander), 136–137
Dzerzhinsky, Feliks, 979(illus.)

Earnings, 792–793, 854–855, 856. *See also* Wage system
Earth, 626. *See also* Astronomy
East: Roman Empire in, 236, 249, 250–254; Orthodox Christianity in, 255, 276; monasticism in, 256; Islamic, 268–275; Polo's travels to, 478–479. *See also* Asia
East Anglia, 284
East Asia, 920(map), 1050(map), 1114
East Berlin, revolt in, 1098
East-central Europe: after World War I, 962; democracy and authoritarianism in, 969; political movements in, 1014; Nazi-Soviet Pact and, 1024–1025; Soviets and, 1052; buffer zone in, 1061; Iron Curtain and, 1062–1063; Soviet bloc in, 1097–1098; destruction of communism in, 1121–1132; ethnic conflict in, 1132, 1134(map). *See also* De-Stalinization; Eastern Europe; specific countries
Easter, 216
Eastern empire, *see* Byzantine Empire; East; Roman Empire
Eastern Europe: Christianity in, 297; trade and, 298; Slavs in, 337–339; in Middle Ages, 413–414; Ottoman Turks and, 423–427, 426(map); Reformation and, 532–533; peasants in, 550; Habsburgs and, 573(map); Poland-Lithuania in, 605–607; powers in, 606(map); Russia and, 608–611; Crimean War and, 814; Jews in, 869; autocracies in, 905–909; after World War I, 945–948 and *map*. *See also* East-central Europe; Mongols; specific countries
Eastern front, in World War I, 925 and *illus.*
Easter Rebellion, 927
East Frankish Kingdom, 296, 320
East Germany, 1062, 1085, 1098, 1101, 1127–1128. *See also* Germany
East India Company, 732
East Indies, 1089
Eastman, George, 870
East Prussia, 525
Ebert, Friedrich, 970, 971
Ebla (Tell Mardikh), Syria, 33–34
Ebro River, as boundary, 172
Ecclesiastical courts, 360
Ecclesiastical History of the English People (Bede), 287
Ecerinis, The (Mussato), 441
Ecloga (Leo), 279
Economic and Monetary Union (EMU), 1137 and *illus.*
Economic Consequences of the Peace, The (Keynes), 950
Economic integration, 1094–1097, 1095(box), 1136–1139
Economics: liberalism in, 747–748, 796–797; socialism and, 749–750; revolutions of 1848 and, 762–763; Marx and, 802–805; imperialism and, 887

Economic thought, 663, 664
Economy, 619–620; in Lagash, 14; Athenian, 91; Hellenistic, 127–128; in Ptolemaic Egypt, 129; women and, 141; Roman, 175–176, 197–199, 204–205, 231; Constantine and, 233; in Middle Ages, 298–299, 310–311, 370–372; decline in, 396; change in, 417–422; new elites and, 548–549; common people and, 549–550; trade and, 683–685; of Atlantic region, 684(map); expansion of, 687–689; growth in, 689–690, 811; immigration and, 897; between world wars, 941–942, 964–965; inflation and, 964–965; in democracies, 968; Great Depression and, 996–1000; in Scandinavia, 998–999; after World War II, 1061; in Western Europe, 1079–1080; international groupings, 1096(map); of communist bloc, 1103; oil crisis and, 1105–1106; welfare state and, 1106; in democracies, 1115–1117; after communism, 1130–1131; worldwide, 1139–1140. *See also* Economic integration; specific countries
ECSC, *see* European Coal and Steel Community (ECSC)
Eden, Anthony, 1089
Edicts: of Maximum Prices, 231; of Milan, 234, 237; of Philip IV (France), 386–387; of Nantes, 564, 592, 602
Education: in Sparta, 86, 87; Aristotle on, 110; at Alexandrian Museum, 135; in Rome, 185; of women, 242; Augustine on, 261; Cassiodorus and, 261; under Charlemagne, 294–295; in Middle Ages, 339; universities and, 379; in Italy, 439; humanistic studies and, 442–444; in liberal arts, 445(box); Feltre and, 463; U.S. state universities, 831; of middle-class women, 854; for working class, 857; opportunities in, 863–864; upward mobility and, 1117. *See also* Higher education; Universities
Edward I (England), 363, 366, 386, 402
Edward II (England), 403
Edward III (England), 403, 404, 462
Edward IV (Black Prince, England), 405, 409
Edward V (England), 409
Edward VI (England), 529–530, 565
Edward the Confessor, 330
Edwin Smith Papyrus, 32
EEC, *see* European Economic Community (EEC, Common Market)
Eggley, Ann, 792
Egypt, 4, 10, 22(map), 29(box), 35(map), 732, 889, 943; authority in, 11; to 1100 B.C., 21–33; international system and, 36; Assyria and, 47; Ptolemaic, 119, 124, 126, 129–132 and *illus.*, 131(box); Cleopatra and, 150–151, 150(illus.), 151(illus.); Ptolemaic, 175; cults of, 220; Crusades and, 378; Ottomans in, 762; anticolonialism in, 960; independence of, 1089; Suez Canal and, 1089. *See also* Pyramids
Egyptian Empire, *see* Egypt
Eichmann, Adolf, 1042
Eighteenth Dynasty (Egypt), 28–30
Einhard, 289(box), 291, 294

Einstein, Albert, 884, 1077
Eisenhower, Dwight D., 1056
Eisenstein, Sergei, 967
El Alamein, Battle at, 1051
Elba, Napoleon at, 727
El Cid, see Díaz de Vivar, Rodrigo ("El Cid")
Eldorado, 499
Eleanor of Aquitaine, 329, 364
Elections: in Roman Republic, 163; episco-
    pal vs. canonical, 326; of popes, 359; in
    Paris, 719; universal-manhood (France),
    764–765; in U.S., 831; in Britain, 834
Electors, 523–524, 575, 719
Electricity, 862, 865
Elements (Euclid), 138
Elijah (prophet), 54
Eliot, George (Mary Ann Evans), 746
Eliot, T. S., 1077
Elites: in Greece, 82; in Athens, 99; Hel-
    lenistic, 126, 139; in Rome, 158–159, 166,
    190–191 and illus., 199, 237, 240; Cicero
    and, 187; in Late Antiquity period, 229;
    as Christians, 239–240; after Rome, 262;
    Muslim, 272; under Charlemagne, 292;
    medieval, 300, 311–314; economic
    change and, 548–549; religious unrest
    and, 557(box); Locke and, 650; French
    Revolution and, 729, 730; non-Western,
    959–960. See also Aristocracy; Nobility
Elizabeth I (England), 528, 530–531,
    530(illus.), 565–569, 567(illus.), 581,
    582(box), 843
Elizabethan Settlement, 530–531
Ellul, Jacques, 1150, 1151
Emancipation, see Serfs and serfdom;
    Slaves and slavery
Emancipation Proclamation (U.S.), 831
Embargo, on oil, 1105
Emigration, 126. See also Immigration;
    Migration
Emile (Rousseau), 670
Emirate, of Cordoba, 282
Emirs, 272
Emperors, see Empires; specific emperors
    and empires
Emperor-worship, 199
Empires, 811, 886–898. See also Anticolo-
    nialism; Dynasties; Imperialism; Inde-
    pendence and independence move-
    ments; Nationalism; Supranational
    empires; specific empires
Empirical method, 634
Employment, 420, 421(illus.), 747. See also
    Unemployment
Ems dispatch, 823, 836
Encomendero and encomienda, 498–499, 500
Encyclopedia (Diderot), 664–665, 664(illus.)
Endgame (Beckett), 1075
Energy, 781, 846, 865, 884. See also Nuclear
    power; Oil
Engels, Friedrich, 790(box), 802
Engines, 784. See also Steam engine
England (Britain), 943; Stonehenge in, 9;
    Germanic invasions of, 247; during
    early Middle Ages, 284–287; Vikings
    in, 297; trade and, 298; Jews in, 320;
    Anglo-Saxon, 329–330; in Middle Ages,

329–332; Celts in, 335–336; monarchy
    and government of, 364–366, 403,
    404(illus.), 589; Magna Carta and, 366;
    society in, 395–396; Hundred Years' War
    and, 402–407 and map, 409; France and,
    404–405, 407; Statute of Laborers in, 419;
    cloth trade and, 420; Rising of 1381 in,
    423, 424(box); exploration by, 491; Refor-
    mation in, 527–531; Spanish Armada
    and, 559–560; religious and political
    crises in, 565–571; economy of, 568–569;
    civil war and revolution in (1642–1649),
    598–603; Interregnum in, 600–601; re-
    ligion in, 602; Glorious Revolution in,
    602–603; overseas trade of, 612; Dutch
    and, 615; North American colonies of,
    618(map); science and revolution in,
    638–639; scientific societies in, 642;
    Voltaire on, 662(box); during Enlighten-
    ment, 672–675; Hanoverian monarchs
    in, 673, 685; Scotland and, 673–674,
    673(illus.); Atlantic trade of, 682–683;
    Caribbean colonies of, 683; France and,
    685, 686–687; North American holdings
    of, 688(map); American Revolution and,
    700, 701–702; European revolutionary
    movements and, 700–701; Napoleon
    and, 722, 724, 725, 730–733; dominance
    of seas by, 725; colonies and, 730, 758;
    economy in, 732; expansion of, 732–733;
    Methodism in, 743; unrest and reform
    in, 753–757; rail system in, 777(box);
    industry and, 779–780, 779(illus.), 782,
    783–784; cities in, 788; child labor in,
    793–794 and box; Crimean War and,
    812–813; North American territories
    of, 829; Victorian period, 833–834; view
    of Parliament, 833(box); royal family
    in, 842–843 and illus.; urban reform in,
    860–861; church attendance in, 869–870;
    literature in, 871, 873; Crystal Palace
    exhibition in, 876–877 and illus.; social-
    ism in, 880–881; India and, 888(illus.),
    894–895; imperialism of, 889; as democ-
    ratic power, 899–900; constitutional crisis
    in, 900; women's suffrage movement in,
    900, 901(illus.); alliances and, 909; Ger-
    many and, 910; in World War I, 925; econ-
    omy in, 928, 929, 964; Arab policy of,
    942–943; anticolonialism and, 960; power
    of, 962; society in, 968; Great Depression
    and, 996; unemployment in, 997(illus.);
    Mussolini and, 1013–1014; Battle of Britain
    and, 1034–1035 and illus.; U.S. and, 1048;
    and Yalta, 1052–1055, 1053(illus.); after
    World War II, 1063; Palestine and, 1065–
    1066; society in, 1080–1082; decoloniza-
    tion and, 1089, 1091; welfare state in, 1106;
    Thatcher in, 1119–1120. See also Churchill,
    Winston; Monarchs and monarchies; World
    War I; World War II; specific monarchs
Enkheduanna, 15–16
Enlightened despotism, 675–677
Enlightenment, 659, 660–671. See also
    Voltaire
Enlil (god), 15, 17
Enmebaragesi of Kish, 14

Entente (Britain-France), 909
Enterprise, see Business
Entertainment, 957–959. See also Leisure
Entomology, 641(illus.)
Entrepreneurs, 176, 420, 782–783
Environment, 1107; early humans and, 5;
    industrialization and, 795–796; urban,
    861; science of, 864; global, 1139; technol-
    ogy and, 1144. See also Cities and towns;
    Geography; Urban society
Epaminondas (Theban leader), 103
Epic literature, 19, 35, 64
Epic of Gilgamesh, 19, 20(box), 51
Epicurus and Epicureans, 141, 143–144, 187
Epidauros, 106
Epidemics, 501, 753, 791. See also Black
    Death
Epirus, kingdom of, 128
Episcopal elections, 326
Epistle to the Romans (Barth), 986
Epitome (Zonaras), 170(box)
Equality, 665–666, 832
Equestrians, 168, 181–182
Equiano, Olaudah, 685(box)
Equinoxes, 628
Erasistratus of Ceos, 139
Erasmus, Desiderius, 458, 459–461
Eratosthenes of Cyrene, 138
Eremitic monasticism, 256, 315
Erfurt Union, 819
Erinna (poet), 141
Eroticism, 137, 139. See also Sex and sexuality
Escorial, 560
Essais (Montaigne), 578
Essay Concerning Human Understanding
    (Hume), 664
Essay on Human Understanding (Locke), 649
Essay on the Inequality of Human Races
    (Gobineau), 883
Essay on the Principle of Population, An
    (Malthus), 747
Essays, of Montaigne, 580
Essenes, 147, 214–215
Estado da India (India Office), 486
Estates, 176, 293, 299, 318, 330, 419, 613. See
    also Manors
Estates General (France), 423, 590, 672, 704.
    See also French Revolution
Estates of Transylvania, 533
Este family, 455; Obizzo d', 410; Isabella d',
    444 and illus., 464, 465(box)
Esterhazy, Marie-Charles-Ferdinand-Walsin
    (Major), 901
Esterhazy family, 850
Estonia, 611, 1033
Ethelred II (England), 311, 329, 343
Ethical dualism, 63
Ethics, 143(box), 371–372
Ethiopia, 478, 1014
Ethnic Germans, 1020, 1040, 1060
Ethnicity and ethnic minorities, 947;
    in Austria-Hungary, 827, 905; self-
    determination and, 942; in east-central
    Europe, 948(map), 1132; Germany and,
    1021; conflict and, 1132, 1134(map)
Etruria, 155
Etruscans, 155–157

Euboea, 81

Eucharist, 340, 516

Euclid, 138

Eugénie (France), 867

Eugenius IV (Pope), 468

Euhemerus of Messene, 144

Eumenides (Aeschylus), 112

Eupatrids, 89, 90, 95–96

Euphrates River valley region, 4, 10–11, 268. *See also* Mesopotamia

Euripides, 98(box), 112

Eurocentrism, 1147–1149

Eurocrats, 1094

Europe, 4–5, 9–10; expansion of, 307–311; in Middle Ages, 326–335, 354 (map); Celtic realms in, 335–336; states in, 336(map); central governments in, 360–369; papacy and, 401–402; Italy and north, 439; Renaissance courts of, 462–468; as Old World, 475–476; navigation in, 476–477; contacts beyond Christendom, 477–479; geography and, 479–480; exploration by, 480–491; Spanish colonies and, 491–500; Columbian Exchange and, 500–504; religious wars in, 547–548; Spanish Habsburgs in, 554(map); in Thirty Years' War, 571, 573–578, 575(map); after Thirty Years' War, 576–578; absolutism and, 590–597; revolution in England, 597–604; rulers in central and eastern, 604–611; overseas trade and, 611–620; Enlightenment rulers and society in, 671–680; revolutionary period in, 699–733, 724(map); political system in, 739; in 1815, 740(map); search for stability in, 741–742; concept of European republic, 747; revolutions of 1848 in, 762–770; industrialization in, 787–796; political shifts in, 811–812; railroads in, 848(map); population of, 879; new imperialism of, 886–898; migration from, 897–898 and *map*; territorial settlement in, 946(map); popular culture in, 957–958; power of, 959–960; Nazi "New Order" in, 1037–1046, 1038(map); spheres of influence in, 1052; World War II and, 1055–1056, 1055(map), 1059; Cold War and, 1073–1107; American culture and, 1077–1079, 1141–1144, 1143(box); economy, democracy, and society in West, 1079–1086; Soviets and, 1097–1098; unemployment in, 1115; past vs. present in, 1115(illus.); after Cold War, 1126(map). *See also* Central Europe; East-central Europe; Eastern Europe; Northern Europe; World War I; World War II; specific countries

European Coal and Steel Community (ECSC), 1094, 1136

European Commission, 1137

European Community (EC), *see* European Union (EU)

European Court of Justice, 1136

European Economic Community (EEC, Common Market), 1094. *See also* European Union

European Parliament, 1136

European theater, in World War II, 1036(map), 1048

European Union (EU), 1094, 1136–1139

Euthanasia program, Nazi Germany and, 1012, 1040

Evangelical Christians, 511

Eve (biblical), 56

Everyday life, *see* Lifestyle

Evolution, 3, 491

Evolutionary Socialism (Bernstein), 881

Evolutionary theory, 864–865, 866(box)

Exchange, *see* Columbian Exchange; Trade

Excommunication, 323–324, 325, 360, 515

Executive branch, 98, 163

Exhibitions, *see* Crystal Palace exhibition

Existentialism, 1075–1076, 1075(illus.), 1076(box)

Exodus, 51–52

Expansion, 33, 589–590; Egyptian, 28–30; Assyrian, 168–171, 174(map), 175–176, 204; of Christianity, 219–220; Germanic, 247–249; of Islam, 269(map), 271–273; of Europe, 307–311; by England, 568, 732–733; of United States, 829–830 and *map*; new imperialism and, 886–898; German, 1008; of Nazi Germany, 1024(map). *See also* Germanic peoples

Experimental procedure, 638–639, 643

Exploration: of New World, 474(map), 475–476, 480–486; winds, currents, and, 481(map); voyages of, 484(map); by Spain, 486–491; new imperialism and, 887

Exports, 198, 420. *See also* Trade; specific industries

Expressionism, 885, 950(illus.)

Extermination camps (Nazi Germany), 1011–1012, 1032, 1040–1043, 1042(illus.), 1070–1071 and *illus. See also* Holocaust

Eyre system, 403

Ezekiel, 56

Ezra, 56

Fabian Society, 881

Factories, 781–782, 792, 793–794 and *box*, 800, 862, 965. *See also* Industry and industrialization

Factory system, 797, 801(box)

Fairs, commerce and, 371

Fairy tales (Grimm), 746

Faisal ibn-Husayn, 943, 944(box), 945(illus.)

Faith, 259, 340, 360

Falange, 1018

Fallada, Hans, 998

Families and family life, 6; in Homeric society, 73; in Rome, 159–160, 236; women and, 301–302; size of, 308; nobility and, 312; economic change and, 549; industrialization and, 793–796; middle-class, 852–853 and *box*; marriage, sexuality, and, 965; in Nazi Germany, 1011; declining role of, 1119

Famine, 396, 415, 1002

Fanon, Frantz, 1093 and *box*

Faraday, Michael, 865

Farms and farming, 9, 176, 414, 688–689, 856, 857. *See also* Agriculture

Farrell, Thomas F., 1031

Fascism, 974–975, 981, 982–984, 982(box), 996, 1013–1014, 1060; popular fronts and, 1015; Spanish civil war and, 1016–1018. *See also* Authoritarianism; Nazis and Nazism; Totalitarianism

Fathers, 159–160. *See also* Families and family life; Men

Fatima, 275

Faust (Goethe), 745

Fealty, 313(box)

Fedele, Cassandra, 445(box)

Federal leagues, *see* entries under League; Hanseatic League

Federal Republic of Germany (West Germany), 1062. *See also* West Germany

Federici, Silvia, 1150, 1151

Felix, Julia, 220

Feltre, Vittorino da, 442, 463

Feminism, 1083(box), 1106, 1118–1119; in Enlightenment, 665, 666(box). *See also* Abortion rights; Women

Ferdinand I (Holy Roman emperor), 524, 527, 572

Ferdinand II (Castile), 367

Ferdinand II (Holy Roman emperor), 572–573, 575

Ferdinand VII (Spain), 741, 757–758

Ferdinand of Aragon, 427, 429–430, 499

Ferry, Jules, 887

Fertile Crescent, 7, 8(map)

Fertility, 308

Fertilizers, 856

Festivals, in Egypt, 24–25

Feudalism, 312–313 and *box*, 317–318, 328, 330

Fichte, Johann Gottlieb, 746

Ficino, Marsilio, 446, 448

Fiefs, 312, 313, 330, 332, 335, 356, 365

Fifth Crusade, 378

Fifth Lateran Council, 535

Fifth Republic (France), 1085–1086

Film, 967, 1010, 1028–1029

"Final Solution," 1040

Finances, 60, 233, 274, 362–363, 568–569, 827–828

Fine art, 1110. *See also* Art(s)

Finland, 534, 741, 1033

Fire at Sea (Turner), 743

First Book of Maccabees, 146

First Consul, *see* Napoleon I

First Crusade, 320, 344–346, 347(box), 361, 377, 378(map)

First Estate (clergy), 704

First Great Northern War, 605, 607, 608(illus.)

First International, 882

First Jewish Revolt, 216

First Punic War, 172

First Triumvirate, 184

First World War, *see* World War I

Fishing, 419

Five Good Emperors, 204

Five Pillars of Islam, 270–271

Flagellants, 416

Flanders, 334(map), 363, 370, 420, 422, 461, 522. *See also* Belgium; Low countries; Netherlands

Flaubert, Gustave, 871, 874

Flavian dynasty, 203–204
Flemish arts and people, see Flanders
Floods, Nile River and, 21
Flood story, 51
Flora, Columbian Exchange and, 502
Florence, 370, 411, 412, 439; Medici bank in, 418; humanistic studies in, 442; Niccolò Niccoli's library in, 444–446; art in, 450–453, 451 and illus., 455, 470–471. See also Renaissance
Florentine Codex, 503
Flowering Light of Divinity, The (Mechtild of Magdeburg), 386
Fluitschip (flyship), 611
Foch, Ferdinand, 939
Folk culture, 671
Fontenelle, Bernard de, 651(illus.), 652
Food, 308–310; distribution of, 551(illus.), 552; production of, 688–689; transportation of, 847–848. See also Agriculture; Crops; Diet; Farms and farming
Food riots, 551–552
Ford, Henry, 965
Foreign affairs, 161–162, 582
Foreign policy, see Diplomacy; Foreign affairs; International relations
Fortifications, see Bastions; Castles; Defense; Forts
Forts, French North American, 686(illus.), 687
Fourier, Charles, 750, 802
Fourteen Points, 937, 938(box)
Fourth Crusade, 377–378, 379
Fourth Dynasty (Egypt), 23, 24
Fourth Lateran Council (1215), 386
Fourth Republic (France), 1085
Fragonard, Jean-Honoré, 670
France, 290(map), 943; Vikings in, 297; Jews in, 320; Capetian, 326–328; territorial principalities of, 327–328, 327(map); Normans in, 337; vernacular literature in, 343; monarchy and government of, 361–363, 364(box); England and, 362, 365; Henry II and, 364–365; culture in, 384; taxation of clergy in, 386–387; society in, 395–396; papacy and, 396; Pragmatic Sanction of Bourges and, 402; Hundred Years' War and, 402–407 and map; monarchs in, 403–404 and illus., 589; English claims in, 404–405, 407; consolidation of, 409; trade in, 418–419; revolts in, 422–423; exploration by, 491; Reformation in, 531–532; religious and political crises in, 562–565; royal succession in, 563(illus.); religious toleration in, 564; royal authority in, 564–565; Louis XIV and, 589–597; absolutism in, 590–597; Dutch and, 595; Spain and, 595; Nine Years' War (King William's War), 596–597; territorial gains of, 596(map); eastern border of, 597; colonies of, 618–619, 618(map); science and, 635–638, 642–643; Enlightenment in, 671–672; economy in, 672, 722, 751–752, 785–786; colonization by, 683; Britain and, 685, 686–687; North American forts of, 686(illus.), 687; American Revolution and, 701–702; An-

cien Régime in, 702–704; Austria and, 713–714; churches in, 718–719, 722; impact of Revolution in, 728–729; restoration and reform in, 739, 751–753; Quadruple Alliance and, 741–742; freedom of press in, 754(box); revolution of 1848 in, 763–766; women's rights in, 764, 766(box); industrialization in, 784–786; cities in, 788; labor in, 794, 800–801; factory system in, 797; riots in, 799; Crimean War and, 812; Paris Commune in, 836; Third Republic in, 836–837; literature in, 871, 873–874; socialism in, 881–882; imperialism of, 888, 889, 891; Vietnam and, 889; as democracy, 900–903; Dreyfus affair in, 901–903; Morocco and, 909–910; World War I and, 911, 921, 923, 937; war effort in, 939; Alsace, Lorraine, and, 945; power of, 962; inflation in, 964–965; society in, 968; Communist party in, 977; Mussolini and, 1013–1014; left-right conflict in, 1014–1015; popular front coalition in, 1018–1020; fall of, 1033–1034; Vichy regime in, 1033–1034; in World War II, 1051; postwar period in, 1079–1080, 1085–1086; women in, 1082; nuclear weapons in, 1087, 1095–1097; colonies of, 1089–1090; Days of May uprising in, 1104; Muslims in, 1112(illus.), 1113–1114, 1141; higher education in, 1117; German reunification and, 1133–1135; EU and, 1137; immigration and citizenship in, 1140; socialism in, 1145. See also European Union (EU); French Revolution; World War I; World War II; specific monarchs and leaders
Franche-Comté region, 595
Franchise, in France, 719, 764–765
Francis I (Austria), 682, 758
Francis I (France), 461, 522, 532
Francis II (France), 562
Francis V (Habsburg), 814
Franciscans, 374–375, 499–500
Francis Ferdinand (Austria), 911
Francis Joseph (Austria-Hungary), 824–827, 905
Francis of Assisi, 352(illus.), 353, 374–375, 375(illus.)
Franco, Francisco, 1017, 1104
Franco-Austrian War, 820
Franconia, 320
Franco-Prussian War, 822–824, 836, 910
Franco-Russian Alliance, 909
Franke, Fritz, 924(box)
Frankfurt assembly, 768, 769, 770
Frankish peoples and kingdoms, 211, 247, 282, 296, 297–298. See also Carolingian Empire
Franklin, Benjamin, 659, 702
Frederick (Denmark), 675
Frederick (Palatinate elector), 575, 673
Frederick I (Barbarossa, German Empire), 355–356, 367–368
Frederick I (Denmark), 534
Frederick II (German Empire), 355, 357–359
Frederick II (Prussia, "the Great"), 676, 682
Frederick of Saxony, 523

Frederick William (Great Elector, Brandenburg-Prussia), 605, 676
Frederick William IV (Prussia), 768, 769–770
Free Corps (Germany), 970
Free Democratic party, 1084
Freedmen, in Italy, 199
Freedoms, see Censorship; Press; Rights
Free French troops, 1051
Free-market economies, 1139. See also Market economy
Freemasons, 760
Free trade, 997–998. See also Laissez faire; Trade
French Académie des Sciences, 642–643, 646 and illus.
French and Indian War, see Seven Years' War
French Congo, 891
French Empire, 723–725, 834–836
French Revolution, 698(illus.), 699–700, 704–710, 714(illus.); first phase of (1789–1791), 710–713; Second, and foreign war (1791–1793), 713–715; republic and Terror in, 715–719; Thermidorian Reaction and Directory in, 719–720; Napoleon I and, 720–728; impact in France, 728–729; political symbolism in, 729, 734–735 and illus., 734(illus.); impact overseas, 729–730; socialism and, 749–750. See also France; Napoleon I
Freud, Sigmund, 884, 986
Friars Minor, see Franciscans
Friendly societies, 798, 800
Froben, Johannes, 456
Fronde (French revolt), 590
Frontier regions, 276–277, 296–297, 320, 889. See also Provinces
Fronts: in World War I, 919, 920(map); in World War II, 1048, 1050–1051
Fugger family, 419
Führer, Hitler as, 1010
Fulbert of Chartres, 339
Fur trapping, 683

Gadsden Purchase, 829
Galápagos Islands, 864
Galatia, 126
Galen, 380, 416, 628, 640–641
Galicia, 767
Galileo Galilei, 624(illus.), 625, 630, 632–633 and box, 635, 647–648
Gallican church, 402
Gallican jurisprudence, 458
Gallienus (Rome), 211–213
Gallus, Trebonianus, 210(illus.)
Gama, Vasco da, see Da Gama, Vasco
Gamond, Zoé Gatti de, 750
Gandharan sculpture, 134, 135(illus.)
Gandhi, Mohandas, 948, 960, 1000, 1001(box), 1058, 1063
Gangs, political, 186
Gardens, 694–695, 694(illus.)
Garibaldi, Giuseppe, 816–817, 818(illus.)
Gascony, 327, 363
Gaslights, 862
Gaugamela, Battle at, 122
Gauguin, Paul, 886, 895

Gaul, 175, 184, 244, 245, 247, 273. *See also* Celts

Gay, Peter, 993

Gelasius I (Pope), 255

Gender, 1081–1082; Israelites and, 56–57; learning and, 242; in sciences, 643–644, 645(box); political thought and, 651–652; welfare issues and, 1081–1082; society and, 1118–1119. *See also* Men; Sex and sexuality; Women

General Workers' Brotherhood, 800

Genghis Khan, *see* Jenghiz Khan

Genoa, 334

Genocide, *see* Holocaust

Gentiles, 147, 217, 219

Gentleman, concept and behavior of, 464–466, 467(box), 593

Gentry, 548–549. *See also* Classes (economic and social)

Geoffrey of Anjou, 332

Geoffrin, Marie-Thérèse, 668

Geography, 478, 479–480, 487. *See also* specific countries and regions

Geology, 864

Geometry, 20, 94, 108, 138. *See also* Mathematics; Science

Geopolitics, *see* World-view

George I (England), 673

George II (England), 673

George III (England), 842

George IV (England), 842

Gérard, François, 714(illus.)

Gerbert of Aurillac, 339

Géricault, Théodore, 744, 772–773 and *illus.*

German Confederation, 741, 759, 819

German Democratic Republic (East Germany), 1062. *See also* East Germany

German Empire, 355–360, 400; in Middle Ages, 320–326; Holy Roman Empire and, 412–413; William I of, 810(illus.). *See also* Germany

Germanic peoples, 229; Rhine River as frontier, 199; Roman Empire and, 211, 233, 240; expansion of, 243–250; kingdoms of, 249(map); Spain and, 281; in Italy, 282

Germanicus, 202

German People's Party (DVP), 971

Germany, 290(map); clergy in, 316; Jews in, 320; duchies and, 320–321 and *map;* Saxons in, 320–323; Salian dynasty in, 323; investiture controversy in, 323–326; Mongols and, 368; Russia and, 368–369; Holy Roman Empire and, 412–413; Scandinavia and, 413; territories in, 413; trade of, 419; revolutions in, 423; peasant revolt in, 517–519, 517(illus.); religious reform in, 518(map); Reformation and, 521–522; politics in, 523–525; religious settlement in, 525–527; Habsburgs and, 575; Thirty Years' War and, 576; France and, 596–597; Napoleon and, 723, 725, 726; nationalism in, 746; states of, 758–759; revolutions of 1848 and, 768–770; industrialization in, 786–787; cities in, 788; workers in, 799, 800; Bismarck in, 819–820; unification of, 819–824, 821(map), 825(box); social welfare programs in, 862–863; socialism in,

881, 918; imperialism of, 888–889; autocracy in, 904–905; before World War I, 909–910, 911; Balkan region and, 911; economy in, 927; antiwar sentiment in, 937; peace and, 938–939; Russia and, 939; warfare in 1918, 939–940; constitutional monarchy in, 940; military defeat and political change in, 940–941; World War I settlement in, 943–945; in 1920s, 959; power of, 962–963; inflation in, 964; movies in, 967 and *illus.;* Weimar Republic in, 969–974; alienation in, 986; Great Depression and, 997; Hitler and Nazism in, 1005–1013; fascist Italy and, 1013–1014; before World War II, 1020–1021; Soviet Union and, 1023–1024, 1037–1046, 1051; expansion of, 1024(map); after World War II, 1052, 1056–1057; Allied bombings of, 1055; borders with Poland, 1057; zones in, 1057; division of, 1061–1062; economy in, 1079; government of, 1084; Berlin Wall in, 1101, 1128 and *illus.;* Green movement in, 1106; terrorism in, 1106; reunification of, 1132, 1133; EU and, 1137; immigration to, 1140. *See also* East Germany; German Empire; Holy Roman Empire; Nazis and Nazism; Socialist party (Germany); West Germany; World War I; World War II; specific German states

Germs, Lister and, 867

Gestapo, 1007, 1010–1011

Ghana, 477, 1091, 1092

Ghent, 370, 422

Ghettos, Jewish, 1040

Ghiberti, Lorenzo, 450, 451–452, 451(illus.), 455

Ghirlandaio, Domenico, 467

Gibbon, Edward, 229

Giberti, Gian Matteo, 535

Gilgamesh of Uruk, 14. *See also Epic of Gilgamesh*

Gil Robles, José Maria, 1016

Giolitti, Giovanni, 903, 981

Giotto di Bondone, 375(illus.), 450–451, 450(illus.), 454

Girls, *see* Women

Girondins, 713, 714, 716, 717–718

Giza, 24

Glaber, Ralph, 307, 311

Gladstone, William, 834, 835(illus.), 889, 899

Glasnost (openness), 838, 1122

Glazar, Richard, on Holocaust, 1070–1071

Global issues, 1139–1141, 1144–1146, 1147–1149, 1148(box)

Global village concept, 1114, 1116

Glorious Revolution (England), 602–603

GNP, *see* Gross national product

Goa, 485

Gobineau, Arthur de, 883

Godfrey of Bouillon, 346

Gods and goddesses, 10; of Sumer, 14; Sargon and, 15; of Mesopotamia, 17–19, 18(illus.); of Egypt, 24, 27, 30; of Hittites, 35; Yahweh as, 43, 52; of Assyrians, 45; Greek, 69–71, 92–93, 106; mystery cults and religions, 144, 220; Roman,

162; Carthaginian, 173(illus.); Bacchus and, 191; of Islam, 269; of Aztecs, 493, 497. *See also* Hebrews; Israel; Jews and Judaism; Religion; Theology

Goebbels, Joseph, 1010

Goethe, Johann Wolfgang von, 743

Gold, 482, 498, 811, 847

Gold Coast, 482, 960, 1091

Golden Bull, 413

Golden Horde, 368, 369(box)

Gold standard, 964, 997

Golgotha (Calvary) Hill, 216

Gomulka, Wladislaw, 1099

Gonzaga family, 442, 462, 463–464; Gianfrancesco, 463; Lodovico, 463; Francesco, 464

Goodbye to All That (Graves), 951

Good Government of Siena (paintings), 455

Good Shepherd, Christ as, 215(illus.)

Gorbachev, Mikhail, 1122, 1124, 1125, 1127, 1130

Gordon, Charles, 889

Gordon, George, *see* Byron, Lord (George Gordon)

Gorze reform, 315

Gospel According to the Silver Marks, The, 385

Gospels (Christian), 213, 216

Gothic style, 244(illus.), 355, 375(illus.), 379, 381–384, 383(illus.), 744, 895(illus.)

Goths, 211. *See also* Ostrogoths; Visigoths

Gouges, Olympe de, 712(box)

Government: Hammurabi and, 16–17 and *box;* Plato on, 109; Aristotle on, 110 and *box;* of Hellenistic world, 126; under Justinian, 251; of Islam, 274; by medieval nobility, 314; central, 360–369; urban growth and, 370; medieval, 402–414; of churches, 516–517; of cities, 549; poverty relief and, 552; Hobbes on, 649; Locke on, 649–651, 650(box); Rousseau on, 665–666; in Enlightenment, 671–680; legitimacy of, 729; liberal ideology and, 749; revolutions of 1848 and, 763; laissez faire and, 796; civil service and, 851; welfare policies of, 862–863; colonial, 891; democracies, 898–904; autocracies, 904–909; and business, 998; role of, 1118, 1119–1120; after communism, 1130–1132. *See also* Democracies (nations); Kings and kingdoms; Monarchs and monarchies; Power (authority); specific city-states and countries; specific countries; specific types of governments

Gozzoli, Benozzo, 455

Gracchus family: Gaius, 178, 181–182; Tiberius Sempronius, 180–181 and *box*

Grammar, 340, 380, 442

Gramsci, Antonio, 1077

Granada, 367, 429, 560

Grand Armée, 725

Grand Duchy of Moscow, 369, 414

Grand National Consolidated Trades Union, 800

Grand princes, of Russia, 338

"Grand Remonstrance," 571

Granicus River, Battle at, 122, 124(map)

Gratian, 237, 340
Grave Circles A and B, 67, 68(illus.)
Gravelines, Battle at, 560
Graves, Robert, 951
Gravitation, 639–640
Great Britain, *see* England (Britain)
Great Depression, 973, 996–1000
Greater East Asia Co-Prosperity Sphere, 1048
Great Interregnum (Germany), 359
Great Lakes region, 618 and *map*, 683
Great Northern War, 675; First, 605, 607, 608(illus.); Second, 611
"Great Patriotic War," *see* World War II
Great Powers, 739, 741–742, 762, 888–889, 909. *See also* World powers
Great Pyramids, 23, 24, 25(illus.)
Great Reform Bill of 1832, 755, 757
Great Reforms, in Russia, 906
Great Schism, 396, 398–401, 399(box)
Great Unwashed, The, 802
Great War, 918. *See also* World War I
Greece, 33, 906, 1063; Egypt and, 23; Athens and, 43; Minoan civilization in, 64–66, 65(map); Mycenaean civilization in, 67–69; Homer and, 69–71; *demos* (people) in, 71; polis in, 79–81; archaic and classical, 80(map), 81–95, 83(map), 84(illus.), 87(illus.), 88(box), 90(illus.), 104–113; classical Athens, 95–100; struggle for hegemony in, 100–104; in Peloponnesian War, 104(map); expansion of, 119–120; Hellenistic period in, 119–147; Rome and, 155–156, 174(map), 175, 176–180, 179(box), 190, 191(illus.); mystery cults of, 220; Islamic culture and, 275; Byzantine Empire and, 276; Renaissance study of, 442; astronomy in, 626; nationalism in, 746; Ottomans and, 762; in World War II, 1035; democracy in, 1104. *See also* Hellenistic world; Magna Graecia; Philosophy
Greek church, *see* Orthodox Christianity
Greek Dark Ages, 69
Greek fire, 276, 277(illus.)
Greek language, 126, 208. *See also* Bible
Greek leagues, 128–129
Greenland, 337
Green movement, 1106, 1144
Gregorian calendar, 628
Gregory I (Pope), 283 and *illus.*, 319, 390
Gregory VII (Pope), 323–326, 325(box), 330
Gregory IX (Pope), 360
Gregory XI (Pope), 398
Gregory XII (Pope), 401
Gregory XIII (Pope), 628
Grey, Earl, 755
Grey, Edward, 910
Grimm, Jacob and Wilhelm, 746
Groener, Wilhelm, 940, 970
Groote, Geert, 512
Gropius, Walter, 987, 992, 993, 1077
Gross national product, 787(illus.)
Grotius, Hugo, 582
Grounds of Natural Philosophy (Cavendish), 643
Grufydd ap Cynan (Wales), 336
Guadeloupe, 687, 730

Guarino of Verona, 442
Guernica (Picasso), 470, 1017, 1018
Guernica (town), 1017–1018
Guesde, Jules, 881, 882
Guiana (Suriname), 619
Guicciardini, Francesco, 448, 534
Guilds, 370–371, 420, 421(illus.), 422, 455, 549, 798. *See also* Labor
Guillotine, *see* French Revolution
Guiscard, Robert, 333
Guise family, 562, 563
Guizot, François, 749
Gulags, 1077
Gulf of Finland, 607, 610, 611
Gulf War, *see* Persian Gulf War
Gunpowder Plot, 569
Guomindang (Kuomintang), 961
Gustav I (Sweden), 534
Gustav III (Sweden), 675–676
Gustav Adolf (Sweden), 576, 577(illus.), 607
Gutenberg, Johann, 456
Gutenberg Bible, 456
Gutian Empire, 16
Gymnasium, women in, 140–141
Gypsies, 1043

Habsburg family, 413, 521(illus.), 522–523, 554(map), 682, 814; Holy Roman Empire and, 571–573; in Austria, 573(map); power of, 575–576, 603–604; Spanish throne and, 597; in Austria-Hungary, 905; after World War I, 941, 942. *See also* specific rulers
Habsburg-Valois Wars, 412, 522, 562
Hadith, 271
Hadrian (Rome), 204
Hadrian's Wall, 204
Hagia Sophia, 251, 252–254, 254(illus.), 301
Haig, Douglas, 925
Haiti, 730, 731(box)
Hamlet (Shakespeare), 580
Hammurabi's Code, 16–17 and *box*
Handbook for Merchants (Pegalotti), 479 and *box*
Hanging Gardens of Babylon, 48
Hannibal, 172, 173
Hanover (Germany), 686, 759
Hanover family, in England, 673
Hanseatic League, 419
Hanukkah, 146
Harald Bluetooth (Denmark), 329
Harald Hardrada (Norway), 330
Harams (sanctuaries), 268–269
Hargreaves, James, 779
Harnack, Adolf von, 930
Harnesses, 310
Harold of Wessex, 330, 331(illus.)
Harun-al-Raschid, 274
Harvey, William, 641–642
Hasmonean family (Maccabees), 146
Hatshepsut (Egyptian queen), 29, 30(illus.), 151
Hattians, 35
Hattusas (Boghazköy), 34
Hattusilis III (Hittite king), 35, 36
Haussmann, Georges, 858–859, 858(illus.), 860(box)

Havel, Václav, 1123 and *box*
Hawaii, *see* Pearl Harbor attack
Hawkwood, John, 407–408
Haydn, Franz Josef, 671
Health, 415–417, 415(illus.), 778, 861–862; influenza pandemic and, 941. *See also* Disease; Epidemics; Medicine
Health Act (England), 860
Hebraic studies, 459
Hebrews, 15, 51, 19, 43–44, 50–57, 217. *See also* Jews and Judaism
Hecale (Callimachus), 139
Hedonism, 144
Hegel, Georg Wilhelm Friedrich, 743, 802, 803
Hegemony, 87, 100–104
Heidegger, Martin, 1075
Heidelburg, university at, 458
Heliocentrism, 138, 627, 632
Hellenic League, 101
Hellenic period (Greece), 119
Hellenism, 126, 176–180. *See also* Greece; Roman Republic
Hellenistic world, 130(map); Greece in, 119–120; Philip II of Macedon and, 120–121; Alexander the Great and, 121–124; kingdoms in, 125–134, 125(map); Seleucids and, 132–133; Greco-Indian interaction in, 133–134; philosophy in, 134; Alexandrian movement in, 134–142; philosophies and religions of, 142–147; Judaism in, 145–147, 146(box); Cleopatra and, 150–151
Hellespont, Battle at, 103
Helmholtz, Hermann von, 865
Heloise, 341
Helots, 86
Helsinki Accords, 1103–1104, 1122
Henotheism, 27, 51
Henry (prince of Wales), 634
Henry I (England), 331, 336
Henry I (Germany), 320
Henry II (England), 332, 336, 361, 364–365
Henry II (France), 522, 562
Henry III (England), 366
Henry III (France), 563
Henry III (Germany), 323
Henry IV (England), 409
Henry IV (France), 563, 582
Henry IV (Germany), 323–326, 324(illus.), 325(box)
Henry V (England), 407, 409
Henry V (Germany), 325–326
Henry VI (England), 407, 409
Henry VI (German Empire), 356–357
Henry VII (England), 402, 409–410
Henry VII (Holy Roman emperor), 413
Henry VIII (England), 402, 410, 459, 527–529, 565
Henry of Anjou, *see* Henry II (England)
Henry of Navarre, 563
Henry of Saxony (Germany), 320
Henry "the Lion" of Saxony, 356
Henry "the Navigator" (Portugal), 482
Heracleitus of Ephesus, 94–95
Heraclius, 276
Herculaneum, 224, 225

Hattians, 35
Hattusas (Boghazköy), 34
Hattusilis III (Hittite king), 35, 36
Haussmann, Georges, 858–859, 858(illus.), 860(box)

Herder, Johann Gottfried, 746, 747
Heresy and heretics, 234–235; Arianism as, 239; monophysitism as, 239; Berengar and, 340; Roman church and, 360; Albigensians, 363, 372–373; catharism, 363, 372–373; Waldensians and, 372; Hus and, 400; Wyclif and, 400; Joan of Arc and, 407; Beguines and, 512. *See also* Albigensians; Arians and Arianism
Hermeticism, 638
Hermetic magic, 448
Hermit, 256
Herod Antipas, 214
Herodotus, 26, 59, 89, 102, 113
Heroes, of Homer, 44, 71–73
Herondas, 137
Herophilus of Chalcedon, 138–139
Herzegovina, 828, 829
Herzl, Theodore, 883
Hesiod, 35, 69, 82, 91
Hesse-Cassel, 759
Hevellus, Elisabetha and Johannes, 644(illus.)
Heydrich, Reinhard, 1040
Hezekiah (Judean king), 53
Hierarchical society, 240–243, 315
Hieroglyphics, 31, 130
High Council (France), 591
Higher education, 1104–1105, 1117. *See also* Universities
Highlands (Scotland), 671, 673–674, 673(illus.)
High Renaissance period, 450
Hijra, 269
Hilda (Britain), 285, 286(box)
Hildebrand, *see* Gregory VII (Pope)
Hildegard of Bingen, 340–341, 342(box)
Himmler, Heinrich, 1007, 1040, 1041(box)
Hindemith, Paul, 986
Hindenburg, Paul von, 923, 925(illus.), 940, 971, 1007
Hipparchia of Maroneia, 141
Hipparchus of Nicaea, 138
Hippias, 91
Hippocrates, 107, 380
Hippocratics, 107
Hiram of Tyre, 50
Hirohito (Japan), 1058
Hiroshima, 1031, 1058
Hispaniola, 488, 731(box)
Historical and Critical Dictionary (Bayle), 652
Histories (Tacitus), 209–210
Histories, The (Herodotus), 113
History and historians, 178, 470–471, 867. *See also* specific historians
Hitler, Adolf, 969, 974, 996, 1005–1013, 1028–1029 and *illus.*, 1028(illus.), 1056. *See also* Germany; Nazis and Nazism; Third Reich; World War II
Hitler Youth, 1009
Hittites, 4, 33, 34–36, 35(map), 36(illus.)
Hobbes, Thomas, 649
Ho Chi Minh, 1089
Hohenzollern family, 605, 824; Albrecht von, 525
Holland, 613–615, 741. *See also* Netherlands
Holocaust, 1011–1012, 1032, 1040–1043, 1042(illus.), 1070–1071

Holstein, 575, 820
Holy books, 257–258. *See also* Bible
Holy Land, 317, 333, 346, 377–379. *See also* Crusades; Jerusalem
Holy Roman Empire, 397, 412–413, 571–578; Spain and, 429; Charles V and, 509, 521–527; religion and, 525–527; Spain and, 561; Napoleon and, 723; Germany and, 819. *See also* Austria; German Empire; Germany
Home front (World War I), 926–927
Homer, 43, 44, 64, 69–71, 71–73, 76, 91
Homeric poems, 43–44
Home rule: for Ireland, 899–900; for India, 948
Hominids, 4
Homo erectus, 4
Homosexuals and homosexuality, 92, 139, 1043
Honecker, Erich, 1127
Hong Kong, 1048
Hooker, Richard, 531
Hoover, Herbert, 998
Hoplite phalanx, 83–85, 84(illus.), 90, 96, 120, 158, 168
Horace, 200, 201
Hormuz, 485
Horses, 34, 309
Hortense (Rome), 185
Hospitallers, *see* Knights
Hospitals, 863
Höss, Rudolf, 1042
House, Edward, 879
Household, 159–160, 319(box), 549
House of Commons (England), 571, 833, 900. *See also* Parliament
House of Hanover, *see* Hanover family
House of Islam, 273
House of Lords (England), 571, 833, 900. *See also* Parliament
House of Orange, *see* Orange family
House of War, 273
House of Wisdom, 275
Housing, 311(illus.). *See also* Castles
Howell the Good, 319(box), 335
Huamán Poma, 495(box)
Hugenberg, Alfred, 1007
Hugh Capet, 328, 404
Hugh of Cluny, 324(illus.)
Hugo, Victor, 744, 747, 835
Huguenots, 531–532, 533(box), 562, 565, 618
Humanists and humanism, 438–449, 443(box), 628; Jews and, 447(box); Renaissance and, 456–461. *See also* Erasmus, Desiderius; More, Thomas; Renaissance; Scholasticism
Human rights, 1103–1104, 1122, 1132
Humans: evolution of, 3, 4; early, 4–10, 40–41 and *illus.*; deification of, 106
Human sacrifice, 493
Hume, David, 664
Hunchback of Notre Dame, The (Hugo), 744
Hundred Years' War, 395–396, 405–410, 405(illus.), 406(map)
Hungary, 337, 603, 677, 767, 942, 943, 1121, 1122; Protestantism in, 533; Austria and, 604, 767, 824–827, 905; communism in,

942; revolts in, 1099–1100, 1101(illus.); Soviet Union and, 1124; anticommunist revolution in, 1127. *See also* Austria-Hungary
Hunnic kingdom, 245
Huns, 236, 244, 246(box), 247, 930
Hunt, Holman, 870
Hunter-gatherers, 5; in Americas, 491
Hunting, 7
Hurrian kingdom, 29, 33, 34, 35
Hus, John, 400, 514
Husite movement, 400–401
Hutter, Jakob, 521
Huygens, Christiaan, 638
Hygiene, 861
Hyksos, 28
Hypatia of Alexandria, 242
Hyperinflation, 964, 969

Iberia, 282, 332, 429, 430
Iceland, 337, 534
Iceman, The (prehistoric human), 40–41 and *illus.*
Icon, 277, 279(illus.), 280
Iconoclastic controversy, 277–280
"Iconoclastic fury," 556
Idealism, of Plato, 108
Ideal Marriage (Van de Velde), 965
Ideograms, 11, 68
Ideology, *see* Philosophy; Political thought; Politics; Religion; Revolutionary period; specific ideologies
Ides of March, 185
Idiot, The (Dostoyevsky), 872
Il Galateo (Sir Galahad) (Casa), 467
Iliad (Homer), 64, 69–70, 73
Illness, *see* Disease
Illuminated manuscripts, 258(illus.), 285–287, 304–305 and *illus.*, 304(illus.)
Imago Mundi (Ailly), 487
Imams, 270
Imitation of Christ, The, 512
Immigration, 1139; in Hellenistic world, 126–127; to New World, 491; urbanization and, 788–789; of farm workers, 857; in Britain, 1120; citizenship and, 1140–1141. *See also* Migration
Imperator, Octavian as, 196–197
Imperial council (Germany), 523
Imperialism, 886–898, 892(box); of Egypt, 30; of Spain, 553–561; British, 568, 732–733; French, 683; renewal of, 886–898; racism and, 890; European migration and, 897–898; of Italy, 903; after First World War, 959; protests against, 963(illus.); East Asia and, 1000; neocolonialism and, 1092. *See also* Colonies and colonization; Decolonization; Empires; specific empires
Import Duties Act (Britain), 997
Impressionism, 870
Incas, 492, 494, 495(box), 498
Income, *see* Earnings
Indentured servants, 616–617
Independence and independence movements: among Jews, 145; Portugal and, 561; American colonies and, 700, 701–702; after French Revolution, 730; in Latin

Independence and independence movements *(cont.):* America, 758; in Ottoman Empire, 828–829; Arabs and, 943, 944(map), 945(illus.), 1066; in India, 960, 1058, 1063; after World War II, 1063; Israel and, 1064–1066; decolonization and, 1087–1093, 1088(map); Egypt and, 1089; North Africa and, 1090; Vietnam and, 1090; in sub-Saharan Africa, 1090–1092; for Soviet republics, 1129–1130. *See also* specific countries and regions
Independent Labour party, 881
Independent Socialist party (Germany), 937
Index of prohibited books, 536, 665
India, 4, 732; Zoroastrianism in, 63; Gama and, 483; Portuguese in, 486 and *illus.;* British-French conflict in, 687; England and, 888(illus.), 891–892, 894–895; Westernization in, 895(illus.); Gandhi and, 948; nationalism in, 960; Great Depression and, 1000; independence of, 1058, 1063
Indian Ocean region, 483, 732
Indians, *see* Amerindians
Indigenous peoples, 491–494, 616. *See also* Amerindians
Indigo, 683
Indika (Megasthenes), 134
Indochina, 887, 888, 889, 891, 1047, 1089–1090
Indo-European languages, 34, 155
Indonesia, 1092
Inductive reasoning, 634
Indulgences, 514
Indus River region, 134, 273
Industrialists, 850
Industrial Revolution, *see* Industry and industrialization
Industry and industrialization, 774(illus.), 775–805, 785(map), 808–809; trade and, 310–311; growth of, 689–690, 848–849; in England, 755; depression and, 763; steel, 846; transportation and, 847–849, 848(map); agricultural, 857; Crystal Palace exhibition and, 876–877; imperialism and, 889–890; after World War I, 964, 968; mass production and, 965; in Soviet Union, 980, 1002–1003; in Great Depression, 998; in East Germany, 1098; "third industrial revolution" and, 1115–1117, 1116(box). *See also* Marx, Karl; Marxism
Inertia theory, 632
Infant mortality, 778
Infantry, *see* Military; Soldiers
Infection, 867
Infidels, 273
Inflation, 211, 231, 499, 548, 568, 964
Influenza pandemic, 941
Information revolution, 5
Ingrès, Jean, 744
Inheritance, 301–302, 312
Innocent III (Pope), 357 and *illus.*, 358(box), 360, 366, 373, 377, 378
Innovation, 355, 371, 476–477, 690, 965–967. *See also* Inventions
Inquiry into the Nature and Causes of the Wealth of Nations, An (Smith), 663, 747, 748(box)

Inquisition, *see* Spanish Inquisition
Inquisitors, in Roman church, 360
Institute for Social Research (Frankfurt), 987
Institutes (Justinian), 251
Institutes of Oratory (Quintilian), 444
Institutes of the Christian Religion (Calvin), 519, 531
Insurrections, *see* Revolts
Intellectual thought, *see* Philosophy; specific topics
Intermarriage, 123–124
International law, 582
International Monetary Fund, 1124, 1139
International organizations, *see* specific organizations
International relations, 812–833; between world wars, 972; in 1930s, 995–996; Hitler and, 1007–1009, 1008(box); of Western Europe, 1086–1097, 1096(map); Helsinki Accords and, 1103–1104; after Soviet breakup, 1133–1136. *See also* specific treaties and wars
Internationals (socialist), 882, 918, 975–977 and *illus.*
International style, *see* Bauhaus; Design
International system, 33, 35(map), 36–37
Interregnum (England), 600–601
Intervention, in Russia, 942, 975, 976(map)
Inventions, 308–310, 476–477, 782–783. *See also* specific inventions
Investiture controversy, 323–326, 325(box)
Investment, 371–372
Ionia, 94, 100, 132
Iran, 7, 47. *See also* Persia and Persian Empire
Iraq, 44–48, 943, 949, 1133. *See also* Mesopotamia
Ireland, 247, 571, 899; Saint Patrick in, 284; Christianity from, 285; Vikings in, 297; Celts in, 335; England and, 336, 364, 732; Elizabeth I and, 568; Charles I and, 598; Cromwell and, 600–601; reform movement in, 700–701; Easter Rebellion in, 927; conflicts in, 1140
Irene (Byzantine Empire), 280, 281(box)
Ireton, Henry, 599(box)
Irnerius, 340
Iron Age, 44
Iron Curtain, 1062–1063, 1064(box)
Iron industry, 780–781
Iron law of wages, 747
Irrationality and uncertainty, 884–886
Isabella of Castile, 427, 429–430, 488
Isaiah (prophet), 45, 54
Ishtar Gate (Babylon), 49(illus.)
Isidore of Miletus, 251, 252
Isidore of Seville, 259, 281–282
Isis, 145, 220
Islam, 268–275; Dome of the Rock and, 53(illus.); Muhammad and, 269–271; expansion of, 270(map), 271–273; frontier against Byzantine Empire, 273; Umayyad rule in, 273; law in, 274; Abbassid rule in, 274–275; religious split in, 275; Spanish invasion by, 282; Mongols and, 479. *See also* Muhammad; Muslims
Islamic Empire, 273. *See also* Islam

Islands, *see* specific islands
Isocrates, 126
Isolationism, 23; in U.S., 949
Israel, 50–57, 54(map), 883; Ten Lost Tribes of, 46–47; kingdom of, 147; modern state of, 1064–1066, 1067(map), 1089
Israelites and Israelite culture, 51, 56, 57. *See also* Hebrews
Issus, Battle at, 122
Istanbul, 427. *See also* Constantinople
Isthmus of Panama, 490
Italian Alps, Iceman in, 9, 40–41 and *illus.*
Italian language, 818–819
Italian League, 412
Italy, 276, 297, 943; Greek colonization in, 82; geography of, 155; early period in, 156(map); Rome and, 167(map), 168–171; Ostrogoths in, 248; Germanic peoples in, 282; Lombards in, 282; Christian kingdom in, 282–283; in Middle Ages, 332–335; communal movement in, 334(map); Frederick I (Germany) and, 356; Lombard League in, 356; Henry VI (Germany) and, 356–357; German Empire and, 356–359; government and monarchy in, 367–368; population of cities in, 370; in Middle Ages, 410–412; French invasion of, 412; economy in, 418; Ciompi revolt in, 423; humanism in, 438–449; Renaissance arts in, 450–456; Renaissance courts in, 462; trade and, 478–479; Holy Roman Empire and, 522; Spanish rule and, 527, 553; Napoleon and, 723; Congress of Vienna and, 741; nationalism in, 746; restoration and reform and, 759; revolutions of 1848 and, 767–768; industrialization and, 787; unification of, 814–819, 817(map); imperialism of, 888–889; as democracy, 903–904; World War I and, 919; after World War I, 964, 980–981; fascism in, 982–985, 1013–1014; World War II and, 1035–1037; resistance in, 1044; Allied invasion of, 1051; postwar government in, 1086; politics and terrorism in, 1106; corruption scandal in, 1145
Ivan III (Russia, "the Great"), 414, 608
Ivan IV (Russia, " the Terrible"), 608–609
Ivanhoe (Scott), 744
Ivory Coast, 891

Jackson, Andrew, 831
Jacobins (France), 710, 713, 716, 720
Jacobite church, 255
Jacquerie movement, 423
Jamaica, slave revolt in, 756
James I (Aragon), 367
James I (England), 569, 575
James II (England), 602
James IV (Scotland), 410
James VI (Scotland), *see* James I (England)
James of Compostella, 332
Jamestown, 491, 616
Janissaries, 426–427, 761
Jan of Leiden, 520
Japan, 959; trade with, 477; view of British Parliament, 833(box); Great Depression

Japan (cont.), and, 1000; atomic bomb and, 1031, 1057–1058; World War II and, 1032, 1046–1048, 1050(map); "Pan-Asianism" of, 1049; Yalta conference and, 1053. See also Asia
Jaruzelski, Wojciech, 1125–1127
Jaurès, Jean, 881–882, 881(illus.)
Java, 730
Jazz, culture and, 1147
Jefferson, Thomas, 695, 748–749, 829
Jem (Ottoman), 427
Jenghiz Khan, 368, 478
Jeremiah (prophet), 54
Jericho, 7, 13
Jerome, 258
Jerusalem, 48, 52, 53(illus.), 55, 146, 147, 213–214, 271(illus.), 377; First Crusade and, 346
Jesù (church), 538, 539(illus.)
Jesuits, 536, 572, 648(box)
Jesus Christ, 213–216, 215(illus.); dating methods and, 4; language of, 60; divinity of, 234–235. See also Christianity
Jewish France (Drumont), 883
Jews and Judaism, 43, 44, 55–56; ancient Israel and, 50–57; return to Judea, 60; in Hellenistic world, 126, 142, 145–147, 146(box); Christianity and, 213; rabbinic, 213; Christ and, 214–216; Paul of Tarsus and, 217–219; women and, 219, 242; in Middle Ages, 300, 318–320; social position and, 312; in society, 318–320; expulsion from Spain, 332, 423, 429–430 and illus.; Crusades and, 379; plague and, 416; in Ottoman Empire, 427; Spanish Inquisition and, 430–431; humanism and, 447(box); in France, 722; Disraeli and, 834; in Germany, 850, 979; tolerance and, 869; Zionism and, 883, 943; anti-Semitism and, 883–884; Hitler and, 1008 and box, 1009, 1011–1012; in fascist Italy, 1014; Holocaust and, 1040–1043, 1042(illus.); after World War II, 1059–1060; modern Israel and, 1064–1066. See also Anti-Semitism; Hebrews; Holocaust; Nazis and Nazism
Jihad, 273
Joanna (prophet), 798
Joanna (Spain), 522
Joan of Arc, 407, 408(box)
Jobs, 414, 850–851. See also Labor; Wage system
Joffre, Joseph, 921
John (England), 362, 365–366
John, duke of Braganza, 561
John II (Castile), 429
John IV (Portugal), 561
John XXII (Pope), 397
John XXIII (antipope), 400
John XXIII (Pope), 1117
John Chrysostom, 259
John of Damascus, 280
John of Salisbury, 316
John Paul II (Pope), 1124, 1132
Johnson, Samuel, 775
John the Baptist, 214, 418(illus.)
John the Cappadocian, 251
Joinville, Jean (sire de), 364(box)

Jones, John Paul, 700, 702
Jordan, 7. See also Moab
Joseph Bonaparte, see Bonaparte family
Joseph II (Austria), 677
Joséphine de Beauharnais, 720
Josiah (Judean king), 53
Joule, James, 865
Juan Carlos (Spain), 1104
Judah, 48, 50, 52–53, 54(map), 55
Judea, 56, 103, 145, 199, 213–214
Judgment day, 147
Judgment of Corah, The (Botticelli), 468
Judicial review, in France, 703
Judiciary, 98, 163. See also Courts
Julia (Augustus' daughter), 193, 199, 201–202
Julian, 236, 237
Julian calendar, 184, 628
Julian of Norwich, 512
Julio-Claudians, 201–203, 202(illus.)
Julius II (Pope), 535
July Monarchy, 752–753, 764, 801
June uprising, in Paris, 765
Junkers, 759, 820
Jupiter (planet), 632
Jurisprudence (Gallican), 458
Jury duty, 96
Justice, 14, 93
Justinian, 251–254, 264, 275; Code of, 251
Jutland, Battle of, 921
Juvenal, 209

Kaaba, 269
Kádár, János, 1100, 1124
Kadesh, Battle at, 36
Kafka, Franz, 986
Kalahari Desert, 5
Kamikaze, 1057
al-Kamil, Malik, 353
Kandinsky, Wassily, 886
Kant, Immanuel, 664
Kapp Putsch, 970, 971
Kassite kingdom, 33
Kautsky, Karl, 881, 978(box)
Kay, John, 779
Kempe, Margery, 512
Kennedy, John F., 1102
Kent, Duke of, 842
Kenya, 1091
Kepler, Johannes, 630–631
Kerensky, Alexander, 934
Ketteler, Wilhelm von, 863
Keynes, John Maynard, 950
Khadija, 269
Khanates, 368
Khartoum, 889
Khepren (Egyptian king), 24
Khrushchev, Nikita, 1072(illus.), 1073, 1098–1101, 1100(box), 1102
Khufu (Cheops, Egypt), 24, 25(illus.)
Kiefer, Anselm, 1142(illus.), 1144
Kiev, 337, 338, 368
King of Kings (Persia), 60–63
Kings and kingdoms: in Hellenistic world, 125–134, 125(map); in Roman Empire, 199; Germanic, 245–250, 249(map); Christian, 280–287; Anglo-Saxon, 284; social

status of, 312; medieval government power and, 402–414. See also Empires; Monarchs and monarchies; Pharaoh; specific rulers and kingdoms
Kingsley, Mary, 891, 892(box)
King Solomon's mines, 487
King William's War (Nine Years' War), 596–597
Kinship, in Rome, 160
Kipling, Rudyard, 890
Kirov, Sergei, 1004
Kish, king of, 14
Klaus, Václav, 1131
Knights, 314, 316(illus.), 317, 344, 345, 346, 462, 464
Knossos, 65–66 and illus.
Knowledge, see Humanists and humanism; Wisdom
Knox, Robert, 883
Koch, Robert, 866
Koestler, Arthur, 1077
Kohl, Helmut, 1133
Kolchak, Alexander, 976(map)
Kopelev, Lev, 1003(box)
Kosciuszko, Tadeusz, 701, 729
Kristallnacht (Crystal Night), 1011
Kronstadt naval base, 978
Krupp, Alfred, 877
Kublai Khan, 479
Kun, Béla, 942
Kuomintang, see Guomindang
Kursk-Orel, Battle at, 1044
Kush, 47
Kuwait, 1133
Kwasniewski, Alexander, 1131

Labé, Louise, 578
Labor, 419–420; specialization in, 7, 8; by months, 300(illus.); social position and, 312; corvées and, 317–318; women and, 420; economy and, 421–422; for sugar industry, 482; for Spanish colonies, 498–499; indentured servants as, 616–617; Africans as slaves, 619; changes in, 689–690; socialism and, 749–751; Chartism and, 757; revolutions of 1848 and, 762; industrialization and, 778; solidarity of, 797–798; collective action and, 799–802; Marx and, 802–805; during World War I, 926; mass society and, 965–967; women and, 1011, 1082; decline of organized, 1117. See also Cotton and cotton industry; Serfs and serfdom; Slaves and slavery; Strikes (labor); Wage system; Workers; specific countries
Labor unions, 800, 802, 1117, 1120; Solidarity and, 1124–1127, 1125(illus.). See also Labor; Workers
Labour party (Britain), 968, 1080–1081
Lafayette, Madame de, 593
Lafayette, Marquis de (Marie-Joseph), 702, 704, 728
Lagash, 14
Laissez faire, 747, 796–797. See also Free trade
Lamartine, Alphonse de, 764
Lancastrian kings (England), 409

Land(s): in Athens, 90; Rome, 180–181 and *box*; in Rome, 198–199; increased cultivation of, 308; conversion to grazing, 422; industrialization and, 795–796. *See also* Agriculture

Land bridge (Bering Strait), 491

Landscape gardens, 694–695 and *illus.*, 694(illus.)

Lanfranc, 330, 340

Lang, Fritz, 967(illus.)

Langland, William, 440

Language(s): Akkadian, 14, 15; Sumerian, 14; Semitic, 16, 34; Indo-European, 34; Hebrew, 51; of Persians, 59; Aramaic, 60; words derived from Greek, 82; Greek vs. Aramaic, 126; in Seleucid kingdom, 132; Indo-European, 155; Latin, 155; of Roman Empire, 208; Christianity and, 213; of Germanic tribes, 243–244; vernacular, 308; Latin culture and, 339–341; literature in Latin and vernacular, 384–386; in Scandinavia, 413; classical, 458; Nahuatl, 492. *See also* Writing; specific languages

Langue d'Oc, 363

La Nouvelle Héloïse (Rousseau), 670

Laodike III (Seleucid queen), 141(box)

La Pasionaria, *see* Pasionaria, La

La Rochelle, 564–565

Las Casas, Bartolomé de, 500 and *illus.*

Lascaux caves, 6

Las Navas de Tolosa, Battle at, 366–367

Lassalle, Ferdinand, 881

Last Judgment (Zoroastrianism), 63

Last Judgment, The (Michelangelo), 453

Late Antiquity, *see* Roman Empire

Late Middle Ages, *see* Middle Ages

Late Neolithic Age, *see* Copper Age

Lateran Councils, 360, 535

Latifundia (estates), 176

Latin America, 758, 1000. *See also* Americas; Central America; Mexico; South America

Latin church (West), 255. *See also* Catholicism and Catholic church

Latin language, 155, 208, 339–341, 384–385. *See also* Bible; Vernacular

Latin League, 169–170

Latin peoples, 158, 169

Latium, 155, 157(map)

Latvia, 1033. *See also* Livonia

Laud, William, 569, 570

Laval, Pierre, 1043

Law(s): Hammurabi and, 16–17 and *box*; in Egypt, 24; Ten Commandments and, 52; Israelite, 57; Persian, 60; in Sparta, 86; Twelve Tables, 161, 166; Roman, 183, 187, 199, 253(box); legal science and, 187; *Constitutio Antoniana*, 208; in Germanic kingdoms, 250; codes of, 251, 677, 680, 722, 725, 728; Islamic, 274; in Byzantine Empire, 277; canon, 295; in Middle Ages, 340; common, 366; Magna Carta and, 366; in Spain, 367; Golden Bull and, 413; Gallican jurisprudence and, 458; Grotius and, 582; court depositions and, 586; in Russia, 680. *See also* Courts

Law courts, in France, 672

Law of Suspects, 719

Law of the Maximum (France), 715, 718

Lawrence, T. E., 942, 943

Laws (Plato), 109

Laws (scientific), 631–632, 639–640

Laws of Ecclesiastical Polity (Hooker), 531

Lays (literary forms), 385

Lead poisoning, 792

League of German Cities, *see* Hanseatic League

League of Nations, 948, 949–950, 972, 1014, 1061

League of Schmalkalden, 527

Learning, *see* Culture; Education; Pergamum; Scholars and scholarship

Lebanon, 943

Lebensraum (living space), 1008

Le Corbusier (Charles-Édouard Jeanneret), 988

Ledru-Rollin, Alexandre, 764

Lefèvre d'Étaples, Jacques, 458, 532

Left (political), 969–970, 1014–1015. *See also* Communism; Germany; Russia; Socialism; Soviet Union

Legal science, 187. *See also* Law(s)

Legates, 324

Léger, Fernand, 988, 989(illus.)

Legionnaires, 168–169 and *illus.*

Legions, Roman, 169

Legislation, 855, 863

Legislative Assembly (France), 712–713, 714

Legislature, 97, 163, 164–165, 719, 768–770. *See also* specific legislative bodies

Legnano, Battle at, 356, 368

Leisure, 798, 799(illus.), 852, 855 and *illus.*, 965. *See also* Entertainment

Lend-lease Act, 1048

Lenin, Vladimir, 907–908, 907(box), 932, 933(illus.), 936(box), 977, 978–979

Leningrad, 1004; Battle at, 1039, 1046. *See also* Petrograd; St. Petersburg

Leninism, 1005. *See also* Lenin, Vladimir; Marxism-Leninism

Leo I (Pope), 239, 244

Leo III (Byzantine Empire), 276–277, 279, 280

Leo III (Pope), 267, 291

Leo IX (Pope), 345

Leo X (Pope), 509, 514

Leoba (Britain), 286(box)

Leonardo da Vinci, 452–453, 452(illus.), 461

León-Castile, 332

Leonidas (Spartan king), 101

Leopold I (Austria), 603, 604 and *illus.*

Leopold I (Holy Roman Emperor), 597

Leopold II (Belgium), 887, 889, 891

Leopold of Austria, 413

Leovigild (Visigoth king), 281

Lepanto, Battle of, 560

LePen, Jean-Marie, 1141, 1145

Lérins, monasticism in, 256

Lesbia, *see* Clodia (Rome)

Less developed countries (South), 1114

Letter of Paul to the Ephesians, The, 218(box)

Letter on Toleration (Locke), 652

Letters, *see* Culture; Scholars and scholarship

Letters of Illustrious Men, The (Reuchlin), 459

Letters of Obscure Men, The (satire), 459

Letter to the Grand Duchess Christina (Galileo), 633

Lettres philosophiques (Philosophical Letters) (Voltaire), 661, 662(box)

Leuctra, Battle of, 103–104

Levant, 22(map), 51

Levelers, 598, 599(box), 600, 638

Leviathan (Hobbes), 649

Lévi-Strauss, Claude, 1092–1093

Libation Bearers (Aeschylus), 112

Liberal arts, *see* Education

Liberal capitalism, *see* Capitalism

Liberal party (Britain), 899–900

Liberals and liberalism, 700, 730, 747–749, 757, 764, 796–797, 820, 880

Liberators, 185, 187, 195

Liberty, 700, 735 and *illus.*

Liberty Leading the People (Delacroix), 745

Library, 135, 444–446, 446, 863–864, 876

Libya, 47, 903, 906

Lichtenstein, Roy, 1110

Lidice, 1044

Liebknecht, Karl, 940, 970

Lieferinxe, Josse, 434–435 and *illus.*

Liege homage, 405

Life expectancy, 792, 819

Life of Anthony, 256

Life of Charlemagne (Einhard), 289(box)

Lifespan, 308

Lifestyle: religious, 241–243, 258–259, 538–540; of women, 302; after French Revolution, 744–745; of workers, 791–793; middle-class, 851–854; in countryside, 857. *See also* Rural society; Urban society; specific countries

Lighting, 862

Lightning war, *see* Blitzkrieg

Lima, 498

Lincoln, Abraham, 830, 832

Lindbergh, Charles, 967

Lineages, 312

Linear A, 64–65

Linear B, 68

Linguistic studies, 458

Lister, John, 867

Literacy, 667–668; Hellenistic, 135; literature and, 578–580; impact of, 586–587. *See also* Printing; specific countries

Literature, 578–580; *Epic of Gilgamesh*, 19, 20(box); Egyptian, 31; Hittite, 35–36; *Iliad, Odyssey*, and, 43; Hebrew Bible, and, 43–44, 50; in Greece, 91–92, 93; in Alexandria, 136–137; Hellenistic, 139; Latin, 177–178; in Roman Empire, 209–210; medieval, 300; in Latin and/ or vernacular, 308, 342–343, 384–386, 439–440; monks and writers of, 340; in Middle Ages, 355; courtly, 385; popular, 386; humanism and, 438; national, 580; in France, 593; public opinion and, 667–668; cult of sensibility in, 670–671; realism in, 871–874; about World War I, 951; between world wars, 985–987; surrealism in, 987; women and, 987, 988(box). *See also* Poets and poetry; Romanticism; Vernacular; Wisdom literature; specific writers

Lithuania, 413–414, 607, 1033, 1129. *See also* Poland-Lithuania
Little Man, What Now? (Fallada), 998
Liverpool, 788, 789, 790
Lives of Illustrious Men, The (Petrarch), 441
Livia, 193, 201–202
Living conditions, 854–856, 1102. *See also* Lifestyle
Livius Andronicus, 178
Livonia (Latvia), 607, 611
Livy, 158, 179(box), 190, 200, 201, 441
Lloyd George, David, 900, 928, 943
Locarno Agreement, 972
Locke, John, 649–651, 650(box)
Locomotives, 784
Logic, 340, 380, 438
Logos, 95, 142
Lombard, Peter, 380
Lombard League, 356
Lombards, 282
London, 439, 788, 789, 790(box), 858, 876–877 and *illus.*
London, Treaty of, 919, 935
Longitude, on maps, 480
Long Parliament, 571, 598, 601
L'opinion des femmes, 766(box)
Lord Protector, 601
Lordship, defined, 313
Lord's Supper, 219
Lorenzetti, Ambrogio, 455
Lorraine, 320, 945. *See also* Alsace and Lorraine
Lothair, 291, 296
Louis VI (France), 329
Louis VII (France), 329, 361, 377
Louis VIII (France), 363
Louis IX (Saint Louis, France), 363, 364(box), 387
Louis XI (France), 408–409
Louis XIII (France), 564, 565, 576
Louis XIV (France), 588(illus.), 591–597, 593(box), 596(map), 671, 672, 703; science and, 646 and *illus.*
Louis XV (France), 672, 703
Louis XVI (France), 672, 702–704, 707, 708–710, 711, 713–714, 713(illus.), 715, 727. *See also* French Revolution
Louis XVIII (France), 727, 729, 739, 741, 751, 752(illus.)
Louisiana Purchase, 829
Louis Napoleon, *see* Napoleon III (France)
Louis of Aquitaine, 291
Louis Philippe (France), 752–753, 764, 800, 836
Louis the German, 296, 320
Lourdes, 869
Louvain, 458, 920(illus.)
Louvre, 669, 864
Love, *see* Poets and poetry; Romantic love
Low Countries, 527. *See also* Netherlands
Loyalists, in Spain, 1017–1018
Loyola, Ignatius, 536, 537(box)
Lucan, 209
Lucian, 209
Lucilius, 177
Lucretia, rape of, 158, 159(box)
Lucretius, 187

Ludd, Ned (character) and Luddites, 799
Ludendorff, Erich, 923, 925(illus.), 926, 938, 1006
Ludwig I (Bavaria), 768
Ludwig II (Bavaria), 759
Lueger, Karl, 883
Lukács, Georg, 987
Lumber industry, 311
Lusitania (ship), 926
Luther, Martin, 510, 512–515 and *box*, 521–522, 532. *See also* Christianity; Reformation
Lutherans and Lutheranism, 526(map). *See also* Luther, Martin
Lützen, Battle of, 576
Luxemburg, house of, 413
Luxemburg, Rosa, 940, 970
Luxury goods, 176, 190–191 and *illus.*, 298
Lycurgus, 86
Lydia (kingdom), 85
Lyell, Charles, 864
Lyon, 199
Lyric poetry, 91–92. *See also* Poets and poetry
Lysander, 103, 106
Lysistrata (Aristophanes), 113

Maastrict agreement, 1136–1137
MacAlpin, Kenneth, 335
Macao, 485
Macbeth (Shakespeare), 580
Maccabees, First Book of, 146
MacDonald, Ramsay, 968
Macedon and Macedonians, 280, 344–345, 906; Philip II and, 119, 120–121; expansion and, 119–120; after Alexander, 124, 128–129; Rome and, 174(map), 175. *See also* Alexander the Great
Machiavelli, Niccolò, 448–449 and *illus.*
Machines and machinery, 139, 781, 856(illus.), 857. *See also* Industry and industrialization; Mechanization
Macinghi-Strozzi, Alessandra, 444
McLuhan, Marshall, 1116(box)
Madame Bovary (Flaubert), 871
Madeira Islands, 482
Mad hatters, 792
Magdeburg, Battle at, 577
Magellan, Ferdinand, 484(map), 490–491
Magenta, Battle at, 815, 817(map)
Magi, 64, 411(illus.)
Magic, 26, 33, 552
Maginot Line, 962, 1033
Magistrates (Rome), 163–164
Magna Carta, 366
Magna Graecia, 82, 155
Magnetism, 865
Magyars, 297–298, 320, 337–338, 533, 767, 824–825
Mahmud II (Ottoman Empire), 761
Maid, the, *see* Joan of Arc
Maiestas Domini, 295(illus.)
Maistre, Joseph de, 742–743
Maize, 502
Malaya, 1048
Malay Peninsula, 485
Males, *see* Men
Male suffrage, in France, 719
Mali, 477

Malintzin (Doña Marina), 496
Malta, 9–10 and *illus.*
Malthus, Thomas, 747
Mamluk Turks, 427
Manchester, 788, 790
Manchuria, Japan and, 1000, 1046
Mandates (League of Nations), 949
Mandeville, John, 478
Mandrake Root, The (Machiavelli), 448, 449
Manet, Edouard, 837(illus.)
Manetho, 131
Manfred (German Empire), 356
Manhattan Project, 1058
Mani (Persia), 373
Manichaeism, 221
Manifest Destiny, 829
Manners, 622–623 and *illus.*
Manors, 299, 301, 317
Mansa Musa, 477
Mantegna, Andrea, 463
Mantua, 410. *See also* Gonzaga family
Manufacturing, 786–787, 1116–1117
Manuscript book, 304–305 and *illus.*, 304(illus.), 305
Manutius, Aldus, 456
Manzikert, Battle at, 345
Mao Zedong (Mao Tse-tung), 1000, 1066
Map, Walter, 361
Maps, 480, 488(illus.)
Maranos, 430
Marat, Jean Paul, 716
Marathon, 99; Battle at, 100
Marcel, Étienne, 423
Marcellinus, Ammianus, 246(box)
March Revolution (Russia), 931–933
Marcus Aurelius, 204, 210
Marcuse, Herbert, 1077
Margaret of Angoulême, 532
Margaret of Denmark, 413
Margaret of Parma, 556, 557, 581
Margaret Tudor, 410
Marguerite of Porete, 440
Mari, conquest of, 33
Maria Theresa (Austria), 677, 682
Maria Theresa (Spain), 591
Marie Antoinette (France), 702, 703(illus.), 717
Marie de France, 385
Marie de l'Incarnation (Marie Guyart), 619(illus.)
Marie de' Medici, *see* Medici family
Marie Louise (Austria), 726
Marie of Champagne, 385
Marina, Doña, *see* Malintzin
Maritain, Jacques, 1077
Marius, Gaius, 182
Market economy, 747, 748(box), 797, 1120, 1131
Markets, 549, 887
Marne, Second Battle of, 940
Marozia, 323
Marriage, 178–180, 241–242, 301–302, 420, 793, 854, 1011
"Marseillaise," 699
Marseille, 791
Marshall Plan, 1079
Marston Moor, Battle at, 598

Martel, Charles, 288
Martianus Capella, 478
Martin, Pierre, 846
Martin V (Pope), 401 and *illus.*
Martinique, 730
Martin of Tours, 256
Martyrdom, Jews and, 147
Marx, Karl, 751, 765, 802–805, 803(illus.)
Marxism, 802–804, 881, 978(box), 987, 996;
  Russia and, 907–908, 932, 934; fascism
  and, 974; intellectual thought and,
  1076–1077. *See also* Communism; Russia;
  Soviet Union
Marxism-Leninism, 1000, 1005
Mary, *see* Virgin Mary
Mary (Queen of Scots), 559, 568
Mary II (England), 602–603, 615, 672
Mary Magdalene (basilica), 306(illus.), 307
Mary of Oignies, 376
Mary Tudor (Mary I, England), 528, 530,
  559, 565
Masaccio, 451, 452
Masons, 760
Massachusetts, 617
Massachusetts Bay Company, 617
Massacre of the Champ de Mars, 711
Massacres, *see* Saint Bartholomew's Day
  Massacre
Mass culture, 885, 1110–1111
Mass killings, *see* Extermination camps;
  Holocaust
Mass media, *see* Media
Mass production, 965; consumerism and,
  965–967
Mass society, 963–969, 966(box), 985–988,
  989(illus.)
Masters of the Soldiers (German), 250
Materialism, 845, 872–874, 873(box), 890.
  See also Age of Optimism; Realism; Wealth
Mathematical Principles of Natural Philosophy
  (Newton), 640
Mathematics, 19–20, 31, 48, 95, 138. *See also*
  Astronomy; Science
Matignon Agreement, 1019
Matilda (England), 332
Matilda of Tuscany, 324(illus.)
Matriarchy, 7
Matteotti, Giocomo, 984
Matter, 633–634, 639–640
Matthias (Holy Roman emperor), 575
Maupeou, Nicolas de, 672
Maximilian II (Holy Roman emperor), 572
Maxwell, James Clark, 865
Maya, 496
Mazarin, Jules, 590
Mazowiecki, Tadeusz, 1127
Mazzini, Giuseppe, 746, 747, 767, 814
Mecca, 269, 477
Mechanics, 632–633, 636–637
Mechanistic world order, 649–652
Mechanization, 690. *See also* Industry and
  industrialization
Mechtild of Magdeburg, 386
Medea (Euripides), 112
Medes, 47, 59
Media, 963. *See also* Film
Medici family, 412, 418, 420; Lorenzo de',

411, 470–471; Piero, 411, 412; Cosimo de',
  411 and *illus.*, 418, 632; Giovanni de',
  418; Catherine de', 562; Marie de', 564
Medicine, 628, 866–867; Mesopotamian, 21;
  in Egypt, 31–33; Hippocratic, 107; Hellenistic, 138–139; study of, 380; bubonic
  plague and, 416; women and, 550(box);
  Galen and, 640–641; Harvey and, 641–642;
  professionalization of, 851; psychoanalysis and, 884. *See also* Health
Medieval period, *see* Middle Ages
Medina, 269
Meditations (Descartes), 636
Meditations (Marcus Aurelius), 204
Mediterranean region, 34, 35(map), 334,
  732; Sea Peoples of, 37; Phoenicians and,
  48–49, 83(map); Greeks and, 82, 83(map);
  Macedon and, 120–124; eastern,
  130(map); Rome and, 175; Christianity
  in, 262; trade and, 298, 477; Spain and,
  560; industrialization and, 787; Barcelona
  conference and, 1141
Medusa (ship), 772–773 and *illus.*
Megasthenes, 134
Megiddo, Battle of, 29, 36
Mehmed II (the Conqueror, Ottomans), 424,
  426, 427
Mein Kampf (Hitler), 1006, 1008(box)
Melanchthon, Philip, 525–527
Melania the Younger, 242, 256, 257(box)
Memoirs of World War I, 951
Memphis (Egypt), 23
Men: in ancient groups, 5; Jewish, 56; in Is-
  raelite culture, 57; in Sparta, 86; in Athens,
  99; in Hellenistic art and society, 139–142;
  in Roman society, 162–163; in urban soci-
  ety, 319
Menander (dramatist), 136–137, 178
Menander Soter Dikaios, 134
Mendeleev, Dmitri, 865
Mendicants, 373–375, 499–500
Menes (Egyptian king), 23
Mennonites, 521
Mensheviks, 907, 932. *See also* Kerensky,
  Alexander
Mercantilism, 591
Mercenaries, 407–408
Merchant marine, 691
Merchants, 300, 370–371, 418, 419, 420,
  478–479. *See also* Commerce; Trade
Mercia, 284
Merian, Maria Sibylla, 641(illus.), 643
Mérimée, Prosper, 746
Merikare (Egyptian king), 29
Merneptah (Egyptian king), 51
Merovingian kingdom, 247, 287–288
Mesopotamia, 4, 9, 10, 11, 12–21, 12(illus.),
  943; Sumer and, 12–14; Akkadians and,
  14, 15–16; religion in, 17–19, 18(illus.);
  arts and sciences in, 19–21, 20(box); Hur-
  rians in, 33; Parthians in, 133; as Roman
  province, 204; trade and, 298. *See also*
  Babylonia
Messalla, 201
Messenians, 86
Messiah, 147, 201, 213–214
Mesta brotherhood, 427–428

Metals and metalworking, 7, 44. *See also*
  Gold; Mining; Silver
Metaphysics, 628, 643. *See also* Astronomy;
  Science
Methodism, 743, 798
Methodius, 297
Metics (resident aliens), in Athens, 99
Metric system, 718
Metropolis (movie), 967 and *illus.*
Metternich, Clemens von, 741, 742(illus.),
  758, 759, 766
Mexico, 493(map); Aztecs in, 492–494; Cortés
  in, 494–498; diseases in, 499; shrine of
  Virgin of Guadalupe in, 506–507; United
  States and, 829
Michael (Russia), 609
Michelangelo Buonarroti, 451, 452, 453
Middle Ages: early civilizations in, 267–268;
  trade and commerce in, 298–299; society
  in, 299–302; agriculture and business
  in, 308–311; social order and classes in,
  311–320; Celtic lands in, 335–337; Slavic
  world in, 337–339; culture in, 339–344;
  First Crusade in, 344–346; castles in,
  350–351, 350(illus.), 351(illus.); society
  in, 353–355, 395–396; Europe during,
  354(map); German Empire and papacy
  in, 355–360; governments in, 360–369,
  402–414; guilds in, 370–371; economic
  life in, 370–372; culture in, 379–386;
  Gothic architecture in, 381–384, 383(illus.),
  390–391 and *illus.*; Western Christian
  church in, 396–402; economy and society
  in, 414–423; church in later period, 511–512;
  romantic movement and, 744. *See also*
  Architecture; Clergy; Nobility; Peasants;
  Women; specific countries
Middle classes, 850–854, 907. *See also*
  Classes (economic and social)
Middle East: before Muhammad, 268–269;
  during and after World War I, 920(map),
  942–943, 944(box), 946(map); World
  War II and, 1035–1037; Palestine and,
  1064–1066; oil crisis and, 1105; Persian
  Gulf War and, 1133; Western views of,
  1148(box). *See also* Arab-Israeli conflicts;
  Crusades; First Crusade; Western Asia
Middle Kingdom: in Egypt, 23, 28, 31,
  32(box); Hittite, 34; Carolingian, 296
Midway, Battle of, 1049
Migration, 589–590; by early humans, 5–6,
  491; Germanic, 243–244; by nationality,
  897; European, 897–898 and *map*; of
  refugees after World War II, 1060; intellectual, 1077–1079. *See also* Immigration
Milan, 410, 412, 442, 462, 553, 560
Miletus, 94, 100
Militarism, of Rome, 168–169
Military, 551; of Sargon, 15; Assyrian, 45–46
  and *box*; hoplite phalanx and, 83–85,
  84(illus.); in Sparta, 86, 87; in classical
  Athens, 96; Delian League and, 101; of
  Macedon, 120, 121–122; Roman, 168–169,
  170(box), 180, 182, 199, 208, 211, 231, 233,
  236, 249; Byzantine, 276–277; nobility
  and, 314; medieval castles and, 350–351,
  350(illus.), 351(illus.); French, 408, 595,

Military (cont.), 718; Janissaries and, 426–427; Netherlands revolt and, 557–558; changes in, 595; in England, 598; in Russia, 609, 838, 840; conscription and, 681; of Napoleon, 725; at beginning of World War I, 919; in Germany, 970, 1011. See also Conscription; Napoleon I; Navy
Military draft, see Conscription
Military orders, 317, 427
Militia, see National Guard
Mill, John Stuart, 749, 797, 834
Millet, Jean-François, 870
Milo, Cicero and, 186(box)
Milosevic, Slobodan, 1135
Miltiades (Greek general), 100
Milvian Bridge, Battle at, 234
Mining, 310, 996. See also Gold; Silver
Minoan civilization, 64–66, 65(map)
Minorities, 427, 827. See also Ethnicity and ethnic minorities; specific groups
Minos (Minoan king), 65
Miracle stories, 243
Mirror for Simple Souls, The (Marguerite of Porete), 440
Mishnah, 219
Missiles, nuclear, 1102
Missions and missionaries, 499–500, 502, 890
Mississippi River region, 618 and map
Mitanni, kingdom of, 29, 34
Mithraism, 220–221, 220(illus.)
Mithridates, 183
Mitterrand, François, 1107, 1145
Moab (Jordan), 58
Mobilization of enthusiasm, 929–931
Moctezuma II (Aztecs), 493, 496–497
Modernism, 958, 965–967, 987–988, 989(illus.), 992–993 and illus., 992(illus.), 1144
Mogul Empire, 687
Moguls, 483
Mohács, Battle of, 573(map)
Moldavia, 762, 828
Molière (Jean-Baptiste Poquelin), 593–594
Molotov, Vyacheslav, 1065(box)
Moltke, Helmuth von, 918
Molucca Islands, 490. See also Spice Islands
Monarchs and monarchies: spread of, 339; contract with people, 581; resistance to, 582; enlightened despotism and, 675–677; workers and, 800–801. See also Constitutional monarchy; French Revolution; Government; Kings and kingdoms; Queens; Revolutionary period; specific dynasties, empires, and rulers
Monasteries and monasticism, 255–257, 314, 315; cenobitic, 256; eremitic, 256, 315; women and, 256, 257(box); in Britain, 285; of Hilda and Leoba, 286(box); Carolingian, 292–293; convents and, 301; monks and writers, 340. See also Clergy; specific orders
Monet, Claude, 870
Money, 86. See also Coins
Mongols and Mongol Empire, 355, 368, 369(box), 478, 479–480, 479(box); and Russia, 368–369, 414, 608–609
Monks and monasteries, 256–257. See also Monasteries and monasticism

Monnet, Jean, 1079, 1094, 1095(box)
Monophysitism, 239, 252
Monopolies, 569, 570(illus.), 797
Monotheism, 27, 43–44, 51–54, 57, 63–64
Montaigne, Michel de, 578–580, 579(box), 637
Monte Cassino, 256–257
Montenegro, 828, 829
Montesinos, Antonio, 499
Montesquieu, baron of (Charles de Secondat), 663
Monteverdi, Claudio, 464, 581
Monticello, 695
Montmorency family, 531
Montpellier, university in, 380
Morality, 652, 842–843, 852
Moral living, see Christianity; Lifestyle; Morality
Moravia, 297, 298
Moravian Societies, 521
More, Hannah, 742
More, Thomas, 458, 459, 528, 749
Moreau, Gustave, 886
Moriscos, 430
Morisot, Berthe, 870
Moro, Aldo, 1106
Morocco, 889, 909–910, 1090
Morrill Land Grant College Act (1862), 831
Mortality: bubonic plague and, 426. See also Death
Mosaics, in Ravenna, 264–265 and illus.
Moscow, 368, 369, 414, 610, 975; Napoleon and, 726. See also Russia
Moses, 50, 51–52, 55(box)
Moslems, see Muslims
Mosques, 270, 299
Motion, 636, 639–640
Mound-builder societies, 492
Mountains, see specific ranges
Movies, see Film
Mozambique, 1091
Mozart, Wolfgang Amadeus, 671
Mu'awiya, 273
Muhammad, 268, 269–271, 271–272. See also Islam; Muslims
Mühlberg, Battle of, 527
Mule (machine), 779
Müller, Hermann, 973
Multinational corporations, 1139
Mummy (Tutankhamon), 27(illus.), 28
Munch, Edvard, 886 and illus.
Munich conference, 1022–1023
Municipal Corporation Act (Britain), 755
Municipia, in Rome, 170–171
Münster, Anabaptists in, 520–521
Müntzer, Thomas, 520
Muscovites, see Moscow
Museums, 135, 864, 914–915 and illus.
Music, 538, 581, 671, 743, 986
Muslims: people of the Book and, 50; Islam and, 268–275; Shi'ite and Sunni, 275; Byzantine Empire and, 276; in Spain, 282, 322, 332, 367; trade and, 298; cities of, 299; Rome and, 322–323; removed from central Mediterranean, 334; Crusades and, 345, 377–379; poetry of, 385; Ottoman Turks and, 423–427; in Iberia,

429, 560; trade and, 477, 479–481, 482; in France, 1112(illus.), 1113, 1141. See also Islam; Moguls; Mongols and Mongol Empire; Ottoman Empire; Turks
Muslim Turkish Empire, 396
Mussato, Albertino, 441
Musset, Alfred de, 746
Mussolini, Benito, 982–984, 983(illus.), 1013–1014. See also Italy
Mycenaean civilization, 67–69
Mystery plays, 386
Mystery religions, 144–145, 220–221
Mysticism, 377, 535–536, 540
Mythology, 26–28, 69–71. See also Gods and goddesses; Religion

Naevius, Gnaeus, 178
Nagasaki, 1031, 1058
Nagy, Imre, 1099, 1124
Nahuatl language, 492, 498
Naipual, V. S., 1151
Names (personal), in Roman Empire, 208
Nancy, Battle of, 413
Naples, 282, 412, 553, 560, 723, 816
Napoleon I (Napoleon Bonaparte, France), 720–728, 721(illus.), 724(map), 727(illus.)
Napoleon III (France), 766, 768, 812, 815, 835–836, 890–891
Napoleonic Code, 722, 725, 728
Napoleonic wars, 723–727
Naram-sin, 15 and illus.
Narváez, Ramón, 758
Naseby, Battle at, 598
Nasser, Gamel Abdul, 1089, 1092
Nation, concept of, 746
National Assembly (France), 705, 707–708, 710, 711, 729, 765
National Assembly (Germany), 768
National Banking Act (U.S.), 831
National Convention (France), 715, 719
National Guard (France), 708, 709, 751, 764
National Health Service, 1081
Nationalism, 739, 746–747, 963(illus.); Germany and, 759, 768–770, 819–824; in Russia, 760; in Balkan region, 761–762; in Austrian Empire, 767; Italy and, 767–768, 814–819; in Austria-Hungary, 827, 905; in Ottoman Empire, 828–829, 828(illus.); new imperialism and, 887–889; in Germany, 905; in China, 960, 961(box); in non-Western world, 960; pan-Arab, 1089, 1090. See also Nationalists
Nationalists: in Spain, 995, 996, 1017–1018; in China, 1066–1067. See also Nationalism
Nationalities, see Ethnicity and ethnic minorities; Self-determination; specific nationalities
Nationality Act (Britain), 1120
National literatures, 580
National Socialist German Workers' party (NSDAP, Nazis), 973
National Society (Italy), 815
Native Americans, see Amerindians
NATO, see North Atlantic Treaty Organization (NATO)
Naturalism, of Giotto, 450(illus.)
Natural law, 187

Natural resources, 5, 783
Natural selection, 797, 865
Natural truths, 381
Nature, 106, 139, 634–635 and *illus.*, 671, 694–695 and *illus.*, 694(illus.), 743
Navarino Bay, Battle at, 762
Navarre, 332, 564
Navigation, 371, 476–477, 481(map), 483, 487
Navy: Athenian, 96; Persian, 101; in Punic Wars, 172; of Aragon-Catalonia, 367; Portuguese, 486; Spanish Armada as, 559–560; Battle of Lepanto and, 560; in France, 591; in Russia, 611; Dutch, 615; French, 702; British, 730–732, 910, 919, 925–926; German, 910, 919, 925–926
Nazarenes, 216–217
Nazis and Nazism (Germany), 969, 973–974, 996, 1005–1013, 1011–1012, 1043–1044, 1140; Italy and, 1013–1014; expansion of, 1024(map); films and, 1028–1029 and *illus.*, 1028(illus.); World War II victories of, 1032–1037; "New Order" in Europe, 1037–1046, 1038(map), 1041(box). *See also* Germany
Nazi-Soviet Pact, 1023–1024
Neandertals, 5
Near East, *see* Western Asia
Nebuchadrezzar II (Nebuchadnezzar), 47–48, 49(illus.)
Nefertiti (Egyptian queen), 30
Nehemiah, 56
Nehru, Jawaharlal, 1092
Nelson, Horatio, 724, 730–731, 732(illus.)
Neo-Babylonians, 47–48, 55; Jews and, 55–56
Neocolonialism, 1092
Neoexpressionism, 1144
Neo-Hittite era, 34
Neolithic era, in Egypt, 22
Neolithic Revolution, 7–9, 9–10. *See also* Copper Age
Neo-Platonism, 628
Neoromanticism, 884, 885–886
Neri, Filippo, 535
Nero (Rome), 202, 203, 209
Nerva (Rome), 204
Nervo-Trajanic dynasty, 203
Netherlands, 556(map), 595–597, 603, 613(illus.); Spain and, 553; revolt of, 553–559; France and, 562, 723, 724; Elizabeth I and, 568; Louis XIV and, 595; trade and, 611, 613, 616; commerce of, 612(map); Golden Age of, 613–615; North American colonies of, 619; science and, 638; political crisis in, 701; Dutch East Indies and, 1089. *See also* Low countries; Thirty Years' War; William of Orange
Networks, *see* Trade
Neutrality pact, Soviet-Japanese, 1046–1047
New Amsterdam, 619
New Atlantis (Bacon), 634
Newcomen, Thomas, 781 and *illus.*
New Deal, 998
New Economic Policy (NEP), 978–979
New Experiments Physico-Mechanical (Boyle), 638
Newfoundland, 491, 616
New France, 618

New Harmony, Indiana, 750
New imperialism, *see* Imperialism
New Kingdom (Egypt), 23, 28–30, 31. *See also* Egypt
New Kingdom (Hittite), 34
New Lanark, Scotland, 750
New Laws, 500
"New man," in Rome, 185
New Model Army, 598
"New Order," of Nazis, 1037–1046, 1038(map), 1041(box)
New Plymouth, 617
New right, 882
"New Rome," Constantinople as, 250
New Spain, 491
New Testament, 213, 238, 446, 460, 515
Newton, Isaac, 636, 639–640, 639(illus.), 660
"New woman" concept, 999(box)
New World, *see* Americas; Colonies and colonization; North America; Old World; specific countries
New York: as art capital, 1077
New Zealand, immigration to, 897
Nicaea, *see* Council of Nicaea
Niccoli, Niccolò, 444–445
Nice, 815
Nicene Creed, 235, 262
Nicetas (bishop), 373
Nicholas I (Russia), 760–761 and *illus.*, 814
Nicholas II (Russia), 906, 908–909, 931
Nicholas V (Pope), 446, 466
Nietzsche, Friedrich, 884
Niger Delta, 482
Nigeria, 960
Nightingale, Florence, 813 and *box*, 851
Nihilism, 884
Nijmegen, Peace of, 595
Nile River region, 4, 9, 10–11, 21–22, 118(illus.), 889. *See also* Egypt
Nineteen Eighty-Four (Orwell), 1077
Ninety-five Theses (Luther), 514
Nineveh, 47
Nine Years' War, 596–597
Nivelle, Robert, 625
Nkrumah, Kwame, 1092
NKVD (secret police), 1010–1011
Nobel, Alfred, 847
Nobel Peace Prize, in 1926, 972
Nobility, 312–314, 328, 409, 413, 548–549, 551, 562, 592, 622–623, 672. *See also* Aristocracy; Barons
Nogarola, Isotta, 444
Nomads, 51, 268
Nonalignment, 1092
Nonintervention policy, 1020
Nonviolence, Gandhi on, 1001(box)
Non-Western world: World War I and, 917, 948–949, 959–960; Great Depression and, 1000; after World War II, 1060; West and, 1112(illus.), 1113–1149. *See also* Third World; Western world
Nördlingen, Battle at, 576, 577(illus.)
Norman Conquest, of England, 330–331 and *illus.*, 336
Normandy invasion, 1051
Normandy region, 297, 328, 329, 365
Normans, 330, 332, 333

North (developed countries), 1114, 1139
North (U.S.), 829–831
North Africa, 909–910; Rome and, 175; Vandals in, 247; Islam and, 273, 275, 332; Berbers in Spain and, 282; gold trade and, 482; imperialism in, 889; World War II and, 1035–1037, 1050–1051; French colonies in, 1089; independence in, 1090
North America: exploration of, 491; colonies in, 616–619; trade with, 682–685. *See also* Americas; Exploration; specific countries
North Atlantic Treaty Organization (NATO), 1086–1087, 1096(map), 1136
Northern Europe, 439, 457–459, 461–462. *See also* Europe; Renaissance
Northern Hemisphere, *see* Europe
Northern Ireland, conflicts in, 1140
North German Confederation, 822
Northmen, 297, 339
North Sea region, 419
Northumbria, 284, 336
North Vietnam, *see* Vietnam
Norway, 296, 337, 413, 534, 741. *See also* Scandinavia
Noske, Gustav, 970
Notre-Dame of Paris, 383 and *illus.*, 384(illus.)
Nova Scotia, 616
Novels, 871–874, 872(box), 951
November Revolution (Russia), 934–935
Novgorod, 338, 368, 414
Novikov, Nikolai, 1065(box)
Novum Organum (Bacon), 634
Nubia, 23, 47
Nuclear power, 1129, 1144
Nuclear weapons, 1032; atomic bomb and, 1030(illus.), 1031, 1057–1058; arms build-up and, 1087; in France, 1095–1097, 1136; Cuban missile crisis and, 1102; in former Soviet Union, 1129–1130. *See also* Weapons and weaponry
Numeration systems, 19–20
Nuns, 314, 377
Nuremberg trials, 1060
Nursery schools, 1118
Nursing, 851. *See also* Nightingale, Florence
Nystadt, Treaty of, 611

Obelisks, 31
Obrenovich, Milosh, 761
Observatories, 630, 631(illus.)
Obsidian, 7
Occupation zones (Germany), 1057, 1061–1062
Oceans, currents, 481(map), 483
Ockham's razor, 511
O'Connor, Rory, 336
Octavian, *see* Augustus
Oder-Neisse line, 1085
Odes (Horace), 201
Odoacer, 247, 248
Odyssey (Homer), 64, 69–70
Oedipus the Tyrant (Sophocles), 112
Offa (Mercia), 287
Oil, 1055, 1105–1106, 1105(illus.)
Okinawa, 1057
Old-age pensions, 862

Old Babylonian period, 17–19
Oldenburg, Claes, 1110 and *illus.*
Old Kingdom: in Egypt, 23, 31; Hittite, 34
Old Stone era, *see* Upper Paleolithic era
Old Testament, 213, 258 and *illus. See also* Bible
Old World, 4, 475–476, 503(box)
Oleg of Novgorod, 338
Oligarchs, in Sparta, 86
Oligarchy, 34, 95, 183
Olivares, Gaspar de (Count), 561
Olmütz, 819, 820
Olympian gods, 92–93
Olympias (queen), 140
Omdurman, Battle of, 891
Omnibus, 861
On Agriculture (Cato), 178
On Anatomical Procedures (Galen), 640
On Architecture (Alberti), 466
On Christian Doctrine (Augustine), 261
On Christian Freedom (Luther), 514
On Divine and Human Readings (Cassiodorus), 261
On Duties (Ambrose of Milan), 258
One-Dimensional Man (Marcuse), 1077
O'Neill, Hugh (lord of Tyrone), *see* Tyrone, lord of
On Liberty (Mill), 749
"On My Own Ignorance and That of Many Others" (Petrarch), 443(box)
On the Babylonian Captivity of the Church (Luther), 514
On the Civil War (Caesar), 184
On the Contempt of the World (Innocent III), 360
On the Diseases of Women (Trotula of Salerno), 280
On the Donation of Constantine (Valla), 446
On the Fabric of the Human Body (Vesalius), 641
On the Gallic War (Caesar), 184
On the Motion of the Heart (Harvey), 641
On the Nature of Things (Lucretius), 187
On the Origin of Species by Means of Natural Selection (Darwin), 866
On the Revolution of Heavenly Bodies (Copernicus), 628, 629(box)
On the Subjection of Women (Mill), 749
OPEC, *see* Organization of Petroleum Exporting Countries
Opera, 464, 581
Oppian Law, 190
Optimates, in Rome, 182
Optimism, *see* Age of Optimism
"Oracle of the Potter, The," 130, 131(box)
Oracles, 93
Oral communication, 587
Oral tradition, Homer and, 70–71
Orange family, 613, 701; William of Orange (Netherlands), 557. *See also* William of Orange (England)
Oratorian order, 535
Oratory, of Cicero, 185
Orchestra of the Paris Opera (Degas), 870
Order of Preachers, *see* Dominicans
Order of the Garter, 462

Orders: military, 317; of knights, 462. *See also* Clergy
Ordinances of 1311 (England), 403
Ordinances of Justice (Florence), 411
Oregon territory, 829
Oresteia trilogy (Aeschylus), 112
Orfeo (Monteverdi), 581
Organization of Petroleum Exporting Countries (OPEC), 1105
Organizations, *see* Associations; Labor; Labor unions; Workers
Organized labor, *see* Labor; Labor unions
Orientalism (Said), 1148 (box)
Orient Express, 847
Original sin, 259
Origines (Cato), 178
Orloff, Count, 850
Ortega y Gasset, José, 985
Orthodox Christianity, 255, 276, 339, 345, 533, 761
Orwell, George, 1077
Ossian, 671
Ostpolitik, 1084, 1085, 1103
Ostracism, 96
Ostrogoths, 244, 247–248, 282
Oswy (Northumbria), 285
Otto I (Germany), 320, 322, 323
Otto II (Germany), 320, 322
Otto III (Germany), 320, 322 and *illus.*, 323
Otto IV (Germany), 362, 365
Ottoman Empire, 426–427, 426(map), 761–762, 827–829, 941; in Middle Ages, 423–431; minorities in, 427; Hungary and, 604; Peter the Great and, 611; unrest in, 761–762; Crimean War and, 812–813, 814; nationalism in, 828–829, 828(illus.); autocratic government of, 905–906; World War I and, 919; end of, 942–943. *See also* Ottoman Turks; Turks
Ottoman Turks, 423–427, 426(map), 480, 532; Italy and, 412; expansion of, 481; Suleiman and, 522–523; behavior of, 524(box); Spain and, 560
Otto of Brunswick, 357
Overpopulation, famine and, 415
Overseas trade, *see* Trade
Ovid, 201, 385
Oviedo, 282
Owen, Robert, 750, 800, 862
Owen, Wilfred, 954–955
Oxford University, 380, 458

Pachomius, 256
Pacific region, 476, 490, 1032, 1046–1049, 1050(map), 1052, 1058
Pacific rim countries, 1114
Pact of Steel, 1014
Paganism, 64
Painting, 870, 1077–1078; cave art and, 6; Romanesque style in, 322(illus.); in Renaissance, 437, 450–453; portraiture as, 456; late baroque, 670; romantic, 743, 744; impressionist, 870; realism in, 870; neoromantic, 886; surrealism in, 987; modernism in, 988; American leadership in, 1077–1079; pop art and, 1110–1111

and *illus.*, 1110 (illus.); neoexpressionism in, 1144. *See also* Art(s)
Pakistan, 4, 122, 134
Palaces: at Sussa and Persepolis, 62–63; in Crete, 65–66 and *illus.*; Mycenaean, 68; papal, at Avignon, 397(illus.). *See also* Louvre
Palatinate, 575
Palatine Hill (Rome), 154
Paleography, 304
Paleolithic period, *see* Upper Paleolithic era
Palestine, 7, 35(map), 48, 943; Egypt and, 28; city-states of, 33–34; as Canaan, 34; international system and, 36–37; Hebrew conquest of, 52; Christianity and, 213; First Crusade and, 346; after World War II, 1064–1066; partition of, 1067(map)
Palestrina, Giovanni, 535
Palmyra, 211
Pamela (Richardson), 670
Panaetius, 178
Panama, Isthmus of, 490
Panama City, 498
Pan-Arab nationalism, 1089
"Pan-Asianism," of Japan, 1049
Panegyric on the City of Florence (Bruni), 442
Pan-Europeanism, 1094
Pankhurst, Emmeline, 900, 902(box)
Pannonia, 247
Pannonian plain, 244
Papacy, *see* Papal States; Popes and papacy
Papal bulls, 386, 387, 388, 402, 490
Papal legates, 324
Papal States, 283, 368, 402, 410, 767
Papen, Franz von, 1007, 1011
Papyrus, 31
Paracelsianism, 638
Paracelsus (Philippus von Hohenheim), 628
Paraguay, 730
Parallel Lives of Noble Greeks and Romans (Plutarch), 210
Paris, 362(illus.); population of, 299; university in, 379, 380, 458; treaty of (13th century), 404–405; French Revolution and, 706–707; Thermidorian Reaction and, 719; July Revolution (1830) in, 752; revolt in, 765; renovation in, 858–859, 858(illus.), 860(box); liberation of, 1051
Paris Commune (1871), 836, 837(illus.)
Paris Exhibition (1937), 1017(illus.)
Paris Peace Conference, *see* Paris peace settlement
Paris peace settlement (World War I), 943–950, 944(box), 960–963
Parlements (France), 408–409, 590, 672, 703
Parliament (Austria-Hungary), 905
Parliament (England), 366, 753, 754–755, 833–834; power of, 403; Puritans in, 567–568; Gunpowder Plot and, 569; James I and, 569; Short and Long, 570–571; monarchy and, 597–603, 674; Charles II and, 602; James II and, 602–603
Parliament (European), 1136
Parliament (France), 753, 836, 837. *See also* Parlements (France)
Parliament (Germany), 820
Parliament (Spain), 757, 758

Parliament (Sweden), 534, 675
Parliamentary government, 900, 903, 964
Parma, duke of (Alexander), 558, 559–560, 568
Parmenides, 95
Parthenon (Athens), 105(illus.), 116–117, 116(illus.), 117(illus.)
Parthia (Persia) and Parthians, 133–134, 184, 199, 204, 211
Pascal, Blaise, 150, 637
Pasion (former Greek slave), 100
Pasionaria, La (Dolores Ibarruri), 994(illus.), 995
Passchendaele, Battle of, 925
Pasteur, Louis, 867
Pasteurization, 867
Pastoral Rule (Gregory I), 283
Pastoral Symphony (Beethoven), 743
Paterfamilias, in Rome, 159–160
Paterna, Caelia, 219
Patriarchal society, 76
Patriarchs, 51; of Alexandria, 255
Patricians, 157, 165–166
Patrick, *see* Saint Patrick
Patriot party, in Netherlands, 701
Patristic writings, 258, 262
Patronage, 160–162, 240–241, 409–410, 453–456, 591
Patrons, scientific, 643
Paul (apostle), 226
Paul III (Pope), 536
Paulette, 564, 590
Pauline Christians, 217
Paul of Tarsus, 213, 216–219, 218 (box)
Pavia, 282; Battle at, 522
Pax Mongolica, 478
Pax Romana, in, 195, 203–210. *See also* Augustus; Roman Empire
Paxton, Joseph, 876, 877
Peace, 937, 942–943; World War I settlement, 943–950; after World War II, 1061–1062
"Peace" (Brooke), 955
"Peace in our time," 1023
Peace of Alais, 565
Peace of Augsburg, 527, 571
Peace of Constance, 356, 368
Peace of Lodi, 412
Peace of Lübeck, 576
Peace of Nijmegen, 595
Peace of Paris: of 1763, 687; of 1856, 828
Peace of Prague, 576
Peace of the Pyrenees, 591, 595
Peace of Utrecht, 597, 603
Peace of Westphalia, 577, 595, 603
Pearl Harbor attack, 1048
Peasants, 301, 317–318; in Rome, 198–199, 241; social position of, 312; in Russia, 414, 680, 838, 908, 909, 932–933; economy and, 421–422, 549–550; revolts by, 517–519, 620, 692; in Brandenburg-Prussia, 605; in Denmark, 675; French Revolution and, 707–708; Greek, 762; Soviet collectivization and, 1000–1002. *See also* Land; Serfs; Soviet Union
Peasants' Revolt (England), *see* Rising of 1381
Peel, Robert, 754

Pegalotti, Franceso, 479 and *box*
Peisistratids, 91
Peisistratus (Athens), 43
Pelopidas (Theban leader), 103
Peloponnesian League, 87–88, 100
Peloponnesian War, 87, 99, 103, 104(map)
Peloponnesian War, The (Thucydides), 113
Peloponnesus region, 85–89
Penitential acts, 511
Pen names (women writers), 745–746
Pensées (Thoughts) (Pascal), 637
Pensionary, in Holland, 613
Pensions, 862
People of the Book, 50, 273
People's Republic of China, 1067. *See also* China
Pepin III (king of Franks), 282, 288
Perception, Descartes and, 637
Perestroika (restructuring), 1122
Pergamum, 120, 126, 132–133
Pergamum Altar, 133 and *illus.*
Pericles, 96–97, 106
Periodic table, 865
Persepolis, 60, 62 and *illus.*
Persia and Persian Empire, 45(map), 57–64, 273, 276, 909; soldiers of, 44; religions in, 55, 59–60, 63–64; Greece and, 100–101, 102(box); Peloponnesian War and, 103; Alexander the Great and, 121–122; Parthians and, 133–134; Roman Empire and, 236; Safavid dynasty in, 427. *See also* Sassanid dynasty
Persian Gulf region, 485
Persian Gulf War, 1133
Persian Wars, 100–101
Persis (Anshan), 59
Perspective, in arts, 451, 452
Peru, 494(map)
Perugino, Pietro, 465(box), 467–468 and *illus.*
Pétain, Philippe, 923–924, 925, 939, 962, 1033, 1043
Peter, 238, 239
Peter I (Russia, "the Great"), 603, 609–611, 609(illus.), 610(box)
Peterloo Massacre, 755(illus.)
Peter of Holstein-Gottorp, 678 and *illus.*
Petition of Right, 570
Petrarch, Francesco, 398, 441–442, 443(box)
Petri, Olaus, 534
Petrine theory of papal primacy, 239
Petrograd, 931, 934–935. *See also* Leningrad; St. Petersburg
Petrograd Soviet, 932
Phalanx, *see* Hoplite phalanx
Pharaoh, 24, 26(box)
Pharisees, 147, 215, 216, 217
Pheidon, 85
Philike Hetairia (Society of Friends, Greece), 762
Philip II (Augustus, France), 361, 362–363, 365
Philip II (Macedon), 119, 120–121; conquests of, 124(map)
Philip II (Spain), 499, 503, 522, 553, 554(map), 559, 560, 568
Philip III (France), 363

Philip IV ("the Fair," France), 363, 386–389, 396, 402
Philip IV (Spain), 561
Philip V (Macedon), 175
Philip V (Spain), 597
Philip VI (France), 402, 404
Philip of Anjou, *see* Philip V (Spain)
Philip of Habsburg, 429, 522
Philip of Hesse, 525
Philip of Swabia, 357
Philip of Valois, *see* Philip VI (France)
Philippides, 144
Philippines, 490, 1048
Philistines, 52
Philo of Alexandria, 143
Philosophes, 660, 663
Philosophical Dictionary (Voltaire), 660–661
Philosophy, 380; Greek, 94–95; origins of Western, 94–95; Socrates and, 105, 107; Sophists and, 106–107; Aristotle and, 107, 109–111; Plato and, 107–109; idealism as, 108; Stoic, 128, 178; skepticism as, 134; Cynic, 141; Epicurean, 141; Hellenistic, 142–144; Descartes and, 637; mechanistic world view, 649–652; of Voltaire, 660–663; reason vs. emotion in, 884; after World War II, 1075–1076. *See also* Enlightenment; Metaphysics; specific philosophies and philosophers
Phoenician (Canaanite) cities, 34
Phoenicians, 44, 48–50, 82, 83(map)
"Phony War," 1032–1033
Photography, 813, 870
Physicians, *see* Medicine
Physics, 94, 637, 639–640, 865, 884
Physiocrats, 663
Physis (nature), 106
Pi (mathematics), 31
Picasso, Pablo, 470, 895, 1017(illus.), 1018
Pico della Mirandola, Giovanni, 446–447, 459
Pictographs, 11, 12 and *illus.*
Pictor, Quintus Fabius, 178
Piedmont, 767, 768, 814, 815, 817–818, 817(map), 819
Piedmont-Sardinia, 741, 759
Piers Plowman (Langland), 440
Pilate, Pontius, 216
Pilgrimages, 346, 511, 512
Pilgrims, 617
Pilsudski, Josef, 969
Piracy, 690
Pisa, 334, 370; Council of, 399–400
Pisae-Ariminum line, 171
Pisanello (Antonio Pisano), 463
Pissarro, Camille, 858(illus.), 870
Pius IV (Pope), 538
Pius IX (Pope), 767, 814, 869
Pizarro, Francisco, 498
Plague, *see* Black Death (plague)
Planck, Max, 884
Planetary motion, 626, 628–629, 631–632, 639–640. *See also* Astronomy
Plantation system, 482, 499, 616, 730, 731(box)
Plants, Columbian Exchange and, 501–502, 501(illus.)

Plataea, Battle at, 101
Plato, 107–109, 446, 749
Platonic Theology (Ficino), 446
Plautus, Titus Maccius, 178, 190
Plays, *see* Drama
Playwrights, *see* Drama
Plebeians, 158, 165–166
Plebiscites, 721–722, 835, 836, 1023
Plenis, 127
Pliny the Elder, 209
Pliny the Younger, 209, 219
Plotina, 204
Plotinus, 134
Plows, 13, 309–310, 309(illus.)
Plutarch, 88, 181(box), 210
Pocket boroughs, 674–675, 755
Podestàs, in Italy, 368
Poets and poetry, 578; Enkheduanna and,
16; Babylonian, 19; epic, 19, 20(box);
Homer and, 43, 44, 64, 69–71, 76, 91;
Alcaeus, 83; Tyrtaeus, 84; Greek, 91–92,
104–105; Alexandrian, 137; Hellenistic,
139; *Distaff*, 141; Virgil and, 153; in Rome,
177–178, 200–201; Lucretius and, 187;
Balbilla and, 204; Latin, 209; Dante
Alighieri and, 379; of Archpoet, 384–385;
of Muslim Spain, 385; Ovid, 385; in ver-
nacular, 385–386; Shakespeare and, 580;
Donne and, 647; romantic, 743; of World
War I, 954–955 and *illus.*; surrealism and,
987. *See also* specific poets
Pogroms, 869, 1060
Poincaré, Raymond, 939, 962
Poitiers, Battle at, 288, 405
Poitou, 329
Poland, 337, 414, 603, 945, 1103, 1121, 1122;
castle in, 338(illus.); Protestantism and,
532–533; Sobieski in, 604, 607; Prussia
and, 605; Baltic region and, 605–607;
Sweden and, 607; Vasa in, 608; Peter
the Great and, 611; Russia and, 678–679,
760; partition of, 679(map); reform and,
701; French Revolution and, 729; Con-
gress of Vienna and, 741; after World
War I, 969; Germany and, 972; World
War II and, 1023, 1024, 1032, 1039–1040,
1044; Soviets and, 1055; borders with
Germany, 1057; after World War II, 1060;
demonstrations in, 1099; Solidarity in,
1124–1127; privatization in, 1130–1131;
after communism, 1131; Germany and,
1133
Poland-Lithuania, 605–607
Pole, Reginald, 530
Police forces, 862. *See also* Secret police
Polis (in Greece), 79–81, 82–83, 85, 110(box)
Political nationalism, 746. *See also*
Nationalism
Political parties, 674, 862–863, 1084. *See also*
specific countries and parties
Political power, *see* Power
Political system, 729, 833–834, 899. *See also*
Government
Political Testament (Richelieu), 566(box)
Political thought: Hittite, 35–36; humanism
and, 448–449; Hobbes and, 649; Locke
and, 649–651; of Voltaire, 662–663; of

Montesquieu, 663; Enlightenment ideas
and, 668–669; liberalism and, 748–749;
irrationality, uncertainty, and, 884
Politics: in Greece, 81–91; in Athens, 96;
Stoic, 143(box); in Rome, 160, 163–165,
180–185, 186, 236; Carolingian fragmentation and, 296–297; women and, 314;
in England, 365, 674–675; in Germany,
523–525; in France, 561–565; after Thirty
Years' War, 577–578; women and, 712;
after French Revolution, 729; symbolism
in, 729, 734–735 and *illus.*, 734(illus.);
culture and, 880–886; in democratic soci-
eties, 968–969; in Italy, 981–984, 1106;
in 1930s, 995–1026, 1028–1029. *See also*
Government
Politics (Aristotle), 110(box)
Pollock, Jackson, 1077, 1110
Pollution, 795–796. *See also* Environment
Polo family, 478; Marco, 477(illus.), 478–479
Polybius, 163, 178
Polyglot Bible, 458
Polytheism, 50, 162, 220
Pompeia Paulina, 209
Pompeii, 205(illus.), 224–225 and *illus.*,
224(illus.)
Pompey the Great, 183, 184
Pontiff, *see* Popes and papacy
Pontius Pilate, *see* Pilate, Pontius
Poor Clares, 376
Poorhouses, 552, 690
Poor Law (Britain), 755
Poor relief, 552
Pop art, 1078, 1110–1111 and *illus.*, 1110(illus.)
Popes and papacy, 162, 238, 869, 1117;
power and theories of, 239; authority of,
255, 386–388, 398–399, 401–402; rule in
Italy, 282–283; Carolingians and, 288;
Charlemagne and, 291; investiture con-
troversy and, 323–326; France and, 329;
First Crusade and, 345–346; German Em-
pire and, 355–360; Frederick I (Germany)
as vassal of, 356; characters and activities
of, 359–360; in Avignon, 396, 397–400;
crisis and reform of, 396–402; Babylonian
Captivity and, 397–400; claimants to,
399–400; *Donation of Constantine* and, 446;
court of, 462; in Renaissance, 466–468;
ambassadors from, 478; Council of Trent
and, 537–538; modernization and, 1117.
See also Catholicism and Catholic church;
Clergy; Rome; specific popes
Popolo (Italy), 335, 410
Popolo d'Italia, Il (newspaper), 983
Popular culture, 957–958, 963–969
Populares, in Rome, 182
Popular front coalitions, 1014–1015, 1017,
1018–1020
Popular sovereignty, 835
Population: of cities and towns, 207, 237,
299, 370, 438–439, 489, 788, 789(map);
growth of, 308, 396, 414–417, 468; bubonic
plague and, 415–417; of Americas, 492; in
Spanish America, 499; economic change
and, 548; of British North America, 683;
growth of, 687–688, 739–741, 879; Malthus
on, 747; industrialization and, 778; of

Britain, 784; of France, 784–785; of Italy,
819; rural, 857; in less developed coun-
tries, 1114; baby boom and, 1117; density
of, 1138(map)
Portolan, 480
Portraiture, in Renaissance, 456
Portugal, 332, 476, 480–486, 485(box), 490;
Spain and, 553, 560; war of independence
in, 561; Dutch trade and, 616; decoloniza-
tion and, 1091; democracy in, 1104
Portuguese Empire, 483–486
Positivism, 884
Postal service, 848, 851
Postindustrial society, 1115–1117, 1116(box)
Postmodernism, 1144
Postwar world, after World War II,
1060–1068, 1072–1108
Potato, 502, 688–689
Pot of Gold (Plautus), 191
Potsdam conference, 1056–1057, 1058, 1062
Po Valley, 282
Poverty, 199, 371, 550–552, 690, 747, 755,
856. *See also* Mendicants; Social welfare
Power (authority): in Mesopotamia, 11; in
Egypt, 24; of Persian kings, 62–63; in
Sparta, 86; in Athens, 96, 99; of Ptolemies, 130; of
women, 141; in Rome, 163, 164(illus.);
165–166, 232–233, 236; public, 241; state
vs. church, 255; in Islam, 273; in Germany, 322, 523–524, 824, 962, 974; in
France, 329, 564–565, 962; of popes, 356,
357, 358(box), 396, 398–401; of churches,
360, 396, 510; in England, 366, 403, 409,
962; monarchies and, 396; of medieval
governments, 402–414; in Italy, 410, 411,
1013; in Spain, 428–429, 553–561; Renaissance courts and, 462–468; of Habsburg
family, 575–576; of sovereign, 581–582;
in Central and Eastern Europe, 603–605,
606(map); in Baltic region, 605–608; of
Napoleon I, 721–723; shifts in Europe,
811–812; international relations and,
812–814; of United States, 829–833; of
Europe, 959–960. *See also* Church and
state; Elites; Government; Monarchs and
monarchies; Nobility
Power (energy) sources, 781
Pragmatic Sanction of Bourges, 402
Pragmatism, of Aristotle, 110
Prague, 400, 573
Prague Spring, 1103, 1122
Praise of Folly (Erasmus), 460
Praxiteles, 140(illus.)
Prayer, 315, 316(illus.)
Precious metals, *see* Gold; Silver
Prehistory, 4–10, 40–41 and *illus.*
Presbyterianism, 570, 598
Press, 754(box), 812–813. *See also* Censorship
Press gangs, 691
Prester John, 478
Priam, *see* Trojan War; Troy
Prices, 548, 857
Pride, Thomas, 600
"Pride's Purge," 600
Priesthood, 162, 234, 514. *See also* Clergy;
Popes and papacy
Primavera (Botticelli), 452, 470–471

"Primitive" peoples, 890
Primo de Rivera, José Antonio, 1018
Primogeniture, 312, 784
Primrose League, 891
Prince, The (Machiavelli), 448–449
Princess of Cleves, The (Madame de Lafayette), 593
Principalities (France), 327–328, 327(map)
Principate, 205, 211
Principia Mathematica (Newton), 639(illus.), 640
Principles of Political Economy (Mill), 797
Principles of Political Economy (Ricardo), 747
Printing, 456–457 and *map*, 516
Prison Notebooks (Gramsci), 1077
Prison reforms, in Britain, 754
"Pristine Theology," 447
Privateers, 557, 690
Privatization, 1130–1131
Privy Council (England), 674
Procopius, 338
Production, 778–787. *See also* Putting-out system
Products, *see* Trade
Professionals and professionalism, 642–644, 850, 851, 867
Progress, 864, 873(box)
Proletariat, Marx on, 803–804
Prometheus Unbound (Shelley), 745
Propaganda, 264–265 and *illus.*, 929–931, 1010, 1028–1029, 1028–1029 and *illus.*, 1028(illus.)
Propaganda trials, in Soviet Union, 1004
Property, 301–302, 319(box), 552, 680, 710, 749. *See also* Land
Prophets, 50, 53–54, 268, 269–271
Prose, 94, 178. *See also* Literature
Proslogion (Anselm), 351
Prosperity, 964–965, 1115–1117
Prostitution, 854(illus.)
Protagoras, 106
Protectorate of Bohemia and Moravia, 1023
Protectorates, 600–601, 894(box)
Protestant, use of term, 510–511
Protestantism, 510, 526(map); Luther and, 510, 512–515; in Zurich, 517; Calvin and, 519–520; in England, 527–529, 530–531, 565–568, 569–571; in France, 531–532, 562–565, 722; in Eastern Europe, 532–533; in Scandinavia, 534; types of, 534–535; Saint Bartholomew's Day Massacre and, 546(illus.), 547, 562–563; in Netherlands, 556; science and, 647; Ireland and, 700, 899; in Germany, 904. *See also* Christianity; Protestantism *(cont.)*, Presbyterianism; Religion; Thirty Years' War
Protests, 1099–1100, 1104–1105, 1104–1107
Protoindustrialization, 778
Provisional government (Russia), 931–933
Prussia, 413, 676–677, 713, 759, 768, 769, 821; Hohenzollerns in, 525; duchy of, 605; economy in, 676–677; power of, 682; Congress of Vienna and, 741–742; riots in, 799–800; German unification and, 819, 820–824, 825(box); Bismarck and, 819–820; war with France, 836; industrialists in, 850. *See also* Brandenburg-Prussia

Psychoanalysis, Freud and, 884
Ptolemaic Egypt, *see* Egypt
Ptolemies, 119, 135. *See also* Cleopatra; specific Ptolemies
Ptolemy I (Egypt), 129, 135
Ptolemy V Epiphanes, 130
Ptolemy XII (Egypt), 150
Ptolemy XV Caesar, 151
Ptolemy of Alexandria, 478, 626, 627
Public art, 454–455
Public Health Bill (England), 860
Public life, 105, 301, 442
Public opinion, 666–669, 703–704
Public services, 859–862
Public speaking, 106. *See also* Rhetoric
Public transportation, 861 and *illus.*
Public works, 199, 835
Puduhepa (Hittite queen), 35, 36
Pugachev rebellion (Russia), 692–693
Punic Wars, 172–175
Punishment, in Mesopotamia, 16–17
Punjab, 134
Punt, land of, 29–30
Purges, 1004–1005, 1007
Puritans, 567–568, 569, 598, 617, 638
Putney debates, 599(box)
Putting-out system, 690, 762, 778, 857
Pylos, 69
Pyramids, in Egypt, 23, 24, 25(illus.)
Pyrrho of Elis, 134, 144
Pyrrhus of Epirus, 171
Pythagoras of Samos, 20, 95
Pythagorean theorem, 95

Qadi, 274
Quadruple Alliance, 741
Quakers, 600 and *illus.*, 783
Quantum theory, 636
Queens, 29, 30(illus.), 34, 35, 140, 150–151. *See also* specific queens
Quetzalcoatl, 497
Quintilian, 444
Qumran, 147, 215
Quran, 270–271, 272(box), 273, 275
Quraysh, 269

Rabbis, 217–219
Race and racism, 868, 883, 890, 1008 and box, 1009, 1011–1012. *See also* Slaves and slavery
Racine, Jean, 594
Radicals and radicalism, 520–521, 598–600, 1005–1006. *See also* France, popular front coalition in; French Revolution
Raft of the "Medusa" (Géricault), 744, 772–773 and *illus.*
al-Rahman, Abd, 275
Railroads, 777(box), 778, 784, 847–848 and *map*
Ramesses II (Egyptian king), 31, 36
Ranke, Leopold von, 867
Rape of Lucretia, 158, 159(box)
Raphael, 452
Raphia, Battle of, 130
Rasputin, Grigori, 931
Ras Shamra, *see* Ugarit
Rathenau, Walther, 927, 970

Rationality, 636–637. *See also* Reason; Reasoning
Ravenna, 264–265 and *illus.*, 282
Raw materials, in Germany, 927
Re (god), 27
Reactionaries, 751, 757–758
Reading, *see* Literacy; Literature
Reagan, Ronald, 1119(illus.), 1146(box)
Realism, in arts, 92, 870–874
Reality, Parmenides and, 95
Realpolitik, 812
Rearmament, in Germany, 1011, 1020, 1086
Reason, 636–637, 649, 660, 718–719. *See also* Enlightenment
Reasoning, 634, 637
Rebel, The (Camus), 1076
Rebellions, 103, 517–519, 517(illus.), 551–552, 556–558, 692–693, 730
Reccared (Visigoth king), 281
Reconquista (Spain), 332, 333(map), 366, 367, 427
Reconstruction, 831, 832
Recreation, 90(illus.). *See also* Leisure
Red Brigades, 1106
Red Cross, 815
Reds, in Russia, 942, 975, 976(map)
"Red Shirts," 818(illus.)
Reed, John, 936(box)
Reflections on the Revolution in France (Burke), 742
Reform: in Egypt, 30; of Solon, 90–91; in classical Athens, 96–97; under Caesar, 184; under Diocletian, 229–231, 232(box); of Constantine, 231–233; military, 237; Carolingian, 292–293; in Catholic church, 307–308; spiritual, 315; in France, 363, 703–704, 711, 718–719, 751–753, 836–837; mendicant orders and, 373–375; of papacy, 401–402; in Christianity, 457–459; in Russia, 680; in Britain, 753–757, 900; in 1848–1849, 763(map); in Ottoman Empire, 827–828; women and, 854 and *illus.*; in Italy, 903; in east-central Europe, 1122–1127. *See also* Reformation
Reformation, 509–510; movements toward, 510–521; in Germany, 518(map); Anabaptists and, 520–521; Holy Roman Empire of Charles V and, 521–527; in England, 527–531; in France, 531–532; in Eastern Europe, 532–533; in Scandinavia, 534; late period in, 534–540; woodcut from, 542–543 and *illus. See also* Calvin, John; Counter-Reformation; Luther, Martin
Reform Bills (Britain), 755, 757, 834, 863, 899
Reformed church, 519–520, 527
Reform movements, 700–701, 1102–1103
Regulation, as global issue, 1139
Reichstag (Germany), 824, 973–974, 1006, 1007
Reinsurance Treaty, 909
Relativism, Plato and, 108
Relief, for poverty, 552, 862–863
Relief sculpture, 21
Religion: Sargon and, 15; in Mesopotamia, 17–19; in Egypt, 24, 26–28; in New Kingdom, 30; Canaanite, 34; Hittite, 35; Cyrus

Religion (cont.): and, 59–60, 61(box); in Greece, 92–94, 105–106; Pythagoras and, 95; women and, 99–100, 511–512; Indian, 134; mystery, 144–145, 220–221; Hellenistic, 147–148; in Rome, 162, 199, 220, 237; in Pompeii, 225; Justinian and, 251–252; in pre-Islamic Arab world, 268; in Byzantine Empire, 273; in Persian Empire, 273; medieval clergy and, 314–317; spiritual reform and, 315; church vs. state, 323–326; as social movement, 375–377; in Ottoman Empire, 427; Christian concept of death and, 434–435; humanism and, 438; transfer to New World, 476; exploration and, 480–481; Aztec, 493; Inca, 494; Columbian Exchange and, 502; Reformation and, 509–540; in Saxony, 524–525; in Germany, 525–527; in England, 528–529, 565–571, 602, 674; Saint Bartholomew's Day Massacre and, 546(illus.), 547, 562–563; witch-hunts and, 552–553; of Netherlands, 556; in France, 561–565, 592; Thirty Years' War and, 571–578; Peace of Westphalia and, 577; in Austria, 604; in Poland-Lithuania, 605, 607; Poland vs. Sweden, 607; in Holland, 613–614; in New France, 618; science and, 646–648; political thought and, 652; in Russia, 679–680; nonconformity in, 783; working class and, 798; evolutionary theory and, 865; challenges to, 868–870; loss of faith and, 886; Barth's concepts and, 986; renewal of, 1077; secularization and, 1117–1118; in Poland, 1132. See also Afterlife; Churches; Clergy; Gods and goddesses; Missions and missionaries; Mythology; Secularization; specific religions, religious leaders, and religious thinkers

Religious orders, see Monasteries and monasticism; specific orders
Religious Peace of Augsburg, 527
Religious toleration, 61(box), 237, 427, 564, 582, 601, 869. See also Religion
Remarque, Erich Maria, 951
Rembrandt van Rijn, 615 and illus.
Remedello culture, 41
Renaissance, 437–438; Carolingian, 293–296; educational reform in, 442–444; arts in Italy, 450–456; printing and, 456–457; spread of, 456–462; and court society, 462–468; papacy in, 466–468; Florentine art during, 470–471. See also Art(s); Humanists and humanism; Reformation
Renoir, Auguste, 870
Reparations, 943–945, 971–972, 1062
Republic (Plato), 109
Republicanism, 715, 753, 835–836
Republicans, in Spain, 995, 1017–1018
Republics, 412, 600–601, 715–719, 752, 764, 768–769, 836–837, 975, 1015–1016
Reshid Pasha, Mustafa (Ottoman Empire), 827
Resistance, to Nazis, 1043–1044
Resorts, 852, 855
Resources, 548, 591–592. See also Natural resources

Restoration (England), 601–602
Restoration (France), 739, 751–753
Resurrection, 147
Retailing, in France, 844(illus.), 845
Reuchlin, Johannes, 459
Reunification, see Germany
Revealed truths, 381
Revolt of the Masses (Ortega y Gasset), 985
Revolts: popular, 422–423; in Netherlands, 556–558; in France, 590, 597; in Poland-Lithuania, 607; peasant, 620, 692; July Revolution (Paris, 1830), 752; in Russia, 760, 761; against Turks, 762; by laborers, 799–800; Paris Commune (1871) as, 836. See also Revolution(s); Riots
Revolution(s): in Sparta, 129; in Roman Republic, 180–182; Abassid, 274–275; in England (1642–1649), 598–603; American, 700, 701–702; French, 704–720; of 1848, 738(illus.), 762–770, 763(map); in Paris (July, 1830), 752; socialism and, 881; anarchism and, 882; in Russia, 925, 931–935; unrest in Germany, 970; anticommunist, 1127–1132. See also Reform; Russian revolutions; Science; specific revolutions
Revolutionary period, 699–733
Revolutionary Tribunal (France), 719
Revolutionary War in America, see American Revolution
Revolution of 1905 (Russia), 908
Rhetoric, 106, 178, 210, 380, 438
Rhineland region, 244, 822, 972, 1020
Rhine River, 199, 320, 820, 945
Rhodes, 128
Rhodes, Cecil, 887
Rhodesia, 1091
Rhodri the Great, 335
Rhône region, trade and, 298
Riasanovsky, Nicholas V., 610n
Ricardo, David, 747
Ricciardi family, 418
Rice production, 683
Rich, see Elites; Wealth
Richard I ("the Lionheart," England), 365
Richard II (England), 407, 409
Richard II (Shakespeare), 580
Richard III (England), 409
Richardson, Samuel, 670
Richelieu, Cardinal (Armand-Jean du Plessis), 565, 566(box), 590
Riefenstahl, Leni, 1028–1029
Right (political), 1141, 1145; conflict with left, 1014–1015
Rights, 499–500, 665, 722, 749, 832–833. See also Equality; Women's rights
Riksdag (Sweden), 413, 534, 675
Riots, 551–552, 799, 940. See also Paris Commune; Revolts; Violence
Rising of 1381, 423, 424(box)
Risorgimento, 814
"River of Gold," 482
River valley civilizations, see Egypt; Mesopotamia; specific river regions
Rivière, Henri, 889
Roads and highways, 60, 171(illus.), 310, 371, 778

Roanoke Island, 491
Robert the Pious, 328
Robespierre, Maximilien, 716–717, 716(box), 718(illus.), 719
Robin Hood, 365
Rocco, Alfredo, 982(box)
Rocket (locomotive), 847
Roger II "the Great" (Italy), 333–334
Röhm, Ernst, 1007
Rollo (Norway), 337
Roman Catholic church, 285, 297, 345. See also Catholicism and Catholic church; Christianity
Romance, 355, 385
Roman Empire, 192(illus.), 193–221, 194(map); defense of, 199; law in, 199; Rhine River as German frontier, 199; culture under Augustus, 200–201; Julio-Claudians in, 201–203, 202(illus.); Flavians and "Good Emperors" in, 203–204; Pax Romana in, 203–210; ordinary people in, 206(box); 3rd century crisis in, 210–213; Persia and, 211, 212(box); Christianity and, 213–221; Constantine and, 227–229, 231–233; Late Antiquity period of, 227–261; Diocletian and, 228(map), 229–231, 232(box); division of, 229(map), 230(illus.); eastward power shift in, 232–233; in 4th century, 235–243; East and West, 236; Huns and, 236; Persian threat to, 236; Visigoth threat to, 236; administration of, 236–237; hierarchical society in, 240–243; Germanic peoples and, 243–250; in West, 243–250; barbarians in, 245; sack of Rome and, 245; treaty with Visigoths, 245; Huns and, 246(box); Britain and, 247; "fall" of, 247; Germanic kingdoms in, 248–249; in East, 250–254; Justinian and, 251–254; Christianity, 254–261; Byzantine Empire and, 275, 276. See also Byzantine Empire; Roman law; Roman Republic; Rome; specific rulers
Romanesque style, 308, 322 and illus., 343–344 and illus., 343(illus.)
Roman History (Livy), 441
Romania, 204, 533, 811, 828, 829, 945, 948, 1101, 1127. See also Moldavia
Roman law, 253(box). See also Law(s)
Romanov family: Alexis, 609; Michael, 609; Peter "the Great," 609–611, 609(illus.), 610(box)
Roman Republic, 154, 167(map); founding of, 158–162; Twelve Tables in, 161, 166; religion and world-view in, 162–163; power in, 163, 164(illus.); government and society in, 163–166; conquest of Italy by, 168–171, 170(box); Punic Wars and, 172–175; expansion of, 174(map); Hellenistic east and, 175; society and economy of, 175–176; Greek impact on, 176–180; attitudes toward conquered in, 179(box); politics in, 180–185; luxury goods in, 190; restoration of, 197. See also Roman Empire; Rome
Romanticism, 743–746, 772–773 and illus. See also Neoromanticism
Romantic love, 92, 139

Rome, 153, 157(map), 193(illus.), 205, 412; calendar in, 31; conquest of Greece, 129; Attalid kingdom and, 132; Forum in, 152(illus.); founding of, 154; before republic, 154–158; monarchy in, 157–158; fire in, 203; Visigoth sack of, 245, 259; Vandal sack of, 247; Italian dominance and, 282–283; Muslim raid of, 297; population of, 299; attacks on, 322–323; Great Schism and, 396; papacy and, 398; history of, 441; in Renaissance, 466; population of, 468; sack of (1527), 522; as part of Italy, 818. See also Italy; Roman Empire; Roman Republic
Rome, Treaty of, 1094
Rome-Berlin axis, 1014
Rommel, Erwin, 1037, 1050–1051
Romulus, 154
Roosevelt, Franklin, 998, 1048, 1051, 1052–1055, 1053(illus.)
Rosetta Stone, 130
Roswitha of Gandersheim, 339
Rothko, Mark, 1110
Rotten boroughs, 755
Rousseau, Jean-Jacques, 665–666, 667(box), 670–671, 743
Rouvray, Madame de, 731(box)
Royal courts, 292, 293, 365
Royal demesne, 363
Royalists, 742–743, 764. See also French Revolution
Royal Road (Persia), 60
Royal scientific societies, see Scientific societies
Royal Society of London, 638, 642, 643
Royalty, 581–582
Rubens, Peter Paul, 583–584, 583(illus.)
Rubicon, Caesar and, 184
Rudolf II (Holy Roman emperor), 572, 573
Rudolph of Habsburg, 413
Rufus, Servius Sulpicius, 187
Rühle-Gerstel, Alice, 999(box)
Rule of Saint Augustine, 374
Rule of St. Benedict, 295
Rules (Christian), 256–257, 295
Rump Parliament, 600, 601
Rural society, 299, 317–318, 549–550, 856–857. See also Society
Ruskin, John, 873
Russell, Bertrand, 1087(illus.)
Russia, 414, 605, 607, 814, 1129; Vikings in, 297, 337; government and monarchy in, 368–369; caravans to, 480; Protestantism and, 533; Baltic region and, 605; expansion of, 608–611; Second Great Northern War and, 611; during Enlightenment, 677–680; Poland and, 678–679 and map, 701; churches in, 679–680; Pugachev rebellion in, 692–693; serfs in, 693 and box; Napoleon and, 723, 725–726, 727(illus.); French Revolution and, 729–730; Congress of Vienna and, 741–742; social unrest in, 760–761; industrialization and, 787; Crimean War and, 812–813; Moldavia, Wallachia, and, 828; Ottoman war with, 829; reforms in, 837–840; agriculture in, 857; pogroms in, 869, 883; litera-

ture in, 872; anarchism and, 882; imperialism of, 889; modernization of, 906; autocratic government in, 906–909; Revolution of 1905 in, 908; Austria and, 910; Germany and, 910, 933–935; Balkan region and, 911; Revolution of 1917 in, 925, 931–935; Bolsheviks in, 933–935; communism in, 942, 975–977; foreign intervention and civil war in, 942; territorial shield against, 947–948; economy and government of, 1131–1132; NATO and, 1136. See also Commonwealth of Independent States; Soviet Union; Tsars (Russia); World War I; specific rulers
Russian Empire, 677–680
Russian revolutions, see Russia
Russian Social Democratic party, 907–908, 907(box)
Russo-Japanese War, 908
Ruth (biblical), 57, 58(box)
Ryswick, Treaty of, 596–597
Ryutin, M. N., 1003

SA (Sturmabteilung), 1006, 1007
Sabina, 204
Sabines, 155
Sack of Kiev, see Kiev
Sack of Rome, see Rome
Sacraments, 259, 511, 514
Sacred writings, Christian, 257–258
Sacrifice, Aztecs and, 493
Sadducees, 147, 215–216
Sadler, Michael, 794(box)
Sadowa, Battle at, 822, 823(illus.)
Safavid dynasty, 427
Safety, of highways, 310
as-Saffar, Muhammad, 754(box)
Said, Edward, 1147, 1148(box)
Sailors and sailing, 48, 483, 690, 691–692 and illus. See also Navigation; Ships and shipping
Saint(s), 301, 434–435 and illus., 511. See also specific saints
Saint Bartholomew's Day Massacre, 546(illus.), 547, 562–563, 581
Saint-Domingue, 731(box)
St. Giles, London, 789, 790(box), 791(illus.)
St. Helen, Napoleon at, 728
St. John, Bayle, 593(box)
St. Lawrence River region, 491, 616, 618, 683
St. Patrick, 284
St. Peter, church of, 538
St. Petersburg, 610, 931. See also Leningrad; Petrograd
St. Sebastian Interceding for the Plague-Stricken (painting), 434–435 and illus.
Saint-Simon, Henri de, 750, 802
Saladin, 377
Salamis, 101
Salerno, university in, 380
Salian dynasty, 323
Salic Law of Franks, 250
Salisbury, Lord, 890
Sallust, 187
Salons (intellectual), in Paris, 668, 710
Salutati, Coluccio, 442
Salvation, 324, 510, 511, 513, 514, 519

Samaria, 52
Samnites, 155, 168
Samnite Wars, 171(illus.)
San Bernadino of Siena, 455
Sancho I (Navarre), 332
Sand, George (Amandine-Aurore Dupin), 745–746
San Francisco, conference in, 1061
Sanger, Margaret, 965
Sanitation, 790
Sans-culottes (France), 714
San Stefano, Treaty of, 829
San Vitale (church), 264–265 and illus.
Saône region, trade and, 298
Sappho of Lesbos, 92
Sarajevo, 1135
Saratoga, Battle of, 702
Sardinia, 412
Sargon (of Agade), 14, 15–16, 15(illus.), 57
Sargon II (Assyria), 45
Sartre, Jean Paul, 1075 and illus., 1076(box)
Sassanid dynasty, 211
Satellites, see Space exploration
Satellite territories, 1039–1040, 1121–1127
Satires (Juvenal), 209
Satrapies, 60
Saul, see Paul of Tarsus
Saul (Israelite king), 52
Savonarola, Girolamo, 412
Savoy, 815
Saxons, 247, 320–323
Saxony, 320–321, 326, 524–525, 576, 604, 605, 759. See also German Empire
Scaevola, Quintus Mucius, 187
Scandinavia: Carolingian Empire and, 296; in Middle Ages, 337; government of, 413–414; Protestantism and, 534; Napoleon and, 723; Great Depression and, 998–999; Hitler and, 1033; social welfare in, 1080. See also Denmark; Norway; Sweden
Scapegoat, The (Hunt), 870
Scapegoats, Christians as, 219
Scene of Shipwreck, see Raft of the "Medusa"
Schacht, Hjalmar, 998, 1014
Schiele, Egon, 886
Schism, see Great Schism
Schleicher, Kurt von, 1007
Schleswig-Holstein, 820
Schlieffen Plan, 921
Schliemann, Heinrich, 76–77
Scholars and scholarship, 133, 300, 339–341, 342(box), 379, 456–457. See also Humanists and humanism
"Scholars' Revolt," 891
Scholasticism, 355, 380–381, 438, 458–459
Scholastics, 511
Schön, Erhard, 542–543 and illus.
School of Athens (Raphael), 452
Schools, 294–295, 339–341, 370, 379, 857. See also Education; Higher education; Universities
Schools of thought, 628. See also specific schools of thought
Schuman Plan, 1094
Schwarzenberg, Felix von, 767
Science, 626–642; Mesopotamian, 19–21; in Neo-Babylonian empire, 48; Ionians and,

Science *(cont.)*, 94; nature and, 106; Aristotle and, 109; Hellenistic, 138–139; study of, 380; Scientific Revolution and, 625–652; society and, 642–652; women and, 643–644; evolutionary theory and, 864–865, 866(box); physics, chemistry, medicine, and, 865–867; social, 867–868; Einstein and, 884; space exploration and, 1094. *See also* Industry and industrialization; Technology; specific sciences
Scientific professionalism, 642–644
Scientific rationalism, 476
Scientific Revolution, *see* Science
Scientific societies, 643–644
Scipio Aemilianus, 178
Scipio Africanus, Publius Cornelius, 173
Scotland, 247, 284, 335, 671, 673–674, 673(illus.); Normans and, 336; England and, 364, 366, 410, 673–674; rebellion in, 570, 571; Enlightenment in, 668; poetry of, 671; clans in, 689. *See also* Mary (Queen of Scots)
Scott, Walter, 744
Scott, William Bell, 774(illus.)
Scribes, 304
Script, 294, 304–305. *See also* Manuscript book; Writing
Scriptures, learning and, 380–381
Sculpture: Neolithic and Copper Age, 9–10 and *illus.*; Akkadian, 15(illus.); Mesopotamian, 21; Egyptian, 31; human body in, 92; in classical Greece, 106; of Gandharan school, 135(illus.); Augustan, 201; Antonine, 210; in Renaissance, 450, 451. *See also* Art(s); Chartres cathedral
"Sea Beggars," 557
Seafarers, 82. *See also* Phoenicians; Sea Peoples
Sea Peoples, 37, 48, 52, 69
Secondary education, 863
Second Balkan War, 919
Second Battle of the Marne, 940
Second Crusade, 377
Second Estate (nobles), 704
Second front (World War II), 1048, 1050–1051
Second Great Northern War, 611
Second Industrial Revolution, 846–847
Second International, 882, 918
Second Isaiah, 43, 56
Second Punic War, 173
Second Reform Bill (Britain), 834, 863
Second serfdom, 422
Second Sex, The (Beauvoir), 1083(box)
Second World War, *see* World War II
Secret police, 760, 979(illus.), 1007, 1010–1011, 1098
Sectionalism (United States), 829
Secularization, 525, 679–680, 1117–1118
Security Council (UN), 1066
Seleucia, Mesopotamia, 120
Seleucids, 124, 126, 127, 128, 132–133, 141(box), 175
Seleucus, 132
Self-determination, 701, 942, 945
Self-Help (Smiles), 797
Self-rule, 827. *See also* Independence and independence movements

Selim (Ottoman emperor), 427
Selim III (Ottoman emperor), 761
Selkirk, Lord, 700
Semitic languages, 16, 34, 44, 60
Senate (France), 837
Senate (Rome), 163, 164, 183, 184, 197
Senators (Rome), 157, 231, 237
Seneca the Elder, 209
Seneca the Younger, 209
Sennacherib (Assyria), 45
Separation of powers, 672
Septimius Severus, 210–211
Serapis, cult of, 145
Serbs and Serbia, 338, 425, 761, 828–829, 906, 911; revolt by, 761; independence of, Serbs and Serbia *(cont.)*, 829; World War I and, 919; Bosnia war and, 1132, 1134(map), 1135–1136
Sereny, Gitta, 1070, 1071
Serfs and serfdom, 422, 605, 680, 693 and *box*, 708, 760–761, 838
Sermon on the Mount, 216
Servan-Schreiber, Jean-Jacques, 1141–1142, 1143(box)
Servants, 851–852, 855
Servetus, Michael, 520
Servilia, 184
Servius Tullius, 158
Settlements, Germanic, 245
Seven Years' War, 682, 686, 687, 701
Severan dynasty, 210–211
Sewage systems, 861
Sex and sexuality, 92, 139, 553, 745–746, 965. *See also* Gender
Sextus Empiricus, 144
Sextus Tarquinius, 158, 159(box)
Seymour, Edward, 529
Sforza family, 411–412, 455; Ludovico, 412
Shaftsbury, Lord (Anthony Ashley Cooper), 649
Shakespeare, William, 580
Shapur I (Persia), 212(box)
Sheep, in Spain, 428
Shelley, Percy Bysshe, 745
Shelter, of ancient humans, 6
Sheriffs, in England, 365
Sherman, John, 831
Shi'a (Party of Ali), 273
Shi'ite Muslims, 275
Ships and shipping, 476–477, 847; Phoenician trade and, 48; of Carthage, 172; trade and, 298; lumber industry and, 311; in Middle Ages, 371; of Dutch, 611; in Russia, 611. *See also* Navigation; Navy; Trade
Shires, 320
Short Parliament, 570–571
Shrines, 317, 506–507, 511
Siam (Thailand), 889, 949
Sicily, 82, 103, 172, 276, 282, 297, 356–359, 412
Sicily and Naples, king of, 368
Sidereus Nuncius, see Starry Messenger, The
Sidney, Henry, 568
Sieges, in Netherlands, 558
Siemens, William, 846
Siemens electrical company, 993 and *illus.*
Siena, 370, 454–455

Siete Partidas (Alfonso X), 367
Sieyès, Joseph Emmanuel (Abbé), 704
Sigismund (Holy Roman emperor), 400
Sigismund II (Poland-Lithuania), 607
Sigismund Vasa (Sweden and Poland), 608
Signatures (book segments), 586–587
Silesia, 682
Silk, 298, 967
Silone, Ignazio, 1077
Silver, 498, 499
"Silver Age," in Roman Empire, 209
Simons, Menno, 521
Sin: original, 259; plague and, 416; Luther on, 513
Sino-Soviet split, 1102
Sisley, Alfred, 870
Sistine Chapel, 453, 454(illus.), 466–468 and *illus.*
Six Acts (Britain), 753
Six Books of the Republic, The (Bodin), 581
Sixth Crusade, 378
Sixtus IV (Pope), 402, 430, 467, 490
Skeptic philosophy, 134, 142, 144
Skinheads, 1140
Slaves and slavery: in Sumer, 14; in Sparta, 86–87; in Athens, 100; in Hellenistic world, 128; technology and, 139; in Rome, 176, 178, 241; social status of, 301; Portugal and, 482; Spain and, 498; African, 499, 501; Indian, 500; France and, 718, 730; British abolition of, 755–756 and *box*; in United States, 830–831, 832. *See also* Labor; Slave trade
Slave trade, 48, 498, 616, 683–685, 684(map), 685(box), 772–773 and *illus. See also* Slaves and slavery
Slavic lands and peoples, 276, 296–297, 320, 337–339, 911, 1040. *See also* Czechoslovakia; Poland; Russia; Yugoslavia
Slovak peoples and language, 337, 1132
Slovenia, 338
Slums, 789–791, 790(box), 860
Sluter, Claus, 461
Small Catechism (Luther), 539
Smallpox, 494, 501, 867
Smelting, 780
Smiles, Samuel, 796–797
Smith, Adam, 663–664, 747, 748(box), 797, 998
Smith, John, 617(box)
Smoot-Hawley Tariff Act (U.S.), 997
Snowstorm, Steamboat off a Harbour's Mouth (Turner), 743, 745(illus.)
Sobieski, Jan, 604, 607
Social classes, *see* Classes
Social Contract, The (Rousseau), 665–666, 667(box)
Social criticism, 872–874
Social Darwinism, 797, 890, 1009
Social Democratic Party (Germany), 881, 937, 940, 1084
Social imperialists, 887
Socialism, 749–751, 880–882, 1145; Marxism and, 802–804; worker welfare and, 862; World War I and, 918; Bolshevism and, 934; in Germany, 940, 970, 974; after World War I, 942; in Italy, 981–982, 1086;

Socialism (cont.), in Soviet Union, 1002(illus.); popular fronts and, 1015, 1018–1020; French intellectuals and, 1105; in Western Europe, 1107. See also Communism; Internationals; Marx, Karl; Marxism

"Socialism in one country" (Soviet Union), 1000

Socialist party (France), 882

Socialist party (Germany), 904, 905. See also Social Democratic Party (Germany); Socialism

Socialist party (Russia), 907–908, 907(box)

Socialist Revolutionary party, 932, 934

Social responsibility, 863

Social security system, 862

Social sciences, 867–868

Social Statics (Spencer), 797

Social status, see Classes; Elites

Social War, in Rome, 182

Social welfare, 862–863, 900, 998–999, 1080–1082, 1106, 1119–1120

Society: ancient, 2(illus.), 3–4; Upper Paleolithic, 5, 7; in Mesopotamia, 13–14; Greek, 71–72, 81–91; phalanx and, 83–85; of Sparta, 86; Athenian, 90; Hellenistic, 139–142; Roman, 158, 160, 163–166, 175–176, 197–200, 208–209, 240–243; church and state in, 291, 315–316; in Middle Ages, 299–302, 311–320, 355, 395–396; townspeople and Jews in, 318–320; economic life and, 370–372; in England, 403; in Russia, 414; in Middle Ages, 414–423; in Renaissance courts, 462–468; in Americas, 492–494; state and, 548–553; culture and, 578–584; end of traditional, 619–620; table manners and, 622–623; science and, 634–638, 642–652; mechanistic world order and, 649–652; in Enlightenment, 671–680; agriculture and, 689; industrial growth and, 689–690, 787–796; of U.S., 832; in Russia, 838–840; changing conditions in, 849–857, 929; state welfare and, 862–863; educational and cultural opportunities, 863–864; anthropological view of, 868; immigration and, 897; between world wars, 963–969, 985–988, 989(illus.); in democracies, 968–969; in Germany, 969–970, 1009–1013; in Soviet Union, 980, 1102; Great Depression and, 998–1000; social movements in, 1106; postindustrial, 1115–1117, 1116(box); affluence and secularization in, 1117–1118; gender issues and, 1118–1119; government's role in, 1119–1120. See also Classes; Mass society; Social welfare

Society of Jesus, see Jesuits

Socioeconomic change, 929

Sociology, study of, 868

Socrates, 105, 106–107, 108(box)

Socratic method, 107

Soldiers, 44, 83–85, 84(illus.), 126–127, 168–169 and illus., 237, 919(illus.). See also Casualties; specific wars

Solferino, Battle at, 815, 817(map)

Solidarism, 862

Solidarity movement (Poland), 1124–1127, 1125(illus.)

Solomon (Israelite king), 50, 52, 487

Solomon Islands, 1049

Solon, 90–91

Solzhenitsyn, Alexander, 1077

Somalia, 29

Some Reflections on Marriage (Astell), 666(box)

Somme River, Battle at, 924–925

Song of Roland, 343, 385

Sophists, 106–107

Sophocles, 105, 112

Sorbonne (Paris), 532

Sorrows of Young Werther (Goethe), 743

South (less developed countries), 1114, 1139

South (U.S.), 829–831

South America, 490, 491, 685

Southeast Asia, 1089–1090

Southern Hemisphere, 483

Southern Rhodesia, 1091

Southern Slavs, 338

South Vietnam, see Vietnam

Sovereignty, 581–582, 828–829, 831

Soviet bloc, Helsinki Accords and, 1103–1104

Soviets (councils), 932

Soviet Union, 975–980, 979(illus.); Stalin and Stalinism in, 980, 996, 1000–1005; opposition in, 1003–1005; ideology of, 1012(illus.); Czechoslovakia treaty and, 1022; Nazi-Soviet Pact and, 1023–1024; World War II and, 1032, 1033, 1037–1046; Japan and, 1046–1047; Britain, U.S., and, 1048; westward advance of, 1051; and Yalta, 1052–1055, 1053(illus.); victory in Europe, 1056(illus.); post-war Germany and, 1057, 1062; buffer zone and, 1061; Iron Curtain and, 1062–1063; Cold War and, 1065(box); Khrushchev and, 1072(illus.), 1073–1074; forced-labor camps in, 1077; NATO and, 1087; communist bloc and, 1097–1104, 1121–1127; satellite states of, 1122–1127; Gorbachev and, 1128–1129; dissolution of, 1129. See also Cold War; Commonwealth of Independent States; Russia; specific leaders

Space exploration, 1094

Spain: Vandals in, 247; Justinian and, 251; Islam and, 273, 274–275; as Christian country, 281–282; Visigoths in, 281–282; Muslim-Christian conflict in, 282; Jews in, 320, 423, 429–430 and illus.; Reconquista in, 332, 333(map); government and monarchy in, 366–367; woolen trade in, 420; economy in, 427–428; union of Aragon and Castile in, 427–431; exploration by, 475, 476; New World and, 494–500; Holy Roman Empire and, 522; trade of, 553–554; Netherlands and, 553–559; empire and power of, 553–561, 555(map); Habsburgs in, 554(map), 597; Thirty Years' War and, 575–576; France and, 591, 595, 597; colonies and, 616, 683, 685, 730; France and, 723; restoration and reform in, 757–758; industrialization and, 787; Hohenzollerns and, 824; North American territories and, 829; democracy to civil war in, 1015–1018, 1016(map);

minorities in, 1140. See also Spanish civil war; specific rulers

Spanish America, 499, 730. See also Central America; Latin America; North America

Spanish Armada, 559–560, 568

Spanish civil war, 994(illus.), 995, 996, 1015–1018, 1016(map), 1020

Spanish Empire, 396, 423–431, 553–561, 758

"Spanish Fury," 558

Spanish Inquisition, 402, 430–431

Spanish Netherlands, 595, 597, 603. See also Netherlands

Sparta, 85–89, 87(illus.), 88(box), 100; Hellenic League and, 101; Peloponnesian War and, 103, 104(map); empire of, 103–104; religion in, 106; Macedon and, 121; in Hellenistic world, 129; revolution in, 129

Speeches, see Rhetoric

Speer, Albert, 1055

Spencer, Herbert, 797

Spengler, Oswald, 986

Spheres of influence, 943, 1032, 1052

Sphinx, 24

Spice Islands (Moluccas), 479, 485

Spice trade, 485–486, 612

Spinning jenny, 779

Spinoza, Baruch, 652

Spirit of the Laws, The (Montesquieu), 663

Spiritual Exercises (Loyola), 536, 537(box)

Sputnik I, 1094

Spy planes, 1074

SS (Schutzstaffel), 1007, 1040, 1042–1043

Stadholder, 613

Stagflation, 1105

Stakhanovism, 1002

Stalin, Joseph, 979(illus.), 980, 1051, 1052–1055, 1053(illus.), 1098, 1099, 1100(box). See also Stalinism

Stalingrad, Battle at, 1044, 1045(box)

Stalinism, 996, 1000–1005, 1003(box)

Standard of living, 812, 851

Stangl, Franz, 1070

Stanley, Henry, 887

Starry Messenger, The (Galileo), 632

State (nation): Plato on, 109; church and, 255, 291, 315–316, 323–326; in Europe, 336(map); society and, 548–553; science and, 645–646; Hobbes on, 649; Locke on, 649–651; Rousseau on, 665–666; warfare in, 680–687; Hegel on, 743; role in society, 851. See also Church and state; Government; Nation; specific states and nations

Status, see Classes; Elites

Statute in Favor of the Princes, 357

Statute of Laborers (England), 419

Staufen dynasty, 355, 357, 359

Steam engine, 779, 780, 781 and illus., 782

Steamships, 847

Steel industry, 846

Stephen of Blois (England), 332

Stern, Daniel (pen name), 791

Stöcker, Adolf, 883

Stoic philosophy, 128, 142–143, 143(box), 178, 187

Stolypin, Peter, 909

Stone Breakers, The (Courbet), 871(illus.)

Stone engravings, 6–7

Stonehenge, 9
Storing (Norway), 413
Story of Sinuhe, The, 31, 32(box)
Strafford, earl of (Thomas Wentworth), 571
Strait of Magellan, 490
Strategic concerns, 733, 889. *See also* Defense
Stravinsky, Igor, 986, 1077
Stresa, meeting at, 1013–1014
Stresa Front, 1014
Stresemann, Gustav, 971–973, 972(illus.)
Strikes (labor), 691, 799, 800, 903, 906, 926, 1017, 1120. *See also* Labor; Labor unions; Workers
Structuralism, 1092–1093
Stuart family, 674
Subinfeudation, 330
Submarines, 926, 1034
Sub-Saharan Africa, independence movements in, 1090–1092
Suburbs, 852, 861–862
Succession, 521(illus.), 563(illus.)
Sudan, 889, 891
Sudetenland, 1021, 1023, 1060
Suez Canal, 847, 849(illus.), 889, 1089
Suffrage, 749, 901(illus.); in France, 719, 751, 752, 764; in Britain, 753, 755, 899; in German states, 768; in Italy, 819; in U.S., 832 and *illus.*; for women, 834, 900, 965; in France, 835. *See also* Elections; Voting and voting rights; Women's suffrage
Sugar industry, 482, 499, 616, 730
Suger, Abbot, 381–383
Sukarno, Achmed, 1092
Suleiman (Ottoman Turks), 522–523
Sulla (Lucius Cornelius Sulla Felix), 183
Sully, duke of, *see* Béthune, Maximilien de
Sumer and Sumerians, 3, 12–16. *See also* Sargon
Summa Contra Gentiles (Thomas Aquinas), 381
Summa Theologiae (Thomas Aquinas), 381
Sunna, 271, 275
Sunni Muslims, 275
Sunspots, 632
Sun Yixien (Sun Yat-sen), 960, 961(box)
Supercontinent, 491
"Superman," Nietzsche and, 884
Superpowers, 1092
Suppliant Women, The, 98(box)
Supply and demand, 747
Supranational empires, 824–829
Supranational issues, 1139–1140
Suras, 270, 272(box)
Surgery, 867
Suriname, *see* Guiana
Surrealism, 987
Survival of the fittest, 797
Susa palace, 62–63
Suttee, 894
Sutton Hoo, 284, 285(illus.)
Suzdal, 368
Swabia, 320, 323, 326, 355
Swastika, 1010. *See also* Nazis and Nazism
Sweden, 337, 413, 605, 675–676; Russia and, 368–369; Reformation and, 534; Thirty Years' War and, 576; relationship of Poland with, 607; Second Great Northern War and, 611; Dutch and, 614–615; Napoleon and, 723; Congress of Vienna and, 741;

social welfare in, 1080, 1081(illus.), 1106. *See also* Scandinavia
Swein (Denmark), 329, 330
Swing, The (Fragonard), 670(illus.)
Swiss Confederation, 413
Switzerland, 413
Sykes-Picot Agreement, 943
Syllabary, 64–65, 68
Syllabus of Errors (Pius IX), 869
Symbolism (political), 729, 734–735 and *illus.*, 734(illus.), 1010
Symbolists, 885
Symeon (Bulgar Khan), 338
Synagogues, 56
Syncretism, 26–27
Syndicalism, 882
Synod of Whitby, 285
Syphilis, 501
Syracuse, 108, 138
Syria, 35(map), 132, 762, 943; Ebla in, 33; Hurrians in, 33; city-states of, 33–34; Ugarit and, 34; international system and, 36–37; Rome, Persia, and, 212(box); Islam and, 273
Syro-Palestinian city-states, 4

Table manners, 622–623
Tacitus, 197, 198(box), 209–210
Tahiti, 895
Taínos, 488–489
Taiwan, 1066
Talleyrand, Charles, 741
Tanks, 921, 1033
Tannenberg Forest, Battle at, 414
Tanzimat reform movement, 827
Tariffs, 887, 1094
Tarquinius Superbus, 158
Tatars, 680
Tatlin, Vladimir, 977(illus.)
Taurus Mountains, 7
Taxation: in Roman Empire, 231, 237; in Germanic kingdoms, 250; in Byzantine Empire, 277; Danegeld as, 320; of church, 386–387; common people and, 551; of Netherlands, 555; Parliament and, 568; in England, 570; revolts against, 620; in France, 672; in U.S., 831; on imports, 997. *See also* Economy
Taylor, Frederick W., 965
Taylor, Harriet, 749
Teachers and teaching, 380, 851, 854, 857. *See also* Education; Schools
Technocracy, 750
Technology, 5; Stonehenge and, 9; in Uruk Period, 13; of Hyksos, 28; Hellenistic, 139; agriculture and, 308–310; printing and, 456; navigation and, 476–477; military, 557–558; state and, 645–646; mechanization and, 690; Saint-Simonism and, 750; rural society and, 856–857, 856(illus.); aircraft bombing and, 927; after World War I, 964; *Sputnik I* and, 1094; computer and, 1115–1116; environment and, 1144. *See also* Crystal Palace exhibition; Industry and industrialization; Science
Teheran meeting, 1051
Telegraph, 848–849
Teleological view, 109–110

Telephone, 848, 849
Telepinu (Hittite king), 35
Telescope, 630, 632
Tell, William, 413
Tell Mardikh, *see* Ebla
Temples: in Mesopotamia, 11; of Sumer, 14; Egyptian, 31; in Jerusalem, 52, 53 and *illus.*, 55, 146, 147; in Greece, 83, 92–93; Parthenon, 105(illus.); in Hellenistic world, 127; in Rome, 177(illus.)
Tenancies, 299
Ten Commandments, 52
Ten Lost Tribes of Israel, 46–47
Tennis Court Oath, 705 and *illus.*
Tenochtitlán, 492–493, 492(illus.)
Terence (Publius Terentius Afer), 178
Teresa of Avila, 535 and *illus.*, 536
Territoriality, 8
Terror: in Soviet Union, 1003–1005
Terror, the (France), 715–719, 717(box), 735
Terrorism, 1106, 1141
Terrorist societies, 882
Testament of Youth (Brittain), 951
Tetrarchy, 229, 230(illus.)
Teutonic knights, 413, 525
Texas, 829
Textbooks, 294
Textile industry, 793–794 and *box. See also* Cotton and cotton industry; Industry and industrialization
Texts, Christian, 458
Thailand, *see* Siam
Thales, 94
Thasos, 103
Thatcher, Margaret, 1106, 1119–1120, 1119(illus.), 1146(box)
Theater, 580–581. *See also* Drama
Thebes, 87, 103
Theists, 663
Themes (military districts), 276–277
Themistocles, 100
Theocritus, 137
Theodora, 251, 252(illus.), 264
Theodore (archbishop of Canterbury), 285
Theodoric (Ostrogoth), 248; mausoleum of, 248(illus.)
Theodoric I (Visigoth), 245
Theodosian code, 251
Theodosius I, 236, 245
Theodosius II, 236, 250–251
Theodulf, 295
Theogony (Hesiod), 35, 69–70
Theology: Trinitarian, 237, 239; Christology and, 239; Christian belief and, 258; of Augustine, 258–260; Islam and, 275; under Charlemagne, 295; humanism vs. scholasticism and, 459; of Luther, 510–511, 513–514; in late medieval period, 511–512; Zwingli and, 517; of Calvin, 519–520; in England, 531; in France, 532; of Catholic reformation, 535–536; separation of Catholic and Protestant, 538; anxiety and, 986. *See also* Heresy; Humanists and humanism; Reformation; Religion; Renaissance; specific religions
Theophrastus, 135
Thera, 66
Theresienstadt, 1043

Thermidorian Reaction, 719–720
Thermodynamics, 865
Thermonuclear fission, 1057
Thermopylae, 101
Thespian (term), 111
Thiers, Adolphe, 836
Third Crusade, 365, 377
Third Dynasty (Egypt), 23
Third Estate (commoners), 704
Third Intermediate Period (Egypt), 47
Third (Communist) International, 975, 977(illus.). *See also* Comintern
Third Punic War, 175
Third Reich (Germany), 969, 1060. *See also* Germany; Hitler, Adolf
Third Republic (France), 836–837, 900–903, 1020
Third World, 1092. *See also* Non-Western world
Thirteenth Sibylline Oracle, 212(box)
Thirty Years' War, 561, 571, 573–578, 575(map), 595, 603, 607
Thomas à Kempis, 512
Thomas Aquinas, 355, 381, 382(box)
Thomas-Gilchrist method, 846
Thrace, 120
Thraysbulus of Miletus, 85
Three Emperors' League, 909
Three-field system, 310
Thresher, 856(illus.), 857
Thucydides, 82, 113
Thule Society, 1006
Thutmose III (Egyptian king), 29, 30
Tiananmen Square, 1127
Tiberius, *see* Gracchus family
Tiberius (Augustus' successor), 202, 203
Tiglath-pileser III (Assyria), 45
Tigris River valley region, 4, 10. *See also* Mesopotamia
Tilsit, Treaty of, 723
Timbuktu, 477
Time of Troubles (Russia), 609
Timon (philosopher), 136
Tito (Josip Broz), 1044, 1098
Titus (Rome), 203, 204
Tobacco industry, 616, 683
Tocqueville, Alexis de, 765, 831–832
Tokyo, bombing of, 1058
Toledo, Spain, 281, 332
Toleration, *see* Religious toleration
Tolstoy, Leo, 872
Tombs, 9, 24, 31
Tools, 7, 856–857
Torah, 50, 56, 217–219
Tordesillas, Treaty of, 490
Tories (England), 674
Toscanelli, Paolo, 480, 487
Totalitarianism, 996, 1025–1026
Total war, World War I as, 926–931
Toulouse, 245
Tourism, 852
Toussaint-Louverture, François Dominique, 730
Trade: in Mesopotamia, 13; of Sumer, 13–14; of Ugarit, 34; Phoenicians and, 48–50; Mycenaean, 68–69; ancient Greek, 81–82; Hellenistic, 127–128; of Carthage, 172; Arab, 268–269; in Middle Ages, 298–299,

355, 371, 417–419; Scandinavians and, 337; in Russia, 338; cross-Channel, 363; woolen, 420; beyond Christendom, 477–479; in gold, 482; with Asia, 482–483; by Da Gama, 483; Spain and, 553–554; in France, 591; in Baltic region, 605; overseas, 611–620; Netherlands and, 613–615; Atlantic region and, 616–619, 682–685; society and, 619–620; triangle trade, 683–685, 684(map); industry and, 690, 778; Napoleon and, 725; British, 732, 783; French-English, 836; new imperialism and, 887; Great Depression and, 997–998; Common Market and, 1094. *See also* Commerce
Trade routes, 371, 490–491. *See also* Caravans and caravan routes
Trade Union Congress, 800
Trade unions, 800, 1124–1127. *See also* Labor unions
Trading firms, 485–486
Trafalgar, Battle at, 723, 725, 730, 732(illus.)
Tragedy, 111–112
Trajan, 204
Transhumance, 41
Transportation, 310, 777(box), 778, 847–849, 855, 861 and *illus. See also* Industry and industrialization; specific forms of transportation
Transylvania, 533
Trasformismo, 819
Travel, 371, 477–478, 477(illus.), 478–479, 479(box)
Travels (Polo), 477(illus.)
Travels of Sir John Mandeville, 478
Treaties: Ebla-Ashur, 33; from international system, 36–37; Roman-Visigoth, 245; after Thirty Years' War, 577–578; Treaties *(cont.):* French-English trade, 836; of Versailles, 943; between France and Czechoslovakia, 1022; Nazi-Soviet Pact and, 1023–1024; by West Germany, 1084–1085. *See also* Peace of Constance; specific treaties
Treblinka, 1070
Trench warfare, 921, 922, 923(illus.), 924(box)
Trent, *see* Council of Trent
Trials, after World War II, 1060
Triangle trade, 683–685, 684(map)
Tribal assembly, 164, 165
Tribes, 243–244, 268. *See also* Ancient world; Germanic peoples
Tribonian, 251
Tribunes (Rome), 165–166. *See also* Gracchus family
Trinitarian theology, 237, 239, 276
Trinity, 258
Trinity (Masaccio), 452
Triple Alliance, 909
Triple Entente, 909, 919, 935–939, 980
Tristan, Flora, 750
Tristes Tropiques (Lévi-Strauss), 1092
Triumph of the Will (movie), 1028–1029 and *illus.*, 1028(illus.)
Trojan War, 70, 73, 76–77
Trotsky, Leon, 934, 979 and *illus.*, 980, 1003
Troubadours, 385

Troy, 70, 76–77, 76(illus.), 77(illus.). *See also* Trojan War
Troyes, Treaty of, 407, 409
Truman, Harry, 1056, 1058
Truman Doctrine, 1063
Truths, natural and revealed, 381
Tsars (Russia), 414, 608. *See also* specific rulers
Tudor family, 409; Henry VIII, 527–529; Mary I, 528. *See also* Elizabeth I (England); Henry VII (England)
Tuileries Palace, 711, 714(illus.), 715
Tunisia, 889, 1090
Turkey, 7, 522–523, 943. *See also* Ottoman Turks; Turks
Turks, 274, 345, 423–427, 427, 604, 762, 905–906. *See also* Ottoman Empire; Young Turks
Turner, Joseph, 743, 745(illus.)
Tuscany, 412
Tutankhamon (Tutankhaton, Egypt), 27(illus.), 30
Twelve Tables, 161, 166
Twenties, culture in, 957–959
Two-party system, 1107
Two Treatises on Government (Locke), 649
Tyche, cult of, 144
Tyche of Antioch, 144
Tyler, Wat, 423
Tylor, Edward, 868
Typhoid fever, 791
Tyranny, 85, 91
Tyrants, 25–26, 85, 410–411
Tyre, 49
Tyrone, lord of (Hugh O'Neill), 568
Tyrrhenian Sea, 155
Tyrtaeus, 84

Ucello, Paolo, 436(illus.), 437
Ugarit (Ras Shamra), 33, 34, 35(map), 48
Ukraine, 604, 607, 609, 939, 975, 1129
Ulama, 275
Ulbricht, Walter, 1098, 1101
Ulfilas, 237
Ulster (Ireland), 899. *See also* Ireland
Ultra-royalist ideology, 742
Umar, 272–273
Umayyads, 273, 274
Umberto I (Italy), 903
Umma, 273
Unalienable rights, 749
Unam sanctam (Boniface), 388, 401
Unemployment, 968, 997(illus.), 998, 1106, 1115, 1120, 1145. *See also* Economy; Employment
Unification, of Italy, 814–819, 817(map), 819–824
Union, *see* North (U.S.)
Union of Kalmar, 413, 534
Union of Soviet Socialist Republics (U.S.S.R.), *see* Soviet Union
Union of Utrecht, 558
Unions, *see* Labor unions
United Kingdom, *see* England (Britain)
United Nations (UN), 1053, 1061, 1066, 1085
United Nations Monetary and Financial Conference, 1061

United Provinces, 558–559, 561
United States, 943; Constitution of, 702;
Spanish Latin American colonies and,
758; territorial expansion of, 829–830 and
map; as world power, 829–833; slavery
in, 830–831; Civil War and, 831; democracy in, 831–833; immigration to, 897;
World War I and, 925, 939–940; League of
Nations and, 949; Great Depression and,
998; World War II and, 1046, 1048–1050,
1059; Japan and, 1047, 1048; and Yalta,
1052–1055, 1053(illus.); intellectual thought
and culture in, 1077–1079; Vietnam and,
1090; Cuban missile crisis and, 1102;
Americanization and, 1141–1144. *See also*
American Revolution; Cold War; Mass
culture
United States Constitution, 700
Universal Church, *see* Catholicism and
Catholic church
Universe, 94, 626–628, 636–637. *See also* As-
tronomy; World-view
Universities, 370, 379–380, 458, 503, 854,
1117–1118. *See also* Higher education
Upper Paleolithic era, 5–7
Uppsala, university at, 458
Uprisings, *see* Revolts
Ur, 2(illus.), 14, 16
Urban II (Pope), 329, 345, 346
Urban VI (Pope), 398
Urban VIII (Pope), 633
Urban society, 788–791; Greek, 82–83,
85; Hellenistic, 140–141; in Roman
Empire, 199; in Middle Ages, 318–320,
355; economic life and, 370–371,
548–549; protests in, 551–552; growth
of, 689; city planning, renovation, and,
857–859, 860(box). *See also* Cities and
towns; Industry and industrialization;
Society
Urkesh, 34
Ur-Nammu, 16
Uru-inim-gina of Lagash, 14
Uruk, 14, 18(illus.)
Uruk Period, 13
U.S.S.R. (Union of Soviet Socialist Republics),
see Soviet Union
Ustashe, 1044
Usury, 371
Uthman, 272, 273
Utjest, duke of, 850
Utopia (More), 459, 749
Utopias, 750
Utrecht: Union of, 558; Peace of, 597, 603
U-2 spy plane, 1074

Vaccination, 867
Vacuum, Boyle on, 638–639
Valencia, 367
Valens (Rome), 236
Valentinian, 236, 237, 243, 250
Valentinian III, 236, 247
Valerian, 211
Valla, Lorenzo, 446, 460
Valois family, 556, 563(illus.)
Van Artevelde, James, 422
Vandals, 247
Van de Velde, Theodore Hendrik, 965

Van Eyck, Jan, 460(illus.), 461
Vasa, Gustav, 534
Vasa family (Sweden), 608
Vasari, Giorgio, 437, 450
Vassals, 292, 301, 312–313, 320, 328, 330,
332, 355–356, 361, 362
Vassy, Protestants killed at, 562
Västerås Ordinances, 534
Vatican, 446, 452, 453, 454(illus.), 466–468
and *illus.,* 538, 819, 985
Vega, Lope de, 580
Vehicles, 310
Venetia, 818, 825
Venice, 334, 377, 411, 412, 478–479
Verdun: Treaty of, 290(map), 296, 320; Bat-
tle at, 923
Vernacular, 308, 342–343, 384–386, 439–440
Verne, Jules, 847
Verres, Gaius, 175
Versailles, 694, 695, 708–709 and *box,*
708(illus.), 960–963; Treaty of (1919), 943
Versailles palace, 593
Vesalius, 641
Vespasian (Rome), 203–204
Vespucci, Amerigo, 490
Vestal Virgins, 162
Vesuvius, Pompeii and, 225
Vezelay, 306(illus.)
Vichy, 852, 1033–1034, 1043
Victor Emmanuel II (Italy), 767, 817
Victor Emmanuel III (Italy), 1051
Victoria (England) and Victorian Age, 791,
834, 842–843, 852, 876–877, 888(illus.),
894(box).
Vienna, 458, 522, 767, 883
Vietnam, 889, 1089–1090
Vikings, 287, 297, 320, 337
Villages, 7, 9, 318
Villani, Filippo, 450
Villani, Giovanni, 439
Vindication of the Rights of Woman, A (Woll-
stonecraft), 665
Violence, 273, 378–379, 407, 550–552, 620,
900, 902–904, 908, 909, 973, 981. *See also*
Wars and warfare
Virgil, 153, 200–201, 386
Virginia, 616, 617(box)
Virginia Company, 616
Virgin Mary, 511
Virgin of Guadalupe, shrine of (Mexico),
506–507
Virtuous life, 448–449
Visconti family, 411–412, 442
Visigoths, 236, 237, 244, 245, 247, 250, 259,
281–282
Vladimir (Russia), 338
Vladimir-Suzdal, 338
Voice of Women, The (France), 764
Volcanic eruptions, 66
Volcanoes, *see* Vesuvius
Volksgemeinschaft (racial community), 1009
Voltaire (François-Marie Arouet), 658(illus.),
659, 660–663
Volunteer Movement (Ireland), 700
Volunteers, 863
Voting and voting rights, 86, 170, 719, 755,
764–765, 831, 832 and *illus.,* 834, 965. *See
also* Suffrage; Women's suffrage

Voyages, *see* Exploration; Sailors and sail-
ing; Ships and shipping
V-2 rocket bombs, 1057
Vulgate Bible, 258, 446, 458, 460, 536
Vytautus (Lithuania), 414

Wage system, 747, 795, 808–809 and *illus.*
See also Earnings; Industry and
industrialization
Wagram, Battle of, 723
Waiting for Godot (Beckett), 1075
Wake Island, 1048
Waldensians, 372
Waldo, 372
Waldseemüller, Martin, 490
Wales, 284, 319(box), 335, 336, 364, 366
Walesa, Lech, 1124–1127, 1125(illus.),
1131
Walhalla (Bavaria), 759
Wallachia, 762, 828
Walpole, Robert, 674
War and Peace (Tolstoy), 872
War communism, 978
War crimes, 1060
Warhol, Andy, 1110, 1111 and *illus.*
War of Austrian Succession, 673, 682
War of Spanish Succession, 597
Warriors, Aztec, 497(illus.)
Wars and warfare: Neolithic, 8–9; in
Sumerian city-states, 14–15; international
system and, 36–37; Assyrians and, 45–46
and *box;* Greece and, 84, 87–89; Persian,
100–101; Punic Wars, 172–175; Roman,
182–183, 244; jihad as, 273; Albigensian,
363; between England and Scotland, 366;
humanists and, 448; of Aztecs, 493–494;
religious, 547–548; Netherlands revolt
and, 556–558; Spanish Armada and,
559–560; religious upheavals, 561–565;
under Louis XIV, 594–597; during Enlightenment, 680–687; British-French,
686–687; France and Austria, 713–714; of
France, 715; Napoleonic, 721, 723–727;
for German unity, 820–824; of Ottoman
Empire, 829; imperialist conquests and,
891–892; trench warfare and, 921; total
war and, 926–931; Nazis and, 1012–1013;
in Bosnia, 1132, 1134(map), 1135–1136,
1135(illus.); ethnic, 1132, 1134(map). *See
also* Civil wars; Militarism; Navy; Revo-
lution(s); World War I; World War II;
specific wars
Warsaw, duchy of, 723
Warsaw Pact, 1096(map), 1098, 1099
Wars of Austrian Succession, 686
Wars of the Roses (England), 409
Washington, George, 702
Wassermann, Jakob, 986
Water, 225, 790, 795–796, 860–861
Water frame, 779
Waterloo, Battle of, 728
Water power, 781
Water pump, 781
Watt, James, 779, 781, 782, 783
Wazir, 274
Wealth, 129, 176, 190–191, 371, 499, 548–549,
792–793, 852. *See also* Classes (economic
and social); Merchants; Poverty

Wealth of Nations, see Inquiry into the Nature and Causes of the Wealth of Nations, An (Smith)

Weapons and weaponry, 8–9, 351, 681, 921, 923, 927, 1033. *See also* Atomic bomb; Bombs and bombing; Nuclear weapons

Wedgwood, Josiah, 782

Weimar Republic, 969–974, 986, 1006, 1007, 1083–1084

Weizmann, Chaim, 943

Welfare, *see* Social welfare

Wellington, duke of (Arthur Wellesley), 726

Weltpolitik, 905

Wentworth, Thomas (earl of Strafford), *see* Strafford, earl of

Wesley, John, 743

Wessex, 284, 287

West (U.S.), 832(illus.)

West, the, *see* Western world

West Africa, 1091

Western Asia, 7, 8(map), 298. *See also* Arabs and Arab world; Islam; Middle East

Western bloc, 1084

Western civilization, 1150–1151

Western Europe, 308, 869; economy and society in, 1079–1086; and world, 1086–1087. *See also* Central Europe; Cold War; Eastern Europe; Europe; Western world; specific countries

Western European Union (WEU), 1136

Western front (World War I), 922–923, 922(map), 940

Westernization, 891–896, 1151

Western Slavs, 337

Western world, 1114–1120; emergence of United States and, 829–833; non-Western world and, 961(box), 1112(illus.), 1113–1149; after World War II, 1063–1067; political alienation in, 1104–1107; debate over Western civilization, 1150–1151. *See also* Democracies (nations); Europe; Non-Western world; specific countries

West Frankish Kingdom, 296, 326, 327(map)

West Germany, 1062, 1079 and *illus.*, 1080, 1082–1085, 1107, 1117. *See also* Germany

West Indies, 488, 494, 495

Westphalia, 723; Peace of, 577, 603; Treaty of, 607

What Is the Third Estate? (Sieyès), 704

"What Is to Be Done?" (Lenin), 907(box)

Wheel, 13

Whigs (England), 674

"White Man's Burden" (Kipling), 890

White Mountain, Battle of, 575

White people, 832 and *illus.*, 890

Whites (Russia), 942, 975, 976(map)

Whitney, Eli, 780

Whore of Babylon (Dürer), 462

Why God Became Man (Anselm), 341

William I (Prussia, German Empire), 811, 819, 824, 904

William II (England), 331

William II (Germany), 904–905, 904(illus.), 939, 940

William IV (England), 842

William IX of Poitou, 385

William Frederick IV (Prussia), 759

William of Aquitaine, 313(box), 315

William of Malmesbury, 314

William of Nassau, *see* William of Orange (Netherlands)

William of Normandy ("the Conqueror"), 330

William of Ockham, 511

William of Orange (England), 596–597, 602–603, 615, 672. *See also* Orange family

William of Orange (Netherlands), 557

William of Rubruck, report on Mongols, 369(box)

Williamsburg, Virginia, gardens in, 694–695, 694(illus.)

Wilson, Woodrow, 879, 926, 936–937, 938(box), 943, 948, 949

Wind power, 781

Winds, 481(map), 483

Winkelman, Maria, 643

Winthrop, John, 503

Wisdom, 94

Wisdom literature, 19

Witch-hunts, 552–553

Wittelsbach family, 413

Wittenberg Castle church, 510, 514

Wollstonecraft, Mary, 665

Wolsey, Thomas, 402

Women: in ancient groups, 5; as Sumerian rulers, 14; Enkheduanna, 16; in Mesopotamia, 17; in *Epic of Gilgamesh*, 20(box); Egyptian, 28; Hatshepsut, 29; as queens, 34, 35; in Israelite culture, 56–57; in Homeric society, 73; in Sparta, 87 and *illus.*, 88(box); Sappho of Lesbos, 92; sexuality of, 92; in Athens, 99–100; Hellenistic, 139–142; economic power of, 141; in Rome, 160, 162, 178–180, 183–184, 190–191, 207, 241; education of, 185; Five Good Emperors and, 204; Christian, 219; Jewish, 219; learning and, 242; Deborah (Old Testament) and, 242(box); Melania and, 256; monasticism and, 256; Carolingian, 293(box); social status of, 301, 312; birthrate and, 308; noble, 314; in society, 318, 319; medieval guilds and, 370–371; Albigensian movement and, 373; religious communities of, 375–377; universities and, 380; plague and, 416; employment of, 420, 421 and *illus.*; status of, 420–421; writers, 440 and *illus.*; education of, 443–444, 445(box); as Renaissance portraitists, 456; in Gonzaga court, 464; in late medieval religious life, 511–512; convents and, 540; economic change and, 549; as healers, 550(box); armies and, 551; literature of, 578; as preachers, 600(illus.); in sciences, 643–644 and *illus.*; equality of, 665; march on Versailles by, 708–709 and *box*, 708(illus.); in France, 712, 718, 719, 722, 764, 765(illus.); political symbolism and, 734–735 and *illus.*, 734(illus.); romantic movement and, 745–746; socialism and, 750; as workers, 792, 795; family and, 793; labor unions and, 802; wages of, 808; as British monarchs, 842–843; in professions, 851; roles of, 852–853

and *box*, 929 and *illus.*; education and careers of, 854; as reformers, 854 and *illus.*; working-class servants, 855–856; volunteer charity work of, 863; colonies and, 891, 892(box); domestic mobilization and, 928(box); voting rights of, 965; in arts, 987; in literature, 987, 988(box); in Spanish civil war, 995; "new woman" concept, 999(box); in Nazi Germany, 1011; in French resistance, 1044; welfare issues and, 1081–1082; gender issues and, 1118–1119. *See also* Abortion rights; Feminism; Women's rights; Women's suffrage

Women's rights, 764, 766(box), 902(box)

Women's Social and Political Union, 900

Women's suffrage, 766(box), 834, 900, 901(illus.), 965

Wood, *see* Lumber industry

Woolen trade, 420

Woolf, Virginia, 987, 988(box)

Wool industry, 591, 690

Wool trade, 363

Word of God, 517

Wordsworth, William, 743

Workers: social position of, 312; peasants as, 317–318; second serfdom and, 422; industrialization and, 692; socialism and, 749–751; Chartism and, 757; in Britain, 783–784, 854–856; living conditions of, 790, 791–793; family life and, 793–795; solidarity among, 797–798; leisure of, 798, 799(illus.); collective action and, 799–802; political action by, 800; Marx and, 802–805; wages of, 808–809 and *illus.*; in France, 835; state and, 862–863; education, culture, and, 863–864; in Italy, 903–904; in Russia, 906, 908 and *illus.*; in Germany, 940–941; mass society and, 965–967; Nazism and, 1005–1006; in France, 1019, 1020; women as, 1081–1082; in Germany, 1101; in Soviet Union and East Germany, 1103. *See also* Economics; Industry and industrialization; Politics; Socialism

Workers' Union (Tristan), 750

Working class, *see* Classes (economic and social); Labor; Workers

Workmen's compensation, 862

Works and Days (Hesiod), 82

Workweek, length of, 855

World Bank, 1124, 1139

World-view, 162–163, 625–652, 1007–1009

World War I, 909–911, 917–951, 928(box); stalemate in, 918–926; fronts in, 920(map); as total war, 926–931; destruction in, 930(illus.); Russian Revolution and, 935; in 1917–1918, 935–941; costs of, 941–942; settlement after, 943–950, 946(map), 960–963; writings about, 951, 954–955 and *illus.*; West after, 959–963. *See also* Eastern front; Western front; specific countries

World War II, 1030(illus.), 1031–1068; events leading to, 1020–1025; "Phony War" in, 1032–1033; fall of France in, 1033–1034; Battle of Britain in, 1034–1035 and *illus.*; Italy and, 1035–1037; European theaters in, 1036(map); Holocaust and,

World War II *(cont.)*, 1040–1043; Soviet Union in, 1044–1046; U.S. and, 1046; in Pacific region, 1046–1049, 1050(map); second front in, 1048, 1050–1051; invasion of Italy in, 1051; Normandy invasion in, 1051; Allied victory in, 1051–1060; Yalta conference and, 1052–1055, 1053(illus.); impact in Europe, 1055(map); end in Europe, 1056; end of war with Japan, 1058; results of, 1058–1060, 1059(illus.); postwar world and, 1060–1068. *See also* Atomic bomb; Cold War; Nazis and Nazism; specific countries

Worms, Concordate of, 326, 355

Wretched of the Earth, The (Fanon), 1093 and box

Writing: in Mesopotamia, 11–12 and *illus.*; in Egypt, 31; hieroglyphs, 31; in Crete, 64–65; Linear A, 64–65; Linear B, 68; Caroline minuscule (script), 294, 304–305; about World War I, 951; of women, 987. *See also* Language(s); Literacy; Literature; Novels; Poets and poetry

Writs, 329

Wyclif, John, 400, 514

Xerxes (Persia), 57, 59, 62, 101, 102(box)

Yagoda, Genrikh, 1004

Yahweh, 43, 52

Yalta conference, 1052–1055, 1053(illus.)

Yeltsin, Boris, 1129, 1130(illus.), 1131, 1132

Yorkists (England), 409

Yorktown, Battle at, 702

Young, Arthur, 702

Young, Owen D., 972

Young Europe, 747

Young Germany group, 747

Young Italy group, 747

Young Plan, 972

Young Turks, 827, 905–906

Ypres, 422; Battle at, 925

Yudenich, Nicholas, 976(map)

Yugoslavia, 942, 945, 1044, 1063, 1096(map), 1098, 1133–1135, 1134(map)

Yukichi, Fukuzawa, 833(box)

Zadruga, 339

Zagros Mountain region, 7, 59

Zama, Battle at, 173

Zarathustra (Zoroaster), 63

Zealots, 216

Zemstvos, 839

Zeno, 142

Zenobia, 211

Zhukov, Georgi, 1056, 1098

Ziegler, Anton, 738(illus.)

Ziggurat, 48

Zionism, 883, 943, 1064–1066

Zodiac, 48

Zola, Emile, 871, 872(box), 874

Zollverein (customs union), 822

Zones, in Germany, 1057, 1061–1062

Zoroaster and Zoroastrianism, 44, 57, 63–64. *See also* Zarathustra

Zurich, church reforms in, 517–518

Zweig, Stefan, 966(box)

Zwingli, Huldrych, 517

Zyuganov, Gennady, 1131